D1222490

HARPER
ENCYCLOPEDIA
OF THE
MODERN WORLD

A 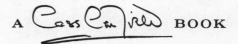 BOOK

HARPER ENCYCLOPEDIA OF THE MODERN WORLD

A CONCISE REFERENCE HISTORY
FROM 1760 TO THE PRESENT

EDITED BY

RICHARD B. MORRIS

AND

GRAHAM W. IRWIN

1817

HARPER & ROW, PUBLISHERS

NEW YORK, EVANSTON, AND LONDON

R
903
H293m

138603

MOUNT UNION COLLEGE
LIBRARY

Exclusive of those on pages 8, 226, 227, and 512,
the maps are copyright © 1967, 1970 by Lilli Tanzer

HARPER ENCYCLOPEDIA OF THE MODERN WORLD. *Copyright © 1970 by Harper & Row, Publishers, Incorporated. Printed in the United States of America. All rights reserved. No part of this book may be used or reproduced in any manner whatsoever without written permission except in the case of brief quotations embodied in critical articles and reviews. For information address Harper & Row, Publishers, Incorporated, 49 East 33rd Street, New York, N.Y. 10016. Published simultaneously in Canada by Fitzhenry & Whiteside Limited, Toronto.*

FIRST EDITION

LIBRARY OF CONGRESS CATALOG CARD NUMBER: 73-81879

CONSULTANT EDITORS

Africa: K. ONWUKA DIKE, formerly Vice-Chancellor, University of Ibadan, Nigeria

China: K. O. HSIAO, Far Eastern and Russian Institute, University of Washington, Seattle, Wash., U.S.A.

Class, Labor, and Social Thought: RALF DAHRENDORF, University of Konstanz, Federal Republic of Germany

Communist World: PHILIP E. MOSELY, School of International Affairs, Columbia University, New York, U.S.A.

Constitutional Development: LOUIS HENKIN, School of Law, Columbia University, New York, U.S.A.

Economic Development and Technology: W. W. ROSTOW, University of Texas, Austin, Tex., and MIRA WILKINS, Smith College, Northampton, Mass., U.S.A.

Education: LAWRENCE A. CREMIN, Teachers College, Columbia University, New York, U.S.A.

Europe to 1914: JEAN-BAPTISTE DUROSELLE, Sorbonne, Paris, France

Europe since 1914: MARTIN GILBERT, Merton College, Oxford, England

India: S. P. SEN, Institute of Historical Studies, University of Calcutta, Calcutta, India

Japan: YOSHITAKE OKA, University of Tokyo, Tokyo, Japan

Latin America: GILBERTO FREYRE, University of Recife, Pernambuco, Brazil

Middle East: BERNARD LEWIS, School of Oriental and African Studies, University of London, London, England

Science: I. I. RABI, Department of Physics, Columbia University, New York, and BRUCE S. EASTWOOD, Clarkson College of Technology, Potsdam, N.Y., U.S.A.

Southeast Asia: WANG GUNGWU, Australian National University, Canberra, Australia

CONTRIBUTORS

Basic Chronology

OMONIYI ADEWOYE
SUSAN ASHLEY
ANTHONY M. BERRETT
MARTIN J. BRESNICK
JOHN O. DWYER
NICHOLAS B. FESSENDEN
JOHN F. FLYNN
R. LUCINDA GOKEL
MARIAN KIRSCH
KATHARINE LEAB
JAMES LoGERFO
EDWARD L. McGOWAN
ANNA MACIAS
MAO CHUN-FAN
LINDA C. ROSE
JAMES T. SABIN
PAUL I. SHERMAN
BENTON C. STARK
KEYVAN TABARI
JUDITH WALSH

THOMAS J. ARCHDEACON
CLINTON BAILEY
MARIO BICK
RENATE BRIDENTHAL
RONALD L. ERNHARTH
GEOFFREY FIELD
FRANCIS C. FOLDVARY
LOIS HAGER
DANIEL J. LEAB
BERNADETTE LI
PATRICK MACFADDEN
SUSAN McNAMARA
MARTIN MANTELL
DAVID W. ROBINSON
HARRY KENNETH ROSENTHAL
LOUISA SCHELL
MARGARET SMITH
EDWARD R. STEHLE
ROYALL TYLER
ALEXANDER W. WILDE

Topical Chronology

Art: SARAH FAUNCE
Constitutional Order: FRANK J. MACCHIAROLA
Economic Development and Technology: MIRA WILKINS
Education: CHARLES H. LYONS
Literature, Theater, etc.: ROBERT MOSS
Medicine: MARILYN LAVIN
Music: BERENICE ROBINSON MORRIS and WILLARD RHODES
Philosophy and Psychology: THEDA SHAPIRO
Religion: JAMES T. SABIN
Science: BRUCE S. EASTWOOD
Social Order: DANIEL CHIROT

CONTENTS

II. TOPICAL CHRONOLOGY

ECONOMIC DEVELOPMENT AND TECHNOLOGY IN AN AGE OF REVOLUTION • 655

MAPS

CHARTS

ABOUT THIS BOOK

The *Harper Encyclopedia of the Modern World* provides a summary of the essential facts of world history during the past two hundred years. It is divided into two parts: a "Basic Chronology," which deals with political, military, and diplomatic history by state, region, and area; and a "Topical Chronology," in which are handled, on a world-wide basis, economic, social, and constitutional history, and the history of science, thought, and culture.

"The Modern World" may be defined in many different ways: as the result of the victory of man over his environment, as the product of a gradual change from communal to individual life styles, as a final coalescing—because of the recent revolutions in communications and technology—of many civilizations into one. However defined, modernity did not come to all areas of the world simultaneously, and today the continents and the great geographic regions within the continents stand at markedly different stages of historical development. Yet in a very broad sense the modern world may be said to have emerged in the half-century following 1750, with its initial impact in the Western world.

In Europe and North America the second half of the eighteenth century saw the culmination of the Enlightenment and the Age of Reason, as well as the beginnings of the Industrial Revolution. The period also witnessed the Era of Democratic Revolutions, notably the American and the French, with their twin impact on the rise of nationalism. The emergence of Russia as a world power may also be said to date from this time.

In other areas the modern world began to emerge in the late eighteenth century and during the early nineteenth. In Latin America, for example, the last years of the eighteenth century saw the gathering of revolutionary forces which loosened the Spanish and Portuguese hold, although the revolutions themselves did not start until 1810.

The profile of Africa began to change in the early nineteenth century, with the abolition of the (legal) slave trade, the establishment of effective Christian missions, the penetration of the interior of the continent by European explorers and traders, the great Moslem jihads in the Sudan, the founding of modern Egypt under Mohammed Ali, and the spread of white settlement following the French conquest of Algiers (1830) and the Great Trek in South Africa (1836–37).

The same period was marked in Asia by a rapid increase in the volume and value of Asian trade with the West, which signalled the beginning of the extraversion of the Asian economies that was to mark the Age of Imperialism. In China, cracks in the Manchu governmental structure appeared, with peasant revolts starting as early as 1774 and foreign encroachments beginning in earnest with Lord Macartney's mission of 1793. The rise of "modern Japan" may be dated from the late Tokugawa period, which saw increasing maritime contacts with the outside world (despite an official seclusion policy) and the gradual spread of Western learning via translations from the Chinese and Dutch.

The emergence of a Second British Empire, with India rather than America as its main focus, followed the general settlement achieved after the War of the American Revolution. In India, the elimination of the French as rivals for power, the transformation of the East India Company from a trading concern into a territorial power, and the victory over Tipu Sultan of Mysore in 1799 established the British as unchallenged overlords, if not yet proprietors, of the subcontinent. In Southeast Asia, British penetration into Malaya and French into Indochina came with the nineteenth century. In Indonesia, the demise of the Netherlands East India Company (1799), the reduction of the Javanese states to submission by the successor Dutch colonial government, and the inauguration of the highly profitable "Culture System" of agricultural exploitation brought about major changes. Finally, in Australia, first discoveries and colonization along the eastern seaboard coincided with the last years of the American Revolution and the emergence of the Second British Empire.

The present work is a "world" encyclopedia in a special sense. The political and economic domination of the Western over the non-

Western world, which has been so marked a feature of the last century and a half, resulted in ethno-centric attitudes on the part of the West which were reflected in its historiography. Although the decolonization process ushered in by the Second World War is now almost complete, and although there has been a revolution in the writing of the history of the non-Western world during recent decades, much of the former bias still persists, particularly in works of reference. In the present volume, therefore, the attempt has been consciously made to set the record straight, to provide a balanced presentation shorn of the prejudices which accorded to the activities of non-Westerners a very minor role during the era of imperialism and colonialism. This is true not only of the politically-oriented Basic Chronology, but also of the Topical, where non-Western economic, social, and cultural achievements are given their just due.

Throughout the volume events and sequences of events are arranged chronologically. For convenience, however, an entire story has sometimes been told under one key year or group of years. For this reason, among others, an exceptionally full Index has been provided. Reference to it will enable the reader to locate the page or pages on which the major description of an event appears, as well as the pages containing additional or subsidiary entries. In other cases it has been found appropriate to divide a subject into several entries by country and chronological segment. The Congress of Vienna, for example, which is described in the "Nationalism, Liberalism, and Reaction in Europe, 1800–71" section of the Basic Chronology, appears under "The Hapsburg Lands, 1800–15," but also under "The Italian States and the Risorgimento, 1800–15," under "Russia, 1809–14," and "Russia, 1815–25," under "The Unification of Germany, 1807–15," and under "Great Britain and Ireland, 1815–15." Here again, reference to the Index, and also to the Contents, which is comprehensive, will enable the reader to make sure that he has not missed any vital entries.

Because the feature which distinguishes the modern age most sharply from its predecessors is the technological revolution, a major portion of the Topical Chronology is devoted to the section entitled "Economic Development and Technology." Within this section, the subject matter is handled by major time segments for major world areas, the latter arranged according to their relative status on the economic development scale. Headings within subsections follow the same order throughout: agriculture (and animal husbandry), raw materials, labor, energy, manufacturing and industry, transportation, communications, finance, foreign trade, foreign investment, business organization, government policy, and "other factors." This style of arrangement means that the reader may skip, tracing a particular theme for one country, group of countries, or the whole world from 1760 to the present, or, if he wishes, read straight through to gain a perspective of world-wide economic development and technological change (or lack of it) during a series of particular time spans.

All dates are by reference to the modern Western (Gregorian) calendar. For the Western world itself, this has been simple to achieve, since all the countries of Europe and the Americas, except Russia, had adopted the Gregorian system by 1760, the starting date of the encyclopedia. Russian Old Style dates (to 1917) and dates taken from sources which employed non-Western calendars, eras, and annual reckoning systems have been converted to their Gregorian equivalents.

The work is designed to be read as well as referred to. To this end some repetition has been permitted, in the belief that the reader will not wish to be burdened with a multiplicity of cross-references. In a few cases, where large topics fell naturally under more than one heading, and where duplication would have been unreasonably wasteful of space, cross-references have been supplied.

Foreign personal and place names appear in the text in the forms most likely to be familiar to the general reader. Where these forms, because of the development of modern scientific systems of transliteration, have become obsolete, the more correct versions have been added, where the name first occurs in each case, in parentheses: thus, "Muscat (Masqat)." Both forms, cross-referenced where necessary, appear in the Index.

The editors wish to express their gratitude to Cass Canfield, of Harper & Row, who initiated the project, to the late James Fergus McRee, copyeditor, who detected many errors and inconsistencies, and to Beulah Hagen, who saw the work through the press. Lilli Tanzer drew the maps from the designs of Susan McNamara. John C. Caldwell supplied the information upon which the world demography maps are based. Our thanks are also due to the editorial consultants and to more than fifty contributors and research and editorial assistants. A world encyclopedia of this scope and complexity could not have been produced in four years without their sustained and dedicated labor.

R.B.M.
Columbia University   G.W.I.

I

BASIC
CHRONOLOGY

THE DEMOCRATIC REVOLUTION
IN THE WESTERN WORLD,
1760–1825

The United States and Europe, 1760–99

THE AMERICAN REVOLUTION

THE COLONIAL POWERS IN COLLISION. By the middle of the 18th cent. 3 major European powers appeared solidly entrenched in the Western Hemisphere. The vast Spanish Empire embraced all of South America (save for Portugal's Brazil and the British and Dutch Guianas), all of Central America (save for British Honduras), major islands in the Caribbean, and on the North American continent the Floridas, California, and the Southwest. France held Canada and certain islands in the Caribbean, while the world-wide British Empire numbered some 31 colonies, extending from Hudson Bay to Borneo, from the Honduran logwood coast to the Bay of Bengal, and embracing almost 15 m. people. Some of these colonies, those involving control over non-English peoples (United East India and Royal African Companies) or over vast largely unpopulated domains (Hudson's Bay Co.), were administered by private business companies chartered by the crown. Others were owned and governed by private proprietors (Maryland, Pennsylvania, and Delaware). Two colonies, Connecticut and Rhode Island, managed to hold on to their original self-governing status. However, a clear trend toward the setting up of royal provinces had emerged. The royal colonies, numbering 8 of the original North American 13 (including Georgia after 1732) along with the British West Indian islands, were ruled by governors named by the king. Other instruments of British colonial control were the Board of Trade (1696), which after 1748 emerged as a central agency of colonial supervision, such crown officials as the Secretary of State for the Southern Department (special Colonial Secretary created 1768), the Admiralty, the War Office, and the Privy Council, which reviewed colonial laws and acted as the highest court of appeal from the colonies.

The original 13 colonies had long enjoyed a considerable measure of self-government. Their assemblies, like the House of Commons, played an indispensable role in raising colonial revenue, and by 1750 had wrested control over expenditures from the governors, as well as much of the appointing power.

2ND 100 YEARS' WAR. 1689–1763. During the period, Great Britain and France (along with other European powers) fought 4 wars to maintain that delicate balance of power both in continental Europe and in the colonial world deemed necessary to survival as 1st-rate powers. Allies of the major antagonists switched sides as their own interests dictated. These wars resulted in France being stripped of her empire in America. By the Treaty of Utrecht, 1713, Britain won Newfoundland, Acadia, and Hudson Bay from France, and from Spain the cession of Gibraltar and the island of Minorca. By the Treaty of Paris, 1763, ending the Seven Years' War, 1756–63, which began in America in 1754 as the French and Indian War, Britain acquired Canada and all of France's territorial claims east of the Mississippi except New Orleans. In exchange for East and West Florida, captured in the war, Britain returned Cuba to Spain; France, to compensate Spain for her substantial losses, gave her New Orleans and the Louisiana Territory, retaining only the two fishing islands of St. Pierre and Miquelon and privileges of fishing off the Grand Banks.

The financial burdens imposed upon Britain both by the war and by the new responsibilities of the peace gave rise to a new issue of taxation in the colonies, while at the same time the expulsion of the French from North America freed the colonists from fear of foreign aggression and the need for protection by the British Empire.

1763

PROCLAMATION OF 7 OCT. In process of formulating a policy for the newly acquired territory in North America, the crown issued a proclamation forbidding settlement west of the Alleghenies, ordering colonists already there to leave, and placing the area under the control of the British military commander in America. The proclamation also established English law and royal governments for the new provinces of Quebec, East Florida, West Florida, and Grenada.

PONTIAC'S REBELLION. 7 May–28 Nov. The British acquisition of the old Northwest posed problems of relations between Indians and white settlers. Numerous grievances, including a British refusal to supply the Indians with ammunition, incited the Ottawa chief Pontiac and his followers to revolt. Beginning in May 1763, the Indians destroyed every British post west of Niagara until Col. Henry Bouquet defeated them at Bushy Run, thereby saving Ft. Pitt. Many tribes signed treaties at Presque Isle, 12 Aug., with Col. John Bradstreet, and in Nov. Pontiac lifted a 5-month siege of Detroit; he finally made peace at Oswego, 24 July,

1766, with the Indian Commissioner Sir William Johnson (1715–74).

1764

AMERICAN REVENUE ACT (SUGAR ACT). 5 Apr. This measure, the first aimed specifically at raising a crown revenue in the colonies, was proposed by the Chancellor of the Exchequer, Lord Grenville, to assure that the Americans would shoulder the heavy fiscal burden of colonial defense. It increased duties on non-British products imported into the colonies, added to the list of "enumerated" goods (sent only to England), and levied a 3d. per gal. tax on foreign molasses. Grenville ensured enforcement by overhauling the inefficient customs service and establishing a vice-admiralty court (no jury) at Halifax.

CURRENCY ACT. This act extended to all the colonies the ban on legal-tender paper money in effect in New England since 1751. Virginia, which had emitted £250,000 in paper, was the main target. Colonial opposition to this deflationary measure and to the Sugar Act forecast trouble for the coming years.

STAMP ACT. 22 Mar. The Stamp Act was the first direct tax imposed by Parliament on America. It sought to raise £60,000 annually for colonial defense by a levy on newspapers, legal documents, ships' papers, licenses, etc. The tax evoked united opposition throughout the colonies.

TAXATION AND REPRESENTATION. Lawyer Daniel Dulany of Maryland argued (*Considerations*) that Parliament could not levy internal revenue taxes like the Stamp Act on colonies which could not feasibly be represented in it. In Virginia the House of Burgesses asserted that only the provincial legislature could tax Virginia.

STAMP ACT CONGRESS. 7–25 Oct. Delegates from 9 colonies met in New York and adopted John Dickinson's (1732–1808) moderate "Declaration of Rights and Grievances," 19 Oct., which asserted that the Stamp Act violated the colonists' right as British subjects to be taxed only by bodies in which they had representation.

PRESSURES FOR REPEAL. To hasten redress of their grievances, merchants in New York, Philadelphia, and Boston banned the purchase of European goods (nonimportation), and the other colonists ceased transactions requiring stamps or openly violated the law when it became inoperative, 1 Nov. British merchants, whose exports to America plummeted from £2,249,710 worth in 1764 to £1,944,108 worth in 1765, also sought repeal from the Rockingham ministry, which had replaced the Grenville government, 10 July.

1766

REPEAL. 18 Mar. Parliament responded by repealing the offensive legislation, but passed the Declaratory Act, 18 Mar., which asserted its jurisdiction over the colonies "in all cases whatsoever."

TRADE LAWS MODIFIED. 1 Nov. Parliament set a 1d. per gal. duty on all molasses and removed export duties on British West Indian sugar.

NEW YORK AND THE QUARTERING ACT. In Jan. the assembly refused to comply fully with Parliament's Quartering Act, Mar. 1765, which required the colonies to provide barracks and provisions for British troops. A clash, 11 Aug., between redcoats and citizens exacerbated the situation, and Governor Sir Henry Moore prorogued the recalcitrant legislature, 19 Dec. Under threat of parliamentary suspension, the assembly appropriated £3,000, 6 June, 1767.

1767

TOWNSHEND ACTS. 29 June. A number of acts proposed by Charles Townshend, Chancellor of the Exchequer in the Chatham government, levied supposedly acceptable external taxes (import duties on glass, lead, paints, paper, and tea) on America to defray the costs of the military, judiciary, and civil government there. Another measure established new vice-admiralty courts and an American Board of Customs Commissioners in Boston to assure true compliance.

1768

MASSACHUSETTS CIRCULAR LETTER. 11 Feb. This letter, drawn up by Samuel Adams (1722–1803) and circulated by the assembly, attacked the Townshend Acts as violating the principle of no taxation without representation, and denounced any attempt to make colonial governors and judges independent of the people. Governor Francis Bernard dissolved the legislature, and he also dissolved the next one when it voted 92–17 not to rescind the letter, 30 June. Seven "rescinders" lost their seats in the 1769 election.

BRITISH TROOPS IN BOSTON. 1 Oct. The presence of the frigate *Romney* in Boston Harbor emboldened the harassed customs commissioners to seize, 10 June, the sloop *Liberty* in which John Hancock (1737–93) allegedly was smuggling Madeira wine. Fearing the angry townsmen, the customs officials took refuge next day in Castle William and called for troops. Two infantry regiments landed unopposed, 1 Oct., despite threats of violence by the Sons of Liberty.

PROGRESS OF NONIMPORTATION. Boston merchants, 1 Aug., banned the importation of Townshend-taxed items until repeal, and of most other British goods from 1 Jan., 1769, to 1 Jan., 1770. New York, 28 Aug.; Philadelphia, 10 Mar., 1769; and Baltimore, 30 Mar., merchants also reached nonimportation agreements of varying stringency. By the end of 1769 only New Hampshire remained aloof from nonimportation.

1769

VIRGINIA RESOLVES AND ASSOCIATION. On 16 May the House of Burgesses resolved that only the governor and provincial legislature could tax Virginians, and, 17 May, established the Virginia Association, forbidding the import of dutied British goods (except paper), slaves, and many European luxury items. The spread of the association was rapid, with Maryland, South Carolina, and Georgia endorsing similar programs. Delaware, Connecticut, and Rhode Island residents pledged nonimportation, and the New Jersey assembly voiced support. British exports to America declined from £2,157,218 in 1768 to £1,336,-122 in 1769.

1770

TAX TEA ONLY. 12 Apr. Lord North came to power, 31 Jan., and, pledging that he would levy no new taxes on America, withdrew all the Townshend duties except that on tea. The collapse of nonimportation quickly followed. New York's defection, July, from the various associations prompted Philadelphia, Sept.; Boston, Oct.; South Carolina, Dec.; and Virginia, July 1771, also to withdraw.

UNREST IN NEW YORK. Several people were seriously injured in a clash, 16 Jan., between Sons of Liberty and redcoats in New York ("Battle of Golden Hill"). Alexander McDougall, a leader of the Sons, was imprisoned by the assembly for contempt, 13 Dec., 1770–27 Apr., 1771, after he attacked it in a broadside for appropriating £2,000, 15 Dec., 1769, in compliance with the Quartering Act.

BOSTON MASSACRE. 5 Mar. The incident known as the Boston Massacre was the culmination of several clashes between townsmen and redcoats. About 9 P.M. on 5 Mar., at the command of a person never identified, a detachment of soldiers fired into a mob of taunting civilians, killing 5. Charged with murder and defended by patriot lawyers John Adams (1735–1826) and Josiah Quincy (1744–75), 5 redcoats were acquitted and 2, pleading clergy, were burned in the hand for manslaughter.

1772

THREATS TO HOME RULE. After nightfall on 9 June the merchant John Brown led some men in burning the customs schooner *Gaspee,* which was aground near Providence. A commission of inquiry learned nothing from the unco-operative Rhode Islanders. Announcements that the crown would henceforth pay the Massachusetts governor, 13 June, and judges, Sept., thus rendering them independent of the General Court, aroused concern.

NEW COMMITTEES OF CORRESPONDENCE. Samuel Adams, through the Boston town meeting, set up a standing committee of correspondence, and other towns in the province followed Boston's example, as did every colony except North Carolina and Pennsylvania by Feb. 1774.

1773

TEA ACT. 10 May. Parliament rescued the nearly bankrupt East India Company by allowing it to sell tea directly to consignees in the colonies, and by remitting fully all British duties on the product when exported there. Thus, despite a 3d. per lb. import duty in America, the company could undersell both honest colonial merchants and smugglers. The colonists, who especially feared the monopolistic aspects of the Tea Act, managed by threats and persuasion to procure the resignations of the tea consignees in Philadelphia, Oct., and New York, 1 Dec., but not in Boston.

BOSTON TEA PARTY. 16 Dec. Trouble resulted when Governor Hutchinson refused, 16 Dec., to allow the ship *Dartmouth,* which lay in Boston Harbor, to return to England without paying duty. Bostonians disguised as Mohawk Indians boarded the ship and dumped all the tea (342 chests) overboard. Charleston's consignment was landed without opposition, 22 Dec., and stored until the patriots seized and sold it in July 1776. On 22 Apr., 1773, some New York "Indians" (Sons of Liberty) held a tea party, and Annapolis men burned the *Peggy Stewart* and her tea cargo on 19 Oct.

1774

COERCIVE ACTS. 31 Mar., 20 May. George III and Parliament sought to punish Boston for her tea party. The

Boston Port Bill virtually closed the port until the town compensated the East India Company and the customs. The Administration of Justice Act, 20 May, allowed crown officers indicted in Massachusetts for capital offenses committed in quelling riots or collecting revenue to stand trial in England. The Massachusetts Government Act empowered the king to appoint the Council (previously elected by the Assembly), gave him and the governor control of judicial selections, and required the governor's approval for town-meeting agendas.

QUEBEC ACT. 20 May. This act established a permanent Canadian civil government, with a crown-appointed legislative council, the taxing power reserved to Parliament, and the rights of Catholics guaranteed. The colonists, who inaccurately counted it among the "Intolerable" (Coercive) Acts, disliked these alien features and the extension of the Canadian boundary to encompass lands claimed by Virginia, Connecticut, and Massachusetts.

COLONIAL PROTEST. The Boston town meeting demanded immediate economic sanctions against Britain, but moderates in Philadelphia, 21 May, and New York City, 23 May, suggested instead an intercolonial gathering. The General Court agreed, and during the summer all the colonies except Georgia nominated delegates to a congress to be held in Philadelphia in Sept.

1ST CONTINENTAL CONGRESS. 5 Sept.–26 Oct. Radicals like the Adamses (Mass.) quickly convinced the 56 delegates meeting in Carpenters Hall to endorse the Suffolk Resolves, adopted earlier in Massachusetts. These resolutions advised the populace to disobey the unconstitutional Coercive Acts, form a government to collect and withhold taxes from the crown, raise a militia, and enforce economic sanctions against Britain.

GALLOWAY'S PLAN OF UNION. 28 Sept. The delegates defeated the plan of the Pennsylvania conservative Joseph Galloway (1731–1803) to establish a subordinate American branch of Parliament, composed of a president-general appointed by the king and a council periodically elected by the assemblies, whose consent as well as Parliament's would be necessary for any law dealing with America.

DECLARATION AND RESOLVES. 14 Oct. The Congress denounced numerous parliamentary acts for violating colonial rights, including the assemblies' exclusive control, subject to royal veto, of taxation and internal policy.

CONTINENTAL ASSOCIATION. 18 Oct. The delegates pledged their colonies to start nonimportation of British goods and of slaves, 1 Dec.; nonconsumption, 1 Mar., 1775; and nonexportation to British areas, 1 Sept., 1775. Extralegal local committees were to enforce the association, a modified version of which even Georgia adopted. After sending an address to Americans, Britons, and the king, the Congress adjourned, 26 Oct., 1775.

WAR PREPARATIONS IN NEW ENGLAND. The Massachusetts House constituted itself a provincial legislature, 7 Oct., and empowered a Committee of Safety under John Hancock to call out the militia. In Portsmouth, N.H., patriots confiscated arms and ammunition, without bloodshed, from Ft. William and Mary.

1775

CONCILIATION PLANS. Feb. The Lords rejected Chatham's suggestion, 1 Feb., that Parliament, in return for a voluntary revenue and acceptance of her supreme legislative authority, should recognize the Continental Congress and pledge not to raise a revenue in America. However, the Commons endorsed, 27 Feb., North's proposal that Parliament "forbear" from levying revenue taxes on colonies whose assemblies voluntarily contributed money.

CRISIS IN NEW ENGLAND. Massachusetts' 2nd Provincial Congress met, 1 Feb., to prepare the colony for hostilities which Patrick Henry (1736–99) prophesied as imminent in his famous "Liberty or Death" speech, 23 Mar. Parliament declared Massachusetts to be in rebellion, 9 Feb., and Lord Dartmouth, Secretary of State for the Colonies, authorized General Thomas Gage (governor since May 1774) to use force, if necessary, against the inhabitants.

LEXINGTON AND CONCORD. 19 Apr. Gen. Gage, 18 Apr., detailed Lt. Col. Francis Smith's 700 men to destroy patriot supplies at Concord. Paul Revere, dispatched along with William Dawes by Boston's Committee of Safety to give the alarm, warned Sam Adams and John Hancock at Lexington, where the next morning 70 "Minute Men" confronted the advancing British. The patriots were obeying Maj. John Pitcairn's order to disperse when his men, hearing the report of an unidentified firearm, opened fire

without orders; 8 Americans died in the ensuing skirmish. Smith went on to accomplish his mission at Concord, but paid a heavy price to colonial snipers, who killed 73 and wounded 174 of his men on the road back to Charlestown. The Americans, who had lost 93 killed, wounded, and missing, then began a siege of Boston which lasted until Mar. 1776.

CAPTURE OF FORT TICONDEROGA. 10 May. Ethan Allen's "Green Mountain Boys" captured Ft. Ticonderoga on Lake Champlain by surprise, 10 May. Benedict Arnold (1741–1801), instructed by the Boston Committee of Safety to take Ticonderoga, accompanied Allen. Americans also seized Crown

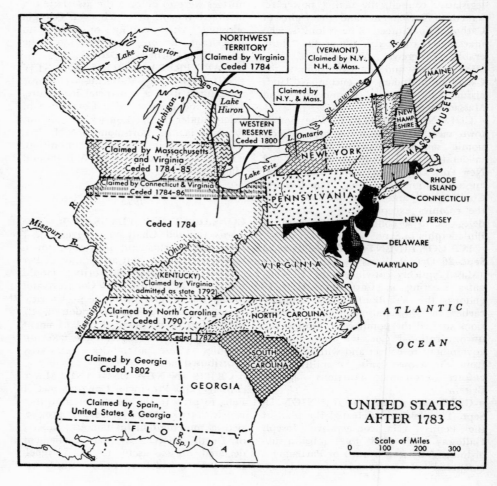

UNITED STATES
AFTER 1783

Point, N.Y., 12 May, and St. John's, Canada, 16 May.

WASHINGTON NAMED COMMANDER. 15 June. Congress accepted the troops besieging Boston as a Continental Army, and arranged to raise money and more men, 10–22 June. On Thomas Johnson's (Md.) motion, which John Adams seconded, Congress unanimously named George Washington (1732–99) commander in chief, 15 June, and appointed Artemas Ward, Charles Lee, Philip Schuyler, and Israel Putnam major generals, 17 June.

BUNKER HILL. 17 June. The Americans, discovering Gen. Gage's plans to occupy Dorchester Heights overlooking Boston on 18 June, countered by fortifying Breed's Hill on the Charlestown peninsula on the night of 16–17 June. Gage decided to send Maj. Gen. William Howe with 2,400 men to dislodge the 1,600 colonists under Col. William Prescott. After 2 unsuccessful frontal assaults, Howe's men, reinforced by troops of Maj. Gen. Henry Clinton, dropped their heavy packs and routed the powderless patriots from Breed's Hill and Bunker Hill with a bayonet charge. British casualties of 1,054 (many of them officers) as opposed to 397 American losses made it a Pyrrhic victory.

OLIVE BRANCH PETITION. 5 July. This petition, written by John Dickinson and adopted by Congress, expressed Americans' devotion to George III and their desire for a peaceful reconciliation. Before adjourning, 2 Aug., Congress also endorsed, 6 July, a "Declaration of the Causes and Necessities of Taking Up Arms" by Thomas Jefferson (1743–1826) and Dickinson, and rejected, 31 July, Lord North's reconciliation plan.

EXPEDITIONS AGAINST QUEBEC. Aug.–Dec. When Gen. Schuyler fell ill at St. John's, Gen. Richard Montgomery became commander of an expedition from New York designed to prevent an attack from Canada. Montgomery drove the British commander, Sir Guy Carleton, back to Quebec, Nov., and there joined Benedict Arnold, 3 Dec., who had arrived, 13 Nov., with troops from Cambridge. They launched a disastrous attack against Quebec, 31 Dec., in which nearly 100

Americans were killed or wounded, including Montgomery (killed) and Arnold (wounded), and over 300 were captured.

CONGRESS RECONVENES. 12 Sept. Learning, 9 Nov., that George III had rejected the Olive Branch Petition and declared the colonies to be in rebellion, 23 Aug., Congress, with Georgia present, disavowed allegiance to Parliament, 6 Dec.

NAVY ESTABLISHED. 13 Oct. Congress authorized a navy of 2 (later 4) ships of 10 guns each; adopted regulations for it, 28 Nov.; and commissioned officers, 22 Dec., naming Esek Hopkins (R.I.) commodore. It also encouraged privateering, issuing letters of marque and reprisal, 23 Mar., 1776.

COMMITTEE OF CORRESPONDENCE. 29 Nov. A Committee of Correspondence was established by Congress to contact friends of America in Europe.

HOSTILITIES IN THE SOUTH. 11 Dec. At Great Bridge angered colonists defeated and drove from Virginia the Loyalist forces of Governor Dunmore, who had offered, 17 Nov., freedom to slaves deserting rebel masters.

1776

MILITARY BALANCE SHEET. When hostilities commenced, each side had certain advantages and certain weaknesses. The patriots, armed with the superior American rifle and fighting on their own soil under George Washington's excellent leadership, lacked training, supplies, and naval support. The professional British army, well-equipped and financed, was tactically inflexible, far from home, and failed adequately to mobilize Loyalist assistance.

"COMMON SENSE." 9 Jan. The appearance of Thomas Paine's (1737–1809) pamphlet, *Common Sense,* which denounced George III and the institution of monarchy, brought many Americans to favor independence.

BRITISH EVACUATION OF BOSTON. 17 Mar. In early Mar., the colonists set up Gen. Henry Knox's artillery on Dorchester Heights, thus making Boston untenable. Gen. Howe, commanding the

British since 10 Oct., 1775, embarked his soldiers and 1,000 Loyalists on troopships, 17 Mar., and sailed to Halifax.

FRENCH AID. Apr.–May. The French foreign minister, Comte de Vergennes, seeking to weaken Britain, persuaded Louis XVI to give the Americans 1 m. livres in munitions, 2 May, through a fictitious company headed by French agent Pierre Caron de Beaumarchais. Meanwhile, the Americans, 6 Apr., opened their ports to all nations except Britain.

RETREAT FROM CANADA. May–July. After unsuccessfully besieging Quebec, Arnold's troops, under Gen. John Thomas, began to retreat, May. Harassed by Carleton's men, they joined Arnold at St. John's and reached Ticonderoga in July. Both sides began to build fleets to control Lake Champlain.

HOSTILITIES IN THE SOUTH. June. Gen. Henry Clinton's British expeditionary force arrived off the coast of Charleston, S.C., 1 June, where Gen. Charles Lee assumed command, 4 June. Clinton failed to capture the city as Col. William Moultrie's men, inflicting over 200 casualties, smashed an assault by Sir Peter Parker's warships on nearby Sullivan's Island, 28 June.

MOVEMENT TOWARD INDEPENDENCE. June. On 7 June, Richard Henry Lee (Va.) offered a resolution that the United Colonies "are, and of right ought to be, free and independent States," and Congress, postponing a decision, named, 11 June, Jefferson, Benjamin Franklin (1706–90), John Adams, Robert Livingston (1746–1813), and Roger Sherman to draft a Declaration of Independence. Jefferson, drawing upon the "natural rights" political philosophy, drafted the document.

DECLARATION OF INDEPENDENCE. Independence was voted by Congress as 12 colonies approved Lee's resolution of 7 June. The New York delegation, under instructions, 11 June, from the Provincial Congress, abstained. The same colonies voted, 4 July, to endorse an amended version of Jefferson's Declaration. New York's Provincial Congress approved the Declaration, 9 July, and Congress ordered the document engrossed and signed by the delegates, 19 July. Hancock (president) and Thomson (secretary) had signed it on 4 July, and most affixed their signatures on 2 Aug., but some, like Matthew Thornton (N.H.), did so later.

BATTLE OF LONG ISLAND. 27 Aug. Anticipating Gen. Howe's selection of New York City as his base, Washington brought his army there from Boston, 21 Mar.–13 Apr. From July to Aug., Howe landed 32,000 troops on Staten Island and brought 20,000 of them to Long Island, 22–25 Aug. On 27 Aug., Howe captured Gen. Sullivan and inflicted 1,500 casualties on the Americans, who fled to Brooklyn Heights, from where Washington stealthily shipped them by night, 29–30 Aug., to Manhattan.

STATEN ISLAND PEACE CONFERENCE. 11 Sept. This conference, requested by the king's commissioners, Gen. William and Adm. Richard Howe (brothers), was fruitless as Franklin, John Adams, and Edmund Rutledge rejected the British *sine qua non*, withdrawal of the Declaration of Independence.

BRITISH OCCUPATION OF NEW YORK CITY. 15 Sept. Howe landed troops at Kips Bay, and occupied New York City. Washington, fearing that he and his men would be trapped, retreated to Harlem Heights, where he repelled a British assault, 16 Sept.

BATTLE OF VALCOUR BAY. This battle, 11 Oct., and that of Split Rock, 13 Oct., resulted in defeats for Arnold's outgunned Lake Champlain fleet at the hands of Carleton's sailors. Winter's approach forced Carleton to return to Canada, 3 Nov., without attacking Ticonderoga.

RETREAT ACROSS NEW JERSEY. 18 Nov.–20 Dec. Washington withdrew to White Plains, 23 Oct., and, after the British had captured the high ground there, 28 Oct., retreated to North Castle, 1 Nov. In Manhattan, Howe's troops captured 2,818 patriots in Ft. Washington, 16 Nov., and two days later Gen. Cornwallis' approach forced Gen. Greene to abandon Ft. Lee, N.J. Meeting at Hackensack, Greene and Washington retreated across New Jersey into Pennsylvania, 11 Dec. After giving Washington almost dictatorial powers, Congress prudently removed itself to Baltimore.

COUP AT TRENTON. 26 Dec. Returning to New York, Howe left only a few small garrisons in New Jersey. Washington crossed the Delaware River by night, 25 Dec., and surprised the Trenton detachment, capturing 918 Hessians, while suffering only 5 casualties. He returned to Pennsylvania and then reoccupied Trenton, 30–31 Dec.

1777

COUP AT PRINCETON. 3 Jan. Howe quickly sent troops to Trenton, 1 Jan., and they made light contact with the Americans, 2 Jan. Cornwallis planned to attack the next day, but Washington slipped away by night to Princeton, where he routed, 3 Jan., a British column which had attacked his vanguard, and then led his men to winter quarters in Morristown.

FOREIGN AFFAIRS. Congress reconvened in Philadelphia on 12 Mar., and reconstituted the Committee for Secret Correspondence as the Committee for Foreign Affairs. Also it appointed several commissioners to represent America abroad, sending Arthur Lee, 1 May, to Spain; Ralph Izard, 7 May, to Tuscany; and William Lee, 9 May, to Vienna and Berlin. Foreign officers contributing their talents to the American cause included (date of commission in parentheses) Maj. Gens. the Marquis de Lafayette (31 July) and "Baron" Johann de Kalb (15 Sept.), Col. of Engineers Thaddeus Kosciusko (18 Oct., 1776), and Inspector Gen. Baron Friedrich Wilhelm von Steuben (5 May, 1778).

FALL OF PHILADELPHIA. 23 July– 26 Sept. Leaving New York, 23 July, Howe landed 15,000 men at Head of Elk, 25 Aug. He defeated Washington at Brandywine Creek, 11 Sept., and Gen. Anthony Wayne at Paoli, 21 Sept., and occupied Philadelphia, 26 Sept. Congress fled to Lancaster, 19 Sept., and then to York, 30 Sept.

BATTLE OF GERMANTOWN. 4 Oct. Washington's army suffered 700 casualties in a futile attack on the main British encampment at Germantown. He withdrew and took up winter quarters at Valley Forge, mid-Dec. Cornwallis forced the evacuation, 20 Nov., of Ft. Mercer, thus clearing the Delaware as far north as Philadelphia for British vessels.

NORTHERN CAMPAIGN. Gen. John Burgoyne put his plan of 28 Feb. into operation. This plan envisaged a 3-pronged attack on New England. Burgoyne himself drove south from Canada, 17 June, and seized Mt. Defiance overlooking Ft. Ticonderoga, 2 July, which Gen. Arthur St. Clair evacuated, 5 July.

Col. Barry St. Leger, leading the 2nd prong east from Oswego, besieged Col. Peter Gansevoort's men in Ft. Stanwix, 3 Aug. Mohawk chief Joseph Brant inflicted heavy casualties on Gen. Nicholas Herkimer's men coming to relieve Stanwix, 6 Aug., but St. Leger retreated to Oswego, 22 Aug., as Arnold approached with 1,000 men.

Burgoyne sent Lt. Col. Baum to capture badly needed supplies stored at Bennington, Vt., but Gen. John Stark's patriots mauled the attackers, 16 Aug. Nevertheless, Burgoyne pressed on to attack Bemis Heights, where the American commander, Gen. Horatio Gates, with 6,000 men repulsed him at Freeman's Farm, 19 Sept. Gens. Daniel Morgan and Ebenezer Learned checked Burgoyne's assault on the American left, 7 Oct., and a daring charge by Benedict Arnold drove the British back on Bemis Heights, from where they retired to Saratoga, 8 Oct.

The attack's 3rd prong, a drive up the Hudson, never materialized, as Howe was in Pennsylvania and Gen. Henry Clinton ventured north only to Esopus. His situation hopeless, Burgoyne asked for terms, 13 Oct., and by the Convention of Saratoga, 17 Oct., his 5,700 men laid down their arms.

ARTICLES OF CONFEDERATION. 15 Nov. A committee led by Dickinson had proposed Articles of Confederation on 12

July, 1776. On 15 Nov., 1777, they were adopted by Congress and submitted for ratification. Each state was to have one vote in the Confederation Congress and was to share proportionately the expenses of government.

1778

FRANCO-AMERICAN ALLIANCE. 6 Feb. The French, who feared the possible effect of new British peace proposals offered after the defeat of Burgoyne, finally recognized American independence in two treaties (1) of amity and commerce and (2) of alliance, 6 Feb., the latter setting forth war objectives and a formal agreement not to make a separate peace. Conrad Gérard became French minister to the U.S., Mar., and Congress ratified the treaties, 4 May, naming Franklin minister to France, 14 Sept.

CARLISLE PEACE COMMISSION. 12 Apr. Lord North, hoping to prevent congressional ratification of the Franco-American alliance, pledged, 16 Mar., to repeal the Tea and Coercive Acts and levy no revenue taxes in America. Furthermore, Parliament commissioned, 12 Apr., the Earl of Carlisle, William Eden, George Johnstone, and the Howe brothers as peace emissaries, empowered, if necessary, to promise suspension of all acts passed since 1763. When the negotiators arrived, 6 June, Congress informed them, 17 June, that it would discuss only the withdrawal of British troops and the recognition of American independence. When the commissioners' Manifesto and Proclamation, 3 Oct., appealing directly to the people, also came to nothing, they returned to England, 27 Nov.

JOHN PAUL JONES'S RAIDS. Apr. Privateers were the mainstay of the American naval effort, taking 733 prizes by 1778. The exploits of Capt. John Paul Jones's *Ranger* were especially daring. Roaming the Irish Sea, Jones captured 2 ships, 14–17 Apr., burned another, spiked the guns of the fort at Whitehaven, England, 23 Apr., and defeated the British sloop *Drake* off northern Ireland, 24 Apr.

BATTLE OF MONMOUTH. 28 June. Distressed by rumors of an approaching French fleet, Clinton, who had replaced Howe on 8 May, abandoned Philadelphia, 18 June, and withdrew across New Jersey with Washington pursuing from Valley Forge. The American vanguard caught Clinton at Monmouth Court House, 28 June, but fled in confusion as Gen. Charles Lee's leadership proved inadequate. Washington regrouped the patriots, and they managed to hold off repeated British assaults. That night Clinton slipped his men away to New York.

CAPTURE OF KASKASKIA. 4 July. Encouraged by Governor Patrick Henry (Va.), the Kentucky militia leader George Rogers Clark drove into the Northwest against enemy forces terrorizing the frontier. Clark took numerous posts, including Kaskaskia, 4 July; he also captured Lt. Gov. Henry Hamilton at Vincennes, 25 Feb., 1779.

FRANCO-AMERICAN ATTACK ON NEWPORT. 29 July–29 Aug. Comte d'Estaing's French fleet arrived near Newport, R.I., 29 July, but the appearance of Admiral Howe's ships, 10 Aug., prevented an attack, and a storm scattered both fleets, 11 Aug. Without naval support, Gen. Sullivan's assault on Newport, 29 Aug., was unsuccessful.

1779

WAR IN THE SOUTH. Jan.–June. The British moved their operation south with much success. After taking Savannah, 29 Dec., 1778, Lt. Col. Campbell captured Augusta, 29 Jan. Moultrie's patriots successfully defended Port Royal, S.C., 3 Feb., and Col. Andrew Pickens defeated Loyalists at Kettle Creek, Ga., 14 Feb., but Gen. John Ashe's attempt to recover Augusta ended in disaster at Briar Creek, 3 Mar., and Gen. Augustine Prevost decisively beat Gen. Benjamin Lincoln's Continentals at Stono Ferry, 19 June.

WAR IN THE NORTH. June–Sept. American success continued in the north as Gen. "Mad Anthony" Wayne recaptured, 15 July, and dismantled the fort at

Stony Point, N.Y., taking almost 700 prisoners. Maj. "Light Horse Harry" Lee drove the British from New Jersey by capturing Paulus Hook, 19 Aug. Avenging frontier massacres, especially those at Wyoming, 3 July, 1778, and Cherry, 11 Nov., 1778, Valleys in Pennsylvania, Gens. John Sullivan and James Clinton defeated, 29 Aug., Indians and Loyalists under Sir John Johnson and Joseph Brant at Newtown (Elmira) and ravaged 40 Iroquois villages.

SPANISH DECLARATION OF WAR. 21 June. In accordance with the Convention of Aranjuez, 12 Apr., with France, Spain entered the war, 21 June, after Britain had rejected her demand for Gibraltar and an ultimatum, 3 Apr. However, fearing for her colonies, Spain refused to recognize American independence.

"BONHOMME RICHARD" AND "SERAPIS." Capt. Jones sailed from France, 14 Aug., in a rehabilitated vessel he renamed *Bonhomme Richard* to honor Franklin. Near England, 23 Sept., he defeated Capt. Pierson's *Serapis*, transferred his crew to it from his own sinking ship, and brought it to port, 6 Oct.

FAILURE AT SAVANNAH. 9 Oct. Admiral d'Estaing and Gen. Lincoln joined forces, 23 Sept., but their attack on Savannah, 9 Oct., failed. The British again took the offensive as Clinton withdrew his troops from Rhode Island, 11 Oct., and left New York, 26 Dec., to attack Charleston.

1780

LEAGUE OF ARMED NEUTRALITY. Catherine II of Russia proposed a League of Armed Neutrality, 28 Feb., declaring that her navy would protect neutral Russian trade. Vergennes encouraged the League, and Denmark, Sweden, the Netherlands, Austria, Portugal, the Kingdom of the Two Sicilies, and Prussia became members.

FALL OF CHARLESTON. 12 May. Clinton besieged Charleston from early Feb. until Lincoln surrendered the city and its 5,400-man garrison, 12 May. Corn-

wallis took command there when Clinton returned to New York, 5 June.

BATTLE OF CAMDEN. 16 Aug. Gen. Gates, who was commissioned by Congress, 13 June, to oust the British from South Carolina and Georgia, decided to strike with his Southern Army at Cornwallis' supply depot at Camden, S.C. Gates made contact, 16 Sept., but fled 160 miles back to Hillsboro, N.C., when Col. Banastre Tarleton's cavalry smashed his rear. Gen. Nathanael Greene replaced Gates, 14 Oct., and assumed command of the army in the south, Dec. Cornwallis invaded North Carolina, 8 Sept., but turned back when guerrillas under Cols. Isaac Shelby and William Campbell defeated and captured Maj. Patrick Ferguson's 1,100 Loyalists at King's Mountain, 7 Oct.

TREASON OF ARNOLD. 21 Sept. Benedict Arnold, convicted, 26 Jan., for abusing his powers as commander of Philadelphia, resumed, May, a subversive correspondence which he had carried on with Clinton in 1779. Arnold took command of West Point, 5 Aug., and gave Clinton's adjutant, Maj. John André, plans showing the weaknesses of the post, 21 Sept. André, imprudently wearing civilian clothes, was captured, 23 Sept., and executed as a spy, 30 Sept. Arnold, who fled to the warship *Vulture* in the Hudson River, 25 Sept., became a brig. gen. in the British army and took part in several actions against the patriots.

1781

PENNSYLVANIA MUTINY. 2,400 disgruntled veterans decided to march on Philadelphia, 1 Jan. Joseph Reed, president of the Pennsylvania Executive Council, negotiated with them, 7 Jan., and managed to get almost half to return to service. Executions of several malcontents crushed insurrections by New Jersey, late Jan., and Pennsylvanian, May, troops.

ROBERT MORRIS, SUPERINTENDENT OF FINANCE. During a period of acute financial distress Congress appointed Robert Morris (1734–1806) superintendent of finance, 20 Feb. By 1780, Congress had issued $191,500,000 in paper money, which had depreciated drastically. Congress virtually repudiated these "Continentals" by allowing, 18 Mar., 1780, states to use them at one-fortieth of their face value to pay their debts to the central government. Morris improved the situation by (1) having Congress approve, 26 May, a national bank, the Bank of North America; (2) supplying the army by contract rather than requisition, June; and (3) obtaining money from France, May, and the Netherlands, 5 Nov.

RATIFICATION OF ARTICLES OF CONFEDERATION. Maryland signed, 27 Feb., after all the states, including Virginia, 2 Jan., had renounced their claims to western lands, thus completing the ratification of the Articles of Confederation.

WAR IN THE CAROLINAS. Gen. Greene's army re-entered South Carolina, where, with few losses, Gen. Morgan and Col. William Washington's cavalry crushed Tarleton at Cowpens, 17 Jan. Retiring to Virginia, Feb., the patriots returned to North Carolina with 4,400 men. Cornwallis won a Pyrrhic victory at Guilford Courthouse, 15 Mar., and retreated to Wilmington for reinforcements. Despite setbacks at Hobkirk's Hill, 19 Apr.; Ninety-Six, 22 May–19 June; and Eutaw Springs, 8 Sept., by autumn Greene had isolated the British in Charleston.

U.S. PEACE NEGOTIATIONS. Congress appointed John Jay (1745–1829), 13 June, Franklin, Henry Laurens, and Jefferson, 14 June, to assist John Adams to negotiate peace. Advised by the French minister, Chevalier de la Luzerne, Congress, 15 June, reduced its essential demands to independence and sovereignty, and instructed the commissioners not to act without French consent.

INVASION OF VIRGINIA. Cornwallis attacked American bases in Virginia, which were undermining British control of the Carolinas. 7,500 redcoats raided extensively until the junction of the forces of Lafayette, reinforced by Wayne, 10 June, and von Steuben, 19 June, led

Cornwallis to retire to Yorktown, 1 Aug., where he could establish sea communications with New York. Washington and Rochambeau, who had reached Newport, 11 July, 1780, with 5,000 French troops, met at Wethersfield, Conn., and decided to attack New York. When Washington learned, 14 Aug., that de Grasse intended to operate in the Chesapeake area instead of supporting the attack, he switched his target to the British positions in Virginia. Feinting toward Staten Island, Washington put the Franco-American army in motion, 21 Aug., south through New Jersey.

YORKTOWN CAMPAIGN. 30 Aug.– 19 Oct. Arriving 30 Aug., de Grasse landed his 3,000 troops to join Lafayette near Yorktown. He engaged Adm. Thomas Graves's fleet, 5 Aug., which retired to New York, 10 Aug., after Count Barras's squadron reinforced de Grasse, 9 Aug. French ships fetched Washington's and Rochambeau's soldiers, 14–24 Sept., to Williamsburg, from where they approached Yorktown, 28 Sept. The allies pounded British interior positions with artillery, 9 Oct., and took 2 key redoubts, 14 Oct. Cornwallis asked for terms, 17 Oct.; capitulated, 18 Oct.; and had his 8,000 men lay down their arms, 19 Oct. Washington renewed the siege of New York, to which Clinton, after arriving belatedly off Chesapeake Bay, 24 Oct., with 7,000 reinforcements, had returned.

1782

FALL OF LORD NORTH'S MINISTRY. 20 Mar. Frustrated by British defeats, the Commons rejected further prosecution of the American war, 27 Feb., and authorized negotiations with the rebels, 5 Mar. Rockingham replaced North, 22 Mar., and Sir Guy Carleton became British commander in New York, 4 Apr., to which all British forces were withdrawn.

EARLY PEACE NEGOTIATIONS. 12 Apr.–27 Sept. Richard Oswald met Franklin in Paris, where negotiations began, 27 Sept., after Shelburne, who had replaced the deceased Rockingham on 1 July, virtually authorized recognition of American independence, 19 Sept. Jay arrived from Spain, 23 June, and Adams from the Netherlands, 26 Oct., having obtained Dutch recognition of the U.S., 19 Apr. Laurens, released from prison in England, took little part in the discussions, and Jefferson declined serving.

PRELIMINARY ARTICLES OF PEACE. Deciding not to keep the French, whom they distrusted, fully informed, Jay, Adams, and Franklin presented, 5 Nov., to Henry Strachey and Oswald suggestions which became the basis of the preliminary articles, 30 Nov., and of the definitive peace treaty, 3 Sept., 1783. The stipulations included (1) recognition of U.S. independence; (2) generous American boundaries, including the Mississippi in the west; (3) a guarantee of the right of Americans to fish off Newfoundland and Nova Scotia and of their privilege to dry fish in certain areas; (4) validity of debts owed among nationals of the two countries; (5) exhortation of the states to restore Loyalist property and rights; and (6) withdrawal of British troops from America.

1783

PEACE. Britain signed preliminary treaties with France and Spain, 20 Jan., and declared an armistice, 4 Feb.

TREATY OF PARIS. The Preliminary Articles of Peace were ratified by Congress on 15 Apr., and the definitive Treaty of Paris, 3 Sept., on 14 Jan., 1784.

DEPARTURE OF LOYALISTS. Nearly 100,000 harassed Tories fled the American Revolution. Numerous states disfranchised, removed from office, and even exiled those who would not repudiate George III. By 1782 all the states, complying with a congressional recommendation, 27 Nov., 1777, had confiscated Loyalist property, prompting the British to grant £3,292,452 in compensation by 1790.

RESULTS OF THE REVOLUTION. A vast, independent republic was established. Democracy and liberty were promoted directly or indirectly by the overthrow of the royal and proprietary ruling classes, by property confiscation, by the abolition of primogeniture and entail,

and by the disestablishment of the Anglican Church where tax-supported. Massachusetts, New Hampshire, Pennsylvania, Connecticut, and Rhode Island ended slavery, 1780–84, and 11 states prohibited or heavily taxed the slave trade. (Cont. p. 202.)

THE FRENCH REVOLUTION

In theory, mid-18th-cent. France was an absolute monarchy. All laws emanated from the king, and the powerful royal intendants administered the provinces. France was the richest and most populous country in Europe. Her population (80% rural) increased from 20 to 25 m. during the 18th cent., which also saw an unprecedented increase in French commerce and industry.

In spite of France's riches, her government was unable to mobilize sufficient resources either to carry out a successful foreign policy or to solve problems of finance. Governmental action was impeded by competition between overlapping ecclesiastical, administrative, and fiscal agencies. Except for a free-trade area in the French heartland, trade was hampered by innumerable tolls. Government revenues were inadequate, due to an inefficient tax-farming system and to exemptions from taxation won in earlier times by the nobility, the church, and various regions and municipalities. The burden of taxation fell mainly on those least able to pay. Moreover, the government's efforts to abolish privilege were usually thwarted by the 13 *parlements* (royal law courts). The judges of the *parlements* bought their offices, and considered themselves guardians of privilege and of the French "constitution." They claimed the right to veto royal legislation, and with popular support successfully nullified attempts to tax privileged groups.

The second half of the 18th cent. was also marked by the emergence of the *philosophes,* of whom the most important were Voltaire (1694–1778), Jean-Jacques Rousseau (1712–78), and Denis Diderot (1713–84). These and other *philosophes* believed in the primacy of reason, and demanded that the state be just, humane, and rationally organized. They advocated the abolition of privilege and the elimination of clerical influence in government. Their influence was widespread and helped to undermine the position of the privileged orders.

1763

TREATY OF PARIS. The weakness of the French government was demonstrated by the Seven Years' War, 1756–63. In Germany, French armies were stalemated by those of petty princelings, while England (a third the size of France in population) seized practically all the French colonies. By the Treaty of Paris, 10 Feb., 1763, France lost to Great Britain Canada, most of her Indian possessions, and 4 West Indian islands. She earlier had had to cede Louisiana to Spain, 3 Nov., 1762.

1764–70

MINISTRY OF CHOISEUL. The Duc de Choiseul (1719–85) had become secretary of state for foreign affairs in Dec. 1758, and later took over the War and Navy ministries as well. He built France up again after the disasters of the Seven Years' War, and reinvigorated the French army and navy. He failed, however, to effect any financial reforms. He fell, Dec. 1770, when Louis XV (ruled 1715–74) vetoed his policy of defending Spanish claims to the Falkland Islands against those of Britain.

1771–74

MAUPEOU'S REFORMS. René Nicolas de Maupeou (1714–92), who became keeper of the seals in 1763 and chancellor in 1768, and Abbé Joseph Marie Terray (1715–78), *contrôleur-général* from 1769 to 1774, believed that the French state could be rejuvenated only by eliminating the *parlements,* which had previously obstructed all reforms. On their advice, Jan. 1771, Louis XV abolished the *parlements* and established new courts, whose justices he himself nominated and could dismiss. The new system functioned successfully up to the death of Louis, 10 May, 1774. Freed from the obstructionism of the *parlements,* Terray was able to invalidate many tax exemptions and privileges.

1774–77

MINISTRY OF TURGOT. Louis XVI (ruled 1774–92) recalled the *parlements* and replaced Terray with Anne Robert Jacques Turgot (1727–81). Turgot cut back pensions and government expenditure, improved the postal services, and allowed limited freedom in the grain trade. In Jan. 1776 he promulgated the Six Edicts, which abolished the guilds and substituted a general tax on land (to finance road building) for the *corvée* (which drafted peasants for work on the roads). Court intrigue and the opposition of the *parlements* caused his fall, May 1776.

1778–83

AMERICAN WAR OF INDEPENDENCE. France joined the American colonists in their struggle for independence from Britain early in 1778. After the British were defeated in North America, peace was made at Versailles, 3 Sept., 1783, France receiving St. Lucia and Tobago in the West Indies and Sénégal and Gorée Island in West Africa.

1783–88

MINISTRY OF CALONNE. The expenses of the American war further weakened French state finances. Charles Alexandre de Calonne (1734–1802), *contrôleur-général* from 1783 to 1787, tried to save the government from bankruptcy by borrowing. When this failed, he proposed a general land tax. In an attempt to bypass the *parlements,* he convoked an Assembly of Notables, Feb. 1787, hoping that this body would approve his proposal. The Assembly, however, came out against a land tax, and Calonne was dismissed, 8 Apr.

MINISTRY OF BRIENNE. Under pressure from the queen, Marie Antoinette (1755–93), Louis XVI then appointed Loménie de Brienne *contrôleur-général* and *premier ministre,* May 1787. Brienne submitted new tax proposals to the Parlement of Paris, which rejected them. Soon the provincial *parlements* joined in harassing the government, and the tax-collecting system began to break down. The keeper of the seals, Lamoignon, decided to solve the crisis with Maupeou's methods. On 8 May, 1788, he suspended the *parlements* and established new law courts.

The church, whose senior offices were staffed wholly by nobles, and the nobility protested. The provincial *parlements* organized popular uprisings against royal authority. On 8 Aug., Louis capitulated to what had become a nation-wide revolt of the privileged orders by recalling the *parlements* and granting their chief demand: the convocation of the Estates-General by 1 May, 1789. On 25 Aug., 1788, Jacques Necker (1732–1804), a Genevan banker who had directed the finances of the French government from 1776 to 1781, was reappointed minister of state.

BALANCE OF POWER IN THE ESTATES-GENERAL. The Estates-General had not met since 1614–15. On that occasion the three estates (clergy, nobility, and commons) had met separately, and no bill could become law unless all three ratified it. The Parlement of Paris declared, 25 Sept., 1788, that the Estates-General should function as they had in the 17th cent. It soon became clear to the urban middle classes, who had previously supported the *parlements* as champions of the rights of the people (or of their own rights), that the *parlements* were willing to act only in defense of aristocratic privilege. The middle classes therefore demanded double representation and voting by head, not by order. If granted, this would have allowed the commons (98% of the population) to hold half the seats in a unicameral legislature. After several provincial riots and a deluge of pamphlets, Necker and the royal council granted, 27 Dec., double representation for the Third Estate, but not voting by head.

POPULAR UNREST. Political crisis coincided with economic crisis. A bad harvest in 1788 sent bread prices up, and widespread suffering was caused. Moreover, from 1787 onward, industry had slumped, due in part to the import of cheap British goods following a lowering of French tariffs in accordance with the Anglo-French Treaty of 1786. In Apr. and May 1789, popular uprisings, provoked by countless grievances both immediate and long-standing, broke out all over France.

1789

MEETING OF THE ESTATES-GENERAL. The Estates-General met at Versailles, 5 May. The clergy and nobility had c. 300 representatives and the commons 600, 65% of whom were lawyers and minor officials. Throughout May, debate centered on whether the Estates-General should vote by head (as advocated by the Third Estate) or by order (as demanded by clergy, nobility, and court). On 10 June, the Third Estate declared that all estates should meet together, and invited the other 2 orders to join it. By 15 June, 12 priests had done so.

NATIONAL ASSEMBLY. On 17 June, the Third Estate renamed itself the National Assembly as an expression of its national rather than class representation. It immediately claimed control over taxation and the right to recast the constitution. Louis XVI retaliated on 20 June by locking the representatives out of the assembly hall. They met in a nearby tennis court, where they swore not to dissolve before writing a constitution (the "Tennis Court Oath"). By 25 June a majority of the clergy (two-thirds of the clerical representatives were priests of humble origin who sympathized with the Third Estate) and 47 nobles had joined the Third Estate. Finally, 27 June, the threat of an uprising in Paris forced the king to order the remaining nobles and churchmen to join the Third Estate.

PARIS COMMUNE AND NATIONAL GUARD. Paris "electors" joined the existing government of that city to form the Commune, 13 July, with Jean Sylvain Bailly (1736–93) as mayor. Marie Joseph, Marquis de Lafayette (1757–1834) became commander of a newly organized militia, later, 10 Aug., sanctioned on a national scale as the National Guard. This "municipal revolution" occurred in similar fashion in all French cities.

STORMING OF THE BASTILLE. The presence of troops around Paris and the dismissal of the popular minister, Necker, 11 July, led to a general insurrection. The Bastille, an arms depot as well as a prison, was attacked in the search for arms, 14 July, and the prisoners inside were freed. Louis withdrew his troops, recalled Necker, and acknowledged the revolutionary tricolor. Some nobles began to emigrate.

THE GREAT FEAR. The rural insurrection of Apr. and May continued sporadically throughout June and July and was intensified by a nation-wide panic in late July and early Aug., the "Great Fear" of imaginary brigands in the service of an aristocratic conspiracy. By this time most peasants were refusing to pay taxes, dues, or tithes. In some regions they attacked châteaux and burned manorial records.

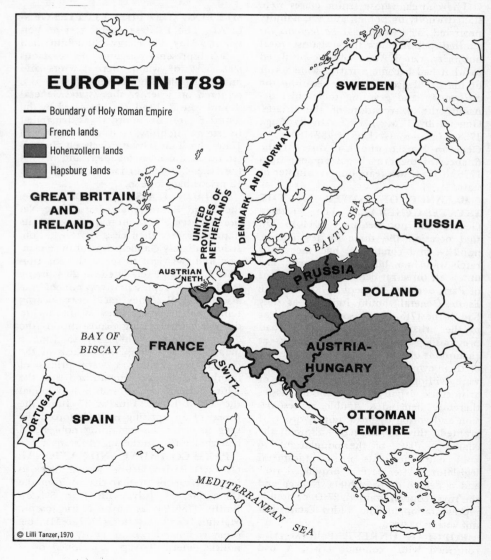

EUROPE IN 1789

— Boundary of Holy Roman Empire

French lands

Hohenzollern lands

Hapsburg lands

GREAT BRITAIN AND IRELAND

SWEDEN

DENMARK AND NORWAY

UNITED PROVINCES OF NETHERLANDS

AUSTRIAN NETH.

BALTIC SEA

RUSSIA

PRUSSIA

POLAND

BAY OF BISCAY

FRANCE

SWITZ.

AUSTRIA-HUNGARY

PORTUGAL

SPAIN

OTTOMAN EMPIRE

MEDITERRANEAN SEA

© Lilli Tanzer, 1970

NIGHT OF 4 AUG. On a single dramatic evening, 4 Aug., the Assembly abolished most feudal privileges, although this legislation was modified later, 5–11 Aug. In sum, the Assembly decreed legal and fiscal equality, redemption of seigneurial dues for an indemnity, abolition of labor services and personal dues without compensation, and abolition of tithes and corporate, municipal, and provincial privileges.

DECLARATION OF THE RIGHTS OF MAN. Prior to drafting a constitution, the National Assembly drew up a statement of principle, 26 Aug. It declared as "natural rights" the right to liberty, property, and security, freedom of opinion and the press, and religious toleration, and declared that sovereignty resided in the nation. On 10 Sept. the Assembly decided on a unicameral legislature with a suspensive veto for the king, by which he could delay a measure for 2 successive legislatures. He could not declare war or make treaties without the Assembly's consent.

MARCH ON VERSAILLES. The refusal of the king to sanction the Assembly's decrees, the high price of bread, and the news that royal troops had arrived in Versailles provoked a mass march led by women on Versailles, 5–6 Oct. They broke into the palace and forced the king to sanction the Assembly's legislation, provide grain, and move to Paris. 200 members of the National Assembly resigned; the rest followed the king to Paris.

CONFISCATION OF CHURCH LANDS. To meet the financial crisis the Assembly nationalized all church property, 2 Nov., and used it as security for *assignats,* bonds bearing interest at 5% and redeemable for land.

REORGANIZATION OF LOCAL GOVERNMENT. A decree of 14 Dec. granted communes the right to elect municipal officials. The former provinces were replaced by 83 departments (named on 26 Feb. of the following year) and divided into districts. Each district and department was to have an elective assembly and an elective "directory." A dis-

tinction, based on tax payments, between "active" and "passive" citizens restricted the franchise for local elections to about 4 m. out of 6 m. male French adults. There were higher property qualifications for electors to the Legislative Assembly.

1790

CIVIL CONSTITUTION OF THE CLERGY. All monastic institutions except those dedicated to education and charity were dissolved, 13 Feb. The state assumed the debts of the church, and undertook to maintain its function and pay clerical salaries. Many church, as well as royal, lands were confiscated and nationalized. On 14 May the Assembly decreed the auction of nationalized lands in large blocks, which benefited the wealthy bourgeois and peasants, thus securing their loyalty to the revolution. Agrarian unrest continued among large numbers of small peasants and day laborers. On 12 July, dioceses were made coterminous with departments and subordinate to 10 metropolitan areas, headed by archbishops who were to assume the functions of the Holy See in the matter of confirming bishops. All clerics having official functions were to be elected. The bishops and many of the lower clergy opposed these decrees and announced that their approval of them would be contingent on that of the pope. On 27 Nov. the Assembly imposed an oath to uphold the Civil Constitution of the Clergy with the object of bringing recalcitrant clerics into line. All except 7 bishops and half the lower clergy refused to swear this oath.

1791

PAPAL BULL "CARITAS." Confirming an earlier pronouncement, 10 Mar., Pope Pius VI condemned the principles of the revolution and the Constitution of the Clergy by the bull *Caritas,* 13 Apr. To reduce religious discord, however, the Assembly permitted, 7 May, nonjuring priests to conduct services. On 24 May the papal nuncio left France.

THE FLIGHT TO VARENNES. Louis XVI decided on counterrevolution to restore his power and halt the Assembly's attack on the church. He planned to flee France, hoping to enlist the aid of his brother-in-law, the Emperor Leopold II of Austria. He reached Varennes (about 40 miles from the border of the Austrian Netherlands) before being arrested and brought back to Paris, 25 June. There he was suspended, rather than deposed, to prevent foreign intervention; the royal family became virtual prisoners in the Tuileries.

DECLARATION OF PILLNITZ. Leopold II and Frederick William II of Prussia declared their willingness to protect Louis, provided all other European sovereigns agreed, 27 Aug. It was known that Britain would not join in any guarantee of this kind, so the agreement was a dead letter. Both monarchs were hoping to satisfy the demands for intervention being made on them by French émigrés in their lands. The Declaration of Pillnitz aroused public opinion in France against both Austria and Prussia.

CONSTITUTION OF 1791. The Assembly incorporated the legislative decrees of 1789–91 as a constitution, 3 Sept., which the king accepted, 14 Sept. The Civil Constitution of the Clergy was detached from this constitution so that it could be amended (as the constitution could not) and so that nonjuring priests could swear allegiance to the new state. On 30 Sept., after disqualifying themselves in respect of the coming elections to the Legislative Assembly, the members of the National Constituent Assembly voted to dissolve.

CONVENING OF THE LEGISLATIVE ASSEMBLY. The seating arrangements in the Legislative Assembly, convened 1 Oct., gave rise to the custom of relating political opinions to location (Right, Left, Center). Of the 745 deputies elected, 264 belonged to the Feuillants, a moderate political club; they joined the Royalists on the Right side of the Chamber. Led by Bailly and Lafayette, they hoped to establish a 2nd chamber, abolish the Civil Constitution of the Clergy,

reconcile the émigrés to the regime, and avoid war with Austria; they kept close contact with the court. The highest seats on the Left (later known as the "Mountain") were occupied by members of the radical Jacobin Club. These were divided into the supporters of Jacques Pierre Brissot (1754–93) and Pierre Victurnien Vergniaud (1753–93), who advocated war with Austria, and those of Maximilien Robespierre (1758–94), who recommended consolidating the Revolution before engaging foreign powers. The unorganized Center or "Plain" tended to follow the Feuillants on domestic issues and the Brissotins or Girondists on foreign policy.

1792

OUTBREAK OF WAR. Most émigrés had fled to the Rhineland, where they vociferously demanded Austrian and Prussian intervention designed to restore the old order and Louis's powers. French relations with Austria deteriorated throughout Jan., and by 7 Feb. Leopold II had decided that war was probable and made a defensive alliance with Prussia. On 1 Mar., Leopold died, and his more bellicose son, Francis II, ascended the throne. In France a Brissotin ministry was formed, headed by Jean Marie Roland (1734–93) and Charles François Dumouriez (1739–1823). On 20 Apr. the Assembly declared war on Austria, but poor preparation and discipline and a lack of leadership (half the officers had emigrated) turned the first encounter, 29 Apr., into a French defeat. At home the reaction was to tighten security. Two decrees, 27 and 29 May, ordered the deportation of refractory priests denounced by at least 20 "active" citizens and the dismissal of the King's Guard. On 13 June, Louis dismissed the Roland ministry. This angered the Girondins, who, 20 June, incited a crowd to invade the Tuileries.

With the 1st allied entry into France, 11 July, the Assembly proclaimed "the fatherland in danger" and called up all able-bodied Frenchmen for military service. Defeat in war and high bread prices had increased radical feeling in Paris. "Passive" citizens were admitted to the sectional assemblies of the 48 electoral and administrative districts of the capital, and the Assembly, 25 July, permitted them to meet daily. On 30 July, "passive" citizens were allowed into the National Guard.

BRUNSWICK MANIFESTO. On 27 July the Duke of Brunswick, commander in chief of the Austro-Prussian forces, threatened Paris with destruction should harm come to the royal family. This action inflamed French public opinion still further. Delegates from the Parisian sections overthrew the municipal government, 9 Aug., and established a more powerful Commune as a rival authority to the Legislative Assembly.

STORMING OF THE TUILERIES. On 10 Aug. a radical crowd invaded the royal palace and killed the Swiss Guards. This marked the beginning of the "2nd French Revolution." The Assembly suspended the king and established a provisional executive council of 6 ministers, headed by Georges Jacques Danton (1759–94). It also summoned a National Convention, to be elected by universal manhood suffrage.

SEPTEMBER MASSACRES. In Paris hysteria mounted as Lafayette defected to the Austrians, 19 Aug.; the frontier fortress of Longwy fell, 23 Aug.; and Verdun capitulated, 2 Sept. The Paris crowd got wind of an imaginary prison plot, attacked the prisons, and slaughtered 1,200 inmates, only 25% of whom were political prisoners. A French victory at Valmy, 20 Sept., halted the allied invasion, and the panic in Paris abated.

CONVENING OF THE NATIONAL CONVENTION. The National Convention met, 20 Sept. The Girondins, led by Roland, had a majority and controlled the ministry. The more radical Mountain, led by Danton and Robespierre, represented the Jacobin Club and drew support from the Parisian sans-culottes (artisans and small tradesmen), so called because they wore long trousers instead of the knee breeches of an aristocrat.

PROCLAMATION OF THE REPUBLIC. On 21 Sept. the Convention abolished the monarchy, and proclaimed a French republic on the 22nd.

FRENCH VICTORIES. In Sept. and Nov. the war began to go better for France. French armies overran Savoy, 22 Sept., and Nice, 29 Sept. General Custine invaded the Rhineland, taking Speyer, 30 Sept., Mainz, 21 Oct., and Frankfurt. Kellermann recaptured Verdun, 8 Oct., and Longwy, 22 Oct., while the Austrians gave up their siege of Lille, 8 Oct. Dumouriez defeated the Austrians at Jemappes, 6 Nov., and occupied all of the Austrian Netherlands. On 27 Nov., at its own request, Savoy was annexed to France.

1793

EXECUTION OF THE KING. The Convention tried Louis XVI, from 11 Dec., 1792, to 14 Jan., 1793, for treason for summoning the aid of France's enemies. It unanimously adjudged him guilty and by a vote of 361–321 sentenced him to death. He was executed, 21 Jan.

WAR DECLARED ON BRITAIN AND THE NETHERLANDS. Britain and the Netherlands had been affronted by France's opening of the Scheldt Estuary to international trade, 16 Nov., 1792, in violation of the Treaty of Westphalia. Britain mobilized, and the Convention declared war on her and on her Dutch ally, thus beginning the War of the 1st Coalition, 1 Feb., 1793–17 Oct., 1797.

FRENCH ANNEXATIONS. In Jan. France annexed Nice, and in Mar. Belgium, the Rhineland, and the Bishopric of Basel.

FRENCH REVERSES. The allies defeated Dumouriez at Maastricht, 1 Mar.; Neerwinden, 18 Mar.; and Louvain, 21 Mar. After failing to persuade his troops to march on Paris and install a constitutional monarchy there, he defected to the Austrians, 5 Apr. The allies also defeated Custine near Mainz, 14 Apr. On 7 Mar. France declared war on Spain, which had been mobilizing. Also in Mar. a counter-revolutionary rebellion began in the Vendée in western France, provoked by the government's decision to call up 300,000 men for the army.

IMPOSITION OF STRICTER GOVERNMENT CONTROLS. On 9 Mar., 80 members of the Convention were endowed with full powers and sent to the provinces to check laxities in administration. On 9 Apr., others were dispatched to the armies to enforce discipline. A Revolutionary Tribunal, a special court which had operated during the first crisis between 17 Aug. and 19 Nov., 1792, was reinstituted, 10 Mar. On 28 Mar., the Convention declared *émigrés* "civilly dead," and confiscated their property. The Convention also imposed the death penalty on anyone advocating in print the dissolution of the Convention or the restoration of the monarchy. On 6 Apr., the executive functions of the ineffectual Committee of General Defense, created 1 Jan., 1793, were transferred to a new Committee of Public Safety, which consisted of 9 (later 12) members, elected monthly. The Committee of Public Safety deliberated in secret and at first had limited powers. On 4 May, because of pressure from the Paris sections and from the Commune, the Convention established price controls for grain, based on average market values. On 21 May, the Convention set up a Commission of 12, composed mostly of Girondins, to investigate sectional disorders and sans-culotte agitation, and on 24 May this commission arrested Jacques René Hébert (1755–94), a popular radical journalist, and 3 other sans-culottes. A large crowd of sans-culottes forced the Convention, 31 May, to abolish the Commission of 12, and 2 days later secured the arrest of 31 Girondin deputies, thus leaving the "Montagnards" in control of the Convention.

FEDERALIST REVOLTS. A number of Girondin deputies fled to the provinces, where they encouraged uprisings against the dominance of Paris. By mid-June, 60 departments, especially those in the south and west, were in revolt. The Convention tried to win over the poorer peasants by decreeing, 3–10 July, the sale and rental of *émigré* lands in small lots and the optional division of common fields. By the end of the year, government forces were in control of the provinces.

CONSTITUTION OF 1793. To ease radical pressure the Jacobins wrote a more democratic constitution, providing for popular referenda of legislation, direct election of the national assembly, and an executive council of 24. Although ratified by 2 m. voters, 24 June, and promulgated, 10 Aug., it was never put into effect.

REORGANIZATION OF THE COMMITTEE OF PUBLIC SAFETY. Absorbing the functions of both the Convention and the Commune, the Committee of Public Safety evolved into a centralized dictatorship, although deputies on mission and local revolutionary committees remained relatively independent. The committee was the first efficient executive of revolutionary France. It suppressed domestic opposition and secured military victory. Danton ceased to be a member, 10 July, and Robespierre became one, 28 July.

ASSASSINATION OF MARAT. 13 July. The murder of Jean Paul Marat (1743–93), a radical publicist, aroused fears of a Girondin resurgence among the Hébertistes and Enragés, who demanded adoption of Marat's programs. To placate them, the government imposed the death penalty on hoarders of food, 26 July, established public granaries, and allocated 100 m. livres for grain purchase, 9 Aug.

LEVÉE EN MASSE. Condé, Mainz, and Valenciennes fell to the allies, 10, 23, 28 July. Troops had to be diverted to the Vendée, 1 Aug., and to Lyons, 4 Aug., to subdue internal revolt, while Toulon fell to the British, 29 Aug.

To meet a growing foreign and internal threat, the government decreed the conscription of single men between 18 and 25, and organized married men, women, and children for the production and transportation of matériel. The victories of the following year were due to the strength and high morale of a new mass army of nearly 1 m. men.

THE TERROR. On 5 Sept. the sansculottes invaded the Convention and demanded further measures to ward off famine and tighter security to prevent counterrevolution. The Revolutionary Tribunal, in consequence, was enlarged and reorganized to expedite trials. Thus began the Terror, which lasted until July 1794 and claimed 40,000 victims, mostly royalist and federalist rebels. On 17 Sept. the Convention passed a law defining suspects very broadly and making them liable to arrest by local Watch Committees.

REPUBLICAN CALENDAR. The Gregorian Calendar was replaced, 6 Oct., by a secular calendar which divided the months into 3 *décades* of 10 days each. The first year of the republic was dated from 22 Sept., 1792. The months were renamed after the seasons, 24 Oct., and the days according to their order in the *décade*.

THE REVOLUTIONARY GOVERN-MENT. The Convention suspended the Constitution of 1793, and declared, 10 Oct., that the provisional government headed by the Committee of Public Safety would be "revolutionary until peace."

EXECUTION OF THE GIRONDINS. Girondin opposition was broken by the execution of 21 deputies and the arrest of 73, 31 Oct.

CAPITULATION OF LYONS. After a 2-month siege Lyons surrendered to the Republican army, 9 Oct. By Mar. 1794, 1,667 of the Lyons rebels had been executed.

DECHRISTIANIZATION. The religious Terror was sponsored by the Hébertistes rather than by the government. The archbishop of Paris was forced to resign, 7 Nov., and the Cathedral of Notre Dame was converted into a Temple of Reason. A "Festival of Reason" was held there on 10 Nov. On 23 Nov. the Commune closed the churches of Paris.

LAW OF 14 FRIMAIRE, YEAR II. On 4 Dec. the Committee of Public Safety assumed power to appoint and dismiss all local officials, and set up administrative machinery to put France under a revolutionary dictatorship.

FRENCH VICTORIES. With victories at Hondschoote, 8 Sept., and Wattignies, 16 Oct., the French halted the allied

invasion. They recaptured Toulon from the British, 19 Dec., and at the end of that month re-entered Germany.

1794

ELIMINATION OF GOVERNMENT OPPOSITION. Concerned about the effect of dechristianization on the loyalty of devout Catholics, Robespierre had Hébert and 17 others arrested, 14 Mar., and executed, 25 Mar., on charges of complicity in a foreign plot. Robespierre then turned on Danton, who had supported him against Hébert. Charged with subversion and financial fraud, Danton and his followers were arrested, 30 Mar., and guillotined, 5 Apr.

CIVIC RELIGION. On 7 May the Convention proclaimed a kind of state deism, recognizing a Supreme Being and the immortality of the soul. Previously, 26 Mar., the Convention had suspended payment of clerical salaries. The new religion was inaugurated, 8 June, by a Festival of the Supreme Being with Robespierre conducting the services, but the new cult never won a mass following.

LAW OF 22 PRAIRIAL. This law destroyed judicial guarantees for accused persons by refusing the appointment of counsel for defendants, and allowing only two judgments, acquittal or death, 10 June. In Paris during June and July there were more executions than during the earlier Terror (Sept. 1793–July 1794). By the new law, deputies could be tried without prior impeachment by the legislature. This frightened some members of the Convention, who began to plot against Robespierre.

9 THERMIDOR. Robespierre's speech of 26 July to the Convention, threatening proscription of unnamed suspects, galvanized the deputies into self-defense. On the next day, 9 Thermidor, they impeached him and his 2 main supporters on the Committee of Public Safety, Saint-Just and Couthon. An abortive insurrection of the Commune to save Robespierre failed. On 28 July he was guillotined with 21 of his supporters, and 86 other adherents met the same fate during the next 3 days.

THERMIDORIAN REACTION. Between the fall of Robespierre and the dissolution of the Convention (26 Oct., 1795) occurred the "Thermidorian Reaction." The Convention persecuted the Jacobins and dismantled the machinery of the Terror. It relaxed economic controls; permitted the revival of Catholic worship; repealed the law of 22 Prairial, 28 July; released many prisoners; and abolished the Paris Commune, 27 July. On 24 Aug. it resumed control over internal affairs from the Committee of Public Safety, but left the committee with power over war and foreign affairs. On 12 Nov. the Jacobin Club in Paris was closed.

PROGRESS OF THE WAR. French victories during the year (the invasion of Catalonia in May and the reconquest of Belgium in July) had helped to make the dictatorship of Robespierre and the Committee of Public Safety seem unnecessary. Successes continued on all fronts. The French captured Fuenterrabia and San Sebastián in Spain, Aug.; took Mannheim, Dec.; and invaded the Netherlands.

1795

TREATY OF LA JAUNAIE. By agreeing to the Treaty of La Jaunaie, 17 Feb., the Convention tried to pacify the Vendée, where bloody guerrilla warfare had succeeded the defeat of a royalist army. The Convention conceded an amnesty for rebels, religious freedom for nonjuring clergy, and indemnities for war damage. These concessions, however, gained only a short truce for the Convention.

FREEDOM OF WORSHIP. Following the unofficial opening of some Catholic churches in Jan., the Convention reaffirmed the separation of church and state (as proclaimed on 18 Sept., 1793) and religious liberty. Ceremonies were to remain private, and the clergy had to swear allegiance to the republic.

UPRISINGS OF GERMINAL. High food prices caused by the severe winter and near famine of 1794–95 and the Convention's trial of former terrorists angered the sans-culottes. On 21 Mar. they demonstrated, demanding "Bread and the Constitution of '93" and "Liberty for the Patriots." On 1 Apr. they invaded the Convention, but were quickly dispersed by the National Guard. The government deported 4 members of the Committee of Public Safety, executed 16 former officials of the Revolutionary Tribunal, and arrested the deputies who had supported the demonstration.

UPRISING OF PRAIRIAL. On 20 May, a crowd invaded the Convention and killed 1 deputy, but were dispersed by the National Guard. The next day an insurrection broke out in the working-class sections of Paris. It was quelled by troops in 2 days, but furnished a pretext for the "White Terror," conducted against the supporters of the "Red Terror" of 1793–94. A military commission condemned 30 insurgents, including 6 Montagnard deputies. Hundreds more were arrested. In the south and west, vigilante groups like the "Companies of Jehu," in collusion with government agents, massacred suspected Jacobins.

REOPENING OF CHURCHES. The Convention permitted unsold confiscated church buildings to be reopened for worship on citizens' petitions, 30 May.

ABOLITION OF THE REVOLUTIONARY TRIBUNAL. After having ordered 326 post-Thermidorian executions, the Revolutionary Tribunal came to an end, 31 May. Henceforth treason was to be tried in ordinary courts.

DEATH OF "LOUIS XVII." After the death of the Dauphin (1785–95) ("Louis XVII") on 8 June, the Comte de Provence (1755–1824), brother of Louis XVI, took the title of Louis XVIII to maintain continuity of the monarchy. On 24 June he issued a manifesto from Verona declaring his intention to restore the old order and punish the revolutionaries. On 12 June the government had dropped the designation "revolutionary," which it had held since 10 Oct., 1793.

CONSTITUTION OF 1795. A new constitution was ratified, 22 Aug. Resembling the constitution of 1791, it restored indirect elections and property qualifications for voting and officeholding. The legislative branch consisted of a Council of 500 to propose legislation and a Council of 250 Elders (who had to be over 40 years of age) to adopt or reject it. The executive consisted of 5 directors, nominated by the 500 and selected by the elders. The Directory appointed ministers, officials, and army officers, and could declare war or conclude peace with the legislature's consent. Annual elections were to be held to renew the councils by one-third and to replace one director. The lack, however, of a mechanism to settle disputes between the two branches of government resulted in frequent coups and ultimate dictatorship.

TWO-THIRDS DECREE. Fearing a royalist or Jacobin electoral victory, the Convention decreed the re-election of its own members to two-thirds of the seats in the new legislature, 30 Aug. This action was ratified by the voters by only a small margin.

VENDÉMIARE UPRISING. Angered by the Two-Thirds Decree and by the rearming of the sans-culottes, a crowd of about 25,000, consisting of monarchists, bourgeois, and members of the National Guard, attacked the Convention, 5 Oct. Government troops, led by Barras and Napoleon Bonaparte (1769–1821), crushed the revolt. Bonaparte was then appointed commander in chief of the "Armée de l'Intérieur." The Convention disarmed the National Guard, halted the White Terror, and adjourned, 26 Oct.

THERMIDORIAN DIPLOMACY. By the Treaty of Basel, 5 Apr., France withdrew from the right bank of the Rhine in exchange for Prussian recognition of French claims to the left bank at a general peace, at which time dispossessed German princes would be compensated elsewhere in the empire. By the Treaty of The Hague, 16 May, France withdrew from the Netherlands and the 2 states concluded an offensive and defensive alliance. Spain withdrew from the war, 22 July, ceding her half of Santo Domingo (in the West Indies) to France.

War continued, however, with Britain. The British fleet landed an expedition of *émigrés* at Quiberon Bay in Brittany, 27 June, where they joined the Vendeans in a revolt which the government quickly suppressed. War also continued with Austria as the French reannexed Belgium, 1 Oct., and Austria retook the Rhineland, Oct. and Nov.

GOVERNMENT OF THE DIRECTORY. During its 4 years of power, 2 Nov., 1795–9 Nov., 1799, the Directory succeeded in creating a measure of order and prosperity out of political and economic chaos. Aiming at moderation, it forestalled coups from the Right and the Left, thus losing the support of both. Weakened, it increasingly had to rely on military support, and ultimately succumbed to Napoleon's dictatorship.

INAUGURATION OF THE FIRST DIRECTORY. The first directors, La Revellière-Lépeaux, Reubell, Letourneur, Barras, and Carnot, inaugurated, 2 Nov., expressed their conservative republicanism in a manifesto, 5 Nov. The elections of 12 Oct. had increased royalist strength in the councils to 158, as against 305 republicans and 228 moderates.

1796

SUPPRESSION OF UPRISINGS. In Mar. General Hoche checked federalist and royalist insurgents in the Vendée, Normandy, and Brittany.

CONSPIRACY OF "EQUALS." A union of former Jacobins and protosocialists, led by François Émile Babeuf (1760–97), engaged in a conspiracy which ended with Babeuf's arrest, 10 May. His followers tried to free him by attacking the military camp at Grenelle, 9–10 Sept., but failed when the soldiers refused to fraternize as expected. Babeuf and Darthé were executed, 17 May, 1797; Buonarroti and others were deported.

FINANCIAL MEASURES. On 19 Feb. the Directory discontinued printing *assignats,* which had fallen to 1% of face value, stabilized them at 3%, and replaced, 18 Mar., about half of these at a rate of 30 to 1 with *mandats territoriaux,* notes redeemable for public land. Within the year this new paper currency had depreciated to 2% of value.

ITALIAN CAMPAIGN. The Directory planned to drive Austria out of the war by an offensive in Italy and in Germany.

French armies failed to advance in Germany, but Napoleon invaded Piedmont and forced its government to hand over 8 fortresses to France and recognize the annexation of Nice and Savoy. On 10 May, Napoleon defeated the Austrians at Lodi, and took Milan 5 days later. He besieged an Austrian army in the fortress of Mantua for 8 months, beating off all Austrian attempts to relieve it. The rest of the Italian states withdrew from the war against France.

WAR WITH BRITAIN. France wrested Corsica from Britain, Oct., but the British continued to maintain a blockade of French ports. As Anglo-French peace talks held at Lille, Nov. and Dec., foundered, Hoche led an expedition, Dec., to aid an Irish uprising, but was kept from landing by a storm.

1797

FINANCIAL MEASURES. The depreciation of the *mandats territoriaux* to the level of *assignats* led to the repudiation of all paper money, 4 Feb. On 30 Sept. the Directory passed the Law of the Consolidated Third, a virtual repudiation of two-thirds of the internal debt.

The March elections for one-third of the legislature resulted in an overwhelming victory for the Right, but the royalists were too disunited to overthrow the Directory. In the Directory, Barthélemy, a constitutional monarchist, replaced Letourneur, 20 May, and the Prince de Talleyrand (1754–1838), a former bishop, became minister of foreign affairs.

PROGRESS OF THE WAR. On 2 Feb. Napoleon took Mantua and advanced on Vienna. Ignoring the Directory's treaty-making prerogatives, he made a preliminary peace with Austria at Leoben, 18 Apr.; the Austrians agreed to cede Belgium and Lombardy, for which Napoleon secretly promised compensation in Venice.

COUP OF 18 FRUCTIDOR. Fearing a monarchist coup, Barras, Reubell, and La Revellière appealed for help to Napoleon. On 4 Sept. Napoleon dispatched General Augereau, who, at the head of the National Guard, forestalled the imminent impeachment of the 3 republican directors by invading the Council of 500 and impeaching 177 of its members. Barthélemy, who was deported, and Carnot, who fled, were replaced by Merlin de Douai and François de Neufchâteau. The new Directory assumed dictatorial powers, suppressing 42 newspapers and imposing press censorship for 1 year. It ordered returned *émigrés* to leave France within 10 days or be executed. Both parliamentary government and the counterrevolutionary threat came to an end.

TREATY OF CAMPO FORMIO. By the terms of this treaty, 17 Oct., Austria ceded Belgium to France and received Istria, Dalmatia, and Venetia. Austria also recognized the French annexation of the left bank of the Rhine, less Cologne.

1798

DECISION TO OCCUPY EGYPT. France remained at war only with Britain. Instead of attempting a direct invasion of the British Isles, Napoleon and Talleyrand decided to wrest Egypt from Turkey, thus cutting Britain's most important route to India.

COUP OF 22 FLORÉAL. In the spring elections, 11 May, of 437 councilors (the normal one-third plus a further 177 to fill vacancies created by the coup of 18 Fructidor), a Jacobin victory gave promise of future conflict between the 2 branches of government. In order to obtain a pliable legislature, the Directory had the outgoing councils annul the election of 106 deputies and return government candidates instead. Teilhard succeeded François de Neufchâteau as director, 15 May. This 2nd violation of the constitution further reduced the popularity of the Directory.

PROGRESS OF THE WAR. On 19 May Napoleon sailed from Toulon with 38,000 men. He took Alexandria, 1 July, defeated the Mamelukes (Mamlūks) in the Battle of the Pyramids, 21 July, and entered Cairo next day. Admiral Horatio Nelson, however, surprised and destroyed the French fleet at Abukir (Aboukir) Bay, thus destroying Napoleon's communications with France.

In Aug. General Humbert led a small expedition to aid the Irish rebels, but Cornwallis captured the French invaders, 8 Sept.

On 9 Sept. Turkey declared war on France and allied herself to Britain and Russia. Czar Paul I feared a French-supported resurrection of Poland and opposed French expansion in the Middle East.

By a decree of 25 Nov. the Directory attempted to tighten its control over the military by re-establishing the office of Commissioners to the Army. This measure, opposed by the generals, was instrumental in turning them against the Directory.

1799

SYRIAN CAMPAIGN. In Feb. Napoleon attempted to prevent a Turkish invasion of Egypt by attacking Syria. After taking Gaza and Jaffa, he began a siege of Acre, 19 Mar. Plague and low supplies and the news that the British fleet was transporting Turkish troops to the Nile forced him to raise the siege, 20 May, and return to Egypt.

CONSCRIPTION LAWS. With the French armies everywhere outnumbered, the Directory passed 2 conscription laws in Apr. and June, designed to increase the number of men under arms by 175,000.

COUP OF 30 PRAIRIAL. In the mid-April elections for the renewal of one-third of the councilors, the Jacobins and democrats triumphed. Sieyès replaced Reubell as director. The new Councils unconstitutionally forced the resignations of Teilhard, La Revellière, and Merlin de Douai, 18 June–30 Prairial, and replaced them with Gohier, Ducos, and Moulin. Many former Jacobins joined the administration. The reconstituted Directory restored freedom of the press, and radical newspapers proliferated, re-establishing the mood of 1793, when military defeat and the threat of invasion had led to demands for tighter internal security against counterrevolution.

LAW OF HOSTAGES. A law of 12 July empowered the government to intern relatives of *émigrés* in certain restless departments, and to deport 4 such hostages if a "patriot" was murdered.

On 6 Aug. the Directory decreed a forced loan, but only a third of the expected sum could be collected.

On 5 Aug. a royalist insurrection broke out in southern France. Government troops subdued it within 2 weeks. In Oct. the Chouannerie again rebelled, but was soon quelled.

Still aiming at moderation, the Directory deported the staffs of 50 royalist and Jacobin newspapers. French victories in the autumn, however, removed the threat of foreign invasion, and Jacobin agitation subsided.

PROGRESS OF THE WAR. The transfer of Austrian troops from Switzerland to the Rhineland left the Russians to face the French by themselves. A Russian army under Korsakov was defeated by Masséna in the 2nd Battle of Zurich, 25–27 Sept. French arms were also successful in the Netherlands, where a British invasion force was defeated, and by the Convention of Alkmaar, 18 Oct., the allies agreed to evacuate the Netherlands. Disappointed by defeat and angered by Austria's desertion in Switzerland, Czar Paul I withdrew from the coalition, 22 Oct.

EGYPTIAN CAMPAIGN. Returning from Syria, Napoleon defeated at Abukir, 25 July, a Turkish army which had just landed in Egypt. Napoleon realized, however, that he was fast becoming a prisoner of his own conquests. He was without a fleet and received reports of rising domestic disorder in France. He left Egypt, 24 Aug., and landed at Fréjus, 9 Oct.

COUP OF 18 BRUMAIRE. Arriving in Paris, 16 Oct., Napoleon joined his brother Lucien, president of the Council of 500, Talleyrand, the Directors Sieyès and Ducos, and Minister of Police Fouché in a plot to overthrow the government. On 9 Nov. (18 Brumaire) the Council of Elders (sitting without many unco-operative deputies who had been invited too late for them to attend) voted to move the legislature to St.-Cloud outside Paris on the pretext of an imminent Jacobin uprising. The Directory resigned, though

Gohier and Moulin had to be detained before they agreed to abdicate their power. At St.-Cloud on the following day troops surrounded the councils and, after a stormy scene between Napoleon and the enraged republican deputies, disbanded them. A rump reassembled that evening to legitimize the end of the Directory and establish a provisional executive consulate consisting of Napoleon, Sieyès, and Ducos. (*Cont. p. 131.*)

THE SISTER REPUBLICS

The so-called sister republics owed their existence to French arms and represented the ideological and military expansion of the French Revolution. Their territories served as buffers protecting the frontiers of France, and their human and material resources were indispensable to the French war effort. Yet each of these republics had indigenous revolutionary origins, and foreign exiles in Paris played an important part in convincing the revolutionary government to overcome its initial reluctance to intervene in the domestic affairs of other countries. Unstable mixtures of native initiative and foreign domination, the sister republics were tied to the fortunes of revolutionary France.

The Netherlands

1760–76

SEVEN YEARS' WAR. During the Seven Years' War, 1756–63, the United Provinces of the Netherlands were torn between taking a neutral position, in exchange for commercial commitments from France, and actively siding with Britain in accordance with long-standing treaty obligations. Neutrality was in the end preferred, and when at the Paris peace conference, 1763, the Netherlands tried to act as mediator, it was treated as inconsequential and virtually ignored during the negotiations. Between 1763 and 1776 the Netherlands retained some prosperity as the financial capital of Europe, and Dutch funds underwrote many British and French commercial enterprises.

1776–84

WAR OF AMERICAN INDEPENDENCE. When the British North American colonies rebelled, Dutch sentiment was with them, for the Dutch saw in the colonists' revolt a similarity to their own in the 16th and 17th cents. against Spain. They also hoped that a colonial victory would open markets that had hitherto been closed to them by the British Navigation Acts. While the Stadholder Willem V (ruled 1751–1806) was deciding what policy to pursue, the Dutch Caribbean islands of Curaçao and St. Eustatius were already being used as centers of illicit trade with the American colonies. Dutch trade, however, was subject to constant British harassment, and in 1778 the States-General authorized war vessels to accompany Dutch merchantmen, thus beginning a policy of armed neutrality. Naval clashes and diplomatic blundering led Britain to declare war on the United Provinces, 20 Dec., 1780, thus ending a century-old friendship. Unable to match the British superiority in men-of-war, the Dutch shipping industry, chief source of the nation's wealth, declined precipitously. At the conclusion of peace, 15 May, 1784, the United Provinces lost several Caribbean and East Indian colonies, and had to cede trade advantages to the British in Asian waters.

1785–91

THE PATRIOT MOVEMENT. In the 1780's proposals for governmental reform stressed the need to expand political privilege within established forms rather than a resort to revolution. Anti-Orangist regents and Patriot burghers joined forces to oppose the stadholder's 2 chief prerogatives: the right to make appointments to town councils and provincial estates and command of the army. In Feb. 1785 the burghers of Utrecht demanded greater participation in the municipal government (conceded in Mar. 1786). The States-General established a "com-

mission of defense" to rival the stadholder's Department of War, May 1785,
and in Sept. of that year the Patriots of
Holland deprived him of his command of
the garrison at The Hague.

**BRITISH AND PRUSSIAN INTER-
VENTION.** Fearing that his prerogatives
would be further whittled away, the
stadholder sought the protection of
Britain, and the British ambassador to
the United Provinces assumed unofficial
direction of a counterrevolution. Frederick William II of Prussia, brother to
Princess Wilhelmina of Orange, also
offered support. When the princess was
detained against her will at Woerden by
Patriot elements, both Britain and
Prussia, 10 July, 1787, demanded redress.
The following Sept., 20,000 troops commanded by the Duke of Brunswick
crossed the frontier and occupied
Utrecht, The Hague, and Amsterdam.
Persecution of Dutch democrats followed,
and 40,000 emigrated. Strengthened by a
defensive alliance with Britain and Prussia, 15 Apr., 1788, and by an Anglo-Prussian alliance, 13 Aug., for the protection
of the Dutch Republic, the Orange regime was able to stifle all opposition.

1792–95

FRENCH INVASIONS. The outbreak of
war in 1792 encouraged Dutch exiles in
France to seek French aid for a revolution
in Holland. A Batavian Legion was
formed, July 1792, and, led by Herman
Willem Daendels, joined Dumouriez'
army in the attack on Belgium. A Batavian Revolutionary Committee was established in Paris, 22 Oct., and made contact
with the reactivated political clubs in the
United Provinces, preserved since 1787 as
reading societies.

On 2 Feb., 1793, the Committee of
Public Safety declared war on the United
Provinces, and French forces invaded the
Netherlands, 16 Feb. After sustaining
some reverses, they were able to enter
Amsterdam, 19 Jan., 1795. As they did so,
the Amsterdam Revolutionary Committee
declared the establishment of a "Batavian
Republic." The stadholder fled to Britain,
where he virtually gave away the Dutch

colonies by ordering, 7 Feb., their governors to admit British ships and troops as
allies.

1796–99

THE BATAVIAN REPUBLIC. The
next few years witnessed a protracted
constitutional crisis. Dutch moderates
preferred a federalist, decentralized form
of government, while radical democrats,
organized in political clubs, pressed for a
unitary, centralized state. The issue was
resolved by French intervention. With
help from Delacroix, the Assembly was
purged and a "rump" devised a new constitution which was ratified, 23 Apr., 1798,
by a popular vote of 153,913 to 11,597.
The constitution was highly democratic
in tone. It provided for universal manhood suffrage and amendment by popular
initiative. The former provinces were replaced by 8 departments of equal population, further subdivided into circles and
communes. Feudal rights were abolished,
as were guilds and other corporations.
The Reformed Church was disestablished. Finance was nationalized, and
debts and revenues consolidated.

Meanwhile, the war continued. When a
British fleet landed in northern Holland,
27 Aug., 1799, a mutiny compelled its
commander to surrender the bulk of the
Dutch navy to the British. An Anglo-
Russian invasion commanded by the
Duke of York was thrown back at Bergen,
19 Sept., and Castricum, 6 Oct., and by
the Convention of Alkmaar, 18 Oct., foreign troops agreed to evacuate the Netherlands. (*Cont. p. 180.*)

The Italian Peninsula

1760–91

THE PAPAL STATES. In 1760 the
Papal States included Umbria, the
Romagna, and the Patrimony of St. Peter,
around Rome. They were ruled directly
by the popes. During the pontificates of
Clement XIII (ruled 1758–69) and Clement XIV (ruled 1769–74), a major
concern of the papacy was the conflict
over the Jesuits, who had in the opinion

of the Catholic monarchs insinuated themselves too deeply into secular political affairs. The popes were also deeply troubled by the ecclesiastical reforms introduced by these monarchs to curtail the power of the church within their realms. Preoccupied with external affairs, the popes had little time to devote to the proper administration of their own domains. Poverty was widespread, there was little commerce and less industry, and agriculture was neglected. Pius VI (ruled 1775–99), however, sponsored the draining of the Pontine Marshes and improvements to the Vatican museums.

THE VENETIAN REPUBLIC. The ruling oligarchy of the Venetian Republic was hostile to the new ideas of the Enlightenment. Would-be constitutional reformers were imprisoned. The mainland provinces were poorly administered, and their residents had fewer political rights than did the inhabitants of the city. The structure of Venetian society became increasingly rigid and corrupt. The army and navy decayed, and the Republic's shipping became the helpless prey of Barbary pirates. Commerce and industry declined. Venice had become no more than a resort for wealthy vacationers from other parts of Europe.

GENOA. Although nominally a republic, Genoa was ruled by an aristocracy as defensive against and hostile to reform as the Venetian oligarchy. Political unrest in Genoa's largest province, Corsica, manifested itself in full-scale rebellion from 1735 until 15 May, 1768, when, no longer able to subdue the dissidents led by Pasquale di Paoli, Genoa ceded the island province to France by treaty.

SAVOY AND SARDINIA. Savoy and Sardinia had had reform-minded monarchs in the earlier decades of the century, Victor Amadeus II and Charles Emmanuel III (ruled 1730–73), who had reduced the privileges of the clergy and nobility, established a single legal code, and promoted agriculture, industry, and education. But their successor, Victor Amadeus III (ruled 1773–96), neither continued the reformation of society nor carried out the reforms instituted by his predecessors. Instead, he spent much of his time and money on the army, which

he attempted to mold after the Prussian fashion.

MODENA, REGGIO, AND MILAN. Modena and Reggio were ruled by Francesco III d'Este (ruled 1737–80) and, in the last half of the century, by Ercole Rinaldo IV (ruled 1780–96). Both rulers were lethargic, avaricious, and oblivious of their duties, though Francesco III introduced a Code of Constitutional Laws for Milan, 1771. Milan was under the Hapsburgs.

TUSCANY. The Grand Duchy of Tuscany was ruled by the Hapsburgs, though not as part of the Holy Roman Empire. During the reigns of Francis of Lorraine, husband of Empress Maria Theresa, who ruled until 1765, and his son Peter Leopold (ruled 1765–90), Tuscany enjoyed many of the same reforms that had been introduced in Austria by Maria Theresa: its administration was reorganized, a census was taken periodically to distribute the burden of taxation more equitably, improvements were made in judicial procedure, the death penalty and the Inquisition were abolished, the universities were reformed, and corporations enjoying special or unjust privileges were suppressed. In 1790, on the death of his brother Joseph II, Peter Leopold became emperor and was succeeded in Tuscany by his son Ferdinand III (ruled 1790–1801), who continued his father's reform programs.

NAPLES. Many reforms were introduced in the Kingdom of Naples by its Bourbon rulers. The reforms of Ferdinand IV (1759–1825) were halted, however, when his wife, Maria Caroline (1752–1814), a daughter of Maria Theresa, insisted on a pro-Austrian policy, and had the king dismiss his progressive but pro-Spanish ministers. Programs of civil and ecclesiastical reform were then virtually abandoned.

1792–1800

THE FRENCH INVASIONS. In Sept. 1792, French armies occupied Savoy and Nice, which were subsequently annexed to France. Sardinia then entered into a military alliance with Austria, May 1794, against France, and continued to fight against France until 15 May, 1796

(Treaty of Paris). Genoa and Venice desired to remain neutral and maintain normal relations with both sides. Tuscany was coerced by Britain into joining the allied coalition, Oct. 1794, but chose to make peace with France, 9 Feb., 1795. Despite the seizure of ecclesiastical property in France and the promulgation of the Civil Constitution of the Clergy, Pius VI at first refused to join the anti-French coalition. He did not do so until 1797. Ferdinand IV of Naples hesitated to join the coalition out of fear of an imminent French naval invasion, but concluded a treaty with Britain, July 1793, and fought against France. In June 1797, Genoa, under French pressure, dissolved its ancient republic and established the Bonaparte-inspired Ligurian Republic. In Oct. of the same year Austria and France signed the Treaty of Campo Formio, which created the Cisalpine Republic out of Modena, Reggio, Bologna, Ferrara, Milan, and part of Venetia. The remainder of Venetia, including the city of Venice, was given to Austria. The French military occupation of Rome forced the creation of the Roman Republic, 15 Feb., 1798. Pius VI was deported to France. After the French fleet had been destroyed by the British Admiral Nelson off Egypt, Naples, which had earlier made peace with France, rejoined the coalition and marched on Rome. But the Neapolitan army was again defeated, and French forces subsequently occupied Naples and created the Parthenopean Republic, 24 Jan., 1799. Some part of the populations of all the new republics remained hostile to French-inspired and -controlled governments, and continued to offer armed resistance to them and to the occupation forces. With help from an irate citizenry, the allies were able to embark on the reconquest. In June 1799, Naples was restored by Admiral Nelson and, by 1800, only Genoa remained under French control. (*Cont. p. 147.*)

THE ENLIGHTENED DESPOTS AND REVOLUTION

The United States, France, and certain areas of Western Europe contiguous to France experienced the direct effects of the Democratic Revolution on their own soil. Other parts of Europe, while not experiencing a violent overturning of their political, legal, and social institutions, nevertheless felt the impact of the 18th-cent. Enlightenment, and bent to winds of change that blew strongest in America and France.

Germany

GERMANY IN 1760. In 1760 the Germanies totaled over 300 independent states and many independent territories. Formally these diverse polities were united in the Holy Roman Empire of the German Nation, whose Diet met at Regensburg in Bavaria and whose emperor, usually a Hapsburg, was elected by 9 electors. Actually, most of the German states pursued independent courses of action, the majority striving to reproduce the grandeur of the French court at Versailles. Some had direct foreign connections: Hanover was joined in personal union with Great Britain and Saxony with Poland. The 2 strongest powers were Brandenburg-Prussia, the chief Protestant state of Germany, and Austria, the chief Catholic state. Brandenburg-Prussia was ruled by the Hohenzollern line, and Austria by the Hapsburgs. The possessions of the Hohenzollerns included territory in the east (East Prussia), in the center (Brandenburg), and in the west (Cleves, etc.) of Germany. Given the title "King in Prussia" in 1701, the Hohenzollerns preferred it to that of Elector of Brandenburg.

1760–86

REIGN OF FREDERICK II (THE GREAT). In 1760 the king of Prussia was Frederick II (1712–86), who had been on the throne since 1740. Regarding himself as the first servant of the state, he strove to increase its strength, devoting his energies to building up the army, reconstructing areas of his dominions devastated by war, sending Germans to colonize Silesia (recognized as Prussian by the Treaty of Hubertusburg, 15 Feb., 1763, which ended the Seven Years' War), and encouraging industry and commerce.

"Enlightened Despot" par excellence, he had a strong propensity for French models, and regarded Voltaire and other *philosophes* as his mentors and colleagues. The bulk of his reforms were enacted during the period 1746–56, but in 1766 he introduced the French tax-farming system, importing French officials to bring it into operation, and continued to seek greater efficiency in government by the creation of specialized departments of administration.

1ST PARTITION OF POLAND. By agreement with Austria and Russia, Prussia absorbed, 1772, West Prussia (the connecting link between East Prussia and the central Hohenzollern lands), but was denied the cities of Danzig and Thorn.

WAR OF THE BAVARIAN SUCCESSION. With the death of the Elector Maximilian Joseph, 30 Dec., 1777, the Bavarian ruling house of Wittelsbach died out, and Bavaria was inherited by Karl-Theodor of Sulzbach, elector palatine (1724–99). Austria claimed a third of the Bavarian inheritance and, with the consent of Karl-Theodor, Jan. 1778, occupied the territories in dispute. The protests of the next heir, Duke Karl of Zweibrücken-Birkenfeld, supported by Prussia, resulted in the War of the Bavarian Succession between Austria and Prussia, 1778–79.

FÜRSTENBUND. The Hapsburg emperor, Joseph II, planned to exchange Belgium for Bavaria. Fearing an increase of Hapsburg power in western Germany, Prussia organized, July 1785, a League of German Princes (initially Prussia, Saxony, and Hanover but later including many smaller states) and frustrated Joseph's intentions.

1786–99

REIGN OF FREDERICK WILLIAM II. Frederick II of Prussia died on 17 Aug., 1786. His successor was Frederick William II (1744–97), who proceeded to spend for his personal benefit the funds Frederick II had left in the Prussian treasury, neglected the army, reduced French influence in the Berlin Academy, and called into question Prussian tolerance in religious matters by opposing freethinkers and seeking the re-establishment of the pure Protestant faith. He died on 16 Nov., 1797, and was succeeded by Frederick William III (1770–1840).

PRUSSIAN INTERVENTION IN THE NETHERLANDS. In 1787 the attempt of the Dutch Patriot Party to oust Stadholder Willem V of Holland provoked Prussian intervention, since the Stadholder's wife was a sister of the Prussian king. In Sept. a Prussian army entered the Netherlands and restored the Stadholder's authority. To secure it, an Anglo-Prussian convention was signed, Oct.; a Prusso-Dutch treaty of alliance, 15 Apr., 1788; and an Anglo-Prussian mutual-defense treaty, 13 Aug., 1788.

CONVENTION OF REICHENBACH. On 31 Jan., 1790, an agreement was signed between Prussia and Turkey by which Prussia promised to enter the Russo-Turkish War on Turkey's side by the spring of the following year. Faced with this threat, Austria (also engaged in war with Turkey) was obliged to make peace and renounce her territorial gains in the Balkans. In return Prussia recognized Austrian possession of Galicia and promised not to aid the rebellious Low Countries against the Hapsburgs.

2ND PARTITION OF POLAND. By the 2nd Partition of Poland, 23 Jan., 1793, Prussia gained the cities of Danzig and Thorn and the territory between Silesia and West Prussia including Poznań (Posen) and Kalisz.

TREATY OF BASEL. Because of the failure of Prussian arms against France, Prussia was obliged to conclude a separate peace at Basel, 5 Apr., 1795. By this treaty Prussia withdrew her opposition to a French annexation of the left bank of the Rhine.

3RD PARTITION OF POLAND. On 24 Oct., 1795, Prussia, Russia, and Austria agreed to liquidate the Polish state. Prussia's share included the territory around Warsaw.

REIGN OF FREDERICK WILLIAM III. On the death of Frederick William II, 16 Nov., 1797, Frederick William III succeeded to the Prussian throne. He had begun taking steps to end the financial abuses characteristic of his father's reign when Prussia, together with other German states, became involved in the wars of Napoleon. (*Cont. p. 185.*)

The Hapsburg Lands

THE HAPSBURG DOMINIONS IN 1760. The area around Vienna, Styria, Carinthia, Carniola, and the Tyrol formed the predominantly German core of an empire whose Hapsburg ruler was German and usually Holy Roman Emperor. At the end of the 17th cent., after a Turkish army had failed to capture Vienna, 1683, and the Austrians had driven the Turks back, the Hapsburgs by the Treaty of Karlowitz, 1699, took possession of Hungary and Transylvania. In 1718 the Hapsburgs extended their rule in the Balkans when Turkey acquiesced in their seizure of parts of Serbia and Wallachia by the Treaty of Passarowitz. In the west the War of the Spanish Succession placed a Bourbon on the Spanish throne, but the Hapsburgs won the Spanish Netherlands (Belgium) and Spanish possessions in Italy (Treaties of Utrecht, 1713, and Rastatt, 1714).

Eighteenth-cent. Hapsburgs were therefore faced with the difficult task of keeping these disparate lands together. For Charles VI (ruled 1711–40) the problem was complicated by the fact that his successor would be a daughter, Maria Theresa (1717–80). His answer, the Pragmatic Sanction (the pledge of most of Europe to acknowledge Maria Theresa's rule), failed to prevent Frederick II of Prussia from seizing Silesia in 1740. Maria Theresa's attempts to recover her lost territory led to the Seven Years' War, 1756–63.

1760–65

CREATION OF THE STAATSRAT. In 1760, a State Council of 6 members was created, and began to function in 1761. It was dominated by Wenzel Anton von Kaunitz (1711–94), who had been given special responsibility for foreign affairs in 1753 and emerged as the most influential of Maria Theresa's advisers.

CREATION OF THE HOFSKANZLEI. In 1761 the Vereinigte Böhmisch-Österreichische Hofskanzlei replaced the Direktorium as the administrative agency for the central German and Czech lands. Other centralizing decrees included (1) the reinstatement of the Hofkammer as the central financial agency, (2) the subjection of the Gubernium (representing the high provincial nobility) to the administration in Vienna, and (3) the appointment of district officials to supervise the execution of the central government's orders.

TREATY OF HUBERTUSBURG. On 15 Feb., 1763, the Treaty of Hubertusburg was signed, ending the Seven Years' War and confirming Frederick of Prussia's seizure of Silesia.

ACCESSION OF JOSEPH II. On 18 Aug., 1765, the Holy Roman Emperor Franz Stefan, husband of Maria Theresa, died. He was succeeded as emperor by his son, Joseph II (1741–90), whom Maria Theresa designated as coruler of her Hapsburg lands.

1766–79

REDUCTION OF PEASANT OBLIGATIONS. The decree *Urbarium,* 1769, gave peasants in Hungary leasehold tenure and freedom to leave the land. Their feudal obligations were reduced and enforcement of their remaining obligations was placed in the hands of officials of the central administration. Burdens on the peasantry were reduced in Austrian Silesia, 1771; Lower Austria, 1772; Bohemia and Moravia, 1775; and Styria, 1778. In 1776 torture as a tool of the law courts was abolished.

CONTROL OF THE CHURCH. In 1767 the church was forbidden to acquire property in the Duchy of Milan, and from 1768 onward clergy could be taxed by the state. In 1769 some monasteries were dissolved and the remainder regulated, 1771.

BAVARIAN SUCCESSION. On 3 Jan., 1778, Karl-Theodor, heir to the Bavarian throne, recognized the Hapsburg claim to a share of his inheritance. The next heir after him, Duke Karl of Zweibrücken-

Birkenfeld, protested, and Prussia readied her army to oppose this proposed increase of Hapsburg power in Germany. After a war without significant fighting, the Hapsburgs received by the Treaty of Teschen, 13 May, 1779, the Innviertel (that part of Bavaria bounded by the rivers Inn, Danube, and Salza).

1780–90

RULE OF JOSEPH II. Maria Theresa died, 29 Nov., 1780. Of strong Catholic faith, she had nevertheless acted against the church when necessary to protect her inheritance. Her son, Joseph, espoused the Enlightenment and bent his attention to the task of strengthening and unifying the diverse territories under his rule.

UNTERTANSPATENT. 1 Sept., 1781. Peasants in the German core lands, Bohemia, and Galicia were permitted to appeal to the Kreisamt, the local office of the central government, in the event of disputes with their lords.

TOLERANZPATENT. 13 Oct., 1781. Full rights of citizenship, including those of buying land and holding government posts, were extended to non-Catholics in the German, Bohemian, and Polish areas. Protestants were permitted to conduct private religious services.

MITIGATION OF SERFDOM. 1 Nov., 1781. Peasants in certain areas were granted the right to marry, learn a craft, and change domicile without the prior permission of their lords. Between 1781 and 1785 these privileges were extended to all Hapsburg lands.

FURTHER RESTRICTIONS ON THE CHURCH. 12 Jan., 1782. The emperor, in an action to be repeated in 1785 and 1786, ordered the closing of more monasteries. His religious program discouraged meditative monasteries but encouraged the pastorate. Monasteries allowed to continue in existence were forbidden to communicate with the headquarters or branches of their orders in other lands. Papal bulls and briefs could not be published in Hapsburg territories without government approval, and all appeals to Rome were forbidden.

PROMOTION OF THE GERMAN LANGUAGE. German was declared the official language of Hungary, 6 Mar., 1784, and all officials there were ordered to master it within 3 years.

PEASANT REVOLT IN TRANSYLVANIA. In Nov. 1784 a peasant revolt broke out in Transylvania. Rumanian peasants slaughtered their lords until halted by imperial troops.

UNIFICATION OF THE LAW. The publication of the *Allgemeines Gesetzbuch* in 1787 provided a unified body of criminal law for the German, Bohemian, and Polish territories of the empire.

REGULATION OF LABOR SERVICES. In 1787 the *Robotpatent* of 1775, which had set for Bohemia a limit on the amount of labor a lord could exact from his peasants, was extended to Hungary and Galicia.

NEW TAX STRUCTURE. 1 Nov., 1789. Peasants were ordered to surrender 30% of their earnings in the proportion of 12.2% to the state and 17.8% to their lords.

DEATH OF JOSEPH II. 20 Feb., 1790. Emperor Joseph II had striven to unify his territorial possessions under 1 central authority, and in so doing had inflamed religious and local opinion. At his death Belgium was in open rebellion, Hungary was restive, Austrian troops were fighting with no great success against the Turks in the Balkans (war declared Feb. 1788), and the French Revolution was threatening the old order in the Hapsburg Empire as elsewhere. He was succeeded by his brother, Leopold II (1747–92).

1790–99

RULE OF LEOPOLD II. Leopold II, ruler of Tuscany since 1765, had used gradualist methods to reform that duchy. He had restricted church ownership of land, forbidden payments to Rome, removed the right of church asylum, abolished the Inquisition, put the clergy under secular law for secular offenses, reduced the number of priests and the power of the nobility, and introduced peasant reforms. He employed similar gradualist methods in his relations with the territories of the empire, adding to the powers of the regional diets and encouraging them to promulgate reforms of their own.

CONVENTION OF REICHENBACH. 27 July, 1790. By this convention Leopold renounced territorial gains made by Austrian troops in the Balkans in exchange for Prussian promises not to aid rebellious Belgium. In Dec., imperial troops entered Belgium.

WAR WITH TURKEY. An Austro-Turkish armistice was concluded on 19 Sept., 1790, and the Treaty of Sistova, 4 Aug., 1791, finalized the war. The Turks received Belgrade in exchange for agreeing to an adjustment of the northern border of Bosnia in Austria's favor.

LEGAL REFORMS. In 1790–91, Leopold ameliorated the harsh criminal code decreed in 1787; secured passage of a habeas corpus law, Feb. 1791; and reduced the independence of the Ministry of Police.

RULE OF THE EMPEROR FRANCIS. On the death of Leopold II, 1 Mar., 1792, his son, Francis (1768–1835), succeeded him, and was elected Holy Roman Emperor, 5 July. In 1784 Francis had been brought to Vienna to study under the supervision of Joseph II, but few of his uncle's ideals or beliefs in "Enlightened Despotism" impressed him. During a period when Austria was involved almost continuously in war for more than 2 decades, he worked to preserve, not transform, the Hapsburg monarchy.

WAR WITH FRANCE. On 27 Aug., 1791, Leopold II and Frederick William II of Prussia had issued the Declaration of Pillnitz in which they stated that the situation of Louis XVI (virtual prisoner of the French Assembly) and the need to restore order and sound government in France were objects of concern for all European monarchs. France responded by declaring war, 20 Apr., 1792. A Hapsburg-Prussian alliance had been signed on 7 Feb. of that year, and the forces of the 2 powers jointly invaded France during the summer.

TREATY OF CAMPO FORMIO. 17 Oct., 1797. After an initial period of success, the Hapsburg armies were defeated by the French in France, Belgium, and northern Italy. By the Treaty of Campo Formio, Austria gained the Venetian Republic, Istria, and Dalmatia, but France assumed control over Belgium and the left bank of the Rhine (at Prussia's expense) and won recognition of her client Cisalpine and Ligurian republics in northern Italy. War between Austria and France (War of the 2nd Coalition) broke out again in 1799. (*Cont. p. 160.*)

Russia

RUSSIA IN 1760. From 1741 to 1762, Russia was ruled by Elizabeth (1709–62). The state she governed was largely the creation of her father, Peter the Great (1672–1725), who had built a new capital at St. Petersburg, symbol of the enforced westernization of the country. Peter, whose own son opposed his reforms, had made the crown nonhereditary, giving each successive ruler the right to choose his heir. In practice, the result had been that the Guards regiments in St. Petersburg became the controllers of the succession.

The leading positions in the administration and the army were filled by the gentry, who under Peter had formed a class open to talent and required to give a lifetime of service to the state. Under Peter's successors, the position of the gentry had been strengthened, nongentry being denied the right to own serfs, 1746, 1758, and the term of compulsory service being reduced to 25 years, 1737.

Beneath the gentry there was a small class of free peasants, but the mass of agricultural workers were serfs. A large number of these were state peasants, who paid a fixed rent to the government and could not be separated from the land they worked. The majority, however, were privately owned, owing their masters either rent or service and almost completely subject to their power. Russian serfs could be sold separately from the land they lived on and there were many household serfs.

In foreign affairs Peter had transformed Russia into a major European power. The policy of the country was determined by its relations with its 3 neighbors, Sweden, Poland, and Turkey. In the north Peter had seized the Baltic coast and part of Finland from Sweden, and it was generally assumed that Russian expansion in that direction would continue. In the center Poland, which held territories to which Russia had historical claims, was a weak country with an elective monarchy and an almost impotent central Diet. In the south the territory of the Ottoman Turks barred Russia from the access she desired to the Black Sea. In the normal state of affairs, these 3 powers were opposed to Austria, and Russia was therefore usually friendly to that state. During the Seven Years' War, 1756–63, Austria and France fought Prussia and Great Britain. Russia entered the war on the Austrian side and inflicted serious defeats on Prussia, occupying East Prussia and raiding Berlin.

1762

RULE OF PETER III. Elizabeth died, 5 Jan., 1762, and was succeeded by her nephew, Peter III (1728–62). Of German birth, Peter seemingly placed greater value on his German duchy of Holstein-Gottorp, which he had inherited from his father, than on his Russian domains. He never accepted Russian ways, and his attempts to alter Orthodox practices to bring the Russian Church closer to Lutheranism created great opposition. On 1 Mar., 1762, he ended compulsory service for gentry. Although welcomed by the gentry, this decree created unrest among the serfs, who expected a 2nd measure abolishing their service to the gentry.

The war with Prussia ended in May 1762. Frederick II of Prussia was saved from the full effects of his defeats by Peter's high regard for him. All territories captured by the Russians were unconditionally restored, and a Russo-Prussian alliance signed. In addition Peter, who as duke of Holstein-Gottorp had claims on the Danish duchy of Schleswig, prepared for war against Denmark.

ACCESSION OF CATHERINE II (THE GREAT). Peter III was killed by government officials and Guards officers who considered him incapable and hostile to Russia's true interests, and his German wife, Catherine (1729–96), was proclaimed empress, 9 July, 1762. Catherine took the throne in her own name and, since she had no claim to it, was dependent throughout her reign on the support of leading elements among the gentry. She ended the threat of war against Denmark, arranging instead for an alliance with that state, and withdrew completely from the Seven Years' War.

1763–74

THE POLISH SUCCESSION. Stanislas Poniatowski was elected king of Poland, 6 Sept., 1764. On the death of the previous king in 1763, Frederick II had agreed to support Poniatowski, who was Catherine's candidate for the throne and her former lover. Russian troops entered the country and forced Poniatowski's election on the Diet, Poland thereby falling under Russian domination.

REIGN OF CATHERINE II. Catherine had been influenced by the works of the French *philosophes* and as empress engaged in correspondence with Voltaire and welcomed Diderot to Russia. For a Legislative Commission she established in Dec. 1766, she prepared a lengthy "Instruction" which showed the influence of the Enlightenment on her, based as it was largely on the works of Montesquieu and Beccaria. She expressed her opposition to torture and capital punishment, favored a division of powers within the government, and stated that all citizens should be subject to the same laws. At the same time, she insisted that the government must be headed by an absolute ruler. In the original draft she had voiced strong feelings against serfdom, but these sections were deleted or much toned down by her advisers.

Serfdom was a problem for Catherine throughout her reign, for though she opposed it and tried to ameliorate its influence by a decree, 1762, the over-all effect of her period of rule was to strengthen and enlarge the institution. She extended serfdom to the Ukraine, made large gifts of crown lands (converting the state peasants on them into privately owned serfs), gave landlords the right to send serfs to Siberia without trial or right of appeal, 1765, and denied serfs the right of petition against wrongs committed by their masters.

LEGISLATIVE COMMISSION OF 1767–68. The Legislative Commission, intended by Catherine to revise and codify Russian law, met from Aug. 1767 to Dec. 1768. It consisted of 564 delegates, 28 appointed and the rest elected by the various classes of the population (gentry, townsmen, state peasants, Cossacks, nationalities), with the exception of the serfs and the clergy. The delegates brought petitions from their constituencies and there was much debate on them, but the large, unwieldy body could not arrive at any conclusions and was finally prorogued.

INTERVENTION IN POLAND. After making Poniatowski king of Poland, Frederick and Catherine had insisted on religious freedom for Protestants and Orthodox Christians in Poland. The Polish Diet resisted this demand until Mar. 1768, when it was forced to give in. The result was an anti-Russian revolt in the country, which forced the government to request Russian aid in suppressing it, May. Although the Russians had superior military force, the pacification of Poland required several years of campaigning.

RUSSO-TURKISH WAR. Fearing Russian expansion, and urged on by their French and Polish allies, the Turks took advantage of the Russian war with Poland to attack southern Russia from the Crimea, Oct. 1768. In 1769–70 the Russians regained the initiative, capturing the Danubian principalities, Moldavia and Wallachia, and pushing the Turks back in the Crimea. At the same time the Russian fleet sailed from the Baltic to the eastern Mediterranean, and destroyed the Turkish fleet in the Bay of Chesme, July 1770.

1ST PARTITION OF POLAND. By the 1st Partition of Poland, 1772, Russia acquired White Russia as far as the Dnieper and Dvina rivers. In Sept. 1773, at Russian insistence, the Polish Diet accepted the partition.

PUGACHEV'S REBELLION. A Don Cossack, Emilian Pugachev, declaring himself to be Peter III, began a revolt among the Ural Cossacks, May 1773. The revolt spread rapidly among the agricultural and industrial serfs of southeastern Russia, who lived in great hardship. At its height it threatened Moscow, and Pugachev established his own court and government and abolished serfdom within the area he controlled. In 1774, however, the government was able to bring greater military force to bear, and in the summer of that year Pugachev's army was scattered and the movement quickly collapsed. Pugachev himself was surrendered by his own forces and executed, Jan. 1775.

TREATY OF KUCHUK KAINARJI. The war with Turkey ended with the signing of the Treaty of Kuchuk Kainarji (Küçük Kaynarca), 16 July, 1774. Russia obtained part of the northern coast of the Black Sea and returned Moldavia and Wallachia to Turkey. The Crimea was made independent and the Russians were given the right to commercial navigation in Turkish waters and the position of protector of Orthodox Christians in Turkey.

1775–96

ADMINISTRATIVE REFORMS. By a decree of 18 Nov., 1775, the huge provinces into which Russia had formerly been divided were replaced by smaller units, numbering 50 by the end of Catherine's reign. They were drawn without reference to historical boundaries. An elaborate bureaucracy was created with a separation of administrative and judicial functions. Power was decentralized and the gentry were allowed a degree of self-government, including the right to elect some officials and deputies to local assemblies.

ANNEXATION OF THE CRIMEA.
The formal annexation of the Crimea, Aug. 1783, followed the effective seizure of the area by troops under Grigori Potemkin (1736–91), another of Catherine's lovers. As governor general and viceroy of southern Russia, he created the port of Sevastopol, 1784, and developed Russian naval power in the Black Sea. Catherine, who had named her grandsons Alexander (1777–1825) and Constantine (1779–1831), dreamed of creating a new Christian empire based on Constantinople and subservient to Russia. To further this goal, an anti-Turkish alliance had been made with Austria, 1781.

CHARTER OF THE NOBILITY.
May 1785. The gentry were given legal status as a class and the right, which no other group had, of presenting mass petitions to the monarch. Members of the gentry could not lose their estates, rank, or lives without trial by their peers, and they were declared exempt from personal taxes, compulsory service, and corporal punishment.

RUSSO-TURKISH WAR. Protesting Russian annexation of the Crimea, a protectorate established by Russia over Georgia, and interference in Moldavia and Wallachia, the Turks imprisoned the Russian envoy and attacked the Crimea, Aug. 1787. They were defeated by Gen. Alexander Suvorov (1729–1800), and the Russians, aided by the Austrians, then took the offensive in the Black Sea area and in the Balkans. The allies made some progress, but their advance was slow, and in 1790, after the death of the Austrian emperor, Joseph II, the Austrians withdrew their forces.

WAR WITH SWEDEN. June 1788–Aug. 1790. Taking advantage of Russian involvement with Turkey, Gustavus III of Sweden attacked Russia through Finland. For a time St. Petersburg was threatened, but the Swedish attack was stopped by a Russian naval victory and the entry of Denmark, a Russian ally, into the war. In 1790, peace was made with no territorial changes.

TREATY OF JASSY. 9 Jan., 1792. The Turkish war ended with Russia obtaining the Black Sea coast between the Bug and Dniester rivers and Turkey recognizing the annexation of the Crimea.

2ND PARTITION OF POLAND. 23 Jan., 1793. By the 2nd Partition of Poland, Russia obtained most of Lithuania and the western Ukraine. In addition the Polish Diet, which had to accept the terms of the partition, Sept. 1793, agreed to Russian control over Polish foreign policy and the Polish army.

3RD PARTITION OF POLAND. Oct. 1795. On 24 Mar., 1794, a revolt broke out in Poland led by Thaddeus Kosciusko (1746–1817). It achieved momentary success, the Russians being forced out of Warsaw and their subsequent siege of that city being broken. Russian forces under Suvorov, however, recaptured the city in Nov. 1794, and the final partition of the country followed. Austria, Prussia, and Russia participated, the latter obtaining the remainder of Lithuania and the Ukraine and the duchy of Courland.

1796–99

REIGN OF PAUL I. Catherine the Great died 17 Nov., 1796, and was succeeded by her son Paul I (1754–1801). She had felt him incapable of ruling and had kept him from positions of power all his life, even though he was her designated heir. Paul, in turn, had opposed all her policies and was determined to reverse them. On coming to power, he released the prisoners of the Polish revolt of 1794, ordered his father, Peter III, disinterred and buried beside Catherine, and imposed Prussian military regulations on the army. Paul was by nature arbitrary and erratic, and those who worked for him were in constant fear of his absolute power.

NEW SUCCESSION LAW. 16 Apr., 1797. At his coronation Paul proclaimed that the Russian throne would henceforth be inherited by promogeniture in the male line.

LIMITATION OF THE SERVICE OF SERFS. 16 Apr., 1797. The emperor also decreed that those serfs owing an obligation of service should not work more than 3 days a week for their masters. In the same year he restricted the rights granted the gentry in 1785, taking away their exemption from corporal punishment, Jan., and the corporate right of petition, May. Like Catherine, however, he continued the expansion of serfdom by large gifts of crown lands and peasants and by extending the institution of serfdom to the new lands in southern Russia.

WAR WITH FRANCE. At first Paul remained aloof from the wars of the French Revolution, but in 1798 he reversed this policy, making treaties with Turkey, Aug., and Britain, Dec., and promising Russian troops to Austria, Oct. A joint Russo-Turkish force captured the Ionian Islands, Sept. 1798–Mar. 1799, and an Austro-Russian army under Suvorov won major victories in northern Italy, Apr.–Aug. 1799. Suvorov's victories were accompanied by military and political disputes with the Austrians, who opposed the Russian policy of restoring the *status quo* in Italy. Suvorov was ordered to Switzerland, from which he was forced to retreat by the defeat of other allied armies, and by late 1799 it had been decided to bring him back to Russia. Relations with Britain also worsened with the failure of an Anglo-Russian attack on the Netherlands, Sept.–Oct. 1799, and British refusal to co-operate with Russian forces in the Mediterranean. (*Cont. p. 167*.)

Spain and Portugal

SPAIN

1760–77

REIGN OF CARLOS III. Carlos III (1716–88), formerly duke of Parma and king of Naples, became king of Spain in 1759. He strengthened the authority of the central government, reformed the bureaucracy and the army, and, adopting policies advocated by the economist Pedro Rodríguez de Campomanes, brought new economic prosperity to his country.

FAMILY PACT. When the Seven Years' War began, 1756, Spain remained neutral, but by the Family Pact, 15 Aug., 1761, Carlos renewed the alliance between the Spanish and French Bourbons. France agreed to support Spain against Britain in return for a Spanish promise to enter the war if peace had not been made by 1 May, 1762.

WAR WITH BRITAIN. On 2 Jan., 1762, Britain declared war on Spain. Portugal, allied to Britain, was invaded, but the Spaniards achieved only minor successes. A Spanish force captured the Portuguese colony of Sacramento (Itatupã), in present Brazil, but lost Havana (Cuba) and other West Indian possessions, together with Manila in the Philippines, to the British.

TREATY OF PARIS. 10 Feb., 1763. Spain ceded Florida to Britain in exchange for Havana and Manila, returned Sacramento to Portugal, allowed the British logwood-cutting rights in Honduras, and surrendered her claims to fishing rights in the Newfoundland fisheries. By a separate agreement she received New Orleans and Louisiana west of the Mississippi from France.

MADRID RIOTS. Mar. 1766. The immediate cause of serious rioting in Madrid was a government attempt to prohibit the wearing of the round *chambergo* hat and long cape associated with Hapsburg times. In addition the Bourbons were still considered a foreign dynasty, and Charles's reliance on 2 Italian ministers, the marquises of Grimaldi and Squillace, created resentment. Higher taxes and steadily rising food prices also caused dissatisfaction. The riots forced the dismissal of Squillace, and the count of Aranda (1718–99) became the king's chief adviser.

EXPULSION OF THE JESUITS. The Jesuits were accused of instigating the riots of 1766. In addition, they were charged with being a divisive force both at home and in the colonies. On 27 Feb., 1767, Carlos signed the order for their expulsion. The Spanish government also pursued an anti-Jesuit policy in Rome, and José Moñino (1728–1808) was made count of Floridablanca for his part in obtaining papal suppression of the Society of Jesus in 1773.

1778–83

DECREE OF FREE TRADE. 12 Oct., 1778. This decree was the last in a series, begun in 1765, that had progressively broken the monopoly of Seville and Cádiz over the colonial trade. Direct trade among almost all major Spanish and colonial ports was now permitted.

WAR WITH BRITAIN. A Spanish declaration of war against Britain, 23 June, 1779, followed a secret alliance between Spain and France made in Apr. 1779. Although Spain refused openly to recognize the independence of the British North American colonies, she gave them secret aid. Spanish forces occupied Florida, the Bahamas, and Minorca, but a planned Franco-Spanish invasion of Britain did not materialize and a siege of Gibraltar had to be raised.

TREATY OF VERSAILLES. 3 Sept., 1783. Spain retained Minorca and Florida, but returned the Bahamas to Britain and renewed British logwood-cutting rights in Honduras. The Spanish economy had suffered from the wartime disruption of colonial trade, but the postwar period was one of great prosperity and economic expansion.

1788–99

REIGN OF CARLOS IV. Carlos IV (1748–1819) became king of Spain in Dec. 1788. A weaker man than his father, he was strongly under the influence of his wife, María Luisa of Parma. The count of Floridablanca, who had been first secretary of state since 1776, was Carlos' chief minister.

RELATIONS WITH FRANCE. Floridablanca attempted to keep the French Revolution out of Spain. He took extreme measures, including the suppression of all newspapers except the official press, to prevent news of events in France from gaining circulation in Spain. So aggressively did he support the rights of Louis XVI against the French Assembly that it was feared his policies were endangering that monarch rather than helping him. In 1792 the count of Aranda became first secretary. Aranda adopted a more moderate stance toward the French Revolution, a policy that became more difficult to maintain as the Revolution became more extreme.

WAR WITH FRANCE. In Nov. 1792, Manuel Godoy (1767–1815) became first secretary. Godoy was a 25-year-old former Guards officer, and a personal favorite of both the king and queen. He tried to defend Louis XVI while avoiding war with France, but failed in both aims. On 7 Mar., 1793, France declared war on Spain. The war aroused considerable patriotic enthusiasm and Spanish armies invaded France, only to be obliged to retreat in 1794 in the face of a strong counterattack by the French.

TREATY OF BASEL. France evacuated Spain in return for the Spanish (eastern) half of the island of Santo Domingo. For his part in arranging this treaty, 1795, Godoy was given the title Prince of Peace.

TREATY OF SAN ILDEFONSO. 18 Aug., 1796. Spain allied herself to France and placed her fleet in the French service. On 14 Feb., 1797, the main Spanish naval force was defeated by the British off Cape St. Vincent. (*Cont. p. 141.*)

PORTUGAL

1760–76

RULE OF POMBAL. José I (1715–77), of the house of Braganza, became king of Portugal in 1750. His chief minister and the real ruler of the country was Sebastião José de Carvalho e Mello (1699–1782), who in 1770 was made marquis of Pombal. Pombal's power became almost absolute after an attempt on the king's life in 1758 resulted in the imprisonment or execution of many of the higher nobility and the expulsion of the Jesuits, 1759. Corrupt, merciless, and dictatorial, Pombal did much to promote industry, commerce, and education, and was the main force behind the rebuilding of Lisbon after the great earthquake of 1755.

WAR WITH SPAIN. When Spain entered the Seven Years' War on the side of France, she tried to make the Portuguese break their alliance with Britain.

The Portuguese refused, and Spanish troops crossed the frontier, 30 Apr., 1762. With timely British aid, the Portuguese were able to prevent more than minor penetrations of their country.

1777–99

REIGN OF MARIA I. Maria I (1734–1816) became queen of Portugal, 24 Feb., 1777. One of her first acts was the dismissal of Pombal. The nobles he had imprisoned were released and in 1781 he himself was found guilty on criminal charges. Maria was subject to periodic fits of insanity and in Jan. 1792 it became necessary for her son, João (1767–1826), to take control of the government. In 1799 he assumed the title of prince regent.

WAR AGAINST FRANCE. In July 1793, after allying herself with Britain and Spain, Portugal sent troops to support the Spanish invasion of France, Sept. The Spaniards were defeated and made peace with France, July 1795, but the Portuguese persisted in their friendship with the British and their enmity toward the French, thus setting the scene for the Peninsular War. (*Cont. p. 145.*)

Scandinavia

SWEDEN

1760–70

THE "CAPS" AND THE "HATS." In 1760 the king of Sweden was Adolphus Frederick (1710–71) of Holstein-Gottorp (acceded 1751). His realm included Finland, which had been an integral part of Sweden since the 13th cent. The king of Sweden was virtually a figurehead, the country being governed by the Riksdag, an assembly of 4 estates (nobles, clergy, burgesses, and peasants). Within the Riksdag there were 2 parties, the Caps and the Hats, the latter having been in power since 1739. During the Seven Years' War, the Hats followed a pro-French policy and engaged in futile attacks on Prussia, 1757–62, which brought no territorial gains and resulted in a large national debt and a ruinous inflation.

In consequence, the Caps came to

power in 1765. They freed the press and favored economic retrenchment, a lessening of government interference in the economy, and closer ties with Russia and Britain. Their economic policies, however, created even greater hardship in the country than had those of their predecessors. By their failure to increase the power of the king, they lost the support of the court party and fell from power in 1769.

1771–79

RULE OF GUSTAVUS III. In 1771, Gustavus III (1746–92) came to the throne. He was influenced by the French *philosophes* and believed in an "enlightened," but strong, monarchy. On 19 Aug., 1772, he engineered a coup, as a result of which the members of the council were arrested and the Riksdag dismissed. A new constitution was adopted under which the powers of the Riksdag were reduced to control over taxation and the state bank, the sole right to declare war, and an equal voice with the king's over legislation. Gustavus III reformed the civil service, the law courts, and the army, abolished torture, and increased religious freedom, but his absolutist views were reflected in the press law of 1774 and in his reliance on informal, personal advisers in place of the council set up by the constitution to assist him.

1780–90

LEAGUE OF ARMED NEUTRALITY. In 1780 Sweden joined Denmark and Russia in the League of Armed Neutrality, designed to protect neutral commerce during the War of American Independence.

WAR WITH RUSSIA. In 1788 Gustavus III invaded Russia without securing the prior approval of the Riksdag. Not only did the assault fail but Sweden was in turn attacked by Russia's ally, Denmark. Following British and Prussian intercession, the Danes withdrew, and the Russian war was ended by the Treaty of Värälä, Aug. 1790, which restored the *status quo*.

ACT OF UNION AND SECURITY.
Gustavus' unsuccessful and unconstitutional attack on Russia increased the already existing opposition to him within the nobility. Taking advantage of the Danish attack to arouse patriotic feeling, he allied with 3 lower houses of the Riksdag to force changes in the constitution at the nobility's expense. By the Act of Union and Security, Feb. 1789, he was granted virtually absolute powers, while many offices and privileges that had been reserved to nobles were thrown open to all classes.

1791–99

RULE OF GUSTAVUS IV. In Mar. 1792, Gustavus III was assassinated by Jakob Anckarström, a former army officer and a member of a conspiracy of nobles opposed to the new regime. He was succeeded by his son, Gustavus IV (1778–1837), whose uncle, Duke Charles, ruled until 1796.

In 1794 a treaty of neutrality was negotiated with Denmark. The 2 countries agreed to remain neutral in the wars of the French Revolution, and to adopt joint measures for the protection of their commerce. (*Cont. p. 176.*)

DENMARK AND NORWAY

1760–65

RULE OF FREDERICK V. Frederick V (1723–66), of the House of Oldenburg, had become king of Denmark in 1746. His realms included the Kingdom of Denmark itself, consisting of Jutland and the Danish islands; the Duchy of Schleswig, which had been Danish territory since 811 but was not part of the kingdom; the Duchy of Holstein, a part of the Holy Roman Empire, of which the king of Denmark had been duke since 1460; and the Kingdom of Norway, which had been joined in a personal union with Denmark since 1380. Frederick V was an absolute monarch. His principal ministers were Adam Gottlob Moltke, chief marshal, and John Hartvig Ernst Bernstorff (1712–72), foreign minister.

ALLIANCE WITH RUSSIA. In the 16th cent., the Duchy of Holstein-Gottorp had been created out of parts of Schleswig and Holstein. As a result of the Northern War, 1700–21, the ducal portion of Schleswig had been taken by the king of Denmark. In 1762 the then duke of Holstein-Gottorp became Czar Peter III of Russia, and he immediately began preparations to regain his lost territory. War between Russia and Denmark seemed certain when Peter was deposed by his wife, Catherine II. The czarina was more concerned with the Baltic than with Germany, and desired a Danish alliance against Sweden. Treaties were therefore arranged (the final ones were signed in 1773) providing for an alliance against Sweden and for the surrender of the Holstein-Gottorp claims in Schleswig and Holstein in exchange for Oldenburg and Delmenhorst.

1766–72

RULE OF STRUENSEE. In Jan. 1766, Christian VII (1749–1808) succeeded his father, Frederick V. The new king was subject to fits of insanity, and came under the influence of a German doctor, Johann Friedrich Struensee (1737–72). Between 1770 and 1772, Struensee controlled Denmark. A freethinker, strongly influenced by the French *philosophes,* he instituted a program of extreme reform. The privileges of the nobility were attacked, the administration completely reorganized and centralized, and freedom of the press established. On 17 Jan., 1772, however, Struensee was overthrown by a coup led by the queen dowager, Juliane Marie, on behalf of her son, Frederick (1768–1839).

1772–99

MODERATE REFORM AND NEUTRALITY. From 1772 to 1784 the queen dowager, Crown Prince Frederick, and Minister Ove Höegh-Guldberg imposed a regime of extreme conservatism on Denmark. But when on 14 Apr., 1784, Frederick came of age and took power with his father's consent, he ousted the conservatives and installed a new ministry led by Andreas Peter Bernstorff (1739–97). A period of reform followed, during which estate owners were deprived of their judicial authority, 1787; the peasants were given freedom to leave their land, 1788; and the slave trade was abolished, 1792.

In Sept. 1788, Denmark invaded Sweden. Sweden had attacked Russia, and the latter invoked the treaty of 1773 to obtain Danish aid. Britain and Prussia intervened and peace was restored. During the wars of the French Revolution, Denmark remained neutral. (*Cont. p. 177.*)

Poland

1760–73

POLAND IN 1760. In 1760 Poland was the largest country in Europe (282,000 sq. mi.) apart from Russia. Its population numbered some 12 m., some 40% of whom were White Russians, Ukrainians, and Lithuanians, while Germans and Jews formed sizable minorities.

The Polish government was practically powerless. The central Diet (*Sejm*), composed of delegates chosen by provincial diets, elected the king who, in order to become eligible for the throne, had to swear to respect the rights of the nobility (*pacta conventa*). Exercise in the central Diet of the *liberum veto*, a single negative vote, could bar the passage of any bill. Moreover, any group dissatisfied with the conduct of affairs by the central government could form its own organization, known as a "confederation," and conduct its own foreign policy. Poland's powerful neighbors, Russia, Austria, and Prussia, financed such factions for their own ends, and all sought to keep Poland weak.

Most of the inhabitants of the country were rural serfs. The towns were insignificant; total urban population was barely half a million, and the towns had no representation of their own in the central Diet. Landed magnates dominated public life.

SUCCESSION CRISIS OF 1763. The death of King Augustus III, 5 Oct., 1763, ended the Saxon line. During the interregnum that followed, the Czartoryski family (known as "The Family") persuaded the Diet to limit the exercise of the *liberum veto*. Russia and Prussia, however, agreed by the Treaty of St. Petersburg, 11 Apr., 1764, to press for an annulment of this limitation and for the election of Stanislas Poniatowski (1732–98), a former lover of Catherine II and a Czartoryski, to the Polish throne. The Czartoryskis had to abandon their reform plans, and Poniatowski became king of Poland.

CONFEDERATION OF RADOM. In 1766, Russian influence again secured the Diet's rejection of a proposal to abolish the *liberum veto* in relation to tax matters. To safeguard the privileges of the nobility, the elective monarchy, and the *liberum veto*, the Confederation of Radom was formed, 23 June, 1767. In 1768 the Diet yielded to the Confederation's demands, thus weakening the central government still further, and also lifted the disabilities on Dissidents. (Dissidents were non-Catholics: Orthodox Ukrainians and White Russians in the East, and Protestant Prussians in the north and west.)

CONFEDERATION OF BAR. 29 Feb., 1768. The Confederation of Bar was formed in Podolia in the Ukraine to defend Polish independence against Russian encroachment and to revoke the rights granted to Dissidents. The Confederation's troops fought spasmodically against the Russians, who were soon preoccupied with the war against Turkey, 1768–74.

1ST PARTITION OF POLAND. Meanwhile, in 1769, Austrian troops occupied the enclave of Zips (Spisz), which had once belonged to the Kingdom of Hungary. In 1770, on the pretext of protecting it from a cattle plague, Prussia cordoned off West Prussia. When Russia began making gains in her war with Turkey, Austria became nervous over Russian ambitions in the Balkans and demanded compensation. Frederick II of Prussia then suggested that all 3 powers should seek compensation in Poland; he had long coveted West Prussia, which lay between East Prussia and Pomerania.

Russia agreed to Frederick's proposal, 17 Feb., 1772, and Austria followed, 5 Aug. Austria received Galicia (32,000 sq. mi. and 2.7 m. inhabitants), Prussia annexed West Prussia (14,000 sq. mi. and 580,000 inhabitants), and Russia obtained 36,000 sq. mi. of White Russia with 1.3 m. inhabitants. Thus Poland lost 30% of her territory and 35% of her population. Threatened by a Russian army, the Polish Diet ratified the partition, 18 Sept., 1773.

1773–91

INFLUENCE OF THE ENLIGHTENMENT. An educational reform program was instituted, 1773, with the dissolution of the Jesuit order (which had dominated Polish education since the 16th century) and the establishment of an Education Commission (*Komisja Edukacji Narodowej*) which administered and expanded Polish education and was the first ministry of education in Europe. The king encouraged Polish and foreign *philosophes* to join his court and advise him on matters of national policy.

4 YEARS' DIET. A Diet strongly under the influence of reformers opened on 6 Oct., 1788. Russia was engaged in another war with Turkey, 1787–92, and with Sweden, 1788–90, and was unable to interfere decisively in Polish affairs, and Poland gained the benevolent support of Prussia by a defensive alliance signed on 29 Mar., 1790.

On 3 May, 1791, the Diet promulgated a new constitution which was in time approved by both Prussia and Austria. It provided for a hereditary monarchy and for a bicameral legislature chosen by direct elections. Towns were granted self-government and representation in the legislature. Urban dwellers received the right to buy land, hold most offices, and become noble. Catholicism was declared the state religion, but other religions were to be tolerated. Both the *liberum veto* and the confederations were abolished.

1792–99

2ND PARTITION OF POLAND. Catherine II of Russia, however, opposed the Polish reform movement and organized the Confederation of Targowica, 14 May, 1792. Russian troops invaded Poland. Frederick William II of Prussia, alarmed at the possibility of Russian control over the whole country, sent troops into Poznań. But, since he wished to avoid a confrontation with Russia while his forces were engaged in France, he renounced the treaty Prussia had made with Poland, 1790.

Russian and Prussian forces soon overwhelmed the small Polish army. On 23 July, 1792, the Polish government yielded to a Russian demand that all reforms should be annulled and the old constitution restored. On 23 Jan., 1793, Prussia and Russia agreed to a further dismemberment of Poland: Prussia annexed Poznań (1 m. inhabitants and 22,000 sq. mi.), while Russia took 97,000 sq. mi. of Lithuania, White Russia, and the Ukraine. Surrounded by Russian troops, the Diet ratified the partition on 23 Sept.

UPRISING OF 1794. In Mar. 1794 a rebellion against foreign occupation, led by Thaddeus Kosciusko (1746–1817), broke out. In Apr. the citizens of Warsaw ejected the Russian garrison, and soon all foreign troops had been cleared from Polish territory. By Nov., however, the allies had succeeded in crushing the uprising.

3RD PARTITION OF POLAND. In Oct. 1795, Prussia, Austria, and Russia agreed to a 3rd partition. Prussia received Warsaw, Austria Cracow and Lublin, and Russia Vilna, Grodno, Brest, the rest of Lithuania, White Russsia, and the Ukraine. The king of Poland abdicated on 27 Nov., 1795.

GREAT BRITAIN AND IRELAND

1760

ACCESSION OF GEORGE III. On assuming the throne, 25 Oct., George III (1738–1820) had 2 principal aims: to replace the Whig ministry with a nonpartisan one of his own choosing, and to conclude the French phase of the Seven Years' War, for he could not expel the Whigs while they successfully pursued it. He was willing to make sacrifices to end the German phase of the war, for its indecisiveness had made it unpopular. George III was advised by Lord Bute (1713–92), who, 25 Mar., 1761, became a secretary of state.

1761–62

DECLARATION OF WAR ON SPAIN.
4 Jan., 1762. Spain objected to British settlements in Yucatán, the condemnation by British courts of captured Spanish ships, and the denial to Spain of Newfoundland fishing rights. The Bourbon Family Compact and the Franco-Spanish Convention of 15 Aug., 1761, pledged Spain to declare war on Britain by 1 May, 1762. On 7 Oct., 1761, William Pitt (1708–78) resigned after the cabinet rejected his proposal for an immediate preventive war. On 2 Nov., Britain heard officially of the Franco-Spanish treaties; Spain refused to clarify them, and Britain declared war.

BUTE MINISTRY. Bute's growing influence drove the Duke of Newcastle (1693–1768), prime minister since July, 1757, to resign, 26 May, 1762. Bute succeeded him, 29 May.

1763–64

TREATY OF PARIS. 10 Feb., 1763.
Signed by Britain, France, and Spain, the Treaty of Paris confirmed Britain's colonial supremacy in North America, in India, and on the seas. (The Treaty of Hubertusburg, 15 Feb., ended the German phase of the Seven Years' War.) France ceded Acadia, Canada, Cape Breton, and the islands of the St. Lawrence to Britain, gained St. Pierre and Miquelon, and retained fishing privileges off Newfoundland. She further yielded all territory east of the Mississippi except New Orleans. In the Caribbean, Britain regained St. Vincent, Dominica, Tobago, and the Grenadines; France regained St. Lucia, Guadeloupe, Marie Galante, Désirade, and Martinique. Spain granted Britain East and West Florida and logwood-cutting rights in Honduras. Cuba and the Philippines were restored to Spain. In East India, France and Britain mutually restored all post-1749 conquests.

In Europe, France destroyed her fortifications at Dunkirk, reobtained Belle Isle, restored Minorca to Britain, and with Britain withdrew from Germany. In Africa, Britain returned Gorée to France, and France ceded her Sénégal.

THE GRENVILLE MINISTRY. Bute resigned, 8 Apr., 1763, and George Grenville (1712–70), whom George III disliked, succeeded him, 16 Apr.

THE WILKES CASE. On 30 Apr., 1763, John Wilkes (1729–97) was arrested for seditious libel by a general warrant for his attack in No. 45 of the *North Briton* on George III's defense of the Treaty of Paris. Wilkes questioned the legality of the general warrant and claimed parliamentary immunity as an M.P. Chief Justice Pratt declared the general warrant illegal in May and discharged Wilkes, who fled to France, 24 Dec., after the Commons took further action against him. On 20 Jan., 1764, the Commons expelled Wilkes; he was convicted of seditious libel, Feb., and outlawed, Nov. His challenge to the government won him a reputation as a libertarian.

1764–66

GRENVILLE'S ECONOMIC MEASURES.
Grenville's Budget Speech of 9 Mar., 1764, proposed no new taxes in Britain, but stressed the need for additional revenues to maintain the empire. Such subsequent legislation as the American Revenue Act and the Stamp Act, the first revenue measures applied to the colonies, aroused American hostility. In 1766, Parliament repealed the Stamp Act, but passed a Declaratory Act that asserted Parliament's full authority to make laws binding the colonists "in all cases whatsoever."

ROCKINGHAM MINISTRY. George III, anxious to be rid of Grenville, experiencing a crisis over a regency bill, 10 July, disdaining Newcastle, and unable to obtain Pitt, on 13 July, 1765, appointed the Marquis of Rockingham (1730–82) to head a ministry.

CHATHAM MINISTRY. Rockingham's ministry collapsed when Pitt refused to enter it; on 30 July, 1766, Pitt, now Earl of Chatham, formed a ministry which, because of his ill health, was led by the Duke of Grafton (1735–1811) as first lord of the treasury and Charles Townshend (1725–67) as chancellor of the exchequer.

ROCKINGHAMITE OPPOSITION. Rockingham decided that he could not overthrow the Chatham ministry; his followers then went into opposition, which lasted until 1782. During this period, they formulated such governmental principles as the concept of "party," which Rockingham's private secretary Edmund Burke (1729–97) outlined in his *Thoughts on the Cause of the Present Discontents,* 1770.

1767

GRAFTON MINISTRY. On 13 Oct. Chatham resigned when Grafton considered the dismissal of Shelburne (1737–1805). Grafton became prime minister, with Lord Frederick North (1718–93) as chancellor of the exchequer and ministerial spokesman in the Commons. On 20 Jan., 1768, Lord Hillsborough assumed the new office of secretary of state for the colonies.

1768–69

MIDDLESEX ELECTION DISPUTES. Following John Wilkes's election to Parliament, Mar. 1768, riotous celebrations occurred. In May, troops quelling the Wilkesite demonstrations killed several people, an action Wilkes denounced in the *St. James Chronicle,* 8 Dec. The violence of his attack united his opponents, and the Commons expelled him, 3 Feb., 1769. Wilkes was re-elected on 16 Feb., 16 Mar., and 13 Apr., but on 15 Apr. the Commons declared his opponent elected. A pro-Wilkes petitioning movement ensued.

1770

NORTH MINISTRY. The cabinet was split by the Wilkes case and by the Townshend duties, passed, 1767, to main- tain British officials in America. On 27 Jan., 1770, Grafton resigned; North replaced him, 31 Jan. North won passage of a bill for the withdrawal of all the Townshend duties except the tea duty, retained as a symbol of British authority; the repeal measure received royal assent, 12 Apr.

1771–72

FREEDOM OF THE PRESS. The post-1767 defiance of prohibitions concerning the publishing of parliamentary debates led Parliament, 15 Mar., 1771, to send a messenger to arrest an offending printer in hopes of ending this practice. The London aldermen arrested the messenger for infringement of privilege of the City. After this incident, with few exceptions, the press freely published parliamentary debates. Meanwhile, the publisher John Almon had led a press campaign against the government, and Lord Mansfield (1705–93) had ruled, 9 Dec., 1769, in connection with the anonymous and virulent *Letters of Junius,* that juries could not judge seditious libel. Chatham's and Rockingham's challenge of this decision on grounds that the administration had abused the libel laws for political purposes met parliamentary defeat, Jan. 1772. It was not until 1792 that a bill awarding libel cases to juries was passed.

1774–76

REACTION TO AMERICAN UNREST. Both Chathamites and Rockinghamites favored conciliating the disaffected colonies, but the 1774 elections returned a parliamentary majority that endorsed George III's wish to punish Massachusetts for the Boston Tea Party and for general intransigence, and that passed the Coercive Acts, 31 Mar., 20 May. The cabinet advocated both economic strangulation and a land war to restore order. Troops were ordered to America in 1775, and the Prohibitory Bill, 22 Nov., established a blockade of the colonies. Treaties of 9 Jan., 15 Jan., and 5 Feb., 1776, hired mercenaries from Brunswick and Hesse-Cassel to supplement the British forces. Rockingham, convinced of the futility of his opposition to the "Intolerable Acts," retired from parliamentary participation, and Charles James Fox (1749–1806) became opposition leader.

1777–79

CONSEQUENCES OF DEFEAT AT SARATOGA. Gen. John Burgoyne's surrender at Saratoga, Oct. 1777, convinced the cabinet of the difficulty of subduing the colonists. North considered resigning and began preparing a series of bills for effecting reconciliation with America; he introduced these in the Commons, 17 Feb., 1778, and they passed, 16 Mar. Also in Mar., Britain learned of the Franco-American alliance, formed 6 Feb., and broke relations with France. One of North's bills created the Carlisle peace commission, which reached Philadelphia on 6 June and requested, 9 June, a conference with the Congress. On 17 June, Congress demanded recognition of U.S. independence and withdrawal of British forces as the basis of negotiation. The peace mission ended in failure.

NAVAL AFFAIRS. Anglo-French naval hostilities began 17 June, 1778. Admiral Keppel blamed his defeat off Ushant, 27 July, on Sir Hugh Palliser, a subordinate officer. A court-martial acquitted both men, but Keppel resented having been tried. Many young officers sympathized with him against the Admiralty under the Earl of Sandwich (1718–92), whom the Rockinghamites, Keppel's backers, wanted removed. As a result of this affair, many officers refused to command the Channel Fleet under Sandwich when a Franco-Spanish fleet threatened to invade England in the summer of 1779. The crisis ended when France abandoned the invasion.

1780

REFORM MOVEMENTS. In Dec. 1779, Burke had initiated his Economical Reform Movement and a Yorkshire freeholders' meeting had resolved to establish a more representative Parliament and a national Petitioning Movement for reform. On 13 Mar., 1780, the Commons abolished the Board of Trade, but the economical reform movement collapsed, 21 Mar., when the Commons defeated Burke's attempt to decrease the King's Household. Scarce attendance at the petitioners' national congress in London, 11 Mar., dashed their hopes of creating a national assembly. On 6 Apr. the Commons approved their petitions to diminish royal power, but refused, 24 Apr., to remain sitting until reform was effected. Thereafter the movement declined.

GORDON RIOTS. On 2 June, Lord George Gordon (1751–93), leader of the London Protestant Association, petitioned Parliament to repeal the Roman Catholic Relief Bill of 1778; from then until 7 June, nominally anti-Catholic riots raged in London. Mob violence directed against Catholics and the rich caused many propertied people to support the *status quo*, thereby strengthening North's ministry.

DECLARATION OF WAR ON HOLLAND. Anglo-Dutch relations had become strained because of Holland's trade with Britain's enemies. On 17 Apr., Britain declared Dutch ships subject to search. Fearing that Holland would join Russia's League of Armed Neutrality to protect neutral shipping, the cabinet declared war, 20 Dec.

1782

ROCKINGHAM MINISTRY. The capture of Cornwallis' entire army at Yorktown, 19 Oct., 1781, and defeats by the French in the West Indies dashed British hopes for victory in America. The Commons unrelentingly attacked the North ministry, and on 20 Mar. North resigned. Rockingham succeeded him, 22 Mar., with Fox as foreign secretary and Shelburne as home secretary. Under Burke's influence, this ministry disenfranchised revenue officers, excluded government contractors from the Commons, and secured sinecure reform. Peace talks with the Americans began at Paris, 12 Apr. Rockingham's death, 1 July, led to Fox's resignation and the formation of a ministry under Shelburne in which the younger William Pitt (1759–1806) was chancellor of the exchequer.

IRISH REFORMS. The American Revolution had provided Irish Protestants with a pretext for the formation of the supposedly defensive Ulster Volunteer Corps, which had soon become a powerful political force for free trade and Irish legislative independence. With this group behind him, Henry Grattan (1746–1820) obtained trade concessions and secured the repeal of the Drogheda statutes of 1494 (Poynings' Law), which subjected the actions of the Irish Parliament to the English Privy Council and made all laws passed in England applicable to Ireland. The new Irish Parliament, though independent, was limited to Protestants.

1783

TREATY OF PARIS. The preliminary Anglo-American treaty signed 30 Nov., 1782, was not to become effective until settlement with France had been reached. On 20 Jan., 1783, Britain concluded preliminary treaties with France and Spain. The Anglo-French treaty was an avowal of Britain's loss of power and prestige since 1763, but the only substantive changes in territorial disposition were made in the West Indies and Africa. Spain reacquired Minorca and the Floridas. On 3 Sept., definitive treaties were signed at Paris. An Anglo-Dutch treaty giving Britain Negapatam and free navigation of the Moluccas, and providing for mutual restoration of other conquests, was ratified in 1784.

FOX-NORTH MINISTRY. Shelburne's unpopular peace settlement caused cabinet disaffection. On 17 Feb., Fox and North defeated the preliminary treaty in the Commons, and Shelburne resigned, 24 Feb. George III acquiesced in the Fox-North coalition, 2 Apr., and they became secretaries of state in a ministry nominally headed by the Duke of Portland (1738–1809). The ministry lost support after agreeing to the same peace terms it had condemned Shelburne for accepting; it fell over Fox's East India Bill, which was considered a patronage scheme and was defeated in the Lords, 17 Dec. On 19 Dec., Pitt became prime minister.

1784–85

PITT MINISTRY. Pitt's administration was strengthened by the long-postponed general election of 1784, in which Fox's supporters lost over 100 seats. An India Bill was passed, 13 Aug. Pitt attempted to apply the ideas of Adam Smith and restore Britain to financial soundness. His Commutation Bill of 1784 reduced the tea duty to end smuggling. The Board of Taxes, created in 1785, centralized the receipt of revenues. The sinking fund, introduced 11 Apr., 1785, utilized the annual surplus to pay the national debt; by 1792 it had restored national credit.

1786

EDEN TREATY. Article 18 of the Treaty of Paris provided for a new Anglo-French commercial treaty, which William Eden negotiated, 26 Sept. It contained provisions for equal navigation, trade, and travel rights between Britain and France, religious freedom for the subjects of each state in the other, and procedures for settling contraband disputes. The treaty, effective 10 May, 1787, was abrogated during the French Revolution.

1788

ANGLO-DUTCH TREATY. After an unsuccessful attempt by France and the Netherlands to rescind the stadholder's powers, Pitt, fearing French encroachments in the Netherlands that would jeopardize British safety and prosperity, guaranteed Dutch territorial integrity by treaty, 15 Apr.

ANGLO-PRUSSIAN TREATY. For protection in case of a war with France, Britain concluded a treaty with Prussia, 13 Aug. It guaranteed mutual aid in a

European defensive war and the territorial integrity of the Netherlands.

1789

REGENCY CRISIS. George III had become violently insane in Nov. 1788. On 5 Feb., 1789, Pitt submitted a Regency Bill to the Commons; it granted the Prince of Wales restricted royal power. The king's recovery stopped debate, 19 Feb., but the bill served as the basis of the Regency Act of 1810, when George III became permanently insane.

1790

NOOTKA INCIDENT. The controversy over Spain's seizure of the Nootka trading post in 1789 was ended by the Nootka Convention, 24 Oct., 1790, whereby Spain recognized Britain's right to settle and trade on the north Pacific coast of North America.

1791

BIRMINGHAM RIOTS. Riots broke out, 15 July, during the Birmingham Nonconformists' celebration of the fall of the Bastille. Three days of disorder testified to the widespread fear that Nonconformists were revolutionaries.

1793

THE FIRST COALITION. On 25 Mar., Lord William Grenville (1759–1834), foreign minister since Apr. 1791, concluded the Anglo-Russian treaty establishing the First Coalition. Russia agreed to supply troops, prevent neutrals from aiding France, and grant Britain a favorable commercial treaty. Prussia, 14 July, and Austria, 30 Aug., joined the coalition, promising troops in exchange for British subsidies. Similar treaties were concluded with Hesse-Cassel, 10 Apr.; Sardinia, 25 Apr.; Spain, 25 May; and Naples, 12 June.

WAR WITH FRANCE. Distrust of France had increased in 1792 when she opened the Scheldt, 16 Nov., and prom-

ised, 19 Nov., support to any revolutionary people. On 4 Jan., 1793, the Commons passed the Aliens Bill to restrict the activities of foreigners, and on 24 Jan. George III expelled the French ambassador. On 1 Feb., France declared war on Britain and the Netherlands. Pitt's intention was to protect the Low Countries; George III's to defend monarchy.

1794

ANTITREASON MEASURES. The Traitorous Correspondence Bill, Apr. 1793, which prohibited intercourse with France, reflected fear that the Revolution might spread. On 17 May, 1794, at Pitt's request, the Commons suspended the Habeas Corpus Act. The suspension passed with the support of the Old Whigs, who defected to Pitt to form a national party of opponents of Jacobinism. On 7 July the Whig Portland became home secretary and William Windham (1750–1810) secretary for war. The suspension supported Pitt's arrest of the leaders of the Society for Constitutional Information and the London Corresponding Society, whom he suspected of plotting a national convention to replace Parliament. Their acquittal in Oct. made Pitt's antitreason measures appear subversive of popular liberty, but on 6 Nov., 1795, the Lords passed his Treasonable Practices Bill, which defined treason to include criticism of the government; and the Commons approved a Seditious Meetings Bill, which restricted public gatherings.

1795

FITZWILLIAM AFFAIR. On 4 Jan., Lord Fitzwilliam (1748–1833) became viceroy of Ireland. His advocacy of seating Catholics in Parliament (they had obtained the vote in 1793) and his opposition to the powerful Irish Protestants led to his replacement, 19 Feb.

TRIPLE ALLIANCE. On 18 Feb., Britain concluded a defensive alliance with Russia; Austria joined on 20 May. With these pacts Britain hoped to defeat

France quickly, but the agreement collapsed with Catherine II's death, 16 Nov., 1796.

1796

ANGLO-SPANISH HOSTILITIES. Since the beginning of the slave revolts in the West Indies, Spain and Britain had contended for France's possessions there; on 5 Oct., Spain declared war.

FINANCIAL CRISIS. The war greatly strained Britain's financial resources. To stave off bankruptcy Pitt, 5 Dec., 1796, took the unusual step of floating a public loan to meet the government's £18 m. deficit, but in Feb. 1797 a run on the bank occurred and the specie in the Bank of England fell to £1,272,000. Thereafter the government curtailed its foreign loans and subsidies, but the crisis continued. Pitt's Financial Bill, Jan. 1798, established increased and graduated assessments, a progressive income tax, and a "patriotic contribution." In addition, he floated a £3 m. loan and converted the land tax into a parish tax.

1797

BATTLES OF CAPE ST. VINCENT AND CAMPERDOWN. On 14 Apr., Sir John Jervis (1735–1823) defeated the Spanish off Cape St. Vincent, revealing Spain's naval weakness and ending the Franco-Spanish invasion threat. The Franco-Dutch threat ended with the defeat of the Dutch fleet off Camperdown, 11 Oct.

SEAMEN'S MUTINY. Many of Britain's sailors were pressed into service; their food, pay, and leave time were inadequate. Discontent led to the mutinies of 15 Apr. and 7 May at Spithead and the 10 May mutiny at Sheerness. The Spithead mutinies ended by 17 May after the government promised reform, but the Sheerness mutiny had to be suppressed by force.

1798–99

THE IRISH REBELLION. The League of United Irishmen was organized in 1791 to gain Irish independence. After 1793, France aided the insurgents, most notably with the unsuccessful expedition of Lazare Hoche (1768–97) of Dec. 1796. On 23 May, 1798, a rebellion broke out in Ireland, but it was crushed at Vinegar Hill, 21 June. Smaller uprisings took place throughout the summer.

BATTLE OF ABUKIR BAY. On 1 Aug., 1798, Lord Nelson (1758–1805) defeated the French fleet at Abukir Bay, making Britain supreme in the Mediterranean.

ANGLO-RUSSIAN ALLIANCE. On 29 Dec., 1798, Britain concluded an anti-French agreement with Russia. After their joint expedition against the Dutch coast failed at Bergen, 19 Sept., 1799, Russia withdrew from the failing coalition. (Cont. p. 193.)

Latin America and the Caribbean, 1760–1825

THE SPANISH COLONIAL EMPIRE, 1760–1808

1761

SEVEN YEARS' WAR. Carlos III, king of Spain (ruled 1759–88), concluded a defensive alliance, the 2nd Family Compact, with France, 15 Aug., and the following year joined the struggle against Britain. The involvement of Spain and her colonies on the losing side in the Seven Years' War later stimulated important economic, fiscal, commercial, military, and administrative reforms in Spanish America.

1762

CAPTURE OF HAVANA. Having seized the Philippines and Cuba, Britain immediately opened Havana to all British vessels. Within a year 100 ships entered

Havana, as against only 5 or 6 per annum previously.

1763

TREATY OF PARIS. 10 Feb. Spain recovered Cuba and the Philippines, lost Florida and Minorca to Britain, and gained Louisiana from her ally, France. The acquisition of Louisiana, with its long land frontier, was no boon for Spain, since it merely increased the costs of empire. At the same time, the British capture of Havana had indicated that Spain would have to spend more on defense in the future if she were not to run the risk of losing her empire altogether.

1765

THE GÁLVEZ MISSION. On 4 Mar., Carlos III commissioned José de Gálvez (1729–87) to conduct a general investigation in New Spain and to institute such changes as would (1) increase the royal revenues derived from the mines, the tobacco industry (soon to become a government monopoly), the turnover tax, the customs dues, and other sources; (2) end the contraband trade in Spanish America; (3) strengthen the colonial defenses by establishing a standing army and a militia; and (4) improve the quality of government while reducing its costs. Gálvez reached Veracruz on 18 July. His mission was not completed, however, until 1771.

1767

EXPULSION OF THE JESUITS. The Society of Jesus was the only religious order operating in the colonies that had remained independent of the crown. In Apr. 1767 the king ordered all Jesuits out of Spanish America. The royal order was carried out secretly, swiftly, and without regard for public opinion. Some 10,000 Spanish and Spanish-American Jesuits were deported to Rome. Their removal seriously damaged the educational system, but both Carlos III and his successor, Carlos IV (ruled 1788–1808), promoted educational reform in the colonies by encouraging the study of the exact sciences; by contributing funds for the setting up of mining schools, schools of fine arts, botanical gardens, etc.; and by sending mining, botanical, and other scientific missions to America. Many of these missions were led by foreigners of such distinction as Alexander von Humboldt and Baron von Nordenflicht.

1768–78

FREEDOM OF TRADE. In 1765 the crown had opened the main West Indian islands to individual sailings, i.e., to ships on private registry. In 1768 this privilege was extended to Louisiana, in 1770 to Yucatán, and in 1776 to New Granada. By 1778 virtual free trade was permitted within the Spanish dominions. By that year 200 Spanish vessels were employed in the trade with Cuba alone.

During the next decade the value of the entire trade between Spain and her colonies increased by 700%. Whereas colonial industries such as textiles, hats, pottery, and glass could not compete with lower-priced European goods, the production of raw materials for overseas consumption was greatly stimulated by the new policy.

1780

THE REVOLT OF TUPAC AMARÚ. In Peru, under the leadership of José Gabriel Condorcanqui Noguera (1742–81), a lineal descendant of the last Inca emperor and known as Tupac Amarú II, thousands of Indians rebelled against the oppressive and rapacious rule of the local Spanish officials (corregidors). The revolt lasted 3 years. At least 80,000 Indians perished, and the leaders were brutally put to death. It was at first believed that English *provocateurs* had instigated the rebellion, but after the Treaty of Versailles was signed more rational counsels prevailed, and the need for instituting political reforms on the regional level in Peru and elsewhere was generally recognized. The revolt of Tupac Amarú helped to trigger the adoption of the

COLONIAL
LATIN AMERICA

© Lilli Tanzer 1970

intendancy system of local government in Spanish America.

1781

THE COMUNERO REVOLT. While the revolt in Peru was in progress, creoles supported by mestizos and Indians in many towns in the neighboring viceroyalty of New Granada rebelled against increased taxation (especially the anti-contraband tax), increased prices (of tobacco, sealed paper, etc.), corrupt and ruthless royal officials and churchmen, and a discriminatory policy that excluded most native-born Americans from all but minor posts in government. The demands of the commune delegates were accepted by the local authorities, but quickly repudiated once the chief leaders of the revolt had been captured and executed.

1783

THE TREATY OF VERSAILLES. 3 Sept. In June 1779, Spain had entered the War of American Independence on the side of France and against Britain. At the peace treaty Spain regained Minorca and Florida, which had been lost to Britain at the end of the Seven Years' War.

1786

THE INTENDANCY SYSTEM. The French intendant system had been experimentally introduced into Cuba in 1764, and extended to the La Plata region in 1782 and to Peru in 1784. In Dec. 1786 it was adopted throughout the viceroyalty of New Spain and in Chile, and by 1790 had become the rule throughout Spanish America. The chief aim of the new system was the centralizing of the administration for the sake of greater efficiency. Hundreds of provincial officials, the corregidors and *alcaldes mayores,* had previously cheated the crown and oppressed the Indians. These were now replaced by a few dozen intendants. The intendant's most important function was to collect and augment the royal revenues, but he was also the chief military, political, and judicial officer in his district. In addition,

intendants were expected to foster the growth of agriculture, industry, and commerce, improve municipal services, and encourage the arts and sciences. While several intendants appointed after 1786 proved to be good administrators (e.g., Flon and Riaño in New Spain) and greatly increased the economic prosperity of their districts, others were less successful. A serious deficiency of the system, moreover, was that the officials subordinate to the intendants, known as subdelegates, received no fixed salary. As a result, they almost of necessity swindled the poor and trafficked in justice.

1789–1808

DECLINE OF SPANISH POWER. During the Revolutionary and Napoleonic wars, Spain's power to control Latin America was gradually whittled away. Santo Domingo was lost to France, 1795, and Trinidad to Britain, 1797. A large part of the Spanish fleet was destroyed at the battles of Cape St. Vincent, 1797, and Trafalgar, 1805. When the British invaded the viceroyalty of La Plata in 1806–7, it was not royal officialdom but the local residents who resisted and eventually expelled the intruders from Buenos Aires. These events revealed to all, and especially to disaffected Spanish Americans, the almost total impotence of Spain. However, while a legitimate monarch ruled, no scheme for severing the ties between colonies and mother country made any headway in the Americas.

THE MIRANDA EXPEDITION. Francisco Miranda (1750?–1816), a native of Caracas who had traveled widely in the U.S.A. and Europe between 1783 and 1805 seeking support for Spanish-American independence, sailed in Feb. 1806 from New York to Venezuela in command of a filibustering expedition of 200 men, mostly North Americans. Aided by British officials at Barbados, he landed at Coro, Venezuela, in the summer of the same year, but failed to obtain significant local assistance. He was forced to abandon his enterprise, and returned to England to await a more propitious time.

ANNEXATION OF SPAIN BY NAPOLEON. The accession of Napoleon's brother, Joseph, to the throne of Spain, 6 May, 1808, made it possible for Spanish-American patriots to rebel against royal authority with a clear conscience. From now on, they reasoned, the viceroys and other royal officials in the colonies would be taking orders from a French usurper. The annexation of Spain by France thus signaled the beginning of the effective Spanish-American independence movement.

THE SPANISH-AMERICAN WARS OF INDEPENDENCE AND THE CREATION OF NEW STATES, 1808–25

Mexico

1808–11

MIGUEL HIDALGO. On 15 Sept., 1808, loyalist Spaniards deposed José de Iturrigaray, viceroy of New Spain, because they feared he was plotting with local creole leaders to declare New Spain independent from French-occupied Spain. Two years later, 16 Sept., 1810, Miguel Hidalgo y Costilla (1753–1811), a creole parish priest, raised the banner of revolt in the name of the captive King Fernando VII (ruled 1808; 1814–33). Hidalgo was soon joined by thousands of mestizos and Indians. However, the disorders accompanying his rebellion alienated most creoles, and he found it impossible to organize a disciplined army or orderly government. After suffering several defeats at the hands of royalist forces, led mostly by Spanish officers but made up mainly of Mexican recruits, Hidalgo and his followers were captured, 21 Mar., 1811, as they tried to escape to the U.S.A. He and other leaders of the rebellion were executed on 26 July, but the revolt continued.

1812–15

JOSÉ MARÍA MORELOS. In Nov. 1812 a mestizo priest, José María Morelos y Pavón (1765–1815), captured the provincial capital of Oaxaca. By some he was hailed as Hidalgo's successor, but other followers of Hidalgo refused to recognize him. He accordingly planned to legalize his claims to leadership by convening a national congress, to meet in Chilpancingo. At Morelos' instigation the Chilpancingo Congress issued a declaration of complete independence from Spain, 2 Nov., 1813. In Dec., however, Morelos was decisively defeated at Valladolid (Morelia) by a creole officer, Agustín de Iturbide (1783–1824).

On 22 Oct., 1814, the Congress of Chilpancingo promulgated Mexico's first constitution, based largely on French and Spanish models, in an effort to rally support for the rebellion. But in Nov. 1815, Morelos was captured by the royalists and executed, 22 Dec. The revolution degenerated into petty quarrels among innumerable guerrilla leaders.

1817

XAVIER MINA. Revolutionary ardor had waned in Mexico after the restoration of Fernando VII in May 1814. This was conclusively demonstrated in 1817 by the outcome of the attempt of a Spanish liberal, Xavier Mina (1789–1817), to free Mexico from what he regarded as Fernando's reactionary rule. By most Mexican *guerrilloeros* Mina was regarded with suspicion. He was defeated, captured, and finally shot by the royalists on 11 Nov., 1817.

1821–23

AGUSTÍN DE ITURBIDE. The reestablishment of a constitutional monarchy in Spain following a barracks revolt of Jan. 1820 caused many conservative royalist sympathizers in Mexico to change sides and press for independence. Agustín de Iturbide, formerly a determined persecutor of independence leaders, assumed leadership of the new revolt and at the town of Iguala issued a plan for an independent Mexico. This was accepted by the other revolutionary leaders. By the Treaty of Córdoba, 24 Aug., 1821, the last viceroy of New Spain, Juan O'Donojú (1755–1821), aware that all classes of

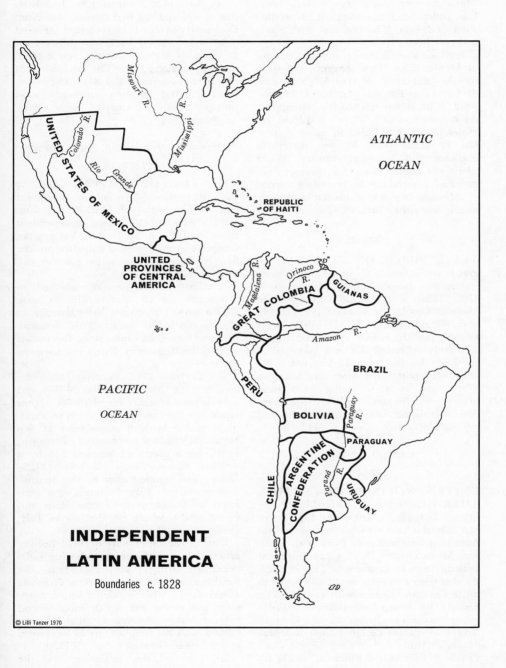

ATLANTIC

OCEAN

REPUBLIC
OF HAITI

UNITED STATES OF MEXICO

Missouri R.

Mississippi R.

Colorado R.

Rio Grande

UNITED
PROVINCES
OF CENTRAL
AMERICA

Magdalena R.

Orinoco R.

GREAT COLOMBIA

GUIANAS

Amazon R.

BRAZIL

PERU

BOLIVIA

Paraguay R.

PARAGUAY

PACIFIC

OCEAN

ARGENTINE
CONFEDERATION

Paraná R.

URUGUAY

CHILE

INDEPENDENT

LATIN AMERICA

Boundaries c. 1828

© Lilli Tanzer 1970

Mexicans were now united in their desire for independence, accepted Iturbide's Plan of Iguala. The last link with Spain had now been cut.

Iturbide assembled a National Congress at Mexico City. This congress, giving in to the demands of Iturbide's troops, declared him Emperor Agustín I, 24 Feb., 1822, of an independent Mexican empire. As emperor, Iturbide was lavish in his expenditures, but failed to pay his army. On 19 Mar., 1823, he was forced to abdicate and left the country. While plans were being made for the establishment of a republic, he secretly returned to Mexico, but was captured and summarily shot on 19 July, 1824.

1824–25

THE REPUBLIC OF MEXICO. A federal republic, made up of 19 autonomous states, was established in Mexico on 4 Oct., 1824. Two military followers of Morelos, Guadalupe Victoria (1789–1843) and Nicolás Bravo (1787?–1854), were elected president and vice-president respectively. Although Victoria managed to serve out his full term (a feat not to be achieved again until after the Mexican War), the years following 1824 were marked by frequent military uprisings, economic dislocation, financial chaos, and political bickering. (*Cont. p. 234.*)

Central America
1823–25

UNITED PROVINCES OF CENTRAL AMERICA. Under the leadership of José Matías Delgado, a lawyer and priest of San Salvador and a proponent of Central American independence from both Spain and Mexico since 1811, a constitutional assembly met in Guatemala City in 1823. By this time Iturbide, who had sought to unite Central America with the Mexican Empire by force, had abdicated. Freed from Mexican domination, Central-American leaders declared their independence, 24 June, and created "The United Provinces of Central America," made up of Guatemala, San Salvador, Honduras, Nicaragua, and Costa Rica.

By Nov. 1824 a constitution had been drawn up, and the first Central American Congress convened and elected Manuel José Arce (1783?–1847), a follower of Delgado, as president of the new confederation, 25 Feb., 1825. The establishment of a new government did not bring peace, however, and military uprisings soon plunged Central America into chaos. (*Cont. p. 250.*)

Colombia, Venezuela, and Ecuador
1811–18

THE RISE OF BOLÍVAR. Led by Caracas patriots, Venezuelan insurgents convened a congress in Mar. 1811, and on 5 July declared Venezuela independent from Spain. On 21 Dec. a Venezuelan Congress promulgated a constitution, the first patriotic group in the Spanish colonies to do so.

A disastrous earthquake occurred in Venezuela on 28 Mar., 1812. It took 20,000 lives, but caused little damage in royalist-controlled areas. This demoralized the insurgent cause, since the masses viewed the disaster as divine chastisement of the rebels.

On 25 July, 1812, Francisco Miranda, leader of the Coro expedition of 1806 and by this time commander of the insurgent armies in Venezuela, was forced to capitulate to the Spanish commander at San Mateo. Miranda was suspected of treason; seized by a group of patriots led by a wealthy creole, Simón Bolívar (1783–1830) ; and handed over to the Spanish authorities, 31 July. Miranda was confined in dungeons in Puerto Rico and Cádiz, Spain, where he died on 14 July, 1816.

During the latter part of 1812 Bolívar assumed leadership of the faltering independence struggle and moved to the neighboring viceroyalty of New Granada (Colombia), where independence sentiment was strong. Having defeated several royalist armies in New Granada, he returned with his companions to Venezuela and occupied Caracas, 4 Aug., 1813.

In Jan. of the following year he founded the 2nd Venezuelan Republic, and assumed the title of Liberator.

Meanwhile Fernando VII had been restored to the throne of Spain. This led to a resurgence of counterrevolutionary forces in Venezuela. The royalists were led by the brutal but able José Tomás Boves, whose *llaneros* (plainsmen) defeated Bolívar in several engagements, and were able to take Caracas. Once again Bolívar had to flee to Colombia. Counterrevolutionary sentiment was strong everywhere except in Argentina, however, and he was obliged to leave even Colombia. In May 1815 he sought refuge in Jamaica.

It was not until early 1817 that Bolívar was able to return to the mainland. Once there, with the aid of the patriot *llanero* leader, José Antonio Páez (1790–1873), he gradually regained control of the interior of Venezuela. On 24 Nov., 1818, a new congress reaffirmed Venezuelan independence.

1819-25

REPUBLIC OF GRAN COLOMBIA. Aided by a large army of British soldiers of fortune, Bolívar defeated the royalists at the Battle of Boyacá, 7 Aug., 1819, paving the way for the occupation of Bogotá, Colombia. In the same month the Republic of Colombia was proclaimed. On 17 Dec. a constituent assembly promulgated a constitution for a "United States of Colombia," to include both Colombia and Venezuela, with Bolívar as president. After the Battle of Carabobo in Venezuela, 24 June, 1821, a decisive victory for the patriot forces, the struggle against Spain in the northern part of South America had been won.

Ecuadorian patriots had first risen in 1809, but not until they were helped by Bolívar and San Martín, the Argentinian liberator of Chile, was independence secured in Ecuador. Royalist resistance ended there after the Battle of Pichincha, 24 May, 1822, won by Bolívar's subordinate, Antonio José Sucre (1795–1830).

Bolívar went to Quito and convinced Ecuadorian patriots that they should join with Colombia and Venezuela in the creation of a "Republic of Gran Colombia," 16 June, 1822. From this time until

his death on 17 Dec., 1830, Bolívar strove to keep in being the republic he had created. (*Cont. p. 237.*)

Argentina and Chile

1810

REVOLT IN BUENOS AIRES. In 1810, Argentine creoles, many of whom had taken part in repelling the British attacks on Buenos Aires of 1806–7, demanded that the viceroy of La Plata resign. Led by Manuel Belgrano (1770–1820), the creoles met so little opposition that the viceregal government was overthrown bloodlessly. It was replaced by a junta, or governing council, 25 May, 1810, which ruled in the name of the captive King Fernando. Independence, however, was the ultimate aim, as the junta's appeal for aid from Great Britain showed. From Buenos Aires armed forces were sent to Bolivia, Paraguay, and Uruguay (all parts of the viceroyalty of La Plata), but in each instance either strong royalist opposition (in Bolivia) or unwillingness to remain part of the La Plata viceroyalty (in Uruguay and Paraguay) frustrated the plans of the Buenos Aires patriots to incorporate the other provinces in a united front against Spain.

1816-21

ASCENDANCY OF SAN MARTÍN. While the creole leaders (*porteños*) in Buenos Aires argued whether they should adopt a monarchical form of government and retain some ties with the mother country or establish a completely independent republic, delegates from 13 interior Argentinian provinces met at Tucumán, organized themselves into the "United Provinces," and declared their independence from Spain, 9 July, 1816. Spain sent no army to reconquer the La Plata region and, in the absence of a common enemy, the port city of Buenos Aires and the provinces of the interior found it impossible to agree on anything except the desirability of independence. The *porteños* insisted on establishing a strong central government with its seat at

Buenos Aires, while the patriots of the interior were equally insistent on a loose confederation. Fighting soon broke out between the 2 factions. Whereas the aristocratic creoles of Buenos Aires sought to establish a prosperous and orderly government on the coast, the interior fell under the sway of regional military chieftains (*caudillos*).

In the midst of this bickering, a Spanish-trained creole officer, José de San Martín (1778–1850), concentrated on the military task of freeing the neighboring territory of Chile from royalist control. Having trained an army for 2 years in the Andean city of Cuyo, he crossed the high Andes into Chile and on 12 Feb., 1817, decisively defeated the royalists at the Battle of Chacabuco. He then unexpectedly refused to assume political leadership in Chile, making way for Bernardo O'Higgins (1778–1842), Chilean patriot whose father had served as viceroy of Peru. O'Higgins completed the liberation of the rest of Chile by winning the Battle of Maipú, 5 Apr., 1818. He ruled Chile as virtual dictator until 28 Jan., 1823, when, discouraged by constant uprisings, he resigned and retired to Peru.

With the assistance of the brilliant British Admiral Thomas Cochrane (1775–1860), San Martín sailed from Chile in Aug. 1820 with a large army. His object was to extend the revolution to Peru, which had remained the center of royalist strength in South America. A year of fruitless negotiations between San Martín and the viceroy of Peru went by. Ultimately San Martín forced his way into Lima, 9 July, 1821, and in Aug. assumed political power as "Protector" of Peru. (*Cont. p. 242.*)

Peru and Bolivia

1822

GUAYAQUIL CONFERENCE. Bolívar, coming from Quito, and San Martín, coming from Lima, met at the coastal city of Guayaquil, Ecuador, to make plans for the final conquest of Peru and Bolivia, which were still largely royalist in sym-

pathy. What precisely transpired at the Guayaquil Conference, 26–27 July, 1822, is not known. It appears, however, from San Martín's subsequent departure (he returned to Buenos Aires and from there embarked for France) that he and Bolívar could not agree on fundamentals and that, to avoid future disputes, San Martín chose to withdraw altogether.

1824

INDEPENDENCE OF PERU AND BOLIVIA. With San Martín out of the way, Bolívar and his follower, Sucre, continued the campaign in Peru. They defeated the royalists at the Battle of Junín, 6 Aug. At Ayacucho, south of Lima, 9 Dec., was enacted the last major confrontation between royalists and patriots in Spanish America. The victory of the patriots ensured the independence of Peru and Bolivia. (*Cont. p. 240.*)

Paraguay and Uruguay

1811–13

PARAGUAYAN CONSTITUTION OF 1813. Paraguayan patriots, having established a governing junta after the overthrow of the royalists on 14 May, 1811, accepted a treaty of alliance with Buenos Aires, 12 Oct. A Congress succeeded the junta, and in 1813 adopted a constitution which gave considerable powers to 2 consuls, who were to alternate in authority every 4 months. This arrangement reflected the commanding positions of 2 junta members, Fulgencio Yegros and José Gaspar Rodríguez Francia (1761?–1840). At the same time, the Congress of Asunción, unwilling to send troops to Argentina, abrogated the military alliance of 1811, and declared Paraguay independent from all countries.

1814–25

DICTATORSHIP OF FRANCIA. In Oct. 1814, Francia prevailed on a newly elected congress to end the 2-man consulship and appoint him sole chief executive of Paraguay. Thus was initiated the dictatorship which lasted until his death in 1840.

URUGUAYAN INDEPENDENCE. Uruguay was not to achieve independence as easily or as quickly as Paraguay. Despite the vigorous leadership of a Spanish-trained creole officer, José Gervasio Artigas (1774–1850), both Argentina and Brazil sought to annex the strategically placed "Banda Oriental," as Uruguay was then called. In 1824 Brazil succeeded in doing so, which led to the outbreak of war between Brazil and Argentina with Uruguay as the prize. (*Cont. p. 246.*)

COLONIAL BRAZIL, 1760–1808

1760–77

ADMINISTRATION OF POMBAL. Sebastião José de Carvalho e Mello, Marquês de Pombal (1699–1782), minister to King José of Portugal from 1750 until the latter's death in 1777, introduced many changes in Brazil. One of his first acts was to expel the Jesuits as enemies of royal absolutism. This deprived the country of some of its best teachers, and led to a decline of the missions to the Indians. In order to centralize government, Pombal designated Brazil as a viceroyalty, and moved the capital from tropical Bahía to the more temperate Rio de Janeiro, 1763. Before his time there were still 11 private captaincies, but he purchased or confiscated all of them, creating in their place two new crown captaincies (Maranhão and Pará). These were ruled directly from Lisbon until 1774, when they became part of the viceroyalty. Pombal also established a new system of superior courts at Bahía and Rio, and curbed the powers of the military officers in charge of districts. He was equally zealous in promoting fiscal, commercial, and economic reforms. In 1765 the annual commercial fleets were abolished, and from that time onward individual sailings were permitted. Two monopolistic commercial companies were created to operate in the economically backward northern regions, one for Pará and Maranhão and another for Pernambuco and Paraíba. Until 1771 the rich diamond fields were worked by individuals granted contracts by the crown. In that year, however, Pombal brought all the Brazilian diamond fields under the direct control of royal agents. Crown revenues increased following the introduction of more efficient extractive processes in the gold-mining industry.

1778–1806

ADMINISTRATION IN THE REIGN OF MARIA I. Pombal lived until 1782, but was removed from office at the accession of Queen Maria I (ruled 1777–1816) because his dictatorial methods had alienated Portuguese and Brazilians alike. His basic policies, however, were continued by the queen's new ministers, as is evidenced by a decree, 1785, prohibiting factories in Brazil as a protection for Portuguese industry. Similarly, the crown continued to guard its financial interests in Brazil by imposing severe penalties on diamond poachers, tax dodgers, and smugglers.

MINAS GERAES CONSPIRACY. In 1789 resentment against crown policy came to a head in the economically depressed region of Minas Geraes. A small group of Brazilian intellectuals, imbued with the ideas of the French *philosophes* and the Constitution of the U.S.A., began to rally support for a rebellion against Portugal. The plot was soon uncovered by local authorities, the orders for collecting overdue taxes that had inspired the conspiracy were rescinded, and the leading conspirators arrested. One of them, Joaquim José da Silva Xavier, known as Tiradentes ("Tooth Puller") because of his informal practice of dentistry, assumed major responsibility for the revolt. Captured in Rio, 10 Apr., 1789, he was executed, 21 Apr., 1792, after a long trial. In time he came to symbolize the dream of an independent, republican Brazil.

1807–8

TRANSFER OF THE COURT. In 1807 Napoleon decided to conquer Portugal in retaliation for her continued alliance with Britain. When French forces approached Lisbon, Nov. 1807, British advisers prevailed on Prince Regent João, son of the insane Queen Maria, to embark for Brazil to escape capture. On 25 Jan., 1808, the regent, his mother the queen, his wife Carlota (daughter of Carlos IV of Spain), and some 15,000 Portuguese notables arrived at Bahía aboard British and Portuguese vessels. The Portuguese court established itself at Rio and remained there for the duration of the French occupation of Portugal.

BRAZILIAN INDEPENDENCE, 1808–25

1808–16

RULE OF JOÃO VI. Having established his court at Rio de Janeiro on 8 Mar., 1808, following his escape from the French in Portugal, the prince regent, João, won the hearts of both the literate creoles and the illiterate masses of Brazil by his enlightened rule and his obvious liking for the country. He opened the ports to unrestricted foreign trade; founded educational institutions; established the first printing press, a central bank, a mint, hospitals, and a national library; and encouraged foreign immigration. On 16 Dec., 1815, he elevated Brazil from the status of colony to that of realm and, on the death of his mother, Queen Maria, 20 Mar., 1816, he assumed the title of King João VI (ruled 1816–26), king of Portugal, Brazil, and Algarves. He resisted, however, all efforts to persuade him to return to Portugal.

1820–25

THE EMPIRE OF BRAZIL. In 1820 the royal, British-dominated government of Portugal was overthrown by a popular revolt. In order to ensure the survival of the Braganza dynasty, João had at last to return home. To act in his stead in Brazil he designated his 21-year-old son, Dom Pedro.

Through their new Parliament, the Portuguese people demanded that Pedro also return to Portugal, but he, with full support from Brazilian patriots, led by José Bonifacio de Andrada e Silva (1763?–1838), declared that he would remain in Brazil. On 9 Jan., 1822, he reiterated his determination to govern the country without interference from Portugal by assuming the title of Perpetual Defender and Protector of Brazil, and by calling a constituent congress in June. On 7 Sept. the third step toward Brazilian independence was taken when Pedro announced his intention to fight for independence if need be. His cry of "Independence or Death" in answer to yet another summons to return to Lisbon is known as the "cry of Ypiranga." Fortunately, the Portuguese government did not choose to fight, and Brazilian independence was achieved with little bloodshed. On 12 Oct., 1822, Dom Pedro was proclaimed constitutional emperor of Brazil and crowned on 1 Dec. A constitution for the new empire was adopted in 1824. (*Cont. p. 247.*)

THE COLONIES OF THE CARIBBEAN, 1760–1825

1760–83

IMPACT OF EUROPEAN WAR. The islands of the Caribbean, colonized by Spain, Britain, France, and other European powers in the 16th and 17th cents., subsisted in 1760 chiefly by exporting sugar, which was produced on plantations by imported African slave labor. War in Europe led to frequent changes of ownership in the West Indies. In Jan. 1762 Britain declared war on Spain and captured Martinique, St. Lucia, St. Vincent, and Grenada. In Aug. Havana fell to a British fleet, and in Oct. Carlos III of Spain sued for peace. By the Treaty of Paris, 10 Feb., 1763, Britain restored Martinique, Guadeloupe, and St. Lucia, but kept St. Vincent and Dominica. Peace brought greater prosperity to Spanish Cuba and the French islands, but the British islands declined.

The outbreak of the War of American Independence caused near starvation in the British West Indies, many portions of which were occupied by French and Spanish forces between 1778 and 1782. The Treaty of Versailles, 3 Sept., 1783, restored the *status quo,* except that Florida was ceded to Spain and Tobago to France. Since after 1783 the U.S.A. was a foreign power so far as the British were concerned, American ships could no longer trade in British West Indian ports as they had before the war. Recourse was had to smuggling, but the islands did not recover their prosperity.

1784–1806

DECLINE OF SPANISH POWER. In 1796 Spain was drawn into the European war on the side of France. For Spain's possessions in the West Indies the result was disastrous. Communications with Europe were cut and the Spanish islands laid open to enemy attack. In 1797 Trinidad was seized by the British.

REVOLT OF SAINT-DOMINGUE. The most valuable French possession in the Caribbean was Saint-Domingue (Santo Domingo), the western half of the island of Hispaniola. In 1789, French planters there sent delegates to the Estates-General, as did the planters of Martinique and Guadeloupe. These were the first colonial representatives to sit in a metropolitan legislative body. The delegates' concept of liberty, equality, and fraternity, however, did not extend to the slaves or mulattoes of their islands, and by 1791 the *colons* of the West Indies were being assailed by the French abolitionist society, the Amis des Noirs. On 15 May of that year the vote, previously held only by the planting class, was granted to mulattoes in the French West Indies by the French National Assembly.

Influenced by revolutionary fervor, the huge slave population of Saint-Domingue grew restive. In Aug. 1791 a large-scale slave revolt broke out in the northern part of the island. By the end of Sept. some 10,000 slaves and mulattoes and 2,000 whites had lost their lives. In Paris the Jacobins gained control, and on 4 Apr., 1792, granted the vote to free Negroes as well as mulattoes, sending an expeditionary force of 6,000 men to enforce their decrees, Sept.

TOUSSAINT L'OUVERTURE. By 1793 both Britain and Spain were at war with France, and both sent expeditionary forces to Saint-Domingue. Port-au-Prince fell to the British, May 1794. Meanwhile, Toussaint L'Ouverture (1743–1803), a former African slave, who had entered the Spanish service in 1793 and built up a force of 4,000 men, deserted the Spaniards and joined the forces of Republican France to prevent the possible restoration of slavery that he believed would result from a British take-over of Saint-Domingue. Beset by Toussaint's troops and suffering from yellow fever, the British were compelled to withdraw from the island. Toussaint also expelled the representatives of France, Aug. 1797. By 1801 he felt secure enough to declare himself governor general over the whole island (the eastern half of which had been ceded by Spain to France by the Treaty of Basel, July 1795). Next year, however, Napoleon dispatched a force of 20,000 men under Gen. Charles Victor Emmanuel Leclerc (1722–1802), who defeated Toussaint in the field, and then kidnapped and deported him to France, where he died, Apr. 1803. The French army began to suffer from yellow fever in its turn, and the resumption of hostilities in Europe following the expiration, 16 May, 1803, of the Truce of Amiens made it difficult for Napoleon to send it reinforcements. The evacuation of Hispaniola was accordingly ordered, and on 8 Oct., 1804, Jean Jacques Dessalines (1758–1806), Toussaint's successor, had himself proclaimed Emperor Jacques I of an independent state. Following the assassination of Jacques I, 17 Oct., 1806, Henri Christophe (1767–1820) assumed control of the northern part of the island and Alexandre Pétion (1770–1818) of the south.

1807–25

POSTWAR SETTLEMENT. At the end of the Napoleonic Wars, Britain retained St. Lucia, Tobago, and Trinidad, and purchased from the Netherlands the

South American territories of Demerara, Essequibo, and Berbice, which became British Guiana. Martinique and Guadeloupe reverted to France and the eastern half of Saint-Domingue to Spain.

REPUBLIC OF HAITI. The emperor of Saint-Domingue, Henri Christophe (Henri I) died on 8 Oct., 1820, and in 1822 the 2 parts of the island were united as the Republic of Haiti under President Jean Pierre Boyer (1776–1850). (*Cont. p. 251.*)

THE ASIAN AND AFRICAN WORLDS, 1760—1870

East Asia

CHINA

CHINA IN 1760. Chung-kuo (meaning "Central Country") is commonly known to the West as China, after the ancient kingdom of Chin which unified the several states into a great empire in 211 B.C. From that year to the end of the Ch'ing ("Clear") dynasty in 1912, China, except for a few lapses (the Three Kingdoms and Western Tsin, A.D. 220–317; the Five Dynasties and Ten States, A.D. 907–960), remained a unitary empire which claimed universality. The Ch'ing dynasty was founded in 1644 through military conquest by the Manchus, an alien people from Manchuria outside the Great Wall. Once in power, the Manchus, while striving to preserve their identity, saw the wisdom of taking over the Chinese form of government, as well as Confucian ideology, virtually intact.

IDEOLOGY. The Chinese political system was largely based upon control through ideas. For 2 millenniums the political and ethical ideas of the Confucian school dominated Chinese politics. Fundamental to the Confucian philosophy was the concept that heaven (e.g., seasons), earth (e.g., resources), and men (e.g., government) formed an eternal trinity; consequently the close affinity of universe, state, family, and man (the ruler as "Son of Heaven" and "king-father," the ministers as "parent-officials," the people as "children-people"). Another important Confucian concept was the idea of the perfectibility of human nature and the corresponding concept of the duty of government to bring it to fruition. Thus, the whole Confucian ideology was one of order and education (or indoctrination), and government by merit. The recruitment of officialdom was made mainly through civil-service examinations based on Confucian literature (the Four Books and the Five Classics), the cornerstone of scholarship and bureaucracy. Thus, equal opportunities were provided for all qualified persons who would rule by merit.

EMPEROR. Theoretically, the emperor was an absolute monarch vested with all legislative, executive, and judicial powers. He was the source of authority, the defender of orthodoxy, the fountainhead of honor and privilege, the head of armed forces, and the dispenser of tax revenues. In practice, however, imperial power was limited by Confucian ideology, tradition, and established rules of the dynasty, the complexity of state affairs, the dimension of the empire, the admonition of the censors, and, above all, the pressure of public opinion reinforced by the concept of *t'ien ming* ("mandate of heaven"), with its implied right of rebellion against the misuse of power.

CENTRAL GOVERNMENT. The important agencies in the central government were the Grand Secretariat (*Nei-ko*), composed of 6 Grand Secretaries; the Grand Council (*Chün-chi chu*), the most important agency, established in 1730 as a temporary military office with a varying number of councilors; the Censorate (*Tu-ch'a Yüan*), the "eyes and ears" of the emperor. All these agencies had important deliberative and advisory functions. Of the regular administrative agencies, the most important were the 6 ministries or boards: Civil Service, Rites, Revenue,

War, Justice, and Public Works. Each was headed by 2 ministers and 4 vice-ministers. The central government was a dyarchy, with roughly equal numbers of Chinese and Manchu high officials. The administration of dependencies (Mongolia, Chinese Turkestan (Sinkiang), Kokonor, Tibet) came under the jurisdiction of the Colonial Office; that of minority groups, under the Ministry of War.

LOCAL GOVERNMENT. China proper (c. 1.5 m. sq. mi.) consisted of 18 provinces: Chihli, Shantung, Shansi, Honan, Shensi, Kansu, Kiangsu, Anhwei, Kiangsi, Fukien, Chekiang, Hupeh, Hunan, Szechwan, Kwangtung, Kwangsi, Yunnan, Kweichow. (The number was increased to 22 with the additions of Sinkiang in 1884 and of Fengtien, Kirin, and Heilungkiang in 1907.) They were provided with 8 governors general, 18 governors, 19 finance commissioners, 18 judicial commissioners, 92 circuit intendants, 185 prefects, and 1,545 district magistrates. The chief functions of local government were the collection of revenues and the maintenance of peace. Other functions—settlement of legal disputes, public construction, relief work, maintenance of educational facilities—were rather limited in scope. Because of the vastness of the empire and the small number of officials, local governments enjoyed considerable autonomy within an over-all centralized political system. Many functions were assumed by the village, the family, and the trade association.

MILITARY FORCES. The banner forces of the Manchus were placed under command of Manchu generals in chief. Banner garrisons of c. 4,000 men were established at Peking, in capitals and other strategic spots in the northwestern and southern provinces, and in major Chinese centers of population. The remnants of the Ming system and new recruits were reorganized as a Chinese constabulary known as the Army of the Green Standard which was used to suppress banditry.

WORLD CONCEPT. Influenced by the Confucian philosophy of "one sun in the sky and one sovereign over humanity," the Chinese conducted their foreign relations on a principle of the inherent inequality of nations. All people beyond the pale of Chinese civilization were considered barbarians; all states other than China were regarded as Chinese tributary states. This claim of universality and cultural superiority remained unchallenged until the mid-19th century, when China began to decline under the impact of western expansion.

1760–92

CONSOLIDATION OF THE EMPIRE. Under Hung-li (1711–99), the Ch'ien-lung emperor (ruled 1736–95), the Chinese Empire attained its maximum territorial expansion. In 1750 he had re-established political control in Tibet by giving the Dalai Lama full temporal authority under the general supervision of 2 imperial residents at Lhasa. Ch'ien-lung's "10 Great Campaigns" included 2 against the Dzungars (a western Mongol tribe) in the Ili region, 1755, 1756–57; the conquest of Chinese Turkestan (Sinkiang) and its Moslem inhabitants, 1758–59; the subjugation of the Burmese, 1766–70; 2 campaigns against the Chin-ch'uan aborigines in western Szechwan, 1747–49, 1771–88; the subjugation of Annam, 1788–89; and 2 campaigns against the Gurkhas, 1792, to repel an invasion of Tibet and to extend Chinese suzerainty to Nepal. The most important victories were the conquests of Ili and Chinese Turkestan, which greatly increased the size of the empire and eliminated the possibility of invasion by Mongols and Turks. All these campaigns took place on the edges of the empire under the command of Manchu generals, and all required large expenditures which tended to weaken the central government.

1793–1824

RISE AND FALL OF HO-SHEN. In the last few years of his reign, the Ch'ien-lung emperor was preyed upon by Ho-shen (1750–99), who had become his chief minister in the 1780's. Corruption and nepotism spread throughout the government as Ho-shen placed his men in key positions and exacted large bribes from officials. The disintegration of civil and military administration permanently damaged the foundations of the Ch'ing dynasty. On 15 October, 1795, the Ch'ienlung emperor abdicated. His son Yungyen (1760–1820) became the Chia-ch'ing emperor, 9 Feb., 1796, but was not allowed to assume real power. After the Ch'ienlung emperor died, 7 Feb., 1799, the Chiach'ing emperor arrested Ho-shen, 12 Feb., confiscated his property, and forced him to commit suicide.

REBELLION OF THE MIAO TRIBESMEN. 1795–97. Miao tribes living in the Kweichow-Hunan-Szechwan border area seized several cities, 1795. Ho-shen's brother Ho-lin and Fu-k'ang-an were ordered to suppress them. Their halfhearted campaign was a pretext for appropriation of military funds by themselves and Ho-shen. In 1796 both commanders died, probably of malaria, and E-le-teng-pao (1748–1805) succeeded them, pacifying most of the Miao tribes by 1797.

WHITE LOTUS REBELLION. 1796–1804. The White Lotus Society (*Pai-lien chiao*), a religious cult active in the late Yüan and Ming periods which had become a secret society, led peasant disorders in Hupeh, 1796. Under the slogan "the officials have forced the people to rebel," the insurrection, led by Liu Chih-hsieh (d. 1800) and Yao Chih-fu (d. 1798), spread to Honan and Szechwan, becoming violently anti-Manchu. Inefficient imperial forces recovered several cities, but failed to take Hsiang-yang, Hupeh, the rebel headquarters, 1797–98. Costs rose and military supplies became inadequate because of Ho-shen's exactions. After the Chia-ch'ing emperor came to power, the war entered a new phase. Imperial forces and local militia in the rebellious provinces of Szechwan, Shensi, Kansu, Hupeh, and Honan were placed under the command of Le-pao (1740–1819), whose policy of arming the peasants and fortifying the villages enabled him to suppress the rebels in northeast Szechwan. In Sept. 1799, E-le-teng-pao became commander in chief; and in Oct., Te-leng-t'ai (1745–1809) was made assistant commander. They successfully enforced Le-pao's policy in Shensi and Szechwan. Liu Chih-hsieh was captured and executed, 1800. The rebels gradually lost ground, and the rebellion ended in 1804. However, the Manchu military establishment had shown itself to be weak, which thus encouraged further rebellion.

CRUSHING OF COASTAL PIRATES. 1800–1809. Another symptom of decline was the increase of piracy on China's southeast coast in the late 1700's. The Manchus had no central naval force, and pirates took advantage of the inability of provincial flotillas to cross jurisdictional lines. Chinese pirates joined with Annamese in raids and received rewards from the Annamese government. The 2 leading Chinese bands of Ts'ai Ch'ien (d. 1809) and Chu Fen (d. 1809) continued to plunder after the Annamese pirate fleet was damaged by a typhoon, 11 Aug., 1800, and destroyed by the forces of Chekiang naval commander Li Ch'ang-keng (1750–1808). They finally were suppressed in 1809.

REBELLION OF THE HEAVENLY REASON SOCIETY. 1813. The leaders of the secret organization known as the Heavenly Reason Society (*T'ien-li chiao*), Lin Ch'ing (d. 1813) of Peking and Li Wen-ch'eng (d. 1813) of Hua-hsien, Honan, had acquired wealth through divination and a large following among officials, military officers, and court eunuchs. After their influence had spread to Honan, Shantung, and Chihli, they decided to incite an uprising in Peking. The magistrate of Hua-hsien learned of the plan and arrested Li. While 3,000 rebels attacked the Hua-hsien government office and freed him, partisans seized several cities in Chihli and Shantung. Li proclaimed his intention to restore the Ming dynasty. With the aid of officials and eunuchs, 200 rebels entered the Forbidden City, 8 Oct. The heir to the throne, Min-ning (1782–1850), staved off the rebels until imperial troops arrived. Lin Ch'ing was arrested and executed. The Manchu general Na-yen-ch'eng (1764–1833) received command of Chihli, Shantung, and Honan forces and quelled the rebellion by year's end.

A NEW EMPEROR. On 2 Sept., 1820, the Chia-ch'ing emperor died at Jehol, and on 3 Oct. Min-ning ascended the throne as the Tao-kuang emperor. He embarked on a policy of frugality, reducing palace expenses and admonishing officials to economize.

1825–32

MOSLEM REBELLION IN CHINESE TURKESTAN. Moslem (Muslim) dissatisfaction with the corrupt practices of Ch'ing frontier officials was exploited by Jehangir (d. 1828), a descendant of the ruling Hodjas of Turkestan. After an unsuccessful attempt to seize Kashgar, 1820, in alliance with Buriat Mongols, he continued to harass border patrols and incite dissension. The Tao-kuang emperor appointed Ch'ang-ling (1758–1838), a general of Mongolian origin, military governor at Ili in 1825. In March 1826, Ch'ang-ling assumed office. Jehangir led his men across the border, July 1826, and took Kashgar, Yarkand, and Khotan. Imperial troops recovered Kashgar, 28 Mar., 1827, but Jehangir escaped. After recovering the other cities, the Ch'ing commanders spread a false rumor of their departure from Kashgar. Jehangir soon crossed the border. He was pursued by Manchu troops, captured, Feb. 1828, and executed in Peking, June.

1833

END OF THE ENGLISH EAST INDIA COMPANY'S MONOPOLY. From the mid-17th cent. to 1834, China's relations with the West and with the British East India Company were essentially identical. Foreign trade had been limited to Canton in 1757, and a group of security merchants at Canton, the Co-hong, had become the sole Sino-foreign trade and communications link. Merchant dissatisfaction with the tariffs and restrictions on the trading system had led the British government to dispatch the Macartney, 1793, and Amherst, 1816, missions to Peking, but they had been regarded as unsatisfactory tribute bearers and their requests had been ignored. The development of the opium trade after 1773

(illegal after 1796) served only to aggravate the situation as addiction increased and China experienced a drain on silver. In 1833 the English East India Company's charter expired, and Parliament chose not to renew it. Thus, the China trade was thrown open to all. To replace the East India Company's chief factor at Canton, Lord Napier (1786–1834) was given a royal commission, 10 Dec., as first superintendent of trade at Canton.

1834–37

THE STRUGGLE FOR DIPLOMATIC EQUALITY. The British government made 2 major attempts to use the Canton superintendency to establish direct communications with Chinese officials on terms of diplomatic equality. In 1834 Lord Napier went to Canton, 25 July, without Chinese permission and attempted to communicate with the governor general by letter rather than by sending a petition through the Co-hong. His violations of Chinese regulations and precedents caused a temporary suspension of trade, threats of military action, and his withdrawal to Macao, 26 Sept. In 1837, Capt. Charles Elliot (1801–75) won the right to communicate by sealed document and to come to Canton whenever business required his presence, but made no progress in securing direct cummunication.

1838

ATTACK ON THE OPIUM TRADE. The shifting of opium traffic to the Kwangtung and Fukien coastal areas—an action necessitated by new anti-opium campaigns—caused a sharp decline in prices. The Tao-kuang emperor approved, Oct., legislation (15 June, 1839) to punish by death both opium smoking and selling. Foreign opium traders would be pardoned upon voluntary surrender before Jan. 1841; thereafter, they would be executed. In Dec. opium belonging to a British merchant was seized, and foreign trade at Canton was suspended. Some British ships bearing opium ignored

Elliot's orders, 18 Oct., to leave the Bogue (Hu-men-chai), forcing him to avoid conflict by petitioning Chinese officials to co-operate with him in suppressing opium smuggling. Trade was resumed on 30 Dec.

1839

LIN TSE-HSÜ AT CANTON. The imperial commissioner assigned to destroy the opium trade, Lin Tse-hsü (1785–1850), arrived at Canton on 10 Mar. He ordered, 18 Mar., foreign merchants to surrender all opium in their possession within 3 days and to file a bond declaring that they would refrain from importing opium on pain of death. Lin rejected the merchants' compromise proposals, suspended trade, 24 Mar., and blockaded the foreign settlement. On Elliot's orders c. 20,000 chests of opium were surrendered, Apr.–May, and all British subjects left the city. Elliot insisted that the merchants not sign bonds, but a few defied him in the hope of resuming trade.

OUTBREAK OF THE 1ST OPIUM WAR. On 7 July, a party of drunken British sailors killed a villager, Lin Wei-hsi, at Chien-sha-tsui, Kowloon. The Chinese authorities and Elliot soon clashed over the matter of who had criminal jurisdiction. When Elliot failed to surrender the culprits to him for trial, Lin Tse-hsü cut off provisions to the British at Macao, 15 Aug., causing them to withdraw, first to their ships and then to Hong Kong. In Sept. a brief skirmish between Chinese and British ships occurred after Elliot had led a fleet to Kowloon to demand supplies and the Chinese had refused to provide them. As a result of a more serious Sino-British engagement, 3 Nov., at Chuenpi (Ch'uan-pi), in which 15 Chinese were killed and 4 junks damaged, the Chinese authorities declared that trade with Britain would cease permanently.

1840

1ST BRITISH EXPEDITION. In a dispatch of 18 Oct., 1839, Lord Palmerston had informed Elliot of his decision to send an expeditionary force to blockade Canton with the aim of securing the establishment of satisfactory diplomatic and commercial relations with China. In Apr. 1840, Parliament authorized military expenditures, and an expeditionary force was sent to Canton. It blockaded Canton in June; sailed north along the coast; passed through Amoy, 2 July; reached Chusan Harbor, 4 July; and took Ting-hai, Chekiang, 5 July. By 28 July, it had blockaded Ningpo and the mouth of the Yangtze. The Manchu official Ch'i-shan (d. 1854) was ordered to negotiate with the British. On 11–12 Aug. the British fleet arrived at Taku, and Ch'i-shan met with Elliot. In mid-Sept., Ch'i-shan persuaded the British to return to Canton for negotiations. He was appointed to replace Lin Tse-hsü and to conduct the negotiations. Ch'i-shan reached Canton on 16 Dec.

1841

CHUENPI CONVENTION. The British became impatient with the Canton negotiations and seized the forts at Chuenpi on 7 Jan. On 20 Jan., Elliot and Ch'i-shan signed a convention which provided for the cession of Hong Kong, diplomatic equality, the payment of indemnity, and the reopening of Canton to trade before 1 Feb. However, both the British and the Chinese governments disavowed the settlement. Ch'i-shan was cashiered, and Elliot was soon recalled.

STRUGGLE FOR CANTON. On 26 Feb. the British seized the forts at the Bogue. Sino-British negotiations were re-opened, 5 Mar. A large Chinese force reached Canton, 14 Apr., and hostilities resumed, 21 May. By 25 May, the British had seized all forts surrounding Canton. On 27 May, a truce was concluded which provided for the ransoming of Canton and the exchange of prisoners.

2ND BRITISH EXPEDITION. An expeditionary force led by the British plenipotentiary, Sir Henry Pottinger (1789–1856), reached Macao, 10 Aug. Elliot left for England, 24 Aug. The British force seized Amoy, 26 Aug.; Ting-hai, 1 Oct.; Chinhai, 10 Oct.; and Ningpo, 13 Oct.

1842

TREATY OF NANKING. After reinforcements had arrived from India, the British forces captured Chapu, 18 May; Woosung, 16 June; Shanghai, 19 June; and Chinkiang, 21 July. On 5 Aug. Pottinger arrived at Nanking to open negotiations with the Chinese representatives Ch'i-ying (d. 1858), I-li-pu (d. 1843), and Niu Chien (d. 1858). He required them to accept his draft treaty without modification. On 29 Aug. the Treaty of Nanking was signed aboard the British warship *Cornwallis*. Its 13 articles (none of which dealt with the opium trade) provided for the cession of Hong Kong, the opening to foreign trade of 5 ports (Canton, Amoy, Foochow, Ningpo, Shanghai), the payment of Mex. $21 m. as an indemnity, the establishment of diplomatic communication on the basis of equality, and the promise of a "fair and regular tariff." The signing of this treaty marked the end of the tribute system and the crumbling of China's traditional world concept.

1843

TREATY OF THE BOGUE. On 26 June, Ch'i-ying, now governor general of Liang-Kiang and imperial commissioner, and Sir Henry Pottinger exchanged ratifications of the Treaty of Nanking at Hong Kong, that day declared a British crown possession with Pottinger as its governor. In the Supplementary Treaty of the Bogue of 8 Oct., the British introduced the "most favored nation" principle, by which they secured automatically all privileges which might henceforth be granted to any other country. Thereafter, all Sino-western treaties contained this clause.

1844

TREATY OF WANGHIA. Signed by American commissioner Caleb Cushing

(1800–79) and Ch'i-ying on 3 July, this treaty gave the U.S.A. all treaty rights enjoyed by Britain with 2 additional provisions: (1) a clear stipulation that the principle of "extraterritoriality" applied to both civil and criminal cases; (2) the right to revise the treaty after 12 years.

TREATY OF WHAMPOA. This treaty, signed 24 Oct. on board the French corvette *Archimède*, resembled the British and American treaties. These treaties created a new legal structure, a treaty system cemented by most-favored-nation clauses. Because the treaties were forced upon China and gave her no reciprocal concessions, they were termed "unequal" or "semicolonial."

TOLERATION OF CHRISTIANITY. French efforts resulted in an imperial decree, Dec., granting toleration to Roman Catholic missions, proscribed in 1724. Catholic missionary activity had continued on a reduced scale. Protestantism had been brought to Canton by the British missionary Robert Morrison (1782–1834) in 1807 and by such Americans as the educator Elijah Bridgman (1801–61) and the medical missionary Peter Parker (1804–88). Ch'i-ying on 22 Dec. extended the toleration edict to Protestantism. Missions were opened at the 5 treaty ports.

1846

RESTORATION OF CHUSAN. Kulangsu and Chusan, occupied by the British, were to be restored to China on completion of the indemnity payment stipulated by the Treaty of Nanking. Although China paid the last installment on schedule, 22 Jan., Chusan was not restored until 25 July and only after Ch'i-ying had signed, 4 Apr., a convention promising that Chusan would not be given to any other foreign country. This guarantee was known as a "nonalienation agreement."

1847

CANTON CITY QUESTION. Canton had lost its virtual monopoly of foreign trade with the opening of Amoy, 3 Nov., 1843; Shanghai, 17 Nov., 1843; Ningpo, 1 Jan., 1844; and Foochow, 1 July, 1844, as treaty ports. The Cantonese, already plagued by unemployment, refused to allow the British into their walled city. On 3 Apr. the British captured the principal forts at the Bogue, rendering them useless. The British governor of Hong Kong, Sir John Davis (1795–1890), forced Ch'i-ying to sign an agreement, 6 Apr., that promised entry at the end of 2 years.

1848–50

ADDITIONAL INCIDENTS AND FURTHER POSTPONEMENT. In June 1848, Davis' successor, Samuel G. Bonham (1803–63), wrote to arrange the 1849 entrance into Canton. After a meeting at the Bogue, Feb. 1849, Ch'i-ying's successor, Hsü Kuang-chin (d. 1858), informed him, 1 Apr., of an imperial rescript declaring the emperor's inability to overcome the unanimous opposition of the Cantonese. Formal protests in 1849 and 1850 had no effect. Bonham's successor, Sir John Bowring (1792–1872), made further requests of Hsü's successor, Yeh Ming-ch'en (1807–69), without success.

1850–56

ONSET OF THE TAIPING REBELLION. While Chinese officialdom was preoccupied with foreign affairs, uprisings occurred every year between 1841 and 1850 as a result of governmental corruption, natural catastrophes, rapid population growth, overtaxation, the formation of secret societies and local defense units, and ethnic rivalries. In this restive atmosphere there began in Kwangsi a protest movement which in the 1850's attempted to destroy the political and social foundations of Confucian China and replace them with a totalitarian theocracy. The Taiping Rebellion was a near revolution which brought the Ch'ing dynasty to the brink of destruction.

A PROPHET-IDEOLOGUE AND A PROPAGATOR-ORGANIZER. The Tai-ping Rebellion was generated by 2 village schoolmasters, Hung Hsiu-ch'üan (1814–64) and Feng Yün-shan (1822–52). Hung, who came from a Hakka family in Hua-hsien, Kwangtung, decided after a long illness, 1837, and a reading of Christian tracts, 1843, that he was a son of God, a new messiah called to destroy demons and to establish the Kingdom of God on earth. His early convert Feng Yün-shan founded the Hakka-dominated God Worshipers Society (*Pai-Shang-ti-hui*), with headquarters at Tzu-chin-shan in Kwangsi. The God Worshipers became known for their militancy as well as for their religious fervor.

PLOT FOR REVOLUTION. By 1850 there were over 10,000 God Worshipers. Their 6 leaders were Hung, Feng, Yang Hsiu-ch'ing (d. 1856), Hsiao Ch'ao-kuei (d. 1852), Wei Chang-hui (d. 1856), and Shih Ta-k'ai (d. 1863). These 6 self-styled Sworn Brothers of the Heavenly Family plotted the establishment of a new dynasty. The real basis of their authority was their home-made Christianity, which caught the imagination of their followers. The God Worshipers were summoned, July, to Chin-t'ien village in Kueip'ing for an organizational meeting. All their belongings were placed in the general treasury, in which they shared equally. Hung and Feng retired to Hua-chou village for safety reasons, but they were besieged by government troops, Dec. A company of God Worshipers rescued them, killing a junior officer, 2 militia leaders, and a number of soldiers.

GOVERNMENT RESPONSE TO UPRISINGS. The Tao-kuang emperor died on 25 Feb., leaving his son I-hsin (1831–61), the Hsien-feng emperor, a legacy of maladministration and discontent. When petitions regarding Kwangsi riots reached Peking that summer, he sent officials and troops to Kwangsi to quell the disturbances. However, neither he nor they understood the dynastic aspirations of the God Worshipers until too late.

OUTBREAK OF HOSTILITIES. On 11 Jan., 1851, Hung Hsiu-ch'üan's 37th birthday, the formal beginning of the Taiping Rebellion was marked by the declaration of the establishment of the *T'ai-p'ing T'ien-kuo* (Heavenly Kingdom of Great Peace), with Hung as *T'ien Wang* (Heavenly King). The rebels advanced to Ta-huang-chiang, 13 Jan., where they won a battle, 18 Feb., with imperial troops commanded by Hsiang Jung (d. 1856). With the arrival, Apr., of reinforcements commanded by Sai-shang-a (d. 1875), the new imperial commissioner, the rebels were forced to retreat to Tzu-chin-shan, but they escaped to Yung-an in Sept. While the imperial forces were regrouping, the Taipings at Yung-an organized their kingdom. On 17 Dec., Hung conferred the title of *wang* (king) on the 5 other leaders.

FROM YUNG-AN TO CH'ÜAN-CHOU. Early in 1852, imperial forces besieged Yung-an, but the Taipings escaped, 6 Apr., and moved north to attack Kweilin, 18 Apr.–19 May. Having failed to take Kweilin, they proceeded to Hsingan, 22 May, and Ch'üan-chou, 25 May, which they intended to by-pass on their way to Hunan. However, after Feng Yün-shan was wounded by artillery fire, they attacked Ch'üan-chou, captured it, 3 June, and slaughtered its inhabitants.

DEFEAT AT SO-I FERRY. When the Taipings took Ch'üan-chou, Chiang Chung-yüan (1812–54), leader of a local corps known as the Hunan Braves, hastened to So-i Ferry to ambush the rebels before they reached Changsha. The Taipings were taken by surprise, 8 June, 1852, and defeated in a 2-day battle. At least 1,000 well-disciplined officers and soldiers in the Taiping army were killed. Among the casualties was Feng Yün-shan, the only Taiping leader who might have held the leadership together and have checked the religious fanaticism that later proved distasteful to most Chinese. The battle demonstrated the ability of such highly trained local forces as the Hunan Braves to overcome the insurgents, and it gave Changsha much-needed time to prepare its defenses.

SIEGE OF CHANGSHA. The Taipings spent about 2 months at Taochow regrouping. Bandits, secret-society members, and peasants joined them by the thousands. After capturing Ch'enchow, 16 Aug., Hsiao Ch'ao-kuei led a small detachment against Changsha, 11 Sept. He was fatally wounded on 5 Oct. The main Taiping force besieged Changsha until 30 Nov. without success. The Taipings then crossed the Hsiang River and took Yiyang, 3 Dec., and Yochow, 13 Dec. With captured boats and munitions, they sailed down the Yangtze. After taking Hanyang, 19 Dec., and Hankow, 29 Dec., they crossed the river to attack Wuchang, the capital of Hupeh.

FROM WUCHANG TO NANKING. The Taipings blew up the city walls and took Wuchang, 13 Jan., 1853. Enriched by tributes and the provincial treasury, the rebels, now estimated at 1 m., decided to abandon Wuchang. Moving east along the Yangtze, they took Kiukiang, 18 Feb., and Anking, 24 Feb. They reached the outer defenses of Nanking on 8 Mar. and captured the city on 19 Mar. Having decided to make Nanking the seat of their kingdom, they renamed it T'ienching (Celestial Capital). Thus the movement was transformed into a stationary organization. In May, expeditions were dispatched north and east, but neither was a real success. The first conquering drive of the Taipings had come to an end, giving the Ch'ing government time for the reorganization of old forces and the gentry time for the creation of new ones.

TSENG KUO-FAN AND THE HUNAN ARMY. To meet the Taiping threat, the Ch'ing government had decided to establish reliable local forces, under gentry leadership. On 29 Jan., 1853, Tseng Kuo-fan (1811–72) assumed the responsibility of recruiting and drilling a Hunan militia. However, he decided to go beyond the government plan and create a provincial force, trained by him and responsible to him. The Hunan Army (*Hsiang-chün*) included such local units as the "Hunan Braves" of Chiang Chung-yüan. Tseng decided to train his men thoroughly in military tactics and Confucian teachings and to give them experience in battle with local bandits before sending them against the Taipings. His force was more highly paid than the imperial troops and was funded by the gentry. Tseng also began to organize a naval force, Aug., in hopes of driving the Taipings off the Yangtze. Despite reprimands from the emperor, he refused to send his men to the aid of Hupeh in 1853, saying that they were not ready.

1ST HUNAN ARMY BATTLES. Early in 1854, the Hunan Army clashed with the Taiping West Expedition forces and was defeated. However, on 1 May, Tseng's men forced the Taipings at Hsiang-t'an to flee the area. Another victory, at Yüeh-chou in July, cost the Taipings more than half their fleet and control of the central Yangtze. On 14 Oct., Tseng's forces entered Hupeh, where they recovered Wuchang (later recaptured by the Taipings) and Hanyang.

TAIPING REFORM PROGRAMS. The structure of the Taiping political system was set forth in the "Land System of the Celestial Dynasty," promulgated early in 1854. The population was to be organized into a system of military units similar to that set forth in the *Chou-li,* a classical Chinese text. However, the military leaders were also to be responsible for political, social, and religious life in a totalitarian extension of the system. Property, land use, and economic distribution all came within this communal framework. Although this extraordinary law was not put into practice in most Taiping areas, some of its provisions influenced later movements in China.

POWER STRUGGLE IN NANKING. In 1856, Yang Hsiu-ch'ing attempted to usurp the position of Hung Hsiu-ch'üan. On 2 Sept., Wei Ch'ang-hui, at Hung's instigation, assassinated Yang and slaughtered all of his family and followers at Nanking. Wei then plotted to destroy Shih Ta-k'ai, but Shih learned of the plan and escaped. When Wei assassinated Shih's family and supporters, Shih, who had rejoined his troops, decided to march on Nanking, Nov. Hung Hsiu-ch'üan then ordered the assassination of Wei Ch'ang-hui, his family, and his adherents.

Shih returned to Nanking and served as chief of staff and administrative head of the government, but he later, May 1857, left the capital and the Taiping movement. Of the original leaders, only the increasingly mad Hung Hsiu-ch'üan was left at Nanking, and the Taiping movement soon lost all coherence and direction.

ATTEMPTS AT TREATY REVISION. Both the American and the French treaties of 1844 called for revision in 12 years. Applying the most-favored-nation principle, the British maintained that the Treaty of Nanking had been subject to revision since 1854 and that other treaties, therefore, should be revised. The Ch'ing government evaded negotiations.

THE "ARROW" AFFAIR. On 8 Oct. the lorcha *Arrow,* a Chinese-owned vessel registered at Hong Kong and captained by an Englishman, was boarded by Chinese police, who arrested 12 Chinese and lowered the British flag. British Consul Harry Parkes (1828–85) and Sir John Bowring demanded redress and apology. Dissatisfied with Yeh Ming-ch'en's response, they sent naval forces upriver to Canton, 23–27 Oct. The attack produced no results, and they withdrew, after which Cantonese destroyed the foreign business ghetto, 14 Dec. The British decided to launch a full-scale expedition, allegedly to protect the treaty system, and the French announced their willingness to co-operate after a French missionary had been killed in Kwangsi.

1857

ANGLO-FRENCH CAPTURE OF CANTON. Rebellion in India made it necessary to divert there troops intended for China. Lord Elgin (1811–63) reached Hong Kong in July. He and Jean Baptiste Louis Gros (1793–1870) were the high commissioners authorized to submit final demands to Yeh Ming-ch'en. Anglo-French forces at Hong Kong declared Canton under blockade, Nov., and final demands were made, Dec.: treaty revision, payment of an indemnity, and access to Canton city. Yeh replied with a promise to resume trade. On 29 Dec., Canton was seized. Yeh, captured on 5 Jan., 1858, was sent to Calcutta, where he died, 1859. Canton was placed under a Chinese governor and an Anglo-French commission.

1858

LOSS OF TAKU AND THE TREATIES OF TIENTSIN. Their request that the Ch'ing court commission a plenipotentiary to confer with them at Shanghai having been refused, Lord Elgin and Baron Gros sent their fleets north in Apr., accompanied by U.S. envoy William Bradford Reed (1806–76) and Russian envoy Adm. E. V. Putiatin (1803–83). These forces sacked the forts at Taku, 20 May, causing the Ch'ing court to send Kuei-liang (1785–1862) and Hua-sha-nai (1806–59) to arrange a truce at Tientsin. The 56-article Anglo-Chinese treaty, 26 June, gave the British the right to maintain a resident envoy at Peking and to travel in the interior of China. The Yangtze was to be opened to foreign trade; Newchwang, Tengchow, Taiwan, Swatow, and Kiungchow were to be opened as trade ports; and the tariff rates were to be revised. An indemnity was to be paid for losses and military expenses. A similar Sino-French treaty, 27 June, contained provisions for the opening of Nanking as a trade port and the right of missionaries to have access to all of China. Treaties also were signed with Russia, 13 June, and the U.S.A., 18 June.

1859

RESUMPTION OF HOSTILITIES. With the departure of the western forces, the Ch'ing government decided against permitting foreign envoys in Peking and opening the Yangtze. At Shanghai tariff conferences, Kuei-liang unsuccessfully offered the abolition of tariffs on all foreign goods in return for annulment of these treaty provisions. When British and French representatives arrived off Tientsin on their way to Peking for treaty ratifications, they were refused passage, June. On 25 June, they tried to force passage, but were repulsed.

1860

OCCUPATION OF PEKING. Anglo-French forces landed at Pei-t'ang, 1 Aug.; defeated imperial forces under Seng-ko-lin-ch'in (d. 1865); and entered Peking, 13 Oct., the emperor having fled to Jehol, 22 Sept. On 18 Oct., Elgin destroyed the Summer Palace (*Yüan Ming Yüan*) in retaliation for the execution of 21 members of a 39-man Anglo-French negotiation party seized 18 Sept. (The survivors had been released on 8 Oct.) On 24 Oct., Elgin and Gros exchanged ratifications of the 1858 treaties and signed new conventions with the emperor's brother I-hsin (1833–98), Prince Kung. The British secured the Kowloon Peninsula, and the French won the right for Catholic missions to hold property in the interior. These conventions opened all of China to the West.

RUSSIAN TERRITORIAL EXPANSION IN MANCHURIA. Beginning in 1854, Russians had founded posts along the northern bank of the Amur to Khabarovsk. The Treaty of Aigun, 16 May, 1858, had ceded to Russia the northern bank of the Amur and given her joint possession of the area between the Ussuri River and the sea, but Peking had rejected it, 1859. The Sino-Russian Treaty of Peking, 14 Nov., 1860, confirmed the Treaty of Aigun and gave Russia the area where Vladivostok had been founded in July 1860.

UNIFICATION OF ANTI-TAIPING COMMAND. In May 1860, after the Taipings destroyed the government forces known as the Great Camp of Kiangnan, Tseng Kuo-fan was made governor general and imperial commissioner for the suppression of the Taipings in south China. He was given full power to deal with all matters relating to the campaign, including the levy of funds.

1861

TSUNGLI YAMEN. On 20 Jan., 1861, Prince Kung received approval for creation of a foreign office, known as the Tsungli Yamen, through which the

Ch'ing government became versed in western diplomacy. It worked to uphold treaties; established the foreign-run Maritime Customs Service, 1861, and a school (the *T'ung-wen Kuan*) to train young men in foreign languages, 1862; and generally promoted knowledge of the West.

RECOVERY OF ANKING. Tseng Kuo-ch'üan (1824–90), a brother of Tseng Kuo-fan, had begun the siege of Anking on 17 May, 1860. In early 1861 the Taiping commanders Li Hsiu-ch'eng (d. 1864) and Ch'en Yü-ch'eng (d. 1862) harassed Tseng Kuo-fan at Ch'i-men in southern Anhwei in the hopes of drawing Tseng Kuo-ch'üan away from Anking. When this maneuver failed, Ch'en unsuccessfully attacked Tseng Kuo-ch'üan in Apr., May, and Aug. Tseng finally took Anking, 5 Sept. It became a base for the recovery of Nanking.

TSENG KUO-FAN'S CAMPAIGN STRATEGY. Soon after Anking was captured, Tseng Kuo-fan decided that he should attack the Taipings on 3 fronts in a campaign that would encompass all of central China. Tseng Kuo-ch'üan would move the Hunan Army downriver to Nanking; Tso Tsung-t'ang (1812–85) would retake the important supply areas in Chekiang; and Li Hung-chang (1823–1901) would campaign in the Shanghai-Soochow area.

DEATH OF THE HSIEN-FENG EMPEROR. On 22 Aug., the Hsien-feng emperor died at Jehol, having named his son Tsai-ch'un (1856–75) emperor and appointing an 8-man regency whose actions were subject to approval by Yehonala (1835–1908), known as the Empress Dowager Tz'u-hsi, and Niuhuru (1837–81), the Empress Hsiao-chen. Prince Kung was in charge of affairs at Peking. With Prince Kung's help and that of his brother I-huan (1840–91), Tz'u-hsi overthrew the 8 regents in Nov. and established the reign period known as *T'ung-chih,* meaning "joint rule."

1862

LI HUNG-CHANG AND THE HUAI ARMY. Li Hung-chang, who had left Tseng Kuo-fan's service early in 1861, was persuaded by Tseng to recruit a force in Anhwei and go to Shanghai as acting governor of Kiangsi. With his new Huai Army and a detachment of Tseng's veterans, he reached Shanghai in Apr., the trip having been paid for by the western powers. He found foreign forces commanded by British Adm. James Hope (1808–81) and French Adm. Léopold Auguste Protet (1808–62) defending the city against the Taiping Gen. Li Hsiu-ch'eng, and a foreign-officered Chinese brigade helping the imperial forces. After Charles George ("Chinese") Gordon (1833–85) reorganized the latter force, it became known as the Ever-Victorious Army. It spearheaded Li's later campaigns on T'ai-ts'ang, K'un-shan, Chiang-yin, and Soo-chow. The Ever-Victorious Army was disbanded after the capture of Ch'ang-chou, 11 May, 1864. Li Hung-chang's position at Shanghai was particularly important to Tseng's campaign because he could provide customs and tax revenues for the support of Tseng's armies.

1863–64

SIEGE OF NANKING AND COLLAPSE OF THE HEAVENLY KINGDOM. Tseng Kuo-ch'üan had encamped at Yü-hua-t'ai under the walls of Nanking on 31 May, 1862, and Li Hsiu-ch'eng had attacked him day and night from 12 Oct. to 26 Nov. before giving up the siege of his camp. From 31 May, 1863, to 19 June, 1864, Tseng worked to strengthen his camp and to encircle the city. Li advised Hung Hsiu-ch'üan to march out of Nanking, but Hung, counting on God's help, refused to leave. There was almost nothing to eat in Nanking, and the Taipings became desperate. Hung died in June, perhaps by suicide. His son Hung Fu (1849–64) succeeded him, with Hung Jen-kan (1822–64), a cousin of Hung Hsiu-ch'üan, as regent. On 19 July, Nanking fell. Mass suicide and slaughter ensued, leaving too few Taipings to carry on the movement. The Ch'ing government crushed the Taiping Rebellion, but it lost much power to such regional leaders as Tseng Kuo-fan in the process.

1865–68

THE NIEN REBELLION. Taiping remnant troops gave new impetus to the Nien disturbances on the borders of Kiangsu, Anhwei, Honan, and Shantung. The Nien were secret-society bandit gangs which had worked together after 1853 and had co-operated with the Taipings for a time. Their leader, Chang Lo-hsing (d. 1863) had shaped them into an effective army by mid-1856. In June 1865, Tseng Kuo-fan was ordered to Shantung, where Seng-ko-lin-ch'in had been killed, May 1865, while fighting Nien bandits. On 12 Dec., 1866, after an unsuccessful campaign, he recommended that Li Hung-chang succeed him. The Nien split into 2 bands. Under Li Hung-chang's direction, the Huai Army destroyed one band in Jan. 1868 and the other in Aug. 1868.

THE "SELF-STRENGTHENING" MOVEMENT. The western powers' obvious military superiority impelled such Chinese generals as Li Hung-chang and Tseng Kuo-fan to seek the introduction of western technology into China. The "self-strengthening" (*tzu-ch'iang*) movement began the westernization of China with the establishment of arsenals to make guns and ships.

1870

TIENTSIN MASSACRE. Believing rumors that the French Sisters of Charity extracted the eyes and hearts of orphans entrusted to their care, a mob gathered at the Catholic church in Tientsin, 21 June, 1870. The French consul intemperately shot at a Chinese official and wounded his servant. The infuriated mob killed the consul and 20 other foreigners, including 10 nuns. The incident revived Sino-foreign tensions after a decade of comparative calm, and caused a resurgence of hope in China that foreigners might be excluded. Tseng Kuo-fan investigated the case and temporized with the French until France's defeat in the Franco-Prussian War left her powerless to threaten China. (*Cont. p. 306.*)

JAPAN

JAPAN IN 1760. In 1760 the government of Japan had been stable for 160 years. Tokugawa Ieyasu (1542–1616) had won the battle of Sekigahara in 1600 and thereby established himself as the most powerful leader in Japan. He built his capital at Edo, now Tokyo. Like his warrior predecessors, he did not aspire to usurp the imperial throne. Instead, he obtained from the emperor the title of shogun, or generalissimo, which became *de facto* hereditary in the Tokugawa family. In theory the shogun was the emperor's deputy; in fact he ruled in his own name. The emperor was confined to his palace in Kyoto and performed only ceremonial functions.

The shogun's government was called the Bakufu, or Camp Government, alluding to its military origin. The Bakufu ruled directly about a quarter of Japan. The other three-quarters were parceled out among feudal lords called daimyo. Hence, the Tokugawa regime has been described as centralized feudalism. There were 3 types of Tokugawa vassals. The tozama (outside lords), whose domains were remote from Edo, had sworn loyalty to Ieyasu only after the Battle of Sekigahara. Satsuma in Kyushu and Choshu in western Japan were powerful tozama domains. The fudai (hereditary vassals) had sworn loyalty before Sekigahara. Most were quite small landholders, and many of them were enfeoffed around the Tokugawa lands in central Japan. The shimpan (related lords) were junior members of the Tokugawa family itself. Kii, Owari, and Mito were the greatest shimpan domains.

The domains of the daimyo were called han. There were about 250 han. They were to a large extent autonomous in their internal affairs, and the Bakufu had no power to levy taxes upon them. The shogun lived off revenue from his own lands, as the other daimyo did. However, the Bakufu had regulations to keep the han under control. The most important of these was the sankin-kotai (alternate attendance) system. Each daimyo was required to maintain a mansion in Edo and to spend time there every other year in nominal attendance on the shogun. He was also obliged to leave his wife and his heir in Edo whenever he returned to his han. Heavy sankin-kotai expenses kept many han budgets unbalanced.

The early shoguns ruled personally, but later power passed more and more into the hands of the Roju (elders), the highest administrative-legislative body in the Bakufu. The Roju were usually selected from the most powerful fudai families. The tozama lords had no voice in the Bakufu councils. Shimpan daimyo did not regularly participate in policy decisions, but could be called on for advice. In the 19th cent. rivalry arose between the entrenched fudai bureaucracy and those tozama and shimpan daimyo who desired to have more say in national affairs.

By shogunal edict, Japan was isolated from all contact with foreign countries. The only exception was a small and tightly controlled trade with Holland and China through Nagasaki. When western knowledge began to spread in the late 18th cent., those few who carried it were called "Dutch scholars." By the 19th cent., the seclusion policy, reinforced by Japan's natural insularity, had become almost sacred. Hence its breakdown under western pressure caused great internal stresses.

In the long peace of the Tokugawa period, history moved slowly. The ideal of Tokugawa statesmen, steeped in Confucian thought, was a simple agrarian economy. The whole political structure was based on a land tax calculated in units (koku) of rice. But money and commerce spread, and local industries gradually arose. Thus traditional economic ideas slowly became antiquated. Society was, according to official teaching, divided into 4 classes (excluding the remote emperor and his court): samurai (warriors), farmers, artisans, and merchants. The samurai lived off rice stipends from their lords. But with prices rising steadily, they fell deeper and deeper into debt to the merchants, while some merchants bought samurai status. Farmers suffered from oppressive conditions in the countryside and fled. And the despised merchants, at the bottom of the social hierarchy, became wealthy, although politically powerless.

By the late 18th cent., Japan was ready for overt social, economic, and institutional change. Not long after seclusion became a serious issue, direct and all-embracing loyalty to the emperor—rather than the traditional chain of loyalty through the daimyo to the shogun—became a burning issue as well. The latter was summed up in the slogan "sonno" ("Revere the emperor"); the former, in the slogan "joi" ("Expel the barbarians"). The two were often fused as the battle cry of the rebellious in the last years of Tokugawa rule.

1760–86

GOYOKIN. In 1761–62, the Bakufu extracted the first recorded goyokin (a forced loan in lieu of taxation) from the merchants of Japan's commercial center, Osaka. Commercial activity itself was not taxed.

OPPOSITION TO THE BAKUFU. In 1767, Yamagata Daini (b. 1725) was executed in Edo for having expressed opposition to the Bakufu and for having advocated exclusive loyalty to the emperor. Takenouchi Shikibu (1712–67), a man known to hold similar views, was exiled. These two were unique in an age when Tokugawa authority was unquestioned.

RISE OF TANUMA OKITSUGU. In 1769 Tanuma Okitsugu (1719–88) was appointed a provisional Roju and given the title of court chamberlain. Henceforth Tanuma, who had risen from low status in the samurai class, was the most powerful figure in the Bakufu. He became a full Roju in 1772.

TEMMEI FAMINES. The famines of 1783–87 (named for the Temmei year period, 1781–89) devastated much of Japan. Bad weather was compounded by the eruption of Mt. Asama in 1784, when large areas were covered with infertile ash.

"TANUMA PERIOD." The Shogun Ieharu, with whom Tanuma's fortunes were linked, died in 1786 and Tanuma was deposed shortly thereafter. Tanuma is known in Japanese history for greed and corruption. But in fact he was progressive in that he did not fight the trend toward increased commercial activity and was not prejudiced in favor of an agrarian economy. He had encouraged land reclamation and riparian works; promoted foreign trade through Nagasaki; developed a broad colonization plan for Hokkaido; consolidated existing Bakufu monopolies and created new ones; promoted the licensing by the Bakufu of large merchant associations; taxed trade and transportation, although irregularly; and tried to make the Bakufu and not the Osaka merchants the chief lending agency to the daimyo. There is even some evidence to suggest that he was considering modifying the seclusion policy.

1787-93

KANSEI REFORM. Shogun Ienari (1773–1841) succeeded Ieharu in 1787. Matsudaira Sadanobu (1758–1829), a conservative, replaced Tanuma as the chief Bakufu official. His program is known as the Kansei reform (from the Kansei year period, 1789–1801). Matsudaira Sadanobu re-established agriculture as the sole permissible base of Bakufu finances. He enforced reductions in government spending and consumption, set up a famine storehouse system, discouraged foreign trade, and tried to reverse the tide of emigration from the villages to the cities. He also canceled or reduced the debts of Tokugawa vassals below daimyo rank. These highly traditional measures helped for a while to stabilize the Bakufu, but in the end weakened it by preventing it from adapting to the times.

PROHIBITION AGAINST NON-ORTHODOX TEACHINGS. Matsudaira Sadanobu forbade, 1790, the pursuit of nonorthodox studies in Bakufu schools. The prohibition was later extended to the han. Only the official Confucianism taught by the Hayashi family was allowed. Matsudaira Sadanobu was dismissed in 1793.

RUSSIAN VISIT. The Russian Erik Laksman (1737–1796) visited Nemuro in Hokkaido in 1792 to open trade. He left when told he would have to visit Nagasaki in order to make contact with the Bakufu.

1794-1829

INCREASE IN WESTERN CONTACTS. In 1804, Nikolai Rezanov arrived in Nagasaki as ambassador from Russia. He wished to propose trade, and carried a letter from Alexander I. After lengthy delays he was sent away. The rebuff resulted in a number of Russian raids in Hokkaido and the Kuriles. In 1808, H.M.S. *Phaeton* entered Nagasaki and, with the menace of her guns, forced the authorities to grant her provisions. The governor of Nagasaki committed suicide. In 1811, Vasilii Golovnin (1776–1831) landed with peaceful intent on Kunashiri in the Kuriles, but was captured and held for 2 years.

Reacting to these foreign incursions, the Bakufu published the "No Second Thought" edict, 1825. It required that all foreign vessels approaching Japan's shores be destroyed and their crews killed if they tried to land.

REFORM IN SATSUMA. Zusho Hiromichi (1776–1848) was appointed, 1827, to carry out a reform program in Satsuma. Satsuma owed huge sums to the merchants of Osaka; Zusho simply canceled the debt. He also enforced very tight control over the han's sugar monopoly, thereby securing for Satsuma a lucrative income source.

REFORM IN MITO. Tokugawa Nariaki (1800–1860) became daimyo of Mito, north of Edo, 1829. He set about strengthening his domain's defenses and reviving the martial spirit of its samurai.

1830-45

TEMPO FAMINES. After a period of prosperity, the Tempo famines (from the Tempo year period, 1830–44) caused great suffering, 1832–36. Peasant revolts became commonplace.

REVOLT IN OSAKA. Oshio Heihachiro (1793–1837), a minor Bakufu official, led an abortive uprising in Osaka, Mar. 1837. While it lasted, it glaringly revealed the weakness of the Bakufu's troops.

"MORRISON" EXPEDITION. The U.S. ship *Morrison* entered Edo Bay ostensibly to return castaways, Aug. 1837. Actually, the mercantile interests behind the voyage hoped to obtain a coaling and provisioning agreement, to secure good treatment for shipwrecked U.S. seamen, and to open trade. But the *Morrison* was fired on both at Uraga, in Edo Bay, and at Kagoshima in Kyushu, the Satsuma capital, and was unable to approach the land.

REFORM IN CHOSHU. Murata Seifu (1783–1855) was appointed to carry out a reform program in Choshu, 1838. He brought the han budget under tight control; stressed promotion of men of ability rather than of birth; redeemed the debts of the han and of its samurai at rates close to cancellation; and abolished the han's commercial monopolies (except for a warehousing operation at Shimonoseki) on the grounds that they benefited the merchants and not the han.

IMPACT OF THE OPIUM WAR. When Great Britain defeated China in the Opium War of 1839–42, informed Japanese took the event as a very menacing demonstration of western intentions and of western military might. They feared Japan might have to defend herself against the same menace. In 1841, Takashima Shuhan (1798–1866), an expert in western gunnery, was invited to demonstrate his art in Edo.

THE TEMPO REFORM. Mizuno Tadakuni (1794–1851) became the principal Roju. To retrieve the Bakufu from grave financial trouble, Mizuno undertook the highly conservative Tempo reform, July 1841. He curbed consumption through the usual sumptuary edicts, cut Bakufu expenses, and reduced the debts of the lower-ranking Tokugawa vassals. He abolished merchant associations and tried to enforce price controls. He attempted to redistribute the shogun's lands more evenly around Osaka and Edo, and prohibited peasants from migrating to the cities. But his policies were unrealistic and had little effect. In 1842, Mizuno relaxed the "No Second Thought" edict out of fear of foreign reprisals. He ordered daimyo to supply foreign ships with requested provisions and to advise them to leave. In Nov. 1843 he was dismissed.

1846–52

WESTERN ARMS. In 1846 western gun-manufacturing techniques were introduced to Satsuma. The western han felt keenly the need for defense preparations.

In Oct. 1847, Komei became emperor.

THE BIDDLE EXPEDITION. Two American warships under Commo. James Biddle (1783–1848) entered Edo Bay, June 1846. Biddle's goals were the same as those of the *Morrison* expedition. The Bakufu refused to negotiate and Biddle was sent away.

ARMS PURCHASE BY SATSUMA. In 1848 Satsuma concluded an arms deal with a French ship that called at the Ryukyu Islands. The Bakufu had prohibited the purchase of foreign arms, but was powerless to stop Satsuma.

INCREASE IN DEFENSE MEASURES AGAINST THE WEST. In June 1849 the Bakufu sent a report to the daimyo on recent entries of foreign ships into Japanese waters. The Bakufu wished to have the daimyo increase their military preparedness against the foreign threat, in concert with the Bakufu's own stepped-up defense preparations.

Japan's first successful reverberatory furnace went into operation in Hizen, the han adjacent to Nagasaki, in 1850. It was used to manufacture cannon.

1853–54

PERRY'S 1ST VISIT. On 8 July, 1853, Commo. Matthew Calbraith Perry (1794–1858) anchored off Uraga in Edo Bay with 4 warships. His mission was to secure good treatment for U.S. sailors and to obtain facilities for navigation and trade. His instructions, which he had insisted on writing himself, allowed him to act in whatever manner he deemed most effective to achieve these goals. When the Japanese procrastinated, Perry sent surveying missions close to Edo. Within a week he obliged the Japanese to receive from him, in a formal ceremony at a place ashore of his own choosing, a letter from President Fillmore to the shogun. The letter contained the U.S. demands. Perry left on 17 July, after informing the Japanese that he would return for an answer the following spring.

THE SUCCESSION DISPUTE. Shortly after Perry's visit, Ieyoshi (12th shogun, ruled Oct. 1837–July 1853) died. The 13th shogun, Iesada (1824–58), had no heir and was unlikely to have one. Hence a crucial succession dispute arose. Most fudai daimyo and high-ranking Bakufu officials backed Tokugawa Yoshitomi (1846–66), Iesada's first cousin and, like Iesada, a nonentity. The other candidate was Hitotsubashi Yoshinobu (1837–1913), the 7th son of Tokugawa Nariaki. Yoshinobu was a vigorous and promising young man. He was supported by many non-fudai daimyo who believed that the Bakufu should consult all men of ability (especially themselves) and not rely solely on the entrenched bureaucracy. Tokugawa Nariaki was the leader of this faction.

REQUEST FOR OPINIONS ON PERRY'S DEMANDS. The chief Roju Abe Masahiro (1819–57) had a translation of President Fillmore's letter sent to all daimyo and solicited their opinions, Aug. 1853. The object of this unprecedented step was to obtain a national consensus on policy. It has since been interpreted as a sign of weakness and indecision on the part of the Bakufu. Of the most important daimyo, about a third favored trade in some form. One of the most prominent of these was Ii Naosuke (1815–60) of Hikone. Another third wished to avoid war only in order to gain time for further defense preparations. Tokugawa Nariaki was the most prominent member of this group. He saw the crisis as a great chance to rally the martial spirit of the Japanese people. A final third advocated rejecting the U.S. demands outright. The consensus favored rejecting a treaty but avoiding war—an untenable compromise. Shimazu Nariakira (1809–58) of Satsuma stood alone, advocating trade with China and India but not with the U.S. In Oct. the Bakufu lifted its long-standing prohibi-

tion on the building of ocean-going ships, and in Dec. a Bakufu edict admitted the inadequacy of Japan's defenses and called for peace through delaying tactics.

PERRY'S 2ND VISIT. Perry returned with 8 warships, Feb. 1854, and insisted on carrying on the negotiations at Kanagawa, closer to Edo than the Bakufu would have liked. On 8 Mar. he received the shogun's answer to President Fillmore's letter.

TREATY OF KANAGAWA. By the Treaty of Kanagawa, 31 Mar., 1854, (1) coal and provisions were to be made available after 1 year at Hakodate, on Hokkaido, and at Shimoda, on the tip of the Izu Peninsula on Honshu; (2) adequate treatment of distressed seamen was promised; and (3) a consul could be appointed to reside at Shimoda after 18 months. In Oct. Great Britain obtained a treaty allowing her ships to call for supplies at Nagasaki or Hakodate.

1855–58

TREATY OF SHIMODA. The Russian Adm. Evfimii Putiatin (1803–83) concluded the Treaty of Shimoda with the Bakufu, Feb. 1855. Russia obtained coaling and refreshment rights at Nagasaki as well as at Hakodate and Shimoda, the boundary between Japan and Russia was drawn through the Kurile Islands, and Russia obtained extraterritorial status for Russians in Japan. In Nov. the Bakufu signed a trade agreement with the Netherlands.

INTERNAL CHANGES. During 1855, a power struggle developed between Tokugawa Nariaki and Abe Masahiro. Nariaki succeeded in forcing the resignation of 2 Roju. For the sake of closer supervision, Hakodate was annexed to the Tokugawa domains from Matsumae han, Apr. In Sept., the Bakufu opened a naval training school in Nagasaki, with Dutch instructors. In Nov., Abe Masahiro was succeeded by Hotta Masayoshi (1810–64).

APPOINTMENT OF TOWNSEND HARRIS. Townsend Harris (1804–78) arrived as U.S. consul in Shimoda, Sept. 1856, with the mission of concluding a commercial treaty. He was not welcomed, for the Japanese text of the Treaty of

Kanagawa required the consent of both countries to the appointment of a consul; the U.S. had followed the English text, which allowed unilateral appointment. In Nov. the Bakufu appointed a commission to study the possibility of trade with the U.S.

HARRIS CONVENTION. A convention proposed by Harris was signed in June 1857. It provided for the opening of Nagasaki as an additional port of call for U.S. ships; extraterritorial status for U.S. residents in Japan; the right for Americans to reside, lease property, and construct buildings; and an equitable discount rate for currency exchange.

TREATIES WITH THE NETHERLANDS AND RUSSIA. A treaty with the Netherlands was signed in Nagasaki, Oct. 1857. The Bakufu approved it after the fact. It permitted unlimited trade at Nagasaki and Hakodate by private merchants under Bakufu supervision. Putiatin signed a similar treaty for Russia a few days later.

HARRIS' AUDIENCE IN EDO. After lengthy procrastination, Harris was received in audience by the shogun in Edo, Dec. 1857. He presented his credentials and a letter from the U.S. president, in accordance with diplomatic practice.

1858–60

U.S. TRADE TREATY. The trade treaty proposed by Harris was ready for signature by Feb. 1858. It provided that a U.S. minister would reside in Edo; that trade would be carried on free of official intervention; that Nagasaki and Kanagawa would be opened to the U.S. in 1859, Niigata in 1860, and Hyogo (the present Kobe) in 1863; and that traders would be permitted to live in Edo in 1862 and in Osaka in 1863. But there was strong opposition to the text, so that signature was postponed until the emperor could be persuaded officially to approve it.

JAPANESE REACTION TO THE TREATIES. Hotta Masayoshi went to Kyoto, Feb. 1858, to obtain the emperor's approval of the Harris treaty. But the emperor felt that Osaka and Hyogo were too close to Kyoto, and also gave considerable weight to the opinions of the daimyo opposed to trade. The emperor refused. A decree, Apr., forced through the imperial council as a compromise, recognized the Bakufu's responsibility for foreign affairs. But Emperor Komei then advertised the fact that he had been coerced, thus rallying antiforeign, anti-Bakufu sentiment.

THE REGENCY. Alarmed at the crisis over the treaty and at the strength of the faction behind Hitotsubashi Yoshinobu, Ii Naosuke had himself appointed tairo (regent). From this exalted office, which was seldom filled, Ii was able to run the Bakufu firmly. In July 1858, he had the U.S. treaty signed without imperial approval, thus incurring the wrath of the imperial loyalists.

ANSEI PURGE. In Aug. 1858, Ii announced his decision in favor of Tokugawa Yoshitomi, the future Iemochi, as the shogun's heir. Iesada died and Iemochi became shogun. Ii dismissed Hotta and one other Roju. He ordered retirement or house arrest for Tokugawa Nariaki, Tokugawa Yoshikatsu (1824–83) of Owari, Shimazu Nariakira (1809–58) of Satsuma, Yamanouchi Yodo (1827–72) of Tosa and Matsudaira Yoshinaga of Echizen (1828–90). This was the beginning of the Ansei purge. It left Yoshinobu's backers disorganized and made Ii a quasi dictator within the Bakufu.

TREATY RATIFICATION. The Dutch, the Russians, and the British obtained treaties similar to the U.S. treaty, Aug. 1858, and France obtained a similar treaty, Oct. A Bakufu representative again went to Kyoto to obtain approval of the treaties, but the emperor still refused. In Feb. 1859, in a compromise decree, the court promised forbearance and the Bakufu undertook to prevent the opening of Hyogo and Osaka. Both committed themselves to revoke the treaties at some time in the future. Finally, in July, the treaties became effective, and foreign diplomats took up residence in Edo.

EXECUTION OF YOSHIDA SHOIN. Yoshida Shoin (b. 1830) was executed by the Bakufu, Nov. 1859. In later years, Shoin became a national hero. He started out as a military expert, a fervent advocate of Japanese self-strengthening, but not an opponent of the Bakufu. But after 1858 he became violently anti-Tokugawa. He was an inspiring teacher and writer. Several of the greatest Meiji-period leaders studied at his school in Choshu.

MISSION TO THE U.S. In 1860 an official Bakufu mission was sent to Washington to exchange ratification of the Harris treaty. The members of the mission were much impressed by Japan's backwardness relative to the U.S.

In Mar. 1860, Ii Naosuke was assassinated by a group of Mito warriors.

1860–63

INTERNAL POWER STRUGGLES AND DETERIORATION OF JAPANESE-WESTERN RELATIONS. In May 1860, the Bakufu proposed that the shogun marry Princess Kazunomiya, the emperor's sister. The court agreed, on the condition that the Bakufu undertake to cancel the treaties or expel the foreigners forcibly within 10 years.

The Bakufu granted monopoly rights for export consignments of many products to certain Edo wholesalers. This attempt at official control of trade was widely evaded.

Harris' secretary, Heusken, was murdered by extremists in Edo, Jan. 1861. Harris offered to ease the Bakufu's difficulties with the court by postponing the opening of Edo, Hyogo, Osaka, and Niigata. These had been due to open at the beginning of 1863.

In Mar. 1861, the Bakufu announced that a mission would visit the countries with which Japan had treaties in order to obtain their agreement to postpone the opening of the ports. The British minister, Sir Rutherford Alcock (1809–97), was gradually won over to support this plan. In July, extremists attacked the British legation, wounding 2 men.

In Jan. 1862, the mission to Europe departed.

THE LONDON AGREEMENT. The Bakufu mission concluded the London Agreement, June 1862. Edo, Osaka, Hyogo, and Niigata were to be opened only on 1 Jan., 1868. Japan promised full compliance with the treaties at the ports

already open. Russia, France, and Holland agreed later in 1862.

Urged by Satsuma and Choshu, the court demanded that Hitotsubashi Yoshinobu and Matsudaira Yoshinaga of Echizen be given high posts, and that the shogun visit Kyoto in order to discuss the expulsion issue.

Extremists attacked the British legation a 2nd time, killing 2 men.

In Aug. Yoshinobu was made the shogun's guardian.

THE RICHARDSON MURDER. Charles Richardson, a British visitor from China, was murdered by members of a Satsuma contingent at Namamugi, near Yokohama, Sept. 1862. Britain demanded an indemnity.

EXTREMIST CONTROL OF KYOTO. The Satsuma force which killed Richardson returned from Edo to Kyoto. On arrival, it found Kyoto under the control of extremists from Choshu, Satsuma, and Tosa. It therefore returned to Kagoshima, the Satsuma capital, leaving extremists in control of the court.

In Oct. 1862 the time required in Edo under the sankin-kotai system was cut down and the requirement that the wife and heir of each daimyo be left in Edo was abolished.

In Nov. the court appointed Sanjo Sanetomi (1837–91), an extremist court noble, as an envoy to the Bakufu to demand the expulsion of the foreigners.

1863–64

DEMANDS TO EXPEL WESTERN BARBARIANS. Great Britain served the Bakufu with an ultimatum to pay an indemnity of £100,000; to apologize for the Richardson murder; and to make Satsuma pay a £25,000 indemnity and execute the murderers, Mar. 1863.

The shogun went to Kyoto to discuss the right time and method for expelling the foreigners, Apr. Once he was back in Edo, however, the Bakufu announced that it was unable to carry out the emperor's expulsion order. The Bakufu and the han were to be put into effect the court's expulsion order on 25 June, 1863, but the Bakufu did nothing. Only Choshu took action, firing on an American steamer in the Shimonoseki Straits. Subsequent Choshu action rendered the straits impassable to foreign ships by the end of July.

BOMBARDMENT OF KAGOSHIMA. A British squadron bombarded Kagoshima, Aug. 1863, in order to enforce Britain's demands for justice in the Richardson affair. Much of Kagoshima was destroyed. The demands were eventually settled and Satsuma established close relations with Great Britain.

SATSUMA-AIZU COUP. Satsuma and Aizu troops seized the imperial palace gates and took control of Kyoto away from the Choshu-backed extremists, Sept. Sanjo Sanetomi and other radical nobles took refuge in Choshu. The shogun agreed again to visit Kyoto, this time as an indication of strength. This was the height of the kobu-gattai (union of court and Bakufu) movement promoted by Shimazu Hisamitsu (1817–87) of Satsuma and his allies.

In Feb. 1864, Hitotsubashi Yoshinobu, Matsudaira Yoshinaga of Echizen, Matsudaira Katamori (1835–93) of Aizu, Yamanouchi Yodo of Tosa, and Date Munenari (1818–92) of Uwajima formed a council which consulted regularly with the emperor. This was a completely unprecedented phenomenon. The council was dominated by Satsuma.

BREAKUP OF THE COALITION. The shogun, Iemochi, arrived in Kyoto. Disagreement over the policy he should adopt broke up the daimyo coalition, Feb. 1864. Shimazu wanted him to convince the emperor of the impracticability of expelling the foreigners, while Hitotsubashi Yoshinobu advocated compromise and the closing of Yokohama as evidence of Bakufu sincerity. All the daimyo except Yoshinobu returned to their han by early Apr. Yoshinobu came increasingly to favor the Bakufu, Shimazu to oppose it.

In Aug. a Choshu force of 2,000 men tried to seize control of Kyoto, but was repulsed, and in Aug. Choshu was declared in rebellion by the court.

BOMBARDMENT OF SHIMONOSEKI. A joint naval force of the treaty powers bombarded Shimonoseki, Sept., landed troops, and dismantled the gun batteries. This was in reprisal for Cho-

shu's attacks on foreign shipping. In Oct. a convention was signed, settling the Shimonoseki affair. Japan was given the choice of paying a $3 m. indemnity or of opening another port in the Inland Sea to trade.

1865–66

DECLINING POWER OF THE BAKUFU. In Mar. 1865 irregular military units under Kido Takayoshi (1833–77) and Takasugi Shinsaku (1839–67) overthrew the pro-Bakufu government of Choshu and defied the Bakufu. In Feb. the Bakufu had ordered the formation of a 2nd punitive expedition against Choshu, under the shogun's personal command. But most pro-Bakufu daimyo were by this time reluctant to participate.

Increased foreign pressure obliged the Bakufu to extract from the emperor formal approval of the 1858 treaties, Nov. 1865.

SATSUMA-CHOSHU ALLIANCE. Satsuma and Choshu concluded a formal, but secret, alliance, Mar. 1866. Satsuma agreed to strive to restore Choshu to favor at court and to support Choshu against the impending attack of the Bakufu.

The Bakufu sent an ultimatum to Choshu, demanding a drastic reduction of territory and the retirement of the daimyo. Choshu ignored the ultimatum, and in July a Bakufu force attacked it.

The death of Iemochi, Sept., gave the Bakufu a pretext to call a truce. In fact, the Bakufu force had been defeated. Choshu's troops were better equipped and trained than the Bakufu's. They included many peasants, a radical innovation.

Hitotsubashi Yoshinobu was named shogun.

1867–68

ACCESSION OF THE MEIJI EMPEROR. Komei died, Jan. 1867, and was succeeded by his 15-year-old son, the Emperor Meiji.

FURTHER DECLINE OF BAKUFU PRESTIGE. In Mar. the shogun and the French minister, Léon Roches (1809–

1901), met at Osaka. Roches proposed a complete reform program to modernize the Bakufu. Most of his measures were considered too radical, but those few that were implemented alarmed Satsuma and Choshu with the prospect of a Bakufu resurgence.

In June the shogun and the great daimyo met in Kyoto. They decided to open Hyogo to trade. The shogun pressed for punishment of Choshu, while most of the daimyo objected. A compromise declaration promised "lenient" treatment of Choshu. The ability of the Bakufu to force a compromise greatly disappointed the daimyo.

RESIGNATION OF THE SHOGUN. In Nov., Yoshinobu submitted to the court his resignation as shogun. Tosa, which stood aside from the Satsuma-Choshu alliance, had feared losing all influence if either the clans opposed to the Bakufu (the "Allies") or the Bakufu won decisively. Hence Goto Shojiro (1838–97) of Tosa had proposed that Yoshinobu should become simply the president of an imperial council of daimyo. Yoshinobu had agreed, but the Allies would not accept him as president of the imperial council, or consent to his retention of the Tokugawa estates. Satsuma and Choshu had already agreed secretly to use force against him. In Dec., Iwakura Tomomi (1825–83), a radical court noble, informed Owari, Tosa, Hiroshima, and Fukui han of the Allies' decision to act. Rather than be left out, the four han joined the Allies.

THE RESTORATION. Troops under Saigo Takamori (1827–77) of Satsuma seized the Imperial Palace gates. A council was convened. It removed Yoshinobu's lands and office and returned administrative responsibility to the emperor, 3 Jan., 1868.

Choshu moved troops to Kyoto while Yoshinobu withdrew to Osaka. Yoshinobu's main supporters, Aizu and Kuwana, were urging him to fight, but Owari and Fukui sought a compromise.

The emperor assumed power over the same social and political structure as before. He had at this time no treasury, no authority to levy taxes, and few experienced administrators in his service.

THE NEW GOVERNMENT. The imperial council appointed new court advisers. Their head was an imperial prince, with Iwakura and Sanjo as deputies. The other councilors were divided into gijo (senior councilors) and san'yo (junior councilors). The gijo consisted of 3 court nobles, 2 imperial princes, and the 5 daimyo whose troops were at the palace gates: Satsuma, Tosa, Hiroshima, Owari, and Fukui. The san'yo consisted of minor court nobles and 3 samurai each from the above 5 han plus Choshu.

CIVIL WAR. Aizu and Kuwana troops marched on Kyoto, 26 Jan. The next day, Satsuma and Choshu troops drove them back to Osaka. Yoshinobu fled to Edo and the court pronounced him a rebel.

SHINTO AS STATE RELIGION. In Feb., 7 administrative departments were created. One of these was the Department of Shinto. At the same time that Shinto was placed under state patronage, Buddhism was partially (and temporarily) disestablished. The department heads were gijo, with san'yo as assistants.

RELATIONS WITH THE OUTSIDE WORLD. In Feb., the new government issued a proclamation in which it declared its determination to hold fast to the decision to open Japan to the world.

SURRENDER OF YOSHINOBU. The imperial troops occupied Edo after an easy march from Kyoto. Saigo Takamori persuaded Yoshinobu to accept the emperor's terms of surrender, Apr.: Yoshinobu was to retire and his successor was to retain only 700,000 koku of estates. (Lands were measured in terms of revenue rather than of area.) In turn, pardon was promised to all Tokugawa adherents who swore allegiance to the new government.

THE "CHARTER OATH." The emperor's "Charter Oath," drafted by Iwakura Tomomi, Kido Takayoshi, and Fukuoka Takachika (1835–1919), was promulgated, 6 Apr. Its 5 articles called for the establishment of an "assembly widely convoked" and for stress on "public discussion," for the abandonment of all "absurd usages," and for a search for knowledge throughout the world in order to strengthen the "foundation of the Imperial Polity." The call for "public discussion" did not imply democracy, but broad participation for all daimyo and samurai in policy deliberations.

THE "1ST CONSTITUTION." In June the imperial government adopted the Seitaisho, generally known as Japan's first constitution. It recognized in principle the separation of the legislative, executive, and judicial powers. However, these powers were all loosely delegated to the Dajokan (Council of State). They were to be exercised by a bicameral assembly, the Dajokan, and the executive departments, all of which interlocked.

Official posts, especially at the san'yo level, were redistributed. Many court nobles were removed and samurai membership was restricted to fewer han. In Sept. Edo was renamed Tokyo (Eastern Capital) and later became the imperial capital.

1869

SURRENDER OF THE HAN REGISTERS. Satsuma, Choshu, Tosa, and Hizen, the most powerful han in the new government, submitted their han registers to the emperor, Mar. Thus they acknowledged the emperor's sovereignty over their territory and laid the basis for true centralized rule. Kido Takayoshi and Okubo Toshimichi (1830–78) of Satsuma were the main promoters of this move. In July all daimyo were ordered to surrender their han registers to the emperor. The daimyo were at the same time appointed governors in their own territories. The new administrative units thereby created were known as ken (prefectures).

GOVERNMENT REORGANIZATION. In Aug. the government was reorganized and given the form that it would retain until the adoption of a cabinet system in 1885. The Dajokan was headed by Sanjo. Its members supervised 6 executive departments: Civil Affairs, Finance, War, Justice, Imperial Household, and Foreign Affairs. All ministers were given samurai assistants and only samurai were appointed as sangi (councilors) to the Dajokan. Thus power gradually passed into the hands of a small

number of samurai from Satsuma, Choshu, Tosa, and Hizen. (*Cont. p. 313.*)

KOREA

1760–1800

REIGN OF YONGJO. In 1760, Korea was under Chinese suzerainty, though not directly ruled by the Chinese government. The reigning periods of Kings Yongjo (1724–76) and Chongjo (1776–1800) of the Yi dynasty are known in Korean history as the Yongjong Era. The era was marked by efforts to eliminate the power struggle between the traditional factions in the country of which the Noron (Old Doctriners), Soron (Young Doctriners), Namin (Southerners), and Pugin (Northerners) were the most important.

King Yongjo led the Tangyongchaek reform movement. He opened government positions to the developing middle class and to illegitimate children of the upper class, who were now allowed to compete in the government examinations. The military tax was applied to all irrespective of class or status, and the land tax was increased. Restrictions on freedom of speech were imposed as a check on factionalism. A government agency, Cheonsa, was established to foster irrigation and reforestation.

REIGN OF CHONGJO. Under Chongjo (ruled 1776–1800), the Kyujanggak (Royal Academy) was established with the duty of ensuring better living conditions for the poor. The arts, particularly literature, showed marked development. There emerged for the first time a literature written in the vulgar script, and a commoner literature written by commoners. Although Chinese Confucianism continued to exert a strong influence, the influence of China herself declined. Trade, manufacturing, and mining increased, encouraged by the Silhak school of learning which advocated social reform and the Swiak (Western Learning) school which introduced European knowledge, particularly Catholic Christian doctrine and the natural sciences.

PERSECUTION OF CHRISTIANS. Catholicism came to Korea without benefit of missionaries. The first convert was Yi Sunghun. The new religion, however, soon conflicted with indigenous ancestor worship, and from 1785 the Korean government began to discourage the spread of Christianity. In 1791 active persecution began, with the execution of Yun Chijung, the 1st Christian martyr. Other executions followed, Catholic books were burned, and the government refused to allow the import of more books from Peking, the major source of Christian influence. Catholicism was driven underground. In 1792 the pope put the Korean Church under the bishop of Peking, and in 1795 a Chinese priest, Shou Wen-mou, was smuggled into Korea, followed by a number of French missionaries.

1801–59

REIGN OF SUNJO. On the death of Chongjo, King Sunjo (ruled 1801–34) succeeded to the throne. Religious persecutions continued. Severe restrictions were placed on Christian missionaries, and a number of Catholic Namin leaders were executed (Sinju Massacre). During this period a Naron (anti-Catholic) faction took power from the pro-Catholic Namin. A leading Namin, Hwang Sayong, sent a message to the foreign missionaries in Peking requesting that a fleet should be sent to force the government of Korea to grant freedom of religion. His plea was intercepted, and further repressions resulted. In 1831, however, Pope Gregory XVI made Korea a bishopric.

REIGN OF HONGJONG. Sunjo died in 1834 and was succeeded by King Hongjong (ruled 1834–49). In 1837, by which time there were 9,000 Christian converts, 3 French priests entered Korea in disguise. In 1839 the government learned of the presence of the missionaries and, partly to distract attention from the general suffering being caused by a drought, initiated once again a policy of severe repression of Christianity. On 21 Sept., 1839, the 3 French priests were executed (Kihae Massacre). Despite the persecutions, by the end of Hong-

jong's reign the number of converts had risen to 13,000 and there were 12 French priests in the country.

In 1849 Hongjong was succeeded by his nephew, King Choljong (ruled 1849–63).

1860–70

TONGHAK MOVEMENT. In 1860, Choe Cheu founded the nationalistic Tonghak school of learning (the eastern sect). This was a synchretist apocalyptic movement based in the south, and combining Taoist, Buddhist, Neo-Confucian, Catholic, and native Songyo shamanist elements. It seems to have been inspired partly by direct western influences and partly by news of the Taiping Rebellion and of foreign invasions of China. The movement obtained a large following, and in 1862–63 a Tonghak-inspired peasant-based revolt broke out. In 1864 the leader of the revolt was killed and the uprising suppressed.

CONSERVATIVE REFORM UNDER TAEWONGUN. In Jan. 1863, when King Choljong died without male issue, his great-great-grandson, Yongjo, succeeded as King Kojong (ruled 1864–1907). The boy's father, Prince Hungson, known as Taewongun, became regent. Taewongun instituted a conservative reform program, which included an attempt to restore the traditional Korean "three systems" (land tax, grain relief, military service). He tried to wipe out factionalism by closing all private academies (*sowon*), depriving the Censors of their power, and directly taxing the *yangban* (noble) class. Recruiting talent more widely than ever before, he reorganized the central administration and revised the law codes. He also tried to increase Korean military strength. His foreign policy was anti-Catholic and exclusionist.

MOUNTING FOREIGN PRESSURES. In Jan. 1866 a Russian gunboat entered Wonsan Harbor and tried to establish trade relations. Korea claimed to be a vassal of China, and referred the Russians to Peking. A Catholic delegation led by Nam Chongsam suggested to the regent that Korea enter into an alliance with Britain and France against Russia. Taewongun's response was to order a purge of Catholics. Nam Chongsam and 9 French priests, including Bishop Berneux, were beheaded (Pyongin Massacre).

In Sept. 1866 the U.S. merchantman *General Sherman* sailed up the Taedong River to Pyongyang seeking trade. A fight broke out, and the ship was burned and all its crew killed.

Reacting to the Pyongin Massacre, the French dispatched 7 warships under Adm. Roze. The expedition entered the Han River, attacked Chong-jok Fortress on Kangwha Island, Aug.–Oct. 1866, but was driven off.

Between 1866 and 1870 (with a peak in 1868 due to a tomb desecration) c. 8,000 Catholics were put to death in Korea; the total number of persons killed or injured during these years was 30,000. (*Cont. p. 319.*)

MONGOLIA

1760–1850

ISOLATION OF MONGOLIA. Mongolia was brought under the control of the Ch'ing (Manchu) Empire of China between 1736 and 1796. The Manchus followed a policy of nonintervention in Mongolian affairs. They ruled the region indirectly, encouraged Lamaism, forbade their Chinese subjects to colonize, prohibited intermarriage between Mongols and Chinese, and made an effort to protect the Mongols from Chinese traders.

1851–70

MONGOLIAN MILITARY LEVIES. Following the outbreak of the Taiping Rebellion, 1851, Mongol feudal levies were summoned to serve the Manchu emperor. Mongol soldiers also fought against the Nienfu peasant rebels in the northern Chinese provinces in the 1850's and 1860's, against the British and French in 1860, and against the Moslems of the southwest in the 1860's and 1870's.

GROWTH OF RUSSIAN INFLUENCE. By the Russo-Chinese Treaty of

Peking, 14 Nov., 1860, Russia received the right to station consuls at Urga, Ili (Kuldja), Chugachak, and Kashgar, and Russian merchants began to enter Outer Mongolia. By another agreement concluded at Peking, 8 Feb., 1862, Russians were allowed to trade throughout the whole of Mongolia. On 7 Oct., 1864, the Protocol of Chuguchak (Boundary Treaty of Tarbagatai) was concluded, stipulating a Russian–Outer Mongolian boundary running through the Sayan Mts. Finally, by the Treaty of Uliassutai, 1870, the frontier between Russia and Outer Mongolia was more closely delineated. During the 1860's Manchu control over Outer Mongolia became generally weaker, and Russian influence increased.

TIBET

1760–73

TIBET IN 1760. In 1760 Tibet was under Chinese suzerainty, 2 high commissioners having been appointed by the Manchu emperor in 1725 to supervise the country's secular affairs. The religion of the people was Buddhism, and there were 2 principal religious leaders, the Dalai Lama and the Panch'en Lama. Regencies were frequent, since new spiritual heads of Tibetan lamaism were usually "discovered" when the candidates were infants.

The 7th Dalai Lama, Kasang Gyatso, had died on 22 Mar., 1757, and Demo Trulku Jampel Delek (High Lama of the Drepung Monastery) had been appointed regent. In 1762 the 8th Dalai Lama (Jampal Gyatso) was discovered in Tsang and the regent brought him to Lhasa, the Tibetan capital.

1774–86

RELATIONS WITH THE ENGLISH EAST INDIA COMPANY. Misunderstanding the intent of a communication sent to India by the Panch'en Lama, Warren Hastings, governor of Bengal, sent George Bogle to Tibet to obtain permission to initiate trade. Bogle arrived at Shigatse, Oct. 1774. He reached Tashil-hunpo the following year and gained the friendship of the Panch'en Lama, Lob-sang Palden Yeshe, but failed to establish a commercial connection between Tibet and India. The Panch'en Lama died on a visit to Peking, 27 Nov., 1780.

On 21 July, 1781, the 8th Dalai Lama assumed power from the regent, Ngawang Tsultrem, who had taken over from Demo Trulku in 1777. In 1782 the British in India learned of the change, and once again Warren Hastings tried to establish trade between Bengal and Tibet, sending Lieut. Samuel Turner to Tashi-Lhunjso in 1783. However, due to Chinese pressure and also to the opposition of the regent in Lhasa, Turner was denied access to the capital.

In 1783 the 4th Panch'en Lama was discovered in Tsang.

1787–93

GURKHA INVASIONS. In 1787 the Gurkhas invaded Tibet from Nepal, claiming trade frauds as justification. The Chinese sent military assistance to the Tibetans, 1788, but their aid was ineffective. The war ended after Chinese mediation had procured a treaty highly unfavorable to Tibet, which was obliged to pay a large indemnity to Nepal. In July 1791 the Gurkhas again invaded Tibet when the Dalai Lama, claiming that he had never approved the treaty, failed to pay the indemnity. Gurkha forces captured and looted Shigatse and the Tashil-hunpo Monastery, and the Panch'en Lama fled. At the Battle of Debung, 4 Sept., 1792, the Tibetans, with the help of a Chinese army under Gen. Fu K'ang-an, defeated the Gurkhas and drove them back to Nepal. The ensuing treaty, 1793, was much more favorable to Tibet, and also to China. Chinese control over the country was strengthened, and the Manchus, acting through their officials (ambans) introduced a number of reforms: the selection of a new Dalai Lama, when there were a number of candidates, to be by lot; an agreement to exclude foreigners; the fixing of boundaries between Tibet and Nepal, Sikkim, and Bhutan; and the stationing of an imperial resident and a large Chinese standing army in Tibet.

1794–1854

CHANGES OF GOVERNMENT AND EROSION OF CHINESE INFLUENCE. The 8th Dalai Lama died on 19 Nov., 1804, and the regent, Tenpai Gonpo Kundeling, took control of the country. Growing external pressures on the Manchus obliged them to reduce their military garrison in Tibet.

Following a dispute, 1807, over the claims of 2 candidates for the position of Dalai Lama, the 9th Dalai Lama, Lung-tok Gyatso, was finally enthroned in 1808.

In 1811 the first Englishman to penetrate to Lhasa, Thomas Manning, was granted an audience by the Dalai Lama.

On 6 Mar., 1815, the 9th Dalai Lama died. By 1817, 3 candidates for the office had appeared and it was not until 1822 that the 10th Dalai Lama, Tsultrem Gyatso, was chosen. He died in 1837, and the 11th Dalai Lama, Khedrup Gyatso, was enthroned in 1841.

During the 1840's Chinese influence in Tibet was reduced, due to incompetent and corrupt residents and to the distractions of the Opium War. In 1841 tribesmen from Ladakh invaded Tibet. They were eventually driven out, and a treaty signed at Leh, the capital of Ladakh, by which boundaries were clarified and promises of friendship exchanged. The Chinese were not party to these negotiations.

1855–70

RENEWED GURKHA INCURSIONS. In 1855 the Gurkhas again invaded Tibet, claiming ill treatment of their nationals and violations of trade agreements. By a treaty of 24 Mar., 1856, the Tibetans agreed to pay an annual tribute to Nepal and also to grant the privileges of extraterritoriality and freedom of trade to Nepalese merchants.

The 11th Dalai Lama was enthroned on 1 Mar., 1855, but died in 1856.

FURTHER DECLINE OF CHINESE INFLUENCE. During the 1850's and

1860's Chinese authority in Tibet continued to decline. In 1858 the regent, Rating, arranged a lottery, by which the 12th Dalai Lama, Trinley Gyatso, was chosen. But in 1862 Shatra proclaimed himself Desi (prime minister) and took power. The regent fled to China, where he died. On 25 Sept., 1864, the Desi, Shatra, also died. In 1868 Paldin Dandup assumed effective power in Tibet as lord chamberlain.

South Asia

INDIA

DISINTEGRATION OF THE MUGHAL EMPIRE. With the death of the Emperor Aurangzeb (Aurangzīb) (ruled 1658–1707), the power of the Mughal Empire, which had covered almost the entire subcontinent, began to decline. In 1759 the emperor, Alamgir (Ālamgīr) II (b. 1699), was put to death, and his son fled to Bihar, where he had himself proclaimed Shah Alam ('Ālam) II (ruled 1759–1806). Local Mughal officials, taking advantage of the collapse of the central government, established personal power over their principalities in Bengal, Oudh, Rohilkhand, and Hyderabad.

Among the indigenous non-Moslem factions competing for regional power at this time, the most important were the Sikhs, the Rajputs, the Jats, and the Marathas. South of Delhi was Bharatpur, a kingdom of Jats, a landowning, peasant caste, founded in the early 18th cent. and ruled in 1760 by Suraj Mal. In the Punjab to the northwest were the Sikhs, the descendants of disciples of a 15th-cent. religious leader, Nanak, and, since 1750, under Afghan control. Southwest of the Punjab were the lands of the Rajputs, a warrior caste, whose kingdoms had been allied with the Mughals since the 16th cent.; alienated by the aggressive religious policy of Aurangzeb, the Rajputs had since held aloof from Mughal affairs. To the south, in the area of the Western Ghats, the Maratha peoples had emerged in the 17th cent. as an independent power: in 1758, when for a brief period they held the Punjab, their power stretched from the Himalayas almost to the tip of the peninsula, those areas not under their direct control paying them tribute. In south India, on the Malabar Coast, was the Hindu kingdom of Mysore. Hyder Ali ('Alī) (1717–82), a Moslem soldier risen to prominence in the army of the raja, succeeded by 1761 in becoming chief minister and de facto ruler of Mysore.

EUROPEAN TRADING COMPANIES. By 1760 the settlements of the Portuguese, Dutch, and Danish trading companies in India were negligible. The 2 major trading companies were those of the British and the French. The English East India Company possessed the 3 independent presidencies of Bombay, Madras, and Bengal. The nawab of Bengal's attack on the British settlement at Calcutta in 1756 had resulted in a British victory at Plassey, 23 June 1757, under Robert Clive (1725–74), and supremacy for the English Company in Bengal.

The French East India Company held the islands of Mauritius and Réunion off Madagascar and in India had factories in Bengal, the Deccan, and on the Malabar Coast. A French army under Gen. Charles Joseph Bussy (1718–85) was maintained at Hyderabad; since 1749 the French had been deeply involved in the internal politics of the Carnatic and of the Hyderabad court.

1760

BATTLE OF WANDIWASH. When news of the Seven Years' War arrived in India in 1756, fighting had broken out between the British and the French, mainly in the Carnatic. Gen. Thomas de Lally (1700–66) was sent from France to defeat the British; Bussy was recalled from Hyderabad to join him. In 1759 the French siege of Madras failed, and Masulipatam in the Deccan was taken by the

British. On 22 Jan., 1760, at the Battle of Wandiwash, the last pitched battle of the war, the French were defeated and Bussy captured. When, after an 8 months' siege, Lally surrendered Pondicherry, 16 Jan., 1761, the war was over.

1761

BATTLE OF PANIPAT. The Maratha capture of Lahore in the Punjab brought renewed invasion by Ahmad Shah Abdali (1724–1773), the Afghan leader, who retook the city. Maratha forces, including the powerful chiefs Holkar and Sindhia, gathered to challenge the Abdali. The Rajputs sent irregular cavalry, and Jat troops from Bharatpur came under Suraj Mal, although both Rajputs and Jats left before the final battle because of quarrels. The peshwa, Balaji Baji Rao (Bālājī Rāo) (ruled 1740–61), appointed his young son Viswas Rao nominal head of the joint army, naming Sadashiv Rao Bhao his adviser and actual leader of the expedition. To oppose the Marathas the Abdali had his own forces, the Rohilla troops, and at least the nominal support of the ruler of Oudh.

The 2 armies were in contact from the late summer of 1760, but the decisive battle occurred on 14 Jan., 1761, at Panipat. The Marathas were besieged in this town, but starvation forced them to abandon it and attack the Afghans. In the fighting, possibly due to a confusion of orders between Sadashiv Bhao and Holkar, a large portion of the Marathas fled the field. Maratha casualties were extremely high. Holkar and Mahadji Sindhia escaped, but both Viswas Rao and Sadashiv Bhao were killed. Although Ahmad Shah Abdali was victorious, a mutiny among his troops forced him to leave India. He turned the rule of Delhi over to an Afghan, who was to rule in the name of Shah Alam ('Ālam) II. The shah was by this time living in Bengal, and now became the Abdali's vassal.

1762–64

DEFEAT OF MIR QASIM, NAWAB OF BENGAL. After Plassey, Mir Jafar (Mīr Ja'far) (1691–1765), installed by Clive as nawab (nawāb) of Bengal, had exempted the private trade of Company servants from transit duties if they had an official pass. But after the deposition of Mir Jafar, the new nawab, Mir Qasim (Mīr Qāsim) (ruled 1760–63), objected to this practice. His protests were overruled by the Calcutta Council, and in retaliation Mir Qasim abolished all duties. The result was war. Between 10 June and 5 Sept., 1763, Maj. Adams, the English commander, won 4 pitched battles over the nawab's forces. At Patna, Mir Qasim, after executing 2 Indian bankers, the former ruler of Bihar, and his English prisoners, fled to Oudh. In July 1763, having agreed to the council's demands regarding duties on private trade and having paid over substantial amounts in presents to the council, Mir Jafar was restored as nawab of Bengal. On Oudh, Mir Qasim obtained the support of Shuja-ud-daula (Shujā-ud-daula) (ruled 1754–75), the nawab wazir of Oudh, and of Shah Alam II. Their forces met the Company's at Buxar, 22 Oct., 1764. Mir Qasim was decisively defeated, and fled the battlefield. Shah Alam II submitted to the British. The nawab of Oudh, who retreated to Rohilkhand, submitted only in the following year when British forces overran Oudh.

1765

GRANT OF THE DIWANI OF BENGAL. Clive returned to Bengal in 1765 for his 2nd term as governor. On 16 Aug., 1765, by the Treaty of Allahabad, he came to terms with the losers of Buxar, Shuja-ud-daula and Shah Alam II. Oudh was restored to Shuja-ud-daula on certain conditions, but 2 of its districts were turned over to the shah for use as his personal residence. In exchange the emperor formally granted the diwani (dīwānī) of Bengal, Bihar, and Orissa to the English East India Company. The Company thus became the official revenue administrator of all 3 territories. In order to continue in this position, the Company had to pay the nawab of Bengal 53 lakhs of rupees per year and the emperor 26 lakhs. Mohammed (Muhammad) Reza Khan was appointed to administer the

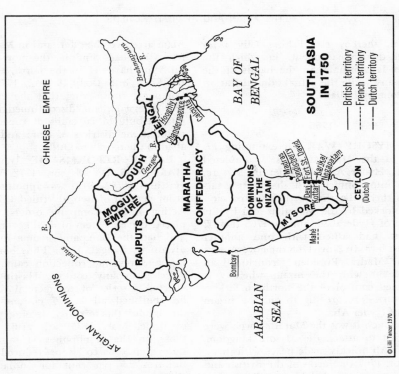

SOUTH ASIA IN 1750

CHINESE EMPIRE

AFGHAN DOMINIONS

Indus R.

Brahmaputra R.

MOGUL EMPIRE

RAJPUTS

OUDH

Ganges R.

BENGAL

Chandernagore
Hooghly
Calcutta

BAY OF BENGAL

MARATHA CONFEDERACY

DOMINIONS OF THE NIZAM

Madras
Pondicherry
Fort St. David
Karikal
Nagapatam

MYSORE

Devi Kottai

CEYLON (Dutch)

Bombay

Mahé

ARABIAN SEA

— British territory
-- French territory
-·- Dutch territory

© Lilli Tanzer 1970

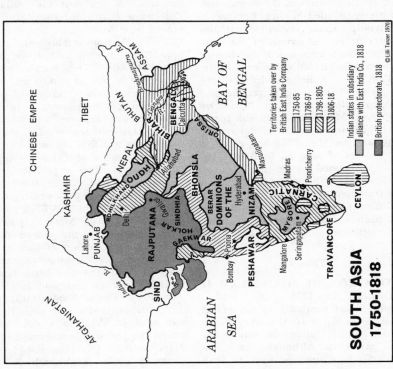

SOUTH ASIA 1750-1818

CHINESE EMPIRE

TIBET

AFGHANISTAN

Indus R.

KASHMIR

NEPAL

BHUTAN

ASSAM

Brahmaputra R.

PUNJAB

Lahore

ROHILKHAND

OUDH

Delhi

Ganges R.

BIHAR

BENGAL

Calcutta

ORISSA

BAY OF BENGAL

PESHAWAR

SIND

RAJPUTANA

Gwalior

SINDHIA

HOLKAR

GAEKWAR

BERAR

BHONSLA

DOMINIONS OF THE NIZAM

Hyderabad

Masulipatam

Bombay

Poona

NIZAM

CARNATIC

Madras

Pondicherry

Mangalore

Seringapatam

MYSORE

TRAVANCORE

CEYLON

ARABIAN SEA

Territories taken over by British East India Company

1750-85
1786-97
1798-1805
1806-18

Indian states in subsidiary alliance with East India Co., 1818

British protectorate, 1818

© Lilli Tanzer 1970

diwani, thereby establishing Clive's so-called dual government, in which the power lay formally in the hands of the Company while the actual administration was done by Indians.

1766–69

1ST MYSORE WAR. In extending his rule to the Malabar Coast (completed 1762), Hyder Ali, the ruler of Mysore, came into contact with the British factories there. To the north his expansion was blocked by the Marathas and by the nizam of Hyderabad, and by 1766 these 2 powers had allied with one another against him. In Nov. 1766 the government of the Madras Presidency concluded an agreement with the nizam whereby it obtained control of the northern Sirkars in return for agreeing to aid the nizam against Hyder Ali.

Although it was the Marathas who were the first to attack the Mysore kingdom, Hyder Ali quickly made peace with them. In Apr. 1767 the forces of the British and of the nizam invaded Mysore. Because of an intrigue involving Hyder's agent, the elder brother of the nawab of the Carnatic, the nizam abandoned the British and allied himself with Hyder Ali. In Feb. 1768, after 2 British victories, the nizam switched sides again, reaffirming his original alliance with the British by the Treaty of Masulipatam. British forces briefly held Mangalore, but Hyder retook the city, and by Mar. 1769 had come to within 5 miles of Madras. In Apr. 1769, Hyder Ali dictated peace terms to the British, providing for a mutual restoration of conquests and stipulating a defensive alliance in accordance with which the British promised to aid Mysore if Hyder Ali were attacked.

1770–73

RESTORATION OF SHAH ALAM II TO DELHI. In 1771 the Marathas occupying Delhi proposed to the exiled emperor, Shah Alam II, that they escort him back to his capital in return for certain payments. Although the Company's officials argued against it, Shah Alam accepted the offer, and in May 1771 left Allahabad. Sindhia, the most powerful Maratha chief in the north, escorted the Shah into Delhi, 6 Jan., 1772. The Company, considering that the emperor had deserted them, discontinued the annual tribute of 26 lakhs of rupees, and restored the districts of Kora and Allahabad to the nawab of Oudh.

EARLY REFORMS OF WARREN HASTINGS. On 13 Apr., 1772, Warren Hastings (1732–1818) was appointed governor general of Bengal (ruled 1772–85). Acting under Company orders, he replaced Clive's system of dual government, and had the Company assume fully the diwani of Bengal, 1772. Thus both civil law and revenue collection came under direct Company control. Hastings also effected a series of commercial reforms: he abolished all but 5 custom houses throughout the territory, freeing passage of trade, Mar. 1773; all tariffs except those on the monopolies of salt, betel nut, and tobacco were reduced to a uniform 2.5 per cent for Indians and Europeans alike; and the Treasury was moved from Murshidabad to Calcutta. In Calcutta, Hastings established 2 courts of appeal, 1 for civil and 1 for criminal cases, 11 Apr., 1780. But, although he attempted to put an end to private trade and to restrict the receiving of presents, both practices continued. A number of land revenue reforms were also tried during Hastings' tenure. The auctioning of revenue was first attempted, and later the employment of Company-appointed collectors. Neither experiment worked satisfactorily, and during Hastings' time no definite revenue policy emerged.

INTERNAL MARATHA STRUGGLES. Four major Maratha powers had been united under the peshwa (peshwā) at Poona: the Gaekwar (Gāikwār) family in Gujarat, the Bhonslas (Bhonslās) at Nagpur, and the northern houses of Holkar (Indore) and Sindhia (Sindhiā) (Gwalior). The peshwa's death, 18 Nov., 1772, inaugurated a long period of internal struggle. A conflict developed between the peshwa's brother and successor, Narayan Rao (Nārāyan Rāo), and the peshwa's uncle, Raghunath Rao (Raghoba) (Raghunāth Rāo, or Raghobā). As a result of the latter's machinations, Narayan Rao was murdered, 30 Aug., 1773. But on the birth of a posthumous son to the peshwa, a council headed by the Brahmin minister Nana Fadnavis recognized the son as peshwa and set up a regency with Nana himself as regent.

1774–83

1ST MARATHA WAR. Raghunath Rao appealed to the British at Bombay for assistance against Poona. The Bombay Presidency agreed to help in return for the concession of certain maritime territories. Raghunath Rao signed the Treaty of Surat, 7 Mar., 1775, agreeing to these provisions, and with the British army's aid defeated the Poona forces, 18 May, 1775.

The Bombay Presidency, however, had acted without the knowledge of the governor general at Calcutta. Hastings' Council condemned the Presidency's action, repudiated the Treaty of Surat, and ordered negotiations with the Poona government. Although the talks resulted in a treaty signed at Purandhar, 1 Mar., 1776, neither side was farther forward, for the court of directors of the East India Company in London upheld the actions of Bombay and approved the Treaty of Surat. The Bombay Council consequently realigned with Raghunath Rao and reopened the war. In this it was unwise, for it was soon defeated and had to sign the Convention of Wadgaon, 13 Jan., 1779, which restored to the Marathas all territory lost by them since 1773, obliged the British to pay an indemnity, and provided for the handing over of 2 British hostages and the yielding up of part of the Bombay revenues.

The Convention of Wadgaon, however, was repudiated by Hastings, and the war began once again. The British capture of Sindhia's fort at Gwalior, long thought impregnable, 3 Aug., 1780, together with other Company victories, led Sindhia to seek an alliance with the British. Through his aid as intermediary, the Treaty of Salbai was signed by the British

and the Marathas, 17 May, 1782 (ratified 26 Feb., 1783). The British gained the island of Salsette, Madhava Rao Narayan (Mādhava Rāo Nārāyan) was recognized as the rightful peshwa, Raghunath Rao was pensioned off, and Sindhia recovered his territories west of the River Jumna.

2ND MYSORE WAR. Relations between Hyder Ali and the British, strained by the Madras Presidency's failure either to implement the provisions of the 1769 treaty or to negotiate a new treaty, deteriorated further in 1778 when war between France and Britain broke out in Europe. The British seized the French settlement at Mahe, 19 Mar., 1779, which was within Hyder Ali's jurisdiction. Full-scale war began in July 1780, when Hyder Ali invaded the Carnatic. The British there were overwhelmed, and in Oct. Hyder took Arcot and gained control of the whole territory. Hastings was able to detach the raja of Berar, Sindhia, and the nizam of Hyderabad from their alliances with Hyder Ali, but in 1782 the latter received the aid of both a French fleet and a French infantry force. The coming of peace, however, between Britain and France in Europe led to the withdrawal of the French to Mauritius.

After Hyder Ali's death, 7 Dec., 1782, the war was continued by his son and successor, Tipu (Tippoo) Sultan. A British attack on Tipu's capital at Seringapatam was about to be launched when the troops were abruptly recalled. The recall was prompted by the desire of Lord Macartney (1737–1806), governor of Madras, 1781–85, to negotiate peace with Tipu. The result was the Treaty of Mangalore, signed 11 Mar., 1784, which temporarily ended the Anglo-Mysore conflict by providing for a mutual restoration of conquered territory and the liberation of prisoners.

1783–99

THE BLINDING OF SHAH ALAM II. From 1772 onward, Shah Alam II had been dependent on Maratha forces to maintain himself at Delhi. In Oct. 1784 he gave control of Delhi to Sindhia in order to obtain help against a provincial revolt. Sindhia was then appointed regent of the Mughal Empire.

In 1787 a minister of the emperor, wishing to end Sindhia's control over Delhi, encouraged the ambitions of a local Rohilla noble, Ghulam Qadir. Financial difficulties and military defeats had temporarily weakened Sindhia's power. His unpaid garrison in Delhi rebelled, and his 2 ministers fled the city. On 5 Sept., 1787, Ghulam Qadir entered Delhi and was appointed regent by the emperor.

Ghulam Qadir, however, was not long content with a regency. On 18 July, 1788, after overcoming the weak resistance offered by the emperor's forces, he forced his way into Delhi. On 30 July he deposed Shah Alam II, and on 10 Aug. he had him blinded. But in 1789, with the aid of reinforcements supplied by Poona, Sindhia retook Delhi, disposed of Ghulam Qadir, and reseated the emperor on his throne. This was the beginning of Sindhia's reassertion of his power in the north. With his defeat of the Rajputs in 1790 and his conquest of his rival, Holkar, in 1792, he established his supremacy in northern India.

3RD MYSORE WAR. By 1785, Tipu Sultan, the most ambitious of the rulers of southern India, had become involved in a competition for power with the nizam of Hyderabad and with the Marathas. In 1787 he sent envoys to both France and Constantinople in search of new allies. In 1788 Lord Cornwallis (1738–1805), governor general, 1786–93, abrogated the 1784 treaty by omitting Tipu's name from a list of allies of the Company given to the nizam. Tipu's attack, 29 Dec., 1789, on a long-time British ally, the raja of Travancore, reopened the war. The Madras government at first refused to aid the raja, but Cornwallis reversed this decision. To assist in the prosecution of the war with Mysore, Cornwallis allied the Company with the nizam on 1 June, 1790, and with the Marathas on 4 July.

In the 1st campaign of the war, Tipu completely outmaneuvered the British forces. In Dec. 1790 Cornwallis himself took command, and came within 9 miles of Tipu's capital at Seringapatam before supply shortages and the onset of the rainy season compelled him to withdraw. In the summer of 1791 an army led by Cornwallis finally reached Seringapatam, and Tipu was obliged to negotiate. By the Treaty of Seringapatam, 19 Mar., 1792, Tipu paid an indemnity of £3 m., and surrendered 2 of his sons to the British as hostages. One half of his territory was annexed and subsequently divided between the British, the nizam, and the Marathas.

THE PERMANENT REVENUE SETTLEMENT. By 1786 the directors of the Company in London had become convinced that the solution to the problem of revenue collection in Bengal lay in a "permanent" revenue settlement designed to give security to landowners by fixing their rents in perpetuity. Under the Mughals the peasants had paid a share of their produce to hereditary tax collectors known as zamindars (zamīndārs), who in turn paid a fixed proportion of what they collected to the government. Cornwallis was now directed to fix the annual revenue rates for a 10-year period. He complied, but in his own view was establishing them in perpetuity. The zamindars were to be regarded as landowners and, through British collectors and subcollectors, were to pay nine-tenths of a fixed rent to government. The Permanent Settlement of Bengal became law on 22 Mar., 1793.

The Settlement did not work well, and was not extended to other parts of India. In Madras and later in Bombay, a system based on direct periodic assessment of the ryots (raiyat, peasant) was put into effect. Still later, in northern India, revenue was levied by assessments on village units.

THE CORNWALLIS CODE. During his first few months in India, Cornwallis suspended the entire Board of Trade in Calcutta. Most of its members were subsequently dismissed. Under Cornwallis the prohibition on private trade was rigidly enforced. Such strictness was now possible because the Company was at last providing adequate salaries for its employees. Cornwallis also initiated the policy of employing Indians in subordinate positions only, the more responsible posts being reserved for Englishmen.

Cornwallis' administrative reforms separated the Company's government into commercial and revenue branches. The administration was headed by a Governor General in Council, a Board of Trade, and a Board of Revenue, each board presided over by a member of council. The commercial branch, headed by the Board of Trade in Calcutta, arranged with commercial residents for the Company's exports. The new arrangements for the revenue branch built on the existing structure of local government, whose basic unit was the district. Officers in charge of districts had 3 duties: to keep the peace, collect the revenue, and administer justice. In Cornwallis' scheme these duties were now divided between a magistrate/collector and a judge. This reformed system of administration, including the Permanent Settlement, was embodied in a series of regulations passed on 1 May, 1793, and known to history as the Cornwallis Code.

4TH MYSORE WAR. Fear of French expansion into India precipitated the 4th Mysore War. In Apr. 1798, as a result of a French-Mysore alliance, a small number of French troops from Mauritius landed at Mangalore.

Lord Wellesley (1760–1842), gov. gen., 1798–1805, at once sought an alliance with the nizam of Hyderabad and with the Marathas. Whereas the peshwa refused to commit himself and remained neutral, the nizam in Sept. 1798 agreed to a "subsidiary" alliance. Wellesley then demanded that Tipu repudiate the French treaty. Tipu's refusal signaled the outbreak of war. Under Wellesley's command, an attack against Mysore was launched, 22 Feb., 1799, from both Bombay and Madras. On 5 Mar. and 27 Mar., Tipu was defeated by British troops, and retreated to Seringapatam. The siege of the capital began, 17 Apr., 1799. After Tipu had refused British terms, the city was seized and plundered, 4 May, 1799. Tipu himself was killed during the fighting. The members of his family were sent to Vellore. In recognition of help granted, the nizam received territory lying on the northeastern border of his state. The Company annexed the lands encircling Mysore, concluded a subsidiary alliance with that state, and restored the 5-year-old heir of the former Hindu ruling dynasty as ruler.

1800–1805

BRITISH EXPANSION UNDER WELLESLEY. The governor generalship of Marquis Wellesley saw the expansion of the Company's power in India by means of "subsidiary" alliances or treaties. By this type of agreement the British undertook to provide a state with Company troops for its protection; in return the ruler agreed to pay for the maintenance of these troops. The state was thus protected against external enemies, but came under British control.

On 1 Sept., 1798, Wellesley concluded a subsidiary treaty with the nizam of Hyderabad. Similar treaties were negotiated with Tanjore, Surat, the Carnatic, and Oudh. By 1801 the rulers of all these states, except Oudh, had been pensioned off and their territories brought under direct Company administration.

On the death of Nana Fadnavis, 1800, the Peshwa Baji Rao (Bājī Rāo) accepted the protection of the Company by the Treaty of Basein, 31 Dec., 1802. British troops installed him at Poona. The peshwa's subsequent actions offended the Marathas, however, and Wellesley found it necessary to declare war on the houses of Sindhia and Bhonsla, defeating both and concluding subsidiary alliances with them: the Bhonslas on 17 Dec., 1803, and Sindhia on 27 Feb., 1804. A 3rd Maratha house, the Gaekwars, was already under British protection. The last Maratha chief, Holkar, refused to come to terms, and in Apr. 1804 Wellesley declared war on him also. In the ensuing struggle the British suffered a series of reverses, and the home government, deciding that Wellesley's policies had become both expensive and unsuccessful, ordered him recalled.

1806–14

TREATY OF AMRITSAR. The annexation by the Company of the Delhi territory had brought it into contact with the Sikh leader Ranjit (Ranjīt) Singh (1780–1839). From 1792, when he succeeded to the headship of a small Sikh tribe, Ranjit Singh's power had been steadily growing, until in 1805 he was the strongest Sikh leader in the Punjab. To Lahore in that year Holkar came seeking refuge, but Ranjit Singh refused to ally himself with Holkar against the Company. The Treaty of Lahore, 1 Jan., 1806, won the Sikhs the friendship of the British, and excluded the Marathas from the Punjab.

Between Ranjit Singh's lands and the Company's lay the so-called Cis-Sutlej States, ruled by Sikh chiefs. Quarrels among these chiefs became the occasion for intervention by Ranjit Singh in their affairs. In 1806 he took Ludhiana. Charles Metcalfe (1785–1846) was sent by Lord Minto (1751–1814), gov. gen., 1807–13, to negotiate an offensive and defensive alliance with Ranjit. The resulting Treaty of Amritsar, 25 Apr., 1809, guaranteed Ranjit Singh against interference in his activities north of the Sutlej, but he abandoned his claims to the Cis-Sutlej States, which came, unofficially, under British protection.

1815–18

THE PINDARI WAR. The Pindaris were marauding tribes made up of landless, casteless men, who frequently were used in war by Maratha chiefs such as Holkar and Sindhia. They roamed through central India in search of plunder. Their main leaders were Chithu, Wasil Khan, and Karim Khan. By 1812, when they raided 2 districts in Bihar, the Pindaris had become a danger to the British. In 1815–16 they raided the nizam of Hyderabad's lands twice and looted the northern Sirkars, netting £100,000 worth of booty. In 1817 Lord Hastings (1754–1826), gov. gen., 1813–23, decided on a large-scale campaign to destroy the Pindaris. An army of over 100,000, divided into a northern division under Hastings himself and a Deccan division under Thomas Hislop (1764–1843), was sent into the field. Hastings' plan to encircle the Pindaris was successful, and by Jan. 1818 they were almost all exterminated, their chiefs dead or in flight, and the remaining tribesmen scattered.

THE LAST MARATHA WAR. Although the Maratha Confederacy had been dissolved in 1802, the peshwa at Poona tried to organize them against the British. Pressure was accordingly brought to bear on him, and on 13 June, 1817, the British envoy, Mountstuart Elphinstone (1779–1859) induced him to sign the Treaty of Poona, by which he renounced the headship of the Maratha Confederacy. On 5 Nov., 1817, however, a party of the peshwa's men sacked the British Residency at Poona. In this last struggle of the Marathas against the British, Sindhia, Holkar, and the Bhonsla house were involved on the peshwa's side, but the Gaekwar house abided by its earlier agreements with the Company. After 3 defeats in battle, the peshwa surrendered, 3 June, 1818. The peshwaship was abolished, and Baji Rao II received a pension from the Company. The Bhonsla house and Holkar were both defeated in battle. Sindhia capitulated without fighting.

Except for the principality of Satara, which was given to the descendants of Shivaji, the peshwa's lands went to the Company and became part of the Presidency of Bombay. Treaties were signed with the chiefs of Rajputana who accepted British paramountcy. The result of these conflicts was the establishment of British power throughout India as far as the Sutlej River. The Company's frontiers were now Assam and the Himalayas to the north, and the border of Ranjit Singh's Sikh kingdom in the Punjab to the northwest.

1819–35

FOUNDATION OF THE BRAHMO SAMAJ. The founder of the Brahmo Samaj was Rammohan Roy (1772?–1833), a Bengali Brahman. Roy was an accomplished linguist, knowing Sanskrit, Persian, Arabic, English, Greek, and Hebrew. He had studied Islam and Christianity and was influenced in his religious beliefs by the English Unitarians. He re-examined the ancient Hindu texts, and found in them a theism which in his belief had been overlaid and corrupted by modern Hindu practice. In 1828 he founded the Brahmo Sabha, later Brahmo Samaj, as a Hindu society for those who wished to return to this earlier theism. Roy wanted to abolish certain Hindu practices such as idolatry, suttee (satī) , and polygamy, and he favored the spread of English education. The Brahmo Samaj and Roy himself were factors in bringing about the reforms of Lord Bentinck. In the mid-19th cent. the reformist aims of the Brahmo Samaj were furthered by its later leaders, Devendranath Tagore and Keshub Chander Sen.

THE BENTINCK REFORMS. Lord William Cavendish-Bentinck (1774–1839) became governor general in July 1828. During his administration an attack was launched on 2 long-standing Indian customs, the practices of thuggee (thagi) and suttee. The thugs were groups of men bound together by vows to the goddess Kali. They engaged in ritual murder and robbery. In 1829 Bentinck had a special department organized to campaign against thuggee. During the first 6 years of operations over 1500 thugs were caught. In 1836 an act ordering life imprisonment for all thugs was passed and strictly enforced thereafter.

Suttee was the practice by which widows burned themselves on their husbands' funeral pyres. From 1820 legislation against it was urged by reform-minded Hindus like Rammohan Roy. Earlier the Bengal government had legalized voluntary burnings. But in 1828 the directors ordered Bentinck to deal firmly with the problem, and in 1829 suttee was made illegal in all 3 presidencies. Indian reaction was minimal. The only protest took the form of an appeal against the law to the Privy Council in Britain, which was considered and dismissed. This was the 1st instance of deliberate, legal interference on the part of the Company with the established customs of the country it was governing.

MACAULAY'S MINUTE ON EDUCATION. In 1813 a provision had been written into the East India Company's Charter Act authorizing 1 lakh of rupees to be set aside for educational purposes in India. No further action was taken until 1823, when a Committee of Public Instruction was formed. A division appeared within the committee between what came to be called the "Orientalists," who wanted classical subjects of the country, like Sanskrit, to be taught, and the "Anglicists," who favored an emphasis on the teaching of English subjects and the English language. In 1834, Thomas Babington Macaulay (1800–59) was appointed legal member of the governor general's Council and president of the Committee of Public Instruction. In 1835 he presented his "Minute on Education," 2 Feb., which argued for the teaching of western literature and science through the medium of the English language on the grounds that such education would be of greater use to students than a study of Indian subjects. Macaulay's minute carried the day. On 7 Mar., 1835, the Council decided that the available funds should be spent on English-type education.

1836–47

1ST AFGHAN WAR. Fearing an Afghan alliance with Russia, Lord Auckland (1784–1849) , gov. gen., 1836–42, arranged a Tripartite Treaty, June 26, 1838, between the British, Ranjit Singh, and Shah Shuja (Shujā) (1780?–1842), a former ruler of Afghanistan. Under this treaty Shah Shuja was to be restored to his throne, replacing Dost Mohammed (Muḥammad) (1793–1863) , who had seized the region in 1826.

Initially the resultant war went well for the British. In Aug. 1839, Shah Shuja entered the city of Kabul, and Dost Mohammed withdrew, surrendering in 1840. But Shah Shuja proved unpopular among the Afghans, and only stayed in power because of the presence of a British garrison in his city. In Nov. 1841 a revolt broke out in Kabul. Under pressure the British agreed to withdraw, and on 6 Jan., 1842, their 16,000 troops left the city. On their way south they were decimated by Afghan attacks and bitter weather. Only 1 man in the main column, Dr. Bryden, survived to reach the city of Jalalabad, 13 Jan., 1842.

Shah Shuja was murdered, Apr. 1842, and Lord Ellenborough (1790–1871), gov. gen., 1842–44, abandoned Auckland's plans to conquer Afghanistan. Ellenborough ordered the British in the area to withdraw. In an attempt to preserve their military reputation, the British retook Kabul, Sept., and withdrew from Afghanistan in Oct., leaving a son of Shah Shuja in power. But in 1843 Dost Mohammed regained the throne of Afghanistan. He maintained friendly relations with the British until his death in 1863.

ANNEXATION OF SIND. Although a treaty of 20 Apr., 1832, between the Company and the Amirs, the rulers of Sind, provided for the preservation of Sind's independence, this treaty was set aside when the British discovered a need for Sind to provide access to Afghanistan. The Amirs were ordered to pay arrears of tribute to Shah Shuja, despite their earlier release from these obligations by the shah himself in 1833. On 11 Mar., 1839, a new treaty was forced on the Amirs. It ordered them to pay 3 lakhs a year and to enter into a subsidiary alliance with the Company.

After the Afghan War, during which, in the British view, the Amirs had taken up an unfriendly attitude, Ellenborough decided to annex part of their territory. Sir Charles Napier (1782–1853) was given the task of effecting this policy, 1 Sept., 1842. Napier offered the Amirs treaty terms, but proceeded as though these had been rejected. He seized the lands that had been demanded, and in Jan. 1843 destroyed a fortress at Imamgarh. The final defeat of the Amirs took place at Miani, 17 Feb., 1843, and they were exiled. Sind was declared annexed, 12 Mar., and Napier was appointed governor.

1ST SIKH WAR. After the death of Ranjit Singh in 1839, succession disputes raged among the Sikh chiefs. Dalip (Dalīp) Singh (1837–93), a minor, was recog-

nized as paramount ruler, but the real power lay with the Khalsa army. Fear of what this army might do led the supporters of Dalip Singh to urge a war against the British. On 11 Dec., 1845, the Khalsa army crossed the Sutlej into Company territory, and on 13 Dec. Sir Henry Hardinge (1785–1856), gov. gen., 1844–48, declared war. At the Battle of Sabraon, 10 Feb., 1846, the Sikh forces were defeated.

On 9 Mar., 1846, the Treaty of Lahore was signed. By this treaty the Sikh army was limited to a specified size; Kashmir, its dependencies, and the Jallandar Doab were ceded to the British (who promptly sold Kashmir to Gulab Singh, a neutral, for a million pounds); and the Sikhs had to pay an indemnity of £500,000. Dalip Singh was recognized as maharaja, with his mother as regent. A British resident, Sir Henry Lawrence (1806–57), was sent to Lahore, and it was agreed that a British army would be stationed there until the end of 1846 to provide protection for the young maharaja.

In Dec. 1846, at the request of the Sikhs, the treaty was revised. A Council of Regency, consisting of 8 sirdars (sardārs) with Lawrence as president, was to rule the Punjab, and the British forces were to remain at Lahore and be paid for by the Lahore government. The agreement was to remain in effect until the maharaja attained his majority in 1854.

1848–49

2ND SIKH WAR AND ANNEXATION OF THE PUNJAB. In 1848 several Sikh chiefs rebelled against the Lahore government. On 10 Dec. of that year Governor General Lord Dalhousie (1812–60), gov. gen., 1848–56, declared war against them. British forces crushed the Sikh army in the Battle of Gujarat, 21 Feb., 1849, and on 30 Mar. Dalhousie proclaimed the annexation of the Punjab. Dalip Singh and his mother received pensions, and were sent to England. For the next 4 years the Punjab was governed by a board consisting of Henry Lawrence as president; his brother, John Lawrence (1811–79); and Charles G. Mansel (1806–

86). In 1853 the board was abolished, and John Lawrence became chief commissioner for the Punjab.

1850–56

ADMINISTRATION OF LORD DALHOUSIE. By employing the doctrines of "paramountcy" and "lapse," Dalhousie greatly extended British administrative power in India. The doctrine of paramountcy stated that the paramount power (the Company) might interfere in the internal affairs of subordinate states if they were being misgoverned. On this pretext Mysore had been brought under direct Company administration in 1831. Now in 1856 Oudh was annexed.

The doctrine of lapse declared that, if the direct ruling line of a subordinate state failed, that state lapsed to the paramount power; the device of adopting a son so that the line might be continued could be regarded as valid only if the paramount power approved. Under this doctrine the Maratha states of Satara, Jhansi, and Nagpur and several smaller states fell to the Company. Dalhousie also abolished the "titular sovereignties" he considered obsolete; thus the titles of nawab of the Carnatic, raja of Tanjore, and peshwa were abolished on the death of their holders.

In 1854 Dalhousie had inaugurated a Public Works Department. During 1855 and 1856 there was a sharp rise in the construction of roads and irrigation channels. The postal system was reformed, and a beginning made in the construction of the Indian telegraph and railroad networks. A new general-education policy was adopted, promoting elementary education in the vernacular and higher education in English.

1857–58

THE SEPOY MUTINY. The Sepoy Mutiny, which began in 1857, mainly involved the army of the Bengal Presidency, the armies of Madras and Bombay being hardly affected. The Bengal army consisted of 151,000 men, of whom only 23,000 were Europeans. The Indian soldiers were mainly of high caste, Brahmans and Rajputs. Discipline was lax. There had been 4 mutinies within the previous 13 years. The sepoys, moreover, were nervous about possible assaults on the rules of their castes. In 1857 the army issued cartridges which had been greased with the fat of cows and pigs; such cartridges were offensive to both Hindus and Moslems, since the ends of the cartridges had to be bitten off before they could be used. At first it was denied that animal fats had been used. Later the cartridges were withdrawn.

Barrackpore, near Calcutta, was the first scene of unrest. At Meerut a group of sepoys refused to use the cartridges and were jailed. On 10 May, 1857, other sepoys at Meerut mutinied, shot their officers, released their imprisoned comrades, and set off for Delhi. At Delhi the Indian forces joined the mutineers. The city was seized, and the 82-year-old emperor, Bahadur Shah II, was restored to the dignity of sovereign ruler.

Troops in Rajputana, Gwalior, Lucknow, Cawnpore, and the United Provinces then mutinied. European officers and civilians were killed. Effective British authority ceased throughout an area from Rajputana to Bihar.

On the death of the peshwa in 1853, the Company had refused to transfer his pension to his adopted son, the Nana Sahib (1820?–1859?). In 1857, therefore, the Nana Sahib emerged as the natural leader of the mutinous troops at Cawnpore. In June the British in Cawnpore, commanded by Sir Hugh Wheeler (1789–1857), were besieged. On 26 June, Wheeler accepted the offer of a safe conduct from the Nana Sahib for his soldiers and for the British women and children in the town. The offer was then rescinded. The soldiers were murdered, and the women and children, after being held prisoner for a time, were killed.

At Lucknow, after the June mutiny, Henry Lawrence and the British forces under him had taken refuge in the Residency buildings. Early in July, Lawrence died of wounds. The remaining forces were relieved in Nov. by a column commanded by Sir Colin Campbell (1792–1863).

In the Punjab the neutrality of the Afghans and the loyalty of the Sikhs enabled John Lawrence and his staff to crush the mutiny by disarming the rebellious regiments. Lawrence organized a column and sent it to Delhi. In Sept. Delhi was recaptured. The emperor was taken prisoner, and some 30,000 mutineers fled the city, which was then sacked and its inhabitants massacred by the victorious British troops.

On 3 Apr., 1858, Jhansi was retaken, and on 20 June Gwalior fell. The mutiny was now almost at an end. Campbell drove the remaining rebels, including the Nana Sahib, into the Nepalese borderlands. Tantia Topi, leader of the Gwalior forces, was captured and subsequently hanged. The Mughals lost their royal status, Bahadur Shah II being exiled to Burma. On 8 July, 1858, Lord Canning (1812–62), gov. gen., 1856–62, proclaimed peace, and by refusing to allow uncontrolled vengeance earned the title, at first derogatory, of "Clemency" Canning.

GOVERNMENT OF INDIA ACT. On 2 Aug., 1858, the British Parliament passed an Act for the Better Government of India. As a result of the mutiny, public opinion in Britain came to view the East India Company's rule in India as an anachronism. By the Act of 1858, the authority of the directors and of the Board of Control was transferred to a secretary of state, a member of the cabinet, responsible to Parliament. The governor general received the additional title of viceroy. To advise the secretary, a Council of India was established, consisting of 15 members, 8 appointed by the crown and 7 at first by the directors and later by the Council itself.

1859–70

INDIAN COUNCILS ACT. The 1853 Charter Act had constituted a Legislative Council for the Government of India. Before this, all legislation had been promulgated by the governor general and his Executive Council. By the Indian Councils Act of 1 Aug., 1861, this Executive Council was reformed: a fifth member was added; the "portfolio" system, whereby members were given charge of specific departments, was introduced; and experts might be appointed to departments requiring their specialized knowledge.

Provision was made for the nomination by the governor general of from 6 to 12 additional members to the Legislative Council for 2-year terms, not less than half of them as "nonofficials." Provincial Legislative Councils were also created. Although no rule was established that the additional members of the Legislative Councils had to be Indians, the measure taken stemmed from an attempt to secure Indian representation in some form within the government. Indians were appointed to Legislative Councils at both the central and provincial levels. (*Cont. p. 329.*)

CEYLON

1760–95

THE ESTABLISHMENT OF DUTCH CONTROL. In the 16th cent. there were 3 indigenous centers of political power in Ceylon: Kotte, Kandy (Kandi), and Jaffna. Kotte in the south and southwest was the major seat of Sinhalese power. The Kotte kingdom claimed supremacy over Kandy, also a Sinhalese kingdom, but its claim was only nominal. Jaffna, the third kingdom, was a Tamil power independent of the other 2.

In 1505 the Portuguese landed at Colombo and negotiated a trade agreement with the king of Kotte. The internal struggles of Kotte brought about the political involvement of the Portuguese in the affairs of the island, and resulted in their ascendancy and the resultant disintegration of the Kotte kingdom. Portuguese power then expanded into the Jaffna kingdom, which was annexed in 1619. This left only Kandy in the central highlands and eastern coast independent of and coexisting with the Portuguese.

The ambition of the Kandyan king to expel the Portuguese led him to conclude a trade agreement with the Dutch, and resulted in the eventual ousting of the Portuguese from the island and the conclusion of a formal treaty between the Dutch and Kandy. By the middle of the 18th cent. the Portuguese had only a few trading stations on the coast, and the Dutch had established their control over both the island's trade and its political affairs. They continued to exercise this power until 1796.

1796-1801

THE ESTABLISHMENT OF BRITISH CONTROL. The need to protect British interests in India against the French led to British involvement in Ceylonese affairs. In 1782 the British had briefly occupied the port of Trincomali, but had been driven away by a French-Dutch coalition. On 16 Feb., 1796, however, British forces expelled the Dutch from the island for good. A treaty with the king of Kandy, 12 Feb., 1796, established the British as the protectors of the Ceylonese coast, and granted them the trading privileges formerly held by the Dutch, but was not ratified in the end by Kandy.

Initially Ceylon was made a part of the Madras Presidency, but when the policies pursued by a representative of Madras provoked a general rebellion, East India Company rule was abolished and the island became a crown colony. The first governor, Frederick North (1766–1827), landed in Oct. 1798. North abolished the taxes proclaimed by his predecessor, Robert Andrews, and temporarily reestablished the Dutch system of revenue collection on instructions from the Company issued 5 May.

1802-18

THE CONSOLIDATION OF BRITISH RULE. In 1802, as a result of the machinations of a court minister, a breach in relations occurred between the British and the king of Kandy. British troops seized the capital of Kandy, 20 Feb., 1803, and then withdrew, leaving a small force to protect a newly appointed puppet king. The successful reassertion of the minister's power led to the death of the king and the massacre of the British troops, 23–24 June. In 1804 and again in 1812 the British were involved in unsuccessful attempts to overthrow the Kandyan kingdom.

In 1815 an attack by the king of Kandy, Vikrama, on a party of British merchants prompted the governor, Sir Robert Brownrigg (1759–1833), to send a retaliatory force into the interior. In the ensuing struggle Vikrama was obliged to abandon his capital, and on 14 Feb., 1815, the British took possession. The king was later captured and sent to Vellore in India, where he died in Jan. 1832.

On 2 Mar., 1815, the Kandyan Convention, by which all chiefs in the island made formal submission to the British, was signed. The governor of Ceylon now ruled Kandy through a resident at the royal court. The chiefs, however, were to retain their traditional offices and privileges. The preservation of the Buddhist religion was guaranteed, and the country was to continue to be governed according to tradition. In 1818 a final rebellion was put down by the British. Chiefly powers and privileges were curtailed, the provinces were brought more firmly under control, and British agents were appointed to the various provincial centers.

1819-70

THE COLEBROOKE REPORT. A commission headed by W. M. G. Colebrooke was appointed to report on conditions in Ceylon and make recommendation for their improvement. The Colebrooke Report of 1831–32 was the result.

The report recommended a redivision of the colony. The old racial and cultural divisions were to be abandoned, and a new and uniform political and judicial administration set up. Ceylon was to be divided into 5 provinces. The governor's advisory council was to be replaced by an Executive Council.

In Mar. 1833 a Legislative Council was established, consisting of the members of the Executive Council, plus 9 official and 6 nonofficial members; 3 of the nonofficials were Ceylonese, nominated by the governor on a communal basis from the Sinhalese, Sinhalese-Kandyan, and Tamil populations.

ECONOMIC CHANGE. As a result of the Colebrooke Report, the traditional Rajakariya system was finally destroyed. Under this system all tenants on crown lands had had to perform compulsory services for the state. More plantation

land, too, was being opened up. In 1848, however, the sale of jungle land previously used by peasants and the imposition of new taxes led to rioting.

In the 1860's there was an increase in road construction and government-sponsored irrigation schemes, and the benefits of public works began to extend to the hitherto neglected northern and eastern parts of the island. (*Cont. p. 329.*)

Southeast Asia

BURMA

1760–94

WARS WITH SIAM AND CHINA. Under Alaungpaya (d. 1760), Naungdawgyi (ruled 1760–63), and Hsinbyushin (ruled 1763–76), the Burmese waged successful struggles against the Siamese, besieging Ayut'ia in 1760 and in 1767. Between 1766 and 1769, they also repulsed a series of Chinese expeditions in Kengtung and across the Yunnan frontier. The victories over the Chinese, resulting in the Kaungton Treaty of 1770, restored trade and cordial Sino-Burmese relations. The wars with Siam, however, brought only defeat. Hsinbyushin died in 1776 and was succeeded by his son Singu, who was deposed by one of his uncles, Bodawpaya (ruled 1782–1819). Wars against the Siamese continued under him, and, though retaining their independence during the invasions of the 1780's, the Siamese lost Arakan in 1784–85. The 1794 revolt in Arakan brought the Burmese in contact with the British, owing to the flight of refugees north from Arakan toward Bengal.

1795–1819

SYMES MISSION. In 1795 the British sent Capt. Michael Symes (1753?–1809) on a mission to Burma to discuss the problem of the Arakanese refugees, which led to a worsening of British relations with the Burmese. The raids of refugees against the Burmese were thought to be

aided by the British, and the inactivity of the British in the Chittagong region gave the Burmese an exaggerated sense of their own strength.

1819–26

1ST BURMA WAR. Bodawpaya's successor, Bagyidaw (ruled 1819–37), sent an army to occupy Assam and Manipur, and made preparations for an attack on Chittagong and Bengal. This resulted in the 1st Burma War of 1824–26. The British attacked the weakest part of the kingdom by sea and were victorious. The Company acquired by the Treaty of Yandabo, 24 Feb., 1826, Arakan, Assam, Manipur, and the Tenasserim provinces, while the Burmese kept upper and central Burma, Pegu, and the mouths of the Irrawaddy River.

1826–39

BURMESE ISOLATIONISM. Defeat by the British dealt a tremendous blow to the pride of the dynasty and encouraged resentment of and isolation from the changing world around it. Placing a resident at the court, the British hoped, would give the Burmese a chance to restore good relations with the outside world, but the opposite resulted. Until Maj. Henry Burney (1792–1845) arrived in 1830, there were no firm negotiations. Burney achieved some success, but his health was bad, and he left Burma in 1834. In 1837, Bagyidaw was deposed by his brother, Tharrawaddy (ruled 1836–46), who repudiated the Treaty of Yandabo. Burney's last replacement, Capt. William McLeod, left the court at Ava in 1839.

1839–53

2ND BURMA WAR. Tharrawaddy died in 1846, and the atrocities of his successor, Pagan Min (ruled 1846–53), caused an almost complete breakdown in central authority. The attitude of the court was reflected in the actions of the local officials who dealt with British traders in Rangoon. In judging these activities, Governor General Dalhousie's concern was to maintain British prestige. This led to the 2nd Burma War in 1852, and the annexation of Pegu and a year later of Toungoo. The new Burmese king, Mindon Min (ruled 1853–78), refused to recognize these acquisitions, since they meant the loss to Burma of its entire coastline, of a province disputed for centuries, and of considerable face. The king of Burma would never willingly sign away territory to a foreign power.

1853–70

BURMESE-BRITISH   RELATIONS. Pegu was administered by a commissioner appointed by the governor general. The other administrators came primarily from the Indian service, and so the Indian model tended to be followed. In 1862, Arakan, Tenasserim, and Pegu were consolidated into British Burma, with Rangoon as the capital. Mindon Min created a new capital at Mandalay, and sought better relations with the British even during the Sepoy Mutiny of 1857. He agreed to commercial treaties in 1862 and 1867 to implement British trade with China up the Irrawaddy River. Relations with the British deteriorated in the latter part of his reign because (1) royal monopolies hindered traders in Rangoon, and (2) the king tried to assert his independence by developing relations with other European powers. (*Cont. p. 347.*)

INDOCHINA

1760–73

RELATIONS WITH SIAM. With the death of King Alaungpaya of Burma, 1760, Vietnamese expansion reached a turning point. In 1767, Mac Thieu Tu unwisely supported a pretender to the Siamese throne. The wrath of P'ya Taksin of Siam destroyed Ha-tien, and Taksin was soon supporting his own claimant at Phnom Penh. The Vietnamese retaliated by invading Cambodia and reinstalling Ang Tong on the Cambodian throne. In 1773, however, Ang Tong abdicated in favor of the Siamese choice, Ang Mon. Mac Thieu Tu made peace with Taksin and both withdrew from Cambodia to prepare for another round.

1773–77

TAY-SON REVOLT. In 1773, however, a rebellion began in the Tay-son district led by Nguyen Van Nhac, Nguyen Van-Lu, and Nguyen Van-Hué, 3 brothers unrelated to the ruling dynasty, who were incensed at the greed of the regent, Truong-Phuc-Loan. In 1774, the Trinh invaded from Tongking, and the following year seized Hué. Trinh Sum's avowed intention was to help the Nguyen, but he did little beyond occupying Hué. Van-Nhac attempted to seize Hué, but failed. In 1776, Van-Lu had captured and then lost Saigon to Mac Thieu Tu who was aiding the Nguyen cause. By 1777, the Tay-son rebels had killed all but one of the Nguyen. The survivor, Nguyen Phuc-Anh (1762–1820), was aided in his escape by a French priest.

1777–87

RISE OF NGUYEN ANH. After the main part of the Tay-son army had left Saigon, Nguyen Anh returned to the city and with his supporters gained possession. In 1779, Do Thanh-Nhon, a supporter of Anh, successfully aided the Cambodians in replacing Ang Mon with

Ang Eng on the Cambodian throne. The next year Siam predictably invaded Phnom Penh, but the armies were withdrawn in 1781. By senselessly having Do Thanh-Nhon killed, Nguyen Anh lost many supporters, as well as Saigon once again to the Tay-son rebels. The brothers then divided Annam, Tongking, and Cochin China among themselves.

1787–1820

THE EMPIRE OF VIETNAM. In 1787, Nguyen Anh asked for French aid, which helped him retain Saigon the next year. Not until 1801 did the Nguyen forces finally capture the northern province of Annam. By July 1802, Anh had regained Tongking, assuming the title Gia-Long, emperor of Vietnam (ruled 1802–20). He then turned his attention to internal reconstruction.

1820–41

REIGN OF MINH-MANG. Minh-Mang (ruled 1820–40) succeeded Gia-Long. He refused in 1825, 1827, and 1831 to enter into commercial treaties with France, and in 1826 broke off diplomatic relations. He also began persecuting Christians, reversing his father's policy. In the late 1830's, he seems to have become aware that British and French activities in Southeast Asia made his isolationism very dangerous. However, he died in Jan. 1841, and Thieu-Tri (ruled 1841–47) followed Minh-Mang's earlier policies.

1841–48

FRENCH ATTACK ON TOURANE. In Feb. 1843, a French ship secured the release of 5 condemned missionaries in Hué. This happened again later in that year and in 1845. In 1847, the French sent 2 ships to Tourane to demand extraterritorial privileges for French nationals. Thieu-Tri attempted to trick the French captains, kill them, and burn their ships, but the plot failed and many Vietnamese vessels were burned in the fight before the French left.

1848–62

FRENCH ANNEXATION OF COCHIN CHINA. The Emperor Tu-Duc (ruled 1848–83) was more isolationist than his 2 predecessors. He ordered the violent destruction of all Christian settlements, and the banishment of all converts. Thousands of people died, victims of mistreatment. In 1851–52, 2 French missionaries were killed. The ignoring of a French protest led to a more violent assault on Tourane than before. Another French missionary was killed in 1856, as was the Spanish bishop of Tongking in the following year, providing pretexts for French and Spanish annexation attempts. After a British and French force took Canton early in 1858, a combined Spanish and French fleet reached Tourane, 31 Aug., 1858, and landed an occupation force. The fleeing Annamese had taken all food and supplies, however, and Tourane had to be abandoned. Saigon was captured in Feb. 1859, but nothing further was done until Peking was taken in Oct. 1860. By Nov. 1861, the French controlled the whole of lower Cochin China. The following May, Tu-Duc asked for terms. On 5 June, 1862, a treaty was signed by which (1) the 3 eastern provinces of Cochin China were ceded to France, (2) Tu-Duc was to pay an indemnity over 10 years, (3) the Catholic religion was to be tolerated, and (4) the ports of Tourane, Balat, and Kuang-An were to be opened to French trade. In Dec. 1862 a series of revolts erupted after Vietnamese mandarins had replaced French residents in the administration. Because of this, Tu-Duc refused ratification of the treaty, and had to be pressured by threats of aid to the Tongking rebels.

1863–70

STRUGGLE FOR CAMBODIA. The French governor, Adm. Pierre de Lagrandière (1807–76), decided to extend French influence in Cambodia, and King Norodom placed his kingdom under French protection, 17 Apr., 1864. Siamese influence was retained somewhat when Mongkut insisted that Norodom be crowned by both Siam and France. But in 1867 Siam gave up all claims to Cambodian suzerainty in exchange for the provinces of Battambang and Angkor. (*Cont. p. 349.*)

SIAM (THAILAND)
1760–82

REIGN OF P'YA TAKSIN. From 1768 to Sept. 1776, P'ya Taksin was the leader of the Siamese forces struggling against a series of invading Burmese armies, and had to deal with revolts within his kingdom. The strain of these campaigns obliged him to transfer much of his power to a subordinate, Gen. Chakri. In 1781, a rebellion in favor of Chakri deposed Taksin, and in 1782, Taksin was killed, Chakri becoming King Rama I (ruled 1782–1809).

1782–1809

REIGN OF RAMA I. Rama I succeeded in maintaining Siam's independence against the incursions of the new Burmese ruler, Bodawpaya. He did not reply in kind when the Burmese king invaded in 1785, but concentrated on internal affairs. He founded modern Bangkok, and so strengthened his hold on Menam, the central part of the kingdom, that he was not beset by the rebellions and civil wars that plagued his neighbors. In fact, domestic strife in Burma and Indochina gave him a chance to extend Siam's area of control. The Tay-son rebellion in Vietnam strengthened Siam in Cambodia because the young king Ang Eng was a refugee in Bangkok. Rama restored him to his throne with Siamese influence as the price. In 1802, however, with the creation by Gia-Long of a Vietnamese empire, Cambodia sent tribute to both Bangkok and Hué, and Rama I forbore to interfere.

1809–21

REIGN OF RAMA II. In 1812, Rama II (ruled 1809–24) unsuccessfully supported a brother of the Cambodian king Ang Chan, and Siamese influence waned. Two years later, however, a Siamese army occupied a large slice of territory in northern Cambodia, and in 1828 absorbed the kingdom of Vientiane.

The other major foreign problem of Rama II's reign concerned the sultan of Kedah, whom the Siamese had not forgiven for ceding Penang, 1786, and Province Wellesley, 1800, to the British. In 1821, a Siamese invasion forced the sultan to flee to Penang.

1821–50

THE BRITISH AND SIAM'S EXTERNAL TRADE. By the efforts of her leaders, Siam had remained independent, and British policies had supported these efforts. In the early 19th cent., Britain was unwilling to extend her commitments to the mainland of Southeast Asia, particularly since a number of the states involved were vassals of China, the source of the East India Company's tea. The British were hesitant about sending missions to Bangkok, fearing that Siamese suspicion of the Company's intentions might produce not the hoped-for commercial advantages but an incident leading to violence. The mission of John Crawfurd (1783–1868) in 1822 produced neither concessions nor incidents.

Rama III (ruled 1824–51) was also highly suspicious of British intentions. He refused to join Britain in the war with Burma, but did sign a commercial treaty, 20 June, 1826, with Capt. Henry Burney (1792–1845).

Altered conditions in the 1840's, especially Siam's re-establishment of state commercial monopolies and the end of the East India Company's monopoly of trade with China, resulted in a change in British policy. In 1849, Sir James Brooke (1803–68) was rebuffed in his attempt to negotiate a new commercial treaty. He recommended a decisive move to secure British influence by deposing Rama III and replacing him with Prince Mongkut. However, desiring peace with Siam, the British government decided against these moves.

1851–70

THE BOWRING TREATY. In 1851, Rama III died and Mongkut became Rama IV. On 18 Apr., 1855, Sir John Bowring (1792–1872) was able to negotiate for the British a Treaty of Friendship and Commerce which (1) established 3% customs duties, (2) permitted the import of opium, (3) allowed British subjects to purchase or rent land near the capital, (4) established a system of extraterritoriality, and (5) permitted a British consul to exercise civil and criminal jurisdiction over British subjects in Siam. Soon treaties were made with France, the U.S., Denmark, Portugal, Holland, and Prussia, inaugurating substantial commercial involvement in, and development of, Siam by Europeans. Siam's independence was, however, maintained. Mongkut died in 1868. His son, Chulalongkorn, became Rama V (ruled 1873–1910), but the country was ruled by a regency until he attained his majority in 1873. (*Cont. p. 354.*)

THE MALAY PENINSULA

1760–1819

EXPANSION OF JOHORE. In 1760 the power of the Sultanate of Johore began to revive. Its ruler demanded and received homage from the sultan of Perak, but the sultan of Kedah refused the same demand, and was deposed and exiled. In 1771, the English East India Company declined to guarantee the independence of Kedah, when it learned that this meant military aid. Raja Haji of Johore and his brother, the sultan of Selangor, thus gained control of Kedah and its trade. Johore at this time was strongly under the influence of Bugis seafarers from Celebes.

DUTCH-JOHORE RELATIONS. Johore maintained good relations with the Dutch until 1782, when Bugis pirates began to raid in the Malacca Straits. In 1783, Raja Haji besieged Malacca at a time of Dutch weakness, but the Dutch broke the siege in June 1784. In Aug. the Dutch expelled the Bugis from Selangor,

and in Oct. from Riau, where a resident was established in June 1785. By 1787, however, the Bugis had recovered Selangor. When Dutch power in the East Indies declined following the outbreak of war in Europe, the Bugis were able to regain control of Riau, Raja Ali displacing the rightful ruler, Tengku Hussein.

PENANG AND SINGAPORE. In 1784, Capt. Francis Light (1740–94) suggested that the English East India Company acquire the island of Penang as a naval base. Penang was accordingly occupied, 11 Aug., 1786, by agreement with the sultan of Kedah, and on 7 July, 1800, a stretch of territory on the mainland (Province Wellesley) was also obtained. On 28 Jan., 1819, Thomas Stamford Raffles (1781–1826) and R. J. Farquhar landed on the island of Singapore. Raffles acquired the island for the East India Company by recognizing Tengku Hussein as sultan of Johore and having him sign a treaty, 6 Feb., 1819.

1820–70

TREATY OF 1824. Singapore grew at a rapid rate and by 1820 was paying its own way. On 2 Aug., 1824, Sultan Hussein allowed it to be alienated permanently in return for a large sum immediately and a pension for life. On 17 Mar. of that year, the British and the Dutch had signed an agreement (Treaty of London) which defined their separate spheres of influence in the Malay Archipelago. Commercial clauses bound the 2 countries to respect each other's trade in India, Ceylon, and the East Indies, and both countries agreed to work to suppress piracy. Malacca became British. In essence, the British now held the Peninsula, and the Dutch the Archipelago. Penang in the north and Singapore in the south grew rapidly in commercial importance, while the Malay mainland remained undeveloped. On 1 Aug., 1826, the administration of Malacca and Singapore was combined with that of Penang and Province Wellesley to form the Straits Settlements. In 1832 Singapore became their capital.

SIAM AND THE MALAY STATES. During this period Britain did not interfere in the internal affairs of the Malay states, but there was considerable commercial penetration, by both Chinese and European merchants, from the Straits Settlements. Siam also, having recovered from her 18th-cent. wars, began to assert her ancient claims to the Peninsula. In 1821, the sultan of Kedah was forced to flee to Penang when his refusal to go to Bangkok resulted in Siamese devastation of his land. John Crawfurd was sent by the British to Bangkok to negotiate about Kedah because food from that state was necessary to Penang's survival, but his mission failed, 1822. On 31 July, 1825, Capt. Henry Burney negotiated a treaty with the raja of Ligor to prevent him from attacking the sultans of Perak and Selangor. In return the British promised not to interfere in Kedah. Burney was then sent to Siam, where he negotiated a treaty, 20 June, 1826, preserving the *status quo,* except that Britain gained somewhat favorable trade conditions, and the sultan of Kedah was removed to Malacca. When Siam disregarded the treaty and threatened Perak, Capt. James Low made a treaty with the sultan of Perak, 18 Oct., 1826, guaranteeing British protection, and though the government of India never ratified it, its provisions were honored in 1844, 1853, and 1874. Siam then put pressure on Trengganu and Kelantan, but was finally rebuffed in her efforts to gain control.

On 1 Apr., 1867, the Straits Settlements were transferred from the India Office to the Colonial Office. This pleased many who favored a policy of direct intervention in the Malay states. (*Cont. p. 346.*)

NETHERLANDS EAST INDIES

1760–1811

DECLINE OF THE NETHERLANDS EAST INDIA COMPANY. In 1760 the Netherlands East India Company ruled Java and dominated the seaways and coastlines of the Indonesian Archipelago. The Company's monopoly policies were causing poverty and retarding economic progress, and it had ceased to make annual profits. Made bankrupt by the disruption of trade caused by the Anglo-

Dutch War of 1780–84, it was allowed to expire on 31 Dec., 1799.

RULE OF H. W. DAENDELS. By this time the status of Dutch possessions in the East Indies had changed. On the establishment of the Batavian Republic in 1795, Stadholder Willem V, the nominal sovereign of Dutch possessions overseas, escaped from the Netherlands to England and ordered officials of the Company to surrender its possessions to his ally, the British, on demand. This led to the transfer of Malacca, Amboina, Banda, and forts on the west coast of Sumatra to the English East India Company. After the setting up of the Kingdom of Holland under Louis Bonaparte, 1806, Herman Willem Daendels (1762– 1818) was sent out to Java to prevent that island too from falling to a British attack. Daendels' reorganization of the administration did much to improve efficiency and he was able to reduce corruption, but his authoritarian handling of the Javanese earned him their dislike. When the expected British assault came, 4 Aug., 1811, therefore, the Javanese did not rise to the defense of their Franco-Dutch masters. The island surrendered on 17 Sept., and Thomas Stamford Raffles became its lieut. gov.

1811–16

THE BRITISH INTERREGNUM. Raffles established British authority and then proceeded to effect administrative reforms. By making the government the owner of the soil and then imposing a general tax on land, he hoped to abolish forced labor. For lack of revenue, however, compulsory services continued to be exacted, particularly in coffee-producing areas, and Raffles' innovations did not bring the desired results. Some of his liberalizing measures nevertheless continued in force when Java was restored to the new Kingdom of the Netherlands on 19 Aug., 1816.

1817–70

THE CULTURE SYSTEM. For a decade the Dutch sought by a variety of means to make the Netherlands East Indies profitable again. They were hindered by their own indecision about which policy to pursue and by the ravages of the Java War, 1825–30. It was not until the appointment of Johannes van den Bosch (1780–1844) gov. gen., 1830–33, that the tide turned. Van den Bosch instituted the Culture (Cultivation) System, by which the peasants of Java were required to grow export crops (sugar, coffee, indigo, tea, cotton, pepper, cinnamon, and cochineal) as directed by, and for the benefit of, the government. The system was a huge financial success, but resulted in great hardship for the Javanese. During the 1850's and 1860's it was gradually abandoned in favor of export agriculture organized on the basis of free capitalist enterprise. (*Cont. p. 344.*)

PHILIPPINES

1760–1806

BRITISH OCCUPATION OF MANILA. The Philippine Islands had been ruled by Spain since the 16th cent., though the whole archipelago had not been brought under Spanish control. On 6 Oct., 1762, a British force captured and occupied Manila. At the same time, a serious Filipino rising occurred in the Ilokano section of Luzon, posing a considerable threat to the Spanish government. The British occupation lasted until June 1764, without extension of British influence far outside Manila. The Treaty of Paris, 10 Feb., 1763, provided for a British withdrawal.

CLERICAL REFORMS. On the accession of King Carlos III, a series of reforms were instituted for the Philippines. The first of these involved restrictions on the clergy, beginning with the expulsion of the Jesuits in 1768. In 1770, the privileged position of friars was attacked by Simón de Anda, (1709–76), gov., 1770–76, with the support of the archbishop of Manila. Their objects were (1) to secularize the properties of the religious orders and (2) to reassert the powers of visitation over parishes by the archbishop. Royal sanction was given for these reforms in 1774, but the attempt was abandoned when Anda died in 1776.

ECONOMIC REFORMS. To make the Philippines economically self-sufficient, José Basco y Vargas (gov., 1778–87) proposed in 1778 measures to improve agriculture, industry, and trade. In 1781 he set up the Economic Society of Friends of the Country, which later established an agricultural school in Manila. In 1785 the Royal Company of the Philippines was formed to direct trade away from overburdened Acapulco (Mexico) and toward Spain by encouraging the use of the route west around Africa. In 1789, Manila became an open port for Asian goods.

1807–50

EARLY 19TH-CENT. DECLINE. After the disintegration of Spain's empire in America, Manila had to direct its trade toward Europe. In 1811, the last Spanish galleon left Manila for Acapulco and 4 years later the last ship from Acapulco arrived in Manila. Soon British and American ships outnumbered Spanish and Chinese. Peninsular Spaniards arrived to engage in private trade, bringing with them new ideas. By 1840, a number of Spanish commercial companies had been formed in Manila. But in 1842, the Treaty of Nanking between Britain and China opened 5 new ports on the South China coast. By 1850 Manila was nearly bankrupt. Economic deterioration was accompanied by social and moral decline as well. The large numbers of regular clergy who entered the Philippines in the 1820's and 1830's had a profound impact on this decadent society. Some of these clergy were Jesuits returning to their former endeavors on the Mindanao frontier; others were refugees from the suppression of certain monasteries in Spain, 1835. The rivalries of Spanish and Filipino clergy flared up again.

COMPETITION FOR THE SOUTHERN ISLANDS. Spanish influence in the southern islands, which were mainly Moslem, had never been strong. The French became interested in the Sulu Archipelago in 1844. This obliged the Philippine government to conduct an expensive holding operation there until 1878, when the sultan of Sulu acknowledged Spanish overlordship, 22 July.

CLERGY-INSPIRED REBELLIONS. The 1st of a series of Filipino clergy-led rebellions occurred in 1843, resulting from resentment against over-all Spanish discriminatory practices and the lack of educational and professional opportunities for Filipinos. The clerical establishment was attacked on moral, racial, economic, and social grounds by the Filipino clergy; by 2 newspapers, *El Diario de Manila* and *El Commercio* (founded in 1848 and 1850, respectively) ; and by Father Peláez and Father Opolinario de la Cruz. The latter formed his own order in 1841, the Colorum, which denied membership to both Spaniards and mestizos. Though not originally or primarily political, the Colorum became so, and Father Opolinario was its first martyr. This led other rebels to use its name.

1851–70

RISE OF NATIONALISM. Nationalist sentiment and unrest built up during the period between 1850 and 1870, but gained real momentum after the opening of the Suez Canal, 1869, which brought the Philippines much closer to the rest of the world, and after the revolution of the same year, which exiled Queen Isabella II of Spain. (*Cont. p. 350.*)

Central Asia

AFGHANISTAN
1760–1808

AFGHANISTAN IN 1760. Following centuries of dominance by Persia and India, an independent Afghan state was established under Ahmad Shah (ruled 1747–73), founder of the Durrani (Durrānī) dynasty. Between 1748 and 1767 the Afghans invaded India 9 times, defeating Mughal, Maratha, and Sikh armies, and gaining temporary control over the Punjab and Kashmir. At the Battle of Panipat, 14 Jan., 1761, which marks the high point of Afghan power in India, they permanently checked Maratha ambitions to rule the subcontinent.

AFGHAN PRESSURE ON INDIA. On the death of Ahmad Shah, his son Timur (Timūr) Mirza (Timur Shah, ruled 1773–93) succeeded to the throne, and moved the capital from Kandahar to Kabul. In 1774, 1779, 1780, 1785, and 1788, Timur invaded India in reaction against military challenge from the Sikhs.

Zaman (Zamān) Shah (ruled 1793–99) , son of Timur Shah, tried to centralize all power in his own hands. His efforts led to constant domestic discord.

Mahmud (Mahmūd) Shah (ruled 1799– 1803, 1809–19) overthrew his half-brother, Zaman Shah; quelled a Ghilzai tribal uprising, 1801; and made successful war on the Uzbegs, 1802.

On 29 Dec., 1800, the British signed a treaty with Persia containing a clause requiring Persia to discourage Afghan incursions into India. In 1803 a revolt dethroned Mahmud Shah, and he was succeeded, amidst dynastic struggles, by Shah Shuja (Shujā) (ruled 1803–9) .

1809–34

TREATY WITH BRITISH. The first official mission to Afghanistan sent by a European power was led by Mountstuart Elphinstone (English East India Company) . A treaty was negotiated, 12 Mar., 1809, providing for Afghan aid to the British in case of an invasion of India by the French. In the same year Mahmud Shah returned to power after overthrowing Shah Shuja, who in turn made numerous efforts to regain his throne, only abandoning them in 1813.

AFGHAN CIVIL WAR. In 1813, Mahmud Shah turned over real power to Fath Khan, who in 1818 was blinded on Mahmud's orders. This act touched off a civil war between the ruling Durrani dynasty (Saddozais) and the supporters of Fath Khan (Mohammedzais). The war lasted from 1819 to 1835 and ended with the fall of the Durrani dynasty.

In 1819, the Sikhs conquered Kashmir, and in Mar. 1823 defeated the Afghans in the Battle of Nowshera. Between 1824 and 1826, Dost Mohammed (Muḥammad) Khan, the youngest of the Barakzai (Barakzāi) brothers (Mohammedzais), gained control of Kabul and Ghazni. In 1833 the Persians unsuccessfully attacked Herat, and Shah Shuja, with British aid, invaded Afghanistan from India. He laid siege to Kandahar in 1834, where on 29 Jan. Dost Mohammed, aided by a British assurance of noninterference, defeated Shah Shuja. Meanwhile the Sikhs occupied Peshawar, and extended their rule to the mouth of the Khyber Pass. By 1835, Dost Mohammed was strong enough to establish the Mohammedzai dynasty.

1835–55

DOST MOHAMMED AND THE BRITISH. Dost Mohammed Khan (ruled 1835–39, 1842–63) was crowned Commander of the Faithful (Amīr al-Mu'minīn) in 1837. He defeated the Sikhs at the Battle of Jamrud, but failed to regain Peshawar. With British approval, a Russian commercial agent, Capt. Vitkavich, settled at Kabul. Also at this time, the Persians demanded control of Herat.

On 26 June, 1838, the British, Sikhs, and Shah Shuja signed the "Tripartite Treaty." By this agreement Shah Shuja relinquished Afghan claims to Sikh-held territory, and, in return, the Sikhs and British promised to provide military support for Shah Shuja's efforts to regain the Afghan throne. On 1 Oct., Lord Auckland, viceroy of India, issued the Simla Manifesto, in which he justified the use of British military forces under the command of Sir Willoughby Cotton (1783–1860) in the struggle between Shah Shuja and Dost Mohammed Khan.

1ST ANGLO-AFGHAN WAR. On 24 Apr., 1839, Kandahar was captured by the British. On 6 Aug., Shah Shuja entered Kabul and mounted the throne as a British puppet. During his reign the British controlled foreign, military, and tribal affairs. Dost Mohammed Khan surrendered on 12 Nov., 1840, and went into exile in India. On 2 Nov., 1841, a British agent, Alexander Burns, was killed by the Afghans during an insurrection in Kabul. On 25 Nov. negotiations began for a British withdrawal, and on 11 Dec. a treaty between the British and the insurgent Afghan chiefs was signed, by which the British agreed to leave Afghanistan.

The British evacuated Kabul, 6 Jan., 1842, but during their march south were repeatedly attacked. This led Lord Ellenborough, viceroy of India, to decide to take retaliatory action, 15 May. On 5 Apr., Shah Shuja was killed. On 16 Sept., the British destroyed Kabul and massacred the refugees from there who had fled to Istalif. The British army finally departed from Afghanistan beginning 12 Oct., demolishing Jalalabad on its way out, but before it reached India it was decimated in the Khyber Pass. Only 1 Englishman of the main column survived. The Anglo-Afghan War caused long-term Afghan xenophobia and deep anti-Christian sentiment. In Jan. 1843, Dost Mohammed Khan returned to Afghanistan and regained his throne at Kabul.

IMPROVEMENT IN ANGLO-AFGHAN RELATIONS. In 1848, war having broken out between the British and the Sikhs, the Sikhs ceded Peshawar to the Afghans in return for Afghanistan's aid against the British. On 21 Feb., 1849, the British defeated both Afghans and Sikhs at the Battle of Gujarat, and took over Peshawar. Beginning in 1850, Dost Mohammed Khan reconquered Balkh, Khulm, Kunduz, Badakhstan, and in 1855 regained control of Kandahar. On 30 Mar., 1855, he signed a 3-point treaty with the British providing mutual guarantees of territorial integrity.

1856–70

REPULSE OF PERSIAN THREAT. In Oct. 1856, the Persians seized Herat, and on 26 Jan., 1857, Dost Mohammed signed a 2nd Anglo-Afghan treaty, confirming the treaty of 1855. The new treaty included a British promise of aid in case of attack on Afghanistan, and the Afghans in turn agreed to allow British officers into their territory for the duration of the Anglo-Persian War. For the rest of his reign Dost Mohammed maintained amicable relations with the British.

DYNASTIC STRUGGLES. Shortly before his death in May 1863, Dost Mohammed had entered Herat and re-established the boundaries of his kingdom. When he died, Shere Ali (Shēr 'Alī) Khan (ruled 1863–67, 1869–79) ascended the throne. Between 1864 and 1865, he had to deal with serious revolts by his brothers. In July 1865, Abd-ar-Rahman ('Abd-ar-Rahmān) Khan led a further revolt; by 24 Feb., 1866, he had occupied Kabul, and on 9 May he defeated the army of Shere Ali Khan at the Battle of Sheikhabad. This loss was followed by another defeat, Jan. 1867, at the Battle of Kalat-i-Ghilzai, and yet another one in Sept. Following these losses, Afzal Khan (ruled 1867–68) became amir, only to die soon afterward. He was succeeded by Azim Khan (ruled 1868–69). In 1869, however, Shere Ali Khan regained the throne, and Abd-ar-Rahman Khan fled from Afghanistan to seek refuge in Russia.

SINKIANG

1760–1824

ESTABLISHMENT OF CHINESE RULE. By 1760 the Ch'ing Empire of China had smashed the power of the western Mongols in the Ili Valley. From this conquest a new province called Sinkiang (New Dominion) was created by uniting Dzungaria and the Tarim Basin. Criminals and political dissenters were exiled to this area. In 1759–60 the Khaja rulers were driven out of the oases of Yarkand and Kashgar as the conquest of the region was consolidated. In 1776 an imperial edict promised a subsidy to Chinese peasants who would settle in Sinkiang.

1825–59

MOSLEM REVOLTS. The 2nd quarter of the 19th cent. was marked by a series of Moslem rebellions in Sinkiang. In 1826–27 Khokand aided one of the Khojas (Jehangir) to launch a holy war against the Ch'ing, who responded by invading Kashgaria. In 1830 another rebellion broke out, but was quickly suppressed. In 1851 the Chinese and Russians signed the Kuldja Convention, which gave the Russians greater freedom of trade at Kuldja, in the upper Ili Valley, and also at Tarbagatai, and awarded them the right to station a consul at Kuldja. Another abortive Moslem uprising took place in 1857. In the same year the Russians, Valikhanov and Semanov, explored Kashgar and the T'ien Shan area.

1860–70

TREATY OF PEKING. On 2 Nov., 1860, the Treaty of Peking was signed, the 1st of a series of agreements by which China and Russia delineated the frontier between Sinkiang and Russian Turkestan. The treaty also gave Russia the right to place a consul at Kashgar.

REVOLT OF YAKUB BEG. In 1864 the warrior-leader, Yakub Beg (1820–77), appeared in Sinkiang as chief of staff of an army recruited by a descendant of the former Khoja ruling house of Kashgar who wished to re-establish Khoja power. The following year this army captured Kashgar and Yarkand. Yakub Beg soon replaced the Khoja leader and reconquered eastern Turkestan by seizing Aksu, Khotan, and Urumchi. In 1866, Ili tribesmen set up an independent Moslem state. This was followed by a rising by Dzungari tribes who gained control of Sinkiang, overran Kansu province, and penetrated into Shensi and Hopei provinces in China proper. By the late 1860's Beg had gained political and military control of the whole of Sinkiang. His territory became the prize of Chinese, Russian, Turkish, and British rivalries, but he was eventually conquered by a Chinese army in 1877.

STEPPE AND DESERT LANDS

1760–1820

TURKESTAN IN 1760. By the mid-18th cent. the lands of the Central Asian nomads had been divided from those of Russia by a line of forts running from the mouth of the Or to the upper Irtysh, and controlled from Orenburg. The Russians felt the need to protect their territories against possible movements of population resulting from the Chinese advance into Sinkiang. The largest states of the area were Khiva, Bokhara, and Khokand.

EDUCATIONAL POLICY. The charter of religious toleration issued by Catherine II in 1785 led to the opening of schools for the Kirghiz peoples and to the publication of books in the vernacular. Islam advanced in the region at the expense of shamanism.

1820–70

RELATIONS WITH KHIVA. In 1824, attempts were made to protect trade caravans from the attacks of Khivan marauders, The policy failed, however, and in 1839 a military expedition, commanded by Gen. Count Perovski (1794–1857), gov. gen. of Orenburg, was sent against Khiva. By a treaty signed in 1842 the Khivans agreed to refrain from attacks on Russians and to stop selling prisoners of war into slavery.

CONTROL OF THE ARAL SEA. In 1847 a Russian force penetrated to the Syr Darya River close to where it empties into the Aral Sea. The fortress of Aralsk was built at this place, and Russian gunboats began patrolling the waters. Incursions by Khokandians led to a 2nd military expedition under Perovski and to the capture of the fort of Ak-Masjid (later, Petrovsk) in 1853. The occupation of the Lake Balkash basin followed, and the line of frontier forts was extended from the Irtysh to Semirechie.

CONQUEST OF TURKESTAN. Turkestan was valuable to Russia as a consumer of manufactured goods and as a producer of raw cotton for the Russian textile industry. It was of strategic importance, since the Ili Valley in the east provided access to and from the Gobi Desert and China. Trade in the region could not flourish until the nomads of the desert had been brought under control. For these reasons Czar Alexander II authorized the conquest of Turkestan.

Military operations began in 1860. Tashkent was taken on 26 June, 1865, and the amir of Bokhara declared holy war. He was defeated after heavy fighting and had to surrender his main stronghold of Khodjent. In 1866 the governor generalship of Turkestan was created. Failure by Bokhara to pay an agreed indemnity led to renewed hostilities and the capture of Samarkand. By treaty, 5 July, 1868, the amir recognized the czar as his suzerain and Bokhara and Khokand were added to the Russian Empire. The submission of Khiva followed, 24 Aug., 1873.

Middle East and North Africa

PERSIA

1760–1801

PERSIA IN 1760. Between A.D. 636 and 651, Arab invaders ended the Sassanian Empire of Persia (226–651), and Islam soon replaced Zoroastrianism as the dominant Persian religion. The country was subsequently ruled by the Arab caliphates of Medina, Damascus, and Baghdad, various regional dynasties, Turkish, Mongol, and Turcoman dynasties from the 11th to the 15th cents. In c. 1500 the Safavi dynasty was established, the first national dynasty to rule all Persia in nearly 8 centuries. Although only a minority of Persians adhered to the heterodox Shiite (Shīʿa) doctrines of Islam, the Safavis made Shiah Islam the official state religion. The foremost Safavi emperor, Shah Abbas (ʻAbbās) the Great (1587–1629), reunited the ancient domains of

Sassanian Persia, including Christian Georgia and Armenia. When the Safavi dynasty ended in 1722, its territories were largely dismembered. The Persia of Shah Abbas was reunited, however, under Nadir (Nādir) Shah, a former Safavi officer, who ruled the country from 1736 to 1747.

ESTABLISHMENT OF THE ZAND DYNASTY. From 1747, when Nadir Shah died, Persia underwent a period of anarchy. Princes and ex-officers fought for supreme authority from their various bases of power. Karim (Karīm) Khan (ruled 1751–79), of the Zand tribe, defeated all other contenders, and reunited almost all of Persia under one rule. His capital was Shiraz, where he had been governor.

ENGLISH EAST INDIA COMPANY AT BUSHIRE. The East India Company had been trading in Persia since 1616, but the privileges it had gained lapsed after the fall of the Safavi dynasty. On 2 July, 1763, however, Karim Khan, hoping to stimulate commerce in his domains, re-awarded the Company its former privileges and extended them. He also authorized it to build and fortify a factory at Bushire. During the 19th cent. this port became the headquarters of Britain's political and commercial activity in the Persian Gulf area.

ESTABLISHMENT OF THE QAJAR DYNASTY. In 1779 Karim Khan died. Civil war again ensued, regional governors vying for supreme power. In 1785, Aga Mohammed (Āghā Muḥammad), head of a Turcoman tribe, the Qajars (Qājārs), which held sway in the Caspian area, emerged as the ruler of Persia. He made Teheran his capital.

TREATY WITH BRITAIN. In 1798, Napoleon revealed his intention of striking at Britain in India, and invaded Egypt as a first step. Persia thus became an area of strategic interest to Britain (1) because Napoleon might send an expedition into India via Persia, and (2) because Afghanistan was threatening to attack the Punjab. The dispatch of Capt. John Malcolm (1769–1833) to Teheran led to an Anglo-Persian treaty of alliance, 28 Jan., 1801 (never ratified), by which Persia promised to exclude any French military or diplomatic presence from her territory and to restrain Afghanistan from attacking India. Britain undertook to supply arms and military advisers in the event of Afghan or French attacks on Persia. This treaty marked the beginning of British political interest in Persia.

1802–20

WAR WITH RUSSIA. In 1801, Russia annexed the predominantly Christian Georgia under an agreement with its titular monarch and began occupying the independent khanates. Georgia, with short interruptions, had been a tributary of Persia since the 16th cent. In 1804, when a Russian force entered Georgia to take control, an 8-year Russo-Persian war broke out.

TREATY OF FINKENSTEIN. Persia requested aid in her war with Russia from Britain, but the British, unwilling to antagonize Russia, their natural ally against Napoleon, refused. Fath Ali ('Alī) Shah (ruled 1797–1834) therefore turned to France, which had been seeking an understanding with him since 1802. He sent an envoy to Finkenstein, Poland (Napoleon's temporary headquarters), and a treaty of alliance was signed there, 4 May, 1807. Napoleon recognized Georgia as Persia's possession, and undertook to supply arms and engineers, infantry, and artillery officers to the Persian army. Persia agreed to declare war on Britain and attack India. Although a French military mission was immediately dispatched, the Treaty of Finkenstein was short-lived, because France contracted an alliance with Russia, at Tilsit, 7 July, 1807.

TREATY OF GULISTAN. In 1812 the Russo-Persian war ended in Russia's favor. The Treaty of Gulistan, 30 Sept.– 12 Oct., 1813, awarded Georgia, and 9 other provinces tributary to Persia, to Russia. Russia also received the exclusive right to maintain ships-of-war on the Caspian Sea. This treaty served as a lever for later Russian expansion at Persia's expense.

ALLIANCE WITH BRITAIN. When Persia's treaty with France became a dead letter, Britain attempted to re-establish her previous position in Persia by sending military training missions to replace the

French mission. A defensive alliance was concluded, 25 Nov., 1814, by which Persia could request either British military aid or a subsidy if she were attacked. In return she undertook to prevent armies hostile to Britain from marching through Persia to India.

BRITISH PREDOMINANCE IN THE PERSIAN GULF. After punitive actions, from 1806 onward, to end piracy in the Persian Gulf, Britain imposed the Treaty for Suppressing Piracy and the Slave Trade, 8 Jan., 1820, on the Arab tribes of the area. She thereby assumed exclusive responsibility for the security of the Gulf, and gained a position of great power in relation to Persia.

1821–70

TREATIES OF TURKMANCHAY. Mutual dissatisfaction with the Treaty of Gulistan caused another war between Persia and Russia, 1826–28. Persia hoped to regain Georgia, and Russia wanted to extend her territory to the Aras River, a natural boundary. By Oct. 1827, the Russians had reached Tabriz, and the war was halted. By the treaty of peace, signed at Turkmanchay village, 10–22 Feb., 1828, Russia received all of Persia's territory north of the Aras River, and reaffirmed her exclusive right to maintain a navy on the Caspian Sea. Simultaneously she was awarded commercial and extraterritorial privileges. Britain gained comparable privileges by agreements dated 5 May, 1836, 28 Oct., 1841, and 4 Mar., 1857 (Treaty of Paris).

ANGLO-PERSIAN WAR. During the period 1826–56 Persian relations with Russia were good. This intimacy was especially apparent when Persia twice besieged the Afghan city, Herat, 1837 and 1856, at Russian instigation. The Russians were themselves expanding in Central Asia. Britain, fearing Russian designs on India, forced the Persians out of Herat, 1837, with a warning. In 1856, however, the warning went unheeded, and a British force attacked Persia. The shah, Nasr-ed-Din (Nāsir al-Dīn) (ruled 1848–96), now sued for peace, and an envoy to Paris signed a treaty, 4 Mar., 1857, with the British ambassador. Persia relinquished her claims on Afghan territory, and accorded Britain most-favored-nation status. Britain thus gained in Persia an equal status with Russia in extraterritorial and consular matters.

TELEGRAPHIC CONVENTION. The Sepoy Mutiny of 1857–58 convinced Great Britain that telegraphic communication with India was imperative for effective control. On 17 Dec., 1862, and 23 Nov., 1865, the British reached agreements with Persia for the construction of telegraph wires from the Ottoman border down to Bushire, from where an underwater cable was laid to India. With the execution of this agreement, Britain acquired a "telegraphic interest" in Persia, in addition to her commercial, political, and strategic interests. Rapid communication with India, as well as with the Australasian colonies, depended on these wires as well as on those running through Constantinople, Baghdad, and Basra. (Cont. p. 358.)

CAUCASIAN LANDS
1760–1828

CAUCASIA IN 1760. Caucasia, inhabited by a great variety of tribes, both Christian and Moslem, had been under Persian political and cultural domination for nearly 2,000 years. During the 18th cent., however, the impact of Ottoman power was increasingly felt, especially in the northern and western regions. More significantly, the expanding Russian Empire became involved in Caucasian affairs, initially as the protector of the area's Christians against the 2 Moslem powers.

RUSSIA AND TURKEY. An active phase of the struggle between Turkey and Russia for influence in Caucasia began in 1769. In 1770 the Russians, for the first time, crossed over the Caucasian mountain ranges. The Turko-Russian Treaty of Kuchuk Kainarja, 21 July, 1774, assured Russian control over Kabarda. In 1783 the Georgian kingdoms of Kartli and Kakheti invited Russian protection against Turkey. The Ottomans' renewed challenge of 1787–91 to Russian predominance in the northern Caucasus proved abortive. In 1801, Kartli and Kakheti were absorbed as Russian provinces. Establishing their hold over Osseti in 1803, the Russians proceeded to dominate Imerti in 1810, and Mingrelia.

RUSSIA AND PERSIA. Aga Mohammed Khan, the founder of the Qajar Dynasty in Persia, wished to re-establish his country's hegemony in Caucasia. Thus, in 1795, he occupied Tiflis and most of Kakheti and Kartli. Within a year, however, troops dispatched by Catherine the Great succeeded in bringing the whole of eastern Transcaucasia under Russian control. After Catherine's death, 1797, Czar Paul withdrew these troops, but the Russians held Georgia for a time. In 1804, Aga Mohammed Khan's successor renewed the war with Russia, in order to regain control of Georgia. To that end he entered into alliance with Napoleon, 4 May, 1807, who promised Persia French military equipment and advisers. The war was terminated by the Treaty of Gulistan, 12 Oct., 1813, which was negotiated through the good offices of Britain. Persia formally acknowledged Russian sovereignty over Georgia and Karabagh, as well as other districts in eastern Caucasia between Lankuran and Derbent. The fighting was resumed 13 years later. According to the new peace treaty (signed in Turkmanchay, Feb. 1828), Persia ceded to Russia the additional territories of Erivan, Nakhichevan, and Talyche.

1829–70

RESISTANCE TO RUSSIAN RULE. By the Treaty of Adrianople, 14 Sept., 1829, which terminated a year-long war with Russia, Turkey abandoned all claims to sovereignty in Circassia. Russian efforts, 1832–39, to subjugate the independence-seeking Moslem Cherkess tribes of the area, however, were hampered by the intensification of a resistance movement initially centered in Daghestan. There, in 1829, Kazi Mullah, the murshid (leader) of the Murids, a military Moslem order with puritan and egalitarian beliefs, had declared a holy war against the Russians. After Kazi Mullah was killed, 1832, his son and the 3rd murshid, Shamyl, led the Murids. Recruiting his supporters from the tribes of the Daghestan and Chechnia regions, Shamyl distinguished himself as one of the greatest guerrilla commanders in the history of war. Only by capturing Shamyl, 6 Sept., 1859, could the Russians put an end to the Murids' resistance. During the next 5 years, under Russian pressure some 200,000 Circassians emigrated to Turkey, preferring Ottoman rule to Russian.

OTTOMAN EMPIRE

1760–1807

THE OTTOMAN EMPIRE IN 1760. In the 11th and 12th cents., Moslem Turkish tribes from Central Asia swept through the Middle East and into Asia Minor, settling and eventually establishing empires. The Seljuk (Seljūq) Sultanate of Rum (Rūm, c. 1077–1300) was limited to Anatolia. The successors of the Seljuks, the Ottomans ('Uthmānlis), extended their power into Europe, Asia, and Africa, and by 1600 governed the largest empire in the world. Nearly all the Arab lands from Iraq to Algiers, as well as the Christian lands of the Balkans and Danube Valley, owed allegiance to the Ottoman government in Istanbul. By 1700, however, Ottoman power had begun to decline, and during the 18th cent. both internal administrative inefficiency and the threat of external encroachment increased. Beginning with Peter the Great (1672–1725), the czars of Russia sought a warm-water port on the Ottoman-controlled Black Sea.

TREATY OF KUCHUK KAINARJA. A 6-year war between the Ottoman Empire and Russia ended in a Turkish defeat in July 1774. By the Treaty of Kuchuk Kainarja, 21 July, 1774, Russia gained a territorial outlet on to the Black Sea and the right to send ships through the Dardanelles Straits. From this time onward, Russian policy aimed at weakening the Ottoman Empire and at gaining outright control of the Dardanelles. Russian ambitions, on the one hand, and the efforts of other European powers to check them, on the other, produced the diplomatic problem known as "the Eastern Question."

1808–49

RULE OF MAHMUD II. The Ottoman Empire was in a turbulent state when the 20-year-old Mahmud (Maḥmūd) II became sultan, 1808, following the assassinations of his 2 immediate predecessors, Selim (Selīm) III (ruled 1789–1807) and Mustafa (Muṣṭafā) IV (ruled 1807–08). The young sultan was convinced that the conservatism of the military and religious establishments was weakening the empire relative to the increasing strength of Europe. Consequently, he abolished the powerful Janissary Corps, an elite military caste, 1826, and reorganized the army along European lines. In the religious domain he disbanded the influential Bektashi dervish order, and built Turkey's 1st medical school based on European rather than Moslem learning. Although Mahmud's modernization measures proved superficial and many Moslems considered him an infidel, he removed important institutional barriers to reform and opened the door to further westernization.

GREEK INDEPENDENCE. In Apr. 1821 a revolt broke out in the Morea (Peloponnese) against Turkish rule. The Powers, dedicated to maintaining the *status quo,* at first refrained from entering the conflict. However, the serious losses which an Egyptian army under Ibrahim (Ibrāhīm) Pasha (1789–1848) inflicted on the Greeks, 1825–27, aroused European public opinion and compelled the Powers to act. The Tripartite Treaty of London, 6 July, 1827, provided for the dispatch of British, Russian, and French warships to the eastern Mediterranean, and at the Battle of Navarino, 20 Oct., 1827, the Turko-Egyptian fleet was destroyed.

Russia then attacked Turkey, Apr. 1828, achieved rapid victory, and by the Treaty of Adrianople, 14 Sept., 1829, extracted from Turkey autonomy for Serbia though not for Greece. Western European opinion, however, favored Greek

independence, and both Russia and the Ottomans concurred in the acceptance of the throne of Greece, May 1832, by the king of Bavaria on behalf of his son, Otho (1815–67).

EGYPTIAN INDEPENDENCE. Ottoman military disasters and political weakness in the 1820's encouraged rebellions in other parts of the empire. Mohammed Ali (Muḥammad 'Alī) (1769–1849), the governor of Egypt, who had long wished to acquire Syria, sent a force led by his son Ibrahim (Ibrāhīm) Pasha, 1831, against Acre. By July 1833, Ibrahim's army had penetrated Asia Minor as far as Kutahya, a town just west of present-day Ankara. Sultan Mahmud sought desperately for allies, but found Britain indifferent and France supporting Egypt. Russia then made an offer of aid which led to a Russo-Turkish treaty of defense, signed at Unkiar-Skelessi (Hunkiâr Iskelesi), 8 July, 1833.

Mohammed Ali's increasing disregard of the wishes of his nominal master, the Ottoman sultan, provoked an attack by Turkish forces on Syria, Apr. 1839, then being ruled by Ibrahim Pasha. The sultan's army was routed at the Battle of Nezib, June, and in July the Ottoman fleet deserted, preferring to side with Mohammed Ali. The Powers then presented a note, 27 July, 1839, to the Ottoman government at Istanbul, and by the Quadruple Agreement of 15 July, 1840, Mohammed Ali was constrained to withdraw from his Asian conquests, but obtained the promise that he and his descendants would be recognized as hereditary rulers of Egypt. This arrangement was accepted by the Ottoman government, 13 Feb., 1841.

TANZIMAT REFORMS. Sultan Abdul Mejid ('Abd al-Majīd) II (ruled 1839–61) was 16 years old at his succession, and the government passed into the hands of the reforming minister, Mustafa Rashid (Muṣṭafā Rashīd) (1802–58), formerly Ottoman ambassador in London. Mustafa Rashid knew that the Powers would only guarantee the Ottoman Empire's continued existence if it reformed itself. Accordingly, in 1839 he drew up a plan of reorganization (Tanzimat) which envisaged a more efficient administration and reformed the legal code. Like the reforms of Mahmud II, those of Mustafa Rashid did not result in basic changes, but showed the Ottoman government's willingness, at least, to modernize.

1850–70

CRIMEAN WAR. A quarrel between Catholic and Eastern Orthodox monks over the guardianship of the holy places in Palestine precipitated the Crimean War, fought by Britain, France, and the Ottoman Empire against Russia. Napoleon III and Czar Nicholas made representations to the sultan on behalf of the respective disputants, and the Ottoman government devised certain compromise concessions, Feb. 1852. But Russia remained dissatisfied, and raised her demand to a protectorate for herself over all of the empire's Orthodox Christians (about 40 % of the Ottoman population). The Russian case was based on an article in the Treaty of Kuchuk Kainarja of 1774 giving them a right of protection over one Orthodox church in Istanbul. When the Ottomans rejected the demand, Russia withdrew her diplomatic staff from Istanbul and sent an army into the Turkish Danubian provinces. The sultan demanded their removal, which was not forthcoming, and the war began, 23 Oct., 1853.

The British and French, fearing the collapse of the Ottoman Empire, declared war on Russia, 28 Mar., 1854. Hostilities lasted until the armistice of 25 Feb., 1856, and resulted in a Russian defeat. By the Treaty of Paris, 30 Mar., 1856, the Ottoman Empire was formally admitted into the Concert of Nations, the signatories pledged themselves to guarantee the empire's independence and integrity, warships were forbidden in the Black Sea, and the Ottomans recovered territory in southern Bessarabia and in the Danube estuary.

HATT-I-HUMAYUN   REFORMS. During the Crimean War the Powers brought pressure to bear on the Ottoman Empire to modernize its legal and administrative systems. They also demanded complete equality for non-Moslem sections of the population. On 18 Feb., 1856, on the eve of the Paris Peace Conference, Sultan Abdul Mejid issued the Hatt-i-Humayun (Imperial Rescript) Reforms, which guaranteed security of life and property to his Christian subjects. As in the past, these changes were resented by the conservative Moslem element and tension increased throughout the empire, finally erupting in the slaughter of thousands of Christians in Syria and Lebanon, 1860. The Powers again intervened, and secured a large measure of autonomy for the Christian population of Lebanon, 1861. (*Cont. p. 355.*)

ARABIA

ARABIA IN 1760. After terminating the Mameluke Empire, 1517, and conquering Iraq, 1639, the Ottoman Turks had established their rule over nearly all of the Arabic-speaking world. Their control was, however, especially tenuous in Arabia. The rulers of the Hejaz (Ḥijāz) acknowledged Turkish suzerainty, but Yemen (Yaman) re-established its independence, 1635, and the Bedouins of the hinterland never really lost theirs. (*Cont. p. 360.*)

The Saudi Empires

1760–1823

RULE OF MOHAMMED IBN SAUD. Originally a petty chief, ruling Dariya (Darʿīya) in Wadi Hanifa, ibn Saud (Suʿūd) became the disciple and protector of Mohammed ibn Abdul-Wahab (Muḥammad ibn ʿAbd al-Wahhāb) (1703–92). The latter, a well-traveled jurist from Najd, was the founder of a rigid, puritan religious revival movement, the Wahabis (Wahhābīs). Highly critical of contemporary beliefs and rituals of Islam, and inspired by the teachings of ibn Hanbal (Ḥanbal) (the founder of one of the 4 orthodox schools of Islamic law), ibn Abdul-Wahab was determined to restore Islam to its primitive strictness. Ibn Saud, crusading for the new movement, succeeded before his death in 1765 in bringing all of eastern and central Arabia under his rule.

WAHABI EXPANSION. While ibn Abdul-Wahab remained the guiding religious spirit of the realm, ibn Saud's son and successor Abdul-Aziz ('Abd al-Azīz) I expanded the empire, with notable assistance from his own son, the future Saud II.

The aggressiveness of the Wahabis, and especially their attacks on pilgrim caravans, alarmed the Ottoman sultan. Turkish troops invaded al Hasa (Ḥasā) in 1798. But in 1801 the Wahabis captured Karbala in Iraq and, in a demonstration of their zeal, sacked that Shiite holy city. In revenge a Shiite assassin took the life of Abdul-Aziz I in 1803.

EGYPTIAN INVASION. Saud II captured Mecca in 1803 and again in 1806, and Medina in 1804. The Ottoman sultan assigned the viceroy of Egypt, Mohammed Ali (Muḥammad 'Alī) Pasha, to the task of crushing the Wahabis. Thus in 1811 Saud, by now engaged in a military campaign aimed at Baghdad, had to alter his plans and face an Egyptian expeditionary force led by Mohammed Ali's son, Tusun (Ṭūsūn). In his first battle with Saud, Tusun was severely defeated, but after receiving reinforcements captured Mecca and Medina, 1812–13. In 1813 Mohammed Ali assumed personal command of the invasion. The following year Saud once more inflicted a serious defeat on the Egyptian troops led by Tusun in the vicinity of al Taif (Ṭāïf). Soon thereafter Saud died in Dariya.

DESTRUCTION OF THE 1ST SAUDI EMPIRE. Abdullah ('Abdullāh) I (ruled 1814–18), Saud's son and successor, made a truce with Tusun, 1815, whereby he acknowledged Ottoman suzerainty and the Egyptians withdrew from Nejd (Najd). But Mohammed Ali denounced this truce, and in 1816 Ibrahim Pasha, another of Mohammed Ali's sons, led a new Egyptian invasion into Arabia. Ibrahim skillfully obtained the support of many local tribes. A 4-month siege of al Raas proved abortive, but he captured al Qasim's 2 major cities, Unaiza ('Unaiza) and Buraida, as well as al Shariga

(Shāriqa). In Apr. 1818, supported by several major tribes, he began a siege of Dariya. Six months later, Abdullah was taken prisoner and sent to Istanbul, where he was executed. Many prominent Saudis were put to death. A few escaped, but the rest were sent to Egypt as prisoners. Having terminated the Wahabi empire, the Egyptians became the new rulers of Arabia.

1824–70

RESISTANCE TO EGYPTIAN RULE. In 1824, Turki (ruled 1820–34), a grandson of Mohammed ibn Saud, succeeded in driving the Egyptians out of Riyadh (Riyāḍ). By consenting to pay yearly tribute to Egypt, whose nominal suzerainty he acknowledged, Turki gained time to build a new Wahabi regime based at Riyadh. He was murdered in 1834 by his cousin, Mishari (Mishārī), who was in turn toppled and killed by Turki's son, Faisal (Faiṣal). When Faisal refused to continue the payment of tribute to Cairo, the Egyptians forcibly replaced him with his brother, Khalid (Khālid), 1838. Faisal was sent to Egypt as a prisoner. The increasing unpopularity of Khalid's subservience to Egypt enabled his cousin, Abdullah ibn Thunaiyan ('Abdullah ibn Thunaiyān), to stage a successful revolt and become the new ruler of Najd, 1841.

2ND SAUDI EMPIRE. Faisal escaped from Egyptian captivity and, deposing Abdullah, 1843, regained the throne and ruled until 1865. Posing as the protector of the Wahabi faith, he expanded his empire. His authority reached to Buraimi and the Omani ('Umāni) hinterland. His influence was felt as far as the frontiers of Yaman and Hadhramaut (Haḍramaut). Northern Arabia, ruled by the house of Rashid, although virtually independent, acknowledged Faisal's suzerainty. Even the British at the Persian Gulf felt the impact of Faisal's extended influence. Following a British naval action, provoked by the plunder of property at the port of Sur (Ṣūr) by tribes allied with the Wahabis, 21 Apr., 1866, Abdullah ('Abdullāh) (ruled 1865–71, 1874–84), Faisal's son and successor, promised that he would refrain from harming British interests. *(Cont. p. 360.)*

Muscat

On 12 Oct., 1798, the English East India Company concluded an agreement with the Imam of Muscat (Masqat) by which the French were excluded from his territory. This agreement, designed to counter Napoleon's Egyptian campaign and threat against India, was the first of a series that eventually placed most of the principalities on the southern and eastern shores of Arabia under varying degrees of dependence on Britain. In 1798, Persia leased, to the sheik (shaykh) of Muscat, Bandar Abbas ('Abbas) and the islands of Hurmuz and Qishm—all previously important sites for European trade. The lease remained valid until 1868. A British base was established at Qishm and became the headquarters of the British forces assigned to suppress piracy and the slave trade and to oversee the maritime truce in the Persian Gulf. On 31 May, 1839, Muscat entered into a series of agreements with Britain. But through other such agreements with the U.S.A., 21 Sept., 1833, and France, 17 Nov., 1844, the ruler of Muscat demonstrated that he was not as dependent on the British as were his neighboring sheiks. *(Cont. p. 360.)*

The Omani Coast and Bahrain

SUPPRESSION OF PIRACY AND THE SLAVE TRADE. During the period 1806–20, forces under the command of the English East India Company took punitive measures against Arab pirates harassing British ships in the Persian Gulf. The rulers of the Omani coast and Bahrain (Bahrayn, Bahrein) signed agreements with Britain, 1820, pledging themselves against piracy and slave trading. For Britain this was the beginning of a formal responsibility for security in the Gulf. On 4 May, 1853, the sheiks of the Omani coast entered into an agreement with Britain never to engage in naval warfare in the Persian Gulf. Thus was made permanent a promise made in a

series of temporary agreements, dating back to 1835, designed to halt armed disputes over rights to the Gulf pearl fisheries—war among the signatories not having been prohibited by the 1820 treaty for the suppression of piracy.

CLARENDON NOTE. In response to a Persian protest against increasing British association with the sheiks of Bahrain, which Persia considered as its domain, the British foreign secretary, Lord Clarendon, clarified the British position on the question, 29 Apr., 1869. The Clarendon Note, however, was later to be subject to differing interpretations by Britain and Persia. *(Cont. p. 360.)*

Aden

Britain established political relations with the rulers of the Aden area in 1799 as a precautionary measure against French moves in the Indian Ocean. On 6 Sept., 1802, a commercial treaty was signed between the East India Company and the ruler of the port of Aden, the sultan of Lahij. Britain forcibly occupied Aden, 19 Jan., 1839, after failing to persuade the sultan to sell it. Possession of the port was desired to facilitate a British steam service between India and Egypt, as well as for strategic reasons against the presence of Egyptian troops in Arabia. On 11 Feb., 1843, the sultan, having been unsuccessful in attempts to recapture the port, formally recognized British control in Aden. *(Cont. p. 360.)*

EGYPT AND THE SUDAN

1760–97

EGYPT IN 1760. The Ottoman Turks conquered Egypt in 1517 but retained the old ruling class, the Mameluke beys, as governors of districts under an Ottoman pasha. The beys' power steadily increased, however, and by the 18th cent. the pasha had become no more than a figurehead.

REVOLT OF ALI BEY. Ali ('Alī) Bey (1728–73), who had held the office of *Shaykh al-balad* (the highest Mameluke office under the Ottoman rule) since 1760, had by 1769 overcome all his rivals in Egypt, and deposed the pasha. Intervening, at the Ottoman sultan's request, in a dynastic quarrel in the Hejaz, he sent an expeditionary force under his retainer, Abu al-Dhahab (Abū al-Dhahab), which took Mecca in 1770. Abu al-Dhahab was then sent into Syria in 1771 to co-operate with the ruler of Acre, Dahir al-Umar (Ẕāhir al-'Umar) against the Ottoman governor at Damascus. Subsequently Abu al-Dhahab entered into an alliance with the Ottomans against Ali. When Ismail (Ismā'īl) Bey, who was dispatched by Ali to halt the advance of Abu al-Dhahab toward Cairo, also defected and joined Abu al-Dhahab, Ali took refuge in Acre, Apr. 1772. There he received arms and men from Russia and returned to fight Abu al-Dhahab. Defeated in battle on 1 May, 1773, he was captured and died soon afterward.

RULE OF IBRAHIM AND MURAD. Egypt was again a dependency of the Ottoman Empire, and Abu al-Dhahab launched a campaign against Dahir al-Umar during which he died, 1776. Ismail took over as *shaykh al-balad*, but he was opposed by Ibrahim (Ibrāhīm) Bey and Murad (Murād) Bey, former lieutenants of Abu al-Dhahab, who proceeded to rule conjointly. In 1786 the Ottoman government dispatched a force against these renegade Mamelukes, and succeeded in installing a new Ottoman pasha and reinstating Ismail Bey as *shaykh al-balad*. However, after the Ottoman withdrawal, 1787, and the death of Ismail, Jan. 1791, Ibrahim and Murad resumed their joint rule.

1798–1802

FRENCH OCCUPATION. In July 1798, Napoleon Bonaparte landed at Alexandria with an expeditionary force to conquer Egypt. This he regarded as the principal step toward undermining British influence in Asia. He tried to maintain cordial relations with the Ottomans, and appealed to the Egyptian people to help him replace the corrupt and exploitative rule of the beys with a truly Islamic and egalitarian regime. He defeated the forces of Murad and Ibrahim, and obtained Egyptian acquiescence in his rule. But on

1 Aug., 1798, Adm. Horatio Nelson destroyed the French fleet at the battle of Abukir Bay. The French also failed in a campaign to capture Murad Bey. On 22 Oct., 1798, dissatisfaction with the taxes and innovations imposed by Napoleon produced a popular revolt in Cairo which was led from the Mosque-University of al-Azhar. The revolt was promptly suppressed, but its causes persisted. In early 1799 Napoleon made an abortive expedition to Syria, and in July of that year the Ottomans, with British naval support, landed an army at Abukir, but suffered a serious defeat at Napoleon's hands. Appointing Gen. Jean Baptiste Kléber (1753–1800) governor of Egypt, Napoleon left for France Aug. 1799.

Ottoman military pressure forced Kléber to agree, 24 Jan., 1800, to evacuate Egypt. But when the British demanded that the French soldiers be treated as prisoners, Kléber resolved to fight on. In June he was assassinated by an al-Azhar student. The new French commander, Gen. Jacques François de Menou (1750–1810), had gained some popularity in Egypt for having professed Islam, but in Mar. 1801 the British landed at Abukir and began advancing toward Alexandria. The French were forced to agree to evacuate Cairo, 30 May, 1801, and Alexandria, 30 Aug., and their army embarked for France in Sept. Napoleon's Egyptian expedition awakened Europe to the area's strategic value in time of war.

1803–48

ACCESSION OF MOHAMMED ALI. After the French departed, the Ottomans took measures to eradicate the power of the Mamelukes. But the British, who did not leave Alexandria till Mar. 1803, provided protection for many of the beys. In May 1803, a revolt of the Albanian soldiers against the Turkish pasha, Mohammed (Muhammad) Khosrev, forced the pasha to flee Cairo. In the ensuing struggle with the Turks, the commander of the Albanians, Mohammed Ali (Muhammad 'Alī) (1769–1849), made an alliance with the Mameluke beys. The allies defeated Khosrev Pasha at Damietta and Ali ('Alī) Pasha Jazairli (the new Ottoman governor of Egypt) at Rosetta. In the struggle for power between Mohammed Bey al-Alfi and Osman ('Uthmān) Bey al-Bardisi, the Albanians sided with the latter, while yet a third Ottoman governor, Khurshid (Khūrshīd) Pasha, endeavored to enforce his authority. Although the Mamelukes now closed ranks, they were unable to overcome the forces of the pashas, and retreated to Upper Egypt. On 12 May, 1805, a delegation of ulema complained to the judge against the misconduct of Khurshid and his troops, and on 14 May another delegation invested Mohammed Ali with vice-regal powers, which he accepted.

DECLINE OF MAMELUKE POWER. Khurshid opposed Mohammed Ali's rule and asked the beys for support. Fighting in Cairo did not cease until the Ottoman government confirmed Mohammed Ali as governor of Egypt. Outside Cairo, Mohammed Ali's authority continued to be challenged by the beys, by the forces that had fought under Khorshid, and by many Albanians who deserted Mohammed Ali to join his rivals. On 17 Aug., 1805, Mohammed Ali caused the slaughter of many beys whom he had tricked into coming to Cairo by false promises of safety. The Ottoman government's support of the Mamelukes became less firm when Mohammed Ali sent large tribute payments to Istanbul.

BRITISH INVASION. On 17 Mar., 1807, the British landed 5,000 men in Alexandria, expecting to join forces with a leading Mameluke, al-Alfi, against Mohammed Ali. Learning that al-Alfi had died on 30 Jan., they sought the co-operation of the other beys. Most beys, however, chose to side with Mohammed Ali against the invaders. The British suffered a serious defeat at Rosetta, and after costly battles at Hamad and Alexandria evacuated Egypt on 14 Sept., 1807.

CAMPAIGN AGAINST THE MAMELUKES. Despite Mohammed Ali's concessions to the Mameluke beys, they continued to resist him. On 2 occasions in 1811 he caused the massacre of a number of prominent beys whom he had deceived into coming to Cairo as his guests. He then ordered the indiscriminate killing of Mamelukes throughout the country. Some fled south to Nubia, only to be attacked by forces sent after them, 1812. The survivors retreated farther south to Dongola.

INVASIONS OF ARABIA. In 1811 Mohammed Ali, following the order of his sovereign, the Ottoman sultan, sent an expeditionary force to subdue the Wahabis in Arabia. His troops occupied the Hejaz, and in 1813 he himself visited Mecca, and deposed the newly restored Sherif (sharīf). In 1815 a truce with the Wahabis suspended hostilities. In 1816 he sent a new expedition to Arabia led by his son Ibrahim (Ibrāhīm). In 1818 Ibrahim defeated and captured the Wahabi ruler, and suppressed opposition to Egypt's supremacy in Arabia.

INVASION OF THE SUDAN. In 1820 Mohammed Ali decided to conquer the Sudan to obtain control of the lucrative caravan trade passing through the area, and to exploit the reputed gold mines of the Funj Sultanate of Sennar (Sennār). He also saw in this campaign an opportunity to employ his dissatisfied troops and to obtain slaves to build a new army. He conquered Nubia, Sennar, and Kordofan, founded Khartoum, and temporarily gained control of the ports of Suakin and Massawa.

AGRARIAN REVOLT. Peasant reaction to Mohammed Ali's rule was demonstrated by risings in Upper Egypt, 1820–24, as well as by flight to other villages, to the towns, and even across the frontier to Syria.

CAMPAIGN IN GREECE. To suppress the Greek revolution for independence, the Ottoman government sought Mohammed Ali's assistance. In Mar. 1825, Egyptian troops led by Ibrahim landed in the Morea. The Egyptian navy wrested control of the sea from the Greeks, and on land the Greeks were overwhelmed by the Egyptian army. On 20 Oct., 1827, a combined British-French-Russian naval force destroyed the Turko-Egyptian fleet at Navarino. In Aug. 1828 Britain sent a fleet to Alexandria and induced Mohammed Ali to withdraw his army from Greece.

OCCUPATION OF SYRIA. In return for Mohammed Ali's support against the Greeks, the Ottoman government had promised him the government of Syria and the Morea. When this promise was not fulfilled, Mohammed Ali's forces invaded Syria, 1831. On 27 May, 1832, Acre was captured and on 21 Dec. the Ottoman forces under the grand vezir were defeated at Konya in Asia Minor. Active intervention by the Powers produced the Agreement of 14 May, 1833, between Mohammed Ali and the sultan. This agreement conferred on Mohammed Ali the governorship of Syria. An Ottoman attempt to regain control of Syria in the spring of 1839 was frustrated by the Egyptians. Egyptian successes were threatening the very survival of the Ottoman Empire, and the Powers again decided to intervene. On 13 Feb., 1841, the sultan appointed Mohammed Ali, who agreed to withdraw from Syria, governor of Egypt and the Sudan for life. Another royal decree, 1 June, 1841, made the government of Egypt hereditary in Mohammed Ali's family.

Old age incapacitated Mohammed Ali before his death on 2 Aug., 1849; his son, Ibrahim, assumed the government, Sept. 1848. Chief among the accomplishments of Mohammed Ali was the creation, by 1823, of a European-style military force, with the aid of French advisers. To sustain his army and navy, and to enrich himself, Mohammed Ali launched an impressive program of economic development and industrialization. He promoted, beginning in 1822, the cultivation of cotton in the Delta. He made major contributions to the introduction of a European system of education in Egypt.

1848–70

RULE OF ABBAS I. Ibrahim Pasha died in Nov. 1848, and was succeeded by Abbas ('Abbās) I (ruled 1848–54). Disliking European ways, the new ruler tried to halt, and even reverse, the process of modernization. Yet in 1851 Abbas was induced by Britain to grant George

Stephenson a contract to build Egypt's first railway, between Cairo and Alexandria. In July 1854, Abbas was murdered by his guards.

RULE OF SAID. Abbas' successor was Mohammed Ali's son, Said (Sa'īd) Pasha (ruled 1854–63). In 1854 Said gave permission for the opening of the British Bank of Egypt, and in 1856 he granted a Frenchman, Ferdinand de Lesseps (1805–94), a concession to build a Suez canal. Said's borrowing from European financiers started Egypt's national debt. He died Jan. 1863.

RULE OF ISMAIL. Ibrahim Pasha's son, Ismail (Ismā'īl) (ruled 1863–79), succeeded Said. By increasing his tribute to the Ottoman government, in 1866 Ismail obtained the right of primogeniture for his family. In 1867, as a sign of further independence, he received from the Ottoman sultan the title of khedive of Egypt. Ismail had been educated in Europe and made strenuous efforts to modernize his country with the help of European and American advisers. Many construction projects were given to European contractors. On 17 Nov., 1869, the Suez Canal was opened. The modernization program, and the heavy costs of ruling and garrisoning the Sudan and of opposing Ethiopia to the south, rapidly exhausted the country's resources, forcing it into more and more borrowing from Europe. (*Cont. p. 360.*)

NORTH AFRICA
1760–1829

NORTH AFRICA IN 1760. In the 18th cent., North Africa (less Morocco) was nominally part of the Ottoman Empire, but in fact almost entirely independent of Turkish control. Tripoli was ruled by the Qaramanli family, Tunis by the beys of the Husainid dynasty, and Algiers by a dey. During the 18th cent. there was a decline in prosperity. Privateering became more difficult and less rewarding, and the rulers pressed more heavily on the population. Distress was increased by plague and famine.

From 1666 Morocco had an indigenous ruling dynasty, the Alawite. Of the Arab-

Berber indigenous population of the Maghrib (North Africa), the Moroccans were perhaps the most resistant to foreign rule. The Alawite dynasty, over the years, established commercial relations with Britain, France, and Spain, thus enhancing the international status of Morocco as a sovereign state.

FOREIGN RELATIONS. The Maghrib offered commercial attractions to the countries of Europe and, after 1786, to the U.S. The region, particularly Morocco, also increased in strategic importance. The rulers of the Maghrib similarly found relations with Europe beneficial. Sidi Mohammed ibn Abd Allah (Sīdī Muḥammad ibn 'Abd Allāh) (ruled 1757–89) of Morocco signed a treaty with Spain, 28 Mar., 1767, and Ali ('Alī) Pasha of Tripoli a treaty with France, 12 Dec., 1774. Morocco was the 1st country in the Maghrib to recognize the U.S. in a treaty of amity signed 28 June, 1786. By 1817, European diplomatic agents were established at Tangier, Morocco. Algiers also had diplomatic relations with Britain, Portugal, France, and the U.S. by the beginning of the 19th cent.

BARBARY CORSAIRS. European commercial relations with the Maghrib were complicated by the presence of the Barbary corsairs. From the days of the Barbarossa brothers in the 16th cent., the Mediterranean Sea had been infested by pirates. Many were European renegades. Their activities extended as far as the North Sea and even Iceland, and so serious was the menace they posed that the subjects of European states ventured into the Mediterranean only after meeting the demands made by the rulers of the Maghrib for substantial annual tributes. The 1st serious attempt to subdue the pirates was in Aug. 1775, when a Spanish fleet, under Count Alexander O'Reilly (1722–94), an Irish soldier of fortune, stormed Algiers. The U.S. began a policy that broke the tradition of paying tributes by going to war with Tripoli, 1801–5, and with Algiers, 1815. In Aug. 1816 British and Dutch ships, under Lord Exmouth (1757–1833) and

Baron van der Capellen, bombarded Algiers, Tunis, and Tripoli, releasing over 3,000 European slaves.

1830–70

FRENCH CONQUEST OF ALGIERS. The French invasion of Algeria was undertaken by Charles X as a safety valve for political discontent in France. The immediate causes were a financial dispute with the dey of Algiers and an alleged insult to the French consul, Pierre Deval. After blockading Algiers for over 2 years, a French expedition under Gen. Louis Bourmont (1773–1846) landed at Sidi Ferruch, 14 June, 1830. The dey capitulated 5 July, 1830. On 22 July, 1834, King Louis Philippe declared Algiers a French possession.

ABD AL-QADIR. The indigenous Arab-Berber population of Algeria resisted the French invasion, particularly resenting the expropriation of the land by European settlers. Under Abd al-Qadir ('Abd al-Qādir) (b. 1808), a resistance movement developed. He was proclaimed sultan by his followers, 22 Nov., 1832, and was recognized by the French as an independent sovereign, 26 Feb., 1834. By this time more than two-thirds of Algeria was under his control. He established a kind of federal government, based on tribal equality, and divided the country into eight *khalifaliks* (provinces) with a hierarchy of administrative officers. From 1835 on, he launched a full-scale war against the French, formally proclaiming the jihad (jihād, holy war) in Nov. 1839. In Oct. 1847, however, he was obliged to surrender and was exiled to France. He failed because of the superiority of the French military forces led by Gen. Thomas Robert Bugeaud, and because his centralizing policies caused resentment and suspicion. Few Algerians shared his vision of a unified state. Resistance against the French continued after 1847, especially among the Kabyles.

ALGÉRIE FRANÇAISE. The French invasion of Algeria was followed by formal colonization, beginning in 1840 with the appointment of Thomas Robert

Bugeaud (1784–1849) as gov. gen. Bugeaud began the policy of "l'Algérie Française." Central to this policy was the granting of Algerian land to European settlers (colons). European immigration was encouraged, free grants of land were made, and the army helped in building roads and in planting settlements. By 1847 there were 110,000 colons, made up of French, Spanish, Italian, Maltese, German, and Swiss elements. A decree of 4 Mar., 1848, made Algeria an integral part of France, and colonization increased rapidly after that date. Although Algerian indigenous inhabitants were, in 1863, recognized as the rightful owners of the land, and some attempts were made to safeguard their communal and individual rights, their hostility to the encroachments of the Europeans steadily increased. A decree of Oct. 1870 put the administration of Algeria directly under 3 departments of the French Ministry of the Interior.

MAINTENANCE OF MOROCCAN INDEPENDENCE. The French occupation of Algeria had repercussions elsewhere in the Maghrib. Support given to Abd al-Qadir by Morocco led to war with France, 1844, and the Moroccans sustained defeat at the Battle of Isly, 14 Aug. Spain, concerned for the safety of her Moroccan fortresses, also declared war, inflicting a heavy defeat on the Moroccans, and exacted an indemnity of some £4 m. Britain's concern for Moroccan integrity and her commercial interests

there made it possible for the Moroccan government to raise loans in London to pay off the Spaniards. The defeats suffered by Morocco led to some efforts at military and administrative reforms under Sultan Mohammed Abd al-Rahman (Muhammad 'Abd al-Rahmān) (ruled 1859–73).

TUNIS PUBLIC DEBT. France supported internal liberal reforms in Tunis, 1857 and 1861, although these remained largely on paper. Increasing demands for taxes to meet the bey's deteriorating financial situation led to revolts, 1864–67. Loans were raised in Europe, and as the financial position of the Tunis government worsened, France, Britain, and Italy established an International Commission, 1869, to take charge of the bey's finances.

THE SANUSIYYA. In Mar. 1835, Turkey reasserted her control over Tripoli. The Qaramanli dynasty was removed and a new governor appointed, directly responsible to the Ottoman sultan at Istanbul. This 2nd Turkish regime did not succeed any better than the 1st in exercising control over the interior. The Sanusiyya (Sanūsiyya) brotherhood, established in 1843 in Cyrenaica by al-Sayyid Mohammed ibn Ali al-Sanusi (Muhammad ibn 'Alī al-Sanūsi) (1791–1859), galvanized tribal life. The brotherhood established over 100 zawiyas (lodges) throughout Cyrenaica, Tripolitania, and the Fezzan, which served as centers of learning, culture, and commerce. (Cont. p. 333.)

Tropical Africa

WESTERN SUDAN

1760–1825

ASCENDANCY OF THE FULBE. The late 18th and early 19th cents. saw the creation of Moslem theocratic states throughout the western Sudan. Leadership for the jihads (jihāds, holy wars) that produced these states was drawn mostly from the clerical caste of the Fulbe

(Fulani, Peul) people, who had been migrating eastward from their area of origin in the basin of the Sénégal to the Niger Bend, into Hausaland and Bornu, and as far as Adamawa (Adamāwa). By the 18th cent. the Fulbe consisted of 2 distinct groups: town dwellers (predominantly Moslem) who provided the political and economic leadership, and pastoral nomads (not yet Islamized) who supplied, when it was required, most of the Fulbe cavalry.

RISE OF GOBIR. In Hausaland there were many independent states, the strongest being Kano and Gobir. Wars among them were frequent and indecisive, but Gobir's conquest of Zamfara, 1764, increased its power and made it a threat to its neighbors.

JIHAD IN FUTA JALON. Toward the end of the 18th cent., the Fulbe of Futa Jalon (northern Guinea) attained dominance over the local peoples due to the efforts of the cleric, Ibrahim Musa (Ibrāhīm Mūsā), and the war leader, Ibrahim Sori (Ibrāhīm Sōri) (d. c. 1784). The followers of these men formed 2 competing parties which fought a series of civil wars in Futa Jalon to determine who should hold office as patriarch (al-māmi). In 1837 a compromise was agreed on: patriarchs elected by each party were to exercise power turn and turn about. Continuing dissensions, however, weakened Futa Jalon later in the 19th cent.

JIHAD IN FUTA TORO. A theocratic state was founded in Futa Toro (Sénégal) by clerics led by Tyerno Sulaiman Bal (Tyērno Sulaimān Bal) (d. 1776). Bal's successor, Abd al-Qadir ('Abd al-Qādir) (c. 1728–1806), defeated the Trarza Moors of Mauritania, 1786–87, and established Futa Toro rule along the left bank of the River Sénégal.

JIHAD OF UTHMAN DAN FODIO. A Fulbe cleric in Gobir, Uthman ('Uthmān) dan Fodio (1754–1817), accused the kings of Hausaland of laxity in their Islamic observances. Attacked by the *sarki* (king) of Gobir, he escaped, 21 Feb., 1804, and proclaimed the jihad, issuing flags to all who were willing to strike down the infidels and bring about a Moslem reformation movement. Kebbi and Zaria fell to Uthman's flag bearers in 1805, Katsina in 1807, Daura and Gobir in 1808, and Kano in 1809. By 1810 the Fulbe and their allies controlled the whole of Hausaland.

RULE OF AL-KANEMI. When the Fulbe attempted to conquer Bornu and succeeded in taking the capital, N'gazargamu, 1808, and driving out the *mai* (king), Bornu's independence was maintained by the Kanembu cleric, Mohammed al Amin (Muḥammad al Amīn), known as al-Kanemi (al-Kānemī) (d. 1835), who became its de facto ruler. He built his own capital at Kukawa (Kūkawa), 1814, and defended Bornu against further attacks by the Fulbe and by Wadai, 1824.

THE EMPIRE OF SOKOTO. Uthman dan Fodio's conquests were ruled by his son, Sultan Mohammed (Muḥammad) Belo (d. 1837), from Sokoto (founded 1809) and by his brother, Abd Allah ('Abd Allāh) (1766–1829), from Gwandu. Together the 2 regions constituted the Sokoto Empire. Under Sokoto's control trade flourished and the influence of Islam spread widely.

KINGDOM OF MASINA. The Fulbe leader Seku Ahmadu (Shaikh Ḥamad, 1775–1844) declared jihad against both Gurari Dyalo (Dyālo), king of Masina, and Da Dyara (Dyāra), king of Segu, defeated them, and established the Fulbe theocratic state of Masina, with its capital at Hamdullahi (Ḥamdullāhi, founded 1815).

1826–70

TUKOLOR EMPIRE OF AL-HAJJ UMAR. Umar ibn Said Tal ('Umar ibn Sa'īd Tal) (c. 1797–1864), a Tukolor cleric born in Futa Toro, after a prolonged visit to the Holy Places of Islam, 1826–34, and residence in Sokoto, 1835, and Masina, 1838, established a military base at Dingiray in northern Guinea in 1845. He recruited followers and bought arms and ammunition with funds obtained from exploiting the gold mines of the area and from trading in religious objects. In 1853 he felt strong enough to declare the jihad. He captured Nyoro in Karta (Kārta) in 1854, Segu in 1861, and Masina in 1862. Much of his support came from the Tijaniyya (Tijāniyya) religious brotherhood, of which he was khalifa for the western Sudan. The struggle against Masina, however, overtaxed his resources. He was besieged in Hamdullahi and managed to escape south to

Bandjagara (Bandjāgara), but died there in 1864. His son, Amadu Seku, succeeded to the Tukolor Empire. (*Cont. p. 335.*)

ETHIOPIA

1760–1840

ETHIOPIA IN 1760. The 18th cent. saw the collapse of the Ethiopian monarchy and the division of the empire into a number of independent provinces. Of these the most important were Tigre (Tigrē) in the north; Wag-Lasta, Simen (Simēn), Begemdir (Bēgēmdir), Gojam, and some smaller provinces in the center; and Shewa in the south. In the past outside support had helped to bolster the dynasty (which claimed descent from King Solomon and the Queen of Sheba) against intrusions from the Moslem kingdoms of Somalia and from the Funj Sultanate of Sennar. But from the expulsion of the Jesuits in 1632 onward, the rulers of Ethiopia discouraged contact with outsiders.

ZEMENE MESAFINT. The "age of princes" (*Zemene Mesafint*) in Ethiopian history began in 1769 when Ras Michael (Mīka'ēl) Sihul of Tigre murdered 2 kings of the royal line within 6 months and became the most powerful man in the kingdom. He ruled from the capital, Gonder, and was visited there, 15 Feb., 1770, by the Scottish explorer, James Bruce. Ras Michael never succeeded in establishing a centrally organized state, and was continuously involved in political and military struggles with other provincial governors. The enthronement and deposition of rival puppets drawn from the Solomonic line continued for 100 years. One of these, Tekle Giyorgis (Gīyorgīs) Fiqr Segid, for example, was put on the throne and removed from it 6 times during the period 1779–1800.

1841–70

RISE OF KASA. A minor Kwara chief, *lij* Kasa (b. c. 1820), unified Ethiopia after many decades of confusion and civil war. In Oct. 1846 he invaded and pillaged Dembiya and in Jan. 1847 occupied Gon-
der, the capital. At the battle of Iloha, 18 June, 1847, he defeated the forces of Menen, queen mother of Gonder, and on 27 Nov., 1852, those of *dejazmach* Goshu of Gojam. On 12 Apr., 1853, he overcame the combined armies of Ras Ali of Gonder and *dejazmach* Wibe (Wibē) Hayle Maryam of Simen, burned Ali's capital in May, and on 29 June defeated Ali again at the Battle of Ayshal. When on 9 Feb., 1855, he once again beat Wibe at the Battle of Deresge (Deresgē), he became master of the whole country. Two days later, 11 Feb., he was crowned King of Kings of Ethiopia as Theodore (Tēwodros) II.

RULE OF THEODORE II. Theodore was a brave war leader and a fanatical supporter of the Ethiopian Church. He began the process of Ethiopian modernization, outlawing many antiquated practices and breaking up independent provinces into smaller units of administration ruled by his own nominees. But his government rested entirely on force. Toward the end of his reign (1855–68) he became increasingly authoritarian and arbitrary.

BRITISH INVASION. A series of diplomatic blunders led to the imprisonment of a number of Englishmen at Magdala (Meqdela), Theodore's capital. Sir Robert Napier (1810–90) commanded a British rescue expedition. After a march of great difficulty, Napier's army of 2,000 men met 4,000 Ethiopians on the plain of Aroge (Arogē) below Magdala fortress. The Ethiopians faced modern weapons with great bravery, but were defeated, 10 Apr., 1868. Theodore withdrew into the fortress and, when the British entered it, shot himself. Napier made no attempt to settle the succession, freed the prisoners, and withdrew from Ethiopia at the end of May.

STATES OF THE WESTERN FORESTS AND COASTS

1760–1870

WEST AFRICA IN 1760. In the 18th cent. the peoples of the West African coasts and forests were closely involved in the slave trade. Profits were so great that competition among them was intense. This was particularly true in the forest states, which were dependent on middlemen for export of slaves and import of European goods. European knowledge of the interior of West Africa was limited to the Senegambia region, where the French had been active since the 17th cent.

Senegambia to the Ivory Coast

COLONY OF SENEGAMBIA. Commercial rivalry in the Senegambia region between the French and the British was always strong and, in time of war, violent. At stake were the profits from the export of slaves, gum, and wax, and both contestants hoped eventually to control the gold mines of the interior. After the outbreak of the Seven Years' War (1756–63), the British navy conquered the most important French posts in the region, 1758, and on 19 Apr., 1764, the British Company of Merchants Trading to Africa was given permission to govern them. In 1765, mismanagement caused Parliament to institute a government based on that of the Crown Colonies of America. French traders undermined the colony, however, because those responsible on the British side failed to integrate the hinterlands with the coast. During the American Revolutionary War, the French navy recaptured the former French posts, and by the Treaty of Versailles, 20 Jan., 1783, Britain ceded them to France.

PROVINCE OF FREEDOM. When the Mansfield Decision, 1772, freed slaves in Britain, the proposal was made that, since the large numbers of unemployed former slaves were a threat to law and order, they should be transported. Under the auspices of a committee led by Granville Sharp (1735–1813), 400 settlers established the "Province of Freedom" at St. George's Bay, 15 May, 1787. Plagued by disease, crop failure, and the hostility of the local Temne, the experiment was terminated in 1790.

COLONY OF SIERRA LEONE. Granville Sharp, together with other abolitionists, such as Thornton, Wilberforce, and Clarkson, then formed the Sierra

Leone Company. In Feb.–Mar. 1792, 1,100 former slaves and 100 whites were settled at Freetown. The company attempted to correct many of the mistakes of 1787, but friction continued between colonists and Temne. A French naval attack of 28 Sept.–13 Oct., 1794, destroyed much of Freetown. In 1800 the colonists were in open rebellion against the Company, and in 1801-2 a war was fought with the Temne. When Britain prohibited the slave trade for British subjects, 25 Mar., 1807, it became desirable for the British navy to have a harbor and refreshment station on which an antislave-trade naval squadron could be based. On 1 Jan., 1808, therefore, Sierra Leone, with its excellent harbor at Freetown, became a British crown colony. The population of Sierra Leone Colony was augmented by (1) the "Nova Scotians" (loyalist ex-slaves freed after the American Revolutionary War); (2) the "Maroons," former runaway slaves from Jamaica; and (3) slaves freed by the British navy from captured slave ships and taken to Freetown.

FOUNDATION OF LIBERIA. The example of Sierra Leone appealed to a number of American opponents of slavery. In Feb. 1816, Capt. Paul Cuffee landed 34 black settlers from the U.S. at Freetown. An American Colonization Society was formed, 28 Dec., 1816, and, in Mar. 1820, 80 colonists attempted to settle at Sherbro Island. The land, however, was found unsuitable for cultivation, many settlers died from disease, and the remainder were driven away by the indigenous inhabitants. A further 33 settlers arrived at Freetown, Apr. 1821. Through determination and the use of force, the American Colonization Society secured a treaty, 15 Dec., 1821, from local chiefs, and the 1st effective colonization of what was to become Liberia took place at Cape Mesurado early in 1822. The settler population of Liberia grew from 150 in 1824 to 2,000 in 1834.

REPUBLIC OF LIBERIA. During the 1830's, separate and competing settlements were being formed in Liberia. Despite British rejection of the American Colonization Society's claim to possess sovereign rights over a portion of the

West African coast, the U.S. government refused to annex Liberia as a colony, and the Society was finally forced to abandon its responsibility for the settlers, who proclaimed their independence, 26 July, 1847. American diplomatic recognition was withheld until 21 Oct., 1862. Meanwhile Liberia gradually enlarged itself by purchase and conquest of territory from surrounding tribes.

FRENCH ACTIVITIES. In 1817 the French regained the control of the trading posts in the Sénégal which they had lost during the Revolutionary and Napoleonic wars, and extended their commercial activities southward during the 1830's and 1840's. Édouard Bouët secured rights of occupation for France from chiefs on the Ivory Coast and in Gabon. In Dahomey, the Marseille firm of Régis reopened commercial ties at Whydah.

FAIDHERBE IN SÉNÉGAL. Louis Léon César Faidherbe (1818–89) was appointed governor of Sénégal in 1854. He saw the need to free the trade routes to the interior from imposts and tolls if French mercantile activity was to prosper. By 1861, through persuasion and force, he had come to terms with al-Hajj Umar (al-Ḥājj 'Umar), deposed some unco-operative rulers of coastal states, secured various trade routes, and constructed a number of forts in the interior. The French thrust into the western Sudan dates from his 2nd term of office, 1863–65.

Gold Coast to the Oil Rivers

ASHANTI AND THE BRITISH. In the mid-18th cent. the Ashanti of the Gold Coast, like other forest dwellers of West Africa, competed for the profits of the slave trade. The Fon kingdom of Dahomey, the Yoruba kingdom of Oyo, and the city-states of the Oil Rivers were all engaged in a continuing economic and political rivalry. Under the *asantehene* (king of Ashanti) Osei Kojo (ruled 1764–77), the Ashanti won a number of battles against states to their south, but failed to clear the routes to the coast of toll collectors. The Ashanti were able, however, to secure a steady supply of arms and ammunition. Between 1807 and 1816, under the *asantehene* Osei Bonsu (ruled c. 1801–24), they won decisive victories over the coastal Fanti and over the Akim, Akwapim, and Wasa. In 1817 a British mission to Kumasi, the Ashanti capital, secured a treaty of friendship, 7 Sept. A second treaty was negotiated, 23 Mar., 1820, but was not ratified.

On 3 July, 1821, the British crown assumed control over the Gold Coast forts from the Committee of Merchants. War broke out between the British and Ashanti in June 1823, due mainly to jurisdictional conflicts and to a misunderstanding of Gold Coast affairs by the new British governor, Sir Charles MacCarthy. In 1824, MacCarthy took the field in person against the Ashanti army and was defeated and killed at the Battle of Bonsaso, 21 Jan. On 7 Aug., 1826, the British avenged this loss by overwhelming the Ashanti at the Battle of Katamanso. In 1828, responsibility for the administration of Gold Coast forts was returned by the crown to the Committee of Merchants.

GEORGE MACLEAN AND THE BOND OF 1844. George Maclean (1801–47), appointed president of the Council of Merchants on the Gold Coast, 8 Jan., 1830, saw the need for a just treaty with the Ashanti, and on 27 Apr., 1831, arbitrated an agreement which ensured an extended period of peace. His forceful and persuasive personality aided him in creating an informal protectorate over the coastal areas, and some Fanti chiefs acknowledged the extension of British jurisdiction into the interior. By 1840, Maclean's influence had helped to treble the trade of the Gold Coast. Maclean had his detractors, however, in both Britain and the Gold Coast, and on 24 Aug., 1843, the crown resumed responsibility for the area. A bond signed, 6 Mar., 1844, between Britain and the Fanti chiefs provided legal justification for British sovereignty.

DECLINE OF OYO AND THE YORUBA WARS. The Empire of Oyo (western Nigeria) declined during the late 18th and early 19th cents. The revolt of Afonja, 1824, led to Fulbe (Fulani) control over Ilorin and the imperial capital, Old Oyo, was abandoned c. 1835. The Fulbe were, however, thrown back by the Yoruba at the Battle of Oshogbo, c. 1840. Meanwhile Oyo's former Yoruba vassal states had begun fighting among themselves. The Owu War, c. 1820–26, and the Ijaye War, 1860–62, were the main engagements, the latter being fought between the Ibadans and the Egba of Abeokuta.

DAHOMEY UNDER GEZO. At the death of King Abandozan (ruled 1797–1818), Gezo (ruled 1818–58) attained power in Dahomey, helped by the Portuguese mulatto slave dealer, Francisco de Souza. Gezo participated in the illegal slave trade and intervened in the Yoruba civil wars, attacking Abeokuta in 1851.

OIL RIVERS OF NIGERIA. Following the prohibition of the British slave trade in 1807, British commercial interests in the Oil Rivers (Niger Delta) encouraged the transition from the slave to the "legitimate" trade. Palm oil, the main product of the region, was in heavy demand in Britain. Attempts were made to restrain the illegal slave trade by inducing local rulers, such as King William Dappa Pepple (1817–66) of Bonny, to sign treaties, but with little effect. The appointment of John Beecroft as British consul for the Bights of Benin and Biafra, 30 June, 1849, however, signaled increasing official British concern, and in 1852 the British government agreed to subsidize steamers plying regularly between West Africa and Liverpool.

COLONY OF LAGOS. Beecroft and others were convinced that Dahomey could be prevented from trading in slaves if support were given to the Egba of Abeokuta in their struggle against King Gezo. The position of British missionaries and merchants, moreover, would be strengthened if a port on the coast of Yorubaland were under British control. Accordingly, a British force landed at Lagos, Dec. 1851, deposed the *oba* (king) Kosoko, and replaced him with the more pliable Akitoye, who signed a treaty accepting British protection, 1 Jan., 1852. Trade

between the Lagos coast and Yorubaland, however, did not flourish. To enforce more favorable commercial conditions the British annexed Lagos, 6 Aug., 1861, and made it a crown colony.

PARLIAMENTARY SELECT COMMITTEE, 1865. Despite the many increases in British influence on the West African coast during the first half of the 19th cent., the British Parliament remained reluctant to add to these responsibilities. The Colonial Office refused to accept territories newly acquired by the government of Sierra Leone. On the Gold Coast, officials temporized with the Ashanti problem, violating the spirit of Maclean's treaty of 1831, and in 1863 their inept diplomacy provoked another war in which the Ashanti defeated the British government's allies. A parliamentary select committee recommended, 26 June, 1865, that Britain should gradually withdraw from her West African possessions, except Sierra Leone. No action was taken, however, and both Britain and West Africa were soon to become involved in the "Scramble for Africa." (*Cont. p. 335.*)

STATES OF THE EAST AND CENTER

East Coast

1760–1826

THE EAST COAST IN 1760. During the 18th cent. the Arabs of Oman in the Persian Gulf established control over the ancient commercial city-states of the East Coast of Africa. Toward the end of the century, however, many local governors were able to make themselves virtually independent, and the traditional authorities of the area found Omani rule to be oppressive. The sultan of Kilwa appealed to Goa and Mozambique for protection, but the Portuguese were not strong enough to dominate the northern East African Coast.

FRENCH TREATY WITH KILWA. The French needed additional labor for their sugar, coffee, and cotton plantations on Réunion and Île de France. By an agreement of 14 Oct., 1776, the sultan of Kilwa agreed to provide a French trader, Morice, with 1,000 slaves per year.

IMMIGRATION FROM INDIA. Indian traders, on the coast since c. 1500, began to settle in ever-increasing numbers, particularly at Zanzibar. By 1811 the Indians were such an important sector of the commercial community that Capt. Smee protested their taxation, as they were British citizens.

SAYYID SAID. In 1806 Sayyid Said (Saʿīd) ibn Sultan (ruled 1806–56) succeeded to the throne of Oman. His East African domain, over which his predecessors had exercised only indirect control, was secure only at Zanzibar, Pemba, Mafia, and Kilwa. In 1814, the Mazrui rulers of Mombasa, a dynasty which had first asserted its independence from Oman in 1741, defied Sayyid Said, and appealed for protection to the British at Bombay. By 1822 the sultan's forces had secured the coastal islands of Pate, Brava, and Lamu.

OWEN'S PROTECTORATE. On 22 Sept., 1822, Said agreed to a treaty making illegal the sale of slaves in his dominions to the subjects of Christian powers. The treaty also provided for a British agent to be posted at Zanzibar and implied British recognition of Said's East African domain. On 7 Feb., 1824, Capt. William Owen (1774–1857) arrived off Mombasa while Said's fleet was bombarding the Mazrui stronghold of Fort Jesus. Hoping to aid in halting the slave trade, Owen intervened and established a protectorate, 9 Feb., 1824. The Mazrui only wanted British protection of their slaving activities, however, and the British could not afford disruption of their relations with Said in the Persian Gulf. After prolonged negotiations, the British forces withdrew, Oct. 1826.

1827–70

DEFEAT OF THE MAZRUI. Soon after the British withdrawal, Sultan Said sent a fleet to Mombasa, but secured only the temporary submission of the Mazrui. An-

other attempt in 1829 also failed. The next visit of the sultan, in 1832–33, included a futile plea to Madagascar for troops. Finally, in 1837, he secured the downfall of the Mazrui at Mombasa by fraud rather than force and had the family deported to the Persian Gulf. Said was now master of the coast. In 1841 he settled permanently at Zanzibar.

RELATIONS WITH FOREIGN POWERS. On 21 Sept., 1833, Said signed a treaty of friendship and commerce with the U.S.A. and on 17 Nov., 1844, a similar agreement with France. In 1841 a British consul was stationed at Zanzibar.

TRADE WITH THE INTERIOR. Arab trading caravans had begun moving inland from the coast c. 1780. By the 1830's, Sultan Said was sending regular trading expeditions hundreds of miles into the interior. Independent traders joined the caravans for protection. In 1844 contact was made with the capital of Buganda, and by 1851 the caravans were moving west of the Great Lakes. The trade was largely financed by the Indian moneylenders at Zanzibar, who were encouraged by Said. Between 1840 and 1860, the Indian population of the island increased from 1,000 to 6,000.

CHRISTIAN MISSIONS. Johann Ludwig Krapf (1810–81) of the Church Missionary Society arrived in East Africa in 1844 and was welcomed by Sultan Said. His activities were restricted mainly to Mombasa, but he and his associate, Johann Rebmann (1820–76), became the first Europeans to sight Mts. Kenya and Kilimanjaro. In 1860 a French Catholic mission, which included 2 Holy Ghost fathers, arrived. This was followed by a party of the United Methodist Free Churches in 1862 and by the Universities' Mission to Central Africa in 1864.

RULE OF MAJID. In 1856 Sultan Said died and his son, Majid (1835–70), succeeded to a throne that was now separate from that of Muscat and Oman. Zanzibar's importance as a commercial center at this time is shown by the fact that total revenues exceeded £50,000 by 1859. They had steadily increased during Said's reign: 1828, £10,000; 1834, £20,000. The primary exports were ivory, cloves, gum copal, cowries, and sesame; imports included cottons, rice, beads, brass wire, gunpowder, muskets, and provisions. During Majid's reign, British influence in Zanzibar increased considerably.

The Interior

THE STATE OF BUGANDA. The most powerful state in the interior of East Africa was Buganda, lying to the north of Lake Victoria. *Kabaka* (King) Semakokiro (ruled 1797–1814), according to tradition, became extremely wealthy through the ivory trade. Buganda had expanded considerably by his time, and was moving from a feudal to a bureaucratic state system. Semakokiro's royal monopoly over the ivory trade produced greater centralization, as the monarch could reward loyal supporters with goods as well as land. Although the *kabaka's* rule was autocratic, Buganda's society was fluid, allowing commoners to advance in wealth, power, and prestige. The Baganda were thus receptive to Moslem and Christian influences in the 19th cent., and conditions were favorable for material and social change.

TRADE IN THE INTERIOR. The 1st direct contact between Buganda and the coastal Arabs took place in 1844 during the reign of *Kabaka* Suna (ruled 1836–56). The main exports were ivory and slaves, and the main imports were cloth and guns. Other tribes of the interior were involved in commercial ties to the coast in the early 19th cent. Primary among them were the Nyamwezi, who controlled the route east from Lake Tanganyika. Ivory and slaves were their main exports, but some copper found its way to the coast from Katanga. By the mid-19th cent., however, the Zanzibaris controlled most of the trade, for they had guns and access to credit.

MUTESA OF BUGANDA. Mutesa (ruled 1856–84) made the role of *kabaka* of Buganda almost completely secure through sophisticated political maneuvering. His kingdom's expansion was virtually complete at this date; he sought only

internal prosperity and political influence over his neighbors.

KABAREGA OF BUNYORO. One of Buganda's rivals, situated to the north, was Bunyoro. By 1869, the date of the accession of Kabarega to the throne of Bunyoro, that kingdom had largely recovered from earlier economic and political impoverishment. Trade contacts with "Khartoumers" (merchants from the basin of the Upper Nile) began a period of intense rivalry with Buganda and involvement with foreign intruders of all kinds.

Bantu Migrations

MFECANE. About 1816, the Zulu chief, Chaka (1773–1828), began a war of conquest against other Nguni peoples living in coastal southeast Africa. The resulting disturbances (*mfecane*) caused large-scale migrations of Bantu peoples.

SWAZI. The Ndwandwe, led by Sobhuza (d. c. 1840), moved north and established the Swazi kingdom, named for Sobhuza's successor, Mswati.

GAZA. Another Nguni migration, led by Soshangane, penetrated southern Mozambique and resulted in the Gaza state, founded c. 1830.

NGONI KINGDOMS. The Jere, under Chief Zwangendaba, passed through Mozambique, and destroyed the kingdom of the Mwane Mtapa, c. 1833. Picking up recruits on the way and now known as the Ngoni, Zwangendaba's following crossed the Zambezi River, 19 Mar., 1835, and moved north of Lake Malawi to the vicinity of Mapupo. After Zwangendaba's death, c. 1848, the Ngoni split up and established 5 separate kingdoms located in various parts of East and Central Africa between Lake Victoria and the Zambezi.

KOLOLO. A group of Sotho, driven out by invasions from Nguniland, migrated north under Chief Sebetwane into Barotseland. There they conquered the Lozi kingdom, but after Sebetwane's death, 1851, the state they formed lost coherence and, following a rebellion of the indigenous Lozi, 1860, and the death of Sebetwane's successor, 1864, a period of anarchy ensued. Order was restored by the great Lozi king, Lewanika.

NDEBELE. An Nguni group, led by Chief Mzilikazi, crossed the Drakensberg Mts.; devastated the central Transvaal, 1824–34; and were defeated by Boers at the Battle of Mosega, Jan. 1837. Determined to seek his fortune farther north, Mzilikazi established the Ndebele state in Matabeleland. At his death, 1868, he was succeeded by Lobengula. (*Cont. p. 335.*)

THE AGE OF WESTERN
NATIONALISM, 1789–1914

Nationalism, Liberalism, and Reaction in Europe, 1800–1871

FRANCE FROM NAPOLEON I TO NAPOLEON III

1800–1802

INTERNAL CONSOLIDATION. After dissolving the legislative councils in the coup of 9–10 Nov., 1799, Napoleon became First Consul at the head of a provisional government, which drew up a constitution, known as the Constitution of the Year VIII. It was promulgated on 25 Dec. and ratified in a national plebiscite in Feb. 1800. The new constitution provided for 3 consuls appointed for 10-year terms (Napoleon remained First Consul), 7 ministries, and a Council of State (all appointed by Napoleon). The legislative branch consisted of a Senate, Tribunate, and Legislative Body; the Senate was ornamental, the Tribunate discussed proposed legislation without voting, and the Legislative Body could only accept or reject proposed measures without debate. All departmental and local administration was run by the Ministry of Interior through prefects.

Napoleon permitted most *émigrés* to return, pacified the Vendée, stabilized the currency, and made a concordat with Pope Pius VII, 15 July, 1801. The concordat stipulated that the French government would pay clerical salaries and nominate bishops, who would then be consecrated by the pope. The pope recognized the sale of church lands, and Catholicism was declared the religion of most Frenchmen. By a plebiscite, 2 Aug., 1802, Napoleon was elected Consul for life.

COLLAPSE OF THE 2ND COALITION. After the French reverses of 1799, Napoleon invaded Italy and defeated the Austrians at Marengo, 14 June, 1800. Following a short armistice, Moreau defeated the Austrians at Hohenlinden, 3 Dec., forcing Austria to sign the Treaty of Lunéville, 9 Feb., 1801, by which she agreed that France should have a free hand in Italy west of Venetia; Austria also had to recognize the French "Sister Republics."

Abandoned by all her allies, Britain signed the Treaty of Amiens, 27 Mar., 1802, which gave tacit recognition to France's conquests in Europe and permitted Britain to retain Ceylon and Trinidad, though obliging her to yield Malta, Elba, Minorca, and the Cape Colony.

1803–5

THE EMPIRE. Napoleon proclaimed the French Empire and crowned himself emperor, 2 Dec., 1804. The legislative bodies became ornamental, while the real power of administration remained in the hands of the Council of State, the ministries, and the prefects. Napoleon promulgated a series of codes, which unified the legal structure of the country and abolished the patchwork of laws left over from the Old Regime. The codes consisted of the Civil Code, 1804, known as the Code Napoléon; the Commercial Code, 1807; the Penal Code, 1810; and codes for civil and criminal procedure. Under these codes all citizens received legal equality and property rights were guaranteed. The Napoleonic codes were widely imitated in parts of Europe and in the rest of the world.

WAR OF THE 3RD COALITION. France and Britain renewed the war in May 1803, because of a British refusal to evacuate Malta. By 1805, Napoleon had assembled a large army at Boulogne to invade Britain. Britain, however, succeeded in gaining Russia, 11 Apr., 1805, and Austria, 9 Aug., as allies, forcing Napoleon to send his invasion force to the east in late Aug. to meet this new coalition. However, Adm. Horatio Nelson ended Napoleon's invasion plans by destroying two-thirds of a combined French-Spanish fleet at Trafalgar, 21 Oct.

The French armies, however, surrounded and captured a large Austrian force at Ulm, 15–20 Oct.; occupied Vienna, 13 Nov.; and smashed an Austro-Russian army at Austerlitz in Moravia, 2 Dec. Francis I, the Austrian emperor, by the Treaty of Pressburg, 26 Dec., yielded Venetia, Istria, and Dalmatia to France, and Tirol and Vorarlberg to Bavaria, while receiving the archbishopric of Salzburg.

1806–9

DEFEAT OF PRUSSIA. Napoleon induced most of the newly enlarged German states to withdraw from the Holy Roman Empire and form the Confederation of the Rhine, 1806, under his protection, thus eliminating Prussian influence from western and southern Germany. Franco-Prussian relations deteriorated. The Prussian army advanced into Thuringia, 13 Sept. (War of the 4th Coalition). The French mobilized, routed the Prussians at Jena and Auerstadt, 19 Oct., and rapidly captured all important Prussian fortresses west of the Oder and Neisse rivers.

Napoleon arrived in Berlin, 27 Oct.,

and issued a proclamation, 21 Nov., excluding all British trade and all British subjects from the Continent, thus inaugurating the Continental System. Meanwhile, Frederick William III and the remainder of the Prussian army fled to East Prussia. A combined Russian-Prussian force stalemated the French at Eylau, 7–8 Feb., 1807, but new French levies arrived in the spring, enabling Napoleon to defeat the Russians at Friedland, 14 June.

TREATY OF TILSIT. 7–9 July, 1807. Prussia ceded all her west-Elbean possessions to France's German satellites and yielded the Polish territories of the 2nd and 3rd Partitions to the newly constituted Grand Duchy of Warsaw. Prussia joined the Continental System, and French garrisons remained in Prussia until Napoleon's defeat in 1813. Czar Alexander recognized all French conquests and satellites and joined the Continental System.

FRENCH INVASION OF SPAIN. Napoleon was determined to control Spain to round out the Continental System. He forced King Carlos IV and his son, Fernando, to abdicate, May, and sent an army into Spain, while proclaiming his brother, Joseph (1768–1844), king of Spain. French troops occupied Madrid, 20 July, 1808, but Spanish forces rallied and drove the French from the city. Napoleon led a new army of 200,000 into Spain, Nov., and retook Madrid, Dec. French troops managed to occupy most of Spain and Portugal, but guerrilla resistance developed and a British expeditionary force tied down a considerable part of the French army. When Napoleon diverted men from Spain to Germany in 1813, the Spanish and British were able to take the offensive, cleared Spain of French troops, and invaded southern France.

1809–10

AUSTRIAN WAR OF LIBERATION. Encouraged by French difficulties in Spain, Francis I of Austria embarked on a war of liberation to free Germany from French domination, Apr. 1809 (War of the 5th Coalition). The Austrians invaded

Bavaria, a French ally, but Napoleon mobilized French troops rapidly and defeated the Austrians in East Bavaria, 19–23 Apr., entering Vienna on 13 May. Nevertheless, the Austrian army arrived on the opposite side of the Danube and drove back the French at Aspern and Essling, 21–22 May. After receiving reinforcements, Napoleon crossed the Danube and defeated the Austrians at Wagram, 5–6 July, forcing Francis to sue for peace. By the Treaty of Schönbrunn, 14 Oct., Austria ceded territory to Bavaria, the Duchy of Warsaw, and the French-administered Illyrian provinces. Austria also made an alliance with France, sealed by the marriage of Marie Louise (1791–1847), daughter of Francis I, to Napoleon, 11 Mar., 1810. Napoleon had divorced his 1st wife, Joséphine de Beauharnais, the previous year.

1811–12

RUSSIAN CAMPAIGN. The Franco-Russian alliance of Tilsit, reaffirmed at a meeting in Erfurt, Sept.–Oct. 1808, disintegrated when Alexander withdrew from the Continental System, 31 Dec., 1810, and when Napoleon dispossessed the czar's uncle by annexing Oldenburg. Napoleon assembled a Grand Army of approximately 500,000 men and invaded Russia, 24 June, 1812. The Russian army avoided its enveloping maneuvers, but offered battle at Borodino, 75 mi. west of Moscow, where it was decisively defeated, 7 Sept. The French entered Moscow 1 week later, and the city was soon destroyed by fire. Napoleon spent 5 weeks in Moscow waiting for peace overtures which never came, then ordered a retreat, 19 Oct. Lack of supplies, harassment by Cossacks, and the winter cold nearly destroyed the Grand Army.

1813–14

WAR OF LIBERATION. Encouraged by the destruction of the Grand Army, Frederick William of Prussia made an alliance with Russia and declared war on France, Mar. 1813. Napoleon, however, raised an army of 200,000 in France and marched into Germany in mid-Apr. He drove the Prusso-Russian army out of Saxony by victories at Lützen (Gross-Görschen), 2 May, and Bautzen, 20–21 May. Heavy losses, however, induced him to agree to an armistice, 4 June, during which both sides wooed Austria. Metternich, the Austrian foreign minister, agreed to join the allies, 27 June, if Napoleon would not accept his conditions for peace: the frontiers of France to be fixed at the Rhine, the Alps, and the Pyrenees. Napoleon refused, and Britain assured all 3 allies of subsidies. The armistice expired, 10 Aug., and Austria immediately declared war (War of the 6th Coalition). For the first time, Napoleon faced all the four Great Powers at once. After 2 months of indecisive campaigning, the allies succeeded in concentrating their numerically superior forces around the French at Leipzig, where they decisively defeated Napoleon in the *Völkerschlacht* (Battle of the Nations), 14–19 Oct. The remnants of Napoleon's army retreated across the Rhine 2 weeks later.

ALLIED INVASION OF FRANCE. The allies began an invasion of France in Dec. 1813. Napoleon's opposing strategy was masterly, but the allies, possessing numerical superiority, were able to occupy Paris, 31 Mar., 1814.

BOURBON RESTORATION. With allied troops on French soil, the French armies near defeat, and the French people anxious for peace, the Imperial Senate, 2 Apr., proclaimed the fall of Napoleon. Napoleon abdicated unconditionally, 6 Apr., and the same day the Imperial Senate called Louis XVIII (1755–1824), younger brother of Louis XVI, to govern France. The allies and the French fixed the terms of Napoleon's exile to Elba in the Treaty of Fontainebleau, 11 Apr., and on 23 Apr. signed an armistice.

On 24 Apr., King Louis XVIII entered France. Proceeding to Paris, he set forth in the Declaration of Saint-Ouen, 2 May, the bases of a constitution.

1ST TREATY OF PARIS. 30 May. Intent upon making France a force for international stability, the allies negotiated a moderate settlement that imposed no indemnity, gave France roughly the boundaries of 1792, and restored some former colonies.

CHARTER OF 1814. 4 June. Granted by Louis XVIII, the charter represented a compromise between divine-right monarchy and the Revolution. It promised freedom of religion and the press, guaranteed legal equality, secured the land settlement of the Revolution, and maintained in substance the Napoleonic Code Civil. Rejecting the principle of popular sovereignty, the charter established a system of shared powers subordinating the bicameral legislature (Chamber of Deputies, Chamber of Peers) to the crown.

1815

100 DAYS. Napoleon escaped from Elba, 27 Feb., landed in France, 1 Mar., and rapidly pushed northward. With the defection of Marshal Ney and his army, 13 Mar., any effective opposition dissolved.

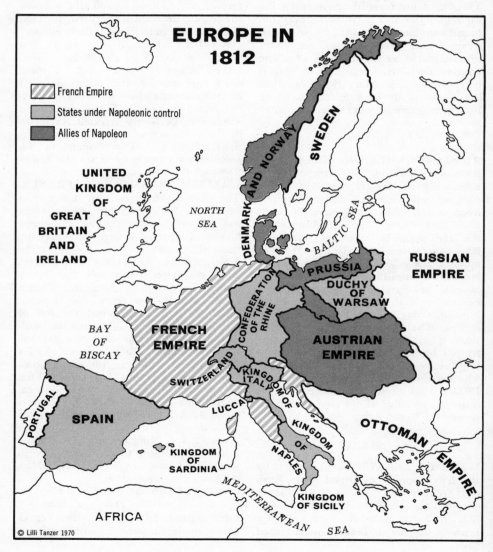

EUROPE IN 1812

French Empire
States under Napoleonic control
Allies of Napoleon

© Lilli Tanzer 1970

As Louis fled to Ghent, 20 Mar., Napoleon entered Paris, issued the *Acte Additionnel,* a constitution modeled on the charter, then marched into Belgium to fight the allies. Defeated at the Battle of Waterloo, 18 June, Napoleon abdicated, 22 June. Louis XVIII re-entered Paris, 8 July, and appointed, 9 July, Talleyrand and Joseph Fouché (1759–1820) heads of the newly unified cabinet, thus initiating the Second Restoration.

TALLEYRAND-FOUCHÉ MINISTRY. The 100 Days left France isolated diplomatically and deeply divided internally. The White Terror, a violent royalist repression of Bonapartists and former revolutionaries, erupted in the south. The election, 14–22 Aug., of an ultraroyalist-dominated Chamber of Deputies, dubbed the *Chambre introuvable,* climaxed the royalist reaction. The cabinet resigned, 21 Sept., before the Chamber met.

RICHELIEU MINISTRY. The duc de Richelieu (1766–1822) followed, 24 Sept., Talleyrand and Fouché, heading a moderate cabinet. The reactionary *Chambre introuvable,* intent on repression, suspended individual liberties, passed stiff sedition legislation, and established extraordinary courts.

2ND TREATY OF PARIS. 20 Nov. The allies, determined to punish France, imposed a harsh peace: the loss of some border territory, 3 years of occupation, payment of 700 m. francs indemnity.

1816

DISSOLUTION OF THE CHAMBRE INTROUVABLE. 5 Sept. The moderate cabinet battled the increasingly ungovernable ultraroyalist parliamentary majority until Louis, prodded by the allies, dissolved the Chamber, 5 Sept. New elections, Oct., returned a more manageable moderate royalist majority.

1817

ELECTORAL SYSTEM ESTABLISHED. 5 Feb. Tax qualifications reduced the electorate to some 90,000 out of a population of 26 m., giving wealthy landowners and the urban middle class political supremacy. Voters met annually to elect one-fifth of the deputies.

The ultraroyalists on the extreme right opposed compromise with the Revolution and favored a strong monarchy closely allied with the Catholic Church. At the center, the constitutional or moderate royalists supported the charter compromise. The doctrinaires, a clique of left-tending constitutionals, provided the philosophical justification of the charter system. The independents or liberals, anticlerical champions of limited popular sovereignty and individual liberties, constituted the extreme left. These political groupings lasted until 1830.

1818

END OF FOREIGN OCCUPATION. Through foreign and domestic loans, the government collected sufficient funds to pay the indemnity. At the Congress of Aix-la-Chapelle, the allies agreed, 9 Oct., to withdraw all troops and invited France to rejoin the Concert of Europe.

RESIGNATION OF RICHELIEU. 26 Dec. The gains of the left in the elections of Nov. 1818 divided the cabinet, some seeking alliance with the ultraroyalists, others with the left center. Unable to impose a solution, Richelieu resigned, 26 Dec.

1819

DESSOLLES-DECAZES MINISTRY. 20 Dec. With the government of Gen. Jean Dessolles (1767–1828) (Council President, Foreign Affairs) and the Duc Decazes (1780–1860) (Interior, Police), power shifted from the right center to the left center. Louis packed, 4 Mar., the ultraroyalist Chamber of Peers with moderate appointments and on 4 May the government lifted censorship. But liberal gains in the legislative elections prompted Decazes (Council President since Nov.) to renounce efforts to reconcile the left.

1820

2ND RICHELIEU MINISTRY. 21 Feb. The murder of Louis XVIII's nephew, the duc de Berry (1778–1820), 13 Feb., by a fanatic, Louvel (1783–1820), provoked an ultraroyalist reaction that forced the king to abandon his favorite, Decazes, and recall Richelieu, 21 Feb.

RESURGENCE OF THE ULTRA-ROYALISTS. In the heat of reaction, the moderates abandoned the center, reducing the Chamber to 2 warring factions. The right prevailed, suspending individual liberties, Mar.; imposing press censorship, 31 Mar.; and passing a reactionary electoral law, 19 June, the Law of the Double Vote, which gave the richest electors the right to vote twice. The legislative elections, 4 and 13 Nov., crushed the left, consummating ultraroyalist control.

VILLÈLE MINISTRY. Unable to maintain a moderate royalist right-center position against the ultraroyalists, Richelieu resigned, 12 Dec., 1820, to be replaced, 15 Dec., by the comte de Villèle (1773–1854), parliamentary leader of the ultras.

1822

THE LEFT SILENCED. After its electoral defeat in 1820, the left regrouped in secret societies, notably the Carbonari, and abandoned legality for insurrection, 1821, 1822. But repeatedly abortive coups, repressive legislation, and infighting gradually reduced the left to silence.

1823

MILITARY INTERVENTION IN SPAIN. At the Congress of Verona, Oct. 1822, the allies authorized France to suppress revolt in Spain. French forces invaded, Apr., quickly defeated the liberals, 31 July (Battle of Trocadero), and restored the legitimate monarch, Fernando VII. Intervention secured French status as a guarantor of the Vienna settlement.

1824

ULTRAROYALIST CABINET, CHAMBER, AND KING. Profiting from the success of the Spanish campaign, the government dissolved the Chamber, 24 Dec., 1823. New elections, 26 Feb., 6 Mar., produced an overwhelmingly rightist Chamber that promptly secured a 7-year mandate by substituting integral renewal every 7 years for partial annual renewal (Law of the Septennat, 8 June).

On 16 Sept. Louis XVIII died. The ultraroyalist comte d'Artois (1757–1836) succeeded his brother as Charles X.

1825

REGIME OF REACTION. The Chambers voted, 27 Mar., to indemnify the *émigrés*, thus finalizing the Revolutionary land settlement. As a protestation of faith, they voted the death penalty for theft of holy vessels (Law of Sacrilege, 20 Apr.), a measure that only stimulated mounting popular anticlericalism.

1826–27

CONSOLIDATION OF OPPOSITION. Freed from censorship, Sept. 1824, a virulent liberal press aroused public opinion. The moderate peers defeated government legislation (laws of succession, press censorship) judged dangerously reactionary. The government's dissolution of the National Guard after a display of antigovernment sentiment, 30 Apr., 1827, and the reimposition of censorship, 24 June, compounded public hostility. Hoping to solidify his majorities, Villèle announced, 6 Nov., the addition of 76 peers and dissolved the Chamber. But new elections, 17, 24 Nov., registered significant gains for the liberals and nascent counteropposition, forcing Villèle to withdraw, 3 Jan., 1828.

1828

MARTIGNAC MINISTRY. 4 Jan. The next cabinet, unofficially headed by the vicomte de Martignac (1778–1832), attempted unsuccessfully through concessions to the liberals (abolition of censorship, 18 July) to reforge a moderate royalist center majority.

INTERVENTION IN GREECE. To counterbalance the Russian invasion of the Balkans (spring), the French government abandoned Villèle's noninterventionism and invaded, Sept., the Greek peninsula, forcing the Egyptians and Turks to evacuate, Dec. Military victory and diplomatic success inaugurated a period of French activism in foreign affairs.

1829

POLIGNAC MINISTRY. 9 Aug. Unsupported by the king and repeatedly defeated by the combined extreme-right and liberal oppositions, the Martignac government was dissolved, 8 Aug. Determined to defy the left and to rally the divided right, Charles X formed, 9 Aug., an ultraroyalist-dominated government headed by the unpopular prince de Polignac (1780–1847).

1830

ADDRESS OF THE 221. 16 Mar. After months of inactivity, the government convoked the Chamber of Deputies, 2 Mar. The address to the throne (Address of the 221), claiming the nation's right to influence the choice of ministers, requested dismissal of the Polignac cabinet. Charles X riposted, dissolving the Chamber, 18 May.

CAPTURE OF ALGIERS. 5 July. Hoping for public support, Polignac, 25 May, dispatched an expedition to capture Algiers, 5 July. He did not save his regime, but secured a French foothold in North Africa.

REVOLUTION OF 1830. The elections (23 June; 3, 13, 19 July) returned a clearly antigovernment majority. Refusing to yield, Charles X, invoking emergency powers, published the July Ordinances, which imposed press censorship, dissolved the newly elected Chamber, and ordered new elections under a more restricted suffrage. Opposition exploded into popular insurrection, 28 July, as rioters, led by republicans, gained control of Paris, 29 July (the July Days).

A group of liberal deputies, overriding the republicans, extended the lieutenant generalship to the duc d'Orléans (1773–

1850) on 31 July, and on 2 Aug. Charles X abdicated. The July Revolution, defeating republic and legitimate monarchy alike, secured a quasi-legitimate parliamentary monarchy controlled by the propertied middle class, the former liberal opposition.

LOUIS PHILIPPE, KING OF THE FRENCH. The deputies called, 7 Aug., the duc d'Orléans, head of the younger, Orleanist branch of the Bourbon line, to the throne as Louis Philippe I (ruled 1830–48). He swore, 9 Aug., to uphold the Charter of 1814, revised, 7 Aug., to increase parliamentary prerogatives and to prevent royal abuse of power.

1831–35

RESISTANCE VS. MOVEMENT. Although Orleanists shared bourgeois, antilegitimist, and anticlerical attitudes, they disagreed on the significance of the July Revolution. The forces of "resistance," viewing the Revolution as a dynastic change only, defended the domestic and international *status quo.* For the partisans of "movement," the Revolution inaugurated a regime dedicated to political democratization and hostile to the international settlement of 1815. These forces dominated parliamentary politics until 1848.

TRIUMPH OF RESISTANCE. Neither the appointment of a liberal banker, Jacques Laffitte (1767–1844) as council president, 2 Nov., 1830, nor the trial and condemnation of Charles X's ministers, 15–21 Dec., ended popular unrest. The forces of movement failed to translate reforming aspirations into a legislative program, and the initiative passed to the forces of order under Casimir Périer (1777–1832) on 13 Mar. The legislative elections, 5 July, gave the conservatives a power monopoly they held until 1848.

BOURGEOIS MONARCHY DEFINED. Under Périer, 13 Mar., 1831–16 May, 1832, minimum reforms guaranteed power to the propertied middle classes. In 1831 the deputies sanctioned election of town councils, 21 Mar.; authorized a bourgeois-dominated national guard to protect the regime, 22 Mar.; gave more propertied bourgeois the vote, 19 Apr.; and abolished the hereditary peerage, 29 Dec.

The subsequent ministry, under Marshal Nicolas Soult (1769–1851), organized colonial government, 24 Apr., 1833, and reformed education, requiring public authorities to maintain schools and establishing standards for teachers, 28 June.

INSURRECTION AND REPRESSION. The government checked serious industrial disturbances in Lyons, Nov. 1831, and political insurrection in Paris, June 1832. A royalist revolt in the South, May–June 1832, collapsed, weakening the legitimist cause.

With conservatives in power, the republicans intensified pressure for social and political reform (1832–34). Striking at the political clubs, centers of republican activity, the government restricted associations, 10 Apr., 1834. The army bloodily repressed ensuing insurrections in Lyons and Paris, 12 Apr.

A prolonged cabinet crisis, Apr. 1834–Mar. 1835, weakened the government and enabled Louis Philippe to gain domination. But the duc de Broglie (1785–1870) restored strong conservative leadership, 12 Mar., 1835.

After an attempt on Louis Philippe's life, 28 July, 1835, the government passed the "September Laws," repressive measures including juridical short cuts and press restrictions, which silenced the republican left.

The monarchy successfully defended, the conservative majority disintegrated. De Broglie withdrew, 5 Feb., 1836, and Adolphe Thiers (1797–1877) formed a government, 22 Feb., without a fixed majority or a specific program.

FOREIGN POLICY. With the exception of military action to secure Belgian independence, Aug. 1831, the French government followed pacific, noninterventionist policies. In this period France generally supported Britain against the legitimate monarchs.

1836

REGIME OF PERSONAL POWER. Breaking with Thiers, Louis Philippe called on the more pliable duc de Molé (1781–1855). The weak Molé cabinet, 6 Sept., and a fluid Chamber majority permitted Louis Philippe to govern. In an atmosphere of political apathy, an abortive coup by Louis Napoleon (1803–73), nephew of Napoleon I, at Strasbourg, 30 Oct., stirred little response.

1837–40

AGITATION FOR REFORM. Relative calm, domestically and internationally, fostered prosperity in France. Molé dissolved the deputies, 3 Oct., 1837, to strengthen the government majority. But an antiministerial coalition was formed to challenge Louis Philippe's regime of personal power. Popular demands for political democratization and electoral reform increased, 1838–40; and, as France became industrialized, Utopian Socialism spurred proletarian class consciousness.

Parliamentary elections, following dissolution, 2 Feb., 1839, forced Molé out of office, 8 Mar. Popular unrest in Paris (Société des Saisons revolt, 12 May) forced a solution to a prolonged cabinet crisis, 8 Mar.–12 May.

Thiers replaced Soult, 1 Mar., 1840. He granted minor concessions to the left, but rejected electoral reform. Louis Napoleon's second attempted coup, at Boulogne, 5–6 Aug., 1840, failed.

MIDDLE EAST CRISIS. The Treaty of London, 15 July, 1840, directed against France and its Egyptian ally, broke the Anglo-French entente and outraged public opinion. Thiers threatened war, but Louis Philippe, intent on peace, secured acceptance of the treaty, 8 Oct. Thiers' clash with the king precipitated his withdrawal, 29 Oct. The incoming cabinet headed by Soult but dominated by François Guizot (1787–1874) governed with minor changes until 1848.

1840–47

GOVERNMENT OF GUIZOT. With Guizot's co-operation, Louis Philippe again achieved a regime of personal power dedicated to the maintenance of the *status quo.* The left center under Thiers and the left under Odilon Barrot

(1791–1873) joined to attack government corruption and demand parliamentary and electoral reform, 1840–42. Elections, 9 July, 1842, following dissolution returned a favorable conservative majority which Guizot maintained by intrigue and favors. Guizot pledged, 1842, state subsidies for railroad construction, stimulating industrial expansion, 1842–46.

Divided since July 1842, Thiers and Barrot reunited to attack government immobility. Guizot dissolved the Chamber, 6 July, 1846, and, despite the solidarity of the left, the conservatives gained in the ensuing elections.

FOREIGN POLICY. To end France's diplomatic isolation, Guizot engineered an entente with England, 1841, confirmed by the exchange of royal state visits, 1843, 1844. Although shaken by the Pritchard affair (ejection of a British missionary from Tahiti), 1843, and by French military activity in Morocco, 1844, the alliance held. Anglo-French rivalry in Spain (the Affair of the Spanish Marriages) broke the alliance, 1846.

DESTABILIZING CONDITIONS. As bad harvests and an industrial depression, 1845–47, exacerbated popular discontent, the dynastic left organized political banquets to mobilize public opinion for reform.

1848

THE FEBRUARY REVOLUTION. Cancellation of a political banquet touched off mass demonstrations in Paris, 22 Feb. As barricades went up, Louis Philippe dismissed Guizot, 23 Feb.; summoned Thiers, 24 Feb.; and then, failing to rally even the bourgeois National Guard, abdicated, 24 Feb.

Moderate and social republicans joined forces in a provisional government, 24 Feb., which proclaimed the Republic, 25 Feb.; created National Workshops to reduce unemployment, 26 Feb.; adopted universal manhood suffrage, 2 Mar.; and opened the National Guard to workers. The moderate republicans, opponents of fundamental social change, won control of the newly elected Constituent Assembly, 23 Apr. An Executive Commission

replaced the provisional government and managed to restore order.

THE JUNE DAYS. The National Workshops, conceived but not directed by Louis Blanc (1811–82), deteriorated into mere charity. But when the government, alarmed by renewed social unrest, 15 May, abolished them, 21 June, workers took to the barricades, 23–26 June. General Louis Eugène Cavaignac (1802–57) smashed the uprising, turning the working class against the bourgeoisie.

GOVERNMENT OF CAVAIGNAC. A grateful assembly made Cavaignac president of the Commission. Blaming the socialists for the June Days, the Assembly banned political meetings and tightened press laws.

PRESIDENT BONAPARTE. The Constituent Assembly promulgated, 20 Nov., a constitution that divided power between a unicameral legislature and a president elected by universal suffrage. Backed by the forces of order, Louis Napoleon Bonaparte became president, 10 Dec. Louis Napoleon sought to reconcile popular government and order. He embraced the Republic, 20 Dec., but appointed an Orleanist cabinet headed by Odilon Barrot.

1849–50

INTERVENTION IN ITALY. Courting Catholic support, Louis Napoleon sent an expeditionary force to destroy the Roman Republic and restore the pope to Rome, 25 Apr. This force remained in Rome until 1870.

REPUBLICAN DECLINE. Although the forces of order (mainly monarchists) won control of the new Legislative Assembly, 13 May, 1849, the radical left, the "Mountain," also gained. An abortive insurrection in Paris, 13 June, 1849, caused 33 leftist members to be expelled from the Assembly, 8 Feb., 1850, but the Mountain regained all but 10 seats, 10 May. Alarmed, the majority imposed new curbs on political freedom: a 3-year residence requirement for voters, 31 May, which affected mainly the workers, and a restrictive press law. As a further guarantee of order, the Assembly allowed church representation on school governing councils and permitted the establishment of private schools (Loi Falloux, 15 Mar., 1850).

1851

COUP D'ÉTAT OF LOUIS NAPOLEON. Unsuccessful in his attempt to extend his term of office legally, 15 July, Louis Napoleon planned a coup d'état. On 2 Dec., the anniversary of the Battle of Austerlitz, he imposed military control on Paris, dissolved the Assembly, restored universal suffrage, and called for a plebiscite on a new constitution.

Resistance was short-lived in Paris, 3–4 Dec. In the provinces, the government countered resistance with mass arrests (c. 27,000). Nevertheless, "yes" votes outnumbered "noes" in the plebiscite: 7½ m. to 600,000, 21 Dec.

1852–57

IMPERIAL CONSTITUTION. Louis's constitution, 15 Jan., 1852, divided limited legislative authority among an appointive Council of State and Senate and a popularly elected Legislative Body, but reserved virtually all power to the president, elected for 10 years. Government management assured "official" candidates' control of the Legislative Body. The people approved by plebiscite, 21 Nov., the transformation of republic to empire, and on 2 Dec. the president took the title Napoleon III.

ALLIANCE WITH BRITAIN. Seeking an alliance with the British, Napoleon III joined Britain (Entente of 24 May, 1853) in resisting Russian intervention in the Ottoman Empire. When hostilities broke out between the Russians and the Turks, 4 Oct., 1853, France and Britain declared war on Russia, 28 Mar., 1854, and concluded a formal alliance, 10 Apr.

CRIMEAN WAR. Popular opposition increased as French troops (80,000 strong) suffered heavy casualties (siege of Sevastopol, Sept. 1854–Sept. 1855). Following allied military success, the emperor presided over the peace conference. The war increased French prestige, but the Treaty of Paris, 30 Mar., 1856, brought France no concrete gains.

ECONOMIC   EXPANSION.   The political stability of the empire nurtured speculative financial ventures, which found backing in newly established joint-stock banks: the Crédit Foncier, Feb. 1852, for real estate, and the Crédit Mobilier, Nov. 1852, for commerce and industry.

For its part, the government encouraged corporate organization (limited-liability law, 1863), subsidized railroad and steamship companies, and accelerated public construction, especially in Paris. There the emperor, together with Baron Georges Haussmann (1809–91), prefect of the Seine, directed sweeping alterations. In addition, the government sponsored efforts to improve workers' conditions.

Although the Paris Exhibition of 1855 revealed French progress in industrialization, bad harvests, 1853–55; outbreaks of cholera, 1853, 1854, 1855; and the depression of 1857 postponed real prosperity. Political life stagnated as the government harassed newspapers, prevented political demonstrations, and intervened in elections.

1858–59

ORSINI ASSASSINATION ATTEMPT. An unsuccessful attempt to assassinate the emperor, 14 Jan., 1858, traced to an Italian patriot, Felice Orsini (1819–58), pushed Napoleon III toward intervention in Italy.

LIBERATION OF LOMBARDY. At a secret meeting with Cavour at Plombières, 20 July, 1858, Napoleon agreed to help Sardinia drive Austria from Lombardy. Cavour provoked Austria into aggression; France declared war, 3 May, 1859; and won Lombardy (Battle of Solferino, 24 June). Discouraged by heavy casualties and afraid that Prussia might invade France, the emperor signed an armistice at Villafranca, 11 July, later ratified as the Treaty of Zurich, 10 Nov. To compensate the French, Sardinia authorized, 24 Mar., 1860, plebiscites in Nice and Savoy; both approved annexation to France.

MOUNTING OPPOSITION. Already in trouble with conservatives over the Italian war, the emperor alienated Catholics by suggesting, 22 Dec., 1859, that the pope's temporal domain could be reduced without jeopardizing his spiritual position.

1860–70

COBDEN TREATY. An advocate of free trade, Napoleon concluded a tariff-lowering treaty with England, 23 Jan., 1860, which pleased liberals but antagonized French industrialists, threatened by British competition.

LIBERALIZATION MEASURES. To appease liberal opinion in the country at large, Napoleon conceded to the Legislative Body the rights to debate imperial addresses, 24 Nov., 1860, and pass on the budget, 31 Dec., 1861. The emperor also approved modification of the Combination Act, 1864, granting workers the right to strike.

INTERVENTION IN MEXICO. France with Britain and Spain intervened to force Mexico to honor its debts, 1861. Then, Napoleon, courting the favor of the church, launched a 2nd expedition, 1862, overthrew the Mexican Republic, June 1863, and installed Archduke Ferdinand Joseph Maximilian (1832–67) as emperor. However, the costs of occupation and diplomatic pressure from the U.S. forced Napoleon to withdraw support. Napoleon's prestige reached a low point when Maximilian was captured and executed, 19 June, 1867.

CONSTITUTION OF 1870. The failure of the Mexican venture and the Prussian defeat of Austria, July 1866, weakened the emperor's resistance to the demands of the moderate opposition, the Third Party, for further liberalization. He granted Parliament the right to interpellate the ministers, 19 Jan., 1867, and augmented the power of the Senate, 14 Mar., 1867. Liberalization of press and public-meeting laws, 1868, gave the opposition new forums.

In the elections of 1869, the opposition (Monarchists, Republicans, and the Third Party) won a potential majority. Succumbing to Third Party pressure, the emperor accorded additional powers to the Legislative Body, 6 Sept., 1869, and named Émile Ollivier (1825–1913), Third Party leader, to head a responsible ministry, 2 Jan., 1870.

A new constitution, 20 Apr., created a parliamentary empire. Appealing to the people by plebiscite, 8 May, Napoleon won overwhelming support for liberalization and the new constitution. (*Cont. p. 282.*)

SPAIN AND PORTUGAL

Spain

1800–1815

TREATY OF SAN ILDEFONSO. 1 Oct., 1800. Spain gave France Louisiana and the services of 6 warships on the condition that Napoleon enlarge the Duchy of Parma, ruled by Italian Bourbons. The condition was met in 1801 by the creation of the Kingdom of Etruria, and further agreements early the same year provided for Spain to bring pressure on Portugal to break its British alliance.

EFFECTS OF THE EUROPEAN WAR ON SPAIN. During the War of the Oranges, May–June 1801, France and Spain invaded Portugal and forced it to close its ports to the British. At the Truce of Amiens, Mar. 1802, Spain ceded Trinidad to Britain but regained Minorca. In Oct. 1803 Spain was forced to pay a monthly tribute to France; this was in response to Napoleon's demand for aid in his renewed war with Britain. The Spaniards were later forced to open their ports to French warships. In Dec. 1804 Spain declared war on Britain; considering Spain no longer neutral, the British had attacked Spanish treasure ships in Oct., prompting Spanish action. At the Battle of Trafalgar, 21 Oct., 1805, a French and Spanish fleet was virtually destroyed by a British force under Adm. Nelson.

TREATY OF FONTAINEBLEAU. 27 Oct., 1807. This treaty provided for the invasion of Portugal by France and

Spain; Portugal was to be divided into several smaller kingdoms.

"ESCORIAL AFFAIR." Oct.–Nov. 1807. The "Escorial Affair" was part of a struggle between the heir to the throne, Fernando (1784–1833), and the royal favorite, Manuel de Godoy (1767–1851). Fernando had been in communication with Napoleon, and an anonymous letter accused him of plotting against Godoy and the queen. The king ordered his son arrested for treason, but the charge was quickly dropped and Fernando's popularity with the people, who detested Godoy, increased.

FRENCH INVASION OF SPAIN. Oct. 1807–Mar. 1808. Supposedly part of the invasion force for Portugal, French troops in Spain totaled over 100,000 by Mar. 1808. In Feb. 1808 Joachim Murat (1767?–1815) was placed in command of them and in Mar. he entered Madrid. Napo-

leon then demanded the cession to him of Spain's northern provinces. Godoy advised the royal family to leave Madrid in order to escape the French, and the monarchs moved to Aranjuez in preparation for a longer move to the south of Spain.

ABDICATION OF CARLOS IV. 19 Mar., 1808. Believing that the move south was part of a plot by Godoy, and that the French were coming to put Fernando on the throne, the latter's supporters rioted, 17 Mar., in Aranjuez and forced the dismissal of Godoy. Rumors that Godoy would escape trial brought further riots, and Carlos was forced to abdicate in favor of his son.

THE BAYONNE ABDICATIONS. May 1808. Fernando, expecting Napoleon's support, was enticed to meet him at Bayonne. There he was forced to restore the throne to his father, who in

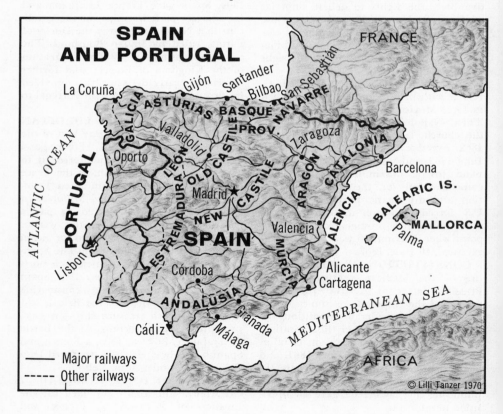

turn surrendered his rights to Napoleon. Joseph (1768–1844), Napoleon's brother and former king of Naples, was proclaimed the new king of Spain on 6 June, 1808. Fernando was held at Valençay in France.

UPRISING IN MADRID. 2 May, 1808. An anti-French uprising was caused by attempts by the French to remove Fernando's brother to Bayonne. It was put down easily and Murat took savage measures of reprisal, but *Los Dos de Mayo* (the 2nd of May) became the symbol of Spanish revolt against French dominion.

REVOLTS AGAINST THE FRENCH. As news of the Madrid uprising and the Bayonne abdications spread, revolts broke out in unoccupied Spain, May–June 1808, and provincial juntas were established which declared war on France and made alliances with Britain. Fernando was proclaimed king, and to the Spanish people he became known as *El Deseado* (the Desired One). In July 1808 the French were defeated at Bailén. A general French retreat resulted and Madrid was evacuated. On 25 Sept., 1808, a Central Junta was organized. Meeting at Aranjuez, it took control of the country in the name of Fernando, and on 14 Nov., 1808, declared war on France.

RESTORATION OF FRENCH CONTROL. Nov. 1808–Jan. 1809. Napoleon took command and, employing heavily reinforced armies, quickly reversed the trend of the war and reoccupied Madrid, Dec. 1808. In Jan. 1809 he defeated a British army under Sir John Moore (1761–1809) at La Coruña (Corunna) and forced it to evacuate Spain. The French then occupied the greater part of the country and the Spanish government retreated to the besieged port of Cadiz.

A fierce guerrilla war continued, however, and was a constant drain on French strength, 1809–11.

CONSTITUTION OF 1812. The Cortes of Cadiz, which had convened on 24 Sept., 1810, promulgated, 19 Mar., 1812, a constitution which provided for a liberal constitutional monarchy, with a unicameral annual assembly to which ministers of the government would be responsible.

WAR WITH FRANCE. Wellington won the Battle of Salamanca, 22 July, 1812. As a result, the entire French position in Spain was threatened and Madrid had to be temporarily evacuated. Later in the year the French managed to restore their position, but Wellington resumed the offensive in 1813. He defeated Joseph at Vittoria, 21 June, 1813, and in Oct. the allied armies invaded France.

RESTORATION OF FERNANDO VII. On 2 Feb., 1814, Fernando was informed that he would only be recognized as king if he accepted the constitution of 1812. On 7 Mar., 1814, Napoleon freed Fernando VII, and on 22 Mar. he entered Spain after 6 years' captivity in France. On 4 May Fernando repudiated the constitution. The Cortes was dissolved, its acts declared null and void, and the liberal members arrested. Absolute monarchy was thus re-established. In order to prevent any opposition, Fernando created a police state. There were sporadic revolts, but these were easily put down.

1816–43

REVOLUTION OF 1820. Units of an army that had been concentrated around Cadiz for transport to South America rebelled. Under the leadership of Colonel Rafael Riego (1785–1823), the troops demanded restoration of the constitution of 1812. Riego was defeated, but the revolt spread to other army units and to Madrid, and in Mar. Fernando agreed to the rebel demands. The constitution was re-established and a Cortes convened in July.

FRENCH INTERVENTION. Apr.– Sept. 1823. At the Congress of Verona, 20 Oct.–14 Dec., 1822, all the powers, except Britain, gave approval to action by France against the revolutionary government. An army commanded by the duc d'Angoulême (1775–1844) overthrew the Cortes and restored Fernando to full power. Ignoring French pleas for moderation, Fernando reinstituted the police state.

SUCCESSION CRISIS. A daughter, Isabella (1830–1904), was born to Fernando on 10 Oct., 1830. Fernando's brother, Don Carlos (1788–1855), disputed her right to the succession, claiming that the Salic Law applied in Spain and a female could not rule. Fernando supported his daughter's claim, and to cover just such a case had issued a pragmatic sanction the previous Mar., setting aside the Salic Law. Isabella was also supported by the moderates and liberals, who feared Don Carlos as an extreme absolutist. In Sept. 1832 the king was thought to be on his deathbed, and Don Carlos nearly succeeded in having the pragmatic sanction of 1830 set aside. Fernando recovered, however, but to safeguard Isabella's claim was forced to accept a more moderate ministry and to purge the army of its Carlist elements. On 29 Sept., 1833, Fernando VII died. By his will his wife, María Cristina de Borbón (1806–78), was appointed regent for their daughter.

CARLIST WARS. On the death of the king the supporters of Don Carlos rose in rebellion. The Carlist movement had its greatest strength in the Basque provinces, Navarre, Aragon, and Catalonia. It reached its high point in 1837, when Carlist armies threatened Madrid. From then on, however, it declined, and in Aug. 1839, by the Convention of Vergara, the chief Carlist army surrendered. Gen. Baldomero Espartero (1792–1879) was made Duke of Victory for his conduct of the final campaign.

ROYAL STATUTE OF 1834. In order to gain support, the government granted, Apr. 1834, a constitution patterned after the French Charter of 1814. The liberals split between the Moderados who accepted the constitution and the Progresistas who demanded the constitution of 1812.

QUADRUPLE ALLIANCE. Britain, France, Spain, and Portugal formed an alliance, Apr. 1834, to support the claims to the throne of Isabella in Spain and Maria da Glória in Portugal against the pretensions of their uncles, Don Carlos and Dom Miguel (1802–66), respectively.

SERGEANTS' MUTINY. Sergeants of the Royal Guard forced María Cristina, Aug. 1836, to restore the constitution of 1812, and to summon a constituent Cortes, Oct.

CONSTITUTION OF 1837. Although written by the Progresistas, the constitution of June 1837 was not as radical as the 1812 constitution. It provided for a bicameral legislature, but left much power in the hands of the monarch.

RULE OF ESPARTERO. A Moderado-controlled Cortes passed a municipal government bill which decreased democratic control of town and city government. Despite rioting against the bill, María Cristina signed it. Gen. Espartero, who was a Progresista, then forced her to resign as regent, 12 Oct., 1840, and assumed power himself. For the next 3 years Espartero ruled as virtual dictator of Spain, but in 1843 the army overthrew him. Isabella, then 13 years old, was declared to be of age and began to rule in her own right.

1844–70

RULE OF NARVÁEZ. From 1844 to 1851 Gen. Ramón Narváez (1800–1868), a Moderado, governed Spain with an iron hand, his power being interrupted only in 1846–47.

THE SPANISH MARRIAGES. In Oct. 1846 Queen Isabella II married Francisco de Asís, duke of Cadiz (1822–1902), and her sister, the Infanta Luisa (1832–97), married the duc de Montpensier (1824–90), a son of Louis Philippe of France. A diplomatic crisis was created because France and Britain had previously agreed that the Infanta would not marry a French prince until the queen had herself married and borne an heir to the throne.

RULE OF O'DONNELL. In June–July 1854, Gen. Leopoldo O'Donnell (1809–67) led a revolt. The ministry was forced to resign and O'Donnell, a Moderado, entered a coalition government with Gen. Espartero. A new, more liberal, constitution was adopted in 1856 but never promulgated, as the queen forced Espartero out of the government, July 1856. In Oct. 1856 O'Donnell was forced out, in turn, and Narváez instituted a more conservative and repressive government. But in June 1858 O'Donnell organized a government based on Moderado and Progresista support. This government enjoyed the longest continuous term of office of any during Isabella's reign. O'Donnell engaged in various foreign ventures, conducting a victorious war against Morocco, 1859–60; temporarily reannexing Santo Domingo, 1861–65; and joining France and Britain in their Mexican venture, 1861–62. Under the strain of domestic, economic, and religious issues, however, the coalition supporting him disintegrated and he was forced to resign, 27 Feb., 1863. Convinced that the queen would never give them political power, the Progresistas decided to boycott all political activities. O'Donnell attempted, 1865, to bring the Progresistas back into politics, but they refused. With this failure, followed by his death in 1867, the queen lost the one loyal supporter who might have created a government with popular appeal.

DICTATORSHIP OF NARVÁEZ. Narváez returned to power, 1866, and, supported by Luis González Bravo (1811–71), instituted a military dictatorship that attempted to save the faltering monarchy. Growing opposition to the queen was increased by her scandalous personal behavior. In Apr. 1868 Narváez died. Bravo, who replaced him, had no influence over the army.

REVOLUTION OF 1868. On 18 Sept., 1868, a revolution was organized by Adm. Juan Topete (1821–85) at Cadiz. The royal army was defeated by the rebels at Alcolea, 28 Sept., and Isabella fled Spain.

CONSTITUTION OF 1869. A constitution promulgated in June 1869 provided for a continued monarchy, but excluded Isabella. Gen. Francisco Serrano (1810–85) was made regent and Gen. Juan Prim (1814–70) prime minister. On 16 Nov., 1870, Amadeo (1845–90), son of King Victor Emmanuel of Italy, was elected king of Spain. The assassination of Gen. Prim, however, 27 Dec., 1870, foreshadowed the failure of Amadeo to establish himself on the throne. (*Cont. p. 297.*)

Portugal

1800–1815

WAR WITH FRANCE. Spain and France invaded Portugal, May–June 1801. They forced the Portuguese to close their ports to the British, grant commercial concessions to France, and pay an indemnity. By an ultimatum of 12 Aug., 1807, the 2 powers demanded that Portugal should declare war on Britain, arrest all Englishmen in Portugal and confiscate their goods, and close Portuguese ports to British ships. All demands were refused. By the Treaty of Fontainebleau, 27 Oct., 1807, France and Spain agreed on the invasion and partition of Portugal. The invasion began in Nov. and an army commanded by the French Gen. Andoche Junot (1771–1813) took Lisbon with little opposition. The Portuguese royal family established a Council of Regency and fled to Brazil. In June 1808, simultaneously with the revolts in Spain, there were uprisings in Portugal and a provisional junta was established in Oporto. Central Portugal threw off French rule.

CONVENTION OF SINTRA. 30 Aug., 1808. In early Aug. 1808, British troops under Sir Arthur Wellesley landed in Portugal and defeated the French. By the Convention of Sintra (Cintra), Junot's army was returned to France on British ships.

PENINSULAR WAR. In 1809 the French invaded Portugal a 2nd time and Marshal Nicolas Soult (1769–1851) captured Oporto. Wellesley again landed with British troops and forced the French to retreat to Spain. In July he defeated them at Talavera. French concentrations then forced him to withdraw to Portugal. In July 1810 a French force under Marshal André Masséna (1758–1817) invaded Portugal and forced Wellesley, now the Duke of Wellington, to retreat to prepared positions at Torres Vedras. From 9 Oct. to 14 Nov. the French attacked, but they failed to take the British positions and were forced to retreat because of lack of supplies. Wellington pursued and by May 1811 the French had been driven out of Portugal.

1816–34

ACCESSION OF JOÃO VI. In Mar. 1816, Maria I died, and the prince regent became king as João VI (ruled 1816–26). Despite the defeat of the French, the court remained in Brazil, where it was welcomed by the Brazilians, who gained many advantages from being at the center of the Portuguese Empire.

REVOLTS IN OPORTO AND LISBON. A revolt in Oporto, 24 Aug., 1820, led to a rebel demand for a Cortes and for the return of João VI. On 15 Sept. a revolt in Lisbon ousted the Council of Regency. On receiving the news of the uprisings, João sanctioned a Cortes and pardoned the rebels. The Cortes convened in Lisbon on 24 Jan., 1821.

RETURN OF THE COURT FROM BRAZIL. In July 1821, João VI returned to Portugal. He had to accept the work of the Cortes. He left his elder son, Pedro (1798–1834), as regent in Brazil, but his younger son, Miguel (1802–66), returned to Spain.

CONSTITUTION OF 1822. João VI accepted a new constitution in Sept. 1822. It provided for a unicameral Cortes which the crown could not dissolve. After the Spanish Cortes had been overthrown by French intervention, conservative uprisings broke out in Portugal, 1823, and João forced the Cortes to dissolve and held the constitution in abeyance. Miguel had played a major part in the uprisings and in Apr. 1824 attempted a coup, but was defeated and sent out of the country.

INDEPENDENCE OF BRAZIL. In Sept.–Oct. 1822, Brazil declared its independence, and Pedro was proclaimed its constitutional emperor. In 1825 João accepted the independence of Brazil, partly to safeguard Pedro's claim to the Portuguese throne.

João VI died, 10 Mar., 1826. Pedro IV was proclaimed king without dispute, his sister Maria Isabel (1797–1827) serving as regent.

CONSTITUTION OF 1826. On 29 Apr., 1826, Pedro IV granted a new constitution. Known as the "Charter," it provided for a Cortes with the upper house appointed by the king for life and the lower house indirectly elected. Pedro also declared that he would abdicate in favor of his daughter, Maria da Gloria (1819–53), if Miguel were betrothed to her and agreed to support the constitution.

THE MIGUELITE WARS. In Feb. 1826 Miguel returned to Portugal. Appointed lieut.-gen., he used his power to put his own supporters in office and call a new Cortes, which declared him the legitimate heir of João VI. In May an uprising in behalf of Pedro in Oporto was easily quelled, and on 11 July, 1828, Miguel was crowned king of Portugal. In Apr. 1831 Pedro returned to Europe from Brazil to safeguard his throne. He left Brazil to his son, Pedro II of Brazil, and declared his intention of securing the throne of Portugal for his daughter.

In July 1832 Pedro captured Oporto, but was besieged there by the Miguelites. The stalemate was broken in June–July 1833, when Pedro's fleet defeated Miguel's at Cape St. Vincent and he took Lisbon. Miguel still controlled the countryside, but his cause became hopeless when Spain withdrew its support from him and gave it to Pedro by the Quadruple Alliance, 22 Apr., 1834, between France, Britain, Spain, and Portugal. On 26 May, 1834, Miguel surrendered at Évora-Monte and accepted exile.

1835–70

SEPTEMBER REVOLUTION. Liberals, demanding a return to the constitution of 1822, won elections in Oporto and forced the dismissal of the ministry, Sept. 1836. Taking control of the government, they adopted the constitution of 1838, which democratized the governmental system to some degree, and made the upper house of the Cortes elective.

RULE OF DA COSTA CABRAL. Following elections in Jan. 1842, which revealed a conservative trend in Oporto, the minister of finance, Antônio Bernardo da Costa Cabral (1803–89), put himself at the head of a conservative movement which overthrew the government and the constitution of 1838. The Charter of 1826 was restored, 10 Feb. In 1846–47 the Septembrists attempted to regain power, but were defeated by the intervention of the Quadruple Alliance powers.

ADDITIONAL ACT. 5 July, 1852. By this act the charter was liberalized. The Additional Act and a new electoral law were part of the "regeneration" program of João Carlos, duke of Saldanha (1791–1876). Supporters of the amended charter became known as the Regenerators, while their more liberal political opponents were known as the Historicals.

RULE OF PEDRO V. 1853–61. Pedro V (1837–61) succeeded Maria II on the throne. Her eldest son, he was 16 at her death and his father, Ferdinand of Saxe-Coburg-Gotha (1816–85), acted as regent until 1855. During Pedro's reign, power alternated between the Regenerators (1851–56, 1859–60) and the Historicals (1856–59, 1860–65).

RULE OF LUIS I. When Pedro V died of typhoid fever, 11 Dec., 1861, Luis I (1838–89) came to the throne. From 1865–71 the country was ruled by a succession of coalition governments. (*Cont. p. 298.*)

THE ITALIAN STATES AND THE RISORGIMENTO

1800–1815

TREATY OF LUNÉVILLE. In early 1800, Austrian troops occupied all of Italy except Genoa. Napoleon, however, defeated the Austrians at Marengo, 14 June, 1800, and the Austrian forces abandoned Italy west of the Adige to the French armies. By the Treaty of Lunéville, 9 Feb., 1801, after protracted negotiations, Austria recognized the Ligurian and Cisalpine republics while retaining Venetia. Napoleon concurred in the restoration of Pope Pius VII (reigned 1800–23) to Rome and Ferdinand IV (1751–1825) to Naples. Lucca, Piedmont, and Parma remained under French military occupation. The Bourbon Prince of Parma, Louis, was granted Tuscany, renamed the Kingdom of Etruria.

EXTENSION OF NAPOLEON'S IN-FLUENCE. Napoleon continued to strengthen his hold on the Italian peninsula. By the Treaty of Florence, 28 Mar., 1801, he forced Ferdinand IV to allow French garrisons in the Kingdom of the Two Sicilies and to close his ports to British ships. On 26 Jan., 1802, delegates of the Cisalpine Republic chose Napoleon as president, and renamed their state the Italian Republic. In Sept. 1802 Napoleon annexed Piedmont to France.

In 1805 Napoleon changed the Italian Republic to a kingdom with himself as king. After his coronation on 26 May, he appointed his stepson, Eugène de Beauharnais (1781–1824), as viceroy. One month later Napoleon annexed the Ligurian Republic to the French Empire. By the Treaty of Pressburg, 26 Dec., 1805, which followed his victory over Austria, he gave Venetia to the Italian Kingdom. Because of Ferdinand's intrigues with Austria in 1805, Napoleon declared him deposed, and dispatched his brother Joseph (1768–1844) to Naples, where the latter was crowned king on 30 Mar., 1806. Ferdinand IV fled to Sicily, which he was able to retain with help from the British.

In 1808 Napoleon subdued the sole remaining independent power in Italy, the papacy. Even though the French emperor had cultivated good relations with Pius VII and had negotiated the important Concordat of 15 July, 1801, with him, he was angered by the pope's refusal to grant his brother Jérôme (1784–1860) a divorce, and wanted to perfect the Continental System by the acquisition of central Italy. In Feb. 1808, French troops occupied Rome and exiled Pius. The province of Latinum was incorporated into the French Empire. In Mar. 1808 Napoleon annexed Tuscany, which 1 year later was turned into a principality for his sister, Maria Anna Elisa Bonaparte (1777–1820). Parma was then annexed, while the Papal Marches on the Adriatic coast were incorporated into the Italian Kingdom. In 1808, when Joseph Bonaparte became king of Spain, he was succeeded in Naples by Joachim Murat (1767?–1815), husband of Napoleon's sister, Carolina. In 1810 the Italian Kingdom acquired South Tirol, after Napoleon's forces had subdued the Tirolean uprising of the preceding year.

NAPOLEON'S IMPACT ON ITALY. Napoleon governed the territory incorporated into the French Empire directly. No representative institutions were permitted, only Assemblies of Notables whose power was consultative. The emperor did apply to Italy some of the reforms associated with the French Revolution. The Civil and Criminal Codes were promulgated; all feudal dues, services, restrictions, and privileges were abolished; and some of the church lands and latifundia (large estates) were confiscated and sold. Napoleonic officials also engaged in road-building and other public-works projects in order to stimulate commerce. Generally speaking, the reforms were more lasting in the north of Italy than in the south.

In the long run, however, the French alienated even the most Francophile Italian liberals by treating Italy as a conquered province. To finance his wars Napoleon increased taxes and conscripted an estimated 120,000 Italians, half of whom were killed. Moreover, the French opened Italian markets to French goods, thus hurting local industries, while the Continental System ruined the considerable Italian sea trade.

Throughout the Napoleonic period the peasantry remained largely passive. Many urban liberals, who had originally supported the French Empire, turned against Napoleon when they realized that he was using Italy for his own and France's benefit. Especially after Napoleon's defeat in Russia in 1812, they formed anti-French secret societies such as the Adelfi, Guelfs, and *Carbonari* (charcoal burners).

ITALY AND SWITZERLAND

ITALY
— State boundaries, 1815
Kingdom of Italy, 1861
Kingdom of Italy, 1866
Kingdom of Italy, 1870
— Boundary, 1866

SWITZERLAND
— Boundaries of cantons
Sonderbund, 1845-48
--- Boundary of Switzerland, 1848

© Lilli Tanzer 1970

These societies demanded independence from France. They were not militarily dangerous, but they helped to undermine the French regime.

FALL OF THE FRENCH EMPIRE. After Austria joined the 6th Coalition against Napoleon, 12 Aug., 1813, an Austrian army of 70,000 immediately invaded the Italian Kingdom. Eugène de Beauharnais's small army slowly retreated as the Austrians advanced. Meanwhile, on 14 Nov. Joachim Murat defected to the allies, and agreed to supply 30,000 troops to be deployed against Eugène if his throne could be guaranteed. When Eugène received word of Napoleon's surrender, 6 Apr., 1814, he agreed to an armistice (the Convention of Schiarino-Rizzino, 16 Apr.). On 20 Apr. a revolt against the government of the Italian Kingdom broke out in Milan, and Austrian troops quickly occupied the city and the rest of Lombardy.

SETTLEMENT OF VIENNA. Before Austria joined the 6th Coalition, the allies had agreed to grant Austria Venetia (Treaty of Reichenbach, 27 June, 1813). In late Apr. 1814 the allies in Paris awarded Lombardy to Austria as well, thus disappointing the hopes of the Italian liberals for an independent constitutional northern Italian state. The settlement of Vienna, 1815, restored Victor Emmanuel I (1759–1824) to Piedmont-Sardinia and awarded him Genoa. Pius VII returned to the Papal States, and Ferdinand III (1769–1824) and Francis IV (1779–1846) (both Hapsburg archdukes) to Tuscany and Modena, respectively. Marie Louise (1791–1847), Napoleon's 2nd wife and a Hapsburg princess, received Parma and Piacenza, while María Luisa (1782–1824), a Spanish Bourbon princess, received Lucca.

THE DOWNFALL OF MURAT. When it became clear that Austria was becoming dominant in the peninsula, Murat, still king of Naples, plotted to expel the Austrians and become king of a united Italy himself. After Napoleon's return to France in Mar. 1815, he marched north and issued a manifesto proclaiming Italian independence and unity, 30 Mar. But Austrian troops defeated his army in May, and he was deposed, Oct. 1815, and eventually shot. Ferdinand IV, changing his title to Ferdinand I, returned to Naples.

THE RESTORATION GOVERNMENTS. Generally speaking, the restored rulers except Pius VII and Victor Emmanuel retained most of the administrative and judicial reforms of Napoleon. The pope did, however, restore the Jesuit order, 1814, which had been dissolved in 1773. All rulers imposed a political absolutism, and refused to allow any representative institutions in their dominions. All imposed strict censorship except Ferdinand III of Tuscany, which became a resort of Italian liberals.

1816–47

BEGINNING OF THE STRUGGLE AGAINST AUSTRIA. The *Risorgimento* (resurgence) was the name given to the 19th-cent. Italian movement toward national unification and constitutional government. The ideals of the movement were held by only a portion of the educated urban upper and middle classes. The peasantry remained bound to old traditions and customs and was hardly influenced by the new ideology. Since Austria under Metternich and Austria's satellite Italian states were all opposed to unification and constitutional government, the goals of the *Risorgimento* could be reached only by defeating Austria and overthrowing her conservative allies.

THE UPRISING OF 1817. The first attack on Hapsburg power in Italy came from the secret societies which had originally been organized to fight against Napoleon. In June 1817 the Guelfs rose at Macerata in the Papal States, but were easily suppressed.

CARBONARI UPRISING OF 1820. Inspired by the Spanish revolution of early 1820, the *Carbonari*, who had infiltrated the Neapolitan army, staged a successful coup in July against Ferdinand I. Under the leadership of General Guglielmo Pepe (1783–1855), they forced Ferdinand to swear loyalty to a democratic constitution. Ferdinand then left for the Congress of Laibach, 16 Jan.–12

May, 1821, where he pleaded for Austrian intervention against Pepe's liberal regime. Austrian troops marched south and annihilated Pepe's untrained militia at Rieti, 7 Mar., 1821, and for the 4th time Ferdinand returned to his throne.

PIEDMONT UPRISING OF 1821. Three days after the debacle at Rieti, a group of Piedmontese officers led by the *Carbonaro* General Santarosa (1783–1825) rebelled, demanding a constitution and war against Austria. Victor Emmanuel abdicated in favor of his younger brother, Charles Felix (1756–1831), who was in Tuscany at that time. Victor Emmanuel's son, Charles Albert (1798–1849), became regent, and agreed to Santarosa's demands. Charles Felix, however, annulled the regent's actions, and asked Austria to crush the revolt, which was done. Charles Felix took the throne and ruled for 10 more years.

CARBONARI REVOLT OF 1831. After the establishment of the ideologically liberal July Monarchy, the *Carbonari* attempted a revolt in the northern cities of the Papal States, 2 Feb., 1831, hoping that France would prevent Austria from intervening. By 26 Mar., however, the Hapsburg armies had crushed the rebels. This was the last of the *Carbonari* revolts.

ATTITUDE OF THE ITALIAN RULERS. Italian liberals were discouraged not only by the failure of the *Carbonari* but also by the refusal of the 4 major powers in Italy (Austria, Piedmont, Naples, and the papacy) to allow any constitutional reforms during the period 1815–46. Metternich (1809–48), the Piedmontese kings, including Charles Albert (1831–49), Naples under Ferdinand I (1788–1825, with interruptions), Francis I (1825–30), and Ferdinand II "Bomba" (1830–59) all opposed unification of the peninsula and all liberal reform. Ferdinand II from 1836 and Charles Albert, however, did pursue a foreign policy independent of Austria.

The popes, Pius VII (1800–1823), Leo XII (1823–1829), Pius VIII (1829–30), and Gregory XVI (1831–46), were likewise generally conservative. Gregory is remembered for his famous encyclical, *Mirari vos*, 1832, which condemned the liberal Catholic movement in France.

MAZZINI. Giuseppe Mazzini (1805–72), renowned as a political thinker, saw all Italian rulers as hopelessly reactionary, and advocated a unitary democratic and republican Italy. He sought to achieve this goal by direct popular revolution, and organized the conspiratorial Young Italy group, Oct. 1831, to begin a revolution. His attempt to overthrow Charles Albert in 1834, however, failed miserably, and a later uprising by Young Italy enthusiasts in Sicily in 1844 was likewise suppressed. Revolts in the Papal States in 1843 and 1845 and in Sicily in 1837 and 1841, unconnected with Young Italy, all similarly failed. They demonstrated that, although many were discontented with the established order, no revolution could succeed in Italy unless the Hapsburg armies were first expelled from the Peninsula.

NEO-GUELFISM. The failure of Young Italy and other popular revolts led some politically minded Italians to propose unification by a confederation of Italian states under the leadership of the papacy. Vincenzo Gioberti (1801–52) in *Il Primato* (On the Moral and Civil Primacy of the Italians) in 1843 and Cesare Balbo (1789–1853) in *Le Speranze d'Italia* (Italy's Hopes) in 1844 advocated this policy, which became known as "Neo-Guelfism." The authors of it did not explain how Austria could be persuaded or forced to accept their proposals. With the election of the liberal Giovanni Maria Mastai-Ferretti (1792–1878) to the papacy as Pius IX (reigned 1846–78) in June 1846, the Neo-Guelfs expected the fulfillment of their hopes.

THE REFORMS OF 1846–47. Pius IX immediately promulgated a series of reforms: a political amnesty, provincial and communal administrative reforms, relaxation of press restrictions, plans for railroad construction, the formation of a civil guard. These reforms reverberated throughout Italy. Florence obtained a free press, May 1847, as did Piedmont, Oct. Charles Albert also allowed communal elections and abolished the extraordinary courts.

1848–49

THE REVOLUTION. The agitation throughout Italy against the Old Regime and Austrian dominance culminated in violence at the beginning of 1848. On 12 Jan. Palermo rebelled. A Sicilian provisional government declared Sicily independent. On 29 Jan. Ferdinand II proclaimed a constitution in Naples to forestall a revolution. On 8 Feb. Charles Albert promised a constitution, and on 4 Mar. it was promulgated as *Il Statuto*, similar in content to that of the July Monarchy and providing for 2 chambers, 1 nominated by the king, the other elected by a restricted franchise. Tuscany proclaimed a constitution, 11 Feb., and the pope promised one 4 days later. When the Milanese heard of Metternich's flight from Vienna, they drove the Austrian garrison under Josef Wenzel Radetzky (1766–1858) out of the city in the 5 Days' Revolt, 18–22 Mar. Likewise, Daniele Manin (1804–57) in Venice began an insurrection on 17 Mar. which expelled the Austrian troops. Francis V (1819–75), who had succeeded his father Francis IV in 1846, and Prince Charles fled from Modena and Parma respectively.

WAR WITH AUSTRIA. Charles Albert immediately put himself at the head of the revolutionary movement by declaring war against Austria and by invading Lombardy. Radetzky retreated to the Quadrilateral, four fortresses in western Venetia, and awaited reinforcements from the Austrian government, which had also been rocked by revolution. The Piedmontese army, swelled by volunteers from all over Italy, advanced to the Quadrilateral and captured 1 fortress, Peschiera, in late May, but otherwise failed to dislodge Radetzky. Meanwhile, Pius IX had removed himself from the leadership of the liberation movement by declaring, 29 Apr., that he could not take sides in a war of Catholics against Catholics. This killed Neo-Guelfism, and papal units withdrew from the Piedmontese army. Ferdinand of Naples, moreover, soon discovered that the majority of his people, apart from the

Liberals and Sicilians, was loyal to him. He used a riot on 15 May as an excuse to disregard the constitution, and withdrew his army from northern Italy.

In a series of plebiscites held between late May and July, all the northern Italian states except Tuscany voted for union with Piedmont. Radetzky, however, received reinforcements, and attacked the Piedmontese army, which had been weakened by the removal of the papal and Neapolitan troops. The Piedmontese, after a 5-day battle around Custoza, 23–27 July, were forced to disengage. Charles Albert agreed to an armistice, 9 Aug., which restored the *status quo*.

THE RADICALS IN ROME AND TUSCANY. Owing to the increasing republican agitation stimulated by the presence of Mazzini, Pius IX left Rome on 24 Nov. for Gaeta, a town in the Kingdom of Naples near the border of the Papal States. By 9 Feb., 1849, an elected Chamber in Rome had declared the pope dispossessed and established a republic. In Tuscany, too, Grand Duke Leopold II (1797–1870), who had succeeded his father, Ferdinand II, in 1824, departed for Gaeta, 30 Jan., 1849, leaving power in the hands of the Radical, Francesco Guerrazzi (1804–73), who soon proclaimed a republic.

2ND WAR AGAINST AUSTRIA. Public opinion pushed Charles Albert into another war against the Hapsburgs, which began on 20 Mar., shortly after the expiration of the 9 Aug., 1848, armistice. Radetzky invaded Piedmont, and won decisively at Novara on 23 Mar., 1849. The same night Charles Albert abdicated in favor of his son, Victor Emmanuel (1820–78), and left the kingdom. He died 4 months later in Lisbon. Peace was signed, 6 Aug., in Milan, and the *status quo* was once again restored. Victor Emmanuel paid an indemnity, and was allowed to retain *Il Statuto*.

REPUBLICAN DEFEAT AT FLORENCE. The Sardinian-Piedmontese defeat at Novara also sealed the fate of the republicans of central Italy. On 12 Apr., 1849, a moderate faction seized power in Florence, and asked Leopold to return. On 1 May Leopold appointed the moderate, Luigi Serristori (1793–1857), to re-store order. Later in the same month, Austrian troops occupied Florence, and Leopold returned himself in July.

THE FALL OF ROME. Pius IX asked the Catholic powers to restore him to his throne. Louis Napoleon, president of the 2nd French Republic, dispatched a force under Gen. Nicolas Oudinot (1791–1863) to occupy Rome and, perhaps, reconcile the pope and the republicans. After much negotiation and bitter fighting, Oudinot took Rome, 2 July. Pius returned shortly thereafter, and re-established his old government.

By 15 May, Neapolitan forces had subdued all of Sicily, and the sole remaining republican outpost was Venice. This city surrendered on 22 Aug. Thus by Aug. 1849 the Hapsburgs had crushed the Italian independence movement.

1850–61

THE RISE OF CAVOUR. Camillo Benso di Cavour (1810–61), a scion of a Piedmontese noble family, had proved himself an excellent manager of his family's estates and a promoter of scientific farming, railroads, and steamboats. Elected to the Piedmontese parliament in 1849, he became minister of agriculture, commerce, and the marine in Oct. 1850 in the cabinet of the liberal Massimo d'Azeglio (1798–1866). He lowered tariffs by agreement with England and France, while also securing a large loan from London. In Nov. 1852 he replaced d'Azeglio as premier.

CAVOUR'S POLITICS. Cavour's goal was Italian unification under Victor Emmanuel. He realized that this could be achieved only through the expulsion of Austria from the Italian peninsula. Charles Albert had believed: *Italia farà da sé* ("Italy will do it herself"). Cavour, on the other hand, sought French and British support in the task of driving Austria from Italy. He hoped to establish sound and progressive government in Piedmont (thus providing a contrast with retrograde Austria), and during the first 2 years of his ministry concentrated on building railroads and improving trans-portation generally in order to establish a firm commercial base for a new war against Austria.

SICCARDI LAWS. In Mar. 1850 the Siccardi Laws (named after the then minister of justice) abolished ecclesiastical courts and mortmain, and prohibited the church from acquiring land by wills without state approval. In 1855, Cavour sponsored a law dissolving 55% of the monasteries in Piedmont, while making the state responsible for priests' salaries. These laws were designed to modernize Piedmont and remove traditionalist influences. Pius IX refused to recognize them. In 1854 he promulgated, without conciliar approval, the dogma of the Immaculate Conception of the Blessed Virgin. This action was interpreted by contemporaries as a step toward papal absolutism.

CRIMEAN EPISODE. In Jan. 1855 the French and British, engaged in the Crimean War against Russia, accepted Cavour's offer of 18,000 Piedmontese soldiers. By these means Cavour hoped to gain the good will of France and Britain, and perhaps receive Parma as compensation. At the Paris Peace Conference in the spring of 1856, Austria vetoed a Piedmontese acquisition of Parma, but Cavour nevertheless had the opportunity to state Piedmont's case, and received a sympathetic hearing from the French and British.

AGREEMENT OF PLOMBIÈRES. For 2 years Cavour negotiated with Louis Napoleon to secure French aid in a war against Austria. The French cabinet and French clerical opinion decidedly opposed any such undertaking. Nonetheless, Louis Napoleon wanted to continue the Napoleonic tradition by securing another victory for French arms. He also wanted to replace Austrian influence in Italy with French. Finally, Cavour and the emperor met secretly at Plombières in the Vosges Mountains in July 1858, and came to the following understanding: (1) Cavour would find a nonrevolutionary *casus belli* with Austria the next spring, and Austria would appear the aggressor; (2) France would supply 200,000 troops, and would receive Savoy and perhaps Nice; (3) Piedmont would receive Lombardy, Venetia, Parma, and Romagna, and Tuscany, Umbria, and the Papal Marches would be offered to the duchess of Parma, while the pope would retain Latinum and Ferdinand II Naples; (4) Napoleon's cousin would marry Victor Emmanuel's 15-year-old daughter, Clothilde. Piedmont and France signed a formal treaty of alliance on 19 Jan., 1859.

WAR OF 1859. All 3 powers began to mobilize early in 1859. Despite British pressure for a congress, tension mounted, and on 23 Apr. Austria sent an ultimatum to Piedmont, demanding her disarmament within 3 days. On 26 Apr. Cavour refused, and 3 days later Austrian troops crossed the Piedmont frontier. France dispatched troops to Piedmont on 3 May.

The combined Franco-Piedmont army defeated the Austrians at Magenta, 4 June, forcing the Hapsburgs out of Lombardy. The allies won a bloody victory at Solferino 20 days later, but the Austrian armies were still intact and still in possession of the fortresses of the Quadrilateral.

ARMISTICE OF VILLAFRANCA. On 24 June Prussia mobilized on the Rhine. Because of his exposed position Napoleon III could not risk continuing the war. Without Cavour's knowledge he negotiated an armistice agreement with the Austrian emperor, Francis Joseph, at Villafranca, 6–12 July. It was provided that Piedmont would annex Lombardy, but otherwise no change was envisaged.

PIEDMONTESE ANNEXATION OF CENTRAL ITALY. Cavour's reaction to Louis Napoleon's betrayal was to resign. Nevertheless, even though the terms of Villafranca were confirmed in the Treaty of Zurich, 10 Nov., 1859, the Old Regime in Italy was crumbling fast. By June all the princes of central Italy had fled. Bettino Ricasoli (1809–80), a supporter of Cavour, took over the provincial government of Tuscany, while Luigi Farini (1812–66), another Cavour agent, seized control of Modena, Romagna, and Parma, which he united into a province that was called Emilia.

On 16 Jan., 1860, Cavour returned to the premiership. He gained Louis Napoleon's approval for the annexation of Tuscany and Emilia, which annexation was ratified by a plebiscite, 13–15 Mar. In return, on 24 Mar., Cavour allowed Savoy and Nice, after a plebiscite, to be annexed by France.

GARIBALDI AND THE 1,000. Popular opinion insisted on the unification of the whole of Italy. Cavour, however, could not openly attack the Kingdom of Naples without provoking an Austrian reaction, nor could he attack Rome without clashing with the French troops there. He therefore acquiesced when Giuseppe Garibaldi (1807–82), the hero of the Roman Republic of 1848–49, set out on an unofficial expedition to Sicily. Garibaldi left with his 1,000 volunteers on 5 May. The British navy protected him, since the British believed that a united Italy would be less susceptible to French influence than a small kingdom of central and northern Italy under Victor Emmanuel. By the beginning of Aug. Garibaldi had secured Sicily. On 7 Sept. he was in Naples. Cavour now feared that Garibaldi might not turn his conquests over to Victor Emmanuel or that he would march on Rome, thus provoking a war with France. With Napoleon's consent Cavour sent an army through the Papal States to head off Garibaldi before he reached Rome. The remnants of the Neapolitan army delayed Garibaldi's advance, and Victor Emmanuel met him at Teano, 26 Oct. There he handed over all his conquests to his sovereign. Plebiscites in southern Italy, the Marches, and Umbria ratified the annexation of these areas by Victor Emmanuel's kingdom. Now all Italy save Latinum and Venetia had been unified.

1861–71

CONSOLIDATION OF THE ITALIAN KINGDOM. Elections for an all-Italian parliament took place during Jan. 1861. The suffrage was limited to 500,000 voters, who returned a majority favorable to Cavour. Subsequently the constitutional kingdom was proclaimed. Cavour died, 6 June.

The parliament of the new Italian

Kingdom decided on a prefectural administrative system with little local autonomy. By a series of measures the legal code, the railroads, the currency system, and weights and measures were unified.

ROME AND THE CONVENTION OF SEPT. 1864. Italian nationalists were unreconciled to the exclusion of Latinum and Venetia from the new Italian state, while Pope Pius IX refused to accept his territorial losses and bitterly opposed Italian unification. In order to retain Catholic support in France, Louis Napoleon could not abandon Rome to the Italian nationalists. The Italian government hoped to obtain Latinum and Venetia eventually, but did not wish to provoke either France or Austria. Consequently, when Garibaldi attempted another march on Rome, the Italian army captured his small force at Aspromonte, 29 Aug., 1862, in southern Italy. Public outcry against so "unpatriotic" a government forced Premier Rattazzi to resign.

At last, in Sept. 1864, the Italian government under Premier Marco Minghetti (1818–86) agreed with Louis Napoleon that it would guarantee Rome against attack if France would withdraw within 2 years.

CHURCH AND STATE. The intransigence of Pius IX was demonstrated by his famous encyclical of 1865, *Quanta Cura,* with its appended *Syllabus Errorum.* The pope condemned nationalism, parliamentary government, civil liberties, and other modern institutions. Moreover, the Vatican Council of 1870 declared the infallibility of the pope when speaking *ex cathedra.* The Italian government, on the other hand, continued its anticlerical policies by dissolving 2,400 monasteries in 1866 and by making civil marriage legal.

WAR OF 1866. As tension between Austria and Prussia increased, early 1866, the Italian government under Gen. Alfonso La Marmora (1804–78) agreed to declare war on Austria if hostilities should break out between Austria and Prussia. In return Italy would receive Venetia.

Prussia declared war on Austria, 16 June, and Italy followed 4 days later. On 24 June, Austrian forces defeated a larger Italian army at Custoza. After the Prussian triumph at Sadowa, 3 July, the Hapsburg forces in Venetia withdrew northward, and the Italians were able to occupy Venetia. On 20 July the Italian fleet suffered a disaster at Lissa. Prussia made peace 6 days later. In spite of her 2 serious defeats, Italy received Venetia in the final settlement.

ACQUISITION OF ROME. In Oct. 1867 an attempt by Garibaldi and a few volunteers to capture Rome was foiled when Napoleon III sent a French army there. Garibaldi was defeated by papal and French troops at the Battle of Mentana, 3 Nov. The Italian government, under the conservative Gen. Luigi Menabrea (1809–96), remained passive.

On 2 Aug., 1870, because of the war with Prussia, the French contingent was withdrawn from Rome, and Louis Napoleon and the Italian premier, Giovanni Lanza (1810?–1882), agreed to reinstate the Convention of September. But by 2 Sept., Louis Napoleon had surrendered, and 2 days later the 3rd French Republic was proclaimed; the Convention of September thus became a dead letter. Lanza then circulated a statement among the Powers promising to respect the spiritual independence of the pope. Italian troops entered the Holy City, 20 Sept., and no Catholic power protested.

FINAL SETTLEMENT. A plebiscite ratified the annexation of Rome and Latinum, but Pius IX still refused to recognize the loss of his temporal power. In May 1871 the Italian government granted him the tax-free ownership of certain buildings in Rome, a sum for expenses, and complete freedom in spiritual matters and in making ecclesiastical appointments. The papacy, however, remained unreconciled to the new conditions until the Concordat of 1929. (*Cont. p. 298.*)

THE BALKANS

1800–1815

CONCESSIONS BY TURKEY TO RUSSIA. With Turkey and Russia allied against France in the Mediterranean, the czar obtained an agreement, 23 Oct., 1802, from the Ottoman sultan that the Greek hospodars (princes) of the principalities would be appointed for 7-year terms and would not be removed without Russian approval.

REVOLT IN SERBIA. Feb. 1804. In 1801 the moderate governor of the Pashalik of Belgrade (northern Serbia) was killed by Janissaries, who then began a reign of terror against the native population. Led by George Petrovich (1766?–1817, known as Kara George), the Serbs revolted and quickly confined the Turks to control of a few fortresses. Negotiations with the sultan broke down on the question of guarantees and because of the insistence of the Serbians on retaining their arms. An appeal for Russian aid failed, but in 1805–6 the Serbs were able to repel Turkish invasions and establish virtual independence.

RUSSO-TURKISH WAR. 1806–12. The French, who were now allied with the Turks, persuaded the sultan to dismiss the hospodars of the principalities without Russian approval. The czar answered by occupying the principalities and in Dec. 1806 Turkey declared war. The sultan offered conciliatory terms to the Serbs, but they preferred an alliance with Russia, and by agreement, 10 July, 1807, a Russian protectorate over Serbia was established. The war was not pursued with great vigor by either side for many years, but in 1811 the Russians gained victories on the Danube and peace was made by the Treaty of Bucharest, 28 May, 1812. The Russians were preparing for a French invasion, and did not make great demands on Turkey, annexing only Bessarabia. The treaty also provided for an amnesty and autonomy in Serbia, with the Turks regarrisoning the fortresses, but the provisions were vague and the Russians had all but abandoned the Serbs. There were many disputes over the implementation of the treaty of Bucharest, and in 1813 the Turks again invaded Serbia, this time successfully. In Oct. Kara George fled the country and Turkish rule was re-established, accompanied by massacres and great destruction.

2ND SERBIAN REVOLT. 1815. A new leader emerged in Milosh Obrenovich (1780–1860, ruled 1817–39, 1858–60), who raised the standard of revolt on Palm Sunday, 1815. He won 4 quick victories over the Turks, and the sultan, fearing Russian intervention now that the Napoleonic wars were over, agreed to a settlement. By a decree of Dec. 1815 Milosh was recognized as the leader of Serbia and the Serbs were allowed to retain their arms and hold a national assembly. In Nov. 1817 the Serbs made Milosh's status as chief hereditary, and the sultan granted Serbia limited autonomy.

UNITED STATES OF THE IONIAN ISLANDS. By agreement of the Great Powers, 5 Nov., 1815, the Ionian Islands, which had been Venetian during the 18th cent., were made an independent state under a British protectorate.

1816–30

REVOLT IN THE PRINCIPALITIES. Mar.–June 1821. The secret *Philike Hetairia* (Society of Friends) had been organized in 1814 to promote a Greek revolt, and in 1820 Alexander Ypsilanti (1792–1828), a Greek who had become a general in the Russian army, became its head. On 6 Mar., 1821, he led a revolt in Moldavia, apparently having decided to begin operations there in order to be near Russian aid. His action, however, was repudiated by the Russian czar, and he aroused little support from the people of the principalities, who considered themselves oppressed by the Greek hospodars who ruled them. Ypsilanti's forces were defeated by the Turks in Wallachia and by June the revolt was over. The major result was a decision by the sultan, June 1822, to appoint native Rumanians as hospodars.

REVOLT IN GREECE. Mar. 1821. A war between the sultan and Ali Pasha ('Alī Pasha), his vassal in southern Albania and northern Greece, which began in 1820, offered the Greeks an opportunity for revolt. Sporadic uprisings in the Morea (Peloponnesus), in Mar. 1821, quickly spread and became a general revolution. While the Turks were able to suppress the revolt in Macedonia and Thessaly, the Greeks, by 1822, were able to win the Morea, many of the islands, and part of continental Greece south of Thessaly. In Jan. 1822 a constitution was promulgated and a national Greek government created. It was, however, plagued by factionalism and, on occasion, civil war, and was never able fully to assert its authority.

EGYPTIAN INVASION OF THE MOREA. Feb. 1825. Despite the disunity among the Greeks, the Turks were unable to recover the Morea and only partially recovered continental Greece. The sultan was obliged to make an agreement with Mohammed Ali (Muḥammad 'Alī), the pasha of Egypt, promising him Crete for himself and the Morea for his son, Ibrahim (Ibrāhīm), in return for aid. Ibrahim suppressed the revolt in Crete and then invaded the Morea, defeating the Greek army there. He combined with the Ottoman Gen. Reshid Pasha (1802–58) to capture Missolonghi, Apr. 1826, and then returned to the Morea while Reshid Pasha completed the conquest of continental Greece by taking the Acropolis in Athens, 5 June, 1827.

CONVENTION OF AKKERMAN. 7 Oct., 1826. A Russian ultimatum forced the Turks to agree to Russian demands in the principalities and Serbia. The hospodars were to be elected for 7 years by boyar (noble) assemblies, and their election could not be vetoed, nor could they abdicate or be deposed without Russian approval. In addition, a settlement of outstanding questions with Serbia, including a grant of autonomy, was to be made.

MEETING OF GREEK NATIONAL ASSEMBLY. Mar.–May 1827. Facing defeat, the various Greek factions united and elected Count John Capodistrias (1779–1831), formerly Russian foreign minister, president of Greece. Despite Ibrahim's victories, he could only control the area his army actually occupied, and the Greeks continued their struggle for independence.

TREATY OF LONDON. 6 July, 1827. At first the great powers had taken little interest in the Greek revolt, but they had been forced to change their policies by public support for the Greek cause and by the severe measures of reprisal taken by the Turks. On 4 April, 1826, Britain and Russia agreed on representations to the sultan favoring the creation of an autonomous Greek state. They then joined with France in the Treaty of London, 6 July, 1827, made an offer of mediation, and demanded an immediate armistice. If this was not accepted by Turkey, the 3 powers were to establish consular relations with Greece and prevent, as far as possible, further hostilities. The latter provision resulted, when the Turks refused the armistice, in the blockading of a Turko-Egyptian fleet in Navarino Bay by a combined allied fleet. On 20 Oct. the allied fleet entered the bay and the Turkish fleet was destroyed.

RUSSO-TURKISH WAR. 1828–29. As a result of the Battle of Navarino, the sultan voided the Convention of Akkerman, Dec. 1827, and Russia used this action as an occasion for war (declared 26 Apr., 1828). The principalities were occupied, but Turkish resistance on the Danube was greater than had been expected and the Russians made no major advance until 1829, when they crossed the Balkan mountains and captured Adrianople, Aug. By the Treaty of Adrianople, 14 Sept., 1829, Russia acquired the mouths of the Danube and was to occupy the principalities until an indemnity had been paid. In addition, the principalities were given internal autonomy, with the hospodars elected for life, and Serbia was again promised autonomy. The Turks were forced to accept the Treaty of London and the terms of a 3-power protocol, dated 22 Mar., 1829, establishing the frontiers of an autonomous Greek state.

GREEK INDEPENDENCE. By an agreement between Great Britain, France, and Russia, 19 July, 1828, the French were to occupy the Morea. The Egyptians agreed to a peaceful evacuation, which was completed by Oct., and on 16 Nov. the Morea and the Cyclades Islands were put under the protection of the 3 powers. The withdrawal of Turkish troops, caused by the war with Russia, permitted the Greeks to reoccupy part of the mainland, and on 22 Mar., 1829, the powers extended the frontiers of Greece to include the island of Euboea and continental Greece south of a line running from the Gulf of Arta to the Gulf of Volo. However, after the acceptance by the Turks of these terms, in the Treaty of Adrianople, the British began to fear that an autonomous Greece would become dependent on Russia for the protection of its rights. On 3 Feb., 1830, therefore, the 3 powers declared for the creation of an independent Greece, with its northern frontier reduced by the exclusion of Aetolia and Acarnania. Prince Leopold of Saxe-Coburg was selected as its ruler, but Capodistrias persuaded him to reject the crown on the grounds that the proposed frontiers were unacceptable to the Greeks.

SERBIAN AUTONOMY. Oct. 1830. In accordance with the Treaty of Adrianople, the sultan issued a firman (imperial rescript) to Serbia, granting internal autonomy and making Milosh the hereditary prince.

1831–43

ASSASSINATION OF CAPODISTRIAS. 9 Oct., 1831. A patriotic and energetic leader, Capodistrias had nevertheless aroused opposition by his autocratic manner, his arbitrariness, and his attempts to strengthen the central authority. He was killed by members of a family whose head he had imprisoned, and his death was followed by anarchy in Greece.

ORGANIC STATUTES FOR THE PRINCIPALITIES. 1831–32. Adopted in July 1831 in Wallachia and in Jan. 1832 in Moldavia, the Organic Statutes were written by the Russians and provided for a division of power between the hospodars and the boyar assemblies. In addition, the boyars were made, for the 1st time, the legal owners of the land and peasant landholdings were decreased by more than 50%, while the services they owed were increased.

THE "BAVARIAN PROTECTORATE." 1833–43. After Leopold's refusal of the Greek throne, the powers offered it to Prince Otho (1815–67, ruled 1832–62), 2nd son of the king of Bavaria. By treaty

dated 7 May, 1832, Otho accepted the offer and the northern frontier of Greece was restored to the Arta-Volo line of the protocol of 22 Mar., 1829. From Feb. 1833 to June 1835, Greece was ruled by 3 Bavarian regents in Otho's name. A strongly centralized system was established, as opposed to the traditional municipal freedom of Greece. Both the regents and Otho, when he reached his majority, tended to ignore native Greek institutions and native Greek leaders, thereby creating much opposition.

ABDICATION OF OBRENOVICH. 13 June, 1839. Milosh Obrenovich's autocratic rule led to opposition and the demand for a constitution. In 1835 he granted Serbia a constitution, but abrogated it almost at once. In Dec. 1838 the sultan, with Russian support, created a 17-member senate, with extensive powers and appointed for life. Milosh attempted to fight this dilution of his power and, when he was defeated, abdicated. He was succeeded by his younger son, Michael (1825–68, ruled 1839–42), because of the death of his eldest son, Milan (1819?–39), shortly after his abdication.

ACCESSION OF ALEXANDER KARAGEORGEVICH. Sept. 1842. Michael was unable to create a stable government, and in Aug. 1842 was overthrown. A national assembly elected Alexander (1806–85, ruled 1842–58), the son of Kara George, to succeed him as Prince of Serbia.

REVOLUTION IN GREECE. Sept. 1843. An uprising by the Athens garrison on the night of 14–15 Sept., 1843, forced Otho to accept a constitution and dismiss most of the foreigners in his service. A national assembly was called, meeting 20 Nov., and a constitution adopted which provided for a bicameral legislature with the lower house elected by manhood suffrage and the upper house appointed for life by the king.

1844—52

REVOLTS IN THE PRINCIPALITIES. 1848. Responding to the revolutionary atmosphere of 1848, liberal revolts occurred in both principalities. The revolt in Moldavia in Apr. was quickly put down, but in Wallachia the hospodar was forced to accept a constitution on 23 June, after which he fled, leaving a provisional government in control. The revolutionaries were strongly anti-Russian, and the Russians, after occupying Moldavia in July, demanded that the Turks overthrow the provisional government in Wallachia. A joint Russo-Turkish occupation resulted in the Convention of Balta Liman, 1 May, 1849, between the 2 powers by which the hospodars were to be again appointed for a 7-year term by the sultan, with Russian approval, and the elected boyar assemblies were replaced by appointed councils.

REFORM CONSTITUTION IN THE IONIAN ISLANDS. 26 Apr., 1849. Granted by the British, the constitution provided for a biennial legislature with a directly elected lower house and an upper house chosen by the high commissioner from the lower house. It had limited powers, but became a vehicle for the expression of Ionian public opinion, in particular the desire for union with Greece.

ABOLITION OF MONTENEGRIN THEOCRACY. 1852. A new prince-bishop, Danilo II (1826–60, ruled 1859–60), converted Montenegro into a hereditary, temporal principality by transferring his religious functions to an archbishop. The Turks attempted to prevent the change, but were stopped by threats of Austrian intervention.

1853–56

CRIMEAN WAR. Disputes between Catholic and Orthodox Christians over control of the Holy Places in Jerusalem led to a Russian demand for a protectorate over all Orthodox Christians in the Ottoman Empire. Backed by Britain and France, the Turks refused to comply and, in July 1853, the Russians occupied the principalities. Efforts at mediation failed, and in Oct. war between Russia and Turkey broke out. The destruction of a Turkish fleet at Sinope, 30 Nov., aroused British public opinion, which already had a strong anti-Russian bias,

and the British fleet was ordered to patrol the Black Sea and protect Ottoman territory. In Mar. 1854 Britain and France declared war when the Russians did not respond to their demand for evacuation of the principalities. However, a combination of Turkish victories and Austrian demands forced the Russians to withdraw from the principalities, Aug. 1854, after which they were occupied for the duration of the war by the Austrians, in accordance with an Austro-Turkish agreement of 14 June, 1854. The focus of the war then shifted to the Crimea, where the allies landed, Sept. 1854, taking Sevastopol, after a long and difficult siege, Sept. 1855. The threat of Austrian intervention then brought Russian agreement on the basic terms of peace and a peace conference opened in Paris, Feb. 1856.

TREATY OF PARIS. 30 Mar., 1856. All war gains were canceled, and Russia ceded southern Bessarabia and the mouth of the Danube to Moldavia. The Danubian principalities were placed under the control of an international commission and the Black Sea was neutralized, both fleets and fortifications on it being prohibited. Turkey was admitted to the Concert of Europe and the special relationship between Russia and the autonomous areas of the Balkans was eliminated, the independence and territorial integrity of the Ottoman Empire and the rights of Serbia and the principalities being placed under the joint guarantee of all the powers. In the principalities, elected assemblies were to meet to express their views on their future organization. A Turkish firman, 18 Feb., 1856, granting liberty of worship and civil equality to all, was noted and approved of, but the powers expressly rejected the right to interfere in the internal affairs of the Ottoman Empire.

1857–64

UNION OF THE PRINCIPALITIES. 1857–61. The assemblies provided for in the Treaty of Paris met in Oct. 1857, and both declared in favor of a 4-point program of union, autonomy, a foreign prince, and representative government.

By the Paris Convention, 19 Aug., 1858, the powers created the "United Principalities of Moldavia and Wallachia," but provided that they were to have different princes and separate assemblies, with a central commission to propose laws in areas of common concern. The principalities responded by electing the same man, Col. Alexander Cuza (1820–73, ruled 1859–66), as prince of both (17 Jan., 1859, in Moldavia; 5 Feb. in Wallachia). In Sept. the powers and the sultan accepted his election on condition that the other provisions of the Paris Convention would remain in force and that no precedent would be established. There was continued agitation for union, however, and in Dec. 1861 the sultan gave permission for the union of the ministries and assemblies of the principalities for the period of Cuza's reign only.

ABDICATION OF ALEXANDER KARAGEORGEVICH. 3 Jan., 1859. Alexander Karageorgevich had aroused opposition by his failure to support a revolt, 1848, of the Slavs in the Hapsburg lands and by his neutrality during the Crimean War. A struggle between Alexander and the senate resulted in the convening of a national assembly, elected by taxpayer suffrage, which demanded his abdication, and Milosh Obrenovich was recalled to the throne.

DEATH OF MILOSH OBRENOVICH. 26 Sept., 1860. Milosh was succeeded by his son Michael, who promised a rule of law and did much to modernize the country. He ended the last vestiges of Ottoman control by obtaining the evacuation of the Turkish quarter of Belgrade, Sept. 1862, and the removal of the remaining Turkish garrisons, 3 Mar., 1867.

REVOLUTION IN GREECE. 1862. Otho's popularity had increased during the Crimean War, when the western powers had to intervene to enforce neutrality on Greece. But it had again declined during the Austro-Italian War (1859), when he had favored Austria while the people sympathized with Italy. His hold on the throne was further weakened by the fact that he had no heir and other Bavarian princes were disinclined to convert to Orthodox Christianity, as required by the constitution. Military uprisings in Feb. 1862 were put down, but the king unwisely decided to make a tour of the provinces. In Oct. revolts erupted again, and before he could return to Athens that city was under the control of the revolutionaries and he was forced to abdicate. Prince William George (1845–1913), the 2nd son of the heir to the Danish throne, was offered the crown, and by a treaty, 13 July, 1863, between Denmark and the 3 protecting powers (Britain, France, and Russia) he became George I, king of the Greeks (ruled 1863–1913). In 1864 a new constitution was adopted providing for a constitutional monarchy, with a unicameral legislature elected for 4 years by universal suffrage.

TURKISH ATTACK ON MONTENEGRO. 1862. In 1861 an anti-Turkish revolt occurred in Herzegovina, and although Montenegro remained neutral the Turks invaded that country as soon as they had put down the rebellion. The Turkish army cut Montenegro in half and forced the Montenegrins to accept the terms of an ultimatum issued at Scutari, 31 Aug., 1862, by which they promised not to support further revolts in the Ottoman Empire and were prohibited from erecting frontier fortresses.

CESSION OF THE IONIAN ISLANDS TO GREECE. 29 Mar., 1864. The treaty of 29 Mar., 1864, carried out an agreement made by the British that they would cede the islands in return for a promise that Greece would not promote revolts in the Ottoman Empire. The formal transfer took place on 2 June.

COUP BY ALEXANDER CUZA. 14 May, 1864. The assembly of the United Principalities, controlled by the boyars, had refused to pass an agrarian reform law and Cuza dissolved it on 14 May, 1864, clearing the chamber with the use of troops. At the same time he called for a plebiscite on a new electoral law and constitution. Under the new system, which was approved by a large majority, the prince was to have the sole right of legislative initiative and the legislature was to consist of an upper chamber appointed by him and a lower chamber elected on a greatly increased suffrage. In Aug. 1864 Cuza promulgated, on his own authority, an agrarian reform law that abolished forced labor, the tithe, and all other feudal dues and gave land to the peasants, in return for an annual payment for 15 years. Other major accomplishments of Cuza's reign were the secularization of the property of the "dedicated monasteries," Dec. 1863, which had owned a large part of the arable land in the principalities, and the establishment, at least in theory, of free and compulsory public education, 1864.

1865–70

ABDICATION OF CUZA. 23 Feb., 1866. The desire of the principalities for a foreign prince, expressed in 1857, continued, and formed a basis for opposition to Cuza. In addition, his arbitrary measures and the increasing corruption and inefficiency of his government united liberals and conservatives against him. On the night of 22–23 Feb., 1866, army officers staged a palace revolt and forced his abdication. Prince Charles of Hohenzollern-Sigmaringen (1839–1914) was chosen to succeed him and on 10 May was proclaimed hereditary prince of Rumania. The sultan was brought to accept the change of ruler and his hereditary status, Oct. 1866, but still refused to accept the name Rumania (Romania). A new constitution, based on the Charter for Belgium of 1831, established civil liberties and an indirectly elected, bicameral legislature, with the prince retaining an absolute veto on legislation.

ASSASSINATION OF MICHAEL OBRENOVICH. 10 June, 1868. Despite the many accomplishments of his reign Michael Obrenovich was killed, and many believed that the Karageorgevich family was responsible. A provisional government was formed and acted quickly to prevent a coup, choosing Milan Obrenovich (1854–1901), Michael's 14-year-old cousin, as prince. A 3-man regency was established, which in July 1869 put a new constitution into effect. A single chamber legislature was created, with 3/4 of its members elected and 1/4 appointed by the prince. Its powers were extremely limited, since it was able only to accept or reject bills proposed to it, and the prince could convene or dissolve it at will.

EXARCHATE OF BULGARIA. 11 Mar., 1870. The creation of a national Bulgarian church (exarchate) by a Turkish decree, was the 1st great victory of Bulgarian nationalism. It came despite long opposition from the Greek Orthodox Church, mainly on the question of jurisdiction, especially in Macedonia. As constituted the Bulgarian church could expand to any area in which it was supported by a vote of 2/3 of the population. The Turks had probably created it in the hope of dividing the Balkan Christians, and they succeeded when the Greek patriarch declared the Bulgarian Church heretical, Feb. 1872. (*Cont. p. 299.*)

THE HAPSBURG LANDS

1800–15

FRENCH INVASION. In May 1801, continuing the expansion of the French Empire, Napoleon invaded the northern Italian provinces of the Hapsburg lands. French victories allowed Bonaparte to dictate severe terms in the Treaty of Lunéville, 9 Feb., 1801; the Hapsburg ruler, Francis (1768–1835), gave up sections of Italy and the left bank of the Rhine to French domination.

CREATION OF THE AUSTRIAN EMPIRE. In May 1804 Napoleon assumed the title "Emperor of the French"; in response, Francis declared himself Francis I, emperor of Austria (ruled 1804–35). This action strengthened his position by making the Hapsburgs hereditary Austrian emperors as well as elected Holy Roman emperors.

3RD COALITION. Austria joined Russia and Britain in a Third Coalition to oppose France. Napoleon responded by an invasion of Austria, which ended in French victory at Austerlitz, 2 Dec., 1805. By the Treaty of Pressburg, 26 Dec., Austria ceded Venetia and Dalmatia to France and Tirol to Bavaria, recognized

Napoleon as king of Italy, and granted sovereignty to Bavaria and Württemberg, which had aided France in the war.

END OF THE HOLY ROMAN EMPIRE. Napoleon organized Bavaria, Württemberg, and several other German states into a Confederation of the Rhine under French protection, thus bringing all the Germanies except Prussia and Austria into the French system. In recognition of his loss of influence, Francis dissolved the Holy Roman Empire, Aug. 1806.

WAR OF 1809. After the defeat of 1805, the Archduke Karl Ludwig (1771–1847) worked to refashion the Austrian army, while sentiment grew in Austria for a war of revenge against France. The minister of foreign affairs, Johann Philipp von Stadion (1763–1824), was one of the supporters of war. In June 1808, Austria began to train a citizen militia of all men between 18 and 45. On 12 Apr., 1809, the Austrians invaded Bavaria and followed this attack with offensives in northern Italy. But Napoleon moved quickly to break the center of the Austrian forces, and the French army entered Vienna, 13 May. The reunited Austrian divisions took a position opposite Vienna and repulsed the French attack at Aspern, 21–22 May, with heavy losses on both sides. On 5–6 July, Napoleon attacked again, with superior numbers, and gained victory at Wagram. Stadion resigned, to be replaced by Klemens Metternich (1773–1859); Archduke Charles retired and Francis agreed by the Peace of Schönbrunn, 14 Oct., 1809, to give up Salzburg, the Innviertel, and western Galicia, as well as the south Slav lands, from which Napoleon created Illyria. Five months later, on 11 Mar., 1810, the emperor of the French married Marie Louise (1791–1847), daughter of Francis I.

DEFEAT OF NAPOLEON. As France and Russia drifted toward war, Austria on 14 Mar., 1812, was obliged by her alliance with France to agree to supply troops for Napoleon's forthcoming Russian campaign. Metternich privately assured the Russians that at most only 30,000 Austrian soldiers would march

with Napoleon, and they would avoid serious fighting. As the French retreated from Russia after their defeat, the Austrian government approved, Jan. 1813, a truce with Russia, in defiance of treaty obligations to France. In May, Austria attempted to arrange peace between France and Russia. When the Congress of Prague failed to produce a peace treaty, Austria joined Russia and Prussia in the war against France, 10 Aug. By the Treaty of Teplitz, 9 Sept., the allies declared their intention to restore a balance of power in Europe. The allies pressed forward against Napoleon, inflicting a crushing defeat on him at Leipzig, 16–19 Oct., and advanced into France. On 1 Mar., 1814, Austria, Prussia, and Britain by the Treaty of Chaumont pledged to agree to peace with France only when a balance of power had been established in Europe. On 31 Mar., allied troops entered Paris; Napoleon abdicated on 4 Apr. The 1st Treaty of Paris, 30 May, formally declared peace between France and the victorious powers, including Austria. The powers decided to hold a congress in Vienna to round out a general peace settlement.

CONGRESS OF VIENNA. The peace conference at Vienna opened formally on 2 Nov., 1814, and closed on 11 June, 1815. In the distribution of territory, Francis I gave up those Hapsburg possessions which were separated territorially from the principal domain; these included Belgium and the Swabian lands in southwest Germany. Austria received Galicia (except Cracow, which became an independent city-state), Dalmatia, and the Italian provinces of Lombardy and Venetia. In addition, Hapsburg monarchs ruled in Tuscany and Modena, giving Austria a predominant influence in Italy. The Vienna Congress also created, 8 June, 1815, the *Deutscher Bund,* a loose union of 39 German states constructed to replace the Holy Roman Empire; Austria was by statute the presiding power in its Diet. A final result of the Congress was the Holy Alliance, which took shape during the Vienna deliberations and was declared on 26 Sept., 1815, with the Russian, Prussian, and Austrian monarchs as its principal signatories.

QUADRUPLE ALLIANCE. The return and final defeat of Napoleon resulted in a harsher 2nd Treaty of Paris, 20 Nov., 1815. On the same day, Austria joined with Britain, Russia, and Prussia in a Quadruple Alliance to perpetuate by armed force for 20 years the terms established by the treaties of Chaumont, Vienna, and Paris. The alliance provided

that representatives of the 4 powers would meet periodically to consider measures to maintain peace; these measures formed part of a conservative and repressive policy maintained by the rulers over the next several years.

1816–47

RISE OF NATIONALISM. The Napoleonic Wars stimulated nationalism in the

AUSTRO-HUNGARIAN EMPIRE 1803-1914

The Empire in **1803**
1810   **1866**
1815   **1914**

© Lilli Tanzer 1970

Hapsburg lands. Political ideas were reinforced by the influence of German romanticism with its emphasis on folk culture, and a corresponding interest in vernacular languages. In 1814 Stefanović Vuk Karadžić (1787–1864) began to lay the foundations of the modern Serbian literary language; over several years he published a Serbian grammar and dictionary and collections of Serbian folk tales, songs, and poetry. Between 1816 and 1819 Václav Hanka (1791–1861) publicized his "old" Czech texts in the hope of creating a Czech national epic. The Austrian dramatist Franz Grillparzer (1791–1872) wrote, 1822, his 1st historical drama, *König Ottokars Glück und Ende,* a realistic tragedy about the 1st Hapsburg emperor. In 1824 the Slovak poet and scholar, Ján Kollár (1793–1852), published *Slávy dcera,* a cycle of sonnets glorifying the Slavic past and future. Kollár became the leader of romantic Pan-Slavism, publishing collections of Slavic folk songs, works on Slavic archaeology, and, in 1837, a treatise on improving cultural relations among the Slavs. In 1825 a Rumanian dictionary appeared. In the same year Josef Jungmann (1773–1847) published his *Historie literatury české;* he later assembled a 5-vol. Czech dictionary, 1834–39, and translated many works into Czech. In Hungary, Count István Széchenyi (1791–1860) offered a year's income toward the founding of a Hungarian academy; in 1833 he published demands for reforms in the backward Hungarian part of the Hapsburg monarchy. He was also a leading influence in the establishment in 1837 of a National Theater in Pest.

The Slovak scholar Josef Pavel Šafařík (1795–1861) published his *Geschichte der slawischen Sprache und Literatur nach allen Mundarten,* 1826. In 1831 *Matice česká,* a Czech organization, was founded. The Czech historian František Palacký (1798–1876) began, 1836, his *Geschichte von Böhmen;* after 1848, he wrote a Czech version of this history of Bohemia. In Hungary, the Diet declared Magyar to be the language of the schools, law courts, and legislation, 1843. In 1845 L'udovít Štúr (1815–56) published an article in a new Slovak language which he had created using a middle Slovak dialect. Jozef Miloslav Hurban (1817–88) and Michal Miloslav Hodža (1811–70) supported Štúr in his campaign to create a Slovak literary language.

REPRESSION OF NATIONALISM. Metternich acted as far as it was in his power to suppress liberal movements wherever they occurred. In 1819, in reaction to student demonstrations, the *Deutscher Bund,* at Metternich's urging, approved the Karlsbad (Carlsbad) decrees which regulated the German press and universities. In July 1820, revolution in the Kingdom of the Two Sicilies forced King Fernando to grant a liberal constitution, but in Oct. the monarchs of Austria, Prussia, and Russia met at Troppau in a conference dominated by Metternich, and agreed on the right of the powers to intervene in states which had undergone a change of government due to revolution which threatened other states. In Jan. 1821 the conference, which now included the Italian princes as well, met at Laibach and decided that Austria should send an army to suppress the Italian rebels. The Austrians entered Naples in Mar. 1821, bringing the revolution to an abrupt end. The army then turned north to put down the rebellion which had meanwhile broken out in Piedmont; the revolutionaries there were defeated in Apr. and Austria emerged more powerful than ever.

During the Italian campaign, Metternich had called for recruits from Hungary and had attempted to reform the system of taxation there. The rising Magyar nationalism took the form of resistance to the Austrian demands, until finally the national Diet was convened, 1825, for the 1st time since 1812. Széchenyi addressed the assembly in Magyar instead of the conventional Latin. This Diet of 1825 forced the Hapsburg emperor to agree to observe Hungarian rights and to call the Diet at least once every 3 years. Revolutions again broke out in Italy, 1830–31. Metternich assured himself of the backing of Russia and Prussia in order to forestall French intervention on behalf of the rebels. Then, in 1831, Austrian troops restored order in Parma, Modena, and the Papal States.

ACCESSION OF FERDINAND I. Ferdinand I (1793–1875, ruled 1835–48) became emperor of Austria upon the death of his father Francis I. Ferdinand's ability to rule was questioned, since he suffered from periods of insanity. He therefore permitted a state conference of the ministers Metternich and Franz Kolowrat-Liebsteinsky (1778–1861) and the Archdukes Ludwig (1784–1864) and Franz Karl (1802–78), to act as the governing body of the empire. The members of the conference disagreed, however, and little was accomplished.

NATIONALIST RESURGENCE IN HUNGARY. József Eötvös (1813–71), journalist and member of the Diet, published articles, 1839–40, revealing the shortcomings of the traditional county administration and advocated a general demand for ministerial responsibility, equality before the law, and universal taxation (which would include the previously exempt nobility). Liberal members of the Diet, led by Ferencz Deák (1803–76), also called for the release of political prisoners, including Lajos Kossuth (1802–94). Kossuth, who had earned the wrath of the government by publishing accounts of parliamentary activities during the 1830's, was freed in 1840. Between 1841 and 1844, Kossuth edited the journal *Pesti Hirlap.* He demanded the abolition of entail and other feudal remnants and the taxation of the nobility. He stressed Magyar superiority over other nationalities in the Hungarian part of the empire, and in 1844 founded the National League to oppose the government in Vienna.

The Polish and Ukrainian peasants in Galicia rose in rebellion against the Polish nobility, 1846. In Nov. 1846 Austria put down the revolt and annexed Cracow.

1848

REVOLTS OF 1848. On 11 Mar. students in Vienna demonstrated for the freedom to speak, learn, teach, believe, and publish according to their own desires, and for the right of representation. In Prague, a mass petition demanded the abolition of the *Robot* (peasant labor due the lord under feudal law), liberal reforms, and the union of Bohemia, Moravia, and Silesia. On 13 Mar. a crowd formed in Vienna and forced Metternich to resign and flee from Vienna. Students armed, and a national guard was formed. On 15 Mar. the Hapsburg court promised the Austrian people a constitution. On 17 Mar. Daniele Manin (1804–57) led an uprising in Venice; he became president of the new Republic of Venice 5 days later. On 18 Mar. street fighting erupted in Milan, ending Austrian occupation there. On 25 Mar. a Croatian Diet convened at Agram under Josip Jelačić (1801–59), who was *Ban* (governor) of the Kingdom of Croatia, Slavonia, and Dalmatia. The representatives put forward national and liberal demands. On 29 Mar. a 2nd petition in Prague emphasized Czech national demands.

Apr. On 10 Apr. a new Hungarian constitution became law, abolishing feudal relationships and establishing a national guard. The Hapsburg emperor recognized the independent government and agreed that in his royal dignity he constituted the major link between the government of Austria and the new government of Hungary. The president of the first Hungarian ministry was Lajos Batthyány (1806–49), who favored maintaining ties with Austria. Other members included Deák as minister of justice, Eötvös as minister of education, Széchenyi as minister of ways and communication, and Kossuth as minister of finance. On 17 Apr. Governor Stadion of Galicia abolished the *Robot* in his province, with compensation by the state to the lords.

May. Transylvanian Rumanians held a meeting at Blaj and agreed on the need for an autonomous Rumanian territory. Serbs gathered at Karlowitz to demand Serbian autonomy. The Magyar reaction led to brutal struggles with both these nationalities. On 28 May, the Hungarian-dominated Transylvanian Diet voted to unite Transylvania with Hungary. In Prague, František Palacký presided over a Slavic Congress.

June. Czech radicals engaged in street fighting in Prague. The Austrian army, under General Alfred Windischgrätz

(1787–1862), restored order in the city, 16 June.

July. As a result of the new constitution, an Austrian parliament was elected by universal suffrage. This Reichstag met in Vienna, 22 July, with a Slavic majority. On 25 July, at Custoza, General Josef Radetzky (1766–1858) led the Austrians to victory over the Piedmontese army, which had come to the aid of other Italian insurrectionists.

Sept. On 7 Sept. the emperor gave his consent to parliamentary legislation abolishing feudal remnants with compensation to the lords for services due them under the old order. The leading parliamentary sponsor of this bill had been Hans Kudlich (1823–1917). At the end of the month, Austrian troops crossed into Hungary; they were supported against the Magyars by the national minorities, notably Croatian forces under Jelačić. The Hungarians formed a Committee of National Defense with Kossuth as president.

Oct. On 6 Oct. a city crowd rose in Vienna and murdered the minister of war, Latour. On 7 Oct. the emperor fled Vienna for Olomouc, and the Austrian parliament soon followed to the nearby town of Kremsier, 22 Oct. On 19 Oct., Felix zu Schwarzenberg (1800–1852) was empowered to form a government. On 28 Oct. Windischgrätz attacked Vienna, and captured the city, 31 Oct.

Nov. On 21 Nov. Schwarzenberg became prime minister. He formed a ministry, retaining for himself the direction of foreign affairs.

Dec. Emperor Ferdinand abdicated in favor of his nephew Francis (1830–1916), who ruled as Francis Joseph I.

Mar. 1849. On 4 Mar. Francis Joseph approved the Kremsier constitution, which established autonomy for the various parts of the empire and equality for its nationalities. On 7 Mar. he dissolved parliament.

1849

RESTORATION OF HAPSBURG POWER. On 23 Mar., 1849, Radetzky's victory over Piedmont at Novara ended Italian hopes of immediate unity. In January, the Austrian troops under Windischgrätz had occupied Budapest. The Hungarian Diet withdrew to Debrecen, where, 13 Apr., it declared Hungary an independent republic with Kossuth as president. General Arthur Görgey (1818–1916) led the Hungarian army, supported by the Polish general Jósef Bem (1795–1850); together they achieved substantial success in resisting Austria. But they were forced to surrender at Világos, 13 Aug., to a Russian army which came to aid the Austrians. Görgey was captured but his life was spared at Russian insistence. Kossuth escaped to Turkey and from there to the West.

1850

NEW DEUTSCHER BUND. In Nov. 1850 at Olomouc, Prussia agreed to acknowledge the authority of a reconstituted *Deutscher Bund* under Austrian leadership. Schwarzenberg demanded the inclusion of the entire Austrian Empire, not just the German and Bohemian lands, in the *Bund* and in the German *Zollverein* (customs union). To facilitate this project he abolished the customs barriers between Hungary and the rest of the empire. Under Schwarzenberg's vigorous leadership, Austria now held a dominant position in Germany and in Italy, though she was not admitted to the Zollverein.

1851

ANNULMENT OF THE KREMSIER CONSTITUTION. On 31 Dec., 1851, encouraged by its own strength and by the return of absolutist regimes in other parts of Europe, the Austrian monarchy declared null and void the Kremsier constitution, which had never actually been put into force.

1852

THE BACH SYSTEM. Schwarzenberg died suddenly on 5 Apr., 1852. Francis Joseph appointed no one in his place, instead assuming a more personal control of government himself. But since the emperor was interested primarily in foreign policy, the direction of internal affairs fell to Alexander von Bach (1813–93), minister of the interior since 1849. Bach was faced with the necessity of instilling a sense of Hapsburg citizenship in all the residents of the empire, including the newly freed serfs. The system which he developed during the 1850's involved complete centralization of government through a bureaucracy which extended downward from Vienna to small primary administrative districts, in which the district officials combined administrative and judicial functions. The empire was ruled as one indivisible state, through an army of officials loyal to the bureaucracy rather than to the often hostile residents of the districts to which they were sent.

1853–60

CRIMEAN WAR. Austria attempted to maintain a policy of neutrality, but actually leaned toward the West. She demanded that Russia withdraw from the Rumanian principalities of Moldavia and Wallachia and occupied them, Dec. 1854. Austria further antagonized Russia by supporting, Dec. 1855, British and French demands for a peace treaty.

WAR IN ITALY. War broke out in Apr. 1859 between Austria and Piedmont. Under the terms of a secret treaty of 1858, France came to the aid of the Italians. Despite Austrian defeats at Magenta, 4 June, and Solferino, 24 June, the Armistice of Villafranca, 11 July, would have allowed Austria to retain membership and power in a new Italian Confederation. Italian nationalists therefore rebelled again. By the Peace of Zürich, 10 Nov., Austria ceded Lombardy to France, which gave it to Italy.

OKTOBER-DIPLOM. At the end of 1859 Agenor Goluchowski (1812–75) replaced Bach as minister of the interior. The Bach system had aroused discontent throughout the empire, and a meeting of the enlarged administrative Reichsrat from Mar. to Sept. 1860 attempted to reconstruct the system of government. The resulting Oktober-Diplom represented a compromise between centralists and federalists, providing for a division of power between the central Reichsrat and the various provincial diets, thus pleasing no one.

1861–62

FEBRUARPATENT. In Jan. 1861, Anton von Schmerling (1805–93) succeeded Goluchowski; in Feb., the Februarpatent superseded the Oktober-Diplom. The patent permitted each province to send delegates to the central Reichsrat, where real power resided. This satisfied the Germans, but the Hungarians refused to participate. Under Deák's leadership, they continued to insist on the individuality of Hungarian rights and interests.

1863

CONGRESS OF GERMAN PRINCES. In order to counteract Prussia's increasingly independent policies, Francis Joseph called for a congress of princes to discuss extension of the functions of the Deutscher Bund. On 17 Aug., 1863, all the German princes met at Frankfurt except the Prussian king, who refused to attend. Although the princes did agree on a federal constitution for a new Germany, they were reluctant to enforce it against Prussian opposition.

1864–65

SCHLESWIG-HOLSTEIN QUESTION. After the failure at Frankfurt, Austrian policy shifted to an attempt at co-operation with Prussia. Austria joined Prussia in a short war with Denmark over the duchies of Schleswig and Holstein. On 30 Oct., 1864, Denmark ceded the duchies to Austria and Prussia in common; on 14 July, 1865, after several disagreements, the 2 victors signed the Treaty of Gastein, which settled the administration of Schleswig and Holstein.

1866

WAR WITH PRUSSIA. On 8 Apr., 1866, Bismarck concluded a secret offensive alliance with Italy against Austria. As tension increased, the *Bund* on 14 June adopted an Austrian motion to mobilize the confederate army against Prussia. Prussia seceded, declared the *Bund* dissolved, and war began. Although Austria defeated the Italians at Custoza, 24 June, the Prussian victory at Sadowa, 3 July, decided the outcome of the war. By the Peace of Prague, 23 Aug., Austria was excluded from Germany; by the Peace of Vienna, 3 Oct., Austria ceded Venetia to France, which gave it to Italy.

1867-70

DUAL MONARCHY. More or less secret discussions had been going on between the Hapsburg court and the Hungarians since 1864. After the Austrian defeat in 1866, negotiations began in earnest between Count Gyula Andrássy (1823-90) of Hungary and Count Friedrich Ferdinand Beust (1809-86), the new foreign minister of Austria. Under the *Ausgleich* (Compromise) of 1867, Francis Joseph, Feb., bowed to the Hungarian demands as outlined by Deák. The 2 parts of Austria-Hungary were each to have their own parliament and ministry, which would govern all matters except military and foreign affairs and the financing of common expenses. Delegations from the legislative bodies of the 2 parts were to meet on matters of joint concern, and a customs union was arranged under a compromise which had to be renegotiated every 10 years. Francis Joseph was crowned king of Hungary on 8 June. Within Hungary, Andrássy headed a government which consolidated Magyar power. In Nov. 1868, Hungary reached a compromise with Croatia which permitted a Croatian Diet but required appointment of a governor by the Hungarian ministry. In Austria, the Slavic proposal for a federal state was overridden by German opposition and by the objections of the Magyars, who feared that federalism in Austria would undermine the integrity of Hungary. But the Austrian constitution which was finally adopted, 31 Dec., 1867, was more liberal than its Hungarian counterpart; it provided for equality of nationalities, preservation of national languages, and a bill of rights. (*Cont. p. 299.*)

RUSSIA

1800-1801

LEAGUE OF ARMED NEUTRALITY. This agreement between Russia, Sweden, Denmark, and Prussia, 1780, renewed in Dec. 1800, was intended to protect the rights of neutral commerce against the British navy. It was part of the growing anti-British policy of the Russian czar, Paul I (1754-1801, ruled 1796-1801). Relations between Russia and its former ally had almost reached the breaking point in the fall of 1800, when the Russians placed an embargo on British shipping, froze British funds, and imprisoned British sailors in response to British seizure of Danish ships and refusal to permit Russian participation in the occupation of Malta.

ASSASSINATION OF PAUL I. 23 Mar., 1801. The coup was the result of a plot between high court officials and guards officers who considered Paul mad and lived in terror of his use of the absolute power he possessed. Paul's son, who succeeded as Czar Alexander I (1777-1825, ruled 1801-25), was aware of the plot and consented on condition that his father not be killed. On taking the throne, however, he took no action to punish the small group of conspirators who had killed his father.

RULE OF ALEXANDER I. Alexander released from prison and recalled from exile large numbers of men, restored the rights of the gentry which had been taken away by his father, lifted restrictions on foreign travel, ended the use of torture, and relaxed the censorship. He had been educated by the Swiss liberal, Frédéric César de La Harpe (1754-1838), and with the advice of an "unofficial committee" of liberal friends hoped to institute a period of major reform in Russia. However, Alexander proved to be hesitant about putting his theories into practice and the committee existed for only a short time and produced little.

CONVENTION OF ST. PETERSBURG. 17 June, 1801. In response to the League of Armed Neutrality the British bombarded Copenhagen, 2 Apr., 1801, and forced Danish withdrawal from the League. Anglo-Russian talks resulted in the Convention of St. Petersburg by which friendly relations were restored and the issues involved in the rights of neutral commerce settled on a compromise basis.

PEACE WITH FRANCE. 8 Oct., 1801. Continuing the negotiations his father had begun, Alexander made peace with Napoleon and established Russian neutrality in the European conflict.

1802–9

MINISTERIAL SYSTEM. 20 Sept., 1802. Replacing the colleges established by Peter the Great, which had been headed by committees, 8 ministries were set up, headed by individual ministers who combined to form a committee of ministers on matters of interdepartmental concern.

VOLUNTARY EMANCIPATION OF SERFS. 4 Mar., 1803. Alexander I was opposed to serfdom and stopped the practice of his predecessors of making large gifts of state land and peasants to private landowners. He hesitated, however, to take direct action against serfdom and hoped that it would be gradually eliminated by a program of voluntary emancipation. This did not happen, as relatively few serfs were freed under the provisions of the decree.

WAR WITH PERSIA. The Persians declared war, 1804, as a result of the Russian annexation of Georgia, 1801. The Russians were victorious and by the Treaty of Gulistan, 12 Oct., 1813, Russian annexation of Georgia was recognized and Russia received territories in the Caucasus.

3RD COALITION AGAINST FRANCE. In 1804 diplomatic relations between France and Russia were broken as the result of incidents growing out of Napoleon's seizure of the duc d'Enghien and his assumption of the title of em-

peror. In 1805 Alexander made treaties of alliance with Britain, Apr.; Sweden, June; and Austria, Aug. In Sept. hostilities began between France and Austria, and Russian troops were sent to the aid of the latter. Napoleon invaded Austria and at Austerlitz, 2 Dec., 1805, defeated a combined Austro-Russian army and forced Austria to make peace. Prussia had joined the coalition in Nov., but had given no aid to its allies, and after the defeat of Austria allied with France. Napoleon's German policy, however, forced Prussia into opposition to him again, and in July 1806 a secret treaty of alliance was made between Russia and Prussia. In Oct. Prussia declared war on France and the Prussian army was defeated before the Russians could come to their aid. A series of inconclusive battles between the French and the Russians followed, the major one being a bloody draw fought at Preussisch-Eylau, 8 Feb., 1807. The 2 armies finally fought a decisive battle at Friedland, 14 June, 1807, where the Russians were defeated and agreed to an armistice.

TREATIES OF TILSIT. After the meeting of Napoleon and Alexander on a raft in the middle of the Niemen River, 25 June, 1807, the treaties of Tilsit were signed, ending the war between France and Russia, 7 July, and France and Prussia, 9 July. At the insistence of Alexander, Prussia was not destroyed, but was greatly reduced, the Grand Duchy of Warsaw, under French domination, being created out of Prussian Poland. Alexander recognized all the changes Napoleon had made in the map of Europe and agreed to support his Continental System against Britain in return for acceptance of Russian expansion at the expense of Sweden and the Ottoman Empire. The agreements were reaffirmed at Erfurt, Oct. 1808, at which time Alexander also agreed to aid Napoleon against Austria.

WAR WITH TURKEY. The French, taking advantage of a dispute between Russia and Turkey over the rights of the principalities of Moldavia and Wallachia, used their influence to induce the Ottoman sultan to declare war on Russia, Dec. 1806. The Russians occupied the principalities, but neither side pursued the war with vigor for many years. In 1811, however, General Michael Kutuzov (1745–1813) defeated the Turks on the Danube and captured Bucharest, Dec. The Russians, who were preparing for war with France, proposed moderate peace terms and by the Treaty of Bucharest, 28 May, 1812, Russia obtained Bessarabia, the autonomy of Serbia was recognized, and the rights and privileges of Moldavia and Wallachia were reaffirmed.

WAR WITH SWEDEN. In Feb. 1808 the Russians invaded Swedish Finland and by the end of the year had completely occupied it. In 1809 Sweden proper was invaded and, after a domestic revolution in which the Swedish king was overthrown, the war ended. By the Treaty of Fredrikshamn, 17 Sept., 1809, Russia received Finland, the Åland Islands, and a northeastern strip of Sweden. Even before the conclusion of the war, Finland had been established as an autonomous grand duchy, with the czar as grand duke; and a Diet elected by the estates of Finland, Mar. 1809, had pledged loyalty to the czar in return for his promise to respect the existing fundamental laws of the country.

1809–14

ADMINISTRATIVE REFORMS. Alexander's major adviser during this period was Michael Speransky (1772–1839), the son of a rural cleric. By a decree of 18 Aug., 1809, a university degree or the passing of an examination was required for the holding of the higher civil positions. By decrees of 6 Aug., 1810, and 7 July, 1811, the ministries were reorganized with a more careful delimitation of their functions, administrative functions were separated from judicial, and precise and comprehensive rules for administration formulated. These latter decrees remained the basis of the Russian bureaucracy until 1917.

ESTABLISHMENT OF THE COUNCIL OF STATE. 13 Jan., 1810. With its members appointed by the czar, the Council of State was established to examine all proposed laws and make recommendations to the czar before he took action on them. It did not have the right to initiate legislation, however, and its function was purely advisory.

FRENCH INVASION. 24 June, 1812. Relations between France and Russia were increasingly characterized by suspicion and fear. Russian aid to France during a war with Austria, 1809, had been purely nominal and trade decrees of 1810 virtually withdrew Russia from the Continental System while excluding luxury French imports. Russian fears of a Polish revival were increased by the transfer of West Galicia to the Duchy of Warsaw (Treaty of Schönbrunn, Oct. 1809), and Alexander was greatly offended by Napoleon's annexation of the Duchy of Oldenburg, whose royal house was closely related to the Romanovs. At the beginning of 1812 France made alliances with Prussia and Austria, while Russia allied with Sweden in order to protect its northern frontier. On 24 June Napoleon, who had assembled an international Grand Army drawn from almost every nation of Europe, crossed the Niemen River with approximately 420,000 men and forced the much smaller Russian forces to retreat.

BATTLE OF BORODINO. 7 Sept., 1812. Russian armies under Prince Michael Barclay de Tolly (1761–1818) and Prince Peter Bagration (1765–1812) had retreated before Napoleon without fighting a major battle. They united near Smolensk, where a series of rear-guard engagements were fought, 17–18 Aug., and the Russians again retreated. The combined army was now placed under the command of General Kutuzov and it was decided to make a stand at Borodino in order to protect Moscow. There, after a bloody battle in which the Russians suffered over 50% casualties, it was again decided to retreat, although the Russians were in control of the field at the end of the day.

FRENCH RETREAT FROM MOSCOW. After his victory at Borodino, Napoleon entered Moscow and made peace offers to Alexander. The latter, to Napoleon's surprise, refused all proposals for negotiations and declared he would continue the fight to the end. The destruction of Moscow by fire deprived the French of supplies and winter quarters, and Napoleon was forced to order a retreat, 19 Oct., 1812. At Maloyaroslavetz,

24 Oct., French forces suffered a defeat that forced them to retreat along the same routes they had used on the advance to Moscow. Crossing country that had already been stripped of all supplies, harassed by both the Russian army and guerrilla forces, with their supply system collapsing and winter setting in, the French retreat quickly turned into a rout. The Grand Army was almost totally destroyed, with only 30,000 to 50,000 men surviving the Russian campaign.

COALITION AGAINST FRANCE. Although some of his generals were satisfied with having driven the French from Russian soil, Alexander insisted that the retreating army be pursued beyond Russia's borders and Napoleon totally defeated. In 1813 treaties of alliance were made with Prussia, Feb.; Britain, June; and Austria, June. On 16–19 Oct. the allies won a major victory at Leipzig. After allied peace offerings were refused, France was invaded, Paris fell, 31 Mar., 1814, and Napoleon was forced to abdicate, 4 Apr.

CONGRESS OF VIENNA. Sept. 1814– June 1815. By the 1st Treaty of Paris, 30 May, 1814, France had been substantially limited to her borders of 1792. The Congress of Vienna was called by the powers to consider the disposition of the other European territories that Napoleon had controlled. Alexander desired the conversion of the Duchy of Warsaw into a Kingdom of Poland, united in personal union with Russia. He was supported by Prussia, which would receive Saxony in compensation, but opposed by Britain, Austria, and the restored French Bourbons. A serious conflict between the powers was imminent when Napoleon's escape from Elba, Mar. 1815, reunited them. The final treaty, signed 9 June, 1815, provided for a smaller Kingdom of Poland under the czar, with Posen returned to Prussia and West Galicia to Austria.

1815–25

HOLY ALLIANCE. In Sept. 1815 Alexander sponsored the Holy Alliance. This agreement, which was eventually acceded to by all of the rulers of Europe except the pope, the sultan, and the king of England, provided for the conduct of international relations on Christian principles and in peaceful ways.

THE CONGRESS SYSTEM. Alexander believed that alliances should form the basis for a system of international cooperation which would ensure peace. At the Congress of Aix-la-Chapelle, Sept. 1818, to which France was admitted on a basis of equality with the other powers, he proposed the creation of an international army, but this was not given serious consideration. At Troppau, 1820, the alliance was converted into a system for the internal control of the nations of Europe when Austria, Prussia, and Russia, with Britain opposed and France neutral, declared that they would take joint action against revolutions anywhere. At Laibach, 1821, and Verona, 1822, Russia supported action against revolutions in Italy and Spain; but with the division among the powers, the Congress system had become meaningless.

POLISH CONSTITUTION. 27 Nov., 1815. This constitution provided for a Diet with an upper house appointed for life by the czar and a lower house elected partly by the landed nobility and partly by the burghers. The constitution was considered a liberal document, providing for freedom of worship, of the press, and of the person, and granting Poland its own army, an independent administration run by Poles, and the use of the Polish language in the government. Alexander did not completely abide by it, however, the real power in the country being held by his brother, the Grand Duke Constantine (1779–1831), who was commander in chief of the Polish army, and Nicholas Novosiltsev (1761–1836), the imperial representative in Warsaw. In addition, censorship was imposed, 1819, and meetings of the Diet were delayed.

BALTIC SERF EMANCIPATION. The Baltic provinces were more subject to western influence than the rest of Russia, and in 1804–5 the status of the serfs in Estonia and Livonia had been regulated at the request of the landowners. These regulations proved unsatisfactory to all parties and, again at the request of the gentry, the serfs were freed, without receiving land, in Estonia, 1816; Courland, 1817; and Livonia, 1819. It was hoped that these provinces would provide the example for emancipation throughout Russia, but, both because of their isolation and the pitiful condition into which the landless peasants sank, this did not happen.

REVOLT IN THE SEMENOVSKY REGIMENT. Oct. 1820. Although directed solely against a dictatorial colonel, this revolt in Alexander's favorite regiment of the Guard, combined with liberal revolts in Italy and Spain in the same year, turned him against reform in the final years of his reign. Gen. Alexis Arakcheev (1769–1834), the minister of war, was Alexander's chief adviser and the dominant figure of the period, during which censorship was made harsher and greater government control over schools and universities was imposed.

SUCCESSION CRISIS OF 1825. On 1 Dec., 1825, Alexander I died. His brother Constantine, who was next in line to the throne, had renounced the succession in 1822. In Aug. 1823 Alexander prepared a manifesto declaring his next older brother, Nicholas (1796–1855), the heir, but kept its existence a secret. The result was great confusion on his death, with Nicholas taking the oath of loyalty to Constantine and refusing to assume the throne himself unless Constantine officially renounced it again. Constantine, who was in Warsaw, considered his action of 1822 sufficient and refused to repeat it. Nicholas finally decided that he had no choice but to assume the throne and ordered the St. Petersburg garrison and the government to take the oath of loyalty to him, 26 Dec.

DECEMBRIST UPRISING. 26 Dec., 1825. There were in the Russian army many officers who had been influenced by liberal thought while in western Europe during the campaigns against Napoleon. They had organized groups to promote liberal thought, and in 1825 2 secret army societies existed, one in the St. Petersburg garrison and the other in the army headquarters at Tulchin in southern Russia. The views of these officers varied greatly—

there were both republicans and constitutional monarchists among them—but they agreed on the need for action by the military to bring about a liberalization of Russian institutions. When Nicholas ordered the taking of the oath to him, the northern group decided to refuse and demanded the appointment of a provisional government which would convene a constitutional assembly. The troops controlled by the rebel officers gathered on the Senate Square, where they were quickly surrounded by larger numbers of loyal troops and, after a day-long stalemate, dispersed by artillery fire. An uprising by the southern group was also defeated, Jan. 1826. The leaders of both groups were tried and in the summer of 1826 5 were executed, 102 sent to Siberia for varying terms, and 13 demoted to the rank of private.

1826–35

CODIFICATION OF THE LAWS. The last codification of Russian law had been done in 1649 and the system was, therefore, chaotic. Nicholas restored Michael Speransky to a position of authority, and Speransky was responsible for the compilation, beginning 1826, of a 45-vol. collection of all Russian laws issued between 1649 and 1825 and a 15-vol. code of active laws which was put into effect in Jan. 1835.

CREATION OF THE "3RD SECTION." Nicholas made great use of "His Imperial Majesty's Own Chancery," which he had expanded from the czar's private secretariat to a major organ for the development and implementation of policy. The 2nd Section of the chancery had been created to codify the laws and the famous 3rd Section was formed to control a corps of gendarmes (political police) established at the same time. Nicholas, who sought to regulate the smallest details of Russian life, gave this section, July 1826, power to inquire into "all happenings without exception," and it probed every aspect of the public and private lives of the people.

WAR WITH PERSIA. The Persians renounced the Treaty of Gulistan, declared war on Russia, June 1826, and were again defeated. By the Treaty of Turkmanchay, 22 Feb., 1828, the Russians received the Armenian provinces of Brivan and Nakhichevan and the exclusive right to maintain a navy on the Caspian Sea.

WAR WITH TURKEY. Russian ships participated with British and French in the naval defeat inflicted on Turkey at Navarino, 20 Oct., 1827, and on 26 Apr., 1828, Russia officially declared war. Moldavia and Wallachia were occupied, May 1828. The Russian campaign during the remainder of that year did not gain any major success, but in 1829 their forces crossed the Balkan mountains and captured Adrianople, Aug. By the Treaty of Adrianople, 14 Sept., 1829, the Russians received the mouth of the Danube and territories in the Caucasus, including the eastern Black Sea Coast. The autonomy of Moldavia, Wallachia, and Serbia was reaffirmed, under the sovereignty of the sultan and the protection of the Russians, and Greece was established as a virtually independent state. Russian merchant ships were also given the right of free navigation in Turkish waters.

REVOLT IN POLAND. The Poles were dissatisfied with the treaty arrangements of 1815, desiring the re-creation of an independent Poland with its 1772 boundaries. Reacting to the revolutionary atmosphere of 1830, a group of conspirators attempted to assassinate Constantine on the night of 29 Nov., forcing him to withdraw from Warsaw with the troops loyal to him. A provisional government, supported by the Polish army, was established and, 25 Jan., 1831, deposed Nicholas and declared Polish independence. Russian forces invaded Poland and, though at first unsuccessful, defeated the Poles at Ostroleka, May, and retook Warsaw, Sept., restoring Russian authority throughout the country by the end of Oct. The constitution of 1815 was revoked and replaced by the Organic Statute of Feb. 1832. The Polish Diet and army were abolished, but the Poles were to retain their special criminal codes, local self-government, and the use of Polish language in their courts and administration. The statute, however, re-

mained a dead letter. Nicholas imposed martial law and put into effect a program of extreme Russification.

TREATY OF UNKIAR-SKELESSI. 8 July, 1833. Mohammed Ali (Muhammad 'Alī), the governor of Egypt, had rebelled against the Ottoman sultan and had defeated the Turkish army, Dec. 1832. It was Russian policy at this time to maintain the Ottoman Empire in existence, and when the Turks requested aid, a naval squadron was sent to Constantinople, Feb. 1833, followed by troops. The other European powers were alarmed at the appearance of Russian forces at the Straits and intervened to settle the Turko-Egyptian war. The Russian forces were withdrawn, but not before an 8-year treaty of alliance had been made with Turkey which provided for Russian aid to Turkey in return for a Turkish promise to close the Straits to foreign warships when Russia was at war.

CONVENTION OF BERLIN. 15 Oct., 1833. Signed by Austria, Prussia, and Russia, the Convention was part of a conservative alliance of the 3 eastern courts designed to prevent further revolutions in Europe. It had been preceded by an Austro-Russian agreement at Münchengrätz, 18 Sept., 1833, by which Austria and Russia agreed on support for the continued existence of the Ottoman Empire and for mutual action against a Polish revolution. At Berlin the 3 powers declared that every sovereign had the right to call on other sovereigns for aid, and that the 3 courts would regard as an act hostile to all of them any attempt by another nation to prevent one of them from providing such aid.

1836–49

PEASANT REGULATIONS. New regulations dealing with the status of state peasants were promulgated, 12 May, 1838. In May 1836, Gen. Count Paul Kiselev (1788–1872), who was responsible for them, had been appointed to head the newly created 5th Section of His Imperial Majesty's Own Chancery, concerned with the status of state peasants, and had ordered a detailed survey of peasant conditions. In Dec. 1837 control of the peasants had been transferred to the Ministry of State Domains, also headed by Kiselev. Under the regulations of 1838, the peasants were given a degree of self-government on the village and town level, and government officials were appointed to aid them in establishing schools, providing medical care, procuring food in time of crop failure, improving local communications, and generally improving the state of the peasant economy. Nicholas was opposed to serfdom in theory, but hesitated to take any positive action because rumors of emancipation might lead to peasant unrest. He made minor efforts to ameliorate the effects of the institution, but in general they were not enforced.

STRAITS CONVENTION. 13 July, 1841. In 1839 the war between Egypt and Turkey had been renewed, again bringing the intervention of the powers. By the Treaty of London, 15 July, 1840, Austria, Prussia, Russia, and Britain had agreed with Turkey on terms to be offered Egypt. In return for their undertaking to force Egypt to accept these terms, the Turks agreed to close the Straits to all foreign warships as long as Turkey was at peace, in effect internationalizing the Treaty of Unkiar-Skelessi, which was about to expire. After the Turko-Egyptian War had been settled, France, which had supported Egypt, joined the other powers in a restatement of the principle of the closure of the Straits which became known as the Straits Convention.

INTERVENTION AGAINST THE REVOLUTIONS OF 1848–49. The revolutions of 1848 left Nicholas as one of the few rulers of Europe with undiminished power, and Russian troops were used, in co-operation with the Turks, to put down a revolt in Moldavia and Wallachia, 1848, and to suppress the Hungarian Revolution, 1849. Within Russia Nicholas adopted more repressive measures, tightened censorship, stepped up political arrests, virtually shut down the universities, and forbade travel abroad.

1850–62

WAR WITH TURKEY. There were continuous disputes between Catholic and Orthodox Christians in Jerusalem over control of the Holy Places. In 1850 France reasserted her position as the protector of Catholic interests, and in 1852 the sultan decided in favor of the French and Catholic claims. The czar responded with an ultimatum to Turkey; and whereas the issues of the Holy Places were settled by talks, Feb.–May 1853, the sultan, with the backing of France and Britain, refused to recognize the czar's claim to be the protector of all Orthodox Christians in the Ottoman Empire. As a result, the Russians broke off talks and occupied Moldavia and Wallachia, July. In Oct. the Turks declared war and permitted a Franco-British fleet to enter the Straits. The defeat of the Turkish fleet at Sinope, 30 Nov., aroused public indignation in Britain and an allied fleet entered the Black Sea, Jan. 1854.

WAR IN THE CRIMEA. In Mar. 1854 Britain and France declared war on Russia, Sardinia joining them in Jan. 1855. Austria remained neutral, but demanded the withdrawal of Russian troops from Moldavia and Wallachia, June 1854, and occupied them herself by agreement with Turkey. This action removed the one area where the land forces of the opposing sides were in contact and left it up to the western powers, with their naval superiority, to choose the field of action. In Sept. 1854 they landed at Eupatoria in the Crimea and, after defeating the Russians at the Alma River, laid siege to Sevastopol, Oct. The Russians attacked the allies at Balaclava, 25 Oct., and Inkerman, 5 Nov., but failed to dislodge them. In Sept. 1855 Sevastopol fell, after a siege, marked by great suffering, which revealed the inefficiencies of both armies. The Russian defeat was partially offset by their capture of the Turkish fortress of Kars in the Caucasus, 28 Nov., 1855.

ACCESSION OF ALEXANDER II. On the death of Nicholas I, 2 Mar., 1855, his son, Alexander II (1818–81), became czar. Alexander lifted the severer restrictions on the universities, the press, and travel that his father had imposed. Nicholas had agreed to negotiations on the basis of allied proposals which involved the surrendering of Russia's protectorate over Orthodox Christians in Turkey and over the principalities and Serbia, free navigation of the Danube, and the limitation of Russian strength in the Black Sea. Alexander carried out this agreement, but talks in Vienna, Mar.–June 1855, broke down on the question of the Black Sea.

TREATY OF PARIS. 30 Mar., 1856. In Dec. 1855 the Austrians threatened to declare war if the Russians did not agree to reopen negotiations on the original allied conditions plus the cession of part of Bessarabia. Talks were resumed, Feb. 1856, and the Treaty of Paris ended the war. The Crimea was returned to Russia in exchange for Kars, the mouth of the Danube and southern Bessarabia being given to Turkey. Navigation of the Danube was opened equally to all nations, and coastal fortifications and fleets were prohibited on the Black Sea. The special relationship between Russia and the Ottoman Empire was ended, the czar giving up his claim to a protectorate over Orthodox interests. The rights of Moldavia, Wallachia, and Serbia were placed under the joint guarantee of all the powers, and Turkey was admitted as an equal partner with the other powers, with her independence and integrity guaranteed by all of them.

1863–70

EMANCIPATION OF THE SERFS. In Apr. 1856 Alexander II announced to the gentry of Moscow that serfdom would have to be ended, and at the close of the year he appointed a committee to consider the question. No action resulted, and it seemed that the usual pattern would be repeated, until the gentry of Lithuania, in 1857, requested that serfdom be ended in their area without the serfs receiving land. By a decree dated 2 Dec., 1857, Alexander ordered the Lithuanian gentry to develop a plan for emancipation based on giving land to the serfs and organizing them into peasant communes. This decree was sent to the provincial governors with the suggestion that all provincial gentry assemblies take similar action. In 1859 the various proposals were sent to an editing commission for study and codification, and the co-

mission produced, Oct. 1860, a draft that became the basis for the emancipation decrees. The decrees were signed on 3 Mar., 1861, and provided for the liberation of the serfs by 3 stages. The serfs were freed immediately from their personal dependence on the landowners. By 3 Mar., 1863, plans were to be completed, under the supervision of government-appointed arbitrators, for the allotment to the peasants of that portion of the land that they were working as their own, with maximum and minimum allotments established for the various regions of the country. Then would begin the period of "temporary obligation," during which the peasants would pay a fixed amount in rent or services for the use of the land. This would be followed by the redemption period, which would begin at no set time but depended on the acceptance by the landowner of a redemption agreement. The state would pay the landowners for the land in treasury bonds and in turn be recompensed by the peasants over a period of 49 years. The peasants could, on agreement with the landowner, take $1/4$ of the maximum land allotment and pay nothing for it. The landowners were not compensated for the freed serfs, but generally received inflated prices for the land. The land was not given to the peasants directly but to the communes, which were responsible for collecting the payments due and, depending on local practice, either divided it permanently or allocated its use among members of the commune. Although free from personal obligation to the landowner, the peasant was still not the equal of other citizens, since he was controlled by the commune, which he could not leave without permission. He was also subject to a special system of customary law. In addition, emancipation did not improve his economic condition, since he was left with a heavy burden of debt and inadequate resources.

REVOLT IN POLAND. In 1861–62 Alexander restored a certain degree of Polish autonomy, in effect putting the Organic Statute of 1832 into practice. However, unrest continued in Poland, stirred up by various patriotic and religious demonstrations. In the hope of removing an unruly element from the cities, a levy of conscripts was ordered, Jan. 1863, but it became instead the signal for revolt. As there was no standing Polish army, the revolt took the form of guerrilla warfare, which spread to Lithuania and White Russia. It took the Russians until May 1864 to suppress it. During this period the only power that supported Russia was Prussia, which by the Alvensleben Convention, 8 Feb., 1863, promised any aid needed. Britain, France, and Austria attempted, unsuccessfully, to force the Russians to bring the issue of the revolution to a European congress. After the revolt was put down, the Kingdom of Poland was liquidated, its provinces becoming the Vistula region within the Russian empire, with Russian administration and an intensive Russification program. The peasants, who had not joined the revolt, were rewarded by being given land on much more favorable terms than in Russia proper.

CONVENING OF THE FINNISH DIET. Alexander II had attempted to amend the laws of Finland in order to introduce reforms there. The Finns protested, however, that according to their constitution, which had been accepted by the czar in 1809, the laws could not be changed without the approval of the Diet. Alexander gave in, and the Finnish Diet met, Sept. 1863, for the 1st time since 1809. After this it was called regularly, and in 1869 Alexander accepted a law establishing its power over legislation and obliging him to convene it at least every 5 years.

ADOPTION OF ZEMSTVO SYSTEM. 13 Jan., 1864. The zemstvo system provided for local self-government on the provincial and district level. The zemstvo district assembly delegates were elected by the landowners, towns, and peasant communes, and in turn elected delegates to the provincial assemblies. The zemstvo assemblies also elected executive boards to carry out their policies. They were given control over health, education, insurance, roads, and emergency food reserves. The zemstvo system was handicapped by lack of funds and the fact that the assemblies had to rely on the ordinary

police to enforce their measures. The system was put into effect slowly, being instituted in 19 of the provinces of European Russia in 1864, in 9 more in 1866, and in a further 6 in 1867–75.

REFORM OF THE JUDICIAL SYSTEM. 2 Dec., 1864. The legal structure of Russia was antiquated, chaotic, and corrupt, but in 1864 a group of decrees created an entirely new system. Trial by jury was introduced, with an open court and legal representation for both sides. The judiciary was separated from the rest of the administration and made independent of outside control. The new court system was to apply equally to all, the only exceptions being the retention of military, clerical, and township courts, the latter to handle petty cases involving the peasants. In practice, however, the system was limited by the continued use of extrajudicial administrative penalties, especially in political cases. The decrees were put into effect slowly, being introduced at first, 1866, only in the judicial districts that included Moscow and St. Petersburg and never being fully applied throughout the country.

ATTEMPT ON THE CZAR'S LIFE. 16 Apr., 1866. Despite the program of reform, unrest continued. The terms of the peasant emancipation were generally disappointing to intellectuals and there was some demand, notably from the St. Petersburg zemstvo, for national zemstvo institutions. The period 1861–62 was particularly noted for unrest, with student demonstrations, a series of unexplained fires in St. Petersburg, and a large circulation of illegal pamphlets. In 1866 this reaction reached its extreme point when a student, Dmitri Karakozov, attempted to assassinate Alexander. The result was a slowing down of reform and an increase in conservative influence in the government, most notably in the case of Count Dmitri Tolstoy (1823–89), who became minister of public education and imposed extremely repressive measures on the schools.

GRANT OF LAND TO STATE PEASANTS. 6 Dec., 1866. The state peasants were given permanent use of the land they were working, in return for a fixed rent. In general they received larger allotments at lower rates than the private serfs.

MUNICIPAL GOVERNMENT ACT. 28 June, 1870. Town councils and town boards were created with powers similar to the zemstvo institutions. The councils were elected on a 3-class voting system, with the ballot weighted in relation to taxes paid, and in turn elected the town mayors and boards. They were given control over local administration, public works, municipal services, and public health.

ABROGATION OF THE BLACK SEA CLAUSES. Taking advantage of the preoccupation of the other powers with the Franco-Prussian War, Russia unilaterally announced, 31 Oct., 1870, the abrogation of the clauses in the Treaty of Paris which forbade coastal fortifications or fleets in the Black Sea. Faced with a *fait accompli,* the other powers accepted the abrogation by the Treaty of London, 13 Mar., 1871. (*Cont. p. 291.*)

SCANDINAVIA

Sweden

1800-1815

WARS WITH FRANCE AND RUSSIA. The renewal of the League of Armed Neutrality, Dec. 1800, designed to protect the commerce of the northern states during the Napoleonic Wars, broke down because of British naval reprisals against Denmark and the death of Czar Paul I of Russia. In 1805 Sweden joined in an alliance with Britain and Russia, and entered the war against France because of her dislike of Napoleon, which was greatly heightened by the execution of the duc d'Enghien. Gustavus IV (ruled 1792–1809) persisted in the war despite French occupation of Swedish Pomerania, 1807, and Napoleon's alliances with Russia, July 1807, and Denmark, Oct. 1807. In Feb. 1808 Russia attacked Finland. In Mar. Denmark also declared war. By Nov. the Russians had captured Finland and in 1809 they attacked Sweden proper.

ACCESSION OF CHARLES XIII. On 13 Mar., 1809, Gustavus was overthrown by a coup. Duke Charles (1748–1818), his uncle, became regent and the Riksdag was convened. A new constitution, similar to the one of 1772, provided for a strong monarch with a Riksdag that had veto powers over legislation and the right to impeach the king's ministers. Duke Charles became king as Charles XIII (ruled 1809–18). As he had no heir, Christian August of Denmark (1768–1810) was chosen as crown prince.

TREATY OF FREDRIKSHAMN. Sept. 1809. Russia received Finland, the Åland Islands, and a northeastern strip of Sweden. Sweden joined the French alliance system, making peace with Denmark, Dec. 1809, and with France, Jan. 1810, on condition that she break off trade with Britain in return for the restoration of Swedish Pomerania.

RULE OF PRINCE BERNADOTTE. In Aug. 1810 Jean Baptiste Bernadotte (1763–1844) was chosen crown prince. Christian August of Denmark having died, it became necessary to choose a new heir to the throne. There were several candidates, but it was suggested that the choice of a French marshal would guarantee Napoleon's good will, and Bernadotte was selected. He arrived in Sweden, Oct. 1810, and, as Crown Prince Charles John, became the effective head of the government. From the first he was independent of French control, permitting secret trade with Britain which brought French reprisal in the form of the occupation of Swedish Pomerania.

RUSSIAN ALLIANCE. In Apr. 1812 Sweden allied itself with Russia. Giving up hope of recovering Finland, Charles John secured a promise, Aug. 1812, of Russian aid in an invasion of Norway. Britain and Prussia later approved of the Swedish claim on Norway, but refused to permit the diversion of forces against Denmark. Charles John was placed in command of the northern army attacking the French in Germany. After the battle of Leipzig, Oct. 1813, he detached his Swedish army and attacked Denmark through Holstein.

TREATY OF KIEL. Jan. 1814. Norway was ceded to Sweden, but without its dependencies, Iceland, Greenland, and the Faroe Islands; Denmark received Swedish Pomerania and joined the anti-French coalition.

NORWEGIAN CONSTITUTION. Objecting to the Swedish union, a Norwegian assembly met at Eidsvold, Apr.–May 1814, adopted a liberal constitution, and chose Christian Frederick of Denmark (1786–1848) as king. Charles John put down the revolt, but granted easy terms to the Norwegians; the new constitution provided for an indirectly elected Storting which would choose an upper house from among its own members. The Act of Union, Aug. 1815, provided for Norwegian independence in everything but foreign policy, with the king exercising only a suspensive veto on legislation.

1816–54

RULE OF CHARLES XIV. When Charles XIII died, 1818, Charles John became king as Charles XIV (ruled 1818–44). As time passed, he became more conservative and absolutist, and a liberal middle-class opposition developed which demanded a parliamentary form of government. In the 1840–41 Riksdag, the liberals had sufficient strength to force changes in the government.

RULE OF OSCAR I. Oscar I (ruled 1844–59) was not as conservative as his father, Charles XIV. He admitted liberals to the government; did away with restrictions on freedom of the press, 1844; passed new poor-relief laws, 1847 and 1853; and made humanitarian changes in the penal code. At the end of his reign, he became more conservative and dismissed the liberals from the government.

1855–70

ALLIANCE WITH BRITAIN AND FRANCE. Nov. 1855. Moving away from the Russian alliance, Oscar I made a treaty by which Britain and France guaranteed Sweden against Russian attack. The treaty was seen as a prelude to Swedish entry into the Crimean War, but peace was made before any action could be taken.

REFORMS OF DE GEER. When Charles XV (ruled 1859–72) became king, he appointed a new council with Louis de Geer (1818–96) as minister of justice. De Geer became the leader of the government and instituted a large number of reforms, including the abolition of corporal punishment of servants; freedom of religion; the democratization of local government, 1862; a new penal code, 1864; and internal free trade, 1864.

REFORM OF THE RIKSDAG. One of the principal liberal demands had been for a change in the basis of representation in the Riksdag. In 1823, 1828, 1844, and 1858, minor reforms had been made, but the 4-estate system remained. Now, under de Geer's leadership, this was changed and a 2-house legislature, the upper indirectly elected, the lower directly, was created, 1865. A property qualification existed for voting and under the new laws about 1/4 of adult males could vote.

COMMERCIAL TREATY WITH FRANCE. 1865. Similar to the Anglo-French Cobden Treaty, this agreement embodied the principle of free trade and was part of the victory of liberal economic doctrines.

RISE OF THE AGRARIAN PARTY. The first Riksdag elected under the new constitution, 1866, was dominated by a newly formed Agrarian Party, led by Count Arvid Posse (1820–1901), which was supported by the peasants in the lower house and by the landowners in the upper. They demanded an end to the old system of land taxes and to the military system by which the army was quartered on the land. Opposing de Geer's policies, they prevented the enactment of further reforms. (*Cont. p. 297.*)

Denmark

1800–1820

WAR WITH BRITAIN. The British regarded the renewal of the League of Armed Neutrality, Dec. 1800, by Denmark, Sweden, Prussia, and Russia as a hostile act. On 2 Apr., 1801, a fleet commanded by Sir Hyde Parker bombarded Copenhagen. Denmark was forced out of the league, which collapsed after the assassination of Czar Paul I, 23 Mar., 1801. As the Napoleonic Wars continued, Danish neutrality became more difficult to maintain. After the Franco-Russian Treaty of Tilsit, July 1807, Britain, fearing that the Danes were about to join the French alliance, seized Danish ships, July 1809, and captured Copenhagen and the Danish fleet, 7 Sept. The Danes responded by signing the Treaty of Fontainebleau with France, 31 Oct., and declaring war on Britain.

TREATY OF KIEL. 14 Jan., 1814. On 12 July, 1813, by a treaty of mutual assistance with France, the Danes renewed their French alliance despite Napoleon's setbacks. Sweden, meanwhile, had joined the anti-French coalition, and after the Battle of Leipzig, Oct. 1813, the Swedish army detached itself from the allied army and invaded Holstein. Peace was eventually made with Sweden and Britain by the Treaty of Kiel. The British retained Heligoland; Sweden received Norway

SCANDINAVIA

+++++++ Major railways

ATLANTIC OCEAN

NORWAY

SWEDEN

FINLAND

GULF OF BOTHIA

Bergen

Oslo

Helsinki

Stockholm

Tallinn (Reval)

USSR

ESTONIA

Göteberg

Riga

LATVIA

DENMARK

BALTIC SEA

LITHUANIA

Malmo

Copenhagen

Kaunas

Kaliningrad

Vilnius

KALININGRAD

NETH.   GERMANY   POLAND

© Lilli Tanzer, 1970

without its dependencies, Iceland, Greenland, and the Faroe Islands; Denmark was given Swedish Pomerania, which it later, June 1815, exchanged with Prussia for the Duchy of Lauenburg. Denmark also joined the coalition against France.

1821-47

ESTABLISHMENT OF PROVINCIAL ASSEMBLIES. 15 May, 1834. Carrying out a policy announced in 1831, separate assemblies were established for the islands, Jutland, Schleswig, and Holstein. They were purely advisory and there was a landed-property qualification for voting.
RULE OF CHRISTIAN VIII. 1839-48. Christian resisted growing demands for a national constitution and assembly, but did reform the army, 1842, institute a regular budget, establish parish and county self-government, 1841, and re-establish the Icelandic assembly, 1843. At the end of his reign he had a constitution drafted, but died before he could take action.

1848-50

SCHLESWIG-HOLSTEIN REVOLT. In Jan. 1848 Frederick VII (ruled 1848-63) became king. One of his first acts was to proclaim a draft constitution that was to be submitted to a constituent assembly. It provided for a single assembly for Denmark proper (Jutland and the islands), Schleswig, and Holstein. A ministry with a liberal majority took office. In Mar., however, a revolt broke out in Schleswig and Holstein. The large German population in the duchies objected to incorporation into Denmark, and demanded instead a common constitution and the admission of Schleswig to the German Confederation, to which Holstein already belonged. A provisional government was established and an appeal made to the German Confederation for aid.

German troops responded to this appeal, and in the war that followed (broken by Truce of Malmö, Aug. 1848-Apr. 1849) they drove the Danish forces from Schleswig and Holstein. The Danes won the Battle of Fredericia in Jutland, 6 July, 1849, after which an armistice was concluded. By the Treaty of Berlin, 2 July, 1850, the war ended with all the parties retaining their prior rights. The German powers remained in possession of Holstein, but withdrew their support from the provisional government in Schleswig, which was then overthrown by the Danes.

CONSTITUTION OF 1849. The work of a constituent assembly which had been meeting since the prior Oct., the constitution adopted in June 1849 did not apply to the duchies. It was a liberal document that established freedom of the press, abolished the privileges of the nobility, and created an annual, bicameral assembly (the Rigsdag). All male heads of household were given the vote, the lower house (*Folketing*) being elected directly and the upper house (*Landsting*) indirectly.

1851-62

MANIFESTO OF 1852. Frederick VII announced, 28 Jan., 1852, his intention of proposing a new constitution providing for joint control over foreign affairs, finance, and defense by Denmark and the duchies while establishing separate ministries and assemblies for Schleswig and Holstein-Lauenburg to handle all other matters. This was accepted by the German powers and Holstein was evacuated.
LONDON PROTOCOL. 8 May, 1852. Signed by Britain, France, Russia, Sweden, Austria, Prussia, and Denmark, the protocol provided that Prince Christian of Glücksburg (1818-1906) should be the heir to all of the domains of the Danish monarchy, Frederick VII having no heir. The claims of Duke Christian of Augustenborg (1798-1869), who had been a leader in the revolt in the duchies, had been settled for a money payment.
JOINT CONSTITUTION. 2 Oct., 1855. The Constitution of 1855 applied to both Denmark and the duchies and provided for a royal council which was to be partly elected and partly appointed by the king. The constitution and the manifesto of 1852 represented the policy of conservative Danes favoring a tripartite state in which Holstein, Schleswig, and the kingdom would remain separate under a joint government. The duchies protested that

the constitution had not been submitted to their assemblies for approval and, after a German ultimatum, Mar. 1857, the Holstein assembly was convened. That body rejected the constitution on the ground that it did not give the duchies equal powers with the kingdom in the government. In Nov. 1858 the constitution was rejected in Holstein. The situation was still not acceptable to the duchies, which feared that Denmark was adopting the policy of isolating Holstein while bringing Schleswig within the kingdom. The duchies insisted that they had been made inseparable by the act of 1460 by which the king of Denmark became duke of Holstein. In addition, language ordinances designed to strengthen Danish influence in Schleswig were protested and made the justification for German involvement in that duchy.

1863–70

MANIFESTO OF 1863. Relying on the diplomatic isolation of Prussia resulting from the Polish revolution, the Danish government announced, Mar. 1863, that a new constitution would be drafted and would apply to the kingdom and Schleswig but not to Holstein. Believing, incorrectly, that they would be supported by the other powers, the Danes persisted in their course despite vigorous German protests, and the new constitution was adopted by the Rigsdag 13 Nov., 1863.

ACCESSION OF CHRISTIAN IX. On 15 Nov., 1863, Frederick VII died, and, in accordance with the London Protocol, Prince Christian became king as Christian IX. On 18 Nov. he signed the new constitution. At the same time the son of the Duke of Augustenborg, Frederick of Nör (1829–80), claimed the title of duke of Schleswig-Holstein on the basis of rights given him by his father.

WAR WITH PRUSSIA AND AUSTRIA. In Dec. 1863 federal German troops occupied Holstein, and Prussia and Austria demanded, 16 Jan., 1864, the immediate withdrawal of the constitution of 1863. War followed in which the Danes were quickly forced back to Jutland. A conference in London arranged an armistice, 12 May, 1864, and agreement was reached on the division of Schleswig. A precise dividing line could not be agreed on, however, and the war was renewed, 26 June. Continued Austro-Prussian victories forced Denmark to accept the Treaty of Vienna, 30 Oct., 1864, by which all of Schleswig, Holstein, and Lauenburg were ceded to Austria and Prussia, the claims of Frederick of Augustenborg being brushed aside.

CONSTITUTION OF 1866. As a result of the war the National Liberal government fell, and was replaced by an Agrarian government, led by Count Christian Frijs (1817–96). The constitution of July 1866 was similar to that of 1849 except that part of the *Landsting* was to be appointed by the king. Danish politics now entered a period of instability, with shifting alliances between peasants, landowners, and liberals until the formation of a stable conservative government in 1875. (*Cont. p. 297.*)

THE LOW COUNTRIES AND SWITZERLAND

The Netherlands

1800–1812

THE NAPOLEONIC KINGDOM. On 27 Mar., 1802, peace with Britain was concluded at Amiens, by which the Netherlands East Indies, except for Ceylon, were returned to the Batavian Republic, and the former Stadholder, Willem V (1748–1806), was permitted to rule over secularized church lands on the southern border of the Netherlands. When in 1803 war against Britain was resumed, the republic had to furnish France with troops and a fleet. In 1805 Napoleon, now emperor of the French, had the executive power of the republic conferred on a single person, Rutger Jan Schimmelpenninck (1765–1825), with the title of council-pensionary. Soon after his appointment, Schimmelpenninck's physical health deteriorated, and Napoleon used this as a pretext to establish a Kingdom of Holland, June 1806, with his brother Louis (1778–1846), as 1st king (ruled 1806–10). The number of political subdivisions was expanded from 8 to 11, with the department of Vlissingen (Flushing) being ceded to France. Although he was endowed with almost absolute power in the Netherlands, Louis was in fact a vassal of the French emperor.

Louis determined to improve the condition of his adopted country. He introduced a variation of the Code Napoléon, uniting in 1 instrument numerous local laws and customs; he had many damaged dykes and waterways reconstructed; and he created, 4 May, 1808, the Royal Netherland Institute for Science, Letters, and Fine Arts. In 1810, after French accusations of Dutch violations of the trade embargo against Britain, Louis was forced, as a penalty, to cede Brabant and Zeeland to France. A few months later, 9 July, the Netherlands were deemed within the natural frontiers of France and, as such, were annexed. Police spies, press censorship, and military and naval conscription were introduced.

1813–47

RESTORATION OF THE HOUSE OF ORANGE. Local uprisings and Bonaparte's defeats in 1813 made possible the restoration, 2 Dec., 1813, of Willem V's son, Willem of Orange (1772–1843). He was proclaimed sovereign-prince of the Netherlands, 30 Mar., 1814. On 16 Mar., 1815, he assumed the title of king as Willem I (ruled 1815–40). The Congress of Vienna awarded the Austrian Netherlands to the new kingdom, to be united in a "perfect amalgamation." Luxembourg, which had been a province of the Austrian Netherlands, was now constituted as a separate grand duchy, with Willem as first grand duke.

REVOLUTION OF 1830. Friction soon developed between the Dutch-Flemish and French-speaking areas of the united kingdom, based primarily on the fear of religious persecution of Catholics by a Calvinist king and government. All ministries were located in The Hague, the promise to convene the legislature in Brussels in alternate years was not kept, and all military establishments were located in the north. Although the Walloon population was numerically superior, civil and military appointments were distributed on a 10-to-1 basis in favor of the Dutch. The imposition of Dutch as the single official language of the kingdom, and Willem's desire to control the education of Catholic priests, prepared the way for the Belgian revolution. The revolt began on 25 Aug., 1830. The king appealed to the powers to help to restore order in the southern provinces, but Dutch excesses in attempting to suppress the rebellion made peaceful reconciliation impossible. The powers, meeting in London, 20 Jan., 1831, authorized the independence of Belgium, placing on the throne Leopold of Saxe-Coburg-Saalfeld (1790–1865), a member of a minor branch of the Prussian royal house.

1848–70

CONSTITUTIONAL REVISION OF 1848. In 1840 Willem I replied to public pressure for liberalization of the constitution with several reforms, including acceptance of the principle of ministerial responsibility. Rather than reign under the new system, however, he abdicated in favor of his son, Willem II (ruled 1840–49). Willem II (1792–1849) prevented the spread of the revolutionary fervor of 1848 to the Netherlands by yielding some of his authority to the States-General by the Constitutional Revision of 1848.

REIGN OF WILLEM III. Willem III (1817–90, ruled 1849–90) reluctantly applied the principle of ministerial responsibility and allowed Jan Rudolf Thorbecke (1798–1872), leader of the Liberal majority in the States-General, to form a government. During Thorbecke's first ministry, 1849–53, the Netherlands reached an agreement with the Vatican, 1852, permitting a native hierarchy for Dutch Catholics; and government subsidies were provided for Catholic as well as Calvinist schools. Papal attempts to advance Catholic interests still further brought an outcry from Dutch Protestants, with whom Willem associated himself, April 1853. In the face of hostile public opinion, Thorbecke resigned, to be followed by conservative coalition

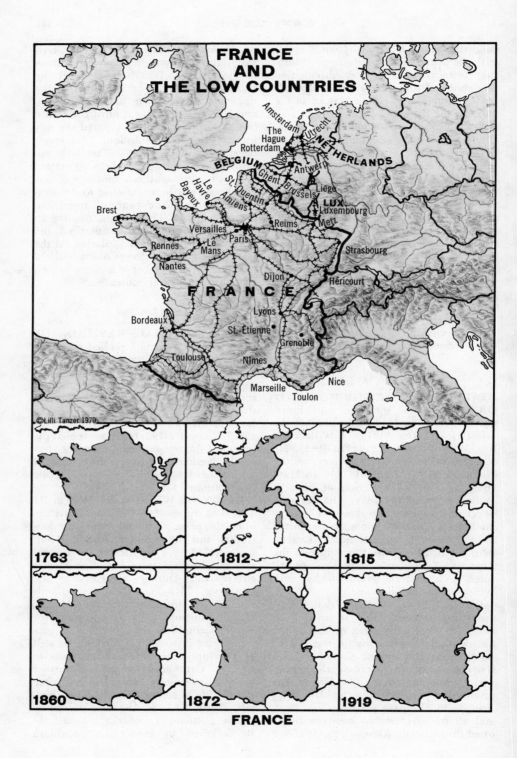

FRANCE AND THE LOW COUNTRIES

Brest
Bayeux
Le Havre
St. Quentin
Amiens
Reims
Versailles
Paris
Rennes
Le Mans
Nantes
Dijon
Strasbourg
Héricourt
Bordeaux
Lyons
St.-Étienne
Grenoble
Toulouse
Nîmes
Marseille
Nice
Toulon

Amsterdam
The Hague
Rotterdam
Utrecht
NETHERLANDS
BELGIUM
Ghent
Antwerp
Brussels
Liège
LUX.
Luxembourg
Metz

F R A N C E

©Lilli Tanzer 1970

1763 **1812** **1815**

1860 **1872** **1919**

FRANCE

ministries. In 1861, with a Liberal majority controlling the States-General, funds were voted for the construction of an extensive railway system. From 1862 to 1866 Thorbecke again served as premier; during 1863 free secondary and technical education was authorized, and slavery abolished in the West Indian colonies. Early in 1867 Willem, as personal sovereign of Luxembourg, negotiated with Napoleon III to sell the grand duchy to France; but Prussia, which maintained a garrison in Luxembourg, saw the need for a buffer fortress against France and opposed the sale. On 11 May, 1867, a conference of European powers produced the Treaty of London, by which Prussia withdrew her troops and the independent neutrality of Luxembourg was guaranteed by the powers. The conservative government of the Netherlands fell because of this diplomatic embarrassment; and after 2 years, 1868–70, of government by a group of younger Liberals, Thorbecke returned, Jan. 1871, as premier for the third time, to deal with the emergency created by the Franco-Prussian War. (*Cont. p. 297.*)

Belgium

1800–1813

NAPOLEONIC RULE. In 1800 Belgium (then known as the Austrian Netherlands) formed part of the French Empire. Belgian Catholics supported the Napoleonic regime after the Concordat of 1802 between France and the papacy, and Belgians of all classes appreciated the economic prosperity which derived from war profits and from access to the European market. Out of Belgium's already advanced agricultural and industrial sectors grew a new social class composed of wealthy burghers, large capitalists, nobles, and landed proprietors, who would later provide the leadership for an independent nation. Support for France began to dissipate in 1809. Napoleon's break with the pope in that year caused the disaffection of the Catholic hierarchy; continued military conscription and increasingly arbitrary police control deepened Belgian

alienation. Allied troops entered Belgium without resistance in Dec. 1813.

1814–30

THE KINGDOM OF THE NETHERLANDS. In 1814 the Congress of Vienna agreed that Belgium should be joined in "perfect amalgamation" with Holland to form the Kingdom of the Netherlands. Belgian economic interests favored the union, which offered Dutch colonies as a replacement for the lost European market for Belgian metal and textile production; and King Willem I encouraged industrial development, notably by the establishment of the industrial bank, the Société Générale des Pays-Bas, 1822. Catholics, however, opposed the constitutional provisions for freedom of religion, and during the 1820's the Catholic clergy came under increasing persecution as they continued religious teaching in defiance of Willem's attempts to establish state schools. In addition, the Belgian provinces, whose population exceeded that of the Dutch, opposed the granting of equal representation for the 2 groups in the States-General and the disproportionately large number of Dutch civil servants. Willem's declaration in 1819 that after 1823 Dutch was to become the administrative language throughout the Netherlands was viewed as another attempt to exclude Belgians from political and cultural life.

REVOLUTION OF 1830. The direct impetus for the revolution came from political agitation of young people influenced by French radical thought, acting on a laboring class which was caught in a trap of fixed low wages, rising prices, and increasing unemployment resulting from mechanization. A proletarian uprising in Brussels, 25 Aug., 1830, grew to full-scale revolt against the hated Dutch and ended with a declaration of Belgian independence, 18 Nov., 1830.

1831–70

REIGN OF LEOPOLD I. On 31 July, 1831, with the approval of the European powers, the Belgian congress installed

Leopold of Saxe-Coburg-Saalfeld as King Leopold I (ruled 1831–65). The monarch's power was limited under the new constitution; all his actions required approval by a bicameral parliament elected by the people. But Leopold, as head of the army, was able to exercise authority against various political groups; and his close dynastic ties to major European royal houses enabled him to control Belgian foreign relations personally and effectively.

From 1830–35 the new nation faced an economic depression caused by the loss of Dutch markets and of water routeways to Germany. A public program of railway construction provided new access to European markets and increased industrial and commercial activity by 1840. The laboring class, however, failed to share in the prosperity. Between 1835–50 wages fell to 75% of the 1830 level, while the cost of living rose continuously. Dissatisfied workers, forbidden to strike, struck illegally in 1846 but were quickly suppressed and sentenced to prison.

The elections of 1847 returned the first all-Liberal government, whose effective leader was Hubert Joseph Walther Frère-Orban (1812–96). During the revolutionary uprisings of 1848, he maintained order in Belgium by extending the suffrage. He initiated a policy of free trade which reduced tariffs and the cost of living. His government fell, 1852, because of Catholic opposition to his attempt to establish public schools. Succeeding governments continued the free-trade policies, and in 1857 the Liberals returned to pass a series of laws limiting the power of the Catholic Church. Frère-Orban's government refused, however, to extend the franchise to the working class. The Catholic Center Party, representing workers' interests, achieved power in 1863 and began to reduce taxation and military expenditures.

ACCESSION OF LEOPOLD II. At the accession of Leopold II (1835–1909, ruled 1865–1909), the Belgian working classes were feeling the full effects of industrial expansion: prices fell and wages rose slowly; bread and wool were easily accessible. The new king was convinced that such good conditions could continue only if Belgian industry had easy access to raw materials. He therefore began planning for an overseas colonial empire. (*Cont. p. 296.*)

Switzerland
1800–1829

HELVETIC REPUBLIC. The massacre of the royal Swiss Guards in Paris, Aug. 1792, had angered the Swiss people, as also had the subsequent seizure, 1793, by the French Revolutionary government of episcopal lands in Basel. No war ensued between the Swiss Confederation and France, however, although the allies were permitted to recruit mercenaries within the Confederation's territories. In Oct. 1797 Napoleon annexed 3 cantons to the Cisalpine Republic. In Feb. 1798 a Helvetic Republic was proclaimed: the number of cantons was increased from 13 to 23; the government centralized; a bicameral legislature established, to be elected by manhood suffrage; and an executive body of 5 directors created. In Apr., Geneva, the only part of the Confederation which had accepted and practiced the doctrines of the French Revolution, was annexed to France.

PERIOD OF FRENCH DOMINATION. As a French satellite, Switzerland was invaded by an Austro-Prussian army which unsuccessfully confronted French forces at Zürich, June 1799. Stubborn resistance to French domination, and general dissatisfaction with the constitution, moved Napoleon to impose another, 30 Sept., 1802. The number of cantons was reduced to 19, and the ancient powers of the cantons over education, ecclesiastical property, the coinage of money, and the postal systems were restored to them. The Swiss, however, had to supply 16,000 troops to the French armies, and were subjected to the Continental System, which greatly reduced the volume of trade and of industrial production.

ASSERTION OF NEUTRAL STATUS. When the Napoleonic Empire began to crumble, 1813, Switzerland declared its neutrality for the remainder of the war. The Congress of Vienna affirmed and guaranteed Swiss neutrality, 1815. Using Napoleon's last revision as a basis, the Swiss modified their constitution to end the subordination of smaller cantons to large ones, and the army was accepted as the only federal institution and charged with the defense of federal borders. The inviolability of the Swiss frontier led many advocates of ideas that were unpopular in other European countries to seek asylum in Switzerland. Two notable examples were Giuseppe Mazzini (1805–72) and the future Napoleon III of France. Both used Switzerland as a base for their respective revolutionary activities.

1830–70

INFLUENCE OF FRENCH REVOLUTIONARY IDEAS. Revolutionary enthusiasm in France, July 1830, inspired Swiss intellectuals to demand greater democratization of their society. Agitation resulted in the passage of laws protecting female and child labor and creating teacher training schools and new universities in Berne and Zürich in order to provide easier access to educational opportunities. By Nov. 1830 the traditional patrician regimes in the cantons, which had been restored in 1815, were undermined by constant factional bickering and reformist agitation. Twelve Cantons adopted liberal constitutions, but 7 preserved the old order.

WAR OF THE SONDERBUND. In 1845 the 7 conservative cantons, which were predominantly Catholic in religion, seceded from the Confederation and formed the Sonderbund, 11 Dec. In Nov. 1847 the federal Diet declared the Sonderbund dissolved. The Jesuits, who were considered by liberals the instigators of the secession, were permanently expelled from Switzerland by decree of the Diet. The Sonderbund did not accept the dissolution, however, and resisted by force. Within a year the Federal army, led by Gen. Guillaume Dufour (1787–1875), suppressed the rebellion. After the war the Diet granted generous peace terms, and

Protestant cantons helped to pay the war debts of the losers. The tragedy of war, and the influence of nationalist ideas in neighboring states, resulted in the erection of stronger central authority.

CONSTITUTION OF 1848. A new constitution, promulgated 12 Sept., 1848, provided the federal government with new or increased powers over the army, the budget, the judicial system, and popular welfare. A tradition of civic responsibility, cantonal autonomy, and a reluctance to apply all the revolutionary ideas of 1848 at once permitted the new Swiss Republic to remain exceptionally stable. As a result of this stability, Switzerland became the seat of numerous international banking and humanitarian organizations, and continued to serve as a refuge for advocates of revolutionary and unorthodox political behavior. (*Cont. p. 297.*)

THE UNIFICATION OF GERMANY

1800–1807

THE NAPOLEONIC REORGANIZATION. In 1800 the Holy Roman Empire contained over 300 separate sovereignties. The south German states supported Austria against France, but Prussia under Frederick William III (ruled 1797–1840) remained at peace. The Austrians and their allies suffered severe defeats at Marengo, 14 June, 1800, and Hohenlinden, 3 Dec., 1800, before accepting a peace at Lunéville, 9 Feb., 1801. France obtained the left bank of the Rhine, and Austria had to surrender her power in Italy beyond the River Adige. Moreover, Napoleon pressed for a congress to secularize ecclesiastical territory within Germany. As guardian of sovereign rights within the empire, Austria tried to avoid this, but met opposition from other German states, especially in the south, which stood to gain from a rearrangement of lands. The accession of Czar Alexander I brought peace between France and Russia, Oct. 1801, rendering further Austrian resistance impossible. Finally, a plan for secularization was accepted by Austria and by the Federal Diet (*Reichsdeputa-*

tionshauptschuss), Apr. 1803. As a result some 112 states were dissolved, and numerous cities and towns absorbed into neighboring areas, 1803.

During 1803–6 Germany attempted to work the new system, redistributing the Reichstag votes and. revising defense quotas. West of the Rhine, French legal codes and administrative techniques were introduced. The European war, which reopened 16 May, 1803, underlined German impotence. The French made sallies into Hanover and kidnapped the duc d'Enghien from German soil. Prussia pledged neutrality while Bavaria and Baden accepted a French alliance.

CONFEDERATION OF THE RHINE. With the defeat of the Allied Coalition at Austerlitz, 2 Dec., 1805, Napoleon completed his reorganization of Germany. The lands of the Imperial Knights were granted to the rulers of Bavaria, Württemberg, Baden, and Hesse-Darmstadt, and these states were linked together in a Confederation of the Rhine, 12 July, 1806. This replaced the old Confederation, and was calculated to provide Napoleon with troops and money and act as a pro-French buffer against the Hapsburgs. Soon afterward, Emperor Francis I of Austria acknowledged the situation with a proclamation dissolving the Holy Roman Empire, 6 Aug., 1806.

DEFEAT OF PRUSSIA AND PEACE OF TILSIT. The Prussian king had avoided military engagements from 1795 to 1806. He had eventually sided with the Coalition, but never actively involved the Prussian army. Napoleon, for his part, was ready to use Hanover as a pawn for bargaining with Britain. An economic recession intensified the opposition felt by Prussians to their king's passivity over Hanover, and by Oct. 1806 war had broken out. Prussia, without allies, was rapidly and decisively defeated at Jena, 14 Oct., 1806. Frederick William continued the war, but Austria could offer no assistance, and after a short alliance Russia was forced to withdraw her forces beyond the Niemen. Prussia and Russia were then compelled to accept a peace at Tilsit, 7–9 July, 1807.

The peace maintained Prussia between the French and Russian empires as a concession to the czar. Prussia lost her possessions west of the Elbe, including Magdeburg and Altmark. Napoleon created in the west a Kingdom of Westphalia, to be ruled by his brother, Jérôme (1784–1860). In addition, Prussian Poland was incorporated into the Grand Duchy of Warsaw, and an indemnity levied on the remaining Prussian territory. French troops remained in occupation until the end of 1808.

1807–15

PRUSSIAN REFORM MOVEMENT. There had been signs of reform in Prussia before 1806. A financial commission and a statistical bureau had been set up. Internal tariffs and the salt monopoly were modified, while on crown lands peasants were granted greater freedom. But only after the disaster of Jena was there a widespread recognition of the need for far-reaching changes. The reforms of 1807–13 were largely associated with 2 men: Baron Heinrich von Stein (1757–1831) and Baron Karl August von Hardenburg (1750–1822), who controlled Prussian policy during these years.

LAND EMANCIPATION EDICT. 9 Oct., 1807. This edict ended most personal services connected with land, and granted peasants freedom to marry and to leave a domain without the prior consent of their lords. Land could henceforth be bought and sold like any other commodity, and prohibitions against peasant or middle-class acquisition of noble land ended. Initially, efforts were made to prevent the continued growth of large estates and the dispossession of peasants. But modifications of the edict, especially in 1816, resulted by the 1820's in the creation of a large landless proletariat. The nobility remained exempt from land tax until 1861 and retained their manorial police powers until 1872.

REFORM OF TRADE AND INDUSTRY. In Dec. 1808 provincial governments were directed to free food and textile industries from guild restrictions. By an edict, Nov. 1810, and an Industrial Law, Sept. 1811, Hardenburg extended this policy, trying to stimulate trade at a time of great economic difficulty and dislocation.

ARMY REFORMS. The Military Organization Commission was dominated by Gens. Gerhard von Scharnhorst (1775–1813) and August von Gneisenau (1760–1831). It urged the introduction of a national service system without any exemptions. Army commissions were to be awarded on merit and by examinations. Discipline was made less brutal and living conditions for soldiers improved. Officer schools were set up and tactics revised. To circumvent Napoleon's restriction of the Prussian forces to 42,000 men, a short-service system was instituted, eventually resulting in a trained reserve of 150,000 men. By 1814, with Hermann von Boyen (1771–1848) as war minister, the Prussian army had become one of the most efficient in Europe.

ADMINISTRATIVE REFORMS. In Dec. 1808 Stein established 5 ministries to

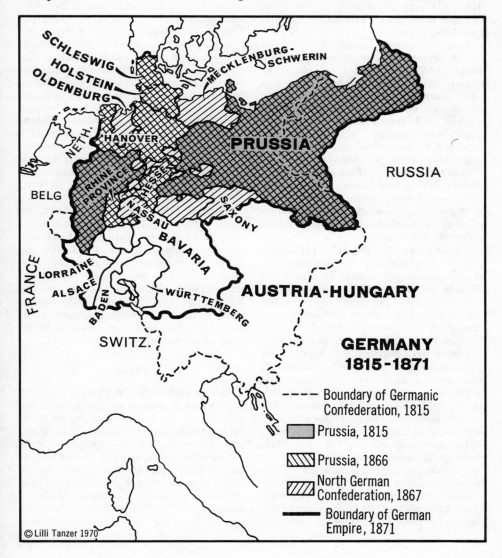

© Lilli Tanzer 1970

GERMANY 1815-1871

- – – – Boundary of Germanic Confederation, 1815
- ▨ Prussia, 1815
- ▨ Prussia, 1866
- ▨ North German Confederation, 1867
- ▬▬ Boundary of German Empire, 1871

handle finance, foreign affairs, domestic affairs, war, and justice. The ministries were co-ordinated by a Council of State. A prior edict, Nov. 1808, had extended the rights of towns to self-government, and had made their administration more uniform. Later, 1812, Hardenburg set up elected councils for rural communities.

EDUCATIONAL REFORMS. Wilhelm von Humboldt (1767–1835) transformed the Prussian educational system, 1809–10. He was strongly influenced by Johann Pestalozzi (1746–1827) and the example of the newly created educational system in France.

Johann Gottlieb Fichte (1762–1814), in his *Addresses to the German Nation,* 1807–8, had emphasized the role of schools in creating national spirit, and von Humboldt brought all education under state authority. Elementary schooling was made compulsory, and secondary schools were founded both for the humanities (*Gymnasien*) and for a more practical training (*Realschulen*). In 1810 a university was established in Berlin, and by 1812 school-leaving examinations (necessary for university entrance) had been created. These measures helped to produce a marked revival of German universities after 1815.

REFORMS OUTSIDE PRUSSIA. French influence and the Prussian example encouraged reform in the south German states. A Bavarian constitution was published, May 1808, replacing the old Estates with a single-chamber legislature. Press laws were liberalized, and the independence of the courts safeguarded. Attempts were also made to modify serf obligations and decrease ecclesiastical powers over education. In Baden the Napoleonic legal code was adopted and, as in Württemberg and Hesse-Darmstadt, various financial and administrative reforms were undertaken. Whereas most of Germany suffered reaction after 1815, these south German states were to retain, for a time, constitutions modeled on the Bourbon Charter of 1814.

GERMANY AND THE VIENNA SETTLEMENT. The Continental System and repeated exactions of men and money fanned a growing nationalist movement in Germany and intensified resentment against French rule. In 1809 alone there were 5 attempts to overthrow the government of Westphalia. When Napoleon invaded Russia, June 1812, he received aid from many German states. In the War of German Liberation following the French retreat from Moscow, Prussia took the lead. In Oct. 1813 Napoleon was defeated at Leipzig, and on 30 May, 1814, the 1st Treaty of Paris was signed. By this treaty France retained some of her wartime conquests in Germany, but the problem of the future of Saxony was postponed. At the Congress of Vienna, Nov. 1814–June 1815, Austria and Britain successfully thwarted Prussia's attempt to retain the area. Prussia gained ⅖ of Saxony (instead of the whole) and received compensation in the Rhineland and Westphalia, also retaining Posen. After Napoleon's return from Elba, 1 Mar., 1815, and defeat at Waterloo, 18 June, 1815, the Prussians hoped for Alsace and Lorraine, but received only the Saar region (2nd Treaty of Paris, 20 Nov., 1815).

PREDOMINANCE OF PRUSSIA. In June 1815 the old Federal Diet was re-established under Austrian presidency, and the Confederation of the Rhine dissolved. Germany now contained less than 40 states and Prussian power had been considerably enhanced. Gains in the Rhineland made her the main buffer against further French encroachments, and these same lands were soon to be of great economic value.

1816–47

KARLSBAD DECREES. During 1814 and 1815 many monarchs in South Germany and the King of Prussia promised their subjects more representative institutions, and after the Vienna settlement new constitutions were enacted in south Germany. There was a considerable liberal-nationalist movement, especially in the universities, which manifested itself in societies (*Burschenschaften*), founded first at Jena and then elsewhere. These groups held a general meeting at Wartburg, 1817, and soon afterward a General German Students' Union was established as a nationwide body.

Dissent was increased by economic difficulties and bad harvests. To meet it a conservative reaction spread throughout Western Europe. In 1818 the Prussian king refused to implement previous promises of constitutional reform. In July 1819 the Karlsbad Decrees were pushed through the Federal Diet by Metternich after August von Kotzebue, a reactionary journalist, had been murdered by a student. The decrees provided for (1) more stringent press censorship, (2) officials to investigate the universities, and (3) a Central Investigation Committee at Mainz to co-ordinate the repression of liberal and ultranationalist sentiment. The Vienna Act, 1820, further deterred individual states from adopting constitutions. The Germanies thus became rigidly controlled police states.

6 ARTICLES. 28 June, 1832. In 1830 liberal-nationalist revolutionary movements erupted in France, Belgium, Poland, and Italy. Metternich, with Prussian co-operation, was successful in suppressing revolt within Germany. The 6 Articles gave the Federal Diet more control over the internal affairs of the states, and tightened restrictions on the press and public assembly. Württemberg and Baden alone retained a semblance of liberalism. On 18 Sept., 1833, Russia, Austria, and Prussia signed the Treaty of Münchengrätz, guaranteeing the *status quo* in Poland and cementing their general alliance against political change.

ZOLLVEREIN. Economic conditions varied in the different German states, but most people were engaged in agriculture. The first half of the 19th cent. saw modifications in the serf system in many areas and a shift to a more capitalistic utilization of the soil. Farms were smaller in the west, especially in those areas which had experienced direct French rule. A crucial economic problem was caused by rapid population growth: 23 to 35 m. between 1800 and 1850.

After the Vienna settlement Prussia, under Hardenburg's ministry, embarked on financial and tax reforms. In 1818 the Maassen Tariff was introduced to rationalize the multitudinous existing duties on imports and exports. It laid down uniform duties on the import of foreign manufactured goods and agricultural products, while raw materials entered free of charge. There were no export duties. Heavy tariffs on goods imported for consumption outside Prussia encouraged other German states to join a Prussian customs union. Other groups of states banded together in the late 1820's, but could not compete. By Jan. 1834 most of the German states (but not Austria) belonged to the *Zollverein,* a Prussian customs union which created an internal free-trade area of 163,000 sq. mi. The exchange of goods and development of industry were further facilitated by railway construction which began in the 1840's.

ACCESSION OF ERNST AUGUSTUS OF HANOVER. The accession of Victoria to the British throne, 1837, brought Ernst Augustus (1771–1851, ruled 1837–51) to the throne of Hanover, since Salic Law prevailed there. Ernst Augustus abolished the constitution and dismissed 7 University of Göttingen professors who protested this action.

GERMAN LIBERALISM. During the 1840's there were some signs of a revival of liberal and nationalist ideas. In their *Staatslexikon,* 1834–49, Karl von Rotteck (1775–1840) and Karl Welcker (1790–1869) tried to synthesize Kantian philosophy and the political ideals of the French Revolution. In 1841 Friedrich List (1789–1846) in his *National System of Political Economy* called for a national economy and a climate of freedom in which ideas and innovations could gain swift recognition. The accession of Frederick William IV of Prussia (ruled 1840–61) also revived nationalist hopes. In 1841 he planned a National Diet for Prussia, but was persuaded to shelve the scheme. It was only in 1847, when money was needed to construct a railway to East Prussia, that a United Diet was finally called. During the 1840's Prussian influence over German defense and trade increased. By 1847, when economic recession and bad harvests multiplied demands for reform of the Federal Diet, many looked to Prussia for leadership.

1848–49

OUTBREAK OF THE REVOLUTIONS OF 1848. When the United Diet was summoned in Prussia in 1847, German liberals and radicals held conferences questioning the existing structure of the German Confederation. The Prussian Diet was soon dissolved, but revolution in Paris, Feb. 1848, touched off unrest throughout Europe. Popular discontent and palace intrigue brought Metternich's downfall, 13 Mar., which was followed by revolution in Hungary and Italy. With Austria preoccupied elsewhere, the fate of Germany lay in the hands of Frederick William IV of Prussia. When rioting occurred in Berlin, he decided to withdraw his troops, appoint a liberal ministry, and pledge himself to constitutionalism and the cause of national Germany, 18 Mar. Elsewhere German princes hastened to appease their subjects by granting constitutions.

The economic causes of the revolution were a severe slump in trade and industrial production, together with disastrous harvests and a potato blight. Mass misery in the towns and countryside endowed the middle-class political movement with real strength. Widespread rural riots against manorial dues and rents occurred during the spring. Peasants were starving while landlords exported their excess produce at vastly inflated prices. Craftsmen in the towns—factory workers were small in number and played no real part in the unrest—centered their demands around the necessity of returning to a guild system with guaranteed prices, wages, and employment. But the middle class, which led the revolution, did not heed mass demands, and adhered firmly to its belief in property rights and economic liberalism.

NATIONAL ASSEMBLY AT FRANKFURT. On 31 Mar. the German governments allowed a preparliament (*Vorparlament*) to meet at Frankfurt to prepare for elections to a National Assembly. Eventually it was decided to elect delegates according to the franchises of their individual states instead of by universal manhood suffrage. This effectively excluded workers and peasants from the National Assembly, which convened at Frankfurt, 18 May. Its 330 delegates were of the middle class except for 4 master artisans and 1 peasant. The Assembly concentrated on constitutional and legal issues and made no real effort to come to grips with urban and rural distress. It found its power challenged by the separate state governments and was itself deeply divided. Having no machinery for raising taxes and no army, it was forced to rely on Prussian and Austrian troops to quell minority movements among the Czechs and Poles. When the Danes threatened to annex Schleswig, which, together with Holstein, was under Danish rule but mainly German-speaking, the Assembly encouraged Prussian intervention.

FAILURE OF THE REVOLUTION. By June 1848 the revolutionary impetus had begun to wane in France and in central Europe. Prince Alfred Windischgrätz (1787–1862) suppressed the Pan-Slav movement in Prague and then occupied Vienna with the imperial army. By Nov. Prince Felix zu Schwarzenberg (1800–52) controlled Austria, while in Prussia Frederick William IV brought his army back to Berlin and appointed a conservative ministry under Friedrich von Brandenburg (1792–1850) and Otto von Manteuffel (1805–82). In Dec. 1848 a very limited constitution was granted in Prussia as a sop to the middle classes (and in May 1849 the "3-Class System" of voting further increased the power of the Prussian nobility). By the end of 1848, therefore, power had returned to the regional centers and the Frankfurt Assembly was soon to be deserted by all but the extreme left. But first, 28 Mar., 1849, it was decided to offer the crown of a united Germany, excluding the Hapsburg lands, to the king of Prussia. Frederick William refused a crown proffered by the people, but for a time toyed with his own schemes for unity, inviting the German princes to meet at Erfurt. But Austria, having recovered her position in Italy and, with Russian aid, in Hungary, was now able to press for a return to the old Confederation. Further risings in May 1849, largely in the south, were repressed by Prussian forces. Tension and rivalry between Austria and Prussia mounted, but finally Prussia declined a confrontation and at Olmütz, 29 Nov., accepted a restoration of the 1815 Diet.

The handicraftsmen, unrepresented at Frankfurt, held their own congresses. In Prussia and Austria, governments enacted manorial reforms to appease rural dissatisfaction, and this was rapidly copied elsewhere. In the towns also, the new conservative governments established public works schemes and new guilds to win over working-class support.

By 1848 the liberal solution for German unity had failed. Individual governments and princes had shown no willingness to subordinate themselves to a central authority. The middle-class revolt stepped into a vacuum of power: Austria was distracted elsewhere and Frederick William IV had chosen to join the movement. But the forces of reaction were not defeated, and by Nov. 1848 had reasserted themselves without difficulty. The revolution had, however, re-emphasized the predominant role Prussia would have to play in future efforts toward German unification.

1850–60

ECLIPSE OF AUSTRIAN INFLUENCE. After 1850 Austria tried to recover her economic and political power in Germany. Olmütz was followed by the attempt of Schwarzenberg and Karl von Bruck (1798–1860), the Austrian finance minister, to push the whole Hapsburg Empire into the *Zollverein*. Prussian resistance and the death of Schwarzenberg in 1852 defeated these aims in 1853 and again in 1862.

ECONOMIC ADVANCE IN GERMANY. A marked revival of prosperity in the 1850's set the seal of success on economic liberalism, and most of the restored guilds were dissolved. Joint-stock companies proliferated and long-term industrial investment by banks, e.g., Schaafhausen and Darmstadt, supplied capital for interstate railway lines and a rapid acceleration of industrial output. A severe economic crisis in 1857, however, temporarily checked this growth, and provided the social conditions for an enlargement of the liberal opposition in Prussia and other states.

ITALIAN WAR. In 1859 France, allied to Sardinia, declared war on Austria. The Hapsburgs were defeated, and in the subsequent peace were forced to give up Lombardy. The war divided German opinion and acted as a catalyst for liberalism and nationalism. The Italian success led to the foundation of a German National Association by Rudolf von Bennigsen (1824–1902) and other liberals. But while some saw Austria as the common enemy of Italian and German unification, others, desiring a large Germany, including Austria, called for a demonstration of unity against France. The Prussian leader, Otto von Bismarck (1815–98), wanted to use the occasion to extract gains for Prussia in north Germany, but Austria hastened to sign an armistice with the French to avoid the necessity of such concessions.

CONSTITUTIONAL CRISIS OF 1860. The insanity of Frederick William IV of Prussia led to the regency of his brother, William (1797–1888), who appointed, Nov. 1858, a liberal cabinet under Prince Karl Anton of Hohenzollern (1811–85). But the country was soon in crisis over the Army Bill of 1860. The inefficiency of the Prussian mobilization in 1859 led Albrecht von Roon (1803–79), the war minister, to propose drastic reorganization. The standing army was to be increased from 200,000 to 370,000 men, and the service period extended from 2 to 3 years. The strength and importance of the militia (of great sentimental importance to Prussians) were greatly decreased in favor of a larger and more professional army, which was to cost an extra 9.5 m. thalers annually. Prussian liberals, fearing an increase in the power of the king and the military class, tried to gain concessions. But William, who became king in

1861, was inflexible. A Progressive Party was formed to oppose the army budget, and the liberals were victorious in the elections of Dec. 1861. They demanded an itemized budget and restriction of military service to 2 years, but parliament was again dissolved. A further liberal electoral victory, May 1862, only strengthened the king's resolve. On Roon's advice he now appointed Bismarck minister-president, Sept. 1862. Bismarck ruled and raised necessary revenue in spite of parliament.

1861–71

FURTHER DIMINUTION OF AUSTRIAN INFLUENCE IN GERMANY.

Austria, after the Italian War, began to work for a revision of the federal structure. In 1859 she failed to extract aid from the German states and now, under Anton von Schmerling (1805–93), an attempt was made to push the Hapsburgs back into German affairs politically and via the *Zollverein*. The Austrian emperor summoned a meeting of the German princes at Frankfurt, Aug. 1863. At Bismarck's insistence the Prussian king did not attend. Moreover, in 1862 Bismarck had used the signature of a trade agreement between Austria and France to block Austrian efforts to enter the *Zollverein*.

SCHLESWIG-HOLSTEIN.

Christian IX of Denmark promulgated, Nov. 1863, a new constitution incorporating Schleswig into the Danish state. Ties with Holstein, the duchy belonging to the German confederation, were to remain purely personal. This action was a breach of the London Protocol of 8 May, 1852, which had patched up Danish-German relations by guaranteeing the *status quo*. The new constitution threatened to end all hope of bringing Schleswig into the German Confederation. To the latter end the Diet supported the Duke of Augustenborg's claims to rule the duchies.

Bismarck used this situation to acquire the duchies for Prussia. He persuaded Austria to accept an alliance and oppose the Danish constitution on the grounds of the London Protocol, thus circumventing the Federal Diet, which supported Augustenborg. The Danes resisted, and war broke out in which, without assistance, Denmark was quickly overrun. By Oct. 1864, after the failure of a London Conference of the Powers, the duchies were ceded to Austria and Prussia.

AUSTRO-PRUSSIAN WAR.

Bismarck was determined to build up Prussian political power in central Europe to match her rapidly growing economic strength. Immediately after the peace with Denmark, he began to Prussianize the duchies. Austrian policy wavered, but after considerable tension it was agreed by the Treaty of Gastein, Aug. 1865, that Austria should rule Holstein and Prussia Schleswig. Soon, however, Bismarck accused Austria of furthering the claims of Augustenborg, and the threat of war grew. Bismarck made the necessary diplomatic preparations for such a conflict by talks with Napoleon III at Biarritz, Oct. 1865, and by making a political alliance with Italy, Apr. 1866. He even made contact with Hungarian separatists and was ready to foment revolution in the Hapsburg lands. Hatred of Austria among Prussian liberals eased his position within Prussia, where the military were prepared if the need for war arose. Within the Confederation, Bismarck tried to gain support by proposing a national parliament elected by universal manhood suffrage. In view of Bismarck's unconstitutional rule in Prussia, German liberals treated this with skepticism. Austria decided to place the fate of the duchies before the Frankfurt Diet. Prussia regarded this as a violation of the Treaty of Gastein, and invaded Holstein. Austria then called for federal action against Prussia, June 1866.

Most German states supported Austria, despite their membership in the *Zollverein*, while Prussia gained aid from Italy and from a few minor states in north Germany. The 7 Weeks' War displayed the military efficiency of Prussia, culminating in the victory of Sadowa, 3 July, 1866. The swiftness of the action prevented French interference, and the peace granted at Prague, 23 Aug., 1866, was moderate. Prussia gained both duchies but made no other territorial demands on Austria. There was a small indemnity, and Bismarck agreed to the continued existence of Saxony and the southern states. But north Germany was reorganized into a confederation under Prussia, which annexed Hanover, Hesse-Cassel, Nassau, and Frankfurt.

The victory greatly enhanced Bismarck's position in Prussia. Elections, held the day after Sadowa, increased conservative representation, and parliament accepted a bill of indemnity for the illegal collection of taxes since 1862. By Nov. 1866 the liberals were deeply divided. A National Liberal Party was formed to support Bismarck and his foreign policy.

NORTH GERMAN CONFEDERATION. The North German Confederation possessed both a Reichstag, elected by universal manhood suffrage, and a 2nd chamber representing the state governments. But real power lay with Prussia, and the Reichstag had little influence. After 1871 the Confederation constitution was extended to fit all Germany.

FRANCO-PRUSSIAN WAR. After Sadowa only France acted as a bulwark against further German unification. Napoleon III's failure to intervene in 1866 diminished his support at home, while fear of Prussia led to a series of army reforms and a conviction that further unification in Central Europe could not be tolerated. For the moment Napoleon made unsuccessful and politically damaging efforts to gain compensation in the Rhineland and Luxembourg. This merely facilitated Bismarck's negotiations with the south German states for military alliances.

In July 1870 Franco-Prussian relations were suddenly inflamed because of the offer of the vacant Spanish throne to Prince Leopold of Hohenzollern (1835–1905). Bismarck, hoping for political gain, pressed for acceptance. France, fearing encirclement, threatened war, and Leopold decided to decline the Spanish crown. But the French badly needed a diplo-matic victory and demanded guarantees from the Prussian king that there would be no renewal of the candidature. King William, who was staying at Ems, telegraphed these demands to Bismarck, who proceeded to print his own version (the Ems Telegram). Prussia was ready for war, and the public version of the telegram was calculated to push an insulted French nation into conflict with Prussia. Militarily and diplomatically, the French were unprepared. Russia was unlikely to intervene, and the Austrian government was preoccupied with running a reconstructed empire, the Dual Monarchy having been set up in 1867. War was declared in July 1870. A Prussian victory at Sedan, 2 Sept., was followed by a long siege of Paris, 19 Sept., 1870–28 Jan., 1871, before the war ended, 10 May, 1871.

UNIFICATION OF GERMANY. On 18 Jan., 1871, at Versailles the ruling princes offered William of Prussia the crown of a united Germany. The North German Confederation, enlarged to include south Germany, became a Prussian-dominated federation with only a façade of representative government. Added to Germany were the regions of Alsace and most of Lorraine, taken from a defeated France. A united Germany had been created, without Austria, and as a result of the exercise of Prussian military superiority. (Cont. p. 286.)

GREAT BRITAIN AND IRELAND

1801

UNION OF GREAT BRITAIN AND IRELAND. On 21 April, 1800, the House of Commons approved the Act of Union (effective 1 Jan., 1801), which created the United Kingdom. At Westminster the Irish gained representation with 4 spiritual and 28 temporal lords and 100 members of the Commons. The established churches of the 2 countries were united into a single Protestant Episcopal Church. This union was the cause of considerable discontent among the Irish, who increasingly favored national independence.

PITT'S RESIGNATION. William Pitt (1759–1806) resigned on 3 Feb. over Catholic disabilities. On 5 Feb. Henry Addington (1757–1844) formed a weak ministry; the ensuing period of ministerial instability lasted until 1812.

BRITISH NAVAL VICTORIES. British naval supremacy was established by Aberdeen's capture of the French fleets at Cairo, 22 June, and Alexandria, 27 Aug., and by Nelson's destruction of the Danish fleet at Copenhagen, 2 Apr.

1802

HEALTH AND MORALS OF AP-PRENTICES ACT. The movement toward government supervision of labor conditions began with the Health and Morals of Apprentices Act, 22 June. It forbade the employment of pauper children in cotton mills until age 9, limited their workday to 12 hours, and prohibited their employment at night.

TREATY OF AMIENS. On 27 Mar. Britain and France signed the Treaty of Amiens, which was born of the 2 countries' mutual exhaustion. Except for Trinidad and Ceylon, Britain agreed to return all conquests to France and her allies.

1803

OUTBREAK OF WAR OF THE 3RD COALITION. The Treaty of Amiens did not guarantee the independence of the countries surrounding France. By an ultimatum of 4 Apr., Britain agreed to recognize France's reorganization of Italy if France withdrew from Holland and Switzerland and recognized Britain's retention of Malta, a strategic island in terms of naval power. France refused, and on 16 May war resumed.

1804

WAR WITH SPAIN. To hinder Spain from joining France, Britain captured Spain's South American treasure fleet, 5 Oct., leading Spain to declare war, 12 Dec.

PITT'S RETURN TO POWER. Pitt succeeded Addington on 10 May. Factionalism within the cabinet reached a crisis when Pitt's friend Viscount Melville (1771–1851), first lord of the Admiralty, was impeached. Addingtonians bitterly attacked Melville during his trial (9 Apr., 1804–12 June, 1806). Pitt's subsequent hostility toward the Addingtonians led to the resignations of Addington (now Lord Sidmouth) and the Earl of Buckinghamshire (1760–1816) on 7 July, 1807.

1805

FORMATION OF THE 3RD COALITION. Fear of France drove Russia to conclude a compact with Britain on 28 June. Britain promised Russia and Austria £1,250,000 as a subsidy for 1,000 troops per year.

BATTLE OF TRAFALGAR. On 21 Oct., Adm. Pierre de Villeneuve (1763–1806), blockaded at Cadiz since Mar., slipped out of the harbor, but met Nelson off Trafalgar, 21 Oct. The Franco-Spanish fleet lost 19 ships in the battle, and the British lost none, although Nelson was killed.

1806–9

MINISTRY OF ALL THE TALENTS. Pitt's death on 23 Jan., 1806, led to the formation of the Ministry of All the Talents under William Grenville (1759–1834). Its major accomplishment was the abolition of the slave trade, 25 Mar., 1807. On 24 Mar., 1807, the ministry resigned over a dispute with George III about Catholic disabilities.

ORDERS IN COUNCIL. Britain responded to the Continental System with the orders in council of 11 and 21 Nov., 1807, which blockaded the ports of France and her allies and restricted neutral trade.

THE PORTLAND AND PERCEVAL MINISTRIES. The Duke of Portland (1738–1809) replaced Grenville as prime minister in 1807, but the initial setbacks in the Peninsular campaign and the failure of the Walcheren campaign brought

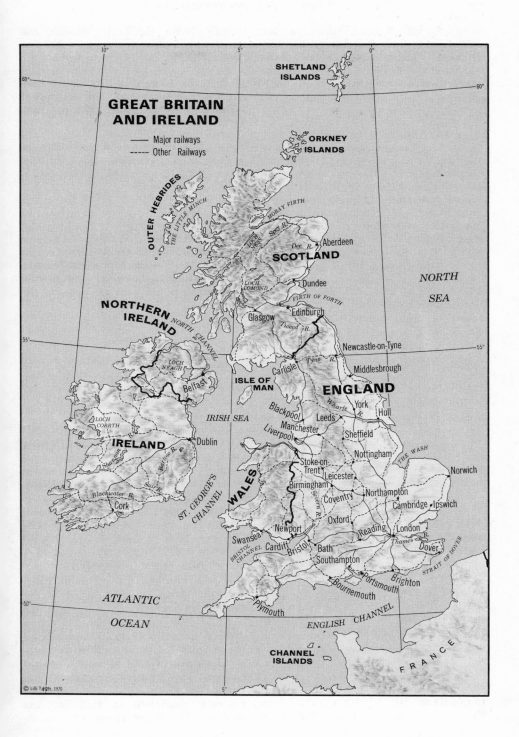

GREAT BRITAIN
AND IRELAND

—— Major railways
---- Other Railways

about the fall of this ministry. In Oct. 1809 Lord Spencer Perceval (1762–1812) replaced Portland, with Hawkesbury (1770–1828, later Lord Liverpool) as minister for war.

1810

THE REGENCY. In the autumn of 1810 George III became permanently insane and the Prince of Wales (1762–1830) became-regent according to the provisions of the 1787 Regency Bill, which prevented him from assuming full power until 18 Feb., 1812. Whig hopes of gaining office were thwarted because the regent supported the Perceval ministry.

1812

THE LIVERPOOL MINISTRY. The assassination of Perceval, 11 May, made Liverpool prime minister. His ministry, which lasted 15 years, ended instability by attracting to itself factions that had competed for power. George Canning (1770–1827) joined it in 1814, the Duke of Wellington (1769–1852) in 1818, and Marquis Wellesley (1760–1842) and the Grenvilles in 1821. Liverpool also attracted young talents like Lord Palmerston (1784–1865), Robert Peel (1788–1850), and William Huskisson (1770–1830).

1813

THE FINAL COALITION. Lord Castlereagh (1769–1822), the foreign secretary, was the principal architect of the 1812–14 coalition. On 15 June, 1813, Britain signed the Treaty of Reichenbach with Russia and Prussia, binding them not to conclude a separate peace. Austria's adhesion to the treaty, 24 June, marked the 1st time since 1789 that all 4 major powers had united against France.

1814–15

CONGRESS OF VIENNA. The First Treaty of Paris, 30 May, 1814, gave Britain Malta, the Ionian Islands, and Heligoland in Europe; St. Lucia, Tobago, and Trinidad in the West Indies; the Cape of Good Hope in Africa; and Ceylon, the Deccan, and the upper Ganges Valley in South Asia. The Congress of Vienna tacitly recognized Britain's mastery of the seas by not debating the question.

CORN LAW. To rescue British agriculture from depression, the Corn Law was passed, 11 Mar., 1815. It imposed a duty on foreign grain.

1816

ABOLITION OF INCOME TAX. The Commons abolished the wartime income tax, 18 Mar., exacerbating the government's financial difficulties and placing the burden of the national debt on the poor.

1819–20

FACTORY ACT. The ineffective Factory Act of 14 June, 1819, restricted child labor to 12 hours per day, but applied only to the cotton industry and did not provide for inspectors.

PETERLOO, THE 6 ACTS, AND THE CATO STREET CONSPIRACY. In Dec. 1818 economic conditions deteriorated and disturbances, accompanied by demands for political reform, ensued. On 16 Aug., 1819, the local magistrates dispersed a peaceful rally at St. Peter's Field, Manchester, with troops. The "Peterloo Massacre" ended with 11 dead and over 400 wounded. Between 23 Nov. and 29 Dec. the government carried the 6 Acts, which further curtailed public meetings, prohibited training in the use of firearms, empowered magistrates to search out and seize firearms, placed a stamp duty on all political literature, increased the penalties for seditious libel, and provided for speedy trial in cases of misdemeanor. The resultant government unpopularity abated with the improved economic conditions of 1820 and the abortive Cato Street Conspiracy, an attempt by 20 extremists to murder the cabinet and establish a republic, 23 Feb., 1820. The plot renewed fears of radicalism and revolution and hindered the cause of moderate reform.

ROYAL DIVORCE CRISIS. On 29 Jan., 1820, the prince regent succeeded his father, becoming George IV (ruled 1820–30). On 5 July he forced the cabinet to introduce a bill to obtain for him a divorce from his estranged wife, Caroline (1768–1821). On 10 Nov. the cabinet dropped the bill in the face of its certain defeat in the Commons, and Caroline accepted a settlement, Jan. 1821.

BRITISH RESPONSE TO CONGRESS OF TROPPAU. At the Congress of Troppau, Castlereagh in his state papers of 5 May and 16 Dec., 1820, illustrated the growing divergence between Britain and the eastern monarchies by asserting that the Alliance powers were not entitled to interfere in the internal affairs of other states solely to maintain the monarchical *status quo*.

1821–22

CABINET RECONSTRUCTION. Because of George IV's hostility toward him, Liverpool reorganized his cabinet between 5 and 9 Dec., 1821, replacing Sidmouth with Peel as home secretary. From this time until his suicide on 12 Aug., 1822, Castlereagh's influence was dominant in the cabinet. On 11 Sept., 1822, Canning became foreign secretary and leader of the Commons. He combined Castlereagh's policy of active interest in continental affairs with popular demagogy. He gained the support of the commercial class through such measures as the remission or reduction of many assessed taxes, tariff reduction, abolition of the tariff barrier between Great Britain and Ireland, 5 July, 1825, and the conclusion of numerous commercial reciprocity treaties, thereby giving the ministry a "liberal Tory" outlook.

CONGRESS OF VERONA. Canning was unsympathetic toward the alliance system, and on 20 Nov., 1822, at the Congress of Verona Wellington refused British support for the allies' plan to intervene in Spain. On 30 Nov. Wellington withdrew from the congress.

1824

COMBINATION ACTS. Repeal of the Combination Acts of 1800 on 21 June, 1824, resulted in the rapid growth of unionism. Strikes and violence led to the passage of a new Combination Act, 6 July, 1825, which specifically forbade such actions.

1827

CANNING MINISTRY. On 17 Feb. Liverpool was stricken with apoplexy; Canning replaced him on 12 Apr. Peel and Wellington resigned, and Canning effected an alliance between the liberal Tories and the Whigs, paving the way for Catholic emancipation and the reforms of the 1830's.

1828

WELLINGTON MINISTRY. Canning's death on 8 Aug., 1827, led to the creation of the short-lived Goderich ministry, which was dismissed on 8 Jan., 1828, and succeeded by Wellington's ministry. Though Wellington's political ineptitude and penchant for reaction caused the liberal Tories to resign, the beginnings of reform occurred under his ministry.

CORN LAW. The 1st reform measure was the new Corn Law, passed on 15 July; it provided for a sliding scale of grain duties.

EAST RETFORD DISPUTE. Wellington's 1st political dispute as prime minister occurred over the boroughs of Penryn and East Retford, which were found to be steeped in corruption. Huskisson and the Canningites wanted their franchises transferred to Leeds and Manchester. The Lords refused to enfranchise Manchester, and Huskisson and his allies resigned in May.

1829

CATHOLIC EMANCIPATION. On 9 May, 1828, the Test and Corporation

Acts, which denied Nonconformists public office, were repealed. The election of Daniel O'Connell (1775–1847) to Parliament in 1828 brought the issue of Catholic emancipation to a head; he could not take his seat in Parliament as a Catholic, but to deny it to him would court revolution in Ireland. In Mar. 1829 the government backed emancipation, which was passed, 13 Apr., enabling Catholics to vote, sit in Parliament, and hold any office except lord chancellor of England and lord lieutenant of Ireland.

1830

WILLIAM IV AND THE GREY CABINET. The elections of 1830, marking the accession of William IV (1765–1837) to the throne on 26 June, were fought over the reform issue. Wellington's opposition to it forced his resignation on 16 Nov., ending a half-century of almost uninterrupted Tory rule and bringing the Whigs to power under Lord Grey (1764–1845).

1832–33

THE GREAT REFORM ACT. In 1830 no more than ⅓ of the members of the Commons were freely chosen. Ancient provisions and population shifts due to the Industrial Revolution had resulted in gross electoral inequalities. The Grey ministry's 1st reform bill, though popular outside Parliament, was defeated in the Commons, 19 Apr., 1831; on 22 Apr. William IV prorogued Parliament. The ministry gained a sweeping victory in the May elections. In Oct. the Lords defeated the 2nd reform bill, and Parliament was prorogued, 20 Oct. Under threat of the creation of new peers, the 3rd reform bill finally passed the Lords, 4 June, 1832. The Reform Act revolutionized the British electoral system, disenfranchising 56 rotten boroughs and pocket boroughs. It reduced to 1 representative apiece 32 small boroughs and redistributed the 143 vacant seats among growing towns, underrepresented counties, and Scotland and Ireland. The franchise was confirmed for £10 householders in the boroughs and in the counties for 40s. freeholders, £10 copyholders, freeholders, and leaseholders for 60 years, and for £50 tenants at will and leaseholders for less than 60 years. Between July and Sept., 1832, similar legislation was extended to Scotland and Ireland. The Reform Act gave the industrial and commercial classes electoral dominance.

REBELLION AND REFORM IN IRELAND. Irish resentment of the Episcopal Church sparked the Tithe War of 1831. To restore order, the Commons passed the Coercion Bill on 1 Apr., 1833, giving the lord lieutenant unlimited power to suppress public meetings and impose martial law. Reforms also were granted; the Irish Church Temporalities Bill, enacted 2 Aug., 1833, abolished 10 of the 22 Protestant bishoprics in Ireland and taxed clerical incomes.

ABOLITION OF SLAVERY IN THE COLONIES. On 23 Aug., 1833, the campaign against slavery, begun in the 1790's, was completed with the abolition of slavery in the colonies. The bill provided for the immediate emancipation of children under 6 and for apprenticeship for those over 6.

FACTORY ACT. The inadequacies of earlier legislation led to the passage, 29 Aug., 1833, of a more stringent Factory Act. It prohibited the employment of children under 9, restricted the workweek of those between 9 and 13 to 48 hours, demanded 2 hours' daily schooling for children under 13, and provided for a system of paid inspectors.

1834

NEW POOR LAW. According to the New Poor Law of 14 Aug., relief was to be administered by a general Board of Commissioners; the dole was to be limited to the sick and the aged; able-bodied paupers were to be employed in workhouses.

1ST MELBOURNE MINISTRY. A divided cabinet forced Grey's resignation, 9 July. Lord Melbourne (1779–1848) replaced him, but William IV's disappointment in Melbourne resulted in the latter's resignation, 15 Nov. Whig strength, steadily declining since 1832, was dissipated under Melbourne. There followed a period of political instability, during which the old party designations of Whig and Tory were replaced by those of Liberal and Conservative.

1835-36

THE 1ST PEEL AND 2ND MELBOURNE MINISTRIES. Peel replaced Melbourne and set out his program in the Tamworth Manifesto, 17 Dec., 1834, proposing that the new Conservatives accept the Reform Act and follow it with a program of "judicious reform." Peel thus gained the support of both Whig and Tory moderates, but his ministry fell, 7 Apr., 1835, over the Irish question. Melbourne replaced him.

REFORMS OF THE MELBOURNE ADMINISTRATION. The Municipal Corporations Act, 9 Sept., 1835, reformed the corrupt municipal governments by establishing uniform administration for all boroughs and cities—except London and 67 small boroughs—creating town councils, consisting of a mayor (chosen annually), councilors (elected triennially), and aldermen (chosen sexennially). The Marriage Act, 28 June, 1836, legalized civil marriages; provided for local registration of births, marriages, and deaths; and permitted dissenters to marry in their own chapels. The Ecclesiastical Commission forbade plural benefices over 2 mi. apart, augmented stipends for parish priests, and reduced large episcopal incomes.

1837

ACCESSION OF QUEEN VICTORIA. William IV died, 20 June. He was succeeded by his 18-year-old niece, Victoria (1819–1901), whose reign marked the entrenchment of responsible parliamentary government in England.

1839

JAMAICA CRISIS AND THE 3RD MELBOURNE MINISTRY. Economic conditions in Jamaica worsened after emancipation, and the planters attempted to subvert the government's reforms. The Commons approved, 9 Apr., by only 5 votes the suspension of the Jamaican constitution. The closeness of the vote caused Melbourne to resign, 7 May. When Victoria asked Peel to form a new ministry, he insisted that she dismiss some of her Whig bedchamber attendants. The "Bedchamber Question" infuriated Victoria, who recalled Melbourne on 10 May.

CHARTIST MOVEMENT. Dissatisfied with the limited reforms of the Whigs and the failure of the union movement, the laboring classes had founded the London Working Men's Association in 1836. They composed a charter—hence their designation as Chartists—which demanded manhood suffrage, vote by ballot, abolition of property qualifications for membership in Parliament, salaries for members of Parliament, equal electoral districts, and annual Parliaments. They presented the charter to Parliament on 13 May, during their national convention in London. After its rejection, the convention retired to Birmingham, and activists under Feargus O'Connor (1794–1855) gained predominance, instigating riots in July. After the suppression of the 4 Nov. riot in Newport, Wales, the Chartists resumed a more moderate course. In July 1840 O'Connor founded the National Charter Association. It drafted the 2nd charter, which Parliament rejected, 3 May. Chartism, undermined by factionalism, the growth of trade unions, and the Anti-Corn Law League, languished until 1848.

1840

MARRIAGE OF VICTORIA AND ALBERT. On 10 Feb. Victoria married her cousin Albert of Saxe-Coburg-Gotha (1819–61). The marriage was unpopular, and not until 1857 was Albert named prince consort, though Victoria's devotion to him already had made him de facto coruler.

1841

2ND PEEL MINISTRY. Melbourne's resignation, 28 Aug., brought in the 2nd Peel ministry, which included William

Gladstone (1809–98). Peel's budget of 1842 began the era of liberal budgets in England, and his 2nd Free Trade Budget, 1845, eliminated export duties.

1842–44

LABOR LEGISLATION. The Coal Mines Act, 5 July, 1842, prohibited women and boys under 10 from working underground, and the Factory Act, 22 Mar., 1844, fixed 6½ hours as the maximum workday for children, and 12 hours the maximum for women.

1846

ABOLITION OF THE CORN LAW. The National Anti-Corn Law League, founded 20 Mar., 1839, gained nationwide importance in 1841, when it began contesting elections. The struggle over the Corn Law split the Conservatives, with Peel supporting free trade and Benjamin Disraeli (1804–81) opposing it. Wellington induced the Lords to accept repeal of the laws, and on 26 June repeal was enacted. The Customs Law, passed at the same time, abolished livestock duties and duties on many manufactured goods.

FALL OF THE PEEL MINISTRY. Peel resigned, 29 June, and Lord Russell (1792–1878) replaced him, with Palmerston as foreign secretary.

1847–48

THE TEN HOURS' BILL. Passed on 17 May, 1847, this bill limited the workday for women and young persons aged 13–18 to 10 hours.

YOUNG IRELAND INSURRECTIONS. The Young Ireland Party, founded in 1840 by William O'Brien (1803–64), had become the principal Irish nationalist organization by 1847. The potato famine of the 1840's increased Irish discontent and culminated in the agrarian crimes of the autumn of 1847 and the unsuccessful Tipperary Insurrection, 29 July, 1848.

"KENNINGTON COMMON FIASCO." This abortive demonstration accompanied the presentation of the 3rd charter to Parliament in 1848. The 10 Apr. outbreak marked the end of Chartism.

1850

DON PACIFICO AFFAIR. Dissatisfaction with Palmerston's bellicose foreign policy came to a head with the Don Pacifico affair. Don Pacifico, a Portuguese Jew with British citizenship, pressed claims he had against the Greek government until, Dec. 1849, a mob attacked his house in Athens. Palmerston supported him by seizing Greek vessels at Piraeus, Jan. 1850, thus compelling Greece to recognize Don Pacifico's claims. Palmerston defended his actions before Parliament, 29 June, but he promised Victoria, 14 Aug., that henceforth he would not act without informing her.

1851–52

GREAT EXHIBITION. Held in Hyde Park, 1 May–15 Oct., 1851, and organized by Prince Albert, the Great Exhibition demonstrated Britain's technological achievements and industrial strength.

FALL OF PALMERSTON AND RUSSELL. Palmerston's precipitate approval of Louis Napoleon's coup d'état of 2 Dec., 1851, led Russell, who had long disapproved of Palmerston's foreign policy, to instruct the ambassador in Paris, 5 Dec., to withhold recognition of the new regime, thereby preparing the way for Palmerston's dismissal, 9 Dec. On 20 Feb., 1852, however, Palmerston brought about Russell's fall. Lord Stanley (later Lord Derby, 1799–1869) replaced him with a short-lived Conservative ministry that included Disraeli.

ABERDEEN MINISTRY. On 28 Dec., 1852, Lord Aberdeen (1784–1860) formed a coalition ministry that included Palmerston, Russell, and Gladstone.

1854–57

CRIMEAN WAR AND 1ST PALMERSTON MINISTRY. Britain entered the Crimean War on 28 Mar., 1854. Public dissatisfaction forced Aberdeen's resignation and Palmerston's accession to the prime ministership, 5 Feb., 1855. He soon faced the Sepoy Mutiny in India, 1857, and the war in China, 1856–57.

1858

2ND DERBY MINISTRY. After the Orsini bomb plot, which was planned in England, Palmerston introduced a bill increasing the penalty for conspiracy to murder. Its defeat brought about his resignation, 22 Feb., and the return of the Derby-Disraeli ministry, 25 Feb.

PARLIAMENTARY QUALIFICATIONS. Parliament discontinued property qualifications for its members, 15 June, and removed Jewish disabilities, 23 July.

1859

2ND PALMERSTON MINISTRY. On 18 June Palmerston replaced Derby with a Liberal ministry which included Gladstone. Political factionalism now stabilized into 2 camps, the Conservatives under Derby and Disraeli and the Liberals in alliance with the Radicals.

1860

COBDEN-CHEVALIER TREATY. Signed between Britain and France on 23 Jan., the treaty provided for mutual tariff reductions to encourage commerce and appeared to herald an era of free trade.

1861

THE "TRENT" AFFAIR. On 8 Nov., 2 Confederate envoys on the British steamer *Trent* were abducted by a Union naval vessel. Prince Albert modified Palmerston's strident ultimatum to the Union, thereby averting a crisis.

DEATH OF PRINCE ALBERT. On 14 Dec. Prince Albert died, and the bereaved Victoria withdrew from public life.

1865–66

2ND RUSSELL MINISTRY. Palmerston died, 18 Oct., 1865, and Russell, his successor, was beset with urgent demands for electoral reform. The Reform Act of 1832 notwithstanding, only 1 man in 6 could vote and electoral anomalies remained. On 26 June, 1866, Russell resigned after the defeat of his reform bill.

1867

2ND REFORM ACT. The 3rd Derby-Disraeli ministry took office, 6 July, 1866. It passed the 2nd Reform Act, 15 Aug., 1867, which doubled the electorate to 2 m. by extending the franchise to all householders paying the poor rate, to £10 lodgers in the boroughs, and to £5 land-owners and £12 occupying tenants in the counties. Boroughs of less than 10,000 received only 1 representative; Manchester, Birmingham, Leeds, and Liverpool were given 3; 9 new boroughs and 25 new county seats were created. The Scottish Reform Act, 13 July, 1868, extended similar reforms to Scotland, but the Irish Reform Act of that date merely reduced the borough franchise.

1868

1ST DISRAELI MINISTRY. On 29 Feb. Disraeli replaced Derby as prime minister, but on 9 Dec. Gladstone succeeded Disraeli after a Liberal victory in the Nov. elections.

1869–70

IRISH REFORMS. Gladstone attempted to pacify Ireland, where the Fenian Brotherhood, founded 1858, was fomenting revolution. The Disestablishment Act, 26 July, 1868, affected the Episcopal Church in Ireland as of 1 Jan., 1871. The Irish Land Act, 1 Aug., 1870, entitled tenants to compensation for unjust eviction and provided government loans to encourage peasant proprietorship, but failed to curb the landlords' rights to unimpeded disposal of their property, rent increases, and sudden eviction.

EDUCATION ACT. Passed on 9 Aug., 1870, this act attempted to end the chaos in English education. It continued the voluntary schools that were in good standing, but denied them funds from local rates. Board schools, controlled by locally elected school boards, were established. They obtained funds from government grants, parents' fees, and local rates. The most controversial feature of the act was the provision permitting religious education in voluntary schools only.

CIVIL SERVICE REFORM. An order

in council, 4 June, 1870, directed the use of competitive examinations, at the discretion of department heads, to fill posts in the government bureaucracy. (*Cont. p. 277.*)

The Growth of the United States, 1784–1877

THE BUILDING OF THE AMERICAN NATION

1784–85

TREASURY BOARD. On 28 May, 1784, a Treasury Board was established. Samuel Osgood, Walter Livingston, and Arthur Lee became commissioners. A Dutch loan enabled Robert Morris to resign, 1 Nov., leaving a $21,000 surplus despite the inefficient requisition system that had operated through much of the war.

MT. VERNON CONFERENCE. Commissioners from Virginia and Maryland met at Washington's home, settled certain mutual navigation problems, and advised their legislatures to adopt uniform imposts, currency, and commercial regulations, and to join with Pennsylvania in establishing water communications between the Chesapeake and the Ohio. Delegate Madison had Virginia request, 21 Jan., 1786, an interstate commercial convention at Annapolis, Sept.

JAY-GARDOQUI NEGOTIATIONS. Congress authorized Jay, 20 July, 1785, to negotiate with Spanish Minister Don Diego de Gardoqui on his country's rejection, 1784, of America's right to free navigation of the Mississippi. Both nations were adamant until Congress, 29 Aug., 1786, voted to defer pressing navigation rights in return for a favorable commercial treaty. Lacking the 9 votes necessary for treaty ratification, however, the talks broke down.

1786

RELIGIOUS FREEDOM. The Virginia Statute for Religious Freedom, based on Jefferson's draft of 1779, was adopted on 16 Jan. It ended compulsory church

support and attendance and discrimination based on religion.

TREATY WITH MOROCCO. Thomas Barclay gave $10,000 in gifts to the sultan of Morocco in exchange for a treaty, 28 June, protecting American shipping from the Barbary pirates. The U.S. made similar agreements with Algiers, 1795; Tripoli, 1796; and Tunis, 1797.

PROPOSALS TO REVISE THE ARTICLES. 7 Aug. Prodded by Charles Pinckney's (S.C.) motion, 3 May, Congress considered reorganizing the government. A committee advised, 7 Aug., congressional control of foreign and domestic commerce and improvement of the requisition system, but Congress never ventured to submit these recommendations for ratification.

ANNAPOLIS CONVENTION. 11–14 Sept. Called by Virginia, 21 Jan., this convention was attended by only 12 delegates from Delaware, New Jersey, New York, Pennsylvania, and Virginia. The other states failed to act or their representatives arrived too late. The delegates, led by John Dickinson (Del.), adopted, 14 Sept., Hamilton's call for another convention to render the Constitution adequate to the Union's needs. Congress cautiously approved, 21 Feb., 1787, a convention "for the sole and express purpose of revising the Articles."

SHAYS' REBELLION. Aug. 1786–Feb. 1787. Faced with foreclosures, debt-ridden Hampshire County (Mass.) farmers convened, 22–25 Aug., to denounce the government for their plight, and armed men closed the courts at Northampton, 31 Aug., and Worcester, 5 Sept. Daniel Shays' (1747–1825) band closed the Supreme Court at Springfield, 26 Sept., despite the presence of Gen. William Shepherd's militia sent there by Gov. James Bowdoin. After the capture of Job Shattuck, 30 Nov., ended the insurrection in the east, Shays still menaced the government in western Massachusetts. On 26 Dec. he marched to join Luke Day and attack Springfield's federal arsenal, but was routed by Shepherd's artillery, 25 Jan. Dispatched by the governor, Gen. Lincoln arrived in Springfield, 27 Jan., and pursued the insurgents. Day fled to New Hampshire, and Shays to Vermont after Lincoln had defeated him at Petersham, 4 Feb. The legislature eased taxes, made reforms, and pardoned all except Shays, Day, and 2 others. Shays was pardoned later, 13 June, 1788.

1787

OPENING OF CONSTITUTIONAL CONVENTION. The Constitutional Convention began 11 days late, with a quorum of 7 states. Only New Hampshire and Rhode Island had not appointed representatives; New Hampshire did so in June, but Rhode Island boycotted the convention. James Madison (1751–1836), who kept notes of the proceedings, and Mason (Va.), Gouverneur Morris and James Wilson (Pa.), Roger Sherman (Conn.), and Elbridge Gerry (Mass.) were the most active of the 55 delegates. Washington was president and William Jackson secretary of the convention, whose proceedings were secret.

VIRGINIA PLAN. 29 May. Edmund Randolph's (1753–1813) Virginia Plan envisioned a strong national government. Randolph desired that a popularly elected lower house select an upper house from nominees proposed by the state legislatures. Both houses would choose the executive, who, together with some judges, could veto legislation.

NEW JERSEY PLAN. William Paterson's New Jersey Plan, 15 June, reflected small states' opposition to Randolph's plan for apportioning both houses by population. He offered Congress the right to tax and regulate foreign and interstate commerce. The convention voted 7 to 3

basically to follow the nationalist Randolph, 19 June.

NORTHWEST ORDINANCE. 13 July. Based on a Jefferson plan, 23 Apr., 1784, and a committee report, 19 Sept., 1786, the Northwest Ordinance was adopted by Congress on 13 July. It affected the territory north of the Ohio. Congress would appoint a governor, secretary, and 3 judges; a legislature would be elected when there were 5,000 free adult male residents. Congress was eventually to create 3 to 5 states equal to the original 13. Slavery was outlawed and individual rights protected.

CONNECTICUT COMPROMISE. 16 July. Working from a proposal of 13 June by Roger Sherman (Conn.), the convention decided that each state would be represented in proportion to its population in the lower house, 12 July, and would have an equal vote in the Senate, 16 July.

FINAL STAGES. 6 Aug.–28 Sept. The convention debated a preliminary draft of the Constitution presented by a Committee of Detail, 6 Aug.–10 Sept., and appointed, 8 Sept., a Committee on Style and Arrangement (Hamilton, William Johnson, Rufus King, Madison, and Gouverneur Morris). Morris wrote the final draft presented on 12 Sept. It was approved by 12 states, 17 Sept., but Gerry (Mass.), Randolph (Va.), and Mason (Va.) refused to sign the document. Congress received the Constitution, 20 Sept., and submitted it for ratification by state conventions, 28 Sept.

"FEDERALIST PAPERS." 27 Oct. 1787–2 Apr. 1788. The "Federalist Papers," by Hamilton (1755–1804), Madison, and Jay, appeared in New York newspapers. These 77 essays, which supported ratification of the Constitution, appeared with 8 more in *The Federalist,* Mar.–May 1788.

1788

RATIFICATION OF THE CONSTITUTION. Delaware, 7 Dec.; Pennsylvania, 12 Dec.; and New Jersey, 18 Dec., had already ratified the Constitution the previous year. Georgia ratified on 2 Jan., and was followed by Connecticut, 9 Jan., and Massachusetts, 6 Feb. With Federalist (pro-Constitution) acquiescence, 30 Jan., Massachusetts proposed 9 amendments, including reserving to the states all powers not explicitly granted to the federal government.

Over Federalist objections, rural opponents of the Constitution submitted it to a popular referendum in Rhode Island, 24 Mar. Rhode Island decisively rejected it, but finally ratified on 29 May, 1790.

Maryland ratified on 28 Apr. and South Carolina on 23 May. New Hampshire, proposing 12 amendments, cast the 9th and deciding vote for ratification, 21 June.

Madison obtained Virginia's ratification on 25 June. Hamilton and Jay used New Hampshire's and Virginia's decisions to wrest control of the Poughkeepsie Convention from Governor Clinton's Antifederalists, and New York ratified on 26 July.

North Carolina withheld ratification until Congress' submission of a bill of rights, 25 Sept., 1789, prompted her to approve the Constitution on 21 Nov.

THE NEW GOVERNMENT. Congress made New York the capital on 13 Sept., and set dates for the appointment of presidential electors, 7 Jan., 1789; their balloting, 4 Feb.; and the 1st Congress, 4 Mar.

1789

GOVERNMENT IN OPERATION. Jan.–Apr. 69 Presidential electors, popularly chosen or appointed by the legislatures, 7 Jan., voted on 4 Feb. Lacking a quorum, Congress delayed opening; the House organized, 1 Apr., and the Senate counted the electoral ballots, 6 Apr. Washington was unanimously elected President, and John Adams (1735–1826) Vice-President. Adams having taken his seat, 21 Apr., New York Chancellor Robert R. Livingston (1746–1813) administered the oath of office to Washington at Federal Hall on 30 Apr.

BILL OF RIGHTS. 25 Sept. Federalist leaders and Washington were willing to add the constitutional amendments proposed by 5 state ratifying conventions. Prompted by Madison, 9 Sept., Congress submitted 12 of them for ratification, 25 Sept. The states ratified 10, which became the Bill of Rights of the Constitution, 15 Dec., 1791.

EXECUTIVE DEPARTMENTS. Congress appointed Henry Knox (1750–1806), 7 Aug.; Hamilton, 11 Sept.; and Jefferson, 26 Sept., as secretaries of war, the treasury, and state respectively. Samuel Osgood became postmaster general, 26 Sept., and Congress organized the Post Office, 8 May, 1795. Having established courts by the Federal Judiciary Act, 24 Sept., Congress, 26 Sept., made Jay chief justice and Randolph attorney general.

1790

HAMILTON'S FISCAL PROGRAM. A factor in the rise of parties, the financial proposals of Hamilton were announced in 3 messages to Congress. The Report on the Public Credit, 14 Jan., concerning the national and state debts, recommended funding the foreign ($11,710,378) and domestic ($44,414,085) debt at par, and assuming $21,500,000 of the states' $25,000,000 Revolutionary debt. These measures would revive the public credit and confidence in the government at home and abroad, and bind the creditor class to the federal government. Debtor and agrarian groups that had sold depreciated securities to speculators opposed funding the domestic debt. States, especially Virginia, which had paid their debts and feared an increase of federal power, had the House reject, 12 Apr., the assumption of state debts.

SECTIONAL COMPROMISE. Hamilton agreed with Jefferson and Madison, c. 20 June, to have Congress situate the national capital in the South in return for southern votes for assumption. Congress located the permanent capital along the Potomac, 10 July, and passed assumption, 26 July. Funding became law on 4 Aug. Southern fears were expressed by Patrick Henry when he attacked assumption, 16 Dec., as establishing a money interest, as inimical to agrarianism and republicanism, and beyond Congress' constitutional powers.

1791

BANK OF THE UNITED STATES. As requested by Hamilton in his report on banking, 13 Dec., 1790, the Bank of the U.S. was chartered on 25 Feb. Before signing the bill, Washington asked his cabinet's opinion on the constitutionality of a national bank. Jefferson argued against, 15 Feb.; Hamilton, 23 Feb., asserted the bank's constitutionality on the basis of the "implied powers" of the Constitution.

EMERGING POLITICAL ALIGNMENTS. Jefferson and Madison toured New York and New England, May–June, seeking aid, especially from the Clinton-Livingston-Burr faction, in establishing an Antifederalist coalition against Hamilton's fiscal program. Jefferson and his Democratic-Republicans believed in a democratic, agrarian society of broadly diffused wealth under popular, representative, decentralized government. Hamilton and his Federalists desired strong government by the elite which would produce a balanced, diversified economy by aiding manufacture and commerce. Jefferson's principles were expressed in Philip Freneau's antiadministration newspaper, the *National Gazette*, est. 31 Oct., and Hamilton's in John Fenno's *Gazette of the United States*, est. 15 Apr., 1789.

1792

RESISTANCE TO THE WHISKY TAX. 21 Aug.–29 Sept. As Hamilton requested, 13 Dec., 1790, Congress passed a revenue tax on distilled liquors, 3 Mar., 1791. At Pittsburgh, 21 Aug., Albert Gallatin (1761–1849) and incensed farmers who disposed of their surplus grain by distilling threatened legally to obstruct collection, but Washington pledged, 29 Sept., to enforce the excise.

JEFFERSON-HAMILTON FEUD. Attacked in the *National Gazette*, Hamilton anonymously asserted in Fenno's newspaper, July–Dec., that Jefferson was an Antifederalist intriguing against the administration's programs. Washington wrote to Jefferson, who was contemplating retirement, 23 Aug., and Hamilton, 26 Aug., but their replies, 9 Sept., revealed his failure to heal the rift.

1793

FRENCH REVOLUTION AND NEUTRALITY. 22 Apr. The French Revolution proved a divisive political issue. Jefferson and Hamilton, favoring France and Britain respectively, both desired neutrality, but the latter also wanted to repeal the 1778 treaties with France. Instead, Washington's Neutrality Proclamation, 22 Apr., declared Americans at peace with both Britain and France.

GENÊT AFFAIR. "Citizen" Edmond Charles Genêt (1763–1834), French Girondist minister to the U.S., arrived in Charleston, 8 Apr., and began commissioning privateers to prey on British vessels. Washington received him coolly, 18 May, and, through Jefferson, advised him, 5 June, that he had violated U.S. sovereignty, and ordered his ships to leave American waters. Instead, Genêt threatened to appeal directly to the people, and sent to sea the privateer *La Petite Démocrate*. Jefferson and Madison agreed that Genêt harmed the Antifederalists, and the cabinet decided, 2 Aug., to demand his recall. His Jacobin successor, Joseph Fauchet, sought to arrest Genêt, 1794, but Washington let him stay in the U.S.

JEFFERSON'S RESIGNATION. 31 Dec. Anglophobic Republicans sympathized with France, but Federalists feared her alleged atheism and anarchism. When Washington turned more toward Hamilton and his cohorts, Jefferson resigned, 31 July, effective 31 Dec. Edmund Randolph became secretary of state, 2 Jan., 1794.

1794

WHISKY INSURRECTION. The "Whisky Insurrection" resulted from enforcement of the excise. When western Pennsylvania farmers ignored his order, 7 Aug., to disperse, Washington dispatched, 24 Sept., Henry Lee, accompanied by Hamilton, with 15,000 militia. The rebellion was easily suppressed.

JAY'S TREATY. 19 Nov. Britain's retention of the Northwest posts, allowing her to control the fur trade and impede western settlement, and her orders in council, 8 June, 6 Nov., 1793, authorizing seizure of U.S. vessels and impressment of their crews, upset the Americans. Yet tariffs on British goods were vital to Hamilton's fiscal program, and so Washington, with Senate approval, 19 Apr., sent Jay to England to ameliorate the situation. By Jay's Treaty, 19 Nov., the British promised to leave the Northwest by 1 June, 1796, ended discrimination against American vessels in the British East Indies, and, provided Americans ceased carrying certain staples, opened the West Indies to American ships not exceeding 70 tons. The U.S. granted Britain most-favored-nation trade status, and the questions of illegal seizures and (to the distress of many, especially Virginians) pre-Revolutionary debts were referred to joint commissions. Articles written by "Camillus" (Hamilton) defended the treaty from attacks by Republicans, Southerners, and northern mercantile interests, and the Senate, dropping the West Indies provision (Art. XII), ratified it on 24 June, 1795.

1795

CABINET TAKE-OVER BY FEDERALISTS. Timothy Pickering became secretary of war, 2 Jan., and Oliver Wolcott, Jr., replaced Hamilton, who resigned, 31 Jan. Suspected of collaboration with the French against the Jay Treaty, Randolph resigned, 19 Aug., and Pickering succeeded him as secretary of state, James McHenry becoming secretary of war, 27 Jan., 1796.

TREATY OF SAN LORENZO (PINCKNEY TREATY) 27 Oct. After negotiating with Thomas Pinckney at Madrid, Spain recognized the U.S. boundaries established by the Treaty of Paris,

1783, and granted Americans free navigation of the Mississippi.

1796

WASHINGTON'S FAREWELL ADDRESS. 17 Sept. Written with the aid of Madison, 1792, and Hamilton, 1796, Washington's Farewell Address explained the President's refusal of a 3rd term; warned against parties, especially sectional ones; and advocated avoiding permanent foreign alliances.

PRESIDENTIAL ELECTION. 7 Dec. John Adams (Federalist) was elected President, and Thomas Jefferson (Democratic-Republican) Vice-President.

1797–99

XYZ AFFAIR. 18 Oct., 1797. Adams dispatched, 31 May, Charles Cotesworth Pinckney (1746–1825), John Marshall (1755–1835), and Elbridge Gerry (1744–1814) to improve deteriorating relations with France. In Paris, 3 agents (later called X, Y, and Z) of Talleyrand, the French foreign minister, demanded a loan to France and a $240,000 bribe, 18 Oct. Marshall rebuked them, 17 Jan., 1798, and Adams announced, 19 Mar., to outraged Americans the collapse of negotiations.

QUASI-WAR WITH FRANCE. 1798–1800. Opposing the prowar Federalist faction, Adams sought peace while having Congress act, 27 Mar.–17 July, 1798, to bolster American defenses. He appointed Benjamin Stoddert, 21 May, secretary of the new, 3 May, Navy Department and made Washington, 2 July, army commander. A 2-year undeclared naval war followed Congress' abrogation of the alliance treaties with France, 7 July, 1798.

ALIEN AND SEDITION ACTS. As relations with France worsened, the Alien and Sedition Acts were passed by the Federalists. The Naturalization Act, 18 June, 1798, raised the residency requirement to 14 years (repealed in 1802). The Alien Act, 25 June, authorized deportation of aliens suspected of treasonous activities (expired in 1802). The Alien Enemies Act, 6 July, authorized the banishment in wartime of subjects of enemy powers. The Sedition Act, 14 July, prohibited unlawful combinations to prevent execution of federal laws and false and malicious publications about the government (expired 3 Mar., 1801). All 10 persons convicted under the Sedition Act were Republican publicists, including James Thomas Callender and Matthew Lyon. Republican President Jefferson subsequently pardoned all, and Congress repaid their fines with interest.

KENTUCKY AND VIRGINIA RESOLUTIONS. These resolutions advocated the compact theory of government and denounced the Alien and Sedition Acts as unconstitutional. The Kentucky legislature's resolves, framed by Jefferson, claimed, 16 Nov., 1798, that each state could identify and redress federal usurpations of undelegated powers. Madison's Virginia declaration urged, 24 Dec., states to resist unconstitutional measures. When Northerners proclaimed the Supreme Court as arbiter of constitutionality, further Kentucky resolutions, 22 Nov., 1799, advocated state nullification of unconstitutional enactments.

FRIES' REBELLION. Feb. 1799. John Fries, opponent of the direct federal tax on property, raised a rebellion in Pennsylvania and was sentenced to death for treason, but pardoned by Adams.

On 14 Dec., 1799, George Washington died at Mt. Vernon.

1800–1801

CONVENTION OF 1800. When Talleyrand promised to receive respectfully a U.S. minister, Adams nominated, 18 Feb., 1799, William Vans Murray, who, with Oliver Ellsworth and William R. Davie, negotiated the Convention of 1800 (Treaty of Morfontaine, 30 Sept., 1800) releasing America from its French alliance. Discovering intrigue, Adams ousted prowar Hamiltonians from the cabinet. He requested McHenry's resignation, 6 May, 1800, and appointed John Marshall, 13 May, to replace the dismissed, 12 May, Pickering.

PRESIDENTIAL ELECTION. Federalists Adams and Charles C. Pinckney (S.C.) and Republicans Jefferson and Aaron Burr (1756–1836) (N.Y.) ran for President and Vice-President, 3 Dec., 1800. The Alien and Sedition Acts and British impressment tactics were key issues. Jefferson and Burr each obtained 73 electoral votes. The House, influenced by Hamilton, elected Jefferson President, 17 Feb., 1801. The 12th amendment (ratified 25 Sept., 1804) separated the balloting for President and Vice-President. Jefferson's conciliatory inaugural address, 4 Mar., 1801, stressed the need for limited government, states' rights, civil liberties, and peace. Innovating, he wrote his annual message (8 Dec.) instead of addressing Congress.

1802

JUDICIARY ACT. On 8 Mar. the Judiciary Act of 27 Feb., 1801, was repealed, and a Republican Judiciary Act, 29 Apr., 1802, again reorganized the courts.

FINANCIAL POLICY. Jefferson's policy of cutting taxes and spending reduced the national debt from $83 m. to $57 m. between 1802 and 1809.

1803

MARBURY v. MADISON. 24 Feb. Refusing William Marbury's request for a writ of mandamus against Madison, Chief Justice John Marshall (appointed 20 Jan., 1801), establishing a precedent, declared unconstitutional Congress's empowering, 1789, of the Supreme Court to issue such writs.

LOUISIANA PURCHASE. Napoleon's secret acquisition of Louisiana from Spain by the Treaty of San Ildefonso, 1 Oct., 1800, threatened American security and commerce. When Spain temporarily suspended, 16 Oct., 1802–19 Apr., 1803, the right of deposit at New Orleans, Jefferson sent James Monroe (1758–1831) 12 Jan., 1803, to Paris to help Robert R. Livingston negotiate an agreement on the use of the Mississippi. Napoleon, seeking funds for an impending war with Britain, had Talleyrand offer, 11 Apr., all Louisiana to the American negotiators, who, although authorized only to pay $10 m.

for New Orleans and West Florida, purchased the 820,000 sq. mi. between the Mississippi and the Rockies for $15 m., 2 May. For once Jefferson broadly interpreted the Constitution, which did not explicitly authorize acquiring foreign territory, and the Senate approved, 20 Oct.

LEWIS AND CLARK EXPEDITION. Meriwether Lewis (1774–1809) and William Clark (1770–1838) stimulated western settlement and commerce by their overland trek to the Pacific, 31 Aug., 1803–7 Nov., 1805, and return to St. Louis, 23 Sept., 1806.

1804

BURR-HAMILTON DUEL. Burr killed Hamilton in a duel, 11 July, after the latter's comments, 16 Feb., helped defeat him in the New York gubernatorial election, 25 Apr.

PRESIDENTIAL ELECTION. 5 Dec. Jefferson won re-election over Charles Cotesworth Pinckney, and Republican George Clinton defeated Rufus King for Vice-President.

1805–6

COMMERCE AND NEUTRAL RIGHTS. Britain's sea power enabled her to impress American seamen and seize neutral shipping trading with her enemy France. British Justice William Scott's "continuous voyage" decision in the *Essex* case, 23 July, 1805, reversed the "broken voyage" doctrine of the *Polly* case, 1800, which permitted American vessels to carry goods from the French West Indies to France provided they 1st passed through U.S. customs. Congress retaliated with the Nicholson Non-Importation Act, 18 Apr., 1806 (effective 15 Nov.), which Jefferson suspended from 19 Dec., 1806, to 22 Dec., 1808. Britain, 16 May, and France (Berlin Decree) 21 Nov., declared each other's European dominions blockaded.

MONROE-PINKNEY TREATY. 31 Dec., 1806. Monroe and William Pinkney, in London negotiations with Lord Holland, 27 Aug., obtained such an unfavorable agreement from the British on maritime policies that Jefferson dared not submit it for ratification.

ECONOMIC WARFARE. Britain forbade European coastal trade with France, 7 Jan., and required ships trading with the Continent to pass 1st through a British port, 11 Nov. Napoleon's Milan Decree, 17 Dec., ordered seizure of any ships complying with Britain's orders.

BURR'S "CONSPIRACY." 19 Feb.– 1 Sept. Burr's "conspiracy" either to separate treasonously the western states from the U.S. or to conquer Spanish territory was betrayed by his associate Gen. James Wilkinson (1757–1825) to Jefferson, who forbade anti-Spanish actions, 27 Nov., 1806. Burr, leading an expedition southwest from his accomplice Harman Blennerhassett's island in the Ohio, then fled. Captured in Alabama, 19 Feb., 1807, and indicted for treason, 24 June, Burr was acquitted in Richmond's Circuit Court by Marshall, who clarified America's treason law.

1807–9

"CHESAPEAKE"-"LEOPARD" AFFAIR. 22 June, 1807. Relations with Britain deteriorated sharply when fire from the *Leopard* caused 21 American casualties on the *Chesapeake,* whose commander had refused to surrender 4 alleged British deserters.

EMBARGO. Hoping to influence the belligerents by economic measures, Jefferson obtained an imprudent Embargo Act, 22 Dec., 1807, forbidding American vessels to leave for foreign ports. Britain received necessary supplies from South America and profited from the decline of the American carrying trade, while France, under the Bayonne Decree, 17 Apr., 1808, seized $10 m. in U.S. goods and ships. The Enforcement Act, 9 Jan., 1809, intended to counter increased smuggling, intensified the opposition of New England Federalists, eastern Republicans, and John Randolph's (Va.) dissident "Quids." Men like Governor Jonathan Trumbull (Conn., 23 Feb., 1809) and Timothy Pickering advocated nullification, but Federalist Massachusetts District Judge Davis upheld the embargo. Jefferson's Non-Intercourse Act, 1 Mar., reopened trade with all nations except England and France. Madison rescinded, 9 Aug., an order of 19 Apr. resuming trade with Britain when Foreign Secretary Canning disavowed British Minister Erskine's promise of repeal of the orders in council of 1807 which applied to the U.S.

SLAVE-TRADE PROHIBITION. The African slave trade was prohibited by Congress, 2 Mar., 1807, effective 1 Jan., 1808.

ELECTION. 7 Dec., 1808. James Madison defeated Federalist Charles Cotesworth Pinckney and anti-embargo eastern Republican George Clinton for the Presidency. Clinton defeated Rufus King for the Vice-Presidency.

1810

MACON'S BILL NO. 2. 1 May. This bill authorized a resumption of trade with England and France, stipulating that if either belligerent ameliorated its maritime policy before 3 Mar., 1811, the President could institute nonintercourse against the recalcitrant nation.

FRENCH ATTACKS ON U.S. TRADE. Napoleon decided, 5 Aug., to offer revocation of the Berlin and Milan decrees provided the U.S. declare nonintercourse with Britain. Foreign Minister Duc de Cadore informed the American Minister John Armstrong that the decrees had been suspended. Madison reopened trade with France, 2 Nov., and Congress sanctioned nonintercourse against Britain, 2 Mar., 1811. America's next minister to France, Joel Barlow, discovered that Napoleon had in fact not ceased his attacks on American commerce.

ANNEXATION OF WEST FLORIDA. 27 Oct. The annexation was announced by Madison after southern expansionists established an independent state, 26 Sept. Congress incorporated the region into the Mississippi Territory, 14 May, 1812, and the Peace of Ghent confirmed U.S. possession, 1814.

FLETCHER v. PECK. Marshall voided as a contract violation the Georgia legisla-

ture's rescinding, 1796, of its predecessor's fraudulent $500,000 sale to legislators and others of 35 m. acres in the Yazoo River area of Mississippi and Alabama.

1811

END OF 1ST BANK OF U.S. 4 Mar. Despite Treasury Secretary Gallatin's pleas, conservative "Old Republicans," Anglophobes upset by heavy English investment in the bank, and supporters of state banks defeated the rechartering of the U.S. Bank. In the House, 24 Jan., Clinton cast the deciding Senate vote against recharter, 20 Feb.

TECUMSEH. 31 July–8 Nov. Shawnee Chief Tecumseh's (1768?–1813) attempts to organize the Indians against white encroachment prompted fearful frontiersmen to request protection, 31 July. Leaving Vincennes, 26 Sept., Indiana Territorial Governor Gen. William H. Harrison (1773–1841) earned a costly victory at the Battle of Tippecanoe, 7 Nov., and razed the Indian capital, 8 Nov. British assistance to Tecumseh heightened animosity toward Britain.

"WAR HAWKS." 4 Nov. Americans elected several bellicose Republicans to the 12th Congress. Mostly Southerners and Westerners, they included Speaker Henry Clay (1777–1852) (Ky.) and Foreign Relations Committeemen John C. Calhoun (1782–1850) (S.C.), Felix Grundy (Tenn.), and Peter Porter (N.Y.). Dubbed "war hawks" by John Randolph, they were extremely conscious of the national honor and desired expansion toward Canada and the West. No "war hawk" himself, President Madison eventually supported their program.

1812

OUTBREAK OF THE WAR OF 1812. A 90-day general embargo became law, 4 Apr., and Congress authorized the President, 10 Apr., to call up 100,000 militia. When Foreign Secretary Lord Castlereagh reasserted Britain's refusal to withdraw her orders in council, Madison, claiming France had canceled the Berlin and Milan Decrees, drafted a war message.

Too late, 16 June, Britain terminated the orders. On 18 June Congress declared war on Britain, with maritime New England, New York, New Jersey, and Delaware dissenting. Madison's message, 1 June, mentioned impressment and violations of neutral rights as causes.

A 3-pronged drive against Canada, the main U.S. objective, fared badly. Gen. William Hull entered Canada, 12 July, but returned to Detroit, 8 Aug., and, fearing an Indian massacre of noncombatants, surrendered it to Gen. Brock, 16 Aug. Gen. Stephen Van Rensselaer's men occupying Queenstown Heights, 13 Oct., were crushed when New York militia refused to enter Canada to reinforce them. Gen. Henry Dearborn's attack from Plattsburg also collapsed, 19 Nov., when militiamen refused co-operation. The victories at sea, however, of the *Constitution,* 19 Aug., and *United States,* 25 Oct., over the *Guerrière* and *Macedonian* bolstered American morale.

ELECTION. 2 Dec. Madison was re-elected President over the Federalist candidate, antiwar Republican De Witt Clinton (N.Y.). Elbridge Gerry became Vice-President.

1813

BRITISH BLOCKADE. The British navy closed American ports by 1814 and harassed the seaboard. Although domestic manufacturing increased, the nation suffered severe economic hardships. The capture of 825 vessels by American privateers, 1814, had little retaliatory effect. On 1 June, Capt. P. V. B. Broke's *Shannon* captured Capt. James Lawrence's U.S. frigate *Chesapeake* near Boston.

LAKE ERIE. Gen. Harrison was commissioned, 17 Sept., 1812, to free Detroit, but British control of Lake Erie frustrated his efforts, 1813. In a bloody battle, 10 Sept., Capt. Oliver Perry's 10 vessels (55 guns) defeated Capt. Robert H. Barclay's 65-gun squadron, clearing the British from Lake Erie. His flagship *Lawrence* destroyed, Perry reported, "We have met the enemy and they are ours."

BATTLE OF THE THAMES. 5 Oct. Harrison defeated Gen. Henry A. Proc-

tor's men, who had fled Detroit. Tecumseh's death in this engagement ended the Indian menace.

ATTACK ON CANADA. Dearborn's troops raided, 27 Apr., York (Toronto), burned public buildings, and returned to Niagara, 8 May. Col. Winfield Scott (1786–1866) forced the British to abandon Fort George, 27 May, but Gen. Vincent defeated him at Stony Creek, 6 June.

Although War Secretary John Armstrong ordered him to assist Gen. Wilkinson in an attack on Montreal, Gen. Wade Hampton returned to Plattsburg after nearing Canada, 19 Sept. Learning this, Wilkinson, defeated near Chrysler's Farm, 11 Nov., established winter quarters, 13 Nov. Capturing Fts. George and Niagara, 18 Dec., the British burned Buffalo and Black Rock, 29–30 Dec.

PEACE PROPOSALS. 4 Nov. Castlereagh, rejecting Russian mediation, suggested direct peace talks. The Senate authorized J. Q. Adams, J. A. Bayard, Jonathan Russell, Clay, 18 Jan., 1814, and Gallatin, 8 Feb., to negotiate with Lord Gambier, Goulburn, and W. Adams.

1814

WAR EMBARGO. Madison obtained a war embargo, 17 Dec., 1813, to interdict New York and New England trade with the enemy. Recognizing their small value, Madison, 14 Apr., ended commercial restrictions.

CREEK WAR. War against the Creek Indians began with the Fort Mims (Ala.) massacre, 30 Aug., 1813. At Horseshoe Bend, 27 Mar., 1814, Gen. Andrew Jackson (1767–1845) subdued the Creeks, who signed the Treaty of Fort Jackson, 9 Aug. Harrison's Treaty of Greenville, 22 July, pacified the northwestern Indians.

NORTHERN CAMPAIGN. Following a military reorganization, Jan.–Feb., Gens. Jacob Brown and Winfield Scott, responsible for the Niagara sector, seized Fort Erie, 3 July. Scott crushed Gen. Sir Phineas Riall at Chippewa Plain, 5 July, and Brown fought Riall and Gen. Gordon Drummond to a draw at Lundy's Lane, 25 July. Lacking naval support from Commodore Chauncey, U.S. troops returned to Fort Erie and drove off Drummond's besiegers, 21 Sept. Erie's evacuation, 5 Nov., ended the drive on Canada.

Sir George Prevost drove south from Canada and halted below Plattsburg, 6 Sept., to await Capt. George Downie's supporting vessels. Capt. Thomas Macdonough destroyed Downie's fleet, 11 Sept., in the Battle of Lake Champlain, forcing Prevost to withdraw to Canada.

WASHINGTON AND BALTIMORE. 19–22 Aug. Sir Alexander Cochrane landed, 19 Aug., Gen. Robert Ross's 4,000 British veterans at Benedict on the Patuxent River. Ross routed Gen. William Winder at Bladensburg, 24 Aug., and proceeded to Washington, where the White House, Capitol, and other buildings were burned, 24–25 Aug., to avenge York. Madison, replacing Secretary of War Armstrong with Monroe, re-entered Washington, 27 Aug., after the British had embarked for Baltimore. There stout defenses stood off British attacks, 12–14 Sept., and the British sailed for Jamaica, 14 Oct.

NEW ORLEANS. When the British fleet with Sir Edward Packenham's troops approached New Orleans from Jamaica, Jackson hastened, 15 Dec., there from Baton Rouge. Fighting, 8 Jan., 1815, 2 weeks after the peace treaty, Jackson's men, suffering 21 casualties, inflicted 2,036 on the enemy, who re-embarked, 27 Jan.

PEACE OF GHENT. 24 Dec. The treaty ending the War of 1812 provided for a return to the *status quo* except that the U.S. retained West Florida taken from Spain. The numerous maritime issues which generated the conflict were not mentioned. The Senate ratified the treaty on 15 Feb., 1815.

NATIONALISM, SECTIONALISM, AND EXPANSIONISM

1815

MILITARY ESTABLISHMENT. On 27 Feb. Congress ordered the navy's gunboats sold and Great Lakes vessels decommissioned. The House, 3 Mar., limited the army to 10,000 men.

NORTH AFRICA TREATIES. 3 Mar.–5 Aug. Stephen Decatur's (1779–1820) fleet, commissioned by Congress, 3 Mar., to stop the Barbary pirates' seizures of American ships and seamen, successfully exacted treaties from Algiers, 30 June; Tunis, 26 July; and Tripoli, 5 Aug.

1816

2ND BANK OF U.S. 10 Apr. Wartime monetary chaos prompted Treasury Secretary Alexander Dallas to request a national bank with a $50 m. capitalization under which the President could suspend specie payments. Madison, who approved such a bank in his annual message, 5 Dec., 1815, vetoed an unsatisfactory congressional version, 20 Jan. Calhoun, with the support of Clay, who saw the bank as a fiscal necessity, proposed, 8 Jan., an institution like that desired by Dallas. Although Daniel Webster (1782–1852) (Mass.) opposed it, the national bank was established, 10 Apr., and opened 1 Jan., 1817. The government subscribed 1/5 of its $35 m. capitalization and appointed 5 of its 25 directors. Langdon Cheves, 1819, and Nicholas Biddle (1786–1844), 1822, succeeded in turn the incompetent 1st president, William Jones.

PRESIDENTIAL ELECTION. 4 Dec. Republican James Monroe (Va., 183 votes) crushed Federalist Rufus King (N.Y., 34 votes). Republican Daniel D. Tompkins (N.Y.) became Vice-President.

1817

BONUS BILL VETO. 3 Mar. Arguing from the Constitution's "general welfare" clause, Calhoun proposed, 4 Feb., that the government devote the $1.5 m. bonus paid by the 2nd U.S. Bank for its charter privileges and any dividends from the institution's stock to internal improvements to promote unity and security. Madison advocated such measures in his annual message, 3 Dec., 1816, but felt they required a constitutional amendment and therefore vetoed the bill, 3 Mar.

"ERA OF GOOD FEELINGS." This phrase, coined by Boston's *Columbian*

Centinel, 12 July, has inaccurately described Monroe's presidency, which was really a period of sharp factional politics and social change.

RUSH-BAGOT AGREEMENT. 28–29 Apr. Acting Secretary of State Richard Rush and British Minister to America Charles Bagot completed an agreement conceived by Madison and Castlereagh to limit the naval force their nations could deploy on waterways between the U.S. and Canada.

1818

SEMINOLE WAR. When conflict ensued with Indians and runaway Negroes after Americans had destroyed their refuge at Fort Apalachicola, Spanish Florida, on 27 July, 1816, Andrew Jackson proposed seizing Florida to Monroe ("Rhea Letter," 6 Jan.) . Without administration authorization, he captured St. Marks, 7 Apr., and Pensacola, 24 May, and executed Arbuthnot and Ambrister, Englishmen accused of aiding the enemy. The popular general escaped punishment despite denunciations by the House, 12 Jan., 1819; Senate, 24 Feb., 1819; and cabinet, except for Secretary of State John Quincy Adams (1767–1848) . Asserting that the U.S. acted in self-defense, Adams advised Spain to control Florida or cede it to America.

CONVENTION OF 1818. 20 Oct. This agreement established the 49th parallel as the northern U.S. boundary from Lake of the Woods to the Rockies, leaving unsettled the demarcation line west of the mountains.

1819

PANIC OF 1819. Financial panic, caused by inflation, speculation, and credit contraction due to Congress' demand, 1817, for specie payment resumption, resulted in debtor relief legislation and aroused resentment against the mismanaged National Bank.

ADAMS-ONÍS TREATY. Adams concluded a treaty (ratified 24 Feb.) with Spanish Minister Luis de Onís by which the U.S. surrendered its Texas claims,

and Spain East Florida and its claims to the Pacific Northwest. Final exchange of ratifications occurred 22 Feb., 1821.

DARTMOUTH COLLEGE CASE. 2 Feb. When the state court upheld the New Hampshire legislature's alteration, 1816, of Dartmouth College's 1769 charter, the trustees, with Webster as counsel, appealed to the Supreme Court. Marshall found for Dartmouth, stating that a private institution's charter was an inviolable contract under the Constitution.

M'CULLOCH v. MARYLAND. 6 Mar. Marshall upheld the constitutionality of the Bank of the U.S. and declared unconstitutional any state taxes on the bank.

1820

MISSOURI COMPROMISE. 3 Mar. The populous 11 free states controlled the House while the 11 southern slave states protected their interests with their equal Senate vote. The question of the admission of Missouri to the Union threatened this balance. The Senate rejected, 27 Feb., 1819, Representative James Tallmadge's (N.Y.) proposal, 13 Feb., prohibiting the introduction of more slaves into Missouri and providing that the children born of slaves in the state after its admission should become free at age 25. When Congress next met, the Senate accepted, 17 Feb., 1820, Jesse B. Thomas' (Ill.) amendment to admit Missouri with slavery while banning the institution in the Louisiana Purchase north of Arkansas's northern boundary (36° 30′) , and agreed to admit Maine as a free state, 18 Feb. Although it balked at first, the House enacted, 3 Mar., the compromise's provisions. Maine achieved statehood 15 Mar.

Antislavery congressmen disliked the Missouri Constitution's banning of free Negroes and mulattoes, 19 July. Clay's "2nd Missouri Compromise," 2 Mar., 1821, forbade Missouri's admission until its legislature guaranteed individual rights. Missouri agreed, 26 June, and became a state, 10 Aug.

SLAVE TRADE. On 15 May engaging in the African slave trade was declared piracy, and Americans importing slaves became subject to the death penalty.

1821

NEW YORK'S CONSTITUTIONAL CONVENTION. 28 Aug.–10 Nov. Despite objections by conservatives like Chancellor James Kent, the New York Constitutional Convention abolished property requirements for voting.

1822

CUMBERLAND ROAD BILL. This bill, which authorized road repairs and tolls, was vetoed by Monroe, 4 May, who believed an internal-improvement program required constitutional reform.

LATIN AMERICA. The House readily supported, 28 Mar., Monroe's proposal, 8 Mar., to recognize newly independent Spanish American republics, as Clay had proposed, 1818 and 1821. Recognition was quickly granted to Colombia, 19 June; Mexico, 12 Dec.; and other nations.

1823

RUSSIAN TERRITORIAL CLAIMS. After Adams had stated, 17 July, that the continent was closed to further European colonization, Russia, which claimed, 4 Sept., 1821, American territory south to 51°, agreed, 17 Apr., 1824, to a 54° 40' boundary.

MONROE DOCTRINE. 2 Dec. When France, a member of the Quadruple Alliance, which had promised to restore Fernando VII of Spain to full authority (Congress of Verona, Nov. 1822), refused to renounce territorial ambitions in Latin America, Britain felt concern for her commercial interests. Foreign Secretary Canning proposed joint Anglo-U.S. opposition to any allied intervention in Spanish America to the American Minister Richard Rush, who informed Washington. Jefferson and Madison advised Monroe to co-operate with Britain, but Adams, skeptical of British motives, preferred that the U.S. act alone. British interest waned when France renounced

(Polignac Agreement, 9 Oct.) all intentions to conquer or annex Spanish-American colonies, and Monroe followed Adams' advice. In his annual message, 2 Dec., Monroe declared that while the U.S. would not interfere with existing European colonies in America, it would view any further colonization attempts as a threat. Lacking the force of international law, the Monroe Doctrine received little contemporary attention, but later played a central role in shaping U.S. policy.

1824

"THE AMERICAN SYSTEM." 30–31 Mar. Clay proposed protective tariffs and internal improvements (the "American System") to make the U.S. more self-sufficient. Congress passed the General Survey Bill, 30 Apr., making possible surveys and estimates of roads and canals necessary for the national interest.

PRESIDENTIAL CAMPAIGN. The Tennessee legislature, 20 July, 1822, nominated Andrew Jackson; Kentucky named Clay, 18 Nov., 1822; and a Boston meeting selected J. Q. Adams, 15 Feb. Crawford, nominated by a congressional caucus of only 66 of 216 Republicans, was eliminated by a heart attack. "King Caucus" and the "American System" were important issues.

ELECTION. 1 Dec. Calhoun became Vice-President, but the House had to elect the President as Jackson received only a plurality (99) of the electoral votes. Supported by Clay, Adams won, 25 Feb., 1825. Jacksonian charges of a "corrupt bargain" gained credence when Clay became secretary of state.

1825

CIVIL SERVICE. Adams' refusal to oust incumbents from patronage jobs decreased his political leverage. Furthermore, these appointees often opposed his policies.

OPPOSITION. Adams' annual message, 6 Dec., supporting an extensive American System outraged states'-righters. Calhoun filled important Senate posts with anti-administration men, but Adams' New

England–West coalition retained the initiative over the divided Southerners.

1826

PANAMA DEBATE. When Adams nominated 2 delegates, 26 Dec., 1825, to attend a Panama Congress of Latin American nations in 1826 as consultants, Calhoun and Sen. Martin Van Buren (1782–1862) of New York attacked him for accepting the invitation from Colombia and Mexico without Senate approval, and argued that attendance would compromise U.S. sovereignty. The Senate nevertheless sanctioned the mission, but delegate Richard C. Anderson died en route, 24 July, and John Sargeant failed to arrive in time.

1827

CHANGES IN THE FRANCHISE. Democracy expanded as property, taxpaying, and religious qualifications for voting disappeared. The number of elective offices increased, and by 1828 the people rather than the legislatures chose presidential electors in all states except South Carolina and Delaware.

TARIFF DISPUTE. Calhoun's vote in the Senate defeated a bill (introduced 10 Jan.) seeking prohibitive duties on woolen goods to protect northeastern textile interests. The agricultural South opposed tariffs which raised the cost of manufactured items.

1828–29

TARIFF OF ABOMINATIONS. 19 May, 1828. Jacksonians, confident of southern loyalty to their leader, proposed, 31 Jan., a tariff which levied high duties on iron, hemp, and raw materials while neglecting woolens. They hoped New England, Adams' power base, would defeat the measure and alienate the vital Middle States. However, the bill, which accepted the protective principle, passed with New England support. Jacksonians of the western and Middle States voted for the tariff, thus depriving Adams of a party issue. South Carolina protested the tariff, 19 Dec., and Calhoun, now a sectionalist,

anonymously issued his *South Carolina Exposition and Protest* advocating nullification.

ELECTION OF JACKSON. Andrew Jackson, the frontier military hero, and Calhoun became the "democratic" candidates in a bitter personal contest against Adams and Richard Rush (Pa.), nominees of the "National Republicans." On 3 Dec. Jackson (178 votes) defeated Adams (83). Van Buren's "Albany Regency" won New York for Jackson. Calhoun remained Vice-President. Jackson's inaugural address, 4 Mar., 1829, pledged economy and states' rights. A group of his political friends (the "Kitchen Cabinet") advised Jackson until he organized a regular cabinet in 1831. Jackson increased significantly the use of patronage for party purposes (the "Spoils System"), but did not make wholesale political removals.

1830

WEBSTER-HAYNE DEBATE. 19–27 Jan. When Sen. Robert Y. Hayne (S.C.) attacked federal power, 19 Jan., Daniel Webster denounced southern indifference toward the Union. Hayne advocated nullification, 21, 25 Jan., but Webster defended the sovereignty of the national government and of the Constitution as interpreted by the courts, eloquently praising "Liberty *and* Union, now and forever, one and inseparable," 26, 27 Jan. Webster denied, 27 Jan., Hayne's contention that the Constitution was a compact between the states.

MAYSVILLE ROAD VETO. 27 May. Jackson, who doubted the constitutionality of federal internal improvements, vetoed a bill subscribing $150,000 to build the 60-mi. Maysville Road, lying entirely within the borders of Kentucky.

1831

JACKSONIAN DIPLOMACY. Jackson announced, 5 Oct., 1830, that the U.S. and Britain had agreed to reopen the West Indian trade (closed, 1826–1827). William C. Rives negotiated a treaty, 4 July, whereby France agreed to pay 25 m. francs in compensation for Napoleonic naval depredations, and the U.S. 1.5 m. francs for commercial violations of the Louisiana Treaty. After some difficulties, France began payments by May 1836.

ANTI-MASONIC PARTY. America's first 3rd party, the Anti-Masonic Party, emerged after revelations, 1827–31, that almost all New York officeholders and Jackson belonged to the secret Order of Freemasons.

ABOLITIONISM. William Lloyd Garrison (1805–79) began publishing *The Liberator,* 1 Jan., and founded the New England Antislavery Society, 1831, and the American Antislavery Society, 1833. He opposed political action and desired to end the union with the slaveholding states. Theodore Weld of Oberlin College (Ohio) and philanthropists Arthur and Lewis Tappan established the American and Foreign Antislavery Society, which broke with Garrison, 1840.

1832

INDIAN POLICY. Jackson refused to enforce Marshall's decision (*Worcester* v. *Georgia,* 3 Mar.) voiding a Georgia law requiring whites who settled land reserved by treaties for the Cherokee to swear allegiance to the state. He preferred to move Indians to areas west of the Mississippi. The Creeks, Choctaw, and Chickasaw moved, and the Cherokee submitted, 29 Dec., 1835. The Black Hawk, Apr.–Aug., and 2nd Seminole, Nov. 1835–Aug. 1843, wars resulted when some tribes balked.

NULLIFICATION. The protective nature of the lower 1832 tariff enabled a convention of South Carolina extremists, 24 Nov., to nullify the act. Jackson's "Proclamation to the People of South Carolina," 10 Dec., drafted by Secretary of State Livingston, asserted federal sovereignty and denounced the state's threatened secession as treason. Jackson requested, 16 Jan., 1833, authorization to use force to collect the revenue, and Calhoun, who resigned as Vice-President, 28 Dec., to enter the Senate, opposed it unsuccessfully. Jackson signed the Force Bill, 3 Mar., and a compromise tariff introduced by Clay, 13 Feb. South Caro-

lina ended the controversy by rescinding its nullification order, 15 Mar., but nullified the Force Bill, 18 Mar., to save face.

BANK VETO. 10 July. The effective U.S. Bank was disliked by debtors, state bankers, and states'-righters. When Jacksonian Sen. Thomas Hart Benton (Mo.) attacked the Bank, Feb. 1831, Clay advised President Biddle immediately to request a renewal of the charter due to expire in 1836. Arguing that the Supreme Court's position on the Bank's constitutionality did not bind the President, Jackson acted to strike against monopoly by vetoing recharter, 10 July.

PRESIDENTIAL ELECTION. The Anti-Masons nominated, 26 Sept., 1831, William Wirt (Md.) and Amos Ellmaker (Pa.); the National Republicans, 12 Dec., 1831, Clay and John Sergeant (Pa.); and the Democrats, 21–22 May, Jackson and Van Buren. The Bank was the overriding issue. On 5 Dec., 1832, Jackson was reelected (219 votes) over Clay (149) and Wirt (7). Van Buren became Vice-President.

JACKSON'S ATTACK ON THE BANK. Removal of the Bank's deposits became Jackson's goal. He appointed Attorney General Roger B. Taney secretary of the treasury, 23 Sept., replacing William Duane, who opposed removal. Taney announced, 26 Sept., that the government would cease deposits 1 Oct., and began placing the public funds in "pet" state banks. Jackson defended himself, 3 Dec., claiming that the Bank engaged in politics. Biddle had actively supported Clay in 1832 and was tightening credit to bring the administration to terms. The Senate adopted, 28 Mar., 1834, Clay's resolution of 26 Dec., 1833, censuring Jackson, and Benton's efforts to expunge it were unavailing until 16 Jan., 1837.

The Deposit Act, 23 June, 1836, required that a deposit bank be designated in each state, and distributed the $5 m. surplus among the states.

1834

WHIG PARTY. Led by Clay and Webster, the Whigs were an anti-Jackson coalition of National Republicans, pro-Bank former Democrats, and Anti-Masons. Many of Calhoun's nullifiers also joined.

1835

ABOLITIONIST MOVEMENT. Abolitionist propaganda prompted southern states to expel antislavery editors. Postmaster General Kendall condoned southern interception of antislavery propaganda, and Jackson advocated, 2 Dec., banning it from the mails. The Senate rejected Calhoun's bill authorizing postmasters to seize publications illegal in their states.

LOCO-FOCOS. 29 Oct. Successors of the New York Workingman's Party, the Loco-Focos nominated a primary slate. These radical urban Jacksonians opposed monopoly and privilege, and favored hard money, popular elections, free trade, and strict construction.

1836

TEXAS. Stephen F. Austin (1793–1836), carrying out his father Moses' plan, began American settlement in Texas, Aug. 1821. The Federal Republic of Mexico, which incorporated Texas as a state, 7 May, 1824, encouraged colonization, 24 Mar., 1825, but later outlawed slavery and further American settlement, 8 Apr., 1830. Relations worsened with Santa Anna's Centralist Party, and conventions of Texans renounced Mexican sovereignty, Oct.–Nov. 1835, and declared independence, 2 Mar. Santa Anna slaughtered 187 Texans under William B. Travis at the Alamo in San Antonio, 23 Feb.–6 Mar. Sam Houston (1793–1863) defeated and captured Santa Anna at San Jacinto, 21 Apr., and became president of the Texas Republic, 22 Oct. Congress rejected, 25 Aug., 1837, Texas' annexation request, 4 Aug., 1837.

SPECIE CIRCULAR. 11 July. On Jackson's order the Specie Circular was issued to arrest the inflation and land speculation sparked by excessive use of paper money. Requiring that gold or silver be used for purchasing public lands, it strained the pet depositories and undermined confidence in the state banks. Jackson pocket-vetoed, Mar. 1837, a measure rescinding the Circular, but repeal came by joint resolution, 21 May, 1838.

PRESIDENTIAL ELECTION. The Democrats nominated, 20 May, 1835, Van Buren and Richard M. Johnson (Ky.). Hoping to throw the election into the House, the opposition ran sectional favorites Webster, Harrison (Ohio), and Hugh L. White (Tenn.). On 7 Dec. Van Buren was elected (170 votes). No vice-presidential candidate having a majority, the Senate elected Johnson, 8 Feb., 1837.

1837

PANIC OF 1837. Reckless speculation caused New York banks and others to cease specie payments, 10 May. Cotton prices and land sales fell precipitously. Van Buren advocated, 5 Sept., specie currency and Treasury depositories independent of state banks.

ABOLITIONIST CONTROVERSY. Abolitionist petitions, 1836, against slavery in the District of Columbia inflamed southern congressmen. The Senate received the petitions, but automatically rejected them. The right of petition was ardently defended by former President J. Q. Adams, now a representative from Massachusetts. Henry L. Pinckney's (S.C.) special House committee recommended a "gag rule" (adopted 26 May, 1836) ordering antislavery memorials tabled. The House resolved it lacked jurisdiction over slavery in the states and declared interference with it in the capital inexpedient. The next session adopted, 19 Dec., a stricter gag rule after Representative William Slade (Vt.) presented more abolitionist petitions. Calhoun responded to Sen. Benjamin Swift's (Vt.) arguments against slavery extension, 19 Dec., by proposing, 27 Dec., 6 resolutions, several of which were adopted, including a confirmation of the compact theory of the Union and an attack on abolitionist efforts in Washington. Clay, seeking to dissociate the Whigs from the extremists, denounced abolitionism, 7 Feb., 1839. When Sen. Preston (S.C.) advised Clay that he might have antagonized northern Whigs, the Kentuckian retorted: "I had rather be right than President."

1838

U.S.–CANADIAN RELATIONS. Already existing tension between the U.S. and Canadian governments was aggravated by neutrality and border disputes. Canadians burned, 29 Dec., 1837, the *Caroline*, which American Anglophobes used to supply rebel William Lyon Mackenzie's post on the Niagara River's Navy Island, and both sides called up their militias. Gen. Winfield Scott arranged a truce, Mar. 1839, and no blood was shed in this "Aroostook War."

1840

INDEPENDENT TREASURY. 4 July. Clay and Webster opposed Van Buren's independent treasury plan, 5 Sept., 1837. The Senate approved it, 4 Oct., 1837, but the House rejected it, 25 June, 1838. Calhoun's supporters, opposing the Whigs' nationalism, rejoined the Democrats, and the subtreasury bill, requiring the government to take care of its own funds, passed the 26th Congress, 1840.

PRESIDENTIAL ELECTION. Rejecting the controversial Clay, the Whigs' Harrisburg Convention, 4 Dec., 1839, nominated William H. Harrison (Ohio), a popular military hero without political qualifications or enemies, for President and states' rights adherent John Tyler (1790–1862) for Vice-President. The Democrats renominated Van Buren, 5 May. In its use of slogans, emblems, and rallies, the 1840 campaign set the style of later presidential campaigns. The Whigs exploited a derisive remark in the Democrats' Baltimore *Republican*, 23 Mar., associating Harrison with log cabins and hard cider, to portray their candidate as a man of the people. On 2 Dec. Harrison was elected (234 votes) over Van Buren (60). Tyler became Vice-President. On 4

Apr., 1841, Harrison died of pneumonia, and the "old Republican" Tyler became the first Vice-President to succeed to the presidency.

1841

INDEPENDENT TREASURY ACT. On 13 Aug. the Whigs repealed the Independent Treasury Act, as Clay requested, 7 June, preliminary to establishing another national bank.

BANK VETOES. 16 Aug., 9 Sept. Tyler vetoed, 16 Aug., a Whig bill to establish a "Fiscal Bank of the U.S.," and also rejected, 9 Sept., a modified version which omitted his stipulation that the bank obtain permission from a state before establishing a branch there.

CABINET RESIGNATIONS. 11 Sept. Every cabinet member except Webster resigned to protest Tyler's bank vetoes. Frequent cabinet changes characterized Tyler's presidency. Calhoun's appointment as secretary of state, 6 Mar., 1844, replacing the deceased Abel Upshur, marked the ascendancy of the South in the Democratic Party.

1842

WEBSTER-ASHBURTON TREATY. 9 Aug. Negotiated by Webster and Sir Robert Peel's envoy, Alexander Baring, Lord Ashburton, this treaty gave the U.S. 7,000 of the 12,000-sq.-mi. disputed region between Maine and New Brunswick, navigation of the St. John's River, other boundary concessions, and an informal apology for the *Caroline* incident. The Senate ratified on 20 Aug.

DORR'S REBELLION. Rhode Island severely restricted the suffrage. Dissidents framed, Oct. 1841, a People's Constitution providing white manhood suffrage, and elected, 18 Apr., Thomas W. Dorr (1805–54) their governor. Having unsuccessfully attacked the state arsenal, 18 May, Dorr was sentenced to life imprisonment by Samuel W. King's legal government, 25 June, 1844, but received a pardon in 1845. A new constitution, Apr. 1843, liberalized the suffrage.

1843

NATIVISM. Anti-Catholicism and heavy Irish immigration prompted formation of the American Republican Party in New York, June, and Philadelphia, Apr. 1845, and a national Native American Party, July 1845. Often supporting Whigs, they opposed voting and office-holding privileges for Catholics and foreigners.

1844

OREGON DISPUTE. The Convention of 1818, renewed 6 Aug., 1827, provided for joint occupation west of the Rockies between 42° and 54° 40′ N. The U.S. based its claims partially on Capt. Robert Gray's discovery of the Columbia River, 1792, and the presence of American settlers in the Willamette Valley; Britain on voyages by Cook, 1778, Vancouver, 1792, and Mackenzie, 1793. Desiring the Columbia River area, Britain rejected U.S. offers to fix the boundary at 49°. Tension mounted as American settlers adopted a provisional government, 5 July, 1843, and petitioned Congress for territorial status.

TEXAS. When abolitionist forces prevented U.S. annexation of slaveholding Texas, President Mirabeau B. Lamar (1798–1859) led the republic along an independent course. The U.S., upset by Texas' close relations with Britain and France, told Texan Minister Isaac Van Zandt, 16 Oct., 1843, that it desired to reopen annexation discussions despite Santa Anna's bellicose warnings, 23 Aug., 1843. Sam Houston, president since Dec. 1841, fearing the loss of British support, held off until Secretary of State Upshur gave assurances, 16 Jan., of Senate acceptance of annexation. Houston accepted annexation provided the U.S. defend Texas against Mexican attack, and Secretary of State Calhoun signed the agreement, 12 Apr. Calhoun's note, 18 Apr., defending slavery and Tyler's remark, 22 Apr., that annexation would protect the institution impelled northern senators to reject the treaty, 8 June.

PRESIDENTIAL CAMPAIGN. Denouncing any extension of slavery, the Liberty Party nominated, 30 Aug., 1843, James G. Birney and Thomas Morris (Ohio). Silent on Texas, the Whigs selected Clay and Theodore Freylinghuysen (N.J.) on 1 May. The Democrats chose, 29 May, James K. Polk (1795–1849) (Tenn.), whom Jackson supported over Van Buren for President. George M. Dallas (Pa.) received the vice-presidential designation after antislavery Van Burenite Silas Wright declined it. Robert J. Walker (Miss.) formulated the platform, which demanded reoccupation of Oregon and reannexation of Texas. On 4 Dec. Polk was elected. Birney's incursions cost Clay New York and the election.

1845

ANNEXATION OF TEXAS. 1 Mar. Tyler requested, 2 Dec., 1844, the annexation of Texas by a joint resolution, which, unlike a treaty, required only a majority in both houses and the President's signature. The Senate, 27 Feb., and House, 28 Feb., complied, extending the 36° 30′ compromise line to include Texas, and offering her admission. Texans ratified, 13 Oct., a convention's acceptance, 4 July, and entered the Union, 29 Dec.

ANTIRENT WAR. 1839–46. Agrarian uprisings in New York like the "Helderberg War," 1839–40, resulted from dissatisfaction with perpetual leases. The introduction of fee-simple tenure under the 1846 constitution ameliorated the situation.

POLK DOCTRINE. 2 Dec. Reinforcing the Monroe Doctrine, the Polk Doctrine forbade European interference in the American continent's affairs, including U.S. annexations.

"MANIFEST DESTINY." This rallying cry for U.S. continental domination 1st appeared in John L. O'Sullivan's *United States Magazine and Democratic Review*, July–Aug.

BREAK WITH MEXICO. Mexico suspended relations with the U.S., 28 Mar., and prepared to resist annexation. Gen.

Zachary Taylor (1784–1850) was ordered into Texas, 15 June, and established a defensive position at the Nueces, 31 July, which the Mexicans claimed was the Texas boundary. Ordered forward by Washington, 13 Jan., 1846, Taylor arrived at the Rio Grande, 24 Mar., claimed by Texans as their border. Taylor rejected Gen. Pedro de Ampudia's demand, 12 Apr., that he withdraw to the Nueces.

SLIDELL MISSION. When Foreign Minister Manuel de Peña y Peña said, 15 Oct., that Mexico would negotiate the Texas boundary, Polk dispatched John Slidell with instructions, 10 Nov., to offer $5 m. for New Mexico and $25 m. for California in return for a Rio Grande settlement. Unfavorable public opinion forced President José J. Herrera to decline to receive Slidell, 16 Dec. Learning this, Washington ordered Taylor to the Rio Grande, 13 Jan., 1846. Gen. Mariano Paredes, who overthrew Herrera, 31 Dec., pledged to defend Mexican territory and refused to receive Slidell, 12 Mar., who then returned home.

1846

OREGON SETTLEMENT. 15 June. On 21 May, Polk gave the British the 1-year notice of termination of joint occupation of Oregon required by the renewed Convention of 1818. The U.S. refused to repeat its 49th-parallel compromise offer, but promised to resume negotiations if Britain took the initiative. When Lord Aberdeen, foreign secretary in the conciliatory Lord Russell ministry, submitted a draft treaty locating the border at 49°, Polk presented it to the Senate, 10 June, which ratified it, 15 June.

INDEPENDENT TREASURY ACT. This act, repealed in 1841, was repassed by the Democratic Congress on 6 Aug.

OUTBREAK OF MEXICAN WAR. Gen. Mariano Arista informed Taylor, 24 Apr., that he considered hostilities as having begun. When Mexican cavalry crossed the Rio Grande and attacked an American reconnaissance unit, 25 Apr., Taylor reported, 26 Apr., the start of hostilities.

Polk requested, 11 May, a declaration of war against Mexico, which he charged had "shed American blood on the American soil," and Congress complied, 13 May. Whig opposition to a military appropriation bill foreshadowed their increasing hostility to the administration.

COURSE OF THE WAR. While suffering very light losses, Taylor's 2,300 troops inflicted some 350 casualties on Arista's 6,000-man force at Palo Alto, 8 May, and over 700 at Resaca de la Palma, 9 May. The 36,000-man Mexican army was poorly equipped and commanded. Inadequate communications and sanitation hindered the 100,000 American soldiers, whose generals could not work harmoniously together or with the administration. Many future Civil War commanders, however (e.g., Grant and Lee), saw action. Stephen W. Kearny was ordered to occupy New Mexico and California, and Winfield Scott to attack Veracruz and seize Mexico City.

Santa Anna became president of Mexico on 6 Dec.

CALIFORNIA. Polk ordered, 17 Oct., 1845, American Consul Thomas O. Larkin secretly to encourage Californians to enter the Union. When American settlers under William B. Ide declared their independence, 14 June, Capt. John C. Frémont (1813–90), who received still mysterious instructions, 9 May, supported this "Bear Flag Revolt" and became leader of the California Republic, 5 July. Commodore Robert F. Stockton, replacing the ill John D. Sloat, who raised the flag at Monterey, 7 July, seized Los Angeles, annexed California, 17 Aug., and declared himself governor. However, José María Flores recaptured California south of San Luis Obispo, 22–30 Sept.

Reaching Las Vegas, 15 Aug., Kearny annexed New Mexico. He took Sante Fe, 18 Aug., and defeated, 6 Dec., Mexicans at San Pascual, Calif. Stockton and Kearny took Los Angeles, 10 Jan., 1847, and the remaining Mexicans capitulated by the Treaty of Cahuenga, 13 Jan., 1847.

WILMOT PROVISO. 8 Aug. David Wilmot (Pa.) proposed banning slavery from territory acquired from Mexico. The

House added, 15 Feb., 1847, the proviso to the "$3 m. Bill" appropriating money for negotiations with Mexico, but the Senate rejected it, 1 Mar., 1847. Attacking the Proviso, Calhoun asserted, 19 Feb., 1847, that Congress, the agent of the states, could not interfere with slavery or prevent slave states from sharing in U.S. territorial acquisitions.

MONTERREY. 25 Sept. Taylor began ascending the Rio Grande, 6 July, and proceeded to Monterrey. While Gen. William North captured, 21–22 Sept., Federation and Independence Hills, the western approaches, Taylor entered the city, 21 Sept. The Mexicans, who suffered 367 casualties against the Americans' 488, surrendered, 25 Sept.

1847

DONIPHAN'S EXPEDITION. Col. Alexander W. Doniphan left Santa Fe, Oct. 1846, and entered Chihuahua, 1 Mar., having lost 1 man while killing 300 at the Battle of the Sacramento, 28 Feb.

BATTLE OF BUENA VISTA. 22–23 Feb. Violating Scott's order, 3 Jan., to remain on the defensive, Taylor advanced to a position near Buena Vista, 21 Feb. His defeat of Santa Anna's 15,000 troops, who suffered 1,500 casualties, ended hostilities in northern Mexico.

VERACRUZ. 22–27 Mar. Gen. Scott arrived at Tampico, 18 Feb., to prepare the U.S. expedition against Veracruz. His 10,000 troops and Commo. Conner's fleet bombarded the city, 22 Mar., forcing the Mexicans to surrender, 27 Mar. American losses totaled 82; Mexican, c. 180.

INLAND CAMPAIGN. 18 Apr.–6 Sept. Driving inland, Scott's 9,000 troops defeated Santa Anna's 13,000 at Cerro Gordo, 18 Apr., capturing 204 officers and 2,837 men. Reinforced by Gen. Franklin Pierce (1804–69) at Puebla, 6 Aug., Scott inflicted over 7,000 Mexican casualties at Contreras and Churubusco, 19–20 Aug., and then granted an armistice, 24 Aug., to allow peace discussions. Chief State Department Clerk Nicholas P. Trist, dispatched by Polk, 15 Apr., negotiated unsuccessfully with a Mexican peace commission headed by ex-President Herrera, 27 Aug.–6 Sept.

MEXICO CITY. 8–14 Sept. Gen. Worth killed or wounded c. 2,000 Mexicans at the Battle of Molina del Rey, 8 Sept., and Gens. John A. Quitman and Gideon J. Pillow routed 5,000 at Chapultepec, 13 Sept. Scott entered the capital by night, 13–14 Sept. President Pedro María Anaya requested negotiations, 22 Nov., with Trist despite the fact that Polk had recalled him, 16 Nov.

1848

DISCOVERY OF GOLD. 24 Jan. James W. Marshall's gold find on Johann Augustus Sutter's land in the lower Sacramento Valley started the California gold rush.

TREATY OF GUADALUPE HIDALGO. 2 Feb. The U.S. obtained Texas with the Rio Grande as boundary, New Mexico, and California, a total of 1,193,061 sq. mi. The Senate, over the objections of those who wanted to annex Mexico, ratified it, 10 Mar., after rejecting a motion to add the Wilmot Proviso. Mexico ratified 25 May. 1,721 Americans had died of wounds and 11,155 of disease.

OREGON TERRITORIAL ORGANIZATION. 14 Aug. When Sen. Jesse Bright (Ind.) proposed extending the 36° 30' Compromise to the Pacific, Calhoun denied, 27 June, congressional jurisdiction over slavery in the territories. The House tabled, 28 July, Sen. John M. Clayton's (Md.) Compromise, which validated Oregon's provisional law against slavery and forbade New Mexico and California to legislate on the institution, and organized Oregon without slavery, 2 Aug. The Senate concurred, 13 Aug., and Polk signed, 14 Aug.

PRESIDENTIAL ELECTION. When Polk declined renomination, the Democrats selected, 22 May, Lewis Cass (Mich.), who supported local determination of the status of slavery ("squatter sovereignty"), and Gen. William O. Butler (Ky.), and expressed opposition to congressional interference with slavery in the states. The Whigs chose the Mexican War hero

Gen. Zachary Taylor and Millard Fill-more (1800–74), 7 June. New York's Barnburners bolted the Democratic con-vention and, joining with the Liberty Party and New England's "Conscience Whigs," nominated, 9 Aug., Martin Van Buren and Charles Francis Adams (1807–86) (Mass.) as candidates of the Free-Soil Party. Supporting the Wilmot Proviso, the party advocated "Free soil, free speech, free labor, and free men." On 7 Nov. Taylor was elected (163 votes) over Cass (123). Van Buren's large vote in New York contributed much to Cass's defeat.

1849

"ADDRESS OF THE SOUTHERN DELEGATES." 22 Jan. Issued by Cal-houn on behalf of southern congressmen, the address denounced northern enact-ments against slavery expansion.

CALIFORNIA AND NEW MEXICO. The slavery issue prevented Polk from getting California and New Mexico or-ganized. A California convention, 1 Sept.–13 Oct., adopted an antislavery constitu-tion which the citizens ratified, 13 Nov. With Taylor's support California applied for admission, 12 Mar., 1850. Its petition threatened the existing balance of 15 free and 15 slave states.

1850

COMPROMISE OF 1850. 29 Jan.–20 Sept. To ease sectional animosities, Clay urged, 29 Jan., California's admission as a free state and New Mexico's organization without restrictions on slavery. He pleaded for mutual concessions by North and South, 5–6 Feb., but the dying Calhoun, speaking through James M. Mason (Va.), demanded, 4 Mar., an equal share of the territories for the South and an amendment restoring the equilibrium between the sections. Daniel Webster spoke eloquently, 7 Mar., for the Union, arguing that the geography of the terri-tories made congressional legislation to preclude slavery unnecessary. William H. Seward (1801–72, N.Y.) condemned, 11 Mar., any compromise with slavery.

With the support of Fillmore, who suc-ceeded to the presidency upon Taylor's death, 9 July, Clay and Stephen A. Douglas (1813–61, Ill.) pushed through Congress a bill ending the slave trade in the District of Columbia, 20 Sept., and an "Omnibus Bill" on the territories. Cali-fornia was admitted as a free state, 9 Sept., and New Mexico and Utah, carved from the rest of the acquired Mexican territory, were authorized, 9 Sept., to establish their own positions on slavery ("popular sovereignty"). A Fugitive Slave Act was passed, 18 Sept., authorizing special U.S. commissioners, after a sum-mary hearing at which the claimant's affidavit was adequate proof of owner-ship, to issue certificates returning run-away slaves. A commissioner received $10 if he issued a warrant, but only $5 if he refused. Those who aided fugitive slaves were made liable to imprisonment and a $1,000 fine.

CLAYTON-BULWER TREATY. 19 Apr. British establishment of a protecto-rate over Central America's Mosquito Coast and seizure from Nicaragua, Jan. 1848, of the San Juan River area threat-ened U.S. plans for an isthmian canal. Tensions eased when Secretary of State John M. Clayton and British minister Henry Lytton Bulwer negotiated a treaty providing that any isthmian canal would be neutral, not exclusively controlled, and open equally to citizens of both nations.

NASHVILLE CONVENTION. 10 June. Rejecting extremist Robert Barn-well Rhett's (S.C.) secessionist views, 9 slave states convening at Nashville re-quested only the extension of the Mis-souri Compromise line to the Pacific.

GEORGIA PLATFORM. 13–14 Sept. Georgia's state convention expressed southern Unionists' acceptance of the 1850 Compromise but threatened seces-sion if Congress interfered with the inter-state slave trade or fugitive-slave legis-lation.

HÜLSEMANN LETTER. 21 Dec. When Austria protested the Taylor ad-ministration's sympathetic assurances to Hungarian rebels, Secretary Webster wrote to Austrian chargé Chevalier Hül-semann defending U.S. interest in European revolutions based on the principles of the American Revolution.

1851

LÓPEZ FILIBUSTERING EXPEDITIONS. Southern annexationists aided refugee Gen. Narciso López' attempts to overthrow Cuba's Spanish government. Cuban authorities executed, 13 Aug., López and 50 Southerners at Havana after his 3rd filibustering venture failed to spark a popular revolution.

1852

"UNCLE TOM'S CABIN." Harriet Beecher Stowe's novel, a devastating and emotional attack on slavery, was published, 20 Mar.

PRESIDENTIAL ELECTION. The Democrats nominated, 1 June, Franklin Pierce (N.H.) and William R. King (Ala.), and the Whigs, 16 June, Winfield Scott and William A. Graham (N.C.). Both parties praised the 1850 Compromise, but the Free-Soilers, who selected, 11 Aug., John P. Hale (N.H.) and George W. Julian (Ind.), condemned it. Pierce was elected, 2 Nov., by 254 votes over the candidates of the declining Whig (42) and Free-Soil parties.

1853

GADSDEN PURCHASE. 30 Dec. James Gadsden obtained Mexican cession of 29,640 sq. mi. in present-day southern New Mexico and Arizona.

1854

KANSAS-NEBRASKA ACT. 30 May. Proposed by Sen. Stephen A. Douglas (Ill.), the act organized these territories on the basis of popular sovereignty, thus voiding the 1820 Compromise. Several factors may have influenced Douglas: belief in self-government and that geography prohibited slavery's expansion, desire for southern support for his presiden-

tial ambitions, and the need to stimulate western settlement to promote the building of a transcontinental railroad west from Chicago.

MASSACHUSETTS' EMIGRANT AID SOCIETY. 26 Apr. Founded by Eli Thayer, the society brought 2,000 antislavery settlers to Kansas by 1857 to guarantee that it would become a free state. Its methods were imitated by proslavery groups from Missouri.

FOUNDING OF THE REPUBLICAN PARTY. The Republican Party was founded at a Ripon, Wis., convention, 28 Feb., of Whigs, Free-Soilers, and Democrats opposed to the Kansas-Nebraska Act. Throughout the North and West, men demanded the repeal of the Kansas-Nebraska and Fugitive Slave Acts.

KNOW-NOTHING PARTY. The Know-Nothing, or American, Party, feeding on anti-Catholic and anti-immigrant sentiment, achieved its peak in 1854–55. The members split over slavery and many became Republicans.

OSTEND MANIFESTO. 18 Oct. Advocating the acquisition of Cuba by purchase or force as necessary for the protection of slavery, the Ostend Manifesto resulted from a meeting of Pierre Soulé, John Y. Mason, and James Buchanan, U.S. ministers to Spain, France, and Britain respectively. Although Secretary of State Marcy disowned the manifesto, the Republicans used it to show that the administration supported slavery extension.

1855

"KANSAS QUESTION." Proslavery and antislavery groups battled to control Kansas' territorial government. Intimidation by armed Missouri "Border Ruffians" resulted in the election of a proslavery territorial delegate, John W. Whitfield, 29 Nov., 1854, and legislature, 30 Mar. Proslavery forces replaced Gov. Andrew H. Reeder, appointed June 1854, with Wilson Shannon, 31 July. Antislavery Kansans formed, Sept.–Oct., a Free State Party; elected Reeder territorial delegate, 9 Oct.; framed the Topeka Constitution excluding Negroes from the territory, 23

Oct.–2 Nov.; and elected a separate governor and legislature, 15 Jan., 1856.

NICARAGUA FILIBUSTERING EXPEDITION. American adventurer William Walker, supported by the Accessory Transit Co., which had interests in the isthmus, seized control of Nicaragua during a civil war, June–Oct. 1855. Walker opened the area to slavery, but neighboring republics, encouraged by Cornelius Vanderbilt, who took over Accessory Transit, ousted him, 1857.

1856

"BLEEDING KANSAS." President Pierce's denunciation, 24 Jan., of the Topeka government disclosed his support of the proslavery forces. Civil war flared in the spring as proslavery Kansans and Border Ruffians outraged northern opinion by pillaging the Free State town of Lawrence. The fanatical John Brown (1800–1859), in an act disowned by antislavery Kansans, retaliated by executing 5 proslavery Kansans in a midnight raid near Pottawatomie Creek, 24–25 May. Peace temporarily returned when Gov. John W. Geary (Pa.) prevented an attack on Lawrence by 2,500 Border Ruffians.

Congress failed to act before adjournment on Kansas' application for statehood, 4 Mar. The House never considered Sen. Robert Toombs's (Ga.) measure, 2 July, requesting free elections for a Kansas constitutional convention. The Senate rejected a House proposal, 3 July, to admit Kansas under the Topeka constitution. Southerners praised and Northerners decried Rep. Preston S. Brooks's (S.C.) assault, 22 May, on Sen. Charles Sumner (1811–74, Mass.) for remarks the latter made about his uncle, Sen. Andrew P. Butler (S.C.), in an antislavery speech on Kansas, 19–20 May. Sumner was disabled until Dec. 1859.

PRESIDENTIAL ELECTION. The nativist American (Know-Nothing) Party, 22 Feb., and the Whigs, 17 Sept., nominated Millard Fillmore (N.Y.) and Andrew J. Donelson (Tenn.). The Democrats selected, 2 June, James Buchanan (1791–1868) (Pa.) and John C. Breckinridge (Ky.), and the Republicans John C.

Frémont (Calif.) and William L. Dayton (N.J.). "Bleeding Kansas" was the chief issue. On 4 Nov. Buchanan was elected (174 votes) over Frémont (114) and Fillmore (8).

1857

DRED SCOTT DECISION. 6 Mar. Negro slave Dred Scott began suit for his freedom in 1846, basing his claim on his residence between 1834 and 1838 in areas where the Missouri Compromise prohibited involuntary servitude. When the case reached the Supreme Court, Chief Justice Roger B. Taney (1777–1864) and the majority found (*Dred Scott* v. *Sandford*) that (1) slaves were not citizens and could not sue in federal courts; (2) Scott's status was his legal one in the state wherein he resided when he brought suit (Mo.); and (3) the Missouri Compromise unconstitutionally deprived people of their property. This was the first time since *Marbury* v. *Madison* (1803) that the Court declared a congressional act unconstitutional. Northern reaction was highly unfavorable.

LECOMPTON CONSTITUTION. 19 Oct.–21 Dec. The proslavery legislature meeting at Lecompton, Jan.–Feb., called a 15 June election for a constitutional convention. The Free State victory in the election for the legislature, 5 Oct., demonstrated that a proslavery constitution would not be ratified, so the convention, 19 Oct.–8 Nov., limited the people's choice either to vote for slavery or to forbid the further introduction of slaves into Kansas. The constitution was ratified, 21 Dec., because its opponents boycotted the voting. Northerners denounced the document, and the Democratic Party began to crumble as Douglas broke with Buchanan when the President supported it. The antislavery legislature held another election, 4 Jan., 1858, which almost unanimously rejected the entire Lecompton Constitution.

1858

DOUGLAS AND LECOMPTON. Douglas attacked the Lecompton Constitution as a violation of popular sovereignty. Over his objections Congress accepted, 30 Apr., administration Democrat William H. English's (Ind.) compromise proposal that the whole Lecompton Constitution be popularly ratified, with rejection delaying Kansas' admission until it had achieved a population of approximately 90,000.

"A HOUSE DIVIDED AGAINST ITSELF CANNOT STAND." 16 June. Senatorial nominee Abraham Lincoln (1809–65) predicted at the Illinois Republican Convention at Springfield that slavery would eventually exist in every state or in none. Republican presidential hopeful William H. Seward's (N.Y.) "Irrepressible Conflict" speech, 25 Oct., shared Lincoln's view.

LINCOLN-DOUGLAS DEBATES. 21 Aug.–15 Oct. Lincoln won national prominence during 7 campaign debates with Douglas. The latter alienated southern supporters with his "Freeport doctrine" that, despite the Dred Scott decision, slavery could not exist unless local legislatures enacted necessary police regulations. Lincoln, who declared slavery immoral, gained more popular votes than Douglas, who evaded the moral issue, but the legislature elected the Democrat.

Campaigning against the Lecompton Constitution, Republicans won every northern state election except in Illinois and Indiana, and took 18 additional congressional seats.

1859

JOHN BROWN. 16–18 Oct. Brown's raid against Harper's Ferry, Va., was intended to spark slave revolts throughout the South. Captured by Col. Robert E. Lee (1807–70), Brown was hanged, 2 Dec., for treason against Virginia. Conservative Northerners denounced the attack, which Southerners attributed to abolitionists and Republicans.

AFRICAN SLAVE TRADE. The Southern Commercial Convention at Vicksburg, Miss., 9–19 May, advocated reopening the African slave trade. President Buchanan opposed it, and promised, 19 Dec., to use all legal means to prevent slave importations.

1860

DAVIS RESOLUTIONS. 2 Feb. Sen. Jefferson Davis (1808–89, Miss.) successfully proposed several proslavery resolutions. One denounced states' attempts to thwart the Fugitive Slave Law and another stated that Congress had to protect slavery in the territories.

SECESSION THREATS. Several state legislatures in the Lower South advocated secession if a Republican became President. The Upper South had more faith in the benefits of the Union.

PRESIDENTIAL CAMPAIGN. The Democrats met at Baltimore, 18 June, and chose Douglas (Ill.) and Herschel V. Johnson (Ga.). When the party refused to advocate slavery in the territories, southern delegates seceded and nominated, 28 June, John C. Breckinridge (Ky.) and Joseph Lane (Ore.). Former Whig and American party members selected, 9 May, John Bell (Tenn.) and Edward Everett (Mass.) as candidates for their compromising Constitutional Union Party. The Republicans nominated, 16 May, Lincoln (Ill.) and Hannibal Hamlin (Me.), and supported internal improvements and homesteads, while opposing slavery in the territories.

ELECTION OF LINCOLN. 6 Nov. Lincoln received 180 votes (18 free states) over Breckinridge (72, 11 slave states), Bell (39), and Douglas (12). Douglas closely followed Lincoln's 1,866,352 popular votes with 1,375,157.

CIVIL WAR AND RECONSTRUCTION

1861–77

SECESSION CRISIS. 20 Dec., 1860–1 Feb., 1861. Denouncing the election of the sectional Republican Party's antislavery presidential candidate, South Carolina's state convention voted unanimously, 20 Dec., to secede from the Union. Mississippi, 9 Jan.; Florida, 10 Jan.; Alabama, 11 Jan.; Ga., 19 Jan.; Louisiana, 26 Jan.; and Texas, 1 Feb., quickly followed. In the Upper South, Arkansas, North Carolina, Tennessee, and Virginia remained loyal, but threatened secession if the federal government resorted to force. Buchanan accepted Attorney General Jeremiah S. Black's position that the government could not use force to prevent secession.

ESTABLISHMENT OF THE CONFEDERACY. 4 Feb. The Montgomery (Ala.) Convention of the seceding states established a provisional government. The Confederate Constitution resembled the U.S. one, but stressed states' sovereignty and outlawed slave importations. Jefferson Davis (Miss.) and Alexander H. Stephens (Ga.) were elected, 9 Feb., provisional President and Vice-President of the Confederacy.

Federal forts and arsenals were then seized throughout the South. Buchanan refused, 31 Dec., to surrender federal forts, but South Carolina seized, 30 Dec., the U.S. arsenal at Charleston. That city's batteries drove off, 9 Jan., an unarmed ship bringing provisions and reinforcements for Maj. Robert Anderson's men in Fort Sumter.

OUTBREAK OF CIVIL WAR. Lincoln's announcement, 6 Apr., that he would provision Fort Sumter prompted South Carolina to demand, 11 Apr., its immediate surrender. Maj. Anderson complied, 13 Apr., only after Gen. Pierre G. T. Beauregard's batteries bombarded, 12 Apr., the installation. Lincoln called for 75,000 volunteers to put down the "insurrection," 15 Apr.

BORDER STATE CRISIS. Claiming Lincoln's call for volunteers presaged an invasion of the South, Virginia seceded, 17 Apr., and Richmond became, 21 May, the Confederate capital. Arkansas, 6 May; Tennessee, 7 May; and North Carolina, 20 May, followed suit. Virginia's mountainous western sector balked and organized, 11 June, a Union government under Francis H. Pierpont. West Virginia became a state, 20 June, 1863. Slaveholding Delaware unanimously rejected secession, 3 Jan. In Maryland, Gov. Thomas Hicks and a majority of the populace were Unionists, but the legislature was willing to accept southern independence. The federal government secured Maryland in mid-1861 by suspending habeas corpus and imprisoning numerous officials. Kentucky's legislature proclaimed, 20 May, neutrality, and Lincoln promised not to send in troops. However, when Confederates occupied Hickman and Columbus, Gen. Ulysses S. Grant (1822–85) took, 6 Sept., Paducah, and the legislature, 11 Sept., called for the Confederates' ouster. Kentucky contributed 75,000 men to the Union army. Civil war raged in Missouri, where the defeat of secession-minded Gov. Claiborne F. Jackson at Pea Ridge, Ark., 6–8 Mar., 1862, guaranteed Union control of the state.

OPPOSING FORCES. The 23 Union states, with a population of 22 m. and a balanced economy supported by an extensive railroad system and merchant marine, had numerical and material superiority. The 11 Confederate states had a population of 9 m., including 3 m. slaves, and a staple agricultural economy which lacked industry, banking, and railroads. Despite these disadvantages the South chose secession believing that the North would not fight and that Britain, dependent on southern products, would give the Confederacy material aid. Southerners also viewed as advantages their control of the mouth of the Mississippi, defensive role, and excellent officer corps.

The Union and Confederate armies enlisted 1,556,678 and 1,082,119 men respectively. The North fought to restore the Union and, after 1862, to free the slaves; the South for the independence and sovereignty of the Confederacy.

STRATEGY. The North planned to use 1 army to capture Richmond and another to capture the Mississippi and Tennessee rivers. These forces would then join to crush the Confederacy. The South hoped to capture Washington and invade Pennsylvania to force a divided North to request peace.

1ST BULL RUN. 21 July. Popular demands for action prompted the dispatch of Gen. Irvin McDowell's unseasoned troops to attack Beauregard at Manassas Junction, Va. McDowell's attack, 21 July, seemed successful until reinforcements and Gen. Thomas J. "Stonewall" Jackson's stand enabled Beauregard to drive the Northerners back to Washington in disorder.

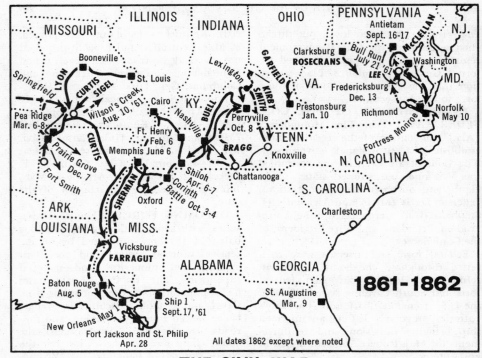

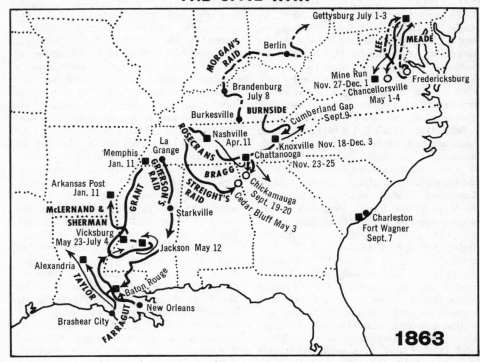

THE CIVIL WAR

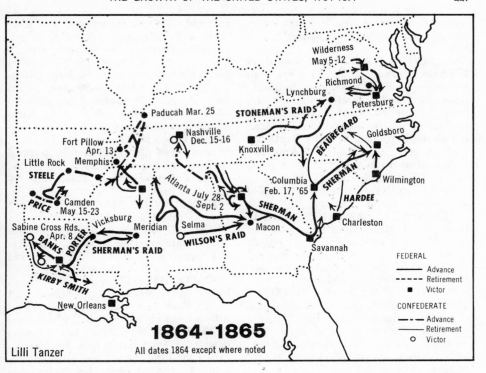

Wilderness
May 5-12

Richmond

Lynchburg

STONEMAN'S RAIDS

Petersburg

Paducah Mar. 25

BEAUREGARD

Goldsboro

Nashville
Dec. 15-16

Knoxville

Fort Pillow
Apr. 13

Little Rock

Memphis

STEELE

SHERMAN

Wilmington

Atlanta July 28-
Sept. 2

Columbia
Feb. 17, '65

HARDEE

Camden
May 15-23

PRICE

SHERMAN

Sabine Cross Rds.
Apr. 8

Vicksburg

Meridian

Selma

Macon

Charleston

BANKS

PORTER

SHERMAN'S RAID

WILSON'S RAID

Savannah

KIRBY SMITH

FEDERAL

——— Advance
- - - - Retirement
■   Victor

New Orleans

CONFEDERATE

— · — · Advance
——— Retirement
○   Victor

1864-1865

All dates 1864 except where noted

Lilli Tanzer

ASSUMPTION OF COMMAND BY McCLELLAN. 24 July. Maj. Gen. George B. McClellan, whose victory at Philippi, 3 June, cleared the Confederates from the Valley of the Kanawha in western Virginia, replaced McDowell. McClellan became general in chief, 1 Nov., when Gen. Winfield Scott retired.

NAVAL BLOCKADE. Lincoln ordered, 19 Apr., the 3,500-mi. southern coast blockaded to starve the Confederacy. Relying heavily on Nassau in the Bahamas for supplies, the rebels cleared approximately 600 ships during the first year of the blockade instead of the usual 6,000. Federal capture of Forts Clark and Hatteras, N.C., 28–29 Aug., Port Royal, S.C., 7 Nov.; Roanoke Island, 8 Feb., 1862; New Orleans, 29 Apr., 1862; and other coastal locations significantly increased the blockade's effectiveness.

ANGLO-U.S. RELATIONS. Britain's upper class and commercial interests supported the Confederacy, while the lower class favored the Union. Her declaration of neutrality, 13 May, angered the Union

by mentioning the South's belligerent status, but Lord John Russell promised American Minister Charles Francis Adams that Britain would not deal with Confederate agents.

TRENT AFFAIR. Capt. Charles Wilkes of the *San Jacinto* removed, 8 Nov., Confederate commissioners James M. Mason and John Slidell from the British steamer *Trent,* but Secretary of State Seward eased the situation by releasing them.

JOINT COMMITTEE. 20 Dec. A joint committee on the conduct of the war was established by a Congress displeased with Lincoln's vast powers. Radical Republicans like Thaddeus Stevens (1792–1868, Pa.) dominated it.

1862

WAR IN THE WEST. Gen. U. S. Grant and Commodore A. H. Foote captured Fort Henry on the Tennessee, 6 Feb. Grant took 14,000 prisoners at Fort Donelson on the Cumberland, 16 Feb., forcing Confederate Gen. Albert S. Johnston to abandon Nashville, which fell 25 Feb.

SHILOH. 6–7 Apr. Grant moved to Pittsburg Landing, Tenn., to prepare an attack on Confederates under Johnston, Beauregard, and Polk at nearby Corinth, Miss. The rebels smashed into Grant's inadequately defended position, 6 Apr., but Grant, reinforced by Gens. Buell and Wallace, emerged victorious, 7 Apr. The 63,000 Northerners suffered 13,000 losses and the 40,000 Southerners 11,000.

On 26 Apr. New Orleans was occupied by Gen. Benjamin F. Butler.

PENINSULA CAMPAIGN. Lincoln removed, 11 Mar., McClellan, who had ignored his 22 Feb. command to launch an offensive, as gen. in chief, and ordered the Army of the Potomac, minus McDowell's corps, against Richmond.

"MONITOR" AND "MERRIMAC." 9 Mar. In the first battle of ironclads, the U.S.S. *Monitor* fought the *Virginia* (formerly *Merrimac*) to a draw. The *Virginia* withdrew for repairs to Norfolk, where she was scuttled when the city fell, 10 May.

McCLELLAN'S ADVANCE. 17 Mar.– 31 May. Having occupied Yorktown, 4 May, McClellan, despite his overwhelming strength, stopped 20 mi. from Richmond at White House to await McDowell's corps.

JACKSON'S VALLEY CAMPAIGN. 23 Mar.–9 June. Stonewall Jackson's 18,000 troops kept 2½ times as many Union soldiers engaged in the Shenandoah Valley. He routed Gen. Banks at Winchester, 24 May, driving the Northerners across the Potomac.

SEVEN PINES (FAIR OAKS). 31 May–1 June. Gen. Joseph E. Johnston attacked 2 of McClellan's corps isolated on the south bank of the Chickahominy River, but another corps rescued them. Union losses totaled 6,000, Confederate 8,000.

7 DAYS' BATTLE. 26 June–2 July. Robert E. Lee, commander of the Army of Northern Virginia, engaged McClellan's forces for 7 successive days starting 26–27 June at Mechanicsville. McClellan

battered the Confederates until Lee withdrew to Richmond, 2 July, after unsuccessfully attacking at Malvern Hill, 1 July. Union losses in the Peninsula Campaign reached 15,849, Confederate, 20,614.

2ND BULL RUN. 29–30 Aug. When Gen. Pope, under orders from Gen. in Chief Halleck, prepared to attack Richmond, Lee reacted quickly. Jackson destroyed Pope's base at Manassas Junction, 26 Aug., and the Confederates trapped counterattacking Union forces. Maj. Gen. James Longstreet drove Pope back toward Bull Run.

INVASION OF MARYLAND. When Lee invaded Maryland, 14–15 Sept., McClellan defeated him at South Mountain and Crampton's Gap, 14 Sept., but Jackson captured, 15 Sept., 11,000 men and the supply depot at Harper's Ferry.

ANTIETAM. 17 Sept. The war's bloodiest day produced 11,657 Union and 11,729 Confederate casualties. McClellan won a technical victory as Lee withdrew to Virginia, 18 Sept. The Union's success deterred France and Britain from recognizing the Confederacy, and enabled Lincoln to issue, 22 Sept., his Preliminary Emancipation Proclamation freeing as of 1 Jan., 1863, slaves in rebellious areas.

WESTERN THEATER. Gen Braxton Bragg advanced from the Confederate base at Chattanooga into central Tennessee, but withdrew after a bitter battle with Rosecrans at Murfreesboro, 31 Dec.– 3 Jan., 1863, which produced 9,220 Union and 9,239 Confederate losses.

FREDERICKSBURG. 13 Dec. Lincoln replaced, 7 Nov., the frustratingly cautious McClellan with Ambrose E. Burnside. At Fredericksburg, Burnside's 113,000 troops lost 1,284 in attacking 75,-000 rebels who only lost 595. Joseph Hooker replaced Burnside, 25 Jan., 1863.

1863

EMANCIPATION PROCLAMATION. 1 Jan. Congress freed, 17 July, 1862, the slaves of traitors and of those supporting the rebellion, and abolished slavery in the Capital, 16 Apr., 1862, and the territories, 19 June, 1862. Lincoln, who had not requested abolition lest the border states revolt, saw that European and popular opinion was becoming more radical and issued his Emancipation Proclamation, 1 Jan. This statement, which declared slaves in rebellious areas free, went no farther than previous legislation and applied only to places where the federal government exercised no control.

MILITARY DRAFT. Under Congress' 1st Conscription Act, 3 Mar., males 18–35 were liable to the draft but could escape by paying $300 or finding a substitute. This inequitable system provoked the New York City Draft Riots, 13–16 July, in working-class districts. Four drafts raised only a small part of the Union army. The Confederacy drafted, 16 Apr., 1862, white men 18–35 for 3 years. Some Southerners questioned the constitutionality of this corruptly administered act, which exempted many occupations and allowed substitution. Desertions on both sides reached approximately 10%.

FINANCING THE WAR. Congress's National Banking System, 25 Feb., required national banks to invest 1/3 of their capital in U.S. securities and authorized them to issue notes based on these bonds. The Confederacy issued over $1 billion in paper, which depreciated to $1 = ¢1.6 by the end of the war.

HOME FRONT. Northern prices (117%), production, and profits rose significantly, while wages (43%) lagged. Immigration, c. 800,000, and increased mechanization of industry and farming replaced the man power lost to the military. In the South women filled supervisory positions and most slaves remained loyal.

FOREIGN AFFAIRS. Seward rejected, 6 Feb., Napoleon III's offer of mediation and Congress denounced, 3 Mar., such "foreign intervention."

CONFEDERATE RAIDERS. 4 Apr. British-built Confederate raiders like the *Alabama* dealt severely with Union shipping, destroying 257 vessels. Upon U.S. Minister Charles Francis Adams' protest, the British government seized, 5 Apr., the newly constructed *Alexandra*, but the courts released her.

CHANCELLORSVILLE. 2–4 May. Lee's 60,000 troops won a costly victory over Hooker's 130,000. Jackson, who lost his life, surprised and routed the Union right. Hooker retreated, 5 May, across the Rappahannock. Union deaths totaled 1,575, Confederate 1,665.

VICKSBURG CAMPAIGN. Leaving Memphis, 29 Mar., Grant crossed the Mississippi and proceeded down the Louisiana coast to a point south of the strategic citadel of Vicksburg. He ferried across, 30 Apr., and approached the city with 20,000 men. Grant besieged Vicksburg, 22 May–4 July, and Gen. John C. Pemberton surrendered its 40,000-man garrison, 4 July, giving the Union control of the Mississippi. Union casualties reached 9,000, Confederate 10,000.

GETTYSBURG CAMPAIGN. 27 June–4 July. Lee moved his army up the Shenandoah, and by 23 June Gen. Richard S. Ewell's cavalry had approached Chambersburg, Pa. Undetected, Hooker pursued Lee and established headquarters at Frederick, 27 June. Maj. Gen. George G. Meade replaced Hooker, who resigned, 28 June, after disputes with Halleck.

Confederate Gen. Ambrose P. Hill's fortuitous clash with John Bedford, 30 June, at Gettysburg prompted a showdown. The Southerners drove the Northerners, 1 July, back upon Cemetery and Culp's hills. Gens. Jubal A. Early, Longstreet, and Ewell failed, 2 July, to take Cemetery Ridge, Little Round Top, and Culp's Hill respectively. Lee had Longstreet send, 3 July, 15,000 men under Pickett, Pettigrew, and Trimble against the main federal positions, but the superior fire power of the more numerous Northerners mauled them. The flooded Potomac blocked Lee's retreat, 4 July, but bad weather prevented pursuit and he reached Virginia, 13 July. Union losses totaled 3,155 killed, c. 20,000 wounded or missing; Confederate 3,903 killed, c. 24,000 wounded or missing. Lincoln's most memorable speech helped dedicate, 19 Nov., a cemetery at Gettysburg.

Gettysburg ended southern hopes for European aid. When Adams threatened war, Britain seized Confederate iron-clads ("Laird rams") under construction. Napoleon halted ship sales to the South.

CHICKAMAUGA. 19–20 Sept. Reinforced by Longstreet, Bragg, whom Rosecrans maneuvered out of Chattanooga, 9 Sept., smashed the Northerners at Chickamauga. The stand of Gen. Thomas, the "Rock of Chickamauga," saved the Union forces, which retired into Chattanooga. Union dead totaled 1,657, Confederate 2,312.

CHATTANOOGA.   23–25   Nov. Thomas replaced Rosecrans and, reinforced by Hooker, took the offensive. He drove Bragg off Lookout Mountain, 23 Nov., and routed his forces from Missionary Ridge, 25 Nov. Union dead totaled 753, Confederate 361. The Northerners could now march through Georgia to the sea.

PRESIDENTIAL   RECONSTRUC-TION. 8 Dec. Lincoln announced his plan to grant amnesty to Southerners who swore loyalty and to recognize state governments where 10% of the 1860 electorate took the oath and which agreed to emancipation.

1864

THE WILDERNESS. 5–6 May. Grant, now supreme military commander, utilized his 100,000-man Army of the Potomac to batter Lee. Crossing the Rapidan, 4 May, he entered the Wilderness. Attacking his flank, Lee's 60,000 troops, suffering 10,000 casualties, inflicted 18,000.

SPOTSYLVANIA. 8–12 May. Lee inflicted some 12,000 more Union casualties when Grant's maneuvers failed at Spotsylvania Court House.

COLD HARBOR. 1–3 June. Engagements on 3 June cost Grant 12,000 casualties. In the month ending 12 June, Confederate losses totaled c. 30,000, an unbearable blow despite the Union's almost 60,000 casualties.

PETERSBURG. 15–18 June. Grant moved to Petersburg, 20 mi. below Richmond, to isolate the Confederate capital. Losing 8,000 men, 15–18 June, he began siege operations.

EARLY'S RAIDS. 2–13 July. Confederate Gen. Early, raiding in Maryland, neared Washington, D.C., but was repulsed, 13 July. Gen. Philip H. Sheridan defeated him at Winchester, 19 Sept.; Fisher's Hill, 22 Sept.; and Cedar Creek, 19 Oct., and devastated the Shenandoah Valley.

INVASION OF GEORGIA. 7 May–2 Sept. Gen. William T. Sherman's 100,000 troops left Chattanooga, May. Joseph E. Johnston harassed him, inflicting 2,000 casualties at Kenesaw Mountain, 27 June, while suffering only 270. Unsatisfied with his defensive strategy, Davis replaced Johnston with John Bell Hood. Sherman entered Georgia, inflicting heavy losses on Hood, 20, 22 July, and took Atlanta, 1 Sept.

MARCH TO THE SEA. 14 Nov.–22 Dec. With 60,000 men, Sherman drove 300 mi. across Georgia, capturing Savannah, 22 Dec. Living off the land, the Northerners devastated an area 60 mi. wide along their route.

NASHVILLE. 15–16 Dec. Hood's strategy was to cut Sherman's long communication lines, but Gens. Thomas and John M. Schofield destroyed his army at Nashville.

PRESIDENTIAL ELECTION. The Republicans nominated, 7 June, Lincoln and War Democrat Andrew Johnson (1808–75, Tenn.). The Democrats selected, 29 Aug., Gen. McClellan and George H. Pendleton (Ohio). War frustrations and Radical denunciations for his veto of the stringent Wade-Davis Reconstruction Bill hurt Lincoln's chances, but Sherman's successes reunited the party and boosted the nation's morale. Lincoln was re-elected by 212 votes to 21, but with a narrow popular margin.

1865

WEAKENING OF THE CONFEDERACY. Transportation disruptions, devastation, federal occupation, and the blockade produced hunger in the South and lowered morale. Disunionist tendencies appeared, protest riots shook southern cities, and ⅔ of the soldiers left the ranks. Davis desperately authorized arming the slaves, 7 Nov., 1864, and the Congress belatedly agreed, 20 Mar., 1865.

SHERMAN IN THE CAROLINAS. 16 Jan.–21 Mar. Sherman's men ravaged South Carolina, taking the capital, Columbia, 17 Feb., and Charleston, 18 Feb. In North Carolina, Johnston, restored to command by Lee, who was now leader of all Confederate forces, slowed Sherman's progress.

PETERSBURG AND RICHMOND. 2 Apr. Battered by Grant's 115,000 troops, Lee attacked at Five Forks, 1 Apr., but Sheridan repulsed him. Lee evacuated Petersburg and Richmond to join Johnston in North Carolina.

APPOMATTOX COURTHOUSE. 9 Apr. Having surrounded Lee, Grant asked him to surrender, 7 Apr., and they reached terms, 9 Apr., at Appomattox Courthouse, Va. Lee's approximately 30,000 soldiers were paroled to return home with their private horses and mules.

LINCOLN'S ASSASSINATION. 14 Apr. John Wilkes Booth shot, 14 Apr., Lincoln at a performance of *Our American Cousin* at Ford's Theater, Washington. Lincoln died the next morning and Andrew Johnson became President. Booth died trapped in a barn near Bowling Green, Va.; 4 other conspirators were executed, 4 imprisoned, and 1 man, John H. Surratt, was acquitted.

FINAL CAPITULATION. 26 Apr.–26 May. Johnston surrendered, 18 Apr., to Sherman, and agreed to terms, 26 Apr. Gen. Kirby Smith surrendered to Gen. Canby at New Orleans, 26 May, ending Confederate resistance. Jefferson Davis was captured, 10 May, in Georgia.

CASUALTIES. Union losses totaled 359,528 dead and 275,175 wounded; Confederate, 258,000 dead and at least 100,000 wounded.

RECONSTRUCTION UNDER JOHNSON. Johnson recognized loyal governments in Arkansas, Louisiana, Tennessee, and Virginia. He established provisional governments for the other 7 states, and announced, 6 Dec., restoration of the Union when they abolished slavery and repudiated their state war debts.

RADICAL REACTION. The Radical Republicans refused to endorse Johnson's actions and claimed Congress alone could reconstruct the conquered provinces or seceding states. They established a Joint Committee of 15, dominated by Radical Thaddeus Stevens (Pa.), to study Reconstruction problems.

ABOLITION OF SLAVERY. 18 Dec. Slavery was abolished by the 13th Amendment to the Constitution.

1866

NEW FREEDMEN'S BUREAU BILL. 19 Feb. To counteract repressive Southern Black Codes, Congress, over Johnson's veto, authorized the Freedmen's Bureau (est. 3 Mar., 1865) to try by military commission persons accused of violating freedmen's civil rights.

CIVIL RIGHTS ACT. 9 Apr. Passed over Johnson's veto, the act granted Negroes citizenship and equal rights.

14TH AMENDMENT. 16 June. Proposed because of doubts about the constitutionality of the Civil Rights Act, the 14th Amendment established Negro citizenship and guaranteed constitutional rights against infringement by the states. Ratification, a congressional condition for restoration to the Union, came 28 July, 1868.

CONGRESSIONAL REPRESENTATION AND ELECTIONS. A joint committee denied, 20 June, that the South merited representation. Congress restored Tennessee, 24 July, when it ratified the 14th Amendment. The Republicans campaigned as the party of the Union, while identifying Johnson with ex-rebels and Copperheads (pro-southern Democrats). Radical Reconstruction became inevitable when the Republicans won 2/3 of each house.

1867–68

1ST RECONSTRUCTION ACT. 2 Mar., 1867. The South was divided into 5 military districts. Constitutional conventions were to ratify the 14th Amendment and grant Negro suffrage. Supplementary Reconstruction Acts, 23 Mar., 19 July, 1867; 11 Mar., 1868, expedited enforcement of the first.

MILITARY RECONSTRUCTION. Johnson unenthusiastically enforced these laws. 20,000 troops oversaw the establishment of Radical southern governments by southern "scalawag" whites, northern "carpetbaggers," and southern Negroes.

ALASKA. 9 Apr., 1867. The Senate ratified Secretary Seward's treaty acquiring Alaska from Russia for $7.2 m.

FOUNDATION OF GRANGER MOVEMENT. 4 Dec., 1867. The Patrons of Husbandry ("Grangers") and numerous independent farmers' parties opposed monopolies and sought regulation of certain public utilities. Illinois passed the 1st Granger legislation, 7 Apr., 1871, establishing a railroad and warehouse commission to fix maximum rates.

OMNIBUS ACT. 22–25 June, 1868. Arkansas, Alabama, Florida, Georgia, Louisiana, North Carolina, and South Carolina were restored to the Union after they had framed acceptable constitutions. Mississippi, Texas, and Virginia ratified the 15th Amendment (proposed 26 Feb., 1869) guaranteeing Negro voting rights, and gained readmission by 1870. Congress ousted Georgia for expelling, Sept., Negroes from the legislature, but readmitted her when she restored them and ratified the 15th Amendment, 15 July, 1870.

IMPEACHMENT OF JOHNSON. 24 Feb.–26 May, 1868. Congress, in special session, passed, 2 Mar., 1867, the Tenure of Office Act forbidding the President to remove, without Senate consent, appointees confirmed by that body. When Johnson removed, 21 Feb., 1868, Secretary of War Edwin M. Stanton, the House's Covode Resolution, 24 Feb., impeached him. Chief Justice Salmon P. Chase presided at the Senate trial, 30 Mar.–16 May, which acquitted Johnson. 35 Senators, 1 short of the necessary ⅔, voted, 16 May, finding Johnson guilty of high misdemeanor.

PRESIDENTIAL ELECTION. The Republicans nominated, 20–21 May, 1868, U. S. Grant and Schuyler Colfax (Ind.). The Democrats selected, 9 July, Horatio Seymour (N.Y.) and Francis P. Blair (Mo.). The Republican campaign centered on waving "the bloody shirt of the rebellion." On 3 Nov. Grant was elected, 214–80. 500,000 Negro votes decided the contest.

SUPREME COURT AND RECONSTRUCTION. Fearing that the justices would invalidate Reconstruction legislation, the Radicals denied, 27 Mar., 1868, the Court jurisdiction in *ex parte McCardle*. The Court, however, upheld Congress' right to reconstruct the South (*Texas* v. *White,* 1869).

1869

PUBLIC CREDIT ACT. 18 Mar. This act provided for the payment of government obligations in gold.

"BLACK FRIDAY." 24 Sept. The government's sale of $4 m. in gold stymied Jay Gould's and James Fisk's attempt to corner that metal.

1870–71

SANTO DOMINGO. The Senate defeated, 30 June, 1870, a Grant-supported treaty to annex Santo Domingo.

KU KLUX KLAN ACTS. 31 May, 1870, and 20 Apr., 1871. These acts, which were declared partially unconstitutional, 1876 and 1883, sought to enforce the 15th and 14th Amendments respectively against the terrorist activities of the white supremacist Ku Klux Klan organization.

TWEED RING. 8 July, 1871. George Jones's revelations in *The New York Times* of the Tammany machine's corrupt practices led to the conviction of William Marcy ("Boss") Tweed, 5 Nov., 1872.

1872

"ALABAMA" CLAIMS. An international arbitration tribunal established by the Treaty of Washington, 8 May, 1871, ordered Britain to pay, 25 Aug., 1872, the U.S. $15.5 m. for damages done by British-built Confederate raiders.

CRÉDIT MOBILER EXPOSÉ. Vice-President Schuyler Colfax and other important politicians were accused of corrupt practices in relation to the Union Pacific Railroad's construction.

PRESIDENTIAL ELECTION. The Liberal Republicans nominated, 1 May, Horace Greeley (1811–72) and B. Gratz Brown (Mo.) on a reform platform, and the Democrats followed suit, 9 July. The Republicans nominated, 5 June, Grant and Henry Wilson (Mass.). Grant was re-elected, 286–66.

1873

"THE CRIME OF 73." 12 Feb. Labeled by its detractors as a crime, the Coinage Act demonetized silver.

PANIC OF 1873. 18 Sept. When Jay Cooke's banking firm collapsed, a financial panic ensued. The government issued $26 m. in greenbacks to offset its effects.

1875

SPECIE RESUMPTION ACT. 14 Jan. The panic weathered, Congress ordered specie payments resumed by 1 Jan., 1879, and greenbacks in circulation reduced to $300 m.

CIVIL RIGHTS ACT. 1 Mar. The Act of 1875 forbade discrimination in public accommodations.

WHISKY RING. Formed by revenue officers and distillers to defraud the government, a whisky ring was uncovered, 1 May, and Grant's private secretary, O. E. Babcock, implicated.

1876

BELKNAP'S IMPEACHMENT. War Secretary William W. Belknap resigned when impeached for receiving bribes in the sale of Indian Territory trading posts.

PRESIDENTIAL ELECTION. The Republicans nominated, 16 June, Rutherford B. Hayes (1822–93, Ohio) and William A. Wheeler (N.Y.). James G.

Blaine (1830–93), a leading contender, was eliminated when accused, 31 May, before the House of unethical dealings with the Union Pacific Railroad. The Democrats selected, 27–29 June, Samuel J. Tilden (1814–86, N.Y.) and Thomas A. Hendricks (Ind.). In the election, 7 Nov., Tilden won the popular and apparently the electoral vote. However, Florida, Louisiana, South Carolina, and Oregon, where Republicans disputed Tilden's victory, reported, 6 Dec., 2 sets of election returns.

1877

ELECTORAL COMMISSION. 29 Jan. An Electoral Commission of 5 Democratic and 5 Republican congressmen and 5 Supreme Court justices, including 2 Democrats and 2 Republicans, was established to resolve the dispute. Independent David Davis (Ill.) was supposed to be the fifth justice, but Republican Justice Bradley was chosen when Davis became U.S. senator. Voting straight party lines, the commission awarded, 9, 16, 23, 28 Feb., Hayes all the doubtful votes.

ELECTION OF HAYES. 2 Mar. Hayes was declared elected, 185–184. Southerners adopted the commission's decision, and in return Hayes withdrew, Apr., federal occupying forces; appointed, 5 Mar., David M. Key (Tenn.) postmaster general; and promised to support southern internal improvements.

END OF "BLACK RECONSTRUCTION." Extravagance and malfeasance plagued Radical governments in the South. However, the need to rebuild that devastated area and to provide hitherto neglected services like schools and hospitals justified many expenditures. Georgia, North Carolina, Tennessee, and Virginia, 1869–71; Alabama, Arkansas, Mississippi, and Texas, 1874–75; and Florida, Louisiana, and South Carolina, 1877, ousted the Radicals. (*Cont. p. 300.*)

Latin America and the Caribbean, 1825–1914

MEXICO

1825–34

ERA OF SANTA ANNA. President Guadalupe Victoria, 1824–28, who represented the Liberals and Federalists, was a soldier rather than an administrator. He suppressed an uprising led by his Conservative vice-president, Nicolás Bravo. Victoria should have been followed by Manuel Gómez Pedráza, a moderate backed by the Conservatives, who won a narrow victory in the elections of 1828. But the results were challenged by Antonio López de Santa Anna (1795?–1876), whose domination of the political scene for the next 2 decades nearly destroyed Mexico. Liberal Vicente Guerrero, the defeated candidate, became president, 1829, but his term was soon interrupted by an army revolt, led by Santa Anna, fresh from an easy victory over a Spanish force at Tampico. Guerrero was replaced by his Conservative vice-president, Anastasio Bustamante, 1829–32, who was in turn under the thumb of the foreign minister, Lucas Alamán. Although an economic reformer, Alamán was a fervent Conservative in politics and religion. Sensing a reaction against Alamán's dictatorial policies, Santa Anna overthrew Bustamante and permitted Gómez Pedráza to complete his term. Santa Anna then became president himself, 1833–35, but he left the government to the vice-president, Valentín Gómez Farías, the leader of Mexican liberalism during this period. Gómez Farías curtailed the privileges of the church and the army. When a cholera epidemic touched off widespread discontent with the oligarchy, however, Santa Anna returned to office and repealed Gómez Farías' progressive measures.

1835–45

CONSERVATISM AND REGIONAL REVOLTS. Unable to control his hand-picked Conservative congress, Santa Anna again retired from the government. The Congress then drew up a new centralist constitution, 1836, which established a 5-member council as a counterweight to the power of the Presidency. Meanwhile, the Texans, discouraged by Gómez Farías' refusal to give them self-government and antagonized by Santa Anna's plan to enforce centralization, declared themselves independent, 2 Mar., 1836. Santa Anna sought to revive his waning popularity by subduing Texas, but he was defeated at the battle of San Jacinto, 21 Apr. Bustamante again became president, 1837–39, but his power was threatened by regional revolts, directed against the political and economic hegemony of central Mexico. Santa Anna finally atoned for the Texas fiasco by defeating a small French invasion at Veracruz, the "Pastry War," and embarked on a new presidential term, 1839–40. The peace was soon disturbed, however, by an attempted Liberal uprising in Mexico City, led by Gómez Farías. As a compromise, Bustamante became president, 1840–41, but not for long. His government was overthrown by a trio of generals: Mariano Paredes, Gabriel Valencia, and Santa Anna. Under a new Conservative constitution, Santa Anna returned to power, 1841–44, but, lacking money to pay his followers, could not maintain order. Paredes revolted and Congress named the moderate José Joaquín Herrera, president (1844–45).

1846–54

WAR WITH THE U.S. President Polk's annexation of Texas and Slidell's offer to buy the Southwest were exploited by Paredes to overthrow Herrera. Following an attack on U.S. troops in disputed territory, war was declared, May 1846. U.S. victories in the north and Paredes' incapacity provoked a revolt, which restored Gómez Farías and the federalist Constitution of 1824. Lack of anyone better qualified forced Gómez Farías to give Santa Anna command of the army. When Gómez Farías made himself unpopular by taxing the church to finance the war, he was easily unseated by Santa Anna, returning from what he claimed was victory at Buena Vista, 22–23 Feb., 1847. Despite an 11th-hour co-operation between the political factions, U.S. forces occupied Mexico City. The Maya Caste War in Yucatán and new threats of secession from the north prompted the moderates to conclude a quick peace. The Treaty of Guadalupe Hidalgo, 2 Feb., 1848, gave the U.S. nearly half of Mexico: California, New Mexico, Nevada, Utah, Ari-

zona, part of Colorado, and, of course, Texas. This huge loss of territory intensified the desire of the reformers to reorganize the country. The postwar moderate Conservative presidents, Herrera, 1848–50, and Mariano Arista, 1851–53, were conscientious but were confronted by overwhelming problems of finance and the maintenance of order. Alarmed by the growing liberal movement, the Conservatives under Alamán once more put Santa Anna in the presidency, 1853–54, hoping to re-establish a centralized, and ultimately monarchical, government. Alamán's death, however, gave Santa Anna a free hand. Mexican politics reached a

MODERN LATIN AMERICA

0 500 1000
Scale of Miles (Approx.)

© Lilli Tanzer 1970

new low level with his sale of the Mesilla Valley to the U.S. (Gadsden Purchase, 30 Dec., 1853).

1854–61

THE REFORMA. The Indian leader Juan Álvarez and a group of distinguished Liberal intellectuals proclaimed the Plan of Ayutla, 1 Mar., 1854, calling for a constitutional convention, and led a revolt against Santa Anna. Santa Anna fled, leaving the government to the Liberals. Álvarez became provisional president, 1855, but, lacking political skill, he was unable to ride the tide of criticism provoked by the *Ley Juarez,* which abolished church and army courts. A moderate, Ignacio Comonfort, 1855–58, became president under the theoretically federalist and congressionalist Constitution of 1857. Although the *Ley Lerdo,* which forced the church and other corporate bodies to sell their property, was passed during Comonfort's term, his vacillations displeased both Liberals and Conservatives. An uprising under Felix Zuloaga and Miguel Miramón brought the Conservatives to power in Mexico City. Comonfort's vice-president, the Indian lawyer Benito Juárez (1806–72), proclaimed himself president and a civil war, 1858–61, ensued. A final wedge was driven between the 2 sides by Juárez' Laws of Reform, 1859. All church property became liable to confiscation without compensation, and church and state were separated. A Liberal victory kept Juárez in the presidency for a while, 1861–63, but Liberal opposition in Congress, rebellious Conservative army detachments, and a French invasion drove him out again.

1862–67

FRENCH IMPERIAL ADVENTURE. Suspension of service on foreign debts led to the arrival of a British, Spanish, and French expeditionary force to obtain financial satisfaction. French plans also included conquest, and Prince Maximilian and his wife Charlotte (Carlota), who it was hoped would found a new French dynasty, were installed in Mexico City, 1864–67. Maximilian re-established a centralized government and an imperial court, but his efforts to conciliate the Liberals and his taxation of the church angered the Conservatives, who had originally invited him. Napoleon III soon had to withdraw the French forces, leaving Maximilian to face the Liberals alone. Defeated, he was executed by Juárez, 19 June, 1867.

1867–76

LIBERAL RULE. Juárez returned to the presidency, 1867–71, now a popular symbol of nationalism and liberalism. He sought to unify the country, but years of fighting had brought the habit of violence and had produced economic stagnation. Juárez tried to normalize political life, but his increasingly highhanded rule and his reduction of the army earned him many Liberal as well as Conservative enemies. He died shortly after his re-election, 1872, which had been the occasion for a revolt by one of the defeated candidates, the Liberal General Porfírio Díaz (1830–1915). Vice-President Sebastián Lerdo de Tejada finished Juárez' term, 1872–76. He followed Juárez' policies, incorporating the Laws of Reform into the constitution, but he lacked political skill and appeal. When he was re-elected, Díaz harnessed the diverse opposition factions and with army support overthrew him. The *Reforma* had provided a Liberal program for Mexico, but its leaders had not been able to implement it.

1876–1910

ERA OF PORFÍRIO DÍAZ. From 1876 to 1910 Díaz was president, except for a brief period, 1880–84, when the office was held by Gen. Manuel González. Without changing the Constitution of 1857, Díaz imposed a centralized, 1-party regime, permitted the church to regain its former position, gave the military special benefits, and helped the already wealthy landowners to increase their holdings. Order and material progress were achieved, but at the price of complete domination of the economy by foreign interests and the lack of educational and other reforms benefitting the lower classes. Governmental oppression gradually provoked a violent reaction, ushering in the 1st of the 20th-cent. social revolutions.

1910-14

REVOLUTION. The elections of 1910 saw the appearance of an opposition candidate, the idealistic Liberal, Francisco Madero (1873-1913). Díaz' willingness to share power with a vice-president had stimulated hopes of political change, but these were dashed when Díaz was reelected. Issuing the Plan of San Luís Potosí, 5 Oct., 1910, Madero then called for Díaz' resignation and joined the popular revolts which broke out under Pancho Villa (1877-1923) and Emiliano Zapata (1879?-1919). The Díaz political machine, old and weakened by years of internal feuding, was incapable of meeting the challenge. Riots in Mexico City forced Díaz' resignation, 1911. Madero was elected 1st revolutionary president, Nov. 1911-Feb. 1913. Well-intentioned but too weak for such violent times, Madero could not control the opportunists and his program of political reform did not satisfy the popular leaders, who wanted, above all, land redistribution. Madero was murdered by Victoriano Huerta, who succeeded him, Feb. 1913-July 1914. Huerta was a corrupt counter-revolutionary dictator, with no program which could win him popular support. Thus, Zapata and Villa continued their campaigns, now joined by Venustiano Carranza and Álvaro Obregón, who called for constitutional government. Aided by the U.S. occupation of Veracruz, the insurgent forces seized power, Aug. 1914, and called a convention at Aguascalientes to organize a government. The revolutionaries were divided, however, Villa and Zapata remaining in Mexico City while Carranza and Obregón retired to Veracruz. The struggle among the victors had begun. (*Cont. p. 450.*)

COLOMBIA AND VENEZUELA

1825-30

DISSOLUTION OF GRAN COLOMBIA. President Simón Bolívar (1783– 1830) of Gran Colombia was at odds with Francisco de Paula Santander (1792–1840), his vice-president and the leader of those who opposed Bolívar's centralist, authoritarian, somewhat anticlerical regime. The Santander group also disliked Bolívar's use of Colombian men and money in "foreign" wars. The Constitutional Convention of Ocaña, Mar. 1828, called to heal this rift, failed to do so; and Bolívar became dictator. Santander, accused of complicity in an attempt on Bolívar's life, was exiled. Meanwhile, Bolívar's plan for Pan-American co-operation, the Congress of Panama, 22 June–15 July, 1826, had also failed. Regional uprisings in Venezuela, Colombia, Ecuador, and Peru led to another unsuccessful convention, Jan. 1830, and to the resignation of Bolívar. Joaquín Mosquera (1787–1877) was elected president of Gran Colombia, May, but at that moment Venezuela and Ecuador seceded. Overwhelmed by these difficulties, Bolívar died, 17 Dec.

1831-49

SANTANDER AND THE CREATION OF COLOMBIA. Santander, the "Man of Laws," became president, 1832–37, under a new centralist, conservative constitution. Personally a moderate, Santander appeased the Liberals by curbing the power of the church to some degree and by emphasizing education. His successor, José Márquez, continued Santander's policies, 1837–41, but was more anticlerical, provoking a civil war, 1839–41, in which the Conservatives defeated the federalist Liberals.

PÁEZ AND THE BIRTH OF VENEZUELA. Conservative José Antonio Páez, president, 1830–34, under the 1st Venezuelan constitution, typified the backlands leaders whom the Wars of Independence had brought to power in many Latin American countries. He was, however, more successful than most. A moderate centralist, Páez maintained order and fostered economic progress; he continued state support of the church, but curtailed some of its privileges and made concessions to the Liberals in education and civil liberties. When his successor,

José Vargas, 1835, was overthrown by the army, Páez intervened and had a civilian, Carlos Soublette, finish Vargas' term. Páez was then re-elected, 1839–43. At this point his power was challenged by a new Liberal Party, but Soublette succeeded in returning to the presidency, 1843–46.

CONSERVATIVE RULE IN COLOMBIA. Pedro Alcántara Herrán and his minister, Mariano Ospina Rodríguez, presided, 1842–45, over a prosperous but repressive regime. By the Constitution of 1843 the church was restored to its former powerful position. The election of the opportunistic Tomás Cipriano de Mosquera meant the continuation of this program for a while, but growing Liberal opposition pushed Mosquera into a more tolerant, anticlerical position. During his administration, 1845–49, the Bidlack Treaty was signed with the U.S., 1846, guaranteeing Colombian sovereignty over the Panama Isthmus.

1849–80

THE RULE OF THE LIBERALS. In Colombia the Liberals were strong enough to elect José Hilario López to the presidency, 1849–53, and to promulgate the extremely anticlerical, democratic, and federalist Constitution of 1853. José María Obando, 1853–54, and Manuel María Mallarino, 1855–57, tried to give effect to these reforms, but constant disorder and a deteriorating economic situation enabled the Conservatives to come to power for a brief period. Ospina Rodríguez, 1857–60, seemed willing to compromise on federalism; the new Constitution of 1858 was even more decentralized, but the Conservatives maintained their determination to curb the states. This provoked another civil war in which Mosquera, now a declared Liberal, returned to power. In 1863, a truly radical constitution was passed which, repeating previous federal and anticlerical provisions, stressed civil liberties and provided for a 2-year presidential term. Mosquera, 1861–64, 1866–67, became increasingly repressive, however, and was finally overthrown. Between 1867 and 1880 the congress and the states ruled Colombia, a period punctuated, however, by continuous Conservative revolts.

In Venezuela, José Tadeo Monagas was elected president as a Conservative, but turned into a self-styled Liberal once in power, and defeated 2 revolts against him led by Páez. Little was done during his rule, 1846–51, 1855–58, and that of his brother José Gregorio, 1851–55, apart from the establishment of a dictatorship, whose severity finally led to its overthrow. A civil war broke out between Liberals and Conservatives and Páez returned to the presidency, 1861–63. This time he imposed an authoritarian, clerical regime, but could not crush the Liberals. Páez was unseated by Juan Falcón, 1863–68, who promulgated a democratic, federalist constitution, 1864. Disorder continued, however, allowing José Tadeo Monagas, and then his son, Ruperto, to return to office—this time as Conservatives, 1868–70.

1880–1914

"REGENERATION" AND DICTATORSHIP. Although elected as a Liberal, 1880–82, Rafael Núñez of Colombia turned into a dictatorial Conservative during his 2nd term, 1884–94. Exploiting the centralist constitution adopted in 1886, a concordat, 1887, and the power of his National Party, a coalition of moderate Liberals and Conservatives, Núñez restored both the church and the presidency to their former powerful positions, but with enough concessions to the Liberals to unify the country, at least during his lifetime. Under his successors, Miguel Caro, 1894–98, Manuel Sanclemente, 1898–1900, and José Manuel Marroquín, 1900–3, the Conservatives managed to stay in power. The party was badly shaken, however, by a protracted Liberal revolt, 1899–1903, which culminated in the humiliating loss of Panama. The Conservative Rafael Reyes ruled as a dictator, 1904–9, but by fostering economic development and by giving the Liberals some representation in the government, he reached a party settlement which lasted 20 years. Opposition finally led to his resignation. Carlos Restrepo continued his predecessor's compromise policy, 1910–14, though with greater emphasis on civil liberties and a weak presidency.

In Venezuela, "Regeneration" began earlier than in Colombia. Seizing power as a Liberal, Antonio Guzmán Blanco imposed on Venezuela a repressive, centralized regime, liberal only in its strong anticlericalism. Despite corruption at all levels, the economy prospered and a sense of national unity, based partly on official glorification of Guzmán Blanco, was created. Sometimes ruling in person, 1870–77, 1879–84, sometimes from Paris through puppet presidents, Guzmán Blanco finally lost popularity and was overthrown. Out of the ensuing civil war, one of Guzmán Blanco's puppets, Joaquín Crespo, emerged as victor. Also theoretically a Liberal, Crespo, 1892–98, was preoccupied with a boundary dispute with British Guiana, which was settled somewhat favorably for Venezuela. Crespo's successor was overthrown by a Conservative provincial cattleman, Cipriano Castro, who instituted a corrupt and oppressive dictatorship, 1899–1908. Having no domestic program, Castro concentrated on nationalism. When Britain, Germany, and Italy blockaded Venezuela to enforce the repayment of her debts, 1902–3, Castro gained popularity by resisting "the Powers." His actions were eventually sanctioned by the International Court. Juan Vicente Gómez, Castro's vice-president, seized power in 1908. Political skill and money, derived initially from coffee and cattle, and after 1918 from oil, enabled Gómez to impose a harsh and efficient dictatorship. With the support of a modernized army and foreign investors, Gómez repressed political opponents and successfully ignored demands for social reform. (Cont. p. 454.)

ECUADOR

1825–30

INDEPENDENCE. Ecuador formed part of Bolívar's Gran Colombia, but the continuing presence of Colombian soldiers, bureaucrats, and tax collectors, plus the example of opposition to Bolívar pro-

vided by Venezuela and Colombia, fed a nationalist reaction. A war between Gran Colombia and Peru, 1828–29, increased instability. Finally, Juan José Flores (1800–64), one of Bolívar's generals, threw his military support to the separatists, and Ecuador declared itself independent, 13 May, 1830.

1830–45

RULE OF FLORES. Flores, a Venezuelan, became president, and imposed his own dictatorial rule. Nationalist and civilist resentment against him led to a revolt under Vicente Recafuerte, but the outcome was merely an arrangement whereby the 2 leaders agreed to alternate in the presidency. Recafuerte promulgated an anticlerical, somewhat liberal constitution, but, due partly to the influence of Flores, few reforms were realized. Upon Flores' return to office, 1839–45, a new constitution was drafted, and Flores had himself re-elected for an 8-year term. He was finally overthrown by a group of nationalists and antimilitarists from Guayaquil.

1845–60

RULE OF THE LIBERAL GENERALS. Despite the civil aims of those who had ousted Flores, Ecuador continued to be ruled by a series of nationalistic, anticlerical generals, of whom Vicente Roca, 1845–49; José Urbina, 1851–56; and Francisco Robles, 1856–59, were the most important. The domestic confusion, aggravated by interference from other countries, was epitomized by the cession of Guayaquil to Peru by the provincial boss, Guillermo Franco. At this point Gabriel García Moreno (1821–75) seized power.

1860–75

DICTATORSHIP OF GARCÍA MORENO. García Moreno, 1860–65, believed that only Catholicism could unite Ecuador. By the constitutions of 1861 and 1869 and the Concordat of 1863 he imposed a Conservative, centralist government, which gave the church great power and even deprived non-Catholics of citizenship. Moreno was followed in the presidency by 2 puppets, Jerónimo Carrión, 1865–67, and Javier Espinosa, 1868–69, returning to power himself in 1869. Despite material progress, Liberal opposition grew, culminating in García Moreno's assassination, 5 Aug., 1875.

1875–1914

OLIGARCHS VS. REFORMERS. Ignacio Veintimilla overthrew the moderate but weak Antonio Borrero, and imposed a corrupt military dictatorship. Presidents José Caamaño, 1884–88; Antonio Flores Jijón, 1888–92; and Luís Cordero, 1892–95, attempted to return the country to a clerical, authoritarian, civilian regime, but with limited success. Eloy Álfaro seized the presidency, 1895–1901. He and especially Leonidas Plaza Gutiérrez, 1901–5, introduced educational and anti-clerical reforms. The Liberal program was embodied in the Constitution of 1907, passed during Álfaro's 2nd term, 1906–12, but rule by the oligarchy continued. Álfaro's attempt to stay in power touched off a civil war in which he was killed. Plaza returned to office, 1912–16. Meanwhile, Ecuador had lost territory to Brazil, 1904. (*Cont. p. 454.*)

PERU

1825–35

RULE OF BOLÍVAR'S GENERALS. Bolívar's departure from Peru, 1826, was followed by a struggle for power among the "Marshals of Ayacucho." Andrés Santa Cruz, Bolívar's appointed successor, was a capable president, but soon suffered electoral defeat at the hands of the Liberal, José de Lamar, 1827–28, who launched attacks against Bolívar's troops in Ecuador and Bolivia. Defeat in Ecuador led to the ousting of Lamar by Agustín Gamarra, 1829–33, a Conservative. Luis Orbegosa, a more liberal figure, followed Gamarra in the presidency, 1833–35.

1835–45

IDEA OF CONFEDERATION. Threatened by revolts led by Gamarra and Felipe Salaverry, Orbegosa requested the aid of Santa Cruz, the president of Bolivia. Santa Cruz defeated the rebel generals and then established the Peruvian-Bolivian Confederation, 1836–39, a union between the states of North Peru, South Peru, and Bolivia with Santa Cruz as lifetime "Protector." Despite the advantages of and historical justification for the Confederation, it was opposed by those local leaders who resented Santa Cruz's assumption of power and by Peruvians who considered him a foreign invader. The Confederation's most determined enemies, however, were Argentina and, especially, Chile. Chile declared war, 1837–39, and defeated Santa Cruz's forces at Yungay, 20 Jan., 1839. The Confederation was dissolved, and Gamarra recaptured the presidency, 1839–41. Reversing the policy of Santa Cruz, he started a war to annex Bolivia, but was defeated at Ingaví, 18 Nov., 1840. This temporarily ended foreign wars, but the struggles among Peruvian generals continued.

1845–62

CREATIVE ORDER UNDER CASTILLA. Ramón Castilla (1797?–1867), a Conservative who made some concessions to the Liberals in education and religious matters, gave Peru a much-needed period of stability and progress, 1845–51. He allowed José Echenique to succeed him, 1851–55, but Echenique proved so corrupt that Castilla brought about his deposition, and took power again himself, 1855–60. The Constitution of 28 July, 1860, embodied Castilla's presidentialist but relatively enlightened program.

1863–72

WAR AND CORRUPTION. The Spanish seizure of Peru's guano-rich Chincha Islands, 14 Apr., 1864, theoretically to enforce payment of claims, provoked a diplomatic and political crisis in Peru. After concluding an unpopular treaty with Spain, Juan Pezet, 1863–65, was displaced by Mariano Prado, 1865–68. Meanwhile, as a result of a Latin American Congress held at Lima, a Quadruple Alliance was formed, consisting of Chile, Peru, Ecuador, and Bolivia. The Alliance declared war on Spain, 14 Jan., 1866. After a defeat at Callao, Spain withdrew. The Liberal, Prado, was replaced by a Conservative, Pedro Díaz Canseco, 1868. Canseco's successor, José Balta, 1868–72, symbolized the confusion of that decade. Persuaded by his finance minister, Nicolás de Piérola, Balta embarked on an extravagant program of public works, which further corrupted politics and dissipated Peruvian resources.

1872–83

CIVILIAN RULE AND THE WAR OF THE PACIFIC. The newly formed Civilist Party succeeded in electing Manuel Pardo president, 1872–76. Pardo favored economic nationalism, decentralization, and educational reform, but was hindered by an economic recession. His policies were not continued by his successor, Mariano Prado, 1876–79. Fighting between the Civilists and the Democrats, a radical party led by Nicolás Piérola, weakened Peru, and helped to contribute to her defeat by Chile in the War of the Pacific, 1879–83. During this international crisis, provoked by Chile's desire to exploit the nitrates on Peruvian and Bolivian soil, the presidency was occupied successively by Prado, Piérola, García Calderón, and Montero, 1879–82. Finally, Miguel Iglesias, representing northern Peru, signed the Treaty of Ancón, 20 Oct., 1883, by which Peru ceded the provinces of Tarapacá, Tacna, and Arica to Chile, the latter 2 for 10 years, after which a plebiscite was to be held.

1884–94

THE GENERALS RETURN. With the Civilists discredited by Peru's disastrous defeat, Andrés Cáceres, the leader of guerrilla resistance during the war, seized power, 1884–90. Cáceres and Remigio Morales, 1890–94, helped to reconstruct the country, but their dictatorships drove the political parties into opposition.

1895–1908

PARLIAMENTARY OLIGARCHY. In 1895 Piérola seized the presidency and ruled until 1899. A popular figure, supported by both Democrats and Civilists, he introduced reforms and stimulated the economy. Under Eduardo Romaña, 1899–1903, and José Pardo, 1904–8, there was further progress along these lines.

1908–14

THE SOCIAL QUESTION. Augusto Leguía, 1908–12, encouraged economic development and promised a pro-Indian social policy, but his autocratic methods antagonized both parties. His successor, Guillermo Billinghurst, 1912–14, relied on popular support. Billinghurst was overthrown, however, when he tried to weaken the powers of the oligarchic Congress. (*Cont. p. 453.*)

BOLIVIA

1825–29

INDEPENDENCE. After defeating the last royalist forces at Tumulsa, 2 Apr., 1825, Antonio José de Sucre (1795–1830) remained in charge as Bolívar's representative. Against Bolívar's wishes, independence was declared, 6 Aug., and Sucre became president, 1826–28, under a constitution especially designed for the new nation by Bolívar. This constitution, which specified a lifetime presidency and created a Chamber of Censors, indicated to what degree Bolívar had become a conservative thinker. Sucre ruled well, but fell victim to an anti-Colombian reaction, led by rival Bolivian leaders and assisted by a Peruvian invasion.

1829–41

ERA OF SANTA CRUZ. Andrés Santa Cruz (1792?–1865), a Bolivian, was elected president, 1829–39. A constructive dictator, Santa Cruz established the foundations of the Bolivian state. His continuing interest in Peru, where he had been president, finally led to his creation of the Peruvian-Bolivian Confederation, 1836–39, but when the Confederation was defeated by Chile he fell with it.

1841–80

NATIONAL UNIFICATION AND POLITICAL UNREST. After rallying the country to defeat the Peruvian invasion, José Ballivián became president, 1841–47. Ballivián was autocratic but progressive, and Bolivia under his rule achieved some advances. In 1848 Manuel Belzú seized the presidency and instituted a kind of popular dictatorship, encouraging the urban workers to riot against the upper classes. Belzú's chosen successor, Jorge Córdoba, proved incompetent. He was overthrown by José Linares, the first civilian to be president, 1857–61, but Linares' attempt to impose administrative reforms soon led to his downfall. José María de Achá, a moderate but weak president, followed him, 1861–63.

Under the administration of the ignorant and brutal Mariano Melgarejo, 1864–71, Bolivian political life reached its nadir. Completely irresponsible, Melgarejo ceded rich rubber lands to Brazil, and gave Chile a nitrate concession. He was finally unseated by another violent soldier, Agustín Morales, 1871–72. A breathing space was obtained during the terms of Adolfo Ballivián and Tomás Frías, 1873–75, both civilians and reformers. But Hilarión Daza's seizure of power, 1876–80, meant a return to reckless military dictatorship. Daza's attempt to renege on previous nitrate agreements with Chile, 1866, 1872, 1874, provoked the disastrous War of the Pacific, 1879–83, as a result of which Bolivia lost control of her nitrate deposits and all coastal territory. Accused of treason after Bolivia's defeat, 1880, Daza was overthrown.

1880–1914

GOVERNMENT BY PARTY. The War of the Pacific, temporarily settled by a truce with Chile, 4 Apr., 1884, served as an issue around which Conservative, Liberal, and Democratic parties were formed. Narciso Campero, Daza's successor, was followed in the presidency by the Democrat Gregorio Pacheco, a wealthy mineowner, 1884–88. Political stability continued under the clerical and authoritarian, but economically progressive, regimes of the Conservatives Aniceto Arce, 1888–92; Mariano Baptista, 1892–96; and the less competent Severo Fernández Alonso, 1896–98.

In 1899 José Pando exploited the issue of the location of the capital to attain power, ruling until 1904. The federalist system he proposed was not implemented. Bolivia lost the rich Acre rubber territory to Brazil by the Treaty of Petropolis, 17 Nov., 1903. Under the Liberal Ismael Montes, 1904–8, however, anticlerical laws were passed. In a final treaty with Chile, Bolivia recognized the loss of her coast in exchange for 2 free ports, 20 Oct., 1904. After the term of Eliodoro Villazón, 1909–13, Montes returned to office. (*Cont. p. 453.*)

CHILE

1825–41

FOUNDATION OF THE CONSERVATIVE REPUBLIC. Supreme Director Ramón Freire was unable to control the warring Liberal and Conservative factions, and accomplished little, 1823–26. Resigning, he was replaced by Francisco Pinto, 1826–29, who first tried to govern through the federalist Constitution of 1826 and then through the centralist Constitution of 1828. Liberal disunity finally enabled the Conservatives under Joaquín Prieto to overthrow Pinto at Lircay, 17 Apr., 1830. Prieto became president, 1831–41, but the real ruler of Chile was Diego Portales Palazuelos. Using the Constitution of 1833, Portales Palazuelos imposed an authoritarian, centralist, clerical regime. This system, at least for a time, was well suited to the social structure of the country and, because of Portales' moderation, his control of the army, and his emphasis on economic development, formed the basis for the stability which distinguished Chilean politics. But Portales Palazuelos was assassinated, 6 June, 1837, during the war against the Peruvian-Bolivian Confederation, 1837-39.

1841-61

THE LIBERAL REACTION. Victory brought national self-confidence and the election of Manuel Bulnes, the hero of the war, 1841-51. A period of efficient government ensued, and there was a minor relaxation of Portales' authoritarianism. The growing Liberal Party, however, was not appeased. Manuel Montt, the 1st civilian president of Chile, 1851-61, had a farsighted educational and economic program. But his determined opposition to political reforms infuriated the Liberals, who rebelled twice during his term, 1851, 1859. Montt's insistence on the supremacy of the state over the church during the Affair of the Sacristan, 1856, lost him much Conservative support. Liberals and Conservatives, uniting in opposition to the ruling Nationalist Party, eventually formed the Fusion Party, 1858.

1861-76

PARTY POLITICS AND LIBERAL RULE. Impressed by the strength of the Fusion Party, Montt chose a moderate, José Joaquín Pérez, to succeed him, 1861-71. Pérez proceeded to introduce minor political and religious reforms, eventually turning from the Nationalist Party to the Fusion for support. Meanwhile, Liberals dissatisfied with the Fusion had broken away to form a Radical Party, 1863. The only violence which occurred during Pérez' "Era of Good Feeling" was the Spanish bombardment of Valparaíso, 1865. During the term of Pérez' successor, Federico Errázuriz Zañartu, 1871-76, the Fusion split over the issue of church control of education. Errázuriz then relied on a coalition of Liberals, Radicals, and Nationalists to put through a program which curbed the power of both the president and the church.

1876-86

WAR OF THE PACIFIC. The Liberal Aníbal Pinto, 1876-81, was chiefly concerned with an economic crisis and the war against Peru and Bolivia, 1879-83. Basing her attack on Bolivia's violation of previous treaties, Chile was technically right, but fought the war in fact to wrest from Peru and Bolivia their valuable nitrate deposits. Despite early naval victories won by Chile, 1880, Peruvian resistance postponed peace until 1883, when the Treaty of Ancón, 20 Oct., 1883, was signed. Victory greatly enriched Chile, increased self-confidence and prestige, and fortified the power of the Liberals. Thus, when Domingo Santa María was elected president, 1881-86, he approved all the anticlerical legislation desired by the Liberals, except for the separation of church and state. Progress was achieved in economic development. Political reforms limiting the power of the executive were also enacted, but these had little practical effect.

1886-91

REVOLUTION. General opposition to President José Manuel Balmaceda's progressive program of government planning, economic nationalism, and social reform, 1886-91, and the failure of the Liberal majority in Congress to support him, led Balmaceda to try authoritarian methods to realize his aims. His attempt to override Congress on the budget issue, however, led to his deposition, and the government's troops were defeated by a navy-Congress coalition, probably backed by British nitrate interests. Balmaceda's fall meant the end of the presidentialist, Santiago-based government created by Portales, and the beginning of a decentralized, parliamentary, but even more oligarchical, political system.

1891-1914

THE FUTILE YEARS. Under Jorge Montt, 1891-96, and Federico Errázuriz Echaurren, 1896-1901, both backed by Conservative-led coalitions, there was some economic growth, and constitutional liberties were maintained. The number and power of the parties, however, led to extreme ministerial instability and, consequently, the lack of any constitutional program. Political life became increasingly corrupt and opportunistic. Germán Riesco, 1901-6, a moderate Liberal, achieved diplomatic settlements with Argentina, 20 Nov., 1902, and Bolivia, 20 Oct., 1904, but accomplished little else. Neither Pedro Montt, 1906-10, nor Ramón Barros Luco, 1911-15, dealt with the pressing political issues of labor reform and sustained economic development. These matters became rallying cries for the Radicals and for the Socialist Labor Party, formed in 1912. (*Cont. p. 452.*)

ARGENTINA

1825-29

THE FAILURE OF LIBERALISM. The war with Brazil over the possession of what became Uruguay, 1825-28, brought home to the disunited provinces of Argentina the need for national government. Bernardino Rivadavia (1780-1845), a Liberal from Buenos Aires, was elected president, 1826-27. Though extremely capable, Rivadavia pleased neither the interior provinces, which opposed his centralist constitution, liberal political ideas, and mild anticlericalism, nor Buenos Aires, which disliked his financial policies and the federalization of the city. Failure to win the war finally led to Rivadavia's downfall. The central government was dissolved, each province governing itself as the struggle continued between the Federalists on one side and the Unitarians, supporters of a centralized government based on Buenos Aires, on the other. Neither of the next 2 governors of Buenos Aires, the Federalist Manuel Dorrego, 1827-28, nor the Unitarian Juan Lavalle, 1828-29, could impose order on the country.

1829-35

ROSAS' 1ST TERM. Juan Manuel de Rosas (1793-1877), a wealthy cattleman,

seized the governorship of Buenos Aires in 1829. He defeated the Unitarians, and signed a loose pact of union with 3 other provinces. This pact officially recognized the right of Buenos Aires to conduct foreign affairs, 4 Jan., 1831. Still resisted by some Liberals, Rosas refused to serve again, and led a series of Indian campaigns in the south, increasing his popularity. Meanwhile, his Sociedad Popular Restauradora harassed the governors who succeeded him.

1835-52

DICTATORSHIP OF ROSAS. Rosas was finally granted full powers, which he used to establish a clerical, Conservative, and highly oppressive regime, 1835-52. Refusing to set up a national constitutional government, he styled himself a Federalist. In fact, his personal power together with his friendships with provincial leaders permitted him to control the country. His economic policies benefited mainly Buenos Aires. He relied on his popularity, and on an aggressive foreign policy, in his campaign to unify, and perhaps expand, Argentina. An attack on the Peruvian-Bolivian Confederation failed, 1837, but he had more success in his resistance to the French and British blockades of Buenos Aires, 1838-40, 1845-50, provoked by Argentina's interference in the affairs of Uruguay. In the end Rosas was defeated at Caseros, 3 Feb., 1852, by a coalition of provincial governors led by Justo José Urquiza (1800-1870), by Unitarians and Liberal intellectuals at home, and by Brazil and Uruguay abroad. Rosas had created a nation, but at the price of arbitrary dictatorship and rule by the cattle barons of Buenos Aires.

1852-62

THE 2 ARGENTINAS. Urquiza now ruled as a provisional president. His gaucho background and his federalism, however, antagonized Buenos Aires, which demanded special status for itself. The other provinces formed the Argentine Confederation under Urquiza, 1854-60, and adopted the Constitution of 1853, a pro-church, nominally federalist, document. At Cepeda, 23 Oct., 1859, the 1st clash between the 2 Argentinas, Urquiza triumphed, but Buenos Aires remained the richest and most populous province. At Pavón, 17 Sept., 1861, the Confederation, now under Santiago Derquí, withdrew from association with Buenos Aires, leaving Bartolomé Mitre (1821–1906) provisional president, 1860–62.

1862–68

WAR OF THE TRIPLE ALLIANCE. Bartolomé Mitre, 1862–68, the 1st of a group of progressive presidents, set up a Liberal National government, and reached a compromise on the issue of the status of Buenos Aires, but was soon diverted by the War of the Triple Alliance, 1865–70, in which Brazil, Argentina, and Uruguay fought Paraguay. Intervention by all three countries in the affairs of Uruguay caused this costly and unpopular war. Territorially, Argentina profited little from participation in it.

1868–80

THE SCHOOLMASTER PRESIDENTS. During the administration of the brilliant and energetic Domingo Faustino Sarmiento, 1868–74, a provincial sympathetic to Buenos Aires, education and immigration were emphasized. Sarmiento also used the power of the central government to repress provincial revolts. In 1874 dissension in Buenos Aires again enabled a provincial, Nicolás Avellaneda, to win the presidency, 1874–80. Avellaneda's term was one of increasing prosperity for the country. The status of Buenos Aires was finally settled in 1880, when Julio Roca, backed by Avellaneda and the provinces, defeated the Buenos Aires candidate, federalized the city, and created a new provincial capital.

1880–90

THE CORRUPT OLIGARCHY. During the term of Julio Roca, 1880–86, of the landowners' Partido Autonomista Nacional (PAN), Argentina experienced a booming prosperity, which stimulated much speculation in land and railroads.

Anticlerical laws were passed at this time, 1884. Unfortunately Roca's successor, Miguel Juárez Célman, 1886–90, allowed corruption and reckless financing to produce a serious economic crisis. Economic difficulties and the iron rule of the PAN party machine provoked a revolt by the newly formed Radical Party under Leandro Alem, 1890. The Radicals were defeated, but Juárez Célman was forced to resign.

1890–1904

THE FLEXIBLE OLIGARCHY. Vice-President Carlos Pellegrini, 1890–92, who succeeded Célman, was no reformer, but by trying to stabilize the economy and reduce corruption he revealed the readiness of the oligarchy to adapt itself to change. This ability and the divisions among the Radicals made possible the election of another Conservative PAN candidate, Luis Sáenz Peña, 1892–95. A sick man and without party support, Sáenz Peña had to contend with both a reaction in Congress against the power of the president and with another Radical revolt, 1893. Resigning, he was replaced by Vice-President José Uriburu, 1895–98. It was not until the re-election of Roca, 1898–1904, that the oligarchy really recovered from the crisis of 1890. Despite the growing power of the Radicals, now under Hipólito Irigoyen, and the existence of a Socialist Party, another wave of prosperity permitted Roca to reimpose his centralized, corrupt, and rather autocratic style of rule. This time his term was enhanced by a favorable settlement with Chile, 1902, and the enunciation of the Drago Doctrine, 1904, the internationally agreed principle that foreign debts could not be collected by force.

1904–14

THE RADICAL MOVEMENT. Conservative Presidents Manuel Quintana, 1904–6, and José Figueroa Alcorta, 1906–10, continued to ignore the Radicals and their demands, despite another revolt, 1905. By 1910, however, lower- and middle-class pressure made PAN realize that some compromise was required.

Roque Sáenz Peña, a Conservative with a reform program, became president, 1910–16. His electoral law, signed in 1912, guaranteed universal male suffrage and the secret ballot, and eventually enabled the Radicals to come to power legally. (*Cont. p. 451.*)

PARAGUAY

1825–40

THE HERMIT DICTATOR. Dr. José Gaspar Rodríguez Francia (1761?–1840), in breaking the power of the church and upper classes, imposed an iron dictatorship on Paraguay, 1814–40. Fearing the threat to his position which immigration and foreign trade might bring, he completely isolated his country from the outside world. This policy fostered national unification, but kept Paraguay backward.

1841–62

RULE OF CARLOS LÓPEZ. Carlos Antonio López, 1844–62, more progressive but less honest than Francia, allowed external trade, conciliated the church, and sought to increase national prestige by creating a powerful army and by pressing claims against foreign powers.

1862–76

WAR OF THE TRIPLE ALLIANCE. Francisco Solano López, 1862–70, the son of Carlos López, thought of himself as the arbiter, and perhaps one day the conqueror, of the La Plata region. When his diplomatic attempts to curb Brazilian and Argentinian intervention in Uruguay were rebuffed, López attacked both countries, initiating the War of the Triple Alliance, 1865–70. That Paraguay survived a crushing defeat was due only to the rivalry between the victors, for she had lost nearly half her population and a great deal of territory. Under a new constitution, Cirilo Antonio Rivarola became president, 1870. Brazilian troops did not leave Paraguay until 1876.

1876–1914

THE PERIOD OF INSTABILITY. In reaction to 62 years of dictatorship, Paraguayan politics now entered a period of almost continuous disorder. The party of the Conservatives ruled, led by Bernardino Caballero and then by Patricio Escobar. A revolt, 1904, brought the Liberals to power, but the change meant little for the people of Paraguay. (*Cont. p. 453.*)

URUGUAY

1825–35

INDEPENDENCE. The war between Brazil and Argentina was ended by Great Britain, which proposed the creation of a new state out of the disputed territory, 27 Aug., 1828. Independence was guaranteed by the Constitution of 1830, and José Fructuoso Rivera (1790?–1854) became the first president of Uruguay, 1830–35. Unwilling to surrender power to a successor, Manuel Oribe, 1835–39, Rivera led a revolt. From this struggle emerged Uruguay's 2 traditional parties, the conservative, rural, clerical *blancos,* led by Oribe, and the liberal *colorados,* under Rivera.

1836–63

CIVIL WAR AND FOREIGN INTERVENTION. Despite Rosas' backing of Oribe, aid from many quarters (Brazil, certain Argentine provinces, the Unitarians, and France) put Rivera back into the presidency, 1839–46. When the French withdrew, Oribe renewed his offensive, which culminated in the siege of *colorado*-controlled Montevideo, 1843–51. The French and British blockade of Buenos Aires, 1845–49, helped Rivera somewhat, but it was the forces of Brazil and the Argentinian, Urquiza, that raised the siege and defeated Oribe. Despite a compromise between the parties, the *colorado* President Venancio Flores, 1851–55, was soon faced with a *blanco* revolt, which even Brazilian aid could not quell, and the *blancos* seized power, 1855–63. Stable government, however, was rendered impossible by continuing pressure from Buenos Aires and Brazil.

1863–71

WAR OF THE TRIPLE ALLIANCE. An invasion in support of Flores, backed toward the end by Brazilian troops, overthrew the *blanco* President Anastasio Aguirre, 1865, and provoked Paraguay's attack on Brazil. This was the 1st stage of the War of the Triple Alliance. Despite the assassination of President Flores, 1868, the *colorados* remained in control, defeating the *blancos* again in a new civil war, 1870–71.

1872–90

RULE OF THE COLORADO GENERALS. A postwar settlement gave the *blancos* a subsidy and control of 4 of Uruguay's 15 departments. This assured the peace needed for economic progress. The gaucho leaders gave way to a series of army generals: Lorenzo Latorre, 1876–80, autocratic but interested in education; Máximo Santos, 1882–86, unpopular and dictatorial; and Máximo Tajes, 1886–90, who tried to curb the army and conciliate both political parties.

1890–1903

RULE OF THE COLORADO CIVILIANS. Julio Herrera y Obes, 1890–94, worked to establish competent civilian government, but the highhanded methods of his successor, Juan Idiarte Borda, 1894–97, provoked another *blanco* revolt. The *colorados* promised concessions, but these were not implemented by Juan Cuestas, 1897–1903, who instituted a reasonably progressive though authoritarian regime.

1903–14

BATLLE AND THE BIRTH OF MODERN URUGUAY. During his 1st term José Batlle y Ordóñez, 1903–7, was preoccupied with another *blanco* revolt, which he settled by substituting proportional representation for the old system of *blanco* control of rural departments. With the country more unified, his successor Claudio Williman, 1907–11, and later Batlle himself, 1911–15, were able to introduce a program of social welfare reform, economic nationalism, state-owned corporations, and increased political democracy, including the establishment of a biparty plural executive. (*Cont. p. 451.*)

BRAZIL

1825–31

REIGN OF DOM PEDRO I. Due to the peaceful transition from colony to empire, 1822, the advice of capable ministers, and Pedro's own efforts, Brazil remained a unified, relatively stable state during the first difficult post-Independence years. But Pedro's failure to work within the framework of the Constitution of 1824 and his extravagance made him increasingly unpopular. Nativist feeling was aroused by his appointment of Portuguese to high office and by the way in which he involved Brazil in Portuguese dynastic struggles. A treaty with Great Britain, 23 Nov., 1826, promising to end the slave trade antagonized the planters. Finally, the unsuccessful war against Argentina to retain Uruguay as a Brazilian province, 1825–28, weakened Pedro's position. He was forced to abdicate in favor of his 5-year-old son, 7 Apr., 1831.

1831–41

THE REGENCY. During the first years of Pedro II's minority, a 3-man regency governed Brazil, 1831–35. It was seriously weakened by fighting among the newly emerging national political parties. The chief problem, however, lay in a rash of regional revolts, some military, some popular—both monarchical and republican. The regency responded with the Additional Act, 12 Aug., 1834, which appeased the federalists by giving more power to the provincial legislatures, suppressed the conservative Council of State, and created a single regent. The priest, Diogo Antonio Feijó, the first regent, 1835–37, was capable, but his autocratic measures antagonized Congress without repressing the 2 worst uprisings of the decade: a civil war in Pará, 1835–40, and the Revolução Farroupilha in Rio Grande do Sul, 1835–45, this latter state even declaring itself an independent republic. Under Feijó's successor, the Marquês de Olinda (1793–1870), national unity continued to be threatened by federalist revolts, 1837–40. Both parties agreed that the majority of Pedro II should be proclaimed early in order to strengthen the central government. The regency had avoided both partition and dictatorship, but had been too preoccupied with maintaining order to institute many lasting reforms.

1841–50

CONSOLIDATION. A man of wide intellectual interests and liberal ideas, Pedro II (ruled 1841–89) soon showed himself to be a capable, conscientious emperor. Aided at first by the Conservatives, he pursued a policy of centralization, reversing the Additional Act, 3 Dec., 1841, and successfully repressing a new group of revolts as well as the secession of Rio Grande do Sul, 1845. The political parties also felt Pedro's firm hand. Although he carefully maintained parliamentary forms, the power granted him by the constitution and his own political skill enabled him to control the government. He favored no particular party. Efficient administration gave his regime a progressive reputation.

1850–60

THE TRIUMPHANT DECADE. Due to Pedro's popularity and to the political stability which culminated in the biparty Ministry of Conciliation, 1853, Brazil was able to embark on a period of remarkable economic progress. National self-confidence inspired an aggressive foreign policy. True, Brazil was forced by British military pressure to abolish the slave trade, 4 Sept., 1850, but Brazilian influence continued strong in the La Plata region to the south. The threat posed by Argentina to the independence of Uruguay and the possibility of a denial of free access to the La Plata River system provoked Brazil to join the coalition which overthrew Rosas in 1852. In return Brazil received much disputed territory and a decisive influence in Uruguay, where in 1854 Brazilian troops put the *colorado* party in power.

1860–70

WAR OF THE TRIPLE ALLIANCE. The Christie Affair, 1861–65, a diplomatic clash between Britain and Brazil over a minor incident involving British sailors, showed that Brazil was still not strong enough to resist a great European power. The War of the Triple Alliance, 1864–70, however, proved that Brazil was dominant in Latin America. This war, in which Brazil, Argentina, and Uruguay imposed a crushing defeat on Paraguay, grew out of the rivalry among these countries for effective control of Uruguay, the key to dominion in the La Plata region. Pressured by Rio Grande do Sul interests with investments in Uruguay, Pedro ordered the invasion of that state in support of the *colorados,* who favored Brazil, 1865. This provoked the Paraguayan dictator López to attack Brazil and then Argentina, allegedly in defense of the balance of power. Paraguay's tenacious resistance prolonged the uneven struggle until the death of López, 1 Mar., 1870. The positive results for Brazil were an increase in prestige and territory and a sense of national unity.

1870–80

BREAKDOWN OF THE SYNTHESIS. The formation of a Republican Party, 1870, had its roots in traditional agitation for a more decentralized, democratic government, but it was also a specific protest against the length of the War of the Triple Alliance and Pedro's use of his moderating power to oust a Liberal ministry, 1868. Slavery was challenged, too, receiving its 1st defeat in the Rio Branco Law, 28 Sept., 1871, which freed all future slave offspring, though apprenticing them to their masters until the age of 21. Finally, a quarrel with the church over Freemasonry and the power of the state in religious matters, 1872–75, lost Pedro the support of the Brazilian Church and the religious population.

1880–89

THE COMING OF THE REPUBLIC. Despite the return of a Liberal ministry, 1878, and a more democratic electoral law, 1881, Pedro's power became increasingly resented as he grew out of touch with national problems. Meanwhile the abolitionist movement gained strength, leading 1st to the passage of a law freeing all slaves over 60, 28 Sept., 1885, and ultimately to complete abolition, 13 May, 1888. Since the "Golden Law" granted no compensation to slaveowners, it greatly alienated the planter class from the monarchy. The decisive blow to the empire, however, came from the army, which had emerged from the War of the Triple Alliance with a new sense of professional importance. From 1884 onward, various army officers made determined efforts to win a special political status for the army. When the emperor and the parties resisted these attempts, the officers became republicans. Tacitly supported by other groups which opposed the monarchy, Floriano Peixoto, Deodoro da Fonseca, and the civilian positivist intellectual, Benjamín Constant, forced Pedro to abdicate after an unexpected military coup, 15 Nov., 1889.

1889–98

BIRTH PANGS OF THE REPUBLIC. Deodoro da Fonseca (1827–92), the president of the provisional government, 1889–91, promulgated decrees establishing a federal republic, separating church and state, and widening the electorate, all of which were confirmed by the Constitution of 24 Feb., 1891. Despite these federalist provisions, Fonseca's government was so centralized and presidentialist that, coupled with an economic crisis, it provoked a revolt. Fonseca was forced to resign in favor of his vice-president, Floriano Peixoto, 1892–94. Peixoto proved to be even more authoritarian than Fonseca, but he was also far more capable. He met the growing dissatisfaction with the republic, which culminated in the monarchist uprising supported by the navy and Rio Grande do Sul, 1893–94, by repression. He was respected, however, as a founder of the republic and for permitting Prudente José de Moraes Barros, a civilian, to succeed him, 1894–98. A transitional president, Moraes Barros relaxed Peixoto's tightly centralized control, and made some progress in the fields of finance and foreign relations, reaching a boundary settlement with Argentina, 9 Aug., 1895. But his administration was discredited by its clumsy repression of the revolt of the backland religious community of Canudos.

1898–1914

THE STABLE REPUBLIC. During the administration of Manuel de Campos Salles, 1898–1902, civilian, constitutional government was the rule. Foreign loans helped to finance the bureaucracy, public works, and the army. The Treaty of Petropolis with Bolivia, 17 Nov., 1903, which gave Brazil most of the rubber-rich Acre territory, was one of several favorable boundary settlements with both Latin American states and European colonial powers. The presidencies of Francisco Rodrigues Alves, 1902–6, and Affonso Penna, 1906–9, continued this constructive record. Politics were still quite corrupt, however, and were controlled by the state machines of Rio de Janeiro, Minas Gerais, and São Paulo. The electoral victory of Marshal Hermes da Fonseca, 1910–14, indicated that the army had again replaced the party oligarchies as the arbiter of national politics. Fonseca's corrupt and dictatorial regime ushered in an era of severe economic and political problems for the republic. (Cont. p. 453.)

CENTRAL AMERICA

1825–40

UNITED PROVINCES OF CENTRAL AMERICA. This was a loose federation, comprising Guatemala, Nicaragua, Honduras, El Salvador, and Costa Rica. Manuel Arce (1783?–1847), its 1st President, 1825–29, failed to satisfy either the Liberal or Conservative factions, which soon, 1826, began fighting over the issues of anticlericalism, centralism, and the dominant position of Guatemala. Liberal Honduran Francisco Morazón (1799–1842) was victorious, and during his progressive administration, 1829–39, he sought to realize a program of federal government, economic growth, and, especially, anticlericalism. This last issue eventually provoked Conservative and Indian opposition, led by Rafael Carrera (1814–65). The Union was dissolved, 1838, and Morazón defeated, 1840. Attempts to revive the Confederation were made every decade thereafter, but, except for short-term agreements, they were uniformly unsuccessful.

1840–70

CENTRAL AMERICA IN CONFUSION. During the 30 years after 1840, unstable dictatorships of varying severity and civil wars within the various states between Liberal and Conservative factions were the general rule. The outstanding personalities of the time were the Guatemalan Indian Rafael Carrera, the North American William Walker (1824–60), and the Costa Rican Presidents Braulio Carrillo (1800–1845) and Juan Mora Porras (1814–60). Carrillo, 1835–42, and Mora Porras, 1849–59, in co-operation with a relatively enlightened oligarchy, helped lay the basis for Costa Rica's unusually progressive and democratic political tradition. In Guatemala, Carrera, 1838–65, supported by the Conservatives and his own Indian followers, instituted a clerical dictatorship, which permitted some material progress but gave little real help to the large Indian community. By intervening in neighboring El Salvador and Honduras, Carrera enabled the Conservatives to come to power in those countries. Nicaragua suffered from being the likely site for an interoceanic canal, thereby attracting the attention of foreign powers. The Clayton-Bulwer Treaty between the U.S. and Britain, 19 Apr., 1850, which followed British occupation of San Juan del Norte, 1848, and the establishment of Vanderbilt's Transit Co. to ferry California gold-rush prospectors, stipulated that neither country was to control a future canal or to occupy any part of Central America. Intervention reached a peak soon after, however, when the U.S. adventurer William Walker made himself president of Nicaragua, 1856–57, with the help of the Liberals. Opposition to him united Central America, but only until his defeat. The Liberals were discredited, and the Conservatives ruled Nicaragua, 1863–93.

1870–1914

RULE BY DICTATORS. Guatemala's next important president, 1871–85, was Justo Rufino Barrios (1835?–85), who came to power as a Liberal but soon instituted another dictatorial, anti-Indian regime. An able administrator, Barrios promoted modernization by means of anticlerical legislation and by encouraging foreign investment. He also tried to revive a Central American Union, but was killed when he invaded El Salvador to impose it. His most notorious successor was the corrupt "Liberal" dictator, Manuel Estrada Cabrera (1857–1924), 1898–1920. Unlike Guatemala, El Salvador was governed during this period by a fairly progressive group of families. Nicaragua, however, suffered Central America's 2 chronic evils: dictatorship and foreign intervention. Conservative disunity enabled the Liberal José Santos Zelaya (1853–1919) to seize the presidency, 1893–1909. His tyrannical and corrupt regime earned him many domestic enemies; his meddling in the politics of Honduras and El Salvador in the name of Central

American unity led to the Washington Conference, 1907, which set up a Central American Court to forestall such aggression.

FOREIGN INTERVENTION. The threat of British intervention in Nicaragua to collect unpaid debts provoked the U.S. to aid the Conservatives in overthrowing Zelaya. A period of U.S. financial and military control followed. Conservative President Adolfo Díaz (1874–1964) was kept in office by U.S. marines, 1912. Honduras was also under the shadow of the United Fruit Co. and the marines at this time. Former President Policarpo Bonilla (1858–1926) was restored to power, 1911–13, with the help of the U.S. The most striking example of U.S. domination, however, was the creation of Panama out of Colombian territory, 1903. The 2nd Hay-Pauncefote Treaty with Britain, 18 Nov., 1901, had granted the U.S. the sole right to construct an interoceanic canal through the isthmus. Colombia refused to ratify the Hay-Herrán Treaty, 22 Jan., 1903. Impatient, the U.S. encouraged Panamanians to revolt, 3 Nov., and by the Hay-Bunau Varilla Treaty, 18 Nov., obtained permanent rights to a 10-mi. zone and permission to intervene in the rest of Panama. Despite the apparatus of a constitutional democracy (Manuel Amador Guerrero [1833–1909] became the 1st president, 1904–8), Panama remained under the rule of a feuding oligarchy, the national police force, and, most important, the U.S.-owned Canal, which opened 15 Aug., 1914. The exception to this gloomy picture was again Costa Rica. Although at first under the dictatorial but economically progressive administration of Tomás Guardia (1832–82), 1870–82, by 1889 the political climate was democratic enough for an opposition candidate to win the presidential election. (*Cont. p. 454.*)

THE CARIBBEAN ISLANDS

1825–44

SPANISH ISLANDS. Cuba's isolated location, the influx of many royalist refugees from mainland Latin America, and the presence of a strong Spanish garrison meant that Cuba, and the similarly situated Puerto Rico, remained loyal to Spain even after her other colonies had declared their independence. Hispaniola, however, comprising present-day Haiti and the Dominican Republic, took the opposite course. Independent since 1804, Haiti was ruled, 1818–43, by the French-educated mulatto, Jean Pierre Boyer (1776–1850). Initially liberal, Boyer became more dictatorial as Haiti's economy and administration deteriorated, a result of the earlier destruction of her educated class and of financial burdens imposed by France in accordance with the 1825 treaty of recognition.

During this period the Dominican Republic was ruled, 1822–44, by Haiti, which occupied it, exploited it economically, and repressed it culturally. Boyer's overthrow gave Dominican revolutionaries the chance to declare independence.

BRITISH ISLANDS. By the Emancipation Act of 28 Aug., 1833, all slaves in the British West Indies under 6 years of age were declared free, the remainder being required to serve a period of apprenticeship: 6 years for field hands, 4 years for others. For field laborers the apprenticeship system was terminated in 1838.

FRENCH ISLANDS. In Martinique slave conspiracies were uncovered in 1822, 1824, and 1833. In 1832, however, the tax on slave manumissions was abolished throughout the French islands, and in 1833 registration of slaves was made compulsory, and mutilation and branding of captured fugitives declared illegal. In 1836 all slaves entering France itself became automatically free.

In 1831 free persons of color were granted full civil rights, and in 1834 Colonial Councils were established for Martinique and Guadeloupe.

1845–99

CUBAN INDEPENDENCE. Increasingly authoritarian rule from Spain, which hurt the sugar industry, finally drove Cuba to rebel. The 1st attempt, the destructive 10 Years' War, 1868–78, was unsuccessful. It did, however, intensify the desire for independence, which increased as administrative reforms and freer trade policy promised by Spain failed to materialize. In 1896 a Cuban government in exile in New York, headed by Tomás Estrada Palma (1835–1908) and the poet journalist José Martí (1853–95), was able to instigate a full-scale revolt. When setbacks threatened another defeat, the U.S. intervened and defeated Spain, 1898. Puerto Rico became U.S. territory and Cuba, as pledged by the Treaty of Paris, 10 Dec., gained its independence.

HAITI. Haiti meanwhile experienced a period of economic and social stagnation under a series of incompetent and tyrannical generals, culminating in the administration, 1847–59, of Faustin Soulouque. The more progressive presidents who followed him, Fabre Geffrard, 1859–67; Lysius Salomon, 1879–88; and Florvil Hyppolite, 1889–96, tried to restore constitutional government, foster the economy, and create foreign ties, but they made little headway.

DOMINICAN REPUBLIC. The Dominican Republic had similar problems plus the extra complication of the threat of another Haitian invasion. This provoked the 2 dictatorial generals who alternated between 1844 and 1878 in the presidency, Pedro Santana (1801–64) and Buenaventura Báez (1810–84), to seek protectorate status for the Dominican Republic. Santana restored it to Spain, 1861–65, but Spanish political, economic, and ecclesiastical control turned out to be distasteful to the Dominicans and also to U.S. investors. Báez looked to the U.S., offering the lease of Samaná Bay and then annexation, an offer declined by the U.S. Senate. The Dominican Republic did, however, become an economic dependency of the U.S. especially during the harsh, efficient dictatorship, 1882–99, of Ulises Heureaux (1846?–99).

BRITISH CROWN COLONIES. Following a revolt in Jamaica, Oct. 1865, the Jamaica Act was passed, 12 Dec., which,

together with an Imperial Act of the following year, removed power from the island's representative Assembly and transferred it to the governor. Crown-colony government was also initiated in the other British islands, except Barbados. On 19 May, 1884, a Legislative Council was created in Jamaica, and on 1 Aug., 1891, a measure of representative government was attained by British Guiana.

1899–1914

U.S. INTERVENTION. During the short period of direct U.S. rule, 1899–1901, Cuba was administered by a military governor, Leonard Wood (1860–1927). A centralized, anticlerical constitution was then promulgated, and Tomás Estrada Palma became president, 1902–6. But the Platt Amendment, which the U.S. insisted be incorporated in the constitution, made Cuba effectively a protectorate, since it provided for U.S. intervention if required and limited Cuba's right to contract debts and to make treaties. When the re-election of Estrada was challenged by the Liberal opposition, he appealed to the U.S., and Charles Magoon, supported by U.S. marines, was sent in as governor, 1906–9. A new election brought José Miguel Gómez (1858–1921) to power, 1909–13. Despite Gómez' Liberal affiliations, this meant another round of venality, violence, sugar prosperity, swollen bureaucracy, and eventual U.S. intervention, 1912. Mario García Menocal continued this unimpressive record, 1913–21.

Puerto Rico remained under the U.S., but after the Foraker Act, 12 Apr., 1900, was governed by civil authorities. The Dominican Republic and Haiti were also occupied by U.S. forces. Continuing disorder hurt North American investments, and failure to satisfy European creditors encouraged foreign intervention. The U.S. first administered the Dominican customs revenues, 1905, and after a brief interval of political calm, 1908–11, under Ramón Cáceres, assumed complete control, 1916. (*Cont. p. 328.*)

The Areas of White Settlement, 1770–1870

CANADA

1760–83

CONQUEST OF FRENCH CANADA. By the Treaty of Paris, 10 Feb., 1763, Britain's conquest of French Canada was confirmed. France also ceded Cape Breton Island, and the Mississippi was recognized as the boundary between Louisiana and the British colonies. After 1763 Britain faced the problem of incorporating a French Roman Catholic colony into a British Protestant system of government; differences in religion, law, and nationality formed the background of subsequent political and social discord.

PROCLAMATION OF 1763. 7 Oct. The former French colony was renamed Quebec (the boundaries roughly those of the seignorial tenures), while, in the south, lands (New Brunswick and Prince Edward Island) still largely unsettled were added to Nova Scotia, and Labrador was placed under the Newfoundland administration. Territory west of a line drawn approximately at the Ottawa River became an Indian reserve, in which land purchases and settlement were prohibited, though trading licenses were freely granted. A governor, with a nominated advisory council of 4 official and 8 nonofficial members, received restricted powers to legislate and create courts of justice until an Assembly could be summoned.

ADMINISTRATION OF GOV. MURRAY. James Murray (gov., 1763–66) set up a judiciary, continuing as far as possible French laws of property and inheritance, and allowed Catholics to sit on juries. He used revenue from customs' dues to defray administrative expenses, which angered the British merchants of Montreal, as also did his refusal to call an assembly because anti-Catholic exclusion laws would have placed the French majority at the mercy of the British minority. The merchants refused to pay duties,

petitioned the Board of Trade in London, and forced Murray's recall, 1766.

Gov. Sir Guy Carleton, Lord Dorchester, built a line of forts along the Lake Champlain route linking Quebec with New York, 1768. By an ordinance of 1770, he established 2 courts of common pleas to take over the jurisdiction of the justices of the peace. Confusion of laws and institutions, the doubtful legality of ordinances, and fiscal measures increased pressure for new legislation.

QUEBEC ACT. 7 Oct., 1774. The western boundaries were redrawn to include land set apart by the Proclamation of 1763, and the Ohio and Mississippi valleys. The territory remained an Indian reserve, but was placed under the colony's jurisdiction. A revised oath allowed Roman Catholics to take office. The governor, with an appointed council of 17–23 members, was granted legislative authority, but without power to tax except for local improvements. Ordinances dealing with religious matters had to have royal consent. The seignorial system was continued, and French law was maintained for civil cases, while British law was to be used in criminal cases. The Quebec Revenue Act, 1774, imposed customs duties, and crown revenues were to pay the costs of civil administration.

WAR OF THE AMERICAN REVOLUTION. 1775–83. Although the Quebec Act removed some French-Canadian grievances, the British minority considered it a punitive measure directed against the American colonies. The 1st Continental Congress appealed, 1774, to Canadians to rebel, and John Brown, a New England lawyer, attempted, Mar. 1775, to win the support of dissatisfied Montreal and Quebec merchants. In May 1775, the "Green Mountain Boys" under Ethan Allen, joined by Benedict Arnold, captured Fort Ticonderoga and Crown Point, Arnold later occupying St. John's.

Montreal was captured, 12 Nov., and Quebec was besieged throughout the winter. The arrival, May 1776, of British reinforcements forced the American troops to retreat, and by the end of the year Lake Champlain was again under British control. By the Treaty of Paris, 6 Sept., 1783, Britain surrendered the country between the Ohio and the Mississippi, and it was provided that the American government would recommend to the individual states appropriate compensation for the Loyalists.

1784–1814

LOYALIST IMMIGRATION. 1783–91. Disenfranchised and dispossessed by the Revolution, Loyalists from the former American colonies moved into Canada. About 35,000 went to Nova Scotia, from which, 1784, New Brunswick was separated under a gov., nominated council, and elected assembly; Prince Edward Island became a separate administrative area under a lieut. gov. Another 20,000 moved to Quebec with the largest settlements on the upper St. Lawrence, Lake

Ontario, Lake Erie, and the Eastern Townships region bordering New York and Vermont. Land grants of 200 acres were given to noncommissioned officers, while privates and civilians received 100 acres, with 50 acres for each additional member of the family. The composition of the Canadian population was altered by the Loyalist immigrants, who increased the pressure for the use of English law and language, and for a representative assembly with powers to tax. Following the *Haldimand* v. *Cochrane* case, the English party forced, 1784, through the Legislative Council an ordinance introducing habeas corpus, and Lieut. Gov. Henry Hamilton, in the absence of Gov. Haldimand, instituted trial by jury, 1785. In 1785, Loyalists petitioned that the settlements above Montreal should be constituted as a separate province.

CANADA ACT. 10 June, 1791. This act divided Quebec at the Ottawa River into 2 provinces, Upper and Lower Canada, each with a Legislative Council nominated for life and an elected Assembly, the crown reserving the right to disallow colonial laws. In Upper Canada,

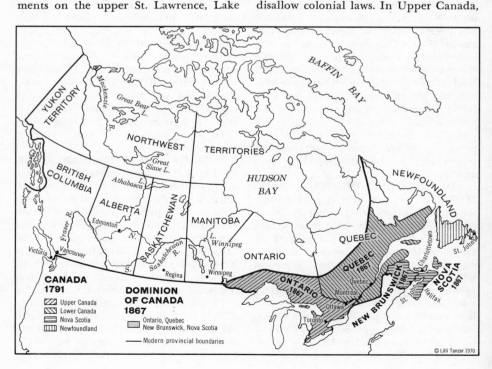

CANADA 1791
▨ Upper Canada
▧ Lower Canada
▤ Nova Scotia
▥ Newfoundland

DOMINION OF CANADA 1867
▦ Ontario, Quebec New Brunswick, Nova Scotia
— Modern provincial boundaries

© Lilli Tanzer 1970

land was to be granted in freehold; in Lower Canada, seignorial tenure was retained unless conveyance by English law was requested. One-seventh of all lands granted was to be reserved for the maintenance of the Protestant clergy (Clergy Reserves), and the rights of Roman Catholics were guaranteed.

WESTERN EXPANSION AND TRADE. Before the British conquest of Canada, British and French fur traders in the western territories had competed for the support of the Indian tribes, on whose co-operation successful trading largely depended. As French competition increased, the Hudson's Bay Co., whose charter of 2 May, 1670, gave it a monopoly and jurisdictional control of the Rupert's Land region, pushed inland to set up trading posts. Subsequent rivalry arose between the Hudson's Bay Co. and Montreal fur traders, who, in 1783, formed the Northwest Co. (merged with Hudson's Bay Co., 1821), which established a network of posts from Lake Superior to the Rockies, while at the same time American traders were coming in from the Ohio area. Peter Pond, 1775–88, re-explored much of the area covered by Sieur de La Vérendrye, 1731–42, and crossed the watershed between rivers emptying into Hudson Bay and the Arctic. Alexander Mackenzie (1764–1820) discovered, 1789, the Mackenzie River, and in 1793, making the 1st overland journey from the east, reached the Pacific coast. At first for the Hudson's Bay Co., and later for the Northwest Co., David Thompson (1770–1857) explored, traded, and surveyed the future Manitoba, Saskatchewan, and Alberta, 1785–1807, and Simon Fraser (1776–1862) with John Stuart (1779–1847) explored the Fraser River.

On the Pacific coast the fur-trading post which had been set upon Nootka Sound was seized by Spain, which, by an agreement with the British, surrendered its claims to the area, 1790. Between 1792 and 1794 George Vancouver explored the coast and circumnavigated Vancouver Island. J. J. Astor's Pacific Fur Co. established, 1811, a trading post at Astoria, near the mouth of the Columbia River. At the same time, Lord Selkirk overcame the opposition of the Hudson's Bay Co., from

which he bought 116,800 sq. mi. of land, and was given a grant, 1812, to settle Scottish immigrants in the Red River Valley. In 1815 and 1816, forcible attempts by the Northwest Co. to oust the colonists failed, and after an investigation, 1817, Selkirk's grant was confirmed and the colony resettled.

JAY'S TREATY. 17 Nov., 1794. Britain, having failed to evacuate the northwestern military posts ceded to the U.S. by the Treaty of Paris, agreed to withdraw by 1796, and a boundary commission was appointed to settle the disputed western and Maine frontiers. But western expansion by both countries, American immigration into Upper Canada, and intrigue for Indian support continued, the British being accused of supplying and inciting the Indians.

WAR OF 1812. U.S. attacks on Canada failed. The Treaty of Ghent, 24 Dec., 1814, restored the *status quo* and provided for a boundary commission to make recommendations regarding the Maine–New Brunswick frontier, but left western and lake problems unsettled.

1815–40

RUSH-BAGOT AGREEMENT. 28–29 Apr., 1817. Resolving the problem of disarmament left unregulated by the Treaty of Ghent, this agreement limited British and American naval vessels on the Great Lakes to 1 ship each on Lakes Champlain and Ontario, and 2 each on the upper lakes, no vessel to exceed 100 tons or to mount more than 1 18-pound cannon.

NORTHWEST BOUNDARY SETTLEMENT. 20 Oct., 1818. The northwest boundary between Canada and the U.S. was established at the 49th parallel from Lake of the Woods to the Rocky Mountains. The region west of the mountains (Oregon Territory) was to be jointly occupied for a 10-year period. The agreement also conceded the U.S: fishing rights off the Labrador and Newfoundland coasts.

FAMILY COMPACT AND CHATEAU CLIQUE. In both Upper and Lower Canada, resentment grew from the constitutional conflict between the elected Assemblies and the dominant administrative cliques (the Family Compact in Upper Canada, the Château Clique in Lower Canada). Under the provisions of the Canada Act, the governor, responsible only to the British government and supported by a nominated Legislative Council, could override the actions of the Assembly. Although between 1791 and 1814 relations with the United States and Britain overshadowed local provincial affairs, the colonists' opposition, which led to the eventual breakdown of government, was based on (1) long-standing disputes about control of patronage and the judiciary; (2) Clergy Reserves, questions of church establishment, and the control of education; (3) settlement, land development, and the provision of public works; and (4) revenue and supply. In Lower Canada, party lines were sharpened by national differences. The administration and Legislative Council were controlled by the British minority, including the merchants, and the Assembly by the French majority with largely agricultural interests.

EXECUTIVE-LEGISLATIVE CONFLICTS. Led by Louis Joseph Papineau (1786–1871; elected Speaker, 1815), the Assembly concentrated its efforts on controlling crown revenues and supply. In 1818 the British government accepted the Assembly's proposal to meet provincial expenses out of the permanent revenues, which, being usually insufficient, had to be supplemented by the legislature, thus opening the way for control of all expenditures. In 1819 the Assembly refused to vote the appropriation until it had examined and voted on each item in both the permanent and supplementary revenues. In 1820 the Assembly refused the request for a permanent civil list and, with its demands becoming more aggressive, Gov. Lord Dalhousie (1770–1838) dissolved the legislature, and after the election refused to recognize Papineau as Speaker. Under Gov. Sir James Kempt, Papineau was again made Speaker, and in 1829 a law was passed increasing the representation from the Eastern Townships. In 1831 the government transferred the crown revenues to the control of the Assembly, which refused the requested civil list. The Assembly of 1834 adopted

Papineau's 92 Resolutions and his party won a huge majority in the election of that year. In 1836 the Assembly voted supplies for a 6-month period only, and in 1837 refused supplies altogether.

GRIEVANCES OF UPPER CANADA. In Upper Canada the postwar depression revived issues of reform, and in 1817 discontent was voiced by Robert Gourlay by means of his 31 Questions, which drew attention to the large undeveloped land holdings in Upper Canada, where there was much speculation, and to the position of the Anglican Church, which was identified with the ruling oligarchy by settlers and traders, most of whom were dissenters. In 1828 the Reform Party, led by Robert Baldwin (1804–58), Marshall Spring Bidwell (1799–1872), William Lyon Mackenzie (1795–1861), and Egerton Ryerson (1803–82), won a majority in the Assembly and passed 58 bills, all of which were rejected by the Legislative Council. Defeated in 1830, when the new Assembly granted his own funds to the governor, Sir John Colburne, the Reformers again won control in 1834 and Mackenzie, as chairman of a committee of the Assembly, issued, 1835, the 7th Report on grievances. In 1836 some moderate reformers, appointed to the Legislative Council by Gov. Sir Edward Bond Head (1793–1875), resigned. The Assembly passed a vote of no confidence and, refusing to vote supplies, was dissolved. Head's part in the ensuing election campaign assured the defeat of the Reformers and the "Bread and Butter" Assembly voted, Nov. 1836, the necessary appropriations.

REJECTION OF BRITISH PLANS FOR UNION. Common provincial concerns led to a British government proposal, 1822, for a Canadian union, designed to satisfy the demands of the British minority in Lower Canada, and to resolve disputes over the distribution of revenue from customs dues. For the proposed bill, rejected in Lower Canada as detrimental to French-Canadian interests, and in Upper Canada as undemocratic, was substituted the Canada Trade Act, 5 Aug., 1822, which apportioned the disputed revenue between the provinces. In 1828 and again in 1834, British parliamentary commissions failed to recommend viable solutions, the main obstacles being demands for an elective council and a permanent civil list. Lord John Russell's 10 Resolutions presented, 6 Mar., 1837, to Parliament rejected Canadian demands for responsible government and authorized the governor to use public funds to carry on the government. The Lower Canada Assembly refused to submit and was prorogued. In Upper Canada, the Resolutions were the occasion for mass meetings. Joint action was agreed on by the radicals in both provinces, while moderate reformers like Baldwin, Bidwell, and John Neilson of Lower Canada withdrew their support from Mackenzie and Papineau, who together signed, 31 July, 1837, the "Declaration of the Reformers of Toronto."

REBELLIONS IN UPPER AND LOWER CANADA. In Upper Canada armed resistance began when Mackenzie's rebels were scattered, 4 Dec., 1837, by Loyalist volunteers at Montgomery's Tavern in Toronto. Mackenzie escaped across the border, and occupied Navy Island in the Niagara River, where a Canadian force burned the American ship, *Caroline,* which was supplying the rebels. Mackenzie evacuated, 13 Jan., 1838, the island and was arrested by U.S. authorities. Throughout the rest of the year his followers, with the help of American supporters (Hunters' Lodges), staged border clashes. In Lower Canada, Papineau, learning that there was a warrant for his arrest, went into exile shortly before rebel forces were routed, Nov.–Dec. 1837, at St. Charles, St. Eustache, and St. Denis.

MISSION OF LORD DURHAM. As a result of the rebellions, the constitution of Lower Canada was suspended, 1837, and Lord Durham (1792–1840) was appointed governor in chief of all 5 British North American provinces, 29 May, 1838. In Lower Canada, Durham established a special governing council, and by ordinance granted a general amnesty except for rebel ringleaders in exile in America and 8 others who, pleading guilty, were banished to Bermuda. Destined to be the scapegoat of British political factions, Durham's policy was unsupported in Parliament and the ordinance was disallowed, and Durham, by his proclamation of 9 Oct., 1838, resigned.

DURHAM'S REPORT. 11 Feb., 1840. Lord Durham's "Report on the Affairs of British North America," published a year and a half after his resignation, recommended a union of Upper and Lower Canada, and responsible government for a united Canada, reserving for the British government control over foreign relations, regulation of trade, disposal of public lands, and the form of the constitution. Revenue bills were to be sponsored by the cabinet and to be presented to the legislature, while in return for a permanent civil list crown revenues were to be in the hands of the colonial government. In Oct. Lord Sydenham (1799–1841) arrived in Quebec as governor in chief to prepare for the union.

ACT OF UNION. 23 July, 1840. The act provided for the union of Upper and Lower Canada (renamed Canada West and Canada East) with a governor, a nominated legislative council of not less than 20 members to hold office for life, and an elected assembly of 84 members divided equally between each of the former provinces. Reports were to be in English, but French could be used in debates; crown revenues were surrendered for a civil list; supply bills were to originate with the governor and be submitted to the Assembly; provincial debts were to be consolidated and assumed by the new union; and existing laws were to continue unless and until amended.

1841–70

MAINE–NEW BRUNSWICK FRONTIER. Unresolved by the Treaty of Ghent and also when submitted, 1827, for arbitration by the king of the Netherlands, the dispute over the Maine–New Brunswick frontier flared up over land grants to British settlers along the Aroostook River. In 1839 Canadian lumberjacks, cutting timber in the disputed areas and refusing to leave, seized the U.S. land commissioner. This marked the beginning of the "Aroostook War." The fracas ended in a truce, with the frontier problem once more referred to a boundary commission. By the Webster-Ashburton Treaty, 9 Aug., 1842, the boundary was drawn at the present line. The U.S. received more than half the disputed territory, but Britain retained a region through which passed a proposed military route from New Brunswick to Quebec.

OREGON BOUNDARY TREATY. In 1845 President Polk claimed the whole Oregon Territory for the U.S. By a treaty of 15 June, 1846, the U.S.–Canadian frontier was fixed at the 49th parallel to the middle of the Vancouver Island Channel, and then through Juan de Fuca Strait. Both countries were guaranteed navigation rights in the Channel, the Strait, and on the Columbia River.

PUBLIC WORKS PROGRAM. Gov. Sydenham (term of office, 1839–41) initiated a program of public works for the completion of the Welland Canal (opened 1829) between Lakes Erie and Ontario, the improvement of navigation, and the construction of roads and bridges, for which the British government guaranteed a loan of £1.5 m. He also guided through the legislature bills dealing with municipal government, disposal and settlement of land, the reform of the criminal law, and the school system.

SYDENHAM-HARRISON RESOLUTIONS. The issue of responsible government, left unclarified in the Union Act, was raised by Baldwin in 1841. He introduced a series of resolutions (Sydenham-Harrison Resolutions) proposing that the governor, while responsible to the crown, should choose as his advisers those having the confidence of the Assembly.

BALDWIN-LAFONTAINE MINISTRY. Sydenham's successors, Sir Charles Bagot (1842–43) and Sir Charles Metcalfe (1843–46), tried to maintain the policy of maintaining a core of moderates in the Executive Council, but problems increasingly revolved around the relationship of the Council to the Assembly, in which political factions were forming. In 1842, moderate reformers under Baldwin combined with the French led by Louis Hippolyte Lafontaine (1807–64) to form a powerful coalition forcing Bagot to construct a ministry under their joint leadership. In 1843 the Baldwin-Lafontaine ministry resigned over the question of patronage, Metcalfe dissolved the Assembly, and after a stormy election, 1844, Metcalfe formed a Conservative ministry with a tiny majority.

GOVERNORSHIP OF LORD ELGIN. Under Lord Elgin (gov., 1847–54) relations between the Executive Council and the Assembly were further defined. After the victory of the reformers in both Canada West and East in the 1847 elections, the Conservatives resigned and Baldwin and Lafontaine again formed a ministry. In the session of 1849 the Assembly enacted legislation for judicial, municipal, and educational reforms, a general amnesty, and the promotion of railroad construction. The membership of the Assembly was increased from 84 to 130. Elgin's policy was tested when he gave his consent to Lafontaine's unpopular Rebellion Losses Bill. The bill provoked a storm of protest, and rioting broke out in Montreal among the anti-French factions, but Elgin was supported by the British Parliament, which refused to interfere in what was now considered a local matter.

ANNEXATION MANIFESTO. 10 Oct., 1849. Repeal of the British Corn Laws, 1846, and Navigation Acts, 1849, caused a sharp economic depression in Canada. Discontent with the British connection therefore increased among the Montreal and Eastern Townships commercial community, and was expressed in a short-lived movement for annexation to the U.S. (Annexation Manifesto, 10 Oct.). To help meet the economic situation, Elgin, with the co-operation of Francis Hincks, conducted a long-drawn-out negotiation with the U.S., and on 5 June, 1854, a Reciprocity Treaty was concluded.

MARITIME PROVINCES. In New Brunswick, Charles Fisher (1808–80) became prime minister of the 1st party government, 1854. In Prince Edward Island, torn by disputes over land tenure, the Assembly voted, 1847, a resolution asserting executive responsibility, and George Coles (1810–75) became prime minister in 1851. In Nova Scotia the hold of the Halifax oligarchy on the Executive

Council (nominated for life) and the governor was broken by the efforts of Joseph Howe (1804–73). By taking advantage of Russell's dispatch of 1839 to Sir John Harvey (gov. of New Brunswick) authorizing Harvey to make changes in his council for "reasons of public policy," Howe succeeded in persuading, 1840, the Assembly to pass a vote of no confidence in the Council. After a period of unsatisfactory coalitions, the Assembly again passed, Jan. 1848, a vote of no confidence, and James B. Uniacke was called on to form the 1st party government, Feb.

COALITION GOVERNMENT. By 1860 nearly half of the clauses of the Union Act had been changed by legislation or modified in practice, including a revision, 1856, making the Legislative Council elective and reducing the number of its members from 60 to 48, 12 chosen biennially for an 8-year term. Between 1854 and 1867, 10 ministries held office and government was brought to a virtual standstill. Sectional interests had given rise to the convention of the "double majority" (the support on important issues of a majority of representatives from each of the old provinces), and any ministry was in effect a coalition of the moderate center. As the population of Canada West outstripped that of Canada East, the radical "Clear Grits" led by George Brown (1818–80) demanded representation by population, a policy opposed by French Canadians, who also opposed nondenominational schools.

WESTERN EXPANSION. Expansion in the northwest, the ineffectual jurisdiction of the Hudson's Bay Co., and the discovery of gold, including the Fraser River deposits, revived the issue of Canadian control in that region. On 19 Nov., 1858, British Columbia was made a separate province. The need for an interprovincial railway system and railway expansion into the northwest, and the financial confusion surrounding railway construction underlined the necessity for comprehensive Canada-wide planning and control.

MOVEMENT TOWARD CONFEDERATION. In 1856 Antoine A. Dorian (1818–91), leader of the French *Rouges,*

suggested federal union; 2 years later Alexander T. Galt (1817–93) presented resolutions also favoring federation; and in the election of 1859, Brown and William McDougall (1822–1905), campaigning on a platform of federation and annexation of the northwest, won a majority. In 1863 the John Sandfield–John S. Macdonald (1812–72) –L. V. Sicotte (1812–89) ministry, committed to the "double majority" principle, was defeated over the issue of the Separate School Bill and its refusal to accept a British government loan to guarantee the costs of the construction of the Intercolonial Railway. With the outbreak of the American Civil War and consequent strained relations with the U.S., problems of imperial defense and neutrality provided an impetus to the federal movement, as did the later repeal, 1866, of the Reciprocity Treaty of 1854 by the U.S., and Irish Fenian raids on the Niagara and Vermont border. After the collapse of the Macdonald-Dorian Ministry in 1864, Gov. Lord Monck was unable to put together another ministry until, under the titular leadership of Étienne Taché, a ministry was formed, committed by Brown, G. E. Cartier (1814–73), and John A. Macdonald (1815–91) to seek federation.

CHARLOTTETOWN AND QUEBEC CONVENTIONS. The question of legislative federation for the Maritime Provinces was raised by Charles Tupper (1821–1915) of Nova Scotia and S. L. Tilley (1818–96) of New Brunswick. They arranged for the Charlottetown Convention, 1 Sept., 1864, which a Canadian delegation asked to attend. Plans were then quickly drawn for the Quebec Convention, 10–28 Oct., which drew up 72 resolutions outlining an Act of Confederation. The resolutions were submitted to each provincial legislature, and in spite of opposition in New Brunswick and Nova Scotia, a delegation went to Britain, where the London Resolutions were published, Dec. 1866.

BRITISH NORTH AMERICA ACT. 28 Mar., 1867. This act of the British Parliament established the Dominion of Canada (Ontario, Quebec, New Brunswick, Nova Scotia) under a bicameral federal government, with an appointed Senate of 24 members each from Ontario and Quebec and 12 each from Nova Scotia and New Brunswick, and a House of Commons with representation by population. Provincial governmental powers were defined, the residual powers being with the federal government. On 1 July, John A. Macdonald became 1st Dominion prime minister, heading a Liberal-Conservative ministry.

RED RIVER REBELLION. By a British Act of 1869, Rupert's Land and the Northwest Territory were bought from the Hudson's Bay Co. for £300,000 and William McDougall was appointed lieut. gov. Subsequent unrest among the population (mostly hunters, trappers, and fur traders) was caused by land surveys, leading to a belief that the land was to be confiscated. Under the leadership of Louis Riel, rebels seized Fort Garry (Winnipeg) and, setting up a provisional government, issued a bill of rights demanding an elected legislature and representation in the Dominion parliament, 1869. A commission under Donald A. Smith pacified the rebels to some degree, but their execution of Thomas Scott, leader of a small English opposition, aroused indignation in Ontario, and the rebels were eventually dispersed by an expedition led by Col. Garnet Wolseley.

MANITOBA ACT. 5 July, 1870. This act constituted Manitoba as a province, and in 1871 British Columbia also joined the Dominion on the understanding that construction of a transcontinental railway would begin within 2, and be completed within 10, years. (*Cont. p. 321.*)

AUSTRALIA

1770–1808

DISCOVERY. From 1596 to the discovery of Van Diemen's Land (Tasmania) by Abel Tasman in 1644, the Dutch, sailing from the East Indies, landed at many points on the north and west coasts of Australia, calling the land New Holland. William Dampier, the English adventurer, anchored at Melville Island, 1688, and Shark's Bay, 1699. On 30 Apr., 1770,

Capt. James Cook (1728–79) landed at Botany Bay, explored northward, and claimed, 23 Aug., for Great Britain the east coast, which he named New South Wales.

1ST CONVICT SETTLEMENT. Influenced by Cook's reports, the British government considered New South Wales as a possible place of settlement for American loyalists, subsequently deciding on a self-supporting penal colony to relieve overcrowding in British jails after the loss of the American colonies made it impossible to send criminals sentenced to transportation to America. On 18 Jan., 1788, Capt. Arthur Phillip arrived at Botany Bay with 11 ships, including 6 convict transports carrying 717 convicts of whom 520 were men, and moved, 26 Jan., to Port Jackson (Sydney). Problems of settlement were compounded by the disorderliness of the convicts and the failure of supply ships to arrive, causing strict rationing of food, 1789–92. A contingent of Marines initially provided protection, but in 1789 the New South Wales Corps was organized on a permanent footing, both officers and soldiers being promised grants of land. Phillip began the practice of giving convicts conditional pardons for good behavior and land grants of up to 30 acres. He also assigned convicts as laborers to private individuals. The 1st free settlers arrived in New South Wales in 1793.

NEW SOUTH WALES CORPS. Phillip's successors in command, Francis Grose and William Paterson, officers of the New South Wales Corps, relaxed controls, permitted land grants (many officers, e.g., John Macarthur [1767–1834], became powerful landowners), and allowed the officers of the Corps to establish a trade monopoly over arriving cargoes, including rum. The officers were also able to call on the unlimited services of convicts. Civil jurisdiction was replaced by military.

ADMINISTRATION OF GOV. HUNTER. Capt. John Hunter (gov., 1795–1800) re-established the civil magistracy, but was unable to break the economic monopoly of the Corps. He supported the efforts of Macarthur, who had

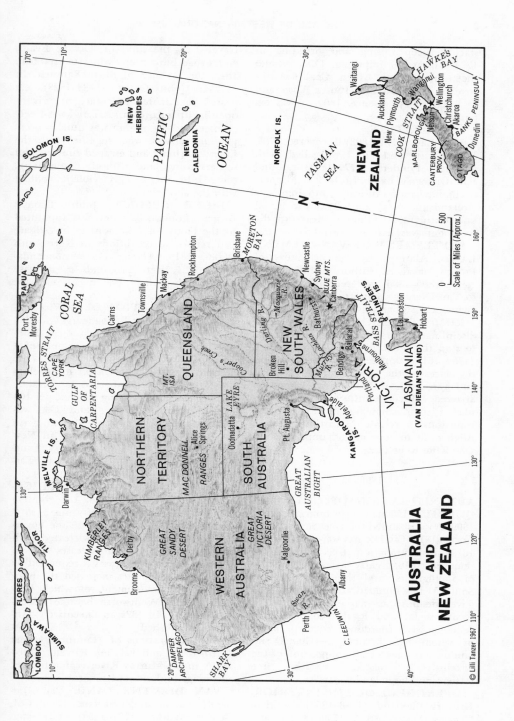

AUSTRALIA
AND
NEW ZEALAND

© Lilli Tanzer 1967

Scale of Miles (Approx.)
0   500

N

NEW ZEALAND

HAWKE'S BAY
Waitangi
Auckland
Wanganui
New Plymouth
Wellington
COOK STRAIT
MARLBOROUGH
Nelson
Christchurch
CANTERBURY PROV.
Akaroa
BANKS PENINSULA
OTAGO
Dunedin

PACIFIC OCEAN

SOLOMON IS.
NEW HEBRIDES
NEW CALEDONIA
NORFOLK IS.

TASMAN SEA

CORAL SEA

Port Moresby
PAPUA

TORRES STRAIT
CAPE YORK

GULF OF CARPENTARIA

MELVILLE IS.
Darwin
130°

TIMOR
FLORES
SUMBAWA
LOMBOK
10°

DAMPIER ARCHIPELAGO
Broome
KIMBERLEY RANGES
GREAT SANDY DESERT

WESTERN AUSTRALIA

GREAT VICTORIA DESERT

Derby
Kalgoorlie
Perth
Swan R.
Albany
C. LEEUWIN
SHARK BAY
30°

NORTHERN TERRITORY
Alice Springs
MAC DONNELL RANGES

SOUTH AUSTRALIA

Oodnadatta
LAKE EYRE
Cooper's Creek

GREAT AUSTRALIAN BIGHT

QUEENSLAND

Cairns
Townsville
Mackay
Rockhampton
Brisbane
MORETON BAY

MT. ISA

Pt. Augusta
Broken Hill
Adelaide
KANGAROO I.

NEW SOUTH WALES
Darling R.
Macquarie R.
Newcastle
Sydney
BLUE MTS.
Bathurst
Canberra
Lachlan R.
Murray R.
Murrumbidgee R.
Bendigo
Ballarat

VICTORIA
Portland
Melbourne

Launceston
Hobart
TASMANIA
(VAN DIEMAN'S LAND)
FLINDERS IS.
BASS STRAITS

170°
10°
20°
30°
160°
150°
140°
130°
120°
110°
40°

started sheep raising and breeding in 1794. Macarthur imported, 1797, merino sheep from South Africa. Coal was discovered, 1797, on the Hunter River and at Botany Bay, whence, 1800, it was exported to India.

EXPLORATION OF COASTS. George Bass (1771–1803) discovered, 1798, Bass Strait, and in 1798 sailed with Matthew Flinders (1774–1814) around Van Diemen's Land. In 1802–3 Flinders circumnavigated Australia, proving New Holland and New South Wales to be all one continent. At Flinders' suggestion the continent was named Australia.

SETTLEMENT OF VAN DIEMEN'S LAND. Alarmed by the proximity of French naval expeditions, Philip King (gov., 1800–1806) ordered an expedition to Van Diemen's Land to establish settlements near Hobart and Launceston.

RUM REBELLION. Appointed as a disciplinarian to control the officers and to stop the traffic in rum, William Bligh (1754–1817) imposed strict penalties on the officers of the New South Wales Corps and ran foul of Macarthur, whom he arrested, 1807. The infuriated officers persuaded their commander, Maj. George Johnston, to release Macarthur, declare Bligh unfit to govern, and imprison him (the Rum Rebellion).

1809–30

ADMINISTRATION OF GOV. MACQUARIE. Lachlan Macquarie (gov., 1809–21) disbanded the New South Wales Corps, 1810. Civil courts were established, 1814; restrictions on free immigration removed, 1816, greatly increasing the flow of immigrants; and the Bank of New South Wales founded, 1817. Macquarie's governorship was marked by efforts to secure social and legal recognition for "emancipists" (pardoned convicts, many of whom had become merchants and landowners) against the opposition of the "exclusives" (officials, wealthy free settlers, and large landowners).

OPENING UP OF THE INTERIOR. Gregory Blaxland (1778–1853), William Charles Wentworth (1790–1872), and William Lawson (1774–1850) crossed the Blue Mountains, 1813. Their route was re-traveled by the surveyor, George Evans, and a road built from Sydney to establish, 1815, the 1st interior town, Bathurst. In 1817–19 John Oxley (1783–1828) explored the Lachlan and Macquarie rivers, opening up grazing lands. Land was freely granted and the region was quickly occupied by settlers, who, together with the squatters (freed and escaped convicts and settlers using land without permission), came into increasingly violent conflict with the aborigines.

BIGGE REPORT. John Thomas Bigge, a London barrister, was appointed by the House of Commons to investigate and report on conditions in New South Wales, 1819. Among his recommendations, 1821, were proposals to increase large land grants and to assign more convict labor.

ADMINISTRATION OF GOV. BRISBANE. Sir Thomas Brisbane (gov., 1821–25) favored large as against small landholdings. Grants up to a maximum of 4 sq. mi. were made according to the amount a settler could invest in development or to the number of laborers he employed, 1 convict being assigned per 100 acres. The Australian Land Co. was formed, 1824, with a grant of 1 m. acres and a monopoly of coal mining in New South Wales. The Van Diemen's Land Co., 1825, received 400,000 acres in Tasmania.

NEW SOUTH WALES JUDICATURE ACT. 19 July, 1823. A Legislative Council was established of from 5 to 7 nominated members to advise the governor. A Supreme Court was created with military juries for criminal cases and an ordinary jury in civil cases if requested by both parties. The act increased the pressure for self-government, of which William Charles Wentworth became a leading advocate. In 1825 an Executive Council was established.

The explorations of Hamilton Hume (1797–1873) and William Hovell (1786–1875) in the Murray River region further encouraged inland settlement.

VAN DIEMEN'S LAND. Van Diemen's Land, under Lieut. Gov. Col. George Arthur (1784–1854), was separated from New South Wales in 1825. A large, unruly convict population and bushrangers (escaped convicts and outlaws) terrorized the countryside, leading to retaliation by the aborigines and causing the Black War. Arthur finally controlled the situation, but failed in his efforts to round up, 1830, the aborigines to ensure their survival. George Robinson, a Methodist minister, eventually took, 1835, the Van Diemen's Land aborigines to Flinders Island, where the last one died in 1860.

LAND POLICY UNDER DARLING. Sir Ralph Darling (gov., 1825–31) approved a land policy which permitted grants of up to 2,560 acres and the sale of crown lands up to 4,000 acres at not less than 5s. an acre. The power of the wealthy landowners increased and the demands of the emancipists, led by Wentworth, for recognition became more insistent. Darling tried to set a policy of limits of location, i.e., concentrated settlement, within the 19 Counties (bounded by a semicircular line around Sydney).

INCREASE IN LEGISLATIVE COUNCIL MEMBERSHIP. An Act of 25 July, 1828, increased the size of the Legislative Council to 18 members, of whom 8 were to be administrative officials and 7 "nonofficials." In practice the nonofficials were always leading exclusives.

DISCOVERIES OF STURT. In 1827 Allan Cunningham explored the Darling Downs region and in 1828 Charles Sturt (1795–1869) discovered the Darling River and traveled, 1829–30, down the River Murray to its mouth. Sturt's journeys opened up a huge new region for pastoral settlement.

FOUNDING OF WESTERN AUSTRALIA. Claimed in 1826 by the British when a military post was set up at King George's Sound, the Swan River was explored, 1827, by Capt. James Stirling (1791–1865), who urged colonization. Initial opposition to the scheme was overcome by Thomas Peel (1795–1864) and by Stirling, and a grant of 1 m. acres was made, Peel being given 250,000 acres for his own use. Immigrants were to receive 40 acres for every £3 they invested in development. On 18 June, 1829, a settlement was made on the Swan River. Inadequate preliminary surveys, insuffi-

cient capital and labor, poor terrain, and geographic isolation from other colonies made life in the new colony difficult, and Western Australia led a precarious existence for many years.

1831–36

LAND POLICY IN NEW SOUTH WALES. In 1831 regulations were issued fixing the price of land at a minimum of 5s. an acre to be sold at auction. Revenue obtained from land sales was to be applied to financing immigration and to public works. Pressure to obtain grazing lands mounted, making it impossible to contain settlement within the 19 Counties. The New South Wales Legislative Council passed, 1836, the Squatting Act, which allowed the occupation of crown lands for an annual fee of £10, with no limit set on the size of runs. This marked the beginning of pastoral expansion, the term "squatter" gradually losing its derogatory meaning as educated, wealthy settlers obtained land.

SYSTEMATIC COLONIZATION. Economic and social conditions in England stimulated interest in "systematic colonization," promoted by Edward Gibbon Wakefield (1796–1862) and his supporters. Wakefield, realizing that successful settlement required adequate land, capital, and labor, developed the theory that if land were sold at a "sufficient price" and the proceeds applied to assist further emigration, there would be a supply of laborers needing to work for several years before they had enough money to buy their own land, and the number of landowners would be restricted to those with capital. By these means a suitable balance would be achieved between land, capital, and labor. Wakefield's adherents formed, 1833, the South Australian Association, with George Fife Angas (1789–1879) a principal investor. The Association received, 1834, a charter to establish a colony with a governor and a Board of Commissioners in London to supervise land sales at not less than 12s. an acre.

FOUNDING OF SOUTH AUSTRALIA. The 1st South Australian settlers landed at Kangaroo Island, soon moving to a mainland site at Adelaide. Despite the work of surveyor William Light (1786–1839), more immigrants were sent out before proper surveys had been made. Land speculation consequently became rife. John Hindmarsh (1782–1860), the 1st governor, was succeeded in 1838 by George Gawler (1795–1869), who combined the offices of gov. and resident commissioner. By accelerating surveys, controlling land sales, and a road-building program, Gawler tried unsuccessfully to overcome the problems. The colony was near bankruptcy when George Grey (gov., 1841–45) was sent out. By an Act of 30 July, 1842, the Board of Commissioners was abolished and South Australia became a crown colony. Grey reduced expenditures and restored solvency. The discovery, 1841–45, of copper and lead-silver mines attracted both capital and immigrants.

SETTLEMENT OF VICTORIA. In 1834, Edward Henty (1810–78) and his brothers began farming at Portland Bay. In 1835 John Batman (1801–39) and his associates arrived from Van Diemen's Land and, having made a treaty with uncomprehending aborigines, settled at Melbourne. A group from Van Diemen's Land, led by John Fawkner (1792–1869), arrived in the same area, and other settlers came overland. The New South Wales Legislative Council passed an act, 1836, prohibiting the occupation of crown lands without permission, but this proved impossible to enforce. The Port Philip District was later administered by Superintendent C. J. Latrobe (1801–75).

1837–50

CESSATION OF TRANSPORTATION. The report of a Parliamentary Committee, 3 Aug., 1838, headed by Sir William Molesworth, led to criticism of the transportation system both in Britain and Australia. On 18 Nov., 1840, transportation to New South Wales ceased. Until 1853 convicts continued to be sent to Van Diemen's Land, and to Norfolk Island until 1855. Convicts were sent to Western Australia from 1850 to 1868.

EXPLORATION OF THE INTERIOR. Edward Eyre (1815–1901) reached the Lake Eyre region, turned south to Streaky Bay on the Great Australian Bight, and then crossed the deserts to reach Albany, 1841–45. Charles Sturt forced his way into the Stony Desert, and Ludwig Leichhardt (1813–48) explored the region from Darling Downs to the Gulf of Carpentaria.

CONSTITUTION ACT OF 1842. An Act of 30 July, 1842, created for New South Wales a 36-member Legislative Council, with 12 nominated and 24 elected members (6 to be from the Port Phillip District), to hold office for a 5-year period. The franchise was to be based on a property qualification. The act also made provision for systems of local government.

LAND POLICY. By an Act of 22 June, 1842, free grants of land were abolished. From then on land was sold by auction at a minimum upset price of £1 an acre throughout all the colonies. In 1844 Gov. George Gipps (1791–1847) of New South Wales levied a squatting fee on each run (a run was to be not more than 20 sq. mi. or carry more than 4,000 sheep) and granted leaseholders the right to purchase their land. A regulation of 9 Mar., 1847, further systematized leaseholding.

AUSTRALIAN COLONIES GOVERNMENT ACT. 5 Aug., 1850. Port Phillip District was separated from New South Wales to form the new colony of Victoria. Each colony could now constitute its own legislature, make its own franchise laws, alter its own constitution, and impose customs duties. The constitution drawn up for New South Wales provided for a Legislative Council appointed for life, an elected Legislative Assembly, and cabinet government. With the exception of Western Australia, the other colonies adopted similar constitutions, though their Councils were elective. Constitutions were adopted by New South Wales, Victoria, and Tasmania (the former Van Diemen's Land) in 1855, and by South Australia in 1856. Manhood suffrage was introduced in South Australia, 1855, Victoria, 1857, and New

South Wales, 1858, and vote by ballot in Victoria and South Australia in 1856, and in New South Wales in 1858.

1851–70

GOLD RUSH. Gold strikes were made at Bathurst (N.S.W.) in 1851 and at Ballarat and Bendigo (Victoria). The rapid inflow of miners and adventurers necessitated government regulation of the gold fields. In 1851 a license fee of 30s. (reduced in 1853 to £1) was imposed. Opposition to fees, problems of collection, and the severity of law enforcement measures caused discontent among the diggers, especially at Ballarat, where Peter Lalor led the easily crushed rebellion at Eureka Stockade, 3 Dec., 1854. In 1855 a Miner's Right, costing £1 a year and entitling the holder to vote, replaced the licensing system. The gold rushes acted as a spur to wheat growers and agriculturalists, who had to feed an increased population, but the influx of diggers and the diversion of labor from towns and farms disrupted the economy, especially in Victoria. As alluvial deposits were exhausted and deep mining became both profitable and necessary, the diggers drifted away from the gold fields, causing problems of unemployment.

CHINESE RESTRICTION ACT. June 1855. This act was passed by the Victoria legislature because of the large Chinese immigration to the gold fields. It imposed a poll tax of £10 on each Chinese and later a yearly residence tax of £4 was required. Despite the opposition of the British government, similar restrictive laws were passed by other colonies.

TORRENS TITLE. The Real Property Act (Torrens Land Transfer Act), 28 Jan., 1858, passed in South Australia, and copied by other colonies, provided for the systematic registration of land transactions.

COLONY OF QUEENSLAND. In 1859 Queensland, the former Moreton Bay penal settlement, became a separate colony. As exploration opened up the interior, immigration into Queensland increased, and it developed into a leading pastoral center.

LAND SELECTION. The Land Acts of 1861, promoted by John Robertson (1816–91) in New South Wales and Charles Gavan Duffy (1816–1903) in Victoria, attempted to help diggers and small farmers, and to break up large squatter-owned leaseholdings by allowing selection of land before survey of from 40 to 640 acres at £1 an acre with a down payment of 5s. on condition of occupancy and development. Abused by squatters turned selectors and also using hired "dummies," the selection laws settled fewer people than predicted. The unpredictable climate and the bringing into cultivation of marginal land militated against the success of small holdings. Revised Acts of 1865 and 1869 imposed stricter laws, but the squatters had already obtained large tracts of freehold land.

KANAKA LABOR. In 1868 Queensland regulated "blackbirding," the importing of Kanaka labor from the Pacific islands for work on the sugar plantations. Inaugurated in 1842 by Robert Towns for cotton plantations, the practice had degenerated into a system close to slavery.

COLONIAL DEFENSE. In 1863 the Duke of Newcastle (colonial secretary) circulated a dispatch laying down the principle of colonial responsibility for local defense. By the Colonial Naval Defence Act of 1865, Australian authorities obtained several ships for coastal and harbor defense. Finally, in 1870, local militia forces were established, and British garrison troops were withdrawn. (*Cont. p. 323.*)

NEW ZEALAND

1770–1839

1ST SETTLEMENTS. Discovered in 1642 by the Dutch Captain Abel Janszoon Tasman, New Zealand was not rediscovered until Capt. James Cook (1728–79) landed, 7 Oct., 1769, on the 1st of 3 voyages, circumnavigated both islands, and claimed them for Great Britain. From 1792 American, British, and French sealing and whaling ships arrived in New Zealand waters with increasing frequency, and eventually established settlements ashore, notably at the Bay of Islands and around Cook Strait. In 1794 the 1st traders from Sydney arrived, seeking timber and flax for the Australian penal colonies. They paid the Maoris with metal tools and firearms. The possession of muskets by the Maoris led to fierce tribal warfare, the campaigns, 1821, of Chiefs Hongi around Auckland and Te Rauparaha from Wanganui to Akaroa causing widespread destruction. Mainly populated by drifters and escaped convicts, the New Zealand settlements became notorious for outlawry.

ESTABLISHMENT OF CHRISTIAN MISSIONS. Samuel Marsden (1765–1838), chaplain of the penal colony at Sydney, decided to protect the Maoris from the evils of colonization. He opened a Church of England mission station at the Bay of Islands and, returning to Sydney, left behind lay missionaries who opened schools, cleared land for farms, and taught European methods of agriculture. In 1820 Thomas Kendall, a schoolteacher, took Chiefs Hongi and Waikato to England in order to have their language transcribed, and in 1827 a Maori translation of parts of the Bible was published by William Colenso. Missionary activity increased with the arrival, 1823, of the 1st ordained Anglican minister, Henry Williams, who worked closely with the Wesleyan mission, opened 1822, at Hokianga. In 1828 the 1st Roman Catholic mission was established at Hokianga. Imbued with the ideals of the humanitarian and evangelical movements, the missionaries opposed colonial expansion and directed their efforts toward keeping the country for the Maoris.

APPOINTMENT OF BRITISH RESIDENT. In 1827 James Busby was appointed as British resident. Since Britain had not claimed sovereignty and was reluctant to do so, Busby had no real powers of law enforcement.

THIERRY LAND CLAIM. In 1835 Baron Charles de Thierry, English-born son of French emigré parents, claimed sovereign rights to territory at Hokianga.

Australian and British speculators and traders were already buying and claiming large tracts of land from the Maoris, while responsible settlers, missionaries, and officials in New South Wales were demanding that the British take steps to control the situation.

NEW ZEALAND COMPANY. In 1837 the New Zealand Land Association was formed by a committee of influential colonial reformers, including Lord Durham and Edward Gibbon Wakefield. The Association urged annexation and planned colonization, a policy opposed by both the Colonial office and the missionaries. In May 1839 the Association was dissolved. Its members reorganized as a joint-stock enterprise, the New Zealand Co., and bought land without waiting for a charter or governmental permission.

1840–55

1ST COLONIZATION. 22 Jan., 1840. The 1st British colonists landed from the ship *Tory* at Port Nicholson (the site of Wellington) in Cook Strait. Capt. William Hobson (1793–1842) arrived as consul, 29 Jan., with instructions to claim British sovereignty over North Island, and to annex the sparsely populated South Island by right of discovery, the country to be a dependency of New South Wales.

TREATY OF WAITANGI. 6 Feb., 1840. This treaty was negotiated between Britain and certain Maori chiefs, with missionaries acting as interpreters. The chiefs' ceded sovereign rights to Great Britain and were guaranteed protection and possession of their lands, although the crown reserved rights of pre-emption. On 21 May Hobson proclaimed British sovereignty and placed the capital at Auckland.

LAND POLICY. In 1841 New Zealand was declared a separate colony with Hobson as governor. Hobson imposed customs duties and, by voiding all land claims until investigated by Land Commissioner William Spain, came into immediate conflict with the New Zealand Company, which, with settlers already arrived and waiting for land, claimed some 2 m. acres under its charter (granted Feb. 1841) and the right to sell land at 5s. an acre, as against the £1 an acre decided on by the government. About 1/6 of the company's claims were eventually recognized.

During 1841 settlements were established at New Plymouth, in Taranaki, and at Nelson under the auspices of the New Zealand Co. Capt. Robert Fitzroy (gov., 1843–45) attempted to solve the land question and acquire revenue by permitting the direct purchase of land from the Maoris on payment of 10s. an acre (early reduced to 1d.) to the government. The measure was disallowed and Fitzroy recalled.

MASSACRE OF WAIRU. At Nelson, colonists under Arthur Wakefield (1799–1843) tried to arrest the chiefs Te Rauparaha and Te Rangihaeata for resisting land surveys, and were murdered at the massacre of Wairu, 17 June, 1843. Gov. Fitzroy condemned the slaughter, but, feeling the settlers were at fault and without military strength, failed to take effective action against the Maori chiefs. At the Bay of Islands, Maori discontent with customs duties and falling profits from trade came to a head when Chief Hone Heke sacked Kororareka (Russell).

ADMINISTRATION OF GOV. GREY. Arriving in New Zealand with a reputation for firmness, Capt. George Grey (gov., 1845–54) quashed Maori unrest in the north; held, 1845, Te Rauparaha in custody; and put down, 1847, an uprising at Wanganui. Grey restored crown control over land transfers, instituting a policy of block purchases from the Maoris. By these means he acquired most of South Island. In 1853 he reduced the price of land to 10s. an acre. His vigorous governorship brought a period of stability.

CONSTITUTION ACT OF 1846. An Act of 23 July, 1846, divided New Zealand into 2 provinces, New Ulster in the north and New Munster (Wellington and South Island), each with a governor, appointed council, and elected assembly. Grey recommended that this elaborate system was premature, and the act was suspended, 1847, for 5 years. In conse-

quence, the colonists' demands for self-government increased.

SOUTH ISLAND SETTLEMENTS. Dealing through the New Zealand Company, the Association of the Scottish Free Church settled Otago (capital Dunedin) in 1878. The Church of England Canterbury Association, led by John R. Godley (1814–61), settled, 1850, Canterbury (capital Christchurch). In these settlements sheep raising soon proved suitable and profitable, and with the grant, 1851, of 14-year grazing licenses the industry grew rapidly in importance.

CONSTITUTION ACT OF 1852. An Act of 30 June, 1852, established 6 provinces, each with an elected superintendent and provincial council. The franchise was to be based on a small property tax. A governor, nominated Legislative Council, and an elected House of Representatives (General Assembly) were to be responsible for general administration, while the Colonial Office, through the governor, retained control of Maori affairs. Grey's delay in summoning, 1854, the General Assembly allowed the provinces to assert their authority. The period of provincial government lasted from 1852 to 1875.

1856–70

RESPONSIBLE GOVERNMENT. Responsible government was granted to New Zealand on 17 Aug., 1857. At the same time the provinces gained control over land sales and revenues. The cost of land purchases was to be met out of central government loans ("Compact of 1856").

NEW PROVINCES. The New Provinces Act, 1858, established Hawke's Bay, 1859; Marlborough, 1859; Southland, 1861 (reunited with Otago in 1870); and Westland, 1873.

MAORI WARS. 1860–72. Expanding colonization with its accompanying demand for land, a growing reluctance to sell on the part of the Maoris, and their doubts about the efficacy of the protection promised them by the Treaty of Waitangi were the main causes of the wars of 1860–72. The situation was aggravated by the Maori "king" movement, a tribal union to achieve self-government, promoted by Wiremu Tamihana; Te Whero Whero was elected king in 1858. In 1862 arose the fanatical Hau-Haus, who combined in their belief system primitive Maori mythology and Judaeo-Christian doctrines. Guerrilla warfare broke out in Taranaki over the land claims long disputed by Te Rangitake. Ineffectual British suppressive campaigns encouraged the more hostile and warlike Waikato tribes, who were not pacified until the defeat, Apr. 1864, of Rewi at the Orakau *pa* (fort), and the capture, June 1864, of Te Ranga and, 1869, Titokowaru at Otauto. With the suppression of Te Kooti, who had escaped from imprisonment on Chatham Island and killed settlers and Maoris at Poverty Bay as he moved inland, the war came to an end. The gradual withdrawal of troops, sent from Australia under Gens. Pratt and Cameron, was completed by 1870.

INCREASES IN SELF-GOVERN-MENT. From 1860 onward, relations between Britain and New Zealand and between the provincial and central governments became more clearly defined. During Grey's 2nd term as governor, 1861–67, the colony became, 1862, responsible for native affairs, the crown abandoned its rights of pre-emption, and by the New Zealand Settlement Act, 1863, the colony was able to assert a policy of "self-reliance" and assumed responsibility for the conduct of the Maori Wars.

ECONOMIC DEVELOPMENT. The discovery of gold in Otago, 1861, and Westland, 1865, tripled the population of South Island, greatly increasing its prosperity. Almost untouched by war, the southern provinces embarked on programs of public works. The 1st railroad, Christchurch to Ferrymead, opened in 1865. The northern provinces, disrupted by the fighting, were less prosperous.

SEPARATISM. In the 1860's a separatist movement developed, especially in South Island. Provincialist and centralist factions appeared, with problems of military and native affairs further confusing the issues by cutting across party lines. In 1865 Wellington replaced Auckland as

the capital to meet South Island complaints that the government was not centrally located. The decline in gold discoveries, growing unemployment, and a diminishing revenue fanned discontent. (*Cont. p. 325.*)

BOER AND BRITON IN SOUTH AFRICA

1770–95

SOUTH AFRICA IN 1770. Founded in 1652 as a refreshment station for ships of the Netherlands East India Company, by 1770 Cape Colony extended north to the Orange River and east to the Great Fish River. Dutch-speaking Boers (cattle farmers) lived in the frontier regions in isolation from the Company's administration at Cape Town. They had driven the nomadic Bushmen from their hunting grounds, were already employing cattle-herding Nama (Hottentots) on interior farms, and the struggle with the Bantu (black African) peoples living east and north of the Great Fish River had begun.

GRAFF-REINET REBELLION. In 1785, on petition of the colonists, the area of Graff-Reinet was made a separate administrative district. Adriaan van Jaarsveld, who had routed, 1781, the Bantu Xhosas, became border commandant. Honoratus Maynier was then given orders to settle disputes, and successfully negotiated treaties with the Xhosas. Bantu infiltration and raids persisted, however, and, evicting Maynier, the colonists set up, June 1795, their own government under van Jaarsveld. The district of Swellendam also rebelled.

END OF COMPANY RULE. In Cape Town demands for reform increased, and petitions were sent to the Company's directors in the Netherlands seeking an equal number of civilians on the High Court of Justice, representation on the Council of Policy, and permission to trade freely and export produce to the Netherlands. Forestalling seizure by the British during the American War of Independence, the French stationed, 1781–83, a fleet at the Cape, inducing a temporary prosperity which, on their leaving, was quickly followed by a slump. In great financial distress owing to the wars in Europe, British naval supremacy, and outworn financial policies, the Company appointed 2 special commissioners to investigate the situation at the Cape, but in 1795 it went bankrupt. At this time the population of the colony was about 45,000, of whom some 20,000 were slaves.

1795–1806

1ST BRITISH OCCUPATION. In 1795 the British ordered a fleet under Adm. Sir George Elphinstone and a military force led by Maj. Gen. James Craig to occupy the Cape, and by the Capitulation of Rustenburg, 16 Sept., the Dutch garrison surrendered. As 1st British gov. of Cape Colony, Craig followed a conciliatory policy, replacing the Committee of the High Court with a nominated burgher Senate of 6 members. Earl Macartney,

who succeeded Craig in 1797, introduced judicial reforms and abolished monopolies.

RESTORATION OF DUTCH RULE. Under the Treaty of Amiens the British returned the Cape to the Netherlands (Batavian Republic), 1803. A Dutch commissioner-general, Jacob de Mist, tried to establish a centralized administration, creating 2 new districts, codifying the functions of the landdrosts (sheriffs) and heemraaden (justices of the peace), and adding civil duties to the military ones already possessed by the field-cornets. Liberal in outlook, de Mist tried to protect Hottentots by registration and supervision of labor contracts, and allowed Johannes van der Kemp of the London Missionary Society to establish, 1803, a Hottentot reserve at Bethelsdorp. Other London Society missionaries helped to settle a mixed Hottentot-European people (Griquas) under Andries Waterboer along the Orange River with headquarters at Griquatown.

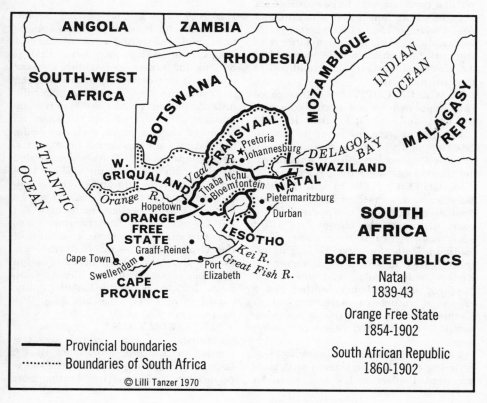

© Lilli Tanzer 1970

2ND BRITISH OCCUPATION. Following the expiration of the Truce of Amiens, the Dutch garrison, by the Capitulation of Papendorp, 10 Jan., 1806, again surrendered to the British, who acquired permanent possession of Cape Colony under the terms of the Convention of London, 13 Aug., 1814.

1807–19

HOTTENTOT ORDINANCES. The abolition of the slave trade throughout the British colonies threatened a labor shortage, a result of which in the Cape was a greater demand for Hottentot workers, whom the colonists accused the missionaries of protecting in the mission stations. By the Hottentot Code, proclaimed, 1809–11, by the Earl of Caledon (gov., 1807–11), Hottentots were required to have a fixed place of abode registered with the landdrost, and a pass if they moved beyond the district boundaries. Written contracts were to be required for terms of service longer than a month, and wages were to be paid. Further ordinances, 1812, 1819, permitted farmers to apprentice the children 8–18 years old of the Hottentot workers, and landdrosts to apprentice orphans.

BLACK CIRCUIT. An ordinance of 1811 appointed annual circuit courts to try civil and criminal cases. In 1812 circuit judges were instructed to investigate complaints of abuses against Hottentots. Most accusations proved unfounded, but the incident angered the Boers.

SLACHTER'S NEK. In 1815 Frederik Bezuidenhout, accused of ill-treating Hottentots and of failing to appear before a court to answer the charge, was killed while resisting arrest by a white officer leading a Hottentot corps. Having unsuccessfully tried to stir up revolt among the Xhosas under Gaika, and among the burghers, Bezuidenhout's brother and a group of insurgents were arrested at Slachter's Nek. At their trial 6 were condemned to death and others to banishment.

FRONTIER POLICY. On the frontier, believing that close permanent settlement was needed to secure law and order, Sir John Cradock (gov., 1811–14) cleared the Xhosas from the Zuurveld, where many farms had been abandoned. By a proclamation of 1813, Cradock tried to encourage voluntary change of loan farms from leasehold to perpetual, hereditable quitrent, accompanied by accurate land surveys. The policy proved ineffective and farmers again left their farms. Lord Charles Somerset (gov., 1814–26), revising Cradock's plan of separation of Boer and Bantu, tried, 1817, at the Kat River Conference with the Xhosas to promote co-operation, and recognized Gaika as paramount chief. During a feud with his uncle, Ndlambi, Gaika appealed for help. British and burgher forces repulsed, 1819, a Xhosa attack on Grahamstown, and Gaika was restored to the chieftaincy. The region between the Fish and Keiskamma rivers was declared a neutral zone, the Ceded Territories.

1820–36

1820 SETTLERS. The postwar depression in Britain acted as a spur to emigration, and the withdrawal of trained troops from the Cape provided additional backing for a plan to establish a buffer settlement of British immigrants between the Bantu and the discontented Boer colonists. Parliament voted £50,000 to pay the passages of groups of not less than 10, organized under a leader, each man being entitled to a quitrent grant of 100 acres. Approximately 4,000 British were settled in the Zuurveld (Albany). The land turned out to be unsuitable for agriculture and a 3-year drought added to the difficulties of the settlers, many of whom left for the towns. Settlers' complaints, the deteriorating economic condition of the Cape, and pressure from the missionary Dr. John Philip of the London Missionary Society led to the appointment, 1823, of a commission of inquiry, consisting of J. T. Bigge and Maj. William Colebrooke.

"ANGLICIZATION." Problems of government revolved around the economic and strategic importance of the Cape, the conflicting demands of a sparse population (British settlers wanting more effective government and Boers wanting less regulation), and relations between Africans and Europeans. English became the official language of government, 1824, and of the courts, 1828. The governor's autocratic powers were modified by the establishment, 1825, of an Advisory Council of 4 official members, and the colony was divided into 2 provinces, Andries van Stockenstroom becoming commissioner-general of the Eastern District. In 1833, letters patent and supplementary instructions issued to Sir Benjamin D'Urban (gov., 1834–38) ordered the setting up of an Executive Council of official members and a Legislative Council comprising 5 official and from 5 to 7 nominated unofficial members, all legislation to be initiated by the gov. only.

JUDICIAL REORGANIZATION. A Charter of Justice was issued (1828; revised, 1832; promulgated in final form, 1834), whereby the gov. ceased to be the final court of appeal, judges had to be barristers appointed by and responsible to the crown, and Roman-Dutch law was to continue as the basis of the law, but with English practices and rules of court. At the same time the landdrosts and heemraaden were replaced by civil commissioners and magistrates. Somerset's Ordinance of 1823 covering the treatment of slaves was followed, 1824, by the 19th Ordinance (issued by Acting Gov. Richard Bourke), which allowed slaves to give evidence in criminal cases. These regulations were consolidated by orders in council, 1830 and 1831.

50TH ORDINANCE. Desiring to ameliorate the condition of the Hottentots, Philip and other missionaries pressed for improvements. The 50th Ordinance canceled civil restrictions, abolished the pass system, and allowed Hottentots to buy land. In 1829 the Kat River Settlement was established for Hottentots under the guidance of the mission societies.

BANTU INVASIONS. It had been recognized that the colonists' northward movement and unrest among Africans living beyond or in any one section of the border produced repercussions along the whole frontier. During the 1820's impis (regiments) commanded by the Zulu king, Chaka, conquered much of Natal, driving many of the inhabitants of the area southward and also westward across the Drakensberg Mts. Northern expansion by white colonists was thus blocked. Frustrated in the east, the Boers tried to find pastures and permanent settlements in Griqualand, but the Cape government refused to allow any further extension of the frontier. Raiding and counterraiding by both Xhosa and Boers continued. In 1835 D'Urban ordered troops to push the Xhosa back across the Kei River, and named the region Queen Adelaide Province. The Colonial Office disallowed this action, however, and the attempt to control the province was abandoned, Dec. 1836.

The Cape of Good Hope Punishment Act, 1836, made British subjects liable to punishment on their return to the Colony for crimes committed south of Lat. 25° S., though to neither colonists nor Bantu did the Cape government provide adequate protection along the frontiers.

1836–53

GREAT TREK. Stirred by dislike of government policies, especially those influenced by the humanitarian movement and missionary support of African rights, and by the introduction during a period of drought of a new land policy of sale by auction, the Boers began to look for new lands and freedom from government interference. Acting on reports that most of the population had been cleared from the High Veld by Chaka's depredations, exploring parties went out, and in 1835 Louis Trigardt led a small group of trekkers as far as Zoutpansberg. The following year a large trek under Andries Hendrik Potgieter (1792–1852) established itself at Thaba Nchu, where it was joined by a trek from Graff-Reinet led by Gerrit Maritz. The trekkers elected a Volksraad (combined legislature and court), and appointed Maritz as landdrost with Potgieter as commandant. After the arrival of Piet Retief's trek in 1836, Retief (1780–1838) was chosen both gov. and commandant-general.

Dissension among the trekkers caused the parties to separate. Potgieter defeated the Ndebele at the Battle of Marico River, Nov. 1837, and, crossing the Vaal River, claimed the region (Transvaal). Retief led his party into Natal, where, during negotiations with Dingaan, the Zulu king, he and his men were murdered, Feb. 1838. Regrouping under Andries Pretorius (1798–1853), the Boers defeated Dingaan at Blood River, 16 Dec., settled in Natal, and formed, 1839, the first Boer republic, with its capital at Pietermaritzburg.

FOUNDING OF BRITISH NATAL. The British withdrew their troops from Port Natal, 1839, but, because of continuing Zulu incursions and unrest among other eastern tribes due to the trekker policy of segregation, British troops reoccupied, May 1842, the port after quelling trekker opposition. Many Boers left Natal to return to the High Veld. In 1843 Natal became a British possession, and was organized, 1845, as a district of Cape Colony with a separate administration.

BOER-AFRICAN RELATIONS. In the northeastern region, to keep order among the trekkers, Africans, and Griquas under Adam Kok at Philippolis, Sir George Napier (gov., 1838–44) made treaties with Kok and with Moshesh, the Sotho king. Both undertook to maintain order and to enforce the Punishment Act, which had the effect of putting trekkers under African governments. In June 1845 Napier's successor, Sir Peregrine Maitland (gov., 1844–47), summoned the Trans-Orangian chiefs to a conference at Touwfontein, where each agreed to divide his territory into an alienable area available for European settlement and an inalienable area reserved for Africans, with a British resident at Bloemfontein to handle European affairs.

ORANGE RIVER SOVEREIGNTY. A 2nd trek was set in motion by the Napier treaties and by the assertion of British authority over Natal. Potgieter negotiated the cession of Portuguese territory in the eastern Transvaal and, failing to secure Trans-Orangia, followed other trekkers north to set up, 1845, a capital at Andries-Ohrigstad. After the War of the Axe,

1846–47, Sir Harry Smith (appointed both gov. and high commissioner with powers to deal with affairs beyond the colonial frontier) (1847–52) annexed the Ceded Territory, naming it Victoria East and settling Fingos (refugees from Natal) in its northern half, and also annexed the former Queen Adelaide Province as a separate dependency and an African reserve (British Kaffraria). While still negotiating with the Natal Boers under Pretorius, Smith proclaimed, Feb. 1848, British sovereignty over the region between the Orange and Vaal rivers and the Drakensberg. In protest Pretorius marched south, but was defeated at Boomplaats, 29 Aug. Smith once again proclaimed the Orange River Sovereignty.

SAND RIVER CONVENTION. 17 Jan., 1852. Intermittent strife persisted between the Orange River Sovereignty, the Basutos, the Griquas, and the Transvaal. Despite an agreement, 1849, to elect a single Volksraad, religious separatism and an inadequate revenue and police force prevented unity among rival Boer groups. On the outbreak of the War of 1850–53 along the eastern frontier, the British sent special commissioners to investigate. At the Sand River Convention these commissioners met with delegates from the Transvaal, agreed to recognize the independence of that territory, and disclaimed alliances with tribes north of the Vaal River.

CONSTITUTION ORDINANCE. 11 Mar., 1853. Although an ordinance of 1836 had established municipal districts and although the synods of the Dutch Reformed Church had been freed, 1843, from state control, racial friction and prejudice, the expense of the military establishment, and increasing rivalry between the East and West Districts hindered the further development of representative government in the Cape. Confidence in the Legislative Council, in which the unofficial members could be outvoted, declined. Anticonvict demonstrations, 1848, caused the nominated members to resign. Proposals for reform deadlocked the Council until 1853, when the Constitution Ordinance finally passed. The ordinance provided for 2 elective houses, equal representation for East and West, voting by word of mouth, and a franchise based on so low a property qualification that 80% of the adult male population became entitled to vote regardless of race. The 1st parliament, 1854, divided Cape Colony into municipal and rural units of local government and extended trial by jury to civil cases.

1854–70

BLOEMFONTEIN CONVENTION. 13 Feb., 1854. Continued guerrilla warfare, the defeat of a British force under Lieut. Gen. George Cathcart (gov., 1852–54) by the Basutos at the Berea, Dec. 1852, the cost of maintaining troops, and reluctance to accept the responsibilities of expansion caused the British government to reconsider its frontier policies. A new special commissioner, Sir George Clerk, was sent with instructions to abandon, if necessary, the Orange River Sovereignty. In the face of some burgher opposition, the British government agreed by the Convention of Bloemfontein to withdraw from the Sovereignty and to refrain from interference beyond the Orange River. Relations with the Griquas and Basutos were left undefined. The Orange Free State was established with a president and Volksraad, 1854.

BRITISH EXPANSION IN THE EAST. Following a policy of interspersing white colonists and Africans in tribal areas, Sir George Grey (gov., 1854–61) settled German immigrants in regions depopulated by cattle killing and famine in British Kaffraria. In 1860 Grey decided to extend the frontier to link up with Natal, which had been made a crown colony, 1856, and started to import indentured Indian labor, 1860. He also persuaded Adam Kok to surrender the Philippolis lands to the Orange Free State and accept instead Nomansland (Griqualand East). In 1864 Sir Philip Wodehouse (gov., 1862–70) abandoned the Transkei lands and British Kaffraria was annexed to the Cape.

SOUTH AFRICAN REPUBLIC (TRANSVAAL). Marthinus Pretorius was elected president of the Transvaal, 1853. Hoping for a single Boer Republic, he also accepted, 1859, the presidency of the Orange Free State. Opposition in the Transvaal forced him to resign from the presidency of that region, to which, however, he was re-elected in 1864. Seeking an outlet to the coast, Pretorius bargained with the Zulu king, Cetewayo, who ceded, 1861, a strip of land along the Blood River. Natal protested the annexation and the British government immediately claimed a prior right to Delagoa Bay. Although wars and burgher disaffection had broken out in the Zoutpansberg region, following the discovery of gold, 1868, in the northwest, Pretorius issued a proclamation annexing territory in that area and also a corridor of land down the line of the Maputa River to Delagoa Bay.

ORANGE FREE STATE–BASUTO WAR. Land hunger and the undefined boundaries of both Basutoland and the Free State continued to cause border conflicts. In 1858 the Free State lost a war against the Basutos. Further encroachments by white colonists caused the outbreak of a 2nd war, which had repercussions in the Cape, the Transvaal, and Natal, and helped to deepen a general commercial depression. Moshesh petitioned unsuccessfully for annexation by the British and, threatened by famine, was forced to agree to cede, by the Treaty of Thaba Bosigo, Apr. 1866, most of his people's arable land. Recurring commando raids and growing dissatisfaction with the policy imposed by the Conventions pushed the British government into a decision to authorize the attachment of Basutoland to Natal. Wodehouse, however, distrusting Natal's native policy as carried out by Theophilus Shepstone, annexed, 1868, Basutoland to the crown. (It was transferred to Cape Colony in 1871.) The Orange Free State acquired only part of the arable lands. Land losses caused the Basutos to supplement their agricultural production by working as laborers for whites.

DISCOVERY OF DIAMONDS. When diamonds were discovered at Hopetown and on the lower Vaal, 1868, 3 problems arose: (1) who was to supervise the diggings; (2) where did the frontiers lie as between Boers, Griquas, and Tswanas; and (3) who should control the "Missionaries' Road" to the north? Negotiations concerning the Griqua Campbell lands were conducted by David Arnot, who, deserting Adam Kok, claimed them for Nicolaas Waterboer. They were thus denied to the Free State, which, however, seized them in 1871. First attempts at arbitration failed, and Sir Henry Barkly (gov., 1870–77) and Pretorius agreed to joint control of the diamond fields until the settlement of claims could be decided by a commission headed by Lieut. Gov. Robert Keate of Natal. Jan Brand, on the other hand, president of the Free State, insisted on foreign arbitration. In Oct. 1871 Keate awarded in favor of the African chiefs. Soon afterward Barkly annexed Griqualand West, which included the diamond fields, and proclaimed the boundary at the Keate Award line. (*Cont. p. 326.*)

THE FRENCH IN NORTH AFRICA
1770–1830

TURKISH RULE IN ALGERIA. Turkish military officers, acting autonomously but receiving the approval of the Ottoman sultan, governed northern Algeria until 1830 as a regency of Constantinople. The dey succeeded to office by the election of his fellow officers or the assassination of his predecessors, and ruled Algiers Province by means of Turkish civil subordinates, Turkish military garrisons, and indigenous chiefs. He received regular taxes and customs from the 3 other provinces or beyliks: Oran (west), Titteri (interior center), and Constantine (east). Each of these was controlled by a bey assisted by a similar structure of Turks together with Kulughis (descendants of Turkish men and indigenous women) and makhzan (proadministration) tribes. However, most of northern Algeria escaped effective Turkish administration, and serious revolts by non-makhzan tribes and religious leaders punctuated the early decades of the 19th century.

FRANCO-ALGERIAN DISPUTE. Members of the Bacri and Busnach families, Jews of Livornese origin, had acquired most of the carrying trade of Algiers by 1800. By 1819 the Bacri had obtained a monopoly and were collaborating closely with Marseille merchants, the French government, and the French consul in the regency capital. An argument between Dey Husayn and Consul Pierre Deval, 1829, led to French demands for an apology and a French blockade of the port. The Polignac cabinet of 1830, anxious to increase its prestige and win the national elections in France, invoked the "insult" of 1827 as the principal cause of its expedition against Algiers.

1830–48

CONQUEST OF THE COAST. In the summer of 1830, 37,000 men under Gen. Louis Bourmont (1773–1840) took control of Algiers and most of the surrounding province; they soon occupied Bône and Oran as well. Subsequent French rule was plagued by political controversies within the army over the 1830 Revolution in France, frequent changes in command, and the beginnings of resistance in Titteri Province and at Bône. Nonetheless, by 1834 the army had "pacified" Titteri; spread its control to Bougie, Arzew, and Mostaganem; and established the 1st "Arab Bureau," the primary instrument of information and administration in the interior.

"LIMITED OCCUPATION." The French government and army embarked in 1834 on their first Algerian policy, "limited occupation." This policy involved control of the coast, interior garrisons in selected positions, and the use of whatever existing indigenous structures (often the makhzan tribes) were available A gov. gen. commanded the operation from Algiers. Inconsistencies in application, the brutalities of some soldiers, and indigenous resistance to Christian European control made this policy fail and brought on the plan of total conquest in the 1840's.

DEFEAT OF BEY AHMAD. In the eastern province the French tried to dominate the interior and encountered the resistance of Bey Ahmad (Ahmad) at

Constantine. After defeating Gov. Gen. Bertrand Clauzel (1772–1842), 1836, Ahmad succumbed to Clauzel's successor, Sylvain Charles Valée (1773–1846) in the following year and withdrew to the Awras (Awrãs) mountains to conduct a much more limited campaign until his surrender in 1848.

JIHAD OF ABD-EL-KADER. A more dangerous opposition arose in the western and central provinces in the form of a loose tribal confederation headed by Amir Abd-el-Kader ('Abd al-Qãdir) (1807–83). From the time of his election as amir, 1832, until his declaration of the jihad against the French, 1839, Abd-el-Kader focused his attention against the land and privileges of the makhzan tribes and on consolidating his strength in the west and at the garrisons of Mascara, Saida, Boghari, and Takdempt, his capital in the Tell Atlas Mountains close to the Oran-Titteri provincial boundary. From 1839 until his surrender in 1847, the amir was the "Commander of the Faithful" combating the European.

Abd-el-Kader signed a treaty, 1834, with Gen. Desmichels, and a secret pact, 1837, with Gen. Bugeaud, both designed to preserve order and recognize the respective spheres of control in the interior and along the coast. The amir was able to consolidate and develop a thriving arms trade through Morocco and Tlemcen, but he encountered significant indigenous opposition in some quarters, such as that expressed by the Tijaniyya (Tijãniyya) Moslem center at Ain Mahdi on the Saharan border. The march of French troops through the central interior in 1839 in violation of the 1837 accord was the occasion of the amir's declaration of holy war. Subsequently, the rapid loss of European control and prestige made it imperative that the French either evacuate or subdue the interior.

DEFEAT OF ABD-EL-KADER. France and the new gov. gen., Thomas Robert Bugeaud (1784–1849), opted for conquest and increased their forces to over 72,000 men, including both indigenous and French contingents of cavalry and infantry. Through devastation, the deposition and replacement of chiefs, and the construction of forts, Bugeaud managed to end the control of the amir's coalition in the center and west and, by 1844, to drive Abd-el-Kader into Morocco.

The Moroccan sultan, Abd-er-Rahman ('Abd al-Rahmãn), had tended to support the amir and now responded to a French advance into his "sphere" by attacking a reconnaissance unit. The French reacted quickly, defeated the Moroccan army decisively at Isly, 14 Aug., 1844, and signed the Tangiers Treaty and the Lalla Maghnia Convention of the same year. These agreements forbade Moroccan intervention in "Algerian" affairs and drew a boundary between the 2 areas. France's reluctance to continue the penetration of Moroccan territory was partly due to her desire to avoid conflict with the strong British interests in the Sultanate.

The 1845 revolt of Bu Maza, a religious leader in Oran Province, and other uprisings provided Abd el-Kader with an opportunity to reorganize in the west. His effort was short-lived and the French captured him, 1847, and exiled him to Damascus.

1848–70

ADMINISTRATION AND COLONIZATION. The army administered the 3 provinces (Oran, Algiers, and Constantine) from its headquarters at Algiers until the influx of civilian Europeans (beginning in 1835 and expanding in the 1840's) necessitated substantial changes. By 1847, 110,000 Europeans inhabited Algeria, $6/7$ in urban centers. 50% were French. Spaniards predominated in and around Oran and Maltese at Bône, and there were many Italians, Germans, and Swiss. By this time Bugeaud's efforts at military colonization of the land had failed and civilians, both individual and corporate, had taken over many of the best farming areas of the coastal plains under spoliation laws passed in 1844 and 1846.

In this situation the administrative reforms of 1845, 1847, and 1848 were passed, dividing each Algerian province into civil territories under prefects and military ones under generals. The former included most of the coastal cities and some of the European plantations; in 1848 they became French departments. The latter included the indigenous and "mixed" areas, utilized old Turkish institutions and Arab bureaus, and fell under the jurisdiction of the gov. gen. The growing civilian population continued to feel, however, that the military dominated Algeria.

In 1858–60, Napoleon III removed the military areas temporarily from the control of the Army Ministry and put them under a Ministry for Algeria and the Colonies. Although he attempted to protect tribal or collectively owned lands through the *senatus consultum* of 1863, the over-all effect of his policies was to favor great concessions to large companies and consequently to continue the dismemberment and expropriation of indigenously held land. The *senatus consultum* of 1865 gave Algerians the option of French nationality, but few were willing to take the necessary step of abandoning their Moslem identity.

FRENCH ENTRY INTO THE SAHARA. Led by Jacques César Randon (1795–1871; gov. gen., 1851–58), the army took the northern Saharan centers of Laghouat, Wargla, and Touggourt in successive years, in response to the resistance of Mohammed ibn-Abdullah (Mu-hammad ibn 'Abd Allah), and in an effort to develop influence in the Sahara and attract its trade back to Algerian ports. Subsequently the French expressed their interest through explorations like those of Henri Duveyrier in 1860 in Tuareg country, but did not expand again militarily until the late 19th cent.

CONQUEST OF THE 2 KABYLIAS. Rivalries and disagreements among officers and strong Kabylian resistance extended the conquest of these areas and made the operation more brutal than it might otherwise have been. By 1854, the French controlled Little Kabylia around Bougie and Djidjelli, but only after the suppression of the revolt of the Rahmaniyya (Rahmāniyya) brotherhood and other Kabylians in 1857 was European influence firmly imposed in Greater Kabylia around Dellys.

RESISTANCE TO FRENCH RULE. In 1859 the Banu Snassen of Oran Province attempted to unite groups in Algeria and Morocco, but succumbed to the campaign of Gen. Martimprey. The same officer put down a revolt of the Awlad (Awlād) Sidi Shaykh in the southwest, 1864–65, in protest against abuses by the Arab bureaus. Epidemics of cholera, typhus, and famine reached serious proportions in Constantine Province in 1866–69, probably killing at least ⅕ of the population. (*Cont. p. 333.*)

THE AGE OF IMPERIAL RIVALRY, 1870–1914

The Preponderance of the West

GREAT BRITAIN AND IRELAND

1871

ARMY REGULATION BILL. 17 Aug. Introduced by the secretary for war, Edward Cardwell (1813–86), the bill initiated short-service enlistment, established the "linked-battalion" system, abolished the practice of purchasing commissions, and equipped the infantry with breech-loading rifles. Through these and other reforms, Cardwell transformed the British army into an efficient, modern force.

UNIVERSITIES TESTS ACT. 16 June. Men of all creeds could now hold teaching posts at Oxford and Cambridge Universities.

TRADE UNION ACT. 29 June. This act protected union funds and held that a trade union could not be declared illegal simply because it might be in restraint of trade. Strike enforcement, however, was denied unions by the Criminal Law Amendment Act, 21 Aug., which strengthened the Combination Act of 1825 by increasing the penalties for picketing and coercion.

1872

BALLOT ACT. 18 July. Voting by secret ballot was established.

1873

IRISH UNIVERSITY BILL. An attempt to create a religiously integrated university, Gladstone's Irish University Bill was defeated in the Commons, 12 Mar. Gladstone resigned, but Disraeli forced him to continue in office by refusing to accept the prime ministership.

JUDICATURE ACT. 5 Aug. This sweeping reform remodeled the court system and fused the common law and the rules of equity into a single system. One supreme court of judicature was established, under which were a High Court of Justice and a Court of Appeal. The High Court's 3 subdivisions were Chancery, Queen's Bench, and Probate, Divorce, and Admiralty.

1874

2ND DISRAELI MINISTRY. Disraeli came to power with an overwhelming Conservative majority in the Feb. general election. An independent Irish party, an unexpected result of the Ballot Act, appeared at Westminster; 59 Home Rulers were led by Isaac Butt (1813–79).

1875

PARNELL'S TACTICS. Charles Stewart Parnell (1846–91) was elected to Parliament as member for Meath. He· perfected a technique of obstructionism to draw attention to the Irish question.

DOMESTIC LEGISLATION. Home Secretary Richard Cross (1823–1914) introduced a series of acts designed to better the conditions of life and labor.

The Conspiracy and Protection of Property Act, 13 Aug., legalized peaceful picketing and collective bargaining. The Public Health Act, 11 Aug., consolidated earlier sanitary laws and laid new responsibilities on local authorities for the provision and maintenance of sewers and drains. The Artisans' Dwelling Act, 19 July, gave local authorities the right to condemn holdings and whole areas as unfit.

SUEZ CANAL SHARES. In Nov. Disraeli acted to purchase 176,602 ordinary shares in the Suez Canal Co., representing a 44% interest, from the Khedive Ismail of Egypt. The British were thereby enabled to reduce merchant shipping rates, and Disraeli's action paved the way for the subsequent British occupation of Egypt.

1876

ROYAL TITLES BILL. Interest in the East was heightened by the conferring, Apr., upon Queen Victoria of the title of empress of India.

TRADE UNION AMENDMENT ACT. 27 June. This act provided a legal definition of a trade union.

MERCHANT SHIPPING ACT. 15 Aug. Passed as a result of the efforts of Samuel Plimsoll (1824–98), the Merchant Shipping Act prohibited the overloading of ships and the use of unseaworthy vessels.

1877–79

IRISH LAND WAR. The Fenian Michael Davitt (1846–1906) founded the Irish National Land League, 21 Oct., 1879, to prevent eviction, reduce rents, and gain Irish ownership of tenanted land. Parnell, now leader of the Irish party in Parliament, served as the League's president. The League was suppressed in 1881, and its leaders arrested. Simultaneously a Land Act was passed which instituted a system of dual ownership, created a special court to determine fair rent, and gave tenants the right to sell their interest in holdings to the highest bidder.

1880

2ND GLADSTONE MINISTRY. Gladstone's continued criticism of the "imperial idea" helped to unseat Disraeli. The Mar. general election brought the Liberals to power, and Gladstone took office on 28 Apr.

1881

BRADLAUGH INCIDENT. Charles Bradlaugh (1833–91), newly elected to the Commons, refused to take the oath of allegiance on the grounds that he was an atheist, and offered instead an affirmation of allegiance. An opposition group led by Lord Randolph Churchill (1849–95) raised the cry of "Bradlaugh and Blasphemy" and twice prevented passage of an Affirmation Bill, 1881, 1883. In 1886 the question was withdrawn as being outside the competence of the Commons, but in 1888 Bradlaugh succeeded in legalizing affirmation, thus removing the last trace of religious discrimination from Parliament.

1882

KILMAINHAM TREATY. Gladstone made peace with Parnell, who was released from Kilmainham Prison on 2 May. Lord Spencer (1835–1910) became viceroy of Ireland and Lord Frederick Cavendish became chief secretary.

PHOENIX PARK MURDERS. On 6 May, Cavendish and Thomas Burke, his undersecretary, were murdered in Phoenix Park, Dublin, by a group known as "the Invincibles."

1883

CORRUPT AND ILLEGAL PRACTICES ACT. 25 Aug. This act limited the total amount permitted to be spent by all parties in a general election to £800,000 and ruled out all forms of bribery and undue influence.

1884–85

FRANCHISE ACT. New Radical demands for social legislation resulted in the introduction of a Franchise Act, which passed the Commons early in 1884, but was held up in the Lords pending redistribution measures. As passed on 6 Dec., 1884, the Franchise Act fully extended the franchise to Ireland.

REDISTRIBUTION ACT. Passed in June 1885, the Redistribution Act introduced virtual manhood suffrage and created a system of single-member constituencies. Counties and boroughs ceased to be the basis of representation in the House of Commons.

1ST SALISBURY MINISTRY. Gladstone's failure to rescue General Gordon at Khartoum damaged his prestige, and an opposition amendment to his budget led to his defeat, 8 June, 1885. Lord Salisbury (1830–1903) formed a minority government on 24 June. His administration tried to gain Irish support in the Commons by passing the Ashbourne Act, Aug. 1885, which provided a £5-m. loan fund to assist Irish tenants to purchase land.

1886–87

3RD GLADSTONE MINISTRY. Gladstone returned to power, 13 Feb., with Liberal and Irish support. On 8 Apr. he introduced a Home Rule Bill. It was defeated, 8 June, and the "Liberal Unionists" bolted the Liberal Party. A general election called in July resulted in a severe defeat for Gladstone.

2ND SALISBURY MINISTRY. Salisbury assumed office on 26 July. His nephew Arthur Balfour (1848–1930) became chief secretary for Ireland, Mar. 1887, and supported a new Crimes Bill to suppress dissent in Ireland. Passage of this bill was aided by the Pigott forgeries. In Apr. 1887 *The Times* published a letter, allegedly written by Parnell, con-

doning the Phoenix Park murders. A special commission discovered the letter to be a forgery by Dublin journalist Richard Pigott, exonerated Parnell, and ordered *The Times* to pay the cost of the inquiry.

LABOR AGITATION. A huge Socialist meeting in Trafalgar Square, 13 Nov., became a battle between the police and the crowd in which 2 were killed and over 100 injured. The day became known as "Bloody Sunday."

1889

LONDON DOCK STRIKE. 15 Aug.–16 Sept. The movement to organize unskilled labor began with this strike, led by Ben Tillett, with the aid of Tom Mann and John Burns. The dockers demanded and won a standard wage of 6d. an hour.

1890

FALL OF PARNELL. Divorce-court proceedings revealed, 17 Nov., Parnell's adulterous liaison with the wife of Capt. W. H. O'Shea. As a result, Justin McCarthy (1830–1912) succeeded him as leader of the Irish party, 6 Dec. Parnell died, 6 Oct., 1891.

1892

4TH GLADSTONE MINISTRY. After assuming office, 18 Aug., Gladstone drafted a 2nd Home Rule Bill, which passed the Commons, 1 Sept., 1893, but failed to pass the Lords, 8 Sept., 1893. When Gladstone resigned, 3 Mar., 1894, Victoria chose Lord Rosebery (1847–1929) to succeed him.

1893

INDEPENDENT LABOUR PARTY. An avowedly socialist organization, the I.L.P. was established, Jan., by Keir Hardie (1856–1915), 1 of 2 socialists elected to Parliament in 1892. Its membership benefited from the industrial unrest and rioting that marked 1893, especially in the Midlands.

GAELIC LEAGUE. Douglas Hyde formed the Gaelic League to restore Irish as the spoken language of Ireland. Though nonpolitical, the League was revolutionary in its separatist implications.

1894

DEATH DUTIES. A new direct tax was created with the levying of death duties on all forms of property.

1895

3RD SALISBURY MINISTRY. After Secretary for War Henry Campbell-Bannerman (1836–1908) was censured by the Commons, 21 June, for failing to provide the army with sufficient cordite, the cabinet resigned. Salisbury formed a Conservative cabinet which included such Liberal Unionists as Joseph Chamberlain (1836–1914), who became colonial secretary.

1897

WORKMEN'S COMPENSATION ACT. 6 Aug. Employers were made directly responsible for injuries suffered by their workers.

1900

LABOUR REPRESENTATION COMMITTEE. Trade unionists and Independent Labour Party members formed the Labour Representation Committee in Feb. to increase their representation in Parliament. The leader in creating this precursor to the Labour Party was Keir Hardie. The committee's secretary, J. Ramsay MacDonald (1866–1937), later became the first Labour prime minister.

1901

TAFF VALE CASE. Legal action was brought by the Taff Vale Railway Co. of South Wales against the Amalgamated Society of Railway Servants for damage done to railway property during a strike. The union was found responsible for its members' actions and was ordered to pay damages and costs. Trade unionists regarded the decision as an attack on the right to strike.

DEATH OF VICTORIA. Queen Victoria died, 22 Jan., after a brief illness, and her son, Edward VII (1841–1910), became king.

1902

BALFOUR MINISTRY. On Salisbury's resignation, 11 July, Balfour became prime minister.

EDUCATION ACT. Framed by R. L. Morant (1863–1920), the Education Act of 1902 abolished the school boards established by the Education Act of 1870, and made county and borough councils responsible for primary and secondary education. Voluntary as well as board schools were brought under the authority of the councils' Statutory Education Committees. Despite Nonconformist objections to the financing of church schools by rate payers, the Education Act became law in Dec.

1903

TARIFF REFORM LEAGUE. Joseph Chamberlain resigned, 18 Sept., over Balfour's refusal to restore duties on imported foodstuffs. The Tariff Reform League was organized, and Chamberlain toured the country preaching protectionism.

1904

MILITARY REFORMS. Balfour reactivated the Committee of Imperial Defence, giving it a permanent secretariat. Sir John Fisher (1841–1920), 1st sea lord, and the Earl of Cawdor (1847–1911), 1st lord of the admiralty, worked to counter German naval strength by redistributing the fleet—the sea routes to the Far East were no longer considered to be endangered by France because of the Anglo-French Entente of 8 Apr.—and by laying down the battleship *Dreadnought* and the battle cruiser *Invincible,* the 1st all-big-gun ships.

1905

SINN FEIN. Founded by Arthur Griffith (1872–1922), the Sinn Fein ("We Ourselves") advocated the establishment of a separate Irish state, politically and economically self-sufficient.

CAMPBELL-BANNERMAN MINISTRY. Balfour resigned, 4 Dec., and Campbell-Bannerman succeeded him, 5 Dec. The Liberals won an overwhelming majority in the general elections of Jan. 1906.

1906

TRADE DISPUTES ACT. 21 Dec. Trade unions were made immune from actions of tort. The Taff Vale ruling was thereby reversed.

MILITARY REORGANIZATION. Secretary for War R. B. Haldane (1856–1928) undertook massive military changes, beginning with the creation of a general staff.

1907–8

LLOYD GEORGE'S REFORMS. David Lloyd George (1863–1945), president of the Board of Trade, was responsible for such reforms as the Merchant Shipping Act, 1906; the Act for Taking a Census of Production, 1906; and the Patents Act, 1907. Through his efforts, the Port of London Authority was established, 1908, to bring order to the docks.

ASQUITH MINISTRY. Campbell-Bannerman resigned, 6 Apr., 1908, and died on 22 Apr. Herbert Asquith (1852–1928) succeeded him. The new administration passed the Old-Age Pension Bill, effective 1 Jan., 1909, which provided 5s. per week to persons over 70 whose incomes did not exceed 10s. per week.

1909–10

PEOPLE'S BUDGET. Lloyd George, now chancellor of the exchequer, wished to reduce the national debt and provide for defense needs. His 1909 budget increased income tax and tobacco, liquor-license, and death duties. These measures were unpopular with the upper classes, especially because they included a land tax that required a national land survey. The budget passed the Commons, 4 Nov., but was rejected by the Lords, 30 Nov. Asquith denounced the Lords' action as unconstitutional, 2 Dec. A general election was fought on this issue and on the Home Rule question, and the Liberals won. The Commons passed the budget on 27 Apr., 1910, and the Lords immediately let it pass.

ACCESSION OF GEORGE V. Edward VII died, 6 May, and George V (1865–1936) ascended the throne.

1911–12

PARLIAMENT ACT. 18 Aug., 1911. The Parliament Bill deprived the House of Lords of veto power over money bills; provided that other bills would become law, even if rejected by the Lords, if they had passed the Commons 3 times and if 2 years had lapsed since introduction; and reduced the duration of Parliament from 7 to 5 years. The bill passed the Commons, 15 May, 1911, and, under the threat of the creation of 250 Liberal peers, was passed by the Lords on 10 Aug., 1911.

NATIONAL INSURANCE ACT. Passed in Dec. 1911, this act provided health insurance for all workers and unemployed insurance for some. Both schemes were to be financed by contributions from employers, employees, and the government.

INDUSTRIAL UNREST. A wave of strike and riot activity by dock workers and railwaymen began in the summer of 1911, and 850,000 coal miners struck in Mar. 1912. A Minimum Wage Law, Mar. 1912, brought temporary quiet.

ULSTER OBSTRUCTIONISM. The Ulster party, led by Sir Edward Carson (1854–1935) joined with Conservatives in opposition to Asquith's Home Rule Bill. The measure passed the Commons twice, but was rejected by the Lords. In July 1912 the Ulstermen pledged to oppose Home Rule by every means, including armed insurrection. The government, which needed Irish party support, was thus gravely embarrassed politically.

1913–14

SUFFRAGETTES. Militant action to secure the vote for women was led by Emmeline Pankhurst (1858–1928), who had joined with her daughters, Cristabel and Sylvia, in forming the Women's Social and Political Union in 1903. Her violent tactics led to her arrest and imprisonment on several occasions. In 1913 a follower, Emily Davidson, flung herself under the king's horse at Epsom, and died. Women over 30 were enfranchised in 1918, and women between 21 and 30 in 1928.

DUBLIN STRIKE. In Aug. a bitter strike began in Dublin, led by James Connolly (1870–1916) and James Larkin. By Sept., 24,000 people were unemployed. The 8-month strike, though inconclusive, led to the growth of the Irish Citizen Army.

HOME RULE. On 25 May, 1914, the Commons gave Asquith's Home Rule Bill a 3rd reading. The Lords demanded that Ulster be given permanent exclusion. With this disagreement still unresolved, George V signed the Home Rule Bill on 10 Sept., and it was ratified by Parliament the following day. Because of the deteriorating situation in Europe, however, it was put in abeyance for 1 year, and was then postponed until the end of World War I. (*Cont. p. 401.*)

FRANCE

1870

FRANCO-PRUSSIAN WAR. The announcement, 2 July, 1870, that Prince Leopold of Hohenzollern was a candidate for the Spanish throne awakened French fears of encirclement by Prussia. Protesting to Emperor William I, French diplomats obtained assurances that Leopold's name would be withdrawn. But when Napoleon III insisted on guarantees, William refused, 13 July, and Chancellor

Bismarck published an inflammatory account of the French setback (Ems Telegram, 13 July). The message aroused French opinion. Over the objections of the extreme left and without firm commitments from allies, the Ollivier government, pushed by the bellicose foreign minister, the duc de Gramont, declared war, 19 July.

The French had superior infantry weapons but lacked the artillery, the imaginative leadership, and the organization of the Prussians. Disastrously chaotic mobilization left France ill-prepared to resist invasion.

Defeated in Alsace, 6 Aug., the emperor retired to Metz to regroup his forces, while Right and Center legislators brought down the Ollivier ministry, 9 Aug.

Napoleon relinquished command, but stayed in the field as French armies suffered decisive defeats near Metz, 14, 16, and 18 Aug. Taking refuge at Sedan, the emperor and his troops came under German artillery fire, 1 Sept. He ran up the white flag and capitulated, 2 Sept.

GOVERNMENT OF NATIONAL DEFENSE. When news of Sedan reached Paris, crowds overthrew the empire and established a republican "Government of National Defense" (Revolution of 4 Sept.). Failing to obtain acceptable armistice terms, the new government ordered war to the bitter end.

On 18 Sept. Prussian troops reached Paris and began a siege, 19 Sept., which lasted until 28 Jan., 1871. Léon Gambetta (1838–82), war minister, ordered, 5 Nov., an offensive to relieve Paris. The French recaptured Orléans (Battle of Coulmiers, 7 Nov.), but Prussian troops, strengthened after the fall of Metz, 27 Oct., forced the French into retreat. In 3 battles—St.-Quentin, Le Mans, Héricourt, Jan. 1871—the Prussians defeated the main French armies. With Paris close to starvation, the government capitulated, 28 Jan.

1871

BORDEAUX ASSEMBLY. Parliamentary elections, 8 Feb., returned a provincial, royalist majority determined to end the war. Adolphe Thiers, designated, 17 Feb., "Chief of the Executive Power," negotiated peace terms: Prussian annexation of Alsace and part of Lorraine and occupation of territory held in France until payment of a 5,000-m. franc indemnity (Treaty of Frankfurt, ratified 21 May).

PARIS COMMUNE. 18 Mar.–28 May. Assembly decisions to transfer the capital to Versailles, to end the wartime moratorium on debts and rents, and to suspend National Guard payments, Mar., stirred intense popular resentment in Paris. Violence broke out when government troops attempted to remove stockpiled cannons, 18 Mar. Thiers ordered withdrawal, 18 Mar., and began to mass troops for assault. Paris organized for civil war, electing, 26 Mar., a municipal council, self-christened the "Commune."

Although Karl Marx immortalized the Commune as a Socialist-directed class war, its leaders, Jacobin-inspired revolutionaries, fought to defend the republic and municipal rights. Intent on war and conscious of legality, the Commune produced no significant socialist legislation.

On 21 May government troops entered Paris through an unguarded gate. As they advanced, the Communards countered with a ferocious but futile defense (Bloody Week, 21–28 May). Summary executions and mass deportations left the working class without leaders.

1871–73

GOVERNMENT OF THIERS. The monarchist Bordeaux Assembly, divided between Orleanists and Legitimists, postponed establishment of permanent political institutions. Thiers continued without specific term as "President of the Republic" (Rivet-Vitet Law, 31 Aug., 1871).

Benefiting from rapid economic recovery, France paid the indemnity due to Prussia by 1873 and ended Prussian occupation.

Suspicious of Thiers's preference for the conservative republic, the monarchists united to force his resignation, 24 May, 1873. Marshal MacMahon (1808–93), a royalist, accepted the presidency, 24 May.

REPUBLIC BY DEFAULT. The monarchists appealed to the Legitimist pretender, the Comte de Chambord (1820–83), but his refusal, 14, 27 Oct., 1873, to accept the tricolor flag made his accession impossible. Prospects for restoration died as republican gains in by-elections, 1871–73, and royalist divisions threatened the monarchist majority. To guarantee a conservative executive, the royalists voted a 7-year term for MacMahon (Law of the Septennate, 20 Nov., 1873).

1874–79

CONSTITUTION OF 1875. After months of indecision, the Assembly established a republic, with a president elected by a 2-chamber legislature (Wallon amendment, 30 Jan., 1875). Additional constitutional laws created extensive presidential powers, a responsible cabinet, and an indirectly elected Senate to balance a Chamber of Deputies elected by universal suffrage.

THE "REPUBLICAN REPUBLIC." Although after the elections of 1875, Republicans controlled the Chamber, MacMahon forced out, 16 May, 1877, the Republican minister, Jules Simon (1814–96) and called on the royalist, de Broglie. Dissolution followed, 25 June, but the Republicans, organized under Gambetta, maintained their majority following the elections of 14 and 28 Oct. The "May 16 Crisis" established cabinet responsibility to parliament alone, opening the way to legislative predominance. Henceforth, no president dared dissolve the Chamber on his own responsibility.

On 30 Jan., 1879, MacMahon resigned and was replaced, 30 Jan., by the conservative republican Jules Grévy (1807–91). With victory at the senatorial elections, 5 Jan., 1879, Republicans controlled the republic.

1880–85

REPUBLICAN REFORMS. In order to end clerical domination of education, the Republicans established free, 16 June, 1881, secular, and compulsory, 28 Mar.,

1882, primary schools. Republican governments accomplished other long-promised reforms: amnesty for Communards, July 1880; freedom of public meeting, 30 June, 1881, and of the press, 29 July, 1881; legalization of trade unions, Mar. 1884; decentralization of local administration; and abandonment of life senatorships.

FROM BOOM TO SLUMP. Government spending (Freycinet plan, 1878) sparked a boom that ended with the crash of the Union Générale, a Catholic bank, Jan. 1882. Economic stagnation and a series of bad harvests hit France.

POLITICAL DEVELOPMENTS. "Opportunist" Republicans, advocates of gradual reform, held power, while "Radical" Republicans urged faster change. Dormant since 1881, the Conservatives gained strength in the elections of 1885. An expanding Socialist movement split, 1882, into the Marxist Parti Ouvrier Français, under Jules Guesde (1845–1922), and the more moderate Possibilist party.

Republican divisions necessitated coalition governments which were a prey to shifting majorities. Few governments lasted long enough to implement solid programs.

1886–89

BOULANGER CRISIS. A scandal involving Grévy's son-in-law Daniel Wilson, forced the president's resignation, 2 Dec., 1887. Government immobility, economic downswing, and a surge of nationalism focused on the recovery of Alsace-Lorraine fed the opposition.

The discontented rallied to Gen. Georges Boulanger (1837–91), minister of war, Jan. 1886–May 1887. But, despite an impressive electoral mandate, Boulanger refused to seize the government, 27 Jan., 1889, and fled France, 8 Apr.

The elections of 22 Sept., 1889, confirmed Republican control of the Chamber. Moving out of opposition, the Radicals co-operated in a government of "republican concentration," dominated by the Moderates.

1890–96

THE RALLIEMENT. Convinced of the futility of the monarchist cause, Pope Leo XIII urged French Catholics to accept the republic, Feb. 1892. The order split the Conservatives. Some obeyed and rallied to the republic, but others remained unreconciled.

PANAMA CANAL SCANDAL. The builder of the Suez Canal, Ferdinand de Lesseps, organized a company, 1880, heavily backed by the small French investor, to dig a canal in Panama. In serious financial difficulty, the company bought journalistic silence and parliamentary support for a new loan, which failed, forcing the company to admit ruin, Feb. 1889. Exposure of the scandal, 1892, by revealing the involvement of important Republican officials and deputies, undermined confidence in the republic.

PROTECTIONISM. Pressure from industrialists and the fall of agricultural prices converted a reluctant majority from free trade to protection (Méline Tariff, Jan. 1892). High tariff barriers contributed to a revival of industry, 1895, which in turn stimulated general prosperity.

FRANCO-RUSSIAN ALLIANCE. To escape the isolation imposed by the Triple Alliance, France made overtures to Russia, 1890–91. An entente, 1891, prefaced the secret adoption of a mutual-defense pact, Dec. 1893 and 4 Jan., 1894. Although conceived largely as the instrument of an anti-German policy, the alliance forced France to follow Russia into closer relations with Germany.

SOCIALIST GAINS. Criticizing the *"embourgeoisement"* of the Possibilist deputies, the Allemanists (under Jean Allemane), working-class militants, broke away, Oct. 1890, forming the Parti Ouvrier Socialiste Révolutionnaire. Trade union organization progressed, and the Socialists made gains in municipal elections. As parliamentary Socialist representation increased, a group of gifted

Socialist deputies emerged: René Viviani (1863–1925), Alexandre Millerand (1859–1943), and Jean Jaurès (1859–1914).

In 1896 most Socialist factions adopted a common minimum program, 30 May, advocating the destruction of capitalism by reform, not revolution.

ANARCHIST VIOLENCE. Following a new wave of terrorism in 1892, anarchists bombed the Chamber, 9 Dec., 1893. Repressive legislation did not prevent the assassination of President Sadi Carnot, Jules Grévy's successor, by an anarchist, 24 June, 1894. Measures to limit revolutionary activity passed after violent opposition from the left, July 1894. The Radicals broke with the Moderates and cemented ties with the Socialists.

POLITICAL INSTABILITY. Ministerial crises multiplied as the Left intensified pressure on shaky governments, 1893–95. Jean Casimir-Perier (1847–1907), Carnot's successor, resigned, 17 Jan., 1895, and was replaced by Félix Faure (1841–99). An all-Moderate ministry under Jules Méline (1838–1925) restored some stability, Apr. 1896–June 1898.

1897–99

DREYFUS AFFAIR. The army accused Capt. Alfred Dreyfus (1859–1935), a Jew, of passing military documents to the Germans and condemned him on flimsy evidence to life imprisonment on Devil's Island, Dec. 1894. Although re-examination of the evidence incriminated Maj. Esterhazy, a military court acquitted him, Jan. 1898. Émile Zola's *J'accuse*, 13 Jan., 1898, riveted public attention on the "Dreyfus Affair."

Conservatives, nationalists, and anti-Semites, the anti-Dreyfusards, insisted on the preservation of the army's authority and honor. The Dreyfusards, liberals and intellectuals, defended justice and demanded a revision of the Dreyfus judgment.

President Faure died, 16 Feb., 1899, and was replaced by Émile Loubet (1838–1929). As anti-Republican attacks increased, René Waldeck-Rousseau (1846–1904) formed a government of Republican Defense, 22 June, supported by Radicals and Socialists. Breaking a precedent, the Socialist, Millerand, entered the cabinet.

At the long-anticipated retrial, judges found Dreyfus guilty, 11 Sept., 1899, but reduced his sentence to 10 years. President Loubet pardoned Dreyfus, 19 Sept., and in 1906 he was fully exonerated. The Dreyfus Affair had divided France and had badly shaken the republic.

1900–1905

SEPARATION OF CHURCH AND STATE. Striking at clerical sources of anti-Republican activity, the Waldeck-Rousseau government, by the Associations Law, 1 July, 1901, required all religious orders to obtain state authorization.

The 1902 elections confirmed a shift of power from the Moderates to the Radicals and Radical Socialists, spokesmen of the lower middle classes. Socialists joined Radicals in a Bloc des Gauches. Backed by a solid anticlerical majority, the Émile Combes (1835–1921) government, June 1902–19 Jan., 1905, barred religious orders from public-school teaching, 1904. Formal separation of church and state followed, 9 Dec., 1905. The state relinquished control over the appointment and payment of church officials, provided that lay organizations take over church property, and guaranteed freedom of conscience.

MILITARY REFORMS. Gen. Louis André (1838–1913), war minister, directed the republicanization of the army, 1900–1904, until the opposition discovered his reliance on Masonic information and forced him to resign, 15 Nov., 1904 (*Affaire des Fiches*). In Mar. 1905 the Chamber established 2-year military service for all, without exception.

SOCIALIST UNITY. In 1902 French Socialists split on the issue of support for bourgeois governments. But under orders from the Socialist International, meeting in Amsterdam, Aug. 1904, the Socialists united in the Parti Socialiste Unifié (S.F.I.O.) and adopted the principle of nonco-operation with bourgeois governments, Apr. 1905.

TRADE UNION MOVEMENT. The major trade union organizations merged with the Confédération Générale du Travail (C.G.T.) in 1902. Revolutionary syndicalist leadership committed the C.G.T. to political neutrality, the general strike, and social revolution.

ANGLO-FRENCH ENTENTE. France and Britain signed a convention, 8 Apr., 1904, regulating outstanding colonial differences. France accepted British occupation of Egypt and obtained recognition of its interests in Morocco.

1ST MOROCCAN CRISIS. William II, the German emperor, speaking in Tangier, challenged French claims to special interests in Morocco, 31 Mar., 1905. Théophile Delcassé (1852–1923), foreign minister since 1898, urged resistance to Germany, but the cabinet, afraid of war, accepted the international conference demanded by the Germans (Algeciras Conference, 16 Jan.–7 Apr., 1906). Delcassé resigned, 12 June.

1906–11

RETURN TO POLITICAL INSTABILITY. Armand Fallières (1841–1931), Bloc des Gauches candidate, succeeded the outgoing president, Loubet, 17 Jan., 1906. The 1906 elections crushed the Conservative opposition and strengthened the Bloc des Gauches. But, when Radical governments under Clemenceau and Briand used force to restore order during a prolonged period of strikes, 1907–10, the Socialists abandoned the Bloc. The emergence of 2 oppositions forced a reversion to Center governments and cabinet instability.

2ND MOROCCAN CRISIS. Germany pressed for compensation for French gains in Morocco. When negotiations lagged, Germany dispatched the gunboat *Panther* to Agadir, 1 July, 1911, ostensibly to protect German property. The French agreed to buy German acceptance of French special interests in Morocco with a slice of the Congo, 4 Nov.

1912–14

DOMESTIC DISINTEGRATION. To restore stability, the Chamber called on Raymond Poincaré (1860–1934) to form a government, 14 Jan., 1912. He resigned, 18 Jan., 1913, to become president of the republic. As the Radical majority disintegrated, cabinet instability intensified. Voted on the eve of war, a law increasing military service from 2 to 3 years aroused the violent opposition of the Left, pushing the Radicals and Socialists together. The elections of 26 Apr.–10 May, 1914, delivered the Chamber to the Radicals, Radical Socialists, and Socialists. (*Cont. p. 401.*)

THE GERMAN EMPIRE
1871

FOUNDING OF THE EMPIRE. On 18 Jan. in the Hall of Mirrors at Versailles (symbolizing the victory over France by the German princes united under the Hohenzollerns) King William I of Prussia was crowned emperor of Germany. The states which constituted this new empire were the North German Confederation, dominated by Prussia, and the southern kingdoms of Bavaria, Baden, Hesse-Darmstadt, and Württemberg. On 14 Apr. the Reichstag adopted an Imperial Constitution, framed by Otto von Bismarck, by which the king of Prussia received the hereditary right to the German throne. As emperor of Germany, the Prussian king represented the Reich in foreign affairs and commanded the armed forces. He presided over the Bundesrat (Upper House), in which the individual German states were represented, with Prussia dominant; and he convened and adjourned the Reichstag (Lower House), whose 397 members were elected by all German men over 25 years of age. The only all-German minister was the imperial chancellor. The chancellor appointed heads of department for Reich affairs, but the individual state governments retained responsibility for most domestic matters. The chancellor was responsible to the emperor, not to the Reichstag, and a vote of no confidence or a defeat in the Reichstag did not necessarily affect his position. In 1871 Bismarck held the chancellorship, as well as the influential post of minister-president of Prussia.

POLITICAL PARTIES. Bismarck's power was further enhanced by the division of the Reichstag into several conflicting parties. To the far right were the Conservatives, mostly Prussian landowning aristocrats, whose major interests were the preservation of Prussian traditions and protection of their own agricultural livelihoods. An offshoot of the Conservatives, under the leadership of Wilhelm von Kardorff (1828–1907), was the Free Conservative Party, or Reichspartei, which drew into its membership nobles from other parts of the empire as well as from Prussia. These nobles owned industrial as well as agricultural enterprises, and the Free Conservatives had therefore a wider, more liberal orientation. The National Liberal Party represented chiefly business and professional interests. Its leaders included Rudolf von Bennigsen (1824–1902) and Eduard Lasker (1829–84). Its members had the typical 19th-cent. liberal sympathy for national unity, free trade, material progress, and anticlericalism. The Progressive Party, which fluctuated greatly in strength from one election to the next, drew its main support from the commercial middle classes, lower officials, and intellectuals; its members, led by Eugen Richter (1838–1906), demanded a full-fledged parliamentary state. The Center Party, led by Ludwig Windthorst (1812–91), was unique in that its basis lay not in class or ideology but in religion. As the representative of German Catholic interests, it attracted members from all classes and geographic areas of the empire who supported federalism, autonomy for the church, and freedom of religious education. Finally, the Social Democrats represented the German working classes.

In addition to these parties, the Reichstag contained a few representatives of dissident minorities, including Poles, Guelph Party supporters of the former king of Hanover, and Danes from North Schleswig. On 10 May, 1871, another minority group reluctantly joined the empire when the Peace of Frankfurt, which officially ended the Franco-Prussian War, transferred Alsace-Lorraine from France to Germany.

1871–88

KULTURKAMPF. On 8 July, 1871, Bismarck abolished the special division for Catholic affairs in the Prussian Ministry for Public Worship and Education. This action marked the beginning of the *Kulturkampf* (cultural struggle) against the Catholic Church in Germany. During the previous decade the church, under the direction of Pope Pius IX, had taken a more aggressive attitude than in the past, culminating in a definition of papal infallibility in 1870. Bismarck, supported by the National Liberals, saw the Catholics as a menace to German unity. Not only were Catholic Germans sympathetic to Catholic Poles and Hanoverians within the empire, but on the international level there was a danger that German Catholics might unite under papal leadership with their Catholic neighbors in France and Austria. Bismarck attacked the Center Party in the Reichstag, and on 4 July, 1872, obtained a law dissolving the Jesuit order. Most of the other anti-Catholic laws were passed in Prussia under the direction of Adalbert Falk (1827–1900), Prussian minister for public worship and education. The "May Laws," passed in 1873, 1874, and 1875, provided for state supervision over education and the appointment of clergy, made civil marriage compulsory, and placed ecclesiastical discipline under state control. By 1876 many Prussian bishops and priests were in prison and opposition was increasing to Bismarck's policies, as Liberals became alarmed at restrictions on basic liberties and Conservatives began to worry that similar action might be taken against the Lutheran Church. Bismarck, searching for a way to retreat, was helped by the accession in 1878 of a new pope, Leo XIII. The 2 men held direct negotiations which led to the gradual repeal over the next decade of most of the anti-Catholic laws. Falk resigned in 1879.

LEAGUE OF THE 3 EMPERORS.
Bismarck's foreign policy after the Franco-Prussian War attempted to maintain the *status quo* through a complex system of defensive alliances. Friendship with France was impossible so long as Germany held Alsace and Lorraine; Bismarck therefore aimed to isolate France, and particularly to prevent any kind of Russo-French alliance which might lead to Germany's having to fight a war on 2 fronts. In Sept. 1872, Emperor William I met in Berlin with Alexander II of Russia and the Hapsburg Emperor Francis Joseph. Their cordial discussion of European affairs led, Oct. 1873, to the formation of the 3 Emperors' League, by which they pledged themselves to co-operate in the preservation of the European peace. This peace was disturbed briefly in the spring of 1875 by the "war in sight" crisis. Alarmed at France's quick economic recovery and plans to increase her army, Bismarck made angry statements, while the German press published excited articles, climaxed by the headline "Is War in Sight?" At this point both Britain and Russia intervened, and Germany backed down.

CONGRESS OF BERLIN. 13 June–13 July, 1878. A more serious situation arose in the Balkans, where Austria and Britain opposed Russia's domination after her defeat of Turkey in 1877. Bismarck refused to support the Russian position, instead offering to serve as "honest broker" at an international congress. The congress met in Berlin, and the disgruntled Russians saw their gains reduced. Bismarck turned toward Austria, with whom he signed a secret defensive treaty against Russia, Oct. 1879. But Russia, facing a chaotic domestic situation at the time, preferred a peaceful course in her foreign relations. Her conciliatory attitude allowed a re-establishment of the 3 Emperors' League in June 1881.

RISE OF THE SOCIAL DEMOCRATS. In the 1874 elections to the Reichstag the Social Democrats won 9 seats, and in May 1875 Social Democrats of various persuasions came together at Gotha to form a united party. The Gotha program represented a compromise between the followers of Karl Marx and of Ferdinand Lassalle: it called for an economy of productive co-operatives financed by the state, in order to emancipate labor and construct a society in which exploitation would cease. In the 1877 elections, Social Democratic strength increased to 12 seats. Bismarck viewed this new, class-based, internationally oriented party with alarm. In 1878 there were 2 attempts, May and June, to assassinate the emperor. Bismarck accused the Social Democrats and dissolved the Reichstag; in the new elections the Conservatives gained strength while the Social Democrats lost 3 seats. The Reichstag passed an anti-socialist law, 19 Oct., 1878, which gave the government authority to suppress labor organizations and socialist activities of all kinds. During the next decade, Bismarck attempted to substitute his own kind of social reform, through sickness insurance, 1883; accident insurance, 1884; and old-age and incapacity insurance, 1889. Under these acts employers, employees, and the state contributed in various proportions to compulsory insurance schemes. In spite of this social legislation, the Social Democratic Party continued to grow, and after 1890 the anti-socialist laws were not renewed.

INDUSTRIALIZATION. The boom after the Franco-Prussian War was followed by depression in Germany in 1873, but by 1880 the economy had revived and continued to grow until World War I. Improvements in canals extended the already well-developed transport system; increasing coal and iron production formed the basis for new manufactures; and the textile, chemical, and electrical industries all expanded. Along with industrial growth came a growth in banking facilities. The Reichsbank, or central bank, was established in 1875. Banking institutions had a powerful role in financing German industry, and between banking and industry a system of interlocking directorates developed. German industry, moreover, tended to develop by means of cartels, or combinations controlling prices and production for a horizontal or vertical group of products.

During the 1870's German producers debated the question of free trade vs. protection. Responding to the demands of both farmers and industrialists, the Reichstag adopted a protective tariff, 12 July, 1879. That year also marked a change in the direction of German politics, since Bismarck turned away from the Liberals in order to get Conservative and Center support for passage of the tariff. This alliance persisted until the debate in 1887 over the Septennate, a bill to increase army strength by 10% for a period of 7 years. The Center opposed the bill, but Bismarck achieved its passage with support from an alliance of conservative parties and the now demoralized National Liberals.

RELATIONS WITH RUSSIA. In May 1882 Bismarck attempted to make Germany's international position even more secure by joining with Austria and Italy in a Triple Alliance directed against France. In the mid-1880's another Balkan crisis strained this new alliance system. Russia, at odds with Austria, withdrew from the 3 Emperors' League, 1887; but to replace the League, Czar Alexander agreed to a Reinsurance Treaty with Germany. This secret treaty committed each of the 2 states to benevolent neutrality if the other fought a war, except if Germany began a war against France or Russia began hostilities against Austria. Germany further pledged diplomatic support for Russian ambitions in the Balkans, a pledge which conflicted with the spirit of German agreements with Austria.

COLONIAL POLICY. Until the 1880's Bismarck refused to join in the European imperial scramble, although north-German merchants were eager for overseas expansion. The Deutsche Kolonialverein (German Colonial League) was founded, Dec. 1882. In the following year Bismarck reversed his policy and began to support German imperial ventures. In 1884 Adolf Lüderitz signed treaties resulting in the creation of a German protectorate in Southwest Africa. Also in that year Germany acquired Togoland and the Cameroons. In 1885 an official protectorate was declared in East Africa as a result of the efforts of Karl Peters (1856–1918), founder of the Gesellschaft für Deutsche Kolonisation (Society for German Colonization). During these same years Germany obtained possessions in the Southwest Pacific, including a part of New Guinea, the Bismarck Archipelago, and the Marshall and Solomon islands.

1889–1914

FALL OF BISMARCK. Emperor William I died on 9 Mar., 1888, to be succeeded by his son, Frederick III (1831–88). Through his wife, Victoria, eldest daughter of Queen Victoria of Great Britain, Frederick had been exposed to liberal British influences and had become the hope of German liberals. But by the time of his accession to the throne he was mortally ill with cancer of the throat. Unable to take any active part himself, he left the conduct of affairs to Bismarck. On his death, 15 June, 1888, the crown passed to his son, William II (1859–1941), a man of very different views. Within the next year an inevitable conflict arose between the 74-year-old chancellor and the 29-year-old emperor, who was determined to exercise his own rule. Moreover, the Reichstag elections of 1890 resulted in a defeat for Bismarck's supporters and an increase in strength for the left. Bismarck resigned as chancellor, 18 Mar., 1890, and was replaced by Gen. Leo von Caprivi (1831–99).

RULE OF WILLIAM II. After Bismarck's retirement there occurred some decentralization of the power which had formerly rested with the chancellor alone. The emperor now took a more active part in policy formation, as also did various secretaries of state. William leaned toward liberalism at the beginning of his reign, supporting progressive laws passed to improve factory conditions and soften the treatment of minority groups. But these measures failed to reduce socialist and minority opposition to the central government. The Social Democrats met at

Erfurt, Oct. 1891, and adopted a new program which emphasized class struggle. They dropped their former demands for state-financed producers' associations, which represented an ideological switch from Lassalle to Marx. In reaction to the liberal measures of the government, the conservatives started their own propaganda leagues and pressure groups. In Apr. 1891 the organization which later took the name Alldeutsche Verband (Pan-German League) was formed; its members advocated union of all German ethnic groups in one pan-German state which, in the end, would rule the world. In Feb. 1893 the Prussian landowners joined in the Bund der Landwirte (Agrarian League) to protect agrarian interests and oppose Caprivi's policy of lower tariffs. In the same year the Ostmarkenverein (Eastern Marches Association) was formed to protest against concessions to the Poles. By this time the emperor had become disenchanted with liberalism and was allowing his innate conservatism to come to the fore. He encouraged Caprivi to push through the Reichstag a bill to increase the size of the army, 1893, and declined to support his chancellor against attacks from the conservative agrarians. In Oct. 1894 he accepted Caprivi's resignation and appointed as his successor the 75-year-old Prince Chlodwig zu Hohenlohe-Schillingsfürst (1819–1901).

NAVAL EXPANSION. Hohenlohe remained chancellor until 1900, when he was replaced by Prince Bernhard von Bülow (1849–1929), who held the post until 1909. Both men pursued a generally conservative policy, which tried to contain the increasing agitation of Social Democrats and trade unions. William, an ardent yachtsman, was preoccupied with building a great German navy. In 1897 he appointed as state secretary for naval affairs Adm. Alfred von Tirpitz (1849–1930), who shared his enthusiasm for naval expansion. In 1898 the Reichstag passed a costly bill for ship construction, and further appropriations followed in 1900. In 1898 also the Flottenverein (Naval League) was founded to generate

patriotic propaganda for the navy. Like the other propaganda leagues, it drew membership and financial support from the great industrialists, who in turn made large profits from the military expansion programs.

INCREASING STRENGTH OF THE LEFT. In 1909 Theobald von Bethmann-Hollweg (1856–1921) succeeded Bülow as chancellor, to serve until 1917. During his term industrialization and urbanization increased, and the strength of the trade unions and socialists grew. In 1910 Berlin had more than 2 m. residents, and over 50% of the German population lived in urban areas. Membership in the Free Trade Unions had passed the 2-m. mark, and in the election of 1912 the antigovernment Social Democrats became the largest single party in the Reichstag.

GERMAN WELTPOLITIK. Under the inconsistent and often irresponsible direction of William II and his advisers, Germany became increasingly isolated from all other European nations except Austria, her one remaining dependable ally by 1914. In June 1890, acting on advice from Baron Friedrich von Holstein (1837–1909), permanent counselor at the Foreign Office, William decided not to renew the German-Russian Reinsurance Treaty. In the same year Germany appeared to move closer to Britain, following an agreement which defined boundaries of German and British territories in East Africa and gave Zanzibar to Britain in exchange for German possession of Helgoland. But subsequent German policy served increasingly to alienate Britain as well as other states. William was determined to pursue a policy of *Weltpolitik* (world politics) which would make German influence felt everywhere. In 1895, after the Jameson raid against Johannesburg, William sent President Kruger of the Transvaal a telegram congratulating him on the defeat of the British invaders. This incident inflamed British public opinion. In addition, the continued build-up of the German navy presented a serious threat to Brtain.

In 1897 Germany used the murder of 2 German missionaries as a pretext for landing at Kiaochow and demanding from China a 99-year lease of the Shantung Peninsula, despite previous Russo-Chinese negotiations for Russian control in that area. In 1900 Germany took the lead in sending an international army to put down the Boxer Rebellion in China. Meanwhile, Germany was also active in the Middle East, where in 1903 the promoters of the Berlin-Baghdad railway obtained from the Turkish government wide concessions for their project, which antagonized the Russians. In 1905 William met Nicholas II of Russia at Björkö in the Baltic, and reached agreement on a mutual-aid treaty between their countries. Neither Foreign Office would ratify the treaty, however, and Russia's ally France rejected the idea of a Russo-German accord completely.

MOROCCAN CRISIS. In 1905 William II traveled to Tangier to challenge French influence in Morocco. At the ensuing international conference at Algeciras, 1906, Russia and Britain backed France. The event forced the resignation of Holstein. It also drew Russia and Britain closer, and by 1910 Europe had become divided into 2 opposed and increasingly armed camps: a Triple Entente of Britain, France, and Russia faced the Triple Alliance of Germany, Austria and Italy. The general staffs of the various powers busied themselves formulating strategies in case of war. In Germany the plan which had been worked out under Count Alfred von Schlieffen (1833–1913) anticipated simultaneous war against Russia and France. In this event Germany must first crush France by an attack through neutral Belgium and Luxembourg, and then turn east to meet the Russians, who would have taken longer to complete their mobilization. In 1911 another crisis occurred in Morocco when Germany sent the cruiser *Panther* to the port of Agadir in order to protest French military action in the sultanate. Negotiations resulted in German agreement to a French protectorate in Morocco in exchange for French cession to Germany of a part of the Congo.

OUTBREAK OF WORLD WAR I. During 1912 and 1913 local wars in the Balkan Peninsula increased tension between Russia and Austria, the 2 major powers with interests in the area. Germany took no part except to stand behind her ally Austria. In July 1914, as he departed for his summer cruise, William agreed to back Austria in any action she wished to take against Serbia in retaliation for the assassination of the Archduke Francis Ferdinand. Russia in turn declared her solidarity with Serbia. Within the next few weeks, the crisis widened as all the major European powers were drawn in to support their various allies. Bethmann-Hollweg, realizing finally the seriousness of the situation, tried to moderate Austrian policy, but without success. Austria declared war on Serbia, 28 July, 1914. Russia responded with an order for general mobilization, 29 July. By this time foreign policy had become subordinate to military strategy. Following the dictates of the Schlieffen Plan, Germany mobilized, and declared war on Russia, 1 Aug. On 3 Aug. she declared war on France, and German troops invaded Belgium next day. (*Cont. p. 401.*)

THE RUSSIAN EMPIRE

1871–78

3 EMPERORS' LEAGUE. After a meeting in Berlin of the Russian, Austrian, and German emperors, Sept. 1872, agreements were made between Germany and Russia, May 1873, and Austria and Russia, June 1873, providing for a loose alliance between the 3 powers. The league was never put to effective use and broke down because of Austro-Russian rivalry in the Balkans.

ARMY REFORM. 13 Jan., 1874. The old Russian army, composed of long-term peasant conscripts, was replaced by one based on a universal system of military obligation, with a lottery used to choose recruits who then served 6 years on active duty and 9 years in the reserve. The term of service was reduced in proportion to the conscript's level of education, university graduates serving only 6 months.

FOUNDING OF THE "LAND AND LIBERTY" SOCIETY. The main aim of the "Land and Liberty" Society, a populist, revolutionary organization, founded 1876, was the distribution of all land to the peasants. When its members, mainly urban intellectuals, found their propaganda efforts among the peasants ineffectual, a number of them turned to the use of terror as a political weapon. In 1879 the society split into those who still favored propaganda activities and those who were self-conscious terrorists, the latter forming the "People's Will," an organization committed to assassination with the czar as a major target.

RUSSO-TURKISH WAR. Revolts in Bosnia, Herzegovina, and Bulgaria, 1875–76, were put down with great ferocity by the Turks, causing Serbia and Montenegro to declare war on the Ottoman Empire, 1876, and arousing strong pan-Slavic feeling in Russia. When the Turks refused great-power intervention on behalf of the Christian population of the Balkans, Russia declared war, 24 Apr., 1877. After initial successes the Russians were stopped at Pleven, 20 July, and did not capture it until 10 Dec. They then crossed the Balkan highlands and, with their armies threatening Constantinople, were able to negotiate the Treaty of San Stefano, 3 Mar., 1878. The Turks recognized the independence of Rumania, Serbia, and Montenegro, with the latter 2 regions gaining territory; agreed to the creation of an autonomous principality of Bulgaria, including Macedonia; promised reforms in Bosnia and Herzegovina; and ceded to Russia part of the Dobruja (the area between the lower Danube and the Black Sea) and districts in the Caucasus.

TREATY OF BERLIN. 13 July, 1878. British and Austrian objections to the Treaty of San Stefano led to a great-power conference in Berlin to revise its terms. Macedonia and a new province of Eastern Rumelia were detached from Bulgaria, the former being returned to full Turkish rule while the latter was made administratively autonomous under the political and military control of the sultan of Turkey. The territorial gains of Serbia and Montenegro and of Russia in the Caucasus were reduced, and Russia ceded the Dobruja to Rumania in exchange for southern Bessarabia. Austria was given control of Bosnia and Herzegovina and authorized to maintain garrisons in the sanjak (district) of Novi Pazar.

1879–87

SPECIAL COMMISSION AGAINST TERRORISM. 25 Feb., 1880. The terrorist activities of the "People's Will" led to the appointment of a special commission, headed by Count Mikhail Loris-Melikov (1825?–88), with almost unlimited powers to deal with the problem. The police forces were reorganized and Loris-Melikov, who believed it necessary to resume the reform efforts of the 1860's, forced the more conservative ministers out of the government, notably the minister of education, Dmitri Tolstoy (1823–89). By Aug. 1880 the danger had seemingly been greatly reduced, and the commission was ended, Loris-Melikov becoming minister of internal affairs.

ASSASSINATION OF ALEXANDER II. 13 Mar., 1881. The "People's Will" was on the verge of extinction, but its remaining members made 1 last effort to kill the czar, and succeeded. The same day he had signed a proclamation announcing his acceptance of a proposal by Loris-Melikov for the creation of commissions, including zemstvo representatives, to propose reform measures. His son, Alexander III (1845–94), rejected the plan, and on 11 May, 1881, announced his commitment to unlimited autocracy, causing Loris-Melikov to resign.

RENEWAL OF THE 3 EMPERORS' LEAGUE. 18 June, 1881. A 3-year agreement between Germany, Austria, and Russia provided for the benevolent neutrality of the other 2 if 1 of them was at war, with the exception of a war with Turkey. It was renewed, 1884, but allowed to lapse, 1887, due once again to Austro-Russian disagreements in the Balkans.

ISSUE OF THE "TEMPORARY REGULATIONS." 26 Aug., 1881. These regulations, which actually remained in force until 1917, provided that when a state of emergency had been declared in any area, local officials should have greatly increased powers over all types of gatherings and administrative powers of search, arrest, and deportation. In Sept. 1882 the censorship was also greatly strengthened.

REDEMPTION OF PEASANT LAND. 9 Jan., 1882. By the emancipation decrees, the start of the period of re-

demption of peasant land had depended on voluntary agreements between the landowner and the peasants. By imperial decree redemption was now to begin in cases where such agreement had not been reached, and all redemption payments were to be reduced. In June 1886 payments by state peasants were changed from rent to a redemption payment, and the peasants were given ownership of the land they occupied.

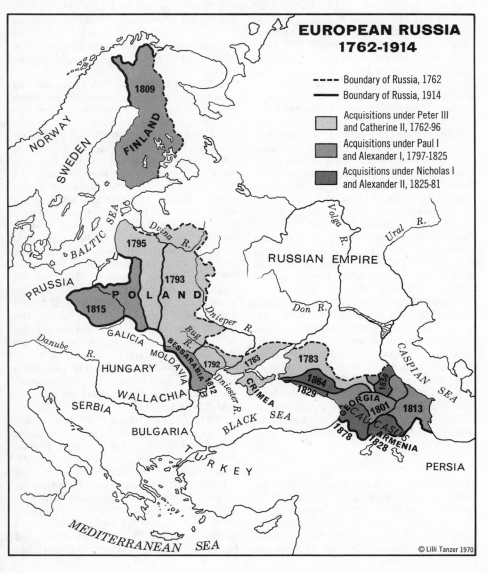

EUROPEAN RUSSIA 1762-1914

- - - - Boundary of Russia, 1762
—— Boundary of Russia, 1914

Acquisitions under Peter III and Catherine II, 1762-96

Acquisitions under Paul I and Alexander I, 1797-1825

Acquisitions under Nicholas I and Alexander II, 1825-81

© Lilli Tanzer 1970

REINSURANCE TREATY WITH GERMANY. 18 June, 1887. Replacing the 3 Emperors' League, a new 3-year agreement was made, providing for neutrality on the part of Russia if Germany was involved in war, and vice versa, except in the case of an aggressive war against either France or Austria.

1888–99

FRANCO-RUSSIAN ALLIANCE. 27 Aug., 1891. France and Russia agreed on mutual consultation in international affairs. A military convention, 17 Aug., 1892, provided for military co-operation against any threat from the Triple Alliance (Germany, Austria, and Italy), and was ratified by an exchange of diplomatic notes, 27 Dec., 1893, and 4 Jan., 1894.

RULE OF NICHOLAS II. As committed as was his father to autocracy, Nicholas II (1868–1918), who became czar on 1 Nov., 1894, was a much weaker ruler. During his reign, the industrialization of Russia proceeded at a greatly increased rate, particularly as a result of the policies of the minister of finance, Sergei Witte (1849–1915), between 1892 and 1903. The creation of an urban working class plus widespread crop failures in the early 1890's led to the reappearance of political unrest, which had been largely absent during the reign of Alexander III.

REDUCTION OF FINNISH AUTONOMY. By decree, Feb. 1899, imperial laws were given precedence over Finnish in areas of imperial concern. In addition, after the appointment of Gen. Nicholas Bobrikov (1839–1904) as gov., Aug. 1898, a policy of Russification was followed. The attempt to turn Finland into a Russian province resulted in the growth of a revolutionary movement in what had been a peaceful and loyal area.

1900–1905

FOUNDING OF THE S.R. The Socialist Revolutionary Party (S.R.), founded 1901, inherited the traditions of Russian populist radicalism and favored communal ownership of all land by the peasants. The party revived the use of political assassination as a revolutionary technique and was the cause of numerous murders between 1902 and 1907.

2ND CONGRESS OF THE S.D. 30 July–23 Aug., 1903. Founded in 1898 by the union of various Marxist groups, the Russian Social Democratic Labor Party (S.D.) had no real existence until its 2nd congress, held in 1903 in Brussels and London. It was split into 2 factions, which formed 2 almost separate parties: the Bolsheviks, led by Lenin (born Vladimir Ilyich Ulyanov, 1870–1924), favoring a small, centrally controlled party of professional revolutionaries, and the Mensheviks, favoring a broader, freer party.

RUSSO-JAPANESE WAR. Russia had created a sphere of influence in Manchuria, obtaining a concession for the Chinese Eastern Railway, 1896, and a lease on Port Arthur, 1898, and occupying Manchuria after the Boxer Rebellion, 1900. Here and in Korea the Russians were in conflict with the Japanese. In Feb. 1904 the Japanese broke off diplomatic relations and attacked the Russian naval squadron in Port Arthur. The war consisted of a series of Russian defeats: on the Yalu River, May 1904; at Liaoyang, Aug.–Sept.; at Port Arthur, which fell Jan. 1905; and at Mukden, Feb.–Mar. 1905. On 27 May a fleet which had sailed from the Baltic was destroyed by the Japanese at the Battle of Tsushima Strait. President Theodore Roosevelt of the U.S.A. acted as mediator, and the Treaty of Portsmouth, 5 Sept., 1905, ended the war. Japan's sphere of influence in Korea was recognized, both powers evacuated Manchuria, and Japan received a lease on Port Arthur and the southern half of Sakhalin Island.

"BLOODY SUNDAY." 22 Jan., 1905. Defeat in the Far East brought increased unrest and demands for change in Russia. A meeting of zemstvo leaders, Nov. 1904, demanded a representative assembly and was supported by widespread expressions of public opinion. In Jan. 1905 an ironworkers' strike in St. Petersburg developed into a general strike in favor of political reform. When the workers, led by Father George Gapon (1870?–1906), joined in a mass demonstration, 22 Jan., to present a petition to the czar, they were fired on by troops and hundreds were killed and wounded.

REVOLUTION OF 1905. "Bloody Sunday" was followed by uprisings and strikes throughout the country. The government attempted to quiet unrest with vague promises of popular participation in the government, 3 Mar., but with little effect. A revolt on the battleship *Potemkin,* June, indicated that even the loyalty of the armed forces was uncertain. On 19 Aug. the czar created a state Duma, but gave it only consultative powers and excluded the urban working class and most professionals from the suffrage. This was unacceptable to the opposition and a railway strike in Moscow, Oct., resulted in a general strike movement throughout the country and the creation of the St. Petersburg Soviet (council) of Workers' Deputies. In the same month the liberal Constitutional Democratic Party (Cadets) was organized, with a program favoring parliamentary government and economic and social reform. On 30 Oct. the czar issued a manifesto, based on proposals made by Sergei Witte, granting civil liberties and a Duma, elected on a broadened franchise, with control over legislation and the ministries. Witte was made head of the newly created Council of Ministers, in effect becoming prime minister. In Nov. peasant redemption payments were abolished, effective 1907, and the autonomy of Finland fully restored. Radical opposition continued, but the government was now strong enough to regain the initiative. In Dec. the members of the St. Petersburg Soviet were arrested and an uprising in Moscow put down by force, after which the revolutionary ferment in the country subsided.

1906–14

CODE OF FUNDAMENTAL STATE LAWS. 6 May, 1906. The decrees establishing the Duma were codified and, in some degree, changed by a new Code of Fundamental Laws. Almost universal manhood suffrage was introduced, but with a complicated system of indirect elections. The Duma was chosen for 5 years, but the czar could dissolve it earlier provided he called for new elections at the same time. The Council of State was made an upper legislative house, half its members appointed by the czar and half elected by various public bodies. Laws could be initiated by either house and required the approval of both houses and of the czar. The Duma had the right to question ministers, but no power over them, and about ⅓ of the budget was excluded from its control. The czar retained full authority over the administration, the armed forces, and foreign policy, and the government could issue temporary emergency decrees which had the force of law. At the same time as the code was issued, Witte, whom the czar distrusted, was replaced by I. L. Goremykin (1839–1917). Peter A. Stolypin (1863–1911) became minister of internal affairs.

1ST DUMA. 10 May–21 July, 1906. The members of the 1st Duma were almost all in opposition to the government, the Cadets, the largest single party, dominating the proceedings, since the S.D. and S.R. had both boycotted the elections. An address was adopted calling for further constitutional changes and the division of large estates among the peasants. This was rejected by the government, and as cooperation between it and the Duma proved impossible, the czar, after considering the creation of a Cadet ministry, dissolved the Duma.

RULE OF STOLYPIN. Stolypin was appointed head of the government, 21 July, 1906. He retained the Ministry of the Interior, and attempted both reform and the repression of radical groups at the same time. An emergency decree, 1 Sept., permitted local officials to use field courts-martial for the summary trial and execution of revolutionaries. On the other hand, a decree removed most of the remaining legal disabilities of the peasants, 18 Oct. On 22 Nov. a decree was issued permitting peasants to leave their communes and retaining and consolidating their land holdings.

2ND DUMA. 5 Mar.–16 June, 1907. The S.D. and the S.R. took part in the election which led to the 2nd Duma, while the government gave active support to rightist groups, notably the Union of the Russian People. The result was a strengthening of both left and right at the expense of the center parties. Stolypin proposed a program of reform, but the opposition did not accept it and the Duma was again dissolved.

ELECTORAL LAW. 16 June, 1907. In order to secure a conservative Duma, the representation of the national minorities was decreased by a new franchise law, while greatly increased weight was given to landowners and wealthy city dwellers.

ANGLO-RUSSIAN ACCORD. Conflicts in Persia, Afghanistan, and Tibet were settled by an agreement between Russia and Britain, 31 Aug., 1907. This accord, combined with the Franco-British *entente cordiale* formed in 1904, resulted in the de facto creation of a Triple Entente in opposition to the Triple Alliance, although no formal alliance or military agreement was ever made between Russia and Great Britain.

3RD DUMA. The revised electoral law resulted in a greatly decreased leftist representation in the 3rd Duma, which lasted from 1907 to 1912. The largest party was now that of the Octobrists, a liberal group somewhat to the right of the Cadets and composed of landowners and commercial and industrial leaders. Stolypin was able to work with a coalition of Octobrists and some rightists, and his peasant reforms were confirmed and extended by laws of 27 June, 1910, and 11 June, 1911. Stolypin also supported Russification in the border areas, and by a law of 30 June, 1910, the Finnish Diet was subordinated to the Russian Duma and Finnish autonomy ended. Stolypin aroused the distrust of the rightists and the czar and was on the verge of being dismissed when he was assassinated, Sept. 1911.

AUSTRIAN ANNEXATIONS IN THE BALKANS. Although the annexation by Austria of Bosnia and Herzegovina, Oct. 1908, represented only a formal change in the status of the provinces, the Russians suffered a major diplomatic defeat when they were forced, by German threats, to accept it without the *quid pro quo* they desired, the opening of the Dardanelles to Russian warships.

LENIN AND THE S.D. Taking advantage of the dominance of his supporters at a congress of the S.D. held in Prague and convened by him, Lenin formally expelled, Jan. 1912, all those who differed from him ideologically. The opposition, divided into many factions, was unable to develop a united front against him.

BALKAN WARS. Montenegro, Bulgaria, Serbia, and Greece defeated Turkey, Oct. 1912–May 1913, and then, following a dispute over the spoils, Serbia, Greece, Rumania, and Turkey defeated Bulgaria, June–Aug. 1913. Russia, in concert with Austria, attempted to prevent these wars and then, after the 1st of them, acted to stop Bulgarian annexation of Constantinople. The wars caused a great increase in tension in the area, with Bulgaria becoming an Austrian ally, while Serbia and Rumania were allied to Russia.

4TH DUMA. In the 4th Duma, 1912–17, the right had greater representation than in the 3rd, and the Octobrists, who were reduced in strength, tended to move into opposition to the government. This reflected a general conservative reaction in the country which led Nicholas to give serious consideration to reducing the Duma to the status of a consultative body. The royal family at this time was strongly under the influence of Gregory Rasputin (1871–1916), a semiliterate "holy man," who apparently had the power to control the bleeding of the heir to the throne, Alexis, who suffered from hemophilia. (*Cont. p. 425.*)

THE SMALLER STATES OF EUROPE

1870–1914

BELGIUM. Leopold II (ruled 1865–1909) built a great and prosperous state on the foundations laid by his predecessor. He established companies all over the world, acquired a vast colonial empire in the

Belgian Congo, and made Brussels a magnificent capital. A principal domestic political issue in Belgium, the question of religious education, contributed to the establishment of the rival Liberal and Catholic parties. The Catholic Party gained control of Parliament in 1884, and during its 30-year rule restored religious education in most of the public schools and removed property qualification for voting. King Albert I succeeded Leopold II in 1909.

THE NETHERLANDS. When Willem III (ruled 1840–90) died without a male heir, his widow Emma served as regent until her daughter, Wilhelmina (ruled 1890–1948), came of age in 1898. Although the franchise was greatly extended in 1867 and 1896, universal suffrage was not enacted until 1918. A law establishing compulsory education at some schools, passed in 1900, partially resolved disputes between Catholics and Calvinists about the control of elementary education.

LUXEMBOURG. On the death, 1890, of King Willem III of the Netherlands, who was also the grand duke of Luxembourg, the grand duchy passed to Adolphus of Nassau (ruled 1890–1905). Luxembourg thus became independent, and its territorial integrity and neutrality were guaranteed by the European powers.

SWITZERLAND. Switzerland underwent a constitutional revision in 1874 which introduced the principle of the referendum and also enlarged the powers of the Confederation. In 1891 the initiative was adopted, resulting in a great deal of popular legislation for all of Switzerland. To provide for defense, compulsory military service was established in 1874 and subsequently strengthened, particularly in 1907. Switzerland developed economically as a result of industrialization and an ever-growing tourist trade.

SCANDINAVIA. The reign of King Christian IX of Denmark, 1863–1906, was marked by a constant struggle between the lower house of Parliament on the one side and the monarch and upper house on the other. The constitution was ignored between 1892 and 1901, when the

king ruled without restraint. In 1901 the middle class, augmented by economically well-off peasants, succeeded in forcing the king to recognize a ministry representative of the Liberal majority in the lower house. Demands for the democratization of political institutions resulted in constitutional amendments, 1914–15, which lowered the voting age from 30 to 25, extended the vote to all men and most women, and abolished the appointive seats in the upper house.

The enforced union of Sweden and Norway in 1815 was dissolved by action of the Norwegian Parliament in 1905, which unanimously decreed the complete separation of Norway and Sweden, and deposed the king of Sweden in favor of the 2nd son of the king of Denmark, who became Haakon VII (ruled 1905–57). When a Norwegian plebiscite ratified the decree, it was reluctantly accepted by the Swedish government.

Universal male suffrage was introduced in Norway in 1898. Direct elections rather than indirect came in 1906. Women with property qualifications received the vote in 1907, and all such qualifications were removed, and the royal veto abolished, in 1913.

The Swedish King Oscar II (ruled 1872–1907) was succeeded by his son Gustavus V in 1907. Shortly thereafter, proportional representation in both houses of Parliament was adopted and universal manhood suffrage established for elections to the lower chamber.

SPAIN. Amadeo I, duke of Aosta (1845–90), the 2nd son of Victor Emmanuel II of Italy, became king of Spain in 1870. Having the support of only a fraction of the Spanish people and constantly frustrated in his attempts to govern, he abdicated in 1873. Parliament declared the throne vacant and established a republic. Anarchy ensued, and Alfonso XII (1857–85), son of Isabella II, was put on the throne to restore order. His strong government was ably directed by the prime minister, Cánovas del Castillo (1828–97).

The Spanish Constitution of 1876 established a bicameral Parliament and limited the king's power, but popular government was curbed by an agreement between the 2 parties that they would alternate control of the government. The nobility, the army, and the Catholic Church all opposed the rise of popular government. Much emigration to Latin America ensued, leaving illiterate masses behind. María Cristina (1858–1929) acted as regent for her son after the death of Alfonso XII in 1885 until the accession of Alfonso XIII (1886–1941) in 1902. María Cristina's reign was marred by the Spanish-American War of 1898 and the loss of Cuba, Puerto Rico, and the Philippines, Spain's last colonies of any importance.

PORTUGAL. The reign of Louis I, 1861–89, saw the decline of civil war and some progress toward constitutional government, but, as in Spain, the government was controlled by the wealthy, the church, and the bureaucrats. Chaos and corruption returned after the accession of Carlos I (ruled 1889–1908). Carlos was assassinated in 1908 and Manuel II ruled for only 2 years. A revolution, Oct. 1910, established the Portuguese Republic.

ITALY. The formal political unity of Italy was attained in 1870 when King Victor Emmanuel II (ruled 1861–78) used the Franco-Prussian War to enable him to overpower the pope and take Rome. In practice the king's powers were exercised by a ministry responsible to a 2-chamber Parliament. In view of the history of the Catholic Church in Italy, the royal government decided to keep Catholicism as a kind of national institution by paying the salaries of the clergy and permitting religious instruction in the schools, while concurrently reducing the number of monastic establishments, confiscating church property, and tolerating anti-Catholic propaganda. Pope Pius IX refused to accept Italy's proposed "law of papal guarantees" and insisted on viewing himself as a prisoner and calling on foreign governments to come to his aid. By forbidding Italian Catholics to vote or hold office under the royal government, the pope alienated a large number of patriotic Italians from the church and deprived Italy of the services of many Italians who were obedient to him.

Italy had 2 main political groups, the Right and the Left. The Right was in power, 1870–76, and various groups of the Left were in power, 1876–96, under the leadership of Agostino Depretis (1813–87) and Francesco Crispi (1819–1901). The Right assumed control again, 1896–1903, and then the Left regained power, 1903–13, generally under a coalition headed by Giovanni Giolitti (1842–1928). The major changes which occurred when a ministry moved from Right to Left were in patronage, not in policy.

Italy's nationalistic ambitions led to an increase in and reorganization of the Italian army after compulsory military service was enacted in 1875, and also to the building of fortifications and the creation of a navy. These military costs and the resulting colonial empire were paid for by increased taxation which ultimately led to bankruptcy and cuts in social and educational services. Popular unrest resulted, indicated by emigration from Italy, by movement from the southern to the northern part of the country, and by the spread of socialism. A Socialist Party in Milan, founded in 1891, elected 12 members to the Chamber of Deputies in 1895. Another reaction to unrest was anarchism, which resulted in the assassination, 1900, of King Humbert I (b. 1844), who had succeeded Victor Emmanuel II in 1878.

Soon after the Ethiopian setback and the retirement of Crispi, 1896, movements were made toward internal reform. These included old-age pensions, workmen's accident insurance, nationalization of private insurance companies, nationalization of railways, municipal ownership and operation of public utilities, and the legalization of trade unions.

The property qualification for voting was reduced somewhat in 1882, but a literacy test and some property qualifications remained until 1912. The general election of 1913 resulted in a large increase in Socialist representation. The bourgeois-Left coalition group under Giolitti resigned and was replaced by a nationalist ministry under Antonio Salandra (1853–1931).

AUSTRIA-HUNGARY. In the Austrian part of the Dual Monarchy rapid industrialization and commercialization occurred. During the 1870's the industrial and financial *bourgeoisie* exerted power through the Liberal Party, enacting laws favorable to their interests, establishing public schools, and countering church influence. The Christian Socialist Party, organized by Karl Lueger (1844–1910), gained influence in the 1880's by attracting the lower middle class of the cities and the peasantry. Emphasizing social legislation and political democracy, the Christian Socialists regulated factories and mines, forbade work on Sundays, limited the employment of women and children, legalized unions, instituted accident and sickness insurance for workers, enlarged the number of parliamentary electors, 1896, and enacted universal manhood suffrage, 1907. By the turn of the century the influence of the Christian Socialists was declining, primarily because of the adherence of young intellectuals and the urban proletariat to Marxist socialism and the Social Democratic Party, which increased its representation in Parliament from 11 to 87 in the 1907 general election. Increasing democratization provided opportunities for Austria's subject minorities—Rumanians, Italians, Czechs, Slovaks, Poles, Croats, Serbs—to press for greater cultural freedom and autonomy, which Emperor Francis Joseph would not consider. In Hungary, the Magyar aristocracy refused to share power even with the Magyar masses, much less with the subject nationalities. The large landed estates remained intact; Hungarian was used in the public schools throughout the kingdom; the Slovaks in the north and the Serbs in the south were subjected to repeated attempts at Magyarization; and local autonomy was abolished in largely Rumanian Transylvania, and also in Croatia in the west. There was no extension of the suffrage, and property qualifications were so high and voting laws so intricate that only 1 in 20 could vote in 1910. Although the Magyars represented only about half the population, Parliament consisted almost entirely of Magyar representatives. Hungary's agricultural development mainly benefited the large landowners and led to large-scale emigration, 1896–1910, and popular agitation for electoral reform.

GREECE. Under King George I (ruled 1863–1913) Greece made some progress in spite of political and financial difficulties. Since most ethnic Greeks still lived under the Ottoman Empire, efforts were made in 1897 to remove Crete from Turkish rule. The attempt was unsuccessful, but the leader of the insurgents, Eleutherios Venizelos (1864–1936), attained such popularity that George I had to invite him to form a government, 1910, on mainland Greece. By reforming the government and reorganizing the army and navy, Venizelos prepared Greece for national unification.

RUMANIA. In 1878, after the Russo-Turkish War, Rumania became 1st an independent state and then a kingdom, 1881, with a German prince of the family of Hohenzollern-Sigmaringen as King Carol I (ruled 1881–1914). Rumania was faced with a complex national unification problem since Rumanians were scattered through the Ottoman Empire, the Russian province of Bessarabia, the Hungarian province of Transylvania, and Austrian Bukovina. A Rumanian alliance with Austria-Hungary resulted in a preponderance of German influence and modeling of political institutions on those of Prussia. Under Carol I agricultural progress was made, foreign markets encouraged, and mineral resources exploited. The failure of the peasantry to share in the affluence touched off anti-Semitism, emigration, and rioting.

SERBIA. Serbian politics revolved around the rivalry between the family of Karageorge, the original peasant leader of the Serbian rebellion against the Ottoman Empire, and the family of Milo Obrenović, the soldier who secured autonomy for Serbia. The Obrenovićs were in power from 1859 to 1903, sustaining occasional pro-Karageorge insurrections and assassinations.

Prince Milan Obrenović (1854–1901)

transformed Serbia into a kingdom, 1882, and, after losing the Serbo-Bulgarian War of 1885, fell under the control of the Austrian Hapsburgs and had to impose heavy taxes to pay war debts. In an attempt to regain popularity, he instituted a democratic constitution, 1889, and then abdicated in favor of his son, Alexander I, who reigned until murdered in 1903. The grandson of Karageorge, Peter I (1844–1921), then became king. He restored the Constitution of 1889 and chose his ministers from the majority party in Parliament. (*Cont. p. 415.*)

THE UNITED STATES OF AMERICA

1878–79

SAMOA. 12 Jan., 1878. The U.S. acquired by treaty nonexclusive rights to a naval station at Pago Pago.

CURRENCY PROBLEMS. Sought by western silverites and inflation-minded farmers and laborers, the Bland-Allison Act, 28 Feb., 1878, ordered the monthly purchase and conversion into currency of $2 m. to $4 m. in silver. A Greenback Labor Party, a prolabor and proinflation organization led by James B. Weaver (Iowa), won 14 congressional seats. On 1 Jan., 1879, specie payments were resumed without difficulty, as greenbacks reached their gold face value, 17 Dec., 1878.

1880

PRESIDENTIAL ELECTION. 2 Nov. Republicans James A. Garfield (1831–81, Ohio) and Chester A. Arthur (1830–86, N.Y.) defeated (214–155) Democrats Winfield Scott Hancock (Pa.) and William H. English (Ind.) by less than 10,000 out of 9 m. votes.

CHINESE TREATY. 17 Nov. The U.S. decided to limit the immigration of Chinese laborers. The Exclusion Act, 1882, stopped this influx for 10 years.

1881

ASSASSINATION OF GARFIELD. Garfield, supported by the "Half-Breeds," wrested N.Y.'s patronage from Sen. Roscoe Conkling's "Stalwart" machine. On 19 Sept. he died of wounds inflicted, 2 July, by a disappointed "Stalwart" office seeker, and was succeeded in the presidency by Arthur.

1883

PENDLETON ACT. 16 Jan. Sen. George H. Pendleton (Ohio) sponsored a bill establishing the principle of competitive examinations for federal civil-service positions.

1884

PRESIDENTIAL ELECTION. 4 Nov. Republican James G. Blaine (Me.) faced Democratic Gov. Grover Cleveland (1837–1908) (N.Y.), who had independent Republican ("Mugwump") support. Rev. Samuel D. Burchard's remark, 29 Oct., associating Democrats with "Rum, Romanism, and Rebellion," cost Blaine New York and the election (219–182).

1886

PRESIDENTIAL SUCCESSION ACT. 19 Jan. This act arranged the heads of the executive departments in the line of succession behind the Vice-President.

"STEEL NAVY." Navy Secretary William C. Whitney launched the construction of a modern steel navy built in U.S. shipyards.

1887

ELECTORAL COUNT ACT. 3 Feb. Each state became the judge of its electoral returns.

INTERSTATE COMMERCE ACT. 4 Feb. Prompted by the Supreme Court's Wabash decision, 1886, which undermined states' authority to regulate railroads, the Interstate Commerce Act forbade numerous unjust practices and established the Interstate Commerce Commission (I.C.C.) to oversee the industry. Operators circumvented the ambiguous law and the Supreme Court (Alabama Midlands Case, 1897) emasculated the commission.

1888

CANADIAN FISHERIES. The Republican Senate rejected, 21 Aug., the Anglo-U.S. Bayard Chamberlain Treaty, but an accompanying *modus vivendi* granting Americans privileges in Canadian ports regulated use of the fisheries until 1923.

PRESIDENTIAL ELECTION. 6 Nov. The Democrats nominated Grover Cleveland and Allen G. Thurmond (Ohio), and the Republicans Benjamin Harrison (1833–1901) (Ind.) and Levi P. Morton (N.Y.). Campaigning for a high protective tariff and soldiers' pensions, Harrison won (233–168).

1889

SAMOA. A conference in Berlin, 14 June, established a tripartite (U.S., Britain and Germany) protectorate guaranteeing the independence and sovereignty of the islands.

LATIN AMERICAN CONFERENCE. 2 Oct., 1889–19 Apr., 1890. Attended at Washington by all the hemispheric nations except Santo Domingo, this conference paved the way for reciprocal tariff agreements. Secretary of State James G. Blaine had unsuccessfully called a similar meeting, 1881, when he held the same post under Garfield.

1890

DEPENDENT PENSION ACT. 27 June. Under Harrison annual pension expenditures leaped from $81 m. to $135 m.

SHERMAN ANTITRUST ACT. 2 July. When state antitrust laws proved inadequate to regulate the interstate industrial combinations developing in America, Congress passed the Sherman Antitrust Act outlawing consolidations in restraint of trade. This ambiguous act was ineffective.

SHERMAN SILVER PURCHASE ACT. 14 July. Requiring the monthly purchase and conversion into redeemable notes of 4.5 m. ounces of silver, this act increased the money supply and weakened the federal gold reserves.

1891

U.S.-CHILE RELATIONS. A Valparaiso mob killed, 16 Oct., 2 American sailors. Harrison virtually asked, 25 Jan., 1892, Congress for war. Chile finally apologized and paid a $75,000 indemnity.

1892

BERING SEA DISPUTE. 29 Feb. Britain and the U.S. agreed to submit the latter's claim to exclusive sealing rights in the Bering Sea to international arbitration. The U.S. lost the case, 15 Aug., 1893.

PEOPLE'S (POPULIST) PARTY. Disgruntled farm and labor groups established, 22 Feb., the People's Party of the U.S.A. and nominated, 2 July, James B. Weaver for President. The Populists demanded free silver coinage at 16 to 1 and government ownership of transportation and communication lines.

PRESIDENTIAL ELECTION. 8 Nov. Cleveland (277) was elected over Harrison (145) and Weaver (22). Opposition to the high McKinley Tariff, 1890, and Cleveland's support of the gold standard were important factors.

1893

HAWAII. American sugar planters under Sanford B. Dole, supported by the U.S. minister, John L. Stevens, overthrew Queen Liliuokalani's autocratic government and requested annexation, Feb. President Cleveland's investigator, Congressman James H. Blount (Ga.), found that most Hawaiians opposed annexation, but the President, declining to use force when the Dole government refused to step down, recognized the Republic of Hawaii, 7 Aug., 1894.

FINANCIAL PANIC. The Panic of 1893 forced Cleveland to have the Sherman Silver Purchase Act repealed, 1 Nov., thus splitting the Democratic Party.

1894

"COXEY'S ARMY." Led by Populist Jacob S. Coxey (Ohio), 400 jobless men demonstrated in Washington, 30 Apr., but dispersed when their leaders were arrested, 1 May, for trespassing.

1895

"APPEAL OF THE SILVER DEMO-CRATS." 5 Mar. Framed by Representatives William Jennings Bryan (1860–1925, Neb.) and Bland, the appeal advocated free silver.

GOLD RESERVE. When the public failed to subscribe to government bond issues, Treasury Secretary Carlisle obtained loans from bankers, including J. Pierpont Morgan, Feb., to protect the gold reserve. Political opponents attacked this action, which gave the bankers a $1,500,000 profit on a $62-m. loan.

VENEZUELAN BOUNDARY DISPUTE. When Britain rejected a U.S. offer, Feb., to arbitrate her long-time quarrel with Venezuela over the British Guiana boundary, Secretary of State Richard Olney, invoked, 20 July, the Monroe Doctrine, and Cleveland proposed, 17 Dec., an independent commission whose decision the U.S. would enforce against Britain. Desirous of American friendship, Britain co-operated, and the commission supported, 3 Oct., 1899, most of her claims.

1896

PRESIDENTIAL ELECTION. 3 Nov. The Republicans nominated William McKinley (1843–1901, Ohio) and Garret A. Hobart (N.J.) on a gold-standard and high-tariff platform. The Democrats and dissident National Silver Republicans selected William Jennings Bryan and Arthur Sewall (Me.), and advocated free silver at 16 to 1. The Populists nominated Bryan and Thomas E. Watson (Ga.). McKinley won, 271–176.

1898

OUTBREAK OF SPANISH-AMERICAN WAR. Relations between the U.S. and Spain deteriorated after the Cubans revolted, 24 Feb., 1895. The American "yellow press" and expansionist Republicans demanded action even after Spain

recalled brutal Gen. Valeriano "Butcher" Weyler. William R. Hearst's N.Y. *Journal* printed, 9 Feb., Spanish Minister Dupuy de Lôme's private letter stating that McKinley was vacillating.

When an explosion sank, 15 Feb., the *Maine* in Havana Harbor, killing 260 Americans, McKinley, under powerful pressures, reversed his pacific course and requested, 11 Apr., U.S. intervention. Congress agreed, 20 Apr., pledging (Teller Amendment) that the U.S. had no goal except Cuban independence. Spain declared war 24 Apr. and the U.S. 25 Apr.

MANILA BAY. 1 May. America's excellent navy gave her a decided advantage. Commodore George Dewey's Asiatic Squadron, suffering 8 wounded, destroyed the Spanish fleet at Manila Bay, killing 381. After a blockade of Manila, the Spanish surrendered, 14 Aug., the Philippines.

CUBAN EXPEDITION. Gen. William Shafter's 17,000 troops arrived off Santiago, 20 June. The Americans were victorious at San Juan Hill, 1 July, where dismounted "Rough Riders" under Lt. Col. Theodore Roosevelt fought. On 3 July the Spanish fleet was destroyed as it tried to escape Rear Admiral William T. Sampson's fleet blockading Santiago. Admiral Cervera suffered 474 casualties, the Americans 2. Santiago surrendered 17 July.

On 7 July, the war having shown its strategic value, Hawaii was annexed. By the Treaty of Paris, 10 Dec., Spain agreed to relinquish Cuba and to cede Puerto Rico, Guam, and the Philippines to the U.S.

1899

PHILIPPINE QUESTION. Their hopes for immediate independence dashed, Filipinos under Emilio Aguinaldo revolted, 4 Feb., against U.S. rule. The rebellion lasted until 1902.

1ST HAGUE CONFERENCE. 18 May–29 July. With U.S. support, the conference established the Permanent Court of International Arbitration.

PARTITION OF SAMOA. 2 Dec. Samoa was divided between Germany and the U.S. American Samoa became a strategic naval base.

1900

CURRENCY (GOLD STANDARD) ACT. 14 Mar. This act declared the gold dollar of 25.8 grains the standard U.S. unit of value.

OPEN DOOR POLICY. 20 Mar. Announced by Secretary of State John Hay, the policy provided for equal commercial access to China for all nations.

BOXER REBELLION. When traditionalist Chinese tried to oust foreigners, an international expedition, including U.S. troops, suppressed them. The Boxer Protocol, 7 Sept., 1901, demanded a $333-m. indemnity from China.

PRESIDENTIAL ELECTION. 6 Nov. Stressing prosperity, the Republicans nominated William McKinley and Theodore Roosevelt (1858-1919, N.Y.). The Democrats selected William Jennings Bryan and Adlai E. Stevenson (Ill.), and denounced imperialism. McKinley won 292-155.

1901

PLATT AMENDMENT. 2 Mar. Drawn up by War Secretary Elihu Root (1845-1937), the Platt Amendment authorized U.S. intervention to protect Cuban independence and maintain law and order. Cuba had to include this in her constitution, 12 June, before U.S. troops would leave.

ASSASSINATION OF McKINLEY. On 14 Sept. Roosevelt succeeded McKinley, who died of wounds inflicted, 6 Sept., by anarchist Leon Czolgosz.

HAY-PAUNCEFOTE TREATY. 18 Nov. British agreement was obtained for the construction by the U.S. of a neutral isthmian canal open to all nations on equal terms.

1902

ROOSEVELT TRUST POLICY. Roosevelt's policy was to regulate the monster corporations rather than destroy them, although he did successfully have the Northern Securities Co., a railroad holding company, dissolved, 1904.

REFORM. The Reform states, notably Wisconsin under Robert M. La Follette (1855-1925), instituted broad administrative and legislative reforms in this period.

1903

HAY-HERRAN CONVENTION. 22 Jan. Colombia was offered $10 m. and a $250,000 annual rental for a 6-mi.-wide strip for an isthmian canal through its province, Panama. Colombia's Senate delayed action to obtain more money.

MUCKRAKERS. Between 1903 and 1910 numerous writers exposed corruption in business and politics and attacked social evils. Ida M. Tarbell's *History of the Standard Oil Company*, 1903, exemplified the genre.

ELKINS ACT. 19 Feb. This Act defined unfair discrimination between shippers and provided punishments for giving or receiving rebates.

PANAMA REVOLT. 3 Nov. With tacit U.S. approval, Panama declared herself independent of Colombia.

HAY-BUNAU-VARILLA TREATY. 18 Nov. Panama received $10 m. and a $250,000 annual rental for a 10-mi.-wide canal strip.

ALASKAN BOUNDARY DISPUTE. An Anglo-U.S. commission, influenced by Roosevelt's threat of force, awarded the U.S. control of disputed ocean inlets in the Alaskan Panhandle.

1904

PRESIDENTIAL ELECTION. 8 Nov. Republicans nominated Theodore Roosevelt and Charles W. Fairbanks (Ind.), and the Democrats, whose platform denounced trusts, chose Alton B. Parker (N.Y.) and Henry G. Davis (W. Va.). Roosevelt won 336-140.

ROOSEVELT COROLLARY TO THE MONROE DOCTRINE. 6 Dec. The bombardment by Britain and Germany of Venezuelan ports, Dec. 1902, for nonpayment of debts made clear the possibility of European intervention in Latin America. Consequently, when Santo

Domingo became involved in similar difficulties, Roosevelt enunciated his doctrine that the U.S. would act as an international peace force in cases of flagrant wrongdoing or impotence in the Western Hemisphere. The U.S. took over, 1905, the management of Dominican debt payments.

1905

PORTSMOUTH (N.H.) PEACE CONFERENCE. 9 Aug. Suggested by Roosevelt, the conference ended the Russo-Japanese War. Roosevelt did not desire the complete defeat of either power lest it upset the Asian balance and endanger U.S. interests.

1906

HEPBURN ACT. 29 June. The I.C.C. was authorized to set maximum railroad rates and made its orders binding pending court action.

PURE FOOD AND DRUG ACT. 30 June. Adulterated products were banned from interstate commerce.

1907

GENTLEMAN'S AGREEMENT. 24 Feb. The influx of Japanese laborers stirred antagonism on the West Coast. Japan agreed, 24 Feb., to withhold passports from laborers emigrating to the U.S., and recognized America's right to prohibit Japanese from entering on passports originally issued for travel to any other country.

2ND HAGUE PEACE CONFERENCE. 15 June–15 Oct. The conference adopted the Drago Doctrine that European nations should not use force to collect debts owed by American nations.

PANAMA CANAL. Construction began under Lt. Col. George W. Goethals (1858–1928). The canal from Cristobal to Balboa was opened 15 Aug., 1914.

1908

WHITE HOUSE CONSERVATION CONFERENCE. 13 May. The conference expounded the necessity of preserving the nation's natural resources and led to the establishment, 8 June, of the National Conservation Commission under Gifford Pinchot.

ALDRICH-VREELAND ACT. 30 May. This act established a National Monetary Commission whose report, 1912, contained proposals that contributed to the Federal Reserve Act, 1913.

PRESIDENTIAL ELECTION. 3 Nov. The Republicans nominated Roosevelt's choice, William H. Taft (1857–1930, Ohio) and James S. Sherman (N.Y.), and pledged antitrust enforcement and conservation. The Democrats chose Bryan and John W. Kern (Ind.). Taft won 321–162.

ROOT-TAKAHIRA AGREEMENT. 30 Nov. The U.S. and Japan recognized the Pacific *status quo* and upheld the Open Door policy.

1909

"DOLLAR DIPLOMACY." The policy of President Taft and Secretary of State Philander C. Knox, which sought to increase U.S. trade by supporting American enterprises abroad, aggravated international relations in China. Wilson ended Taft's policy.

1910

TRUST POLICY. Taft's administration started 90 antitrust proceedings (compared to Roosevelt's 44) and obtained Standard Oil's dissolution, 1911.

MANN-ELKINS ACT. 18 June. The I.C.C. was granted jurisdiction over telephone, telegraph, cable, and wireless companies.

REPUBLICAN INSURGENCY. Progressive Republicans led by Sen. Robert M. La Follette (Wis.) opposed Taft's signature, 1909, of the Payne-Aldrich Tariff. House insurgents deprived Speaker Joseph G. Cannon (Ill.) of his power to appoint the Rules Committee.

1911

U.S.-CANADIAN RELATIONS. The Reciprocity Agreement was terminated, 26 Jan., when Canadians, upset by Taft's talk of annexation, elected the antireciprocity Conservatives to power.

NICARAGUAN INTERVENTION. The Knox-Castrillo Convention, 6 June, with Nicaragua authorized U.S. intervention and a customs receivership to refund the national debt. Although the U.S. rejected the agreement, dissatisfied Nicaraguans revolted, and U.S. marines landed, 14 Aug., 1912, to protect American interests.

1912

SOCIAL LEGISLATION. State action characterized the Progressive era. Maryland's workmen's compensation law, 1902, and Massachusetts' minimum-wage law, 1912, were notable firsts.

ROOSEVELT'S CANDIDACY. Alienated from Taft and supporting the New Nationalism, Roosevelt entered the race, 24 Feb., for the Republican presidential nomination.

LODGE COROLLARY. 2 Aug. Prompted by a Japanese syndicate's attempt to buy a site in Lower California, the Lodge Corollary extended the Monroe Doctrine to non-European nations and to foreign companies.

PRESIDENTIAL ELECTION. 5 Nov. When conservative Republicans renominated Taft and Sherman, a Progressive ("Bull Moose") Party chose Roosevelt and Hiram W. Johnson (Calif.). The Democrats selected Gov. Woodrow Wilson (1856–1924, N.J.) and Thomas R. Marshall (Ind.). Wilson's "New Freedom" sought the abolition of monopolies, while Roosevelt's "New Nationalism" demanded their regulation. Wilson (435) defeated Roosevelt (88) and Taft (8).

1913

MEXICAN REVOLUTION. Taft recognized the democratic reformer, Francisco I. Madero, who overthrew long-time dictator Porfirio Díaz, 25 May, 1911, but not the reactionary Gen. Victoriano Huerta, who had Madero assassinated, 22 Feb.

Wilson asked Huerta to resign, 7 Nov., and allowed arms to go to rebels under Venustiano Carranza.

CONSTITUTIONAL AMENDMENTS. The 16th Amendment, authorizing a federal income tax, took effect, 25 Feb. The 17th, authorizing popular elections of U.S. senators, took effect 31 May.

PUJO REPORT. 28 Feb. Representative Arsène Pujo's (La.) committee's report on the increasing concentration of money and credit aided Wilson's banking and reform program.

FEDERAL RESERVE (OWEN-GLASS) ACT. 23 Dec. Designed to control credit and ensure a flexible currency, the act established a Federal Reserve Board and 12 Federal Reserve Banks which could issue notes based on cash deposits of member banks.

1914

VERACRUZ INCIDENT. 21 Apr. Huerta broke relations with the U.S. when troops bombarded and occupied Veracruz to prevent a German munitions delivery.

ABC CONFERENCE. 20 May–30 June. Although Mexico rejected the peace plan of Argentina, Brazil, and Chile, moral pressure forced Huerta to accept its provision that he resign, 15 July. The U.S. withdrew its troops, 23 Nov., and recognized, 19 Oct., 1915, Carranza as *de facto* President.

FEDERAL TRADE COMMISSION ACT. 26 Sept. The act established a bipartisan board to investigate and stop unfair competition in interstate commerce.

CLAYTON ANTITRUST ACT. 15 Oct. This act forbade price discriminations to create monopolies, some interlocking directorates, and stock acquisitions lessening competition. The law made corporation officers individually responsible, but exempted agricultural and labor organizations. (*Cont. p. 440.*)

The Reaction of the East

REFORM AND REVOLUTION IN CHINA

1870–95

WEAKENING OF MANCHU POWER. In the early years of imperialist pressure on China, the western powers sought economic and commercial privileges rather than territory. Moreover, they hoped to maintain the authority of the Manchus, with whom the "unequal treaties" had been concluded. After the collapse, 1864, of the Taiping Rebellion, however, which had threatened Manchu power, the western nations exploited China's weakness by nibbling at her dependencies and outer territories. The activities of the Russians in Turkestan, the British in Burma, and the French in Indochina seriously weakened Manchu control over the outer regions of the Chinese Empire. It was Japan, however, that posed the greatest threat to China.

LOSS OF RYUKYU ISLANDS. A Sino-Japanese Treaty, 13 Sept., 1871, provided for reciprocal extraterritorial rights, but did not satisfy Japan's desire for a privileged position, especially most-favored-nation treatment, similar to that enjoyed by the western powers in China. In 1872 the Japanese brought the king of Okinawa, who traditionally paid tribute to both China and Japan, to their country to pay homage to the Meiji emperor. This was a first step toward bringing the Ryukyu (Liuchiu) Islands, of which Okinawa was the most important, under Japanese control. A few years later, the murder of some shipwrecked Ryukyu islanders by Formosan natives brought a Japanese expedition to occupy part of Formosa. Although China did not administer the area occupied by the Formosans, Britain intervened to demand Japanese withdrawal from Formosa. An article in the ensuing Sino-Japanese agreement, however, tacitly reaffirmed Japanese claims to the Ryukyu Islands.

INDEPENDENCE OF KOREA. A much more serious Japanese provocation arose as a result of Japan's challenge to China over Korea. In 1875 the Japanese sent a survey party to Korea, and a naval clash occurred. When China disclaimed responsibility for such incidents, the Japanese sent a strong naval force to Korea, forcing that country, 1876, to sign a treaty of independence, thus denying Chinese suzerainty. The treaty also accorded Japan extraterritoriality in Korea, the opening of several Korean ports, and the establishment of diplomatic relations.

BRITISH INTERVENTION IN SINKIANG. In 1872 the Russians signed a trade agreement with Yakub Beg, commander of the Khojan army, which opened eastern Turkestan to Russian commerce. In 1873 Yakub's nephew, Saiyed Yakub Khan Tora, arrived in India, where he received a warm welcome from the British and a promise of arms. With the approval of the Indian government, a trading company was formed to carry on commerce with Sinkiang. From India, Tora went to Istanbul, where he was welcomed by the sultan of Turkey. In 1874 the sultan conferred on Yakub Beg the title of "Commander of the Faithful," signed a trade treaty with Sinkiang, and agreed to send arms. Tora returned to Sinkiang accompanied by the British agent, T. Douglas Forsyth, who concluded a commercial agreement with Yakub Beg. Yakub also received the right to exchange ambassadors with India. In 1876 the government of India ratified the treaty of 1874.

CHINESE RECONQUEST OF SINKIANG. Noting the increase in foreign influence in Sinkiang, the Manchu government appointed, 1876, Tso Tsungt'ang as commander in chief of a military expedition designed to reconquer Sinkiang. During the same year a Russian mission under Gen. Aleksei Nikolaevich Kuropatkin demanded control of certain strategic posts in the mountain passes west of Kashgar. Yakub acceded to these demands. As clear indications of Manchu efforts to regain Sinkiang appeared, a conference of high czarist officers concerned with Siberia and Turkestan was held in St. Petersburg, Mar. 1876. The Russians decided that they would abide by the Kuldja agreement of 1851, that the Tekes River Valley should remain within the Russian Empire, and that the Manchus must grant commercial privileges to Russian traders and pay an indemnity to Russia for losses suffered during the recent upheavals. In 1877 a Manchu army under Tso captured Tien Shan, Khara Shahr, Toksun, and Turfan; Yakub Beg committed suicide or was assassinated. By the autumn of 1877, Kucha, Bai, Aksu, and Uch Turfan had also fallen before the Manchu advance. The power of Yakub Beg and the independence of Sinkiang had been destroyed.

GROWTH OF REGIONALISM. The Chinese central government never recovered its strength after suppressing the Taiping rebellion. Moreover, the Manchus crushed the Taipings at the cost of their own administrative disintegration: military officials dispatched to wrest certain regions from the rebels remained there and built up their own political and military machines. The central government was compelled to name these officials as governors general of the provinces they controlled. Possessing considerable military and financial resources, the regional officials had to be consulted by the throne on all major policy issues, and many even dealt directly with foreign powers. Significantly, most of these officials, being Chinese, contributed to the rise of a Chinese nationalist movement directed against the Manchus. The growth of regional power in China was a major characteristic of periods of dynastic decline.

INCREASE IN FOREIGN FINANCIAL CONTROL. The new commercial activity in the western-dominated treaty ports provided Chinese provincial officials with an important source of revenue and a field for patronage. The regional leaders worked closely with the new Chinese business class which had arisen in the treaty ports and thus remained outside the jurisdiction of the central government. China's problems were further complicated by financial difficulties; since the "unequal treaties" provided for fixed tariff levies on imports, China could not collect enough revenue from her trade to cover rising government expenditures. The Manchus were thus forced to rely increasingly on loans from western banks and governments, a situation which rendered China still more vulnerable to outside pressure.

Thus, by the closing decades of the 19th cent., China, while not strictly a colony, was no longer an independent state in control of her own fate. Far from being able to play one imperialist power off against another, she was compelled to grant to all any concessions she granted to one. In short, China suffered most of the disadvantages of the colonial system, especially the plunder of her resources by foreigners, without benefiting from its advantages, such as protection by a metropolitan country and assistance toward economic development.

SINO-JAPANESE WAR. The Chinese had long maintained Korea as a tributary state, but the vagueness of the tribute system in contrast to western concepts of international law meant that China could retain her position in Korea only so long as she was strong enough to exclude outside interference. When Japan opened Korea in 1876, China's protests were unavailing, and the western powers quickly signed their own treaties with Korea. In 1885, after several coups and countercoups in Seoul, Li Hung-chang for China and Ito Hirobumi for Japan concluded a treaty by which both countries obtained the right to send troops to Korea when necessary, provided they gave notification in advance. A lull followed this treaty, but in 1894 the outbreak of the Tonghak Revolt threatened the Korean government. The king of Korea requested Chinese military assistance, though the revolt had petered out before the troops arrived. Japan also sent troops, and the Japanese claimed that China's notification of her intention to send them was dispatched too late and contained an unwarranted reference to the suzerainty of the Manchus in Korea. The Japanese then sank a ship bringing Chinese reinforcements, and thus launched a full-scale Sino-Japanese war. Japan won a rapid series of victories and, when Japanese troops seemed ready to march on Peking, China sued for peace. By the Treaty of Shimonoseki, 17 Apr., 1895, China had to relinquish all claims to suzerainty over Korea, whose independence was thus reaffirmed, cede the islands of Formosa and the Pescadores to Japan, and pay a huge indemnity. In addition, Japan obtained extraterritorial rights for her subjects in China, as well as most-favored-nation treatment, thus acquiring a status and commercial privileges in China equal to those of the western powers.

1896-1901

THE "SLICING OF THE MELON." Defeat in the war against Japan placed in doubt China's continued existence as an independent state, and invited the imperialist powers to begin the "slicing of the melon," i.e., the carving up of her territory. Aware of western intentions, the Chinese approached Russia for support. A secret Sino-Soviet military alliance was signed, 1896; but, since Russia's role was prompted by her own expansionist designs in Manchuria, the alliance failed to benefit China. In fact, its terms gave Russia the right to build a railway through northern Manchuria. In 1898 Russia extended her railway rights, and also obtained the Kwangtung "leased territory," including the strategic port of Dairen and the naval base of Port Arthur. The British, too, added the Kowloon territories to the Crown Colony of Hong Kong, and received assurances that China would reserve for Britain the dominant position she held in Shanghai and in the Yangtze Valley provinces. France also joined the scramble for Chinese territory; she forced the Chinese, 1895, to agree not to alienate Hainan Island to anyone but the French, and in 1898 received special mining and railway privileges in southern China, preferential customs rates for goods from French Indochina, and a 99-year lease on Kwangchow Bay. In the same year Germany received the "leased territory" of Kiaochow, and secured mining and railway priorities in the Shantung Peninsula. The Japanese forced China to agree, 1898, not to alienate Fukien Province, opposite Japanese-occupied Formosa, to anyone but Japan. By the end of the century almost every Chinese province, harbor, and economic concession had become a "leased territory" or "sphere of influence," the former usually implying a larger degree of political as opposed to purely economic control.

THE 100 DAYS. Beset with administrative collapse and foreign encroachments, the young Manchu emperor, Kuang-hsü (1871–1908), turned in desperation to K'ang Yu-wei (1858–1927), the last important thinker in the Confucian tradition, to devise a program of reform that would preserve Chinese independence. K'ang aimed to transform China into a constitutional monarchy, eliminate the swollen and corrupt bureaucracy, and regain control over the provincial and district administrations. A series of imperial edicts laid the foundation for K'ang's reform program. He advocated abolition of the traditional examinations for government officials and a complete renovation of China's educational system in order to introduce liberal arts and sciences on the western model alongside the Chinese classics. He also proposed the creation of agricultural and technical schools throughout China. The new educational system had a dual purpose: to equip officials with the knowledge and techniques of the modernization process, and to instill information on public affairs as a first step toward representative government. Establishment of newspapers and the training of journalists were also to contribute to the public educational process. To encourage popular participation in government, district and provincial assemblies were to be elected which would, in turn, select delegates to a national parliament. In the economic sphere K'ang advocated state support of industry, the creation of a modern banking system, the establishment of bureaus to encourage mining and improve agriculture, the introduction of a modern national budget, and the construction of more railways to facilitate commercial transportation and thus stimulate trade. His major problem was the speed at which his reforms, if they were to be successful, had to be carried out. His measures did not have time to mature, and aroused the opposition of powerful vested interests, particularly among the scholar-gentry class.

Those opposing the reforms found their champion in the empress dowager, Tz'u-hsi (1835–1908), the former regent for her nephew and still a strong behind-the-scenes influence at court. K'ang advised the emperor to call in Yüan Shih-k'ai, China's strongest military leader at the time, to arrest the chief military supporters of the empress dowager. Yüan, however, revealed K'ang's plan, and the latter had to seek refuge in Hong Kong. The empress dowager then took the emperor prisoner, and resumed power herself under a new regency. K'ang's reform edicts were rescinded, and China relapsed into weakness and confusion. The failure of the "100 Days" deprived her of her last chance, under the monarchical system, to modernize her institutions.

THE "OPEN DOOR." China's increasing vulnerability to western encroachments and her inability to prevent them undermined the traditional U.S. policy of protecting Chinese independence and assuring equal economic opportunity for all foreign powers in China. The American secretary of state, John Hay, sought to bolster this policy by issuing the so-called Open Door Notes to Britain, France, Germany, Russia, Italy, and Japan. The notes demanded that no foreign power interfere with the rights and privileges of other powers in China by establishing economic and commercial monopolies or by discriminating in railway rates or harbor dues. American insistence that the Chinese government collect its own revenues emphasized the authority of that government and the territorial and administrative integrity of China. Only the Russians hesitated, announcing that they would respect the Open Door provided

the other powers did the same, but, while promising to treat citizens of all countries equally, they omitted a pledge to accord them equal status with Russian subjects. Russia's negative attitude automatically released all other powers from adherence to the Open Door, but, since no nation was willing to deny its commitment publicly, Hay was able to pretend that his notes had been accepted. In fact, the Open Door policy had some success in stopping the trend toward foreign monopolies in China.

BOXER REBELLION. Foreign influence seeped into China not only in the form of economic and territorial concessions but also through missionary activity. Hatred of the missionaries provided the driving force behind the Boxer Rebellion, 1899–1901. The members of the "Society of Righteous Harmony," a peasant-based secret society in north China, were called Boxers because their stylized physical exercises resembled boxing. In many areas the Boxers were primarily an antigovernment organization; but in places where there was widespread missionary activity, they adopted a xenophobic attitude as well. Christian converts had been denouncing certain aspects of village life as "pagan," thus arousing the anger of other peasants. Local officials then attempted to divert blame for the villages' economic ills away from themselves and on to the missionaries and their disciples. Reactionary court officials saw in the Boxer movement an opportunity to focus responsibility for China's difficulties on foreigners. These officials, ignorant of the true strength of the foreign powers, even believed that the Boxers might free China from the imperialist grip. The empress dowager herself harbored a grudge against the powers for preventing her from formally deposing the emperor and for refusing to surrender K'ang Yu-wei and other escaped leaders of reform.

Thus encouraged from many sides, the Boxers launched their uprising in Shantung, 1899, by attacking isolated missionaries, foreigners employed on railroads and other enterprises, and Chinese converts to Christianity. The attacks spread

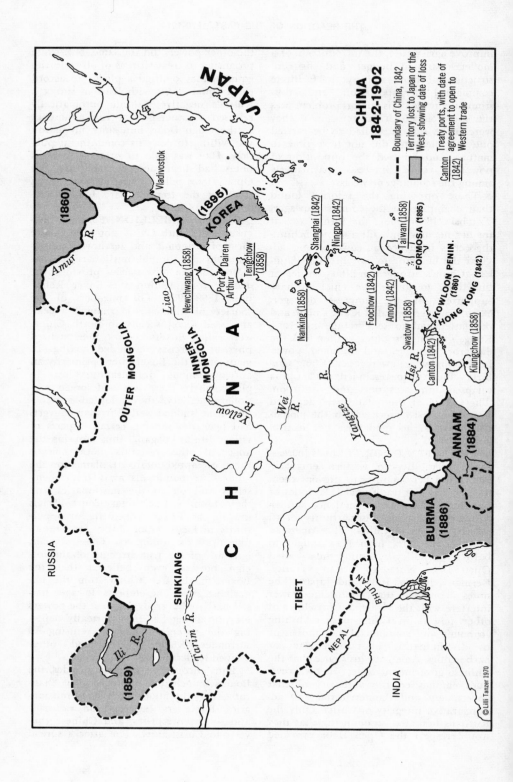

JAPAN

CHINA 1842-1902

– – – Boundary of China, 1842

▨ Territory lost to Japan or the West, showing date of loss

Canton (1842) Treaty ports, with date of agreement to open to Western trade

(1860)

Amur R.

Vladivostok

(1895)
KOREA

OUTER MONGOLIA

Liao R.

Newchwang (1858)
Port Arthur   Dairen

Tengchow (1858)

INNER MONGOLIA

Yellow R.

Wei R.

Nanking (1858)

Shanghai (1842)
Ningpo (1842)

Taiwan (1858)
FORMOSA (1895)

Foochow (1842)
Amy (1842)
Swatow (1858)
Hsi R.
Canton (1842)

KOWLOON PENIN.
(1860)
HONG KONG (1842)

Kiungchow (1858)

C H I N A

Yangtze R.

RUSSIA

SINKIANG

Tarim R.

Ili R.

(1859)

TIBET

BHUTAN

NEPAL

INDIA

ANNAM (1884)

BURMA (1886)

© Lilli Tanzer 1970

into other areas of China and culminated, May 1900, in the siege of the foreign legation quarter in Peking. The Boxers murdered the head of the Japanese legation, and the German minister to Peking was later killed by a Manchu sergeant. An international military expedition, composed of Japanese, British, French, Italian, Russian, and American troops, arrived at Peking, Aug., to relieve the legations, and a German unit joined the occupation forces later. Negotiations to end the fighting dragged on for nearly a year because of disputes among the occupying powers on the size and distribution of the indemnity. Finally, 7 Sept., 1901, the Boxer Protocol was signed. Its most important provisions were the imposition of a huge indemnity, to be paid out of China's maritime customs and salt gabelle (tax), and the granting to the powers of a right to station troops between Peking and Tientsin. This right the Japanese later exploited in their campaign for control of northern China. The Boxer Protocol also required that China apologize for the murder of the Japanese and German officials, cease the importation of arms and war matériel or their manufacture for at least 2 years, fix customs dues at 5% ad valorem, punish officials responsible for the Boxer insurrection, destroy certain forts, and establish a western-style ministry of foreign affairs. The powers would have liked to abolish the imperial government, but the Boxer rising indicated the difficulties such a course might encounter; they therefore allowed the empress dowager to remain in power.

1902–14

REFORM UNDER THE EMPRESS DOWAGER. The decade between the Boxer Protocol and Sun Yat-sen's revolution witnessed a mounting struggle between regional authorities and the Peking-based central government. Having finally realized that only basic reforms could preserve its position, the Manchu dynasty, headed by the empress dowager, instituted some of the programs first put forward by K'ang Yu-wei; any relationship between them, however, was firmly denied. Unlike K'ang's reform program, the measures now taken were piecemeal and designed to meet an immediate threat rather than to modernize China. By far the most significant reform was the abolition, 1905, of the traditional examination system. Since the examinations had determined membership in the scholar-gentry class, this class, the very backbone of the dynasty, soon disappeared. Thus the death knell of traditional Chinese society sounded, and the way was paved for an attack on Confucian philosophy itself. The introduction of western-type educational institutions led to a demand on the part of students—supported by provincial leaders wishing to limit the power of the throne—for a constitution and representative government. After much hesitation, the empress dowager announced, 1907, a 9-year program during which a representative governmental system would be created. Both she and her imprisoned nephew, the emperor, died the following year.

MOVES TOWARD REPRESENTATIVE GOVERNMENT. In 1909 the provincial assemblies, organs designed to advise provincial governors general but not to legislate, convened for the first time. The constitutional assembly convoked in 1910 witnessed an intense struggle between the delegates representing provincial assemblies and those appointed by the central government. The government was forced to shorten the period of preparation of a constitution to 5 years and to promise that a national parliament would be created by 1913.

REGIONAL CHALLENGES TO MANCHU AUTHORITY. Yüan Shih-k'ai and other regional leaders, meanwhile, continued to strengthen their power against both the central government and Japanese and western encroachments. Manchu attempts to play the provincial leaders off against one another reaped little success. The climax of the struggle between the regional authorities and Peking occurred in 1909–11 over railway policy. Having lost most of its authority over military and financial resources, the central government placed great importance on its control of railways. In 1911 the Manchus proposed a plan to finance a centrally controlled railway using provincial capital, which was to be paid back through interest-bearing government bonds. Large demonstrations and strikes greeted the announcement of this plan in Szechwan, and Peking was forced to dispatch troops to the rebellious province. The Szechwan uprising initiated the republican revolution.

RISE OF SUN YAT-SEN. Born of peasant stock, Sun Yat-sen (1866–1925) received a western education in a British missionary school in Hawaii, where he adopted Christianity, and later in Hong Kong. The shock of China's defeat in the Sino-Japanese War set him seriously working for the overthrow of the Manchu government. In 1894 he founded a secret revolutionary group, the "Revive China Society," which staged an abortive uprising in Canton, 1895. Forced to flee, he became a fugitive from the Chinese government with a price on his head. He traveled widely abroad, collecting funds and recruiting members for his group. At a meeting in Tokyo in 1905, several secret societies joined with Sun's group to become the T'ung-meng-hui (Combined League Society). Sun remained head of the new group. Its program was vague, the only definite goal being the overthrow of the Manchu dynasty and the creation of a Chinese republic. Support for the T'ung-meng-hui came from cadets of regional military schools sent overseas to study; among these cadets was Chiang Kai-shek (b. 1886), sent to Japan by Yüan Shih-k'ai's military academy. Men like Chiang created a link between the T'ung-meng-hui and regional groups within China struggling against the Manchus.

REVOLUTION OF 1911. On 10 Oct., 1911, the date regarded as the start of the Chinese Revolution, an explosion ripped apart a house in Wuhan where T'ung-meng-hui members manufactured bombs. Police seeking the cause of the explosion discovered a list of the society's members and local army officers. Fearing reprisals, these officers forced their commander to lead an uprising against Manchu troops. The insurrection quickly spread to other cities in central and southern China. The Manchus called on Yüan Shih-k'ai, who commanded the loyalty of the powerful northern army. In exchange for the post of governor general in the central Yangtze Valley and other concessions, Yüan agreed to lead a campaign against the revolutionaries. Faced by Yüan's superior military force and their own divided leadership, the revolutionary groups negotiated a settlement, Feb. 1912, by which Sun surrendered his leading role to Yüan in return for the latter's promise to end Manchu rule. Having yielded its effective power to Yüan, the Manchu dynasty had no choice but to abdicate the throne and transfer authority to him in exchange for a guarantee of personal protection and a financial settlement. Many leaders of the T'ung-meng-hui served in Yüan's first cabinet, but it collapsed, Aug. 1912, as a result of a struggle between Yüan and the society.

FOUNDATION OF THE KUOMINTANG. Sung Chiao-jen (1866–1918) amalgamated, Aug. 1912, the T'ung-meng-hui with 4 other political groups to form the Kuomintang (Nationalist Party). Unlike the T'ung-meng-hui, the Kuomintang was an open political party; Sun Yat-sen himself opposed its foundation, preferring a closed, secret-society type of organization loyal to himself. The parliamentary elections of 1913 made the Kuomintang the strongest single party in China, but the parliamentary cause suffered a severe blow when Yüan, jealous of Sung's growing power and popularity, engineered the latter's assassination. After Sung's death, parliament became the scene of a struggle between Yüan, who favored a strong presidential system of government, and a group advocating the election of a prime minister responsible to a parliamentary majority. When Yüan sought to enhance his power by replacing pro-Kuomintang military officials in the Yangtze Valley with his own supporters, the Kuomintang staged an open rebellion, Aug. 1913. Yüan quelled this uprising and, 3 months later, outlawed the Kuomintang. (*Cont. p. 479.*)

THE MODERNIZING OF JAPAN
1870-76

THE MEIJI ERA. 1870 can be taken as the year in which the basic trends of the Meiji period began to emerge. By 1869 the government had taken the form it was to retain until 1885, under a Dajokan (Council of State). In keeping with the restorationist mood, the titular heads of the major government bodies were court nobles. However, it was their samurai assistants who held the real power. The most prominent of these samurai were from the former feudal domains of Satsuma, Choshu, Tosa and Hizen in Kyushu, Shikoku, and southern Honshu. Among them were Okubo Toshimichi (1830–78), Kido Takayoshi (1833–77), Ito Hirobumi (1841–1909), Yamagata Aritomo (1833–1922), Okuma Shigenobu (1832–1922), Itagaki Taisuke (1836–1919), and Saigo Takamori (1827–77). Some became oligarchs, ruling in the name of Emperor Meiji, and some became opponents of the regime. But all made an indelible mark upon Japanese history.

ABOLITION OF THE FEUDAL DOMAINS. In Aug. 1871 the former feudal domains were completely abolished and their armies disbanded. The move had not been possible until Saigo and other conservative leaders were won over to the modernizing cause. Japan was divided into ken, or prefectures.

IWAKURA MISSION. A mission headed by Iwakura Tomomi (1825–83), the only court noble with real power, left for a long tour of the U.S.A. and Europe, Dec. 1871. The avowed purpose of the mission was to seek revision of the unequal treaties, but every government turned it down on this issue. Instead the mission members, including Okubo, Kido, Ito, and other leaders, were able to see with their own eyes the technological superiority of the modern West. This educational experience had a profound impact on their later policies.

NEW SOCIAL ORDER. In early 1872 the new Japanese social order was given its final 3-class form: aristocrats, gentry, and commoners. In practice, the gentry (former samurai) had no useful advantages over the commoners. Japan's small eta (pariah) class was also legally emancipated by this time, being placed on a level with the commoners. Social equality was further promoted in 1872 by the announcement of plans for a system of compulsory primary education. By 1906, 98% of all Japanese children attended primary schools.

CONSCRIPT ARMY. The establishment of a conscription system, Jan. 1873, for the army shattered Japan's aristocratic warrior tradition. All ranks were thrown open to men of every social origin. The great leader behind Japan's military modernization was Yamagata.

LAND-TAX REFORM. A radical land-tax reform, July 1873, provided the government with a uniform and dependable source of revenue. The tax was to be paid in cash, instead of in kind, at the yearly rate of 3% of the market value of the land. The new tax weighed heavily on the farmers, for it allowed no leniency in bad years; nor could the farmers always obtain cash advantageously.

STATUS OF SAMURAI. In Dec. 1873 the government allowed former daimyo and samurai to commute their feudal stipends for a lump sum. This was a step toward relieving the government of an unproductive financial burden. In 1876 all former samurai were forbidden to wear their swords in public and were forced once and for all to commute their stipends for government bonds. This settlement was generous to the daimyo, but far less so to the regular samurai.

KOREAN QUESTION. In 1872 Japan had sought, without success, to open Korea to trade. The Japanese had strategic designs on Korea, and the rebuff wounded their pride. Hence a faction led by Saigo came to press for war. Its members, mostly from Hizen and Tosa, were those who were losing out to men of Satsuma and Choshu in the contest for power, and therefore advocacy of war was also a move in a domestic power struggle.

Most of the top Stacho (Satsuma and Choshu) leaders had gone abroad with the Iwakura mission, leaving Saigo as the head of a caretaker government. Although of Satsuma himself, Saigo was a conservative and deeply worried about the fate of the samurai; he saw war as a chance to revive them. In the summer of 1873 he obtained approval for a campaign. The Iwakura mission then returned, and in Oct. the plan was canceled. Okubo argued that Japan was not strong enough for war; that she should concentrate on internal strengthening and reform; and that she should not give the western powers any excuse for action against her.

With the victory of the Satcho clique headed by Okubo, Saigo, Itagaki, Okuma, and their followers resigned. Some became involved in armed rebellion; others turned

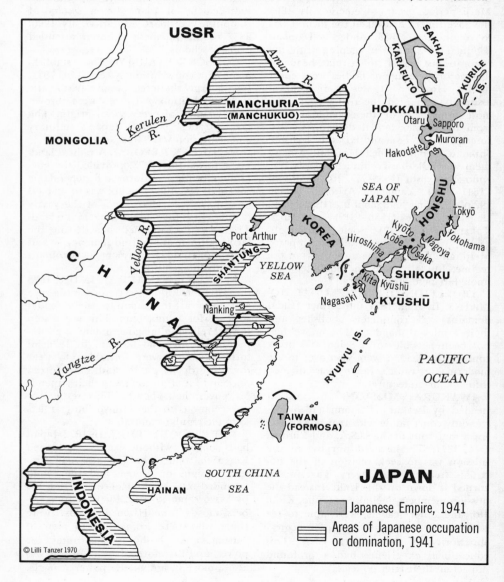

JAPAN

Japanese Empire, 1941

Areas of Japanese occupation or domination, 1941

© Lilli Tanzer 1970

to political opposition. Okubo soon became Japan's first home minister, an extremely powerful position. Satcho domination of the government was now secure.

MOVEMENT FOR REPRESENTATIVE GOVERNMENT. In Jan. 1874 Itagaki and Goto Shojiro, in a memorial, denounced the oligarchs for ruling without regard to the emperor or to the people. They proposed a popularly elected assembly so as to unify public opinion and save the state from decay. The government rejected the proposal, but at least referred it to a committee for study. Thus began an enduring debate over representative government. The oligarchs felt, in view of the vehemence of the "popular rights movement," that the creation of an assembly might tame the opposition, but that such an assembly should be given no real power.

In Feb. 1875 the government called a conference with the political opposition at Osaka. It agreed to create a Genro-in (Senate) and a supreme court, and to call prefectural assemblies. However, these bodies were to represent only a very small part of the population, and were to be advisory only.

FORMOSA EXPEDITION. The murder of some Ryukyuans by Formosan natives provided the Japanese with the occasion for a punitive expedition. The expedition employed many former samurai and released some of the tension created by the Korean issue. In Oct. 1874 China's agreement to pay an indemnity amounted to tacit recognition of Japanese sovereignty over the Ryukyu Islands. In 1879 Japan incorporated them as Okinawa Prefecture.

FOREIGN RELATIONS. In May 1875 Russia recognized Japanese sovereignty over the Kuriles, while Japan recognized Russian sovereignty over Sakhalin. In Feb. 1876 the Treaty of Kanghwa opened 2 Korean ports besides Pusan to trade with Japan. China, however, refused to recognize Korea's competence to conclude a treaty, since Korea had always been a vassal state. Thus Japan did not obtain an implied recognition by China of Korean independence, as she had hoped to do.

1877-89

SATSUMA REBELLION. After his resignation Saigo had returned to Satsuma and established private schools for the samurai there. He was profoundly admired by many former samurai, who were deeply dissatisfied with the policies of the government, especially its failure to launch an expedition against Korea. A threatening situation thus developed in Satsuma. In Jan. 1877 the government tried to remove the contents of an arsenal in Kagoshima, the Satsuma capital. Saigo's followers promptly seized the arsenal and began a march on Tokyo. Saigo himself had no thought of armed rebellion, but placed himself at the head of the march out of loyalty to his men. The march was blocked at Kumamoto, immediately to the north, but it was not until Sept. 1877 that the rebellion was finally put down. Saigo died as Kagoshima fell. The new conscript army had proved its worth.

CONSTITUTIONAL PROPOSALS. In Tosa, his home province, Itagaki had formed the Risshisha (Society for Striving toward a Definite Aim) to aid the samurai and to promote his political views. In June 1877 the Risshisha submitted to the government a memorial bitterly attacking the oligarchs and demanding the creation of a diet. The government turned the proposal down. The Genro-in had in fact been preparing an English-style constitution since 1876. In May 1878, Okubo was assassinated because of his dictatorial methods of administration, and Ito replaced him as home minister. Ito favored extreme caution in granting a constitution.

POLITICAL REPRESSION. In response to the rapidly growing movement for representative government a law was enacted, 1880, placing political meetings under police supervision and forbidding members of the armed forces, teachers, and students to attend such meetings. Political groups were forbidden to advertise or to correspond with one another. This law was one of several enacted over the years to repress the political opposition.

FALL OF OKUMA. The future outline of the Meiji government emerged clearly from the crisis that brought about the expulsion of Okuma from the government. Being from Hizen, he was not of the Satcho clique, and was in fact Ito's rival for power. He had withheld his views on a constitution, although the other oligarchs had long since declared cautious approval. In Mar. 1881 he challenged Ito by demanding the introduction of a constitutional form of government in which the cabinet would be responsible to a parliament with real authority. Moreover, he demanded that the 1st elections be held in 1882. These proposals were rejected. After a time serious governmental corruption in Hokkaido was brought to light, and the government came under severe public criticism. The oligarchs assumed that Okuma was trying to exploit the scandal and stir up trouble in order to overthrow the Satcho clique. Accordingly, they ousted Okuma, Oct. At the same time it was announced that a diet would be created by 1890. By this action those in power hoped to reduce the strong anti-government feelings that had been aroused.

FOUNDING OF THE POLITICAL PARTIES. Itagaki founded the Jiyuto (Liberal Party) before the end of 1881, in anticipation of the opening of the diet. The Jiyuto was supported mainly by rural interests and imbued to some extent with the ideas of French radicalism. Okuma founded the Kaishinto (Progressive Party), based more on urban interests and influenced by English liberalism, in early 1882.

PREPARATION FOR THE CONSTITUTION. In 1882, Ito left for Europe to study suitable models for the constitution, and spent nearly all his time in Berlin and Vienna. The political parties became fragmented and weakened by repressive laws. Violence provoked by the drastic retrenchment of 1881 discredited them further. In late 1884 the Jiyuto was dissolved. It did not re-form until just after the first elections. In 1885 the first Japanese cabinet replaced the Dajokan. In 1886 Ito began drafting the constitu-

tion, in complete secrecy. The draft was submitted to the Privy Council in May 1888. The Privy Council had been created to review the draft, and lived on as the highest advisory body in the government. It was totally removed from public scrutiny.

LI-ITO CONVENTION. By the Li-Ito Convention, 1885, Japan and China undertook to withdraw their troops from Korea and to notify each other of any intention to intervene there. Japan was biding her time before a showdown.

PROMULGATION OF THE CONSTITUTION. 11 Feb., 1889. The emperor of Japan bestowed the constitution on his subjects. The text reserved to him all sovereign powers such as the declaration of war and the conclusion of treaties. He exercised legislative power "with the consent of the Imperial Diet" (as the parliament was called). He alone could initiate amendments to the constitution, and he had extensive powers of ruling by ordinance. He was the direct commander of the military services, which placed the services on a level with the premier himself. The constitution did not mention a cabinet, for each minister was in theory responsible to the emperor alone. The Diet consisted of an appointed House of Peers and an elected House of Representatives. It could be dissolved at will by the premier and was powerless to enforce a vote of no confidence. Its budgetary powers were very limited. The constitution also provided for a supreme court.

As between executive, legislature, and judiciary, the executive branch was clearly dominant. The constitution provided for the basic rights of the people, but all were made subject to law. It laid clear and positive stress on the duties of the emperor's subjects.

1890–99

EDUCATIONAL POLICY. The Imperial Rescript on Education, Oct. 1890, set a lofty moral tone for all of Japanese education until 1945. It exalted the emperor as the father of the nation, and required of his subjects selfless devotion toward him and filial piety toward their parents.

FUNCTIONING OF THE IMPERIAL DIET. The 1st Diet opened in Nov. 1890. It proved hostile to the government even though only 1.24% of the population was qualified, on the basis of property, to vote. The Diet demanded drastic budget cuts, and the government was barely able to reach a compromise. But a lasting peace proved impossible. Yamagata resigned in May 1891; Matsukata, his successor, had to dissolve the Diet in Dec. In the election that followed, the government tried to influence the vote by violence. 25 people were killed, but the new Diet was still hostile. Characteristically, it was not the ensuing furor which felled Matsukata, but the resignation of the war and navy ministers. They were protesting the removal of a protégé, the home minister responsible for the violence. Ito himself then became premier and frustrated a Diet attempt to impeach him. More dissolutions and elections followed. A stalemate had been reached, but it could not be broken to the Diet's advantage.

EXTRATERRITORIALITY. In July 1894 Japan and Great Britain signed a treaty to abolish extraterritoriality, which was to become valid with the adoption of Japan's new civil code, 1899. The government had been trying for many years to have the unequal treaties abolished, and the parties had turned its lack of success into a powerful political weapon. Public indignation had wrecked a compromise settlement in 1889, and Okuma, the foreign minister, nearly lost his life to an assassin.

SINO-JAPANESE WAR. In June 1894 the Tonghak Rebellion broke out in Korea. When the king of Korea called in Chinese troops, Japan quickly sent her own, and demanded acceptance of a sweeping Japanese-oriented reform program. For once both Diet and oligarchs were of one mind in desiring a settlement. In Aug. Japan declared war and, to the surprise of the European powers, rapidly gained control of Korea, the Liaotung Peninsula, and the adjacent seas.

With 7 divisions poised to march on Peking, China was obliged to come to terms.

TREATY OF SHIMONOSEKI. 17 Apr., 1895. China recognized the independence of Korea, opened certain commercial ports to Japan, and agreed to pay an indemnity of 200 m. taels. Japan received Formosa, the Pescadores Islands, and the Liaotung Peninsula.

THE TRIPLE INTERVENTION. Within a week, Russia, France, and Germany—all powers with important interests in China—advised Japan, Apr. 1895, to retrocede Liaotung, and Russia threatened force. Japan was obliged to comply. It was a bitter blow to the entire nation, and in the end served only to rally Japan's nationalistic feelings—especially since Russia herself moved into the Liaotung Peninsula in 1898. Partition of China seemed increasingly likely at this time, and Japan bitterly resented being prevented from taking no more than the other powers were taking for themselves. In the Rosen-Nishi Agreement of Apr. 1898, however, Russia recognized Japan's claim to economic preference in Korea.

PARTY ALLIANCES WITH THE OLIGARCHS. After the Sino-Japanese War, the Diet turned hostile again. However, in seeking a way out of their dilemma, the parties began to ally themselves with key oligarchs. In 1895 Ito gained the support of the Jiyuto and persuaded Itagaki to accept the Home Ministry. Okuma's party soon gave its support to Matsukata. Yamagata remained aloof. The parties were soon disillusioned. In 1898 Itagaki and Okuma joined forces to achieve the main goals of the liberal movement: party cabinets and a cabinet responsible to the Diet. Ito, the premier, withdrew, and allowed Okuma and Itagaki to form a joint cabinet. They soon split hopelessly and, in Oct., resigned. Yamagata then took over and restored oligarchic rule.

1900–1905

YAMAGATA-ITO RIVALRY. By 1900, 2 broad factions existed within the oligarchs. Yamagata commanded the support of the military services, while Ito, more flexible, was aligned with the highest civilian members of the government. One important move in this power struggle was an imperial ordinance issued, May 1900, under the premiership of Yamagata. It required that the war and navy ministers be drawn only from among high-ranking generals and admirals on active duty. Thus a service could order its minister to resign and the whole cabinet would fall. Then a successor could be withheld until the new cabinet suited the service concerned.

FORMATION OF THE SEIYUKAI. In Sept. 1900 Ito moved to compromise with the party movement by forming a party of his own: the Seiyukai (Society of Political Friends). For his patronage Ito demanded obedience to his orders and conceded nothing to liberal ideals. Yamagata immediately resigned. Ito succeeded him, but was unable to establish control over the Yamagata faction. He resigned as premier in May 1901, and as party president in July 1903. He was the last of the original Meiji oligarchs to hold the office of premier. The Seiyukai was taken over by Saionji Kimmochi (1849–1940), his friend, and developed into a major political force. The Yamagata-Ito rivalry continued, but indirectly through Saionji and Katsura Taro (1847–1913), Yamagata's protégé. From 1901 to 1913, the 2 alternated as premier, evidencing the stalemate that existed between the factions.

A Social-Democratic Party was founded, 1901, and was instantly banned by the police. The socialist movement itself, however, was not suppressed.

POWER OF THE GENRO. The Genro (Elders) took on added importance. The Genro were a strictly unofficial group of the emperor's top advisers. No longer overtly active in politics (Ito was the last of them to retire), they continued to rule from behind the scenes and to decide the highest issues of state.

ANGLO-JAPANESE ALLIANCE. Russia did not withdraw her troops from China after the Boxer Rebellion, and pressured the Chinese for concessions in Manchuria. It took vigorous protests from the powers to check her. Japan and Great Britain both feared Russian expansion in Manchuria, and Katsura, unlike Ito, was strongly anti-Russian. Thus an Anglo-Japanese alliance was signed, Jan. 1902. It recognized Japan's special interest in Korea, and guaranteed the neutrality of either power if the other was at war with any single enemy in the Far East. The alliance was a triumph for Japan, since it placed her on an equal footing with Britain and strengthened her in her rivalry with Russia.

RUSSO-JAPANESE WAR. Russia had agreed to withdraw from Manchuria, but by 1903 she showed signs not only of staying but of advancing. When Japan protested, Russia gave a harsh reply. Katsura needed no further provocation. In Jan. 1904 Japan delivered an ultimatum to Russia and, when it was ignored, declared war, 10 Feb. By mid-1904 the Japanese had taken Port Arthur. They captured Mukden after a long siege, Mar. 1905, and, in May, destroyed the Russian fleet off Tsushima in the Korean Strait. However, Japan was approaching the limit of her strength. She asked President Theodore Roosevelt of the U.S.A. to mediate.

TREATY OF PORTSMOUTH. 5 Sept., 1905. The treaty ending the Russo-Japanese War, signed at Portsmouth, N.H., recognized Japan's paramount interest in Korea and ceded to her the leasehold of the Liaotung Peninsula, the southern portion of the Eastern Chinese Railway, and the southern half of Sakhalin. Japan pressed for an indemnity and for all of Sakhalin, but was not strong enough to prevail over Russia's flat refusal. The Japanese public, which saw only a total victory over a major European power, was outraged at this retreat, and there were riots in the streets. But the treaty stood, marking for Japan a great step toward major-power status.

1906–14

ANNEXATION OF KOREA. In Nov. 1905 Japan established a virtual protectorate over Korea. Ito became the first resident general. June 1906 saw the founding of the South Manchuria Railway Co., with both government and private capital. The company enjoyed very broad economic rights in southern Manchuria, and played an essential role in administration and policy formulation for the area. The first governor general of Kwantung (the Liaotung area) was appointed, Aug. 1906, and Korea became a full protectorate in July 1907. Russia recognized the protectorate in a secret convention. The Root-Takahira Agreement, Nov. 1908, between the U.S.A. and Japan, tacitly acquiesced in Japan's actions in Korea. There remained the final step: outright annexation. Ito steadfastly opposed it, and resigned as pressure for annexation became strong. In Oct. 1909 he was killed by a Korean assassin at Harbin. The Treaty of Annexation was signed, 22 Aug., 1910, under the next resident general, Gen. Terauchi Masatake (1852–1919).

THE "TAISHO CHANGE." During the habitual alternation between Katsura and Saionji the Diet resolutely opposed military pressure for greater armaments. The death of Emperor Meiji, 30 July, 1912, ended the most momentous reign in Japanese history. Katsura, leading his 3rd cabinet, met with strong opposition from the political parties. He sought to overcome Seiyukai opposition by having the new emperor Taisho order Saionji to support the government. But he failed, and antigovernment riots broke out in Tokyo and other big cities. Katsura resigned, Feb. 1913, but he had been obliged to recognize the power of the parties. Increasingly, the parties came to be seen as respectable wielders of political influence. Katsura was followed briefly by Adm. Yamamoto Gombei (1852–1933). Okuma was appointed premier in Apr. 1914. The army's drive for expansion had resumed, and Okuma saw no reason to stop it. He dissolved the Diet when it once more opposed the plan to increase the size of the army. The next Diet, however, co-operated willingly, and the stage was set for Japan's entry into World War I. (*Cont. p. 487.*)

KOREA

1870–83

INCREASE IN JAPANESE INFLUENCE. In 1873 King Kojong of Korea reached maturity and the regent, Tai-won-kun, was forced to retire. Power now accrued to the faction of Queen Min, which was more amenable to the West than the regent's had been. In 1874 a Japanese mission under Moriyama Shigeru failed to negotiate a trade treaty. In Sept. 1875 a Japanese gunboat, supposedly engaged in marine surveys off the Korean coast, provoked an incident and was fired upon. The Japanese sent a mission to Peking to seek a definite Chinese avowal of Korean independence. They were told that in domestic and foreign affairs Korea was self-governing, and Li Hung-chang agreed to aid the Japanese to secure a friendly reception at Seoul. At the same time he advised the Koreans to negotiate and modernize.

KANGHWA TREATY. The Japanese then sent an expeditionary force to Korea and, despite opposition from Tai-won-kun, extracted the Kanghwa Treaty from the Korean government, 26 Feb., 1876. This treaty provided for Japanese diplomatic representation at Seoul, for the opening of 3 ports to trade, and for extraterritorial rights for Japanese residents. Between 1876 and 1883 Pusan, Inchon, and Wonsan were opened for trade. The treaty resulted in the rise of a pro-Japanese faction in Korea opposed to the factions of Tai-won-kun and the queen.

CHEMULPO TREATY. In July 1882 the Yi (Tai-won-kun's) faction, aided by military rioters, unsuccessfully attacked Queen Min and the Japanese legation. Chinese and Japanese troops arrived to settle the affair, Aug. On 30 Aug. the Japanese negotiated the Chemulpo Treaty, an agreement which provided for an indemnity and punishment of the guilty, as well as further trade privileges for Japan. The Japanese also obtained the right to station troops in Seoul and to travel in the interior. To assert their suzerainty the Chinese kidnapped Tai-won-kun and imprisoned him in Tientsin for 3 years. In 1882 they obtained a treaty which gave Chinese discriminatory advantages over other foreigners in matters of residence, travel, trade, and import duties. These Chinese actions left in power the Queen Min faction, which had become conservative, antireform, and pro-Chinese.

1884–93

LI-ITO CONVENTION. On 4 Dec., 1884, Korean progressives led by Kim Ok-kiun and Pak Yong-hio, with assistance from the Japanese, attempted a coup against the pro-Chinese conservatives, and seized the king. The insurgents called for Japanese military protection, but Chinese troops under Yüan Shih-k'ai drove the Japanese to the coast and restored the king to the throne. The leaders of the revolt fled to Japan.

Against this background on 18 Apr., 1885, the Japanese, represented by Ito Hirobumi, and the Chinese by Li Hung-chang signed the Li-Ito Convention, also known as the Treaty of Tientsin. By this agreement both powers decided to withdraw their troops from Korea and announced they would consult one another before sending troops there again. Japan thus gained equality with China in the matter of intervention in Korea.

1894–1904

SINO-JAPANESE WAR. In 1894 insurrections in protest against taxation occurred in Chonju, Iksan, and Kobu. These were soon followed by the Tonghak Rebellion, which called for the extirpation of all foreigners. Government forces sent to put down the rebels were defeated. On 6 June, 1894, by request of the Korean government, the Chinese sent in 1,500 troops, informing Japan of their action. Invoking the Li-Ito Convention, the Japanese dispatched 400 troops, 9 June. On 20 July the Japanese government sent an ultimatum to the Korean government, demanding reform, and on 23 July Japanese forces seized the king,

threw out the Min faction, and recalled Tai-won-kun to power. The Japanese then fired on a Chinese warship, 25 July, and captured Seoul and the royal palace. On 26 July a Special High Commission was appointed to prepare government reforms, and the Japanese took control of government appointments. Under strong Japanese pressure, Korea declared war on China, 27 July. On 1 Aug. the Japanese declared war on China themselves, and during July and Aug. their forces defeated the Chinese at battles at Asan, Pyongyang, and Yalu. On 16 Aug. a provisional treaty was signed by which Japan guaranteed Korean independence but stipulated that Japanese advice and aid must be sought by the Korean government. On 17 Apr., 1895, the Treaty of Shimonoseki was negotiated by Ito Hirobumi and Li Hung-chang. China now finally renounced her suzerainty over Korea.

GROWTH OF RUSSIAN INFLUENCE. On 8 Oct., 1895, Queen Min was assassinated, and next day a pro-Japanese cabinet took office. The Japanese government, however, disclaimed responsibility for the queen's death. On 11 Feb., 1896, King Konjong took refuge in the Russian embassy, and yet another cabinet was formed, with Pak Chongyang as prime minister. During 1896–98 American-influenced reformers led by Dr. Philip Jaisohn (So Chae-p'il, 1868–1951) founded the Independence Society, and published the 1st modern newspaper in Korea, the *Independence News*. To counter the reformers the government organized the Hwangguk Society, and by the end of 1898 the reform movement had been suppressed and its leaders, including Jaisohn and Syngman Rhee (1875–1965). were in exile. The movement did, however, succeed in extracting some reforms from the government.

RUSSO-JAPANESE RIVALRY. On 9 June, 1896, the Yamagata-Lobanov Agreement was signed in Moscow, Japan and Russia agreeing to support the Korean king's efforts to restore and maintain order, and guaranteeing foreign loans so that an adequate police force could be maintained. A secret article provided that, in case it became necessary to send troops to Korea, the 2 powers would consult with a view to fixing a neutral zone between their spheres of action. Korea thus became virtually a joint protectorate.

In Feb. 1897 King Konjong returned to his palace, and on 12 Aug. he assumed the title of emperor, since that of king (wang) had become secondary. In the same month the name of the country was changed from Chosen to Taehan (Great Han Empire).

In Apr. 1898 the Nishi-Rosen Protocol was signed. It provided for Japanese and Russian recognition of Korean independence, a mutual agreement not to assist the Korean army or engage in financial reorganization, and Russian recognition of Japanese commercial and industrial interests in Korea.

RUSSO-JAPANESE WAR. Early in 1903 the Russians moved troops to the mouth of the Yalu River, and in July the Japanese opened direct negotiations with them on both Manchuria and Korea. These negotiations lasted from Aug. 1903 to Feb. 1904. The Japanese sought recognition of their interests in Korea; the Russians offered commercial and industrial supremacy for Japan in the southern part of the peninsula and neutralization of the northern. The Japanese would not accept the Russian proposals.

On 8 Feb., 1904, Japanese forces occupied Seoul, and 2 days later declared war on Russia. Japan and Korea signed a protocol, 23 Feb., guaranteeing Korean independence and territorial integrity in return for acceptance by the Koreans of Japanese advice. By the Treaty of Portsmouth, 5 Sept., 1905, which ended the war, Russia acknowledged Japan's "paramount interests" in Korea. The Japanese assumed police responsibility in Seoul, placed a resident general there, and stationed their own police inspectors in all provinces. In Nov. Korea officially became a Japanese protectorate.

1906–14

JAPANESE ANNEXATION. In June 1907 the Korean emperor sent a secret mission to the 2nd Hague Peace Conference seeking aid against Japanese exploitation. Although his request was virtually ignored, the Japanese in retaliation forced him to abdicate, 19 July, in favor of his son, Sunjong (ruled 1907–10), and tightened their control of Korea under the direction of Resident General Ito. On 1 Aug. they ordered the disbanding of the Korean army. Korean resistance continued, however; between 1908 and 1910, 12,000 rioters were killed by Japanese police and troops. On 26 Oct., 1909, Ito, who had resigned as resident general and who opposed complete annexation, was assassinated in Harbin by Korean nationalists. In response, Japan annexed Korea, 22 Aug., 1910. The royal family were given Japanese titles of nobility and a financial settlement, and lesser leaders were bribed or terrorized into accepting the *fait accompli*. On 30 Sept., effective 1 Oct., the new system of government was promulgated. (*Cont. p. 486.*)

The Imperial and Colonial Worlds

THE BRITISH DOMINIONS

Canada

1870–85

RED RIVER REBELLION. When government forces under Col. Garnet Wolseley (1833–1913) put an end to the Red River Rebellion of the métis (half-Indian, half-French), Manitoba became an equal, self-governing province of Canada, 15 July, 1870. The métis had united under Louis Riel (1844–85) to protect their land. The rebellion was rapidly suppressed, but not before Thomas Scott, a government agent, had been killed. Riel was bribed to leave the country in order to minimize the Anglo-French friction this incident created.

TREATY OF WASHINGTON. 8 May, 1871. Sir John Macdonald (1815–91), representing Canada on a team of British negotiators, signed the Treaty of Washington with the U.S.A. Although major Canadian questions were not discussed, e.g., Fenian Raid damages, it was the first time that Canada had been recognized at a diplomatic conference table.

DEVELOPMENT OF THE WEST. British Columbia joined the Confederation, 20 July, 1871, on the strength of a promise that the central government would begin a transcontinental railway within 2 years and finish it within 10. Although other provinces were to be added (Prince Edward Island and Nova Scotia, 1873) or organized out of existing territory (Alberta and Saskatchewan, 1905), with the addition of British Columbia, Canada stretched from ocean to ocean. On 7 Nov., 1873, Canada's 1st prime minister, the Conservative Macdonald, was forced to resign over a railway scandal that grew out of the feverish bidding for the Intercolonial Railway to the Pacific. The Northwest Mounted Police, forerunners of the Royal Canadian Mounted Police, were formed at this time to control the Indians and prepare the west for settlement. The Liberal ministry of Alexander Mackenzie (1822–92) organized the Northwest Territories in 1875.

"NATIONAL POLICY." Macdonald and the Conservatives triumphed in the elections of 1878 with an appeal to nationalism and protective tariffs, known as the "National Policy." In the next few years Macdonald consciously set out to lay the foundations of the Canadian nation and to stir up a sense of patriotism among Canadians. In 1879 the post of high commissioner was created to represent Canadian interests in London.

CANADIAN PACIFIC RAILWAY. By an imperial order in council, 31 July, 1880, all British possessions in North America, except Newfoundland and its

dependencies, were annexed to Canada. The same year the Canadian Pacific Railway Co. was awarded a generous contract ($25 m., 25 m. acres of land, and monopoly of the trade) to build a line to the West Coast. As more and more money was poured into the C.P.R., the Canadian public began to doubt the wisdom of the scheme. Only the return of Louis Riel to lead the 2nd Métis Rebellion, 1885, saved the railway. The swift movement of troops to the troubled area justified present and future outlay on the grounds of national security. The capture and execution of Riel also had the effect of aggravating Anglo-French enmities.

1886-99

INTERPROVINCIAL CONFERENCE. In 1887 the Interprovincial Conference, under the leadership of Honoré Mercier (1840–94) and Oliver Mowat (1820–1903), met at Quebec. It was symbolic of the growing discontent with the power of the central government under Macdonald. It pondered a general revision of the constitution, especially the clauses that permitted the federal authorities to disallow provincial legislation. This meeting, like its successor of 1906, achieved no practical results, mainly because it was so predominantly a 1-party organization, "a Liberal Party gathering."

INCREASE IN IMMIGRATION. The McKinley Tariff of 1890, passed by the U.S.A., aggravated a Canadian economic depression which had begun in 1873 and caused a revival of the old Liberal demands for a reciprocity agreement, while strengthening Canadian ties with Britain. By 1896, however, general prosperity was beginning to revive, a prosperity which was both caused by and the cause of an influx of settlers into Canada, attracted by her new rail links with the Far West and her liberal land policy. Above all, the American West had now reached the saturation point, and potential immigrants were deflected to America's northern neighbor. Canada became a melting pot as millions of settlers flowed in from the continent of Europe, the United

Kingdom, and the United States—a total of 2.5 m. between 1896 and 1914. The Conservative Party, which had declined steadily under competent but unspectacular successors to Macdonald, lost the elections of 1896 to the Liberals under (Sir) Wilfred Laurier, one of the few men in Canada who combined in his person the attributes of the many warring factions of society, being a lawyer, a scholar, a Roman Catholic, and of French origin.

IMPERIAL PREFERENCE. At Laurier's suggestion the Colonial Conference of 1897 accepted a system of preferential tariffs within the British Empire. Preferring economic to political union of the empire, as proposed by the British colonial secretary, Joseph Chamberlain, Laurier saw this as a way to improve Canada's economic position in relation to both the U.S. and Europe.

SOUTH AFRICAN WAR. The sending of Canadian troops to the South African War in 1899 caused great controversy in Canada. The French-speaking inhabitants of Quebec, identifying with the Boers, demanded the return of the Canadian contingent. Laurier circumvented the problem by dispatching only volunteers and having them maintained by Britain, though the South African War still cost Canada some $2.5 m.

1900–1914

CANADIAN-U.S. BORDER PROBLEMS. One of the last great outbursts of anti-American feeling in Canada resulted from negotiations concerning the Alaskan boundary line. The court of arbitration that made the binding decision was composed of 3 Americans chosen for their outspoken pro-U.S. stance, 2 Canadians, and Lord Alverstone for the United Kingdom. Smooth Anglo-American relations were preserved, as had often happened before, at the expense of Canada, as Alverstone, under American and British pressure, voted for the U.S. Better American-Canadian relations followed in the wake of the International Waterway Commission, 1905, and, especially, the

Boundary Waters Treaty, 1909, which set up a permanent board to decide all future border questions.

INDEPENDENCE OF CANADIAN FOREIGN POLICY. In an attempt to assert herself within the British Empire, Canada, which had won the right to withdraw from commercial treaties negotiated by London on her behalf in 1899, gained the more sweeping right, 1908, to decide whether any kind of treaty should be binding on her or not. Laurier's next step was to establish a Department of External Relations.

ROYAL CANADIAN NAVY. A law was passed, 1910, to provide for a small Canadian navy. But a later attempt, 1913, to contribute 3 dreadnoughts to the Royal Navy was rejected by the Liberal Senate on the grounds that Canada still had an inadequate voice in imperial policy making.

CANADIAN-U.S. RECIPROCITY. Due to internal political considerations in the U.S.A., the American Congress passed legislation enabling a reciprocity agreement to be negotiated between the U.S. and Canada. The Liberal Party seized on this long-desired panacea, but Canadians were no longer charmed by it, and in the elections of 1911 voted against the Liberals, thus ending the possibility of reciprocity. (*Cont. p. 476.*)

Australia

1870–89

THE AUSTRALIAN CONTINENT. By 1870 Australians were beginning to think continentally. In that year, as part of a steadily improving communications and transportation network, the 1st transcontinental telegraph was completed. By 1872 there was a regular cable service to both Europe and Asia. Expeditions under John Forrest, 1873–74, and Ernest Giles, 1875, continued the work of exploring and mapping the interior.

TRADE UNIONISM. Labor unions, which had been struggling for recognition, held the 1st Australian Trade Union Congress in 1878–79. The unions not only demanded regulated wages, an 8-hour day, and decent working conditions but also hoped to restrict the employment of Chinese immigrants as laborers. The 2nd Congress was held in 1884 and, except for the turbulent, strike-ridden period 1891–98, annually thereafter, thus giving the Australian workingman a sense and symbol of unity amid intercolonial rivalries.

BEGINNING OF THE FEDERATION MOVEMENT. Sectionalism and friction between the colonies increased during the prosperous 1870's, as each colony asserted itself at the expense of the others. The 1st conference called to discuss federation thus failed, 1880. But the pressures that would eventually bring about union were increasing. Gold was discovered at Kimberley and silver at Broken Hill, and the tide of immigrants continued to flow in. The resources of the colonial governments proved inadequate. Such events, moreover, as the completion of the railway joining Victoria and New South Wales, 1883, were concrete examples of the benefits to be derived from co-operation. To foster that co-operation the imperial government established a permanent body, the Federal Council, to meet every 2 years and decide intercolonial questions. A meeting of the Council in 1888 approved more stringent measures against Asian immigrants. These were subsequently adopted by the colonies, and boosted the growing prejudice in favor of a "White Australia."

ANNEXATION OF PAPUA. An early spur to federation was the realization that Australia was an isolated and militarily weak island in an age of German, French, and Japanese expansion in the Pacific. Australian public opinion therefore rallied behind the policy of preventative expansion espoused by Sir Thomas McIlwraith (1835–1900), premier of Queensland, who annexed Papua (southern New Guinea) in 1883. As had happened 10 years earlier, when the claims of Capt. John Moresby (1830–1922) to New Guinea were disavowed by the imperial government, London at first rejected McIlwraith's move, only agreeing to it,

1884, after the Germans had already occupied much of the northern coast.

1890–99

PRELIMINARIES TO FEDERATION. The failure of the great New Zealand–Australian maritime strike, 1890, convinced many trade union leaders that the road to reform lay along parliamentary channels. They tended, therefore, to support the federation of the Australian colonies. A severe financial crisis and depression, 1893, indicated the futility of tariff barriers between the colonies. This combined with a growing fear of Japanese imperialism (the "Yellow Peril") resulted in a Federal Convention held in Hobart, 1897–98. Delegates from all colonies attended and drew up a constitution, though they could agree on little other than the basic need for federation. There was to be a bicameral, directly elected parliament under the crown as represented by an appointed governor general. The 1st Federal Referendum to decide on the constitution showed that the necessary majorities in all colonies except New South Wales were willing to accept it, 1898. At a meeting of premiers, amendments to the constitution concerning surplus revenues and the powers of the Upper House were adopted, and the constitution was ratified by a 2nd Federal Referendum. Western Australia, 90% of whose revenues came from customs dues, was for this reason reluctant to turn power to levy customs over to a federal government as the constitution provided. However, a compromise was reached, and Western Australia joined in return for a federally financed railway and the right to levy her own customs dues for 5 years after the federation came into being.

1900–1914

COMMONWEALTH OF AUSTRALIA. 1 Jan., 1901. The Commonwealth of Australia began its existence under a government led by the protectionist, Sir Edmund Barton (1849–1920). Because voting strength in parliament was almost evenly divided among 3 rival factions, no party had a clear majority (until the 2nd Fisher government in 1910). This resulted in political instability, and there were 9 separate governments during 1901–14. The best organized of the parties, the Labour Party under J. C. Watson (1867–1941), was able to exert a pressure for reform greater than its size warranted.

SOCIAL LEGISLATION. Both the main programs of the Labour Party—social welfare and restriction of Chinese labor—had long traditions of acceptance in the individual colonies. In 1885 Victoria had set up a board to fix wages in "sweated" industries, extending its competence to other industries in 1896. South Australia enfranchised women, 1894, and other colonies followed suit (Western Australia, 1899; New South Wales, 1902). New South Wales set up conciliation and arbitration courts in 1901, copying those established in South Australia, 1894. From 1902 onward, women could vote in Commonwealth elections. A federal law of the same year limited Asian immigration, and from 1905 onward Anglo-Saxon immigration was actively encouraged. Old-age pensions, available in New South Wales from 1901, were established by federal law for all residents over 65 who had lived in Australia for at least 25 years.

In 1908 Canberra was chosen as the federal capital city. The selection of this site—within the territory of New South Wales—was part of the compromise that won that colony over to the idea of federation.

DEFENSE POLICY. The role of the new Australian Commonwealth in the British Empire was marked as much by co-operation as by self-assertion. Australia participated in the various Empire and Colonial Conferences—1887, 1899, 1902, 1907, 1909, 1911—accepted imperial preference, and supported the British naval squadron deployed in the Pacific. However, just as the danger to Australian security became greatest, British ships were withdrawn for service elsewhere. Thus in 1909 Australia set about con-

structing its own navy, and instituted compulsory military service along the lines laid down by Lord Kitchener's "Report on Australian Defences" of the same year. (*Cont. p. 477.*)

New Zealand

1870–89

ECONOMIC EXPANSION. The ambitious plans proposed by the colonial treasurer (Sir) Julius Vogel (1835–99), 1870, based on borrowing £10 m. in 10 years, helped New Zealand to lay the foundations for future economic expansion and prosperity. Extensive public-works projects, especially railway construction, were accompanied by new external trade arrangements, such as the establishment of a regular steamship service to and from San Francisco, 1870, and the founding of the New Zealand Shipping Co., 1873. In addition, new laws eased land sales, 1873, and attracted settlers. By 1875, however, it was evident that the scramble by individual provincial governments for large loans and for the profits to be derived from land speculation bred inefficiency and corruption, and was mainly responsible for the economy failing to respond satisfactorily to the influx of new capital.

UNIFICATION. The provincial governments were abolished, 1 Nov., 1876, and the central government began to replace divergent provincial schemes with others designed for the welfare of New Zealand as a whole. Railway routes were organized on a master plan to avoid duplication of services. Free, secular, and compulsory education was established, 1877. Trade unions received legal recognition, 1878. All male residents over 21 were enfranchised and, on the Australian model, Asian immigration was restricted in 1881 and again in 1899.

ECONOMIC DOWNTURN AND THE RISE OF LABOUR. The extended depression of the 1880's, due in part to overspeculation and the heavy borrowing of Vogel, was only somewhat relieved by the introduction of successful refrigeration vessels, 15 Feb., 1882, which in time enabled New Zealand's meat and dairy products to reach world markets. During the decade of the 1880's there was an almost "continuous ministry" of the Conservative Sir Harry Atkinson (1831–92), for no opposition offered coherent alternative policies. But the depression itself, with accompanying mass unemployment, encouraged the Labour Movement, which first asserted itself when it supported the passage of New Zealand's 1st protective tariff, 1888.

1890–1906

SOCIAL WELFARE. Labour, having turned from striking as a tool of reform after the failure of the maritime strike of 1890, joined the Liberal Party to bring in a coalition government under John Ballance (1839–93). The election of 1890 was the 1st held under a system of universal manhood suffrage. Combining Labour and Liberal social-welfare programs, Ballance placed graduated taxes on income and on the unearned increment from land, 1891, and had the 1st of 3 sets of Factory Acts, 1891, 1894, 1901, passed to protect the workers.

Richard John Seddon ("King Dick," 1845–1906), who became premier on the death of Ballance in 1893, continued his program by extending the vote to women, 1893. By 2 acts in 1894 the Bank of New Zealand, which had been on the point of collapse, was virtually taken over by the state. In the same session was passed the Industrial Conciliation and Arbitration Act, under which all future industrial disputes were to be settled without immediate recourse to striking. This was followed by a law enabling the central government to buy large estates at a reasonable price and to divide them for resale. The Shops and Shop Assistants Act, 1894, imposed a compulsory early closing time, while the Family Housing Protection Act of the same year set out to secure additional housing and to protect homeowners from forced sale for debt. Further acts included the abolition of a property qualification for voting in national elections, 1896; the establishment

by law of an 8-hour day, 1898; and the introduction of old-age pensions, 1898. These various measures combined with the Government Accident Insurance Office, 1899, and State Fire Insurance, 1903, to form one of the world's most comprehensive social-welfare systems.

1907–14

DOMINION STATUS. New Zealand was granted the status of a dominion in the British Empire, 1907, partly because of her many manifestations of loyalty, including the dispatching of troops to the South African War, 1899; participation in imperial preference, 1903; and support for the British naval squadron in the Pacific. Universal military training was introduced in 1911.

REFORM PARTY. When the Liberal-Labour coalition disintegrated after the death of Seddon, 1906, the Conservative Party was revived as the "Reform Party." Labour set up its own separate representative organizations, the Federation of Labour, 1907, and the Labour Party, 1909.

William Ferguson Massey (1856–1925), who created the Reform Party from old-guard Conservatives and dissatisfied farmers, became prime minister, 1912, and implemented his principal program of turning all crown leases into freeholds. His 1st major problem was with the trade unions, which abandoned the Arbitration Act of 1894 in a series of strikes, 1912–13, in the gold mines and on the docks of Auckland and Wellington. This action culminated in an unsuccessful attempt at a general strike organized by the newly formed United Federation of Labour, 1913. (*Cont. p. 478.*)

The Union of South Africa

1870–94

GRIQUALAND WEST. When the Keate Award, 1871, gave the newly discovered diamond-rich area around Kimberley to the Griqua leader, Nikolaas Waterboer, the territory was taken over by Britain, under pressure from Cape Colony and

London business interests, as the province of Griqualand West. It was made a crown colony in 1873.

SEPARATISM VS. UNION. Basutoland was annexed to Cape Colony in 1871. The Colony, on being granted responsible government, chose (Sir) John Molteno (1814–86) as its first prime minister, 1872. Molteno put all telegraph lines and railways under government control, 1873–74; and adopted a policy opposed to the unification of British territories in South Africa. He and his colleagues rejected the plans for closer union put forward, 1875, by Lord Carnarvon, the British colonial secretary, and symbolized by the appointment of the pro-union Sir Henry Bartle Frere (1815–84) as governor and high commissioner at the Cape, 1876.

SOUTH AFRICAN REPUBLIC. As a further step toward unification, Sir Theophilus Shepstone (1817–93), with official approval, annexed the Transvaal, 1877. This and other early British moves toward union underestimated the extent of separatism and divisive racial policies in South African society. The discovery of many new gold and diamond deposits during the last quarter of the 19th cent. brought in a steady stream of European settlers and adventurers who, in a series of minor wars, clashed with Africans fearful of losing their land. Boer-British antagonisms grew. Taking advantage of British preoccupation with the Basuto "War of the Guns" and restlessness in Zululand, the Boers in the Transvaal rebelled against the British, won a brief war against them, and set up the South African Republic. By the Convention of Pretoria, 3 Aug., 1881, the Transvaal (South African Republic) was given complete self-government subject to the "suzerainty" of the British Crown.

GERMAN SOUTH-WEST AFRICA. German trading interests headed by F. A. E. Lüderitz (1834–86) acquired land at Angra Pequena, 1883, a territory on the southwest coast vaguely under British control. In 1884 the German imperial government announced that it would protect this area, and in 1892 took it over officially. The injection of a colonial

Germany into South African affairs caused renewed imperial activity by Britain: Basutoland was separated from Cape Colony, 1884, and made subject to the British home government, as also was Bechuanaland, 1885. Zululand was annexed in 1887.

RULE OF KRUGER IN THE TRANSVAAL. Following a convention signed in London, 27 Feb., 1884, Paul Kruger (1825–1904), president of the Transvaal, was granted a freer hand in negotiating with the African tribes, and the powers of the British resident appointed to the Transvaal were greatly reduced while all mention of British "suzerainty" was dropped. In return, all European settlers were to have their civil rights protected, and there were to be no discriminatory tax levies at the expense of *uitlanders* (non-Boer residents). British goods, moreover, were no longer to be at a disadvantage in the Transvaal's markets because of extra tariffs or special taxes.

In 1889 a customs union was set up between Cape Colony and the Orange Free State, and the frontiers of German South-West Africa were defined, 1890.

BRITISH SOUTH AFRICA CO. Cecil John Rhodes (1853–1902), important in Cape affairs since helping to found the De Beers Diamond Co., 1880, an avowed imperialist, and head, from its foundation in 1889, of the British South Africa Co., became political leader of the Cape Colony, 1890. The function of the B.S.A. Co., as Rhodes saw it, was to explore and settle the area north of Cape Colony, thus containing the Transvaal and hindering its expansion.

1895–1902

JAMESON RAID. 29 Dec., 1895–2 Jan., 1896. President Kruger closed to British and Cape traders the overland routes through the Transvaal. Anti-Boer elements in Cape Colony, led by Dr. Leander Jameson (1853–1917), then staged a raid on Johannesburg which was quickly repulsed. The emperor of Germany, moreover, congratulated Kruger by telegram, 3 Jan., 1896, for repelling the invasion. Kruger continued a program of discrimination against the *uitlanders*. On 26 Sept., 1896, the Alien Expulsion Act was passed, and on 26 Nov. the Immigration Restriction Act. Restrictions on the freedom of the press and on the right of assembly were strengthened. On 17 Mar., 1897, Transvaal and the Orange Free State renewed their 1889 defensive alliance.

SOUTH AFRICAN WAR. The *uitlanders* addressed a petition of grievances to Queen Victoria, 24 Mar., 1899. Between 31 May and 5 June, Kruger and the governor of the Cape, Sir Alfred Milner (1854–1925) held a series of discussions at Bloemfontein. When these failed, the Boers presented an ultimatum to the British government. This ultimatum was rejected, and war began, 11 Oct., 1899, between Britain and the Transvaal and Orange Free State. Although some 448,000 troops from all over the empire were used against 87,000 Boers before the war was over, in 1899 there were only 25,000 British troops in South Africa. This initial numerical advantage, coupled with other factors like familiarity with the terrain and interior lines of supply and movement, gave the Boers an edge at the start. Thus the Boer Gen. Petrus Joubert (1834–1900) won easy victories at Laing's Nek, 12 Oct., and Nicholson's Nek, 30 Oct., and by 2 Nov. was besieging Ladysmith. The appointment early in 1900 of new British generals (Roberts and Kitchener) and the employment of larger forces enabled the British gradually to turn the tide.

TREATY OF VEREENIGING. 31 May, 1902. In return for Boer acceptance of British sovereignty, the Transvaal and the Orange Free State accepted the status of crown colonies, received a rehabilitation grant of £3 m., and were promised representative institutions as soon as practicable. Responsible government was granted to the Transvaal in 1906 and to the Orange River Colony in 1907.

1903–14

INTERCOLONIAL CUSTOMS CONFERENCE. All tariff barriers were abolished, 1903, between Cape Colony, Natal, the Orange Free State, the Transvaal, Southern Rhodesia, and the High Commission Territories. It was also decided that in future intercolonial conferences of this type should handle relationships with the indigenous Africans.

ESTABLISHMENT OF THE UNION. 31 May, 1910. A national convention met at Durban, 12 Oct.–15 Nov., 1908, Cape Town, 22 Nov.–18 Dec., 1908 and 11 Jan.–3 Feb., 1909, and Bloemfontein, 3–11 May, 1909, to draw up a constitution for a union of the South African territories. The constitution provided for 2 houses: the Lower, with 150 members popularly elected, and the Upper, chosen by provincial councils voting alongside their members in the Lower House. Enabling legislation, the South Africa Act, was passed by the imperial government and in May 1910 the Union of South Africa came into existence, with Louis Botha (1862–1919) as its 1st prime minister.

IMMIGRATION, LAND, AND LABOR. The Immigration Act, 1913, limited the influx of Asians, and by the Native Land Act, 1913, both Europeans and Bantu were forbidden to buy land in each other's areas. At this period the trade unions were beginning to organize and to assert themselves. In an effort to win recognition, benefits, and concessions, they declared a series of strikes, 1913, in the gold mines and on the railways. (*Cont. p. 474.*)

The British West Indies
1870–89

DECLINE OF SUGAR INDUSTRY. When the British Empire abolished slavery and adopted free trade, the traditional staple crop of the British West Indies, sugar, began to be uneconomic. Profits on sugar had been dependent on a fertile soil, cheap labor, and a protected market. Years of inefficient farming had exhausted the soil. Attempts were made to diversify the economy of the islands, and by 1870 bananas had become Jamaica's chief export.

CROWN COLONY GOVERNMENT. In 1871 the ruling oligarchy of British Honduras, rather than see former slaves enfranchised, requested crown colony status, thus surrendering a 100-year-old tradition of limited, but free, democracy. Most of the other colonies had made, or would make, the same request: Grenada, St. Vincent and Tobago, 1876, and Antigua, 1898, until by 1914 only Barbados, Bermuda, and the Bahamas retained democratic institutions.

In preparation for an eventual closer political union of the British West Indies, British Honduras was detached from Jamaica, 1884, and Barbados from the Windward Islands, 1885, while Tobago was united to Trinidad, 1889. Except in the latter case, where economic hardship dictated union, all attempts at federation were thwarted by vested interests in each colony.

In 1891 a measure of democracy was introduced in British Guiana. The franchise was very limited, but this was the 1st such experiment in the colony's history.

1890–1914

EDUCATION POLICY. The census of 1890 revealed that half the West Indian population was under 5 years of age. In Jamaica a Board of Education was established, 1893, and fees in the elementary school system were abolished. A "house tax" was imposed to finance the schools.

SOCIAL-WELFARE POLICIES. The social-welfare program, mainly associated with the Liberal colonial secretary, Joseph Chamberlain, was based on the recommendations of the Royal Commission of 1896–97. The commission had called for improved transportation facilities, better rural credit, the division of large estates into small farms, and systematic agricultural education. Accordingly, a scheme was adopted in Jamaica whereby crown lands were sold to settlers, 1896. An agricultural research center was established, and a system of tariff reductions under imperial preference applied to aid the sugar industry, 1897.

In 1902, £250 m. was granted by the imperial government to West Indian sugar interests in an effort to counter temporarily the effects of a new U.S. tariff

wall and of competition from government-subsidized beet sugar industries being developed in Europe.

JAMAICAN EARTHQUAKE. In 1907 Jamaica was struck by an earthquake which damaged every building in Kingston and killed over 800 people. (*Cont. p. 473.*)

INDIA AND CEYLON

1870–84

ARYA SAMAJ. Dayananda Sarasvati (1824–83) founded the first Arya Samaj in Bombay, 10 Apr., 1875. Popular among Hindus in Oudh, the Punjab, and Northwest Frontier Provinces, where many Moslems (Muslims) and Sikhs lived, the Samaj taught that pure Hinduism was derived from the Vedas, that Hinduism was superior to all other religions, and that lapsed Hindus should be reconverted. Moslems felt threatened by the organization, the tone of whose doctrines enabled it to be used by Hindu extremist politicians in the early 20th cent. under the inspiration of Lajput Rai (1865–1928).

MOSLEM EDUCATIONAL FOUNDATIONS. Sir Syed Ahmed Khan, a Moslem modernizer convinced that Moslems could overcome their economic and political disabilities only by gaining a western education and abstaining from active politics, opened a school at Aligarh for Moslems, 24 May, 1875. To appease the ulema ('ulamā, Moslem scholars), who opposed western studies, the school included religious education in its curriculum. On 8 Jan., 1877, Lord Lytton (viceroy, 1876–80) laid the foundation stone of the Mohammedan Anglo-Oriental College, later to be raised to the status of a university.

BUDDHIST THEOSOPHICAL SOCIETY. Founded in Ceylon by H. S. Olcott, the Buddhist Theosophical Society ineffectively challenged during the 1870's the Christian missionaries who were taking over the educational functions of the bhikkus (Buddhist monks).

INDIAN ASSOCIATION. Influenced by Mazzini, Surrendranath Bannerjee, a former civil servant, founded the Indian Association at Calcutta, 26 July, 1876. The Association was an overtly political organization for western-educated Bengalis. It protested, among other matters, the 1876 regulation lowering the maximum entrance age into the I.C.S. (Indian Civil Service) from 21 to 19.

INDIAN EMPIRE. Queen Victoria assumed the title of empress of India, 1 Jan., 1877. This signified the paramountcy of British power in India, including the princely states.

VERNACULAR PRESS ACT. 14 Mar., 1878. The Viceroy's Executive Council passed a Vernacular Press Act subjecting vernacular newspapers to confiscation if they printed material considered seditious. The Indian Association protested against this act, and also against the Arms Act of Apr. 1878, which imposed a heavy import duty on arms and required universal licensing of guns, but exempted Englishmen from compliance. On 10 Jan., 1882, on the initiative of Lord Ripon (viceroy, 1880–84) the Legislative Council repealed the Vernacular Press Act. The act had never been invoked to close down a newspaper.

ILBERT BILL. Sir Courtney Ilbert introduced in the Legislative Council, 2 Feb., 1883, a bill to remove discrimination against certain Indian judges in the districts by enabling them to try Englishmen as well as Indians. The viceroy, Lord Ripon, strongly supported the bill, but agitation against it by British plantation owners and judges resulted in a compromise bill, which provided that a European on trial in any court could have a jury, half of whose members must be European. The new bill was enacted, 25 Jan., 1884. The Ilbert Bill controversy led to the worst racial antagonism since the Mutiny.

1885–98

NATIONAL CONFERENCE. The 1st session of the National Conference was held at Calcutta, 28–30 Dec., 1883. Called by the Indian Association, the conference was intended to be an India-wide political organization. Its 2nd, and final, session was held at Calcutta, 25–27 Dec.,

1885. Delegates from northern India were attracted to the meeting.

INDIAN NATIONAL CONGRESS. The 1st session of the I.N.C. (Indian National Congress) was held at Bombay, 28 Dec., 1885. Largely inspired and organized by Alan Octavian Hume (1829–1912), a retired I.C.S. officer who feared revolution if responsible Indians did not have a forum in which to vent their grievances against the government, the I.N.C. began as a small group of western-educated persons of the middle class interested in administrative and constitutional adjustments. In 1886 the Congress demanded the expansion and strengthening of the legislative councils and the election of at least half their members. Its membership gradually increased, and it began to meet annually at different cities.

After the founding of the I.N.C., Moslem fears of Hindu domination, as well as Hindu revolutionary exasperation with the servility and gradualness of meliorists and reformers, led to an intensification of communalism and to severe strains within the Congress itself. Unable to satisfy any party, the Indian government's attitude approximated the reformist position.

UNITED INDIAN PATRIOTIC ASSOCIATION. Syed Ahmed Khan, who declared at Lucknow, 28 Dec., 1887, that Moslems and Hindus were 2 different nations and that representative institutions would only result in the subjugation of Moslems to Hindus, founded the United Indian Patriotic Association in Aug. 1888. The establishment of the U.I.P.A. emphasized that the I.N.C. did not represent the views of all Indians.

AGE OF CONSENT BILL. Influenced by Behranji Merwanji Malabai, a Gujarati Parsi, and some Hindu reformers, a bill was introduced in the Legislative Council, Jan. 1891, to raise the minimum age of marriage from 10 to 12 years. Bitter controversy ensued, especially in Maharashtra, where the Chitpavan Brahmin, Bal Gangadhar Tilak (1856–1920), newspaper editor and teacher, attacked the bill on the grounds that foreign rule should not interfere with the Hindu social structure and that the measure was unnecessary. Although the bill passed, 19 Mar., Tilak's revolutionary nationalism, couched in terms of adherence to traditional Hindu social norms, was to continue.

INDIA COUNCILS ACT. 26 May, 1892. Enacted by the imperial parliament, the India Councils Act enlarged the central and provincial legislative councils and enhanced their powers by allowing members to put questions and discuss financial matters. Although not recognizing the principle of election, the act did permit municipal corporations and certain associations to nominate members of council, thus granting the principle of representation of particular interests. The I.N.C. criticized the act for not granting elections.

TEMPERANCE CAMPAIGN IN CEYLON. During the 1880's and 1890's Buddhist nationalists reacted against a British policy of selling liquor licenses by conducting a fervent temperance campaign. Both the Buddhist Theosophical Society and the temperance movement evidenced the frustration felt by the bhikkhus because of their declining importance in political and social life.

GANAPATI FESTIVAL. Following communal riots in Maharashtra, Tilak and Annasabib, an orthodox Brahmin, organized in Poona, Sept. 1893, the 1st annual public Ganapati festival, an event which gave Hindus a popular deity to venerate at a time when otherwise they might have joined Moslems in the Mohurram festival. During a similar festival at Poona in 1894, a communal riot erupted when a mela (religious gathering), disobeying the law, played music outside a mosque.

NATIONAL SOCIAL CONFERENCE. A split in the I.N.C. between reformists and Maharashtrian revolutionaries was avoided, Dec. 1895, when Gopal Krishna Gokhale, a Chitpavan Brahmin, and M. G. Ranade gave in to Tilak's insistence that the National Social Conference (founded by Ranada, 1887), a social-reformist organization, be prohibited from using the I.N.C. tent after a meeting at Poona.

SHIVAJI FESTIVAL. Tilak's inauguration, 15 Mar., 1895, of the Shivaji festival in Raigarh and Poona, honoring the Maratha soldier who killed Aurangzeb's general, Afzul Khan, in 1659 and became the 1st Maratha king, heightened the mass revolutionary character of the Maharashtrian nationalist movement.

CONVICTION OF TILAK. The Bombay High Court tried and convicted Tilak, 8–14 Sept., 1897, for seditious editorial writing in his paper, *Kesari,* the previous 15 June. Tilak's sentence of 18 months, later reduced to 12, led even moderates to protest the injustice of the sentence.

1899–1914

VICEROYALTY OF LORD CURZON. Lord Curzon (viceroy, 1899–1905) took office on 6 Jan., 1899. He instituted a policy of administrative efficiency, creating, 1901, the Northwest Frontier Province and reducing the area of the Punjab. During Curzon's viceroyalty, the incongruity of British policy and Hindu nationalist expectations and demands contributed to the inability of I.N.C. moderates to mollify the extremists. Moslem separatist aspirations aggravated already strained communal relations.

PROPOSED PARTITION OF BENGAL. Curzon announced, 7 Dec., 1903, that, to improve administrative efficiency, Bengal would be divided: Chittagong, Dacca, Mymensingh, and the Tippera Hills would be transferred to Assam, and Chota Nagpur to the Central Provinces, with some parts of the Central Provinces and Madras going to Bengal. The proposed arrangements would have reduced the population of Bengal from 78.5 m. to 67.5 m., and the new province of East Bengal and Assam would have had a Moslem majority. On 19 July, 1905, Curzon, with the reluctant approval of the India Office, published the official decision to divide Bengal. Surrendranath Bannerjee led a mass meeting at Calcutta, 7 Aug., which resolved to boycott British goods. Antipartition activity also included the Swadeshi movement, designed to promote indigenous production of cloth and other goods and a national education program. On 16 Nov., 1905, Bengali nationalists established the National Council of Education, which sponsored the Bengal National College, 1 June,

1906. Nationalist agitation led to communal riots. Antipartition activity was not confined to Bengal; Tilak promoted the Swadeshi movement in Maharashtra.

MOSLEM POLITICAL DEMANDS. Led by the Aga Khan and Nawab Moshin-ul-Mulk, 35 Moslems presented, 1 Oct., 1906, to Lord Minto (viceroy, 1905–10) at Simla a set of political demands, including separate Moslem electorates for the municipalities and legislative councils. Minto gave a sympathetic reply.

ALL-INDIA MOSLEM LEAGUE. Responding to the proposal of Nawab Salimullah Khan of Dacca that Moslems form an overtly political organization, Moslem leaders met at Dacca and established the All-India Moslem League, 30 Dec., 1906. The League's constitution, drafted in 1907, proclaimed as its goals the promoting of constitutional and administrative changes favorable to the Moslem community and encouraging Moslem loyalty to British rule.

DEPORTATION OF NATIONALIST LEADERS. Peasant unrest in the Punjab due to dissatisfaction with the Punjab Colonization Bill, which permitted land inheritance by the soldier pensioners in Chenab Colony only by primogeniture, led to the arrest and deportation, 9 May, 1907, of Lajput Rai, who had spoken in opposition to the bill, on charges of sedition. On 3 June, Ajit Singh, another agitator, was similarly deported. The viceroy disallowed the bill, May, and released the deportees, 18 Nov.

I.N.C. SPLIT. When, in Dec. 1906, the extremists failed to elect their candidate president, and when, as president, Dadabhai Naoroji proclaimed India's birthright to be *swaraj* (self-rule), the I.N.C. was held together only by its capacity to live with the moderates' and extremists' divergent interpretations of its goals, and also by an ability to tolerate differing interpretations of the resolution upholding the legitimacy of the Swadeshi movement in Bengal. On 26 Dec., 1907, at Surat the extremists, frustrated by the moderates in an attempt to nominate Lajput Rai as president, fearful that the moderates would soften the 1906 resolution on the Swadeshi movement, and enraged by the refusal of the chairman of the Reception Committee, N. Malvi, to recognize Tilak for the floor, bolted the meeting. Not until 1916 was the I.N.C. reunited.

INDIA COUNCILS ACT. 25 May, 1909. The India Councils Act of 1909 (Morley-Minto Reforms) (1) increased the number of elected and nominated members of the central and provincial legislative councils (with a majority of nonofficials in the provincial councils); (2) enhanced the powers of these councils by permitting elected members to table resolutions and ask supplementary questions; and (3) extended the number of interest groups represented in the councils. Although the announcement, 1 Nov., 1908, of impending reforms was welcomed by I.N.C. moderates, the regulations, which included the retention by the viceroy of power to disqualify any person from membership in any council, were attacked at the 1909 I.N.C. meeting at Lahore.

McCALLUM-CREWE REFORMS. In Ceylon several small reform societies organized by western-educated Ceylonese pressed demands for constitutional reform, 1910, including power for Ceylonese in the Executive Council and elections to the Legislative Council. Sir Henry McCallum (gov., 1907–13) rejected most of these demands mainly on the ground that they came from atypical Ceylonese who, in contrast to himself who could rely on the reports of the government agents, had no contact with the masses. Nevertheless, the McCallum-Crewe Reforms introduced the principle of election to the Legislative Council by giving Ceylonese who had a yearly income of Rs. 1,500 and who could pass the Senior or Junior Cambridge Examination or a comparable examination the right to elect 1 member to the Legislative Council. The burgher member was to be elected by burghers, and one European urban member and one European rural member were to be elected by their constituencies. There were to be 10 nonofficial members (6 nominated to represent communal groups as well as the 4 elected members) and 11 official members.

DELHI DURBAR. Dec. 1911. At a durbar in Delhi, attended by the new King-Emperor George V and Queen Mary, the emperor announced (1) the repeal of the partition of Bengal, which had the effect of reuniting the 2 Bengals, reducing the status of Assam to a chief-commissionership, and creating a new province, Bihar and Orissa; (2) the raising of the status of Bengal to that of a governorship; and (3) the transfer of the capital of British India from Calcutta to Delhi. (*Cont. p. 455.*)

FRENCH NORTH AFRICA

1870-99

REVOLT IN THE KABYLIAS. As a result of a reduction in strength of French garrisons during the Franco-Prussian War and of a reaction against land expropriation and Jewish naturalization (by the Crémieux Decrees, 1870), the Moqrani family and the Rahmaniyya Order led a revolt in the Kabylias (Algeria) in 1871. Adm. Louis Henri de Gueydon (1809-86), the French commander, needed 80,000 soldiers to suppress the revolt. The Kabylians had to pay indemnities, abandon 500,000 more hectares of land, and, in some cases, suffer criminal penalties.

GROWTH OF CIVILIAN POWER IN ALGERIA. The civilian population of the Algiers area expelled the military in 1870 and temporarily established the revolutionary government of the "commune" of Algiers. Although a military regime returned the following year, the authority of the governor general was reduced, civilian territory steadily grew in extent, and "mixed communes" began to replace the Arab bureaus. The influence of Archbishop (later Cardinal) Lavigerie (1825-92), who had arrived in Algeria in 1867 and founded the White Fathers order soon afterward, was significant in these changes.

DEBT QUESTION IN TUNISIA. The Husaynid (Ḥusaynid) beys, nominally pashas of the Ottoman sultan, progressively lost their autonomy to Europeans during the later 19th cent.

Under Mohammed as-Sadiq (Muḥammad as-Sadīq) (ruled 1859-82), haphazard efforts at modernization by the Turkish elite continued, and the tax burden on the peasants grew heavier. The expanding power of Prime Minister Mustafa Khaznadar (1837-73) meant increasing corruption and indebtedness to European interests, and helped bring about the creation, 1869, of a Financial Commission for the Tunisian Debt composed of French, Italians, Maltese, and Tunisians. Efforts to reform and to renew ties with Constantinople by Prime Minister Khayr ad-Din (ad-Dīn), 1873-77, failed, mainly because of sharpening rivalry between France and Italy in Tunisia as represented by their respective consuls, Roustan and Maccio. In 1878 the Financial Commission collapsed, and France obtained British and German acquiescence in the event she decided to declare a protectorate; Italian power was unable to check the ambitions of the dominant French.

RULE OF SULTAN HASSAN OF MOROCCO. In spite of his reputation in Europe as an admirable ruler, Sultan Mawlay Hassan (ruled 1873-94) was not able to arrest the decline of the Moroccan economy and independence. Plagued by inadequate finances and a weak army, he exerted little sustained control over the mountainous and southern portions of his kingdom, and could not protest the Madrid Convention, 1880, by which European states joined Britain and France in receiving rights to most-favored-nation treatment and a guarantee of protection for their nationals in Morocco.

ESTABLISHMENT OF THE TUNISIAN PROTECTORATE. An incursion into Algeria by mountain brigands provided the pretext for French occupation of Tunisia in 1881. There was no resistance, and the Treaty of Kassar Said (Le Bardo), signed in May, temporarily authorized the French resident minister to handle external affairs and assist the bey in financial matters. After an uprising in the center and south under Ali ben Khalifa ('Alī ibn Khalīfa), France signed the La Marsa Convention, 1883, which committed the bey to administrative, judicial, and financial reforms suggested by the French government; this declaration contained no time limit.

FRENCH RULE IN TUNISIA. As minister of foreign affairs, president of the bey's council, and commander of virtually all military forces in the country, the French resident general became the real ruler of Tunisia. The beylical family received a subsidy and continued to hold office until 1957. French civil controllers oversaw the existing Tunisian provincial administrations, while French technicians and teachers immigrated in increasing numbers to man the developing modern sectors of the economy and society. The traditional sectors declined in importance. In 1883–84 France guaranteed the Tunisian debt and abolished the Financial Commission, and the European powers renounced their consular jurisdictions. In 1891 France replaced the piaster with the franc, and instituted, 1892, compulsory military service in a Tunisian army, a tradition resulting in significant Tunisian participation (involving the death of 10,000 troops) in World War I. The customs privileges of the European powers were revoked, 1896–97, but Italy continued to possess some special rights and was able to exert great influence because of large-scale Italian immigration into Tunisia. The Italian press, banks, schools, and private organizations were powerful.

FRENCH EXPANSION IN THE SAHARA. French interest in a trans-Saharan railway linking her North and West African possessions rose sharply in the late 1870's, but declined again after the massacre of the Flatters exploratory mission, 1881, by Tuareg and Chamba Arab tribesmen. Also in 1881 a fraction of the Awlad (Awlād) Sidi Shaykh revolted in the northwestern Sahara under Bou Amama (Bu ʿAmāma), but were suppressed by a large French force the following year. Later in the decade France successfully discouraged Moroccan claims to the Tawat (Tawāt) oases, but limited her own expansion to the capture of El-Goléa, 1891. In 1899 the French took In-Salah, a commercial center on the edge of

Tawat. The military expedition led by Foureau and Lamy, 1898–1900, crossed the Sahara via the Hoggar (Ahaggar) to join in a convergence of French columns around Lake Chad. The Hoggar Tuareg officially submitted to French control, 1905. During 1906 the completion of the railway from Oran to Colomb Bechar in the northwestern Sahara provided 1 base for eventual French rule in Morocco.

1900–1914

ECONOMIC DEVELOPMENT OF ALGERIA. In 1900 the departmental structure in Algeria was abolished and the territory received full administrative and financial autonomy. The governor general's powers were increased and the *délégations financières,* a group representing various Euro-Algerian economic interests, obtained the authority to decide on budgets. Under the impetus of this autonomy and through the application of new techniques, the production of grapes and wine, citrus fruits, and other agricultural commodities increased markedly, and the European and especially the indigenous population grew at a rapid rate.

GROWTH OF FRENCH INFLUENCE IN MOROCCO. During the dictatorial regency of Vizir Ba Ahmad ben Musa, 1894–1900, and the efficient reign of Mawlay Abd al-Aziz (ʿAbd al-ʿAziz), 1900–1909, customs revenues from European trade probably constituted more than half the government revenue of Morocco. The influence of France grew relative to that of the other European powers. At the turn of the century France was consolidating her position in the western Algerian Sahara and regulating her border disputes with Morocco. By 1905 Italy and Britain had acquiesced in French preponderance in the sultanate, and Spain had agreed to a parallel hegemony for herself in the northern zone. France increasingly determined the general conduct, customs policy, and budget of the Moroccan state.

By contrast the domain of the Sultan and his makhzan (administration) was shrinking, and revolts were increasing in frequency and seriousness. Bou Amama, Raisuli, Ma al-Ainin (Aīnin) and his son al-Hiba (Hība), and others were all active in attacking the sultanate or the Europeans from bases in the mountains or the south.

RISE OF TUNISIAN NATIONALISM. A demand for reform, 1906, by a group of "Young Tunisians" developed by 1908 into a movement for a constitution. In the tense atmosphere resulting from the Italian occupation of Tripolitania in 1911, anti-European sentiment increased, and erupted into protests and riots in and around Tunis, 1911–12. This proto-nationalist activity was confined to the capital and subsided during World War I.

GERMAN INTERVENTION IN MOROCCO. In order to embarrass France and win economic advantages, Germany challenged French preponderance in Morocco on 3 occasions between 1905 and 1912. In 1905–6 she disputed the 1904 agreements substantiating French hegemony, but obtained only an ineffectual statement (Algeciras, 1906) on the internationalization of Morocco. During 1906–8 French troops intervened to quell disturbances at Oujda and Casablanca. Reaction against this helped Mawlay Hafid, whose sympathies were pro-German, to emerge as the new sultan, 1908–9. The stage was now set for the 2nd crisis, 1909, when Germans encouraged French Legionnaires in Casablanca to desert. The resulting controversy was settled in favor of France by the International Court at The Hague. Soon, however, revolts spread throughout the country, and Mawlay Hafid had to request the assistance of French troops against the threat of a rival sultan. The last Franco-German controversy over Morocco followed the arrival, 1911, of the gunboat *Panther* in Agadir Harbor. After an argument, an accord cleared the air, and the 1912 convention establishing a French protectorate over Morocco became possible. Gen. Louis Lyautey (1854–1934) and the new sultan, Mawlay Yusuf (Yūsuf) (ruled 1912–27), then instituted a system of indirect rule and began a slow "repacification."

SPANISH MOROCCO. After the massacre of some Spanish miners near Melilla, 1910, Spain conquered Larache and Alcazarquivir (al-Ksar al-Kabīr). The following year she signed a convention with France creating Spanish Morocco, selecting a khalifa (khalīfa) (lieutenant) nominally responsible to the sultan, and projecting the construction of a jointly controlled railway from Tangiers to Fez. (*Cont. p. 469.*)

THE PARTITION AND COLONIZATION OF TROPICAL AFRICA

TROPICAL AFRICA IN 1870. Alien rule in tropical Africa in the 1870's was generally restricted to a very few coastal enclaves. The French were an exception in that they had penetrated into the interior behind Senegal, and Pierre Savorgnan de Brazza (1852–1905) was in the process of securing treaties on their behalf with chiefs in the River Ogooué region. Elsewhere, the French occupied coastal trading posts along the Ivory Coast and Dahomey, and had a settlement at Gabon. The Portuguese had tried unsuccessfully to extend their trading activities into the interior of Mozambique and Angola. They also controlled the islands of São Tomé and Fernando Po in the Bight of Biafra and had some influence in Portuguese Guinea, south of Senegambia. Britain had de facto control over the Sultanate of Zanzibar, but had no plans for any official assumption of sovereignty in East Africa. The British West African colonies of Lagos, Sierra Leone, and the Gambia were surrounded by viable African states. On the Gold Coast, however, British administration extended over large numbers of coastal peoples.

The Congo

1870–85

INTERNATIONAL AFRICAN ASSOCIATION. At a meeting in Brussels, Sept. 1876, King Leopold II of the Belgians (1835–1909) took the 1st step toward making himself the personal ruler of the Congo. The delegates he persuaded to come to the Brussels meeting were not government representatives but distinguished Europeans and Americans from many fields. They agreed to establish an International African Association. At its 1877 meeting the Association declared its goals to be the suppression of the slave trade and the gathering of scientific information.

STANLEY EXPEDITION. Henry Morton Stanley (1841–1904), who had traced the Congo from the Lualaba to the Atlantic, 1874–77, was recruited by a special committee of the Association to "open up" the region, Aug. 1879. He stayed and worked almost continuously in the Congo until 1884, building roads, establishing settlements, and making treaties with local chiefs.

DE BRAZZA EXPEDITION. From 1879 de Brazza, who had explored the Ogooué, 1875–78, became an official French agent. He reached the north bank of the Congo, 1880, and obtained numerous treaties, 1880–82. The French government endorsed his work and financially supported it. The result was French control of the north bank of the Congo, while Stanley's activities gave Leopold's Association control of the south bank.

ANGLO-PORTUGUESE TREATY. Becoming alarmed at the activities of Stanley and de Brazza, the Portuguese pressed their claims northward from Angola to the Congo mouth. Negotiations with Britain began, Nov. 1882, and the 2 countries signed a treaty, Feb. 1884. An Anglo-Portuguese Commission was to guarantee freedom of navigation on the Congo to all nations, and Britain was to recognize Portuguese claims as far as the Congo estuary and also a Portuguese right to the enclave of Cabinda to the north. The treaty was roundly condemned both in Britain and on the Continent, and was shelved when Portugal failed to convene an international conference on the issue.

BERLIN WEST AFRICA CONFERENCE. 15 nations attended a conference summoned by Bismarck to Berlin, Nov. 1884–Feb. 1885. The Congo basin was declared a free-trade area, all rivers in the region were to be open to all, and international action was to free the area from the slave trade. Throughout the continent, notice was to be given of new annexations, and occupation, to be valid, must be effective.

INDEPENDENT STATE OF THE CONGO. The Berlin Conference recognized the possessions of the International African Association as the Independent State of the Congo and guaranteed the new state's neutrality. King Leopold became its sovereign, Apr. 1885. Initially the activities of Leopold's agents were confined to the lower Congo, where a railway from the coast to Léopoldville was begun, while the eastern Congo was left in the hands of Arab-Swahili slavers from Zanzibar.

1886–1914

COMPETITION FOR KATANGA. The Katanga region of the interior, even then famed for its rich mineral deposits, was ruled by Msiri, who directed a commercial empire whose influence extended from the Indian to the Atlantic Ocean. The activities of missionaries at Msiri's capital inspired fears on Leopold's part that another European power might be about to secure the region. His apprehensions were justified, since representatives of the British South Africa Co. were making determined efforts to persuade Msiri to sign away his sovereignty. The company's diplomacy failed, however, 1890, and the Belgians were on the scene in 1891, offering protection to Msiri. The chief refused and, when civil war broke out in Katanga, suspected the Belgians of intending to join an alliance against him. He therefore attempted to open negotiations with Rhodes's agent once again, but his letter was intercepted by W. G. Stairs, an agent of Leopold. Stairs arranged to have Msiri killed, and Katanga became part of the Congo Independent State. By 1894 Belgian military operations had driven the slavers from the eastern Congo, though fighting and rebellions continued to c. 1900, after which Leopold's control over the region became firm.

CONGO ATROCITIES. King Leopold's commercial enterprises required African labor, and the conditions under which Africans were forced to live and work in the Congo were seen to be no better than the slavery against which the International African Association originally campaigned. European and American humanitarians became concerned over reports of atrocities in the 1890's, and a report by Roger Casement (1864–1916), the British consul, forced Leopold to take action in 1904. A commission investigated and reported, but outrages continued.

ESTABLISHMENT OF THE BELGIAN CONGO. International pressure overcame Belgian opposition to an assumption by the Belgian home government of responsibility for the Congo Independent State. Leopold surrendered control of the Congo to the Belgian parliament, 18 Oct., 1908, and died the following year.

RAILWAY TO KATANGA. Belgian administration in the Congo continued to concern itself more with the exploitation of the country's resources than with the improvement of the human condition. Foreign firms and concessionnaires benefited from improvements in transport, and the completion of the railway to Elisabethville, 1910, permitted an ever-increas-

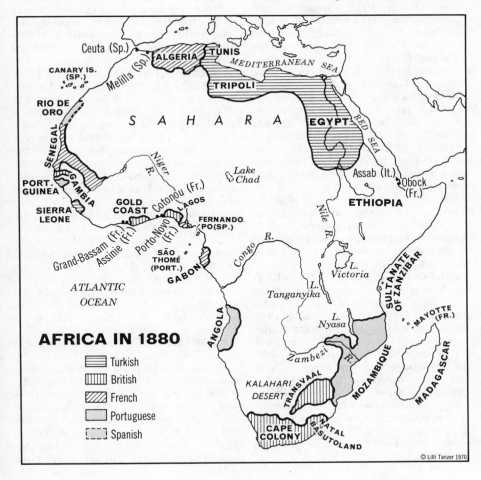

AFRICA IN 1880

Legend:
- Turkish
- British
- French
- Portuguese
- Spanish

© Lilli Tanzer 1970

ing extraction of the mineral wealth of Katanga. (*Cont. p. 473.*)

Central Africa

1870–90

DEATH OF LIVINGSTONE. The last journey of David Livingstone (1813–73) began from Zanzibar in 1867. He traveled into the interior behind Lakes Nyasa and Tanganyika in the hope of finding the source of the Congo, which he believed might also be the true source of the Nile. By 1871 he had reached the Lualaba, out of which the Congo flows, and later in that year was "found" by H. M. Stanley. Together the 2 men disproved any connection between Lake Tanganyika and the Nile system, but Livingstone, sick in body and mind, continued alone on a last journey south toward Katanga, where he still hoped to find the ultimate sources of both great rivers. He died near Lake Bangweulu, May 1873.

MISSIONARY ACTIVITY IN NYASALAND. Livingstone's example and the lingering message of Thomas Fowell Buxton (1786–1845) encouraged the forces of "Christianity and Commerce" to labor for civilization in Central Africa. Commercial concerns soon joined missionaries in attempting to rid the region of the slave trade, exploit its resources, and convert the population. The missions acted independently of European governments, and established in the 1870's networks of hospitals, schools, and trading posts.

ANGLO-PORTUGUESE RIVALRY. The Portuguese considered the region inland from Mozambique to be their own and, after 1880, began pressing their claims. The missionaries asked for British protection, and the British government sent its 1st consul to the region in 1883. The Portuguese were not deterred, however, and throughout the 1880's they attempted to secure treaties with African chiefs and to interfere with the passage of goods and equipment to the traders and missionaries near Lake Nyasa. Britain refused to heed the missionaries' call for a protectorate.

RUDD CONCESSION. Lobengula (1833–94), ruler of the Ndebele state, the most powerful African polity in the area, made treaties of friendship with the Transvaal, 1887, and with Cape Colony, 1888. He also signed over to a representative of Cecil Rhodes, 30 Oct., 1888, exclusive mineral rights to Matabeleland. Rhodes's task was then to secure the concession against Portuguese and Afrikaner counterclaims, an aim shared by the British government.

B.S.A. CO. CHARTER. Rhodes proposed to the British government that the British South Africa Co. be allowed to colonize and administer Bechuanaland and Matabeleland, and to build rail and telegraph lines north to the Zambezi. The company received a royal charter, 29 Oct., 1889. Rhodes agreed to support the efforts of (Sir) Harry Johnston (1858–1927), appointed consul for the Nyasaland region.

DECLARATION OF BRITISH PROTECTORATE. Johnston declared a protectorate over the Shire highlands, 14 May, 1891, and proceeded to negotiate a number of agreements with chiefs beyond the Shire. These were used to support British claims against Portugal, and the British government, early in 1890, threatened to dispatch gunboats to Mozambique. The Portuguese withdrew from the Shire.

LOCHNER TREATY. In Barotseland, west of the River Kafue, Lewanika (c. 1843–1916), *litunga* (king) of the Lozi, ruled a large area. Rhodes wanted to secure mineral rights in the region, and Lewanika was content with the prospect of a British presence between his people and the Ndebele of Lobengula. He therefore signed a treaty with Rhodes's representative, Frank Lochner, 27 June, 1890.

PIONEER COLUMN. Lobengula still controlled Matabeleland and Mashonaland, but Rhodes proposed to settle white farmers in the region in order to safeguard the mineral rights he had acquired against any move by the Portuguese or Afrikaners. South Africans and Britons, led by Dr. Leander Starr Jameson (1853–1917), crossed into Mashonaland, 1890, bypassed Lobengula's capital near Bulawayo, and established Fort Salisbury. Other whites soon followed, and Rhodes's grip on Mashonaland was consolidated.

1891–1914

CONQUEST OF THE NDEBELE. Although the whites from the south attempted to avoid conflict with Lobengula in Matabeleland, the proximity of the 2 groups produced considerable tension. War finally broke out, 1893, and the Ndebele proved no match for the cannon and machine guns brought against Lobengula's capital. After the conquest, both the Ndebele and the Shona peoples were subjected to humiliations at the hands of the whites.

REVOLT OF NDEBELE AND SHONA. African resentments culminated in revolt, 1896, and the whites were forced to fight on 2 fronts. Rhodes personally convinced the Ndebele to lay down their arms and accept company rule, but various Shona chiefs were not subdued until 1897. Atrocities were committed on both sides before the settlers confirmed their military superiority.

BRITISH RULE IN CENTRAL AFRICA. Although Central Africa was the domain of both the B.S.A. Co. and the British government, the lot of the Africans differed little from one part of the region to another. Land was alienated, reserves created, taxes imposed, and labor conscripted. Railway extensions contributed to economic development, both of agriculture and mining, but the Africans, subjected to the humiliations of racial segregation, did not appreciate the improvements.

AFRICAN PROTEST. African dissatisfaction with white rule was demonstrated primarily through the agency of separatist Christian churches. These churches were evangelistic, and charismatic preachers bewailed African suffering and condemned European duplicity. John Chilembwe (1871?–1915), a Nyasa separatist leader who actively opposed British policy, was particularly outraged when Africans were forced to fight against the Germans in Tanganyika. In 1915 he organized an unsuccessful revolt against the British government of Nyasaland. British policy remained unchanged. (*Cont. p. 471.*)

East Africa

1870–95

SUPPRESSION OF THE SLAVE TRADE. Sultan Barghash (ruled 1870–88) was placed on the throne of Zanzibar by the British on the death of Sultan Majid, and Sir John Kirk (1832–1922), the British consul, pressed the new ruler to abolish the slave trade. Barghash resisted because of the dependence on the trade of Zanzibar's economy. In 1873, however, the threat of force by a special British envoy, Sir Bartle Frere, and the persuasive powers of Kirk convinced the sultan of the need to sign a treaty abolishing the slave trade, 5 June, 1873. The British aided Barghash in putting down the various revolts which followed the proclamation suppressing the trade. At this period the British government refused to assume territorial commitments, but dominated the sultanate so completely that it was able to prevent Sir William Mackinnon (1823–93) from accepting a private concession offered him by Sultan Barghash in 1877.

GERMAN COLONIZATION. Returning to Germany from Britain in 1883, Karl Peters (1856–1918) formed, together with other imperialists, a Society for German Colonization. Without the sanction of his government, Peters and his party traveled to Zanzibar, 1884, soon crossed to the mainland, and proceeded inland beyond Bagamoyo. By Dec. 1884 they had secured 124 treaties with African chiefs. Germany had thus unwittingly fallen heir to responsibility for some 2,500 sq. mi. of eastern Tanganyika. Bismarck recognized Peters's acquisitions at the end of the Berlin West Africa Conference, 1885.

ANGLO-GERMAN AGREEMENT OF 1886. German activities in East Africa extended to the Kilimanjaro area and to Witu, north of the Tana River, 1885. The British remained reluctant to act, but when German warships appeared in Zanzibar Harbor they changed their minds. Britain, France, and Germany, conferring together in the "spirit of Berlin," decided that the sultan of Zanzibar's authority extended for a depth of 10 mi. along the East African coast between the Ruvuma (Rovuma) and Tana Rivers. On 7 Dec., 1886, Germany and Britain determined their respective spheres of influence, which Sultan Barghash reluctantly accepted.

IMPERIAL BRITISH EAST AFRICA CO. The government of Lord Salisbury, realizing that the British occupation of Egypt was to be a long-term affair, decided that no other European nation must be allowed to control any part of the Nile valley. The Mahdi's forces held the middle reaches of the river in the Sudan, but religious and political strife still divided the state of Buganda at the headwaters of the Nile on Lake Victoria. Salisbury therefore granted a charter, but no financial support, to Mackinnon's Imperial British East Africa Co., 3 Sept., 1888, which received from the sultan of Zanzibar authority over his coastal possessions. Also in 1888, the German East Africa Co. prevailed on the sultan to lease to it his mainland strip in Tanganyika, and both companies looked toward the wealth and strategic position of Buganda in the interior.

RELIGIOUS RIVALRIES IN BUGANDA. In 1888 the Kabaka (king) Mwanga of Buganda attempted to deprive the contending religious factions at his court of their growing influence. The Moslems, Catholics, and Anglicans united against him, however, and he was temporarily deposed. The Moslems then turned the Christians out of Mengo, the capital. In 1889 Mwanga mobilized Christian support and ousted the Moslems. The latter were soon joined, however, by the forces of the Omukama (king) Kabarega of Bunyoro, Buganda's traditional enemy. Once again Mwanga and his Christian supporters were turned out, only to return, 1890, to occupy Mengo.

ANGLO-GERMAN TREATY OF 1890. The activities of Karl Peters forced the British to take seriously the German threat to the Nile. During the struggles in Buganda, Peters had secured Mwanga's signature to a treaty of friendship with the German emperor. The I.B.E.A. Co.'s representatives were not able to match its terms, and the British government grew alarmed. While the company sent Capt. Frederick Lugard (1858–1945) at the head of a small armed force to establish its authority in Buganda, Salisbury entered into negotiations with the Germans. By giving up the strategic North Sea island of Helgoland and all remnants of Johnston's and Rhodes's Cape-to-Cairo dream, Britain acquired the future Uganda, the German protectorate at Witu, and recognition of her protectorate in Zanzibar, 1 July, 1890. The Germans, though facing active resistance in all parts of the country during the 1890's, were soon in control of the future Tanganyika. Britain had successfully prevented the intrusion of other Europeans into the region of the headwaters of the Nile.

ACTIVITIES OF LUGARD. The I.B.E.A. Co., with headquarters in Mombasa, engaged in little commercial activity in Buganda. Lugard made a show of force there, 1890, and convinced Mwanga and his chiefs to grant "suzerainty" to the company for 2 years. In 1891, although he failed to reconcile the Anglican and Catholic factions, Lugard led a Christian force against the Moslems, defeated them, and temporarily united the Christians. While Lugard was securing further protectorates in the Ankole and Toro regions to the west, the company failed in its appeals for parliamentary support and decided to withdraw from East Africa. Before the withdrawal could be effected, however, Lugard seized the opportunity to overwhelm Mwanga and the Catholics, and prepared to leave behind an Anglican establishment. In the autumn of 1892 an intense public-opinion campaign in Britain was partially successful in turning the attention of the cabinet to Uganda. Lord Rosebery, the foreign secretary, sent the British consul in Zanzibar, Sir Gerald Portal (1858–94), to conduct an investigatory mission in Uganda.

UGANDA PROTECTORATE. Portal's mission succeeded so well that, on 1 Apr., 1893, the Union Jack was raised at Kampala. Portal made sure that the Catholic party regained some measure of equal status with the Anglicans, and proposed that Uganda be retained because of Britain's strategic interest in Egypt. The British parliament approved, 27 Aug., 1894.

EAST AFRICA PROTECTORATE. Convinced of the need for an East African Railway if Uganda's resources were to be exploited, Parliament declared a protectorate, 18 June, 1895, over the region where it would have to be built. The East Africa Protectorate later became Kenya.

1896-1914

EXTENSION OF BRITISH AUTHORITY IN UGANDA. In 1893 the remaining British forces in Uganda had helped the Christians put down a Moslem revolt which had spread westward into Toro. A prolonged war culminated in the flight of Kabarega of Bunyoro and the alienation of much of his land. Mwanga, meanwhile, had become little more than a figurehead under British control, and he fled from Mengo, 1897, to conduct yet another battle to regain power in his capital. His Christian chiefs supported the British, however, and Mwanga was soon forced into exile. His infant son was placed on the throne of Buganda, and the *katikiro* (prime minister), Apolo Kagwa (1869-1927), carried the most influence among the Council of Regents. As the British extended their authority beyond Buganda, they ruled either directly as administrators or through Ganda proconsuls.

BUGANDA AGREEMENT. In 1899 Harry Johnston was sent to Uganda to report on administrative developments and plans. His primary concern was financial, and his 1st proposals regarding land reform favored influential chiefs. The establishment of the *lukiko* (parliament) increased the political power of the appointees of the kabaka and gave Buganda a special position within the Uganda Protectorate, 10 Mar., 1900. Ganda bureaucrats controlled a secular oligarchy which ran the country.

EAST AFRICAN RAILWAY. The British used Indian army troops to disperse African peoples who were obstructing work on the railway inland from the coast. At a cost of almost £8 m., the route was finally completed as far as Lake Victoria, 1901. In 1902 Uganda's eastern province was transferred to the East Africa Protectorate, thus placing the railway under a single colonial administration.

ALIENATION OF KIKUYU LAND. Sir Charles Eliot (1862-1931), commissioner for the East Africa Protectorate (later Kenya), was responsible for making the new railway pay, and he decided on a scheme of white settlement. The highland region was considered to be relatively uninhabited and highly suitable for European farming. The Protectorate government ignored African land rights, and by 1904 had allotted nearly 1 m. acres to fewer than 400 white settlers. Many Africans, meanwhile, were assigned to "reserves." In 1908 taxation of Africans was proposed in order to make them sell their labor to white farmers.

MAJI-MAJI REBELLION. The Maji-Maji Rising, 1905, was the most serious of several faced by the German administration of Tanganyika. It reflected a deep resentment against the uprooting of African traditions, and spread quickly. Leaders distributed *maji* (water), or medicine, which was said to make believers immune to European bullets. The Germans moved systematically to prevent the larger tribes in the west from joining the revolt, and the troubles were over by Jan. 1907. African casualties were very high and a severe famine resulted from the dislocations of war.

INAUGURATION OF THE LEGISLATIVE COUNCIL. Control of the East Africa Protectorate passed from the Foreign to the Colonial Office in 1905, and the commissioner, Sir James Hayes Sadler (1851-1910), became governor. An 8-member Legislative Council 1st met in 1907. The views of the white settlers were well represented in the Council by their leader, Lord Delamere (1870-1931).

SYSTEMATIC ADMINISTRATION AND ECONOMIC DEVELOPMENT. In both the German and British areas efficient administrative procedures were instituted. Railway lines were rapidly extended and cash crops introduced. In Tanganyika the value of sisal exports increased from more than 1 m. marks in 1906 to more than 7 m. in 1912. Coffee, cotton, rubber, hides, and skins replaced ivory as East Africa's staple export, and livestock were introduced on the European farms in the highlands. In Uganda cotton was so successful that by 1915 the imperial grant-in-aid could be withdrawn. (*Cont. p. 471.*)

West Africa

1870–84

FANTI CONFEDERATION. After the announcement of the decision that Britain would withdraw gradually from the Gold Coast (recommended by a Parliamentary Select Committee in 1865), local British administrators decreased their activities. A number of Fanti chiefs reached an agreement to defend their own interests against their common enemy, Ashanti. On 24 Nov., 1871, 31 signatories to a Confederation Agreement envisaged the union of their states, a common assembly, and a constitutional monarchy. They planned a wide range of governmental services under the protection of the British crown. The British administration, however, took offense and charged the Fanti leaders with conspiracy, thus ending the proposed confederation.

WAR BETWEEN BRITAIN AND ASHANTI. Frequent disturbances caused the Gold Coast government to seek to subdue the Ashanti. A force under Sir Garnet Wolseley (1833–1913) looted and burned Kumasi, 6 Feb., 1874, but did not depose the *asantehene* (king of Ashanti).

FRENCH THRUSTS INTO THE INTERIOR. From Senegal, where Brière de l'Isle became governor in 1876, the French turned toward the Sudan to prevent the British from securing rights in the interior. In 1878 Capt. Joseph Galliéni (1849–1916) won victories, built a fort in Tokolor country, and concluded treaties naming France protector of the region. After 1880, at the urging of de

l'Isle, the French began to construct a railway from Dakar to St.-Louis. By 1881–82 Col. G. Borgnis-Desbordes had led a force up the Senegal to forestall the British on the Niger, and French traders were competing energetically with the British all along the Gulf of Guinea.

COMPETITION ON THE COAST. The United African Co. of George Goldie Taubman (1846–1925), active on the Niger from the Delta to the Benue confluence, became the operational base for British interests. Meanwhile, French merchants were gaining influence in the interior of the Ivory Coast, beyond their posts at Assinie and Grand Bassam. The French navy occupied Porto Novo and Cotonou on the Dahomey coast, 1883, in order to challenge the British at Lagos. German missionaries and merchants had long been active in most of these places and, by 1883, controlled the trade of the Togo region. German firms had also prospered in Cameroon, and in both areas merchants were urging their government to annex their holdings. Annexation became possible after Bismarck had taken the 1st step toward the creation of a German overseas empire in South-West Africa in early 1884.

BRITISH EXPANSION IN THE NIGER REGION. Goldie's continued struggle with French competitors on the Niger and the appearance of Imperial Germany at Cameroon led the British government to order its consul, Edward Hewett, to secure treaties along the coast, 1884. Joseph Thompson, acting for Goldie's new National African Co., secured an agreement with the sultan of Sokoto, 1 June, 1885, in the north.

1885–1914

FRENCH CAMPAIGNS IN WEST AFRICA. After the Berlin Conference of 1884–85, the grand design of the French was to join their African possessions together at Lake Chad. Control of the upper and middle Niger was essential to this end, and campaigns were waged during the following years against resisting Africans. In 1887 French forces conquered the Futa Jallon and secured the headwaters of the Gambia, Senegal, and Niger rivers. French generals met stronger opposition, however, from Samori Touré, a Mande (Mandingo) chief who had been building an empire in the western Sudan for 20 years. After being defeated by the French in battles in 1886 and 1889, Samori avoided capture and retired to regroup his forces. From France's equatorial territory, de Brazza's followers were slowly moving north to the Ubangi, Chari, and Adamawa regions by continuing to make treaties with local chiefs. From her stations on the Slave Coast, France gradually took over the state of Dahomey. On the Niger, French forces occupied Segu in 1890, and forced Ahmadu, the son of al-hajj Omar (al-ḥājj 'Umar) , to flee.

BRITISH CONSOLIDATION ON THE NIGER. As a result of the agreements at Berlin, the British declared a protectorate over the lower Niger in 1885. This protectorate extended along the coast from Lagos to Cameroon and included the Niger posts from the Delta to Ibi on the Benue. On 10 July, 1886, Goldie's company was given a royal charter to administer the protectorate. The British government was firmly behind the Royal Niger Co., and when the interests of British merchants were threatened London came to their aid. The most striking example of such British government action was in the case of Ja Ja, the ruler of the Opobo Kingdom of the Delta. His sin was success, for his control over the palm-oil trade was held an obstruction to freedom of commerce. Harry Johnston, then a vice-consul in the Cameroon, captured Ja Ja, who was tried and deported to the West Indies.

West of the Delta, Lagos was suffering both from the disruption of trade caused by warfare in Yorubaland and from the competition of the French in Dahomey. After 1891, when the British annexed several small states surrounding Lagos, their control was extended northward by force and persuasion. The conquest of Oyo completed the subjection of Yorubaland. In the Oil Rivers of the Delta, armed launches patrolled the creeks and removed unco-operative chiefs. When a British expedition to Benin was ambushed, 1897, British troops retaliated, 1898, by destroying Benin City and its surrounding villages and towns.

COMPLETION OF FRENCH CONQUEST. The French needed only an excuse to make total their control over the Fon Kingdom of Dahomey. They found it in 1892, when the king of Dahomey fired on a French exploratory mission, and later in the year France occupied Abomey, the Fon capital. On the Niger, progress was steady as the French conquered Jenne and Masina, 1893, and entered Timbuktu, 1894, where they were to battle sporadically with the Tuareg for a dozen years. French forces occupied Mossi strongholds to the south, 1896–97. By 1900 Gao had been reached, and the French were marching beyond Zinder toward Lake Chad. Samori continued to harass them in the western Sudan throughout the 1890's, but was finally captured, 1898. In the same year Capt. Marchand's attempt to cut across the Nile and link France's West African empire with her small post at Djibouti met its end in the confrontation with Kitchener at Fashoda. In 1900 a 3-pronged attack on the Sudanese adventurer, Rabah, of the Darfur-Wadai region at last allowed the French to link up their Sudanese and Equatorial empires.

CONQUEST OF ASHANTI. Britain's colony on the Gold Coast prospered only during times of peace with Ashanti, and these periods were few. The *asantehene's* domain had not been pacified by Wolseley's expedition of 1873–74, and civil war erupted there in 1886–87. For almost a decade British governors tried all means short of force to bring the Ashanti under their protection, but the *asantehene* either actively resisted or engaged in lengthy procrastination. In 1895 Sir William E. Maxwell (gov., 1895–97) , needing a pretext to intervene, laid down an ultimatum to the Ashanti. When it was rejected, 3,000 troops marched to Kumasi and occupied the city, 1896. Once again the Ashanti question was thought to have been solved. The way to the north was no longer blocked, and British troops were able to man posts in what became the Northern Territories by 1898, thus preventing the feared encirclement of the colony by the French and Germans. In 1900 the British governor asked for the Golden Stool, the revered symbol of Ashanti unity, and the Ashanti rebelled. Ashantiland was annexed as a crown colony 26 Sept., 1901 (effective 1 Jan., 1902).

CONQUEST OF NORTHERN NIGERIA. France and Britain agreed, 26 June, 1891, to remain on the northern and southern sides, respectively, of a line drawn through Hausaland and Bornu (the Say-Barrua Line), but the middle Niger region remained to be won. Capt. Frederick Lugard reached Borgu in 1894, and Britain gained the upper hand. Various British-led forces then proceeded against the Fulani strongholds, and Bida and Ilorin were occupied, 1897. In 1898 another Anglo-French agreement determined spheres of interest in the middle Niger: France was to control northern Dahomey and Britain northern Nigeria. Lugard then completed the conquest of the city-states: Kontagora and Nupe fell in 1901, whereupon some emirs peacefully accepted British protection. Others resisted, and Kano and Sokoto refused to relinquish their independence. In 1903 these last 2 Moslem strongholds, together with Katsina, succumbed to Lugard's forces and the conquest of northern Nigeria was complete.

COLONIAL ADMINISTRATION. By 1906 the British West African colonies had been pacified, but the French continued to expand northward into the Sahara and conducted campaigns against rebellious Africans. Lugard, theorist and practitioner of "indirect rule," returned to the governor generalship of northern and southern Nigeria in 1912, and effected the unification of the 2 colonies on 1 Jan., 1914. Cocoa, in the Gold Coast, became the most successful of the new cash crops, and rail systems were rapidly built from coast to interior in the British, French, and German colonies. (*Cont. p. 471.*)

SOUTHEAST ASIA

Netherlands East Indies

1870–99

SUGAR AND AGRARIAN LAWS. The Sugar Law, 1870, decreed that the Netherlands Indian government would gradually end forced sugar cultivation and permit the free sale of sugar in Java. The Agrarian Law of the same year allowed capitalists to obtain heritable leases from the government for up to 75 years and to hire land from Javanese owners. The 2 measures marked a decisive stage in a process that had begun with the promulgation of the Regeeringsreglement (constitutional regulation) of 1854. The culture system was progressively abandoned in favor of free enterprise.

SUMATRA TREATY. As the competition among European powers for overseas colonies increased, the Dutch were compelled to strengthen their position in the Indonesian Archipelago to forestall rival claims. Outside Java, Dutch officials concentrated most attention on Sumatra, where piracy jeopardized normal trade. However, Dutch attempts to enforce control there harmed the operations of Malacca and Singapore merchants, who urged London to intervene. The resulting Anglo-Dutch negotiations led to the Sumatra Treaty, 1871, by which, in return for ceding their positions on the Gold Coast of Africa to Britain, the Dutch gained freedom of action in Sumatra. The treaty also stipulated that Britain was to enjoy equal trade opportunities with the Netherlands throughout the archipelago.

WAR WITH ACHIN. A new Dutch expansionist movement followed the Sumatra Treaty. One of its earliest manifestations was the long war against the sultanate of Achin (Atjeh). Achin, strategically located on the northern tip of Sumatra, had long resisted Dutch control, while its pirates wreaked havoc in the archipelago. When attempts at negotiations failed, the Dutch declared war in 1873. The Achinese, motivated largely by Moslem fanaticism against the "infidel," resorted to guerrilla warfare, which continued for more than a quarter of a century. Besides tightening their control over Sumatra, the Dutch in the late 19th cent. extended effective rule over several other outer possessions of the East Indies.

1900–1914

ETHICAL POLICY. Strong pressure developed within the Dutch Parliament and among the Dutch people after 1900 in favor of increased attention to the welfare of the Indonesians. The Ethical Policy, officially launched in 1901, advocated increased spending on welfare and education. At the same time, a process of administrative decentralization was inaugurated. In practice, however, the governor general remained under the complete control of the home government until communications were severed dur-

ing World War I. Similarly, an elaborate scheme of village self-government led to such excessive interference from above that village opposition to Dutch rule grew. As for welfare programs, a rapid population increase offset much of the progress they achieved.

RISE OF NATIONALISM. Awakening nationalism in the Dutch East Indies was centered chiefly in Java, which contained about 2/3 of the colony's population. An important milestone in the nationalist movement occurred in 1900, when the Javanese princess, Raden Adjeng Kartini, championed education for women. Her efforts led to the founding of Kartini schools for girls in Java. In 1908 Dr. W. S. Usada, who shared Kartini's view of western education as the means by which Indonesians would enhance their status, founded the Dutch East Indies' first nationalist organization. Called Budi Utomo (High

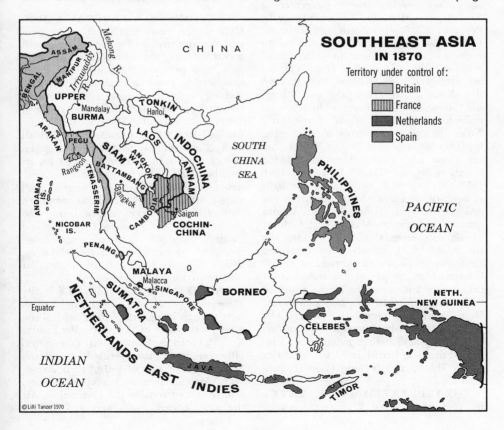

SOUTHEAST ASIA
IN 1870
Territory under control of:
Britain
France
Netherlands
Spain

© Lilli Tanzer 1970

Endeavor), it aimed to establish schools on a national basis. Finally, in 1911, Sarekat Islam, which was to become the colony's chief vehicle of nationalism, was founded. Although it began as a group of Javanese batik traders seeking protection against Chinese exploitation, it had acquired a broad popular base by the eve of World War I. (*Cont. p. 461.*)

Malaya
1870–1905

PANGKOR ENGAGEMENT AND START OF THE RESIDENT SYSTEM. Following the Sumatra Treaty, the British as well as the Dutch undertook a forward movement in Southeast Asia. Britain abandoned its traditional policy of nonintervention in Malay affairs, most notably through the Pangkor Engagement, Jan. 1874, with the sultan of Perak. This agreement provided for a guarantee of British protection, and for acceptance by Perak of a British resident, whose advice had to be sought and followed in all matters other than those involving Malay religion and custom. In Feb. Selangor accepted a British resident, and in Apr. the chiefs of Sungei Ujong and Linggi did likewise. The murder of the 1st resident of Perak, J. W. W. Birch, on 2 Nov., 1875, led to a crisis in that state, but the dispatch of a British expeditionary force and tactful handling of the situation by Sir Hugh Low (resident, 1877–89) restored order and brought prosperity to Perak. In many areas the resident had to contend with serious quarreling between Malays and Chinese immigrants, especially those working the tin mines. Such quarrels, by impeding economic development, threatened British interests. As time passed, the residents became more and more the actual rulers of their states. The British also established State Councils with legislative powers. The various Malay sultans served as presidents of these councils, whose members also included the local British resident, the major Malay chiefs, and leading Chinese businessmen.

THE FEDERATED MALAY STATES. By 1896 there were 4 protected states: Perak, Selangor, Pahang, and the confederation of Negri Sembilan. Because the residents in the respective states pursued unco-ordinated policies, the 4 areas diverged increasingly in such important matters as taxation and land settlement. A plan of co-ordination was formulated in the Treaty of Federation, which united the 4 protected states under a resident general. The Malay sultans lost much of their power but retained their titles and received larger incomes. The position of the State Councils also declined. The British created a large, centralized administrative structure at Kuala Lumpur. The Federation was formally inaugurated 1 July, 1896. As government efficiency improved, prosperity grew and the output of tin and rubber, Malaya's 2 principal industries, expanded dramatically.

1906–14

CREATION OF A FEDERAL COUNCIL. British fears that the resident general was not under effective control, guilt about ignoring the sultans' administrative role, and pressure from new industrial, commercial, and agricultural interests seeking a voice in government all contributed to the decision to establish a Federal Council in Malaya, 1909. The Council had for its president the British high commissioner, who was also governor of the Straits Settlements, and for its members the resident general, the residents of the 4 protected states, each state's sultan, and 4 unofficial members. Although the sultans enjoyed no veto power over decisions of the Federal Council, they continued to exercise some authority through the State Councils, which kept a free hand in matters of Malay religion and custom.

ANGLO-SIAMESE TREATY. By agreement with Siam, 1909, the British were able to bring under their control the 4 northern states of the Malay Peninsula: Kedah, Perlis, Kelantan, and Trengganu. However, these states refused to join the Federation for fear of losing their autonomy, particularly in fiscal matters. Johore, too, remained outside the Federation. All the unfederated states accepted British advisers; but, in contrast to the residents, an adviser enjoyed only the right to be consulted by the local ruler and was forbidden to issue orders. (*Cont. p. 462.*)

Borneo

1870–1914

THE WHITE RAJAS. When the first White Raja of Sarawak, Sir James Brooke (1803–68), handed over his state to his nephew, Charles Brooke (1829–1917), he passed on a territory which had been greatly expanded and had received a British consul, but which was still without international recognition. Brooke asked the sultan of Brunei for more land, but was rebuffed.

BRITISH NORTH BORNEO COM-PANY. After various trading companies had attempted to establish Bornean settlements, Baron von Overbeck and Alfred Dent obtained a lease of northern Borneo from the sultan of Brunei, 29 Dec., 1877. Since part of the region was under the sultan of Sulu's nominal control, Overbeck also concluded an agreement with Sulu, 22 Jan., 1878. Early in 1879, however, Overbeck withdrew from the enterprise, which was taken over by the firm of Dent Bros. On 1 Nov., 1881, the Dent firm, having by this time transferred its Bornean holdings to a "British North Borneo Provisional Association," received a royal charter as the British North Borneo Co. This was the 1st of a group of chartered companies created by Britain in the 1880's for the commercial exploitation of overseas territories. Two major factors motivated London to grant a charter to the Association: fear that other European colonial powers would annex parts of northern Borneo, and a desire to keep the company's activities under a modicum of British government control.

BRITISH PROTECTORATE POL-ICY. A series of agreements, 1888, with North Borneo (Sabah), Sarawak, and Brunei made all these areas British protectorates. Such an arrangement, London believed, would restrain French and German expansion in Southeast Asia and would also prevent Brunei from soliciting the aid of foreign powers against either Sarawak or the British North Borneo Co. The sultan, for his part, welcomed British protection against foreign pressure. (*Cont. p. 462.*)

Burma

1870–84

RULE OF KING MINDON. Burma's king, Mindon, took offense at a British decision, 1871, to conduct future relations with Burma through the viceroy of India. Although Britain had created the province of British Burma, comprising most of Lower Burma, in 1862, Mindon still controlled Upper Burma. He made his capital at Mandalay and sought to maintain good relations with the British authorities at Rangoon. However, he resented being treated like the ruler of a native Indian state. His resentment, coupled with a desire to counter British influence in his kingdom, led him to cultivate friendly ties with France and Italy and to invite French and Italian missionaries, engineers, and government experts to work in Burma. In 1872 Mindon sent his chief minister on a visit to London; en route, the minister stopped in Paris to seek a full-scale alliance. The treaty never materialized, but Britain reacted angrily to the negotiations.

FORSYTH MISSION AND THE "SHOE QUESTION." Anglo-Burmese relations further deteriorated as a result of friction between the king and the business community in Rangoon, which opposed Mindon's commercial methods, especially his retention of royal monopolies. In order to improve Anglo-Burmese relations, Sir Douglas Forsyth led a mission to Mandalay on behalf of the government of India, 1875. Upon his return to Calcutta, however, he complained about the Burmese custom of making foreign envoys remove their shoes and sit on the floor at royal audiences. Later in the year, the government of India ordered the British resident at Mandalay no longer to remove his shoes in the king's presence. Since Mindon could not yield to this demand, the resident lost the valuable personal contact he had maintained with the king.

RULE OF KING THIBAW. When Mindon died, 1878, Burmese officials plotted to make Prince Thibaw, a nonentity king, in order to create a constitutional monarchy. Thibaw, however, came under the influence of his strong-willed queen, who persuaded him to massacre many members of the royal family and place her minions in key government posts. Meanwhile, a Kachin revolt, forays by Chinese guerrillas, and a renunciation by the Shans of allegiance to the Burmese king plunged Upper Burma into chaos. Continuing slaughters at Mandalay prompted the British trading community in Rangoon to demand a change of government in Upper Burma or its annexation.

1885–1914

BRITISH ANNEXATION OF UPPER BURMA. Thibaw, meanwhile, sought to play Paris off against London, which was increasingly worried about French activities in Southeast Asia. In 1885 Britain learned that France had secretly promised arms and munitions to Burma. British diplomatic pressure led to a French disavowal; but no improvement in Anglo-Burmese relations ensued, for Thibaw framed a case against the Bombay Burma Trading Corp. He fined the corporation, which worked Burma's teak forests, for the alleged illegal export of teak logs. Believing that a French syndicate would take over the corporation's operations, Thibaw refused British pleas for arbitration. The government of India then delivered an ultimatum to Mandalay, demanding, among other things, that Burma submit all foreign-policy questions to India. When Thibaw refused, British troops invaded Upper Burma and occupied Mandalay. Britain planned to make the territory a protectorate and place an approved member of the royal family on the throne. However, when no acceptable candidate could be found, Thibaw's territories were annexed to the British dominions in Jan. 1886. A nationwide reaction developed against foreign rule and Burmese troops moved into the jungles to conduct guerrilla warfare against the British forces, who required many years to pacify the land.

REFORMS IN VILLAGE ADMINISTRATION. For the sake of administrative convenience, Burma was made a province of British India, Feb. 1886. This arrangement led to neglect of Burma's distinct history and culture. The Upper Burma Village Regulation of 1887 and the Burma Village Act of 1889 were prime examples of the unfortunate effect of Burma's artificial connection with India. By these decrees, the British broke up the circle (Burma's largest indigenous social and political unit) into villages. The plan aimed to strengthen the village as an administrative unit and use it to restore law and order in the country. However, the reform replaced the circle headman, a local resident, with a village headman serving as a British civil servant. British administrators also adopted a negative attitude toward Buddhism. London's reluctance to become embroiled in religious matters after the Sepoy Mutiny in India, 1857, led to refusal to sanction Burma's ecclesiastical code regulating discipline in Buddhist monasteries. Lacking authority to enforce discipline, Burmese Buddhist leaders stood helpless as unruly monks roamed the country preaching sedition.

LEGISLATIVE AUTONOMY. Promotion of the chief commissioner of Burma to the rank of lieut. gov. and appointment of an advisory Legislative Council to assist him, 1897, marked the prelude to a great expansion of government functions. As elsewhere in Southeast Asia, so in Burma, the colonial power abandoned laissez faire and sought actively to promote governmental efficiency and social welfare. Bureaucratic government flourished as a new secretariat arose in Rangoon. Attempts to institute local self-government had begun as early as 1874, when Municipal Committees were nominated for some Burmese towns. However, the ethnic diversity of the urban population made joint action difficult. In rural areas self-government was characterized by inefficiency and corruption and by a frequent transfer of officials. Only in Rangoon, where sizable communities of Europeans and educated Asians resided, was self-government meaningful.

YOUNG MEN'S BUDDHIST ASSOCIATION. Originally organized to revive Buddhist values in the context of western learning, the Y.M.B.A. (founded 1906) was composed primarily of students of religion. By the time of World War I, however, a General Council of Buddhist Associations was assembling regularly, and religious discussions gradually shaded off into political ones. The awakening of Burmese nationalism dates from this period. (*Cont. p. 462.*)

Indochina

1870–83

FRANCIS GARNIER AT HANOI. Interested in opening a trade route to western China via Tongking's Red River, French merchant Jean Dupuis sought to exchange products from Yunnan for salt from Hanoi. When Hanoi's mandarins refused to abandon their salt monopoly, Dupuis and his followers seized part of Hanoi and appealed to the French authorities at Saigon for help. Based at Saigon was Adm. Dupré, governor of French-controlled Cochin China, who saw in Dupuis's grievance a pretext for intervention in Tongking. Against Paris's orders, he sent a naval officer, Francis Garnier, to Hanoi with a small force to arbitrate between Dupuis and the mandarins. When Garnier arrived, 1873, Tongking was infested with so-called Black Flags, a force including local pirates and remnants of China's Taiping rebels. Garnier, finding the mandarins adamant, seized Hanoi's citadel; but the mandarins requested help from the Black Flags, who killed Garnier, Dec. 1873.

TREATY WITH TU-DUC. Having disavowed Garnier's seizure of the citadel at Hanoi, Paris sent an official, Philastre, to negotiate a settlement with the court of Hué. The resulting treaty, 15 Mar., 1874, pledged Emperor Tu-Duc to recognize French sovereignty over Cochin China; accept a French resident at Hué; open 3 ports, including Hanoi, to French trade; permit free navigation of the Red River as far as Yunnan; and guarantee freedom for Christians in his dominions. For her part, France canceled the unpaid balance of an indemnity owed by Tu-Duc and offered him arms to ward off the Black Flags. In Vietnam's eyes, however, the Philastre–Tu-Duc treaty appeared as a sign of French weakness; and as soon as French forces left Tongking, the emperor violated many of the pact's terms. Furthermore, Tu-Duc renewed his declaration of allegiance to the Chinese emperor and dispatched an embassy to Peking with tribute.

RENEWAL OF FRENCH EXPANSIONISM. On the twin pretexts that Tu-Duc had failed to abide by the treaty and that Black Flag activities threatened French citizens in Hanoi, the French government sent Capt. Henri Rivière at the head of an expeditionary force to Tongking. Ostensibly aiming to halt the Black Flag menace to French shipping on the Red River, Rivière's real goal was to pursue the conquest of Tongking where Garnier had left off. In Apr. 1882 Rivière's troops seized Hanoi, but he himself was killed by Black Flags. By this time Jules Ferry, a chief exponent of colonial expansionism, had become France's prime minister. He insisted not only on the seizure of Tongking but also on the submission of the court of Hué to French control. After he sent another strong force to the area, an armistice was finally signed on 25 Aug., 1883, in which, among other things, Vietnam accepted protectorate status.

1884–1914

SINO-FRENCH WAR OVER INDO-CHINA. Since Peking had claimed Vietnam as a protectorate, it warned that the treaty was not valid without Chinese approval. When France ignored this warning, China sent troops to Vietnam, and an undeclared Sino-French war erupted. By the Treaty of Tientsin, 9 June, 1884, China conceded French protectorate claims to Vietnam and pledged withdrawal of Chinese troops from Tongking.

CONSOLIDATION OF FRENCH CONTROL IN ANNAM AND CAMBODIA. As a result of palace intrigues at Hué, the French placed their own candidate, Dong-Khanh, on the throne there, 1884. He permitted France to install residents in each of Annam's provinces. That same year, the governor of Cochin China used alleged abuses by Cambodian mandarins as an excuse for forcing the Cambodian king to accept administrative reforms. A *résident supérieur* assumed the real power in Cambodia, and every Cambodian province received a French resident with authority over native officials. The outcome was a popular revolt led by a Cambodian prince.

UNION INDOCHINOISE. As an attempt at administrative improvement, the French united Cochin China, Annam, Tongking, and Cambodia into an Indochinese Union supervised by a civilian governor general, Oct. 1887. However, each unit maintained an autonomous structure and a separate budget.

FRENCH COUP IN LAOS. Having strengthened her control over the rest of Indochina, France moved to challenge Siamese overlordship in Laos. The French response to the ouster of 2 agents from Siam in 1893 was to claim the entire left bank of the Mekong River and to send gunboats to Bangkok. Although the Laotian king at Luang Prabang continued to reign, the rest of Laos became in effect a group of French provinces.

PAUL DOUMER AND ADMINISTRATIVE REFORM. Paul Doumer (gov. gen., 1897–1902) fashioned the definitive French administrative system in Indochina. Technically, Cochin China was the only 1 of the 5 divisions of Indochina which ranked as a colony; Tongking, Annam, Cambodia, and Laos were all protectorates. Throughout the Indochinese Union, however, assimilation was the key to French policy, which spurned self-government. Although the Annamese, Cambodian, and Laotian kings and courts continued to function, real control in each case was vested in a *résident su-*

périeur. Day-to-day administration was carried out by native officials under the guidance of French representatives. In Cochin China a governor general was the top official. To preserve a façade of democracy in Indochina, the French created a Consultative Native Assembly, whose job it was to assist the *résident supérieur*. However, its members were elected by a small group of officials of trusted loyalty, and it was forbidden to debate political subjects.

EDUCATION AND NATIONALISM. In 1906 an educational system based on the village elementary school was inaugurated; but private education prevailed in Annam and Tongking, while monastic schools provided the sole elementary education in Cambodia and Laos. The University of Hanoi was founded in 1907, but soon closed as the French crushed political dissent among its students. This was the era of nascent nationalism, though the nationalist movement was confined to the Vietnamese, the most numerous people of Indochina. By the eve of World War I, France's contradictory policy of trying to make Frenchmen out of the Vietnamese while keeping them in a subservient position had stimulated nationalist sentiment. (*Cont. p. 463.*)

Philippines

1870–97

REVOLUTION IN SPAIN AND REPERCUSSIONS IN THE PHILIPPINES. The revolution in Spain which replaced the regime of Isabella II with a republic, 1868, had impact on the Filipino nationalist movement, which already possessed a common cultural heritage (thanks to Spain) and ethnic origin and common hatred of Spanish rule. Although the Spanish Republic lasted only 3 years, that period witnessed an influx into the Philippines of colonial officials with democratic ideas. They introduced a degree of administrative autonomy, permitted the circulation of publications containing liberal ideas, and fostered free political discussion. When the Spanish Republic collapsed in 1871, a reactionary governor general arrived in the Philippines to reverse these policies.

MUTINY AT CAVITE. A mutiny of Filipino soldiers, Jan. 1872, in which local clergy were also involved was magnified by Spanish authorities into an attempted revolution. Spanish repression took the form of the judicial murder of 3 Filipino priests, deportation of various Filipino leaders to penal colonies, and persecution of intellectuals, many of whom fled to Europe, including Madrid. From there they conducted a publicity campaign called the Propaganda Movement. Its adherents were loyalists who sought reform, not revolution. They advocated assimilation of the Philippines as a Spanish province and also voiced such moderate demands as Filipinization of the parishes and freedom of speech, press, and assembly.

JOSÉ RIZAL. Dr. José Rizal, who as a student in Spain had encountered liberal opinion, became the leader of the Propaganda Movement. In 1887 he published in Berlin *Noli Me Tangere* (Touch Me Not), a book describing Filipino suffering under Spanish rule. Four years later, Rizal's publication *El Filibusterismo* (trans. as The Reign of Greed) appeared in Ghent. These books circulated secretly in the Philippines and inflamed nationalist sentiment.

FOUNDING OF LIGA FILIPINO AND KATIPUNAN. Upon his return to Manila in 1892, Rizal established the Liga Filipino, an organization dedicated to the social and political advance of Filipinos, but he was soon deported to Mindanao. Both the Propaganda Movement and the Liga soon died out for want of support. The way was then paved for real revolutionaries like Andrés Bonifacio to move to the forefront. In July 1892, in Manila, Bonifacio founded a secret society, the Katipunan (Sons of the People), which aimed to win independence by force.

OUTBREAK OF REVOLUTION. In 1896, Katipunan leaders contacted Rizal at Mindanao, but he warned against a premature revolution. Meanwhile, however, the government had become aware of Katipunan. When Spanish officials began rounding up its leaders, sporadic fighting erupted and a nationwide rebellion ensued. The government responded with a reign of terror, including the shooting of Rizal on charges of sedition. Although Rizal's martyrdom helped the rebels' cause, they could not hold Manila. Bonifacio took refuge at Tejeros, where he set up a revolutionary government.

PACT OF BIACNABATO. Bonifacio's influence was quickly overshadowed by that of Emilio Aguinaldo, whom the revolutionary assembly named president of the newborn Philippine Republic, Mar. 1897. When Aguinaldo's forces failed to defeat the Spanish troops, he signed the Pact of Biacnabato, Dec., agreeing to end revolutionary activities and to the dispatch of the leaders to voluntary exile in Hong Kong. The Spaniards, for their part, offered to pay the rebels for the surrender of their weapons and to grant compensation to families who had suffered during the uprising. As a result of bad faith on both sides, however, the pact soon collapsed.

1898–1914

SPANISH-AMERICAN WAR AND ANNEXATION OF THE PHILIPPINES. The Spanish-American War revived Aguinaldo's career. Commo. Dewey, having destroyed the Spanish fleet in the Bay of Manila, 1 May, 1898, lacked enough troops to capture the city. He therefore contacted Aguinaldo in Hong Kong, allegedly promising Philippine independence in return for help against Spain. Aguinaldo led a new nationalist revolt and in June proclaimed the country's independence. However, the Americans, denying any commitment to the rebel leader, annexed the Philippines.

SCHURMAN COMMISSION. It took the Americans more than a year to capture Aguinaldo, 23 Mar., 1901, and some of his followers continued guerrilla operations until 1907. Meanwhile, Washington sent a fact-finding commission headed by President Jacob Schurman of Cornell University to the Philippines, 1899. Concluding that the Filipinos desired independence but could not yet govern themselves, the commission advocated local participation in municipal and provincial government, a vast educational campaign, and other steps to prepare Filipinos for self-government.

TRANSITION FROM MILITARY TO CIVILIAN RULE. The 1st American-sponsored civilian regime in the islands, inaugurated 4 July, 1901, was headed by Judge William H. Taft, who proclaimed equality of rights for all Filipinos, separation of church and state, and freedom of press and assembly. Taft's 5-man commission, which later added 3 Filipino members, began implementing the Schurman resolutions.

PHILIPPINE ORGANIC ACT. Congressional passage of the Philippine Organic Act, 1 July, 1902, assured increased self-government. The bill provided for a popular assembly, with the commission becoming the upper house of a bicameral legislature. Executive power was to be vested in a governor general. The Organic Act also declared that all lands owned by religious orders belonged henceforth to the Philippine government to sell or lease, preferably to the actual occupants. However, there was no serious attempt at agrarian reform. The U.S. maintained a virtual monopoly of Philippine trade. Culturally, the Philippines remained isolated from Southeast Asia, as they had under Spanish rule.

1ST PHILIPPINE GENERAL ELECTIONS. The Nacionalista Party, whose supreme goal was immediate independence for the Philippines, won a resounding victory in the 1st general elections, 1909. The newly elected Philippine Assembly received a large voice in domestic legislation. At the Assembly's inauguration, the U.S. promised independence as soon as the Filipinos were capable of ruling themselves. By the eve of World War I, both legislative houses enjoyed a Filipino majority. (*Cont. p. 463.*)

OCEANIA

1870–1914

THE PACIFIC BASIN IN 1870. Before the 1870's there were few outright European possessions in Oceania. Because of her naval power, Britain held almost undisputed sway in the Pacific, but the Colonial Office in London did not take the opportunity to acquire islands. Instead, Britain's possessions were usually annexed at the insistence of the Australasian colonies, or when there was clear evidence that another power, often Germany, was interested enough to take political action. There were British, Australian, New Zealand, German, French, and American traders and missionaries in all parts of the Pacific in increasing numbers at this time, and their activities were in large part responsible for the incorporation of the islands into the respective European empires and for the mosaiclike fashion in which this was done.

CHRONOLOGY OF THE ANNEXATIONS. A native government was set up in Fiji, 1870, and in the same year a Colonial Conference in Melbourne demanded its annexation, which was refused by the Colonial Office. A German consul was stationed in Samoa, 1871. The Pacific Islanders Protection Act was passed, 1872, giving the supreme courts of all the Australian colonies power to try British subjects accused of illegally enlisting natives as laborers. In 1873 Commo. Goodenough and E. L. Layard were appointed to report on the situation in Fiji, and Capt. John Moresby annexed a number of islands off the coast of New Guinea. Fiji was annexed by Britain, Oct. 1874. In 1875 a Reciprocity Treaty was signed by the U.S. and Hawaii, Spain claimed the Carolines, and Queensland demanded the annexation of New Guinea.

In 1877 the Germans surveyed parts of New Guinea, and concluded a treaty with Samoa giving them the right to establish a coaling station and naval depot there. The following year the U.S. concluded a treaty with Samoa entitling her to a naval station at Pago Pago, and the Germans began to consolidate their interests in the Marshall Islands. In Jan. 1879 Germany signed another treaty with Samoa, and Britain did likewise in Aug. France annexed Tahiti, 1880.

In 1881 Britain annexed Rotuma. Queensland unilaterally annexed New Guinea, Apr. 1883, but the action was subsequently disallowed in London. Also in 1883 the Anglo-French agreement of 1878 recognizing the independence of New Hebrides was renewed. The Germans stationed a consul in New Britain, 1884. Britain declared a protectorate over southern New Guinea, 6 Nov., 1884, and Germany claimed the remainder of the island and the Bismarck Archipelago, Dec. Boundaries in New Guinea were settled the following year.

In 1886 Britain and Germany concluded a treaty recognizing each other's Southwest Pacific spheres of influence. France took Wallis Island, 1887; the next year Britain annexed a number of small islands for cable stations. The Berlin Conference on Samoa, 1889, decided to recognize Samoa's independence.

In 1893 Queen Liliuokalani of Hawaii was deposed. In the same year Britain annexed the Solomon Islands. A republic was proclaimed in Hawaii, 1894.

A British protectorate was declared over the Gilbert and Ellice Islands in 1892 and they were annexed as Crown Colonies in 1915. Following the Spanish-American War, 1898, the U.S. took Hawaii, Guam, and the Philippines. In 1899 Germany purchased the Carolines and Marianas from Spain. Britain declared a protectorate over Tonga, 1900. In 1901 the Cook Islands and Niue were absorbed by New Zealand. The Pacific cable was completed, 1902.

On 20 Oct., 1906, Britain and France signed the New Hebrides Convention, which provided that neither power should exercise separate control but rather that each should be responsible for its own nationals. With the outbreak of war in 1914, New Zealand forces occupied Samoa and an Australian force took German New Guinea and parts of the Bismarck Archipelago.

The Areas of Economic Dependence

CENTRAL ASIA

1870–1914

ESTABLISHMENT OF RUSSIAN GOVERNMENT. After the conquest of Turkestan (Tashkent, 1865; Samarkand, 1868; Khiva, 1873; Kokand, 1875), further areas were absorbed into the Russian Empire. Turkmen resistance was broken at Geok-Tepe, Jan. 1881, and the region brought under control; Transcaspia was declared an *oblast*, 6 May, 1881; and additions of territory were made at the expense of Afghanistan, 1885 and 1895. The governor-generalship of Turkestan was created on 11 July, 1867, and that of The Steppes in 1882. By 1898 Turkestan consisted of the *oblasts* of Syr Darya, Fergana, Samarkand, Semirechye, and Transcaspia, while The Steppes comprised Akmolinsk and Semipalatinsk *oblasts*. The regions of Ural'sk and Turgai were separately administered under the Ministry of the Interior. Khiva and Bukhara also had a distinct status, being regarded as vassal states rather than as dependencies.

ADMINISTRATION. A commission headed by Count N. P. Ignatiev drafted, 1884, regulations for Central Asia (the Turkestan Statute went into effect, 1 Jan., 1887), providing for a regional council to assist the gov. gen. and for an independent judiciary. An investigation by Count K. K. Palen, 1908, disclosed much corruption in the Turkestan administration, 2/3 of the officials serving in Transcaspia being convicted of crimes against the state. No significant administrative reforms, however, were carried out before the Revolution of 1917 disrupted the governmental system.

Nevertheless, in both Turkestan and The Steppes there was religious toleration, light taxation, no poll tax or *corvée* (though unpaid labor was employed in railroad and canal construction), and no compulsory military service before 1916.

COLONIZATION. After a slow start Central Asia became an important Russian area of settlement. Peasants were encouraged to take up land, particularly in the The Steppes governor generalship. Resettlement Acts of 1889, 1896, and 1904 and the famine of 1890–91 helped to drive the peasants eastward. During 1893–1905 some 400,000 peasant immigrants took up land in The Steppes, and a further 1.5 m. during 1906–12.

In Turkestan a higher proportion of Russian immigrants were urban dwellers rather than peasants. By 1889 there were c. 20,000 Russians resident in Tashkent and 47,500 (out of a total population of 234,000) by 1904.

ECONOMIC DEVELOPMENT. A railroad running eastward from the Caspian Sea was begun in 1881, the 1st train arriving in Samarkand on 15 May, 1888. Samarkand, Tashkent, and Andizhan were connected by rail, 1895–99, and the link joining Tashkent and Orenburg was completed, 1900–1905. Canals and irrigation dams were constructed, the most important being the Romanov Canal (begun 1900, opened 20 Oct., 1913) and the Sultan-belt and Hindu Kush dams (completed 1890 and 1895 respectively). Many new crops were introduced into Central Asia following the Russian conquest, including silk, grapevines for wine, sugar beets, and various cereals and fruits. By far the most valuable crop, however, proved to be cotton. American cotton plants were imported in the early 1880's and prospered in the fertile Fergana Valley. Between 1886 and 1890 the total acreage under cotton in Turkestan increased sixfold. By the end of the 19th cent. Russia had become the 4th largest textile manufacturing country in the world (after Britain, the U.S., and Germany) with 6 m. spindles and 200,000 power looms, more than half of the latter located in the Moscow area.

INTERNATIONAL RELATIONS. The military conquest of Central Asia by Russia inevitably brought about friction with Persia and Afghanistan and strained relations with the British in India. A Russo-Persian treaty of 1869 confirmed the hold of Persia on the lands south of the Atrek River and prohibited Russia from constructing forts in that region, and another agreement, 1881, established the frontier between the 2 countries. A Russo-Afghanistan boundary agreement was reached, Jan. 1873. No less than 6 Anglo-Russian frontier protocols were negotiated between 1884 and 1895. Finally, a treaty between Britain and Russia, 1907, delineated the respective zones of influence of the 2 powers in Persia, Afghanistan, and Tibet.

SIAM (THAILAND)

1870–1914

RULE OF CHULALONGKORN. The accession to the Siamese throne of Chulalongkorn (Rama V) in 1873 marked the start of a determined attempt to maintain the country's independence through reforms designed to strengthen its resistance against European encroachments. The new king carried out reforms of 2 kinds: symbolic, such as the abolition of compulsory prostration in the royal presence, and substantive. Included in the latter category were steps toward the abolition of slavery, fiscal reforms, ending of forced labor by the lower classes for the army and crown, considerable freedom of the press, decrees on religious toleration, reorganization of the legal system, and public-works projects. Chulalongkorn considered educational improvements essential, and one of his earliest measures provided for the aristocracy to send its sons to special palace schools with a European curriculum or to Europe itself. To further speed Siam toward modernization, Chulalongkorn hired European advisers. Siam also benefited after 1870 by sharing in the vast expansion of European trade resulting from the opening of the Suez Canal. British and French commercial firms and banks dotted Bangkok.

FRENCH PRESSURE ON SIAM. The French conquest of Indochina impeded Siam's eastward expansion. After Vietnam became a French protectorate in 1883, Siam sought to tighten control over Laos. However, the court of Hué, inspired by France, claimed Luang Prabang, while the French worked to increase their influence at the expense of that of Siam among the Lao peoples.

SIAMESE ADMINISTRATIVE RE-FORMS. One of Chulalongkorn's major reforms, 1892, was the centralization of the administrative system and a reduction in the powers exercised by provincial governors. At the same time, local administrative changes designed to give the Siamese people some degree of autonomy were introduced.

PAKNAM INCIDENT. By 1893 France had made it clear that she regarded all territory on the left bank of the Mekong as belonging to Vietnam. When Siam expelled 2 French agents, the French sent troops to occupy land along the lower Mekong and later announced that 2 French gunboats would anchor at Paknam. Siamese pilots were ordered to bring them to Bangkok. Siam refused to provide pilots, but played into French hands by firing first in an engagement with the boats at the Paknam fort, July 1893. Paris then delivered an ultimatum demanding all territory on the Mekong's left bank, payment of an indemnity, and punishment of the Paknam officers who had fired at the French gunboats. London, though alarmed at French expansionism, was fearful of provoking war with Paris and therefore advised Chulalongkorn to accept the ultimatum.

ANGLO-FRENCH AGREEMENT ON SIAM. After much friction, the British and French finally regulated their conflicting claims in the area of Siam, Jan. 1896. In return for renouncing its claims to territory east of the Mekong, Britain won French approval for a joint guarantee of the independence of the Menam River Valley. This provision, by defining Siam's boundaries in terms of the valley, assured the country's independence while also giving it one of the richest areas of the Indochinese Peninsula. Furthermore, Britain and France pledged to seek no exclusive privileges in Siam.

SIAMESE ACCORD WITH FRANCE AND BRITAIN. The years 1904 and 1907 saw Franco-Siamese treaties dealing with territorial claims in Laos and Cambodia. In 1909 an Anglo-Siamese agreement ended British extraterritorial rights in return for Siamese abandonment of 4 Malay states—Kelantan, Trengganu, Kedah, and Perlis—where Siam's rights had been vague and costly to maintain. (Cont. p. 464.)

OTTOMAN EMPIRE

1870–99

BLACK SEA CONFERENCE. In 1870 Russia declared that she would no longer observe the provision of the Treaty of Paris of 1856 limiting the number and size of Russian warships in the Black Sea. This decision was accepted by an international conference held in London, 17 Jan.–13 Mar., 1871. The conference also lifted the restrictions on Turkish ships, but retained the prohibition on the passage of warships through the Straits.

RULE OF ABDUL-AZIZ. The global depression which began in 1873 deprived the Turkish sultan, Abdul-Aziz ('Abd al-'Azīz) (ruled 1861–76), of foreign credit. To meet the deficits caused by his extravagance, he had to increase taxes and this led to internal unrest. On 6 Oct., 1875, the Ottoman government defaulted on payments of interest and amortization of its foreign debts. Another factor which made the western powers hostile to Turkey was the Ottoman government's harsh suppression of rebellions in Bulgaria in the summer of 1876.

NEW OTTOMAN MOVEMENT. On 30 May, 1876, Abdul-Aziz was dethroned in accordance with a fatwa (fetva) ordering the establishment of a constitutional regime. This was a victory for Midhat Pasha and the Young Ottomans. The Young Ottomans were constitutionalists who had hitherto operated clandestinely or from exile. Among them were the great poets, Namik Kemal Bey and Ziya Pasha.

ACCESSION OF ABDUL-HAMID II. Murad (Murād) V, the direct successor to Abdul-Aziz, was deposed, 31 Aug. 1876, after suffering a nervous breakdown. He was replaced by his brother, Abdul-Hamid ('Abd al-Hamīd) II (ruled 1876–1909). On 12 Dec., 1876, an international conference was convened in Istanbul on the initiative of Britain to settle the Bosnian, Serbian, and Bulgarian questions which were threatening to cause a war between Turkey and Russia. On 23 Dec., 1876, the Turkish sultan proclaimed a constitution adapted in part from the Belgian model. This constitution included what was in effect a pledge to safeguard the rights of the Christian subjects of the Ottoman Empire, and had the effect of rendering futile the efforts of the Istanbul Conference.

Abdul-Hamid did not implement all the promised reforms, ignored the constitution, and concentrated on establishing an absolute monarchy. To retain the allegiance of non-Turkish elements within

BALKAN PENINSULA 1800-1914

---- State boundaries, 1914

AUSTRIA-HUNGARY

RUSSIA

BESSARABIA
MOLDAVIA
Danube
BOSNIA
RUMANIA
WALLACHIA
HERZEGOVINA
SERBIA
R.
BULGARIA
MONTENEGRO
EASTERN RUMELIA
ALBANIA
MACEDONIA
Maritza R.
THESSALY
IONIAN IS.
MOREA
AEGEAN SEA
ADRIATIC
SEA
ITALY
IONIAN SEA
BLACK SEA
TURKEY
RHODES
CRETE
MEDITERRANEAN SEA

---•--Limit of Ottoman Empire, 1800
To Russia, 1812
To Austria-Hungary, 1908
Independent states in 1830
Independent states in 1878
Independent states in 1914

© Lilli Tanzer 1970

his empire, he tried to revive the influence of the Caliphate.

RUSSO-TURKISH WAR. On 30 June, 1876, Serbia, at Russian instigation, declared war on Turkey. Montenegro followed. The collapse of Serbian arms led Russia to declare war on Turkey, 24 Apr., 1877. Failing to receive any support from the European powers, Turkey suffered defeat, and agreed to a truce, 31 Jan., 1878, and to the preliminary peace treaty of San Stefano, 3 Mar. Concessions exacted by Russia at San Stefano alarmed the British, who were concerned about the Russian threat to their imperial communications in the Middle East. On 4 June, 1878, Turkey, in return for granting a lease of Cyprus, concluded a defensive alliance with Britain.

CONGRESS OF BERLIN. Convened at Bismarck's instigation, the Congress of Berlin terminated Turkey's dispute with Russia by treaty of 13 July, 1878. This Berlin agreement was more favorable to Turkey than the San Stefano treaty had been. But Turkey had to pledge herself to introduce reforms in certain of her provinces which had Christian inhabitants.

OTTOMAN PUBLIC DEBT. Negotiations between the Ottoman government and representatives of the European bondholders led to the formation of a Council of Administration of the Ottoman Public Debt, with European directors, to ensure the payment of Turkey's debts. By a ferman of 20 Dec., 1881, several categories of Turkish government revenues were assigned to the Council.

REVOLTS AGAINST TURKISH RULE. Following a bloodless revolution in Eastern Rumelia, Sept. 1885, Turkey appointed a Bulgarian governor for that province, 1886, thus tacitly accepting its annexation by Bulgaria. In 1889 a rebellion against Turkish rule began in Crete. In 1894 Armenian mountaineers of the Sassun region also rose against the Turks. The violent suppression of this Armenian revolt prompted Britain and France to force Turkey to promise reforms, May 1895. The sultan did not carry out his promises, the powers failed to take any

measures against Turkey, and Armenians in many areas continued to rebel. Some 80,000 of them were killed. On 17 Apr., 1897, Turkey declared war on Greece, whose government she held responsible for the renewed revolt in Crete. The powers came to the rescue of the Greeks against the advancing Turks. Concessions were made to Turkey, but Crete was placed under international control.

GROWTH OF GERMAN INFLUENCE. Germany opposed the anti-Turkish settlement of the Cretan question. The German government had become keenly interested in acquiring new markets in the Ottoman Empire. Abdul-Hamid also preferred the Germany of William II to liberal Britain and France. In 1899 he granted to the Deutsche Bank a concession to build a railway to Baghdad.

1900-1914

YOUNG TURK MOVEMENT. While Abdul-Hamid ruled despotically, the Young Turks, successors to the Young Ottomans, agitated (especially among students) by means of clandestine publications and through secret societies for the restoration of the Constitution of 1876. In 1907, in Salonika, Talaat Bey and Rahmi Bey formed the secret Society of Union and Progress. Liaison was maintained with the Turkish revolutionaries in Europe who were led by Ahmad Riza. In June 1908 many officers of the Macedonian army, aroused by reports (later proved false) that Britain and Russia were planning to partition Turkey, joined hands with the Society of Union and Progress. Among them were Niazi, Mustafa Kemal, Enver, and Jemal Pasha. A rising led by Niazi, June 1908, ignited several other revolts, and forced Abdul-Hamid to restore the constitution, 23 July. The rebellious Christian groups in the Turkish Balkans now joined the Union and Progress movement. Racial, religious and national differences, however, made cooperation difficult.

FALL OF ABDUL-HAMID II. Russia and Austria, both of whom considered a strong Turkey adverse to their interests, co-ordinated their plans against the Ottoman Empire in a meeting on 15 Sept., 1908. Turkey was forced to recognize the Austrian annexation of Bosnia and the independence of Bulgaria. Rebellions by Armenians, Kurds, and Nestorians followed. A revolt in Yemen was settled by agreement with its imam, 1911.

The "reactionary" opposition to the Young Turks culminated in a military coup, 14 Apr., 1909. Abdul-Hamid sided with the reactionaries. But a Young Turk army under Mahmud Shevket Pasha arrived from Salonika and captured the capital, 24 Apr. Abdul-Hamid was deposed, and Mohammed (Mehmed) V became sultan, 27 Apr.

INDEPENDENCE OF THE BALKANS. On 28 Sept., 1909, Italy demanded from Turkey the cession of Tripoli and Cyrenaica. In the war that ensued the Turks scored some victories, but their troubles in the Balkans compelled them to sue for peace. The Treaty of Lausanne signed 18 Oct., 1912, gave Italy control over Tripoli, Cyrenaica, and Rhodes.

In 1912 a 2-year-long negotiation between Turkey and the powers on the status of Christian subjects of the Ottoman Empire broke down. Thereupon, Oct. 1912, a Balkan alliance of Bulgaria, Greece, Serbia, and Montenegro, supported by Russia, attacked Turkey. Despite some naval successes, the Turks had to retreat. In Dec. 1912 a peace conference was convened in London. The resulting agreement displeased the Young Turks, who then staged a coup against the Liberal Unionist government of Kiamil (Kâmil) Pasha, Jan. 1913. Mahmud Shevket was installed as premier. But even this new government had to accept, 30 May, the Enos-Midia line as the western frontier of Turkey. In the summer of 1913 a war among the Balkan allies over the division of the spoils taken from Turkey permitted the latter to regain some of the territory lost. Peace treaties were signed with Bulgaria, 29 Sept., 1913; with Greece, 14 Nov., 1913; and with Serbia, 14 Mar., 1914. Greece received Crete and most of the Aegean Islands. But Edirne was given back to Turkey, whose frontiers were now moved to the Maritsa River.

PROBLEM OF TURKISH UNITY. The modernizing efforts of the Young Turks were in part successful, especially in the fields of finance and education. But they were disturbed to find that their liberalism and constitutionalism failed to forestall demands for self-determination on the part of non-Turkish elements of the empire. The Young Turks reacted by abandoning the ideals of the 1908 revolution and pursuing more exclusively nationalistic policies. For a time support for Pan-Islam gained ground in Turkey, but this soon gave way to the greater enthusiasm generated by the Pan-Turkish movement, which was led by Enver Pasha and had as its goal the union of all Turkish-speaking peoples under the Osmanli Turks. Another movement of the period, espoused by Ziya Gökalp, advocated the directing of all efforts toward building a Turkish national state. (*Cont. p. 465.*)

MIDDLE EAST

Persia

1870–1904

EXTERNAL RELATIONS. In 1872 the Sistan Arbitration Commission partially settled a Persian-Afghanistan dispute over Sistan by dividing that province between the 2 countries. Settlement of a boundary question betweeen Persia and British Baluchistan followed. In 1879 Persia agreed to accept Russian officers to train and command the Persian Cossack Brigade. Russia thus came to control Persia's only effective military force. Russia's conquest of Geok Tepe, 1881, and Merv, 1884, made her Persia's sole neighbor to the north and northeast.

RULE OF NASIR ED-DIN SHAH. Nasir ed-Din Shah (ruled 1848–96) visited Europe, 1873, 1878, and 1889. The nature and tempo of his Europeanization program was much influenced by these trips. The concessions he granted to foreigners, especially the tobacco *régie* (monopoly), 8 Mar., 1890, made him unpopular, and he was assassinated, 1 May, 1896.

RULE OF MUZAFFAR ED-DIN SHAH. Nasir ed-Din's successor was his son, Muzaffar ed-Din Shah (ruled 1896–1907). On 28 May, 1901, Muzaffar ed-Din granted an oil concession to a British citizen, William Knox D'Arcy (1849–1917), which became the model for later oil concessions in the Middle East.

1905–14

CONSTITUTIONAL REVOLUTION. In 1905 a group of merchants took sanctuary in a Teheran mosque to protest the shah's lavish spending and the corruption and mismanagement of his government. Some ulema ('ulamā) joined the protesting merchants, but all were soon forced to leave the mosque. They then took sanctuary in the shrine of Shah Abdul Azim ('Abd al-'Aẓīm), near Teheran. To disperse them, the shah promised to dismiss 'Ayn al-Dawla, his unpopular sadr-i azam (sadr-i a'zam) (prime minister), and to establish an Idalat Kahanah ('Adālat Khāna, House of Justice). When he failed to carry out these pledges, a large group of Teheran ulema, as a further gesture of protest, journeyed to the holy city of Qum. In Teheran a crowd of some 12,000 merchants and clergy took sanctuary in the British Legation grounds and demanded the removal of 'Ayn al-Dawla and the return of the ulema from Qum. The shah agreed to dismiss his sadr-i azam, 30 July, 1906, but the protesters were also demanding a written constitution. To this the shah reluctantly agreed, 5 Aug.

INAUGURATION OF THE MAJLIS. In Oct. 1906 the first Majlis (the lower house of parliament) was inaugurated. On 30 Dec. the shah signed a law which promulgated the draft of the Fundamental Law (constitution) prepared by a committee of Majlis deputies.

RULE OF MOHAMMED ALI SHAH. On 8 Jan., 1907, Muzaffar ed-Din Shah died. His son and successor, Mohammed Ali Shah (Muḥammad 'Alī Shāh) (ruled 1907–9), was determined to suppress the constitution. But in Aug. 1907, 'Ayn al-Dawla, who had been reappointed sadr-i azam by the new shah, was assassinated, and in Oct. Mohammed Ali yielded to the pressure of public opinion and signed a Supplement to the Fundamental Law.

GROWTH OF EUROPEAN INFLUENCE. On 31 Aug., 1907, Britain and Russia, prompted by a common fear of Germany, agreed to settle their differences in Western Asia. Their agreement divided Persia into a Russian (northern) and a British (southern) sphere of influence, with a neutral "independent" zone in between. The agreement outraged the Persians; the Constitutionalists especially felt betrayed by Britain.

COUNTERREVOLUTION OF 1908. In Nov. 1907 Mohammed Ali Shah reaffirmed his loyalty to the constitution. But in June 1908 he used the Cossack Brigade to attack the Majlis building. Some deputies were killed and others injured, a number were later captured and executed, and a few succeeded in taking refuge in the British Legation. On 27 June the shah declared the Assembly dissolved and the constitution abolished. In protest an uprising took place in Tabriz which was quelled only with the active support of Russian troops in Apr. 1909.

CONSTITUTIONAL REGIME. Antishah tribes from the areas of Rasht and Isfahan united in a march on Teheran, July 1909, which met only feeble resistance. The shah was granted asylum in the Russian Legation, and was deposed in favor of his son, Ahmed (Aḥmad), by the leaders of a new regime.

In 1911 the Majlis granted vast powers to an American, William Morgan Shuster (1877–1960), to administer Persia's finances. The need for foreign advisers stemmed from the Constitutionalists' desire for financial and administrative reform and from their own lack of expertise in these fields.

Mohammed Ali Shah returned from his Russian exile, 1911, and attempted to regain his throne. But his army was defeated by Constitutionalist troops, who also put down a related revolt in Kurdistan led by Mohammed Ali's brother.

In Nov. 1911, 2 Russian ultimata demanding the dismissal of Shuster were rejected by the Majlis, whereupon Russian troops invaded northern Persia. The regent, Nasir al-Mulk, used force to close a recalcitrant Majlis, 24 Dec., and then asked the Shuster Mission to leave. Britain, needing Russian co-operation against Germany, acquiesced in Russia's interference in Persia. (*Cont. p. 466.*)

Arabia

1870–1914

RULE OF SAUD III. In 1871 the Saudi chief, Abdallah ('Abd Allah) II (ruled 1865–71, 1874–84), was defeated by his brother, Saud (Su'ud) III (ruled 1871–74). The Ottoman Turks responded to Abdallah's call for assistance by entering Arabia and bringing the district of al-Hasa under their control. A struggle for leadership produced a period of instability in the Saudi domain. In 1874 Saud III died, and Abdallah returned to the throne.

RASHIDI DOMINATION. Soon after regaining control, however, Abdallah lost it to Mohammed ibn Abdallah (Muḥammad ibn 'Abd Allah) al-Rashid of the Shammar tribe. Abdallah was kept in the Rashidi capital until 1889, when, ailing, he was allowed to return to Riyadh. He was succeeded after his death in the same year by his son, Abd ('Abd) al-Rahman (ruled 1886). Rebelling against Rashidi domination, Abd al-Rahman was defeated and forced to flee to Kuwait. The Rashidis now incorporated the Wahabi realm into their own domain.

In 1900 Sheikh Mubarak of Kuwait and Abd al-Rahman staged an abortive military uprising against the Rashidis.

RULE OF ABD AL-AZIZ. In 1901, Abd al-Rahman's son, Abd al-Aziz ('Abd al-'Azīz) (ruled 1902–53), led a group of 40 young supporters in a march toward Riyadh. By the time this force reached the Saudi capital, Jan. 1902, it had grown to 200. Abd al-Aziz invaded the city, 15 Jan., and defeated and replaced the Rashidi governor of Riyadh. In 1904 Abd al-Aziz defeated an army of Rashidis and their Turkish allies, after which Turkey withdrew from central Arabia. In 1906 the chief of the al-Rashid tribe was killed in a battle with Abd al-Aziz. This ended the Rashidi bid for power at the expense of the Saudis.

In 1910 Abd al-Aziz organized the first Ikhwan (brethren) group in order to revive the ideals of the Wahabi movement. Groups of Bedouins were settled in agricultural colonies, and served Abd al-Aziz as a dedicated and effective military force in the years to come. In 1913 Abd al-Aziz defeated the Turks and annexed the district of al-Hasa to his kingdom.

BRITAIN AND THE PERSIAN GULF SHEIKDOMS. On 22 Dec., 1880, the sheik of Bahrain; on 20 Mar., 1891, the sheik of Muscat, and on 23 Jan., 1899, the sheik of Kuwait in separate agreements surrendered their external sovereignty to Britain. (*Cont. p. 469.*)

Egypt

1870–82

SOUTHWARD EXPANSION. Egyptian forces annexed the former sultanate of Darfur in the Sudan, 1874; occupied Zaila; and took Harar in Ethiopia, 1875. But the invasions of Ethiopia, 1875–76, proved abortive.

FINANCIAL CRISIS. On 8 June, 1873, an Ottoman firman confirmed special privileges, amounting to virtual autonomy, previously conferred on Ismail (Isma'il), the khedive of Egypt. By 1875 Ismail's lavish spending had so depleted Egypt's treasury that he could not even pay the interest on his country's foreign debt. He was therefore compelled to sell his shares in the Suez Canal Co. to the British government, Nov. 1875. On 2 May, 1876, Ismail issued a decree establishing a Public Debt Commission. British dissatisfaction with certain provisions of this decree led him to issue a new one, 18 Nov., 1876, which put the revenues and expenditures of the Egyptian government under the dual control of Britain and France.

On 7 Apr., 1879, Ismail dismissed his British minister of finance and his French minister of public works in an attempt to lessen international control over Egypt's finances. The Ottoman Porte, responding to pressure from Britain and France, deposed Ismail, 26 June, in favor of his son, Mohammed (Muḥammad) Tawfiq. Anglo-French control over Egypt's finances was reinstated, Sept.

RISE OF NATIONALISM. In 1879 Jamal al-Din Afghani, who had been making speeches urging the Egyptians to resist the West, if necessary by violence, was expelled from Egypt. In the same year a mutiny by Egyptian officers indicated the extent of their resentment against foreign domination in the army. In 1882 the khedive felt compelled to appoint a nationalist cabinet, in which the minister of war was Ahmad Urabi ('Urābī), a colonel who had become the leader of Egyptian opposition to foreign control. On 7 Feb., 1882, the khedive ordered the establishment of an assembly of deputies and declared Arabic the official language.

To strengthen the khedive against the nationalists, France and Britain dispatched fleets to Alexandria, May 1882. Alexandria was bombarded by the British, 11 July. The French and Italians having declined to join in, a British invading force defeated Urabi's army, Sept. The British then reinstated the khedive.

1882–1914

BRITISH OCCUPATION. On 20 Sept., 1882, the Egyptian army was dissolved. In Dec. the British began organizing a new army under British officers. On 3 Jan., 1883, the British foreign secretary outlined British policy for Egypt: Britain would hold supreme authority during the period of her occupation, which initially was expected to be short. On 11 Jan. the dual-control system came to an end, and a law of 1 May established consultative councils in Egypt's provinces and 2 assemblies in Cairo. In Sept. Sir Evelyn Baring, later Lord Cromer (1841–1917), arrived in Egypt as British agent and consul general to administer the country.

On 20 Nov., 1883, France acceded to a British demand that the number of British representatives on the Suez Canal control board should be increased from 3 to 10. By means of the London Convention, 18 Mar., 1885, the powers reduced Egypt's national debt and allowed additional borrowing. By a further convention on Egypt, 24 Oct., 1885, Britain and the Ottoman Empire agreed that each would appoint a high commissioner to study the Egyptian situation. The 2 states signed an agreement, 22 May, 1887, but this was never ratified by the Porte. On 29 Oct., 1888, a convention providing for free navigation of the Suez Canal was signed by the Ottoman Empire and the European powers.

On 7 Jan., 1892, on Tawfiq's death, his son, Abbas ('Abbās) II (ruled 1892–1914), succeeded him. On 15 Jan., 1893, the new khedive replaced an Anglophile prime minister with the pro-French Husayn Fakhri Pasha who was sympathetic to the nationalists. In 1894 Mustafa Kamal founded the Hizb al-Watani (National Party). On 12 Nov., 1895, Abbas reappointed the pro-British Mustafa Fahmi prime minister, thus indicating his acquiescence in British domination in Egypt.

INTERNATIONAL RELATIONS. In 1898 French forces occupied Fashoda. The British claimed that the area belonged to Egypt, and the French withdrew. On 19 Jan., 1899, Britain and Egypt signed an agreement that they would rule the Sudan as a condominium, and France formally abandoned her claims in the Nile Valley, 21 Mar. On 8 Apr., 1904, France and Britain agreed to recognize each other's spheres of influence in Morocco and Egypt respectively. In return for greater financial independence, the khedive acknowledged Britain's special position in Egypt, 1 Jan., 1905. On 1 Oct., 1906, the Porte and Egypt agreed that south Sinai should remain under the suzerainty of the Ottoman Empire, while continuing to be administered by Egypt.

EGYPTIAN NATIONALISM AND BRITISH REACTIONS. In 1899 Mohammed Abduh (Moḥammad 'Abduh), a disciple of Afghani, was appointed chief mufti, the highest religious office under the state. Despite strong opposition from conservative ulema, Abduh pressed for an extensive modernization of Islam. An incident in June 1906 between some British officers and the inhabitants of the village of Dinshaway became a key factor in uniting the peasants with the nationalists who opposed the British occupation.

In Apr. 1907 Lord Cromer resigned. The new British administration, under Sir Eldon Gorst (1835–1916), was intended to be more liberal, but failed to satisfy the nationalists. On 10 Feb., 1910, a Moslem nationalist assassinated the prime minister, Butros Ghali, who had angered the nationalists by asking the Legislative Assembly, unsuccessfully, to approve an extension of the Suez Canal Co.'s concession. In Sept. 1911 Lord Kitchener (1850–1916) was appointed head of the British administration in Egypt. (Cont. p. 466.)

THE ERA OF WORLD WAR, 1914–1945

The War of 1914–1918

OUTBREAK OF THE WAR

1914

ASSASSINATION OF FRANCIS FERDINAND. 28 June. In Sarajevo, capital of the recently annexed province of Bosnia, on Sunday morning, 28 June, after an abortive bombing attempt by his co-conspirators, Gavrilo Princip (1894–1918), a Serbian nationalist, fatally shot Archduke Francis Ferdinand, the heir to the Austrian and Hungarian thrones, and his wife. Six of the 7 assassins, members of a Serbian secret society, were caught. One was executed; the others, all under age, were sentenced to long terms in prison.

The Sarajevo murders brought to a head a long-standing antagonism between Austria-Hungary and Serbia. In the week following the assassinations, it seemed that no major crisis would result from the incident, but Count Leopold von Berchtold (1863–1942), the Austrian foreign minister, presupposing Serbian complicity (little evidence of which ever came to light beyond possible foreknowledge of the event), determined to make use of the murders to crush once and for all Serbian competition in the Balkans.

THE "BLANK CHECK." 5 July. Berchtold sent an envoy to Berlin and Emperor William II assured him, 5 July, that Germany would fully support any action the Dual Monarchy might undertake against Serbia because of the assassinations. Chancellor Theobald von Bethmann-Hollweg (1856–1921) officially reiterated this promise of unconditional support, 6 July. Historians differ greatly about the purposes motivating this "blank check." The proponents of German war guilt consider it a proof of Germany's desire for immediate hostilities; other historians consider it at worst diplomatic folly.

AUSTRIAN ULTIMATUM TO SERBIA. 23 July. Berchtold overcame internal opposition to his policy and by 19 July an ultimatum had been drawn up. Its presentation to Serbia was postponed until 6 P.M., 23 July, so that the French president, Raymond Poincaré (1860–1934), and premier, René Viviani (1863–1925), would have left St. Petersburg, where they were on a state visit to their Russian ally, to whom the Serbs looked for support. Berchtold thought it better to wait until the French leaders had departed so that no prompt concerted reaction could be forthcoming. The ultimatum, which called for an answer within 48 hours, included de-

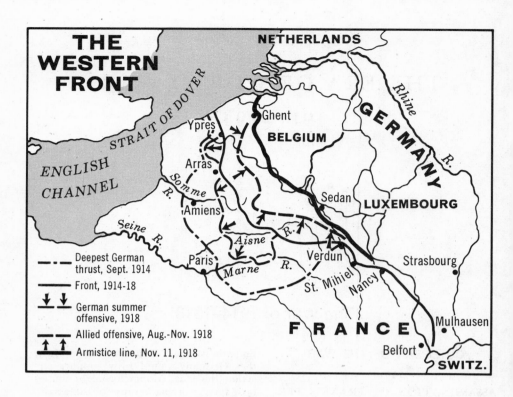

THE WESTERN FRONT

NETHERLANDS

ENGLISH CHANNEL

STRAIT OF DOVER

Ypres

Ghent

BELGIUM

GERMANY

Rhine R.

Arras

Somme R.

Amiens

Seine R.

Aisne

Paris

Marne

R.

Sedan

LUXEMBOURG

Verdun

R.

St. Mihiel

Nancy

Strasbourg

Mulhausen

Belfort

SWITZ.

FRANCE

Deepest German thrust, Sept. 1914

Front, 1914-18

German summer offensive, 1918

Allied offensive, Aug.-Nov. 1918

Armistice line, Nov. 11, 1918

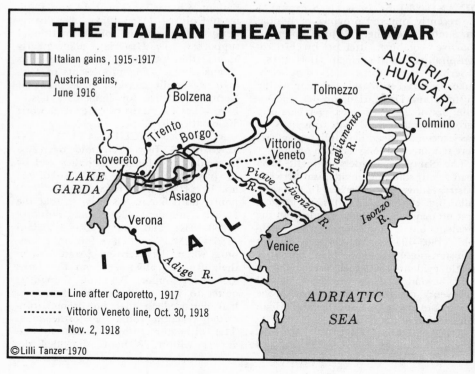

THE ITALIAN THEATER OF WAR

Italian gains, 1915-1917

Austrian gains, June 1916

AUSTRIA-HUNGARY

Bolzena

Tolmezzo

Tolmino

Trento

Borgo

Rovereto

LAKE GARDA

Asiago

Verona

Vittorio Veneto

Piave R.

Livenza R.

Tagliamento R.

Isonzo R.

ITALY

Adige R.

Venice

ADRIATIC SEA

Line after Caporetto, 1917

Vittorio Veneto line, Oct. 30, 1918

Nov. 2, 1918

© Lilli Tanzer 1970

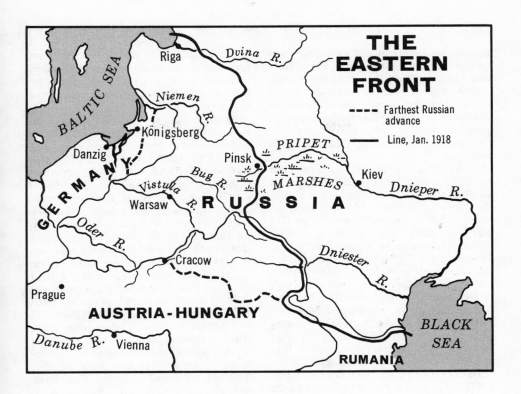

THE EASTERN FRONT

- - - - - Farthest Russian advance

——— Line, Jan. 1918

BALTIC SEA

Riga

Dvina R.

Niemen R.

Königsberg

Danzig

GERMANY

PRIPET

Pinsk

MARSHES

Kiev

Dnieper R.

Vistula R.

Bug R.

Warsaw

RUSSIA

Oder R.

Cracow

Dniester R.

Prague

AUSTRIA-HUNGARY

Danube R. Vienna

BLACK SEA

RUMANIA

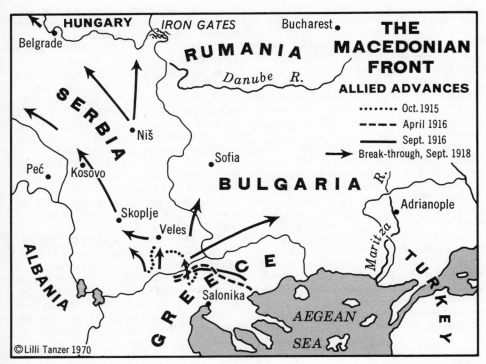

THE MACEDONIAN FRONT

ALLIED ADVANCES

········· Oct. 1915

- - - - - April 1916

——— Sept. 1916

→ Break-through, Sept. 1918

HUNGARY

IRON GATES

Bucharest

Belgrade

RUMANIA

Danube R.

SERBIA

Niš

Sofia

Peć

Kosovo

BULGARIA

Maritza R.

Adrianople

Skoplje

Veles

GREECE

TURKEY

ALBANIA

Salonika

AEGEAN SEA

© Lilli Tanzer 1970

mands that Serbia formally condemn and end all Pan-Serb propaganda, expel from office anyone fomenting it, instigate legal action against certain officials whom Austria-Hungary would name, and allow agents of the Dual Monarchy to participate on Serbian soil in inquiries and proceedings concerning the Sarajevo murders.

A few minutes before the time limit expired, Serbia replied, 25 July, in a manner that was conciliatory but clearly did not meet Berchtold's demands, although the Serbs had gone far in that direction and were willing to submit points remaining in contention to the International Tribunal at The Hague. The reply was rejected and Austria-Hungary broke diplomatic relations with Serbia, which, anticipating this, had earlier that afternoon decreed general mobilization. At 9:23 P.M. Austria-Hungary ordered a countermobilization; 27 July was ordered as "alarm" day, and 28 July as the 1st day of actual mobilization.

DIPLOMATIC NEGOTIATIONS AND MILITARY PREPARATIONS. 25 July–1 Aug. From the time the ultimatum was issued, the statesmen of the Great Powers sought delay or compromise. This failing, other attempts at peaceful settlement were tried; but once the 1st mobilization had begun, steps in the direction of war took on increasing importance. Each country's mobilization was tied to a strict timetable, and none wanted to be unprepared in the event of hostilities.

Sergei D. Sazonov (1861–1927), the Russian minister for foreign affairs, attempted to have the ultimatum's time limit extended, 25 July. At the same time Russia put into effect the necessary military measures preparatory to mobilization.

British Foreign Secretary Sir Edward Grey (1862–1933), whose earlier attempts at mediation failed, proposed a 4-power conference, 26 July. Germany declined; France hesitatingly accepted; Russia agreed in principle, though preferring to rely on direct negotiations with the Dual Monarchy. Meanwhile the Admiralty

ordered the British fleet not to disperse for maneuvers, as planned, and the German fleet was ordered, 27 July, to concentrate off the Norwegian coast and return to base at Kiel.

Alarmed at the warlike course of events, William II interrupted a cruise and returned to Berlin, 27 July.

AUSTRO-HUNGARIAN DECLARATION OF WAR. 28 July. Berchtold thought a *fait accompli* would undercut Russian or other Great Power intervention. Although gunboats bombarded Belgrade, the Serbian capital, the next day, 29 July, the Dual Monarchy's military chiefs estimated that they would need until 12 Aug. to complete their mobilization.

The Austro-Hungarian action caught the Germans by surprise, as they had not believed hostilities would commence until mobilization was complete; William II had just put forward a peace plan which called for occupation of Belgrade as a Serbian pledge for fulfillment of its commitments as well as guarantees of that country's territorial integrity. The declaration of war ended Austro-Russian talks, begun 26 July. French support for Russia was reiterated in conversations between Sazonov and the French ambassador.

RUSSIAN MOBILIZATION. 29–30 July. Czar Nicholas II, under pressure from his military advisers, who argued that Russia needed a very long time to mobilize fully, ordered a general mobilization, 29 July. Telegraphic exchanges between the czar and William II, in which Russia was assured that Austria would be restrained, caused Nicholas to suspend the order and direct only partial mobilization against Austria-Hungary. On 30 July in the late afternoon, the military and Sazonov prevailed on the czar to renew the mobilization order, which was to go into effect on 31 July.

BELGIAN NEUTRALITY QUESTION. 29 July. Germany made a bid for British neutrality in the event of war, but in so doing indirectly admitted that the neutrality of Belgium (established by international treaty in 1839) would not be respected. Upset, Grey the next day, 30 July, requested France and Germany to respect Belgian neutrality. France answered that she would, and Germany refused, 31 July.

OTHER MOBILIZATIONS. Austria-Hungary ordered general mobilization, 31 July. At 1 P.M. on the same day, Germany proclaimed a state of "threatening danger of war" (*drohendes Kriegsgefahr*), the preliminary step to complete mobilization. By midnight a 12-hour ultimatum had been delivered to Sazonov, requiring that Russia suspend all war measures or face the consequences. The same afternoon Germany demanded to know the French position in case of a Russo-German conflict. If, contrary to Germany's expectations, France chose to remain neutral, she should turn over the fortresses at Toul and Verdun, which would be held as pledges and returned after the end of hostilities in the East.

About 4:45 P.M., 1 Aug., Central European Time, France ordered a general mobilization. About a quarter-hour later the Germans mobilized and that evening declared war on Russia, having received no reply to their ultimatum.

BEGINNING OF HOSTILITIES. Germany declared war on France, 3 Aug., using as a pretext alleged border violations. In reality, strategic considerations dictated this move; German military plans called for a quick victory in the West before turning to face an eastern foe.

Although the course of events on the Continent had become plain, the British cabinet, in a series of long and acrimonious meetings, 2 Aug., failed to resolve upon any clear-cut course. The decision to assure France that the Channel coast and North Sea shipping would be protected against German naval attack (according to Grey, a moral obligation arising out of joint naval and military staff arrangements) caused the resignation of 2 cabinet members.

On the night of 1–2 Aug. the Germans marched into Luxembourg and in the early evening of 2 Aug. they demanded transit across Belgium, guaranteeing that country's territorial integrity. On 3 Aug., at 7 A.M., Belgium rejected the demand

and appealed for help. That afternoon the Germans invaded Belgium, although they did not declare war until 4 Aug.

Grey went before Parliament, 3 Aug., and received support for his policies. An ultimatum was sent to Berlin demanding German withdrawal from Belgium. It was at this time that the German chancellor made the unfortunate reference to the 1839 treaty as "a scrap of paper." By midnight, 4 Aug., Great Britain was at war with Germany, partly because honor demanded the action after Belgium's neutrality had been violated, partly because it was a firm principle of British policy that no Great Power should control the Low Countries.

The war spread rapidly. Only Italy among the important members of the original alliance blocs stood aside. She did so on the grounds that she was under no alliance obligation since Austria-Hungary's ultimatum to Serbia was an offensive act.

OPPOSING FORCES. (1) Armies. Germany, considered to have the best military machine in the world, mustered over 2 m. men. Headed by the redoubtable general staff, which had probably the best grasp of the effects of new weapons on battlefield movement, the German divisions were well equipped with artillery and machine guns. Austria-Hungary, which militarily lagged far behind its ally, mobilized over 2,700,000 men when it went on to a full war footing. The Dual Monarchy's heavy artillery was excellent, but training was insufficient, staff work incompetent, supply indifferent, and often a German-speaking officer could not make himself intelligible to his men because only 1 soldier in 4 spoke German. Bulgaria and Turkey, which joined the Central Powers after hostilities had begun, added little military strength beyond numbers since their armies were woefully deficient in equipment and training.

France had only 60% of the potential military man power of Germany and in 1914, to mobilize an army of 1,650,000, found it necessary to call up a larger number of reserves. Although lacking in artillery and machine guns, the French were imbued with a philosophy of attack (*attaque, attaque, toujours l'attaque*), a policy which was to cost their armies dearly. The Russians, who mobilized over 4 m. men in the 1st year of war, relied almost wholly on numbers, but behind the Russian "steamroller" lay technological backwardness, wholesale graft, and almost incredible deficiencies in supply, armament, and training. Great Britain, whose military planners had always emphasized sea power, possessed a small, highly trained, professional army, and initially could put into the field only 125,000 men with limited but good equipment. The Belgian and Serbian armed forces, each numbering about 185,000, although consisting of brave fighters, were equipped very primitively.

TOTAL MOBILIZED MAN POWER
OF ALL BELLIGERENTS,
1914–18

*Allies and
Associated
Powers:*

Russia	12,000,000
France (incl. colonial troops)	8,410,000
Great Britain (incl. colonial troops)	8,095,000
Italy	5,615,000
U.S.A.	4,355,000
Japan	800,000
Rumania	750,000
Serbia	707,000
Belgium	267,000
Greece	230,000
Portugal	100,000
Montenegro	50,000
Total	41,379,000

Central Powers:

Germany	11,000,000
Austria-Hungary	7,800,000
Turkey	2,850,000
Bulgaria	1,100,000
Total	22,750,000

(2) **Navies.** The war at sea was to be primarily a contest between Great Britain and Germany, whose respective comparative strengths were: large warships, 156 and 87; destroyers, 218 and 142; subma-

rines, 55 and 28. Although the Russian navy was confined to the Baltic and Black seas, the Central Powers were hopelessly outclassed on the high seas. Germany's first-rate navy was superior in many technical features of gunnery and damage control, but her allies had only meager sea forces, while Great Britain, the greatest naval power in the world, could count on the assistance of the French and Japanese navies.

The Central Powers were also greatly inferior in commercial shipping. The allies had over 4 times their gross tonnage.

(3) **Air Forces.** When hostilities began, military aviation was still in its infancy, and reconnaissance was considered the main function of the airplane. Such small bombs as might be carried were dropped over the side; armament, usually only for defensive purposes, meant a rifle or a revolver. Planes were quite crude, with "doped" fabric wings and 70-hp engines capable of producing speeds of 60–70 mph. The Germans had about 380 planes and 30 dirigibles, also called Zeppelins after their designer, Ferdinand von Zeppelin (1838–1917); the French had approximately 120 planes and 10 dirigibles; the British had about the same number of planes, of which some 60 were assigned to the British forces in France. Russia and Austria-Hungary each had a few planes.

(4) **Economic Potential.** With the exception of Russia, which was to require major economic assistance to meet her commitments, the highly industrialized economies of the major allied powers enabled them to meet all war requirements. Of the Central Powers, only Germany was heavily industrialized, and her economy had to bear the burden of supporting her allies; Turkey and Bulgaria rapidly became almost entirely dependent on Germany for war materials.

Germany lost her colonies during the 1st few months of the war, and the Central Powers were hemmed in by an effective allied naval blockade. But they, especially Germany, made up most of their deficiencies through territorial conquests which in the West placed them in control of the facilities of Belgium and industrialized northern France, and in the East gained them Balkan resources and man power as well as some of the Russian granaries. The Russian collapse in 1917 brought the Germans further economic advantages.

Despite intense allied economic warfare against them, the Central Powers held their own economically until the U.S.A., with its great resources and industrial capacity, actively entered the war.

STRATEGY. (1) The Western Front. Germany's Schlieffen plan, the essentials of which were formulated in 1905 by Alfred von Schlieffen (1833–1913), chief of the general staff, 1891–1906, called for an immediate offensive against France while remaining on the defensive against Russia. Believing victory possible within 6 weeks, he planned that an overwhelmingly strong right (northern) wing would crash through the Low Countries, capture the Channel ports, bear down on Paris from the west, and trap the French armies against the Swiss borders and their own fortifications in the Vosges Mts. area. A weak left wing would further unbalance the French by enticing them to liberate Alsace-Lorraine. Reportedly, Schlieffen's dying words were, "Keep the right wing strong." By 1914 Moltke had seriously modified this plan. Russia's rapid recovery from the travails of 1905 and the increased importance of the Rhineland industrial area to Germany led him to change the 7:1 troop ratio favoring the right wing to less than 4:1. He also decided not to violate Dutch neutrality, thus forcing the German armies to pass through the fortified Belgian area at Liège.

The allies had no precise plans. Belgium, which prized its neutrality, had not wished to endanger it by any joint war planning with any of its neighbors. If invaded and hard-pressed, the Belgians anticipated withdrawing into the fortress area of Antwerp—as was done. The British general staff had expected that if war came, a British Expeditionary Force (B.E.F.) would be called upon to fight the Germans on the Continent, but its ulti-

mate destination was not clear. French War Plan XVII, drawn up in 1913 by Gen. Joseph Joffre (1857–1931), chief of the French general staff from 1911 to 1916, unwittingly played into the hands of the Germans in that it called for drives into German territory on both sides of Metz to liberate Lorraine. Joffre's plan recognized that Germany might invade Belgium, but mistakenly assumed that, owing to lack of troops, German operations would remain east of the Meuse, and that if necessary the French could extend their battle lines. The French also counted on a Russian offensive to divert German troops eastward.

(2) Eastern Fronts. Austria-Hungary's war plans assumed that the war with Serbia could be settled before Russia could fully mobilize and open another front. The Dual Monarchy, unaware of Germany's total commitment to an offensive against France, also planned for joint operations against the 250-mile-deep salient formed by Russian Poland, which threatened East Prussia on the north and Austrian Galicia on the south. The Russian offensive plans, which went into effect when the Germans' main drive was made against the French, called for pincer movements from Poland into these areas, where the Russians hoped to envelop their enemy.

The Serbs planned purely defensive campaigns. If hard-pressed, they intended to retire into the mountains and await help—which they did in 1915.

THE WESTERN FRONT AND ITALY

1914

GERMAN SWEEP THROUGH BELGIUM. 4–20 Aug. Crossing into Belgium had begun during the early morning of 4 Aug., and within 24 hours German troops had reached Liège, one of the strongest fortresses in Europe. The city was captured, 7 Aug., but the 12 forts surrounding it held out. Heavy 420-mm. siege howitzers were brought in, 12 Aug., and the forts, which had been built to withstand only 210-mm. fire, fell one by one, the last on 16 Aug. The timetable of the not yet completely mobilized Germans had not been greatly delayed. Namur, invested 19 Aug., fell 6 days later. Meanwhile the remaining Belgian forces, under command of King Albert (1875–1934), withdrew north to Antwerp, completing this move by 20 Aug. The same day the Germans entered Brussels.

BATTLE OF THE FRONTIERS. 14–25 Aug. The French, whose limited thrust into Alsace, 7–9 Aug., failed, went on the offensive into Lorraine, 14 Aug. The Germans gave ground according to plan until 20 Aug., when in heavy fighting they mauled the French, who by 24 Aug. had retreated to Nancy. A French attempt in the Ardennes also fared badly, 22–25 Aug., and, having suffered enormous losses, 2 French armies fell back to the western side of the River Meuse. Another French army supporting the Belgians along the River Sambre was also forced to withdraw, 22–24 Aug. The B.E.F., commanded by Sir John French (1852–1925), had moved, 22 Aug., into position at Mons in support of the Belgians. Heavy fighting, 23 Aug., was followed by a retreat, 24 Aug., precipitated by French withdrawal on the B.E.F.'s southern flank. In the battles the French suffered appallingly (over 300,000 casualties), and Moltke, who believed the war won, allowed the detachment of 2 corps from the right wing to East Prussia, then being invaded by Russia. With other corps detached to hold the Belgians at Antwerp, the strong right wing upon which Schlieffen's plan depended had been so emasculated that in some areas the French had achieved numerical superiority.

ALLIED RETREAT. 25 Aug.–4 Sept. The Germans continued their advance. In the Battle of Le Cateau, 26 Aug., part of the B.E.F. was badly defeated. A French counterattack, 29 Aug., resulting in the Battle of Guise, held up the German 2nd Army for 36 hours and also caused the tip of the right wing (the 1st Army) to turn south, 30 Aug., while still east of Paris.

1ST BATTLE OF THE MARNE. 5–9 Sept. The day, 5 Sept., before Joffre's planned counteroffensive was to begin, the Germans made contact with the built-up French forces by the River Ourcq. Heavy fighting ensued, 6–8 Sept. On 6 Sept. the French began their offensive; complicated German and allied maneuvering led to a widening gap between the German 1st and 2nd Armies, which the B.E.F. slowly exploited. Meanwhile, a little farther south, a battle in the Marshes of St.-Gond raged fiercely as the French, under command of Gen. Ferdinand Foch (1851–1929), wavered but held. The Germans, unsuccessful in their attacks and fearing the gap in their lines, began retreating, 10 Sept., 40 miles north to the River Aisne, where by 14 Sept. they had consolidated their positions. That day Gen. Erich von Falkenhayn (1861–1922) secretly replaced Moltke (no public announcement being made until Nov.).

1ST BATTLE OF THE AISNE. 14–18 Sept. This contest marked the transition from a war of maneuver to trench warfare. The allied offensive, with the B.E.F. making the main effort, failed against the entrenched Germans and the front in this area stabilized, with the B.E.F. transferring north to Flanders.

FALL OF ANTWERP. 9 Oct. Fearing a thrust on their flanks, the Germans had begun siege operations against Antwerp at the end of Sept. After the city's fall, the Belgian army retreated along the Channel coast to the River Yser.

BATTLE OF YSER AND 1ST BATTLE OF YPRES. 12 Oct.–22 Nov. A B.E.F. drive, begun on 12 Oct. against the Germans in Flanders, quickly stalled. On 20 Oct. the Germans launched an offensive against the Belgians along the Yser. By 24 Oct. they were across the river, but the battered Belgians hung on grimly, and on 27 Oct. opened the flood gates at Nieuport. Sea water slowly inundated an area 2 miles wide from Diksmuide (Dixmude) to the coast, halting the German advance. Meanwhile, farther south the Germans began a drive for Ypres, 20 Oct., held in the main by the B.E.F., and fighting continued until 31 Oct., when the heaviest German drive failed. On 11 Nov. another massive drive to take Ypres barely failed; indecisive fighting continued. The 1st Battle of Artois, a French offensive near Arras, 14–24 Dec., was inconclusive.

TRENCH WARFARE. The front line established at the end of 1914, which did not vary more than 10 miles in either direction until 1917, left the Germans in control of almost all Belgium and the richest part of France. On this immobile front the troops dug in and a line of trenches stretched from Switzerland to the sea with the enemies only a few hundred yards apart, in places as close as 30 yards. Casualties had been tremendous. The British had 50,000 casualties in the Ypres battle alone. During 1914, France suffered almost 1 m. casualties and Germany slightly fewer.

1915

OPPOSING STRATEGIES. During 1915, the Germans remained generally on the defensive in the West while attempting to defeat Russia in the East. The allies continued to concentrate on the 1 big push they believed could win the war, but the Western Front remained stable.

BATTLE OF NEUVE-CHAPELLE. 10–13 Mar. Sir John French believed that, since the French provided the bulk of the fighting forces on the Western Front, the B.E.F. should be as offensive-minded as possible. Joffre, for his planned offensive, needed to pull out the French troops at Ypres, and Sir John decided that once the B.E.F. had relieved these troops he would be unable to support the French offensive. He therefore ordered an attack. Surprise helped the B.E.F. to overrun the German position, 10 Mar., but bad staff work enabled a German counterattack, 11 Mar., to limit the B.E.F. to a gain of about 1,000 yds. on a 1¼-mile-wide front. The British and the Germans each suffered about 13,000 casualties.

ST.-MIHIEL SALIENT. 6–24 Apr. Also known as the Battle of the Woëvre, this operation was designed by Joffre, with the main drive to come from forces south of the salient. The French achieved negligible results at the cost of high casualties.

2ND BATTLE OF YPRES. 22 Apr.–25 May. The 1st gas attack of the war occurred here. About 5 P.M., 22 Apr., the Germans, making use of a favorable wind, released chlorine gas from cylinders in their own trenches. Directed at French colonial troops, it caused them to panic and leave a large gap in the allied lines which the Germans were unprepared to exploit fully. On 24 Apr. a 2nd gas attack gained a little more ground for the Germans, this time at the expense of the Canadians. On 27 Apr. the British field commander considered it best to withdraw the B.E.F. 2½ mi. to Ypres. The French, learning of this order, relieved him, but his successor issued the same order, and the withdrawal took place, 1–3 May. Heavy fighting continued until the Germans abandoned the attack, 25 May. Casualties: British, 60,000; French, 10,000; Germans, 35,000.

2ND BATTLE OF ARTOIS. 9 May–18 June. On 9 May the French at Souchez and the British at Festubert made simultaneous attacks. The British failed almost immediately; a shell shortage prevented them from conducting more than an insufficient 46-minute artillery bombardment, and without gaining a yard they suffered 10,000 casualties, 9 May. Intermittent heavy fighting took place, 15–27 May, as the British gained half a mile at very high cost. The French, especially in the center under Gen. Henri Phillippe Pétain (1856–1951), managed to gain about 2½ miles, but then the German line held fast despite murderous fighting. Casualties: French, over 100,000; Germans, 75,000.

ENTRY OF ITALY. 23 MAY. After the outbreak of hostilities, both sides courted Italy; but as she eyed mostly Austrian territory, the allies could more easily meet her demands. By 10 May the Germans had convinced Austria-Hungary to meet the Italian demands, but it was too late. On 26 Apr., Britain, France, Russia, and

Italy had concluded the secret Treaty of London which promised Italy the Trentino, the Tyrol to the Brenner Pass, Trieste, Gorizia, Gradisca, the Istrian Peninsula, Dalmatia, and such ports on the Adriatic not already assigned to Montenegro or Serbia. The treaty also recognized Italian sovereignty over the Dodecanese Islands (occupied in 1912), gave Italy the Turkish province of Antalya when and if Turkey was partitioned, and promised her a share in any colonial or financial spoils. In return Italy bound herself to enter the war 1 month from the date of signing. On 3 May the Italian government denounced the Triple Alliance. Although considerable antiwar sentiment existed in the country, the interventionists managed to win a majority in parliament, and war was declared on Austria, 23 May. Italy did not declare war on Germany until 28 Aug., 1916.

Italy entered the war with an army of 875,000, poorly led, deficient in heavy artillery and machine guns, and whose war material had been largely consumed in the Libyan war of 1911–12 against Turkey. The Italian navy was weak, and economically the country proved to be a heavy burden to the allies.

Ringed by mountains on their northern border, the Italians, having to fight their way up from the plains, were in a poor strategic position. They carried on their campaign in the least mountainous region near the River Isonzo. Under the command of Gen. Count Luigi Cadorna (1850–1928), they fought 4 battles there (23 June–7 July, 18 July–30 Sept., 18 Oct.–4 Nov., 10 Nov.–2 Dec.) in 1915, gaining little ground or strategic advantage in desperate fighting that cost them over 250,000 casualties. Austrian casualties totaled about 165,000.

2ND BATTLE OF CHAMPAGNE. 22 Sept.–8 Nov. The Western Front had been quiet during the summer as the allies prepared for a major autumn offensive. One of the war's heaviest bombardments, 22–25 Sept., preceded the French attack, but to little avail as the 1st wave penetrated about 5,000 yds., after which the attackers came to a standstill, 27 Sept. Joffre futilely kept up a war of attrition

until 8 Nov., at a cost of 145,000 men as against 113,000 for the Germans.

3RD BATTLE OF ARTOIS. 25 Sept.– 30 Oct. This battle was fought mainly as a diversion designed to draw off German forces from Champagne. The British, making use of gas for the 1st time, 25 Sept., attacked Loos over particularly difficult terrain. In a battle that dragged on until 14 Oct. the British, losing some 60,000 men to the Germans' 20,000, managed to capture Loos, but failed to reach Lens, their main objective. Dissatisfaction over the use of reserves in this battle led to the replacement, Dec., of Gen. French by Sir Douglas Haig (1861–1928) as B.E.F. commander. On 25 Sept. the French attacked Vimy Ridge, almost winning the crest during the first 3 days before being halted. Fighting continued until 30 Oct.

1916

VERDUN. 21 Feb.–18 Dec. Falkenhayn, who planned to bleed France white in a war of attrition, attacked Verdun, knowing that the French would fight to the last for this famous fortress. Located at the head of an awkward salient split by the Meuse, Verdun offered the French poor lines of communication. Joffre, convinced that fortresses were useless, had stripped the area's forts of their guns and, preoccupied with the Somme offensive, had disregarded warnings of a German attack.

An extremely heavy bombardment, 21 Feb., surprised the French and created havoc. A German attack along the east bank of the Meuse gained ground, and the Germans captured Ft. Douaumont, 25 Feb., a key fort whose skeleton garrison had not been reinforced. Pétain was placed (midnight, 25 Feb.) in command of reinforcements rushed to Verdun and he reorganized the French forces.

The Germans renewed the attack, 6 Mar., this time from both sides of the salient, and bloody fighting raged almost continuously into the summer. The Germans gained little ground, but did take at great cost the hill Le Morte Homme, 31 May, and Ft. Vaux, 7 June. Despite a heavy artillery and gas barrage, 22 June, utilizing the newly perfected and more deadly phosgene gas, a supreme German effort to capture Ft. Souville failed, as did a lesser attempt on 10 July. The Germans went on the defensive, 15 July.

Limited French attacks in Aug. and Sept. and major offensives launched on 24 Oct. and 15 Dec. won back a large portion of the lost ground, including Fts. Douaumont, 24 Oct., and Vaux, 2 Nov.

Fighting stopped on 18 Dec. after the French had suffered about 400,000 casualties and the Germans over 350,000 in the longest battle of the war.

THE SOMME OFFENSIVE. 1 July–18 Nov. The other major operation of 1916, the Somme offensive, was much affected by Verdun. French appeals for help caused the date of the attack to be moved forward a month to 1 July, and French participation was reduced to a small force on the British right flank as Joffre diverted troops to Verdun. This transformation of the offensive into a mostly British operation meant that the area chosen as the objective, heavily fortified by the Germans and of no real strategic value, no longer had any purpose as a field of battle, since it originally had been chosen because it facilitated a joint Anglo-French offensive.

A heavy but ineffectual artillery bombardment, 24 June–1 July, preceded the attack, 1 July, which, without gaining a yard, cost the British 60,000 casualties on the 1st day, the greatest loss ever sustained in a single day by a modern army. The British failure caused the French to halt their advance for fear of being outflanked.

In heavy fighting the British managed slowly to push forward, 2–10 July, and a surprise early morning attack, 14 July, gained them 5 mi. before it bogged down. Heavy fighting continued into the fall.

On 15 Sept. Haig used a new weapon, the tank (so called because during its secret development the vehicle traveling under canvas could be said to be a water carrier or tank). Some ground was gained, but Haig has been criticized for dissipating the surprise value of the tank by not waiting until he had more than the 36 used in the initial action.

The battle churned on in the mud as the autumn rains fell until, after a last British attack, 13 Nov., it petered out, having developed into an even greater struggle of attrition than Verdun. The allies had conquered about 125 sq. mi. of territory of little strategic value at huge cost in casualties: British, over 400,000; French, 200,000. The Germans lost about 450,000 men.

CHANGES IN COMMAND. The campaigns in 1916 on the Western Front had been costly, arduous, and inconclusive, and resulted in no real changes except in the German and French high commands. Dissatisfaction with Falkenhayn's policies led to his replacement, Aug., by the Hindenburg-Ludendorff partnership with Field Marshal Paul von Hindenburg (1847–1934) as chief of the general staff and Gen. Erich Ludendorff (1865–1937) as first quartermaster general. Joffre was replaced, Dec., by Gen. Robert Nivelle (1858–1924), who had distinguished himself at Verdun.

5TH BATTLE OF THE ISONZO. 9–17 Mar. Undertaken at the request of Joffre, who pleaded for diversions to relieve the pressure at Verdun, this Italian offensive bogged down in bad weather and cost many casualties.

AUSTRIAN ASIAGO OFFENSIVE. 15 May–17 June. To get behind the Italian forces on the Isonzo, Austria-Hungary attacked south from the Trentino toward the key rail center of Padua. Initially the Austrians did well, capturing Asiago and Arsiero, 30–31 May, but difficult terrain, lack of strength, and a rapid shifting of Italian troops all joined to stop them by mid-June.

ITALIAN COUNTERATTACK. 16 June–7 July. Helped by the moving of Austrian troops to the East to meet a Russian threat, the Italians forced a withdrawal which set the Austrian forces back almost to their original positions. Casualties: Italians, 147,000; Austro-Hungarians, 81,000.

ISONZO CAMPAIGN. 6 Aug.–14 Nov. In the 6th Battle of the Isonzo the Italians captured Gorizia, 8 Aug., but then failed to advance despite bloody fighting. The 7th (14–26 Sept.), 8th (10–12 Oct.), and 9th (1–14 Nov.) battles of the Isonzo were all marked by heavy fighting and small Italian gains at the cost of large casualty lists.

1917

ENTRY OF THE U.S.A. At the instigation of Ludendorff, a conference of German political and military leaders at Pless, 8–9 Jan., Hindenburg's field headquarters, determined that a policy of unrestricted submarine warfare should be followed. The German high command gambled that if as a result the U.S. entered the war, Germany could win it before American forces became a factor in the struggle. On 31 Jan. the U.S. was notified that, effective 1 Feb., a policy of unrestricted U-boat warfare would be in force. On 3 Feb. the U.S. broke diplomatic relations with Germany.

ZIMMERMANN NOTE. The Zimmermann Note, intercepted by British intelligence, 17 Jan., was a message from the German foreign minister, Arthur Zimmermann (1864–1940), to Mexico. It proposed, in the event of war between Germany and the U.S.A., that there should be an alliance between Germany and Mexico. It offered Mexico financial support and the promise of the restoration of Texas, Arizona, and New Mexico. It also asked Mexico to try to get Japan to change sides. Britain waited until 24 Feb. before transmitting the note to the U.S. and the State Department released it, 1 Mar. U.S.-German relations were further exacerbated by U-boat sinkings of American merchantmen, and on 2 Apr. President Woodrow Wilson (1856–1924) asked Congress for a declaration of war, saying that the "world must be made safe for democracy."

U.S. DECLARATION OF WAR. 6 Apr. The U.S. did not formally join the allies, but remained an "associated power." The U.S. brought fresh manpower and economic resources into the war, but it was to be some time before these could be brought to bear against Germany.

ALLIED PLANS. During 1917 a series of French disasters led to the burden of fighting being placed on the British as the allies continued to attempt the 1 big push on the Western Front believed necessary to win the war. Very attack-minded, Gen. Nivelle planned a great French offensive in Champagne with a joint French-British drive along the Somme as a preliminary diversion. At a series of conferences, Jan.–Mar., his plan was accepted, and it was agreed that Gen. Haig, subject to the right of appeal, would act under Nivelle's direction in the forthcoming offensive. Friction between the 2 generals delayed the attack after Ludendorff effected, 24 Feb.–5 Apr., a strategic withdrawal to strengthen the German lines. The Germans retrenched on a 65-mile front from Soissons to Arras with an average depth of 20 miles. They desolated the area they left and retired behind well-fortified positions known as the Hindenburg Line. This move invalidated Nivelle's strategic premises, but, despite objections by British and French officers and officials, he insisted that the attack take place.

BATTLE OF ARRAS. 9 Apr.–3 May. Designed to draw the German reserves, the British offensive had great initial success, though the 60 tanks used proved ineffectual. By 12 Apr. the Canadians had secured Vimy Ridge, but stiff resistance ended the advance and Haig continued the battle only to help Nivelle's attack along the Aisne.

2ND BATTLE OF THE AISNE. 16 Apr.–9 May. In most of this area the French troops, to reach their objectives, had to cross steep ridges, cut by ravines and heavily overgrown with shrubs and forest. Poor security, including the capture of a French soldier, 4 Apr., carrying the complete battle plans, led to the Germans' making the natural barriers even more formidable. Nivelle had promised easy victory, and pledged to cease the attack within 48 hours if it failed. When the French went forward, 16 Apr., they were massacred, but nonetheless Nivelle ordered successive futile, costly attacks which resulted in very limited gains.

MUTINY IN THE FRENCH ARMY. May. Nivelle's promises had carried the exhausted French troops beyond the breaking point. Widespread mutiny occurred. At one time 54 divisions were refusing to obey orders. Thousands deserted and great areas of the front went undefended, although the Germans did not learn of this. Pétain replaced Nivelle, 15 May, and by July had laboriously restored discipline. 100,000 French soldiers were court-martialed. Officially only 55 were shot, but many more were executed without sentence. Pétain personally visited most of the disaffected troops and improved conditions of service (e.g., leave, rations, etc.). To allow the French army time to convalesce, he appealed to the British to keep the Germans engaged.

MESSINES RIDGE. 7–8 June. From this ridge the Germans could perfectly observe behind the British lines and watch attacks being prepared. In a sharp, well-planned and executed operation (making use of tons of mines buried during 2 years under the German positions), the ridge was quickly captured.

3RD BATTLE OF YPRES. 31 July–15 Nov. Against considerable opposition Haig, partly in pursuit of his own strategic concepts and partly in response to Pétain's pleas, conducted an offensive in Flanders. A series of 9 bloody attacks (much of the time fought over muddy and waterlogged terrain) resulted in the advance of the British line about 9,000 yds. and caused 300,000 casualties. After the Canadians' capture of Passchendaele, 6 Nov., the battle petered out in the cold.

FRENCH VICTORIES. At Verdun, 20–26 Aug., and Malmaison, 23 Oct.–2 Nov., Pétain conducted 2 small, perfectly organized, and successful attacks.

BATTLE OF CAMBRAI. 20 Nov.–7 Dec. Over 300 massed tanks surprised the Germans and gained initial spectacular success. Failure to exploit this breakthrough properly stalled the British advance, and heavy fighting ensued. A German counterattack, 30 Nov., drove the British back in some places beyond their starting positions. This battle was the 1st convincing demonstration of what tanks could achieve if efficiently employed.

10TH AND 11TH BATTLES OF THE ISONZO. 12 May–8 June, 18 Aug.– 15 Sept. Further fruitless attempts by the Italians to break into the mountain barrier cost many casualties and weakened the now exhausted Italian troops.

CAPORETTO CAMPAIGN. 24 Oct.– 26 Dec. A tired Austria-Hungary needed help, and Ludendorff decided to send German troops to the Italian front to be the backbone of a joint offensive designed to knock Italy out of the war. The German troops shattered, 24–27 Oct., the Italian 2nd Army, whose commander, although warned of the impending offensive, failed to take adequate defense measures. The front broke and, in what at times was a rout, the Italians retreated 70 miles south until they succeeded, 10–12 Nov., in stabilizing their lines along the River Piave, as Austrian and German troops, outrunning their supply lines, had to slow down. The Italians repulsed a number of attempts to cross the river. Gen. Armando Diaz (1861–1920) replaced Cadorna. Fearing the worst, the allies sent 11 divisions from the Western Front to Italy.

SUPREME WAR COUNCIL. Established on 27 Nov., the Supreme War Council was an inadequate attempt to unify allied strategy. It grew out of a conference called to consider the Italian situation, 5 Nov. The important civil and military men on the Council failed to end the bickering, especially on the Western Front, among the allies.

1918

OPPOSING STRATEGIES. The Bolshevik Revolution having led to Russia's withdrawal from the war, Germany's military leaders decided to throw everything they had against the allies on the Western Front and defeat them before effective U.S. forces could arrive. The allied leaders planned to initiate no major action until they could make decisive use of U.S. manpower and economic resources.

STATEMENTS OF ALLIED WAR AIMS. Allied leaders believed that publication, Dec. 1917, by the Bolsheviks of the texts of secret treaties concluded earlier in the war (e.g., the Treaty of London) by the allies made necessary public declarations that would counter any unfavorable impressions. The first to speak out, 5 Jan., 1918, was the British prime minister, David Lloyd George (1863–1945), who produced a statement of war aims that sounded moderate and idealistic and included the restoration to their inhabitants of Belgium, Montenegro, Serbia, and the occupied parts of France, Italy, and Rumania, the establishment of an independent Polish state, and "a reconsideration" of the wrong done France by Germany in 1871. President Wilson issued a statement of his own views, 8 Jan., which set forth 14 points as "the only possible" peace program from the U.S. standpoint. The "14 Points" demanded an end to secret treaties and diplomacy, freedom of the seas in peace and war, removal of barriers and inequalities in international trade, reduction in armaments, colonial readjustments, evacuation of occupied territory, self-determination of nationalities and a redrawing of European boundaries along national lines, and the establishment of an international organization to prevent war. Indicative of Wilson's desire for a peace without victors or vanquished, the 14 Points were privately disliked by Allied leaders (the French premier remarked, "The Lord God had only ten"), but publicly they did not dispute them.

U.S. WAR EFFORT. At the time of her entry into the war, the U.S.A. had only a small army short of war material and armed with antiquated weapons. By the end of 1918, the American armed forces had expanded to over 4 m., and 2 m. military personnel had been sent to Europe, of whom about 1,100,000 were combat troops. Until U.S. war production could be sufficiently expanded, the allies had to provide the American Expeditionary Force (A.E.F.) with much of its equipment, and for some items like heavy artillery and tanks the allies continued until the end of the war to be the A.E.F.'s main source of supply. The commander of the A.E.F. was Gen. John J. Pershing (1860–1948). The first U.S. troops arrived in France 28 June, 1917, and the 1st to go into action did so the following Oct.

GERMAN OFFENSIVES. During the winter Ludendorff planned a series of hard blows whose ultimate object was to split the allies and drive the British into the sea. Troop transfers from the East gave the Germans a 10% advantage in combat personnel, but they lacked reserve strength. Ludendorff relied on surprise and new tactics (partially tested at Caporetto): a short artillery barrage which included a high proportion of gas shells designed to knock out enemy guns and observation posts, after which would come a rolling barrage (usually advancing at 1 kph) with the infantry following closely behind; field commanders in full control of units; strongpoints by-passed and left for follow-up units to deal with; and an emphasis on the light machine gun as an offensive weapon. Expecting stiff resistance, Ludendorff cannibalized front-line units to form special divisions and trained them for the new type of operation.

SOMME OFFENSIVE. 21 Mar.–8 Apr. Surprise and a dense fog made it easier for the Germans to pierce the British lines along a 41-mi. front on both sides of the Somme. The Germans broke into the open and gained ground rapidly. By 26 Mar. Amiens, a major link between the allied forces, was in peril, but near Abancourt a hastily improvised force stopped the advance, 28–30 Mar., and 2 other German attacks along the line proved futile. The German drive had been a major tactical success, achieving a penetration 40 mi. in depth. Altogether the Germans overran some 1,250 sq. mi. of territory, captured about 80,000 prisoners and 1,100 guns, and inflicted nearly 200,000 casualties. But their own losses had almost equaled those of the allies, and German manpower could not be replaced, so in a strategic sense the drive was ultimately a failure.

ALLIED UNITY OF COMMAND. During the crisis the British got some help from Pétain, but he insisted that, if the German advance continued, French forces would have to retreat southwest to cover Paris even though this meant leaving a gap between the allied armies. The allied leaders assembled at Doullens, 26 Mar., and Gen. Foch was entrusted with the "co-ordination of the Allied armies." On 3 Apr., after another conference at

Beauvais, he was charged with strategical direction of military operations, and on 14 Apr. he received the title "commander in chief of the allied armies in France." Pershing placed U.S. troops at the disposal of Foch, but he continued to insist on a separate U.S. army, and had a reference thereto included in an interallied agreement signed at the Beauvais conference.

LYS OFFENSIVE. 9–29 Apr. Still hopeful of smashing the British, Ludendorff attacked in Flanders toward the vital rail center of Hazebrouck. A Portuguese unit in the center of the British line gave way and the Germans rushed through. Foch sent some French troops, and this help plus the tenacity of the British in holding on combined to stop the Germans. Passchendaele and Armentières fell to the Germans, but their 15-mi. advance up the Lys River valley cost them irreplaceable casualties.

BATTLE OF CHEMIN DES DAMES. 27 May–6 June. Attempting to unbalance the allies, Ludendorff decided to attack along the River Aisne to draw off reserves from Flanders. A secret shifting of German troops caught the allied forces by surprise, and the Germans penetrated 13 mi. the 1st day. This success led Ludendorff to postpone his Flanders offensive and allow the attack to run its course. By 31 May the Germans were on the Marne about 40 mi. from Paris. U.S. troops were hurriedly rushed to Château-Thierry to aid in the defense and with the French held, 1–4 June, the south bank of the Marne against repeated German attacks. The offensive proved to be another tactical success of little strategic value; Ludendorff's drive had netted him a vulnerable salient at the cost of considerable casualties.

NOYON-MONTDIDIER OFFENSIVE. 9–13 June. Ludendorff planned a new drive to connect the 2 salients formed by the earlier offensives, but the attack failed.

2ND BATTLE OF THE MARNE. 15 July–6 Aug. Despite a severe worsening of German morale, Ludendorff started a fifth and last attack, 15 July, from both sides of Rheims. By 17 July it too had proved a failure, and the initiative now passed from the Germans, who had lost more than 800,000 men in their 5 drives. Meanwhile Foch, who had been planning his own offensive, used the opportunity that came with the slackening of the German effort. His 1st objective was the Marne salient and, on 18 July, 4 French armies, including some British and American divisions, attacked along this perimeter. The Germans conducted a fighting withdrawal as they attempted to save their supplies. By 3 Aug. they were in a strong position at the base of the salient along the rivers Aisne and Vesle, from which attacks to dislodge them failed.

REDUCTION OF THE AMIENS SALIENT. 8 Aug.–25 Sept. A surprise British attack spearheaded by over 450 tanks, 8 Aug., cracked the German lines, gaining 5 mi. before noon. Ludendorff called this "the black day" of the German army, not so much because of the defeat, but because for the 1st time the spirit of whole divisions gave way; men would not fight and many officers could not control their units. On 15 Aug. Foch broadened the attack to include the front from Arras to Soissons. In heavy fighting the Germans fell back step by step, finally retreating behind a strengthened Hindenburg Line from which their first drive had been made in Mar.

REDUCTION OF THE ST.-MIHIEL SALIENT. 12–16 Sept. Created during the German 1914 offensive, the St.-Mihiel Salient had been generally quiet ever since. The Germans had begun withdrawing, 8 Sept., before an attack, 12 Sept., launched by U.S. troops, the 1st major offensive conducted largely by the A.E.F. Within 36 hours the salient had been reduced, and by 16 Sept. the front line had been straightened and the attack stopped.

FINAL ALLIED OFFENSIVE. 26 Sept.–11 Nov. Foch's general plan was to capture the key railroad centers of Aulnoye and Mézières, whose loss would deprive the Germans of the principal capabilities for supply as well as withdrawal. The plan called for a giant pincers movement having 2 major converging offensives, with their starting times staggered so as to upset the employment of their limited reserves by the Germans. A Franco-British drive would advance on Aulnoye and Maubeuge from the west, and a Franco-U.S. drive would move on Mézières from the south.

The battle began, 26 Sept., in the U.S. sector of the front between the Argonne Forest and the Meuse. Over extremely rugged country, American troops attacked a well-entrenched and still determined enemy, and by 3 Oct., despite an 8–1 numerical superiority, had made only slight progress. By 31 Oct., at the cost of many casualties, the U.S. forces had cleared the Germans out of the Argonne Forest. Confusion as command lines broke down led Pershing to give up field leadership, 16 Oct., and limit himself to an over-all command role; a 2nd U.S. Army was created, 12 Oct. In its final drive, 1–11 Nov., the U.S. 1st Army advanced rapidly north, capturing the northern end of the Côtes-de-Meuse and reaching Sedan. The 2nd U.S. Army attacked in the general direction of the Briey iron basin east of the Meuse.

To the north the British launched a heavy assault, 27 Sept., in Picardy between Péronne and Lens; King Albert and the Belgians attacked in the coastal lowlands, 28 Sept.; and the British right wing joined with the French, 29 Sept., in massive attacks all along the front from Péronne to La Fère. Fighting was fierce, but by 5 Oct. the British had breached the last position of the Hindenburg Line, although unusually heavy rain bogged down the attack in the lowlands for almost a week thereafter. By 11 Nov. the Belgians had taken Bruges and Ghent, British forces held Aulnoye and Maubeuge, and the French had made gains in the center of the line.

GERMAN PEACE MOVES. Although dispirited and suffering heavy casualties, the Germans had withdrawn in fair order and kept Foch from closing the pincers. But their leadership cracked. On 29 Sept. Ludendorff's nerve gave way and he asked that an armistice be arranged on the Western Front without delay. This led to the resignation as chancellor, 30 Sept., of Count Georg von Hertling (1843–1919) and to his replacement, 3 Oct., by the liberal Prince Max of Baden (1867–1929). Prince Max asked Wilson, 4 Oct., for an armistice preliminary to a conference which would negotiate a peace on the basis of the 14 Points. Three exchanges of notes, 4–23 Oct., took place between Washington and Berlin as Wilson wanted to be sure that the character of the German government had changed and truly represented the people, and as the allies proved reluctant to accept the 14 Points as the basis of peace.

On 4 Nov. the allies, under the threat of a separate U.S. peace, formally accepted the 14 Points, with the 2 vital reservations that freedom of the seas be discussed at the peace conference and that Germany pay reparations. Wilson transmitted these conditions to the Germans, 5 Nov., and thereafter the actual negotiations were left to Foch.

Meanwhile Ludendorff had regained some of his composure and, while no longer predicting victory, talked of a defensive war. On 26 Oct. he was dismissed. Recognizing the hopelessness of their cause, the Germans realized the need for an armistice. On 3 Nov. mutiny broke out in the German fleet at Kiel and spread to much of northwest Germany. On 7 Nov. revolution broke out in Bavaria. Had the emperor not proved so stubborn, the monarchy might have been preserved, but, as it was, Prince Max's unauthorized announcement of abdication, 9 Nov., came too late. A republic was proclaimed, and the Kaiser fled to Holland, 10 Nov.

BATTLE OF THE PIAVE. 15–24 June. The Germans, in desperate need of manpower, urged the Austrians to attack and put Italy out of the war so that Austrian troops could serve on the Western Front. Crossings of the River Piave were effected at 3 points, but after fierce fighting the Austrians proved unable to maintain their offensive and ordered a retreat, 22–23 June, back across the river.

BATTLE OF VITTORIO VENETO. 24 Oct.–4 Nov. After extensive preparations and much urging by the allies, Gen. Diaz, with the aid of allied troops, launched an offensive which for 3 days, 24–26 Oct., seemed to be inconclusive as the Austrians fought back fiercely. By 27 Oct., however, 3 small bridgeheads had been established across the Piave. As the collapse of the Dual Monarchy became clear to the troops, the Austrians then fell back and resistance had virtually ceased by the night of 30–31 Oct. On 3 Nov. Trent (Trento) was occupied and the Italians landed at Trieste.

END OF THE HAPSBURG MONARCHY. Charles I (1887–1922) had come to the Austro-Hungarian throne in 1916 and, recognizing the war's deleterious effect on his lands, had unsuccessfully attempted peace negotiations. On 4 Oct. he sent a note to the U.S. requesting negotiations on the basis of the 14 Points, to which the U.S. replied, 18 Oct., that it could no longer agree to mere autonomy for the nationalities within the empire. Concurrently, the empire began to fragment. On 15 Oct. Poland declared itself an independent state. On 19 Oct. an assembly of Serbs, Croats, and Slovenes at Zagreb asserted its sovereignty over the South Slav portion of the Dual Monarchy. The Czechs in Prague carried out a bloodless revolution, 28 Oct., and on 30 Oct. in Vienna a German National Council was formed to speak for the German provinces. On 1 Nov. Charles acceded to a request made on 25 Oct. for an independent Hungary. Confronted with this breakup, the government of the empire abandoned all hope of a negotiated peace and offered, 27 Oct., an armistice on almost any terms. On 3 Nov. an armistice was signed between the allied powers and the high command of Austria-Hungary, to go into effect 4 Nov., calling for complete demobilization of the armies of the Dual Monarchy; surrender of half its artillery; evacuation of all occupied territory; the right of free movement for the allies over all roads, railways, and waterways; surrender of much of the fleet; and occupation by the allies of such strategic points as they deemed necessary. Austria-Hungary had ceased to exist.

ARMISTICE IN THE WEST. At Compiègne a commission headed by Matthias Erzberger (1875–1921) negotiated with Foch, 8–11 Nov. The allied terms, designed to make Germany helpless, included German evacuation of occupied territory; evacuation of the left bank of the Rhine and establishment of bridgeheads at Mainz, Cologne, and Coblenz, which would be occupied by allied troops; surrender of all submarines and internment of much of the German fleet; repatriation of all allied prisoners and deported civilians; surrender of considerable military equipment as well as 5,000 locomotives, 5,000 motor lorries, and 150,000 wagons.

The Germans signed at 5 A.M., 11 Nov. At 11 A.M. on that day, except for some isolated incidents, the war on the Western Front ended.

THE EASTERN FRONT

1914

OPPOSING STRATEGIES. Russia mobilized faster than expected, but the mobilization was only partially completed when, much to her later regret, she succumbed to French pleas for an early offensive to divert German forces from the West. The Russians suffered from lack of mobility (their different-gauge railroad equipment was useless on the German railways), inefficient command (their army commanders, jealous of each other, did not work well together), and poor communications (orders were habitually transmitted uncoded).

The Russian strategy called for a 2-pronged assault on East Prussia: the 1st Army to advance from the east and the 2nd to attack from the south. The Germans, operating with limited forces, planned to make use of their superior mobility to defeat the unco-ordinated Russian assaults one at a time.

BATTLE OF STALLUPÖNEN. 17 Aug. The Russian 1st Army, whose advance began 13 Aug., was defeated when it crossed the border by forces under Gen. Hermann von François (1856–1933), who independently had decided to stand and fight to prevent violation of Prussia's "sacred soil." Tactically sound, François's action upset the planned German strategy of timed counterattacks.

BATTLE OF GUMBINNEN. 20 Aug. François urged the German commander in chief, Gen. Maximilian von Prittwitz

(1848–1929), to launch a counteroffensive, but this attack from positions around Gumbinnen resulted in piecemeal assaults which the Russians repulsed. The ensuing stalemate unnerved Prittwitz, especially after he learned that on the same day the 2nd Russian Army had entered East Prussia from the southeast. Telephoning Moltke, he said he planned to withdraw to the River Vistula, but even there doubted if he could hold without reinforcements. On 23 Aug. Hindenburg and Ludendorff took command in East Prussia with the former as senior officer.

BATTLE OF TANNENBERG. 26–29 Aug. Prittwitz's brilliant operations officer, Gen. Max Hoffmann (1869–1927), had the opportunity between 20 and 23 Aug. to develop and put into effect a new strategic plan which was approved by Hindenburg and Ludendorff. German forces, making use of the excellent railroads, were shifted south to face the Russian 2nd Army, while only a cavalry division and a brigade were left to delay the slow-moving Russian 1st Army. On 24 Aug. the Russian 2nd Army met heavy resistance at Frankenau, but, believing the Germans in flight, the Russian commander announced that 25 Aug. would be a day of rest. On 26–27 Aug. the Russian 2nd Army's flanks were defeated and driven back and its center exposed. Finally, the Russian center was surrounded and crushed, 28–29 Aug.

At 11:30 A.M., 29 Aug., the Russians realized their predicament and ordered a general retreat, but it was too late; the Russian 2nd Army had fallen into a German trap and was almost wholly surrounded. The Russian commander committed suicide. Russian killed and wounded reached staggering numbers: the Germans captured 125,000 men and 500 guns and suffered only about 13,000 casualties themselves.

MASURIAN LAKES CAMPAIGN. 9–14 Sept. The Germans now turned on the Russian 1st Army and, augmented by reinforcements from the Western Front, attacked. During 9–10 Sept. they secured the Russian southern flank near Lyck, making the invaders' position untenable

and forcing a withdrawal. To protect this retreat and avoid envelopment, the Russians launched, 10 Sept., a stiff counterattack between Nordenburg and Angerburg which surprised the Germans and caused them to move forward more cautiously. Although suffering heavy losses, the Russian commander managed to save most of his army by forced marches of as much as 55 mi. in 50 hours. After 13 Sept. the German pursuit slackened. Although not put out of the war, Russia had suffered a severe defeat, and her much-vaunted steamroller had proved a failure.

GALICIAN AND POLISH CAMPAIGNS. Initially, the vast forces of the Austrians and Russians were locked in confused conflict in the south as in the great empty spaces armies wandered in search of their opponents, encircled one another, and were encircled in turn themselves. The Austrian plans called for part of the Dual Monarchy's forces to invade Serbia, but for the bulk to be deployed, with German support, against the Russians. For their part, the Russians planned a drive against Galicia to protect their Polish salient. Reconnaissance was poor on both sides, and on 23 Aug. the Russians and the Austrians unexpectedly collided at Kraśnik. In the ensuing battle, 23–25 Aug., the Russians, whose forces were not yet ready for combat, retreated after desultory fighting. At the Battle of Komarov, 26 Aug.–1 Sept., the Austrians scored limited gains. Meanwhile, to the east a major Russian attack caught the Austrians unprepared and they were routed at the Battle of the Gnila Lipa, 26 Aug.–1 Sept. Trying to aid their retreating forces, the Austrians moved troops to the Gnila Lipa front, leaving a 40-mi. gap in the line in the Komarov area. The Russians exploited this situation and in a series of engagements, the Battle of the Rawa Ruska, 5–11 Sept., heavily defeated the Austrian forces.

AUSTRIAN RETREAT. 11–28 Sept. Realizing the precariousness of their situation, the Austrian high command ordered a general withdrawal, 11 Sept., first to the River San (reached 16 Sept.), and then to a line at the Carpathian Mts., 100 miles to the rear of the front. Over

100,000 men were left in the fortress of Przemysl, all of whom were lost together with many stores when, after a long siege, the fortress surrendered, 18 Mar., 1915. Of the 900,000 Austrians operating in Galicia, over 250,000 were killed or wounded.

GERMAN FORCES IN POLAND. 28 Sept.–24 Nov. In an attempt to aid the sagging Austrians, the Germans detached 4 corps from their forces in East Prussia and, constituting them the German 9th Army, invaded southern Poland, 28 Sept.–12 Oct. At its farthest point the German drive was only 12 mi. from Warsaw, but the overwhelming numerical superiority of the Russians forced a withdrawal, 17 Oct.–1 Nov., which was swift and smooth and accompanied by a thorough devastation of the country as the Germans returned to their starting line. On 3 Nov. the decision was made to have the 9th Army invade Poland from the north. By 10 Nov. the Germans had shifted the whole force (once again taking advantage of their superior lines of communication) and begun the offensive. In 4 days they advanced 50 miles and commenced encircling the Russian forces around Lodz. The Russians suffered heavy losses in the bitter fighting which took place in mud and snow as very cold weather hampered both sides. Finally, reinforced by divisions from the Western Front, the Germans took Lodz, 6 Dec., and the Russians fell back to rearrange their lines.

THE BALKANS. The 1st Austro-Hungarian invasion of Serbia failed. The Battle of the Jadar, 16–19 Aug., ended with the invaders defeated, and by 24 Aug. the last Austrian forces had been driven back across the border. A 2nd invasion, launched 8 Sept., was halted by a strong Serbian counterattack, 16 Sept., though the Austrians retained bridgeheads on the rivers Drina and Sava. To shorten their lines, the Serbs then withdrew to higher ground. On 5 Nov. the 3rd Austrian invasion began. Valjevo was captured, 15 Nov., and Belgrade evacuated, 29 Nov. On 3 Dec., inspired by a personal plea from their king, the Serbs counterattacked and after prolonged and savage fighting the Austrians had to yield. The last Austrian forces left Serbia on 15 Dec.

1915

OPPOSING STRATEGIES. The Russians planned a break-through in Silesia as well as an offensive north toward East Prussia from the Polish salient. The German high command lacked a central plan as Falkenhayn, who believed that the war must be won in the West, clashed with Hindenburg and Ludendorff, who believed Russia could be quickly knocked out of the war.

WINTER BATTLE OF MASURIA. 7–21 Feb. Part of a joint offensive with the Austrians, who attacked the Russian flank in the south, 23 Jan., the 1st German attack of 1915 took place in severe winter weather and began after the end of a 2-day blizzard. The Russians were taken unaware and beaten back, and the 20th Russian Corps was encircled in the Forest of Augostow. Although in the space of 2 weeks the Germans advanced over 70 miles, killing almost 100,000 of the enemy and capturing over 110,000 prisoners and more than 300 guns, the attack proved of negligible strategic value because the vast manpower of the Russians still gave them a numerical superiority. The Germans were not able to follow up their advance and had to shift troops south, where the Austrian offensive was faring badly.

GORLICE-TARNOW BREAK-THROUGH. 2–4 May. In response to strong pleas for an offensive from the south, Falkenhayn decided against another double offensive, and Hindenburg and Ludendorff's forces were relegated to a subsidiary operation. Drawing troops from France, the Germans formed a new army under Gen. August von Mackensen (1849–1948) to spearhead the drive. Meanwhile, 16 Apr., German forces in the north attacked as a diversion, but made an advance of 75 miles into Lithuania, entrenching themselves along the River Dubissa before later joining in the general advance. At 6 A.M. on 2 May, almost 1,000 guns began a 4-hour heavy-artillery bombardment along a 30-mi. front between Gorlice and Tarnow. Taken by surprise, the Russians panicked. By 4 May the Germans and Austrians were through the Russian defensive positions.

AUSTRO-GERMAN ADVANCE. 4 May–1 Oct. All through the spring, summer, and early fall, the Germans and Austrians, with but brief pauses, kept up the attack and forced the Russians back. Much of the Russian infantry was poorly trained; many soldiers were sent into combat without rifles and had to snatch them from the hands of dead and dying comrades. Poor communications, an ammunition shortage, and inept leadership further hampered the Russian defense. By 11 May the Russian line was on the River San, 80 miles to the rear. On 17 May the Russians were forced back from this line, and on 2 June the Germans captured Przemysl. On 22 June, Lemberg fell; 30 July, Lublin; 5 Aug., Warsaw; 20 Aug., Novogeorgievsk; 25 Aug., Brest-Litovsk; 16 Sept., Pinsk.

At the end of Sept., Gen. Falkenhayn ordered a halt to the advance. Both Germans and Austrians had outrun their lines of communication. Poor roads, which all along held up the advance, had made supply difficult, and the approach of winter necessitated consolidation. The Russians had retreated 300 miles, and suffered enormous casualties (400,000 Russian soldiers were taken prisoner), had given up more territory than the whole of France, and had lost stores and guns equivalent to what had been on hand at the outbreak of the war. Russia, however, was not yet out of the fight. The bulk of the Russian army had escaped the enemy's successive enveloping movements. On 8 Sept. the czar took over personal command of the army, and it held on. By the end of the year a stable line had been created running from the eastern end of the Carpathian Mts. in the south to Riga on the Baltic Sea.

THE BALKANS. Turkey's need for supplies made the Germans decide to reopen the rail line through Serbia and Bulgaria to Constantinople. A campaign to crush Serbia was therefore planned. From the outbreak of hostilities, both sides had wooed Bulgaria with offers of territory and money. Ferdinand (1861–1948), the pro-German Bulgarian king, hoping to avenge his country's humiliation in the 2nd Balkan War, accepted the Central Powers' overtures. Even before the signing of a convention, the Central Powers had forced Turkey, 22 July, 1915, by a treaty, ratified 22 Sept., to cede to Bulgaria the land west of the River Maritsa as well as both banks of that river except for Adrianople, and had extended, 8 Aug., a loan of 400 m. francs. On 6 Sept. Bulgaria signed a treaty with Germany and Austria which, in return for active participation in an invasion of Serbia during the following month, promised her Serbian Macedonia and the northeastern portion of Serbia as far as the River Morava as well as other territories in Rumania and Greece, should these countries join the Allies.

ALLIED FORCES IN SALONIKA. On 21 Sept. the Bulgarians began to mobilize. Serbia appealed to the allies for aid, and they decided to send troops, initially 1 division each from France and Britain. The pro-allied Greek prime minister, Eleutherios Venizelos (1864–1936), secretly consented to a landing at Salonika, 3–5 Oct., but his attempt to bring Greece into the war on the side of the allies resulted in the enforcement of his resignation, 5 Oct., by the pro-German King Constantine (1868–1923).

Moving up the Vardar Valley 40 miles beyond the frontier to near Veles, the French attempted to join up with the Serbians, but their efforts proved inadequate, and by the end of Dec. the allied army had retired on Salonika. The British wanted to re-embark, but the French, who insisted on staying, won their point. Over the next 15 months the allied force grew in numbers, reaching by 1918 500,000 men from 6 different nationalities, but otherwise stagnated, serving no useful function and initiating offensive action only twice before the autumn of 1918. The Germans wryly called Salonika their "largest internment camp."

CONQUEST OF SERBIA. About 375,000 Central Powers troops along a vast front faced a Serbian army of about 200,000, which had recently suffered severely from a typhus epidemic. On 6 Oct. German and Austrian forces crossed the River Sava. By 7 Oct. they were over the Danube, and on 9 Oct. Belgrade fell. The Bulgarians along Serbia's eastern frontier invaded, 11 Oct. Overwhelmed, the Serbs fell back, blowing up stores and depots, while all able-bodied men joined the colors to halt the invader. Realizing that they could expect little effective help, the Serbs decided, 24 Nov., to conduct a fighting retreat toward the Adriatic Sea. In the face of severe hardships, they withdrew along 3 principal routes through Montenegro and Albania to the coast, from which the allies evacuated about 130,000 of them to Corfu, 15 Jan., 1916. There they were re-equipped and took up positions on the Salonika front. Because of political considerations, Falkenhayn halted the Central Powers forces at the Greek frontier. The Austrians, who quickly crushed Montenegro (which surrendered, 17 Jan., 1916), spent the rest of the war skirmishing in the mountains of Albania with the Italians.

1916

OPPOSING STRATEGIES. The Russians, after conferences with the other allies, agreed to mount an offensive during 1916 no later than 15 June. The Germans planned to concentrate on the Western Front, while the Austrians contemplated an offensive against Italy.

RUSSIAN OFFENSIVE AT LAKE NAROCH. 18–28 Mar. This offensive was undertaken by the Russians, who had been slowly rebuilding and re-equipping their armies, in response to French pleas to create a diversion to draw off the Germans from Verdun. On 18 Mar., after 2 days of artillery bombardment, the Russians launched a hastily conceived and poorly executed attack along a 90-mi. front on both sides of Lake Naroch. Stiff German resistance as well as mud from the spring thaws caused the attack to bog down by 26 Mar. The Germans had regained all lost ground by 30 Mar. and fighting soon died away. This offensive

did not help the French and cost the Russians over 100,000 casualties.

BRUSILOV OFFENSIVE. 4 June–20 Sept. During the spring the Russians resumed their preparations for a summer offensive. Austrian attacks on the Italian front led Italy to appeal to Russia for assistance. The Russian commanders north of the Pripet Marshes declared themselves unprepared to advance the date of the planned offensive, but Gen. Aleksei Brusilov (1853–1926), commander of the Russian forces along the southwestern front, said he could launch an attack, which began on 4 June. Brusilov achieved complete surprise and a tremendous initial success. On 6 June the Russians captured Lutsk. By 10 June the Austrian front had been breached to a depth of 50 mi., and on 17 June the Russians took Czernowitz. By 20 June over 200,000 of the enemy had become prisoners of the Russian armies.

Brusilov had counted on support from the Russian forces to the north of him, but only small operations were undertaken by them, 13 June and 2 July, against Baranovichi, and these failed completely. Meanwhile, his own offensive had lost momentum, and the Germans and Austrians were able to bring in reinforcements from the Western Front, from Italy, and from the northern part of the Russian front.

On 28 July Brusilov renewed the offensive, and when this drive failed after a few days because of ammunition shortages and poor communications, he started yet another one, 7 Aug. Stiff fighting went on through Aug. and into Sept., but the Russians made only small gains. The Russian railroads once again proved inferior to the German-Austrian lateral communications network, and more and more Central Powers troops were brought to bear against Brusilov's forces, which received supplies and reinforcements fitfully. By 20 Sept. the Russians could no longer maintain the momentum of attack and the Brusilov offensive ended. Quiet was generally maintained along the front for the rest of the year.

The Russians had inflicted heavy casualties, capturing upward of 400,000 prisoners and over 500 guns, and the front line had been rolled back to the Carpathians in the south and to a line running from Stanislav to Pinsk further north, but the drive had exacted a very heavy toll from the Russians. It cost them 1 m. men, and exhausted almost all their available supplies. Austrian losses were so great as to preclude any further offensive action in the East and the Austrian drive against Italy had to be halted; 15 German divisions had to be transferred from the West to the East, thus hampering the effort at Verdun; Russia's fighting spirit had been undermined and the demoralized remnants of her armed forces were ripe for revolution; and Rumania, believing the Central Powers defeated, entered the war on the side of the allies.

ENTRY OF RUMANIA. From the outbreak of the war, both the Central Powers and the allies had wooed Rumania, but she followed a policy of opportunistic caution until Aug. 1916. An allied offer to Rumania of Bukovina, Transylvania, the Banat of Temesvar, Maramures, and Crisana, as well as the apparent success of the Brusilov drive, combined to bring Rumania to sign, 17 Aug., the Treaty of Bucharest, which called for a prompt Rumanian attack on Austria-Hungary. On 27 Aug. the Rumanians entered the war, rich in natural resources, but with a poorly trained 560,000-man army short of rifles, machine guns, and artillery and with only a 6 weeks' supply of munitions.

DEFEAT OF RUMANIA. 28 Aug.–7 Jan., 1917. The Rumanians began a drive, 28 Aug., into Transylvania, which by mid-Sept., when it was halted, had over a 200-mi. front achieved a penetration of about 40 mi. in the center. Meanwhile in the south a mixed force (Bulgarians, Turks, Austrians, and Germans) under Mackensen's command had crossed the Rumanian frontier, 1 Sept., and made considerable gains up to mid-Sept., when it was halted by a Russo-Rumanian army. Resumed shortly afterward, the Central Powers' advance continued, and on 23 Oct. Constanza, the main seaport, fell. Falkenhayn had been placed in command of the Central Powers

forces, and he began an offensive in the north, 26 Sept., which by 10 Oct. had cleared the Rumanians from Transylvania. After having failed to breach a number of other passes, Falkenhayn's forces began a successful attack, 10 Nov., through the Vulcan Pass into Rumania. This attack turned the defenses of the other passes. Mackensen co-ordinated his drive with that of Falkenhayn. On 23 Nov. Mackensen's forces crossed the Danube above Sistova and joined up with the other invading groups, 26 Nov. The Rumanians fought back stoutly, but gave ground as they retreated east. On 6 Dec. Bucharest fell. Heavy rains then slowed the pursuit. The Rumanians withdrew across the River Sereth (Siret), and were able, with the aid of heavy Russian reinforcements, to hold that line. On 7 Jan., 1917, the Germans suspended operations.

Rumania had been completely overrun except for Moldavia in the northeast; her armies had been reduced to about 150,000 men; and her granaries and oil fields had been damaged, though not destroyed, and were in the hands of the Central Powers. The country, for all practical purposes, had been eliminated from the war.

SALONIKA. Gen. Maurice Sarrail (1856–1929), the titular head of the allied forces at Salonika, because of the diverse instructions sent directly to the commanders of each national contingent by their superiors, had much difficulty in exercising command over his force, which was now called the "Armées Alliées en Orient."

The Greeks generally showed themselves indifferent to the allied cause. On 26 May they surrendered a key stronghold, Ft. Rupel, to the Bulgarians without a fight. In Aug., as the Bulgarians moved to forestall any relief offensive that might accompany Rumania's intervention, Greek forces holding forts on the coastal strip of Kavalla similarly surrendered, 24 Aug., without firing a shot. Meanwhile, the Serbs had been driven back from Florina.

The allies, fearful that the Greeks might join the Central Powers, interfered with that country's internal affairs. Gen. Sarrail supported Venizelos, who formed a provisional government, 29 Sept., in Crete. This government, which moved to Salonika, 9 Oct., created an army to fight the Central Powers. The French seized the Greek fleet, 11 Oct. Later, when as a token of good faith they asked King Constantine for the surrender of 6 mountain batteries and these were not forthcoming, British and French marines landed at Pireaus, 1 Dec., and fought with the Greeks before embarking again.

A limited allied offensive was launched from Salonika, 10 Sept., in support of the Rumanians. The left wing, mostly Serbs, gained about 25 miles by 19 Nov., and drove the Bulgarians from Monastir, but the right wing failed to advance and as winter set in the fighting petered out except for skirmishes. The Rumanians received no help. Casualties: allies, about 50,000; Central Powers, about 60,000.

1917

PROVISIONAL GOVERNMENT IN RUSSIA. On 12 Mar. the Russian Duma formed a provisional government. On 15 Mar. Nicholas II abdicated in favor of his brother, who refused the crown, 16 Mar. The provisional government then headed Russia, though because of the general disruption its authority was limited.

RUSSIAN JULY OFFENSIVE. The government decided, despite the war-weariness of its people, to uphold its military obligations, hoping also that a successful military effort would galvanize support for itself. Alexander Kerensky (b. 1881), minister of war after 19 May, attempted through rousing speeches and an inspection tour of the front, including the most forward lines, to inspire the soldiers to fight. Brusilov assembled a force of some 200,000 men in the Galicia sector, mostly Finns, Poles, and Siberians. He knew an offensive had only a limited chance of success and his plan was simple: to strike for the nearest place of importance, Lemberg. On 29 June a preliminary artillery bombardment began. Then came the attack, 1 July, and by 8 July the use of additional forces had broadened the front to 40 miles. The Russians scored initial gains against the Austrians, but on 19 July the Germans counterattacked, and the Russian offensive ground to a halt. The poorly equipped Russian troops, many of whom had shown little inclination to fight even when successful, now deserted. ("The army voted for peace with its feet," said Lenin.) By mid-Aug. the Russians, with most of their forces in a state of complete disorganization, had been pushed back behind the offensive's starting line. The Germans checked their drive because they felt confident that there was now little to fear from the crumbling Russian army.

GERMAN DRIVE AT RIGA. 1–21 Sept. The German high command believed that by attacking Riga and thus threatening Petrograd 300 miles away, the new Russian government could be unnerved and peace could be forced. In a surprise attack, 1 Sept., which came after only a few hours of artillery bombardment, the Germans breached the Russian lines. On 3 Sept. Riga was occupied. The Germans advanced, facing almost no opposition as the Russian troops melted away, until 21 Sept. when a halt was called to the operation.

The Germans also took the islands of Oesel (Saare), 16 Oct.; Moon (Muhu), 17 Oct.; and Dagö (Hiiumaa), 18 Oct., in the Gulf of Riga, thus gaining control of the eastern Baltic.

PEACE NEGOTIATIONS. The Bolsheviks seized power in Russia on 7 Nov. Under the new regime, ending the war seemed more a matter of course than ever before. As part of their peace drive, the Bolsheviks made public over the ensuing few weeks the secret diplomacy which had preceded the outbreak of hostilities. On 8 Nov. a radiogram was addressed to all nations calling for an immediate armistice based on the right to self-determination and on the repudiation of all secret and open claims to annexations and indemnities. On 20 Nov. all allied ambassadors received notes calling for an immediate armistice. Formal application was made to the German high command, 26 Nov., for an immediate armistice, and the next day Germany said she was ready to negotiate. The allies were asked by the new Russian regime, 30 Nov., if they were prepared to open negotiations in co-operation with Russia; if they were not, Russia would negotiate alone.

TRUCE TALKS. Talks with the Central Powers opened, 3 Dec., at the Polish fortress town of Brest-Litovsk. On 5 Dec. the discussions recessed for a week while the Soviet delegates sought instructions, and were renewed, 12 Dec. On 15 Dec. a truce was agreed on for 28 days as from 17 Dec., during which time the terms for a final settlement would be worked out. On 22 Dec. peace negotiations proper began at Brest-Litovsk.

At the 1st round of discussions, the Soviets and the Central Powers could not agree on any basis for a settlement. Adolf Joffe (1883–1927), the head of the Soviet delegation, thought he had won the Germans to accept the Russian demand for peace without annexations and indemnities, but he was mistaken. On 28 Dec. the negotiations were adjourned while delegates returned to their respective capitals for instructions.

RUMANIA. With the aid of a French military mission, the Rumanian forces in Moldavia were reorganized, and on 22 July they joined with the Russians in launching a diversionary attack between the fortress of Focsani on the River Sereth and the Carpathians, a front of some 60 miles. On 6 Aug. Mackensen's forces, mostly German, counterattacked, and the Russo-Rumanian armies fell back. The Central Powers could not spare the troops necessary for decisive success, but the collapse of Russia forced the Rumanians, 6 Dec., to sign a truce ceasing all hostilities.

GREECE. A probing operation, Mar., around Lake Prespa by allied forces soon bogged down, achieving nothing but casualties. Abortive night attacks, 24 Apr., 8 May, by the British gained no ground and cost over 5,000 men. On 9 May Sarrail began his long-heralded spring offensive, but stiff resistance forced its abandonment, 21 May.

OVERTHROW OF CONSTANTINE. Charles Jonnart (1857–1927), a Frenchman, was sent to Athens as allied high commissioner to demand that Constantine abdicate. He arrived, 9 June, and the next day French troops landed at Corinth and Thessaly, encountering resistance. Late on 11 June, Constantine abdicated in favor of his 2nd son, Alexander (1893–1920), and left the country, 14 June. On 22 June Venizelos was made prime minister, and Greece formally joined the allies, 2 July.

1918

PEACE NEGOTIATIONS. The Brest-Litovsk conference was reconvened, 9 Jan., with Leon Trotsky (1874–1940) heading the Soviet delegation. A stalemate ensued as Trotsky, hoping the revolution would spread and save Russia, stalled and would not accept any of the demands (including autonomy for Poland, the Ukraine, and the Baltic provinces, and continued occupation of Russian territory) put forward by the heads of the German delegation, Gen. Hoffmann and Baron Richard von Kühlmann (1873–1949), the German foreign minister. Divisions existed among the Central Powers. In contrast to German civilian officials, the high command wanted harsh terms imposed. The Austrians, in need of grain from the East to stave off famine, were desperate for peace.

There was a further recess, 18–30 Jan., as Trotsky returned to Petrograd for conferences. On 1 Feb. the Central Powers recognized the independence of the Ukraine for which a delegation from that area had been agitating at Brest-Litovsk. On 2–7 Feb. came another adjournment while Austro-German talks took place in Berlin. Negotiations resumed, 8 Feb., and next day the Central Powers signed a separate peace at Brest-Litovsk with the Ukraine, the "bread peace," the effect of which was theoretically to leave the Ukraine an independent and neutral state, while actually it became a granary and storehouse for the Central Powers. On 10 Feb. Trotsky, who refused to accept the Central Powers' conditions, announced that Russia would neither sign a peace treaty nor continue fighting ("no peace–no war"), and the Russian delegation went home.

The German government was at first

taken aback, but, 18 Feb., terminated the armistice and ordered an advance. The remnants of the Russian army offered almost no resistance. In the north the advance halted near Narva and at Pskov. In the south the Germans, continuing on even after peace had been signed, penetrated into the Crimea and beyond Rostov, almost 600 miles within the old frontier. The allies used this advance as an excuse to send troops which later supported the Bolsheviks' enemies.

On 19 Feb. the Germans received a telegram from Lenin accepting the earlier terms, but they delayed answering until the advance in the north was almost completed. A German ultimatum was then transmitted to the Soviets, 23 Feb., and next day the Russians gave in, as Lenin, who feared for the revolution, won out over those who wanted to carry on the war. The ultimatum allowed only 3 days for talks and these began on 1 Mar.

TREATY OF BREST-LITOVSK. 3 Mar. The Soviets agreed to recognize the independence of Georgia and the Ukraine; to leave Poland, Estonia, Latvia, and Lithuania to the disposition of Germany and Austria-Hungary; to reaffirm Finland's independence; to hand over Kars, Ardahan, and Batum to Turkey; to halt all propaganda activity in Central Europe; and to open immediately commercial relations with the Central Powers. The territory of Russia was reduced by over 1,200,000 sq. mi. and her population by 62 m. Lost were 32% of the country's arable land, 26% of the railroads, 33% of the factories, and 75% of the coal and iron mines. For the Russians it was a sad ending to a war in which 2 m. Russian soldiers had been killed, over 4 m. wounded, and nearly 3 m. made prisoner. On 15 Mar. the Soviets ratified the treaty. Supplementary treaties signed on 27 Aug. further defined the terms of the peace.

PEACE WITH RUMANIA. The Treaty of Bucharest, 6 May, imposed by the Central Powers on Rumania, included provisions for a long-term German lease on the Rumanian oil fields, cession of Dobruja to Bulgaria, and the payment of indemnities in goods by Rumania. On 9 Nov. Rumania re-entered the war on the allied side with the backing of a French military mission.

ALLIED BALKAN OFFENSIVE. Under Gen. Marie Louis Guillaumat (1863–1940), the Salonika front was reorganized: forces were reassigned, the Greek army was made battleworthy, and the Serbs received replacements from troops who had been moved from Russia. In June Guillaumat was recalled to France to serve as governor of Paris, and Gen. Franchet d'Esperey (1856–1942) replaced him.

D'Esperey's well-equipped army of 350,000 men faced a mostly Bulgarian force, low in morale, weak in equipment, and reduced to about 310,000 when the Germans moved most of their forces to the Western Front. D'Esperey's attack was planned in conjunction with the allies' main drive in France. On 1 Sept. the British feinted in the Vardar Valley, and on 15 Sept. the Serbs and French attacked along a 7-mi.-wide front at Dobropolye. By 17 Sept. the allies had penetrated 20 miles and the front had widened. On 19 Sept. the Serbs crossed the Vardar and the enemy retreated in disorder. The French entered Prilep, 23 Sept., and next day the Serbs captured Gradsko. Meanwhile, 22 Sept., the Bulgarian forces, under heavy pressure on the right, had begun to retreat, closely followed by the British and the Greeks.

COLLAPSE OF BULGARIA. The position of the Bulgarians was now hopeless. The front had been cut in 2 and the halves were being driven in different directions. On 26 Sept. they asked for an armistice, repeated the request, 28 Sept., and were granted one, 29 Sept., to go into effect at noon on 30 Sept. They agreed to surrender all arms and weapons of war, evacuate all Greek and Serbian territory, demobilize most of their army, order other Central Powers troops out of their country, and allow the allies full use of Bulgarian facilities to prosecute the war further against Germany, Austria-Hungary, and Turkey.

END OF THE WAR IN THE EAST. 30 Sept.–11 Nov. Allied forces continued their advance, encountering some fierce resistance from hastily mustered German and Austrian troops. On 12 Oct. the Serbs retook their ancient capital of Nish, reoccupied Belgrade, 1 Nov., and crossed the Danube. Mackensen's troops began a rapid retreat through Transylvania. Meanwhile the French had occupied Sofia, joined the Serbs on the Danube, and later occupied part of Hungary.

THE TURKISH FRONT

1914

TREATY OF BERLIN. 2 Aug. Within the government of Young Turks which ruled Turkey, a small clique headed by the pro-German minister of war, Enver Pasha (1881–1922), feared (not without reason) that the allies intended to partition the Ottoman Empire. They believed that the best chance for Turkey's survival lay in an alliance with Germany. In July Enver Pasha went to Berlin and there negotiated a secret treaty, known only to 4 or 5 Turkish government officials, obligating Turkey to enter the war on the side of the Central Powers in return for the promise of conquered Russian territory. However, with the consent of its allies, Turkey postponed entering the war for 3 months in order to complete needed military preparations.

"GOEBEN"-"BRESLAU" AFFAIR. Two German cruisers, *Goeben* and *Breslau*, which were caught in the Mediterranean when war broke out, bombarded Bône and Philippeville in French North Africa, 4 Aug., before steaming for Constantinople. Their determined commander, Vice-Adm. W. A. T. Souchon (1869–1940), escaped a trailing British squadron and other allied vessels sent in pursuit, reaching the Dardanelles, 10 Aug., and after receiving permission from the Turks to pass through anchored in the Bosporus.

International law held that a belligerent's vessel could find only 24 hours' sanctuary in a neutral port before either sailing out or being interned. Neither happened. The Turks announced that the German cruisers had been sold to Turkey, but this was a fictitious sale. The *Goeben* and *Breslau*, renamed *Selim*

Yavuz and *Midilli*, respectively, continued to be officered by Germans and almost entirely manned by them (with German sailors wearing fezzes and playing at being Turks).

ENTRY OF TURKEY. Despite German pressure for Turkish fulfillment of treaty commitments, a desire for peace prevailed in Turkey except among the Enver Pasha group. Souchon, who had been made commander of the Turkish navy, was ordered by the German emperor to attack the Russians. On 29 Oct., with the connivance of Enver Pasha, Souchon took his 2 cruisers and some smaller Turkish vessels and shelled the Black Sea ports of Novorossisk, Feodosiya, Sevastopol, and Odessa. Russia accordingly declared war on Turkey, 1 Nov., and on 5 Nov. Great Britain and France followed suit. On 14 Nov. the sultan, as caliph, called all Moslems to a jihad (holy war) against those making war on Turkey or her allies.

Turkey had an army of some 500,000 men. Many of its technical and staff officers were Germans, who had arrived, Dec. 1913, with Gen. Otto Liman von Sanders (1855–1929), who had been hired to reorganize the remnants of the Turkish armed forces shattered in the Balkan Wars. Artillery and other equipment were fair; communications were execrable. The most immediate effect of Turkey's entry into the war was the closure of the Black Sea straits and the isolation of Russia, which could neither export her wheat nor import needed munitions via this route. The Turks began military operations in the Caucasus.

CAUCASIAN FRONT. Despite the difficulty of transporting troops to the front (they had to march at least 250 mi. from the nearest railhead), Enver Pasha chose to inaugurate a campaign against Russia with, as a 1st step, the envelopment of the fortress of Kars. During Nov. light encounters took place along the border. On 21 Dec. Enver himself arrived in the Caucasus and the Turks attacked in force. They were hampered by a rigorous terrain and by their commanders' inefficiency. During 29 Dec.–3 Jan., 1915, the Russians won a great victory at Sarikamis, 33 mi. southwest of Kars. Perhaps 50,000 Turkish troops froze to death, and the Turkish 3rd Army was almost annihilated. The most important result of the campaign was a Russian request delivered in London, 2 Jan., 1915 (before the Russian victory had become clear), asking for action against the Turks elsewhere to ease the Caucasus situation. From this resulted the allied attempt to force the Straits in 1915.

MESOPOTAMIAN FRONT. Initiated by the government of India and carried out by troops of the Indian army, allied action in Mesopotamia was designed to support friendly Arabs against the Turks and safeguard British oil interests. On 23 Oct. Indian army troops took up stations at the British-held island of Bahrain in the Persian Gulf. The Turkish forces in Mesopotamia, about 90% of whom were Arabs, and unreliable from the Turkish point of view, were poorly armed. Between 6 Nov. and 8 Dec., the British occupied the area at the head of the Persian Gulf, entering Basra, 23 Nov., after hard fighting and reaching Al Qurna, 8 Dec. Numerous small inconclusive actions were fought.

1915

CAUCASIAN FRONT. On 10 July the Russians launched an attack on the hills northwest of Lake Van. A Turkish counterattack, 16 July, pushed them back, and on 26 July the Turks occupied Malazgirt. A new Russian drive, 4–8 Aug., forced the Turks back, causing heavy casualties, not less than 10,000 being killed and wounded and over 6,000 being taken prisoner. The Russians, however, did not have the strength to follow up, and consolidated their position along a line from Vastan on the southeast corner of Lake Van to Tutak.

ARMENIAN MASSACRES. At the beginning of the war, the Christian Armenian minority in Turkey numbered about 1,500,000, located mostly in Aleppo and in the 8 Anatolian vilayets of Erzerum, Van, Bitlis, Kharput, Diyarbakir, Sivas, Adana, and Trebizond (Trabzon). Near Van the Armenians rose, 13 Apr., and seized the fortress, which they turned over

to the Russians, 19 May, who later evacuated, 4 Aug., and then recovered it, 8 Aug. In June, claiming that the Armenians were aiding the Russians, the Turkish government decreed that all non-Moslems must be transported from points of military concentration and away from lines of communication. Put into effect with unreasonable cruelty, this order resulted in the death of tens of thousands of Armenians. Marched off into the desert, they died from exposure and starvation as well as from attacks by marauders encouraged by members of the government. Death was the fate of most Armenian men; rape, forced conversion to Islam, and slavery the plight of the women. Altogether, during 1915–16 an estimated 1 m. Armenians perished; by the end of the war only a remnant remained in Asia Minor, and these mostly in refugee camps.

EGYPTIAN FRONT. On 3 Feb. an attack was made by the Turks on the Suez Canal. A force of some 22,000 men under the command of Jemal Pasha (1872–1922), the minister of marine, whose chief of staff was a Bavarian, Friedrich Kress von Kressenstein (1870–1924), had been conveyed secretly and efficiently across the Sinai Peninsula. The force attacked near Tussum, halfway between Lake Timsah and the Great Bitter Lake, and although a few boats got across the Canal the attack failed, and the Turks, who lost about 2,000 men, retreated. Except for some raids back and forth the front was quiet in this area during the rest of 1915. The main result of the Turkish attack was that the British, fearing repetitions, kept large numbers of troops in Egypt which might have been employed elsewhere.

SANUSSI RISING. The Sanussi, a powerful Moslem brotherhood, rebelled, Nov. 1915, in the Western Desert near the Nile Delta. Several hard-fought actions, Wadi Majid, 25 Dec., and Halazin, 23 Jan., 1916, interspersed with long and trying desert pursuits, ended with Turkish victory at Agagiya, 26 Feb., 1916.

GALLIPOLI CAMPAIGN. 19 Feb.–9 Jan., 1916. The Dardanelles are a 40-mi.-long channel, in places only 2 to 3 mi. wide, connecting the Mediterranean with the entrances to the Black Sea. A plan was evolved to force them, and thus free the Russian fleet. On 13 Jan. the decision was taken that the British Admiralty should prepare a naval expedition to breach the Dardanelles and bombard Constantinople. A strong advocate of this project was the 1st lord of the Admiralty, Winston Churchill (1874–1965), who argued that the navy could force the Dardanelles. On further consideration it was decided, 16 Feb., that the shores of the Dardanelles would have to be held if the fleet passed through. On 19 Feb. Australian and New Zealand troops (Anzac), who had been sent to Egypt for training, were assigned to Gen. Ian Hamilton (1853–1948), who had been appointed to command.

NAVAL ACTIONS AT THE STRAITS. 19 Feb.–18 Mar. A powerful allied naval squadron bombarded the outer forts, beginning 19 Feb., and landed marines to blow up abandoned guns. The final attack was on 18 Mar., commanded by Vice-Adm. John de Robeck (1862–1928). The Narrows forts were successfully reduced, and Turkish munition supplies gave out. In all likelihood an allied fleet could have passed through the next day unopposed. But the attack had cost 6 out of 16 capital ships and, despite the urging of his staff officer, Commo. Roger Keyes (1872–1945), de Robeck decided against renewing the attack. Hamilton, who had just arrived and concurred in this decision, discovered that the transports carrying his troops had been loaded so capriciously that it would be wiser to retire to Alexandria and repack. The Turks used the respite granted them to strengthen their defenses.

1ST LANDINGS. 25 Apr. The 1st troops were disembarked at Cape Helles and at Ari Burnu, 25 Apr., while the French made a feinting attack at Kumkale. The Russians bombarded the Bosporus ports and Liman von Sanders rushed to Bolayir, thinking the allied assault would take place there. The surprise effect was wasted, however, because of the mistakes made in the landings, especially at Helles, where a sickening slaughter ensued. At Ari Burnu a naviga-

tion error put the Anzacs ashore a mile north of the intended beach among steep ridges, but the determined attackers fought their way ashore and almost carried the heights above. They were stopped by Mustafa Kemal (1880–1938), later known as Kemal Atatürk, who saved the situation for the Turks by committing his whole division, though lacking authority to do so. The troops on the rocky beachheads suffered terribly, being constantly exposed to Turkish fire. All their supplies, even water, had to be brought ashore. The threat of submarines dictated that the supporting fleet stay mainly in the protected harbor at Moudros Bay, Lemnos, which reduced the allies' already limited artillery support. Despite the harrowing conditions, fighting continued. Breakouts were attempted at Helles three times, 6 May, 4 June, and 12 July, with little success, the total gain being 3 mi.

SUVLA BAY LANDINGS. 6 Aug. By now the Gallipoli campaign was receiving heavy support in munitions, even being given priority over the Western Front. Fresh troops were sent in, and a plan evolved calling for a landing at Suvla Bay, a little to the north. A force landing here would join forces with the Anzacs and cut across the peninsula, while the troops at Helles attacked at the same time. The Suvla affair started perfectly, with the troops landing and achieving surprise, but the advantage was soon dissipated; one column got to within a quarter of a mile of the heights with only 20 Turks ahead of them when they sat down for breakfast. Elsewhere hard fighting failed to make gains, 8–10 Aug. Further attacks, 15 and 21 Aug., also failed, and at Suvla Bay the fighting degenerated into bitter trench warfare. The Gallipoli enterprise was seen to be a disaster.

EVACUATION FROM GALLIPOLI. 10 Dec.–9 Jan., 1916. By 20 Dec. all troops were evacuated from Suvla and the Anzac zone without a casualty. On 9 Jan., 1916, the British completed the evacuation of Helles. The costs of the Gallipoli campaign were enormous, both sides together suffering over 500,000 casualties. Its effect on the war as a whole was slight.

MESOPOTAMIAN CAMPAIGN. During early Apr. 1915 the British anticipated a Turkish advance in Mesopotamia, and constructed an entrenched camp at Shaiba, about 10 mi. southwest of Basra. On 12–14 April the Turks attacked, but were repulsed, losing some 6,000 men. The British occupied Ahwaz, 16 May. A Turkish force besieged them, but was driven off and by the end of May Turkish troops had been cleared from the area. The British continued a somewhat haphazard policy of advancing up the Tigris and Euphrates rivers. On 3 June they captured Amara on the Tigris and An Nasiriya on the Euphrates, 25 July. They met considerable opposition, but under Maj. Gen. Charles Townshend (1861–1924) pushed on. Kut was captured 28 Sept., and on 5 Oct. the British reached Al Aziziya. They assaulted Ctesiphon, 22–23 Nov., in the hope of taking Baghdad, but casualties proved too heavy, and they withdrew to Kut, 25 Nov., which was invested by the Turks, 7 Dec.

1916

CAUCASIAN FRONT. The Russians under the able and vigorous Gen. Nikolai Yudenich (1862–1933) began an advance on 17 Jan. By 26 Jan. the Turks had been driven back 50 mi. along a 7-mi. front. On 12 Feb. the Russians renewed their drive, capturing Erzerum, 16 Feb. During Mar. they moved slowly along the Anatolian coast and on 17 Apr., captured Trebizond, an important Turkish military center and the best roadstead in northern Anatolia. Turkish counterdrives at the end of May and in June, using troops released by the allied evacuation of Gallipoli, had limited initial success and eventually petered out. On 2 July Yudenich launched another offensive, capturing Erzincan, 25 July, and the Turks replied by taking Mus and Bitlis, 6 Aug. By the end of Sept. the Turks had been forced to retreat after suffering heavy losses: 30,000 casualties out of an effective strength of about 100,000. The winter of 1916–17 came early and was bitterly cold. By Oct. conditions were such that all fighting ceased except for patrol activity.

EGYPT AND PALESTINE. The British under Gen. Archibald Murray (1860–1945), by building a water pipeline and a railway, began, May, a step-by-step advance from Egypt through Sinai toward the Palestinian frontier. On 23 Apr. the Turks raided Qatia and Duedir, causing heavy casualties but delaying the construction work by only a few days. On 4–5 Aug. Kress von Kressenstein, leading 16,000 Turkish troops supported by German machine-gun companies, attacked at Rumana. He was defeated with losses of almost 50%. The British attacked the outpost camp of Magdhaba, 23 Dec., and after hard fighting captured most of its garrison. Meanwhile they had occupied El Arish, 20 Dec., 27 mi. from the Palestinian frontier.

HEJAZ REVOLT. The Hejaz revolt began, 5 June, with an unsuccessful attack by Arabs on the Turkish garrison at Medina. On 7 June Hussain ibn Ali ('Alī) (1856–1931), sherif of Mecca, proclaimed the independence of the Hejaz, and on 10 June the Turkish garrison at Mecca surrendered.

MESOPOTAMIAN FRONT. The siege of Kut lasted from 7 Dec., 1915, to 29 Apr., 1916. The British made 3 attempts to lift it (9–21 Jan., 7–16 Mar., and 5–23 Apr.), but all failed. Kut, which had supplies for only 2 months, managed to hold out for 5 before surrendering. The British suffered nearly 22,000 casualties in attempting relief, and the captured garrison, which had endured great hardship, numbered about 10,000. The rest of 1916 was spent by the British in defense, as they improved their communications. Meanwhile a Russian advance on Baghdad had failed, June, and the Russians retreated north. On 13 Dec. the British began a slow drive against Kut.

1917

CAUCASIAN FRONT. Only the outbreak of the Russian Revolution saved the Turks from complete disaster in Asia Minor. The winter had been very hard and the Turkish forces suffered more than the Russians from disease, lack of winter equipment, and desertion. When the czar's government fell, the Russian troops initially stood fast, but by the early summer of 1917, though the process of disintegration was more gradual and less dramatic than on the main Russian front, the Russian army in the Caucasus was falling apart. Gen. Yudenich resigned in June. The Bolshevik seizure of power accelerated the breakup, and by the end of the year self-demobilization had led to the complete disintegration of the front. The debilitated Turks, whose manpower by this time amounted to only some 20,000 riflemen, remained inactive except for the reoccupation of the Lake Van area, from which the Russians had withdrawn.

EGYPT AND PALESTINE. Continuing their advance across the desert, the British crossed the Palestinian frontier, 8 Jan., and captured Magruntein and Rafa, 9 Jan. They then continued north up the coast, and on 28 Feb. took the small village of Khan Yunis. The Turks retreated to a defense line running from Gaza to Beersheba.

Murray's assignment, the clearing of the Sinai Peninsula, had stemmed from the British need to defend the Suez Canal. Now the British high command decided to push on in order to keep the Turks occupied.

1ST BATTLE OF GAZA. 26–27 Mar. Gaza, gateway to Palestine, was a formidable objective, even though held by only some 4,000 men. The terrain made it a natural fortress. The British plan called for a cavalry screen to hold off the Turks on the east and southeast, while infantry attacked from the south. To be effective the plan had to be carried out quickly, since communications were stretched and the cavalry's horses could be watered only in Gaza. The starting point of the attack was Wadi al-Ghazze, 6 miles south of Gaza. Heavy fog on the morning of 26 Mar. hampered the attackers but the troops captured the ridges 3 miles south of the town and the cavalry found water there. Bad staff work, however, led to the withdrawal of the cavalry at a critical moment because it was believed the infantry attack had failed. The next day the Turks closed in and took the British troops in enfilade with artillery fire, forc-

ing them to retreat back to their starting point. Casualties: British, about 4,000; Turkish, about 2,400.

2ND BATTLE OF GAZA. 17–19 Apr. Under Kress von Kressenstein the Turks had carefully fortified their positions, making them much stronger, and they had dug in along the Gaza-Beersheba road. The new British plan required an attack on this position along a 2-mi. front, beginning 2 mi. southwest of Gaza. The approach to the Turkish position was almost a glacis and made the advance very hazardous. Despite the courage with which the British attacks were pressed, they failed to pierce the Turkish lines. The British had 6,500 casualties as against 3,000 suffered by the Turks.

In June, Gen. Sir Edmund Allenby (1861–1936) was appointed to command the British forces. Allenby demanded and received reinforcements, and by Oct. the British ounumbered the Turks 2 to 1 in infantry, 8 to 1 in cavalry, and 3 to 1 in guns.

3RD BATTLE OF GAZA. 31 Oct.–7 Nov. Allenby planned a feint at Gaza while Beersheba and its vital water wells were attacked by troops who had circled to the east. The Turks, caught by surprise, put up a good fight; but although they could have destroyed the wells, failed to do so. By 1 Nov. Beersheba was in British hands and the British had begun to roll up the Turkish line. Meanwhile, 2 Nov., a British attack secured the outlying Turkish positions at Gaza, and on the night of 6–7 Nov. the Turks evacuated the town. The British gained a decision at Gaza but did not destroy the Turkish forces.

BATTLE OF JUNCTION STATION. 13–14 Nov. As the British fought their way up the coastal plain (the "Plain of the Philistines") the Turks took up positions in front of Junction Station. After 2 days of fighting it was captured with its steam water-pumping plant intact. This meant that for the first time water in large quantities was available. On 16 Nov. Jaffa was occupied.

OCCUPATION OF JERUSALEM. Part of Allenby's force had wheeled into the Judaean hills, where Falkenhayn, in command of the *yilderim* (lightning) divisions (units put together by Enver Pasha to fight in Mesopotamia but sent to Palestine because of the impossibility of transporting them to Mesopotamia), harassed it. Finally, on 8 Dec. Allenby was able to mount an attack on Jerusalem mainly from the west, with a secondary assault from the south. On 9 Dec. the municipal authorities to whom the Turks had handed over the city surrendered to Allenby. Under Falkenhayn's command the Turks attempted to recapture Jerusalem, 26–30 Dec., but they lacked the strength and a British counterattack drove them back. Over-all casualties for the whole campaign: British, about 18,000; Turkish, about 25,000.

HEJAZ REVOLT. Arab activity was not of major importance during 1917, but raids by Arabs along the Hejaz railway strained Turkish resources and caused troops to be diverted there from elsewhere. The Arab revolt was strongly influenced by T. E. Lawrence (1888–1935), an Englishman with a genius for organizing the Arabs and utilizing their strength.

MESOPOTAMIAN FRONT. Although the British drive on Kut bogged down because of the winter rains, the Turks were driven out of their Khudhaira Bend positions, 6–19 Jan., and by 16 Feb. the whole south bank of the Tigris had been cleared. On 17 Feb. an assault on Sannaiyat was thrown back in disorder, but the British heavily outnumbered the Turks and renewed the attack, 22 Feb. On 25 Feb. Kut was found deserted and in ruins. By 7 Mar. the British pursuit of the Turks had reached Diyala, on the Tigris 10 mi. below Baghdad. The Turkish positions were now outflanked, and on 11 Mar. the British entered Baghdad unopposed.

The British had taken 9,000 prisoners and an immense quantity of military material, and the Turks had lost their best base of operations in Mesopotamia. The British now drove in 3 directions to clear away the remaining Turkish opposition: east into Persia, north of the Adheim, and along the Tigris and Euphrates rivers. On 29 Sept. they occupied Ramadi,

capturing most of its garrison, and on 9 Dec. drove the Turks from Khanaqin.

1918

CAUCASIAN FRONT. The Treaty of Brest-Litovsk, which gave the Turks some Russian territory, ended the war in the Caucasus, but hostilities continued as Enver Pasha, in pursuit of his trans-Caucasian ambitions, involved the Turks in the confusion of the civil war in Russia. For their efforts the Turks gained little, and transfers of troops weakened them on other fronts.

PALESTINE AND SYRIA. Bad winter weather which washed out communications stalled Allenby's offensive plans, and by the end of Mar. the German attacks on the Western Front had necessitated sending nearly 60,000 men from Palestine to France. Allenby received replacements, but these came slowly and were raw. He was able to strike twice, 22 Mar.–2 Apr. and 29 Apr.–3 May, in the Jordan Valley, but strong Turkish resistance was met. The only other important actions took place in the south, where the Arabs hacked away at the Hejaz railway, and finally completely destroyed a long stretch of it. To assist them Allenby provided regular British forces, including armored cars and machine-gun companies.

BATTLE OF MEGIDDO. Allenby planned to break through the Turkish right flank along the coastal plain using naval guns in support. A feint in force was made by the Arab Northern Army at Dera Junction on the other side of the River Jordan, 16–17 Sept. The Megiddo attack, 19 Sept., was a considerable success; before nightfall the Turkish lines had been pierced, and Nazareth, the general headquarters of Liman von Sanders, was captured next day. Haifa fell on 23 Sept. and Samakh on 25 Sept. The Turkish forces west of the Jordan were in a state of collapse.

Meanwhile, on the east side of the river, Anzac troops had captured Amman, 25 Sept., taking 10,000 prisoners, and Lawrence, leading the Northern Army, took Dera Junction, 27 Sept.

PURSUIT OF THE TURKS. The Turkish forces had now almost disintegrated. Damascus was taken, 1 Oct. Malaria and influenza broke out among the British cavalry, but the advance continued, Homs being entered on 15 Oct. Aleppo, over 300 mi. from the offensive's starting point, fell on 26 Oct. 75,000 prisoners were captured, while British casualties were about 5,700. An encounter at Haritan, 26 Oct., where troops under Mustafa Kemal checked the advance of 2 Indian regiments, was the last action before an armistice (signed 30 Oct., effective next day) ended the fighting on this front.

MESOPOTAMIAN FRONT. With the collapse of Russia the Germans and the Turks raced each other on either side of the Black Sea for the Baku oil fields and for Persia. On 18 Jan., Gen. L. C. Dunsterville (1865–1946) had been appointed chief of a British mission charged with reorganizing the scattered remnants of Russian, Caucasian, and Armenian troops into an effective force with which to halt the Turko-German advance. He failed to get through, established himself at Hamadan (about 400 mi. south of Baku), and gradually built up a British force known as "Dunster Force." At the end of July the local government in Baku, fearful of the Turkish advance, revised its earlier anti-British attitude and appealed for aid. Small forces began landing there, 4 Aug., until by the end of the month about 2,000 British troops were in Baku. Turkish attacks began, 20 Aug. The British, who received little assistance from the local government, held on against very superior forces until 15 Sept., when they re-embarked and sailed across the Caspian Sea to Enzeli (Pahlevi).

Meanwhile on the Euphrates Hit was taken, 9 Mar., by the British, and other local actions at this time harassed the Turks. Operations then virtually ceased until the autumn. On 23 Oct. the British began yet another offensive along the Tigris. The Turks withdrew to the Little Zab River, 50 miles to the north, but the British pursued them at great speed, at one point covering nearly 80 mi. in 39 hours. The ensuing Battle of Sharqat ended, 29 Oct., when the British broke through the Turkish defenses, and the Turkish commander, realizing the hopelessness of his position, surrendered the next morning. This ended hostilities on the Mesopotamian Front and an armistice came into effect the following day.

Anxious to occupy the oil fields of Mosul, the British moved on despite the armistice and entered the city, 3 Nov. After some delay British troops also reoccupied Baku, 17 Nov.

ARMISTICE. Bulgaria's surrender on 29 Sept. had isolated Turkey. The Turkish armies had collapsed and allied forces were pressing northward in Syria and Mesopotamia. On 13 Oct. the sultan dismissed Enver Pasha and the other Young Turk ministers, and a new cabinet appealed for an armistice, 14 Oct. Negotiators met, 26–30 Oct., on the British warship *Agamemnon* in Moudros Bay, Lemnos Island, with Adm. Arthur Calthorpe (1864–1937) representing the allies.

Signed on 30 Oct. to go into effect at noon the following day, the armistice called for the Turks to open the Dardanelles, demobilize their army, surrender all war vessels, facilitate the clearing of mines from the Straits, withdraw all forces from northern Persia and the Caucasus, permit allied occupation of strategic points in Turkey, and surrender all garrisons in Tripolitania, Cyrenaica, Arabia, Syria, and Mesopotamia.

THE WAR IN THE COLONIES
1914–18

GERMAN OVERSEAS EMPIRE. In 1914 Germany had a colonial empire over 1 m. sq. mi. in extent. In Africa, her colonies were Togo, Cameroons, South-West Africa, and German East Africa; in the Pacific, the Bismarck Archipelago, North-East New Guinea (Kaiser-Wilhelmsland), Western Samoa, the Caroline and Marshall Islands, and parts of the Solomon and Mariana Islands. In China the Germans held a 99-year lease, obtained in 1898, on Kiaochow. Germany's overseas territories had a total population of about 15 m., of whom only about 25,000 were Germans.

KIAOCHOW. German Kiaochow consisted of about 200 sq. miles on the south coast of the Shantung Peninsula. Tsingtao, its excellent port, was located at the end of a small subsidiary peninsula 3½ mi. wide at the isthmus. By 1914 Tsingtao had been turned into a strong, modern fortress protected by heavy guns covering the coast and by well-fortified defensive zones across the neck of the peninsula. The regular garrison of about 4,000 German marines had been augmented by some 2,500 reservists, Germans and Austrians who had gathered there at the outbreak of war.

On 15 Aug., 1914, Japan demanded that the Germans evacuate the area. Receiving no suitable reply, the Japanese declared war, 23 Aug. On 27 Aug. a Japanese fleet invested the port, but too late to prevent the escape of the German Far Eastern naval squadron. Japanese troops landed at Lungkow, 2 Sept., on the far side of Shantung, and came into contact with German outposts, 14 Sept. Another landing was made, 18 Sept., this time closer to the defensive zone. On 23 Sept. British forces from Hong Kong landed at Laoshan Bay. By 15 Oct. allied troops (about 30,000 Japanese and 1,500 British) were within 5 mi. of Tsingtao. On 31 Oct. bombardment by land and from the sea began as regular methods of siege warfare were adopted. On the night of 6–7 Nov. a general assault captured the infantry redoubts, and at 6:20 A.M. on 7 Nov. the German governor hoisted a white flag. German losses were 199 killed and about 500 wounded; Japanese casualties were 1,800 and British 70.

THE PACIFIC. The German islands in the Pacific fell an easy prey to the allied forces. On 30 Aug., 1914, a New Zealand force occupied Western Samoa, and on 11 Sept. the Australians landed on New Britain in the Bismarck Archipelago. German and indigenous forces in North-East New Guinea surrendered, 21 Sept. On 7 Oct. the Japanese occupied the Marshall and Caroline Islands, and on 9 Dec. an Australian force moved on the Solomon Islands. Little fighting accompanied these actions.

TOGO. German Togoland was a strip of territory in West Africa about 90 mi. wide and 300 mi. deep. Some 100 mi. inland, at Kamina, there was a powerful wireless station, which served as the chief German radio link between Europe and Africa. On 7 Aug., 1914, small Anglo-French forces, pushing in from both sides, captured Lomé, the port. The allied force then moved north, and on 27 Aug., after blowing up the Kamina wireless facilities, the German force there surrendered.

SOUTH-WEST AFRICA. The Germans had few troops in South-West Africa, since they anticipated receiving help from Boers rebelling against the British in South Africa. British South African forces took Lüderitz, 19 Sept., 1914, but further action had to await the suppression by Gen. Louis Botha (1862–1919) of a rebellion, Oct. 1914–Feb. 1915, which involved some of the commanders and troops intended for the South-West African campaign. Botha took command, and the South Africans renewed their assault in Jan. 1915. The campaign was mainly a struggle against nature and the climate rather than against a hard-fighting enemy. 60,000 South Africans moved against the Germans from 4 directions. 20,000 under Botha landed at Swakopmund, 25 Dec., 1914; proceeded against Windhoek, the capital; and captured it, 12 May, 1915. Another force of 24,000 advanced inland from Lüderitz. A third force of 8,000 moved north over the River Orange, and a fourth of about 2,000 crossed the border from the east. The Germans retreated inland to Otavi, at the end of the railway line. Surrounded, they asked for terms, 6 July, and capitulated, 9 July. German casualties, exclusive of indigenous troops, were 1,200; South African losses were 275 killed and 318 wounded.

CAMEROONS. Here German plans called for withdrawal of all forces to Yaoundé, some 200 mi. inland from the coast. On 20 Aug., 1914, a French force, including a Belgian contingent, invaded from the southeast. British troops crossed the frontier from Nigeria, 25–27 Aug., but were soon driven back. On 26 Sept. a joint Anglo-French amphibious expedition attacked Duala, 20 mi. up the River Wuri. Duala surrendered the next day, though most of its garrison escaped.

Allied pursuit resulted in the capture of Edia, 35 mi. to the southwest, on 26 Oct., but again the bulk of the German forces got away. After an unsuccessful counterattack the Germans retreated to Yaoundé. Beset by German guerrilla action and ambushed by hostile Africans, the allies took over a year to reach Yaoundé, and when, 1 Jan., 1916, the British entered it, they found it empty. The German forces had evacuated the town, and had begun a 125-mi. trek to neutral Spanish Guinea, which they ultimately reached successfully. By the end of Feb. all German garrisons had been cleared from Cameroons. Battle losses were small on both sides, disease being the main killer.

GERMAN EAST AFRICA. German East Africa (Tanganyika) was the largest and richest of the German colonies as well as the most difficult to conquer. A German force of about 3,500 whites and 12,000 Africans was skillfully led by Gen. Paul von Lettow-Vorbeck (1870–1964). On 8 Aug., 1914, British cruisers bombarded Dar-es-Salaam, the chief port. During Sept. Lettow-Vorbeck directed a series of raids across the borders of British East Africa and Uganda, at one time threatening Mombasa. On 2 Nov. Indian troops landed at Tanga, but German attacks as well as harassment from wild bees caused severe losses, and reembarkation took place, 4–5 Nov. The year 1915 was spent in sporadic and indecisive fighting along the lakes and frontiers. The Germans seized portions of the Uganda Railway. The conquest of German South-West Africa allowed many of the South African troops there to be transferred for operations against German East Africa. Gen. Jan Christiaan Smuts (1870–1950), who had under his command about 20,000 men, moved south against Lettow-Vorbeck, while other columns converged from Uganda in the east and Rhodesia to the south. The Germans rarely stood and fought; when confronted by superior numbers they scattered into the bush and proved very elusive. Meanwhile the South Africans, unused to the climate, suffered severely from disease and were slowly replaced by Nigerian troops. During 1916–18 British battle

casualties were 10,717, but nonbattle casualties totaled 336,940. Despite his elusiveness Lettow-Vorbeck was gradually pushed into a corner. Smuts left, Jan. 1917, for an Imperial Cabinet post in London, but his successors continued the offensive. The main German force of 5,000 men was surrounded near Mahenge and surrendered, 28 Nov., 1917, while Lettow-Vorbeck, with about 1,300 troops and now commanding the only German force left in the field, withdrew south across the Portuguese frontier. For the remainder of the war Portuguese and British troops pursued him as he led them a hard chase through Mozambique, back into German East Africa, and then into Northern Rhodesia. He surrendered, 23 Nov., 1918, at Abercorn, only after having been informed of the armistice.

THE WAR AT SEA

1914–18

NAVAL STRATEGY. 1914. In late July 1914, as the Serbian crisis deepened, the British and German fleets were mobilized and concentrated in home waters. British naval strategy throughout the war aimed at forestalling a German invasion of Britain, preventing war materials from reaching the Central Powers by sea, and containing the German High Seas Fleet by stationing fleets in the North Sea and the English Channel. German strategy was to wear down British sea power through raids and submarine and mine warfare until the British fleet could be engaged with good prospects of a successful battle.

NORTH SEA AND ENGLISH CHANNEL OPERATIONS. 1914–15. When hostilities broke out, 4 Aug., the British Grand Fleet under Admiral Sir John Jellicoe (1859–1935) began the 1st of its sweeps through the North Sea. Between 5 and 23 Aug. the British Expeditionary Force was convoyed to France without loss. British units raided the German coast on the night of 28–29 Aug., trapping a German patrol in the Battle of the Helgoland Bight. The Germans lost 3 light cruisers and a destroyer. The Germans now intensified their mine and submarine operations around the British Isles. On 22 Sept. the *U-9* sank 3 British cruisers within an hour. Following this action, new orders were issued limiting the use of heavy ships on patrol in submarine waters. In late Sept. British naval units escorted troops to Antwerp, and through Oct. supported the withdrawal down the Belgian coast. The fear of submarine penetration of Scapa Flow led to the movement of the Grand Fleet to Lough Swilly, 20 Oct., where it remained until defenses at Scapa Flow were improved. The battleship *Audacious* was destroyed by a mine, 27 Oct. On 2 Nov. the North Sea was declared a military area, and all neutrals were warned that travel outside prescribed routes was at their own risk. German cruisers raided Gorleston, 3 Nov., while Scarborough and Hartlepool were bombarded, 16 Dec. British battle cruisers forestalled another raid when they defeated a German squadron, 24 Jan., 1915, in the Battle of the Dogger Bank. During the rest of 1915 the German fleet put to sea only to support minelaying operations.

CRUISER AND RAIDER CAMPAIGN. 1914–15. At the beginning of the war there were 13 German cruisers detached from the High Seas Fleet, along with 7 gunboats; 5 armed merchantmen also put to sea. Aside from the cruisers *Goeben* and *Breslau,* which were able to elude the British Mediterranean squadron and escape to the Dardanelles, 10 Aug., the rest of these German ships were neutralized by early 1915.

The German light cruiser *Emden* was able to slip away from Tsingtao in early Aug. and reach the Indian Ocean. Before the *Emden* was sunk, 9 Nov., she had destroyed 15 ships. The rest of the German Far East Squadron under Adm. Count Maximilian von Spee (1861–1914) was able to evade allied forces in the Pacific and make for South America. After bombarding Papeete, 22 Sept., and cutting the British cables at Fanning Island, Spee's cruisers rendezvoused with the *Dresden,* from the West Indies, and the *Leipzig,* from the California coast. The enlarged squadron sank 2 British

cruisers in the Battle of Coronel, 1 Nov., off the Chile coast. British squadrons were quickly concentrated in the Southern Pacific and Atlantic. On 8 Dec. Spee's cruisers were sighted, and 4 of his 5 ships were lost in the Battle of the Falkland Islands. The remaining cruiser, the *Dresden,* was hunted down and destroyed, 14 Mar., 1915.

The cruisers *Karlsruhe* and *Königsberg* had successful careers as raiders until the *Karlsruhe* blew up at sea, 4 Nov., and the *Königsberg* was discovered and destroyed in the Rufiji River, 11 July, 1915.

Of the German commercial raiders, the *Kaiser Wilhelm der Grosse* was sunk off Rio de Oro, 26 Aug., 1914, while the *Cap Trafalgar* was sunk off Trinidad, 14 Sept. The *Kronprinz Wilhelm* was interned at Newport News, 8 Apr., 1915, as was the *Prinz Eitel Friedrich,* 12 Mar. During their short campaign the German cruisers and raiders were able to sink about 2/3 of 1% of British commercial shipping.

NAVAL SUPPORT OF LAND CAMPAIGNS. 1914–15. Action in the Pacific centered around the successful Anglo-Japanese amphibious attack on German Tsingtao, 2 Sept.–7 Nov., 1914. The Australian squadron assisted in the conquest of German Samoa, 30 Aug., and German New Guinea, 11–15 Sept. British naval units assisted in the capture of Douala, 27 Sept., and were employed in blockade duties and river warfare throughout the Cameroons campaign. British battleships and cruisers helped the South African army occupy Walvis Bay and Swakopmund, German South-West Africa, Jan. 1915. Units from the Indian squadron were involved in the abortive amphibious operations at Tanga, 2–5 Nov., 1914, and in the blockade of German East Africa begun in Mar. 1915.

SUBMARINE WAR ON COMMERCE. 1915–16. On 4 Feb., 1915, the German government declared a submarine blockade of Great Britain beginning 17 Feb. Strong U.S. protests against the sinking of the *Lusitania,* 7 May, and the *Arabic,* 19 Aug., led to a revision of German submarine policy. On 1 Sept. the German government announced that no more passenger liners would be sunk without warning and without provision for the safety of noncombatants. Following the announcement, 21 Feb., 1916, that armed merchantmen would be treated as cruisers, the Germans began a period of unrestricted submarine warfare. When the *Sussex* was sunk, 24 Mar., 1916, with the loss of American lives, the U.S. government issued a virtual ultimatum which temporarily ended unrestricted submarine warfare, 10 May.

MEDITERRANEAN AND DARDANELLES CAMPAIGNS. 1914–16. Initially, operations in the Mediterranean were limited to transporting French North African forces to Europe, early Aug. 1914. A French blockade was established over the Austrian fleet in the Adriatic, 16 Aug., while the Dardanelles were blockaded by the British, 29 Oct., following a German-Turkish naval raid on the Russian Black Sea coast.

In early 1915, Russian appeals for relief of the pressure on the Caucasus front led to the attempt to penetrate the Dardanelles. Naval operations began, 19 Feb., but the Anglo-French fleet could not silence the Turkish shore batteries or sweep the mine fields. On 18 Mar. a concerted attack was launched, but it was beaten off with the loss of 1 French and 2 British battleships. The failure of the fleet to force a passage through the Straits led to the Gallipoli Campaign, 25 Apr., 1915–9 Jan., 1916. During this operation, 3 more British battleships were lost.

After the failure of the Dardanelles campaign, emphasis shifted back to blockading the Adriatic and the Dardanelles. After Italy entered the war, May 1915, a combined Anglo-Italian fleet was responsible for containing the Austrian fleet. Utilizing Austrian and Greek ports, German and Austrian submarines ranged all through the Mediterranean, preying upon commerce and supply vessels bound for Salonika and the Near East.

NORTH SEA OPERATIONS. 1916. In early 1916 Adm. Reinhard Scheer (1863–1928) was given command of the German High Seas Fleet and adopted a new activist policy. German destroyer groups put to sea more often. Yarmouth and Lowestoft were bombarded by German battle cruisers, 24 Apr., 1916. The High Seas Fleet sailed, 30 May, to trap part of the British Grand Fleet. The British under Adm. Jellicoe were alerted, and the 2 battle fleets engaged in the Battle of Jutland, 31 May. British losses were heavier—3 battle cruisers, 3 cruisers, and 8 torpedo boats against 1 battleship, 1 battle cruiser, 4 light cruisers, and 5 torpedo boats for the Germans—but the British Grand Fleet retained control over the North Sea. Another fleet encounter was narrowly averted by the Germans, 19 Aug. The British lost 2 cruisers, while 2 U-boats were sunk. German destroyer flotillas raided the Strait of Dover, 26–27 Oct., sinking 2 British destroyers.

UNRESTRICTED SUBMARINE WARFARE. 1917–18. By late 1916 German U-boats were sinking some 300,000 tons of shipping a month. In an attempt to cut Britain off from her overseas suppliers and thereby end the war, the Germans declared a policy of unrestricted submarine warfare after 1 Feb., 1917. The U.S. soon broke diplomatic relations, and on 6 Apr. declared war on Germany. Although the German campaign reached a peak of 875,000 tons destroyed in Apr. 1917, the introduction of convoys, 10 May, and the increased use of antisubmarine craft began to turn the tide. By early 1918 the allies were launching more new tonnage than was being destroyed.

THE MEDITERRANEAN. 1917–18. Allied shipping losses to German and Austrian submarines became serious by mid-1917. In Aug. protection of trade was placed under the control of a single British commander at Malta, while a convoy system was begun under British and Japanese destroyer protection. The German cruisers *Goeben* and *Breslau* raided into the Mediterranean, 20 Jan., 1918. After destroying 2 British monitors, the *Breslau* was blown up by a mine, and the severely damaged *Goeben* retired to the Dardanelles.

Austrian attempts to pierce the Adriatic blockade, Apr. and June, failed. On 31 Oct., 1918, Italian torpedo craft were able to enter the Austrian base at Pola, where they sank the battleship *Viribus Unitis.*

NORTH SEA OPERATIONS. 1917–18. British and German destroyer groups clashed in raids off the Dover and Dutch coasts, 23 Jan., 17 Mar., 20 and 26 Apr., 2 May, 1917; 17 Nov., 14 Jan., and 15 Feb., 1918. German light cruisers attacked the Scandinavian convoy, 27 Oct., 1917, sinking 2 British destroyers and 9 merchantmen. After the raid of 12 Dec., in which a destroyer and 4 armed trawlers were sunk, the British strengthened the escorts and reorganized the Scandinavian routes.

British attempts to blockade German submarines in their bases led to attacks on Zeebrugge and Ostend, 22–23 Apr., 1918. While the entrance to Zeebrugge was partially blocked, the attempt at Ostend failed. Another attack on Ostend, 9–10 May, also was unsuccessful. Both submarine bases were finally overrun in the British land offensive, 17–20 Oct., 1918.

DESTRUCTION OF THE HIGH SEAS FLEET. In late Oct. 1918 plans were laid by the Germans for a last raid into the English Channel. As the High Seas Fleet began to get under way, 29 Oct., mutiny broke out, and the fleet was immobilized. Under the terms of the 11 Nov. armistice, the Germans were to surrender 10 battleships, 6 battle cruisers, 8 light cruisers, 50 destroyers, and all their submarines. These terms were complied with, 20–21 Nov. Following the imposition of the naval clauses of the Versailles Treaty, an additional 8 battleships, 8 light cruisers, and 92 destroyers and torpedo boats were surrendered. On 21 June, 1919, most of the ships of this fleet were scuttled by their crews at Scapa Flow.

THE PEACE

1918–21

PARIS PEACE CONFERENCE. Following the armistice of 11 Nov., 1918, representatives of the major allied and associated powers held preliminary meetings, and on 12 Jan., 1919, the Council of 10, consisting of 2 delegates each from France, Britain, Italy, Japan, and the U.S., was organized to formulate the terms of the peace. Representatives of the other states which had fought against the Central Powers or had broken off diplomatic relations with them were each given a vote in the plenary sessions. Neutral states were permitted to attend those sessions to which they were summoned by the Council of 10.

At the 1st plenary session, 18 Jan., 1919, it became clear that the small powers would act only to approve the decisions reached by the Council of 10. Georges Clemenceau was elected president of the conference. The secretary general selected by the Council of 10 was appointed, and a drafting committee whose members represented the 5 major powers was approved.

The work of the conference was divided between a number of commissions. A Supreme Economic Council was established, 8 Feb., 1919, to advise the conference on economic measures needed until the peace negotiations were completed. Commissions were also created to investigate war guilt; reparations; the establishment of a League of Nations Covenant; international labor legislation; international control of certain ports and transportation networks; economic, financial, and territorial questions; inter-allied military affairs; and aeronautics. On all these commissions, representatives of the 5 major powers constituted a majority. The Supreme War Council, which sat at Versailles under the presidency of Marshal Foch, supervised the execution of the terms of the armistice.

During Feb. and Mar. 1919 the Council of 10 was gradually abandoned in favor of a Council of 4, consisting of Clemenceau, Lloyd George, Orlando, and Wilson. The Japanese plenipotentiary attended only those meetings which dealt with matters of concern to Japan. The ministers of foreign affairs of these states met as a Council of 5 to work out minor technical and executive matters.

ISSUES BEFORE THE CONFERENCE. The main issues confronting the Council of 4 were French attempts to separate the territory east of the Rhine and the Saar from Germany, French insistence that Germany be held responsible for reparations up to the limit of its capacity to pay, and Polish claims to Danzig. Following Wilson's threat to abandon negotiations and return to the U.S., 7 Apr., 1919, the deadlock on these matters was broken and compromises were reached. The Rhineland was demilitarized, while control of the Saar was vested in the League of Nations for 15 years, after which a plebiscite would decide whether the territory would remain under League control, join France, or rejoin Germany. French views prevailed in the matter of reparations. Danzig was made a free city under the League's protection, and Poland was guaranteed access to the Baltic Sea. The Covenant of the League was made an integral part of the treaty and was approved by the conference, 28 Apr., 1919.

Lesser crises developed over Italian, Yugoslavian, Belgian, and Japanese claims. Italy's demands for territories up to the Brenner Pass were met, but its claims on the eastern shore of the Adriatic, including Fiume, were left unresolved. While Yugoslavian indemnity claims were dismissed, Belgium was assured preferred treatment on reparations. Japanese resistance to Wilson's attempts to return German Shantung to China resulted in a compromise by which Japan pledged to restore Chinese sovereignty over Shantung as soon as possible.

On 7 May, 1919, the draft treaty was presented to the chief German delegate, Count Ulrich von Brockdorff-Rantzau (1869–1928). Although the German delegation vehemently protested the reparations clauses as too severe and the other terms of the treaty as inconsistent with the pre-armistice agreement, only minor revisions were conceded. The treaty was signed, 28 June, 1919.

THE TREATY. The Treaty of Versailles consisted of 15 parts, with 440 articles. Part I set forth the Covenant of the League of Nations. Germany's frontiers were redrawn in Parts II and III, the Rhineland was demilitarized, and schedules for plebiscites in the Saar, Schleswig, East Prussia, and Upper Silesia were outlined. In Part IV Germany ceded all its overseas territories, which were given over to the allies as mandated territories,

and Germany's special rights in China, Siam, Egypt, Morocco, and Liberia were canceled. The military clauses of Part V reduced the German army to 100,000 men, disbanded the general staff, severely limited the size of the German navy, and prohibited any military air forces. Part VI provided for the return of prisoners of war and the maintenance of graves. Provisions to punish Kaiser Wilhelm II and other Germans accused of war crimes were outlined in Part VII. Germany's responsibility, along with that of its allies, for the war was set forth in Part VIII along with the reparations procedures. Parts IX and X dealt with financial questions and the restoration of commerce. By Part XI the allies were given full liberty to fly over Germany until 1 Jan., 1923. Part XII guaranteed Czechoslovakia access to the sea; recognized the Rhine, Elbe, Oder, Niemen, and Danube as international waterways; and established commissions to govern them. The International Labor Organization was created by Part XIII. Procedures to guarantee Germany's compliance with the treaty were set out in Part XIV, and a number of miscellaneous matters occupied Part XV.

RATIFICATION OF THE TREATY. Germany ratified the treaty, 9 July, 1919; Britain followed, 31 July; Italy, 7 Oct.; France, 13 Oct.; and Japan, 27 Oct. The U.S. Senate rejected the treaty, 19 Nov., 1919. Germany agreed to give compensation for the scuttling of its fleet in a separate protocol, 10 Jan., 1920. Ratifications were exchanged, 10 Jan., and the League of Nations was formally inaugurated, 16 Jan., 1920.

FORMATION OF THE LEAGUE OF NATIONS. The League grew out of efforts to provide for a postwar system of mutual security, and to create mechanisms for international social and economic co-operation. The Covenant of the League, as set forth in Part I of the Treaty of Versailles, established the constitutional basis of this new system. Membership was to consist of the allied signatories of the treaty, and of 13 neutral states. Other states could be admitted after approval by a 2/3 majority of the Assembly. The League Covenant provided for 3 major organs. The Assembly, comprising representatives of all the members, could deal with any matters within the League's competence. The Executive Council, composed of representatives of France, Britain, Italy, Japan, and the U.S. as permanent members, and 4 others elected by the Assembly, was to have primary responsibility for peacekeeping. Both the Council and the Assembly were to act by unanimous vote. A permanent secretariat was created, and its expenses were to be borne by the member states.

The Covenant provided for disarmament and established procedures for the peaceful settlement of disputes or the implementation of sanctions. It also provided for a permanent international court, the registration and publication of all treaties, and the operation of the mandate system.

Although the U.S. Senate rejected the Versailles Treaty containing the Covenant, both became effective for other signatories, 10 Jan., 1920, and the 1st meeting of the Executive Council followed on 16 Jan. The 1st Assembly convened in Geneva on 15 Nov. A number of subsidiary organs were established, including 2 commissions on military affairs, the Economic and Financial Committees, the Communications and Transit Organization, and the Health Organization. The Permanent Mandates Commission and the Refugee Organization followed in 1921. The International Labor Organization, created by Part XIII of the Versailles Treaty, began independent operation. Established on 21 Jan., 1920, a Conference of Ambassadors (representing the allies) paralleled the League in its early years.

Europe Between the Wars

WESTERN EUROPE AND THE RISE OF FASCISM

1918–24

POSTWAR ELECTIONS. In Great Britain, efforts to keep the tripartite wartime coalition together failed as the Labour Party and part of the Liberal Party refused to continue under Lloyd George's leadership. What remained of the coalition campaigned on a platform of: Germany "must pay to the uttermost farthing," and Britain must be made a land "fit for heroes to live in." The new Conservative-dominated coalition won, 14 Dec., 1918, an unexpectedly decisive victory (c. 500 out of 707 seats).

In Germany, National Constituent Assembly elections were held on 19 Jan., 1919, 4 days after the violent suppression of the "Spartacist Week" demonstrations, 6–15 Jan., had ended with the murder of the Spartacist (now Communist) leaders, Karl Liebknecht and Rosa Luxemburg. The German electorate, now consisting of the entire adult population (universal suffrage adopted 24 Oct., 1918), repudiated extremist agitation. The 3 parties supporting the republic without apol-

ogy—the Majority Socialists (moderate Social Democrats), Catholic Centrists, and Democrats—won 326 of 421 seats.

In France, a large multimember district system with no second ballot was adopted, 12 July, 1919. The comparative unity of the conservative National Bloc enabled it to take advantage of this proportional representation system, and gain 376 or two-thirds of the Chamber of Deputies seats, 16 Nov.

Italy did not receive the Dalmatian coast as promised by the Treaty of London, 26 Apr., 1915, and Premier Vittorio Orlando (1860–1952) was forced to resign, 19 June, 1919, for alleged mismanagement of the peace negotiations. Francesco Nitti (1868–1953), who succeeded him, called a national election. On 16 Nov., under a new proportional representation system, adopted 2 Sept., the trend away from coalitions and toward parties adamant on principles became clear. Socialists with 156 and Christian Democrats with 100 seats constituted more than half the Chamber of Deputies.

WEIMAR CONSTITUTION. 31 July, 1919. Germany was declared a federated nation, political authority being executed in national affairs by the national government and in state affairs by state governments. The Legislature was to consist of the Reichsrat, representing the states, and the Reichstag, representing the people as a whole. The president was to be elected by popular vote for a 7-year term. Article 48 gave the president the power in case of emergency to take all necessary measures to restore public order, including the suspension of civil rights stipulated in the constitution.

BRITISH INDUSTRIAL UNREST. In Britain labor stoppages took place, the most serious being the coal miners' strike of 24–29 Mar., 1919. Many Britons considered too limited such government measures as the Housing and Town Planning Act (Addison Act), 31 July, 1919, and the 1920–22 Unemployment Insurance Acts.

IRISH INDEPENDENCE. On 7 Jan., 1919, 26 of the 73 Irish M.P.'s in the British House of Commons met in the Mansion House, Dublin, to establish an independent assembly, the Dail Eireann. An undeclared state of war followed between the I.R.A. (Irish Republican Army) and the R.I.C. (Royal Irish Constabulary). Fighting continued despite passage of the Better Government of Ireland Act, 23 Dec., 1920, by the British Parliament. The Irish Free State was officially established in Jan. 1923.

WEAKNESS OF THE WEIMAR REPUBLIC. In Germany, a large segment of the population continued to oppose the republic. On 13 Mar., 1920, Wolfgang Kapp (1858–1922) led a *Putsch* in Berlin in the name of the monarchy, forcing the government to flee first to Dresden and then to Stuttgart. Kapp capitulated, 17 Mar., after a paralyzing general strike by Berlin workers. That dissatisfaction with the republic was not confined to disgruntled soldiers was evidenced by the election of 6 June, 1920, in which the strength of the "Weimar Coalition" parties fell to only half the Reichstag seats. On 10 May, 1921, right-wing terrorists began a campaign against republican notables by assassinating Karl Gareis (1844–1921), leader of the Bavarian Independents and vocal opponent of the "free corps" associations. Other victims were

Matthias Erzberger (1875–1921), 26 Aug., 1921, and Walther Rathenau (1867–1922), 24 June, 1922.

FRENCH ATTITUDE TO GERMANY. In France, although some became interested in the Soviet experiment and joined the Communist Party, most people were preoccupied with the problems of securing France against the German invasion of revenge which they were certain would come. France had suffered most from the war: 1,654,550 lives lost, and $10 billion in property damage. The legislature, dissatisfied with the provisions of the Treaty of Versailles regarding geographical security and fearing the ambitions of Premier Georges Clemenceau, denied him the presidency, 17 Jan., 1920. Political success accrued to those adopting a hard line on Germany. When Premier Aristide Briand (1862–1932) showed a willingness to grant a moratorium on German reparation payments during the Cannes Conference, 6–13 Jan., 1921, severe opposition from President Alexandre Millerand, the legislature, and the press forced him to give way to Raymond Poincaré (1860–1934).

RISE OF MUSSOLINI. In Italy, severe economic difficulties and wounded national pride were the basic causes of postwar unrest and extremism. Peasants seized areas promised them during the war. On 31 Aug., 1920, a breakdown of wage negotiations in the metallurgical industry led to a lockout. Workers responded by occupying some large northern factories, remaining there for 8 weeks. Premier Giovanni Giolitti (1842–1928) refused to use force, and the incident was cited by such right-wing groups as the Fascist Party of Benito Mussolini (1883–1945) as an example of the Socialist danger. Giolitti's nonintervention gave new confidence to labor, and 1920–21 saw a rash of work stoppages. Party leaders, unable to cope with the situation, further weakened themselves by continuing to express their dissatisfaction with the peace settlement, thus magnifying their own failures. On 12 Sept., 1919, Gabriele D'Annunzio (1863–1938) took over Fiume and established a petty dictatorship. Giolitti secretly supported him for a time, but on 27 Dec., 1920, the D'Annunzio regime was brought to an end by Italian troops. Giolitti signed the Treaty of Rapallo with Yugoslavia, 12 Nov., 1920, and alienated the upper classes and the church by his plan to make bondholders register and pay taxes. He was compelled to seek new support through a national election. On 15 May, 1921, with the Fascists included in the Giolitti bloc, the election brought Mussolini 35 seats in the Chamber and political respectability. The Socialists forced out Giolitti's successor, Ivanoe Bonomi (1873–1951), on 2 Feb., 1922, and Luigi Facta (1861–1930) became premier, 25 Feb. A vote of no confidence caused Facta's fall, 21 July, but because only Mussolini was willing to form a government, he resumed office, 31 July. Finally, with the government completely debilitated, a curiously hesitant Mussolini agreed to the Fascist "March on Rome," 27 Oct. King Victor Emmanuel III (ruled 1900–1946), fearing the royal aspirations of his cousin the Duke of Aosta, would not proclaim martial law, and Mussolini's "black shirts" took control of Rome. On 31 Oct. Mussolini was appointed premier, and on 25 Nov. he received dictatorial powers until 31 Dec., 1923, to restore order and enact reforms.

WAR REPARATIONS. Although a Reparation Commission was created by Art. 233 of the Treaty of Versailles to calculate the total war damage for which Germany was to be held responsible, allied statesmen decided that the issue was diplomatic as well as economic, and held 8 meetings before the final decision date stipulated by the treaty, 1 May, 1921. At a London meeting, 21 Feb.–14 Mar., 1921, a German counterproposal on reparations provoked the allies into drawing up a list of alleged German treaty defaults and an ultimatum of acceptance of allied reparation terms, drafted at a conference in Paris in Jan., or military sanctions. When the German delegation balked, the threatened military occupation of Düsseldorf, Duisberg, and Ruhrort on the rim of the Ruhr Basin was carried out, 8 Mar., 1921. On 27 Apr. the Reparation Commission announced the total bill: 132 billion gold marks. Failing to secure concessions, German Chancellor Konstantin Fehrenbach (1852–1926) resigned, 4 May. The allies issued, 5 May, an ultimatum giving Germany a week to accept the announced sum or face occupation of the Ruhr. Josef Wirth (1879–1956) of the Catholic Center Party, with the support of the Weimar coalition, formed a government, 10 May, and yielded, 11 May.

REPARATIONS DIPLOMACY. After paying the 15 July and 15 Oct., 1921, installments, concluding the Loucheur-Rathenau or Wiesbaden Agreement, 6 Oct., for the direct supply of reparation material, and delivering bond payments, 28 Oct., Germany requested a moratorium for the part of her debt due on 15 Jan. and 15 Feb., 1922, because of the Nov. 1921 collapse of the mark. A conference of allied leaders at Cannes, 6–13 Jan., 1922, reviewed the request. Simultaneously, Briand and Lloyd George attempted to heal the postwar breach in Anglo-French relations caused by British failure to ratify a treaty of guarantee against a German invasion of France, disputes over the meaning of the plebiscite in Upper Silesia, 20 Mar., 1921, and such other matters as the French insistence during the Washington Naval Conference, 12 Nov., 1921–6 Feb., 1922, on construction of a submarine fleet and the British refusal to become involved in the affairs of France's ally, Poland. A proposed Anglo-French defensive alliance failed because of French popular dissatisfaction with Briand's willingness to accept the reparations moratorium, although at the conclusion of the conference the moratorium was granted.

To examine the general economic situation in Europe the allies called the Genoa Conference, 10 Apr.–19 May, 1922, to which the Soviet Union was invited. To the surprise of the allies, on 16 Apr. at Rapallo German Foreign Minister Rathenau and Soviet Foreign Minister Chicherin signed a treaty restoring diplomatic relations and renouncing all past financial claims. This treaty led to a secret arrangement whereby Germany's tank and air forces were to be allowed to train in Russia (a violation of the Treaty of Versailles) in return for an annual payment and the use by the Soviet Union of German military experts. The Genoa Conference was paralyzed by Poincaré's adamant insistence on the payment by the Soviet Union of prewar debts.

GERMAN INFLATION. The continued fall of the mark resulted in a cessation of timber deliveries to the German government, which in turn caused it to default in reparations (sawn timber and telegraph poles). The French, Italian, and Belgian representatives on the Reparation Committee judged, 26 Dec., 1922, Germany in default, despite British opposition to the motion. The French, who considered Germany deliberately unco-operative, used this ruling as an excuse, and French and Belgian troops began to occupy the Ruhr, 11 Jan., 1923. German Chancellor Wilhelm Cuno (1876–1933) adopted a policy of passive resistance, and French and Belgian technicians had to be brought in to operate mines and railways. In an effort to subsidize those most directly involved in passive resistance, Germany printed additional paper money, precipitating an inflation so extreme (DM 2,520 billion to U.S. $1 on 15 Nov.) that barter replaced money as a system of exchange. Gustav Stresemann (1878–1929) of the People's Party replaced Cuno, 13 Aug., and ended the policy of passive resistance, 26 Sept.

The franc had also fallen and Frenchmen were tiring of Poincaré's futile display of strength. In the elections of 11 May, 1924, the Cartel of the Left won enough seats to displace Poincaré. The last of the occupation troops left the Ruhr, 31 July, 1925. Meanwhile the German monetary crisis had been ended by the issue of the *Rentenmark*, based theoretically on the country's total industrial and agricultural resources. The formulator of this scheme was Hjalmar Schacht (b. 1877), appointed president of the Reichsbank, 22 Dec., 1923.

BRITISH LABOUR GOVERNMENT. In Britain, 15 Nov., 1923, national elections called by the Conservative Stanley Baldwin (1867–1947), who had taken over as prime minister from his colleague Andrew Bonar Law (1858–1923), 22 May, were held. Baldwin had gone to the country on the issue of a protective tariff which he wanted as a means of combating unemployment. His party, which had a majority of 87 seats, lost 90, and Ramsay MacDonald (1866–1937) came in at the head of a Labour ministry. MacDonald extended Britain's postwar policy of international co-operation to such previously taboo areas as the establishment of diplomatic relations with the Soviet Union, 1 Feb., 1924. He was forced into calling new elections, however, by a vote of censure, 8 Oct., on the government's handling of the "Campbell Case," an affair involving a Communist editorial urging British workers not to participate in wars against other workers. On 25 Oct., 5 days before the election, a letter purporting to be from the Comintern chief, Grigori Zinoviev, suggesting means whereby the Labour Party might be taken over and a revolution precipitated, appeared in the Conservative *Daily Mail*. The result was a Conservative election victory and the return of Baldwin. Austen Chamberlain (1863–1937) became foreign secretary and continued the MacDonald policy of international co-operation.

HERRIOT MINISTRY. In France, Edouard Herriot (1872–1957), leader of the victorious left coalition, refused to take over from Poincaré unless President Alexandre Millerand, who had publicly favored the right, resigned. Millerand bowed, and Gaston Doumergue (1863–1937) replaced him, 13 June, 1924. With Herriot as premier, French foreign policy became more flexible, as exemplified by the 28 Oct. recognition of the Soviet Union; nevertheless, the question of security against Germany in the form of the active maintenance of France's defensive alliances with Belgium, 7 Sept., 1920, Poland, 19 Feb., 1921, and Czechoslovakia, 25 Jan., 1924, continued to be of the utmost concern.

RULE OF STRESEMANN. In Germany, Chancellor Stresemann, once a firm monarchist and opponent of the Treaty of Versailles, now believed that Germany must co-operate with France in order to end mutual suspicion and rebuild the Reich. However, he was faced with various problems resulting from the Ruhr crisis: a French-supported Rhineland separatist movement, serious Communist advances in Saxony and Thuringia, and extreme-right activity in Bavaria. One aspect of the Bavarian problem was the abortive revolution, 8–9 Nov., 1923, staged by the Nazi (Nationalsozialistische Deutsche Arbeiterpartei) Party leader, Adolf Hitler (1889–1945), who was given a lenient sentence of 18 months in Landsberg Prison by a sympathetic German judiciary. Rhineland separatism failed, and the army suppressed Communists in Saxony and Thuringia. Stresemann's delicate treatment of the rightist threats and his thorough subduing of leftist actions brought a no-confidence vote in the Reichstag, 23 Nov., compelling him to resign. Centrist Wilhelm Marx (1863–1946) succeeded him, 30 Nov., though Stresemann remained as foreign minister and immediately illustrated his policy of co-operation with the allies by supporting the suggestions of the Dawes Commission (plan announced 9 Apr., 1924, accepted by the Reichstag 28 Aug.) concerning rearrangement of the reparations schedule and acceptance of an allied loan of 800 m. gold marks.

FASCIST RULE IN ITALY. Unlike other major Western European nations, Italy did not experience changes of political personnel in the early 1920's, but she did undergo a change of attitude toward existing policies. The Fascist regime became entrenched. On 14 Nov., 1923, the Acerbo electoral law gave ⅔ of Chamber seats to a party obtaining a plurality, providing that the number of votes was at least a quarter of all votes cast. In the Fascist-directed elections of 6 Apr., 1924, Mussolini's coalition received 65% of the vote and 375 of the 403 seats. Fascist terror methods had become familiar to Italians, but the senseless murder of the outspoken opposition deputy, Giacomo Matteoti (1885–1924), 10 June, 1924, shocked them into a clearer realization of the nature of the Fascist regime. Opposition deputies withdrew in protest from the Chamber, 15 June, in the so-called "Aventine secession." On 3 Jan., 1925, Mussolini brazenly announced that he accepted full responsibility for the murder.

1925–29

GERMAN PRESIDENTIAL ELECTION. 26 Apr., 1925. To succeed President Ebert (d. 28 Feb.) the Social Democrats nominated the Prussian premier, Otto Braun; the Communists nominated the former Hamburg transport worker, Ernst Thälmann; a coalition of parties including Democrats and Nationalists nominated the mayor of Duisburg, Karl Jarres; and the Centrists nominated Wilhelm Marx. In the election, 29 Mar., Jarres received the most votes, followed in order by Braun, Marx, and Thälmann. But Jarres had not received an absolute majority, and a runoff election was called. The Social Democrats, Centrists, and Democrats (the old Weimar coalition) united to form the "People's Bloc," supporting Marx. To combat this union, the Nationalists, People's Party, Bavarian People's Party, and Nazis threw their support behind Hindenburg, who reluctantly accepted after an appeal by Admiral von Tirpitz. Thälmann was again the Communist candidate. In the 26 Apr. election Hindenburg received 14,655,766 votes to Marx's 13,751,615 and Thälmann's 1,931,151.

LOCARNO AGREEMENTS. 16 Oct., 1925. On 9 Feb. Stresemann revived the offer previously rejected by Poincaré of a treaty to preserve the *status quo* in the Rhineland. The major stumbling block in the negotiations that followed was Briand's stipulation that Germany enter the League of Nations without reservations, which meant acceptance of sanctions under Art. 16 and the possibility of Germany having to aid in the protection of Poland. This difficulty was overcome by making co-operation under Art. 16 dependent on geographical position and state of armaments. On 16 Oct. Germany, France, Belgium, Britain, and Italy initialed the Locarno Agreements: (1) mutual guarantee of the Franco-German and Belgo-German frontiers by Britain and Italy; (2) Franco-German and Belgo-German arbitration conventions; (3) Germano-Polish and Germano-Czech arbitration conventions; and (4) Franco-Polish and Franco-Czech treaties of assistance in the event of German aggression. Because of the threat of rejection in the Reichstag, the allies offered to evacuate Cologne. The vote was held on 27 Nov., and the pacts ratified, 271–174, opposition coming from Nationalists, Nazis, and Communists. Hindenburg, to the surprise of many, promptly approved, and the signing took place in London, 1 Dec.

DETENTE IN INTERNATIONAL AFFAIRS. The Locarno Agreements marked the beginning of 4 years of relaxation of international tensions. This turn of events was primarily the work of Stresemann of Germany, Briand of France, and Chamberlain of Britain.

The promised evacuation of the Cologne area was accomplished, 30 Jan., 1926, and Germany applied for admission to the League of Nations, 10 Feb. Unexpected delay was encountered when Poland, Czechoslovakia, Spain, Brazil, China, and Persia demanded permanent seats on the League Council if Germany was admitted to this directing body. A compromise solution raising the number of nonpermanent seats from 6 to 9 soothed most feelings, but Brazil protested and filed notification of withdrawal from the League. On 8 Sept., 1926, Germany was admitted to the League and the Council on a permanent basis. The Allied Military Control Commission was withdrawn from Germany, 31 Jan., 1927, and supervision of the Versailles armaments limitations was entrusted to the League Council. The League's Preparatory Disarmament Commission worked toward an international conference to limit armaments of all member nations. On 24 Sept., 1927, the League Assembly unanimously adopted a Polish resolution prohibiting wars of aggression and, 27 Aug., 1928, the Kellogg-Briand Pact outlawing war as an instrument for settling international disputes was signed by 9 nations, including the U.S.A., France, Britain, Germany, Italy, and Japan. In a short while it was accepted universally. On 16 Sept., 1928, agreement was reached for the complete evacuation of the Rhineland and the final settlement of repara-

tions. The consequences of these agreements were the Young Plan (announced 7 June, 1929, accepted by the Reichstag 12 Mar., 1930), which set a 59-year period for reparations while reducing the total debt and giving Germany the responsibility for transfer; and the Hague Conference of 6–31 Aug., 1929, which arranged for the evacuation of the Koblenz, 30 Nov., 1929, and Mainz, 30 June, 1930, occupation zones.

Although this was a time of relative international good will, the problem of security remained. France signed a defensive alliance with Rumania, 10 June, 1926, and a similar pact with Yugoslavia, 11 Nov., 1927. The French legislature voted, 28 Dec., 1929, credits for the Maginot Line, a series of fortifications to protect the Alsace-Lorraine area and give France time to mobilize her reserves. Germany reaffirmed the 1922 Rapallo agreement with the Soviet Union by the Treaty of Berlin, 24 April, 1926, which contained a promise that each would remain neutral if the other signatory were attacked by a third power and that neither would support an economic boycott directed against the other.

ECONOMIC REVIVAL. Partly because of a lack of co-operation from the Bank of France, Herriot could not stem the fall of the franc. Consequently, Poincaré formed, 28 July, 1926, a National Union ministry with 6 former premiers as ministers. Taxes were increased, government expenditure reduced, and confidence restored so that capital returned from abroad and hiding and the franc checked at $.039, or 20% of its prewar value. By 1930 production and trade totals had reached record levels, to some degree because of the recovery of the textile mills of Alsace and the iron-ore and steel plants of Lorraine, and temporary coal deliveries from the Saar. Another contributory factor was industrial modernization.

U.S. and to a lesser extent British loans were chiefly responsible for Germany's prosperity in these years. Some of these loans were returned as reparations payments; others went to support government and industry. Germany's production rose so rapidly that she achieved a position second only to the U.S.A. By 1928 unemployment was only 650,000. However, criticism of the amount of nonproductive spending in the form of large national subsidies and high unemployment payments was made, 10 June, 1927, by the allied agent-general for reparations, S. Parker Gilbert.

Britain's recovery was less marked than that of France and Germany. The postwar building boom and new communications and transportation industries gave the economy a boost, but Britain's older industries failed to regain important prewar markets. Unemployment never fell below 1 m., and confused government labor policies brought on such difficulties as the general strike of 3–12 May, 1926.

Italy recovered from her immediate postwar depression, in 1926 reaching prewar levels of production and rates of consumption. On 6 May, 1926, the Bank of Italy was made sole bank of issue in the creation of a central banking system. In 1926–27 a deflation policy caused a sharp dip in the economy, with production and trade down and unemployment up. On 3 Apr., 1926, the Rocco Law on Corporations began centralizing the economy with the creation of 13 trade unions (6 for labor, 6 for employers, and 1 for intellectuals and professionals). Disputes were to be settled by the minister of corporations, and strikes and lockouts were not to be permitted. On 21 Dec., 1927, the lira was stabilized at 19 to U.S. $1. In 1928–29 production recovered and crops were good, but trade decreased substantially because of the too-favorable rate Mussolini had fixed for the lira. The establishment of the corporative state envisioned in the Rocco Law was finally completed, 20 Mar., 1930.

FASCIST ITALY. Mussolini continued his assertive foreign policy. On 27 Nov., 1927, he signed a Treaty of Mutual Assistance with Albania which amounted to formal establishment of an Italian protectorate. On 5 Apr., 1927, and 6 Feb., 1930, he signed treaties of friendship with Hungary and Austria respectively, hoping to become the leader of the revisionist states. At home, on 31 Jan., 1926, Mussolini gave himself the right to issue decrees having the force of law. The

Fascist Grand Council received, 12 May, 1928, the power to choose the legislative candidates for public office from a list drawn up by the unions of workers and employers. The slate had to be accepted or rejected as a whole by an attenuated electorate of men over 21 who paid taxes or union dues of not less than 100 lira. An 8 Dec., 1928, law gave the task of choosing the head of government to the Fascist Grand Council, making it the chief organ not only of the Fascist Party but also of the Italian political system. Mussolini also ended the estrangement between the Italian state and the Catholic Church; the Lateran Accords, 11 Feb., 1929, provided for recognition by Pius XI (pope, 1922–39) of the state, recognition by Italy of Catholicism as the state religion, the establishment of Vatican City as an independent state, and an indemnity to the pope in money and state bonds of 1,750 m. lira for the papal territory taken by the Italian state in the 19th cent.

NAZI LEAN YEARS. In Landsberg Prison, Hitler wrote the first part of *Mein Kampf*, and on 20 Dec., 1924, he was amnestied. The Nazis, who had won 32 Reichstag seats in the 4 May, 1924, elections during the brief agitation over the Dawes Plan, could hold only 14 of them in the 7 Dec. elections. A struggle for control of the disintegrating party developed between Hitler and Gregor Strasser (1892–1934), who emphasized the socialist aspects of the Nazi doctrines. By Feb. 1926 Hitler had won over Joseph Goebbels (1897–1945), Strasser's most able supporter. Appointed by Hitler editor of the Berlin publication, *Der Angriff*, Goebbels made full use of his talent for propaganda. In 1925 Hitler began to expand the S.S. (defense corps) to rival the S.A. (storm troops), headed by the increasingly powerful Ernst Roehm (1887–1934). On 6 Jan., 1929, Heinrich Himmler (1900–1945) was made S.S. leader, and its numbers and importance in the Nazi movement grew rapidly. After the 19 May, 1928, elections the Nazi contingent in the Reichstag, headed by Hermann Göring (1893–1946), numbered only 12.

EFFECTS OF THE U.S. DEPRESSION. Hardest hit because of her financial dependence on the U.S.A. was Germany. By 1932 production was off by ½ and unemployment had reached 6 m. France, due to a relatively balanced economy, was not severely affected until 1931–32, when production dropped by ⅕; those seeking unemployment relief in 1935 numbered 503,502 (as against 1,000 in 1930). In Britain ¼ of the working force was on the dole. However, the British economy managed to level off in 1933, and by 1937 production was ⅕ higher than in 1929. Italy was able to weather some of the disaster by public works programs such as the reclamation of the Pontine Marshes.

1930–33

END OF MINISTERIAL RESPONSIBILITY IN GERMANY. The cabinet of the Social Democrat, Hermann Mueller (1876–1931), the last in which Stresemann (d. 3 Oct., 1929) served, resigned, 27 Mar., 1930, because of its inability to get a satisfactory increase in unemployment insurance from the Reichstag. The chairman of the Centrist Reichstag contingent, Heinrich Brüning (b. 1885), succeeded Mueller. After failing to obtain Reichstag support for financial reforms, Brüning was authorized by Hindenburg, invoking Art. 48 of the constitution, to institute his program by decree. On 16 July the financial decrees were issued, and ministerial responsibility was at an end. A motion, principally instigated by Social Democrats, for the recall of the decrees was passed, 18 July. Brüning's answer was to use the weapon of dissolution also given him by Hindenburg.

REICHSTAG ELECTION OF 1930. Nazis and Communists vied for the many German voters made ripe for extremist solutions to Germany's problems by the depression. However, the Communists, instructed by the Soviet Union to attack the Social Democrats, at times co-operated with the Nazis, who were able to mount an extremely effective campaign using donations from such industrial magnates as Fritz Thyssen (1873–1951) of the United Steel Works and Emil Kirdorf (1847–1938) of the Rhenish-Westphalian coal syndicate. The result was a great Nazi success in the election of 14 Sept., 1930: 6,409,600 votes and 107 deputies (an increase of 95). Only the Social Democrats had more seats (143). The Communists increased their 54 seats to 77; the Catholic Center won 68 seats, an increase of 7; and the Nationalists won only 41 seats, a loss of 37.

AUSTRO-GERMAN CUSTOMS UNION PROPOSAL. On 5 Sept., 1929, Briand had proposed a scheme for European federal union, the emphasis of which was economic. Using the Briand proposal as justification, Austrian Vice-Chancellor and Foreign Minister Johann Schober (1874–1932) and German Foreign Minister Julius Curtius (1877–1948) negotiated a customs union (announced 21 Mar., 1931), which seemed to be a step toward total merger (*Anschluss*) of the 2 countries, though such an act was forbidden by Art. 80 of the Treaty of Versailles and by Art. 88 of the Treaty of St.-Germain. France, Italy, and Czechoslovakia protested, and Britain asked the League Council to make a judgment on the matter. The Austrian government agreed, 17 Apr., to do nothing until the Council ruled. On 11 May Austria's Credit-Anstalt began to falter, and France, in retaliation for the proposed customs union, aggravated the situation by putting financial pressure on the bank. On 3 Sept. the abandonment of the customs-union idea was announced by Schober. The League Council's decision, 5 Sept., now meaningless, upheld the legality of the union by an 8–7 vote.

"NATIONAL GOVERNMENT" IN BRITAIN. The British general elections of 30 May, 1929, returned Ramsay MacDonald to the prime ministership. However, when it became clear that the Labour government did not have the confidence of important foreign financial institutions, MacDonald reorganized his cabinet, 25 Aug., 1931, to include Conservatives and Liberals. The new "National Government" was unacceptable to Labour Party executives, and on 28 Aug. Arthur Henderson was elected party leader in MacDonald's stead. MacDonald and his followers reorganized as the National Labour Party. In the 27 Oct. general election the government coalition won 556 seats (471 of them Conservative) to Labour's 52.

The National Government was responsible for the Statute of Westminster, 11 Dec., 1931, which put into effect the Imperial Conference (12 Oct.–18 Nov., 1926) decisions giving autonomy and equal status to the dominions and abandoning free trade, 4 Feb., 1932. To protest the latter decision Liberals led by Herbert Samuel (1870–1963) left the government coalition, 28 Sept., 1932. In 1933–34 the fiction of MacDonald directing a coalition government wore thin, and it was recognized that Baldwin and the Conservatives were in command.

FRENCH POLITICAL CHANGES. In France President Doumergue's 7-year term of office ended in 1931. The logical successor, Briand, was passed over in favor of Paul Doumer (1857–1932) because of Briand's conciliatory policy toward Germany. Doumer's tenure and life were ended, 6 May, 1932, by an assassin, and Albert Lebrun (1871–1950) was chosen to take over the presidency, 10 May. The legislative elections of 8 May (single-member districts had been re-adopted, 13 July, 1927) gave power to the Cartel of the Left: Socialists won 131 Chamber seats, Radicals took 160, and other leftists 43. Herriot formed a ministry, 3 June, but, following tradition, without Socialist participation. But Herriot, abused for his proposal to pay the war-debt installment owed to the U.S.A., soon resigned. He was succeeded, 18 Dec., 1932, by Joseph Paul-Boncour (b. 1879).

RE-ELECTION OF HINDENBURG IN GERMANY. In Germany President Hindenburg's 7-year term ended in 1932. Brüning, hoping to avoid the dangers of an election in extremist-ridden Germany, asked Hitler to consent to the extension of Hindenburg's term until the depression had been brought under control. Hitler refused, deciding to challenge Hindenburg for the office. The Communists again chose Thälmann, and the Nationalists nominated Theodor Duesterberg (1875–1950). In the 13 Mar., 1932, election Hindenburg received 18,661,736 votes to Hitler's 11,338,571, Thälmann's 4,982,079, and Duesterberg's 2,553,976, but failed to receive a majority of the votes by 4/10 of 1%. In the runoff, 10 Apr., the candidates remained the same except for Duesterberg, who was ousted by the Nationalists' resolve to support Hitler. Hindenburg received 19,360,000 to Hitler's 13,400,000 and Thälmann's 3,700,000. A decree was signed by Hindenburg, 13 Apr., dissolving the S.A. and S.S. as agents inimical to the public safety.

ACCESSION TO POWER OF ADOLF HITLER. Putting the finishing touches to the efforts of Kurt von Schleicher (1882–1934) and Ruhr industrialists who resented the government's attempts to keep prices down, Brüning advocated the partitioning of insolvent East Prussian estates. Hindenburg, who owned an East Prussian estate himself (Neudeck), was sensitive about such suggestions, and Brüning was asked to resign, 30 May, 1932. Schleicher advanced Franz von Papen (b. 1879) for the chancellorship, and Hindenburg concurred, 31 May. On 4 June the Reichstag was dissolved. Papen counted on Germany's gratitude for the role of his government's representative in the permanent fixing of the 6 July, 1931, Hoover Moratorium during the Lausanne Conference (16 June–9 July, 1932), and its insistence on armament equality at the Disarmament Conference. The election campaign was savage, as Communists and Nazis battled. One of these battles, at Altona, 13 July, served as justification for Papen to take over the governing of Prussia, 20 July. The election, 31 July, gave the Nazis 230 seats, the Social Democrats 133, the Communists 89, the Centrists 75, and the Nationalists 37.

Although the election was a repudiation of Papen's aristocratically composed "Cabinet of Barons," he refused to resign. However, he realized the need for some sort of popular support and asked Hitler to become vice-chancellor, 13 Aug. Hitler declined. Hitler's assertive behavior in an interview with Hindenburg that day endangered his chances of being offered the chancellorship. He also hurt his cause by a violent attack on Papen and an expression of eagerness at the prospect of Hindenburg's apparently imminent death in a manifesto protesting the death sentence given 5 Nazis accused of murdering a Communist worker. Papen hoped to force the Nazis into submission by a policy of draining the party economically through repeated elections. On 12 Sept., after a farcical parliamentary duel about rules with Reichstag speaker Göring, Papen had the legislature dissolved and funds from his industrialist friends cut off from Nazi election coffers. The election, 6 Nov., seemed to mark the beginning of Nazi decline: Nazis, 196 Reichstag seats (loss of 34); Social Democrats, 121 seats; Communists, 100 seats (gain of 11); Centrists, 70 seats; and Nationalists, 51 seats (gain of 14).

Schleicher, now minister of war, forced Papen into the tactical move of resigning, 17 Nov., believing that Papen would be recalled in a stronger position. But Hindenburg, displeased with this maneuvering, instead gave, 2 Dec., the burden of the chancellorship to Schleicher, depriving him of his former freedom to responsibility. The Nazis were divided between the Gregor Strasser position of co-operation with Schleicher and the Göring, Goebbels, and (after some hesitation) the Hitler position of continued opposition. On 8 Dec. Strasser resigned from the apparently sinking Nazi Party. Papen then made his bid to harness what remained of Nazi strength. On 4 Jan., 1933, he arranged a meeting with Hitler at the home of the Cologne banker, Baron Kurt von Schroeder (b. 1889). Hitler agreed to support a cabinet headed by someone else if the minister of war was to his liking. Papen's moneyed friends paid most of the Nazi debts. However, Nazi successes in the Lippe election, 15 Jan., 1933, gave Hitler enough confidence to renege on his promise and reassert his demand for the chancellorship. Failing to receive Hindenburg's approval for a dissolution of the Reichstag to prevent opponents of his program from holding it up, Schleicher resigned, 28 Jan. On 30 Jan., with the opportunistic Papen as vice-chancellor and supposedly the real director of the cabinet, Hitler, through legal appointment by Hindenburg, became chancellor of the German republic.

CONSOLIDATION OF NAZI POWER. On 27 Feb., 1933, the Reichstag burned. Whatever the extent of their guilt for the act, the Nazis took immediate advantage of it by accusing a half-witted Dutch Communist, Marinus van der Lubbe, of the crime, and by obtaining from Hindenburg an emergency decree, 28 Feb., for the suspension of constitutional liberties, control over the states, and the death sentence for "serious disturbances of the peace." Thus the Nazis were able to suppress campaigns for the 5 Mar. elections. Nevertheless, they obtained only 288 Reichstag seats to 52 for the Nationalists, 120 for the Social Democrats, 81 for the Communists, and 74 for the Centrists. The combined Nazi-Nationalist strength was not sufficient to implement Hitler's plan to have the Reichstag vote itself a vacation until 1 Apr., 1937, and turn its authority over to him. However, with the promise that the presidential veto would be respected, Centrist leader Monsignor Ludwig Kaas (1881–1952) threw his party's support behind this "Enabling Act," and it passed on 23 Mar.

1934–36

STAVISKY AFFAIR. Serge Stavisky had been held by the French police for various criminal financial dealings, but had never been brought to trial. In Dec. 1933 an enterprise he was involved in collapsed and he escaped to the Alps. When he was found dead, suicide was assumed; but when the body of a government lawyer involved in the case was found soon afterward, suspicions were aroused. The Radical Party, which had been in power since the May 1932 election and was headed by Premier Édouard Daladier (b. 1884), was the target of abuse by extreme right-wing organizations such as Action Française and the Croix de Feu, which held, 6 Feb., what developed into bloody demonstrations in the Place de la Concorde and around the Chamber of Deputies. Daladier resigned, 7 Feb., and Doumergue formed a ministry of "National Union," 8 Feb.

PURGE OF THE S.A. Honoring his part in a pact made, 11 Apr., 1934, on the cruiser *Deutschland* with the commander of the German army, Gen. Werner von Fritsch (1880–1939), and the commander of the navy, Adm. Erich Raeder (1876–1960), who gave him their support in the Hindenburg succession—Hindenburg died 2 Aug., and Hitler then styled himself Führer, or leader—Hitler launched a purge of the S.A., 30 June. Together with Roehm and Edmund Heines (1897–1934), such figures as Schleicher and the Catholic Action leader, Erich Klausener (1885–1934) and, indeed, anyone else the Nazis wished removed were liquidated. The S.S. was Hitler's instrument on this "Night of the Long Knives." Estimates of the number murdered range from 400 to over 1,000.

NAZI FOREIGN POLICY. Hitler had indicated the style of his foreign policy by announcing, 14 Oct., 1933, Germany's withdrawal from the League of Nations and the Disarmament Conference. In an effort to separate Germany's allied neighbors, France and Poland, and to ease suspicions concerning plans for the controversial Germano-Polish frontier, Hitler signed a 10-year nonaggression pact with Poland, 26 Jan., 1934. On 13 Jan., 1935, he scored his first territorial success when 90% of the inhabitants of the Saar in a plebiscite conducted by the League of Nations chose reunion with Germany rather than union with France. Hitler took his first calculated risk in defiance of the Treaty of Versailles on 16 Mar., 1935, when he issued a decree for universal military service, thus exceeding the treaty limit of a 100,000-man army. He concluded, however, a naval agreement with Britain, 18 June, by which the German fleet was to be maintained at no more than 35% of the British.

REACTIONS TO HITLER'S GERMANY. A British White Paper of 4 Mar., 1935, affirmed Britain's decision to rearm. The French foreign minister, Pierre Laval (1883–1945), signed an agreement with Mussolini, 7 Jan., to settle disputes over colonial matters and, by inference, to cooperate in European matters as well. That Germany was worrying Mussolini was evidenced by his sending troops to the Brenner Pass to stop a possible German-inspired take-over in Austria following the assassination of the Austrian chancellor, Engelbert Dollfuss (b. 1892) by Austrian Nazis on 25 July, 1934. On 15 Mar., 1935, French legislators agreed to a 2-year military service bill, reversing the trend set by the 18-month service act of 1 Apr., 1923, and the 1-year service act of 28 Mar., 1928. On 2 May, 1935, France signed a mutual-assistance pact with the Soviet Union, a member of the League of Nations since 19 Sept., 1934. At the Stresa Conference, 11–14 Apr., 1935, France, Britain, and Italy agreed to follow a common policy with regard to Germany.

ITALIAN INVASION OF ETHIOPIA. Trumping up a dispute over the Wal-Wal oasis on the Ethiopia-Somaliland border, Mussolini sent troops into Ethiopia. Emperor Haile Selassie (b. 1891) appealed to the League, and economic sanctions were declared, 11 Oct. 1935. On 7 Dec. the French premier and foreign minister, Laval, and the British foreign secretary, Sir Samuel Hoare (1880–1959), agreed on a plan to save some independence for Ethiopia by dividing it into spheres of influence. However, the French press learned of the plan prematurely, and the consequent indignant popular reaction wrecked it. Hoare was replaced, 22 Dec., by Anthony Eden (b. 1897), and Laval was followed by the Radical, Albert Sarraut (1872–1962), 24 Jan., 1936. On 5 May, 1936, Addis Ababa fell, and on 9 May Ethiopia was formally annexed by Italy. The League's ineffective economic sanctions were discontinued, 4 July.

GERMAN REOCCUPATION OF THE RHINELAND. The Franco-Russian alliance, after a delay of almost a year, was presented to and ratified by the French Chamber, 27 Feb., 1936. On 7 Mar. Hitler used this treaty as an excuse to denounce the Locarno Agreements and to order 3 battalions into the demilitarized Rhineland in violation of the Versailles Treaty. French Premier Sarraut consulted his cabinet, and the chief of the French general staff, Gen. Maurice Gamelin (1872–1958) presented the alternatives of total mobilization or total inaction; the latter policy was adopted. On 11 Mar.

the French foreign minister, Pierre Flandin (1889–1958), went to London to get assistance from Britain, a guarantor of the Locarno Agreements, but the British wanted to review German notes to the British, French, and Belgian ambassadors offering a 25-year nonaggression pact to France and Belgium, an agreement for the demilitarization of both sides of the Franco-German border, and a German promise to return to the League. Because demilitarization would constrain France to disassemble the Maginot Line, French resolve to take no action strengthened. On 14 Mar. the League Council declared Germany guilty of violating international agreements. Perturbed by these events, Belgium withdrew, 14 Oct., from its 1920 alliance with France and reasserted its neutrality, making the northeastern frontier of France extremely vulnerable.

FRENCH POPULAR FRONT. In the wake of the 6 Feb., 1934, rightist demonstrations in Paris, French Socialists, along with the C.G.T. (the Socialist trade-union confederation), called a strike for 12 Feb. When the Communists agreed to cooperate, the power of a united working-class movement was evidenced. On 27 July, Socialists and Communists signed a pact of united action against "fascist" organizations. However, further moves toward Socialist-Communist association came only after the Franco-Russian alliance of 2 May, 1935, gave Moscow-oriented Communists an ideological stake in French national defense. By the elections of 3 May, 1936, Socialists, Communists, Radicals, and other leftists had agreed to join in a "popular front," and the result was a victory: Socialists, 146 Chamber seats; Communists, 72; Radicals, 116; and other leftists, 36. The Socialist Léon Blum (1872–1950) formed a ministry of Socialists and Radicals, 4 June, the Communists refusing to accept governmental responsibility. Nevertheless, at the 2–8 Mar. congress at Toulouse, the C.G.T.U. (Communist trade-union confederation) reunited with the C.G.T. This leftist victory was met by a series of sit-down strikes, a development rightist governments had escaped. Blum conferred with employers and employees, 7–8 June, at the Hotel Matignon, and the

"Matignon Accords" were reached, providing wage increases and the safeguarding of collective bargaining. Legislation for a 40-hour week, obligatory paid vacations, and compulsory arbitration followed. Other measures taken by the Blum government included nationalization of certain aircraft plants and extension of a measure of state control over the Bank of France.

SPANISH CIVIL WAR. His financial schemes having collapsed and his army support gone, the Spanish dictator, Gen. Primo de Rivera (1870–1930), who had taken over on 13 Sept., 1923, abjured his office on 28 Jan., 1930, and died, 16 Mar. On 14 Apr., 1931, King Alphonso XIII was forced to leave Spain. On 9 Dec. a republican constitution was adopted by a revivified Cortes. The republic, however, was hamstrung from the beginning by uncompromising leftists and rightists. On 10 Aug., 1932, military royalists under Gen. José Sanjurjo revolted and took Seville before they were suppressed; in 1933, anarcho-syndicalists organized a series of urban revolts. Separatist difficulties also plagued the republic as Catalans forced the government to accept their Charter of Autonomy, 25 Sept., 1932. Other separatist movements, encouraged by this success, increased their agitation. On 6 Oct., 1934, the Catalans proclaimed their independence, but government troops held Spain together, also putting down a serious Communist uprising in Asturias. The rightist-dominated Spanish parliament was dissolved, 6 Jan., 1936. In the ensuing elections, 16 Feb., the leftist "Popular Front" won 278 Cortes seats, the rightist "National Front" won 134, and the center won 55. On 13 July the rightist political spokesman José Calvo Sotelo was assassinated. Meanwhile, the rightist Gens. Emilio Mola (d. 3 June, 1937) and Francisco Franco (b. 1892) were planning a coup d'état. During the night of 17–18 July an assault on the republic began in Spanish Morocco. Burgos became the rebel headquarters on the mainland, and on 1 Oct. Franco was made rebel chief of state. He was aided by Italian and German "volunteers," while the Soviet Union sent supplies to the republican government, headed by the Socialist Largo

Caballero (1869–1946), which also received assistance from the "International Brigade" of men of various nationalities who sought, unsuccessfully, to restore the balance upset by the Fascist and Nazi forces. French Premier Blum called for nonintervention in the Spanish conflict, 1 Aug., 1937. Britain and the Soviet Union concurred, as did Germany and Italy. Britain and France kept their pledge, but Germany and Italy, which had formed an "axis" of co-operation, insisted that their nationals in Spain were volunteers. The Soviet Union also continued to intervene, but only with supplies and technical assistance. Franco's forces slowly pushed back those of the government, now headed by the Socialist premier, Juan Negrín (1894–1957). On 28 Mar., 1939, Madrid was overrun, and the National Defense Council, formed after the fall of Negrín, 6 Mar., by Gen. José Miaja, surrendered. On 7 Apr. the Franco regime signed the Anti-Comintern Pact previously agreed to by Germany and Japan on 17 Nov., 1936, and by Italy on 6 Nov., 1937.

BRITISH ABDICATION CRISIS. On 20 Jan., 1936, King George V, who had been on the throne since 6 May, 1910, died. The new king, Edward VIII, told Prime Minister Baldwin, 16 Nov., that he intended to marry Mrs. Wallis Warfield Simpson, an American recently divorced from her 2nd husband. Baldwin rejected Edward's suggestion that legislation be introduced to allow a morganatic marriage because, among other things, of the unanimous opposition of the Dominion governments. On 10 Dec. an abdication bill passed the Commons, 403 votes to 5, and the king signed it the following day. He was succeeded by his brother, George VI (reigned 11 Dec., 1936–6 Feb., 1952). Baldwin himself resigned and was succeeded by Neville Chamberlain (prime minister, 28 May, 1937–10 May, 1940).

1937–39

THE ANSCHLUSS. The first move toward union of Austria and Germany came on 11 July, 1936, when the Austrian chancellor, Kurt von Schuschnigg (b. 1897) agreed to conduct his country's foreign policy in general conformity to that of the German government in return for a promise by Hitler to respect Austrian independence. On 5 Nov., 1937, at a meeting at the Reich chancellery, German military leaders were informed (according to the notes of Hitler's military adjutant, Col. Friedrich Hossbach) that Hitler was considering invading Austria and Czechoslovakia. Nazi terror within Austria increased, and when Austrian police raided the "Brown House" Nazi headquarters, 25 Jan., 1938, documents were found outlining a plan to use the German army to compel Schuschnigg to relinquish power to Austrian Nazis. Minister Extraordinary Franz von Papen, abruptly recalled, convinced Hitler that Schuschnigg must be persuaded to speak with Hitler directly. Schuschnigg consented and met Hitler at Berchtesgaden, 12 Feb. After much intimidation Schuschnigg was given a list of demands: the Nazis Arthur von Seyss-Inquart (1892–1946), Edmund Glaise-Horstenau, and Hans Fischboek were to head the ministries of the interior, war, and finance; a system of officer exchanges was to be established for closer co-ordination of the armed forces of the 2 countries; and the ban on the Austrian Nazi Party was to be lifted and all Nazi prisoners amnestied. Under threat of invasion the terms were met by Schuschnigg and President Wilhelm Miklas (1872–1956). On 9 Mar. Schuschnigg announced a 13 Mar. plebiscite in which Austrians would decide on the continuance or otherwise of an independent Austria. As for the guarantors of Austrian independence, the British made it clear that they would not intervene; at the time there was no effective government in France (Premier Chautemps had resigned on 10 Mar.); and Mussolini told Hitler's messenger Philip of Hesse, 11 Mar., that the fate of Austria was immaterial to him. On 12 Mar. the German army marched into Austria. The new Austrian chancellor, Seyss-Inquart, signed a document, 13 Mar., declaring in effect the union of Austria and Germany.

CZECHOSLOVAKIAN CRISIS. On 4 separate occasions the British government learned from German sources that aggression against Czechoslovakia was being planned for the autumn of 1938. On 12

Sept. Hitler made a violent speech concerning the allegedly oppressed German minority in Czechoslovakia which sounded ominously like a pretext for imminent action. The German population of the Sudetenland, the region over which the dispute raged, staged a 2-day revolt. On 15 Sept. Chamberlain flew to Berchtesgaden, where Hitler demanded the cession to Germany of the Sudetenland. Chamberlain gave his personal assent, but added that the matter had to be discussed with his government and with the French, who were formally allied to Czechoslovakia. French Premier Édouard Daladier went to London, 18 Sept., and agreed that the cession had to be made. An Anglo-French note containing the cession proposal was sent to the Czech government, 19 Sept., but was rejected. However, after threats of no assistance in the event of a German invasion (upon which contingency the Russo-Czech alliance of 16 May, 1935, would not go into effect), President Eduard Beneš (1884–1948) acceded, 21 Sept. Chamberlain again met Hitler, 22–23 Sept., this time at Godesberg, and informed him of the Czech agreement. Hitler demanded that the cession be fully completed by 1 Oct. On 25 Sept. French and British leaders received a formal Czech rejection of the Godesberg terms. Hitler, however, accepted a British-inspired offer made by Mussolini to mediate the problem at a general conference to be held in Munich. Invitations were sent to Britain, France, and Italy, but not to Czechoslovakia or the Soviet Union. The Munich Conference, 29–30 Sept., accepted a solution to the Sudetenland problem drafted by Göring and other Nazi officials. German occupation was to begin on 1 Oct. and end by 10 Oct. The Czech government accepted the Munich agreement "under protest to the world," 30 Sept. Taking advantage of Czech impotence, Poland seized a 650-sq.-mi. area around Teschen, 1 Oct., and Hungary received, 2 Nov., a 7,500-sq.-mi. piece of southern Slovakia. The rest of Czechoslovakia was converted, 19 Nov., into a federal state, consisting of Bohemia and Moravia, autonomous Slovakia, and autonomous Ruthenia. Slovakia, headed by Mgr. Josef Tiso (1887–1947), demanded, 9 Mar., 1939, from the central Prague government permission for a separate army and diplomatic corps. On 10 Mar. President Emil Hácha (1872–1945) dismissed Tiso and ordered troops into Slovakia. Tiso rallied the Slovakian Diet into declaring independence, 14 Mar. Hácha then went to Berlin to appeal to Hitler; instead of receiving assistance, he was bullied into placing his country under the "protection" of Germany, 15 Mar. That day German troops occupied Prague. On 15 Nov. Ruthenia was annexed by Hungary, and on 16 Nov. Slovakia too became a German protectorate.

POLISH CRISIS. Hitler made clear the aggressive nature of his plans by coercing the Lithuanian government into ceding to Germany the port of Memel, 23 Mar., 1939. The next target was Poland, where the free city of Danzig and the Polish Corridor separating East and West Prussia were, in the German view, unsettled matters. On 31 Mar. Chamberlain formally abandoned the "appeasement policy" by announcing in the Commons that Britain and France would aid Poland if her independence were threatened. Nevertheless, it was not until 25 Aug. that an Anglo-Polish pact was signed, by which time Germany had strengthened herself by the offensive-defensive "Pact of Steel" with Italy, 22 May, which had conquered Albania on 7 Apr. More importantly, Germany had outbid the western powers and reached agreement with the Soviet Union. The "Hitler-Stalin Pact," 23 Aug., publicly consisted of a mutual pledge of nonaggression, the maintenance of neutrality in the event of the other signatory becoming involved in armed conflict, and nonparticipation in groupings of powers directed at the other signatory. A secret protocol, however, divided up the Baltic states and Poland "in the event of a territorial and political transformation." On 28 Aug. the British government proposed direct discussions of Germano-Polish disputes. Hitler consented, provided that a Polish representative arrive by the evening of 30 Aug. This ultimatum startled the Polish government into declaring a partial mobilization on 31 Aug. On 1 Sept., without a declaration of war, Germany invaded Poland. The British and French reacted cautiously, stating their willingness to discuss the situation provided German troops and planes were withdrawn. On 2 Sept. Mussolini tried to slow developments by proposing a 5-power conference. Hitler, however, refused to withdraw his forces, and on 3 Sept. Britain and France declared war on Germany. (*Cont. p. 516.*)

(*Cont. p. 516.*)

EAST CENTRAL EUROPE AND THE BALKANS

Austria

1918–19

END OF THE DUAL MONARCHY. After a series of military setbacks stemming from the deteriorating morale of the troops and the growing food shortage in several cities, Emperor Charles I, in a last desperate effort to save the empire from disintegration, issued a manifesto, 16 Oct., 1918, calling for reconstruction of the monarchy on a federalized basis. But the irreversible demands of the subject nationalities for complete independence forced Charles to abdicate, 11 Nov., 1918, only 8 days after the armistice with Italy had been signed. With this act, the Hapsburg dynasty, which had reigned in Europe since 1282, came to an end.

PROCLAMATION OF THE REPUBLIC. Prior to the abdication of Charles, the German deputies of the imperial Reichsrat, inspired by Bohemian and Hungarian deputies, constituted a Provisional National Assembly and declared the independence of "German-Austria" (Deutschösterreich), 21 Oct., 1918. On 12 Nov., 1918, the Assembly adopted a temporary constitution, proclaimed German Austria a republic, and declared its desire to form a union (*Anschluss*) with Germany.

During the next 4 months, a bloodless power struggle ensued between extremist and moderate elements. The struggle was finally resolved in the elections of Feb. 1919, when a moderate coalition government, composed of urban Social Democrats and agrarian Christian Socialists (Pink Coalition), replaced the provisional government. This coalition was also effective in preventing the establishment of a Soviet-type republic despite Russian and Hungarian efforts to that end.

CREATION OF THE FEDERAL REPUBLIC. A newly elected Constitutional Assembly adopted a permanent constitution, 1 Oct., 1920, and, at the instigation of the Christian Socialists, transformed the country into a federal republic of 9 provinces (*Länder*). The constitution also provided for a government consisting of a president, chancellor, and a bicameral legislature, the latter comprising the Federal Assembly with the power to elect the president. Two months later, in Dec. 1920, Austria was admitted to the League of Nations.

TREATY OF ST.-GERMAIN. 10 Sept., 1919. The boundaries and the political form of the new state were defined in the Treaty of St.-Germain. This treaty forbade any political or economic union with Germany without the consent of the League and compelled the Austrians to change the name "German Austria" to "Republic of Austria." In total, the Austrian half of the Dual Monarchy was reduced in area and population by 75%: to Italy, Austria had to cede the predominantly German-Austrian-inhabited South Tyrol, the Trentino, Trieste, Istria, and some Dalmatian islands; to the newly created Czechoslovakia, Bohemia, Moravia, part of Lower Austria, and most of Austrian Silesia; to Poland, Austrian Galicia and part of Teschen (Těšín); to Rumania, South Bukovina; to newly created Yugoslavia, Bosnia, Herzegovina, and Dalmatia. Austria also lost her entire naval force and her army was reduced to 30,000 volunteers. She received, however, Burgenland in western Hungary, the only territorial award granted by the allies to a defeated power.

1920–38

ECONOMIC PROBLEMS. As a result of the war and the terms of the peace treaty, Austria was reduced to a landlocked and homogeneous country with a German-speaking population. Her new boundaries left her without significant raw materials, food, industry, or foreign markets; her economy, virtually self-sufficient under the Dual Monarchy, became completely dislocated. As a result, she had to face the prospects of prolonged starvation and chaotic internal conditions.

After having failed to carry through a proposed currency and customs union with Italy, Chancellor Ignaz Seipel (1876–1932) appealed for help to the League of Nations, Sept. 1922. The League undertook the country's rehabilitation by granting a loan equivalent to (U.S.) $135 million, 4 Oct., 1922. By June 1926 Austria had achieved a balanced budget, but the coming of the world depression forced her to turn to the League again. Although the League granted a 20-year loan of $42 million in 1932 (Lausanne Protocol), a pledge not to enter into any union with Germany was extracted from her in return.

HEIMWEHR vs. SCHUTZBUND. Austria's economic problems were greatly compounded by a growing rivalry for political control between two militant organizations, each having its own well-armed militia: the *Schutzbund* and the *Heimwehr*. The Socialist *Schutzbund* drew its strength of about 90,000 men from among Social Democrat workers in and around the industrial districts of Vienna (Red Belt); the conservative *Heimwehr* had its power base largely among fascist, anti-Socialist, and reactionary monarchical groups in the rural areas. The *Heimwehr*, numbering some 60,000 men, was largely financed by Prince Ernst von Starhemberg (1899–1956).

The frequent clashes between the 2 militias during the 1920's and 1930's seriously sapped the strength and authority of several governments, headed 1st by the Social Democrat Karl Renner (1870–1950) and later by Social Christian and Pan-German coalitions under Johann Schober (1874–1932) and Seipel respectively. During a demonstration by Viennese workers on 15 July, 1927, 85 persons died in a clash with the police. The subsequent general strike, called by the Social Democrats, was broken by the army, aided by the *Heimwehr*. Strife between the rightists and moderates led to a civil war, 12 Feb., 1934. Finally, on Mussolini's advice, Chancellor Engelbert Dollfuss (1892–1934), who had come to power in 1932, decided to enlist *Heimwehr* aid again to crush what was believed to be a Socialist conspiracy.

ASSASSINATION OF DOLLFUSS. In attempting to fight on 2 fronts while confronting at the same time the rapid growth of Nazism, the country under Dollfuss slowly drifted toward the establishment of a corporate Fascist state. After the abolition of the Social Democratic Party, Apr. 1934, Dollfuss introduced an authoritarian constitution, 1 May. Once the Social Democrats had been crushed, the local Nazis, aided by those in Germany, staged a *Putsch*, 25 July, 1934. Although the Nazi take-over attempt was foiled, Dollfuss, who had opposed the Nazis as well, was killed in his office.

BANNING OF THE HEIMWEHR. In Apr. 1936 Chancellor Kurt von Schuschnigg (b. 1897), successor to Dollfuss, whose policies he followed, outlawed the *Heimwehr* and, repudiating a provision of the Treaty of St.-Germain, introduced compulsory military service.

ANSCHLUSS OF 1938. The *Schutzbund* and the *Heimwehr* eliminated, the country's position deteriorated fast as a result of Mussolini's shift toward Hitler and the ever-worsening economic conditions. Following an ultimatum given him during a visit to Hitler, Feb. 1938, Schuschnigg responded by calling for a plebiscite (for 13 Mar.) on the issue of *Anschluss*. Two days prior to the plebiscite, Hitler threatened to invade unless it was canceled. On 12 Mar., 1938, Interior Minister Dr. Arthur von Seyss-Inquart (1892–1946) assumed power from Schuschnigg (who had resigned the day before) and invited the German army to "maintain order." The *Anschluss* went into effect the same day. (*Cont. p. 526.*)

Hungary

1918–21

END OF THE DUAL MONARCHY. Amidst the great turmoil which befell the Austro-Hungarian Monarchy in the closing months of 1918, Hungary experienced a violent transformation. What emerged at the end was far different from what until then had been known as the kingdom of historic Hungary. Following the proclamation, 16 Oct., 1918, of the federalizing manifesto by Charles I (Charles IV as king of Hungary) —an act which Hungary considered as terminating the 1867 Compromise (*Ausgleich*) —events in quick succession led to an internal crisis which lasted until Nov. 1919.

ESTABLISHMENT OF A LIBERAL REGIME. Upon the outbreak of revolutionary ferment in Budapest, King Charles IV named the liberal Count Mihály Károlyi (1875–1955) to form a new government, 31 Oct., 1918. Trying desperately to preserve the country within its historic borders, Károlyi declared, 16 Nov., 1918, a republic and promulgated long-overdue social and political reforms, including federative status for the minorities. In the meantime, however, both internal and external pressures prevented him from implementing his ambitious program, and the nationalities, refusing to accept his federalizing scheme, attacked the country from 3 directions. Since the Hungarian army had earlier been demobilized, the allied ultimatum drawing the new border with Rumania at the Tisza River found Károlyi unprepared and, sensing the failure of his pro-allied policy, he went into exile, Mar. 1919.

THE SOVIET REPUBLIC. A Soviet-type republic, attended by widespread terror, was proclaimed, Mar. 1919, under the leadership of Béla Kun (1885–1937). An ex-officer in the Austro-Hungarian army, but one who had been captured, trained, and then returned by the Bolsheviks, Kun hoped, with promised Soviet-Russian aid, to repel the invading Rumanian armies. After initial success against the Czechs in Upper Hungary, the Hungarian Red Army without Russian help—which was not forthcoming—could not withstand the Rumanians. Before the Rumanians captured Budapest in Aug. 1919, Kun had fled the country.

TREATY OF TRIANON. 4 June, 1920. During the 3-month-long pillaging of the capital by the Rumanian army, the allies were searching for a government which could sign the peace treaty that had been delayed by the chaotic situation. In Nov. 1919, Miklós Horthy (1868–1957), a rear adm. of the former Hapsburg navy, entered the capital at the head of counterrevolutionary forces; on 1 Mar., 1920, the National Assembly, elected earlier in the year, chose Horthy to act in the absence of the king for the new Hungary. The "new" Hungary, as one of the successor states to the Hapsburg Monarchy, was defined by the Treaty of Trianon.

According to the treaty, Hungary had to cede Slovakia (in the north) and Ukrainian-inhabited Ruthenia (in the northeast) to form Czechoslovakia; Transylvania proper and some purely Magyar-inhabited areas extending into the Great Plain and part of the Banat of Temesvar in the south went to Rumania; and the other half of the Banat, Backa, Slovenia, and Croatia, went to form the new state of Yugoslavia. With a slice of western Hungary having been awarded to Austria proper, Hungary had ceded substantial territory to all her neighbors. Despite repeated pleas for plebiscites, the only case where one was granted was in the city of Sopron (Burgenland), which voted to remain within Hungary, 1921.

As a result, Hungary lost 71.4% of her territory and about 60% of her population, including about 3.5 m. Magyars, nearly 2 m. of whom had lived in areas adjacent to her new borders. Having lost her access to the Adriatic Sea, Hungary was reduced to a landlocked country without most of her natural resources and communication and cultural centers. Her army was also limited to 35,000 men.

HAPSBURG RESTORATION ATTEMPTS. Twice during 1921, King Charles IV attempted to reclaim the Hungarian crown. On 26 Mar., 1921, Charles returned to Hungary, but Horthy, fearing allied reaction, refused to yield without the consent of the Assembly. In Oct. 1921 Charles, with the aid of a small loyalist force, tried again to march on Budapest. The Little Entente mobilized, and pro-Horthy forces captured Charles before he could reach the city. Thereafter Charles was exiled by the British to Madeira, where he died in 1922. In response, the Little Entente forced Hungary to pass a dethronement act deposing the Hapsburgs.

1922–44

THE HORTHY REGIME. Among the 1st acts of the provisional Horthy government had been to hold elections for a Constituent Assembly in early 1920. Although no single party received a majority, the assembly agreed to restore the monarchy and to nullify all acts that had been passed under both the liberal Károlyi and the Communist Kun regimes.

The period between 1921 and 1931 was dominated by Horthy's appointee, Count István Bethlen (1874–1947), under whose premiership the country reverted to a generally conservative rule. The relative financial stability—achieved in part through the help of the League of Nations—which characterized these years was greatly offset by the absence of much-needed land and social reforms. During the premiership of Gyula von Gömbös, 1932–36, the country embarked upon a strongly revisionist policy for which the help of Fascist Italy was enlisted.

Progress toward parliamentary democracy was also made with the passage of the Electoral Reform Bill of 1938. The bill provided for secret balloting and introduced near-universal suffrage.

Although the successive governments of Kálmán de Darányi, 1936–38, Béla Imrédy, 1938–39, and Count Pál Teleki, 1939–41, were successful in checking the local Nazi movement, the country was drawn ever closer toward the Axis powers as the surest way to regain the territories lost in 1920.

FOREIGN POLICY. Hungary's foreign policy during the entire interwar period remained one of open irredentism toward her neighbors in the little Entente. In this goal, Hungary had no effective ally until Apr. 1927, when the conclusion of a friendship treaty with Italy paved the way for secret rearmament.

In Feb. 1934, Hungary both recognized the Soviet Union and concluded a trade agreement with Germany. On 17 Mar. Hungary, Italy, and Austria signed the Rome Protocol.

Following the Vienna Awards—the 1st returning Upper Hungary, Nov. 1938, and the 2nd returning northern Transylvania, Aug. 1940—Hungary became irrevocably indebted to the Axis powers.

In Apr. 1941, when in order to attack Yugoslavia Germany requested troop passage through Hungary, Teleki committed suicide, 3 Apr., rather than abrogate the treaty of "eternal friendship" which he had signed with Yugoslavia in Dec. 1940. (*Cont. p. 533.*)

Czechoslovakia

1918–39

CREATION OF CZECHOSLOVAKIA. As 1 of the successor states to the former Austro-Hungarian Empire, Czechoslovakia received Silesia, Bohemia, and Moravia from Austria and Slovakia and Ruthenia from Hungary under the Treaties of St.-Germain and Trianon respectively. In all, the population of the new state was made up of 5 nationalities: Czechs and Slovaks, comprising 2/3, and Germans, Magyars, and Ukrainians, comprising 1/3.

Considered as perhaps the most fortunate of the successor states, Czechoslovakia received most of the monarchy's industry, connected by an excellent railway system, as well as some agricultural areas growing hops, fruit, and sugar beets. Unlike any of the new or greatly enlarged states in predominantly agricultural Central Europe, Czechoslovakia as a result of her gains inherited a stable and balanced economy and experienced hardly any of the financial problems which beset Austria and Hungary.

PROCLAMATION OF THE REPUBLIC. Thomas G. Masaryk (1850–1937), a former professor in Prague, and Eduard Beneš (1884–1948), his student, are regarded as the founding fathers of Czechoslovakia. Their ambitious nationalistic campaign gained them early allied support and led to the declaration of an independent state of Czechs and Slovaks in Paris, 18 Oct., 1918, just 2 days after Emperor Charles I announced his manifesto envisaging a federalized empire.

On 14 Nov., 1918, the Provisional Assembly sitting in Prague declared the state a republic; it also designated Masaryk as president, 1918–35, Beneš as foreign minister, and Karel Kramář (1860–1937) as premier.

In Feb. 1920, the National Assembly adopted a democratic constitution which provided for a centralized bicameral legislature (whose joint session elected the president). The centralized constitution was adopted despite protest from the Slovaks, who demanded a federalized state which had been agreed upon in the Pittsburgh Pact, 30 June, 1918, stipulating the terms of the Czech-Slovak union.

LAND REFORM AND MINORITY PROBLEMS. To obtain broad support from the people, the new government embarked upon an extensive land reform, particularly in Slovakia, where large estates had been concentrated in the hands of the Slovak Catholic Church and the Magyar nobility. Another urgent task was to bring about reconciliation between the ethnic minorities. Despite guarantees of equality prescribed in a minorities treaty, signed in Paris in 1919, the minority issue contined to plague the government through the 1930's; exacerbated by foreign agitation, it became one of the major causes for the collapse of Mar. 1939.

NAZI AGITATION. Some 3.3 m. German-speaking people, living largely in compact groups along the mountainous border regions of Bohemia-Moravia as well as in inland Bohemia, constituted the largest minority in the new state and proved to be the most susceptible to Nazi propaganda. Beginning in 1932 and gradually gaining momentum, a pro-Nazi party, the Sudetendeutsch Party, became a growing threat to the country's internal stability under the extremist leadership of Konrad Henlein (1898–1945). In the elections of May 1935, the party gained a numerical majority despite attempts by the government to both suppress and appease its opponents.

To counter the new danger, the government tried to disarm the Sudetendeutsch Party by offering far-reaching concessions in cultural and economic matters. Henlein, however, emboldened by Hitler's 1933 victory, rejected the offer as inadequate and pressed for complete autonomy.

With the absorption of Austria by Germany in Mar. 1938, stepped-up Nazi propaganda succeeded in convincing most of the other, smaller German-speaking splinter groups to join the Sudetendeutsch Party. Having thus enlarged his following, Henlein demanded full political as well as ideological autonomy, Apr. 1938. When Prague refused to comply, the stage was set for Hitler to force the issue.

FORMATION OF THE LITTLE ENTENTE. The leaders of Czechoslovakia early realized that the country's continued existence depended on the maintenance of the Central–East European *status quo* as dictated at the Paris Peace Conference in 1919. Under Foreign Minister Eduard Beneš, a series of negotiations were initiated, 1920–21, which led to the formation of a regional bloc known as the Little Entente. Throughout its existence the Entente guarded against Hungary's openly revisionistic policies and hindered attempts to restore Hapsburg rule.

The Entente was based on 3 bilateral treaties: (1) Czechoslovakia-Yugoslavia, 14 Aug., 1920; (2) Czechoslovakia-Rumania, 23 Apr., 1921; and (3) Rumania-Yugoslavia, 7 June, 1921. On 21 May, 1929, the alliance was tightened by an agreement which made the renewal of the alliances automatic at the end of each 5-year period. The Entente drew its members even closer when Hitler came to power in 1933; in Feb. of that year, a permanent office in Geneva was set up which housed a council of the 3 foreign ministers; but in 1938 it proved too weak to withstand the subversive pressure of Germany.

THE MUNICH AGREEMENT. 29 Sept., 1938. Since the Little Entente was designed primarily against Hungary, Czechoslovakia looked elsewhere for support against possible aggression by Germany. A Czecho-Polish treaty of neutrality was signed, 1921. An accord of formal alliance with France was concluded, 25

Jan., 1924. Although the Czechs also entered into alliance with the Soviet Union, 16 May, 1935, neither Soviet nor French aid was forthcoming when it was most needed. In Sept. 1938, the leaders of France, Britain, Italy, and Germany signed an agreement in Munich which sanctioned the union of the Sudetenland with Germany; in Mar. 1939, Hitler occupied the remaining Czech lands and made northern Slovakia into an autonomous protectorate. (*Cont. p. 531.*)

Rumania

1918–40

TERRITORIAL GAINS. The territories awarded to Rumania by the Treaties of St.-Germain, Trianon, and Neuilly—the 3 together increasing the country by over half its original size—exceeded the expectations of her most rabid nationalists. From Hungary, Rumania gained Transylvania, Partium (part of east Hungary proper), and the eastern zone of the Banat of Temesvar (the other half going to Yugoslavia); from Austria, the province of Bukovina; possession of south Dobruja, which she had gained in the 2nd Balkan War, was confirmed and, in addition, she acquired Bessarabia by seizure from Russia.

MINORITIES PROBLEMS. With these territorial gains, Rumania was transformed from a country of homogeneous people into one with a population of which nearly ⅓ consisted of minorities. Among the complaints by the minorities, especially from Transylvanian Hungarians, were allegations of discriminatory applications of land reform, 1921. The ceiling for landholdings set by the reform was much higher in the old kingdom (1,250 acres) than in Transylvania (300 acres), where much of the land was in the hands of the Hungarian minority of 1.5 m. The Magyars also resented the suppression of their 1,000-year-old cultural institutions as well as the imposition of unsympathetic Rumanian officials from the old kingdom. Rumania also encountered resistance to her nationalistic policies from her Ukrainian (1 million), German (750,000), and Bulgarian (250,000) minorities.

ELECTORAL REFORM. Retaining the monarchical form of government under King Ferdinand (ruled 1914–27), Rumanian internal developments, 1918–27, were dominated by the prewar Liberal Party under the control of the Bratianu family. Despite the carrying out of far-reaching land reforms, 1921, and the granting of universal suffrage, 1923, the Liberal regime of Ion Bratianu (1864–1927) became associated with the pursuit of an extreme nationalistic policy and was accused of corruption at the expense of the peasantry and the minorities. Opposition to Bratianu was further increased when an electoral law granting parliamentary control to the party which obtained 40% of the electoral vote was passed, 1926.

THE MANIU REGIME. Following the death of Ferdinand, 1927, who was succeeded by his grandson Michael, Iuliu Maniu (1873–1951), leader of the National Peasant Party, was appointed premier in 1928. Despite his progressive legislation abolishing press censorship and martial law and curbing the oppressive police, Maniu was ousted by King Carol II in 1930. (Carol, after returning from exile, had deposed his son Michael the same year.)

THE IRON GUARD. During the next 7 years, personal intrigue, corruption, and mismanagement under a series of governments led to a tactical coalition between the opposition National Peasant Party and the Iron Guard, a terroristic, anti-Semitic, and Fascist group under the leadership of Corneliu Zelea-Codreanu (?1899–1938). The defeat of the incumbent Tatarescu government in the Dec. 1937 elections by a Maniu-Codreanu coalition prompted Carol to promulgate a new constitution, Feb. 1938, which outlawed all political parties and granted him virtual dictatorial powers. Although outlawed and its leaders executed, Nov. 1938, the Iron Guard continued to challenge Carol's personal rule until, in 1940, accused of "treachery" for the territorial losses to Hungary, the Soviet Union, and Bulgaria the same year, he was forced to abdicate.

FOREIGN RELATIONS. As 1 of the victorious powers, Rumanian foreign policy during the interwar years was governed by her concern to preserve her territorial gains against the irredentist policies of Hungary, the Soviet Union, and Bulgaria. For this reason she joined both the Little and the Balkan Ententes. She also concluded a treaty of alliance with Poland, 3 Mar., 1921, to safeguard against the possible loss of Bessarabia to the Soviet Union. As a double guarantee, Rumania also entered into a nonaggression pact with the Soviet Union in 1933.

As a result of the failure of the Little Entente to protect Czechoslovakia against Hitler as well as the tendency of Hungary to look to Germany to realize her revisionist designs, Rumanian foreign policy during the last few years before the outbreak of World War II became increasingly pro-Axis. (*Cont. p. 537.*)

Yugoslavia

1917–41

CORFU MANIFESTO. Overcoming longstanding differences in customs, culture, and religion which had separated them for centuries, representatives of the South Slavs—Serbians, Croats, and Slovenes—met on allied-held Corfu and proclaimed a union, 20 June, 1917, under the Serbian King Peter I. Montenegro also joined the union, 26 Nov., 1918, after her National Assembly deposed King Nicholas I for opposing the union under Serbia.

Although—according to the manifesto—the 3 national groups were to "rank equally" in the projected federal state, the South Slavs split into 2 factions when the Hapsburg Monarchy finally disintegrated in Oct. 1918. One faction, headed by the Serbian national leader Nikola Pašić (?1845–1926), advocated a strong centralized state; the other, led by the Croatian Stefan Radić (1871–1928), demanded a large degree of autonomy for all constituent members in a federal

union. Finally, on 4 Dec., 1918, the "Kingdom of the Serbs, Croats, and Slovenes" was formally proclaimed.

CENTRALISM vs. FEDERALISM. The domestic affairs of the new state remained confused and explosive throughout most of the interwar period. The issue which most prevented it from achieving a semblance of national unity was that of centralism vs. federalism.

A long-postponed election for a constituent assembly was held in late 1920 and, after much Croatian opposition and the subsequent boycott of the proceedings by 50 Croatian deputies, a centralist constitution was adopted, 28 June, 1921. Designed to do away with traditional localism and regional differences, the constitution replaced the provincial diets (parliaments) with one central Parliament (*Skupshtina*) in the Serbian capital, Belgrade. The Croatian Peasant Party under Radić, however, was determined to pursue an obstructionist policy until its avowed goal of complete autonomy was achieved.

The internal situation came to a crisis, 8 Aug., 1928, when Radić died of wounds he had received on 20 June for venturing to attack the Serbian-dominated government in Parliament. The Croatians then responded by convoking a separate Parliament in Zagreb, 1 Oct., 1928. To head off the collapse of the state, King Alexander I (ruled 1921–34) proceeded to dissolve the Parliament and instituted a dictatorship, 5 Jan., 1929. During the next 3 years, the state was ruled by decrees aimed at erasing particularism. In Oct. 1929, by royal proclamation the name of the state was changed to "Kingdom of Yugoslavia."

The adoption, Sept. 1931, of a new constitution ended the monarchical dictatorship. The new constitution, providing for a parliamentary procedure to ensure victory for the government party, was, however, rejected by the Croats, who viewed it as yet another attempt at "Serbianization."

ASSASSINATION OF ALEXANDER. Serbo-Croat antagonisms culminated in the assassination of King Alexander in Marseilles, 9 Oct., 1934, while on a state visit to France. Although new elections were held, May 1935, under the boy King Peter II (b. 1923), all oppósition members boycotted the Parliament to protest repressive campaign tactics.

SERBO-CROATIAN ACCORD. It was not, however, until 24 Aug., 1939, that an accord between the Serbian and Croatian leaders was reached. The agreement, prompted by the growing alarm at Hitler's *Drang nach Osten,* provided for full autonomy in all matters but defense, internal and foreign affairs, foreign trade, and communications. At the same time, the Yugoslav government was also reorganized so as to allow greater Croatian representation; Vladko Machek, who succeeded Radić as head of the Peasant Party, became vice-premier.

FOREIGN RELATIONS. Yugoslav foreign relations in the 1920's were dominated by a conflict with Italy over the latter's ambitions to gain Dalmatia and the port city of Fiume (based on secret promises by the allies during World War I). The conflict was settled in the Treaty of Rapallo, 1920, making Fiume a free port, and later modified by the Treaty of Rome, 1924, which gave the city to Italy but granted Yugoslavia access to the port for 50 years.

Since Yugoslavia was created largely at the expense of her former enemies Hungary, Austria, and Bulgaria, she entered into alliances with Rumania and Czechoslovakia, thus forming under French tutelage the Little Entente, 1921. Relations with Hungary became especially tense in 1934, when that country, in pursuing a revisionist policy, exploited Serbo-Croatian antagonism and, as a consequence, found herself implicated in King Alexander's assassination. Yugoslavia subsequently retaliated by deporting a number of Hungarian nationals across the border. In a gradual shift to a policy of *rapprochement* with her former enemies under Prince Paul (acting as regent for King Peter II), Yugoslavia first signed on 12 Dec., 1940, a "Treaty of Eternal Friendship" with Hungary and the next year in Mar. Premier Dragisha Tsvetkovich visited Vienna and signed the Tripartite Pact formally joining Yugoslavia to the Axis powers.

Within two days, however, the military opposing the pro-Axis drift executed a *coup d'état* which, in turn, provided Hitler with a pretext to invade the country in April 1941. (*Cont. p. 539.*)

Bulgaria

1919–39

TREATY OF NEUILLY. 27 Nov., 1919. As a member of the defeated Central Powers, Bulgaria signed the Treaty of Neuilly by which she ceded western Thrace to Greece—thereby losing her access to the Aegean Sea—and 4 other smaller areas to the newly created Yugoslavia. The treaty also limited her army to 20,000 men; her navy was reduced to 4 torpedo boats and 6 motor boats, "all without torpedoes." South Dobruja was confirmed as a Rumanian possession.

RULE OF BORIS III. Blamed for joining the defeated Central Powers, King Ferdinand was forced to abdicate in 1918 in favor of his son Boris III (ruled 1918–43). With the fall of the existing cabinet as well, Aleksandr Stamboliski (1879–1923), the Agrarian Party leader who had dared to oppose Ferdinand on the war issue, was named premier, Oct. 1919. He remained in power until 9 June, 1923, when a *coup d'état* ousted him for ruthlessly suppressing all but the peasantry. In the following years, Aleksandr Tsankov (1879–1959), the new prime minister, had to combat repeated Communist attempts at establishing a Soviet-type republic. Finally on 19 May, 1934, fear of Communism led to a military *coup d'état* under Kimon Georgiev; the following year Boris III introduced a personal dictatorship.

SUPPRESSION OF IMRO. In addition to the increasing Communist activity, Bulgaria's internal situation was made more difficult by the presence of some 200,000 World War I refugees from Serbian and Greek Macedonia. The well-armed Internal Macedonian Revolutionary Organization (IMRO), founded in 1893, constituted a constant source of embarrassment to Bulgarian governments because of its guerrilla activities—fanned by Communist agitation—against Greece and Yugoslavia. Already torn by internal dissension, IMRO, along with all other political parties, was finally suppressed in a *coup d'état* in 1934. Once the Macedonian exiles had been checked, the way was cleared for Bulgaria to join the Balkan Entente on 31 July, 1938 (Treaty of Salonika).

NAZI INFLUENCE. Not unlike the other states of Eastern Europe, Bulgaria also was affected by the spread of Nazism. Although officially outlawed in 1938 and 1939, the Nazi movement continued its activity under the leadership of former premier Tsankov. (*Cont. p. 530*.)

Albania

1920–39

PRESERVATION OF ALBANIAN INDEPENDENCE. Albania's independent status, which she had gained during the Balkan War of 1912, was confirmed by the allied powers at the Paris Peace Conference after World War I. A national congress (*Lushnje*) in 1920 also reasserted national independence and moved the capital to Tirana. Real independence, however, did not come until, in the fall of 1920, the Italian occupation troops left the country. Albania was admitted to the League of Nations in Dec. 1920.

ACCESSION OF ZOG I. With the election early in 1921 of a Council of Regents (acting for King William I), Albania remained a monarchy. During 1921–25, however, Albanian politics was characterized by a power struggle fought between various minorities, tribes of mixed origin and following different religions. From the beginning, the political situation was dominated by the personality of Ahmed Bey Zogu (1895–1961), a nationalist of long standing. The conflict turned into violence when, after the elections in 1924, the defeated candidates, followers of Zogu, resorted to arms to contest the results. After a brief sojourn in Yugoslavia, Zogu returned before the year was out and, with the aid of his faction, established himself president. Three years later, however, the monarchy was restored when, 1 Sept., 1928, Zogu was proclaimed King Zog I. In his attempt to introduce

the country to the modern age, he ruled over his kingdom with an iron hand and maintained a semblance of order.

GROWTH OF ITALIAN INFLUENCE. Italian domination over Albania began to increase after the signing of the Treaty of Tirana in 1926; King Zog looked to Italy for financial, technical, and military aid, and, in order to gain a long-coveted foothold in the Balkans, Italy willingly complied. Under cover of the treaty, Italian influence continued to grow until, on Good Friday of 1939, the Italian army occupied the country outright. Zog fled and Albania, under King Victor Emmanuel III, was joined to Italy in a personal union. (*Cont. p. 529*.)

Greece

1921–40

GRECO-TURKISH WAR OF 1921–22. World War I fighting between Greece and Turkey was to have ended along the lines laid down in the Treaty of Sèvres of 10 Oct., 1920. Although the treaty was accepted by the government of Sultan Mohammed VI at Istanbul, a rival nationalist government under Kemal Atatürk proceeded to repudiate its terms. Despite initial successes due to British backing, Greece in the end lost the war and was obliged to sign, Oct. 1923, the Treaty of Lausanne which restored the Maritsa River in Thrace as the Greco-Turkish border. The new treaty also stipulated an exchange of population which left Greece with about 1.2 m. Greek refugees to assimilate. Greco-Turkish relations thereafter remained at best cool until 1930, when the 2 signed a treaty of friendship.

ROYALISTS vs. REPUBLICANS. The war with the Turks exacerbated an already tense internal situation. King Constantine, who had been deposed for his neutrality in 1917, was recalled after the death of his son King Alexander in 1920. Since his reign was too closely associated with military defeat by the Turks, Constantine was forced to abdicate again, 1922. Although he was succeeded by his son George II, defeat by the Turks shifted public sentiment toward the anti-royalist party and a republic was proclaimed, 1924, following the expulsion of George II in 1923.

The republican years 1924–35 were filled with political feuds, *coup d'états*, and countercoups, with Adm. Pavlos Koundouriotis, 1924–29, Eleutherios Venizelos, 1928–33, and Panagis Tsaldaris, 1933–35, among the chief political figures. In 1935, a plebiscite organized to decide the monarchy issue—which in the meantime had been revived—was canceled as a result of a *coup d'état* engineered by former War Minister Gen. Georgios Kondylis. In quick succession, Kondylis, now acting both as premier and regent, defeated the forces of Venizelos, ousted Premier Tsaldaris, and restored the monarchy under a reinstated King George II in Nov. 1935. Within less than a year, however, King George removed Kondylis for nonco-operation, Aug. 1936, and restored the 1911 constitution. A dictatorship was introduced under Gen. Joannes Metaxas (1871–1941). Death within 3 months eliminated Kondylis, Venizelos, and Tsaldaris; in 1938 Metaxas was named premier for life.

FOREIGN RELATIONS. In addition to the Turkish war, Greek foreign affairs in the 1920's were complicated by strained relations with Bulgaria over Greek minorities within Bulgarian Macedonia and Bulgarian aspirations for an outlet to the Aegean Sea, with Italy over Corfu, and with Yugoslavia over mutual ambitions to control Yugoslavian Macedonia.

When a Greek army contingent invaded parts of Bulgarian Macedonia in retaliation for alleged atrocities against Greek nationals, the League of Nations intervened on Bulgarian request and, scoring one of its few successes, arbitrated against Greece. Thereafter, relations between Greece and Bulgaria continued to improve until, in 1938, Bulgaria joined the Balkan Entente.

BALKAN ENTENTE. The Balkan Entente was a loose alliance created in 1934 by Yugoslavia, Rumania, Greece, and Turkey to secure their territorial integrity against Bulgarian and Hungarian revisionism.

Despite Greek neutrality at the outbreak of World War II, Italy, in Oct. 1940, invaded Greece. (*Cont. p. 527.*)

Poland

1918–39

REBIRTH OF HISTORIC POLAND. Although there had been faint attempts by the Central Powers and Russia to give Poland independence, 1914–16, the Polish nationalists, especially General Józef Piłsudski (1867–1935), soon realized that only through their own efforts could real independence be achieved. After the defeat of the Central Powers and with the support of the allies, the various nationalist factions arrived at a compromise and proclaimed an independent and united Poland, 9 Nov., 1918. On 16 Nov. Poland was declared a republic.

ESTABLISHMENT OF THE POLISH FRONTIERS. Recognizing the existence of an independent Poland, the allied powers by the Treaty of Versailles of 1919 fixed her boundaries according to economic, strategic, and ethnographic considerations, at least to the extent that these principles could be reconciled. On the west, Poland was given from Germany western Prussia, comprising an area stretching from Silesia to the Baltic Sea (Polish Corridor); and on the south, she received from Austria Teschen and Galicia. From the Soviet Union on the east, she was to receive parts of the former eastern provinces of historic Poland (which were inhabited mainly by White Russians and Ukrainians). But since the eastern border envisaged by the treaty (known as the Curzon Line) would have given Russia the easternmost parts of historic Poland, war ensued between Polish forces under General Piłsudski and the Red Army of Soviet Russia. It was not until 1921 that the Treaty of Riga fixed a border approximating that of 1772, as claimed by Poland.

Territorial disputes with the newly independent states of Lithuania (over the city of Vilna) and Czechoslovakia (over formerly Austrian-held Teschen) were prolonged throughout most of the interwar period.

MILITARY DICTATORSHIP. After his release from German imprisonment, Piłsudski appeared in Warsaw, took command of the army, and declared himself chief of state, 10 Nov., 1918. (Another national leader who had been active in promoting the Polish cause in allied circles in Paris, Ignacy Paderewski [1860–1941], became premier in Jan. 1919.) Piłsudski, after the adoption of a republican constitution, Mar. 1921, and its confirmation by a plebiscite, Nov. 1922, temporarily retired from public life.

Despite attempts by various cabinets at financial and agrarian reforms during the following 4 years, protracted parliamentary infighting between radicals and conservatives resulted in corruption and ineffectual government which, in turn, led Piłsudski to engineer a *coup d'état* on 11 May, 1926. With the ouster of Premier Wincenty Witos (1874–1945), Piłsudski named his friend Ignacy Mościcki (1867–1946) as president of Poland. The 2 cooperated in forming what came to be regarded as a virtual military dictatorship, which lasted until Piłsudski's death in May 1935. Following the adoption of another constitution, which reduced the Parliament to the role of a rubber stamp, Mościcki, under the tutelage of the military, continued in power until 1 Sept., 1939. On the outbreak of World War II, invasion by Germany and the Soviet Union led to the partitioning of Poland for the 5th time.

MINORITY PROBLEMS. The new state's non-Polish national minorities of Germans, White Russians, Ukrainians, and Jews—together comprising ⅓ of the population—made the task of establishing political harmony very arduous. Constant friction between government and minorities led to incidents which precipitated intervention by the League of Nations. The latter, however, tried in vain to enforce special treaty statutes designed to protect the minorities which Poland had been required to sign in 1919; by the 1930's, Poland became more and more associated with anti-Semitic policies.

BORDER SECURITY. As a new country wedged in between 2 major powers, Poland's principal concern during the inter-war years was to ensure her security through alliances. After settling the border conflict with the Soviet Union in 1921, she signed the same year treaties with 3 other countries. A treaty of alliance was negotiated with France and Rumania to guard against the Soviet Union and Germany, and a treaty of neutrality was concluded with Czechoslovakia. Both treaties were motivated by Poland's desire for friendly relations with the Little Entente without actually joining it, while enabling her to retain amicable relations with her traditional friend Hungary.

In 1929 Poland joined Finland, Latvia, Estonia, Rumania, and the Soviet Union in signing the Litvinov Protocol, which in turn activated the Briand-Kellogg Pact, Aug. 1928, designed to outlaw war as a means of settling conflicts between states. Poland also concluded nonaggression pacts with the USSR in 1931 and with Germany in 1934. (*Cont. p. 535.*)

The Growth of Russian Power

LENIN AND THE BOLSHEVIK REVOLUTION

1917

THE FEBRUARY REVOLUTION. A new era in Russian history dawned in 1917, when the Romanov dynasty, which had ruled the country for more than 3 centuries, was overthrown. Although the Romanov regime had already been gravely undermined by World War I, the immediate spark which ignited the February Revolution was the shortage of bread in Petrograd, at that time the Russian capital. On 12 Mar. (27 Feb. by the old Russian calendar), in the midst of bread riots, Czar Nicholas II (1868–1918) was forced to abdicate. A Provisional

Government set up by the Duma (parliament) and headed by Prince Georgi Lvov (1861–1925) superseded the monarchy. Meanwhile, more radical revolutionaries organized a Soviet of Workers' and Soldiers' Deputies, modeled on a similar institution which sprang up in St. Petersburg during the Revolution of 1905. Other soviets followed. Thus in the aftermath of the February Revolution a system of dual power prevailed in Russia, and the soviets proclaimed many decrees which directly contradicted the policies of the Provisional Government.

Vladimir Ilich Ulyanov, known as Nikolai Lenin (1870–1924), was in exile in Switzerland when the February Revolution occurred. With German approval he returned to Russia secretly via Germany in a sealed train. On arrival he promulgated the "April Theses," which called for opposition to the "bourgeois" Provisional government and assumption of power by the soviets.

Meanwhile, the Provisional Government had failed to stabilize itself, and attempted to postpone most vital decisions until a Constituent Assembly could be convened. In July Alexander Kerensky (b. 1881), a member of the Social Revolutionary Party (SR), became head of the Provisional Government. Kerensky dealt severely with the Bolsheviks after they staged a large demonstration in the capital, and Lenin was forced to flee to Finland. An important turning point for the Provisional Government was the Kornilov mutiny, Aug. The specter of military dictatorship frightened many, and the Bolsheviks were able to claim most of the credit for preventing counterrevolution. The soviets made no move to seize power, and control over them gradually passed from the Mensheviks and SR's to the more radical Bolsheviks. By Sept. the soviets in Moscow and Petrograd (the name of St. Petersburg from 1917 to 1924, when it became Leningrad), were under Bolshevik control.

THE OCTOBER REVOLUTION. Although the Bolsheviks remained a minority in most soviets, Russia's military situation became desperate in the autumn and peasant riots erupted throughout the country. In such an atmosphere Lenin was able to return from Finland and prepare an armed insurrection. His plan was opposed even by some of his intimate associates, notably Grigori Zinoviev (1883–1936) and Lev Kamenev (1883–1936), who argued that conditions in Russia were not yet ripe for a socialist revolution. These objections were voiced at a secret meeting of the Bolshevik Central Committee, 23 Oct., but Lenin overrode the protests. At this meeting the Bolshevik Party's first Political Bureau, its chief policy-making body, was selected. It consisted of Lenin; Lev Davydovich Bronstein, known as Leon Trotsky (1877–1940); Josif Vissarionovich Dzhugashvili, known as Joseph Stalin (1879–1953); Zinoviev; Kamenev; Grigori Sokolnikov (b. 1888); and Andrei Bubnov (1883–1940). The revolution began before dawn on 7 Nov. (25 Oct. by the old calendar), when military detachments loyal to the Bolsheviks seized key installations in Petrograd. In the late evening the Bolsheviks moved against the Provisional Government, whose headquarters were in the Winter Palace. The Bolsheviks simply entered the palace through a poorly guarded back door and arrested the government ministers. The change of government was virtually bloodless and resistance minimal.

CONGRESS OF SOVIETS. On 8 Nov. the 2nd Congress of Soviets convened and named a Council of People's Commissars with Lenin as chairman. (The terms "cabinet" and "prime minister" were rejected as bourgeois labels.) Trotsky was chosen foreign commissar and Stalin commissar of nationalities. The government was virtually a Bolshevik dictatorship, since the Bolsheviks refused to heed Menshevik and SR demands for a broad socialist regime, and provoked a walkout by these two groups. The Congress of Soviets also passed a Decree of Peace, proposing an end to World War I, "without annexations and indemnities," and a Decree on Land, which announced the abolition of private property in land and the transfer of private and church lands to special committees of the Soviets of Peasant Deputies for distribution to the peasantry. The Congress' last act was the election of a new Central Executive Committee composed of Bolsheviks and leftist SR's, with the former in a majority.

1918–21

CONSTITUENT ASSEMBLY. After assuring himself that all soviets were under Bolshevik domination, Lenin turned to the Constituent Assembly, which convened, Jan. 1918, with an SR majority. He would have preferred the Assembly not to convene at all, but strong popular support for it forced his hand. He therefore allowed it to meet, but dispersed it by force with the aid of Bolshevik-led sailors. Thus the last political institution around which the opponents of Bolshevism might have rallied was destroyed. Lenin was now free to construct a "dictatorship of the proletariat," which meant in practice dictatorship by the Bolshevik (renamed Communist in 1918) Party.

BOLSHEVIK PROGRAM. "Peace! Land! Bread!" These were the slogans with which the Bolsheviks had sought popular support in the prerevolutionary period. Peace was secured through the Treaty of Brest-Litovsk with Germany, 3 Mar., 1918. As for the land slogan, many acres were distributed to the peasants, and private property in land was formally abolished. The new regime at first left the peasants undisturbed in the use of the land. Early economic measures in the cities included the inauguration of an 8-hour working day, the establishment of "workers' control" through workers' committees given the right to oversee production, the creation of a Supreme Economic Council to supervise the entire economy, the nationalization of banks, and, June 1918, the nationalization without compensation of all major industries.

CIVIL WAR. Fulfillment of the Bolshevik program was impeded by the outbreak of civil war between "Reds" and "Whites," which lasted more than 3 years and almost destroyed the Russian economy. The White armies began to form in the winter of 1917–18 in peripheral areas of the former Russian Empire and planned thrusts toward the center to destroy the Bolshevik regime. The fact that they had to operate on the periphery placed the Whites at a severe military disadvantage, since their communications and supply lines were overstretched. Another major weakness was lack of unity among the Whites: all agreed on the immediate objective, to overthrow Bolshevik power, but their plans for a postwar government were vague and contradictory. Nor did the Whites possess a leader who could unify their movement on a nationwide basis. Their generals, indeed, lacked political experience. Still another White handicap was, ironically, allied intervention on their side. The 14 nations contributing troops or other assistance to the Whites failed to do enough to turn the tide of battle against the Reds, yet they provided the Bolsheviks with a valuable propaganda weapon by enabling them to pose as champions of the defense of the fatherland against foreign invaders. As a result thousands of Russians ignorant of or hostile to Communist ideology nevertheless fought on the Red side to preserve their country's territorial integrity. Trotsky, who became war commissar after Brest-Litovsk, created the victorious Red Army.

ESTABLISHMENT OF THE COMINTERN. While the civil war was in progress, Lenin sought to promote world Communist revolution. In Mar. 1919 he established the Comintern (Third International) as the vehicle for spreading revolutionary propaganda. In Apr. a Communist regime headed by Béla Kun seized power in Hungary, and soon afterward Bavaria came under Communist control. The Comintern played no significant role in these events, however, and both regimes were short-lived. Similarly, when Finnish Communists seized Helsinki in 1918, they were soon driven out by anti-Communist Finns. During 1920–21, Bolshevik troops brought the newly independent Transcaucasian republics of Georgia, Armenia, and Azerbaijan back under Russian control. The Red Army met more determined resistance in the free Baltic republics, however, and Latvia, Lithuania, and Estonia retained their independence until World War II. During a brief war with Poland, 1920–21, the Red Army failed to install a Communist regime in Warsaw.

CONSOLIDATION OF THE COMMUNIST REGIME. On the home front Lenin's main problem was to preserve his infant regime, which he had barely begun to consolidate when the civil war erupted. In particular he had to ensure the flow of grain from the countryside to the urban workers and the soldiers in the Red Army. His solution was to inaugurate the system of War Communism. Its chief feature was forcible requisitioning of the peasants' crops by the state. After grain had been distributed in urban and war zone areas, the remainder was to be divided among the peasants. The peasants resisted War Communism, however, by hiding grain and by refusing to produce more than their own subsistence required. Numerous peasant uprisings occurred during the summer and autumn of 1918. Shortages became so extreme that money lost all value and most workers had to be paid in kind.

Lenin also took steps to subordinate Russian trade unions to Communist Party control. Moreover, the power of workers' committees was steadily curtailed by political appointees stationed in industrial enterprises. Meanwhile, opposition to Bolshevik policies rose to dangerous heights. In Mar. 1918 the representatives of the Left SR's, the Bolsheviks' junior partners in the coalition government, resigned in protest against the Treaty of Brest-Litovsk. At the Fifth Congress of Soviets, held in June of the same year, Left SR's denounced the practice of requisitioning grain. In July a Left SR named Jacob Blumkin killed the German ambassador, Count von Mirbach, in hopes of provoking renewed Russo-German hostilities. In Aug. a group of Left SR's inflicted on Lenin an injury from which he never fully recovered, and assassinated 2 other Communist leaders.

In reply the Communists unleased a Red Terror under the aegis of the Cheka, the first of a series of names for the secret police. Lenin also used the atmosphere of civil war as a pretext for eliminating all real or potential enemies of the Communist Party. Among the victims were the entire imperial family, who were executed in July 1918. The first Soviet constitution, promulgated in the same month, guaranteed civil rights, but Lenin was already tightening the noose around dissenters. Mensheviks and orthodox SR's were expelled from the soviets, June 1918, and similar action was taken against the Left SR's after the Mirbach assassination. Even within the Bolshevik ranks opposition to Lenin was sharply curtailed.

NEW ECONOMIC POLICY. Red victory in the civil war was purchased at the price of the complete collapse of the Russian economy, widespread famine, and severe tensions in every segment of society. A revolt by sailors at the Kronstadt naval base, Mar. 1921, symbolized the mounting opposition to Lenin's regime. The men of Kronstadt, a bulwark of Bolshevik support during the revolution, now called for "Soviets without Communists!" Even as Lenin quelled the revolt, he realized that it reflected rising discontent throughout Russia.

To relax tensions, stimulate production, and achieve some measure of popular support, Lenin inaugurated the New Economic Policy (NEP), 28 Apr., 1919. The government retained control over the "commanding heights" of industry, but it now allowed a limited degree of freedom to peasants and small businessmen. The NEP abandoned forced requisitioning of crops, the peasants being required to pay the state only a tax in kind based on a certain percentage of output and receiving permission to sell the remainder of their produce on the free market. The Communist theoretician, David B. Goldendach, known as David Riazanov (1870–1942), termed the NEP the "peasant Brest-Litovsk," since it involved a temporary retreat from Communist principles and the granting of concessions to the peasants (like those at Brest-Litovsk to the Germans) and gave Lenin's regime time to strengthen itself. While urging the peasants to increase production, Lenin had to offer them consumer goods for which to trade their surplus grain. He thus focused on reviving industry. In consequence, small businessmen in particular benefited from the NEP; they gained permission to hire labor and to trade with relative freedom in the goods produced. In its early phase, the NEP encouraged the development of small industries, whether private or co-operative enterprises. The government promised new industries freedom from nationalization, while it leased to former owners or producers' co-operatives many small enterprises which had been nationalized previously. The NEP also stimulated trade. A class of so-called "NEP men" arose, operating through their own private trading concerns or as agents of state trading organizations. Many Communists looked suspiciously on the NEP men as an incipient capitalist class. But on the whole the NEP proved successful, both in its economic aspect of stimulating industrial and agricultural production, regaining financial stability, and generally repairing the war damage to the economy and in its political aspect of improving the attitude of social groups, especially the peasants, toward the Communist regime. Nevertheless, the peasant problem continued to haunt Lenin and the Party; they ruled an overwhelmingly peasant country with an ideology which stressed industrialization and glorified the proletariat.

1922–28

CONSTITUTION OF THE SOVIET UNION. While Lenin was introducing greater economic freedom in Russia, he was at the same time sharply reducing political freedom and seeking to eliminate all obstacles to Communist domination. The Tenth Party Congress in 1921, which had ratified the NEP, also banned factionalism within the Party. Shortly after this congress Lenin purged about ⅓ of the Party's membership. Beginning in 1922, any form of Menshevik, SR, or other anti-Communist political activity was labeled counterrevolutionary and was ruthlessly eliminated. Also in 1922 the GPU replaced the Cheka and, unlike the latter, obtained the right to arrest Communist Party members. A new Soviet constitution was promulgated in 1922, but did not differ significantly from the 1918 charter. Basic freedoms such as speech, press, and assembly were proclaimed, but only for the "working class." The constitution declared the separation of church and state, but guaranteed religious freedom as well as antireligious propaganda. Discrimination against national minorities was forbidden. The constitution formally instituted the Union of Soviet Socialist Republics (USSR). It contained a clause providing for the right of the constituent republics to secede, but this right existed only in theory. While the constitution described the USSR as a federation, in practice it became a union dominated by the Russian Republic. Surprisingly, the constitution did not even mention the Communist Party, which in fact was the fountainhead of power in the nation. The apparatus of the state was wholly subordinate to the parallel apparatus created by the Party at every level of administration.

FOREIGN POLICY. In part, the NEP symbolized a Soviet retreat in the face of the failure of Communist revolutions to materialize in the West. Unable to rely on economic assistance from western comrades, Lenin resorted during the NEP period to attempts to attract outside capital by granting concessions to foreign entrepreneurs. More significant, however, was his over-all policy of peaceful coexistence with capitalist nations. Lenin never ceased to believe in the inevitability of world revolution, which he held necessary for the building of socialism in Russia. After the collapse of Communist coups in Hungary and parts of Germany, however, he realized that world revolution would be delayed, and conceded that capitalism had entered a period of temporary "stabilization." He therefore took steps to end Russia's isolation. Already in 1920 the Russian government had signed peace treaties with Latvia, Lithuania, and Estonia; the following year witnessed treaties of friendship and commerce with Persia and Afghanistan. An Anglo-Russian commercial agreement negotiated in 1921 marked the beginning of a series of

© Lilli Tanzer, 1967

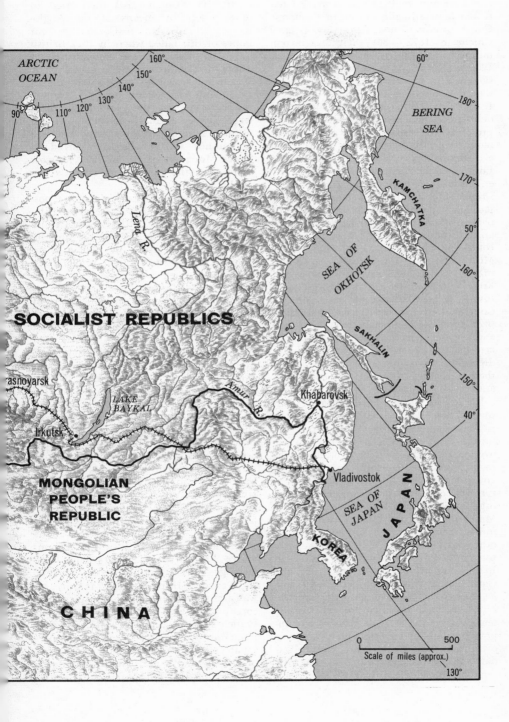

ARCTIC
OCEAN

160°
150°
140°
130°
120°
110°
90°

60°

BERING
SEA

180°

170°

KAMCHATKA

50°

SEA OF
OKHOTSK

160°

Lena R.

SOCIALIST REPUBLICS

SAKHALIN

150°

asnoyarsk

LAKE
BAYKAL

Amur R.

Khabarovsk

40°

Irkutsk

MONGOLIAN
PEOPLE'S
REPUBLIC

Vladivostok

SEA OF
JAPAN

JAPAN

KOREA

CHINA

0   500
Scale of miles (approx.)

130°

trade accords with Britain, Italy, France, and Germany. In 1922 Russia was invited to participate in the European Economic Conference at Genoa, Apr.–May. Grigori Chicherin (1872–1936), then foreign commissar, met his German counterpart, Walther Rathenau, at Rapallo, where they signed a treaty, 16 Apr., canceling Russian reparations claims from World War I in return for cancellation of czarist debts to Germany. The Treaty of Rapallo provided the Soviet Union with much more than economic benefits. It initiated a rapport between the 2 outcasts of Europe, ended their isolation, and greatly enhanced their diplomatic bargaining position. The treaty also marked Soviet Russia's 1st major success in the use of balance-of-power tactics; the accord guaranteed that no united capitalist world could launch an attack on the USSR. Most important, the Rapallo agreement inaugurated a shift away from British and French predominance in Europe and toward a new balance of power on the Continent. A Russian-German neutrality pact, 24 Apr., 1926, marked another step away from Soviet isolation. Several western nations accorded the Soviet Union diplomatic recognition in the 1920's, though the U.S.A. withheld recognition until 1933.

While the Foreign Commissariat pursued "peaceful coexistence" with capitalist governments, the Comintern, the second arm of Soviet foreign policy, worked by both secret and public means to prepare the overthrow of the same governments. An important new departure in Comintern policy occurred at the organization's 3rd Congress in 1921, when Moscow authorized the formation of united fronts between Communists and other parties. The united-front policy was put into effect during the 1920's in Britain and China. In Britain, 1924, the Conservative Party published the "Zinoviev Letter," a message allegedly sent by Zinoviev, then president of the Comintern, urging British Communists to support the Labour government in order to overthrow it at some future, unspecified date. The letter contributed to that government's downfall; it had recently estab-

lished diplomatic relations with the USSR. The Communists then tried to seize power by means of the Anglo-Russian Trade Union Committee, but hopes of this faded when in 1927 British unionists dissolved the committee. In China the Comintern inaugurated a policy of collaboration with the Kuomintang in 1923. Four years later, however, Chiang Kai-shek ordered the liquidation of a large number of Chinese Communists and virtually annihilated their party. The sole Communist success abroad occurred in Outer Mongolia, where in 1924 Moscow established the Mongolian People's Republic.

RISE OF STALIN. Lenin alone possessed the stature and prestige to hold the competing factions in the Russian Communist Party in check. From the time he suffered his 1st stroke in 1922 a fierce struggle for the succession took place. He never designated a successor, but made clear his belief that Trotsky and Stalin were the party's 2 most capable leaders, at the same time deploring the bitter antagonism between them. The greatest achievement of Trotsky was the creation of the Red Army which won the civil war. Stalin, lacking Trotsky's intellectual and military prowess, made his mark by performing routine administrative chores scorned by more theoretically minded Bolshevik leaders. The most important of these chores involved liaison between the party's Politburo and the Orgburo, which assigned personnel to carry out Politburo directives. Stalin thus obtained a unique opportunity to staff the Party apparatus with his own supporters. He also held the post of commissar of nationalities, enabling him to exercise influence in the non-Russian republics, containing about $\frac{1}{2}$ of the population of the Soviet Union, where his party adversaries had little leverage. As Commissar of the Workers' and Peasants' Inspectorate (*Rabkrin*), he was also responsible for efforts to combat corruption and inefficiency in all branches of government. He thus had numerous pretexts for dismissing his personal enemies on grounds of corruption or poor performance. Finally, he was a member of the Politburo and General

Secretary of the Communist Party's Central Committee. The latter post made him head of the Party's powerful Secretariat, its major administrative organ.

DEATH OF LENIN. After suffering a 2nd stroke in Dec. 1922, Lenin wrote his will, in which he criticized Stalin for overzealousness in the use of power. On 4 Jan., 1923, Lenin added a postscript to the will, urging the Central Committee to remove Stalin from the post of general secretary. Lenin later wrote to Stalin saying he was severing all personal relations with him. Lenin intended to culminate his assault on Stalin at the 12th Party Congress, scheduled for the spring of 1923; in Mar. of that year, however, he suffered a 3rd stroke, from which he never recovered although he clung to life until 21 Jan., 1924. Meanwhile, Lenin's will in its entirety was known only to his wife, Krupskaya, and his secretaries; knowledge of his personal break with Stalin was shared only by a few top Communist leaders.

STALIN-TROTSKY RIVALRY. With Lenin incapacitated, power passed into the hands of a triumvirate composed of Stalin; Zinoviev, then chairman of the Petrograd Soviet and president of the Comintern; and Kamenev, chairman of the Moscow Soviet and, like Zinoviev, a noted Communist theoretician. These 3 men, members of the Bolshevik Party from its birth in 1903, united against Trotsky, a relative newcomer to the party. Trotsky's brilliance, charismatic personality, and military achievements aroused jealousy among the triumvirate, which further added to their resentment against him. The party's 12th Congress in 1923 marked the triumvirate's victory over Trotsky and others, who denounced the "bureaucratic degeneration" of the party and vigorously opposed continuance of the NEP, which they saw as a virtual return to capitalism. Trotsky retained tremendous popularity in the Party, and especially in the Red Army he had created. At the time of Lenin's death, however, he was ill and away from Moscow. Stalin took advantage of this by posing as the sole defender of the Leninist tradition. Five days after Lenin died,

Stalin delivered a eulogy in which he vowed to fulfill Lenin's behests. Although Zinoviev, because of his presidency of the Comintern, enjoyed international prestige unmatched by Stalin, and although both Zinoviev and Kamenev were regarded as Communist theoreticians in a way that Stalin was not and were both Russians while Stalin was a Georgian, the latter skillfully outmaneuvered his fellow triumvirs. An important turning point came in May 1924, when Lenin's will was read aloud to the Party's Central Committee. Zinoviev pointed to the smooth operation of the triumvirate as evidence that Lenin's fears of Stalin as general secretary were groundless. More important, the decision was taken not to publish the will.

As the struggle for power developed from 1924 onward, it involved both personal rivalries and controversies over the best and fastest way to realize Communist domestic and foreign goals. The 1st aim of the triumvirate was to eliminate Trotsky as a contender for power. Trotsky proved peculiarly unable to resist pressures on him, as was shown when Zinoviev demanded that he retract his "errors" at the 13th Party Congress, May 1924. Trotsky succumbed, declaring that one could be right only within the Party, not against it. This cry of "my Party, right or wrong" rendered Trotsky morally vulnerable to his opponents, who justified their actions in the name of the Party. The controversy between Trotsky and the triumvirate then took a theoretical turn. In the fall of 1924 Trotsky published *Lessons of October,* a restatement of his theory of "permanent revolution" with its emphasis on the necessity of world revolution and aid from the international proletariat if socialism in Russia was to survive. *Lessons of October* also reopened an ugly wound between Trotsky and 2 of the triumvirs by recalling the opposition of Zinoviev and Kamenev to Lenin's decision to launch an insurrection in 1917. Stalin used the appearance of *Lessons of October* to reiterate once again that Trotsky was a relative newcomer to the Bolshevik ranks, thus implying that he was unqualified to assume Lenin's mantle. More important, however, Stalin fashioned his own theoretical platform from which to challenge Trotsky. His *Problems of Leninism,* published in 1924, set out the theory of "socialism in one country," in direct contradiction to Trotsky's insistence that the preservation of socialism in the Soviet Union necessitated Communist revolutions in the West. Since the prospects of world revolution appeared dim at this time, Stalin's treatise generated a great psychological impact. Lenin and Trotsky both believed that construction of a socialist society could begin in the Soviet Union; what Stalin now asserted was that it could be successfully completed there as well, because of the country's natural wealth and the protection from outside interference offered by its great size. Stalin added that if the Soviet Union did not push on toward socialism despite the lack of Communist revolutions elsewhere, it would soon be unable to abandon the NEP and prevent a return to capitalism. Lenin himself had regarded the NEP as only a temporary expedient designed to spur recovery of the economy after World War I and the civil war. The question therefore arose of how and when to abandon this stage and build socialism and Communism.

ASCENDANCY OF STALIN. Meanwhile, the struggle between Trotsky and the triumvirate continued. In 1925 Trotsky was removed as war commissar. Shortly afterward, however, the Party's formal adoption of "socialism in one country" gave Stalin the influence needed to break up the triumvirate. Zinoviev and Kamenev had been too preoccupied with their struggle against Trotsky to notice the threat from Stalin's increasing power. Kamenev's attack on Stalin at the 14th Party Congress late in 1925 led to his demotion from full to candidate member of the Politburo. In the reconstituted Politburo which emerged from this Congress, 3 Stalin henchmen held full membership. After the Congress, Leningrad remained the only stronghold of resistance to Stalin, who therefore removed Zinoviev as Party leader there. Not until 1926, when the supporters of all 3 had been dismissed from positions of authority, did Zinoviev and Kamenev make common cause with Trotsky against Stalin. Even then, although all 3 opposed the continuation of the NEP, their personal antagonisms made their alliance extremely unstable. By this time Stalin had found new allies in Alexei Rykov (1881–1938), Lenin's successor as chairman of the Council of People's Commissars; Michael Tomsky (1880–1936), leader of the trade unions; and Nikolai Bukharin (1888–1938), a former Left Communist who now headed the Rightists. While Zinoviev, Kamenev, and the other Leftists advocated the abandonment of the NEP, the Right argued that it was successful and should continue. Bukharin championed a "snail's pace" construction of socialism, and told the peasants, "enrich yourselves." Stalin was later to champion the program of Trotsky and the Left, but felt this could not be implemented until the state had accumulated enough power to push it through against the peasants' will. Meanwhile Stalin used his allies on the Right to discredit the Left on both domestic and international issues. In July 1926 he engineered Zinoviev's expulsion from the Politburo; 3 months later he removed Trotsky from the Politburo and Zinoviev from the presidency of the Comintern, which Bukharin inherited. In 1927 Stalin plotted the removal of Trotsky and Zinoviev from the Central Committee on charges of attempting to overthrow the government; when the 2 men led street demonstrations on the 10th Anniversary of the Bolshevik revolution later that year, they were expelled from the Communist Party. At the 15th Party Congress, Dec. 1927, Stalin was able to oust the opposition from the Party en masse. By this time the Soviet united-front policy had collapsed. For this setback Stalin used Trotsky as a scapegoat, although the latter had cautioned against Communist dependence on an alliance with the Chinese Nationalists. The situation in Europe was equally bleak; Britain had severed diplomatic relations with the USSR in the wake of sharp political conflicts over Soviet policy in the Middle East and China, France followed with a *de facto* break in relations, and the Soviet minister in Warsaw was assassinated. Stalin shrewdly conjured up a "war scare" to rally the Party behind him, divert attention from his foreign-policy failures, and further consolidate his power. At the 15th Congress Zinoviev and Kamenev renounced their earlier views, and were permitted to re-enter the Party. Trotsky, however, refused to submit to his critics, and was exiled to Alma-Ata in Soviet Central Asia.

The way was now clear for Stalin to attack the Rightists. Having packed the Politburo with more of his henchmen at the Congress, he isolated Rykov, Tomsky, and Bukharin. He then launched a frontal assault on the concept of a "snail's pace" construction of socialism, calling instead for a rapid economic transformation and an end to the independence of the peasantry. Having made this *volte-face* in policy, he then proposed an alliance with the followers of Trotsky and Zinoviev, who had previously advocated the course he was now proposing. At the end of 1928 Stalin staged a test of strength with the Rightists; Bukharin lost the Comintern presidency and Tomsky the leadership of the trade unions. The following year Stalin expelled Bukharin from the Politburo. Tomsky and Rykov suffered the same fate in 1930, at which time Rykov was replaced as chairman of the Council of People's Commissars by Vyacheslav Mikhailovich Molotov (b. 1890).

Stalin now abandoned the myth of "collective leadership" and emerged as the unchallenged dictator of the Soviet Union. His victory in the succession struggle was based on several major factors: his skillful use of the party machinery, his ability to capitalize on the concept of Party loyalty instilled by Lenin, and his own shrewd sense of timing. Not until several years later, however, did he follow up the political liquidation of his opponents with their physical extermination. Trotsky, Stalin's prime rival, was deported from the Soviet Union in 1929, and ultimately enjoyed more years of freedom than did Stalin's foes who remained behind. During his years of exile he edited the *Bulletin of the Opposition,* copies of which found their way to Moscow. Although he denounced "bureaucratic degeneration" in the Soviet Union, Trotsky remained convinced that attempts to overthrow Stalin would merely benefit the cause of counterrevolution. He retained a substantial body of adherents, who built up parties in many countries, and sought in vain to affiliate them in a 4th International. The Trotskyite schism plagued international Communism from that time onward. Trotsky himself moved to various places, but Stalin's hired assassins finally caught up with him in Mexico, where one of them killed him, 21 Aug., 1940, with an icepick.

THE SOVIET UNION UNDER STALIN

1928–34

NATURE OF THE STALINIST REGIME. By 1928 Stalin was the unchallenged master of the Soviet Union. He had defeated his Party opponents, both Left and Right. He had been able to silence all opposition in the secret police, army, and trade unions, and to bring these bodies more closely under the Party's, and his own, surveillance. The Cheka had been virtually independent of Party control, but the GPU (Gosudarstvennoe Politicheskoe Upravlenie), as the Cheka was renamed, was directly subordinated to the Commissariat of Interior. Trotsky's ouster as war commissar had been followed by the installation of Stalin's henchmen as political commissars and by the tightening of Party supervision over the military. Stalin had also destroyed the considerable independence enjoyed by trade unions during the NEP period, and transformed them into organs of state control over industrial workers.

1ST 5-YEAR PLAN. Having secured his power in the Party and government apparatus, Stalin launched the 1st 5-Year Plan, covering the period 1928–32. The aim of the plan, which signaled the end of the NEP and of compromise with the peasantry, was to industrialize rapidly, and simultaneously to bring about a basic socioeconomic transformation by converting the entire urban and rural labor force into employees of state-controlled enterprises. Stalin presented his rationale for speed in 1931, when he declared: "We are 50 to 100 years behind the advanced countries. We must cover this distance in ten years . . . or they will crush us."

ENFORCED COLLECTIVIZATION. The socioeconomic transformation was most profound in the countryside, where the independent peasant producers constituting the great bulk of the Soviet Union's population were herded into collective farms, there to become a landless agricultural proletariat with the duty of providing the lion's share of the capital needed for industrialization. Stalin sought to foment class war in the villages by calling on "poor peasants" to "liquidate the kulaks [richer peasants] as a class." In practice, government officials brought class war to the villages from without and, by defining "kulaks" in accordance with arbitrary criteria, attacked all peasants who opposed socialism, i.e., the great majority of the peasantry. Faced with peasant unwillingness to join collectives, the state imposed its will by force. Stalin thus not only adopted the basic domestic program of his defeated Left opponents but ignored Lenin's warning that a proletarian-peasant alliance was indispensable to Communism's survival in Russia. Stalin expected some resistance in the campaign against the peasants, but the extent of the defiance, in which peasants slaughtered their own livestock and burned crops rather than deliver them to the state, took him unawares. From 5 to 10 m. peasants died in the process of collectivization and in the resultant famine of 1932–33; millions more were conscripted into industry.

SOVIET TOTALITARIANISM. Despite the disastrous economic consequences of the collectivization drive, its political results were far-reaching. In fact, collectivization ushered in the real beginning of Soviet totalitarianism. A powerful state was the prerequisite for a socioeconomic revolution from above (i.e., against

the peasants rather from below, with their support), but this revolution, in turn, presupposed an authoritarian state to maintain the peasants in subjection. Such a system was required in the cities as well, where workers were assigned to jobs in state-owned enterprises, punished drastically for absenteeism or tardiness, deprived of collective bargaining through their trade unions, forced to engage in campaigns of "socialist emulation" to raise productivity still higher than the already inflated norms of the 5-year plans, and obliged, as were all social groups, to carry internal passports. The technique underlying the 5-year plans involved permanent intimidation of both the urban and the rural labor forces; such a tactic, coupled with the inefficient nature of Soviet planning and the substitution of political fanaticism for rational principles of management, undermined the success of the plans. In 1932, after $4\frac{1}{4}$ years had elapsed, the government announced that the 1st plan had been fulfilled, and 1933 witnessed the promulgation of the 2nd, covering the years 1933–37. The new plan was formally adopted at the 17th Party Congress in Jan. 1934.

By 1934, 99% of all industry was controlled by the state, and collective farms covered 90% of the country's arable land. The only private enterprise remaining in the Soviet Union was the sale of crops grown on the peasants' small garden plots. However, as a result of peasant resistance, collective farms (*kolkhozy*), in which peasants owned all land and farm implements in common and divided their profits, far outnumbered state farms (*sovkhozy*), in which the state owned all land, equipment, and livestock, and hired the peasants as wage laborers. What has been called the "second revolution" or Russia's "Iron Age" involved much more far-reaching economic and political consequences than the Bolshevik Revolution of 1917. For the first time, the Soviet totalitarian structure extended into every corner of every citizen's life. Far from "withering away," as Marx and Lenin had predicted, the state had become stronger than ever. Stalin justified this development by a theory of "capitalist encirclement," implying that the state would remain until Communists controlled the entire world.

FOREIGN POLICY. In 1927, a decade after the Bolshevik Revolution, Soviet foreign policy was at a low ebb. Comintern-sponsored coups and united fronts had failed, and Britain and France, then Europe's leading powers, had assumed a hostile stance toward Moscow. Stalin told the 1927 Party Congress that the era of "stabilization" of capitalism was ending and that the "imperialist" powers were plotting anew against the Soviet Union. The following year the 6th Comintern Congress adopted this interpretation by abandoning the concept of united fronts of Communists and other leftist groups and advocating an attack on all bourgeois political groups, including Social Democrats, who were labeled "Social Fascists." This policy reaped the most dire results in Germany, where the Communists not only assailed the Social Democratic policy of improving relations with the western powers but also aided Hitler's rise by refusing the pleas of many Social Democrats to make common cause against him. Hitler, once in power, repaid the favor by destroying the German Communist Party.

The Comintern's ineptitude stemmed not only from ideological rigidity—Stalin, professing that Nazism represented the highest stage of capitalism in Germany, claimed that it would soon be superseded by a Communist regime—but from Stalin's transformation of the International from a vehicle of world revolution to an instrument of Soviet foreign policy. At the 1928 Party Congress the preservation of the world's first Socialist state, the USSR, was proclaimed as the foremost duty of Communist parties everywhere. Stalin also purged and Russified the Comintern staff. The hard line imposed on the Comintern in 1928 found a certain parallel in Soviet foreign policy on the level of relationships with individual states. Moscow continued, as under Lenin, to regard Britain (held to be the strongest capitalist power) as the main enemy and to play the anti-Versailles powers against Britain and France in the European power balance. At the same

time, however, Stalin was forced by the Soviet Union's isolation and the internal difficulties accompanying the 1st 5-Year Plan to pursue a cautious foreign policy. He was particularly anxious to neutralize the countries on the Soviet Union's western borders to prevent their being used by the capitalist powers as a potential staging area for an invasion of Russia. This was the chief motive behind the so-called Litvinov Protocol, named for Foreign Commissar Maxim Litvinov (1876–1951), and signed on 9 Feb., 1929, by the Soviet Union, Poland, Rumania, the 3 Baltic republics, Turkey, Persia, and the Free City of Danzig. Continuing domestic troubles and anxiety over rising German nationalism also led the Soviet Union to conclude nonaggression treaties with Poland, the Baltic states, Finland, and even France.

Meanwhile Moscow, although the USSR was not a member of the League of Nations, participated in many League-sponsored committees seeking to reduce international tensions. The Soviet Union also sought wider diplomatic recognition. Anglo-Soviet relations were renewed in 1929. In 1933 the U.S.A. accorded recognition. Sino-Soviet ties, severed in 1929, were revived in 1932 as a response to Japanese aggression in Manchuria. Mounting anxiety over Nazism in Germany and militarism in Japan led the Soviet Union to join the League of Nations, 17 Sept., 1934, and to veer away from the Comintern hard line toward bourgeois governments. What became known as the Comintern's "Popular Front" policy received its first trial in France in 1934, though the policy was not officially inaugurated until the following year.

1934–39

THE GREAT PURGES. The extent to which Stalin had disposed of all opposition to his regime was revealed at the 17th Party Congress held in Jan. 1934. At this "Congress of Victors," ostensibly so named to celebrate the achievements of the 1st 5-Year Plan, Stalin declared that "there is nothing more to prove and, it seems, no one to fight." On 1 Dec., 1934, however, Sergei M. Kirov (b. 1888), Zinoviev's successor as Leningrad Party chief, was assassinated. Stalin reasoned that since the assassin, Leonid V. Nikolaev, had had close ties with Zinoviev, the latter was "objectively" responsible. Beginning early in 1935, large numbers of real and alleged supporters of Zinoviev, Trotsky, and other "Leftists" were deported to Siberia. A more ominous development occurred in Aug. 1936, when 16 distinguished Old Bolsheviks, including Zinoviev and Kamenev, were placed on public trial, forced to fabricate confessions of their "errors," and executed. That same year N. I. Yezhov (1895–1938), the "bloodthirsty dwarf," became head of the NKVD, successor of the GPU, and the purges rolled to their peak. In Jan. 1937, 17 leading Communists were condemned to death at the trial of the so-called "Anti-Soviet Trotskyite Center." Marshall Mikhail Tukhachevsky (1893–1937), chief of the army general staff, together with most of the army's top generals, were tried and shot, June 1937. In Mar. 1938 the major leaders of the Right Opposition, including Bukharin and Rykov (Tomsky committed suicide), perished. Yezhov himself was executed after being replaced by Lavrenti P. Beria (1899–1953), Dec. 1938.

Beria's accession to leadership of the police signaled the end of the mass purges and show trials, although numerous arrests and exiles continued. The NKVD became, in fact, the Soviet Union's largest individual employer in the 1930's; perhaps as many as 10 m. persons toiled in its forced labor camps. The purge victims included Lenin's entire Politburo (Trotsky was tried *in absentia*) except Stalin himself, the whole Bolshevik Old Guard, 70% of the members and candidates of the Central Committee elected at the 1934 Congress, and the cream of the leadership of the army, economy, trade unions, and secret police. Reportedly, the police were empowered arbitrarily to arrest a certain percentage of the entire population of the Soviet Union; an estimated 8 m. people were thus affected.

The Great Purges fatally undermined the degree of independent action still left to Soviet institutions, which now became pliant instruments of Stalin's will. Younger and presumably more reliable men, who had spent their formative years under the Stalinist system, replaced the purge victims in key posts. All owed their careers, and some their lives, to Stalin. The totalitarian state structure was now complete. Stalin ignored even his own Party in reaching decisions; 13 years elapsed between the 18th and 19th Party Congresses, held in 1939 and 1952 respectively, and during those years Stalin consulted the Central Committee and even the Politburo ever more infrequently. He had become the infallible *vozhd* (leader), and the "cult of personality" rolled into high gear.

CONSTITUTION OF 1936. In Nov. 1936 Stalin promulgated a new constitution. He explained that the Soviet Union had now completed the building of socialism ("from each according to his ability, to each according to his work," as opposed to Communism, "to each according to his need") ; exploitation of man by man had ended (allegedly because there was no more private ownership of the means of production) ; and antagonistic classes had disappeared (what remained were "friendly classes"—workers and peasants—and a "stratum"—the intelligentsia). Unlike the old constitution, which provided for indirect suffrage weighted in favor of the proletariat, the new document pledged equal, secret, and direct voting. (In fact, secret balloting was regarded with the utmost suspicion, while direct voting meant merely the fruitless and risky option of crossing out the name of the Party nominee on the ballot paper.) The new constitution guaranteed freedom of speech, press, and assembly, and even permitted "street processions and demonstrations." In fact these rights were lacking throughout the Stalin era. Soviet "federalism" and the right of union republics to secede were emphasized in the constitution, but still had no meaning in reality. The most glaring contradiction between the constitution and the facts of Soviet life was that the document merely mentioned the Communist

Party, the true center of power in the country (though naming it "The guiding force"), and omitted any mention of Marxism-Leninism, the official state ideology.

POPULAR FRONT POLICY. At its 7th Congress in the summer of 1935 the Comintern formally adopted the Popular Front policy, which proclaimed the willingness of all Communist parties to cooperate with any political group, whether Socialist or Rightist, which struggled against Fascism. Soviet entry into the League of Nations, implying that Moscow would respect the norms of international behavior, particularly necessitated such a Comintern shift. The major applications of the Popular Front policy occurred in France, Spain, and China.

In the French elections of May 1936 the Communists contributed to the Socialist leader Léon Blum's victory, and supported his government while refusing to enter it. Later, however, the French Communist Party helped to undermine the government through strikes and other tactics. The Communists repeated the same pattern until 1938, by which time the Popular Front policy in France had run its course.

In Spain the Socialists and Communists, both on the Republican side in the Spanish Civil War, formed a Popular Front government with Communist participation, Sept. 1936. Moscow, however, ordered the NKVD to arrest and execute Trotskyites, anarchists, and many Socialists in Spain. Stalin also began sending Soviet aid to the Spanish Republicans; by the summer of 1938 the Communists exercised a strong influence over what was left of the republican regime. Shortly afterward the Soviet Union cut off its aid; unable to secure British or French aid for the Republicans, Stalin hesitated to overcommit Soviet resources and prestige unilaterally, and feared a confrontation with Nazi Germany, which supported Franco's forces. Nevertheless, Stalin managed to delay Franco's victory until he had reaped the maximum advantage from the Popular Front policy; moreover, the experience in warfare and political infiltration gained by Soviet agents in Spain

was to serve Stalin well in his Communization of Eastern Europe. On the other hand, Soviet intervention in Spain increased western distrust of Moscow.

A Popular Front appeared in China in 1937, when the Nationalists and Communists agreed to make common cause against the Japanese. The 2 groups cooperated sporadically over the next few years, but both took advantage of the united front to strengthen their respective positions. Since Communist-Nationalist collaboration heightened Chinese resistance to Japanese aggression, it served to protect the Soviet Union's eastern frontier.

INTERNATIONAL   RELATIONS. The Popular Front policy gained Moscow little security, which Stalin was obliged to seek through conventional diplomacy. Once the Soviet Union had joined the League of Nations, it became a leading advocate of League action to maintain the peace. At the same time Stalin, ever fearful of Soviet isolation and hoping to divert world attention from the Great Purges, sought closer bilateral contacts with other European countries. In 1935, mutual assistance pacts were signed with France and Czechoslovakia. The latter pact obligated the Soviet Union to aid the Czechs only if France did likewise; this escape clause allowed Stalin to remain inactive after France and Britain had surrendered Czechoslovakia to Hitler. Soviet feelings of insecurity deepened in 1936, when Germany and Japan signed the Anti-Comintern Pact, 25 Nov., 1936. In 1937 the Soviet Union concluded a nonaggression treaty with the Chinese Nationalists, then engaged in a full-scale war with Japan. Soviet advisers poured into China, and limited Russian military aid to Chiang Kai-shek's forces continued until Germany invaded Russia in 1941. To some extent the Soviet Union used both bilateral pacts and the Popular Front policy, which had won Communism its greatest international influence up to that time, as diplomatic bargaining counters. As late as 1938, however, both the western democracies, which still believed appeasement of Hitler would work, and the Axis powers virtually ignored the Soviet Union. Then, in the spring of 1939, both sides began to court Moscow, which had meanwhile grown disenchanted about collective security as a result of the Munich agreement and had decided to draw closer to Hitler.

NAZI-SOVIET PACT. During the spring and summer of 1939 the Russian government was simultaneously negotiating openly with the western powers and secretly with the Nazis. Although Stalin regarded both western and Axis coalitions as anathema and hoped they would mutually exhaust each other in war, he aimed to prevent either from attacking the Soviet Union and to secure the highest possible price for adhering to one or the other. Molotov's replacement of Litvinov as foreign commissar, May 1939, symbolized Soviet intentions, for Litvinov had become identified with the policy of collective security against Nazism. Molotov immediately insinuated that Britain and France were not sincere in their negotiations with the USSR and were encouraging Hitler to expand eastward. Not until 5 Aug. did the British and French dispatch a military mission to Moscow, however, and then by ship and without providing it with written authorization to make political decisions. When talks finally began, 12 Aug., the Westerners proved unable and unwilling to meet Stalin's price for a pact—a free hand in the Baltic states and the right to send troops into Poland if Germany attacked. The Nazis, on the other hand, wanted an accord guaranteeing Soviet neutrality before they activated their planned invasion of Poland. On 23 Aug. Foreign Ministers Molotov and Ribbentrop signed the Nazi-Soviet Pact. Its public text was simply an agreement on nonaggression and neutrality; a secret protocol, however, divided Eastern Europe into "spheres of influence" by which the Soviet Union was to receive Finland, Estonia, Latvia, and Bessarabia. Furthermore, the Nazi-Soviet Pact was accompanied by a trade treaty and arrangements for a large-scale exchange of raw materials and arms. The pact, embodying the unusual provision that it was to take effect immediately, enabled Stalin to obtain temporary immunity against Nazi attack and to remain neutral in the 1st stage of the war, which he labeled an imperialistic conflict for the redivision of the world. (*Cont. p. 540.*)

The United States in Crisis and Recovery

EMERGENCE OF THE U.S. AS A WORLD POWER

1914–18

INTERVENTION IN HAITI. The U.S., holding large financial interests, intervened in strife-torn Haiti, 29 July, 1915. President Dartiguenave signed a treaty, 16 Sept., making Haiti a virtual U.S. protectorate. American troops left on 6 Aug., 1934.

BRYAN-CHAMORRO TREATY. 18 Feb., 1916. By this treaty the U.S. granted Nicaragua $3 m. in return for exclusive rights to a canal route and naval base.

MEXICAN BORDER CAMPAIGN. Pancho Villa's marauders killed 18 Americans, 18 Jan., 1916, at Santa Ysabel, Mexico, and 17, 9 Mar., at Columbus, N.M. President Wilson dispatched 15,000 men under Gen. John J. Pershing across the border to pursue Villa. The troops were withdrawn by 5 Feb., 1917. The U.S. recognized Carranza, who became president, 11 Mar.

INTERVENTION IN SANTO DOMINGO. Domestic difficulties in Santo Domingo further increased that country's national debt, and forced the Dominican president to resign, May 1916. The U.S. declared full military occupation, 29 Nov., and U.S. naval officers took over internal administration. The American marines withdrew, July 1924, when Gen. Horacio Vásquez became constitutional president.

WAR PREPAREDNESS. The war in Europe prompted individuals like Theodore Roosevelt and organizations like the National Security League to demand military readiness. Wilson resisted until the *Lusitania* incident, 7 May, 1915. On 3 June, 1916, the National Defense Act was passed. It expanded the army and authorized a 450,000-man National Guard.

PRESIDENTIAL ELECTION. 7 Nov., 1916. The Republicans nominated Supreme Court Justice Charles E. Hughes (N.Y.) and Charles W. Fairbanks (Ind.). Despite Roosevelt's support of Hughes, Wilson and Marshall, campaigning on a peace platform, won a close election, 277–254. (For entry of U.S. into World War I, see p. 374.)

WAR LEGISLATION. The Liberty Loan Act, 24 Apr., 1917, authorized the public sale of war bonds and loans to the allies to buy food and war matériel. The Selective Service Act, 18 May, established a military draft for men between 21 and 30 (later 18 and 45); 2,810,296 men were called. The War Industries Board was established, 28 July, to maximize efficiency in the nation's war industries. The Lever Food and Fuel Control Act, 10 Aug., empowered the President to control the production and distribution of food and fuel necessary for the war. An Act of 6 Oct. prohibited trading with the enemy. On 26 Dec. Wilson placed the railroads under emergency federal control with Secretary of the Treasury William Gibbs McAdoo (1863–1941) as administrator. The Sedition Act, 16 May, 1918, forbade statements detrimental to the war effort or attacking the American form of government.

1919–32

REJECTION OF LEAGUE OF NATIONS MEMBERSHIP. Wilson submitted to the Paris Peace Conference, 14 Feb., 1919, a draft covenant for a League of Nations, and then returned to the U.S., where 39 Republicans had signed Henry Cabot Lodge's senatorial "round robin" denouncing the League's proposed form. On his return to Europe, Mar.–Apr., Wilson agreed to certain compromises regarding reparations, the wording of the convenant, etc. After the signing of the

Treaty of Versailles, 28 June, with its accompanying covenant, opposition to ratification broke out in the U.S. Senate. Wilsonian Democrats supported immediate ratification; Lodge's moderates had reservations; "irreconcilables" led by Hiram Johnson and William E. Borah opposed it. Wilson was adamant. Democrats and moderate Republicans defeated the Foreign Relations Committee's "irreconcilable" amendments, and Democrats and irreconcilables rejected Lodge's reservations, 19 Nov. The League Covenant was rejected and the U.S. did not become a member of the League.

WASHINGTON ARMAMENT CONFERENCE. 12 Nov., 1921–6 Feb., 1922. The conference reduced naval armaments and considered East Asian problems. Five powers agreed not to build capital ships for 10 years and to apportion capital tonnage among themselves at the ratio of 5 (U.S.) : 5 (Britain) : 3 (Japan) : 1.67 (France) : 1.67 (Italy). They also limited submarine warfare and outlawed asphyxiating gases. Nine powers reaffirmed the Chinese Open Door policy.

INTERALLIED WAR DEBTS. Wilson refused British and French arguments in favor of cancellation of interallied war debts. Congress established the World War Foreign Debt Commission, 9 Feb., 1922, which negotiated agreements based on the debtor nations' ability to pay. The European financial situation led the U.S. to reduce drastically the debt's principal, 1925–26, but U.S. insistence on partial payment generated anti-American feeling abroad and isolationism at home.

DAWES PLAN. 9 Apr., 1924. President Calvin Coolidge (1872–1933) appointed, 15 Dec., 1923, a commission under Charles G. Dawes to investigate why Germany had defaulted on her reparations payments. The resulting Dawes Plan advocated reorganizing the Reichsbank under allied supervision and a schedule of graduated reparations payments.

POLICY TOWARD THE LEAGUE OF NATIONS. The U.S., though not a member, was represented at numerous League gatherings, including the International Opium Conference, 1924. Five U.S.

officials represented American interests at
Geneva.

WORLD COURT. Despite Senate approval, 27 Jan., 1926, U.S. reservations
prevented her from joining the Court of
International Justice proposed in the
League Covenant. Elihu Root (1845–
1937) formulated a plan, 1929, which
prohibited the Court from rendering advisory opinions, without American consent, on matters involving U.S. interests.
The Senate did not act, and later, 1935,
rejected membership.

**KELLOGG-BRIAND PACT. 27 Aug.,
1928.** The French foreign minister, Aristide Briand, submitted a bilateral treaty,
20 June, 1927, outlawing war. Secretary of
State Frank B. Kellogg made the agreement multinational, and 14 nations
signed the Kellogg-Briand Pact.

RELATIONS WITH NICARAGUA.
Henry L. Stimson (1867–1950) negotiated,
1927, an agreement between warring Liberal and Conservative factions in Nicaragua, and Liberal José Moncado was
elected president, 4 Nov., 1928, at a U.S.-
supervised election. American marines,
dispatched in 1926, withdrew in 1928.

YOUNG PLAN. A plan put forward by
Owen D. Young, 1929, reduced German
reparations to $8,032,500,000, payable
over 58½ years at 5½% interest. The
Lausanne Conference canceled, 16 June,
1932, over 90% of this obligation.

**LONDON NAVAL CONFERENCE.
21 Jan.–22 Apr., 1930.** The U.S., Britain,
and Japan agreed to limit cruiser construction at the ratio of 10–10–6. Neither
France nor Italy signed the more important provisions of the treaty, which was to
expire on 31 Dec., 1936.

**HOOVER DEBT MORATORIUM.
20 June, 1931.** The desperate world economic situation prompted acceptance of
President Hoover's 1-year moratorium on
both interallied debts and reparations.

STIMSON DOCTRINE. Arising out
of Japan's attack on Manchuria, 18 Sept.,
1931, the Stimson Doctrine declared, 7
Jan., 1932, U.S. opposition to any agreement impairing China's sovereignty or
integrity. After Japan's attack on Shanghai, 29 Jan., the League endorsed the
Stimson Doctrine.

1933–39

"GOOD NEIGHBOR POLICY." President Franklin D. Roosevelt pledged a
"Good Neighbor policy" toward Latin
America, 4 Mar., 1933, and rejected, 28
Dec., the idea of armed intervention.

RECOGNITION OF SOVIET RUSSIA. 16 Nov., 1933. Notes were formally
exchanged as the USSR agreed not to
interfere in U.S. domestic affairs and to
extend religious freedom to Americans in
Russia.

HEMISPHERIC SOLIDARITY. Various Pan-American conferences met in
response to the threat of European Fascism: the Montevideo Conference outlawed, 26 Dec., 1933, outside interference
in internal affairs, and the Lima Conference's "Declaration of Lima" expressed,
24 Dec., 1938, the Americas' determination to resist foreign intervention.

COLONIAL POLICY. The Philippine
legislature accepted the Tydings-McDuffie
Act, which provided, 24 Mar., 1934, for
eventual Philippine independence and
promised removal of U.S. military posts.
Roosevelt approved a Philippine constitution, 8 Feb., 1935, and Manuel Quezon
(1878–1944) became president of the
Philippines, 17 Sept. An Organic Act, 22
Jan., 1936, established a territorial legislature in the Virgin Islands.

DECLINE OF DOLLAR DIPLOMACY. Ambassador Sumner Welles
(1892–1962) negotiated a treaty, 29 May,
1934, with conservative Carlos Mendieta's
Cuban government abrogating the Platt
Amendment. Roosevelt allowed, 17 Oct.,
1933, Panama more equitable commercial
rights in the Canal Zone (ratified 1939),
and withdrew U.S. troops from Haiti,
1934.

NEUTRALITY ACTS. As Europe
moved toward war, Americans became
increasingly isolationist. The Neutrality
Act of 1935 authorized a temporary embargo on arms shipments to all belligerents. The 1936 Act outlawed loans or
credits to belligerents. Neutrality Acts in
1937 forbade munitions shipments to
either side in the Spanish Civil War,
empowered the President to list other

commodities to be paid for on delivery, and made travel on belligerents' ships illegal.

RELATIONS WITH JAPAN. The Japanese sank, 12 Dec., 1937, the U.S. river gunboat *Panay* in China, but quickly apologized, 14 Dec. However, they rejected, 18 Nov., 1938, the Open Door policy.

MEXICAN EXPROPRIATION CONTROVERSY. President Lázaro Cárdenas nationalized most of the properties of American oil companies operating in Mexico, 18 Mar., 1938. Secretary of State Cordell Hull (1871–1955) insisted that fair compensation was due, and the governments eventually agreed that Mexico should pay American claims in return for financial aid.

RELATIONS WITH EUROPE. The British prime minister, Neville Chamberlain, rejected Roosevelt's proposal of 11 Jan., 1938, for a world conference to reduce armaments. Hitler denied hostile intentions when Roosevelt asked, 15 Apr., 1939, Germany and Italy to pledge themselves not to attack 31 specified European and Middle Eastern nations.

DOMESTIC ISSUES

1919

PROHIBITION. The 18th Amendment to the Constitution, prohibiting the manufacture and sale of alcoholic beverages, and submitted for ratification, 18 Dec., 1917, was ratified on 29 Jan., 1919. The National Prohibition Enforcement (Volstead) Act, 28 Oct., 1919, passed over Wilson's veto, defined any beverage with more than half of 1% of alcohol as an intoxicant.

1920

ECONOMIC LEGISLATION. The Esch-Cummins (Transportation) Act, 28 Feb., returned the railroads to private control, strengthened the I.C.C., and established a Railroad Labor Board. The Jones (Merchant Marine) Act, 5 June, ended wartime shipping legislation. The Water Power Act, 10 June, established a Federal Power Commission empowered to authorize construction to improve navigation and develop power resources.

WOMEN'S VOTE. The 19th Amendment to the Constitution, giving the vote to women, was ratified, 26 Aug.

"RED RAIDS." The success of Russia's Bolshevik Revolution prompted mass arrests and deportations of political and labor agitators by A. Mitchell Palmer's Justice Department.

PRESIDENTIAL ELECTION. 2 Nov. The Republicans nominated Sen. Warren G. Harding (Ohio) and Gov. Calvin Coolidge (Mass.), attacked the proposed League of Nations, and promised a "return to normalcy." The Democrats chose Gov. James M. Cox (Ohio) and Franklin D. Roosevelt (N.Y.), and supported the League. Harding won, 404–127.

1921

ECONOMIC RECESSION. A recession, bringing unemployment to 4,750,000 persons, was caused by tight credit, a glutted domestic market, and a decline in exports. Agriculture began a downward spiral which lasted through the depression.

BUDGET AND ACCOUNTING ACT. 10 June. This act created the Bureau of the Budget. The President was instructed to report annually to Congress on the government's fiscal status.

PACKERS AND STOCKYARDS ACT. 15 Aug. Unfair and monopolistic practices in the livestock, poultry, and dairy industries were prohibited.

1922-23

KU KLUX KLAN. The K.K.K., a fundamentalist, racist, and nativist organization, was revived in 1915 and grew in membership to 5 m. by 1922. Newspaper revelations, 1923, of its vicious tactics and the conviction of Indiana Grand Dragon David C. Stephenson for murder, 1925, caused its decline.

ACCESSION· OF COOLIDGE. When Harding died, 2 Aug., 1923, of embolism,

Calvin C. Coolidge (1872–1933) became President. Coolidge's annual message to Congress, 6 Dec., advocated government economy and aid to business.

1924

HARDING ADMINISTRATION SCANDALS. Several departments of government were shaken by exposures of corruption in Harding's administration. Interior Secretary Albert B. Fall was jailed after Sen. Thomas J. Walsh's (Mont.) committee discovered that Fall had secretly leased naval oil reserve lands at Teapot Dome, Wyo., and Elk Hills, Calif., to oil operators Harry F. Sinclair and Edward L. Doheny. Attorney General Harry M. Daugherty resigned after revelations that he had received money from prohibition legislation violators.

SOLDIERS' BONUS ACT. 19 May. The World War Adjusted Compensation (Soldiers' Bonus) Act, passed over Coolidge's veto, provided 20-year endowment policies to veterans below the rank of major.

PRESIDENTIAL ELECTION. 4 Nov. Republicans nominated Coolidge and Gen. Charles G. Dawes (Ill.) and endorsed the high Fordney-McCumber Tariff. Democrats, split between the supporters of William G. McAdoo (Tenn.) and Alfred E. Smith (N.Y.), nominated John W. Davis (W. Va.) and Gov. Charles W. Bryan (Neb.), and advocated a competitive tariff. A farmer-labor Progressive Party chose Sen. Robert M. La Follette (Wis.) and Sen. Burton K. Wheeler (Mont.). Coolidge (382) defeated Davis (136) and La Follette (13).

1925–29

SACCO-VANZETTI CASE. Italian anarchists Nicola Sacco and Bartolomeo Vanzetti were executed, 23 Aug., 1927, for 2 murders committed in 1920. Liberals claimed their Massachusetts trial was prejudiced, but a Massachusetts commission sustained the verdict, 27 July, 1927.

PRESIDENTIAL ELECTION. 6 Nov., 1928. Republicans nominated Commerce Secretary Herbert Hoover (Calif.) and Sen. Charles Curtis (Kan.), and supported prohibition and the protective tariff. Democrats chose Gov. Alfred E. Smith (N.Y.) and Sen. Joseph T. Robinson (Ark.), and supported farm relief and collective bargaining for labor. Hoover (444) defeated Smith (87), whose Roman Catholicism and anti-prohibition views cost him votes.

EXPORT DEBENTURE PLAN. This plan, approved in 1929, provided for export bounties on certain agricultural commodities to be paid in debentures receivable in payment for import duties. Senate support collapsed when Hoover announced he would veto the measure.

AGRICULTURAL MARKETING ACT. 15 June, 1929. This act created a Federal Farm Board to promote the marketing of farm commodities through agricultural co-operatives and price stabilization corporations.

PANIC OF 1929. The stock market collapse of 1929 ended a period of unparalleled U.S. prosperity and touched off a worldwide depression.

1930–31

HOOVER RELIEF POLICY. Opposing direct federal relief to alleviate the depression, Hoover proposed federally aided local public-works projects to help the unemployed.

WICKERSHAM REPORT. 19 Jan., 1931. George W. Wickersham's Law Observance and Enforcement Commission advocated revision of the unpopular Prohibition Amendment. Hoover opposed repeal, 20 Jan.

VETERANS' BONUS. Over Hoover's veto, Congress authorized, 27 Feb., 1931, loans of up to 50% of veterans' bonuses.

1932

RECONSTRUCTION FINANCE CORPORATION. The R.F.C. was established, 2 Feb., to revive the economy by extending credit to banks, life insurance companies, building and loan societies, railroads, and farm mortgage associations.

GLASS-STEAGALL ACT. 27 Feb. An expansion of credit was encouraged by the allocation of $750 m. in government gold for business needs.

RELIEF AND CONSTRUCTION ACT. 21 July. The R.F.C. received authorization to lend $300 m. to states unable to finance economic relief themselves.

FEDERAL HOME LOAN BANK ACT. 22 July. Discount banks for home mortgages were established. The aims were to curtail foreclosures and encourage construction.

"BONUS ARMY." 28–29 July. In June 17,000 veterans camped around Washington to demand cash payment of their bonuses. Gen. Douglas MacArthur commanded troops who forcibly removed 2,000 veterans who had remained through July.

PRESIDENTIAL ELECTION. 8 Nov. The Republicans renominated Hoover and Curtis. The Democrats nominated Gov. Franklin Delano Roosevelt (1882–1945) (N.Y.) and John Nance Garner (Tex.). Both parties advocated cuts in government spending and a balanced budget, but Roosevelt pledged a "New Deal" for Americans and help for the "forgotten man at the bottom of the economic pyramid." Hoover attacked as radicalism ideas for government economic regulation proposed by Roosevelt's "Brains Trust," which included Rexford G. Tugwell and Adolph A. Berle, Jr. Roosevelt (472 electoral votes, 42 states) defeated Hoover (59), and the Democrats took both houses of Congress by substantial margins.

1933

THE NEW DEAL. Between Roosevelt's election and his inauguration the economic crisis became desperate. By 4 Mar. almost every state had closed its banks. On 5 Mar. Roosevelt called a special session of Congress for 9 Mar., and declared a bank holiday until then. Almost at once 75% of the Federal Reserve System banks reopened and stock prices began to rise. The "Hundred Days" session of Congress, 9 Mar.–16 June, produced the following relief and recovery measures:

9 Mar. An Emergency Banking Relief Act approved Roosevelt's emergency actions, enlarged his control of monetary policy, and authorized the Treasury to call in all gold.

20 Mar. An Economy Act, to balance the budget, reduced government salaries and veterans' benefits.

22 Mar. The Beer-Wine Revenue Act legalized and taxed beverages containing 3.2% or more of alcohol.

31 Mar. The Civilian Conservation Corps Reforestation Relief Act provided work for 250,000 young men developing the nation's natural resources.

19 Apr. The U.S. abandoned the gold standard. Stock and commodity prices rose.

12 May. A Federal Emergency Relief Act, administered by Harry L. Hopkins (1890–1946), authorized outright grants to local governments for relief purposes.

12 May. The Agricultural Adjustment Act (AAA) sought to restore prosperity by establishing parity prices for basic commodities based on farmers' 1909–14 purchasing power. It also authorized government subsidies for farmers who voluntarily limited production, and established the Agricultural Adjustment Administration.

18 May. Sen. George W. Norris (Neb.) proposed that the government reopen its First World War power plant at Muscle Shoals, Ala., to service inhabitants of the Tennessee River Valley. Hoover and Coolidge had vetoed the measure, but Roosevelt established the Tennessee Valley Authority (TVA) to sell electricity and fertilizer and develop the area, and serve as a "yardstick" to judge fair power rates.

27 May. A Federal Security Act required that prospective purchasers receive full information on securities issues.

13 June. A Home Owners Refinancing Act sought to save other than farm residences from repossession by refinancing mortgages through the Home Owners Loan Corporation (HOLC).

16 June. The Glass-Steagall (Banking) Act established the Federal Deposit Insurance Corporation (FDIC) to safeguard bank deposits under $5,000.

16 June. The Farm Credit Act provided low-interest, long-term mortgage refinancing by extending short-term production and marketing credits.

16 June. The National Industrial Recovery Act (NIRA) authorized the President to prescribe industrial fair-trade codes, exempt from antitrust legislation, in order to stimulate business. The act guaranteed labor's right to collective bargaining, and established Harold L. Ickes' Public Works Administration to promote recovery through construction programs. The Supreme Court (*Schechter* v. *U.S.,* 1935) declared the National Recovery Administration unconstitutional.

LATER NEW DEAL LEGISLATION. 18 Oct. The Commodity Credit Corporation attempted to raise farm prices by extending loans to enable farmers to retain their crops.

8 Nov.–Mar., 1934. The Civil Works Administration (CWA) put 4 m. jobless to work on government projects.

5 Dec. The 21st Amendment to the Constitution repealed the 18th (Prohibition) Amendment.

1934

30 Jan. The Gold Reserve Act enabled the government to control dollar devaluation by empowering the President to set the value of the dollar in relation to its gold content.

2 Feb. The Export-Import Bank encouraged overseas commerce by extending short- and long-term loans to American exporters.

15 Feb. The Civil Works Emergency Relief Act appropriated $950 m. for civil works and direct relief in fiscal 1935.

28 Mar. Independent Offices Appropriations Act. Congress overrode Roosevelt's veto to restore the expenditures reduced by the 1933 Economy Act.

7 Apr. The Jones-Connally Act and the Jones-Costigan Sugar Act placed additional crops under the AAA.

21 Apr. The Cotton Control (Bankhead) Act provided for compulsory limitation of the cotton crop.

6 June. The Securities Exchange Act created the Securities and Exchange Commission to license stock exchanges and regulate trading in securities.

7 June. A Corporation Bankruptcy Act enabled corporations to reorganize if ⅔ of their creditors agreed.

19 June. The Communications Act established the Federal Communications Commission to regulate interstate and foreign telegraph, cable, and radio communications.

19 June. The Silver Purchase Act, designed to please farm and silver interests, authorized an increase in the Treasury's silver holdings until they reached ⅓ of the value of its gold stocks.

28 June. A Federal Farm Bankruptcy Act (Frazier-Lemke Bankruptcy Act), later declared unconstitutional, 1935, enabled farmers to secure credit extensions.

28 June. The National Housing Act established a Federal Housing Authority (FHA) to encourage home construction.

28 June. The Tobacco Control Act imposed compulsory crop limitations in the tobacco industry.

1935

2ND NEW DEAL. On 4 Jan. a 2nd New Deal, containing social-reform legislation, was promised by Roosevelt.

8 Apr. The Emergency Relief Appropriation Act, relegating direct relief to the states, established Harry L. Hopkins' Works Progress (later "Projects") Administration (WPA) to employ the jobless in a national works program. By 1943 the WPA had employed 8,500,000 individuals in manual labor and the arts.

27 Apr. A Soil Conservation Act established the Soil Conservation Service.

1 May. The Resettlement Administration (RA), under Rexford G. Tugwell, conducted conservation projects and moved poor laborers and farmers to better housing, sometimes in government-built "greenbelt towns."

11 May. The Rural Electrification Administration (REA), intended to bring electricity to isolated rural areas, was founded.

22 May. The Patman Bonus Bill, authorizing cash payment of World War I bonuses, was vetoed as inflationary.

7 June. A National Resources Committee was created to plan the development of America's natural resources.

26 June. The National Youth Administration (NYA), under Aubrey Williams, provided part-time employment for needy school, college, and graduate students.

5 July. The National Labor Relations Act (Wagner-Connery Act) created a National Labor Relations Board (NLRB) and guaranteed workers' rights to organize and bargain collectively.

OPPOSITION TO THE NEW DEAL. An anti-New Deal coalition developed in 1934–35. Business interests established the Liberty League. Dr. Francis E. Townsend's Old Age Revolving Pension Plan, Sen. Huey Long's (La.) and Rev. Gerald L. K. Smith's Share-Our-Wealth program, and Rev. Charles E. Coughlin's National Union for Social Justice also opposed Roosevelt's policies.

SOCIAL SECURITY ACT. 14 Aug. This act established a federal-state system of unemployment insurance financed by a payroll tax, old-age and survivors' insurance financed by a tax on employers and employees, and appropriations to help states pay their own old-age pensions and help the destitute.

BANKING ACT OF 1935. 23 Aug. The ex-officio members were removed from the new 7-man Board of Governors of the Federal Reserve System.

PUBLIC UTILITY HOLDING COMPANY ACT (WHEELER-RAYBURN ACT). 28 Aug. Gas and electricity companies were placed under federal regulation and holding companies had to justify their existence or dissolve.

WAGNER-CROSSER ACT. 29 Aug. Retirement pensions were provided for railroad employees.

GUFFEY-SNYDER BITUMINOUS COAL STABILIZATION ACT. 30 Aug. This act, known as the "little NRA," applied NRA-type codes to the coal industry. It was later, 1936, declared unconstitutional.

REVENUE ACT (WEALTH TAX ACT). 30 Aug. This act increased the tax rate on incomes over $50,000, corporate earnings over $50,000, estates, and gifts.

1936

UNCONSTITUTIONALITY OF THE AAA. On 6 Jan. the AAA was struck down by the Supreme Court.

ADJUSTED COMPENSATION ACT. 24 Jan. This act authorized, over Roosevelt's veto, immediate cash payment of veterans' bonuses.

SOIL CONSERVATION AND DOMESTIC ALLOTMENT ACT. 29 Feb. This act replaced the AAA by granting benefit payments to farmers who conserved soil by restricting production.

REVENUE ACT. 22 June. Among other provisions the act levied an undistributed profits tax on corporate incomes.

MERCHANT MARINE ACT. 26 June. Government subsidies were authorized to develop the U.S. merchant marine.

PRESIDENTIAL ELECTION. 3 Nov. Republicans nominated Gov. Alfred M. Landon (Kan.) and Col. Frank Knox (Ill.); they condemned the New Deal and claimed regulated monopoly had replaced free enterprise, but did not predict repeal of Roosevelt's legislation. Fr. Coughlin's supporters endorsed Republican Representative William Lemke (N.D.) and Thomas C. O'Brien (Mass.) for the Union Party. Democrats renominated Roosevelt and Garner. Roosevelt attacked the "economic royalists" who opposed his policies and won a smashing victory, receiving 27,751,612 popular and 523 electoral votes (46 states) to Landon's 16,681,-913 and 8.

1937

SUPREME COURT FIGHT. 5 Feb.–22 July. The Supreme Court's frequent invalidation of New Deal legislation prompted Roosevelt to suggest increasing its membership to 15 if justices refused to retire at age 70. Opponents attacked

F.D.R.'s attempt to "pack" the Court, and some New Dealers like Sen. Wheeler (Mont.) supported them. Chief Justice Charles E. Hughes' denunciation, 21 Mar., of Roosevelt's claim that more justices were needed to handle the case load and the Court's decisions sustaining New Deal measures, including the Social Security and Wagner Labor Relations Acts, doomed the bill, which had irreparably split Democratic ranks, to languish in committee. Roosevelt appointed 7 justices during the next 4 years through normal procedures.

GUFFEY-VINSON BITUMINOUS COAL ACT. 26 Apr. By this measure the unconstitutional Guffey-Snyder Act was re-enacted, except for its wages-and-hours clause.

BANKHEAD-JONES FARM TENANT ACT. 22 July. Forty-year, low-interest loans were authorized to enable farm tenant laborers and sharecroppers to buy farms.

MILLER-TYDINGS ENABLING ACT. 18 Aug. This act legalized contracts to maintain the resale price of branded nationally advertised products traded in interstate commerce.

NATIONAL HOUSING (WAGNER-STEAGALL) ACT. 1 Sept. The U.S. Housing Authority (USHA) was established to extend 60-year, low-interest loans to local governments for slum clearance.

1938

LUDLOW RESOLUTION. 10 Jan. A resolution put forward by Rep. Louis Ludlow (Ind.) proposed an amendment requiring a national referendum before war could be declared, except if American territories were invaded. Roosevelt opposed and the House returned the resolution to committee.

AGRICULTURAL ADJUSTMENT ACT. 16 Feb. The AAA was reconstituted without the objectionable processors' tax. The Secretary of Agriculture was authorized to set acreage allotments if 2/3 of the farmers agreed to a marketing quota. The act authorized loans based on surpluses

which would be stored until they could be sold at parity.

BUSINESS RECESSION. 14 Apr. Roosevelt expanded the WPA and authorized the Federal Reserve System to follow a loose-money policy to stimulate business.

HOUSE UN-AMERICAN ACTIVITIES COMMITTEE. 26 May. The committee was created to investigate Nazis, Fascists, Communists, and other "un-American" organizations.

REVENUE ACT. 27 May. Passed over Roosevelt's veto, the Revenue Act of 1938 lowered taxes on large businesses and raised them on small ones to stimulate the economy.

TEMPORARY NATIONAL ECONOMIC COMMITTEE. 16 June. The TNEC, headed by Sen. Joseph O'Mahoney (Wyo.), investigated the effects of monopolies on the economy. Its report, 31 Mar., 1941, advocated strengthening the Clayton Act and the FTC and passing legislation prohibiting corporations from acquiring the assets of large competitors.

FAIR LABOR STANDARD ACT (WAGES AND HOURS LAW). 25 June. A 40-hour week was established and also a minimum wage of 40 cents an hour.

CONGRESSIONAL ELECTIONS. 8 Nov. Roosevelt's attempt to "purge" conservative Democratic congressmen was generally unsuccessful, although he ousted Rep. John J. O'Connor (N.Y.). The Democrats lost 7 Senate and 80 House seats.

1939

DEFENSE POLICY. 12 Jan. Roosevelt requested a $525-m. emergency defense appropriation, and later asked for additional funds, 4 Mar. and 29 Apr.

ADMINISTRATIVE REORGANIZATION ACT OF 1939. 3 Apr. This act streamlined governmental bureaucracy, which had proliferated since the early 20th cent. A presidential order, 1 July, created the Federal Security, Federal Works, and Federal Loan Agencies, and another, 8 Sept., reorganized the President's Executive Office.

EMERGENCY RELIEF APPROPRI-ATION ACT. 30 June. Continuous WPA employment was limited to 18 months. Despite Roosevelt's wishes, lack of funds necessitated cutbacks in WPA jobs.

HATCH ACT. 2 Aug. It became illegal for non-policy-making federal office-holders to campaign politically and to take contributions from relief employees.

SOCIAL SECURITY AMEND-MENTS. 10 Aug. The Social Security Act increased the federal contribution to state aid to dependent children, the number of occupations covered, and granted supplementary benefits to aged wives. Social Security Acts in 1950, 1952, 1954, 1956, and 1960 further liberalized the law. (*Cont. p. 598.*)

Latin America in Transition

LATIN AMERICA BETWEEN THE WARS

1914–30

THE NEW POLITICS. Although Latin America remained militarily aloof from World War I, the area could not isolate itself from the war's economic effects. Disruption of former trading patterns led to greater trade with the U.S.A. and stimulated local light manufactures. The change, however, was more apparent than real. The U.S. began to replace Great Britain as principal foreign investor, more than doubling direct private investment, 1914–29 (to $3.5 billion), but Latin America's economy remained largely semicolonial, dependent upon the export of agricultural and subsoil primary products.

The war itself had less political impact than the convergence of long-term social and economic change. Explosively in Mexico and more or less peacefully in Uruguay, Argentina, and Chile, the economic development of 4 decades combined with immigration and urbanization (in the southern countries) to produce a new politics. The urban middle sectors, with the support of awakening working classes, successfully challenged traditional landholding forces for control of the government. Elsewhere in Latin America, where socioeconomic change had been less extensive, established elites maintained their dominance—at least until the depression.

URBANIZATION IN ARGENTINA AND CHILE

	Urban (%)	Pop. (m.)
Argentina:		
1869	24.0	1.7
1895	31.8	4.0
1914	40.4	7.9
Chile:		
1875	17.2	2.1
1895	24.1	2.7
1920	32.2	3.7

NOTE: "Urban" defined as 20,000 pop. or over; based on Philip M. Hauser, ed., *Urbanization in Latin America* (New York, UNESCO, 1961), p. 98.

1930–45

EFFECTS OF THE DEPRESSION. The world depression dramatically demonstrated the vulnerability of Latin America's monocultural economies. In 1929–32 exports were down c. 60%, imports c. 75%. Foreign investment dried up almost completely until the end of World War II; U.S. direct private investment was $3.5 billion in 1929, but only $2.7 billion in 1943. The trade drop directly undercut governmental capabilities by shutting off crucial customs revenues. Latent social problems were sharply exacerbated and suddenly thrust upon traditional political systems quite unprepared to cope with them. The immediate political result almost everywhere was a military coup; only Colombia, Costa Rica, and

Uruguay had civilian-controlled governments in the early 1930's. Economic nationalism and "statism" were the typical response of the reformers to the crisis. The coming of the war, with its increased demand for Latin American raw materials, contained the new pressures for a time. But by the end of the war a new series of revolts signaled the beginnings of an agonizing adjustment to the modern era.

MEXICO

1914–17

THE MEXICAN REVOLUTION. On 20 Nov., 1910, Francisco Madero (1873–1913) launched an essentially liberal political revolt which succeeded in ousting, 25 May, 1911, the dictator Porfirio Díaz. The effect of Madero's assassination, 22 Feb., 1913, by Victoriano Huerta was to destroy central authority and broaden the conflict into a full-scale social revolution, the 1st in the Americas. By late 1915 Venustiano Carranza (1859–1920), together with his able general, Álvaro Obregón (1880–1928), had asserted military control over the other principal regional leaders, Emiliano Zapata (?1877–1919) and Francisco (Pancho) Villa (1877–1923) and secured de facto recognition, 19 Oct., 1915, from the U.S. and 5 Latin American countries. Carranza was elected president, 11 Mar., 1917, ending a 4-year constitutional interregnum. During the conflict the U.S. exacerbated the new Mexican nationalism by clumsy diplomacy, armed intervention at Vera Cruz, 21 Apr.–23 Nov., 1914, and the punitive Pershing expedition, 16 Mar., 1916–5 Feb., 1917.

CONSTITUTION OF 1917. A new constitution, written at Querétaro and reflecting the social as well as the political goals of the revolution, was promulgated, 5 Feb., 1917. Socialistic, nationalist, anticlerical, it was the vision of the new Mexico. Its views that the state should intervene actively in the economy, that property had an inherent social function, and that labor was not a commodity but a way of life were to have great influence elsewhere in Latin America. It struck at the power and property of the church (Art. 130) and established an exclusively, and militantly, secular public elementary educational system (Art. 3). In Art. 123 it encouraged labor union organization and set conditions for wages and hours, etc. Art. 27 provided for the breakup of large estates in favor of small and communal holdings and curbed foreign ownership of land, mines, and oil fields.

1918–34

RULE OF OBREGÓN. President Carranza was deposed, May 1920, by Gen. Obregón (ruled 1920–24), organizer of the last successful coup d'état in modern Mexican history. Subsequent revolts in 1923, 1927, and 1929 were all put down, though Obregón survived the one headed by Adolfo de la Huerta, 1923–24, only with the aid of the U.S. and armed workers and peasants. Obregón presided over a great flowering of cultural nationalism which glorified Mexico's Indian heritage (indigenismo). The minister of education, José Vasconcelos, sponsored muralists such as Diego Rivera, José Clemente Orozco, and David Alfaro Siqueiros, who, like the revolution itself, blended Marxism and indigenismo. Educational "missionaries" were sent out by the thousands to bring modernity to the parochial countryside.

RULE OF CALLES. In an effort to disguise a lack of fundamental reform, President Elías Calles (ruled 1924–34) began a campaign of strident anticlericalism. In the Cristero rebellion the church in effect went on strike for 3 years, performing no sacraments and stirring up rural violence against the government. In 1929 Calles created the National Revolutionary Party (PNR; since 1946, PRI) in an attempt to maintain personal control of the government and various regional elites—without actually succeeding himself in office. In this he was successful until 1934. In subsequent years a unique single-party system developed which, while not allowing democratic alternation in office, did provide stability with some representation and civil liberties.

1934–45

PRESIDENCY OF CÁRDENAS. Although chosen by Calles within the PNR, Lázaro Cárdenas (ruled 1934–40) soon proved as president to be his own man, conciliating the church and emphasizing the economic reform Calles had neglected. Cárdenas, more than any other president, strove to realize the social goals of the revolution. He distributed to peasants almost twice as much land, nearly 50 m. acres, as had been given away by all governments since 1916. Much of this (22.2% of the land area of Mexico by 1940) went into *ejidos,* traditional communal Indian holdings which Cárdenas believed distinctively valuable for agrarian Mexico. He fought for the country's "economic independence" by expropriating the foreign-owned railroads, 23 June, 1937, and oilfields, 18 Mar., 1938. The forbearance of the U.S. on the latter issue under the principles of the Good Neighbor policy (negotiated settlement, 17 Apr., 1942) was largely responsible for the warm ties which in the 1940's replaced the previously acrimonious relations between the 2 countries.

On 30 Mar., 1942, Mexico declared war on the Axis powers and subsequently gave the U.S.A. vital economic support. (*Cont. p. 609.*)

URUGUAY

1914–45

RULE OF BATLLE Y ORDÓÑEZ. During the 19th cent. Uruguay's history was full of civil strife, but José Batlle y Ordóñez (president, 1903–7, 1911–15) led the country to democratic stability through a uniquely peaceful social revolution. He was able to establish a working relationship with his opponents, the rural Blanco Party. His dominant, urban, middle-sector Colorado Party gained civilian control of the military, minimized the influence of the church, and established full civil liberties. Batlle early foresaw the need for a nation to control its own economic development. He instituted high tariffs to protect local industry and began the gradual nationalization of key foreign-dominated structures (railroads, electric power plants, telephone services, meat-packing plants, etc.). The state fostered labor organization and implemented some of the most advanced social security and welfare legislation anywhere in the world at that time. Batlle hoped to create lasting political stability by replacing the office of president with a plural executive of 9 men, an idea derived from his study of Swiss democracy. A modified version of this was embodied in the Constitution of 1 Mar., 1919.

CONSTITUTION OF 1934. President Gabriel Terra (ruled 1931–38) found his powers inadequate to deal with the effects of the depression. He therefore staged a bloodless coup, 1933, and wrote a new constitution, 1934, restoring presidential dominance. He and his successors continued to pass progressive social legislation. (*Cont. p. 606.*)

ARGENTINA

1914–30

IRIGOYEN AND MIDDLE-SECTOR REFORM. The Sáenz Peña law of 1912 made possible the free and representative election which, in 1916, brought Hipólito Irigoyen's party (UCR) to power. Under Irigoyen (ruled 1916–22, 1928–30) the urban middle classes proved no more effective in social reform than the landed *estancieros* had been. Education did improve, literacy rose, and the university reform movement, designed to give students and faculty a greater voice in university affairs, spread from Argentina throughout the continent. But the Radicals neglected fundamental social and economic problems. The government violently suppressed labor unrest during the *Semana Trágica,* Jan. 1919, and in the following decade failed to implement significant labor or welfare legislation. The prosperity derived from cereal and meat exports, begun during World War I, was largely taken for granted, and little thought was given to the need to develop an indigenous industrial base (although the national oil authority, YPF, was established in 1922).

1930–43

CONSERVATIVE RESURGENCE. Ending more than 75 years of civilian rule, Gen. José F. Uriburu deposed the aging Irigoyen, 6 Sept., 1930, amidst economic chaos. President Augustín P. Justo (ruled 1932–38), heading a conservative civilian coalition, revived the economy, but at the cost of dependence on Britain (Roca-Runciman Agreement, May 1933), thus offending Argentinian nationalist sentiment.

1943–45

PERÓN AND MILITARY NATIONALISM. The army returned forcefully to politics when a group of pro-Axis, nationalist officers (GOU) seized the government, 4 June, 1943. Juan Domingo Perón (b. 1895), who as labor minister skillfully built support among the neglected working classes, had gained effective control of a semi-Fascist regime by mid-1944. Argentina was the last Latin American state to declare war on Germany, 27 Mar., 1945. (*Cont. p. 605.*)

CHILE

1914–25

RULE OF ALESSANDRI. Arturo Alessandri Palma (1868–1950) was elected president in 1920 at the head of a distinctively middle-sector reformist coalition. The backlog of social and economic problems (collapse of the nitrate market after 1910, declining real wages, etc.), the dogged obstruction of a malapportioned Senate, plus the ineptitude of his own administration, proved too much for him. After instituting a moderate income tax and a progressive labor code (comparable to those of Mexico and Uruguay), he was forced from office, 1924, by junior military

officers impatient with the slow pace of reform. This was the army's first intervention in Chilean politics for almost a century.

CONSTITUTION OF 1925. In a brief return to office Alessandri pushed through a modern constitution, 18 Sept., 1925, which strengthened the presidency, ended some 35 years of parliamentary dominance, separated church and state, and committed the government to an active role in economic development.

1926–45

IBÁÑEZ DICTATORSHIP. After several years of confusion Col. Carlos Ibáñez (1877–1960) became president (ruled 1927–31). He did not come to power to impede reform but to speed it. His action reflected the changed social composition of the army and anticipated the similar interventions that occurred in Brazil, 1930; Cuba, 1933; and Bolivia, 1936–39, and which became common toward the end of World War II. Benefiting from a large influx of foreign capital and the worldwide prosperity of the late 1920's, Ibáñez carried out extensive public works. His political repressiveness and the effects of the depression brought his downfall.

CONSERVATIVE REGIME OF ALESSANDRI. Following a brief and chaotic "socialist republic," Dec. 1931–Sept. 1932, Alessandri returned to office and restored political stability, 1932–38. His able finance minister, Gustavo Ross, successfully achieved economic recovery, but at the cost of growing social and political unrest.

THE POPULAR FRONT. The Socialists and Communists joined the Radicals to elect Pedro Aguirre Cerda (1879–1941) to the presidency by a narrow margin over Ross, 1938. The European-style Popular Front suffered from internal bickering but managed to beat back pro-Axis pressures and to benefit the lower- and middle-income groups that were its chief support. The Development Corporation (CORFO, 1939) was a major step toward a planned economy. (*Cont. p. 606.*)

BRAZIL

1914-30

THE OLIGARCHICAL REPUBLIC.
From its late birth as a republic, 15 Nov., 1889, to 1930 Brazil was dominated by the powerful landowners (*coroneis*) of the states of Minas Gerais and São Paulo, with significant army influence. For Brazil, an immense and highly regionalized country, urbanization and national unity came more slowly than for the nations to the south. Army revolts in 1922, 1924, and 1927, and a 2-year harassment, 1924–25, by a guerrilla band led by Luis Carlos Prestes indicated strong dissatisfaction with the traditional leadership among reformist junior army officers (*tenentes*). When the overproduction of coffee and the depression produced economic chaos, Getulio Vargas (1883–1954), governor of the state of Rio Grande do Sul, supported by the *tenentes* among others, rebelled, 3 Oct., 1930, and succeeded to the presidency, 3 Nov., 1930.

1930–45

VARGAS AND BRAZILIAN NATIONALISM. During the following 15 years of moderate, personalist dictatorship, Vargas led Brazil along a unique path toward modernity. He held no elections, abolished all parties, 1937, but quadrupled the electorate by 1945. He organized labor for the 1st time, but kept it under close government control. Symbolized by the corporatist (but little-implemented) *Estado Novo* constitution of 1937, the state was at the center of a drive for national integration. Economic independence was to be won by government-sponsored industrialization; tariffs were raised to protect domestic industry; state-financed institutes were founded to control vital commodities (coffee, sugar, cotton, etc.); and a base of heavy industry was begun, epitomized by the national Volta Redonda steel plant, 1942. In 1943 total industrial output reached $1.4 billion ($153 m. in 1920). Although always ambivalent in his attitude toward World War II, Vargas joined the allies and sent troops to Europe. (*Cont. p. 608.*)

BOLIVIA

THE CHACO WAR. A 50-year period of comparative stability and growing tin prosperity was ended by the Chaco War, 1932–35. Great social currents were set in motion, and the mobilization of highland Indians as soldiers began finally to break down their castelike segregation from national life. Bolivia's defeat, at a cost of 60,000 lives, turned junior army officers decisively against the nation's traditional political leadership.

MILITARY RADICALISM. Col. José David Toro (president, 17 May, 1936–14 July, 1937) and the more radical Germán Busch (ruled 1938–39) dominated a period of modernizing military dictatorship, during which oil was nationalized, miners were organized, and attempts were made to establish public control of tin.

VILLARROEL. After a conservative resurgence and increasing agitation on both left and right, Maj. Gualberto Villarroel (ruled Dec. 1943–July 1946), with the aid of the radical Nationalist Revolutional Movement (MNR), established a socialist Perónist-leaning government. (*Cont. p. 606.*)

PARAGUAY

CHACO WAR AND ITS EFFECTS. The most traditional country in South America, Paraguay was little changed by its 3-year conflict with Bolivia over the Chaco, 1932–35. A brief modernizing regime led by Col. Rafael Franco, Feb. 1936–Aug. 1937, which initiated economic nationalism and state intervention, was quickly followed by a return to more conservative authoritarianism. (*Cont. p. 606.*)

PERU

INFLUENCE OF THE APRA. A "Progressive" dictatorship by Augusto B. Leguía (ruled 1919–30) was distinguished chiefly by its (largely U.S.-financed) material prosperity and unenforced social legislation. In 1924 Víctor Raúl Haya de la Torre (b. 1895) founded the Revolutionary Popular Alliance (APRA), which was to be the dominant force in Peruvian politics for the next 40 years, though rarely in power. *Aprismo* was a kind of native socialism which sought to end the "Indian problem" (the exploitation and isolation of the Indian from national society) by glorifying *indigenismo* as the cornerstone of Peruvian (and Latin American) cultural identity. APRA's economic nationalism drew wide support from the urban middle sectors. Victorious in the 1931 presidential election, Haya de la Torre was kept from office and APRA suppressed until the final years of World War II. (*Cont. p. 607.*)

ECUADOR

INSTABILITY AND LACK OF CHANGE. Although the breakdown of cocoa prosperity after 1916 created an economic crisis, Ecuador produced no leaders equal to its problems. Between 1931 and 1940 a succession of 14 men filled the presidency. The Indian remained outside national life. Dictator Carlos Arroyo del Rio (ruled 1940–44) brought some tranquillity, but lost scarce national territory in a disastrous war with Peru, 1942. (*Cont. p. 607.*)

COLOMBIA

CONSTITUTIONALISM. After a predominance which had lasted since 1880, the Conservative Party split in 1930 and allowed the moderate Liberal, Enrique Olaya Herrera (1881–1937), to be elected. The peaceful transfer of power, although rightly distinguished from the coups so common elsewhere in Latin America during these years, in effect involved only a shift within the same ruling stratum.

ALFONSO LÓPEZ AND LIBERAL REFORM. Olaya's successor, Alfonso López Pumarejo (ruled 1934–38, 1942–45), personified an attempt by the most progressive part of the traditional ruling group to meet the social and economic crisis of the times. López' 1936 constitutional amendments echoed the rhetoric (labor code, statism, agrarian reform, etc.) of the Mexican constitution without implementing its substance. Although labor unions were gathered into a national federation (CTC), it was essentially an appendage of the Liberal Party. Opposition to the *Revolución en marcha* within López's own party and from the Conservatives had, by 1938, recaptured the initiative, electing the moderate Eduardo Santos (ruled 1938–42) and causing López to resign early in his second term. (*Cont. p. 607.*)

VENEZUELA

THE LEGACY OF GÓMEZ. The ruthless dictatorship of Juan Vicente Gómez (ruled 1908–35) brought Venezuela some stability and an oil-based prosperity. Stimulated by huge North American, British, and Dutch investments after 1918, Venezuela had by 1928 become the 2nd oil-producing nation in the world. That this wealth was of small benefit to the masses and did not promote economic diversification was of somewhat more concern to Gómez' 2 authoritarian successors—not enough, however, to forestall the rapid growth of nationalist and democratic ideas. (*Cont. p. 607.*)

MIDDLE AMERICA

U.S. DOLLAR DIPLOMACY. The small countries of Central America and the Caribbean were largely dominated by the U.S. under the "international police power" asserted by the Roosevelt Corollary of 6 Dec., 1904. U.S. military interventions and direct occupations (notably in Nicaragua, 1912–25, 1927–33; Haiti, 1915–34; and the Dominican Republic, 1916–24) gave short-run stability but did little to change fundamental conditions or prepare the countries concerned for self-rule. Although the Good Neighbor policy withdrew U.S. troops; renounced interventionism, 1933; and abrogated special controls over Cuba, 1934, and Panama, 1939, its effect, following the older policy, was often to help U.S.-tutored military men to establish long-term dictatorships, e.g., those of Rafael Leonidas Trujillo (1891–1961), Dominican Republic, 1930–61, and Anastasio Somoza (1896–1956), Nicaragua, 1936–56. Repressive regimes also existed in Honduras (Tiburcio Carías Andino, 1932–48) and El Salvador (Maximiliano Hernández Martínez, 1930–44), the downfall of the latter being brought about by a spontaneous general strike. Costa Rica was notable for its stable constitutionalism and peaceful social reform, particularly during the enlightened rule of Ricardo Jiménez (ruled 1924–28, 1932–36).

CUBA. Even after abrogating the right of political intervention, the U.S.A. dominated Cuba economically. By 1929, 29% of all U.S. direct private investment abroad was in Cuba, mostly in sugar. The brief regime of Ramón Grau San Martín, 10 Sept., 1933–15 Jan., 1934, put in power by a junior officers' coup, 5 Sept., 1933, led by Sergeant Fulgencio Batista (b. 1901), threatened U.S. influence momentarily, but was forced out by diplomatic pressure. Batista, who held power for the next 10 years, moved his army-labor-based government gradually to the left, cooperating with the Communist Party. His progressive 1940 constitution, although frequently violated in practice, voiced the aspirations of a new generation. Batista accepted his candidate's defeat in the 1944 election at the hands of Grau San Martín and the *aprista* Auténtico Party.

GUATEMALA. The long-time dictatorship of Gen. Jorge Ubico (ruled 1931–44) was ended, 1 July, 1944, by a general strike in the capital. The victory of junior officers in the ensuing power struggle, 20 Oct., released pent-up social pressures and led to the election of the radical reformer Juan José Arévalo, Dec. 1944. (*Cont. p. 609.*)

The Rise of Nationalism in the Dependent World

SOUTH ASIA

India

1914–26

INDIA IN WORLD WAR I. British policy in India during and immediately after World War I had 2 strands. While the British took steps to suppress all revolutionary activity, they had nevertheless to promise further constitutional reforms leading to eventual self-government because of their ideological position in the war and because of the military exigencies of both recruiting Indians into the army and winning battles. The strands refused to intertwine when nationalists saw that the implementation of the former together with the apparent lack of fulfillment of the latter were oppressive. Nationalists were, however, divided, both in their perception of British policy goals and in the tactics they wished to adopt to achieve self-rule.

On 8 Sept., 1914, the Imperial Legislative Council at Simla expressed loyalty to the British cause and resolved to contribute to war expenses. During the war some 800,000 troops and 400,000 noncombatants participated in the war effort. India also supplied arms, ammunition, and other materials at an annual cost of c. £20 m.

GHADR MOVEMENT. Har Dayl began the Ghadr (Mutiny) Movement in California, U.S.A., by urging Indians resident there to return home and rebel. Early in 1914 it was arranged for a Japanese ship, the *Komagata Maru,* to carry 351 Sikhs and 21 Punjabi Moslems from Hong Kong to Vancouver to test Canadian immigration laws, which made it difficult for relatives of Indians in Canada to join them there. The ship arrived at Vancouver, 23 May, stayed in harbor for 2 months, during which time only a few passengers were admitted to Canada, and was forced to sail for India, arriving 29 Sept. 300 Sikhs refused to board a special train for the Punjab and marched to Calcutta; they were repulsed by force. This incident created an impetus for violence in the Punjab, 1914–15. Several thousand Indians returned home from the U.S. and Canada at this time.

BRITISH COUNTERREVOLUTIONARY LEGISLATION. On 5 Sept., 1914, the Ingress Ordinance was enacted to give the government of India power to jail or restrict to their villages Indians returning from overseas. The Defense of India Act, Mar. 1915, empowered the government to intern alleged revolutionaries and try them by special tribunals.

MONTAGU-CHELMSFORD REFORMS. When Lord Chelmsford (1868–1933) became viceroy, Apr. 1916, he solicited opinions regarding postwar methods of government. The 19 elected members of the Imperial Legislative Council submitted a proposal, Oct. 1916, calling for greater legislative authority and autonomy for the Indian vis-à-vis the British home government. With some changes these proposals were accepted by the Indian National Congress (INC) and by the Moslem League at a joint meeting in Lucknow, Dec. 1916. Included in the joint Congress-League scheme were (1) acceptance of communal electorates for central and provincial legislative councils, and (2) approval of the principle of "weightage," whereby minority communities would have more legislative seats than their population alone justified.

On 8 July, 1918, Montagu and Chelmsford published a report which was to be the basis of the Government of India Act, 23 Dec., 1919. The major elements of their reforms were (1) decentralization of authority, with the provinces receiving control of law and order, some classes of revenue, education, agriculture, and public health; (2) changes in the central government, with the creation of a bicameral legislature consisting of a Council of State with a 5-year life and 60 seats, 27 of which were for government-nominated members, and a Legislative Assembly with a 3-year life and 40 of its 140 seats for government nominees; (3) changes in the composition of the provinces, 5 chief commissioner's provinces being created and 10 governor's provinces (including Burma which, following the 1935 consti-

tution, was separated from India in 1937) ; (4) the principle of dyarchy in the provinces, whereby the governor had some "reserved" powers, e.g., control of law and order, land revenue, canals, and finance, while the legislative councils acquired jurisdiction over "transferred" functions, e.g., education, agriculture, and public health; and (5) the extension of communal representation to include the Sikhs in the Punjab, Marathas in Bombay, non-Brahmins in Madras, and Europeans, Anglo-Indians, and Christians.

Bal Gangadhar Tilak, who controlled the INC by 1917, attacked the proposed reforms mainly because of the retention of overarching power by the governor general. Moderates who approved the report withdrew from the INC and, under the presidency of Surrendranath Bannerjee (1848–1925), held the 1st session of the All-Indian Conference of Moderates (changed to the National Liberal Federation of India, 1921) at Bombay, 1 Nov., 1918.

ROWLATT ACT. 18 Mar., 1919. Whereas the Montagu-Chelmsford Report seemed inadequate, at best, to Indian nationalists, the Rowlatt Act (after Sir Sidney Rowlatt, the British judge who chaired a Sedition Committee which reported on 19 July, 1918) antagonized almost all Indians. The act prolonged the wartime legal devices by which suspected revolutionaries could be interned and tried before a court of 3 High Court judges with no appeal. The INC had denounced the report, Dec. 1918.

GANDHI AND "SATYAGRAHA." Mohandas K. Gandhi (1869–1948), who returned to India from South Africa, 9 Jan., 1915, helped to recruit soldiers for the army during the war. Not yet a powerful figure in the INC, he initiated early in 1915 his 1st national *Satyagraha* (lit., "truth-force") campaign, aimed against the Rowlatt Act and other repressive laws, including the salt-tax law and prohibitions on some literature. The campaign opened with a nonviolent *hartal* (general strike) in Delhi, 30 Mar., and in other cities, 6 Apr. It consisted of mass nonco-operation with the government of India and civil disobedience against selected laws by those who had made the special *Satyagraha* pledge and had observed a 24-hour fast. The *hartal* was generally successful in closing down shops, but violence erupted in Delhi, Ahmedabad, Lahore, and Amritsar, as well as in several smaller towns.

AMRITSAR MASSACRE. At Amritsar, 9 Apr., the government arrested 2 INC leaders, provoking mob violence, 10 Apr. On 12 Apr., Gen. Edward H. Dyer arrived to take command. He banned public meetings, but the order was not widely publicized. On 13 Apr. a crowd gathered at Jallianwalla Bagh, a closed-in, courtlike area with few exits, to hear speeches. Without first warning the meeting to disperse, Dyer ordered his soldiers to open fire on the crowd, and about 379 were killed and 1,200 wounded. Martial law was imposed, and Dyer ordered all Indians to crawl when passing along a lane where an Englishman had been killed.

NON-CO-OPERATION. Gandhi won his first fight for control of the INC at Amritsar, Dec. 1919. He persuaded the INC, against Tilak's objections, to support the Montagu-Chelmsford reforms, which had been passed the previous day. However, the leniency of the recommendations of a commission appointed to inquire into the Amritsar Massacre, Mar. 1920, which merely censured Dyer, and the approval given Dyer's action by the House of Lords in Britain, repelled Gandhi. He turned to active nonco-operation, initially in conjunction with the Moslem Khilafat movement led by Mohammed and Shaukat Ali with the aim of persuading the British to amend the peace imposed on the Ottoman Empire.

The Non-Co-operation Movement began 1 Aug., 1920, and consisted of a boycott of British courts, schools, goods, and the Nov.–Dec. 1920 elections held under the 1919 Government of India Act. The movement was generally successful so far as the electoral boycott was concerned; some 75% of the electorate abstained. However, Gandhi canceled, 8 Feb., 1922, a planned civil disobedience campaign in Bordeli county in the Bombay Presidency, when he learned that on 5 Feb. an Indian crowd in Chouri Chaura, United Provinces, had killed police who had fired on them. By this time the Non-Co-operation Movement was dying. Without the threat of mass civil disobedience the government felt safe in arresting Gandhi, 10 Mar. He was tried at Ahmedabad, 18 Mar., for writing seditious editorials in *Young India* (19 Sept. and 15 Dec., 1921, and 23 Feb., 1922) and sentenced to 6 years in prison.

GROWTH OF INC MEMBERSHIP. The INC was restructured to enhance the mass character of its political activity, while facilitating centralized control. In Dec. 1920 it not only ratified its Sept. decision to nonco-operate but also, at Gandhi's urging, transformed its constitution to allow for mass participation. 21 Provincial Congress Committees (PCC's), based on linguistic divisions, were created, their members to be elected respectively by district, town, and village committees. An All-India Congress Committee (AICC), which theoretically was to conduct business between the annual sessions and to elect the real decision-making body, the Working Committee, was to be composed of delegates of the PCC's. The appeal to the masses was heightened by a change in the INC goal from "self-government within the Empire" to "*swaraj . . . by all legitimate and peaceful means*," thus making a Hindi word the key word. Because of this obvious appeal to Hindus, M. A. Jinnah (1876–1948) left the INC.

1927–39

SIMON COMMISSION. Sir John Simon (1873–1954), chairman of the Indian Statutory Commission, arrived in India early in 1928 to study the functioning of the 1919 constitution and to recommend improvements. Because his 7-man commission excluded Indians, the INC, at its Madras session in 1927, had decided to boycott it and organize *hartals* in the major cities as the members of the commission visited them.

NEHRU REPORT. An All-Parties Conference, Aug. 1928, adopted a report drafted by Motilal Nehru (1861–1931), which proposed the creation of 4 Moslem provinces, the retention of a strong central government, and the acceptance of dominion status within the British Empire. Dominion status was disapproved of by leftists like Jawaharlal Nehru (1889–1964) and Subas Bose (1897–1945). In Dec. 1928 the INC at Calcutta accepted a compromise resolution submitted by Gandhi, who called for a mass civil disobedience movement if Britain did not grant India independence by Dec. 1929.

At a meeting in Lahore, Dec. 1929, the INC, insisting on *purna swaraj* ("full independence"), called for a boycott of the legislatures and civil disobedience campaigns as decided upon by the AICC. Within a short time 172 Congress members had resigned from the central and provincial legislatures.

SALT MARCH. 12 Mar., 1930. Gandhi, with 78 followers, began the "Salt March" of 241 miles from Ahmedabad to Dandi, on the Arabian Sea, where, 5 Apr., he took salt from the sea, thus violating the salt-tax law. Both the method and the goal had mass appeal, and widespread boycotts of British goods and civil disobedience, including several instances of violence, followed. The government arrested some 60,000 persons, including the Nehrus and Gandhi, and initiated piecemeal measures to quell the agitation.

DELHI PACT. 5 Mar., 1931. By this pact Gandhi agreed with the viceroy to discontinue civil disobedience in return for efforts to rectify some of the repression resulting from nationalist agitation. Without the prior consent of the INC Working Committee Gandhi accepted the principle of a federal constitution (rather than the unitary constitution proposed by the Nehru Report). This federal constitution had been accepted by the 1st Round Table Discussion in London, 1930, at which the INC was not represented. The Delhi Pact achieved at least a moratorium during which the government and the INC could bargain.

2ND ROUND TABLE DISCUSSION. Gandhi was the sole INC representative at the 2nd Round Table Discussion, 1931, attended by British officials, Indian princes, and representatives of communal groups. The talks ended in a deadlock over the question of communal representation.

NO-TAX CAMPAIGN. In the United Provinces, Autumn 1931, a "no-tax campaign" was mounted by peasants who claimed they were unable to pay even half the usual land revenue tax. They were supported by the U.P. Congress Committee, and the protest spread to the North-West Frontier Province and Bengal. The government arrested all INC leaders, Dec. 1931–Jan. 1932, and passed emergency acts to halt the campaign.

FAST BY GANDHI. On 17 Aug., 1932, Prime Minister Ramsay MacDonald announced that the new constitution proposed for India would provide separate electorates for Harijans (untouchables). Arguing that this would only increase the rift between Harijans and caste Hindus, Gandhi stated from Yeravda Prison, 13 Sept., that, beginning 20 Sept., he would fast unto death unless the decision was reversed. On 26 Sept. his fast ended when the British cabinet approved a compromise between him and the Harijan leader B. R. Ambedkar, whereby Harijan representatives would be elected to reserved seats by the entire Hindu electorate after having been nominated by Harijans alone. If he had not done so before, by his fast Gandhi created a charismatic relationship between most Hindus and himself. He was released from prison, 8 May, 1933.

GOVERNMENT OF INDIA ACT. 4 Aug., 1935. This act, comprising the last constitution given India by the British, introduced the principle of federation: (1) the provinces were granted autonomy, and 3 lists of subjects—provincial, central, and concurrent—defined the limits of their authority; (2) when princes governing one half of the population of princely states acceded to the union, the central legislature would take responsibility for defense and foreign relations in those states. The suffrage was extended to about a sixth of the adult population, communal representation was retained, and reserved powers were granted to the governor general and the provincial governors. Since responsible government was not granted, the INC and the Moslem League were hostile to the new constitution.

ELECTIONS OF 1937. Elections held in the autumn of 1937 were contested mainly by the Moslem League and the INC. Both had organizational structures capable of reaching the masses. The INC captured 7 provincial governments, including the N.W.F.P., a Moslem majority province, but failed to win majorities in the Punjab, Bengal, Sind, and Assam. The elections demonstrated the weakness of the League's appeal to Moslems, and Nehru's reneging on a tacit agreement to form a coalition government with the League in the U.P. demonstrated to Jinnah the precarious position of a minority party in a parliamentary system. In Oct. 1937, in a presidential address, Jinnah made clear that the League must struggle against the INC.

1939–45

INDIA IN WORLD WAR II. On 3 Sept., 1939, without consulting the Legislative Assembly, the viceroy declared India a participant in the war. In Oct., INC ministers resigned after the viceroy had refused to promise independence immediately after the war in return for INC support of the war effort.

On 22 Mar., 1940, the Moslem League passed the "Lahore Resolution," demanding a separate Moslem state. Taking a pacifist line, Gandhi, 13 Oct., 1940, called for individual *satyagraha* by INC leaders to protest the war. About 14,000 were arrested.

With the Japanese threatening Burma and eastern India, Prime Minister Churchill sent Sir Stafford Cripps (1889–1952) to India, Mar. 1942, with an offer of immediate Indianization of the Executive Council, an Indian constituent assembly elected by provincial legislative assemblies, optional dominion status after the war, and the right of a province to secede from the union. The latter was an obvious sop to the League and encouraged Jinnah to strengthen his demand for partition. On 11 Apr. the Congress Working Committee rejected the Cripps offer because it recognized separatism and failed to give Indians control of defense. According to Gandhi, the offer was "a post-dated cheque on a failing bank."

On 8 Aug., 1942, the AICC passed the "Quit India Resolution," promising support for the war in return for independence. It sanctioned mass civil disobedience. On 9 Aug. the members of the Working Committee were arrested. News of the arrests prompted widespread demonstrations and violence, which the government dealt with by emergency measures, including the outlawing of the INC. This enabled the Communist Party to assert control over the hitherto INC-dominated All-India Trade Union Conference, and helped the League to expand its membership on a mass basis.

Assuming that the war with Japan would last at least another year, the viceroy called a conference, 25 June, 1945, at Simla of 21 Indian leaders, including the Congress Working Committee and the heads of the Moslem League, to work out an immediate political settlement. On Jinnah's insistence that the League nominate all the Moslem members, the conference foundered, 14 July. (*Cont. p. 564.*)

Ceylon

1914–25

COMMUNAL VIOLENCE. Fighting between Buddhists and Moslems erupted in Kandy and Gompala, 28 May, 1915, due to the playing by Buddhists of music in front of mosques. With the spread of violence into 5 provinces, the governor declared martial law, 2 June. Although the agitation was quelled within a week, martial law, including courts-martial for civilians, remained in force for 3 months. D. S. Senanayake (1884–1952), a western-educated Buddhist, was among those mistakenly arrested.

CEYLON REFORM LEAGUE. In 1917 educated Tamils and Sinhalese united in the Ceylon Reform League, with Ponnonbalam Arunachalom (1853–1924) as 1st president. In Dec. 1917 the League presented to the British colonial secretary a scheme of constitutional reform: (1) abolition of nominated members of the Legislative Council; (2) an elected majority with an elected speaker; and (3) reduction of the number of official members of the Executive Council and introduction of more elected, non-official members.

CEYLON NATIONAL CONGRESS. The 1st session of the Ceylon National Congress, which incorporated the Reform League and the National Association, was held, 11 Dec., 1918, under the presidency of Sir Ponnonbalam Arunachalom. It pressed for constitutional reforms.

CONSTITUTION OF 1920. Without making significant reforms the constitution introduced in 1920 increased to 37 the number of seats in the Legislative Council. Government officials and nominated members, however, still retained a majority. Congress rejected the constitution as inadequate, but co-operated to make it function in return for a promise by Sir William Manning (gov. 1918–25) that revisions would be considered in a year. At this time the complexion of the Congress changed because of the resignation of most of its Tamil members, who claimed that the Sinhalese had allowed Britain to impose a constitution that failed to make provision for Tamil representation in the Western Province. In Jaffna the Tamil association "Mahajana Sabha," with the goal of adequate Tamil representation, was founded.

CONSTITUTION OF 1924. The Legislative Council was expanded to 49, with a majority of unofficial, elected members, 23 of whom were elected by territorial constituencies and 11 by communal electorates (3 Europeans, 2 burghers, 2 Indian Tamils, 3 Moslems, 1 Western Province Ceylon Tamil). While there was no significant change in the composition of the Executive Council, members of the Finance Committee did gain the right to discuss with department heads their budgets, thus acquiring some power to participate in the executive machinery.

1926–45

CONSTITUTION OF 1931. A royal commission chaired by the Earl of Donoughmore (1875–1948) visited Ceylon, Nov. 1927–Jan. 1928, to consult with various groups on the functioning of the 1924 constitution. In its reports, submitted to the British government in July and published in Sept. 1928, the commission recommended significant changes, which were incorporated in the 1931 constitution. Elections based on territorial constituencies completely replaced communal representation, on the grounds that the latter only reinforced social stratification. Universal adult suffrage was instituted. The 1931 elections were, however, boycotted by Tamil leaders, with the result that the 4 Northern Province seats were uncontested.

Under the 1931 constitution important social legislation relating to education, public health, and unemployment was passed. In Mar. 1933, to correct the inequality in the civil service, in which out of 123 members in 1928 only 35 were Ceylonese, the State Council passed a resolution restricting entry into the civil service to Ceylonese unless no Ceylonese had the qualifications to fill a particular post. By that time the University College, founded in 1921, was graduating students with a British education. In 1934 the State Mortgage Bank was established so that landowners could borrow money at low interest. In 1938 the Bank of Ceylon was set up.

LANKA SAMU SAMAJA. The Lanka Samu Samaja Party (LSSP) was founded, 18 Dec., 1935, by young socialists—in particular, by Phillip Gunawardena, N. M. Perera, Colvin de Silva, and Leslie Goonewardena—who had been studying in Britain and the U.S.A. at the beginning of the depression. Although during the 1932 Spinning and Weaving Mills Strike they had failed to take over the leadership of the labor movement from H. E. Goonesinha, who organized urban workers in the 1920's and founded the Ceylon Labour Party, 1927, they worked hard in the countryside during the 1934–35 malaria epidemic. The LSSP, which won 2 seats in the State Council in 1936, was the only political party in Ceylon with any semblance of discipline or mass appeal. In 1939 it expelled its Stalinist members, who founded the Communist Party of Ceylon in 1944.

CEYLON IN WORLD WAR II. On 5 Sept., 1939, Gov. Sir Andrew Caldecott announced to the State Council that Ceylon would participate in the British war effort. The Council expressed its loyalty, and in June 1940 voted Rs. 5 m. for war expenses. On 5 Mar., 1942, Adm. Sir Geoffry Layton (1884–1964) became commander in chief, and exercised all necessary political power.

SOULBURY COMMISSION. On 26 May, 1943, the British government announced that a draft constitution for after the war and leading toward responsible government would be examined by a commission. By Feb. 1944 this draft constitution had been drawn up, and the colonial secretary disclosed, 5 July, 1944, that a commission would go to Ceylon to discuss it with various groups. When the Soulbury Commission arrived, 22 Dec., however, the Board of Ministers boycotted it because its members declined to base their report solely on the Board's draft. In July 1945 the Commission's report was presented to the colonial secretary, who then negotiated for its acceptance with the Ceylonese nationalist leader, D. S. Senanayake. On 31 Oct. a White Paper was published, incorporating both the Soulbury Commission's and Senanayake's constitutional proposals. The main features of the constitution finally promulgated were (1) retention of universal suffrage, (2) representation of constituencies delimited by both territory and population, (3) retention by the governor general of responsibility for defense and foreign affairs, (4) responsible cabinet government, and (5) establishment of a House of Representatives, composed of 95 elected members and 6 representatives of special interests, and of a Senate of 30 members, 15 elected by the House and 15 nominated by the governor general. (*Cont. p. 564.*)

SOUTHEAST ASIA

Netherlands East Indies

1914–27

COMMUNISM VS. SAREKAT ISLAM. In 1914 a Dutchman founded the Indies Social-Democratic Association, the first Marxist organization in Southeast Asia. Since a European-led party attracted little Indonesian support, it pressed for a common front with the more popular Sarekat Islam (SI). In 1920 the Association changed its name to the Indonesian Communist Union (later PKI), which joined the Comintern the following year. Friction between the PKI and SI became so serious, however, that a split developed. The Communists then created mass organizations to rival those of SI and temporarily emerged as the vanguard of the Indonesian nationalist movement.

OPENING OF THE VOLKSRAAD. The Volksraad (People's Council), reluctantly created by the Dutch, 1918, was not a true representative body; it had a European majority, and its powers were limited to offering advice which the government could ignore. Although more Indonesian delegates were chosen during the 1920's, the Volksraad's powers remained very slight.

ABORTIVE COMMUNIST REVOLUTION. From the time they split with SI, the Communists pursued extremist tactics that culminated in uprisings in Java and Sumatra, 1926–27. Lack of popular support and splits within the Communist leadership assured the defeat of the revolts. The Dutch then outlawed the PKI and deported or imprisoned most of its members. SI was thus left as the main vehicle of the Indonesian nationalist movement.

1928–45

SUKARNO AND THE NATIONALIST PARTY. Sukarno (b. 1902), a Dutch-trained Javanese engineer, founded the Indonesian Nationalist Party, 1929, with the aim of rallying all nationalist groups into a large nonco-operation movement. However, the Dutch quickly arrested Sukarno. Early in the 1930's Sutan Sjahrir (b. 1909) and Mohammed Hatta (b. 1902) sponsored a moderate Socialist Party, but they, too, were imprisoned.

PERIOD OF JAPANESE RULE. Having occupied the Netherlands East Indies, 1942, the Japanese freed Sukarno, Hatta, and Sjahrir. Sukarno and Hatta opted for co-operation with the Japanese, while Sjahrir's group organized an underground resistance movement. In Sept. 1943, as the tide of war turned against the Japanese, they sought popular support by naming Sukarno to head a Central Advisory Council in Java. In 1944 Japan made further concessions, including a qualified promise of Indonesian independence. An Independence Preparatory Committee was formed, Aug. 1945. (*Cont. p. 568.*)

Malaya

1914–29

CHINESE RADICAL ACTIVITY. By 1920 Chinese immigrants into the Malay States and Straits Settlements had organized branches of the Kuomintang, which adopted an anti-British stance during the period of Kuomintang-Communist cooperation in China. Chinese Communist agents helped to create radically oriented youth and labor organizations in Malaya. After the Kuomintang-Communist split in China in 1927, however, the Kuomintang branches in Malaya could no longer provide cover for Communist activity.

1930–45

ECONOMIC DEPRESSION AND COMMUNIST REVIVAL. A Malayan Communist Party (MCP) was founded in 1930, most of its members being Chinese. During the difficult post-depression years the Communists fomented numerous strikes. In 1937 the MCP, following the new line of its Chinese counterpart, called for a united front of all Malayans against the Japanese.

ADMINISTRATIVE DECENTRALIZATION. A major step toward governmental decentralization occurred in 1936, when the office of federal secretary was created. The secretary's duties consisted of liaison and co-ordination among the states. Each federated state remained a British protectorate under the high commissioner. Beneath the federal structure were state governments consisting of a sultan or raja, a resident and a State Council with an advisory role.

JAPANESE OCCUPATION. Efforts by Japanese occupation forces, 1942–45, to stir up Malayan hostility against the British proved largely fruitless. Communists formed the backbone of the underground resistance movement. As Japanese military fortunes decayed, the occupation authorities vainly sought popular support by creating a Malayan Consultative Council at Singapore. (*Cont. p. 569.*)

Burma

1914–29

CONSTITUTIONAL CHANGES. In 1923 Burma became a "governor's province" on the Indian pattern. Burmese ministers responsible to the Legislative Council were to handle such issues as education and public health, while the governor of Burma retained veto power over matters of defense policy, law and order, finance, and revenue. The People's Party, headed by U Ba Pe, became the dominant group in the Legislative Council. The party advocated educational preparation of the people for self-government, rapid Burmanization of the public services, and curtailment of foreign economic exploitation. By the mid-1920's most Burmese leaders favored full responsible government and separation from India.

1930–45

THAKIN PARTY. Frustration over inadequate education and job opportunities led a militant group of Burmese students to create the nationalistic Thakin Party, 1930. Five years later this party joined with another organization to form the "We Burmans Association," whose members addressed one another as *thakin* (master) to symbolize their aim of being masters in their own country. Led by Aung San (1914–47), the Thakins staged a successful student strike at the University of Rangoon, 1936.

GOVERNMENT OF BURMA ACT. The Government of India Act, 1935, promised the complete separation of Burma from India on 1 Apr., 1937. A Government of Burma Act, 2 Aug., 1935, provided for a cabinet led by a prime minister and responsible to a bicameral legislature. The governor remained solely responsible for finance, defense, foreign affairs, and minority groups, but was to act on the advice of his ministers on all other issues. Dr. Ba Maw was chosen prime minister, but by 1939 student strikes, industrial strife, and opposition pressure forced him to resign. His party then joined with the Thakins to form a "Freedom Bloc," which he headed. The Bloc's anti-British and antiwar agitation led to the jailing of Ba Maw and others, 1940.

JAPANESE INVASION. A puppet government headed by Ba Maw was established by the Japanese invaders, 1942, and the following year he became president of an "independent" Burma. By that time, most of the Thakins had joined an underground resistance movement. In 1944 Aung San and his followers secretly organized a nationwide Anti-Fascist People's Freedom League (AFPFL). Ba Maw's escape with the retreating Japanese armies into Thailand left Aung San and the AFPFL as the leading political force in Burma. (*Cont. p. 570.*)

Indochina

1914–40

INDOCHINA IN WORLD WAR I. French wartime policies, particularly unfulfilled promises of democracy for Indochina and the recruitment of Vietnamese youth for military service in Europe, intensified nationalist feelings among the Vietnamese. Ho Chi Minh (b. ?1891) traveled to France during the war; there he joined the French Socialist Party and, 1920, became a charter member of the French Communist Party. Meanwhile French opposition to the demands of moderate political parties in Indochina paved the way for extremist groups there. **FOUNDING OF THE COMMUNIST PARTY.** In 1930 Ho Chi Minh directed the merger of several Communist factions into an Indochinese Communist Party. Communism was not the only threat to French colonial rule in Indochina, however; the Nationalist Annamite

Party, organized in 1927, pursued a terrorist policy culminating in an ill-prepared mutiny at Yenbay, 9–11 Feb., 1930. Severe French countermeasures annihilated the party, but anti-French activities continued.

1941–45

FOUNDING OF THE VIETMINH. Ho Chi Minh founded the Communist-dominated Vietminh, 1941, as an instrument to drive the French from Indochina. In an effort to rally all anti-imperialist groups around the Vietminh, Ho eschewed Communist propaganda and spoke only of a united, independent Indochina. French intransigence allowed Ho and the Communists to gain control of the Vietnamese nationalist movement.

REPUBLIC OF VIETNAM. Originally an anti-French organization, the Vietminh moved to the allied side after Hitler's invasion of the Soviet Union, 1941. In 1943 the French promised autonomy for Indochina within the French Union, but by this time the Vietnamese nationalists were fully committed to independence. At the end of 1944 a Vietnam Liberation Army was formed to wage guerrilla warfare against the Japanese. When the Japanese ousted the French, Mar. 1945, the emperor of Annam, Bao Dai (ruled 1932–45), declared the country's independence. Ho Chi Minh ignored him. Shortly after the Japanese surrender, Ho convened a congress of the Vietminh and was named head of the Vietnam People's Liberation Committee. On 25 Aug., 1945, Bao Dai abdicated, and on 2 Sept. Ho proclaimed the Republic of Vietnam with a Provisional Government at Hanoi. Although the French reoccupied Saigon, the southern Vietnamese countryside remained largely in the hands of nationalist guerrillas. (*Cont. p. 567.*)

Philippines

1914–45

JONES LAW. Promising independence to the Philippines as soon as stable government could be established, the U.S. government's Jones Law, 29 Aug., 1916,

accorded the islands substantial autonomy. Executive power was vested in a governor general, legislative prerogatives in a
bicameral body, and judicial power in a
Supreme Court. Despite the retention of
some reserved powers by the U.S.A., from
this time onward the Filipinos effectively
controlled their domestic affairs.

**TYDINGS-McDUFFIE ACT. 24 Mar.,
1934.** Passed by the U.S. Congress, the
Tydings-McDuffie Act called for creation
of a Commonwealth of the Philippines
on 4 July, 1936, to be followed 10 years
later by an independent republic. During
the decade of the Philippine Commonwealth, U.S. forces would remain in the
islands and Washington would control
foreign relations and defense. Headed by
Manuel Quezon (1878–1944) as president
and Sergio Osmeña (1878–1961) as vice-
president, the commonwealth was essentially a one-party state, since no opposition parties possessed significant support.

JAPANESE OCCUPATION. When
Japanese forces seized Manila, 1942,
Quezon's government escaped to Australia. In Oct. 1943 Japan proclaimed an
"independent" republic of the Philippines, headed by puppet President José
P. Laurel. The Filipinos created a resistance movement, whose backbone in
Luzon was the Communist Hukbalahap
organization. Quezon's government in
exile later moved to Washington, where
Quezon died, Aug., 1944, and was succeeded by Osmeña. (*Cont. p. 630.*)

Siam (Thailand)

1914–32

SIAM IN WORLD WAR I. Chulalongkorn's successor, King Vajiravudh (ruled
1910–25), personally sympathized with the
allies in World War I. However, popular
anti-French sentiment and a pro-German
faction in the army prevented him from
declaring war on Germany until 1917,
when Siamese protests against submarine
warfare tactics were rebuffed. Adherence
to the winning side gained Siam many
diplomatic benefits, the most important
being membership in the League of Nations and abolition of extraterritorial

treaties with western powers during the
1920's.

REIGN OF PRAJADHIPOK. King
Prajadhipok (ruled 1925–35) faced serious
economic problems bred by his predecessor's fiscal mismanagement and aggravated by the depression. A series of
austerity measures, particularly the prun-
ing of the civil service and salary cuts
among junior Siamese officials, many of
whom had returned from European study
with an aversion to monarchy, helped to
pave the way for the 1932 revolution.

REVOLUTION OF 1932. Pridi
Banomyong, a law professor, became the
leader of discontented factions in Siam
and, with military assistance, seized control of Bangkok in a bloodless coup, 24
June, 1932. The king bowed to a constitution which severely curtailed his powers. Pridi's People's Party took over the
government but named P'ya Manopakorn
as prime minister to placate conservative
groups. A new constitution promulgated
in Dec. 1932 reflected the conservative
influence in the government and restored
some of the powers the king had lost 6
months earlier.

1933–45

RISE OF P'IBUN SONGGRAM. Competition between Pridi and P'ya led the
latter to publicize his rival's program for
a planned economy as Communistic.
Pridi was forced into exile, but returned
shortly afterward following a coup by his
supporters. Toward the end of 1933 the
king's cousin led an abortive military
revolt in Bangkok. Although the king
himself remained neutral, rumors insisted
that he had given moral and financial
backing to the rebels. The government
became divided between followers of
P'ibun Songgram, who had restored order
after the abortive military coup, and
those of Pridi. P'ibun gained the upper
hand and became prime minister, 1938.
The hallmark of his regime was intense
nationalism marked by restrictive measures against aliens, reservation of certain
occupations for Siamese, patriotic propaganda, and, symbolically, a change in the

country's name from Siam to Thailand in 1939.

THAILAND IN WORLD WAR II. P'ibun's government developed close economic ties with Japan and signed a pact with the Japanese, Dec. 1940, in the belief that they would win the war. Thailand declared war against the U.S.A. and Britain, 1942, but P'ibun's pro-Japanese policy proved unpopular and he was forced to resign, 1944, when Japan's defeat became certain. Meanwhile Pridi had organized an underground movement which maintained secret liaison with a Free Thai Movement abroad. Once P'ibun fell, Thailand was free to seek accommodation with the western powers. (*Cont. p. 630.*)

THE MIDDLE EAST

Turkey

1914–23

TURKEY AFTER WORLD WAR I. By the armistice signed on 30 Oct., 1918, the government of the Ottoman Empire, discredited by defeat, placed the lands it had ruled virtually at the mercy of the allies. British and French forces landed in Anatolia and occupied it temporarily, Jan. 1919. With Anglo-French encouragement the Greeks landed at Izmir, 14 May, 1919. Resistance to these incursions led to the formation of Societies for the Defense of Rights which, under the leadership of Kemal Pasha (1881–1938), later known as Atatürk, set themselves up in opposition to the government in Constantinople.

ESTABLISHMENT OF THE TURKISH REPUBLIC. On 23 July, 1919, a congress was held at Erzerum which formulated a program, known as the "National Pact," for an integrated Moslem Turkey and resistance to the partition of its territory. The national legislature adopted this pact, 28 Jan., 1920. The British, disturbed at the political complexion of the new legislature, reoccupied Constantinople, Mar. 1920. On 23 Apr. Kemal organized a Grand National Assembly in Ankara, setting up a provisional government and declaring the sultan a "captive" of the allies. The signing of the Treaty of Sèvres, 10 Aug., 1920, by which Turkey was obliged to give up all non-Turkish provinces of the empire as well as a good deal of territory in Anatolia, increased nationalist resistance to the old regime, and on 1 Nov., 1922, the sultanate was abolished and Turkey declared a republic. A new peace treaty was signed, 24 July, 1923, incorporating Turkish aims as stated in the National Pact and abolishing the Capitulations.

1924–45

REFORMS OF KEMAL. Sweeping changes were made in Turkey under the leadership of Kemal. On 13 Oct., 1923, the capital was moved from Istanbul (name changed from Constantinople, 1930) to Ankara, indicating the new Turkish orientation of the country. On 3 Mar., 1924, the caliphate was abolished and Atatürk elected president of the Republic. A new constitution, 20 Apr., 1924, stated that Turkey was an Islamic state, but this article was expunged in 1928. The drive toward modernization and westernization led to measures such as the banning of the traditional headgear, the fez, 25 Nov., 1925, and the replacement of the Islamic by the Gregorian calendar, 26 Dec., 1925. By 1926 the law of the land had been secularized to a great degree with the adoption of an Italian penal code, a Swiss civil code, and German commercial law. On 3 Nov., 1928, the Latin alphabet was adopted in place of the Arabic one, and an effort was made to eliminate Arabic and Persian words from the vocabulary. Women were ordered to unveil and in Dec. 1934 received the vote. A law of 28 June, 1934, made the adoption of Turkish surnames compulsory by 1 Jan., 1935. The new regime involved itself closely with the economic development of the country by means of a series of 5-year plans, the first of which was issued 9 Jan., 1934. Atatürk died on 10 Nov., 1938, and was succeeded as president by Ismet Inönü (b. 1884), a close associate.

TURKEY IN WORLD WAR II. On 19 Oct., 1939, Turkey signed a treaty of alliance with Britain and France, but remained officially neutral in World War II until 23 Feb., 1945, when she declared war on Germany. (*Cont. p. 620.*)

Persia (Iran)

1914–45

INTERNATIONAL RELATIONS. British troops occupied parts of Persia during World War I, although the country was nominally neutral. On 9 Aug., 1919, an agreement was signed putting the country under preferential treaty relations with Britain and providing for a British loan of £2 m. The Majlis (legislature), however, refused to ratify the agreement, and it never came into effect. In May 1920 a Soviet republic, Gilan, was set up on the southern shore of the Caspian Sea, but it collapsed after the withdrawal of Red Army troops, Oct. 1921.

On 16 May, 1928, a treaty with Britain was signed, but in 1932 relations between the 2 countries became strained due to the shah's cancellation of the concession granted the Anglo-Persian Oil Co. The case came before the League of Nations and was finally settled by a new agreement, 29 Apr., 1933, which gave a larger share of oil profits to Persia.

RULE OF REZA KHAN. On 21 Feb., 1921, Col. Reza Khan (1877–1944) took over the government, and on 26 Feb. signed an agreement with Russia. Reza Khan remained the foremost power in the country, first as minister of war, then as prime minister. On 31 Oct., 1925, the Majlis deposed the shah and elected Reza Khan in his place, 13 Dec. The new shah was an admirer of Atatürk and attempted, on a somewhat smaller scale, to institute similar reforms. He introduced a French judicial system, 1927, and in 1928 abolished the Capitulations. In Mar. 1935 the name of the country was changed from Persia to Iran.

IRAN IN WORLD WAR II. With the advent of World War II, Iran proclaimed her neutrality, but in 1941 Britain and Russia requested rights of transit through Iranian territory. Permission having been refused, the 2 powers occupied Iran, 25 Aug., and divided it into 2 zones, Russian and British. The shah abdicated in favor of his son, Mohammed Reza Pahlavi (b. 1919), and a tripartite treaty was signed, 29 Jan., 1942, which specified that British and Russian forces would leave Iran within 6 months after the end of the war. On 9 Sept., 1943, Iran declared war on Germany, and on 1 Dec. the Teheran Declaration issued by Roosevelt and Churchill reaffirmed the independence and sovereignty of Iran. (*Cont. p. 621.*)

Egypt

1914–45

KINGDOM OF EGYPT. The years 1918–22 witnessed a great deal of nationalist agitation in Egypt, resulting in a unilateral abolition of the British protectorate, 28 Feb., 1922. In Mar. 1922 Sultan Fuad proclaimed himself king, and on 19 Apr., 1923, a constitution was inaugurated. The 1st elections, held in Jan. 1924, resulted in a large majority for the Wafd Party, around which the nationalist agitation had taken place. The king, however, wishing to curb the power of the Wafd, engaged in a continuing struggle with it which resulted in his dissolving parliament and revoking the constitution early in 1930. On 22 Oct., 1930, a new constitution and a new electoral law, providing for a system of indirect election, were promulgated, but in 1935 the king first suspended the constitution of 1930 and then, 12 Dec., 1935, restored that of 1923.

RELATIONS WITH BRITAIN. Negotiations with Britain for a treaty to define the relations between the 2 countries went on until 1930. On 8 May of that year they broke down over the question of the Sudan, and remained suspended for the next 5 years. On 26 Aug., 1936, an Anglo-Egyptian treaty was finally signed. It provided for the termination of the British military occupation, but Britain retained the right to maintain military forces in the Suez Canal Zone for defense of the Canal. The question of the Sudan was left largely unsettled. During World War II Egypt was the principal allied base in the Middle East, and the Middle East Supply Center was located there. (*Cont. p. 621.*)

Iraq

1914-45

CAMPAIGN FOR IRAQI INDEPEN-DENCE. At the end of World War I the British were in occupation of Mesopotamia (Iraq), and on 25 Apr., 1920, they received a mandate over the territory from the League of Nations. On 23 Aug., 1921, Faisal, a son of the sherif of Mecca, was crowned king of Iraq. Relations between the new kingdom and Britain were established on the basis of a treaty negotiated on 10 Oct., 1922, and ratified by the Iraq Constituent Assembly, 27 Mar., 1924. The treaty was originally to last for 20 years, but was subsequently limited to 4 by a protocol signed in 1923. On 10 July, 1924, a constitution was promulgated. Further treaties with Iraqi independence and the termination of the mandate as objectives were signed, 13 Jan., 1926, and 14 Dec., 1927, but it was not until 30 June, 1930, that the final treaty was concluded, providing for a 25-year alliance. By the terms of this treaty Iraq became fully independent and entered the League of Nations, 3 Oct., 1932. The British retained rights to 2 air bases and freedom of transit across Iraq for their armed forces.

FOREIGN RELATIONS. On 31 July, 1928, the "Red Line" Agreement, which regulated the interests of the various companies involved in the development of Iraqi oil, was signed. Oil production began in 1930. On 29 Oct., 1936, a coup resulted in the establishment of a military dictatorship, but its leader was assassinated, 11 Aug., 1937, and moderates returned to power. Still another coup, 3 Apr., 1941, in this case with a pro-Axis coloration, led briefly to the exile of the king, crushed by British troops. On 16 Jan., 1943, Iraq declared war on Germany and on 22 Jan. signed the United Nations Declaration, the first Arab state to do so. (*Cont. p. 622.*)

Transjordan

1914-45

ESTABLISHMENT OF THE KING-DOM. The Emirate of Transjordan was, in effect, an accidental creation arising out of the situation in the Middle East at the end of World War I. On 27 May, 1921, Britain recognized Abdullah ('Abd Allah), son of the sherif of Mecca, and brother of King Faisal of Iraq, as the ruler of this territory. Britain's chief purpose in doing so was to prevent him from carrying out a threatened attack on the French in Syria. Transjordan formed part of the British mandate over Palestine, and Britain saw the establishment of Abdullah in this area as a way of controlling it indirectly. Transjordan was consequently excluded from the area of Jewish immigration.

RELATIONS WITH BRITAIN. On 25 May, 1923, the provisional agreement of 1921 was made permanent on the condition that a constitutional regime be set up and a treaty concluded with Britain. This treaty was finally signed, 20 Feb., 1928, and left the British with a large measure of control, especially over foreign affairs. The British agreed to contribute, through loans or grants, to the Transjordanian treasury. The agreement was amended, 2 June, 1934, and 19 July, 1941. On 16 Apr., 1928, an Organic Law was promulgated. During World War II the Arab Legion, created in 1921, played a valuable role on the allied side. (*Cont. p. 623.*)

Palestine

1914-45

BALFOUR DECLARATION. The so-called "problem of Palestine" originated with the Balfour Declaration, 2 Nov., 1917, by which the British, responding to pressures of Zionists (founder, Theodor Herzl (1860–1904), committed themselves to support the creation of a Jewish "national home" in the area. The differing interpretations which could be given to this phrase lay at the heart of the problem. A build-up of tension between Jews and Arabs in the years immediately following World War I came to the surface, Apr. 1920, with violent disturbances in Jerusalem. On 1 July, 1920, Sir Herbert Samuel (1870–1963), himself a Jew, became British high commissioner in Palestine. In Feb. 1922 an Organic Law was enacted, providing for an administration including a partially elected Legislative Council; but due to an Arab refusal to participate in the elections, this provision was never activated. The Arabs wished an end to both Jewish immigration and land sales to Jews, and throughout the period between the wars concentrated their efforts on achieving these ends.

ARAB-JEWISH CONFLICT. The 1st attempt by the British to define the "national home" came in the Churchill White Paper of 1 July, 1922, in which it was taken to mean cultural autonomy without political overtones. Riots in 1929 which were set off by a dispute about rights at the Wailing Wall in Jerusalem led to yet another elaboration of British policy involving stricter limits on immigration and land acquisition. Neither the Arabs nor the Jews were satisfied with the British measures, and the relative calm of the next few years was shattered in 1936 by a new series of riots. On 22 Apr., 1936, the Arabs called a general strike to underline their demands. A British commission, set up to investigate the situation, recommended partition, 7 July, 1937, but on 9 Nov. a report on the projected partition rejected it as unworkable. A conference was held in London, 7 Feb.–17 Mar., 1939, to which Arab and Jewish representatives were invited, and was followed, 17 May, by the issue of another White Paper specifying that Jewish immigration would end after 1944 and envisioning the establishment of an independent state within 10 years with provision for minority rights for Jews. The exigencies of war caused a temporary slowdown of Jewish and Arab efforts to gain their objectives, but this was merely a lull, and beginning in 1943 Jewish terrorist activities com-

menced as a prelude to the postwar struggle. (*Cont. p. 624.*)

Syria and Lebanon
1914–45

ESTABLISHMENT OF THE MANDATES. France had long had an interest in Syria and Lebanon, and this was reflected in her assumption of a mandate over these territories after World War I. King Faisal, who had been placed on the throne of Syria by the Arabs after the war, was expelled from Damascus, 24 July, 1920, by the French. France then took direct control over the whole of what was to become Syria and Lebanon. In 1925 and 1926 there were risings in Syria, but these were put down. In 1928, at the direction of the French high commissioner, a Constituent Assembly was called which drew up a constitution. It did not, however, receive the approval of the French government, and in May 1930 the high commissioner dissolved the Assembly and issued a constitution by decree. This was accepted by the Syrians, and elections were held, Jan. 1932.

Developments in Lebanon followed a similar pattern. In May 1926 a constitution drafted by the Lebanese Representative Council was promulgated and gave Lebanon parliamentary institutions. On 9 May, 1932, the high commissioner suspended this constitution, and on 2 Jan., 1934, a new one was issued.

INDEPENDENCE MOVEMENTS. Negotiations for a treaty to replace the mandates went on for 4 years and led to an agreement, 9 Sept., 1936, under the terms of which Syria was to become independent within 3 years. A similar treaty was signed with Lebanon, 13 Nov., 1936. France did not, however, ratify these agreements, and on 7 July, 1939, the president of Syria resigned. On 10 July the high commissioner suspended the constitution and dissolved the Assembly in Syria and, on the outbreak of war, did the same in Lebanon.

BRITISH CONQUEST. After the fall of France, Syria and Lebanon came under the Vichy government, and on 8 July, 1941, British troops invaded Syria. On the same day the commander of the Free French issued a proclamation promising an end to the mandate and independence. The British troops were victorious, and on 14 July an armistice was concluded and the British occupation of Syria and Lebanon instituted. On 28 Sept. Gen. Georges Catroux, sent by the Free French to negotiate treaties with the 2 countries, announced the independence of Syria, and on 26 Nov. that of Lebanon. In Mar. 1943 the suspended constitutions were reinstated and elections held, and on 22 Dec. an agreement was signed relating to the transfer of power to the Syrian and Lebanese governments. (*Cont. p. 623.*)

Arabian Peninsula

1914-45

PERSIAN GULF AND YEMEN. In contrast to the other Arab lands, the Arabian Peninsula was under less direct European control in the interwar period. The various sheikdoms along the Persian Gulf and the coasts of southern Arabia continued their long-established quasi-protectorate relations with Great Britain. Yemen claimed its independence, and negotiations with Britain led finally to recognition of this by the treaty of 11 Feb., 1934.

SAUDI ARABIA. The bulk of the peninsula was united under Ibn Saud, originally the ruler of the Najd, who founded the Kingdom of Saudi Arabia. A treaty with the British, 20 May, 1927, confirmed him in his possession of the Hejaz and Najd and its dependencies. The outside world's concern with Ibn Saud's kingdom related mainly to its oil resources. On 29 May, 1933, the Standard Oil Co. of California, obtained a 60-year oil concession. In 1934, with the addition of a 2nd company, the consortium became known as the Arabian-American Oil Co. (Aramco). A new concession was signed, 31 May, 1939. In 1943 an agreement was concluded with the U.S. permitting the latter to construct an air base at Dhahran. (*Cont. p. 624.*)

AFRICA

Morocco

1914-33

PACIFICATION. French military operations in the Rif Mountains, which had been interrupted by World War I, were resumed, 1920, by the resident general, Marshal Louis Lyautey (1854-1934). The resistance led by Abd-el-Krim (1885-1963) was finally overcome in 1926.

BERBER DAHIR. By this decree, 16 May, 1930, the French government transferred Berber tribes from the jurisdiction of Moslem law to tribal custom. Urban Moroccans protested against what they regarded as an attempt to undermine the unity of an Islamic Morocco.

1934-45

FOUNDING OF POLITICAL PARTIES. In May 1934 Sultan Sidi Mohammed (Muhammad) ibn Yusuf (ruled 1927-61) received a tumultuous welcome on a visit to Fez, and riots broke out when the French shortened his stay. In Sept. a group of young Moroccans, calling themselves the Committee for National Action, drew up a plan of reform calling on the French to modify their direct administration and establish a protectorate system. In 1937 the committee formed the National Action Bloc under the Islamic scholar Allal al-Fassi (b. 1906). Amidst popular agitation al-Fassi was exiled to Central Africa, where he remained until the end of World War II. Some other Moroccan leaders escaped to Switzerland, and nationalist activity was much reduced for the next several years.

ISTIQLAL. In Jan. 1943, shortly after the Anglo-American landings in Morocco, President Roosevelt met privately with the sultan in Casablanca. Both Moroccans and French came to the conclusion that the President had assured the sultan of American hopes for Moroccan freedom. In Dec. the Istiqlal (Independence) Party was formed, regrouping most of the old National Action Bloc. In Jan. 1944 Istiqlal published a manifesto calling for negotiations to end the protectorate. The sultan allied himself informally with the nationalists by refusing to countersign French decrees. (*Cont. p. 573.*)

Algeria

1914–39

BEGINNINGS OF NATIONALISM. During World War I thousands of Algerians gained experience of European life as soldiers and as workers in French factories. After the war some 70,000 Algerians remained in France, to be stimulated by the postwar intellectual climate there. In 1919, as a reward for war services, the French government allowed some increase in Moslem representation on local bodies in Algeria and Moslem participation in local elections. Municipal elections in Algiers, 1920, brought victory to the Emir Khaled, who called for equality of rights with Frenchmen for all Moslems. French settlers denounced the elections and the results were invalidated. In 1923 Moslem workers in France formed L'Étoile Nord-Africaine, which included Khaled as an honorary president. Beginning as an organization to defend the interests of North African workers in France, the ENA under Messali Hadj evolved into a nationalist movement which demanded Algerian independence. In 1936, after the ENA had been banned, Messali formed the Parti du Peuple Algérien (PPA).

Meanwhile a contrasting movement was growing up among intellectuals in Algeria, who called for assimilation of all Moslems to French civilization. The assimilationists formed an association under Ferhat Abbas (b. 1899) in 1927. Reaction to assimilationist ideas took the form of Moslem-Arab nationalism under the leadership of Sheik Abd al-Hamid ben Badis. In 1935 ben Badis founded the Association of Algerian Ulema, which aimed to revive pure Islam and the Arabic language. The conflict became explicit in 1936, when Abbas denied the existence of an Algerian fatherland and called for emancipation of the Moslems so that they could be worthy of the name of Frenchmen. In return ben Badis declared that Algerian Moslems had their own history and culture distinct from French, and that they were not French and did not want to be.

1940–45

NATIONALIST UNITY. During World War II Algerian Moslems again came into contact with Europe, this time as witnesses to a French defeat. The illiterate mass of Algerians listened to allied broadcasts containing news of the Atlantic Charter and resistance to foreign invasion. In 1943 Abbas turned away from assimilation and presented a "Manifesto to the Algerian People," which asserted the right of Algerians to manage their own affairs under a constitution recognizing the equality of all residents of the country, French and Moslems alike. Gen. de Gaulle responded with the Ordinance of 7 Mar., 1944, which granted voting rights to certain categories of Moslems. The PPA and the ulema joined Abbas in rejecting the ordinance as inadequate. (*Cont. p. 573.*)

Tunisia

1914–33

DESTOUR. In 1920, inspired by President Wilson's declarations, the Young Tunisians joined with some of their more traditional countrymen to form a political party, the Destour (Constitution). Under the direction of Sheik Thaalibi, the Destour demanded the emancipation of Tunisia as a nation. The French resident general, Lucien Saint, responded with a blend of repression and minor reforms. The policy succeeded in dividing the nationalists and weakening their movement for several years.

1934–45

NEO-DESTOUR. In Mar. 1934 the young lawyer and writer Habib Bourguiba (b. 1904) led a group of his own generation out of the Destour to form a new party, the Neo-Destour. He actively sought mass support, but was deported by the French, Sept. 1935. Returning to Tunisia, 1936, Bourguiba traveled throughout the country, addressing workers and peasants in local dialects and organizing the Neo-Destour into local committees which held discussions on the nation's political and economic problems. The nationalists began a campaign of civil disobedience which included a general strike, 1937, and culminated in riots in Tunis, Apr. 1938. Bourguiba and other Neo-Destour leaders were arrested and brought to a trial which was still pending at the outbreak of war in 1939. The prisoners were held in France and Italy until their return to Tunisia, Mar. 1943. After the arrival of the allies in May, Bourguiba began a series of unsuccessful appeals for Tunisian independence. Unable to achieve his ends, he escaped in disguise to Egypt in 1945, while Salah ben Yusuf (1910-61) took over the organization of the party in Tunisia. (*Cont. p. 573.*)

French Black Africa

1914-45

RESISTANCE TO FRENCH RULE. Between the wars the French administration was faced with sporadic revolts against conscription, taxation, and forced labor: by the Dogon (French Sudan), 1918; the Tuareg (Niger), 1918-23; the Lobi (Upper Volta), 1919; etc. By 1930, however, all areas of French Black Africa were under civil rule. French policy made African chiefs civil servants. Representational politics were limited to the 4 communes of Senegal, which were represented in the French Assembly in Paris by an African, Blaise Diagne (1872-1934), 1914-34.

French forced labor policies provoked strikes on the Kayes-Thiès railroad, 1925, while the building of the Congo-Ocean railroad, 1922-34, cost the lives of thousands of Africans, provoking a revolt in

1928. In 1938-39 Africans in Ubangi-Shari rebelled against forced labor. In Jan. 1944 Gen. de Gaulle convened a conference at Brazzaville, French Congo, of French administrators in Africa, which foresaw African representation in the metropolitan Assembly. (*Cont. p. 575.*)

British Africa

1914-45

BRITISH WEST AFRICA. In 1917 J. E. Casely Hayford (1867-1930), a Gold Coast lawyer, founded the interterritorial National Congress of British West Africa, which held its 1st meeting at Accra in 1920. The Congress sought ultimate self-determination and an immediate increase in African representation in colonial Legislative Councils. African chiefs and some wealthy non-chiefs gained seats in these Councils: Nigeria, 1922; Sierra Leone, 1924; Gold Coast, 1925. J. E. K. Aggrey (1875-1927) returned from the U.S.A., Oct. 1924, and, preaching racial co-operation, worked successfully with Gov. Gordon Guggisberg (1869-1930) of the Gold Coast to achieve educational reforms. In 1922 Herbert Macaulay (1864-1946), a Nigerian engineer, founded the Nigerian Democratic Party. In London, Ladipo Solanke founded the West African Students' Union, 1925, in which the Gold Coast lawyer, Joseph B. Danquah (1895-1965), was prominent. All these organizations pressed for constitutional evolution.

In 1929 there was a major outbreak of opposition to colonial rule in Southern Nigeria, while in 1931 a tax strike was organized in Sierra Leone. In the Gold Coast an African Cocoa Growers' Association was formed, 1930, to withhold cocoa from a depressed market, an effort which was renewed, 1937-38, against the formation of a buyers' pool. In 1937 B. N. Azikiwe (b. 1904) returned to Nigeria after an American education to found a chain of newspapers, notably the *West African Pilot,* which asserted African values and pressed for more rapid constitutional reform. Azikiwe was active in the

Nigerian Youth Movement, founded in 1936, with Obafemi Awolowo (b. 1909) a leading Yoruba member. In 1944 Azikiwe formed the National Council of Nigeria and the Cameroons.

BRITISH EAST AFRICA. In 1920 Kikuyu chiefs in Kenya founded the Kikuyu Association and the following year Harry Thuku (b. 1895) formed the Young Kikuyu Association, militant in its protests against racial discrimination; Thuku was arrested and deported in 1922. Despite the opposition of white settlers, who looked to eventual self-governing status for Kenya, the British government declared African rights paramount in East Africa (Devonshire Report, 1923). By that date some 2,000 white settlers owned 40% of the land of Kenya. Land acquisition by whites remained a core problem for the British administration, as the African population had to live within ever-decreasing territorial limits. In 1929 the Kikuyu Central Association was formed, with Jomo Kenyatta (b. 1893) as secretary; Kenyatta was sent to London to protest against the policies of the Kenya government.

Uganda was the scene of sporadic violence, 1929–34, following a fall in world cotton prices.

THE RHODESIAS AND NYASALAND. In 1915 John Chilembwe, an African Christian minister, led a rebellion in Nyasaland, which was rapidly crushed. From 1917 the Kitawala (Watchtower) movement in Northern Rhodesia preached an African millennium, and resisted British attempts to crush it. In 1922 white settlers in Southern Rhodesia voted to become a colony and against joining South Africa, and the following year the territory became an internally self-governing colony, with a franchise that excluded virtually all Africans. The Land Apportionment Act of 1930 assigned half the land to whites, while the Industrial Conciliation Act, 1936, explicitly excluded Africans from the collective-bargaining process. Settlers pressed increasingly for federation of the 3 territories and Africans vigorously opposed it. The rapid development of the mining industry of the Copperbelt after 1929

caused an inflow of African workers; in May 1935 and Apr. 1940 they staged strikes, which developed into riots, against low wages, increased taxes, and the settlers' "civilized labor" policy. In 1944 J. P. Sangala (b. 1900) founded the Nyasaland African National Congress.

SUDAN. The working of the Anglo-Egyptian Condominium in the Sudan did not satisfy Egypt, and after the achievement of Egyptian independence, 1922, demands grew for a closer union of Egypt and the Sudan. On 19 Nov., 1924, the British governor general of the Sudan was assassinated in Cairo. The British replied by effectively removing Egyptians from the administration of the Sudan. A growing group of educated Sudanese demanded union with Egypt, and formed the Graduates' General Congress in 1938. Ismail al-Azhari (1900–1969) emerged as leader of the pro-Egyptian wing. (*Cont. p. 574.*)

Ethiopia

1914–45

RULE OF HAILE SELASSIE. In Sept. 1916 a group of chiefs rebelled against Lij Yasu, and seized Addis Ababa. Zauditu was made empress and Ras Tafari (b. 1892) regent. Ras Tafari attempted to institute reforms, e.g., abolition of slavery, 1926, but met conservative opposition. In 1923 Ethiopia joined the League of Nations. In 1928, after putting down a revolt, Ras Tafari took complete control, and on 2 Nov., 1930, became emperor of Ethiopia as Haile Selassie I. Further revolts were crushed in 1931–32.

ITALIAN CONQUEST. In late 1934, Italian troops began to provoke incidents on the Ethiopian-Somaliland border, and in Oct. 1935 invaded Ethiopia. Ethiopian troops resisted fiercely, but after the loss of the Battle of Mai-Tchew, 25 Mar., 1936, Haile Selassie left Addis Ababa, 5 May. Ethiopia was joined to Eritrea and Italian Somaliland to form Italian East Africa, with the king of Italy as emperor of Ethiopia. Ethiopian guerrilla resistance continued. After Italy entered the war, June 1940, allied troops captured Italian

East Africa. Haile Selassie returned to Ethiopia, 5 May, 1941. (*Cont. p. 618.*)

Belgian Congo and Liberia

1914-45

BELGIAN CONGO. Africans having no political rights in the Belgian Congo, their opposition to colonial rule often took religious form, notably in the movement led by Simon Kimbangu (?1881–1951). There were major risings in Kasai, 1931–32, and Equateur, 1932–33.

LIBERIA. During World War I the Kru people rebelled against the ruling Americo-Liberians. The U.S.A. supplied arms to help put the rising down, and sought internal reforms. Liberia was deeply in debt, and in 1926 accepted a loan, granting a large land concession to the Firestone Rubber Co. in exchange. A League of Nations mission found evidence of forced labor and maladministration. In 1944 William V. S. Tubman (b. 1895) was elected president. (*Cont. p. 577.*)

THE CARIBBEAN ISLANDS

1914-34

ECONOMIC CHANGE. World War I stimulated the economies of the Caribbean islands to some extent, though permanent economic improvements were not yet in sight. Reliance on sugar production was relaxed as some islands began to diversify: Grenada, cocoa and nutmeg; Dominica, citrus products; St. Vincent, arrowroot and cotton; British Guiana, rice. The price of sugar rose rapidly after the war, but when the market crashed in 1923 there were many bankruptcies among the planters. The depression hit the West Indies severely and, in the early 1930's, induced a general apathy and listlessness.

PUERTO RICO AND VIRGIN ISLANDS. In 1917 the U.S. Congress passed the Organic Act, 2 Mar., which made Puerto Ricans U.S. citizens. The Danish Virgin Islands were purchased, 4 Aug., 1916, to prevent a possible German takeover.

1935-45

RISE OF POLITICAL PARTIES. Riots for higher wages and better living conditions began in St. Kitts, 1935, with a strike of sugar workers, and led a few months later to the formation of the St. Vincent Workingmen's Association. Bloodshed occurred in Trinidad, and spread to Barbados. There were disturbances in Guiana and Jamaica, June 1938. Labor unions grew out of these troubles and some of their leaders, Robert Bradshaw in St. Kitts, Vere Bird in Antigua, Grantly Adams in Barbados, and Alexander Bustamente and Norman Manley in Jamaica, were able to transform the labor organizations they controlled into political parties.

FEDERATION. Attempts at federation between the wars among various of the British West Indian islands failed because of lack of popular support, jealousy among political leaders, and the fear of the more economically self-sustaining islands that they would have to support the less developed ones.

MOYNE COMMISSION. The Moyne Commission Report, 1938, recommended (1) the setting up of a West Indian Welfare Fund to disburse £1 m. a year for 20 years, (2) that as many nominated members as possible of the colonial Executive Councils should be replaced by elected members, (3) the granting of universal adult suffrage, and (4) gradual political advance.

FRENCH WEST INDIES. The French followed a policy of centralization in Martinique, Guadeloupe, and French Guiana. The French islands sent soldiers to fight in both world wars, and developed parties and factions corresponding to those in France. The islands were governed by Vichy supporters until 1943, when governors loyal to Charles de Gaulle took over.

DUTCH WEST INDIES. In 1922 a new Netherlands Constitution Act had made Curaçao and Surinam integrated territories of the Kingdom of the Netherlands. In Dec. 1942 the Dutch Empire was divided into 4 coequal parts, with 3 votes each for Curaçao and Surinam, and 15 each for the Netherlands in Europe and the Netherlands East Indies. Representatives to the States-General, however, were not chosen by the people in the Caribbean colonies but by the crown. Surinam and Curaçao, as well as the other Dutch possessions—St. Eustatius (Statia), Saba, and the southern half of St. Martin—were ruled paternalistically, though with a slight democratic façade. (*Cont. p. 570.*)

The British Dominions

UNION OF SOUTH AFRICA

1914–25

SOUTH AFRICA IN WORLD WAR I. When Great Britain declared war on Germany, 4 Aug., 1914, there was no automatic necessity for the self-governing dominions of the British Empire to follow her lead. Canada, Australia, and New Zealand realized that a German victory in Europe would be followed by invasions of other areas, and unhesitatingly joined the war effort. But South Africa demurred, announcing that she would provide only for her own defense. South Africa was the only dominion with German forces on her frontier, yet she was faced with a more truculent domestic opposition to the war than any of the other three. In Apr. 1915 the prime minister, Gen. Louis Botha (1862–1919), suppressed a revolt of intransigent Afrikaners who considered the war another British war of conquest and hoped a German victory would mean independence from Great Britain. Two weeks later the government reversed an earlier decision, and South African forces invaded the neighboring German colony of South-West Africa. The Germans capitulated, 15 July. South African troops were then dispatched to fight in East Africa and France.

LABOR CONTROVERSIES. The South African economy was heavily dependent on gold mining and on the use of cheap African and Asian labor. Botha, who had forged the Union of South Africa in the period after the Boer War, tried to overcome jealousies and hatreds between British and Afrikaners and between Europeans and Africans. A government commission, however, advised, 1916, that if whites were to prevent black Africans from competing against them for jobs, the blacks would have to be confined to reserves. In 1918 Africans organized their first mass action, a boycott of public utilities. The following year Klements Kadali (1896–1951) formed the Industrial and Commercial Workers' Union for Africans, which instigated dock and railroad strikes to obtain better conditions.

SMUTS REGIME. In July 1919 Botha and the deputy prime minister, Gen. Jan C. Smuts (1870–1950), signed the Treaty of Versailles as representatives of a separate and independent nation. South Africa received a mandate from the League of Nations to govern South-West Africa. After Botha's death, 28 Aug., Smuts succeeded to the premiership and sought to strengthen South Africa's ties with the British Empire, resolve domestic racial problems, reduce the high cost of living, and deal with disruptive Afrikaner nationalism.

RISE OF THE NATIONALIST PARTY. In Dec. 1921, white mine workers on the Rand began an armed rebellion against a government policy of using Africans in semiskilled positions; it was suppressed at a cost of over 200 lives. In 1923 the Urban Areas Act restricted urban Africans to living in designated "locations." The Nationalist Party and the Labour Party, which took no position on the national question as they wanted to improve the standard of living of white workers, then united against the ruling South African Party of Smuts because of the latter's policy of lowering color restrictions. After an unsuccessful attempt, 1922, to have Southern Rhodesia join the Union to help thwart the effect of this alliance, Smuts was subsequently defeated in a general election, 1924. He was succeeded as prime minister by the Nationalist leader, J. B. M. Hertzog (1866–1942), who formed a ministry based on the enforced separation of whites and blacks in employment, habitation, and government, and on the loosening of imperial ties to Britain.

1926–45

IMPERIAL CONFERENCE OF 1926.

The official declaration of the Imperial Conference of 1926, drafted by Lord Balfour (1848–1930), acknowledged that the 4 British dominions had reached a stage of total independence, equal in status to Great Britain and to one another, and in no way inferior to one another in any aspect of their domestic or external affairs. They would remain united under the crown by common allegiance and as "freely associated members of the British Commonwealth of Nations." Because of her peculiar history, geographical position, resources, and population, Britain would continue to bear the greater part of the burden of imperial defense, investment, and trade. Equality in status did not mean equality of function.

STATUTE OF WESTMINSTER. The decisions of the Imperial Conference of 1926 were given statutory force by Britain by the Statute of Westminster, 11 Dec., 1931. The crown renounced its right to legislate for the dominions except at their request and with their consent; but a dominion could still not pass laws repugnant to existing British laws applying to that dominion. These concessions were almost gratuitous, since Britain had not exercised her right of interference for decades.

NATIONALIST POLICIES. A series of laws closed skilled trades to Africans (Mines and Works Act, 1926), extended the pass laws, and instituted a "civilized labor" policy (Industrial Conciliation Act, 1924). A distinctive South African

flag was adopted, 1927, and a Native Administration Act of the same year increased the government's power to restrict the rights and mobility of Africans. In 1929, to affirm her independence in foreign relations, South Africa appointed her own ambassadors to the U.S.A., Italy, and the Netherlands. The franchise was extended, 1931, to all adult white men and women; Bantu and Coloreds could vote only if they satisfied rigid educational and property qualifications.

THE DEPRESSION. The depression was beginning to have serious effects on the South African economy by 1931. The world market for timber and minerals had declined considerably, and widespread unemployment resulted among both whites and Africans, a situation exacerbated in the following year when Britain and other western countries abandoned the gold standard, causing a diminished demand for South African gold. To achieve greater political stability during the period of economic crisis, Smuts joined Hertzog in a coalition government, 1933.

DOMESTIC LEGISLATION. Continuing its policy of loosening Commonwealth ties, the government passed a Status Act, 1934, by which it attained full control over all domestic and foreign policy. The Native Laws Amendment Act, 1937, compelled South African cities to effect the complete separation of their white and nonwhite residents. In passing this law the Hertzog government also recognized the need to provide government funds for the education and housing of nonwhites. Despite this and other attempts to improve the lot of nonwhites, however, the disparity between the relative standards of living of the 2 groups gradually became more and more pronounced.

SOUTH AFRICA IN WORLD WAR II. When Britain declared war on Germany, 3 Sept., 1939, Hertzog asked the legislature to state that the European war was of no concern to South Africa. Smuts strenuously opposed Hertzog's indifference, and ultimately succeeded in having the House of ·Assembly declare war, 5 Sept., on the grounds that common ideals and institutions would otherwise be jeopardized. Smuts then assumed the leadership of a new coalition ministry composed of members of the United, Labour, and Dominion (formerly South African) Parties, and South Africa contributed over 300,000 men, ⅓ of whom were nonwhite, to serve in various theaters of war. In the general election of 1941 the coalition was returned with a greater majority than it had had before. Smuts helped to draft and, on South Africa's behalf, signed the United Nations Charter, 1945. (*Cont. p. 616*).

CANADA

1914–28

CANADA IN WORLD WAR I. Unlike South Africa, Canada unhesitatingly declared war on Germany, Aug. 1914. In the early years of the war the army filled its quotas with volunteers, but, to maintain a satisfactory rate of replacements, the Conservative government of Prime Minister Robert Borden (1854–1937) found it necessary to adopt military conscription, 1917. Later in the same year the Canadian army, which initially had been under the British, became a separate command under Gen. Sir Arthur Currie (1875–1933).

INDUSTRIAL RELATIONS AND AGRICULTURAL DEPRESSION. In 1919 the violent Winnipeg metal workers' strike was broken only by the arrest of the strike leaders. The strike helped to arouse public sympathy for labor's right to collective bargaining. By the end of 1920 the postwar economic slump, which had seriously affected other major countries, also began to be felt in Canada. The prairie farmers were the hardest hit, with the price of wheat falling from a 1919 high of (Can.) $2.15 per bushel to $0.60 in 1920. Since wheat was a major export, the effects of the slump were widespread. Farmers' co-operative organizations, which had been introduced earlier in the century, now became a vehicle for assisting farmers to maintain a minimum income. By 1923 the Liberal ministry of W. L. Mackenzie King (1874–1950) had completed the nationalization

and merger into the Canadian National Railway of the former Canadian Northern and Grand Trunk Railways, which had fallen into bankruptcy. Later in the year the government reduced the high tariffs and internal taxes and subsidies to industry which had been introduced 3 years earlier to combat the postwar depression. In the years following, the rate of business expansion increased sharply, particularly in the textile industry. A government coalition which had come to power in 1921, the nadir of the slump, resigned, Mar. 1926, and in the general elections held some months later the Liberal Party gained a clear majority. Mackenzie King formed a new ministry which lasted until 1930.

FOREIGN POLICY. In foreign affairs Canada, a separate signatory of the Versailles Treaty and an independent member of the League of Nations, continued to pursue its own policy in the interwar period. In 1921, with the concurrence of the U.S.A., Canada influenced Britain to renounce her 19-year old treaty of alliance with Japan. The Canadian Government also declined to sign the Geneva Protocol, 1924, and the Locarno Pact, 1925.

1929–45

THE DEPRESSION. When the stock exchanges of Montreal, 29 Oct., 1929, and Toronto, 13 Nov., crashed, the federal government began an unprecedented program of aid to individual provinces according to their needs. With the worldwide fall in agricultural prices affecting them, the wheat-producing provinces were again the hardest hit. Revaluation by the U.S.A. of the price of gold from $20 an ounce to $35 helped the Ontario and Quebec mining industries to endure the depression, and in turn helped the federal government to bear the cost of its provincial-aid programs. The grave economic situation spawned additional political parties: the Co-operative Commonwealth Federation, a farm-labor group, and the Social Credit Party, which advocated monetary reform as a means of ending the depression and, 1935, won a majority of seats in the provincial legislature of Alberta.

CANADA IN WORLD WAR II.

When the European war broke out in 1939, Canada delayed her declaration of war against the Axis powers for one week after the British declaration of 3 Sept. to emphasize the divisibility of the king of England's sovereignty. Canada signed agreements with the U.S.A., 1940, to share military and commercial transport routes across the Atlantic, and U.S.–Canadian relations remained at a high level of amity throughout the war. (*Cont. p. 602.*)

AUSTRALIA

1914–28

AUSTRALIA IN WORLD WAR I. During World War I Australia gave complete control over her land and naval forces, amounting to more than 300,000 men, to Great Britain for deployment against the German Empire. Australian and New Zealand troops fought first in Egypt and then took part in the Gallipoli campaign. They spent the last years of the war in France and Belgium, distinguishing themselves for gallantry at Ypres and Passchendaele. The ruling Labour Party under Prime Minister William M. Hughes (1864–1952) had tried unsuccessfully, 1916, to introduce military conscription to prevent war industries from draining off volunteers for the army.

FALL OF THE LABOUR GOVERNMENT. In 1923 Labour Prime Minister James H. Scullin (1876–1953) claimed and won the right from the crown to name the Commonwealth's governor general. But in the same year Labour lost power to a new coalition of Country and Nationalist Parties representing rural interests which had suffered during the postwar economic recession.

ECONOMIC POLICY UNDER BRUCE. The new prime minister, Stanley M. Bruce (b. 1883), sought to accelerate the development of industry through the use of extensive foreign loans. Bruce also took part in an Imperial Economic Conference held in London, 1925, to study market patterns and promote imperial trade. By 1926 his agricultural policies had raised butter to one of the country's major exports. The following year a government commission's inquiry into the necessity of protection concluded that high tariffs had been beneficial in raising the standard of living but were now costing certain sectors of the economy too much.

As the economy expanded, the Labour movement tried to organize more trades, meeting with mixed success. The maritime workers struck in 1925, and in 1929 strike action secured the right to collective bargaining for workers in the timber industry. A significant change in the constitution was effected, 1928, when the Commonwealth government assumed all the debts of the individual states, receiving in turn the prime taxing power.

1929–45

THE DEPRESSION. In Aug. 1929 the world price of wool, Australia's chief export, suddenly fell, and London bankers insisted on prompt payment of outstanding commercial and government debts. The depression soon aggravated the financial instability of the country. As a solution to the problem the Bank of England proposed balanced budgets and a reduction of 50% in wages and salaries. Australian economists had suggested a reduction of 10%, but in any case by 1932 the national income and standard of living were 30% lower than they had been in 1929. It was ultimately only through reducing costs that Australia narrowly avoided bankruptcy.

AUSTRALIA IN WORLD WAR II. On 3 Sept., 1939, when Britain declared war on Germany, Australia followed suit without opposition from either Parliament or the public. The economy was quickly put on a war footing, with a powerful government agency controlling and organizing industry for efficient war production. In Sept. 1940 Robert Menzies (b. 1894), a Liberal, headed a reorganized war cabinet. The Labour Party under Prime Minister John Curtin (1885–1945), whose ministry succeeded that of Menzies in 1941, introduced conscription (though not for overseas service) for the 1st time, 1942, and by the end of the war over 600,000 men and women had served in the armed forces. Unlike the pattern which followed World War I, the readjustment to postwar conditions was accomplished without inflation and with no substantial unemployment. (*Cont. p. 631.*)

NEW ZEALAND

1914–45

NEW ZEALAND IN WORLD WAR I. New Zealand entered World War I under a coalition government representing the Liberal and Reform Parties and headed by the Liberal leader, W. F. Massey (1856–1925). The nation's wartime military commitment was met by volunteers, although conscription was approved, 1916, as a stand-by measure. The country's chief natural resources, gold and agricultural products, were put at the disposal of Britain. Having signed the Treaty of Versailles and joined the League of Nations, New Zealand received the former German colony of Western Samoa under mandate from the League. The major piece of social legislation passed during the war provided for a triennial referendum on the question of national prohibition of alcoholic beverages, replacing the previous system of local options. Demobilized soldiers received either pensions or land grants from the government.

ECONOMIC POLICIES. The postwar period witnessed excessive speculation in rural land, which was ended only by a sudden fall in land prices, 1921. The Conservative Party victory in the general election of 1925 returned J. G. Coates (1878–1943) as prime minister. Coates's government encouraged the development and expansion of New Zealand's major exports, mutton and dairy products. Because of the success of this program and the nature of the products (which always retain a minimum level of demand), and also because of a sound financial system, New Zealand's economy did not suffer as severely during the depression as did those of the other dominions, whose markets diminished precipitously. New Zealand was not entirely immune from

the world crisis, however, and adopted a series of laws, 1930–35, aimed at countering the effects of low prices and unemployment: many taxes were reduced or abolished, interest rates were lowered, subsidies were paid to farmers, and a reduction of 10% was made in wages, salaries, and pensions.

FOREIGN POLICY. Although New Zealand signed the Pact of Paris, 1928, and the London Naval Treaties, 1930 and 1936, and continued with the other dominions to emphasize her independence from Britain, she nonetheless was reluctant to accept too separate a role in foreign affairs, looking to Britain as guide and provider. She joined with Australia and Newfoundland in asking the British Parliament to allow the Statute of Westminster, 1931, to become operative only when ratified by individual dominion legislatures, which did not occur in New Zealand until 1941, 10 years later.

DOMESTIC LEGISLATION. In 1932 New Zealand participated in the general tariff reductions adopted by Commonwealth countries. The Labour Party returned to office in 1932, with M. J. Savage (1872–1940) heading the government. In the following year the Reserve Bank of New Zealand, founded in 1931, was nationalized. Legislation passed in 1933 fixed minimum wages, provided a 40-hour workweek for industrial workers, and began a program of free secondary education. The Social Security Act, 1938, offered health and medical benefits in addition to providing old-age pensions. The electorate expressed its approval of the establishment of the welfare state by returning Savage and a clear Labour majority in the general election of 1938.

NEW ZEALAND IN WORLD WAR II. Like the other dominions, New Zealand declared war on Germany in 1939 without being subjected to aggression herself, but made clear that she was acting as an independent power. In Sept. 1940 Peter Fraser (1884–1950), who had succeeded Savage as prime minister in Mar., formed a war cabinet on the British model, with members of other major parties holding important portfolios. (*Cont. p. 632.*)

East Asia

THE NEW CHINA

1914–18

RULE OF YÜAN SHIH-K'AI. In 1914 Yüan Shih-k'ai (1852–1916) dissolved parliament and had himself elected president of China for life. Aiming to establish a constitutional monarchy with himself at its head, he called a convention of "citizens' representatives" who, surrounded by armed soldiers, voted in favor of monarchy. Yüan, however, underestimated the opposition to such a move, especially from regional military leaders who viewed a strong centralized monarchy as a threat to their power. After Yüan's death, 1916, his republican opponents reconvened parliament, but in the summer of 1917 a group of provincial military governors seized Peking and parliament was again disbanded.

WARLORDISM AND THE ECLIPSE OF SUN YAT-SEN. The next decade in China's history has been called the "warlord period." Since no single military official was strong enough to dominate the rest, the leaders quarreled among themselves while the central government at Peking became a pawn in the hands of regional military forces. Sun Yat-sen and his followers were powerless to combat the military governments. During 1913–16 Sun lived in Japan, seeking financial support for his campaign against Yüan. After Yüan's death Sun returned to China, and became involved in warlord politics when military officials at Canton permitted him to establish a government there. At the end of World War I Sun's party was at the nadir of its influence.

THE 21 DEMANDS. While the western powers were preoccupied with the war in Europe, Japan seized the opportunity to further her expansion in China, particularly Manchuria. The Anglo-Japanese alliance called for Japan's participation in the war, and Japanese troops captured the German-leased territory of Kiaochow as well as the German-owned Marshall, Mariana, and Caroline Islands in the Pacific. In 1915, when Yüan's government challenged the Japanese occupation of Shantung, the Japanese refused to leave and instead presented China with the "21 Demands."

The Demands were divided into 5 groups, the first 4 dealing with the extension of Japanese rights in Manchuria, Shantung, and Fukien and with the need for increased control over the Hanyehp'ing Ironworks. The 5th group, which set out a scheme for Japanese domination over Chinese police forces and administration, demanded virtual Japanese control of China. Unable to oppose the 21 Demands by force, China revealed them to the world in the hope that the western powers would object. Anglo-American pressure led Tokyo to postpone the 5th and harshest set of demands, but China was compelled to conclude several treaties and exchange notes with Japan which seriously compromised her sovereignty. Most important, China was forced to agree in advance to any arrangements Japan might make in the peace treaty with Germany at the end of the war.

WESTERN FAILURE TO SUPPORT CHINA. The 1915 treaties and notes gave Japan a special position in China far exceeding that held by any of the western imperialist powers. A secret Russo-Japanese treaty of 1916 recognized Japan's new status in China in return for Japanese recognition of Russia's advance into Outer Mongolia. In 1917 Britain, France, and Italy secretly promised Japan that the peace treaty would recognize her new gains on the Asian mainland and in the Pacific. The U.S.A. was the chief opponent of Japanese expansionism, and reiterated American rights and the Open Door policy. When the U.S.A. entered the war in 1917, however, she sought assurance that the Japanese would not take advantage of her preoccupation with Europe to expand further in Asia. The Lansing-Ishii Agreement, 2 Nov., 1917, exchanged Japanese respect for the Open Door for U.S. recognition of Japan's "special interests" in China. Moreover, the U.S.A. agreed to recognize the gains already made by Japan in China in return for a Japanese pledge not to take any further territory.

CHINESE PARTICIPATION IN WORLD WAR I. In 1917 the Americans, believing that Chinese membership in the wartime alliance would strengthen China's voice at the peace table, and the British, wishing to eliminate German commercial rivalry in Chinese ports, both sought to bring China into the war. Parliamentary groups in China insisted that the western powers implement their promises on tariff revision, suspend demands for payment of the Boxer indemnity, and grant other financial concessions before China became a belligerent. The military goverment, however, succumbed to foreign pressure and declared war on Germany without securing these conditions.

1919–27

CHINA AT THE PEACE CONFERENCE. China's diplomatic weakness was clearly illustrated at the Paris Peace Conference. The Chinese delegate raised the question of the validity of the Sino-Japanese treaties and notes of 1915, particularly with regard to Shantung. When the Japanese threatened to leave the conference unless the Shantung question was decided in their favor, the other powers yielded. But China refused to sign the Treaty of Versailles.

TRENDS IN THE CHINESE NATIONALIST MOVEMENT. During the war years Chinese nationalism expressed itself in a series of boycotts against Japanese and western goods. China's failure at Versailles to recover her rights in Shantung gave a new impetus to the nationalist movement, whose backbone was the new intellectual elite. In the eyes of this western-educated group the collapse of the Manchu dynasty and China's continuing weakness discredited the traditional

Confucian philosophy. The attack against the Confucian tradition merged with the so-called "literary renaissance." This began as an attempt to eradicate the old written language and replace it with one capable of expressing the concepts gained through western education. Hu Shih (1891–1962), an American-educated philosophy student, became the chief proponent of the new writing, which spread rapidly among educated Chinese and served as the vehicle of the new nationalism. Nationalist activity culminated on 4 May, 1919, when China's failure at Versailles led to a large demonstration by students and professors at Peking University. Intellectuals throughout the country followed suit. In the period after the "May 4th Movement," as it became known, virtually every school of western philosophy penetrated China. John Dewey's lectures at Peking, 1919–20, gained him many adherents, but his emphasis on gradualism and pragmatism displeased many Chinese intellectuals impatient for social change.

ORIGINS OF CHINESE COMMUNISM. A large number of intellectuals became attached to Communism, which promised rapid, "scientific" solutions to social and economic problems and offered a historically determined role of leadership for an intellectual vanguard. Lenin's theory of imperialism supplied a convincing explanation for China's exploitation by rival imperialist powers. The Bolshevik Revolution, too, with its promise to lift Russia out of backwardness, inspired those hoping to steer China toward modernization. Moreover, the new Soviet regime declared its readiness to surrender all czarist rights and privileges in China, denounced the secret treaties of World War I, and proclaimed its support of Chinese efforts to regain full sovereignty and equality. In 1918 Ch'en Tu'hsiu (1879–1942), head of the literature department at Peking University and a leader of the May 4th Movement, established a Society for the Study of Marxism. Two years later the Comintern sent 2 agents to China, where they contacted Ch'en and organized the 1st Communist cells in Chinese cities. In 1921 Ch'en officially founded the Chinese Communist Party (CCP) in Shanghai.

COMMUNIST-KUOMINTANG UNITED FRONT. Having vainly sought western help in building a Chinese republic, Sun Yat-sen accepted Soviet offers of assistance, 1923. This was the period of Communist-sponsored united fronts between Communists and other left-wing groups. In Jan. 1923 Sun and Comintern representative Adolf Joffe (1883–1927) issued a joint statement in Canton which marked the start of co-operation between the Kuomintang (KMT) and the CCP. The 2 men agreed that conditions in China were not conducive to the creation of a Soviet-type system, and that the chief goal should be attainment of national unification and independence from the imperialist powers. Comintern agent Mikhail Borodin (1884–1953) cemented the KMT-CCP alliance by reorganizing the KMT along the lines of the Russian Communist Party. He also urged Chinese Communists to align themselves with the KMT without, however, merging with it or abandoning the organizational unity of the CCP.

APPLICATION OF THE "3 PEOPLE'S PRINCIPLES." A program based on Sun Yat-sen's "3 People's Principles" was adopted at Borodin's suggestion. The Principles, though vague, appeared to share many of Communism's ideals. Nationalism, Sun's 1st principle, was used chiefly to symbolize China's struggle for freedom from imperialism. The 2nd principle, democracy, was best illustrated by Sun's statement that "on no account must we give more liberty to the individual; let us secure liberty instead for the nation." Sun thus favored an "authoritarian" or "guided democracy," in which a small educated elite governed in the name of the masses. Sun's 3rd principle, livelihood, was primarily concerned with what he called "equalization of land ownership."

KUOMINTANG PROGRAM. In Jan. 1924 Borodin wrote the official program of the KMT, which guaranteed freedom of speech, the press, association, and religion, but declared that only those "who are really loyal to anti-imperialism will enjoy all rights and privileges." In the economic sphere Borodin interpreted Sun's 3d principle as requiring equalization of landholdings but not nationalization without compensation. The program empowered the government to tax the land of private owners and reserved the option to purchase it in the future. Private industries, whether Chinese or foreign-owned, were to be nationalized if they assumed the nature of monopolies or if they were "beyond the capacity of private individuals to develop, such as banking, railroads, and navigation." The program's foreign policy advocated the abolition of "unequal treaties," foreign concessions, extraterritoriality, and foreign control of customs.

Soviet influence in Canton grew when the KMT created a special military academy at Whampoa. Russian military experts played an important role at Whampoa, as well as serving as advisers for the Nationalist army as a whole. Many KMT leaders were eager to launch a "Northern Expedition" to reunify China by freeing her central and northern regions from the warlords and by seizing arsenals in order to reduce Nationalist dependence on Soviet arms. Borodin worked to delay the expedition until he had completed the reorganization of the KMT along Communist lines and had ensured Soviet control over the Chinese revolution.

RISE OF CHIANG KAI-SHEK. Communist penetration of the KMT led to a split between its right and left wings. The schism widened after Sun's death in 1925, since the KMT possessed no leader of comparable prestige to succeed him. In Mar. 1926 Borodin left Canton temporarily, leaving a triumvirate which included Chiang Kai-shek (b. 1886), commander of the Whampoa Academy, in control. Chiang took advantage of Borodin's absence to stage an anti-Communist coup and arrested the Russian military advisers. After Borodin's return, however, a compromise was reached which reflected the desire of each side to maintain co-operation until it was strong enough to eliminate the other. Borodin now shifted his attitude to one of favoring the Northern Expedition, which he saw as an opportunity for the Communists to gather recruits among the proletariat and poor peasantry in the Yangtze provinces.

NORTHERN EXPEDITION. The Northern Expedition began, mid-1926, under Chiang's command. Communist agitators had arranged strikes and peasant revolts behind enemy lines and had even infiltrated the northern armies. Chiang's forces were received by the civilian population as an army of liberation, and deserters from warlord armies swelled his ranks. As the expedition continued, Chiang led 1 column to Nanking, while the other column, including Borodin, the Communists, and the Left KMT, took Hankow. The expedition halted while each group tried to force the other to come to its headquarters. On 10 Mar., 1927, the Hankow group called a meeting which deprived Chiang of his chairmanship of the standing committee of the KMT's Central Executive Committee as well as his military command.

KMT-COMMUNIST SPLIT. In the ensuing power struggle Chiang emerged as victor. He had the support of non-Communist labor leaders, Chinese businessmen and bankers, and the foreign community in Shanghai, all of whom were disturbed by the anti-imperialist attitudes adopted by the KMT under Borodin and were relieved by the Right KMT's break with the Communists. In Apr. 1927 Chiang's troops arrested and executed large numbers of Communists in Shanghai. In July the Left KMT at Hankow repudiated its alliance with the Communists because of CCP attempts to implement radical land reforms and encourage peasant uprisings. The Left KMT expelled the Chinese Communists from Hankow and deported the Russian advisers. Moscow then purged Ch'en Tu'hsiu, making him the scapegoat for the failure of the KMT-CCP alliance, and ordered the CCP to shift to a policy of fomenting strikes in urban areas. China's small proletariat, however, displayed more interest in negotiating for economic benefits than in revolution.

EARLY YEARS OF MAO TSE-TUNG. Born in 1893 of a fairly well-to-do peasant family in Hunan province, Mao Tse-tung was working in the library of Peking University at the time of the May 4th Movement. There he met Ch'en Tu'hsiu, and later became a charter member of the CCP. After the collapse of the KMT-CCP alliance he was sent to his native Hunan to foment peasant insurrections. His "Autumn Harvest Uprisings," named for the season when collection of rents and taxes by landlords aroused peasant hostility, failed miserably, and he was dismissed from the Politburo of the CCP. But Mao was so impressed by the possibilities of peasant revolts against landlords that he decided: "Without the poor peasants there will be no revolution." The Comintern, however, condemned the "excesses" of the peasant movement while the KMT-CCP alliance remained in force.

CANTON COMMUNE. In Dec. 1927 Communist forces, assisted by a local warlord, seized key installations in Canton and created a Soviet of Workers', Soldiers', and Peasants' Deputies. This regime, known as the Canton Commune, lasted only a few days. By the end of 1927, Communist influence in China was at a low ebb, and Chiang Kai-shek was preparing to set up a unified Nationalist government at Nanking.

1928–35

CONSOLIDATION OF THE NATIONALIST GOVERNMENT. In 1928 Chiang resumed the Northern Expedition and brought Peking and Manchuria under at least nominal control. He then established a KMT 1-party regime, for which he invoked the political philosophy of Sun Yat-sen, still revered as the hero of the revolution. Sun's political program had envisaged 3 steps: military unification of China; a period of "tutelage," in which the KMT monopolized power and educated the people in public affairs; and democracy, as defined by Sun.

Chiang's unification of the country was followed by the promulgation, Oct. 1928, of the Organic Law of the Nationalist government. The Political Council of the KMT's Central Executive Committee became the chief policy-making body of the new government, which also consisted of

5 *Yüan,* or branches—Executive, Legislative, Judicial, Examination, and Control —to implement the Council's directives. A president, who also held the posts of head of state in foreign relations and commander in chief of the military forces, headed the government.

RULE OF CHIANG KAI-SHEK. Since, as president, the limits of Chiang's power were undefined, he became a virtual dictator. In 1931 the Organic Law was replaced by a constitution, which retained the same government apparatus but added a bill of rights and weakened the president's power. Chiang resigned the presidency in favor of Lin Sen, who died in 1943, at which time Chiang again became president.

Although Chiang held many party and government posts after resigning the presidency, his real base of power remained the national army, which, in turn, was the instrument by which the Nationalist government exerted authority over military leaders who retained private armies after joining the KMT. Chiang created the Central Military Academy, whose graduates, as well as those from Whampoa, remained personally loyal to him. After the KMT's Russian advisers were expelled, Chiang invited German military experts to help him build a professional army, but he continued to promote officers on the basis of personal loyalty rather than ability. Next to the army the most important pillar of Chiang's power was his relationship, cemented by marriage to Soong Mei-ling (b. 1898), with China's major financial corporations.

Under Chiang the Nationalist government instituted such major reforms as the establishment of a sound currency system, a national budget, and modern economic accounting procedures, improvements in transportation and communications, the introduction of western-style law codes, and the spread of education. The government's critical weakness was its neglect of agrarian problems, particularly widespread tenancy and absentee landlordism. The Communists skillfully exploited agrarian discontent.

NEW LIFE MOVEMENT. Chiang sought to strengthen his rule by an ideological program of his own, the "New Life Movement," inaugurated in 1934. Emphasizing the Confucian virtues of propriety, righteousness, and sense of shame, the movement sought to reform daily living habits, strengthen Chinese moral character, and instill respect for the government's authority. It collapsed largely because of its incompatibility with the new western-inspired values of young Chinese, who rejected Confucianism.

OPPOSITION TO THE CHIANG REGIME. Chiang faced considerable opposition from political rivals within the KMT. The two Ch'en brothers, members of the party's right wing, were Chiang's chief supporters in the intraparty struggle. Known along with their adherents as the "C.C. Clique," the Ch'ens controlled the "Blue Shirts," a secret group charged with maintaining party discipline and weeding out opponents.

Outside the party Chiang's main enemies were the warlords, Communists, and Japanese. Since the Nationalist government firmly dominated only the lower Yangtze Valley, it was vulnerable to challenge by warlord regimes in the rest of China. The Japanese invasion of Manchuria, 1931, forged a temporary unity among rival forces in China. The Tangku armistice, 25 May, 1933, ended the fighting over Manchuria, which came under firm Japanese control.

CHINESE SOVIET REPUBLIC. In addition to fighting the warlords and the Japanese, Chiang's army staged several "extermination campaigns" against the Communists, who in the winter of 1927 retreated, under Mao's leadership, into the Chingkan Mountains in southeastern China. The regular CCP leaders remained in Shanghai, where they continued to obey the Comintern policy of armed insurrection in the cities. The CCP finally admitted the failure of this policy, and accepted Mao's theory of a rural base and peasant support, Nov. 1931, when the Chinese Soviet Republic was created at Juichin, in Kiangsi Province, under Mao's chairmanship. This regime issued a constitution and a land law providing for redistribution of land to the poorest peasants. Mao did not wish to break openly with the Comintern, however, until he had consolidated his power and could present Stalin with a *fait accompli*.

THE LONG MARCH. Thanks to the Japanese invasion of Manchuria and the resulting concentration of Nationalist energies against the threat this posed, the Communists won time to strengthen their republic. The Tangku armistice, however, left Nationalist forces free to attack the Communists again. In late 1933 Nationalist troops surrounded Communist-held territory, setting up a blockade which prevented the Communists from obtaining supplies. By Oct. 1934 the latter's position had become untenable. The result was the famous "Long March," in which the Communists broke free of their enemy's stranglehold and marched over 6,000 miles from southeast to northwest China. In Jan. 1935, in the middle of the Long March, the CCP held a conference at Tsun-yi at which Mao was elected party chairman. Mao thus became the first Communist to reach a top leadership position without formal investiture from Moscow. In Oct. 1935 the Communists established new headquarters at Yenan in Shensi Province. Although this was not far from the Sino-Soviet border, Stalin offered the CCP little assistance.

1936–45

FORMATION OF THE UNITED FRONT. Alarmed by Nazism in Germany and militarism in Japan, the Soviet Union ordered the Comintern to adopt a united-front policy, 1935. The CCP independently followed the same line: a party conference issued a resolution, 1 Aug., 1935, urging united resistance against Japan. Chiang and many CCP members remained wary of co-operation, but Japanese incursions near Yenan, 1936, led the Communists to reiterate the need for a united front. Chiang continued to resist the idea. In Dec. 1936 he ordered the troops under Chang Hsüeh-liang, warlord of Manchuria, to attack the Communists. These troops, however, had been driven out of Manchuria by Japanese forces and were garrisoned at Sian, not far from Yenan. They were thus susceptible to Communist propaganda advocating

an anti-Japanese alliance and disobeyed Chiang's order. When Chiang personally flew to Sian to enforce his wishes, he was kidnapped by Chang's troops. Communist mediation was instrumental in Chiang's release; although he was their chief opponent, the Communists believed his leadership indispensable to a successful united-front policy. On 21 Aug., 1937, a Sino-Soviet treaty of nonaggression was signed at Nanking, and supplementary accords provided for substantial aid to China.

A month later the CCP issued a manifesto proclaiming a CCP-KMT alliance against Japan. The manifesto pledged a number of concessions, the most important of which was reorganization of the Red Army under Nationalist supervision, but Mao insisted on CCP independence within its own territory and autonomy within the united front to a degree still consistent with anti-Japanese unity. On 23 Sept. Chiang issued a statement welcoming the Communist proclamation and promising to cease military suppression of the CCP in favor of joint efforts against the Japanese.

In the 1st year of its existence the united front functioned smoothly. By mid-1938, however, cracks in its structure were apparent. From then on each side accused the other of violations of the 1937 agreements, and clashes between Communist and Nationalist forces increased. A serious military confrontation between the 2 sides in Jan. 1941 led the Nationalists to reimpose a blockade of Communist-held territory.

SUCCESS OF COMMUNIST POLICIES. The years 1941–42 were difficult ones for the Communists, but in mid-1943 a period of rapid Communist territorial expansion began. Japanese puppets ruled most of north China's cities, but the poorly garrisoned small towns and the vast countryside were a military and political vacuum which the Communists filled. The people of north China at first accepted Japanese rule willingly, but Japan's brutal occupation tactics alienated the villagers in time and paved the way for Communist-sponsored rural mobilization on the basis of peasant nationalism and hatred of the Japanese. The theoretical basis of the Communist program was Mao's *On the New Democracy*, 1940. It envisaged a "joint dictatorship of all revolutionary classes" under Communist leadership to lead China through the "bourgeois-democratic" and later the "socialist" stages of the revolution. In order to allay the fears of non-Communist groups, Mao suggested that the bourgeois-democratic stage, which was directed against imperialism and feudalism, would be prolonged and would permit private enterprise and expansion of capitalism. Whenever the Communists entered a village, they attracted peasants to their cause by persuading landlords to reduce rents. This policy also induced landlords to co-operate with the CCP in order to avoid confiscation of their land. The Communists distributed to the peasants land belonging to absentee or collaborationist landlords. One of the CCP's most successful policies during this period was the "Production Movement," which began as a reaction to the KMT blockade of Communist-held areas and aimed to make every such area self-sufficient in agriculture and industry. As the Sino-Japanese war progressed, people in Communist-administered regions came to enjoy a higher standard of living than their counterparts in Kuomintang areas. The Communists built people's militia units so that villagers could participate directly in the fight against the Japanese. These units, whose greatest contribution was gathering military intelligence, complemented the Communists' own regular and guerrilla troops.

COMMUNIST METHODS OF GOVERNMENT. The CCP introduced democracy in the form of elective village and town councils. Although all anti-Japanese political parties, including the KMT, were legalized, the Communists' position of leadership was not jeopardized but rather exercised through "mass organizations" of women's, farmers', youth, and other groups. The Communists also initiated a veritable social revolution in the "liberated areas," including introduction of free and compulsory education, enforcement of monogamy, reform of the legal code, and publication of vast quantities of newspapers and magazines as media for the spread of propaganda,

which, however, never mentioned the word "Communist." Communist-held areas expanded from c. 35,000 sq. mi. containing about 1½ m. people in 1937 to c. 300,000 sq. mi. and 95 m. people in 1945. Similarly, the number of Communist troops increased from approximately 100,000 regulars in 1937 to 900,000 plus 2 m. in the people's militia by 1945.

In order to maintain party discipline in the midst of a vast influx of new members, Mao conducted *cheng feng*, or ideological remolding campaigns. He also emphasized the need to "Sinify" Marxism-Leninism, i.e., adapt it to Chinese conditions. This policy, moreover, did not entail repudiation of the Soviet line; when Stalin dissolved the Comintern in 1943, he urged each Communist Party to attune itself to local conditions. On international issues Mao continued to obey Stalinist dictates. In the spring of 1945 the CCP held its 7th Congress, the 1st since 1928. Its highlight was Mao's speech "On Coalition Government." He called for a "provisional, democratic coalition government—including representatives of all parties and groups" to initiate democratic reforms and mobilize all anti-Japanese elements. He made clear, however, that his ultimate goal was a Communist China.

DECLINE OF THE KUOMINTANG. In sharp contrast to the increased popularity and influence of the CCP, the KMT wallowed in stagnation and corruption. The KMT was never a mass organization, but rather an elite party enjoying passive acceptance, not active support, from the Chinese people. As war gripped China, the KMT abandoned whatever reform programs it may have harbored and, under the leadership of Chiang and the right wing, became increasingly autocratic. It alienated more and more social groups and then resorted to repression to ensure loyalty; repressive measures resulted, in turn, in further disaffection.

Before the war the KMT depended for political and financial support on western-oriented businessmen, industrialists, and financiers in the coastal cities. When the Japanese captured the coastal provinces, this support, as well as the important revenue from maritime customs, was lost.

The war also generated spiraling inflation, which turned many middle-class and wealthy elements against the government. As the Japanese penetrated inland, the Nationalists had to evacuate Nanking and move the capital to Chungking, where conservative landowners provided a basis of support and land tax became the chief item of government revenue. Since the KMT could not afford to alienate the large landlords by promulgating land reforms, the Communists attracted millions of propertyless peasants to their cause.

Chiang's answer to Mao's *On the New Democracy* was *China's Destiny,* 1943. In contrast to Mao's promise of a bright revolutionary future, Chiang envisaged a paternalistic regime. Whereas Mao offered all classes an opportunity to co-operate in China's reconstruction, Chiang scolded western-oriented intellectuals for disloyalty to China, condemned businessmen for profit-seeking, and alienated the youth with his emphasis on frugality and obedience. He disregarded completely the widespread popular support for the CCP, and argued that a military defeat of its forces would dispose of the Communist menace. This attitude led him to scorn the idea of basic reforms and to commit his best troops against the Communists rather than against the Japanese. Despite Chiang's intransigence, negotiations between the CCP and the KMT were held in Chungking in the autumn of 1942. In 1944 talks were resumed, but at the war's end the 2 sides were no closer to agreement. Neither was willing to abandon the 1-party control each enjoyed in its own territory. The surrender of Japan, Aug. 1945, freed both Communist and Nationalist troops for exclusive use against each other and for full-scale civil war. (*Cont. p. 545.*)

KOREA

1914–29

GROWTH OF KOREAN NATIONALISM. During 1918–19 Gen. Yi Tong-hwi organized an embryonic expatriate Korean Communist Party in Khabarovsk and Vladivostok, which sought Soviet arms and aid. On 1 Mar., 1919, the nationalist Samil movement was founded, and held a peaceful nationwide demonstration to indicate nationalist sentiment. The demonstration was brutally suppressed by the Japanese; 6,670 Koreans were killed, 14,611 wounded, and 52,770 arrested. Between 1919 and 1921, An Ch'ang-ho tried to set up a Provisional Government of the Korean Republic, and meetings in support of the attempt were held in Shanghai and Seoul, but no lasting interest was aroused. On 1 Mar., 1919, a Declaration of Independence was signed by 33 patriots and the Mansei movement, nationalist in tone, was formed (and soon suppressed by the Japanese). Anti-Japanese sentiment increased as the Japanese government expropriated the property of Korean farmers. Between 1910 and 1920, 400,000 Japanese moved to Korea.

KOREAN COMMUNISM. In 1925 the Korean Communist Party was inaugurated in Seoul. Between 1927 and 1931 a coalition of Communists and Nationalists formed the Shinganhoe (New Korea Society), but all subversive activities were put down by the Japanese. The year 1929 was marked by a general strike of factory workers in Wonsan and by the Kwangzu student revolt. During the 1920's Communism was a major focus for Korean anti-Japanese activities, in part because only the Soviet Union seemed willing to support such activities. The same period, however, was also marked by efforts on the part of the Japanese in the direction of liberalism, conciliation, and reform, under the leadership of Adm. Saito Minoru. These efforts had small result, but many Koreans were persuaded to collaborate with the Japanese.

1930–45

JAPANESE ECONOMIC EXPLOITATION. During the 1930's half the rice crop of Korea was exported to feed Japan, while the per capita consumption of rice by the Koreans themselves fell by 45%. Japanese liberal policies withered as militarism in the homeland gained sway.

The occupying power installed an excellent network of railways and roads as well as postal services, telecommunications, hydroelectric plants, mines, and some modern industries, but Korean living conditions remained poor, and Japanese large-scale landlordism increased greatly. By 1936, ⅔ of the government bureaucrats in Korea were Japanese, and the use of the Korean language was proscribed.

KOREA IN WORLD WAR II. In 1942 Korea became an integral part of Japan, though Koreans did not automatically acquire Japanese citizenship. Korean youths were conscripted into the Japanese army. On 1 Dec., 1943, at the Cairo Conference, Roosevelt, Churchill, and Chiang Kai-shek issued a statement proclaiming that "in due course Korea shall become free and independent." In Feb. 1945 at the Yalta Conference the Soviet Union agreed to declare war on Japan in return, *inter alia,* for the right to occupy the northern half of Korea pending the establishment of Korean independence. On 26 July at the Potsdam Conference the allies again pledged Korean independence. On 9 Aug. the Russians occupied North Korea, and U.S. troops soon afterward moved into South Korea. The 38th parallel was accepted as the boundary between the 2 occupation zones. (*Cont. p. 587.*)

JAPAN IN AN AGE OF MILITARISM

1914–20

JAPAN IN WORLD WAR I. Japan saw the war in Europe as a chance to improve her position in China. On 23 Aug., 1914, when the Germans ignored a Japanese ultimatum to withdraw their military and naval forces from China and yield up their leased territories, Japan declared war. By 1915 the Japanese had occupied all German-leased territory and the German-owned islands in the Pacific. They then presented to China the 21 Demands, and enforced acceptance of most of them, May 1915. During 1916–17 they consolidated their gains in China by means of a series of secret treaties with the European powers. Japan still lacked U.S. acquiescence in her China position, but the Lansing-Ishii Agreement, 2 Nov., 1917, recognized that "territorial propinquity" gave her a special interest in China. She therefore felt that her position was assured at the coming peace conference. Meanwhile she quietly pushed her economic penetration of China by means of the "Nishihara loans," 1917–18.

SIBERIAN EXPEDITION. When the success of the Bolshevik Revolution raised the possibility of allied intervention in Russia, Japan saw an opportunity to further her interests in Siberia and northern Manchuria. It happened that in June 1918 the Czech army, which had rebelled while returning home via the Trans-Siberian Railroad, captured Vladivostok. The U.S.A. wanted to support the Czechs, and requested Japan's help. The Japanese government favored modest action and adherence to the principle of self-defense. It was in this spirit that Japan assented to the American request. The Japanese army, however, followed its own plan and soon occupied Siberia from Lake Baikal to Vladivostok. Japan gained nothing from the venture, though her troops remained in Siberia until 1922.

PREMIERSHIP OF HARA TAKASHI. The economic boom caused by the war dramatically reversed Japan's unfavorable balance of payments and brought over-all prosperity. But it also caused a very sharp rise in prices. Widespread unrest resulted. The nearly nationwide rice riots of Aug. 1918 caused Premier Terauchi Masatake (1852–1919), a moderate general, to resign. He was followed by Japan's 1st "commoner" premier, Hara Takashi (1856–1921). Hara was not from Satsuma or Choshu, and had refused an appointment to the peerage. He was the president of the Seiyukai, the majority party in the Diet, and his cabinet was composed almost entirely of party men. But Hara was either unwilling or unable to promote strong party rule, and preferred to conciliate the military, the bureaucracy, business interests, and the Genro (Elder Statesmen). It was his party that defeated in the Diet a bill to introduce universal male suffrage. In 1921 he was assassinated by a rightist.

PARIS PEACE CONFERENCE. At Versailles, where she sat on the Council of 10, Japan obtained recognition of her rights in Shantung over bitter Chinese protests. She also received as mandates the former German islands north of the Equator. She failed, however, to obtain in the Covenant of the League of Nations a statement upholding racial equality. Considerable disillusionment in Japan was the result.

1921–31

WASHINGTON DISARMAMENT CONFERENCE. The U.S.A. called the Washington Disarmament Conference, 12 Nov., 1921–6 Feb., 1922, to discuss naval disarmament and the complexities of the China issue. Japan consented to a warship ratio in the proportion of 5 each for the U.S.A. and Britain to 3 for herself. However, she retained effective control over the Western Pacific. Japan also committed herself to returning Shantung to China. The latter concession, honored in 1922, was a signal example of the conciliatory China policy which became identified with Shidehara Kijuro (1872–1951), the foreign minister during much of the 1920's.

PREMIERSHIP OF KATO TAKA-AKI. An earthquake destroyed vast areas of Tokyo in 1923. In 1924 Matsukata Masayoshi, the last of the senior Genro, died, the only Genro left was Saionji Kimmochi. Between 1921 and 1924, 3 brief nonparty cabinets succeeded one another. Then in June 1924 Kato Takaaki (1860–1926), president of the Kenseikai Party, was named premier. In May 1925 Kato succeeded in having the Diet pass the Universal Manhood Suffrage Act. However, the Diet also passed a stringently antisubversive Peace Preservation Law. Kato died in 1926 and was succeeded by Wakatsuki Reijiro (1866–1950). In Apr. 1927 Gen. Tanaka Giichi (1863–1929) took office as premier. Wakatsuki lost influence following the bank panic of early 1927

and Tanaka was selected as president of the Seiyukai, even though it was the minority party at that time.

INTERVENTION IN MANCHURIA. In June 1928, elements of the Kwangtung Army (the Japanese army in Manchuria) murdered the Manchurian warlord Chang Tso-lin (b. 1876) because he would not co-operate with Japan. As premier, Tanaka could not condone this act. But he was powerless to punish it, and eventually had to resign. His successor was Hamaguchi Osachi (1870–1931), the leader of the Minseito, the successor party to Kato's Kenseikai. Hamaguchi renamed Shidehara foreign minister and worked to cut expenditures and extend the real power of the legislative branch. Over stiff military opposition he obtained Privy Council approval of the further limitations imposed upon Japan by the London Naval Treaty, 1929. In Nov. 1930 he was shot and critically wounded by an assassin. Wakatsuki, who followed him, was unable to resist military pressure. The ultranationalist views of men like Kita Ikki (1883–1937) were inspiring a rash of assassination plots among young officers and rightists. Then on 18 Sept., 1931, the Kwangtung Army engineered a minor explosion on a Japanese-controlled railway line in Manchuria, thus providing the pretext for an instant take-over.

1931–41

INCREASE IN EXPANSIONIST PRESSURES. In Feb. 1932 Manchukuo, the Japanese puppet state in Manchuria, declared itself independent.

On 15 May, 1932, Inukai Tsuyoshi (b. 1855), Wakatsuki's successor as premier, was assassinated. He was the last party premier prior to the American occupation. Under his successor, Adm. Saito Makoto (1858–1936), the military pressed harder still for expansion on the Asian mainland and for greater control at home. On the continent the army did indeed expand, causing international protests which provoked Japan to walk out of the League of Nations, Mar. 1933.

At home factional struggles within the

army were approaching a climax. The contenders were the Kodo-ha (Imperial Way Faction), representing young officers and such senior extremists as War Minister Araki Sadao and Mazaki Jinzaburo, and the Control Faction, representing in general higher-ranking officers who were more moderate as to means, if not to ends. On 26 Feb., 1936, Imperial Way adherents tried to seize control of Tokyo and assassinate key members of the government. The coup was swiftly crushed. Its effects were to strengthen the Control Faction and allow it to pose as the savior of the nation.

1ST KONOYE CABINET. The expansionist mood of Japan's leaders was not shaken by the Diet election returns of Apr. 1937, which overwhelmingly favored moderates. Prince Konoye (Konoe) Fumimaro (1891–1945), inaugurated as premier in June, took the 1st positive steps toward a decisive effort on the continent. A Cabinet Planning Board was created to coordinate and direct the activities of the various branches of government. This board was an important example of several advisory bodies established in the late 1930's. They were meant to allow the government complete control over economic, political, and military activity, but none was entirely successful.

SINO-JAPANESE WAR. The Sino-Japanese war began with a clash at the Marco Polo Bridge near Peking, 7 July, 1937. In Dec. the Japanese took Nanking, whereupon Chiang Kai-shek removed his government inland instead of surrendering. Japan's stated objective had been only to obtain Chiang's recognition of her tutelary position vis-à-vis China. Now the Japanese army was to become bogged down in China's vast interior until 1945.

NATIONAL MOBILIZATION. A National General Mobilization Bill, drafted by the Cabinet Planning Board, was passed by the Diet in Mar. 1938. The bill provided for all measures necessary in the event of a national emergency. For the time being, however, it was not to be fully implemented. A new 5-Minister Conference (premier, war, navy, foreign affairs, finance), entrusted with the most urgent matters of state, was dominated by the military. But the most powerful civilians shared the goals of the army and navy.

THE NEW ORDER. On 3 Nov., 1938, Konoye issued a statement on "A New Order in East Asia." The statement looked to the integration of Japan, China, and Manchukuo under Japanese leadership, and to the eventual expulsion of western influence from the area. It had been drafted by a highly distinguished group of civilian intellectuals, not by outright militarists.

MAINLAND EXPANSION. Through the cabinet's Manchurian Affairs Board and the General Affairs Board controlled by the Kwangtung Army, the economies of Japan and Manchukuo were virtually integrated. For China a China Affairs Board in Tokyo and a series of Japanese-owned regional development corporations attempted to achieve the same results. Japan also exerted military pressure to reduce the western presence in China, occupying Hainan Island (French), Feb. 1939, and blockading the British concession in Tientsin, June. But damaging clashes with Soviet troops on the Korean border, July 1938, and on the Mongolian-Manchukuo border, Aug. 1939, alarmed the Japanese government. On the outbreak of war in Europe, Sept. 1939, Japan declared that she would not become involved, but would concentrate on settling the war in China. Negotiations staved off war with the USSR. In Mar. 1940 the Japanese-sponsored Wang Ching-wei government was established in Nanking, and in June Japan forced Britain to close the Burma Road.

DOMESTIC POLITICAL CONSOLIDATION. Konoye's 1st cabinet lasted until Jan. 1939. In July 1940 he was once more the only premier acceptable to all groups. This time his war minister was Gen. Tojo Hideki (1884–1948), Japan's principal wartime leader. Konoye's 4-point program included alliance with the Axis and a planned national economy. The Axis alliance was signed, Sept. 1940, but national economic planning was a vastly more complex problem. The natural and industrial resources available to Japan were widespread geographically and under very different types of control, from full Japanese sovereignty (Korea) to a sovereignty that was officially nominal (Manchukuo) . Moreover, the huge family combines (*zaibatsu*) still resisted full state control. By Oct. 1941 the political parties had been dissolved and the Imperial Rule Assistance Association was established under the premier.

1941–45

PEARL HARBOR. Japan realized that among the western powers only the U.S.A. and the USSR could take action against her, although the Netherlands East Indies had done their best, Sept. 1940, by refusing Japan's demands for oil. In Mar. 1941 Japan obtained a nonaggression treaty from the USSR. From Apr. to Dec. 1941, Ambassador Nomura and Secretary of State Cordell Hull negotiated in Washington, but without result. Japan would not withdraw her troops from China, as Hull demanded, nor give up her alliance with the Axis powers. In June Germany invaded the USSR, prompting the summoning of a Japanese Imperial Conference, 2 July, 1941. At this conference Japan's leaders decided to move into Siam and Indochina even at the risk of war with the U.S.A. In mid-July Konoye removed Foreign Minister Matsuoka Yosuke, believing that Matsuoka was an obstacle preventing smooth negotiations between Japan and the U.S. On 29 July Japanese troops entered Indochina. The U.S.A. immediately froze Japanese assets. On 18 Oct. Tojo became premier. It was soon decided that Japan would make war on the United States and Britain if negotiations broke down. They did break down, and Japan attacked Pearl Harbor, Hawaii, 7 Dec., 1941.

PACIFIC WAR. By May 1942 Japan controlled East Asia from Burma and the Netherlands East Indies to Manchuria, and the islands of the Pacific from the Gilberts to the Aleutians. Her most immediate interest in this vast area was economic exploitation. Politically she hoped to set up "independent" friendly regimes. In Nov. 1942 the Greater East Asia Ministry was created to co-ordinate the exploitation of conquered areas. In Nov. 1943, allied victories like Guadalcanal forced creation of a Munitions Ministry, which finally achieved total economic control over Japan. By Feb. 1944 Tojo was premier, war minister, and chief of the general staff. But the capture of Saipan, July 1944, forced him to resign. He was replaced by Gen. Koiso Kuniaki (1880–1950) . Aug. 1944 saw the formation of a Supreme Council for the Direction of the War, a final effort to co-ordinate all vital government functions. Its chairman was the emperor. In Apr. 1945 Okinawa fell, and Koiso was replaced by Suzuki Kentaro (1867–1948), who favored, in private, termination of the war. By July Japan had asked the USSR to secure a peace short of unconditional surrender.

POTSDAM DECLARATION AND SURRENDER OF JAPAN. On 26 July, 1945, the allies issued the Potsdam Declaration, which called for the unconditional surrender of Japan, to be followed by her occupation, demilitarization, and democratization. Japan did not reply. On 6 Aug. Hiroshima was destroyed by an atomic bomb. On 8 Aug. the USSR declared war on Japan, in accordance with the Yalta Agreement of Feb. 1945. It was the latter that Japan felt as the more crushing blow. On 9 Aug. the Supreme Council met and became deadlocked between those who favored immediate acceptance of the Declaration and those who insisted that Japan should not be occupied and that the emperor's status should not be changed. The atom bombing of Nagasaki on the same day did not break the deadlock. At last, the emperor himself voted for surrender. When the allies rejected a reservation about preserving the emperor's position, the emperor had again to order capitulation. President Truman accepted Japan's surrender on 14 Aug., 1945. The formal surrender was signed aboard U.S.S. *Missouri,* 2 Sept. (*Cont. p. 560.*)

The War of 1939–1945

AXIS-SOVIET PARTITION OF EASTERN EUROPE

1939–41

GERMAN INVASION OF POLAND. After the failure of Nazi efforts (begun 24 Oct., 1938) to gain Polish agreement to the return of the Free State of Danzig to the Reich and the construction of a German extraterritorial road and railway across the Polish Corridor to connect with East Prussia, Hitler secured his eastern flank through the Nazi-Soviet Non-Aggression Pact, 24 Aug., 1939. The German invasion of Poland began on 1 Sept., 1939. The German Luftwaffe gained complete air superiority by destroying the bulk of the Polish Air Force on the ground, and then disrupted lines of communication, thereby crippling Polish mobilization and deployment. Simultaneously the German Army Group North (630,000 men) struck from Pomerania and East Prussia and Army Group South (890,000 men) attacked from Silesia and Slovakia to encircle the hard-fighting but poorly equipped Polish Army (1 m. of its 1.7 m. men mobilized). On 3 Sept. Great Britain and France declared war on Germany, but sent no troops to Poland.

DEFEAT OF POLISH ARMIES. Aided by Poland's decision to make a stand near the frontier so as to protect Polish industry, the Germans quickly broke through everywhere, and by 7 Sept. were 25 miles from Warsaw. An attempted breakthrough, 9 Sept., to Warsaw by the by-passed Poznán Army (100,000 men) forced some German divisions to about-face, but finally the Poznán Army surrendered, 19 Sept. The rapid Polish withdrawal to the southeast compounded German fuel shortages, but on 17 Sept. the pincers of the envelopment closed at Wlodowa. Lvov fell on 21 Sept., Warsaw on the 28th, and the surrender of Kock, 6 Oct., ended organized resistance. The campaign proved the correctness of the German offensive concept of employing large armored striking forces with good close air support, rather than parceling armor out for infantry support. Against Germany the Poles lost 700,000 captured and 66,000 killed. The Germans suffered 44,000 casualties, including 14,000 killed.

NAZI-SOVIET PARTITION OF POLAND. Despite German prodding, the Soviet Union was so unprepared for the rapidity of the German advance that she was unable to invade Poland until 17 Sept. Thereafter the Russians met little resistance, and were mainly concerned with shunting the Germans out of the Soviet sphere guaranteed by the Nazi-Soviet Pact. The Russians captured 220,000 Polish troops, many of whom were to fight the Nazis again, but 4,000 Polish officers were slaughtered in the Katyn forest near Smolensk.

In dividing the spoils the Germans agreed to Stalin's request that no Polish rump state be created (which Stalin feared the Nazis might use against him), and that Lithuania be transferred to the Soviet sphere of control. In return territorial compensations gave Germany almost all ethnically Polish territory, and while the Russians refused to yield any of Poland's oil they did promise to supply Germany with the equivalent of the annual Polish output (300,000 tons of crude oil). Germany now possessed 22 m. and Russia 13 m. of Poland's prewar population. Some ethnically disputed Polish territory was given to Lithuania (including Vilna) and to Slovakia. On 28 Sept., 1939, a new treaty was signed and a joint statement issued calling for an end to the war between Germany and the western powers.

The USSR signed "mutual assistance" pacts, providing for military bases in the Baltic states (with Estonia, 28 Sept.; Latvia, 5 Oct.; and Lithuania, 10 Oct.).

RUSSO-FINNISH WAR. On 22 Oct., 1939, the Soviet Union opened negotia-

tions with Finland, demanding a mutual
assistance pact, a 30-year lease on a naval
base at Hangö, and cession of most of the
Karelian Isthmus, islands in the Gulf of
Finland, and the western half of the
Rybachi Peninsula. The Finns balked
over Hangö and the Karelian Isthmus,
and after voiding the Russo-Finnish Non-
Aggression Treaty, 28 Nov., the Soviet
Union opened the Russo-Finnish War, 30
Nov., with ground attacks all along the
border and the bombing of Helsinki. The
Russian proclamation of a puppet People's Democratic Republic of Finland
failed to take sufficiently into account the
determination of the Finns, who had
completed mobilization (begun 14 Oct.)
and built the "Mannerheim Line" (not
nearly as formidable as Russian propaganda later claimed) across the Karelian
Isthmus.

Finland initially mobilized 9 divisions
and never had more than 210,000 men,
including 11,000 foreign volunteers, while

the USSR attacked with 30 divisions (1 m. men). To the world's surprise, Soviet efforts to sweep north of Lake Ladoga met with disaster as Finnish *motti* tactics isolated and literally chopped the Russian forces to pieces in the dense forests. The Soviet offensive in the Isthmus also stalled. Meanwhile, 14 Dec., the USSR was expelled from the League of Nations for her aggression. In Feb. 1940 the Russians began a massive battering offensive in the Karelian Isthmus which ground slowly forward. Finally, 4 Mar., Soviet armor began to cross the frozen Viipuri Bay, and the Finns, faced with a hopeless situation, sued for peace, 6 Mar. Increased Russian demands now included Finland's 2nd largest city, Viipuri (Viborg).

By the Treaty of Moscow, 12 Mar., 1940, Finland ceded 12% of her territory, from which 420,000 refugees had to be absorbed into the badly shaken Finnish economy. The Finns had lost 23,150 killed and 43,500 wounded and the Soviet forces lost 200,000 men killed.

Stalin rounded out his Baltic holdings when he ordered his troops to engineer Communist coups in Lithuania, Latvia, and Estonia, which were then absorbed into the USSR (15 June–16 Aug., 1940). Following the Nazi conquest of Norway, Apr.–June 1940, the Finns agreed, 12 Sept., to permit German troops, as a counterbalance to Soviet influence, to cross into Norway via Finland (which had been assigned to the Soviet sphere by the Nazi-Soviet Pact).

PARTITION OF THE BALKANS. Alarmed at the rapidity of Hitler's victory in the West, Stalin turned to Rumania, and informed the Germans, 23 June, 1940, that the USSR would demand not only Bessarabia (assigned to Russia by the Aug. 1939 pact) but also Bukovina. Both of these regions had large Ukrainian populations. To cool Hitler's displeasure Stalin agreed, 26 June, to limit his Bukovina claim to the northern part, and on 27 June demanded the cession of this area from Rumania, effective 28 June. It was Hitler's turn to be dismayed, and he decided to block further Soviet advances in the Balkans. Outstanding ethnic claims

against Rumania were settled when Bulgaria received the southern Dobruja (lost in the 2nd Balkan War, 1913) by the Treaty of Craiova, 23 Aug., 1940, and Hungary obtained northern Transylvania (predominantly Magyar, but with a million Rumanians) by the Vienna Award, 30 Aug. In return Hitler guaranteed Rumania's borders, obviously against further Russian claims. In 2 months Rumania had lost ⅓ of her territory and population. On 20 Nov. Hungary joined the Tripartite Pact (concluded originally between Germany, Italy, and Japan, 27 Sept.), and Rumania and Slovakia followed suit, 22 Nov. While Hitler had ordered plans to be made for a possible invasion of the USSR, 21 July, he made one last attempt, in a meeting with the Russian Foreign Minister Molotov, 12–13 Nov., to direct Soviet interest away from the Balkans and south toward the Indian Ocean. But the Russians were adamant, and reaffirmed their interest in Bulgaria and the Dardanelles, while demanding withdrawal of German troops from Finland and revocation of the guarantee of Rumania's borders. Hitler now definitely decided on war, and approved Operation Barbarossa, 18 Dec., which provided for an invasion of Russia on 15 May, 1941.

INVASION OF GREECE AND YUGOSLAVIA. Meanwhile Mussolini, jealous of Hitler's successes, attacked Greece, 28 Oct., 1940, without warning the Germans. To the Duce's chagrin the defiant Greeks soon routed the Italians and mounted a counterinvasion of Albania which was not halted until 1 Mar., 1941. Hitler now had to cover his southern flank, and despite Soviet objections moved German troops into Bulgaria (following Bulgaria's adherence to the Tripartite Pact on 1 Mar.). Yugoslavia was also cowed into signing the pact, 25 Mar., but Serb patriots overthrew the regency of Prince Paul and proclaimed young King Peter of age, 26–27 Mar. Although the new Yugoslav government signed a friendship pact with the USSR, 4 Apr., and Molotov informed the Germans that Russia expected Germany to remain at peace with Yugoslavia, the German Balkan campaign began, 6 Apr., with a simultaneous invasion of Yugoslavia and Greece. Belgrade was devastated, 6 Apr., by German bombers and, aided in the north by widespread mutiny by Croat units whose members resented past Serb domination, the Nazis overran Yugoslavia by 17 Apr., on which date the Yugoslav army surrendered.

YUGOSLAV PARTISAN ACTIVITIES. Yugoslavia was now partitioned, with Croatia independent under the Fascist Ustaši regime of Ante Pavelić, and Germany, Italy (and her puppet, Albania), Hungary, and Bulgaria annexing all but a German-occupied Serbian rump state roughly the size of Serbia before the Balkan Wars of 1912–13. Large-scale Croat, Hungarian, Albanian, and German atrocities against the Serbs followed, partly as retaliation for the 1st serious guerrilla uprisings in Europe by Serbian Chetniks under Col. Draža Mihailović (1893?–1946). A Yugoslav Communist Partisan movement led by Tito (Josip Brož, b. 1892) next arose, and a 3-cornered struggle ensued in which Mihailović sometimes received Axis aid against the Partisans. Though staunchly anti-Axis, Mihailović distrusted the Communists and feared further genocidal reprisals against the Serbs. The ensuing fall-off in Chetnik activity, contrasted with unabated Partisan operations, caused a complete switch of western support to Tito by late 1943.

GERMAN CONQUEST OF GREECE. The Germans also overran Greece, taking Athens, 27 Apr., 1941, and a hastily contrived British expedition, which arrived on 5 Mar., suffered heavy casualties when forced to withdraw, 17 Apr.–1 May. A German airborne invasion took Crete, 20–31 May, suffering 6,600 casualties as against 18,000 British, but Hitler believed his losses were too high and that the surprise factor had been lost, so that he decided against paratroop operations for the rest of the war. Italy annexed the Ionian Islands, and Bulgaria that part of Macedonia and Thrace lost to Greece in 1913. While the Barbarossa Plan allowed for the Greek invasion, the Yugoslav campaign forced a critical postponement of the invasion of Russia to 22 June,

1941. The partition of Eastern Europe was complete.

NAZI SWEEP THROUGH WESTERN EUROPE

1940

INVASION OF DENMARK AND NORWAY. Hitler's expansionist ambitions were directed toward the east, and he hoped that the British and French would recognize his conquest of Poland as a *fait accompli*. In a Reichstag address of 6 Oct., 1939, he stated that the return of Germany's pre-World War I colonies was his only remaining claim, and called for a peace conference, but such pleas were ignored. During the Russo-Finnish War the British and French made an unsuccessful diplomatic attempt to establish a presence in Norway and Sweden, which would not only have aided the Finns but would also have cut the Nazis off from Sweden's high-quality iron ore being shipped from the Norwegian port of Narvik. Allied efforts to block such shipments culminated in the British mining of Norwegian coastal waters, 8 Apr., 1940.

Hitler responded with the simultaneous invasion of Denmark and Norway, 9 Apr. Faced with a hopeless situation, the Danish government agreed to the German occupation of Denmark a few hours after the invasion. Hitler hoped for an equally quick victory in Norway by landing 27,000 troops in the 1st week, and 40,000 soon afterward by warship. The Germans ran into difficulty at Oslo, where the Oscarsborg fort held off the invaders for a day, sinking several warships and allowing the government to escape. But half the 15,000-man Norwegian army was stationed in the Arctic because of the Russo-Finnish War. On 9 Apr. the Germans captured much military equipment and all key communication centers, and soon only 1 Norwegian division remained under central control to block the German advance north from Oslo.

TRONDHEIM AND NARVIK. Between 16 and 23 Apr. Anglo-French forces numbering 12,000 landed at Andalsnes to the south and Namsos to the north of

Trondheim. But following the defeat of a British brigade south of Andalsnes, the allies evacuated the Trondheim area, 3 May. The Germans faced their greatest difficulty at Narvik, which could be reached by land only from Sweden and was at the maximum air-support range. Here the German navy suffered heavy losses (10 destroyers), but the 2,000 German mountain troops landed were thereby reinforced by 2,600 sailors. Allied landings began on 14 Apr. and by the end of May built up the Anglo-French-Norwegian force to 25,000 men who finally drove the Germans from Narvik. The allied collapse in France, however, forced the evacuation of Norway, 4–8 June, and on 9 June the Norwegian army surrendered. Although Britain occupied the formerly Danish Iceland, 10 May, Greenland, and the Faroe Islands, the conquest of Norway gave Hitler naval bases on the North Atlantic and a secure monopoly of Swedish iron ore.

GERMAN INVASION PLANS FOR WESTERN EUROPE. After the failure of his Oct. 1939 peace overtures, Hitler ordered planning for an invasion of the west, *Fall Gelb* (Case Yellow—twice postponed, Nov. 1939 and Jan. 1940, due to bad weather). Army Group B or Belgium (variously 37–43 divisions, including 8 armored) was to swing through Belgium north of Liège, while Army Group A or Ardennes (22–27 divisions, no armor) moved through the heavily forested Ardennes region of Belgium and Luxembourg. The allies also believed the Liège route the more logical and therefore probable, since the formidable Maginot Line and the Ardennes obstructed a direct invasion of France, while northern France was unfortified because the allies planned to defend forward in Belgium. Aided by the barriers of the Ardennes, Meuse River, Liège forts, the supposedly impregnable Fort Eben-Emael, and the Albert Canal, the Belgians were expected to delay the Germans until the British and French reached the Schelde River (Plan E). German delay later led to the shifting of this forward position to the Dyle River (Plan D). Meanwhile the suggestions of Gens. Karl von Runstedt

(1875–1953) and Erich von Manstein (b. 1887), commander and chief of staff respectively of Army Group A, that the main attack be through the Ardennes were accepted by Hitler. Army Group B was reduced to 28 divisions (3 armored), while Army Group A now had 44 divisions (7 armored) with which to drive to the English Channel. In May 1940, 136 German divisions opposed 94 French, 10 British, 22 Belgian, and 9 Dutch divisions. The Germans had 2,440 tanks to the allies' 2,690, but German armor was faster and as in the East concentrated for rapid offensive breakthroughs.

CONQUEST OF THE NETHERLANDS. The opening of Hitler's offensive in the West, 10 May, toppled Neville Chamberlain, who was replaced by Winston Churchill (1874–1965) as British prime minister on the same day. The Netherlands were quickly overrun. On 10 May paratroops captured key bridges and airfields near Rotterdam and The Hague, while the German 18th Army broke through the Maas (Meuse) River defenses in the southern Netherlands. French reinforcements arrived at Breda, 11 May, to stiffen the retreating Dutch, but were forced to fall back toward Antwerp, 13 May. Meanwhile the German army linked up with the paratroop forces, the Dutch government fled to England, and the remnants of the Dutch army withdrew into their final defensive line, the Fortress of Holland. On 14 May the Luftwaffe leveled the business district of Rotterdam as a warning to cease resistance, and the Dutch surrendered the same day.

SURRENDER OF BELGIUM AND THE BRITISH EVACUATION. In Belgium the German 6th Army drove across the Meuse and the Albert Canal north of Liège, 10 May, and then swung southwest. Meanwhile German parachute and glider troops captured Fort Eben-Emael, 11 May. Liège was occupied, 12 May, and by 15 May the 6th Army had concentrated against the Dyle Line, while the 18th Army moved against the Belgian left flank near Antwerp. In the meantime Army Group A required the entire 10th of May to cross the difficult Ardennes in northern Luxembourg. Hard fighting ensued before the Meuse could be crossed near Sedan, 14 May, but the shallow French defenses permitted a deep German penetration which threatened to outflank the allies in Belgium. Allied forces fell back to the Schelde while the Germans raced for the English Channel, which they reached near Abbeville, 20 May. Meanwhile Antwerp fell, 18 May, and hesitant allied efforts to break out south from Belgium, 21–23 May, failed, leaving 40 divisions trapped. A thrust to cut the allies off from the sea seemed likely when the German armor was suddenly halted, 23 May, due to Hitler's desire to husband his depleted tank strength for a drive southward to prevent the French from stabilizing their front as in 1914. King Leopold surrendered Belgian forces on 28 May, and the British Expeditionary Force completed its withdrawal via the port of Dunkirk on 4 June, evacuating 355,000 men (⅔ British).

CAPITULATION OF FRANCE. Having already lost half their armed forces and several bridgeheads across the Somme River portion of their new defense line, the French were unable to prevent a decisive breakthrough by Army Group B, 8 June, northwest of Paris. Meanwhile Mussolini had decided to share in the spoils, and declared war on France and Britain, 10 June. The French fell back behind the Marne, 11 June, and on 14 June the Germans entered the open city of Paris while in the east Army Group C quickly breached the demoralized Maginot defenses. Although Premier Paul Reynaud (b. 1878) considered continuing the fight from North Africa and Churchill offered, 16 June, a union with Britain, a new French government under Marshal Henri Pétain (1856–1951) sued for peace, 17 June. The armistice was signed, 21 June, at the same place, the forest of Compiègne, and in the same railway dining car in which the German capitulation had occurred in 1918. The French suffered 100,000 killed and 1½ m. captured (mostly in the mop-up stage of the campaign), while the British had 70,000 casualties and lost the bulk of their weapons and equipment. Germany lost 27,000 dead, 18,000 missing, and 110,000 wounded. Peace terms provided for Ger-

man occupation of northern and western France, with the remainder under a government at Vichy headed by Pétain, and for the demobilization of the French fleet.

BATTLES OF BRITAIN AND THE ATLANTIC

1940–45

ANGLO-GERMAN STRUGGLE FOR AIR SUPREMACY. When the British did not come to terms, Hitler ordered, 2 July, 1940, planning for an invasion of Britain (Operation Sea Lion). Aerial supremacy was necessary for such an invasion, and the battle for command of the air began, 13 Aug., ending a preliminary phase which had concentrated on Channel shipping and nuisance targets. Until 6 Sept. the Luftwaffe struck against British airfields, aircraft factories, and communications, but the British Fighter Command refused to accept decisive battle against German fighter sweeps. Instead the RAF (Royal Air Force) concentrated against the bomber formations, inflicting heavy losses. Moreover, the British Spitfire fighter had better armament and maneuverability than the German Messerschmitt 109, and the Germans also faced British radar and antiaircraft artillery. In a further attempt to force a decision the Germans began to attack London, 7 Sept., and inflicted severe damage, but as before German losses exceeded those of the British. On 17 Sept. Operation Sea Lion was postponed indefinitely.

By mid-Nov. the Germans had switched entirely to less costly night raids, which continued until mid-May 1941, when the Luftwaffe began to move the bulk of its forces east for the Russian campaign. Despite heavy RAF losses, those of the Germans had been greater (5–3 ratio), and the survival of Fighter Command made the Battle of Britain a British victory. German air raids, including those by V-1 (subsonic) and V-2 (supersonic) rockets later in the war, killed 60,000 British civilians, but as elsewhere conventional bombing demonstrated nowhere near the knockout capability claimed by aerial enthusiasts before 1939.

BATTLE OF THE ATLANTIC.

When the war broke out, the British and French together possessed overwhelming naval superiority over Germany (battleships and cruisers, 103 to 9; aircraft carriers, 9 to 0; submarines, 131 to 57). Only 22 of the German submarines were equipped for Atlantic operations. The German surface fleet proved no match for the allies, as the pocket battleship *Graf Spee* had to be scuttled in Montevideo Harbor, Uruguay, 17 Dec., 1939, and the battleship *Bismarck* was sunk on 26–27 May, 1941, on her maiden voyage.

Soon after the beginning of hostilities the British revived the convoy system, and the Germans responded, late 1940, with submarine wolf packs. In July 1941 the U.S. Navy began convoying merchant vessels bound for Britain part way across the Atlantic, and on 11 Sept. American escorts were ordered no longer to await hostile action but to "shoot first." Allied shipping suffered its heaviest losses in 1 month in Nov. 1942, but stringent anti-submarine measures (escort carriers, destroyer groups, radar, sonar, radio direction finding) turned the tide decisively by mid-1943. The invention of the snorkel and increased U-boat production in 1944 were unable to effect a reversal. Allied and neutral shipping losses amounted to 23 m. tons (⅔ to submarines) during the war, but the German U-boat campaign never came close to winning the Battle of the Atlantic.

INCREASING U.S. WAR INVOLVEMENT AND LEND-LEASE. On 20 July, 1940, President Roosevelt signed a bill providing for a 2-ocean navy and 200 new warships. Increased American war preparedness was further demonstrated when U.S. aircraft production reached 900 per month in Aug. On 3 Sept., 1940, Roosevelt, by executive order, agreed to provide Britain with 50 overage destroyers in return for a 99-year rent-free lease of naval and air bases in Newfoundland, Bermuda, the Bahamas, Jamaica, St. Lucia, Trinidad, Antigua, and British Guiana. On 16 Sept. the U.S. instituted her first peacetime draft, under the Selective Service Act.

By the Lend-Lease Act, 11 Mar., 1941, the President obtained complete freedom to provide the allies with war matériel, including the power to waive repayment (initial appropriation, $7 billion). On 9 Apr., to forestall any German take-over, the U.S. occupied Greenland, and on 7 July took over from Britain the defense of Iceland. Meanwhile, 14 June, all German and Italian assets in the U.S.A. were frozen. Hitler's attack on the Soviet Union soon brought U.S. ships to Soviet ports carrying war matériel.

On 12 Aug., off the coast of Newfoundland, Roosevelt and Churchill signed the Atlantic Charter as a gesture of solidarity and outline of the world peace to be established "after the final destruction of the Nazi tyranny."

INVASION OF RUSSIA

1941–43

OPERATION BARBAROSSA. As originally conceived by the Germans, Barbarossa had 2 phases: to destroy as much of the Russian army as possible close to the border to prevent any delaying withdrawal into Russia's vast interior, and then to drive rapidly to a line running from Arkhangelsk in the north to the Volga. The Germans assigned 152 divisions, including 19 Panzer divisions (3 m. men), to the invasion, opposing a Soviet force in western Russia of 118 infantry and 20 cavalry divisions, and 40 mechanized and armored brigades (2.3 m. men). German allies furnished 16 Finnish (the only immediately significant allied force), 15 Rumanian (initially to pin down Russian forces), and, after the invasion began, several Hungarian, Italian, and Slovak divisions. Armored striking power was even further concentrated by creating Panzer groups (the largest armored force up to this time having been the Panzer corps). German tanks numbered 3,350 compared to 10,000 Russian, most of which were equal to the German, while 2,000 Luftwaffe aircraft faced 6,000 Soviet planes, most of which were obsolete. The Russians had made a better showing since Finland by thwarting a Japanese incursion into Outer Mongolia during an undeclared war, May–Sept. 1939. While Stalin's annexations in Eastern Europe provided a buffer, they also led his army to fight forward of the Stalin **Line** (fortifications built behind the pre-1939 Soviet border).

1ST GERMAN OFFENSIVE: SUMMER 1941. To placate Hitler with a show of good will, Stalin kept promised raw materials rolling into Germany until the very eve of the Nazi attack. Finally, on the night of 21 June, the USSR got wind of the planned invasion, but it was too late to take any real countermeasures before the Nazis struck early on 22 June. The German Army Group North advanced from East Prussia toward Leningrad, and by the end of June had destroyed 14 Soviet divisions. On 10 July it reached Pskov, while the Finns advanced into the Karelian Isthmus on the same day. Army Group Center attacked toward Moscow via Smolensk (as had Napoleon), and by early July had encircled large numbers of Soviet troops at Bialystok and Minsk. Army Group South, though meeting stiff resistance, advanced steadily toward Kiev. These easy initial victories convinced Hitler and his generals that the campaign had been won. Certainly Stalin's rigid tactics, which equated withdrawal with treason, helped yield a huge bag of prisoners for the Germans.

Stalin made a radio appeal, 3 July, for allied aid, proclaimed a "scorched earth" policy to deny sustenance to the invader, and appealed to Russian nationalism. But the Germans continued to advance. By 5 Aug., Army Group Center had captured 100,000 prisoners near Smolensk while Army Group South destroyed 20 trapped Russian divisions near Uman. By mid-Aug. the 1st phase of the Barbarossa Plan had been accomplished, but, contrary to an initial total estimate of 200 Soviet divisions, the Germans had already identified 360.

At this point, instead of advancing on Moscow, where his generals believed the Russian army would fight the decisive battle, Hitler diverted forces from Army Group Center to help seize Leningrad, the Donets Basin industrial area, and the Crimea. On 19 Sept. Army Group South captured Kiev, and on 24 Sept. completed the disarming of no less than 660,000

trapped Soviet troops. Meanwhile to the north the Finns took Viipuri, 29 Aug., and on 31 Aug. reached their pre-1940 border. On 8 Sept. Army Group North cut Leningrad off from any land connection with the rest of Russia. Leningrad would probably have fallen had Hitler not ordered that the city be surrounded rather than attacked directly, and had the Finns not decided to remain on their old borders (so as to refute past Soviet arguments that Finland's boundaries threatened Leningrad).

ASSAULT ON MOSCOW. Hitler now decided to concentrate against Moscow, 6 Sept. Confident of victory, he also cut back German war production, which did not again reach its maximum until mid-1942. But valuable time had been lost. (Napoleon had reached Moscow on 14 Sept.) On 2 Oct. Army Group Center renewed the offensive after having refitted its armor, and on 19 Oct. completed the capture of 670,000 Soviet soldiers. The Soviet government moved east to Kuibyshev on the Volga, 19 Oct., but Stalin remained in Moscow to stiffen the defense. Then the fall rains turned the Russian roads into seas of mud and Army Group Center slowed to a crawl. The advance of Army Group South had meanwhile taken Kharkov, and on 20 Nov. seized Rostov, only to be driven out of the city, 28 Nov., by the first successful Soviet counteroffensive. Army Group North struck across the Volkhov River, 16 Oct., but rain falling on already marshy terrain slowed the advance so that Tikhvin was reached only on 8 Nov. By mid-Dec. the Russians had forced the Germans back to the Volkhov.

Freezing weather now set in, and while no one wanted to fight in the Russian winter there was disagreement within the German military as to whether Moscow could be taken in time. Hitler gave the go-ahead, and in clear weather Army Group Center began a double envelopment of the city, 15 Nov. But although only 20 mi. from Moscow, snow, fog, and extreme cold brought the German offensive to a halt on 5 Dec., 1941. The Germans had overrun most of the Soviet Union's coal and iron resources and 35 m. people. The

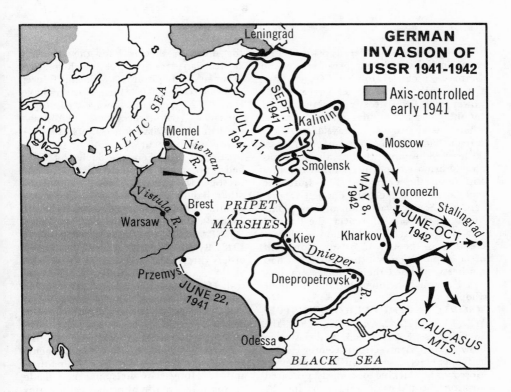

GERMAN INVASION OF USSR 1941-1942

▨ Axis-controlled early 1941

BALTIC SEA

Leningrad

Memel
Nieman R.

SEPT. 1, 1941

JULY 17, 1941

Kalinin

Moscow

Smolensk

Warsaw

Vistula R.

Brest

PRIPET MARSHES

MAY 8, 1942

Voronezh

Stalingrad

JUNE-OCT. 1942

Kharkov

Przemysl

JUNE 22, 1941

Kiev

Dnieper R.

Dnepropetrovsk

Odessa

CAUCASUS MTS.

BLACK SEA

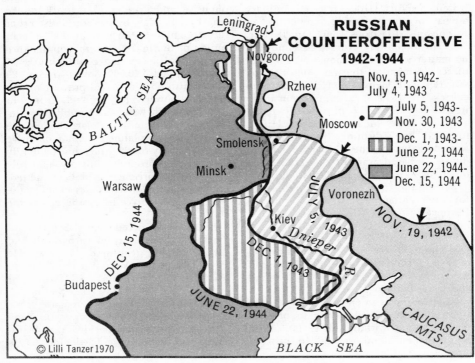

RUSSIAN COUNTEROFFENSIVE 1942-1944

▨ Nov. 19, 1942-July 4, 1943

▨ July 5, 1943-Nov. 30, 1943

▨ Dec. 1, 1943-June 22, 1944

▨ June 22, 1944-Dec. 15, 1944

BALTIC SEA

Leningrad

Novgorod

Rzhev

Moscow

Smolensk

Minsk

Warsaw

DEC. 15, 1944

Voronezh

JULY 5, 1943

NOV. 19, 1942

Kiev

Dnieper R.

DEC. 1, 1943

Budapest

JUNE 22, 1944

CAUCASUS MTS.

BLACK SEA

© Lilli Tanzer 1970

USSR had thus far suffered losses of 5 m. men including 3 m. prisoners, while German casualties totaled 740,000. But the strength of the Soviet government's power had been grossly underestimated by the Germans. Only in the Ukraine, where dissidence had always been widespread, had there been a Soviet collapse. At least 280 infantry and cavalry divisions and 44 armored and mechanized brigades still faced the Germans. The Luftwaffe had failed to strike hard enough to prevent the Soviet evacuation of war plants by rail to the east. Moreover, the Russian war effort received a $1-billion lend-lease credit from the U.S.A., 6 Nov. Confident of a rapid victory, the Germans had neither winterized their vehicles nor provided adequate winter clothing for their troops.

SOVIET COUNTEROFFENSIVE: WINTER 1941–42. On 6 Dec., 1941, the Soviet West Front struck a devastating blow against Army Group Center, which had spent its reserves in the drive on Moscow and, lacking previously prepared positions, could not entrench in the frozen terrain. Hitler rejected military advice to retreat, fearing a repetition of Napoleon's disastrous rout. On 18 Dec. German forces were ordered to stand fast, no matter what. Hitler now took real and direct command of the war when he himself replaced Gen. Heinrich von Brauchitsch (1881–1948) as army commander in chief, 19 Dec. Meanwhile, after the Japanese attack on Pearl Harbor, Hitler, followed by Mussolini, though neither was obligated by the Tripartite Pact to do so, declared war on the U.S.A. His object was to show solidarity with the Japanese and to vent his ire on America for intervening more and more in the European struggle. In turn the U.S.A. declared war on Germany and Italy on the same day, 11 Dec. Thus Hitler recklessly brought the world's strongest industrial power directly into the European war at a time when the Nazi forward march was faltering.

Russian efforts to encircle Army Group Center finally forced Hitler to order a major German withdrawal, 15 Jan., 1942, to a line some 80 mi. west of Moscow. But the situation worsened for the Germans as Russian troops ripped a huge gap between Army Groups North and Center and encircled 100,000 men south of Lake Ilmen. The Germans, however, employed "hedgehog" tactics successfully (withdrawing into communication centers as strong points which, if cut off, could be supplied by air). By mid-Feb. the Soviet offensive had run down, but Russian military prestige was greatly increased. On the other hand, Hitler had demonstrated a seeming ability to overcome overwhelming odds.

GERMAN SUMMER OFFENSIVE: 1942. By spring 1942 Hitler was issuing orders directly to units at the front, and Stalin maintained a similarly tight control. Hitler now planned to strike in the south toward Stalingrad (Volgagrad) and the Caucasus oil fields, thereby drawing in and destroying the Soviet man-power reserves. Although the Germans had suffered 1.2 m. casualties, replacements and allied forces (including 27 Rumanian and 13 Hungarian divisions) had made up the losses. Stalin also planned a major offensive, and a preliminary attack to take Kharkov, 12 May, by the Southwest Front ran straight into the jaws of the German build-up. Stalin refused to countenance retreat, and a German counterattack, 17 May, trapped 240,000 Soviet troops, 25 May. Stalin now increased pressure on the western powers for a 2nd front in Europe, which was finally publicly promised, 11 June, to take place before the year's end. The planned German offensive got under way on 28 June, and by 6 July had taken Voronezh. But by mid-July only 100,000 prisoners had been netted, for new elastic Soviet tactics enabled the bulk of their forces to escape across the Don.

Hitler now ordered Army Group A and the 4th Panzer Army to turn south and cut off Rostov (captured 23 July). He then, 23 July, transferred a Panzer corps from 4th Panzer Army to 6th Army and ordered the latter to take Stalingrad. Army Group A was ordered to cover tremendous distances and clear the Caucasus. Finally, Hitler decided that Stalin would fight a decisive battle for Stalingrad, and ordered 4th Panzer Army to reverse direction and move on the city from the south, 31 July. August brought the Germans empty victories and few prisoners. The oil fields at Maikop were found destroyed, 9 Aug., and although the swastika was planted on Mount Elbrus the Caucasus passes remained in Soviet hands. The armored drive on Grozny was halted by gasoline shortages. The 6th and 4th Panzer Armies lost momentum as they neared Stalingrad. It also became increasingly necessary to fill the expanding front with allied troops. On 19 Aug. 6th Army began its attack on Stalingrad in the teeth of fanatical Russian resistance, and by mid-Oct. the German offensive had ceased everywhere except in this decisive area.

STALINGRAD. The Soviet Union was now copying the Germans and building armored armies, while at the same time it fomented a large-scale guerrilla movement behind German lines, mostly in the north and center. By now the Germans were losing the battle of numbers, even with the use of *Osttruppen* from captured Soviet territory (reaching a maximum of 1 m. troops), some of whom, mostly Cossacks and Moslems, even served in the front line. But early Nazi racist policies had destroyed any chance of enthusiastic support from the Slav population of Russia. By the beginning of the Soviet Stalingrad offensive, 19 Nov., Russian forces in the vicinity amounted to 12 armies. The Soviet 5th Tank Army broke through the Rumanian 3rd Army north of the city in a few hours, and a Rumanian corps south of Stalingrad suffered a similar fate, 20 Nov. The Russians closed the pincers at Kalach, 22 Nov., trapping 6th Army and half of 4th Panzer Army (20 German and 2 Rumanian divisions, some 270,000 men in all). Employing the same policy as during the previous winter, Hitler refused to let 6th Army break out to the west. On 19 Dec. a German relief column drove to 30 miles of its beleaguered comrades, but was soon forced back. To the north of Stalingrad the Russians first destroyed the Italian 8th Army, mid-Dec., and the Hungarian 2nd Army, mid-Jan. 1943, and by 28 Jan. had surrounded 2 corps of the German 2nd Army, opening an enormous gap in the Axis lines. To the south a Russian drive cut off most of Army Group A (400,000 men) in the Caucasus. Hitler promoted Gen. Friedrich von Paulus (1890–1957), 6th Army commander, to field marshal, 30 Jan., in the hope that he would fight to the last man. But Paulus surrendered, 31 Jan., with 90,000 of his men still alive, only 5,000 of whom would survive their march east into the cruel Russian winter and captivity. The Soviet advance continued until a German counterattack, the last German victory in the East, retook Kharkov, 11 Mar., and Belgorod, 18 Mar., stabilizing the front, except for a Russian salient around Kursk, near where the Germans had started in May 1942.

JAPANESE ADVANCE IN THE EAST

1940–42

SINO-JAPANESE WAR. After seizing Manchuria, 1931, and setting up the puppet state of Manchukuo, 1932, the Japanese invaded much of northern China, 1937, and destroyed most of Generalissimo Chiang Kai-shek's German-trained forces. Although by 1939 Japan had struck the Chinese Nationalist regime a crippling economic blow by seizing all the key coastal ports, Chiang stubbornly fought on from his inland capital of Chungking and brought in supplies via Burma, Indochina, and Russia. Meanwhile the Japanese lived off the land and the Chinese Communists under Mao Tsetung steadily increased their domains in the north.

DETERIORATION OF WESTERN-JAPANESE RELATIONS. Hitler's victories of spring 1940 in Western Europe gave Japan a seemingly wide-open opportunity to expand into Southeast Asia. On 20 June the Vichy French government accepted Japanese demands that trade with Nationalist China be halted and that Japanese military observers be permitted to ensure this provision. The British signed an agreement with Japan, 17 July, halting for 3 months the shipment of war matériel, including oil and trucks, via the Burma Road and Hong Kong to China. U.S. opposition to Japanese policies was soon obvious when, after the signing of the 2-ocean-navy bill on 20 July (aimed at enabling the U.S.A. to deal with both a Japanese and a German naval threat simultaneously), President Roosevelt placed an embargo on 1 type of scrap iron and on aviation fuel and lubricants, 26 July. After an ultimatum the Japanese invaded Tongking Province in Indochina, 23 Sept., and the U.S.A. retaliated with a further loan to China, 25 Sept., and a total embargo on scrap iron, 26 Sept. In turn Japan signed the Tripartite Pact with Germany and Italy, 27 Sept.

DIPLOMATIC PRELUDE TO PEARL HARBOR. Japan had meanwhile encouraged Thailand to demand disputed provinces from Indochina and had forced Vichy to accept Japanese mediation, 11 Mar., 1941. On 13 Apr. Japan secured her northern flank by means of a 5-year nonaggression treaty with Russia. Finally, 24 July, Japan began to occupy the remainder of Indochina. The United States now froze Japanese funds, 25 July, and Britain and the Netherlands followed suit. The Dutch also embargoed oil shipments and the U.S.A. and Britain restricted the issue of export licenses to achieve the same result unofficially. The Japanese government soon decided that its dependence on foreign imports obliged it to try to work out some easing of the American ban. If such attempts failed, expansion to the southeast and war with the U.S.A. was the only acceptable alternative. On 20 Nov., 1941, the Japanese offered to cease expansion in Southeast Asia and the South Pacific and to withdraw from southern Indochina on the signing of a treaty, and from Annam when the war with China was over. In return they asked for a free hand in China and the end of the embargoes (including that of the Dutch in the East Indies). On 26 Nov. the U.S.A. rejected this offer, and suggested instead that, in return for the requested concessions from the American side, Japan evacuate China (except Manchuria) and

Indochina immediately and recognize the Chinese Nationalists as the legal government of all China. On 1 Dec. a Japanese Imperial Conference decided on war with the U.S.A.

ATTACK ON PEARL HARBOR. The Japanese planned to fight a limited war for the economic resources of the Southern Region of their planned "Greater East Asia Co-Prosperity Sphere." They intended first to knock out Pearl Harbor, the base of the potentially dangerous U.S. Pacific Fleet, and seize the Southern Region. A defensive perimeter would then be extended and strengthened so that the U.S.A. would see the futility of attacking such a bastion and make peace on the basis of the *status quo*. The Japanese Combined Fleet included 6 aircraft carriers, 2 battleships, 2 cruisers, and several destroyers. The U.S. Pacific Fleet had, on 7 Dec., 1941, 8 battleships, 9 cruisers, 29 destroyers, and 5 submarines, but its 3 carriers were on detached duty. The Japanese struck in 2 waves, at 7:59 and 8:40 A.M. respectively. Surprise was complete, since the 1st planes sighted were believed friendly. Only 4 U.S. aircraft got off the ground and were quickly shot down, while the remainder were strafed on the field. Of 360 Japanese planes only 29 were lost. The Americans lost 3 battleships sunk, 1 capsized, 1 severely damaged, and 3 able to return to the U.S.A. for repairs. In addition 3 cruisers were damaged, 2 destroyers badly damaged, and 2,400 men killed. The Japanese unwisely failed to destroy Pearl Harbor's nearly 5 m. barrels of oil, so as to force the U.S. fleet back to the American coast. Instead the U.S.A. had been humiliated by a "sneak attack" from which she could fairly soon recover.

CONQUEST OF SOUTHEAST ASIA. Also on 7 Dec., 1941, Japanese destroyers heavily damaged the U.S. air base on Midway Island. On 8 Dec. Japan exchanged declarations of war with the U.S.A. and Great Britain, and bombed unfortified Wake Island. Wake's defenders beat off 1 invasion attempt, 11 Dec., but were overwhelmed on 23 Dec. Guam fell quickly, 10 Dec., and the Japanese also took Tarawa and Makin in the Gilbert Islands. The invasion of Hong Kong began on 8 Dec., with the garrison finally surrendering, 25 Dec.

Meanwhile the Japanese 25th Army had seized control of Thailand, occupying Bangkok on 8 Dec. and making landings on the Kra Isthmus the same day. The meager British air forces in the Malaya-Singapore area were quickly destroyed, but a shock went through Britain when the only British capital ships in the Pacific and Indian Oceans, the battleship *Prince of Wales* and the cruiser *Repulse,* were destroyed by Japanese aircraft, 10 Dec. Weak British and Commonwealth forces were quickly pushed into Singapore, 31 Jan., 1942, and Japanese landings from Malaya, 8 Feb., forced the British to surrender, 15 Feb. Dutch forces in the East Indies numbered 40,000 Dutch and 100,000 badly equipped Indonesians. The Japanese landed on Borneo and Celebes, 11 Jan., and on 9 Mar. the Dutch had to surrender. Japan rounded out the southern boundaries of her defensive perimeter, 23 Jan.–mid-Mar., by seizing New Britain and New Ireland in the Bismarck Archipelago (Australian mandate) and Bougainville in the Solomon Islands (British), and by making landings in northeast New Guinea (Australian mandate).

Burma had meanwhile been invaded, 16 Dec., 1941, and the Japanese 15th Army took Moulmein, 31 Jan., 1942, and then advanced to the Sittang River, 24 Feb. Concerned with the threat posed to the Burma Road, Chiang Kai-shek sent the Chinese 5th and 6th Armies under U.S. Gen. Joseph Stilwell (1883–1946), but to little avail. Rangoon fell, 7 Mar., and on 29 Apr. the Japanese cut the Burma Road at Lashio. By the end of May Japan had taken its western objectives with the conquest of Burma and the Andaman and Nicobar Islands, and now threatened India.

CONQUEST OF THE PHILIPPINES. The Philippines were defended by 13,500 American soldiers, 12,000 reliable Philippine Scouts and 3,000 Constabulary, and 100,000 ill-prepared Philippine Army troops all commanded by Gen. Douglas MacArthur (1880–1964). His command

also had 140 combat-ready aircraft and a small naval force. MacArthur planned to defend Luzon, the largest and most important of the Philippine Islands. Bad weather delayed the Japanese air attack, 8 Dec., 1941, which proved a stroke of luck, for American planes which had been searching for the enemy since dawn were caught on the ground refueling. Soon U.S. air power was destroyed. Japanese diversionary landings, 10–12 Dec., at each tip of Luzon failed to deceive the Americans. The main landings of the 100,000-man invasion force came with a division set ashore at Lingayen Gulf, 22 Dec., and another at Lamon Bay, 24 Dec. The Japanese began to converge on Manila, and by 7 Jan., 1942, 15,000 American (including aviation personnel) and 65,000 Philippine troops had withdrawn into the Bataan Peninsula (plus 25,000 unexpected refugees). Stubborn resistance held off the Japanese, but starvation began to take its toll as rations were reduced to ½ and then to ⅓, 11 Mar.

Pursuant to orders from President Roosevelt, MacArthur arrived in Australia 17 Mar. to assume command of allied Southwest Pacific forces, and Gen. Jonathan Wainwright (1883–1953) took command. On 9 Apr. the Bataan force surrendered, with 45,000 Philippine and 9,300 American soldiers completing the famous death march, the rest having died in the Bataan fighting or on the march. The Japanese now turned on Corregidor Island, which dominated Manila Bay, and, after a fierce artillery bombardment, gained a beachhead, 5–6 May, forcing the surrender of all Philippine forces, 6 May.

WESTERN COUNTERATTACK IN THE MEDITERRANEAN

1940–45

AFRICA AND THE MIDDLE EAST. After the fall of France the British sank part of the French fleet at Oran, 3 July, 1940, to prevent it from falling into German hands. But an attempt by British and Free French forces to land at Dakar in West Africa, 23–25 Sept., failed. Meanwhile the Italians advanced 60 miles into

Egypt, 13–18 Sept. On 11 Nov. British planes severely damaged half the Italian fleet at Taranto. In Egypt the British finally counterattacked, 9 Dec., and achieved spectacular success, taking Bedafomm deep in Libya, 7 Feb., 1941; 130,000 prisoners were captured at a cost of only 555 British killed. Britain now halted the advance to aid Greece. Meanwhile British forces moved into Iraq, 17 Apr., to oust pro-Axis political leaders and reinstate a pro-western government, 31 May. To prevent any German take-over the British also defeated Vichy forces and occupied Syria, 8–14 June. In Eastern Africa the Italians had early success, capturing British Somaliland by 19 Aug., 1940. But in Feb. 1941 the British counterattacked, and by 6 Apr. had taken Addis Ababa. Italian resistance ended in the Horn of Africa, 27 Nov., with the fall of Gondar in Ethiopia.

CYRENAICAN CAMPAIGNS. Meanwhile Hitler had decided to form the Afrika Korps under Lt. Gen. Erwin Rommel (1891–1944), who arrived in Tripoli on 12 Feb., 1941. The speed of Rommel's 1st offensive caught the British flatfooted, and by 3 Apr. Benghazi had been retaken. Nevertheless the successful defense of outflanked Tobruk and the Egyptian border enabled the British to counterattack, 15 June. But the offensive failed almost immediately with the lopsided loss of 90 British tanks compared to 12 German. During the ensuing lull Britain and Russia, in order to forestall possible Axis intrigue and gain a Persian Gulf supply route to Russia, occupied Iran, mid-Sept. Finally the British again attacked, 18 Nov., and in fierce fighting pushed the Axis forces back to El Agheila by mid-Jan. 1942, but with a heavy loss of armor (750 British to 340 German tanks). At almost the same time, 1 Jan., 26 nations, including the U.S.A., Soviet Union, Britain, Free France, and China, signed the Declaration of the United Nations in Washington, promising an all-out effort against Germany, Italy, and Japan, and no separate peace.

EL ALAMEIN AND ALLIED NORTH AFRICAN LANDINGS. Rommel now drove the British back to the El Gazala–Bir Hacheim line, 21–28 Jan., where another pause followed. On 27 May his forces renewed the attack, meeting stubborn resistance. A German attack on Alam el Halfa, 31 Aug., was turned back. Eleven British divisions (3 armored) now opposed 13 Axis (4 German) divisions, 4 of which were armored (2 German). The British, under Lt. Gen. Bernard Montgomery (b. 1887), attacked, 23 Oct., and began to force Rommel back from El Alamein.

Far to the west an allied landing, 8 Nov., commanded by U.S. Gen. Dwight D. Eisenhower (1890–1969), soon seized Algiers, Oran, and Casablanca. On 10 Nov. Adm. Jean Darlan (1881–1942) ordered the end of French resistance in North Africa and called on the French fleet in Toulon to defect to the allies. But by the end of Nov. the Germans had occupied all of France and the fleet at Toulon had been scuttled by its crews. On 11 Dec. the Axis forces halted the allied advance at Medjez-el-Bab in Tunisia.

TUNISIAN CAMPAIGN. Churchill and Roosevelt met at the Casablanca Conference, 14–24 Jan., 1943, and decided to invade Sicily but delay the invasion of France, and to force unconditional surrender on the Axis powers. By now Hitler realized the gravity of his situation and rapidly built up his forces, as did the allies. On 14 Feb. Rommel attacked U.S. forces in Tunisia and seized the vital Kasserine Pass, 20 Feb., but soon, 22 Feb., was driven back through the Pass. To the east the British had continued to advance, seizing Benghazi, 20 Nov., and Tripoli, 23 Jan., 1943. On 7 Apr., 1943, allied troops, converging from east and west, linked up northeast of Gabès, and soon a final offensive, 4–13 May, captured 250,000 Axis troops, half of them German, trapped in Tunisia.

INVASION OF ITALY AND SOUTHERN FRANCE. At the Trident Conference (Washington, 12–25 May), Churchill and Roosevelt agreed to invade the Italian peninsula after Sicily, postponing the invasion of France to 1 May, 1944. The 350,000 Axis troops in Sicily included 75,000 Germans. The 1st major allied paratroop operation of the war was marred as the troop-carrying aircraft were fired on as they overflew the invasion fleet without prior clearance, but the resulting random landings confused the defenders. The 140,000-man seaborne landing had little difficulty, however, and by 17 Aug. had eliminated resistance. Allied casualties totaled 20,000, while Axis losses, including prisoners, numbered 165,000 (32,000 German).

On 25 July, 1943, Mussolini had been replaced by Marshal Pietro Badoglio (1871–1955) as premier of Italy, and on 3 Sept. a secret armistice was signed by Italy with the allies (announced 8 Sept.). The British 8th Army crossed the Strait of Messina, 3 Sept., and quickly moved north up the peninsula. On 9 Sept. the Taranto naval base fell, and on 11 Sept. the Italian fleet surrendered itself at Malta. The U.S. 5th Army landed at Salerno, 9 Sept., and by 1 Oct. had taken Naples. Meanwhile Sardinia, 19 Sept., and Corsica, 4 Oct., fell. On 13 Oct. Italy declared war on Germany, and by 8 Nov. the allies had reached the German Gustav Line defenses. A landing at Anzio, 22 Jan., 1944, to outflank the Germans proved abortive when the invaders delayed too long in consolidation, thus permitting the Germans to pen up the beachhead. The Gustav Line was not cracked until Monte Cassino fell, 18 May, when the advance again picked up momentum. Rome, declared an open city by the Germans, fell unscathed, 4 June. The allies reached the Gothic Line north of Florence, 11 Aug.

At the Teheran Conference, 8 Nov.–1 Dec., 1943, Roosevelt, Churchill, and Stalin agreed to follow up the Normandy invasion with a landing in southern France. Landings began, 15 Aug., 1944. Toulon and Marseilles were soon captured, and the allies moved up the Rhone to the Belfort Gap. Meanwhile the Gothic Line had been forced, 24 Aug.–28 Sept., though with heavy casualties. In Greece, after the German withdrawal, the British landed, 3 Oct., took Athens, 14 Oct., and put down a Communist-backed uprising. Back in Italy progress was slow until 9 Apr., 1945, when the allies launched an offensive which broke into the north Italian plain. The Germans began to collapse, and on 28 Apr. Mussolini and his mistress were killed and mutilated by partisans. On 2 May, 1945, the German commander in Italy unconditionally surrendered his 1 m. men, ending the war in the Mediterranean.

THE SECOND FRONT

1944

NORMANDY LANDINGS. The German Commander in Chief West, Field Marshal Karl von Rundstedt, possessed 58 divisions of varying quality. His 7th Army occupied Brittany and most of Normandy, and the 15th Army the Pas de Calais. Both armies formed Army Group B under Field Marshal Rommel. While Rundstedt preferred a mobile defense, Rommel believed that overwhelming allied air superiority would block reinforcements, and therefore built strong coastal defenses to stop the invaders on the beaches. The allies duped the Nazis into believing that the main invasion would come in the Pas de Calais and would be commanded by Gen. George S. Patton (1885–1945). The German 15th Army therefore waited vainly while the decisive battle was fought in Normandy.

Gen. Eisenhower's 45 divisions (2.9 m. men) were originally to land on 5 June, 1944, but bad weather led him, 4 June, to postpone the invasion to 6 June. At 6:30 A.M. American troops landed at Omaha Beach, where they met the toughest opposition encountered by any of the landings, and at Utah Beach, where resistance was the lightest. British and Canadian landings at Gold, Juno, and Sword beaches linked up with the American ones by the end of the day. By 27 June the Americans had taken Cherbourg and the British Bayeux, but the British were stalled before Caen. The U.S. 1st Army fought across the defensively ideal hedgerows, suffering heavy casualties, but took St.-Lô on 18 July. Assisted by heavy bombing, the British took half of Caen, 8 July, but an attack toward Falaise gained only 6 mi., 18 July. By this time well over a million allied troops had been landed, against no serious counterattack (because of the Calais ruse and complete allied air superiority).

BOMB PLOT OF JULY 20. Rommel had meanwhile been seriously injured by a strafing attack, 17 July, and remained unaware of a conspiracy which attempted to overthrow Hitler, 20 July. Col. Claus von Stauffenberg had placed a bomb in Hitler's conference room in the Wolfs-schanze at Rastenburg, East Prussia. But a heavy wooden table beam saved Hitler from the full force of the explosion, and he retaliated with the execution of those involved and many merely suspected. Rommel was forced to take poison, and others were garroted on meat hooks.

THE BREAKOUT. Aided by a massive carpet (4,000 tons) of bombs, 25 July, U.S. forces drove a huge gap, 27 July, in the German lines near St.-Lô and seized Avranches, 31 July. A drive into Brittany captured St.-Malo, 17 Aug., and Brest, 18 Sept., but both ports had been very badly damaged by the retreating Germans. Meanwhile to the east Le Mans had been taken, 8 Aug., and in a desperate attack designed to cut off the allied advance the Germans struck at Mortain, 7 Aug., toward Avranches. The U.S. 3rd Army under Gen. Patton now turned north from Le Mans and neared Argentan, 13 Aug.

From the north the Canadian 1st Army reached Falaise, 17 Aug., leaving only the gap to Argentan through which the Germans trapped in the Falaise pocket could escape. The gap closed, 20 Aug., netting 50,000 prisoners. Gen Eisenhower, desiring to concentrate on purely military objectives, favored bypassing Paris, which Hitler ordered defended to its destruction. But Gen. Charles de Gaulle (b. 1890), leader of the Free French, wanted Paris for its prestige value and to establish his government there. Faced with a spontaneous uprising, the German commander in Paris, Gen. Dietrich von Choltitz (1894–1966), refused to destroy the city and made a truce with the rebels. Franco-American forces liberated Paris finally on 25 Aug., 1944, and allied troops reached the line of the Seine. The drive north up the Rhone Valley seized Lyons, 3 Sept., but the Germans succeeded in stabilizing this front at the Vosges Mountains. However, most of France was again in allied hands.

EAST ASIA AND THE PACIFIC

1942–45

THE BURMA ROAD. American naval victories in mid-1942 in the Pacific lessened the Japanese threat to India, but the U.S.A. and Britain were still faced with the problem of reopening the Burma Road to supply China. Work began, Dec. 1942, on a new road from Ledo in India across northern Burma to intersect with the old Burma Road near the Chinese border. Until the completion of the Ledo Road the only supply route to the Chinese was by air over the 500-mile Himalayan Hump between Assam Province in India and Kunming in China, a most dangerous and costly route. Meanwhile the British in Oct. 1942 launched an offensive in Burma which captured Maungdaw, 17 Dec., but failed to reach Akyab. In Feb. 1943 a specially trained British brigade, the Chindits, struck deep into the Burmese jungles, but were surrounded and lost a quarter of their 3,000 men before infiltrating back. The Japanese also counterattacked from Akyab, Mar., and retook the British gains around Maungdaw, May.

ALLIED POSTWAR PLANS FOR ASIA. At the Cairo Conference, 22–26 Nov., 1943, Roosevelt and Churchill met with Chiang Kai-shek and recognized China as one of the great allies, promising also to send more supplies across the Hump. The Cairo Declaration, 1 Dec., announced U.S., British, and Chinese resolve to strip Japan of all former Chinese territory—including Manchuria, Taiwan, and the Pescadores—and of all Pacific islands acquired since 1914, and to set up an independent Korea. During the Moscow Foreign Minister's Conference, Oct. 1943, Stalin had promised to enter the war against Japan once Germany had been beaten, and at the Teheran Conference, 28 Nov.–1 Dec., he confirmed this

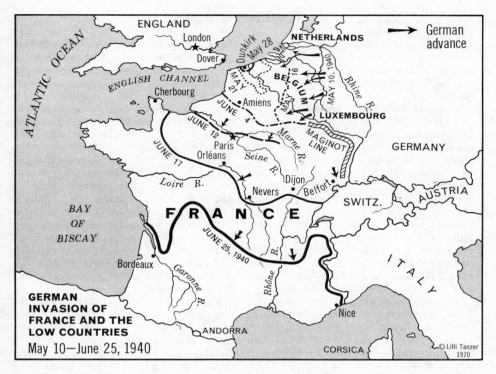

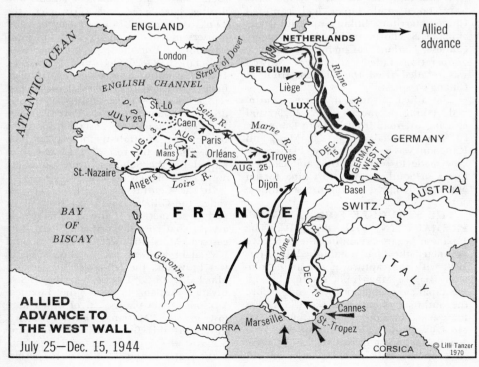

agreement. He also expressed hope for the cession to Russia of southern Sakhalin Island and the Kurile Islands, and for the use of the Manchurian railways and Dairen.

ALLIED ADVANCE IN BURMA. In late Jan. 1944 the Japanese attacked British forces moving down the coast toward Akyab, but, despite early successes, the Japanese effort collapsed, and by Apr. the British were within 30 mi. of Akyab. Another Japanese offensive cut the Imphal road, 29 Mar., but by the end of June the Japanese, short of food and supplies, were in retreat. Meanwhile the allies pushed forward and the American version of the Chindits, Merrill's Marauders (5307th Composite Unit), took the vital Myitkyina airfield, but could not seize the town itself until 3 Aug.

The relatively inactive Chinese front flared up when the Japanese moved to eliminate a series of airfields established by U.S. Gen. Claire Chennault (1890–1958) to support the Chinese. Between Apr. and mid-Dec. all but 2 of the bases were taken and Japan had captured Chinese territory linking up with Indochina. U.S. efforts, mid-1944, to promote Chinese Nationalist-Communist military co-operation failed, and Gen. Stilwell was recalled from the Chinese front at Chiang's request.

The allied advance in Burma continued, taking Akyab, 3 Jan., 1945, and clearing the road from Ledo to Kunming, 20 Jan. Mandalay fell, 20 Mar., and Rangoon was taken, 3 May. Plans were now made to send all U.S. and Chinese forces in Southern Asia to China for an offensive designed to capture a Chinese port.

THE STRUGGLE FOR NAVAL SUPREMACY IN THE PACIFIC. The Japanese began expanding the defensive perimeter they had established by Mar. 1942 with the capture of the main Solomon Islands, May–June. Having broken the Japanese communications code before the outbreak of the war, the U.S.A. was forewarned of a projected landing at Port Moresby, Papua. The Battle of the Coral Sea, 8 May, was a draw, but the Japanese gave up the attempted landing. On 3–7

June the Japanese attacked Dutch Harbor and seized Kiska and Attu in the Aleutians. But intercepted messages prepared the U.S. for Japanese plans to invade Midway. The first wave of Japanese aircraft hit the island at 6:30 A.M. on 4 June, but before the second wave could attack U.S. torpedo planes struck. They were driven off, suffering heavy losses. But the defending Japanese fighters could not regain height, and between 10:20 and 10:25 A.M. U.S. dive bombers turned 3 Japanese heavy carriers into flaming hulks. A 4th Japanese carrier and the U.S.S. *Yorktown* were eliminated that afternoon. Due to Japanese overconfidence, and to U.S. possession of the code and some luck, the Japanese abruptly lost their naval superiority in the Pacific and never regained it.

PACIFIC ISLAND CAMPAIGNS. An American invasion of Guadalcanal and Florida islands, 8 Aug., led to Japanese alarm and the futile reinforcement of Guadalcanal. Japanese efforts to reassert their naval predominance failed, and during late Sept. and early Oct. the "Tokyo Express" of destroyers and cruisers moving at night built up Japanese forces. But the Japanese counterattack failed, 23–26 Oct., and by 9 Feb., 1943, Guadalcanal was entirely in U.S. hands. Meanwhile the Japanese had seized Buna in Papua, 22 July, 1942, and drove to almost 30 mi. of Port Moresby. But despite fanatical resistance Buna was retaken by Australian forces, 22 Jan., 1943. During the rest of 1943 the allies moved up the Solomons and along the north coast of New Guinea.

In the Central Pacific the U.S.A. invaded the Gilbert Islands, 21 Nov., 1943, and were met on Tarawa with suicide attacks that cost 1,000 Marine lives. The eastern Marshalls were by-passed and Kwajalein was seized, 1–8 Feb., 1944, as was Eniwetok, the largest of the western Marshalls, 18–23 Feb. When the U.S.A. invaded Saipan, 15 June, the Japanese sent out carrier planes, 227 of which were lost in the "Marianas Turkey Shoot." Moreover, this Battle of the Philippine Sea cost the Japanese 2 carriers to submarine attack and 1 to aircraft, permanently neutralizing the Japanese carrier force. Fanatical resistance on Saipan cost the U.S.A. 3,000 dead as opposed to 30,000 Japanese. Nearby Tinian was quickly taken, 24 July–1 Aug., and Guam also fell, 21 July–10 Aug.

RECAPTURE OF THE PHILIPPINES. The U.S.A. began her reinvasion of the Philippines with landings on Leyte, 20 Oct., but the naval Battle of Leyte Gulf almost turned the invasion into a disaster. While the U.S. fleet was decoyed away, the Japanese 1st Attack Force steamed through San Bernardino Strait and suddenly came upon a weak U.S. naval force. But instead of pressing the attack and destroying unprotected shipping in Leyte Gulf, the Japanese reversed direction. Despite heavy losses the Japanese reinforced Leyte, but to no avail, and by the end of 1944 the Leyte campaign was over. Japanese casualties numbered 70,000 to 16,000 American. Luzon was invaded at Lingayen Gulf, 9 Jan., 1945, and, despite bitter resistance, Clark Field and Fort Stotsenburg had been captured by 31 Jan. Manila was reached, 2 Feb., but the Japanese fought on in the capital for another month, and resistance continued in the interior until the end of the war. The result of Japanese suicide tactics was reflected in the relative casualties: 170,000 Japanese killed as against 8,000 Americans.

DEFEAT OF NAZI GERMANY

1943–45

GERMAN OFFENSIVE IN THE EAST: SPRING 1943. As usual, Hitler ordered planning for a spring offensive (Operation Citadel). Meanwhile the starving Polish Jews, crowded into Warsaw's ghetto preliminary to extermination, rose up in a desperate frenzy of the doomed, 6 May, 1943. Despite fierce resistance the 50,000 remaining inhabitants were wiped out by SS troops. Earlier, 13 Apr., the Germans had discovered the mass graves of the Poles executed by the Russians at Katyn, and when the Polish government in exile called for an investigation Stalin broke off relations. Hitler's offensive to-

ward Kursk, 5–15 July, soon proved abortive.

SOVIET COUNTERATTACK. The Russians launched a counterattack, using a by now typical strategy of following a tremendous artillery barrage with a steamroller attack on a broad front. On 5 Aug. Soviet forces captured Orel and Byelgorod. Soon a broad gap opened in the German lines on this front, but Hitler maintained his policy of obstructing the timely withdrawal of German forces. When he did permit retreats, either it was too late or his troops were too exhausted to hold the planned line. By the end of Oct. the Russians had crossed the Dnieper and had cut off the German 17th Army in the Crimea. On 6 Nov. Kiev fell. By this time 5.6 m. Russians faced 4 m. Axis troops in the eastern theater. The Russians were far superior in quantity of tanks and artillery, and were more mobile, with wider-tracked tanks and U.S. 4-wheel-drive trucks. On 4 Jan., 1944, they crossed the 1939 border, at Sarny. An attack begun on 4 Mar. soon had them across the Bug, Dniester, and Prut rivers. When they halted in mid-Apr., they had reached the Carpathians.

ADVANCE INTO POLAND. To the north the previously static front near Leningrad was attacked, 15 Nov., 1943, and on 20 Nov. Novgorod was captured by the Russians. The Moscow-Leningrad railroad was cleared, and by 1 Mar. the Germans had been forced back to the Panther Line centered on Pskov, where they held. The next major Russian offensive surprised the Germans by striking Army Group Center, 22 June, 1944, which had sent most of its armor south. The German front disintegrated, and by 3 July Army Group Center had lost $2/3$ of its divisions. On 29 July the Russians reached the Baltic Sea south of Riga and cut off Army Group North. Meanwhile a deep thrust, begun 13 July, took Lublin, 24 July, and then drove along the Vistula toward Warsaw. With the Russians on the outskirts and the Soviet "Kosciuszko" radio station calling for an uprising, the Polish underground took up arms to seize Warsaw, 1 Aug. But Stalin now saw an opportunity to let the German SS destroy a pro-western resistance movement, and made no further move to advance on the Polish capital. Not only did he refuse any support but he also banned western overflights (intended to drop supplies to the rebels) from landing in Soviet territory. After extremely bloody fighting which destroyed most of Warsaw, the Polish Home Army surrendered, 2 Oct.

Meanwhile Army Group Center had opened a corridor, mid-Aug., which permitted Army Group North to escape before the Russians counterattacked, 14 Sept. But when the Russians reached the Baltic north of Memel, 10 Oct., Army Group North was again cut off.

ADVANCE INTO THE BALKANS. In late Aug. a Russian offensive forced the collapse of the Axis southern front, and Rumania surrendered, 23 Aug., and declared war on Germany, 25 Aug. The Russians captured the Ploesti oil fields, 30 Aug.; Bucharest, 31 Aug.; and then invaded Bulgaria, 8 Sept., which also sued for peace and declared war on Germany. Outflanked, the Germans were forced to abandon Crete, Greece, and Albania. Belgrade fell, 20 Oct. The Horthy regime in Hungary had attempted, 15 Oct., to take Hungary out of the war, but the Nazis quickly installed a puppet regime. A Soviet-supported Hungarian government declared war on Germany, 29 Dec., but, although surrounded, the Germans fought on in Budapest.

To the north the Finns had been driven back to the 1940 frontier by mid-July 1944, and on 2 Sept. sued for peace (signed 19 Sept.). The German 20th Mountain Army now had to retreat into northern Norway. After several armed clashes the Finns gave up trying to disarm the Germans in accord with the Soviet armistice, and Finland declared war on Germany, 3 Mar., 1945.

ALLIED PURSUIT IN THE WEST. Gen. Eisenhower planned to advance on a broad front rather than try a daring breakthrough. His main effort was to be by Gen. Montgomery's 21st Army Group through Belgium into the Ruhr. In light of the apparent German collapse Eisenhower tried to satisfy Montgomery's demands for a strengthening of his forces by

also sending the U.S. 1st Army north of the Ardennes. 21st Army Group captured Brussels, 3 Sept., 1944, and Antwerp, 4 Sept. Meanwhile the U.S. 1st Army took Mons, 3 Sept.; Liège, 7 Sept.; Luxembourg, 10 Sept.; and then crossed the German frontier, 11 Sept. South of the Ardennes, Gen. Patton's U.S. 3rd Army seized Rheims, 29 Aug.; Verdun, 31 Aug.; and crossed the Moselle south of Metz, 7 Sept.

Despite these reverses the Germans, through the use of 8 m. foreign laborers, were able to maintain an army of 10 m. men. German war production was still high, and Hitler looked for some miracle weapon like the jet plane (which he had earlier neglected) to save the Reich. On 25 Sept., 1944, he ordered the raising of a *Volkssturm* by calling up all able-bodied males between 16 and 60, thus mobilizing Germany's last manpower reserves.

The rapid allied advance now began to outrun its supplies, which could not be moved forward fast enough even by the one-way "Red Ball Express" truck route. Both Montgomery and Patton thought that their forces should receive the bulk of the available supplies to strike Germany a death blow. Eisenhower now authorized an airborne assault to leap the formidable Dutch river net along the lower Rhine (Operation Market) for 17 Sept. But the linking ground attack by the British 2nd Army (Operation Garden) was slowed by heavy resistance, so that the 1st Allied Airborne Army was badly mauled by enemy armor before it could be rescued. Meanwhile the Scheldt Estuary was finally cleared and the port of Antwerp opened, 28 Nov.

GERMAN ARDENNES OFFENSIVE. With the allied offensive bogged down, Hitler decided to attempt a last desperate counteroffensive through the Ardennes to Antwerp. Maintaining the greatest secrecy, and aided by fog, snow, and English-speaking infiltrators in allied uniforms, the German armored attack, 16 Dec., gained complete surprise. But although the Nazis surrounded the U.S. 101st Airborne Division at Bastogne and drove almost to Dinant, clearing weather, which permitted allied air strikes, and

German fuel shortages helped bring the offensive to a halt. The last phase of the Battle of the Bulge consisted of allied elimination of German gains, completed by the end of Jan. 1945. A lesser German attack in Alsace had little success, Jan. 1945, and the allies countered by reducing the German pocket around Colmar, 20 Jan.–9 Feb.

SLOWING OF THE GERMAN WAR MACHINE. With Germany's reserves spent, collapse was imminent. From Western European bases allied bombing was turning Germany into rubble. German oil production was down to a trickle, with tanks being hauled into action on the Eastern Front by oxen in order to save fuel. Chemical production was crippled, and artillery shells were ¾ filled with rock salt. Dwarfing the earlier fire bomb raid on Hamburg, 24 July–3 Aug., 1943, in which 50,000 were killed, a British incendiary raid on Dresden, 13–14 Feb., 1945, packed with refugees from the East, left 135,000 dead.

YALTA CONFERENCE. Meanwhile Roosevelt, Stalin, and Churchill met at Yalta in the Crimea, 4–11 Feb., 1945. Earlier, at the Quebec Conference, 12–16 Sept., 1944, Roosevelt and Churchill had accepted the proposal of U.S. Secretary of the Treasury Henry Morgenthau, Jr., that Germany be converted into "a country primarily agricultural and pastoral," but quickly abandoned this scheme as unrealistic. At Yalta Stalin suggested that Germany pay $20 billion in reparations through the dismantling of heavy industry, half the proceeds of which would go to war-ravaged Russia. There had never been any doubt among the Big 3 that Germany would be occupied after the war. The British Attlee Committee had, in 1943, devised a partition of Germany into 3 occupation zones and, during preliminary negotiations in 1944, the Soviets had adopted this plan as their own. At Yalta the same plan, except for the addition of a French zone created out of U.S. and British territory, was formally adopted. Berlin was also to be divided into sectors.

THE DRIVE FOR BERLIN. In the west the allies advanced toward the Rhine. Trier fell, 2 Mar., and Cologne, 7 Mar. To the south the Ludendorff railroad bridge at Remagen, which due to an error had not been blown up on time, was captured intact, 7 Mar. In the east Warsaw fell, 17 Jan., and a decisive breakthrough by the Russians reached to the Oder by the end of the month. By mid-Mar. Silesia and the right bank of the Oder had been cleared. Budapest was finally taken, 13 Feb., and the Russians continued into Austria, capturing Vienna, 13 Apr.

The western allies had meanwhile, by 25 Mar., cleared the Saar and Palatinate. Crossings were effected with increasing frequency all along the Rhine. The Ruhr was enveloped, 1 Apr., trapping 325,000 Germans. The advance was now extremely rapid and resistance light, except in a few diehard areas like the Harz Mountains, Kassel, and Heilbronn. In the Netherlands the Germans stubbornly held on and, to prevent the imminent starvation of the Dutch, an agreement, 22 Apr., was made halting the fighting and promising allied food for the inhabitants in return for German agreement not to flood the country. False rumors of a Nazi "National Redoubt" in the Alps led to a drive south. On 22 Apr. Stuttgart fell, on 30 Apr. Munich, and on 4 May Salzburg and Pilsen. No effort was made to seize the Czech capital of Prague, although, unlike Germany, no agreement on zones of occupation had been made.

GÖTTERDÄMMERUNG. The final Soviet offensive encircled Berlin by 24 Apr. Hitler ordered a desperate last-ditch stand, seeing in the death of Roosevelt, 12 Apr., 1945, the counterpart of the demise of Czarina Elizabeth, which disrupted the coalition facing Frederick the Great in the 7 Years' War. Hitler's scorched-earth orders were generally disregarded. But when Marshal Göring radioed a suggestion that he take charge of the government in place of the trapped Führer, Hitler had him arrested for treason. Adm. Dönitz was then designated by Hitler in his will as his successor. Blaming defeat on an unworthy German people, Hitler committed suicide, 30 Apr. Berlin fell, 2 May. Mean-

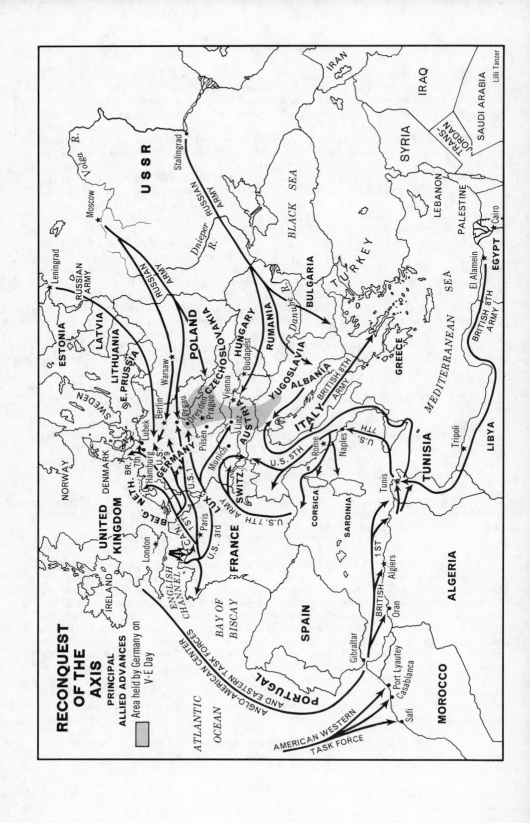

RECONQUEST OF THE AXIS

PRINCIPAL ALLIED ADVANCES

Area held by Germany on V-E Day

Lilli Tanzer

ATLANTIC OCEAN

ANGLO-AMERICAN TASK CENTER AND EASTERN TASK FORCES

AMERICAN WESTERN TASK FORCE

USSR

Volga R.
Stalingrad
Moscow
Leningrad
RUSSIAN ARMY
RUSSIAN ARMY
RUSSIAN ARMY
Dnieper R.
Danube R.

BLACK SEA

TURKEY

IRAN
IRAQ
SYRIA
TRANS-JORDAN
SAUDI ARABIA
LEBANON
PALESTINE
EGYPT
Cairo
El Alamein
BRITISH 8TH ARMY

ESTONIA
LATVIA
LITHUANIA
E. PRUSSIA
SWEDEN
NORWAY

POLAND
Warsaw
Berlin
Orgau
Dresden
Prague
CZECHOSLOVAKIA
Pilsen
Linz
Vienna
AUSTRIA
HUNGARY
Budapest
RUMANIA
BULGARIA
YUGOSLAVIA
ALBANIA
GREECE

DENMARK
Lubeck
Hamburg
GERMANY
Munich
SWITZ.
U.S. 9TH
U.S. 7TH
U.S. 1
LUX.
NETH.
BELG.
BR. 7th

UNITED KINGDOM
IRELAND
London
ENGLISH CHANNEL
BAY OF BISCAY

FRANCE
Paris
U.S. 3rd
U.S. 7TH ARMY
1ST CAN.

ITALY
Rome
Naples
U.S. 5TH
U.S. 7TH
BRITISH 8TH ARMY

CORSICA
SARDINIA

SPAIN
PORTUGAL
Gibraltar

MEDITERRANEAN SEA

Tripoli
LIBYA

TUNISIA
Tunis
Algiers
Oran
BRITISH 1ST

ALGERIA

MOROCCO
Port Lyautey
Casablanca
Safi

while the world was exposed to a series of shocks by the uncovering of Hitler's extermination camps. Dönitz, concerned to prevent German troops from falling into Russian hands, encouraged local surrenders such as those in Italy, Denmark, and the Netherlands, 4 May, and in Bavaria by Army Group G, 5 May. But Eisenhower demanded simultaneous surrender on both fronts of the remainder, threatening to halt any further westward flow of refugees and soldiers. The Germans signed an unconditional surrender on 7 May. Victory in Europe (V-E) Day was proclaimed, 8 May, and a 2nd surrender ceremony took place in Berlin with the Russians present on 9 May, 1945. All Western Europe was now free of Axis control.

CASUALTIES. Greater than the enormous material losses of the European war was the human loss. Soviet dead amounted to some 20 m. (7 m. military). Including *Volksdeutschen,* the Germans lost 6.5 m. lives (3.5 m. military). 4.5 to 6 m. Jews were exterminated at Hitler's order. In Nazi-occupied Europe, Poland, with its large Jewish population, and Yugoslavia, where heavy guerrilla fighting and atrocities against the Serbs took place, suffered the highest casualties. The U.S. lost 405,000, Britain 330,000, and France 270,000 total military dead, primarily in the European theater.

THE DEFEAT OF JAPAN

1945

DRIVE ON THE JAPANESE HOME-LAND. The captured Mariana Islands (Guam, Tinian, and Saipan) furnished bases for increasingly heavy air raids on Japan. The next step was to invade Iwo Jima, 19 Feb., 1945, to provide an intermediate base for emergency bomber landings and fighter cover. Marines raised the U.S. flag on Mount Suribachi, 23 Feb., and organized resistance on Iwo (the most strongly fortified island subdued by U.S. forces during the war) ended on 16 Mar. Practically the entire 22,000-man Japanese force fought to the death, while

6,800 Americans were killed. Okinawa, the largest island in the Ryukyus, on the edge of the Japanese homeland, was the next U.S. target. The assault began, 1 Apr., with the Japanese defending at inland positions rather than on the beaches. *Kamikaze* (divine wind) aircraft raids against supporting U.S. naval forces caused some losses but never seriously threatened the invasion. On 7 Apr. the Japanese Imperial Navy committed hara-kiri when, with the last 2,500 tons of fuel available to it, a suicide attack was mounted off Okinawa. The battleship *Yamato* and 4 destroyers were sunk at a cost of only 10 U.S. planes.

BOMBING OF JAPAN. Mass B-29 (range: 1,600 miles) high-altitude precision air raids on Japan, begun in Nov. 1944 from the Marianas, had poor results. But 21st Bomber Command switched to low-level attacks, and then turned to incendiary raids on Japanese cities with their numerous wooden structures. The 1st night fire bombing raid, 9 Mar., 1945, on Tokyo seared nearly 16 sq. mi. of the city and killed 83,793 persons. Similar attacks spread all over Japan, and Japanese air defense was so poor that soon the Americans were dropping warning leaflets in advance.

POTSDAM CONFERENCE. Meanwhile at the Yalta Conference, 4–11 Feb., 1945, in return for Soviet entry into the Japanese war after Germany's defeat, the USSR had been promised southern Sakhalin, the Kuriles, a lease of Port Arthur, pre-eminence in an internationalized Dairen, and the use of the Manchurian railways. After the fall of Okinawa the Japanese government began to seek a way out of the war, and secretly asked the Soviet Union to mediate. But the Russians stalled, and at the Potsdam Conference, 17 July–2 Aug., 1945, President Harry S Truman (b. 1884) only learned of these feelers second hand from Churchill. (Churchill's Conservative Party was defeated in a British election, 26 July, and Clement Attlee [1883–1967] became prime minister, leaving Stalin the last of the Big 3 war leaders.) The Potsdam Declaration, published on 26 July, called

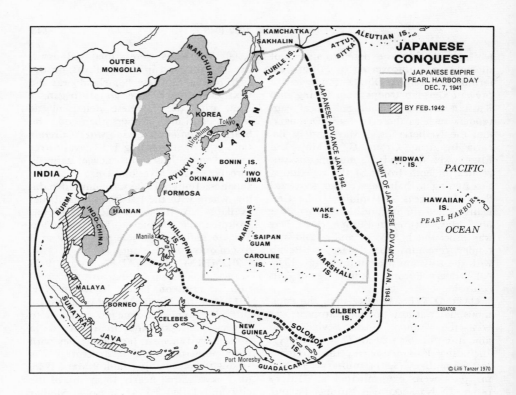

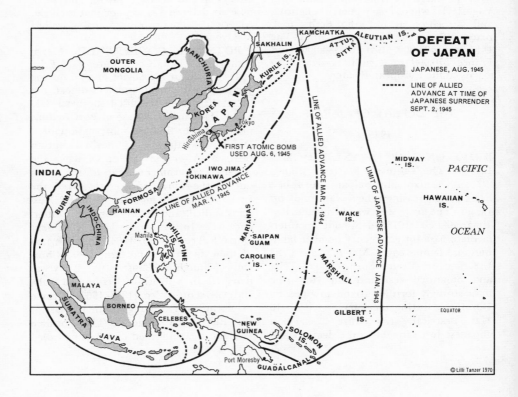

for immediate Japanese capitulation and spelled out the terms of unconditional surrender.

JAPANESE SURRENDER. Since 1942 the U.S. "Manhattan Project" had been working to develop an atomic bomb, and the 1st was exploded at Alamogordo, N.M., on 16 July, 1945. When the Japanese balked at surrendering with the emperor's status unclear, the Hiroshima bomb was dropped, 6 Aug., 1945, killing 71,379 people. On 8 Aug. Stalin declared war, and Russian forces invaded Manchuria, Korea, and southern Sakhalin. The Japanese had, since Okinawa, been withdrawing to the Chinese coast in order to free troops for the defense of the home islands, so the Russians met little resistance. On 9 Aug. another atomic bomb was dropped, this time on Nagasaki. The Japanese now sued for peace. But the atom bombs were only the final blow, for the vulnerable Japanese economy was reduced to a shambles, due not only to air attack but even more to the destruction by submarines of Japan's merchant marine. The formal surrender of the Japanese Empire took place, 2 Sept., 1945, aboard the U.S. battleship *Missouri*, and the 5-m.-strong Japanese army was quickly disarmed. Total military casualties in the Asian war were much lighter than in Europe, with 2.2 m. Chinese dead, 1.5 m. Japanese, and 55,000 Americans.

THE POSTWAR WORLD,
1945–1968

The New Europe

RECONSTRUCTION AND CHANGE IN THE WEST

France

1945–58

FOUNDING OF THE 4TH REPUBLIC. Following the nationalization of the coal mines, 14 Dec., 1944, the provisional government of Charles de Gaulle created the Comités d'Entreprises, 22 Feb., 1945, and Air France, 26 June, and passed social security legislation, 11 Oct. It also purged Vichy collaborators: Pétain was sentenced to death, 14 Aug. (sentence later commuted to detention for life), and Pierre Laval (b. 1883) was executed, 16 Oct. Elections were held for an assembly, 21 Oct.: the Communists and the United Movement of the French Resistance won 152 seats; the Socialists 152; the new Popular Republican Movement (MRP), founded by Georges Bidault (b. 1899), 141; and other groups 110. De Gaulle was elected head of the provisional government, 13 Nov., with Bidault as foreign minister, René Pleven (b. 1901) finance minister, and the Communist leader Maurice Thorez (1900–1964) minister of state.

ECONOMIC LEGISLATION. On 21 Dec. plans were announced for the establishment of a Planning Commission; Jean Monnet (b. 1888) was named to head it, and the 1st plan was published, 3 Jan., 1946. On 25 Dec., 1945, the franc was devalued, the new rate being frs. 119.1 to (U.S.) $1. On 1 Jan., 1946, the Bank of France was nationalized. On 20 Jan. de

Gaulle abruptly resigned, protesting against the weakness of the executive in the proposed constitution, and a new Socialist, MRP, and Communist coalition was formed. On 8 Apr. the gas and electricity industries were nationalized, followed by insurance, 25 Apr., and credit, 17 May.

THE SEARCH FOR STABILITY. The new constitution, providing for an all-powerful National Assembly, was rejected by referendum, 5 May, and on 2 June a new Constituent Assembly was elected, with the MRP as the largest bloc. Bidault formed a new coalition. On 16 June, de Gaulle made a speech at Bayeux, in which he decried party factionalism and called for a presidential type of government. A new constitution with a weak executive was, however, adopted by referendum, 13 Oct. After elections in Oct., from which the Communists emerged as the largest party, Vincent Auriol (1884–1966) was elected president of the Republic, 16 Jan., 1947. On 14 Apr., 1947, de Gaulle formed the Rally of the French People (RPF). Failing to hold down prices—by Jan. 1948 the price level was 13 times that of 1939—the government was faced with frequent strikes for higher wages, which it resisted. Finally, the Communists supported a strike of Renault auto workers, Apr., and joined a no-confidence vote against the government, 4 May. On 9 May Communist cabinet ministers were dismissed. A new liberal statute for Algeria was voted, Aug., but was not implemented. In municipal elections held in Oct. the RPF emerged as the main party, and de Gaulle called for new general elections. The center parties replied by creating a "Third Force" of parties hostile to both Communists and RPF. On 26 Jan., 1948, the franc was again devalued, to frs. 214.4 to $1. In new elections, 17 June, 1951, the Third Force parties gained 404 out of 625 seats.

DECLINE OF THE 4TH REPUBLIC. The MRP proposed a law designed to give financial aid to Catholic schools, Sept. 1951, but Radicals and Socialists

opposed it. The law (Loi Barangé) was eventually passed with MRP and RPF votes. Antoine Pinay (b. 1891) formed a new cabinet, May 1952, preaching financial austerity, and the "Pinay Miracle" (the achievement of national economic health) followed. Divisions of opinion on the conduct of the Indochinese war and on the proposed European Defense Community (EDC) provoked frequent ministerial crises, until on 18 June, 1954, Pierre Mendès-France (b. 1907) became premier on a pledge to end the war. This he

EUROPE IN 1948

Allied Occupation Zones in Germany

Soviet Zone

British Zone

American Zone

French Zone

© Lilli Tanzer 1970

succeeded in doing, but on 1 Nov. rebellion broke out in Algeria. Mendès-France's government fell, 5 Feb., 1955. In elections held on 2 Jan., 1956, Pierre Poujade (b. 1920), leading a new party of small businessmen, won 13% of the votes. The Socialist Guy Mollet (b. 1905) formed a new cabinet. He at once visited Algiers, but his conciliatory statements provoked settler opposition. Reversing himself, he adopted a hard line, dispatching military reinforcements to Algeria. On 30 Oct., 1956, Mollet joined British Prime Minister Eden in sending an ultimatum to Egypt (the Suez Crisis). Facing increasing financial problems and with no success in Algeria, Mollet's government fell, 21 May, 1957. Succeeding governments were no more successful in dealing with the problem. On 13 May, 1958, settlers in Algeria, suspecting that the government was preparing to make a deal with the nationalists, rebelled, and were soon calling for the return of de Gaulle.

RECALL TO POWER OF DE GAULLE. As revolt spread throughout Algeria and to Corsica, de Gaulle was invested as prime minister, 1 June, with power to rule by decree for 6 months and to draw up a new constitution. He visited Algiers, but spoke in generalities. A commission under Gaullist Michel Debré (b. 1912) was set up to draft the new constitution. The draft of this document, providing for a strong presidency, was adopted by referendum, 28 Sept., in France and in all French overseas possessions except Guinée; it replaced the French Union with the French Community. A new National Assembly was elected, Nov., the new Gaullist "Union for the New Republic" (UNR) winning 189 out of 465 seats and the Communists only 10. De Gaulle was elected president, 21 Dec.

1959–68

THE 5TH REPUBLIC. Finance Minister Pinay devalued the franc, 27 Dec., to frs. 493 to $1. Debré was appointed prime minister, 8 Jan., 1959. On 16 Sept. de Gaulle recognized the right of the Algerians to self-determination, and

launched the Constantine Plan. On 24 Dec. a new law vastly increased state aid to Catholic schools. In Jan. 1960 discontented army officers staged a revolt in sympathy with the settlers in Algeria, but it was soon put down. A referendum, 8 Jan., 1961, endorsed the principle of Algerian self-determination. In Apr. there was another army revolt, which also collapsed, and de Gaulle invoked emergency powers. The war in Algeria and the increasing violence led to widespread protests in France. In the fall of 1961 the settler Secret Army Organization (OAS) began a campaign of terror in France and Algeria. A referendum, 8 Apr., 1962, endorsed agreements reached at Évian, and Algeria became independent, 3 July.

THE GAULLIST REGIME. On 14 Apr., 1962, Georges Pompidou (b. 1911) replaced Debré as prime minister. The opposition, protesting a planned referendum for the direct election of the president, defeated the government, which resigned, 6 Oct. In the referendum on 28 Oct., however, the voters endorsed direct presidential elections. In national elections in Nov. Gaullists gained an overall majority. During Mar.–Apr. 1963 there was a wave of strikes calling for higher wages, and on 21 Apr. the government announced a price freeze, followed by a stabilization plan, Sept., to counter inflation.

In June 1965 proposals for a federation of non-Communist left-wing parties proposed by Socialist presidential candidate Gaston Defferre (b. 1910) failed, and Defferre withdrew. In the presidential elections, Dec. 1965, de Gaulle only beat François Mitterand (b. 1916) in a runoff. In Dec. 1966, Socialists and Communists agreed to co-operate in national elections. In the elections held in Mar. 1967 the Gaullists won a slim majority. The government acquired power to make certain economic and social changes by decree for 6 months.

MAY 1968 RIOTS. In May 1968 student rioting, beginning 2 May at the new Faculty of Letters at Nanterre and spreading to the Sorbonne and to provincial universities, touched off a month-long social and economic crisis. The students, led by Daniel Cohn-Bendit (b. 1945), protested against police brutality and called for a radical transformation of French society and for educational reforms. They rioted repeatedly, setting up barricades in the Latin Quarter and fighting with police. They occupied the Sorbonne from 14 May to 16 June. Workers went on strike for one day, 13 May, in sympathy with the students, then more extensively, demanding fewer working hours and higher minimum wages. By 20 May, 7–10 m. workers ($\frac{1}{3}$ of France's labor force) were on strike and transportation, communications, and production were at a standstill. On 24 May, de Gaulle proposed a referendum to decide upon his continuance in office. The "general strike" began to break, 31 May, as workers began making wage settlements with their employers. Normalcy was re-achieved only on 6 June.

RETENTION OF POWER BY DE GAULLE. Parliamentary elections were held 23 and 30 June instead of the proposed referendum. De Gaulle's Union for the Defense of the Republic won an absolute majority for the 1st time, taking votes away from the Communists and from Mitterand's Federation of the Democratic and Socialist Left. On 10 July Maurice Couve de Murville (b. 1907) replaced Pompidou as premier. On 11 Oct. a sweeping educational reform bill was passed, decentralizing the university system and providing for student participation in academic administration. A monetary crisis developed, caused by the "events of May" and the ensuing flight of capital. On 24 Nov., de Gaulle refused to devalue the franc, but announced instead a program of austerity: a wage and price freeze, budgetary cuts, and better administration of the tax laws.

Great Britain and Ireland

1945-63

LABOUR ELECTION WIN. In the elections of 5 July, 1945, the Labour Party won a landslide victory on a platform of full employment, social reform, and nationalization of key industries.

Clement Attlee (1883–1967) became prime minister, Ernest Bevin (1881–1951) foreign secretary, Hugh Dalton (1887–1962) chancellor of the exchequer, Herbert Morrison (1888–1965) leader of the House of Commons, and Aneurin Bevan (1897–1960) minister of health. The sudden ending of lend-lease, announced by the U.S.A. on 24 Aug., made rapid demobilization essential. Faced with a massive housing shortage, the government took compulsory purchase powers. The U.S.A. granted Britain a loan of $3,750 m., 6 Dec.

NATIONALIZATION LEGISLATION. The nationalization of the Bank of England became effective 14 Feb., 1946, and that of civil aviation 1 Aug. The harsh winter of 1946–47 provoked a severe fuel crisis. The Transport Act of 1947 nationalized railroads, canals, and the trucking industry. On 1 Jan., 1948, the coal industry was nationalized. On 5 July, 1948, the National Health Service began, providing free medical care for all. In response to continuing adverse trade balances the government devalued the pound sterling by $\frac{1}{3}$, 18 Sept., 1949. In elections held on 23 Feb., 1950, Labour retained a bare majority. The steel industry was nationalized, 15 Feb., 1951. On 16 Apr. Bevan and Harold Wilson (b. 1916) resigned in protest against the rearmament program.

CONSERVATIVE RETURN TO POWER. Elections held on 25 Oct., 1951, were won by the Conservatives. Churchill returned to power as prime minister with Eden as foreign secretary and R. A. Butler (b. 1902) as chancellor of the exchequer. Faced with a new balance of payments problem, the government imposed higher taxes and cut construction programs. On 6 May, 1953, road transport was denationalized, and iron and steel followed suit, 13 July. Food rationing ended, 4 July, 1954. After improving during 1953–54, the payments position worsened in 1955 as speculation began on a return to sterling convertibility. On 5 Apr., 1955, Churchill retired and was replaced by Eden, with Harold Macmillan (b. 1894) as foreign secretary. The Conservatives increased their majority in elections held on 26 May. On 7 Dec. Attlee resigned and was succeeded by Hugh Gaitskell (1906–63) as Labour Party leader. The discount rate had again to be raised, 1956. Eden resigned, 9 Jan., 1957, following the Suez war, and Macmillan succeeded him. On 4 Apr. new defense plans were announced ending the draft and reducing the armed forces to 375,000 men. During 1958 there emerged a Campaign for Nuclear Disarmament, led by Bertrand Russell (b. 1872) and seeking British renunciation of atomic weapons. The issue figured in the elections of 8 Oct., 1959, which the Conservatives won, but not until Oct. 1961 did Labour finally reject nuclear disarmament as a party policy.

ECONOMIC POLICY. In Apr. 1960 the government instituted a credit squeeze, and in July 1961 called for a wage pause, simultaneously again raising the discount rate. On 20 Dec., 1960, plans for a drastic reorganization of the railways were announced. A rapidly growing rate of Commonwealth immigration led the government to impose controls, 27 Feb., 1962. In July 1962, in the wake of by-election losses, Macmillan shuffled his cabinet, making Reginald Maudling (b. 1917) chancellor of the exchequer. In Jan. 1963 Harold Wilson was elected leader of the Labour Party. During the spring of 1963 the government was badly shaken by a series of spy leaks and associated scandals, notably the "Profumo Affair." On 10 Oct. Macmillan resigned and Sir Alec Douglas-Home (b. 1903) replaced him.

REPUBLIC OF IRELAND. With the coming of peace, normal relations between Ireland and Britain were gradually restored. On 31 May, 1948, prewar trade links were re-established. In elections held on 4 Feb., 1948, de Valera's Fianna Fáil emerged as the largest party, but de Valera rejected a coalition, and Fine Gael leader John Costello (b. 1891) became premier. On 21 Dec., 1948, a law was passed withdrawing Ireland from the Commonwealth, and the Republic of Ireland was proclaimed, 17 Apr., 1949. Following new elections, May 1951, de Valera became premier, but was replaced by Costello in 1954. Costello's coalition was divided over economic policy and

what attitude to adopt toward the I.R.A. (Irish Republican Army), which used terrorism to advance the reunion of Northern Ireland and the south. De Valera returned to power, Mar. 1957, and was elected president, 17 June, 1959. Sean Lemass (b. 1899) became premier and James Dillon (b. 1902) leader of the opposition. Slow moves began toward normalizing relations with Northern Ireland.

1964–68

2ND POSTWAR LABOUR GOVERNMENT. In elections held on 15 Oct., 1964, Labour won a narrow victory, and Wilson became prime minister with George Brown (b. 1914) as his deputy. The new government was faced with a massive sterling crisis, halted for the time being by large borrowings from the International Monetary Fund. On 26 Oct. a 15% surcharge was imposed on imports. In Sept. 1965 a national development plan was published. On 2 Nov. the Race Relations Act went into effect, outlawing racial discrimination in public. New elections, Mar. 1966, increased Labour's majority. Following yet another run on sterling, the government imposed a freeze on all wage increases, July, and cut expenditure heavily. Unemployment figures began to rise.

The steel industry was renationalized, 28 July, 1967. Both in 1963 and in 1967 de Gaulle vetoed British entry into the EEC, ECSC, and Euratom. The sterling crisis worsened and the pound was devalued, 18 Nov., 1967, to £1=$2.40. The Bank of England's discount rate was raised to 8% and government spending was reduced in order to restore confidence in the pound.

Germany

1945–49

DIVISION OF GERMANY. On 5 June, 1945, the allied powers occupying the 4 zones into which Germany had been divided constituted themselves the supreme authority in Germany. A 3-power conference at Potsdam, 17 July–2 Aug., decreed the extirpation of Nazism, the abolition of Nazi organizations and laws, the disbandment of German armed forces, the trial of war criminals, and allied control of education, democratization, and decentralization of government.

POLICIES IN THE ZONES. The borders between the occupation zones tended rapidly to become frontiers and each zone self-sufficient, as each occupying power carried out the Potsdam agreements in its own way. The French sought the separation of the Ruhr and the Rhineland from Germany. In Nov. 1945 the British took over the Ruhr mines and Krupp factories. In the Russian zone the Communist Party flourished under Wilhelm Pieck (1876–1960) and Walter Ulbricht (b. 1893). On 20 Dec. the Communists and Socialists in the Russian zone merged to form the Workers' Party, but Socialists in other zones refused to be associated with it. The Russians confiscated all landholdings over 100 hectares in size, dissolved the big trusts, and removed goods and machinery to the Soviet Union as reparations. The British and Americans united their zones economically to form the "bizone," 1 Jan., 1947. The U.S.A. made Bavaria the first German-controlled area, June 1947; it was soon followed by the united state of Baden-Württemberg and an enlarged Hesse. By the end of 1947 each zone had an elected government. Faced with severe shortages of food and housing, unemployment, and an influx of refugees from the east (c. 10 m. by 1947), the U.S.A. and Britain steadily modified limitations on German industry. On 7 June, 1948, the western powers announced their intention to create a federal state in their zones and to institute a currency reform. The latter came into effect, 20 June, but the Russians rejected it and instituted a land blockade of Berlin.

1949–63

CREATION OF THE FEDERAL REPUBLIC. In the west a parliamentary council drafted a new constitution which, at allied insistence, was to be federal. The task was completed in May 1949, and the constitution promulgated, 23 May. It created a federal system, with a ceremonial president, a powerful chancellor elected by the lower house (itself proportionally elected), and an upper house representing the constituent states.

Elections were held, 14 Aug. Of 402 seats the Christian Democratic Union (CDU), founded by Konrad Adenauer (1876–1967), won 139 and the Socialists, led by Kurt Schumacher (1895–1952), won 131. Theodor Heuss (1884–1963) was elected president of the republic, 12 Sept., and Adenauer formed a CDU-Free Democrat coalition, with Ludwig Erhard (b. 1897) as economics minister.

ADENAUER REGIME. Adenauer's policy called for friendship with France and the U.S.A., an end to the occupation, and German reunification, while Erhard sought economic growth through liberal capitalism. In July 1951 the western powers ended the state of war with Germany. Agreements to terminate the occupation were signed, 26 May, 1952, and Germany entered the EDC, 27 May. In general elections, 6 Sept., 1953, the CDU gained an over-all majority. By the beginning of 1955 industrial production was double that of 1936. On 5 May the Paris Agreements became effective and Germany regained her sovereignty. In the 1957 elections the CDU increased its majority. At their Bad Godesberg convention, 1959, the Socialists reversed their policy on nationalization, accepting the principle of private ownership. Willy Brandt (b. 1913) was elected the Socialists' leader. Adenauer announced his intention to seek the presidency, but later withdrew. In 1961 the CDU lost its majority, and Adenauer formed a coalition with the Free Democrats. In Oct. 1962 the government was shaken by the *Spiegel* affair, and Defense Minister F. J. Strauss (b. 1915) had to resign. Adenauer resigned, 11 Oct., 1963, and Erhard succeeded him.

1964–68

ACCESSION OF KIESINGER. On 27 Oct., 1966, the 4 Free Democrat cabinet ministers resigned over a budgetary dispute, and Erhard refused to seek a vote of confidence. The CDU replaced him as chancellor by Kurt Kiesinger (b. 1904), who formed a coalition with the Social Democrats, Brandt becoming vice-chancellor and minister of foreign affairs, Strauss finance minister, and Gerhard Schröder (b. 1921) defense minister.

GROWTH OF RIGHT AND LEFT RADICALISM. The National Democratic Party (NPD), a rightist, "neo-Nazi" organization founded in 1964 by Adolf von Thadden, became an active force in German politics, capturing 6 to 10% of the vote in elections for various provincial parliaments, 1966–68. The Sozialistischer Deutscher Studentenbund (SDS), led by Rudi Dutschke (b. 1940), demonstrated repeatedly in major cities, calling for educational reforms and diplomatic recognition of East Germany, and opposing the influence on public opinion of conservative publisher Axel Springer. On 14 June, 1968, the much-opposed Emergency Powers Bill was passed, providing for the suspension of civil liberties in time of national danger. With the bill's passage, the western allies relinquished their occupation rights in West Germany to the German government.

Italy

1945–63

CREATION OF POLITICAL PARTIES. Following the capitulation of German troops, 2 May, 1945, large areas of Italy remained outside government control, and there was widespread settling of accounts by Resistance groups. New parties emerged, notably the Christian Democrats, led by Alcide de Gasperi (1881–1954) ; the Social Democrats, led by Giuseppe Saragat (b. 1898) and Pietro Nenni (b. 1891) ; and the Communist Party, led by Palmiro Togliatti (1893–1964). An all-party government was formed, June 1945, but Liberals and Labor Democrats resigned, Nov., and de Gasperi formed a new coalition, with Nenni as vice-premier and Togliatti as justice minister.

THE REPUBLIC. In a referendum held on 2 June, 1946, the voters opted for a republic. A Constituent Assembly was elected, with 207 Christian Democrats, 115 Socialists, and 104 Communists out of a total membership of 556. A new constitution created a decentralized political system under a figurehead president and a premier who had to obtain investiture by both a senate elected for 6 years and a chamber elected for 5. Roman Catholicism remained the state religion, and the 1929 Concordat with the Vatican was retained. From the Fascists the republic inherited the Institute for Industrial Reconstruction (IRI), whose head, Enrico Mattei (1909–62), originally appointed to liquidate it, made the IRI a powerful instrument of industrial progress.

POLITICAL INSTABILITY AND ECONOMIC ADVANCE. On 13 Jan., 1947, the Socialists split apart. Refusing to work with the Communists, the right wing under Saragat formed a new Social Democratic Party. In May Communist ministers resigned, and de Gasperi formed a new coalition. Severe inflation led to a general strike, Dec. 1947. In elections held on 18 Apr., 1948, the Christian Democrats won 307 out of 574 seats. In 1949 there was unrest in Calabria, and on 1 July, 1950, the Cassa per il Mezzogiorno was set up to promote investment in southern Italy.

Deflation proved a successful stimulant of production, and the economic situation improved during 1950–51, sparked by oil discoveries and an upturn in tourism. In elections held in June 1953 the governing parties lost votes and a period of government instability followed the resignation of de Gasperi, July 1953, with the Christian Democrats allied sometimes with the Monarchists and sometimes with the Social Democrats. The Christian Democrats split into factions, a conservative group being led by Giuseppe Pella (b. 1902) and a reformist one by Amintore Fanfani (b. 1908), who was party secretary general. On 5 Oct., 1954, the Trieste dispute with Yugoslavia was finally settled. In Feb. 1955 oil was discovered in the Abruzzi, and Mattei arranged for IRI to exploit it.

Following the Russian denunciation of Stalin, the 2 Italian socialist parties began to move closer together. On 26 Jan., 1959,

Fanfani resigned as premier, and on 31 Jan. as secretary general of the Christian Democrats. A number of short-lived cabinets then held office. In Jan. 1962 the Christian Democrat party congress approved a Fanfani plan to negotiate with the Nenni Socialists, and Nenni agreed to support a left-of-center government, 19 Feb. In Dec. 1962 the government nationalized the electricity industry. The right wing gained strength, however, in the elections of Apr. 1963, and Fanfani resigned, 16 May. In June a government of administrators was formed, provoking left-wing protests.

1963-68

ECONOMIC AUSTERITY. In Sept. 1963 an austerity program was launched to check inflation. On 4 Dec. a new coalition took office, with Aldo Moro (b. 1916) as premier and Nenni as vice-premier. New austerity measures were introduced, 22 Feb., 1964, and on 14 Mar. an international loan was floated. In June Moro was defeated over a plan to aid Catholic schools. On 29 Jan., 1965, a 5-year development plan was adopted, based on a projected 5% annual growth rate. Fanfani again became premier, 5 Mar., resigning on 28 Dec. In July 1966 the two socialist parties, Nenni's Socialist Party and Saragat's Democratic Socialist Party, agreed to reunite.

The parliamentary elections held on 19–20 May, 1968, resulted in small gains for the Communists and Christian Democrats and losses for the Socialists and Liberals. A lengthy political crisis developed when the Unified Socialist Party pulled out of the coalition, opposing the unwillingness of the Christian Democrats to reform the pension, tax, and educational systems and to speed economic development in the south. Moro resigned, 5 June, and a minority Christian Democratic government under Giovanni Leone (b. 1908) was named until a coalition could be formed. Leone's government fell, 19 Nov., and it was not until mid-Dec. that a new coalition of Christian Democrats and Socialists took office under Mariano Rumor (b. 1915).

The Low Countries, Scandinavia, and Finland

1945-68

BELGIUM. A Catholic-Socialist-Liberal-Communist coalition under Achille van Acker (b. 1898) was formed, 11 Feb., 1945, with Paul-Henri Spaak (b. 1899) as foreign minister. Following the elections of 7 Apr., 1946, the Catholic Christian Socialists emerged as the largest party. The Communists left the cabinet, Mar. 1947, and Spaak formed an all-Socialist ministry.

The country was divided on the "royal question," which also heightened Flemish-Walloon differences, the largely Christian Socialist Flemings supporting the unconditional return of Leopold III and the largely Socialist Walloons wanting to make his return conditional. This provoked ministerial crises and street violence. Finally a plebiscite was held, 12 Mar., 1950, which resulted in a vote of 57% for the king's return and 42% against it. The king was restored to the throne, 22 July, and delegated his powers to his son, 31 July, who became Baudouin I on 7 Sept., 1951.

In elections held on 11 Apr., 1954, the Christian Socialists lost the majority they had acquired in 1950, and a Socialist-Liberal Coalition was formed. In the spring of 1955, Catholics demonstrated against a proposal to lower subsidies to private schools, but the bill passed, 13 June. On 3 Feb., 1958, Belgium signed an economic union treaty with the Netherlands and Luxembourg, but the resulting "Benelux" never became fully effective.

Following riots in the Belgian Congo, Jan. 1959, African problems began to dominate government activity, a situation which continued through 1960. In Feb. 1959, strikes broke out in the Belgian coal mines, and in Jan. 1960 there was a general strike in favor of economic and social reforms. In Dec. 1960 the Loi Unique was proposed, reducing state expenditure, increasing taxes, allowing greater investment, and seeking to promote financial stability. The law provoked widespread strikes, but was voted, 13 Jan., 1961.

Walloon demands for constitutional reform provoked another government crisis, and the Christian Socialists lost votes in the elections of 26 Mar. Theo Lefevre (b. 1914) formed a Christian Socialist-Socialist coalition. In Oct. 1961, Flemish and Walloon demonstrators clashed in Brussels. On 15 Feb., 1962, Parliament passed a bill defining the linguistic boundaries of Belgium and making Brussels bilingual, but Flemish-Walloon disputes continued, especially at the University of Louvain. In Apr. 1964, doctors went on strike to protest against a new government medical-care program. At a round-table conference, Jan. 1965, the parties agreed on constitutional reforms designed to prevent one language group from dominating the other, but in elections held on 23 May the governing parties lost votes to the "linguistic extremists." In Feb. 1966, Socialist ministers resigned, and in Mar. a new cabinet was formed of Christian Socialists and members of the Party for Liberty and Progress. Paul van den Boeynants' cabinet fell, 7 Feb., 1968, over linguistic disputes and student riots at the University of Louvain. The king dissolved Parliament in preparation for elections, 1 Apr., in which the Flemish Nationalist Party gained votes. A new coalition of Social Christians and Socialists was formed under Gaston Eyskens (b. 1905).

NETHERLANDS. The Netherlands suffered greatly in the last months of the war. Wide areas were flooded, and many people starved. Queen Wilhelmina returned, 3 May, 1945. From elections held on 17 May, 1946, the Catholic People's Party and a new Labor Party emerged as the strongest groups, forming a coalition, 2 July, which lasted until 1958. Following widespread flooding, 31 Jan.–2 Feb., 1953, a Delta Plan was launched to seal off several estuaries from the North Sea.

Gradually government reconstruction plans led to higher wages and, as the country industrialized, to a decline in unemployment. On 11 Dec., 1958, Premier Willem Drees (b. 1886) resigned. Following elections, 12 Mar., 1959, a

Catholic-Protestant coalition was formed under Jan de Quay (b. 1901). On 15 Aug., 1960, natural gas was discovered in Groningen. On 7 Mar., 1961, the florin was revalued to fl.3.80 to (U.S.) $1. In the elections of 15 May, 1963, left-wing neutralists took votes from the Labor Party, and Victor Marijnen (b. 1917) formed a new coalition, 24 July. On 29 Feb., 1964, labor and management agreed on a 10% wage raise. The 1966 budget proposed a similar increase in government expenditures and on 23 May, in the face of balance-of-payments deficits, a 2-month wage freeze was imposed. In June 1966 there were riots in Amsterdam, originally of workers, and later of "provos." The government fell, 14 Oct., as Parliament refused to increase government spending. In the elections of 15 Feb., 1967, the Catholic and Labor Parties lost votes. Piet de Jong (b. 1915) formed a new coalition government, 3 Apr., 1967.

NORWAY. The Labor Party gained an absolute majority in the elections of 7 Oct., 1945, and retained it in the 1949 and 1953 elections. Vidkun Quisling (b. 1887) was executed, 24 Oct., 1945. By autumn 1946, production surpassed prewar figures. On 22 Jan., 1955, Einar Gerhardsen (b. 1897) returned to office as premier, and on 23 Mar., 1956, the government froze prices. In July 1957 there were strikes for higher wages in the forestry, paper, and construction industries. On 1 Mar., 1959, the workweek was fixed at not more than 45 hours.

On 15 Apr., 1961, a neutralist Socialist Party was formed of dissident Labor members, and Labor lost its majority, 11 Sept., 1961. A 4-year plan issued in 1962 foresaw a 17% increase in production. On 5 Jan., 1962, price controls were reimposed. Gerhardsen resigned, 24 Aug., 1963, but the conservative government that replaced him was short-lived, and he returned to power, 25 Sept. On 23 Apr., 1964, Parliament adopted a law authorizing compulsory wage arbitration by the National Wages Board.

SWEDEN. On 6 Oct., 1946, Tage Erlander (b. 1901) became premier. His government faced pressure to raise wages and had to introduce austerity measures to limit imports. On 1 June, 1955, compulsory health insurance was introduced. The Socialists lost their majority in the elections of June 1958, and Erlander formed a minority government. On 15 Dec., 1965, a law was adopted providing for state subsidies to political parties.

DENMARK. After the elections of 30 Oct., 1945, the Social Democrats remained the largest party. On 23 Mar., 1948, the Faroe Islands were granted internal autonomy. A new constitution with a single chamber came into force, 5 June, 1953. On 30 Sept., 1953, an all-Socialist cabinet under Hans Hedtoft (1903–55) was formed. On Hedtoft's death, H. C. Hansen (1906–60) succeeded him.

In Mar. 1956 a major series of strikes erupted, but were settled by wage increases, 12 Apr. On 20 Feb., 1959, Denmark became a member of the European Free Trade Association (EFTA), though much of her trade was with the EEC. Viggo Kampmann (b. 1910) replaced Hansen as premier, 19 Feb., 1960. On 31 July, 1962, Jens Otto Krag (b. 1914) became premier. On 12 Mar., 1963, Parliament voted to extend existing wage contracts for 2 years and freeze both prices and wages. The Socialists lost votes in the elections of Nov. 1966. On 2 May, 1967, the government announced that Denmark remained a candidate for membership in the EEC.

FINLAND. The Social Democrats and the Communists emerged as the main parties from the elections of Mar. 1945. J. K. Paasikivi (1870–1956) formed an all-party cabinet. A purge was instituted of individuals responsible for the anti-Soviet policy of 1939–40. On 19 May, 1948, Parliament censured a Communist minister and, following losses by them in the elections of July, the Communists were not included in the new cabinet. A nonaggression pact with the Soviet Union, 6 Apr., 1948, was complemented by a trade agreement, 13 June, 1950. The USSR became Finland's best customer.

In Mar. 1950 Urho Kekkonen (b. 1900) formed a new coalition, and was elected president, 15 Feb., 1951. In Mar. 1956 a general strike protested against repeal of the Emergency Powers Act, which tied wages to the cost-of-living index. In the elections of July 1958 the Communists emerged as the strongest party, but were unable to form a coalition, and minority governments continued to rule. On 27 Mar., 1961, Finland became an associate member of EFTA. Kekkonen was re-elected president, Feb. 1962, following Soviet indications that his re-election would be welcomed by the USSR. In Jan. 1964 a wage freeze was imposed for 6 months. After the elections of Mar. 1966 a coalition was formed which included Communists for the 1st time since 1948.

Spain and Portugal

1945–68

SPAIN. On 19 July, 1945, Gen. Franco reorganized his cabinet to include a Catholic Action leader. United Nations attempts to isolate Spain proved abortive, but Spain did not become a member of the UN. On 31 Mar., 1947, a new constitution was promulgated, making Spain a monarchy and giving the Caudillo power to nominate his successor. The constitution was denounced by the pretender to the Spanish throne, Don Juan, but was adopted by a referendum, 6 July.

In the spring of 1951, strikes erupted in Catalonia and the Basque country in protest against low wages and lack of political liberty. The strike leaders were jailed. A new concordat, 26 Sept., 1954, ensured state control of the church.

Prices continued to rise, and riots broke out in Madrid, Feb. 1956. In July 1959 the peseta was devalued, the new rate being 60 to (U.S.) $1, and Spain joined the Organization for European Economic Cooperation (OEEC). The steady growth of tourism (1 m. visitors in 1953, 8 m. in 1961) improved the country's balance of payments. In Sept. 1960, strikes and sabotage increased, and many intellectuals were arrested. On 23 Apr., 1962, the Asturias miners ceased work and their strike movement spread, as liberal church organizations supported the strikers. Arrests were made, and a state of emergency declared, 4 May, but

on 24 May miners' wages were raised and
the strikes ended early in June. On 14
Dec., 1966, a referendum endorsed a new
Organic Law providing for the appointment of a premier and guaranteeing
religious freedom for non-Catholics.

PORTUGAL. After the war the Portuguese government under Antonio de Oliveira Salazar (b. 1889) held elections on
18 Nov., 1945, and eased censorship. Left-
wing parties formed a "Movement of
Democratic Unity" to oppose the government, and censorship was re-established.
In Oct. 1946 a group of army officers
failed in an attempt to seize control of
the state. Arrests for what the government
regarded as "subversion" were frequent.
The opposition boycotted the elections of
1949 as it had those of 1945.

In elections held on 8 June, 1958,
however, Umberto Delgado (1906–65) did
not withdraw, but stood on a platform of
free elections in Portugal. Popular
demonstrations in his favor led to police
action and casualties. He won 23.5% of
the vote, and his popularity grew. Fearing
arrest by the government, he fled the
country.

In Mar. 1959 an uprising was attempted in Lisbon, but it failed. On 23
Jan., 1961, a group of Portuguese hostile
to Salazar seized control of the ship *Santa
Maria* in an attempt to arouse support
for Delgado. In the Portuguese African
territories rebellion broke out in Angola,
Mar. 1961. The Portuguese government
sent troops to Angola, and to Mozambique
and Portuguese Guinea in 1963. In Aug.
1963 the Social Democratic Action Movement was founded in opposition to the
regime. It called for the easing of repression, democratization of the republic, and
self-determination for the overseas territories. The dead body of Delgado was
found, Apr. 1965, in Spain, where he was
presumed to have come to contact members of the Portuguese opposition. The
Action Movement took part in the campaign for the general elections of 7 Nov.,
1965, but withdrew from the ballots,
leaving Salazar's National Union in control of all 130 seats. In Sept. 1968 Salazar
had a brain hemorrhage and was replaced
as premier by Marcelo Caetano (b. 1906).

Austria and Switzerland
1945–68

AUSTRIA. On 29 Apr., 1945, the Russians installed a Populist–Social Democrat–Communist provisional government
headed by Social Democrat Karl Renner
(1870–1950), which Britain and the U.S.A.
recognized. On 25 June Austria was partitioned into 4 occupation zones. In all
zones, especially the Russian, intensive
anti-Nazi measures were taken. Elections
were held, 25 Nov., giving the People's
Party 85 seats, the Socialists 76, and the
Communists 4. Leopold Figl (1904–65)
became chancellor of a 3-party cabinet,
and Renner was elected president, 20
Dec.

The government outlined a program of
de-Nazification, the nationalization of key
industries, and the return to Austria of
the South Tyrol. The U.S.A., Britain, the
United Nations Relief and Rehabilitation
Administration (UNRRA), and the European Recovery Program (ERP) aided
Austria, which had also to cope with over
600,000 displaced persons.

Austrian sovereignty was restored, June
1946, though a final peace treaty waited
on allied agreement. The Communists
left the government, Nov. 1947. In Mar.
1955 the new chancellor, Julius Raab
(1891–1964), visited Moscow, and the
Russians subsequently agreed to make a
treaty with Austria. A State Treaty between the allies and the Austrian Republic was signed on 15 May, 1955, and
provided for Austrian neutrality and the
withdrawal of foreign troops (completed
Oct. 1955).

Raab resigned, 11 Apr., 1961, and was
succeeded by Alfons Gorbach (b. 1898).
On 15 Dec., 1961, Austria asked for
negotiations to enable her to become
associated with the EEC. On 31 May,
1963, the Supreme Court ruled that Otto
von Hapsburg could return, but the
Socialists rejected its decision. On 2 Feb.,
1964, Gorbach resigned, and was replaced
by Josef Klaus (b. 1910). In elections held
on 6 Mar., 1966, Klaus's People's Party
won absolute control of Parliament—the

1st time a single party had had a majority since 1945. On 17 Dec., 1966, Austria and the EEC agreed to a tariff cut on industrial products; but on 29 June, 1967, Italy opposed Austrian entry into the EEC and ECSC because of terrorist attacks against the Italian South Tyrol which were thought to have been perpetrated by Austrians.

SWITZERLAND. After the war Switzerland declined to join the UN, but kept in a high state of military readiness and actively contributed to peaceful international activities. On 11 July, 1958, the government announced that it favored the acquisition by Switzerland of nuclear weapons. On 1 Apr., 1962, a Socialist-sponsored referendum to prohibit all nuclear weapons in Switzerland was defeated. The government restricted the admission of foreign workers, 1 Mar., 1963. By Aug. of the previous year the number of these had risen to 645,000.

Greece

1945–49

CIVIL WAR. After the evacuation of German troops, Sept.–Nov. 1944, most of Greece was controlled by guerrilla forces, especially by the largely Communist ELAS. On 18 Oct., 1944, George Papandreou (b. 1888), a centrist, was made head of a national unity cabinet, but its ELAS members soon resigned. Civil war began as ELAS members attacked right-wing and British occupation forces. Negotiations led to the Varkizoi Agreement, 14 Jan., 1945: the government promised free elections, the basic freedoms, and an end to martial law; and dissidents promised to surrender their arms.

During 1945 there were 6 cabinets. In May 1945, workers in Athens struck in protest against low wages and high prices. Elections, 31 Mar., 1946, were won by the right-wing Populist Party, and a plebiscite, 1 Sept., voted to recall King George II.

In the fall of 1946, charging nonimplementation of the Varkizoi accords, the Communists renewed the civil war. With British, and later American, assistance the revolt was crushed by 1949. Between 1945 and 1949, 45,000 people were killed.

1950–68

POLITICAL INSTABILITY. In elections held on 16 Nov., 1952, the right-wing Greek Rally of Alexander Papagos (1883–1955) won 239 out of 300 seats, and Papagos became prime minister. He was succeeded, Oct. 1955, by Constantine Karamanlis (b. 1907). By 1954 the drachma was at 84,000 to the pound sterling (as against 600 in 1945). Karamanlis' National Radical Union won the elections of 19 Feb., 1956. From 1956 to 1958 the problem of Cyprus dominated Greek politics. In Feb. 1961 Papandreou formed the Center Union, which won 100 seats to the NRU's 176 in the elections of the following 29 Oct. The opposition claimed the elections were fraudulent, and accused the king of meddling in politics. Karamanlis resigned, 11 June, 1963, and the Center Union won most seats at the next election, 3 Nov. Papandreou was named prime minister but, refusing Communist support, resigned, 24 Dec. He won a landslide victory, however, at the elections of 16 Feb., 1964, and became prime minister. On 27 Apr. he amnestied 450 political prisoners, and on 14 July dissolved several right-wing organizations.

The NRU now began to accuse the Papandreou regime of preparing a Communist coup. In May 1965 the "Aspida Affair" broke, in which the right wing accused a number of officers of preparing to take over the army. In July Papandreou proposed the dismissal of the minister of defense. The king refused, and formed a new government which excluded Papandreou. On 14 Apr., 1967, Parliament was dissolved and new elections called, but on 21 Apr. a military coup was staged. The constitution was suspended and numerous arrests made. On 29 Apr. the government, led by Col. George Papadopoulos (b. 1919), abolished the pro-Communist United Democratic Left; on 4 May, 280 liberal and leftist organizations were banned. A law of 3 Nov. abolished jury trials for all common and political crimes and for press offenses. King Constantine XIII appealed, 13 Dec., to his countrymen to join him against the military junta. The countercoup failed and Constantine fled to Rome, 14 Dec. The government named Lt. Gen. George Zoitakis regent with the full powers of the king.

The junta promised to return Greece to civilian rule as soon as the aims of the revolution (to prevent Communist uprisings) should be achieved, and the draft of a new constitution was presented, 11 July, 1968. It provided for a reduction in the king's powers, a strengthened executive, press censorship, and a Constitutional Court which could deprive individuals of their rights and ban political parties. The constitution was overwhelmingly approved in a referendum, 29 Sept.

EAST CENTRAL EUROPE AND THE BALKANS

1945–68

EASTERN EUROPE AFTER 1945. With the exception of Greece, Yugoslavia, and Albania, the destinies of the states of Eastern Europe after World War II were largely determined by the fact that they had been liberated from German domination by the forces of the Soviet Union. Greece, which alone among the countries of Eastern Europe had been occupied by British forces in the wake of the retreating German army, continued to remain under the influence of the western powers. Although both Yugoslavia and Albania had freed themselves from Axis domination through their own partisan forces, they could not extricate themselves from the influence of the USSR until 1948 in the case of Yugoslavia, and until 1960 in the case of Albania. Both countries, however, remained under Communist, albeit dissimilar, rule throughout the 1950's and 1960's under the leadership of Josip Broz Tito (b. 1892) of Yugoslavia and Enver Hoxha of Albania. The rest of the countries—Czechoslovakia, Hungary, Poland, Rumania, and Bulgaria—were required by the Soviet Union for both strategic and ideological reasons to act as a cordon sanitaire to prevent the area from becoming the staging ground for another invasion attempt from the West.

Changes in the monolithic structure binding the satellite countries to the USSR did not occur until after 1953, the year Stalin died. After 1953 the process of de-Stalinization, and the concomitant relative ideological uncertainty set against a background of continuous power struggle, produced a number of ideological and foreign policy shifts. In addition to the factors which were rooted in tradition and national character, it was the process of Soviet-led de-Stalinization which produced, Oct.–Nov. 1956, a political upheaval in Poland and outright revolt in Hungary. Following the control of the Polish ferment and the bloody suppression by Soviet tanks of the Hungarian uprising, a relative stability ensued in Eastern Europe. By the early 1960's, it became increasingly evident, however, that the idea of "several roads leading to Communism," 1st enunciated by N. S. Khrushchev, would remain a permanent feature of East European political developments.

In Czechoslovakia the process of de-Stalinization, controlled tightly under the leadership, 1958–68, of Antonin Novotný, led to Novotný's ouster and subsequently to the implementation of a bold "liberalization" program under the new and reformist leadership of Alexander Dubček in early 1968. The far-reaching ferment of Czechoslovak life culminated in a Soviet-led invasion of the country by 5 of its Warsaw Pact allies, Aug. 1968.

WARSAW TREATY ORGANIZATION (WARSAW PACT). Signed in Warsaw, 14 May, 1955, a military pact created a mutual defense alliance between Albania, Bulgaria, Czechoslovakia, East Germany, Hungary, Poland, Rumania, and the USSR. The treaty, binding for 20 years, was to lapse in the event of the conclusion of a collective European security system; it provided for the reorganization of the armed forces of the member nations under a unified military command, with headquarters in Moscow. The pact also formally legalized the presence and future stationing of Soviet troops in some of the member states. (The signing ceremony took place just 1 day prior to the signing of the Austrian peace treaty, which voided the legality of the presence of Soviet troops in Hungary and Rumania.)

According to the Soviet Union, the treaty was made necessary by the creation of the North Atlantic Treaty Organization (NATO) ; it was a direct response to the inclusion in NATO of a remilitarized West Germany under the Paris Pacts of 1954.

In 1962 Albania became a nonactive member of the alliance, partly because it sided with Communist China in the Sino-Soviet dispute. As a result of the Soviet-led invasion of Czechoslovakia, Aug. 1968, Albania formally withdrew from the organization the same month.

COUNCIL FOR MUTUAL ECONOMIC AID (COMECON). Known as COMECON, the council was founded, Jan. 1949, to act as an instrument of greater economic integration between the USSR and the satellite states of Eastern Europe. Largely neglected till 1954–56, its role thereafter was gradually expanded until, in 1959, it adopted a new charter which elevated it to a status similar to that of the Common Market. The charter claimed to be the answer to the West's Marshall Plan, and provided for increased economic, commercial, and industrial collaboration not only between the USSR and the member states but also among the member states as well.

The added goal of industrial specialization, envisaged as being based on the availability of natural resources within each state, soon led to opposition, especially from Rumania after 1962. Albania, apparently because of the support extended to Communist China in the latter's polemics against the USSR, was excluded from council sessions beginning 1961. The Mongolian People's Republic was admitted into COMECON in 1962.

Albania

1945–68

VICTORY OF THE NATIONAL LIBERATION FRONT. The major Albanian partisan group, the National Liberation Front, was dominated by Communists under the leadership of

Enver Hoxha. Supported by Tito of Yugoslavia, the front shortly after the departure of the German forces, Nov. 1944, took control of the country. The Communists, working under cover of the front, which was renamed, 1945, the Albanian Democratic Front, polled 93% of the votes cast in the elections on 2 Dec., 1945; on 11 Jan., 1946, the Communist-dominated legislature proclaimed the country a People's Democratic Republic with Hoxha as premier and Koçe Xoxe as vice-premier and interior minister.

Following the mining of 2 British warships near Corfu Island in the Adriatic, Britain and the U.S. broke off relations with Albania.

SPLIT WITH YUGOSLAVIA. Since attaining its independence in 1912, Albania had been dominated by one protector after another. Yugoslavia, which replaced Italian domination late in World War II, showed increasing interest in the country's affairs. For one thing Yugoslavia opposed U.S.-Albanian diplomatic ties; Yugoslavia also hoped to control Soviet-Albanian relations in the postwar period. As a result, Albania looked to the USSR for the protection of her independence; consequently, the rift between Tito and Stalin in the summer of 1948 was seized upon as an opportunity vigorously to denounce the former.

INTERNAL DEVELOPMENTS. Using police terror and political purges as a means to maintain control, the Albanian government after 1945 followed the example set by the other satellite states of Eastern Europe. Interior Minister Xoxe, who had been one of the leaders of the liberation movement during the war, was tried and executed for "Trotskyite and Titoist activity," May 1949. Later in 1961, Liri Belishova, a member of the Central Committee, and Teme Sejko, a Soviet-trained admiral, were executed for "treasonable activities." A constitution on the Soviet model was adopted in 1950.

FOREIGN AFFAIRS. Albania joined COMECON, Feb. 1949, and became a founding member of the Warsaw Pact in 1955. The same year Albania was admitted to the UN.

From the period following Tito's excommunication from the Cominform in

1948 until shortly after the suppression of the Hungarian Revolution in 1956, Albania was one of the most loyal of Soviet satellites. Although Albanian-Yugoslav relations improved, at least superficially, as a result of the 1955 *rapprochement* between Yugoslavia and the Soviet Union, the Tirana government did not cease to fear Tito's influence. Thus during 1956–58, when relations between Khrushchev and Tito deteriorated, Hoxha renewed his attack on Tito.

ALBANIAN-SOVIET SPLIT. Already deteriorating in 1959, Albania's relations with the USSR became progressively worse during the 1960's. The main cause of tension was the renewal of Khrushchev's *rapprochement* with Tito. In Nov. 1960, at a meeting in Moscow of representatives of 81 Communist parties, both Hoxha and Premier Mehmet Shehu openly charged Khrushchev with treason and "revisionism." At the 4th Congress of the Albanian Communist Party, Feb. 1961, Albania openly supported Communist China in her clash with the Soviet representative; in June, Adriatic-based Soviet submarines left Albania, and this was followed by the withdrawal of all economic assistance to Albania by the Soviet Union and other East European satellites. Following Khrushchev's open attack on the Albanian party at the 22nd Soviet Party Congress, Oct. 1961, as "dogmatist," Albania openly counterattacked, charging the Soviet leader with yielding to Yugoslav "revisionism" and collaborating with U.S. imperialism. In Dec. 1961, the USSR severed diplomatic relations with Albania. Thereafter, Albania became Communist China's mouthpiece in the latter's polemics against the USSR, and represented the Communist Chinese viewpoint at the UN General Assembly.

Bulgaria

1945–68

DOMESTIC ISSUES. After World War II Bulgaria went through a period of coalition government during which non-Communist representation was gradually eroded with Red Army assistance. First the monarchy was abolished in favor of a People's Republic, Oct. 1946, with power in the hands of a Communist-dominated Fatherland Front. The years 1944–47 were marked by a series of violent purges in which opposition parties and factions were destroyed. Nikola Petkov, leader of the opposition Agrarian Party in the Fatherland Front, was tried and hanged, Sept. 1947, shortly after a U.S.-Bulgarian peace treaty had been ratified. Other trials followed, and in Dec. 1947 the Sobranie (Parliament) adopted a new constitution modeled on the Soviet Constitution of 1936. By early 1948 Bulgaria was under a 1-party system ruled by the Communists led by Georgi M. Dimitrov, a former Comintern leader.

POST-STALIN ERA. After 1953 Bulgaria permitted only a limited degree of relaxation of political terror, despite promises made in response to pressure from the intellectuals and despite the resentment of the collectivized peasantry. In the party leadership, the Stalinist Vlko Chervenkov, successor to Dimitrov in 1949, was forced to give up his posts as general secretary of the Party in 1954 and as prime minister in 1956; finally, 1962, he fell victim to the 2nd de-Stalinization purge and was expelled from the Party. The political vacuum created by Chervenkov's fall was filled by a younger and native Communist, Todor Zhivkov. As a protégé of Chervenkov, Zhivkov succeeded him as party 1st secretary in 1954 and, in 1962, he also assumed the post of premier; thereafter Zhivkov remained the undisputed leader of Bulgaria, even weathering the fall of Khrushchev, who had been his mainstay till 1964.

Despite the emphasis on heavy industry, Bulgaria economically remained largely an agricultural country confronted with serious problems: in Sept. 1961 food rationing was introduced and on 1 Jan., 1962, the currency had to be revalued. In the late 1960's Bulgaria's rate of economic growth showed marked improvement.

FOREIGN RELATIONS. The Paris Peace Treaty of June 1947 allowed Bulgaria to keep South Dobruja but forced her to yield Thrace and Yugoslav Macedonia. During the period after 1944 and before the ouster of Tito from the Cominform in June 1948, a South Slav federation, which would have comprised Bulgaria, Yugoslavia, and, possibly, Greece, was contemplated by both Tito and Dimitrov. The 2 leaders agreed on a customs union and the abolition of their borders at Bled (Bled Agreement) in Aug. 1947. Stalin's opposition to a larger political unit in the Balkans and Tito's defiance of the Comintern, June 1948, scuttled the plan. Although the federation issue was buried, the Macedonian problem continued to plague Yugoslav-Bulgarian relations; during 1967–68 Bulgaria appeared to be renewing her old claim to Yugoslav Macedonia.

After Stalin's death Bulgarian relations with Greece and Turkey improved somewhat, despite a threat to expel all Turkish nationals, 1950–51. In 1955 Bulgaria joined the Warsaw Pact and was admitted to the UN; she had been a member of COMECON since Jan. 1949. As a member of the Warsaw Pact, she participated in the Soviet-led invasion of Czechoslovakia, Aug. 1968. In general, Bulgaria dutifully followed Soviet foreign policy shifts.

Czechoslovakia

1945–53

RESTORATION OF CZECHOSLOVAKIA. With the exception of Ukrainian-speaking Ruthenia—which was ceded to the USSR to create a common Soviet-Hungarian border—Czechoslovakia's pre-1938 borders were restored at the 1945 Potsdam Conference of the "Big 4"; Britain had already recognized the country's prewar borders, 5 Aug., 1942, when she repudiated the 1938 Munich agreement which dismembered Czechoslovakia. At Potsdam, Czechoslovakia was also authorized to expel some 2.5 m. Sudeten Germans—her main liability during the interwar years—and to enforce on Hungary an exchange of Hungarians in return for Slovaks; the latter move led to considerable friction between the 2 govern-

ments during the immediate postwar years. Left with a reduced minority of some 500,000 Germans and some ½ m. Hungarians (in Slovakia), Czechoslovakia became a near-homogeneous state after World War II.

Following the occupation of post-Munich Czechoslovakia by Germany, a government in exile under Eduard Beneš (1884–1948) was set up in London which, unlike that of Poland, was recognized by Moscow as well as the other allies. Though subjected to Nazi terrorism, Czechoslovakia suffered no major disruption of her economy during the war; Czechoslovak units fought with the allies under Gen. Ludvík Svoboda.

Early in Apr. 1944, a coalition government headed by Beneš accompanied the Soviet forces which entered the country through eastern Slovakia; American forces entered Bohemia from the west and Prague was liberated, 12 May, 1945. Both the U.S. and the Soviet forces left Czechoslovakia in Dec. of the same year.

COUP OF FEB. 1948. Already a legally functioning political party before the war, the Czechoslovak Communist Party in a free and secret election became the strongest party in the country when, 26 May, 1946, it polled 38% of the votes cast. Beneš, who became president of the republic, called upon Klement Gottwald, a pro-Moscow Communist, to form a coalition government; the Communists gained control of key portfolios, including the interior ministry under Vacláv Nosek.

Although the coalition worked well initially, the slow penetration by the Communists into all branches of the state apparatus led to increasing friction between them and the other parties in the coalition. By early 1948 Communist popularity was on the wane. Fearing the loss of its parliamentary strength at the approaching general elections, the Communist Party decided to seize power through a *coup d'état*. The decisive issue was the control of the police forces, especially those of Prague. After the resignation, 21 Feb., 1948, of 12 non-Communist ministers to protest a police purge, Premier Gottwald formed another cabinet, 25

Feb., rather than dismiss Interior Minister Nosek—responsible for the purge of the police—or advance the date of the election, as had been expected by the non-Communist faction. In anticipation of resistance by supporters of the "bourgeois" parties, the Communist Party, using armed Workers' Militia, staged repeated demonstrations in major cities. President Beneš, hoping to avoid civil war, approved the new government, thereby making the transfer of power constitutional.

GOTTWALD-ZÁPOTOCKY RE-GIME. After the Communist takeover, the National Assembly adopted a new constitution—a replica of the 1936 Soviet constitution—on 9 Mar., 1948. The Slovaks obtained greater autonomy. The next day, Foreign Minister Jan Masaryk (b. 1886), son of the founder-president of Czechoslovakia, Tomas G. Masaryk, was found dead at his office. In the elections, which followed on 30 May, only a single slate of National Front candidates was allowed to run. The new government was headed by the Communist Antonin Zápotocký, a former trade union leader; Gottwald succeeded President Beneš, who had resigned on 6 June.

The opposition silenced, the new regime enacted a program of rapid industrialization (at the expense of consumer industry) and proceeded to nationalize all industrial plants employing more than 50 workers; land collectivization was also pressed, but not as forcefully as in other satellite countries, such as Bulgaria and Hungary. The new regime closely aligned its foreign policy to that of the Soviet Union.

In order to rid the party of its dissenters, as well as in response to Tito's defiance of Stalin, 1948, a series of show trials was held between Mar. 1950 and Jan. 1954. The purges culminated in the arrest of Foreign Minister Vladimir Clementis (Slovak) and Communist Party Secretary General Rudolf Slánský (Czech Jew); both were executed, 3 Dec., 1952.

1953–68

NOVOTNÝ REGIME. Antonin Novotný became party 1st secretary, Mar. 1953, and president in 1957. Partly responsible for the purge of Slánský and Clementis, he ruled with an iron hand and paid only lip service to the Soviet-inspired policy of de-Stalinization in the late 1950's. To camouflage his own complicity in the purges, he purged as scapegoats 1st Deputy Premier Rudolf Barák, Feb. 1962, and then Premier Viliam Siroký, Sept. 1963, both on false charges. These purges greatly strengthened Novotný's hand in his fight against the pressures for liberalization, resurgent Slovak nationalism, and demands for a drastic overhaul of the deteriorating economy.

A new constitution adopted in 1960 declared the state a Socialist Republic. Slovak autonomy, provided for under the 1948 constitution, was curbed in the new one; the Slovak National Council in Bratislava was made subservient to the National Assembly in Prague. This action, among others, led during the late 1960's to a renewal of the prewar antagonism between Czechs and Slovaks.

From 1963 onward, Czechoslovakia underwent a protracted process of cultural thaw, illustrated especially in the field of education and the revival of the once-famed Czechoslovak film industry. In 1965 an increasing demand for economic reform led to the adoption of a plan giving greater autonomy to local managers and making profitability a criterion of economic efficiency. At the same time foreign trade with nations other than Czechoslovakia's COMECON partners and the encouragement of tourism were stepped up.

The growing freedom of speech and the press, however, gave rise to ever bolder criticism of the Novotný regime. At the Congress of the Czechoslovak Writers' Union, July 1967, a coalition of anti-Novotný forces accused him of anti-Slovak sentiments and charged him with blocking the implementation of the 1965 economic reforms. During a stormy meeting of the Central Committee, Dec. 1967, his ouster was prevented only through the intervention of Leonid I. Brezhnev, the Soviet party leader. In Jan. 1968, however, Novotný was deposed as 1st secretary and was succeeded by the Slovak party leader, Alexander Dubček, who had previously attacked Novotný for relegating Slovakia to the status of a 2nd-class province.

LIBERALIZATION AND SOVIET OCCUPATION. Under Dubček's leadership, Czechoslovakia embarked upon a bold liberalization program—known as the "Action Program"—setting as its goal "to give Communism a human face." As part of the "Action Program," the reformist Dubček leadership released all political prisoners, allowed broad criticism of the party, and proceeded with the long-postponed rehabilitation of the victims of the previous political trials. In foreign policy, Czechoslovakia contemplated the resumption of diplomatic relations with West Germany and closer ties with non-Communist nations, especially with those of Western Europe.

Preceded by veiled and open criticism and warning, especially from the Soviet Union and East Germany, 5 Warsaw Pact allies of Czechoslovakia invaded the country on the night of 20–21 Aug., 1968. The invasion precipitated one of the broadest international condemnations of the Soviet Union and its more loyal allies— East Germany, Poland, Bulgaria, and Hungary. The occupation initially failed in its alleged objective of unseating the Dubček leadership (many members of which had 1st been abducted to the Soviet Union and then returned). Although Czechoslovakia was forced to legalize the Soviet troops' presence, some of the reforms, among them press freedom, survived until the liquidation of the Dubček regime by the spring of 1969. Rumania, a Warsaw Pact partner of Czechoslovakia, refused a Soviet demand to participate in the invasion; Yugoslavia also denounced the invasion.

Hungary

1944–49

DEFEAT IN WORLD WAR II. As a reluctant ally, Hungary joined Germany in the attacks on Yugoslavia and the USSR in 1941. After severe losses on the Russian front, however, the regime of Miklós Horthy (1868–1957) tried to take

the country out of the war, 15 Oct., 1944; the ill-prepared attempt failed and he was 1st arrested and then deported to Germany. Unlike Czechoslovakia, Hungary became the scene of a devastating campaign waged by the retreating German forces against the Red Army, Oct. 1944–Apr. 1945. A provisional government, formed of 4 coalition parties, Dec. 1944, signed an armistice with the Soviet Union in Moscow, Jan. 1945.

The peace treaty, signed in Paris in 1947, forced Hungary to give up territories regained during the war; the treaty also called for $500 m. reparation payments to the USSR, Czechoslovakia, and Yugoslavia.

GOVERNMENT BY COALITION. For 3 years after the war, Hungary was ruled by a series of coalition governments which came increasingly under the domination of the minority Communist Party. Formed after free and secret elections, 4 Nov., 1945—which had returned the non-Communist Smallholder Party with a 59% majority against 17% polled by the Communists—the new coalition regime proceeded to implement wide-ranging social and land reforms. In addition, it passed other important measures aimed at the reconstruction of the economic, cultural, and social life of the war-torn country. In Jan. 1946 Hungary adopted a republican constitution.

COMMUNIST ASSUMPTION OF POWER. Although a minority party (but backed by the occupying Soviet army), the Communists, led by Mátyás Rákosi, were able to eliminate their coalition partners through the application of the famous "salami tactics." One by one, they 1st broke the Smallholder Party, 1948, through terror and blackmail, and then proceeded to absorb the Social Democrats, Jan. 1948. In Feb. 1949 the Communists merged all other opposition parties into the People's Independence Front, and on 15 May they held an election where Communist-approved candidates, without opposition, polled 95.6% of the votes. In Aug. 1949, a new constitution, patterned after the 1936 Soviet model, proclaimed Hungary a "People's Democracy."

1950–56

THE STALINIST PHASE. The opposition eliminated and the population intimidated, the country came under the virtual dictatorship of Rákosi, secretary general of the Hungarian Workers' (Communist) Party, 1944–56. He carried out drastic purges of the rank and file and eliminated all real and potential rivals and opponents.

All private industrial firms with more than 10 employees were nationalized; freedom of religion, the press, and assembly were greatly curtailed. At the same time, discontent grew: among the industrial workers because of the imposition of high work norms and wage and price controls; among the peasantry because of the forced collectivization of land just distributed. The chronic economic difficulties stemming from forced industrialization, and compounded by growing peasant resentment, led to a crisis situation by 1953.

THE "NEW COURSE." Imre Nagy, who had been minister of the interior and of agriculture in the early postwar coalition government, replaced Rákosi as premier on Soviet demand on 4 July, 1953, just 4 months after Stalin's death. Nagy, whose rise—and fall—closely paralleled that of Georgi Malenkov in the USSR, quickly embarked on the implementation of the so-called "new course," which, in effect, was the repudiation of most of the policies pursued by Rákosi. Nagy reversed the previous economic policy by emphasizing consumer-goods production as against the previously stressed heavy industry; the forced collective farms were dissolved and thousands of political prisoners were released.

Utilizing the brief power vacuum which existed in the USSR between Malenkov's fall, Feb. 1955, and Khrushchev's denunciation of Stalin, Feb. 1956, Rákosi began a counteroffensive against Nagy. The latter's "new course" policy was condemned as "right-wing deviationism"; in Apr. 1955 Nagy was removed as premier and, Nov., expelled from the Party. Most of the laws promoting collectivization were restored.

Following Khrushchev's denunciation of Stalin and his methods at the 20th Congress of the Soviet Communist Party, Feb. 1956, Hungarian intellectuals—many of them Communists—called for a similar investigation into Rákosi's own misdeeds and demanded the rehabilitation of victims sentenced on fabricated charges. Rákosi's attempt to arrest Nagy and some 400 intellectuals and thus to consolidate his position was blocked by the USSR; he was replaced as 1st secretary, July 18, by one of his most hated collaborators, Ernö Gerö.

1956–68

REVOLT OF 1956. Although Gerö tried to contain the growing cultural and political ferment which followed Rákosi's ouster, a peaceful mass demonstration, staged in support of Poland's confrontation with the USSR, erupted into a massive popular uprising, 23 Oct., 1956. The involvement in the street fighting of Soviet forces, whom Gerö had called upon to restore order, further exacerbated the antagonism between rebellious students and workers on the one hand and the pro-regime secret police on the other. Fighting did not abate until after Nagy had returned to the government and Soviet forces had withdrawn from Budapest, both demanded by the rebels. The Communist Party had disintegrated in the process and Gerö, who had been replaced by János Kádár, fled to the USSR.

Pressed by a progressively radicalized public opinion, Nagy formed a new coalition government, including Kádár, and withdrew from the Warsaw Pact, declared Hungary's neutrality, and appealed to the UN for help and a guarantee of independence. In the meantime, international tension rose as a result of a split between the U.S. and her European allies over the Suez crisis.

Meanwhile Kádár, who had secretly quit Nagy's cabinet to form a countergovernment, asked the USSR for armed support. On 4 Nov., 1956, the Soviet Union launched a 2nd, more massive military attack on Hungary. A short-lived armed resistance and the general strike which followed brought great economic hardship; nearly 200,000 refugees fled the country, leaving it faced with a severe skilled man-power shortage.

Nagy and some of his aides, who had been abducted by Soviet secret police despite Kádár's promise of safe conduct, were interned in Rumania and, after secret trial, executed in June 1958.

KÁDÁR REGIME. After the uprising, Hungary continued under the regime established by Kádár, whose prime goal for several years was to restore the country's economic and social life (aided by the infusion of massive Soviet-bloc financial help), and to bring about a reconciliation between his regime and the population, especially the intellectuals. In these tasks he was aided by the presence of the Soviet troops stationed in Hungary since World War II. Kádár also reorganized the Communist Party (renamed the Hungarian Socialist Workers' Party after Nov. 1956) along new lines: he purged the party of many diehard Stalinists (among them Rákosi and Gerö), whom he had accused of harsh practices, and made them quasi-responsible for the uprising. Kádár carried out severe reprisals against thousands of alleged participants in the revolt, many of whom were executed and imprisoned despite his promises to the contrary. Compulsory collectivization, which had been stopped in 1956, was resumed again in 1958–59.

By 1962, however, a general shift in party policy ("he who is not against us is with us"), a general amnesty (including pardon for political prisoners), the curbing of the secret police, and the encouragement of a liberalized cultural and economic life combined to help overcome the post-1956 antagonism of the population toward Kádár and his regime. In 1964, an accord giving more religious liberty to both the Catholic laity and the clergy was concluded between the regime and the Vatican.

In 1965, Kádár gave up his post as premier, though he retained the more important 1st secretaryship; he was succeeded by Gyula Kállai and then by Jenö Fock.

Broad economic reforms, introduced as the "New Economic Model," 1 Jan., 1968, provided for far-reaching decentralization of the hitherto bureaucratically planned economy by upgrading the role of management and introducing the profit motive in a limited way.

Hungary's foreign policy after 1956 remained closely aligned to that of the rest of the Soviet bloc, but diplomatic and trade relations with Yugoslavia and western countries—including the U.S.—steadily improved. As a member of the Warsaw Pact, Hungary reluctantly provided token forces for the Soviet-led occupation of Czechoslovakia, Aug. 1968.

Poland

1945-56

VICTORY OF THE LUBLIN GOVERNMENT. In accordance with an agreement reached at Yalta, Feb. 1945, the western powers awaited the creation of a coalition government based on the 2 governments in exile: 1 in London and the other, dominated by Communists, in Lublin. The USSR withheld recognition from the London government until July, when Stanislaw Mikolajczyk, leader of the main opposition Peasant Party, was included in the Lublin government. Although the Lublin government was nominally led by a Polish Communist, Władislaw Gomulka, as secretary general of the Communist Party, 1943–48, the real power lay with the Russian, Boleslaw Bierut, as head of state, 1944–47. Tension within the coalition came to a head in Jan. 1947, when, on Communist insistence, a single electoral list was proposed for the upcoming elections. Postponed by the Communists for tactical reasons for nearly 2 years, the elections and the preceding campaign were held under the most unfavorable conditions for the non-Communist parties, which had been required to give advance support to the Communists in return for being allowed to participate. Mikolajczyk refused the single list and was forced to flee the country in Oct. the same year. Despite terror tactics, the government coalition gained only 394 seats out of a total of 444. In Dec. next year, the Socialist Party was forced to fuse officially with the Communists (renamed thereafter the Polish United Workers Party): Josef Cyrankiewicz, the pro-Communist leader of the Socialist Party, was given the post of prime minister, 1947–52, in the new government.

THE NEW POLAND. Before the end of the war, Poland had lost to the USSR some of her eastern provinces (c. 70,000 sq. mi.) in return for former German (Prussian) territories (c. 39,000 sq. mi.) lying east of the rivers Oder (Odra) and Neisse (Nysa), including the former Free City of Danzig. A new border settlement, reached at the Potsdam Conference, Aug. 1945, also authorized Poland to expel some 8 m. Germans from the acquired areas. Although the USSR recognized as permanent Poland's new western frontier, the Potsdam agreement merely placed the newly acquired territories under Polish administration pending a German peace treaty.

STALINIST PERIOD. In the late 1940's and early 1950's, the Communist-dominated government carried out a land reform and nationalized all large enterprises. No longer hampered by opposition, the government liquidated the last elements of the wartime "underground." The Catholic Church, with a following among 95% of the population, was subjected to persecution and its leader, Stefan Cardinal Wyszynski, the primate of Poland, was arrested just after Stalin's death (26 Sept., 1953), despite the 1950 accord with the government guaranteeing freedom of religion. As a result of rapid but irrational industrialization, living standards suffered. A new constitution adopted in 1952 made Poland into a "People's Republic." In 1949, Poland joined COMECON. In Nov. of the same year Soviet (though Polish-born) Marshal Konstantin Rokossovsky was made minister of defense and commander in chief of the Polish army.

PURGE OF GOMULKA. A Communist who had opposed the indiscriminate copying of Soviet economic planning, as well as the denunciation of Tito's defiance of Stalin as necessarily bad, Gomulka found himself at odds with the pro-Moscow faction of the Polish Communist Party. Denounced on charges of having committed a "nationalist deviation," Gomulka was stripped of his posts: in Sept. 1948 as general secretary, and in Jan. 1949 as vice-premier. Finally, July 1951, he was imprisoned.

POST-STALIN REACTION. Reflecting the unsettled power struggle in the Kremlin that followed Stalin's death in 1953, the political situation in Poland remained confused. Unlike Hungary, Poland did not embark upon the implementation of a "new course." Only in Mar. 1954 did Bierut give up his position as premier (while retaining the more important post of leader of the Party). Though freed from prison in Dec. of the same year, Gomulka's release was not made public until Apr. 1956, the year of crisis. Uncertainty was added to the already confused situation created by the denunciation of Stalin's personality cult by Khrushchev, Feb. 1956, when Bierut died suddenly, 14 Mar. He was succeeded by Edward Ochab as party 1st secretary (till Oct. 1956).

1956–68

RETURN OF GOMULKA. An already volatile situation, created by growing criticism of the Stalinist era by numerous political clubs throughout Poland, was further exacerbated, June 1956, when riots broke out in Poznán and had to be put down by the army. First demonstrating against low living standards and then for more freedom, Poznán students and workers were initially denounced by the government as having been incited by foreign influences. As discontent became increasingly vocal and widespread, the government reconsidered its position, which in turn resulted in open division among the leadership. The situation was resolved, without bloodshed, when, after Stalinists had been ousted from the Politburo, Gomulka accepted the post of Communist Party 1st secretary.

SOVIET INTERVENTION. In the meantime, the Soviet leadership, alarmed by the growing anti-Soviet sentiment throughout the country, suddenly appeared in Warsaw to forestall Poland's defection, and the city, surrounded by Soviet contingents which had been stationed in the country since World War II, became tense. Receiving promises that Poland would remain within the bloc, the Soviet leaders—Khrushchev, Mikoyan, Kaganovich, and Molotov—departed. Following elections to the Politburo, 19 Oct., Rokossovsky was ousted and had to leave Poland.

NEW POLICY FOR POLAND. The main features of the new policy that was implemented in Poland after Oct. 1956 included (1) the disappearance of police terror, (2) relative freedom of cultural and creative activity, (3) a *modus vivendi* between church and state, and (4) a guarantee of private ownership in agriculture. In foreign policy, too, Poland was given freer rein in dealing with the West, including the U.S. At the same time she retained close relations with the USSR.

GOMULKA REGIME. During the late 1950's and 1960's Gomulka came under increasing attacks from both liberals and diehard neo-Stalinists, between whom he continued to attempt to strike a middle course. Although he had received important support from the Catholic Church at the critical moment in Oct. 1956, relations with the church during the 1966 millenary celebrations of Poland as a Christian nation became strained. The most liberal Communist state of Eastern Europe in the early 1960's, Poland after 1963 appeared to have lost much of the freedom she had gained in Oct. 1956. During early 1968, after weeks of student rioting in major Polish cities, the Polish government embarked upon an increasingly anti-Zionist campaign; thousands of persons of Jewish origin were purged from their positions. As Czechoslovakia in early 1968 embarked upon a bold liberalization program, Poland became alarmed. A member of the Warsaw Pact, Poland participated in the Soviet-led invasion of Czechoslovakia on 20–21 Aug., 1968. Despite renewed attacks from younger nationalist-minded Communists demanding more freedom of action from the USSR, Gomulka's position, backed by the Soviet Union, was confirmed at the Communist Party's 5th Congress, Nov. 1968.

Rumania

1944–68

POSTWAR RUMANIA. To avoid an anticipated Soviet occupation of his country, Rumania's King Michael, 23 Aug., 1944, overthrew the Fascist Antonescu government in a *coup d'état* and, 2 days later, declared war on Germany and opened the country to the Red Army. The king's move in switching sides before liberation by the Soviet Union proved to be the decisive factor in Rumania's reacquisition of all of Transylvania from Hungary. The Paris Peace Treaty of 1947 restored prewar Rumania except for northern Bukovina and Bessarabia, which were transferred to the USSR, and south Dobruja, which was retained by Bulgaria. The treaty also required Rumania to pay the USSR large sums in war reparations.

COMMUNIST TAKEOVER OF 1948. Following a brief rule by a coalition government named by King Michael, the Communist Party, backed by the Red Army, pressured him into the appointment, 6 Mar., 1945, of a Communist-dominated cabinet, 1945–52, under the pro-Communist Petru Groza. Despite repeated western protests at Yalta and Potsdam against the composition and methods of the Groza cabinet, the Communist Party had liquidated most opposition by Mar. 1948. After a sham election, 19 Nov., 1946, to confirm the Groza cabinet, the Communists, under the pro-Moscow leadership of Ana Pauker, staged in early 1947 a wave of mass arrests and forced the abdication of Michael, 30 Dec. Following the proclamation of a republic, the already purged Socialist Party was absorbed by the numerically much smaller Communist Party, Feb. 1948. A "People's Republican" constitution was adopted by the National Assembly, Apr. 1948, which had been elected in the absence of opposition, 28 Mar. This constitution was replaced by one more closely in line with the constitution of the USSR of 1936; adopted in Sept. 1952, it gave considerable regional autonomy to the large Hungarian minority in Transylvania.

GHEORGHIU-DEJ REGIME. Although already head of the small Communist Party in 1945, Gheorghiu-Dej's power became more real with the liquidation of a number of pro-Moscow party leaders in 1952, 1 year before the Soviet leadership launched its "new course" following Stalin's death. The ouster of Foreign Minister Ana Pauker (a Jew) and Justice Minister Vasile Luca (a Hungarian) was claimed by Gheorghiu-Dej during the 1st de-Stalinization period in 1956 as having been made in anticipation of that policy 4 years before it was launched. With the exception of a show of discontent among the Transylvanian Magyars, the Hungarian uprising of 1956 was weathered by the Rumanian leadership without any significant upheaval. During the uprising, Rumania fully supported the Soviet position of intervention. In recognition of Rumanian loyalty the USSR withdrew the Soviet garrisons in 1958. In 1961, the year Khrushchev launched his second de-Stalinization drive, Gheorghiu-Dej became president of the newly created state council and until his death, Mar. 1965, he ruled Rumania unchallenged. During his regime, but especially after the withdrawal of Soviet forces in 1958, Rumania showed signs of independence both in economic and foreign affairs while maintaining close affinity with the USSR in matters of ideology.

INCREASE IN INDEPENDENCE FROM THE USSR. Long considered 1 of the most docile of the Soviet satellites, Rumania in the 1960's began to oppose the USSR on a variety of issues involving the Soviet bloc and also relations with Communist China. Among these were her role within COMECON, the Warsaw Pact, cultural and economic ties with the West, and her apparently neutral stance in the deteriorating Sino-Soviet ideological dispute.

Beginning in 1963, and increasingly so thereafter, Rumania came to regard the inferior role assigned to her by the Soviet Union within COMECON as inhibiting her desire to industrialize. Envisaged by COMECON as a producer of raw materials and a manufacturer of oil-drilling and refinery equipment, Rumania refused to co-operate and instead looked to the West for capital to develop her heavy industry based on the untapped resources of Transylvania. Gaining much-needed concessions, Rumania signed trade agreements with the U.S., Britain, and West Germany; in 1967, she established diplomatic relations with the latter, the only East European country beside the USSR and Yugoslavia to do so. Championing the cause of national sovereignty, she refused to participate in the Sino-Soviet dispute and, instead, attempted to assume the role of umpire; China, in return, openly supported Rumania's aspirations. In foreign policy matters, Rumania twice defected from the common Soviet-bloc stand: during the 1967 Arab-Israeli war, she refused to condemn Israel and withheld support from Soviet-sponsored resolutions in the UN debate on the war: in 1968 she supported unconditionally the Czechoslovak liberalization drive and, when asked to participate in the invasion of that country, Aug. 1968, refused.

Rumania remained far behind such countries as Czechoslovakia, Hungary, and Poland in relaxing the Communist Party's hold on the population until 1965, when the death of Gheorghiu-Dej catapulted into prominence Nikolae Ceauşescu. A protegé of Gheorghiu-Dej, Ceauşescu began a partial rehabilitation of some of the purged leaders and even denounced his mentor for Stalinist practices. During the 2nd half of the 1960's, he abolished some of the most Stalinist features of his government, curbed the secret police, launched a cautious program of de-Russification of Rumanian cultural life, and called for the abolition of all military blocs, including the Warsaw Pact. Maintaining a strict observance of orthodox Marxist principles with regard to building Communism—a new constitution proclaiming a "Socialist Republic" was adopted in 1965—Rumania during the late 1960's appeared to be on the way to independence.

Yugoslavia

1945–68

VICTORY OF THE PARTISANS. At the conclusion of World War II Yugoslavia along with Greece and Albania were the only countries of Eastern Europe that were under the control of their own resistance movements dominated by Communists. Yugoslavia's postwar political development was largely determined by the fact that both the Soviet Union and the western allies granted recognition and support to the apparently more popular leftist partisan movement led by Josip Brož Tito as against the rightist Chetniks under Draža Mihajlović (1893?–1946).

ACCESSION OF TITO. Having made himself premier, Mar. 1945, of a government in which there was token representation of the rightist government in exile, Tito took control of the country, Jan. 1946, without Soviet assistance. In 1946 a constitution drafted on the 1936 Soviet model declared Yugoslavia a Federal Republic composed of 6 republics with nominal autonomy; actual power was vested in the Communist Party controlled by Tito.

WAR GAINS. The peace treaty of 1947 gave Yugoslavia the eastern part of Venezia Giulia, though Trieste, the area's most coveted portion, was made into a free territory. A subsequent agreement, 1954, divided the port city between Yugoslavia and Italy.

POSTWAR RECONSTRUCTION. After the war, Tito proceeded to implement Communist policies. A vigorous drive was undertaken toward socialization and industrialization under the dictatorship of the proletariat. With extensive aid from the western allies, and as a founding member of the UN in 1945, Yugoslavia received substantial financial aid for postwar reconstruction of her war-torn economy. Internally, the government eliminated opposition; the Roman Catholic Church was curbed by the imprisonment of Archbishop Stepinac of Zagreb,

1946 (released in 1951), and the execution of Mihajlović, 1946.

BREAK WITH THE USSR. The allegiance of Yugoslavia to the USSR was broken in 1948, when Tito's refusal to accept the unconditional supremacy of Stalin and the Soviet Union precipitated his country's expulsion from the Cominform. The rift with the Soviet Union, which with minor variations lasted throughout the post-Stalin era as well, freed Tito to build "national" Communism and enabled him to establish closer ties with the West and receive financial and political assistance when needed.

POST-STALIN PERIOD. Shortly after Stalin's death, May 1953, the Soviet Union resumed diplomatic relations with Yugoslavia. Especially after his assumption of full power in 1954, Khrushchev made serious efforts to heal the ideological breach created by his predecessor. Despite the drastic change in Soviet orientation in Feb. 1956, when Stalinist policies and methods—including those affecting Yugoslavia—were repudiated, Tito did not return to the Soviet-led bloc of nations as a full member. Although Yugoslav-Soviet relations deteriorated after the suppression of the 1956 Hungarian Revolution, they never again hit the low point of the Stalinist era. During the late 1950's and in the 1960's, Yugoslavia formed with such countries as the United Arab Republic and India the so-called nonaligned bloc, while relations with Czechoslovakia, Hungary, and especially Rumania were continuously improving.

Supporting the Soviet concept of peaceful coexistence between states with different systems, Yugoslavia in the 1960's sided with the Soviet Union in the Sino-Soviet dispute. In a show of token support of the USSR, Milovan Djilas, one of the severest critics of Soviet Communism, was rearrested in 1962. In 1964 Yugoslavia, in another token gesture of good relations, became an affiliate member of COMECON.

PURGE OF THE SECRET POLICE. The disclosure in 1966 of an extensive eavesdropping system by the secret police, headed by Alexander Ranković, led to a broad reorganization of the Communist Party and to a series of political purges of members closely connected with the police. Ranković, who had been considered Tito's heir apparent, was removed from his post in 1966; the same year Djilas was released from jail as a gesture to appease the party's liberal faction.

DENUNCIATION OF THE INVASION OF CZECHOSLOVAKIA. The Soviet-led invasion of Czechoslovakia, 20–21 Aug., 1968, seriously strained Yugoslavia's relations not only with the Soviet Union but with the other participants in the invasion as well. Shortly before it began, Tito had personally given his support to Alexander Dubček and the Czech liberalization policies during a visit to Prague, 9–11 Aug. Following the enunciation of the so-called "Brezhnev doctrine," Sept. 1968, which attempted to justify the right of the Soviet Union to invade any member of the "Socialist Commonwealth" in defense of socialism, Tito declared his determination to fight with force any unsolicited assistance from any source. As a Warsaw Pact member but not party to the invasion, Rumania drew closer to Yugoslavia by also denouncing as unjustified the invasion of Czechoslovakia.

THE SOVIET UNION

1945–50

THE USSR AFTER WORLD WAR II. The conclusion of the European war, 7 May, 1945, seemingly signaled the emergence of a new era in the lives of the Soviet people. Capped by Stalin's toast to the Russian people at a meeting of the senior Soviet military, 24 May, this triumph made the Japanese surrender of 2 Sept. an anticlimactic event. The deprivations of the anti-Nazi war, which left 25 m. homeless and some 20 m. civilian and military dead in its wake, were balanced by national pride in the USSR's world-power status and the expectancy that a better life was in the offing. The Communist Party, through expansion of its total membership from some 3,900,000 to 5,700,000 in the war years, had taken a step in the direction of becoming more and more representative. The Patriarchate of the Russian Orthodox Church had been restored, Sept. 1943, after 18 years in official limbo. Other signs of normalcy were the elections to the Supreme Soviet (legislature), 10 Mar., 1946, the 1st held since 1937. In the same month, the Council of People's Commissars was renamed, more universally, the Council of Ministers, with Joseph Stalin appointed its chairman (prime minister) and Vyacheslav M. Molotov, the foreign minister, his deputy.

RESTORATION OF AUTHORITARIAN RULE. Events, however, soon muted these widespread expectations among the populace. The 4th 5-Year Plan, launched in Mar. 1946, called for complete industrial recovery from the effects of the war and, in some capital sectors, for a surpassing of the 1941 economic developmental levels, all to the detriment of the long-neglected consumer sector. Agricultural recovery was set back by the drought of 1946, which resulted in continued grain rationing throughout 1947 and led to food riots in Kharkov over the winter of 1946–47. Further adverse indicators were the "anticosmopolitan" chauvinistic pronouncements, Sept. 1946, of Stalin's literary and cultural affairs chief, Central Committee Secretary Andrei A. Zhdanov (1896–1948). The commander in chief of the Soviet armed forces and military hero, Marshal Georgi Zhukov, was dismissed, Nov. 1946, and relegated to a minor post. The draconian labor law of 1940, freezing all workers in their positions and raising the workweek from 40 to 48 hours, remained in force. In agriculture, the Council on Kolkhoz Affairs, established 8 Oct., 1946, initiated measures to reduce the acreage of private peasant plots, which had swollen beyond control during the war, and within a year some 14 m. privately tilled acres had been brought back into the state sector. Taxes on farmers' non-Kolkhoz earnings rose to confiscatory levels through increases instituted in 1948, 1950, and 1951. Religious convictions soon became incompatible with advancement through the Komsomol (Party Youth Organization) and the

Party. Grandiose power and irrigation projects were projected in the Volga and Dnieper regions, spearheading Stalin's "nature transformation" program.

REJECTION OF WESTERN INFLUENCES. In the later 1940's conformity to conservative, xenophobic dictates became the rule. Dimitri Shostakovich (b. 1906) and other prominent Soviet musicians were called to heel for cosmopolitanism in their music and forced to recant, Feb. 1948. At an academic assembly on biological science, Aug.–Sept. 1948, Trofim D. Lysenko's (b. 1898) genetic theories (the outdated Michurin school), sponsored by Stalin, as applied to agrobiology, triumphed in a clash with Soviet "Mendelists"; Mendel's theses did not conform to the Stalinist manipulative concept of nature. Nikolai A. Voznesensky (1903–50), chairman of the State Planning Commission, went into sudden eclipse for his allegedly voluntarist approach to economics and was later shot, Sept. 1950; his advocacy of rational planning had failed to coincide with Stalin's turn to a deterministic emphasis on the dominant substructure (productive forces) in society. 1950 was also marked by the reinstatement, Jan., of the death penalty (abolished in 1947) for broadly interpreted subversive activities.

1950–53

AGRICULTURAL POLICY. A decree of the Council of Ministers on agriculture, 7 June, 1950, heralded a drive, sponsored by Nikita S. Khrushchev (b. 1894), to amalgamate Kolkhoz holdings; this was by 1953 to reduce the number of 1950 Kolkhoz units from 252,000 to 92,000 with a rise in average acreage from 2,800 to 20,000. The 5th 5-Year Plan, approved in 1952, called for completion of the Dnieper and Volga projects by the mid-1950's.

STALIN'S "LAST TESTAMENT." The long-range portents of the above became clearer with the publication of Stalin's "last testament" just prior to the 19th Party Congress of 5–14 Oct., 1952. His "Economic Problems of Socialism in the USSR" in essence called for a concerted drive to complete the socialist phase and defend the USSR as socialism's motherland from a hostile capitalist world—i.e., to perfect the garrison state on its road to communism.

19TH PARTY CONGRESS. The 19th Congress formalized Stalin's moves to assure the implementation of his directives for the future. The older guard, original Bolsheviks and the careerists of the 1930's alike, such as Molotov and Beria, had been stripped of their state posts and limited to Politburo posts close to Stalin's elbow. The Congress created a new, expanded Party Politburo, renamed Presidium, in which the older lieutenants were outnumbered by more pliable newcomers. Organizational and ideological educational reforms portended the further indoctrination of holders of important Party and state posts in the reasserted orthodox tenets of Stalin. The Doctors' Plot accusations of 13 Jan., 1952, implicating 10 Jewish Kremlin physicians in the deaths of Zhdanov, Aug. 1948, and high military figures, seemingly augured a thoroughgoing repurging of the Party and state structures. Then, on 5 Mar., 1953, Stalin died at 74.

1953–57

POST-STALIN RELAXATION. Soon after announcing Stalin's death, the new Party Presidium's reduced membership (representing again only the older leaders) implemented relaxation measures: in quick succession, a wide political amnesty, 29 Mar.; a drop in basic food prices, amounting to 50% for some vegetables, 1 Apr.; and a denunciation of the Doctors' Plot accusations, 4 Apr., ensued. With lightning speed Beria, reappointed head of the reconstituted Ministry of Internal Affairs (secret police), was purged by a Central Committee announcement of 10 July as an "enemy of the [Communist] Party and the Soviet people," seemingly because he had made a move for sole power at a hypersensitive time. Georgi M. Malenkov (b. 1902), Stalin's apparent chosen successor, had abandoned his dual Party-state leadership status in mid-Mar., retaining only the premiership. As 1953 progressed, Khrushchev, the senior Party secretary and main counterweight to Malenkov's political preeminence, gradually became his major rival.

MALENKOV-KHRUSHCHEV RIVALRY. Malenkov had moved to secure his position by (1) presiding, as prime minister, over a centralized Council of All-Union "superministries" in Moscow, which had been reduced from 51 to 25 ministries at Stalin's death; (2) inaugurating, 8 Aug., 1953, a "new course" aimed at increased development of consumer industries, while holding capital industrial development constant; (3) increasing investment in agriculture.

Khrushchev eventually undermined these bids through 1953 and 1954. At the 3–7 Sept., 1953, Central Committee Plenum, which officially appointed him 1st party secretary, he sketched a devastating picture of Soviet agriculture, revealing that in the areas of grain and livestock production the USSR was lagging behind pre-1917 levels. This directly refuted Malenkov's situation report at the 19th Congress. Organizationally, he undercut Malenkov by increasing the presence of the Party's local secretaries at the rural grass roots, in violation of the 19th Congress rules. He further counterattacked, 24 Feb., 1954, by unveiling a grandiose Stalinlike "Virgin Lands" project, which called for the expansion of (mainly grain) cultivated areas by 31 m. acres into marginal, hitherto unutilized sections in the eastern and southern USSR. Malenkov had advocated more intensive rational use of the land under cultivation. High yields in 1954 seemingly bore out Khrushchev's optimistic long-range agricultural prognostications.

FALL OF MALENKOV. On 21 Dec., 1954, *Pravda* and *Izvestia* (the Party and state dailies, respectively) carried contradictory editorials on the priorities to be assigned to heavy and consumer industry, reflecting personal policy differences in the leadership. Soon Khrushchev had gained support from the heavy industrial and military leaderships; at the 8 Feb. Supreme Soviet session, Malenkov resigned as premier and was succeeded by Nikolai A. Bulganin (b. 1895), a member of the Presidium; Marshal Zhukov, who replaced him as defense minister, headed the military elements in the coalition which brought Malenkov down.

Over the years 1955–57 there occurred a series of policy initiatives and modifications, reflecting struggles in the leadership, which reached a *dénouement* in the Anti-Party Group affair of mid-June, 1957, when Khrushchev, through skillful politicking, assembled a coalition to beat back his opposition.

20TH PARTY CONGRESS. The most dramatic moment in this sequence of events was the Secret Speech delivered by Khrushchev at the 20th Party congress, 14–25 Feb., 1956, during the final 2 days. In it he made a violent break with the Stalinist past, calling attention particularly to the excesses of the mass purges of the 1930's. The speech precluded any future attempts at internecine struggle at the leadership level, as well as indiscriminate use of mass terror. The Congress also created a Central Committee Bureau for the RSFSR, to become a preserve for Khrushchev appointees, and co-opted Leonid I. Brezhnev (b. 1906) and Zhukov (in candidate status) to the Presidium and the former to the Secretariat as well. On 5 June, Molotov was succeeded as foreign minister by Dimitri N. Shepilov (b. 1905), a Party secretary since July 1955.

GROWTH OF KHRUSHCHEV'S POWER. Early 1957 marked the announcement of sweeping economic organizational reforms: the Supreme Soviet's resolution of 10 May abolished 140 All-Union, Union-Republic, and Republic industrial ministries and established 105 Regional Economic Councils (*sovnarkhozy*), operating on regional economic principles. This move, coupled with Khrushchev's appeal to the consumer instincts of the populace and his liberalization of Soviet-bloc and East-West relations, crystallized against him a variegated Presidium majority, led by Molotov, Malenkov, and Lazar M. Kaganovich, which eventually mustered 7 of the 11 votes in that body. Khrushchev thwarted their move by throwing the conflict into the wider Central Committee arena for discussion; in this countercoup, he was abetted by the military faction. Zhukov rose to full membership in the Presidium and Aleksei N. Kosygin (b. 1904) to candidate status in the wake of the expulsion of the opposition's leadership from their high posts. Other key events during 1957 were the launching of Sputnik I, and the sudden eclipse of Zhukov, 31 Oct.

1958-64

THE KHRUSHCHEV ERA. Khrushchev became premier in late Jan. 1958, succeeding Bulganin, who was later identified as an "anti-Partyite." Until his own departure from politics in Oct. 1964, he followed a policy of constant reform in all areas of national life, designed to keep his opposition in the leadership off balance and to preserve his own position at the summit of power. Economic efficiency and Party involvement in economics were emphasized. The abolition of the Machine Tractor Stations (MTS's), Feb. 1958, made the Party more responsible for agricultural production; from May 1958 on, with indifferent success, greater investments were diverted into the chemical fertilizer industry. A main objective of the reform of Nov. 1962, the splitting of both Party and state into separate industrial and agricultural hierarchies, was to solve the chronic ills of Soviet agriculture. However, the highly touted Virgin Lands program proved undependable, with the harvests of 1955 and 1957 plummeting below half of those of 1954. The USSR was forced to import grain in the summer of 1963.

The *sovnarkhoz* decentralization move of 1957 was countered by a reassertion of economic centralization in Mar. 1963 through creation of a new superplanning agency, the Supreme Council of National Economy, which in part redressed the losses of the heavy-industry interests and authoritarian centralizers who had earlier been undercut.

RESISTANCE TO KHRUSHCHEV'S POLICIES. Within the Party itself, Khrushchev failed to achieve 2 primary goals after 1957—the total discrediting of the anti-Partyites and identifying himself as the great "de-Stalinizer" of Soviet life. The Extraordinary 21st Congress of Jan.–Feb. 1959, intended to read the 1957 opposition out of the Party, resulted in

desultory denunciations and ambiguous criticisms. Only in Apr. 1964 was it announced that "Molotov and others" had been expelled from the Party. Likewise, a renewal in Oct. 1962 of the anti-Stalin campaign, sparked by a Khrushchev-approved poem, *Stalin's Heirs,* by Evgeni Evtushenko (b. 1933), was climaxed by Khrushchev's forced turnabout in midstream and his denunciation of liberal intellectuals and artists, 8 Mar., 1964. The Party-state reform of 1962, moreover, served to alienate the politically oriented Party bureaucrats at lower levels by its emphasis on economic production.

ANTAGONISM OF THE MILITARY. Khrushchev progressively disenchanted another important group, the conservative military, by his calls both early in 1960 and again in 1964 for a reduction in the size of the standing army. As with other reforms, he was forced to backtrack on these demands as cyclical tensions in international relations, such as Berlin (1958 and 1961), the U-2 and Paris Summit crises (1960), and Cuban crisis (1962), seemingly justified the "military preparedness" line of the traditional military.

FALL OF KHRUSHCHEV. Moves, only partly achieved, to enlist popular support by raising the Soviet system's status as a democratic and economic world power ultimately left the citizenry indifferent. These started with Khrushchev's promises at the 20th Congress on overtaking the U.S. by 1970 and ended with his famous "goulash communism" statement in Hungary, Apr. 1964. At the 22nd Congress, Oct. 1961, Stalin's class-struggle concept (dictatorship of the proletariat) was replaced with that of "the state of the whole people." There was increased public participation in government, e.g., the legal reinstatement, 1961, of the Comrades' Courts (these had atrophied in the 1930's), which provided for trial by 1 judge and 2 lay assessors. Official support was given to voluntary "vigilante" groups (*druzhiniki*) intended to preserve public order. These innovations implicitly called for the withering away of the state on the road to Communism. In Jan. 1960 a Commission for Constitutional Reform was instructed to draw up a new constitution to replace that of 1936 with its discredited Stalinist associations.

Khrushchev's fall was directly triggered by his summoning, Sept. 1964, of a mixed Party-state consultative assembly, with many outside "experts," to discuss increased investment allocations to the consumer sector. An alliance of alienated key groups voted him out of his leading Party and state positions, 14 Oct., 1964.

1964-68

ACCESSION OF BREZHNEV AND KOSYGIN. Brezhnev, as new Party first secretary, and Kosygin, as premier, led the institution of a wave of measures aimed at restoring stability in place of the administrative chaos created by Khrushchev's organizational reforms. In Dec. 1964, the functional division of the Party was abolished. A decree of Sept. 1965 completely dismantled the *sovnarkhoz* structure, which in Nov. 1962 had been reduced to some 40 territorial councils. Throughout 1964-65 the slogan of "the state of all the people" and the goals set by the 22nd Congress' program became progressively muted. Members of the Khrushchev "clique," such as Aleksei Adzhubei (b. 1924), his son-in-law and editor of *Izvestia,* and Leonid F. Ilichev (b. 1906), Party secretary, were demoted and replaced soon after Khrushchev's fall. A reassertion of the demand for ideological conformity underlay the Sinyavsky-Daniel trial of Feb. 1965, the 2 writers being sentenced to terms in corrective labor camps.

23RD PARTY CONGRESS. These calls for political and ideological uniformity were re-echoed by the Party at the 23rd Party Congress, 29 Mar.–8 Apr., 1966, which signaled the major themes of the post-Khrushchev style of leadership. Frequent references underlined the Party-state consensus on continued, but less erratic and inconsistent, change. The renewal of membership in the Central Committee touched only 20% of its 1961 members—a low turnover for the post-Stalin period (cf. 50% in 1961). Speeches emphasized a businesslike approach in contrast to Khrushchev's proposals for dramatic 1-shot panaceas. On the perennial economic allocations problem, continued stress was laid on heavy industry's investment priority, while consumer industries, though slated to grow, were to do so more gradually. Kosygin emphasized more the application of rational methods to stimulate industrial growth than increased investments to expand production. Notably missing were denunciations of the Stalinist era's excesses, a sign of tacit consent to shelve the anti-Stalin campaign. Although Khrushchev was not mentioned by name, it was unmistakably he at whose doorstep blame was laid for the shortcomings of the recent past. In failing to be re-elected to the new Central Committee, he lost his last important Party post.

ECONOMIC POLICIES. That the problems of the early 1960's had not vanished with the appearance of a new leadership was soon evident. Though the draft of the 5-Year Plan for 1966-70 had been approved by the Party in Mar. 1966, Kosygin announced, Sept., a delay in its implementation, and the Supreme Soviet ratified, Dec., only a truncated version for 1967.

The industrial reform announced in Jan. 1966, emphasizing greater profitability, material incentive, and autonomy for plant managers, had by Oct. 1967 been extended to some 5,500 industrial enterprises, or $\frac{1}{3}$ of the total. Industrial growth, 1960–67, by official admission had slowed to a rate of 6%, as against 8.2% in 1956–60. In Soviet industry, the output of the average worker remained at only $\frac{1}{3}$ of his U.S. counterpart. The minimum monthly wage was fixed by the Sept. 1967 Party Plenum for most white- and blue-collar workers at 60 rubles (U.S. $66), with the national nonagricultural average 100 rubles ($110). In the same month the legislature approved a higher growth rate for consumer industries than for heavy industry (8.6% vs. 7.9%) for 1968–69. In Jan. 1968, the country went on a 5-day, 41-hour week.

AGRICULTURAL POLICIES. In agriculture, efforts were made to draw the farmers into the productive process via the introduction of a minimum wage and pension plans. The relative share of state farms (*sovkhozy*—the preferred, more "advanced" socialist farms) in production had dramatically increased from 1940 to 1966 (e.g., from 3 to 42% of eggs, 10 to 54% of grain, 16 to 51% of vegetables produced) and their acreage climbed from 13% to 25% of total cultivated area between 1953 and 1958. However, private peasant plots, comprising only 3% of the cultivated land, contributed 13% of all marketed and 33% of total produce output.

INTELLECTUAL DISSENT. In Jan. 1968 the trial of 4 writers on charges of anti-Soviet activities sparked a new wave of intellectual dissent within the Soviet Union. Petitions and letters of protest against the trial led Communist Party General Secretary Brezhnev to call for "iron discipline" within the Party. Soon after Brezhnev's 29 Mar. warning, a number of Soviet scholars and writers were expelled from the Party.

DOCTRINE OF THE "COMMUNIST COMMONWEALTH." In an attempt to justify the Aug. 1968 invasion of Czechoslovakia, a new doctrine of intervention was advanced in *Pravda,* 26 Sept., 1968. It asserted that the sovereignty of individual countries in the world socialist community must be subordinated to the common welfare of that community, and that the community had the right to intervene when, in a fraternal socialist country, socialism was threatened.

Revolution in East Asia

THE PEOPLE'S REPUBLIC OF CHINA (MAINLAND)

1945–49

CHINA AFTER WORLD WAR II. After Japan was defeated in 1945, the civil war in China which had been temporarily and partially suspended broke out again, despite U.S. efforts to mediate. Mismanagement and corruption resulted in widespread popular discontent with the Nationalist regime and allowed the Communists to extend their influence in the country. By the end of 1948 they controlled Manchuria and were poised for the conquest of the rest of the mainland.

COMMUNIST MILITARY VICTORY. In Jan. 1949 Peking, which under the Communists again became the capital of China, was surrendered. During the next 10 months Communist armies moved south and southwest, taking the cities of Hankow, Wuchang, Shanghai, Canton, and Chungking. Finally, the Nationalist government was forced to flee to Taiwan, 7 Dec.

ESTABLISHMENT OF COMMUNIST GOVERNMENT. While the military conquest proceeded, the Communists prepared to set up a new government. Years of civil war and foreign invasion had made the people unused to functioning as one political unit. To help integrate them into a single polity and tie them as individuals to the regime, "mass organizations" were instituted for labor, peasants, women, youth, literary and art circles, etc.

The form of government was also designed to integrate the people. In July its principles were articulated in a speech by Mao Tse-tung, head of the Chinese Communist Party (CCP), entitled "On People's Democratic Dictatorship." The "people" (workers, peasants, petty bourgeoisie, and national bourgeoisie) would run the democratic government, but would impose a dictatorship on "enemies of the people" (landlords and counterrevolutionaries).

In late Sept. a national representative conference of the "people" was convened at which the form of government pending the promulgation of a constitution was adopted. On 1 Oct., 1949, The People's Republic of China (PRC) was inaugurated. Mao Tse-tung headed the new government with Chou En-lai (b. 1898) as his premier. The façade of democratic coalition was maintained by giving non-Communists prestigious government posts, but in reality the whole government structure acted as the administrative arm of the CCP and CCP members held all key posts.

INTERNATIONAL RELATIONS. Although a new government had been formed, the regime still faced severe economic problems, especially inflation, and still had to complete the conquest of Hainan Island, Taiwan, and Tibet and "mop up" Nationalist troops in west China and Sinkiang.

Mao had defined the PRC's international position in his July speech when he announced that the new state would "lean to one side," i.e., toward the Communist bloc. The USSR recognized the PRC, 2 Oct., 1949, and in Dec. Mao left for negotiations in Moscow. In addition to the Communist bloc, Burma, India, Indonesia, Switzerland, Sweden, Denmark, Pakistan, Ceylon, Afghanistan, Norway, Finland, the U.K., the Netherlands, and Israel also recognized the new government during 1949 and 1950.

1950–52

SINO-SOVIET TREATY. 14 Feb., 1950. Mao returned to China from Moscow soon after signing a 30-year Sino-Soviet Treaty of Friendship, Alliance, and Mutual Assistance. The negotiations had formalized the "lean to one side" policy and had guaranteed the infant Communist state a degree of security which would otherwise have been impossible in the largely non-Communist world. Agreements providing for Soviet economic and technical aid were also concluded.

KOREAN WAR. Meanwhile, the Communist armies took new territory. Hainan Island was captured, Apr. 1950, and preparations for the invasion of Taiwan were then begun. Success seemed assured because the Nationalists were defeated and disorganized and in Jan. the U.S. had denied a commitment to Taiwan's defense. The start of the Korean War, June, changed the situation radically. President Truman's 27 June statement that American security would be endangered by an attack on Taiwan and the subsequent presence of the U.S. 7th Fleet in the Taiwan Straits precluded any Communist action there. By fall UN victories in Korea threatened Chinese security and in early Oct. Chou En-lai asserted that China would intervene if UN troops crossed the 38th parallel. On 7 Oct. the troops did cross it and on 25 Oct. China announced that "Chinese People's Volunteers" were being sent to aid North Korea. By 1953 up to 1 m. Chinese troops had gone to Korea. In Oct. Tibet's "liberation" was also begun.

AGRARIAN REFORM LAW. 30 June, 1950. This measure aimed at eliminating the power of the landlord-gentry class. The program involved confiscation and redistribution of land and physical elimination of the landlords. The "rich peasants" were exempt to avoid disrupting the economy too severely. Class conflict, with the lower classes judging and punishing the upper ones, was an integral part of the drive. This had the dual advantage of encouraging peasant activism and committing the peasants to the reforms by making them responsible. Inflation had been curbed by the end of 1950.

CONQUEST OF TIBET. By Apr. 1951 the conquest of Tibet had been completed. Representatives of the Dalai Lama, Tibet's traditional ruler, signed an agreement in Peking incorporating Tibet into China as an autonomous region. (The PRC was to be responsible for Tibetan foreign affairs, but there was an independent local government.)

CONSOLIDATION OF CCP CONTROL. During 1951 several campaigns in addition to land reform were mounted, all aimed at consolidating the Communists' economic and political control. In Mar. a Party rectification campaign which lasted 2 years and involved a reinvestigation and reregistration of all members was begun. The "Resist-America, Aid-Korea" campaign and the campaign against counterrevolutionaries were conducted in conjunction with the Korean War. The former, stressing a presumed U.S. design to invade China, served both to arouse nationalism and eliminate "bourgeois" pro-western attitudes. The campaign against counterrevolutionaries, imposing a reign of terror on the urban population, resulted in mass executions of those accused of actively opposing the regime. The "3-Anti Campaign" (against corruption, waste, and bureaucratism) was begun experimentally, Aug., in Manchuria to increase discipline in Party and government organizations. In Dec. it was expanded into a nationwide drive and, in addition to its original purposes, became a tool to fight "bourgeois" and "rightist" thought. The campaign lasted through the following spring. Chou En-lai initiated the Ideological Reform Campaign, Sept., at a mass meeting of teachers and professors. It was originally planned as a 4-month drive to force intellectuals, through the use of criticism and self-criticism, to accept Marxism-Leninism and CCP rule. Because considerable passive opposition remained, this movement was combined with the 3-Anti Campaign late in the year.

5-ANTI CAMPAIGN. By 1952 most sectors of the economy had reached or surpassed pre-1949 levels and, although consumer goods were still in short supply, communications had been considerably improved and the economy had been centralized. However, despite the 3-Anti Campaign there continued to be some corruption, especially in economic circles. To combat this a nationwide "5-Anti Campaign" (against bribery, tax evasion, theft of state assets, cheating in labor or materials, and stealing state economic intelligence) was conducted among the bourgeoisie, especially the urban merchants and manufacturers, Jan.–Mar. The campaign was similar to the one against counterrevolutionaries in that it encouraged class warfare, public denunciations, and abject confessions, but it was carefully controlled by the Party and there were no mass executions. When it had run its course the influence of the old business class had been destroyed and what remained of the private sector was firmly under Party and government control. By this time most foreign investors had left China because of extremely strict government policies.

LAND POLICY. On 30 June the regime announced that land reform had been largely completed. By Aug. the 2nd step toward developing socialist agriculture was begun; the Ministry of Agriculture announced that 40% of the peasants in China belonged either to mutual-aid teams or agricultural producers' co-operatives. In the former, several families co-operated on a year-round basis, but each family retained its own land and received the produce raised on it. The latter included more families. In addition to a small private plot, each family owned shares in the rest of the land, which was farmed collectively. The income from the crop was divided according to the shares held and wages were paid according to work performed. Under both systems participation was voluntary but strongly urged.

1953–57

INCREASE IN SOVIET AID. The period of reconstruction which had begun with the Communist conquest in 1949 was basically complete by 1953. In Mar. of that year Stalin died, after which Soviet aid to China was substantially increased. A Soviet commitment to finance 91 new industrial and other projects was made in Sept. The Korean truce, July, gave the economy a further boost.

INDUSTRIAL POLICY. During the 1st part of the year industrial development was emphasized. However, by June 1953 management problems were evident and that month a national labor discipline campaign was launched. Cadres were widely criticized for poor management and organization. In mid-July the *People's Daily,* the regime's semiofficial newspaper, cited cadre mistakes as the main cause of serious target underfulfillment in state-operated factories. In Sept. a campaign to increase production and practice economy was begun.

AGRICULTURAL POLICY. Problems were also apparent in the agriculture sector. On 15 Feb., 1953, a Party decision ordered moderation in establishing new co-operatives. The cadres had

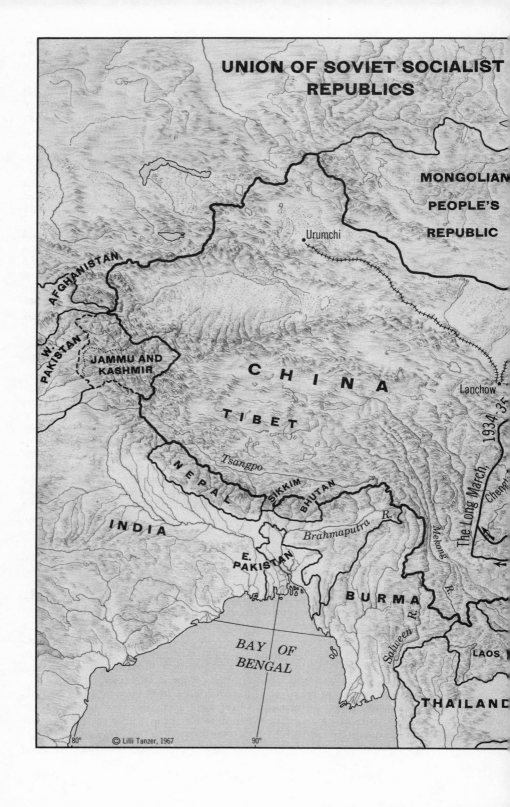

UNION OF SOVIET SOCIALIST
REPUBLICS

MONGOLIAN

PEOPLE'S

REPUBLIC

Urumchi

AFGHANISTAN

W. PAKISTAN

JAMMU AND
KASHMIR

C H I N A

Lanchow

T I B E T

The Long March, 1934-35

Tsangpo

Chengtu

N E P A L

SIKKIM

BHUTAN

INDIA

Brahmaputra R.

R.

Mekong

E.
PAKISTAN

B U R M A

R.

Salween R.

LAOS

BAY OF
BENGAL

THAILAND

80°   © Lilli Tanzer, 1967   90°

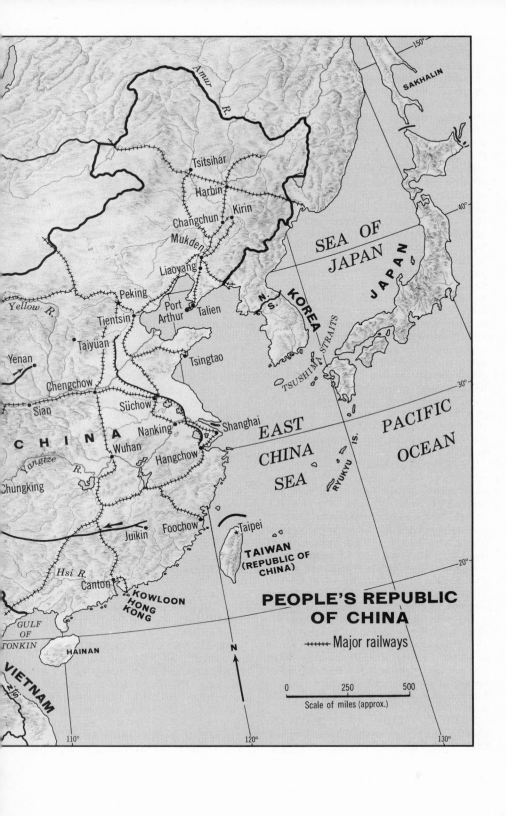

PEOPLE'S REPUBLIC
OF CHINA

++++ Major railways

0   250   500

Scale of miles (approx.)

apparently been pushing the program very hard and their zeal was resented by peasants who, having finally gained their own land, were not anxious to give it up. Disliking regimentation by the cadres, many were migrating to the cities. Measures to relieve the situation were taken in Apr. The peasants were ordered to remain in rural areas and a campaign to educate cadres in the Russian experience of industrialization and co-operativization was begun. As late as mid-Sept. the theme that co-operatives had been set up too rapidly was reiterated. However, on 1 Oct. a *People's Daily* editorial on the "general line of the state during the period of transition" explained that China had entered the transition to socialism and that nonsocialist sectors of the economy (including agriculture and industry) would be reformed. A nationwide movement to study the general line was launched and co-operatives were again encouraged. In mid-Dec. the Party called for the number of co-operatives to be increased from 15,000 to 35,000 in 1954. Preparations for a constitutional government were begun in mid-Jan., when a Committee to Draft the Constitution was set up. In July a national census was ordered.

INTERNATIONAL RELATIONS. In 1954 there was a general relaxation of tension between the Communist bloc and the rest of the world. The idea of a 3rd, neutral bloc subject to growing Communist influence began to gain acceptance in China. One of the earliest indications of the new policy was the Chinese role in the Geneva Conference which met to seek a settlement of the Indochina and Korean issues, Apr.–July. Agreement on Korea was not reached, but Chou En-lai played a key role in formulating the cease-fire agreement for Indochina. In Apr. China also negotiated an agreement with India in which Chinese sovereignty over Tibet was acknowledged and the 5 principles of "peaceful coexistence" on which Chinese foreign policy was based in following years were 1st outlined.

POLICY TOWARD TAIWAN. Shortly after returning from Geneva, Chou called for the "liberation" of Tai-

wan and attacked plans for the formation of SEATO. Chou's speech initiated the 1st Taiwan Straits crisis, which lasted into 1955. On his arrival in Peking, late Sept., Khrushchev lent his verbal support to the campaign. China condemned the mutual-defense treaty signed by the Nationalists and the U.S. late in the year as aggression.

PARTY PURGES. The only important Party purges between 1949 and the mid-1960's occurred at a Party conference in early Feb. 1954. Although it was not announced until a year later, at this time Kao Kang and Jao Shu-shih, the Party leaders in Manchuria and east China, were ousted for violating Party discipline and trying to create "independent kingdoms." Their removal was followed by a campaign for Party unity and collective leadership which lasted until summer.

ADOPTION OF THE CONSTITUTION. In Mar., Mao Tse-tung presented a draft constitution to the Committee for Drafting the Constitution. It was accepted by the temporary government, mid-June 1954, and shortly thereafter the completion of the basic-level elections and the national census was announced. The population of mainland China (excluding Taiwan and the overseas Chinese) was said to be 583 m. The 1st National People's Congress was held, 15–28 Sept., and formally adopted the constitution. A government reorganization followed. Mao Tse-tung, Liu Shao-ch'i (b. 1898), and Chou En-lai were elected to the top posts.

PEASANT CO-OPERATIVES. The co-operative movement grew rapidly in 1954. In late Mar. there were 91,000 co-operatives, 4 times the goal set for the whole year. Although in Aug. most of them were called failures, by late Dec. the figure was about 400,000.

BANDUNG CONFERENCE. In the early months of 1955 the Taiwan Straits crisis continued with Chou En-lai condemning UN efforts for a cease-fire as interference in China's internal affairs. The tension was finally relaxed when the Asian–African Conference was held in Bandung, Indonesia, 18–24 Apr. Like the 1954 Geneva Conference, the Bandung

Conference demonstrated China's new foreign policy of wooing the "3rd bloc." During the conference Chou En-lai said China was willing to discuss the Far East situation with the U.S., although he maintained a few days later that the Taiwan Straits problem was an internal one. A treaty concerning nationality was signed with Indonesia.

In late Apr. China's prestige was further enhanced by a nuclear-aid agreement with the USSR and in late July it was announced that ambassadorial-level talks between the PRC and the U.S. would be held in Geneva. As a symbol of the new diplomatic approach, a Chinese embassy was opened in Afghanistan, July, and diplomatic relations were established with Nepal, Aug.

POLICY TOWARD INTELLEC-TUALS. In early Feb. 1955 another campaign to reform intellectuals was undertaken. It centered around writer Hu Feng, who was accused of ignoring Marxist-Leninist principles. By May it had expanded into a general movement against "counterrevolutionaries."

5-YEAR PLAN. After a Party Conference in Mar. 1955, the 1st 5-Year Plan was finally announced. The plan covered the period 1953–57 and emphasized industrial development. During the year merchants and peddlers in rural areas were urged to join the co-operative movement. Between mid-Feb. and mid-Nov. the number of co-operatives jumped from about 600,000 to almost double that number. A Party conference in early Oct. hailed the approaching "high tide of socialization in rural areas." In 1956, however, it was revealed that the 1st 5-Yr. Plan was suffering severe maladjustments, at least some of which were due to a lack of enthusiasm on the part of the peasants, workers, and intellectuals. A Party conference held in Jan. 1956 considered how to increase Party control over the intellectuals and enlist their support for national construction and socialism.

"HUNDRED FLOWERS" SPEECH. On 2 May, 1956, Mao gave his famous address entitled "Let a Hundred Flowers Blossom, Let a Hundred Schools of Thought Contend" which outlined a new policy of encouraging free expression and creative thinking in order to deal with the country's problems. In spite of repeated urging throughout the year, the intellectuals did not take advantage of their new freedom, apparently preferring the safety of silence.

SINO-SOVIET RELATIONS. The 20th Congress of the Communist Party of the USSR was held in Feb. 1956 and 2 important issues were raised: the denunciation of Stalin and the admission that there are "many roads to socialism." The Chinese press did not comment on the Congress until early Apr., when it noted that Stalin had made some mistakes, but refused to condemn him entirely, presumably because Mao's position could be considered analogous to Stalin's. On the question of diverse patterns of socialist development, leeway in domestic policy was supported, but the need for a common foreign policy was also maintained. Thus China encouraged Poland and Hungary to assert domestic independence in the summer and early fall. However, during the Oct. Polish and Hungarian uprisings China supported the Poles, but opposed the Hungarians, the difference being that the Poles only wanted increased domestic freedom while the Hungarians threatened to leave the Communist bloc. The CCP played a major role in the negotiations and decisions made during this period of crisis. The competition and policy disagreements which led to the Sino-Soviet split may have begun at this time.

"HUNDRED FLOWERS" CAMPAIGN. The "Hundred Flowers" campaign was newly emphasized in early 1957. In a speech, Feb., entitled "On the Correct Handling of Contradictions Among the People," Mao outlined a policy for dealing with domestic dissent and reiterated the need to loosen controls over free expression of opinion. From then until late May the people were invited to express their suggestions and criticisms. Simultaneously, a national cadre rectification campaign was carried out, the implication being that the cadres were inhibiting free comment. Finally, in May and early June the response came with both basic and violent criticism of the CCP. Its intensity apparently took the Party by surprise, threatening to undermine the whole power structure. In early June the Party retaliated with a massive "antirightist" campaign which continued into 1958. In July and Aug. there were widespread arrests of "counterrevolutionaries." Thus the "Hundred Flowers" campaign was brought to a sudden halt.

BEGINNING OF THE SINO-SOVIET SPLIT. The fall of 1957 was another turning point in Chinese foreign policy. In late Aug. the USSR tested its 1st ICBM and agreed to help China build its own nuclear deterrent. Early the following month the 1st sputnik was launched. Then in early Nov. Mao made his 2nd trip to the USSR and met with the world's other Communist leaders. In a speech at one conference Mao maintained that the Russian scientific achievements gave the Communist world a strategic advantage which should be pushed immediately. He insisted that "the east wind prevailed over the west wind," and recommended aggressive action. The Russians apparently disagreed, cautioning against the dangers of nuclear war with the U.S. This basic strategy disagreement has persisted ever since and from it has developed the Sino-Soviet split, the Chinese accusing the Russians of holding "revisionist" attitudes toward "imperialist" states and the Russians accusing the Chinese of being unrealistic about the possible alternatives in the nuclear era. The theoretical question involved is said to turn on the inevitability of war.

1958

THE "GREAT LEAP FORWARD." In the early months of the year the antirightist and rectification campaigns continued and violent attacks on Yugoslav "revisionism" were made. (The latter were veiled criticisms of the USSR.) Then, in the summer, China launched a radically new program for speeding industrial development, abandoning the Soviet model and initiating the Great Leap Forward. The co-operative movement had been growing since 1952 and now the co-operatives were merged into multifunctional communes, averaging about 5,000 households each. The administration of each commune was responsible for the political, economic, and military organization of its members. Land was owned by the commune, but for production purposes the communes were subdivided into brigades (equivalent to the old co-operatives) and teams (equivalent to the old mutual-aid teams). In the movement's early stages communal living was encouraged with the establishment of central mess halls, child-care centers, etc. Although wages were paid, there was an effort to implement a free supply system based on the Communist precept "to each according to his needs." In addition to agriculture, the communes were expected to undertake industrial production. The small-scale steel plants established at this time have become a symbol of the economic disaster that the Great Leap brought.

Much of the commune movement apparently began without the specific orders of the top Party leaders, and in early Aug. Mao reportedly toured the communes to inspect the results. On his return, an important Party conference was held at Peitaiho and the communes were declared the best form for socialist construction and the transition to Communism. In the following months, as the movement spread, claims were made that China was rapidly approaching Communism (having outdistanced the Soviet Union in this respect) and had now become the true leader of the Marxist-Leninist revolution throughout the world. However, by late Nov. another Party conference seriously reviewed the movement and began to restrain it, announcing that the transition from socialism to Communism was in the very distant future. Economic dislocations had already become evident as a result of uneconomical production methods, particularly with reference to modern industry, and the crash programs implemented by the communes.

2ND TAIWAN STRAITS CRISIS. Simultaneously with the height of the Great Leap there occurred the 2nd Taiwan Straits crisis, which began in Aug. 1958 and was virtually over by Oct., but which was much more severe than the earlier one. The Communists blockaded one of the offshore islands and then extended their territorial limit to 12 mi. in order to cut off supplies. The U.S. refused to recognize the 12-mi. limit, escorting supply ships to the conventional 3-mi. limit and breaking the blockade. On 6 Sept. Chou En-lai offered to resume talks with the U.S. in Warsaw and in early Oct. the shelling of the island was temporarily halted. The USSR did not protest U.S. actions until after 6 Sept., suggesting that it was unwilling to support Chinese militancy. Thus the Chinese were forced to back down in the face of superior U.S. strength and new fuel was added to the smoldering Sino-Soviet dispute.

1959-61

REBELLION IN TIBET. In Mar. 1959, with the Tibetan rebellion, the regime faced the 1st serious threat to the unity of the Chinese state since it came to power in 1949. The revolt was speedily crushed and the Dalai Lama sought asylum in India. Because of his presence there, Apr., the Chinese accused India of expansionism and interference in Chinese internal affairs. By fall, border clashes which continued through Dec. began to occur between Indian and Chinese troops. Perhaps the most significant aspect of the conflict with India was the lack of support China received from the USSR, which apparently again refused to underwrite Chinese militancy. It was learned later that in 1959 the Russians had also abrogated their nuclear-aid agreement with China. This had serious implications for future Chinese security and further intensified the dispute with the USSR.

PROMOTION OF LIU SHAO-CH'I. At the 2nd National People's Congress, Apr. 1959, Mao was not re-elected chairman of the PRC, although he continued to head the Party. Instead, Liu Shao-ch'i was named to the post, implying that he would later succeed Mao as the most important leader of China.

MODIFICATION OF THE COMMUNE POLICY. From June 1959 onward, retreat from the excesses of the Great Leap became evident. Decentralization was urged for some aspects of commune work, the free supply system was limited, and efforts to develop small-scale modern industry in the agricultural setting were scrapped. In Aug. and Sept. announcements were made of deflated production statistics for 1958, thus discrediting the exaggerated claims for the "Great Leap Forward," and scaled-down targets were belatedly announced for 1959. However, the official explanation of economic setbacks caused by the Great Leap was that China suffered serious droughts and floods between 1959 and 1961, and in the last part of 1959 a campaign against the "rightist" critics of the Great Leap was waged.

RENEWED EMPHASIS ON AGRICULTURE. The retreat from the Great Leap was even more obvious in 1960. On 1 Jan. an article in the Party journal *Red Flag* announced that agriculture would be the foundation for economic growth during the year. (During the Great Leap, industry had been given priority.) A 12-year National Agricultural Program was ratified, Apr., and during July and Aug. a nationwide campaign to make agriculture the basis of the economy was conducted. Decentralization in the communes to increase popular enthusiasm and encourage better management was begun. Despite reorganization of rural communes, in Mar. and Apr. urban communes to organize neighborhood industry, household services, and welfare projects were promoted. However, it was stressed that most property would remain private and participation would be voluntary.

ARMY POLICY. Early in 1960 there was a move to prepare the militia to assume an economic role and a stress on the possibilities of a successful "people's" war against other states with highly developed weapons. (The latter was probably related to the Soviet withdrawal of nuclear aid.) In Oct. Defense Minister Lin Piao began to stress political indoctrination for the army, foreshadowing the nationwide campaigns of the following years.

SINO-SOVIET SPLIT. During 1960 the Sino-Soviet dispute became public. *Red Flag* articles, Apr., asserted that tactical maneuvers by imperialists did not change imperialism's basic nature and that so long as imperialism existed wars were inevitable. The Russians maintained that some wars could be avoided. In June, at a Conference of Communist Parties in Bucharest, a violent, personal exchange occurred between the CCP representative and Khrushchev, each accusing the other of poor judgment. In July the USSR withdrew all its experts and aid from China.

INCREASE IN FOREIGN ALLIANCES. As the Sino-Soviet dispute intensified, so did competition for allies in the Afro-Asian states. As a series of African states became independent in 1960, China quickly recognized them. (This was also part of China's effort to deprive Taiwan of votes on the China issue in the UN.) In Jan. the instruments of ratification for the Sino-Indonesian Dual Nationality Treaty signed in 1955 were finally exchanged, and a Treaty of Friendship and Mutual Non-Aggression was signed with Burma. Boundary and aid agreements with Nepal, Mar., a Friendship and Non-Aggression Treaty with Afghanistan, Aug., and a boundary treaty with Burma, Oct., were also signed. One desired effect of these agreements was to isolate India from her neighbors.

ECONOMIC DECENTRALIZATION. A Party meeting in Jan. 1961 announced the virtual abandonment of Great Leap economic policies. Between Jan. and June 1961 the value of the experience of old peasants, the importance of rural trade fairs to the economy, and the necessity of private plots and individual family sideline enterprise to supplement the collective economy were all stressed. By June decentralization of production decision-making to the team level had apparently been accepted. All of these trends indicated a reversion to co-operatives and in some cases mutual-aid-team levels of co-operation. Starting in Sept. there were campaigns to increase production and quality in light industry and to improve standards and systems of accounting in all enterprises.

A further deterioration in Sino-Soviet relations took place when Khrushchev made a violent attack on the Albanians at the 22nd Communist Party Congress of the USSR in Oct. Chou En-lai, who headed the CCP delegation, criticized the attack and then left the meetings.

During the year contacts between Japan and the PRC grew, particularly in the field of trade.

1962–65

SOCIALIST EDUCATION CAMPAIGN. Efforts for economic stabilization and commune decentralization continued in 1962. In the early months of the year there was also evidence of a new emphasis on Party discipline and effectiveness, but it was not until a Party conference in Sept. that this was clearly defined. With Mao presiding and delivering an important speech on class struggle, the conference marked the beginning of a nation-wide effort to strengthen support for the regime and rectify Party work styles in order to guarantee the continuation of the revolution. At the conference the Party decided to conduct a Socialist Education Campaign and afterward several local ones were begun experimentally in the rural areas. Their results showed that, since the failure of the Great Leap, the rural population had increasingly reverted to "capitalist" forms such as private plots and individual marketing. Many had left farming for more lucrative jobs in business. The cadres had lost their revolutionary zeal to the point of being unable to control, and in some cases even encouraging, these tendencies. In short, the revolution was at stake.

CONFLICT WITH INDIA. In mid-Apr. 1962 the border conflict with India was renewed with each side accusing the other of aggression. By Oct. there was fighting between Chinese and Indian troops. The USSR continued military aid to India throughout, earning new denunciations from the CCP. The Russian handling of the Cuban missile crisis in the fall was especially criticized. On 1 Dec. China announced that her troops would withdraw from the Indian border unilaterally. They did conduct a partial withdrawal, but remained in what had been considered Indian territory.

IDEOLOGICAL REFORM CAMPAIGNS. Although the Socialist Education Campaign was not openly discussed until late in 1963, political drives which were related to it were begun. Socialist indoctrination for everyone was stressed with the dual goal of increasing class consciousness and collective production enthusiasm. One of the basic techniques was to make people compare their present lives with how they had lived before the Communists took over and to recall how they had suffered at the hands of the "exploiting classes." Early in the year a campaign to emulate the self-sacrificing spirit of an army martyr named Lei Feng was carried out. By June cadres were being urged to participate in physical labor to increase their ties with the general population.

In Sept. 1963 it was announced that the economy had recovered from the "natural disasters" of 1959–61.

INTERNATIONAL RELATIONS. Although China announced in Mar. that its withdrawal from Indian territory was complete, tensions along the Sino-Indian border were increased that month when the Dalai Lama announced a new Tibetan constitution to be implemented after the Chinese were driven out of Tibet. Efforts to isolate India continued as China signed new boundary agreements with Nepal, Jan., Pakistan, Mar., and Afghanistan, Nov. In 1965 the Chinese issued an ultimatum demanding Indian withdrawal from "Chinese" territory, but they later backed down.

The main preoccupation of Chinese foreign policy during 1963 was the dispute with the USSR and competition for leadership of the world Communist movement. As the U.S. and the USSR approached agreement on a partial nuclear test ban, Chinese accusations of Soviet "revisionism" became increasingly violent. Talks held in Moscow, July, between Soviet and Chinese Party leaders led nowhere. When the treaty was signed, late July, the Chinese condemned it and in the following months bitter personal attacks were leveled at Khrushchev in an effort to undermine his leadership.

EXPANSION OF THE SOCIALIST EDUCATION MOVEMENT. Efforts to increase socialist consciousness and collective production enthusiasm and improve cadre work styles were continued in 1964 while the Socialist Education Movement was considerably expanded. At various times nearly every other campaign was said to be part of this general one. In Jan. 1964 a nationwide production drive was launched in industry and commerce, called the campaign "to compare with, learn from, and overtake the advanced and help the backward." At the same time a movement to "Learn from the PLA" (the Chinese army) was begun. The political indoctrination which had been carried out in the army since 1961 was held up as an example for the rest of the country as all were urged to study Mao's works. By fall, the Socialist Education Movement had been extended to the cities and a new attack on intellectuals who allegedly denied the necessity of continuing class conflict was launched.

RELATIONS WITH THE USSR. Verbal attacks on the USSR intensified in the first half of 1964. When Khrushchev proposed, June, a meeting of all Communist parties, the Chinese called it an effort to further split the Communist movement by attacking the CCP. Khrushchev's unwillingness to give up his plan exacerbated the dispute and probably also contributed to his removal from power in mid-Oct. Then, 16 Oct., the PRC exploded its first atomic bomb, thereby gaining considerable international prestige and increasing China's bargaining power with the USSR. Since Soviet aid for Chinese nuclear development had been withdrawn in 1959, the Chinese could take much of the credit for the obvious technological advance. After these 2 events the dispute temporarily subsided. In Nov. Chou En-lai led a delegation to Moscow and Khrushchev's fall was hailed in the Chinese press as a great victory for Marxism-Leninism against "revisionism."

RECTIFICATION CAMPAIGNS. In Jan. 1965 Mao apparently personally ordered a reorientation of the Socialist Education Movement to deal with the few people in the Party who had been influenced by capitalism. In spite of this, the tendency to expand the campaign continued. For instance, national conferences on conducting political work in industry and communications and in agriculture and forestry were held. Rural and urban part-work, part-study schools whose programs were to be co-ordinated with the local socialist education campaigns were promoted. Thousands of people (particularly students) were sent into the countryside to help with the various campaigns and to gain an increased commitment to socialism in the process. By fall cadres above the basic levels were being held responsible for the morale problems lower down in the scale. A campaign to rectify county Party officials resulted. They were accused of enjoying a soft life, ignoring Party policy, and losing contact with real situations. The following year it was revealed that many cadre members had lost their posts during this period. Also in the fall, another campaign was begun among the intellectuals. Various writers were accused of allegorically opposing the regime. From these 1st criticisms in Nov. and Dec. the Cultural Revolution developed.

FAILURE OF THE 2ND AFRO-ASIAN CONFERENCE. The pause in the Sino-Soviet dispute was only temporary. In mid-Feb. 1965 Kosygin, the new Soviet premier, visited Peking. Shortly thereafter, the Chinese again began to comment on Soviet "revisionism" and, late May, accused Khrushchev's successors of continuing his line, only more subtly. The 2nd Afro-Asian Conference, the successor to the one held in Bandung in 1955, was scheduled to be held in Algeria in mid-1965. When the issue of Soviet participation arose, the Chinese were strongly opposed. Ultimately, the conference was "indefinitely postponed."

RELATIONS WITH INDONESIA. By 1965 the Afro-Asian states were seriously reconsidering their relations with China. The failure of the Great Leap, the militant Chinese stand on war, the Sino-Soviet split, and the confrontation on the Indian border had all engendered mistrust. An attempted coup in Indonesia, mid-Sept., in which Chinese Communists

were implicated, was a final blow to the "peaceful coexistence" image. From this time, Indonesia, which had been one of China's firm supporters, began to harass Chinese in Indonesia until, 1967, diplomatic relations were suspended.

1966–68

START OF THE CULTURAL REVOLUTION. By early 1966 frequent references to the Socialist Education Campaign had ceased, but the political indoctrination campaign became even more massive. The slogans "Bring Politics to the Fore" and "Study Mao's Works" were nationally adopted. The "little red book," *The Quotations of Mao Tse-tung*, which was to become the symbol of the Red Guard, began to be generally distributed. Attacks on leading writers grew in number and severity. Their writings were condemned as "poisonous weeds" which advocated a return to the capitalist system and the overthrow of the regime. In mid-Apr. 1966 the 1st references to the Great Proletarian Cultural Revolution began to appear. They seemed to refer initially to the campaign against writers, but by June university faculties and Party personnel were also coming under fire. In mid-June university enrollment was postponed.

LIN PIAO AND THE RED GUARDS. Liu Shao-ch'i figured prominently as a leader of the movement until the Party conference in early Aug. over which Mao presided. The conference adopted a decision on the Cultural Revolution which stressed that the main problem was to purge the Party of a few members who had "taken the capitalist road." After this, a series of mass rallies was held in Peking with Mao often presiding. Defense Minister Lin Piao (b. 1908) usually appeared with him and, although Liu Shao-ch'i was generally present, he stayed in the background. By mid-Aug. Lin Piao was credited with correctly interpreting Mao's works and Red Guard units made up of teenagers were being formed on a national scale. The Red Guards, with the regime's blessing, temporarily ran wild, changing road and store names to more "revolutionary" ones and attacking and humiliating people for having "bourgeois" household goods or clothing. However, by early Sept. there were efforts to curb these excesses, the Red Guards being cautioned to use reason rather than force.

INTERNATIONAL RELATIONS. While the Cultural Revolution raged domestically, Chinese foreign relations steadily deteriorated. In Jan. 1966 both Dahomey and the Central African Republic broke diplomatic relations with the PRC. In Feb. the Chinese embassy in Indonesia was attacked and the Cuban regime was accused of being anti-Chinese. In Mar. the Chinese refused to attend the 23rd Russian Communist Party Congress and in Oct. Ghana suspended diplomatic relations with the PRC. During Dec. the Chinese began to put pressure on Macao, accusing the Portuguese authorities there of atrocities.

EFFECTS OF THE CULTURAL REVOLUTION. In 1967 the stability which had characterized the CCP for so long seemed to have completely broken down as the Cultural Revolution broadened and deepened, spreading to rural areas as well as cities and including more and more people. In the course of the year some of the Party's oldest and most powerful leaders, notably Liu Shao-ch'i, were denounced, but some subsequently reappeared without seeming to have lost their positions. Revolutionary committees to conduct the Cultural Revolution were set up at all levels of society and in the early months of the year they were urged to seize power from those following the capitalist road. This seemed to imply that the regime was trying to circumvent the Party apparatus. "Economism," encouraging production but overlooking politics, was attacked. By May there were reports of fighting in several provinces as Maoist and anti-Maoist factions apparently struggled to gain control. This continued sporadically through Sept. In that month Mao toured several provinces and afterward the Cultural Revolution seemed to slacken. Fighting broke out again, however, in a number of provinces in Dec. 1967, and

continued through the summer of 1968. During this period the anti-Maoist faction continued to be purged. By the summer 34 of 63 active members of the 1965 Central Committee of the CCP had been removed, and 9 had been publicly criticized. Of 72 active alternates to the Central Committee, 27 had been purged and 29 publicly criticized, while only 9 of the 45 1st and 2nd secretaries of regional party organizations were still active. On 31 Oct., 1968, the Central Committee announced that Liu Shao-ch'i, earlier labeled as "the top Party person in authority taking the capitalist road," had been removed from his post as chief of state.

INTERNATIONAL RELATIONS. During 1967 pressure on Macao continued and a similar campaign against the British in Hong Kong was begun in the late spring. Diplomatic incidents involving many countries which had previously been relatively sympathetic toward China occurred. These ranged from a near rupture of relations with Britain over physical attacks on British diplomatic personnel to a squabble with Ceylon over the distribution in that country of Mao buttons. In 1968 the pressure against Hong Kong continued, and relations with India further deteriorated because of alleged Chinese assistance to the Naga rebels.

THE REPUBLIC OF CHINA (TAIWAN)

1949

LOSS OF THE MAINLAND. The Communist armies moved south from Manchuria in early Jan., forcing negotiations for the surrender of Peking. On 21 Jan. President Chiang Kai-shek announced his retirement from office and made Vice-President Li Tsung-jen (b. 1890) acting president. In the following months other major cities fell to the Communists. In mid-Oct. the Nationalist government was moved from Canton to Chungking, but in late Nov. Chungking also fell. In early Dec. Li Tsung-jen left for the U.S.A., the seat of government was moved to Taipei,

Taiwan, 7 Dec., and Chiang himself fled to Taipei.

Although the Nationalists now ruled the equivalent of only 1 Chinese province, the national structure of government was maintained. Government practice has since remained static; in spite of democratic forms, the real decisions are made by Chiang and his advisers, the provincial administration is mainly staffed with Nationalist refugees rather than Taiwanese, and public expression of opinion is tightly controlled. While this has created certain problems for the regime, thus far Chiang's power has not been seriously challenged and attention has been focused on economic development and foreign relations, especially the recovery of the mainland.

1950-53

THE KOREAN WAR. In Jan. 1950 the U.S. denied any commitment to the defense of Taiwan, and on 1 Mar. Chiang resumed his duties as president in Taipei. By late spring Communist troops were massing on the Chinese coast opposite Taiwan in preparation for invasion, but the Korean War broke out before the invasion was begun, causing President Truman to announce in late June that the 7th Fleet would neutralize the Taiwan Straits. In exchange, the Nationalist government agreed not to try to retake the mainland.

U.S. support for Taiwan continued during the next few years. In Jan. 1951, military aid to the Nationalists was resumed. In the following May, the U.S. said that it would aid Taiwan and refuse recognition to the Communist regime.

In Dec. 1951 a Taiwan Provincial Assembly was set up, but it has never exercised real power. Li Tsung-jen continued to claim the presidency, but in Jan. 1952 he was impeached *in absentia* for violating the nation's laws and was ousted from the Nationalist Party (KMT).

In the early months of 1952 there was a dispute between the Nationalists and the Burmese over Nationalist forces who had escaped into Burma and were using it as a safe base for operations against the Communists. Burma, fearing Communist retaliation, attacked these forces.

After President Eisenhower took office, he stated in early 1953 that the 7th Fleet's neutralization of the Taiwan Straits would be ended. With U.S. aid Taiwan was developing economically and it was felt that the neutralization protected the Communists more than the Nationalists. However, the decision was never implemented.

1954-55

1ST TAIWAN STRAITS CRISIS. In Mar. 1954 Chiang won his 2nd 6-year term as president. The following Aug. Communist Premier Chou En-lai called for the "liberation" of Taiwan, initiating the 1st Taiwan Straits Crisis, which lasted into 1955. Tensions in the Straits increased in the following months and on 3 Dec. the Nationalists signed a Mutual Defense Treaty with the U.S. which committed the U.S. to the defense of Taiwan and the Pescadores Islands. In Jan. 1955 it was noted that, by the defense treaty, the Nationalists agreed not to attack the mainland without previous U.S. approval. The UN Security Council voted, Feb., to discuss a cease-fire in the Taiwan Straits and to invite the Communists to participate. When the Communists refused the invitation, UN efforts were abandoned. The same month the Tachen Islands, which were difficult to defend because of their distance from Taiwan, were evacuated by the Nationalists with the help of the U.S. 7th Fleet. However, the Nationalists pledged continued defense of the other islands. By spring the crisis was passing as the Communist regime offered to negotiate with the U.S.A. on the Far Eastern situation.

1956-57

ECONOMIC POLICY. Although there were still guerrilla efforts to infiltrate the mainland and the ultimate goal of return was not renounced, from 1956 the Nationalists appeared to concentrate increasingly on economic development. The 1st 4-year program for development ended in 1956 and the 2nd began in 1957. By 1957 U.S. economic and technical aid since 1949 had exceeded $770 million. Public criticism of the administration indicated some relaxation of censorship.

In June 1956 Chou En-lai's offer to negotiate directly with the Nationalists over Taiwan's "peaceful liberation" was quickly rejected. In May 1957 there were anti-U.S. riots in Taipei and the U.S. embassy was burned after an incident involving the killing of a Chinese by a U.S. serviceman.

1958

2ND TAIWAN STRAITS CRISIS. By 1958 Taiwan's economy had progressed considerably, but it remained dependent on U.S. aid, which since 1949 had exceeded $1 billion. New strains were put on development in the summer when the 2nd Taiwan Straits Crisis began. The Communists blockaded Quemoy, one of the offshore islands, in late Aug., whereupon the U.S. reaffirmed its commitment to the islands as they related to the security of Taiwan. When the Communists declared, Sept., that their territorial waters extended 12 mi. from their shores (including Taiwan) instead of the usual 3 mi., the U.S. responded by escorting supply ships for Quemoy to the 3-mi. limit. This continued for a month, after which the Communists temporarily suspended the shelling of the island and then resumed it on alternate days. The problem was not solved, but the peak of the crisis had passed.

1959–64

ECONOMIC DEVELOPMENT. After 1959 Taiwan's economic development proceeded rapidly, achieving an annual growth rate of 6% by 1964. In 1959 a 10-year development program was outlined, and by 1964 the government had apparently shifted its emphasis from militarily recovering the mainland to attracting the mainland Chinese through economic prosperity.

Although guerrilla activities and some shelling of the offshore islands continued, there was only 1 major build-up of Communist forces opposite the Nationalist-held islands, mid-1962.

INTERNATIONAL AFFAIRS. Competition between the Communists and the Nationalists for support in Africa grew as it became clear that African nations could control the crucial votes on the question of Communist China's admission to the UN, which had become increasingly closely contested in the early 1960's. The Nationalists used aid, trade, and personal diplomacy to gain support among the African states and were relatively successful. One setback occurred in Jan. 1964, when France forced Taiwan to break diplomatic relations by denying that the Nationalists represented China in Paris.

TAIWANESE INDEPENDENCE MOVEMENT. During this period there were renewed efforts by the Taiwanese to gain independence from Chinese rule, or at least increased democracy, but little progress was made. In 1960 Taiwanese parties agitated for a place on the ballot in local elections. Fearing the formation of a united Taiwanese Party (the China Democratic Party), the KMT sought a coalition with 2 other Chinese parties, the Democratic Socialists and the Young China Party. The government said it would not recognize the new party if it were formed. Then, Sept. 1960, a publisher who was a leader of the new party was arrested for sedition and given a long prison sentence, Oct. The controversy continued into 1961 and 1962, and opposition leaders were arrested. The movement did not keep Chiang from being elected for a 3rd presidential term, Mar. 1960.

1965–68

U.S.-TAIWAN RELATIONS. A major turning point in U.S.-Taiwan relations was reached in 1965, when in July it was announced that U.S. economic aid was being phased out. In Aug., after over a

decade of negotiation, a Status of Forces
Agreement was reached between the 2
states providing for Nationalist jurisdiction over crimes committed by U.S. servicemen in Taiwan.

The economy was aided by U.S. purchases in Taiwan for the Vietnam War.
The Nationalists strongly supported the
war, but were not asked to contribute
troops because of the implications it
might have for Communist Chinese involvement.

RE-ELECTION OF CHIANG.
Chiang's position remained secure. In
1965 one of the leading advocates of
Taiwan's independence returned there
from Japan calling for unity in opposition to the Communist mainland regime
and consequently weakening the independence movement. In Mar. 1966
Chiang was elected, at the age of 79, to a
4th 6-year term as president.

JAPAN

1945-46

SURRENDER. Japan formally surrendered on 2 Sept., 1945, aboard the battleship *Missouri* anchored in Tokyo Bay.
Gen. Douglas MacArthur and Foreign
Minister Shigemitsu Mamoru were the
principal signers. Shortly before this, Mac-
Arthur had landed in Japan as the
Supreme Commander for the Allied
Powers (SCAP). It soon became clear that
the Japanese were stunned and disillusioned and wished genuinely to co-operate with the occupation forces. Moreover,
they were impressed by the occupation's
constructive goals: the elimination of
militarism in Japan, the guaranteeing of
human rights, and the achievement of
basic democratic reforms.

1ST OCCUPATION MEASURES. On
4 Oct., 1945, SCAP published what has
been called the Japanese Bill of Rights. It
abolished laws restricting human rights,
ordered the release of political prisoners,
and deprived the Home Ministry of many
of its powers. State Shinto was disestablished. A Trade Union Act gave workers
the right to organize. On 1 Jan., 1946, the
emperor published a rescript denying his
divinity.

**PROMULGATION OF THE CON-
STITUTION.** Premier Shidehara Kijuro
(1872–1951) formed a commission to draft
a new constitution. The resulting draft
was presented to SCAP on 1 Feb., 1946.
SCAP found it too conservative, and
MacArthur immediately ordered the Government Section of his General Headquarters to draft another. The new draft,
written at a feverish pitch, was presented
to the Japanese cabinet on 13 Feb. SCAP
representatives and the cabinet discussed
it for 2 exhausting days, and a partial
revision was made. On 6 Mar. the draft
constitution was published with the strong
endorsement of the emperor and of SCAP.

One reason for MacArthur's haste was
fear of interference from the Far Eastern
Commission (FEC). The FEC was an 11-
nation body sitting in Washington, formally charged with establishing occupation policy. It met for the 1st time on 26
Feb., 1946. But MacArthur maintained his
autonomy in the matter of the constitution, as in nearly everything else. In Nov.
1946 the constitution was approved nearly
intact by the Diet. It became effective, 3
May, 1947.

**PROVISIONS OF THE CONSTITU-
TION.** The new constitution abolished
the fiction that the emperor was the
actual head of the government and
placed genuine responsibility on the Diet
and the cabinet. The Diet is supreme. It
consists of the House of Councilors and
the House of Representatives. Both are
elected, but the latter is clearly stronger.
The House of Councilors has 250 members who sit for 6 years; 60% of them
represent prefectures, while 40% are
elected by the nation at large. The House
of Representatives has 467 members from
118 electoral districts, elected for 4 years
each. The Diet elects the premier from
among its members. It originates constitutional amendments. In legislative and
budgetary matters, the representatives can
overrule the councilors.

Although the constitution is unclear on
the issue, it is agreed that the head of
state is the premier. The emperor is

described as the "symbol of the State and of the unity of the people," deriving his position from the will of the people with whom resides sovereign power. A Supreme Court is established to run the judiciary and to pass on the constitutionality of laws. The rights of the Japanese people are defined clearly and in detail, even to the optimistic "right to maintain the minimum standards of wholesome and cultured living." No form of discrimination based on sex is recognized. Lastly, Art. 9 specifies that Japan "renounces war as a sovereign right of the nation." This article was added with MacArthur's backing.

1946-48

DOMESTIC POLITICS. The 1st postwar elections—the 1st in Japan's history under universal adult suffrage—were held in Apr. 1946. The contending parties were the Liberals, the Progressives, the Social Democrats, and the Communists. Postwar political freedom had allowed the Japanese Communist Party (JCP) to become very active. One of its top leaders, Nosaka Sanzo (b. 1896), had returned from refuge in China to promote his own "peaceful revolution" line. The JCP obtained 5 seats, although its influence outside the Diet was stronger than this. The Social Democrats, who represented labor and urban intellectuals, won 93 seats. The Progressives, a conservative party descended mainly from the prewar Minseito and led by Shidehara, obtained 94. The Liberals, who came from the old Seiyukai, gained 139 seats. Shidehara was obliged to resign in favor of the Liberals' president, Yoshida Shigeru (b. 1878). Yoshida, a former diplomat, had escaped being purged because of his pro-peace stand during the war. Now he faced grave inflation, scarcity of food, and economic disruption, as well as the difficulty of dealing with SCAP. Labor discontent mounted and a massive strike planned for Feb. 1947 was only averted by last-minute fiat from MacArthur. In the elections of Apr. 1947, the Liberals obtained only 132 seats, and Katayama Tetsu (b. 1887) became premier at the head of a Socialist-

Conservative coalition. However, he could not put his economic policies into effect over conservative opposition. In Feb. 1948 he resigned and was replaced by Yoshida.

REPARATIONS. Basic occupation policy required the exaction of reparations, and yet Japan was obviously unable to pay any. In the end the U.S. renounced any claim, while some surplus industrial facilities were distributed among 6 allied nations, especially China.

WAR CRIMES TRIALS. For the trial of suspected war criminals, a military tribunal was set up in each major area where Japanese troops had operated. In Tokyo, 28 major war criminals including former premiers Tojo, Koiso, and Hirota were tried by the International Military Tribunal for the Far East. The trials began in May 1946 and the sentences were handed down in Nov. 1948. Seven of the defendants were hanged.

LAND REFORM. In Oct. 1946 the Diet passed 2 radical land-reform bills sponsored by SCAP. Before the war, 46% of the land had been cultivated by tenants. The land reform reduced tenancy to 10% and placed the remaining tenants in a far more advantageous position than before. Absentee landlords were obliged to sell most of their land to the government for resale to their tenants on easy terms. Owner-cultivators were restricted to a maximum allowable holding. The reform was completed by 1950 and brought genuine improvement in the countryside.

THE PURGES. In 1946 highly placed individuals in all fields who had been active in Japan's war effort were purged. They were removed from their positions and forced into inactivity. In 1947 the purge was expanded, striking individuals down to the local level. This stage of the purge was mechanically applied and caused much confusion, though it undoubtedly brought new blood into many organizations. By 1951 most public figures had been "de-purged" and were able to resume their careers.

REFORM OF EDUCATION. The occupation stressed eliminating prewar nationalistic ethics and instilling the democratic ideals of individual initiative, academic freedom, and educational opportunity. The school system was decentralized and government control over it was eliminated. The pattern of elementary, secondary, and college education was modified to resemble more closely that of the U.S.A.

POLICE REFORM. In Dec. 1947 the Home Ministry, long associated with prewar police controls, was abolished. The police were decentralized and reorganized as local, municipal, and national rural police. But such extreme decentralization gradually proved unsuitable in a small country like Japan.

ECONOMIC DECENTRALIZATION. Japan's ability to wage war had depended on her modern industry, which was controlled by the *zaibatsu,* the great family combines peculiar to Japan. Hence, SCAP felt that the *zaibatsu* bore much of the responsibility for the war and attempted to dissolve them. The biggest were in fact broken up, but U.S. policy turned against the reform before long, on the grounds that Japan needed strengthening, not further curbing.

1948–50

YOSHIDA'S 2ND CABINET. Yoshida replaced Katayama as premier, Oct. 1948. In Jan. 1949 the Liberals won the 1st clear majority in the Diet since the war. At the same time the JCP won 35 seats and 10% of the vote. Thus there appeared a trend toward polarization in politics, with conservatism clearly dominant.

Another trend was called the "reverse course": reversal of occupation reforms. Conservatives objected most to the decentralization of the bureaucracy and the police, but they also disliked the educational reforms. But public pressure forestalled several government-sponsored threats to these reforms. Occupation policy changed too. Complete political freedom had allowed leftist-directed labor agitation to become highly effective. Hence SCAP acted to restrict political activity on the part of labor and in 1949 began a drive against the JCP which ended with the banning of top JCP officials, 1950. The JCP went underground for several years. The U.S. now preferred to think of Japan as an ally against the Communist threat in the Far East, and wished to end the occupation.

1950–52

THE PEACE TREATY. The outbreak of the Korean War, June 1950, strengthened the U.S. desire for peace with Japan. Already in 1947 the U.S. had tried to call a peace conference, though Soviet opposition had foiled the attempt. Negotiations for the treaty began in Oct. 1950 under John Foster Dulles. Dulles proceeded on the principle that the peace should be liberal and that Japan would of her own will prefer to join the free world. The free world allies were cooperative, but the USSR raised objections, the principal of which was that China should be represented by the regime in Peking. The San Francisco Peace Conference began 4 Sept., 1951, and 4 days later was signed by all nations attending, except the Soviet bloc. Peking was not represented. The treaty ended the state of war and the occupation, and recognized Japanese sovereignty. It also provided for a special agreement regarding Japan's security. Japan renounced all claim to Formosa, the Pescadores, the Kuriles, southern Sakhalin, and the mandated islands of the Pacific. UN trusteeship was established over the Ryukyus and the Bonin and Volcano islands.

REARMAMENT AND THE MUTUAL SECURITY PACT. From the start of the peace negotiations, Dulles encouraged Japan to rearm. Yoshida was willing, but the issue was highly controversial in Japan. The 1st step toward rearmament was the creation, July 1950, of a 75,000-man Police Reserve by directive of SCAP. In Mar. 1954 the U.S.-Japan Mutual Defense Assistance Agreement, covering equipment, goods, and services, was signed. In 1960, the Police Reserve was renamed the National Self-Defense Force with land, sea, and air arms.

Perhaps even more significant was the signing of the Mutual Security Pact in Sept. 1951, on the same day as the peace treaty. It became effective, Apr. 1952. The pact provided for the continued presence in Japan of U.S. forces and bases, thus defending Japan against any aggressor and at the same time serving U.S. strategic interests in the Far East.

1952–54

FALL OF YOSHIDA. Yoshida and the Liberals were confirmed in power by the elections of Oct. 1952. At the same time, the JCP lost all its seats. This was the price it paid for having switched from peaceful to violent tactics, thereby antagonizing the public. The labor demonstrations and riots of May Day 1952 were the work of the JCP, and resulted in the passage of a dangerously vague antisubversive-activity law. The Socialists were also weakened, having split in half over the question of whether or not to support the peace treaty. The 2 Socialist factions together received only 111 seats. But despite success in this and subsequent elections, Yoshida began to lose ground. There was much opposition to his "1-man cabinet" style of government and to his rearmament policy. Moreover, the Korean War had given a valuable boost to the Japanese economy. When the war effort ended, July 1953, the boom flagged too, reflecting unfavorably on Yoshida.

In the summer of 1954, the passage of a new law recentralizing the police and of enabling legislation related to the Mutual Defense Assistance Agreement intensified the opposition. Then Hatoyama Ichiro (1883–1959) bolted the Liberals and formed his own Democratic Party. Hatoyama had been purged from the office of Liberal Party president, and Yoshida had taken over with the understanding that he would return control to Hatoyama as soon as possible. But Yoshida would not step down. Hatoyama's move brought Yoshida's resignation and soon won him the premiership.

1954–57

THE HATOYAMA AND ISHIBASHI CABINETS. In Apr. 1955 the Democratic Party obtained only a plurality over the Liberals, thus forcing a coalition. When the 2 Socialist factions reunited, Oct. 1955, in the hope of making a serious bid for power, they alarmed the conservatives into merging. The result was the Liberal-Democratic Party (LDP) which has maintained control over the government to date. Under Hatoyama the Socialists reached essentially the same balance with the LDP that exists at the end of the sixties: $\frac{1}{3}$ of the seats in both houses. They have constituted a kind of perpetual opposition. This fact has driven them to resort frequently to strikes, petitions, and demonstrations in order to put pressure on the Diet from outside. The JCP has held a few seats in the Diet ever since 1955. In that year the Communists showed signs of returning to the peaceful policy of Nozaka, who came out of hiding to lead the party openly.

Japan further normalized her international position in Oct. 1956 by exchanging diplomatic representatives with the USSR and by signing a trade agreement. The territorial issue, however, was not settled, for the USSR refused to consider Japan's claim to those of the Kurile Islands that lie closest to her shores. Shortly after this agreement the USSR withdrew her veto, in force since 1952, and Japan was admitted to the UN.

In Dec. 1956 Hatoyama resigned because of illness. His successor, Ishibashi Tanzan (b. 1884) lasted only 2 months before his health failed too. He was followed by Kishi Nobusuke (b. 1896).

1957–60

THE KISHI CABINET AND THE RENEWAL OF THE SECURITY PACT. Since the occupation the Japanese have been uneasy about their position in the world, often fearing harmful involvement in the struggle between the blocs. They have generally approved and yet resented Japan's dependence upon the U.S.A. Some have urged Japan to stand with her Asian neighbors for pacifism and neutrality. The government itself has preferred to restrict Japan's international role to trade. Thus in 1957 Japan responded to business pressure by relaxing restrictions on trade with Communist China.

The biggest popular drive for neutrality was the campaign in 1960 to block renewal of the Security Pact. The pact had no term, but both Japan and the U.S. felt that it needed modification. Kishi obtained some control for Japan over the purpose to which U.S. bases in the country might be put, and hoped this would be enough to ensure quiet passage of the treaty. But when the agreement was put before the Diet in May 1960, violent student demonstrations broke out. The Socialists boycotted the Diet and picketed the House of Representatives. Left alone, LDP forces ratified the treaty. This action led to huge demonstrations on 26 May and after. The public disorder was so serious that on 16 June the cabinet had to ask President Eisenhower to cancel his forthcoming visit. On 18 June the ratification took effect. Kishi resigned immediately and was replaced by Ikeda Hayato (1899–1965).

1960–68

THE IKEDA AND SATO CABINETS. Ikeda quickly struck the keynote of his policy by promising to double the income of every Japanese in 10 years. By the late '60s Japan's prosperity suggested that his goal was not unrealistic. In Oct. 1960 occurred the sensational assassination of the Socialist leader Asanuma Inejiro (1898–1960). Asanuma was notorious for his pro-Peking leanings, which the Socialists have generally retained. The JCP has, after a violent internal struggle, rejected China and aligned itself with the USSR. The LDP's basic orientation reflects Japan's extremely close ties, especially economic ties, with the West. However, the LDP is obliged to remain sensitive to pressure for pacifism and neutrality and for increased contacts with Communist countries.

In Nov. 1964 Ikeda resigned for health reasons. He was followed by Sato Eisaku (b. 1901), Kishi's younger brother. In Feb. 1965 Japan and the Republic of Korea signed a Treaty on Basic Relations, the crucial step toward the normalization of relations between the 2 countries. Korean-Japanese normalization had been a highly controversial issue throughout the early 1960's. In the Jan. 1967 elections, the LDP for the 1st time obtained slightly less than 50% of the vote, though it only lost 1 seat in the House of Representatives. The LDP was under a cloud due to exposure of serious corruption among its officials. However, the Socialists made no significant gains on that score. The Komeito (Clean Government Party), the party sponsored by the militant Soka Gakkai (Value Creation Society) won 5.4% of the vote in this, its 1st election.

In elections to the upper chamber of the Diet, 7 July, 1968, the Komeito continued to show its strength by gaining 4 new seats. The LDP, however, was able to maintain its majority. Premier Sato retained his hold over the LDP in party elections, 27 Nov., 1968. He pledged strong leadership in dealing with the main problems confronting Japan: regaining Okinawa, the continuation or abrogation of the American-Japanese security treaty, and student unrest.

Retreat from Empire

INDIA, PAKISTAN, AND CEYLON

1945

COMMUNAL ANTAGONISMS. On 14 June, the British government announced its intention to form an Executive Council consisting of Indian leaders, with equal representation for Moslems and Hindus. At the suggestion of Lord Wavell (viceroy, 1943–47) a conference of Indian leaders met at Simla, 25 June. They were invited to submit nominations to the Council. The conference failed because of Jinnah's insistence that the League nominate all the Moslems, 14 July. Elections for the Central and Provincial Legislative Assemblies were announced, 21 Aug. Congress fought the election on the issue of independence, the League on that of Pakistan. Communal rioting was widespread. On 19 Sept., Wavell announced his intention to call a constitution-making body. In the Central Assembly elections, Nov.–Dec., the League won all the Moslem seats and Congress all the open seats.

1946

ALL-INDIA INTERIM GOVERNMENT. In the provincial elections, Jan.–Apr., Congress won 80% of the general votes cast, and the League 74% of Moslem votes cast. A British cabinet mission arrived, 23 Mar., talked with leaders, and convened a conference at Simla for 5 May, hoping to induce agreement to co-operate on constitutional progress. The conference broke down, 12 May, and the mission published its own plan, 16 May, proposing (1) an all-India interim government; (2) the grouping together of provinces desiring it, with their own legislatures and executives; (3) a decentralized federal system; and (4) the election of a Constituent Assembly. Both the League and Congress accepted these proposals, but interpreted them differently. In June both agreed to work in the interim government. Wavell formed a caretaker government, 29 June. Claiming Congress did not accept the mission plan, the League withdrew its own acceptance, 29 July, and named 16 Aug. "Direct Action Day," which was marked by riots and several thousand deaths in Calcutta. On 2 Sept. an all-Congress interim government was sworn in, including Nehru, Vallabhbhai Patel (1875–1950), Rajendra Prasad (1884–1963) and Rajagopalachari (b. 1879). In elections for a Constituent Assembly, held in July, Congress won all the open seats except 9 and the League 73 of 78 Moslem seats. After strong appeals from Wavell and Nehru, Jinnah agreed to join the interim government, 13 Oct., but kept up Direct Action and maintained the boycott of the Con-

stituent Assembly when it met, 9 Dec., amidst spreading violence.

1947

PARTITION. On 22 Jan. the Assembly adopted a resolution submitted by Nehru to create an independent republic. With the League refusing to join the Assembly and Congress threatening to leave the government if the League remained in it, the British announced, 20 Feb., that they would transfer power in India before June 1948 and appointed Lord Mountbatten (b. 1900) viceroy. After consultations in India and London, Mountbatten formulated a plan which was put to Indian leaders at a meeting on 2 June which agreed to (1) partition; (2) consultation with communally mixed provinces (Punjab, N.W.F.P., Sind, Baluchistan, and part of Assam), and their partition if their people desired it; (3) the convening of a Pakistan Constituent Assembly; and (4) independence on 15 Aug., 1947.

INDEPENDENCE OF INDIA AND PAKISTAN. Under Mountbattan's guidance the subcontinent was divided between India and Pakistan. The Punjab and Bengal decided to partition themselves. A Boundary Commission delimited a provisional frontier on purely religious lines, thus splitting the Sikh area in 2, and the Sikhs turned to violence. Mountbatten convened a conference of Indian princes, 25 July, and urged them to opt for one dominion or the other. By 15 Aug., only Kashmir, Hyderabad, and Junagadh had not made their decision. Jinnah was named governor general of Pakistan and Mountbatten of India. Independence was declared, 15 Aug., in the two dominions, with millions of Hindus fleeing to India and millions of Moslems to Pakistan. Junagadh's Moslem ruler opted for Pakistan, but, his people being mainly Hindu, Nehru ordered in Indian troops, 9 Nov., and incorporated it after a plebiscite, Feb. 1948. Hyderabad declared its own independence, but was occupied by Indian troops, Sept., 1948.

INDEPENDENCE OF CEYLON. On 9 Oct., 1945, the Soulbury Commission pro-

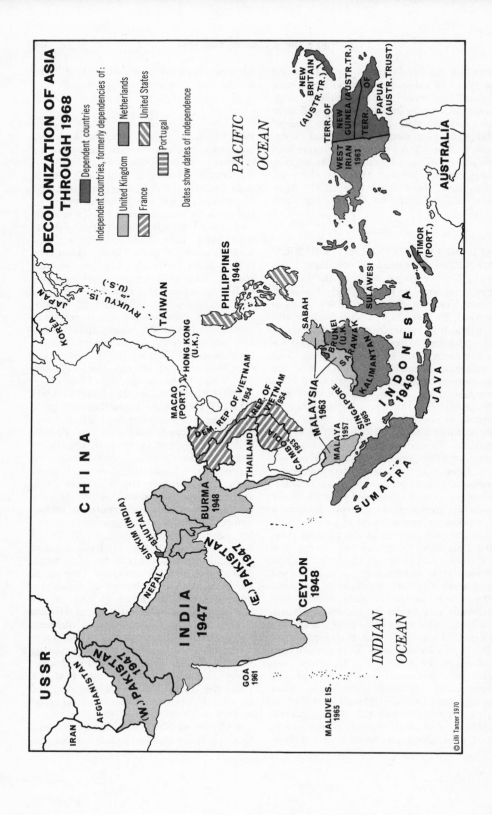

DECOLONIZATION OF ASIA THROUGH 1968

Independent countries, formerly dependencies of:

- Dependent countries
- United Kingdom
- Netherlands
- France
- United States
- Portugal

Dates show dates of independence

PACIFIC OCEAN

NEW BRITAIN (AUSTR. TR.)

TERR. OF NEW GUINEA (AUSTR. TR.)

TERR. OF PAPUA (AUSTR. TRUST)

WEST IRIAN 1963

AUSTRALIA

JAPAN

KOREA

RYUKYU IS. (U.S.)

TAIWAN

PHILIPPINES 1946

TIMOR (PORT.)

SULAWESI

SABAH

HONG KONG (U.K.)

MACAO (PORT.)

DEM. REP. OF VIETNAM 1954

REP. OF VIETNAM 1954

CAMBODIA 1955

THAILAND

BRUNEI (U.K.)

SARAWAK

KALIMANTAN

INDONESIA 1949

JAVA

CHINA

MALAYSIA 1963

SINGAPORE 1965

MALAYA 1957

SUMATRA

BURMA 1948

SIKKIM (INDIA)

BHUTAN

NEPAL

(E.) PAKISTAN 1947

CEYLON 1948

USSR

IRAN

AFGHANISTAN

(W.) PAKISTAN 1947

INDIA 1947

GOA 1961

MALDIVE IS. 1965

INDIAN OCEAN

© Lilli Tanzer 1970

posed responsible government for Ceylon, and on 17 May of the following year Britain published a new constitution, providing for full internal self-government. After elections held Aug.–Sept. 1947, D. S. Senanayake (1884–1952) was named prime minister. Ceylon became independent in the Commonwealth, 4 Feb., 1948.

SOUTHEAST ASIA

Indochina

1945–50

RESTORATION OF FRENCH INFLU-ENCE. On 9 Mar., 1945, the Japanese ousted the Vichy government of Indochina and united Tongking and Annam in the state of Vietnam under Emperor Bao Dai. Cochin China was added, 14 Aug. Bao Dai, however, was forced to abdicate, 26 Aug., and on 2 Sept. Ho Chi Minh proclaimed the Democratic Republic of Vietnam (DRV) in Hanoi, having already created a provisional Committee of the South in Saigon, which was challenged by the Cao-Dai and Hoa-Hao sects. On 12 Sept. British and Indian troops arrived south of the 16th parallel, while Chinese troops entered northern Vietnam in support of the DRV. On 23 Sept. the French, with British support, seized control of Saigon by force.

VIETMINH-FRENCH RELATION-SHIPS. On 31 Oct., 1945, Adm. Thierry d'Argenlieu arrived in Saigon as high commissioner for Indochina, and promised wide-reaching autonomy. In Nov. Ho Chi Minh dissolved the Indochinese Communist Party and formed a national government of Vietminh and Chinese-supported groups. After prolonged negotiations Ho and the French reached agreement, 6 Mar., 1946, whereby France recognized the DRV as an autonomous state within an Indochinese Federation which was itself to belong to a future French Union, and promised to withdraw French troops from the country within 5 years. French forces then entered Hanoi. At the Dalat Conference, 18 Apr.–11 May,

1946, Ho and the French failed to agree on an interpretation of the March Accords, especially the status of Cochin China. On 1 June d'Argenlieu established Cochin China as a state within the French Union. A conference at Fontainebleau, July–Aug., also failed to produce an agreement.

OUTBREAK OF WAR. On 23 Nov., 1946, the French bombarded Haiphong, killing several thousand persons. The Vietminh attacked the French in Hanoi, 19 Dec., and full-scale war broke out, the Vietminh troops being led by Vo Nguyen Giap (b. 1912). French reinforcements were brought in and, after heavy fighting, Dec. 1946–Feb. 1947, the French retook Hanoi. On 5 June, 1947, after long negotiations with Bao Dai, the French recognized the independence of Vietnam and its membership in the French Union by the Bay of Along Accords. On 8 Mar., 1949, the Élysée Agreements provided for the unification of Vietnam as an associated state in the French Union under Bao Dai, and agreements with Laos, 19 July, and Cambodia, 8 Nov., constituted these areas also as associated states.

1951–54

NEGOTIATIONS FOR INDEPEN-DENCE. On 3 Mar., 1951, the Indochinese Communist Party was reconstituted in the DRV as the Vietnam Workers' Party. A Vietminh offensive, Sept.–Oct. 1950, drove the French from northern North Vietnam, but French troops repulsed a Vietminh attack on the Red River Delta, May–Oct. 1951. In Apr. 1953 the Vietminh invaded Laos, overrunning the north and east of the country. On 13 June the king of Cambodia removed to Siam in protest against a French refusal to grant his country full independence. On 3 July the French announced plans to "complete" the independence of Indochina, and their proposals were accepted by Bao Dai, 28 Aug. A National Congress which met on 12 Oct., however, proceeded to call for independence before negotiations. A set of Franco-Laotian agreements, 23 Oct. provided for the independence of Laos.

DIEN BIEN PHU AND THE GENEVA CONFERENCE. In Jan. 1954 the Vietminh blockaded Dien Bien Phu, a strongpoint from which the French had hoped to protect Laos. By 21 July French forces had suffered 72,000 casualties, the Vietminh about 500,000, and some 250,000 civilians had died. On 26 Apr. the Geneva Conference on East Asian Affairs opened, and on 4 June France and Vietnam initialed agreements providing for Vietnamese independence. The final declaration of the Geneva Conference (not signed by any party) called for (1) the temporary partition of Vietnam at the 17th parallel, (2) the withdrawal of French troops from North Vietnam and Vietminh troops from the South, (3) the holding of elections in 1956, (4) the withdrawal of the Vietminh from Laos and Cambodia and recognition of the independence of both, and (5) the creation of an International Armistice Control Commission to supervise the arrangements made. (*Contd. p. 591.*)

Netherlands East Indies (Indonesia)

1945–49

PROCLAMATION OF THE INDONESIAN REPUBLIC. On 17 Aug., 1945, Sukarno declared the Republic of Indonesia in Batavia (Djakarta) with himself as president and Mohammed Hatta (b. 1902) as vice-president. On 28 Sept. British troops landed with orders to suppress the Republic, and on 30 Sept. the returning Dutch announced their unwillingness to negotiate with it. A series of engagements followed between allies and Indonesian forces, notably the Battle of Surabaya, Nov., in which the Indonesians held off the British for 10 days. By Dec., however, the allies controlled all of the East Indies except Sumatra and most of Java.

LINGGADJATI AGREEMENTS. On 25 Nov., 1946, after prolonged negotiations, the Dutch and Indonesians signed the Linggadjati Agreements, by which (1) the Dutch recognized the Republic of Indonesia as the *de facto* government of Java and Sumatra, and (2) a United States of Indonesia was to be set up, consisting of the Republic and East Indonesia, which would form a union with the Netherlands. The 2 sides interpreted the Linggadjati Agreements differently, and they were not ratified until 25 Mar., 1947.

1ST "POLICE ACTION." On 20 July, 1947, the Dutch, dissatisfied with the Indonesian interpretation of Linggadjati, resorted to arms. On 30 July India and Australia took the Indonesian case to the UN Security Council, which set up a Consular Committee, 25 Aug. (replaced by a Good Offices Committee, Sept.), to oversee a cease-fire and work toward a definitive solution. The Dutch continued their advance and created new "states" in areas brought under their control. On 17 Jan., 1948, the Good Offices Committee was able to arrange the Renville Agreements between the Dutch and Indonesians and a truce was agreed.

2ND "POLICE ACTION." A Communist-inspired rebellion, Sept. 1948, was suppressed by the Republic, Nov., but the Dutch and Indonesians continued to disagree over the distribution of power between the proposed United States of Indonesia and the proposed Union. On 18 Dec. the Dutch denounced the truce; took Djakarta; imprisoned Sukarno, Hatta, and other leaders; and overran the major population centers of Java and Sumatra. On 24 Dec. the Security Council called for a cease-fire and release of the Indonesian leaders.

INDEPENDENCE OF INDONESIA. While the Dutch procrastinated over compliance with the Security Council's resolution, guerrilla activity against them increased. On 28 Jan., 1949, the Council again called for a cease-fire, the release of all prisoners, and the transfer of sovereignty to the Republic by 1 July, 1950. Under U.S. pressure, the Dutch reluctantly agreed to stop the war, effective 3 Aug., 1949. The Indonesian leaders were released, and a Dutch-Indonesian conference met on 23 Aug. Agreement was reached on Indonesian independence and the creation of a Netherlands-Indonesian Union. Sukarno became president of the United States of Indonesia, 16 Dec., which achieved independence, 27 Dec. It consisted of all the former Netherlands East Indies except West New Guinea (West Irian). (*Contd. p. 627.*)

1961–68

WEST IRIAN DISPUTE. Indonesia maintained its claim to West Irian, and when the Dutch inaugurated a partly elective New Guinea Council, 5 Apr., 1961, the Indonesians began landing troops there, Jan. 1962. As Dutch-Indonesian troop clashes spread, the UN persuaded the two sides to talk, and it was agreed to transfer sovereignty to a temporary UN administration and then to Indonesia. The UN took over West Irian on 1 Oct., 1962, and relinquished it to Indonesia on 1 May, 1963. A plebiscite was agreed for 1969.

Malaysia

1945–48

MALAYAN UNION. On 10 Oct., 1945, the British government announced plans to create a Malayan Union, and on 1 Apr., 1946, the Union was inaugurated. It comprised the former federated and unfederated Malay States, but Singapore became a crown colony. The Malays, fearing the loss of their privileged status to the Chinese, opposed the Union, and formed the United Malays' National Organization (UMNO) under Dato Onn bin Ja'afar (b. 1895).

FEDERATION OF MALAYA. Following consultations with UMNO, the Federation of Malaya was created, 1 Feb., 1948. The Malays retained certain citizenship privileges and their sultans their prerogatives. In June a Communist-led rebellion broke out, and on 12 July a state of emergency was declared. The emergency lasted until 1960, although the political appeal of the insurgents declined after the promise of Malayan independence in 1956. A total of 11,000

lives were lost during the period of the emergency.

1949–63

INDEPENDENCE OF MALAYA. On 24 May, 1954, the Alliance Party (a merger of UMNO and the Malayan Chinese Association) under Tunku Abdul Rahman (b. 1904) called for elections. When the British government refused, the Alliance boycotted the administration. The impasse ended, 7 July, when elections were announced for 25 July, 1955. The Alliance won 51 out of 53 elective seats and called for self-government. Anglo-Malayan talks held in Jan. 1956 produced a promise of independence by 31 Aug., 1957, and set up the Reid Commission to make constitutional proposals. The Commission recommended, 20 Feb., 1957, dual citizenship for British subjects in Malaya, which the Alliance rejected, and the inclusion of Penang and Malacca (but not Singapore) in the Federation, which was approved. On 3 July a new constitution was promulgated for Malaya which preserved Malay citizenship privileges, and Malaya became independent, 31 Aug., 1957.

INDEPENDENCE OF SINGAPORE. A constitution promulgated in Feb. 1955 created a Council of Ministers, and elections held on 2 Apr. made the Labour Front the leading party. Its leader, David Marshall (b. 1908), became chief minister and called for immediate self-government. Anglo-Singaporean constitutional talks broke down, however, 5 May, and Marshall resigned, 7 June, to be replaced as chief minister by Lim Yew Hock (b. 1914). On 4 Apr., 1957, an agreement was reached with the British government by which Singapore would become self-governing after 1 Jan., 1958. The elections of 31 May, 1959, resulted in a victory for the left-wing People's Action Party, whose leader Lee Kuan Yew (b. 1923) became prime minister. Self-government was finally achieved on 3 June, 1959.

CREATION OF MALAYSIA. A proposal to create a "Greater Malaysia" of

Malaya, Singapore, Brunei, North Borneo (Sabah), and Sarawak was put forward by the Malayan prime minister. The government of Singapore endorsed the suggestion, as did the Singaporean electorate in a referendum held on 1 Sept., 1962. A commission of inquiry discovered majority pro-Malaysian sentiment in Sarawak and North Borneo, Aug. 1962. On 8 Dec., 1962, an Indonesian-aided anti-Malaysian rebellion broke out in Brunei, whose sultan had accepted membership in Malaysia. On 8 July, 1963, the governments of Malaya, Singapore, Sabah, and Sarawak agreed on a constitution for Malaysia. Brunei did not join. A UN mission confirmed that majority opinion in Sabah and Sarawak favored the membership of those countries, and Malaysia came into existence, 16 Sept., 1963. (Contd. p. 628.)

Burma

1945–48

DOMINANCE OF THE AFPFL. On 27 Mar., 1945, the Burmese National Army rebelled against the Japanese and joined the allies. On 17 May the British promised eventual dominion status for Burma, but argued that this must be delayed until war damage had been repaired. An Executive Council of 9 British and 3 Burmese was appointed, 1 Nov., after the Anti-Fascist People's Freedom League (AFPFL), led by Aung San (1915–47), had refused to co-operate with the British administration without a definite promise of independence. Discontent with British procrastination led to a strike, Aug. 1946, and a guarantee of independence was obtained.

INDEPENDENCE. An interim Burmese government and the summoning of a Constituent Assembly were agreed to by the British, Jan. 1947, and in elections held the following Apr. AFPFL candidates won 172 out of 182 noncommunal seats. On 19 July Aung San and 6 other Burmese ministers were assassinated. U Nu (b. 1907) formed a new government, and on 11 Oct. the independence agreements were signed by Britain and Burma. On 4 Jan., 1948, Burma became independent, and elected not to remain a member of the Commonwealth. (Contd. p. 629.)

THE CARIBBEAN

British West Indies

1945–66

FEDERATION PROPOSALS. On 15 June, 1945, the British government announced acceptance of the idea of a West Indian federation if the people of the West Indies favored it. In Jan. 1947 the Windward and Leeward Islands agreed to set up a federation. On 9 Sept. representatives of all British West Indian territories met at Montego Bay, Jamaica. They agreed on the desirability of federation but disagreed on its form. The Standing Closer Association Committee set up by the conference called for a federation in its report of 10 Mar., 1950. During 1951–52 all territories except British Guiana, British Honduras, the Virgin Islands, and Barbados accepted the idea in principle. A conference on federation met, 13 Apr., 1953, and agreed on a capital in Grenada. Universal suffrage was progressively introduced in the British colonies: in Barbados in 1951, where elections were won by the Barbados Labour Party led by Grantley Adams (b. 1898), and in British Honduras and British Guiana in 1953.

GUIANA CRISIS OF 1953–54. Elections in British Guiana, Apr. 1953, were won by the People's Progressive Party (PPP), led by Cheddi Jagan (b. 1918), with 18 out of 24 seats. In Oct., the British government sent military reinforcements to Guiana and, 9 Oct., suspended the constitution and dismissed the government, claiming Jagan and his colleagues were Communists. On 20 Oct., a British White Paper claimed that the PPP government had shown no concern for the people's welfare, had used strikes for political purposes, had been under Communist influence, and had been promoting violence. On 2 Dec., the Robertson Commission was charged with recommending modifications to the Guiana constitution, and an interim government of officials was appointed, 27 Dec. On 18 Feb., 1954, Jagan was arrested for disobeying an order confining him to Georgetown and, 12 Apr., was jailed for 6 months. On 2 Nov. the Robertson Commission reported that the Jagan government had made the Guiana constitution unworkable, and recommended slowing down the colony's progress toward self-government.

FEDERATION OF THE WEST INDIES. In Feb. 1956, a further conference on federation met in London but failed to resolve renewed disagreement over the site of a capital. Elections in Trinidad, 24 Sept., were won by the People's National Movement (PNM) of Eric Williams (b. 1911). In Jan. 1957, a British Colonial Office commission named Barbados as the site for the capital of the federation. On 3 Jan., 1958, the Federation of the West Indies was inaugurated, consisting of all the British territories except Guiana and Honduras, with a capital in Trinidad. The 1st federal elections, 25 Mar., were won by the Federal Labour Party, led by Manley, Williams, and Adams, over the Democratic Labour Party of Bustamante. Adams became federal prime minister. In September 1959, a federal constitutional revision conference opened, with Jamaica insisting on representation in the legislature on the basis of population; no agreement was reached. On 3 Aug., 1960, the Federation received internal self-government.

INDEPENDENCE OF THE ISLAND COLONIES. In May 1961, Bustamante announced that he would oppose the Federation. In May–June 1961, a Federal Constitutional Conference agreed on independence for the Federation on 31 May, 1962, and revised the constitution to make the federal government very weak. In a referendum, 19 Sept., the Jamaican electorate voted to leave the Federation. Williams won elections in Trinidad, 4 Dec., 1961, and decided to leave the Federation. After talks held on 1–9 Feb., 1962, Jamaica and Britain agreed on independence for that colony on 6 Aug. During Feb.–Mar. 1962, delegates from the Leeward and Windward Islands and Barbados met to plan a little federation.

The West Indies Federation was dissolved, 31 May, 1962. On June 8, Trinidad and Britain agreed on independence on 31 Aug., 1962. In the Bahamas self-government was introduced, 7 Jan., 1964. In Nov. 1964, agreement was reached on a federation of Barbados, Antigua, Dominica, Montserrat, St. Kitts, St. Lucia, and St. Vincent. On 30 Dec., 1965, the British government proposed that the Leeward and Windward Islands become associate states of the United Kingdom. By early 1967 all had accepted this status except Montserrat.

BRITISH HONDURAS. Elections in British Honduras, 28 Apr., 1954, were won by the People's United Party (PUP), led by George Price, whose success was repeated in the 21 Mar., 1957, elections. Price called for closer co-operation with Central America. Constitutional talks with Britain broke down in Nov., however, when Price was found to be holding secret talks with a Guatemalan official. On 6 Dec. Price was expelled from the Legislative Council, and next day British troops landed at Belize. On 11 Dec. Mexico laid claim to British Honduras.

In the elections of Mar. 1961 the PUP won all seats, and Price became 1st minister. Internal self-government was introduced, 1 Jan., 1964.

SELF-GOVERNMENT IN GUIANA. In Feb. 1955 the PPP split as Jagan expelled a group led by Forbes Burnham (b. 1923). In Apr. 1956, despite Jagan's opposition, the British government established a Legislative Council composed of an equal number of nominated and elected members. In Mar. 1960 the governments of Britain and Guiana agreed on internal self-government for the colony during 1961.

Elections were held under a new constitution, Aug. 1960. The PPP won 20 seats to 11 gained by Burnham's People's National Congress. Jagan became prime minister and demanded full independence for Guiana. A proposed tax increase led to riots in Georgetown, Feb. 1962. Britain again sent troops to restore order, but a general strike lasted from 13 to 19 Feb. A constitutional conference, Oct.–Nov., failed to reach agreement. On

22 Apr., 1963, the British Guiana Trades Union Congress called a general strike to protest expected government action against trade unions. The strike produced violence, which took an increasingly racial turn, and lasted until 8 Aug. Further racial clashes, in which over 100 were killed, were associated with a sugar workers' strike, Jan.–July 1964, and an emergency was declared, 24 May. Citing the failure of Jagan and Burnham to agree on Guiana's constitutional progress,

the British imposed a new constitution based on proportional representation. Elections held on 7 Dec. gave the PPP 24 seats, the PNC 22, and the European United Force 7. Jagan refused to resign, calling the elections fraudulent. On 12 Dec. Burnham was summoned to form a government. The PPP boycotted the Assembly until 18 May 1965. Constitutional talks in London, 2–19 Nov., which Jagan would not attend, resulted in agreement that the colony, to be known as Guyana,

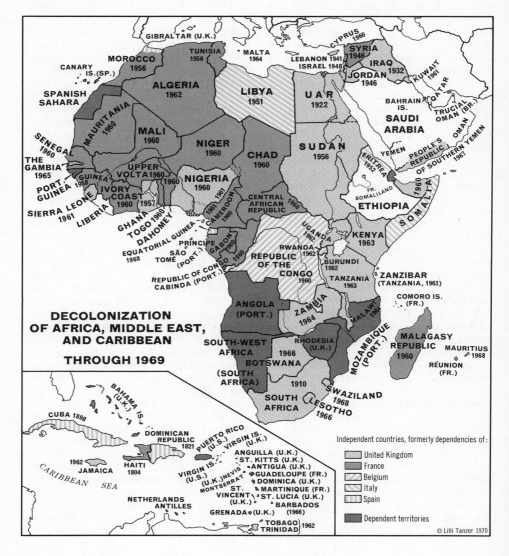

DECOLONIZATION
OF AFRICA, MIDDLE EAST,
AND CARIBBEAN

THROUGH 1969

Independent countries, formerly dependencies of:

United Kingdom
France
Belgium
Italy
Spain

Dependent territories

© Lilli Tanzer 1970

would become independent on 26 May, 1966. (*Contd. p. 610.*)

Other Territories

1945–61

FRENCH COLONIES. In accordance with the postwar French constitution, the colonies of Guadeloupe, Martinique, and French Guiana became departments of France by a law of 19 Mar., 1946. Each colony was to have an elected General Council and could send deputies to the metropolitan Parliament. In July 1961, a separatist movement, the Antillan and Guyanan Autonomy Front, was outlawed by the French government. Separatist activity continued, however, led by Aimé Césaire (b. 1913).

DUTCH COLONIES. On 3 June, 1954, representatives of the Netherlands, the Netherlands Antilles, and Surinam agreed on a constitution for a tripartite Kingdom of the Netherlands, with each region to control its own affairs and to be on an equal footing with the others. These arrangements became effective on 29 Dec.

PUERTO RICO. On 3 July, 1950, U.S. Public Law 600, ratified by the people of Puerto Rico by referendum on 4 June, 1951, went into effect: the law abolished the Organic Act of 1917 and authorized the Puerto Ricans to draw up a new constitution. This constitution, which gave Puerto Rico commonwealth status in relation to the U.S.A., was adopted by popular vote on 3 Mar., 1952, and became effective on 25 July. On 5 Nov., 1953, Luís Muñoz Marín, leader of the Popular Democratic Party, was elected governor.

AFRICA

French North Africa

1945–62

MOROCCO. Sultan Sidi Mohammed ben Youssef (1910–61) joined the *Istiqlal* call for independence in 1947. The French proposed minor reforms, but these were rejected as inadequate. Widespread vio-lence followed, resulting in the banning of the *Istiqlal* in 1952. In 1953 the sultan was deposed by the French and exiled. Continued violence led to his recall, Nov. 1955. A new, predominantly *Istiqlal* government negotiated for independence, which was promulgated on 2 Mar., 1956.

TUNISIA. Habib Bourguiba (b. 1903), expecting little from the French after the war, settled in Cairo and campaigned for a sovereign Tunisia. In 1949 he returned to Tunisia, but reforms were blocked by French settlers. The French government moved too slowly for the Tunisian nationalists, who increased their agitation, and Bourguiba was arrested, Jan. 1952. Violence erupted throughout Tunisia, and the government of Premier Mendes-France permitted his return, June 1955, after initiating negotiations, completed 3 June, designed to lead to Tunisian internal autonomy. Bourguiba suppressed dissidence in the nationalist ranks and Tunisia became independent, 20 Mar., 1956.

ALGERIA. Police suppression of riots in Setif, May 1945, led to the death of thousands of Moslems. Ferhat Abbas (b. 1899) was elected to the French Constituent Assembly. His UDMA (*Union Démocratique du Manifeste Algérien*) campaigned for a federal relationship between France and Algeria. The government of the 4th Republic, however, created an Algerian Assembly (Law of 20 Sept., 1947), elected, half by 1,300,000 Moslem voters and half by 370,000 French and 60,000 assimilated Moslem voters. The militant nationalists of Messali Hadj's PPA (*Parti Populaire Algérien*) founded, Oct. 1946, the MTLD (*Mouvement pour le Triomphe des Libertés Démocratiques*). The UDMA representatives lost their seats in the corrupt elections of 1948 and the MTLD became the dominant nationalist force. Abbas' continued efforts to negotiate with the French failed, while, within the MTLD, those favoring violent action in the face of French repression initiated "the Revolution," 1 Nov., 1954, and created the FLN (*Front de Libération Nationale*).

The French government replied with force, but terrorism spread, leading to

French and settler reprisals. The French army in Algeria reached 450,000 men. In 1956, the French by a ruse arrested and imprisoned 5 nationalist leaders, including Ahmed Ben Bella (b. 1916). Amidst growing international pressure for a settlement, the European settlers, fearing a compromise on the part of France, rebelled, May 1958. De Gaulle returned to power. In Sept. 1958 the nationalists set up a Provisional Government in Exile (GPRA) in Tunis with Abbas, who had joined the revolution in 1956, as president. (He was replaced by Youssef Ben Khedda, Aug. 1961.) In Sept. 1959 de Gaulle recognized the right of Algerians to self-determination. He repressed settler and military revolts, Jan. 1960, Dec. 1960, and Apr. 1961. After preliminary negotiations between the French and the FLN at Mélun, June 1960, had failed, a settlement was reached at Évian and a cease-fire declared, 18 Mar., 1962. In a referendum, 1 July, 1962, Algerians voted overwhelmingly for independence, which was proclaimed. (*Contd. p. 611.*)

British West Africa

1945–65

GOLD COAST. A new constitution was introduced in 1946 (the Burns Constitution), but was ill-received by nationalists because it retained a majority of indirectly elected chiefs. Discontented intellectuals united under Joseph B. Danquah (1895–1965) to form the United Gold Coast Convention (UGCC) to press for rapid constitutional progress. Danquah called Kwame Nkrumah (b. 1909) from London to be secretary of the UGCC, 1947. A UGCC-organized boycott led to rioting in urban centers, Feb. 1948. The Watson Commission recommended social, political, and educational reforms. Nkrumah rejected compromise and broke away from the UGCC to form the Convention People's Party (CPP), June 1949, calling for "self-government now." He organized a strike and was imprisoned, Jan. 1950. In elections held under a new constitution, Feb. 1951, the CPP won and Nkrumah was released to lead a new government. In 1954 constitutional

changes provided for direct elections to all seats and the CPP won 72 out of 104 seats contested in the elections of that year. Conservative opposition parties emerged to press for a federal form of government. This was rejected, and after new elections had indicated the continued majority of the CPP, the Gold Coast became independent as Ghana, 6 Mar., 1957.

NIGERIA. The Richards Constitution, 1946, provided for a federal Legislative Council dominated by traditional and official members and also for regional advisory bodies. Awolowo agreed to work with it, but Azikiwe boycotted it, pressing for a new constitution and Africanization of the civil service. The MacPherson Constitution, June 1951, set up a strong federal government, but soon proved unworkable. In 1951 Awolowo founded the western-based Action Group (AG), while in the north the conservative Northern People's Congress (NPC) emerged. In 1953 the British called a conference of Nigerian leaders, which worked out a new constitution (effective Oct. 1954). The NPC, dominated by Ahmadu Bello, *sardauna* of Sokoto (1909–1966), declined to heed a southern call for independence, 1956. The eastern and western regions became self-governing in 1957, and the northern in 1959. Further constitutional reforms provided for a federal prime minister, and Abubakar Tafawa Balewa (1912–66), vice-president of the NPC, was appointed to that office, 1957, heading an AG-NPC coalition. Elections in 1959 confirmed the power of the AG in the west, the NCNC in the east, and the NPC in the north; the new government was an NPC-NCNC coalition. Nigeria obtained her independence on 1 Oct., 1960.

SIERRA LEONE AND THE GAMBIA. Constitutional progress in Sierra Leone was hindered by the division between the colony and the protectorate. Internal self-government was granted, 1957, to a government led by Milton Margai (1895–1964), leader of the conservative, protectorate-based Sierra Leone People's Party, which led the country to independence, 27 Apr., 1961.

Proposals for a union of the Gambia

with Senegal failed, and the colony became independent within the Commonwealth, 18 Feb., 1965. (*Contd. p. 613*).

French Tropical Africa

1945-66

RISE OF NATIONALIST MOVEMENTS. The constitution of the 4th Republic made African subjects French citizens but retained the 2-college system for elections and gave only a limited number of citizens voting rights. It created territorial assemblies with federal Grand Councils for both West and Equatorial Africa; the territories elected deputies to the National Assembly in Paris.

At the initiative of Ivory Coast planter Félix Houphouet-Boigny (b. 1905) African leaders met in Bamako, Oct. 1946, and founded the interterritorial *Rassemblement Démocratique Africain* (RDA), 1947, to press for wider reforms. RDA worked with the Communists in the National Assembly and was repressed in Africa by the French administration.

In the late 40's many Africans were killed in political riots and many imprisoned. In Madagascar, there was a revolt, beginning in Mar. 1947, which took a year to suppress and resulted in many thousands of dead.

LOI-CADRE OF 1956. In Oct. 1950 Houphouet-Boigny broke with the Communists, but despite this the RDA was defeated in the elections of June 1951, leaving the IOM (*Indépendants d'Outre-mer*), led by Léopold Senghor (b. 1906) of Senegal, as the main African party in that colony. The French reversed their policy and began to work with a more moderate RDA; the franchise was gradually widened, and reforms culminated in the Loi-Cadre, enacted June 1956, in effect Feb. 1957. The Loi-Cadre provided for adult suffrage, for elections to the territorial assemblies, and for each assembly to elect a responsible Council of Government with an African vice-president and wide powers.

ACHIEVEMENT OF INDEPENDENCE. Togo became an autonomous republic within the French Union, Aug. 1956. The legislature of the French Cameroons received increased powers and the French initiated strong military action against the rebellion of the *Union des Populations du Cameroun,* a dissident branch of RDA.

In the territorial elections of Mar. 1957 the RDA won outright control in the Ivory Coast, Sudan, and Guinea. Houphouet-Boigny, a French minister since 1956, called an RDA conference at Bamako, Sept. 1957, at which disputes over federation with France were not resolved.

In the referendum on the new constitution of the 5th Republic, Sept. 1958, all territories voted for autonomy within the new French Community, except Guinea, where Sékou Touré (b. 1922) opted for independence. Attempts to refederate the territories, opposed by Ivory Coast, led to the creation of the Federation of Mali by Senegal and Sudan, 1959, while Ivory Coast, Upper Volta, Dahomey, and Niger formed the Council of the Entente, 1959. Mali demanded independence, Sept. 1959, and Malagasy did the same. All territories became independent in 1960.

French Somaliland, Réunion, and the Comoros remained as France's only African possessions after the independence of Algeria, 1962. In August 1966 de Gaulle's visit to Djibouti sparked proindependence riots. France announced a referendum on independence. (*Contd. p. 613.*)

British East Africa

1945-63

UGANDA. Buganda separatism was strong after the war, and the Baganda, rejecting any diminution of the powers of their Kabaka, Frederick Mutesa II (b. 1924), opposed increased African elected representation in the Legislative Council. In 1953 the Buganda legislature, supported by the Kabaka, asked for separate independence. The British refused and deported the Kabaka. He was allowed to return, Oct. 1955, after reforms had been negotiated providing for an enlarged Legislative Council, a ministerial system, and a promise of Baganda co-operation. African parties remained weak until the amalgamation of non-Baganda parties,

1960, to form the Uganda People's Congress (UPC) under Milton Obote (b. 1924) and the invigoration of the Democratic Party, founded 1956, by Benededicto Kiwanuke (b. 1922). In the elections of 1962, the UPC won in alliance with the Kabaka's party and Uganda became independent, 9 Oct., 1962.

KENYA. White settlers opposed the moderate reforms demanded by the Kenya African Union led by Jomo Kenyatta (b. 1893). Pressure on land and political frustration among the Kikuyu led to the growth of secret societies, culminating in the Mau Mau uprising, 1952–56. Between 1952 and 1955, 10,173 Mau Mau members were killed; terrorists killed 32 Europeans, 24 Asians, and 291 Africans. Kenyatta was arrested, found guilty of leading Mau Mau, and imprisoned. As the rebellion faded out, constitutional reforms widened African representation on the Legislative Council. The Kenya African National Congress (KANU) was founded, 1960, and Kenyatta took over its leadership after his release, Aug. 1961. KANU won the elections of May 1963, and Kenyatta led Kenya to independence, 12 Dec., 1963, as prime minister.

TANGANYIKA AND ZANZIBAR. Tanganyika, a UN trust territory, progressed toward independence as the British government came under increasing UN pressure. The Tanganyika African National Union (TANU) was founded, 1954, by Julius Nyerere (b. 1921) and soon had the support of virtually all Tanganyikans. Tanganyika became independent, 9 Dec., 1961.

In Zanzibar, rivalry between the dominant Arab group and the African population produced frequent clashes. At independence, 10 Dec., 1963, the Arabs retained power. (*Contd. p. 618.*)

British Central and Southern Africa

1945–68

FEDERATION OF RHODESIA. European settlers, whose numbers rose sharply after 1945, pressed the British government to create a federation of Northern and Southern Rhodesia and Nyasaland, where African rights were very limited. At the Victoria Falls Conference, 1949, white leaders, including Roy Welensky (b. 1907) and Godfrey Huggins (b. 1883), agreed on a federation, which the British government accepted. African opposition was strong and organized in the Northern Rhodesia African National Congress, led by Harry Nkumbula (b. 1916); the Southern Rhodesia African National Congress, led by Joshua Nkomo (b. 1917); and the Nyasaland African National Congress, inspired from London by Hastings Banda (b. 1902). Over African opposition, the Federation was created, 1953, with 6 Africans representing in Parliament 8 m. Africans and 29 whites representing 300,000 whites.

INDEPENDENCE. African opposition to the Federation continued and, despite settler pressure, Britain introduced electoral reforms in Nyasaland and Northern Rhodesia. Banda returned to Nyasaland, 1958, to fight federation. The federal government banned the Nyasaland ANC, 1959, and arrested Banda. The ANC was replaced by the Malawi Congress Party which won 90% of the vote in the elections of 1961. The Northern Rhodesia ANC was banned in 1959 and replaced by the United National Independence Party (UNIP), led by Kenneth Kaunda (b. 1924). In 1960 the British-appointed Monckton Commission proposed that each territory be empowered to leave the Federation, and the Federation was dissolved, 1963, after the departure of Nyasaland and Northern Rhodesia. New constitutions introduced in those territories provided for elected African majorities, and independence was granted. In Southern Rhodesia a new constitution had been imposed in 1961, providing for gradually increasing African rights. The settlers pressed for independence, but the British government refused. The settlers, led by Ian Smith (b. 1919), declared unilateral independence, Nov. 1965.

SOUTH-WEST AFRICA. In 1946 Chief Hosea Kutako rejected South African proposals to incorporate South-West Africa, a former League of Nations mandated territory, in the Union, and asked the UN to terminate the mandate. South Africa rejected this course. In 1950, the

International Court of Justice advised that the General Assembly had supervisory rights over South-West Africa. On 18 July, 1966, the International Court declared that Ethiopia and Liberia, which were trying to have the Court rule on whether or not South Africa had violated the mandate by imposing apartheid in South-West Africa, had no standing in the matter.

HIGH COMMISSION TERRITORIES. In 1950, the United Kingdom government banished the Bamangwato chief in Bechuanaland, Seretse Khama (b. 1921), but, at Bamangwato insistence, allowed him to return in 1956. In July 1958, the Cowen Report recommended the creation of elected organs of government in Basutoland. In local elections, 1960, the Basutoland Congress Party, led by Ntsue Mokhlehle (b. 1918), won 73 out of 162 seats. The 1st general elections in Bechuanaland, Mar. 1965, were won by Seretse Khama's Bechuanaland Democratic Party; he was named prime minister, and Bechuanaland became the independent Republic of Botswana, 30 Sept., 1966. Basutoland elections, Apr. 1965, were won by the Basutoland National Party whose leader, Leabua Jonathan, became prime minister; Basutoland became independent Lesotho on 4 Oct., 1966. The 3rd High Commission Territory, Swaziland, became independent on 6 Sept., 1968.

The Sudan and Ex-Italian Africa

1945–60

ANGLO-EGYPTIAN SUDAN. Anglo-Egyptian talks to revise the Condominium failed, Jan. 1947. Egypt demanded the union of Egypt and the Sudan, and in 1951 abrogated the condominium arrangement unilaterally. Union with Egypt was advocated by Ismail al-Azhari (b. 1902), leader of the National Unionists Party (NUP), whereas the Umma ('Umma) Party of Abdullah Khalil (b. 1888) rejected union. Under nationalist pressure, Britain evolved a Self-Government Statute, 1952, but the new Neguib government of Egypt and the NUP pressed for changes, which were incorporated in an Anglo-Egyptian agreement of 12 Feb.,

1953. The NUP won the elections of 1953, and al-Azhari became prime minister. The Sudan became independent on 1 Jan., 1956.

EX-ITALIAN COLONIES. Failing agreement among the Big 4, the disposal of the Italian colonies was referred to the UN General Assembly, as agreed at the Yalta Conference. In Libya, nationalists led by Sayyid Idris (b. 1890) pressed for independence. In 1949, the UN Assembly called for the union of Cyrenaica, Tripolitania, and the Fezzan in an independent state, and in 1950 a National Assembly was convened, which drew up a constitution. Libya became independent, 24 Dec., 1951, with Sayyid Idris as king. The Assembly sent a commission to Eritrea, which failed to agree on recommendations. In Nov. 1950, the Assembly called for the federation of Eritrea with Ethiopia, and this went into effect, 15 Sept., 1952. In Somalia, the Somali Youth League (SYL, founded 1943) opposed an Italian trusteeship and called for independence within 10 years and the formation of a Greater Somalia. The Assembly voted to create an Italian trusteeship, which began on 1 Apr., 1950. The Italians encouraged the creation of parties. In municipal elections, 1954, the SYL remained the leading party. In 1956 the 1st general elections in Somalia under universal suffrage were won by the SYL, whose leader, Abdullahi Issa (b. 1922), became prime minister. Somalia united with British Somaliland and became independent, 1 July, 1960, with Aden Abdullah Osman (b. 1908), president of the SYL, as president.

Belgian and Portuguese Africa

1945–62

BELGIAN AFRICA. In 1955 a Belgian liberal manifesto called for a program leading to Congolese independence in 30 years. The 1st municipal elections in the Congo were held in 1957, and the *Mouvement National Congolaise* of Patrice Lumumba (1925–1961) achieved national prominence. Riots in Léopoldville, Jan. 1959, were followed by further reforms. In Jan. 1960 Belgian and Congolese leaders met in Brussels and agreed on 30 June, 1960, as independence date. After elections in May a government was formed with Lumumba as prime minister and Joseph Kasavubu (b. 1910), leader of ABAKO, as president.

The Belgian change of policy also affected Ruanda-Urundi. In 1959 in Ruanda, the Bahutu overthrew the ruling Batutsi and created a republic. Belgian trusteeship ended, 1 July, 1962, and Ruanda (Rwanda) and Urundi (Burundi) became separate independent states.

PORTUGUESE AFRICA. In June 1951 Portugal declared her African colonies integral parts of Portugal, though less than 0.50% of the African population had gained *assimilado* status. A develop-

ment plan was launched and settlement by Portuguese encouraged. (The white population of Angola rose from 44,000 in 1940 to 200,000 in 1959.) African nationalist activity was not tolerated. In 1961 a revolt broke out in Angola, led by the Union of Angolan Peoples under Holden Roberto (b. 1925). In 1963 revolts broke out in Portuguese Guinea led by Amilcar Cabral (b. 1927) and the African Party for the Independence of Guinea and Cape Verde (FLING), and in Mozambique led by the Front for the Liberation of Mozambique (FRELIMO) under Eduardo Mondlane. The Portuguese sent large armies to all 3 countries, but failed to suppress the uprisings.

THE EVOLUTION OF DEPENDENT TERRITORIES

1945		1968	
Name	*Status*	*Name*	*Status*
Africa			
Algeria	Part of France	Algeria	Indep. (3 July, 1962)
Angola	Port. colony	Angola	Overseas territory of Portugal (11 June, 1951)
Basutoland	Br. colony	Losotho	Indep. (4 Oct., 1966)
Bechuanaland	Br. protectorate	Botswana	Indep. (30 Sept., 1966)
Cameroun (Fr.)	Fr. trust territory	Cameroun	Indep. (1 Jan., 1960)
Cameroons (Br.)			
Southern	Br. trust territory	—	Part of Cameroun (1 Oct., 1961)
Northern	Br. trust territory	—	Part of Nigeria (1 June, 1961)
Congo, Belgian	Belg. colony	Congo (Kinshasa)	Indep. (30 June, 1960)
Cape Verde Is.	Port. colony	Cape Verde Is.	Overseas territory of Portugal (11 June, 1951)
Comoro Is.	Fr. colony	Comoro Is.	Overseas territory of France (internal self-government, 22 Dec. 1961)
Eritrea	Ex-Ital. colony under Br. administration	—	Part of Ethiopia (11 Sept., 1952)
Fr. Equatorial Africa:			
Chad		Chad	Indep. (11 Aug., 1960)
Gabon	Fr. colony	Gabon	Indep. (17 Aug., 1960)
Moyen-Congo		Congo (Brazzaville)	Indep. (15 Aug., 1960)
Ubangui-Chari		Central African Republic	Indep. (13 Aug., 1960)

1945		1968	
Name	*Status*	*Name*	*Status*
Fr. West Africa: Dahomey		Dahomey	Indep. (1 Aug., 1960)
French Guinea		Guinea	Indep. (2 Oct., 1958)
French Sudan[a]		Mali	Indep. (20 July, 1960)
Ivory Coast	Fr. colony	Ivory Coast	Indep. (7 Aug., 1960)
Mauritania		Mauritania	Indep. (28 Nov., 1960)
Niger		Niger	Indep. (3 Aug., 1960)
Senegal[a]		Senegal	Indep. (20 July, 1960)
Upper Volta[b]		Upper Volta	Indep. (5 Aug., 1960)
Gambia	Br. colony	The Gambia	Indep. (18 Feb., 1965)
Gold Coast	Br. colony	Ghana	Indep. (6 Mar., 1957)
Kenya	Br. colony & protectorate	Kenya	Indep. (12 Dec., 1963)
Libya	ex-Ital. colony under Br. and Fr. adminstration	Libya	Indep. (24 Dec., 1951)
Madagascar	Fr. colony	Malagasy	Indep. (26 June, 1960)
Mauritius	Br. colony	Mauritius	Indep. (12 Mar., 1968)
Morocco (Fr.)	Fr. protectorate	Morocco	Indep. (2 Mar., 1956)
Morocco (Sp.)	Sp. protectorate	—	Part of Morocco (7 Apr., 1956)
Mozambique	Port. colony	Mozambique	Overseas province of Portugal (11 June, 1951)
Nigeria	Br. colony and protectorate	Nigeria	Indep. (1 Oct., 1960)
Northern Rhodesia	Br. colony	Zambia	Indep. (24 Oct., 1964)
Nyasaland	Br. protectorate	Malawi	Indep. (6 July, 1964)
Port. Guinea (Bissau)	Port. colony	Port. Guinea	Overseas province of Portugal (11 June, 1951)
Réunion	Fr. colony	Réunion	Overseas department of France (1 Jan., 1947)
Ruanda-Urundi	Belg. trust territory	Rwanda	Indep. (1 July, 1962)
		Burundi	Indep. (1 July, 1962)
St. Helena	Br. colony	St. Helena	Br. colony
São Tomé and Principe	Port. colony	São Tomé and Principe	Overseas territory of Portugal (11 June, 1951)

1945		1968	
Name	*Status*	*Name*	*Status*
Seychelles	Br. colony	Seychelles	Br. colony
Sierra Leone	Br. colony and pro-tectorate	Sierra Leone	Indep. (27 Apr., 1961)
Somaliland (Br.) c	Br. colony	—	Part of Somalia (1 July, 1960)
Somaliland (Fr.)	Fr. colony	Fr. territory of the Afars and Issas	Fr. overseas ter-ritory (2 July, 1967)
Somaliland (ex-Ital.) d	Ex-Ital. colony under Br. ad-ministration	Somalia	Indep. (1 July, 1960)
South-West Africa	South African mandate	South-West Africa	South African mandate
Southern Rhodesia	Br. colony	Rhodesia	Br. colony; *de facto* indep. (11 Nov., 1965)
Sp. Equatorial Africa	Sp. colony	Equatorial Guinea	Indep. (12 Oct., 1968)
Sudan (Anglo-Egyptian)	Anglo-Egyptian condominium	Sudan	Indep. (1 Jan., 1956)
Swaziland	Br. colony	Swaziland	Indep. (6 Sept., 1968)
Tanganyikae	Br. trust territory	Tanzania	Indep. (9 Dec., 1961)
Tangier	International city	—	Part of Morocco (29 Oct., 1956)
Togoland (Br.)	Br. trust territory	—	Part of Ghana (6 Mar., 1961)
Togoland (Fr.)	Fr. trust territory	Togo	Indep. (27 Apr., 1960)
Tunisia	Fr. protectorate	Tunisia	Indep. (20 Mar., 1956)
Uganda	Br. protectorate	Uganda	Indep. (9 Oct., 1962)
Zanzibare	Br. protectorate	—	Part of Tanzania (26 Apr., 1964)
The Americas			
Alaska	U.S. territory	—	Part of U.S.A. (3 Jan., 1959)
Bahamas	Br. colony	Bahamas	Br. colony
Barbados	Br. colony	Barbados	Indep. (30 Nov., 1966)
Bermuda	Br. colony	Bermuda	Br. colony
Br. Guiana	Br. colony	Guyana	Indep. (26 May, 1966)
Br. Honduras	Br. colony	Br. Honduras	Br. colony
Cayman Is.	Br. colony	Cayman Is.	Br. colony
Falkland Is. and Dependencies	Br. colony	Falkland Is. and Dependencies	Br. colony
Fr. Guiana	Fr. colony	Fr. Guiana	Overseas depart-ment of France (11 June, 1947)
Greenland	Danish colony	—	Part of Denmark (5 June, 1953)
Guadeloupe	Fr. colony	Guadeloupe	Overseas depart-ment of France (1 Jan., 1947)

1945		1968	
Name	*Status*	*Name*	*Status*
Leeward Is.[f] Antigua St. Kitts-Nevis- Anguilla Montserrat	} Br. colony	Leeward Is.	Associated states of the U.K. (27 Feb., 1967, for Antigua and St. Kitts-Nevis-Anguilla)
		Montserrat	Br. colony
Martinique	Fr. colony	Martinique	Overseas department of France (1 Jan., 1947)
Jamaica	Br. colony	Jamaica	Indep. (6 Aug., 1962)
Neth. Antilles	Dutch colony	—	Part of Kingdom of the Netherlands (29 Dec., 1954)
Newfoundland	Br. colony governed by commission	—	Part of Canada (31 Mar., 1949)
Panama Canal Zone	U.S. leased territory	Panama Canal Zone	U.S. leased territory
Puerto Rico	U.S. colony	Puerto Rico	Commonwealth (3 July, 1952)
St. Pierre and Miquelon	Fr. colony	St. Pierre and Miquelon	Overseas dept. of France (1 Jan., 1947)
Surinam	Dutch colony	—	Part of Kingdom of the Netherlands (29 Dec., 1954)
Trinidad and Tobago	Br. colony	Trinidad and Tobago	Indep. (31 Aug., 1962)
Turks and Caicos Is.	Br. colony	Turks and Caicos Is.	Br. colony
Virgin Is. (Br.)	Br. colony[g]	Virgin Is. (Br.)	Br. colony
Virgin Is. (U.S.)	U.S. colony	Virgin Is. (U.S.)	U.S. colony
Windward Is.[h] Dominica Grenada St. Lucia St. Vincent	} Br. colony	Windward Is.	Associated states of the U.K. (1 Mar., 1967, for St. Lucia and Dominica; 3 Mar., 1967, for Grenada)
Asia Aden Colony	Br. colony	—	Part of People's Republic of Southern Yemen
Aden Protectorate	Br. protectorate	People's Republic of Southern Yemen	Indep. (28 Nov., 1967)
Brunei	Br. protectorate	Brunei	Br. protectorate
Burma	Br. colony	Burma	Indep. (4 Jan., 1948)
Ceylon	Br. colony	Ceylon	Indep. (4 Feb., 1948)
Christmas Is.	Br. colony	Christmas Is.	Australian dependency (11 Oct., 1958)
Cocos Is.	Br. colony	Cocos Is.	Australian dependency (3 Nov., 1955)
Cyprus	Br. colony	Cyprus	Indep. (16 Aug., 1960)

1945		1968	
Name	*Status*	*Name*	*Status*
Fr. India: Chandernagore Karikal Mahé Pondichérry Yanaon	Fr. Colony	— — — — —	Part of India (9 June, 1952) Part of India (28 May, 1956)
Fr. Indochina Cambodia		Cambodia	Indep. (9 Nov., 1953)
Laos	Fr. Colony	Laos	Indep. (29 Dec., 1954)
Vietnam		North Vietnam	Indep. (declared 2 Sept., 1945; Geneva Agreement, 21 July, 1954)
		South Vietnam	Indep. (29 Dec., 1954)
Hong Kong	Br. colony	Hong Kong	Br. colony
India	Part of Br. Empire	India	Indep. (15 Aug., 1947)
		Pakistan	Indep. (15 Aug., 1947)
Korea	North, under Russian occupation	People's Republic of Korea	Indep. (8 Sept., 1948)
	South, under U.S. occupation	Republic of Korea	Indep. (15 Aug., 1948)
Kuwait	Br. protectorate	Kuwait	Indep. (19 June, 1961)
Macao	Port. colony	Macao	Overseas territory of Portugal (11 June, 1951)
Malayan Union[l]	Br. colony	Malaysia	Indep. (31 Aug., 1957)
Maldive Is.	Br. protectorate	Maldive Is.	Indep. (26 July, 1965)
Neth. East Indies[j]	Dutch colony	Indonesia	Indep. (27 Dec., 1950)
North Borneo	Br. protectorate	Sabah	Part of Malaysia (16 Sept., 1963)
Palestine[k]	Br. mandate	Israel	Proclaimed (14 May, 1948)
Philippines	U.S. colony	Philippines	Indep. (4 July, 1946)
Port. India (Goa, Daman, Diu)	Port. colony	—	Part of India (20 Dec., 1961)
Port. Timor	Port. colony	Port. Timor	Overseas territory of Portugal (11 June, 1951)
Ryukyu Is.	U.S. military occupied territory	Ryukyu Is.	U.S. administered territory (8 Sept., 1951)
Sarawak	Br. protectorate	Sarawak	Part of Malaysia (16 Sept., 1963)
Sikkim	Br. protectorate	Sikkim	Indian protectorate (15 Aug., 1947)

1945		1968	
Name	*Status*	*Name*	*Status*
Singapore[1]	Br. colony	Singapore	Indep. (16 Sept., 1963)
Transjordan	Br. mandate	Jordan	Indep. (22 Mar., 1946)
Trucial Oman	Br. protected state	Trucial Oman	Br. protected state
Europe			
Gibraltar	Br. colony	Gibraltar	Br. colony
Malta	Br. colony	Malta	Indep. (21 Sept., 1964)
Oceania			
Amer. Samoa	U.S. territory	Amer. Samoa	U.S. territory
Fiji	Br. colony	Fiji	Br. colony
Fr. Polynesia	Fr. colony	Fr. Polynesia	Fr. overseas territory (13 Oct., 1946)
Gilbert and Ellice Is.	Br. colony	Gilbert and Ellice Is.	Br. colony
Guam	U.S. territory	Guam	U.S. territory
Hawaii	U.S. territory	Hawaii	Part of U.S.A. (11 Mar, 1959)
New Caledonia	Fr. colony	New Caledonia	Fr. overseas territory (13 Oct, 1946)
New Hebrides	Anglo-Fr. condominium	New Hebrides	Anglo-Fr. condominium
Solomon Is.	Br. protectorate	Solomon Is.	Br. protectorate
Tonga	Br. protectorate	Tonga	Br. protectorate
Western Samoa	N.Z. trust territory	Western Samoa	Indep. (1 Jan., 1962)

a French Sudan and Senegal became independent as Mali, 20 July, 1960; the federation broke up, 22 Aug., 1960.

b Upper Volta was recreated as a distinct unit, 4 July, 1947, out of areas of the Ivory Coast, French Sudan, and Niger.

c Br. Somaliland became independent, 26 June, 1960, and joined Ital. Somaliland when it also achieved independence, 1 July, 1960.

d Ex-Ital. Somaliland became an Ital. trust territory before achieving independence as Somalia.

e Zanzibar became independent, 10 Dec., 1963, and united with Tanganyika, 26 Apr., 1964. The union was named the United Republic of Tanzania, 29 Oct., 1964.

f The Leeward Is. Federation was dissolved, 1 Jan., 1960. Antigua and St. Kitts-Nevis-Anguilla acquired self-government, 27 Feb., 1967, within the West Indies Associated States.

g Until 1 July, 1956, administered as part of Leeward Is.

h The Windward Is. Federation was dissolved, 1 Jan., 1960.

i The Malayan Union, formed Sept. 1945, was replaced by the Federation of Malaya, 31 Aug., 1957, which in turn became the Federation of Malaysia, 16 Sept., 1963.

j West New Guinea (West Irian) remained under Dutch control and did not become part of Indonesia until 1 May, 1963.

k Following the 1st Arab-Israeli War, Dec. 1948, Transjordan incorporated Arab Palestine and changed its name to Jordan, 2 June, 1949.

l Singapore joined Malaysia at its inception, 16 Sept., 1963, and left the Federation to become a sovereign state, 9 Aug., 1965.

The Cold War

THE COLLAPSE OF THE WARTIME ALLIANCE

1945

THE ALLIANCE IN 1945. It was President Roosevelt's hope that the alliance of Britain, the U.S., and the Soviet Union would continue into the postwar world. The newly formed United Nations, with its numerous supporting agencies, was intended both as a forum in which disputes might be settled peacefully and an effective means whereby postwar recovery might be carried through.

In this perspective, the Yalta Agreements were designed to allow France a powerful voice in Western Europe and Britain a commanding role in the Mediterranean world; the Soviet Union's influence in Eastern Europe was recognized and all 4 wartime partners would combine in controlling Germany.

The defeat of Germany and Japan served to loosen the bonds among the wartime allies. President Roosevelt died, April 1945; the subsequent years witnessed a gradual return to the hostile atmosphere of an earlier period. The

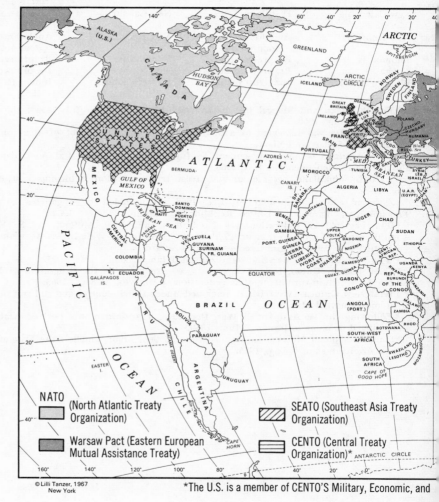

NATO (North Atlantic Treaty Organization)

Warsaw Pact (Eastern European Mutual Assistance Treaty)

SEATO (Southeast Asia Treaty Organization)

CENTO (Central Treaty Organization)*

© Lilli Tanzer, 1967
New York

*The U.S. is a member of CENTO'S Military, Economic, and

competing pressures of 2 rival world systems definitively stamped the postwar decade as a period of Cold War tensions.

1946–47

THE IRON CURTAIN. In a speech at Fulton, Mo., 15 Mar., 1946, Sir Winston Churchill, while noting Russia's anxiety "to be secure on her western frontiers by the removal of all possibility of German aggression," called for closer Anglo-American co-operation to meet the challenge of a situation in which "from Stettin in the Baltic to Trieste in the Adriatic, an Iron Curtain has descended across the Continent."

TRUMAN DOCTRINE. In Mar. 1947 President Truman enunciated in a speech to the American Congress a policy later to be known as the Truman Doctrine. In a clear warning to the USSR he announced that for the future the U.S. "would support free peoples who are resisting subjugation by armed minorities or by outside pressure."

RIVAL POLITICAL PARTIES IN GERMANY. In Germany, a primary area of conflict, attempts at a quadripartite administration were defeated by Soviet refusal to co-operate in furnishing information and statistical returns. In Apr. 1946 the Communist Party in the Soviet zone formed an alliance with the Social Democrats in a new German Socialist Unity Party (*Sozialistische Einheitspartei Deutschlands*, SED) . During 1946–47 elections were held in all zones of Germany. The SED won in the Soviet zone, and in the American, French, and British zones

THE COLD WAR
Members of Politico-Military Alliances

WEU (Western European Union)

ANZUS

ASPAC (Asian and Pacific Council)

ASEAN (Association of Southeast Asian Nations)

Counter-Subversion Committees

the Christian Democratic and Social Democratic parties topped the polls.

OCCUPATION ZONE POLICIES. In May 1946 General Lucius Clay (b. 1897), the American commander, suspended reparation deliveries to the Russian zone in retaliation for Soviet intransigence. Secretary of State James F. Byrnes announced at Stuttgart, Sept. 1946, the pending fusion of the American and British zones; and on 2 Dec. an agreement was signed between Byrnes and British Foreign Secretary Ernest Bevin. The Soviet zone gradually became a Communist state. The Junker estates in East Prussia were divided up, and a "People's Police" was armed as a paramilitary force.

WESTERN EUROPEAN ECONOMIC RECOVERY. On 10 Mar.–24 Apr., 1947, the Council of Foreign Ministers of the great powers met in Moscow to draft peace treaties for Austria and Germany, but no agreement was reached. On 12–15 July, 16 West European delegates and 9 from the Soviet bloc met in Paris to discuss plans for European recovery (the Marshall Plan). The ministers agreed to draft a European Recovery Program (ERP), the Soviet bloc declining to join on the grounds that such a plan depended on American financing. After the withdrawal of the Soviet and East European delegates, Austria, Belgium, Britain, Denmark, Ireland, France, Greece, Iceland, Italy, Luxembourg, the Netherlands, Norway, Portugal, Sweden, Switzerland, and Turkey set up a Committee of European Economic Co-operation (CEEC). The Committee's report (the Paris Report) outlined a scheme of exchange control and tariff reduction among the members and special dollar credits were made available by the U.S.

ESTABLISHMENT OF THE COMINFORM. In Sept. 1947 a Warsaw Conference of the Communist parties of the Soviet Union, Poland, Czechoslovakia, Hungary, Rumania, Bulgaria, Italy, and France established the Communist Information Bureau (Cominform), which, with headquarters in Belgrade, would serve as an "exchange of experience and the coordination of activities."

A further meeting of the Big 4 foreign ministers, 25 Nov.–15 Dec., failed to agree on a German settlement, and the Foreign Ministers' Council adjourned indefinitely.

1948–49

BRUSSELS TREATY AND OEEC. In Feb. 1948 the U.S., Britain, and France conferred in London on the question of German participation in the ERP. On 17 Mar. the Brussels Treaty was signed by Britain, France, and the "Benelux" countries (Belgium, Netherlands, and Luxembourg). It provided for a 50-year defensive alliance against armed attack in Europe and set up a Permanent Military Committee in London. On 20 Mar. Soviet Commander-Marshal Sokolovsky resigned from the Allied Control Council, and on 16 Apr. the 16 nations of the ERP established the Organization for European Economic Co-operation (OEEC).

BERLIN BLOCKADE. On 18 June, 1948, currency reforms were instituted in the western zones of Germany. The new Deutschemark was established in West Germany and in the western sector of Berlin. It was banned in the Soviet zone as well as in Soviet Berlin. From Jan. 1948 onward French, British, and American traffic to and from Berlin, which lay in the Soviet zone, was being stopped and searched. Gradually a blockade of Berlin cut all access by canal, road, and rail, thereby necessitating the Berlin Airlift, which carried tons of supplies daily to the city.

On 31 July diplomatic talks between the West and the Soviets began; by the end of Aug. a draft directive on a currency for Berlin was agreed on but broken almost immediately. In Feb. 1949 the U.S. and British forces set up a blockade to halt all traffic across the eastern boundaries of their respective zones.

ESTABLISHMENT OF NATO. On 4 Apr., 1949, a North Atlantic Treaty was signed in Washington by Britain, Belgium, Italy, the Netherlands, Denmark, Luxembourg, Portugal, Iceland, Norway, Canada, and the U.S.; it promised mutual assistance against the Soviet Union in a defensive pact under the guidance of a North Atlantic Council.

In May 1949 the Soviet government raised the Berlin blockade after 18 months of the airlift. The same month saw elections in the Soviet zone of Germany and a government under predominantly Communist leadership. The zone was renamed the German Democratic Republic (GDR), 5 Oct., 1949.

Western foreign ministers meeting in New York, 12–19 Sept., agreed to include West Germany in the system of western defense. Soviet Deputy Premier Molotov met at Prague, 20 Oct., with the foreign ministers of the GDR, Bulgaria, Hungary, and Rumania, and denounced West German participation in military alliances. On 20 Dec., 1949, the Brussels Treaty powers fused their military arrangements with those of the North Atlantic Treaty Organization (NATO).

1950–64

THE BERLIN WALL. In June 1961 the Cold War over Berlin took a serious turn. At the Vienna meeting of President Kennedy and Chairman Khrushchev, the Soviet leader called for a separate treaty with the GDR, leaving the West to negotiate arrangements with the East German government on the use of road, canal, and railway routes. Secretary of State Dean Rusk rejected these terms at a NATO Council meeting, 11 June.

In the first 10 days of July, over 1,000 refugees flooded daily into West Berlin from the east. Food and fuel rationing were introduced by the East German government. By the end of July over 13,000 had crossed. Checks and controls were increased on road and rail links. On 1 Aug. East Berliners working in West Berlin had their identity cards confiscated, and on 13 Aug. the borders were closed. This closure was made permanent, 18 Aug., by the erection of a 5-ft. concrete wall topped with broken glass and barbed wire. On 22 Aug. all crossing points except one were closed to "foreigners." A Soviet note, 23 Aug., accused the western powers of violating the 1945 agreements and called

for 4-power (including Soviet) control of the air corridors. The 3 western powers replied, 26 Aug., and denied any "competence of the Soviet Union" to discuss the use of the air corridors. On 13 Sept. a Soviet statement denied that the suggestion for a separate Soviet–East German peace treaty was an "ultimatum." A 300-ft. zone along the 25-mi. frontier between East and West was bulldozed. On 25 Oct. American tanks moved up to the checkpoint and British and French troops arrived at the border; Soviet tanks also moved up, 27 Oct., only to withdraw after 16 hours; this was followed shortly afterward by the withdrawal of U.S. tanks. The year ended with a continuing series of harassing incidents.

An agreement was eventually negotiated permitting West Berliners to visit East Berlin during Christmas 1963, and a pass accord was agreed upon, Sept. 1964, which allowed West Berliners to visit the other sector of the city on certain fixed occasions.

KOREA

1945–49

ESTABLISHMENT OF NORTH AND SOUTH KOREA. At the Cairo Conference, 1943, the U.S., Britain, and China had declared for Korea's independence, later confirmed at Potsdam, 1945. On 9 Aug., 1945, Soviet troops entered Korea and accepted the surrender of Japanese forces north of the 38th parallel, 15 Aug. U.S. troops arrived, 8 Sept., to accept the Japanese surrender in the south. A temporary military arrangement was agreed, using the 38th parallel as a dividing line.

On 8 May, 1946, the U.S. and the USSR negotiated unsuccessfully to form a national Korean government. The USSR sponsored elections in North Korea, Nov., and set up an administration under the Communist leader Kim Il Sung (b. 1912). A meeting of a U.S.-USSR commission on Korea which began 13 May, 1947, broke down on 8 July. On 14 Nov., over Soviet objections, the UN decided to send a commission to Korea to supervise elections. Under the chairmanship of India's Krishna P. S. Menon, the commission met in Seoul, 12 Jan.-14 Feb., 1948. On 23 Jan., UN sources disclosed that it had been refused entry into North Korea.

On 16 Feb., 1948, a broadcast from Pyongyang stated that a North Korean "people's army" had been formed. In Apr. an "All-Korea Joint Political Conference," meeting in Pyongyang, announced its determination to prevent the holding of elections in South Korea. Despite serious disturbances, however, and the disruption of some railways and the government's communications system, elections were held, 10 May. They resulted in a victory for 2 "rightist" parties, headed by Syngman Rhee (1875–1965) and Kim Sung Soo. Rhee was elected president, 20 July. The Republic of Korea (southern part of the country) was proclaimed, 15 Aug., 1948. On 8 Sept. the northern part became the People's Republic of Korea.

1950–59

OUTBREAK OF THE KOREAN WAR. On 25 June, 1950, hostilities began. The UN commission reported that South Korea had been invaded by North Korean forces. A Security Council emergency meeting called for immediate cessation of fighting and withdrawal of northern forces. North Korea's failure to comply resulted in a Security Council resolution, 27 June, 1950, asking members to aid South Korea "to repel the armed attack." On 7 July the Security Council established a unified UN Command under the U.S. to send aid to South Korea. This was endorsed by 53 member states. Gen. Douglas MacArthur was appointed commander in chief of UN forces in Korea.

COURSE OF HOSTILITIES. South Korean territory was almost completely overrun in the initial engagements and U.S. casualties were heavy. The North Korean push was halted 50 mi. from Pusan on the south coast. On 14 Sept., 1950, an American army landed at Inchon and retook the old capital of Seoul. Each

side reverted to the 38th-parallel demarcation line, and Gen. MacArthur delivered a surrender ultimatum to the North Korean forces. This was rejected and U.S. troops crossed the parallel, 9 Oct., took Pyongyang, the northern capital, and by Nov. had reached the Yalu River between North Korea and Manchuria.

Chinese forces intervened in considerable numbers; Seoul was captured by North Korean and Chinese troops, 4 Jan., 1951, but was retaken in Mar. by forces under Gen. Matthew B. Ridgway.

DISMISSAL OF MacARTHUR. Gen. MacArthur, without authorization from his government, declared himself prepared to negotiate with the commander of the Chinese and North Korean forces. He warned China she faced military extinction if the U.S. extended the war to Chinese coastal and interior bases. Secretary of State Dean Acheson characterized the threat as "unexpected and unauthorized" and Gen. MacArthur was relieved of his command, 11 Apr. He addressed a joint session of Congress, 19 Apr., criticizing the administration's handling of the war.

KAESONG AND PANMUNJOM TALKS. North Korean and Chinese armies began a spring offensive, 15 May. They sustained heavy losses and were forced to withdraw. Armistice negotiations began at Kaesong on the parallel in July and continued until 5 Aug., when Gen. Ridgway broke them off, charging violation of demilitarization regulations. The talks continued at Panmunjom, 25 Oct., mainly on the question of repatriation of war prisoners. An armistice was signed 26 June, 1953, with an uneasy truce continuing thereafter. A U.S.–South Korean mutual defense treaty went into effect 17 Nov., 1954.

SUPERVISORY COMMISSION. The armistice ended the war but the political differences remained. In Feb. 1954 a Geneva Conference of Foreign Ministers failed to agree on reunification procedures. The Neutral Nations Supervisory Commission was set up to carry out the armistice agreements, but was finally withdrawn in 1956.

1960–68

THE 2 KOREAS. In Mar. 1960 President Syngman Rhee of South Korea was re-elected, but the elections were subsequently declared fraudulent; student rioting followed and Rhee was forced to resign, Apr. 1960. In July 1960 new elections brought the opposition party, the Conservative Democrats, to power. The National Assembly chose as premier Dr. J. M. Chang (1899–1966) and as president Yun Po Sun (b. 1897), a rival of Chang's. The new administration promised economic reform, but large-scale unemploy-ment and inflation reduced the effectiveness of the new government. On 16 May, 1961, the military overthrew the civilian government. Gen. Chung Hee Park (b. 1916) emerged as the dominant military figure, and in 1964 resigned from the army to be elected president. Park was faced with an increased number of border skirmishes, which were attributed to South Korean involvement in the Vietnam War. In Jan. 1968 North Korean infiltrators penetrated to Seoul in an attempt to assassinate Park. On 23 Jan., 1968, the U.S. Navy intelligence ship *Pueblo* was seized by North Korea,

THE KOREAN WAR

CHINA

Tumen R.

Changjin

Yalu R.

Nov. 1950

Pungsan

NORTH KOREA

SEA OF JAPAN

Taedong R.

Chongju

Wonsan

P'yongyang

Kosong

Armistice Line

Kaesong

Kangnung

SOUTH KOREA

Seoul

Han R.

Jan. 1951

Naktong R.

Sept. 1950

YELLOW SEA

Taegu

Pohang

Chinju

Pusan

↓↓ Line of farthest southern retreat

↑↑ Line of farthest northern advance

/////// Demilitarized zone

CHINA

BURMA

Dien Bien Phu

Red R.

Xuan Mai

Hanoi

Haiphong

GULF OF TONKIN

Mekong R.

LAOS

HO CHI MINH

NORTH VIETNAM

Vinh

Dong Hoi

THAILAND

Demilitarized zone

Khesanh

Conthien

Hué

Danang

TONLE SAP

Kong R.

TRAIL

Quangngai

Dakto

Kontum

Pleiku

CAMBODIA

Mekong R.

Quinhon

Ban Me Thuot

Taninh

Dung R.

SOUTH VIETNAM

Saigon

MEKONG DELTA

THE WAR IN VIETNAM

© Lilli Tanzer 1970

which charged that the vessel had been engaged in electronic spying within its territorial waters. Despite intensive U.S. diplomatic efforts the *Pueblo*'s 83-man crew were not released until Dec. 1968, and the ship herself remained in North Korean hands.

CUBA

1953–68

THE CASTRO REVOLUTION. On 26 July, 1958, Fidel Castro (b. 1927) with 170 followers attacked the Moncada Barracks at Santiago de Cuba. This event marked the beginning of the Cuban revolt against dictator Fulgencio Batista, who had come to power in a coup on 10 Mar., 1952.

Although the attack was a failure, it brought Castro recognition. In Sept. 1956 he traveled to the U.S. to collect support and funds for another rising. On 2 Dec. he landed in Oriente Province with 82 followers; they were discovered by Batista forces and only 12 escaped to the Sierra Maestra. During Aug.–Sept. 1958 Castro's lieutenant, Ché Guevara (1928–67) led a successful uprising in Las Villas Province. On 5 Nov. Castro emerged from the mountains and launched a military operation designed to take over the island. Santa Clara fell to Guevara, 31 Dec., and underground Castro supporters rose to take Havana. In Jan. 1959 Batista fled Cuba and Castro became premier, 16 Feb.

The beginning of Castro's rule was marked by an agrarian reform program and widespread executions of Batista officials. Criticism of the revolutionary tribunals carrying out these punishments led to their dissolution, May 1959.

U.S.-CUBAN RELATIONS. During 15–20 Apr., 1959, Castro visited the U.S., where his statements suggested a desire to maintain friendly relations and win the support of moderate elements. After the agrarian reform law of 2 June, however, there was a marked change in U.S.-Cuban relations. The new law allowed the government direction of the national economy and was the 1st step toward a socialist state in Cuba.

On 27 June the U.S. charged that Cuba was adding to tensions in Latin America. U.S.-owned oil refineries were nationalized, 29 June, and on 3 July Congress voted to cut the Cuban sugar quota. In Oct. 1960 the U.S. imposed an embargo on all exports to Cuba except unsubsidized food and medical supplies. Cuban trade with Communist countries served to fill the gap left by U.S. withdrawal: 700,000 tons of sugar rejected by the U.S. in July 1960 were bought by the USSR and China also became a customer. On 7 Aug. all major enterprises controlled by U.S. subjects in Cuba were nationalized.

Relations with the U.S. became further strained over the question of the U.S. naval base at Guantánamo, held under a U.S.-Cuban treaty of 1903. (Cuban water supplies to the base were cut off, 6 Feb., 1964, in reprisal for U.S. seizure of 4 Cuban fishing boats off the coast of Florida.)

On 3 Jan., 1961, Cuba ordered U.S. embassy personnel limited to 11, the size of Cuban representation in the U.S. The U.S. broke off all diplomatic relations, American interests in Cuba being represented by the Swiss.

BAY OF PIGS INVASION. On 17 Apr., 1961, 1,200 anti-Castro Cuban activists, who had been trained in Guatemala by the U.S. Central Intelligence Agency, landed with U.S. military supplies and support facilities at the Bay of Pigs, Cuba. They encountered severe resistance and were defeated in a few days. Most of them were taken prisoner and later ransomed with funds raised in the U.S. On 31 Jan., 1962, Cuba was expelled from the Organization of American States (OAS).

CUBAN MISSILE CRISIS. President Kennedy, in an address to the nation, 22 Oct., 1962, demanded the withdrawal of Soviet missiles from Cuba. An air and naval quarantine was ordered, 24 Oct. On 27 Oct. Kennedy rejected a Soviet proposal to withdraw missiles from Cuba in exchange for a withdrawal of U.S. missiles from Turkey. On 28 Oct. Chairman Khrushchev agreed to dismantle and remove Soviet rockets and Kennedy agreed not to invade Cuba. A joint U.S.-USSR note to UN Secretary General U Thant, 7 Jan., 1963, officially declared the crisis resolved.

DEATH OF GUEVARA. Cuba's efforts to export its revolution to other Latin American countries through the clandestine shipment of arms and the training of guerrillas continued to be largely unsuccessful. The U.S. accelerated its training of Latin American military men in counterinsurgency warfare, and on 9 Oct., 1967, these efforts bore fruit when Ché Guevara was killed while leading a guerrilla group in Bolivia.

VIETNAM

1954

GENEVA CONFERENCE. 26 Apr.–21 July. The Geneva Conference originally had been called to effect a political settlement in Korea as well as to resolve the Indochina war. The talks on Korea, involving 19 nations, quickly stalemated and ended, 15 June, without any results. The U.S., Britain, France, Russia, and Mainland China also took part in the talks on Indochina, the other participants being the French-sponsored State of Vietnam, the Democratic Republic of Vietnam (the Vietminh), Laos, and Cambodia. This phase of the conference opened, 8 May, coincident with the French surrender, a few hours earlier, of Dien Bien Phu—a military defeat which made clear the bankruptcy of France's policy and position in Indochina. The talks made little progress until after 18 June, when Pierre Mendès-France (b. 1907) became French premier and promised to end the war by 20 July.

GENEVA ACCORDS AND FINAL DECLARATION. 20–21 July. The Accords were signed cease-fire agreements between representatives of the forces fighting in Indochina. The Vietnam agreement included provisions calling for a temporary demarcation line (the 17th parallel) with a buffer or demilitarized zone 5 km. wide on either side designed to permit regrouping of forces, each signatory party to administer its half of the country pending general elections which would bring about unification, a ban on the introduction of new military personnel or matériel, a 300-day period during which Vietnamese would have free choice to decide which part of the country they wished to live in, and supervision by the International Control Commission (India [chairman], Canada, Poland) of the agreement. The Final Declaration, 21 July, endorsing the Accords as well as adding that the unification elections should take place within 2 years, was orally assented to by all but the State of Vietnam and the U.S., although U.S. delegate Undersecretary of State Walter B. Smith (1895–1961) declared formally the U.S. would "refrain from the threat or use of force to disturb" the agreements, but would view "any renewal of the aggression . . . with grave concern. . . ."

1954–56

RISE OF DIEM. On 17 June, 1954, Bao Dai (b. 1913), head of the State of Vietnam, appointed Ngo Dinh Diem (1901–63) prime minister (invested formally 5 July). Diem, supported by various American interests, rapidly consolidated his power. American influence became paramount as by Apr. 1956 Diem had ended almost all official French presence in South Vietnam. Using cash and force of arms, he broke, 1955–56, the power of the politico-religious sects. He used an engineered referendum, 23 Oct., 1955, to depose Bao Dai and as a basis for the declaration, 26 Oct., of the Republic of Vietnam under his presidency. A Constituent Assembly, elected, 4 Mar., 1956, in polls which allowed for no real opposition, drafted a constitution (promulgated 26 Oct., 1956) which transformed it into a National Assembly and which confirmed Diem's power.

THE DVR AND UNIFICATION ELECTIONS. In the north the Democratic Republic of Vietnam, under the leadership of Ho Chi Minh (b. c. 1890), attempted to straighten out its economic difficulties (agrarian unrest led to a peasant rebellion which was brutally crushed in Nov. 1956), reorganized its government structure, and prepared for the unification elections. Most observers have agreed with the Vietminh's assumption that it would have won the elections handily. The Diem government, with American support, rejected attempts, 1955–56, to have these elections, declaring it had not signed and therefore was not bound by the Geneva Accords, and that conditions for free elections must 1st be evidenced in North Vietnam. The unification elections were never held.

FOREIGN SUPPORT FOR SOUTH VIETNAM. A protocol to the Southeast Asia Collective Defense Treaty, 8 Sept., 1954, extended its provisions to include Cambodia, Laos, and "the free territory under the jurisdiction of the State of Vietnam." On 1 Oct. U.S. President Eisenhower (1890–1969) wrote Diem (letter delivered 23 Oct.) offering U.S. assistance "in developing and maintaining a strong, viable state, capable of resisting attempted subversion or aggression. . . ."

1957–60

RENEWAL OF HOSTILITIES. At the end of 1956, Communist guerrillas (Vietcong, as they came to be called, from the words *Viet-Nam Cong-San* meaning "Vietnamese Communists") began sporadic terrorist activity in South Vietnam. The 1st U.S. military casualties occurred, 22 Oct., 1957, when a bomb exploded in the quarters of U.S. Military Assistance and Advisory Group personnel. The guerrilla campaign, constantly growing in scope and apparently receiving increasing encouragement from the north, reached its 1st peak in Jan. 1960, when the Vietcong overran some Army of the Republic of Vietnam (ARVN) posts. The U.S. announced, 5 May, 1960, that at the request of South Vietnam the number of U.S. military advisers would be raised from 327 to 685 by year's end.

The increasingly authoritarian (opposition winners in the 30 Aug., 1959, National Assembly elections were not allowed to take their seats), corrupt, and nepotistic Diem government had proved unable to counter the Vietcong's impact

despite generous U.S. aid which some observers calculated averaged as high as $300 million annually. In a lengthy night meeting, 19–20 Dec., 1960, the National Liberation Front of South Vietnam (NLF) was formed, including both Communist and non-Communist anti-Diem insurgents.

1961–64

GROWTH OF COMMUNIST STRENGTH. In 1961 the annual death toll (c. 500) of Vietnamese friendly to the Diem regime and to the U.S. was 10 times greater than it had been in 1959. The strength of the Vietcong (est. 15,000) had trebled since 1959. Infiltration from the north of former Vietminh personnel was on the rise. Much of the countryside (estimates ran as high as 80%) had fallen under NLF sway. On 9 Apr., 1961, Diem, who had overcome, Nov. 1960, a coup directed against him, was re-elected, but despite the government's control of the polls the results demonstrated his limited support. On 18 Oct., 1961, he proclaimed "a state of emergency" (extended 26 Oct., 1962, for 12 more months).

AMERICANIZATION OF THE WAR. Three American missions visited South Vietnam during 1961, and U.S. President Kennedy (1917–63) reaffirmed, 14 Dec., the U.S. commitment to the country. Although Kennedy decided against sending large numbers of troops to Vietnam, 1,500 additional advisers were sent who now were permitted "to advise in battle mission." Two U.S. army helicopter companies, the 1st direct U.S. military support for battle against the NLF, arrived in Saigon, 11 Dec., 1961. During 1962 the situation continued to deteriorate despite massive American financial support. Great emphasis was placed on the "strategic hamlet" idea (1st used in the late summer of 1961), but by year's end maladministration had indicated the ultimate failure of this policy. Diem promised the U.S. that he would implement all sorts of needed reforms, but failed to do so effectively.

The by now 4,000 American military personnel (as of 8 Feb. under the direction of a new U.S. Military Assistance Command, Vietnam) chafed at their inability to do more than advise the ARVN, which in a series of supposed mopping-up operations demonstrated its incompetence. On 10 Mar. the U.S. admitted that American pilots were flying some combat missions in South Vietnam. On 31 Dec., 1962, U.S. forces numbered 10,000.

During 1963, although U.S. policymakers continued to affirm support for South Vietnam, their disenchantment with the Diem government rose perceptibly as it proved incapable either of dealing with the enemy or of winning over the citizenry. On 2 Jan., 1963, at Ap Bac, a fortified village in the Mekong Delta, in the war's 1st "stand and fight" battle, 200 Vietcong held their ground against 2,000 ARVN with armor and air support. Throughout the year the Vietcong, increasingly reinforced from the north, stepped up the number and intensity of their raids as the ARVN proved unable to deal with them.

BUDDHIST CRISIS. May–Sept. 1963. Diem, a Catholic, had received considerable support from the 900,000 mostly Catholic refugees who had fled south in 1954–55. Friction had arisen between the Diem government and the leaders of the Buddhist majority of the population at first because of apparent favoritism toward Catholics and then, 1962–63, because of religious oppression apparently instigated by Diem's brother Ngo Dinh Nhu (d. 1963), the head of the secret police. The climax came after police in Hué, governed by another Diem brother, fired, 8 May, into a crowd protesting against not being allowed to fly Buddhist flags during a religious festival. Demonstrations spread to Saigon. A Buddhist monk immolated himself in protest, 11 June, the first of 7 persons to do so. Increasing unrest forced Diem to proclaim, 21 Aug., martial law (ended 16 Sept.). In apparent indifference to all that had gone on, the government held elections, 27 Sept., in which all candidates had to be approved in advance.

END OF DIEM GOVERNMENT. 1–2 Nov., 1963. With American foreknowledge and probable connivance a group of South Vietnamese armed forces leaders carried out, 1 Nov., a coup against the Diem government, murdering, 2 Nov., Diem and Nhu, and establishing junta rule.

PLEDGE OF SUPPORT BY JOHNSON. In 1964 the official U.S. position continued to be that the war was strictly a Vietnamese conflict, but in practical terms the U.S. was taking over increasingly both its direction and prosecution, especially as the leaders of the South Vietnamese armed forces jockeyed with each other for control of the government. Coups followed each other so rapidly that no government lasted more than 5 months. On 1 Jan. U.S. President Johnson (b. 1908) reaffirmed the U.S. commitment in South Vietnam and promised the government there: "We shall maintain in Vietnam American personnel and matériel as needed to assist you in achieving victory."

INCREASED NLF ACTIVITY. The NLF again stepped up its activity (according to U.S. sources the total number of "incidents" went from 19,500 in 1963 to 25,500 in 1964). Increasingly terrorist operations were directed against Americans (most notably a raid on U.S. barracks in Kontum, 2 Feb., bombings of Saigon hotel billets, 25 Aug. and 24 Dec., and an attack on the U.S. air base at Bien Hoa, 30 mi. from Saigon, 1 Nov.)

TONKING GULF INCIDENT. 2–7 **Aug., 1964.** Apparently as an aftermath of a South Vietnamese raid, 30–31 July, on North Vietnamese naval installations, North Vietnamese PT boats attacked, 2 Aug., the U.S. destroyer *Maddox* on patrol in the Gulf of Tonking. President Johnson ordered, 3 Aug., the patrol reinforced; and although exactly what happened remains unclear, the destroyers *Maddox* and *C. Turner Joy* reported, 4 Aug., a North Vietnamese PT-boat attack. In reprisal U.S. planes for the 1st time bombed North Vietnamese bases. Johnson appealed to Congress for support and it approved, 7 Aug. (House: 416–0; Senate: 88–2), a resolution authorizing the President "to take all necessary measures to repel any armed attacks against the forces of the U.S. and to prevent future aggression." By 31 Dec., 1964, U.S. forces in South Vietnam numbered 23,000. The North Vietnamese army was estimated to have 1,000–5,000 troops in South Vietnam.

1965

ACCESSION OF THIEU AND KY. Although not officially, U.S. policy during 1965 shifted from support of democratic government in South Vietnam to defeat of North Vietnam.

Successive coups continued to disrupt the South Vietnamese government, Jan.–June, 1965, and the situation did not stabilize until 19 June, when in another coup Gen. Nguyen Van Thieu (b. 1923) and Air Vice-Marshal Nguyen Cao Ky (b. 1930) became head of state and premier in the 9th regime since the fall of Diem.

ESCALATION. Deeper U.S. involvement began ostensibly in response to a Vietcong attack, 7 Feb., on U.S. personnel at Pleiku which resulted in retaliatory air strikes against North Vietnam, 7, 8 Feb., as did, 10 Feb., a raid on U.S. barracks at Quinhon. On 24 Feb. U.S. bombers for the 1st time attacked Vietcong targets in South Vietnam. President Johnson announced, 28 Feb., a policy of continuous air strikes against North Vietnamese military targets to force the enemy into "a negotiated settlement." On 7–9 Mar. 3,500 U.S. marines landed at Da Nang to guard the U.S. air base there. This raised U.S. forces in South Vietnam to 26,500, which reinforcements by June had raised to 34,000, all technically still advisers. On 9 June U.S. troops were officially committed to field operations, taking part in their 1st major offensive, in Zone D, on 28 June. During July to Dec. increasing numbers of U.S. troops (31 Dec., 175,000) became involved in heavy combat operations throughout South Vietnam. U.S. casualties in 1965: 1,350 dead, 5,300 wounded, 148 missing or captured.

Despite the influx of U.S. troops, NLF operations continued (U.S. sources estimated 26,500 incidents). Estimates of North Vietnamese troops in south at year's end ranged from 11,000 to 40,000.

PEACE OVERTURES. On 24 Feb., 1965, UN Sec. Gen. U Thant (b. 1909) announced that his determined efforts, Sept. 1964–Jan. 1965, to arrange peace talks had failed, and indicated the fault lay with the U.S. On 8 Apr., North Vietnam put forth a 4-point program which in effect called for U.S. withdrawal, neutralization of a peacefully united Vietnam, and settlement of South Vietnam's internal affairs "in accordance with the program of the NLF." The U.S. termed the program unacceptable. A U.S. halt of air raids on North Vietnam, 13–19 May, elicited no response satisfactory to American policymakers. Tortuous negotiations, Nov.–Dec., involving Italian officials came to an abrupt and unsatisfactory end, 15 Dec., when U.S. planes for the 1st time bombed a major North Vietnamese industrial target. Other more informal attempts during the year by various parties, including the Russians, the pope, and French President de Gaulle to arrange peace talks also failed.

In the U.S. many disagreed with the escalation policies of the Johnson administration, and teach-ins, mass protests, and open letters expressed their dissatisfaction. On 15–16 Oct., 1965, there were nationwide antiwar demonstrations in which thousands participated.

1966

CONDUCT OF THE WAR. Despite heavy losses (600 planes between Feb. 1965 and Oct. 1966), the U.S. extended the air war over North Vietnam with multiplane missions (some from bases in Thailand) and a growing list of targets. On 29 June occurred the 1st U.S. bombing of installations near Hanoi, North Vietnam's capital, and Haiphong, its key port; 1st U.S. bombing of the demilitarized zone, 30 July.

On the ground, taking over the bulk of the offensive fighting from the dispirited ARVN, U.S. troops (by 31 Dec. nearly 380,000 strong, with another 30,000 in Thailand) engaged in "search and destroy" missions as well as larger actions in pursuit of a policy of attrition against the enemy. Despite impressive numbers of kills as well as a continued troop build-up, the U.S., even with the support of nearly 30,000 South Koreans, smaller contingents of Australian and New Zealand forces, and the ARVN, could not achieve the 10:1 ratio military experts considered necessary to control guerrilla operations. Vietcong recruits and North Vietnamese infiltrators kept the ratio at about 3:1.

PEACE OVERTURES. All attempts by interested parties (including U Thant, 24 May; de Gaulle, 1 Sept.; and the pope, 4 Oct.) to achieve some kind of settlement foundered on the divergent views of the U.S. and North Vietnam on the status of the NLF. The U.S. said it would not, as North Vietnam demanded, recognize the NLF's separate status.

Political unrest continued in South Vietnam as Buddhists confronted, Mar.–June, the government, which agreed to elections (held 11 Sept.) for a Constituent Assembly, although the electoral laws enacted assured Ky and the military junta of victory.

On 6–8 Feb., President Johnson met with Ky in Honolulu, and on 24–25 Oct. with the leaders of Australia, New Zealand, the Philippines, South Vietnam, Thailand, and South Korea (all countries directly involved in the war). These conferences resulted in declarations and afforded the U.S. President a chance, 26 Oct., to visit South Vietnam, but otherwise had little effect on the war.

In the U.S. antiwar protests continued. On 25–27 Mar. there was an international protest weekend.

1967

CONDUCT OF THE WAR. Events followed what had become a familiar pattern. A holiday truce, 31 Dec., 1966–2 Jan., 1967, as well as a Lunar New Year bombing halt, 8–12 Feb., resulted in no positive steps toward peace. The U.S. and North Vietnam expanded their efforts. On 22 Feb. U.S. artillery for the 1st time fired accross the demilitarized zone into North Vietnam. On 26 Feb. U.S. warships, which had done so, sporadically, in the past, began shelling targets in North Vietnam on a continuing basis without restrictions. U.S. planes began to mine North Vietnamese rivers, 27 Feb. On 11 Aug. U.S. planes began bombing within 10 mi. of the China border and the Chinese began to claim violations of their air space.

The ground war continued to be fought fiercely. U.S. forces, numbering, Feb., more than 400,000, and augmented contingents from South Korea (45,000), Australia (4,500), and New Zealand (360), were engaging an increasingly large enemy force. (The infiltration from North Vietnam was estimated as high as 7,000 a month.) On 19 May U.S. and ARVN forces moved into the southern portion of the demilitarized zone.

ELECTIONS IN SOUTH VIETNAM. In South Vietnam the military continued to dominate the political scene. Despite the presence of 20 eminent Americans, sent by President Johnson to observe the polling, campaign laws and practices made it evident that Thieu and Ky, the junta's candidates for president and vice-president, would win the elections, 3 Sept. They did so, but only with a plurality.

PEACE OVERTURES. International proposals for settlement of the war gave way to appeals for an end to hostilities, especially the bombing of the North, which North Vietnam indicated must be granted unconditionally before any talks could begin. The U.S., within which antiwar sentiment was sharply on the rise, came under renewed criticism internationally for its policies in Vietnam. The *détente* with the Soviet Union became strained as the latter increased its assistance to North Vietnam; on 23 Sept. the USSR formally signed an aid pact with the DRV.

1968

RIVAL POLICIES AND STRENGTHS. At the beginning of 1968 the dominant issues remained unchanged: North Vietnam insisted on an unconditional halt to the bombing as a preliminary to peace talks of any sort; the U.S. insisted on reciprocity. North Vietnam continued to demand NLF representation at any peace talks; the U.S. refused to accept the NLF as more than an expedient creation of North Vietnam. On 1 Jan., 1968, U.S. troop strength was 475,000 men, about 2,000 more than the peak U.S. strength during the Korean War. By Dec. 31 there were approximately 550,000 U.S. servicemen in South Vietnam.

TET OFFENSIVE. 30 Jan.–25 Feb. The NLF, using Vietcong guerrillas and North Vietnamese regulars, launched, 30 Jan., widespread co-ordinated attacks on major urban areas throughout South Vietnam. Coming on what was supposedly the 1st day of a mutually agreed upon Tet, or Lunar New Year, truce, this offensive had considerable success. In Saigon, Vietcong commandos occupied U.S. embassy buildings for 6 hours before being wiped out. In Hué, block-by-block fighting lasted until 24 Feb. Other cities also fell into Communist hands for a short time. Although U.S. military spokesmen said the offensive had failed to make any lasting military headway, they admitted it had a strong propaganda impact, since it came in many areas which had been said to be secure from such attacks.

On 31 Mar. President Johnson announced halting of the bombing north of the 21st parallel and asked for a response from North Vietnam.

PEACE TALKS. On 3 May, after 5 weeks of wrangling about the location, both sides finally agreed on Paris as the site for talks preliminary to peace negotiations. Preliminary talks, 10 May–1 Nov., failed, as North Vietnam continued to insist on an unconditional halt to the bombing and the U.S. continued to demand reciprocity. On 1 Nov. the U.S. ceased aerial, naval, and artillery bombardment of North Vietnam. Wrangling over the shape of the conference table, Nov.–Dec., an apparent detail related to the status of the NLF delayed the beginning of formal peace talks.

CONDUCT OF THE WAR. The war continued unabated while negotiations went on. From Jan. to 5 Apr., NLF forces besieged 6,000 U.S. marines at Khesanh. On 8 Apr., U.S. and allied forces launched "Operation Complete Victory," announced as "the biggest drive of the war so far," in an attempt to clean up Communist forces in the 11 provinces around Saigon. On 5–13 May the Communists' 2nd major offensive of the year throughout South Vietnam hit hard at Saigon, and the city was struck again, 3–15 June. Savage fighting broke out again in July in various provinces and continued into the fall.

On 23 June, 1968, the undeclared war in Vietnam became the longest sustained military action ever fought by the U.S. It had lasted 6 years, 6 months, and 1 day since the death of the 1st U.S. serviceman at the hands of the Vietcong on 22 Dec., 1961. Total U.S. casualties since then, as of 31 Dec., 1968: 29,000 dead, 185,000 injured, 950 missing, 350 captured. Deaths since 1 Jan., 1961, of other forces: ARVN, 73,000; allied forces, 2,500; enemy (U.S. and South Vietnam estimates), 414,000.

THE NUCLEAR ARMS RACE

1945–68

U.N. ATOMIC ENERGY COMMISSION. Atomic bombs dropped on Hiroshima, 6 Aug., and Nagasaki, 9 Aug., 1945, ushered in an international debate on the control of atomic armaments. On 24 Jan., 1946, the UN Atomic Energy Commission was established. It consisted of 1 representative from each Security Council nation and a Canadian representative.

EARLY ARMS CONTROL PROPOSALS. A Soviet motion at UN General Assembly, 1946, proposed a general reduction of armaments by all the major powers. A counterresolution submitted by Britain sought to extract details of all armed forces and verification of figures. The USSR insisted on the inclusion of armament details as well. A compromise resolution, 14 Dec., asked the Security Council to decide what information should be provided by each state. During 1947–48, however, discussions on the control of arms foundered. The USSR insisted in the UN General Assembly, 18 Sept., 1948, that primary importance must be attached to the banning of atomic weapons—on which the West then had a monopoly. No agreement could be reached on inspection procedures.

RESUMPTION OF THE ARMS RACE. 1949–50 were years of national rearmament, with wars taking place in Malaya, Indochina, and Korea. The production of more effective atomic bombs was announced, 1 Aug., 1949, by the U.S. Atomic Energy Commission. On 20 Sept., 1949, the 4th UN General Assembly met against a background of reports of an atomic explosion in Siberia and of a new U.S. weapon, the hydrogen bomb. On 28 Jan., 1950, the Russians claimed parity with the U.S. in the atomic field. The decision to rearm West Germany inside NATO, 19 Dec., 1950, and the Korean War prevented serious disarmament negotiations.

REJECTION OF DISARMAMENT PROPOSALS. In Oct. 1951 the USSR exploded another atomic bomb. An Atomic Energy and Conventional Armaments Commission of the 4 Big Powers was established, Dec. 1951, to draft a treaty providing for regulation and reduction of all armed forces as well as abolition of weapons of mass destruction. The USSR announced a successful hydrogen bomb test, 20 Aug., 1953. A Russian resolution on disarmament was defeated in the General Assembly, 27 Nov. On 8 Dec., President Eisenhower proposed an international pool of atomic materials, but this was rejected by the Soviet Union, 22 Dec.

INCREASE IN WEAPONS TESTING. U.S. Secretary of State John Foster Dulles spoke of the need for "massive retaliatory power," 12 Jan., 1954. American nuclear tests carried out in Mar. injured Japanese fishermen. Prime Minister Nehru of India called for a halt to all testing, 22 Apr.

A conference of heads of state and foreign ministers in Geneva, 18–23 July, 1955, saw the beginning of a letup in the arms race. No definite agreement was reached, however, and the USSR resumed testing of nuclear weapons, 24 Aug., 1956. Another call for the halting of tests was put forward, 2 July, 1957, by Canada, France, Britain, and the U.S.

All of these moves and countermoves were overshadowed by the growing tension in Europe. The Berlin crisis heralded resumption of heavy testing by the Soviet Union—a series of 30 tests from Aug. to Oct. 1961. U.S. testing resumed on 15 Sept.

BAN ON ATMOSPHERIC TESTS. On 5 Apr., 1963, the Soviet Union accepted a U.S. proposal for direct communication between the 2 heads of state—the "hot line." President Kennedy announced, 10 June, a moratorium on nuclear testing in the atmosphere. Three-power talks in Moscow (USSR, U.S., and Britain) began, 15 July, and produced the 1st Test Ban Treaty by which no tests might be conducted in the atmosphere, in outer space, or under water. The treaty was signed in Moscow, 5 Aug., and ratified by the U.S. Senate, 24 Sept. Neither China nor France subscribed to the treaty, although 99 other countries did so. On 20 Apr., 1964, President Johnson announced plans to cut back the production of materials for manufacturing nuclear weapons.

FRANCE AND CHINA AS ATOMIC POWERS. France became the world's 4th nuclear power when she exploded an atomic bomb on 14 Feb., 1960. In the following years France developed an independent nuclear striking force, and on 24 Aug., 1968, tested her 1st hydrogen bomb. In Oct. 1964 China tested her 1st nuclear device. U.S. Defense Secretary Robert McNamara warned, 7 Mar., 1966, that China would have warhead delivery capability in 2–3 years. China tested her 3rd nuclear weapon, 9 May, 1966, in Sinkiang. On 11 May the State Department revealed that the U.S. had rejected a Chinese suggestion that both countries pledge not to use nuclear weapons against each other. On 27 Oct., 1966, China announced the successful launching of a nuclear missile, and on 17 June, 1967, tested its 1st hydrogen bomb.

NUCLEAR MISSILE TREATIES. A U.S.-USSR agreement was signed, 27 Jan., 1967, which banned the placing of mass-destruction weapons in outer space. Although a nuclear nonproliferation treaty was signed, 1 July, 1968, by the United States, Soviet Union, Britain, and 59 other nations, West Germany, France, and China were not among the signatories.

Economic Development and Triumphant Nationalism

NORTH AMERICA

United States

1945–50

RELIEF AND RECONSTRUCTION. On 21 Aug., 1945, lend-lease terminated, having disbursed $50.6 billion in aid. President Truman announced, 27 Dec., 1946, that 7 nations had made settlements. Immediately after the war the U.S. gave over $116 billion in UNRRA, etc., loans, mostly to Eastern Europe. By a presidential directive of 22 Dec., 1945, 42,000 refugees gained admittance to the U.S.; 205,000 visas were granted for displaced persons. Secretary of State George C. Marshall proposed, 5 June, 1947, that the U.S. rebuild the world economy to enable free institutions to flourish. The resulting Marshall Plan Conference, 12 July, of 16 nations established the Committee for European Economic Cooperation, which relied heavily on U.S. support. A Foreign Aid Act, 17 Dec., 1947, granted relief to Austria, China, Italy, and France. Truman submitted to Congress, 19 Dec., a $17 billion European Relief Program (ERP). The "Point 4" program, also outlined by Truman, provided economic assistance to underdeveloped nations.

ANTI-INFLATION MEASURES. Price and wage controls, except those on rent, sugar, and rice, were ended by 9 Nov., 1946. Truman called, 26 July, 1948, a special session of Congress which enacted, 16 Aug., an Anti-Inflation Act. The Defense Production Act, 8 Sept., 1950, authorized Truman to fix prices and wages.

DEFENSE. On 1 Aug., 1946, the McMahon Act established the Atomic Energy Commission. The National Security Act, 26 July, 1947, combined the army, navy, and air corps into a National Military Establishment (later Department of Defense, 1949) under a cabinet-rank secretary of defense. Military appropriations remained high in the postwar period. The Defense Reorganization Act of 6 Aug., 1958, subordinated the uniformed services to a central civilian authority.

INTERNAL SECURITY. Truman's Loyalty Order, 22 Mar., 1947, provoked an investigation of subversive activities in the Executive Branch. On 3 Aug., 1948, ex-Communist Whittaker Chambers stated that Alger Hiss had been a Communist and had given him State Department papers. Hiss received 5 years for perjury, 17 Nov., 1949. Julius and Ethel Rosenberg were convicted, 29 Mar., 1951, of atomic espionage and were executed at Sing Sing Prison, 19 June, 1953. The Internal Security (McCarran) Act, 23 Sept., 1950, passed over Truman's veto, ordered the registration of Communist organizations, the internment of Communists in national emergencies, and prohibited the immigration of anyone who had belonged to a totalitarian organization. Puerto Rican nationalists Oscar Collazo and Griselio Torresola failed in an attempt to assassinate Truman, 1 Nov., 1950. Subsequently, a Communist Control Act, 24 Aug., 1954, deprived the Communist Party of its rights, privileges, and immunities.

TAFT-HARTLEY ACT. 23 June, 1947. Passed over Truman's veto, this act outlawed the closed shop, instituted a mandatory 60-day "cooling-off" period before strikes, and permitted employers to sue for strike damages.

PRESIDENTIAL ELECTION. 2 Nov., 1948. Republicans nominated Govs. Thomas E. Dewey (b. 1902), N.Y., and

Earl Warren (b. 1891), Calif. Democrats selected Truman and Sen. Alben W. Barkley (1877–1956), Ky. Rebellious southern Democrats nominated Gov. J. Strom Thurmond (b. 1902), S.C., for the States' Rights ("Dixiecrat") Party. Truman (303) surprisingly defeated Dewey (189) and Thurmond (39). The Democrats regained both houses.

1951–64

22ND AMENDMENT. 26 Feb., 1951. The 22nd Amendment to the Constitution limited presidents to 2 terms in office.

PRESIDENTIAL ELECTION. 2 Nov., 1952. Gen. Dwight D. Eisenhower defeated Sen. Robert A. Taft (1889–1953), Ohio, for the Republican presidential nomination. Sen. Richard M. Nixon (b. 1913), Calif., became the vice-presidential candidate. Republicans opposed Truman's China and Korea policies, supported the Taft-Hartley Law, and took an ambiguous stance on Negro rights.

Truman declined to run for re-election, 30 Mar., and the Democrats nominated Gov. Adlai E. Stevenson (1900–1965), Ill., and Sen. John J. Sparkman (b. 1899), Ala. The Democrats attacked Taft-Hartley, supported the New and Fair Deals, and advocated federal civil-rights legislation. Eisenhower (442) soundly defeated Stevenson (89) by more than 6 m. votes. The Republicans won both houses.

"CAPTIVE PEOPLES" RESOLUTION. Congress shelved, 7 Mar., 1953, an administration resolution attacking Soviet subjugation of free peoples. Eisenhower urged, 16 Apr., Eastern European independence, but, despite East German rioting, 18–24 June, announced, 1 July, that the U.S. planned no physical intervention in Eastern Europe.

ESTABLISHMENT OF HEW. On 1 April, 1953, a new federal government department, Health, Education, and Welfare, was established.

FARM PROGRAMS. On 11 Jan., 1954, Eisenhower proposed a system of flexible price supports based on an updated parity. Legislation to this effect became law, 28 Aug. The Soil-Bank Bill, 28 May, 1956, compensated producers who kept their 1956–59 crops below their allotments. The Agriculture Act of 28 Aug., 1958, gave farmers a choice between modified price supports and increased crop quotas.

McCARTHY HEARINGS. Republican Sen. Joseph R. McCarthy's (1908–57), Wis., Permanent Investigating Subcommittee's hearings on Communist activities in government stirred much controversy. McCarthy attacked the Democrats, 4 Feb., 1954, for "20 years of treason." He charged that Army Secretary Robert T. Stevens and Brig. Gen. Ralph W. Zwicker had suppressed evidence of espionage at Fort Monmouth's (N.J.) Signal Corps Engineering Laboratories. Eisenhower's denunciation, 14 June, 1953, of "book burners" spurned McCarthy's tactics. The Senate "condemned," 2 Dec., McCarthy after Sen. Arthur V. Watkins', Utah, committee unanimously recommended that he be censured for contempt of the Senate Privileges and Elections Subcommittee.

OPPENHEIMER CASE. The Atomic Energy Commission suspended, Dec. 1953, Dr. J. Robert Oppenheimer (b. 1904) as a security risk. To Gordon Grey's special AEC Committee Oppenheimer admitted having aided Communist causes, but denied being a Communist. Nuclear physicist Edward Teller (b. 1908) testified that Oppenheimer had actively opposed the H-bomb project. The committee cleared him as "loyal" but found him lacking in "enthusiasm" for the H-bomb project. As a result, he was not reinstated, 12 Apr., 1954.

HOUSING LEGISLATION. The Housing Act of 2 Aug., 1954, authorized construction of 35,000 houses for people uprooted by slum clearance. It also raised maximum permissible mortgages and lowered down payments. 1955, 1957, and 1958 Acts liberalized the law, and Eisenhower assigned $650 m. for urban renewal, 24 Sept., 1959.

DIXON-YATES CONTRACT. Joint congressional hearings revealed that Budget Bureau consultant Adolph H. Wenzell, a vice-president of Dixon-Yates' financial agency, had taken part in negotiations which authorized, 5 Oct., 1954, the Dixon-Yates group to build a power generating plant to supply Memphis, Tenn. Eisenhower canceled the contract, 11 July, 1955.

CIVIL RIGHTS. A bus boycott by black citizens of Montgomery, Ala., led by Rev. Dr. Martin Luther King (1929–68) began, 1 Dec., 1955. In accord with a Supreme Court order, 13 Nov., 1956, desegregated bus service began in Montgomery, 21 Dec.

The Civil Rights Act of 9 Sept., 1957, created a 6-man bipartisan Civil Rights Commission to investigate unconstitutional denials of voting rights and authorized federal district courts to issue injunctions against interference with voting.

When a federal district court nullified a state court's injunction against the integrating of a high school at Little Rock, Ark., Arkansas Gov. Orval Faubus called out the National Guard, 24 Sept., 1957, and prevented the registration of 9 black students. Rioting erupted, 23 Sept., when Faubus withdrew the troops after a federal court order not to obstruct blacks. Eisenhower sent in 1,000 airborne troops. The black students entered the school, 25 Sept. Integration, however, progressed slowly in the South.

President Kennedy used federal troops to enable a black student, James Meredith, to register at the University of Mississippi, 30 Sept.–1 Oct., 1962; ordered an end to discrimination in federally financed housing, 20 Nov., 1962; and called, 19 June, 1963, for an Omnibus Civil Rights Law.

A Civil Rights Law of 2 July, 1964, protected the right to vote and outlawed discrimination in employment and places of "public accommodation."

HIGHWAY PROGRAM. The Federal-Aid Highway Act, 29 June, 1956, provided $32.5 billion for the construction of 42,000 miles of interstate highways and to complete the federal-aid highway system.

PRESIDENTIAL ELECTION. 6 Nov., 1956. Democrats nominated Adlai E. Stevenson for president. Sen. Estes Kefauver (1903–63), Tenn., narrowly defeated Sen. John F. Kennedy, Mass., for the vice-presidential position. Republicans renominated Eisenhower and Nixon. The party platforms were quite similar, though Stevenson proposed an international ban on H-bomb testing which Eisenhower opposed. Eisenhower won (457–74) by over 9,500,000 votes, but the Democrats took both houses.

U.S. INTERVENTION IN LEBANON. The "Eisenhower Doctrine," promulgated 5 Jan., 1957, warned that the U.S. would permit no Communist conquests in the Middle East. Modifying a resolution by Rep. Thomas A. Gordon, Ill., the Senate authorized aiding Middle East nations to develop economic and military power. When rebellion erupted in Lebanon, 9 May, 1958, U.S. marines landed, 15 July, at President Camille Chamoun's request for aid under the provisions of the Eisenhower Doctrine.

CIVIL LIBERTIES. A restriction of the use of F.B.I. files, 30 Aug., 1957, permitted the introduction in court only of material relating to a witness' testimony.

EURATOM. The European Atomic Energy Community Act, 2 July, 1958, authorized the exchange by the U.S. with its allies of atomic information and materials.

NATIONAL DEFENSE EDUCATION ACT. 2 Sept., 1958. This act authorized $295 m. in 3% loans to college students and 5,500 graduate fellowships for future college teachers.

LABOR MANAGEMENT REPORTING AND DISCLOSURE ACT. 14 Sept., 1959. This act sought to ensure fair union elections and end corruption, and forbade all unions to use the secondary boycott.

MEDICARE. A Medical Care Bill, 13 Sept., 1960, established a federal-state program to provide medical care for the needy aged.

1960 PRESIDENTIAL ELECTION. 8 Nov., 1960. Democrats nominated Sens. John F. Kennedy and Lyndon B. Johnson (b. 1908), Tex., and advocated medical care for the aged under Social Security. The Republicans selected Richard M. Nixon and Henry Cabot Lodge (b. 1902), Mass. Kennedy defeated Nixon, but by only 112,881 out of 68,800,000 votes cast. The official vote count, 6 Jan., 1961, gave Kennedy 303 and Nixon 219 electoral votes. Kennedy's Inaugural Address, 20 Jan., 1961, pledged action against tyranny, poverty, disease, and war.

THE "NEW FRONTIER." Kennedy's "New Frontier" brought intellectual enthusiasm and appointees like Defense Secretary Robert S. McNamara and Labor Secretary Arthur J. Goldberg to Washington. However, Congress rejected much of his program, including medical aid for the aged.

ASSASSINATION OF JOHN KENNEDY. 22 Nov., 1963. Lee Harvey Oswald allegedly shot Kennedy as he rode in a motorcade in Dallas, Tex., and was himself killed by civilian Jack Ruby while in custody. Vice-President Johnson succeeded Kennedy.

ECONOMIC OPPORTUNITY ACT. 30 Aug., 1964. This act established a youth Job Corps to implement Johnson's "war on poverty."

PRESIDENTIAL ELECTION. 3 Nov., 1964. Conservative-dominated Republicans nominated Sen. Barry M. Goldwater (b. 1909), Ariz., and Rep. William E. Miller, N.Y. Democrats nominated Johnson and Sen. Hubert H. Humphrey (b. 1911), Minn. Johnson crushed Goldwater by approximately 16 million votes. In his State of the Union Message, 4 Jan., 1965, Johnson called for redoubled efforts against poverty, disease, discrimination, and ignorance, in order to achieve a "Great Society."

1965–68

VIETNAM. The U.S. assumed the major responsibility for defending South Vietnam's government against the Vietcong. In Feb. 1965 President Johnson authorized bombing attacks on North Vietnam. By 1968 more than 500,000 American soldiers were in Vietnam. The war became increasingly unpopular as U.S. combat deaths rose, and many condemned it as an unnecessary, imprudent, and even immoral involvement in non-American affairs. Opponents of the war frequently demonstrated in the nation's cities (*pp. 591–596 above.*)

U.S.–COMMUNIST RELATIONS. The Vietnam war slowed the trend to-

ward better relations with the Communist world, but both sides acted with restraint. In the 6-day war, June 1967, the U.S. supported Israel while the USSR encouraged the Arab states, but the leaders of the superpowers maintained direct communications to avoid a confrontation. President Johnson and Premier Aleksei Kosygin held a summit meeting at Glassboro, N.J., 23–25 June, 1967, which helped to reduce tensions. North Korea's seizure of the U.S. Navy intelligence ship *Pueblo* and its 83-man crew exacerbated deteriorating relations between the countries; the crew was released, 22 Dec., 1968, after 10 months of negotiations and a U.S. apology, later retracted, for spying. Russia's invasion of Czechoslovakia, Aug. 1968, led the U.S. Senate to delay consideration of the pending Nuclear Nonproliferation Treaty.

GREAT SOCIETY. Large Democratic majorities in both houses of the 90th Congress gave President Johnson legislation which he deemed necessary to create the "Great Society" promised in his State of the Union Message, 4 Jan., 1965. "Medicare," financed through Social Security, provided hospital insurance for those Americans over age 65. The Voting Rights Act authorized the attorney general to send federal registrars to enroll Negroes in states which violated the 15th Amendment. A new immigration act replaced the national-origins quota system with a less ethnically discriminating scale of priorities. Republican gains in the 1966 elections and the increasing costs of the Vietnam war reduced the output of domestic legislation in the latter half of the Johnson years.

BLACK AMERICA. Younger black leaders, like Stokely Carmichael, H. Rap Brown, and Eldridge Cleaver, called for "Black Power," a slogan expressive of black pride and militancy. Riots in the ghettos emphasized Negro dissatisfactions. Los Angeles, Aug. 1965, Cleveland, July 1966, and Detroit and Newark, July 1967, suffered scores of deaths and millions of dollars in property damage due to racial disturbances. President Johnson's Special Advisory Commission on Civil Disorders reported, Feb. 1968, that white racism underlay problems which threatened to tear the nation asunder. Black Americans made some gains as the Republican, Edward Brooke, was elected Senator for Mass., and as black Democrats Carl Stokes and Richard Hatcher won election, Nov. 1967, as mayors of Cleveland, Ohio, and Gary, Ind., respectively.

POLITICAL ASSASSINATIONS. Murderers continued to fell American public leaders. Black Muslims allegedly shot, 21 Feb., 1965, Malcolm X, leader of the rival Black Nationalists, as he spoke in Harlem. On 4 Apr., 1968, Rev. Martin Luther King, Jr., a moderate Negro leader, was shot to death in Memphis, Tenn., where he was encouraging support for the city's striking sanitation men, mostly blacks. James Earl Ray, a white American, was later extradited from London and convicted of the crime. On 5 June, 1968, Sen. Robert F. Kennedy (N.Y.) was fatally wounded in the Ambassador Hotel in Los Angeles as he left celebrations of his Democratic presidential primary victories in California and South Dakota. Bystanders captured his alleged assailant, Sirhan B. Sirhan, a Jordanian immigrant.

DEMOCRATIC PRESIDENTIAL NOMINATION. Sen. Eugene McCarthy (Minn.), an opponent of the war in Vietnam, stunned President Lyndon B. Johnson by gathering 42% of the vote, 12 Mar., 1968, in New Hampshire's Democratic primary. Sen. Robert F. Kennedy, another critic of the administration, soon entered the contest, 16 Mar. When the President surprisingly withdrew, 31 Mar., from the race, his Vice-President, Hubert Humphrey, announced his candidacy, 27 Apr. Sen. George McGovern (S.D.), another "dove," joined the fray after Kennedy's assassination, 5 June. Meeting at Chicago, 26–29 Aug., the Democrats nominated Humphrey and Sen. Edmund T. Muskie (Me.). The convention endorsed President Johnson's Vietnam policy while police clashed with antiwar demonstrators in the streets of Chicago.

PRESIDENTIAL ELECTION. At Miami Beach, Fla., Republicans nominated, 8 Aug., former Vice-President Richard M. Nixon with Maryland Gov. Spiro T. Agnew as his running mate. Although more conservative, the Republican platform was similar to the Democratic on the issues of war, the urban crisis, and law and order. Nixon won the election, 5 Nov., with only 43.4% of the popular vote, as an ultraconservative 3rd party, running former Alabama Gov. George C. Wallace and retired Air Force Chief of Staff Gen. Curtis LeMay, gathered 13.5%. Nixon received 302 electoral votes, Humphrey 191, and Wallace 45. The Democrats retained control of both houses of Congress.

SPACE EXPLORATION. In June 1965 Maj. Edward White left the Gemini 4 capsule commanded by Maj. James McDivitt for 20 minutes, thus becoming the 1st American to "walk" in space. Lt. Col. Gordon Cooper and Lt. Comm. Charles Conrad established several space endurance records during an 8-day flight in Aug. 1965. On 1 June, 1966, the U.S. "soft-landed" Surveyor 1, a research craft, on the surface of the moon. Tragedy struck, 27 Jan., 1967, when a fire in the Apollo I capsule killed astronauts Virgil Grissom, Edward White, and Roger Chaffee during a launch practice. The U.S. achieved a great space triumph in Dec. 1968, when Col. Frank Borman, Capt. James Lovell, and Maj. William Anders took Apollo 8 into orbit around the moon, at a distance of less than 70 miles from its surface. They ended their 6-day journey on 27 Dec., landing safely in the Pacific Ocean (moon landing, p. 652).

Canada

1945–47

1945 ELECTIONS. On 2 Feb., 1945, Prime Minister W. L. Mackenzie King's government received a setback with the defeat of Defense Minister A. G. L. McNaughton (1887–1966) in a parliamentary by-election. On 23 Feb. the government canceled 9 parliamentary by-elections due on 23 Apr. in favor of general elections in the summer. Elections in June gave the Liberal Party 119 seats. Parliament opened on 6 Sept.

ROSE CASE. In Feb. 1946, Fred Rose, Polish-born Communist M.P., was arrested and charged with violating the official-secrets acts by turning over secret information to the Russians. He was convicted on 15 June.

RELAXATION OF WARTIME CONTROLS. On 31 Jan., 1946, the government lifted price ceilings on over 300 consumer goods and relaxed controls over wages of office workers and factory workers. On 10 July the government took over the Dominion Steel and Coal Corp., the Steel Company of Canada, and Algoma Steel Corp., to meet strike threats. On 29 Nov. wartime controls on wages and salaries were removed, but price controls were retained. During the period 10 Apr.–15 May, 1947, there was a 400,000-man drop in unemployment. On 25 May a strike of 13,000 coal workers in Nova Scotia ended with a pay raise. On 30 Sept., all army, naval, and air forces changed from a wartime to a peacetime footing and the army changed its name from Canada Active Service Force to Canada Army Active Force. During 1947, price controls were removed from many items—household articles, fresh vegetables, fruit and fish, dairy products, restaurant meals, textile and leather products, bakery items, tea, and coffee. By Sept. most curbs were off. Canada also passed regulations relating to the immigration of displaced persons during 1947.

1948–55

ST. LAURENT REGIME. In Sept. 1948 Lester Pearson (b. 1897) became state secretary for external affairs, and Louis Stephen St. Laurent (b. 1882) served as acting premier and justice minister while King was abroad. On 15 Nov., King resigned and St. Laurent became prime minister. On 3 Aug., 1949, it was announced that "Dominion" had been dropped from the name of Canada on government letterheads and official documents. On 17 Oct. all wartime controls on foods ended.

On 27 June, 1949, St. Laurent's Liberal Party won 193 of the 262 seats in Commons, the Progressive Conservatives winning only 45. In Oct. parliamentary by-elections gave the Liberals 4 seats, the Independents 3, and the Progressive Conservatives 1. The fiscal year ending 31 Mar., 1950, showed a \$111-million budget surplus and a dollar exchange reserve of more than \$1.24 billion. A deadline of Apr. 1951 was set for the ending of rent control.

On 15 Sept., 1950, Parliament adjourned after a 16-day special session in which it (1) doubled the defense budget to \$850 million, (2) called all of the country's regular armed forces to active duty, (3) gave the government power to control essential materials and services, and (4) approved government restraints on consumer installment buying as an anti-inflationary measure.

In Jan. 1951 Canada's population exceeded 14 million for the first time, and Canadian exports achieved a peacetime record of \$3,118.4 million. On 26 Apr. the Liberal Party won elections in Prince Edward Island. On 25 June Conservative candidates unseated 4 Liberals in parliamentary by-elections by assailing the government for the high cost of living. The Commons now had 185 Liberals, 46 Progressive Conservatives, 13 Co-operative Commonwealth Federalists, 10 Social Credit Party members, 4 Independent Liberals, and 4 independents.

The national elections of 10 Aug., 1953, were won by the Liberals, their 5th consecutive victory. The House of Commons now consisted of 171 Liberals, 50 Conservatives, 23 Co-operative Commonwealth Federalists, and 15 members of the Social Credit Party.

VALUE OF THE CANADIAN DOLLAR. On 19 Sept., 1949, the Canadian dollar was devalued from U.S. \$1.00 to U.S. \$.90. On 30 Sept., 1950, it was freed to find its own level on the world market. By 5 Oct. it had risen on the New York exchange to U.S. \$.94½. The Canadian dollar was freed because of the country's strong gold reserve of \$1,798 million, up \$534 million during the preceding 3 months.

APPOINTMENT OF MASSEY AS GOV. GEN. On 24 Jan., 1952, Vincent Massey (1887–1967), Canadian high commissioner in London, 1935–46, and chancellor of the University of Toronto since 1947, was appointed to succeed Field Marshal Viscount Alexander as gov. gen. Massey was the 1st Canadian appointed to the post.

1956–62

CONSERVATIVE VICTORY OF 1957. On 30 Oct., 1956, the Progressive Conservatives won the provincial elections in Nova Scotia for the 1st time in 23 years. On 14 Dec., John Diefenbaker (b. 1895) was elected leader of the Progressive Conservative Party at a convention in Ottawa. National elections held on 10 June, 1957, resulted in the loss of the Liberals' 170-seat majority in the Canadian Federal House of Commons. The Liberals won 104 seats and the Conservatives 109. Diefenbaker formed a new government on 17 June.

AWARD OF NOBEL PRIZE TO PEARSON. On 14 Oct., 1957, ex-External Affairs Secretary Lester B. Pearson won the 1957 Nobel Peace Prize. Although no reason was given by the committee, it was understood that he was honored principally for his efforts in 1950–53 to halt the Korean War, for his leadership in creating the UN Expeditionary Force to enforce the truce in the Middle East, and for efforts to strengthen the military and nonmilitary functions of NATO.

DIEFENBAKER REGIME. On 16 Jan., 1958, Pearson succeeded St. Laurent as Liberal Party leader. Elections held on 30 Mar. resulted in an overwhelming victory for Diefenbaker's Conservatives over Pearson's Liberals. On 8 Apr. the Gordon Commission, set up by Parliament to survey Canada's economic future, reported that Canada's trade would be primarily geared toward the U.S. within the next 25 years, to the detriment of her sales to Britain and Europe. On 18 Jan., 1960, Prime Minister Diefenbaker, in his 1st major message to Parliament, called for alterations in the British North America Act designed to broaden Canada's right to amend its constitution without the sanction of the British Par-

liament. On 4 Aug. a Canadian Bill of Rights was approved unanimously by the House of Commons.

NEW DEMOCRATIC PARTY. At a convention in Ottawa, 31 July–4 Aug., 1961, the New Democratic Party was formed by an amalgamation of the 1-million-member Canadian Labor Congress, members of the old Socialist Farmers' Co-operative Commonwealth Federation, and various intellectuals dissatisfied with both the Conservative and Liberal parties.

IMMIGRATION LAW. 19 Jan., 1962. New immigration regulations were issued, abolishing discrimination based on race, color, or religion. Immigrants now were to be judged solely on education, training, and skills.

MACKENZIE TERRITORY. The Northwest Territories Council (Little Parliament of the North) approved, 1962, a proposal to create by 1964 within its own 1.3-million-sq.-mi. territory a new 580,000-sq. mi. self-governing area to be called Mackenzie Territory. This territory would have its own governing council and a resident commissioner.

FALL IN FOREIGN RESERVES. In June 1962 the government devalued the dollar to a par value of U.S. $0.92½. The step was taken to discourage the continual drain on foreign-exchange reserves. On 24 June Diefenbaker announced plans to borrow $1 billion abroad to bolster the Canadian dollar and an austerity plan designed to reduce the budget deficit and the deficit in Canada's balance of payments.

1963–68

FALL OF THE DIEFENBAKER GOVERNMENT. On 5 Feb., 1963, Diefenbaker's Conservative government was overthrown by a vote of no confidence. The defeat resulted from a bitter domestic and U.S.-Canadian dispute begun by a statement, 30 Jan., by the U.S. State Department which was critical of Ottawa's reluctance to accept American nuclear weapons for joint U.S.-Canadian defense of North America and for Canadian units in NATO forces. Diefenbaker was overthrown by a Social Credit Party motion, approved by a 142–111 vote, which stated that his government had failed to give a clear statement of Canada's national defense policy. A Liberal motion of no confidence was then passed by the same 142–111 vote. In elections held 8 Apr. the Liberals fell 5 votes short of the majority required before they could automatically replace the Conservative government. The Liberals won 128 seats to the Conservatives' 96. Diefenbaker resigned, 17 Apr., and Pearson was sworn in, 22 Apr., as prime minister.

NEW CANADIAN FLAG. On 15 Feb., 1965, the new maple-leaf flag was raised for the 1st time. It was meant to symbolize the desired unity between French- and Anglo-Canadians.

POLITICS IN QUEBEC. 1966. On 16 June Daniel Johnson (1915–68) of the conservative Nationale Union replaced Jean Lesage (b. 1912) as premier of Quebec. In the 108-seat Quebec Legislative Assembly, there were now 55 Nationale Union members and 51 Liberals. In a news conference, Sept., Johnson discussed his "2-nation" theory and asked for more internal control for Quebec.

EXPO 67. A highly successful international exposition was held in Montreal, 1967.

ACCESSION OF TRUDEAU. On 6 Apr., 1968, Justice Minister Pierre Elliott Trudeau (b. 1921) was elected leader of the Liberal Party and sworn in as prime minister, 20 Apr. He dissolved Parliament, 23 Apr. In the general elections held on 25 June, the Liberals won a decisive victory.

LATIN AMERICA

Argentina

1945–55

THE AGE OF PERÓN. After demonstrating his overwhelming support among the ragged masses (*descamisados*), Juan Domingo Perón was elected, 24 Feb., 1946, president of Argentina. Perón in-augurated one of the most remarkable regimes in the history of Latin America. Under the cloudy ideology of *justicialismo*, Peronism proved a semifascist variant of extreme nationalism, built upon the twin pillars of labor (with mass involvement) and the army. Its nationalism took diplomatic ("3rd position") and economic forms (nationalization of telephones, 1946; railroads, 1948). Its statist economic policies, bent on industrialization at all cost, disastrously neglected agriculture, the source of nearly all foreign exchange. Wheat production declined from 8.2 metric tons in 1941 to 2.3 in 1950; agricultural and pastoral production declined 50%, 1946–52. Perón tolerated no organized opposition of any kind.

Until her death (26 July, 1952) Perón's wife, María Eva Duarte de Perón, was nearly his coruler, with labor unions, newspapers, and state welfare under her personal control. His (unsuccessful) attempt to impose her as his vice-president, 1951, alienated part of his crucial military support. The effects of his calamitous economic policies, his turning to foreign capital in an attempt to solve them (Standard Oil of Calif., 1953), and his growing anticlericalism (after an earlier harmonious relationship with the church) solidified opposition against him. He was deposed by a military coup, 19 Sept., 1955.

1955–68

THE LEGACY OF PERÓN. Neither Perón's military nor civilian successors were able to deal with his working-class supporters, who remained loyal, a source of continuing indigestion in the body politic. After the military regime of Gen. Pedro E. Aramburu, 1955–58, attempted to disperse the *peronistas* by suppression, civilian Radical Arturo Frondizi, 1958–62, tried to reintegrate them into traditional politics (while seeking to stabilize and reinvigorate the economy). After elections, 18 Mar., 1962, which demonstrated *peronista*-bloc strength, the military judged the attempt a failure and ousted Frondizi, 29 Mar. The army remained the arbiters through the uneasy administration of Arturo Illía, 1963–66, finally unseating him, 29 June, 1966, and installing Gen. Juan Carlos Onganía, 30 June, at the head of a new repressive dictatorship.

Chile

1942–64

THE POLITICS OF INFLATION. A runaway inflation, beginning during World War II and accelerating during the 1950's, reflected fundamental structural problems within Chile's democracy. Neither the governments of traditional politicians—Radicals Juan Antonio Ríos, 1942–46; Gabriel González Videla, 1946–52; and Liberal Jorge Alessandri Rodríguez, 1958–64—nor of a former dictator, now elected president—Carlos Ibáñez, 1952–58—could simultaneously achieve development and stability. The economy was not strong enough to support the demands that the government was too weak to refuse. Inflation masked the neglect of basic social and economic problems.

1964–68

EDUARDO FREI AND CHRISTIAN DEMOCRACY. As the long economic crisis wore on, Chile's electorate grew increasingly disenchanted with its traditional politicians of the center and right. In the 1958 elections, they had narrowly selected Alessandri over Salvador Allende, candidate of the Marxist FRAP coalition. In 1964, they turned massively to the progressive Christian Democrats and Eduardo Frei Montalva, who, in an essentially 2-man race with Allende, was the 1st president in the century to win more than 50% of the vote. The effect of this, and subsequent congressional elections, 1965, was to break the mold of traditional politics. Despite stiff opposition from the combined right and left, the Christian Democrats, a nonclerical reformist Catholic party, began a frontal assault on fundamental problems. The purpose of "Chileanization" of copper, Dec. 1964,

principal source of foreign exchange, was to assure adequate funds for development. The government assumed greater control, but did not nationalize the U.S.-run mines, in exchange for promises of $500-m. new investment and doubled production by 1970. Important land reform, education, and community development legislation was enacted.

Uruguay and Paraguay

1945–68

STABILITY AND STAGNATION IN URUGUAY. In 1952 Uruguay replaced its presidential form of government with a 9-man executive National Council, which was operative until 1966, when the more conventional executive was restored. In the 1958 election the Nationalist Party (Blancos) ousted the Colorados from control of the national government for the 1st time in 93 years. The Colorados returned to power in 1966. Neither party under either constitutional arrangement seemed able to halt spiraling inflation (the price index rose from 100 in 1958 to 393 in 1963), the drain of the state's welfare burden, economic stagnation (especially wool and meat production), and the concomitant social unrest and frequent strikes.

PRAETORIAN STATE IN PARAGUAY. Ruled since 11 July, 1954, by Gen. Alfredo Stroessner, Paraguay continued as an isolated, backward, peaceful dictatorship.

Bolivia

1945–64

THE MNR AND SOCIAL REVOLUTION. On 9–11 Apr., 1952, a widespread popular uprising led to the recall from Argentina of Víctor Paz Estenssoro, exiled leader of the Bolivian National Revolutionary Movement (MNR). In the following decade the MNR presided over and partially directed the beginnings of a painful transformation of this poorest of South American countries. In his 1st term

Paz Estenssoro made suffrage universal; disbanded the army and armed a civilian militia; nationalized the tin mines, source of foreign exchange (COMIBOL, Oct. 1952) ; and, partially compelled by Indian uprisings, instituted an important land reform, 2 Aug., 1953. The social goals— rapid economic development and the integration of the Indian into national life—were laudable and supported financially by the U.S. The economic effects of revolutionary policies, however—declining agricultural production and an unparalleled inflation (average of 57.3% per year, 1951–60) —created grave new social problems and sharp rifts within the MNR. President Hernán Siles Zuazo, 1956–60, and Paz in his 2nd term, 1960–64, forced by economic necessity to austerity measures, were increasingly repressive. In 1963 labor leader Juan Lechín withdrew from the MNR. On 4 Nov., 1964, Gen. René Barrientos Ortuño headed a junta that ousted Paz and he assumed the presidency, 6 Nov.

1964–68

THE MILITARY IN POLITICS. Despite armed clashes between the army and tin miners, 1965, Ortuño was able to consolidate his hold over the government, and he was elected president in the national election held on 3 July, 1966. Ortuño's government was shaken by the publication of the captured war diary of Ché Guevara, who was killed by Bolivian troops, 9 Oct., 1967. Following the disclosure that a government minister had released the diary, a state of siege was declared, and on 27 July, 1968, an all-military cabinet was appointed.

Peru and Ecuador

1945–62

APRISTA INFLUENCE IN PERU. Although representing a majority of popular opinion in the country and with the fundamental support of President José Luis Bustamante, 1945–48, the Aprista Party was unable to carry through its

economic or social legislation against the dogged opposition of Peru's traditional oligarchy. Gen. Manuel Odría (president, 1948–56) deposed Bustamante, outlawed the Apristas, and ruled without pretense of democracy. His elected successor, Manuel Prado, 1956–62, lacked the political advantage of high export prices from which Odría had benefited and ran into increasing economic difficulties.

1963–68

BELAÚNDE TERRY. After the military annulled the results of the 1962 presidential elections (in which Aprista leader Haya de la Torre had a plurality), another election was held, 9 June, 1963, and Fernando Belaúnde Terry of Acción Popular was elected. Lacking the traditional military enmity toward Haya, Belaúnde was able to enlist the support of progressive elements within the armed forces for social programs often largely appropriated from the Apristas. Belaúnde's inability to cope with a severe financial crisis and his imposition of a settlement with American oil interests, which offended nationalist army officers, led to a coup on 3 Oct., 1968. The civilian government was replaced by a "Revolutionary Government" composed of military men.

INSTABILITY IN ECUADOR. The apparent beginnings of constitutional succession begun by the reformist and democratic administration of Galo Plaza Lasso, 1948–52, were ended by a series of military coups in the 1960's. The Indians remained unintegrated into the nation, the economy underdeveloped, and politics traditionally personalistic and unstable.

Colombia and Venezuela

1946–57

VIOLENCIA IN COLOMBIA. A split in the Liberal Party allowed the Conservative, Mariano Ospina Pérez, to be elected president, 1946. Almost immediately the government began purging Liberal officials, increasingly making use of the army and police. The persecution aroused Liberal resistance and set in motion a dialectic of violence unparalleled in Latin America in the 20th cent. An estimated 200,000 people died in more than a decade of civil war, banditry, and class warfare. The *bogotazo,* an immense riot which destroyed all of central Bogotá ($500 m. damage, 1,500 killed), followed the assassination of the Liberal leader, Jorge Eliécer Gaitán, 9 Apr., 1948. The semifascist repression initiated by President Laureano Gómez, 1950–53, intensified hostilities and finally led to intervention by the army, June 1953. An inept attempt by Gen. Gustavo Rojas Pinilla to reshape Colombian politics in a Peronist mold united students, church, and both parties against him. He was ousted, May 1957.

DEMOCRACY AND DICTATOR-SHIP IN VENEZUELA. After a brief period of reformist rule, 1945–48, the Acción Democrática (AD) party was overthrown by the military, Nov. 1948. Emerging from the ruling junta, Col. Marcos Pérez Jiménez established a personal dictatorship, 1950–58, which was politically brutal and economically irresponsible. On 23 Jan., 1958, Pérez Jiménez fled in the face of overwhelming popular pressure.

1958–68

COLOMBIAN NATIONAL FRONT. The *Violencia* destroyed the fabric of Colombian society without producing a revolutionary government. On 7 Aug., 1958, Liberal Alberto Lleras Camargo, 1958–62, began the unique National Front, a constitutional arrangement for 16 years during which the 2 traditional parties would alternate in the presidency and otherwise divide all political offices equally between them. The agreement did bring greater stability but no concerted action to deal with the effects of the social upheaval. It remained to be seen if the Liberal Carlos Lleras Restrepo, 1966–70, would be more successful in attacking fundamental problems than

the "do-nothing" administration of the Conservative Guillermo León Valencia, 1962–66.

AD AND VENEZUELAN DEMO-CRATIC REFORM. Ruling in coalition with the Christian Democrats (COPEI), AD's Rómulo Betancourt, 1959–64, brought Venezuela planned economic development, significant social reform, and —in the face of guerrilla terror on the left and army pressure on the right—determinedly democratic government. Betancourt cut illiteracy from 50% to 21%, carried out agrarian reform, fostered labor organization and industry profit sharing, built the huge Guayana City industrial complex, and began to utilize Venezuela's enormous oil receipts to diversify the economy. Venezuela's 1st elected civilian president in history to finish his term, Betancourt turned over his office to former AD labor leader Raúl Leoni, 11 Mar., 1964. The coalition government broke down, Mar. 1966, with the AD's partners charging that they were not being permitted a large enough role in the government. Leoni was able to form another government, however, and continued to advance AD programs.

Brazil

1945–54

DUTRA. On 25 Oct., 1945, President Getúlio Vargas was deposed to assure the return of democracy. In Dec. Gen. Enrico Dutra was elected. He proved an unimaginative chief executive. Policy was shaped largely by the clash between the formerly dominant agricultural and mercantile interests and the nationalistic industrialists that had emerged during the Vargas era. The Constitution of 1946 established a federal system but included many provisions for social welfare pioneered by Vargas.

RETURN OF VARGAS. Vargas, reelected president, Oct. 1950, found leading a democratic government, with a hostile Congress, difficult (although he succeeded in founding the state oil monopoly, PETROBRAS, in 1953). Beset by a declining demand for exports and a threatened military coup, Vargas committed suicide, 24 Aug., 1954.

1956–64

KUBITSCHEK AND GROWTH. Juscelino Kubitschek won a narrow plurality in the presidential election of Oct. 1955 and, following a "preventive" coup to ensure his succession, took office in Jan. 1956. He brought the country rapid economic growth, especially of infrastructure (average growth 7.2% per year, 1956–60); built the new national capital of Brasília (dedicated Apr. 1960), opening the interior for development; attacked regional imbalance with a new development agency (SUDENE, headed by Celso Furtado) for the poverty-stricken northeast; and generally favored growth over stability. Brazil paid a price: rapid inflation (cost of living up 211%, 1956–60) and neglect of social development leading to increasing unrest.

DRIFT TO THE LEFT. Elected as a reformer in Oct. 1960 and promising an "independent" foreign policy, Jânio Quadros resigned enigmatically, 25 Aug., 1961. His successor, his leftist and independently elected vice-president, João (Jango) Goulart, took office after strong resistance from the military and amid rising tensions. His inability to deal with the inflation (more than 80%, 1963; 20% per month, 1964) and his drift to the left led to his ouster by the military in a broadly supported coup, 31 Mar.–2 Apr., 1964.

1964–68

"REVOLUTIONARY" GOVERNMENT BY THE ARMY. With the coup the military moved from its position as prompter in the wings, where it had been since 1945, to the center of the political stage. President Humberto Castelo Branco, 11 Apr., 1964–15 Mar., 1967, assumed far-reaching decree powers, deprived of political rights some 9,000 public figures, abolished existing political parties, re-established close ties with the U.S., and adopted conservative austerity remedies for inflation. After the indirect election and installation of Marshal Arthur da Costa e Silva as president, 15 Mar., 1967, there were some signs that the military might relax its direct hold over the nation.

Central America

1945–68

MEXICO. With the governments of Miguel Alemán, 1946–52, and Adolfo Ruiz Cortines, 1952–58, the civilian heirs of the Mexican revolution turned to the right, sacrificing social reform to economic development. The economic results were impressive: the most diversified economy in Latin America, with a high rate of sustained and balanced growth (average, 6.5% per year, 1951–60), and "Mexicanized" control of key sectors. But the level of real wages in 1958 was actually lower than in 1939, and in 1956 46% of school-age children were still not in school. Adolfo López Mateos, 1958–64, reversed the trend somewhat, channeling more of the budget into social investments, stepping up land redistribution more than any president had done since Cárdenas, and instituting profit sharing for labor (though using the army to break a rail strike, Apr. 1959). The guarantee of congressional seats to opposition parties, 1964, by Gustavo Díaz Ordaz (president, 1964–70) emphasized not the liberality of the government party (PRI) but rather its continuing inability to allow genuine democracy.

STUDENT UNREST. Dissatisfaction with heavy-handed police behavior and infringements on student autonomy led to violent street fighting between students and police-military contingents, July 1968. As the fighting extended through the summer into Oct., the demonstrators were able to force a government reappraisal of parts of the penal code, as well as a pledge to uphold university autonomy.

GUATEMALA. The progressive regime of Dr. Juan José Arévalo, 1945–51, began a decade of social change. Arévalo instituted social security and a labor code, restored civil liberties, encouraged the formation of labor and peasant unions, and attempted to integrate the Indians (50% of the population) into the national life. His successor, Col. Jacobo Arbenz Guzmán, 1951–54, moved further left, fell under Communist influence, and repressed opposition. His agrarian reform, July 1952, struck at the extensive holdings of the United Fruit Co., and alarmed the U.S., which helped arm the "liberation army" that overthrew him, June 1954. Between 1954 and 1968, 2 military and 2 civilian regimes have for the most part tried to avoid the problems raised by the revolution. From 1967 onward guerrillas were active in the countryside.

EL SALVADOR. Since a junior officers' coup, 13 Dec., 1948, El Salvador has had moderate military government, with economic development, stability, some social reform, and a degree of political freedom. With the exception of the period 26 Oct., 1960–24 Jan., 1961, when a more extreme military faction seized power, rule was lodged mainly with 2 government parties, PRUD, 1950–60, and PCN, 1961 onward. Resistance from the tiny but entrenched civilian oligarchy, added to the military's own fears of instability, prevented fundamental change.

COSTA RICA. After winning a 2-month civil war, 1948, and restoring the government to the president-elect, José Figueres was himself elected president in 1953. His *aprista*-type National Liberation Party (PLN) implemented a program of agricultural, industrial, and educational development, abolished the armed forces, and democratically turned over office in 1958 when the Conservative opposition (PUN) won a narrow victory. A change of presidents also occurred following the 1962 (PLN) and 1966 (PUN) electoral contests.

NICARAGUA. Despite the assassination of the long-time dictator, Anastasio (Tacho) Somoza in 1956, Nicaragua continued to be run like a private fief by his surviving family.

HONDURAS. Following a coup by restless junior officers, 1956, the Liberal,

Ramón Villeda Morales, 1957–63, instituted a brief period of change in his poverty-stricken country. When his party appeared certain to win re-election, the army, desirous of regaining direct control, staged a coup, 3 Oct., 1963.

PANAMA. After a short period of reform under José Remón, 1952–55, Panama's politics continued to be characterized by electoral successions and extreme personalism. A growing sense of nationalism was demonstrated by the anti-U.S. riots of Jan. 1964. A new Canal Treaty followed, 24 Sept., 1965. In Mar. 1968 the National Guard, which supported the National Liberal Party government, prevented the National Assembly from removing President Robles from office. Robles' candidate in the May elections was defeated, but the National Guard overthrew the victor, President Arnulfo Arias, on 11 Oct., 1968. Charging that Arias had attempted to reshuffle the Guard's leadership, the National Guard replaced the president with a junta of senior officers.

The Caribbean

1945–68

THE CUBAN REVOLUTION. Following the ineffective and corrupt elected regimes of Ramón Grau San Martín, 1944–48, and Carlos Prío Socarrás, 1948–52, Fulgencio Batista, 10 Mar., 1952–31 Dec., 1958, built a dictatorship on the support of the army, organized labor, and the U.S. After 3 years of guerrilla warfare, he was overthrown by Fidel Castro, who gradually instituted the most sweeping social revolution in the history of the hemisphere.

The revolution in Cuba was not so much the events that brought Castro to power as the direction taken thereafter. The Agrarian Reform, 17 May, 1959, was a crucial turning point. It was intended to achieve Cuba's "economic independence" by nationalizing the vital sugar industry and estates (principal source of foreign exchange), diversifying agriculture, and distributing land to the landless. Its excutive agency, INRA, largely run by the revolutionary army, soon assumed the larger task of administering all nationalized properties (Cuban and foreign) and reorganizing the whole economy under state control. Anti-Batista moderates had left all top government posts by July 1959, gradually being replaced by members of the Communist Party (PSP). In July and Oct. 1960 all large foreign and Cuban businesses were nationalized (est. $1 billion U.S. property). The 15 Oct., 1960, Urban Reform limited income from rentals to $600 a month, driving middle-class *rentiers* into exile. But living conditions for the poor improved.

The effect of the U.S.-USSR confrontation over Cuba, 1961–62, was to accelerate its government's movement toward East European Communist models. Castro proclaimed Cuba a "socialist" country, 1 May, 1961, and himself a "Marxist-Leninist," 2 Dec., 1961. In Feb. 1961 a Ministry of Industry had been founded (headed by Ché Guevara) to carry out economic centralization and industrialization. This policy proved a failure. Importing raw materials for Cuban-produced manufactures was more expensive than importing finished goods from abroad. Serious food shortages provoked internal dissention and "Revolutionary Tribunals" were established, May 1962, to deal with economic crimes. But Castro was alert to the dangers of losing the authentically Cuban character of the revolution (and his own leadership of it). He denounced PSP leader Aníbal Escalante, 26 Mar., 1962, when the Communists attempted to co-opt the new single government party (ORI, later PURS). The limits on his control, however, were emphasized by the big-power settlement of the Oct.–Nov. 1962 missile crisis.

Castro's May 1963 visit to Moscow resulted in his reversing Cuba's development priorities. Terming its past policy "economic cretinism," Cuba agreed to return to intensive sugar production (which had fallen from 6.8 m. tons to 3.8 m. during 1961–63). The 2nd Agrarian Reform, 2 Oct., 1963, expropriated the land of some 10,000 medium farmers and shifted the ownership balance to 70% state, 30% private. Cuba's youth, who had taken part in a successful mass literacy campaign in 1961, were subject,

after 12 Nov., 1963, to compulsory military service. The government's purposes were essentially to mobilize a cheap source of labor and to socialize the youth into revolutionary values. After Nov. 1964, more old-line Communist leaders were eliminated from power in government (Castro himself replacing INRA head Carlos Rafael Rodríguez). As of 1968, Castro remained at the center of the revolution, with his vast popular support largely intact.

DOMINICAN REPUBLIC. After the assassination of Trujillo, 30 May, 1961, the Dominican Republic struggled to overcome the effects of his brutal 31-year dictatorship—feeble institutions and powerful armed forces. The reformist democrat, Juan Bosch, landslide victor in the Dec. 1962 elections, was ousted after only 8 months in office, 27 Feb.–25 Sept., 1963. A popular revolt, including junior officers led by Col. Francisco Caamaño Deñó, overthrew the conservative Donald Reid Cabral regime, 24 Apr., 1965. Out of fear of "another Castro," the U.S. encouraged Trujillo's old officers to counterattack, 26 Apr., and then, for the 1st time since 1926, intervened directly, landing marines, 28 Apr. Some 20,000 invasion troops presided over 4 months of civil war (ending 31 Aug., 1965). On 1 Mar., 1966, Joaquín Balaguer, a puppet premier under Trujillo, defeated Bosch in an OAS-supervised presidential election.

HAITI. Beginning in 1957 François Duvalier ("Papa Doc") replaced the traditional dictatorship of the Garde d'Haïti by a reign of terror at the hands of his *Tons-Tons Macoutes* (voodoo secret police), driving foreign capital and the educated elite abroad and intensifying the misery of the masses.

AFRICA

North Africa

1956–68

TUNISIA. On 25 July, 1957, about 1 year after Tunisian independence, the Legislative Assembly abolished the monarchy and appointed Habib Bourguiba head of state pending preparation of a new constitution. Bourguiba initiated social reforms, granting full equality to all citizens and placing persons of all religions under the same secular law. During 1956–57, the state took over religious and tribal lands for distribution to individual farmers; and in Nov. 1958, the government began compulsory repurchase of land belonging to European settlers.

On 1 June, 1959, the constitution established Tunisia as a republic; in the Nov. elections, Bourguiba was returned as president at the head of a Neo-Destour government. Late in 1959, Bourguiba began a labor mobilization program, under which thousands of urban unemployed returned to their home provinces to carry out public works projects.

In 1961, when the French extended their base at Bizerte, Bourguiba called for evacuation and blockaded the base. The French retaliated with a paratroop attack which inflicted heavy casualties on Tunisian troops and prestige. Tunisia then took the case to the UN, which backed her position; and France agreed to evacuation, effective 1963. In Oct. 1964, the Neo-Destour held its 7th congress, at which the party was reorganized and renamed the Parti Socialiste Destourien (PSD). The national elections in Nov. returned Bourguiba as president and approved a single list of PSD candidates for the Assembly.

ALGERIA. Algerian independence, July 1962, came in the midst of an economic crisis resulting from war and from the exodus of the French who had operated the commercial economy. In addition, there was an open split in the FLN. In July the GPRA was established in Algiers with Ben Khedda as premier. But Ben Bella withdrew from the government and, with the support of the army under Col. Houari Boumédienne, organized his own Political Bureau. By Sept. Ben Bella had attained effective control of the country. He initiated a socialist economic policy under which Algerian peasants took over estates abandoned by the French and operated collective farms with the help of state-directed management committees. By the end of 1963, Algeria began to nationalize foreign-owned land and industry, although the economy continued to depend on French aid and French co-operation in exploitation of Saharan oil.

During 1963, Ben Bella consolidated his political position, bringing the Communist Party and the trade unions under FLN control and putting down revolts in the Kabyle region. In Sept. 1963, Algerian voters approved a new constitution which designated the FLN as the sole legal party, with the right to name a single list of candidates for president and National Assembly. In July 1964, revolts broke out again in the Kabyle and Biskra areas, in opposition to the excessive personal power of the president. On 19 June, 1965, Col. Boumédienne removed Ben Bella in a bloodless coup, suspended the constitution and the Assembly, and assumed the presidency at the head of a 26-man Conseil National de la Révolution. Boumédienne began to restructure the FLN and adopted a more gradual economic policy designed to ensure financial stability and attract foreign investment.

MOROCCO. The 1st year of independence, 1956, was devoted to restoration of public order, as the sultan and predominantly *Istiqlal* government put down dissidence in both urban and rural areas. Then the general unrest began to crystallize into organized political movements. Late in 1957, the Mouvement Populaire emerged in rural and Berber regions, advocating a doctrine of "Islamic socialism"; the party received legal recognition after a revolt in the Rif in 1958. Also in 1957, a split began to appear within *Istiqlal;* and in the summer of 1959, Mehdi Ben Barka joined trade unionists and other *Istiqlal* secessionists in the Union Nationale des Forces Populaires (UNFP), which was committed to a more radical economic and social policy than *Istiqlal* under Al Fassi.

Party rivalry brought renewed disorder, until King Mohammed announced, May 1960, that he was taking control of the government. After Mohammed's sudden death in Feb. 1961, the crown prince assumed power as King Hassan II. In Dec. 1962 a popular referendum ratified a new constitution which gave extensive authority to the monarchy and established a Legislative Assembly with limited power.

In preparation for the elections of May 1963, Ahmed Reda Guedira formed a new royalist party, the Front pour la Défense des Institutions Constitutionnelles (FDIC). The FDIC led, but failed to win an effective majority in the elections; and the new government under Prime Minister Ahmed Bahnini met constant challenges from the UNFP, which had boycotted the constitutional referendum, and from *Istiqlal*, which questioned the election returns. Guedira's regrouping of FDIC elements into the Parti Socialiste Démocratique (PSD), Apr. 1964, failed to strengthen his position significantly, and the Assembly continued to debate while economic and social conditions deteriorated. In Mar. 1965 the populace expressed its frustration by riots in Casablanca; in June Hassan suspended the constitution and himself took control as prime minister. He retained this post until July 1967, when he rearranged the cabinet and appointed Mohammed Benhima prime minister.

West Africa

1957–68

GUINEA. Guinea's rejection of the de Gaulle constitution, 1958, led to an immediate withdrawal of French technical and financial aid and consequent deterioration in economic conditions. The country became a 1-party state, Dec. 1958, when opposition parties merged with Sekou Touré's Parti Démocratique de Guinée (PDG). On 1 May, 1959, Guinea entered into a union with Ghana, as part of their common pan-African policy, and received a £10 m. Ghanaian loan. During 1960 Guinea withdrew from the franc zone and signed commercial and cultural agreements with various Communist countries. But nationalization and Communist aid proved largely ineffective; and in Dec. 1961, Touré expelled the Soviet ambassador for alleged plotting against his government. By Dec. 1962 Guinea was

drawing closer to the West again in the hope of developing the country's promising bauxite and iron ore resources, although Touré received a new Soviet ambassador, Mar. 1962, and has continued to insist on Guinean nonalignment. In Mar. 1966 Touré gave asylum to deposed Ghanaian president Nkrumah and designated him co-chief of state, apparently a nominal position.

GHANA. At independence in 1957, Nkrumah's CPP governed Ghana with a program stressing national unity and socialist economic development. Opposition from traditional tribal and religious leaders, private cocoa farmers, and middle-class intellectuals coalesced into the United Party, to which the government responded by trying to concentrate power in the CPP. In 1958 an Industrial Relations Act placed national labor unions under central control, and a Preventive Detention Act set aside the right to free trial. Several opposition leaders were detained under the latter act in 1959.

In Apr. 1960, a plebiscite chose a republican constitution with Nkrumah as president. In 1961 falling world prices for Ghana's principal export, cocoa, increased the balance-of-payments problem and necessitated an austerity budget. In Sept. and Oct. the government repressed protest strikes by railway and dock workers. Nkrumah persisted in his policy of heavy investment in large, long-term development projects, including the Volta River hydroelectric power and aluminum smelter project, begun in 1962, and in spite of pressing domestic problems, he continued to devote considerable attention to leadership in the pan-African movement.

In a Supreme Court trial, Dec. 1963, Chief Justice Sir Arku Korsah acquitted 3 men accused of treason. Nkrumah dismissed Korsah and nullified the court's decision under a new Law of Criminal Procedure Act which was rushed through the National Assembly. On 31 Jan., 1964, a referendum approved constitutional amendments which empowered the president to dismiss judges and named the CPP as the sole national party. The CPP adopted an increasingly militant attitude which placed ideology before reality, while corruption within its ranks undermined popular support.

By 1965 Ghana was heavily in debt abroad; in Dec. Nkrumah negotiated a 2-year moratorium on debts to Communist countries and began seeking similar arrangements with western creditors. On 24 Feb., 1966, while Nkrumah was out of the country, a group of senior army and police officers took control and established a National Liberation Council (NLC) under Gen. Joseph Ankrah. The NLC outlawed the CPP, suspended the constitution, and dissolved the Assembly. It canceled the economic plan and announced a policy of stabilization by reduced government spending. Aid from western countries eased Ghana's balance-of-payments deficit.

NIGERIA. Regionalism continued to dominate Nigerian politics after independence in 1960. Chief Awolowo, leader of the Action Group in the federal Parliament, challenged the regional system when he tried to gather behind him all the more radical elements in the country who opposed the Balewa government's economic program and pro-western foreign policy. Chief Akintola, premier of the Western Region and deputy leader of the Action Group, opposed Awolowo. The party split open in May 1962, when Akintola lost both his positions. During the ensuing violence, the federal government declared a state of emergency in the west and began a long trial which ended with Awolowo's imprisonment for treason, Sept. 1963. Meanwhile, Jan. 1963, Akintola had been reinstated as western premier and had formed the Nigerian National Democratic Party (NNDP), a coalition of his followers and the NCNC.

On 1 Oct., 1963, Nigeria became a federal republic with 4 regions, including the Mid-West Region which had been created in May. The Parliament elected Azikiwe president. Two main groups opposed each other for the 1st national elections, 30 Dec., 1964: the Nigerian National Alliance (NNA), led by Ahmadu Bello, combined the NPC, NNDP, Mid-West Democratic Front, and small eastern opposition parties; and the United Progressive Grand Alliance (UPGA), led by eastern premier Michael Okpara, brought together the NCNC, Action Group, and northern opposition parties. The campaign became a north-south contest, marked by violence, and on 28 Dec. the UPGA announced that it would boycott the elections because of irregularities in nominating candidates in several constituencies. With a fraction of the electorate voting, the NNA won an overwhelming majority. President Azikiwe hesitated to acknowledge these results, but after intensive discussions with various political leaders, he announced, 4 Jan., 1965, that a compromise had been reached whereby Prime Minister Balewa would form a government and supplementary elections would be held in doubtful constituencies. The elections, held 18 Mar., brought UPGA representation in Parliament to 108 against 197 for NNA, but failed to end unrest.

On 15 Jan., 1966, a group of eastern junior army officers carried out a coup in which Balewa, Bello, and Akintola were assassinated. By 17 Jan., Maj. Gen. Johnson Aguiyi-Ironsi, commander in chief of the army, had suppressed the revolt. He banned political parties and established a military government. On 29 July, northern soldiers in a countercoup killed Ironsi and replaced him with Lt. Col. Jakubu Gowon. This action was followed by riots and the slaughter of thousands of easterners living in the north and by a mass exodus of easterners to their home region. Lt. Col. Odumegwu Ojukwu, governor of the Eastern Province, challenged the legitimacy of the new regime; and relations between the federal government and the east deteriorated. On 30 May, 1967, the east seceded and proclaimed itself the independent Republic of Biafra. On 6 July fighting broke out between federal and eastern troops, and continued during the rest of 1967 and throughout 1968.

Democratic Republic of the Congo

1960

SITUATION AT INDEPENDENCE. The Congo became independent on 30 June, 1960, with an excellent economic potential and an explosive political situation. The atmosphere was one of apprehension and mutual suspicion between the Belgian and African communities. In addition, the Africans, with almost no training in western politics and with extravagant expectations of the benefits of "independence," were themselves divided into numerous tribes.

ARMY MUTINY AND BELGIAN INTERVENTION. On 5 July, 1960, African soldiers in Léopoldville and Thysville mutinied against their European officers in protest against their unchanged status and low wages. The next day the prime minister, Patrice Lumumba, promoted all soldiers 1 grade but failed to halt the spread of the mutiny into Lower Congo, where European civilians were attacked. On 7 July frightened Belgians began leaving the Congo. On 9 July, as the mutiny spread to other parts of the country, the Belgian government decided to send troops to protect its citizens; Belgian soldiers arrived the next day in Elisabethville, Luluabourg, and other centers of violence. On 11 July Lumumba and President Joseph Kasavubu, who were touring the disturbed areas trying to restore peace, agreed to accept the Belgian troops if they restricted themselves to protecting Europeans. But on the same day, Belgian ships bombarded Matadi, which had already been evacuated by Europeans; and Belgian forces supported Katanga in a declaration of secession under Moise Tshombe. On 12 July, after they had been refused permission to land at Elisabethville, Lumumba and Kasavubu requested UN intervention against Belgian aggression. The first UN troops arrived, 15 July, the Belgians began to withdraw from Léopoldville, and a measure of order was restored.

FALL OF LUMUMBA. On 5 Sept., 1960, Kasavubu, with UN and western support, dismissed Lumumba, who had been seeking Russian aid to invade Katanga and restore national unity. Lumumba in turn dismissed Kasavubu, and in the resultant confusion Col. Joseph Mobutu of the Armée Nationale Congolaise (ANC) replaced them both, 14 Sept.,

with a College of Commissioners composed of university graduates and students. Lumumba, who opposed the new government, was confined to his residence, while Kasavubu began to come to an understanding with the College. Two of Lumumba's supporters, Antoine Gizenga and Christophe Gbenye, began working in Stanleyville, Nov., to set up a rival government; by the end of the month, they had established control over Orientale Province. Lumumba himself escaped, 27 Nov., but was captured by Mobutu's troops, 2 Dec., and imprisoned at Thysville.

1961–68

KATANGA SECESSION. On 17 Jan., 1961, the Léopoldville authorities transferred Lumumba to Elisabethville, where he was murdered. The event aroused anger throughout Africa and brought a new UN resolution to return the Congo to parliamentary government. President Kasavubu negotiated with Katangans and Lumumbists, and on 2 Aug. a new government was formed with Cyrille Adoula as prime minister and Gizenga as deputy prime minister. During Sept. fighting broke out in Katanga when UN forces under Conor Cruise O'Brien attempted to remove foreign mercenary troops. In Oct., after disagreement with the Adoula government, Gizenga returned to Stanleyville and rallied support in Orientale; but in Nov. some army elements turned against him, bringing about his arrest and imprisonment, Jan. 1962. In Dec. 1961 Adoula met with Tshombe, who consented to Léopoldville's demands for reunification but then delayed implementation of the agreement after returning to Katanga.

UN AND U.S. INTERVENTIONS. In Mar. 1962 Adoula and Tshombe began negotiating again, but the talks broke off without agreement in June. On 3 Sept. Tshombe accepted a UN proposal for reunification, but again postponed implementation. On 28 Dec. UN forces renewed military action, and on 14 Jan., 1963, Tshombe announced the end of Katanga's secession and went into exile.

But unrest continued throughout the Congo. In Apr. trade-union leaders were arrested after the threat ˜ of a general strike. In Sept. Kasavubu declared Parliament closed; and in Oct. several opposition leaders were arrested, while others escaped to Brazzaville, where they formed a Comité National de Libération (CNL) to plot the overthrow of the Adoula government.

During early 1964, insurrections which had begun in Kwilu, Dec. 1963, spread to Orientale and Kivu, where local guerrillas fought the ANC. In June Tshombe returned from exile to announce that he could bring about a compromise. Kasavubu appointed him prime minister, 10 July; but no compromise was reached and, after the rebels captured Stanleyville in Aug., Tshombe requested and received U.S. air support. In Oct. the ANC, reinforced with mercenaries, moved into Eastern Congo; in Nov., with the help of a U.S. airlift of Belgian paratroopers, the ANC took Stanleyville and the rebellion began to peter out.

COUP BY MOBUTU. In Feb. 1965, preparing for the Mar.–Apr. legislative elections, Tshombe joined several parties into the Convention Nationale Congolaise (CONACO). Opposition Lumumbist parties formed the Alliance des Mouvements Nationalistes Congolais Lumumba. Because of voting irregularities in some districts, the opening of the new National Assembly was delayed from 30 June to 20 Sept., during which time a power struggle between Kasavubu and Tshombe grew increasingly evident. When the Assembly did open, a deadlock developed between supporters of the 2 rivals and persisted until 25 Nov., when Mobutu executed a coup. He took power as president and minister of defense, appointed Col. Leonard Mulamba prime minister and commander in chief of the ANC, and announced that he would rule for 5 years by decree subject to parliamentary approval. On 26 Oct., 1966, Mobutu dismissed Mulamba, assumed the functions of prime minister himself under a presidential regime, and began building a new single party, the Mouvement Populaire

de la Révolution (MPR). During the latter half of 1967, a rebellion by white mercenaries temporarily threatened stability, but crisis was averted when the OAU intervened to bring about evacuation of the mercenaries to Ruanda, Oct.

South Africa

1945–68

ADOPTION OF APARTHEID POLICY. At the end of 1947, the National Party published a pamphlet advocating *apartheid,* a policy of "preserving and safeguarding the racial identity of the white population of the country; of likewise preserving and safeguarding the identity of the indigenous peoples as separate racial groups, with opportunities to develop into self-governing national units. . . ." Its principles included segregation of ethnic groups into their own areas, with Africans working in cities regarded as temporary migrants without the political or social rights of white residents. The Nationalists, led by Malan, won the election of May 1948 and replaced Smuts's United Party government. Although his more militant supporters favored complete territorial separation of the races, Malan rejected this policy as impracticable, since the South African economy depended on African labor. Instead, the government initiated legislation for increasingly stricter control over relations among the races, including prohibition of mixed marriages, 1949, population registration, 1950, and provision of separate housing areas, 1950.

REACTION OF NONWHITES. Opposition to this legislation drew together all nonwhites, especially after enactment of the Suppression of Communism Act, 1950, which was so generally worded as to constitute a common threat. On May Day, 1950, the African National Congress (ANC) and the South African Indian Congress joined to sponsor a strike, during which 18 people were killed. In 1951 legislation restricted Africans to unskilled jobs; in 1952 the pass laws were tightened. In 1952 also, ex-Chief Albert

Luthuli, an advocate of racial co-operation, became president of ANC; from June until the end of the year, thousands of African, Indian, and Colored demonstrators violated *apartheid* laws and went to prison in a defiance campaign.

During 1953, new laws segregated transport facilities and schools and forbade Africans the right to strike. In that year, a group of whites split off from the United Party to form the Liberal Party, which demanded a universal franchise and a Bill of Rights. In 1954 Johannes Strijdom, a representative of the more extreme Transvaal branch of the National Party, was elected prime minister. In June 1955 a multiracial Congress of the People met near Johannesburg to demand equal rights and opportunities for all South Africans. Leaders of the Congress, including Luthuli, were among the 156 people arrested for treason in Dec. 1956 and held until their trial ended in acquittal, Mar. 1961. During that time, the revolutionary leadership was immobilized and dissension arose within the movement, culminating in the formation, Apr. 1959, of the Pan-Africanist Congress (PAC), an exclusively African party opposed to co-operation with other racial groups or with the Communists.

BANTUSTAN POLICY. Meanwhile, more restrictive laws were passed. In 1956 Coloreds were removed from the common voters' roll, and in 1957 the Immorality Act provided for stricter regulation of social intercourse. In 1958 Strijdom was succeeded by Hendrik Verwoerd, who advocated a positive approach to *apartheid* through "separate development." The Promotion of Bantu Self-Government Act, 1959, provided for eventual creation of 8 self-governing African territories (Bantustans) and abolished the 1936 agreement which had allowed qualified Africans to elect 3 white representatives to Parliament. Also in 1959, the Progressive Party emerged as another offshoot of the United Party; it called for a universal franchise with high but non-racial qualifications.

SHARPEVILLE. On 21 Mar., 1960, Africans gathered at Sharpeville to demonstrate against the pass laws. Police fired into the crowd, killing 72 people and injuring about 186. The government outlawed the ANC and PAC, proclaimed a state of emergency which suspended habeas corpus, and embarked on mass arrests. On 15 Mar., 1961, South Africa withdrew from the Commonwealth after other members expressed objection to her racial policies; on 31 May the country adopted republican status.

ECONOMIC PROSPERITY AND INTERNAL SECURITY. Outside pressure on the republic increased as more African states gained independence and pressed their case against South Africa in the UN and other international bodies, and provided more bases for African revolutionaries in exile. South Africa stiffened her laws: the Bantu Laws Amendment Act, 1963, further curtailed African rights and the General Law Amendment Act, 1963, allowed detention of persons for 90 days without trial. In addition, the republic pressed on with efforts to attain economic self-sufficiency. The country had achieved spectacular growth in the postwar period: exploitation of rich mineral resources provided export income (particularly from gold, which makes up some 70% of exports) and a basis for industrial development, which was increased by substantial domestic investment and the use of abundant cheap labor. But as of 1968, the economy remained dependent on imports of some industrial supplies and oil; hence, in spite of political differences, South Africa was careful to maintain good economic relations with western nations, which bought her exports and sent in foreign capital.

THE TRANSKEI. In Nov. 1963 the Transkei became the 1st Bantustan, after popular election of 46 of the 109 members of its Legislative Assembly. The Transkei Assembly received jurisdiction over some local matters (subject to approval by the republic), but control of foreign affairs and security remained with the central South African government. The partition of the country under the Bantustan policy was opposed by the United Party and became the major issue in the Mar. 1966 election. But the National Party emerged stronger than ever, with 126 out of 170 seats in Parliament.

ASSASSINATION OF VERWOERD. On 6 Sept., 1966, Verwoerd was stabbed to death, but there was apparently no political motive on the part of the white assassin, who was ruled insane. John Vorster replaced Verwoerd as prime minister.

Other Independent States

1955–68

ZAMBIA. Northern Rhodesia became the Republic of Zambia, 24 Oct., 1964, with Kaunda as president. His UNIP was the only effective political party, holding 55 out of 75 seats in the National Assembly. Copper exports (2nd largest in the world) gave the country a favorable balance of trade, but the resulting income was poorly distributed. Most of the people remained subsistence farmers or unskilled mine workers, while wealth was concentrated in the foreign-controlled Copperbelt. Kaunda's government immediately announced an agreement under which the British South Africa Co., in return for £4 m. compensation, surrendered to the Zambian government the mineral rights which had been yielding some £15 m. a year in royalties. With UN aid, the government was drawing up plans for balanced growth when Rhodesia's Unilateral Declaration of Independence, Nov. 1965, created a new series of economic problems. In 1965 Zambia had depended on the jointly owned Rhodesian Railways to carry copper exports and 96% of imports, among which coal and oil were particularly vital. After UDI, Zambia began to develop domestic coal deposits and sought to reorient trade routes through Tanzania and Congo. By the end of 1968, all Zambian oil imports came on these alternate routes, but some 75% of other imports continued to pass through Rhodesia.

TANZANIA. Just after Tanganyika's independence in Dec. 1961, Julius Nyerere demonstrated his dedication to political party development by resigning as prime minister to devote his full time to leadership of TANU. After he was elected president under the republican constitution which went into effect on 9 Dec., 1962, he continued to work to combine all elements of Tanganyikan society into a single-party structure which would retain the traditional African concept of government by consensus.

In Jan. 1964 a revolution in Zanzibar ended with power in the hands of Abeid Karume's Afro-Shirazi Party, which supported union with Tanganyika. In Mar. the 2 countries joined in the United Republic of Tanganyika and Zanzibar, renamed Tanzania in Oct. Karume was named vice-president, and his party became a branch of TANU.

On 5 Feb., 1967, following a meeting of TANU leaders in Arusha, Nyerere made his Arusha declaration on self-reliance. He stated that the way to economic development in a poor, agricultural country such as Tanzania was not through dependence on foreign capital with its attached conditions, but through hard work in the countryside by the Tanzanians themselves. He then nationalized foreign-owned commercial banks and other firms and large industrial and agricultural establishments, promising fair compensation.

On 1 June, 1967, Nyerere met in Kampala with the presidents of Kenya and Uganda to sign a 15-year East African Co-operation Treaty, which established an East African Community to take over and continue the communications, finance, commerce, industry, and social and research services which had been operated on a regional basis since 1961 by the East African Common Services Organization (EACSO). The treaty also provided for an East African Common Market and Development Bank.

UGANDA. On 9 Oct., 1963, when the post of governor general was abolished, the Kabaka of Buganda, Sir Edward Mutesa II, became president while Obote remained prime minister. The alliance between Kabaka Yekka and UPC continued but grew increasingly uneasy, and

UPC steadily built its strength until by Dec. 1965 it held 67 of the 91 seats in the National Assembly. On 24 Feb., 1966, moving to combat his enemies within the coalition, Obote suspended the constitution, and on 2 Mar. he assumed all powers of government. On 15 Apr., Parliament adopted a new constitution which provided for a president at the head of a unitary state, abolishing the federal status of Buganda and the other kingdoms. Obote was elected president. Upon the outbreak of violence in Buganda, he declared a state of emergency and sent in troops who captured the palace, 24 May, and the Kabaka fled the country. On 8 Sept., 1967, the Assembly approved another new constitution, which made Uganda a republic with a president having broad executive power.

KENYA. Kenya became a republic on 12 Dec., 1964, as a *de facto* 1-party state, since KANU had by then absorbed all opposition parties. Kenyatta was elected president and Oginga Odinga vice-president. During 1965 signs appeared of increasing tension between the radical, anti-western Odinga and the more moderate politicians, particularly Tom Mboya, minister of economic planning and development and secretary general of KANU. At a party conference in Mar. 1966, the post of deputy president, which had been held by Odinga, was eliminated. On 14 Apr. Odinga announced his resignation as vice-president of Kenya; and in the following days, 3 cabinet members and several trade-union leaders and members of the National Assembly resigned from KANU in support of Odinga, who took over as president of a new opposition party, the Kenya People's Union (KPU). Mboya engineered a constitutional amendment requiring the 29 KANU defectors in the Assembly to get affirmation of their constituents' continuing support in special elections which were held in June. KPU, facing the established KANU Party organization, emerged with 9 seats.

ETHIOPIA. The end of World War II found Ethiopian sovereignty completely restored and Emperor Haile Selassie firmly in control, with power to initiate legislation and to appoint the prime minister, senators, judges, and other government officials. In Nov. 1955 a revised constitution provided for election of deputies to the lower chamber of Parliament by universal suffrage. In the elections of 1957, there were still no political parties, but rather factions all of which sought the emperor's help.

In Dec. 1960, during the emperor's absence, some officers of the Imperial Bodyguard attempted a coup which failed when the army and air force opposed them. The populace rejoiced at the return of Haile Selassie, stronger than ever. During 1961 the emperor quieted some of the remaining discontent by distributing several ministerial portfolios, recognizing trade unions, and appointing commissions of investigation into administration and land reform; but modernization in Ethiopia continued to be hindered by feudal, religious, and political institutions and by a traditionalist approach to agricultural production. In 1963 the emperor prevailed upon Eritrea to become an integral part of the empire, giving up the federal status it had held since 1952. Also in 1963, he enhanced his pan-Africanist stature by acting as host to the 1st meeting of the Organization of African Unity at Addis Ababa.

SUDAN. At independence in 1956, Sudan faced serious problems of internal unity: ethnically, culturally, and linguistically, the country was divided between the Arab Moslem north and the tropical African south influenced by Christian missionaries; politically, temporary alliances were formed on the basis of personalities or interest groups, rather than clearly defined party ideologies.

Ismail al-Azhari of the NUP was replaced as prime minister, 5 July, 1956, by Abdullah Khalil at the head of an uneasy coalition between 2 northern conservative parties, Umma and the People's Democratic Party (PDP). In Feb. 1957 the government aroused southern resentment by announcing a policy of cultural integration under which missionary schools would be absorbed into a national system. In 1958 Sudan faced an economic crisis resulting from accumulated unsold stocks of cotton, which normally contributed more than 60% of exports, and falling world cotton prices. On 17 Nov., 1958, with the support of some political leaders, Gen. Ibrahim Abboud occupied government offices in a bloodless military coup. He suspended the constitution, dissolved Parliament and political parties, and established a Supreme Council of the Armed Forces.

The new government survived 3 attempted coups in 1959; but during the next few years, trade unionists, civil servants, and students grew increasingly discontented with the pervasive military rule. Southern opposition and demands for autonomy also increased. Southern leaders in exile in neighboring countries formed the Sudan African National Union (SANU) under William Deng. Inside Sudan, an underground movement, *Anyanya* (a poisonous insect), took shape in the south in 1963; its acts of terrorism in 1964 met with violent repression by the central government. In Oct. 1964, student demonstrations in Khartoum were supported by a Professional Front of civil servants and a general strike. The Abboud regime was replaced by a civilian caretaker government under Sir al-Khatim al-Khalifa, which achieved an interim agreement with the southern provinces and arranged elections for Apr.–May 1965. On 14 June the resulting Constituent Assembly elected Mohammed (Muḥammad) Ahmad Mahgoub of the dominant Umma Party as prime minister.

The Mahgoub government failed to deal effectively with renewed violence in the south and continuing economic and social discontent throughout the country. In July 1966 political infighting brought about Mahgoub's replacement by Umma Party President Saddiq al-Mahdi at the head of a coalition of Umma and NUP. In May 1967 Saddiq's government fell, primarily because of opposition by the various political factions to his plans for a new constitution providing for a strong president elected by direct popular vote. Mahgoub took over again and named a coalition government which included representatives of Umma, NUP, PDP, and the southern parties.

MIDDLE EAST
Turkey
1945–68

DEVELOPMENT OF POLITICAL PARTIES. In Turkey the postwar years witnessed the emergence for the 1st time of opposition parties, the most important of which was the Democratic Party, founded on 7 Jan., 1946. On 14 May, 1950, the 1st completely free elections, contested by several parties, took place, with the Democrats winning a large majority of the seats, thereby ending the almost 30-year rule of Atatürk's Republican People's Party. The fact that the RPP allowed such an election to take place seemed to bode well for democracy in Turkey. Early in 1952 Turkey was admitted to full membership in NATO, underscoring its membership in the European community. On 2 May, 1954, a 2nd election resulted in another victory for the Democratic Party, but in Oct. a split developed in the ranks of the party and led to the formation of the Freedom Party by the dissident elements. The elections of 27 Oct., 1957, reflected the beginnings of dissatisfaction with the Democrats; although the party received a plurality of the seats, it did not have an absolute majority of votes cast.

MILITARY COUP OF 1960. On 27 May, 1960, a coup led by Gen. Gürsel overthrew the regime, and he became president. The leading members of the Democratic Party were tried for treason, and several of them, including Adnan Menderes, the former prime minister, were executed. The military did not, however, wish to remain in power indefinitely, and a new assembly was convened, Jan. 1961, to act as a temporary Parliament until a new constitution was ratified, 26 May. Elections held on 15 Oct., 1961, resulted in the formation of a coalition government in which a new party, the Justice Party, was represented. On 22 Feb., 1962, there was an abortive military revolt by officers in Ankara who wished a military take-over, but this was put down, as was a similar attempt on 21 May, 1963. The Justice Party received a majority in the elections held in 1965.

CYPRUS. The problem of Cyprus, with its considerable Turkish population, was a source of continuous concern to Turkey in the postwar years. The island had become a British crown colony in 1925, and on 16 Aug., 1960, became an independent republic. Growing pressure for the union of Cyprus with Greece resulted in armed clashes between Greek and Turkish Cypriots, and the question came before the UN, which sent an international force, the 1st contingents of which arrived on 14 Mar., 1964. Although this eased the situation somewhat, the next years did not witness any permanent solution of the problem.

Iran

1945–68

RELATIONS WITH THE USSR. The conclusion of World War II found Russian troops still in occupation of the northern part of the country, and in the fall of 1945 there were disturbances in Azerbaijan, which was under Soviet control. On 12 Dec., 1945, the governor of Tabriz was deposed and an autonomous Republic of Azerbaijan proclaimed with Soviet support. At about the same time an independent Kurdish republic was established in Mahabad. On 4 Apr., 1946, Iran came to terms with the Soviet Union, signing an agreement which provided for the withdrawal of the Soviet troops. In return Iran agreed to the establishment of an Iranian-Soviet oil company to develop the northern provinces. On 9 May, 1946, the Soviet army withdrew, and on 15 Dec. the regime in Azerbaijan collapsed. On 22 Oct., 1947, the *Majlis* refused to ratify the agreement, and it remained a dead letter. In Feb. 1950 land reform, which was to continue over the next decade and a half, began with the handing over by the shah of the royal estates for redistribution.

OIL ROYALTIES. Perhaps the most crucial events that took place in Iran in this period revolved around the question of oil royalties. The agreement with the Anglo-Iranian Oil Co., signed in 1933, was revised, 17 July, 1949, but the new agreement was not ratified by the *Majlis*, which felt the increase in the percentage of profits was not large enough. On 20 Mar., 1951, the *Majlis* passed a law nationalizing the oil industry, which the shah was forced to sign. On 29 Sept., after negotiations had failed, Britain took the case to the UN, and on 3 Oct. the last British company personnel were evacuated. The question was finally settled, after the overthrow of the government in Iran by a military coup, 19 Aug., 1953, by a new agreement, 5 Aug., 1954. This provided for a division of the profits on a 50-50 basis.

REFORM POLICIES. Further land-reform laws were passed as part of the so-called "White Revolution" of the shah and his advisers, and on 20 Aug., 1960, the Office of the Land Reform came into being. On 17 Sept., 1963, a new Parliament was elected, and on 21 Jan., 1965, the prime minister was killed by a member of an extremist religious sect, indicating that the reform policy of the shah and the government was not approved in all quarters.

Egypt

1945–68

EXTERNAL RELATIONS. The efforts of Egypt in the years immediately following the war were directed toward achieving the complete withdrawal of British troops from Egyptian soil. A treaty initialed on 25 Oct., 1946, was not signed by the Egyptians because it did not provide for the British to leave the Sudan. Following the defeat of Egyptian forces in the 1st Arab-Israeli War of 1948, an armistice was signed with Israel, 24 Feb., 1949, but a permanent peace settlement was never made. On 15 Oct., 1951, Egypt unilaterally abrogated the Anglo-Egyptian Treaty of 1936, and it was not until 12 Feb., 1953, that an agreement was signed between the 2 powers for self-determination in the Sudan. This was followed on 19 Oct., 1954, by an agreement concerning the Suez Canal Base, under the terms of which British forces were to withdraw within 20 months but retained the right to return under certain conditions.

ACCESSION OF NASSER. Internally Egypt was going through a series of upheavals that resulted in radical changes. Increasing dissatisfaction with the monarchy led on 23 July, 1952, to a coup by a group of colonels in the Egyptian army, and on 26 July the king abdicated. On 18 June, 1953, the monarchy was abolished and Egypt became a republic. Gamal Abdel ('Abd al-) Nasser emerged as the leader of the movement and, assuming the presidency, 14 Nov., 1952, immediately began making changes. On 8 Sept., 1952, an agrarian reform decree was issued, followed by the abolition of the *Waqfs* (lands held in perpetual trust, usually for the ultimate benefit of some religious institution or good work). On 10 Dec., 1952, the old constitution was abrogated, and it was not until 23 June, 1956, that a new one came into existence.

SUEZ CRISIS OF 1956. One of Nasser's most cherished schemes was the construction of a high dam at Aswan to increase the cultivable land of the country. When on 17 July, 1956, the U.S. refused a loan it had earlier promised for the dam, he reacted swiftly and violently. On 26 July he seized and nationalized the Suez Canal. The situation was further complicated on 29 Oct. when Israeli forces invaded Egypt, and on 31 Oct. Britain and France began air attacks which were followed by the landing of troops in the Canal Zone. On 1 Nov. Egypt blocked the Canal, on 6 Nov. a cease-fire was accepted, and a UN force was dispatched, 15 Nov. The dispute over the use of the Canal itself was not settled until 18 Mar., 1957. On 9 Jan., 1960, work was begun, with large-scale Soviet aid, on the Aswan Dam.

ESTABLISHMENT OF UAR. Egypt had long seen itself as the leader of the movement for Arab unity and made several attempts to establish its position formally. On 1 Feb., 1958, the United Arab Republic was formed by a union with Syria which lasted until the withdrawal of the latter, 28 Sept., 1961. On 17

Apr., 1963, an agreement for an Arab Socialist Union comprising Egypt, Syria, and Iraq was signed, but dissensions among the member countries rendered it ineffective. Nasser was re-elected for a 6-year term on 15 Mar., 1965, but with diminished prestige because of the deteriorating economic situation in Egypt and because of the defeat of the Egyptian armed forces in the 3rd Arab-Israeli War, 1967.

Iraq

1945–68

INTERNATIONAL RELATIONS. The evacuation of the last British troops from Iraq, Oct. 1947, marked the real beginning of Iraqi independence, and on 16 Jan., 1948, a treaty was signed between the 2 countries by the terms of which the British were to withdraw from the air bases they had previously held. This treaty was not, however, ratified, due largely to the Arab-Israeli War of 1948. In 1950 a Development Board was set up which was to receive 70% of future oil royalties. These were to be used for land development. On 3 Feb., 1952, a new agreement was signed with the Iraq Petroleum Co. giving Iraq 50% of the profits. On 24 Feb., 1955, Iraq joined a mutual defense pact with Turkey to which Britain adhered, 30 Mar. The Anglo-Iraqi alliance of 1930 was abrogated.

ESTABLISHMENT OF THE REPUBLIC. Iraq was not exempt from the revolutionary fever current in the Middle East, and on 14 July, 1958, the monarchy was overthrown. King Faisal II and his prime minister, Nuri al-Sa'id, were killed and Iraq was made a republic. On 24 Mar., 1959, Iraq withdrew from the Baghdad Pact. In Mar. 1961 the 1st of a new series of Kurdish rebellions that were to continue for the next 5 years broke out. On 8 Feb., 1963, the government of Gen. Kassem was overthrown and Arif, a leader of the Ba'ath Party, became president. On 17 Apr., 1963, Iraq joined with Syria and Egypt in the National Socialist Union, and on 29 Apr., 1964, a new constitution came into being. In June 1966 a cease-fire with the Kurds was effected, and on 30 June, 1966, an attempted coup was put down.

Jordan

1945–68

CREATION OF THE KINGDOM OF JORDAN. On 25 Apr., 1946, the amir of Transjordan took the title of king, and on 15 Mar., 1948, he signed a treaty of alliance with Britain. During the Arab-Israeli War of 1948, Abdullah's forces occupied parts of what had been the Palestine Mandate, and he annexed this territory on 1 Dec., 1948. On 26 Apr., 1949, to underscore this new acquisition Transjordan became the Kingdom of Jordan. On 20 July, 1951, Abdullah was murdered, but the monarchy remained 1st under his son Talal and then under his grandson Hussein. On 2 Jan., 1952, a new constitution was promulgated. On 1 Mar., 1956, King Hussein, in a move to gain popular favor in the face of increasing criticism of Jordanian dependence on Britain, dismissed Gen. Glubb, the commander of the Arab Legion, and on 24 Oct. Jordan signed an agreement with Egypt and Syria which placed the armed forces of these 3 countries under an Egyptian commander in chief. On 7 Apr., 1957, there was an attempted coup against the king, but Hussein put this down, 10 Apr., thereby demonstrating the viability of the monarchy. The Iraqi revolution in July 1958 produced tensions in Jordan, and the British landed forces to protect the country against the threat of external interference, but they were evacuated within a short time.

ARAB-ISRAELI WAR OF 1967. Early in the summer of 1967 Jordanian forces were defeated by Israel, and in the course of the war Jordanian territory, including the old city of Jerusalem, was captured by the Israelis.

Syria

1945–68

POLITICAL INSTABILITY AND MILITARY COUPS. Governmental instability characterized the history of Syria in the postwar years, with a number of coups resulting in frequent changes in government. On 21 June, 1945, Syria, together with Lebanon, issued a declaration releasing all French citizens from service in the 2 countries, and French and British troops were withdrawn from Syria at the end of Apr. 1946. In July 1947, elections took place, but in 1949 there were 3 coups, resulting finally in a military dictatorship under Shishakli that lasted from 29 Nov., 1951, to 25 Feb., 1954. With the coming of a new regime the constitution, suspended in 1950, was restored, and elections held, Sept. 1954.

PARTICIPATION IN THE UAR. On 20 Oct., 1955, Syria signed a mutual-defense pact with Egypt, and on 1 Feb., 1958, in the face of the threat of growing Soviet influence in Syria, concluded a complete union with Egypt with the formation of the United Arab Republic. This union was not, however, a success, due largely to Syria's resentment at finding itself the junior partner in the arrangement and to Syrian dislike of Egyptian economic policies.

BREAKUP OF THE UAR. On 28 Sept., 1961, a coup by the Syrian army led to the dissolution of the United Arab Republic, and on 1 Dec. elections were held for a Constituent Assembly. A new series of coups in 1962 and 1963 led to the formation of a coalition government composed of army elements and members of the Ba'ath Party as well as other elements. A conflict within the Ba'ath Party itself between moderates and extremists has kept the political situation extremely fluid with constant reshuffling of governments.

Lebanon

1945–68

REVOLUTION OF 1952. Unlike its Arab neighbors, Lebanon enjoyed relative stability in the postwar years with 1 major exception. Foreign troops were withdrawn from the country by the end of 1946 and elections held in the spring of 1947. On 18 Sept., 1952, a bloodless revolution ousted President al-Khuri, who had been in office since 1943, and a new president was elected by Parliament. The distinctive feature of Lebanese government derived from the fact that due to the heterogeneous population it had always to be composed along strictly observed sectarian lines, with certain offices traditionally going to members of specified religious groups.

CRISIS OF 1958. The crisis that arose in Lebanon in 1958 occurred over the election of a new president and coincided with the Iraqi revolution. President Chamoun wished to amend the constitution to enable him to run for a 2nd term, a proposition contested by a loosely organized National Front, which included most of the Moslem leaders of the country as well as some Christians and supporters of Arab unity. Egypt supported the rebels, who gained control of not inconsiderable parts of the country. When the outbreak of the Iraqi revolution threatened to aggravate the situation even further, the U.S. acted to preserve Lebanese independence by landing marines on 15 July, 1958. Ultimately the president decided not to seek re-election, the American troops were evacuated, and a compromise candidate was agreed upon for the office. The sectarian system of government was maintained and continued to form the basis of Lebanese stability.

Arabian Peninsula

1945–68

SAUDI ARABIA. Saudi Arabia in the years after the war concentrated largely on the development of its oil resources and on a slow but perceptible process of political and social modernization. On 30 Dec., 1950, the agreement with Aramco was revised to give the government 50% of the company's profits, and in 1956 a government-owned oil company was formed to develop areas not included in the Aramco concession. On 2 Nov., 1964, King Ibn Saud abdicated in favor of his brother Faisal, to whom he had relinquished most of his power earlier in the year. From 1962 onward Saudi Arabia was involved in the conflict in the Yemen through its support of the Royalists there.

YEMEN. Despite several attempted coups the monarchy in the Yemen retained control until Sept. 1962, when a republican revolt broke out led by Col. Sallal. On 8 May, 1965, a republican constitution was proclaimed, but the conflict did not remain an internal one due to the support of the Royalists by Saudi Arabia and of the Republicans by Egypt. Various attempts to settle the question failed, notably at the Khartoum Conference in Sept. 1967, Egypt being anxious to withdraw its troops in the Yemen for possible use against Israel.

Israel

1945–68

ARAB-ISRAELI WAR OF 1948–49. The state of Israel was proclaimed on 14 May, 1948, the day on which Britain officially ended its mandate over Palestine, with Chaim Weizmann (1874–1952) as first president and David Ben-Gurion (b. 1886), prime minister. The new state was immediately invaded by armies from the surrounding Arab countries, but armistice agreements signed between Jan. and June 1949 left Israel in control of a great deal of Palestine. No peace treaties were negotiated, since the Arabs refused to recognize the existence of Israel. The history of Israel since its creation has necessarily been dominated by the fact that it is surrounded by hostile powers whose avowed purpose is to annihilate it.

SUEZ CRISIS OF 1956. Continuing raids by both Arabs and Israelis in the border areas marked the years after 1948, erupting into full-scale war in 1956, as a result of which Israel gained access to the sea through the Strait of Tiran. Over the course of the next decade the situation remained relatively quiet, although the Arabs made no secret of their firm intention to recapture Palestine.

ARAB-ISRAELI WAR OF 1967. On 5 June, 1967, in response to Egypt's blockade of the Strait of Tiran, Israel launched a series of campaigns against Egypt, Syria, and Jordan. In the lightning Six Days'

War, she administered crushing defeats on all 3, capturing considerable teritory and matériel. A cease-fire was arranged under UN auspices, but the problem remained unsolved, the Israelis refusing to give up the positions they had taken and the Arabs still unwilling to negotiate with a government whose existence they would not concede. Meanwhile fighting continued intermittently through 1968 along the new borders.

SOUTH AND SOUTHEAST ASIA

India

1947–58

SITUATION AT INDEPENDENCE. Britain partitioned her Indian empire into predominantly Hindu India and predominantly Moslem Pakistan. India's constitution provides for a federal system, with the central and state governments sharing power. The bicameral central Parliament consists of a House of the People and a Council of States. India's president is largely a ceremonial figure; real power rests in the prime minister, who heads a cabinet responsible to the House of the People.

ASSASSINATION OF GANDHI. Known worldwide for his championship of *Ahimsa* (nonviolence), Mahatma Gandhi (1869–1948) was a prime mover in India's struggle for independence. His appeal for mutual tolerance between Hindus and Moslems alarmed Hindu extremists, one of whom killed him, 30 Jan., 1948.

PANCHA SHILA. As the Cold War intensified, Indian Prime Minister Jawaharlal Nehru pursued a nonaligned foreign policy. At the same time, he worked to promote world peace on the basis of his 5 Principles of Peaceful Coexistence (*Pancha Shila*), endorsed in a joint statement by Chinese Premier Chou En-lai, 1950. In the postwar years India led a nonaligned bloc of states with considerable influence in international affairs.

COMMUNISM IN KERALA. The biggest surprise of the 1957 general elections was the victory of the Communist Party in the southern Indian state of Kerala. This victory was due more to superior organization than to massive popular support. Although the Communist regime did not pursue radical policies, Kerala's Congress Party, churches, and other groups launched a nonco-operation movement which paralyzed the government and forced Indian President Rajendra Prasad to suspend Kerala's government in 1959.

1959–68

SINO-INDIAN BORDER DISPUTE. The Sino-Indian border was never satisfactorily demarcated, and in 1959 military clashes erupted on the Himalayan frontier. A much more serious border crisis occurred in 1962, when Chinese troops staged a limited invasion of India. Continuing Chinese hostility forced India to rely increasingly on Soviet and American military aid, thus undermining Indian nonalignment. Prime Minister Nehru's death, 27 May, 1964, further diminished India's leading role in world affairs. His successor, Lal Bahadur Shastri (1904–66), was virtually unknown to the international community.

WAR WITH PAKISTAN. India fought 2 wars with Pakistan during 1965, 1 in the Rann of Kutch, the other in Kashmir. Militarily the struggles were inconclusive, but the Kashmir conflict led Soviet Premier Aleksei Kosygin to offer to mediate Indo-Pakistani differences at a summit conference in the Soviet city of Tashkent. The Tashkent Declaration, signed in Jan. 1966, pledged mutual withdrawal of forces from the battle zone and settlement of future Indo-Pakistani disputes without resort to force. As he prepared to return home from Tashkent, Prime Minister Shastri died suddenly of a heart attack. His successor was Nehru's daughter, Mrs. Indira Gandhi (b. 1917).

DECLINE OF CONGRESS PARTY. After governing India virtually unchallenged since independence, the Congress Party suffered a serious setback in the 1967 national elections. It barely retained a majority in the central Parliament, and in more than half of the states it actually lost its edge to opposition coalitions ranging broadly over the political spectrum. Regional and linguistic grievances, religious fanaticism, widespread poverty and hunger, and discontent with Congress' increasingly corrupt and ineffective leadership combined to produce the electoral debacle.

Pakistan

1947–60

WAR WITH INDIA. Pakistan achieved independence as a state consisting of 2 regions divided by 1,000 miles of Indian territory. Although both East and West Pakistan adhered to Islam, they differed greatly in geography and climate and in the ethnic and linguistic background of their peoples. The death in 1948 of Mohammed Ali Jinnah, Pakistan's founding father, deprived the new nation of a potent unifying symbol. Pakistan's difficulties were further compounded that year by an undeclared war with India over Kashmir, a state with a predominantly Moslem population and a Hindu ruling class. The Kashmir issue was debated in the UN Security Council, which in 1949 secured a cease-fire and partitioned Kashmir. Pakistan has insisted that India hold a plebiscite permitting the Kashmiris to choose between Indian and Pakistani rule, but India has consistently refused.

PAKISTAN, SEATO, AND CENTO. Pakistan's foreign policy has been motivated primarily by fear of Indian aggression. U.S. offers of weapons in return for Pakistani adherence to the SEATO and CENTO military alliances were therefore well received. Although Washington conceived of both SEATO and CENTO as vehicles for preventing Communist expansion, Pakistan's membership rested primarily not on anti-Communism but on the need for U.S. protection against India.

COUP OF 1958. Party rivalries, cabinet instability, and deterioration of law and order marked Pakistani politics and prompted the army in 1958 to stage a bloodless coup. Field Marshal Moham-

med Ayub Khan became the dominant figure in the new military regime. In an effort to legitimize his government, Ayub in 1959 launched a Basic Democracies plan, providing for the direct election by universal suffrage of 80,000 so-called Basic Democrats who, in turn, would elect Pakistan's president. In 1960 the newly chosen Basic Democrats chose Ayub.

1961–68

DRIFT TOWARD CHINA. Securely in the western camp until 1962, Pakistan then expressed anxiety over large U.S. arms shipments to India in the aftermath of the Sino-Indian border war. Ayub feared these arms would eventually be used against Pakistan. Increasingly skeptical of SEATO's or CENTO's ability to protect her against India, Pakistan sought closer ties with China, most notably through a Sino-Pakistani border agreement signed in 1963. Nevertheless, Pakistan, still dependent on U.S. economic aid, retained membership in the western military pacts, and still outlaws her Communist Party.

GROWTH OF OPPOSITION TO AYUB. For the 1st time in her history, Pakistan in 1965 held direct presidential elections. Ayub was challenged by a coalition of opposition groups whose candidate was Miss Fatimah Jinnah, sister of Pakistan's founder. Ayub won handily, however, and the opposition failed to remain united after the voting. In 1968 rising separatist sentiment in East Pakistan and the growth of opposition sentiment in West Pakistan posed an increasing threat to Ayub's regime.

Ceylon

1948–59

INDEPENDENCE. Ceylon's 1st independent government was headed by Prime Minister Sir John Kotelawala's United National Party. The conservative-oriented UNP, which maintained close ties with the West, remained in power until 1956, its main opposition coming from Ceylon's Marxist groups.

COLOMBO PLAN. A meeting of British Commonwealth Foreign Ministers in Colombo, Ceylon, resulted in the Colombo Plan, a program of regional co-operation in economic aid and technical assistance. The Plan's members include the U.S., Britain, Canada, Australia, New Zealand, and Japan as donors and 17 Asian states as beneficiaries who use the aid for economic development projects.

COLOMBO CONFERENCE. In 1954, representatives from Ceylon, India, Pakistan, Indonesia, and Burma met at Colombo to devise plans to promote economic and political co-operation among themselves and to call for united efforts to preserve world peace. The 5 later sponsored the Bandung Conference, held in Indonesia in 1955. The 5 Colombo Powers, as they were called, gave a major impetus to Afro-Asian co-operation and for a time represented a significant bloc in international affairs.

DEFEAT OF UNP. Having ruled Ceylon since independence, the UNP lost the 1956 elections to the Sri Lanka Freedom Party, led by S. W. R. D. Bandaranaike. The SLFP governed in coalition with a leftist party as the People's United Front until 1959, when conservative SLFP members forced the leftists out of the government.

1960–68

RULE OF BANDARANAIKE. After Prime Minister Bandaranaike's assassination by a Buddhist monk, his widow replaced him in office. Because Mrs. Bandaranaike, the world's 1st woman prime minister, adopted increasingly radical policies, she lost so much support that in 1964 her SLFP was forced to form a coalition government with 3 Communist groups. Her radicalism, reflected at home by confiscation of foreign-owned industries and abroad by the loosening of many western ties in favor of friendship with Communist states, finally generated such opposition from moderates in her party that the government collapsed. The ensuing elections returned the UNP to power under Prime Minister Dudley Senanayake. He advocated a mixed social-ist economy and a return to closer relations with the West.

LANGUAGE RIOTS. Friction between Ceylon's Sinhalese-speaking majority and Tamil-speaking minority had simmered since independence, but in 1966 a decision to permit use of the Tamil language for government business in Tamil areas led to bloody communal riots. A state of emergency was imposed; but the language issue, together with severe economic difficulties, remain the country's most acute problems.

Indonesia

1949–60

NATIONAL ELECTIONS. Indonesia's 1st national elections, 1955, gave the largest number of votes to the Nationalist Party and Masjumi (a Moslem organization), but the Indonesian Communist Party (PKI) captured 4th place. Since staging an abortive coup in 1948, the PKI had been obliged to moderate its tactics.

BANDUNG CONFERENCE. Indonesia's foreign policy remained neutralist, and the Bandung Conference, 1955, of 29 Afro-Asian nations marked her debut as a leader of the nonaligned world. Sponsored by the Colombo Powers, the conference condemned colonialism and urged international co-operation.

"GUIDED DEMOCRACY" AND REGIONAL REBELLIONS. Weak coalition governments and widespread political factionalism led to disillusionment with parliamentary democracy, which Sukarno called unsuitable for Indonesia. In 1957 he advocated "Guided Democracy," featuring a National Advisory Council with functional representation and an all-party cabinet, including Communists. Meanwhile, centrifugal pressures, always strong in Indonesia, exploded in 1958 in rebellions in Sumatra and Sulawesi directed against the Javanese-dominated central government. The army crushed the uprisings. In 1959 the Constituent Assembly rejected Sukarno's plan for "Guided Democracy," whereupon the president dissolved the Assembly by decree. The following year he suspended Parliament and replaced it with a "Mutual Co-operation" Parliament with functional representation. Sukarno formally inaugurated the new system in his Political Manifesto of 17 Aug., 1960.

1961-68

"LIBERATION" OF WEST IRIAN. In 1961 Sukarno severed diplomatic relations with the Netherlands for its failure to hand over West Irian, a part of the former Dutch East Indies, to Indonesia. Threatening to seize West Irian by force, Sukarno authorized guerrilla forays into the territory. When war between the Netherlands and Indonesia loomed, the U.S. intervened to mediate the crisis. In 1962 an accord stipulated that West Irian would revert to Indonesian hands on 1 May, 1963, following an interim UN administration.

CONFRONTATION WITH MALAYSIA. Countering western hopes that the acquisition of West Irian would satisfy Indonesia's nationalist ambitions, Sukarno announced, 1963, his intention to crush the new British-sponsored Federation of Malaysia. As in the case of West Irian, much of the impetus for the campaign came from the Communists, who had successfully exploited Sukarno's growing anti-western orientation to increase their influence in Indonesia. During the anti-Malaysia campaign, Sukarno, having alienated his western friends, pursued an increasingly pro-Chinese foreign policy which culminated, 1965, in Indonesia's withdrawal from the UN.

ABORTIVE COMMUNIST COUP OF 1965. On 30 Sept., 1965, the 3 m.-strong PKI, largest Communist Party outside the Communist bloc, staged an abortive coup which was crushed by the troops of Gen. Suharto. The result was a military takeover of Indonesia and a massacre of Communists.

ACCESSION OF SUHARTO. In Mar. 1966, having already been pressured into banning the Communist Party, Sukarno, whose own connection with the coup remained obscure, reluctantly signed over all executive powers to Suharto. In Mar. 1967, the Provisional People's Consultative Congress named Suharto acting

president. Gravitation of political power to the army has been accompanied by concentration on Indonesia's desperate economic problems and abandonment of foreign adventures such as the Malaysian confrontation. Indonesia rejoined the UN, abandoned the Jakarta-Peking axis, and returned to a neutralist foreign policy. Meanwhile, Sukarno, though shorn of all real power, retained considerable popularity, especially in Java.

On 27 Mar., 1968, Suharto was elected president by the Consultative Assembly. Faced with renewed PKI guerrilla activity (stimulated by discontent because of inflation and rice shortages), the government began to concentrate its energies on a new anti-Communist military campaign.

Malaysia

1957-68

SITUATION AT INDEPENDENCE. After independence, 31 Aug., 1957, Malaya remained in the Commonwealth and permitted Britain to maintain military bases in the country. Independent Malaya was a federal state with an elective monarch (chosen by a conference of rulers for a 5-year term). The cabinet was responsible to a bicameral legislature. Malayan independence was a blow for the Communist rebels, who lost hope of exploiting anti-British nationalist feelings.

FEDERATION OF MALAYSIA. Fears that Singapore, with its predominantly Chinese population, would become an outpost of Peking led the British, 1963, to advocate merger between Malaya and Singapore (independent, 1959). Such a merger, however, would have given the Chinese a racial preponderance. The decision was therefore taken to include the British territories of Sarawak and Sabah in Borneo in the new Federation of Malaysia, along with Singapore. Born on 16 Sept., 1963, Malaysia was immediately threatened with extinction by Indonesia. Not until 1966, when a military regime replaced Sukarno, did a treaty end the undeclared war.

WITHDRAWAL OF SINGAPORE FROM THE FEDERATION. After only 2 years of merger, Singapore, for political and economic reasons as well as personal rivalry between Tengku Abdul Rahman of Malaysia and Lee Kuan Yew of Singapore, seceded from Malaysia, 1965. However, Singapore pledged co-operation with her neighbor in defense and economic matters.

Burma

1947–68

SITUATION AT INDEPENDENCE. After the proclamation of the Republic of the Union of Burma, 1947, and in return for a generous financial settlement from Britain and a British promise to supply military personnel to train Burma's army, Thakin Nu signed a treaty allowing Britain to use Burmese ports and airfields. Burma's constitution embodied a system of parliamentary democracy, cabinet responsibility to the legislature, and separate states or administrative divisions for Shans, Kachins, Karens, and other minority groups.

COMMUNIST REBELLION. A combination of opposition to the agreement with Britain and adherence to the new militancy advocated by the international Communist movement prompted Burma's Communists to rise in rebellion against the central government, 1948. Sporadic violence among Burma's minority groups further weakened the government.

MILITARY COUP OF 1958. Economic difficulties and minority grievances plagued Burma throughout the decade following independence. In 1958 the AFPFL, which still dominated the country's politics, split into 2 factions, of which that headed by U Nu remained in power. Nu, however, resigned and invited Gen. Ne Win to take over the government and pacify the country. Army rule, characterized by efficiency, honesty, and reduction of Communist and other insurgencies, was followed by free elections in 1960. U Nu's wing of the AFPFL won, but its inefficiency and weakness again imperiled national unity.

COUP BY NE WIN. Finally, Ne Win seized power in a military coup, 1962, which ended parliamentary democracy in Burma. He preserved the country from fragmentation along ethnic lines, but his vague ideal of "Burmese Socialism" did little to solve pressing economic problems. In foreign policy the military regime maintained strict nonalignment and pursued an increasingly xenophobic policy.

Vietnam, Laos, and Cambodia

1954–68

GENEVA ACCORDS. The Geneva Conference of 1954, attended by the major world powers and the Indochinese states, established a cease-fire and partitioned Vietnam into a Communist nation under Ho in the north and a French-supported state in the south, with elections to reunify the country scheduled for 1956. The Geneva Conference also dealt with the newly independent states of Cambodia and Laos, where Communists harassed the royal governments. The influence of both the Khmer Issaraks in Cambodia and the Pathet Lao in Laos was greatly curtailed, and the 2 nations committed themselves to neutral foreign policies.

RISE OF THE VIETCONG. Ngo Dinh Diem, who became South Vietnam's president in 1956, refused to hold national elections as stipulated by the Geneva Conference. Thus, the Communist Vietcong, seeing no hope of Vietnamese reunification while Diem ruled, plotted to overthrow his government. Beginning in 1957, the Communists assassinated large numbers of village and hamlet officials. In 1960 their efforts entered a new phase with the creation in Hanoi of the Front for the Liberation of the South and plans for concerted military action.

CIVIL WAR IN LAOS. Indigenous Communists continued to harass the neutralist government of Laos after the Geneva Conference. A triangular struggle among right-wing military forces, the neutralist government, and the Pathet Lao led to full-fledged civil war, 1961. At a new Geneva Conference, 1962, the world powers imposed a settlement along the lines of the 1954 accords, but its terms were not regarded as binding by the Pathet Lao.

ASSASSINATION OF DIEM. President Diem's autocratic regime alienated virtually every segment of South Vietnam's population. His overthrow by a military coup and assassination, 2 Nov., 1963, led to a long series of military juntas apparently more preoccupied in squabbling among themselves than in improving the lot of the peasantry or prosecuting the war against the Vietcong.

ESCALATION OF VIETNAM WAR. The U.S., which formerly had supplied arms, financial aid, and military advisers to South Vietnam, gradually assumed a major combatant role. During 1965, large numbers of American troops entered South Vietnam and U.S. planes began bombing North Vietnam (*pp. 591 ff.*).

Philippines

1946–68

U.S.-FILIPINO RELATIONS. Following Filipino independence, 4 July, 1946, the Philippines received tariff concessions on imports into the U.S., but in return had to accept a "parity clause" guaranteeing American businessmen equal rights with Filipinos to exploit the islands' natural resources. This provision generated much bitterness among Filipinos, as did the Military Bases Agreement, signed in 1947, which granted the U.S. a 99-year lease and full legal jurisdiction over several base complexes.

HUKBALAHAP REBELLION. Having led the anti-Japanese resistance in Luzon during World War II, the Communist Party of the Philippines (CPP) deeply resented the government's refusal to allow its leader, Luis Taruc, to occupy the congressional seat he won in postwar elections. President Manuel Roxas also failed to reach an agreement with the Communists to surrender their arms. In 1948 a full-fledged rebellion erupted, led by the Hukbalahaps, the military arm of the CPP. Two years later, Ramon Magsaysay was named defense minister and placed in charge of anti-Communist operations. Magsaysay intensified military action against the Hukbalahaps, but simultaneously launched a land-reform program to free peasants from the abuses of landlordism. Such measures, coupled with a well-timed police raid on Communist headquarters in Manila, forced the insurgents underground by 1952. Elected president in 1953, Magsaysay continued his agricultural reforms, but they did not survive his death in a plane crash, 1957.

MANILA PACT AND SEATO. Having maintained close links with the U.S. after independence and with the memory of Communist insurgency fresh in mind, the Filipino government welcomed the creation of the Southeast Asia Treaty Organization (SEATO), inaugurated by the Manila Pact, Nov. 1954. Later, left-wing Filipinos advocated renunciation of SEATO and a more independent foreign policy, but Manila continued to support U.S. policy in Asia.

RENEWAL OF COMMUNIST TERRORISM. Although it was outlawed in 1957, the CPP emerged from underground, 1965, to recruit peasant support, denounce the corruption-ridden government, and exploit anti-American sentiment among left-wing students, intellectuals, and others. Hukbalahap terrorists assassinated or threatened many provincial and local officials and big landlords.

CONTROVERSY OVER SABAH. In 1968 the Philippines became embroiled with Malaysia in a war of words over the state of Sabah (formerly North Borneo). The Filipino government claimed the area because Sabah was at one time part of a region the remainder of which is now within the Philippines.

Thailand

1945–68

RULE OF PRIDI. After World War II, Pridi and his colleagues dominated Thai politics. Political instability and widespread corruption and smuggling, however, discredited civilian government. The mysterious death, moreover, of the young king of Thailand, 1946, raised speculation about Pridi's possible complicity.

MILITARY COUP OF 1947. When P'ibun staged a military coup in 1947, he claimed to have saved Thailand from a Communist and republican take-over. Elections in 1948 gave him a mantle of legitimacy both at home and abroad. In 1949 Pridi, backed by some military men, sought to oust P'ibun's regime and reinstate civilian government. When the coup failed, Pridi fled to China.

THAI ACCESSION TO SEATO. In response to police allegations, 1952, of a Communist plot to overthrow the government, P'ibun authorized the arrest of hundreds of resident Chinese and a ban on Chinese newspapers and schools. The regime also promulgated an Un-Thai Activities Act forbidding Communist activity. Thailand's anti-Communism was reflected in foreign policy by adherence, 1954, to SEATO, which established its headquarters in Bangkok.

EXPERIMENT WITH DEMOCRACY. In 1955 P'ibun suddenly announced that democracy would be permitted in Thailand. This decision was due to a combination of factors: a recent trip by P'ibun to the U.S. and Britain, an attempt to gain popular support, and a softening attitude toward China due to Chou En-lai's warmth at the Bandung Conference.

RETURN TO MILITARY GOVERNMENT. Elections held under the new multiparty system, 1957, gave the government a bare majority, but it was widely accused of ballot rigging. When opposition reached threatening proportions, the government declared a national emergency, which ended political democracy in Thailand. Later that year, Gen. Sarit Thanarat staged a bloodless coup, dissolved the legislature, and suspended the constitution. An army-led coalition government was formed, but in 1958 Sarit staged another coup and assumed power at the head of a military junta. His regime renewed suppression of the Communists and other opposition groups.

U.S. GUARANTEE TO THAILAND. Disturbed by Communist successes in the Laotian civil war across Thailand's frontier, Thai Foreign Minister Thanat Khoman signed a joint statement with U.S. Secretary of State Dean Rusk, 6 Mar., 1962, guaranteeing Thailand's security and territorial integrity and pledging U.S. protection of the country from armed attack or "indirect aggression." Two months later, as the Laotian situation deteriorated further, the U.S. landed a marine contingent in Thailand.

COMMUNIST INSURGENCY. As the Vietnam War intensified, the U.S. made increasing use of its military bases in Thailand, while the Thais sent troops to South Vietnam. Such actions angered Peking, which in 1965 announced creation of a Thai Patriotic Front dedicated to the overthrow of the Bangkok regime and elimination of U.S. influence from Thailand. The Communist threat became particularly strong in the northeast, Thailand's most underdeveloped area, whose residents are ethnically similar to the Lao peoples across the Mekong River. In 1967 the military took over complete control of the anti-Communist campaign in the northern provinces, and martial law was declared, 1 Dec., in 5 central and southern provinces.

AUSTRALASIA

Australia

1945–68

POSTWAR POLICIES. On 5 July, 1945, Joseph B. Chifley replaced John Curtin as prime minister. Labour remained in office until 1949, running the country according to principles far different from those employed by prewar governments. The almost immediate achievement of full employment resulted from a sharp increase in consumer demand and not from a healthy balance among various types of industries or from an adequate supply of basic services supporting production growth. As a reaction against having been attacked, Australia was now determined to sustain her position by rapidly increasing her economic strength and by building up her population by encouraging the flow of immigrants from Europe. Though aware of changes in Europe, the Australian government was much more concerned with her neighbors to the north, and Labour's general reaction was to view the rising anticolonialism of the new Asian nations in terms of nationalism rather than Communism, even at the risk of alienating the former colonial powers.

LABOUR PARTY–COMMUNIST CLASH. The Australian Communist Party, having followed a prowar policy, had won control of several important unions, though its numbers remained small. These unions antagonized the Labour government by employing the strike weapon to settle disputes rather than by using the available arbitration machinery. The Communist-inspired strike in the New South Wales coal mines, 1949, brought swift government retaliation. Public reaction to the economic chaos caused by the coal strike and also to Chifley's unsuccessful attempt to nationalize the banks resulted in a victory for the Liberal-Country Party coalition in the 1949 general election.

THE MENZIES ERA. Under Robert G. Menzies (prime minister, 1949–66), Australia entered a new era. To promote economic growth Menzies did not hesitate to borrow abroad. Although in the 1950's there were 3 periods of inflation and 3 of recession, the general trend of the national income was upward. Employment, especially in the steadily growing industrial sector, remained full, and Menzies remained in office. He dealt with the 2 important issues which had defeated Labour by satisfactorily regularizing relations between the Commonwealth Bank and the private trading banks, and by proposing to proscribe the Communist Party. Fearing gross infractions of the civil liberties of all citizens as a consequence of an attempt to silence one group, Labour successfully fought the proscription attempt, but anti-Communism was not thereby abated or the Communist cause noticeably advanced. Though accused of favoring the Communists and badly split when a large Roman Catholic element set up a splinter Democratic Labour Party, Labour candidates

gained 15 more seats in the House in the 1961 elections, reducing the Liberal-CP majority to 2.

FOREIGN AFFAIRS. For Menzies Australia's relations with Britain were of primary importance, and next to them her relations with the U.S. But as the postwar world changed, the Australian government's foreign policy changed likewise to meet new demands. The Commonwealth had to sustain its own position, especially in regard to the U.S. and Asia, and with less dependence on Britain than before the war. Thus Australia refused to recognize mainland China (though Britain did so), was the first UN member to join the U.S. in the Korean War, and sent troops to Vietnam.

On 20 Jan., 1966, Menzies retired and was succeeded as prime minister first by Harold E. Holt (1908–67) and then by John H. Gorton (b. 1911). There has been little change in the government's internal or external policies.

New Zealand

1945–68

INDUSTRIAL RELATIONS. In Feb. 1945 the government substantially altered New Zealand's 3-year-old wage stabilization plan by allowing labor unions dissatisfied with existing wages and scales to apply to arbitration courts for review.

LABOUR VICTORY OF 1946. On 27 Nov., 1946, the Labour government was re-elected, winning 42 parliamentary seats to the National Party's 38.

ECONOMIC POLICY. In Sept. 1947 New Zealand extended butter and meat rationing into 1948 to permit maximum exports to Britain. In Aug. 1948 New Zealand restored currency parity with Britain. In Sept. meat rationing was abolished, with only butter and gasoline remaining. (Butter rationing ended on 4 June, 1950.) New Zealand had record trade totals for the year ending 30 June, 1948. In Sept. 1949 the New Zealand pound was devalued from U.S. $4.03 to $2.80.

NATIONAL PARTY REGIME. In elections held 30 Nov., 1949, Labour (in power 14 years) lost control of Parliament when the National Party won 46 seats to Labour's 34. On 13 Dec. Sidney George Holland (1893–1961), leader of the National Party, became prime minister. In June 1950 Holland announced that the Legislative Council, the upper house of Parliament, would vote itself out of existence after he appointed enough new members to give his National Party a Council majority. Elections in Sept. 1951 increased the National Party's strength— 50 seats to Labour's 30. In the Nov. 1954 parliamentary elections, the National Party won 43 seats to Labour's 37. On 20 Sept., 1957, Holland resigned as prime minister because of poor health and was succeeded by Deputy Prime Minister– Agriculture Minister Keith Jacka Holyoake (b. 1904).

LABOUR VICTORY OF 1957. In Nov. 1957, Labour won the general elections, and Walter Nash (1882–1968) was sworn in as prime minister, 12 Dec. In Jan. 1958 Nash imposed licensing controls on all imports because New Zealand's foreign-payment deficit had increased from $11.2 million in Sept. 1956 to $84 million in Sept. 1957. In Sept. 1959, the government announced a $114-million trade surplus for the year ended 30 June, due to heavy U.S. purchases of beef and wool.

ACCESSION OF HOLYOAKE. In Nov. 1960, Nash's Labour Party was defeated by the National Party led by ex-Prime Minister Holyoake. The National Party won 45 seats to Labour's 35. On 1 Dec., 1963, Holyoake's National Party won another 3-year term, and in 1966 Holyoake won his 3rd 3-year term, indicating public endorsement of his policy of sending combat troops to Vietnam. In 1967, the New Zealand currency was devalued by nearly 20% in response to British devaluation.

Patterns of Regional Organization

THE MOVEMENT FOR EUROPEAN UNITY

1946–54

EARLY PROPOSALS. European union had been discussed among European resistance leaders during the war and by the governments in exile in London. Speaking in Zurich, 19 Sept., 1946, Churchill called for a United States of Europe, with Britain as a sponsor rather than a member. European socialists, especially Paul-Henri Spaak (b. 1899), supported closer union, but British socialists were unenthusiastic. In June 1946 Churchill launched the United Europe Movement.

CONGRESS OF EUROPE. In Dec. 1947, most of the movements for European unity formed the International Committee of the Movements for European Unity; among these were Churchill's United Europe Movement, the European Union League led by Paul van Zeeland (b. 1893), the European Union of Federalists led by Henri Brugmans (b. 1906),

the Nouvelles Équipes Internationales of Robert Bichet (b. 1903), the Socialist Movement for a United States of Europe of Bob Edwards (b. 1906), and the European Parliamentary Union founded on the initiative of the veteran proponent of European unity, Count Coudenhave-Kalergi (b. 1894). The committee convened a "Congress of Europe" at The Hague, 7–10 May, 1948, with 713 participants from 16 countries, including Churchill, de Gasperi, Spaak, and Robert Schuman; it called for an economic and political union of Europe and the creation of a consultative assembly of European parliamentarians and a European Court of Human Rights. These proposals were studied by the Brussels Treaty Permanent Council, while the U.S.A. announced its support for European union.

COUNCIL OF EUROPE. Belgium and France proposed a parliamentary assembly, but Britain rejected this, proposing instead an intergovernmental council of ministers. Meanwhile, the International

Committee formed the European Movement, 25 Oct., as a permanent unofficial group to promote European unity. The British reluctantly agreed to the idea of an Assembly. On 5 May, 1949, the statute creating the Council of Europe was signed by 10 powers in London; it set up a parliamentary Consultative Assembly and a Committee of Ministers meeting in Strasbourg. The Consultative Assembly, whose 1st president was Spaak, attempted at once to strengthen the supranational nature of the Council, but British and Scandinavian members opposed such moves. A European Convention on Human Rights was signed, 4 Nov., 1950, creating a Court and a Commission, and granting the right of individual recourse.

MARSHALL PLAN. On 5 June, 1947, Gen. George C. Marshall, in a speech at Harvard, invited European countries to draw up a recovery program, promising American aid in implementing it. Bevin, Molotov, and Bidault met to discuss the offer 27 June–3 July, but could not agree, Molotov rejecting a collective approach. Britain and France invited other European states to meet to prepare a joint program; 14 non-Communist states attended the Paris Conference, July. The Conference set up a Committee on European Cooperation to construct a joint 4-year program of needs, resources, and requirements; this report was adopted, 22 Sept., and sent to Washington. On 15 Jan., 1948, Britain and France proposed creating a permanent organization to harmonize action; on 16 Apr., 16 countries participating in the European Recovery Program signed the Convention creating the Organization for European Economic Cooperation (OEEC). From 1948 to 1952 OEEC distributed $12 billion of American aid.

EUROPEAN COAL AND STEEL COMMUNITY. On 9 May, 1950, French Foreign Minister Robert Schuman made public a detailed proposal worked out by Jean Monnet (b. 1888) for placing French and German coal and steel under a High Authority which would have directly binding powers, the agreement to be open to other European states. Benelux (the economic union of Belgium, the Netherlands, and Luxembourg, formed 29 Oct., 1947), Italy, and Germany welcomed the plan; the British stood aloof. Within continental Europe, only the Gaullists, Communists, and German Socialists opposed the idea. In the ensuing negotiations among the 6 countries, a Council of Ministers to represent the states was added to the plan. The Treaty of Paris creating the European Coal and Steel Community (ECSC) was signed, 18 Apr., 1951. The High Authority of 9, appointed by but not responsible to the member states, took office under Jean Monnet as president, 10 Aug., 1952; a Common Assembly of 78 parliamentarians designated by each Parliament was empowered to discuss the work of the Community; a Court of Justice adjudicated treaty disputes; and a Consultative Economic and Social Committee advised the Authority. By May 1953 the Common Market in coal and steel was effective.

EUROPEAN DEFENSE COMMUNITY. With the outbreak of the Korean War, the U.S. sought the raising of 12 German divisions. On 11 Aug., 1950, Churchill proposed the creation of a European army; Reynaud, Adenauer, and Schuman supported it. Pressure grew, especially after the adoption, Sept., of a "forward" strategy by NATO. In an effort to prevent the creation of an autonomous German army, René Pleven (b. 1901) proposed, 24 Oct., the creation of a European Defense Community (EDC), on the lines of the ECSC. Benelux, Italy, and Germany accepted. Negotiations led to the signature of the Treaty of Paris instituting EDC, 27 May, 1952; it provided for organs similar to those of ECSC and for the integration of the 6 armies.

EUROPEAN POLITICAL COMMUNITY. On 30 May, 1952, the Common Assembly asked the governments of the 6 to prepare the draft of a European Political Community as foreseen in the EDC Treaty. The 6 foreign ministers invited the Common Assembly to draft such a treaty, 10 Sept.; adding representatives of other member states of the Council of Europe, it formed an Ad Hoc Assembly, presided over by Spaak, which presented its draft for a "European Community," 10

Mar., 1953; it proposed a People's Chamber, directly elected, and a Senate representing the states, an Executive Council responsible for general administration, a Council of national ministers to harmonize national and European policies, a Court of Justice, and an advisory Economic and Social Council. The proposed community would absorb the functions of EDC and ECSC. The other 5 ratified EDC, but when it was put to the French National Assembly, it was rejected on a

technicality, 30 Aug., 1954. Both EDC and EPC therefore died.

1954–68

WESTERN EUROPEAN UNION. Following the French Assembly's action, Eden at once called a conference in London of the 6, Britain, the U.S.A., and Canada, 28 Sept.–3 Oct. Britain declared her willingness to maintain British troops on the Continent. The Conference re-

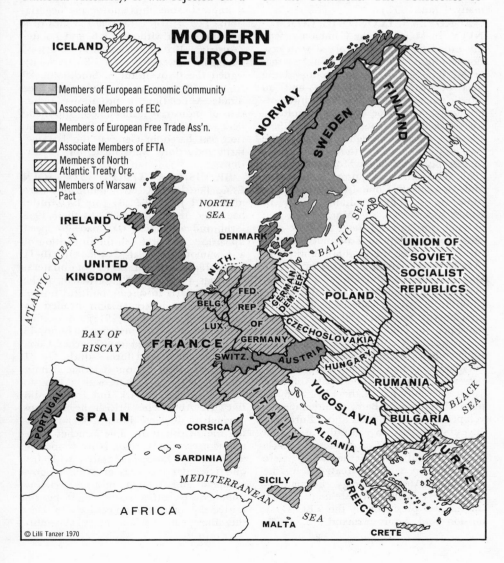

MODERN EUROPE

- Members of European Economic Community
- Associate Members of EEC
- Members of European Free Trade Ass'n.
- Associate Members of EFTA
- Members of North Atlantic Treaty Org.
- Members of Warsaw Pact

© Lilli Tanzer 1970

sumed in Paris, 20–23 Oct., and resulted in the Paris Agreements. These restored German sovereignty; allowed controlled rearmament of Germany; admitted Italy and Germany to a revised Brussels Treaty (renamed Western European Union); prohibited Germany from manufacturing atomic, bacteriological, or chemical weapons; and established a European Statute for the Saar. (The Statute was rejected by the Saar voters, 23 Oct., 1955, and the Saar was incorporated in Germany, 1 Jan., 1957.)

EUROPEAN ECONOMIC COMMUNITY. In May 1955 the Common Assembly called on the 6 to proceed with economic union. The foreign ministers met at Messina, 1–2 June, and endorsed the idea of economic integration and an atomic energy community. An intergovernmental committee (Spaak Committee) was formed and reported in Apr. 1956. Pressure was also brought to bear by the Action Committee for the United States of Europe, founded by Monnet, 18 Jan., 1956. The ministers approved the report and the Spaak Committee prepared a draft treaty. The resultant Treaty of Rome was signed, 25 Mar., 1957, and entered into force, 1 Jan., 1958. It provided for a European Economic Community (EEC); for the gradual elimination over 12 to 15 years of all tariffs among the Six, and the introduction of a common external tariff; for the making of common agricultural, social, trade cycle, transport, and energy policies; and for the free movement of labor, capital, and services. It created a Council of Ministers, an independent Commission of 9, and an enlarged Common Assembly of 142 with powers of discussion. The ECSC Court of Justice became that of the EEC. A European Development Bank to aid underdeveloped areas of the EEC and a European Investment Bank to assist the associated territories of the EEC (colonies of France, Belgium, and the Netherlands) were established. A separate treaty set up the European Atomic Energy Community (Euratom). Walter Hallstein (b. 1901) was named president of the EEC Commission and Louis Armand (b. 1905)

president of the Euratom Commission. Both organizations settled in Brussels.

EUROPEAN FREE TRADE ASSOCIATION. In July 1956 Macmillan proposed to the OEEC that it investigate the creation of an industrial free trade area. A working group reported its feasibility, Jan. 1957. In Sept. negotiations began among the OEEC members in a committee chaired by Reginald Maudling (b. 1916). The French were cool to the proposal, and in Nov. 1958 they declared it impracticable, thus ending the negotiations. The British canvassed the idea of a free trade area without the 6, and 7 states (Austria, Britain, Denmark, Norway, Portugal, Sweden, and Switzerland) signed the Convention of Stockholm, 20 Nov., 1959, creating the European Free Trade Association; a progressive reduction of industrial tariffs among the members was to be instituted. The organization was based in Geneva; the 1st 20% tariff reductions were made on 1 July, 1960.

BRITISH ATTEMPT TO JOIN EEC. The 1st EEC tariff reductions were made on 1 Jan., 1959. By July 1960 duties had been reduced to 80% of their 1958 level, and a decision was made to speed up further cuts and also the institution of a Common External Tariff. On 10–11 Feb., 1961, after a series of bilateral meetings, the heads of government of the 6 met in Paris to discuss political union. They set up a commission headed by Christian Fouchet (b. 1911) to outline proposals. At a 2nd meeting in Bonn, 18 July, they instructed the Fouchet Committee to draw up a formal draft. On 31 July, Macmillan announced that Britain would open negotiations with a view to joining EEC. Denmark and Ireland did likewise, Aug. The British negotiations opened on 10 Oct., Edward Heath leading the British team. The Fouchet Committee presented its plan, Nov., proposing a Union of European States, with frequent regular meetings of heads of government and foreign ministers, acting unanimously; other states might be admitted by unanimous decision. In Dec. the European Parliamentary Assembly called for the inclusion in the plan of a secretary general with powers of initiative and direct elections to the Assembly. After prolonged discussions, the 6 agreed, 14 Jan., 1962, on the broad lines of a common agricultural policy and passage to the 2nd stage of the treaty. Discussions on political union continued, but on 17 Apr., following a British request in the Western European Union Council to take part in them, Belgium and Holland refused to accept a revised French draft plan, and declined further discussions without British participation, which the French in turn rejected. The British negotiations continued, the British insisting on safeguards for their agriculture, Commonwealth trade, and their EFTA partners. De Gaulle made a state visit to Germany, 4–9 Sept. In a press conference, 14 Jan., 1963, de Gaulle stated that he did not deem Britain ready to join the EEC; the negotiations were adjourned, *sine die,* 29 Jan.

DEVELOPMENT OF EEC. On 22 Jan., 1963, de Gaulle and Adenauer signed a Franco-German Treaty of Co-operation, providing for semi-annual meetings of heads of government and more frequent meetings of other ministers. The Bundestag attached a preamble to it on ratification, reiterating Germany's commitment to NATO and belief in British membership in the EEC. On 20 July the 6 signed the Convention of Yaounde with 18 associated states of the EEC, to run to 1969. In Sept., Nigeria asked for association negotiations; the association agreement with Turkey was signed, 12 Sept. On 24 Sept, Tanganyika, Uganda, and Kenya requested negotiations, on 18 Oct. Tunisia, and on 14 Dec. Morocco. On 23 Dec. the Council agreed on basic regulations for certain agricultural products. On 5 Feb., 1964, negotiations opened with Algeria. In a decision, 15 July, the Court of Justice recognized the primacy of Community law over national law. In Sept., the Commission proposed "Initiative 64" to speed up the customs union and remove other trade barriers. On 15 Dec., the Council finally agreed on common cereal prices, the

heart of the agricultural policy, to be effective 1 July, 1967. On 19 Mar., 1965, negotiations on membership began with Austria. On 8 Apr., a treaty was signed for the merger of the executives of the ECSC, EEC, and Euratom. On 30 June, following disagreement on the financing of the agricultural policy, the French decided to boycott Community activities. The crisis was resolved, 28–29 Jan., 1966, when France agreed to resume participation after agreement to disagree on the question of majority voting. On 16 July the association agreement with Nigeria was signed. On 8 Feb., 1967, the Council adopted the 1st medium-range economic program. British Prime Minister Harold Wilson made a new bid to join EEC, 11 May. On 17 May de Gaulle virtually ruled out the possibility of British membership in the foreseeable future.

WESTERN HEMISPHERE CO-OPERATION

1945–68

REGIONAL ORGANIZATION BEFORE WORLD WAR II. "Pan-Americanism," a term much in use before World War II, referred specifically to regional organization which included both the U.S. and Latin America (as distinct from a "Latin Americanism" which concerned Latin nations exclusively). The history of Pan-Americanism dates from the 1st International Conference of American States, 2 Oct., 1889–19 Apr., 1890, which instituted a "Commercial Bureau," renamed the "Pan American Union" in 1910. This limited machinery for diplomatic and economic co-operation could serve no multilateral function, confronted by the overwhelming preponderance of power asserted by the U.S., especially in the Caribbean, 1890–1930. The system was powerless to stop several intraregional conflicts in the interwar period, notably the bloody Paraguay-Bolivia Chaco War, 1932–35. In the early 1920's Latin nations tried, unsuccessfully, to use the League of Nations as an institutional counterweight to the regional organization, which, by the time of the Havana Conference, 1928, they were openly denouncing as a State Department puppet.

U.S. GOOD NEIGHBOR POLICY. Franklin Roosevelt rejuvenated the North-South relationship, ending unilateral U.S. intervention (Montevideo Conference, Dec. 1933), laying foundations for economic co-operation (e.g., Export-Import Bank, 1934), and involving Latin nations in hemispheric defense during World War II (Havana Conference, 1940).

PAN AMERICAN CONFERENCES. Following World War II the range of U.S.-Latin American co-operation broadened, with the periodic grandiose Pan American conferences (the last held in Caracas, 1954) gradually replaced by more frequent and specialized contacts, diplomatic, cultural, military, and economic. Nevertheless, inter-American regional organization remained weak, providing neither the collective security desired by the U.S. nor the economic development wanted by Latin America.

ORGANIZATION OF AMERICAN STATES. U.S. involvement in World War II and the Cold War ended whatever basis the old Pan-Americanism possessed—a common New World isolationism from Europe. The U.S. inevitably saw Latin America as one part of its worldwide commitment. It conceived of regional organization primarily in terms of collective security, with the Rio Pact for mutual defense (2 Sept., 1947) and the Organization of American States (OAS, created Mar. 1948) as its instruments. Latin American nations, the long fight for the principle of nonintervention fresh in their memories, resisted this initiative. They remained largely unresponsive to U.S. appeals for OAS action on Korea, Mar. 1951, Guatemala, Mar. 1954, and Cuba, 1960 onward. In 1965 the U.S. demonstrated its lack of confidence in multilateral military action when it unilaterally invaded the Dominican Republic, 28 Apr., in direct violation of the OAS Charter, only afterward requesting creation of an OAS peace force, which came into existence, 6 May.

ECONOMIC CO-OPERATION. Through the 1950's Latin nations worried less about an external threat from Communism than an internal one from pressing social and economic problems. The violent Latin response to the good-will tour of Vice-President Richard Nixon, 27 Apr.–15 May, 1958; the proposal of "Operation Pan America" by Brazilian President Juscelino Kubitschek, June 1958; and the victory of Fidel Castro in Cuba, 1 Jan. 1959, finally spurred the U.S. to a new kind of regional co-operation. On 29 Dec., 1959, it supported establishment of an Inter-American Development Bank, with $1 billion capitalization. By the Act of Bogotá, 12 Sept., 1960, the U.S. endorsed Latin American social reform and statist economic planning.

ALLIANCE FOR PROGRESS. Proposed, 13 Mar., 1961, by President John F. Kennedy, and chartered at Punta del Este, Uruguay, 17 Aug., 1961, the Alliance for Progress committed the nations of the Americas to a $100 billion 10-year program of tax and land reform and a projected 2.5% annual economic growth. Of the $100 billion, the U.S. pledged $20 billion, with $11 billion of this from government funds at low interest. The results have not been encouraging. Few Latin governments have had either the technical expertise to implement national economic planning or a real commitment to social reforms. For its part, the U.S. has appeared less concerned with social justice than social stability. Despite the creation of an Inter-American Committee for the Alliance, Jan. 1964, the *Alianza* has remained essentially a foreign aid program, based on bilateral bargaining between individual Latin nations and the U.S.

LATIN AMERICANISM. Although efforts were made in the 19th cent., there was no significant intra–Latin American co-operation until the 1960's. Then it was not so much cultural similarities that brought Latin nations together as a common economic dilemma. Through the 1950's the UN's Economic Commission for Latin America (ECLA, headed, 1950–63, by the Argentine, Raúl Prebisch) made them aware of their deteriorating position vis-à-vis the advanced manufacturing nations. Latin America's terms of trade declined by 21% between 1950 and 1962. What was desirable for the developed countries was not necessarily beneficial to them: stripped of protection under the tariff reductions approved by GATT (General Agreement on Tariffs and Trade), intraregional Latin trade dropped from 12.1% of total exports in 1955 to 7.1% in 1961. With the example of the thriving European Economic Community before them, Latin America turned to economic integration.

CENTRAL AMERICAN COMMON MARKET. In the century and a half following independence from Mexico, 1823, 25 unsuccessful formal efforts were made to reintegrate the Central American countries politically. In Dec. 1960, turning to economic co-operation, Guatemala, El Salvador, Nicaragua, and Honduras (joined by Costa Rica, July 1962) signed at Managua, Nicaragua, a General Treaty establishing a customs union. With the elimination of tariff barriers between one another (on 85% of tariff items by mid-1965), intraregional trade rose from $32.7 m. in 1960 to $136.0 m. in 1965. The creation of a common external tariff was 70% complete (by value) by 1966. Some progress had been made on integrated economic planning.

LATIN AMERICAN FREE TRADE AREA. The Treaty of Montevideo (ratified 2 May, 1961) created a free trade area (LAFTA) between Argentina, Brazil, Chile, Mexico, Paraguay, Peru, Uruguay, Colombia (30 Sept., 1961), and Ecuador (3 Nov., 1961), determined "to establish, gradually and progressively, a Latin American common market." This broader commitment was strengthened by the Latin nations at Punta del Este, Apr. 1967, and there endorsed by the U.S., which, although not directly included, stood to gain greatly from expanded markets for U.S.-owned subsidiaries. The gradual elimination by 8% per year of internal tariffs raised intra-LAFTA trade from $299 m. in 1961 to $588 m. in 1964, but Argentina alone reaped almost half this gain. By 1967 LAFTA had achieved neither a common external tariff nor significant economic complementarity and integration. An "Andean Group" (Colombia, Chile, Venezuela, Peru, and Ecuador) was created by the Declaration of Bogotá, 16 Aug., 1966, to counterbalance the economic weight of the 3 largest Latin countries, Brazil, Mexico, and Argentina.

PAN-ARABISM

1945–68

NATURE OF PAN-ARABISM. Pan-Arabism, although it had its roots in the 19th and early 20th cents., is, in political terms, largely a creation of the years since 1945. What began primarily as a cultural movement in the mid-19th cent. and received further stimulus from the Pan-Turkic policy of the Ottoman Empire after the Young Turks' revolution of 1908, emerged as a more recognizably political movement in the mid-1930's mainly as a result of the Palestine Question. The basic components of Pan-Arabism had long been present: a common language and culture as well as a glorious past, the memory of which still produces a strong emotional response. In its early stages, however, Pan-Arabism remained little more than a vague attachment to a culture and language and lacked a concrete program. The first objective of Pan-Arabism was freedom from foreign control, and it was not until the Arabs had attained independence from Ottoman and European overlordship that there could be any real attempt to make Pan-Arabism a meaningful basis for unity within the Arab world.

FORMATION OF THE ARAB LEAGUE. The attempts to make Pan-Arabism a reality have taken several different forms. The earliest and most long-lived of these was the creation of the Arab League, 22 Mar., 1945. Composed originally of 7 states, it has grown to include 13 Arab countries of the Middle East and North Africa. It was envisaged as an organization through which the members could co-ordinate their political activities and make decisions on Arab affairs. The power of the League was limited from the beginning, however, by the proviso that its decisions were only binding on those members who accepted them. The success of the Arab League as an instrument of Pan-Arabism has been confined largely to the nonpolitical sphere. During the Palestine war of 1948 there was dissension in its ranks because of the determination of Jordan to annex parts of what had been Palestine, and the Arab military effort against Israel met with defeat. The armies of the various Arab states participating in the war were unable to co-operate effectively.

ARAB LEAGUE POLICIES. On the positive side the Arab League adopted a cultural treaty, 27 Nov., 1945, providing for exchanges of professors and students and for translations of texts and co-operation between scientists and writers of member countries. In 1950 a joint defense and economic co-operation treaty was signed, and in 1954 an Arab postal union was set up. Jan. 1959 saw the creation of an Arab Development Bank and further economic ties were established, Jan. 1965, with the creation of an Arab common market. The Arab League has also held conferences on common problems such as the division of the Jordan waters. There have, however, been continuous quarrels among its members, leading in some cases to temporary withdrawals from the League, such as those of Iraq and Egypt.

LEADERSHIP OF NASSER. With the emergence of Gamal Abdel Nasser in Egypt after the revolution of 1952, Pan-Arabism found its most powerful exponent. As the spokesman of the Pan-Arab ideal, Nasser had no rival. His personal charisma, coupled with his notable success in dealing with the West, made him the natural leader of the Pan-Arab movement, but even he was unable to preserve for long the ephemeral unions created with Syria in 1958 and with Syria and Iraq in 1963. The United Arab Republic, created by the merger of Syria and Egypt, lasted only until 1961, when Syria withdrew, having disliked the imposition of Nasser's economic policies, which were ill-suited to the Syrian economy, and resenting the almost totally Egyptian personnel

and orientation of the regime. In the case of the UAR practical considerations proved too powerful for Pan-Arab feeling to overcome. The union of the monarchies of Iraq and Jordan, which occurred almost immediately after the formation of the UAR in Feb. 1958, was also short-lived and vanished in the Iraqi revolution of July 1958.

INFLUENCE OF THE BA'ATH PARTY. The projected union of Egypt, Syria, and Iraq, 1963, brought into play the conflict between Nasser and the Ba'ath Party, a socialist organization founded in 1940 and having branches in several Arab countries. At the moment of union, Apr. 1963, the Ba'ath was in power in Syria and Iraq and on good terms with Nasser, and it seemed that the union might have some chance of success. This situation did not last, however, and the union was never implemented. In addition conflict within the Ba'ath organization itself, both in Syria and Iraq, weakened the party's position as a potential basis for Pan-Arab unity. Ba'ath theoreticians have attempted to formulate an ideology for the Pan-Arab movement, but the party has not been able to attain and hold onto political leadership.

PAN-AFRICANISM

1945–58

PAN-AFRICAN CONGRESSES BEFORE WORLD WAR II. The idea of pan-Africanism had its origins in the Western Hemisphere, among black men living in the United States and the West Indies. The 1st Pan-African Congress was convened in London, 1900, by H. Sylvester Williams, a lawyer from Trinidad. About 30 delegates from Britain, the West Indies, and North America met together to express their solidarity as black men in the face of white oppression in America and Africa. They addressed a protest to Queen Victoria about British expansion into African land in Central Africa. It was at this congress that the American intellectual, W. E. B. Du Bois, made his well-known prediction: "The problem of the twentieth century is the problem of the color line."

The 2nd Pan-African Congress met in Paris, 1919, during the Peace Conference. Fifty-seven representatives from the U.S., the West Indies, and various African colonies came together under Du Bois' leadership. This congress adopted resolutions calling for laws to prevent exploitation of Africans and asserting the right of Africans to participate in the government of their own countries.

In 1921, Du Bois presided over the 3rd Pan-African Congress, which met in 3 sessions in London, Brussels, and Paris. The delegates now numbered 113, but the majority were still from America and Europe. The conference called for increased local self-government in colonies and recognition of the equality of all races. These demands were reiterated at the 4th Pan-African Congress in London and Lisbon, 1923. A 5th Congress met in 1927 in New York; it was the last meeting led directly by Du Bois.

PAN-AFRICAN FEDERATION. During World War II, Britain became the center of pan-Africanism. In 1944, several organizations joined to form the Pan-African Federation, whose leaders included the West Indians George Padmore and C. L. R. James and the African Jomo Kenyatta. In 1945, the Federation sponsored the 6th Pan-African Congress in Manchester. Although influential Americans and West Indians were present, this congress was predominantly African. Among its members were such future leaders as Kwame Nkrumah, Chief S. L. Akintola, Jomo Kenyatta, and Wallace Johnson. The resolutions of the Manchester Congress reflected the change in the pan-African movement; the delegates demanded independence for Africa within the world community, and they pledged to use force, as a last resort if necessary, to achieve African freedom.

1958

1ST CONFERENCE OF INDEPENDENT AFRICAN STATES. The 1st pan-African meeting on African soil included all 8 independent African states: Ghana, Liberia, Ethiopia, Sudan, Egypt, Tunisia, Libya, and Morocco. The delegates met at Accra, Ghana, 15–22 Apr., 1958, and declared their opposition to colonialism and their support for Algeria's fight for independence. They adopted a policy of nonalignment and loyalty to UN decisions in foreign affairs, and they agreed to recognize each other's sovereignty and settle differences among themselves by negotiation.

PAN-AFRICAN FREEDOM MOVEMENT FOR EAST AND CENTRAL AFRICA. Political parties in Tanganyika, Kenya, Uganda, Northern and Southern Rhodesia, Nyasaland, and Zanzibar met at Mwanza, Tanganyika, Sept. 1958, to form a loose grouping which aimed to promote continental unity by consolidating regional associations. In 1962, PAFMECA became PAFMECSA with the addition of countries of Southern Africa. The organization became increasingly concerned with assisting liberation movements.

1ST ALL-AFRICAN PEOPLES ORGANIZATION CONFERENCE. The AAPO was a group not of governments but of political parties. The first conference, held in Accra, Ghana, 5–13 Dec., 1958, declared its ultimate objective to be "the evolution of a Commonwealth of Free African States." This aim was strongly supported by Ghana's President Nkrumah, who called for the "total liberation of Africa."

1959–68

CONAKRY DECLARATION. On 1 May, 1959, at Conakry, Guinea, Ghana and Guinea declared the creation of the Ghana-Guinea Union, which was to be the beginning of a Union of Independent African States. In Dec. 1960, Mali joined to form the Ghana-Guinea-Mali Union.

SANNIQUELLIE DECLARATION. In reaction to the Conakry Declaration, Liberia's President Tubman called a meeting with Nkrumah and Touré at the Liberian village of Sanniquellie. On 19 July, 1959, they issued a statement setting

forth the principles which should under-
lie a Community of Independent African
States. In such a community, each state
would maintain its own national identity.

**2ND CONFERENCE OF INDEPEN-
DENT AFRICAN STATES.** The conference met at Addis Ababa, Ethiopia,
15–24 June, 1960, with delegates from 13
countries: Algeria Provisional Government, Cameroon, Ethiopia, Ghana,
Guinea, Libya, Liberia, Morocco, Nigeria,
Somalia, Sudan, Tunisia, United Arab
Republic. The discussion at this meeting
revealed the continuing difference of
opinion between those who would impose
African unity immediately from above
and those who would allow unity to
evolve gradually out of federations of
sovereign states.

BRAZZAVILLE   DECLARATION.
Brazzaville, Republic of Congo, was the
site of a meeting of delegates from 12
former French territories: Cameroon,
Central African Republic, Chad, Republic of Congo, Dahomey, Gabon, Ivory
Coast, Malagasy Republic, Mauritania,
Niger, Senegal, Upper Volta. In addition
to discussing several current political
questions, they declared, 19 Dec., 1960,
their desire for progress in inter-African
co-operation, but they opposed complete
political integration.

CASABLANCA CONFERENCE. Algeria, Ghana, Guinea, Libya, Mali, Morocco, and the United Arab Republic met
at Casablanca, Morocco, 3–7 Jan., 1961, to
express their opposition to the Brazzaville
group's position on the Congo and Mauritania. But on the question of African
unity, although Nkrumah argued for political union, the majority of the Casablanca powers were willing to commit
themselves only to efforts for "an effective
form of co-operation."

MONROVIA CONFERENCE. This
conference met at Monrovia, Liberia,
8–12 May, 1961, in an attempt to reconcile differences among the various groups.
In addition to the 12 Brazzaville states,
Liberia, Nigeria, Somalia, Sierra Leone,
Togo, Ethiopia, and Libya sent representatives. But the absence of most of the
Casablanca group weakened the force of

the Monrovia declaration on principles of
unity.

LAGOS CONFERENCE. From 25–30
Jan., 1962, the Monrovia group met again
in Lagos, Nigeria, with the addition of
Congo (Léopoldville) and Tanganyika
but without Libya, which stayed away
along with the other Casablanca states.
Although this conference also failed to
bring together all African states, it ratified a charter for an Inter-African and
Malagasy States Organization.

**ADDIS ABABA CONFERENCE AND
THE OAU.** Thanks largely to the efforts
of Ethiopia's Haile Selassie, Nigeria's
Abubakar Tafawa Balewa, and Guinea's
Sekou Touré, it finally came about that
almost all the independent African states
met together to form the Organization of
African Unity. On 25 May, 1963, in Addis
Ababa, Ethiopia, 30 states signed a charter which stated that the purpose of the
OAU was "to promote the unity and
solidarity of the African states" and
which pledged members to co-ordinate
various political, economic, and social activities. The Organization was to have an
Assembly of Heads of State and Government meeting annually, and a Council of
Ministers and various special commissions
which were to meet more often to implement Assembly decisions.

During 1963, the Ghana-Guinea-Mali
Union, PAFMECSA, the Casablanca, and
the Monrovia groups all disbanded in
order that their members could concentrate their unity efforts on the OAU. After
some controversy, the Brazzaville group
also agreed, 1964, to cease functioning as
a political body but continued economic
and social co-operation.

The OAU has remained a group of
sovereign states rather than a political
unit. As such it has sometimes suffered
from disputes among its members over
frontier quarrels and interference in one
another's internal affairs. But the Organization has presented a united viewpoint
on such issues as *apartheid,* neocolonialism, and liberation of the remaining
colonies and has thus provided an African voice in international discussion.

Postwar International Co-operation

1945–49

FOUNDING OF THE UNITED NATIONS. During World War II, support for a new organization to prevent recurrence of war developed among the allies. In the Moscow Declaration of 30 Oct., 1943, the Soviet Union, the U.S., and Britain, joined by China, agreed to seek its establishment. A proposal on organizational structure was prepared after a series of conversations held at Dumbarton Oaks near Washington, 21 Aug.–9 Oct., 1944, and agreement on most basic points was secured at Yalta, Feb. 1945. With the approach of European victory, the United Nations Conference on International Organization, representing 50 allied or associated states, met in San Francisco, 25 Apr.–26 June, to draft a Charter. A Steering Committee, composed of all heads of delegations, decided major policy questions. A 14-member Executive Committee supervised routine matters; most drafting was done by 12 technical committees of 4 commissions. The Dumbarton Oaks proposal formed the basis of discussion; few changes were made in its general outlines, since approval by the great powers was vital. Primary political powers were accorded to a General Assembly and a Security Council. The former, representing all members, received extensive powers of discussion and recommendation on international issues. The Security Council was given the responsibility of preserving peace, with real enforcement powers. It was to be composed of 5 Permanent Members: Britain, China, France, Russia, and the U.S., and 6 (later increased to 10) members elected by the General Assembly. Action on substantive matters would require agreement of 7 (later 9) members, including all 5 major states. Other organs were to include the Secretariat, the Trusteeship Council, and the Economic and Social Council. The International Court of Justice was reconstituted by a separate statute. The Conference adopted the Charter, 25 June, and the U.S. joined, 8 Aug. With Soviet accession, 24 Oct., the Charter went into effect.

INTERNATIONAL FINANCE. In 1945 the dollar and the pound were the basic international reserve currencies. On 27 Dec., 1945, the International Monetary Fund was created, a basis being thereby established for co-operation in international monetary matters. On 18 Sept., 1949, the British pound was devalued by 30.5% in relation to the U.S. dollar; within a few days 25 countries devalued their currencies: Australia, Burma, Ceylon, Denmark, India, Ireland, New Zealand, Norway, Sweden, Union of South Africa, 18 Sept.; Canada, Egypt, Finland, Israel, Portugal, 19 Sept.; France, Iceland, Iraq, Netherlands, 20 Sept.; Belgium, 21 Sept.; Greece, Jordan, 22 Sept.; Luxembourg, 23 Sept.; Thailand, 27 Sept.; and West Germany, 29 Sept.; the devaluations involved countries accounting for almost half the world's trade and about 60% of the exports of the industrial countries.

During the 1950's most currencies remained inconvertible. In 1958 convertibility at fixed rates of exchange in the sterling area for nonresidents was introduced, and thereafter convertibility spread and there was a general decline in the restrictions on payments.

On 18 Nov., 1967, the British pound was devalued from $2.80 to $2.40, a change of 14.3%. Ireland followed, devaluing immediately. Other countries devalued: Israel, 19 Nov.; Guyana, Spain, Cyprus, Malawi, and New Zealand, 20 Nov.; Denmark, Jamaica, and Ceylon, 21 Nov.; Sierra Leone and Trinidad and Tobago, 22 Nov.; Iceland, 27 Nov.; and Nepal, 11 Dec.; the devaluations affected countries accounting for only 12% of world trade and only 12% of the exports of the industrial countries.

After the Second World War the world's monetary reserves (dollars, pounds, and gold) did not increase as fast as world trade; because an expansion of international liquidity was considered essential to the continued growth of commerce, world financial leaders gave thought to new means of supplementing existing reserve assets. On 26 Aug., 1967, the "Group of 10," made up of representatives of Belgium, Britain, Canada, France, West Germany, Italy, Japan, Sweden, the Netherlands, and the U.S., agreed to a plan to establish a new kind of international monetary reserve, known as "special drawing rights" (SDR's). At a meeting in Rio, the Board of Governors of the International Monetary Fund resolved that work proceed toward the introduction of SDR's. On 16–17 Mar., 1968, the governors of the central banks of Belgium, Britain, West Germany, Italy, the Netherlands, Switzerland, and the U.S. met in Washington, D.C., and agreed to a "Dual Gold Market"; officially held gold would be used only to effect transfers among monetary authorities, and the central banks were no longer to supply gold to the London gold market or any other gold market. On the free market the price of gold would fluctuate; officially, gold would remain at $35 per ounce. The "Group of 10" met in Stockholm, 29–30 Mar.; with the exception of the French representatives the Ministers and central bank governors in Stockholm agreed to give the necessary authority to the Executive Directors of the IMF to take steps to introduce SDR's. Their hope was that the SDR system would "make a very substantial contribution to strengthening the [world] monetary system."

INTERNATIONAL BANK. On 27 Dec., 1945, the International Bank for Reconstruction and Development (World Bank) was founded. Unlike the IMF, which sought to stabilize currencies, the IBRD's functions were to provide financing for worldwide reconstruction and development. The International Finance Corporation, an affiliate of the World Bank, was established, July 1956. The IFC was especially designed to encourage the expansion of private enterprise in less developed countries. In Nov. 1960 another affiliate of the World Bank was set up—the International Development Association, designed to spur development financing. In 1967 the disbursements of the World Bank group (including IBRD, IFC, and IDA) exceeded $1 billion.

INTERNATIONAL TRADE. After World War II most states had high tariffs, quantitative restrictions, exchange controls, and other restraints on international commerce, and from 1945 onward member states of the UN discussed measures designed to lead to trade liberalization. In 1947 tariff bargaining sessions were held in Geneva. A UN-sponsored international conference on trade was held in Havana, Nov., with 57 countries participating; in Mar. 1948 the conference completed preparation of the so-called Havana Charter, which provided for the establishment of an International Trade Organization to seek reductions in world trade restrictions. The U.S. Congress, however, never accepted the charter and ITO never came into existence.

Meanwhile, Jan. 1948, a General Agreement on Tariffs and Trade (GATT) had been accepted as an interim measure designed to serve until ITO was established; the tariff schedules negotiated in Geneva in 1947 were annexed to the Agreement; since ITO was never created, GATT continued and became an important institution. The 1st round of tariff bargaining under GATT was held at Annecy, France, 1949; the 2nd round was at Torquay, England, 1950–51. Geneva was the site for the 3rd round, 1956, and also for the 4th and 5th rounds, 1960–62. The 4th round involved the application of GATT rules to the European Economic Community and the 5th, the "Dillon Round," involved an exchange of tariff concessions among GATT members and included the formulation of concessions as a result of the Common Market's external tariff. While the Dillon Round was still in progress, the U.S. Trade Expansion Act, 11 Oct., 1962, became law; it provided a basis for further negotiations for the liberalization of trade. After more than a year of preliminary talks, GATT formally launched its 6th round, the so-called Kennedy Round, Nov. 1964. On 30 June, 1967, 46 members of GATT signed the "Kennedy Round Pact," a group of agreements which provided for the gradual cutting of tariffs by as much as 50% over the ensuing 5 years; the average cuts were estimated at 35%, affected almost 6,000 items, and involved $40 billion of world trade in industrial products; the Kennedy Round had achieved the largest tariff reductions ever made among industrial nations. Tariff concessions on agricultural products were also agreed on, as was a world grains agreement which was to guarantee higher minimum trading prices and institute a program of food aid to less developed countries of 4.5 m. metric tons of grain annually.

INTERNATIONAL COMMODITY AGREEMENTS. Of international agreements designed to stabilize commodity prices, those for wheat, sugar, tin, and coffee were the most important.

In 1949 an International Wheat Agreement was signed; the agreement was revised in 1953, 1956, and 1962; and the 1962 agreement was extended, 1965 and 1966. By 1966, exporting countries involved in the agreement included the Big 4—U.S., Canada, Australia, and Argentina—plus France, Sweden, Spain, Italy, Mexico, and the USSR (which joined for the 1st time in 1962) ; importing countries participating numbered 39. The 1966 agreement expired on 31 July, 1967, and an International Wheat and Food Aid Agreement was drafted as part of the GATT Kennedy Round to replace it.

An International Sugar Agreement came into force, 1 Jan., 1954, and covered about 95% of the free world market's sugar supplies. In 1960, owing to events in Cuba, the sugar agreement ran into difficulties; the U.S. government put an end, 16 Dec., to all American purchases of Cuban sugar. In the fall of 1961 international discussions on sugar quotas were held, but no agreement was reached, and on 31 Dec. of that year all regulation of the free market in sugar ended.

On 30 June, 1954, the principal tin producing countries—Malaya, Bolivia, Indonesia, Congo, Thailand, and Nigeria—signed an International Tin Agreement; all the major consuming countries, except

the U.S., also signed; but ratification was delayed and the agreement did. not become operative until 1 July, 1956. Its aim was to create adequate supplies of tin at reasonable, stable prices. In Feb. 1962 a 2nd International Tin Agreement came into effect with much the same participants.

An International Coffee Agreement was signed, Sept. 1962. At that point coffee prices had been declining for 8 consecutive years. The Coffee Agreement succeeded in stabilizing prices, and an International Coffee Organization was established which included 61 countries (exporters and importers) and represented 98% of the world trade in coffee.

NUREMBERG TRIALS. German atrocities before and during World War II led the U.S., USSR, Britain, and France to agree in London, 8 Aug., 1945, to try responsible military, political, and industrial leaders. The agreement included a statute establishing the jurisdiction and functions of an International Military Tribunal, whose members were to be named by the signatories. Twenty-four individuals and 8 organizations were indicted by the allies for conspiracy to wage war, crimes against peace, war crimes, and crimes against humanity. The Tribunal heard prosecution and defense evidence in Nuremberg, 20 Nov., 1945–31 Aug., 1946. Its judgment was delivered, 30 Sept.–1 Oct. Of the 22 who were tried, 19 were convicted. Sentences ranged from 10 years' imprisonment to death; 4 organizations were proscribed. The Nuremberg trials, one of the last joint actions of the allies before the outbreak of the Cold War, was also the precedent for trials held later in Germany and in Tokyo, 1946–48.

UNIVERSAL DECLARATION OF HUMAN RIGHTS. International interest in the preservation of human rights grew during World War II, and the San Francisco Conference incorporated their protection into the UN Charter as one of the organization's purposes. In 1946, the Economic and Social Council created the Commission on Human Rights with Mrs. Franklin D. Roosevelt as its 1st chairman. Eventually the Commission and Council produced a Declaration of Human Rights which was adopted by the General Assembly, 10 Dec., 1948. The Declaration specified many political, social, and economic rights that were to be sought as goals by UN members. Efforts to draft a convention embodying these principles failed at first, partly because of growing tensions between the U.S. and the Soviet Union, partly because of opposition to UN action in domestic affairs. The deadlock continued throughout the Cold War, until 2 conventions were approved by the Assembly, 16 Dec., 1966. Other efforts had more immediate success. The Convention on the Prevention and Punishment of the Crime of Genocide received Assembly approval, 9 Dec., 1948, becoming effective in 1951. The Convention on the Political Rights of Women entered into force in 1954. Slavery and forced labor were also reviewed by the Economic and Social Council, as were the rights of national minorities. In a number of resolutions, the Assembly condemned racial discrimination in South Africa, and the Security Council eventually decreed sanctions against that country for its continued violations of human rights.

REFUGEES. The UN Relief and Rehabilitation Administration (UNRRA) was created, 9 Nov., 1943, to deal with the refugee problem after the Second World War. The war and the flight or expulsion of populations from Eastern Europe produced a vast care and resettlement problem which UNRRA proceeded to meet. Although the organization performed vital services for European and Far Eastern refugees in the postwar world, increasing Cold War tensions led to its dissolution. In its place, the General Assembly established the International Refugee Organization (IRO), 14 Dec., 1946. Lacking general international support, IRO did not complete accepting transferred functions from UNRRA until late in 1948. After substantially completing its work in Europe, IRO was succeeded by the Office of the UN High Commissioner for Refugees, created on 3 Dec., 1949. Becoming operational on 1 Jan., 1951, this Office experienced difficulties in its early years, but eventually

secured broad international backing, and continues the work of UNRRA and IRO throughout the world. In addition to these general organizations, the Assembly created the UN Relief and Works Agency for Palestine Refugees in the Near East (UNRWA), 8 Dec., 1949, to aid those displaced by the Arab-Israeli hostilities of 1948.

1950–59

TRUST TERRITORIES. The UN Conference at San Francisco left disposition of former League mandates and Italian colonies to interstate negotiations, subject to approval by the General Assembly, or the Security Council in the case of "strategic" territories. The UN Trusteeship Council was to supervise administration. By 1 Nov., 1947, the General Assembly had approved agreements covering 9 former mandates; South Africa never accepted UN supervision of South-West Africa. On 2 Apr., 1947, the Security Council approved the "strategic" United States Trust Territory of the Pacific Islands. When negotiations over former Italian colonies failed, their disposition was submitted to the General Assembly for final determination. On 21 Nov., 1949, that body recommended independence for Libya on 2 Jan., 1952, and suggested that Italy should administer Somaliland as a trust territory for 10 years. The Trusteeship Council accepted the terms of the Somaliland agreement, requiring direct supervision by an Advisory Council, and on 2 Dec., 1950, the General Assembly gave final approval, establishing the last UN Trust Territory. Ethiopia received Eritrea on 11 Sept., 1952. In the next decade the Trusteeship Council exercised active supervisory powers, utilizing Visiting Missions, and by 1967 all but 3 Trust Territories were independent.

SPECIALIZED AGENCIES OF THE UN. With the outbreak of the Korean War in 1950, relations between the U.S. and the USSR, and their allies, reached their lowest point. It was in the UN and its specialized agencies that regular cooperative contacts between the eastern and western blocs were maintained.

These agencies were created by intergovernmental agreement and associated with the UN through the Economic and Social Council. Among those created soon after World War II were the Food and Agriculture Organization (FAO), the UN Educational, Scientific, and Cultural Organization (UNESCO), the World Health Organization (WHO), the International Bank for Reconstruction and Development (IBRD), and the International Civil Aviation Organization (ICAO). The World Meteorological Organization (WMO) was formed in 1951. Some of these provide services, like FAO, concerned with increasing food supplies and preventing famine; WHO, combating epidemic diseases and promoting public health; and WMO, providing worldwide weather observations. IBRD aids underdeveloped states financially, and UNESCO promotes literacy, research, and protection of cultural properties. Others are regulatory, like ICAO, which sets standards for international air navigation and transport. The older agencies include the International Labour Organization (ILO), the International Telecommunications Union (ITU), and the Universal Postal Union (UPU). These are primarily regulatory, with the ILO acting through the device of multilateral conventions. In recent years, all agencies have increased their interest in aiding underdeveloped nations through technical assistance.

UN SECRETARIAT. The Secretariat is the administrative arm of the United Nations. Headed by a secretary general chosen by the Security Council, the civil servants of the Secretariat are selected by, and responsible to, him. In carrying out decisions of the political organs, it is presumably impartial; members are expected to serve the organization, not national or ideological interests. The secretary general possesses wide powers of a political nature, including the right to bring issues before the Security Council. The Council and Assembly frequently grant him broad discretion in implementing their decisions, and he exercises independent investigative and diplomatic functions. Trygve Lie of Norway was the 1st secretary general. Elected before the start of the Cold War, he was caught in the middle of the struggle between the U.S. and the Soviet Union. The latter boycotted him after 1951 because of the Korean War; in late 1952 suggestions of Communist infiltration of the Secretariat disturbed the U.S. Unable to ease international tensions, Lie announced his earlier decision to retire, 10 Nov. With the election of Dag Hammarskjold of Sweden, Apr. 1953, an era of activism began, evidenced in the 1958 Lebanon crisis and the 1960 Congo crisis. After Hammarskjold's death, U Thant of Burma was chosen, Nov. 1961, and continued the role of conciliator and mediator between East and West.

ATOMS FOR PEACE. With the end of the Korean War, the atmosphere for international negotiation improved, and the 1st detonation of a Russian hydrogen bomb, 12 Aug., 1953, turned thoughts in the U.S. toward promoting the peaceful applications of atomic energy. The concept of the internationalization of nuclear energy for nonmilitary purposes had first been advanced by the U.S. as part of a comprehensive arms control plan on 14 June, 1946. This Baruch Plan had been almost forgotten when, 8 Dec., 1953, President Dwight D. Eisenhower put forward his "Atoms-for-Peace" proposal in a speech before the General Assembly. International reaction was favorable, after initial Soviet hesitation. Following several years of negotiation, the International Atomic Energy Agency (IAEA) was established as a UN subsidiary, 23 Oct., 1956, with support from both East and West. This organization assists states in their development of nuclear power for peaceful purposes. It operates as a bank through which fissionable materials are provided to nonnuclear powers under adequate safeguards. In addition, it promotes research in the peaceful uses of atomic energy and provides technical assistance in this field to developing nations.

GENEVA CONFERENCE ON FAR EASTERN AFFAIRS. Since 1946, France had been faced with a growing independence movement in Indochina. Attempts to create national regimes linked to the French Community in Cambodia, Laos, and Vietnam had failed. By 1954, the revolutionary forces, including Communists, were steadily gaining strength. On 18 Feb. the Berlin 4 Power Conference of Foreign Ministers agreed to convene a Conference on Far Eastern Affairs under British and Russian cochairmanship in Geneva on 26 Apr. Representatives of 19 countries, including the U.S., mainland China, and France, attended. After Dien Bien Phu fell to Communist-led forces on 8 May, 3 Accords were signed by all participants except the U.S. and the incumbent Vietnamese government on 21 July. They provided for suspension of hostilities, withdrawal of foreign forces, and complete independence for Cambodia, Laos, and Vietnam. Vietnam was partitioned between a Communist regime in the North and the incumbent regime in the South, pending 1956 elections. Simultaneously, the U.S. stated that it would respect the Accords and view their violation with concern. Although the system later broke down, these agreements represented an early effort at stabilization of conflict through direct East-West negotiations.

GENEVA "SUMMIT" CONFERENCE. In the decade following the 1945 Potsdam Conference, the hardened positions and mutual distrust engendered by the Cold War prevented additional direct contacts between the leaders of the U.S. and the Soviet Union. However, partial successes at the 1954 Berlin 4 Power Conference of Foreign Ministers led to increased support for similar meetings at a higher level. The Austrian State Treaty of 15 May, 1955, ending the postwar division and occupation of Austria after years of discussions, showed that agreement was possible. Encouraged by the progress of these negotiations, in early May the western states proposed a 4-nation "summit" conference of heads of government to convene in Geneva on 18 July. When the conference was held, its results were insubstantial; the division between East and West was still too great. Nevertheless, the participants did succeed in lessening tensions to some degree and

obtaining a better understanding of each other than would have been possible at the height of the Cold War. The Geneva Conference of Foreign Ministers, which followed on 27 Oct., was even less successful. German reunification was an obstacle, and renewed acrimony marked the meeting, although agreements on increased cultural exchanges were negotiated.

SUEZ CRISIS. On 29 Oct., 1956, Israel invaded Egypt in retaliation for Egyptian support of terrorist attacks upon Israeli territory. Israeli troops advanced rapidly toward the Suez Canal. By prearrangement with Israel, Britain and France demanded withdrawal of all belligerent forces from the Canal and permission to intervene to safeguard the waterway. When Egypt refused, Britain and France bombed Egyptian airfields, 31 Oct., and on 5 Nov. landed troops near the Canal. International reaction was swift. The Soviet Union, though engaged in crushing a rebellion in Hungary, condemned the invasion. The U.S. also denounced the intervention, and worked to secure withdrawal. More by accident than by design, the U.S. and the USSR voted together in the Security Council to demand withdrawal. When British and French vetoes prevented action, the U.S. supported a Yugoslav resolution transferring the issue to the Assembly. On 1 Nov. the Assembly demanded a cease-fire, and on 4 Nov. it requested the secretary general to establish a UN Emergency Force (UNEF) to police the cease-fire and supervise withdrawal. Faced with opposition by the major powers, on 7 Nov. Britain, France, and Israel agreed to end the fighting. On 14 Nov. units of UNEF, the 1st truly international UN police force, arrived in the Suez area; removal of troops began by 23 Nov. The Suez crisis marked a turning point in the Cold War; relations within and between blocs were never the same again.

INTERNATIONAL GEOPHYSICAL YEAR. Growing demands for planet-wide information by scientific communities of all nations, reinforced by the speed of scientific progress and improvements in information-gathering techniques, led to the institution of the International Geophysical Year (IGY) of 1 July, 1957–31 Dec., 1958. In the 18 months of the IGY, scientists of 66 countries co-operated in research and data-gathering projects on a nonpolitical basis. Studies of the earth, its atmosphere, and outer space were conducted by groups that made their discoveries available to all participants. Exploration of outer space was highlighted by the launching of the 1st artificial earth satellite by the USSR on 4 Oct., outside the framework of the IGY. This was followed by a similar U.S. launching on 31 Jan., 1958. Exploration in Antarctica by scientific teams of several nations laid the foundations for co-operation which later resulted in the 12-state Antarctic Treaty of 1 Dec., 1959, an agreement that demilitarized Antarctica and suspended territorial claims there. The synoptic and interdisciplinary information gathered and made available to the world's scientists in this period was vast; the process of sorting alone required several years.

1ST GENEVA CONFERENCE ON THE LAW OF THE SEA. Under the UN Charter, one of the duties of the General Assembly is that of promoting the development and progressive codification of international law. To accomplish this purpose, the Assembly created the International Law Commission, 21 Nov., 1947. Despite the pressures of the Cold War, the Commission carried out its mandate in many fields. Among its accomplishments, the development of the law of the sea is outstanding. In 1956 the group adopted a proposed convention codifying the law in this field. On 21 Feb., 1957, the Assembly called for an international conference to consider the suggestions, and the 1st Geneva Conference on the Law of the Sea convened, 24 Feb., 1958. Representatives of 86 states, including the Soviet Union and the U.S., attended. Despite the expected disagreement stemming from strongly conflicting national interests in the regime of the seas, the Conference produced 4 multilateral conventions covering the continental shelf, the high seas, fisheries, and territorial waters. The success of the 1st Conference led to the 2nd Conference, 1960, to consider questions that remained

unanswered. Although further agreement was not reached, the 2 Conferences were models of international co-operation in the resolution of conflicting nonpolitical claims.

INCREASING EAST-WEST CONTACTS. In the years after the 1955 Geneva "Summit" Conference, communication between East and West continued to increase. In 1959 this exchange of contacts multiplied. The 24 July–2 Aug. trip of the American vice-president to Moscow for the opening of a U.S. trade fair followed closely upon a visit by the British prime minister. Later, on 15–27 Sept., the chairman of the Council of Ministers of the USSR, Nikita S. Khrushchev, toured the U.S. In this 1st visit by a Soviet Russian head of government to the Western Hemisphere, talks held with President Dwight D. Eisenhower helped reduce some tensions of the period. During these visits, arrangements were made for a 4-nation meeting, to be held in Paris in 1960. Although the Paris "Summit" Conference ended abruptly in failure, official high-level contacts continued. At the same time, the cultural and other exchange programs that had been instituted earlier continued to spread, and East-West trade in nonstrategic goods began to grow. The period also saw increasing numbers of western tourists in Russia, contributing to a decline in the strong popular distrust that had developed in both blocs after World War II.

1960–68

CONGO CRISIS. Belgium granted the Congo independence on 30 June, 1960. During the colonial period, little had been done to prepare the Congolese for self-government, and disintegration soon began. Army mutinies spread, endangering European lives and property, and impelling Belgium to intervene militarily. On 11 July the major province of Katanga seceded. In response to these events, the Security Council, with East-West support, created a UN Force under the direction of Secretary General Dag Hammarskjold, 14 July, to end both intervention and violence. The Congolese central government collapsed into 2 competing factions, 5 Sept., and the neutrality of the secretary general in refusing to recognize the group supported by the USSR led to Soviet demands for a 3-man Secretariat leadership, or "troika." The operation continued, however, and on 21 Feb., 1961, the Council authorized the use of force to prevent civil war. After the central government crisis was resolved on 2 Aug., 1961, in favor of the pro-western faction, Soviet disinterest grew, prompting refusals to pay assessments for the operation. When the secretary general died in a plane accident, 18 Sept., 1961, while in the Congo, "troika" demands were again raised, but the appointment of Secretary General U Thant on 3 Nov., 1961, ended the controversy. Eventually the action was successful in removing a source of tension and preserving Congolese unity; after several minor clashes, Katangese secession ended, 21 Jan., 1963, and troops were withdrawn on 30 June, 1964.

THE DEVELOPMENT DECADE. As old colonial empires dissolved, the number of independent nations increased rapidly. In 1960, a total of 16 states from Africa alone were admitted to UN membership, and in the following years still more were added. Since most of these countries were underdeveloped and in need of assistance to achieve economic viability, demands increased. Early multilateral aid programs had been carried on under the UN through the Expanded Program of Technical Assistance (EPTA), established in 1949, and the Special UN Fund for Economic Development (SUNFED), created in 1956. Additionally, specialized agencies, particularly the International Bank for Reconstruction and Development, had also been established to provide assistance. These international efforts, even when added to the vast American and Soviet bilateral programs, were unable to meet rising demands. These difficulties caused the underdeveloped states to try to use their increased UN voting strength to mandate increasing aid programs. Although this occasionally led to a common U.S.-Soviet front to defeat excessive demands, both supported the General Assembly resolution, 19 Dec.,

1961, declaring the 1960's a "Development Decade." A goal of increasing annual growth rates in underdeveloped nations to 5% was adopted, and developed countries were urged to participate more fully in multilateral efforts. Although the first half of the decade was unsuccessful, the institution of the UN Conference on Trade and Development, 1964, an increasing emphasis on multilateral aid, and the merger of EPTA and SUNFED into the UN Development Program, 1966, gave hope for later success.

NEUTRALIZATION OF LAOS. Although the 1954 Geneva Accords on Indochina resulted in peace in Laos for several years, Communist-led outbreaks against the national government began in 1959. A neutralist government was created in 1960, but pro-western military forces took control later that year. The neutralists allied with the Communist Pathet Lao, and hostilities continued with both sides receiving outside support. On 24 Apr., 1961, Britain and the Soviet Union called for a new Conference on Laos; it opened in Geneva, 16 May, 1961. Representatives of East and West encouraged the leaders of the Laotian factions to agree on a common program, and on 22 June, 1961, they did so. A national government was established under neutralist leadership, June 1962, and a Declaration of Neutrality was made on 9 July. This was incorporated into the Final Declaration of the Conference, 23 July. The attending states, including the U.S. and mainland China, agreed to recognize the independence and neutrality of Laos and to refrain from further intervention. Although unrest continued, it was primarily of local origin, and the Geneva Conference did succeed, at least for a time, in eliminating another point of contention between East and West.

NUCLEAR TEST BAN TREATY. Early disarmament proposals, such as the 1946 Baruch Plan and the 1955 "Open Skies" proposal made at the Geneva "Summit" Conference, were unsuccessful in the years following World War II. Although both the U.S. and the Soviet Union continued to advance suggestions for general and complete disarmament, it became clear that the continuing Cold War made agreement on such proposals unlikely. Instead, the interest of the major powers turned to control of atomic weapons, as a step toward eventual total disarmament. In 1959 and 1960 the USSR and the U.S. suspended nuclear testing temporarily, but the moratorium ended in 1961. Negotiations continued, and agreement on a partial nuclear test ban was reached in Moscow, 5 Aug., 1963. The resultant treaty, effective on 10 Oct., prohibited atomic testing in the atmosphere, under water, and in outer space. Of the nations possessing nuclear capabilities, the U.S., USSR, and Britain acceded to the treaty. France and mainland China, allied respectively with the U.S. and Soviet Union, did not adhere, thus pointing up the growing disunity within the formerly monolithic opposing blocs. Efforts in disarmament continued, directed largely at the problem of nuclear proliferation and the question of eventual total disarmament.

CYPRUS. Strong hostility between the Greek Cypriots, who desired union with Greece, and the island's Turkish minority delayed independence for Cyprus until constitutionally guaranteed privileges for the protection of the Turks were accepted. When Britain granted independence, 16 Aug., 1960, Greece, Turkey, and Britain signed a Treaty of Guaranty with Cyprus to assure its continued existence. Attempted constitutional changes disadvantageous to the minority triggered violence, 21 Dec., 1963, and fear of Turkish intervention led Cyprus to appeal to the Security Council. After an observation mission appointed by the secretary general had reported, the Council acted, 4 Mar., 1964. The vote underlined how greatly the rigidity of the eastern and western blocs had continued to alter over the years. France decided to abstain together with the USSR and Czechoslovakia, while the Soviet Union's allies joined the majority in recommending that the secretary general establish a UN Force to be supported by voluntary contributions. Although the Force formed rapidly and contributed to the maintenance of order, the truce that was established remained uneasy. The secretary general was compelled to request repeated extensions of the life of the Force. Nevertheless, it did constitute an example of a multilateral peacekeeping operation undertaken and continued with Soviet acquiescence.

UNITED NATIONS FINANCES. In the Suez and Congo crises, UN action was based partly upon resolutions of the General Assembly instead of the Security Council. Several states, including the Soviet Union and France, challenged the legality of assessments levied for expenses incurred under these resolutions, and refused payment. By 1964, 16 countries were sufficiently in arrears to fall within the Charter provision requiring that they be deprived of their General Assembly votes. At the 1964 Assembly session, a constitutional crisis was avoided by acting only with unanimous consent, thus making votes unnecessary. A Special Committee on Peacekeeping Operations was established, 18 Feb., 1965, to review the financial problems of the organization and recommend solutions. The committee met during 1965, and on 31 Aug. approved a proposal designed to solve existing difficulties. This compromise provided that the Assembly would proceed normally, and that the question of voting would not be raised. The budget deficit would be met by voluntary contributions, primarily from the developed nations, including the U.S. and the Soviet Union. The compromise was accepted before the 1965 session opened on 21 Sept., and the UN was able to function normally, saved from a constitutional crisis by international co-operation and compromise.

INTERNATIONAL COURT OF JUSTICE. An organ of the UN, the International Court of Justice (ICJ) is composed of 15 judges elected to 9-year terms by the General Assembly and Security Council. Advisory opinions may be requested by other UN units, but only states may refer actual controversies to it. The Court's jurisdiction over such disputes arises from either specific agreements to refer questions or prior acceptance of its compulsory jurisdiction by unilateral declaration. Since its creation as the successor to the Permanent Court of International Justice, the ICJ has acquired compulsory jurisdiction over more than 40 states, some with reservations. When a dispute is brought before the Court, an *ad hoc* judge is named by each party to the controversy. Among the disputes settled by the ICJ were the *Corfu Channel* case of 1949, and the *Asylum* and *Norwegian Fisheries* cases of 1951. In the 1962 opinion on *Certain Expenses of the United Nations,* the Court upheld certain UN peacekeeping operations and assessments to support them as valid, resulting in the 1965 negotiations on UN finances. The 18 July, 1966, decision to reject, on procedural grounds, complaints against South Africa in the *South-West Africa* case illustrated the Court's reluctance to deal with political questions, and its ability to function independently.

PEACEFUL USES OF OUTER SPACE. The international community took an early interest in the exploration and exploitation of outer space. On 12 Dec., 1959, a permanent UN Committee on the Peaceful Uses of Outer Space was created to report on international aspects of space exploration. ITU, WMO, and UNESCO soon became involved with programs in space communications, weather observation, and scientific research; on 20 Dec., 1961, a UN Registry of Space Vehicles was established. The UN played a major role in the development of rules for space exploration. On 17 Oct., 1963, the Assembly urged that states refrain from orbiting weapons of mass destruction, and on 13 Dec., 1963, adopted a declaration of principles governing the exploration and use of outer space. These resolutions were later embodied in a treaty which received Assembly approval on 19 Dec., 1966, and which was signed by over 60 nations, including the U.S. and the USSR, 27 Jan., 1967. Its major provisions restrict military uses of space and call for free access to space installations. Additionally, it provides for peaceful co-operation by setting standards and promoting dissemination of information. Approval of the Outer Space Treaty by the U.S. Senate, 25 Apr., was a landmark of the developing international consensus of the 1960's.

U.S. MOON LANDING. Preparatory to the 1st successful moon landing, the U.S. launched, 11 Oct., 1968, the 1st manned flight of an Apollo spacecraft (Walter M. Schirra, Jr., Donn F. Eisele, R. Walter Cunningham), and the 1st manned voyage around the moon (launched 21 Dec.) was made in Apollo 8 by Frank Borman, James A. Lovell, Jr., and William A. Anders. The U.S.S.R. Soyuz 5 (launched 15 Jan., 1969) rendezvoused with Soyuz 4 (Yeliseyev and Khrunov). U.S. astronauts James A. McDivitt, David R. Scott, and Russell L. Schweikart, in an Apollo 9 space flight, docked with a lunar model (launched 3 Mar., 1969). On 18 May astronauts Thomas R. Stafford, Eugene A. Cernan, and John W. Young descended in Apollo 10 to within 9 mi. of the moon. Climaxing 8 yrs. of manned space flight competition between the U.S. and the Soviet Union, U.S. astronauts Neil A. Armstrong and Col. Edwin E. Aldrin, Jr., taking off 16 July in Apollo 11, touched down on the moon with their lunar module. Armstrong's 1st step on the moon was taken 20 July at 10.56:20 EDT. After taking rock and soil specimens, the pair successfully rendezvoused with Lieut. Col. Michael Collins, navigator of the Apollo craft, and splashed down 950 mi. S.W. of Hawaii, 24 July.

II

TOPICAL
CHRONOLOGY

ECONOMIC DEVELOPMENT AND TECHNOLOGY IN AN AGE OF REVOLUTION

Introductory. The period 1760–1968 witnessed a rapid and unprecedented rise in per capita income in Europe, North America, Australia, and New Zealand. The "West" came to regard economic growth as a normal condition. In the 19th and early 20th cents. relative economic stagnation was replaced by economic growth in many nations—from Argentina to Japan. Changes in the economic structure of nations took place. After World War II, governments throughout the world—in Latin America, Africa, the Middle East, Asia, and also in Europe and the United States—turned their attention to economic development.

1760–1830

The First Industrial Revolution—Great Britain

SCIENTIFIC AGRICULTURE AND ANIMAL HUSBANDRY. The British Industrial Revolution was characterized initially by an agricultural revolution. Jethro Tull (1674–1740) had demonstrated the need for selectivity in the choice of seed, sowing in rows, deep hoeing, and plowing, and had invented the seed drill; his innovations provided new techniques in constant tillage. Charles Townshend (1674–1738) promoted scientific crop rotations and advocated use of the turnip in crop rotation. Robert Bakewell (1725–95) taught improved stock breeding. Arthur Young (1741–1820) popularized new farming techniques and large-scale farming. 1771: John Brand of Lawford (Essex) manufactured the 1st all-iron plow, although by 1830 most English farmers still used wooden plows. 1772: Thomas Coke (1752–1842) in Norfolk started reforms in animal husbandry; later Coke was successful with 4-crop rotation (the "Norfolk System"). C. 1784: Scotsman Andrew Meikle made 1st threshing ma-

chine. 1798: John Wilkinson, British ironmaker, installed a steam-powered threshing machine; he also innovated in land reclamation and reforestation schemes. Before the end of the 18th cent. Irishmen, Scots, Frenchmen, Americans, Germans, and Flemings considered England their agricultural mentor.

New crops: Novel fodder crops—clover and rye grass, alfalfa, roots, swedes, cabbages, carrots as well as turnips tried in crop rotation. 1795–1814: Potato acreage in England increased an est. 60%.

Land reform: The enclosure movement of the 18th cent. involved the fencing and consolidation of medieval open fields, which had formerly been farmed in small, discontinuous strips by peasants who had shared the right of pasture, fuel, and game on common land. It also involved the enclosure of waste lands. Enclosure replaced small holdings with large-scale farming, using advanced methods. 1710–60: Est. 300,000 acres were enclosed; 1760–1843: est. 7 million acres enclosed.

655

1801: Parliament passed the 1st General Enclosure Act.

Agricultural productivity: Because of new agricultural techniques and because enclosures increased the productive land in England, agricultural productivity (output per man) rose sharply. There were food surpluses to meet demands from growing urban centers. Because of enclosures, peasants were turned off the land and became wage laborers and purchasers of food. Increasingly, agriculture became concerned with producing for national markets rather than for local consumption. Rising prices of corn in the 2nd half of the 18th cent. encouraged greater production.

Price rise: 1793–1815: Due to war demands agricultural prices soared, which stimulated the growing of additional crops for sale. Rising prices meant profits for reinvestment in agriculture and industry. The changes in English agriculture caused a breakup of village life and an end to traditional patterns. Estimates indicate that in 1811 and all years prior to that agriculture, forestry, and fishing provided the greatest percentage of British national income. In 1821 and all years thereafter the manufacturing, mining, and building sector exceeded the agricultural sector.

INDUSTRIAL RAW MATERIALS. Britain was well-endowed with raw materials needed for industrialization, namely, coal and iron. Cotton for the textile industry could be imported; the use in the American South of the cotton gin, invented, 1793, by Eli Whitney (1765–1825), sharply reduced the cost of raw cotton.

LABOR. A demographic revolution took place in England and Wales, with population expanding rapidly. Estimates: 1760, 6.6 million; 1830, 16.4 million. The population of England and Wales increased 7% in the decade 1760–70, 11% in the decade 1780–90, and 16% in the years 1810–20. Rising population meant a demand for goods—a market for food and industrial products. Men moved from rural areas to urban centers because of changes in agriculture and because of the pull of industry. 1800: Greater London had a population of 959,000 and was the largest city in the world, but population estimates indicate that the number of inhabitants in rural areas grew almost as rapidly as in the cities. The growth of population was the main reason for labor surpluses from which the industrial labor force could be drawn. Labor became wage labor. Slavery never existed on a large scale in England; in 1772 Lord Chief Justice Mansfield ruled it illegal. Henceforth, all labor was free labor. Education was at a high level in England (compared with the rest of the world) ; literacy was important for the success of the Industrial Revolution.

STEAM POWER. Industry was revolutionized by steam power. 1698: Devonshire inventor Thomas Savery (1650?–1715) patented a steam engine for use in pumping mines; it was not successful for this purpose, but was utilized in water-supply systems. 1712: Blacksmith and ironmonger from Devonshire Thomas Newcomen (1662–1719) built the 1st successful steam engine to be employed in pumping water from copper, tin, and coal mines. 1765: Scotsman James Watt (1736–1819) devised a separate condensing chamber, making the steam engine suitable for more extensive application. 1769, 5 Jan.: Watt patented his 1st engine with the separate condenser. 1774: Hardware manufacturer Matthew Boulton (1728–1809) agreed to finance Watt and to allow

STRUCTURE OF THE BRITISH NATIONAL PRODUCT
(% of national income)

	Agriculture, Forestry, Fishing	Manufactures, Mining, Building	Trade, Transport, and Income from Abroad	Government, Domestic, and Other Services	Housing
1811	35.7	20.8	16.6	21.7	5.7
1821	26.1	31.9	16.9	19.3	6.2
1831	23.4	34.4	18.4	18.1	6.5

the latter to use his employees to perfect the machine. 1776: Watt completed his 1st successful engine at Boulton's Birmingham works. The Boulton-Watt steam engine was the 1st practical steam unit for industrial purposes. Watt adapted the engine to rotary motion, 1781; invented the reciprocating expansion engine, 1782; applied the steam engine to tilt hammers in iron and steel forges, 1784. 1785: Cotton mill at Papplewick was 1st textile plant to use a steam engine. 1775–1800: Boulton and Watt built 289 steam engines (84 for cotton mills, 9 for wool and worsted mills, 30 for coal mines, 28 for foundries and forges, 22 for copper mines, 18 for canals, and 17 for breweries). Steam power made possible urban factories, created innovations in transportation, and had linkage effects in the iron and steel industry. Steam engines required precise working parts, which encouraged the use of new machine-tools to make the parts and encouraged new developments in the metallurgical industries.

INDUSTRIES AND TECHNOLOGICAL ADVANCE. The cotton textile industry: Expansion was stimulated by the demand for cotton textiles whetted initially by imports brought in by the East India Company. 1733: John Kay (1704–64) invented the flying shuttle. 1769: Richard Arkwright (1732–92) patented the water frame, introducing the possibility of power spinning; 1770: James Hargreaves (d. 1778) patented the spinning jenny. 1779: Samuel Crompton (1753–1827) combined the water frame and the jenny in the "mule." 1785: Edmund Cartwright (1743–1823) invented the 1st power loom; 1813: 2,400 power looms in England; 1829: roughly 50,000 power looms in England. After 1785, with the application of steam power to this industry and with the new technology, the mill could be moved from the stream to urban centers, where labor was available. By 1830, cotton textile production was a factory industry; hand spinning had ceased and all processes prior to weaving were done in the factory; weaving took place partly in the factory on power looms and partly still in homes on hand looms. From a relatively insignificant industry in 1760, by 1831 cotton textile production employed over 800,000; cotton textiles had become the major British export. Improvements in this industry were followed (at varying speeds) by producers of wool and other textile fibers. Most important, textiles were a primary manufacturing sector: by 1830, expansion was generating employment in the making of power equipment, machinery, and, in turn, in the basic iron and steel industry.

The revolution in iron: 1589: 1st patent for use of coal in ironmaking. 1709: Abraham Darby (1676–1717) used coal as a substitute for charcoal in smelting iron in blast furnaces. 1776: John Wilkinson (1728–1808) introduced steam blast for smelting iron with coke. 1783–84: Henry Cort (1740–1800) took out 2 patents for "puddling" and "rolling." 1784: The Boulton-Watt steam engine applied to iron production—for the bellows, the hammers, rolling, and slitting. 1786: John Smeaton used blowing cylinders of cast iron at the Carron ironworks. 1827: J. B. Neilson invented the hot blast (patented 1828), which more than cut in half the coal or coke required to smelt iron. The use of coal (instead of charcoal) and steam as a source of power opened the possibility of large, integrated iron works; a single concern could do smelting and refining. 1788: Britain's 59 coke furnaces produced 53,800 tons of pig iron, while 26 furnaces produced 14,500 tons of charcoal iron; 1806: Britain's output of 250,400 tons of pig iron practically all came from coke furnaces. 1830: Production rose to 677,000 tons, due to demands for iron in making steam engines, machinery, apparatus of various sorts, and water pipes. 1805: Because of its use of coal, England became the world's greatest iron producer (surpassing the earlier leaders of 1740, Russia and France).

Steel: Pig iron could be transformed into cast iron in the foundry, into wrought iron by the puddling process, or into steel. Most pig iron was converted into cast or wrought iron and only a small quantity into steel. Blistered steel and sheet steel were made in cement furnaces and used for swords, knives, and razor blades. 1740: Benjamin Huntsman (1704–

76) developed a process for making "crucible" or cast steel. 1787: Some 20 Sheffield steel refiners used this method. 1800: David Mushet (1772–1847) patented a process to make steel directly from bar iron. Innovations made poor-grade iron usable in steel.

The machine-tool industry: 1777: Jesse Ramsden (1730–1800) described a screw-cutting lathe. 1797: Henry Maudslay (1771–1831) invented the carriage lathe; Maudslay was the key maker of industrial lathes in England; his shop was the training ground for English machine-tool builders, among them Joseph Clement (1779–1844), Richard Roberts (1789–1864), Joseph Whitworth (1803–87), and James Nasmyth (1808–90).

The chemical industry: Innovations related mainly to developments in textiles. 1797, 1799: Charles B. Tennant (1768–1838) took out patents for bleaching powder, made by absorbing chlorine in slaked lime.

Gas lighting: 1792: William Murdock (1754–1839) used coal gas to light a room in a home in Redruth, Cornwall (gas lighting had been used earlier in Germany). 1805: Coal gas used in lighting a factory in Great Britain; 1806: in London, German-born Frederick Albert Winsor formed the world's 1st gas co., the National Light and Heat Co. (later the Gas Light and Coke Co.); 1807: gas lighting installed on Pall Mall in London.

Other technological innovations: 1809: The arc lamp invented by Sir Humphry Davy (1778–1829); 1821–31: Michael Faraday (1791–1867) developed the electric motor and generator. 1822: Charles Babbage (1792–1871) developed the principles of a calculating machine. 1760–1830: Rapid rise in number of English patents sealed in each decade: 1760–69, 205 patents; 1780–89, 477 patents; 1800–9, 924 patents; 1820–29, 1,453 patents.

TRANSPORTATION REVOLUTION. Roads: In mid-18th cent., roads in England were inadequate and in poor repair. 1767: A road went down the Taff Valley; earlier coal had been shipped from the Merthyr and Dowlas district along a path on the backs of ponies and donkeys. Three great road engineers, J. Metcalf (1717–1810), Thomas Telford (1757–1834), and John Loudon McAdam (1756–1836), made major improvements. McAdam replaced unbroken flints with a packing of angular granite fragments, which consolidated into a natural concrete (macadam); c. 1815: 1st macadam road completed; the new highways were smooth and well drained. Turnpike companies were formed for road repair and construction. 1784: The 1st mail coach left London for Bristol; the Post Office began to promote road construction. The stagecoach provided regular service and horse-drawn wagons moved goods along the new roads. 1784: James Watt patented a steam-driven carriage; 1800: English engineer Richard Trevithick (1771–1833) invented a steam engine which he used to propel carriages, but steam-propelled road vehicles were not produced commercially.

Inland waterways: In the mid-18th cent. rivers near Wigan and St. Helens were improved to handle the increased coal trade. 1759–61: James Brindley (1716–72) built a canal from Worsley to Manchester for shipments of coal for the coal owner, the Duke of Bridgewater; this "Bridgewater Canal" was the 1st great accomplishment of the "canal age"; the canal "mania" began. 1830: There were 3,639 miles of canals and canalized rivers in England.

Steamships: 1801: First practical British steamboat—the *Charlotte Dundas*—was built by William Symington (1763–1831); 1812: Henry Bell's steamer, the *Comet*, with side paddle wheels appeared on the Clyde. 1814: England had 2 steamers; 1830, 315 steamers. 1826: The British steamer *Enterprise*, en route to India, used steam power on 63 days of 103-day trip. (The rest of the voyage was under sail.)

Railroads: Before 1820, the Newcastle area had some 360 miles of railroad; traction was by cable attached to a fixed engine or to a horse. 1802: Trevithick was the 1st in the world to use a steam-propelled carriage on a railroad. 1814: George Stephenson (1781–1848) built his 1st locomotive. 1825: Stockton and Darlington Railway opened, with Stephenson driving a steam-powered train; this was the world's 1st public passenger-carrying railway, but passenger traffic was by horse-drawn coach until 1833. 1829: Stephenson's *Rocket* demonstrated the superiority of steam locomotion over the horse. 1830, 15 Sept.: Manchester & Liverpool Railway opened; it used locomotive power for traction; it was built to carry passengers as well as freight; it marked the start of the "railway age." The Industrial Revolution was for all practical purposes completed before the introduction of railways using steam power.

FINANCE. 1760: England had the world's highest per capita income. In general capital was invested in government securities and land. Capital had been accumulated by British merchants who accrued large fortunes through foreign trade. Financial intermediaries had developed. Britain had an established system of money and banking. The Bank of England (formed in 1694) was a semipublic, semiofficial institution to lend money to the government, receive deposits, and make commercial loans. The 18th-cent. pound was theoretically based on silver (the pound *sterling*). By the 1760's, there was little silver coin in circulation; actually, but not legally, Britain was on the gold standard. 1816: Gold was made the sole standard and full legal tender; 1821: this took effect, and Britain formally and legally went onto the gold standard. At this time, British banking consisted of the Bank of England, 60 London private banks (without note issue), and roughly 800 private small note-issuing country

banks. Among the most prominent of the London private banks were Baring Brothers, founded in 1770 by Francis Baring (1740–1810), and N. M. Rothschild & Son, founded in 1798, a branch establishment of the House of Rothschild, Frankfurt. 1825–26: Financial crisis resulted in the failure of some 60 country banks. 1826: Parliament passed an act which allowed the Bank of England to establish branches throughout the United Kingdom and which permitted the establishment of joint-stock banks outside of a radius of 65 miles of London. (1833 Act permitted joint-stock banks to be established in London area.) Banking for merchants, manufacturers, and farmers, which had been done mainly by private banks before 1826, came increasingly to be done by joint-stock banks owned by security holders. 1810: Formation of the Ruthwell savings bank in Scotland; the savings-bank concept spread from Scotland to England and Wales. Insurance companies in England provided sources of savings. The last decade of the 17th cent. had seen a money market develop in England and a stock exchange. 1773: London stock-brokers, who had met at Jonathan's Coffee House, in Change Alley, moved to Sweeting Alley; this building became known as "The Stock Exchange Coffee House"—the first use of the phrase "stock exchange." 1802: New stock exchange building opened on Bartholomew Lane; members of the exchange totaled 500.

FOREIGN TRADE. 1760–1830: British foreign trade soared.

BRITISH TRADE EXPANSION
(in millions £ and U.S. $ equivs.)

Year	Imports		Domestic Exports		Re-exports	
	(£)	($)	(£)	($)	(£)	($)
1760	9.8	49.0	11.0	55.0	3.7	18.5
1800	17.8	173.0	12.0	60.0	4.8	24.0
1830	55.9	279.5	38.3	191.5	5.6	28.0

By 1815 British foreign trade was the largest in the world. Tea, sugar, rice, and tobacco were key imports and were not only for the rich but also for the lower classes. 1760: 2.5 million pounds of cotton imported; 1800: 56 million pounds; 1830: 264 million pounds. Cotton became

the largest single import. Imports were mainly raw materials. Manufactured goods were the main export; of these, cotton yarn and cotton manufactures by 1830 comprised more than 50%. The slave trade was lucrative; 1783–93: Liverpool-registered ships carried more than 300,000 slaves—valued at £15,186,850—from the West Coast of Africa to the Western Hemisphere. 1807: Britain abolished the slave trade; smuggling, however, remained a source of revenue. The Napoleonic Wars curtailed certain trade. 1807: Jefferson's Embargo cut commerce with the U.S. In the face of these impediments the British resorted to smuggling, changed markets rapidly, and, when the Napoleonic Wars ended, Britain's trading connections and volume of trade were broader and larger than before. The growth of the cotton textile industry contributed importantly to trade expansion; likewise, freer commerce encouraged more commerce. The age of the great trading companies— with monopoly privileges—was closing. 1793: under its renewed charter, the English East India Co. was required to let certain private merchants trade in India; 1813: Act, renewing East India Co.'s charter, opened Indian trade completely. 1821: End of Co. of Merchants Trading with Africa. 1825: Dissolution of the Levant Co., which had had trading privileges with Mediterranean countries. 1833: Act terminated East India Co.'s monopoly in China and provided that after 22 Apr., 1834, the company should close its commercial business in India. By the early 1830's, with few exceptions, exclusive privileges were annulled. 1824 ff.: William Huskisson (1770–1830), president of the Board of Trade, sponsored measures rationalizing the customs legislation, reducing import duties on manufactured goods, eliminating or lowering import tariffs on raw materials, removing prohibitions on imports, and cutting out bounties and most restrictions on exports. Parliament liberalized the Navigation Acts (which had given preferential treatment to British shipping). 1824 ff.: Britain made a series of treaties, putting foreign ships on an equal basis with British ships in British ports. The expansion in international trade was essential to British economic growth, providing accumulated capital for industrial growth, encouraging the modernization of transportation, aiding the emergence of financial intermediaries, giving access to raw materials, and, most

vital, offering a market for what new industries—especially the textile industry— produced. Foreign trade stimulated the development of the port cities of London, Hull, Newcastle, Bristol, and Liverpool. Foreign trade assisted in the creation of a business environment with values conducive to profit making. It widened the vision of participants.

FOREIGN INVESTMENT. British foreign investments were made by large trading cos.; there were British investments in sugar plantations in the West Indies. Foreign governments floated loans in London; Britishers bought U.S. federal and state securities after the American Revolution. During the wars of 1793–1815 British capital went to Europe as loans or subsidies to allies. British capital financed American trade. From 1806 British moneys went into South American investments. 1815 ff.: Operating through the Barings, Rothschilds, and others, British investors were active in French *rentes*. After the Napoleonic Wars, London replaced Amsterdam as the dominant city in international capital markets. Britain became a creditor nation.

BUSINESS ORGANIZATION. 1720: As a result of the South Sea Bubble, British law passed, requiring all joint-stock cos. to be incorporated by Act of Parliament or chartered by the crown. Cumbersome procedure retarded the use of the joint-stock co. form. The industrialist in Britain was usually an entrepreneur, who employed his own money and skills; he might get others to lend him funds or go into association with friends. He used personal contacts to raise funds. He reinvested profits earned for purposes of expansion. While he devised new forms of business organization, integrating processes of production and marketing, he did not act through the media of the corporate form. Even after 1825, when the 1720 Act was repealed, the corporate form was not associated with industrial investments. Since it was possible to establish joint-stock enterprises by private act before 1825 and without one after 1825, canal, dock, bridge, road, insurance, and banking cos. (which needed to mobilize large amounts of money) did take this form; they had continuity of life, transferable shares, and by the end of the 18th cent. some had even arranged limited liability for their members.

GOVERNMENT POLICY. The role of government in the British Industrial Revolution was one of providing a favorable environment. A series of strong kings had unified the English state; there was a stable political structure, a common law, internal free trade, and patent protection for inventors. 1800: Parliament made it generally illegal for workers to combine to increase wages or reduce hours of work. 1811–12: The Luddite riots (workmen breaking machines) were countered by Parliament in 1812, legislating that machine destruction was a capital felony. Government action in eliminating monopolies cleared the path for the expansion of manufacturing and trade. The government's role was to avoid entanglement in the economic system.

OTHER FACTORS CONDUCIVE TO INDUSTRIALIZATION. 1776: Publication of Adam Smith, *The Wealth of Nations:* expression of sentiment that a nation's resources should be developed without government direction; monopo-

lies at home and abroad should be abolished; trade should be free. Nonconformity in religion in England aided the industrialization process; hard work was not discouraged; thrift was a virtue. The general interest in the nation in science and engineering—whether applied to agriculture or industry—provided a favorable environment for change. England was the leader in scientific inquiry. Innovation was not rejected; innovation was based on new products, new markets, new forms of organization, new sources of raw materials, as well as new production methods. There was the opportunity for an entrepreneur to rise on the basis of his own merits.

THE BUSINESS CYCLE. The first Industrial Revolution took its course through war and sharp oscillations in the business cycle. The American Revolution did not sever America's economic ties with Britain, or retard the change. The Napoleonic Wars aided British prosperity, but with the temporary cessation of hostilities in 1801 there was a depression and in 1811 a deep depression. 1815 witnessed another downturn and not until 1821 was there a slow revival; 1831: recession.

The Beginnings of Sustained Industrialization—U.S. and Western Europe

During 1760–1830 the beginnings of sustained industrialization were evident in the U.S. and in parts of Western Europe. The lead was taken by the U.S., France, and Belgium, while Italy, the German states, Switzerland, Austria, and the Netherlands also showed some signs of change. In the U.S. and in these parts of Europe—as everywhere around the world except in England—agriculture employed the most men and contributed more than any other sector to national income.

AGRICULTURE AND ANIMAL HUSBANDRY. Agricultural improvements: In the U.S. and Europe, British agricultural improvements combined with

indigenous innovation. In the U.S., agriculture ranged from small farms in New England to larger farms in the Midwest to plantations in the South. The most dramatic change in American agriculture was due to Eli Whitney's cotton gin, 1793, which provided a basis for the southern 1-crop economy. The U.S. was in the forefront in the invention and application of new farm machinery. 1797: Charles Newbold patented America's 1st cast-iron plow; it did not win popular acceptance. 1819: Jethro Wood (1774–1834) perfected a 3-piece cast-iron plow with standardized interchangeable parts, which became the most widely used plow in northern farming. With labor shortages and with the high cost of labor, northern farmers were receptive to improvements in agriculture that economized on men. In the South, owing to the cotton economy, slave labor increasingly replaced free labor; mechanization was not widely used. Because there was an abundance of land, Americans paid little attention to conservation, use of fertilizers, or methods involving better utilization of existing lands. The open frontier meant that new land could come under cultivation and the old could be abandoned. On the European Continent progress in agricultural innovation took place more slowly. There was in Western Europe much more interest in British agricultural methods than in the U.S. Crop rotation was adopted by forward-looking landowners on the Continent at the end of the 18th and begining of the 19th cent.; but side by side, old systems of agriculture prevailed. Flanders and Brabant led in intensive scientific farming. In Germany, in the Palatinate, Rhineland, Baden, Nassau, and in the area near Erfurt, Wurzburg, and Augsburg, farming was well advanced. This was also true in Alsace. In Holland, France, Germany, and Sweden marsh- and grassland were reclaimed and put under the plow. In Western Europe more land was put under cultivation. Mechanization of agriculture, occurring in England and the U.S., was slow to take place in Western Europe because of the presence of small landholdings and tenant farming. In some areas in France, grain was still trodden out by oxen as it had been for centuries. Many French landlords, unlike their British counterparts, found attention to the details of scientific agriculture beneath their dignity; French peasants because of their poverty could not afford scientific agriculture.

New crops: Cotton output, after the cotton gin, expanded rapidly in the U.S.

U.S. COTTON OUTPUT
(000 bales)

1790–91	9
1800–01	211
1810–11	269
1820–21	647
1830–31	987

The potato became an important food crop in much of Western and Central Europe. New fodder crops were cultivated. At the turn of the century the sugar beet was introduced in France.

Land reform: America had no peasant economy and no "traditional" medieval landownership structure. Vestiges of the feudal forms that did exist were eliminated: 1779, Virginia and Pennsylvania; 1786, New York abolished quitrents (payments of rents by settlers) . 1776: Virginia ended entail, which had made land inalienable; other states followed. 1777: Georgia eliminated primogeniture, which passed land to the eldest son; other states followed. 1777: Confiscation of Loyalist estates broke up large landholdings. Land Acts of 1785, 1796, 1800, 1804, and 1820 set the terms of sale of western land and opened the way to new settlement and cultivation. In the American South, the size of landholdings grew, as plantations became the means of growing cotton. Land reform in Western Europe involved a sharp change in the traditional pattern. In the 18th cent. French peasants had been tenants under the feudal system. 1789–93: French Revolution freed peasant from his dues and services. Unlike in England, where land reform transformed the peasant into a wage laborer, in France the peasant became a landowner. The French armies during the Revolutionary and Napoleonic period brought French ideas of land reform to Belgium, the Netherlands, Germany, Italy, and Austria-Hungary. 1795–1814: Seigneurial dues were terminated in Belgium and the Netherlands; many peasants became landowners. 1798: French abolished feudalism on the left bank of the Rhine and from 1804 sold property of the church and the emigrés to the peasants. In French-dominated Westphalia and the Grand Duchy of Berg, certain obligations of the peasants to the lord were abolished. In western Germany, as the feudal system was eliminated, peasants became landowners; but in many parts of Germany west of the Elbe, the traditional structure prevailed; 1783: emancipation of serfs in Baden; 1807–9: Baron von Stein (1757–1831) of Prussia freed the serfs; 1808: his edict permitted trade in land and consolidation of holdings; 1811: Karl August von Hardenberg (1750–1822) of Prussia gave peasants the right to become full proprietors, but this edict and a subsequent one, 1816, made it virtually impossible for a peasant to obtain full title without selling some of his land to the lord. Thus there occurred the formation of large landholdings by the Junkers in Prussian territory east of the Elbe. 1808: Serfs emancipated in Bavaria; in Hesse, 1811; in Württemberg, 1819. 1808–9: The French extended land reforms to Italy; peasants got clear title to land, estates of religious orders were seized and sold, and seigneurial obligations were abolished. 1815 ff.: After the overthrow of Napoleon, the manorial system in Italy ended. In northern Italy peasant farming and large farm units remained, whereas in the south large landholdings (latifundia) prevailed, worked largely by hired hands and sharecroppers. 1760's and 1770's: Under Maria Theresa, queen of Bohemia and Hungary, archduchess of Austria, etc., new codes fixed the dues and services of the peasant and number of days of labor service (*robot*) required of him; the peasant was given greater freedom. 1781: Joseph II ended serfdom in Austria; 1782: law extended to Galicia; 1783, Transylvania; and 1785, similar decree issued for Hungary. Reforms by Joseph II, which aimed to replace large landed estates with small peasants' farms, were not successful; the reform movement collapsed because of landlord opposition. 1789, 10 Feb.: Joseph II issued a famous agrarian reform decree which was later withdrawn because of landlord opposition; the peasant remained subject to the lord of the manor. In Denmark enclosure of common lands took place. 1682, 1725, 1769, 1791: Royal government ordinances protected the peasant and secured for the cottager, who lost his rights to common land, sufficient land to keep a cow and pigs. Agrarian reform in Denmark created a nation of peasant owners. In southern Sweden peasants obtained titles to their land.

Productivity: In the U.S. agricultural productivity rose, as agriculture became increasingly efficient. 1789–1830: In France there was little improvement in agricultural productivity. Small peasant ownership did not serve to raise output per man. Elsewhere in Europe, there is little evidence of significant increases in productivity.

Commercialization: American agriculture became commercial agriculture. Stimulated by rising American population as well as by the growth of urban areas in the East and export opportunities, most agricultural output went to market. In Western Europe the trend was to greater commercialization of agriculture. Commercialization was stimulated by rising population, growth of urban areas, ascending agricultural prices (c. 1755 to c. 1817), and improved transportation. Between 1817 and 1850 there was a decline in price levels, but changes that took place in earlier years were not reversed.

Effects of the changes: In the U.S. cotton became a major export crop, capable of aiding American economic development. In Western Europe, the changes in agriculture, which disrupted the old seigneurial land-tenure system, to some extent introduced labor mobility, thus creating preconditions for subsequent economic development. In the U.S. and in Western Europe, the level of agricultural activity was high enough that these countries could feed themselves; none depended on food imports for existence. Judged as a whole, the period 1760–1830 could be considered as a time of agricultural boom in both the U.S. and Western Europe.

RAW MATERIALS. The U.S. had vast areas of timber resources. 1776: roughly $1/7$ of the world's iron supply was produced in the U.S. Coal existed, but the coal industry did not. Total consumption of anthracite coal in the U.S. in 1828 was less than 100,000 tons. (Charcoal rather than coal served as the basic fuel.) The resources of the U.S. were vast, but were unknown and undeveloped. France had large timber resources, which were dwindling as charcoal consumption rose. In Western Europe, the coal and iron region stretched from the British Isles across the English Channel to Scandinavia and Upper Silesia. Sweden had important iron-ore resources, as did Germany and France. France, while it held Belgium (1797–1815), had access to its coal resources. 1800: Belgian coal mining was the most important on the Continent, located at Mons, Charleroi, and Liège. 1800–1830: Belgian coal-mining industry expanded rapidly. 1815 ff.: France's own supplies of coal were inadequate. 1815 ff.: The coal mines of the Ruhr in Germany began to be worked effectively.

LABOR. In the U.S. labor was scarce. Population rose from 1.6 million in 1760 to 12.9 million in 1830, but this still was inadequate. There was a high land-man ratio. Compared with Europe, labor in the U.S. was expensive; this encouraged mechanization and technological advance. In Western Europe, population was also rising, but not as dramatically. France's population rose from 26.9 million in 1801 to 31.8 million in 1831. At the end of the 18th cent., there was abundant cheap labor on the Continent, which may have slowed technological advance. The population of the U.S. was basically rural; in 1800 only 6 cities had populations over 8,000 (Philadelphia, New York, Baltimore, Boston, Charleston, and Salem); France's population was also rural, but in 1801 there were 90 cities with populations over 10,000; in Europe, Paris was 2nd only to London as the largest city. Increasing urbanization occurred in both the U.S. and France; this was less true elsewhere in Europe. In the U.S., compared with Europe, labor was mobile. The freeing of the serf in Prussia, other German states, and Austria increased mobility, but when in the elimination of feudal levies the peasant became an owner of land (as in France), this often reduced the mobility. As the guild system was eliminated in Western Europe, this encouraged labor mobility. In the U.S., Americans were tinkers out of need; slowly they developed industrial skills; American education, especially in New England, was good; literacy was high. France took the leadership in civil engineering and mining schools (1747: École des Ponts et Chaussées and 1794: École Polytechnique were founded); but sec-ondary education and beyond were available only to an elite; elementary education was poor; there was no compulsory system of schooling. 1821: 25,000 communes had no schools of any sort; the majority of the French population was illiterate. The rest of Europe was also lacking in mass education and industrial skills.

ENERGY. Water, wind, and domestic animals were the main sources of power in the U.S. and on the European Continent. The small mill and factory on the small stream were typical in the 13 American colonies and then in the U.S. As late as 1815, horse- or ox-pulled winches were typically used in powering cotton mills in France. 1820–1830: Water power was the usual source of energy for cotton mills in France; industry on the Continent mainly used water power. Steam-power developments in England had impact in the U.S. and on the Continent. 1801: Oliver Evans (1755–1819) built a small, stationary high-pressure steam engine; 1803: he established a shop to manufacture that engine, Mars Iron Works, which marked the beginnings of commercial production in the U.S.; Evans' high-pressure engine was simple, powerful, and cheap; it quickly replaced the imported Boulton-Watt engine for use in American industry. In the U.S. steam came to be employed where water power was not readily obtainable and also in such industries as glass manufacture, bleacheries, and print works, where heat was needed; by 1830, industries in the Middle States were adopting steam power (57 out of the 161 plants in Pennsylvania used steam), while New England still depended on water power. (Only 4 out of 132 Rhode Island textile mills used steam.) On the European Continent, Belgium was most receptive to the adoption of steam power; it was tied in with the mining industry, cotton textiles, and the engineering industry. 1784: Le Creusot iron works in France used a steam engine as motive power for hammers of the forge, for pumping in the mines, and blowing the furnace. 1812: Steam introduced into cotton mills in Alsace, by 1817 in Lille, and in a woolen mill at Louviers; 1817–20: steam employed in cotton-spinning mills of Rouen; 1818: between 150 and 200 steam engines in operation in France, half imported from England. 1819 ff.: Most steam engines were made in France, because of high tariffs. 1830: 625 French establishments possessed steam engines. The German states did not adopt steam power readily; by 1800 only a few Newcomen machines and a few Watt engines were in use, mainly for mining operations. 1812: Freund was 1st Berliner to make a steam engine; 1832: only 30 steam engines in Berlin.

INDUSTRIES AND TECHNOLOGICAL ADVANCE. 1760's: In the American colonies, there was a thriving shipbuilding industry (1760: ⅓ of total British tonnage was colonial-built). Other manufacturing included household products, leather goods, and hats; weaving and shoemaking were done in the home. Mills and factories included lumber, flour, paper mills, and glass manufactories; there were breweries (in New York and Pennsylvania) and sugar refineries (in Pennsylvania); local furnaces and forges produced iron. On the European Continent as in America there existed artisan industries; in Europe, textiles were made everywhere—in France, Switzerland, Italy, Germany, the Low Countries, and in the Hapsburg Empire; local furnaces and forges produced iron. By the end of the 18th cent. France and Italy had glass, paper, metal-working, and sugar-refining industries. 1780–1830: Spread of British technology, despite British legislation prohibiting emigration of mechanics (until 1825) and prohibiting export of drawings, models, or specifications of textile machinery, or the machinery itself (until 1842); Americans, Germans, French, and Belgians learned from the British. In the U.S. and on the Continent, British machinery and workmen aided the diffusion of British methods; British technology meshed with indigenous innovations.

Textiles: 1789: Samuel Slater (1768–1835) came to America; he transferred by memory designs of the spinning frame in Richard Arkwright's and Jedediah Strutt's works in England; he began to build spinning machinery in Pawtucket, R.I.; 1790,

5 Apr.: Slater became partner in firm of Almy & Brown; 20 Dec: spinning began, the 1st spun cotton by power in the U.S. 1793: John and Arthur Scholfield arrived from England; they introduced British methods of wool carding and reduced from hours to minutes the time required to prepare wool fibers before spinning. 1813: Boston Manufacturing Co. was established at Waltham, Mass.—the 1st textile factory to conduct all operations under a single roof, converting with power-driven machinery cotton into cloth (the "Waltham System"); its technology was American rather than British. 1816: American William Gilmour introduced a successful crank-type loom in Rhode Island; Ira Draper, in Massachusetts, patented self-acting loom temples for holding and guiding cloth during weaving, 1823. 1823: Asa Arnold's compound gear for changing velocity for winding cotton filaments; 1828: Charles Danforth invented cap spinner for improving weft; John Thorp invented ring spinning process. By 1830, in the wool industry, America was using power looms. (Here the U.S. was in advance of Great Britain.) On the Continent, Irish engineer John Holker settled in Normandy, France, and introduced British techniques. 1798: Lancashire mechanic William Cockerill made textiles machines at Verviers and later at Liège. C. 1800: The flying shuttle was widely adopted in the French cotton industry; a Scotsman, Norman Douglas, who understood wool carding and spinning machinery, founded a workshop on an island in the Seine (financed by French capital); Hargreaves' spinning jenny was accepted in France; jennies were being used in Alsace, 1803. 1801: Frenchman Joseph Marie Jacquard (1752–1834) exhibited at a Paris industrial exhibition a loom he had invented for weaving figured fabrics. Earlier, Frenchman Jacques de Vaucanson (1709–82) invented a loom; Jacquard saw it in 1803, and incorporated Vaucanson's methods to improve the Jacquard loom. 1823: In the vicinity of Mulhouse, France, experiments began with power looms; by 1830, 2,000 in use. 1830: France was 2nd only to England in world cotton spindleage, but produced only about ¼

as much cotton as Great Britain. (U.S. was in 3rd place in world spindleage.) 1794: 1st German cotton-spinning mill using Arkwright water frame established; progress in German cotton textiles was slow; what cotton textile activity did develop was in the Rhenish provinces at Krefeld and Elberfeld and in Saxony. 1801: In Belgium, a modern cotton textile industry began to develop at Ghent.

Iron industry: By the time of the American Revolution, 1776, there were ironworks in every colony except Georgia and more forges and blast furnaces in the colonies than in England and Wales combined; their output was smaller than that of British industry. 1816: Welsh ironworker Thomas C. Lewis introduced Cort's puddling and rolling processes to American industry. Technical innovation in the U.S. took a different pattern from Britain; in the U.S. the pattern was puddling, rolling, and then utilization of coal. The European Continent followed the British order: coal, puddling, rolling. 1782: At Le Creusot in France 1st blast furnace on the Continent to use coke. Because France lacked good coking coal, progress using coke was slow. 1791–92: 1st coke blast iron was produced from charcoal furnace in royal manufactory at Malapan, Prussia; 1796: coke blast furnace built in Upper Silesia, Germany; the Germans experimented with puddling in 1825; c. 1810: Friedrich Krupp (1787–1826) purchased a small forge in Essen, Germany, and tried to manufacture cast steel; 1815: he put his product on the market without success. 1821: John Cockerill built the 1st coke blast furnace in Belgium.

Factory production: American innovations were in labor-saving devices. 1782 ff.: Oliver Evans created an automated flour mill. (1780's: LeBlanc in France used interchangeable parts in production of firearms, but the system was not developed in France) ; 1798–1800: Eli Whitney developed a system of interchangeable parts in the manufacture of arms; 1799: Simeon North (1765–1852) of Connecticut also used interchangeable parts in manufacture of pistols. C. 1800: Manufacturing of nails standardized; cut rather than hand-wrought nails were an American innovation. 1807–12: Americans Eli Terry (1772–1852) and Seth Thomas (1785–1859) began to make clocks on the basis of machine-made interchangeable parts; 1825: Henry Burden (1791–1871) of Troy, N.Y., made railroad spikes by machine; 1826: Collins Co. was formed in Connecticut to mass produce axes.

Iron Production
(000 tons)

Year	United Kingdom (long)	France (metric)	Germany (metric)	U.S. (long)	World Total (long)
1740	20	26	18	1	160
1790	68	40	30	30	280
1800	190	60	39	40	460
1810	250	85	45	55	620
1820	368	140	89	110	1,010
1830	677	220	118	180	1,590

Gas lighting: 1786: German Johann Georg Pickel, a pharmacologist, lit his laboratory with coal gas—the 1st known application of coal gas to lighting; 1799: German Wilhelm Lampadius did experimental gas lighting of the palace of the Elector of Saxony in Dresden; 1816: Baltimore was 1st American city to have gas lighting.

Other technological innovations: 1785: French chemist Berthollet invented method of bleaching cloth with chlorine. 1791–94: Frenchman Nicolas LeBlanc is credited with being the 1st to succeed in making artificial soda. 1794: Frenchman Claude Chappe (1763–1805) developed semaphore telegraph; the 1st line ran from Lille to Paris and the system spread to other countries. 1799: Frenchman Louis Robert invented a machine to make a continuous web of paper. 1800: Italian Alessandro Volta (1745–1827) made 1st electric battery. 1803: Fourdrinier brothers in France invented papermaking machine. 1809: German Samuel Thomas Sommering invented 1st electric telegraph. 1819: Dane Hans Christian Orsted (1777–1851) discovered electromagnetism. 1820: Frenchman André Marie F. Ampère (1775–1836) applied the discovery of electromagnetism to the telegraph.

TRANSPORTATION. Roads: Often following Indian trails, roads had been built in the American colonial period; local roads were linked for long-distance travel; by 1776 an unpaved road extended from Boston, Mass., to Savannah, Ga. After the Revolution, U.S. turnpike companies were formed to build toll roads; by 1810, thousands of such turnpike companies existed; 1820: all major cities in the eastern and northern states were connected by surfaced roads; after 1825, highway development by private cos. slackened; the roads reverted to state and local governments. 1811–18: Construction of the Cumberland Road, a paved highway, linking Cumberland, Md., on the Potomac River, with Wheeling, W. Va., on the Ohio River, was financed by federal government funds. Horse-drawn wagons and carriages provided the traffic; 1800: American Oliver Evans ran a "steamer on wheels" through Philadelphia, but this did not inaugurate a new age. 1760: France and Italy had a network of Roman roads, some of which had been cared for, many of which were neglected. 1760–89: Road building accelerated in France based on administrative and strategic needs; great highways were constructed between important cities. During the Revolution, French roads were not maintained. 1799 ff.: Napoleon made attempts to build and repair roads; government funds were spent on routes linking Paris with Antwerp, Amsterdam, and Hamburg; with Metz and Mainz; and with Italy via Marseilles and Corniche, via Mont Cenis, and via the Simplon Pass; 1814: there were 16,300 miles of imperial roads; much of Napoleon's expenditures for roads lay outside what became the permanent frontiers of France. 1815–30: roads in France fell into disrepair; only a few were improved. In Belgium and the Netherlands, main roads, paved with stone blocks, were reasonably good. German roads were poor, compared with those in France and the Low Countries. 1815: Prussia benefited by obtaining French-built roads in the Rhenish and Westphalian provinces. Transport was by horse-drawn carriages and wagons. 1769: Frenchman Nicolas Joseph Cugnot (1725–1804) built the world's 1st steam-propelled wagon; it was not developed commercially.

Inland waterways: In America, rivers often provided the best commercial routes. Sailing vessels went up the Mississippi, James, Potomac, Delaware, Hudson, and Connecticut rivers; rafts and flatboats were used to transport produce; where these were not suitable there was an early incentive to apply steam transport. 1787: John Fitch (1743–98) ran 1st U.S. steamboat up the Delaware River; James Rumsey (1743–92) ran his steamboat on the Potomac River. 1807: Robert Fulton's (1765–1815) *Clermont* was 1st successful U.S.-built steamboat; it was demonstrated on the Hudson River. 1813: John Stevens (1749–1838) built 1st ironclad steamboat; 1815–60: the "golden age" of river steamboats. 1816: Steam navigation began on Lake Ontario—and later spread to other lakes. 1819: The American steamship, *Savannah,* crossed the Atlantic. France had many rivers, but some (Loire and Garonne) were irregular in flow; others (the Rhone, for instance) flowed too swiftly; many were too shallow; navigation was not easy. Elsewhere in Western Europe, rivers provided an important form of transportation. 1783: Marquis Jouffroy d'Abbans (1751–1832) operated the 1st paddle-wheel steamboat on the Sâone River. 1821: Steam used on the Calais packets. 1820's: France was slow in adopting river steamers. Before 1825, steam services existed in Danish waters, from Stockholm to St. Petersburg, on the Rhine, and on Swiss lakes.

Canals: 1792–96: 1st canal in U.S. was built at South Hadley, Mass.; by 1800 in the U.S. a handful of successful canals had been built; 1816: about 100 miles of canals existed; 1817: New York state legislature authorized the Erie Canal, a 364-mile canal from Albany to Buffalo, through unsettled country; 1825: canal was completed. Its success triggered a canal-building effort in the U.S., similar to that which had occurred in England after the completion of the Bridgewater Canal. By 1830 total canal mileage in U.S. reached 1,277 miles. Canal construction in Europe had a far longer history. In the Netherlands and Belgium canals had existed for centuries; they were kept in repair; France had started its modern canal system in the early 17th cent.; by 1830 total canal mileage in France was 1,260 miles. Germany was slower in building canals; 1772–75: Bromberg Canal linked the Oder and Vistula rivers.

Tramways and railroads: 1795: Boston Brick Works built 1st U.S. tramway; others carrying freight followed, powered by gravity, horses, mules, or cable attached to fixed engines. 1829: Delaware and Hudson Canal Co. imported 2 English steam locomotives for its new railroad; they proved too heavy and were abandoned. 1830: The Baltimore & Ohio Railroad, the 1st common carrier (carrying both passengers and freight) in the U.S., began operations; it used steam locomotion; the engines were made in New York. The American "railroad age" had begun. 1830: 23 miles of railroads operated in the U.S. There was not a single railroad in operation on the European Continent using steam locomotion.

FINANCE. Sources of capital: In colonial America and in the early history of the American Republic, capital was accumulated mainly through trade and through investments in land. British capital financed trade and to a small extent invested in America. In Europe mercantile capital provided the largest basis for surpluses. 1801: France was the wealthiest nation in the world (in terms of total—not per capita—national income); its net national product in 1801 was £288 million compared with Great Britain's gross national income of £232 million. Yet much of France's resources were devoted to

unproductive use: loans to the state, upkeep of the court and government bureaucracy, and war expenditures.

Financial intermediaries: These developed in the U.S. only after independence. 1781: Bank of North America was founded. 1784: Bank of New York and Massachusetts' Bank of Boston were established. 1791: Bank of the United States was organized as a central bank (not rechartered in 1811). 1816: 2nd National Bank of the United States was chartered (1832: recharter vetoed by President Andrew Jackson; 1836: expiration of charter of 2nd Bank). 1817: 1st savings bank in the U.S. was founded in New York. On the European Continent, banking institutions had a long history. 1609: Bank of Amsterdam was founded (collapsed 1791). Amsterdam was Europe's financial center until it lost its position to England during the Napoleonic Wars; 1814: Netherlands Bank formed; it could control issue of paper currency as well as perform other banking activities. 1619: Hamburg Bank founded (survived until 1875). 1656: Bank of Stockholm established (closed in 1664; refounded 1668 as Bank of Sweden and still exists). 1716: French bank established by John Law (failed in 1720); 1776: Caisse d'Escompte formed (modeled on Bank of England); it had unfortunate history; 1800, 13 Feb.: establishment of Bank of France; 1817 ff.: France set up a number of independent note-issuing banks; 1818: 1st savings bank in France. 1736–1816: Banks to finance the Danish, Prussian, and Austrian governments came into existence. 1736: Courant Bank of Denmark; 1765: Royal Exchange and Loan Bank of Berlin (became the Prussian Bank in 1846); 1816: the Austrian National Bank. 1760's: Meyer Amschel Rothschild (1743–1812) founded the House of Rothschild in Frankfurt. The Hopes, Parish, Bleichröder, and Mallet Frères in Amsterdam, Hamburg, Berlin, and Paris respectively were important private bankers. 1822: Société Générale pour Favoriser l'Industrie Nationale was founded in Brussels; a milestone in continental banking, it combined commercial and investment banking operations, granted loans on current account, discounted commercial paper, accepted drafts, and entered into long-term industrial financing. Despite these many banking activities, banking on the European Continent lagged behind that in Great Britain. While most of Europe was part of a monetary society (some peasants were not), banking facilities did not yet reflect this.

Stock exchanges: 1791: A group of Philadelphia traders organized the 1st stock exchange in the U.S. 1792: A group of 24 curb brokers in New York signed an agreement on methods to be followed in trading stock on Wall Street; 1817: these stockbrokers drafted the constitution and rules of the New York Stock Exchange. In Europe the Amsterdam stock exchange was founded in the early 17th cent.; it held the dominant position in Europe; 1795: it almost completely collapsed when the French conquered Holland. 1724: Stock exchange founded in Paris; it stopped operations during the French Revolution, reopened under the Directory, and was reorganized by Napoleon; 1815: stock exchange listed only government securities. France was far behind England in developing a capital market. Berlin and Frankfurt also had stock exchanges.

FOREIGN TRADE. American trade expanded, despite setbacks immediately after the Revolution and after Jefferson's 1807 Embargo. Imports were mainly manufactured goods; exports were mainly raw materials. After 1793 raw cotton became an important U.S. export, after 1803 the most important single export. The slave trade had been profitable for New England merchants; after it became illegal considerable illicit trade continued. In the colonial period, American trade had been mainly wih England and the West Indies ("triangular trade"); 1776 ff.: trade became more diversified; 1784: U.S. entered profitable Canton trade with voyage of the *Empress of China*. By 1830, U.S. imports were $71 million; exports, $74 million; U.S. was in 3rd place after Britain and France in foreign trade. 1787: French foreign trade totaled livres 1,153.5 m., or $230 m.; it was greater than British foreign

trade. During the Napoleonic Wars, Napoleon hoped for commercial strangulation of Britain by excluding her goods from Europe—the "Continental System." By 1809 he had closed all European ports except those in Turkey, Sicily, and Portugal to British commerce. The Continental System failed; British goods reached Continental Europe through the Greek islands, Malta, the Channel Islands, and Helgoland. Napoleon himself violated the System, clothing his army in Lancashire cloth, selling licenses which exempted traders from the decrees, and attempting to attract profits away from the smugglers. France did not develop her trade and dropped to a position below Britain. 1830: French foreign trade totalled $181 million. The Netherlands, which had a flourishing international trade in the 17th cent., was by the end of the 18th cent. in a poor position. 1782: Dutch East India Co. (founded in 1602) paid its last dividend; 1798: Co. was dissolved; 1792–1820: European nations outlawed the African slave trade, though slaving continued illegally until after the U.S. Civil War, when it dropped sharply.

BUSINESS ORGANIZATION. Structure: In colonial America business organization consisted of family industries (within the household), domestic or "putting-out" systems in textiles and shoemaking (a merchant brought raw materials to the producer; the producer made the product in his home; the merchant marketed it), and mills and factories (usually owned by individual entrepreneurs or their families or partnerships). Trading firms were usually family enterprises. 1776 ff.: manufacturing increasingly went out of the home into the factory.

Guilds: No guilds barred development of business activity in the U.S. 1760: On the Continent, guilds still impeded business enterprise; with the abolition of guilds in France, 1791, ideas on freer enterprise spread with French military might to the Low Countries, western Germany, and Italy. Tuscany, 1770, Sicily, 1786, Lombardy, 1787, and Naples, 1821, abolished guilds. This gave entrepreneurs the possibility of entering into key trades. Private business enterprises in

France, the Low Countries, Germany, and Italy tended to be family units; they sought high profits at the expense of low volume, quality rather than quantity, traditional patterns rather than innovation, security rather than risk-taking.

Adoption of corporate form: In the U.S. manufacturing enterprises were in general unincorporated. Corporations did spread rapidly for use in internal improvements (turnpikes, bridges, canals, etc.), insurance, and banking; in the U.S. the use of the corporate form was more important than in Britain or on the Continent. The French, suspicious of the joint-stock co. form, avoided it, and permission to incorporate was difficult to obtain; up to 1830 there were fewer than 150 *sociétés anonymes* created in France. In Belgium industrial enterprise tended to be unincorporated. 1819: The insurance company Securitas was Belgium's 1st 19th-cent. *société anonyme*. 1822: The *société générale* took this form. In Germany, joint-stock cos., if formed at all, were by special charter; it was not a form much used. This was also true in Italy.

Entrepreneurs: Important early American entrepreneurs included Henry William Stiegel (1729–85), ironmaster (after 1760) and glassware maker (after 1764); ironmakers Peter Hasenclever (1716–93), John Jacob Faesch (1729–99), and William Alexander ("Lord Stirling," 1726–83); merchants John Hancock (1737–93), Stephen Girard (1750–1831), John Jacob Astor (1763–1848), and John P. Cushing (1787–1862). 1801, 21 Apr.: founding papers and articles of incorporation executed in Paris for E. I. Du Pont de Nemours & Co. of Delaware, a company to manufacture military and sporting powder in the U.S. 1806: William Colgate founded a small business in New York to manufacture soap and candles. Among the key European entrepreneurs were the ironmakers: Krupp in Prussia, the Boignes brothers and François de Wendels and his brother in France, and John Cockerill in Belgium.

GOVERNMENT POLICIES. British government policies may have aided economic development in the American colonies; British mercantilism—furnishing preferential markets and protection for shipping—assisted American foreign traders, although British restraints angered the merchants. The British saw the colonies as providers of raw materials and markets for the mother country; British policy was to discourage manufacturing in the colonies; manufacturing developed despite British attitudes rather than because of them. 1789: The U.S. Constitution gave Congress rights to pass laws in the fields of interstate commerce and foreign trade, coinage, weights and measures, contract and property, taxation, disposition of unsettled lands, transportation, and banking. The Constitution stipulated that states could not erect tariff barriers against one another, an essential prerequisite for the creation of a national market. In the early years of the republic, with tariff, patent, and banking legislation, laws for funding the national and states' debts (which established public credit) as well as aid to internal improvements, the U.S. federal government provided foundations for economic development. 1792: U.S. Congress authorized the creation of 2 national armories; subsidies were given to private business to make muskets, pistols, and rifles; these subsidies for national defense purposes were exceptional aids to industrial activity. State governments provided corporate charters to business enterprise; state and local governments in the U.S. promoted internal improvements and education. 1819, 2 Feb.: the *Dartmouth College Case* gave new security to corporate charters, and later aided business enterprise. 1760–1830: The governments in France, Prussia, and Austria were more involved in industrial activity than the U.S. government; they became direct investors in certain industries and also encouraged industrialization through patent legislation, financial aids to research, tax concessions, tariffs, monopoly rights, assurance of supplies and labor, technological aid (which the governments obtained for businesses from abroad), loans at low or no interest, and often outright subsidies. In Western Europe restraints on free enterprise came to be removed; there was clarification and codification of legislation. 1760 ff.: Reforms of Maria Theresa and Joseph II in the Austrian Empire were in the direction of cutting internal tariffs; 1789 ff.: France reduced barriers to trade; weights and measures were standardized; 1791: Loi le Chapelier abolished guilds in France with influence throughout Europe. 1807: Clauses in French Commercial Code set basis for co. laws of Belgium, Holland, Switzerland, Italy, and Spain; under the Code there was the joint-stock co., *société anonyme*, which might or might not have limited liability (according to its charter) and which was subject to government regulation, and the *sociétés en commandite*, which had sleeping partners (with limited liability) and active partners (with no limited liability) and which were not subjected to government supervision since they were not considered legally to be corporations. 1810–11: Prussia abolished guilds. 1819: Maassen tariff in Prussia removed internal barriers.

OTHER FACTORS. The "Protestant Ethic," endorsing thrift, hard work, and personal achievement played a role in American economic development. Americans had some interest in science, but their inventive spirit was more important. America was an "open" society; there were few traditions, tremendous optimism, and new land for settlement. There was the opportunity for individual accomplishment. Success in the American Revolution and the War of 1812 gave the country a sense of optimism. France had many advantages helping her toward industrialization. The French had a tradition of interest in science; there was no absence of invention; what was lacking was the translation of science and invention into profitable opportunities. The French were still fettered by traditional attitudes and values. The Napoleonic Wars also impeded French economic development, depriving the nation of men, capital, and raw materials. 1815: Loss of the French conquests under Napoleon cut off Piedmont, Lombardy, Rhenish Prussia, and Belgium from France, all of which had contributed to French industry: the settlement left an aura of defeat. Lack of political independence may have slowed Belgian development. 1815 ff.: Germany consisted of 38 sovereign states; the political divisions hindered the development of a common market; traditional political and economic patterns continued, despite the changes caused by the French impact, 1790–1815.

The Nonindustrial World

During the period 1760–1830 most of the world's economy was nonindustrial. Nonindustrial societies were heterogeneous. There were areas of western tradition (Eastern Europe, parts of Russia, Spain, and Portugal), of western impact (from Canada, Australia, and New Zealand to Latin America, the West Coast of Africa, and South Africa to the Ottoman Empire, India, Malaya, Java), of eastern tradition (China and Japan), and societies of technologically primitive nonliterates (e.g., North American Indians, Australian aborigines, nomads of the Middle East, Central Asia, Southeast Asia, etc.).

Securing food took priority over other forms of economic activity. Wants were related to survival. In practically all the nonindustrial world, agriculture was the primary mode of existence, employing and supporting most of the population. Exceptions lay in primitive communities: certain North American Indian tribes, the Eskimos, the Bushmen of the Kalahari Desert in Southern Africa, the aborigines of the southeastern coastal lands of Australia, the Negritos, Semang, and Sakai of the Malay Peninsula, plus jungle tribes in Assam, Burma, and Siam; these peoples lived by hunting, plus in some instances fishing, and in all cases collecting wild roots and plants. Other exceptions were the "pastoral nomads"; they domesticated animals—camels, sheep, goats, cattle, or horses; they were present in North Africa, Arabia, Afghanistan, and southern Russia. In most of the world, however, agriculture was practiced.

AGRICULTURE AND ANIMAL HUSBANDRY. Eastern and most of Southern Europe, Ireland: There was little improvement in agricultural methods; innovations taking place in England were known but not applied; in Eastern Europe, the feudal manorial system persisted as did serfdom or the near equivalent, despite the reforms of Joseph II. In Russia the manorial system with serfdom remained unaltered. In Spain, large entailed landed estates prevailed, using low-paid wage labor or, more typically, sharecroppers. In Ireland tenant farming on a subsistence level was the main mode of cultivation.

Canada, Australia, and New Zealand: Two societies coexisted—that of the original peoples and of the immigrants. In Canada settlers rapidly outnumbered the Indian population. Cultivation of the land occurred and a timber industry developed. Lumbering proved a key by-product of general farming. 1788: 1st British settlement in Australia. 1796: 1st plow introduced in Australia by John McArthur of the New South Wales Corps; McArthur became an advocate of sheep breeding, and in 1813 sheep breeding in Australia began to be actively pursued. 1769–70: Capt. James Cook, visiting the islands of New Zealand, found cultivated land "laid out in square plantations." 1826: New Zealand Co., founded in England, dispatched colonists to New Zealand, but these, unimpressed, migrated to Australia. The Maoris (natives of New Zealand) still outnumbered the immigrants; agriculture was primarily native cultivation. None of these "new" countries had the manorial system, serfdom, or the use of slave labor. White settlers had no "traditional agricultural society." There was, moreover, land suitable for cultivation once exploration and transportation opened these regions. In Canada and Australia, changes in agriculture and animal husbandry involved innovations introduced by immigrants. In New Zealand, since Europeans were mainly traders, whalers, and missionaries, most of whom imported food, the effects on agriculture were as yet minimal.

Latin America and the West Indies: Native agriculture coexisted with 2 types of western agriculture. There were the "plantation colonies" in the tropics, where sugar, cotton, and indigo were raised for export; these were characterized by large landholdings and absentee proprietors; most used slave labor. The sugar plantations of the West Indies and of Brazil stand out in this category. Second, there were the "farm colonies" in the temperate zones, established by the Spaniards in Chile and Argentina and by the Portuguese in southern Brazil, and characterized by settlement and freehold land systems. In Jamaica, Barbados, and other British-controlled islands in the 18th cent., British owners had small farms for grazing and breeding animals. The sugar plantations of the West Indies were owned by Britons, Frenchmen, Danes, Dutchmen, and Spaniards and organized to supply the European Continent. In much of Spanish America, the land tenure pattern existing in Spain in the 16th cent. had been introduced—large manorial estates, cultivated by "peons"; entail prevented the dissolution of the estates, which passed generation by generation to eldest sons. Although the church favored the retention by Indians of their land held before the conquest, the church likewise became a large owner of property in Spanish America. By the time of independence, 1810 ff., giant estates in the "plantation colonies" and in the "farm colonies" on the mainland were owned by white or mestizo Latin Americans or ecclesiastical corporations. Landholdings by native villages still existed, but became increasingly less important. Concentration of land ownership, labor by slaves or poorly paid peons, inefficient use of the land (tillage of only part of the land area and primitive agriculture methods), retarded economic progress in Latin America. The political revolutions did not alter the structure of land tenure or the development of agriculture. 1824: Bernardino Rivadavia land law in province of Buenos Aires; 1826: extended to rest of Argentina. Contrary to its intentions, the land law fixed on Argentina the pattern of the latifundia. In subsequent years, large tracts of public land passed into the hands of a few families.

Tropical Africa: Most European settlement in tropical Africa by 1830 was along the coast by merchants. 1817: French officials in Senegal attempted to develop agriculture; they attracted a small group of settlers, who started plantations, tried to grow indigo, sugar, coffee, and cotton, but found the crops not competitive with varieties grown in the West Indies. 1835: The colony of Senegal abandoned its plantations. Outside Senegal, almost all agriculture in tropical Africa was native agriculture; in most of Africa, where the soil permitted, cultivation was practiced. Often there was shifting cultivation: a rotation of farming sites in contrast to a rotation of crops; a group would burn to clear the land, cultivate for several years, and then move on to new land when the soil was exhausted. From the 16th cent., the Portuguese had introduced to West Africa from Latin America such food plants as maize, manioc, sweet potatoes, groundnuts (peanuts), papayas, cayenne pepper, tomatoes, and tobacco. These spread throughout tropical Africa. 1822: The Portuguese introduced cacao from South America to São Tomé; cultivation spread. 1820–30: Cloves were introduced from the Moluccas to the islands of Zanzibar and Pemba. Generally African crops were raised intermingled with one another. Agricultural organization revolved around the village. In some instances, the village "owned land" and in other cases the equivalent of private property existed. In parts of West Africa (for instance in Dahomey, in Hausaland, among the Ibos, etc.), cultivation was done in part by Africans using slave labor. Most agriculture in tropical Africa was on a subsistence basis, but in Hausaland and elsewhere some cash crops were produced. Palm oil became a cash crop in West Africa, but nowhere were specialized, commercial crops the norm. Because of the tsetse fly in much of the African tropics there were no animals for transport, manure, meat supplies, or milk. On the other hand, in parts of East Africa, cattle, sheep, and goats were of primary importance.

Southern Africa: Native agriculture coexisted with the farm communities of the Dutch and British colonists. The latter practiced European methods, while the former farmed in traditional fashion. 1810–11: Travelers to Cape Colony found the Hottentots cultivating vegetables, tobacco, and pumpkins; the Klaarwater Hottentots grew tobacco and used wild leaves for tea; in the early 19th cent. Europeans introduced the plow to the African tribes in the eastern district of the Cape.

Ottoman Empire: In Anatolia farm techniques remained what they had been for almost 1,000 years; village agriculture was on a subsistence basis. Cultivated areas in Iraq, Syria, and Arabia were fewer than in Roman or early Arab times. By the 18th cent. tobacco was being raised for export from Salonica, Syria, and Trebizond, but tobacco exports were still not substantial. Egyptian agricultural developments represented an exception. 1806–1814: Mohammed Ali (Muḥammad ‘Alī) (1769–1849), founder of modern Egypt, introduced land reforms: peasants were required to pay taxes to the government directly instead of to a landlord; he ordered a resurvey of cultivated land; the state acquired large landholdings on which taxes had not been paid or where title deeds were irregular; his followers or relatives were granted large estates; as a substitute for communal ownership, peasants were given *de facto*—not yet legal—ownership of land. New crops were introduced, including cotton, rice, and maize. 1821: Planting of long-staple cotton began in Egypt on a commercial scale. 1820's: Cotton replaced grain as Egypt's chief export. Agriculture in Egypt became more efficient.

India: Agriculture was inefficient and precarious. The soil suffered from exhaustion after centuries of cultivation. Famines followed droughts. 1769 and 1790–92: Widespread famines swept through India, made worse through soil deterioration and overpopulation. Indians cultivated small plots, barely adequate for subsistence. 1793: Lord Charles Cornwallis as gov. gen. of India made landlords of the zamindari (individuals recognized by the Moguls [Mughals] as responsible tax collectors in the villages). The zamindari were to pay the same amount to the government each year (and not have periodic reassessments). Cornwallis hoped the zamindari, with an eye to raising their own incomes, would encourage agricultural improvements (like contemporary English landlords). The system, mainly in operation in Bengal, was not effective. 1812: In southern Madras, the tax payments were fixed for each individual cultivator (ryot) and were to be paid by the occupier of the land to the government (the ryotwari settlement); these arrangements, unlike the permanent settlements with the zamindari, were temporary and subject to reassessments. C. 1818: In Bombay Presidency the peasant was not made an owner (as in Madras) but was given "rights" to his estate; assessments were temporary. The British created a revolution in land tenure in India; throughout the area they ruled, they demanded payment in money and payment in full each year; they established a system of private property in land.

Ceylon: 1824: The 1st British plantation in the East was begun at Peradeniya; coffee was the product.

China: South Chinese farmers had constructed and maintained for centuries elaborate terracing and irrigation systems for wet-rice cultivation. Tea cultivation was widespread in south China. In northern China wheat was the major crop. Throughout China subsistence agriculture predominated; peasants were using iron plows, however crude the wrought iron, while in Europe many peasants still used wooden plows; there were thousands of small isolated villages; Chinese agriculture was commercialized to a certain extent; urban areas requiring foodstuffs meant the presence of a domestic market; tea was the key export crop, and it met with increasing demand in England. In China rising population meant peasants' farms were subdivided into small plots, often insufficient to keep a family alive in the poor seasons. Peasants had to borrow, which in turn led to dispossession from their land. C. 1775: Serious peasant rebellions began, becoming widespread in the following decades.

Japan: Technological (not mechanical) changes took place in Japanese agriculture, based not on western practice but on Japanese and Chinese experience. Miyazaki Antei's *Nogyo zensho,* 1698, was the 1st Japanese treatise on scientific agriculture and had influence throughout the Tokugawa period (to 1868). Other works followed, such as Okura Eijo's *Nogu Benri ron (On the Efficacy of Farm Implements,* c. 1768). Commercial fertilizers (dried fish, oil cakes) were widely used, supplementing the natural fertilizers. These raised crop yields and permitted more intensive use of land. There was improved use of seed varieties. In response to increasing urbanization in Japan in the 18th cent., quantities of grain, rice, fish, timber, and fibers were required to fill basic needs. Prior to urbanization, each region, village, and holding had produced for subsistence. Rice and lesser grains were staples. Each family grew a little fruit and some vegetables, and perhaps tobacco. By the beginning of the 19th cent. Conditions had changed. Except in especially remote, backward locales, peasants specialized according to the soil, climate, and price. Local markets supplied other needs. Cultivation of mulberries and raising of silkworms took place in the valleys of central Honshu, cotton in the same area, sugar cane in southern Kyushu and the islands in the south. Not all crops had become commercial; self-sufficient plots intermingled with cash crops. Much of the agricultural activity had come to involve wage labor. Owing to infanticide, the Japanese population seems to have remained approximately constant, which curbed the excessive subdivision of peasant farms typical of India and China.

Southeast Asia: Commercial agriculture commingled with village subsistence agriculture, with the latter predominant. Rice was the basic crop. In Burma, Siam, and Malaya European trading cos. (by their purchases) encouraged the commercialization of agriculture. The Philippine Islands, Java, and Sumatra also developed commercial agriculture. 1798: The Dutch East India Co. dissolved into bankruptcy and the Dutch government took control over the East Indies; the policy of the

Co. was continued: demands for pepper, coffee, indigo, cotton, and sugar, which were sold in Europe (the "forced delivery system"). Through controls over local rulers, the Dutch fixed prices and restricted trade but did not act directly. In the vicinity of Batavia, Co. employees had started hundreds of private sugar estates, the proprietors of which were Chinese. 1811: Thomas Stamford Raffles (British administrator) took over from the Dutch in Java. Raffles abolished the forced delivery system, hoping farmers would produce for a free market; he collected land taxes in money to encourage more commercialization. 1816: Java returned to the Dutch; they kept Raffles' method in part, but it did not work. Peasants preferred to grow the traditional crop, rice, and to borrow money for land tax payments rather than switch to the more profitable commercial crops. 1830: Raffles' system abandoned in favor of the "culture system."

RAW MATERIALS. Basic raw-material resources in the nonindustrial world were largely unknown and inaccessible. Russia's vast raw-material supplies were in the main unconnected by transportation and undeveloped; there was, however, substantial iron-ore mining in Russia. Spain had iron resources and copper. By contrast the indigenes of New Zealand and Australia did not know how to make bronze or forge iron. The settlers in Australia had not yet uncovered that land's mineral resources, nor had the Canadian settlers in their land. Spain and Portugal in colonizing Latin America invested in mines to obtain precious metals. The colonizers extracted huge quantities of gold and silver from the mines of the New World. 1759–88: During the reign of Carlos II, nearly 500 million pesos in coin and bullion were imported from the American colonies into Spain. 1783: Carlos III promulgated a new mining code for New Spain, which in the next years extended to Venezuela, Guatemala, New Granada, Peru, and Chile. It served as the basic mining law for most of Spanish America until the late 19th cent.; it covered operations of mines, fiscal organization of the industry, regulation of labor, trade in precious metals, banking and credits, technical training for mining engineers, etc. 1800: Spanish and Portuguese American mines were producing 90% of the world's precious metals. It was precious metals rather than industrial raw materials that were developed in Latin America. In most of Africa iron was known and used. Africans had worked the copper deposits in Central Africa and had smelted low-grade copper oxide ores. Gold had long been mined by Africans.

Ottoman Empire: Minerals were undeveloped. The Arab Middle East seemed to lack mineral resources.

Asia: The mining industry, although it had a long history, was still in its infancy; in India, gold, copper, and iron were mined but the volume was negligible; Chinese coal, iron, copper, tin, and silver resources had begun to be developed, but silver in circulation as currency came from the New World via Europe and the Philippines; in Japan, mining enterprises existed in gold, silver, and copper—operated by the shogun or by daimyo; coal was produced as was iron from iron sands, but on a small scale; in Southeast Asia, tin was mined on a small scale in the Red River Valley, the Malay Peninsula, and the islands to the south; iron and gold were mined in the Malay Peninsula; tin was mined on the island of Banka off eastern Sumatra. More important, industrial raw materials other than minerals that were developed in the nonindustrial world included cotton (in India, China, Japan, Egypt, etc.), hemp and jute (in Russia, India, Southeast Asia, and the Philippines), silk (in East Asia), and timber (in Eastern Europe, Russia, Canada, Manchuria, Japan, Korea, southern China, etc.). Massive development of mineral resources of underdeveloped countries awaited exploration, transportation, and capital-intensive investment. None was yet available.

LABOR. Much of Asia was heavily populated, with the population rising in China and India, and fairly stable in Japan. Elsewhere in the nonindustrial world the population was sparse. Australia was being newly settled by convicts transported from England plus some free immigrants; Canada had a slow stream of immigration. In Latin America and Africa, there was no overpopulation, nor was this the case in the Dutch East Indies. Population in the nonindustrial countries was mainly in rural areas. Many Asian cities were large, but only 1% of the entire Asian population (excluding Russia) lived in urban areas. The cities, with their commercialized economies and their accumulations of wealth and also poverty, were in sharp contrast to the prevailing massive poverty of the vast rural areas. Large income differentiations existed throughout the nonindustrial world. With the partial exception of the new white settlers in Australia and Canada, for the most part the nonindustrial world was characterized by a highly structured traditional society; the structure of such societies varied dramatically, but status rather than contract everywhere prevailed; there was, with the exception of Japan, little labor mobility. In Eastern Europe and Russia, the presence of serfdom retarded economic progress. The caste system in India provided a strong bar to change. Slavery in much of the underdeveloped world also provided a block to progress. Abolition of slavery spread slowly: 1826: Chile abolished slavery; 1829: Mexico. Yet slavery remained in much of Latin America, Africa, the Arab world, the British Empire, and Southeast Asia, though its harshness and rigor varied very greatly. Throughout the underdeveloped world, with the exception of Japan, industrial skills and education were lacking; in Japan, industrial skills emerged in rural industries. In India, the British introduced a European educational system; 1813: the East India Co. was ordered to spend £10,000 per year to instruct Indians.

ENERGY. The basic energy resources throughout the nonindustrial world were human power and domestic animals. Wind and water power were used to a small extent.

MANUFACTURING. Manufacturing ranged from the whittled stick for digging to tools of stone, bone, or shell to decorations (necklaces, earrings) to clothing to household goods (pottery, matting, bags, and baskets, etc.) to weapons (clubs, bows and arrows, etc.). Boats were manufactured. In most societies, metals were worked. Wood carvings and leather goods were typical manufactures. No matter how primitive a society, it had some sort of manufacturing. Even economies that were nonexchange societies had manufacturing. There were no known societies that did not have the use of fire, the use of a cutting instrument, or the use of string. Most manufacturing was within the household. In some few underdeveloped countries, factories, forges, and foundries were introduced (they were exceptional). In Russia, Eastern and most of Southern Europe, artisan manufacturing prevailed. 1760: Russia was the world's largest producer of iron; in 1805, Russia's output fell below England's; after 1828, its production was lower than that of France or the U.S. Settlers in Australia and Canada manufactured basic household items; Canadian settlement was of longer duration, and there were an ironworks (at St. Maurice, Que.), shipbuilding, potash works, and a number of sawmills and gristmills; nevertheless, most of the colonists' requirements for manufactured goods were imported from England. New Spain and Peru, under Spanish rule, had cotton and woolen cloth industries; silver, leather goods, hardware, furniture, shoes, and handicrafts were manufactured; food-processing industries had developed; shipbuilding became important in Havana, Guayaquil, and Buenos Aires. Spain discouraged manufacturing in the New World colonies, but by 1800 the Spanish colonies had more extensive industry than their mother country, although the manufacturing was insignificant compared with Northern Europe or the U.S. 1811 ff.: In Argentina, under Rivadavia the state built a foundry for cannon, a powder factory, and a gun works. African manufactures consisted of bags, baskets, hats, nets, cloths, etc.; there were smiths, weavers, potters, woodworkers, ropemakers, and boatbuilders; simple utensils were produced, as were ornaments and weapons. In the Middle East handicraft industries had retrogressed from their level in earlier eras and were still retrogressing; artisan industry in the Moslem (Muslim) world had a higher level of activity in 1760–1830 than after 1830, when European machine-made goods increasingly replaced the handmade products; within the Ottoman Empire cotton, silk, embroidery, Moroccan leather, and cutlery industries existed. In Egypt Mohammed Ali made attempts to start modern industry; 1818 ff.: machinery and technicians were imported into Egypt from Europe; the Egyptian government made direct investments in the factories, trained workers, and sought out raw materials and fuel; by 1830 modern cotton, woolen, silk, and linen textile mills, sugar refineries, glass and paper factories, as well as tanneries existed in Egypt plus a government armament plant complete with a foundry. Egyptian progress was exceptional for the less developed world. India, once a net exporter of manufactured cotton goods, was becoming, 1800–1830, a net importer of cotton goods; India's own handmade product could not compete with British machine-made goods. In China spinning, weaving, and printing cotton was a well-developed art since the 17th cent., an industry of craftsmen; a Chinese silk industry had also emerged. Chinese porcelain was world-renowned. Japan had well-developed rural industries, in cotton and silk and in crafts. In Java Chinese inhabitants made embroidery, dyed cotton, and were tailors, carpenters, joiners, and smiths. In New Zealand the Maoris made clothing from animal skins. In the South Pacific, clothing was manufactured from tree bark. The less developed world—with its range of manufactures and manufacturing methods —was characterized by a low level of technology by comparison with the West. In these years, not a technological innovation of worldwide consequence came from anywhere in the nonindustrial world.

TRANSPORTATION. In the non-industrial world, transportation facilities were poor.

Roads: In Eastern and Southern Europe roads were in disrepair. Road building in Canada and Australia was in its infancy. Rough trails were in evidence in much of Latin America, while footpaths characterized much of Africa and Southeast Asia. In Egypt, under Mohammed Ali attempts were made to build modern roads. Japan had a road system.

Overland transport: Human beings, using their hands, heads, backs, and shoulders (worldwide); mules, donkeys, and llamas (in Latin America); and camels, mules, donkeys, and less often horses (in the Middle East), were beasts of burden. Rough carts drawn by oxen were present in much of the nonindustrial world. Dogs pulled sleds in the Arctic. Caravan travel was typical of arid regions in Asia and Africa.

Water transportation: Use was made, when possible, of navigable rivers. 1812 ff.: British government began to build canals in Canada to avoid the rapids on the St. Lawrence; this was done partly as a measure of defense against the U.S. 1829: Welland Canal completed in Canada, which improved the St. Lawrence Seaway. 1819: Digging of the Mahmudia Canal, connecting the Nile with Alexandria. The Grand Canal in China (on which construction started in the 5th cent. B.C.), covering some 1,200 miles from Peking to Ningpo, was a major transit route. These canals for internal communication were exceptional in the less developed world. For shipping, the nonindustrial world had a wide range of vessels: bark canoes, dugouts, rafts, catamarans, sampans, and a variety of small sailing ships. 1816: 1st steamship launched by Canadians in Lake Ontario. Water transport was developed, often primarily for the purpose of fishing; when used for transport, travel by water was usually superior to and cheaper than overland transit. In short, in the nonindustrial world, transportation facilities were limited, as were the needs for such facilities.

FINANCE. All underdeveloped countries were short of capital.

Financial intermediaries: 1750's: Russia had begun modern banking institutions; 1769: the Russian Note Bank founded; 1817: in Russia, formation of government-owned State Commercial Bank, with specific purpose of granting commercial credits; it was not very active. Spain and Portugal had commercial banking facilities, developed as a result of their long-time trading connections. Initially, Canadians and Australians depended on Great Britain for banking facilities. By the early 1800's, banks were started in Canada; 1817: 1st bank established in Australia. 1808: The Bank of Brazil was founded (failed in 1829). 1825: Argentina organized a national bank (which survived until 1836). These banks were exceptional in Latin America. Before 1810 a bank at the Cape of Good Hope was established. Japan was exceptional in its range of financial institutions; by the end of the 17th cent. a credit system had developed from money changers, merchant bankers, and financiers of the daimyo which was similar to that existing in Europe in that period; by 1760–1830 Japan had substantial urban banking activity. China too had private banking facilities: some were pawnshops, some "cash shops," which changed one kind of money to another; others received deposits, made loans, bought and sold drafts, and issued bills, which served as money in the locale. In India, indigenous banking consisted of native bankers or "schroffs" who dealt in the large commercial centers and in the courts of native rulers; they aided payments by means of their hundis, or bills of exchange. With the exception of Japan, in no case in the underdeveloped world were financial intermediaries well developed. In fact, in the less developed world large segments of the economy were self-sufficient and not part of a monetized economy, or only peripherally part of one. In Australia in the 1790's rum was the medium of exchange for the white settlers. 1810–21: Under Gov. Lachlan Macquarie, Australia developed a more effective monetary system. In primitive societies there would often be a highly developed system of trade and exchange using shell currencies (the Tolai of New Guinea, for instance) or cattle (in East Africa) or brass rods (in much of Africa); barter was common in many transactions.

FOREIGN TRADE. With the exception of Japan, most nonindustrialized countries felt the impact of foreign trade (some to a greater, some to a smaller extent). Foreign trade served (1) to monetize the economy (barter went only so far; traders usually dealt in money); (2) to jar existing traditional systems (even when European, Arab, and Indian traders recruited native intermediaries to act on their behalf, this detached men from their villages); (3) to create urban centers (which were often enclaves isolated from the traditional rural activity of the country); (4) to introduce new machine-made products; (5) to create new wants; and (6) in some countries to retard or wipe out existing handicraft activities. World trade was liberalized. Monopolies held by English companies were abandoned. 1765: Spain opened the Caribbean islands to almost unlimited trade with 9 key Spanish ports; 1770: concession extended to Campeche and Yucatán; 1776–77: New Granada; 1778: extended to all Spanish America with the exception of New Spain and Venezuela; by 1790 traders from any port in Spain could buy and sell anywhere in Spanish America. 1769: Monopoly of French East India Co. abolished. 1798: The Dutch East India Co. dissolved. The result of these measures was a great increase in trade. Liberalization of trade did not mean an end to privilege; instead it meant the assertion of new rights by the leading trading nations. Britain, for example, by Anglo-Portuguese treaties of 1642, 1654, and 1661 had obtained special privileges for her merchants in trading in Portugal. 1810: Britain transferred her old privileges and pre-eminent position in Portugal to the Portuguese colony, Brazil. 1827: After independence, Brazil and Britain concluded a commercial treaty, the new empire accepting Britain as having special privileges (including extraterritoriality, consular concessions, guaranteed low import tariff); Brazil lost its right to set its own tariffs; this treaty expired in 1844 and so did the privileges. In general, nonindustrial nations were exporters of primary commodities, usually agricultural products; the imports of nonindustrial countries were in the main manufactured goods. Russia exported, with rare exceptions, only raw materials (hemp, flax, wood, grain, tallow, hides, and furs); from China it imported tea, silk, jewels, etc., much of which it re-exported. Russia depended on Western European nations for most of its colonial products (sugar, coffee, spices, and drugs) and for most manufactures (textiles, metals, pottery, paper, etc.). Spain imported raw materials and precious metals from Latin America, and re-exported much of what it imported in exchange for manufactured goods. Canada exported mainly furs, fish, and timber. Wheat also became an export (but not yet an important one because of the English corn laws). 1821: New South Wales and Van Diemen's Land (Tasmania) exported 175,433 pounds of fine wool; 1831: the total exports were 2,493,339 pounds, and a major export industry had been launched. Both Canadians and Australians were importers of manufactured goods. Latin America by the close of the 18th cent. exported a greater agricultural output per annum than it did precious metals; imports were mainly manufactured goods. With the official end of the slave trade, trade in palm oil and to a lesser extent groundnuts (peanuts) became a staple of West African commerce. With the Industrial Revolution in England, there was more interest in cleanliness, and the soap industry that developed in Great Britain depended on imports of palm oil. About 1825: Liverpool merchants turned their attention to palm oil, and major exports from West Africa began. Interest also arose in palm kernels; 1822: 1st export of palm kernels from West Africa. The demand for groundnuts was stimulated by the soapmakers. 1830: Groundnuts 1st appeared in the trade returns of Gambia. India, 1760: Chief exports were indigo, saltpeter, and manufactured cotton and silk textiles; imports were specie, woolens, and miscellaneous manufactured goods. 1830: India exported very few manufactured textiles; instead, exports were raw materials; imports were manufactured goods. China exported fine textiles, porcelain, and tea, and imported bullion, some manufactured products, raw cotton, and opium. Southeast Asian commerce and the trade of the East Indies involved the export of tropical crops. From the Spice Islands the main exports had changed to coffee and sugar,

since fresh meat was available in Europe (owing to agricultural improvements), and Europeans no longer needed spices to disguise the flavor of spoiled meat. Foreign trade of Africa and Asia was usually conducted by European traders, although Arab and Indian traders were active in Africa. For the most part, European trading companies were content to remain traders rather than colonizers.

FOREIGN INVESTMENTS. Investing by European countries in less developed regions had begun—in foreign loans, trade, plantations, etc.—but the era of giant foreign investments was still ahead.

BUSINESS ORGANIZATION. Foreign trade was dominated by Europeans. Production was developed, resting on ties of kinship, religion, and social status. Guilds were significant in Latin America and in India, China, and Japan. Practically everywhere business was small business, family enterprise; exceptions were isolated state-owned units (in Egypt and Argentina, for example).

GOVERNMENT POLICY. The policy of the state toward economic growth in nonindustrial countries varied; generally governments did little to aid economic change, except for colonial governments seeking trade expansion, but at the same time discouraged manufacturing. In Australia the early British governors granted land and stock—the initial capital for development—to members of the New South Wales Corps, to freed convicts, and to other settlers; the governors tried to make Australia self-sufficient in agricultural products. In Argentina in the 1820's there were abortive attempts to use the government as an agency for economic growth. In Egypt there was a definite governmental effort to industrialize the nation. But such concerted state measures toward economic development were isolated. Whether tribal authority, government by village elders, or other kinds of local government, order and the *status quo* rather than economic progress and growth were basic.

OTHER FACTORS. Throughout the underdeveloped world, ignorance and poverty created their own vicious circle. In general, the desire for industrialization or for achievement was absent. With the exception of the new settlers in sparsely populated Canada and Australia, traditional patterns (although what was "traditional" varied) were carried on without change or desire for change. Generally, religious and ritualistic customs retarded progress. Practically everywhere in the less developed world, kinship and the extended family took priority over the nuclear family and the individual. Climate played a key role in retarding development in much of the nonindustrial world. Much of the tropics were infested with malaria. Filariasis, hookworm, schistosomiasis, and yaws were dangerous diseases. Exposure to high temperatures sapped energy. The impact of the West through trade provided a basis for change, but change was slow.

1830–1870

The Workshop of the World—Great Britain

AGRICULTURE. British agriculture was the most efficient in the world. 1846: repeal of the corn laws; farmers feared the effects on British agriculture; imports did rise, but there was no fall in wheat prices. Demand for agricultural output grew. 1846–73: "Golden age" of British agriculture. Productivity rose. 1840's: Iron and steel plows substituted for heavy wooden plows; iron tooth and disk implements replaced brush and wooden rollers for harrowing. 1850's: Widespread adoption of planting in drills by machine; the cultivator came into use. 1850's ff.: American innovations of Cyrus McCormick and Obed Hussey in reapers and mowers were employed. Fertilizers were well used. 1839: Imports of Peruvian guano on a commercial scale began; the U.K. became a key importer of Chilean nitrates; c. 1840: John B. Lawes (1814–1900) began to produce phosphate from bones to be used as fertilizer; the employment of chemical fertilizers spread. British agriculture became capital-intensive; there was an increase in the proportion of capital to other inputs. Real wages in agriculture rose. Yet, at the same time, British agriculture came to make an ever-lower percentage contribution to national income; agriculture, forestry, and fishing, which comprised 23.4% of national income in 1831, represented only 14.2% in 1871.

RAW MATERIALS. 1830's: New coal and iron-ore fields were opened in Scotland; 1850's: Cleveland ore field opened; 1860's: Cumberland-Lancashire field developed. 1830–70: Coal output in U.K. rose from 22.4 m. tons to 110.4 m. tons; iron-ore output in 1870 totaled 14.6 m. tons. 1858: Mining and quarrying accounted for about 3.5% of British national income; of this coal mining was 60%, iron ore 9–10%, tin, copper, and lead about 12.5%, and other minerals (including stone, clay, etc.) about 18.5%. The development of mining in Britain was caused by the demands of the iron and steel industry, manufacturing in general, and the growth of railroads. Britain continued to be a large importer of raw cotton, and also of wool, for the textile industry.

ENERGY. The use of the steam engine spread rapidly; steam was the basis for factory industry; it was essential for the "railway age" and significant in ocean travel. 1831: Michael Faraday discovered that electricity could be generated by revolving a copper coil in a magnetic field. 1867: Charles Wheatstone (1802–75) and S. A. Varley invented a dynamo-electric machine, practically simultaneously with Siemens' invention in Germany. These innovations notwithstanding, the age of electricity had not yet arrived.

INDUSTRY. For the 1st time in history a nation was obtaining its major income from manufacturing, machine production.

STRUCTURE OF BRITISH NATIONAL PRODUCT
(as % of national income)

Year	Agriculture, Forestry, Fisheries	Manufactures, Mining, Building	Trade, Transport, and Income from Abroad	Government, Domestic, and Other Services	Housing
1831	23.4	34.4	18.4	18.1	6.5
1851	20.3	34.3	20.7	18.4	8.1
1871	14.2	38.1	26.3	13.9	7.6

Productivity in manufacturing rose, and real wages also rose. British manufactures dominated world markets.

Textiles: The cotton textile industry became increasingly capital-intensive as the use of power machinery spread; by the 1850's handloom weavers contributed little to the output of the industry. By mid-cent., England produced half the world's cotton cloth. 1850's and 1860's: Power looms were widely adopted in the woolen industry.

Iron: The British made heavy investments in the iron industry. 1870: Britain produced 6 m. tons of pig iron (almost half the world's total). Iron was used to make boilers, bridges, rails, buildings, ships, and agricultural implements.

SHARE OF IRON INDUSTRY IN BRITISH NATIONAL PRODUCT
(as % of GNP)

App. Date	Gross Output (Less Coal and Imported Ore)
1831	3.6
1851	6.2
1871	11.6

Steel: 1839: J. M. Heath added manganese to crucible steel while it was smelting and made it easier to weld; this lowered by 50% the cost of the best steels. 1856: Henry Bessemer (1813–98) demonstrated the "Bessemer process" of blowing air through molten cast iron and at the same time removing the silicon and carbon by oxidation; the process required the use of pig iron low in sulphur and phosphorus. 1856: Robert Mushet recognized the need to add manganese after the blowing for deoxidation and recarbonation; 1862: the 1st Bessemer steel rails were laid; 1863: Bessemer steel 1st used in ship construc-

tion. 1856: William Siemens (1823–83), German-born British subject, conceived the idea of a gas regenerative furnace, and by 1861 had built one. 1863: The Siemens regenerative furnace was used at the Martin works in France in connection with an open-hearth bath of molten pig iron and scrap to make steel, thus the Siemens-Martin process. 1867: Siemens started to make steel at Birmingham. 1870: Britain, as the world's largest steel producer, made only 287,000 metric tons.

Chemical industry: In most branches of the chemical industry, Great Britain led. The chemical industry was not a big industry (only 9,172 workers employed in 1851), but it did stimulate scientific inquiry. Britain led in soda manufacture. 1849: Thomas Graham (1805–69) was responsible for the birth of colloidal chemistry. 1856: Mauve, the 1st coal-tar dye, was made in England by William Henry Perkin (1838–1907).

Other technological innovations: 1840: Sir William R. Grove (1811–96) invented the 1st incandescent electric light. 1845: R. W. Thompson invented the pneumatic tire. 1845: I. C. Johnson, manager of Messrs. White & Sons' works at Swanscombe, Kent, produced modern Portland cement.

TRANSPORTATION. Road transport: British roads continued to be improved; early in the 1830's, the steam carriage was heavily taxed. 1835: A Red Flag Law was passed by Parliament, fixing a speed limit of 4 mph on all free-moving self-propelled vehicles and requiring a flagman on foot to walk ahead of the moving vehicle. Thus the steam (and later motor) vehicle industry was retarded and the horse-drawn carriage and wagon prevailed. 1839: Kirkpatrick MacMillan of Dumfries invented the 1st real bicycle.

Railways: From 1830 on canal building declined and railroad building soared.

BRITISH RAILROADS

Date	Miles
1825	26
1844	2,236
1850	6,635
1860	10,410
1870	15,310

1847: Peak of building boom; railway construction equaled c. 12% of national income. 1850: Railways were carrying more goods and passengers than roads and canals.

Transoceanic travel: In international commerce, ocean transit by steamer increasingly replaced the sailing ship. 1834: The East India Co. started to use steamships between Bombay and Suez. 1836: The Oriental Steamship Co. (British) started service to Egypt and Syria; 1838: the British steamer, *Great Western,* was the 1st regular steamship to cross the Atlantic without recoaling. 1839: The Peninsular & Oriental line (P. & O.) established regular steamship service from England to Alexandria to meet ships of the East India Co. which came up the Red Sea. 1840: Samuel Cunard (1787–1865) founded the 1st significant transatlantic steamship line (Cunard Line). 1842: Royal Mail Steam Packet Co. (British) started service to the Caribbean and South America. 1842: P. & O. began to run steamers between Suez and Calcutta; 1845: that co. added a line to Hong Kong. 1845: The *Great Britain* made her 1st voyage; she was the 1st large steamer (over 3,000 tons) to be built of iron and the 1st to introduce the screw propeller in ocean

navigation. 1846: Britain introduced steamer service to West Africa. But of all the transportation innovations, one was outstanding; 1869, Nov. 16: the Suez Canal opened. The canal, built by a Frenchman, Ferdinand de Lesseps (1805–94), and financed by an international company, had a dramatic impact on the organization of British transport. The British Empire became more accessible for trade.

COMMUNICATIONS. 1837: A 5-needle telegraph system was tried on the London & Birmingham Railway, devised by William Fothergill Cooke (1806–79) and Charles Wheatstone (1802–75). 1837: Railways in England were 1st to adopt the telegraph. 1846 ff.: Independent telegraph companies were formed. 1851: The 1st successful submarine telegraph cable was laid across the English Channel, from Dover to Calais. 1866: Transatlantic cable connected America and Europe. 1869: British Post Office bought all existing telegraph lines in Britain.

FINANCE. England was the financial capital of the world. Capital for expansion of industry was practically all internally generated, although industry did resort to some short-term bank financing. Industrial capital was reinvested in more industry; mercantile capital went into industry and transport; funds once invested in land were applied to industry and railroad investments. The government was not an important source of capital. Banking facilities developed rapidly, with joint-stock banks and branches replacing country banks. 1844: Under the Bank Act the Bank of England was divided into 2 separate departments for issue and for banking; no new banks of issue were to be created; the amount of issue of existing

EFFECTS OF THE SUEZ CANAL

	By Cape	By Canal	Nautical Miles Saved (%)
London to:			
Bombay	10,667	6,274	41.2
Madras	11,280	7,313	35.2
Calcutta	11,900	8,083	32.1
Singapore	11,740	8,326	28.8
Hong Kong	13,180	9,799	25.8

banks was not to be increased; country-bank issues were not to be legal tender. The act was designed to eliminate gradually all notes except those of the Bank of England.

FOREIGN TRADE. 1842: Sir Robert Peel secured the reduction of duties on 750 British imports; he reinstated the income tax to make up for loss of revenue. 1845: Peel abolished 430 out of the 813 remaining import duties and eliminated all export duties. 1846, 6 June: Repeal of the corn laws, leaving small duties on grain until 1849 and then only a nominal duty, which was later abolished. The opening of Britain to foreign grain marked her transition from an agricultural to a manufacturing and commercial nation. Foodstuffs would have to be imported from abroad.

BRITISH 10-YEAR IMPORT AVERAGES
($ million at fixed prices)

Year	Grain	Animal Foodstuffs
1830's	10.5	8.5
1840's	31.0	17.0
1850's	55.5	18.0
1860's	100.5	66.5

1849, 1854: Britain finally repealed the Navigation Acts, which had restricted commerce. 1853, 1860: British legislation swept away hundreds of remaining import duties and left Britain a "free-trade" nation. 1860, 23 Jan.: the Cobden Treaty with France was signed, heralding freer trade between Britain and France. 1860 ff.: Britain made treaties with Belgium, Italy, Prussia, the *Zollverein,* Austria, etc., obtaining tariff reductions. The free-trade measures had salutary results. The British government did not have to protect industry since there was no competition from abroad. British factories produced goods at lower costs than handmade products the world over. British foreign trade expanded dramatically; Britain kept her leadership in international commerce. Her foreign trade (exports plus imports) in 1830 was $564 million; in 1870 it was $3,186 million. Foreign trade provided a market for British manufactures; the demand aided in sustaining her industry.

FOREIGN INVESTMENT. 1830's: Some British speculated in American securities (with large losses); 1840's: the British made investments in railroad building in France and Belgium, until crises and revolutions, 1848, slowed this outflow; 1850's: the British made foreign investments in railroads, government securities, and businesses worldwide: in U.S., Canada, Brazil, France, Belgium, Denmark, Sweden, Portugal, Italy, Russia, Turkey, Algeria, British India, and Australia.

BOOK VALUE OF BRITISH FOREIGN INVESTMENT,
1854
($ million)

U.S.	250–350
French, Belgian, Dutch, and Russian govt. sec.	225–275
Spain and Portugal	175–225
Latin America	175–200
French railways	125–150
Belgian railways	25

BUSINESS ORGANIZATION. The predominant form of business organization in Britain remained the partnership or the unincorporated company. 1844: The Companies Act; 1856: the Joint Stock Company Act, establishing limited liability; and 1862: the Consolidated Statute. These acts made the incorporated co. a more feasible way of doing business and the form came more into use. 1830's: Charles Babbage did pioneer work on factory management—making cost studies of the process of production.

GOVERNMENT POLICY. Government policy in Britain was designed to remove barriers to commerce. Government aid to business was through providing political stability, law and order, charters and rights of ways for railroads, and subsidies to the steamer services. 1842: Peel's reintroduction of the personal income tax gave the government new means of meeting expenses (Britain had had general income taxes, 1798–1816, to cope with war needs); 1842 ff.: income tax remained in operation in Britain. Except in the case of the telegraph the British government did not directly participate in domestic business. In the colonies, the British government played a more affirmative role, but there existed in England in these years an unfavorable attitude toward colonies. While Britain's imperial responsibilities increased in Australia, New Zealand, India, Ceylon, Malaya, South Africa, and Canada (until Canada was given dominion status in 1867), the government accepted responsibility in economic matters with grave reservations. Yet improvements in transportation and communication and the 1869 opening of the Suez Canal were factors that forecast greater trade and greater imperial involvement by the British government.

The Spread of Industrialization—U.S. and Western Europe

During 1830–70 industrialization spread to the U.S., Belgium, France, Germany, etc. All (Belgium excepted) were still predominantly agricultural. Yet in these countries the relative importance of agriculture was declining. The gainfully occupied force in agriculture in the U.S. was 70%, 1830, and 53%, 1870; France, 52%, 1860–69; Germany, 47%, 1871.

AGRICULTURE. In the U.S. dramatic changes took place in agriculture. American agriculture moved westward. The fertile prairies of the Midwest came under the plow; large-scale farming operations developed there.

Agricultural innovations: 1830: Chilean nitrate 1st imported into U.S. as fertilizer. 1831: Obed Hussey (1792–1860) of Maryland patented 1st successful reaper. 1831: Cyrus H. McCormick (1809–84) of Virginia established McCormick Harvesting Machine Co., a predecessor co. of International Harvester Co.; 1834: McCormick patented his reaper. 1833: Chicago blacksmith John Lane made 1st steel plow. 1837: John Deere (1804–86) introduced his steel plow; 1847: Deere started a factory in Moline, Ill., to manufacture steel plows; by 1860, the steel plow was standard throughout the American West, but iron plows continued to be used because of the relatively high cost of the steel plow. 1837: Hiram and John Pitts of Maine introduced the 1st successful thresher. 1850: 1st chemical fertilizer plant established in Baltimore, Md. 1854: Ketchum patented his mower. 1856: The Marsh brothers designed a harvester (with hand binding). 1850's: Grain drills began to displace broadcast sowing of wheat in Pennsylvania and in other wheat-growing areas. Everywhere in the North the use of new farm equipment spread, increasing productivity. In the antebellum South the work was done by slave labor and there was no need for mechanization. 1862–63: End to slavery, but with the Civil War and Reconstruction mechanization proceeded slowly. Agricultural innovation also spread in Europe. 1840: German chemist Justus von Liebig (1803–73) published his *Organic Chemistry in Its Application to Agriculture and Physiology,* dealing with soil chemistry; he argued that by adding chemicals, land fertility would be greatly increased. 1840's: Chemical fertilizers began to be sold in France and Germany to a limited extent. French agriculture, on the whole, remained traditional; there was knowledge of British innovation, of foreign competition, and of prices, but still change was tardy. Plows and threshing machines powered by horses or mules were the only types of agricultural machinery commonly adopted, and the number of threshing machines was limited. Horse hoes, drilling machines, reapers, mowers, horse rakes, and haymaking machinery were used only to a modest extent in France. Retarding agricultural advance in France was the presence of small peasant holdings. By the middle of the 19th cent., French peasants still left some of their land fallow, ignoring information on crop rotation well known in England.

German agriculture, likewise, was slow to adopt agricultural implements, yet on the larger farms east of the Elbe better machinery was being adopted. Transportation aided the merchandising of machinery and fertilizer, and also the farms' produce. 1830–65: There seems to have been an increase in agricultural productivity in German states. In Austria the larger farms were the 1st to begin mechanization, but slowly.

New crops: In the U.S. there were no new crops. Cotton production in the South rose steadily before the Civil War; as the Midwest came to be settled grain moved westward; corn and wheat became far more important American crops. 1850's: 72% increase in wheat production, which took place in the Mississippi Valley; 50% increase in corn production. In Europe, sugar-beet production, which had begun in France, spread; 1830's: a boom in sugar-beet growing in Silesia and Saxony; c. 1845: the sugar-beet industry became well established in Germany. Sugar-beet production decreased Europe's dependence on sugar imports from the West Indies and Brazil.

Land reform: In the U.S. the Preemption Act, 1841, gave settlers 1st rights to purchase land on which they squatted. 1854: Graduation Act declared lands not disposed of at the government-prescribed minimum could be sold at lower prices. 1862: Homestead Act gave title to 160 acres (at no charge) to a bona fide settler if he lived on the land and improved it. In Europe, land-reform legislation of earlier years took effect. In France the peasant remained the cultivator. In Germany in the west the peasant got title to his holdings by paying indemnities to the lord over a long period of time. East of the Elbe, peasants, who did not have enough land to support themselves, sold all and migrated to the New World or moved to western Germany to become a pool of labor for industry. Open fields became increasingly a thing of the past. By 1850, large landowners could carry out improvements, unhampered by traditional rights and customs. 1848–49: In Austria peasants secured clear title to their holdings after payment of indemni-

ties; the peasant was a free man. In Austria large estates coexisted side by side with peasant holdings.

Commercialization: In the U.S. and in Western Europe there was increasing commercialization of agriculture. In the U.S. the demand for more food production owing to the growing population, especially the urban population, put new incentives on the development of agriculture; the extension of American transportation facilities enabled specialization and meant American agricultural products could go into domestic commerce; the repeal of the corn laws in England, 1846, opened British markets to American grain. In Western Europe, new transportation connections also increased the specialization and commercialization of agriculture, but the process was slower because of the presence of peasant holdings. When in the late 1840's and early 1850's the British market was opened to Danish grain, butter, and livestock, Danish agriculture prospered.

RAW MATERIALS. 1848: Gold was discovered in California. In the U.S. there was an expansion of mining of basic minerals: coal, iron, and copper (1845: copper output 100 long tons; 1870: 12,600 long tons). 1859: Drilling of Drake's well at Titusville, Pa.; this became the world's 1st commercial oil well. 1859: U.S. petroleum production 2,000 barrels; 1870: 5.3 million barrels; a new industry had been created. 1830's: The French undertook a search for additional coal resources; expansion of production in the Pas de Calais; France was short of coal and yet levied tariffs to protect high-cost domestic production; 1847: discovery of coal fields in the Nord; output expanded. German coal resources were superior. The 3 main coal fields (the great Ruhr field, the Roer field, and the Silesian field, on which mining began in the 1840's) provided a basis for the German iron and steel industry. 1830's: Large-scale mining began in the western fields; by 1846, German coal production was roughly 3.2 m. English tons a year, which was less than the U.S. total of 5.3 m. tons, or the French total of 4.5 m. tons; the Germans still thought their resource base was "limited."

By 1870 Germany's position had improved.

COAL PRODUCTION, 1870
(million metric tons)

Great Britain	112.2
Germany	34.9
U.S.	29.9
France	13.3
Belgium	13.6
Austria-Hungary	8.4

1840's: Belgium was producing more iron than the entire *Zollverein;* 1870: growth of German iron mining. By 1870 German iron-ore production was the greatest on the European Continent. Germany had excellent resources for a chemical industry

—not only coal but potash deposits. 1856: German potash deposits developed in Stassfurt. Sodium chloride, potassium salts, and sulphur could be extracted from German deposits of iron pyrites. The German resource base gave Germany a superior position in the chemical industries. With British free trade, there was a demand for Swedish iron and Sweden expanded its iron-ore production.

ENERGY. 1837: Frenchman Benoît Fourneyron (1802–67) developed the water turbine, with 60 hp. 1840's: Uriah A. Boyden (1814–79) introduced Fourneyron's water turbine to the New England textile industry, thus retarding introduction of steam power. Yet steam as an energy source spread most rapidly.

CAPACITY OF ALL STEAM ENGINES
(million hp)

	U.S.	U.K.	France	Germany	Belgium	Austria	Russia	Italy
1840	.76	.62	.09	.04	.04	.02	.01	.01
1850	1.68	1.29	.27	.26	.07	.10	.07	.04
1860	3.47	2.45	1.12	.85	.16	.33	.20	.05
1870	5.59	4.04	1.85	2.48	.35	.80	.92	.33

1837: Thomas Davenport of Rutland, Vt., was 1st to produce a successful electric motor. 1838: Charles Page of Boston drilled steel plates with a battery-driven motor. 1860–63: Antonio Pacinotti in Italy improved the design of generators. 1867: German Ernst Werner von Siemens (1816–92) announced invention of the electric dynamo. (His work came simultaneously with that of Wheatstone and Varley in England.) 1870: French engineer Z. T. Gramme (1826–1901) made a ring dynamo, the 1st commercially practical generator of direct current.

INDUSTRY. In the U.S. manufacturing in every industry from food processing to lumbering to iron (and steel) to metalworking spread. The U.S. became independent of imports of basic manufactured goods. On the Continent, Belgium became the great manufacturing country, consuming more coal and iron per capita than any country besides Great Britain. 1840's: Expansion of textiles in France; 1850's and 1860's: expansion of iron industry. 1835 ff.: German industrial development accelerated. 1830 ff.: Progress

in Austria in cotton textiles, woolens, silk goods, and paper; development was mainly in lower Austria and Bohemia.

Textiles: The important innovations in the U.S. textile industry had taken place before 1835; the industry (although the largest American industry in terms of assets) became conservative in nature. 1845: Frenchman Josué Heilmann (1796–1856) invented a machine comb for combing cotton and wool. While mechanization of the textile industry increased in France, Belgium, Switzerland, Germany, and Austria, their textile industries did not become a leading sector as had textiles in England. 1850: Raw-cotton consumption in France, Belgium, and the German *Zollverein* combined was far less than half that in Great Britain.

Iron and steel: 1839: 1st successful coke-smelting furnaces in U.S. built in Maryland; success with smelting anthracite on a commercial scale achieved at Pottsville, Pa., under the supervision of English ironworker Benjamin Perry; this marked a new era in American iron technology. 1840: American Henry Burden (1791–

1871) introduced rotary concentric squeezer for working puddled iron free of slag. 1845: Foundation of Trenton Iron Works; 1851: foundation of the Cambria Iron Works; 1853: foundation of Jones & Laughlin, pioneers in the modern American iron industry. 1847: Pittsburgh-born William Kelly (1811–88) refined molten pig iron with a blast of air in an acid-lined vessel. 1856: The 1st Bessemer patents were taken out in the U.S., but the Commissioner of Patents awarded Kelly priority. 1864, Sept.: The 1st production of steel in the U.S. under the Kelly process done at the Wyandotte Works, Mich. 1865: A. L. Holley (1832–82) built at Troy, N.Y., the 1st Bessemer steel works in the U.S.; 1866: Kelly and Bessemer interests merged in the U.S.; 1867: Abram S. Hewitt (1822–1903) acquired American rights to use and license the Siemens-Martin open-hearth process of making steel. 1869: F. J. Slade built the 1st open-hearth furnace for steelmaking in the U.S. for Cooper, Hewitt & Co. Belgium with its well-located coal resources took the lead in the European iron industry; its per capita production continued high, but it was quickly surpassed in total production. France's coal resources were poorer and not well located, and thus it lagged. 1850: France still smelted more than half its iron ore in charcoal furnaces. 1850's and 1860's: France completed the transformation to coke smelting. 1863–67: Bessemer steel converters were adopted in 6 great French ironworks. 1863: Émile and Pierre Martin (father and son) in Sireuil, France, 1st used successfully the open-hearth process; their use of pig iron and scrap steel to make steel became known as the Siemens-Martin process. Germany was slower than France to develop a modern iron industry. 1847: 1st coke blast furnace constructed in the Ruhr. 1867: August Thyssen (1842–1926) founded his works in Duisburg for the manufacture of hoop iron. 1868: For the 1st time German pig-iron production surpassed that of France. 1849: Lohage and Bremme started a company to make steel by puddling, a major advance in producing cheap steel. 1851: Alfred Krupp (1812–87) demonstrated at the Crystal

Palace exhibition in London a 2-ton flawless block of cast steel; his Essen steelworks achieved international fame. Germany took a clear lead in the European steel industry.

PRODUCTION OF PIG IRON AND STEEL, 1870
(000 metric tons)

	Pig Iron	Steel
U.K.	6,061	287
U.S.	1,682	68
Germany	1,391	170
France (incl. Alsace-Lorraine)	1,178	84
Belgium	565	9

Metalworking industries: Americans took the initiative in the metalworking industries. Locomotives: 1832: Baldwin Locomotive Works established in Philadelphia; 1834: Norris Works built to make locomotives. Guns: 1836: Samuel Colt (1814–62) invented the revolver (1853: he built a new armory south of Hartford, Conn. with 1,400 machine tools); 1847: Eliphalet Remington (1793–1861) put Remington pistol on the market (built at Remington's works at Ilion, N.Y., est. 1816). 1860: Oliver F. Winchester (1810–80) introduced repeating rifle; 1862: Richard J. Gatling (1818–1903) invented the revolving machine gun. Printing: 1846: Richard M. Hoe (1812–86) invented the rotary printing press. Sewing machines: 1846: Elias Howe (1819–67) patented the sewing machine; 1850: Isaac M. Singer (1811–75) invented the 1st practical sewing machine; 1858: Lyman R. Blake (1835–83) patented a machine for sewing the tops of shoes to the bottoms; 1862: Gordon McKay (1821–1903) improved Blake's machine. Washing machines: 1847: 228 U.S. patents issued for washing machines. Machine tools: 1848: Frederick H. Howe (1822–91) designed the 1st milling machine manufactured for sale; it was made by the arms maker Robbins & Lawrence Co., Windsor, Vt.; the milling machine was used in production of small arms, clocks, sewing machines, and other light metal products made by mass production; by 1860 it was well established in American shops; 1850 ff.: Americans began to take world leadership in the machine-tool industry. Grinding machines driven by power, lathes, shapers, planers, drill presses became common in American shops; the use of interchangeable parts (machine-made parts of uniform design) in mass production by mid-19th cent. was known as the "American System"; 1855 ff.: specialized tool builders came into being; 1860: Francis A. Pratt and Amos Whitney founded Pratt & Whitney of Hartford, Conn., to make machine tools for guns and sewing machines. Safety pins: 1849: Walter Hunt invented modern safety pin. Elevators: 1852: Elisha G. Otis (1811–61) invented 1st passenger elevator. Railroad cars: 1864: George M. Pullman (1831–97) made 1st railroad car for sleeping. Typewriters: 1867: Christopher Sholes (1819–90) invented 1st practical typewriter. Vacuum cleaners: 1869: I. W. McGaffey patented a suction-type vacuum cleaner. On the European Continent there was no similar large-scale proliferation of metalworking industries. John Cockerill's Belgian engineering works, est., 1817, stood out in the heavy industries; by 1839, it was making locomotives, engines, and machinery of all descriptions and employed 4,320 persons; Belgian machinery was exported to Holland, Russia, and Germany. In France, metallurgical industries consisted of skilled cutlers (who made fine handmade goods), small shops manufacturing specialized machinery and machine tools, manufacture of textile machinery (esp. in the 1860's; Schlumbergers of Mulhouse, Alsace, was the 1st in France and among the 1st in Europe); engineering firms, such as Schneiders of Le Creusot, would make a range of metallurgical products on order, including steam engines and other industrial machinery. 1830: German metalworking industries were mainly artisan industries; 1830–1870: there developed the engineering shops of Harkort, Borsig, Egells, which made locomotives, marine engines, and lathes; Alfred Krupp's Essen works made grinding machines and other machine tools.

Electrical industry: The electrical industry was in its infancy. The 1st applications were to the telegraph. 1847: The German firm of Siemens & Halske was established, one of the world's earliest and most important electrical firms. 1869: In Chicago, Western Electric Co. formed, as a supplier to Western Union.

Chemical industry: 1837: Proctor & Gamble (soap and candles) was established in Cincinnati, Ohio. 1839: American Charles Goodyear (1800–1860) accidentally discovered the process of vulcanizing rubber. 1840: British traveler John Bowring reported of Germany, "Chemical knowledge in its various branches is further advanced than with us." 1840: 1st soda produced in Germany by the Leblanc method. 1840–70: German soda and sulphuric acid production was less than in France; the German chemical industry had diversity; it turned out the rarest pharmaceuticals, alkaloids, and organic acids. 1843 ff.: German A. W. Hofmann made major strides in industrial uses of coal tar; he stimulated the development of industrial chemistry in Germany and England. 1845: A. P. Sharp (later Merck, Sharp & Dohme) opened apothecary shop in Baltimore, Md., 1846: Swiss chemist C. F. Schönbein (1799–1868) discovered nitrocellulose or "explosive cotton wool"; Italian A. Sobrero (1811–70) discovered nitroglycerin. 1849: Chas. Pfizer & Co., fine chemicals, established. 1855: 1st commercial production of aluminum started at Rouen, France (using process developed by Henri Sainte-Claire Deville); sulphuric acid was extracted from zinc ores in Germany; German F. Gaedcke obtained cocaine from coca leaves. 1863: Belgian Ernest Solvay (1838–1922) began to operate process for production of soda. 1865: French chemist Paul Schutzenberger (1829–97) invented "celanese," acetate rayon. 1866: the Swede Alfred Nobel (1833–96) invented dynamite; in U.S., Duffield, Parke & Co. (later Parke, Davis) established. 1869: Celluloid, the 1st successful pyroxylin plastic, manufactured in the U.S. by J. W. & I. S. Hyatt, Albany (patented 1868).

Other industries and innovations: 1851: American Gail Borden (1801–74) began commercial production of condensed milk. 1855: Bunsen burner invented in Germany. 1859 ff.: Kerosene began to be used to light residences and offices in the U.S. and Europe.

% DISTRIBUTION OF WORLD'S
MANUFACTURING PRODUCTION, 1870

U.K.	31.8	Russia	3.7
U.S.	23.3	Belgium	2.9
Germany	13.2	Italy	2.4
France	10.3	Others	12.4

TRANSPORTATION. Roads: In the U.S. and Europe roads were improved. 1845–70: Great age of Prussian roadbuilding.

Canals: 1830: 1,277 miles of canals in the U.S.; 1840: 3,326 miles of canals; 1859: 3,698 miles of canals, the end of the "canal era"; by 1850 there was more abandoned canal mileage in the U.S. than there were new additions. 1830: 1,260 miles of canals in France. 1835–48: 1,200 miles of major canals newly cut in France, linking the Rhine to the Rhone, from the Marne to the Rhine, and from the Aisne (near Berry-au-Bac) to the Marne above Épernay. 1848: End of 1st canal era in France. 1860: Imperial Plan in France: canals and canalized rivers were improved and modernized. 1869: 2,736 miles of canals were open in France. By 1870 most of the German river basins were linked by canal. Other inland waterways were improved in the U.S. and Europe. Steamboat travel became the norm. American entrepreneur Cornelius Vanderbilt (1794–1877) made his fortune out of steamboats.

Railroads: In the U.S. railroads rapidly replaced canals as the typical means of travel. U.S. railroad mileage: 1830, 23; 1840, 2,818; 1850, 9,021; 1860, 30,636; 1870, 52,922. 1869: 1st transcontinental railroad completed in the U.S. America led the world in the construction of railroads. The railroad system in the U.S. was privately owned, but was aided by land grants and subsidies from the government. 1832: 1st steampowered railroad started operations on the European Continent: the French railway line, St.-Étienne to Lyons. 1835: 1st Belgian railway, Brussels to Malines, opened; 1st German railroad from Nuremburg to Fürth covered 5 miles. 1839: 1st Dutch railway, Haarlem-Amsterdam. The 1st French railway was built by private capital; the French state aided private cos.; 1842: the French national railroad program was drafted; 1857: French railroads for the 1st time carried more traffic than French waterways; by 1859, 6 great cos. controlled the French railroad system; the cos.' profits on part of the system were guaranteed by the state; 1860–70: decade of most intensive railroad building in France. 1870: The French railway system was basically complete. The 1st Belgian railroad was state-built, as was the basic system; private cos. were also allowed to construct railroads in Belgium. Railroad expansion in Germany accelerated; in Prussia, private cos., aided by the government, took the initiative (1844, 500 miles in operation; 1860, 3,500 miles in operation); in western and southern Germany, railroads were state-owned from the start. 1840, 92% of German railroads were owned by private cos.; by 1870, 57% were in private hands. 1850–70: The key railroad connections were completed in Western Europe. 1870: Railroad mileage (thousands of miles): U.S., 52.9; Germany, 12.2; France, 10.8; Belgium, 1.9. Railroads in the U.S., Belgium, France, and Germany provided a basis for other industries to develop. Railroads opened new mining regions. Railroads stimulated the iron and then the steel industries, and the metallurgical and timber industries. They encouraged construction. Because they were capital-intensive, they served to attract capital. Railroads, inasmuch as they required new products, spurred innovation. In the U.S. railroads provided a means of extending settlement. Railroads in Germany connected navigable rivers, brought together the German states, linked Germany with Poland and Russia, and gave Germany the opportunity to develop its trade in Central Europe and the Balkans. In every nation, railroads created national unity and a national market, gave industries the possibilities of economies of scale, and provided opportunities for industries to obtain cheaper raw materials. Good transportation links opened the way for more specialization, better utilization of resources, and thus cost advantage; similarly, faster transportation lowered costs and offered economies. 1869: 1st use of refrigeration in railway transit in the U.S., which would in time revolutionize railroad haulage.

Transoceanic travel: Despite the pioneering *Savannah,* Americans were slow to adopt the steamship for ocean transit, clinging to the sailing ship. 1840's: The fastest clipper ships crossed the Atlantic eastbound in about 14 days—as did contemporary steamships. 1844: The *Midas,* owned by Boston merchant R. B. Forbes, left Boston for Hong Kong, arriving 14 May, 1845; the *Midas* was the 1st American steamship in Chinese waters (though she traveled mainly under sail) . 1844 ff.: use of the steamship spread; 1846: Ocean Steam Navigation Co. established in U.S. as a subsidized steamship line, N.Y.-Bremen. (It went out of business in 1857 when its mail contract ran out.) 1847: Collins Line established in U.S. with a mail contract to Liverpool (1858: suspended operations) . Other U.S.-government-subsidized steamship lines developed. European steamship lines also started. 1837: Messageries Maritimes, a French line, introduced a steamer service between Marseilles and Alexandria; 1838: an Austrian steamship line, Lloyd, began a Mediterranean service. 1840: The French government offered to subsidize the establishment of a steamship line between Le Havre and New York and to establish government-owned and -operated lines to the Caribbean and South America. 1847: The Hamburg-Amerika Line founded (1856: adopted its 1st screw-propelled steamer) . 1851: The French Messageries Impériales began operations in the Mediterranean and extended services into the Indian Ocean, to the Far East, and to the South Atlantic. 1861: The Compagnie Transatlantique, founded by the Péreire brothers, connected France and Mexico. 1867: North German Lloyd lines began a weekly service to New York.

COMMUNICATIONS. 1836: Samuel F. B. Morse (1791–1872) invented a practical electric telegraph. By 1846–47, New York was connected to Albany, Boston, Buffalo, Cleveland, Detroit, and Chicago by telegraph. 1861: Telegraph connections in the U.S. made with the West Coast. 1840's: Telegraph lines spread throughout Europe. 1850's: Submarine cables introduced. 1866: Completion of the transatlantic cable.

FINANCE. Capital, although still scarce, became more plentiful in the U.S. as business growth occurred. Foreign capital (mainly British) was invested in the U.S. in the 1830's, and in the 1850's, the late 1860's, and the 1870's. On the European Continent, capital was locally generated and also came from Britain. Financial intermediaries developed. 1833: U.S. federal funds were deposited in state banks, "pet banks." 1834–37: Growth in number of state banks in the U.S. from 506 to 788; by 1860, 1,562 state banks. 1864, 3 June: National Banking Act passed in the U.S., designed to deal with both monetary chaos and fiscal needs; established a national banking system; national banks could issue a uniform paper currency and national bank notes. 1865: Congress placed a 10% per annum prohibitive tax on the notes of state banks, thus effectively giving sole privilege of bank note issue to the national banks; the number of national banks increased, while the number of state banks decreased. Investment banking by J. P. Morgan, A. Belmont (representing the Rothschilds) , and S. G. Ward (representing Baring Brothers) began to make headway in the U.S. On the European Continent modern banking facilities developed. 1835: Banque de Belgique and Banque Liègeoise founded in Belgium; 1841: Bank of Flanders established. These banks along with the Société Générale provided Belgium with banking facilities to aid her industrialization. 1850: The Belgian Parliament reformed the banking system, establishing a central bank, the Banque Nationale, which received a monopoly of note issue. 1830's: The Bank of France, under sound and successful management, expanded steadily; 1848: Bank of France awarded a monopoly of note issue. 1848: Revolution in France destroyed existing credit institutions; the government helped found Comptoir National d'Escompte (collapsed 1889) . 1852: The Crédit Foncier, the famous mortgage bank, founded. 1852: Émile and Isaac Péreire established Crédit Mobilier in Paris for industrial finance (failed 1867) ; while it lasted, Crédit Mobilier financed railroad cos. as well as dock and gas cos. 1855 ff.: the Paris market played a key role in financing European railroads; of importance besides the Péreires, were the Paris Rothschilds. 1859: France's 1st real deposit and loan bank founded, the Crédit Industriel et Commerciel; 1863: Crédit Lyonnais established; 1864: Société Générale pour Favoriser de Développement du Commerce et d'Industrie en France started operations. 1850's and 1860's: Foundation of new era in French banking; industrial banks were important in stimulating growth. 1830 ff.: Frankfurt played an important role in European finance because of the Rothschilds. 1846: Prussian Bank took the place of the previous State Bank, which marked the start of modern banking in Prussia. 1848–56: foundation of important joint-stock banks in Germany: Bankverein of A. Schaaffhausen in Cologne, 1848; the Diskontogesellschaft, 1851; the Bank für Handel und Industrie in Darmstadt, 1853; and the Berliner Handelsgesellschaft, 1856. 1870: Deutsche Bank founded. 1855: The Austrian Kreditanstalt für Handel und Gewerbe was established; it became the largest commercial bank in Austria.

FOREIGN TRADE. After Great Britain, France and the U.S. followed in volume of foreign trade. 1870: French foreign trade (exports plus imports) totaled $1,094 million; U.S. foreign trade, $867.6 million. 1832–60: U.S. tariffs were scaled down or shifted from specific duties to ad valorem duties. 1861: High Morrill tariff passed. 1861–69: U.S. duties increased to an average rate of 47%. 1870: Minor reduction in U.S. tariff. In France, high tariffs remained until c. 1860, when France began to lower tariffs. 1860: France signed commercial treaty with Britain; 1861: trade agreements were made between France and Belgium, Italy, and Switzerland; 1862: trade agreement between France and Prussia, and, 1866, by extension, France and the Zollverein. In Germany, 1 Jan., 1834, Zollverein tariff established, forming into a customs union ⅔ of the German states; other states subsequently joined. 1834–48: The Zollverein tariffs on manufactured goods rose. 1841: Friedrich List's (1789–1846) doctrine of protecting infant industries appeared in Part 1 of his National System of Political Economy; the doctrine had a keen impact on German policy. 1860's: Temporarily, there was a liberalized trade policy. 1863 and 1865: Trade agreements were made between Prussia and Belgium; 1865: trade agreements were made between Prussia and Britain and Prussia and Italy. In short, in the 1860's, when the U.S. was moving toward a higher tariff, France and Germany were, temporarily, moving in the other direction.

FOREIGN INVESTMENT. The U.S. and France were net recipients of foreign investment, while the Dutch were important international investors.

BUSINESS ORGANIZATION. In the U.S. the corporate form came to be used more frequently (the U.S. led the world in the use of this form) ; it was still mainly used for banking, insurance, and public utilities. 1856: Western Union Telegraph Co. became America's 1st giant corporation. In the U.S. most corporations continued to be incorporated by special charter granted by the states, although increasingly states were adopting general incorporation laws. Belgium had taken the leadership on the European Continent in using the joint-stock co. form (société anonyme). 1830's and 1840's: In France the joint-stock co. form was rare and used mainly for banking, insurance, and public utilities. There was far wider use of the société en commandite sur action form. 1850's: The French put such forms under stricter government control. Although the form remained important, the société anonyme form began to be used more frequently. 1863: France created the société à responsabilité limitée, a true limited-liability company. 1867: The need to get individual authorization for every société anonyme was eliminated. 1838: Prussia adopted a railway co. law, based on the French Commercial Code. 1843: Prussia adopted a general law for joint-stock cos. Yet by the 1860's only in

Hamburg and Bremen could a co. come into existence without a special government authorization. The joint-stock co. form was still rare in Germany.

GOVERNMENT POLICY. In the U.S. under Andrew Jackson (President, 1829–1837), the federal government stayed out of business. The Maysville Road veto, the veto of the charter of the National Bank, and the lowering of the tariff were reflections of a laissez-faire philosophy. State and municipal governments, however, contributed to building transportation facilities. 1840's: The U.S. federal government began to subsidize steamship lines. 1850's: the U.S. government started aid for railroad construction. 1861 ff.: Steady rise in U.S. tariff. In France under the July Monarchy and 2nd Empire the government assisted transportation ventures. German industrialization was dependent on political considerations. The German state governments invested directly in railroads. The Prussian state government operated ironworks and leadworks and coal mines. German states brought in technicians to aid development. 1834: The formation of the German *Zollverein*, 1834, and the North German Confederation, 1867, directly aided economic growth by creating a national market. 1834–67: Most customs duties on imports of machinery were used by the *Zollverein* to promote manufacturing—textile mills, paper mills, and sugar-beet plants. German polytechnic schools and universities were state-supported; they provided technical and scientific training which proved a special aid to the chemical and electrical industries.

OTHER FACTORS. From 1839 to 1879 the U.S. GNP is estimated to have grown at 4.3% per year. In France, the Industrial Revolution was gradually effected in an environment of political turmoil. Germany had to await complete unification before its Industrial Revolution could flower. Belgium, once it achieved political independence in 1830, led in the Industrial Revolution taking place on the European Continent.

Economic Change in the Less Developed World

AGRICULTURE AND ANIMAL HUSBANDRY. In most of the nonindustrial world agricultural conditions prevailing between 1760 and 1830 persisted without change. Yet some changes did occur.

Scientific agriculture: 1830's and 1840's: In Egypt land under cultivation increased, owing to large-scale irrigation works. 1830–70: There was increasing application of scientific techniques to Japanese agriculture. 1830: British engineers in India began to reconstruct the Indian canal system (the Western Jumna, Eastern, and Cauvery canals) to provide irrigation. 1836: Surveys were made for the great Ganges Canal (opened 1854); 1846: Godaveri Canal planned, for irrigation; 1850–70: canal making spread over India, penetrating deserts and wasteland to bring water to land to extend cultivation. Australian sheep raising expanded dramatically, using modern methods. When plantation agriculture was introduced by Westerners into the tropics, the techniques were western in origin.

New crops and livestock: Tea: 1834: Lord William Bentinck sent a committee to China to obtain tea seeds and Chinese labor and to introduce the crop in northern India. 1835: Government tea plantations were started in Assam on these Chinese foundations; Assam, however, had a native tea plant; the British tried to market it and were successful. 1850's: cultivation of the native tea plant progressed rapidly in Assam, Bengal, southern India, and Ceylon; the capital promoting the expansion of tea was European. Jute: 1838: The regular export of raw jute from India to Dundee began. Coffee: 1830's: Systematic cultivation of coffee as a plantation industry began in India; it flourished up to 1862, when the deadly borer beetle and leaf blight appeared; 1885: almost complete end to coffee cultivation. 1830's: Crown land sold to planters in Ceylon; 1869: 176,000 acres under coffee; fungus attacked the coffee plant in Ceylon and after 1876 the coffee plantings were ruined. In Java large-scale coffee cultivation developed, as also in Brazil and Colombia; in Brazil coffee was plantation agriculture; in Colombia it was peasant agriculture. In Brazil, as sugar, tobacco, and cotton became less profitable, coffee assumed key importance in the national economy. Sugar-cane cultivation continued in the West Indies and Brazil. In Hawaii, under the impact of Americans, sugar-cane cultivation spread. In Java sugar-cane cultivation, although not new to this period, was greatly enlarged; sugar was grown on the sawah land used for rice cultivation. 1830 ff.: In the Ukraine sugar-beet cultivation began. Quinine: 1865: cinchona (quinine) plantations started in Java. Palm oil and peanut production in West Africa greatly expanded, stimulated by the growth of the European soap industry. Sheep: 1844: 1st sheep station in New Zealand started in the Wairarapa, with sheep imported from Australia.

Landholding: In eastern Europe the feudal manorial system began to break down. By 1850 in Livonia, Hungary, and Rumania large estates were employing wage labor. 1861: End to serfdom in Russia; land reform established a landowning peasantry. In Japan land passed into the hands of the merchants; by 1853, Japanese merchants controlled more than 30% of the cultivated land in that country, acting as rent receivers; among the large landowners were the Konoike and Mitsui commercial houses; there emerged in Japan a wage labor force as a result of peasants losing their land; agriculture became more efficient; intensive cultivation by peasant families proved highly productive in Japan. In India the British land reforms had not made agriculture more productive, since they left virtually unchanged the basic process of production. In China, with no primogeniture, landholdings became more fragmented. There is no indication that agriculture became more efficient; in fact, the op-

posite seems possible. After acquiring Algeria (beginning 1830) the French decided to treat land in that country as private property. A land law, 1863, led to the breaking up of village holdings and the acquisition of about 20% of the best land by European settlers. New European settlement in Canada, Australia, New Zealand, and Latin America meant new landholdings. In Canada settlement extended into more of the country. Land laws in Australia tried to encourage cultivation, but despite the land laws wool remained the staple; farming did not take priority over grazing. 1829: Edward Gibbon Wakefield (1796–1862) in England advocated systematic immigration to Australia and favored land sales at a "sufficient price" within Australia; 1831: land grants were abolished in Australia; all land was sold; 1835: South Australian Co. formed for colonization; 1861: Crown Lands Alienation Act in New South Wales allowed anyone to select 40 to 320 acres of crown land (raised to 640 acres maximum in 1875) and pay £1 an acre (5s. down); similar land acts made available land to settlers in Victoria. 1837 ff.: Traders, speculators, and missionaries began to buy land in New Zealand; 1839: the New Zealand Co. started to sell land in that country at £1 per acre to colonists and investors. Latin America: 1840–60: New public lands were settled in Colombia, and the government distributed them to farmers in medium-sized plots, a policy in sharp contrast to that of the Mexican, Chilean, and Argentine governments, which made huge land grants, continuing the prerevolutionary practice of large landholdings.

Commercialization: Throughout the less developed world, agriculture became more commercial, as transportation facilities made it possible to market crops, as European traders and investors created new means of bringing produce to market, and as the volume of world trade increased. 1830: Johannes van den Bosch, gov. gen. of the Netherlands East Indies, introduced a forced-delivery plan, known as the "culture system"; each peasant, instead of paying a land tax, had to cultivate government-owned export crops on

⅕ of his fields or, alternatively, to work 66 days a year on government-owned estates or other projects; the system was most important in Java, but was also present elsewhere in the Dutch East Indies; the new system, with commercialization as its goal, tested out a wide variety of crops (indigo, sugar, coffee, tea, tobacco, pepper, cinchona, cinnamon, cotton, silk, cochineal) ; coffee and sugar were at first the most successful.

Increase in cultivated land area: With scientific agriculture in some countries, with new crops in others, with changes in the structure of landholdings, with new settlement, and with commercialization, cultivation of lands in the less developed areas was extended. Also encouraging the spread of cultivation was the extension of the railroads. Factors retarding the development of agriculture in the less developed world were (1) use of traditional methods; (2) general absence of mechanization; (3) lack of capital to be applied to agriculture; (4) absence of extensive transportation facilities; (5) absence of a developed marketing structure to encourage surpluses; (6) absence of information (as late as the 1850's and 1860's, there was a widespread belief that a large portion of what is now the Canadian Northwest was unfit for agriculture on account of the climate and the soil) ; (7) absence in some cases of agricultural labor (in Australia and in much of Africa) ; and (8) giant landholdings in much of Latin America (that were not efficiently farmed) and small landholdings in much of Asia (that were too small for efficient farming) .

RAW MATERIALS. The economic development of 2 less developed nations was sharply spurred by the finding of precious minerals: 1851: gold was discovered in Australia (in New South Wales and Victoria) ; 1867: diamonds were discovered in South Africa. Both encouraged immigration to the countries and brought wealth in their train. So great a spur was the discovery of gold in Australia that by 1861 the estimated gross national income per capita was $250; the average for Britain (excluding Ireland) in 1861 was

about $150: Australia had become relatively rich. 1858: Discovery of gold in New Zealand caused a smaller "gold rush." 1830: An English co., the São João d'El Rei Mining Co., leased a mining property in Brazil; later it worked the Morro Velho mine; from 1837 to 1865 its production of gold alone was valued at $18,180,133. The mining of industrial minerals in the less developed nations proved less dramatic. Coal production was concentrated in the important industrial and industrializing nations. Compared with them in 1870, Russia's output of .69 million metric tons, Spain's .66 million metric tons, and India's .61 million metric tons were humble. In Canada, in the 1850's, coal mines in Cape Breton, Maritime Provinces, opened; Cape Breton coal replaced coal imports from England. 1858: The coal fields at Arroio dos Ratos in Brazil began to be worked. Japan had coal adequate to its early needs, and by 1869 the Hizen domain had a modern coal mine in operation, started with British capital and technical assistance. Iron production was concentrated in the important industrial and industrializing countries, although Spain, Algeria, and Cuba had iron-ore resources and were exporters. Russia was known to have good iron resources, but these were not well situated; Russian iron-ore production rose slowly. The Brazilian iron mines of Ipanema were being worked on a small scale; the iron deposits in Minas Gerais were known. Iron mining was done in Canada in Ontario and in New Brunswick. The less developed countries excelled in other metals. Copper: 1850: Chile took the world's leadership in copper production. Tin: While in 1870 Great Britain was the world's largest tin producer, less developed countries followed. In the Malay Peninsula, British and Chinese capital and entrepreneurs developed the tin mines. In the Dutch East Indies the islands of Banka and Billiton were most important as sources of tin. On Banka the mines were controlled by the Dutch government, while on Billiton (where tin was found in 1851) the mines were privately owned. 1849: Tin was discovered in Australia.

Tin Production, 1870
(000 long tons)

U.K.	10.2
Malaya (incl. small output from Thailand)	9.0
Netherlands East Indies	7.3
China	.5
Australia	.2
Bolivia	.1

In the new oil industry, where the U.S. took the leadership, by 1870 Russian production was .21 million barrels; Rumania, in 3rd place, had an output of .08 million barrels. 1859: Oil discovered in Canada, but production was negligible.

LABOR. In much of the less developed world slavery still remained, but was declining in importance. 1833, 23 Aug.: Britain abolished slavery in the British colonies. 1851: New Granada (later Colombia) abolished slavery. 1854: Ecuador and Venezuela ended slavery. 1861: End to serfdom in Russia. Education in the less developed world was generally on a low level, although Japan's urban population was literate; in Japan in the 1860's new schools, teaching western science, opened. China had a scholar aristocracy with the mass of the people uneducated. Missionaries from the western nations created schools and spread education. In the Gold Coast, for example, the Basel Mission trained craftsmen, carpenters, blacksmiths, and mechanics; the Gold Coast would become a recruiting ground for nearby African countries that wanted skilled labor. Missionaries transmitted western ideas and values. Likewise, in areas of new settlement educational standards of the West began to be communicated.

ENERGY. Human and animal power, wind, and water still provided the main sources of energy in the nonindustrial world. Steam had minor impact in some factories and in transportation.

INDUSTRIES. The conditions of 1760–1830 remained in most of the less developed countries. Modern machinery and methods spread slowly. Nowhere was the industrial sector substantial and yet it existed in embryo. In Russia a modern cotton textile industry slowly began to emerge after 1830, primarily in the provinces of Moscow and Vladimir. In 1850 there were 1,300 power looms in the Russian cotton textile industry, and in 1860, 10,000 power looms, but in 1859 Russia had 86,000 handlooms, producing ⅘ of Russian cotton cloth. The Russian wool industry also began to mechanize, but even more casually. 1840: Sugar-beet refineries in the Ukraine began to use steam power; 1861: 85% of Russian sugar production was from refineries using modern machinery. The Russian iron industry grew slowly. Pig-iron production: 1830, 182,953 metric tons; 1870, 359,531 metric tons. By 1857 locomotives were being made in St. Petersburg. In Canada the lumber industry of earlier years expanded; shipbuilding existed based on the wood resources. 1830: The Canadian iron industry was inefficient and on a small scale: stoves, axes, agricultural implements were made in Canada. 1860: 1st Canadian rolling mill opened at Toronto. 1866: Iron and nail works were one of the key industries in Montreal. By 1870 iron products to supply the railroads were produced in Canada and other iron products were made in quantity, but many iron manufactures continued to be imported. Tanneries, whisky distilleries, and breweries sprang up in Canada, as did paper factories and glass manufactories. Woolen and cotton mills also made rough fabrics; their numbers grew. Latin America: 1830: Mexico's modern textile industry started using power-driven machinery. 1850's: Brazil started a modern textile industry; c. 1863: a beef-extract plant was built in Uruguay by the Liebig Meat Extract Co. of London—probably the 1st modern factory in that country; yet throughout Latin America there was little modern industry. 1835: Turkey set up a fez-cap factory (caps of red wool), founded by Sultan Mahmud; other government-sponsored manufacturing enterprises in Turkey included cloth, paper, and glass factories; a foundry and forge were established in Constantinople, which used English engineers, mechanics, materials, and machines. 1838: By an Anglo-Turkish Convention foreign traders were allowed to buy and sell anywhere within the Ottoman Empire, including Egypt;

competition from foreign goods was too much for Egypt's infant industry, which mostly collapsed. Throughout the Ottoman Empire, handicraft manufacturing slumped because of competition from cheap British-manufactured goods. The pressure of imports retarded industrialization in this case. India: 1830's: Rapid decline of native cotton textile industries and crafts with influx of British products. Imports stimulated industrialization. 1854: Parsi merchant Cowasjee Nanabhoy Davar (b. 1815) established the Bombay Spinning and Weaving Mill, marking the start of the modern steam-powered cotton textile industry in India; the capital was Indian and British; the machinery, technicians, and management were all British. 1855: Manufacture of jute on a large scale started at Rishra, near Serampore, India; the machinery, technicians, and management were British; here the stimulus was not imports but potential export demand. 1859: 1st power loom used in jute industry at Barnagore, near Calcutta. Japan: Rural industries manufacturing cotton and silk proliferated. 1854 ff.: After the opening of Japan to the West, the shogun started ironworks and other industrial plants along western lines; both the central government and the daimyo (provincial lords) established arms manufactories along western lines. Foreign advisers were brought in to offer their skills. 1859 ff.: Imports of cheap British machine-made cotton textiles began to disrupt the existing Japanese cotton textile industry. 1863: Prince H. Shimazu at Kagoshima, with the aid of an English engineer, started Japan's 1st cotton spinning by machinery. 1868: After the Meiji Restoration, Japan became fully committed to industrialization. 1870: The Japanese government established factories for silk reeling, following the French and Italian model. Early modern industry in China was in armaments; 1855: Tseng Kuo-fan (1811–72) established small arsenals in Kiangsi; others followed.

TRANSPORTATION. Everywhere in the less developed world transportation was inadequate. Yet it was primarily changes in transportation that created basic conditions for economic growth in much of that world. Commercialization of agriculture depended on transportation; raw material utilization rested on transportation; urbanization and transportation went hand and hand. Innovations in transport, more than in industry, brought steam power to most of the less developed world. Industry would in some cases be stimulated later by the growth of transportation links (in Canada, for instance), but it was also hampered, for cheap machine-made British goods, carried by new means of transport, often put artisan industries out of business. The development of transportation facilities brought foreign capital to less developed nations. Transportation was the basis for the expansion of foreign trade. In these years, only preliminary steps were taken in the transportation revolution.

Roads: Within most less developed countries, roads were inadequate, yet some changes took place. 1834 ff.: Substantial improvements were made on the road from Cairo to Suez, which connected the Red Sea to the Nile. Under Lord Dalhousie, gov. gen. of India, 1848–54, trunk roads for wheeled traffic began to be built in India; it was found that 1st-class roads were almost as expensive to build as railroads, and while the latter brought returns to the builder, the former did not. 1830: There was only a single trunk road into the interior of Java; by 1847, owing to the labor due the Dutch under the "culture system," Java had fine roads and bridges. In Australia, under the influence of Thomas Mitchell and Britisher David Lennox, a student of Thomas Telford, road building made progress; travelers used vehicles that often managed in part without roads. One such was the "bush coach," made and driven by Cobb & Co.; by 1870 Cobb & Co. harnessed 6,000 horses per day and their coaches went 28,000 miles a week.

Inland waterways: Rivers continued to provide important transportation routes in less developed countries. 1852: The Yellow River (a main transportation route in China) broke loose with great damage. Rivers were more important than canals in the less developed countries. "The Age of the Canal"—so significant in the history of transportation in Great Britain, the U.S., France, and on the Continent—was generally bypassed by less developed nations. Canada offered a major exception to this; 1830–40: canal building flourished in Canada. In India canals built for irrigation were used on occasion for navigation; the Godaveri Canal was considered an excellent means of transport; but the irrigation canals, except in the deltas of the rivers, were in general not successful for commerce. The Grand Canal in China continued as an important transport route, but it was hardly a "modern" canal; moreover, the accumulation of silt in the canal made it less suitable for grain transport. Steam slowly made an impact. 1830's: Steamers in Canada regularly plied the rivers. 1839, 1842: 4 British steamers, belonging to the East India Co., sailed up and down the Tigris, the Euphrates, and the Karun, surveying the rivers and carrying passengers and mail; 1860: Britishers obtained rights of navigation and rights for a mail service between Baghdad and Basrah; 1861: the Euphrates and Tigris Steam Navigation Co., Ltd. (British-owned), was incorporated to start a steamship service on both rivers. 1830's, 1840's and 1850's: Latin American countries gave concessions for steam navigation of various rivers; 1837: Brazil introduced regular steamship services along the Atlantic coast and on the Amazon; navigation was restricted to Brazilian ships. 1849: Cornelius Vanderbilt (1794–1877), American steamboat tycoon, got a concession from the Nicaraguan government to provide transit across Nicaragua by canal or carriage road and steamboat; he chose the latter means. 1867: The Amazon was opened to navigation by steamers of all nations. 1841–42: Mohammed Ali authorized the Peninsular & Oriental Co. to run 2 steamships on the Nile as well as steam tugs on the Mahmudia Canal. 1853: Francis Cadell piloted a river steamer (built in Sydney, Australia) up the Murray River; travel by steamer became common in Australia. 1862:

Shanghai Steam Navigation Co. was founded in Shanghai by American trading firm, Russell & Co., a joint venture with Chinese and American capital; it plied the Yangtze River and was important on routes along the China coast. 1866: Steamer service started in Japan between Yokohama and Nagasaki. By the late 1860's, local steam navigation companies, mainly British, were operating water routes to and into every country and major island in East Asia from Burma to Japan. By 1868 the Japanese owned 138 western-type steamships, either imported or built in Japan. Slowly, the steamboat became more in evidence on rivers and lakes around the world, yet it was by no means the typical means of water transport in less developed nations.

Railways: 1830's: Canada and Russia started railroad construction. 1836: St. Johns, Quebec, had 1st Canadian railroad, with horse traction, replaced by steam locomotion in 1837. 1836: 1st railroad completed in Russia, St. Petersburg to Tsarkoe-Selo, but only after Russia's defeat in the Crimean War did railroad construction accelerate. 1837: 1st Cuban railroad built. 1840's: Railroad construction began in Asia. 1845: British cos. were established in India to build railroad lines from Calcutta to Raniganj (coal fields) and from Bombay to the cotton-growing districts (1853: 1st 20 miles of the Great Peninsula Line opened, Bombay to Thana; 1854: 1st part of the East Indian Railroad, Calcutta to Raniganj, opened). 1848: 1st railroad in Spain. 1848–55: Construction of Panama Railroad, by U.S. capital, connecting the Atlantic and the Pacific (opened for passenger traffic, 1851); 1849–52: construction in Chile of 1st railroad from coal-mining town of Copiapo to coast (opened 1851; built by American William Wheelwright and financed by British capital). 1850's: 1st railroads in Africa and Oceania. 1853: 1st railroad in Egypt from Alexandria to Kafr al-Zayyat was completed (1856: extended to Cairo; 1858: Cairo linked by rail to Suez). 1854: 1st railroad in Australia opened, near Melbourne, and 1st railroad in Brazil started

operations (9 mi.) from Rio to Petropolis. 1856–66: European capital built 1st
Turkish railroad, Smyrna to Aydin
(opened 1860). 1857: 1st Argentine railroad opened (6 mi. of track from Buenos
Aires to San José de Flores). 1860: 1st
railroad opened in Cape Colony, South
Africa. 1863: 1st railroad in New Zealand, Christchurch to Ferrymead, started
operations. 1865: Railroad system started
in Ceylon.

RAILROADS IN THE LESS DEVELOPED WORLD,
1870
(000 mi.)

Russia	7.0
India	5.0
Canada	2.5
Latin America	2.4
Africa	1.1
Oceania	1.1
Asia (excl. India and Russia)	0.1

In most of the less developed world (exceptions were Canada, and to a small
extent Russia), all rails and locomotives
for the railroads had to be imported.
Railroad construction, which stimulated
heavy industry in Great Britain, U.S.,
Belgium, France, and Germany, did not
have that effect in most of the less developed world.

Transoceanic travel: Steamship connections between less developed countries
and Europe meant greater foreign trade,
more immigration to areas of new settlement, and the spread of technology, skills,
know-how, and capital. 1833: Canadian-
built steamship, the *Royal William*,
steamed across the Atlantic; she, like
other transoceanic steamers before her,
used sail as well as steam.

FINANCE. Capital in less developed nations was scarce. Modern financial institutions were often absent. Yet they began
to develop; some were indigenous; some
were based on foreign investment. 1860:
State Bank founded in Russia (it was not
a bank of issue; paper currency was
issued by the State Printing Office, on the
basis of an 1843 law); 1864: 1st joint-
stock commercial bank was founded in
Russia—the St. Petersburg Private Com-

mercial Bank. 1841: Savings banks were
legislated for in Russia, but by 1862 only
2 savings banks existed in that country.
In Canada there was a broad development of banking facilities. This was the
case also in Australia. In Latin America,
1851, the 2nd Bank of Brazil was founded
with sole right of issue; 1864: financial
panic in Brazil; while the Bank of Brazil
survived, the right of issue was transferred to the Treasury. In Argentina,
1862–68, under Bartolomé Mitre's government, a national credit bank was founded
and foreign banks were welcomed. Banking in Latin America was in its infancy.
Middle East: 1846: English private banking firms had established themselves in
every Mediterranean port (40 of them)
between Gibraltar to Jerusalem; 1848:
there were 7 British bankers in Alexandria. 1850's: Growth of foreign banking
activities in Egypt. 1855: The Bank of
Egypt was established in Alexandria with
British capital. 1856: The Ottoman Bank
was founded in Constantinople, with
British capital. There were in India several kinds of "European" banks: the
Presidency Banks of Bengal, Bombay, and
Madras, which were to a limited extent
government banks; 1862: the Presidency
Banks were deprived of their privilege of
note issue. In the mid-19th cent. joint-
stock co. banks started under both
European and Indian management; the
rate of failure of both was high. 1850's:
Growth of foreign branch banking activities in India. 1870: Post Office Savings
Bank started. Banking by Indian bankers
charging excessive rates of interest also
continued; it was often difficult to distinguish between the banking, trading,
and moneylending functions of the Indian banker. After the opening of 5
treaty ports in China in 1842, financial
institutions were needed to handle expanding trade; Chinese banks had never
financed foreign commerce; foreign banks
filled the gap. 1845: The British-owned
Oriental Banking Corporation started a
branch in Hong Kong and in 1848 in
Shanghai; this was the 1st foreign bank
in China. 1848–72: A dozen foreign banks
opened branches in Shanghai, among
them 2 key British banks: the Chartered

Bank of India, Australia, and China (chartered in 1853) and the Hong Kong and Shanghai Banking Corporation (est. in Hong Kong in 1864 by British, German, American, Persian, and Chinese merchants; 1865: branch in Shanghai; in time this bank became all British-owned and the largest bank in China). Shanghai became the capital market of China. The foreign banking houses financed Chinese merchants and Chinese banks as well as foreign trade. Japan: While Japan had a history of considerable financial expertise, by the time of the Meiji Restoration the country as yet had no national banking institutions. Locally, however, Japanese merchants, serving as bankers, did channel funds into profitable ventures. Japan had an exceptionally high rate of savings and investment. Japan was by 1870 probably more accustomed to money than any other nation in the less developed world.

FOREIGN TRADE. Commodity exports from underdeveloped nations rose as railroads penetrated the interiors of less developed lands, as steam travel replaced sail, and as the demand for imports increased in the more developed nations, especially Britain. Industrializing nations sought out new markets the world over. World commerce, including the trade of industrializing and less developed nations, rose dramatically.

WORLD TRADE (EXPORTS PLUS IMPORTS)
($ billion)

Year	Value
1830	1.9
1840	2.7
1850	4.0
1860	7.2
1870	10.6

There are no available figures indicating what percentage of this trade involved less developed countries and what percentage was among more developed countries; from qualitative evidence, it seems likely that during 1830–70 a growing volume came to involve the less developed lands. New treaties aided the expansion of trade. Britain made treaties with less developed nations, obtaining trading privileges; other industrializing nations followed Britain's lead, making their own treaties. Such agreements came to be known as the "unequal treaties" (pp. 68–72, 78–80 above). As new areas were opened to trade, commodities from new locales entered into trade and existing commerce expanded. 1830: Exports of nitrates from Chile began (but, 1830–70, copper was Chile's most important export in terms of value); 1830's ff.: wool had become the key item in Australian trade; coffee from Ceylon, Java, and also Brazil took on new significance; opium, carried on British ships from India to China, became important in trade; tea exports from China mounted (there existed a triangular trade involving Britain-India-China); 1838: the regular export of raw jute from India began. 1840 ff.: Egypt became an export-oriented economy with raw cotton the major export; 1846 ff.: after the repeal of the British corn laws grain exports from Canada started to mount. (Forest products were still the most important export from the Canadian colonies.) 1850–60: The value of Australian wool exports doubled (1851: Australia became the world's largest exporter of wool); the export of palm oil from West Africa increased from 30,000 tons, 1851, to over 50,000 tons, 1860; palm oil had become West Africa's major export; the groundnut trade also became important in West Africa's export trade. 1854–55: During the Crimean War Indian jute replaced Russian supplies of flax and hemp in the British market. 1856: Tea became for the 1st time an important item in Indian trade. (China was still the largest supplier of tea for Britain; the British plantations in India and Ceylon were just getting established.) 1857: New Zealand had become a major exporter of wool. 1858 ff.: Raw silk became an important export from Japan. 1860–65: Boom in raw cotton exports from Egypt, India, and Brazil, because of the curtailment of U.S. exports during the American Civil War. 1861: Agricultural exports from Canada for the 1st time exceeded forest exports. 1870: Sugar had become the most important item in the trade from the Dutch East Indies, representing 45% of all exports (coffee represented 43%). For the most part the newer commodities from less developed countries engaged in foreign trade were agricultural. Precious metals in terms of their value were also important in commerce. Industrial minerals were not yet significant in international trade. The expansion of foreign commerce brought less developed nations into closer contact with the industrializing nations. Because in most cases the less developed countries did not provide the banking facilities, the insurance, the shipping, and the marketing of their exports, they did not reap the maximum benefits from this trade.

FOREIGN INVESTMENT. Investment by Europeans in less developed countries included stakes in (1) plantations, (2) railroads, (3) banking, (4) mining, (5) trade, as well as loans to the less developed nations. There were isolated investments in manufacturing.

BUSINESS ORGANIZATION. In most countries the conditions described as applicable during 1760–1830 were still in force. But there also began to develop "dual organizations" in many less developed nations. On the one hand, there was traditional, local handicraft industry, established on a family basis. On the other hand, foreign business organizations operated in these countries. Some of these latter were family firms (trading houses), but many were large-scale concerns creating efficient enclave enterprises. Local and foreign businesses meshed in different fashions. In many areas, foreign business provided capital, management, and machinery as well as marketing, while the local contribution was only labor. In India, the managing-agency system developed. At first managing agents were exclusively British. They promoted new industries, found financing for existing industries, and offered management for companies. In return, they were paid a commission based on production, sale, or profit of the business. Contracts with managing agents assured a commission, even if the firm suffered a loss. The managing agent provided a means of by-passing the traditional caste-structured society, which forbade many

castes in India to engage in industrial activity. In China, before the opening of the treaty ports, all foreign transactions went through the Chinese Hong merchants' monopoly; by 1836 their monopoly had fallen apart. Instead, the comprador system developed; foreign firms employed on contract a comprador to handle the Chinese side of the business (hiring of the Chinese staff and work force, dealing with Chinese merchants, buying and selling). 1831 and 1843: In Japan (before the opening of foreign trade), the shogun abolished by decree all forms of guilds; the effect was so disrupting that in 1851 the government attempted to recreate the guilds; this proved impossible and monopolistic privileges were to be swept away. After the opening of Japan, Japanese business enterprises developed rapidly. Although they used foreign technicians, methods, and machinery, there was no direct domination of Japanese business by foreign capital. In most of the less developed world, entrepreneurship was absent, though there were exceptions. In Canada and Australia, there is evidence of business entrepreneurship. There were some striking examples of entrepreneurship in Latin America. Irineu Evangelista de Souza, Baron of Mauá (1813–89) in Brazil, built roads, canals, railroads, and ports; he invested in shipping; laid telegraph lines; introduced gaslighting in Rio de Janeiro; built textile mills, and owned and operated huge acreages of farm land in Brazil, Uruguay, and Argentina; he organized joint-stock cos. for his ventures, and from 1850–75 (until the financial crash which ruined him) dominated the Brazilian money market. In India, Parsi and Bhatia merchants were key to developing the modern textile industry, because they were not restrained by caste restrictions and taboos. In China, entrepreneurship seemed stifled by governmental bureaucracy, yet the compradores came in time to be transformed into independent entrepreneurs. In Southeast Asia, Chinese immigrants were an important entrepreneurial group. More than anywhere in the East entrepreneurship began to flourish in Japan.

Minomura Rizaemon (1821–77) started as a poor orphan and rose to be general manager of Japan's leading commercial house, Mitsui (founded in the 17th cent. in sake brewing, Mitsui had branched into commerce and banking); Minomura handled Mitsui's relations with the shogunate, and then after the Meiji Restoration undertook banking for the new government. 1860's: Iwasaki Yataro, founder of Mitsubishi, started his career as a leading business entrepreneur. Okura Kihachiro (1837–1928) traded rifles before the Restoration and later went to Tokyo, entering into foreign trade and then into industry. Sumitomo (tracing its origins to the 17th cent.) was another Japanese firm (in copper mining) that later became important.

GOVERNMENT POLICY. The role of government in economic development was still not an important factor in most of the less developed world. That the Ottoman Empire, China, Japan, Siam, and Burma had given up their rights to control their tariffs meant that they had lost a vital instrument for protecting industry and developing fiscal policy; this retarded industrialization. Japan found alternative methods of development and of gaining revenue; the Ottoman Empire, China, Siam, and Burma did not. Throughout the less developed world (with the exception of Japan), governments did not take leadership in industrialization. In Russia the government, frightened by defeat in the Crimean War, was desirous of strengthening the country. Basic reforms were made: 1861: the manor was abolished by imperial decree; serfdom was ended. Yet in the 1860's the Russian government was not committed to industrialization. In Latin America political instability retarded economic growth. In the Ottoman Empire, and also in China, government bureaucracy, inefficiency, and corruption held back development. In India, Great Britain acted to develop the nation as a supplier of raw materials. The British government brought order to much of India, but 40% of the country was left to the personal rule of India's princes.

The British decided not to act in the sphere of religion; thus one of the factors that was retarding economic development in the country continued to operate. The British did bring public-health measures and more education. They arranged for railroads built by private companies to be given land free, a guarantee of 5% interest on the capital, and they were to share with the government any profit over the 5%. The government kept close control over the railroads since it had provided the guarantees. Japan was the only less developed nation where the government took the leadership in industrialization. Even before the Meiji Restoration, 1868, the shogun and the daimyo played an affirmative role; after it, the government acted in an even more positive fashion. The 1867 Confederation of Canada and the 1868 Restoration in Japan provided a base for national unity in each country, aiding economic development.

OTHER FACTORS. Throughout the less developed world inertia, tradition, custom, and existing institutions retarded growth. With the exception of the newly settled countries and of Japan, and with some other minor exceptions, change was regarded with suspicion and distrust. In Latin America, preoccupation with political problems left little time for economic planning or forethought. In Africa most of traditional society remained little altered. Wars, rebellions, and political instability throughout much of the less developed world held back development. 1848–65: The Taiping Rebellion in China impeded industrialization. Practically everywhere in the less developed world, the extended family played an important role in retarding change; for the successful, saving was often impossible because of the nature of the family commitment. Yet the diffusion of the technology, ideas, and institutions of the industrializing countries was taking place. In Australia and Canada all 3 took hold. Japan by the 1850's, if not earlier, showed a propensity to accept innovation. Where the social structure of countries tended to be rigid, the impact of industrializing nations was less. In Australia and

Canada, the newness of the nations made for receptivity. In Japan, while status depended on birth, there was an acceptance of a potential in individuals; personal achievement was recognized; the divisions between samurai and commoner were becoming less sharp as samurai became entrepreneurs or as they were linked by marriage to merchant families.

This flexibility in social structure made Japan more adaptable to ideas from the West. The size of nations affected the receptivity to change. Where nations were large, where there was no political unity or interdependence, where isolation prevailed, the degree of industrialization was slight.

1870–1919

The Drive Toward Maturity—U.S., Britain, and Western Europe

During the years from 1870 to the end of World War I, certain countries—the U.S., Britain, France, Germany, and some other parts of Western Europe—achieved the status of "mature industrial societies."

AGRICULTURE. The percentage of gainfully occupied labor participating in agriculture, forestry, and fishing showed a marked decline in every industrial nation. In the U.S., although agriculture became relatively less important, there was significant expansion in agricultural output.

% Gainfully Occupied Labor Force
in Agriculutre

	U.K.	Germany	U.S.	France
1870–79	15	47	52	53
1880–89	12	42	50	48
1890–99	10	36	42	49
1900–09	9	34	37	42
1910–19	8	n.a.	31	n.a.

Note: Data represent a year or an average of the available years within the time period. N.a. = not available.

U.S. Farming, 1870–1920

	Indexes of Output (1947–49 = 100)	Improved Land (000 acres)
1870	23	188,922
1880	37	284,771
1890	43	357,617
1900	56	414,451
1910	61	478,452
1920	70	505,023

1870–96: American agricultural expansion took place despite the drop in farm prices. 1896–1914: The price index moved upward, and then in 1914–20 prices soared; American agricultural output continued to grow.

Farm Products, U.S. Wholesale
Price Index
1910–14 = 100

1870	112
1880	80
1890	71
1896	56
1910	100
1920	211

America was an exporter not an importer of food products. British agriculture followed a different course. As transportation facilities increased, cheap American and later Canadian, Argentine, Australian, Russian, and Rumanian grain began to enter Britain in quantity. No tariff barred the imports. 1876: British agriculture began to suffer; it was not competitive. 1879: A great depression began in British agriculture. 1875–1908: British wheat acreage fell by ½ as imports substituted for British wheat; imports of animal foodstuffs also rose; Denmark, the Netherlands, and New Zealand provided bacon, eggs, cheese, and ham for the British consumer. With the coming of refrigeration, beef from the U.S., and then Argentine beef and New Zealand lamb became competitive in Britain.

DECENNIAL IMPORT AVERAGES, GREAT BRITAIN
($ million at fixed prices)

	Grain	Animal Foodstuffs
1870's	170.5	123.0
1880's	210.5	185.5
1890's	290.0	316.5
1900's	310.0	464.0

By the last 2 decades of the 19th cent. British agriculture had fallen to a relatively low level of significance; its decline continued. Britain imported more food than it raised. 1914: Great Britain produced only 20% of the wheat and cheese it consumed, 25% of the butter and oleomargarine, and 58% of the meat. 1914–18: The consequences of importing so much from abroad were serious during the war, and there arose widespread sentiment in England for the rehabilitation of agriculture—a policy not followed. A similar crisis threatened other countries in Western Europe. 1873–96: France was affected by the great agricultural depression; agricultural output (measured at constant prices) declined. 1881: France began to restrict the imports of foodstuffs. 1896 ff.: Agricultural expansion resumed, with the recovery due partly to the upturn in prices but mainly to the impact of the

Méline protectionist tariff of 1892; thereafter, French tariffs were further raised. France, as a result, continued to be self-sufficient in bread.

GROSS FRENCH AGRICULTURAL PRODUCT
AT CONSTANT (1905–13) MARKET PRICES
(million 1905–13 francs)

	Gross Product	Geometrical Average of Annual Rate of Growth
1865–74	8,713	0.59
1875–84	8,356	−0.42
1885–94	8,326	−0.04
1895–1900	9,256	1.06
1905–14	10,265	1.04

1870–90: With improvement in sea transportation and railroad lines linking Germany with the Polish and Hungarian plains, the Russian agricultural areas, and the cornlands of Rumania, Germany began to import food. C. 1871–79: Germany shifted from a net exporter to a net importer of food. 1873–96: During the great agricultural depression, prices fell. 1879: Germany, like France, resorted to tariff protection of agriculture. German tariffs were lower than French and, unlike in France, did not result in self-sufficiency.

GERMAN AGRICULTURE
(million metric tons)

	Wheat		Rye		Barley		Oats	
	Crops	Imports	Crops	Imports	Crops	Imports	Crops	Imports
1900–04	3.90	2.03	9.66	.83	3.12	1.17	6.95	.51
1905–08	3.72	2.32	9.94	.55	3.15	1.96	7.95	.62
1911–12	4.21	2.08	11.23	−.32	3.32	3.30	8.11	3.00

1861/65–90: German agricultural production (including the great agricultural depression) rose an average of .7% per year. 1880–1912: Over 4 m. acres were added to the area under main food crops in Germany; 1890–1913: German agricultural production expanded an average of 2% per annum.

Technical innovations: 1870's: In the U.S. and Europe use of wire fencing spread. 1880's: Introduction of barbed wire. American agriculture became mechanized with the introduction of the spring-

tooth harrow, after 1877; twine binder, 1878; gang plow, after 1880; giant combine harvester-thresher, 1880's; corn-shucking and fodder-shredding machine, 1890; corn binder, 1892; and disk harrow, after 1892. The results were large increases in yield per man. 1886: Invention of the steam tractor; 1892: 1st gasoline tractor developed. Tractors in the U.S.: 1910, 1,000; 1915, 25,000; 1920, 246,000. In the U.S. primary power on farms (other than man power) increased from estimated 1.6 hp per worker, 1870, to estimated 4.1 hp per worker, 1920. In the U.S. the use of commercial fertilizer spread.

COMMERCIAL FERTILIZERS CONSUMED IN U.S.
(000 short tons)

1870	321
1880	753
1890	1,390
1900	2,730
1910	5,547
1920	7,176

1920: Mainly because of mechanization, agricultural productivity in the U.S. was from 2 to 6 times that of the main countries of Western Europe. 1870–1920: The more progressive of British farmers increasingly introduced agricultural machinery and commercial fertilizers. France and Germany, which had been much slower than Britain to mechanize, now did so.

AGRICULTURAL IMPLEMENTS
(000)

	Threshers Germany	France	Reapers Germany	France	Sowing Machines Germany	France	Steam Plows Germany
1882	374	211	20	35	64	29	.8
1892		234		62		62	
1895	856		35		169		1.2
1907	1,436		301		290		3.0

NOTE: (Holdings using implements in Germany; number in use in France) .

Unfortunately, statistics do not exist for France during 1892–1919, but after 1905 observers reported a great increase in mechanization in that country. 1911: Threshers were practically universal in France. The use of commercial fertilizers in both France and Germany spread, causing a rise in yield per acre.

Innovations in dairy industry: 1878: Introduction of centrifugal cream separator by the Swede, C. G. P. de Laval (1845–1913) . 1890: Stephen Babcock in Wisconsin perfected a simple butterfat test.

New forms of agricultural enterprises: 1870's ff.: In the U.S., farmer co-operatives spread (1st co-operative was in cheesemaking in Wisconsin, 1841) . In Germany (where the agricultural co-operative movement began in the 1860's) , the number of agricultural societies rose rapidly. 1883: 1st agricultural co-operative founded in France; by 1914, 6,667 such societies existed with member-

ship of over 1 m. In Britain agricultural co-operatives were organized, but co-operation was slow in developing. Co-operative societies in every one of these countries got new impetus with the declining prices at the end of the 19th cent. Co-operatives offered facilities for credit, marketing, purchasing, and often joint processing.

RAW MATERIALS. Coal: Coal output of the major industrial nations expanded rapidly up to the time of World War I, and in some cases into the war. 1919: Fall of world coal production under 1913 level. The greatest percentage growth in coal production had been in the U.S., followed by Germany. The basic raw material for the early Industrial Revolution had been coal, which came from the industrializing nations. Though new sources of energy developed, coal remained essential. 1870–1919: Petroleum also became a vital industrial raw material. With the exception of the U.S.,

COAL PRODUCTION
(million metric tons)

	U.K.	Germany	U.S.	Belgium	France	World Total
1870	112.2	34.2	29.9	13.7	13.3	218
1900	228.8	149.6	244.7	23.5	33.4	767
1913	292.0	277.3	517.1	22.9	40.8	1,341
1919	233.4	210.3	505.5	18.5	22.5	1,173

petroleum was not found in quantity in the leading industrial nations. It was imported, the revolution in transportation making this possible. The U.S. was in 1st place in world petroleum production.

CRUDE-OIL PRODUCTION
(million barrels, 42 U.S. gals.)

	U.S.	World Output
1870	5.26	5.80
1900	63.62	149.14
1913	248.45	385.35
1919	378.37	555.88

Iron: The major industrial nations continued to be large consumers and producers of iron ore. 1876: The Thomas-Gilchrist process made it possible to use high-phosphorous-content iron ores in the making of steel (patented 1878). Germany thus developed the Lorraine iron fields. Until c. 1900 Britain ignored her phosphorous-bearing ores, continuing to import the low-phosphorous ores from Sweden and Spain. In the U.S., the key innovation in iron-ore production was the move of the industry westward. 1909–14: Ore from the Mesabi Range (about 100 mi. long in northeast Minnesota) virtually replaced ore from the Wisconsin and Michigan fields. The growth of the steel industry stimulated iron-ore mining.

Copper, lead, zinc: As electrical industries developed there were new demands for copper. Of the leading industrial nations, only the U.S. developed a major copper industry. 1883: As the Montana copper mines came into production, the U.S. surpassed Chile and became the world's leading copper producer.

PRODUCTION OF COPPER
(000 metric tons)

	U.S.	World Output
1870	13	n.a.
1880	27	156
1890	122	274
1900	275	497
1913	557	1,002
1919	584	1,009

1881–86 and then 1898 ff.: U.S. was the world's largest producer of lead. To 1906:

Germany was the world's leading producer of zinc. 1909 ff.: U.S. was consistently in 1st place in zinc production.

New processing methods: 1877: Bessel brothers introduced flotation, a new means of mineral separation; 1886: Denver schoolteacher Carrie J. Everson patented all the essential elements of the flotation process. 1901–10: With the introduction of froths, produced mechanically with air, use of the flotation method spread. As a result, low-grade sulphide ores—copper, lead, zinc—that had not been economical to mine could now be utilized. 1887: In Glasgow, R. W. and W. Forrest and J. S. MacArthur patented a process using a dilute solution of potassium cyanide as a solvent for gold; use of the "cyanide" process spread, making recovery of gold cheaper and more thorough, thus tremendously increasing the world's gold supply. 1890: German-born British subject Ludwig Mond (1839–1909) developed a nickel-extracting process; German-born American chemist Herman Frasch (1851–1914) patented a hot-water process of sulphur mining (1901: commercial production achieved). 1891: In the U.S. the Orford Copper Co. introduced a new process of treating nickel, the Orford nickel process. Such new methods increased the possibilities of developing new resources on a large scale.

ENERGY. The use of the steam engine for power led men to think of other more efficient means of harnessing energy. Electrical power and the internal combustion engine took on importance.

Electrical power generation: 1881: The 1st public electric power station established at Godalming, England, by Siemens Brothers. 1882: Thomas Edison's (1847–1931) system of central-station power production started. 1884: Britisher Charles A. Parsons (1854–1931) invented a practical steam turbine; it was devised to turn an electric generator, which Parsons himself designed; later, 1887, C. G. P. de Laval, Swede, and, 1898, C. G. Curtis, American, developed variations of the Parsons steam turbine. 1895: Hydroelectric power project completed at Niagara Falls—a pioneer venture in the large-scale development of electrical power.

Power transmission: 1882: Edison's central-station power plant used direct current in transmission. 1885–86: Transformers were developed by William Stanley in the U.S. and Zipernowski, Deri, and Blathy in Hungary. 1886: American George Westinghouse (1846–1914) produced a commercially practical transformer, which cleared the way for alternating-current electrical distribution (the main advantage of a.c. over d.c. was the efficiency of transmission). 1890's ff.: Alternating current began to triumph over direct current in America. 1891: Exhibition at Frankfurt with a demonstration of the long distance over which electric power could be transmitted; this stimulated important developments in the German electrical industry. 1895: Niagara Falls electric power facility used alternating current, indicating the superiority of this system over direct current. The way was set for the growth of large centralized electric utilities in the 20th cent. The central power station with long-distance transmission and versatility as a power source replaced the isolated plant serving a single function. 1904: 1st electric locomotive built.

Internal-combustion engine: The internal-combustion engine also became an important source of power. 1876: German engineer N. A. Otto (1832–91) produced the 1st practical gas engine; 1885–86: German Gottfried Daimler (1834–1900) developed a practical internal-combustion engine, using gasoline; 1895: German Rudolf Diesel (1858–1913) invented a new variety of internal-combustion engine, burning heavy oil. While the Germans took the initiative in all 3 inventions, America, the world's largest petroleum producer, made the most dramatic applications of the internal-combustion engine.

Prime-mover capacity:

TOTAL HORSEPOWER OF ALL PRIME MOVERS IN U.S.
(million)

	Total	Automotive[a]	Work Animals	Factories	Mines	Farms[b]	Railroads	Powered Merchant Ships	Sailing Vessels	Windmills	Electric Central Stations
1870	16.9	—	8.7	2.4	.4	—	4.5	.6	.3	.03	—
1900	65.0	.1	18.7	10.3	2.9	4.0	24.5	1.7	.2	.1	2.4
1920	453.4	280.9	22.4	19.4	5.1	21.4	80.2	6.5	.2	.2	17.0

a Includes passenger cars, trucks, buses, and motorcycles.
b Excludes horses and other work animals in 3rd col.

Comparable figures do not appear to exist for Great Britain, France, or Germany. The following census data probably underestimate the prime-mover capacity:

PRIME-MOVER CAPACITY
(millions hp)

	Country	Total
1907	U.K.	10.7 (tot. cap.)
1907	Germany	8.7 (power prod.)
1906	France	3.5 (tot. cap.)

1870–1920: The major portion of the world's inanimate energy was produced by the U.S., Great Britain, Germany, and France.

INDUSTRY. 1870: Britain was still the leading industrial nation of the world; 1906–10: Britain trailed the U.S. and Germany. France's slow industrial development meant her percentage of world manufacturing output steadily declined. Belgium, a small nation, never had a sizable percentage of world manufacturing, although its manufacturing per capita remained high (1881: 51% of all Belgians were engaged in manufacturing—a higher percentage than in Britain, Germany, France, or the U.S.).

The age of steel: 1878: Two Englishmen, S. G. Thomas (1850–85) and his cousin Percy Gilchrist (1851–1935), introduced a process adapting the Bessemer steelmaking process for use with high-phosphorous-content iron ores. This process, which removed the phosphorous, became the basis of the development of

% Distribution of World's Manufacturing* Production

	U.K.	U.S.	Germany	France	Belgium
1870	31.8	23.3	13.2	10.3	2.9
1881–85	26.6	28.0	13.9	8.6	2.5
1896–1900	19.5	30.1	16.6	7.1	2.2
1906–10	14.0	35.3	15.9	6.4	2.0
1913	14.0	35.8	15.7	6.4	2.1

* Note: Finished products, semimanufactures, as well as manufactured foodstuffs.

European steelmaking. 1880 ff.: Steel production, using the Thomas-Gilchrist method applied to both the Siemens-Martin open-hearth and Bessemer processes, grew rapidly in France, Germany, Belgium, and the U.S. The open-hearth method of steel production was slower than the Bessemer process, but it produced steel almost free of nitrogen and thus more malleable; it also could use a relatively high percentage of scrap instead of pig iron. 1907: World steel output from open-hearth furnaces exceeded that from the Bessemer converters. Until the adoption of the oxygen process (in the 1950's and 1960's), the open-hearth method remained the prime technique for steelmaking. 1879: Werner von Siemens invented an electric furnace, which made possible the production of high-grade steel free from impurities. 1900: Bethlehem Steel Corp. exhibited chromium-tungsten steel at the Paris Exposition; 1904: Vanadium steels 1st developed. 1912: British metallurgist Henry Brearley invented stainless steel. The U.S. steel industry grew most dramatically. 1873 ff.: Andrew Carnegie (1835–1919) devoted himself to steel production. 1901: Carnegie Steel Co.—the largest steel co. in the world—was merged into the newly formed billion-dollar corporation, U.S.

Steel. In the industrial nations most pig iron came to be converted into steel. From railroad tracks to shipbuilding, steel replaced iron. Steel opened the way to a vast new construction industry, and to a variety of new products from machine tools to consumer goods. In the 20th cent. the automobile industry became a major user of steel.

The oil industry: 1870, Jan.: Standard Oil Co. of Ohio incorporated, capitalized at $1 m.—John D. Rockefeller (1839–1937), president. (1863: John D. Rockefeller had joined Maurice B. Clark and Samuel Andrews in operating a Cleveland oil refinery; the firm was Clark, Andrews & Co.; 1865: new firm, Rockefeller & Andrews formed, the direct predecessor of Standard Oil of Ohio.) 1870's: Standard Oil Co. of Ohio expanded its refining facilities; by 1879 it controlled 90–95% of the oil refined in the U.S. 1882, 2 Jan.: Standard Oil Trust Agreement: the shares of the acquired companies were transferred to a trust. 1882: Standard Oil Co. of New Jersey and Standard Oil Co. of New York were incorporated; 1889: Standard Oil Co. of Indiana formed. Shares were held by the trust. 1892: After decision by Ohio Supreme Court, 2 Mar., Standard Oil Trust was dissolved and reorganized; Standard

Pig Iron and Steel Production
(million metric tons)

	Great Britain		United States		Germany		France	
	Iron	Steel	Iron	Steel	Iron	Steel	Iron	Steel
1870	6.06	.29	1.69	.07	1.39	.17	1.18a	.08a
1880	7.88	1.32	3.90	1.27	2.79	.66	1.73	.39
1890	8.03	3.64	9.35	4.35	4.66	2.16	1.96	.57
1900	9.10	5.13	14.10	10.38	7.55	6.64	2.71	1.56
1910	10.17	6.37	27.74	26.51	14.79	13.70	4.04	3.51
1913	10.26	7.66	31.00	31.30	19.00	18.63	5.10	4.64

a 1870 figures include Alsace-Lorraine.

Oil of New Jersey was assigned a leading corporate role. 1899: Standard Oil Co. (N.J.) was reincorporated and served as *the* holding and operating company for the Standard Oil group. 1900: Standard Oil Co. (N.J.) acquired the Pacific Coast Oil Co. (formed in 1879) ; this co. was renamed Standard Oil Co. (Calif.) in 1906. 1911: U.S. Supreme Court decision dissolved the Standard Oil Co. (N.J.) and in its place arose 34 separate companies, among them Standard Oil Co. (N.J.), Standard Oil Co. (N.Y.) —later, 1931, merged with Vacuum Oil Co. to become Socony-Vacuum, then, 1955, Socony-Mobil Oil Co. and, 1966, renamed Mobil Oil Corp., Standard Oil Co. (Ind.), Standard Oil Co. (Calif.). 1901: Oil discovered at Spindletop in Texas; start of Texas oil industry; Gulf Refining Co. of Texas formed (predecessor to Gulf Oil Corp.). 1902: The Texas Co. started (predecessor of Texaco, Inc.). America remained in 1st place in the world's petroleum industry, and in the 1870's and 1880's, U.S. refined-oil exports dominated European markets. 1880's ff.: Foreign investments in Russian oil (mainly by the French Rothschilds and the Swedish Nobel brothers—Robert, Ludwig, and Alfred) developed the Russian oil fields. 1883: Completion of railroad from the Baku oil fields to Tiflis; this made Russian oil available in Europe. 1888 ff.: Standard Oil responded to the competition from Russian oil by establishing affiliates in Europe. 1880: Aeilko Jans Zijlker (1840–90), manager of the East Sumatra Tobacco Co., sent some petroleum to Batavia to be tested; 1890, May: Royal Dutch Co. came into existence to develop the Sumatra fields discovered by Zijlker. 1896: H. W. A. Deterding (1866–1939) joined Royal Dutch, and took charge of the marketing. 1896: The British firm, M. Samuel & Co. (est. 1830), traders in oil and other produce, purchased oil properties in East Borneo. 1897, 18 Oct.: Britisher Marcus Samuel (1853–1927) established the Shell Transport & Trading Co., Ltd. (named after the kerosene brand sold by his M. Samuel & Co.). 1907: Merger of Royal Dutch and Shell Transport and Trading Co.

into the Royal Dutch-Shell group. 1912: American Gasoline Co. established (name changed to Shell Oil Co. of California, 1914), as 1st entry of Royal Dutch-Shell group into the American oil business. 1870–1900: The oil industry's main product was kerosene for lighting; 1880 ff.: kerosene began to meet competition from electricity; 1900 ff: with the automobile, the oil industry began the change-over to gasoline as its main product in the western world; kerosene was still the major export to markets east of Suez. 1914–19: Expansion of the oil industry because of the war, as vehicles powered by internal-combustion engines were used on the fronts, as oil-burning ships were adopted, and as the airplane made its entry on the scene. Likewise, the tractor, more frequently used in farming, called for gasoline.

The electrical industry: 1871: Electric-arc lighting perfected by Ohio inventor C. F. Brush (1849–1929). 1874: Stephen Dudley Field of New York invented the 1st electric streetcar. 1876: Alexander Graham Bell (1847–1922) patented the telephone; Elisha Gray (1835–1901) of Western Electric also patented a telephone; Edison established his laboratory at Menlo Park, N.J. 1877: Edison invented phonograph and microphone. 1879: Edison developed the 1st practical incandescent lamp; Joseph Wilson Swan (1828–1914) in England also developed a practical incandescent lamp; 1st experimental streetcar line built by Siemens and Halske for the Berlin Industrial Exhibition; Elihu Thomson (1853–1937) and Edwin J. Houston (1844–1914) designed an arc-lighting system. 1881: 1st city in the world lighted by electricity, Aurora, Ill.; 1st electric railway opened in Germany for public service. 1882: American Schuyler Skaats Wheeler (1860–1923) invented an electric fan; American Henry W. Seely patented an electric iron. 1883: German Edison Co. founded (name changed to Allgemeine Electrizitäts-Gesellschaft in 1887); Emil Rathenau (1838–1914) was managing director. 1885: 1st electric streetcars operated commercially in the U.S. in Baltimore, Md. 1886, 8 Jan.: Westinghouse Electric Co. incorporated. 1887: Edison invented a motion-picture machine. 1888: Croatian-born American inventor, Nikola Tesla (1857–1943), patented the alternating-current induction motor. (Tesla also invented new forms of dynamos, transformers, induction coils, and condensers, arc and incandescent lamps.) 1889: Singer Manufacturing Co. developed an electric sewing machine. 1891: Edison obtained 1st radio patent in the U.S. 1892: General Electric Co. incorporated, C. A. Coffin (1844–1926), 1st president. 1895: 1st practical wireless telegraphy invented by Italian, G. Marconi (1874–1937). 1896: American William S. Hadaway patented an electric stove. 1897: German-born American inventor, Emile Berliner (1851–1929), developed a commercial product later called a phonograph record. 1902: American Lee De Forest (1873–1961) established the American De Forest (later United) Wireless Telegraph Co. at Jersey City, N.J., which installed for the U.S. Navy the 1st high-power naval radio stations. 1903: The Siemens enterprises in Germany (the Siemens Konzern) reorganized; Siemens & Halske, which had handled all facets of the electrical business, confined itself to telephony and electrochemistry, while Siemens Schuckert Werke now dealt with heavy electrical equipment. 1906, 20 Oct.: De Forest announced his 1st 3-element vacuum tube (filament and 2-plate electrodes). 1907: Hurling Machine Co. (U.S.) developed an electric washing machine. 1913: De Forest presented the oscillating Audion, which gave him the title, "the father of radio broadcasting." 1913: Germany and the U.S. led in world output of electrical products; the British and French electrical industries lagged behind. 1914–18: With the war, the electrical industry's output in the allied countries grew dramatically. 1917: Metropolitan-Vickers acquired Westinghouse's English plant.

The automobile industry: 1875: German Siegfried Marcus made a crude but operable model of a gasoline automobile; it was never manufactured. 1885–86: Germans Gottfried Daimler and Karl Benz (1844–1929) developed practical engines and drove experimental motor-boats, motor cycles, and cars. 1889: Panhard & Levassor in France, using Daimler and Benz patents, manufactured Daimler engines and made the 1st commercial automobiles. 1893: The Duryea car was 1st American gasoline-propelled vehicle to make a verified run. 1896: Highway Act in Great Britain repealed restrictions on self-propelled vehicles; H. J. Lawson formed England's 1st motor-car co., the Daimler Motor Car Co. (using a foreign car); Peugeot established in France. 1896, 4 June: Henry Ford (1863–1945) drove his 1st car on the streets of Detroit. 1899: Louis Renault (1877–1944) began production of the Renault car; 1900: Herbert Austin (1866–1941) in England drove his 1st model. 1903, 16 June: Ford Motor Co. incorporated. 1903: European automobile production was greater than American output. 1908, 16 Sept.: General Motors Co. formed—a holding co., promoted by William C. Durant (1861–1947); 1908–9: General Motors acquired ownership or substantial control of more than 20 American automobile and accessory companies, including Buick, Cadillac, Oldsmobile, and Oakland; 1909: GM became the largest automobile company in the world. 1908: Ford Motor Co. introduced the Model T. 1911, 8 Mar.: Ford Motor Co. (England), Ltd., formed (the successor of an English branch of the Ford Motor Co., organized in 1909). 1911, Nov.: Chevrolet Motor Co. of Michigan founded. 1913–14: Ford Motor Co. introduced the moving assembly line, the basis for mass production. 1913: Ford's Model T sales exceeded those of all General Motors products and became the greatest in the world. By 1913 American automobile production far exceeded that of all of Europe. 1913, Apr.: William Richard Morris, later Lord Nuffield (1877–1963), produced his 1st car in England, the Morris-Oxford; his aim was to rival the Model T. 1915–16: Chevrolet obtained control of the larger General Motors; 1916, 13 Oct.: General Motors Corp. formed, an operating company, which acquired the assets of General Motors Co., and in 1918 the assets of Chevrolet; the Model T Ford, however, remained the largest-selling car in the world and the Ford Motor Co. remained the world's largest automobile company. Using interchangeable parts and the moving assembly line, the American automobile industry had taken world leadership. The French did not adopt mass production; French entrepreneurs admired quality custom-made units, and as a result the French automobile industry fell behind; similarly the German automobile industry tended to be conservative. Percival L. D. Perry (1878–1956; 1938, Lord Perry) of the Ford Motor Co. (England), Ltd., introduced American ideas of mass production to the British industry; Morris was ready to follow. But the U.S. industry surged ahead, in good part because it had economies of scale (the more units made, the cheaper the price per unit) and the American market was large enough to take advantage of these economies. The automobile industry stimulated the steel industry and also encouraged parts manufacturers, glassmakers, rubber-tire producers, electrical-equipment manufacturers, leather and leather fabric industries. The automobile industry, especially in the U.S., prompted a range of services, dealerships, repair shops, service stations, etc.

The chemical industry: 1870: Vaseline 1st produced by R. A. Chesebrough (1837–1933) in U.S. 1871: Carbon black made from natural gas in Pennsylvania and West Virginia—U.S. patent to J. Howarth and S. T. Lamb; salicylic acid synthesized from phenol by German H. Kolbe; sulphuric acid made from copper-ore roaster gases in Germany. 1872: Brunner-Mond founded in England; it became the world's largest producer of alkalies (merging into the Imperial Chemical Industries, Ltd., 1926); 1873: practical ammonia ice machine perfected by American David Boyle; Carl von Linde in Germany invented ammonia refrigeration; 1875: Raoul Pictet in France developed sulphur dioxide refrigeration. 1878: Adolf von Baeyer (1835–1917) in Germany synthesized indigo; Germany took the lead in the world in the manufacture of synthetic dyestuffs. 1879: American Ira Remsen (1846–1927) discovered saccharin. 1870's: Spread of the use of chemical pulp for papermaking in England, and then elsewhere. 1885: American George Eastman (1854–1932) manufactured the 1st commercial film. (1888: Eastman registered the trademark "Kodak" for his new camera.) 1886: Charles Martin Hall (1863–1914), American, and Paul L. T. Héroult (1863–1914) in France independently devised means of electrolytic production of aluminum; this opened up the new field of electrochemistry. 1887: A German co., Aluminum Industrie A.G., formed to work the Héroult process at Neuhausen, Switzerland. (1892, this co. was the largest producer of aluminum in the world.) 1888: Pittsburgh Reduction Co. was founded to develop the Hall process (1907, name changed to Aluminum Co. of America). The new methods of producing aluminum caused a sharp drop in price (1855, when aluminum was produced by the earlier methods, the cost was $90 per lb.; by 1892, it was $.50 per lb.). 1889: Count Louis Marie Hilaire Bernigard de Chardonnet (1839–1924) exhibited in Paris the 1st dress made of "artificial" silk. 1880's and 1890's: The application of chemical methods to the processing of minerals spread. 1891: American Edward G. Acheson (1856–1931) 1st produced carborundum (abrasive, produced by an electrochemical process). 1901: C. von Linde in Germany made liquid oxygen. 1904: F. Stolz in Germany synthesized adrenalin. 1905: F. Rothe in Germany developed cyanamide process for nitrogen fixation; J. C. Wood in England invented safety glass. 1909: The plastic, Bakelite, 1st of the synthetic resins, was discovered by Belgian-born American chemist Leo H. Baekeland (1863–1944). 1912: Development of Haber-Bosch nitrogen fixation process in Germany. 1914: Corning Glass Works (U.S.) introduced pyrex glass. 1914: Despite innovations in the American and British chemical industry, in drugs, coal-tar dyes, and potash production, Germany led. 1914: Germany, with nitrogen fixation from cyanamide, the arc, and the Haber processes, produced 80,631 tons of nitrogen.

PRODUCTION OF SYNTHETIC DYESTUFFS, 1913
(000 short tons)

Germany	150.0
U.K.	5.6
U.S.	3.3
France	2.2

1914: Because of German and British involvement in war, the U.S. chemical industry began to develop products previously imported. 1916: U.S. gave special protection to the American chemical industry, Emergency Dye Tariff, 8 Sept. 1917, 6 Apr.: U.S. entered the war. 1917, Aug.: Alien Property Custodian in U.S. seized German chemical patents and American producers were licensed to produce under them. 1917, 1 Nov.: Union Carbide & Carbon Corp. established (later 1 May, 1957, renamed Union Carbide Corp.), a merger of 4 independent chemical companies. 1918: At war's end the American chemical industry showed new strength; the U.S. coal-tar dye industry was a product of the war; U.S. producers had developed local supplies of potash; nitrogen fixation in the U.S. had begun.

Other innovations: 1871: H. W. Bradley, Binghamton, N.Y., patented oleomargarine. 1873: Remington arms makers began to manufacture the typewriter, invented by Sholes. 1876: Melville R. Bissell, American, invented 1st workable carpet sweeper. 1878: Dayton saloonkeeper James Ritty conceived the idea for a cash register. (1883: National Manufacturing Co. formed to acquire the cash-register patents; 1884, John Henry Patterson [1844–1922] obtained control of National Manufacturing Co. and changed name to National Cash Register Co.). 1884: American Herman Hollerith (1860–1929) developed a system of using punch cards to sort, tabulate, and analyze data; 1st applied to Census of 1890. (1896: Hollerith formed the Tabulating Machine Co., a predecessor company to International Business Machines.) 1886: American Ottmar Mergenthaler (1854–99) patented the linotype. 1888: American William S. Burroughs invented the adding machine. 1889: American Hiram Maxim (1840–1916) designed an automatic machine gun. 1895: "Cinematograph" patented in France.

TRANSPORTATION. Railroads: The railroad age reached its apogee in U.S. and Western Europe.

RAILROAD LINES
(000 mi.)

	1870	1910
U.S.	52.9	240.3
U.K.	15.3	23.4
Germany	12.2	38.0
France	10.8	24.2
Austria-Hungary	6.0	27.6

The vast extension of the railroad shortened distances and tremendously enhanced trade. Use of refrigerated railway cars meant meats and other perishables went into national and then international trade.

Steamships: Steamships connected domestic railroads with foreign lands. 1870's: New steamship tonnage (built and registered) exceeded for the 1st time new sailing-ship tonnage. Refrigerated ocean transport came into use. 1870: U.S. shipments of chilled beef and other foodstuffs were being sent to British and other European ports; 1877: French interests experimented with shipping frozen meats from Argentina to France; 1880: 1st cargo of frozen meat sent from Australia to London; 1882: Australian mutton, beef, poultry, and fish were regularly frozen and shipped to Britain; 1892: transoceanic trade in frozen meats equaled 2 m. carcasses; 1902, 4 m. carcasses. 1885: The 1st ocean-going steam tanker for the transport of refined oil, used by the Nobels, carried 1st cargo of refined oil from Batum to Antwerp. The expansion of the railroads and steamship service put Europe and the U.S. in closer contact with the rest of the world. The opening of the Suez Canal, 1869, and the U.S.-owned Panama Canal, 1914, shortened distances.

Domestic transport (other than railroads): 1880's: Introduction of electric streetcar. The bicycle, invented earlier, was now improved. 1877: Ball bearings were presented; 1885: safety rear driving mirror was 1st marketed (invented 1876 by Englishman H. J. Lawson); 1889: Britisher John Boyd Dunlop (1840–1921) introduced pneumatic tires. 1900: 5 m. bicycles in France, 5 m. in Britain, 4 m. in Germany, and 4 m. in the U.S. Just as the bicycle industry grew, the automobile industry developed. In Europe and the U.S. the automobile began as a "toy" of the rich, but with mass production and with the Model T (introduced 1908), by 1920 in the U.S. the automobile was becoming a popular mode of conveyance.

PRIVATE AUTOMOBILES IN USE
(000)

	U.S.	France	U.K.	Germany
1900	8	3	1a	1a
1910	458	54	53	n.a.
1920	8,123	135	187	60a

a Estimated.

Air transport: 1903, 17 Dec.: Americans Wilbur Wright (1867–1912) and his brother Orville (1871–1948) made 1st successful airplane flight at Kitty Hawk, N.C., 1906: German Count Ferdinand von Zeppelin (1838–1917) flew 1st practical airship (dirigible) at 30 mph (passenger service began, 1910). 1908: Louis Breguet and Charles Richet built a combined helicopter and biplane, which flew 64 ft. 1912: American Glenn Hammond Curtiss (1878–1930) built 1st seaplane. 1913: U.S. total aircraft production, 43 planes. 1914 ff.: World War I provided a stimulus to the airplane industry. 1915: Dutchman Anthony H. G. Fokker (1890–1939) built for the Germans the 1st of his famous planes, with machine-gun fire through a revolving propeller. 1918: U.S. aircraft production, 14,020 planes (of which 13,991 were for military use).

COMMUNICATIONS. Cables: New cable connections linked Europe with North and South America and the Far East.

Telephones: 1876: 1st "long distance" telephone conversation, Cambridge to Boston, Mass. 1879 ff.: The telephone was introduced in Europe. 1892: Europe had 254,900 telephones; U.S., 239,300 telephones. 1898: Number of telephones in U.S. surpassed number in Europe. 1915: 1st transcontinental telephone line

opened between New York and San Francisco. 1920: 1.5 telephones per 100 persons in Europe, 12.4 telephones per 100 persons in the U.S.; the U.S. had 13 million telephones.

FINANCE. Gold and the gold standard: The financial situation worldwide was shaken by the fabulous discoveries of gold in South Africa. 1870–90: World gold production fluctuated between a low of 4.75 m. troy oz., 1883, and a high of 6.05 m. troy oz., 1889. 1890 ff.: Production rose rapidly. 1915: Production 22.72 m. troy oz. In that year, 40.0% of the world's gold supply came from South Africa, 21.2% from the U.S., 8.6% from Australia, and 5.6% from Russia—the leading gold producers. Even before this rise in gold production, in 1871–73 Germany adopted the gold standard and, 1873–74, so did the Latin Monetary Union (including France, Belgium, Italy, and Switzerland); 1875–76: Denmark, Norway, and Sweden followed, and, 1879, the U.S.; Britain had adopted the gold standard much earlier. By 1914 most of the world (China was a key exception) was on the gold standard. 1914–18: With the war, most participants went off the gold standard.

Banking structure: By 1870, in Britain, France, and Belgium a modern banking structure had been erected. 1875, Mar.: German Reichsbank established, based on the Prussian Bank (est. 1846); it controlled note issue throughout the empire, and carried the main cash reserves and provided banking facilities for the entire empire. 1875–1905: The Reichsbank opened nearly 100 main branches and 4,000 subbranches. In the U.S. the Federal Reserve Act, 23 Dec., 1913, established the Federal Reserve System, the 1st central banking structure in the U.S. since the expiration of the 2nd National Bank charter in 1836. Rise of investment banking in U.S. and Germany. In the U.S. investment banking houses such as Jay Cooke & Co. (failed 1873); Drexel, Morgan & Co. (J. P. Morgan & Co. after 1894); Kuhn, Loeb & Co.; Lee, Higginson & Co.; and Kidder, Peabody & Co. played important roles in financing American railroads and industries. J. P. Morgan (1837–1913), particularly, was important in organizing, financing, and obtaining management for consolidations that took place in the U.S. in the 1890's and early 1900's. Germany developed investment banking on a grand scale. Banks of deposit were committed to building industry. 1872: 130 deposit banks in Germany; 1914: almost all the liquid savings and credit resources were in the possession of 12 banks. The major ones had become the "4 D's": the Deutsche (est. 1870), the Dresdner (1872), the Diskontogesellschaft (1851), and the Darmstadter (1853). The banks were noncompetitive, had areas of specialties, and often joined in banking syndicates to finance business expansion. In France there were the private banks (such as the Paris House of Rothschild), which participated in banking syndicates. There were the industrial banks, key among them the Banque de Paris et Pays Bas, the Banque de l'Union Parisienne, the Banque Française pour le Commerce et l'Industrie. There were also the deposit banks, including Crédit Lyonnais, Comptoir Nationale d'Escompte (failed 1889), the Société Générale, and Crédit Industriel et Commerciel. The industrial and deposit banks looked in the main to foreign investment and foreign financing. The deposit banks had started for the most part as industrial banks and then stopped lending to domestic industry. French banks, unlike the German banks, did not concern themselves mainly with the foundation and supervision of domestic industrial enterprises (they tended to issue bonds rather than stock). The industrial banks, when they did finance domestic enterprise, tended to abjure responsibilities for management. Unlike the German banks, they did not take leadership in making industrial enterprises more efficient. It is frequently argued that whereas the German banks served a progressive entrepreneurial function encouraging economic growth, the French banks accepted the passive conservativism of the French people and did not stimulate the latter's industry, inventive talent, or organizing ability. Others counter that the French banks failed to aid French industry because they were

not needed. In Britain private banks were important in underwriting securities, but did not give leadership to British enterprise or control it.

Allocation of savings: In the U.S. domestic savings were practically all reinvested within the country. Capital accumulated in industries was reinvested in industries. Savings in Germany were in the main reinvested in German economic development, but there were also substantial foreign investments. In France savings tended to go into foreign rather than domestic investments in search of higher rates of return, while in Britain, c. 1875 ff., foreign lending also attracted a substantial portion of savings.

Stock exchanges: An American capital market developed. 1908: Foundation of New York Curb Agency by group of street brokers (1952, the Curb became the American Stock Exchange). The Paris Bourse (stock exchange) and the Berlin Börse were both subject to close national governmental control and supervision. 1896: German legislation severely restricted business on the Berlin exchange, to check speculation in stocks. French and German speculators transacted their business abroad, especially in London, Brussels, and Amsterdam. The London market was the greatest in the world, handling securities of nations around the globe.

FOREIGN TRADE. The foreign trade of industrial nations rose. London remained the center of world trade.

VALUE OF FOREIGN TRADE (EXPORTS PLUS
IMPORTS)
($ million)

	1875	1913
U.K.	3,186	6,837
Germany	1,433	4,970
U.S.	1,079	4,392
France	1,430	2,953

Railroads, steamships, and refrigerated transport plus growing world population encouraged the expansion of commerce. The gold standard assured a stability of international exchange rates. The rise of new colonial empires stimulated foreign trade. Industrial nations exported manufactured goods and imported foodstuffs and industrial raw materials. The U.S. was the major exception to this pattern, since it was an important exporter of agricultural products. (1865–75 ff.: American grain began to reach European markets in quantity; 1880's: U.S. became an important exporter of beef and to a lesser extent pork. With the exception of isolated years, raw cotton remained the largest single U.S. export. Petroleum—refined and crude—became a significant U.S. export.) British exports of manufactured goods grew. (Cotton manufactures continued as Britain's largest single export, comprising in 1913 $\frac{1}{4}$ of the volume.) German exports came to compete with British products in many markets. The Germans developed a "double selling price": at home, manufacturers, protected by the tariff and through cartel arrangements, raised domestic prices; overseas, in competitive situations, German goods were often sold below cost. Multilateral trading patterns developed among European nations, Europe and Asia, and North and South America. It has been suggested that the slowing down in the pace of British economic growth at the end of the 19th cent. and start of the 20th cent. was due to the growth of foreign competition at home and in world markets.

Tariff policies. From the repeal of the corn laws to the McKenna duties, 1915, Britain remained committed to free trade. Her free-trade policy had been adopted when she was the workshop of the world. 1915, 21 Sept.: When Britain had fallen behind the U.S. and Germany in industrial productivity, when she required new revenues for wartime needs, she adopted the McKenna duties, placing duties on imports of manufactured goods; the McKenna duties also provided imperial preference. 1870–97: U.S. held to a protectionist tariff policy; although there were occasional reductions in tariff, the trend was upward: 1872, 6 June: 10% tariff reduction in U.S.; 1875, 3 Mar.: 1872 tariff reduction removed; 1883, 3 Mar.: 5% reduction in tariff; 1890, 1 Oct.: McKinley tariff raised duties to new high level, average 49.5%; this tariff had for the 1st time explicit provisions

for negotiations with other nations on reciprocal concessions; 1894, 28 Aug.: Wilson-Gorman tariff lowered duties to average 39.9%; 1897, 7 July: Dingley tariff raised level to new high, average 57%; 1909–19; moderate tariff policy in U.S.; 1909, 9 Apr.: Payne-Aldrich tariff lowered duties to average of about 38%; 1913, 3 Oct.: Underwood tariff decreased levies to average of about 32%; 1916, 8 Sept.: emergency dye tariff designed to protect the new chemical industry. 1870–79: Germany reduced duties. 1873: German duties on iron and shipbuilding materials were abolished; those on iron products were lowered (eliminated, 1 Jan., 1877, but protection remained on certain manufactured goods). 1879: New German tariff raised rates on manufactured imports and also imposed duties on corn imports. The levies on manufactured goods were designed primarily for revenue rather than protection. 1885 and 1888: Germany raised duties higher. In the late 1870's, agricultural imports began to flood into France. 1880's: Restrictions on imports into France; 1881: French government forbade entry of American pork. 1884: France increased taxes on foreign sugar. 1885, 1887: France imposed higher duties on cattle. 1885: Rye, barley, and oats imports were taxed. 1885, 1887: Flour duty raised. 1885: Import duty increased on wheat. 1890–92: General European response to the McKinley tariff in the U.S.: 1890: France raised her tariff. 1892: In France the Méline tariff raised most agricultural duties and also duties on manufactured goods. 1891–1902: Germany raised some duties, but also negotiated treaties reducing key agrarian and industrial tariffs. 1902, 14 Dec.: Germany enacted a new tariff, characterized by (1) higher level of duties on foodstuffs, (2) free entry of raw materials used in manufacture, (3) low duties on partially finished manufactures, and (4) increasingly higher duties depending on how finished a manufactured product was. 1910: France further raised tariffs, but the government could negotiate tariff reductions by reciprocal agreements. The principal object of protectionism in France and Germany was to aid agriculture.

TARIFF COMPARISON (BASED ON 78 ITEMS),
1913
(% ad valorem)

U.S.	32%
France	16
Germany	12
Belgium	6
U.K.	0

Nontariff trade restrictions such as prohibitions of imports and exports, quotas,
exchange controls, and licensing did not
in general exist; most such were outlawed
by trade treaties. Only on occasion, e.g.,
in emergencies, might such restraints be
imposed. 1914–18: Worldwide restrictions were introduced because of wartime
needs; it was expected that after the war
these would terminate. 1914, Aug.:
British blockade of Germany started;
other nations joined blockade. 1917, 6
Oct.: U.S., Trading with the Enemy Act.
1919, 12 July: Allied blockade lifted.

FOREIGN INVESTMENT. 1875:
Book value of existing British foreign investment was estimated at $6 billion—
mainly in bonds of foreign governments
and railway shares and debentures. Of this
about $2.5 billion was invested in Europe
and Egypt and the remainder in the
U.S., India, South America, and the
Dominions and colonies in that order.
1914: Book value of Britain's long-term
foreign investments reached $18.3 billion.
The direction of British new capital out-
flows moved increasingly toward non-European countries; Britain financed new investments in Africa and Asia through
liquidating older investments on the
Continent. Most of the foreign investment involved construction of railroads
and development of natural resources.
1870–1914: British foreign investment
represented a high percentage of current
British savings. (1905–14: British foreign-
investment outflow was over half British
savings.) Britain led in overseas investment, but France too was a large foreign
investor. 1850–1914: ½ to ⅓ of French
savings went to foreign investments. 1914:
Book value of French long-term foreign
investments was estimated at $8.7 billion.
Germany devoted less of its savings to
foreign investment. Yet by the 1880's it

TRENDS IN U.K. CAPITAL FORMATION
AS % EXPENDITURE GENERATING GNP
(decade averages)

	Gross Domestic Fixed Capital Formation	Net Foreign Investment
1870–79	8.1	3.9
1875–84	7.8	3.1
1880–89	6.1	5.9
1885–94	5.7	4.9
1890–99	6.9	3.2
1895–1904	8.5	2.1
1900–1909	7.8	3.9
1905–14	6.0	6.9

had changed from a capital-importing to
a capital-exporting nation. 1914: Book
value of German foreign investments
equaled $5.6 billion. 1914: Belgium, the
Netherlands, and Switzerland together
had foreign investments to the extent of
$5.5 billion, while that year the U.S.
(still a debtor in international accounts)
had some $3.5 billion invested abroad.
The presence of the gold standard and
the stability of foreign exchange rates encouraged international capital flows.
Foreign investment financed foreign
trade. The long-run effects of the large
foreign investment on the British and
French economies are controversial. It
has been argued that in Britain and
France, economic growth was retarded
by the diversion of savings to foreign investment. On the other side, it is claimed
that had there been demand for it capital
would have gone to domestic use and
that the slow economic growth of Britain
and France was a *cause* of the capital
outflow rather than an effect. It is also
argued that foreign investment, by encouraging foreign trade and by the returns through dividends and interest, did
pay. Germany and more so the U.S., both
of which devoted a smaller percentage
of their savings to foreign investment
than Britain and France, used most of
their capital at home. This undoubtedly
contributed to their growth. 1914–18:
Wartime losses (including the repudiation by the Soviet government of foreign
debts to international investors in the
U.K., France, and Germany) came to
about $4–$5 billion each. U.S. losses were
far less. 1914: The U.S. was a debtor
nation in international accounts to the
extent of $3.7 billion. 1914–18: Britain

borrowed from abroad, mainly from the U.S. 1919: The U.S. had become a creditor nation to the extent of the same $3.7 billion and was the largest creditor nation in the world; New York replaced London as the world's financial center.

BUSINESS ORGANIZATION. Limited-liability corporations: 1914: In the U.S. and, to a smaller extent, Britain the limited-liability corporation had become the typical means of doing business not only for public utilities (including transportation) but also for industrial enterprises; in Germany and France the use of this form increased. Limited liability made it easier to attract funds; the corporate form contributed to business expansion; it provided the basis for the separation of ownership and control which came later.

Pools: Associations of otherwise independent businesses to control prices and/or apportion markets were common in the U.S. in the 1870's and 1880's. (1887: The Interstate Commerce Act forbade pooling in American railroads; 1890: Sherman Antitrust Act prohibited agreements to restrain trade; 1899: U.S. Supreme Court case, *Addyston Pipe and Steel Co.* v. *U.S.* [175 U.S. 211] applied the Sherman Act prohibition to pools among manufacturers.) In Britain trade associations of a voluntary nature often served the same function as pools in the U.S. In France agreements to control competition were also evident. In these countries no antipooling measures were taken.

Cartels (Europe and international): Similar to pools, but often more formal, cartels were associations of otherwise independent producers to fix production quotas, prices, and/or market territories; sometimes the German government took direct part as a participant in German cartels. Before 1877, c. 14 cartels in Germany (earliest in 1860's); 1876–77: 1st Rhenish-Westphalian coal cartel agreement. 1879: 1st German potash cartel; 1900: c. 275 cartels in Germany; there was hardly a trade without a cartel. The rational industrial organization created by a cartel was favored by German producers and the government. The cartel was most in evidence in Germany,

although there were cartels in Britain, France, and elsewhere; in Britain agreements establishing a "community of interests" between otherwise independent firms were not uncommon. Under U.S. antitrust legislation the cartel was clearly illegal in America; it was not illegal in Europe. International cartels involved American, German, French, Swiss, Canadian, British, and Dutch businesses. 1883: 1st international cartel (steel rails).

Trusts (U.S. and Europe): Stockholders deposited their stock with trustees, vesting in the latter the right to vote the stock and thus control the policies of the corporations involved. The most important American trusts were the Standard Oil Trust, est. 2 Jan., 1882, the American Cotton Oil Trust, 1884, the National Linseed Oil Trust, 1885, the Sugar Trust, 1887, and the Distillers' and Cattle Feeders' Trust (the Whisky Trust), 1887. Trusts were not incorporated and not subject to state control; they were the focus of much public opposition in the U.S. 1890, Jan.: The Whisky Trust was reorganized as a single corporation; 1891: the Sugar Trust was reorganized as a single corporation (as a result of an 1890 New York state court decision); 1892: the Standard Oil Trust was dissolved, and replaced by single corporations (as a result of 1891 Ohio state court decision). 1890, 2 July: Sherman Antitrust Act forbade "every contract, combination in the form of trust . . . in restraint of trade. . . ." 1895–1902: The trust form, described above and used as a means of combining 2 or more corporations, no longer existed in the U.S.; the term, however, had come to be loosely used to mean large conglomerations of corporate power. In Europe "trusts" were often set up to give shareholders financial returns while depriving them of voting rights; there were not the restrictions upon them that there were in the U.S.

Mergers: Large corporations became the norm in the U.S.; many were formed by mergers of existing cos. 1897–1902: 1st major wave of mergers in the U.S.; some merged units were holding cos. (a single co., holding the shares of other cos.); some were operating cos. (if in a merger the acquired corporations were dissolved and merged into the single co., this unit became an operating co.); others combined the functions of holding and operating cos. There were in the U.S. major consolidations of financial and railway interests. Large industrial cos. in the U.S. were made possible by a joining of financial and industrial interests.

Combines: What was known in the U.S. as a giant corporation, generally formed by mergers, or, in the loose sense of the word, a "trust," was called a "combine" or "trust" in England and on the European Continent. 1890: Royal Dutch formed, which in time became a major European "combine." 1891: Formation in England of United Alkali, including competing alkali firms. 1895–96: Messrs. J. & P. Coats (thread) amalgamated with its 4 chief competitors into an important British combine. 1896–1901: Large (by British standards) combines were formed for the manufacture of Portland cement, wall paper, tobacco, and various facets of the textile industries; by this time Brunner Mond had become another large British "combine." 1903: Krupp enterprises in Germany were a combine. 1906: William Hesketh Lever, Viscount Leverhulme (1851–1925), used Lever Brothers, Ltd., to acquire major competitors and created in Britain the "soap combine." The "combines" in the U.S. were the largest in the world; those in Britain 2nd; Germany was fast catching up; France, for the most part, remained

a country of small business. In some usages, the word "combine" carried the connotation of combination in restraint of trade, but this was by no means the general meaning of the term.

Konzerns: A German form of organization of firms bound together by personal ties, e.g., the Siemens Konzern and the Stinnes Konzern (in steel).

Business entrepreneurs: Characteristic of America, leading business entrepreneurs were Collis P. Huntington (1821–1900), James J. Hill (1838–1916), and Edward H. Harriman (1848–1909) in railroads; Carnegie in steel; Cyrus Hall McCormick, harvesters; John D. Rockefeller, oil; James Buchanan Duke (1856–1925), tobacco; Henry Clay Frick (1849–1919), coke; Philip D. Armour (1832–1901) and Gustavus Swift (1839–1903), meat packing; Arthur Vining Davis (1867–1964), aluminum; Henry Ford, automobiles; Andrew W. Mellon (1855–1937), banking and diversified enterprises; J. P. Morgan, banking. 1880: 100 millionaires in U.S. (est.); 1916, 40,000 millionaires in U.S. (est.). Leading German entrepreneurs included Friedrich Alfred Krupp (1854–1902) and his son-in-law Gustav Krupp von Bohlen und Halbach (1870–1950), August Thyssen, and Hugo Stinnes (1870–1924) in steel; Emil Rathenau and his son Walther Rathenau (1867–1922) and Siemens in electricity. In Britain Alfred Moritz Mond, 1st Baron Melchett (1863–1930), in chemicals, Sir

10 LARGEST U.S. INDUSTRIAL COS., 1 JAN., 1904

	Incorporated	No. of Plants Acquired or Controlled	Stocks and Bonds Outstanding[a] ($ million)
1. U.S. Steel (and controlled properties)	1901	785	1,370
2. Consolidated Tobacco Co. (and affiliated corps.)	1901	c. 150	503
3. American Smelting & Refining Co. (and affiliates)	1899	121	202
4. Amalgamated Copper Co.	1899	11	175
5. American Sugar Refining Co.	1891	c. 55	145
6. United States Leather Co.	1893	25	130
7. International Harvester Co.	1902	6	120
8. Consolidated Lake Superior Co.	1897	16	117
9. Standard Oil Co. (N.J.)	1899	c. 400	97
10. Pittsburgh Coal Co.	1899	c. 207	84

[a] This includes the stocks and bonds in the hands of the public of all subsidiary or controlled corps., as well as of the parent co., at par values.

Thomas Lipton (1850–1931) in tea retailing, and Lever in soap were key entrepreneurs, while Cecil Rhodes was an important British entrepreneur abroad.

General industry associations: 1895: In U.S., National Association of Manufacturers formed. 1916: Federation of British Industries. 1919: Confédération Générale de la Production Française established on the proposal of the minister of commerce "to contribute to the development of the productive power and export trade of France." 1919, Feb.: Reichsverband der Deutschen Industrie founded.

Scientific management: 1911: American Frederick Winslow Taylor (1856–1915) published *Principles of Scientific Management;* this and other volumes by Taylor turned attention to the problems of efficiency in job management, planning the work flow, understanding costs; Henry Lawrence Gantt (1861–1919) and Frank B. Gilbreth (1868–1924) were other American innovators in job management. 1916: In France, Henri Fayol (1841–1925) published his pioneering study of business administration, *Administration industrielle et générale.*

GOVERNMENT POLICY. Protection: Protection of and aid to agriculture became a new function of the governments of industrial nations. The French protection was most significant, but was at a cost, and food prices in France were higher than anywhere else on the Continent. 1889: The British Board of Agriculture was established "to foster and direct the farmer." 1916, 17 July: U.S. Federal Farm Loan Act, 1st step in U.S. aid to the farmer. Protection of industry occurred through tariffs in the U.S. and on the European Continent. The British, committed to a free-trade policy, did not protect their industry until 1915. Until the war emergency, there was virtually no direct aid to or participation in industry in the U.S. or Britain on the part of government. Taxes were low. (There was no income tax on corporations in the U.S. until 1909, and then the so-called "corporate excise tax" was 1% on corporate incomes.) In Germany, on the other hand, profitable private industrial enterprises were fostered by government subsidies; the German dyemakers got subsidies for research, favorable rates on the state-owned railways, and remission of certain taxes; the German automobile industry was subsidized. German states operated state-owned mines and iron works. 1914: Prussia owned some 40 mines and 12 blast furnaces. Municipalities in Germany often owned slaughterhouses and other plants.

Aids to transportation: The U.S. government gave land grants to the railroads. 1914, 15 Aug.: The U.S. government-built-and-financed Panama Canal opened to traffic. 1875, 25 Nov.: purchase of Suez Canal Co. shares by Prime Minister Disraeli; British government later ratified his action. 1870's: French government took part in building and operating certain railroads in France. 1879: Freycinet plan called for French government construction of major public works, including railroads; 1883: railroads built under the plan were in difficulty, and private operations began—although the French government retained a railroad network in southwestern France and guaranteed interest on the capital invested in other railways (railroads paid profits over a certain level to the government) ; 1908: French state took over the Ouest line when it was in difficulty. 1870–1910: Increasing German governmental involvement in railroads; 1910: 94% of German railroads under public ownership. 1885: Germans gave government assistance to steamship services to Eastern Asia and Australia.

Involvement in other public utilities: The British, German, and French telegraph and telephone systems were under government control. In Britain the telephone monopoly belonged to the General Post Office, which initially licensed private companies. 1902: The G.P.O. began to install its own telephone exchanges. 1911: G.P.O. acquired all telephones in Great Britain. In Germany telephones began as a government monopoly; the German government encouraged their introduction. 1881: 1st public telephone service opened in Paris, by private company licensed by the French government; subsequently, the French government introduced telephones; 1889: French government took over the entire telephone system. Throughout Western Europe (Belgium, Holland, Austria, Italy) telephones came into government hands. In Britain municipal ownership of water supplies and gas enterprises grew. In Germany municipalities nationalized electric power plants, gasworks, and waterworks; joint-venture cos. ("mixed ownership cos.") combined private and public ownership in electric power plants, gasworks, waterworks, and traction systems; a private co. would form such enterprises and the municipalities would acquire stock interests in exchange for the granting of franchises.

Involvement in education: In all the industrial nations, governments provided education facilities, which served to raise the standards of the work force. Involvement in social welfare measures moved countries away from free enterprise. (This was especially true in Germany, then in Britain, but to a far less extent in the U.S.)

Aid to business abroad: The growth of colonial empires helped create conditions suitable for British, French, German, Belgian, and Dutch businesses to operate overseas. Cos. chartered to do business abroad were helped by the British, French, German, Belgian, Dutch, and U.S. governments. In their business activities within the empires, European businessmen could count on their governments' support. In the U.S., under the presidencies of McKinley, Roosevelt, and Taft, American businessmen could get aid for defense of their properties abroad; under Woodrow Wilson, there was less enthusiastic support, but in certain instances American businesses asked for and got assistance from their government.

Regulation of business: In an attempt to increase competition, the U.S. Congress passed a series of measures: 1887, 4 Feb.: Interstate Commerce Act established an Interstate Commerce Commission, America's 1st regulatory agency; 1890, 2 July: Sherman Antitrust Act (see above). 1914, 26 Sept.: Congress established the Federal Trade Commission as a powerful regulatory agency. 1914, 15 Oct.: Clayton Act enumerated unlawful restraints of trade. Comparable measures to increase competition were not passed by the European governments. 1888-94: In Britain railroad legislation regulated the rights of railroads to change prices, which decreased rather than increased competition. In the U.S., court decisions as well as legislative acts were designed to increase competition.

The power to tax: 1913, 25 Feb.: Adoption of the 16th Amendment to the U.S. Constitution gave Congress the power to levy taxes on incomes. 1914, 15 July: France for the 1st time passed a law taxing personal incomes. 1920: Germany for the 1st time taxed personal incomes. (German states earlier, 1891 ff., had introduced income taxes.)

Role of government in wartime: 1914-18: In every belligerent nation, government involvement in the economy increased during World War I. Every nation imposed new taxes. 1915, Sept.: British raised taxes sharply and introduced excess-profits tax; every year during the war British taxes rose. 1916, June: Germany imposed new war taxes on profits and business turnover. 1916: French raised taxes and introduced a turnover tax. 1917, 3 Oct.: U.S. War Revenue Act imposed a graduated income tax and an excess-profits tax on corporations. Every nation issued some type of war bonds. Every belligerent nation established new government offices to deal with wartime planning, raw-material procurement, and transport of goods. 1914, 22 May: British government acquired a 51% interest (later raised to 56%) in Anglo-Persian Oil Co., which gave the British navy a major source of fuel oil. 1915, 9 Mar.: Defence of the Realm Act was designed to mobilize Britain's resources; May: British Ministry of Munitions Act placed under government control plants that could be used to produce for the war effort. By 1918 the British government was purchasing 85% of all imported foodstuffs; operated 250 munitions factories; had oil interests; held possession of railroads, coal mines, flour mills, and Irish distilleries; controlled prices on many commodities; and rationed, 14 July, sugar, meat, butter, margarine, bacon, ham, and lard. The French, likewise, introduced extensive economic controls, taking over all the railways, making loans to manufacturers for them to convert their factories to war production, and establishing agencies for the purchase of raw materials. 1917, 28 July: U.S. established War Industries Board to coordinate the nation's war industries; it included agencies for purchase of raw materials. 10 Aug.: Lever Food and Fuel Control Act gave U.S. President the right to issue orders to encourage production and to control food and fuel distribution. 4 Dec.: 1st government contract signed for the government-owned nitrogen fixation plant at Muscle Shoals, Ala.—the only one of 5 different government-owned fixation plants that was in successful operation at the signing of the Armistice. 26 Dec.: President Woodrow Wilson took over the railways. 1918, 5 Apr.: War Finance Corporation created in the U.S. to finance war industries. Among the allies, joint government activities coordinated transport. (The Allied Maritime Transport Council was a multistate authority.) Germany took similar measures; most of the railroads were already in government hands. 1914 ff.: German War Food Administration sought to reduce German food consumption (since many imports were cut off), regulated production and distribution of foodstuffs, gave the individual states power to impose price controls (by war's end price controls covered almost all foodstuffs in nation); 1915, 25 Jan.: Germany introduced rationing. 1914 ff.: The War Raw-Material Office (Kriegs-Rohstoffabteilung —K.R.A.) regulated purchases of raw materials. 1915: German War Industry Administration started. 1915 ff.: New "War Industrial Companies" created mixed government-industry-owned companies, under the supervision of the War Industry Administration. 1916, 5 Dec.: The Hindenburg Plan enacted into law in Germany, with the goal of the complete militarization of the nation's economic life; workshops could be compelled to produce for the war effort, unused machinery could be transferred to workshops where it would be used, workers could be kept on munitions production, and all civilian men between the ages of 17 and 60 were drafted for war work. In every nation it was recognized that the extent of government involvement was temporary.

OTHER FACTORS. 1870: German unification had a highly favorable effect on economic growth in that country. 1870 ff.: The development of nationalism in Germany aided economic development, until the nationalism became so extreme that World War I began; the military interests of the state served to encourage industrialization. 1914–18: World War I stimulated American economic development; industries were built to meet war needs; there was no physical damage in the U.S. In Britain, France, Germany, and Belgium, the war caused major dislocation and slowed economic development. 1870–1919: The revolution in medical science raised health standards in the industrial nations and had a favorable effect on economic development.

MEASURES OF ECONOMIC GROWTH. 1870–1913: From the available statistics on economic growth it is clear that France developed slowly, falling far behind; Britain too, once the workshop of the world, now by her slow growth lost her leadership to the U.S.; the U.S. in particular and Germany, though to a far less extent, had a favorable rate of growth up to World War I.

ANNUAL GROWTH RATES: TOTAL OUTPUT AND OUTPUT PER CAPITA, 1870–1913
(%)

	Total Output	Output per Capita
U.S.	4.3[a]	2.2[a]
Germany	2.9[a]	1.8[a]
Belgium	2.7	1.7
Netherlands	2.2[b]	0.8[b]
U.K.	2.2	1.3
France	1.6	1.4

NOTE: Figures are compound rates.
[a] 1871–1913.
[b] 1900–1913.

Estimated per capita income in 1911: U.S., $368; Great Britain, $250; Germany, $178; France, $161.

The Spread of Industrialization

During the years 1870–1919, industrialization spread into northern Italy, the Hapsburg Empire (notably Bohemia), Sweden, Denmark, Norway, Russia, Japan, Argentina, Australia, Canada, and elsewhere. Most of these regions remained primarily pastoral or agricultural, but c. 1900 in Sweden, Norway, and Denmark there was a shift from the majority of the population being in agriculture to the majority being in other occupations. The agricultural population of Bohemia-Moravia-Silesia was 50% in 1890 and 38% in 1900. Whether agriculture or livestock raising remained the dominant mode of life or whether other activities employed more men, in all of these areas the *relative* employment in agriculture and pastoral activities was declining.

AGRICULTURE. The key change in agriculture and livestock raising was due to the expansion of the railroads, which brought farm produce into international commerce. Moreover, the development of refrigerated railroad cars and ocean transport made possible shipments of meat and other perishables over distances. Steamship travel made bulky commodities easier to ship. Everywhere commercialization of agriculture and specialization spread. In all these countries (Russia excepted), productivity in agriculture or livestock raising increased. In most cases there was more mechanization of agriculture, better breeding techniques, or alternatively (in Japan) the introduction of new seeds and better fertilizers. 1901–11: In Canada machinery used on farms more than doubled. 1884: Australian H. V. McKay invented a stripper-harvester. Wheat became important to the economic growth of Argentina, Australia, Canada, and Russia. Beef became key to the prosperity of Argentina and sheep to Australia and New Zealand. Dairy products were crucial in Denmark's economic development. Japan and Russia used taxes on agriculture as the basic means of financing industrial development. In both countries major agricultural reforms occurred. Japan: 1871: Abolition of fiefs and emergence of national taxation. 1873, July: Land-tax revision which unified revenue collection and modernized the Japanese agrarian system; it provided the government with large tax revenues, placing the burden of capital accumulation on the agricultural sector; inefficient peasants were driven into tenancy and debt (1913: 46% of land was farmed by tenant farmers); many peasants left the farms; but farm output rose, and the tax, designed to enhance agricultural efficiency as well as raise revenues, achieved its end. 1876: land tax in Japan reduced, yet it still remained the only important source of Japanese government revenues. 1885/89–1905/14: Japanese agricultural output doubled. Russia: 1870's: Peasants formed about ⅘ of the Russian population. Since 1861 they were no longer serfs, but they lived in village communes, or mirs; no peasant could leave without communal permission. The land in the commune was subdivided into allotments among peasant households; the peasants paid redemption payments stemming from the 1861 emancipation. The peasant economy was unable to increase its productivity because its income after taxes and the redemption payments did not permit large investments. Taxes were not designed to reward efficiency. 1880's: Deterioration of position of Russian peasant; Russian government policy was to tax the peasant to obtain state revenues used to industrialize; Russian grain output per capita was less than it had been 3 decades before. 1890's: Conditions worsened. 1905: Revolution in Russia accompanied by peasant uprisings. 1906, 22 Nov., and 1910, 27 June: Acts sponsored by prime minister of Russia Peter A. Stolypin (1862–1911) introduced agrarian reforms; peasants were permitted to acquire personal ownership of the land

and to swap strips of earlier allotments into a single consolidated holding; the Russian government no longer accepted the concept of household ownership; the land of peasants who left the village commune went to the head of the household, in private ownership. The way was open for the 1st time for the movement to urban areas of peasants; also for the 1st time, Russian peasants could sell their land and use the proceeds outside of agriculture. Redemption payments were ended. The acts introduced something resembling the British enclosure movement. 1907–14: More than 6 m. households asked for consolidations of allotment land. Stolypin's reforms favored personal initiative. They contributed to industrial growth, since more labor was available for the factories; the reforms also temporarily relaxed the fiscal pressures on agriculture and started to create for the 1st time among the peasantry a group of consumers. After the 1917 Russian Revolution, there were major land reforms. 1917, 8 Nov.: Land Decree ordered immediate partition of large estates and their division among the peasantry. 1918, 19 Feb.: Law for nationalization of the land. 1919: Soviet government attempted to establish state farms; major protests from the peasantry resulted.

Agricultural prices: 1890's: The low worldwide prices of agricultural products affected all these nations, but most of all Australia. The pastoralists faced not only low prices but labor difficulties and droughts, which sharply reduced the number of sheep.

Agricultural co-operatives: 1882: 1st successful Danish agricultural co-operative established; 1918: 90% of the Danish landowners were involved in co-operative societies, including creameries, bacon factories, butter and cattle export societies, and credit unions. Co-operative techniques developed in Denmark were copied throughout Scandinavia and in Canada and Australia. 1891: Cheese and butter factories (built in Canada in the 1880's) were reorganized on a co-operative basis by the Dominion Dairy Commissioner; co-operation spread; 1909: United Farmers of Alberta formed a co-operative to erect its own grain elevators; 1911: Saskatchewan Co-operative Elevator Company followed. 1915: In Australia, as a result of state action, co-operative wheat pools were formed. 1880's: In the Austrian Empire, following the German model, agricultural co-operatives were started; they developed in Italy too, at first for buying supplies and then for processing and marketing fruits, vegetables, milk, and wine. In many instances, the agricultural co-operatives were inaugurated as a response to low worldwide prices.

RAW MATERIALS. The development of industrial raw materials hastened the industrialization process in many nations; improvements in transportation made raw materials more accessible. Northern Italy's industrialization utilized iron deposits around Lake Como, in the Val d'Aosta, on the island of Elba, and at Termi in Umbria; yet the nation was short of iron. Italy produced some coal, but also imported coal from Britain. Rich natural resources existed in Bohemia, Styria, Silesia, and Moravia, and these were the parts of the Austro-Hungarian Empire where industrialization took place. Because of improved transportation, the iron-ore deposits in Krivoi Rog and coking coal in the Donets Basin began to be used for Russian industrialization. 1880's: Important petroleum deposits in the Baku region were developed, and 1883 ff.: oil became a Russian export. Canada's mineral resources were increasingly discovered and developed: copper, lead, zinc, silver, nickel, asbestos, and iron. Canada had adequate coal for domestic use, although it did import some of its coal requirements. Australia had iron and coal, but the iron and steel industry in that country was in its infancy. 1874–82: Australia was the world's largest tin producer. Japan was short of iron, which it had to import; it had coal, but needed to import blending and coking coals from north China for its metallurgical industries; Japan also had copper resources. 1885/89–1905/13: Output from Japanese mines increased tenfold. Nonmineral industrial raw materials were particularly important in the economic development of Australia: Australia had wool, which provided needed foreign exchange. Japan at first used locally grown cotton and silk as basis for its textile industry (by the 1890's, it was an importer of raw cotton). Timber exports from Russia and Sweden were important in their development.

COAL PRODUCTION
(million metric tons)

	1870	1913
Austria-Hungary	8.35	54.11
Russia	.69	32.21
Japan	.25a	19.68b
Canada	.67	14.62
Australia	.90	14.51
Italy	.06	.70

a 1874, earliest available.
b 1914 (1912, 19.50).

ENERGY. In the industrializing nations, the use of coal, petroleum, natural gas, water power, and electricity spread. These nations reflected the trend in the industrial nations away from fuel wood, gas-producer wood, sawmill waste, bagasse, and other vegetable fuels toward solid and liquid fuels, natural gas, and water power (commercial sources). Norway, Sweden, Austria, Canada, and Italy had excellent water resources which could be mobilized for hydroelectric power; development was just beginning. 1914: Russia exceeded France and Germany in terms of horsepower per head of industrial population, although Russia still lagged behind Britain and the U.S. (But Russia was still mainly agricultural and in terms of horsepower per head of total population she followed the world's leaders.)

INDUSTRY. Textiles: The 1st modern industry to develop in most of the industrializing countries was textiles. This was true in Italy, the Hapsburg Empire, Rus-

% DISTRIBUTION OF THE WORLD'S MANUFACTURINGa PRODUCTION

	Russia	Italy	Sweden	Canada	Japan	India	Other Countries
1870	3.7	2.4	0.4	1.0		11.0	
1881–85	3.4	2.4	0.6	1.3		12.1	
1896–1900	5.0	2.7	1.1	1.4	0.6	1.1	12.6
1906–10	5.0	3.1	1.1	2.0	1.0	1.2	12.3
1913	5.5	2.7	1.0	2.3	1.2	1.1	12.0

a Finished products, semimanufactures, and manufactured foodstuffs. See p. 707 above for world leaders; these plus the above add across to 100%.

sia, Japan, Argentina, Australia, and Canada. The development of the silk and cotton industries was particularly important in the history of Japan. 1870: 1st modern silk filature opened in Japan with a French technician as superintendent. 1883: Osaka Spinning Co. established 1st cotton mill in Japan to use modern large-scale production methods. 1885: More cotton cloth was produced in Japan than imported. C. 1896: More cotton was spun by machine than by hand; 1896 ff.: modernization of the cotton industry proceeded rapidly. 1914: In cotton weaving as in spinning a modern industrial organization existed in Japan. Similarly, the silk industry developed; Japan became a major exporter of raw

silk (a semimanufactured product) and also of silk textiles. Of all the newly industrializing nations, Japan alone found in the export of cotton and silk products an important source of foreign exchange; Japan alone of the newly industrializing nations found these industries to be a leading sector. 1870: All the industrializing nations imported textile machinery; 1914: some textile machinery was made in these countries—except in Argentina and Australia, which still remained dependent on imports of machinery.

Iron and steel: Steelmaking techniques spread from Britain, Western Europe, and the U.S. to the industrializing nations. In Russia, under the aegis of government support and with the help of foreign investment, the iron and steel industry developed dramatically; 1880's and 1890's: the small charcoal furnaces of Russia's 18th-cent. iron industry were increasingly replaced by coke-fired furnaces, mainly in the Ukraine. 1914: These new furnaces were larger than the ones in use in Germany or Britain, although smaller than those employed in the U.S. In Russia steel output rose even more rapidly than iron output. Austro-Hungarian iron and steel output also increased, as did production in Canada, Italy, and Sweden. C. 1890–1910: Start of Canadian steel industry (1914, 90%

of Canada's annual consumption of steel rails was produced within the Dominion). 1900, Apr.: William Sandford in Australia established an open-hearth furnace and turned out the 1st Australian steel (co. was Sandfords, Ltd.); 1913: Australian steel production was still negligible. 1901: Start of modern Japanese iron and steel industry with 1st production at government-owned Yawata Ironworks (founded in 1896, mainly for military purposes); before 1913, practically all iron and steel in Japan was produced by this works.

PIG IRON AND STEEL PRODUCTION
(million metric tons)

Year	Austria-Hungary Iron	Steel	Russia Iron	Steel	Sweden Iron	Steel	Italy Iron	Steel	Canada Iron	Steel	Japan Iron	Steel
1870	.40	.04	.36	a	.30	.01	—	—	—	—	—	—
1880	.46	.05	.45	.30	.41	.04	.02	a	—	—	—	—
1890	.96	.50	.93	.39	.46	.17	.01	.11	.02	—	—	—
1900	1.47	1.15	2.89	2.22	.52	.30	.02	.12	.09	.02	.02b	—
1910	2.01	2.15	2.74	2.35	.60	.47	.22	.64	.75	.83	.16c	—
1913	2.31	2.68	4.55	4.82	.73	.59	.43	.85	1.13	1.17	.24	.25

NOTE: See p. 707 for comparisons with major industrial nations.
a Less than 10,000, but some recorded production.
b 1901.
c Est., c. 1912.

1914–18: During World War I the Japanese and Australian iron and steel industries grew, stimulated by the cutting off of imports. 1918: Japanese output of pig iron was .63 m. tons, and .54 m. tons of steel. 1915: Broken Hill Proprietary Co. in Australia entered into iron and steel production at Newcastle, N.S.W., Australia's 1st major iron and steel producer.

Metal-products industries: In Italy metal-products industries flourished. 1870 ff.: The Ansaldo Co., founded by Giovanni Ansaldo (1819–59) in 1852, was building steam engines, then moved into shipbuilding, construction of locomotives, munitions, and, 1914–18, Ansaldo interests began to manufacture airplanes. 1880's: In Italy other general engineering firms came into operation. 1880's and 1890's: Italian bicycle industry developed and then the automobile industry. 1899: Giovanni Agnelli (1866–1945) formed FIAT (Fabbrica Italiana Automobili Torino) to manufacture

automobiles; 1899–1907: c. 40 companies established in Italy to produce automobiles. 1908: Camillo Olivetti (1868–1943) started to make typewriters. In Russia heavy-machinery industry developed rapidly, usually utilizing foreign capital; there were no automobiles or tractors or typewriters made in Russia. In Sweden, engineering industries began. Canada developed a range of metal-products industries, in heavy industries and in consumer products. Many American companies established affiliates or subsidiaries in Canada to manufacture the items they made in the U.S.; indigenous industries also emerged. 1904: Gordon M. McGregor (1873–1922) of Walkerville, Ont., in collaboration with Henry Ford, founded Ford Motor Co. of Canada, Ltd., Canada's 1st significant automobile enterprise. (1905, assembly of automobiles began; 1908, manufacture of automobiles began. Australia lagged behind, because of its less developed iron and steel industry. 1914–18: Stimulation of Australian metal-products industries because of the curtailment of imports. 1917 ff.: Automobile bodies began to be made in Australia (the chassis were still imported). 1893: 1st locomotives made in Japan. 1899: 1st bicycle manufactory established in Japan; it did not prosper. 1914–18: World War I cut off imports of bicycles; a Japanese bicycle industry developed; Japan became an exporter of bicycles to China, India, South Asia, New Zealand, etc. 1906: Horatio Anasagasti started to manufacture automobiles in Argentina (his enterprise was not a success).

Food-processing industries: As wheat, beef, and to a less extent sheep came from the Argentina pampas to Buenos Aires, stockyards, packing houses, and flour mills rose; the expanding food-processing industries led to the growth of Buenos Aires, stimulating the development of other industries, breweries, textile mills, shoe manufacturing, etc.; commerce in food products developed, based on the food-processing industries. Argentina flourished. 1890 ff.: Argentine beef increasingly replaced American beef in European markets. 1880's and 1890's: Denmark mechanized and reorganized her dairy industry, which became the basis for Danish prosperity. Food-processing industries in Australia and New Zealand spurred those nations' development.

Other industries: In most of the newly industrializing nations, breweries and sugar refineries were built, early industries in the industrializing process. Also developed: petroleum refining (Russia, Canada, Japan, Argentina), paper (Russia, Canada, Japan, Italy, Austria-Hungary, Sweden), chemicals (throughout Europe, Canada, and in Japan. 1881–1913: Chemicals were Italy's major growth industry, growing an average of 11.3% per annum). Others: electrical equipment (Russia, Canada, Japan, Italy, Austria-Hungary), rubber goods (Canada, Italy, Japan, Russia), glass (Canada, Italy, Austria-Hungary, Russia, Japan, Australia, and Argentina), and cement (Russia, Canada, Italy, Austria-Hungary, Japan, Australia, and Argentina). Switzerland developed an important watchmaking industry. In all of these nations, there was "import substitution," the increasing replacement by local manufacture of goods previously imported from abroad.

TRANSPORTATION. Canals: 1895: The German-constructed Kiel Canal across the Danish peninsula opened, reducing the time to get from the Baltic to the North Sea. 1901: The Austrian Chamber approved a proposal creating a network of canals, connecting the basins of the Danube, Elbe, Oder, Vistula, and Dniester.

Railroads: The age of the canal was past. Everywhere railroad construction far surpassed canal mileage.

RAILROAD LINES
(000 mi.)

	1870	1880	1890	1900	1910	1914	1920
Russia	7.0	15.0	20.2	31.7	41.2	48.0	36.6a
Austria-Hungary	6.0	11.5	16.8	22.9	27.6		—
Italyb	3.8	5.4	8.0	9.8	10.6		12.7
Canada	2.5	6.9	14.0	17.9	24.8	30.8	39.0
Sweden	1.1	3.7	5.0	7.0	8.7		9.4
Australia	1.1	3.6	9.8	12.6	16.5		24.1
Switzerland	0.9	1.6	2.0	2.4	2.9		3.3
Argentina	0.4	1.4	6.1	10.2	16.5		22.5
Norway	0.2	0.7	1.0	1.3	1.9		2.0
Japan	0	0.1	1.4	3.7	6.1		8.5

a Drop because of changes in territory. b State-owned railroads only.

1872: 1st Japanese railroad opened. 1885: Opening of Canada's 1st transcontinental railroad. 1903: Completion of the Trans-Siberian Railroad, Russia's transcontinental. 1917, Oct.: Opening of East-West Transcontinental Railway in Australia. 1919: After war, revolution, and civil war, about 80% of the railroads in European Russia were damaged and 60% were out of order; moreover, Russia's territorial losses deprived her of considerable railroad mileage. Railroad construction was essential to economic growth in Russia, Canada, Australia, and Argentina. Railroads decreased transportation costs and brought new regions and products into commerce; they made possible the movement of bulky commodities. They served to increase exports. In Russia and Canada the development of railroads stimulated the modern coal, iron, steel, and metallurgical industries. More slowly, in Australia, heavy industry developed, prompted in part by the railroads. By contrast, Argentina, penalized by lack of natural resources (coal and iron), did not develop heavy industries; all the materials for the Argentine railroads had to be imported. In most countries railroads extended the areas of settlement and stimulated construction industries; in Russia and Canada the construction industries were based on locally available raw materials; in Australia this was partially true; in Argentina, steel buildings were imported and not until 1908 did Argentina even have commercial production of cement.

Other overland transportation: 1877–1917: 14-fold rise in number of registered carts pulled by horses, oxen, and men in Japan was indicative of the increase in travel. Bicycles became a common mode of transport in Europe and in Japan; 1917: 1.1 m. bicycles registered in Japan. 1913: Private automobile usage in Canada was 54,000 vehicles; 1919, 342,000 (Canada in 1919 2nd only to the U.S. in private automobile usage). 1913: Private automobile usage in Italy was 20,000 vehicles; 1919, 24,000. 1913: Private automobiles in use in Russia, 7,000—all imported from abroad. 1913: C. 1,000 private automobiles in use in Japan—all imported from abroad; 1917: 3,856 automobiles registered in Japan. 1913: Figures for Australia are not available, but they were far higher than Japan; 1909–12: 2,000 Model T's were sold in Australia, plus a range of other American, British, and continental makes.

Shipping: With the exception of Argen-

tina (because of absence of raw materials) and Switzerland (because it was inland), the industrializing nations all expanded their steamship fleets.

FINANCE. Capital: Capital was short in all the newly industrializing countries, and there was considerable reliance on foreign capital. 1870's ff.: The gold standard was adopted by all; 1914: practically all abandoned it.

Banking structure: Before unification in Italy, states had had separate currency and banks of each state had rights of note issue. 1874: The Sardinian National Bank, which had grown the fastest and had ⅓ more capital than all other banks of issue combined, came to act as a central bank. 1870's: Investment banks in Italy multiplied. 1893: Massive Italian bank failures; 1893, 10 Aug.: the Sardinian National Bank was renamed the Bank of Italy. 1893 ff.: Expansion of investment banking. 1895 ff.: The large Italian banks played important roles in the industrialization of Italy, serving, as in Germany, an entrepreneurial role; the banks did their banking along German lines, making long-term loans to the metallurgical, electrical, and shipping industries. 1914: There was considerable German investment in Italian banking. Italy had an established banking structure. 1897: The Russian State Bank became a bank of issue and was converted into a central bank. 1870–1900: Development of commercial banking, at 1st along British lines. 1900–1913: Growth of large banking institutions in St. Petersburg; St. Petersburg banking developed mainly along German lines. 1913: 50 joint-stock commercial banks in Russia (6 holding 55% of total liabilities); chief among them were the St. Petersburg banks, which eclipsed the Moscow banks. 1908 ff.: Foreign investment in Russian joint-stock banks multiplied. (50.5% of the foreign investment was French, 37.1% German, 9% British, and 3.4% other nationalities.) Whereas in the 19th cent. Russian banks had not invested in industry because of absence of good investment opportunities, low standards of commercial honesty in the country, and inadequate capital, by 1908 ff. the joint-

AIDS TO TRANSPORTATION, 1870–1914

Government	Private Railroads	Government-Owned Railroads
Italy[a]		1884: 2/3 railroads; 1905: 7/8 railroads
Denmark	1870's ff.: Subsidized	1870's: Some; 1880's: commitment to develop state railroads
Russia		1881: Decision on national ownership and, 1881 ff., government bought up practically all privately owned railroads
Japan		1906–9: Nationalization of trunk railroads
Argentina	1850's–1907: Private capital got a guarantee of 7% return on investment in railroad construction, land for right of way, and duty-free imports of all equipment; 1907, 30 Sept.: Mitre Law discontinued 7% guarantee, but railroads were given a 40-year duty exemption on all equipment and materials used on the roads	1870's and 1880's: Provincial government (Buenos Aires) built 726 mi. of railroad; 1889: sold to British co.
Canada	Subsidized	
Australia		1870's: State governments adopted policy in favor of state-owned construction

[a] There was also a small percentage of mixed private-government ventures in Italy.

INVOLVEMENT IN TELEGRAPH AND TELEPHONES, 1870–1914

Government	Telegraph		Telephones
	All Government	Part Government	
Italy	Yes		1907 ff.: Purchase of private cos.
Russia	Yes		
Japan	Yes		Owned and operated
Canada		In sparsely settled communities	
Australia	Yes		Owned and operated

1880's ff.: Telegraph lines on the European Continent were government owned and operated; most telephone systems, started by private enterprise, came to be government owned and operated; Danish and Norwegian telephones remained in the private sector; in Russia telephones were not a state monopoly.

REGULATION OF BUSINESS, 1870–1914

Government	Antitrust Legislation	Other Regulation
Italy	None	Promotion rather than regulation
Russia	None	Promotion rather than regulation
Japan	None	Promotion rather than regulation
Argentina		1907, 30 Sept.: Mitre Law taxed railroads for the 1st time; introduced government's right to regulate railroads
Canada	1889: Act made it illegal to enter into conspiracy in "restraint of trade"—Canada's 1st such measure; 1910: Combines Investigation Act superseded 1889 legislation and authorized investigation of associations whose activities were detrimental to the public good (the act remained in force until 1919, when it was superseded by another, but only one investigation was conducted under it)	
Australia	1906: Industries Preservation Act to prevent monopolies; act was never made effective	

1914–18: With the war, government involvement increased. 1915: A Central Committee of War Industries in Russia sought to co-ordinate that nation's war effort; 22 Aug.: Central Committee for War Mobilization created in Italy. 1916: War profits tax introduced in Italy. In Canada and Australia, the state increasingly participated in economic life. 1917, Nov.: With the Russian Revolution, the Russian state assumed an entirely new role. It undertook land reform and nationalized the banks; a 27 Nov. decree gave workers control over Russian factories; 17 Dec.: church property was confiscated; 18 Dec.: decree established the Supreme Council of National Economy (*Vesenkha*).

OTHER FACTORS. Nationalism became associated with industrialization in the newly industrializing nations. Militarism, in Japan especially but also in Russia,

contributed to the growth of industry. Japanese victory over China and Russia gave that nation new industrial prowess. 1905: Russia's defeat made Russians reexamine their industrial weakness. Political unity in Italy, Japan, Canada, and Australia was an important component in the growth process. Russia, Canada, and Australia had unsettled frontiers, which had impact on economic development. As yet the Russian frontier had little effect on economic growth; the railroad had penetrated Siberia; the frontier meant the possibilities of a national market and rich resources. Wheat made the Canadian West, and the frontier gave vitality to that country; by 1914, most of Canada was settled, and the frontier could be considered "closed." In Australia the open frontier attracted new immigrants, but the growth in output was accompanied by a rise in population, so the growth rate per capita was relatively low. The development process was uneven. There were spurts and then setbacks. 1890's: Russian economy saw rapid industrial growth; 1901–3: serious economic crisis in Russia; then, with the Revolution of 1905 and other disorders, not until 1909 did industrialization again proceed. 1870's and 1880's: Years of rapid development in Australia; 1890's: depression; 1903/04–1913/14: continuous and dramatic rise in real Australian gross domestic product. In Europe the effects of World War I were disastrous. There was a loss of men, of financial assets, and of momentum. In no country was the damage more devastating than in Russia. With the war came a disorganization of production and supply. Industrial output slumped; transportation could not meet national needs. War losses were immense. The revolutions disrupted the Russian economy. With the signing of the Brest-Litovsk Treaty, 3 Mar., 1918, Russia withdrew from the war; the economic losses under this treaty were substantial; Russia gave up large territories, which included 40% of the industry and industrial population of the former Russian Empire, 70% of the iron and steel production, and 90% of the sugar output. Civil war followed, and the Russian economy experienced new setbacks. 1914–18: In Argentina and Australia, with imports curtailed, there were shortages. In Argentina total industrial production and national income went down, while with scarcity prices rose 27%. 1913/14–1919/20: In Australia prices increased 72.6%; in constant prices there was a decline in gross domestic product. Yet in Argentina and Australia, there were import substitutions; after the war, both

countries emerged strengthened. In Japan industry developed new vigor.

MEASUREMENT OF ECONOMIC GROWTH. 1860–1914: Divergent estimates of Russian increases in aggregative national output range from 2.5% per annum (and 1% per capita) to over 3.5% per annum; in Russia the mass of the population was involved in relatively stagnant agriculture, which deflated the aggregative national output figures (1885–1913: annual rate of industrial growth in Russia estimated at 5.7%).

ANNUAL % RATE OF GROWTH
OF TOTAL OUTPUT, 1870–1913
(compound rates)

Japan	4.4a
Canada	3.8
Australia	3.4
Denmark	3.2
Sweden	3.0
Switzerland	2.4
Norway	2.2b
Italy	1.4

a 1880–1913.
b 1871–1913.

ANNUAL % RATE OF GROWTH
OF OUTPUT PER CAPITA, 1870–1913
(compound rates)

Sweden	2.3
Denmark	2.1
Canada	2.0
Japan	1.9a
Norway	1.4b
Switzerland	1.3c
Australia	.8
Italy	.7

a 1880–1913.
b 1871–1913.
c 1890–1913.

Economic Change in the Less Developed World

During the years 1870–1919, in Africa and Asia, nomadic peoples began to settle. Algerian nomads established villages. Yet in the Arabian peninsula, in Persia and Afghanistan, in parts of New

Guinea, and in parts of Africa, nomads still followed the way of life they had pursued for centuries.

AGRICULTURE. Most of the world continued to live by agriculture. In isolated locales little disturbed the traditional patterns. And yet, increasingly, there was a breakdown of isolation, disruption, and change. With the opening of the Suez Canal, the extension of transportation facilities, and the expansion of international trade, new commercialization of agriculture was possible. The many new plantations and new crops caused change. The spread of colonization began to alter the agricultural life of less developed countries; the colonial powers' confrontation with alien patterns of land tenure and their attempts to understand, formalize, or revise these patterns created change. In many areas ideas of private property, wage labor, and cash crops were introduced on a large scale for the 1st time. In the less developed tropical areas there was primitive (subsistence), commercial (within the country), and export agriculture. Primitive agriculture still predominated in most of Africa, Asia, and parts of Latin America; it continued to be shifting or settled, to involve the most rudimentary use of tools, and to be characterized by an absence of specialization. Crop failures, famines, and often starvation continued to be the fate of masses of peoples who lived on a subsistence basis, especially in Asia. Commercial agriculture for domestic consumption was still not widespread in the less developed world, because of lack of markets. Nonetheless, as cultivation of crops for export grew, indigenous growers no longer raised their own food; they began to purchase food; their specialization stimulated domestic commercial agriculture. Likewise, colonial administrators and white settlers were part of a market economy. Urban centers in Asia, Africa, and Latin America depended on food purchases. Paid agricultural labor on plantations had money to buy food. Thus there was being created limited commercial agriculture for domestic consumption. Export agriculture of 2 kinds existed, plantation and native agriculture. Plantations in Asia and Africa were usually foreign owned and managed; in Latin America, many were foreign owned, but many were not. Plantations have been described as "en-

claves" in less developed countries; they used the most advanced knowledge and scientific techniques of the developed nations; in general they employed considerable capital; they were part of a market economy; they specialized in particular tropical export crops. They hired native wage labor. Their modern business organization was in contrast to the backwardness of the societies in which they existed.

Tropical agriculture: The years 1870–1914 were the peak period for Europeans and Americans to organize new overseas plantations. In Ceylon the British started quinine, tea, and then rubber plantations. In Malaya the British began sugar, coffee, and coconut plantations; 1895: rubber started as a large-scale plantation crop in Malaya; investors were British and Chinese. In India, British-owned or -managed tea, quinine, sugar, cotton, and jute plantations multiplied. French investors started plantations in the newly acquired French territory in Indochina. The Dutch government had, in accord with the culture system, created large estates in the Netherlands East Indies; 1870: the Dutch government introduced an Agrarian Land Law, inaugurating the "Corporation Plantation Period" in the history of the East Indies. 1873: 73% of the agricultural exports from the Netherlands East Indies came from private plantations; 19% came from Dutch government plantations; the plantations were in sugar, coffee, tea, quinine, tobacco, sisal, tapioca, oil palm, and even rice; by the turn of the cent., rubber plantations were founded. Thus the plantation system extended throughout the colonial areas of the Far East. It was the same in Africa. In tropical Africa, British, German, Belgian, and French-owned plantations became prevalent. King Leopold and then the Belgian government encouraged private investors to start plantations in the Congo. 1899: In French Equatorial Africa, the French decreed that about ⅔ of the territory would be divided among some 40 French cos.; these cos. got monopoly rights over forest and other products. 1909 ff.: In place of these large concessions (many of which were failures), the French government started to grant smaller concessions for French private rubber, coffee, banana, cocoa, and palm-oil plantations. In German East Africa, as in German West Africa, the Germans granted huge tracts of land to companies, syndicates, and individuals with large amounts of capital for them to establish sisal, coffee, rubber, cotton, cacao, tea, and banana plantations; 1903 ff.: in East Africa, where there were large areas of uncultivated, unsettled land, British investors started sisal, rubber, coffee, and tea plantations. In the Caribbean, especially Cuba, American-owned sugar plantations multiplied, and in Middle America banana plantations were created. In Brazil, coffee, sugar, cacao, tobacco, and cotton plantations continued to be owned by Brazilians. Elsewhere in Latin America, large-scale sugar plantations, owned by wealthy Latin Americans (Peruvians, Colombians, Ecuadorians, Mexicans, etc.), continued. Often the plantations in Latin America would have absentee landownership, but the absentee owner would be a Latin American rather than a European or North American. 1876–1910: In Mexico under Porfirio Díaz, lands of Indians and mestizos and communal lands (ejidos) increasingly went into the possession of large landowners, some of them Mexicans and some foreign; by 1910, 90% of the rural population of Mexico had no land. 1917, 31 Jan.: The new Mexican constitution was adopted; it proclaimed the principles of agrarian reform; yet large landholdings, foreign and Mexican, still persisted in Mexico. Often plantation agriculture stimulated local farming. United Fruit Co. purchased from small farmers; British planters in the West Indies bought, processed, and marketed the output of native sugar-cane growers; similarly, British plantation owners in Ceylon purchased from local tea producers. In Malaya, stimulated by the success of the large rubber plantations, natives planted the same seeds with excellent results. Plantation owners provided marketing outlets and often processing facilities for the local crop. European traders, who were not plantation owners, offered marketing

channels for peasant agriculture. British administrators in West Africa believed that the development of peasant agricultural activities was a natural growth and plantations were an artificial creation (only maintained through organized immigration or some form of compulsory labor), that native agriculture was the cheapest means of producing for export markets, and that peasant output could be increased. Thus the British in West Africa encouraged local production. Native export crops were at first raised, mixed in with traditional crops; initially, they involved no change in the method of cultivation and no new technology. Often, increases in peasant output came simply from the expansion of land under cultivation. Peasant export agriculture grew particularly in areas where there was no population pressure and where there were unused arable lands available. As indigenous farmers developed cash crops, they often came to specialize. Native agriculture for export included the rubber of the Amazon Valley (collected from wild trees by Brazilians): rubber, coffee, and cocoa from the Gold Coast; palm oil throughout British and French West Africa; groundnuts (peanuts) in Gambia and Senegal; cocoa in Guinea; timber from the Ivory Coast; cotton in Uganda; coffee in Colombia and Central America; and rice in Burma and Thailand. In short, crops that were primarily native crops in one country (rubber in Brazil, palm oil in Nigeria, coffee in Colombia, for instance) could be plantation crops in another country (rubber in Malaya, palm oil in the Belgian Congo, coffee in Brazil).

Agricultural research: The colonial powers conducted research into tropical crops and conditions of growing. The British led in establishing botanical gardens, in testing seeds, in introducing agricultural laboratories, in starting government demonstration farms, but the other colonial powers also took similar steps. Studies were made of plant diseases, of methods of obtaining higher yields, and of means of eliminating insects and parasites. The British found agricultural research a profitable proposition; foreign plantation owners also conducted research on their own.

Temperature-zone agriculture: Most of the less developed areas were in tropical climates. In the temperate zones of the less developed regions, changes in agriculture were somewhat different. Whereas in the tropics large foreign investments were made in plantation agriculture, in the temperate areas of the less developed world, although foreign capital often was involved in the commercialization of agriculture, in trade and transportation, there was far less foreign investment in agriculture itself. When there was foreign investment, it was by settlers rather than by large impersonal plantation enterprises. In temperate zones of the less developed world, south of the Tropic of Capricorn, white settlers were common. In Southern Africa, European settlers established corn, wheat, and tobacco farms; in South-West Africa, Europeans became involved in stock raising. In the temperate areas of Latin America that were less developed—in southern Brazil, Uruguay, and south-central Chile—settlers undertook European-style farming. In southern Brazil and Uruguay, stock raising and corn and wheat farming prevailed. Chile, following Iberian-peninsula practices, developed large estates with inefficient farming, but these were owned by settlers in Chile, not foreigners. Agriculture in all these temperate zone nations was largely commercial. It involved agriculture on private property. In the less developed areas of traditional settlement above the Tropic of Cancer some changes took place in agriculture, although these regions in large part were characterized by an absence of change, by a continuation of old forms of cultivation, traditional patterns of land tenure, and subsistence agriculture. Nonetheless, in western Turkey, mechanization of agriculture began. (In Adana, for example, in the early 1900's there were in use 1,000 mowing machines, 100 steam threshers, and 110 steam plows.) Cash crops for export increased; 1884–1911: Turkish tobacco cultivation grew 3-fold (tobacco was Turkey's main export); Turkish cotton output in Adana ex-

panded from 400 tons, 1896, to 33,750 tons, 1911. In Syria (tobacco), Egypt (cotton), Iraq (dates), and Lebanon (silk), as well as wheat and barley in most of these lands, there was an expansion of cash crops for export. The extension of breeding of silkworms in Lebanon provided a basis for considerable prosperity. In general, in the 19th cent. agricultural methods did not alter, but the areas under cultivation rose, causing output to expand. In the early 20th cent. there was some introduction of improved seeds and commercial fertilizer in the Middle East countries; in Lebanon scientific research aided in preventing diseases of the silkworm. Throughout the Ottoman Empire, the substitution of private property for communal or tribal systems of land tenure began to occur. In Iran the output of cash crops rose slowly, but exports were restricted by poor transportation. 1870's ff.: In China attempts to increase areas under cultivation were made, but methods of cultivation remained unchanged. 1878–79: A famine was estimated to have destroyed between 9 to 13 m. persons in China. The Chinese had used the iron plow before Europe; now, as the West switched to steel plows and extensive mechanization, China did not change, believing in its superiority. China's tea production dropped, faced with competition from Indian tea, which was raised on large plantations; China failed to modernize her tea industry, and tea remained a peasant crop. Likewise, cotton in China was a peasant crop. 1900 ff.: Chinese silk suffered a decline, faced with Japanese competition. (Chinese farmers were unable to prevent silkworm disease, or produce as high a quality product as Japan.) Land taxes and land tenure relationships remained basically unaltered in China, although tenant farming increased. 1918: C. 50% of Chinese peasants were occupying owners, 30% tenants, and 20% owned part and leased part of their land. The unit under cultivation remained small. With population rising, in the early 20th cent., landless peasants provided a pool of cheap coolie labor for urban and rural areas (and for emigration) and also a source of recruits for warlord armies. Productivity in Chinese agriculture showed no increase; changes in agriculture did not become aids to economic development. There was no foreign investment in Chinese agriculture.

Relocation of agricultural production: (1) Rubber: 1876: Britisher H. A. Wickham transported rubber seeds from the Brazilian Amazon River to England; 1876–79: some 7,000 plants were raised at Kew Gardens. 1876 ff.: These plants were shipped to the Far East, replanted in government gardens, and then transplanted on plantations; in time the trees began to yield, especially in Malaya and Ceylon; the cultivation of *Hevea brasiliensis* then spread to the Netherlands East Indies. Plantation output rose rapidly in the East, and, 1914, Asian rubber output reached 52.17% of the world's production; Brazilian wild rubber production was eclipsed. (2) Cacao: 1885: 1st export of cacao from the Gold Coast; 1919: the Gold Coast produced half the world's supply. (3) Quinine: 1870's: Increasing production of plantation quinine in Java and India brought the price of quinine planted in Ceylon down to unprofitable levels. (4) Tea: 1870's: British producers of quinine in Ceylon increasingly switched to tea; 1875: barely 1,000 acres planted with tea in Ceylon; 1893: 305,000 acres of tea. (5) Coffee: 1880's: Coffee became a major crop for Colombia. 1885: Coffee cultivation—plagued by the borer beetle and leaf blight—came to an end in India (land was replanted with tea or quinine). As coffee in India and Ceylon declined, Brazilian coffee output grew. 1880–81: Brazilian coffee output 3.7 m. 60-kilo bags; 1901–02: output 16.3 m. 60-kilo bags; Brazil was the world's largest coffee producer. (6) Sisal: 1893: 1st introduced from Mexico into Africa by the Germans. (7) Opium: 1907: British government in India made an agreement with China to cut opium exports to China; this resulted in a reduction of opium cultivation in India.

Agricultural co-operatives: 1904: Co-operative Credit Societies' Act passed in India, allowing credit societies to be formed. 1907: India had 149 co-operatives. 1912: Indian law passed allowing the formation of co-operative societies for other than credit; co-operatives were formed for seed distribution, purchase of manures and implements, cattle insurance, cotton sales, dairying, and cotton ginning; 1918: India had 26,465 co-operatives. Even so, co-operatives did not have significant impact in India—or in other parts of the less developed world.

Effects of change: The consequences of all the changes in agriculture were (1) plantation agriculture disrupted existing traditional society and demonstrated what could be done with agriculture, given sufficient capital and skill; (2) plantations in their demand for wage labor, no matter how small the wage was and no matter if they used immigrant labor, increased the monetization of the economy—an essential precondition for later economic development; (3) plantation agriculture, in that it encouraged native growers to raise and market similar crops, created profitable farming enterprises outside the foreign enclave; (4) commercialization of agriculture in the tropics and in the temperate areas brought increased monetization; (5) agricultural research, to the extent that it existed, served a useful purpose for less developed countries; (6) new crops offered new sources of revenue and more effective use of resources; (7) the agricultural co-operative movement served to spread information about scientific agriculture, and to encourage commercialization of agriculture. These were affirmative aspects of the changes. Attempts at changing or clarifying land-tenure relations seem at this point to have had no clearly positive or negative effect on economic development. What was still absent in all these less developed areas was an effective use of agricultural surpluses for economic development; this did not occur because (1) there were still limited surpluses outside of the plantation economies (which because of their foreign ownership were "capital-autonomous"), and (2) the governments of these countries did not devise fiscal policies designed to tax agriculture for the benefit of economic development, as was done, for example, in Russia and Japan. The co-operative movement did not serve a constructive function in this respect, because of its limited impact. Likewise, in none of the less developed nations did agricultural incomes rise to the point that peasants provided a market for domestically produced industrial products. In India, China, Mexico, and Brazil, incipient industrialization seems to have been retarded by the absence of rural markets. Because a large part of the distribution of export crops was in foreign hands, the profits accrued from the trading activities did not usually go back into the countries' economy and aid their growth. But over time, Asians, Africans, and Latin Americans did participate in the trade and services, with favorable results.

RAW MATERIALS. Diamonds and gold: 1869: Diamonds were discovered in the Kimberley fields in South Africa; 1886: discovery of gold on the Witwatersrand in South Africa. Diamonds and gold spurred immigration to South Africa and created prosperity. Except during the Boer War, South African gold production rose steadily; 1905 ff.: South Africa was consistently the world's largest gold producer; 1913: South African gold output was 8.81 m. troy ounces. Industrial raw materials in the less developed countries were slowly coming into production, but, compared with the industrial nations, output was small.

Coal: Production in 1913 (m. metric tons) : India, 14.9; China, 14.0; South Africa (Transvaal, Natal, and Cape of Good Hope.) 8.8; Mexico, 2.4 (1912). In India the new railroad lines opened the way to develop certain coal-mining areas. The coal fields in Bengal and Bihar were developed by British capital. 1895 ff: Chinese coal attracted foreign capital; 1913: the largest producer was the Kailan Mining Administration, a British-Chinese enterprise. 1905 ff.: Japan, which lacked good coking coal, made investments in Chinese coal mining. 1914 ff.: There was considerable foreign interest in developing Chinese coal mines, but poor transportation and lack of good harbors on the China coast hampered the export trade in coal.

Iron: The iron-ore resources of Brazil were becoming well known, but there was not much development. Iron ore was mined in India. 1905 ff.: In China, the Japanese, who had virtually no iron-ore resources, took leadership in developing Chinese iron mining with the goal of meeting Japanese needs; the 3 largest Chinese iron mines were all financed by Japanese capital. The Japanese invested in iron mining in Manchuria. Iron-ore deposits in North Africa (in Tunisia and Algeria) were developed by European capital. With extension of railroads, new minerals came into production.

Other minerals: Minerals (other than gold, coal, and iron) which provided, or would provide, substantial export industries for less developed nations included nitrates, tin, copper, and oil. (1) Nitrates: Nitrate production in Chile grew steadily; during World War I Chile was under a cloak of prosperity based on nitrate production. Nitrates had been developed mainly by British capital. (2) Tin: 1883: Malayan tin output exceeded Australian production and, 1883–1919, Malaya was 1st in worldwide production. 1889–1904: The Netherlands East Indies was in 2nd place, then, 1904–19, Bolivia held 2nd place, with the Netherlands East Indies in 3rd position. China and Thailand also became substantial producers of tin; 1903 ff.: Nigerian production of tin began, undertaken by British capital; Nigeria became an important producer. (3) Copper: 1878 ff.: Copper in Chile was a declining industry; 1880: Chile produced ⅕ of the copper consumed in the world; 1882: Chile produced less than 1/10 of the world's copper. In the early 1900's American investments in Chilean copper (based on new technology for processing low-grade ores) created new possibilities for that Chilean industry. 1911: Belgian capital started production in the copper mines of the Belgian Congo. 1870–1910: Mexico increased its production of copper, lead, zinc, silver, etc. 1870–1914: Turkey enlarged its production of coal, lead, emery, borax, and chrome.

Oil: While most of the world's oil came

from the U.S. and Russia (until 1917), in underdeveloped countries oil resources began to be developed. 1890: Royal Dutch started to develop oil fields in Sumatra, and other Dutch oil companies got concessions there. 1896: Samuels obtained 3 concessions in East Borneo. 1901: American Edward Doheny started to drill in Mexico; commercial oil production began; 1918: Mexican oil production surpassed Russian output and became 2nd only to U.S. output. (1918: U.S. output, 355 m. barrels; Mexican output, 63 m. barrels.) 1908: Oil was found in commercial quantities in Iran by Anglo-Persian Oil Co. 1914: Commercial oil discovered in Venezuela. The development of mineral resources on a large scale was by foreign capital. Oil production in the less developed countries was in every case financed and managed by foreign enterprises. Whereas in all the industrial and most of the industrializing nations a large percentage of the mineral resources was used domestically to supply domestic industry, in less developed countries the bulk of the mineral resources was exported to industrial nations. Nonmineral industrial resources in the less developed countries often existed in the form of raw cotton, hemp, jute, and timber. Both India and China grew cotton, which provide a basis for their early cotton industries. But by the early 1900's China was importing raw cotton for her industry.

LABOR. Mobility of labor: Demand for wage labor on the plantations and in the mines of the industrializing areas created new labor mobility. In Brazil, the new textile mills in Rio attracted wage labor. The entry of foreign labor—European, Chinese, or Indian—or the migration of African labor over considerable distances within Africa (and the mixing in the labor forces of various African tribes) represented new mobility throughout the less developed world. The continued migration of Arab traders into Africa and of Greeks, Armenians, and Syrians into Egypt was also evidence of mobility. 1878: China lifted official prohibitions on migrations of peasants from northern China to Manchuria. Slavery was being ended in most of the less developed

countries, although it still persisted in much of the Arab world. 1868–1910: Thailand and Cambodia abolished slavery. 1873: End of slavery in Puerto Rico. 1884: Legal status of slavery abolished in Malaya. 1886: Cuba ended slavery. 1884, Nov.–1885, Feb.: The Berlin Conference formally prohibited slavery in the Congo, but King Leopold's subsequent use of enforced black labor virtually voided the antislavery provisions. 1877, Aug.: Egypt and Britain signed a Slave Trade Convention, providing for an end to the slave trade in the Sudan by 1889 (it was not effective). 1888, 13 May: Brazil abolished slavery. 1916: Slavery made illegal in southern Nigeria and in all of Kenya. Tradition remained a key factor inhibiting labor mobility everywhere in the less developed world. The caste system in India was not conducive to labor mobility. In a number of Latin American countries, Ecuador, Peru, Bolivia, and in parts of Central America, Indians and poor mestizos fell into debt to landlords and signed wage contracts to cover the debt that involved debtor servitude; such contracts served to impede labor mobility. Similarly, in exchange for land, certain relationships of servitude or indenture existed in the west-coast countries of Latin America.

Quality of labor: In all the less developed countries, there was a persistent shortage of skilled, literate labor. In India, despite overpopulation, there was an acute shortage of factory workers. Labor was uncommitted to factory work, and served part time in farming. Other less developed countries found similar shortages. On foreign-owned plantations and even more in the mining camps, workers were taught elementary skills which had been lacking. The absence of skilled, literate workers was unquestionably a major factor in retarding industrialization. Even more, the absence of managers and technicians retarded industrialization.

ENERGY. The energy resources of the less developed world remained for the most part undeveloped. The use of steam power in developing modern industry spread slowly in India and China and parts of Latin America. The use of electric power and the power of the internal combustion engine was starting. 1893: 1st use of hydroelectric power in Mexico. 1901: 1st large hydroelectric plant started in Brazil. Human, animal, and water power were, however, still the main sources of energy for most of the less developed world.

INDUSTRIES. Textiles: India's modern textile industry had preceded Japan's, yet it developed more slowly. 1876: India had a million power driven spindles. 1887: Empress Mills Factory started operations in Nagpur, India, founded by Jamsetjee N. Tata (1839–1904); it installed the newest British machinery and was an innovator in the Indian textile industry. Indian cotton textile factories were under the control of Indians, including Parsees, and were located in Bombay and western India. Often they employed British managers. While the Indian industry had difficulty maintaining itself against the pressure of goods imported from Britain and later (in the 20th cent.) from Japan, the industry did develop. 1914: India was the 4th largest cotton manufacturer in the world (following the U.S., Great Britain, and Japan). India likewise developed an important jute industry. 1870's: Boom in jute production; 1908: Calcutta jute output surpassed that of Dundee. 1890: China's 1st modern textile mill was established, the Shanghai Machine Cotton Weaving Co. 1912: China passed the million mark in power spindles; 1913: there were 46 Chinese-owned cotton mills in that country, and a number of others which were financed by foreign capital. In the cotton-producing countries in Latin America, modern textile industries developed. 1909: There were a million power-driven spindles in Brazil. Brazil's textile industry developed slowly because of high production costs. (Transportation of the raw cotton to the factory was expensive, coal for steam power was usually imported, productivity was low, equipment was imported, marketing charges were high with poor transportation, and taxation proved a handicap.) 1880's–1910: Modern textile industries in Mexico, Peru, and to a lesser extent Colombia and Venezuela developed. British

textile machinery and technicians from Lancashire were often imported for the industry. In the Ottoman Empire, there were successful silk factories (in Lebanon), a variety of carpet-weaving plants, and a few cotton-yarn factories. Many of the latter were failures; attempts at modernization were unsuccessful; older handicraft industries disappeared; and the empire became increasingly dependent on imports of cotton yarn and fabrics. Egypt did start a few modern textile plants and 2 spinning mills; it was exceptional on the African continent. South of the Sahara there were no modern textile plants, and increasingly African consumers imported western textiles.

Iron and steel: The iron and steel industries in the less developed countries were in their infancy. 1890: Construction of China's 1st modern iron and steel plant, the Hanyang Iron and Steel Works, began in Hankow (completed 1893); 1914: production, 135,000 tons of steel; that year, the iron and steel firm passed to Japanese financial and managerial control; 1914–18: Japanese influence in the Chinese iron and steel industry grew. 1900–1903: 1st modern steelworks in Latin America built at Monterrey, a joint venture of American and Mexican capital. 1905: Chilean government granted a concession to a French co. to start an iron and steel industry in Chile (the French enterprise was not a success). 1911, Dec.: Operation of Tata Iron and Steel Co. began in Bengal, 155 mi. west of Calcutta, financed by Indian capital but with foreign management; this was India's 1st iron and steel plant; 1914: production: 150,000 tons of pig iron and 75,000 tons of finished steel. 1917, 19 Oct.: 1st successful manufacture of commercial steel in Brazil—in the Engenho de Dentro works of the Central Railroad of Brazil.

Other industries: An assortment of modern industries, all on a small scale, began to develop in India, China, and parts of Latin America (Brazil and Mexico, mainly). In Egypt, under the British occupation, some breweries, cigarette factories, and soap manufactories developed. These were typical early industries. Other early industries included flour milling and sugar refining. In Brazil there were glass and paper factories. 1914: In India cement production started. But industrialization in the less developed world was limited.

TRANSPORTATION. Railroads: Railroad construction expanded in Asia, Africa, and Latin America. Railroads were built primarily by foreign capital; most were designed to bring primary products (agricultural and mineral) into world commerce. Some had as a goal more effective colonial administration. Improved ocean transportation connected with the railroads.

RAILROADS IN THE LESS DEVELOPED WORLD
(000 mi.)

	1870	1880	1890	1900	1910	1920
Latin America	2.4	7.9	34.9	37.5	60.7	69.2
Asia (excl. Russia)	5.1	10.0	20.1	36.5	59.5	59.5
Africa	1.1	2.9	5.9	12.5	23.0	n.a.

1870: Brazil had 650 mi. of railroad; 1920, 17,800 mi.; the railroads were built mainly by foreign capital. 1876, June: 1st railroad opened in China, with capital provided by the British trading house of Jardine, Mattheson & Co. (a short line from Shanghai to Kiangwan); 1876, Aug.: a Chinese was killed on the railroad; 1877: the rails were torn up and shipped to Formosa (where they rusted); 1880: the Tangshan-Hsukochwang railroad was built in China between the Kaiping coal mines and Pei Tang; 1896: China had only 240 mi. of railroad; 1896 ff.: the French, Russians, British, Japanese, and later Americans got concessions to build railroads in China. 1920: Only 5,000 mi. of railroads in China; many provinces had no railroads at all; transportation was inadequate. 1877: Mexico had 417 mi. of railroad; 1920: 13,000 mi., mainly financed by foreign capital. 1885: 1st railroad in Malaya, built to transport tin from the mines; 1st railroad in tropical Africa, connecting Dakar with the Senegal River port of St. Louis. 1888, 12 Aug.: Railroad connections made between Constantinople and Western Europe; 1889: German investors started railroad construction in Turkey; this was the 1st step on a projected Berlin to Baghdad Railroad; large sections of the railroad were built but at the outbreak of war, 1914, the railroad had not been completed. 1890's: Much of African railroad construction was in South Africa; 1892: 1st railroad built in Iran; 1915: Iran had no other railroads; 1916: Russian company completed a line from Dzhulfa to Tabriz. 1893: 1st railroad opened in Thailand. 1896: Kenya-Uganda railroad started, a key East African railroad. 1900–1910: Intensive railroad building in India, based on British capital; 1920: India alone had 37,000 mi. of railroad. 1903: Benguela railroad started in Africa. 1909: British South Africa Co. had provided Southern and Northern Rhodesia with their railroad systems, offering alternative routes to the sea through the Cape or through Beira.

Consequences of railroad building: New areas were opened to development. Agricultural properties and mines were brought into commercial development. Isolation of communities was broken down. Employment on railroads meant the introduction of cash wages and more monetization. Not only did railroads open new sources of supplies but they opened new markets. 1920: Lord Lugard estimated that 1 railroad train in Africa could do the work of 13,000 human carriers at $\frac{1}{20}$ the cost. Locomotives were not bothered by the tsetse fly, which killed draft animals in much of Africa. Thus, with the railroads, large areas in Africa became open to development. But railroad construction in the less developed world was not sufficient to create countrywide markets because of the low per capita income.

Other means of transportation: Despite the development of the railroad, primitive means of transportation still persisted in most of the less developed world. Human carriers were widely used. Where tsetse flies were absent, pack animals were used in many areas. Automobile usage in the less developed nations was low. Internal water transport was aided by the increasing use of steamships, but traditional means of travel by water persisted.

COMMUNICATIONS. Under the aegis of foreign investment and colonial administrators, telegraph lines were introduced worldwide. 1870–71: Cable lines connected Vladivostok, Nagasaki, Shanghai, Hong Kong, and Singapore, and from there telegraph communications went around the world via London and San Francisco.

FINANCE. All the less developed countries were short of capital. They had no domestic capital markets of importance. Many countries borrowed in Europe. With the aid of European entrepreneurs private companies floated their stock in Europe. Colonial governments often became involved in local enterprises because of the absence of available private (foreign or domestic) capital. In China the government took part in Chinese industry. Banking intermediaries (foreign and domestic) came into existence in the less developed areas, but they were inadequate to serve the needs of economic development. Everywhere there were foreign banking houses. 1896: 1st modern Chinese bank established, Imperial Bank of China. 1913: Bank of China started under government auspices; 1914: 17 modern banks in China; modern banking began to replace the old-fashioned Shansi banks. 1915: Chinese government authorized the creation of agricultural banks. In India, banking lagged; the government of India was the key banker in the country; in these years it had its own cash balances and had exclusive right of note issue. 1913: British-owned exchange banks—handling remittances of monies to and from India—numbered 12; there were 18 joint-stock banks in India, with capital and reserves of more than Rs. 5 lakhs (Rs. 500,000) ; there were also the Presidency banks. 1890: Imperial Bank of Persia founded, chartered in England. 1891: Loan Bank of Persia established, as branch of the Russian State Bank. In the Ottoman Empire, foreign banks proliferated; 1888: the government founded an agricultural bank in the Ottoman Empire. In Latin America new banking institutions started; 1871, 17 Aug.: Banco Nacional de Bolivia founded; 1911: Banco Central de Bolivia established. 1882: Banco Nacional Mexicano founded (1884: reorganized as Banco Nacional de Mexico, S. A.). 1888–89: New banks in Brazil multiplied. *In toto,* banking facilities in the less developed world, however, were not plentiful. Moneylenders, charging high rates of interest, continued to be prevalent in all countries.

Stock exchanges: Less developed countries had no domestic capital markets of importance, although stock exchanges were being started. 1892: 1st stock exchange in Chile established in Valparaiso; 1893: stock exchange in Santiago, Chile, begun. 1893: A mercantile exchange, the Royal Exchange, was established in Calcutta. 1899: Indian Share and Stock-Brokers Association formed in Bombay; it dealt in joint-stock co. securities. 1908: The Calcutta Stock Exchange Association was started. Often with the aid of European entrepreneurs, private cos. in less developed countries would sell their securities on European exchanges.

FOREIGN TRADE. Commodity exports from undeveloped nations rose, and European and American businessmen made investments in agriculture, mining, and trade in less developed nations, as Latin America became increasingly settled, as railroads penetrated the interiors of all continents, as port facilities were improved, as the Suez Canal (completed 1869) made transportation between East and West easier and the Panama Canal, opened Aug. 1914, encouraged trade between the U.S. and Latin America, as refrigerated cars aided the movement of tropical output, and as the demands in most developed nations grew, based on higher income in the latter nations.

VALUE OF FOREIGN TRADE IN 1913
(EXPORTS PLUS IMPORTS)
($ million)

British India	1,383
China	750
Brazil	643

Less developed countries were typically exporters of primary materials and importers of manufactured goods. The unequal treaties of earlier years meant that many less developed countries could not place high duties on imports. Some less developed countries, which had in earlier years exported manufactured products, found they could no longer compete in world markets. 1900 ff.: India lost its export markets for cotton goods in the Far East to Japan. Probably the only instance where a less developed country developed a new manufactured product as an important export was India, with its export of manufactured jute. There were some other cases where there were exports of manufactured goods, based on the processing of local raw materials.

Trading cos.: The age of the chartered co. temporarily returned. Having eschewed monopoly privileges and having dissolved the major trading cos. of times past, Great Britain in Africa and in Borneo, and Germany in Africa, re-embarked on a policy of chartering giant trading cos. with special privileges. Outside of Africa and Borneo, however, large trading cos. with monopoly rights and administrative functions were a thing of the past. Trading firms and corporations, without monopolies, handled international transactions.

Consequences of foreign-trade expansion: Increased foreign trade introduced money into less developed countries. Port cities grew up based on foreign trade. The coastal towns remained in sharp contrast to the interiors of many nations where commercialization had not penetrated; yet more and more, Africans and Asians who had never had any contact with money became fewer. Foreign trade introduced new products to the less developed countries. As international trade grew, banking, insurance, shipping, and marketing abroad continued to be handled in large part by foreigners. Thus the benefits of this activity did not accrue to indigenous entrepreneurs. Yet in some countries there developed certain services connected with trade—and moneys were made locally. Chinese merchants—aided by their guild organizations—began to handle the distribution within that country of imported goods. In India and China profits made from these activities were sometimes reinvested within the country. Indian merchants mingled their capital with British money in developing industry. Chinese merchants invested in industries (in joint activities with the government or with foreign capital, and sometimes alone). Yet frequently, in the less developed countries, men who made money did not invest their earnings at home; instead they spent the earnings on articles of consumption imported from abroad. Thus, moneys made from foreign trade did not altogether satisfactorily serve the function of providing domestic investment capital, as had been the case, for example, in Great Britain and the U.S.

FOREIGN INVESTMENT. Foreign investment in the less developed countries played an increasingly important role. In some countries, foreign investment prompted the extension of imperialism. Thus, 1869: the bey of Tunis, who had borrowed heavily in Europe, did not meet his obligations, and Britain, France, and Italy exercised financial control over Tunis; 1881: France occupied Tunis, making it a French protectorate. 1876, 4 Apr.: The British accused the Khedive Ismail of Egypt of poor financial management, and advocated European supervision; 18 Nov., khedival decree appointed British and French controllers to manage the Egyptian debt; 1878, 15 Aug.: Sir Rivers Wilson (an Englishman) made minister of finance and M. de Blignières (a Frenchman) made minister of public works; 1879, 25 June: sultan of Turkey deposed Ismail; 4 Sept.: under new khedive, Tewfik, European controllers were reappointed and their tenure was subject to British and French (not Egyptian) "Anglo-French Dual Control." 1880, 17 July: Law of Liquidation provided that all Egyptian budgetary surpluses should go to service the national debt; 1882, 11 July: after threats to British investment, the British landed troops in Egypt to protect the Suez Canal; 15 Sept.: British occupied Cairo; 9 Nov.: Dual Control of Britain and France ended; the British took charge. 1883–1907: Sir Evelyn Baring (1841–1917; 1892, Lord Cromer), as British Consul-General in Egypt, reordered Egyptian public finance. In short, foreign investment led to British occupation. Similarly, French occupation of Morocco was closely tied to the protection of foreign loans. Foreign investment also led to foreign administration: the British established a number of chartered cos. in Africa, and Britain then followed as colonizer. Because of their foreign debts, some less developed countries lost control of their finances and were faced to greater or less degree with the presence of foreign administrators. 1900, Jan., and 1903–4: Persia pledged its customs revenues at all places except Fars and the Persian Gulf ports to the Russians, and at Fars and the Persian Gulf ports to the British in return for foreign loans. 1917: American financial commission was established in Nicaragua to stabilize that nation's finances. In these cases, political interference followed foreign loans. In other instances, the prior presence of colonial governments created a good environment for foreign investment. Likewise, the foreign-investment climate was improved by the presence of the western powers in China, supported by unequal treaties, extraterritoriality, open ports (1895, 17 Apr.: Treaty of Shimonoseki at end of Sino-Japanese War gave Japanese subjects freedom to engage in manufacturing in open ports and towns in China; other nations got the same advantage under the most-favored-nation clause), spheres of influence (1895, 20 June: treaty between China and France gave France a sphere of influence south to the borders of French Indochina; 1896 and 1899: Russia obtained a sphere of influence in Manchuria; 1898, Feb.: Britain got from the Chinese government the Yangtze Valley as her sphere of influence; 1905, 5 Sept.: in the Treaty of Portsmouth, after the Russo-Japanese War, Russia handed over her sphere of influence in south Manchuria to Japan; 1905: Japan also obtained Shantung as her sphere), and leased areas (1898, 6 Mar.: the Germans leased Kiaochow; 27 Mar. and 7 May: Russians leased the southern part of the Liaotung Peninsula, including Talienwan and Port Arthur; 10 Apr.: France leased Kwangchow; 9 June: Britain secured a lease of Kowloon and Weihaiwei; 1905, 5 Sept.: Japanese took over the Russian lease of the southern part of the Liaotung Peninsula; the leased areas were under the complete control of the foreign power during the term of the lease, in all cases 99 years except in the Russian lease and the British lease of Weihaiwei, which were both 25 years). The political implications of foreign investment were thus extensive; the loss of national sovereignty that might occur after the acceptance of foreign loans or preliminary to foreign investment was feared in less developed countries. Yet there were important benefits that did accrue to less developed regions as a result of the British, Dutch, Belgian, French, German, American, Canadian, Japanese, and Russian investments that went into railroads, port facilities, schools, plantations, mines, public utilities, and banking in less developed regions. Oil production began, based on foreign capital. Foreign investment stimulated trading activities. While there were certain foreign investments in manufacturing in less developed countries, this was not typical, because within the latter there was no large domestic market for locally produced goods; moreover the industrial nations wanted to export *their* products to the less developed countries. Most foreign investments in manufacturing in the less developed countries that did exist were in the processing of materials for export or in manufacturing for the use of the expatriate community of the plantation, in the mining town, or in the foreign concession. Exceptions were foreign investments in cigarette factories that sold their product in the less developed countries. Foreign investments assisted economic progress through the establishment of infrastructure and in the development of primary products for export; foreign investment was not aimed at industrialization of the less developed nations. Industrialization that occurred, based on foreign investment, was an extra bonus rather than an intended consequence. As a result of foreign investment, new resources went into international commerce; in time in many nations this commerce would provide sources of taxable revenue. Foreign investment brought money into the economy, and there were linkage effects; wage laborers had money to spend, no matter how little. Services developed as a result of foreign investment, which provided income for local people. Local farmers produced crops which were sold to the foreign investor. Local mines developed, based on the existence of foreign demand as represented by a new smelter. Foreign investors introduced new skills. Foreign investors in many cases introduced the conception of profit making. Foreign investors demonstrated new standards of health, sanitation, and education. Foreign investment brought in new capital that was not otherwise available. In the Middle East, foreign investment accounted for the greater part of net capital formation. 1900–1914: Annual capital imports into India from Britain came to about 1% of Indian national income. In China, foreign capital dominated the modern sector; it provoked the Chinese government and Chinese people to try to modernize their economy. Foreign investment brought to the less developed countries an obligation to repay the investment which had both positive and negative effects: the negative effects are obvious; the positive effects were that the obligation meant a need to raise revenue which stimulated development. Most important, foreign investment brought with it in every less developed country a disruption of the old economy; new social and cultural patterns as well as political and economic change came with foreign capital.

BUSINESS ORGANIZATION. Traditional family enterprises continued in less developed countries as they had for centuries. Family enterprises ranged from the small subsistence plot (cultivated by the extended family) to a variety of household activities to prosperous family firms. At the other pole, there were modern foreign-owned joint-stock cos. These companies included the limited-liability corporations that by the turn of the century were managing the Dutch plantations in the Netherlands East Indies and the banana plantations in Middle

America, the large companies that ran the Belgian mining enterprises in the Congo, and the American-owned mining enterprises in Latin America. For all kinds of mining ventures in less developed countries, joint-stock cos. were organized and their stock floated on the London market. Other corporations active in less developed countries included such multinational units as Standard Oil, Lever Brothers, and British-American Tobacco. In addition, there were the new British chartered cos. 1884: British North Borneo Co. established (its aim was to develop trade and to make a profit out of land disposal and taxation). 1886: Royal Niger Co. chartered, designed to engage in trade in palm oil and palm kernels; it had monopoly privileges in Northern Nigeria (1899: British government agreed to buy the co.'s monopoly rights and its treaties, land, and mining rights; the co. kept trading posts and warehouses; 1900 ff.: Royal Niger Co. continued as a profitable trading co. with no administrative responsibilities, the British government having taken over the administration of Northern Nigeria); 1888, 3 Sept.: Imperial British East Africa Co. chartered to promote "trade, commerce, and good government" in East Africa; it expanded and established British rule in Kenya and Uganda (it sought to develop the trade routes to Uganda, to put new products into trade, and to make profits out of land sales and taxation; it became overextended; 1894: the British government bought the co.'s assets and took over the administration of British East Africa). 1889, 29 Oct.: British South Africa Co., founded by Cecil Rhodes (1853–1902), chartered by the British government to bring the lands north of the Limpopo River within the reach of miners, farmers, foresters, and traders, but primarily to develop gold mining; it built railroads and carried on the administration of Southern Rhodesia (until 12 Sept., 1923) and of Northern Rhodesia (until 1 Apr., 1924). Between the 2 poles of the various native unincorporated family enterprises and the various foreign incorporated companies were certain indigenous firms in the modern sector, such as the Indian businesses run by managing agencies. 1870's: In China, a form of business organization, the *kuan-tu shang-pan* (the official supervision and merchant system), started new industries; the government would aid a Chinese enterprise, and the merchant would supply the basic capital; it was thought that only with official patronage would Chinese merchants invest in industry. 1894: 1st year in which total capital of new Chinese private enterprises in the modern sector (manufacturing and modern mining) exceeded that of Chinese government and government-private enterprises. 1894 ff.: Private Chinese businesses in modern industries developed (generally within the treaty ports); 1894–95: Sino-Japanese War aided in dissolving the links between the Chinese merchant and the government. Chinese merchants often went into joint ventures with foreign capital. In Latin America modern factory enterprises developed, in textiles, processed foods, and beverages, which were owned and managed by an individual, his family, or a small group of partners. These businessmen might go into several different kinds of enterprises, each on a relatively small scale. They were generally unincorporated.

Entrepreneurship: The development of entrepreneurship in the less developed countries was slow. Risk taking was not a typical attribute. Traditional attitudes and loyalties inhibited entrepreneurial behavior. Indian investors hedged their risks by using management agencies; the Chinese hedged theirs by involvement 1st with the government and then with foreign capital. In India certain groups had special entrepreneurial talents, e.g., the Parsees. A number of compradors in China became leaders in industry, but usually linked with foreign capital and generally in the treaty ports. Foreign firms in China often served entrepreneurial roles, and the Chinese imitated. There was considerable entrepreneurial activity on the part of the Chinese in Southeast Asia, where they developed new industries. In Lebanon and Syria indigenous entrepreneurs emerged to a far greater extent than elsewhere in the Middle East, where entrepreneurship was limited. Lebanese and Syrians also migrated to become entrepreneurs away from home—in Africa and in Latin America. In Latin America successful entrepreneurs were few, but there were some. 1881: Francisco Matarazzo (1851–1937) arrived in Brazil; he was a leading example of the immigrant entrepreneur; he began as a rural store owner, started a lard refinery, then dealt in flour and grain, erected flour mills, moved into manufacture of bags for flour, then into cottonseed oil production, and next into soap and boxes; his operations became among the largest enterprises in South America. Another success was Simón Patiño (1868–1947); born in Cochabama, Bolivia, of humble parents, Patiño acquired a small tin mine in the 1890's; by 1910 he was a millionaire; his interests expanded to include tin properties in Malaya and tin smelters in Germany and England.

GOVERNMENT POLICY. In most less developed countries, governments became involved in economic development.

Colonial governments: British government policy—that colonies must be self-supporting—meant revenues had to be found locally. Since revenues were not easy to come by, British administrators took steps to encourage economic development so that there would be sources of government income. British colonial governments, by building railroads, ports, and public utilities, and by introducing law and order, made important contributions to the development of the colonies. With the exceptions of the railways in India, the Rhodesias, and Nyasaland, the railroads throughout the British tropics were built by British colonial governments. In India, the railroads were subsidized by land grants and the state-guaranteed interest on investments; in time Indian lines came to be built by the British government directly. 1888: King Leopold organized the Comité d'Études du Haut-Congo, designed to develop the Congo with Belgian capital; 1906: Belgium adopted a plan for economic development for the Congo—probably the

1st central-government development plan. The French government provided subsidies to French colonies. Because of their concern for health, education, and commerce and as a result of their sponsorship of agricultural research, the colonial powers played important roles in economic development; they were, however, hesitant about the industrialization of the colonial areas and contributed little to that end. The introduction by the colonial powers of western concepts of law, justice, and contract likewise set a basis for later economic development.

Independent governments—Eastern Hemisphere: In the Ottoman Empire, the Convention of 1838 had deprived the empire of the right to raise tariff duties above 5%; 1862: the empire got the right to raise duties to 8%, but this was inadequate to encourage modern industry. 1873: The Ottoman Empire exempted machines used in industry from duties. 1913: The Ottoman Empire offered special privileges to individuals establishing new industries or expanding existing ones. These measures were not effective. Moreover, the rules, codes, and patterns of law existing within the empire were not conducive to economic development. China too, by the unequal treaties, was deprived of the right to set her tariffs to protect industry or to raise tariffs for revenue purposes. 1870's: The Chinese government sought to promote industrial development. 1872: Li Hung-chang undertook to develop guns, cannons, and armament industries, but this had no substantial effect on economic growth. The government introduced the *kuan-tu shang-pan* system. But, in general, the Chinese government was not successful. The imperial government had no funds for these enterprises; often the enterprises were left to provincial governors. The government-sponsored industries found themselves in financial difficulties. 1882: Chinese imperial government exempted factory-produced cotton goods from inland transit taxes and later applied this policy to all machine-made products (but a large internal market did not develop because of the low standard of living). 1882 ff.: Provincial governments offered monopoly privileges to companies which introduced western-type manufactures. 1898: China for the 1st time permitted the patenting of inventions. 1903: Active government promotion of private industry began in China with the formation of the Ministry of Commerce, yet promotion was limited owing to the bankruptcy of the imperial government. 1912: New republican government in China continued the policy of attempting to promote industry. 1914: Chinese government agreed to guarantee dividends of 5% to 6% of paid-up capital to stockholders in selected industrial corporations. Despite the efforts of the Chinese governments—central and provincial, before and after the revolution—they were unable to spur economic development on a substantial scale. Neither before nor after 1912 did the governments give the Chinese economy a stable set of laws and monetary practices to provide the basis for economic development. Corruption in government served as a drain on efficient use of the few existing government resources. Where industry did develop, it was primarily in the treaty ports, where western standards prevailed.

Independent governments—Western Hemisphere: In Latin America, national governments took initial steps to prompt development. In Mexico Porfirio Díaz subsidized railroads, provided police protection for foreign investors, and granted concessions to those who would build smelters. 1903–9: The Mexican government purchased control of the main railroad lines. 1917: The Mexican constitution set the basis for a far more extensive government role in economic life. 1911 ff.: In Uruguay, President José Ordóñez began to nationalize foreign-owned public utilities. 1870 ff.: Brazil encouraged railway construction through subsidies. 1875: Brazilian government guaranteed 7% return on investment to those sugar planters who modernized production. 1879: Brazilian import tariff increased the protection granted to industry; the policy of protective tariffs was confirmed in the tariff of 1888; 1905: Brazil extended tariff protection to food output. Legislation in Brazil granted duty exemptions on certain industrial equipment and raw materials (although this was erratic and Brazilian industries in this period complained of the tariffs on their imports of equipment). 1906–7 ff.: Coffee Valorization Scheme. The state of São Paulo, Brazil, took the initiative in the world's 1st large-scale attempt to control the world price of a foodstuff; the state, in order to establish a balance between supply and demand for coffee, intervened in the market and purchased surpluses; the plan was financed by foreign capital. Elsewhere in Latin America, governments subsidized railroads and aided in the flotation of railroad securities; they became involved in construction of highway and port facilities, but negligible effort was made by Latin American governments in the direction of industrialization.

OTHER FACTORS. In Asia and Africa there was the broad challenge of the West. With colonization came new ideas on administration, justice, and property. Christian missionaries, who arrived in large numbers with the colonizers (and before), confronted old religious values with new alternatives. Medical practices of the colonists vied with past superstitions. The basic inertia of traditional societies in Asia and Africa was jarred, even when there was no colonization—as in the case of China. Along with the western impact came humiliation; traditional societies had not stood up to the encounter. Whereas in Japan the humiliation of the unequal treaties offered a stimulus for rapid and profound change, in most of the less developed world the humiliation of colonization or of unequal treaties and defeat in war (as in the case of China) did not spur a positive response. The revolution in China and the establishment of the republic, and the achievements of the Young Turks in the Ottoman Empire, were partially successful as attempts at modernization, but unsuccessful as attempts at economic development. Latin America had long since thrown off colonization; in much of the region, however, political instability slowed economic development. Political instability in China had similar effects. Economic development required a concept of progress, and this was absent in much of the less developed world. Likewise, a concept of nationality has served the cause of economic development. Ideas of nationalism were absent in Africa, and in Asia too they were in many cases lacking. China, which had a unity and feeling of national tradition, did not have a central government strong enough to promote political and national unity. Poor communications in most of the less developed world retarded the extension of ideas of "the nation." Throughout the less developed world the vicious circle of poverty, which begot more poverty, provided a seemingly insuperable obstacle to economic development.

1865–1914

The International Economy

INTERGOVERNMENTAL MULTINATIONAL ECONOMIC INSTITUTIONS. 1865: Latin Monetary Union established (treaty took effect, 1866), including France, Belgium, Italy, and Switzerland; 1868: Greece joined; Spain, Rumania, Finland, and several Latin American countries followed the policies of the Union without joining; it established standards of fineness of coins and metal or metals to be used in coinage; 1873–74: it adopted the gold standard; from its adoption the use of the gold standard spread, so that by the end of the 19th cent. every country of importance in world commerce, except China and Persia, had adopted gold as the basis of its currency. 1865: 20 European nations signed international telegraphic treaty, establishing the International Telecommunication Union; 1868: several Asiatic countries joined; 1869: International Office of Telegraphy established at Bern, Switzerland; 1875: International Telegraph Convention signed at St. Petersburg, and revised at Lisbon, 1908; there were 50 signatories to the Lisbon Convention. 1874: Universal Postal Union founded by 21 countries under the Treaty of Bern; other nations subsequently joined; the organization made the world a single postal territory. 1878: Semi-official World Meteorological Organization established. 1879: International Bureau of Weights and Measures founded by convention signed in Paris by 17 nations. 1883: Convention of the International Union for the Protection of Industrial Property signed in Paris, protecting patents and trade marks. 1886: Bern Convention inaugurated international copyright protection. 1912: International Radiotelegraphic Convention signed in London. 1919, 25 Jan.: Resolution of the Peace Conference established the League of Nations; the Secretariat of the League was to collect information dealing with international economic problems.

THE ENERGY REVOLUTION.

WORLD PRODUCTION OF COMMERCIAL SOURCES OF ENERGY
(billion kwh electricity equivalent)

	Coal[a]	Petroleum[b]	Natural Gas	Water Power	Total
1870	1,658	8		8	1,674
1880	2,569	43		11	2,623
1890	3,894	109	40	13	4,056
1900	5,785	213	75	16	6,089
1910	8,724	467	162	34	9,387
1920	9,934	1,046	254	64	11,298

a Includes lignite.
b Includes natural gasoline.

THE TRANSPORTATION REVOLUTION.

SPEED OF TRANSPORT
(mph)

	Horse Coach	Canal Tug	River Boat	Ocean Ship	Railroad	Automobile	Airplane
1880	5	3	8	20	50		
1900	5	4	10	25	60	30	
1920	5	4	11	30	65	55	110

Even more important than speed, the actual existence of steamships, railroads, telegraphs, and cables as well as refrigerated transport provided the basis for a global economy. The airplane made the world still smaller.

WORLD CONSUMPTION OF ENERGY FROM COMMERCIAL SOURCES
(as % of total energy use)

1870	35.4
1880	44.3
1890	53.3
1900	62.5
1910	68.0
1920	72.7

WORLD TRADE (EXPORTS PLUS IMPORTS)
($ million)

1870	10.6
1880	14.7
1890	17.5
1900	20.1
1910	33.6
1913	40.4

1919–1945

The Mature Industrial Society of the West

AGRICULTURE. 1920: In the major industrial nations (except the U.S.), agricultural output was lower than before World War I.

INDEX OF PHYSICAL VOLUME OF
AGRICULTURAL PRODUCTION, 1920
(per capita of total population; 1913 = 100)

Germany	62
Belgium	78
France	83
U.K.	89
U.S.	112

1920–45: agriculture occupied an increasingly less significant role in these economies. 1920's: American agriculture did not share the general prosperity; 1930 ff.: U.S. agriculture felt the depression more severely than did industry. 1940–45: U.S. agriculture prospered. 1920–40: In Western Europe low agricultural prices existed, with the nadir in 1932–33.

Mechanization: Despite economic difficulties on American farms, mechanization increased rapidly.

TRACTORS AND AUTOMOBILES ON U.S. FARMS
(000)

	Tractors	Automobiles
1920	246	2,146
1930	920	4,135
1940	1,545	4,144
1950	2,354	4,148

In Europe, long-distance transmission of electricity and use of tractors, trucks, and, to a far lesser extent, automobiles aided the farmer. Compared with the U.S., European mechanization on the farm proceeded slowly. 1940–45: British and Swedish mechanization especially accelerated.

TRACTORS IN USE
(000)

	1939	1949
Germany	60	75[a]
U.K.	55	280
France	30	89
Sweden	20	52

[a] 70,000 in western zones, 5,000 in Soviet zone.

Self-sufficiency: 1920–45: The U.S. remained self-sufficient in foodstuffs. 1930's: Attempts were made in Britain, France, and Germany to enlarge national food output; in France and Germany, especially, the governments hoped to achieve self-sufficiency.

SELF-SUFFICIENCY IN FOODSTUFFS, 1937

	% total consumption
U.K.	25
Netherlands	67
Germany	
(1934 boundaries)	83
France	83

RAW MATERIALS. Coal: U.S., Germany, and Britain still led in world coal production.

COAL AND LIGNITE PRODUCTION
(million metric tons)

	1920	1930	1938
U.S.	597.2	487.1	355.3
U.K.	233.2	247.8	230.7
Germany	252.4	288.7	381.5
France	25.3	55.0	47.6
World total	1,319	1,416	1,469

1920: European coal production had been sharply affected by the war. The peace settlement provided that the Saar Basin be detached from Germany and the coal mines ceded to France (the coal reserves of the Saar were equal to those in all of France); the settlement also provided that Upper Silesia, the source of 23% of Germany's hard coal, would go to Poland; by the peace settlement, Germany lost c. 36% of its coal reserves. 1923: French occupation of the Ruhr temporarily halved German coal output. 1930: Coal output figures reflected the worldwide depression; increases in German, French, and British output represented recovery from the postwar disorder. 1935, 1 Mar.: After a plebiscite had been held in the Saar Valley, the Saar region was returned to Germany. Germany took advantage of its rights under the peace treaty to repurchase the coal mines; this accounted for the large increase in German coal production in 1938. 1938: Coal production figures indicated German preparation for the war and the waning of U.S. and British coal industries. Liquid fuels, natural gas, and hydroelectrical power began to compete with coal; the shift had been made during World War I from coal-burning to oil-burning ships, eliminating this large source of coal consumption; improved utilization of coal in electrical generation curtailed the demand for coal. 1930's: The British coal industry was in the doldrums, as was the U.S. coal industry.

Oil: With the exception of the U.S., all the mature industrial nations continued to be importers of oil. 1919: U.S. became concerned with the problems of oil shortages; Americans began an intensive search for oil resources abroad; 1930: large east Texas oil discoveries.

OIL PRODUCTION
(million barrels of 42 U.S. gals.)

	1920	1930	1938
U.S.	422.9	898.0	1,213.2
World total	688.9	1,411.9	1,978.3

Iron ore: 1919: When Lorraine was returned to France, Germany lost the source of 74% of its prewar iron ore; Germany had to buy from France. 1930's: German improvements in steelmaking meant it could use previously unutilized ore. 1938–41: German territorial expansion brought huge iron-ore resources under its control. The U.S. remained basically self-sufficient in iron ore. 1938: Great Britain's output of iron ore was 11,800 metric tons; its imports were 5,100 metric tons.

General: 1930's: Key innovations in raw-material usage occurred as a result of the German drive toward self-sufficiency. The Germans developed new chemical industries based on utilization of waste wood and German timber; they put more acreage into such industrial raw materials as flax and hemp; they sought to develop substitutes for basic raw materials.

Synthetics revolution: 1920–45: Increasingly, in the mature industrial nations substitutes for natural raw materials appeared—rayon for silk, plastic for wood, clay, glass, and metals, synthetic nitrates for natural nitrates, and synthetic rubber for natural rubber; research was done on obtaining oil from coal. Such steps made industrial nations less dependent on specific primary products.

ENERGY. Use of electric power and the internal combustion engine created a revolution as great as the one caused by the use of steam in the 1st Industrial Revolution.

ENERGY CONSUMPTION PER CAPITA, 1937
(electricity equivalent in kwh for all energy sources)

	Per Capita Use	Ratio of Inanimate to All Other Sources
U.S.	6,996	97.6
U.K.	5,553	97.9
Germany	3,461	96.2

A substantial portion of the world's energy production was represented by the major industrial nations.

ENERGY PRODUCTION, 1935
(%)

U.S.	37.695
U.K. and Ireland	13.743
Germany (1936)	12.556
France	3.300
World	100.000

SOURCE: Abbott Payson Usher, "The Resource Requirements of an Industrial Economy," *Journal of Economic History,* Suppl. VII (1947), pp. 44–46.

Electric power: New techniques sharply reduced coal consumption in electric generation.

FUEL EFFICIENCY IN THERMAL POWER STATIONS
(kwh per ton of coal)

	U.S.	U.K.	Germany[a]
1920	735	662	
1925	1,102	926	
1930	1,378	1,250	
1935	1,531	1,515	1,469–2,571
1938	1,575	1,587	
1948	1,695	1,587	

[a] Lower and upper limits of power stations.

1920 ff. Application of new techniques involving high-voltage transmission (currents of 100,000 volts or more) extended the distance over which electricity could be distributed.

ELECTRICAL PRODUCTION, 1930–40
(billion kwh)

	1930	1940
U.S.	114.6	179.9
Germany	13.2	25.4
France	8.2	11.5
U.K.	6.9	10.5[a]

[a] Estimated. 1940 figure is not available; 1937, 8.9; 1943, 12.0.

Internal-combustion engine: The internal-combustion engine as a means of powering transport came of age. 1924, 17 Dec.: 1st diesel-electric locomotive put into service in the U.S.

Rocket power: 1919, 28 June: Treaty of Versailles disarmed Germany of its military air force, but did not mention rockets as potential weapons; Germany could develop them without treaty violation. 1923, 1 Nov.: American Robert H. Goddard (1882–1945) successfully operated a liquid oxygen and gasoline rocket motor on a testing frame. 1923: Publication in Germany of Hermann Oberth, *Die Rakete zu den Planetenräumen* (*The Rocket into Interplanetary Space*), which stimulated widespread discussion of rocket propulsion. 1928, 11 Apr.: 1st manned rocket automobile tested by Fritz von Opel, Max Valier, and others in Berlin, Germany. 1930, 17 Dec.:

GROWTH IN ELECTRICITY PRODUCTION PER CAPITA, 1920-47

Kwh per capita

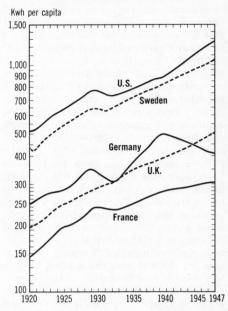

German army decided to develop military missiles. 1930: British inventor Frank Whittle (b. 1907) awarded patents for 1st turbojet engine. 1932: German engineer Paul Schmidt patented a ramjet engine, which was later modified and used in the V-1 flying bomb. 1937, 12 Apr.: Whittle's 1st gas turbine engine, the U-type, was static-tested. 1942, 22 Oct.: Westinghouse Electric Co. got government authorization to build the 1st practical jet engines of wholly American design. 1944, 17 Nov.: Following the success of the German missiles, U.S. Army Ordnance initiated the "Hermes" program for research into and development of ballistic missiles. (When on 31 Dec., 1954, Army Ordnance ended the Hermes project, the latter had developed high-performance liquid-fuel rockets and stabilized platform inertial guidance equipment).

Atomic energy: 1942, 2 Dec.: 1st self-perpetuating nuclear chain reaction (fission of uranium isotope U-235) was achieved at the University of Chicago, under physicists Arthur H. Compton (1892–1962), Enrico Fermi (1901–54), and others. 1945, 16 July: 1st atomic bomb tested at Alamogordo, N.M. (bombs were dropped 6 Aug. on Hiroshima and 9 Aug. on Nagasaki, Japan); the harnessing of the atom opened the way for a new source of industrial energy.

INDUSTRY. 1919: In the U.S. new capacity had been built during the war; many industries in America had not been fully converted to war production and so reconversion was not difficult; there was no physical damage in the U.S. In Europe economic dislocation was immense; nations had to convert from war to civilian production and reconstruct plants damaged during the war. In the U.S. and Europe the war had witnessed inflation, which created adjustment problems in the postwar era; demobilization caused an indigestion of man power. 1920–21: Severe economic downturn in the U.S. and Europe. 1922–24: Rapid recovery in the U.S.; slow recovery in most of Europe,

with France the exception. 1924: Industrial production in France had surpassed the 1913 level; based on 1913 = 100, the index for manufacturing production in France was 117.9, in England only 87.8, while in Germany it was 81.8. 1925–29: Industrial growth in Europe and especially in the U.S. was the norm. 1929–33: During the Great Depression industrial output fell. 1933–39: France remained in general stagnation. 1933 ff.: U.S. witnessed languid recovery, blemished by the depression of 1938, and then followed by an upturn with the war demands; British industrial expansion resumed until 1937, when the recession of 1937–38 slowed development, which restarted with the outbreak of war. German industrial growth, sharply jarred by the depression, moved upward as Germany prepared for war. 1930's: Growth of manufacturing in the mature industrial nations did not keep pace with the world as a whole.

INDEXES OF MANUFACTURING ACTIVITY
(1913 = 100)

	U.S.	Germany	U.K.	France	World
1920	122.2	59.0	92.6	70.4	93.2
1921	98.0	74.7	55.1	61.4	81.1
1922	99.5	81.8	73.5	87.8	99.5
1923	141.1	55.4	79.1	95.2	104.5
1924	133.2	81.8	87.8	117.9	111.0
1925	148.0	94.9	86.3	114.3	120.7
1926	156.1	90.9	78.8	129.8	126.5
1927	154.5	122.1	96.0	115.6	134.5
1928	162.8	118.3	95.1	134.4	141.8
1929	180.3	117.3	100.3	142.7	153.3
1930	140.0	101.6	91.3	139.9	137.5
1931	121.6	85.1	82.4	122.6	122.4
1932	93.7	70.2	82.5	105.4	108.4
1933	111.8	79.4	88.3	119.8	121.7
1934	121.6	101.8	100.2	111.4	136.4
1935	140.3	116.7	107.9	109.1	154.5
1936	171.0	127.5	119.1	116.3	178.1
1937	185.8	138.1	127.8	123.8	195.8
1938	143.0	149.3	117.6	114.6	182.7

SOURCE: League of Nations, *Industrialization and Foreign Trade,* New York, 1945.

In the mature industrial nations innovations were not for the most part in textiles (except for synthetics), or in iron and steel, or in shipbuilding.

Textiles: 1920's: To counteract decline, certain American textile companies trans-

ferred their operations from New England to the South, where labor rates were lower; 1930's: the textile industry in the U.S. floundered. 1920–40: The British textile industry, Britain's great staple in the past, was on the decline; 1924: British

% Distribution of the World's
Manufacturing Production

	U.S.	Germany	U.K.	France
1913a	35.8	14.3	14.1	7.0
1926/29	42.2	11.6	9.4	6.6
1936/38	32.2	10.7	9.2	4.5

a These 1913 figures (unlike those on p. 707 above) are adjusted to represent the frontiers established *after* World War I.

Source: League of Nations, *Industrialization and Foreign Trade,* New York, 1945.

output of cotton textiles equaled £84 million; 1935: British cotton textile output was £40 million. Rayon production in the U.S. and Great Britain grew.

Iron and steel: Basic innovations were absent in iron- and steelmaking, although there were advances in metallurgy and chemistry of steels (new alloys and improvements in old methods: larger ovens, mechanization of rolling mills, and fuel economy); in Germany new processes of producing steel, using low-grade iron ore, were introduced by the state-owned Hermann Göring Works. On the whole, however, the iron and steel industries in the mature nations were not progressive industries and were slow to adopt what technological improvements there were. Growth industries in the mature industrial nations were automobiles, chemicals, and electrical supplies of all kinds. The pattern of development in the growth industries varied by country and by decade.

Automobiles: 1920's: Prosperity in America was linked with the expansion of the automobile industry. 1929: In the U.S., automobile production peaked at an output of 4.5 m. passenger cars, a figure not exceeded again until after World War II; the U.S. automobile industry had 3 large producers, Ford, General Motors, and Chrysler (formed in 1925). 1919 ff.: Europe copied America's mass-production methods; in England, Morris and Austin produced cars by mass production; Ford expanded its output at Manchester, England; in France, Renault and Citroen adopted moving assembly lines. 1924: Adam Opel, A.G., in Germany (which had begun to manufacture cars in 1898) started postwar operations, adopting American mass-production

methods; it made a small car and led in German industry. 1925: General Motors bought the small British producer, Vauxhall Motors, Ltd. 1928 ff.: Ford started construction of the largest automobile plant outside the U.S., at Dagenham, England (1st cars produced in 1931). 1929: General Motors purchased control of Adam Opel, A.G., giving G.M. leadership in the German automobile industry. 1931: Ford started to manufacture at Cologne, Germany. 1934: Ford began to make automobiles in France; Simca (Société Industrielle de Mécanique et Carrosserie), the successor to a Fiat dealership in France, began to produce Fiat cars in France. 1934, 8 Mar.: Adolf Hitler proposed the *Volkswagen,* a cheap mass-produced vehicle. 1934 ff.: British, German, and French automobile output (protected by tariff barriers) rose; in all these countries small cars, locally produced, designed for the European markets, made progress over the imported large American units. 1930's: U.S. automobile production was lower than in the 1920's; in Europe, automobile output exceeded the European levels of the 1920's, but the U.S. industry continued to outproduce all of Europe.

Chemical industry. 1919 ff.: The American chemical industry adopted innovations developed in Europe (rayon, cellophane, etc.). 1920: Standard Oil (N.J.) produced isopropyl alcohol commercially, the 1st chemical from petroleum. 1923: Thiokol, 1st synthetic rubber, discovered by American chemist J. C. Patrick (1892–1965). 1925, 28 Nov.: I. G. Farbenindustrie formed, combining all the major chemical producers in Germany; I. G. Farben diversified into all facets of the chemical industry. 1928, Oct.: Imperial Chemical Industries (I.C.I.) joined together the 4 great British companies manufacturing heavy chemicals, alkalies, explosives, and coal-tar dyes into a new company with an authorized capital of £65 million, a new high in Britain. 1928: Établissements Kuhlmann in France linked the Kuhlmann enterprises (in sulphuric acid), St.-Gobain (heavy chemicals, alkalies, fertilizers, glass, etc.), Pechiney (electrochemicals), and the

Nitrogenous & Composited Fertilizer Co. (synthetic ammonia). 1929: In the U.S., there was no single great chemical company; the leaders in the American chemical industry were Du Pont, Allied Chemical, and Union Carbide; there were a large number of pharmaceutical concerns; the oil companies were becoming interested in the chemical industry. 1920's: The age of synthetics and new chemical processes; synthetic nitrogen increasingly replaced natural nitrates, synthetics challenged wood chemicals, synthetic medicines rose in numbers, synthetic lacquers and resins came into commercial production, the phenolic and cellulosic plastics were widely used, rayon output grew, the petrochemical industries began, and hydrogenation of oil and coal was developed. 1931: Belgian-born American chemist Julius A. Nieuwland (1878–1936) discovered "Neoprene," a synthetic rubber introduced by Du Pont. 1933: I.C.I. made 1st commercially produced synthetic detergent; soapless shampoos were developed in Germany by I. G. Farben. 1934: 1st Buna rubber (S) patented in Germany by I. G. Farben; commercial production of vitamin C began in the U.S. and Europe, the 1st vitamin to be prepared chemically. 1935, 28 Feb.: Nylon discovered by Wallace H. Carothers (1896–1937), American chemists, at Du Pont (1940, 15 May: nylon stockings 1st put on sale). 1936: Leonard Colebrook and Neave Kenny in England introduced sulfanilamide, the 1st of the sulfa drugs. (1938: A. J. Ewins and M. A. Phillips in England synthesized sulfapyridine, the most effective of the early sulfa drugs.) 1937, Mar.: Sun Oil Co. began to operate the 1st fully commercial catalytic cracking unit by the Houdry process, developed by French engineer Eugène J. Houdry (1892–1962); the Houdry process created a revolution in oil refining, producing high-octane gasoline at quality and yields better than ever before. 1938: "Fiberglas" patented by Americans Games Slayter (1896–1964) and John H. Thomas (b. 1907). 1939: Swiss chemist Paul Müller (1899–1965) invented DDT. 1930's: Large expansion in synthetic plastics and abrasives; the Germans maintained superiority in a wide range of chemical products. 1939: The value of chemicals produced by American industry totaled $3.7 billion compared with $454 million in 1920; a chemical revolution had taken place, involving the use of chemicals in many industries and the spread of new chemical processes and new synthetic products. 1930's: In the mature industrial nations, especially the U.S. and Germany, the chemical industries were highly innovative. 1942: Penicillin (discovered in England in 1929) was introduced to the public, the 1st antibiotic to prove useful for injection into the body. 1944: Streptomycin introduced. The age of antibiotics had begun.

Electrical industries: The expanding use of electric power meant a comparable growth in the manufacture of industrial and consumer electrical products. 1919: General Electric Co. formed Radio Corporation of America. 1920's: The radio changed from a toy to a household appliance in all the mature industrial nations. 1924: 1st television system developed. 1925: The 1st 2 theaters in the world to be completely air-conditioned were in New York, the Rivoli and the Rialto; this stimulated the development of air-conditioning equipment by electrical cos.; 1st automatic electric percolator developed in the U.S.; 1926: 1st automatic electric toasters for use in the home produced in the U.S. 1929, Jan.: Formation of Associated Electrical Industries, Ltd. in England, a merger of several of the largest British electrical firms. 1930, July: Schick, Inc., marketed the 1st commercial electric shaver. 1937: 1st fully automatic electrically operated washing machine produced in the U.S. 1938: Introduction of fluorescent lamps in the U.S. 1939: R.C.A. demonstrated 1st color T.V. 1940's: Electronics developed as a subsidiary of the electrical industry. 1944, May: Professor Howard Hathaway Aiken (b. 1900), with the co-operation of International Business Machines, built an automatic sequence-controlled calculator, Harvard Mark I; this was the 1st successful general-purpose digital computer. 1945: John W. Mauchly (b. 1907) and J. Presper Eckert (b. 1919) at the University of Pennsylvania designed and built the Electronic Numerical Integrator and Calculator (ENIAC), the 1st electronic computer. 1945, May: 1st computer program, written by J. von Neumann (1903–57), for the Electronic Discrete Variable Automatic Computer (EDVAC), then under design.

Aircraft industry: An aircraft industry grew in every mature industrial nation.

AVERAGE ANNUAL INCREASE IN
MANUFACTURING, 1933–48
(% per annum)

U.S.	8.1
Belgium	2.4
U.K.	1.5
Holland	1.0
France	.2

SOURCE: UN, *Growth of World Industry—National Tables.*

1938–48: Decline in manufacturing activity in West Germany was equivalent to an average annual loss of 6.9%.

CONSUMER GOODS. 1920's: Revolution in consumer goods industries, especially in U.S.: automobiles, electrical appliances (from radios to refrigerators), cosmetics, etc., were widely available to consumers. Consumer goods were accompanied by consumer credit provisions and new retailing outlets. The U.S. had developed mass-production industries that went far beyond those related to housing, clothing, feeding, and defense. 1930's: Depression temporarily dampened consumer spending. 1939–45: Industries converted from consumer goods to wartime industries.

TRANSPORTATION. Railroads: 1919 ff.: Traffic on the railroads rose steadily in the U.K., France, and Germany. 1919–39: American railroads were eclipsed by the automobile; passenger traffic declined. 1924–41: Transition from steam to diesel and diesel-electric locomotives.

Automobiles, trucks, and highways: 1919 ff.: Automobile travel in the U.S. and Europe grew rapidly, but the private automobile in Europe was not nearly as ubiquitous as in the U.S.; in the U.S. and Europe, the truck began to provide competition with the railroads for freight traffic.

REGISTERED MOTOR VEHICLES
(million)

	U.S.		U.K.		France		Germany	
	Total	Private Autos	Total	Private Autos	Total	Private Autos	Total	Private Autos
1921	10.49	9.21	.46	.25	.23	.17	.09	.06
1926	22.05	19.22	1.04	.68	.89	.54	.32	.21
1930	26.53	23.00	1.52	1.04	1.46	1.10	.68	.43
1935	26.23	22.49	2.04	1.48	2.06	1.50	1.12	.81
1938	29.44	25.17	1.42	1.94	2.25	1.82	1.82	1.30

Expansion of motor vehicle use created a need for new roads and highways. 1930's: Highway construction was a form of public works to use the unemployed, especially in Germany and the U.S. 1933, June: Law passed in Germany authorizing construction of 4,200 miles of Reich motor roads. 1933–40: Germany built a system of expressways (the *Autobahnen*). 1940: In the U.S. the Pennsylvania Turnpike opened, the 1st modern toll road in America.

Air travel: 1919, 5 Feb.: 1st civilian airline with passenger service, Germany's Deutsche Luftreederei, started operations between Berlin, Leipzig, and Weimar; 8–31 May: American Albert Cushing Read (1887–1967) made 1st transatlantic crossing, stopping at 2 islands in the Azores, at Lisbon, and then on to Plymouth, England. 14–15 June: British aviators Capt. John Alcock (1892–1919) and Lieut. Arthur W. Brown (1886–1948) made 1st nonstop transatlantic crossing by airplane (Newfoundland to Ireland, 1,936 mi.—15 hrs. and 57 mins). 1924, 6 Apr.–28 Sept.: 3 U.S. Army planes circumnavigated the globe. 1927, 20–21 May: American Charles

A. Lindbergh (b. 1902) in his monoplane, *Spirit of St. Louis,* made 1st nonstop solo flight from New York to Paris, 3,610 mi.—33 hrs. and 29 mins. 1929, 24 Sept.: American aviator James H. Doolittle (b. 1896) made 1st public all-blind (i.e. instrument) flight, accompanied by a check pilot. 1935, 9 Mar.: Hermann Göring announced the existence of a German Air Force; this meant that Germany was openly violating the Treaty of Versailles; Dec.: U.S.-built Douglas DC-3 made its 1st flight; the DC-3 was one of the most successful aircraft in aviation history. (By 1938 the bulk of air travel in the U.S. was by DC-3.) 1937: Scheduled airlines worldwide transported 2.5 m. passengers. 1938, 10–14 July: American Howard Hughes (b. 1905), with 4 others, flew around the world in 3 days, 19 hrs., and 17 mins. 1939, 20 May: Pan American Airways started regular commercial flights between the U.S. and Europe, by way of the Azores. 1939–45: Air travel for military purposes expanded. 1940, 8 July: Boeing 307-B Stratoliner made 1st commercial flight with a pressurized cabin. Application of new forms of propulsion to air travel: 1926, 16 Mar.: Goddard launched world's 1st liquid-fueled rocket at Auburn, Mass.; it traveled 184 ft. in 2½ secs.; the event was the "Kitty Hawk" of rocket history. 1928, 11 June: Friedrich Stamer in Germany made 1st rocket-powered flight in a tailless glider (1-mi. flight). 1929, 17 July: Goddard fired a liquid-fueled rocket with a camera, thermometer, and barometer and recovered these items intact after the flight; Aug.: 1st recorded jet-assisted take-off of an airplane occurred in Dessau, Germany, powered by a battery of solid-propellant rockets; 30 Sept.: 1st jet-assisted take-off of a glider (powered with 16 rockets of 50 lbs. thrust), which made successful 75-sec. 2-mi. flight in Frankfurt, Germany; Fritz von Opel was the pilot. 1930, 4 Apr.: Formation of the American Interplanetary Society (later American Rocket Society) by David Lasser, G. Edward Pendray, Fletcher Pratt, and 9 others, with the goal of "interplanetary expeditions and travel." 1931, 14 Mar.: In Ger-

many, 1st European-made liquid-fueled rocket was launched (built by Johannes Winkler). 1939, 27 Aug.: 1st complete flight of jet-propelled aircraft, piloted by Erich Warsitz, took place secretly in Germany. 1941, 15 May: 1st official flight of British turbojet (with Whittle's jet engine); July: 1st successful U.S. jet-assisted take-off. 1942, 1 Oct.: 1st U.S. jet-propelled aircraft tested at Muroc, Calif.; aircraft was powered by engines developed by General Electric Co. in the U.S. from the British Whittle model; 3 Oct.: 1st successful experimental launch and flight of 5½-ton German rocket (V-2). 1943, Aug.: Germans launched 1st radio-controlled glide bomb against a British ship—the start of guided-missile warfare. 1944, 8 Jan.: Jet-propelled Lockheed XP-80 made 1st flight (at 500 mph) from Muroc, Calif.; this was the 1st U.S. airplane designed from the start for turbojet propulsion; it was powered by a British engine; 13 June: 1st German V-1 fell on London. 1944, Summer: German program initiated for use of manned V-1's for suicide missions; test flights made in Germany. 8 Sept.: 1st German V-2 rocket (3,400 mph) struck England. 1945, 8 May: At time of German surrender, more than 20,000 V-1's and V-2's had been fired.

COMMUNICATIONS. 1920, 16 July: World's 1st commercial radio telephone service opened between Los Angeles, Calif., and Santa Catalina Island; 2 Nov., Station KDKA, owned and operated by Westinghouse Electric & Manufacturing Co., opened in Pittsburgh—the 1st radio station to broadcast regularly scheduled programs (1st broadcast was the election returns of the Harding-Cox presidential contest). 1922: British Broadcasting Company organized; in the U.S. Albert H. Taylor and Leo C. Young 1st developed "radio detection"—the 1st step in radar. 1923: Charles Francis Jenkins (1867–1934) transmitted pictures of President Harding by radio from Washington to Philadelphia; Apr., 1st sound-on-film talking pictures (vaudeville shorts) shown at Rivoli Theater, New York. 1924: Russian-born American Vladimir K. Zworykin (b. 1889) completed a television system, including an iconoscope (pickup eye) and kinescope (receiving tube) in the Westinghouse research laboratory in Pittsburgh; 1st 3-color traffic lights appeared in the U.S. 1926: Western Electric Co. made sound films commercially practical; British Broadcasting Corp. established, replacing British Broadcasting Co.; in U.S. Gregory Brett (b. 1899) and Merle A. Tuve (b. 1901) developed effective radar detection; in Britain J. L. Baird (1888–1946) demonstrated television in Soho. 1927: New York to London telephone communication established; talking equipment, with simultaneous action and sound, announced in U.S. for motion pictures; 1st transmission of television signals, New York to Washington, by American Telephone & Telegraph Co. 1928, 6 July: 1st all-talking moving picture presented at Strand Theater, New York; the "movie" spread rapidly and movie theaters multiplied; 11 Sept.: Radio Station WGY, Schenectady, broadcast the 1st television play. 1928: American scientist E. F. W. Alexanderson (b. 1878) made 1st demonstration of home television; in Britain J. L. Baird demonstrated color television. 1932, 11 Oct.: Television 1st used in a political campaign in the U.S. 1935: Great Britain had 5 radar detection stations in operation. 1936: Broadcasting by FM (frequency modulation) developed by American Edwin H. Armstrong (1890–1954); 2 Nov.: BBC started television service. 1938: Chester Carlson demonstrated the feasibility of xerography. (1940: Carlson took out his 1st patent; 1944: the Battelle Memorial Institute agreed to develop the invention; 1947: agreement between Battelle and the Haloid Co. (now Xerox Corp.) to further develop the invention; 1960: 1st xerographic copier marketed.) 1941: 1st full commercial television in U.S., but television did not become commonplace in the U.S. until after World War II.

FINANCE. 1919 ff.: Domestic and international finance became interwoven. The mature industrial nations were the principals in international financial relations, involving the entire world. 1919: Disruption of European financial conditions after the war; huge wartime-incurred debts represented peacetime obligations. Wartime inflation had destroyed the value of savings, thus impeding the revival of investment; postwar inflation continued; interest rates on borrowing were high because no one knew the value of money. 1919: U.S. had become the greatest creditor nation in the world; America came out of the war with inflation, but with prosperity. U.S. returned to the gold standard. (1917: U.S had placed an embargo on gold and suspended gold redemption.) 1921: Severe worldwide recession in the U.S. and Western Europe.

German financial crisis: 1921, 30 Apr.: Reparations Commission set German reparation obligations at roughly $32.5 billion; at that point Germany had paid less than half its interim obligations. Germany accepted these reparation terms and raised funds for the initial payment by borrowing in London. German inflation grew, and the German mark lost its value rapidly. 1922, July: Germany requested a 2-year moratorium on reparation payments. The French government refused. 26 Dec. and 9 Jan.: The Reparations Commission declared Germany in default on reparations. 1923, 11 Jan.: As a result, France and Belgium occupied the Ruhr district. Oct.: A new bank, the Rentenbank, was established in Germany to issue new currency. Nov.: German currency reform; new German mark replaced the old mark at the rate of 1 new mark for every 1 trillion old marks. The successful currency reform had been accomplished by Hjalmar Schacht (b. 1877), president of the Rentenbank. 1923: Britain had lent the allies funds during the war, which the latter expected to repay through reparations; the U.S. had lent Britain money during the war, which it expected to have repaid; with the German defaults, the chain of debt repayments broke down. 1924, 9 Apr.: The Dawes Plan issued, prepared by a committee under American Charles G. Dawes (1865–1951); it provided for reorganization of the German Reichsbank under allied supervision, reduction of German reparation payments, a virtual moratorium on German debt payments for 1 year, a loan to Germany of 800 m. gold marks (of which $110 m. would be raised in the U.S.) ; 1 Sept.: the Dawes Plan went into effect; Schacht became president of reorganized Reichsbank (serving until 1930) . 1924: With the Nov. 1923 currency reform and the Dawes Plan, Germany seemed on the route to recovery; the nation returned to the gold standard. 1925, May: Britain went back to the gold standard at the prewar parity in relation to the dollar ($4.86) ; 1926, 25 Oct.: Belgium returned to the gold standard. 1928, 25 June: French legislation brought France back to the gold standard. 1928: Restoration of pre-1914 financial conditions seemed achieved; yet the restoration was precarious.

International indebtedness: International long-term lending on the part of U.S., Britain, and France rose. Germany was by now an important debtor on international account, borrowing from abroad about 3 times as much as she paid out in reparations. The U.S. lent money to Germany for the latter to pay reparations, which allowed European countries to pay their war debts to the U.S. 1929, 7 June: The Young Plan, prepared by American Owen D. Young (1874–1962) , aimed at a final settlement of the reparations question; it reduced German indebtedness to $8 billion, payable over 58½ years. 1929, Oct.: U.S. stock-market crash; Nov. ff.: U.S. stock-market prices continued to fall; U.S. loans to Europe began to dry up. 1930: Bank suspensions in U.S. reached 1,352; losses to depositors, $343.5 million. 1931, Mar.: When Germany made plans for a customs union with Austria, the French in opposition brought financial pressure on Austria and Germany. 11 May: The largest commercial bank in Austria, Kredit-Anstalt, failed. 5 June: German government memorandum mentioned the possibility of discontinuing reparations payments; foreign short-term funds, fearing disaster, fled Germany; Bank for International Settlements (established May 1930) , Bank of England, Bank of France, and the U.S. Federal Reserve System loaned Germany $25 m. to tide her over financial

collapse. 20 June: U.S. President Herbert Hoover proposed a 1-year moratorium on all reparations and war-debt payments. 7 July: French government accepted the Hoover proposal. 12 July: The important German Darmstädter and National Bank failed; run on other German banks; German government decided to close all banks and credit institutions in the country (banks were reopened 5 Aug.) ; Germany froze British short-term assets in Germany. 20–23 July: London conference of representatives of the U.S., Belgium, France, Germany, Italy, Japan, and the U.K. agreed to renew loans to Germany when they expired. July: Britain (because of blocked short-term assets in Germany and Central Europe) became a heavy borrower from abroad. French banks began to withdraw funds from London, as did other foreign banks, when rumors spread of possible financial difficulty. Aug.: Britain's reserves of foreign exchange reached a new low. 23 Aug.: British government resigned. 21 Sept.: Britain suspended the gold standard. 23 Dec.: Committee of the Bank for International Settlements reported Germany would not be able to make payment on reparations, due in July 1932. 1931: 2,294 bank suspensions occurred in the U.S.; losses to depositors came to $391.2 million. 1932, 2 Feb.: Reconstruction Finance Corporation established in the U.S. with authority to provide emergency financing for U.S. banking institutions, life insurance companies, building and loan societies, railroads, and farm mortgage associations; Charles G. Dawes headed the R.F.C. 27 Feb.: In U.S. the Glass-Steagall Act passed, designed to increase the collateral the Federal Reserve could hold against Federal Reserve notes; government bonds as well as eligible paper were to serve as collateral; the act provided aid for individual banks, broadening the conditions under which they could borrow from the Federal Reserve. 16 June: International conference opened at Lausanne to discuss problem of German reparations and interallied debts; plans made were not ratified by governments involved. Germany never resumed reparations payments. 1932: Britain established an Exchange Equalization Account, through the operations of which it attempted to control fluctuations of the pound and the currencies tied to it; Britain, as leader of the so-called sterling bloc, took responsibility for stabilizing the currency of the bloc.

U.S. financial crisis: 1932: 1,456 bank suspensions in U.S.; losses to depositors, $172.5 million. (The existence of the R.F.C. had stemmed the tide of bank failures temporarily.) 1933, Jan.–Feb.: Bank failures in the U.S. mounted; 4 Feb., Louisiana declared a 1-day bank holiday; 14 Feb., Michigan governor called for an 8-day bank holiday; 2 Mar., 21 other U.S. states had suspended or restricted banking operations. 4 Mar.: On Inauguration Day practically every bank in the U.S. was closed or under restriction by state proclamation. 5 Mar., 11 P.M.: The new U.S. President, Franklin Delano Roosevelt, issued a proclamation, dated Mon., 6 Mar., proclaiming a 4-day bank holiday and placing a 4-day embargo on gold, silver, and currency exports; although Secretary of Treasury William H. Woodin declared U.S. had not gone off the gold standard, this effectively took the country off gold, for it put gold out of reach. 9 Mar.: Emergency Banking Relief Act in U.S. approved the national bank holiday and other measures taken by the President; the act provided a plan for the reopening of all sound banks and gave the President broad powers over transactions in credit, currency, gold, and silver. 10 Mar.: U.S. executive order continued the prohibition against gold exports and dealings in foreign exchange, except under Treasury permission. 19 Apr.: Executive order took U.S. definitely off the gold standard, prohibiting gold exports unless they were shown to be "necessary to promote the public interest." 12 May: Thomas Amendment to the Agricultural Adjustment Act authorized U.S. Federal Reserve banks to purchase up to $3 billion of government securities directly from the Treasury, and if they did not the President was authorized to direct the Treasury to issue up to $3 billion in greenbacks; the Thomas Amendment provided for devaluation by presidential proclamation of the gold content of the dollar by a maximum of 50%. 5 June: Gold Clause Repeal Joint Resolution; the gold clause in U.S. federal and private obligations was canceled; contracts and debts became payable in legal tender.

Increase in governmental controls: 1932, 12 June–27 July: World Economic Conference in London, avoiding discussion of the insoluble issues of war debts and reparations, sought to secure agreement on currency stabilization; the U.S. sent representatives, but the U.S. policy—with the removal of the gold standard just before the conference—was more national than international; the conference did nothing to restore international financial stability. 1933, 16 June: U.S. Banking Act (1) created the Federal Bank Deposit Insurance Corporation, for guaranteeing individual bank deposits under $5,000; (2) prohibited the payment of interest on moneys in checking accounts in banks in the Federal Reserve System; (3) raised minimum capital requirements for national banks to $30,-000; (4) allowed branch banking by national banks, where it was permitted to state banks by state law; and (5) extended the open-market operations of the Federal Reserve Board—all of which measures were designed to cope with the U.S. domestic crisis. 25 Oct.: U.S. government set the price of gold at $31.36 an ounce (as compared with $29.01 an ounce on the world markets on 24 Oct). 18 Dec.: Price of gold increased to $34.06. 1933: France remained on the gold standard (until Sept. 1936) ; Germany kept an "artificial" parity and retained foreign-exchange controls. The National Socialist government in Germany completely repudiated its reparation obligations. European nations, which owed the U.S. $10.3 billion (of which $7.1 billion were war debts and $3.2 billion were postwar loans), had repaid less than $3 billion. 1933 ff.: Under Hjalmar Schacht, as president of the Reichsbank (1933–39) and as minister of economics (1934–37), Germany mobilized its finances for rearmament; Schacht printed banknotes, manipulated currency (at 1 point, German currency was estimated to have 237 different values), and created credit within the nation; Schacht was considered to be a financial magician. 1934, 30 Jan.: Gold Reserve Act in U.S. gave the government greater control over dollar devaluation; the act placed the U.S. on a gold-bullion standard internationally and on an irredeemable paper standard domestically; it amended the Thomas Amendment to give the President the power to devalue the dollar to between 50% and 60% of its former gold value. 31 Jan.: President Roosevelt by proclamation officially devalued the dollar to 59.06% of its former value, and Secretary of Treasury Henry M. Morgenthau, Jr., announced that he would buy and sell gold at $35 an ounce plus or minus ¼ of 1% handling charge. 13 Apr.: The Johnson Act in the U.S. prohibited loans by Americans to any foreign government that remained in default in its payments to the U.S. 5 Dec.: German law for regulation of credit put German banks under tight government control. 1935, Mar.: Belgium went off the gold standard, devaluing its currency. 23 Aug.: U.S. Banking Act of 1935—a purely domestic act—provided that (1) the title of the Federal Reserve Board be changed to the Board of Governors of the Federal Reserve System, (2) state nonmember banks having $1 million or more deposits were required to become members of the Reserve System by July 1942 or forfeit their insurance benefits, and (3) an open-market committee composed of the Board of Governors and 5 representatives of the Reserve banks be created; these and other provisions made the Banking Act of 1935 an important step in the direction of central banking in the U.S.— the largest step since the passage of the Federal Reserve Act of 1913. 1936, July: Reform of the Bank of France, under which the French government got a leading voice in bank policies. (7 Aug.–25 Sept.: The Bank of France lost $320 m., principally to the U.S. and England.) 25 Sept.: Tripartite Currency Agreement between France, Great Britain, and the U.S. announced; these countries agreed to co-operate in the stabilization of currencies; this was a key move toward joint action in monetary and exchange matters; 26 Sept.: France virtually suspended the gold standard; 27 Sept.: Holland left gold; 28 Sept.: Switzerland left gold. 1 Oct.: Legislation in France authorized suspension of the gold standard law of 25 June, 1928, thus officially devaluing the franc; U.S. arranged with Great Britain and France for the purchase and sale of gold through stabilization funds of these countries, with the aim of reducing fluctuations between their currencies. 1937, June: Gold began to flee France; the franc declined. 1 July: France removed the legal limits on exchange fluctuations. 1937–38: French franc gained value in late 1937 (with reaffirmation of the Tripartite Agreement), but declined again in 1938. 1939, 20 Jan.: Walther Funk replaced Schacht as president of the Reichsbank in Germany; 24 Mar.: Germany undertook a new inflationary financial program; German foreign-exchange controls remained in force; remittances remained blocked.

World War II measures: 1939, Sept.: With the coming of the war, new controls on foreign exchange were imposed. The British pound, which had declined from $4.86 to $3.20 after the Sept. 1931 devaluation and had risen up to $4.90 before World War II, was now fixed at $4.03. 1940: U.S., France, and Great Britain recognized that to deal with the disruption of trade and payments in the 1930's a properly functioning international payments systems was required; the experiences of the 1930's indicated that the *ad hoc* steps taken by individual states were inadequate, but solutions were not yet at hand. 1940, Apr.: When Germany invaded Denmark and Norway, U.S. froze the assets owned by these countries in the U.S., to prevent American funds and property of these countries being utilized by Germany and to protect them for their owners. (As other areas were occupied by Germany, U.S. followed the same procedure.) June: With German occupation of France, the Tripartite Agreement became inoperative; it had, however, been an early stage in international co-operation. 1942, Aug.: John Maynard Keynes proposed an International Clearing Union, equivalent to an international central bank. 1944, Apr.: Agreement was reached between the U.S. and the U.K. on the establishment of an International Monetary Fund. July: At Bretton Woods, N.H., plans were made by 44 nations for such a fund; plans were also made for a world bank. 1945, 27 Dec.: Articles of Agreement for the International Bank for Reconstruction and Development (the World Bank) and for the International Monetary Fund were signed by 30 countries.

FOREIGN TRADE. 1920's: World War I disrupted commerce. 1920: The current value of U.S. exports reached an all-time high, not to be exceeded until 1948. The high figures reflected postwar inflation and worldwide demand. 1921: With the recession there was a sharp drop in demand. 1924: Measured in terms of *constant* purchasing power (1913 currencies as base), the value of foreign trade of France had risen 9%, 1913–24, while British trade had declined 3% and that of Germany 42%. 1928: All the mature industrial nations were exporting more (in current values) than in 1913; yet Britain, which had in the pre-World War I years depended on foreign trade to stimulate prosperity, was in a poor position; if the export values for Britain are recalculated in terms of 1925–29 prices, then, 1927–29, the average real value of British exports ran to about 84% of the 1913 level. When in 1925 Britain had returned to the gold standard, the pound was overvalued—thus imports were cheap and exports expensive; British goods had difficulty competing abroad. Textile industries in less developed countries and Japanese output created competition with British textiles overseas. British coal exports lagged. By contrast, when France returned to the gold standard in 1926, the franc was undervalued, and French exports rose as a result. 1926–29: U.S. foreign trade exceeded British

foreign trade and the U.S. became the world's largest trader.

Trade restraints in the 1920's: 1920's: Tariffs to some extent impeded the trade of industrial countries, but not in a major fashion. 1920: Britain decided on a complete prohibition of imports of dyestuffs and coal-tar dyes to protect its domestic chemical industry and to bar the revived German industry. 1921, 3 Apr.: France passed a temporary tariff, raising duties 5 times their 1910 level; 27 May: Emergency Tariff Act in the U.S., with dye licensing provisions and embargoes on oxalic and formic acids, amyl and butyl alcohols, butyl acetate, and fusel oil, aimed to protect America's new chemical industry; this act also raised duties on agriculture; the act contained antidumping provisions, which provided for special duties on goods sold in the U.S. at lower prices than they were sold abroad; 12 Aug.: Britain also passed an antidumping act; 1 Oct.: Safeguarding of Industries Act in Britain extended the range of wartime McKenna duties, which were retained; under the new British act, customs duties were collected on 6,000 imported articles. 1922, 21 Sept.: Fordney-McCumber Tariff (U.S.) imposed higher duties on agricultural products, raised other rates, and gave the U.S. President the power to alter duties as much as 50% to equalize foreign and domestic costs of production; this act contained the highest duties in American history. 1924: Minor reductions in duties in England, but duties reimposed in 1925. 1925, 11 Jan.: High tariff protection given to agriculture in Germany, as Germany enacted a tariff of the same type as its 1902 tariff. 1926, Apr.: France raised all import duties by 30%; Aug.: France again raised all import duties by 30%. 1927: Further increase in French duties, but modifications were made through tariff negotiations. 1929: Customs duties had risen in the mature industrial countries well above the 1919 level, but nowhere were the duties prohibitive.

1930's: 1930–33: Sharp decline of trade with worldwide depression. 1933 ff.: Attempts at trade recovery, but in a context of restraint; Britain regained leadership in world foreign trade, followed by U.S., Germany, and France.

Trade restraints in the 1930's: 1930–33: Trend worldwide toward trade restrictions, tariffs, exchange controls, quotas, and licensing. 1930, 17 June: Hawley-Smoot Tariff became law in the U.S.; it increased U.S. tariff rates to their highest level in 20th cent.; this tariff provoked retaliatory action by other countries. 1931, May: France became the 1st nation during the depression to adopt "quantitative restrictions" on trade, i.e., to put quotas on imports. (By 1934, 3,000 articles were on the French quota list.) 1932: U.S. introduced "import excise taxes," which were tariffs by another name, on copper, petroleum, coal, lumber, oils, and fats. 1932, Feb.: With the Import Duties Act, Britain instituted quotas; Britain was finally fully committed to a protective tariff policy; 21 July–20 Aug.: at the Ottawa Conference various parts of the British Empire accepted increased imperial preference; the result of the conference was a higher external tariff for the empire (including Britain). 1932: France gave preferential tariff concessions to its colonies. 1933 ff.: Germany expanded export trade to the Balkans and Latin America. Policies of "bloc trading" came into evidence: Britain with its empire, France with its empire, Germany with selected regions, and the U.S. to a greater extent with Latin America. 1933: With the depression and trade restraints, foreign commerce of the major industrial nations sank to a nadir. 1933: U.S. exports were a mere 37.9% of the 1929 level, while imports were 35.8% of that level. 1933–34: Britain made bilateral commercial treaties to reduce tariff barriers with Scandinavian and Baltic countries. 1934, 12 June: U.S. sought to stem the tide of rising trade barriers with the Trade Agreements Act, a turning point in U.S. tariff history; it authorized the President to enter into reciprocal trade agreements with other governments for reduction of specific duties by as much as 50%. 1934 ff.: U.S., under this act, made a series of bilateral agreements aiming toward freer trade, but the for-

eign trade of the U.S. and of the industrial nations in Europe recovered slowly; economic nationalism was the norm. 1937: British exports reached their peak for the decade (83% of the 1929 level; at no time in the 1930's did British exports exceed their 1913 level). 1938: British exports represented a new low as a percentage of British industrial output: 1924, 27%; 1930, 22%; 1935, 17%; 1938, 15%. German government policy of self-sufficiency discouraged imports; the Germans encouraged exports through (1) direct export subsidies, (2) rewards of various sorts to exporters, (3) barter agreements, and (4) manipulation of exchange rates. Exports did rise as a result. 1939–45: International trade came to be shaped by the patterns of war deliveries. 1940, July: U.S. started export control; 1941, Apr.: almost half of U.S. exports had to be licensed (arms, ammunition, certain machine tools, chemicals, raw materials); Dec.: all U.S. exports became subject to license after U.S. entered the war. Britain and Germany also put on restraints of trade designed to meet wartime requirements.

FOREIGN INVESTMENT. 1920's: The principal capital markets were New York and London. Americans made foreign investments as never before. 1929: U.S. foreign investments had a book value $17.2 billion; those of Britain were $18.2 billion; this total of $35.4 billion represented the bulk of international investments. (France had $3.5 billion invested abroad, the Netherlands $2.3 billion, Germany $1.1 billion, Switzerland $2 billion, and other countries, including Canada, Belgium, Sweden, Japan, India, Australia, and New Zealand, together totaled $5.7 billion.)

1929–33: U.S. capital market evaporated; 1934–40: the U.S. was a net importer of capital. 1932–37: There was a general disenchantment in Britain with foreign investment; Britain became a net importer of capital. 1937: The value of U.S. foreign investments had dropped to $11.8 billion, while British foreign investment (converted at the exchange rate at end of year) had grown slightly to $18.8 billion.

FOREIGN INVESTMENT POSITION, 1938
($ million)

	Credits (Foreign Investments Abroad)	Debts (Foreign Investments Within Nation)
U.K.	22,905	1,299
U.S.	11,491	7,007
France	3,859	559
Germany	676	2,743

1939–45: With the war, Germany lost almost all its foreign assets. At war's end the U.S. and Britain still ranked as the world's largest creditor nations. Together they controlled foreign assets of about $29.5 billion compared with $35.4 billion in 1929 and $34.3 billion in 1938.

FOREIGN AID. 1941, 11 Mar.: U.S. Lend-Lease Act aided Britain in supplying her dollar requirements; goods were supplied to Britain without immediate payment. 1941, 11 Mar.–1945, Aug.: U.S. lend-lease aid came to $43,615 m., of which $30,073 m. went to the British Empire (mostly to Great Britain) and $10,670 m. went to USSR. Reciprocal aid to the U.S. from the British Empire came to $7,567 m.

BUSINESS ORGANIZATION. The methods of business organization developed in the U.S. spread to Europe. 1920's: More use of the corporate form in Euope. The "rationalization" movement assumed popularity in Western Europe, with conferences, discussions, and study groups established to apply the techniques of scientific management; linked with this was the diffusion to Europe of American ideas on mass production of standardized products. In the U.S. innovations in business organization included (1) the increased use of the pyramided holding-company structure in utilities, which served to centralize control; (2) the introduction by Du Pont and General Motors of a form of organization structure for business enterprises—comprising a central staff and multidivisional operating units, designed to provide efficient use of resources within a large corporation; (3) the more frequent use of committees within a business organization, in place of a 1-man decision making system; and (4) the spread of research laboratories

within business enterprises (the earliest ones were before World War I, but only in the 1920's did they become common). 1925–29: 2nd large wave of corporate mergers in the U.S.; the corporate form provided continuity of business organization and a means of facilitating mergers. In the U.S. the corporation had become the way of doing business. 1929: In large American corporations, there was increasingly a separation of ownership and management control. This was more the case in the U.S. than in Europe, because of (1) the greater use of the corporate form, (2) the longer use of the corporate form, and (3) the growth in the U.S. of enterprises to a larger scale. In Europe too the age of the giant enterprise was emerging. 1925, 28 Nov.: Formation of I. G. Farbenindustrie A. G. in Germany. 1926, Oct.: Sir Alfred Mond united Brunner-Mond, United Alkali, British Dyestuffs Corp., and the Nobel Industries into Imperial Chemical Industries, Ltd. 1926: Vickers-Armstrong, Ltd., munitions makers, was founded. 1929, Jan.: Associated Electrical Industries founded in Britain, merging several of the key British electrical companies. 1930: Establishment of Unilever, Ltd. In Germany, the cartel form of operation continued, sometimes encouraged by the German government. International cartels also became more prevalent. International business enterprises—single companies with business stakes worldwide—came into new prominence. 1930's: Americans, seeking explanations for the depression, asked new questions about corporate organizations, concentration of corporate power, and the role of the large business enterprise. 1932: Estimated 2,400 cartels in Germany. 1933 ff.: Under National Socialism in Germany, the tendency of business organization was toward more combination, greater co-operation, and less competition; compulsory cartels became prevalent in Germany. 1930's: The decline of competition was also evident in Britain. In France, with general stagnation there was little change in private business organizations, although the government played a far larger role in business. 1930's: Americans began to fear the decline of competition (pp. 769–770 below).

GOVERNMENT POLICY. General: 1919–26: The French government, expecting Germany to cover the bill (with reparation payments), put large sums of money into reconstruction of devastated areas, which encouraged economic expansion in France.

FRENCH CENTRAL GOVERNMENT EXPENDITURES AS % OF NATIONAL INCOME

Estimates

1920	47.5
1921	28.1
1922	29.6
1926	27.9

In Britain the government played a less significant role in generating investment; after the war, most government intervention stopped. 1922–26: British central government expenditures, however, ran just over 20% of national income, with the expenditures mainly on payments of the national debt, defense, and veterans' pensions. In the U.S., Republican governments held to the motto "less government in business, more business in government"; 1920, 1 Mar.–5 June: Merchant Marine Act (Jones Act) provided for sale of U.S. government-owned ships to private interests. 1922–26: U.S. federal government expenditures were about 4% of national income. Germany, trying desperately to recover from its wartime losses, found its domestic policies shaped by international conditions. 1920: German state railways became the property of the Reich; 1924: on the recommendation of the Dawes Plan, private companies undertook to operate the German railroads on 40-year leases. 1926–29: Except in respect of aid to agriculture, in some

cases tariffs, and in Britain aid to exports, there was no marked increase in governments' role in the economies of the mature industrial nations. 1929–39: With the depression and postdepression attempts at recovery, governments of mature nations took on a more important role, trying for the 1st time to provide extensive aid to the able-bodied unemployed. 1933 ff.: The New Deal in the U.S. inaugurated greater government participation; the National Industrial Recovery Act introduced government-industry planning (which lasted 1933–35). 1933, 1 May: Adolf Hitler outlined Germany's 1st 4-year plan, aiming at lowering unemployment and increasing economic advance. 1935 ff.: In the U.S. government-industry planning was abandoned, and more reliance was placed on the market mechanism, including a government role in regulation and welfare. 1935–36: The British government's activities in supervising, co-ordinating, and planning industrial expansion began to increase. 1936 ff.: In France under the Popular Front government, state intervention took the form of welfare measures and direct participation. 1936, Sept.: Hitler announced Germany's 2nd 4-year plan, which involved more extensive planning than had ever been undertaken in the U.S. or Western Europe; state control and interference sought to make Germany self-sufficient in raw materials, encourage industries, prompt technological changes, and use existing resources efficiently. Hitler and Hermann Göring indicated that the 4-year plan involved sacrifices; workers had to put aside wage increases, business to accept curtailment of freedom of action, everybody to pay higher taxes; in return the state promised Germans security from enemies in time of war, economic strength, and a higher standard of living in the long run. The German 4-year plan was directed toward developing Germany's economic capacity to fight a war. 1938: With the recession in the U.S., President Roosevelt was prepared for the 1st time consciously to employ fiscal policy as an aid to recovery; U.S. regulation of business enterprise increased. 1940–45: Wartime governments' involvement in economic matters soared in the U.S., Germany, and Britain; 1944: after liberation, Ministry of National Economy established in France, and wave of nationalization began.

Aids to agriculture: The pleas of the farmer in the mature industrial nations made government aid seem essential. 1921: U.S. 1st postwar tariff gave special protection to agriculture. 1922, 18 Feb.: Co-operative Marketing Act (Capper-Volstead Act) in U.S. exempted agricultural producers, co-operatives, and associations from antitrust laws. 1923, 4 Mar.: Intermediate Credit Act in U.S. sought to facilitate loans for crop financing; it established 12 intermediate credit banks, each with a capital of $5 million subscribed by the government; each bank was authorized to make short-term loans (6 months to 3 years) to agricultural co-operatives; the act also authorized the creation by private capital of agricultural credit corporations. 1924, 24 Aug.: Agricultural Credits Act provided for government loans to dealers and co-operatives to permit them to withhold commodities from domestic and foreign trade in an effort to prevent bankruptcies and dumping. 1925: German agricultural tariff rose sharply; British Sugar (Subsidy) Act was passed, under which Britain provided subsidies to its beet-sugar industry. 1929: German legislation made provisions for agricultural credits. 1929, 15 June: Agricultural Marketing Act, in U.S., established a Federal Farm Board to promote marketing of farm commodities through agricultural co-operatives and by stabilization corporations. 1930: In U.S., Federal Farm Board created Cotton Stabilization Corp., Grain Stabilization Corp., and Wool Marketing Corp. 1931: British Agricultural Marketing Act established an agricultural marketing board; Wheat Act in Britain guaranteed wheat prices. 1932, 2 Feb.: Reconstruction Finance Corp. in U.S. authorized to loan money to farm mortgage associations. 1933: Agricultural Marketing Act in Britain placed new restraints on agricultural imports; under the act, schemes were established for marketing potatoes, pigs, and milk. 1933 ff.: Under the New

Deal in the U.S. and under National Socialism in Germany, new aids to farmers. 1933 ff.: In addition to high protective duties, France established extensive support programs for wheat, wine, sugar beets, and some other crops. 1933, 27 Mar.: Farm Credit Administration set up in the U.S. by executive decree; 12 May.: Agricultural Adjustment Act in U.S. sought to guarantee a fair return to agriculture and to restore the purchasing power of the farmer; it introduced the concept of parity prices (based on 1909–14 period); it aimed to eliminate surplus crops through compulsory curtailed production; for the 1st time the American farmer was subsidized (1936: Supreme Court ruled the act unconstitutional). 2 June: German Law for the Reduction of Unemployed contained provision for national funds to be spent on agricultural activities; sums spent out of profits for improvement of agriculture were made exempt from income tax. 16 June: Farm Credit Act in U.S. gave the farmer the opportunity to refinance farm mortgages on long terms at low rates. Aug.: U.S. participated in International Wheat Agreement. 18 Oct.: Commodity Credit Corp. established in U.S., authorizing the use of Reconstruction Finance Corp. funds for loans to farmers. 1933–34: German agriculture was completely reorganized under the Food Estate (Reichsnährstand), which included landowners, tenants, cultivators, agricultural workers, processors of foodstuffs, and wholesale and retail traders in agricultural produce, as well as all agricultural co-operative societies and farmers' organizations; German agriculture was rationalized; state control and guidance of marketing associations was established; the Germans sought self-government of agriculture under state supervision. 1934: British introduced subsidies for cattle raisers; Germans started a "battle for production" of agricultural output with extensive government subsidies. 31 Jan.: Farm Mortgage Refinancing Act in U.S. established Federal Farm Mortgage Corp., 23 Feb.: Crop Loan Act in U.S. allocated more funds for loans to farmers. 21 Apr.: Cotton Control Act in U.S. provided for compulsory reduction of surplus cotton crops. 9 May: Jones-Costigan Sugar Act in U.S. sought to limit sugar production. 28 June: Federal Farm Bankruptcy Act in U.S. gave new relief to farmers, providing means of obtaining credit; it suspended bankruptcy proceedings for 5 years (act declared unconstitutional in *Louisville Joint Stock Land Bank* v. *Redford*, 1935). 28 June: Tobacco Control Act in U.S. provided for compulsory reduction of surplus tobacco crops. 1935, 29 Aug.: Farm Mortgage Moratorium Act in U.S. offered a 3-year moratorium on seizure to debt-burdened farmers. 1936, 6 Jan.: In U.S., Agricultural Adjustment Act of 1933 declared unconstitutional (*U.S.* v. *Butler*); 29 Feb.: Soil Conservation and Domestic Allotment Act in U.S. provided benefit payments to growers who co-operated with the government soil-conservation program; payments related to the acreage withdrawn from production (this was designed to replace the unconstitutional AAA legislation); there was to be no compulsion. Sept.: 2nd German 4-year plan aimed at agricultural self-sufficiency, cutting food imports and developing agriculture; government funds were allocated for land improvement; prices of fertilizers were artificially lowered; credits were provided farmers for purchase of machinery and fertilizers; attention was paid to better agricultural practices; agriculture prices were artificially raised to encourage production of potatoes and sugar beets. 1937: In Britain, legislation guaranteed prices for oats and barley; producers of fertilizers were subsidized by the government. 1938, 16 Feb.: New Agricultural Adjustment Act in U.S. sought to curb farm surpluses; the secretary of agriculture could fix marketing quotas and authorize acreage allotments to farmers; as in the 1933 Agricultural Adjustment Act, the parity principle was repeated; this act established the concept of the "ever-normal granary"; the U.S. government would store excess crops and only when the price was above parity would these be marketed; the act authorized the creation of the Federal Crop Insurance Corp.

Aids to industry: 1918, 10 Apr.: Webb-Pomerene Act passed in U.S., an act to promote export trade; it allowed exporters to combine without being subject to U.S. antitrust laws. 1919: German Coal Act was designed to merge the entire German coal industry into a national compulsory cartel, supervised by the German government; under this legislation there was a rationalization of the German coal industry. 1920's: In Britain, where the coal industry was ailing, the government sanctioned restrictive agreements among coal producers and the fixing of production quotas; export subsidies were paid by the government. 1921 ff.: Tariff protection of industry in the U.S. and in Western Europe. 1928: British established an Export Credits Guarantee Department. 1930: Coal Mines Act in Britain endorsed earlier restrictive measures in industry and introduced a marketing scheme for coal, including quotas, export markets, and minimum prices; this amounted to a government-sponsored cartel. 1933, 20 Feb.: Hitler in Germany made promises to industrialists to aid them, and asked that they assist him; Apr.: taxation on all new motor cars removed in Germany to encourage that industry; 2 June: Law for the Reduction of Unemployment in Germany contained tax aids to firms that raised capital expenditures and increased employment. 16 June: National Industrial Recovery Act in the U.S. sought to raise prices and encourage industrial expansion; the act employed the concept of industrial self-regulation (with industry codes) under government supervision; the act created the National Recovery Administration. (1935: The U.S. Supreme Court declared the code provisions of the act unconstitutional in *Schechter Poultry Corp.* v. *U.S.*). 1933 ff.: British government supported rationalization proposals in the shipbuilding, tin-plate, and wool-combing industries. 1934, 2 Feb.: Export-Import Bank established in U.S. to provide industry with credits for exports to the newly recognized Soviet Union (this bank never functioned in this capacity); 12 Mar.: a 2nd Export-Import Bank was established in the U.S. to provide credits for American exports to Cuba and then to other countries (1936, the 2 Export-Import banks became 1). 1935, 21 May: Defense Law passed in Germany (Schacht was appointed plenipotentiary general for war economy) ; under the law, encouragement of industrial development, especially munitions factories and armaments. 1935 ff.: British government began to aid the nation's steel industry. 1936, Sept.: 4-year plan in Germany; Hermann Göring in charge; export subsidies were given to industries and industry was urged to expand. 1937: British steel industry discussed planned price changes with the government's Import Duties Advisory Commission, which favored the industry's needs. 1939: Cotton Industry (Reorganization) Act passed in Britain sought to reduce competition in the British cotton industry. The attempts by government to reduce competition were seen as aids to industry.

Aids to transportation: 1920's: The British subsidized their airlines, as did the U.S. 1928, 22 May: Merchant Marine Act (Jones-White Act) in the U.S. was designed to encourage private shipping. 1933: Road and Rail Traffic Act in Britain sought to reduce competition on the railroads. 1936, 26 June: Merchant Marine Act in U.S. provided outright subsidies to develop domestic shipping. In every mature nation, governments built new highways. 1944: In the U.S., Federal Aid Highway Act provided federal assistance for the building of a national system of interstate highways and federal aid to primary and secondary road construction.

Other government aids: 1919: British passed an act to encourage home building, guaranteeing local authorities against losses on approved municipal projects. 1920, 10 June: Water Power Act in U.S. established a Federal Power Commission, which was authorized to issue licenses (limited to 50 years) for the construction and operation of facilities to improve navigation and to develop and utilize power facilities (such as powerhouses, dams, reservoirs, and transmission lines) on U.S. public lands; the commission was empowered to regulate rates and security issues of such licensees. 1923: Chamber-

lain Act in Britain provided for 20-year annual subsidies of £6 on new (suitable) houses; 1924: Wheatley Act raised the subsidy to £9 per annum for 40 years. 1930: Housing Act in Britain gave financial aid for slum clearance. 1932, 2 Feb.: Reconstruction and Finance Corp. established in U.S., which would provide emergency financing for banking institutions, life insurance companies, building and loan societies, railroads, and farm mortgage associations. 21 July: Relief and Construction Act in U.S. extended the functions of the R.F.C. 22 July: In the U.S., Federal Home Loan Bank Act established a Home Loan Bank Board and authorized the establishment of 8 to 12 banks for home mortgages. 1933, 31 Mar.: Civilian Conservation Corps Reforestation Relief Act in U.S. involved the government in public works programs, designed to cut unemployment. 1 May: German 4-year plan announced by Hitler provided a range of public works measures. 12 May: Federal Emergency Relief Act in U.S. authorized grants to states and municipalities for the administration of relief. 13 June: Home Owners Refinancing Act passed in U.S., which created the Home Owners Loan Corporation; act provided means for refinancing home mortgage debts for nonfarm owners. 16 June: Title II of the U.S. National Industrial Recovery Act provided for a federal emergency administration of public works to be established by the President; Roosevelt set up the Public Works Administration, under Secretary of Interior Harold L. Ickes (1874–1952) ; this section of the act was not considered to be unconstitutional and continued after the code provisions of the act were rejected by the U.S. Supreme Court. 8 Nov.: Civil Works Administration established in U.S. as an emergency unemployment relief program. 1934, 15 Feb.: Civil Works Emergency Relief Act authorized $950 million in U.S. for civil works and direct relief. 27 Apr.: In the U.S., Home Owners Loan Act authorized funds for the refinancing of home mortgages. 28 June: National Housing Act in U.S. was designed to stimulate residential construction; it provided for the establishment of the Federal Housing Administration for the purpose of insuring loans made by banks, trust companies, building and loan associations, and other private lending institutions for new construction and improvements. 1935: Housing Act in Britain authorized local authorities to plan housing projects. 8 Apr.: Emergency Relief Appropriation Act in U.S. provided for the establishment of large-scale public works programs for the jobless; it authorized the establishment of the Works Progress Administration (renamed Works Project Administration in 1939). 26 June: National Youth Administration created as part of the Works Progress Administration to superintend work-relief and employment programs for persons between 16 and 25 years of age. 14 Aug.: Social Security Act broadened the U.S. government's aids to the unemployed and to the aged.

Regulation, rationalization, and control: 1933, 27 May: Federal Securities Act ("Truth in Securities" Act) in the U.S. made corporations disclose in detail relevant information relating to new securities issues offered the public. 1933, 16 June: Under the National Industrial Recovery Act in the U.S., the American government sought to supervise industry, to raise prices, and to develop a system of industrial self government. 1934, June–Dec.: German government sought to control prices of industrial goods; the National Socialist government organized industry into 13 groups, each with subgroups, with the whole structure under the Ministry of Economics; the goal was industrial self-government; the management was left to private enterprise; general direction and planning were by the state; compulsory cartels were formed in Germany in 26 important industries. 16 June: Emergency Railroad Transportation Act in U.S. provided for financial reorganization of the carriers, avoidance of unnecessary duplication of services and facilities, and other means of improving conditions of rail transportation; the act authorized a new office, the Federal Coordinator of Transportation. 1934: Dividends Limitation Law in Germany, designed to encourage industries to reinvest

profits. 6 June: Securities Exchange Act in the U.S. established a Securities and Exchange Commission; act provided for federal regulation of the stock exchanges; all issues of securities offered the public (not just new issues) required full disclosure of relevant information. 19 June: Communications Act in U.S. established the Federal Communications Commission (FCC) for regulation of interstate communication by telephone, telegraph, cable, and radio. 1935, 26 Aug.: Public Utility Holding Co. Act (Wheeler-Rayburn Act) in U.S. put public utilities under federal regulation; all utility holding companies had to register with the Securities and Exchange Commission; the act required utility holding companies to simplify their corporate structure and to eliminate pyramiding; the act also gave the U.S. Federal Power Commission authority to regulate the transmission and sale of electric power in interstate commerce. 1936, 19 June: Robinson-Patman Act in U.S. was designed to protect small retail businesses against the large chain stores; it made illegal price discrimination between different purchasers of commodities of like grades and qualities, where the effect was to lessen competition or to create a monopoly. June: Price regulation adopted in France, in an effort to obtain price stability after the introduction of new social legislation. Sept.: Under a new German 4-year plan there was large increase in government regulation. 1936–37: Enlarged British government regulation, including some price controls. 1937, 17 Aug.: Miller-Tydings Resale Price Maintenance Act in U.S. protected small retailer; it amended the U.S. antitrust laws to legalize contracts made between producers and distributors, which involved maintenance of resale prices of branded nationally advertised goods traded in interstate commerce. 1938, 16 June: Temporary National Economic Committee (TNEC) established in the U.S. to look into concentration of corporate power. 1939 ff.: Department of Justice in the U.S. initiated a series of antitrust suits against giant American enterprises. The attempts of the U.S. government policy, 1936 ff., to protect and encourage small business had no counterpart in Europe, where the thrust of government policy was toward rationalization and elimination of competition. European governments' controls sought larger-scale, more efficient business enterprises, while the U.S. government sought to safeguard competition and return to the classical free-market economy. 1939, spring: French government assumed authority over entire economy, in the belief war was imminent. 24 Aug.: British Parliament passed the Emergency Powers Bill, giving the British government key powers over all facets of the economy; the British Treasury ordered all owners of foreign securities to return their holdings to the Bank of England within 30 days; this gathering of foreign assets was to obtain resources with which to buy needed materials from abroad. 1 Sept.: British Currency (Defense) Bill passed, which provided that funds from the Exchange Equalization Account could be utilized for war needs. Nov.: Britain adopted a broad price-control law, Prices of Goods Act. During the war, for every participant regulation and control expanded.

Direct participation in industry: 1920: The operation of the potash properties in Alsace, returned to France under the Treaty of Versailles, went under a "national industrial office," Les Mines Domaniales de Potasse d'Alsace, administered by a French government office; a French government agency also started to manufacture synthetic ammonia, taking over from a German firm the patents for the Haber process. 1924: French government participated in a group of "mixed" industry-government cos. in the Alsace territory. 1933–34: German government chose the route of supervision rather than direct participation; the state actually divested itself of certain direct participations. 1934, 8 Mar.: Hitler at Berlin automobile show made 1st suggestions for the *Volkswagen*. 1936, Aug.: With the establishment of the Popular Front in France there was accelerated state participation; law in France authorized 3 defense ministries to nationalize enterprises in munitions and aircraft industries. 1936, Sept. ff.: Under 4-year plan in Germany new government-owned enterprises began to make synthetic rubber, textiles, fuel, and other products from Germany's own resources, designed to make Germany self-sufficient; Hermann Göring Works was built by the German government to make steel by a new process from local low-grade ore. 1936: In Britain the Air Ministry started the "shadow factory" plan, new plants to be built by the government and operated by cos. in the automobile industry to manufacture parts for aircraft engines. 1940–45: With the coming of the war, government direct participation increased; the making of the atomic bomb at Oak Ridge, Tenn., was a U.S. federal government project; the German government participated directly in research on and manufacture of V-1 and V-2 missiles. Government and/or government-financed plants to build aircraft existed in all the mature nations. Governments financed new factories to fill war needs. 1940–45: U.S. government financed new plant construction, so that by the end of the war 90% of the plants for synthetic rubber, aircraft, magnesium, and shipbuilding, 70% of the aluminum capacity, and 50% of the machine-tool facilities were U.S. government-owned. 1944–45: Wave of nationalizations in France. 1944, Oct.: The holdings of Louis Renault, who was accused of having collaborated with the Germans, were nationalized; a new co., Régie Nationale des Usines Renault, owned by the state, was established, Jan. 1945. 18 Dec.: Coal-mining companies in northern France were merged into a single public enterprise, Houillères du Nord et du Pas de Calais. French nationalization continued in 1945–46.

Direct participation in other sectors: 1926: Electricity (Supply) Act passed in Britain, establishing a Central Electricity Board, to own and operate a national transmission system known as the "grid"; this spurred development of electric power on a national basis. 1933 ff.: In the U.S. and Germany, governments became involved in large-scale public works programs, designed to eliminate unemployment and revive the economy. 1933, 18 May: Establishment of the Tennessee Valley Authority (TVA) in the U.S. as an independent public corporation, authorized to construct dams and power plants and to improve economic and social conditions in the Tennessee Valley region (including 40,000 square miles in the states of Tenn., N.C., Ky., Va., Miss., Ga., and Ala.) ; this was the U.S. government's 1st entry into electrical power production. TVA would produce, distribute, and sell electric power and nitrogen fertilizer to the region's residents and industry (1933–40: Congress appropriated $270 million for TVA's activities). 1933: Roosevelt authorized the use of Public Works Administration funds for the construction of the Grand Coulee Dam on the Columbia River as part of a plan for the development of the Columbia Valley. 1933–40: Other power developments by the U.S. federal government included the completion of the Boulder Dam on the Colorado River, the Fort Peck Dam on the Missouri River (in Montana), and the Bonneville Dam on the Columbia River. 1935, 11 May: Rural Electrification Administration was established in the U.S., by executive order, to administer a program of generating and distributing electricity in isolated rural areas not served by private utilities. These measures, involving the U.S. in public utilities enterprises, had worldwide impact; from France to Latin America, governments took part in large-scale hydroelectrical developments. 1937, Aug.: Nationalization of the railroads in France; Société Nationale des Chemins de Fer Français established to administer a unified railroad system (51% owned by the state, 49% owned by private capital). 1940–45: General wartime participation of the governments was extensive; 1940–45: In U.S. 3,800 miles of oil pipelines were constructed by the government to carry petroleum to the East Coast, one of many types of direct participation.

OTHER FACTORS. 1936: John Maynard Keynes (1883–1946) published *General Theory of Employment, Money*

and Interest, introducing the "new economics"; using Keynesian ideas, economists in the U.S. and abroad would in time demonstrate a new role for government.

MEASURES OF ECONOMIC GROWTH.

REAL NATIONAL INCOME PER CAPITA, 1920-46

(index 1925-29 = 100)

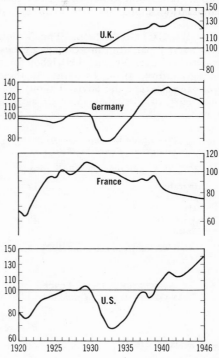

NONMONETARY INDICATORS OF RELATIVE NATIONAL CONSUMPTION LEVELS, 1934–38

	Relative Data (U.S. = 100)
U.S.	100.0
U.K.	75.6
Germany	62.0
France	57.6

NOTE: Includes food, tobacco, medical and sanitary services, education and recreation, transportation, and communication.

SOURCE: M. K. Bennett, "International Disparities in Consumption Levels," *American Economic Review,* Sept. 1951, p. 648.

The Drive Toward Maturity—USSR, Canada, Australia, Japan, Etc.

During the period 1919–45 the Soviet Union, Italy, Canada, Australia, and Japan (and some other countries) took large strides along the path to industrial maturity.

AGRICULTURE. 1919: The USSR, Italy, and Japan (but not Canada or Australia) had over 50% of their labor force in agriculture. 1940: In none of these countries (except the Soviet Union) was over 50% of the labor force in agriculture.

% OF LABOR FORCE INVOLVED IN
AGRICULTURE, FORESTRY, FISHERIES

	1920–29	1930–39
Australia	20	17
Canada	36	32
Italy	56	48
Japan	53	49
USSR[a]	85	59

[a] Soviet figures are for 1925 and 1940.

AGRICULTURAL LABOR FORCE
IN OTHER SELECTED COUNTRIES

	% of Total Labor Force
New Zealand (1945)	20
Denmark (1940)	29
Norway (1930)	35
Czechoslovakia (1947)	38
Austria (1939)	39

Agricultural progress: 1920's: The low agricultural prices experienced by farmers in the mature industrial nations adversely affected the newly industrial nations, with these major exceptions: (1) In Canada and Australia—based on available land— wheat acreage expanded. 1923–28: Canadian wheat acreage grew by 3 m. acres. Costs were low and western Canadian farmers prospered despite similarly low agricultural prices. 1919: 6.5 m. acres were planted with wheat in Australia; 1929, 15

m. acres in wheat in Australia; here too expansion occurred despite lower price. (2) Russian agricultural output began slowly to turn upward, 1922–28 (as the government left the individual farmer on his own). Most of this output was absorbed by domestic consumption. 1927–31: Large rich harvests in Japan sent rice prices down to their nadir. 1929 ff.: All the newly industrialized nations felt the depression severely. 1930: With the virtual closing of the American market for Japanese silk, prices dropped drastically. 1930 ff.: Soviet agriculture stagnated because of the depression and peasant opposition to collectivization. 1932–33: Famine in Russia.

OFFICIAL INDEX OF GROSS AGRICULTURAL
OUTPUT, USSR
(1913 = 100; base refers to geographic area
of Sept. 17, 1939)

1913	100
1920	67
1921	60
1926	118
1928	124
1929	121
1930	117
1931	114
1932	107
1933	101
1934	106
1935	119
1936	109
1937	134
1938	120
1939	121

1930 ff.: Canadian wheat production sank into the doldrums; depression, drought, crop failures, and foreign tariff barriers had a disastrous impact on the wheat farmer. (1929–36: The Saskatchewan wheat crop averaged only 60% of the preceding 5-year period; wheat prices were about 56%.) The plight of the wheat farmer affected the rest of the

Canadian economy, causing the 1930's to be a time of national stagnation. 1930's: Australian acreage in wheat production declined from the 1930–31 high of 18 m. acres to 12 m. acres, 1934–37, and then rose to 14 m. acres, 1938–39. 1930's: Japanese agricultural output rose slowly, aided to a small extent by the government; Italian output in agriculture expanded significantly, mainly because of government assistance and protection. 1930's: On the whole, the decade saw few benefits accruing to the farmer in the newly industrialized nations.

Land reform: 1919, July: Italian war veterans, spurred by talk by socialists and populists about agricultural reform, began to occupy the farming area in the Lazio and then elsewhere; the government gave the prefects power to expropriate holdings and cede them to the new occupants; 1920, 15 Apr.: 27,252 hectares (half in Lazio) had been redistributed in this manner; 1922 ff.: under the Italian Fascist government no attempt was made to change the landholding pattern, but with agricultural distress large landowners frequently sold or rented part of their holdings to small farmers; 1922–40: in Italy there was a rise in number of independent cultivators, who were loyal to the Fascist regime. 1919 ff.: In Eastern Europe (including Czechoslovakia) there were major agrarian reforms, with some 60 m. acres redistributed; these measures created more small farmers. 1919–28: In Russia, despite efforts, 1919–21, to initiate state farming and despite formal "nationalization," most land remained in peasant hands; 1921: under the New Economic Policy in Russia peasants were allowed to hold their land (though title was vested in the state) and to trade in their own produce. 1927: In the USSR all forms of state and co-operative farming included only 2% of the peasants; the number of small farms had increased (1916, 18 m. farms in Russia; 1928, 25.6 m. farms). The Soviet government thought small farming was inefficient. 1928: The Soviet government undertook a new policy of collectivization; to succeed in the other goals of its 5-year plan, it needed labor released from agriculture

to man new factories, large amounts of food to feed the urban labor force, and exportable surpluses to obtain foreign exchange for industrial machinery. It wanted to put unused land into production, to mechanize farming, and to increase productivity. To obtain these benefits and also for ideological reasons (peasants were conservative and hostile to Communist goals), the Soviet government decided to substitute collective farms (*kolkhozy*) for individual peasant farms. 1928 ff.: Collectivization proceeded by force over the violent opposition of the peasants. 1932: Sharp reduction in area seeded. 1933: Under 2nd Soviet 5-year plan peasants were allowed to farm "garden plots" (allocated to them by the collectives) and to sell freely any surplus. 1938: Collectivization in Russia included 19 m. peasant households and 99.3% of cultivated land. 1940: The USSR had more than 236,000 collective farms (with 371 m. acres) and 4,000 state farms (with 4.7 m. acres).

Mechanization: 1919 ff.: In Canada and Australia extensive mechanization of agriculture occurred. 1928 ff.: Russian government policy sought to increase output through mechanization; tractor plants were built as part of the 1st Russian 5-year plan. The low level of mechanization is evident from the table that follows.

NUMBER OF TRACTORS IN SELECTED COUNTRIES (000)

	1939	1949
USSR	483.5	400.0
Canada	131.5	322.9
Australia	50.0a	76.3
Italy	39.0	39.0
Austria	2.2	10.0
Japan	.1	1.8

a 1940–41 figures.

Self-sufficiency: 1930's: Government policy in the maturing nations aimed at agricultural self-sufficiency. Most were or became self-sufficient in foodstuffs: Russia (1937), 100%; Italy (1937), 95%; Japan (1930), 80%. Japan—failing to achieve domestic self-sufficiency—sought self-sufficiency within its empire.

RAW MATERIALS. Coal: 1920: Soviet coal production was 27% of its 1913 value; its coal output was only 6.2 m. metric tons; 1930, 50.4 m. metric tons; 1938, Soviet coal production exceeded that of France, and ranked 4th in world industry (following Germany, U.S., and Great Britain).

COAL AND LIGNITE PRODUCTION, 1938
(million metric tons)

USSR	132.9
Japan	53.0
Poland	38.1
Czechoslovakia	30.5
Australia	14.0
Canada	12.9
Italy	2.2

Canada and Italy had inadequate coal for domestic needs and were importers. Japan needed to import certain coking coals.

Oil: Of the newly industrialized countries, only the USSR was self-sufficient in petroleum. 1920: Soviet oil production was 41% of the 1913 value. 1927: USSR resumed its role as the 2nd largest oil producer in the world. (USSR surpassed Mexican output to achieve that status.) Soviet oil production (in millions of barrels of 42 U.S. gallons) : 1920, 25.4; 1930, 127.4; 1938, 206.2.

Iron ore: USSR and Canada had substantial reserves of iron ore; on the other hand, Italy was an importer of iron ore. Japan had virtually no iron ore, and had to import for its needs.

Other industrial resources: USSR was rich in natural resources of all kinds; Canada too had excellent mineral resources, while Italy and Japan were deficient. Raw silk from Japan—an industrial raw material—continued as an important Japanese export and provided Japan with foreign exchange. 1930's: In the search for self-sufficiency, efforts were made in Italy to develop local resources and also substitutes for certain natural resources. Japan's expansion into Manchuria, 1931, and China, 1937, and then its sweep through Southeast Asia, 1941–42, provided it with basic industrial resources (iron, coal, rubber, and oil).

ENERGY. The energy revolution—the use of electricity and the internal-combustion engine—that had occurred in the mature nations spread to the newer industrial nations. Inanimate sources of energy now did the bulk of the work.

ENERGY CONSUMPTION PER CAPITA FOR PRODUCTIVE PURPOSES, SELECTED COUNTRIES, 1937
(electricity equivalent in kwh for all energy sources)

	Per Capita Use	Ratio of Inanimate to All Sources
Australia	2,971	91.3
USSR	1,380	88.2
Japan	1,251	91.0

1935: Energy production as a percentage of the world total was, with the exception of the USSR, small compared with the leading industrial nations.

ENERGY PRODUCTION, 1935
(%)

World	100.000
USSR	8.584
Japan	2.963
Canada	1.488
Czechoslovakia	1.046
Australia	0.722
Italy	0.675

SOURCE: Abbott Payson Usher, "The Resource Requirements of an Industrial Economy," *Journal of Economic History*, Suppl. VII (1947), pp. 44–46.

Electric power: The surge of industrialization in the newer countries came to be based from the start primarily on electric rather than steam power. In Canada, Japan, and Italy most of the electric production was from hydroelectrical facilities; in the USSR and Australia, the developments were primarily in thermoelectrical plants; 1940: only about 10% of Soviet electrical energy was generated by hydroelectrical stations.

ELECTRICAL PRODUCTION, 1930–40
(billion kwh)

	1930	1940
Canada	18.1	30.1
Japan	15.7	35.5
Italy	10.6	19.4
USSR	8.4	48.0
Australia	2.4	5.1

Internal-combustion engine: Applications of the internal-combustion engine to motor-vehicle transport took place along the same lines (but on a smaller scale) as in the mature industrial nations.

Other sources of energy: 1924, Apr.: Establishment in the USSR of a Central Committee for the Study of Rocket Propulsion. 1932: According to Soviet historians, jet-assisted-take-off-type rockets were 1st used in that country. 1935: Successful flight of Russian liquid-propellant meteorological rocket, designed by M. K. Tikhonravov. 1937: The USSR set up rocket test centers—Kazan, Moscow, and Leningrad. 1941, Nov.–Dec.: The Russians used antiaircraft rockets against German aircraft which were attacking Moscow and also air-to-air rockets on their Stormovik Il-2 fighters. Russian work on rocketry—whether for civilian or military purposes—aided in the development of a powerful propellant to be used in the postwar years.

INDUSTRY. Industrialization occurred in the new industrial nations mainly through the borrowing of techniques developed in the mature industrial nations. 1920's: Canadian industrial progress was significant, following closely the course of U.S. development; U.S. investors in the dominion aided in the growth of the latter's industry. Yet Canadian manufacturing continued to represent only a small portion of world manufacturing. 1930's: With the depression, there was a slowdown in the development of manufacturing in Canada. 1920–40: Italian, Japanese, Soviet, and Australian manufacturing output rose more rapidly than the world average; only Soviet manufacturing, however, came to provide a substantial percentage of *world* manufacturing. 1938: USSR was 2nd only to the U.S. in world manufacturing.

Textiles: Among all the newly industrialized nations, only in Japan did the textile industry act as the leading sector. The Japanese textile industry became increasingly efficient (1920, 91 workers per 100 looms in Japan; 1931, 36 workers per 100 looms); 1927–32: the technical revolution in the Japanese cotton industry gave that nation the opportunity to move into foreign markets formerly served by British goods. 1930's: Japan introduced more precision machinery, improved the quality of its cotton goods, and reduced prices. Although its textile industry became increasingly capital-intensive, wage levels remained low. Japan had the lowest-cost cotton textile production in the world.

INDEXES OF MANUFACTURING OUTPUT
(1913 = 100)

	USSR	Italy	Canada	Japan	Australia	World
1920	12.8	95.2	99.1	176.0	100.5	93.2
1921–25	41.1	124.7	103.9	203.3	125.9	103.2
1926–29	134.9	170.1	147.4	289.8	146.9	138.9
1930	235.5	164.0	147.5	294.8	129.1	136.9
1931–35	393.2	139.7	122.8	365.8	142.9	128.2
1936–38	774.3	186.3	163.6	528.9	188.2	185.0

SOURCE: League of Nations, *Industrialization and Foreign Trade*, New York, 1945.

% DISTRIBUTION OF WORLD'S MANUFACTURING PRODUCTION

	USSR	Italy	Canada	Japan	Other Countries[a]
1913[b]	4.4	2.7	2.3	1.2	18.0
1926/29	4.3	3.3	2.4	2.5	17.7
1936/38	18.5	2.7	2.0	3.5	16.7

SOURCE: League of Nations, *Industrialization and Foreign Trade*, New York, 1945.

a Excludes U.S., Germany, U.K., and France; the latter plus those included in the table above total 100%.

b 1913 figures adjusted to represent the frontiers established after World War I.

Iron and steel:

CRUDE STEEL PRODUCTION, 1938
(million metric tons)

USSR	18.0
Japan	6.5
Italy	2.3
Czechoslovakia	1.9
Australia	1.2
Canada	1.2

SOURCE: United Nations, *Statistical Yearbook 1949–50.*

Utilizing steel, engineering industries developed especially in the USSR and Japan. 1930's: Growth of Japanese and Soviet armaments industries. Automobiles and tractors: 1919: Japanese army authorities ordered trucks from existing private factories; 1919–31: most motor vehicles in Japan were imported; 1931: Japan started to develop an indigenous motor-vehicle industry.

MOTOR VEHICLE PRODUCTION IN JAPAN
FROM HOMEMADE PARTS

1931	434
1932	840
1933	1,612
1934	2,701
1935	5,355
1936	9,632

1923, 4 Mar.: Soviet decree formally established a domestic tractor industry. 1928: 5-year plan endorsed expansion of tractor output. 1930, June: Stalingrad tractor factory opened, the 1st Russian large-scale tractor plant. 1932, Jan.: USSR began to produce the 1st all-Russian-made cars and trucks at a plant in Nizhni Novgorod. 1944: Australia made the commitment to full manufacture of automobiles (not only building the bodies); the Australian government invited foreign automobile makers to submit proposals, which they did.

Other industries: 1920's: Increase in industries processing raw materials (paper and pulp in Canada, especially). 1920–40: Electrical and chemical industries grew. 1930–45: In the USSR, Japan, Italy, Canada, and Australia new aircraft industries began. Petroleum refining became

an important industry in USSR and Canada (the latter based mainly on imported oil). 1930's: In Italy, the state-owned Azienda Generale Italiana Petroli (AGIP), established in 1926, started to build refineries in that country; American cos. also built refineries in Italy. Although Australia had several oil refineries, they were concerned almost entirely with by-products and accounted for only a small fraction of Australian requirements; all automobile and aviation gasoline used in Australia was refined abroad. 1938–48: The war stimulated industrial activity in some cases and destroyed it in others.

AVERAGE ANNUAL RATE OF CHANGE OF
MANUFACTURING ACTIVITY, 1938–48
(%)

Australia	4.5
Canada	6.0
Italy	−0.2
Japan	−4.5

SOURCE: United Nations, *Growth of World Industry—National Tables,* New York, 1963.

TRANSPORTATION. 1920: For practically all the new industrial countries railroad development had been completed; the USSR was the exception. 1920–40: Railroad lines in the Soviet Union increased from 36,600 to 62,500 mi. Automobiles became the main means of transportation in Canada. 1920's: Total private automobiles in use in Canada numbered 2nd only to those in U.S.; 1930's: private automobiles in use in Canada numbered 3rd, after the U.S. and Britain.

PRIVATE AUTOMOBILES IN USE
(000)

	Canada	Italy	Japan	Russia
1921	423	34	8	—
1926	736	105	28	8
1930	1,047	183	56	10
1935	990	244	83	44
1938	1,160	289	59[a]	85

[a] The decline was due to the Japanese government's policy of not granting foreign exchange for imports of private automobiles.

In Japan available transportation ranged from the primitive to the sophisticated.

BICYCLES, CARTS, AND MOTOR VEHICLES
(INCLUDING TRUCKS) REGISTERED IN JAPAN,
1937

Bicycles	7,878,463
Carts for goods, human or animal drawn (excl. horsecarts and oxcarts)	1,519,334
Horsecarts	307,889
Oxcarts	111,146
Motor vehicles (incl. trucks)	128,735
Rickshas	15,376

With the growth of automobile travel came improvements of the roads in all these countries, especially Canada and Italy. Travel by air increased. 1937, 15 July: 3 Russian flyers made a world-distance nonstop record, flying over the North Pole from Moscow to San Jacinto, Calif., in 62 hours. 1941, Aug.: An Italian Caproni-Campini jet-propelled plane, having a conventional engine with ducted fan, was produced and test-flown in Italy; 30 Nov.: Italian jet-propelled Caproni-Campini airplane flew 275 miles from Turin to Rome.

FINANCE. Capital: 1919–39: In the drive to maturity, the new industrial nations generally financed their economic growth out of locally available funds; this was true in the USSR, Italy, and Japan; it was not in large part true in Canada and only partly true in Australia. USSR, because of its refusal to honor previous debts, got virtually no capital from abroad. Italian economic growth was out of reinvested earnings rather than foreign capital. Japan too financed its own development in the main with a high rate of savings and investment. Canada, by contrast, depended on U.S. and to a smaller extent British capital; Australia got considerable capital from Britain.

Banking reform: 1919: In the USSR banking was in disarray following the Revolution, 1917, when it had been nationalized. 1921, 16 Nov.: New Russian state bank (the Gosbank) established. 1919–20: Boom in Japanese banking; 1920–21: failure of a number of Japanese banks; 1923: Kwanto earthquake in Japan meant new calls on banking facilities; moratorium declared as an emergency measure; 1927: Watanabe Bank failed, the Akaji Bank followed,

and a run occurred on Japanese banks; this major banking crisis had come in the wake of the construction boom after the earthquake. 1928, 1 Jan.: as a result of the 1927 crisis, a new Banking Law in Japan provided that all ordinary banks must have capital of more than 1 m. yen (banks in Tokyo and Osaka were required to have capital of more than 2 m. yen, while banks in towns and villages with populations under 10,000 were allowed a minimum capital of 1.2 m. yen); the new Banking Law prompted many bank mergers. 1926, 6 May: When the right of issue was finally confined to the Bank of Italy, Italy at last had a central banking system; 1936, 12 Mar.: in a major reform of the Italian banking system, the Bank of Italy was transformed into a public institution. 1934: Canada established its 1st central bank; the Royal Bank of Canada opened, 11 Mar., 1935.

Stock exchanges: After the Bolshevik Revolution, Russian stock exchanges were closed. 1922, 2 Jan.: Re-establishment in Moscow of a Central Commodity Exchange with a stock-exchange section. 1930: Abolition in the USSR of both the commodity and stock exchange; the spread of government ownership and centralized allocation of capital in the USSR made the use of stock exchanges irrelevant.

Effects of international financial conditions: Unlike the mature industrial countries, the new industrial nations were less active as principals in international financial transactions. The events that stemmed from the establishment of German reparations and German inability to pay, however, ultimately had important worldwide ramifications. While Japan's domestic financial crisis of 1927 anticipated the world crisis, her financial recovery was once more jarred by world conditions, 1929–33. Although there were no bank failures in Canada, Canada felt the world financial crisis in a severe manner, with economic stagnation as a consequence. The Soviet Union, seeking to end her isolation from the world economy, found the curtailment of credit worldwide, affecting her economy. 1929–33: The world crisis left no nation exempt. 1931, 2 Dec.: Japan went off the gold standard. 1934, 26 May.: The Italian government imposed strict control over foreign exchange, and controls continued through World War II. 1936 ff.: Japanese controls on foreign exchange became more extensive.

FOREIGN TRADE. 1920's: Japan depended on imports of essential raw materials and on exports to obtain foreign exchange to import for its needs; textiles continued as the main Japanese export. Italy required imports of iron and oil—basic raw materials; initially, Mussolini's government, 1922 ff., sought to stimulate foreign trade through commercial treaties (1922, 13 Nov.: Italian-French treaty; 1923, 28 Apr.: Italian-Austrian treaty; 1925, 31 Oct.: Italian-German treaty); 1925 ff.: Italy's policy became more nationalist. After the Bolshevik Revolution, Russian foreign trade dropped sharply; 1921 ff.: the Soviet Union sought to reenter international trade, with only minor success. 1920's: Wheat was the basic Canadian export. 1929, Aug. ff.: Wheat prices in Liverpool began to fall sharply; Canada had giant grain surpluses which pushed down prices; there were excellent harvests in Europe; USSR began to export wheat; 1930: Australia had a record wheat crop (214 m. bushels); to add to the depressing influences, European nations erected high tariff barriers, closing off markets to Canadian, Russian, and Australian wheat. The Canadian and Australian economies suffered, as the result of falling export prices. 1931–32: Australian wheat exports were 80% greater in volume than before the depression; butter exports more than doubled; mutton increased nearly 2½-fold; sugar twice over; beef by ⅓, flour by ¼, and wool by ¹⁄₁₀; nonetheless, with the low prices, in value Australian exports were 55% of their 1928–29 value. 1929, Apr.: Export price per 100 *kin* of Japanese silk was 1,420 yen; 1932, June: export price for the same quantity of silk was 390 yen. 1929–33: Italy, Canada, Australia, and Japan followed the international pattern of raising tariffs and imposing restraints on imports. 1932, 21 July–20 Aug.: Ottawa Conference was convened with the goal of reviving trade within the British Empire; the British offered dominion products preferential treatment; such products were guaranteed free entry into Britain for 5 years (except for certain exempted items on which a duty might be applied after 3 years); Britain imposed or raised its duties on foreign goods. In return, the dominions lowered their tariffs on British imports. 1932 ff.: These arrangements notwithstanding, Canadian trade stagnated. Australia lowered its duties in accord with the Ottawa Agreements, but because of imperial preference the Commonwealth became involved in trade disputes with other countries. 1933 ff.: Australia negotiated commercial treaties with Belgium, France, and Czechoslovakia. 1936, May: Australian government adopted the policy of "trade diversion," consisting of discriminatory duties, quotas, and import licenses directed against the U.S. and Japan; the U.S. was subjected to discrimination because it sold far more in Australia than it bought there; the Australians discriminated against the Japanese to protect British trade (Japanese products in Australia competed against British goods); Japan, as a result, stopped buying Australia's major export, wool, which hurt the Australian economy. 1936, Dec.: Australian-Japanese agreement. Japan, however, continued to purchase less from Australia than in the 1920's. 1930's: Australian commerce recovered very slowly from its depression lows. 1930s: In Italy self-sufficiency became the cornerstone of government commercial policy; 1935, 7 Jan.: Count Paolo Taon di Revel, Italian minister of finance, terminated completely the system of multilateral trade and payments negotiations; he imposed added restrictions on trade and foreign exchange transactions; Italy encouraged bilateral agreements and barter plans. 1935: League of Nations declared economic sanctions against Italy after that nation's invasion of Ethiopia (9 Oct., 1935: sanctions declared, to be imposed 18 Nov.); the League urged all countries (1) to end exports of arms and war matériel to Italy; (2) to refuse credit to the Italian government, public agencies, businesses, and private persons in Italian territories; (3) to stop importing Italian goods; and (4) to discontinue exporting raw materials required for Italy's war industries. 1935, 9 Oct.–18 Nov.: Italy bought everything it could before the sanctions went into effect; 18 Nov. ff.: many nations (including U.S., Germany, and Japan) did not follow the League's proscriptions; Italy was able to import sufficient goods. 1936, 15 May: The League's sanctions against Italy ceased; they had been a total failure. Yet Italy continued to pursue a policy of self-sufficiency. 1933: Yardage of Japanese cloth exports exceeded that of Britain for the 1st time. Tariff barriers abroad rose against "cheap" Japanese exports. 1934: Japanese Trade Protection Law gave the government power to retaliate against discrimination against its goods; Japan increasingly turned to "empire self-sufficiency." 1930's: National and empire "self-sufficiency" became common goals. "Bloc trading," such as that within the British Commonwealth and in the Japanese Empire, assumed increasing importance.

Soviet participation in world trade remained low; because of the USSR's continued failure to honor its prewar debts, it was not considered a reliable trading partner. USSR achieved virtual self-sufficiency. 1939 ff.: Canadian exports and imports rose as Canada filled wartime needs; with many imports cut off, Australia moved into more manufacturing. 1941, Dec. ff.: Japanese trade with the allied countries ceased entirely and was confined during the war years to areas under Japanese control. 1943: Under lend-lease Americans made large shipments to Russia for the latter's defense; the USSR's imports rose sixfold over their 1936–40 level; her exports fell by ¼.

FOREIGN INVESTMENT. USSR had renounced her foreign obligations. 1920's: While a few foreign investments were made in the USSR, most foreign investors hesitated; 1928 ff.: USSR stopped trying to encourage foreign investors. There were no important Soviet investments abroad. Japan and Italy were creditors in international accounts, while Canada and Australia were debtors.

FOREIGN INVESTMENT POSITION, 1938
($ million)

	Credits (Foreign Investments Abroad)	Debts (Foreign Investments Within Nation)
Japan	1,230	534
Italy	424	176
Canada	1,855	6,628
Australia	254	3,730

1939–45: Following the war and military defeat, Japan and Italy lost almost all their foreign assets; Canada and Australia continued to be debtors on international accounts.

BUSINESS ORGANIZATION. Canadian and Australian business organizations in all but size bore a clear resemblance to those developed in the U.S. 1928 ff.: In the USSR government participation in business meant an attempt to substitute a "command" economy for one regulated by the market; government-owned business enterprises allocated resources to correspond with prescribed needs (prescribed by the government) rather than market demands;

profit in Russia was not the measure of business performance—as in other contemporary industrial nations. In Japan the *zaibatsu* form of business organization assumed greater importance; 1931: Major Industries Control Law and Industrial Association Law in Japan legalized the existence of cartels; 1930's: the leading giant *zaibatsu* continued to be Mitsui, Mitsubishi, Sumitomo, and Yasuda; other large *zaibatsu* existed; in addition, private Japanese corporations developed outside the *zaibatsu* structure. Also present in Japan were literally thousands of small businesses (of the type prevalent in a backward economy). 1922 ff.: Mussolini's plans for a corporate state in Italy took shape; private businesses were expected to co-ordinate their plans with national goals; yet within the context of the corporate state, private enterprise was given a large measure of freedom. The Italian government encouraged cartelization. 1930's: Increasingly the Italian government became directly involved in industrial enterprises. There do not seem to be any valid generalizations on the path of the newly industrialized nations and forms of business organization; prevailing government attitudes toward competition ranged from acceptance of competition as desirable (in Canada and Australia) to rejection of it as inefficient (in the USSR, Japan, and Italy). The rejection of competition was most complete in the Soviet Union; in Japan, despite government encouragement of cartelization, there seems to have been considerable competitive activity on the part of private businesses; in Italy harmonization took priority over competition.

GOVERNMENT POLICY. 1920–40: As a whole, these decades saw increased government intervention in every industrial nation; there were (1) aid to agriculture, (2) participation in building transportation facilities, (3) aid to and in some instances direct involvement in industry, and (4) in some nations new planning and control.

Aid to agriculture: 1925, 20 June: Mussolini called for higher Italian grain output and urged agricultural self-sufficiency; 1925 ff.: Italian farmers got tariff protection, artificially high prices, and other government assistance; the Fascist state undertook land reclamation and improvement; 1926, 30 Dec.: Italian government aid went to farmers' co-operatives (purchasing, processing, and marketing units); 1927, 29 July: law passed in Italy creating the National Consortium of Agrarian Credit for Improvements, providing loans to farmers. 1936: After the Ethiopian War, the Italian government renewed its efforts toward developing agricultural self-sufficiency; under government sponsorship new crops were introduced. 1928: With government encouragement, Canadian wheat pools held back part of their crop, seeking to avoid price declines.

1930, Nov.: Canadian federal government provided substantial aid to the wheat pools. 1930's: The Japanese government used its funds to attempt stabilization of rice and silk prices, to readjust farm debts, to provide relief to indigent tenant farmers, to control fertilizer prices, and to encourage emigration to Manchukuo. 1931–35: The Australian government subsidized wheat farmers to the extent of £12.5 million; state governments in Australia canceled debts of many wheat growers; 1934: the Australian government imposed high domestic prices on wheat to aid the farmer; the proceeds of a tax on flour were distributed among the wheat growers; similar government support went to the dairying and sugar industries in the Commonwealth.

Transportation: Participation in highway and railroad construction became a common function of all governments. 1920: Formation of Canadian National Railroads, which put the transcontinental railroads in Canada (except for the Canadian Pacific Railway) in government hands; nationalization was not based on principle, but rather to maintain operations on railroads that were not profitable to private investors. 1928: Establishment in Italy of the Autonomous State Agency for Roads, which undertook a large-scale program of building *autostrade* and improving existing roadways. The Japanese railroads and roadways were government-built.

Government aid to and participation in industry: Tariffs and restrictions against imports aided industry; likewise, governments sought to encourage exports. 1919 ff.: Japanese government extended protectionist tariffs to key industries, iron and steel, machinery, and chemical; it encouraged citizens to "buy Japanese." 1931 ff.: Japanese government policy of armament and industrial development went forward with dramatic results. Key officials in the *zaibatsu* took on important roles in shaping government economic policy; the government thus was sympathetic to industry's needs. 1934: Yawata Ironworks (the government-owned iron and steel co.) merged with 6 *zaibatsu* firms to form the Japan Iron Manufacturing Co. (the Japanese government owned 78% of the authorized capital of this firm—the largest iron and steel producer in Japan) . 1937 ff.: After the start of the Sino-Japanese War, the Japanese government undertook extensive direct investment in Japanese business. "National Policy Cos." were formed, owned by the government to expand production for war needs. The Australian government had participated in munitions production during World War I; after the war, some plants were retained by the government; these produced consumer goods until the outbreak of World War II, when they were reconverted into armament facilities. The Australian government, which owned railroads, also manufactured equipment for the railroads; it participated with British oil cos. in joint ventures, refining certain oil products. The Australian government also took part directly in aircraft production and shipbuilding. The Italian government gave aid to industry when it was required. 1933, 23 Jan.: Formation in Italy of the Istituto per la Ricostruzione Industriale (IRI), with capital provided by the state and by the sale of its own bonds; the new IRI was to aid banks and faltering industries. IRI made direct investments in a number of enterprises, providing financing and management; 1936: IRI took over the Italian Line, Lloyd Triestino, Adriatica, and Tirrenia and established, as a shipping subsidiary, Finmare; 1937: IRI created Finsider, a subsidiary, which had holdings in the metallurgical trades, including Italy's major steelworks; IRI also became involved in shipbuilding, machine industries, and munition manufacturing. 1933–41: IRI's net expenditures were 4 billion lire; through its activities what had started as government aid became extensive direct government involvement in industry. This supplemented the Italian government's participation in the petroleum industry and its general controls.

Government planning and control: The most extensive government involvement was in the Soviet Union. 1918–21: Period of "War Communism": the Soviet government attempted to nationalize the means of production and also the service industries; it sought to nationalize land. 1921–28: New Economic Policy (NEP) in the USSR marked a sharp change in policy; about 40% of Russian business was returned to private ownership and operation (this involved mainly enterprises in light industry and trade) ; peasants were allowed to till their own land (although technically the land belonged to the state) ; foreign concessionnaires were invited to invest in USSR. Basic industry and utilities remained nationalized. 1928, 1 Oct.: The 1st 5-Year Plan of the Soviet Union was announced, providing for heavy industry, increased coal and oil production, greater electrical energy output, and automobile, tractor, and machining plants. The plan offered the basis for an industrialized Russia. Renewed emphasis was placed on nationalization of all industry. Foreign technical aid was called in, but foreign capital was not. The 5-Year Plan endorsed collectivization of the land. 1933: By this time all private ownership of Soviet industrial production had ended; with the exception of collective farms and some co-operatives (mainly in retailing), state ownership had become general. 1933: 2nd 5-Year Plan introduced; it stressed the growth of transportation; initially it put emphasis on enlarged consumption. 1933–35: Output of consumer goods increased, so that severe shortages, which occurred under the 1st 5-Year Plan, were in part eliminated. 1936: Emphasis of 2nd 5-Year Plan shifted attention primarily to heavy industry; production for defense began. 1938: USSR inaugurated 3rd 5-Year Plan, concerned mainly with providing for the possibility of war. Italy: 1922–25: "Liberal phase" of Italian Fascist economic policy began: Mussolini, 1922, returned to private ownership all government-owned utilities, reopened to private underwriters the field of life insurance (which had been nationalized in 1912) , issued decrees seeking to attract foreign capital, and eliminated government subsidies to co-operatives; tariffs were moderate; Mussolini's plans for a corporate state began to take shape; the goal was to organize employers and employees into syndicates or "corporations" that would act in harmony in the interest of the total national welfare. 1923, 20 Dec.: Mussolini named a permanent commission of 5 worker and 5 employer representatives to study means of improving relationships between business and labor. 1926, 3 Apr.: Rocco Law on Corporations (written by Alfredo Rocco, minister of justice) was the capstone of the "corporate state"; it created means for the government to use in handling disagreements between employers and workers. The law authorized the establishment of 13 syndicates (6 each for employers and employees plus 1 for professionals and intellectuals); employees had a general confederation and a similar general confederation was projected for employers (the latter never came into existence); at the top of the pyramid was the Ministry of Corporations, which controlled the entire system; the system sought to encourage private initiative; state intervention was to occur only when private enterprise could not act efficiently or when there were political considerations involved. Government intervention could be in the form of aid, regulation, ownership, and control. 1933 ff.: Major increase in Italian government's role. 1934, 4 Feb.: Reform of the Italian corporate state's structure occurred, substituting 9 syndicates for the original 13; the reform introduced 22 new corporations composed of leaders in the 9 syndicates, technicians, workers, co-operatives, and Fascist Party. Members of the 22 corporations formed the National Council of Corporations. 1939, 19 Jan.: Italian Chamber of Deputies replaced by a Chamber of Fasces and Corporations, made up of members of the National Council of Corporations, representatives of the Fascist Party, and the Grand Council of Fascism. The extensive government planning and control in the USSR and the novel role of the government in Italy put these states in a unique peacetime economic position. The Japanese government, in its attempt to build up armaments, did not perhaps take radical departures, although its role was clearly one of increased national involvement. By contrast, the Canadian government sought to promote economic development by maintaining classical competitive enterprises. 1919: Combines and Fair Prices Act and the Board of Commerce Act passed in Canada to cope with postwar profiteering (1921: Privy Council disallowed these measures). 1923: Canadian Combines Investigation Act passed, which became Canada's basic antitrust measure. 1923 ff.: Canada continued to see the role of government as favoring competition rather than co-operation among business enterprises. 1938 ff.: In every newly industrialized nation, as the threat of war grew, government regulation and control became the norm. New government agencies were formed to direct the various economies toward war production. Planning and control came to be linked with national defense and victory.

MEASURES OF ECONOMIC GROWTH. The indexes of manufacturing output indicate that with the exception of Canada (which felt the depression years most severely) the USSR, Italy, Japan, and Australia all grew faster during the interwar years than the world average.

NONMONETARY INDICATORS OF RELATIVE NATIONAL CONSUMPTION LEVELS, 1934–38

	Relative Data (U.S. = 100)
Canada	80.6
Australia	80.0
Czechoslovakia	47.0
Japan	40.0
Italy	39.6
USSR	33.6

NOTE: Includes food, tobacco, medical and sanitary services, education and recreation, transportation, and communication.

SOURCE: M. K. Bennett, "International Disparities in Consumption Levels," *American Economic Review*, Sept. 1951, p. 648.

Economic Change in the Less Developed World

During 1919–45 much of the less developed world remained unchanged. There were still the Bedouins, who moved with their camels and horses over vast territories. Masai cattle breeders in East Africa still wandered over long distances to obtain fresh pasturage. Mongol and Turkish cattle-breeding tribes in Central Asia held to established patterns of migration, returning regularly to the same regions. Change in the lives of most nomads was nonexistent. Yet in some cases change did occur. 1920's: the Siberian reindeer nomads began to adopt a more settled pastoral life. King ibn Saud in Saudi Arabia took preliminary steps to develop agricultural communities and to transform Bedouins into farmers. In Outer Mongolia some nomads began to settle.

AGRICULTURE. For most of the world agricultural conditions—subsistence farming, commercial (domestic and export) farming, and plantation agriculture (for export) —persisted in much the same fashion as in 1870–1919. Typically, a less developed country had more than 50% of its population involved in agriculture, although there were exceptions. 1920–45: Changes in agriculture included spreading use of the plow in agriculture (especially in Africa), increasing monetization of economies (through greater commercialization of agriculture practically everywhere and through more demand for male labor where there were plantations), new lands under cultivation, and some new plantations (but the peak years of starting fresh enterprises, 1870–1919, were past). Efficient plantation agriculture in rubber, quinine, tea (for example) eclipsed indigenous agriculture; 1920's: expansion of rubber plantation economy in Malaya and the Netherlands East Indies. Except for foreign-owned plantations, everywhere agriculture remained undercapitalized. Mechanization (except

AGRICULTURAL LABOR FORCE IN SELECTED COUNTRIES

	Agricultural Labor as % of Labor Force
Thailand (1937)	89
Turkey (1935)	82
Bulgaria (1934)	80
Rumania (1930)	79
Korea (1938)	76
Nigeria (1931)	74
Philippines (1939)	73
Nicaragua (1940)	73
Colombia (1938)	73
Yugoslavia (1948)	72
Guatemala (1940)	71
Egypt (1937)	71
Burma (1931)	70
Netherlands East Indies (1940)	69
India (1931)	67
Brazil (1940)	67
French Morocco (1946)	67
Mexico (1940)	65
Poland (1931)	65
Peru (1940)	63
British Malaya (1931)	61
Ceylon (1921)	54
Greece (1928)	51.8
Chile (1940)	36
Argentina (1946)	36

NOTE: Includes forestry and fishing.

on foreign-owned plantations) proceeded slowly.

Agrarian reform: 1919 ff.: 12 Eastern European nations undertook agrarian reform. 1924 ff.: In Turkey a gradual process of land redistribution began; peasants were given tax relief and encouraged to raise output. In Latin America, where large landed estates, inefficiently farmed, retarded economic progress, land reform began. 1917–34: In Mexico 20 m. acres were returned by the government to Indian villagers and to mestizos; nonetheless, large landholdings persisted. 1934–40: Under the administration of Lázaro Cárdenas in Mexico, millions more acres were redistributed and there

AREA AND BENEFICIARIES OF LAND REDISTRIBUTION IN EUROPE AFTER WORLD WAR I

	Area Redistributed		Area, in Millions of Acres, Allocated to			Plots, in Thousands, Allocated to		
	Millions of Acres	% of All Agricultural Land	State[a]	Former Owners	Other Farmers	New Farmers	Small Farmers	Former Tenants
Finland	3.7	2.1	—	2.2	1.5	22	10	97
East Germany	1.0	—	—	—	1.0	16	28	—
Poland[b]	3.7	6.1	—	—	3.7	109	200	—
Czechoslovakia	9.9	14.1	4.9	0.2	4.7	1.7	303	—
Hungary	1.7	9.7	—	—	1.7	549	113	—
Yugoslavia	4.9	4.6	1.2	2.5	1.2	—	256	—
Rumania	14.8	29.7	2.2	—	12.6	—	1,369	—
Bulgaria	0.5	2.0	—	—	0.5	—	17	—
Greece	3.2	—	—	1.2	2.0	—	229	—
Latvia	9.1	42.4	5.2	0.5	3.5	64	13	7
Lithuania	2.0	17.5	0.2	—	1.7	36	19	—
Estonia	5.7	25.0	2.7	1.2	1.7	33	—	27
Total	60.3	—	16.5	7.9	35.8	—	—	—

SOURCE: W. S. and E. S. Woytinsky, *World Population and Production*, New York, 1953, p. 497.

a Often includes woodlands or wasteland.

b By 1937 about 6.5 million additional acres had been redistributed among some 700,000 purchasers.

was a breakup of the largest landed estates. 1945: By this time the Mexican government had redistributed 76 m. acres to 1.7 m. individuals; land had been given to agrarian communities known as *ejidos,* to the extent of 3 m. acres. Mexican land reform was the most dramatic in Latin America. 1921: Tenancy reform legislation in Argentina sought to protect the tenant by requiring contracts of not less than 5 years' duration and by recognizing certain tenant rights; the legislation was, however, ignored by the large landlords. 1930's: Laws were passed in Argentina, seeking to tax large landowners and aid small farmers; but the legislation was evaded. The Argentine land reforms had no important effects. In much of Asia small peasant plots grew smaller as population increased. Attempts were made in India to consolidate "postage stamp" plots, with little success. 1939: 75% of the landholders in India held less than 10 acres; in many sections of India average farm size was less than an acre. 1929–33: A survey of about 17,000 farms in China in 22 provinces discovered 80% averaged less than 7.17 acres. 1930:

Land Law in China gave the Land Bureau power to take steps for the consolidation of scattered plots into single holdings; success in this effort was minimal. In China, there was no reform of tenancy relations and, at the same time as fragmentation in ownership existed, there were also large absentee landowners. Inequity in land distribution was evident. 1930's: In Tongking (Indochina) 62% of all farm families had less than .9 acres in rice fields (the major crop), while in Annam 69% of the peasants cultivated less than 1.2 acres in rice; little was done to cope with this situation. Egypt had a similar problem, with 70.7% of all farms under an acre in size; on the other hand, Egypt also had huge landholdings. 1938: The average cocoa farm in the Gold Coast was 2½ acres. Land reform in colonial empires continued to involve clarification of land-tenure relations and the introduction of concepts of private property.

Agricultural progress: 1920–45: The perpetuation in many countries of existing agricultural conditions (or the worsening of agricultural conditions with land fragmentation), plus the low level of agricultural technology, did not aid agricultural productivity and served to retard the process of industrialization. One exception was Turkey, where, based mainly on the increase in agricultural output, per capita income rose by over 50% between 1924 and 1938.

RAW MATERIALS. Coal: On the whole, less developed nations were not large producers of coal. 1938: In all South America only 3.3 m. metric tons of coal were produced, while in all Africa (excluding South Africa and Southern Rhodesia) only .5 m. metric tons of coal were mined. In the less developed world, only Poland, India, China, and Union of South Africa developed their coal output so it exceeded that of Australia or Canada. They were exceptional and compared with the leading industrial nations their coal output was low.

COAL PRODUCTION, 1938
(million metric tons)

Poland	38.1
India	28.9
China	27.0[a]
Union of South Africa	16.3
Hungary	9.3
Southern Rhodesia	1.0
Mexico	.9

a Estimate for 1936.

Oil: 1919–40: The major interwar development in the less developed countries was in petroleum. Oil development was by foreign capital. 1919: The largest oil producers were the U.S., Mexico, USSR, and the Netherlands East Indies (in that order); oil production was just starting in Venezuela; the only Middle Eastern countries producing oil were Iran and Egypt. 1940: The largest oil producers were the U.S., USSR, Venezuela, Iran, Netherlands East Indies (in that order); in the interim, key events in the oil industry were: 1927, Oct.: large Kirkuk oil field discovered in northern Iraq. 1932, 1 June: Oil discovered in Bahrain. 1938: Oil discovered in commercial quantities in Saudi Arabia; oil discovered in Kuwait. 1938, 18 Mar.: Mexican government nationalized its oil industry.

Iron ore: In China, India, French Indochina, Brazil, Chile, Union of South Africa, and North Africa, iron-ore mining developed.

Copper: 1930's: In Chile copper replaced nitrates as the nation's major export. Northern Rhodesian mines came into production; output of copper mines in the Belgian Congo rose. The U.S. remained the world's largest producer of copper.

Tin: Tin came almost exclusively from less developed countries, and the world's

OIL PRODUCTION IN LESS DEVELOPED COUNTRIES
(million barrels of 42 U.S. gallons)

	1920	1925	1930	1935	1940
Mexico	157.1	115.5	39.5	40.2	44.1
Netherlands East Indies	17.5	21.4	41.7	47.2	60.8
Iran	12.2	35.0	45.8	57.3	79.3
India (incl. Burma)	8.4	8.3	8.9	9.2	10.1
Rumania	7.4	16.6	42.7	61.8	43.8
Poland	5.6	6.0	4.9	3.8	3.9
Peru	2.8	9.2	12.4	17.1	13.4
Trinidad	2.0	4.4	9.4	11.7	20.2
Argentina	1.6	6.3	9.0	14.3	20.3
Egypt	1.0	1.2	2.0	1.3	5.2
British Borneo	1.0	4.3	4.9	5.5	7.0
Venezuela	.5	19.7	136.7	148.2	186.8
Colombia	—	1.0	20.3	17.6	25.9
Iraq	—	—	.9	27.4	25.7
Bahrain	—	—	—	1.3	7.3
Saudi Arabia	—	—	—	—	5.6

COPPER PRODUCTION
(000 metric tons)

	1920	1925	1930	1935	1940
Chile	99	190	223	267	352
Mexico	45	54	68	42	41
Peru	33	37	48	30	36
Belgian Congo	19	90	139	108	160
Rhodesia					
(primarily Northern Rhodesia)	3	2	8	146	231

largest tin producers were Malaya, Netherlands East Indies, Bolivia, Thailand, China, and Nigeria. World War II resulted in changes of patterns of control over raw materials. The Japanese invasion of Southeast Asia meant that industrial raw materials such as rubber and tin, and to a lesser extent oil, were under Japan's control.

Synthetics: 1919–45: While less developed countries produced increased quantities of industrial raw materials, a challenge to raw-material industries came in the form of synthetics; the develop-

ment of synthetic nitrates put the prosperous Chilean nitrate industry into the doldrums; synthetic rubber presented a potential challenge to natural rubber; synthetic fibers began to offer competition to other industrial raw materials.

ENERGY. In less developed countries, use of electrical power and the internal-combustion engine rose, especially in Latin America. The use of human beings and animals as sources of energy, however, remained common in Asia and Africa.

ENERGY CONSUMPTION PER CAPITA FOR PRODUCTIVE PURPOSES, 1937
(electricity equivalent in kwh for all energy sources)

	Per Capita Use	Ratio of Inanimate[a] to All Sources
Chile	1,162	85.0
Mexico	664	70.9
Argentina	1,600	67.0
Brazil	450	56.6
India	289	35.4
Egypt	242	36.0
Netherlands East Indies	197	30.9
China (excl. Manchuria and Jehol)	164	21.2

[a] Inanimate includes wood, falling water, coal, oil, gas, and electricity.

ENERGY PRODUCTION, 1935
(%)

World	100.000
Latin America	3.626
Asia (excl. USSR and Japan)	4.752
Africa	0.916

SOURCE: Abbott Payson Usher, "The Resource Requirements of an Industrial Economy," *Journal of Economic History*, Suppl. VII (1947), pp. 44–46.

The less developed countries accounted for only small portions of the world's total energy production.

INDUSTRY. The spread of industry to less developed nations was most pronounced in Latin America and Asia (especially India and China); manufacturing in Africa (except for South Africa) remained rudimentary (and mainly of a household sort). 1920–45: In South Africa, substantial development of manufacturing industries. 1920's: In the

Netherlands East Indies attempts made to establish large-scale manufacturing enterprises failed because of the absence of local markets. 1930's: In India, China, and a number of Latin American countries modern industries were established; in the Netherlands East Indies, development of small-scale industry in rural regions; in French Indochina, new industries were established on a small scale, of a native handicraft type. Measures of growth of manufacturing in less developed countries are few.

INDEXES OF MANUFACTURING ACTIVITY
(1913 = 100)

	India	Spain	Rumania	Chile	Greece	South Africa[a]	World
1920	118.4	94.0	—	—	—	312.1	93.2
1921–25	122.1	104.5	75.0	79.5[b]	292.8	342.9	103.2
1926–29	146.6	126.2	122.8	127.7	345.6	477.0	138.9
1930	144.7	131.5	132.5	156.7	363.2	—	136.9
1931–35	174.8	117.0	144.3	147.7	398.3	662.9[c]	128.2
1936–38	230.4	—	178.6	196.5	497.1	998.8	185.0

SOURCE: League of Nations, *Industrialization and Foreign Trade,* New York, 1945.
a Base: 1911 = 100.
b 1922–25.
c 1932–35.

Despite the impressive growth of manufacturing in India, Greece, and South Africa, as indicated above, the manufacturing output of these countries, along with that of other less developed countries, remained low compared with that of the industrial nations. Using a different index, Mainland China's industrial production also showed significant growth.

INDEX OF INDUSTRIAL PRODUCTION OF
MAINLAND CHINA
(1933 = 100)

1920	45.9
1925	64.1
1930	80.2
1933	100.0
1935	119.8
1938	102.3
1940	136.1

NOTE: Index based on net value-added per unit of product, weighted by 1933 net value-added. (This should reflect changes in level of output.)
SOURCE: John K. Chang, "Industrial Development of Mainland China, 1912–1949," *Journal of Economic History,* XXVII, Mar. 1967, p. 66.

Textiles: 1920–40: Indian factory-made cotton cloth replaced imports. 1920 ff.: China's machine-made yarn replaced imports; 1925: China was no longer a net importer of yarn. (1937: China had roughly 5 m. spindles, about half of them in foreign-owned—mainly Japanese —mills.) 1920–40: Modern power looms began to replace handlooms in China; 1937: China's 60,000 power looms were also mainly in Japanese mills; 80% of China's cloth was still woven on handlooms. 1920 ff.: Brazilian cotton textiles became a well-developed factory industry; in Argentina, new textile factories—on a large scale—began.

Iron and steel: 1921: Establishment of Brazil's 1st integrated iron and steel operation, with charcoal blast furnaces, by the Belgo-Mineira Co. (a Luxembourg steel combine) ; 1941: construction started on the National Steel Co. (Companhia Siderúrgical Nacional) works at Volta Redonda (production began 1946) —the true start of Brazil as a steel-producing nation. 1920–40: Expansion of existing iron and steel facilities in India and Mexico. 1934: Establishment in Pretoria, South Africa, of a fully integrated iron and steel industry. 1944: Incorporation of Cia. de Acero del Pacífica, S.A., in Chile, and the start of construction on what would become a large-scale fully inte-

SOURCE OF COTTON CLOTH CONSUMED IN INDIA
(% by source)

	Indian Mill-Made	Women on Handlooms	Imports
1920–25	38	29	33
1931–32	57	30	13
1940–41	65	28	7

grated Chilean steel enterprise. Few underdeveloped countries had steel industries; where steel was made, production was small relative to the industrial nations.

CRUDE STEEL PRODUCTION, 1938
(000 metric tons)

India	982
South Africa	300
Rumania	277
Yugoslavia	227
Brazil	92
Mexico	74
China (excl. Manchuria)	60
Turkey	38

UN figures (except China); Chinese figures are from *Mineral Industry;* they are in gross tons. Turkish figures are for 1940.

Other industries: 1920–45: India developed certain metal products and chemical industries. India's sugar-refining, papermaking, soap, match, cement, rubber, and leather-goods industries developed. In China, factory-made paper, matches, and pottery replaced village industries; 1930's: the main Chinese industrialization took place in Manchuria, which was (from 1931) under Japanese control. 1937: Japan invaded China proper; the effects on industry were twofold: (1) the destruction of industrial equipment, but (2) the rebuilding of industry to meet Japanese requirements. 1920's and 1930's: British firms developed business enterprise in Hong Kong—sugar refining and cement, as well as textiles. 1937: After the Japanese invasion of China, industrialization of Hong Kong (still under British sovereignty) accelerated. 1920's: In Malaya, where there was prosperity based upon rubber and tin, rubber-tire industries and automobile assembly began (based on foreign investment). 1920's: In South Africa, automobile assembly began, 1924; processing of locally produced foodstuffs (flour, cheese, preserved fruit, and sugar) developed as a substantial industry; diamond-cutting workshops were established (1927 for the 1st time); other industries from the making of gasoline pumps to nails and shovels started in South Africa. 1934 ff.: As the South African steel industry developed, metalworking industries expanded, involving engineering industries (including machinery) as well as consumer goods. 1920's: In Brazil, automobile assembly began, 1920; electrical-appliance, cement, and corn-products industries took form. 1930's: In Brazil a variety of new chemical, metal products, and foodstuffs industries started. In Argentina and Mexico similar industries made headway. In many less developed countries factory industries were often confined to textiles, paper, soap, and breweries. In much of Africa even these basic factory industries did not exist. Facilities for manufacturing automobiles, tractors, trucks, or aircraft existed in none of the less developed countries. In none of the petroleum consuming countries in Asia or Africa was there a petroleum refining industry; where petroleum production existed, however, refineries were built, generally by foreign capital, and in some Latin American countries refineries existed running on imported crude oil. 1938–45: World War II stimulated industrialization in Latin America, especially Argentina and Brazil. It also spurred manufacturing in South Africa. In China, after the Japanese invasion, industrial production showed marked annual variations (see table p. 789).

TRANSPORTATION. In most less developed countries, railroad construction continued. Most railroads were built in

Average Annual Rate of Growth of Manufacturing Industries,
World War II Years
(%, compound rates)

	1936/38–48	1938–48	1939–48	1940–48
Argentina			5.8	
Brazil			6.6	
Bulgariaa			8.5	
Chile	4.6			
Colombia		.7		
Greece			—4.6	
India			1.5	
Morocco		4.9		
Rumania		—1.8		
South Africa		6.1		
Spain				1.7

NOTE: These rates are based on *quantity* of production.
SOURCE: United Nations, *Growth of World Industry—National Tables*, New York, 1963.
a Includes mining.

INDUSTRIAL PRODUCTION OF MAINLAND CHINA
(1933 = 100)

1937	110.4
1938	102.3
1939	119.0
1940	136.1
1941	161.6
1942	176.5
1943	157.5
1944	141.3
1945	94.3

NOTE: Index based on net value-added per unit of product, weighted by 1933 net value-added. (This should reflect changes in level of output.)
SOURCE: John K. Chang, "Industrial Development of Mainland China, 1912–1949," *Journal of Economic History*, XXVII, Mar. 1967, p. 66.

RAILROAD LINES: LENGTH BY CONTINENT
(000 mi.)

	1920	1930	1949
Latin America	69.2	84.4	85.2
Asia (excl. USSR)	59.5	82.5	92.1
Africa	23.0a	42.4	42.1

a 1910 figures; 1920 figures not available.

order to carry primary commodities to port cities for export; they did not develop national markets. India with its substantial railroad network still used bullock carts to a large extent for internal transit. 1919: In China most of the major cities were connected by rail; this should have aided development. 1920's: The political chaos in China was not conducive to more railroad building and operations of the existing system were curtailed. 1929 ff.: Chinese government's plans to extend the railroads came to little. 1938: Completion of 865-mi. Trans-Iranian Railway from the Persian Gulf to the Caspian Sea, built with native capital, a major construction feat, designed with national interests in mind rather than as a link with foreign railroads (as had been the case with most Middle Eastern lines). Despite the extension of railroad lines, rail transport remained inadequate in most less developed countries. Nonetheless, railroads did compete with traditional methods of transport, substituting for, in some cases, and supplementing, in other cases, water, animal, and human carriers. Likewise, highways were constructed in less developed countries. 1919 ff.: Highways were built in Iran, Iraq, Turkey, Syria, Egypt, and Arabia; many followed the ancient pilgrim and caravan routes; automobile and truck traffic along the roads increasingly replaced camel caravans. In Africa highways were often built as links connecting with the railroads. Many African roads were built to improve the utilization of human porterage. 1920's and 1930's:

Trucks and cars began to travel African roads; railroad and truck transport (in that order) were far cheaper than the use of humans; 1923: 1st steps taken to build a Pan-American Highway. Late 1920's and 1930's: Provisions for air travel (airline routes, airports, etc.) were introduced into less developed countries; air travel, however, was mainly by foreigners or the select few within these countries. Despite the introduction of modern transportation facilities throughout much of the less developed world, traditional modes of transport persisted as they had for hundreds of years. Yet the basis for a transportation revolution had been set.

FINANCE. All underdeveloped countries were short of capital. They depended to a large extent on foreign investment. Banking facilities were inadequate in most countries. In most less developed lands, foreign banks continued to finance foreign trade and deal in foreign exchange. The major innovation in banking in the less developed countries in the 1920's and 1930's was the spread of central banking institutions. 1920's: In China about 100 local banks (private, provincial, and national) issued large amounts of bank notes, the value of which depreciated rapidly. 1924: Establishment of the Central Bank of China in Canton; 1928: this bank was reorganized and relocated in Shanghai; it was to act as a central bank of issue and a government treasury. China sought to create domestic banks to compete with foreign banks in dealing with foreign exchange (the Bank of China), to aid internal improvements and industry (the Bank of Communications), and to assist the farmer (the Farmers' Bank of China). The 4 major banks—the Central Bank of China, the Bank of China, the Bank of Communications, and the Farmers' Bank of China— all issued notes, and their functions, theoretically distinct, were not so in practice. 1935, Nov.: China nationalized the old silver currency and substituted a uniform paper currency; the notes of the 4 key banks replaced silver and other notes. 1921: The 3 Presidency Banks in India were merged, and the Imperial

Bank of India, a central bank, was created to handle the general banking business of the government of India. 1934: Reserve Bank Act and Imperial Bank of India (Amendment) Act were passed in India; under these measures a central reserve bank (a new central bank) was established and the Imperial Bank of India no longer acted as the government bank; the new Central Bank (which began to function Apr. 1935) controlled credit and currency, regulated exchange, and handled the government's banking business. 1919 ff.: 1st Arab, Egyptian, and Turkish commercial banks established; they were small compared with the European banks operating in these countries. 1920's and 1930's: Establishment in Latin America of added banking facilities, and also of central banks (for example, 1923, 11 July: Banco de La Republica, established in Colombia as a central bank; 1925, 21 Aug.: Banco de Chile established in Chile as a central bank; Sept.: Banco de Mexico, S.A., established as a central bank; 1939, 8 Sept.: Banco Central de Venezuela, S.A., incorporated). 1934, 24 Apr.: Nacional Financiera formed in Mexico to provide a market for Mexican government bonds; 1941: it was reorganized to aid in financing industrial expansion. Stock exchanges in less developed countries were in their infancy. 1933: Formal organization of Mexico City Stock Exchange. By 1939 there were organized stock exchanges in Rio, São Paulo, Pôrto Alegre (government bonds only), Recife, Santos, and Vitoria, Brazil. Stock exchanges existed in other Latin American cities. 1927: Manila Stock Exchange organized.

FOREIGN TRADE. To the extent that less developed countries were involved in world trade, they felt market fluctuations more severely than the industrial nations. 1921: Sharp temporary drop in prices of primary products, but full recovery did not take place. 1920's: Because populations of industrial countries were growing more slowly, demands for primary goods also rose slowly. Prices on primary products showed weakness. Attempts were made to stabilize prices. 1922, 1 Nov.: The British rubber restriction scheme, the Stevenson Plan, sought to curtail output of the rubber plantations in Malaya and Ceylon with an eye to raising the world price of rubber. (Increased rubber production elsewhere brought the plan to failure.) 1923: After overproduction of coffee in Brazil, the Brazilians introduced a coffee valorization plan, which sought to raise the export price of coffee. 1926: Cuba restricted exports of sugar, seeking to raise the price of that commodity; the principal exporters of copper sought to control world prices (on a private basis, without government participation). 1929–32: The Great Depression affected primary producers severely. The terms of trade moved sharply in favor of industrialized countries as prices of primary commodities sank more rapidly than the prices of manufactured items. With prices of primary products reaching new lows, underdeveloped countries erected high barriers to imports—tariffs, quotas, exchange controls, etc. They sought to manufacture for themselves; governments and private interests participated in more concerted attempts to raise export prices. 1931, Feb.: International Tin Restriction Scheme involved the governments of Malaya, Netherlands East Indies, Bolivia, and Nigeria (Thailand joined the agreement, July 1931); May: sugar agreement made between trade associations of exporters designed to raise price of sugar in world markets; 1933, Apr.: International Tea Agreement signed by exporters; the governments of India, Ceylon, and Netherlands East Indies agreed to uphold the agreement; 1934, June: International Rubber Agreement involving the governments of Britain, Holland, Siam, and Indochina sought to regulate rubber exports; 1936: agreement between producers of copper in Chile, Northern Rhodesia, and the Belgian Congo was designed to raise copper export prices. 1933–37: Although the terms of trade swung back slowly in favor of the primary producing countries, the volume of trade remained low. Foreign trade of less developed countries languished. 1938: Terms of trade once more turned against the less developed countries. 1939, Sept.– 1940, May: Prices of primary commodities rose rapidly, stimulated by wartime demands. 1940, May: Following the German invasion of Europe, curtailment of markets for much of the output of primary producers; 1941, Dec. ff.: after Japanese invasion of Southeast Asia, commerce in vegetable-oil seeds from the Philippines, the Netherlands East Indies, and Malaya ceased; the Philippines stopped exporting sugar to the U.S. Britain could no longer buy tea from the Netherlands East Indies and China. Burma, Indochina, and Thailand no longer exported rice. Rubber and tin exports to the allies from Japanese-controlled territories were cut off, as were exports of manila hemp and petroleum.

FOREIGN INVESTMENT. Foreign investment dominated certain economies. 1920–45: Oil in Venezuela and the Middle East was developed by foreign capital; copper in Chile once more became an important export because of American capital; in Northern Rhodesia and the Belgian Congo, copper was found and mined on a substantial scale because of foreign investment. Foreign investment grew in South African mining. 1920's: Railroads, gas, electricity, water supply, river transport, banking, and some factories in the Middle East remained under foreign control; Middle Eastern export trade was handled in the main by foreign concerns; the key interests were the French and British in Turkey (the Germans lost much of their stake after World War I); French, British, and Belgians in Egypt; British in Iran (the Russians retreated from their investments after World War I) and the French in the Levant. In India, large-scale British investments continued to be important. The modern sector in China was both stimulated and dominated by foreign capital; the largest Chinese coal mines were in foreign hands (Japanese and British), the iron and steel industry was under foreign control, modern plants (for export) were under foreign hegemony; in fact, a significant portion of China's transportation, trade, and large-scale banking was owned by foreign capital. In the Netherlands East Indies, rubber, tin, coal, oil, sugar, and tea still attracted giant Dutch investments. Huge British (and Chinese) investments were made in Malayan tin and rubber. French Indochina obtained French (and to a far smaller extent Chinese) investment in rubber, coal mining, and the export trade. The bulk of foreign investment in less developed countries was in primary production or in infrastructure (transportation, port facilities, public utilities, etc.) . 1930's: Opposition in many less developed countries to foreign investment became increasingly apparent. In some countries the opposition came at the same time as these countries were assuming political controls over their own economy; this was not the case in Latin America, where the opposition had nothing to do with the resumption of political sovereignty, although often it was *expressed* in terms of hostility to political intrusions. In Latin America the foreign investor was put under new restraint; profit remittances were blocked; exchange was not granted for imports; hampering restrictions on operations were frequently imposed. 1937: The Brazilian constitution limited foreign investments in water power and mining, banks and insurance cos., and public utilities; oil refining and production in Brazil were confined to Brazilian nationals. Bolivia expropriated the Standard Oil Co. (N.J.) oil refineries; Mexico completed nationalization of railroads. 1938, 18 Mar.: Large-scale expropriations of foreign oil properties in Mexico. Late 1920's: In Turkey, after the Kemalist Revolution, foreign debts were reduced through defaults, negotiations, and some repayments. 1929 ff.: Turkey bought out foreign investments in railways, coal and copper mines, the tobacco monopoly, and a number of public utilities; legislation in Turkey regulated foreign investment, licensed imports, and offered preferential treatment to Turkish business. 1930's: New capital raised in Egypt increasingly came from domestic rather than foreign sources. In India, sentiment turned away from encouraging foreign investment. In Thailand restrictions on foreign control of industries were imposed; the Thai government became involved in many industries in order to forestall and to substitute for foreign investment. In China the government sought alterna-tives to foreign capital. 1930's: The flow of capital from industrial to underdeveloped countries slowed down because of the depression and because of hostility to foreign investment. (Only oil exploration and production continued to attract major foreign investments.) 1938–48: British investment in India declined by over 80%, in large part because of the liquidation of British railway holdings and sterling loans; by 1944, Indian railroads had become the property of the government of India. 1941–45: Introduction of American lend-lease and the financing by the U.S. Export-Import Bank of development in Latin America added a new dimension to foreign investment, the dimension of foreign aid.

Effect of foreign investment: 1919 ff.: Foreign investment, as in previous years, proved highly disruptive to traditional societies. Africans and Asians were thrust into a monetized economy, due in considerable part to the presence of foreign investment. Most Latin Americans were already involved in a money economy, although in the Andes the presence of new and large mining enterprises served to introduce Indians into a commercial economy. Foreign investment introduced new desires for goods, the demonstration of a different pattern of life. It developed previously unused resources. Yet clearly less developed countries were going to carry on their growth with reservations about foreign investment.

BUSINESS ORGANIZATION. Underdeveloped countries generally had a range of business organization, from the labor-intensive, capital-short family unit to the large foreign-owned modern sector establishment (generally involved in extractive industries, plantations, public utilities—transportation and power—and/or distribution) . What was in between depended on the country. In much of Latin America and Asia, indigenous traders and businessmen transferred their activities to the modern sector. Immigrants served to introduce novel business practices. In Latin America and in India, entrepreneurial efforts spread over a variety of ventures rather than being concentrated in a single industry. Entrepreneurship in Latin America was stimulated by Italian immigration (especially in Brazil and Argentina) and also by Jews who left Germany during the Hitler years. In India the Tata family diversified into various ventures in the modern sector. Of the Hindus who entered modern industry, enterprise came to be in the hands of the former bankers, moneylenders, and traders (primarily the Marwaris, the Gujaratis, and the Bhatias). In India commercial commitments began to be transformed into industrial interests. The Birla family, of the Marwaris caste, came to participate in a range of industrial enterprises under the aegis of Ghanshyandas Birla (b. 1894) and B. M. Birla (b. 1904). In India the managing agent system, initially in British hands, came increasingly under Indian control. While the managing agent did direct Indian capital into industrial activities, the system had major inadequacies; it seems to have offered a poor foundation for industrial finance; profits frequently went to the managing agent rather than into the specific industrial enterprise, leaving the latter with insufficient funds for reinvestment. In China the problems of developing nonforeign, modern, efficient industrial business organizations were not surmounted. There emerged in China nothing comparable to the Japanese *zaibatsu* or even to the Indian managing agencies; no entrepreneurs of national stature such as the Tatas or the Birlas existed in China. In Southeast Asia, however, Chinese entrepreneurs continued to play important roles in stimulating business enterprise. Syrians and Lebanese in Africa (as traders rather than in industry) were important entrepreneurs. In East Africa, Indians, mainly in the retail trade, filled entrepreneurial functions. In South Africa, British immigrants created new businesses. In less developed countries, governments started to become involved in industrial activity, especially in Latin America.

GOVERNMENT POLICY. Government efforts to mobilize resources for economic development in some less developed countries began to take shape.

Aid to agriculture: Government aid to agriculture took various forms: (1) in certain countries, land reform occurred, generally designed to assist the small farmer; (2) on occasion, when farmers were hurt by imports, governments imposed protective tariffs (thus, 1931, India placed import duties on wheat); (3) governments (colonial and independent) offered new agricultural credits (from India to China to Mexico to Chile); (4) imports of agricultural implements were made duty-free in countries such as India to encourage their use; (5) governments sought to commercialize agriculture; (6) 1933 ff.: Chinese government planned projects in land reclamation, irrigation, water conservation, and reforestation; the Chinese government sought to introduce scientific methods, but its efforts in this direction were not successful; and (7) when world prices of agricultural commodities declined (in the 1920's, and especially in the early 1930's), governments tried to stabilize prices through participation in worldwide commodity agreements.

Aid to industry: Underdeveloped countries made use of the tariff and other protective devices to encourage industry. 1920's, and especially in the 1930's: In Latin America high protective tariffs became commonplace. 1920's and 1930's: Less developed countries that had been deprived of tariff autonomy by unequal treaties reassumed their right to establish their own tariffs and to protect nascent industry. 1921, June: India obtained fiscal autonomy and for the 1st time had the right to establish her own protective tariff; a Tariff Board was established to consider the need for protective duties. 1920's: Certain Indian industries (steel the most important of them) were given protection from imports; no protection in India was granted to locomotive building, steel casting, or enamelware, for example, because these industries were seen as having little possibility of developing. 1927: Thailand recovered tariff autonomy. 1929: China recovered tariff autonomy effective 1 Jan., 1931: customs duties were increased. 1929, June: High protective tariff introduced in Turkey with the goal of encouraging Turkish industrialization. (The Capitulations had been abrogated in 1914 and Turkey could set its own tariffs.) 1929–33: Practically everywhere in the less developed world, tariffs rose and other restrictions on trade (quotas, prohibitions, exchange controls, etc.) were imposed. 1930's: Latin American governments aided industry through exempting from import duties machinery needed in building plants and by granting other tax exemptions.

Participation in the economy: In the independent nations rather than the colonial countries, governments took on a direct role in the economy. 1920's: A government oil co. in Argentina sought to develop oil resources. 1924 ff.: Turkey began to take over railroads, public utilities, and mines that had previously been in the hands of foreign investors. 1930's: Thai government became directly involved in shipping, in the oil industry, teak lumbering, production of sugar, tobacco, alcohol, silk, and other consumer goods. 1937: Bolivia nationalized Standard Oil Co.'s (N.J.) oil facilities in that country; Bolivia established a national oil co. 1938: A government-owned Mexican oil co. was established to operate the nationalized facilities there. 1939–45: A Chilean government co. participated directly in industry.

Development plans: 1920: The Gold Coast began a 10-year Development Plan, "The Guggisberg Plan," one of the earliest development plans. 1925–41: Riza Pahlavi (1877–1944), shah of Iran, undertook reform programs, resulting in improved public sanitation and education. 1931, Nov.: National Economic Council established in China to draw up a plan of work most needed. 1934: Mexico adopted a 6-year development plan; Turkey committed itself to a 5-year plan, aimed at industrializing the country. 1935, 24 May: Portugal passed a Law of Economic Reconstruction. 1937: Cuba adopted a 3-year plan for economic and social reconstruction. 1938: Venezuela initiated its 1st 3-year plan; in India, a National Planning Committee was established, with Nehru as chairman. 1939: Corporación de Fomento de la Producción (CORFO) established in Chile; this government corporation was designed to plan and promote economic development; 1939–45: CORFO became involved through direct stock participation in min-

ing, steel, agriculture and stock raising, fish packing, radio production, public utilities, electrical products, wine distribution, reforestation, chemicals, pharmaceuticals, dyes, etc. 1940: Colombia adopted a development plan. 1944: Paraguay announced a 5-year plan; Puerto Rico's Planning, Urbanizing, and Zoning Board prepared a development plan.

Problems: Government aid to economic development in the less developed countries was in many instances impeded: (1) In certain countries, chaotic political conditions, lack of full government control, tended to vitiate the power of government; in China, for instance, the failure of government to keep peace and order was an important factor inhibiting economic advance; in many industries, China had the potential of Japan, but did not realize it because of political uncertainties; with life and property in jeopardy in the interior of China, investors were discouraged. Similarly, in other countries where political uncertainty prevailed, economic development was retarded. (2) Corruption and excessive bureaucracy in the governments of many less developed countries tended to slow development. (3) While they sought to create peace and order, while they discouraged corruption, and while they promoted economic development (which would provide more funds to administer the colony and which would utilize unused mineral resources and increase agricultural production), colonial governments in general did not encourage factory industries for fear their development would curtail the colonial powers' exports.

OTHER FACTORS. 1930's: The growth of nationalist feeling occurred in the less developed countries, some of which was due to the new tariffs, behind which the countries developed their own national identity; much of the rise of nationalist feeling stemmed from a hostility to foreign "colonialists." Likewise, the impact of the West on Asia had resulted in many Asians adopting western ideas of nationalism. With World War II, ideas of nationalism were reinforced; in China and Southeast Asia, opposition to the Japanese stimulated national feeling. This would have important impact in the post-World War II years. Likewise, western ideas of modernization spread and had their impact. The demonstration of the material achievements of Europe, the U.S., and Japan had ideological consequences. More important, beliefs in change and progress began to spread in the less developed countries. Traditional societies were increasingly under stress.

MEASURES OF ECONOMIC GROWTH.

NONMONETARY INDICATORS OF RELATIVE NATIONAL CONSUMPTION LEVELS, 1934–38
(U.S. = 100)

Argentina	53.7
Cuba	41.0
Spain	36.8
Brazil	31.6
Mexico	29.0
Poland	28.8
Yugoslavia	27.4
Philippines	25.7
Rumania	25.4
Turkey	24.2
Egypt	22.2
Thailand	21.4
India	20.8
Korea	19.4
Persia	18.2
China	18.0
Nigeria	17.9
Fr. Indochina	17.7
Neth. East Indies	17.0
Fr. W. Africa	15.8

NOTE: Typically 1934–38; deals with food, tobacco, medical and sanitary services, education and recreation, transportation, and communications.
SOURCE: M. K. Bennett, "International Disparities in Consumption Levels," *American Economic Review*, Sept. 1951, p. 648.

1919–1945

The International Economy

ENERGY.

WORLD PRODUCTION OF COMMERCIAL SOURCES OF ENERGY
(billion kwh electricity equivalent)

	Coal[a]	Petroleum[b]	Natural Gas	Water Power	Total
1920	9,934	1,046	354	64	11,198
1930	10,228	2,123	575	128	13,054
1940	11,702	3,120	867	193	15,882

SOURCE: United Nations, *Conference on Peaceful Uses of Atomic Energy*, Geneva, 1956.
[a] Includes lignite.
[b] Includes natural gasoline.

WORLD GENERATION OF ELECTRICITY
(billion kwh)

	World	U.S.	All Other Countries
1920	126	57	69
1925	180	85	95
1930	310	115	195
1935	375	119	256
1940	505	180	325
1942	585	233	352
1944	660	280	380

SOURCE: Edison Electric Institute, *Pocketbook of Electric Utility Industry Statistics*, 1965.

COMMUNICATIONS. 1944: Radio-telephone service connected more than 70 countries; a person in the U.S., if it were not for the war, could be connected by telephone with any one of 93% of the world's telephones.

FINANCE. 1919: Disruption of European finance after the war. 1919: Return to the gold standard by the U.S. 1920–21: Worldwide recession. 1922 ff.: General readoption of the gold standard:
1922: Lithuania and Latvia
1924: Germany, Sweden, and Hungary
1925: Britain, Holland, Neth. East In-

dies, Australia, New Zealand, South Africa, Switzerland, and Austria
1926: Canada, Finland, and Belgium
1927: Denmark, Czechoslovakia, Poland, and Italy
1928: France and Norway.
The key trading countries that did not adopt gold in these years were Brazil, Spain, and Turkey, which kept on an inconvertible paper basis, and China and Persia, which maintained the silver standard. 1929–33: Worldwide depression. 1929 ff.: Departures from the gold standard included:
1929, Dec.: Argentina
1930: Australia and New Zealand
1931, July: Germany, Hungary, and Chile initiated exchange control
1931, 21 Sept.: Britain left the gold standard
1931, 21 Sept. ff.: Denmark, Norway, Sweden, Finland, India, Japan, and Colombia suspended gold payments; Austria, Greece, Czechoslovakia, and Italy introduced exchange control.
1932, Apr.: 24 countries had suspended the gold standard and in 17 countries the gold standard was virtually inoperative. Temporarily, U.S., Belgium, France, Holland, and Switzerland formed a gold bloc. Britain led a sterling bloc, represented by those countries whose currencies were depreciated in terms of gold and in varying manners tied to the pound; the latter countries had most of their monetary reserves in sterling. The bloc included the Commonwealth countries (except Canada, Newfoundland, Hong Kong, and South Africa), the Scandinavian countries, Portugal, Finland, Iran, Greece, Egypt, Iraq, and Siam. Argentina, Bolivia, and Japan came to be on the fringe of the sterling bloc. 1933, Mar.–Apr.: U.S. went off the gold standard. 1935, Mar.: Belgium left the gold standard; 1936, 26 Sept.: France in effect suspended the gold standard. Holland, 27 Sept., Switzerland, 28 Sept., followed. 1930's: General disruption of international finance. 1939: The sterling bloc came to an end, and was replaced by the so-called "sterling area" comprising much the same countries. 1939, Sept.: Free convertibility of pounds into dollars, gold, and other outside currencies was abandoned with the

outbreak of war; exchange controls applied. 1939, Sept.–1945: Disruption of international finance with the war.
TRANSPORTATION.

SPEED OF TRANSPORT
(mph)

	1920	1930	1940	1945
Horse coach	5	5	5	5
Canal tug	4	4	4	4
Passenger ship (river)	11	11	11	11
Ocean ship	30	30	35	35
Railroad	65	70	100	100
Automobile	55	60	75	75
Airplane	110	185	300	500
Rocket	—	—	—	3,400

SOURCE: W. S. and E. S. Woytinsky, *World Commerce and Governments,* New York, 1955, p. 308, with modifications.

FOREIGN TRADE. 1920's: Resumption of world trade after World War I; 1929–33: depression, rise of tariff and other barriers to trade; world trade shrank. 1933 ff.: Economic nationalism spread, and as a result foreign trade stagnated.

WORLD TRADE (EXPORTS PLUS IMPORTS)
(gold U.S. $ billion)

1920	65.8
1921	41.8
1922	45.3
1923	49.7
1924	56.8
1925	64.7
1926	62.0
1927	65.2
1928	67.4
1929	68.6
1930	55.5
1931	39.7
1932	26.8
1933	24.2
1934	23.3
1935	23.8
1936	25.7
1937	31.8
1938	27.7

SOURCE: Woytinsky and Woytinsky, *World Commerce,* p. 39.

FOREIGN INVESTMENT. 1919–45: Foreign investment was keenly affected by slow economic recovery in Europe in the 1920's, depression in the 1930's, and

10 LEADING ARTICLES IN WORLD TRADE, 1937
(value of exports in $ million)

1. Iron and steel products   1,350
2. Machinery (excl. electrical)   1,100
3. Raw cotton   880
4. Cotton fabrics   740
5. Wheat (incl. flour)   710
6. Wool and hair   700
7. Automobiles and parts   640
8. Petroleum products   600
9. Coal   575
10. Rubber (nonfabricated)   520

war in the 1940's. 1944–45: One scholar (W. S. Woytinsky) estimates that in relation to world income, the value of foreign investment was probably not much more than ¼ and certainly less than ⅓ of what it had been in 1914 on the eve of World War I. (His estimate takes into account the lower purchasing power of the dollar, the rise in world population, and the growth in world income.)

INTERGOVERNMENTAL INSTITUTIONS. 1920, 10 Jan.: League of Nations formally came into operation with a membership of 64 nations; the U.S. did not join. 1920 ff.: Economic activities of the League and its committees were undertaken by its Economic and Financial Organization. Conferences held by the League dealt with such economic problems as raw-material resources, statistical co-ordination, simplification of customs formalities, etc. The League undertook special studies of economic problems. The Economic and Intelligence Section of the Secretariat made country data available on a comparative basis for the 1st time. The League's economic activity was mainly in research, but it did take concrete actions: 1922: the League aided in arranging for the post-World War I rehabilitation of Austria, Hungary, Greece, Bulgaria, Estonia, the Free City of Danzig, Albania, and the Saar Territory. 1935: The League advocated economic sanctions against Italy, a highly unsuccessful act. 1943–45: Plans for post-war international institutions multiplied. 1943, May: International conference at Hot Springs, Va., proposed a permanent body to consider problems of an adequate food supply for increasing world population. Such a body (the Food and Agricultural Organization) came into existence in 1945. 1943, Nov.: United Nations Relief and Rehabilitation Association created to arrange supplies of food and clothing to allied nations after their liberation. 1944, summer: Conference at Bretton Woods, N.H.; 2 new institutions were to be created, an International Monetary Fund and an International Bank for Reconstruction and Development; they started operations in 1945. Thus were the foundations for postwar international co-operation in the economic sphere established.

1945–1968

The Industrial Nations

AGRICULTURE. The main trends in agriculture in the industrial nations were: (1) 1945–68: Agriculture represented an increasingly smaller percentage of gross domestic product in the major industrial nations. Only in the USSR did agriculture still involve a substantial portion of GDP. (2) 1945–68: Population participating in farming declined in all the industrial nations. (3) 1945–68: Output per man-hour (productivity) of those individuals employed in agriculture rose, primarily because of increasing mechanization and application of chemical fertilizers, insecticides, and improved seeds. Despite the reduction in farm population, total agricultural output everywhere grew. Yet in some countries the rise was outpaced by the nations' population growth. 1965: For example, per capita output in the Soviet Union was less than in 1958. (4) Agriculture tended to become capital- rather than labor-intensive. (5) 1945–68: No general trend existed in the amount

% OF GDP AT FACTOR COST OF AGRICULTURE,
SELECTED INDUSTRIAL NATIONS

	1950	1953	1958	1965
Australia	29			14
Austria	18			10
Canada	13			6
France	15			8
West Germany	10			4
Italy		23		13
Japan		21		12
USSR			24	22
U.K.	6			3
U.S.	7			4

SOURCE: United Nations, *Statistical Yearbook 1966.*

of land under cultivation. 1945–66: In the U.S. acreage harvested dropped from 354 to 296 m. acres. 1954–57: In the Soviet Union, 90 m. acres of virgin land were put under cultivation, substantially raising the acreage harvested. (6) Attitudes toward conservation: 1945–68: Industrial nations were in general conscious of the need for conservation of land resources; in this respect Soviet agricultural policy was a major failure. 1945 ff.: In an attempt to raise Soviet agricultural output per annum, policies under both Stalin and Khrushchev showed no concern for subsequent harvests or long-run agronomic consequences; crop rotation and soil preservation measures were neglected; farms became denuded of feed and seed grains. 1961, Oct.: Introduction in the Soviet Union of the "plow-up" program, seeking to replace "low-yielding" crops (sown grasses and oats) and fallow with "high-yield" crops (peas, beans, and sugar beets); the plan was a failure. 1964, Oct. ff.: After the fall of Khrushchev, caused in part by his failure in agriculture, more attention was paid in the USSR to providing for long-term agricultural planning and to conservation of farm resources. (7) Land tenure and ownership: With the exception of Japan and to some extent the USSR, there were no major changes in land tenure and ownership relations in industrial nations, although there were alterations in the size of the farm unit under cultivation. Private property in agriculture remained the norm in North America, Western Europe, Japan, and Australia. (In Russia there were some concessions to private property.) In the U.S. large corporate enterprises became involved in agriculture; farm size rose. 1946, Oct.: Farm Land Reform Law passed by the Japanese Diet, a key land reform, insisted upon by the occupation forces: absentee landlordism was prohibited but a landlord might keep up to 2½ acres in the area in which he lived; a cultivator could own as much as 7½ acres for his own use and also could have an additional 2½ acres, which he could rent; under the land reform about 5 m. acres were redistributed and about 2 m. tenants became landowners; the reform removed major inequalities in ownership. In the Soviet Union landownership relations underwent some changes, and important revisions in government policies occurred, including changes in attitudes toward collective farms, state farms, and private plots, changes in the degree of central government control of farm production, greater utilization of economic incentives, and a more favorable attitude toward larger farm units; collective farms that averaged 1,000 acres in the 1930's averaged by the 1960's 15,000 acres (1960's: state farms averaged 30,000 acres). (8) Agricultural self-sufficiency: The U.S., Canada, and Australia had agricultural surpluses, which they exported. Under normal conditions, the USSR was agriculturally self-sufficient but, 1963–65, the Soviet Union made wheat purchases of $1½ billion from Canada, Australia, and other non-Communist countries, which suggested that her agricultural production was deficient. 1958 ff.: The European Common

Market countries together produced a surplus of lard, milk, fruit, potatoes, and vegetables; were self-sufficient in butter and cheese; produced 90–99% of meat, fish, rye, eggs, beet, sugar, and wine; 80–89% of their barley, corn, wheat, and rice; but imported over half their needs for citrus fruits, tobacco, cane sugar, cotton, and dried fruits. Japan required imports of foodstuffs to supplement her home-grown supplies, but her dependence on foreign supplies of food was less than in the pre-World War II years, owing to improvements in Japanese agriculture. Britain continued to be a large importer of foodstuffs. In the West all the industrialized nations subsidized agriculture to keep agricultural output higher than it would be were the market mechanism relied upon. (9) Trade in agricultural produce: 1945–57: Trading patterns for agricultural exports and imports of the industrial countries shifted, but no newly defined trend emerged. 1957–68: The key innovation in commerce in agricultural products came about with the adoption of an agricultural policy for the European Economic Community. 1957, 24 Mar.: By the Treaty of Rome, France, West Germany, Italy, Holland, Luxembourg, and Belgium committed themselves to act in the European Economic Community (EEC) to encourage increased agricultural productivity, to obtain for agricultural workers a fair standard of living, to stabilize agricultural markets, to develop regular and adequate supplies of farm produce, and to assure the consumer agricultural produce at a reasonable price. The EEC had difficulty in formulating the specifics of a common agricultural policy because of differences among the member countries. 1962, Aug.: 1st of the Market's regulations to implement a unified agricultural program came into force, representing the start of common policies on price, community financing, and commercial relationships. 1967, 1 July: A common market for cereals, pork, eggs, and poultry emerged; all restrictions on trade in these farm products among the 6 member nations ceased; external tariffs on these products became uniform. 1968,

1 July: A common market came into existence for all the Community's agricultural output. (10) 1945–68: In the domestic distribution of food products in industrial nations, the spread of the sale of frozen foods to the consumer represented an important trend.

RAW MATERIALS. Coal: 1945–68: Industrial nations remained large producers of coal, but as technology changed and as oil, natural gas, hydroelectric power, and nuclear power became more important sources of energy, coal industries in the U.S., Canada, Britain, and West Germany did not grow.

Oil: With the exception of the U.S. and USSR, the key industrial nations remained importers of oil. The U.S. was —as in the past—the world's largest oil producer; the USSR was in 3rd place after Venezuela. 1961: Oil output in the USSR surpassed that of Venezuela. 1947: Oil discoveries at Le Duc, south of Edmonton, Alberta, Canada, opened up new oil fields in that country.

CRUDE OIL PRODUCTION
(million metric tons)

	1948	1965
U.S.	273.0	384.9
USSR	29.2	242.8
Canada	1.7	39.7
France	.1	3.0
Netherlands	.5	2.4
Italy	a	2.2
World total	467.1	1,511.4

SOURCE: United Nations, *Statistical Yearbook 1966.*
a 9,000 metric tons.

Natural gas: 1945–68: Major deposits of natural gas were located in the U.S. and the Soviet Union. Canada's gas fields in southern Alberta and in the Peace River area on the Alberta-British Columbia boundary came into production. 1950's: Discovery of natural gas deposits in Italy; France had a gas field in the Pyrenean foothills; 1959: discovery of Groningen gas field in the Netherlands; 1966: natural gas discoveries in the North Sea and Britain. Natural gas was expensive to transport and its use depended on its nearness to the consuming markets; thus these discoveries were a boon to Western Europe.

NATURAL GAS PRODUCTION
(billion cubic meters)

	1957	1965
U.S.	300.8	454.2
USSR	18.6	127.7
Canada	6.2	41.6
EEC Countries	6.5	18.0

SOURCE: United Nations, *Statistical Yearbook 1966*.

Iron ore: The major industrial nations were among the largest producers of iron ore. 1950's: Massive development of Canadian iron resources.

IRON-ORE PRODUCTION (IRON CONTENT)
(million metric tons)

	1948	1965
USSR	16.2	89.0
U.S.	50.9	50.5
Canada	1.5	21.7
France	7.5	19.3
Sweden	8.2	17.6
Australia	1.3	4.3
U.K.	4.0	4.2
West Germany	1.8	2.5

SOURCE: United Nations, *Statistical Yearbook 1966*.

Technological changes: In the raw-materials industries, technological changes brought increased mechanization. 1948: Introduction in U.S. of a continuous-mining machine for use in coal mining—a major step in raising productivity. Technological change also improved resource utilization. Natural gas, pumped into oil wells, increased the output of these wells. Deep-drilling and offshore-drilling techniques opened up new oil resources. 1967, 10 Dec.: World's 1st use of a thermonuclear blast to release inaccessible natural gas took place in New Mexico. Late 1950's: As high-grade iron ores in the Lake Superior region became exhausted, Americans began to use formerly neglected taconite ore, which was pelletized by a new process. 1957, 13 Sept.: Large-scale commercial production of taconite

started in the U.S.; this provided the basis for the revival of the Mesabi Range. In nonferrous minerals improved processing methods offered possibilities of using low-grade ores; technological change made it possible to utilize formerly wasted minerals and thus enlarged the resources of developed nations. Slag—once rejected as waste—became of interest to mining engineers. Technological change also altered the demand for minerals; 1950's: uranium, for example, was at a premium because of the requirements of atomic energy.

The synthetics revolution: Despite continuing replacement of primary raw materials by synthetics, there remained many raw materials for which there were no substitutes and industrial raw materials continued in high demand in the industrial nations. Moreover, the chemical industry, in its production of synthetics, began to place new demands on formerly wasted raw materials.

Political problems: 1946, 23 July: Strategic and Critical Materials Stockpiling Act sought to assure the U.S. of essential raw materials. 1950, 9 May: Robert Schuman, then French minister of foreign affairs, proposed that France and Germany put their coal and steel production under a supernational authority: Schuman favored inviting other nations to participate; the so-called Schuman Plan emerged from French concern over the economic revival of Germany. 1951, 18 Apr.: Treaty establishing the European Coal and Steel Community (ECSC) was signed by the foreign ministers of France, West Germany, Italy, Luxembourg, Belgium, and the Netherlands; the treaty—following the Schuman Plan—aimed to eliminate internal trade restrictions for coal and steel products and to encourage free movement of productive resources among the 6 nations. 1953, Feb.: An ECSC free-trade zone, involving iron ore, coal, and scrap, came into existence and all intra-Community tariffs on these commodities were eliminated; the resources of the member nations effectively complemented one another. The ECSC was a predecessor to the EEC.

ENERGY. Fossil Fuels: 1945 ff.: Coal, which once represented the primary source of low-cost energy, increasingly met competition from forms of energy available at still lower cost. Oil provided 1 alternative; natural gas, which on the basis of energy content was substantially cheaper than fuel oil, also competed.

1964: Coal still represented the main primary source of energy in the U.K., Germany, and the USSR, but it no longer held this position in the U.S., Canada, or France, where oil and natural gas stood supreme.

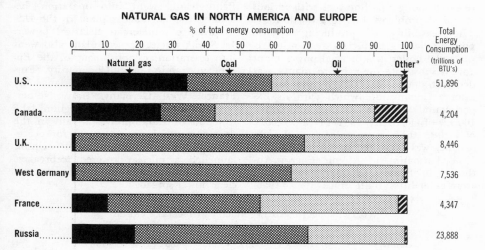

NATURAL GAS IN NORTH AMERICA AND EUROPE

ªHydroelectric power and nuclear energy.
SOURCE: United Nations, Data for 1964, Chase Manhattan Bank, *World Business*, Sept. 1966.

1964–68: USSR shifted increasingly away from use of coal for energy, as did Britain and Germany.

Internal-combustion engine: 1945–68: The internal-combustion engine continued to be the best form of propulsion for automobiles and other motor vehicles. Innovations in the internal-combustion engine consisted primarily of higher horsepower units.

Electrical energy:

ELECTRICAL ENERGY PRODUCTION IN SELECTED
COUNTRIES AND REGIONS
(billion kwh)

	1948	1965
U.S.	336.8	1,157.4
Europe (excl. USSR)	249.0	996.1
USSR	66.3	506.7
Japan	35.6	192.1
Canada	47.2	144.3
Australia	8.3	35.7

SOURCE: United Nations, *Statistical Yearbook 1966*.

1960–68: Stimulated by concern about air pollution, experiments in the U.S., Japan, and elsewhere were made with electric-powered automobiles; storage batteries were given trials but had to be replenished after each discharge by a relatively long process of recharging; fuel cells were devised which continued to function after a few minutes of "refueling"; the work on fuel cells was still experimental, and the advantages of the electric propulsion remained the same as in 1900: short range, low power, high cost, and high weight-to-energy ratio. 1945 ff.: Diesel-electric engines proved the most satisfactory form of propulsion for railroad locomotives.

Rocket power: 1945–68: Rocket power for propulsion came increasingly into use; the turbine-powered automobile, experimented with as early as 1928, was not manufactured commercially, but jet-powered airplanes became commonplace. Rocket power made possible the "space age".

Nuclear power: 1946, 1 Aug.: Mc-Mahon Act in U.S. established the Atomic Energy Commission. 1947: North American Aviation report dealt with the possibility of applying nuclear power to missile propulsion (a nuclear rocket); research along this line met with serious technical problems, but continued. 1951: The feasibility of producing electric power by using a nuclear reactor to replace the boiler in a thermal power plant (or to substitute for a hydro plant) was demonstrated in the U.S. by the Atomic Energy Commission, which with its Experimental Breeder Reactor developed 100 kw of electricity. 1954, 21 Jan.: U.S.S. *Nautilus*, the 1st atomic-powered submarine, was launched at Groton, Conn. 1954: Formation of Atomic Energy Authority in Britain to take over British atomic facilities built since 1945. 1956,

17 Oct.: The world's 1st full-scale nuclear power station opened at Calder Hall, Cumberland, England, and Britain took world leadership in production of electrical power using nuclear energy. 1957: Shippingport Atomic Power Station in Pennsylvania went into operation, becoming the 1st nuclear plant in the U.S. to produce commercial electrical power; 1st Soviet nuclear power plant also went into operation; establishment of the European Atomic Energy Community (Euratom) by Treaty of Rome signed by France, West Germany, Italy, Netherlands, Luxembourg, and Belgium; the function of Euratom was to aid in the development of atomic energy for peaceful purposes. 1958: Soviet Union launched a nuclear-powered icebreaker. 1958 ff.: Production of electricity by nuclear power spread.

WORLD PRODUCTION OF ELECTRICITY BY NUCLEAR ENERGY
(billion kwh)

Country	1957	1960	1965
U.K. (1957)	.409	2.079	15.836
U.S. (1957)	.010	.518	3.657
USSR (1957)	n.a.	n.a.	n.a.
Italy (1963)	—	—	3.510
France (1958)	—	.130	.897
Canada (1962)	—	—	.120
West Germany (1961)	—	—	.112
Belgium (1962)	—	—	.050a
Japan (1963)	—	—	.002a

NOTE: Date in parentheses is when production was 1st recorded in UN *Statistical Yearbook* except for USSR, where date is 1st installed capacity.
SOURCE: United Nations, *Statistical Yearbook 1966.*
a 1964.

1965–66: Cost of generating electricity with nuclear power went down sharply, because of improved reactors and because the cost per kwh declined as nuclear power plants increased their capacity. 1966: 1st year that orders for nuclear power generation equipment in the U.S. exceeded all other types of power facilities.

Other new sources of power: 1950's and 1960's: Work was under way in the U.S. and Britain on magnetohydrodynamics, the process of generating electricity by shooting ionized gas through a magnetic

field. New developments took place in the U.S. and Western Europe and in New Zealand in using tidal energy, wind energy, solar energy, geothermic energy, and thermal energy of the sea. 1955, 31 Aug.: A sun-powered automobile was demonstrated in Chicago; Oct.: 1st solar-powered telephone call made by customer of regular Bell Telephone System. 1957 ff.: Italy, New Zealand, and the U.S. developed electrical production using geothermal energy. Developments in space-age sciences brought forth a new variety of techniques for generating power. 1959, 19 Jan.: U.S. Atomic Energy Commission demonstrated a 5-watt radioisotope thermoelectric generator. 1960, 18 Apr.: National Aeronautics and Space Administration let contracts for an electric rocket; 4 May: tests made in the U.S. at Lewis Research Center of hydrogen-oxygen high-energy engine; 17 June: Lewis Research Center undertook tests of hydrogen-fluorine engines. 1960's: In the U.S. and Western Europe, experiments were made with optical lasers, a potential source of power. 1966: Union Carbide in the U.S. developed a hydrogen-oxygen fuel-cell system used to power an experimental delivery van.

INDUSTRY AND TECHNOLOGICAL CHANGE. Postwar reconstruction: 1945 ff.: Industrial development in Europe and Japan involved rebuilding the damaged industrial plant. In North America and Australasia, by contrast, there was no wartime damage; the task involved conversion to peacetime production. 1945 ff.: American foreign aid contributed importantly to rebuilding Europe and Japan. 1948: Every principal Western European country (except West Germany) had reached or surpassed its 1938 level of production. Late 1947–early 1948: Decision made to let Germany rebuild its industry. SCAP (Supreme Commander of the Allied Powers) in Japan similarly decided to encourage Japan to rebuild. 1951: West Germany surpassed its 1938 level of production; 1953: Japanese manu-

facturing reached the 1938 level. 1950's: Major rebuilding of industry in Soviet Union, parts of Eastern Europe, Western Europe, and Japan.

Automation: 1947: Delmar S. Harder (b. 1892) and John Diebold (b. 1926) used the word "automation." The word came to mean anything from the use of machines to run machines, to a controlled operation of an entire process, involving machines that automatically performed their operations, using an electronic judgment ("feedback"). 1950's and 1960's: The feedback element of automation became crucial—electronic controls inspected, approved, and corrected industrial work in the process of manufacture. Automation came of age with the computer and was applied in most industries.

Steel: 1950 ff.: Worldwide introduction of the basic oxygen process, which refined pig iron into steel by injecting jets of oxygen into a molten pool of pig iron; the process produced high-grade steel, more quickly and efficiently than older methods, at lower investment and operating costs. It was a major innovation. 1950, Nov.: VOEST, a nationalized Austrian steel company, using the patents of German C. V. Schwarz (issued in 1943) and of Belgian John Miles (issued in 1946), completed its tests of the oxygen process. 1952: VOEST was the 1st firm in the world to go into commercial production of steel using the oxygen process. 1954: A Canadian plant, Dominion Foundries & Steel Co., introduced the process in the

INDEXES OF MANUFACTURING ACTIVITY
(base: 1958 = 100)

	1959	1960	1961	1962	1963	1964	1965
World[a]	111	120	127	137	145	157	169
Japan	121	152	182	198	219	257	267
USSR and Eastern Europe[b]	112	125	138	151	163	177	192
U.S.	114	117	118	127	134	143	156
EEC	107	118	124	130	137	147	155
Canada	107	109	113	122	131	143	155
Australia	110	112	111	122	131	139	148
U.K.	106	115	115	115	120	130	134

SOURCE: United Nations, *Statistical Yearbook 1966.*

[a] Excluding Albania, Mainland China, Mongolia, North Korea.

[b] Eastern Europe includes Bulgaria, Czechoslovakia, East Germany, Hungary, Poland, and Rumania.

Western Hemisphere. On the European Continent and in Japan use of the process spread; by the end of the 1950's and 1960's the major American steel cos. had adopted it.

WORLD'S LEADING STEEL PRODUCERS
(million metric tons)

	1948	1960	1965
U.S.	80.4	90.1	119.3
USSR	18.6	65.3	91.0
Japan	1.7	22.1	41.2
West Germany	6.8	34.1	36.8
U.K.	15.1	24.7	27.4

SOURCE: United Nations, *Statistical Yearbook 1966.*

Automobiles: The motor-vehicle industries in the industrial nations grew dramatically.

MOTOR-VEHICLE PRODUCTION
(000)

	1948	1960	1965
Australia			
Cars	—	150.6	334.5
Trucks	—	53.7	69.3
Canada			
Cars	166.8	325.8	710.7
Trucks	96.9	72.0	141.8
France			
Cars	100.1	1,135.6	1,374.0
Trucks	98.3	233.6	242.1
West Germany			
Cars	29.9	1,816.8	2,733.7
Trucks	29.8	237.8	237.7
Italy			
Cars	44.4	595.9	1,103.9
Trucks	15.0	48.9	71.6
Japan			
Cars	.4	165.1	696.2
Trucks	36.8	595.2	1,222.4
USSR			
Cars	20.2	138.8	201.2
Trucks	176.9	501.3	612.6
U.K.			
Cars	334.8	1,352.8	1,722.0
Trucks	173.3	458.0	455.2
U.S.			
Cars	3,909.3	6,674.8	9,305.6
Trucks	1,376.3	1,194.5	1,751.8

SOURCE: United Nations, *Statistical Yearbook 1966.*

1950–68: The largest car producers in the U.S. remained General Motors, Ford, and Chrysler. In Germany, Volkswagen (a nationalized German company, established in the 1930's in response to Hitler's demand for a cheap car) and Opel (a GM subsidiary) led the industry. In Britain the British Motor Corp. (formed in 1952, uniting Morris and Austin) along with Ford Motor Co., Ltd. (a Ford subsidiary), led that nation's industry. In Italy, Fiat was the pace-setter.

Chemicals: 1950's and 1960's: The large petroleum cos. took part in the chemical industry, making a range of petrochemical products. The pharmaceutical industry witnessed a veritable revolution in the manufacture of drugs, serums, and vaccines. With antibiotics, new vaccines, and new methods of treatment, the industry was transformed. The U.S., Britain, and Germany led in the world's chemical industries. Japan also developed a substantial chemical industry; it was especially active in the production of synthetic fibers, but also in other chemicals (see table, pp. 806–807).

Electricity and electronics: 1945–68: Electronics was a major growth industry; innovations were revolutionary; the television set was the most complex electronic product marketed commercially.

PRODUCTION OF TELEVISION RECEIVERS
(000)

	1948	1960	1965
U.S.	975	5,611	10,036
U.K.	91	2,141	1,591
USSR	4	1,726	3,655
France	1	655	1,250
West Germany	—	2,164	2,776
Japan	—	3,578	4,180

SOURCE: United Nations, *Statistical Yearbook 1966.*

1948: Invention of the transistor by Americans John Bardeen (b. 1908) and W. H. Brattain (b. 1902), working under William Shockley (b. 1910) at Bell Telephone Laboratories, was the next stage in the electronics industry. 1950, 1 Mar.: Eckert-Mauchly Computer Co. acquired by Remington-Rand; 1951, 14 June: Remington Rand delivered (to the Bureau of Census) UNIVAC—the 1st production model of an advanced large-scale general-purpose computer—a vacuum-tube computer; this was the 1st commercially produced computer. 1952: Masaru Ibuka, president of the Japanese Sony Co., obtained Bell Lab's transistor patents. 1954–61: Discoveries made by Bell Labs in the field of intermetallic alloys, through which electric current could be conducted without loss ("super-conductors"). 1954: International Business Machines (IBM) demonstrated the 1st large transistorized computer. 1955: Sony turned out the world's 1st transistor radio; 1957: Sony introduced the 1st pocket-sized transistor radio; 1958: Sony presented the 1st transistorized FM radio. Invention in the U.S. of the integrated circuit, which reduced costs of computer operations at a ratio of 3–1 over transistorized computers and increased the speed of calculations. 1959: Sony introduced the 1st all-transistorized television set. Use of vacuum-tube computers—the 1st generation of computers—had practically ceased; 2nd-generation transistorized computers had replaced them; these would now be replaced by the 3rd generation, integrated-circuit computer. (From the vacuum-tube computers of the early 1950's to the integrated-circuit computers of the 1960's, computers' capacity for calculation was increased 1,000-fold). Christopher Strachey, British mathematician, gave 1st public paper on time-sharing. ("Time-sharing" involved the utilization of a single computer by many individuals in diverse locations; 1961, Nov.: 1st demonstration of time-sharing at the MIT Computation Center, using 4 "remote" consoles in the same room.) 1960: Sony introduced the 1st transistorized videotape recorder. 1964: Charles H. Townes (b. 1915), American from MIT, and Russian scientists Nikolai Basov and Alexander Prokhorov won the Nobel Prize in physics for their work on lasers; 1964–68: research into the laser, a device for generating and manipulating light, brought forth varied applications to data display systems for computers, tunnel-boring machines, cancer surgery, plasma diagnosis, 3-dimensional photography, and communications (transmission over a light beam of TV programs). 1965:

Sony introduced the 1st transistor microphone; Union Carbide achieved the most powerful solid-state continuous-wave laser beam yet recorded. 1966: The IBM 360, a multipurpose computer line, using advanced microcircuitry, was introduced; Sony presented the 1st integrated-circuit radio. 1968: Prospects of large-scale (circuit) integration (LSI), with higher speeds, greater reliability, and lower costs, in the 4th generation of computers.

NUMBER OF COMPUTERS INSTALLED IN THE U.S., 1950–68

1950	10–15
1955	1,000
1960	6,000
1965	30,800
1968 (as of 1 Jan.)	40,159

SOURCE: American Federation of Information Processing Societies and *EDP Industry Report*, Jan. 26, 1968, p. 14.

SPACE AGE. Prelude: 1945: The U.S. made the commitment to develop missiles for military purposes; Feb.: "Project Nike" initiated to seek new means of air defense against high-speed, high-altitude bombers, which were beyond the reach of existing artillery; 8 Mar.: 1st test launch of U.S. air-to-air missile; Aug.: components of about 100 V-2 ballistic missiles were shipped from Germany to the U.S. for study; Oct.: Secretary of War Robert P. Patterson (1891–1952) endorsed a plan to bring key German scientists to the U.S. to aid in military research and development; 1946, 22 Mar.: 1st American rocket launched to move outside the earth's atmosphere. 24 Oct.: U.S. launched a V-2 rocket carrying a camera and taking motion pictures of the earth at about 65 mi. above the earth's surface. 1947, 24 Apr.: French government established a rocket test range in Algeria. Sept.: U.S. "Project Rand" report indicated that earth satellites were technically feasible. 1948, 4 Nov.: U.S. Air Force announced the formation of the Rand Corp., successor to Project Rand, to assemble and develop the most advanced scientific, technical, industrial, and military knowledge relevant to Air Force decisions. 1949, 11 May: U.S.

SOME INNOVATIONS IN THE CHEMICAL INDUSTRY, 1945–67

Food	Clothing	Shelter	Health	Transportation and Communications	Tools and Equipment	Packaging
Selective and pre-emergent weed and brush killers	New synthetic fabrics, including, 1950: introduction of "Orlon" acrylic fiber; 1951: introduction of "Dacron" polyester fiber, which became important in "wash and wear" garments; other synthetic fabrics	Silicone products, such as construction sealants, coating and surfacing materials	1945 ff.: New antibiotics, among them, 1948: aureomycin; 1950: terramycin; 1952: chloromycetin	Higher-octane gasolines	Silicones	Polyethelenes for packaging
Defoliation as harvest aid		New paints and pigments	Antihistamines	New lubricants	Low-cost sheet-forming dyes	
New insecticides (1947: 1st use of organic phosphates as insecticide; others followed)		New insulation materials	Synthetic hormones	Nonflammable hydraulic fuel	Nylon machine parts	
Fungicides	Durable-press fabrics	Foamed plastics	Cortisone for arthritis	Range of new coating and insulation materials	Fluorinated hydrocarbons	
Soil conditioners	Inherent colors in man-made fabrics	Synthetic carpeting of tufted plastic	Radioisotopes	Nylon tire cord	Expansion of electrochemical industries, making for better metals for tools and equipment	
Mold inhibitors			1952: Tran-	New uses of plastics in the automobile industry		

1955: Man-made industrial diamonds

Man-made industrial rubies

New synthetic rubber compounds

New resins for reinforced plastics with applications in the utility, outboard motor, and transportation fields

quilizers

1955: Salk vaccine for poliomyelitis

1956: Oral contraceptives; 1961: Sabin vaccine for poliomyelitis could be taken orally

1966: Measles vaccine

1967: **Symmetrel,** 1st oral chemical agent to work efficiently against influenza

1960's: Drugs for treatment of mental illness

Aerosol foam cleaners

Consideration of polymers as "basic structural" materials

New cleaning solvents, introduced into textiles as stain and water repellents

1964: "Corfam," a synthetic material for shoe uppers

Plastic protective helmets

Range of new fertilizers and fertilizer-pesticide mixtures

Synthetic hormones for animals

Animal disease-control agents (including antibiotics, and antioxidants)

Liquid nitrogen systems for in-transit food refrigeration

SOURCE: Adapted from Manufacturing Chemists' Association, *The Chemical Industry Facts Book,* 3rd ed., 1957, with many additions.

President Harry Truman signed a bill providing for a 5,000-mi. guided-missile test range; it was subsequently established at Cape Canaveral (later Cape Kennedy), Fla. 1951, 4 Oct.: M. K. Tikhonravov declared Russian rocket advance equal to or superior to that of the U.S. and that the Russians believed the creation of artificial earth satellites and space flights were feasible. 1954, 29 Apr.: 1st launching in the U.S. of a 3-stage rocket vehicle, including 2 Nike boosters and a Deacon rocket as the 3rd stage; 14 Oct.: 4-stage solid-fuel rocket launched in U.S.; USSR established an Interdepartmental Commission on Interplanetary Communications to develop an earth satellite; 16 Dec.: U.S. Air Force announced that the Atlas Intercontinental Ballistic Missile (ICBM) was being constructed by Convair. 1955, 1 Dec.: Eisenhower gave highest priority to ICBM programs, especially the Thor and Jupiter projects. 1957, spring: Several Russian tests of ICBM's; 26 Aug.: Soviet News Agency announced that the USSR had a "few days" earlier successfully launched a "super long-distance intercontinental multistage ballistic rocket"; 20 Sept.: 1st successful launch of the U.S. Air Force's Thor Intermediate Range Ballistic Missile.

Space research and travel: 1957, 4 Oct.: Soviet Union launched Sputnik I (weighing 180 lbs.)—the earth's 1st artificial moon; 3 Nov.: USSR's Sputnik II (weighing 4 tons) carried a dog named "Laika." 1958, 31 Jan.: U.S. launched its 1st artificial earth satellite, Explorer I (30.8 lbs.); it discovered the presence of a

SEQUENCE OF KEY U.S. MISSILE DEVELOPMENTS

	1st Successfully Launched in U.S.
V-2	1946
Navaho	1950
SNARK	1952
Redstone	1953
Jupiter	1956
Atlas	1957
Thor	1957
Vanguard	1957
Titan	1959
Nike-Zeus	1959
Saturn	1960

radiation belt around the earth. (6 Dec., 1958: Pioneer I, an American satellite, identified a 2nd radiation belt around the globe; these belts were called the Van Allen belts.) 17 Mar.: U.S. launched Vanguard I rocket to test solar cells; as a scientific satellite, it proved that the earth was slightly pear-shaped. 26 Mar.: U.S. launched Explorer III, which produced valuable information on the radiation belt, micrometeorite impacts, and temperatures. 15 May: Soviet Union put Sputnik III into orbit for aerodynamic studies; this satellite weighed about 7,000 lbs. 1 July: Japanese Kappa-6tw 2-stage rocket was flown to the altitude of 30 mi. above the Michikawa Rocket Center, Japan. 27 Aug.: Russians sent 2 dogs to an altitude of 281 mi. and safely returned them to earth. 27 Aug.: President Eisenhower signed Public Law 85–766, which included an appropriation of $80 m. for a National Aeronautics and Space Administration (NASA), including $50 m. for research and development and $30 m. for other expenses. (1 Oct.: NASA officially came into existence.) 7 Oct.: NASA organized Project Mercury to (1) put a manned capsule into orbital flight around the earth, (2) consider man's reactions to and capabilities in space, and (3) find means by which the capsule and the pilot could be recovered without harm to either. 11 Oct.: U.S. launched Pioneer I, a space probe which went 70,700 mi. before returning to earth: it determined the extent of radiation bands, observed the earth's magnetic field, and made 1st studies of the density of micrometeors in space and 1st measurement of the interplanetary magnetic field. 1959, 2 Jan.: USSR put Lunik I into a solar orbit—the 1st man-made object placed in orbit around the sun. 3 Mar.: Pioneer IV was the 1st U.S. satellite to orbit the sun. 2 Apr.: The 1st 7 astronauts were selected in the U.S. for Project Mercury: Capts. Leroy G. Cooper, Jr., Virgil I. Grissom, and Donald K. Slayton; Lieut. Malcolm S. Carpenter; Lieut. Comms. Alan B. Shepard, Jr., and Walter M. Schirra, Jr. (U.S.N.); and Lieut. Col. John H. Glenn (U.S.M.C.). 12 Sept.: Russia's Lunik II launched; Lunik II became the 1st man-made object to hit the moon. 4 Oct.: USSR launched Lunik III, which took the 1st photographs of the hidden side of the moon. 1960, 1 Apr.: U.S. launched 1st weather observation satellite, Tiros I (Television Infrared Observation Satellite), which inaugurated a new era in meteorological observation. 12 Aug.: Echo I, launched in the U.S., demonstrated radio communication by satellite. 19 Aug.: USSR launched into orbit Spacecraft II, weighing 5 tons and carrying 2 dogs and biological specimens; 21 Aug.: USSR announced the safe recovery of the dogs and the biological specimens from Spacecraft II, the 1st successful recovery of living organisms from orbit. 1961, 12 Apr.: Russian Yuri A. Gagarin made a 1-orbit trip in space and returned safely —the 1st man to fly beyond the earth's atmosphere. 5 May.: Astronaut Alan B. Shepard, Jr., was the 1st American in space. 6 Aug.: Maj. Gherman S. Titov, Russian cosmonaut, was launched into orbit in Vostok II; he made 17 orbits and returned to earth safely, 25 hours and 8 minutes later (7 Aug.). 1962, 20 Feb.: Lieut. Col. John H. Glenn, U.S. astronaut, was 1st American to orbit the earth; he orbited 3 times and returned safely; 7 Mar.: solar observatory satellite launched by the U.S. into orbit—the 1st of large 2nd-generation satellites developed by NASA. 26 Apr.: 1st international satellite (Ariel)—a British-American joint venture—launched from Cape Canaveral, with the goal of studying cosmic radiation. 10 July: U.S. launching of Telstar, a communications satellite. 11 Aug. and 12 Aug.: 2 manned Soviet space ships (Vostok III and Vostok IV) were launched into orbit; 12 Aug.: 1st live TV broadcast from a spaceship—from Vostok III. 15 Aug.: Vostok III and IV landed safely, Vostok III after 64 orbits and Vostok IV —6 minutes later—after 48 orbits. 27 Aug.: U.S. launched unmanned Mariner II on its 109-day mission to fly by Venus. (14 Dec.: Mariner II took 1st instrument readings of Venus's temperature, atmosphere, etc., as it flew within 21,100 mi. of the planet; Mariner II radioed these data 36 m. miles back to earth.) 1963, 14 June:

Vostok V, Russian spacecraft, manned by Lieut. Col. V. F. Bykovsky, was launched; 16 June, Russian Valentina Tereshkova, in Vostok VI, was 1st woman in space; 17 June, communications in space between Vostok V and VI. 20 June: Vostok V and VI landed safely; Bykovsky set new record by orbiting the earth 81 times, covering 2 m. miles (Tereshkova orbited 48 times). 16 Oct.: U.S. Air Force launched twin unmanned satellites, designed to detect nuclear explosions in space. 1964, 12 Oct.: Voskhod I was launched by the USSR—the 1st 3-man satellite. 1965, 18 Mar.: Russian Aleksei Leonov, leaving Voskhod II, took the 1st walk in space—duration 10 minutes; 23 Mar.: U.S. spacecraft Gemini III was pilot-maneuvered during orbit by Americans Virgil Grissom and John Young. 3 June: Launch of Gemini IV, U.S. 2-man orbital flight, from which American Edward H. White took a 20-minute walk in space; 15 July: unmanned U.S. Mariner IV (launched 28 Nov., 1964) transmitted 1st photographs of Mars, from 10,500 mi.; subsequent photographs received from the satellite were from as close as 6,118 mi. from the planet. 21–29 Aug.: U.S. spacecraft, Gemini V, with 2 astronauts on board, made new world record—120 orbits. 26 Nov.: 1st French satellite launched. 4 Dec.: Gemini VII, U.S. 2-man orbital flight, launched; it remained in orbit for 14 days, a new record; 15 Dec.: Gemini VII made 1st rendezvous in space (with Gemini VI, launched 15 Dec.). 1966, 4 Feb.: Russian Lunik IX (launched 31 Jan., 1966) was the 1st spacecraft to soft-land on the moon; 1 June: U.S. 3-legged Surveyor I spacecraft landed on the moon. 1967, 27 Jan.: Fire in Apollo spacecraft on the ground killed 3 American astronauts—Virgil I. Grissom, Edward H. White, and R. B. Chaffee. 23 Apr.: Soviet cosmonaut Vladimir M. Komarov crashed on re-entry from space, the 1st known Russian space casualty. 18 Oct.: Russians made the 1st soft-landing of a capsule on the planet Venus; it found temperatures of from 104° to 536° F., and obtained other scientific information, which it relayed back to earth. (For moon landing, see p. 652).

Supersonic transports: Anglo-French agreement to build "Concorde" supersonic airliner (1,400 mph), 26 Mar., 1962. U.S. decided to build prototype SST (1,750 mph), 29 Apr., 1967. On 31 Dec., 1968, Russian SST, TU–144 (1,550 mph), made 1st flight; 1st flight of Concorde, 2 Mar., 1969.

TRANSPORTATION. The dramatic spread of motor-vehicle usage was reflected in the rise of automobile and truck production. Construction of limited access roads accelerated, to meet the demands for new highways. 1964, 1 Oct.: The world's 1st high-speed (125 mph) modern passenger train was introduced in Japan. 1967, 4 Dec.: French wheelless "aerotrain" went 215 mph on a cushion of air—a world record for track vehicles; the train was powered by a turboprop engine. 1950's and 1960's: Growth of pipe-line facilities in major industrial nations to transport oil and gas.

Shipping: 1966: Figures on major nations' merchant shipping are misleading, because many American and other ships sail under foreign flags.

MERCHANT SHIPPING OF LEADING INDUSTRIAL NATIONS
(million gross registered tons)

	1948	1966
World		
Shipping other than tankers	80.3	171.1
Tankers	15.3	60.2
U.K.		
Ships	18.0	21.5
Tankers	3.5	8.0
U.S.		
Ships	29.2	20.8
Great Lakes	2.3	1.9
Tankers	5.5	4.4
Japan		
Ships	1.0	14.7
Tankers	.01	5.1
USSR		
Ships	2.1	9.5
Tankers	.1	2.5

SOURCE: United Nations, *Statistical Yearbook 1966.*

Air travel: 1945 ff.: Airplanes became a common means of traveling; passenger and, to a smaller extent, freight mileage by air mounted. Jet aircraft, used during the war, were improved upon by the

British, Americans, and Russians, initially primarily for military use. 1947, 14 Oct.: U.S. Air Force Capt. Charles E. Yeager made the 1st supersonic flight in a manned aircraft in level or climbing flight; flight was made in a rocket-powered research plane, the Bell XS-1 (later the X-1). 1950, Oct.: U.S. Air Force announced a plan to replace all piston-engined planes with jet aircraft. 1952, 21 Apr.: British Overseas Airways, with the De Havilland Comet, started the 1st jet passenger service—London to Rome. 1958, 4 Oct.: 1st commercial jet airplane crossing of the Atlantic made by BOAC; this inaugurated a new epoch in civilian travel. 1958: 1st year in which total number of transatlantic passengers by air exceeded the number of passengers by sea. 1960: World's scheduled airlines (excluding USSR and Communist China) carried 108 m. passengers.

Communications: 1945 ff. There was a remarkable growth in telephone, radio, and television usage in the industrial world.

TELEPHONES
(no. in use in million units)

	1948	1965
U.S.	38.20	93.66
U.K.	4.87	10.62
Canada	2.45	7.44
France	2.23	6.12
West Germany	1.86	8.80
Sweden	1.43	3.38
Japan	1.31	14.00
Italy	1.01	5.98
Australia	.96	2.81

SOURCE: United Nations, *Statistical Yearbook 1966.*

The field of "telecommunications" blossomed. 1956: Bell Telephone Co. developed a "visual telephone," which would transmit pictures over telephone wires. 1960's: Development of long-distance xerography (introduced Dec. 1962); scanners and printers could operate reliably between cities miles apart; electronic blackboards were developed, which transmitted writing over a long distance on telephone wires (the writing received could be preserved). 1960, 12 Aug.: Echo I, launched in the U.S., demonstrated the

RADIOS
(est. no. in use in million receivers)

	1948	1965
U.S.	74	240
U.K.	11	16
Canada	2	10a
France	6	15
West Germany	7	26
Japan	7	20
Australia	2	3
USSR	11	74

SOURCE: United Nations, *Statistical Year-book 1966.*
a 1964.

feasibility of radio communication by satellite. 1962, 10 July: Launching of Telstar I at Cape Canaveral made possible the 1st transmission of live TV pictures across the Atlantic Ocean. 31 Oct.: President Kennedy signed a communications satellite bill, establishing a private profit-making corporation (50% owned by the general public and 50% owned by utilities) to handle global communications by satellite. 1965, 2 May: TV 1st used "Early Bird," the U.S. Commercial Communications Satellite (Comsat).

FINANCE. International: 1945: U.S. emerged from the war a great creditor nation. Britain, by contrast, had become a debtor nation, as had France. Germany and Japan were in desperate need of foreign funds for revival. American foreign aid came to the assistance of Europe. The International Bank for Reconstruction and Development (established 27 Dec., 1945) had as one of its key purposes financing reconstruction. 1947: 1st IBRD loans went to Belgium, Denmark, Finland, Luxembourg, the Netherlands, and Yugoslavia. In Europe there developed a "dollar shortage," an inadequate supply of dollars at the established rate of exchange. Foreign-exchange controls remained. 1948, June: West German currency reform, wherein the reichsmark was exchanged for a new deutschemark at the rate of 10 to 1. 1949, 1 Apr.–18 Sept.: Britain's reserves declined by over $500 m. 18 Sept.: Britain devalued the pound sterling, from $4.03 to $2.80; other countries followed. 1950, 1 July: European Payments Union (EPU) created to facilitate payments between member countries.

1950's: European nations increased their gold and foreign-exchange reserves; the dollar shortage began to disappear; U.S. balance-of-payments deficits became endemic. 1956, July: Egyptian government nationalized the Suez Canal. Oct.: The Suez Canal and oil pipe lines traversing Syria were closed; 1957, Apr.: reopening of Canal and partial restoration of oil pipe lines; the "Suez Crisis" put a severe strain on European financial resources. The International Monetary Fund played a prominent role in promoting international financial stability—aiding member nations. Nonetheless the franc continued to be weak. Aug.: France devalued the franc; the British pound seemed in jeopardy; Britain raised the bank rate to 7%—the highest level since the early 1920's—and the crisis was averted. 1958, 27 Dec.: Britain announced the immediate convertibility of the pound sterling by residents of countries outside the sterling area; earnings in sterling could thereafter be freely converted into dollars at roughly the official rate of $2.80 per pound. Austria, Belgium, Denmark, Finland, France, West Germany, Ireland, Italy, Luxembourg, the Netherlands, Norway, Portugal, and Sweden made similar announcements. Most nations excluded capital from the convertibility provisions. France devalued the franc from 420 to 493.7 francs to the U.S. dollar. European Monetary Agreement came into force, superseding the now defunct European Payments Union; it aimed to promote convertibility of currencies and aid international trade; it was signed by the OEEC members. 1959–60: The right of convertibility for current transactions was extended by European countries to include their own members; restrictions on capital movements remained. 1961, Mar.: Germany revalued the mark upward. Aug.: The pound sterling was again under pressure and there was a threat of devaluation; again the crisis was averted. 1960's: U.S. balance-of-payments deficits continued; new weakness of the pound. 1967, 18 Nov.: Britain devalued the pound, making it worth $2.40.

Domestic: 1950's: All the industrial nations committed a higher proportion of GNP to domestic investment than ever

GROSS DOMESTIC CAPITAL FORMATION AS A
SHARE OF GNP
(based on totals in current prices)

	Years	% GNP
U.K.	1950–60	15.4
West Germany	1950–60	24.0
Italy	1950–60	20.8
Denmark	1950–60	18.1
France	1950–60	19.1
Netherlands	1950–60	24.2
Sweden	1950–60	21.3
Australia	1950/51–1959/60	28.6
Canada	1950–60	24.8
U.S.	1950–60	19.1
Japan	1950–59	30.2
USSR	1960	32.6a

SOURCE: Angus Maddison, *Economic Growth in the West*, New York, 1964, p. 76, and Simon Kuznets, *Modern Economic Growth*, New Haven, 1966, pp. 236–239.

a Gross national capital formation as % of GNP.

before in their history, the U.S. excepted. (In the U.S. pre-World War I percentages were higher.)

Central Banks: In Europe especially, but also in other industrial countries, central banking policies sought to encourage a high rate of investment. Central banks became of key importance in controlling credit and regulating demand; they became instruments of economic planning.

Other banking facilities: 1945 ff.: Bank of International Settlements became in the postwar years an important European banking institution. 1958, 1 Jan.: In accord with the Treaty of Rome establishing the EEC, a European Investment Bank was founded; it was organized primarily to make loans principally to private enterprises and governmental agencies within the EEC, although it could finance enterprises outside the EEC.

Capital markets: 1945–68: The U.S. was the world's major capital market. In Europe, there were attempts to stimulate capital markets, but by 1967 there was still not complete freedom of capital movement. 1958–59 ff.: There developed in Europe a "Eurodollar market"—a market for lending and borrowing the world's key convertible currencies, mainly dollars, but other currencies as well. 1967:

The Eurodollar market was one of the world's largest markets for short-term funds. 1951–61: The Tokyo Dow Jones average rose from 100 to over 1,800 points. The Japanese stock exchange aided in creating a capital market in that country; for the 1st time in the postwar years, securities of major industrial companies were publicly traded. Trading per day on the Tokyo Exchange rose from an average 2.5 m. shares in 1951 to 100 m. shares in 1961. 1961–65: Decline of Tokyo Dow Jones—from a high of 1,829 to a low of 1,020. 1965–67: sweeping changes in Japan, as the exchange sought to regain public confidence.

FOREIGN TRADE. 1945: After the war, world trade was disrupted. Everywhere there were restrictions on commerce. 1946: Despite the restrictions, U.S. trade boomed; exports were 90% over their 1938 level and imports about 40% over the 1938 level. By contrast, exports of European countries (leaving Germany aside) were about 60% of their prewar (1938) level; German exports were negligible. Financed by loans and grants from abroad, European imports were 80% of their prewar level. Japanese exports were small; Japanese imports were higher than exports. 1947–48: U.S. continued to have large export surpluses; other industrial countries had difficulty exporting because of war devastation; they had difficulty paying for imports because of low exports. 1948: Customs union became effective between the Netherlands, Luxembourg, and Belgium as these nations abolished tariffs among one another and established a common external tariff. 1949: With the devaluation of the pound and other currencies, European exports became more competitive and foreign trade mounted. 1957: Treaty of Rome and formation of European Economic Community, 1 Jan., 1958; the EEC sought to remove all trade restrictions among the member nations (France, West Germany, Italy, Holland, Belgium, and Luxembourg) and to establish a common external tariff; 1968, 1 July: removal of internal tariff barriers and establishment of a common external tariff. 1959, 20 Nov.: Formation of the European Free

Trade Association (EFTA), including Britain, Sweden, Norway, Denmark, Switzerland, Austria, and Portugal. EFTA sought to remove quotas and tariffs among the 7 members, but did not seek to develop a common external tariff; 1967, 1 Jan.: EFTA achieved free trade in manufactured products among its 7 members. 1959 ff.: While no single country in the EEC had a larger foreign trade than the U.S., together they did. So too, the EFTA countries together had larger trade than the U.S. 1960's: The U.S. remained the largest single trading nation; West Germany replaced Britain as 2nd largest. 1962, 4 Oct.: Trade Expansion Act in U.S. committed the U.S. to freer trade worldwide; the U.S. President was given the authority to negotiate tariff reductions. 1964 ff.: Subsequent discussion, known as "Kennedy Round" negotiations, served to lower tariff barriers. 1967: Rise of protectionist sentiment in the U.S., which represented a reversal of entire postwar trend, yet during 1967 this sentiment was not translated into legislation. 1968: Despite the end of tariff barriers in the EEC, France undertook protective measures to safeguard the franc.

FOREIGN INVESTMENT. 1945–68: The U.S. became the world's major foreign investor. 1945: U.S. and Britain together controlled foreign assets of about $29.5 billion. 1966: U.S. alone controlled foreign assets that had a book value of about $111.9 billion. 1945–67: Rapid growth of American business enterprises abroad, especially in Europe. In many major European industries (automobiles, chemicals, oil, computers, etc.), American companies had a crucial role.

FOREIGN AID. 1945, June–1950, June: U.S. foreign aid exceeded $28 billion; included in this total were aid under United Nations Relief and Rehabilitation Administration and its successor programs (about $3.5 billion); aid to civilians furnished by the armed services in occupied countries, mainly Germany and Japan ($5.3 billion); surplus property credits and other credits for reconstruction, recovery, and development (over $10 billion, including the British loan of

MAJOR TRADING REGIONS AND COUNTRIES
(in $ million; exports are f.o.b.; imports are c.i.f.)

	1948	1960	1965
U.S.			
Exports	12.5	20.5	27.1
Imports	7.2	15.7	21.3
EEC[a]			
Exports	6.7	29.7	47.9
Imports	10.6	29.6	49.0
EFTA[a]			
Exports	9.6	18.5	26.1
Imports	12.8	23.0	31.8
U.K.			
Exports	6.3	10.2	13.2
Imports	8.1	12.6	15.6
West Germany			
Exports	.8	11.4	17.9
Imports	1.7	10.1	17.5
France			
Exports	2.1	6.8	10.1
Imports	3.5	6.3	10.2
Japan			
Exports	.3	4.1	8.5
Imports	.7	4.5	8.2
USSR			
Exports	n.a.	5.6	8.2
Imports	n.a.	5.6	8.1
Canada			
Exports	3.8	5.6	8.1
Imports	2.6	5.7	8.0

SOURCE: United Nations, *Statistical Yearbook 1966.*
[a] 1948 figures involve countries that would become part of EEC or part of EFTA.

$3.75 billion in 1946); and the European Recovery Program, exclusive of program credits ($7 billion). 1947, 12 Mar.: President Truman appeared before the U.S. Congress and urged that "it must be the policy of the U.S. to support free peoples who are resisting attempted subjugation by armed minorities or outside pressures" —a policy of containment to prevent Communist aggression against non-Communist states (the Truman Doctrine); 15 May: Passage of Greek-Turkish aid program by the U.S. to assure those countries' peaceful development "free from coercion." 5 June: In a speech at Harvard, U.S. Secretary of State George C. Marshall proposed a European Recovery Program, the "Marshall Plan." 17 Dec.: Adoption in U.S. of an emergency Foreign Aid Act. 1948, 3 Apr.: Economic Co-operation Act in U.S. created the Economic Co-operation Administration (ECA) to develop plans for European economic recovery; subsequent to the passage of the act, 16 European nations formed the Organization of European Economic Co-operation (OEEC) to co-operate with the ECA in developing programs to benefit Western Europe. 1949, 20 Jan.: "Point 4 Program": President Truman in his inaugural address declared, "We must embark on a bold new program for making the benefits of our scientific advances and industrial progress available for the improvement and growth of underdeveloped areas" (Point 4 of the speech). 6 Oct.: Mutual Defense Assistance Act authorized the President of the U.S. to grant military assistance in the form of equipment, materials, and services to nations participating in the North Atlantic Treaty Organization. 1950, 5 June: Act for International Development incorporated Truman's Point 4 Program and represented an important shift in American aid programs from Europe to less developed countries. 25 June: Start of Korean War; foreign aid became increasingly an instrument of defense. 1951, 10 Oct.: Mutual Security Act consolidated most of the current U.S. aid programs into 1 mutual security program; the ECA became the Mutual Security Administration (MSA). 1953, 1 Aug.: Establishment in the U.S. of the Foreign Operations Administration to replace MSA and to handle the aid programs. 1955, 30 June: International Co-operation Administration took over the functions of the FOA; the ICA's main thrust was toward technical assistance, although it did allocate certain aid funds. 1961, 13 Mar.: President Kennedy called for an Alliance for Progress, which committed the U.S. to massive social and economic aid to Latin America. 4 Sept.: Act for International Development in the U.S. created a new Agency for International Development (AID) to co-ordinate the U.S. aid programs. U.S. aid programs were the most extensive in the world (1945, 1 July–1966, 31 Dec.: U.S. net foreign aid totaled $106.9 billion). Other industrial countries saw their responsibility to or their political advantage in

foreign aid programs. 1949, 25 Jan.: In response to the establishment of the OEEC, there was—under Soviet influence —the formation of the Council of Mutual Economic Assistance (COMECON); it included the USSR, Poland, Czechoslovakia, Bulgaria, Hungary, and Rumania (East Germany and Albania joined later; 1962: Albania dropped out; Mongolia was added; 1964, Sept.: Yugoslavia was made an affiliate); COMECON sought to assist socialist planning, commerce, and economic development within, and then outside, Eastern Europe. 1961, 30 Sept.: OEEC was officially replaced by the new Organization for Economic Co-operation and Development (the OECD); the members of the OECD included the former members of the OEEC, plus the U.S. and Canada; Yugoslavia and Finland became involved in certain of its activities (1964: Japan became a member); the OECD sought to aid economic growth of its member nations and of less developed countries; within the OECD was the Development Assistance Committee (formed as the Development Assistance Group in 1960 and incorporated into the OECD in 1961); the DAC aimed to co-ordinate and improve bilateral aid programs of its members. 1950's and 1960's: European nations (in Western and Eastern Europe) and Japan were involved in bilateral foreign aid to less developed countries. Foreign aid also went through various multilateral channels. Foreign aid consisted not only of capital exports but of the export of managers, skills, and technological "know-how."

BUSINESS ORGANIZATION. Significant changes in business organization occurred in every industrial nation.

U.S.A.: 1945–68: As business enterprises in the U.S. grew larger, they tended to diversify their activities; late 1950's and 1960's: a new type of American corporate enterprise came into being, the so-called "conglomerate"; a conglomerate was a corporate enterprise with no *major* product line or industrial specialty; no single industry produced over 50% of its revenues; instead, the conglomerate's output might include a range of products, from ships to typewriters. U.S. antitrust legisla-

OFFICIAL BILATERAL TRANSFERS OF LONG-TERM
CAPITAL AND GRANTS FROM INDIVIDUAL
DEVELOPED MARKET ECONOMIES TO
UNDERDEVELOPED COUNTRIES
($ billion)

	1961–65
U.S.	15.211
France	4.074
U.K.	1.925
West Germany	1.728
Japan	.638

BILATERAL COMMITMENTS OF THE USSR TO
DEVELOPING COUNTRIES
($ billion)

	1954–61	1962–65
USSR	2.684	1.416

NET FLOW OF USSR AID
TO 11 LESS DEVELOPED COUNTRIES IN AFRICA,
ASIA, AND LATIN AMERICA AS REPORTED BY
THESE COUNTRIES[a]
($ billion)

	1961–64
USSR	.3597

SOURCE: All 3 tables, United Nations, *Statistical Yearbook 1966.*
[a] Brazil, Burma, Ceylon, Ethiopia, Ghana, India, Indonesia, Pakistan, Somalia, Sudan, United Arab Republic.

tion, which served to bar large enterprises from expanding in the same line through acquisition, initially did not pose an obstacle to the new conglomerate. Likewise, large American corporations became increasingly "multinational"; they expanded their operations worldwide (except in the Communist countries). Many large American corporations became oriented toward research and development to a greater extent than ever before. For the 1st time in U.S. peacetime history, the federal government became a major customer of American business; the U.S. government underwrote a considerable part of the massive investment in research and development by American corporations. As corporations grew in size, diversified their business activities, expanded overseas, entered into new research projects, and developed new relationships with the U.S. government,

significant changes took place in the management of these large enterprises. Management became professionalized. Businessmen increasingly took professional training courses in management methods. During World War II, the field of "operations research," as applied to military logistics, developed; 1950's and 1960's: operations research was used to handle business problems; mathematical and statistical techniques were applied to business analysis. Likewise, during World War II, again related to military needs, new techniques of financial analysis were developed which had peacetime business applications. 1960's: Use of computers by American business created a revolution in data gathering and analysis. Routine clerical tasks, such as payrolls, were easily handled by a computer. Information could be stored in computers and retrieved in seconds; using techniques of linear programming, the computer could solve certain limited business problems; the consequences of other business decisions could be simulated on the computer. American businesses became "systems-oriented"; i.e., they sought to prepare complete, integrated systems of control of production, inventories, finance, marketing, etc. The "systems approach" involved rigorous analysis of "cost-effectiveness," generally utilizing the computer to digest masses of information and often to simulate the consequences of individual decisions.

Western Europe: In Western Europe the changes in business management were different and less dramatic. 1945 ff.: After the war, the occupation forces in Germany sought to break up the giant cartels. I. G. Farbenindustrie—the largest German combine—with interests in 400 cos. in Germany and 500 foreign enterprises, was the key combine under attack; 1952–53: I. G. Farbenindustrie was divided into 3 separate major groups: the Badische Aniline und Soda Fabrik, the Bayer Werke, and the Hoechst Werke; these became Germany's 3 leading chemical cos. In many parts of Europe, government ownership of key enterprises became common. 1950's and 1960's: European business growth tended to involve increases in scale in the *same* industry, although British enterprises undertook some of the diversification that American cos. were experiencing. 1957, 25 Mar.: The Treaty of Rome, establishing the Common Market, contained antitrust provisions, designed to avoid cartelization, but the idea of antitrust did not have deep roots. 1960–68: The tendency in Europe was away from strong antitrust policies. To meet American competition, European business hoped to grow in size and Europeans tended to encourage rather than to discourage mergers. There was a realization throughout Western Europe that the professionalization of American management gave American cos. a competitive advantage in European markets. Within Europe there was a proliferation of management training programs and an awakened concern for the techniques of management; there came to be a recognition that increases in productivity (output per resource input) came not only from technological change but also from effective management. In Britain, especially, the nation's loss of competitive advantage was blamed on poor management. Major British cos. employed American management consultants. On the Continent, Europeans sought to close the "management gap"—the gap between American and European management methods.

Soviet Union: 1945–68: The means of production in the Soviet Union remained government-owned, but there came to be a separation of ownership and management; a managerial group developed, which ran the state-owned enterprises. 1945: The Soviet Union continued to seek central planning of the entire economy. 1950's and 1960's: USSR began to realize that decentralization of decision-making would lead to more efficient use of resources. Late 1950's and 1960's: Still committed to government ownership and to over-all central planning, the Russians began to make concessions to the market system in running state-owned enterprises. They recognized that the use of money was a good measure of performance (and even considered the use of "profits" as a means of measuring the relationship of inputs to outputs). They introduced economic incentives, which related managerial compensations to increases in productivity. They even began to recognize a need for measuring the cost of money. Writers on the Soviet economy began to talk of a "convergence" in business organization between capitalist and socialist systems: both systems had increasing separation of ownership and control; both developed managerial elites; both had enterprises that seemed to require similar talents for administration; by the mid-1960's the USSR had begun to use techniques similar to those used in the U.S. to measure performance; the USSR, however, was far behind the U.S. in developing "professional management" methods. In Eastern Europe, late 1950's and 1960's, Yugoslavia developed a high degree of decentralization in production, investment decisions, and pricing; it led in this respect in Eastern Europe.

Japan: 1945–47: Under the Supreme Commander of the Allied Powers (SCAP) there was the so-called "*zaibatsu*-busting." 83 *zaibatsu* holding companies were dissolved and were required to sell their stock in the individual companies forming the *zaibatsu* to the general public on the open market. Large fortunes of leading families were confiscated by a capital levy. 1947, 10 Dec.: Law to provide for "deconcentration" of 1,200 Japanese companies; it was not implemented. 1948, Dec.: The *zaibatsu*-busting activities of SCAP tapered off. 1950's and 1960's: Re-formation of the *zaibatsu* in Japan, but on a different basis; no longer were there key families owning these huge organizations. Large *zaibatsu* enterprises, linked by interlocking directorates, were highly diversified units, in a wide variety of industries; 1960's: government policy in Japan was to encourage concentration and amalgamation of enterprises and to avoid "undue competition." Yet at the same time, small business in Japan flourished. The ownership of publicly held securities in businesses became widespread. In Japan there was interest in American management techniques and receptivity to American technology; Japanese management did not rigidly follow American management practices; instead, in many important respects, Japan developed distinctive managerial structures. As for American technology, Japan welcomed it and modified it in a creative fashion.

GOVERNMENT POLICY. Economic role of the state: In every industrial nation, the role of government assumed new significance. In market economies (U.S., Western Europe, and Japan), governments utilized monetary and fiscal policies to promote economic development. In the USSR economic planning continued; in Eastern Europe it began. 1945: The Labour Party took office in Britain; the tone was set for government intervention. 1945–46: France prepared its 1st plan for modernization and equipment. 1946, 20 Feb.: Employment Act adopted in the U.S.; it has been called the "Magna Carta of government interventionism"; the act established the Council of Economic Advisers to prepare "national economic policies to foster and promote free competitive enterprise, to avoid economic fluctuation, and to maintain employment, production, and purchasing power." 1946: Netherlands introduced its 1st Central Economic Plan. Russia adopted its 4th 5-Year Plan, seeking to reconstruct war damages and with an emphasis on industrial development. 1947: Monnet Plan (1947–51, extended to 1953), in France, put emphasis on the development of coal mining, electric power, ferrous metals, cement, agricultural machinery, and domestic transportation; this was the start of so-called "indicative" planning in France—i.e., planning where goals were formulated and government aids for achieving these goals were provided, but there was no direct control over private firms. 1947, late, and 1948: Occupation forces in Germany and Japan took steps to rebuild these devastated countries. 1948 ff.: Under the Marshall Plan each participating nation was required to prepare 4-year and annual plans. Eastern Europe, under Russian influence, began to plan after the Soviet model. 1951: 5th Russian 5-Year Plan was for the 1st time concerned with consumer goods. 1955: Introduction of the Vanoni 10-Year Plan

for Italian economic development; 23 Dec.: Japanese cabinet approved a 5-Year Plan for 1956–60. 1956: 6th Russian 5-Year Plan—in fact, a 7-year plan, emphasizing agriculture, housing, and industry. 1961–68: Using fiscal and monetary policies, along with wage-price guidelines, the U.S. government took steps to promote economic growth; President Kennedy's "New Frontier" and President Johnson's "Great Society" programs demonstrated an enlarged government role. 1966: 8th Russian plan, a 5-Year Plan; the plan put new emphasis on decentralization of industry.

Extension of government ownership: 1945: The wave of nationalizations begun in France in 1944 continued. May: Nationalization of Société des Moteurs Gnome et Rhône. June: Provisional nationalization of Air France. Nov. ff.: The French Constituent Assembly formed after the elections undertook to nationalize (1) the Bank of France and the 4 largest credit institutions, (2) gas and electricity, (3) 34 insurance companies (between 50% and 62% of the total insurance activity), and (4) the remainder of the coal-mining industry (May 1946: Charbonnages de France established as a national corporation to administer the nationalized coal industry). 1945, 19 Dec.: Final passage in Britain of the Bank of England Act (effective 1 Mar., 1946, the Bank of England was nationalized); Dec.: British government introduced the Coal Industry Nationalisation Bill (passed in July 1946; 1 Jan., 1947: the new National Coal Board assumed control over the British coal mines). 1946, 17 Apr.: British government announced it intended to introduce legislation to nationalize the steel industry. (Nov. 1948: A Steel Bill was introduced; 24 Nov., 1949: Steel Bill passed; under its provisions the government-owned Iron and Steel Corp. took over 107 major British steel companies.) Nov.: British government introduced measures to nationalize the railroads, highway freight transportation, canals, and London Transport, which were adopted and became effective 1 Jan., 1948. Dec. 1946: British government introduced a bill to nationalize the electrical utility system in its entirety (13 Aug., 1947: passage of the Electricity (Supply) Act, which nationalized the British electrical utility system, effective 1 Apr., 1948). 1948, Mar.: The French nationalized the Paris transport network. 1948: French government reorganized 2 maritime shipping cos. (Compagnie Générale Transatlantique and Compagnie des Messageries Maritimes), keeping the pattern of mixed ownership; new statutes for Air France changed the ownership pattern from 100% state to mixed ownership. The British Parliament passed an act nationalizing the gas industry (effective 1 May, 1949). 1953: Iron and Steel Act in Britain returned the steel industry to private enterprise; under the Tory government long-distance road transport was also denationalized and the publicly owned railroads were reorganized. Establishment in Italy of Ente Nazionale Idrocarburi (ENI) —a government-owned oil co.; ENI's operations under Enrico Mattei (1906–62) came to be broad in scope and to cover atomic energy as well as petroleum and chemicals; the Italian government-owned IRI continued to expand throughout the postwar years. 1962: Electric power industry nationalized in Italy. 1967, 22 Mar.: British Parliament passed the Steel Nationalization Bill; the 14 major producers were nationalized; 200 small firms were left under private ownership; 28 July: British government took over ownership of 90% of the British steelmaking capacity; the 14 major steel cos. were consolidated into the new British Steel Corp., the largest industrial enterprise in Britain.

Status of government ownership: 1968: In France the government was involved in electric power, gas, coal, atomic energy, motor-car production, banking, railroads, airlines, some shipping lines, radio, television, telegraph, telephone, city transport, and tobacco, plus parts of the insurance, aircraft, armaments, and petroleum industries; the French state was a shareholder in some 500 industrial and commercial enterprises. In Britain, the state was involved in banking, electric power, coal, gas, atomic energy, steel, railroads, airlines, radio broadcasting, telephone and telegraph, and part of the television industry; the government had investments in petroleum. In Italy, the government participated in a wide range of industries and owned electric power, railways, and telephones; certain enterprises in Italy were joint ventures between the government and private enterprise. In the Soviet Union, all basic industry, transportation, communications, and banking were government-owned. The Australian government was involved in railroads, airlines, coastal shipping, and electricity supply (the state governments). The German government was not importantly involved in business, with the exception of the railroads, telephones, and some industrial enterprise, the most important being mining. The Japanese government owned the railroads, radio broadcasting, television broadcasting, telephones and telegraph, and the airlines; it was involved in banking; yet basic industry was in the private sector (the

U.S. FEDERAL ADMINISTRATION BUDGET
EXPENDITURES, 1945–66
($ billion)

	Total	National Defense
1945	98.3	81.3
1946	60.3	43.2
1947	38.9	14.4
1948	32.9	11.8
1949	39.5	12.9
1950	39.5	13.0
1951	44.0	22.5
1952	65.3	44.0
1953	74.1	50.4
1954	67.5	47.0
1955	64.4	40.7
1956	66.2	40.7
1957	69.0	43.4
1958	71.4	44.2
1959	80.3	46.5
1960	76.5	45.7
1961	81.5	47.5
1962	87.8	51.1
1963	92.6	52.7
1964	97.7	54.2
1965	96.5	50.2
1966	107.0	57.7

SOURCE: *Economic Report of the President, 1967.*

public sector in Japan was smaller than it had been before World War II). In the U.S. and Canada there was not widespread government ownership; in the U.S., the government, through agencies such as the Atomic Energy Commission and through NASA, was directly involved in business activity. In Canada certain railroads were publicly owned, and there were some other concessions to public ownership in utilities, but here too basic industry remained in the private sector.

Defense spending: In the U.S. especially, but also elsewhere in the industrial world, defense spending represented a substantial portion of government expenditures. U.S. government expenditures provided a spur to industry.

AVERAGE ANNUAL RATE OF GROWTH OF GROSS DOMESTIC PRODUCT[a]
(%)

| | 1950–60 | | 1960–65 | |
	Total	Per Capita	Total	Per Capita
Australia	4.3[b]	2.0[b]	4.7[c]	2.6[c]
Belgium	3.1[b]	2.4[b]	4.9	4.2
Canada	3.9	1.2	5.5	3.6
Denmark	3.2	2.5	4.9	4.1
France	4.5	3.6	5.1	3.7
West Germany	7.9	6.7	4.9	3.6
Italy	5.5[d]	4.8[d]	5.1	4.4
Japan	9.0[b]	6.4[b]	9.6	8.5
Netherlands	4.8	3.4	5.0	3.6
Sweden	3.3	2.6	5.0	4.3
U.K.	2.8	2.4	3.3	2.5
U.S.	3.3	1.5	4.7	3.1

SOURCE: United Nations, *Statistical Yearbook 1966.*
[a] At constant market prices.
[b] 1953–60.
[c] 1960–64.
[d] 1951–60.

The Developing Countries

AGRICULTURE. 1945–68: Although the agricultural sector continued to represent a substantial portion of the gross domestic product in most developing countries, here as in the industrial nations the percentage of agriculture to GDP (with a few exceptions) declined. Argentina, Brazil, Bulgaria, India, Indonesia, Jordan, and Rumania number among the exceptions; in these countries the contribution of agriculture either rose or remained constant.

In less developed countries a large percentage of the population continued to be involved in agriculture, but as industry developed their proportion declined. As population rose in less developed countries, the latter sought to keep food production rising as fast or faster than the population. The record shows that food production had difficulty keeping pace with rising population.

Much of agriculture in the less developed world remained on a subsistence level. Small plots peripheral to the market economy continued in India, Pakistan, and much of tropical Africa. (1954: Estimated 65–75% of the total cultivated land and 60% of the total adult male labor force in tropical Africa were involved in subsistence agriculture; 1968: most Africans still got their livelihood in this way, although the tendency was toward increasing commercialization of agriculture.) In less developed countries peasants intermingled cash crops with

% OF GROSS DOMESTIC PRODUCT AT FACTOR COST OF AGRICULTURE, SELECTED UNDERDEVELOPED COUNTRIES

	1950 1951	1952 1953	1954 1955	1956 1958	1959 1960	1961 1962	1963 1964	1965
Algeria	34				21			
Argentina	14							16
Bolivia					32			23
Brazil	29						29	
Bulgaria		30						34
Burma	40						33	
Cambodia					46	41		
Chile	14							10
China (Mainland) a		59		48				
China (Taiwan)			39					26
Colombia	38							32
Congo (Dem. Rep. of)	37				28			
Costa Rica	44					31		
Ecuador	39							34
Ethiopia						67	65	
Greece	34							25
Honduras	56							44
Hungary	25							20
India	51						51	
Indonesia		54			56			
Iran					34			30
Iraq		22				16		
Jordan					18			25
Kenya			47					38
Korea (Rep. of)			48					41
Lebanon	20			17				
Malawi			55				47	
Malaysia					37	31		
Mexico	22							17
Nigeria	74					65		
Pakistan	58						48	
Peru	23						20	
Philippines	42							34
Poland				25				23
Portugal	33							21
Rumania	28							30
Spain				26				21
Sudan				61			54	
Tanzania				62				55
Thailand					40			33
Turkey	49							36
Uganda				67				59
United Arab Rep.					33	25		
Vietnam (Rep. of)					34			29

SOURCE: United Nations, *Statistical Yearbook 1966.*

a The structural change that took place in Communist China is better demonstrated by figures given in T. C. Liu and K. C. Yeh, *The Economy of the Chinese Mainland*, Princeton, 1965, p. 66. Their figures are: 1952: agriculture represented 47.9% of net domestic product; 1959: agriculture represented 29.9% of net domestic product.

their subsistence crops; this became the tendency in Africa. There were also peasant export economies specializing in cash export crops; for example, in Burma and Thailand (based on rice) and Ghana (based on cocoa). Often when export cash crops replaced subsistence crops, there was a decline in food production

INDEX NUMBERS OF PER CAPITA FOOD PRODUCTION BY REGION
(1958/1959 = 100)

	1955–56	1956–57	1957–58	1958–59	1959–60	1960–61	1961–62	1962–63	1963–64	1964–65	1965–66
Africa	100	102	99	100	101	104	99	102	102	102	97
Latin America	95	99	99	100	98	96	96	95	97	99	95
Asia											
Near East	91	97	98	100	100	98	96	100	100	97	95
Far East[a]	98	100	97	100	103	104	104	103	103	105	101

SOURCE: United Nations, *Statistical Yearbook 1966.*
a Excluding Mainland China.

for domestic consumption. All these 3 types of peasant agriculture created limits on the rise of agricultural output per capita (because there was no change in traditional methods of cultivation). As urban areas and population expanded, and as peasants moved into producing cash crops for export, a number of countries found they could no longer support their food needs; moreover, famines and starvation once accepted in less developed countries were no longer tolerable by modern standards. Thus many less developed countries became importers of foodstuffs. This was true in parts of Africa; India, in times of natural disasters, became a food importer; Mainland China, 1961–62, became a large importer of wheat; because of large estates and inefficient use of land in Chile, that nation, once self-sufficient in foodstuffs, became a regular net importer of food. Plantation agriculture, which *was* efficient, continued to concentrate on export. With the exception of sugar, there were few plantations growing basic foodstuffs (cereals, rice, potatoes, breadfruit, etc.)

Plantations: 1945–68: Decline of plantation agriculture. In some areas large plantations founded in the past persisted, but few new plantations were established. In Central America, United Fruit moved in the direction of purchasing bananas from small indigenous farmers rather than growing them. In South Vietnam, where the French had had large rice plantations, in 1954–58 the South Vietnamese government purchased the plantations. In Indonesia, 1957, the giant Dutch plantations were expropriated. 1947 ff.: The policies of Asian and African governments favored the small

holders. 1959–60: Nationalization of the large American sugar plantations in Cuba.

Scientific agriculture and mechanization: 1945 ff.: Exhaustion of soil through long use of the land accentuated the difficulties of raising agricultural output in less developed countries, especially in East Asia. In Africa improper use of the land through overgrazing, destruction of growths by fire, overcropping, and poor rotation techniques destroyed land resources. In most of the less developed world, there was an attempt to introduce chemical fertilizers, irrigation, and flood control. 1950's and 1960's: In Communist China, new use was made of electric energy in pumping stations to drain farmlands in time of flood and to irrigate in times of drought (1952–65, est. increase in application of electricity in Mainland China for this purpose 43 m. kwh to 2,500 m. kwh). Mechanization of agriculture in most less developed countries proceeded slowly. Granting technical assistance to developing countries were the Food and Agriculture Organization, ECAFE (Economic Commission for Asia and the Far East), the World Bank, and the International Development Corp. (a World Bank affiliate). Likewise, new regional and national development banks provided capital for transforming agriculture.

Agrarian reform: Many less developed countries took steps toward agrarian reform. Land reform followed 2 paths with respect to the size of the unit under cultivation: (1) the breakup of large estates in the hope of getting more land into production and in the interest of "justice" (this included massive redistribution of land) and (2) the consolidation of small plots into large holdings in the hope of making agriculture more efficient. In addition, land reform involved changes in ownership and land tenure toward (1) more widespread ownership of land, (2) eliminating absentee landlords and protecting tenants and small farmers, (3) freeing small holdings from feudal arrangements, (4) collectivization or socialization of ownership, and/or (5) desocialization of agriculture. Such land reforms were endemic in underdeveloped countries, with certain exceptions. (Most of tropical Africa, Laos, and Cambodia represent exceptions; in these areas, small landholdings predominated, and there was as yet no pressure of overpopulation.) 1945: 1st Agrarian Law was passed in Venezuela (1945–48: 1.17 m. acres distributed to 7,000 families); May: Turkish Land Reform granted small plots to peasants (1950, Dec.: About 1.3–1.4 m. acres had been distributed to the peasants under the Land Reform Act in Turkey; nonetheless, many large estates remained). 1945-49: Socialization of agriculture in Eastern Europe after the Communist governments took over. 1947 ff.: Land reform started in India. (1945: 43% of India's cultivated land was under a zamindari-type system; 1956: only 8.5% was under this system. Land-reform laws in India varied from state to state; in general, the tendency was toward more fragmentation in ownership, which was counteracted by government-sponsored co-operatives to supply to peasant farmers credit, fertilizers, marketing assistance, etc.; 1965: 200,000 co-operatives in India.) 1948: Uruguay organized the National Land Settlement Institute; it sought to buy and redistribute land; lack of funds and other difficulties made its success minimal. Oct.: Land Nationalization Act passed in Burma; under it the government obtained title to all land owned by absentee landlords; the land was to be redistributed among the landless peasants. 1949, June: Land Reform Law in South Korea provided for government purchases of land from landlords and redistribution of the land among tenant farmers. 1950: Agrarian reorganization on the Chinese mainland followed the Com-

munist take-over; an agrarian law authorized confiscation from landlords and rich peasants of almost ⅓ of the cultivated land of the country; the land was redistributed to the poorer peasants, confirming the system of private ownership; Oct.: seizure of all privately owned land in North Korea, and distribution of the land to small farmers (title remained in the hands of the government). 1950–54: Experiments were made on the Chinese mainland with mutual-aid teams, which worked to cultivate the land (by 1954, over ½ the farm households in the nation were involved). Land reform in the Philippines undertaken; peasants who renounced the Hukbalahap were granted landholdings by the government. 1952: Agrarian Law in Guatemala made idle farmlands over 667 acres subject to expropriation and distribution to landless farm workers (1954: Revolution in Guatemala slowed the land-reform activities). Sept.: Egyptian Land Reform sought to improve the position of the small farmer and tenant; large landholdings were confiscated. 1952–53: Desocialization of agriculture in Yugoslavia (although Yugoslavia claimed long-run commitment to socialized agriculture). 1953: Law in Formosa expropriated large estates, involving about 71% of the island's land surface; successful land redistribution followed. Sept.: Agrarian Reform Law in Bolivia provided for extensive land redistribution, settlement of new areas, and improvement in tenancy relations; large haciendas (including ¾ of the nation's crop land) were expropriated; these were divided among small farmers (1952: 50,000 landowners in Bolivia; 1956: 800,000). 1954: Consolidation of mutual-aid teams in China into agricultural co-operatives. 1955–57: Small farm co-operatives in China were merged into large collective farms (by 1957 collectives involved almost all the farms in China); in the collective, manpower was organized into production brigades. 1956: Poland and Hungary desocialized agriculture. (Hungary soon reversed the pattern and resocialized agriculture; Poland did not, although the country remained committed in word to socialized agriculture.) 1958: Introduction of the commune in China, a combination of the large collectives, but with broader functions; the commune assumed local government powers, promoted village manufacture, and sought to communalize the life of its members (1958, Oct.: 98% of all peasant households in China were involved in the 26,500 communes) ; the communes entirely eliminated private property. (1958, Dec.–1959, Aug.: The commune in China became a loose federation of collectives; the "brigade"—equivalent in size to the old collective farm—directed economic activity; many pre-commune forms began to reappear.) 1958 ff.: Under Ayub Khan in Pakistan attempts were made at land redistribution. 1959: After Syria joined with Egypt in the United Arab Republic, 1 Feb., 1958, Syria followed the Egyptian pattern of land reform, breaking up the large estates and redistributing land (after Syria broke away from the UAR, Sept. 1961, the land-reform movement still continued). Iraqi Land Reform involved the dissolution of the large landed estates and redistribution of land. Cuban Land Reform Act sought to break up large estates and to expropriate foreign-held land; in Cuba former owners were permitted to retain a minimum amount of property; each peasant family was to receive 66.6 acres; 1959–60: wholesale expropriation of sugar, tobacco, and cattle lands in Cuba; instead of peasants receiving land, they were drafted to work on large cooperative agricultural enterprises. 1960: Venezuela passed Agrarian Reform Law, aiming to improve the pattern of land tenure and rural living conditions. Iran passed a law restricting private landholdings (the actual large-scale land reform was carried out in Iran in 1963). 1961: As a result of the decline in agriculture, Mainland China revised its system; private plots (aggregating about 5% of the collectively owned land) were returned to peasants; in the commune, production brigades owned the land, while at sublevel production teams directed work. Colombia adopted Social Agrarian Reform Law, which established Colombian Agrarian Reform Institute (INCORA);

the aim in Colombia was to redistribute land to small farmers; INCORA could purchase, expropriate, or cancel ownership of land not worked productively for 40 years. Costa Rica approved Land Settlement Law to give permanent title to squatters, legalize occupancy, and settle idle agricultural land. 1962: Chile passed its 1st agrarian reform law; the government was empowered to expropriate and subdivide large holdings. (1963: Constitutional amendment in Chile authorized the government to pay compensation for expropriated land in installments; 1965: new agrarian reform law submitted to Chilean National Assembly; 1967, July: after 2 years of delay, the Chilean Agrarian Reform Bill became law; the act called for the redistribution of about 15 m. acres of previously privately held land.) Dominican Republic adopted Agrarian Reform Law; its aim was to consolidate small private holdings into more efficient operations; the problem in the Dominican Republic was fragmentation of land into postage-stamp plots; the government also began distribution of publicly held land. Honduras enacted an Agrarian Reform Law which authorized expropriation (with compensation) of unproductive land and a progressive land tax to penalize private owners of unused farmland. Mainland China established "the production team" as the "basic accounting unit" in agriculture; ownership of most land continued to be vested in the production brigade; small private plots continued, but were peripheral to the system. 1963: Nicaragua passed a Land Reform Law; it was to create a more desirable pattern of land distribution and tenure. New land-reform measures introduced in the Philippines, protecting tenant farmers. 1964: Brazil amended its federal constitution to accord with the needs of its land-reform program; Brazilian land statute gave the federal government power to expropriate idle or underutilized farmland with compensation in cash for small holdings and in agrarian bonds for latifundia (large estates). Ecuador adopted Agrarian Reform and Colonization Law, which sought to limit landownership to economically productive units and do away with absentee ownership and semifeudal forms of tenancy and labor; the law banned forced labor. Peru enacted Agrarian Reform Law; this eliminated so-called *feudatorios*—tenants, sharecroppers, and laborers who worked under arrangements similar to indentured labor; aim of the law was to increase agricultural output and productivity; land redistribution was planned; large inefficient private holdings were made subject to expropriation. Mainland China created new communes and acted to make the unit under cultivation smaller (1964: 74,000 communes). 1966: Land reform in North Vietnam—with redistribution of land to the peasants. 1966–67: Algeria took steps in the direction of agrarian reform; it nationalized large estates and redistributed land on a collective basis to landless Algerians. 1967, Nov.: South Vietnamese government committed itself to full-scale land reform.

Agricultural progress: 1945–68: Difficulties in the agricultural sector often held back industrialization. Nations that would have preferred to spend foreign exchange on imports of machinery had to spend it on food. Transforming traditional agriculture into efficient modern agriculture was one of the hardest problems faced by developing countries. The pattern was one of commercialization of agriculture.

RAW MATERIALS. Coal: The most dramatic development was that of Communist China's coal resources. 1960: Com-

COAL PRODUCTION OF SELECTED LESS
DEVELOPED COUNTRIES
(million metric tons)

	1948	1960	1965
Mainland China	32.4	420.0	316.0
Poland	70.3	104.4	118.8
India	30.6	52.6	67.2
North Korea	2.1	6.8	14.9
South Korea	.9	5.3	10.2

SOURCE: United Nations, *Statistical Yearbook 1966*, except for 1965 Mainland China figure, which is an estimate in millions of tons given by W. P. Wang, "The Mineral Resource Base of Communist China," *An Economic Profile of Mainland China*, Washington, 1967, p. 174.

munist China led the world in coal production (420 m. metric tons, compared with 392 m. in the U.S. and 374 m. metric tons in the USSR). 1961–65: Decline in Communist Chinese output, so that the nation dropped behind the U.S. and USSR in production; nonetheless Mainland China continued as a 1st-rank coal producer. 1945–68: Coal production in Latin America and in the developing countries in Africa continued to be small.

Oil: 1945–61: Venezuela ranked after the U.S. as the world's 2nd largest oil producer. (In 1961 it became the world's 3rd largest oil producer, following the U.S. and the USSR.) 1945 ff.: Oil reserves of the Middle East were tapped on a large scale. 1950's: Discovery that Africa, once considered to have little or no oil, had huge quantities of oil in Libya, Algeria, and Nigeria, and possibly elsewhere as well. New techniques for finding oil, along with new means of deep drilling and offshore drilling, served to raise oil reserves and output. Oil production in less developed countries was in large part for export.

KEY OIL-PRODUCING COUNTRIES IN
LATIN AMERICA, ASIA, AND AFRICA
(000 metric tons)

	1948	1965
Venezuela	70,215	182,409
Kuwait	6,393	109,045
Saudi Arabia	19,052	101,033
Iran	25,270	93,454
Iraq	3,427	64,473
Libya	—	58,475
Algeria	—	26,481
Indonesia	4,326	23,925

SOURCE: United Nations, *Statistical Yearbook 1966*.

Natural gas: Natural-gas resources in less developed countries were in general not developed for export because of the transportation expense; natural gas was used to improve the output of existing oil wells, but frequently it was flared—that is, burned and wasted because it was not economical to utilize. Yet in oil-producing nations, where there were natural-gas deposits, attempts began to be made to utilize the natural gas locally or to ship it in liquefied form.

Iron ore: The mining of iron ore in certain less developed countries accelerated or began on the basis of new discoveries. In Communist China, India, and Brazil, the iron ore was in large part used domestically, while iron ore in Venezuela and Liberia was in the main for export. 1960's: Iron-ore resources in many African countries were known to exist, and development was beginning.

KEY IRON-ORE-PRODUCING COUNTRIES IN
LATIN AMERICA, ASIA, AND AFRICA
(IRON CONTENT)
(million metric tons)

	1948	1965
Mainland China	n.a.	39.0 (est.) a
India	1.4	14.3
Brazil	1.1	12.3
Venezuela	—	10.8
Liberia	—	10.3

SOURCE: United Nations, *Statistical Yearbook 1966.*
a Economic Commission for Asia and the Far East, *Economic Survey*, New York, 1966, estimated 1965 production at 50 m. tons.

Copper: Copper exports became an important source of revenue for such less developed countries as Chile, Zambia, and the Democratic Republic of the Congo. 1965: The world's largest producers of copper, in order, were the U.S., USSR, Chile, Zambia (formerly Northern Rhodesia) , and the Democratic Republic of the Congo (formerly the Belgian Congo) .

COPPER PRODUCTION
(000 metric tons)

	1948	1965
Chile	567.4	730.6
Zambia	226.5	695.7
Congo (Dem. Rep. of)	155.5	288.6

SOURCE: United Nations, *Statistical Yearbook 1966.*

Bauxite: As aluminum uses grew in industrial nations, there came to be an enlarged demand for bauxite.

KEY BAUXITE PRODUCERS, 1965
(000 metric tons)

World	34,080
Jamaica	8,722
Surinam	4,360
Guyana	4,302

SOURCE: United Nations, *Statistical Yearbook 1966.*

1950's and 1960's: Development of bauxite resources in Africa; the largest enterprises were in Guinea. Ghana's bauxite resources were known, and development had started. Another mineral that provided important export revenues was tin from Malaysia, Bolivia, Thailand, Indonesia, and Nigeria.

Contribution of raw materials to economic development: 1945–68: The coal and iron-ore output of Communist China and India helped their national development. Other less developed countries began to employ their raw-material resources—once primarily for export—for domestic use. Raw materials that were extracted by foreign investors provided valuable sources of income for the Middle Eastern oil-producing nations, for Venezuela, and for Chile. 1948: Petroleum Agreement in Venezuela resulted in the establishment of the concept of a 50–50 division of profits between the producers and the government as a basic principle. 1950's: The 50–50 principle spread to the oil-producing countries in the Middle East. 1950's and 1960's: Less developed countries began to get more than 50% of the profits from oil production. Revenues from oil particularly, but also from other minerals, provided capital for economic development.

ENERGY. 1945 ff.: Many underdeveloped lands still depended on humans and oxen, especially in Asia and Africa. Yet as countries developed, they increasingly utilized modern forms of energy.

Commercial sources of energy: (1) Fossil fuels. Some less developed countries went through the traditional Industrial Revolution pattern, using coal as the primary energy resource. Late 1950's and early 1960's: Coal represented by far the largest portion of primary energy used in Communist China—roughly 66% of the

Consumption of Energy from Commerical Sources in Relation to Total Energy Consumption in Less Developed Regions, 1952

	%
Asia (excl. China, North Korea, and USSR)	42
Africa	50
South America	55
Central America	65

Source: United Nations, *Peaceful Uses of Atomic Energy*, Geneva, 1956.

fuel and power balance of the country (the rest being composed of brushwood, rice husks, dung, and other local noncommercial fuel) ; as for commercial energy in Mainland China, coal supplied over 90%. Other underdeveloped countries, which were producers of oil and natural gas, based their industrial revolutions on these raw materials rather than coal. (2) Use of the internal-combustion engine in less developed countries spread as automobile registrations increased. (3) Output of electrical energy rose rapidly.

Electrical Energy Production by Region (billion kwh)

	1948	1965
World	809.8	3,339.7
Africa	13.4	56.6
South America	17.9	73.2
Asia (excl. Japan)	23.2	132.9

Source: United Nations, *Statistical Year-book 1966.*

1950's and 1960's: Recognition and some development of large hydroelectrical power potential in Asia and Africa. Some sites were, however, so remote that use of the power was not considered. Development of hydroelectric energy involved tremendous capital. When consumers were not present, development was not economical.

Nuclear energy: 1964, Oct.: Communist China exploded its 1st nuclear bomb; this indicated the potentials for harnessing nuclear energy. 1965: India made contracts for its 1st nuclear power station at Tarapur, near Bombay, and had 2 other proposed nuclear power projects; Pakistan made plans for nuclear power stations in Rooppur in East Pakistan and in Karachi in West Pakistan. The Philippines started an Atomic Research Center.

INDUSTRIES. Industrialization spread in Latin America; 1950–65: Latin American industry grew at an average annual rate of 5.6%. 1955–65: Share of light industry in total production in Latin America decreased from 60% to 51%, while that of heavy industry increased from 40% to 49%. Industrialization in Latin America occurred in large part as a result of government policies of import substitution. Often small high-cost industrial plants were built to serve national markets; the high production costs made most of Latin American industry uncompetitive in world markets. In less developed countries in Asia, industrialization took diverse patterns. Countries such

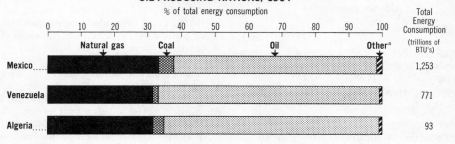

SOURCES OF PRIMARY ENERGY IN SELECTED OIL-PRODUCING NATIONS, 1964

[a]Other-hydroelectric power.
SOURCE: United Nations, *Statistical Yearbook 1964*, and Chase Manhattan Bank, *World Business.*

as India, Mainland China, North Korea, and North Vietnam, where the government role was impressive, emphasized heavy industry—metal and machine building—in order to produce capital equipment to encourage economic growth. On the other hand, Pakistan and China (Taiwan) stressed consumer and intermediate goods; they expected later to move into heavy industry. Malaysia, Singapore, and Hong Kong tended to concentrate on light industry. 1960's: Recognition throughout Asia that nations ought to be self-sufficient in such industries as textiles, steel (in many countries), chemical fertilizers, cement, and petroleum. 1945–68: For developing nations in Asia as a whole there was a shift of emphasis from light to heavy industry; import substitution became the general policy. 1950's and 1960's: Industry in tropical Africa remained rudimentary, though countries began to do more processing of domestic raw materials. Assisted by foreign technical aid and foreign investment, new industries began in tropical Africa. Economists debated whether in their growth less developed countries, which had abundant labor and little capital, should use labor-intensive rather than capital-intensive methods; while economists argued, less developed countries tended in new industries to adopt the most sophisticated technological methods—borrowed from the industrial nations.

Textiles: 1945–68: Most less developed countries had textile industries, ranging from handicraft industries to machine manufacture. Among the less developed countries, Communist China surged ahead in the cotton textile industry. 1965: China had 130,000 automatic looms (compared with 96,000 in Japan and 28,000 in India; the U.S. had 285,000, the USSR 182,000, and Britain 47,000) ; 1960: cotton-yarn production in Communist China (1.6 m. metric tons) was 2nd only to the U.S. (1.8 m. metric tons). Some less developed countries, India, for example, had old-fashioned machinery in their textile industries; the industries were already "mature." Other countries were still seeking self-sufficiency in cotton textiles

(Burma, Ceylon, Indonesia, Cambodia, and Malaysia, for example) . African nations remained large importers of textiles. 1950's and 1960's: A number of less developed countries undertook output of synthetic fabrics (India, Communist China, Brazil, Argentina, for example) .

Steel: Substantial steel industries existed in only a few developing countries.

STEEL PRODUCTION, 1965
(000 metric tons)

Mainland China	15,000a
Poland	9,088
India	6,413
East Germany	3,890b
Spain	3,460
Rumania	3,426
Brazil	2,896c
Hungary	2,520
Mexico	2,403
Yugoslavia	1,769
Argentina	1,360
North Korea	1,230a

SOURCE: United Nations, *Statistical Yearbook 1966.*

a Bureau of Mines estimate; Emery in the *Asian Survey,* June 1966, estimated Communist China's steel production at 10 m. metric tons, while the *Far Eastern Economic Review,* Mar. 31, 1966, p. 623, estimated China's production at 12 m. metric tons.

b Ingots only.

c Excluding alloy steels.

1965: The spread of steel production was evident in that less developed countries with steel production between 500,000 and 1 m. metric tons included Venezuela, Bulgaria, and Turkey; those with production between 500,000 and 200,000 metric tons included Chile, Portugal, China (Taiwan) , Greece, and Colombia; those with production under 200,000 metric tons included Egypt, Rhodesia, Israel, South Korea, Peru, Pakistan, Uruguay, and Thailand. Other nations starting new steel industries were Burma, Ceylon, Indonesia, Malaysia, the Philippines, and Iran. 1965: Communist China began to produce steel tubing for oil-drilling equipment, high-silicon steel rails, and alloy-steel plates for making chemical fertilizer and power generation equipment. Machine tool and equipment industries developed in countries that had steel industries.

Automobiles: Late 1950's: 1st automobile manufacturing in Latin America; 1968: Brazil, Argentina, and Mexico had significant automobile manufacturing industries. India had some motor vehicle production (not on a large scale).

Petroleum refining: 1945–68: Less developed countries with oil production built petroleum refineries; this was not new; the key innovation was the proliferation of refineries based on imported crude oil. New refineries were built in India, China (Taiwan), South Korea, Malaysia, Pakistan, the Philippines, Singapore, Thailand, Rhodesia, Kenya, and Senegal, for example.

Chemicals: In Latin America and Asia, chemical industries developed. Synthetic fabrics, chemical fertilizer plants, heavy chemicals, and pharmaceuticals were among the new industries of the 1950's and 1960's. 1960's: Petrochemical complexes designed to utilize the by-products of petroleum refineries and to use otherwise wasted natural gas were developed in many less developed countries.

Electrical and electronics industries: Electrical-equipment industries proliferated. New activities started in Communist China, India, Brazil, Argentina, Mexico, and Chile. 1960's: Communist China had 2 large facilities to build electrical equipment, 1 in Manchuria (started by the Japanese in the 1930's and, 1953–60, expanded with aid from the USSR) and 1 near Shanghai (1952–55, built with Czech technical aid). In Hong Kong, China (Taiwan), the Philippines, and South Korea, electronics industries developed, turning out TV, radio, and phonograph components and sets, electronic memory units, semiconductors, and other products of the electronics industry. 1965: Reports from Communist China indicated that that nation was building large electronic microscopes and high-speed electronic digital computers.

Other industries: Processing of locally produced minerals in many less developed countries increased. 1956: Opening in Guinea of the 1st alumina plant in Africa (based on locally available bauxite). 1965, Aug.: Opening in Thailand of that country's 1st tin smelter (although the nation had been a tin producer for centuries). New industries in Latin America, Asia, and Africa included, in many countries, cement, paper, and glass enterprises; the countries which had these industries before World War II expanded such industrial activities.

TRANSPORTATION. 1950's and 1960's: Less developed countries pre-

FREIGHT RAILROAD TRAFFIC
(billion net ton-kilo.)

	1948	1965
World	1,804	3,972
Africa (excl. South Africa)	14	31
South America	26	40
Asia (excl. USSR and Japan)	52	377

SOURCE: United Nations, *Statistical Yearbook 1966*.

sented the paradox of using traditional means of transportation (human carriage, animals, etc.) but also the airplane. In practically every less developed country transportation facilities continued to be inadequate. Railroad traffic rose, but with few exceptions (Mainland China and certain African nations) there was little building of new track. Mainland China did build railroad lines into west China, seeking to unify the country; 1966: the entire railroad system of Communist China covered 22,000 miles. India modernized its railroads and made small extensions; India's railway system—the 4th in size in the world after the U.S., USSR, and Canada—equaled (1963–64) 34,500 mi.

Road and highway construction proceeded, though slowly. 1959, Mar.: Plans made and approved by the Economic Commission for Asia and the Far East for an Asian Highway. 1963, 16 Apr.: Pan-American Highway in Central America completed; the highway was at this point passable from Argentina (Tierra del Fuego) to Alaska (Fairbanks) except for a 450-mi. stretch in eastern Panama. For the transportation of oil, oil companies built pipe lines in less developed countries. Water transportation remained important in some nations, especially in Mainland China, where the length of inland waterways suitable for navigation was more than 55,000 mi. (compared with 5,000 mi. in India). 1945–68: Development of port facilities in West Africa and harbor improvements in East Africa.

MOTOR VEHICLES IN USE
(000 units)

	1948	1965
World		
Passenger cars	42,970	139,730
Comm. vehicles	13,050	37,600
Africa (excl. South Africa)		
Passenger cars	226	1,303
Comm. vehicles	176	609
South America		
Passenger cars	650	2,750
Comm. vehicles	520	2,160
Asia (excl. USSR, Japan, Mainland China, North Korea, and North Vietnam)		
Passenger cars	345	1,082
Comm. vehicles	313	1,243

Air travel: The true revolution was in air travel. Most less developed countries had airports, served by the international airlines; many less developed countries started their own airlines. 1960's: An expression of sovereignty in Africa was to have a national airline. The new accessibility of the less developed world, made possible by the jet airplane, was of vast importance in the process of economic development. The knowledge of the industrial world became more readily available in the developing nations.

COMMUNICATIONS. Not only the jet airplane but the appearance in less developed countries of movies, radios, and television demonstrated events in the outside world. Radios—especially after the introduction of the low-priced transistor set—gave illiterate peoples insights that the printed page could not give. 1950's: Introduction of television in major Latin American nations and to some extent in Asia. 1960's: From Congo (Brazzaville) to Ethiopia, from Gabon to Ghana, from Kenya to Liberia, from Malaysia to Indonesia, and from Pakistan to Saudi Arabia, television spread. Such channels of communications gave millions of people access to modern ideas, which contributed to the breaking down of the traditional order.

FINANCE. 1945–68: Among the key innovations was the availability of large amounts of capital to less developed countries for the purpose of economic development. Capital came through bilateral foreign aid programs, through international agencies, and through private foreign investment; by using their power to tax, governments could obtain significant revenues for development—especially governments in the oil-producing states, which put levies on the foreign oil producers. While rich individuals in poor countries built palaces and bought luxuries or dispatched their money abroad for deposit in Swiss banks, increasingly more effective efforts were made by the governments of less developed states to channel the newly available capital into use for development. Capital from foreign sources and from taxing foreign enterprises domiciled within less developed countries opened possibilities to the governments of those nations for planning and organizing their national development. Marketing Boards in Africa were often used to accumulate profits which could be put back into development schemes. 1960's: $\frac{4}{5}$ of the investments being made in less developed countries came from the resources of those countries; the $\frac{1}{5}$ from abroad, however, provided a necessary aid.

Banking: 1945–68: More banking facilities became available in less developed countries—some of them domestic and some foreign. Central banking and development banking institutions emerged. Banks were established to offer agricultural credits. Attempts were made to start savings banks, but in many less developed countries inflationary pressures militated against them. In West Africa traders who accumulated savings frequently did not deposit them in banks for fear of demonstrating their wealth to relatives, who would expect a share.

International banking institutions: 1945–68: Less developed countries could use international banking institutions to aid their economic development. **1959 ff.:** Regional banking facilities were created to meet the needs of developing countries. **1958:** Establishment of the European Development Fund to aid the dependencies of European states associated with the European Economic Community. **1959, Dec.:** Establishment of the Inter-American Development Bank, to aid in financing development in Latin America; all members of the Organization of American States subscribed (1 Oct., 1960: the Bank started operations; 1961, 1st loans were made by the Inter-American Development Bank). **1960, 13 Dec.:** The treaty establishing the Central American Common Market provided for the organization of a Central American Bank for Economic Integration to promote growth within the region. **1964, 1 Jan.:** International Bank for Economic Co-operation started operations in Eastern Europe; it was modeled on the European Payments Union; **Aug.:** the African Development Bank came into existence (1 July, 1966: the African Development Bank started to do business from its headquarters in Abidjan, Ivory Coast); the capital of the African Development Bank was subscribed by some 31 African governments. **1965, 4 Dec.:** Agreement signed in Manila under the auspices of the Economic Commission for Asian Development Bank. **1966, 22 Aug.:** Asian Development Bank officially came into existence. **24–26 Nov.:** Inaugural meeting of the Asian Development Bank held in Tokyo; member countries at this time totaled 30 (18 within and 12 outside Asia); **19 Dec.:** the Bank officially started operations. **1967, 6 June:** The Kampala Treaty included provisions for an East African Development Bank. **Oct.:** Arab economic ministers meeting in Algiers approved the text of an agreement establishing an Arab Development Fund.

Interest rates: For moneys locally available, interest rates in less developed countries tended to be high. Where inflation existed, such as in most of Latin America, exorbitant interest rates held back development. In many countries—especially in Asia and Africa and to a lesser extent Latin America—there existed a financial dualism; on the one hand there were the new modern banking institutions serving the modern sector of the economy, and on the other hand the rural economy still had the old moneylenders who practiced usury. Peasants borrowed from local lenders (village moneylenders, landlords, shopkeepers, etc.) at steep interest rates.

Stock exchanges: Throughout Latin America—in Argentina, Brazil, Chile, Mexico, and Venezuela, for example—large cities had stock exchanges. The number of securities traded rose; yet the volume was small compared with industrial nations. **1956:** Securities (Contracts) Regulation Act in India recognized 7 Indian stock exchanges and was India's 1st attempt since independence to control stock-exchange activities. Stock exchanges that emerged in less developed countries served the same function as they had in the key industrial nations. Major development of stock-market activities in less developed countries was, however, for the most part still in the future.

FOREIGN TRADE. 1948–65: Foreign trade of less developed countries grew, but on the whole the growth did not keep pace with the expansion of world trade, which rose over 3-fold.

Exports: 1945–68: Underdeveloped countries depended as in the past on exports of primary commodities. Some of their exports were challenged by synthetics during World War II. In many uses synthetic rubber replaced natural rubber; synthetic preparations substituted for cotton; paper bags were used instead of jute. Synthetic nitrates (perfected during World War I) almost completely replaced natural nitrates; chicle was no longer required in chewing gum; synthetics took the place of the castor bean in castor oil. Thus countries that had exported these raw materials had to substitute other exports, if possible. Likewise, as industrial nations grew more prosperous, the amount of money they spent on food did not rise as fast as incomes; thus the relative demand for foodstuffs was less. On the other

WORLD TRADE BY REGIONS AND COUNTRIES
($ million; imports are c.i.f.;
exports are f.o.b.)

	1948	1960	1965
World			
Exports	57,500	128,000	186,300
Imports	63,600	135,300	196,800
Latin America			
Exports	6,520	8,560	11,100
Imports	6,180	8,350	9,600
Africa (excl. South Africa)			
Exports	3,030	5,240	7,680
Imports	3,600	6,480	7,860
Asia (excl. Japan and Mainland China)			
Exports	6,490	11,930	15,810
Imports	7,390	13,060	17,240
Mainland China, North Korea, North Vietnam, Mongolia[a]			
Exports	520	2,040	2,000
Imports	740	2,200	2,200

SOURCE: United Nations, *Statistical Year-book 1966*.

[a] Excluding the trade among these Communist countries.

hand, certain raw-material exports were important expanding sources of revenue. In general, however, underdeveloped countries found that what they could buy with a given amount of exports of primary commodities became less; that is, the terms of trade were going against them. (This was not true for every underdeveloped country, nor was it true for all years; in some years the terms of trade shifted in favor of less developed countries; but the generalization is valid for the whole period 1945–68.) In Latin America and Africa, underdeveloped countries had little success in exporting manufactured products. On the other hand, in Asia, certain less developed countries did undertake substantial exports of labor-intensive manufactured goods.

MANUFACTURED EXPORTS AS % OF TOTAL EXPORTS IN SELECTED ASIAN COUNTRIES, 1964

Republic of Korea	46.6
India	42.8
China (Taiwan)	32.0
Pakistan	24.5

SOURCE: United Nations, *Economic Survey of Asia and the Far East*, Bangkok, 1966, p. 190.

In the main, however, underdeveloped countries remained exporters of primary commodities and importers of manufactured articles. Prices of commodity exports fluctuated in world markets and underdeveloped countries sought means of controlling the price and promoting more exports. They entered into international commodity agreements; 1962: UN Conference on Trade and Development (UNCTAD) was organized at the insistence of less developed nations; it considered the problems facing exporters of primary products. Many countries on their own established government export cos. or marketing boards, which sought to promote exports and stabilize the price of the exported commodities. (Examples: 1946, 28 May: Establishment in Argentina of the Instituto Argentino de Promocion del Intercambio—IAPI; 1945 ff.: establishment of Marketing Boards or *caisses de stabilisation* to control marketing of cocoa in Ghana and Nigeria; coffee in Ivory Coast, Uganda, and Kenya; cotton in Nigeria and Uganda; peanuts in Nigeria and Senegal, etc. 1961: Foreign trade became a government monopoly in Egypt.)

Imports: Less developed countries tried to increase exports in order to obtain foreign exchange to buy goods from abroad; as they industrialized, the manufactured goods that they imported showed a definite shift from consumer to producer goods. Often less developed countries maintained barriers against imports to encourage local industry; most protected their indigenous industries with high tariffs. Less developed countries typically had restrictions on imports, including licensing, limitations on the allocation of foreign exchange, multiple exchange rates, and even prohibitions on some imports. 1960's: A few less developed countries had state-owned trading cos., which carried out the major part of the import trade. 1966: Algeria had a number of government-owned units, which had monopolies over imports. The Guinean state enterprise handled a large part of that nation's imports. Imports of jute, sugar, tea, olive oil, and certain medicines were a government monopoly in Iraq, while imports of sugar, salt, tobacco, cigars, and cigarette papers were a government monopoly in Libya. The Ghanaian National Trading Corporation handled much of that nation's import trade. The lowering of restrictions on foreign trade so typical of the industrial nations in the postwar years was less characteristic of the underdeveloped countries, where trade restraints remained the norm. Each nation wanted to protect its own industry and aid its *own* development.

Regional integration: Some attempts were made toward regional integration, but these were on the whole not as successful as the EEC. Latin America: 1960, 18 Feb.: Treaty of Montevideo signed by Argentina, Brazil, Chile, Mexico, Paraguay, Peru, and Uruguay; it established the Latin American Free Trade Association (LAFTA); the treaty took effect 2 June, 1961; 30 Sept., 1961: Colombia joined; 3 Nov., 1961: Ecuador joined; 1966: Venezuela, 11 July, and Bolivia, 12 Dec., joined; the goal of LAFTA was to eliminate internal trade barriers by 1973; 1960–65: trade within the LAFTA countries increased by 86%. 1960, 13 Dec.: General Treaty on Central American Economic Integration, signed at Managua, Nicaragua, by Nicaragua, El Salvador, Guatemala, and Honduras (took effect June 1961); July 1962: Costa Rica accepted the treaty provisions and joined the Central American Common Market; the Central American Common Market showed quick results; 1960–65: trade within the market increased more than 300%. 1966: Establishment of the Andean Group, a subregional group, comprising Chile, Colombia, Ecuador, Peru, and Venezuela (Bolivia joined in 1967). This group of countries, which were also in LAFTA, proposed a customs union and free transit within their region. 1967, 11–13 Apr.: U.S. President Lyndon B. Johnson visited Punta del Este, Uruguay, and met with the Latin American presidents; new plans were made for a Latin American Common Market, with the goal of free internal trade by 1985; under the new plans the 11-nation Latin American Free Trade Association and the 5-nation

Central American Common Market would be merged. Africa: Colonial policy gave a kind of regional integration; there were no tariff barriers between French colonies or between British colonies. Integration, however, was based on the territories of the mother country; French Africa used the franc; British Africa used sterling. Trade between French and British Africa was negligible. Before independence there were some efforts at increased integration; independence meant national policies; some new tariff barriers rose; border crossings became complicated by red tape; coins and bank notes bore new national designations. Yet after independence there were renewed efforts at regional integration, which were challenged by nationalist disintegration, and then once more new attempts were made at integration. The key attempts at economic integration were: 1953–63: the Federation of Rhodesia and Nyasaland provided economic as well as political unity. 1959: 2 customs unions were formed: (1) The Conseil de L'Entente, involving the Ivory Coast, Upper Volta, Niger, and Dahomey (Togo joined in 1964); this customs union was never implemented; and (2) the Union Douanière Économique d'Afrique Équatoriale, involving Congo (Brazzaville), Gabon, Central African Republic, and Chad (1962: Cameroon was also included). 1960, 26 Dec.: Ghana, Guinea, and Mali agreed to coordinate their economic and monetary policies; later Upper Volta endorsed the agreement (this attempt at economic integration failed). 1961, Dec.: East African Common Services Organization united Kenya, Uganda, and Tanganika in a *de facto* common market. 1963, 20 July: Yaounde Convention was signed by 17 independent African states—Burundi, Cameroon, Central African Republic, Chad, Congo (Brazzaville), Congo (Léopoldville), Dahomey, Gabon, Ivory Coast, Mali, Mauritania, Niger, Rwanda, Senegal, Somalia, Togo, and Upper Volta—and Madagascar; the group became associated with the European Economic Community for 5 years (the convention became operative 1 June, 1964). 31 Dec.: The breakup of the Federation of Rhodesia and Nyasaland left intact the regional economic integration among the 3 countries, which was only shattered by the 1965 Unilateral Declaration of Independence from Britain by Rhodesia. 1964, Dec.: The Treaty of Brazzaville authorized an economic union, comprising Congo (Brazzaville), Gabon, Central African Republic, Chad, and Cameroon —nations already in the Union Douanière Économique d'Afrique Équatoriale. 1966, 1 Jan.: Inauguration of the Central African Customs and Economic Union, as authorized by the Brazzaville Treaty. 4 May: 8 East African countries—Burundi, Ethiopia, Kenya, Malawi, Mauritius, Tanzania, Uganda, and Zambia—signed a cooperation agreement as a transition until an East African Economic Community could be created. 3 June: Treaty signed in Abidjan, Ivory Coast, establishing a customs union for West Africa. 15 Dec.: The Abidjan Treaty went into force; included in the new West African Customs Union were Ivory Coast, Upper Volta, Niger, Dahomey, Mauritania, and Senegal; the treaty provided for a common external tariff and discriminatory duties against goods coming from outside the French franc area and the European Economic Community; this superseded the Conseil de L'Entente. 1967, 6 June: Kenya, Tanzania, and Uganda signed a treaty in Kampala, which established an East African Economic Community and Common Market. 1 Dec.: The Kampala Treaty came into effect; it provided for the strengthening of existing common-market ties among the East African nations and the transfer of the headquarters of the East African Common Services Organization from Nairobi, Kenya, to Arusha, Tanzania. Kenya, Tanzania, and Uganda planned to establish a common customs tariff against imports into East Africa; the treaty guaranteed freedom of transit of goods across the national borders within the common market. Middle East: 1964, Apr.: Agreement reached to establish an Arab Common Market (effective 1 Jan., 1965); agreement was signed by Iraq, Jordan, Syria, and the UAR.

FOREIGN INVESTMENT. Less developed countries continued to be recipients of private foreign capital.

NET FLOW OF PRIVATE LONG-TERM CAPITAL FROM DEVELOPED MARKET ECONOMIES TO NEWLY DEVELOPING COUNTRIES, 1956–65 ($ million)

	OECD Estimate	UN Estimate[a]
1956	$2,578	
1957	3,230	
1958	2,717	
1959	2,435	
1960	2,580	
1961	2,593	2,362
1962	1,914	1,600
1963	1,872	1,808
1964		2,009
1965		2,703

SOURCE: Organization for Economic Cooperation and Development, *The Flow of Financial Resources to Less-Developed Countries, 1956–1963*, Paris, 1964, p. 19, and United Nations, *Statistical Yearbook 1966*.

[a] The UN estimates are lower because the UN excludes the flow of resources to Cyprus, Greece, Malta, Spain, Turkey, and Yugoslavia which are included by the OECD. Other adjustments are also made, which add to the discrepancy between OECD and UN estimates.

The flow of private foreign capital to these nations seemed inadequate to supply their needs. The flow was not greater because of the uncertainties of investment in less developed areas and because of the more promising investment possibilities in developed countries. 1945–68: Most less developed countries (except the Communist nations, which expropriated foreign holdings) viewed private foreign investors with mixed feelings. On the one hand, they feared and resented the presence of foreign investment, because (1) it might interfere with national sovereignty (impede national planning, thwart national defense, exercise undue power); (2) aliens pocketed the profits; (3) other benefits—payments of certain wages and salaries, payments for patents, payments for equipment, etc.—went to foreigners; (4) the enterprise might be more in the interest of the investor than the nation where the investment was made; (5) it might destroy local business that could not compete with giant foreign units; (6) it might discourage entrepreneurship, since foreigners took advantage of the opportunities; and (7) it might create new desires for goods that less developed countries did not have and that if obtained would result in a drain of the nation's foreign exchange. Thus, some non-Communist countries attempted to rid themselves of certain existing foreign investments; for example: 1946: Argentine government purchased the assets of the foreign-owned telephone system; 1948: Argentina completed its purchase of the British-owned railroads. 1951, 15 Mar.: Iran nationalized the Anglo-Iranian Oil Co. (1954, Aug., a settlement was reached which allowed foreigners to develop the Iranian oil fields). 1952, 31 Oct.: Bolivian government nationalized the 3 largest tin-mining enterprises (foreign and domestic capital had been intermingled in these ventures). 1956, 26 July: Egypt nationalized the Universal Co. of the Suez Maritime Canal, owned in large part by the British government and French private stockholders (in time, they were reimbursed). 1957, Dec.: Indonesian government took over some 400 agricultural estates as well as a number of banks, industrial firms, and transportation lines owned by Dutch investors. 1958 ff.: A number of countries in Latin America acquired the properties of the foreign utilities there. 1962, 27 Apr.: Ceylon nationalized 83 gasoline stations and other oil facilities owned by 2 American cos. Other countries barred new foreign investment in certain sectors, for example, in oil distribution, refining, and production, in petrochemicals, and in industries whose products were facing stern competition. India, for example, banned foreign investors from industries "reserved as a State responsibility." 1965: Foreign investment in the form of direct equity participation was not allowed in Burma and Indonesia (but with the fall of Sukarno, the situation changed in Indonesia; 1967: Indonesia again desired to attract foreign investment). On the other hand, less developed countries often

greatly desired foreign investors because (1) the latter provided needed capital frequently unavailable elsewhere; (2) they provided required skills, patents, and equipment, plus the knowledge of the functioning of an industrial economy; the last was essential, for projects undertaken by foreign investors were likely to be well formulated and implemented; (3) they could be taxed, and would provide an excellent source of government revenues; (4) by developing natural resources, they gave poor countries the opportunity to earn foreign exchange; (5) they provided employment; (6) they often served not to discourage other industries but, quite the opposite, to stimulate ancillary industrial activities. 1960's: Less developed countries often indicated that they desired certain types of foreign investment and not others. Likewise, as the bargaining power of less developed nations rose, these nations often stipulated as a condition of doing business that the foreign investor make a marked contribution to their economies. In turn, less developed nations actually provided a range of incentives to encourage foreign investors. Such incentives included tax relief, aid in providing overhead facilities, protection from competition, exemptions from duties on capital goods required for the establishment of a plant, and release from payment of duties on certain raw-material imports (if the raw materials were not available locally).

FOREIGN AID. Less developed countries were recipients of foreign aid from industrial nations and international agencies. Foreign aid provided capital for projects that could not otherwise have been undertaken. Technical assistance was an added type of foreign aid, which offered less developed countries skills that they lacked. Foreign aid did not present conflicts for less developed countries that private foreign investment created, although bilateral aid was often considered as politically motivated and created other conflicts. A few less developed countries had their own foreign-aid programs. 1954–65: According to UN statistics, Communist China committed the equiva-

NET OFFICIAL FLOW OF CAPITAL FROM DEVELOPED MARKET ECONOMIES
AND MULTILATERAL AGENCIES TO DEVELOPING COUNTRIES, 1961–65
($ million)

	Bilateral	Multilateral	Total
1961	4,595	224	4,919
1962	4,963	415	5,378
1963	5,272	639	5,911
1964	5,186	725	5,911
1965	5,449	730	6,179

SOURCE: United Nations, *Statistical Yearbook 1966.*

lent of $835 m. to foreign aid. Underdeveloped countries in Eastern Europe— Poland, Hungary, Rumania, and Bulgaria —had small foreign-aid programs. 1960's: Arab oil-producing nations, such as Kuwait, considered foreign-aid programs.

BUSINESS ORGANIZATION. 1945– 68: Key trends involved: (1) More participation by the state in business activities. In less developed countries in Eastern Europe and in Communist China, North Vietnam, and North Korea, all business enterprises came to be owned and operated by the state. In many non-Communist countries governments owned large enterprises. (2) More participation by local entrepreneurs in the modern sector. In Latin America, where the state played a substantial role, private enterprise also flourished. Small businesses run by individuals, families, or partnerships still prevailed in Latin America, yet at the same time many Latin American entrepreneurs managed modern corporations. Large industrial empires existed in Argentina, Brazil, and Mexico, created by entrepreneurs of Italian origin. In Medellín, in Colombia, modern enterprises, run by Colombians, prospered. A substantial middle class was developing in Latin America to provide a basis for the modern business. In Hong Kong, Malaysia, and Singapore, private enterprise prevailed; increasingly, entrepreneurs— many of them Chinese—took part in the modern sector of the economy. In Africa, entrepreneurship was in evidence, although in the growth of modern business enterprises, tropical Africa was far behind Latin America and even far behind most of Asia. In much of Asia and Africa the traditional producing unit, made up of individuals, bound by ties of kinship,

religion, and social status, was challenged by the emergence of modern business enterprise. Widespread use of money in Asia and Africa provided the basis for the growth of business enterprise. (3) Decline of the "managing agent" in India. 1954: Of the total productive assets of companies in India, the Federation of Indian Chamber of Commerce and Industry estimated that nearly 80% were managed by managing agents. 1956: Indian Cos. Act restricted operations of the managing agent. 1956–68: Less use of the managing agent form in India. To some extent, new "management contracts" between Indian enterprises and foreign firms represented an adaptation of the old form. (4) 1950's and 1960's: When large foreign enterprises existed, they often tried to encourage local businesses, providing jobs to local contractors, buying when possible from local suppliers, and utilizing and stimulating local service industries. (5) In many less developed countries new enterprises combined private and public, domestic and foreign capital. There were enterprises that were entirely domestic, which combined government and private funds; there were enterprises that involved co-operation between public-sector cos. and foreign investors; there were enterprises that involved private-sector cos. or individuals and foreign investors. The extent of these combinations was new in less developed countries. (6) Late 1950's and 1960's: In Eastern Europe, there was a marked decentralization of decision-making in state enterprises. 1957 ff.: Mainland China, following the Soviet model, began to decentralize its economic planning; this was not fully implemented. 1961: After the failure of the "Great Leap," indications were that decentralization plans had been abandoned. 1960's: In most non-Communist less developed countries, successful government enterprises seemed to have developed considerable independence from centralized direction. (7) As modern businesses took form in less developed countries, managerial talent was required. 1950's and 1960's: An attempt was made by industrial nations to aid in establishing business schools and training programs in less developed lands. Moreover, literally thousands of students—financed by their governments, by foreign grants, or by foreign companies—went to industrial countries to learn business methods. Managerial contacts served to communicate business methods. There was an injection of western business procedures throughout the world.

GOVERNMENT POLICY. 1945–68: Independent governments of less developed countries accepted the goal of rapid industrialization; they insisted it would not do for their countries to remain producers of primary products and importers of manufactured goods; the commitment to manufacture became general, in Communist and non-Communist developing countries, in former colonial states and long-independent countries. Industrial countries were seen as world leaders; governments of less developed countries wanted to follow the same path. A few governments—such as that of Mainland China—went to the extreme of seeking economic self-sufficiency. Economic nationalism became a key to many governments' policies. In most less developed countries, governments assumed leadership in planning the growth of industry. Development plans were characteristic of less developed countries. Some plans were partial, some were general, but all involved governments in actively promoting economic growth. Some of the early plans were developed by colonial governments in the colonies or in London, Paris, or Brussels; these were designed to encourage economic growth, but did not generally seek to sponsor industrialization; some were influenced by colonial powers; by the 1960's, development plans were prepared by national governments and were practically all devoted to industrialization; as the 1960's progressed, however, planners recognized that effective industrialization also involved planning improvements in agriculture.

Aids to agriculture: Most government plans recognized a need for government aid to agriculture. Aid took the form of assistance in providing chemical fertilizers, irrigation, flood control, and technical advice. Aid occasionally involved rural electrification. The initiation of land reform was designed in part to assist agricultural output (although this was not always the reason for it or the effect of it).

Government-sponsored co-operatives: Governments participated in marketing boards and export cos. which it was hoped would assist agriculture (but did not always do so). Governments were involved in extending agricultural credits. They also took part in negotiations for international commodity agreements which provided aid to agriculture.

Aids to industry: Governments of less developed countries offered aid to domestic industries through such measures as (1) allocation of investment funds; (2) protective tariffs; (3) import quotas and exchange controls, which barred competitive products; (4) outright prohibition of the entry of competitive goods; (5) providing foreign exchange for cos. to import needed (but not locally available) raw materials and machinery; (6) a favorable (often a special) rate of exchange for imports of required raw materials and machinery; (7) exemptions from certain taxes, or tax concessions of various types (including good depreciation allowances); (8) promises to foreign investors that they could transfer their capital and their earnings freely; (9) subsidies to industries that exported; (10) establishment of industrial estates with power, water, transportation, and other facilities; and (11) rarely, monopoly privileges or assurances that no other cos. in the same industry would be allowed to enter the market. In Communist countries, and some non-Communist countries, aids to industry involved allocations of funds to those industries desired under the development plans.

INITIATION OF ECONOMIC DEVELOPMENT PLANS BY DEVELOPING COUNTRIES, 1945–66

1945   Ecuador; British Colonial Development and Welfare Act, leading to development plans for Barbados, Basutoland, British Guiana, British Honduras, Cyprus, Dominica, Gold Coast, Grenada, Jamaica, Leeward Islands, Nigeria, Northern Rhodesia, Nyasaland, St. Kitts-Nevis-Anguilla, St. Helena, St. Lucia, St. Vincent, Seychelles, Sierra Leone, Tanganyika, Uganda

1946   Angola, Argentina, Poland, Sudan; French Plan Pleven for development of French colonies

1947   Bulgaria, Ceylon, Czechoslovakia, French Cameroons, Greece, Philippines, Yugoslavia

1948   Burma, East Germany, Iran, Swaziland; all countries of the French Union

1949   Belgian Congo, Ruanda-Urundi

1950   Colombo Plan, affecting Ceylon, India, Malaya, North Borneo, Pakistan, Sarawak, Singapore

1951   Albania, Antigua, Iraq, Liberia, Macao

1952   Aden, French Guinea, India

1953   Brunei, Capo Verde, Mainland China, Mozambique, North Vietnam, Portuguese Guinea, Republic of China (Taiwan), Timor

1954   Italian Somaliland, Jordan, Kenya, North Korea, Surinam

1955   Guatemala, Pakistan, Syria

1956   Afghanistan, Bechuanaland Protectorate, Cambodia, India, Indonesia, Malta

1957   Ethiopia, South Vietnam

1958   Mainland China

1959   Chad, Iceland, Laos

1960   Chile, Colombia, Guinea, South Korea, United Arab Republic, Venezuela

1961   Bhutan, Cameroon, Congo (Brazzaville), El Salvador, Fiji, India, Mali, Nicaragua, Niger, Senegal, Thailand

1962   Bolivia, Dahomey, Honduras, Lebanon, Mexico, Turkey

1963   Bermuda, Brazil, Congo (Léopoldville), Costa Rica, Federation of South Arabia, Gabon, Haiti, Israel, Libya, Panama, South Africa, Turkey, Upper Volta

1964   Canary Islands, Gambia, South Africa, Spain

1965   Kuwait, Malawi, Uruguay, Zambia

1966   Cameroon, India, Togo, Zambia

Aid to other sectors: Less developed countries were concerned about the development of transportation and port facilities, public utilities, and education. Such activities were in large part undertaken by government bodies. Governments sought out funds from development banks to apply to such infrastructure investments.

Direct participation: 1945–68: Governments of less developed countries generally participated directly in economic development. In Communist nations (in Eastern Europe, Mainland China, North Vietnam, North Korea, Mongolia, and, after 1960, Cuba), government ownership became the rule. Government ownership of large enterprises also became widespread in Latin America. 1966: Chilean government for the 1st time participated directly in the copper industry. 1960's: In non-Communist Asian nations,

GOVERNMENT OWNERSHIP OF THE LARGEST ENTERPRISES IN LATIN AMERICA, 1963

		Rank of the Enterprise by Size in Each Country	% Government Ownership by Enterprise (s)
Petroleum	Argentina	1	100
	Brazil	2	90
	Chile	5	100
	Mexico	3	100
Petrochemicals	Colombia	16	100
	Venezuela	3a	100
Railroads	Argentina	2	100
	Brazil	1	100
	Chile	1	100
	Colombia	1	100
	Mexico	1, 7, 11	100
Electricity	Argentina	3	100
	Brazil	5, 14, 17	15–100
	Chile	4, 7	100
	Colombia	18	100
	Mexico	3, 4, 9	100
	Venezuela	6, 7a	100
Steel	Argentina	4	99
	Brazil	6, 9, 10	60–91
	Chile	13	35
	Colombia	2	4
	Mexico	12	66.8
	Venezuela	2a	100
Banking and Finance	Argentina	5, 8, 20	100
	Brazil	3, 4	56–100
	Chile	6, 15	100
	Colombia	5	100
	Mexico	5, 8, 10, 16, 17	83–100
	Venezuela	10, 19a	100
Automobiles	Argentina	11	23
Telephones	Argentina	16	100
	Brazil	8	100
	Colombia	7	100
	Mexico	12	20
	Venezuela	8a	100
Sugar	Chile	16	100
	Venezuela	15a	100

SOURCE: Based on data compiled by Frank Brandenburg, *Development of Private Enterprise in Latin America*, Washington, 1964.
a Venezuelan rankings exclude privately owned oil companies.

such as Afghanistan, China (Taiwan), Indonesia, Iran, South Korea, and the Philippines, governments assumed an important role in starting such key import-substituting industries as cement, fertilizers, chemicals, rubber tires and tubes, iron and steel, and machinery, textiles, and sugar. In India the government participated directly in iron and steel production; in petroleum production, refining, and distribution; in fertilizer and other chemical industries. The Indian government ran the railroads and produced loco-motives for them. 1961: The Indian government reserved for the state such other industries as arms and ammunition, atomic energy, heavy castings and forgings, heavy plant and machinery, coal and minerals, aircraft and air transport, shipbuilding, telephones and telephone cables, telegraph and wireless apparatus (excluding radio sets), and generation and distribution of electricity. 1960's: The government of Ceylon invested in the nation's nascent steel industry and established a plywood factory, paper factory, vegetable-oil mill, footwear factory, ceramic factory, cement plant, and sugar factories. 1963 ff.: The Burmese government committed itself to bringing about the gradual government ownership and development of the whole industrial sector; it established a steel plant, a pharmaceutical industry, spinning and weaving mills, a brick plant, and cement works. 1950's and 1960's: Throughout the Middle East public-sector operations increased. Middle Eastern governments established government-owned oil and petrochemical companies. 1961, July: United Arab Republic nationalized most of the industry, finance, transport, and foreign trade in Egypt and Syria. 1964, July: Iraq nationalized its key industries and its financial institutions. 1960's: Government ventures in Africa became extensive in Ghana and Tanzania; in many other African countries, governments, through mixed enterprises with foreign capital, became involved in developing industry.

REGIONAL PLANS. Not only did countries develop customs unions and development banks on a regional basis but other attempts were made to create regional economic integration.

Latin America: 1945: Establishment of the UN Economic Commission for Latin America, which did studies of regional development problems. 1948 ff.: The Organization of American States, basically a political organization, had an economic and social council; 1959 ff.: the OAS became more concerned with problems of economic development.

Africa: 1945: Establishment of the UN Economic Commission for Africa, which promoted regional economic development. Pan-Africanist sentiment had impact on regional planning for economic development.

Middle East: 1945, 22 Mar.: Arab League formed; it was basically a political organization, but it also considered economic problems.

Asia: 1945: Establishment of the UN Economic Commission for Asia and the Far East (ECAFE), headquartered in Bangkok, which made studies on means of promoting economic development. 1950, 28 Nov.: Colombo Plan was established to channel funds and technical assistance from the U.S., Canada, Europe, and Australasia to certain South and Southeast Asian nations; it had no funds of its own. 1957, Sept.: Under the auspices of ECAFE, establishment of the Committee for Co-ordination of Investigations of the Lower Mekong Basin after an international agreement was made among the governments of Cambodia, Laos, Thailand, and the Republic of Vietnam to develop water resources in the Mekong Delta. 1961, July: Association of Southeast Asia was established by Malaya, Thailand, and the Philippines; it sought to exchange economic data among these countries. 1964, July: Organization for Regional Co-operation for Development (Turkey, Iran, and Pakistan) formed to co-ordinate the economic planning of all 3 countries. 1965, July: Pakistan and Indonesia created the Indonesian-Pakistan Economic and Cultural Organization. 1967, Aug.: Association of Southeast Asian Nations came into being as a successor to the Association of Southeast Asia; it included Malaysia, Thailand, the Philippines, Indonesia, and Singapore.

OTHER FACTORS. Ideas contributed to economic change. The idea of progress: in many countries for the 1st time there was the possibility of improving the lot of the average individual. The idea that reason, science, and engineering could be applied to control the environment and could substitute for tradition, superstition, and magic was new in many countries.

The concept of equality, the equitable distribution of wealth, provided a basis for land reform, taxation, and many measures that were breaking down the old order and assisting in economic growth. The idea of socialism in some less developed countries—although not in all—provided a break with tradition. The idea of independence from colonial domination and the development of political sovereignty in Africa and Asia offered a basis for industrialization. The idea of nationalism was important in contributing to economic development; industrialization in Germany, Italy, Japan, and Russia, as well as in other countries, had been marked by the growth of intense nationalism; this was also the case in less developed countries. Attempts at regional co-operation among less developed countries met major obstacles because each nation sought its own independent development. This was especially true in Latin America, to some extent in Asia (especially Communist China), while in Africa, national lines were still being defined. The idea of regional co-operation in economic development vied with the idea of nationalism. Regional co-operation had many advantages, and the success of the European Economic Community provided an example of what many less developed nations aspired to achieve. Less developed countries were confronted with the problem of the huge gulf between them and the industrial nations of the world. Even though development was occurring in underdeveloped countries, the gap between them and the industrial nations seemed to broaden. This was a gap between poor and rich nations, the imitators and the innovators in technology, the countries that had to seek out capital and those that had considerable capital resources, those with an unskilled and untrained population and those with a highly trained labor force. Moreover, the gulf between poor and rich nations began to be copied *within* underdeveloped countries, where poverty and wealth stood in contrast, where traditional methods of work vied with new technology borrowed from the industrial nations, where labor-intensive activities provided a sharp contrast with modern sector enterprises financed by foreign investment or foreign aid, and where illiterate majorities stood out in stark contrast to educated nationals of less developed countries. Political instability in less developed countries was another factor which often retarded economic development. Less developed countries—many of them newly freed from colonialism—appeared more prone to *coup d'états* and revolutions than industrial nations; changing governments and civil disorder slowed the development process. The need of a politically stable base for economic development had not been met in many countries.

GOVERNMENT AND SOCIETY
IN AN AGE OF REVOLUTION

The Constitutional Order

THE NATURE OF CONSTITUTIONALISM

INTRODUCTORY. While the meaning of the word "constitution" is not a fixed one, a constitution has generally been regarded as the supreme law of a state, by reference to which all other laws, enactments, actions, and dispositions of the instrumentalities of that state are judged. A constitution usually consists of general principles which are accepted as binding standards of lawful action. Written constitutionalism was formally introduced in the U.S. in 1787, and the U.S. Constitution remains the oldest written constitution in use. In 1789 the French National Assembly adopted a "Declaration of the Rights of Man and of the Citizen," and from that time on state after state has adopted a written document, generally called a constitution, to serve as its basic law.

Some states, however (notably Great Britain), although possessing a constitutional form of government, do not have the fundamental principles by which their citizens live set down in a single document. In the British case a progressive limitation of the prerogatives of the monarch—the Magna Carta, 1215; the Confirmatio Cartarum, 1297; the Petition of Right, 1628; the abolition of the Court of Star Chamber, 1641; the Habeas Corpus Act, 1679; the Bill of Rights, 1689; the Act of Settlement, 1701; and the Act of Union with Scotland, 1707—created constitutionalism without a (single) con-

stitution, since these documents have always been regarded by the British people as compacts of everlasting duration. Their provisions have been respected by later acts of Parliament and have been rendered effective by judicial interpretation.

Modern constitutionalism, as exemplified in the U.S. and France, arose because of the desire of men seeking freedom under law to strike down the pretensions of absolutist monarchies. A republican form of government was sought in order to deny the claims of an unfettered royal prerogative, of a "divine right" of kings, and of the doctrine of *"l'état, c'est moi."* The French Declaration of the Rights of Man drew its inspiration from the theories of the European Enlightenment, from the practical experience of Frenchmen under the *ancien régime,* and specifically from the bills of rights previously adopted by the American states. From the late 18th cent. onward, constitutionalism has sought to articulate the individual freedoms which the citizens of a state feel themselves entitled to demand, and to lay down, permanently and with precision, the limits beyond which the authority of governments may not extend.

ELEMENTS OF A WRITTEN CONSTITUTION: PREAMBLE. The development of constitutional forms has resulted in general agreement on what such a document should contain. Almost every constitution begins with a preamble. Typically, the preamble states the source of the constitution's authority, and sets out its ideals and objectives. The brief

52-word preamble of the U.S. Constitution, 1787, speaks the language of the Enlightenment. The German constitution of 1871, written in the period of national unification, refers to the need to safeguard German territory.

More recent constitutions, such as those of many independent African states, affirm an adherence to broad political and social ideals. The Moroccan, 1962, speaks of the necessity for African unity, while others, e.g., the constitution of the Ivory Coast, 1962, proclaim support not only for the principles of democracy and of the Declaration of the Rights of Man but also for the principles of the UN Charter.

The preamble to the constitution of the Republic of South Africa, 1961, indicates that its people are "convinced of the necessity to stand united." The preamble to the constitution of the People's Republic of China, 1954, describes in detail the "heroic struggle" of the Chinese people to achieve socialism.

FORM OF GOVERNMENT. A constitution also describes the form of government under which the people of the polity to which it applies will live. Constitutions have been written for empires (e.g., the German Empire, 1871) and monarchies (e.g., Italy, 1848), but more often for republics (e.g., France, 1959). In more recent times nations have described their forms of government in terms of social classes. The Italian constitution of 1947 declares: "Italy is a democratic republic based on labor." The constitution of the People's Republic of China, 1954, states that "China is a people's democratic state led by the working class and based on the alliance of workers and peasants." The description in the constitution of the 5th French Republic, 1959, of France as "an indivisible, secular, democratic, and social Republic" has been transferred directly to the constitutions of at least 12 former French African colonies. As independent states they have adopted most of the provisions of the French constitution as their basic law.

SOVEREIGNTY. Constitutions usually also describe the source of sovereign, or ultimate, power. Most declare that sovereignty resides in the people (e.g., the

U.S., 1789, and Belgium, 1831). Others proclaim that it resides in the nation (e.g., Chile, 1925, Burundi, 1962, and Turkey, 1945). Others again ascribe sovereignty to (1) "God alone [but] given by His will as a sacred trust to the State" (Libya, 1951); (2) an emperor (Ethiopia, 1955); (3) "the working people of town and country" (USSR, 1936); and (4) the pope (Vatican City Constitutional Laws, 1929).

STRUCTURE OF GOVERNMENT. Most nations employ written constitutions to establish and delimit their governmental structures. A 3-branch structure (executive, legislature, judiciary) is common. Separate functions result in a separation of powers, while the sharing of many functions results in a system of checks and balances. This form of government, usually with an elected chief of state, and usually therefore republican, is the most widespread. Constitutional monarchies, where surviving, are today generally characterized by the same tripartite division of powers.

The legislative branch, with the principal function of enacting laws, often consists of a 2-house body (U.S., Britain, France), although many nations have a unicameral legislature (Israel, USSR). Popular universal suffrage is the rule.

Some nations elect a president by direct popular suffrage to serve as chief of state and head of government (Brazil). Others elect a president who serves as chief of state, while a prime minister elected by Parliament heads the government (Italy). While the principal function of the executive is to oversee the administration of law, some countries vest much legislative power in the president (France), while in others parliamentary rule is almost complete (West Germany). Party responsibility dominates the British model, which depends on constant majority rule and collective responsibility for governmental action. The U.S. model is marked by a lack of collective party responsibility and by no removal of the chief executive from office following an adverse parliamentary vote.

All nations provide for an instrumentality to adjudicate citizen disputes and legal grievances and to enforce the law of the land. Written constitutionalism has tended to create judiciaries independent of the other branches of government, since they exist by constitutional right and not at the whim of executive or legislative fiat. Strong executive action, however (e.g., Ghana, 1964), can deprive a judiciary of its independence, whether constitutional safeguards are present or not. Many states (e.g., the U.S.) vest powers of review in their highest judicial bodies. Possession of review power enables the judicial branch to pronounce upon the constitutionality of both legislative and executive acts, and strike them down if deemed contrary to the state's fundamental law. Some states, however (e.g., South Africa), forbid constitutional adjudication by their judiciaries.

AMENDMENT. Every constitution makes provision for amending itself, since it is necessary from time to time for a state's fundamental law to be adapted to changing conditions. In the U.S. the constitutional amendment process is formal and arduous. One result of this has been that, since the Bill of Rights, the U.S. Constitution has been amended only 15 times. On the other hand, the U.S. Constitution has readily lent itself to judicial interpretation, and a resort to frequent amendments has not been so necessary as might otherwise have been the case.

India represents the other extreme. The Indian constitution is detailed and contains many provisions usually found in statutes. A relatively simple amending process is therefore appropriate—a ⅔ majority in both houses of Parliament. Certain fundamental provisions of the Indian constitution, however, notably those affecting executive powers, state powers, and property rights, can be amended only by more difficult procedures.

Many countries, particularly those in Latin America, where the average life of a constitution has been less than 20 years, have had numerous constitutions. Venezuela has had 23, the Dominican Republic, 22, and Haiti, 18. France has had, since the Revolution of 1789, 2 empires, 2 kingdoms, and 5 republics.

It is not the rule that constitutional amendment follows constitutional procedure, since constitutional government can be overthrown as well as any other. In Latin America, between Mar. 1962 and Apr. 1964, 7 military coups deposed constitutional, duly elected presidents. In Africa, between June 1965 and Feb. 1966, another 7 governments were overthrown.

HUMAN RIGHTS

THE CONCEPT OF HUMAN RIGHTS. Almost every constitution lays down the fundamental rights of the citizen. The U.S. Constitution lists them, mainly in the form of a group of constitutional amendments commonly designated the Bill of Rights. The American example has been followed by many states.

In the course of time the concept of fundamental human rights, which in the late 18th cent. meant mainly political and religious freedoms, has achieved a broader applicability. Many social and economic rights are now guaranteed constitutionally. Moreover, whereas previously human rights were thought of primarily as those rights which were judicially enforceable, the 20th cent. has witnessed the drawing up of constitutions which establish nonenforceable rights as well. These may be intended to serve as a guide to instrumentalities of government (India, 1949) or to describe the goals of the individual citizen rather than his current situation (Mexico, 1917).

Some nations (e.g., Saudi Arabia, 1926, and South Africa, 1961) are without constitutionally declared rights. On occasion in the past citizens' rights have been deliberately abrogated (Law Centralizing the Administration of Justice, Germany, 1935). Guarantees of human freedom, moreover, are not always enforced even when clearly specified in written constitutions.

PROTECTION OF LIFE AND LIBERTY. Constitutional provisions in the area of the protection of life and liberty are generally designed to safeguard the dignity and worth of the individual. They prohibit slavery and inhumane treatment. The last 200 years have seen a steady erosion of *legally* sanctioned denials of human dignity (slavery, serfdom, outcaste status, etc.) and the appropriate constitutional safeguards are almost universally acknowledged in theory. In practice, however, emergency situations, such as war, and the elevation by some states of the well-being of society as a whole above that of the individual (Law for the Protection of German Blood and German Honor, Germany, 1935) have led to the loss by large numbers of the most fundamental human rights.

FAIR PROCEDURES IN THE ADMINISTRATION OF JUSTICE. Constitutions also commonly stipulate that all citizens shall enjoy the benefits of a fair and impartial system of justice. These may include the right to a jury trial, and usually do include immunity from arbitrary arrest, the right to a speedy trial, the right of a man to face his accuser in a court of law (trials *in absentia* being specifically prohibited), and the right to a legal defense, often provided, if necessary, at state expense. In addition to the traditional protections against double jeopardy and *ex post facto* laws, the more modern constitutions often contain detailed provisions concerning the conduct of trials and limitations on the penalties that may be imposed.

PERSONAL FREEDOMS. Political, social, economic, and religious freedoms are guaranteed by many constitutions. In the period following the French Revolution of 1789 the constitution drafters were most concerned with political and religious guarantees. These included the right of religious observance; freedom of thought and conscience; freedom of speech, of the press, and of assembly; a limited right to vote; and the sanctity of privately owned property. Since then, however, modern constitutions have not only expanded the right to vote and limited the right of property but have greatly extended the scope and number of guaranteed individual rights. In many states these now include the right to an education, the right to work, the right to form political organizations, the right of free marriage, the right to travel, freedom of communication between citizens, and the right to form trade associations. Socialist nations have sharply curtailed private ownership of property (USSR,

1936), while some African nations (particularly those formerly under British colonial rule) have incorporated detailed guarantees of the right to private property (Kenya, 1963). Provisions calling for the social use of property and those in Latin America vesting subsoil mineral rights in the nation (Mexico, 1917) rather than in individuals or corporations have created conflict between capital-exporting and capital-importing nations.

WOMEN'S RIGHTS. The mid-19th cent. saw women uniting for the 1st time in political groups to strengthen their demand for equality with men. From that period onward they began actively seeking higher education and entry into professions previously barred to them. By 1840 the 1st formal women's suffrage movement had been organized, and progress toward constitutionally guaranteed rights for women began. New Zealand was the 1st state to extend the franchise to women, 1893. Women began voting in Britain in 1918 and in the U.S. in 1920. Other states soon followed. Ecuador was the 1st Latin American state to grant the vote to women, 1929, and France permitted them to vote in 1945. In Indonesia and in India, in particular, women played a vigorous role in the struggles for independence and were accorded full political rights after independence had been achieved. Today women vote in almost every state (Switzerland being the most notable exception). The greatest advances in this area, comparatively speaking, have been made in the Communist states, where full employment has meant encouraging female participation, at all levels, in the national work force. The UN enacted a Covenant on the Political Rights of Women in 1952—the 1st instrument of international law aimed specifically at advancing women's rights on a worldwide basis.

THE DEVELOPMENT OF CONSTITUTIONAL GOVERNMENT

1776–1810

UNITED STATES. Modern constitutionalism was born in the U.S. and in France, and tied, initially, to a rejection of monarchical institutions. In the U.S. the British colonial administrations had proved oppressive and were judged intolerable; in France the ruling classes had lost contact with a politically awakening *bourgeoisie.* The result was revolution against the old order in 1776 in the U.S. and in 1789 in France.

The American "Founding Fathers" were profoundly influenced by French political thought and by British constitutional practice and precedent. Rousseau's and Montesquieu's ideas, reinforcing almost 2 centuries of British common-law tradition, were frequently cited as authority for political proposals. The Declaration of Independence, 1776, an assertion of natural rights and a list of the British government's misuses of power, was written and approved of by men conscious of an inherited legal tradition, familiar with the patterns of colonial self-government, and appreciative of the latest modes of political expression.

After a period of ineffective national government under the Articles of Confederation, 1781, a national Constitution was adopted, 1787, which was conservative in tone and reflected the new nation's need for stability, national organization, and order.

FRANCE. The French *philosophes* had intended to correct the abuses of the *ancien régime* by an attack on aristocratic government and by instituting basic changes in governmental structures. They hoped as well to affirm the natural birthright of man to "liberty, property, security, and resistance to oppression" (Declaration of the Rights of Man and of the Citizen, 1789). Further, they built the constitution of 1791 around the need to correct specific abuses of the *ancien régime.*

The 1791 constitution, however, monarchical in form, was doomed to failure by political events, as also were the constitutions of 1793, 1794, and 1795. France was in turmoil and chaos, and while the constitution of 1791 represented a reaction against the *ancien régime,* the more conservative constitution of 1795 was a response to the Reign of Terror and the Jacobin constitution of 1793. In 1795 the constitution makers expounded not on the rights of man, as the Declaration of Rights had done, but also listed his duties; they reposed sovereignty in the people, but limited it as well.

Nevertheless, the French constitutions of 1789–95 established a precedent that has lasted to the present day. Almost immediately constitutions based on the French model (and following in the wake of the French army) were proclaimed in part of Switzerland, 1798, and in the Italian states of Modena, 1796, Milan, 1797, Genoa, 1797, and Naples, 1799.

1810–1914

LATIN AMERICA. From 1810 onward the emergence of the U.S. as an independent nation capable of maintaining its independence served as an example to the Spanish colonies in Latin America. Similarly, the successful operation of the U.S. Constitution during several decades provided political inspiration. All Latin America (save Mexico, 1822–24 and 1862–67, and Brazil, 1824–89) adopted the republican form of government. Most newly independent Latin American states followed U.S. forms and structures of government and passed bills of rights. They also derived inspiration from the egalitarian and republican thought of late 18th-cent. France.

Latin America, however, was basically ill prepared for democracy. Years of tight colonial administration from abroad, regionalism accentuated by poor communications, an unyielding retention of power by the upper classes, fierce and divisive ideological conflicts, and revolutions that did not bring social reform inhibited the development of democratic government under law. Power was frequently seized by a *caudillo,* a regional or national strong man, supported by military force. Such leaders dominated Latin American politics for a century or more. The result was that, even though provided with adequate and sometimes admirable written constitutions, the Latin American states did not achieve the commonly accepted goals of constitutionalism.

INFLUENCE OF NAPOLEON. Soon after revolutionary France began spreading its influence over Europe, Napoleon Bonaparte began exercising his own influence over the revolution. Successively first consul, 1799, first consul for life, 1802, and emperor, 1804, Napoleon, while retaining many of the superficialities of republicanism, turned France full cycle back to monarchy. He made France stable again, but erased most political rights in the process. His administrative, bureaucratic, and military reforms were lasting, but few of the constitutional structures he imposed survived his defeat in 1815.

TRIUMPH OF CONSERVATISM. The fall of Napoleon occasioned the Congress of Vienna, 1814–15, which called for a restoration to their thrones of those European princes who had suffered at Napoleon's hands. Prompted by Metternich and Talleyrand, the Congress attempted to restore much of the old order on the principle of legitimacy. Absolutism was now replaced by constitutionality, but the constitutional states of Europe after 1815 were not legitimized by an appeal to the sovereignty of the people but by a grant delivered out of the hands of a beneficent king. In the period after 1815 a conservative reaction occurred even in Great Britain. The Habeas Corpus Act was suspended, 1816, and from 1819 to 1822 6 Acts of Parliament curbed the long-established rights of freedom of speech, of the press, and of assembly.

GROWTH OF PARLIAMENTARY DEMOCRACY. Despite the strength and initial success of the conservative reaction which followed the Napoleonic Wars, the leaven of French revolutionary ideas continued to work throughout Europe. Kings and subjects alike retained memories of freedoms enjoyed under the republican governments of the Napoleonic era. In Mar. 1822 Fernando VII of Spain was forced to accept reforms demanded by the Spanish Cortes. When Greece won independence from the Ottoman Empire, 1829, a monarchy was set up as a concession to the principle of legitimacy, but the power of the new king of Greece was constitutionally circumscribed. The attempt of Charles X of France to replace legitimist constitutionalism by absolute

rule failed when the revolt of July 1830 claimed his throne. When, in the same year, Belgium broke away from the United Kingdom of the Netherlands, legitimacy sustained another blow. A national Belgian Congress established strong parliamentary government, and Art. 78 of the constitution of 1831 limited the powers of the king to those the state granted him.

In Britain the supremacy of Parliament had already severely reduced the prerogatives of the monarch. The Reform Bill of 1832 increased the franchise, and the Chartist Movement, though defeated by 1848, laid the foundations of the constitutional democracy that was to be achieved in the years ahead: universal manhood suffrage, annual Parliaments, equal parliamentary constituencies, no property qualifications for office, and salaries for members of Parliament.

The aims of the revolutionaries of 1848 included constitutional government, and constitutions were promulgated in Austria, Piedmont, and Switzerland. Even in Asia constitutionalism made its mark. The Japanese constitution of 1889, though almost devoid of citizen guarantees, demonstrated an understanding of the technology of western government, and Sun Yat-sen introduced the concept of western constitutionalism to China after the revolution of 1912.

1914–45

REPUBLICANISM. For the 1st modern constitutional states, the U.S. and France, constitutionalism and republicanism had gone hand in hand. Elsewhere, however, constitutional democracy, where achieved, came about with only a slight reduction in the number of the world's monarchies. The Americas remained the only part of the world where the republican form of government could be regarded as the norm. In Europe, Asia, and Africa only 7 states were republics in 1916: Andorra, China, France, Liberia, Portugal, San Marino, and Switzerland.

The results of World War I, however, were so decisive, and the collapse of 4 great empires—the Austrian, German,

Russian, and Turkish—so complete, that in many areas entirely new states were formed and in others new governments created with wide freedom to fashion new constitutional forms. In Europe 6 new (fully independent) states appeared— Czechoslovakia, Poland, Finland, Estonia, Latvia, and Lithuania—and all were republics, with constitutions based on the principles of 19th-cent. liberalism, i.e., emphasizing political rights and avoiding questions of economic injustice. In all, however, democratic ideas and institutions were protected by constitutional forms. Czechoslovakia, for example, modeled its 1920 constitution on those of the U.S. and France. The depression severely tested the strength of newly won constitutionalism in Europe, and ended it in Latvia, Lithuania, and Estonia. Poland reacted to the threat of Nazi Germany by curtailing parliamentary government and concentrating power in the hands of the president. Only Finland and Czechoslovakia, among the new European republics, were able to maintain constitutionally guaranteed democratic forms between the wars.

In Germany the Weimar Republic was a brief essay in democracy after decades of absolutism. Turkey became a republic but, although its forms of government were strongly influenced by western examples, it soon fell under a 1-party regime. Only Bulgaria, among the states that were on the losing side in World War II, did not undergo radical constitutional transformation after the war ended.

THE SOCIAL CONSTITUTION. While Europe was engaged in war, Mexico was witnessing a period of civil unrest which had not been fully resolved at the time of the adoption of the Mexican constitution of 1917. Europe responded to the postwar challenge by producing political constitutions. Mexico, by contrast, created the world's 1st social constitution, a document that has been widely imitated in Latin America and throughout the world.

Though an intensely nationalistic document, embodying few structural changes, the Mexican constitution was in other respects strikingly innovative. It was the 1st constitution to emphasize the social value of privately owned property, thus laying a foundation not only for future strict regulation (later, nationalization) of private foreign investment but preparing for decades of successful land reform in a country where 25% of the land was once held by slightly more than 100 proprietors. The 1917 Mexican constitution established broad and comprehensive personal guarantees: the right to education, an 8-hour working day, social security, family rights, trade-union rights. It spoke not only of rights to be enforced now, but of the goals a nation should have before it if it is to achieve true democracy.

THE INTERWAR AUTHORITARIAN STATES. The USSR, though possessing a theoretically constitutional form of government, created a political system under which individual rights were subordinated to the demands of the state. In the Stalin era, popular guarantees had meaning only within the context of the requirements of the Communist Party and were limited by the Party's interests. Italian Fascism promised efficient and strong government, industrial peace, prosperity, salvation from Communism, and a revival of the glories of the Roman past. To achieve these ends the Fascists altered the Italian constitution and devitalized Parliament. A "corporate state" was created, 1925, in which labor, industry, commerce, and the arts were wedded to government. Citizens' rights were consciously subordinated to the needs of the corporate state. In Germany, Hitler attained power by constitutional means, but from Mar. 1933 he and his Nazi henchmen ruled dictatorially. All forms of dissent were ruthlessly suppressed, and the most fundamental of human rights, that to life itself, was repeatedly and flagrantly denied during the years of the Nazi tyranny. Authoritarianism and arbitrary governmental action also marked the activities of the Japanese state as, in the period leading up to World War II, civilian agencies of the Japanese administration were increasingly subordinated to control by a militarist elite. By the time the war began, a large part of the world was being ruled by governments which rated state or party interest above constitutionally guaranteed popular rights.

1945–68

THE COMMUNIST STATES. After World War II, Communist governments were established in East Germany, Poland, Czechoslovakia, Hungary, Rumania, Bulgaria, Yugoslavia, and Albania. As satellites of the USSR (Yugoslavia broke away from the Soviet bloc in 1948) these states adopted economic programs in harmony with Soviet policy and united politically with the USSR against the West. Socialist constitutions, modeled on the Soviet constitutions of 1918, 1924, and 1936, were adopted, reposing sovereignty in the working class. Acceptance of the concept of the "unity of the people's power" meant that the classical western constitutionally guaranteed separation of powers was not adopted. Nevertheless, although all Communist states limit personal freedom if that freedom is used, or is likely to be used, for "antidemocratic" purposes, they guarantee many social and economic rights, such as free medical services, free education at all levels, inexpensive housing, and full employment.

NEW NATION STATES IN ASIA AND AFRICA. The end of World War II signaled the beginning of the end of imperial and quasi-imperial rule throughout Asia and Africa. The Islamic states of the Middle East adopted constitutional forms of government on achieving independence, but have not yet seen fit to guarantee full religious freedom or equality between the sexes. The state of Israel, though without a written constitution, guarantees the rights of its citizens in its Declaration of Independence, and possesses a judiciary noted for its vigor in redressing violations of personal liberty suffered by Israeli citizens. In Japan constitutionalism was restored by the U.S. occupation, and an independent judiciary created. Some court decisions, 1960, have limited the freedom of assembly for political purposes.

The constitution of India, 1949, borrowed heavily from the rest of the world. Definitions of fundamental rights were taken from the U.S. Constitution, a federal structure from the Canadian, a parliamentary system from Britain, and the notion of nonjusticiable directive rights from Ireland. Despite serious economic crises India has remained committed to the preservation of democracy, and its citizens' fundamental rights have been construed liberally by zealous courts.

All of Africa, with the exception of Liberia, Egypt, Ethiopia, and South Africa, was under foreign domination until the 1950's. In the period of colonial rule Africans were not without constitutional rights, though their European rulers tended to act more arbitrarily in overseas dependencies than they did at home. As the African states attained independence, they erected their new governments on a firmly constitutional base, accepting in most cases the principles of the separation of powers, the independence of the judiciary, and the need for citizens' guarantees. It was in Africa (Lagos, 1961) that an International Commission of Jurists proclaimed that "fundamental human rights, especially the right to personal liberty, should be written into and entrenched in the constitutions of all countries."

Human rights, however, have often been ignored in independent Africa. Ghana established laws, Sept. 1962, permitting police detention for 28 days without charges being preferred and indefinite "preventive detention" on the authority of the attorney general; Dahomey dissolved all political parties, Nov. 1963, after jailing the president of the supreme court; in May 1966, political parties were outlawed in Nigeria. Numerous military coups—in Algeria, Congo (Kinshasa), Dahomey, the Central African Republic, Nigeria, and Ghana between June 1965 and Feb. 1966 alone—have removed legitimate governments by unconstitutional means.

The Social Order

THE NATURE OF SOCIAL MOD-ERNIZATION. The 2 defining character-istics of a modern society are a high degree of differentiation and of integra-tion.

The former refers simply to specializa-tion. A highly differentiated society is one in which the various tasks necessary for keeping the economic, political, and cul-tural subsystems going are performed by specialized social units. In contrast, in an undifferentiated society particular social units perform a much larger variety of tasks.

A high degree of integration means that most if not all segments of the society interact with each other and are in some way dependent on each other, and that, as a result, they all share a set of common basic cultural principles or values. In a poorly integrated society, various geo-graphical parts may be almost self-suffi-cient and independent of the rest of the society, or particular classes may have value systems basically different from other classes, or they may exist largely outside the economic life of other classes, or they may be barred from power in the political life of the society. In a highly integrated society the elimination of these separations enables the society to effectively mobilize all of its parts when threatened by danger. Class differ-ences are not ended (they may actually be intensified), but classes interact more fully and co-operate more effectively.

The history of social modernization is one of increasing differentiation (which increased social efficiency) and of an ac-companying integration (which was needed to tie the various parts of society together in an age of specialization). In the past, societies that failed to differenti-ate sufficiently also failed to industrialize and keep up economically with more "modern" societies that were quicker to adapt. On the other hand, nations that failed to integrate sufficiently did not hold together; either provinces broke away or else semipermanent class warfare disrupted them as various "out" classes attempted to seize the benefits of "in" classes.

The process of increasing differentia-tion and integration did not go smoothly in all modernizing states. As men were forced into new occupations and life pat-terns, and as they increasingly demanded a share of political, economic, and cul-tural power, tensions inevitably devel-oped. The working out of these tensions produced the social revolution that has created the modern world.

Modernization in the sense here defined began in Western Europe and spread from there during the 19th and 20th cents. to the rest of the world.

RURAL DISLOCATION AND URBANI-ZATION IN THE WEST, 1750–1900

POPULATION. A striking characteristic of the period between 1750 and 1900 in Western Europe and the U.S. was the rapid increase in population (pp. 877 ff. below).

APPROXIMATE TOTAL POPULATION
(million)

	1750	1800	1850	1900
Britain	c. 7.5	10.5	20.8	37.0
France	c. 20.0	27.6	35.8	39.0
Germany	–	24.5	35.4	56.4
U.S.	1.5	5.3	23.2	76.0

As industrialization increased, so did urbanization. By 1871, 61.8% of the population of England and Wales lived in urban districts. Urbanization, though still considerable, was less marked in the U.S., France, and Germany. In 1870, 74% of the U.S. population was classed as rural; 68.9% of the French population, 1872; and 63.9% of the German, 1871.

The populations of the modernizing

states were much affected by migration. Britain and Germany lost many people, mainly to the U.S. and, in the case of Britain, to her dominions (pp. 881–883 below).

TOTAL EMIGRATION FROM BRITAIN AND
GERMANY
(000)

	Britain	Germany
1846–50	199	
1851–60	1,313	622
1861–70	1,572	634

Fewer Frenchmen emigrated, but France suffered a population loss when Alsace-Lorraine was added to the German Empire, 1871.

Over-all population increases in the modernizing nations were made possible

primarily by the rapid advances achieved in agricultural technology (p. 655). But improvements in agriculture also had the effect of making much of the rural population unnecessary for food production. In England, 1740–1830, one result of better rural technology was the enclosure movement (p. 655) in which landlords and prosperous farmers evicted the small peasantry from the land by prohibiting them the traditional usage of common lands. France had no enclosure movement, and there was no direct pressure on the peasantry to abandon the land (which explains the relatively slower rate of urbanization of France compared to that of England and Germany). But France's population, already the densest in Europe in the 17th cent., continued to

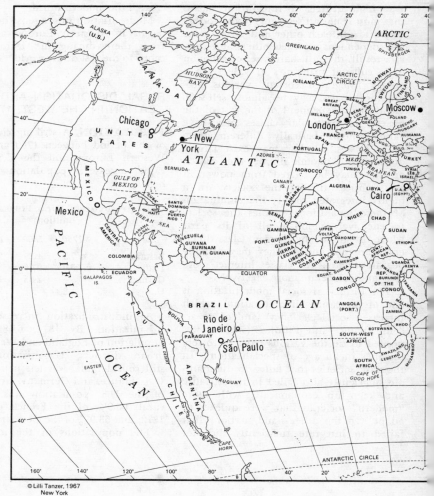

© Lilli Tanzer, 1967
New York

grow well into the 19th. French farms became smaller and smaller, and because land tended to be divided equally among all a farmer's sons, many peasants found themselves with uneconomic holdings and this forced them to emigrate to the cities.

In Germany the formal emancipation of the serfs in 1807 allowed the more efficient landowners to take over the small and inefficient holdings. In the half-century that followed emancipation, the proportion of lands controlled by the big estates grew rapidly. While the East Prussian estates grew most rapidly, most of western Germany did not escape the trend. Marginal peasants were forced off the land and into the growing industrial zones (and many, eventually, to America).

The pattern in the U.S. was exceptional because it was the immense immigration from Europe between 1860 and 1910 and not internal migration that swelled the urban labor force. Meanwhile, the rapid extension of cultivated lands in the West and the improvement of agricultural techniques more than kept pace with the rising food needs of the country. Since it was European social disorders that forced the bulk of the immigrants into the U.S.'s cities, the U.S. profited from these without itself having to experience them.

The population growth and urbanization of Western Europe and the U.S. coincided with a greatly stimulated industrial development.

SOCIAL EFFECTS OF INDUSTRIALIZATION. There had long been cities before the growth of modern industrial

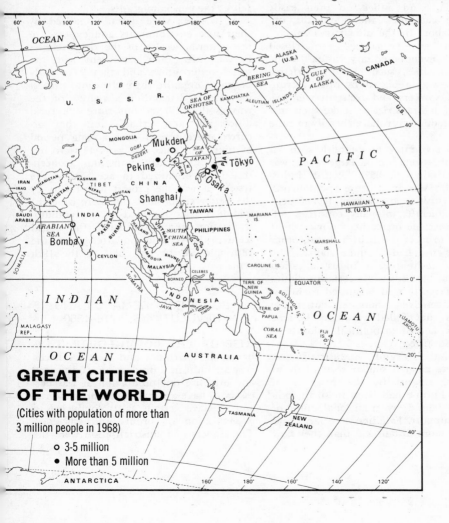

GREAT CITIES OF THE WORLD

(Cities with population of more than 3 million people in 1968)

o 3-5 million
• More than 5 million

% OF POPULATION LIVING IN CITIES
OF MORE THAN 10,000 PEOPLE

	1800	1850	1890
U.K.	20.0	38.5	59.0
France	9.5	14.5	26.0
Germany	7.2a	10.5	30.0
U.S.	3.8	12.0	27.5

a For Prussia only, 1816.

ones, but their economic and social organization was different. Premodern cities were centers of commerce and artisan production, but no city until modern times developed a machine-based production system. The old cities had fairly small-scale units of production which depended on the individual skills of specialized craftsmen. Industrial cities, on the other hand, relied on their easily operable machines and abundant unskilled labor. In the old artisan centers, craftsmen were organized into closed guilds or even hereditary castes. In the industrial cities, such closed, restrictive practices were replaced by open recruitment of workers and constant competition within industries to make their machines produce ever more cheaply to raise profits.

The 1st country to establish such an industrial system on a large scale was Great Britain (p. 657). British industrialization was in a sense spontaneous. But as British exports spread, less efficient local handicrafts in many countries suffered. It became increasingly obvious that in order to meet the British threat, other countries also had to industrialize. The ideas and techniques of industrialization spread quickly. But while certain societies were sufficiently well organized to industrialize themselves, others were not. Those countries that failed gradually became economic, and often political, colonies of the industrialized West.

Urbanization and industrialization everywhere created similar sorts of social problems. Essentially, the peasants of Western Europe had lived in small communities bound by traditional rules of mutual support. Families were large and included more distant kin than they now do. The extended family was committed to supporting its members. Behavior in economic and political activities was also regulated by traditional rules, and each individual had his security more or less assured by the community. But as demographic forces pushed men off the land, the old families and communities broke up and their mutual support functions were not replaced by new institutions. Individuals became isolated and only marginally useful units. The early factory system demanded long working hours in poor conditions, and female and child labor was more cruelly exploited than it had ever been before. Wages were low and workers were reduced to bleak existences further accentuated by the feeling of loss and the frightening uncertainties felt by the new immigrants.

As workers were detraditionalized by their new environments and exposed to the material wealth of the richer classes in the cities, their discontent with the social order grew, and they eventually began to organize themselves into protest movements demanding a redress of the wrongs done them. But since the rural dislocation and urbanization that occurred were spread over a long period of time, and since the workers were not at first sufficiently numerous, concentrated, or organized to act against the system, it was the protest movements by the better established and more coherent middle classes spawned by early industrialization that dominated the social scene in the West in the latter part of the 18th and in the first half of the 19th cents.

BOURGEOIS DEMANDS AND REVOLUTIONS, 1770–1860

RISE OF THE BOURGEOISIE. To finance the machines and factories necessary for industrial production, and to lead and organize this production, it was necessary to have a certain amount of capital and to have certain skills conducive to maximization of profits and efficiency. The leaders of industrialization were the financial and industrial bourgeois, or capitalists.

This group had its antecedents in Western Europe in the commercial middle classes that had dominated European trade for several centuries before industrialization. It was during that period that such financial institutions as joint-stock companies and credit banks had been established, and that the techniques of modern accounting and large-scale organization of production were learned.

But throughout the period of developing commerce that preceded industrialization, there persisted a conflict between the old landowning feudal aristocracy and the rising merchant class. The former felt it deserved a near monopoly of prestige and high political office, while the latter felt that its commercial skills and growing wealth entitled it to a share of prestige and power. The revolutionary wave which began to sweep Europe toward the end of the 18th cent. was essentially a struggle between the old feudal aristocracy and the rising middle classes that wanted to replace it.

The desires of the middle classes between 1750 and 1850 were roughly similar throughout the West. They wanted their societies to promote or at least permit the expansion of the commercial and industrial activity on which they, as a class, depended. This required a sufficiently large market and the possibility of conducting commerce freely within it. It required protection against outside competition. It required at least that modicum of social and political stability that is necessary for commerce and for the defense of property rights. Finally, the middle classes wanted social recognition in the form of high prestige for their most successful members, for this would legitimize the pursuit of profits which had been considered somewhat immoral in earlier European society.

The outcome of the revolutions between 1774 and 1848 was largely determined by the degree to which middle-class demands were met in various western countries. These demands were enshrined in a liberal value system that asked for national unification and the elimination of internal restrictions on trade, government co-operation against threatening outside forces which frequently took the form of militant nationalism, government abstention from regulating society in any way that might preserve artisan production against the more efficient industrial producers, repression of radical anti-property movements such as socialism, and voting rights and democracy for the *bourgeoisie*. The liberal ideology claimed that the less government interference there was, the better, but only up to the point at which government interference became necessary to help the middle class.

There were various middle classes and their interests were not always identical. For example, the old artisan class favored the extension of voting rights, but was resolutely opposed to the development of large-scale industries which put it out of business. This old middle class was gradually pushed down by industrialization and became the most radical of the lower classes in the 19th cent. The rural middle class wanted tariffs against foreign crops but not against outside manufactured goods (which it bought) if these were cheaper than domestic goods. The industrial middle class had precisely the opposite interest. And in all the countries being discussed there were somewhat distinct financial, commercial, and industrial middle classes whose interests sometimes coincided but at other times clashed.

U.S. The 1st of the modern revolutions was the American one. The 13 American British colonies emerged from the war with France, 1757–63, heavily dominated in the North by mercantile interests and in the South by a rural planter class. American society was characterized by the almost total absence of a feudal aristocracy and by the equal absence (with the exception of the southern Negro slaves) of a serf class. Thus the 2 extreme forces that plagued Europe throughout the 19th cent., the diehard reactionary aristocratic element and the uprooted small peasant, were largely absent. From the Boston merchants to the small farmers, the entire society fitted into a sort of all-encompassing middle class with a common liberal ideology. These were the "self-made" men who had achieved whatever position they had through their own work and who naturally felt entitled to rule themselves. On the other hand, these were not the sort of men who felt impelled to achieve a radical transformation of the entire social system, although a change in a more egalitarian direction did come about as a result of the American Revolution.

The British attempt to tighten political control over the American colonists at the end of the French and Indian War led to resentment. The colonists considered taxation without representation to be a grievance, although representation in Parliament was not in fact a colonial demand. But, worst of all, Britain tried to restrain the commerce conducted by the Americans in order to favor British merchants. Simultaneously, the southern planters were heavily indebted to the British merchants from whom they imported their consumer goods, and the small American farmers were increasingly indebted to the coastal American merchants from whom they bought their finished goods and to whom they sold their produce. Almost all segments of the middle class had some sort of grievance against the system, and the middle class was all-pervasive. These grievances were channeled against the British by the revolutionary leaders, who were primarily those men of substance who wished to free themselves in order to attain what they felt to be their rightly deserved position of eminence in the society.

The Revolutionary War ended in 1783, but the internal goals of the Revolution were not yet met. The failure of the colonies to unite effectively and to establish a common legal and monetary system displeased those commercial interests which felt that national integration was a prime requisite for a sound economy. The Constitution of 1787 enshrined liberal values demanded by the middle class and city workers without ending

sources of conflict between the merchant *bourgeoisie,* the planter class in the South, and the interior farmers. The virtue of the Constitution was that it established a system ideally suited to later industrialization with only one major exception, the preservation of slavery. Though the various state constitutions continued to require property qualifications for voting, a substantial proportion of the white males could nevertheless vote. (Yet it was not until 1807 that the 1st state abolished all restrictions on voting for white males and, as late as May 1842, there was an armed rebellion in Rhode Island by forces demanding universal white male suffrage.) A common money, a common foreign policy, and the abolition of internal trade barriers were the other main aspects of the integration demanded by Americans. Aside from this, a common language and a shared implicit belief in the allocation of social prestige by achievement rather than by birth were already part of the American value system.

GREAT BRITAIN. If Great Britain ever had a bourgeois revolution, it took place in the 1640's, not in the 18th or 19th cent. By 1750 British economic and social conditions were already favorable to the growth of a middle class. The nation was politically united and there were no internal restrictions on trade. The government's foreign policy successfully kept outside markets open for English business and the import of primary products from the colonies flowing. Perhaps most importantly, the British aristocracy was a viable and profit-oriented class which saw no objection to rational business activity. This enabled capitalist methods to spread quickly into agriculture and made British agriculture the most efficient in the world.

As Britain industrialized, the business class remained nonrevolutionary. During the wars with France between 1790 and 1815, they felt that the defense of their continental markets by their government against the Napoleonic blockade justified their remaining passive as various radical movements threatened the social order.

revolution from above, which succeeded well enough in reviving Prussian military power and in driving out Napoleon.

After the Napoleonic Wars the aristocracy and the Prussian court reverted to a more natural conservatism, but the social effects of the reform continued. The artisan class declined, the cities grew, and the great industrial bourgeois families of Germany, such as the Krupps, were founded. The various customs unions of the 1830's further stimulated the growth of industry. But the aristocracy retained its political privileges, and at least in Prussia there was no development of constitutional government (though southern German states continued to be more progressive than northern and eastern ones). The period, in fact, was characterized by ostensible tranquillity covering the changes and labeled the Biedermeier era (after an architect whose complacent style epitomized the times).

As in the case of the French revolution of 1848, the mass discontent that exploded in Germany in the same year was largely fed by discontented artisans who were losing their positions to the growing industries. There had been several outbreaks of discontent in the 1820's, 1830's, and 1840's, but the revolution of 1848 was far more serious because it was supported in the countryside by the impoverished peasantry, and, most importantly, it was joined by the middle-class liberals who had long been in the opposition. It was the latter element that seized control of the revolution (p. 190).

The turmoil released by the 1848 revolution, however, separated the *bourgeoisie* from its lower-class supporters. The peasant uprisings destroyed too much property, the artisans asked that industrial freedom be curtailed, and the liberals were alienated. The middle-class response in trying to stop a revolution opened the door for the aristocracy, who regained power by playing, on the one hand, on the dislike of the poor for the *bourgeoisie,* and, on the other, on the *bourgeoisie's* fear of instability and radicalism.

Though the revolution was quickly defeated, the conflicting forces it had brought into play set social policy in Germany for the rest of the century. Toward the poor, the policy was to be fairly generous (by 19th-cent. standards). On 16 May, 1853, child labor was proscribed (at a time when it was still current in Britain and France) in Prussia, and throughout the decade other measures pacified and relieved the poor. For the bourgeois there was nationalism which was translated into German unification, protection from outside competitors, and an aggressive foreign policy. For the bourgeois there was also full industrial freedom and the social acceptance of the wealthiest industrialists into the aristocracy through intermarriage. For the aristocracy, especially for the Prussian Junkers, there was, 1st, the imposition of tariffs against food imports (part of the protectionist policy of 1879) and, 2nd, the maintenance of high social prestige and the senior positions in the army. Binding all this together was an aggressive nationalistic monarchy and a bureaucracy whose top members were largely recruited from the richer classes. The upper middle class won a victory in the economic sphere at the price of surrendering political control to the aristocracy and the monarchy.

OTHER EUROPEAN COUNTRIES. The growth of a middle class, and with it the desire for national independence and integration, took place to a greater or lesser extent elsewhere in Europe.

The case of Austria-Hungary demonstrates what happens to a modernizing society which fails to integrate itself culturally. In 1848 there was no unified Austrian revolution; instead there was a Czech, a Hungarian, an Italian, and an Austrian uprising. The way was paved for the eventual disintegration of the empire.

In Russia there was no middle-class revolution because the middle class remained much too small. In the mid-19th cent. the economic developments which had unbalanced Western Europe had not yet occurred on a large scale in Russia.

In the rest of Eastern Europe the idea of nationalism spread, but the social and economic base of the middle classes was too weak to make its demands a real issue. Rather there was a series of nationalist uprisings against the Russian, Ottoman, and Austrian empires without strong accompanying liberal movements.

At the start of the 19th cent. Italy was as politically disunited as Germany, and throughout the 1st half of the century the goal of national unification was most deeply cherished by middle-class liberal secret societies (p. 149). Since it eventually proved too difficult for these groups to unite their country, there developed, as in Germany, a monarchical-liberal alliance that eventually succeeded in performing the task.

In industrializing countries like Sweden economic progress such as the development of the railway system after 1850 brought with it the eventual triumph of liberalism within several decades. But in countries like Spain (which had little economic development outside of Barcelona) no middle class evolved. The agrarian sector of the society was little changed and political life was more typical of nonmodern societies than of the more developed European nations.

THE WESTERN INDUSTRIAL SOCIETIES, 1860–1914

THE NATURE OF RATIONALIZATION. In those countries where bourgeois revolutions and demands achieved a measure of success, and where there was successful industrialization, there followed certain institutional and value changes. Not only were political structures changed but also the structure of families, religions, and daily work for most people. Attitudes toward these also changed. The ideal of rationalization spread from the economic to other sectors of society as differentiated and specialized institutions were created at all levels to perform tasks previously left to more diffuse structures.

The dominant value of industrialization is rationalism. In business terms this is the capacity to take a given goal (prof-

its) and consciously to examine the most suitable means of attaining it. Nonbusiness considerations such as family ties, religious beliefs, or the host of loyalties and obligations normally held by men must be relegated to a lesser place insofar as economic management is concerned.

Rationality was not "invented" by middle-class entrepreneurs. The origins of western rationality are old and the systematic, rational pursuit of knowledge began in Europe during the Renaissance. Then the idea was to isolate the causes and effects of various natural phenomena from the bundle of religious and moral values of the time. Just as business rationality examines the best means of gaining profits and judges success by the careful accounting of results, so did modern science from the 16th cent. onward judge the validity of its theories by the careful measurement of phenomena to see if the theoretical predictions coincided with observed events. In rational business as in science, when events did not match expectation, new methods or explanations were sought.

The modern period was preceded by the expansion of rationality into religion. A basic idea common to most varieties of Protestantism was that each believer ought to examine the Bible to find in it the correct principles. The means to attainment of proper religious thought were to be chosen and religious success measured by worldly results, not by hypothetical abstraction. Each individual was required to bring his life into harmony with his religion, and success in the former was interpreted as a sign of grace in the latter. Thus the pursuit of business and scientific rationality was in harmony with religious expectations.

The flowering of intellectual rationalism took place in the 18th cent., when the notion of rationality spread to the examination of society and governments. But it was not until the growth and economic triumph of the middle class in the 19th cent. (a little earlier in Britain and the U.S.) that such rationalization spread to the wider society.

The most obvious consequence of

economic rationalization was a vastly increased division of labor. Within factories more and more workers performed smaller and more precise tasks as part of an assembly line. A host of new occupations was created. For example, full-time scientists first appeared in the 19th cent.; before, there had only been amateurs who rarely received their income purely from research. The numbers and types of doctors, lawyers, and engineers vastly increased. Types and varieties of industries multiplied. An index of this large-scale differentiation was the growth of property, contractual, and administrative law and a relative decline in the importance of religious and moral law.

THE FAMILY. A further consequence of industrialization was increased social mobility. Rationality demanded that the best men be picked for the right jobs and, although this principle was very far from being thoroughly carried out in the 19th cent., the need for efficiency at least caused widespread recognition of merit. Through education or business or administrative skills it became possible for men to advance above the positions into which they were born. The expansion of the middle-class "liberal" professions further opened the door to social advancement through education. Even people who did not raise their relative standing in society could realistically hope to raise their material prosperity, and to educate their children sufficiently to raise their standing.

Families had been the principal economic, welfare, and educational units in society. In the industrial cities they ceased to be units of production. Schools took over much of the educational function. Moreover, the dispersion of families through migrations in search of work disrupted the extended family and destroyed its capacity to take care of its old and disabled members. In the new industrial society elders were a drag on a couple's ability to live well and finance an education for their children. Similarly, too many children impoverished a family and made it less likely that the children would be well-enough educated to rise to higher social status.

The destruction of the extended family was not simply the result of economic pressures. The young could escape from the restrictions of their elders and move to the city which had no restrictive traditional obligations. Once married, young people desired to maximize their own enjoyment of material benefits and not to share them with others.

Europe's population through the early 19th cent. had continued to rise because of the decline in death rates due mostly to economic advances. But as the upwardly conscious middle class became an ever larger proportion of the society, the birth rates began to fall (p. 875). Rates fell most sharply among the middle classes, who saw a real possibility of improving their position, or at least their children's, and not so much among the very poor, who had no such hope. It was, moreover, the middle classes who tended to accumulate a certain amount of property and did not want to have to leave it to too many children. Neither the very rich nor the very poor had such concerns.

Not only the industrial and commercial middle class but also the small landowning peasantry, who felt many of the same desires for the preservation of their property, limited the number of their children. In fact, this phenomenon was chiefly one of the lower middle class, landowning peasants, shopkeepers, and lower-level bureaucrats. France, the proverbial nation of little shopkeepers and small farmers, had almost no increase in population between 1870 and 1940.

In many rural areas in Western Europe the increased life expectancy of the old (which meant that they kept control of their farms longer), the lack of new lands, and the increasing capital requirements for running successful farms drove the young to the cities and overseas. Areas that had no industry lost population. For example, between 1848 and 1900 Ireland's population dropped from 8.2 million to 4.5 million. (See further "World Population," pp. 877 ff.)

THE CHURCHES. Along with the family and the economy, religious institutions were also changed by industrialization and the spread of the middle-class ethic. Whereas churches had claimed wide competence outside of strictly religious matters, their field of action was gradually restricted during the 19th cent.

In the first half of that century the bulk of the middle classes in Catholic Europe tended to be pronouncedly anticlerical because of the alliance of the church and the old aristocracy. Even in Protestant countries the middle classes tended toward opposing the power of official churches. In the U.S., for example, religion was excluded from direct interference in politics even though it continued to play a large role in men's personal lives. There was no established church in the U.S.

Bismarck's relations with the Catholic populations and church in the German Empire in the 1870's were conditioned by the church's hostility to industrialization and secularization of the state. His greatest ally in the struggle to destroy the influence of the Catholic Church was the middle class, while the church found support from the working classes as well as from the aristocracy. Though the *Kulturkampf* waged against Catholicism in the 1870's was cloaked in the guise of German nationalism, it was firmly opposed by the Lutheran Church and by the Prussian aristocracy, who saw it chiefly as a drive toward secularization of the schools and the legal system. (For example, civil marriage was introduced in Germany in 1872.)

In France, the early Revolution, 1789–95, had been violently anticlerical. Church lands had been confiscated, clergy persecuted, and ecclesiastical privileges removed. Napoleon was more lenient, but his concordat with Rome, 1801, affirmed the French state's control over the church. Attempts to revive the former power of the church during the Bourbon restoration ended with the revolution of 1830. Thereafter, a combination of rejuvenated church thought and the growing social conservatism of the high *bourgeoisie* (especially after the radical popular excesses of 1848) revived the power of the church. By the 1850's the high *bourgeoisie* had become very Catholic.

In opposition to this, there developed between 1850 and 1900 a powerful, militantly anticlerical Freemasonry, drawing its support mainly from the members of the liberal professions (doctors, lawyers, and teachers) and the lower middle classes who eventually formed the Radical Party. In 1886 this group succeeded in having mildly anticlerical laws passed, designed to weaken the Catholic school system. The church issue, however, continued to divide France until the anticlericals succeeded, Dec. 1905, in formally disassociating church and state from each other by using the passions aroused by the Dreyfus case, 1894–99. The power of the French Catholic Church was broken.

In Italy there occurred a similar growth of anticlericalism in the early 19th cent. among the revolutionary middle classes. In the second half of the century the situation was further exacerbated by the refusal of the papacy to accept the political unification of Italy and the elimination of the secular papal state. It was not until 1929 under Italian Fascism that state and church in Italy finally made their peace.

In Great Britain the dominant religious institution was the Anglican Church, which played a powerful political role in the first half of the 19th cent. Typically, Britain handled her religious reform through parliamentary action. In 1828 the old law which prohibited Protestant Nonconformists and Catholics from holding office (the Test Act) was repealed. Nevertheless, the largely middle-class non-Anglican Protestants continued to be excluded from the universities and to be discriminated against by the Anglican aristocracy. Much of the substance of the disagreement between Liberals and Conservatives in the Victorian period (as it had been between Whigs and Tories earlier) was over religion. The former were largely middle- and lower-class Dissenters (or Nonconformists) who fought the power of an official church as the middle class on the Continent fought the power of the Catholic Church. The universities were finally opened to Dissenters, 1871, and nonchurch primary schools were established (though not in every part of Britain) .

Naturally, these political crises over church-state relations and the weakening of the political power of the official churches furthered the general secularization of values and hastened the decline of religion's influence over everyday life.

BUREAUCRATIZATION AND CENTRALIZATION. The supremely rational management tool is a bureaucracy whose members are chosen and promoted according to their merit (that is, their technical capacity to advance the purposes of the organization) . Bureaucracies are specialized into departments skilled in particular facets of organizational requirements. Such an administrative group is effective in all fields from industrial to military to religious organization. Bureaucracy is not an exclusively modern phenomenon, but it is only in the modern period that it has become so widespread.

During the late 18th cent. governments began to undertake vast new tasks. It was necessary to integrate national economies and cultures, to command large armies to preserve national interests against outsiders, and to maintain internal social calm in the face of increasing social dislocations. To fulfill these tasks governments needed better administrations than they had previously possessed.

The earliest model of an efficient government bureaucracy in modern times was the French Revolutionary–Napoleonic structure whose development was much helped by the previous growth of the administration under the old monarchy. It consisted chiefly of some 90 departments ruled by career bureaucrats appointed by the central government. At the center the administration depended on a number of specially trained, technically proficient bureaucrats. Education was similarly reorganized and the French were the first to establish a series of state schools for the training of centrally controlled teaching cadres. Napoleon also greatly increased the size of the permanent police force.

Britain was far slower to develop a centralized bureaucracy because, by comparison with France, its monarchical institutions had been less centralized. Nevertheless, the British rationalized much of their governing structure during the 19th cent. In 1829 the 1st permanent police force was created in England, largely to control radical mobs. In 1834 central control over the workhouses for the poor was established according to a new set of poor laws (Poor Law Amendment Act) . In 1836 government registration of births, marriages, and deaths was begun to help the government keep track of its population. This served government inspectors in enforcing the factory reform laws of the 1830's. In 1835 municipal government was somewhat standardized by parliamentary law (Municipal Corporations Act) . Bit by bit local tradition and powers were replaced by central-government authority. Under the Liberal Gladstone government, 1871, the army began to be converted into a modern military machine where before it had been officered by gentry who had bought their commissions. In 1870 the civil service was opened to competitive examination. Before the end of the century the government took in hand a number of welfare schemes to satisfy the demands of the working class. But over all, Britain, save for the U.S., remained the slowest of the industrial powers to bureaucratize itself.

The unique characteristic of the German bureaucracy was the remarkable development of a highly rationalized and efficient army ruled by the bureaucracy of the general staff. The German bureaucracy of the 19th cent. had a particularly high reputation for technical competence.

The bureaucracy of the U.S. grew even more slowly than that of Britain because of the decentralized form of government. It was only in the 1880's that large-scale federal bureaucratization began with the creation of the 1st of the federal administrative boards, the Interstate Commerce Commission, 4 Feb., 1887. Only on 16 Jan., 1883, was civil-service recruitment made competitive and, in some degree, by merit.

But in the U.S., as everywhere else in the industrial world, the habits of bureaucratization spread much farther than

merely into the central government. Big
industries, municipalities, and even some
political parties came to be run according
to the rules of bureaucratic efficiency.
This was, however, only an intimation of
what was to come in the 20th cent.

**ECONOMIC AND CULTURAL IN-
TEGRATION.** The entire process of
modernization made the various geographic parts of the western nations ever
more closely bound to each other.
Whereas in medieval times a province
could be detached from a state without
disrupting the economic life of either, this
became increasingly difficult in the 19th
cent.

Similarly, local customs and languages
(or dialects) and loyalties tended to be
increasingly submerged by national language, law, and value systems. Economic
interdependence was much helped by the
need of industries for mass markets and
by the growth of productive capacity.
Improved communications also helped.
Railways, telegraphs, and mass literacy
and the growth of a popular mass press
were the instruments of cultural integration as well as of economic. The notion
of the "nation," though not a novelty in
the 19th cent., was much strengthened.

Conversely, the sprawling multilingual
and multinational empires of Eastern
Europe (the Austro-Hungarian, the Ottoman, and to some extent the Russian)
failed to bind their peoples together, and
became ever more vulnerable in face of
the more modern powers.

**LIMITS OF 19TH-CENT. LIBERAL-
ISM.** The general rationalization of western society brought a large number of
benefits. The standard of living rose to
unprecedented heights after the painful
beginnings of industrialization. The advantages of science, education, and legal
rights were spread to wide sectors of
society which had not previously enjoyed them. Religious intolerance diminished. (For example, the Jews were
emancipated in France on 27 Sept., 1791,
and elsewhere in Western Europe following the Napoleonic conquest.) The political participation of the masses increased.
These advantages may be subsumed

under the title "liberalism," and everywhere liberalism's chief standard bearers
were the growing middle classes.

But middle-class rationalism had distinct limitations. For one thing, with growing prosperity and success the middle
classes in the industrial world began to
worry more about the conservation of
their advantages than about the spread
of these to the less advantaged. In the 2nd
place, the fervent nationalism that accompanied the rise of the middle classes
turned increasingly into chauvinism. This
trend produced the 1st formally racist
ideology in history. In France, Joseph
Gobineau (1816–82) expounded the doctrine of Aryan racial superiority (*Essay
on the Inequality of the Human Races,*
1853–55). In Germany, similar theories
were popularized by Richard Wagner
(1813–83) in his operas. At first such
doctrines appealed mainly to the aristocratic sentiments that opposed the
bourgeois revolutions, but toward the end
of the 19th cent. their assumptions came
to be increasingly adopted by the middle
classes.

France, the most middle class of the
great European powers, came to be politically dominated by the shopkeeper and
small farmer toward the end of the century, and the fear of change felt by these
groups slowed down progress in France
decisively. Small producers and distributors were consistently protected against
their larger and more efficient competitors. This, combined with the lack of
population growth, created a stagnant
French economy that was surpassed by
Germany and the U.S. Of the major industrial nations, France showed the
slowest economic growth between 1870
and 1914 (or for that matter, until 1939).
In other words, where the lower middle
class became too dominant, progress
slowed.

Britain and Germany continued to be
dominated by an alliance of the old aristocracies and the wealthy industrialists
(2 classes that increasingly merged as they
intermarried). The U.S. toward the end
of the 19th cent. became increasingly
dominated by big-business elements, the

1st generation of the great millionaires, Rockefeller, Morgan, Harriman, and others. Where the major industrialists had such control over their nation's economies, they continued to press the expansive industrial growth on which their positions rested.

Though the economies of most of the industrial powers did not fall under the domination of the lower middle classes, the chauvinism of these classes influenced foreign policy. In Britain, at first Disraeli, and then Joseph Chamberlain, rose to power on the nationalism of these elements. Political imperialism and the conquest of colonies was one of the results. This was also the case in Germany, Italy, France, and even the U.S., whose war with Spain carried imperialist overtones.

Toward the end of the century social Darwinism, epitomized by the works of Herbert Spencer (1820–1903) and W. G. Sumner (1840–1910), tended to become popular among the middle classes. This ideology claimed that, as in the plant and animal world, so in the human world, the most capable rise to the top. The most capable were presumed to be the biologically strongest, and therefore, to improve the race, it was necessary to avoid helping the poor, who constituted a weakening element. This sort of reasoning was extended to nationalities. The industrial whites were said to be racially superior to the nonindustrialized peoples outside Europe and the U.S. since the former were materially more successful.

RISE OF WORKING-CLASS MOVEMENTS.

It was not the aim of the middle-class revolutions of the late 18th and 19th cents. to absorb the industrial working class or proletariat into national political life or to spread the material benefits of industrialization to it. Indeed, the standard of life of early British, French, and German workers was low. In Orleanist France, for example, the working day in the new industrial cities was 15 hours. Half a man's wages was spent on bread alone. Meat was almost never available. Conditions in Britain were somewhat better by the 1830's, but child labor, low wages, and wretched living standards were still common. Prostitution, alcoholism, and the other social diseases symptomatic of the bewilderment of uprooted rural folk dumped into the cities abounded. It was reports of these miseries that fueled Marx's revolutionary indignation.

Two sets of factors, however, changed this pattern. First, the increased productivity of industry made it ever more possible to spread material benefits to the workers, and even highly desirable to include them in the rising prosperity in order to expand markets. Second, the numerical growth of the working class, its increased concentration, improved methods of communications, and a higher standard of literacy made it increasingly easier for the working class to organize itself. In the end the threat of violence posed by working-class organizations to the established system at the end of the 19th cent. convinced the higher and middle classes of the industrial nations that it was better to give in to some working-class demands than to face the disruptive effects and possible social chaos that would result from violent confrontation.

Working-class demands were fairly simple: shorter hours, a higher standard of living, the right to form unions and strike, and some sort of welfare scheme to replace the vanished welfare coverage of the rural extended family and to protect workers from the wide economic swings then current.

SOCIALISM. Before the revolutions of 1848 there were intellectual socialist programs, e.g., those of Claude Henri de Saint-Simon (1760–1825), Charles Fourier (1772–1837), Pierre Proudhon (1809–65), and others, several socialist utopian movements (most notably that of Robert Owen, 1771–1858), and a host of proletarian outbursts ranging from that of François Baboeuf (1760–97) during the French Revolution to Chartist agitation in England. But these were only weakly organized movements and there were no real socialist parties; nor was there much trade union activity, since this was illegal in most of the industrial countries.

The abortive national workshops of

1848 France were the 1st serious attempt by an industrializing nation to guarantee fair and full employment to workers. But the defeat of the far left between 1848 and 1850 by an aroused middle class ended this experiment.

In 1864 the 1st Socialist International convened and was dominated by the theories and personality of Karl Marx (1818–83). In 1871 the Paris Commune proved the disruptive potential of the radical left. But in fact the Commune was largely controlled by the followers of Auguste Blanqui (1805–81) and Proudhon, who were more typically small artisans opposed to industrialization than Marxist industrial workers.

In Germany the 1st socialist movement was led by Ferdinand Lassalle (1825–64) and as early as 1866 it received some encouragement from Bismarck, who eventually hoped to use it against possible middle-class opposition. One of the results of this vague alliance was Bismarck's support for universal suffrage (granted in Prussia in 1866). Though formally Marxist, the German Socialist Party (founded in 1875) had an increasing stake in the system against which it preached as its parliamentary representation rose. In 1877 it received 493,000 votes; in 1884, 550,000 votes; in 1887, 763,000 votes; in 1890, 1,427,000 votes; and by 1912 it was the largest single party in Germany. The German labor class was even stronger than these figures indicate since many of the Catholic workers adhered to the Catholic Center Party.

In France the strength of the Socialist Party also gradually rose. In 1884 trade unions were legalized. In 1899 the socialists participated in a government coalition in Parliament for the 1st time (largely because of their pro-Dreyfus, anticlerical, antiarmy, and anticonservative position). But because of the socialist tendency to co-operate with the system, and despite its formal theoretical Marxism, there developed a split in the French working class between the trade unions and the Socialist Party. The trade unions felt that they were not gaining enough concrete benefits, while the socialists

under Jean Jaurès (1859–1914) took an increasingly moderate tack and limited their activity to parliamentary maneuvering. The anarcho-syndicalist movement that developed from the more violence-oriented trade-union movement in France later formed the heart of the French Communist Party (founded in Dec. 1920).

In 1889 the 2nd International was formed. It too was Marxist, but it was ideologically split between the reformists and the revolutionaries. By organizing workmen's benevolent associations and by providing insurance, cultural activities, and even some schooling for the children of their members, the more successful European socialist parties cooled revolutionary ardor. Although from 1890 to 1914 there were frequent strikes and although the myth persisted of the great general strike that would eventually overthrow bourgeois society, strikes tended to be for short-term objectives and not for ultimate political ideals. In 1898 Eduard Bernstein (1850–1932) proposed that the socialist parties abandon their revolutionary ideologies. His ideas were defeated by the orthodox Marxist Karl Kautsky (1854–1938), but while the intellectual aims of the European socialists remained revolutionary, their actions did not. By 1914 French and German socialists were loyal supporters of their governments and the ideals of proletarian internationalism were quite dead (leading Lenin to denounce Kautsky as an archhypocrite and betrayer of Marxism).

BRITISH LABOUR MOVEMENT. In Britain and the United States analogies could be found with continental Europe except that the labor movements began as gradualist reform movements without passing through a prolonged Marxist revolutionary stage.

The almost unique quality of the British Labour movement was its early association with religion. Nonconformist, primitivist Protestant sects filled many of the emotional and social needs of the British working class, and though these sects were frowned upon by the Church of England, they remained nonrevolutionary and absorbed much of the radicalism of the poor. Methodism in Britain grew from 60,000 members in 1790 to about 600,000 in 1850. There were, moreover, other similar sects, though the Methodists were the largest. These sects grew in periods of social and economic turmoil and retreated in periods of stability. For example, the height of Chartist agitation coincided with a rapid increase in their numbers. After 1850 their growth was slowed by the amelioration of working-class conditions, but they continued to grow rapidly in the newly industrialized parts of Britain. Thus as trade unions developed (they were legalized in 1824, 60 years ahead of France), their leaders and membership tended to be more religious than their continental counterparts and consequently less Marxist and revolutionary. (On the Continent there was a tendency outside of Catholic parts of Germany for the churches to leave workers alone, and they in turn were largely agnostic.)

In the 1830's and 1840's a series of laws limited child and female labor in British mines and factories and remedied some of the harsher conditions of working-class life. In 1851 the 1st modern trade union, the Amalgamated Society of Engineers, was formed in Britain. It was the purpose of this union to keep itself out of politics and to work instead for the improvement of its members' standard of life. In 1867 some of the working class were enfranchised by the 2nd Reform Bill (Disraeli felt that he could thereby gain the votes of the workers), and in 1884 the 3rd Reform Bill enfranchised almost all the urban workers. In 1883 the Fabian Society was formed by British intellectuals who felt that evolutionary socialism was desirable. In the 1880's unskilled workers were organized for the 1st time and this produced the successful dock strike of 1889. In 1906 the trade unions and the Fabians united to form the Labour Party.

U.S. TRADE UNIONISM. American trade unionism had its roots in the post-Revolutionary and Jeffersonian eras, enjoyed an efflorescence during the 1830's, but really came to maturity after the Civil War. But the Knights of Labor, founded in 1869, and the National Labor Union

included only a small part of the workers of the U.S. As of 1885 the Knights of Labor engaged in a series of strikes that brought them about 700,000 members. In 1886 the American Federation of Labor was formed, but it was more an organization of skilled craft workers than a mass union trying to include all workers. It was also much less radical than the Knights of Labor, who, however, were too loosely organized to survive the reaction that came in the wake of the Chicago Haymarket Square bombing, 1886, attributed to anarcho-Communists.

Although American labor has always been considered reformist rather than revolutionary, and although the most successful of the labor organizations, the A.F. of L., was always antirevolutionary, the gains made by American labor in the 1880's and 1890's may in part have been the response to a series of violent strikes: Railway strike, 1877, McCormick strike, 1886, Homestead, 1892, Pullman, 1894, coal strike, 1902. In the 1877 railroad strike federal troops were called in, and the government adopted a hostile posture toward radical unionism. But by the Presidency of Theodore Roosevelt (1901–9), a new attitude emerged. Within a comparatively short time progressive labor measures were adopted. In President Wilson's 1st term, 1913–17, a Seaman's Act was passed, 4 Mar., 1915, and child labor was prohibited by Congress, 1 Sept., 1916 —though this act was later declared invalid by the courts. By the Clayton Antitrust Act, 15 Oct., 1914, labor received the right to organize itself, to strike, and to demand collective bargaining.

The partial success of working-class movements in the West up to 1914 legitimized labor organizations and brought certain benefits to the workers. It did not yet lead to what has since become known as the welfare state. By accepting the 1st demands of the working class, however, western societies blunted the revolutionary potential of the labor movements. This was made possible only by the ever rising productive capacity of the industrial economy which made it easier to spread material benefits to all.

THE INDUSTRIAL SOCIETIES, 1914–55

THE EVE OF WORLD WAR I. Between 1890 and 1914 it began to seem as though the industrial countries were entering a period of great stability. The struggle between aristocracies, bourgeois, workers, and peasants was ending. In Germany and Britain the old aristocracies had survived, but they had accepted, though in different ways, industrialization and were merging with the richer industrialists. The middle classes were content with their prosperity, and even the working class had been sufficiently pacified to blunt its revolutionary impact. In France the coalition between the bourgeois and the prosperous farmers and peasants found a new stability following the resolution of the church-state conflict of 1905. Even the radical labor unions were less anarchistic by 1910 than before. In the U.S. the pacification of labor had begun and the reforms of Theodore Roosevelt and Woodrow Wilson had largely placated the populist progressives.

In the nonindustrial world the western powers and Japan had political or economic control. It was only in Eastern Europe, in the Balkans, in the Ottoman Empire, and in Russia that there seemed much potential for instability.

WAR CASUALTIES. World War I destroyed the illusion of tranquillity. The casualty figures alone reveal the extent of the blow, though they cannot measure the moral and economic shock.

APPROXIMATE NUMBER OF DEATHS DURING THE WAR DUE TO FIGHTING, 1914–18

Germany	1,900,000
Russia	1,700,000
France	1,400,000
Austria-Hungary	1,000,000
U.K.	750,000
Italy	500,000
Turkey	400,000
Serbia	400,000
U.S.	115,000

Counting both deaths and serious injuries, the French casualty rate was 25% of the total army. For Serbia, Russia, Germany, and Austria-Hungary, these rates were higher. Death on an appalling scale and the accompanying privations brought old social systems into question. All the major losers went through subsequent revolutions (Germany, Austria-Hungary, Turkey, and Russia, which may be regarded as a loser despite its support for the eventual victors from 1914 to 1917).

POSTWAR GERMANY. During the last 2 years of the war, Germany fell under the total control of the army general staff. Imminent military collapse, Nov. 1918, provoked a revolt in the army and navy among tired and disillusioned soldiers. On 9 Nov., 1918, the German emperor abdicated and the war ended 2 days later.

The Weimar Republic which followed had the general support of the moderate socialists, the Catholics, and most of the middle classes, but it never destroyed the pre-eminence of the big industrialists, of the landowning Prussian Junkers, or of the army. From 1919 to 1923 the government had to rely on the army to crush revolts from the right and left (among them Adolf Hitler's attempted Nazi coup of 8–9 Nov., 1923). By 1922 the German economy had not yet recovered from the war because of the continued occupation of the Rhineland and because of the heavy reparations payments it had to make. From 1918 to Jan. 1923, the value of the German mark deteriorated from a rate of 4 marks to U.S. $1 to over 7,000 to $1. By 1 Nov., 1923, the rate had fallen to 130,000,000,000 marks to $1. While the holders of real property did not suffer, especially those with debts, the middle and lower classes had their savings wiped out. As small businesses collapsed, unemployment rose, and a general depression began. These events so frightened and demoralized the middle classes that they began to turn increasingly toward the radical right, while significant numbers of workers became Communists. From 1924 to 1929 there was a recovery, but the army, the landowners, and the industrialists continued to fear a Communist takeover and thus financed right-wing antidemocratic forces. The depres-

or less effective land reforms. But as Germany regained its economic power in the 1920's and 1930's, the nonindustrial Eastern European countries (and Czechoslovakia was the only well-industrialized one) became increasingly dependent on it. They exported their agricultural produce and raw materials to Germany in return for industrial products, and Germany came to dominate their economies as if they were colonies. This facilitated the rise of fascism, particularly in Rumania and Austria.

PORTUGAL AND SPAIN. In 1933 a fascist corporate state was declared in Portugal, and after a bloody civil war (1936–39) Spain also became a fascist state. These, however, were more agrarian than industrial fascist regimes.

GERMANY UNDER HITLER. Though much more industrialized than Italy, Germany still had a landed aristocracy, a powerful antidemocratic army and bureaucracy, and, most significant, an insecure, disillusioned middle class which had hardly recovered from the financial collapse of 1923 when it was hit by the depression of 1929. Since the working class seemed to be going increasingly Communist, the Nazi Party of Adolf Hitler (1889–1945) gained many adherents from the middle classes. Using the example of Mussolini's fascist toughs of the early 1920's, Hitler created the Brown Shirts (Storm Troopers). By early 1932 there were 300,000 of these (many of them unemployed men), forming a private Nazi army. In 1930 and 1931 in a series of private meetings with German industrialists, Hitler raised much of the money necessary to finance his party. In 1932 he gradually won over the Junker and officer aristocracy by posing as the only bulwark against Communism. On 30 Jan., 1933, after important electoral successes, he came to power. On 23 Mar. (Enabling Law) he received absolute power.

In their drive to power, the Nazis had created not only their own army but also their own administrative structure parallel to the state's. This machinery moved rapidly to take control of Germany after Hitler's accession to power. The semi-decentralized federal structure was dismantled and replaced by full centralization, Jan. 1934. Earlier the Nazis had begun implementing their anti-Semitic policy by removing all state bureaucrats from office if they were Jewish, Apr.–July 1933. All cultural activities were placed under the party, 22 Sept., 1933. In Mar.–Apr. 1934 trade unions were destroyed.

But in the 1st year of Nazi rule there developed a split between the mass revolutionary Nazi movement (whose power base was the Brown Shirts) and the more pragmatic Hitler. The radical Nazis aimed to eliminate the big capitalists as well as the aristocratic elements of the officer corps. Hitler wished to avoid such social upheaval, which might have seriously weakened Germany. On 30 June, 1934, the radical wing of the Nazi Party was violently purged, much to the relief of the German conservatives.

Hitler, however, was not a simple puppet of the old-line conservatives. He continued to move toward the elimination of every independent organization in Germany and to make the entire society subservient to the party. The Christian churches were restricted. A secret police, the Gestapo, placed its agents everywhere to root out subversion. The introduction of so many young Nazi officers amounted to a virtual take-over of the army (thus, on 20–21 July, 1944, when the officer corps tried to overthrow Hitler, it was easily defeated and much of the old Junker high-officer caste was liquidated). In Sept. 1936, Hitler proclaimed a 4-Year Economic Plan which put German industry directly under party control. By that time the Nazi regime had become as "totalitarian" as the contemporary Soviet Russian regime.

TOTALITARIANISM. Dictatorship was not a new phenomenon in history. But until the 1920's and 1930's it had not been technically possible for any state to assume such thorough control of all levels of society. It was only with modern mass communications that there could be the possibility of ever present mass indoctrination. Only a highly efficient bureaucracy could control so many details. This effective control over the totality of German life was what distinguished German fascism from other European fascisms, even Italian fascism, since these had arisen in far less efficient and industrialized societies.

FRANCE IN THE 1930's. Those countries that lacked reactionary military and quasi-feudal elites did not turn to fascism during the depression. In France, it is true, a host of fascist movements developed, of which the Cagoulards (hooded men), the Patriotic Youth, Jacques Doriot's French Popular Party, and the older Cross of Fire were the most important. Doriot's party actually achieved a membership of some half-million at its height in the late 1930's. But unlike Italy, there was no French monarchy to help the fascists into power. Nor was there a Junker class, a hereditary officer caste, or even an antirepublican bureaucracy. The monarchists (chiefly in the Action Française) remained a risible minority of reactionary youth who never played an important role. (It was only the German occupation between 1940 and 1944 that permitted a fascist regime to establish itself in France.)

France's early response to the depression was to seal itself off from the outside world by tariffs, to maintain price supports, and to discourage industrial competition. This kept France safe until 1931–32, when the cheapness of foreign products made it impossible for France to sell goods abroad. Even then unemployment remained low compared to Germany, Britain, or the U.S. Conservative economic policies remained in force until 1936, and prevented a rationalization of the French economy.

In May 1936, the Front Populaire, a leftist coalition of Socialists, Communists, and Radicals (which in France meant moderates), came to power. The Front quickly passed a series of labor reform bills. A 40-hour workweek was instituted. But the economy itself was neither overhauled nor primed by heavy government spending and, predictably, it remained stagnant. The demoralization of France

produced by this stagnation, its declining strength vis-à-vis Germany, and its insistent social and economic conservatism (popular and moderate as it was) led to its startlingly rapid defeat by Germany in 1940.

BRITAIN IN THE 1930's. Great Britain responded to the depression by reversing its century-old free-trade policy in 1932. But since there had been a Labour government in power at the start of the depression, the election of 1931 brought a Conservative victory. Britain thus did not engage in a wholesale program of reform to overcome the depression, and it was not until rearmament for World War II began that, in the late 1930's, it regained its prosperity.

U.S. IN THE 1930's. Of the major western democratic nations, the U.S. carried out the most ambitious program of social reform in response to the depression. The New Deal, as this reform program was called, did not really end the depression (that had to wait until the heavy spending put into rearmament from 1939 on), but it did restore domestic tranquillity and confidence in the government. It also ended many of the most glaring social injustices.

An outstanding feature of the New Deal and of New Deal legislation was the increase it entailed in the activity of the federal government. After Roosevelt's accession to power, 4 Mar., 1933, a flood of federal legislation consciously attempted to correct social injustices and improve the lot of the underprivileged. Acts of Congress and of the executive reformed banking, securities trading, and the currency, created jobs for the unemployed, and regulated housing, agriculture, wages, labor relations, trade unions, pensions, insurance, and taxation (p. 445). Though highly unpopular among many of the affluent in the U.S., these measures saved the old social system by reforming it.

THE ROOTS OF SOCIAL INSTABILITY. Industrialization continued the differentiation and rationalization of society which had started in the 18th and 19th cents. But by 1930 there remained large parts of society for whom new integrative bonds had not yet evolved to replace traditional ones. One indication of the decay of old social bonds was continued urbanization. Another was the continued disintegration of traditional extended families and their replacement by more upwardly mobile, smaller families. The birth rate continued to fall (except for a momentary upward spurt after World War I), and this movement was accelerated by the depression.

FEMINIST MOVEMENT. Yet another element of social change was the new role played by women. Rather than remaining in the traditionally subordinated roles which they had held, some women began to compete with men in political and economic life, a process accelerated by the use of women in factories during World War I. Though the pattern changed slowly for the majority of women (in the 1960's men still held almost all superior positions), there were certain dramatic legal changes such as the extension of the right to vote to women (1918–20 in the U.S., Britain, and Germany, but not until 1945 in France and Japan).

INCREASE IN GOVERNMENTAL ACTIVITY. All these continuing changes increased the problem of the individual's isolation from larger social units which could support him in times of trouble. This made individuals feel more vulnerable to the complex and distant forces that shaped their daily life. In every industrial society in the 1930's, strong pressures arose for increased government action. Were there no longer any extended families to care for the old? Then the government must do it. Did stockmarket speculation bring unemployment? The government must regulate it. And indeed central governments were the only agencies that could effectively deal with the intermeshing world economic and social problems before which local associations were dwarfed.

Government action was not enough. The uprooted also sought to form their own associations for protection and companionship. These tended to play into the hands of political parties which could use them for their own purposes. Thus workers' associations fulfilled more than

political purposes, but they also provided a main base of support for various leftist parties. Early fascist movements were coalitions of similar types of groups. The logical extension of this search for new groupings was the over-all attempt to organize men's lives in the totalitarian states, and it was the need for new organization that allowed totalitarianism to succeed. In countries where economic and social change was sufficiently gradual to allow older associations and groupings to survive, there was less need for government involvement.

WORLD WAR II CASUALTIES. World War II surpassed all previous wars in total casualties. It was at once a racist war (of Germans against Slavs and Jews, of Japanese against whites), an ideological war (of fascism against all other systems), an economic, and a nationalistic war. Technical efficiency made mass slaughter possible, and also involved larger proportions of populations than in any previous war.

MILITARY AND CIVILIAN DEATHS, WORLD WAR II

USSR	20,000,000
Poland	6,000,000a
Germany	5,000,000b
China	1,300,000c
Japan	1,800,000
Yugoslavia	1,600,000
France	540,000d
Rumania	460,000
Italy	450,000
U.K.	420,000
Czechoslovakia	415,000
Austria	380,000
U.S.	350,000

a Incl. c. 3,000,000 Jews.
b Incl. c. 1,100,000 civilians.
c Military deaths only; civilian casualties were much more numerous.
d Incl. c. 330,000 civilians.

RISE OF COMMUNIST POWER. Communists played a leading role in many European resistance movements which arose against the Nazi occupation. This was because the prewar Communist organizations had better prepared their members for clandestine operations than had other political groups. In Yugoslavia the Communists emerged as the only ruling force after the war. In Greece, Italy, France, Czechoslovakia, and Poland they became important components in the postwar political balance. Where the Soviet army could directly assist them, as in Eastern Europe, they took power. Where it could not, they nevertheless remained significant as the representatives of the working class and poor peasants (most notably in France and Italy). In Greece they were defeated in a civil war.

SOCIAL CHANGE IN THE POST-WAR YEARS. In Britain, war suffering created pressures for social reforms. In 1945 the Labour Party took power after winning an overwhelming victory at the polls. A National Insurance Act, 1946, and a National Health Service Act, 1946, were passed and went into effect in 1948. A series of nationalizations of major industries took place. Britain thus became a welfare state (pp. 519, 817–818).

The shock of the 1940 defeat in France and the victory of the Resistance movement against the Vichy government in 1944 had a major effect. Economic planning and rationalization were pushed. Coal, gas, and electric industries were nationalized as well as the largest deposit banks and insurance companies. The social-security system was enlarged. Even the pattern of demographic decline was somewhat reversed by an increased birth rate. Between 1946 and 1958 the 4th Republic ruled over the greatest economic expansion known to France since the 1850's. Many of the old problems remained, however, particularly because of a failure to achieve sufficient concentration of industry through large firms, the persistence of too many small shopkeepers and peasants, and the relative stagnation of southern France. These problems manifested themselves in political instability and persistent hostility between labor and management which helped the French Communist Party to remain strong.

German society was profoundly changed by the war. The Prussian landowners disappeared as their lands were occupied by the Communists. The officer caste (largely decimated by Hitler during the war) went with them. Great prosperity after 1949 discouraged any return to fascism.

Defeated and occupied Japan went through a similar social transformation. The landowners were expropriated by the land reform of 1946. The democratization of Japan, however, did not curb the growth of the *zaibatsu,* who participated in an industrial boom (which made Japan the world's 3rd largest industrial power by 1969). From 1945 to 1955 Japan went through a large-scale modernization which spread the benefits of the economy to the population and brought her into the ranks of the high-mass-consumption industrial nations.

Eastern Europe had entered World War II as a semicolonial area of big landowners. Communist rule decisively broke this pattern; however, it was not enough to do away with landlords. Full modernization presupposes the tightening of internal links within a society and the relative decrease of dependency on outside powers. Until the mid 1950's the Soviet Union acted as a sort of colonial overlord in Eastern Europe. After this period, however, an internal liberalization of East European regimes occurred (with notable exceptions and reversals), accompanied by increasing independence from Soviet domination. Rumania's refusal to adhere to Russia's demands in 1966 that it delay industrialization to continue exporting agricultural and mineral products marked the formal recognition in Eastern Europe that modernization there had to take a path roughly similar to that earlier followed in the West.

By 1955 Soviet Russian industrial production was from 2 to 3 times greater than in 1940. But successful industrialization brought with it the same demands for liberalization which had previously taken place in the West. The managerial class created in the 1930's to run the economy was opposed to irrational police-state methods which put a higher premium on political behavior than on technical efficiency. Stalin's death, 5 Mar., 1953, stopped a planned attack on this growing source of protest. His successors pursued for a time the more rational line of liberalization and a softening of police methods, accompanied by a drive to increase consumer goods and raise the low standard of living. How significantly these reforms have stabilized Soviet society has not been tested in crisis.

THE NONINDUSTRIAL SOCIETIES, 1760–1968

THE SOCIAL ORDER IN THE COLONIAL WORLD. Except for a few peripheral European communities in Canada, Australia, New Zealand, and South Africa (which were not industrialized but whose populations already had semimodernized social structures), the world outside Europe and the U.S. was neither much industrialized nor modernized (with the partial exception of Russia and Japan) before the 20th cent. (p. 740). There was neither the large-scale differentiation and rationalization of society nor the tight integration of states which characterized western nations. The economies of the nonindustrial societies were poor and the middle classes small. Malintegration of these nonmodernized areas left them vulnerable to western interference, which was able to play on regional, political, and cultural differences. Their technological backwardness left them open to economic and military domination by the West. This and the West's aggressiveness produced the age of modern colonialism.

Despite wide differences between the various colonies and semicolonies that arose in Asia, Africa, and Latin America between 1760 and World War I, a general model may be described for them since they shared many characteristics.

Where there was actual domination from the outside (imperialism) rather than commercial exploitation only, some form of cash taxation was imposed on the local population to pay for administration. Taxation often forced peasants to grow cash crops, since they needed money to satisfy the new government's demands. In all colonies the production of cash crops and mineral products which could profitably be exported to the home and other markets was pushed. Everywhere the effect was to discourage the growth of local manufacturing and to strengthen the position of native landowners—unless they were too poorly organized to produce the desired commodities or were expropriated by Europeans. In some areas, e.g., in India, a whole new class of landowners was created. Elsewhere, e.g., in coastal China, a class of middlemen (compradors) used their commercial profits to buy land and transform themselves into a new landowner class which partially replaced the traditional aristocracy. Nearly everywhere, however, native artisans and putative manufacturing middle classes were destroyed or prevented from getting any kind of start.

With colonialism came an improvement in internal communications. This permitted large-scale population migrations which had not before been possible. There developed large commercial and administrative cities, usually along the coasts. The demand for labor in these cities attracted young men from the interior who came to earn tax money and to partake in the pleasures of "modern life." Thus in most colonies and semicolonies there was a rapid growth of cities which were not, however, in most cases manufacturing centers. Urbanization and the growth of a class of uprooted peasants living in cities eventually proved to be major stimulants to revolt against western authority.

European schools were started, either by missionaries to win converts or by administrations to train low-level help. At first the products of these schools in Asia and Africa were docile supporters of the colonial regimes, but as they gradually discovered that impassable race barriers blocked the advancement of "natives," they became leaders of the nationalist, anticolonial protest movements.

The colonizers frequently supported landowners and traditional authorities who shared in the profits of colonial-

TABLE I. ESTIMATED POPULATION BY REGION
(million)

	1750	1800	1850	1900	1940	1950	1960	1965
World total	728	906	1,171	1,608	2,295	2,517	3,005	3,295
North America	1	6	26	81	144	166	199	214
Middle America	5	10	13	25	41	52	68	80
South America	6	9	20	38	89	111	146	166
Europe and Russia	144	192	274	423	575	572	639	676
Asia (excl. Russia)	475	597	741	915	1,244	1,381	1,659	1,830
Africa	95	90	95	120	191	222	277	311
Oceania	2	2	2	6	11	13	16	17

NOTE: Columns may not add up because of rounding.

TABLE II. % DISTRIBUTION OF WORLD POPULATION BY REGION

	1750	1800	1850	1900	1940	1950	1960	1965
World total	100.0	100.0	100.0	100.0	100.0	100.0	100.0	100.0
North America	0.1	0.7	2.2	5.0	6.3	6.6	6.6	6.5
Middle America	0.7	1.1	1.1	1.5	1.8	2.1	2.3	2.4
South America	0.8	1.0	1.7	2.4	3.9	4.4	4.9	5.0
Europe and Russia	19.8	21.2	23.4	26.3	25.0	22.7	21.3	20.5
Asia (excl. Russia)	65.2	65.9	63.3	56.9	54.2	54.9	55.2	55.6
Africa	13.0	9.9	8.1	7.5	8.3	8.8	9.2	9.5
Oceania	0.4	0.2	0.2	0.4	0.5	0.5	0.5	0.5

SOURCE: (Tables I and II): A. M. Carr-Saunders, *World Population*, Oxford, 1936, p. 42 (1750–1900); United Nations, *Determinants and Consequences of Population Trends*, New York, 1953, p. 11 (1750–1900); and *Demographic Yearbook 1966*, p. 95 (1940–65).

TABLE III. RATE OF GROWTH PER ANNUM
(%)

	1750–1800	1800–1850	1850–1900	1900–1950	1950–1965
World total	.4	.5	.6	.9	1.8
North America	3.6	3.0	2.3	1.4	1.7
Middle America	1.4	.5	1.3	1.5	2.9
South America	.8	1.6	1.3	2.2	2.7
Europe and Russia	.6	.7	.9	.6	1.1
Asia (excl. Russia)	.5	.4	.4	.8	1.9
Africa	−.1	.1	.5	1.2	2.3
Oceania	0	0	2.2	1.6	1.8

TABLE IV. RATE OF GROWTH PER ANNUM, 1750–1965
(%)

World total	.71
Areas of European settlement (Europe, the Americas, and Oceania)	.93
All other	.63

SOURCE: (Tables III and IV): Data from Table I. Growth rates derived, using formula $r = \left(\sqrt[n]{\dfrac{x_t}{x_i}} - 1 \right) 100$, where n = number of years; x_t = terminal-year data; and x_i = initial-year data.

type economies, but these tended to be the most conservative elements in their societies. The more modernized, western-educated subjects of colonial regimes naturally opposed these conservative elements who not only served as the tools of imperialism but simultaneously opposed internal modernization.

THE REVOLUTION OF RISING EXPECTATIONS. With the breakup of the European colonial empires after World War II, a host of newly independent states emerged in Asia and Africa. All professed modernization as their goal, but few were able to establish a social order conducive to achieving it. A major source of instability was rapid urbanization. Traditional village and family ties were broken, and individuals were thrown into less secure environments. In consequence, they sought out and created new organizations for moral and economic support. Their requirements were fulfilled by a wide variety of radical political parties as well as by new unions, churches, and other associations. The rise of socialist parties in 19th-cent. Europe may be seen as an analogous development. But whereas the revolutionary potential of the European socialists was blunted by increasing prosperity, the non-industrial world of the mid-20th cent. developed radical mass parties before the onset of industrial maturity. This has

made the satisfaction of radical demands unrealistic.

In 19th cent. Europe, moreover, economic and medical advances lowered the death rate. But within 50 years after the drop in death rates, birth rates also began to drop as increased prosperity and social mobility induced people to have fewer children. In the nonindustrial world of today, however, medical advances imported from the West have reduced the death rates while birth rates have remained very high. Thus population growth has been rapid even though industries have not grown to absorb the extra manpower.

Mobilization for nationalist and modernizing revolutions has increasingly led the masses to demand equality. This has forced leaderships to promise ever greater

TABLE V. CRUDE BIRTH RATES OF SELECTED COUNTRIES PER ANNUM
(rates per 1,000 total population)

	1751–1780 (1)	1781–1810 (2)	1841–1850 (3)	1891–1900 (4)	1920–1929 (5)	1930–1939 (6)	1940–1949 (7)	1950–1959 (8)	1960–1964 (9)
England and Wales	37.2	37.5a	32.6	29.9	19.2	15.1	16.7	15.7	17.9
Belgium	—	—	30.5	29.0	20.0	16.5	15.6	16.8	17.0
France	38.6b	34.7	27.3	22.2	19.2	16.2	17.5	18.9	18.0
Germany*	—	—	36.1	36.1	21.1	17.8	*	16.6	17.5
Netherlands	—	38c	33.0	32.5	25.0	21.0	23.8	21.7	20.7
Russia**	—	43.7d	49.7	49.2	44.4e	37.6e	31.4e	25.8	22.4
Japan	—	—	—	29.8	34.5	30.5	30.1	21.4	17.2
Australia	—	—	—	29.9	23.0	17.4	21.3	22.8	21.9
U.S.	—	55f	44.3g	33	21.4	17.4	21.6	24.5	22.4
Argentina	—	—	—	—	30.9	25.4	24.6	24.5	22.4
Egypt (UAR)	—	—	—	45.2h	43.3	43.2	41.0	42.2	42.8
Chile	—	—	—	38.8h	42.1	38.5	36.1	34.8	34.8
India	—	—	—	46i	46.4i	45.2i	39.9i	41.7i	38.4

SOURCE: Col. 1: Phyllis Deane and W. A. Cole, *British Economic Growth 1688–1959*, Cambridge, 1964, p. 127 (Britain); D. V. Glass, "World Population," in *Cambridge Economic History of Europe*, Cambridge, 1965, VI, p. 101 (France).

Col. 2: Deane and Cole, *op. cit.*, p. 127 (Britain); Glass, *op. cit.*, pp. 101, 97 (France and Russia); Simon Kuznets, *Modern Economic Growth*, New Haven, 1966, p. 43 (Netherlands and the U.S.).

Col. 3: Glass, *op. cit.*, pp. 68–69, 97 (all except U.S.); Department of Commerce, Bureau of the Census, *Historical Statistics of the U.S.*, Washington, 1960, p. 23 (U.S.).

Col. 4: W. S. and E. S. Woytinsky, *World Population and Production*, New York, 1953, p. 144 (all except U.S., India, Egypt, and Chile); Kuznets, *op. cit.*, pp. 42–44 (U.S.; Kuznets gives the Australian birth rate as 42 per thousand.); Glass, *op. cit.*, p. 84 (India); Carlo Cipolla, *The Economic History of World Population*, Baltimore, 1962 (Egypt and Chile).

Cols. 5–9: UN, *Demographic Yearbook 1965*.

a 1781–1800; b 1771–75; c 1813–24; d 1801–10; e 1926–28, 1937–39, 1940–44; f 1790–1800; g 1860; h 1905–9; i est. annual averages for 1891–1901, 1921–31, 1931–41, 1941–51, and 1951–61.

* Germany to 1945; West Germany, 1945–64; 1940–44, 17.4; 1945–49, 13.0.

** European Russia, pre-1920; USSR, 1920–64.

TABLE VI. CRUDE DEATH RATE OF SELECTED COUNTRIES PER ANNUM
(rates per 1,000 total population)

	1751–1780 (1)	1781–1810 (2)	1841–1850 (3)	1891–1900 (4)	1920–1929 (5)	1930–1939 (6)	1940–1949 (7)	1950–1959 (8)	1960–1964 (9)
England and Wales	30.4	27.7a	22.4	18.2	12.2	12.0	11.9	11.6	11.8
Belgium	—	—	24.4	19.2	13.8	13.2	14.2	12.0	12.1
France	—	—	23.2	21.5	17.3	15.8	15.8	12.2	11.2
Germany*	—	—	26.8	22.2	12.9	11.4	*	10.8	11.1
Netherlands	—	—	26.2	18.4	10.5	8.8	9.8	7.5	7.8
Russia**	—	—	—	34.1	22.6b	17.9b	18.0b	8.6	7.2
Japan	—	—	—	20.9	21.4	17.7	16.6	8.6	7.3
Australia	—	—	—	13.0	9.6	9.2	10.4	9.1	8.7
U.S.	—	25c	—	19	11.9	11.0	10.3	9.4	9.5
Argentina	—	—	—	—	13.5	11.6	10.0	8.7	8.5
Egypt (UAR)	—	—	—	26.5d	26.1	27.0	24.9	17.8	16.5
Chile	—	—	—	32.5d	27.8	23.6	18.5	13.0	11.8
India	—	—	—	44e	36.3e	31.2e	27.4e	22.8d	12.9

SOURCE: Col. 1: Deane and Cole, *op. cit.*, p. 127.
Col. 2: Deane and Cole, *op. cit.*, p. 127 (Britain) ; Kuznets, *op. cit.*, p. 43 (U.S.) .
Col. 3: Glass, *op. cit.*, pp. 68–69.
Col. 4: Woytinsky and Woytinsky, *op. cit.*, p. 165 (except U.S., Chile, Egypt, and India) ; Kuznets, *op. cit.*, p. 43 (U.S.) ; Glass, *op. cit.*, p. 84 (India) ; Cipolla, *op. cit.*, p. 78 (Chile and Egypt) .
Cols. 5–9: UN, *Demographic Yearbook 1966.*
a 1781–1800; b 1926–28, 1937–39, 1940–44; c 1790–1800; d 1905–9; e est. annual averages for 1891–1901, 1921–31, 1931–41, 1941–51, and 1951–61.
* Germany to 1945; West Germany 1945–64; 1940–44, 12.2; 1945–49, 11.3.
** European Russia, pre-1920; USSR, 1920–64.

TABLE VII. NATURAL INCREASE IN POPULATION IN SELECTED COUNTRIES PER ANNUM
(rates per 1,000 total population)

	1751–1780 (1)	1781–1810 (2)	1841–1850 (3)	1891–1900 (4)	1920–1929 (5)	1930–1939 (6)	1940–1949 (7)	1950–1959 (8)	1960–1964 (9)
England and Wales	6.8	9.8a	10.2	11.7	7.0	3.1	4.8	3.9	6.1
Belgium	—	—	6.1	9.8	6.2	3.0	1.4	4.8	4.9
France	—	—	4.1	.7	1.9	.4	1.7	6.7	6.8
Germany*	—	—	9.3	13.9	8.2	6.4	*	5.8	6.4
Netherlands	—	—	6.8	14.1	14.5	12.2	14.0	14.2	12.9
Russia**	—	—	—	15.1	11.9b	12.6b	12.1b	12.8	10.0
Japan	—	—	—	8.9	13.1	12.8	13.5	12.8	9.9
Australia	—	—	—	16.9	13.4	8.2	10.9	13.7	13.2
U.S.	—	30.0c	—	14.0	9.5	6.4	11.3	15.1	12.9
Argentina	—	—	—	—	17.4	13.8	14.6	15.8	13.9
Egypt (UAR)	—	—	—	18.7d	17.2	16.2	16.1	24.4	26.3
Chile	—	—	—	6.3d	14.3	14.9	17.6	21.8	23.0
India	—	—	—	2.0e	10.1e	14.0e	12.5e	14.3e	25.5

SOURCE: Tables V and VI, birth rate minus death rate.
a 1781–1800; b 1926–28, 1937–39, 1940–44; c 1790–1800; d 1905–9; e est. annual averages for 1890–1901, 1921–31, 1931–41, 1941–51, and 1951–61.
* Germany to 1945; West Germany, 1945–64; 1940–44, 5.2; 1945–49, 1.7.
** European Russia, pre-1920; USSR, 1920–64.

rewards to maintain popular support. (This double phenomenon is what is often called the revolution of rising expectations.) But the leaders find it ever more difficult to maintain the tight social discipline and economic austerity demanded by early industrialization. Thus a vicious circle has developed of promises followed by disappointments. The resulting instability, with leaders' attempts to put the blame for failure on outsiders by encouraging rabid jingoism, has favored the rise of military regimes which alone have the power to control their populations.

A further problem has been the very existence of highly successful industrial nations. To be sure, these can transfer technology to less favored countries, but they are also a source of almost insurmountable competition in world markets. This has made the development of internal industries increasingly difficult for nonindustrial countries.

Finally, Western Europe, the U.S., Russia, Japan, and China all entered the modern age as fairly coherent cultural units with old intranational links. Most new Asian and African states have not enjoyed a similar advantage.

WORLD POPULATION, 1760–1968

TOTAL POPULATION AND DISTRIBUTION. Between the mid-18th cent. and the present, world population has increased more than 4-fold (see Table I). The distribution of world population altered as indicated on Table II.

POPULATION GROWTH. There has been an acceleration in the rate of the world's population growth (see Table III). While the growth of population has occurred in less developed areas of Asia and Africa as well as in areas of European settlement, the rate of growth has been greatest in the areas of European settlement (see Table IV). In the 20th cent. the rate of growth in Africa exceeded the world rate (see Table III). Between 1950 and 1965 the rate of growth in Asia exceeded the world rate (see Table VI). The rate of growth in less developed areas surpassed that of industrial countries.

BIRTH RATES. Good data are not available to measure the birth-rate pat-

TABLE VIII. INFANT MORTALITY RATES IN SELECTED COUNTRIES, ANNUAL AVERAGE
(deaths under 1 year of age per 1,000 live births)

	1871–1880 (1)	1891–1900 (2)	1920–1929 (3)	1930–1939 (4)	1940–1949 (5)	1950–1959 (6)	1960–1964 (7)
England and Wales	149	153	74	59	45	25	21
Belgium	153	161	105	87	78	41	28
France	172	164	94	76	77	40	25
Germany*	—	207a	113	72	*	43	29
Netherlands	203	158	67	42	41	22	16
Russia (USSR)	266	268	178b	166b	182b	61	32
Japan	—	170	153	117	77	40	26
Australia	—	112	57	41	32	23	20
U.S.	—	162a	73	57	38	27	25
Argentina	—	—	113	97	78	63	60
Egypt (UAR)	—	—	150	163	148	128	117
Chile	—	—	233	209	163	122	115
India	—	—	180c	169c	183d	139d	80e

SOURCE: Cols. 1 and 2: Woytinsky and Woytinsky, *op. cit.*, p. 167; Cipolla, *op. cit.* (Germany and U.S., 1900).

Cols. 3–6: UN, *Demographic Yearbook 1966.*

a 1900; b 1926–28, 1937–39, 1940–44; c British India only; d 1941–51, 1951–61. e 1960–64, but only the "registration area," which comprised a population of about 320 m. in these years.

* Germany to 1939; West Germany, 1946–64; 1946–49, 100.

tern worldwide. The table on p. 875 summarizes some of the available historical information.

As nations industrialized, birth rates witnessed an overall decline. For indus-

trial nations, the lowest years were the 1930's; then there was an upward turn in birth rates, but the birth rates of the 1960's did not reach the levels of before 1900 (before 1929 in Europe). Less de-

TABLE IX. LIFE EXPECTANCY AT BIRTH
(years)

		1875 (1)	1905 (2)	1925 (3)	1950 (4)	1963–65 (5)
England and Wales	M	41a	51b	56c	66	68
	F	45a	55b	59c	71	74
Belgium	M	—	45d	56	62e	68f
	F	—	49d	60	67e	73f
France	M	—	45g	52h	64i	68j
	F	—	49g	56h	69i	75j
Germany*	M	36	45	56	65k	68l
	F	38	48	59	68k	73l
Netherlands	M	—	51m	62n	71o	71p
	F	—	53m	63n	73o	76p
Russia (USSR)	M	—	31q	42	61r	66l
	F	—	33q	47	67r	74l
Japan	M	—	44s	42	56	68t
	F	—	45s	43	60	73t
Australia	M	—	55	63	66u	68v
	F	—	59	67	71u	74v
U.S.	M	—	47	58	66	67t
	F	—	50	61	71	74t
Argentina	M	—	45w	—	57x	63y
	F	—	47w	—	61x	69y
Egypt (UAR)	M	—	—	36z	41e	52aa
	F	—	—	41z	47e	54aa
Chile	M	—	—	40bb	50cc	—
	F	—	—	41bb	54cc	—
India	M	25dd	23ee	27ff	32gg	42hh
	F	25dd	23ee	27ff	32gg	40hh

SOURCE: Col. 1: Glass, *op. cit.*, pp. 72 (England and Wales), 82 (Germany), 84 (India).

Col. 2: Glass, *op. cit.*, pp. 72 (England and Wales), 82 (Belgium, Germany, Russia, Australia), 84 (India); UN, *Demographic Yearbook 1948* (France, Netherlands, Japan); *Historical Statistics of U.S.* (U.S.); UN, *Demographic Yearbook 1957* (Argentina).

Col. 3: UN, *Demographic Yearbook 1957* (England and Wales, France, Netherlands, Egypt, Chile); Glass, *op. cit.*, pp. 82 (Belgium, Germany, Russia, Australia), 86 (Japan), 84 (India); *Historical Statistics of U.S.* (U.S.).

Col. 4: UN, *Demographic Yearbook 1957* (all except U.S. and Egypt), *Historical Statistics of U.S.* (U.S.); UN, *Demographic Yearbook 1966* (Egypt).

Col. 5: UN, *Demographic Yearbook 1966*.

a 1871–80;   b 1901–12;   c 1920–22;   d 1895;   e 1946–49;   f 1959–63; g 1898–1903;   h 1920–23;   i 1950–51;   j 1964;   k 1949–51;   l 1964–65; m 1900–1909;   n 1921–30;   o 1950–52;   p 1961–65;   q 1895;   r 1954–55; s 1899–1903;   t 1965;   u 1946–48;   v 1960–62;   w 1914;   x 1947;   y 1959–61; z 1936–38;   aa 1960;   bb 1930;   cc 1952;   dd 1881–91;   ee 1901–11;   ff 1921–31;   gg 1941–50;   hh 1951–60.

* To 1945, all Germany; after 1945, West Germany only.

veloped countries, with few exceptions, were characterized by high birth rates. Birth-rate figures for poorer countries are incomplete, but from c. 1920 onward there seems to have been the same general decline in the birth rate in poorer countries (as they improved their well-being) as there had been in the case of the leading industrial nations in earlier years. The decline was a slow one.

DEATH RATES. Good data are not available to measure the death-rate pattern worldwide. Table VI summarizes some of the available historical information.

In the leading industrial nations, death rates declined steadily. Evidence for the death rates in most poorer countries in the 18th, 19th, and early 20th cents. is not available. Figures given by Carr-Saunders indicate a rise in death rates in India, 1885–1900. Between 1900 and 1917 death rates in India fluctuated. Because of severe crop failures, causing starvation, and because of the influenza epidemic, death rates in India soared in 1918. An estimated 5 m. deaths occurred in India during 1918–19. In some less developed countries the death rate rose during 1920–40 (see Table VI, data on Egypt) ; in other countries, the death rate declined (see Table VI, data on Chile and India). From 1940 onward there was a sharp drop in death rates in poorer nations, as

TABLE X. AGE COMPOSITION OF WESTERN POPULATIONS AT VARIOUS POINTS OF TIME
(% of total population)

	Age Group	England and Wales	France	Sweden	
Before 1800	(years)	1695	1775	1750	
	0–14	(38)	33.3	33.3	
	15–64	(57)	62.6	60.5	
	65 and over	(5)	4.4	6.2	
	Total	100	100.0	100.0	
1800			1801	1800	
	0–14	—	33.0	32.3	
	15–64	—	61.4	62.0	
	65 and over	—	5.6	5.7	
	Total	—	100.0	100.0	
		Great Britain			U.S.
1850		1851	1851	1850	1850
	0–14	35.5	27.3	32.9	41.6
	15–64	59.9	66.2	62.3	55.5
	65 and over	4.6	6.5	4.8	2.9
	Total	100.0	100.0	100.0	100.0
1900		1901	1901	1900	1900
	0–14	32.6	26.1	32.4	34.4
	15–64	62.7	65.7	59.2	61.3
	65 and over	4.7	8.2	8.4	4.1
	Total	100.0	100.0	100.0	100.0
1950		1951	1950	1950	1950
	0–14	22.5	21.7	23.4	27.0
	15–64	66.7	66.5	66.3	64.9
	65 and over	10.8	11.8	10.3	8.1
	Total	100.0	100.0	100.0	100.0

SOURCE: Glass, *op. cit.*, p. 134.

modern medicine, sanitation, and disease control had their effect.

NATURAL INCREASE IN POPULATION. The figures in Table VII do not reflect the change in population in these countries because they do not take into account international migration. The rate of increase in the U.S., 1790–1800, was due to an extraordinarily high birth rate (see Table V). Natural-increase figures rose sharply, 1960–64, in the UAR, Chile, and India because of sharply falling death rates (see Table VI).

INFANT MORTALITY RATES. From the decade of the 1890's onward, infant mortality rates, in every country in Table VIII, except USSR and India, show a steady and drastic drop. The Soviet rates show a steady drop, except for the World War II years; the Indian rates show an upward turn during 1941–51, but this may be due to changes in the statistical series. There seems ample evidence of a general sharp drop in infant mortality from the late 19th cent. to the mid-20th. Progress in medicine and sanitation plus

TABLE XI. AGE COMPOSITION AROUND 1950 OF POPULATIONS WITH HIGH FERTILITY
(% of total population)

	Age Group (years)	Netherlands 1950	Spain 1950	Portugal 1950	Yugoslavia 1950
Europe	0–14	29.3	26.2	29.5	30.8
	15–64	63.0	66.6	63.5	63.5
	65 and over	7.7	7.2	7.0	5.7
	Total	100.0	100.0	100.0	100.0

		Brazil 1950	Colombia 1950	Venezuela 1950	
Latin America	0–14	41.9	42.0	42.0	
	15–64	55.6	55.1	55.3	
	65 and over	2.5	2.9	2.7	
	Total	100.0	100.0	100.0	

		Ceylon 1946	India 1951	Japan 1950	Mainland China 1953
Asia	0–14	37.2	37.5	35.4	35.9
	15–64	59.3	58.9	59.7	59.7
	65 and over	3.5	3.6	4.9	4.4
	Total	100.0	100.0	100.0	100.0

SOURCE: Glass, *op. cit.*, p. 136.

TABLE XII. CITIES WITH 100,000 OR MORE INHABITANTS BY REGION, 1800, AROUND 1930, AND AROUND 1965

	1800	1930	1965
World total	36	678	1,508
America (N. and S.)	1	162	332
Europe (excl. Russia)	18	248	374
Russia (USSR)	2	56	193
Asia (excl. Russia)	14	193	492
Africa	1	17	103
Oceania	—	2	14

SOURCE: Woytinsky and Woytinsky, *op. cit.*, p. 118 (1800 and 1930); UN, *Demographic Yearbook 1966* (1965).
NOTE: Figures include urban agglomerations, not just cities proper.

better nutrition and standards of living cut down infant mortality just as such progress lowered the death rates.

LIFE EXPECTANCY AT BIRTH. The period shows a steady increase in life expectancy at birth. In 1875 life expectancy at birth in England and Wales was only 41 for men and 45 for women; in India it was 25 for both sexes. By the 1960's, in industrial nations, the life expectancy at birth was 67 to 71 years for men and 73 to 76 years for women. In India, 1950's, the life expectancy at birth was 42 years for men and 40 for women.

AGE COMPOSITION OF THE POPULATION. The data on age composition reflect the aging of western populations since 1850. The aging population so in evidence among western populations was not yet apparent, 1950, among Latin American and Asian populations.

MIGRATION. During the past 2 centuries there has been a tendency worldwide toward greater mobility of population. After c. 1820 the world's main recipient of immigrants was the U.S. Emigration from Europe provided the bulk of U.S. immigrants.

TABLE XIII. IMMIGRANTS TO THE U.S. BY COUNTRY OF LAST PERMANENT RESIDENCE, 1820–1966
All countries, 43,614,313

Europe	35,221,800	Rumania	160,459
Albania	2,242	Spain	201,916
Austriaa	} 4,287,149	Sweden	1,261,768
Hungary		Switzerland	335,818
Belgium	195,319		
		Turkey in Europe	162,412
Bulgaria	66,789	USSRa	3,345,610
Czechoslovakia	130,569	Yugoslavia	73,594
Denmark	357,342	Other Europe	50,261
Estonia	1,021		
Finland	29,559	Asiad	1,242,189
		Chinae	419,643
France	713,532	India	18,502
Germanya	6,862,900	Japan	348,623
Great Britainb	4,711,711	Turkey in Asia	208,415
England	3,014,362	Other Asiad	247,006
Scotland	804,821		
Wales	93,543	America	6,710,846
		Canada and Newfoundland	3,836,071
Greece	514,700	Mexico	1,414,273
Irelandc	4,706,854	Central America	177,641
Italy	5,067,717	South America	400,926
Latvia	2,233	West Indies	777,382
Lithuania	3,533	Other America	104,553
Luxembourg	2,431		
Netherlands	345,036	Africa	59,117
Norway	849,811	Australia and New Zealand	89,928
Polanda	473,670	Pacific Islandsd	22,305
Portugal	305,844	All other countries	268,128

SOURCE: Department of Justice, Immigration and Naturalization Service, *Annual Report; Statistical Abstract of U.S. 1967.*

a 1938 to 1945, Austria included with Germany; 1899 to 1919, Poland included with Austria-Hungary, Germany, and USSR.

b Beginning 1952, includes data for United Kingdom not specified, formerly included in "Other Europe."

c Comprises Eire and Northern Ireland.

d Philippines included in "Other Asia" beginning 1952 and in "Pacific Islands" 1934 to 1951. Prior to 1934, recorded separately as insular travel.

e Beginning 1957, includes Taiwan.

TABLE XIV. EMIGRATION FROM EUROPE, 1851–1960
(000)

	1851–1960	%	1851–1860	1861–1870	1871–1880	1881–1890	1891–1900	1901–1910	1911–1920	1921–1930	1931–1940	1941–1950	1951–1960
British Isles	20,501	33.6	1,313[a]	1,572[a]	1,849[a]	3,259	2,149	3,150	2,587	2,151	262	755[b]	1,454[c]
Sweden	1,265	2.1	17	122	103	327	205	224	86	107	8	23	43
Norway	882	1.4	36	98	85	187	95	191	62	87	6	10[b]	25
Finland	426	.7	n.a.	n.a.	n.a.	26	59	159	67	73	3	7	32
Denmark	575	.9	n.a.	8	39	82	51	73	52	64	100	38[d]	68
France	548	.9	27	36	66	119	51	53	32	4	5	n.a.	155[e]
Belgium	284	.5	1	2	2	21	16	30	21[f]	33	20[g]	29[h]	109
Netherlands	631[i]	1.0	16	20	17	52	24	28	22	32	4[j]	75[k]	341[l]
Germany	6,485	10.6	671	779	626	1,342	527	274	91	564	121[j]	618	872
Austria	4,241[m]	6.9	31	40	46	248	440	1,111	418[n]	61	11[o]	n.a.	53[p]
Switzerland	383	.6	6	15	36	85	35	37	31	50	47	18[d]	23
Spain	5,184	8.5	3	7	13	572	791	1,091	1,306	560	132	166	543
Portugal	2,950	4.8	45	79	131	185	266	324	402	995	108	69[q]	346
Italy	11,511	18.8	5	27	168	992	1,580	3,615	2,194	1,370	235	467	858
Russian	2,238	3.7			58	288	481	911	420	80[s]			
Poland	3,048[t]	4.9								634[t]	164[t]		
Total	61,152		2,171	2,805	3,239	7,785	6,770	11,271	7,791	6,865	1,226	2,275	4,922

n.a. = Not available.

SOURCE: William Woodruff, *The Impact of Western Man*, New York, 1967, pp. 106–7.

a Figures are not available for 1851 and 1852, nor for Irish ports before 1880; b 1946–50; c includes intracontinental emigration from Ireland, 1952–54; d includes intracontinental emigrants, 1941–44; e 1946–59, excludes emigration to French overseas territories; f 1913–18 excluded; g 1940 excluded; h 1941–47 excluded; i until 1940, estimates only; j no estimates for 1937–40 available; k 1946–50 only, excludes emigration to Dutch overseas territories; l excludes emigration to Dutch overseas territories; m figures pre-1930 cover entire Austrian empire; 1921 ff. cover Austrian republic; total refers to all overseas emigrants; figures by decade until 1920 cover only Austrian emigrants; n 1911–13; o 1931–87; p 1954–60; q includes intracontinental emigration, 1941–49; r figures underestimate overseas emigration; s Estonia and Lithuania; t incomplete data.

TABLE XV. INTERCONTINENTAL IMMIGRATION INTO SELECTED AREAS, 1851–1960

(000)

	1851–1960	1851–1860	1861–1870	1871–1880	1881–1890	1891–1900	1901–1910	1911–1920	1921–1930	1931–1940	1941–1950	1951–1960
U.S.	34,711	2,536	2,160	2,433	4,852	3,684	8,666	4,775	2,723	443	804	1,635
Canada	6,156	n.a.	290	220	359	231	947	1,154	987	82	419	1,467
Argentina	7,602	20a	160	261	841	648	1,764	1,205	1,397	310	461	535
Brazil	5,413	122	98	219	525	1,129	671	798	840	239	131	591b
British West Indies	1,030	75	101	98	66	61	170	459	n.a.	n.a.	n.a.	n.a.
Cuba	629	6	13	n.a.	n.a.	n.a.	243	367	n.a.	n.a.	n.a.	n.a.
Mexico	287	n.a.	n.a.	n.a.	n.a.	n.a.	n.a.	107	113	37c	16	14
Uruguay	642	n.a.	85	112	140	90	21	57	21d	57		59e
Australia	4,592						652	1,172	949	143	491	1,185
New Zealand	961	33	69	145	65	35	89	91	116	32	58	228
South Africa	439	n.a.	n.a.	n.a.	n.a.	n.a.	n.a.	71	100	53	97	118

SOURCE: Woodruff, *op. cit.*, pp. 108–9.

a 1857–60; b 1951–59; c 1941–49; d 1920–29; e 1951–58.

The Expanding World of Education

The revolution in education which has occurred during the past 2 cents. can be construed in 3 broad and overlapping phases: (1) the rise of massive publicly supported systems of education in the West, (2) the spread of western ideas about education to nonwestern peoples, and (3) the creation of a world educational community.

THE RISE OF PUBLIC EDUCATION IN THE WEST, 1750–1914

THE CONCEPT OF PUBLIC EDUCATION. In feudal Europe education

tended to be a privilege of the aristocracy and the preserve of the church. During the Renaissance, however, formal education became more secular in nature and more widespread in application. Nevertheless, it remained for the 18th-cent. Enlightenment to stress the democratic idea that education was the right of all men; and for 19th-cent. nationalists to emphasize the republican idea that education, since it was a necessity if a nation was to grow economically and preserve its integrity militarily, was the concern of the state. During this period the role of the church in education progressively

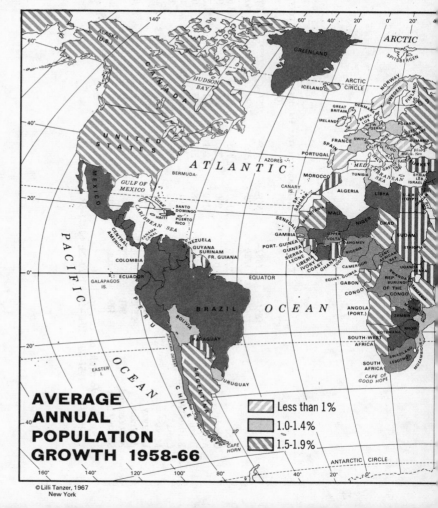

AVERAGE ANNUAL POPULATION GROWTH 1958-66

Less than 1%
1.0-1.4%
1.5-1.9%

© Lilli Tanzer, 1967
New York

diminished, and the classical curriculum, which formed the basis of training for the feudal nobility and those who served it, was de-emphasized in favor of more popular and utilitarian studies.

RUSSIA. Russia was the 1st major European power to begin setting up a state-controlled system of education. As part of his scheme of modernization, Czar Peter the Great (ruled 1689–1725) called for the construction of state schools so that Russia's need for government administrators and military officers could be met. In 1701 he crowned his fledgling school system with the Moscow School of Navigation and Mathematics (now the Naval Academy). In 1755, the University of Moscow was founded. Under Catherine the Great (ruled 1762–96), the Russian state education system received a great impetus. Her Statute of 1786 ordered

that (1) government primary schools be created in district and provincial towns; (2) religion should be taught only in the lower 3 years of those schools; (3) the study of Latin should be de-emphasized in favor of subjects more useful to the state; and (4) the state system should be free and open to all, including serfs. Catherine's educational schemes were greatly extended during the reign of Czar Alexander I (ruled 1801–25), whose Statutes for Vilna, 1803, and the Russian Provinces, 1804, reflected a Utilitarian's concern for education, and whose Ukase Law of 1809 declared that educational attainment be made the key criterion for governmental appointments. Three universities were built during Alexander's reign: Kharkov, 1804; Kazan, 1804; and St. Petersburg, 1819.

Public education suffered a reversal at

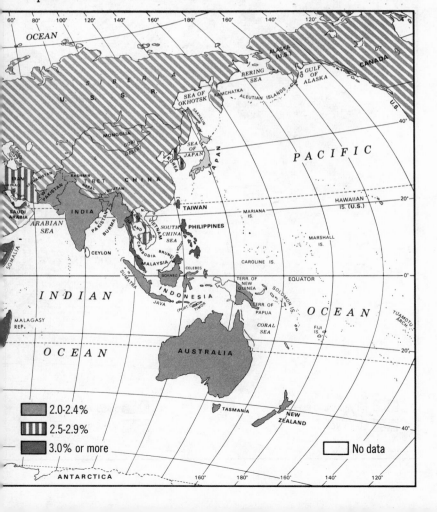

2.0-2.4%

2.5-2.9%

3.0% or more

No data

the hands of Nicholas I (ruled 1825–55).
Frightened lest vast numbers of serfs be
allowed to rise above their stations in life,
he promulgated a statute, 1827, which
effectively barred them from higher
education and re-emphasized the importance of an aristocratic curriculum of
Latin and Greek. In 1861, however, the
serfs were emancipated and all educational restrictions were removed from
them. In reaction to the assassination of
Alexander II, Alexander III (ruled 1881–
94) suspended all educational reforms
and embarked on a plan of Russification.
His Decree of May 1887, which made the
Russian language obligatory in all schools,
was specifically aimed at the Baltic provinces, where (especially at Dorpat University) German was in vogue. Alexander

III's reign was further marked by the
efforts of the procurator of the Holy
Synod, K. P. Pobedonostsev, to turn the
state system into a parochial one, and of
the minister of public instruction, T. D.
Delyanov, to return to the elitist system
of Nicholas I. Such reactionary schemes
were countered when the Duma was
created in 1906. The ill-fated Nicholas II
(ruled 1894–1917), however, turned a
deaf ear to most proposals for educational
reform, thus making the Revolution of
1917 all the more inevitable.

GERMANY. Certainly the most influential and emulated educational system of
the 19th cent. was that of Prussia, whose
1st educational advances came during the
reign of Frederick William I (ruled 1713–
40). In 1717, he ordered all children of

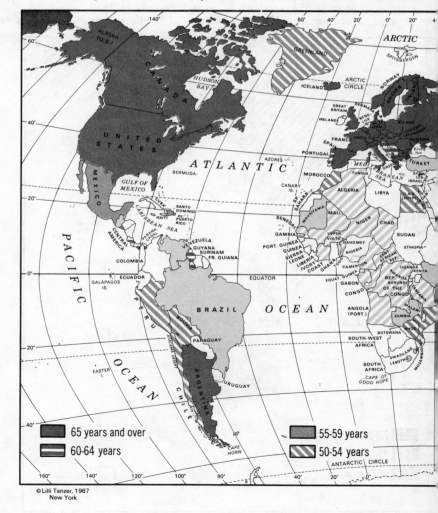

65 years and over   55-59 years

60-64 years   50-54 years

© Lilli Tanzer, 1967
New York

primary-school age to attend school, should one be convenient; and, in 1736 and 1737, he promulgated edicts calling for the erection of schools in certain educationally barren areas. In 1763, his successor, Frederick the Great (ruled 1740–86) laid down the Landschulreglement, an educational code that was to become the basis of Europe's 1st compulsory-education laws. After Prussia's disastrous defeat by Napoleon at Jena, 1806, control over education was given over to the imaginative reformer Wilhelm von Humboldt (1767–1835). Inspired and aided by the nationalistic philosopher, Johann Gottlieb Fichte (1762–1814), Humboldt initiated many reforms: (1) the establishment of a permanent Department of Education, 1808; (2) the

conversion of several old-fashioned grammar schools into more modern Gymnasiums, 1809; (3) the revival of the school-leaving examination, 1812; (4) the gradual institution of local educational authorities; and (5) the revitalization of the German universities. In 1809 Humboldt founded the University of Berlin on the experimental principle of *Lehrfreiheit* (complete academic freedom in teaching and research), a principle which was soon copied in other universities both in Germany (e.g., Bonn, 1818) and abroad (e.g., Athens, 1837). Germany's leading educational philosopher at this time was Johann Friedrich Herbart (1776–1841), whose "culture approach" idea advocated teaching by actual experience. Other educational thinkers (notably

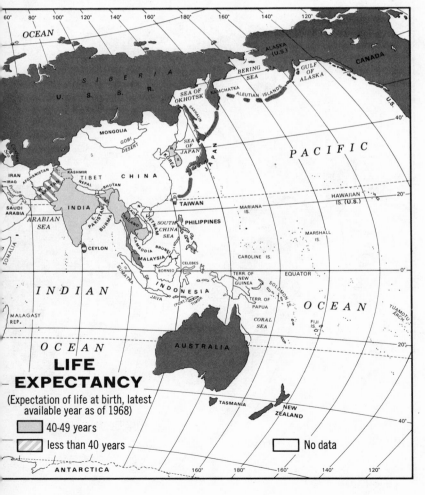

LIFE EXPECTANCY

(Expectation of life at birth, latest available year as of 1968)

40-49 years

less than 40 years

No data

Friedrich Froebel (1782–1852), the founder of the Kindergarten) were profoundly influenced by the ideas of the Swiss educator Johann Pestalozzi (1746–1827), who was in turn influenced by Rousseau's ideas of a natural education.

The events of 1870–71, coupled with Germany's rapid industrialization, caused Germans to re-examine and reformulate their educational policies. The nation's major educational struggle lay between champions of a classical secondary-school curriculum and advocates of a more scientific and nationalistic course of study. Despite the fact that Germany needed more scientists and despite the pronouncement of Kaiser William II at the 1890 Education Conference ("It is our duty to educate young men to become young Germans and not young Greeks and Romans"), the classics retained their social and academic prestige. Not until the Educational Conference of 1900 was a workable truce arranged between the classicists and the modernists.

FRANCE. 18th-cent. France was a place of vast educational ferment as both philosophers and revolutionaries reconsidered the purpose and methods of education. The most influential of the philosophers was Jean Jacques Rousseau, whose *Émile*, 1762, asserted that education should develop the "natural goodness" of the child, an idea that effectively countered many of the then-powerful Christian beliefs which stressed the depravity of the child and the constant need for discipline. Another influential En-

© Lilli Tanzer, 1967
New York

lightenment thinker was Louis René de la Chalotais (1701–85), whose essay *On National Education* was an influential argument for a unified and state-controlled system of education. Though the activists of the French Revolution attempted to create such a system, the Reign of Terror stifled any lasting educational reforms. Thus it remained for the Napoleonic reforms of 1808 to set the foundations of France's modern educational system. These reforms (1) founded the Université de France, a purely administrative organ; (2) reorganized the structure of secondary and higher education into a unified state-controlled system; (3) instituted a state-controlled system of certificates (e.g., *baccalauréat, licence*) which could attest to educational quali-

fications; and (4) created a government system of teacher placement and school inspection.

Although François Guizot (1787–1874) attempted, in the Law of 1833, to extend state control to the primary-school level, his efforts were eventually thwarted by the Loi Falloux, 1850, passed during the 2nd Republic. However, Prussian military successes in 1866 and 1870 (the so-called "victories of the Prussian schoolmaster") jolted many Republican reformers, most notably Jules Ferry (1832–96), into working for the creation of a universal system of state-controlled public education. Thus, there quickly followed the Laws of (1) June 1878, which required each commune to own its own primary school; (2) June 1881, which abolished all fees

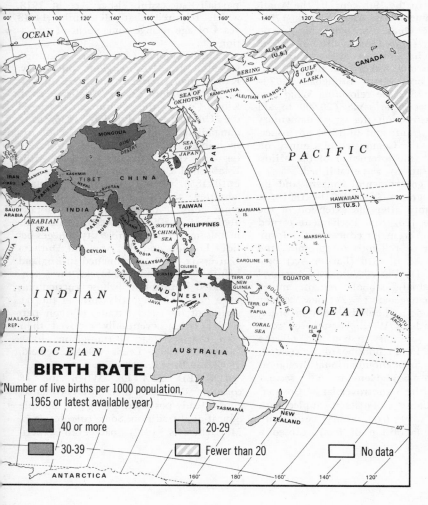

BIRTH RATE

(Number of live births per 1000 population, 1965 or latest available year)

40 or more	20-29
30-39	Fewer than 20
	No data

for primary schools and training colleges; and (3) Mar. 1882, which made education compulsory for all children between the ages of 6 and 13. Church influence in the public schools was greatly restricted by the Law of 30 Oct., 1886 (which forbade clerics to teach in the schools and banned all religious instruction in the primary schools) , and by the Associations Law of 1901 (under which the anticlerical Prime Minister Émile Combes closed some 300 parochial schools, 1902–5, and forbade, 1904, all teaching congregations) .

BRITAIN. Hampered by a severe church-state controversy, Britain was the last of the major European powers to develop a system of public education. The need for establishing one, however, was seen early in the 19th cent. by the Anglican parliamentarian Andrew Bell (1753–1832) , the Quaker schoolmaster Joseph Lancaster (1778–1838) —both of whom claimed to have originated the monitorial, or Lancastrian, system—and the Whig reformer (Lord) Henry Brougham (1778–1868) . In 1832 the reforming Whig government set aside some £20,000 to aid school construction, the 1st parliamentary education grant; and in 1839, an inspection body, the Committee of Council on Education (the forerunner of the Ministry of Education) , was established.

Despite governmental concern and increases in grants (£813,400 by 1861), it was not until after the extension of the suffrage in 1867 that Parliament turned its attention to major educational reform. A product of religious compromise, the Education Act of 1870 (Forster Act) provided that (1) V.A. ("Voluntary Agency," i.e., parochial) schools remain under private management; (2) new secular and rate-aided schools be built in order, in the words of W. E. Forster, to "complete the voluntary system and fill the gaps"; (3) local school boards be created; and (4) nondenominational religious instruction be given in all secular schools (the controversial "Cowper-Temple Clause") . This act, coupled with those of 1880 (compulsory education) and 1891 (abolition of fees), caused a

great increase in school attendance (from 1,168,000 in 1870 to 4,000,000 in 1881) .

Dissatisfaction with the Cowper-Temple Clause and with the inefficiency of a plethora of local boards (over 2,500 by 1900) resulted in the Board of Education Act, 1899, which instituted a unified central control, and the Balfour Act, 1902, which (1) set up a smaller number of Local Educational Authorities (L.E.A.'s) in place of the school boards; (2) brought all schools, including V.A. schools, under varying degrees of control by the L.E.A.'s; (3) abolished the religious requirements of the Cowper-Temple Clause; and (4) recognized, for the first time, that secondary education was a responsibility of the state. The full meaning of this last provision was underscored in the only partially successful Fisher Act of 1918, which required that all youths 14–18 years of age receive some form of education.

The development of higher education was also affected by religious controversy. Rather than charter a dissenters' university in London or an Anglican rival, King's College, the government chartered the University of London, 1836, as a nonaffiliated and nonteaching body responsible for examining and conferring degrees. At Oxford and Cambridge the Established Church remained in control until 1858, when dissenters were finally admitted, and not until 1871 were religious tests at the 2 institutions totally abolished. Further, to meet increasing demand, some 9 other university colleges besides London and the Anglican Durham University, 1837, were opened in England before 1900. Called "red brick," these nonaffiliated institutions (whose curriculums were designed originally to meet the demands of the special trades of their particular cities) eventually received their own charters (e.g., Birmingham, 1900; Liverpool, 1903; Leeds, 1904; Sheffield, 1905; and Bristol, 1909) .

UNITED STATES. When the 13 colonies declared their independence, they already possessed a long and notable educational tradition. Some colonies (e.g., Massachusetts, 1647) had even experimented with compulsory-education laws, and by 1776 the new nation could boast of some 9 colleges (Harvard, 1636). The bulk of this educational activity, however, took place in the semi-theocracies of the northern colonies, where the church was closely identified with the state. Thus the beginnings of modern education in America date not so much from colonial times as from the years directly following the Declaration of Independence, when the church was progressively disassociated from the state, and hence from education. Also, although the Federal Land Grant Ordinances of 1785 and 1787 did contain provisions for education, the control of schools in the U.S. evolved as a function of state rather than federal government. The 1st important laws establishing the right of the state to create a system of "free schools" for all (laws passed over violent religious opposition) were in Massachusetts, 1827; Pennsylvania, 1834; New York, 1867; Connecticut, 1868; and the midwestern states, 1850's. The building of effective systems of public education, necessitated by the advent of Jacksonian democracy (1830's on), was accomplished by the so-called "common school" reformers, e.g., Horace Mann (1796–1859) in Massachusetts and Henry Barnard (1811–1900) in Connecticut. In 1852 Massachusetts became the 1st state to pass a compulsory-education law.

Secondary education, too, expanded in 19th-cent. America. In addition to the traditional Latin schools of colonial times, there arose a multitude of academies which stressed a more modern secondary-school curriculum. By 1850 there were some 5,000 of these schools. From 1860 on, however, the academies were supplanted by the public high school (the 1st established in Boston, 1821), especially after the Kalamazoo Decision of 1874, which held that local school boards did have the right to tax for the maintenance of public secondary schools.

The 19th-cent. witnessed a vast extension of higher education as well. As a result of public demand and religious controversy, hundreds of colleges (most of them denominational and many short-lived) were founded by 1861. The number increased even more after the Morrill Land Grant Act of 1862, which set up public agricultural colleges. Private philanthropy of the Gilded Age resulted in further university growth, e.g., Vanderbilt, 1873; Johns Hopkins, 1876; and Stanford, 1895.

During the Progressive Era a reform movement in education was born. The philosopher John Dewey (1859–1952), who argued that learning must be related to life, was the chief exponent of progressive education. The resultant curriculum reform, begun by the Committee of 10, 1890, culminated in 1918 with the publication of the influential *Seven Cardinal Principles of Secondary Education* (which emphasized civic education) and the passage of the Smith-Hughes Act (which stressed vocational education in the high school).

OTHER WESTERN COUNTRIES. Not all of Europe experienced educational success. In Italy, for example, the Casati Law of 1859, passed originally for Sardinia but later adopted for all of Italy as the basis for that nation's compulsory-education laws, was not very effective; in 1922–23, illiteracy rates ranged from 11% in the north to 70% in the south. The Casati Law also attempted to organize Italy's secondary schools, but they remained in a fairly chaotic state until the Gentile reform of 1923. The most famous of Italy's educational reformers was Maria Montessori (1870–1952), whose pedagogical beliefs roughly paralleled those of John Dewey.

Elsewhere, the European emigrants of the 17th–19th cents. took their educational heritage with them. The 1st schools in Australia (New South Wales, 1803) were Anglican-controlled, and it was not until the Act of 1866 that a free, secular, and virtually compulsory school system was established. Canada was plagued by violent religious controversy. The Quebec Act of 1774 allowed the French Catholic educational system (which began in 1685) to continue, but made no provision to support it. The British North America Act, 1867, placed the control of education in the hands of the provincial governments, but stipulated that they could not interfere with the internal management of parochial schools. Universal free schooling was available in the eastern provinces in 1870, and in the western provinces by 1910.

In Latin America, the educational reform movements prompted by the independence struggles of the early 19th cent. were marked by efforts to remove the church from the classroom and to set up national systems of education. National universities created at this time include Argentina's Buenos Aires, 1821; Colombia's Antioquia, 1822; Peru's Trujillo, 1824; Bolivia's La Paz, 1831; and Chile's Santiago (founded in 1738 but nationalized in 1843). In their efforts to found national systems of education, the reformers of Latin America looked to Europe and America: Argentina's Bernardino Rivadavia and Domingo Faustino Sarmiento, for example, drew their inspiration from England's Lancaster and the U.S.'s Mann, respectively. Argentina, however, was the only South American nation which met with any significant success in eradicating illiteracy.

SPREAD OF WESTERN EDUCATION TO THE NONWESTERN WORLD, c. 1800–1950

The spread of western education to nonwestern peoples came as a result of (1) a direct imposition of European institutions by means of colonization, and/or (2) an expedient adoption of modern education by a country seeking to defend itself against western military or economic encroachment. As was true for Europeans a century or so before, nonwesterners found western education to be a potent force for modernization.

JAPAN. The seeds of Japan's modern system of education were sown at the beginning of the Tokugawa period when the Shogun Ieyasu issued the Buke Shohatto, 1615, which ordered the samurai to devote themselves to learning as well as to warfare. Soon schools of Con-

fucian learning (imported from China) sprouted throughout the land. Into this state system of education the militaristic shogunate of the 18th cent. infused western knowledge. Convinced that his officers should know something of western military sciences, the Shogun Yoshimune ordered, 1740, 2 of his courtiers to study Dutch and then translate works in that language. To further the cause of translating yet more western writings, the shogunate established, 1811, the Bansho Wage Goyo (Office for Translating Barbarian [i.e., Western] Writings), an institution replaced, 1856, by the more important Bansho Toishirabe-dokoro (Institution for the Investigation of Barbarian Languages). Also, 1856, the shogunate opened the Kobusho, a school of western military science, and 3 years later a western-style naval academy was established. Foreign education penetrated to the local level as well. By 1868, among the 300 or so schools run by the feudal lords, there were some 45 teaching Chinese medicine; 12, western medicine; 29, western studies; 3, Dutch studies; and 6, English studies.

The Meiji Restoration of 1868 signaled an acceleration of Japan's educational growth. In 1868, Keio University was founded; in 1877, out of the shogunate's school for western learning, there sprang the Tokyo Imperial University, the pinnacle of Japan's education system; and, in 1882, Waseda University was founded, the 1st of Japan's private universities. Primary education also received emphasis. The Education Law of 1872 stipulated that all people, regardless of sex or social position, should receive a basic education. Popular education was greatly advanced when Japan's 1st "modern" prime minister, Ito Hirobumi, took office in Dec. 1885. Ito promptly appointed the greatest of Japan's ministers of education, Mori Arinori. Mori, who had traveled extensively in and was impressed by Europe, adopted a German organizational and pedagogical pattern for Japan. The Sino-Japanese War, 1894–95, demonstrated to Japan's leaders the strategic value of heavy industry; and to further its development, a Vocational Education Law was passed in 1894. The Meiji emperor was concerned, however, lest this modernizing of education lead to a westernizing of Japan. In 1890, therefore, an Imperial Rescript commanded that Confucian and Shinto values be made the basis for all education. Except for expansion, the Japanese system of education remained in this form until the American occupation.

CHINA. Traditional Chinese education (formalistic and identified with the political service) remained unchanged from the 14th to the mid-19th cent. The 1st western school (a Catholic seminary) was opened in 1852, and shortly afterward a variety of other missionaries opened western-style schools. In 1861, as a result of increasing commercial involvement, the government established 2 colleges (Canton and Peking) for the study of western languages, and from the mid-1880's it started sending students to America and Europe to study. Not until after the Boxer Rebellion, 1899–1900, however, were there any massive governmental reforms, the most important being the establishment of the National University at Peking, 1902, and the modernizing of the civil-service examination requirements, 1905.

Popular education was a great concern of the Nationalists, who, from 1912 on, established a system of education which closely resembled the American pattern. Indeed, the ideas of the American educator John Dewey enjoyed a considerable vogue in the Nationalist period. The greatest problem facing the exponents of popular education was the simplification of the traditional, and very complicated, system of writing. This problem was partially solved by the introduction of the *pai-hua* ("plain talk") system invented by the philosopher Hu Shih. Using such simplified Chinese, James Yang-ch'u Yen organized a massive government literacy campaign in the 1920's and 1930's. (By 1937, 42% of primary-school-age children were in school.) The number of universities also increased: 47 in 1925, and 108 in

1937. During the 1930's the Nationalists tried to bring all schools (including missionary institutions) under a unified central control. World War II laid waste many schools and universities, but this was only a temporary setback; by 1946, some 60 universities, with some 60,000 students, were in operation. After 1949 the Nationalists in Taiwan established a system of education on the Japanese model, while the Communists on the mainland nationalized all schools.

INDIA. Western education was introduced into India in the 18th cent., when Protestant missionaries (e.g., Danish, from 1705; English Baptists, from 1793) 1st arrived. But not until the rise of British ascendancy over the subcontinent at the beginning of the 19th cent. was education officially sponsored. In 1813, prompted by Utilitarian motives, Parliament directed the English East India Co. to set aside a sum each year for the education of Indians; some 10 years later, the Company set up 2 Committees of Public Instruction (at Madras and in Bengal) to supervise this educational effort. The cause of western education in India received its greatest impetus, however, with the publication of Thomas B. Macaulay's *Minute on Education*, 1835. Eloquently arguing the case for Anglicizing the people of India, Macaulay was instrumental in spreading a system of education in which English was the medium of instruction and literary studies were emphasized. The resulting educational policy was not without its defects: (1) it was not at all conducive to the growth of primary education (in 1905, only 1 village in 5 could boast of a school) ; (2) it caused a disproportionate growth of secondary schools and universities (1st university colleges: Calcutta, Bombay, and Madras, 1857; Punjab, 1882; Allahabad, 1887) ; (3) instead of science, it emphasized a literary curriculum which trained students only for a diminishing number of civil-service positions; and (4) it created a special breed of men, at ease neither in eastern nor in western society.

Though the British sponsored numerous commissions of inquiry into the problems of education, it was not until the 20th cent. that anything positive was accomplished in the way of reform. Both the Indian National Congress and the All-India Moslem League were outspoken in their demands for universal primary education and an emphasis on Indian, rather than European, studies. The pace-setting All-India National Education Conference convened by Gandhi at Wardha, 1933, called for the creation of special junior- and senior-level secondary schools in which vocational and technical instruction, and not simply university preparation, would be stressed (a scheme reinforced by the influential Sargent Report of 1944). The Wardha Scheme and the Sargent Report remain the basis of India's present educational system.

MIDDLE EAST. Western education came to the Middle East as a result of both a direct imposition of European control and a conscious adoption by indigenous governments seeking to improve themselves militarily. The latter case is well illustrated by Turkey. During the reign of Selim III (ruled 1789–1807) western education was introduced through military schools staffed with European teachers. During the time of Mahmud II (ruled 1808–39), Turkish students went to study in the capitals of Western Europe for the 1st time, and a Council of Public Instruction was founded, 1838, to lay the basis of a system of public education. In the reign of Abdul Mejid (ruled 1839–61), a reign dominated by the westernized reformer Mustafa Reshid, a modernization plan, the *Gulhanehatti-kumayouni* (which called for education expansion) was drawn up and partially implemented. As a result of the revolt of the "Young Turks," July 1908, the reign of Mohammed V (ruled 1909–18) was marked by a reorganization of military academies and a policy of secularization in government-supported schools. Secularization occurred even more under the republican regime of Mustafa Kemal Atatürk, 1923–38, when even the *medresses* (Islamic colleges) were brought under the Commissariat of Education. Not

until 1948 did the Turkish Assembly soften this hard policy of strict separation between mosque and state.

As had been the case in Turkey, so in Egypt the modernization of the educational system was begun locally, though later it received an impetus from direct European intervention. Following the French occupation, 1793–1801, and the British invasion, 1807, Mohammed Ali (ruled 1805–48) was determined to modernize the Egyptian army. By 1820 he had imported a variety of French instructors (notably Col. Joseph Sèves) and opened a military school at Isna. In addition, Ali sent several officers to Europe (principally France) for study. During the reign of Ismail Pasha (ruled 1863–79), who himself had studied in Europe, government schools patterned after the French *lycées* were established. During the period of direct British control of Egypt, 1882–1919, education did undergo some reform: (1) many foreign schools (chiefly missionary enterprises) were opened; (2) the curriculum of higher educational institutions became Anglo- rather than Francocentric; (3) the ancient Islamic university al-Azhar (founded A.D. 970) was modernized by the Mufti Mohammed Abduh, 1899; and (4) Cairo University was opened at Giza, 1908. There were problems, however. As in India, there were too many unemployed westernized intellectuals, and British efforts to spread primary education were feeble and half-hearted.

In much of the remaining Middle East, French influence predominated (e.g., at the University of St. Joseph, founded at Beirut by French Jesuits, 1881, and the Académie Libanaise, Beirut, 1937). The one major exception to this generally French pattern was the American University at Beirut, founded by missionaries in 1866.

SUB-SAHARAN AFRICA. The 1st main thrust of western education was carried to Africa by missionary societies founded as a result of or in reaction to Pietism in Germany and Wesleyanism in Britain, e.g., the Church Missionary Society (C.M.S.) founded by Anglicans in 1799 and operational in West and East Africa; the Swiss Basel Society, active in the Gold Coast from 1828; and the French Society of Our Lady of Africa ("White Fathers"), founded in 1868 and operational in East and Central Africa. Although influential despite their small numbers, the missionaries' educational effectiveness was confined to a very few areas, e.g., Freetown, Sierra Leone, where in 1816 the C.M.S. opened tropical Africa's 1st secondary school, Fourah Bay College, which, in 1876, offered tropical Africa's 1st university courses. The missionaries sought primarily to increase mass literacy so that the Bible could be read, but they did dispense some advanced literary education to a few of their brighter students. By the 1820's Freetown was sending students to Britain to study the classics, and by 1848 some citizens of Dakar were fully assimilated into French culture.

With the onset of imperialism at the end of the 19th cent., education fell into the hands of colonial governments. But because of the problems connected with establishing colonial rule and the demands of World War I, the organization of education remained in a confused state until the 1920's, when Britain, France, and Belgium each issued a policy statement which set the pattern for the modern development of education in tropical Africa. The British statement, prepared by the Advisory Committee on Native Education, 1925, and prompted by the American Phelps-Stokes Commission to Africa of 1921–22, called for (1) primary education in the vernacular, (2) a stress on vocational (especially agricultural) education, and (3) the planning of a comprehensive system of education that was to culminate eventually in university training and at the same time prevent the creation of an unemployed educated elite. The French policy statement, written by R. Antonetti in 1925, largely echoed the British statement except that French, and not the vernacular, was to be the medium of instruction in the primary schools. The Belgian government's statement of 1925 differed considerably, however. Emphasis was placed only on primary education, which, after the Concordat of 1906, was left largely in the hands of the Catholic Church.

The next set of major reforms came during and after World War II. During 1943–45, Britain's Asquith Commission (for West Africa) and Elliot Commission (for East Africa) planned the development of university expansion (Achimota, Gold Coast, 1948; Ibadan, Nigeria, 1948; Makerere, Uganda, 1949; University College, Khartoum, Sudan, 1951), and a British White Paper, *Education for Citizenship,* 1948, called for primary-school expansion. France's educational reforms were initially outlined at the Brazzaville Conference of 1944, at which de Gaulle promised a vast expansion of primary education. In response to African demands, however, technical and secondary education received the main emphasis in the Colonial Development Plan of 1946. Two years later, the University Institute of Dakar was established. Also in 1948, Belgium issued a 10-year development plan which made provisions for academic secondary schools. In 1954, Lovanium was established as the 1st Congolese university.

THE WORLD EDUCATIONAL COMMUNITY, 1945–1968

The 3rd phase in the development of modern education has been in effective operation only during the past quarter-century or so. In this stage, education became less western and more universal in its appeal and application, its problems and potentialities.

A SIMILARITY OF PROGRAMS. As a relatively homogeneous form of modern education settled over the world, the educational policies of the nations exhibited distinct similarities. For one thing, scientific and technical education received a universal stress. In the U.S. this stress could be seen in the increasing involvement of the federal government in education, e.g., in the large number of grants to universities for scientific research both during and after World War II, and in the National Defense Education Act of 1958 (a product of the "Sputnik Crisis"). In the USSR, as a result of the efforts of Professor A. I. Markushevich, among others, mathematics and science instruction received great emphasis after 1950. In 1953, the Moscow School No. 425 was opened as a specialized scientific school for talented youths (by 1969 there were about 100 schools operating on the No. 425 plan), and soon afterward 4 special boarding schools (Moscow, Leningrad, Kiev, and Novosibirsk) were opened for extremely gifted young scientists. Chinese education also stressed scientific study. Both the speech of Vice-Premier Chen Yi, June 1961, and the *70 Articles Concerning Education,* Fall 1961, called for Chinese schools to produce an increasing number of technical experts and not simply revolutionaries. (This policy, implemented during 1961–66, later came under fire during the Cultural Revolution.) In Britain, technical education at a lower level was sponsored by the Education Act of 1944, and at a higher level by the expansion of the Imperial College of Science and Technology, beginning 1953, and the growth, beginning 1957, of some 14 Colleges of Advanced Technology (C.A.T.'s).

Another similarity in programs can be seen in the efforts of virtually all nations to extend educational opportunities to as many citizens as possible. In the U.S. a considerable expansion took place at the post-high-school level: the number of colleges increased from 9 in 1776 to nearly 700 in 1967, while the number of 2-year "junior colleges" (1st one: Joliet, Illinois, 1902) grew from 74 in 1915 to over 700 in 1967. Britain's Education Act of 1944 promised "secondary education for all" and the British evolved a system of "modern" schools roughly comparable to American general high schools. In the USSR, Khrushchev's educational reforms of 1958–59 planned for (1) an extension of the period of compulsory lower-school attendance from 7 to 8 years, (2) the addition of an extra year to the higher-school curriculum, and (3) a 3-year non-compulsory continuing education scheme

for students not in a higher school. Developing nations have felt keenly the need to extend a basic education to all their citizens. The Indian Constitution of 1949, for example, laid down the principle (not yet converted into the fact) of compulsory education until the age of 14, and the 1961 Conference of African States on the Development of Education placed a high priority on achieving 100% primary-school enrollment by 1980.

A SIMILARITY OF PROBLEMS. Increasingly, nations have discovered that their educational problems are not unique. The relationship of church, state, and education is an example. In the U.S., although both federal and state constitutions stress the necessity of a separation of church and state (the New York Board of Regents barred all forms of prayer from the classroom, June 1962), the hard line of no aid at all to parochial schools has softened somewhat. The Oregon Decision, 1925, recognized the right of churches to maintain separate school systems, and the Everson Decision, 1947, found that the parents of parochial-school children might legitimately be reimbursed for some educational expenses such as school-bus transportation. The Elementary and Secondary Education Act of 1965 provided some federal financial assistance to church schools. In France, too, as a result of de Gaulle's controversial Law of 31 Dec., 1959, some government aid to the parents of children attending religiously sponsored schools was allowed. In Britain the existence of Voluntary Agency schools was much strengthened by the Butler Act of 1944, which institutionalized a dual system of state and church schools. Even such nonwestern areas as tropical Africa have been troubled by the problem of church schools. Though many nationalists (especially Sekou Touré of Guinea, whose government took over the church schools) have attacked mission schools as agents of neocolonialism, most newly independent African countries have chosen not to nationalize their church schools, so great is the cost of any alternative.

Another major area of controversy is the perennial conflict between educational quantity and quality a conflict which in the USSR and the People's Republic of China has taken on the added flavor of an ideological conflict. In an ideal Communist state all students are treated as intellectually equal, and none should be permitted educational advantages denied to others. But, in practice, many planners in the USSR and China have realized the importance of creating an intellectual aristocracy. Thus scholars of the Soviet Academy attacked Khrushchev's reforms of 1958–59, the effect of which was to water down the scientific curriculum in order to reach more students, and also to place a higher value on practical experience than on academic qualifications in university placement. Similarly, scholars of the Chinese Academy came under attack, June 1966, from the forces of the Cultural Revolution.

RISE OF INTERNATIONAL CO-OPERATION. Despite international education conferences at London, 1851, Philadelphia, 1876, and Brussels, 1880, it was not until 1909 that the Belgian, Edward Peeters, set up at Ostend the 1st permanent International Bureau of Education. World War I, however, suffocated this infant society and not until Dec. 1925 was a 2nd Bureau (still in existence) established at Geneva. In addition, under the auspices of the League of Nations a Committee on Intellectual Co-operation was established, 1922. The events of 1936 onward diminished the effectiveness of this committee, but a Conference of Allied Ministers of Education held in London, Apr. 1944, agreed to re-establish an international education body at the war's completion: the United Nations Economic, Scientific, and Cultural Organization (UNESCO), which was established at Paris in 1946.

International educational co-operation, however, has not been limited to multilateral organizations; many individual governments have furthered its cause. For example, Britain's Colonial Development and Welfare Acts of 1940 and 1945 devoted some £7,350,000 toward the construction of universities and technical institutes; France's Plan for Modernization and Equipment, 1946, called for an overall development of education in her overseas possessions; and the U.S.'s Fulbright Act, 1946, and "Point 4" program, 1949, called for an international exchange of students and teachers, and recognized the responsibility of industrial nations to give educational aid to developing areas.

Recent events in the field of international educational co-operation have taken on a variety of new forms. The Soviet-American Cultural Agreement, 1958, provided for educational exchanges between the world's 2 most industrialized countries. Former colonial powers continued to aid their former colonies, but in a different way: e.g., France co-ordinated its educational assistance within the French Community, 1958, while Britain channeled assistance through a newly formed, 1964, Ministry of Overseas Development. Many nations that were not themselves great colonial powers began sending educational aid to the developing world. For example, Canadians are presently teaching in West and East Africa; Chinese and Soviet teachers are now, or have been recently, instructing in Guinea, Ghana, and Tanzania; and the U.S., through the Agency for International Development, 1961, the Peace Corps, 1961, and the International Education Act, 1966, has extended educational assistance into virtually every corner of the "3rd World."

THE REVOLUTION IN SCIENCE

The Philosophical Outlook of Post-Newtonian Science

CARTESIAN DUALISM. From Descartes (1596–1650) to Kant (1724–1804), science and philosophy groped hand in hand for a viable exit from the labyrinth of the mind-body problem set up by Descartes. Cartesian dualism, fully developed in the *Principia philosophiae,* 1644, was a congenial inspiration for scientific methodology, though a metaphysical monster. To treat the physical world as body alone was, for Descartes, to reduce phenomena to extension and motion. This, in turn, should permit a complete mathematization of physics. However, Cartesian mathematics and Cartesian physics were never wedded in the philosophical restatement of Galileo's practical program for physics. Galileo described specific terrestrial motions in detailed mathematical language in his *Discorsi,* 1638. Descartes outlined a universal dynamics, which by its very nature could not be set out satisfactorily in quantitative terms; even the 2nd book of Newton's *Principia* showed the impossibility of developing successfully a fluid mechanics capable of justifying the Cartesian vortexes in mathematical terms. Nonetheless, it was the authority of Descartes more than any other single writer which set the tone and temper for science of the Newtonian era.

Concentrating on body apart from mind was to center on matter alone (in terms of motion and extension). Only the rational soul of man qualified as an inhabitant of the realm of mind. All other activities of living beings could be explained through material actions. The details of these material actions were to be perceived by rules laid down in the *Discours sur la méthode,* 1636, modeled on the methods of Greek geometry and theoretically available to anyone. The method aimed at eliciting clear and distinct ideas about things. Clearness and distinctness led to an assurance of reality; they also led to a determination of true qualities. The only qualities sufficiently clear and distinct were the mathematical ones, extension and motion. This reductive materialism can be found in Galileo's *Saggiattore,* 1623, and in extreme form in Hobbes's *De corpore,* 1655. The complete separation of mind from body led not only to materialism in physics but also to mechanism, since dynamics (physical causality) was of primary concern to Descartes. Purposely eschewing all spiritual and occult forces, he laid out a physics designed to yield clear and distinct cognition of simple causative processes, viz., mechanical, "billiard-ball" situations.

MECHANISM. Mechanism, the primary legacy of Descartes to his scientific contemporaries, spurred both practical and theoretical researches in physics. Since material contact of bodies was the *sine qua non* of a mechanistic model, the problem of impact was the leading question of the day for physicists. Despite their disavowal of Aristotelian-scholastic thought, Cartesians were forced to introduce subtle (ethereal) matter in the place of supposed vacuums. The alternative was empty space through which physical forces were still propagated—such mysterious occurrences could not be allowed! The work of Boyle in pneumatics registered aversion to the existence of an absolute vacuum. In the investigations of Christiaan Huyghens (1629–95) on the nature of light and of gravity, the apex of mechanistic physics was reached. He followed Descartes in analyzing light in terms of impulse transmitted through subtle matter. He surpassed Descartes in developing a theory of "gravific" subtle matter in a spherical vortex; the weight of a body corresponded to the centrifugal tendency of its component subtle matter. In the preface to the 2nd edition, 1713, of Newton's *Principia,* Roger Cotes placed the Cartesian mechanists between the scholastics and Newton in scientific method with the following words: "These [Cartesians] supposed all matter homogeneous, and that the variety of forms which is seen in bodies arises from some very plain and simple affection of the component particles; and by going on from simple things to those which are more compounded, they certainly proved right, if they attribute no other properties to those primary affections of the particles than nature has done. But when they take a liberty of imagining at pleasure unknown figures and magnitudes, and uncertain situations and motions of the parts; and, moreover, of supposing occult fluids, freely pervading the pores of bodies, endued with an all-performing subtilty, and agitated with occult motions; they now run out into dreams and chimeras, and neglect the true constitution of things. . . ." Here Newton parted with the mechanists though he sympathized with their enterprise. For him mechanism was an hypothesis, not a program in physics. Even so, he showed hopes in the General Scholium to the *Principia* that eventually a fully mechanical model of the world might be conceived on the basis of experimental physics.

ABSOLUTISM. Newton was not without metaphysical assumptions. In his absolutist notions of space and time he showed the effects of mechanistic materialism. With matter and motion related mathematically, science moved teleologi-

cal explanation and the use of secondary qualities to a different level of discussion. This naturally led to preoccupation with space and time. Since Descartes, science had been presented with the idea of space as something primary. The Platonist Henry More (1614–87) made it clear that extension need not be equated with matter, and that extension, or space, is real even though uninhabited by matter. Space, in fact, became divine (not deity) in More's view, and possessed the qualities of unity, simplicity, eternity, perfection, incorruptibility, and pure actuality. Like the Jewish mystics, More identified space with God's omnipresence. His influence on Isaac Barrow (1630–77) showed in the latter's geometrical Platonism, and more especially in a common notion of space. Barrow, Newton's mentor, saw space as the presence and potency of God. As a mathematician and physicist he went on to deal with time as well as space, both entities being necessary to motion. "Time," asserted Barrow, "does not denote an actual existence, but simply a capacity or possibility of permanent existence . . . whether things run or stand still, whether we sleep or wake, time flows in its even tenour." Motion served only as a measuring stick for time. In space and time as divine absolutes, Barrow saw the source of mathematics' certitude and lucidity.

Ignoring the religious overtones of his teacher, Isaac Newton (1642–1727) retained the absolutist views of space and time, even attempting to demonstrate the difference between absolute and relative acceleration in his famous bucket experiment. Observing that water spinning in a bucket takes the same shape whether the bucket be moving or still, he concluded that the operative forces cause an accelerated motion relative to absolute space. Not until Ernst Mach (1838–1916) did anyone point out that the water accelerates with respect to the fixed stars, i.e., some other reference frame, not absolute space.

EXPERIMENTALISM. Before Newton, experimentation had usually been called upon for individual cases in evidence rather than for conclusive proof.

The growing interest in experimental approaches to physics was fostered primarily by Francis Bacon (1561–1626) and René Descartes. Bacon, impressed by the image of the craftsman creating tools to control nature, took this image as a key in his program for reforming society through science. Descartes, in less extensive manner than Bacon, set up the craftsman's experience as something close to his clear and distinct ideas necessary for scientific knowledge. In both cases, and generally among succeeding physicists, the experimental approach had meaning only in terms of a dehumanized nature. With the magical element absent from nature, control through rational, manual manipulation made sense. Mechanistic materialism was both symptom and partial cause of this trend. Only through this new philosophical outlook of the 17th cent. did the influence of the craftsman pervade scientific theory and lead to an emphasis on experimentation. Through the programs of scientific academies, e.g., the Accademia del Cimento in Italy, there occurred systematic experimenting on problems such as atmospheric pressure. A leading experimentalist prior to Newton was Robert Boyle (1627–91), but his work was not always systematic, nor was there in it the nice relationship of theory and data found in Newton's work. With Newton, especially in the *Opticks,* a new standard was set for the use of experimental evidence in scientific argument. Theory became dependent primarily upon systematic experiment. This novel view was so unusual that only the Frenchman Pardies among his many critics came to recognize Newton's "New Theory of Light and Colours" as a simple statement of observations. Much given to speculation in more informal contexts, Newton resisted indemonstrable hypotheses in his formal work on optics and mechanics. He saw action-at-a-distance as the result of ignorance of causes, not as a positive hypothesis about nature. The success of Newtonian physics, coupled with the new scientific philosophy, made systematic, experimental science the only respectable sort. The 18th cent. saw a large body of technical and sophisticated experiments devised to particularize and extend Newton's theories; one example was Cavendish's determination of the value of the universal gravitation constant.

THEORIES OF KNOWLEDGE. The epistemology accompanying the new scientific philosophy incorporated the same elements, viz., dualism, materialism, and mechanism. Very few systematic philosophers espoused all these elements, but they formed the central problems in 17th- and 18th-cent. theories of knowledge. Cartesian dualism sprang from Descartes' concern over confused ideas in the mind. Since these perturbations could not be from God, they must be from a nonmental source, the body. The bodily senses were capable of materialistic and mechanistic explanation. Only the human reason, receiving and recognizing clear and distinct ideas, was free of mechanism. These innate ideas were intuitive, rational truths, their reality hanging upon the reality of the ultimate idea, God. On clear and distinct ideas Descartes believed it possible to build certain knowledge. His followers overemphasized the deductive side of the system, and saw in it a geometrical, demonstrative sort of method. As such it inspired skepticism and mysticism in men like Pascal, who saw that metaphysics and empirical studies could never attain the certitude of Euclidean geometry. Spinoza (1632–77) carried the so-called Cartesian method to perfection in his *Ethica,* where a totally Euclidean system of demonstration appeared. In this line of thought Spinoza influenced many, from Leibniz in metaphysics to Pufendorf in political theory.

Spinoza's epistemology solved the mind-body problem by dissolving it: he saw body and soul as 2 aspects of the same reality. The universe, both physical and mental, was described in terms of substance, attributes, and modes. Knowledge of the universe proceeded through 3 grades—opinion, reason, intuition. Observation of particulars gained significance only when such knowledge cohered in a system of truth. Harmony, rather than external correspondence, was the test of truth. His monistic epistemology and ontology determined Spinoza's commitment to a strictly demonstrative methodology, leading from the unitary essence of God to all things.

John Locke (1632–1704) aimed his denial of innate ideas at Platonists like More as much as at the Cartesians. Stressing the empirical grounds of knowledge, Locke conceived the "blank tablet" (a phrase going back to Aquinas) of the mind as gaining knowledge through simple and complex ideas. Simple ideas derived from sensation and reflection, complex ideas from combinations of simple ones. His indecision on the degree of self-activity possessed by the mind during the relating of simple ideas allowed a variety of developments in his name by later philosophers. Also, despite his attempt to leave the existence of inner experience independent of outer, he made sensation so clearly the root of reflection that complete sensualism was the ultimate derivative of his system. It is notable that this 1st systematic attempt at empiricism in modern philosophy, 1690, appeared just 3 years after the 1st systematic attempt at empiricism in modern science—Newton's *Principia*.

George Berkeley (1685–1753), bishop of Cloyne, showed the direction which Locke's views, controlled by Cartesian dualism, were to take. If there is a strict division of mind and matter, Berkeley maintained, then all direct attempts at correlation of sensation and the external world are doomed. Complete certitude is present, according to Descartes, Locke, and Berkeley, only in intuitive knowledge. But Descartes and Locke saw the possibility of an intuition of substantial reality; Berkeley showed that only perception, not an object of perception, can be intuited. Like Hobbes, Berkeley disproved the conception of corporeal substance, yet through nominalism he ended up with no reality beyond perception. Only his development of a spiritualistic metaphysics led him to posit the reality of anything beyond perceptions.

While Berkeley disposed of the Cartesian realm of body in favor of mind, with finite spirits receiving ideas from the infinite spirit, his successor David Hume (1711–76) carried empiricism to its logical end, viz., that neither spirit nor body can be shown to have any objective existence. Both Berkeley and Hume demolished the reality of abstract ideas: both recognized them as general names for groups of individual perceptions. A completely consistent nominalism led Hume to deny reality to mind as well as body; both were no more than complexes of perceptions. The only certain knowledge for Hume was pure mathematics, precisely because it concerns only the possible relations between contents of ideas. Hume's positivistic stand led also to a denial of any perception of cause and effect. The causal relation is no more than an imposition upon what is really sequence and nothing more.

The French temper was more receptive to this positivism than was the English. Étienne Bonnot de Condillac (1715–80) nicely represented the spirit of the French Enlightenment with his positivistic synthesis of sensualism and rationalism. Its sensualistic basis depended on a popular materialism. The detailed development of Condillac's views involved relations of ideas, science being only the result of various transformations of ideas. Simple composition and decomposition sufficed to explain all signs of ideas, thus all knowledge.

By the end of the 18th cent. the various issues raised by Descartes concerning knowledge of the external world had all seen development. Both empiricists and rationalists turned more and more to a recognition of the radical separation of the intellect from the outside world. That mental activity, rather than external reality, was the basis of knowledge emerged in such different philosophies as those of Leibniz and Hume.

OPTIMISM OF THE ENLIGHTENMENT. The optimism of the Enlightenment resulted from all the trends discussed above. The new scientific philosophy's most general impact was a guarantee of certitude. Whether through idealism or materialism, the scientific and philosophical outlook of the period suggested that now, as Pope said of Newton, "all was light." Mechanism in science and determinism in philosophy were taken as favorable signs. In England, the Newtonian universe seemed to prove deism and rational religion in general. The geometrical metaphysics of Spinoza and the harmonic monadology of Leibniz had optimistic outlooks—one for knowledge, the other for ethics. German rationalism led, in the person of Alexander Baumgarten, to a science of aesthetics. Christian Wolff applied the geometrical method of Spinoza and Leibniz to pedagogy in general. Materialistic mechanism was carried to its physiological extreme of mechanistic biology by the physician Pancratius Wolff in Germany along with Hartley and Priestley in England. Heinrich Lambert turned Locke's distinctions, in a more sharply conceived formulation, to good use in the measurement of intensity of illumination of light (*Photometria*, 1760).

The interest in sense perception and its systematization is apparent in the careful aesthetic distinctions of Lessing's *Laocoön* and the sensual bases given to mathematics by Rüdiger and Lossius. La Mettrie's *L'Homme machine* expressed the popular currency in French thought of a strictly materialistic and mechanical world in biology as well as physics. Voltaire increased the popularity of skeptical sensualism with his *Lettres sur les Anglais,* and literature saw the theory canonized in Diderot's *Rêve d'Alembert.* Condillac's brand of empiricism was recognized as the only philosophy by the government during the French Revolution; these views were called "ideology," i.e., the only worthwhile ideology in epistemology, by Destutt de Tracy. Sensualism and mechanism advanced to the extent that Laplace felt free to reply to the emperor that he had no need for the "hypothesis of deity."

Only toward the end of the 18th cent. did disillusionment with the great empirico-rational synthesis of the era appear. Leibniz' concern with feeling was accentuated by Herder in his essay on the soul. The failure of mechanistic biology appeared in the more rational objections of Kant as well as in the mystical tracts of Oken and Schelling. In France, Rousseau's *Émile* and *Nouvelle Héloise* registered the failure of positivistic and mechanistic methods for the improvement of society. The optimism of the 18th cent. was finally swallowed up by the French Revolution.

Astronomy and Cosmology

NEWTON. Newton's *Principia,* 1687, was based upon the establishment of the law of gravitation. The basic relevant problem, as put to Newton by Halley in 1684, was the shape of a planetary orbit wherein the centripetal force varied inversely as the square of the distance from the central body. Newton's proof that conic sections all describe paths involving such a force appeared formally in the 1st 4 sections of the *Principia.* His claim to have worked this out 2 decades earlier remains unproven by external evidence. The problem of mathematically resolving the attraction of a massive body into an attraction by a mass point at the center may have kept him from making his discovery known earlier; this problem was solved by 1686. Positive scientific advances necessary to the law of gravitation, 1st based on the moon's motion, were Galileo's law of falling bodies, Kepler's laws of planetary motion, and Huyghens' law of pendulum motion. To these Newton added basic definitions (primarily mass) and axioms (his 3 laws of motion) plus a highly inventive mathematics. On the basis of fluxions (p. 907, below) Newton blended successive finite rectilinear figures into successions of infinitesimals forming smooth curved surfaces. The 3 books of his major work respectively deal with the motion of bodies *in vacuo,* the motion of bodies in resisting media, and the mathematical system of the world. The *Prin-*

cipia itself proceeds in the form of Euclidean geometry, while employing a mathematics foreign to Greek geometry. For both reasons the *Principia* could never serve as a textbook. Its form was too monumental and its mathematical reasoning was too intuitive. The subsequent development of calculus left the *Principia* standing as a lone pinnacle of human ingenuity and philosophic brilliance, but earthbound by a ponderous mathematics.

BRADLEY. The Newtonian synthesis gave rise to 2 centuries of observational and theoretical developments in astronomy and cosmology. Virtually all of these were elaborations or applications of Newtonian mechanics. James Bradley (1693–1762), 3rd Astronomer Royal, attempted for some time to give the 1 ironclad proof of the heliocentric hypothesis—observation of parallactic displacement of the stars, resulting from the earth's motion in its orbit. When he found the star Gamma Draconis to change as much as 40 min. in position, 1725, he realized that this maximum parallactic displacement should have occurred at a different time of the year than the motion observed. But only in 1728 did astronomical aberration of light occur to him as an explanation. Involving the presumed motion of the earth in its orbit, the explanation depended upon the variations in speed and direction of the earth relative to the light coming from the star. Aberration suggested the heliocentric hypothesis almost as strongly as parallax; only a revolving earth would account satisfactorily for the phenomenon.

In the observations basic to his discovery of aberration, Bradley reported some minor variations not due to this cause. Between 1727 and 1747 he investigated the possibility that the influence of the moon's nodes (intersections of the lunar and earthly orbits) might cause the minute variations. After correlating changes in the moon's orbit with stellar displacement for the 19 years of a lunar nodal period, he showed that nutation accurately accounted for the data. Nutation, an irregularity in the motion of precession, is made up of many gravitational effects, but that identified by Bradley in

1748 is of primary importance. It gave observational evidence of Newtonian gravitational effects of other bodies upon the oblate spheroid of the earth.

KANT. Use of Newtonian mechanical principles was made in a speculative fashion in *Allgemeine Naturgeschichte und Theorie des Himmels,* 1755, published anonymously by Immanuel Kant. Thomas Wright's idea of a disklike form for the Milky Way provided Kant with a basis for hypothesizing an infinite system of such galaxies. Contractions in the rotating nebular disk were made the scientific explanation for the creation and motions of planets, satellites, and rings. This manifestation of 18th-cent. rationalism made Newton's scientific reasons for theism less compelling.

CLAIRAUT. Comets, while generally explained by Newton, still posed problems in astronomy. Alexis Claude Clairaut (1713–65) began theoretical computations on the expected perturbations in the motion of Halley's comet, due to reappear sometime from 1757 on. After laborious computations he reported late in 1758 that Saturn and Jupiter had retarded the comet's motion 100 and 518 days respectively. His resultant prediction for the perihelion of the comet was just 32 days later than the actual occurrence, a margin of error he had explicitly anticipated. This prediction gave another support to the Newtonian gravitational theory on which it was constructed.

BODE. In 1772 Johann Elert Bode (1747–1826) put forth a strange law intended to give some mathematical (not physical) meaning to the positions of the planets. Drawing the law from a recent footnote by J. D. Titius, Bode gave a series of integers representing the locations of the known planetary orbits. Starting with Mercury as zero, the series assigned the consecutive integers to the known succeeding planets (almost) in the general formula Radius $= 0.4 + 0.3 \ (2^n)$. This worked well until $n = 5$, for which no planet existed. When Herschel later discovered Uranus, which fitted into position $n = 8$, a body for $n = 5$ was searched for, and the asteroids were discovered. Neptune was later discovered under the impetus of Bode's law, but its 20% deviation combined with Pluto's 50% deviation showed that the "law" was ultimately numerology.

HERSCHEL. Apparently without stimulation from Bode's law, William Herschel (1738–1822), in examining a section of Gemini with his self-made, superior telescope, noted a body moving along the ecliptic at about 1 min. per day. Since it could be easily magnified and had no tail, his final conclusion was that a new planet had been found. After computing the whole orbit, he found it to be 19 times larger than the earth's orbit. His attempt to name it for King George was ultimately thwarted by foreign insistence on the name Uranus.

In 1784–85 Herschel published 2 papers *On the Construction of the Heavens.* His extensive experience with telescopes brought him to the conclusion that galaxies were simply groups of small stars. He assumed the stars to be equally luminous and essentially equidistant from each other; on this basis he computed the depth of the Milky Way by counting the stars in the field of his telescope. The result was a given magnitude of the galaxy in terms of a mean distance between stars. The dynamic aspects of the universe he drew up in terms of a clustering tendency in nebulae, with the Milky Way as one example of such nebulae. His speculations evolved over the next decades so that in 1811 he maintained that distant, small nebulae were not results of agglomeration but rather the primitive state of thin nebulous matter from which cosmic evolution took place. Herschel's German-bred rationalism, evident in these theoretical works, was not received sympathetically at the Royal Society or the major universities of England.

LAPLACE. Pierre Simon de Laplace (1749–1827) was comparable to Newton in depth and breadth of genius in physics. While owing much to the simultaneous attentions of Lagrange to the same problems, Laplace completed and generalized the theory of lunar and planetary inequalities. Beginning with the distinction of secular and periodic inequalities of motion, he finally realized, 1784, that the perturbations in the orbits of Jupiter and Saturn were periodic, not cumulative, over a long time. Since the times of revolution of Jupiter and Saturn are not quite commensurable (in terms of small whole numbers), disturbances in their motions were found to be repetitive in cycles of about 900 years with a rather appreciable, 3rd-order inequality. In his paper on the long inequality of Jupiter and Saturn, Laplace set down 2 significant relations for planetary motion. With respect to eccentricity he declared: "If the mass of each planet be multiplied by the square root of the axis of its orbit and by the square of the eccentricity, then the sum of these products for all the planets is invariable save for periodical inequalities." For inclination he gave an exactly similar law. It is notable that these statements establish funds of eccentricity and of inclination, which the planets collectively can never overdraw; if one increases its eccentricity, another's decreases.

In line with his discovery of apparently complete periodicity of planetary inequalities, Laplace found, 1787, the so-called secular acceleration of the moon's mean motion to be cyclical as well. He showed that a slowly decreasing eccentricity of the earth's orbit results, via the sun's influence, in acceleration of the moon's average rate of motion. Both variables he proved to be periodic: earth's orbital eccentricity would ultimately begin to increase, and the moon's motion would show deceleration in response.

With the publication of *La méchanique céleste*, 1799–1825, Laplace systematized his various discoveries into a tour de force of scientific and philosophical optimism. The concept of periodic variations was central to his universe, as it thus became predictable, certain, and essentially unchanging. (However, it should be remembered that his mathematics involved neglect of certain small quantities.) To Laplace it seemed that Leibniz' image of a perfectionist clockmaker was more correct than Newton's version of a deity occasionally resetting and rewinding his timepiece.

GAUSS. Karl Friedrich Gauss (1777–1855) added to the mathematical regularization of the solar system by publishing, 1809, a method for calculating the orbit of a planet from 3 complete observations. Each positional observation involves right ascension and declination. The 6 equations based on 3 pairs of such elements allowed quick calculation of bodies difficult to observe. When Ceres, the 1st of the asteroids, was discovered, 1801, it was lost after a few weeks. Gauss applied his method to predict its orbit, and the planetoid was rediscovered about a year later very near the predicted position.

LEVERRIER. Jean Joseph Leverrier (1811–77) represented both the zenith and the nadir of Newtonian mechanics. On the basis of utter faith in the classical system, he considered it necessary to posit, 1846, an unseen planet beyond Uranus to explain the latter's perturbations. Using Bode's law and computations based on the Uranian inequalities, Leverrier assigned a position within 1° of that 1st observed for Neptune later in the year. Unfortunately for the Newtonian system, Leverrier then turned to the observation of 38″ advance in the perihelion of Mercury. His reasoning for the existence of Neptune to explain problems with Uranus was reapplied with disastrous results. The prediction of an intra-Mercurial planet, christened Vulcan, led to a great search and ultimate failure. The presumption of an ironclad Newtonian system was tacitly dropped by Asaph Hall (1829–1907), who suggested a slight departure from the Newtonian inverse square law to explain Mercury. It only remained for Einstein to suggest a more significant departure.

EINSTEIN. The paper of Albert Einstein (1879–1955) on "Die Grundlage der Allgemeinen Relativitätstheorie", 1916, predicted a perihelial advance of 43.03″ ± 0.03″. The amazing correlation between this theoretical statement and observational data served to establish the general theory of relativity's point that the correct form of laws of nature is independent of the motion assumed for the observer. For Mercury's perihelion the theory worked on a basis of the square of the ratio of the planet's velocity and the velocity of light; for other planets the result would be so small as to indicate an imperceptible motion. In 1917 Einstein indicated the cosmological usefulness of general relativity theory. With gravity reduced to local curvatures, produced by matter, in space-time, the primary object of investigation became space itself via non-Euclidean geometry. Since space has a positive curvature in terms of attracting matter, the universe must have a finite content. The model of the universe set out by Einstein, as well as Willem de Sitter's variation on Einstein's model, was static. However, the equations used in the model require a situation without equilibrium. Succeeding cosmologists have generally recognized an expanding universe.

HUBBLE. Edwin P. Hubble (1889–1953) gave some sense of observational order to the concept of an expanding universe when he demonstrated, 1929, that receding nebulae observed by Slipher and Shapley were moving away from us with a regular, linear increase in velocity. The shift toward the red end of the spectrum in analyses of nebular light indicated tremendous outward velocities and millions of light-years in distance.

EDDINGTON. Arthur S. Eddington (1882–1944) 1st computed the forces involved in the massive bodies of radiant stars. For the sun he found a central temperature of 18 million degrees and a central pressure of 9 billion atmospheres. In *The Internal Constitution of the Stars*, 1925, he set out the mass-luminosity law, showing that stellar luminosity is entirely determined by mass and quite independent of the diameter of stars. Eddington had assumed that stellar matter behaved like a perfect gas. When he found no contradictions to this assumption, even in dense dwarf stars, it became evident that centrally located stellar atoms had lost outer electron shells through ionization and thus moved freely despite the extreme internal density of stars like the white dwarfs. Eddington's work on the interior construction of stars has been basic for subsequent cosmology.

MILNE. E. A. Milne (1896–1950) was responsible for an alternative view, developed from 1932 onward, of the cosmos based upon special rather than general relativity theory. Deriving space measures from observable time measures, he constructed a system with every member surrounded by an infinity of others receding with linear increase in velocity. The outermost move with the speed of light and are inaccessible, since the measuring standard (light) puts them an infinite distance away. Nonequivalent particles gather around equivalents to form nebulae. Abandoning the tensor equations of general relativity, Milne made natural laws invariant in transformations between equivalent observers according to special relativity. Though attempting to obviate ambiguities in applications of the general theory, Milne could not easily encompass certain features of gravitation, and his theory has remained peripheral to the major trend in cosmology.

THE EXPANDING UNIVERSE. The problems with which Milne was grappling are the essential characteristics of the cosmic model of Jules Lemaître (b. 1894), proposed in 1927 and developed by himself and George Gamow (b. 1904) since then. Lemaître's expanding universe theory develops from the instability of a world in Einstein's general relativistic model. Galaxies diverge outward from a "primeval atom" because their matrix, space, is constantly expanding with a broadly homogeneous distribution of "matter" therein. The equation of matter with geometrical features of space-time, and the meaning of homogeneity in such a model, prodded Milne to attempt a reformulation of the assumptions of cosmology.

THE "STEADY-STATE" THEORY. The general relativity universe involved certain conclusions which divided theorists in the 1940's. According to orthodox theory, the expanding universe must have had a point of singularity—a point when the density of the universe was infinite. Largely in reaction to this theoretical requirement, the "steady-state" version of the expanding universe was proposed by Hermann Bondi and Thomas Gold in 1948; Fred Hoyle and William McCrea remodeled it in accord with relativity theory. Such a universe had no beginning

and in its expansion was constantly forming new galaxies from hydrogen created in the gaps resulting from expansion. The singularity was thereby obviated, allowing a time-independent mean density as well as other time-independent properties.

QUASARS. Difficulties arose for the steady-state theory in the 1960's with the newly discovered significance of cosmic radio sources. As early as 1931 the appearance of radio signals in space was noticed. After World War II the improved techniques of radar were applied to obtain positions for radio sources in order to direct optical telescopes to these sources. In this way the 1st visible radio source, the Crab Nebula, was discovered, 1949. In the 1950's a number of strong radio emissions were found to correspond to weak light sources and were christened quasi-stellar objects, or quasars. Working in 1962 with the spectrum of one of these objects (3C 273), Maarten Schmidt 1st noted the red shift in quasar spectra. Since then quasars have been observed with red shifts indicating recession speeds over 80% the velocity of light. According to steady-state theory, such objects must be at noncosmological (intragalactic) distances. But it has been found that 3C 273, at least, shows radio emission passing through the Virgo cluster of galaxies, about 40 million light-years from earth. Only if the red shifting is of non-Doppler origin can quasar data fit into steady-state theory.

BLACK-BODY RADIATION. The detection of cosmic black-body radiation, 1965, has been a major blow against the steady-state concept and in favor of some form of "big-bang" theory. About 1950 Gamow spoke of a very dense, extremely hot, early stage of the universe, from which an outward explosion took place. The original thermonuclear explosion would explain the large amount of helium observed today relative to hydrogen. From such an early stage, time would allow the passage to a state of equilibrium between matter and radiation having a black-body spectrum. Such a spectrum would continue and the only change during expansion would be cooling of the radiation. Recent calculations and observations have arrived at a temperature of 3° Kelvin for the current stage. According to steady-state theory there is no explanation for the apparent ubiquity of black-body characteristics of the spectra over a wide range of wave lengths. The theory would seem to demand new radiation with newly created matter, and this new radiation would not be uniformly black-body. Further observation of cosmic black-body radiation, with respect to its uniformity and universality, and with respect to other cosmological characteristics, such as an isotropic universe, will have much to say about the fate of present cosmological theories.

Mathematics

BERNOULLI BROTHERS. When Newton (in the 1660's) and Leibniz (in the 1670's) evolved the calculus, numerous mathematical problems suggested themselves. The Bernoulli brothers, Jakob (1654–1705) and Johann (1667–1748), both found inspiration in the mathematics of Leibniz and corresponded with him. They worked out most of the material contained in modern elementary texts on differential and integral calculus. Superior to his brother in critical power, Jakob followed Leibniz' more cautious view of infinitesimals as only potentially existent. The infinitely small he saw as "a perpetual fluxion toward nothing." Viewing the differential as variable, Jakob associated the calculus more with the method of limits. Johann, the more imaginative, adhered to the more philosophical side of Leibniz on infinitesimals and considered them to be actual. Rather than work toward a limit concept, he considered increase by an infinitesimal to be no increase at all, thereby making omission of higher-order differentials the fundamental procedure. It was, however, partly on the basis of Johann's unpublished treatise on differentiation, 1691–92, that L'Hospital wrote his *Analyse des infiniments petits*, 1696, the 1st published textbook on the subject. L'Hospital's text was highly influential in spreading the new techniques.

TAYLOR AND MACLAURIN. Brook Taylor (1685–1731) is remembered chiefly for his series for $f(x+h)$, published in 1715. His *Methodus incrementorum* interpreted ratios of fluxions in terms of finite differences of moments. Colin Maclaurin (1698–1746), in his *Treatise on Fluxions*, 1742, attempted to satisfy the complaints of Berkeley's *The Analyst*, 1734, against the new analysis. Maclaurin therefore abandoned the infinitesimal as well as Taylor's algebraic tendencies in analysis; instead he developed geometrical demonstrations of analysis, omitting all notation of fluxions until the end of his treatise. His notion of instantaneous velocity for a variable motion was in terms of "the space that would have been described if the motion had continued uniformly" from the reference point. Maclaurin did not conceive of any such notion as the limit of an average rate of change as the intervals approach zero. His elegant geometry was much admired, but it obscured the greater promise of an algebraic approach.

EULER. Leonhard Euler (1707–83), despite his naïve notions of infinity and continuity, contributed extensively to the development of calculus by means of a new, formalistic approach. He freed the new analysis from geometrical limitations by making the subject into a formal theory of functions. Systematically he studied and classified the elementary functions plus their differentials and integrals. In the use of infinite series, Euler warned others to be careful with divergent series, yet made such statements as $1 - 1 + 1 - 1 + \ldots = \frac{1}{2}$. His contributions to trigonometry, theory of numbers, analytical geometry, and other fields all bear the mark of his genius for formalization.

D'ALEMBERT. Jean-le-Rond d'Alembert (1717–83) refused to consider Newton's prime and ultimate ratios of quantities literally, but rather as limits of quantities. Strictly speaking, he decided, the variable quantity only approaches its limit rather than ever coinciding. The differential was simply the limit of ratios of finite differences of 2 variables. D'Alembert likewise defined 2nd- and higher-order differences in terminology similar to the concept of limiting ratios. His geometrical analogies, however, involved paradoxes which dissuaded many mathematicians from abandoning the older view of actual infinitesimals. In various dynamical applications of the differential, he introduced—along with Daniel Bernoulli—the use of partial differential equations.

LAGRANGE. Joseph Louis Lagrange (1736–1813) avoided the imprecise conceptualization of limit given by d'Alembert, turning to Euler's function concept. In so doing Lagrange focused attention on the derivative (*fonction dérivée*). The use of Taylor's series, with some care for considerations of convergence, was basic in Lagrange's work; he assumed that all functions allow such a series expansion. Noting that the coefficients of the powers of h in the series involve the ratios of differentials and fluxions, he saw definition of differentials and fluxions in terms of these coefficients as a way to avoid introducing limits or infinitesimals. The result was a useful, formalized calculus, based on algebraic method. In his *Méchanique analytique*, 1788, the full power of his calculus of variations (developed in 1760–61) appears, with its unification of the varied principles of statics and dynamics.

LAPLACE. In contrast to Lagrange, Laplace (p. 904, above) saw mathematics purely as a tool for solving physical problems. This is evident in his *Méchanique céleste*, which introduced the potential function in the form of a partial differential equation applicable to gravitation, electricity, and magnetism. His *Théorie analytique des probabilités* was based on the method of generating functions, which treated successive values of any function as the coefficients in the expansion of another function with reference to a different variable; the latter is the generating function of the former. Laplace also showed that the most advantageous method, in terms of minimum mean probability of error, for reducing many equations of condition to the number of unknown quantities to be determined was the method of least squares. In general, Laplace synthesized and formalized all prior knowledge on probabilities in a highly original and creative way.

LEGENDRE. Adrien Marie Legendre (1752–1833) made his contributions in the shadows of Laplace and Lagrange. His work on elliptical functions, 1825–26, started with Euler and Lagrange and left the subject in a state unchanged for another 40 years. Beginning with an integral depending upon the square root of a polynomial of the 4th degree in x, Legendre showed that such integrals reduce to 3 canonical forms. In number theory, his other abiding fascination, he did important work, crowned by the theorem of quadratic reciprocity. His formulation, 1806, of the method of least squares was useful to Laplace in probability theory.

GAUSS. Karl Friedrich Gauss (1777–1855) represented a turning point in the history of mathematics. For men like Laplace and Lagrange, mathematics had the service of science as its highest goal. Gauss, while still influenced by this older view, maintained that mathematics was the "queen of the sciences." Especially in number theory was Gauss's genius radiant. His *Disquisitiones arithmeticae*, 1801, gave the 1st rigorous proof of the so-called fundamental theorem of algebra, i.e., that every algebraic equation with real coefficients has at least 1 root and therefore n roots. His 3rd proof of this involved complex integrals. With the theory of quadratic residues, Gauss 1st introduced into number theory complex numbers of the form $a + bi$. This was extended, 1831, into an arithmetic as well as an algebra of complex numbers. Gauss gave remarkable clarification to the notion of complex numbers by representing them by points in a plane. Though contributing important work in calculus of variations, geodesy, etc., Gauss made his most striking discoveries in the realm of arithmetic, his "queen of mathematics."

FOURIER. It was Joseph Fourier (1768–1830), an active participant in the French Revolution, who called attention to the need for rigor in pure mathematics. His *Théorie analytique de la chaleur,* 1822, based on investigations of the propagation of heat in solid bodies, is the source of modern methods for the integration of partial differential equations with fixed boundary values. Objections by Lagrange to the theory did not disturb Fourier, who trusted to his physical intuition for the proper results. For all functions, even the discontinuous and the wholly arbitrary, he used an infinite series of sines and cosines of multiple arcs; the proof he provided in the expansion of an "arbitrary" odd function by a sine series. Earlier Lagrange had constructed by interpolation a finite summation formula from which Fourier's result is obtainable by a jump to infinity. But it required Fourier's lack of pure mathematical conscience to make this transition to an integration formula. Henceforth it was painfully obvious that mathematicians needed clarification of their intuitions of "arbitrary" function, real number, and continuity.

CAUCHY, WEIERSTRASS, AND RIEMANN. Augustin Louis Cauchy (1789–1857) made complex-function theory an independent field of mathematical research. He is responsible for the foundations of the calculus as found in modern textbooks. His extraordinary output included detailed studies of convergence in infinite series. He gave the 1st existence proof for the solution of a differential equation and of a system of such equations. His attention to rigor in the definitions of limit, derivative, differential, definite integral, and continuity established a satisfactory means for dealing with the ancient paradoxes of Zeno, as well as the elements of the classical theory of functions of a real variable. In theories of functions, Cauchy's lectures, 1821, at the École Polytechnique were truly epoch-making. The establishment of complex-function theory on a basis of the

power series was due to Karl Weierstrass (1815–97), who began the reduction of principles of analysis to simple arithmetical concepts. The importance of topology for complex function theory was established by G. F. Bernhard Riemann (1826–66).

ABEL AND JACOBI. To Niels Henrik Abel (1802–29) and Karl G. J. Jacobi (1804–51) belongs the systematic foundation of elliptical functions. In 1827 Abel stood the investigation of elliptical integrals on its head: he considered a as a function of x rather than following the "normal" procedure of seeing x as a function of a. Through this inversion of the integral, he discovered the double periodicity of the elliptical function. Jacobi's classic text, 1829, on elliptical functions made the theory available to the mathematical public. From the details of Abel's and Jacobi's work many new directions appeared in mathematics, e.g., complex multiplication, elliptical theta functions, and elliptical modular functions.

HAMILTON AND GRASSMANN. William Rowan Hamilton (1805–65) was the 1st to publish, 1844, a consistent algebra of rotations and vectors in space. The fundamental formula was $i^2 = j^2 = k^2 = ijk = -1$. The quaternions derived therefrom did not follow the commutative law of multiplication. In successively more sophisticated presentations, 1853 and 1866, Hamilton showed the key importance of quaternions in mathematical physics, but a strong conservative tendency discouraged use of his new tool in physics. The more philosophically based contemporary algebra of Hermann Grassmann (1809–77) was almost totally ignored by physicists except for J. Willard Gibbs (1839–1903). Yet Grassmann's algebra not only dropped the commutative law; it also dealt with space of n dimensions. It included Hamiltonian quaternions as a special case and expanded the results to n-dimensional space. It included the theories of determinants, matrices, and tensor algebra.

NON-EUCLIDIAN GEOMETRY. Janos Bolyai (1802–60), N. I. Lobachevsky (1793–1856), and Riemann all discovered non-Euclidean geometry. Bolyai in 1833 and Lobachevsky in 1826–29 published their independent developments of hyperbolic geometry. In hyperbolic geometry there is more than 1 parallel to a reference line. In Riemann's "spherical" non-Euclidean system, 1854, one finds the additional result that 2 straight lines intersect twice. Thus space becomes unbounded yet finite. In conjunction with abstract algebra, non-Euclidean geometry gave to modern mathematics its reputation as the imaginative creation of mathematicians.

CANTOR. Georg Cantor's (1845–1918) contribution to number theory was through point-set theory. In his arithmetical analysis Cantor derived all rational numbers from natural numbers and then defined irrationals through infinite sequences of rationals. Thus he arithmetized the continuum of real numbers. A 1-to-1 correspondence of points on a straight-line segment and the continuum of real numbers was established. In turn, he proved that all points in a spatial continuum can be put in 1-to-1 correspondence with all points on a straight-line segment. Distinguishing cardinal from ordinal numbers, he showed a significant difference between the 2 in the realm of transfinite numbers. With the transfinite ordinals, one could count well-ordered sets. For cardinal numbers Cantor proved, 1874, the set of all algebraic numbers to be denumerable, and in 1878 he showed how to construct an infinite nondenumerable set of real numbers. Demonstrating the existence but not the identity of any of these transfinite numbers, Cantor was fully in line with the medieval tradition of Adam of Littlebridge and Albert of Saxony.

KLEIN. Felix Klein (1849–1925) represented, in his Erlangen Program, a strong tendency of mathematics toward unification in the later 19th cent. His key to the classification of different fields was the group concept. In his inaugural address at Erlangen, 1872, he declared every geometry to be the theory of invariants of a particular transformation group. His approach to geometries dealt with distinct figures in restricted groups of transformations leaving definitions and theorems in-

variant. Yet it was exactly the geometry where the group is unrestricted and corresponds to identity which suddenly sprang to prominence in 1916 with general relativity theory. This theory showed space to be more than a locus and to have a structure of its own consisting of a set of relations generally not defined in terms of a transformation group. However, for almost half a century, group theory provided the basis for a synthesis of geometry and algebra.

LIE. M. Sophus Lie (1842–99) shared with Klein the honor of unifying mathematics through group theory. While Klein dealt essentially with discontinuous groups, Lie dwelt on continuous groups, writing in 1893 that this "theory of invariants of all continuous groups embraces all theories of invariants hitherto noted." Under continuous-group theory he was able to subsume Newtonian mechanical principles, kinematics, and differential invariants.

POINCARÉ. Henri Poincaré (1854–1912) stands at the pinnacle of 19th-cent. mathematics. In the calculus of finite differences his focal position is paralleled only by Newton's. Poincaré's automorphic functions, 1881–84, uniformized any algebraic curve $f(x, y) = 0$. He profitably applied continuous group theory to linear algebra. His many individual contributions, however, are paralleled by a sense of the unifying trends of late 19th-cent. mathematics, a development from which 20th-cent. mathematics has in great degree been departing. In 1900 he looked to the philosophies of number based on the theory of infinite sets to dispel past difficulties in the continuum of analysis. Though suspicious of logicians, he could not ignore work like Hilbert's postulational discussion of geometry, 1899.

HILBERT. At an international congress of mathematicians in Paris, 1900, David Hilbert (1862–1943) proposed 23 mathematical problems for the 20th cent. He agreed that the arithmetical continuum and non-Euclidean geometry were the 2 greatest achievements of the 19th cent. His 1st problem for the new era dealt with the real-number continuum and related to the axiom of choice of

Ernst Zermelo (1871–1956). It asserted the existence, given a set of mutually exclusive nonempty sets, of a set having only 1 element in common with each of the given sets. Kurt Gödel (b. 1906) proved the consistency of this axiom, 1940, and Paul Cohen (b. 1934) showed its independence of other axioms in a specified system of set theory. Hilbert's 2nd problem raised the question of the consistency of the axioms of arithmetic. Russell's and Whitehead's *Principia mathematica,* 1910–13, showed pure mathematics to be derivable from a few logical principles, but only with Gödel's theorem of 1931 was Hilbert's problem answered. Gödel showed that the axioms of a system are never sufficient to prove or disprove every statement within that system: a metasystem is always required. Hilbert's *Grundlagen der Geometrie,* 1899, provided an axiomatization for geometry to match the earlier development in other branches of mathematics.

BROUWER. From 1907 on L. E. J. Brouwer (1882–1966) attacked the logical and formal bases of mathematics supported by Russell and by Hilbert. Brouwer's intuitionism insisted, for example, that the use of indirect proof in transfinite arithmetic is invalid because uncertain. He denied the logical law of the excluded middle. In 1918 Brouwer was joined by Hermann Weyl (1885–1955), and their attacks could not be met satisfactorily by Hilbert.

LEBESGUE. In a less philosophical vein Henri Lebesgue (1875–1941) eschewed generalism for more detailed development. His most striking creation was the Lebesgue integral, 1902, which reconstructed the field of integration, substituting a sense of point correspondence for smooth variation.

FRÉCHET. With Hilbert, Maurice Fréchet (b. 1878) is responsible for the modern generalizing and abstraction of set theory and of space. From 1904 to 1910 Hilbert developed the formal concept of space named for him. Around 1906 Fréchet generalized the methods of calculus of variations through his functional calculus. Another generalizing tendency was the creation of topology,

especially by Brouwer with his invariance theorems, 1911, and a fusion of methods from Cantor and Poincaré. In the succeeding half-century topology moved from a geometrical character to an algebraic under the influence of work in the U.S. The period between the 2 world wars saw an abstraction in algebra as well. Since World War II the development of homological algebra, a topological version of abstract algebra, has taken place, with the 1st book on the subject, 1955, by Henri Cartan (b. 1904) and Samuel Eilenberg (b. 1913).

PROBABILITY, STATISTICS, AND THE COMPUTER AGE. Perhaps the most popularly known area of modern mathematics is probability and statistics. In 1901 J. Willard Gibbs published his *Elementary Principles in Statistical Mechanics,* and Émile Borel (1871–1956) published a basic text in probability theory in 1909. In physics, genetics, and elsewhere the field found applications as its axiomatic foundations were worked out (Hilbert's 6th project). The use of high-speed calculating machines to solve problems in statistics and probability theory has revolutionized 20th-cent. mathematics. Beginning with the experiments of Charles Babbage in the 1830's, calculators and computers have become progressively more efficient and sophisticated (p. 805, above). Two men deeply involved in generalizing the mathematical implications of the computer revolution were John von Neumann (1903–57) and Norbert Wiener (1894–1964). Neumann assisted in the development of computer capabilities during and after World War II and was largely responsible for the extended application of finite mathematics in the social sciences. Among his earlier work were the recognition of Hilbert space as the framework for quantum theory, the solution of Hilbert's 5th problem for compact groups, and basic work in the foundations of mathematics. His later work included a theory of automata. Wiener had earlier assisted in the creation of the modern theory of linear spaces. His *Cybernetics,* 1948, established a new subject, the study of control and communication in both machines and living beings.

Classical Physics

MECHANICS

NEWTON. The basis of classical dynamics lies in Newton's *Principia,* where one finds under "Definitions" and "Axioms" the fundamentals of the new mechanics. Of 8 definitions, the first 4 define mass, momentum, inertia, and impressed force. There follow descriptions of absolute time and absolute space, necessary prerequisites for the definitions established as the 1st 2 laws, or axioms, of motion. The 1st is the law of inertia; the 2nd finds alteration of motion proportional to the motive force impressed and in the direction of the impressed force. The 3rd law of motion sets action equal to reaction. Determined empirically, this law describes conservation of momentum. In the last book (III) of *Principia,* Newton derived the law of universal gravitation. It was shown to be deducible from Kepler's 2nd and 3rd laws via 4 "Rules of Reasoning in Philosophy." These rules embodied the new world outlook of the 17th cent. While it is possible to see the law of gravitation as a simple deduction from empirical data, it is historically more correct to see Newton's reasoning as a hypothetico-deductive process from the hypothesis of the inverse-square law of gravitation. In any case, he made no special hypothesis for the mechanism of gravitation. More than just a mathematical law, universal gravitation was conceived as a physical hypothesis, a force the detailed explanation of which he guessed at only in the concluding General Scholium of *Principia.*

D'ALEMBERT. One of the quarrels ensuing from *Principia* was the exact nature of "quantity of motion." In the *Traité de dynamique,* 1743, d'Alembert maintained to be fruitless the question whether the force of a body in motion is proportional to mv or mv^2. He not only clarified the difference between the 2; he considered "forces inherent in bodies" to be "obscure and metaphysical." D'Alembert preferred a more positivistic program for mechanics.

D'Alembert's principle was 1st elevated to the status of a unifying principle by its namesake, although it had already been applied in more limited fashion by Hermann, 1716, and Euler, 1740. By this principle the general dynamical problem became the discovery of the motion of each body in a system where a particular motion is impressed on each, while the interference of other bodies prevents direct transmission of the motion. D'Alembert's solution used analysis of each motion into a part having a direct effective transmission and a part effecting no change in the body. The sum of the former parts will describe the collective motions actually occurring in the system of bodies. Lagrange developed a more practical means of applying this principle.

LAGRANGE. Lagrange summarized and analyzed the 4 principles of dynamics. The conservation of *vis viva,* he observed, originated with Huyghens. The conservation of motion of the center of gravity was shown to be Newton's principle. The conservation of moments, discovered by Euler and Daniel Bernoulli, was found to be a generalization of a Newtonian theorem. Maupertius' principle of least action appeared to Lagrange as vague and arbitrary, and he opted for Euler's alternative version, the integration product of $m v d s$.

The basic principle of statics, the principle of virtual displacements, was 1st perceived in its universal applicability by Johann Bernoulli, who mentioned it in a letter of 1717. Lagrange, in his *Mécanique analytique,* 1788, asserted "that all the general principles which may still be discovered in the science of equilibrium, will be only this same principle of virtual velocities." He saw it to be a general formula encompassing all problems of equilibrium. Lagrange's deduction, that $P\alpha + Q\beta + R\gamma + \ldots = 0$ defines equilibrium, used the principle of the pulley.

According to Ernst Mach, the Lagrangian demonstration classifies as discernment of a principle rather than as logical deduction.

HERTZ. Among basic systems of mechanics, that of Heinrich Rudolf Hertz (1857–94) in *Die Principien der Mechanik in neuem Zusammenhange,* 1894, suggested a return to a Cartesian view of the world, wherein the concept of force is eliminated and space, time, and mass alone are the necessary concepts for a mechanics in the world described by Maxwell's equations. The single basic principle of Hertzian mechanics was a combination of the law of inertia and Gauss's principle of least constraint (applied through connection of masses). While the principle was new in form, the origins were in Lagrange's equations. Hertz's geometrical approach to mechanics was the last attempt to carry out a Cartesian program via the traditional concepts of space and time. A revolution in those concepts led the way to the geometrical approach of relativity theory.

PROPERTIES OF MATTER

NEWTON. Perhaps the most controversial property of matter in the Newtonian system was the force of gravitation. Newton himself was rather careful to avoid attributing any such intrinsic force to matter. For him gravitation in "experimental philosophy" was the deduced result from phenomena. Gravitation simply described a situation; the cause of gravitation he professed not to know. His successors were not always as careful. A property of matter of 1st importance in Newton's system was mass, statically defined at the beginning of *Principia.* Ernst Mach supposed a definition of mass to be an undesirable premise and attempted to base the logical deduction of the laws of motion on bodies rather than mass. For Newton acceleration derived from bodies rather than mass would have been a dubious hypothesis. In the law of gravitation Newton finds gravitational mass equivalent to inertial mass almost by accident. This equation is basic in relativity theory.

CAVENDISH. In 1789 the direct, experimental determination of the law of gravitation was made by Henry Cavendish (1731–1810). A simple apparatus gave data for the horizontal attraction of 2 large leaden balls for 2 small spheres suspended from the ends of a bar. In terms of the measured times of oscillation of the suspended spheres, Cavendish was able to compute the density of the earth.

YOUNG. The elasticity of matter, defined by Robert Hooke and put in successively improved mathematical form by Poisson, Navier, and Cauchy, was neatly defined in its common form by Thomas Young, 1807, who coined the phrase "modulus of elasticity." Young's modulus gives characteristic coefficients for materials deformed by tension or pressure, as in a wire or a column; the coefficients relate variation in force applied to change in length of material.

AMPÈRE. André Marie Ampère (1775–1836) was responsible for the 1st clear statement of the formal distinctions between particles, molecules, and atoms as 19th-cent. science understood them. "Particle" referred to the smallest portion of a body still having the same gross characteristics as the body itself (e.g., solidity). Molecules were the subdivisions of particles and were considered to be held in spatial relationships with each other by a combination of attractive and repulsive forces, including gravitation. The atoms were understood as the "material points" from which attractive and repulsive forces in the molecule emanated.

HEAT

BLACK. Beyond such general concepts and experimental determinations of material properties as outlined above, the areas of heat, light, electricity, and magnetism were extensively explored in late 18th- and 19th-cent. physics. As early as Galileo, heat had been explained as the result of atomic motion. On the other hand, Lavoisier had considered "caloric" as a substance, albeit weightless, in his quantitative approach to chemistry. From Joseph Black (1728–99) and his *Lectures on the Elements of Chemistry,* 1803, came accounts of the discovery of specific and latent heats. Recounting his work of 1760, he treated heat as a fluid substance ("caloric"). Clearly distinguishing temperature from quantity of heat, he saw specific heat in terms of the amount of "caloric" necessary to raise the temperature of a certain mass by 1°C. About the same time he recognized the latent heat in bodies, the amount of "caloric" which must be dissipated from a body in one state before it will change to another denser state at the same temperature. However, Black's experiments did not suggest to him the consequent difficulties in maintaining a materialistic, or substantial, theory of heat.

RUMFORD. Benjamin Thompson, Count Rumford (1753–1814) was the 1st to quarrel with the caloric theory of heat. He noted, 1798, the appearance of heat in the boring of cannon, recording the creation of enough heat to boil 18¾ lbs. of water in 2½ hrs. It became apparent that the heat increase was generated by friction alone. He concluded that "any thing which any *insulated* body, or system of bodies, can continue to furnish *without limitation,* cannot possibly be a *material substance:* and it appears to me to be extremely difficult, if not quite impossible, to form any distinct idea of any thing, capable of being excited and communicated, in the manner the heat was excited and communicated in these Experiments, except it be MOTION."

GAY-LUSSAC. Louis Joseph Gay-Lussac (1778–1850), while a demonstrator at the École Polytechnique, showed experimentally, 1802, that any gas between the freezing and boiling temperatures of water will expand or contract at the same rate as any other gas with a given amount of heating. The results encouraged scientists in the current viewpoint that gases are harmoniously and simply elastic. Upon Gay-Lussac's work was founded J. R. Mayer's hypothesis that the work spent in the compression of a gas is exactly the mechanical equivalent of the heat evolved.

DULONG AND PETIT. Further unification of heat theory, in terms of atomic theory, was accomplished by the experiments, 1819, of Pierre Louis Dulong (1785–1838) and Alexis Thérèse Petit (1791–1820) on a selection of solids. The results showed a close correlation of specific heats and relative atomic weights of the various simple substances; the specific heats varied inversely as the relative atomic weights. This led directly to the law adopted by Dulong and Petit that "the atoms of all simple bodies have exactly the same capacity for heat."

FOURIER. Joseph Fourier, following Lavoisier's line of reasoning, tended to see heat as material rather than the product of mechanical forces. Avoiding the question of causes of factors in heating, he observed general relationships among these factors and expressed them in equations analogous to the general equations of dynamics. Experimentally he noted the necessity of temperature difference for the motion of heat. The analogy of heat flow to water flow was unimportant for Fourier's work, but it was central in the genesis of Carnot's *Réflexions sur la puissance motrice du feu,* 1824.

CARNOT. Nicolas Léonard Sadi Carnot (1796–1832) anchored his thought on the notion of the impossibility of a perpetual motion. Thus the transmission of heat from an area of higher temperature to one of lower temperature created work, but at least that much work was required to recreate the original temperature differential. Carnot introduced the idea of a complete cycle of a working material and the correlative reversibility. At the same time he recognized that no engine could have a greater efficiency than a reversible engine: a perpetual motion machine is impossible. Later in life Carnot abandoned the material theory of heat for the mechanical and even calculated a mechanical equivalent of heat. Carnot's work, while referring only to heat, contained the ideas behind the 1st 2 laws of thermodynamics, i.e., the conservation, equivalence, and convertibility of energy, and the availability of energy.

MAYER. Julius Robert Mayer (1814–78) can be credited with the 1st published statement of the equivalence of heat and mechanical energy, 1842, as well as quantitative determinations thereof. Mohr had made a general philosophical statement of the principle in the preceding decade.

Mayer stated that the work spent in compressing a gas is the exact mechanical equivalent of the heat evolved. He based his view on Gay-Lussac's work. The philosophical matrix of Mayer's version of the principle of the conservation of energy caused tardy acceptance of his results.

JOULE. Late recognition was also the response to James Prescott Joule's (1818–89) experimental statement of the mechanical equivalent of heat, 1843, making it clear that the principle of conservation of energy was involved. Yet like Mayer, Joule had to await Kelvin's recognition of his work, 1847, before seeing its wide acceptance. Joule founded his reports on painstaking and extensive experiments—more so than Mayer—and published his most famous and complete memoir on the equivalence of heat and work in 1850.

HELMHOLTZ. Hermann von Helmholtz (1821–94) composed the classic statement of conservation of energy in *Über die Erhaltung der Kraft,* 1847. His pamphlet introduced a correct mathematical expression of the principle and interrelated the various forces studied in physics. The treatise concluded with an assertion of the universality of the principle of conservation of "force," including even the heat of living beings. His paper was refused (as Mayer's had been) by Poggendorff's *Annalen,* because it offered no new data and suggested a return to the more philosophical trend from which physics had so recently escaped. In fact, Helmholtz persisted in the use of the ambiguous term "force," although his mathematical statement was quite clear. Only with Kelvin's adoption of Young's term, "energy," and with Rankine's rephrasing of the principle to one of "conservation of energy" was ambiguity completely removed.

CLAUSIUS. Rudolf Clausius (1822–88) published in 1850 a paper which paralleled Kelvin's contemporary perception of the importance of "loss" of energy. To Mayer, Joule, and Helmholtz, it had not occurred to ask how the loss and waste of power in nature occurs, if energy is not only conserved but converted to work. Only Carnot (after 1824) had faced the problem of the inability to convert all the heat involved into work; it occurred to

him that heat might pass from a hotter body to a colder without the creation of any motion, though he made no real study of this issue. Clausius, however, turned his considerable mathematical skills—he was not a great experimenter—to the problem of energy lost during conversion of energy to work. He pointed out that maximum work is gained by heat flow when the 2 bodies of different temperatures never touch. The full consequences of the 2nd law of thermodynamics, correctly stated by Clausius in 1850, were synthesized in his 1865 paper, which introduced the term "entropy" and developed its properties. Clausius concluded that (1) the energy of the universe is constant, and (2) the entropy of the universe tends toward a maximum.

KELVIN. It was William Thomson, Lord Kelvin (1824–1907), who 1st attempted, 1848, to establish an absolute temperature scale wherein all degrees would have the same value, so that a decrease of a given number of degrees at any temperature would always have the same mechanical equivalent. A more correct scale, that now current, was described by Kelvin in 1851. At the same time he made his own statement of the 2nd law of thermodynamics. Kelvin 1st saw the necessary interrelationship of the 1st 2 laws in physics. Only the acceptance of both at once would explain the impossibility of a perpetual-motion machine, since energy must be available before useful work can be done. Mathematically as well as conceptually he made the issue clear. Along with Clausius, Kelvin saw the universal significance of the constant tendency toward dissipation of energy.

ANDREWS. In experimental physics the work of Thomas Andrews (1813–85) on the continuity of gaseous and liquid states, 1863, was closely related to the mechanical theory of heat, which most English physicists favored. Andrews identified as a "critical temperature" that at which a gas and a liquid appear to form a single-phased fluid, unidentifiable in whole or in part as distinctly gas or liquid. Increase in pressure made no difference.

BERNOULLI AND BROWN. The mechanical theory of heat owed much to the development of a kinetic theory of gases. Daniel Bernoulli (1700–1782) gave the 1st successful application of the kinetic theory in his *Hydrodynamica,* 1738. Giving a quantitative account of the force necessary to compress a gas, he credited the increase by heat of air's elasticity to an increased motion of the particles of air. Observation of the effects of these particulate motions in fluids was made by the botanist Robert Brown (1773–1858), who reported Brownian motion in 1827 on the basis of microscopic observation of the motions of subparticles of pollen.

MAXWELL. In 1860 James Clerk Maxwell (1831–79) published his 1st statement of the distribution of molecular velocities. He later improved on the calculations previously given. With direct reference to heat, "Maxwell's demon" was an instructive device for pointing out the basis in distribution alone for heat "flow."

GIBBS. From 1871 on Josiah Willard Gibbs (1839–1903) developed a very abstract form of thermodynamics, quite independent of any association with heat engines. With respect to systems of different chemical or physical "phases," Gibbs devised his Phase Rule, 1877, $F = C - P + 2$. While Maxwell was aware of Gibbs's work and made good use of the latter's development of 3-dimensional graphing of the different thermodynamic quantities, it was not until Ostwald's translations of 1892 that Gibbs's work became generally available. Meanwhile Maxwell and Ludwig Boltzmann (1844–1906) were developing statistical mechanics on the basis of probability theory, showing the strong tendency of molecules to approach a norm of activity. Improvements by Maxwell and Boltzmann over the former's distribution law of 1860 have become the basis of thermodynamics. In 1877 Boltzmann pointed out the relationship of probability to entropy, a direct and striking relationship, indicating that increase in entropy is the most probable state of the universe.

LIGHT

HUYGHENS. Huyghens' *Traité de la lumière,* 1690, had posited a wave theory of light, but with such flaws that it was overwhelmed by Newton. Huyghens adopted a geometrical view of propagation of light in waves in order to explain the most interesting phenomenon of double refraction in Icelandic spar. Although his theory had the philosophical merit of reinforcing Fermat's mathematical deduction of the law of refraction from the principle of economy, his waves were not periodic and could not account for the extensive phenomena reported by Newton in thin films.

NEWTON. On the other hand, Newton's *Opticks,* 1704, showed in irrefutable experimental fashion the composition of white light and an explanation of Newton's rings which seemed complete. Yet his theory involved a particulate view of light. This required such peculiarities as the "fits" of easy reflection and easy transmission for the rings, the possession of "sides" by light particles to explain polarization, and a mechanism for refraction which made light travel faster in denser media (as with Descartes also). Furthermore, Newton took very poor note of the data of interference patterns described in Grimaldi's *De lumine,* 1665, for Newton reported and explained only the internal fringes.

YOUNG. The interference patterns in thin films and especially in experiments with slits and knife edges were the crucial phenomena leading to the reintroduction of a wave theory by Thomas Young (1773–1829) in his papers of 1801–4. Although Young had a firm grasp of the principle of interference, the key to the success of wave theory, he was widely ignored, because of the authority of Newton, until the appearance of Fresnel's work over a decade later.

MALUS. Between the work of Young and Fresnel there appeared the significant observations of Étienne Louis Malus (1775–1812) on polarized light. Huyghens and Newton, each through his own theory, had observed and explained polarization in connection with doubly refractive crystals. Malus, a Newtonian, showed that polarization occurs in a variety of substances and is even found in reflection as well as refraction. Not until 1817 did it strike Young that a transverse vibration, perpendicular to the direction of propagation, would account for the phenomena in terms of wave theory.

FRESNEL AND ARAGO. Beginning in 1815 Augustin Jean Fresnel (1788–1827) delivered a series of papers on diffraction and the light fringes caused by interference. Pressed by minds like Laplace and Poisson, Fresnel applied mathematical analysis in order to obtain more exact and persuasive results in favor of the wave theory of light. Although Arago sympathized with the undulatory theory, he refused to have his name attached to the article, 1821, resulting from his work with Fresnel on the interference of polarized light. Fresnel's commitment to the notion of a wave transverse to the longitudinal propagation was more than Arago wished publicly to espouse, because of the entailed, paradoxical nature of the ether. The Fresnel-Arago view triumphed, however, even in the face of opposition from scientists such as Biot and Brewster.

RÖMER, FIZEAU, AND FOUCAULT. An important constant in the study of physical optics is the speed of light. Olaf Römer (1644–1710) 1st determined a value by studying the eclipses of Jupiter's moons, 1676; the eclipses occurred late when the earth was farthest in its orbit from Jupiter, and they happened early when the earth was nearest in its orbit to Jupiter. Bradley's discovery and explanation, 1728, of the astronomical aberration of light (p. 903, above) corroborated Römer. In 1838 Arago described a device for measuring the speed of light. Both Fizeau, 1849, and Foucault, 1862, actually constructed measuring devices on the basis of Arago's ideas. The principle behind Foucault's method was the observation of the fixed image of a moving image. His results indicated a velocity of 298,000 km. per sec. By 1926 Michelson had achieved a determination of 299,796 km. per sec.

STOKES. The phenomenon generally known as fluorescence was 1st correctly described by George Gabriel Stokes (1819–1903) on the basis of his experiments with fluorspar and other organic substances. Carefully distinguishing false from true "internal dispersion," Stokes pointed out the change of refrangibility

of light involved. His memoir, 1852, indicated that such a change is always in a direction of less refrangibility; this led him to the discovery of spectral lines for light normally beyond the visible, violet end of the spectrum. On the most basic level Stokes's account suggested a way to understand mechanically the interaction of the ether and the parts of ponderous bodies in the transmission of light.

KIRCHHOFF. A full understanding of spectrum analysis came with the joint paper, 1859, on Fraunhofer lines by Gustav Kirchhoff (1824–87) and Robert Wilhelm Bunsen (1811–99), although Kelvin claimed that Stokes had recognized the relationship of sodium vapor lines and those of the sun's atmosphere as early as 1849. Kirchhoff noted that a sodium flame emits only yellow light, having the same refractive index as the Fraunhofer D line in the solar spectrum. Further experiment proved that sodium vapor absorbs the same light as it emits. While Euler had already speculated on a general law for the relation of emitted and absorbed light, Kirchhoff saw correctly the relevance of a heat law for thermal equilibrium between absorption and emission. He concluded that "colored flames in the spectra of which bright lines present themselves, so weaken rays of the color of these lines, when such rays pass through them, that in place of the bright lines, dark ones appear."

BALMER AND RYDBERG. Johann Jakob Balmer (1825–98) was the 1st to set out a law for the distribution of the spectral lines discovered in the 19th cent. Balmer's formula treated the wave lengths of the 4 prominent lines in the hydrogen spectrum. The ratios of the wave lengths were given by small numbers. A constant was determined as a multiplier for each of the ratios in order to get the wave lengths. From his formula, $m^2 / (m^2 - n^2)$, where m and n are integers, he found a series of ratios defining very closely the 9 spectral lines definitely assigned to hydrogen. Johannes Robert Rydberg (1854–1919) introduced a formula, $n =$

$$n_0 - \frac{N_0}{(m + \mu)^2},$$ in 1890. N_0 represented

the Rydberg constant, applied in common to all elements. This constituted an advance beyond Balmer's formula of 1896, wherein the constants varied with each element.

MICHELSON AND MORLEY.

Among the most well-known experiments on light was the series of attempts made by Albert Abraham Michelson (1852–1931) and Edward Williams Morley (1838–1923) to measure the motion of the earth relative to the ether. Their paper of 1887 posed the problem of explaining astronomical aberration of light in terms of Fresnel's undulatory theory, which required the ether to be at rest except in the interior of transparent media. Aberration could indeed be explained by the theory; Michelson and Morley proposed to test the theory itself. Their results, given in terms of the displacement of interference fringes, indicated displacements much less than $1/8$ of those predicted by theory. The experiments showed a failure of Fresnel's theory to explain aberration and similar failure on the part of alternatives suggested by Stokes and by Lorentz. It should be noted that the Michelson-Morley experiment was not a basis for Einstein's special relativity theory; Einstein became aware of the experiment after formulating his theory.

ELECTRICITY AND MAGNETISM

GRAY. The study of electricity and magnetism became a science only in the 18th cent., and in electrostatics the century saw the establishment of a complete mathematical and physical theory. Stephen Gray (d. 1736) initiated the steps leading to a scientific theory by discovering, 1729, that "electrick vertue" can be transmitted from a charged body to other bodies. The ability of certain substances, especially metals, to conduct electricity was recognized, and Gray showed that "electric fluid" acted only at or near the surface of a conductor.

DU FAY. At midcentury the electric fluid was generally thought to comprise an area, filled with electric effluvium, around the electrified body. Charles François Du Fay (1698–1739) explained the

attraction and, subsequent to contact, repulsion of gold leaf for an electrified glass tube by a 2-fluid theory, 1733–34. He reasoned that the leaf acquired electric force by contact with the glass; the gold leaf then became surrounded by its own effluvium and repelled the effluvium, or vortex, around the glass. Noting, further, that a glass rod and a resinous rod attract each other when electrified and repel their own kinds, Du Fay suggested separate electrics, named vitreous and resinous. The actual flow of electric fluid was suggested by Musschenbroek's discovery, 1745, of the Leyden jar. William Watson (1715–87), a London apothecary, interpreted the shock received in making physical contact between the charged gun barrel and the outside of the jar as a simple transferrence of "electrical aether," 1746. No creation or destruction of electric was suggested, only the accumulation, depletion, and flow of a substance possessed by all bodies.

FRANKLIN. Benjamin Franklin (1706–90) theorized, 1747, that electric charge is conserved when flow of electric takes place. He interpreted his experiments to show that a differential in a single electric accounted for electrical force. Two repelling glass rods were similarly charged, while 2 attracting rods had one with a surplus of electric and the other suffering an actual deficiency. When Franklin recognized that 2 resinous, charged rods also repelled each other, he was disconcerted, for he saw vitreous electricity as a surfeit of electric, while resinous was only an absence. How could 2 bodies repel by virtue of a lack of electric? Franklin also found himself in an ambiguous position over the existence of an electric effluvium, as a means of conveying charge between bodies. His interpretation of the Leyden jar experiment disposed him to an action-at-a-distance theory. On the other hand, the attraction of a charged body for smoke from heated resin suggested that electric did flow into and suffuse the atmosphere around the charged body.

AEPINUS. Problems in Franklin's model of electric action were worked out by Franz Ulrich Theodor Aepinus (1724–1802). Following the 1-fluid theory, he explained repulsion of resinously charged bodies as mutual repulsion by matter itself, since neutral bodies were matter plus electric, and positive charge required a surplus of electric. Aepinus' generalization, 1759, of the observation that glass is impermeable to electric led to dismissal of the effluvial view of propagation of electric force. Noting that air and other bodies were nonconductors, he reasoned that electric, shown by Gray to reside only on the surface of conductors, acts at a distance across intervening air. Action at a distance also was shown to explain electric (electrostatic) induction of charge. Joseph Priestley (1733–1804), reinforced by John Robison in 1769, 1st hypothesized, 1767, electric force to be like gravitation, i.e., inversely proportional to the square of the distance and without effect on a body within the shell of electric charge.

COULOMB. The inverse-square law for the force between magnetic poles was 1st discovered by John Michell (1724–93) in 1750. To an understanding of both electricity and magnetism Charles Augustin Coulomb (1736–1806) made contributions. Using a torsion balance of his own invention, he verified Priestley's inverse-square law. Coulomb, reasoning from the model of physical and chemical processes, revived the 2-fluid theory of electricity in the new terms of Aepinus—action at a distance. In the study of magnetism Coulomb overthrew the vortex theory and verified Michell's law of inverse squares.

POISSON. Mathematical maturity came to electrostatics rapidly through the efforts of Simeon Denis Poisson (1781–1840). Accepting the 2-fluid theory, he applied Lagrange's function for the attraction of spheroids to electrical considerations, 1813. Poisson gave a solution to the electrostatical problem of determining surface density on 2 charged conducting spheres at any distance apart. In the study of magnetism he defined mathematically the magnetic potential and gave a law for induced magnetism in a sphere placed in a magnetic field, 1824. Four years later, George Green (1793–1841) generalized and extended the electrical and magnetical investigations of Poisson.

GALVANI. The distinction of electrostatics from electrodynamics did not take place until the end of the 18th cent., since electrodynamics had not aroused serious interest previously. Luigi Galvani (1737–98), at 1st by accident, 1780, observed the sensitivity of a frog's crural nerve to metallic contact. Thinking at first that electricity caused the muscular contraction, he made repeated experiments to learn, 1786, that a metallic contact between nerve and muscle produced the contraction. While some supposed the effect to be caused by a new, animal electricity, Galvani felt the electric fluid in the nerves was the same as that of the Leyden jar.

VOLTA. Alessandro Volta (1745–1827) refused to countenance the hypothesis of an electrical fluid in the nerves. In 1800 Volta suddenly made galvanic action of more interest by intensifying the electric force. This was accomplished by a connected series of units, each unit comprised of discs of copper, zinc, and wet pasteboard in that order. The resulting "pile," it was observed, gave an indefinite number of shocks in succession, apparently inexhaustible in its electric charge. Volta conceived the charge to be a result of electric tension between the 2 kinds of metal; this "tension" included confusedly the modern notions of charge and potential. The necessity for moist connecting discs he also saw, though not understanding the mechanism of the pile.

As early as 1796 Giovanni Fabroni (1752–1822) noted the partial oxidation of 1 of a pair of metals in a vessel of water with a circuit completed between them; he concluded that galvanic action was connected with chemical action. Learning of Volta's pile, William Nicholson (1753–1815) and Anthony Carlisle (1768–1840) repeated the Voltaic experiments and noticed, 1800, the production of gas where a drop of water was added on the upper plate to secure good contact. Succeeding experiments with the wires from both ends of the pile in a tube of water showed them that hydrogen appeared at 1 wire and oxygen at the other. Late in the same year Humphry Davy (1778–1829) found that pure water permits no current between the plates, thus supporting Fabroni's theory of a necessary connection between chemical and electrical activity. Davy proved that oxidation is necessary for establishment of Voltaic electricity. His explanation, however, was the reverse of actuality, for he believed the chemical changes responsible for restoring an equilibrium of electrical charge, while the contact of metals produced electromotion by disturbing the equilibrium.

OERSTED. From early in the 18th cent. a connection between electricity and magnetism was suspected. In the early 19th cent. Hans Christian Oersted (1777–1862) set out to discover precisely what relationship might exist. By 1820 he was able to announce the qualitative effect of a closed electric circuit on a magnetic needle—the tendency of the current to orient the needle perpendicular to the direction of flow, oppositely as the wire was placed above or below the needle. Oersted explained the effect as the force of electric conflict in space on material magnetic particles, which alone are impenetrable and resistant to that conflict. Later in the same year, Jean Baptiste Biot (1774–1862) and Felix Savart (1791–1841) announced precise results of repetitions of Oersted's experiments. The force on the magnetic pole was found to be exactly at right angles both to a perpendicular from the wire and to the wire itself; the intensity of the force was found to be inversely proportional to the distance. Contrary to Oersted, Dominique François Jean Arago (1786–1853) spoke of action at a distance in reporting, 1820, that iron filings are attracted; that steel can be completely magnetized by a current was also reported. In 1825 Arago described a phenomenon which presented for some time afterward a problem of interpretation. This was the deflection of a magnetic needle by a parallel rotating plate of some conductor; the deflection increased with the velocity of the plate.

AMPÈRE. André Marie Ampère (1775–1836) immediately turned to extending Oersted's discovery when it was announced in Paris. He quickly discovered,

1820, that between parallel currents there is attraction when the currents flow in the same direction, while repulsion occurs if the currents flow oppositely. In 1823 Ampère published a brilliant paper in which he derived a mathematical expression for the force between two elements of circuits, assuming the force to act along the line joining those elements. Regarding his formula as the foundation of quantitative electrodynamics, he saw it as the analogue of the law of gravitation in mechanics. Ampère's assumption of force acting along the line joining 2 elements, embedded in an action-at-a-distance matrix, was exactly what could be shown to be false by 1900. Furthermore, the tendency to discuss discrete electric charges in Ampère's theory was an embarrassment to Maxwell's field theory, despite the success of the latter in predicting a finite velocity of propagation for electromagnetic waves. Finally, Heaviside insisted, 1888, that Ampère's foundation for electrodynamics is not to be found in his law of force between current elements, but in his formula for the magnetic force of an element of a conductor supporting current in a magnetic field. Yet the work of Ampère remained basic; witness its extension in the force laws of Clausius and Lorentz.

SEEBECK. Quite different from Volta's order of electromotive power of metals was the thermoelectric order discovered in 1822 by Thomas Johann Seebeck (1770–1831). He noted that only heat, no intervening liquid, is required to establish a circuit in a ring composed of copper and bismuth, or other pairs.

OHM. Whether thermoelectric or electrochemical, currents were studied more and more for their relative efficacies. Davy's paper of 1821 explored fully the significance of length and cross-sectional area of conductors. It was left to Georg Simon Ohm (1787–1854) to complete a theory of Voltaic circuits by considering the battery's power. On an analogy with heat flow in a wire, Ohm discussed electric flow, leading up to a determination of "driving power" of the battery in terms of a differential between 2 points in a circuit; the analogue was temperature.

Via a confusion of electrostatic potential with electroscopic force of an open pile, Ohm was led to his correct equation of current in a wire with the product of conductivity of the wire and electroscopic differential between the terminals. The analogy between electroscopic difference and temperature was illuminating, and was realized to link electrostatic with electrodynamic theory.

FARADAY. Michael Faraday (1791–1867) is commonly accounted the greatest experimentalist of the 19th cent. in electrical and magnetical research. His *idée fixe* was the lines of force suggested by the curves followed by iron filings on paper over a bar magnet. In 1832 he showed that induction of current is the production of a definite electromotive force, depending only on the intersections of the wire and the magnetic curves: currents induced under the same circumstances in different wires were proportional to the conducting powers of the wires. His explanation of current induction was: "Whether the wire moves directly or obliquely across the lines of force, in one direction or another, it sums up the amount of forces represented by the lines it has crossed . . . the quantity of electricity thrown into a current is directly as the number of curves intersected." In 1833 Faraday showed that all known effects of electricity, whether physiological, luminous, mechanical, or other, could be obtained equally well from static and current electricity. This indicated the similarity of process in the wire of a completed Voltaic circuit and the wire discharging a condenser. Later in the same year he reformed a branch of electrochemistry by proving that the action of the metals in electrodes is not integral to the decomposition of solutions by currents; his theoretical account indicated why the evolved substances appear only at the terminals, why the substances are often not retained at the terminals, and why compounds, not mixtures, are separated by currents. He even speculated that the electricity which flows during decomposition in a Voltaic cell is the exact equivalent of the electric power possessed by the atoms separated at the electrodes. In 1838 Faraday developed a full theory of electrostatic induction on the model of magnetic induction. His explanation involved propagation of electrostatic action via a medium in a way similar to the propagation of currents. After a 4-year interval of rest, he resumed research and entered the field of light polarization. His *Thoughts on Ray Vibrations*, 1846, show a clear tendency toward an electromagnetic theory of light. Faraday's major contributions in the following years were in the area of diamagnetic and paramagnetic action, especially in relation to axial orientations of crystals. The essential thrust of Faraday's work appears in his formation of a clear, physical version of field theory. He came to conceive of all matter as composed of space-filling forces, a so-called atom being no more than a point center for a field of force. Crediting Boscovich with this basic idea, Faraday conceived of no true vacuum and no ultimate particles; action at a distance was discarded.

KELVIN. Although Faraday constantly fell back on his physical model of electric action propagated in a continuum, it was William Thomson (Lord Kelvin) who first introduced this same model, 1842, to mathematical physics. Thomson's argument was by way of analogy between distribution of electrostatic force, traditionally seen as action at a distance, and distribution of heat flow, a phenomenon of continua. His memoir of 1846 suggested a parallel between the propagation of electromagnetic phenomena and the transmission through an elastic solid of changes in elastic displacement.

MAXWELL. From Faraday's models and Thomson's mathematical analogies came the 1st memoir, 1855, of James Clerk Maxwell (1831–79). In this paper Maxwell 1st showed the physical significance of the operators *curl* and *div*, already introduced by Stokes. Maxwell's papers of 1861–62 gave a mechanical picture of the electromagnetic field. Thomson's view of magnetism as rotation was combined with Faraday's tubes of force; each unit tube of force was to be regarded as a single vortex, with the contained medium rotating about the axis of the tube. His mechanism for current, electromotive force, and tension was extended to electrostatic phenomena. The electrostatic state was described as a displacement of particles from equilibrium, constant at a certain value. Maxwell generalized Faraday's displacement concept, which likened electrostatic and electrodynamic phenomena, but only in material dielectrics. For Maxwell displacement exists with electric force not only in material bodies but also in free ether. His full exposition of electromagnetic field theory came in 1864 (modified in 1868). A striking part of his theory was the inclusion of light with electromagnetic phenomena. He applied it accurately to the propagation of light in crystals, metals, and isotropic media. Maxwell's theory was strange and unacceptable to some like Kelvin, who saw electric current as transmission by a wire, rather than by the surrounding dielectric with the wire as no more than a guide for the current. More difficult for many to accept was the notion that all currents are closed, since a displacement current in the dielectric of a condenser would complete an apparently discontinuous current. Only the later success of Maxwell's equations within special relativity theory brought general acceptance of the displacement idea.

Experimental support for Maxwell began to appear in the 1870's. Kerr showed, 1875, that dielectrics under strong electrostatic stress become doubly refractive. In 1875–76 Helmholtz and Schiller showed that the pre-Maxwellian potential theory gave incorrect predictions for the action of a ring magnet on an unclosed current. H. A. Rowland (1848–1901) supported the Faraday-Maxwell equivalence of a moving electrified body and an electric current by his production, 1876, of a magnetic field when a charged plate was rotated (electric convection) parallel to fixed condenser plates above and below. In 1879 Edwin H. Hall demonstrated an additional electromotive force from the action of an electromagnet on a current passing across the lines of force. The details of the Hall effect gave further support to the increasingly accepted hypothesis that magnetism is a rotatory, not a linear, phenomenon.

HERTZ. With Heinrich Hertz (1857–94), Maxwell's theory found its experimental justification. In a series of researches, 1887–90, Hertz studied the propagation of electric waves in air. On the basis of observed interference of electric waves in air and in a wire, he calculated the velocities in each. Electric waves in air were shown to be of finite velocity and of the same order of magnitude as the velocity of light. He also found electric waves to be reflected, refracted, diffracted, and polarized similar to light waves. In 1892 Hertz presented the various possible interpretations of action across free space. He favored the view that only polarizations exist, and such a fundamental state is the cause rather than the effect of electricity. Hertz concluded that Maxwell's position was a combination of this and the view that energy is present only in the medium, not in charges acting at a distance. Since both views are expressed by Maxwell's equations, both views were seen by Hertz as the same theory. Here he engaged in a positivist error, forgetting that there might be testable consequences of one theory differing from the other. In fact, relativity theory gave yet another interpretation of the equations, leading to different consequences from the interpretations of Maxwell and Hertz.

CATHODE RAYS. Under the heading of electrical studies, the investigation of the cathode-ray tube led to a totally different aspect of electrical action, the activity of discrete particles. Johann Wilhelm Hittorf (1824–1914) found, 1869, the cathode ray to be obstructed by metals, deflected by a magnet, and to travel in a straight line. Eugen Goldstein (1850–1930) noted that an extended cathode surface emits rays only as perpendiculars to the surface of the terminal; thus they could be focused. To William Crookes (1832–1919) was due the construction of the tube, thereafter named for him, in its modern shape. His experiments, 1879, showed the cathode ray to carry energy and also, he thought, to have momentum. Crookes's hypothesis, commonly accepted in England, interpreted the cathode ray as a stream of electrically charged gas molecules. The German school of thought adhered to an electromagnetic-wave interpretation. Each school had experimental evidence for support. Against the ethereal-vibration theory were experiments by Jean Perrin (1870–1914) and J. J. Thomson (1856–1940). In 1895 Perrin found that a metallic cylinder which received the rays became charged with resinous electricity. Thomson pointed out that such electrification no longer occurred when a magnet turned the rays so that they no longer entered the cylinder. Yet it remained difficult to explain how charge-carrying particles of the type known could penetrate an aluminum film, as Philipp Lenard had shown cathode rays to do, 1894.

The application of magnetic fields to cathode rays suggested the solution to the dilemma in 1897. J. J. Thomson was impressed by the size of the deflection of the rays by a magnetic field; such particles should be much more massive than atoms. The year before, Lorentz had suggested for the Zeeman effect an electric atom of $\frac{1}{1,000}$ the mass of a hydrogen atom; calculating the theoretical charge-to-mass ratio necessary to produce the effect, Larmor found it 2,000 times too small, since the hydrogen atom was the smallest conceivable particle with mass.

THE ELECTRON. Thomson's experiments, resulting in the epoch-making papers of 1897–99, showed deflection of the rays in an electrostatic as well as a magnetic field and computed the charge and mass of the particle as well as the charge-to-mass ratio. Though accepted with reticence, Thomson's hypothesis of the electron, about 1.4×10^{-3} the mass of a hydrogen ion, was well supported by ingenious experimentation. His model of the atom, 1904, was of a region of uniformly distributed positive charge, regularly interspersed (in terms of mutual repulsion) with the negative electrons. While the model was purely hypothetical, the discovery of subatomic particles was not.

Modern Physics

HEAT AND LIGHT

In 20th-cent. physics, the study of thermal radiation was responsible for initiating the most profound revolution in physical theory since the 17th cent. The relevant problem was a satisfactory theory to explain **black-body radiation.** In 1859 and 1860 Gustav Kirchhoff published papers showing the independence from the nature of bodies of the emission-absorption ratio of radiation. It was this universal aspect which much later attracted Planck. Kirchhoff's 2nd paper introduced the notion of a perfectly absorbent and emissive "black body." Yet not until 1895 were Otto Lummer and others able to construct black-body radiators. In the next few years Lummer and others determined accurately the spectra of black bodies. In 1894 Wien had already developed a theoretical **displacement law,** indicating a general relationship for spectral distribution of black-body radiation with respect to temperature. Wien's radiation law of 1896 applied satisfactorily for high-frequency vibrations, but experiments reported in 1900 proved its incorrectness for low frequencies. Meanwhile, John William Strutt, Lord Rayleigh (1842–1919), made use of the equipartition theorem of statistical mechanics to derive an alternate law for low-frequency vibrations. The resultant **Rayleigh radiation law,** 1900, agreed with Wien's displacement and admirably accounted for the low frequencies where Wien's radiation law failed. But at high frequencies it would lead to the so-called ultraviolet catastrophe (after Ehrenfest, 1911); that is, at higher frequencies the energy density would tend to an infinite maximum. This contradicted experience.

Max Planck (1858–1947) **recognized**

the mutual limitations of Rayleigh's and Wien's radiation laws. His reaction was to interpolate between the 2 and so obtain a law applicable to both high and low frequencies. In its final state, presented to the German Physical Society on 14 December, 1900, Planck's radiation law introduced the universal **quantum** constant h and combined views of continuously and discontinuously varying energy (an inconsistency 1st noted by Einstein in 1906). Most interesting about this revolution in physics—that energy exists in discrete "packets" represented by the constant h—was the tardy recognition of its significance. Planck repeatedly tried to fit the new formula into classical theory; he later referred to the initial postulation of h as "an act of desperation."

In 1907 Einstein applied quantum theory to specific heat and showed its greater usefulness than the previously applied equipartition theorem. While classical theory predicted specific heat of solids to be independent of temperature, Einstein showed clearly that specific heat decreases with temperature and only appears to be independent at higher temperatures. This broadened applicability of quantum theory to molecular kinetic theory was largely responsible for Walter Nernst's support, 1911, of Planck's hypothesis and thereby for the holding of the 1st Solvay Conference, 1911, in Brussels. This conference marked the end of quantum theory as radiation theory. From Nernst's interest in molecular kinetic theory, from Bohr's enthusiasm over the conference proceedings (as reported to him by Rutherford), and from the growing recognition of the significance of Einstein's quantization of light, quantum theory soon became the new basis for the theory of matter.

In 1905 Einstein published a paper "On a Heuristic Viewpoint Concerning the Production and Transformation of Light" in which it was shown that a quantum view of light is the best (not necessarily the only) explanation for the behavior of high-frequency, low-density monochromatic radiation. Thus in the so-called photoelectric effect—the term **photon** was introduced in 1926 by G. N. Lewis—an increase in the frequency of incident light brought an increase in the velocity of ejected photoelectrons; to increase the intensity of incident light gave corresponding increase only in the number of photoelectrons ejected. This theoretical result, suggested by Lenard's experiments of 1902 and verified by A. L. Hughes in 1921, was contrary to all expectations in classical electromagnetic theory. Expansion of this hypothesis of light quanta to a view allowing both particulate and undulatory characteristics for light was tentatively realized by Einstein as early as 1909. His "heuristic viewpoint" was accepted only with great reluctance by physicists like Lorentz and Planck in the years immediately after 1905; as late as 1913, Planck, Nernst, and others recommended Einstein's work very highly in general, but referred to the hypothesis of light quanta as having "missed the target in . . . [its] speculations."

In addition to the photoelectric effect, other experiments contributed to the **wave-particle** dualistic view of light. In 1912 Max von Laue (1879–1950), using the atomic structure of a crystal as a diffraction grating, obtained the 1st observed interference phenomena for X rays. While this also opened up a new field, solid-state physics, its immediate effect was to suggest a wave aspect for X rays, previously considered as particle streams by many. In 1922 Arthur H. Compton (b. 1892) discovered the effect named for him. Inexplicable on the wave theory of light, the scattering of photons by electrons in a way requiring the assignment of mass to light gave additional support to the particle aspect of light. In no other way could physicists explain the difference in frequency between incident and scattered X rays on the 2 sides of a thin material layer. Combination of Laue's and Compton's experiments with X rays produced the same poignant paradox as combination of Fresnel's and Einstein's theories of light, viz., a wave-particle duality.

MECHANICS

The universality of Einstein's thought is suggested by his development of relativity theory in addition to his invaluable contributions to quantum theory. The special theory of relativity, published in 1905, was conceived as a basic theoretical structure for a study "On the Electrodynamics of Moving Bodies." This article postulated (1) that physical laws are the same in all inertial systems and (2) that the velocity of light in an inertial system is independent of the motion of its source. The applicability of these assumptions to the predicament posed by the Michelson-Morley experiments (*pace* D. C. Miller's proposals) was obvious (p. 918 above).

The **Fitzgerald hypothesis**, suggested in 1892, assumed the velocity of the earth relative to the ether to be unmeasurable in principle, for it postulated a contraction of all bodies in the direction of their motions in the ether. The contraction occurred in the ratio of $\sqrt{(1-v^2/c^2)}$:1. In 1895 Lorentz added transformation equations to the Fitzgerald contraction. The transformation regarded time as measurable differently in systems moving with respect to each other; the equations gave length and time measures from 1 system to another. While equivalent to special relativity theory as a method, the Fitzgerald-Lorentz interpretation tended to leave the ether theory in disrepute. If the ether were inconceivable in physical terms and unobservable in principle, it seemed to be a superfluous hypothesis.

Einstein's **special relativity theory** was conceived as a physical application of part of Ernst Mach's philosophy of science. For Mach scientific theory required both economy and generality of explanation. With this in mind, rather than the Michelson-Morley experiments, Einstein conceived space without ether and in which the speed of light was a constant. The result was to eliminate the ether on grounds of methodological economy.

While special relativity related only to uniform, or inertial, motion, Einstein's **general theory of relativity**, 1915, dealt with accelerated motion as well. In the spirit of Mach's philosophy, general relativity made space-time and matter interrelated phenomena, rather than allowing space-time to retain a quasi-absolute status, whereby it would remain independent of contained matter. With non-inertial frames of reference, Einstein was able to show the gravitation of inertial frames (the Newtonian world) to be characteristics of the reference frame alone. Since gravitational acceleration is the same for all masses, a reference frame with such acceleration will show no gravitational effects from an internal viewpoint. Experimentally, gravitational mass and inertial mass can be shown to be equivalent. Einstein considered this to indicate a theoretical equivalence of gravity and inertia. The purpose of general relativity is to provide a field theory of gravitation which will satisfy the idea of equivalence of all reference frames. With space-time itself as the field, the theory defines such characteristics as mass in terms of the geometrical character of space-time. Likewise, the equivalence of energy and mass became apparent through general relativity theory, which was responsible for the famous equation $E = m c^2$. This gives an increasing mass as acceleration occurs and does not admit the oft-heard characterization of Newtonian gravitation as a limited case of general relativity. Also, the Euclidean geometry of space in the Newtonian world disappears in order to retain the general principle of relativity with regard to the velocity of light. Non-uniform gravitational fields, like the sun's, are described by curved, non-Euclidean space. Here the properties of space are determined by the presence and characteristics of matter.

CONSTRUCTION OF MATTER

The construction of matter as viewed theoretically derives essentially from 20th-cent. thinking, developing out of experimental work with subatomic particles and out of the rapidly expanding theory of quanta. J. J. Thomson's discovery of the electron (p. 923, above) was soon followed by W. Kaufmann's experimental discovery, 1910, of variability in the electron's mass, the mass increasing rapidly as its speed approached that of light. Only after the appearance of the relativity theory was this observation correctly explained. Various models of the atom preceded the important Bohr model of 1913. Thomson's model, 1904, spoke of a sphere of positive electrification containing discrete corpuscles of negative electricity, adding that atomic properties depended on the number and distribution of electrons. The 1st really useful **atomic model**, viz., one which accounted for a sufficiently large number of data, was that of Ernest Rutherford (1871–1937), who based his model, 1911, upon extensive work with radioactive particles. The scattering of alpha particles by thin metal foils indicated a concentrated nucleus but a vastly less dense region for the electron population. Rutherford's planetary electrons— the electrons around the nucleus were conceived like planets around the sun— directly contradicted Thomson's model. While Thomson had made a useful determination of charge (c) and mass (m) for the electron, it was the method, 1913, developed by R. A. Millikan which gave the most accuracy. The method hinged on a change in velocity of an oil droplet as it captured ions during its rise and fall between 2 horizontal plates. He showed that units of ionic charge are fixed and always equal, not just statistical means. The completion of pre-quantum atomic theory came with the determination of atomic numbers, indicating the number of positive electric units in the nuclei of atoms. Working in his newly developed science of X-ray spectroscopy, H. G. J. Moseley (1884–1915) found, 1913, that the frequency of a given line in the spectra of atoms successive by weight varied as $(N-b)^2$; b is a constant and N is an integer changing by unity in the succession of elements. N was the **atomic number** and allowed determination of the number of elements possible between any 2 of known atomic number. Elemental properties thus became fixed by atomic number.

The introduction of quantum notions into the theoretical picture of atomic structure occurred with **Niels Bohr's** (1885–1962) reconsideration of the Rutherford model. Rutherford had been able to produce no constant value for the length of an electron from the nucleus. Bohr's addition of Planck's constant h gave the required constant. The most con-

vincing evidence for a quantized atomic model came when Bohr turned his attention to the classification of spectral lines in 1913. Immediately Bolmer's formula struck a harmonic note in his thoughts. Subsequent computation produced Rydberg's formula and the Rydberg spectroscopic constant through use of the quantum constant h. Assuming a nucleus surrounded by normally stable electron orbits, Bohr "explained" the failure of the atom to collapse from constant dissipation of energy by the orbiting electrons; energy could be emitted only in passage of an electron from 1 privileged orbit (in terms of h) to another. This anticlassical conception of the atom, 1913, was rapidly accepted as a result of support from Einstein, Jeans, and Campbell, and because of directly confirming experiments by J. Franck and G. Hertz, 1914, on radiation in the transition of electrons from excited to stable energy levels. The extremely fertile views of Bohr provided adequate ground for both speculative and experimental development over the next decade.

Bohr's model was easily conceivable by the mind, which gave it both appeal and severe limitations. An initial modification was the transition from circular orbits to elliptical electron orbits, suggested by Arnold Sommerfeld (1868–1951). In addition, Bohr calculated the effect of the "perihelial" motion of the electron (analogous to the advance of Mercury's perihelion), according to general relativity theory, and was thus able on purely theoretical bases to explain adequately the fine structure of spectral lines, 1915. Bohr's consciousness of an apparently ineluctable contradiction between classical and quantum notions brought him to the statement, 1918, of the **principle of correspondence**. Considering the case where the frequency v approaches zero, that is, where the energies approach a virtual continuum, Bohr noted that methodologically the classical frequency and the quantum frequency approach identity. This result occurs with very high quantum numbers. Theoretically, however, Bohr appeared to find both quantum and classical theories to be "caricatures," each representing only an extreme region of phenomena. The correspondence principle formed a link between these extremes.

The isolation of Bohr's model from the issue raised by Einstein of wave vs. particle assured, hindsight shows, the downfall of that model. In 1924 Louis Victor de Broglie (b. 1892) set forth in his doctoral dissertation an elaboration of several preceding papers in which he expanded the wave-particle duality proposed by Einstein for light into a wave-particle duality for all matter. Introducing relativistic conceptions as well, Broglie suggested the existence of phase waves (faster than light), many of which composed a wave moving with exactly the speed of the particle concerned, e.g., an electron. He observed the mathematical equivalence of the undulatory principle of least time and the particulate principle of least action. His theory gave a simple, striking vision of the basis for Bohr's permissible orbits. But only with the experimental proof provided inadvertently by Davisson and Germer, 1925, in the Bell Telephone Laboratories was Broglie's new **wave mechanics** given belief. It was shown, to the initial surprise of the experimenters, that electrons (presumably particles par excellence) exhibited diffraction patterns (presumably evidence par excellence for waves). Almost simultaneously, other research led to an explosion of theory development in the mid-20's of this century. In 1925 Wolfgang Pauli (b. 1900) enunciated his **exclusion principle**. Quite simply, it said that no 2 electrons can have the same set of 4 quantum numbers. In the model of the atom the exclusion principle assigned the planetary electrons to their proper positions on a more rational basis than Bohr's previous *ad hoc* arrangement. At the same time, 1925, G. E. Uhlenbeck and S. Goudsmit provided Pauli with a new quantity needed to complete the basis of his exclusion principle. They proposed for the electron a 4th quantum number, realized on the basis of electron spin, introducing an angular momentum and magnetic moment. Spin of the electron accounted for anomalies of the Zeeman effect as well as the fine structure of optical and Röntgen spectra.

Still struggling with the inadequacies of the continually revised Bohr atom, Werner Heisenberg (b. 1901) sought for the 1st time to obviate the use of classical mechanics as a preliminary to the use of quantum theory. Starting with nothing more than direct observation, and ignoring classically based formulas for co-ordinates and velocities of electrons as functions of time, Heisenberg recreated the calculus of matrices as a foundation for an independent **quantum mechanics**, 1925. In this system, multiplication of the quantum values p and q is noncommutative, to wit, $p \times q \neq q \times p$. The matrix mechanics of Heisenberg, in collaboration with Born and Jordan, was within a year converted from its initial unwieldy form to a quantum algebra based on the mathematical formalism of classical Hamiltonian mechanics. This was done by P. A. M. Dirac (b. 1902), who made use of the classical Poisson bracket expression to obtain $pq - qp = \dfrac{ih}{2\pi}[p, q]$. On the basis of this mathematical reasoning, Dirac brought into quantum mechanics all of classical mechanics amenable to Poisson brackets rather than derivatives. By making the basic equation a postulate of the theory, he integrated Bohr's correspondence principle into the heart of the new mechanics, for the new postulate correlated quantum mechanical variables with their classical prototypes.

Before 1926 Broglie and others had not extended the theory of waves in quantum mechanics to the point of introducing a medium. In this year Erwin Schrödinger (1887–1961) gave the initial impetus to what became wave mechanics. His **psi function** related to the motion of a point in many-dimensional space (equivalent to highly complex motions in space of 3 dimensions). It gave a picture of the atom as a system of vibrations. As in acoustics, Schrödinger reasoned, so in a quantum energy transition, the change in frequency can be considered as a "beat" phenomenon. Rather than a jumping of electrons in the atom, he posited a change in vibrational mode, a process continuous in space and time and characteristic of waves. Thinking in terms of Hamilton's optical-mechanical analogy, Schrödinger made use of the already developed notion of wave packets to link particle and wave mechanics. Yet there still remained a basic philosophical problem in 1926. If the methodology seemed acceptable, the epistemology was a paradox. What did the equations signify experientially? Schrödinger attacked Bohr's view of discontinuity and quantum jumps. It was Heisenberg who saw the analogue in the progress of relativity theory. Just as Einstein's new views of space and time formed a conceptual matrix for the Lorentz transformations, Heisenberg looked for a way to fit nature to the situations described by quantum mechanics. His result was the uncertainty relation $\Delta p \Delta q \geq h/2\pi$. That is, as p becomes more definite, q becomes less precise. Thus, in measurements on the order of magnitude of the quantum constant, when position is well determined, momentum is indeterminate, and vice versa. More than any other aspect of quantum mechanics the **uncertainty principle** has excited scientists, philosophers, and laymen in discussions of acausality, free will, determinism, and other similar topics. Finally, in a magnificent attempt at unification, Dirac, followed by Jordan, brought relativity theory into the new quantum mechanics, 1929. For the 1st time, electron spin became intrinsically involved in the equations. The symmetry introduced by relativistic mechanics led to other problems, however. It predicted the existence of particles similar to electrons but with negative mass. This strange result appeared to be a hole in the theory until 1931, when Carl Anderson actually observed these so-called "holes in matter," now referred to as **positrons.** Yet the synthesis of relativity and the quantum, as Broglie observed, 1937, still needed refinement, for the new theoretical predictions for the behavior of the photon did not accord with experiment.

MAGNETISM

The further advance of the physicist's view of the structure of matter is best pursued by review of a separate, though closely related, tradition: the experimental discovery and observation of radioactivity and elementary particles. But before following the experimental extension of the quantum picture of matter, the remarkable advances permitted in the understanding of magnetism on the basis of quantum theory should be outlined.

In the modern (20th-cent.) study of magnetism the preliminary developments grew out of the late 19th-cent. theory of electrons. In 1901–3 W. Voigt and J. J. Thomson restated earlier conceptions of paramagnetism and diamagnetism in terms of electrons; the attempt was made to explain both forms as induced states following collision by spinning electrons. The explanation failed. Only with Paul Langevin's explanation of 1905 was it generally accepted that the magnetic theory of Ampère and Weber could be reformulated through electron theory. Regarding diamagnetism as the immediate and sole effect when 1st applying an external magnetic field, Langevin found that diamagnetism is a general atomic property based on the absence of magnetic moment. **Paramagnetism,** by contrast, appeared as an induced state masking the natural diamagnetism and caused by molecular collisions. Pierre Weiss extended Langevin's work by explaining **ferromagnetism,** 1907. Weiss considered the internal magnetic field in molecular aggregates, using the mutual effect of molecules on each other to account for ferromagnetism and its disappearance above a critical temperature. The explanations of Langevin and Weiss, Bohr wrote in 1911, were derived from failure to apply classical statistics completely; this meant that assumptions of a quantum nature had been made unwittingly.

The development of the Bohr atom, 1913, led physicists to suggest the existence of a distinctive **magnetic moment,** resulting from the quantization of electron orbits. This elementary magnetic moment came to be known as the **Bohr magneton.** In 1918 Bauer and Picard experimentally verified this elementary moment as equal to $he/4\pi mc$ in paramagnetic gases. Sommerfeld's above-mentioned work of 1915 involved the limiting of orientations of the magnetic moments with respect to the field. Only parallel, antiparallel, or perpendicular orientations are possible. Magnetic moment associated with Uhlenbeck's and Goudsmit's 1925 discovery of electron spin explained fine spectral lines. Weiss's proposed internal magnetic field was explained in 1928 by Heisenberg on the basis of electron exchanges in the atom and between atoms. Ferromagnetism, he said, results from the stable parallelism of a number of electron spins, as the electrons exchange positions between atoms. Further understanding of ferromagnetism came from Felix Bloch's postulating a "Bloch wall," 1932, between neighboring domains magnetized in different directions. This wall constituted a transition layer where the magnetic moments were arranged in spiral fashion. In 1934 Bloch suggested **spin waves.** These arose at a certain point when rising temperature caused the directional change of an atomic magnetic moment in a ferromagnetic substance. The originally (at absolute zero) parallel moments would be disturbed by the heat input, and the reorientation of 1 atomic moment would affect nearby atoms, the continuing effect being known as a spin wave.

The attribution of a magnetic moment to the atomic nucleus as well as to the electron 1st occurred with Pauli, 1923, but it was Enrico Fermi (1901–54) who clearly developed and quantitatively defined **nuclear magnetic moment,** 1930. This moment turned out to be on the order of 1/1,000 the value of the Bohr magneton. The possibility of correctly and accurately measuring nuclear magnetic moment arrived with the work of I. I. Rabi, 1934. His method involved quantitative determination of the basic cause of magnetic moment, **precession,** via the effect had by an electromagnetic wave in resonance.

RADIOACTIVITY AND ELEMENTARY PARTICLES

While the rapid development of magnetic theory was a notable result of an effective, matured quantum mechanics, the applicability of the basic laws of the quantum was constantly questioned and stretched by the experimental discoveries of elementary particles. In fact, the very inception of a quantum theory of atomic structure grew out of such discoveries.

The earliest modern curiosity about components of the atom arose with work on radioactivity. From the Crookes tube, Wilhelm Konrad Röntgen (1845–1923) observed a new emission in 1895. This new ray, which he called **X ray,** caused fluorescence of a paper screen washed with barium-platinum-cyanide, and the radiation could penetrate wood, flesh, aluminum, and other materials. However, refraction and other properties of normal rays did not seem to belong to Röntgen's rays. It was known in the Cavendish laboratory at Cambridge that photographic plates were affected by Crookes tubes. The reaction was simply to keep Crookes tubes away from storage areas for photographic plates! The 1st recognition of the importance of such exposure of sealed photographic plates was that of Henri Becquerel (1852–1909), who observed the effects of uranium salts on these plates, 1896. He initially assumed exposure of the uranium to sunlight to be necessary, but soon found that similar results occurred after months of nonexposure. This radiation, like X rays, had the property of discharging electrified bodies by making conductors of insulators. Excited by Becquerel's work, Marie Curie and her husband Pierre began work on radioactive elements. Thorium was found to behave like uranium. A new element, **polonium,** was discovered, 1898. Since both bismuth and barium obtained from pitchblende ore exhibited radioactivity, it appeared that another component of the ore must explain the radioactive properties. In 1898 the separation of a radium salt, and presumably therefore a new element, was announced. Only 4 more years of work enabled the Curies to isolate **radium** in sufficient amount and pure enough to establish unequivocally, 1902, its independent existence and attributes. These 4 years resulted in the collection of one decigram of pure radium chloride.

The continuing emission of energy in radioactivity, especially by radium, raised the problem of conservation of energy. How could this emission continue, apparently undiminished, with no observable change in the radium? It was suggested by Elster and Geitel, 1898, and developed by Rutherford and Soddy on experimental bases, 1902–3, that a radioactive atom is in the process of changing from an unstable to a stable condition. As early as 1900 the rays emitted by radium had been recognized as 3 in type: alpha, beta, and gamma rays, in order of penetrability. In 1903 the **disintegration hypothesis** of Rutherford and Soddy was given experimental support by Ramsay and Soddy, who identified helium spectroscopically as the gaseous emanation from radium bromide. By 1908 Rutherford could recount the recent discoveries in support of the disintegration theory in terms of an established list of parentage from uranium down to radium and on to a variety of subsequent products including lead. The particle experiments of 1908–9 by Rutherford, Geiger, Marsden, and Royds liberated extensive data. An electric method of counting alpha particles was devised and used. Alpha particles were proven to be positively charged helium atoms. The scattering of alpha particles by atoms of a thin plate was observed and quantitatively determined. The appearance of deflections at angles greater than 90° was the basis of Rutherford's important atomic model of 1911. Within a year C. T. R. Wilson had devised the **cloud chamber,** wherein the deflections of alpha particles by single atoms, described by Rutherford, could be photographed and observed.

With the investigation of radioactive breakdown of elements, there emerged the suggestion of atoms chemically identical but physically (by atomic weight) different. By 1913 much experimental data existed supporting this result for radioactive elements. In that year J. J. Thomson, using his "positive-ray analysis" for finding values of m/e, found that neon in his discharge tube produced results for atomic weight 20 and atomic weight 22 also. Both atoms were neon, differing only

in atomic weight. The displacement laws indicating the position in the periodic table of atoms derived from radioactive decay were drawn up by A. S. Russell, K. Fajans, and F. Soddy in 1913. The name **isotope** was given by Soddy to both radioactive and nonradioactive variants of an atom. F. W. Aston (1877–1945) contributed extensively to isotope research. He confirmed the 1913 work of Thomson, assessed the masses of various isotopes with respect to oxygen (the ratios being in whole numbers), and suggested possible methods for separating isotopes, 1919. In 1913 Rutherford had already laid down the theoretical distinction explaining isotopes when he pointed to the positive charge of the nucleus as the fundamental constant determining chemical properties; change in mass alone would have no chemical effect.

In 1919 Rutherford established the **proton.** Explaining the collision of an alpha particle with hydrogen atoms, he showed by measuring deflections in magnetic and electric fields that a hydrogen nucleus of unit positive charge resulted from the collisions. This charged hydrogen nucleus was soon designated by the term proton. Subsequently he directed alpha particles at nitrogen. In 1920 he proved that an occasional particle will actually collide with a nitrogen nucleus and alter the nucleus from charge 7 to charge 8 and from mass 14 to mass 17, i.e., from nitrogen to an isotope of oxygen. Transmutation of matter was thus realized. In 1921 Rutherford and Chadwick noted similar transformations for 5 other elements, the beginning of a continually extended list.

The climactic era of quantum mechanics (c. 1925–28) issued in the unexpected, initially unwanted prediction of a new particle by Dirac's theory of the electron, 1928, which required the existence of a positive election and an antiproton. The positron was discovered in 1932, but it was not until 1955 that the **antiproton** was observed with certainty. While antiparticles were disconcerting, the discovery of newer types of particles left the neat world of the proton and electron (and perhaps their antiparticles) aghast. As early as 1920 Rutherford had postulated the neutron. Bothe and Becker, 1930, discovered the emission by light nuclei of extremely penetrating rays, when bombarded with alpha particles. Attempts to explain the radiation as electromagnetic failed. Using new detecting techniques, Chadwick, 1932, identified the rays of Bothe and Becker as neutral particles, i.e., **neutrons.** The antineutron was not observed until 1956.

From 1930 on the world of elementary particles rapidly came to resemble a zoo —or even a haunted house—as many particles were postulated as necessary and discovered only years later. In order to save the law of conservation of energy, Wolfgang Pauli, 1930, invented the **neutrino.** Maintaining a constant speed, that of light, this particle was without mass or charge. Posited to account for the apparent imbalance of energy in beta radiation, the neutrino was claimed to possess whatever energy the observed beta particles lacked to add up to the loss of energy by the emitting nucleus. The neutrino remained an article of faith with physicists until its experimental detection in 1956. Pauli's idea of an origin within the nucleus was soon discarded by Fermi, 1934. Since the establishment of neutrons, 1932, it seemed unreasonable to suppose electrons within the nucleus. So also for neutrinos, said Fermi. Instead, the electron (beta particle) and its accompanying neutrino are created at the moment of emission; simultaneously a nuclear neutron becomes a proton. Here was the 1st successful theory of creation and destruction of basic matter.

In 1935 Hideki Yukawa predicted the existence of the pi meson, or **pion.** Just as the recent quantum theory of electric and magnetic force had designated photons as the carriers of force, so Yukawa considered a particle exchange as the cause of nuclear force holding protons and neutrons together. Such a force had to be strong enough to overcome the electrical repulsion of protons in the nucleus, but its strength must act only over very short distances, about 10^{-12} cm., the size of the nucleus. The existence of the pion was justified in terms of the uncertainty principle, which defined both the energy limit and lifetime limit of the pion. The occurrence of the particle was explained by collision of 2 highly energetic protons, one of which converted momentarily into a neutron and a pion. The continuing process in protons accounted for the stability of the atomic nucleus. Over a decade passed before this useful particle was actually observed, 1947. In 1936 a particle thought to be the pion was observed in cosmic radiation. However, this newly observed particle turned out to be the **muon,** which is 200 times as massive as the electron, but otherwise essentially identical to it.

From 1934 on, a number of physicists, pre-eminently Fermi, developed the discovery by I. Curie and F. Joliot, 1934, that highly energetic alpha particles will bring about a continuing emission of positrons when nonradioactive elements are bombarded. Fermi turned to the production of neutrons in place of alpha particles and thereby increased greatly the potential for artificial nuclear transmutations, since the neutron is not repulsed by the positive nucleus. This new tool, the bombarding neutron, became the critical tool in producing continuous nuclear fission. By 1939 it was recognized that suitable materials, such as uranium 235 and plutonium, produced much kinetic energy and beta radiation, with the simultaneous release of neutrons providing a basis for further fission. Technical difficulties were surmounted to allow Fermi and his collaborators to produce a "critical" **atomic pile** in late 1942.

In 1941 the divergence difficulties of quantum field theory prompted Wheeler and Feynman to propose the notion of action-at-a-distance as an alternative to that of the field. In terms of particle physics this meant direct particle interaction with no independent field having its own energy and momentum. The approach of Wheeler and Feynman did aid in eliminating divergences (infinite terms), and it also introduced the peculiar notion of advanced potentials (1st suggested by Schwarzschild in 1903). In fact, the 2 men argued that field and action-at-a-distance interpretations are ultimately interchangeable. The union, rather than conflict, of Newtonian mechanics and relativistic, four-dimensional space was the basic direction proposed. The means was a complementary view of particle and field.

From 1947 to 1954 the list of known particles expanded from 14 to 30. In the same time period the available energy in a particle accelerator was increased 30 times. The 16 new particles belonged to 4 families, kaons, lambdas, sigmas, and Xis. Though unpredicted and unexpected, they soon came to be considered the last strongly interacting long-lived particles to be available for discovery. In 1953, Gell-Mann and Nishijima (independently) developed a conservation law in terms of values assigned *ad hoc* to the types of particle. The law predicts whether and what sort of particle can be expected in a strong interaction process. The 4 new types have been found always to be produced in numbers of 2 or more.

In 1956 Tsung Dao Lee and Chen Ning Yang suggested that the previously assumed parity principle might profitably be abandoned in order to solve certain problems. That this spatial symmetry (or parity) could be violated in *weak* interactions was verified in the same year, when it was shown experimentally by Chien Shiung Wu that nature shows a definite preference for emission of beta rays from cobalt 60 in a particular direction. This suggested, theoretically, that the equations for interaction of quantized fields need not be symmetrical with respect to parity and to charge separately. A simpler mathematical expression could be introduced, involving only a combined symmetry in charge and parity. In the mid-1960's workers at the Brookhaven National Laboratory apparently established violation of symmetry (charge-conjugation symmetry) in interactions other than weak ones, specifically in the decay of neutral eta mesons, about 7.2% of the time. However, repetition of the Brookhaven experiments by C.E.R.N. (Conseil Européen pour le Recherche Nucléaire) workers with almost 10 times as many examples failed to confirm the proposal of violation in some strong interactions.

Chemistry

17th and 18th Cents.

BOYLE. The 2 kinds of chemical change most interesting to the alchemists of medieval times were combustion and the calcination of metals. Both involved heating, and both were actually the same sort of reaction. The recognition of the identical nature of these 2 processes marked the initial stage of modern chemistry. That fire was an especially potent agent in chemical change was a truism for the alchemist; witness the stereotype of a practitioner huddled over his retort. In the late 17th cent. Robert Boyle (1627–91) experimented ingeniously with heated compositions. In an evacuated jar he heated tin; after cooling it he opened the jar to weigh the tin, finding that its weight had increased. Because he made the measurement after opening the container, Boyle failed to perceive the equal importance of air in calcination and in combustion. He had noted the failure of heated sulphur to burn in an evacuated jar. But the calcination of tin he explained as passage of igneous corpuscles through the container into the metal, thus adding to the weight. Despite such errors Boyle is remembered as a founder of modern chemistry. He emphasized its theoretical study for no ulterior, i.e., alchemical or iatrochemical, reason; he rigorized experimental method; he gave a clear definition of an element.

STAHL. The problem of "fiery corpuscles" as discussed by Boyle was made elementary in the phlogiston theory of George Stahl (1660–1734), who explained changes accompanied by heat in terms of "the matter and principle of fire." The phlogiston theory presumed to account for combustion and calcination. However, when considerations of weight change were added to this essentially qualitative theory, it was found inadequate—unless phlogiston should sometimes possess negative weight! The centrality of the quantitative question in phlogiston theory led chemical theory in a more mechanical and materialistic direction. The phlogiston theory was never conceived to deal primarily with the question addressed by Lavoisier's oxygen theory—the question of weight changes.

LAVOISIER. Antoine Laurent Lavoisier (1743–94) led a life of varied interests, many of which exhibited his economical approach, as if using a balance sheet to organize the answer to any question. This balance-sheet outlook dominated his chemical work. Along the way, his careful method led him safely past the pitfall of Boyle. Lavoisier weighed his heated tin both before and after opening the exhausted container. He soon had the quantitative aspects of combustion and calcination completely in hand. The theoretical explanation occurred to him only after the suggestion from Priestley that the product of heating a calx (oxide) was dephlogisticated air. Ignoring phlogiston, Lavoisier saw that "purified air" (oxygen) was the product. Subsequent quantitative experiment, including a correct interpretation of Cavendish's combustion of "inflammable air" (hydrogen) to get water, led to the formulation of Lavoisier's oxygen theory of chemical combination.

19th Cent.

DALTON. After Lavoisier, oxidation as such ceased to be the most attractive topic of chemical discussion. Lavoisier stopped short at classification and refused to consider an atomic theory in chemistry, for he saw such a theory as metaphysics. The primary issue leading to atomic theory after Lavoisier was the mechanism of reaction. Whether the structure of matter was continuous or not was argued by Berthollet (continuum) and Proust (discontinuity). J. L. Proust (1754–1826) completely discredited his opponent and set forth the law of fixed proportions in

1799. In the same vein, but in a somewhat forbidding and speculatively mathematical way, J. B. Richter (1762–1807), laid down the law of reciprocal proportions in 1794. The 3rd such law, that of multiple proportions, was given by John Dalton (1766–1844), who realized the full theoretical import of these quantitative laws, each of which showed a preservation of integral amounts of the substances involved. Dalton's atomic theory appears in *A New System of Chemical Philosophy*, 1808. Making the philosophical jump needed to pass beyond the macroscopic laws on proportions, he hypothesized a microscopic world of atoms. For Dalton every atom of a single element was alike; the differences between elements were discontinuous. Like the ancient atomists, he retained a simple mechanical view, implicitly involving himself in the reductionist's difficulty of explaining qualities of the compound not possessed by its constituents.

Dalton's emphasis on simplicity, both mechanically and quantitatively, led to a persistent confusion for another half-century. His atomic theory was based directly on relative weights, whence he considered a compound like water, seen simply as HO, to be made of hydrogen having a weight of 1 and oxygen 8. The principle of economy could hardly have been more misleading.

In 1808 J. L. Gay-Lussac suggested on sound experimental bases integral volume relationships in gas reactions. Based on the equal expansion of gases with temperature increase, his hypothesis should have led chemists to the view that equal volumes of gases have equal numbers of reactive particles. Gay-Lussac noted the ease with which Daltonian atomism fitted into his law, yet Dalton never agreed. Dalton chose to assess the validity of the law via his assumption of monatomic particles in common gases like oxygen. Since this obviously made Gay-Lussac's statements on relative densities of gases seem paradoxical, Dalton blithely assumed Gay-Lussac wrong. Berzelius was able to use Gay-Lussac's hypothesis to define water as H_2O and ammonia as NH_3.

AVOGADRO. Amadeo Avogadro (1776–1856) explicitly resolved the problem in Dalton's thinking. Gay-Lussac had pointed out that 2 volumes of hydrogen and 1 of oxygen give 2 of steam. The implications of this fact and others behind the law of combining volumes were made distinct by Avogadro's hypothesis, 1811. Interested in combining volumes from the chemical rather than physical viewpoint, Avogadro conceived an equal number of molecules in equal volumes of 2 gases. Noting that this required the splitting of molecules into "half-molecules" in such combinations as hydrogen plus oxygen, he explained away Dalton's objections to Gay-Lussac. In 1814 Ampère revived Avogadro's hypothesis, but it was generally ignored for half a century until its usefulness was more obvious to chemists.

BERZELIUS. In the early development of electrochemistry, growing out of the experiments by Galvani, Volta, and Nicholson and Carlisle (p. 919, above), the use of atomic theory and Avogadro's hypothesis did not seem necessary. As early as 1803 Jöns Jakob Berzelius (1779–1848) noted that decomposed salts in electrolysis resulted in acids at the positive pole and bases at the negative. Berzelius, who introduced modern chemical symbolism in 1813, followed up extensive experiments by Humphry Davy and himself with a dualistic theory, 1812. As a synthesis this theory assumed an identity of chemical and electrical attraction. Metals were electropositive; oxygen was strongly electronegative. Chemical combination came from neutralization by oppositely charged elements, but this occurred on a nonquantitative level. A compound could retain over-all charge, so that a substance like copper sulphate exhibited characteristics considered to be electropositive. Michael Faraday (p. 921, above) brought electrochemistry to a more quantitative level. Contemporary with his collaboration (with William Whewell) on the development of a nomenclature for electrochemistry, 1833, Faraday experimented with conductivity and electrolysis. Observations such as the unsatisfactory nature of pure water as conductor resulted. More significantly, he recognized a relationship between amount of electrical current and amount of substance decomposed. The ratios of quantities gave rise to electrochemical equivalents. The potential assistance of this work for solving atomic-weight values was postponed by Berzelius' refusal to accept Faraday's electrochemical laws.

DEVELOPMENT OF ORGANIC CHEMISTRY. The dualistic theory of Berzelius eventually foundered on the growing mass of data from organic chemistry. Rather like animal electricity, animal, or organic, chemistry was considered in the late 18th cent. to be radically different from its mineral, or inorganic, relative. The basically German school of *Naturphilosophie* supported this distinction. The vitalists in biology and medicine also maintained the essential differentiation of living from nonliving matter. Not until 1828 was a crucial blow given to the vitalist view of organic compounds. At this time Friedrich Wöhler (1800–1882) synthesized urea, an animal product, from inorganic substances. The synthesis of organic from inorganic compounds henceforth provided the keystone of antivitalist literature.

The wide variety of organic compounds made up of a small number of chemical elements posed special problems for organic chemists. Gay-Lussac established, 1815, the concept of the radical, "a body which, though compound, acts the part of a simple substance in its combinations with hydrogen and metals." At the same time Michel Eugène Chevreul (1786–1889) studied the composition of fats with the help of the radical concept. He concluded, 1823, that fats were compounds formally analogous to inorganic salts; fats were compounded from organic acids and glycerol. Organic and inorganic substances reacted according to the same laws. The discovery by Wöhler and Liebig, 1832, of the benzoyl radical seemed to confirm the hopes of the organic chemist for the radical concept. By 1830 the significance of structure, introduced implicitly by the radical concept, became clear when Berzelius noted the identity upon analysis of tartaric and racemic acids. That different properties could result from structural variations with the same chemical atoms he indicated by the term "isomerism."

In 1837 Justus von Liebig (1803–73) and J. B. A. Dumas (1800–1884) claimed the radical concept as the final key to organic chemistry. But the simple nature hereby assumed for the organic radical, as a direct analogue of the inorganic element, was soon discredited. In 1834 Dumas reported the substitution of hydrogen by chlorine in the process of chlorinating ethyl alcohol. Auguste Laurent (1808–53) carried this line of questioning far enough to say that chlorine "takes the place of" hydrogen in such reactions; for example, chlorination of naphthalene gave compounds remarkably similar to the original naphthalene. Dumas rejected this extension of the empirical evidence. Forced by later evidence to revise, Dumas went even further and suggested chlorine substitution for the carbon atom as well as the hydrogen, thus prodding Liebig into public ridicule, 1840, of Dumas' overextension of the "type" theory of substitution. Laurent's theory, experimentally based, made untenable Berzelius' attempt to apply dualistic theory to organic chemistry. It also aroused Liebig's ire, since the substitution theory made the simple radical concept unacceptable. The theory of original and derived nuclei (the type theory), begun by Laurent, was a focus of chemical controversy for over a decade. A notable aspect of Laurent's version was the use of a geometrical model to explain substitution.

MOLECULAR STRUCTURE. At mid-century a primary interest was locating the position of radicals in molecules. Various type theories were introduced by Charles A. Wurtz (1817–84), Alexander W. Williamson (1824–1904), and Charles F. Gerhardt (1816–56). These new types had predictive value for indicating substitution products; the older type theory had been only a classifying tool. In 1852 Edward Frankland (1825–99) was able to add the concept of valence to clarify the organic combining capacities of various metals and, by extension, of all atoms.

As early as 1848 Louis Pasteur (1822–95) had given classic demonstration of the importance of structure for understanding chemical compounds on the level of microscope observation. The only difference between levorotatory and dextrorotatory optical activity of salts of tartaric acid was in their crystalline structure. One was the mirror image of the other. J. H. van't Hoff (1852–1911) and J. A. Le Bel (1847–1930) independently explained such behavior, 1874, by noting possibilities for isomerism with tetravalent carbon, having 4 equally spaced (3-dimensionally) positions for attachment. If 4 different radicals were shifted among these 4 positions on carbon, e.g., in lactic acid, 2 different, mirror-image arrangements existed. This was the only difference between the 2 optically active forms of $CH_3 CH (OH) CO_2H$. To Friedrich August Kekulé (1829–96) belongs the credit for making known the ability of carbon atoms to form chains. In 1858, after working on the variety of formulae possible by mixing different types, the idea of multiple carbon chains occurred to him. He thought of the concept when he generalized tetravalence of carbon to include combination between 2 carbons, so that each was left with only 3 positions for attachment of other atoms or radicals. The open-chain, or aliphatic, structure as well as the ring, or aromatic, structure, 1865, were conceived by Kekulé in a modified, 2-dimensional way. Kekulé's "flat" projections were 1st given stereometric interpretation by van't Hoff and Le Bel's conception of the carbon atom's distribution of its 4 bonds in the directions of the corners of a regular tetrahedron, 1874.

The organic synthesis represented by Kekulé, van't Hoff, and Le Bel led to a flowering of analytic work in the field. A. Grum Brown (1838–1922) noted the double bond for ethylene, 1864. Emil Erlenmeyer (1825–1909) conceived the triple bond for acetylene, 1862. Tautomerism, observed in acetoacetic ester as early as 1863, was explained, 1876, by Alexander M. Butlerov (1828–86). Only gradually did the equilibrium between *keto* and *enol* forms of such compounds become apparent. Adolf Baeyer (1835–1917) developed the strain theory, 1885, to explain stability in ring compounds by the distortion of their bonds from the normal tetrahedral arrangement. Victor Meyer's (1848–97) theory of steric hindrance, 1894, appealed to structural considerations to explain the obstruction of substitutions on any carbon atom near another holding large groups. Emil Fischer (1852–1919) was able to make elegant use of stereochemical techniques in characterizing isomeric sugars, 1891.

SYSTEMATIZATION OF INORGANIC CHEMISTRY.

Roughly contemporary with the structural organization of organic chemistry occurred the systematization of inorganic chemistry. Basic to this was Stanislao Cannizzaro's (1826–1910) revival and promulgation of Avogadro's hypothesis via the "Sunto di un Corso di Filosofia Chimica," 1858. Referring atomic weights to the weight of a half-molecule of hydrogen as unity, Cannizzaro gave correct molecular weights for many compounds. With correct molecular weights as the index for establishing elemental interrelationships, progress rapidly appeared. Earlier William Prout (1785–1850) suggested, 1815–16, that atomic weights might be systematized as integral multiples of hydrogen as unity. Johann W. Döbereiner (1780–1849) noticed, 1829, a natural grouping of elements in triads, such as chlorine, bromine, and iodine.

Following the reintroduction of Avogadro's hypothesis, A. E. B. du Chancourtois (1819–86) arranged, 1862–63, the elements in a spiral in terms of atomic weight. John A. R. Newlands (1837–98) also developed the notion of periodic repetition in his law of octaves, 1865, placing all elements in a chart with 8 vertical rows. The most important systems were those of Julius Lothar Meyer (1830–95) and Dmitri Ivanovitch Mendeleev (1834–1907). Both used the atomic weights made possible by Avogadro's hypothesis in order to construct a list of elements in order of increasing atomic weight. Meyer, 1870, emphasized periodicity of physical properties while Mendeleev, 1869, was most struck by the periodicity of chemical properties. Mendeleev stressed the predictive value of the periodic table. Noting 3 empty places on the chart, he predicted the characteristics of the elements which would be found to fit in these places. The subsequent discoveries of gallium, 1874, scandium, 1879, and germanium, 1885, confirmed his speculations. Thereafter the periodic table was widely accepted.

PHYSICAL CHEMISTRY. Physical chemistry in the 19th cent. developed significantly in the areas of kinetic theory, thermodynamics, and electrochemistry. C. L. Berthollet (1748–1822) 1st recognized clearly, 1803, the importance of concentration, or mass, in the extent of a reaction. Gay-Lussac reiterated the idea of mass action. In 1850 Ludwig Wilhelmy (1812–64) found a determinate relationship of rate of reaction and amount of reactant present. The notion of 2 simultaneous and opposite reactions, at equal rates, was pointed out by Williamson, 1850, as characteristic of chemical equilibrium. In 1862–63 Marcellin Berthelot (1827–1907) and L. Péan de St.-Gilles (1832–63) measured the affinity relations in the formation of esters, but failed to study the reverse reaction, hydrolysis, in the equilibrium. Only with Cato Maximilian Guldberg (1836–1902) and Peter Waage (1833–1900) was the law of mass action fully stated and demonstrated, 1863. Showing that equilibrium is achieved in incomplete reactions, they gave a quantitative expression of equilibrium conditions at a given temperature in terms of molecular concentration. Other conditions being equal, the "driving force" for substitution was found to be directly proportional to the product of the masses. Van't Hoff classified reactions in terms of the number of molecules participating, 1877. Svante Arrhenius made it clear that not every molecular collision resulted in reaction, 1889. With the solid basis accumulated by the last quarter of the century, kinetics became a recognized field in chemistry.

For roughly 50 years after Lavoisier, no chemical studies of heat were made. In 1840 Germain Henri Hess (1802–50) established the constancy of heat evolved in a reaction sequence, no matter the number of intermediate steps. Following the initial translations of thermodynamics from physics to chemistry, Josiah Willard

Gibbs made important studies in thermochemistry. In addition to the phase rule, already discussed, he introduced useful concepts like chemical potential.

Prior to Arrhenius, the most important study of ions was that of Johann Wilhelm Hittorf (1824–1914), who studied ion transport in solutions and observed that each ion had a characteristic rate of transport. He concluded that ions in an electrolyte do not exist in a stable, molecular form. Svante Arrhenius (1859–1927) announced the dissociation theory in 1883. Basically, he said that a dissolved electrolyte was immediately dissociated, whether or not current flowed. The theory explained electrolytic conduction; osmosis of aqueous solutions of acids, bases, and salts; and other results in physical chemical research of the period. Extending the dissociation theory, Walther Nernst (1864–1941) explained electromotive force via solution pressure of the electrodes balanced by osmotic pressure of the dissolved ions, 1889. In the same year he conceived the theory of solubility product to explain precipitation reactions.

20th Cent.

PHYSICAL CHEMISTRY. Nernst's 3rd law of thermodynamics, 1906, defined the entropy of a crystal at absolute zero as zero. The theory proved most useful in calculating chemical equilibrium from few physical constants. G. N. Lewis (1875–1946) made current the thermodynamic notion of free energy as maximum work available in a system, 1923. He and others in California have done much to extend the use of the 3rd law of thermodynamics.

In 1913 Max Bodenstein discovered the chain reaction resulting from the bombardment of hydrogen and chlorine by a photon. This along with observation, 1900, of free triphenyl methyl radicals suggested the general existence of free radicals. Spectroscopists' reports along these lines were affirmed in 1925 by Hugh Taylor, who considered free radicals to be frequent participants in chemical reactions.

Chemical kinetics received further interest because of radiation studies. Jean Perrin advocated a radiation hypothesis of reaction, 1918, seeing that frequency of collision in monomolecular reactions did not determine reaction rates. Activation energy was assumed to come from radiation from the walls of the container. The hypothesis forced re-examination of reactions and brought a reassertion by F. A. Lindemann, 1922, of the collision hypothesis. Further study showed that activation energy must be concentrated in a single bond for a monomolecular reaction to take place.

Arrhenius' theory of solutions had raised more questions than it answered; it applied only to dilute solutions and was based only on aqueous solutions. Peter Debye (1884–1967) and Erich Hückel (b. 1896) improved the theory of dilute aqueous solutions by postulating an "atmosphere" of oppositely charged ions for each ion. The atmosphere was used to explain the decrease in mobility of the central ion toward an oppositely charged electrode. Reduction in mobility was made proportional to the square root of concentration. Thomas M. Lowry (1874–1936) and J. N. Brønsted (1879–1947) independently proposed, 1923, a broader acid-base theory in terms of the acceptance (by a base) or loss (by an acid) of a hydrogen ion. The transfer of hydrogen ions was the essential character of acids and bases compared to salts, which were left under the aegis of the Debye-Hückel theory. G. N. Lewis broadened acid-base theory more by considering acceptance or donation of an election pair (rather than loss or acceptance of hydrogen ions or protons) as the characteristics of acids and bases respectively, 1938. This definition of an acid as any molecule or ion with an incomplete election group around 1 of its atoms gave much greater generality to the acid-base theory of solutions.

Following the placement of orbital electrons through the work of Bohr, Sommerfeld, and Moseley (p. 926, above), it was possible for G. N. Lewis and Walther Kossel each to propose the electrovalent theory of chemical bonding, 1916. Since 8 outer-ring electrons were required for stability, as in the rare gases, any deficiency could be filled by the transferring or sharing of electrons apropos of their number of vacancies in the outer shell. In the case of electrovalency, 2 ions are conceived as contributing to each other, as in common salts. Irving Langmuir (1881–1957) further developed Lewis' theory, introducing the term "covalent" to explain more clearly combination in nonmetallic atoms as a bond in which both of a combination pair of electrons come from the same atom, 1919. Nevil V. Sidgwick (1873–1952) 1st called attention to the radical difference of the so-called covalent bond from the electrovalent, 1923. As understood by Langmuir, the covalent bond simply explained combination of incomplete electron shells. Sidgwick recognized the usefulness of what he called the co-ordinate bond to explain co-ordination compounds like H_2PtCl_6, formed by HCl and $PtCl_4$. Alfred Werner (1866–1919) had given the 1st successful account of these formations in 1893. Sidgwick's application of covalent bonds to co-ordinate compounds gave a more suitable mechanism for their occurrence.

With the development of quantum mechanics in the 1920's, physical chemistry saw new vistas opened. Among the early users of the new physics in chemistry was Linus Pauling, who developed the resonance theory, 1931, as a means for treating a nonvisualizable state between 2 conceptual structures. Pauling contributed the concept of electronegativity for explaining partially ionic compounds and assisted in the working out of the notion of hydrogen bonding in liquids such as H_2O, HF, and CH_3CO_2H.

BIOCHEMISTRY. In the 20th cent. biochemistry's most extensive contribution has been in the area of nutrition. In 1906 Frederick Gowland Hopkins (1861–1947) made it experimentally clear that highly refined fats, proteins, carbohydrates, and minerals are insufficient as foods. He pointed out that natural foods obviously contain many other substances essential for health. In 1909 Thomas B. Osborne (1859–1929) and Lafayette B. Mendel (1872–1935) began experiments which showed the wide variety of chemical composition of pro-

teins, especially in terms of amino acids present. The dietary importance of different amino acids became evident as a result of experiments with different proteins.

Casimir Funk (b. 1884) introduced the notion of vitamins in 1912 when he found in rice polishings and in yeast a concentrated pyrimidine which cured beriberi. The original name "vitamine," coined by Funk, meant that the trace nutrients responsible for curing beriberi, scurvy, pellagra, and rickets were amines involved in vital processes. Even though later research showed some to be nonamines, the shortened form, "vitamin," came into use.

E. V. McCollum and M. Davis identified vitamin A as present in the nonglyceride part of fats, in glandular tissues, and in plant leaves, but not present in animal fatty tissues or in vegetable oils. While vitamin A was initially considered a preventive for rickets as well as for the characteristic eye soreness associated with vitamin A deficiency, E. Mellanby, 1919, found rickets in animals fed the vitamin. McCollum, 1922, introduced the term "vitamin D" to explain the prevention of rickets by cod-liver oil even after its vitamin A was destroyed.

Vitamin C, or ascorbic acid (named 1933), was 1st isolated in 1928 by Albert Szent-Györgyi from adrenal glands, orange juice, and cabbage. When Charles G. King found a crystalline substance, 1931, preventing scurvy in guinea pigs, Szent-Györgyi and J. Svirbely identified it as the compound isolated in 1928. Structural analysis and subsequent development of commercial syntheses soon made vitamin C an inexpensive product.

In 1915 McCollum introduced the water-soluble B vitamin concept. As studies progressed, the extensive complex of vitamins involved here became evident. Not until 1926 was the antiberiberi factor isolated in crystalline form. Another decade was required for analysis and commercial synthesis; R. R. Williams, who did this work, named the substance thiamin.

The isolation of vitamin B_2 in the early 1930's was due to the work of many biochemists. Preparation of a yellow oxidation enzyme from yeasts and also from whey powder led Kuhn and Booher to the recognition of a spectroscopic similarity of yellow pigments from yeast, liver, heart muscle, spinach, and eggs. Kuhn and Karrer synthesized B_2 in 1935. In 1936 nicotinic acid was found to be a derivative of the yellow oxidation enzyme from yeasts. By 1937 the usefulness of this substance in curing pellagra was established by Conrad Elvehjem. Throughout the 1930's and 1940's further extension of the B vitamin complex was made, down to the isolation, 1948, of B_{12}, successfully

analyzed via X-ray studies, and usefully applied in the treatment of pernicious anemia.

In addition to vitamin studies, the explorations of effects of inorganic elements made clear by the end of the 1930's the need of animals for such as sodium, magnesium, zinc, cobalt, iodine, and phosphorus. While nutrition studies form only 1 field in modern biochemistry, they serve to illustrate the fruitful interaction of biological, chemical, and medical knowledge found as well in the biochemical studies of metabolism and hormones in the modern era.

Biology

DEVELOPMENT OF RESEARCH TECHNIQUES. The emergence of modern biology, especially zoology, was intimately connected with the Scientific Revolution's themes of experimental method and quantitative investigations. Following the 16th cent. return to an emphasis on direct observation (which Aristotle and Galen had always stressed), a systematic experimental method was not unnatural for biology when such a method was put forth by Bacon and Descartes. William Harvey (1578–1657) showed the advantage of careful, controlled experiment in his inductive reasoning concerning the circulation of the blood. He also made some use of quantitative reasoning, when he wondered what the body could do with such a large quantity of blood as the heart pumps per minute. 17th-cent. mechanistic views were carried to their logical conclusion by Richard Lower (1631–91), who treated the heart as nothing but a mechanical pump. Stephen Hales (1677–1761) carried the quantitative methodology to cruel perfection in his experiments on blood pressure and blood quantity in a horse (*Haemastaticks,* 1733). His earlier work, presented in *Vegetable Staticks,* 1727, provided important quantitative and functional information on plants. Along with Hales, Albrecht von Haller (1708–77)

was one of the few 18th-cent. biologists to continue the experimental tradition of the 17th cent. His distinction of irritability (contractility) from sensibility in the nervous system, 1755, provided an important basis for the flourishing of neurophysiology in the 19th cent.

SYSTEMS OF CLASSIFICATION. Most characteristic of 18th-cent. biology were philosophical discussions over the nature of life and the system of natural order. These discussions were close to the heart of Enlightenment rationalism. One of the more fruitful results of such interest was a useful system of classification. As early as Andrea Cesalpino (1519–1603) a system of plant classes by flower and fruit types had been offered, 1583. Kaspar Bauhin (1560–1624) used part of Cesalpino's scheme and suggested a clearer distinction of genus from species in plants. John Ray (1627–1705) 1st turned to a distinctly "natural" system of classification, 1686. This required that all resemblances be accounted for, rather than an artificially chosen few. Building upon his predecessors, Carl Linnaeus (1707–78) first issued his *Systema naturae* in 1735. His system was essentially that still in use today, involving a hierarchy of class, order, genus, and species. His regular form of description for the parts of plants and animals became standard.

From Linnaeus on it was accepted practice to use a binary name for every plant and animal. Two of the most notable successors to Linnaeus in classifying were A. P. de Candolle (1778–1841), author of a botanical system with better correspondence to nature, 1824–70, and Georges Cuvier (1769–1832), whose *Le règne animal,* 1817, described a nonphilosophic system of life, based on the latest findings in comparative anatomy. Linnaeus, Candolle, and Cuvier provided the essence of modern classification.

NEUROPHYSIOLOGY

THE NERVOUS SYSTEM. The 19th cent. was the heroic age of experimentation on the nervous system. Modern neurophysiology began with Sir Charles Bell's (1774–1842) clear distinction of the anterior and posterior roots of the spinal cord as sources of motor and sensory stimuli respectively, 1811. However, it was necessary for François Magendie (1783–1855) to repeat Bell's demonstration in 1822 before general acceptance was forthcoming. Jean Marie Pierre Flourens (1794–1867) introduced the notion of nervous co-ordination, 1826, via his experiments on a dog and a pigeon deprived of their cerebellums. He also found the dependence of vision on the cerebral cortex and the importance of the semicircular canals of the inner ear for regulating movement. Marshall Hall (1790–1857) applied himself to the study of similar stimuli in a complete and a separated spinal cord. He demonstrated the ineffectiveness of voluntary action beyond the break, although a stimulus applied to the nervous system beyond the break would produce involuntary activity in the muscles, 1833. Pain was not felt in limbs beyond the separation of the spinal cord. Hall's conclusion was the hypothesis of serial segmental reflex arcs, activated by the spinal cord without need of connection to the brain.

Robert Remak (1815–65) contributed to neuroanatomy by describing the 6 cortical cell layers of the cerebrum. He noted the continuity of axons with nerve cells in the spinal cord, and discovered the grayness of the nonmedullated, sympathetic nerve fibers, 1838. Johannes Evangelista Purkinje (1787–1869) described the nuclei and dendrites of nerve cells in 1837. Rudolf Albert von Kölliker (1817–1905) pointed out the primacy of nerve cells over nerve fibers, some of which are processes of nerve cells, 1845.

More general theory appeared in neurophysiology with Johannes Müller (1801–58), whose law of specific nerve energies, 1834–40, laid down a specificity of nerve impulse in terms of the sense organ rather than the stimulus: fire registers heat to the touch and light in the eye, and electric stimuli result in sensations characteristic of the sense organ affected. Emil DuBois-Reymond (1818–96), publishing his *Untersuchungen über Thierische Elektricität* in 1848, was largely responsible for the exact study of electricity applied to animal nervous systems. His interest in this was generated by a vigorous opposition to vitalism; he predicted in this book that physiology would disappear into chemistry and physics, and then reversed himself to speak in 1872 of the inability of a physiochemical view to explain the origins and nature of life.

Otto Dieters' posthumous work, 1865, distinguishing long and short nerve processes (axons and dendrites), pointed out that nerve cells do not form networks. Camillo Golgi (1843–1926) rediscovered, 1873, Dieters' law positing 1 axon and many dendrites per nerve cell. At the same time Golgi reported his method of using silver chromate to stain the nerve elements for microscopic observation. Wilhelm His (1831–1904) showed that axons grow from primitive nerve cells, 1887. The neuron theory was fully stated in 1891 by Heinrich W. G. Waldeyer-Hartz (1836–1921). Foremost in the histology of the nervous system at the turn of the century was Santiago Ramón y Cajal (1852–1934). Ramón and Golgi differed on the neuron theory, the former upholding it. Ramón showed definitely that there is no reticulum, or continuous network, of nerve fibers. The nerve cells were found to be an insulated series with either contact or contiguity, but no continuity, 1889. Ramón's work was based upon improvements on Golgi's staining techniques, allowing Ramón to show the finer structure of the brain far more successfully than ever before.

SHERRINGTON. The high point in neurophysiology came with the work of Sir Charles Scott Sherrington (1857–1952). His general method was to eliminate the brain stem, using a "spinal animal" alone; the primary animal used was the rhesus monkey, with lower animals as controls. Concentrating on spinal reflexes, he postulated the synapse, 1897, a reflex arc consisting of 2 or more neurons, as basic in all spinal reflexes. This brought into consideration the intercellular barrier and required recognition of varying ease of transition of impulses under different conditions. Sherrington's *Integrative Action,* 1906, set forth a brilliantly elaborated theory of integrated nervous action. He built up a complex system of co-ordinated motor behavior based upon the study of reflexes as the simplest expression of integrative action; the primitive elements of the theory were excitation and inhibition of impulses at the synapses. This work constituted the high point in the study of involuntary reflex actions.

CELL THEORY

GLOBULES. Another area of biology which saw its real beginning in 19th-cent. experimentalism was cell theory. Kaspar Friedrich Wolff (1733–94), in the course of his embryological studies, remarked on the microscopic "little globules" constituting all animal organs, 1759; his meaning was vague but suggestive. Of practical value in the prehistory of cell theory was the invention of slicing machines, 1780, capable of cutting as thin as .0005 in. The globular theory, quite distinct from, though ancestral to, cell theory, was advanced by C. F. B. de Mirbel (1776–1854), who observed, 1802, the universality of uniform cells, or globules, in plant structure. Even René Henri Joachim Dutrochet (1776–1847) remained within the confines of globulist theory when he de-

scribed organs as differing in the contents of their cells, but he maintained a very indefinite doctrine of the actual contents or processes of the cells. He did recognize that cells are themselves responsible for growth, 1824. The essential isolation of each cell in plants was stressed by Franz J. F. Meyen, 1830, who participated in the gradual exposition of the various parts of the cell in the 1830's.

THE CELL NUCLEUS. In cytology the 1830's brought the critical point in theoretical development, supported by better microscopy with much greater attention to details. Of primary importance in this era was Robert Brown's (1773–1858) discovery of the cell nucleus in plants. His 1833 paper on Orchidaceae and Asclepiadaceae clearly distinguished the cell nucleus from other structures, and set up the nucleated cell as the botanical unit of structure. Dumortier's observation of algal cell division, 1832, was soon followed by the similar observation, 1837, of Hugo von Mohl (1805–72), who also described in detail some of the steps of mitosis, 1835–39. 1838 saw the 1st full statement of cell theory, by Matthias Jakob Schleiden (1804–81), who conceived of the cell as the essential unit of plant life and the nucleus as its essential internal element. However, Schleiden also believed that the cellular reproduction was by free-cell formation: the nuclear membrane was supposed to become the wall for daughter cells formed within a parent cell, and structures of the parent cell would dissolve to reform in the daughter. By 1844, Mohl's studies of the cell wall and the protoplasm effectively destroyed Schleiden's hypothetical mechanism of cell reproduction. In 1839 Theodor Schwann (1810–82), directly inspired by Schleiden, applied the cell theory to animals, emphasizing that the activity of the total organism is the sum of activities of essentially independent cell units. Of special importance was Schwann's recognition of 2 classes of cell phenomena, those concerning structural change and those concerning metabolic change. With respect to the latter, for example, the importance of cell membranes for separation of chemical substances was stressed, although the mechanism was conceived to be like that of a galvanic pile. Unfortunately, Schwann adopted Schleiden's system of cellular reproduction.

PROTOPLASM. In 1839 Purkinje introduced the term "protoplasm" to describe the initial product in the development of the cell. He represented only the sap and wall of plant cells as results of the protoplasm. Explanation was needed for other contents of the "sarcode" of Félix Dujardin (1801–62), who thus named the moving mass of contents between the food vacuoles of protozoa, 1835. Dujardin was concerned to put to rest the notion that the parts of microscopic animals were parallel to parts of complex, macroscopic animals. Karl Theodor von Siebold (1804–84) 1st made clear the unicellular nature of protozoans and described the function of the cilia as motive parts, 1845. Kölliker the embryologist treated the ovum as a single cell and embryonic development as cellular division, 1844. Max Schultze (1825–74) finally unified the ideas on protoplasm, protozoa, and egg cell with his idea of the cell as "a lump of nucleated protoplasm," 1861; he decided on protoplasm as "the physical basis of life" in 1863. Rudolf Virchow (1821–1902), in his *Die Cellular Pathologie*, 1858, dealt with the structure of the tissues of every bodily organ. His aphorism "every cell from another cell" was, unfortunately, linked to a doctrine of endogenous formation of cells, though the exogenous version of Schleiden was considered untenable. Initial scientific reception tended not only to criticize Virchow's weaker points but to follow traditional views of free-cell formation and spontaneous generation in preference to his improvements. Another couple of decades were needed for general approbation of "every cell from another cell."

In the 1880's Walther Flemming (1843–1915), Eduard Strasburger (1844–1912), Eduard van Beneden (1846–1910), and others worked out the essentials of cell division. Both the full details and the nomenclature for mitosis appeared at this time (1882 on). The high level of individuality in cells was shown by H. V. Wilson, 1907. The appearance of a truly reliable and well-defined technique of culturing cells outside the body came with R. G. Harrison's paper of 1907. Henceforth cytology developed, especially in practical medical directions, with much greater rapidity than before.

MICROBIOLOGY

SPONTANEOUS GENERATION. The realm of microbiology, like many other aspects of biology, was a creation of the microscope. Anton van Leeuwenhoek (1632–1723) stood out among the early microscopists for the accuracy of his observations. Among a mass of reports on different body tissues and animals, his discoveries of infusoria, 1676, and bacteria, 1683, were especially remarkable, considering his use of only a simple lens. The observations of infusoria, apparently generated spontaneously from initially clear infusions of hay, gave rise to controversy over such generation for almost 2 centuries. An important point in this controversy came in the mid-18th cent. John Turberville Needham (1713–81) boiled mutton broth and transferred it to a perfectly sealed container. A few days later he observed that swarms of little animals had appeared in the infusion, 1748. Lazzaro Spallanzani (1729–99) felt that the state of the air in the experiment was crucial. His experiments (published 1767) compared mixtures heated to boiling in open and in closed containers. With sufficient time of heating (over $\frac{1}{2}$ hr.), the sealed containers produced no organisms, no matter how long one waited. Opponents believed Spallanzani had spoiled the air and that spontaneous generation would take place in unheated air.

A new dimension appeared with chemical experiments on fermentation. It was considered to be a strictly chemical process supporting spontaneous generation. In 1836 Charles Cagniard de Latour (1777–1859) claimed that yeast is made of minute organisms, which cause fermentation. Theodor Schwann (1810–82) immediately repeated this claim. Franz Schulze (1815–73) and Schwann experimented (1836 and 1837, respectively) to show that purified air does not support spontaneous generation. These experiments were not conclusive, and during the 1840's the chemist Liebig swayed the field with his view that fermentation was not microbial but rather a chemical process peculiar to organic matter. In 1854 Heinrich G. F. Schröder (1810–85) and Theodor von Dusch (1824–90) succeeded in filtering out bacteria from air by cotton wool. This mechanical method obviated the objections proposed by abiogenists against the use of acid baths or heat to "spoil" the air before introducing it to a boiled infusion. However, modifications of the experiment raised some questions about the universality of Schröder's and Dusch's conclusion.

PASTEUR. It was Louis Pasteur who laid to rest the question of spontaneous generation. Late in life Pasteur set down in a polemical dialogue—following the style of Galileo—the reasons for pasteurizing wines. He began his biological studies in 1854 with fermentation experiments. The ultimate result of the work was not to prove that microbes are involved in fermentation—Schwann had done this—but rather to show that the presence of microbes is the sole condition both necessary and sufficient for fermentation. Pasteur's classic experiments appeared in his *Mémoire sur les corpuscules organisés qui existent dans l'atmosphère,* 1861, where the most convincing display of his theory was made by a flask with a very long, thin, unstopped neck, bent in a horizontal "S." After prolonged heating of a decomposable substance in the flask, no putrefaction or fermentation took place for an extended period of time; yet within a few hours after breaking the neck near the body of the flask, putrefaction appeared. Only the length and angle of the neck prevented bacteria from entering, and this changed when the neck was removed. Even this experiment failed to convince everyone, and the era of belief in spontaneous generation persisted until John Tyndall (1820–93) added further experiments of a most convincing nature in his 1881 *Essay on the Floating-Matter of the Air.*

Microbiological research following Pasteur was able to deal more with questions of detail and less with the basic issue of abiogenesis. Karl Nägeli (1817–91), known for his programmatic lack of interest in Mendel's work on genetics, was able to assert, "I have for 10 years examined thousands of different forms of bacteria, and I have not yet seen any absolute necessity for dividing them even into 2 distinct species." By contrast Robert Koch (1843–1910) made as one of his essential postulates in medical microbiology the complete correspondence of bacteria inoculated and bacteria terminally extracted in assigning the bacterial cause of a disease; extensive data were collected to support the notion of distinct species of bacteria. In 1882 Koch introduced publicly the method of plating bacteria either in (anaerobic) or on (aerobic) a culture solidified with gelatin or agar. Coupled with his perfection of the fixing of bacteria and staining with aniline dyes, Koch's culture method provided a basis essentially unchanged to date for the preparation of bacteria for study. Of special and ironic interest in the study of fermentation was the work of the chemist Eduard Buchner (1860–1917), who resolved the controversy between Liebig and Pasteur by showing fermentation in cell-free extracts. Buchner demonstrated the production of a chemical ferment by the yeast fungi; the ferment could be isolated and still function to give fermentation without the fungi, 1897. Subsequent microbiological work rests more in such areas as disease research and genetics. In the 20th cent. the disappearance of microbiology as an independent field exemplifies the growing tendency toward synthesis of the branches of biology.

EMBRYOLOGY

GERM-CELL THEORY. In the 18th cent. there was disagreement about the nature of the development of the embryo. The preformation theory then held sway in, and *ipso facto* was a discouragement to, embryological research. Why investigate, if everything is ready-made from the beginning? Some preformationists went so far as to imagine miniature but mature figures under their microscopes while examining animal ova. Charles Bonnet (1720–93) rediscovered (after Leeuwenhoek) parthenogenesis in the summerhatched generations of aphids, 1745. This led him to work out a thorough preformation theory, under the influence and with the subsequent support of Albrecht von Haller. As Bonnet saw it, every egg contained within itself all the germs of all individuals to which a mother gave birth and the subsequent generations *ad aevum*. These germs had a noncorporeal aspect in Bonnet's thinking and mirrored rather well Leibniz's monad theory.

Kaspar Friedrich Wolff (1738–94) published in 1759 his *Theoria generationis*, attacking preformation theory and suggesting epigenesis, which had already been the model of Aristotle and Harvey. According to Wolff, generation means creation. By epigenesis he intended the growth of new parts, not actually present to begin with; the arbiter of direction of such growth was an "essential force" in each organism. Spallanzani, a preformationist, discovered the necessity of spermatozoa for gestation to begin in many animals, but he believed the sperms provided no added element to the embryo, only initial stimulation of the process, 1780. His "proof" was the increase in size of a frog's egg before fertilization in the mother. G. R. Treviranus (1776–1837) lent his weight to the side opposite Spallanzani when he treated spermatozoa as the analogue of pollen, 1805; this was done as part of a grand attempt to unify the various sciences of life under the heading of "biology," a term Treviranus originated.

As an age of much more systematic commitment to experimentation, the 19th cent. saw a rapid succession of observations resolving and surpassing the repetitious controversy of the 18th cent. in germ-cell theory. Étienne Geoffroy Saint-Hilaire (1772–1844) made experiments, 1822–26, in which he artificially produced abnormal developments in chicks, thereby arguing against preformation. Jean Louis Prévost and Jean Baptiste Dumas found that filtration destroyed the fecundating power of sperms, 1824. The following year

Dumas repeated and reversed Spallanzani's experiments for preformation. Dujardin, 1827, distinguished spermatozoa from infusoria and showed the production of sperms in the seminiferous tubules. In 1841 Kölliker wrote on the essential place of sperms in reproduction, noting that spermatozoa, like ova, were cellular by nature and origin. George Newport (1803–54) showed the significance of the sperm's entry point for the segmentation of amphibian eggs, 1850–54. In botany Nathaniel Pringsheim (1823–94) went beyond the primitive statement of sexuality in flowers and observed the sexual process in detail in the fresh-water alga *Vaucheria sessilis*, 1855.

In 1859 Darwin's *Origin of Species* suggested by omission a serious problem. If new species occurred, then variation is possible. But if variation is possible, why is it not rampant, and how do we account for the continued transmission of characteristics? Unfortunately, Darwin tried to answer this question—by a theory of pangenesis, 1868. Flying in the face of experimental embryology, Darwin's speculative embryology was little better than a return to the previous century. He theorized that particles from all parts of an organism pass to the reproductive material and thus determine the nature of sperm and egg. Side by side with this turning back of speculative thought, the embryologists continued their observations. In 1875 Oscar Hertwig (1849–1922) described the nuclear fusion in the formation of the zygote, a process brought over from general cytology. Hermann Fol made the 1st actual observation in detail of penetration in *Asterias glacialis* of the ovum by the sperm, 1879, marking the final datum needed to complete Pringsheim's work. Flemming, 1879, began intranuclear research with description of the splitting of chromosomes. In the study of chromosomes Eduard van Beneden demonstrated the equal number of chromosomes in every cell of any body, as well as the production of the haploid stage in meiosis, 1887. By 1892 it was possible for Theodor Boveri (1862–1915) to give the detailed stages of spermatogenesis and oögenesis. August Weismann (1834–1914) combined in himself the knowledge of a skilled experimenter and the ability to generalize shrewdly. His concept of a substance continuous from parent to child was called germ plasm, distinct from general body cells. An elaborate hierarchy of particles and particle groups was conceived to explain heredity, 1892. Despite the perspicacity of Weismann's thinking, his speculative bent disenchanted experimentalists and made it less easy for genetic theories like Mendel's to gain general acceptance when known.

EMBRYONIC DIFFERENTIATION. The exact differentiations involved in embryonic development have been a creation of the late 19th and 20th cents. There was, of course, some speculation in this direction as early as Wolff's *Theoria generationis* in order to support epigenetic theory. Wilhelm His developed a mechanical explanation for all biological phenomena. His student Wilhelm Roux (1850–1924) followed this direction with his program of "mechanics of development." In the spirit of Haeckel, Roux distinguished an initial period of predetermined embryonic development and a 2nd period of functional development. Support for preformation came from the application to this scheme of Roux's famous experiment on a frog's egg, 1888. Destruction of 1 half (a blastomere) left the other uninjured, and it developed as a half-embryo, presumably along a predetermined pattern. Hans Driesch (1867–1941) soon overturned this reasoning and observation by showing that 1 half a sea urchin's egg (a blastomere) will give a complete individual, differing only in size from the normal case, 1891. This same course was later found to apply to the frog as well, if great care were taken in the experiment. The discrediting of Roux's supraexperimental reasoning led to a greater attention to purely experimental results in embryology.

From the end of the 19th cent. to the mid-20th, the organization of knowledge of cell division evolved from a series of ingenious and detailed experiments. Some of these are briefly chronicled below. By constricting a newt's egg Hertwig, 1893, obtained twin embryos. His further studies included centrifuging frogs' eggs so that the yolk collected at 1 pole and the protoplasm at the opposite pole. The result was cleavage and development only at the protoplasm pole, 1897. The various studies of abnormal cleavage were climaxed in the experiment of Jacques Loeb (1859–1924), where an enucleated half of an egg began to develop only after many divisions of the nucleate half and when a nucleus wandered from the nucleate side into the other, 1894. This experiment discredited Weismann's theory of genetic development, whereby nuclei following cell division were considered of more specific developmental potency, incapable of producing a total organism. Loeb's experiment showed the creation of a complete individual from each half of the original egg. In 1899 Loeb went on to suggest that a certain ion concentration in the environment is all the sea urchin ovum needs for parthenogenetic reproduction. From this he concluded that physicochemical explanations may be sufficient to explain embryonic development. Here Loeb indicated one of his abiding interests—the desire to develop a systematically mechanistic view of life processes.

One of the philosophical convictions of Haeckel and Roux was elaborated on an experimental basis by Hans Spemann (1869–1941). By introducing ordinary ectoderm in place of ectoderm specifically destined to form nerve cord in a newt, he observed the completely normal development of the nerve cord in the growth of the newt, 1918. This showed that there is indeed an earlier period when development of the organism seems to take a predetermined pattern, and only later do artificial changes halt or disrupt the normal process. To this discovery was added the climactic concept of an "organizer." In 1921 Spemann showed by comparing frontal and median cleavages in eggs that the gray crescent, or dorsal, region is responsible for organizing an embryonic axis. In embryos deprived of this region, though possessing as much as ¾ of the cleavage nucleus, no more than a ventral fragment ever developed. Stöhr, 1924, found trunk mesoderm to differentiate itself enough to produce an embryonic heart. Vogt, 1925, was able to predict the destinies of various parts of amphibian blastulae. Spemann and others, 1933–34, demonstrated that even cell-free extracts from an organizer area remained capable of controlling development. The influence of biochemistry in the field became paramount about this time. Needham and Waddington found evidence, 1933–35, that the controlling element in organizers was a sterol. Brachet (1938 on) pointed to the importance of RNA (ribonucleic acids) in the development of specialized regions. This was supplemented by his suggestion, 1952, that relocation of microsomes (containing RNA) is involved in neural induction. In the 20th cent. the advance of embryology has become closely related to advances in genetics, for both have focused on intracellular studies, often on a biochemical basis.

GENETICS

MENDEL. The study of genetics probably has fewer precursors, or protogeneticists, in its history than any other area of biology. Before and contemporary with Gregor Johann Mendel (1822–84) the study of variation was conceived essentially as a population rather than an individual phenomenon. The few earlier suggestions of individual change tended to be environmentally based, as with Lamarck, and speculative. No concept of a genetic factor in individuals was previously introduced. Mendel's work appeared in articles of 1866 and 1869. From examinations of pea plants he recorded the appearance of dominant and recessive traits. By inbreeding of not only the 1st filial but succeeding filial generations with dominant and recessive traits, he found that only the recessives bred true. Interpretation of these observations via the construction of a genealogical tree gave a series of statements known as Mendel's 1st law. Wide application of the laws for inheritance of Mendelian (paired and opposed) characters has since been demonstrated. Mendel's 2nd law stated the independence of a given

pair of opposed characters from every other pair. This law has been extensively modified with the 20th-cent. discoveries concerning linked characters. It is remarkable that Mendel's hypotheses were so simple. He excluded the notion that the hereditary contributions of the parents might be unequal. He excluded the possibility of linkage of different inherited factors. Also, in his experiments most of the results were unbelievably more regular than should be expected from the standard deviation in random sampling. Only by these hypothetical and methodological simplifications is it likely that one could have achieved Mendel's results.

The monumental disregard of Mendel's work deserves comment. The journal containing his articles, though obscure, was received by both the Royal Society and the Linnaean Society. The biologist Nägeli, with whom Mendel corresponded extensively on inheritance, continually referred in print to the absence of strict rules for inheritance. W. O. Focke's 1881 publication of *Die Pflanzenmischlinge* referred 15 times to Mendel, but never showed comprehension of the significance of his discoveries. The biologists interested in variation were evolutionists, but they were not seeking a Mendelian type of theory.

CHROMOSOME THEORY. From Mendel to 1900 the best work relevant to genetics was done by embryologists. In 1883 van Beneden suggested genetic continuity of the chromosomes. Theodor Boveri (1862–1915) gave experimental evidence, 1887–1902, to support this, concluding, "for every chromosome that enters into a nucleus there persists in the resting stage some kind of unit, which determines that from this nucleus come forth again exactly the same number of chromosomes that entered it. . . ." The researches of Hertwig and others (1884–88) pointed to the cell nucleus as the basis for inheritance. The individuality of chromosomes was postulated in 1885 by Karl Rabl (1853–1917). It was Boveri's work which shifted biological attention from nucleus to chromosomes. In 1887 Weismann's comprehensive theory of chromosome distribution in cell division appeared. Weismann's theory made direct conversion of observed facts from population studies into factors on the individual level. His speculations were ingenious and predicted certain discoveries, such as the occurrence of meiosis, but the nonexperimental basis of his postulates of biophore, determinant, and id (*Das Keimplasma,* 1892) excited distaste in many thoroughgoing experimentalists. The superficial similarity of Weismann's thought and Mendel's helped delay general acceptance of the latter's work after its rediscovery in 1900.

Exemplary of the evolutionist approach to inheritance was Francis Galton (1822–1911). Taking a hint from the developing field of social statistics, Galton applied statistics to the study of variation. Characteristic of his work was the law of ancestral inheritance, 1889, which predicted for each member of each ancestral generation an arithmetically determined influence on an individual. No correspondence with observed phenomena was given. This "biometrical" approach was opposed by William Bateson (1861–1926), an able polemicist and subsequently a Mendelian, in his 1894 publication of numerous examples of discontinuous variations. Whereas Galton's bell curves of distribution of variations suggested continuity or only minute discontinuity, Bateson's field work led to an emphasis on striking and large discontinuities observed in the field.

1900 marks the rediscovery of Mendel's work. E. Tschermak, Karl Correns, and Hugo De Vries (1848–1935) all published works that year with explicit references to Mendel; Correns and De Vries, when they learned of him, were already well advanced in their own work. Of some relevance is De Vries' study of *Oenothera lamarckiana* (evening primrose) in 1886 and subsequently. The striking variations, including divergent forms like dwarf and latifoliate, he interpreted as new species. He also denied the validity of the law of cleavage (Mendelian) for the primrose mutations. Discrepancies appeared when others repeated his experiments, and it was later made clear that De Vries had failed to distinguish carefully between phenotype and genotype. The weakness of this work brought resistance to Mendel's work, as it was linked initially to that of De Vries. In 1901 Bateson had Mendel's work translated into English, for Bateson saw its significance for natural selection. After his 1904 confrontation with the biometricians at the British Association of Natural Science, Mendelian principles spread rapidly.

The developments of the 1st decade of the 20th cent. served to ensure Mendel's place in the history of genetics. In 1891 H. Henking reported the "peculiar chromatin element," lone and nonpaired in meiosis. In 1905 this was proven to be the sex-determining chromosome by E. B. Wilson (1856–1939) and N. M. Stevens, the 1st case of attribution of a single characteristic to a definite chromosome. Walter S. Sutton (1876–1916) and Boveri pointed out independently, 1903, that heredity particles in general appear to be carried by the chromosomes. The conscious interrelationship of cytology and heredity research dates from Sutton's paper. W. L. Johannsen (1857–1927) substituted mutation theory for natural selection, which had been thought by evolutionists to be an active source of variation, 1903. For some time thereafter the idea of natural selection was completely discredited as a significant part of evolution. From 1905 to 1908 Bateson and R. C. Punnett published experimental studies introducing clearly the notion of particle (gene) interaction and implying by their data, though not consciously realizing, particle (gene) linkage. G. H. Hardy (1877–1947) introduced rigorous statistical reasoning into genetics, giving rise to the field of population genetics, 1908. From Hardy's paper came the awareness of a "gene-pool" concept and of evolution as a result of change in the proportional distribution of genes in a normally unchanging pool. All this was produced by Hardy's simple answer to the question whether a dominant characteristic should be expected to spread through the whole population or not.

GENE THEORY. By 1906 *Drosophila melanogaster,* the fruit fly, was recognized to be virtually "created by God solely for heredity research," as one student put it. In 1910 Thomas Hunt Morgan (1866–

1945) explained the appearance of white eye in *Drosophila* as a sex-linked characteristic. Morgan, trained as an experimental embryologist, had disliked Weismann's theories and Mendel's as well until the work of Sutton and other researchers (mentioned above) convinced him of both Mendel's validity and the significance of the sex chromosome in heredity. Morgan's subsequent gene theory, 1911, brought him a Nobel prize in 1933. The seminal contribution of his 1910 paper was the assignment of a specific gene to a specific chromosome. In 1913 A. H. Sturtevant showed definitely that genetic factors follow a linear arrangement on the chromosome. By 1915 heredity research was sufficiently advanced to see the publication of *The Mechanism of Mendelian Heredity,* a classic, by Morgan, Sturtevant, Bridges, and Muller.

In 1917 Sewall Wright published an article often regarded as a crucial point in genetics. Via his studies of the mechanism of coat color formation in mammals he laid the foundations for physiological genetics. His focus was on how the gene accomplishes its effects rather than on the mechanics of gene transmission. The study of the gene's mode of action has remained the central problem in genetics since Wright and is of critical interest in other areas of biology as well. In actual application, Wright's research direction was exceedingly difficult to prosecute because of use of the mouse. Not until 1941 was an ideal organism, the mold *Neurospora,* found for such studies by G. W. Beadle and E. L. Tatum. Their hypothesis of 1 gene acting as or through 1 enzyme was much strengthened by N. H. Horowitz and U. Leopold, 1951. Among the biochemical studies on microorganisms to determine mode of genetic action, one of the most impressive was that of O. T. Avery, C. M. MacLeod, and M. McCarty, 1944, to show DNA (desoxyribonucleic acid) of primary importance in changing the hereditary make-up of an organism.

In 1921 L. C. Dunn wrote on unit character variation in rodents. Certain mutations, Dunn showed experimentally

for the 1st time, were homologous in different species, thus providing the 1st genetical evidence directly useful in the study of evolution of natural populations.

The view of a genetic effect as due simply to presence or absence of a factor was radically changed by Sturtevant, 1925, in a study of the bar, or narroweyed, character in *Drosophila*. Previously, "crossing over" (exchange of homologous chromosome parts) was thought to involve equal parts. Sturtevant noted unequal crossing over, i.e., a quantitative variation, as cause of the variations in the bar characteristic, though other mutations remained susceptible of qualitative explanation only. One especially interesting result was that ". . . two genes lying in the same chromosome are more effective on development than are the same two genes when they lie in different chromosomes." Supporting the study of mutation in genes was H. J. Muller's application, 1927, of X rays to *Drosophila,* whereupon the mutation rate rose several thousand %. Stadler independently showed the same phenomenon in barley, 1927. This new tool has greatly assisted the study of mutation as such. In 1931 the Sutton-Boveri hypothesis was given overwhelming experimental substantiation by Harriet B. Creighton and Barbara McClintock. Their paper established in classic fashion that "pairing chromosomes, heteromorphic in two regions, have been shown to exchange parts at the same time they exchange genes assigned to these regions." The reality of simultaneous crossing over in cytological and genetic phenomena was thus admirably demonstrated. For the study of chromosomes and chromosome rearrangement and mapping, T. S. Painter introduced an invaluable aid with his discovery, 1933, of the giant chromosomes of the nuclei in *Drosophila's* salivary glands. Since then detailed cytological maps have been constructed for over 5,000 numbered bands, and the positions of genes for 400 mutations have been established.

In 1946 Joshua Lederberg and Edward L. Tatum demonstrated that gene recombination exists in the bacterium *Escherichia coli,* thus indicating sex in bacteria.

The rapid reproduction of bacteria made this discovery important, for new genetic series could be produced rapidly. With N. D. Zinder, 1952, Lederberg found the striking fact of viral transmission of hereditary materials from 1 bacterium strain (*Salmonella typhimurium*) to another, with the acceptance and reproduction of those materials by the 2nd strain. The medical significance of this discovery was immediately recognized.

An obvious classic of recent genetical literature was the model for the structure of DNA proposed by J. D. Watson and F. H. C. Crick, 1953. Their hypothesis, in agreement with all experimental data, involved a bihelical structure with the atomic sequences running in opposite directions. The suggested pairing of atoms in turn has indicated for the 1st time a possible mechanism for self-reproduction of the molecule. With this model to work from, genetics has entered a period of even more detailed and precise experimentation than before.

RADIATION EFFECTS. Genetics has constantly caught the public eye more than any other branch of biology. A notable example of the social concern of geneticists was the 1947 Genetics Conference report on the genetic effects of the atomic explosions in Hiroshima and Nagasaki. A list of 7 recommendations was made to establish a long-term government-supported research study of the affected populations. Another example of increasingly numerous statements by scientists was A. H. Sturtevant's "Social Implications of the Genetics of Man" (*Science*, 1954, pp. 405–7), which indicated the extensive, permanent, and almost totally deleterious effects of radiation on human genetics.

EVOLUTION

PRE-DARWINIAN EVOLUTIONISTS. An area of biology which has become intimately related to genetics from the 1930's, but was initially considered irrelevant to or even antithetical to genetics, is evolution theory. Preceding the notion of biological evolution, there existed a strong sense of cultural evolution. The 17th cent. saw a transition of religious millenary views to secular utopian theories. The correlative idea of secular progress was a strong theme in 18th-cent. Enlightenment thought, embodied earlier in Vico and later in Condorcet. An excellent example of the synthesis of religio-cultural ideas of progress with a biological—and teleological—evolution was the thought of the preformationist Charles Bonnet; his belief in the evolution of species derived from an eschatology of increasing perfection of the world after each of a series of past and future catastrophes.

Georges Louis Leclerc de Buffon (1707–88) laid down a strictly naturalistic evolution, based upon geological evolution (1749 on). Species, he felt, were clearly mutable. Erasmus Darwin (1731–1802), the grandfather of Charles Darwin, was impressed by Buffon and was led to emphasize both variability in the single attributes of species, whether from artificial or climatic or other causes, and the broad similarity among animals. The implication of his work, 1794–96, is evolution by differentiation, via acquired characteristics, from few primitive ancestors. With Buffon and E. Darwin, Jean Baptiste de Monet Lamarck (1744–1829) completed the triumvirate of naturalists most important as precursors of Charles Darwin.

GEOLOGY. An area of scientific thought initially more relevant than natural history to evolution theory was geology. Buffon's *Théorie de la terre,* 1749, made intelligent deductions from the locations of fossil shells to the redistribution of seas in time. His *Époques de la nature,* 1778, reasoned from current tidal deposits to an age of over 75,000 years for the earth, with 6 epochs. Peter Simon Pallas (1741–1811) undertook for Catherine II an exploration of eastern Russia and Siberia, 1768–74, from which he brought back a mine of information, including the discovery of "great animals of India, bones of elephants," etc., in the Siberian ice. Responsible for the 1st geological survey (1746, of France and England) was E. Guettard (1715–86), who noted the continuity of bands of rock on both sides of the Channel and suggested the volcanic nature of mountains in central France. N. Demarest (1725–1815) 1st confirmed the latter. It was William Smith (1769–1839), a drainage engineer, who gave a sufficiently detailed account of British strata and their characteristic fossils, 1815, to initiate serious stratigraphical studies in England. In Switzerland, Horace Benedicte de Saussure (1740–99) established the importance of strata bedding in the Alps, 1786–96, noting that the strata must have been laid down on a level and then forcibly folded into their observed form.

Large-scale controversy in geology emerged in the conflict of Neptunism and Vulcanism. Abraham G. Werner (1750–1817) swayed numerous students at the Freiburg School of Mines with his view that the essential process of formation for all rocks is aqueous, or sedimentary. His diluvial (Neptunist) theory, 1774, was based on data from the Harz Mountains in Saxony and applied universally. The Vulcanist theory of James Hutton (1726–97) appeared in 1795, and can be seen as the 1st scientific geological theory, for it recognized both igneous and aqueous processes and tended much more to limit itself to observable fact. Werner's inability to explain reasonably the known columnar structure of basalt formations was exemplary of the limits of Neptunism. John Playfair's defense, 1802, of Hutton's theory was largely instrumental in its acceptance.

A principal figure in the creation of modern geology was Georges Cuvier (1769–1832), who with Alexandre Brongniart published the 1st systematic account, 1808, of strata—taking note of all fossilized fauna rather than 1 or 2—based on study of the Paris basin. In 1812 Cuvier's *Recherches sur les ossemens fossiles* established the modern science of paleontology on his correlation theory, which required that all elements of an animal's (fossil's) structure be functionally consistent. Introducing the book was Cuvier's catastrophist theory of geological change, designed to explain the marked variation in fossil contents from stratum to stratum.

Epitomizing a continuing tendency to combine good fossil research with extravagant religious history was William Buckland's *Reliquiae diluvianae,* 1823, seeking to give geological support to the Genesis account of the Flood. Élie de Beaumont (1798–1874) represented the updated continuity of catastrophism with his description of mountain building, identifying 4 distinct upheaval systems in Southwestern Europe. Carrying over Hutton's Vulcanist thinking, Charles Lyell (1797–1875) insisted on the absence of variation in the forces bringing change to the earth's crust. His *Principles of Geology,* 1830–33, the origin of uniformitarian theory in geology, was a cornerstone of optimistic materialism's edifice against divine activity in nature.

DARWIN. Lyell's uniformitarian views along with Malthus' *Essay on Population,* 1798, acted as the leaven for biological data provided by the voyage, 1831–36, of the *Beagle,* on which Charles Darwin (1809–82) acted as ship's naturalist. By 1844 Darwin had drawn up his 1st sketch of the transformation of species. In 1858 appeared the joint essays of Darwin and Alfred Russel Wallace (1823–1913), who had independently conceived the theory of natural selection. Finally in 1859 the *Origin of Species by Means of Natural Selection* saw daylight. Its breadth of application made it incontrovertible on the general issue of evolution. That new species appear was thenceforth clear, but the mechanism remained debatable, despite the popular appeal of natural selection (soon current in "social Darwinism"). The problem of finding a suitable mechanism occasioned debate for another 4 decades and more (p. 944, above). The apparent conflict of evolution theory and genetics theory in explaining variation was dissolved only after the temporary replacement of natural selection by Mendelian genetics. When it was realized that each complemented the other, the areas of evolution theory and genetics blended together rapidly. Paralleling Hardy's contribution to genetics were Sewall Wright's studies on the mathematics of evolutionary variation in populations (1930 on). R. A.

Fisher pointed out, 1932, that the dominant characteristics present in wild types are due to natural selection. The study of adaptation and viability in different geographical regions was forwarded by Goldschmidt (1932 on) and Timofeeff-Ressovsky, 1933. Amidst advancing techniques and more detailed studies, Theodosius Dobzhansky's *Genetics and the Origin of Species,* 1937, marked the full integration of 2 long-separated areas. The modern applications of evolution theory have extended as far as scientific anthropology (Robert Redfield) and Catholic theology (Teilhard de Chardin).

Psychology

Interest in human psychology is as old as man himself. From Aristotle until the present, nearly every great philosopher has speculated about the structure and functions of the mind. But only at the end of the 19th cent. did psychology become a subject worthy of study in its own right, due to modern advances in science—improvements in the empirical method, advances in mathematics, and the development of an experimental physiology and of the theory of evolution.

BIRTH OF EXPERIMENTAL PSYCHOLOGY. Throughout the 19th cent., physiologists, developing their experiments on body functions, increasingly turned to psychological problems. Believing that sensations could be measured, several German physiologists performed the 1st experiments in psychology. Working in Leipzig, c. 1830–40, Ernst Heinrich Weber (1795–1878) studied the perception of variations in touch, weight, and vision. He investigated the sensitivity of various areas of the body by measuring the "2-point threshold"—the necessary distance between 2 compass points applied to the skin for each to be felt distinctly (*Der Tastsinn und das Gemeingefühl,* 1846). Gustav Theodor Fechner (1801–87) introduced "psychophysics," the science of the relations between mind and body (*Elemente der Psychophysik,* 1860). Johannes Müller (1801–1858) related further the mind and the body by explaining that nerves are specialized to perform specific functions (*Elements of Physiology,* 1834–40). His pupil, Hermann von Helmholtz (1821–94), did pioneering research on optics (*Physiological Optics,* 1856–66) and acoustics and on "reaction time"—the amount of time which elapses between a stimulus and the response.

ASSOCIATIONISM. In England, the predominating psychology was based on "associationism": experience was held to be the basis of all mental capacity. Alexander Bain (1818–1903) produced the 1st systematization of psychology, along associationist lines. In *The Senses and the Intellect,* 1855, and *The Emotions and the Will,* 1859, he attempted to analyze every mode of experience. In 1876 he founded *Mind,* the 1st journal devoted to psychology.

WILHELM WUNDT. Wilhelm Wundt (1832–1920) is the 1st man who can properly be called a psychologist. He, too, began as a physiologist and philosopher; but he believed that psychology should be freed from metaphysics, and set up psychology as an experimental science by founding the Psychologisches Institut—the 1st formal psychological laboratory—at Leipzig in 1879. Here virtually all the early experimental psychologists were trained; here, too, was founded a 2nd and more important psychological journal, the *Philosophische Studien,* in 1881. Wundt himself rarely conducted experiments, but he always appealed for experimental proof of his theories and readily changed them in response to the results. His major works (*Grundzüge der physiologischen Psychologie,* 1873–74; *Logik,* 1880–83; *Ethik,* 1886; *Einführung in die Psychologie,* 1911) underwent considerable changes from one edition to the next. Wundt considered psychology to be the science of conscious experience. Experience was composed of sensations, images, and feelings. The appropriate method of psychology was introspection (*Selbstbeobachtung*) ; experiment was to proceed by measuring stimuli and responses. At the Psychologisches Institut, notable experiments were performed on sensation and perception.

DEVELOPMENT OF EXPERIMENTAL PSYCHOLOGY.

In 1883, one of Wundt's students, G. Stanley Hall (1844–1924), founded the 1st formal psychological laboratory in the U.S. at Johns Hopkins. In 1887 he began the *American Journal of Psychology*, the 1st U.S. periodical devoted to psychology. His interests were varied, and included child psychology and religious psychology. He was the 1st to use the questionnaire to study children, and later helped introduce psychoanalysis to the U.S.

James McKeen Cattell (1860–1944) was Wundt's 1st laboratory assistant. He did pioneering studies of reaction time, of attention span, and of perception time in reading. He studied the differences between individuals, which Wundt tended to ignore, and in 1894 administered the 1st mental tests to students at Columbia University, N.Y., to measure their memory, associations, and reaction time.

Francis Galton (1822–1911) was early interested in the theories of Charles Darwin. In 1869 he published *Hereditary Genius,* a discussion of the inheritance of brilliance in certain families. He later turned to experimental methods and was a pioneer in the use of statistics for psychological measurement. His *Inquiries into Human Faculty and Its Development,* 1883, described his discovery, while experimenting on association, that subjects allowed to associate freely most often spoke about their childhood and adolescence.

Hermann Ebbinghaus (1850–1909) subjected both learning and memory to quantitative treatment, 1879–84. He was the 1st to take up a psychological problem not derived from physiology. Using nonsense syllables, he studied the difficulties of memorization, the effects of overlearning, and the amount of time saved in relearning (*Memory,* 1885).

Edward Lee Thorndike (1874–1949) studied animal learning, deciding that learning is achieved by trial and error: the animals repeated accidental solving of their tasks until they had learned the solution (*Animal Intelligence: An Experimental Study of the Associative Processes in Animals,* 1898).

WILLIAM JAMES.

A doctor and physiologist at Harvard, William James (1842–1910) was interested in psychology, and in 1875—4 years before Wundt—set up an informal laboratory in which his students could do psychological experiments. He took an interest also in the study of hypnotism and hysteria then going on in France, in the Darwinian theories, and in unexplainable psychic phenomena—telepathy, clairvoyance, etc. In 1884 he founded the American branch of the Society for Psychical Research (founded in England, 1882). In *Principles of Psychology,* 1890, he described mental life as a unity, a total experience which was constantly being transformed ("stream of consciousness"). He denied the possibility of studying psychology by measurement alone. He experimented on emotions and believed they were caused by physiological changes. He made a catalogue of human instincts. In *The Varieties of Religious Experience,* 1902, he made a psychological analysis of conversion, believing that it occurred through the ejection of certain elements of the personality from consciousness and the identification of the self with one purpose.

STRUCTURALISM.

Under the leadership of one of Wundt's students, Edward Bradford Titchener (1867–1927), the structuralists developed experimental psychology along the lines set by the Leipzig laboratory. Titchener began a laboratory at Cornell in 1892 and in 1927 founded the Society of Experimental Psychologists. His published works include *Experimental Psychology,* 1901–5, and *A Textbook of Psychology,* 1909–10.

FUNCTIONALISM.

In opposition to structuralism, which studied mental states, the functionalists concerned themselves with processes, investigating the relationships between mental and organic functions. A group of functionalists formed at the University of Chicago, led by John Dewey (1859–1952) and James Rowland Angell (1869–1949).

WÜRZBURG SCHOOL. In Germany also an antistructuralist tendency developed at the turn of the century. Oswald Külpe (1862–1915), Karl Marbe (1869–1953), and others investigated conscious attitudes which had escaped Wundt's attention: doubt, certainty, affirmation, dissent. They were most interested in the items of experience which are not sensory in nature.

CONDITIONING AND BEHAVIORISM. The work of 2 Russian physiologists led to an entirely new theory of behavior and learning, based on reflexes. Ivan Petrovich Pavlov (1849–1936), professor of physiology at the St. Petersburg Military Medical Academy, received the Nobel prize in 1904 for his work on the physiology of digestion. His research led him to difficult problems of behavior and, in experimenting with dogs, c. 1905, he devised the method of "classical conditioning." If the ringing of a bell constantly accompanied the feeding of a dog, it could eventually cause the dog to salivate, even if no food were presented. Thus a "conditioned reflex" could be induced. Vladimir Michailovich Bekhterev (1857–1927) arrived at similar results while doing independent work (*Objective Psychology*, 1907). He developed a theory of learning through conditioned reflexes (*General Principles of Human Reflexology*, 1917).

John B. Watson (1878–1958) founded the school known as behaviorism, building a new psychological theory around conditioning (*Psychology as the Behaviorist Views It*, 1913). He treated behavior in terms of stimuli and responses alone. More recent experiments in conditioning have been performed by B. F. Skinner (b. 1904). He invented the "Skinner box," a simple rat's cage containing a bar which, when depressed, releases a pellet of food.

GESTALT. While studying the perception of motion, Max Wertheimer (1880–1943) decided that experience had to be studied as a whole, not in terms of each of its parts taken separately. In 1912, with Wolfgang Köhler (1887–1967) and Kurt Koffka (1886–1941), he founded the Gestalt school of psychology, devoted to the study of forms, structures and patterns (*Gestalten*). Köhler applied the principles of Gestalt in his study of anthropoid apes. He discovered that the apes solved problems by sudden insight and not by trial and error: they would respond all at once to an integrated set of clues (*The Mentality of Apes*, 1917). In *The Growth of the Mind*, 1921, Koffka described learning as the progressive realization of forms, rather than an accretion of experiences.

FIELD THEORY. Kurt Lewin (1890–1947) was influenced by Gestalt, by scientific field theory, and by mathematical topology. In *A Dynamic Theory of Personality*, 1935, and *Principles of Topological Psychology*, 1936, he developed the concept of individual action within a field, a "life space" which provided certain barriers to action which could be circumvented only by leaving the field: e.g., by withdrawing into dream or daydream.

STUDIES OF SEXUALITY. Baron Richard von Krafft-Ebing (1840–1902), a German neurologist and psychiatrist, studied the influence of heredity on insanity and sexual deviation. In 1886 he produced the *Psychopathia Sexualis*, a catalogue of sexual deviations. Two common forms of sexual perversity have come to be named for the authors who 1st described them: "sadism," describing sexual gratification obtained through inflicting pain on the love object, after the Marquis de Sade (1740–1814); and "masochism," describing sexual gratification obtained by causing the love object to inflict pain on oneself, after Leopold von Sacher-Masoch (1836–95).

Havelock Ellis (1859–1939) published 7 volumes on sexuality between 1898 and 1928, collectively entitled *Studies in the Psychology of Sex*. His works were the subject of legal proceedings, but he was the 1st to succeed in publicly broaching this delicate subject. He interpreted the vast collection of data at his disposal from a biological, rather than clinical, viewpoint.

The most prominent recent writer on sexuality was Alfred Kinsey (1894–1956), an American zoologist who discovered considerable variation in human sexual behavior among the 18,500 individuals he and his associates interviewed (*Sexual Behavior in the Human Male,* 1948; *Sexual Behavior in the Human Female,* 1953).

PSYCHIATRY. Philippe Pinel (1745–1826) was the 1st to give insanity a medical, rather than demonic, interpretation (p. 963, below). Franz Mesmer (1734–1815) discovered that he could relieve patients of their symptoms by "animal magnetism"—later called "mesmerism" and then "hypnotism." Subsequently, French neurologists began to study neurotic behavior by means of hypnotism. At his neurological clinic in the Salpêtrière in Paris, Jean Martin Charcot (1826–93) and his pupil Pierre Janet (1859–1947) found they could cure patients by means of suggestion while they were under hypnotism. Charcot believed the hypnotic state to be a form of hysteria.

In the 20th cent. psychiatry has used several methods. Adolf Meyer (1866–1950) stressed the importance of biology, psychology, and sociology in understanding and helping patients. He urged psychiatrists to study the life history of each patient; he considered the individual both a victim and a product of his environment and experiences. Psychotherapy was widely used by psychiatrists as well as psychoanalysts. Medical means were also employed. The Viennese psychiatrist Manfred Sakel (1906–1957) began using insulin shock in 1933 to treat schizophrenia. Two Italians, Ugo Cerletti (b. 1877) and Lucio Bini (b. 1908) used electroconvulsive therapy for the 1st time in 1938. Psychosurgery—the cutting of nerve fibers to cure certain neurotic symptoms (lobotomy)—was devised in 1935 by the Portuguese neurologist António de Egas Moniz (1874–1955). New drugs known as "tranquilizers" have largely replaced sedatives. The American Psychiatric Association was founded in 1884.

PSYCHOANALYSIS. Sigmund Freud (1856–1939) was born in Moravia, received his medical degree from the University of Vienna in 1881, and then became associated with the neurologist Josef Breuer (1842–1925). While treating hysteria cases by means of hypnosis,

Breuer had discovered that a cure was often effected by catharsis: by allowing the patient to talk freely about his experiences while in the hypnotic state. Freud studied in Paris with Charcot and Janet, 1885–86, and at the renowned neurological clinic in Nancy. In 1895 Freud and Breuer published *Studies in Hysteria.* They had discovered that the neurotic's symptoms were often caused by the **repression** from consciousness of undesirable memories of thoughts, which the individual either could not remember or refused to recognize. Hypnosis proved useless in effecting lasting cures; furthermore, the patients became emotionally attached to the therapist (**transference**). Breuer felt that the method was discredited and Freud went on alone after 1895. He replaced hypnosis with the method of **free association**: the patient, while in a relaxed state, said anything that occurred to him, however nonsensical or immoral. In this way, repressed material was often brought to consciousness, although **resistances** frequently prevented this. In dreams, however, subconscious material was often allowed to reach consciousness in distorted form. Freud's theory of dream elaboration, **censorship** of the unconscious material, and **symbolism** was published in 1900 (*The Interpretation of Dreams*). By analyzing and discussing his patients' dreams, Freud was often able to bring the repressed memories to consciousness and thus to alleviate the symptoms.

Central to psychoanalysis was Freud's theory of sex (*Three Contributions to the Theory of Sex,* 1905), for he believed that **libido**, sexual energy, was the driving force of life, beginning at birth. The young child went through phases of sexual development, from **autoerotism** (love of his own body), through the **Oedipus** or **Electra complex** (love of parent of the opposite sex and competitive feelings toward the parent of the same sex), homosexuality (attachment to his playmates of like sex), to "normal" heterosexual love. The earlier attachments (**cathexes**) subsisted in weakened form, causing conflicts in the adult which frequently resulted in neuroses. It was, therefore, into their childhood that Freud delved for the solution to his patients' problems.

After 1900, disciples grouped themselves about Freud. He began to teach seminars in psychoanalysis in 1902, continuing as professor of neuropathology at the University of Vienna until he fled the Nazis in 1938. The earliest and most important of his followers were Karl Abraham (1877–1925), Alfred Adler (1870–1937), Sandor Ferenczi (1873–1933), Ernest Jones (1879–1958), C. G. Jung (1875–1961), and Otto Rank (1884–1939). The International Psychoanalytical Association was founded in 1910. The 1st journal of the movement was the *Jahrbuch für psychoanalytische und psychopathologische Forschungen,* 1908–14; the *Internationale Zeitschrift für Psychoanalyse* and *Imago* followed in 1912.

From 1912, Freud began to apply psychoanalysis to the study of society, religion, and anthropology, beginning with *Totem and Taboo,* 1912. Under the influence of World War I, he began to write of a **death instinct** that struggled in every individual against a **life instinct,** causing aggression and war ("Thoughts on War and Death," 1915; *Civilization and Its Discontents,* 1930). In the latter part of his life, Freud attempted to describe the mental forces which struggle against one another in each person. They were 3: the **id,** expressing the instinctual drives of the individual; the **ego,** the reality principle which adapts the individual to the requirements of society; and the **superego,** the reproving parental conscience. These theories were outlined in *Group Psychology and Analysis of the Ego,* 1920, and *The Ego and the Id,* 1923.

Alfred Adler was one of the earliest participants in the psychoanalytic movement. Interested in Freud's theory of **compensation** for deficiencies, he published *A Study of Organic Inferiority and Its Psychical Compensation,* 1907, demonstrating how social, intellectual, or physical inadequacy was compensated for by overt behavior or symptoms. These studies led him to break with the Freudian movement, 1911, and begin the school of "individual psychology." He believed that the driving force in life was the desire for power, not libido. He called admitted inferiority the **inferiority complex** and showed how the attempt to overcome it could lead to aggressiveness.

Carl Jung was also unable to accept the primacy of sexuality as stipulated by Freud and left the psychoanalytic movement in 1913 to practice "analytical psychology." He studied the effects of heredity and of spiritual forces on the mind: he spoke of the "collective unconscious," mythic material which he felt to be inherited by members of a culture. He classified individuals according to basic psychological categories, coining the terms "extrovert" and "introvert" (*Psychological Types,* 1920).

SOCIAL PSYCHOLOGY. William McDougall (1871–1938) was interested in the irrational foundations of behavior. In *An Introduction to Social Psychology,* 1908, he developed a theory of human behavior based on inherited instincts and an acquired superstructure of sentiments. He saw social life as the product of instincts. In *Instincts of the Herd in Peace and War,* 1916, Wilfred Trotter (1872–1939) described World War I as a clash of instincts. McDougall himself began studying abnormal psychology while in the British army during the war. He published an *Outline of Abnormal Psychology* in 1926.

CHILD PSYCHOLOGY. The most important child psychologist of the 20th cent. was Jean Piaget (b. 1896). His major theory (expounded in *The Language and Thought of the Child,* 1923; *The Child's Conception of the World,* 1929; *The Moral Judgment of the Child,* 1932) treats of the child's egocentricity: he accepts his own viewpoint as the objective one and fails to distinguish himself from what is external, so that he attributes life to all he encounters. Piaget considered intellectual development to be a gradual emancipation from the egocentric way of thought.

Child psychoanalysis was developed notably by Anna Freud (*Einführung in der Technik der Kinderanalyse,* 1927) and Melanie Klein (*The Psychoanalysis of Children,* 1932).

INTELLIGENCE AND PERSONALITY TESTING. Alfred Binet (1857–1911) founded the 1st French psychological laboratory at the Sorbonne in 1889 and the 1st French psychological journal, *L'Année psychologique,* in 1895. He devised the 1st intelligence tests for school-children in 1905. The tests, revised in 1908 and 1911, were arranged for the age levels at which the average child could be expected to do them satisfactorily. A child's "mental age" was the level he attained on this scale. The German psychologist Wilhelm Stern (1871–1938) suggested that absolute retardation or advancement in years was less important as a measure than relative retardation or advancement. In 1911 he introduced the intelligence quotient (IQ), determined by dividing mental age by chronological age. The "Stanford revision" of Binet's test, 1916, has been the most widely used of intelligence tests.

The Swiss psychiatrist Hermann Rorschach (1884–1922) began in 1911 to use a group of ink blots in order to compare normal, neurotic, and psychotic personalities. By showing the subject an ink blot and asking him to state what he saw in it, Rorschach was able to classify many personality types. A standard set of "Rorschach prints" has been widely used.

Medicine

EARLY MEDICINE

SYSTEMATIC CLINICAL INSTRUCTION. The establishment of systematic clinical instruction, the hallmark of modern medical education, dates from the 17th–18th cents. The Leiden School in the Netherlands, after Hermann Boerhaave (1668–1738) became a teacher there, 1701, provided the model for modern medical bedside teaching. Early imitators of Boerhaave's methods included Archibald Pitcairne (1652–1713) at the College of Physicians in Edinburgh, founded in 1681, and Gerard van Swieten (1700–1772) at the Old Vienna School, founded c. 1745.

RISE OF SCIENTIFIC PHYSIOLOGY. Boerhaave's *Institutiones medicae,* 1708, were widely adopted, but it was his pupil, Albrecht von Haller (p. 939, above), who started physiology on its modern career with his *Elementa physiologiae corporis humani,* 1757–66. In addition to his work on the nervous system, Haller's studies of respiration, bone formation, and embryology were influential. Combined with the work of Stephen Hales (p. 939, above) on blood pressure, quantity, etc., 1740's, the advances of Boerhaave and Haller marked the rise of scientific physiology.

DEVELOPMENT OF DIAGNOSTIC TECHNIQUES. Basic modern diagnostic techniques were devised in the later 18th cent. Only as a result of the work of Giovanni Battista Morgagni (1682–1771) was morbid anatomy made a regular part of medical analysis. After his time the anatomical location of lesions became a routine concern of pathologists. Leopold Auenbrugger (1722–1809) 1st noted the medical value of the characteristic resonances of various parts of the body. His invention of percussion as a medical device, 1761, was simple and basic. Of similar value was the invention of the stethoscope, 1819, and the practice of auscultation by R. T. H. Laennec (1781–1826). For over half a century, however, the stethoscope remained in its less dependable, monaural form.

BEGINNING OF OCCUPATIONAL MEDICINE. On the Disease of Artificers, the 1st work on occupational disease, was published, 1700, by Bernardino Ramazzini (1633–1714) of Modena. In 1831 Charles Turner Thackrah (1795–1833) published *The Effects of Arts, Trades and Professions on Health and Longevity.* Thackrah's comprehensive study of industrial disease and poverty renewed interest in occupational medicine (which had lapsed since Ramazzini's time) and special attention was given from this time onward to health and safety measures in industry.

BEGINNING OF PEDIATRICS. *A Treatise on the Diseases of Children,* by Michael Underwood (1737–1820), appeared in 1784. The book remained the standard pediatric reference until supplanted, 1848, by *Lectures on the Diseases of Infancy and Childhood,* by another Englishman, Charles West (1816–98). In France the most significant publication in the field was the *Practical Treatise on Diseases of Children* by Frédéric Rilliet (1814–61) and Antoine Barthez (1811–91), 1838–40. In Germany the *Handbuch der Kinderkrankheiten* began publication in 1877. The German immigrant physician, Abraham Jacobi (1830–1919), was the chief pioneer pediatrician in the U.S.

PATHOLOGY AND THE STUDY OF INFECTION. Sir John Pringle (1707–82) recognized the danger of putrefaction, 1750, and managed to have some influence in favor of antiseptics in British military hospitals. It was long, however, before his and similar views were influential (as is shown by the handbooks used by surgeons at the time of the American Civil War, when suppuration and septic conditions were still regarded as normal). James Lind (1716–94) noted the importance of lemon juice as a preventative of scurvy, 1753, and made improvements in shipboard hygiene, 1757, including the drawing up of rules for the prevention of typhus.

CLAUDE BERNARD. The outstanding medical physiologist of the mid-19th cent. was Claude Bernard (1813–78). From him stem 3 discoveries of primary importance. The vasoconstrictor function of the cervical sympathetic nerve was observed in 1852, and vasodilation by nerves like the submaxillary in 1857. By the latter date Bernard had recognized that the vasomotor nerves affect capillaries, not arteries or veins. Bernard's investigations produced 2 especially notable facts about the digestive system. The 1st was the discovery of the digestive function of pancreatic fluid. Comparative anatomical dissections alerted him to the digestion of fat into fatty acid and glycerol below the entrance of the pancreatic duct into the intestine. He also noted production of maltose from starch by the pancreatic juice, 1848. His most outstanding experimental work, however, led to the discovery of glycogen in the

liver, 1857. His experiments were related to the debate as to whether or not animals could synthesize complex substances like fats and sugars. The laboratory procedure of Bernard in investigating the conditions of the existence of sugar in the liver and its possible sources is a classic of experimental procedure. (The ramifications of his discovery have extended as far as the Cori cycle, a biochemical cycle based on glycogen, for which C. F. and G. J. Cori received the 1947 Nobel prize in medicine and physiology.) Bernard's *Introduction à la médicine expérimentale,* 1865, established itself both as a medical and as a philosophical classic. Together with the works of Descartes, the *Introduction* still forms part of a basic education in a French *lycée.*

RUDOLF VIRCHOW. A towering figure among pathologists was Rudolf Virchow, a student of Johannes Müller. Contributing significantly to an understanding of thrombosis and pyemia, Virchow made his greatest contribution as a result of microbiological work (*Die cellular Pathologie,* 1858). This study both demolished unsatisfactory theories of "humors" and prepared the ground for new investigations. The cellular basis for studying inflammation led Virchow to the correct explanation of leukemia and to the distinction between the myeloid and lymphatic types.

THE FIGHT AGAINST COMMUNICABLE DISEASE

SMALLPOX. Smallpox inoculation using serum from mildly infected patients was advocated by Cotton Mather (1663–1728) in the American colonies and was successfully practiced there by Zabdiel Boylston (1679–1766). The inventor of smallpox vaccination, however, was the Englishman, Edward Jenner (1749–1823). Jenner's contribution was his recognition, 1796, of the way in which cowpox disease can pass from person to person indefinitely and in undiluted strength. The use of fluid from a human cowpox pustule became a widespread and effective preventive measure against smallpox.

GERM THEORY. Louis Pasteur's demonstration of the germ-bearing capacity of the air (p. 943, above) was the biological basis for his specialized studies on various diseases, such as the French silkworm disease, 1866, and anthrax. Contemporaneously with Robert Koch (p. 943, above), Pasteur worked out the reasons for the deadly and apparently irrepressible outbreaks of anthrax among European, especially French, cattle. Pasteur had witnessed the forming of bacterial spores in fermentation and in the process of the silkworm disease. It was Koch who 1st worked out the importance of bacterial spores, encysted bodies highly resistant to destruction. The necessity of a minimum heat and an amount of oxygen was established by Koch, 1876, for the production of anthrax spores. The purely microbial origin of anthrax was subsequently clarified by Pasteur, 1877, who learned the possibility of weakening anthrax bacillus to prevent the appearance of spores, thus producing an effective agent for anthrax inoculation, 1880. Pasteur's preparation of a treatment for incipient rabies, 1885, followed the same principles.

DIPHTHERIA. Diphtheria was 1st clearly distinguished from scarlet fever by Pierre Bretonneau (1771–1862) of Tours, France. Its bacterium was discovered by Klebs, 1883, and Loeffler, 1884, and Bela Schick (b. 1877) introduced, 1913, the "Schick test," a skin test which indicates susceptibility to diphtheria. The disease was dramatically reduced in incidence when those showing Schick-positive reactions were immunized with antitoxin serums 1st developed, 1894, by Emil von Behring (1854–1917).

TYPHOID. Typhoid and typhus fever were first clinically differentiated by William W. Gerard (1809–72) in 1837. In the mid-19th cent. William Budd (1811–80) suggested that typhoid was transmitted by the ingestion of infected material and that a contaminated water supply resulting from defective sewers was likely to be particularly responsible for spreading the disease. Further steps toward conquering typhoid, however, could not be taken until Carl J. Eberth (1835–1926) recognized the typhoid bacillus, 1880,

and Georg Gaffky (1850–1918) isolated it in a pure culture, 1884. In 1896 Georges F. Widal (1862–1929) developed a diagnostic test for enteric (typhoid) fever, and in the same year Sir Almroth Wright (1861–1947) discovered the killed-virus vaccine which has had great success in immunizing against the disease. Karl Wilhelm von Drogalski (1871–1950), director of the Saarbrücken Typhoid Station, Germany, discovered, 1903, an individual with no past history of enteric fever excreting the organism. Shortly afterward several other healthy carriers of the disease were also found. "Typhoid Mary," the best-known of these individuals, worked as a cook in the U.S. and infected at least 26 persons with enteric fever between 1900 and 1907.

CHOLERA. The 1st great cholera epidemic swept through Europe in 1831–32. This catastrophe greatly increased interest in public-health measures. Following a cholera epidemic in London, 1848, John Snow (1813–58) suggested that the disease was spread by consumption of contaminated water. Six years later he produced epidemiological proof of this theory by demonstrating that water drawn from a pump in Broad Street, City of London, had been directly responsible for over 500 of the deaths which had occurred during the cholera epidemic of 1854. In 1883 Robert Koch discovered the organism *vibrio cholerae,* which causes cholera. Theobald Smith (1859–1934) proved, 1886, that injection with a filtered virus obtained from infected hogs provided immunization against the disease.

TUBERCULOSIS. In 1859 Hermann Brehmer (1826–89) opened the 1st successful tuberculosis sanatorium at Görbersdorf in Silesia. Similar institutions were soon established in other countries. In the U.S Edward Trudeau (1848–1915) founded the well-known sanatorium, 1884, and laboratory for the study of tuberculosis, 1894, at Saranac Lake, N.Y. In 1865 the experiments of the French military surgeon Jean Antoine Villemin (1827–92) proved tuberculosis to be an infectious disease, and in 1882 Robert Koch (1843–1910) discovered its cause, the tubercle bacillus. Early diagnosis was aided by Röntgen's discovery of the X ray, 1895, and in 1898 Theobald Smith distinguished 2 types of tubercule bacilli, human and bovine. Inoculation against tuberculosis, using live but attenuated tubercule bacilli vaccine, was introduced in France, 1921, by Albert Calmette (1863–1933).

YELLOW FEVER. In 1881 Carlos Finlay (1833–1915) of Havana, Cuba, first suggested that the *Aëdes aegypti* mosquito was the transmitter of yellow fever. Not until 1900, however, did a commission headed by Walter Reed (1851–1902) of the Medical Corps of the U.S. Army prove Finlay's theory by means of massive experiments on volunteer civilians and soldiers. William Gorgas (1854–1920) made the 1st practical application of Reed's findings. In 1898 the extremely high mortality rate from yellow fever among soldiers in Havana caused the U.S. Army to send Gorgas there as its chief sanitary officer. Operating at 1st on the theory that yellow fever was a filth disease, Gorgas initiated measures to improve the city's sanitation. His improvements drastically lowered the incidence of malaria, typhoid fever, and dysentery, but had no appreciable effect on yellow fever. When Reed's findings became known in 1901, Gorgas instituted stringent measures designed to eliminate the mosquito from the environs of Havana. His efforts were highly effective. In 1904 he was placed in charge of a sanitation team charged with eradicating yellow fever from the Canal Zone. In attempting to isolate the microorganism responsible, false starts were made by men as eminent as Hideyo Noguchi (1876–1928), one of many physicians to succumb to yellow fever. Not until 1927 were researchers successful in infecting experimental animals. The virus was found, 1933, to be one of the smallest known. Max Theiler (b. 1899) and others finally produced a satisfactory vaccine, 1937.

MALARIA. Discovered, 1880, by Charles L. A. Laveran (1845–1922), the malaria parasite was observed through its asexual stages in erythrocytes by Ettore Marchiafava (1847–1935) and others. Golgi (p. 940, above) noted the coincidence of the fever phase with rupture of red blood cells, 1885. It was Sir Ronald Ross (1857–1932) who painstakingly dissected anopheles mosquitoes for evidence of malaria as well as culex mosquitoes for bird malaria parasites. In 1898 he observed the complete cycle, both asexual and sexual, for bird malaria, and failed to see each stage in *Plasmodium* only because he was transferred—at the time he was in the India Medical Service of the British army—to another area and assignment. The observations were actually made by Amico Bignami (1862–1929), Giuseppe Bastianelli (1862–1959), and Giovanni Grassi (1854–1925) in all 3 species of *Plasmodium,* 1899. In the same year Ross was able to return to his investigations and verified the work of the Italians. He received the Nobel prize in 1902.

INFLUENZA. In 1946 a World Influenza Center was established in London to prevent a recurrence of the pandemic of 1918–19, when more than 15 m. people died of influenza. By identifying the virus at the time of an outbreak and quickly developing a vaccine to combat it, the Center was able to reduce the fatality rate during the influenza pandemic of 1957–58.

POLIO. In 1949 John F. Enders (b. 1897), Thomas H. Welter (b. 1915), and Frederick C. Robbins (b. 1916) of Harvard Medical School demonstrated that polio virus could be grown in cultures of nonnervous human and monkey tissues in quantities sufficient for use in preparing a vaccine. In 1953 a vaccine was constructed from 3 strains of inactivated polio virus by Jonas E. Salk (b. 1914) and, after successful laboratory tests, 1,830,000 U.S. schoolchildren were vaccinated. Evaluation of this further massive testing showed that the Salk vaccine provided active immunity for at least 6 mos., and that booster injections provided further protection. In 1961 an even more effective live-virus vaccine developed by Albert B. Sabin (b. 1906) was licensed.

SURGERY

STERILIZATION. At the Vienna General Hospital, Ignaz Philipp Semmelweis (1818–65) was aroused by the death rate

(10–30%) in the obstetrics ward. Puerperal fever, he suggested and then proved, 1846, was induced because attending physicians came from the post-mortem room to the maternity patients without any sterilization. The incidence of puerperal fever was reduced to about 1% through his insistence on sterilization, yet the idea aroused opposition and was discarded until the time of Lister. Nor was Semmelweis' article on the disease published until the beginning of the antiseptic era, 1861. That an idea will not prevail in the absence of a proper milieu is indicated by the similar neglect of the work, 1795, of Alexander Gordon (1752–99) stressing the need for sterilization to prevent puerperal fever. It was the public insistence, 1843 and 1855, of Oliver Wendell Holmes (1809–94) which led to adherence, in the U.S., to Gordon's and Semmelweis' recommendations.

JOSEPH LISTER. Joseph Lister (1827–1912) is considered the author of the fundamental revolution in surgery—the antiseptic method. In the mid-19th cent. blood poisoning, erysipelas, pyemia, and gangrene (called "hospital gangrene") were considered normal accompaniments of the healing of a wound. Lister made a preliminary study of the early stages of inflammation in 1858, but it was Pasteur's work on air-borne bacteria that opened his eyes to the medical significance of sterilization. By 1870 he was practicing effective antiseptic surgery and gradually introduced less drastic antiseptics. By 1879 Sir William Macewen (1848–1924) had given up Lister's carbolic spray and had, in fact, been practicing essentially aseptic—as opposed to antiseptic—surgery earlier. The introduction of aseptic surgery was made possible by the same revolution in bacteriology that inspired Lister.

ANESTHESIA. Despite occasional use of nitrous oxide and ether by earlier surgeons, William T. Morton (1819–68) was the 1st to make extensive attempts to inform the medical world of the value of anesthetics, 1846. Sir James Young Simpson (1811–70) sought an alternative to ether, which was favored by Morton, because of its unpleasant effects on some patients. He established chloroform, 1847, as an effective substitute in general anesthesia. From this time onward, neatness and thoroughness could replace speed as the mark of a good surgeon.

APPENDICITIS. Henry Hancock (1809–80), a London surgeon, performed the 1st operation for peritonitis, 1848, although at that time it was not recognized as such. In 1886 Reginald Haber Fitz (1843–1913) of Philadelphia established "appendicitis" as a lesion. In the same year Rudolf Ulrich Krönlein (1847–1910) performed the 1st appendectomy, but credit for the 1st successful operation following the correct diagnosis of a perforated and abscessed appendix goes to the Philadelphian, Thomas George Mason (1835–1903). In 1889 Charles McBurney (1845–1913) of New York recognized inflammation of the lower right abdomen to be a symptom of appendicitis.

CORNEA TRANSPLANTS. The 1st cornea transplants were achieved in 1905. Receiver rejection of the new tissue was not a problem in these early homografts—transplants between 2 unrelated individuals—since the cornea is the transparent cover of the eyeball and has no blood circulation.

HEART SURGERY. The development of various electrical graphing devices (p. 961, below) greatly assisted in the establishment of viable techniques for surgery on the heart. In 1939 Gross began arterial canal surgery, and in 1944 the concept of compensatory heart surgery was put forward by H. Taussig. An early example of the latter technique was Blalock's anastomosis between an aorta branch and a branch of the pulmonary artery, 1945. In 1966 Michael De Bakey, (b. 1908) of Houston, Texas, successfully utilized a "left ventricular by-pass," allowing the device to assume the function usually performed by the left ventricle for 10 days, during which time the patient's heart was able to recover sufficiently to permit removal of the by-pass.

ORGAN TRANSPLANTS. The 1st complete explanation for the major problem in transplant operations, recipient rejection of the donor's tissue, was offered by Sir Peter B. Medawar, 1953, who demonstrated the manner of functioning in this connection of the white blood cells.

aureomycin in 1948, and terramycin was discovered by Finlay's research team, 1950. Both are wide-spectrum and can be taken orally.

MENTAL HEALTH

ABOLITION OF PHYSICAL RE-STRAINTS. In 1788 Vincenzo Chiarurgi (1739–1820) abolished all forms of restraint at the Boniface Asylum in Florence, and in 1793 Philippe Pinel (1745–1826) unshackled the patients at Bicêtre, the Paris asylum for men. Previously, the "treatment" of lunatics had included incarceration and occasional torture. Thomas Kirkbride (1809–83) and Benjamin Rush (1745–1813) followed their example in the U.S., and the Quaker, William Tuke (1732–1822), and his son, Henry Tuke (1755–1814), reduced the use of restraint in England. However, no institution abolished all forms of mechanical restraint until 1839, when the reformer, John Conolly (1794–1866), was appointed resident physician at the Middlesex Asylum at Hanwell, the largest mental hospital in England. The corollary of constant observation was stressed as well. Early publications in the field of mental health include Philippe Pinel, *Medico-Philosophical Treatise on Mental Alienation,* 1801; Jean Étienne Dominique Esquirol, *Des Maladies mentales,* 1838, the 1st true textbook of psychiatry; Vincenzo Chiarurgi, *On Mental Diseases in General and in Particular,* 1793–94; and Benjamin Rush, *Diseases of the Mind,* 1812.

CAMPAIGN FOR BETTER MENTAL HOSPITALS. A memorial to the legislature of Massachusetts, 1843, inaugurated the campaign of Dorothea Dix (1802–87) to obtain better-equipped institutions for the mentally ill. Through her efforts 32 asylums were established or enlarged in the U.S. and Europe.

INFLUENCE OF FREUD. The Viennese physician Josef Breuer (1842–1925) was the 1st to use hypnotism to allow his patient to achieve emotional "catharsis," 1880–82. Following this success, he was joined by Sigmund Freud (1856–1939) and together they published, 1895, their observations on this technique in *Studies on Hysteria.* Breuer failed to pursue these findings, but Freud continued the work. The appearance of his book *Interpretation of Dreams,* 1900, marked the beginning of modern psychoanalysis (p. 954).

SHOCK TREATMENT. Julius von Wagner-Jauregg (1857–1940) 1st used shock therapy, 1917, to treat certain types of severe melancholia and depression. In 1933 Manfred Sakel (1900–1957) of Vienna introduced the use of insulin in shock therapy, and in 1938 2 Italian physicians, Ugo Cerletti (b. 1877) and Lucio Bini (b. 1908), improved the technique by using electricity to produce the necessary convulsive state. In recent years the widespread use of tranquilizers has caused a decline in all types of shock treatment.

LOBOTOMY. Antonio de Egas Moniz (1874–1955), a Portuguese neurologist, performed the 1st prefrontal lobotomy, 1935. This was the 1st time brain surgery had been used to treat mental illness.

Public Health

MEDICAL EDUCATION AND HOSPITALS

LONDON DISPENSARY. In 1696 the London Dispensary, the 1st clinic in the English-speaking world, was opened to dispense medicines to the sick poor. In 1771, 1786, and 1796 similar dispensaries

were founded in New York, Philadelphia, and Boston respectively.

EARLY HOSPITALS. In the 18th and early 19th cents. many of the great hospitals of Britain, the U.S., and Western Europe were either founded or rebuilt: St. Bartholomew's, 1730, and the London Hospital, 1752, in Britain; Allgemeines

Krankenhaus, 1774, in Vienna; Philadelphia General, 1752, New York Hospital, 1771, and Massachusetts General, 1811, in the U.S. The Foundling Hospital of London, the 1st institution for unwanted infants, was opened by Thomas Coram (?1668–1751) in 1739.

MEDICAL EDUCATION IN THE U.S. The 1st medical faculty in the U.S. was established at the College of Philadelphia, 1765. In 1768 medical instruction was given at King's College; 1783, Massachusetts Medical School; 1798, Dartmouth; 1799, Transylvania; 1810, Yale; 1807, College of Medicine (Md.).

GOVERNMENT FINANCING OF HOSPITALS. In 1831 in Denmark and Sweden a hospital system financed by taxes was instituted.

BEGINNING OF NURSING EDUCATION. In Ireland, Catherine McAuley (1787–1841) started the Sisters of Mercy, and Mary Aikenhead (1787–1858) founded the Irish Sisters of Charity, 1834, for the improvement of nursing. Two years later Theodor Fliedner (1800–1864) opened a small hospital in Kaiserwerth, Germany, and began training 6 young "deaconesses" according to the hygienic principles of the English Quaker philanthropist, Elizabeth Fry (1780–1845). Although Kaiserwerth is important in the history of nursing reform, instruction there and at other institutions modeled after it consisted primarily of several months of daily attendance at a hospital where the student learned as much as possible from the untrained nurses on duty. Among the deaconesses trained at Kaiserwerth was Florence Nightingale.

MEDICAL ETHICS. The British physician Thomas Percival (1740–1804) drew up a comprehensive scheme of medical conduct. His work, *Medical Ethics,* remains a standard in the field.

REGULATION OF THE MEDICAL PROFESSION. The British Medical Act of 1838 established a General Medical Council to control entry into the medical register, thereby standardizing medical education and examinations. In the U.S. the Council on Medical Education and Hospitals of the American Medical Association (established in 1847) took on the supervision of the quality of medical education. In most countries today medical education is state-controlled. Only those physicians whom the General Medical Council admits to the register are licensed in Britain and the Commonwealth countries, although in Britain unlicensed doctors are allowed to practice. In most Western European countries, the USSR, China, and Japan, graduation from state-controlled medical schools serves as a license to practice. In the USSR each doctor must also practice in an assigned location for 3 years. Licensing of doctors in the U.S. is controlled by each state; there are no national laws.

WOMEN IN MEDICINE. Elizabeth Blackwell (1821–1910), the 1st woman to receive an M.D. degree, graduated from the Medical School at Geneva, N.Y., 1849. Women's Medical College of Pennsylvania, the 1st medical school to instruct only female students, opened in 1850.

MEDICAL EDUCATION IN VIENNA. The Vienna School of Medicine, founded in the mid-19th cent., continued until World War I to hold a pre-eminent position among world medical schools.

FLORENCE NIGHTINGALE. *Notes on Nursing,* 1860, was published by Florence Nightingale (1820–1910) shortly after her return from nursing activities in the Crimea during the Crimean War. In the same year Miss Nightingale began to put her theories into practice when she became superintendent of the Nursing School at St. Thomas' Hospital in London. Training at this 1st modern nursing school consisted of a 1-year probationary period and 2 years' work as a member of the hospital staff. In 1873 a school following this model was begun at Bellevue Hospital in New York.

MEDICAL BIBLIOGRAPHY. John Shaw Billings (1838–1913), curator of the Army Medical Museum and Library in Washington, D.C., founded the *Index-Catalogue to the Library of the Surgeon-General's Office,* a massive attempt to compile a complete cumulative bibliography of medical literature. The vast amount of medical literature published in recent years throughout the world (more than 5,000 medical journals appeared in 1960) made it impossible to keep the project up to date and it was abandoned in the mid-20th cent. Other indexes are available which catalogue articles from several thousand journals, but they make no effort to present a cumulative compilation.

REGISTRATION OF NURSES. Mrs. Bedford Fenwick (1857–1947) established the British (later Royal) Nurses Association to promote government registration of nurses and standardization of their training in Britain, 1887. In 1901 New Zealand became the 1st state to require the registration of nurses, and shortly afterward the U.S. followed this example. In 1911 a Nurses Registration Act became effective in Britain, and in 1919 another Nurses Act established the General Nursing Council to maintain a register of nurses.

JOHNS HOPKINS MEDICAL SCHOOL. The opening of the Johns Hopkins Medical School, 1893, and Abraham Flexner's (1866–1959) report, *Medical Education in the United States and Canada,* 1910, helped to upgrade the standards of American medical schools. Johns Hopkins required at least a year of undergraduate training in the natural sciences, and combined theoretical scientific education with bedside experience in its 4-year program. Flexner's report emphasized the need for adequate laboratories, frequent contact with patients, and skilled teaching staffs. Johns Hopkins became the model for medical schools throughout the country. However, the rising costs which implementing reform entailed reduced the number of American medical schools: 148 (1910), 76 (1932), 77 (1950), 83 (1962).

WORLD CONFERENCE ON MEDICAL EDUCATION. In 1953 the 1st World Conference on Medical Education was held in London. 600 delegates representing 59 nations considered the problems of undergraduate medical training. Further training to follow graduation from medical school was the main topic of a 2nd conference held in Chicago, 1959.

BIRTH CONTROL

CONTRACEPTION. Jeremy Bentham's recommendations in favor of birth control, 1797, were received without enthusiasm in Britain; but when Francis Place (1771–1854) suggested, 1822, in *Illustrations and Proofs of the Principle of Population,* that contraception might be considered preferable to late marriage as a means of curbing reproduction, his ideas met with a more favorable response.

FAMILY PLANNING. In 1912 a Socialist newspaper, *The Call,* published Margaret Sanger's articles "What Every Woman Should Know," and "What Every Girl Should Know," urging contraception as a means of emancipating women from unlimited childbearing. In 1914 Mrs. Sanger published information about contraception in a pamphlet, *Family Limitation,* and in 1910 she opened the 1st birth-control clinic in the U.S. in Brooklyn, N.Y. Similar clinics opened in other U.S. cities and these formed the National Birth Control League in 1917 and the Planned Parenthood Federation of America in 1942.

Marie Stopes initiated the birth-control movement in Britain, and the 1st clinic opened there in 1921. Sweden, which in the 1930's established tax-supported municipal clinics, was the 1st country to give public assistance to birth control. In other countries family limitation assistance includes legalization of abortion and contraception in Japan, 1948; government support to birth-control campaigns in India, 1950's; re-establishment of "abortion on request" in the USSR, 1955; and support for family planning in Chile, 1963, the 1st predominantly Roman Catholic country to do so.

THE PILL. The U.S. Food and Drug Administration approved the 1st oral contraceptive, 1960, following 5 years of field tests in Puerto Rico, Haiti, Los Angeles, San Antonio, and New York. "The Pill," which was developed during the 1950's by Gregory Pincus, M. C. Chang, and John Rock, has been declared effective in preventing pregnancy if taken according to prescription.

PAPAL ENCYCLICAL. Oral contraceptives, however, were condemned by Pope Paul VI in his encyclical *Humanae vitae,* 29 July, 1967, together with other forms of artificial contraception. The rhythm method, sanctioned by Pope Pius XI (encyclical *Casti connubii,* 1930), remained the only method of contraception approved by the Roman Catholic Church.

PUBLIC-HEALTH LEGISLATION

1ST HEALTH-INSURANCE SCHEME. In 1757 the British Parliament approved an act "for the relief of coal heavers working upon the River Thames." The act required employers to make deductions from the coal heavers' wages. The money was then paid into a common fund from which sick, invalid, and aged workers received benefits. Employer fraud forced the act to be abandoned, 1770, but the system was reinstated, 1792.

SLUM CLEARANCE. The decade of the 1760's saw the 1st attempt at slum clearance in London. Wooden buildings were replaced by brick, and the streets were paved, lighted, and drained in some areas.

GOVERNMENT RESPONSIBILITY FOR HEALTH. Johann Peter Frank (1745–1821) published *A Complete System of Medical Polity* in 1779. Frank, who practiced medicine in 10 different cities in Germany, Austria, and Russia, and served as head of the General Hospital in Vienna, was the 1st to suggest that a government should be responsible for the health of its citizens. Far in advance of his time, he urged international regulation of health and the establishment of national authorities to co-ordinate efforts to improve hygiene and sanitation.

1ST FEDERAL HEALTH PROGRAM IN U.S. In 1798 Congress adopted a plan for the insurance by the state of disabled seamen. The scheme was to be financed by a 20% deduction from mariner's wages.

CHILD LABOR. The British Health and Morals of Apprentices Act, 1802, limited child workers to a 12-hr. day. Although the act was largely ineffective, its approval by Parliament made the British government the 1st to recognize its responsibility for industrial conditions and awakened interest in child-labor reforms in other countries. The Factory Act of 1819 prohibited the employment of children under 9 in British cotton mills, and limited children under 16 working in the industry to a 12-hr. workday. The Factory Act of 1833 forbade the employment of children under 9 in all British textile mills, and restricted those under 13 to an 8-hr. workday and those between 13 and 18 to 12 hrs. Even more important, the act provided for the appointment of 4 factory inspectors to enforce these regulations and made 2 hrs. of schooling each weekday mandatory for all children between the ages of 9 and 13 working in factories.

In the U.S. the 1st child-labor law was enacted in Massachusetts, 1842. Six yrs. later Pennsylvania prohibited children under 12 from working in certain mills and limited their workday to 10 hrs. in other industries. However, loopholes in the act and the mild punishment prescribed for violators rendered this legislation ineffective.

PUBLIC SANITATION. In 1842 Edwin Chadwick (1800–1890) published *Report of an Inquiry into the Sanitary Conditions of the Labouring Population of Great Britain.* Chadwick, who advanced the "sanitary idea" by focusing concern on preventive group measures rather than the cure of individual instances of disease, is often regarded as the founder of modern public-health systems. His report recognized the correlation between poverty and illness, and his recommendations favoring such innovations as daily refuse removal, abolition of cesspools, and a radical redesign of sewers were later adopted.

FEMALE LABOR. In Britain the Mines and Collieries Act, 1842, forbade underground work by women and young children. In 1845 these prohibitions were extended to print shops, in 1860 to bleaching and dyeing works, in 1861 to lace factories, and in 1864, 1867, 1874, and 1878 to many other hazardous industries.

BRITISH PUBLIC HEALTH ACT. 1848. A milestone in public-health legislation, this act established locally elected health boards, each of which appointed a medically trained health officer and created a sanitary code to serve as the standard for remedying sanitation defects. Although the reforms inaugurated were short-lived, the act laid the basis for further public-health legislation.

U.S. BOARDS OF HEALTH. The report of the Massachusetts Sanitary Commission, 1850, by Lemuel Shattuck (1793–1859) recommended the establishment of a state board of health. The *Systematic Treatise,* 1850, by the Ohio physician, Daniel Drake (1785–1852), urged the same reform. However, Massachusetts did not institute such a board until 1869. Most other state and municipal governments took similar action during the 1870's and 1880's, though Texas waited until 1909.

BRITISH FOOD AND DRUGS ACT. 1872. The Adulteration of Food and Drugs Act required inspection and analyses of most foodstuffs and levied a fine of £250 for the 1st violation and 6 mos'. imprisonment at hard labor for 2nd offenders.

BRITISH PUBLIC HEALTH ACT. 1875. This act contained a complete sanitary code which, following necessary adjustments and additions, is still in operation in the U.K.

POLLUTION. The Chicago City Council adopted the 1st smoke ordinance in the U.S. in 1881. In 1912 the 1st federal water-pollution studies were undertaken by the Public Health Service.

In the 20th cent. the increasing danger of air pollution was emphasized by numerous disasters: in the Meuse Valley in Belgium, 1–5 Dec., 1930, contaminants emanating from steel mills, power plants, glassworks, lime kilns, a zinc factory, a sulphuric-acid factory, and a fertilizer plant, all located within a 15-mi. area,

caused, in exceptional atmospheric conditions, over 60 deaths. A meteorological inversion and stagnation over Donora, Pa., U.S., on 27–31 Oct., 1948, resulted in 20 fatalities and 6,000 reported illnesses. On 24 Nov., 1950, a malfunctioning sulphur removal unit at a petroleum refinery in Poza Rica, Mexico, vented large quantities of hydrogen sulphide into the air, killing 22 and hospitalizing 320. A temperature inversion in London, 5–9 Dec., 1952, was responsible for an increase in the death rate by 3,500 during the immediately ensuing months.

COMPULSORY SICKNESS INSURANCE. The 1st compulsory health insurance scheme was originated, 1883, by Otto von Bismarck in Germany. Bismarck's plan provided for free treatment, free medicine, and a cash allowance for industrial and certain other manual workers. It departed from common-law doctrine, since proof of employer negligence was not required before a worker received these benefits. Similar schemes were adopted in Austria, 1888, Hungary, 1891, Luxembourg, 1901, and Norway, 1909. The German plan also served as a model for the British Workmen's Compensation Act of 1907 and for the workmen's compensation laws approved by every state in the U.S. between 1902 and 1948.

U.S. PURE FOOD AND DRUG ACT. 1906. By this act Congress prohibited the manufacture, transportation, or sale of adulterated food. The legislation had minimal effect, however, since the courts narrowly defined "adulteration," and the "distinctive name exemption" was a wide loophole which permitted the sale of virtually anything provided its manufacturer gave it a "distinctive name."

HEALTH EDUCATION. After World War I, health education became a major preoccupation of many governments. The USSR established a department of health education within the Commissariat of Health, the U.S. set up a similar division within the Public Health Service, and the British founded a Central Council for Health Education. Public-health activity, including education, began in India shortly after the Government of

India Act of 1919 placed health administration under the jurisdiction of the provinces.

U.S. SOCIAL SECURITY ACT. 1935. This act included health provisions, such as maternal and child health care, aid to crippled children, child-welfare services, vocational rehabilitation, and assistance to state public-health programs. The plan was financed by equal contributions by employers and employees.

NEW ZEALAND SOCIAL SECURITY ACT. 1938. This New Zealand Act provided completely state-supported hospital and medical care for the entire population. A tax of 1s. 6d. in the pound was approved to pay for the medical attention and other social benefits provided by the act.

U.S. FOOD, DRUG, AND COSMETIC ACT. 1938. Following the deaths of 73 persons who had taken a poisonous drug, elixir sulfanidimide (the Pure Food and Drug Act of 1906 did not prohibit the distribution of poisonous drugs), this act eliminated major loopholes in the earlier legislation.

BRITISH DISABLED PERSONS EMPLOYMENT ACT. 1944. The basis of vocational rehabilitation in Britain, the act provided for employment of the disabled—to be arranged by resettlement officers in the Ministry of Labour—and established the quota of disabled workers each employer was required to engage. Austria, France, Germany, Greece, and Israel, among other countries, adopted similar "quota" arrangements. In the USSR the handicapped are retrained by the Ministry of Social Welfare and employers are required to provide them with suitable work.

BRITISH NATIONAL INSURANCE ACT. 1946. The act insured employees against accidental personal injury and industrial disease arising from their particular employment. Coverage under the act became compulsory; previously, benefit plans had depended on the payment of workmen's compensation insurance.

BRITISH NATIONAL HEALTH SERVICE ACT. 1946. This act provided complete medical care for the entire population of England and Wales. The government had 1st guaranteed sickness benefits to workers in 1911, when the National Insurance Act had been passed. This early act provided treatment, drugs, and cash allowances for nonmanual workers earning less than £160 per year and for all manual laborers. Financed by levies on employers and employees in addition to contributions from the state, it benefited 16 m. workers. The 1946 act fully socialized medicine in England and Wales. Financed by a flat-rate system of payment, the National Health Service was organized to provide medical service for all. Each citizen was to select the doctor by whom he wished to be treated, and the government contracted to pay the doctor a fee for each patient on his list. In 1947 the act was extended to Scotland.

U.S. NATIONAL MENTAL HEALTH ACT. 1946. The Congress approved funds to finance research and training programs and to aid the states in founding community mental-health centers.

CANCER AND CIGARETTE SMOKING. In 1953 Anton Ochsner (b. 1896) in the U.S. released a study showing that cigarette smoking was responsible for an increased incidence of lung cancer. His findings were confirmed by a British government study and by a report by the American Cancer Society, 1954. In 1964 the surgeon general of the U.S. reported that "cigarette smoking is a health hazard of sufficient importance to warrant remedial actions." In response to this, Congress, 1964, approved the Federal Cigarette Labeling and Advertising Act which required the warning "Caution: Cigarette Smoking May Be Hazardous to Your Health" to be printed on all cigarette packages sold in the U.S. after 1 Jan., 1966. Several European countries have since adopted similar measures.

CANADIAN HOSPITAL INSURANCE ACT. 1958. The Canadian government, by the Hospital Insurance and Diagnostic Services Act of 1958, undertook to provide grants-in-aid to the individual provinces, which in turn were to provide unlimited hospitalization in ward beds and hospital outpatient diagnostic services.

BRITISH MENTAL HEALTH ACT. 1959. Passed by Parliament in an effort to eliminate legal and social distinctions between mental and physical illness and to provide care for sick persons not requiring institutionalization, the act made it possible for any mental patient to be treated on an informal basis. Hospitalized patients might have their cases regularly reviewed to determine whether further residential care was necessary. Before this the Mental Treatment Act of 1930, which had relaxed the provisions of the Lunacy Act of 1890 that had made all hospitalized mental patients subject to compulsion, regulated the care of the mentally ill in Britain.

MEDICARE. A Medicare Bill was approved by the U.S. Congress in 1965. Hospitalization benefits under Medicare provide up to 90 days of hospital care to the aged for each spell of illness, with the patient paying the 1st $40 of his hospital expenses and $10 a day after the 1st 60 days. Part of the plan, which became effective in 1967, also pays for up to 100 days of nursing-home care following 3 or more days of hospitalization, and provides up to 100 different medical services (e.g., home nursing) after discharge from a hospital or nursing home. Other benefits include outpatient diagnostic services, with the patient paying the 1st $20 and 20% of the costs from the same hospital during a 20-day period, and a lifetime limit of 190 days of inpatient psychiatric care. This part of the plan is financed by compulsory taxes on earnings, which began in 1966 at $7/10$ of 1% (half paid by the employer and half by the employee) and are scheduled to rise to 1.6% by 1987. A voluntary supplementary plan is also available to individuals 65 or older. Under this option each subscriber pays a $3 monthly fee which is matched by an equal contribution from the federal government. In return, after the patient pays the first $50 of his annual medical expenses, the federal government assumes responsibility for 80% of the fees resulting from physicians' and surgeons' care, up to 100 home health services (without previous hospitalization), lab tests, surgical dressings, etc. Outpatient psychiatric services are limited to $250 or 50% of the expenses, whichever is smaller.

INTERNATIONAL REGULATION OF HEALTH

NEUTRALITY OF MILITARY HOSPITALS. Sir John Pringle (1707–82) recommended in *Observations on the Disease of the Army,* 1752, that the military hospitals of both protagonists during the Battle of Dettingen, 1743, should have been regarded as sanctuaries. His suggestion foreshadowed the plan adopted at the 1st meeting of the Red Cross, 1863.

INTERNATIONAL SANITARY CONFERENCES. The 1st International Sanitary Conference, 1851, marked the beginning of worldwide control of public health. Representatives from Austria, France, Greece, the Papal States, Portugal, Sardinia, Russia, the 2 Sicilies, Spain, the Ottoman Empire, Tuscany, and Britain gathered in Paris to establish minimum quarantine regulations in the wake of the great cholera epidemics then sweeping Europe. Similar conferences met regularly thereafter to ease barriers to trade and protect Europe against exotic pestilences. But not until the 13th International Sanitary Conference, 1903, was sufficient information on cause and control available for adequate plans to be made to cope effectively with the 3 principal epidemic diseases of the time: cholera, plague, and yellow fever.

RED CROSS. Influenced by the widespread suffering of the French, Italian, and Austrian troops during the Battle of Solferino, Jean Henri Dunant (1828–1910) published *A Memory of Solferino,* 1862. His suggestion that a relief organization be founded in peacetime that would be available to aid the wounded in time of war led to the establishment of a committee, 1863, which later became the International Committee of the Red Cross. The 1st national Red Cross societies were founded, 1864, in Belgium, France, Italy, and Spain; by the mid-1960's more than 100 national organizations existed. Originally designed to help victims of war, the Red Cross since the end of World War I has expanded its operations to include peacetime activities such as assistance to the victims of natural disasters.

PAN-AMERICAN SANITARY BUREAU. This bureau, with headquarters in Washington, D.C., was founded, 1902, to work toward the eradication of yellow fever.

BERN CONFERENCES. Conferences held at Bern, Switzerland, in 1905, 1906, and 1913 led to international conventions outlawing the use of white phosphorus in matches, employment of women and children under 16 at night, and stipulating hours of labor for such workers.

DRUG FORMULAE STANDARDIZATION. In 1906 the 1st international agreement was signed for the "Unification of the Formulae of Potent Drugs."

DISSEMINATION OF PUBLIC-HEALTH INFORMATION. In 1909 the Office International d'Hygiène Publique was founded with headquarters in Paris to disseminate public-health information, especially data on communicable diseases.

NARCOTICS CONTROL. The 1st international conference on narcotics control met in Shanghai, 1909. The Hague Opium Convention, 1912, required international control of the production, importation, and export of raw opium and coca leaves and domestic regulation of their manufacture, distribution, and use. These objectives were included in the 1919–20 peace treaty and were upheld by the League of Nations. The Geneva Convention, 1925, attempted to establish an opium production quota system and entrusted the Health Committee of the League with the task of determining which narcotics should be placed under international control.

SOVIET LABOR CODE. 1922. The labor code of the USSR, 1922, theoretically included a comprehensive social-service and medical-aid program financed by heavy taxes levied on employing agencies. Although the constitution of 1936 reaffirmed this plan, it did not go into actual operation until after World War II. Health care in the USSR is standardized, and most services are provided by polyclinics, health centers employing general practitioners, specialists, and public-health experts. 70,000 village and street committees are responsible for sanitary matters and medical care within their individual jurisdictions.

LEAGUE HEALTH ORGANIZATION. In 1923 the Permanent Health Organization of the League of Nations was created, with headquarters in Geneva.

BRUSSELS AGREEMENT. 1924. This agreement introduced free medical care for seamen in major world seaports. It was part of an attempt to prevent the spread of contagious disease and was carried out under the auspices of the Office International d'Hygiène Publique, the League of Nations, the League of Red Cross Societies, the International Union against Venereal Disease and the Treponematoses, and the Belgian government.

INTERNATIONAL SANITARY CONVENTION. 1926. This agreement added smallpox and typhus to the list of quarantinable diseases (the others were malaria, plague, and yellow fever) and made the Office International d'Hygiène Publique a clearinghouse for data on epidemics throughout the world.

INTERNATIONAL PHARMACOPOEIA. In 1929 an international agreement provided for the compilation of an international pharmacopoeia. It was signed by 26 nations.

UNICEF. In 1946 the United Nations International Children's Emergency Fund (UNICEF—after 1953 the UN Children's Fund) was established to aid children in countries devastated by World War II and to promote child health throughout the world after the emergency conditions of the postwar era had passed.

NARCOTICS PROTOCOL OF 1946. This agreement placed all prior narcotics control instruments under the supervision of the UN and replaced the Opium Advisory Committee of the League of Nations by the UN Commission on Narcotic Drugs. A further protocol, 1948, provided the means whereby new drugs might be added to the controlled categories. By 1953 more than 50 nations had agreed to drastic limitations on opium production, and the Single Convention of 1961 codified the provisions of numerous multilateral treaties.

WORLD MEDICAL ASSOCIATION. The World Medical Association for the promotion of closer ties among national medical organizations was established in 1947.

WORLD HEALTH ORGANIZATION. In 1948 the World Health Organization (WHO) was established with headquarters in Geneva. The organization aims to provide the highest possible level of health for all peoples and to increase international co-operation for improved health conditions. A specialized agency of the UN, WHO absorbed the League of Nations Health Organization and the Office International d'Hygiène Publique, but the Pan-American Sanitary Bureau continues to function both as an independent organization and as WHO's regional office in the Western Hemisphere.

INTERNATIONAL SANITARY REGULATIONS. 1951. These regulations were drawn up by the World Health Assembly and replaced a multiplicity of earlier international health conventions. They stipulate the sanitary standards and measures to be enforced against contagious diseases at seaports and airports open to international traffic, and include provisions for sanitary documents such as vaccination and other health certifications.

THOUGHT AND CULTURE IN AN AGE OF REVOLUTION

Religion and Philosophy

RELIGION

Roman Catholicism

18TH-CENT. DECLINE IN THE CHURCH'S POWER. Deism, which spread from England to France in the 18th cent., became an important element in antichurch ideologies. While the deists and the *philosophes* attacked the religious doctrines of the church, Febronianism, Gallicanism, and Josephinism sought to limit the authority of the pope and give the church a local character. Agitation by these groups led to the expulsion of the Jesuits from Portugal, 1759, from France, 1764, and from Spain, Naples, and Parma, 1767. Bowing to diplomatic pressure, Pope Clement XIV (reigned 1769–74) dissolved the Society of Jesus, 9 June, 1773. With the onset of the French Revolution further attempts were made to limit the church's power. The Civil Constitution of the Clergy, 12 July, 1790, sought to reorganize the French Catholic Church, but resulted in a schism. The papal bull *Caritas*, 13 Apr., 1791, condemned the innovations. Persecution of the church in France continued until the Concordat of 10 Apr., 1802.

19TH-CENT. REVIVAL. After the collapse of the Napoleonic Empire, the church began to reassert its power in Europe as well as benefit from a revival of belief. In reaction to the Enlightenment, spokesmen for Ultramontanism such as Joseph de Maistre (1753–1821) and Félicité de Lamennais (1782–1854) em-phasized the infallibility of the church. The 18th-cent. pattern of church-state conflict was replaced by papal concordats with Sardinia and Bavaria, 1817, Naples, 1818, and the Netherlands, 1827. The French concordat was revised, 1819, while special arrangements were worked out with Prussia, 1821, and later with other German states. The revival of faith led to the establishment of a number of new orders. The Society of Jesus was revived, 1814, while missionary orders were established, such as the Oblates of the Blessed Virgin Mary Immaculate, 1816, the Marists, 1817, the Lyons Society of African Missions, 1856, the Fathers of the Holy Spirit, 1848, and the White Fathers, 1868.

CHALLENGE OF LIBERALISM. The revival of faith continued throughout the 19th cent., but the church felt itself threatened by the re-emergence of nationalism and by the development of liberal doctrines which challenged it in matters of marriage, education, and authority. Pius VIII (reigned 1829–30) issued the encyclical *Traditi humilitati nostrae*, 24 May, 1829, to promote Christian education, maintain marriage laws, and oppose secret societies. During the pontificate of Gregory XVI (reigned 1831–46) a number of other encyclicals were issued to counter the wave of liberalism both in the church and in society. Of these *Mirari vos*, 15 Aug., 1832, which denounced the program of the Liberal Catholics, was the most important.

PAPAL INFALLIBILITY. The reign of Pius IX (1846–78) was initially seen as liberal but, following the upheavals of 1848–50, Pius joined the counterrevolution against liberalism and nationalism. He strengthened his hold on the church when he declared the Immaculate Conception of the Blessed Virgin Mary to be dogma, 8 Dec., 1854. This was the 1st time a dogma of the church had been promulgated without consulting a council, and thus served as a demonstration of the pope's authority within the church. In the *Syllabus of Errors,* which was appended to the encyclical *Quanto cura,* 8 Dec., 1864, and in a number of other declarations Pius IX detailed the church's stance against liberalism. The church hierarchy, which was fully under ultramontane control, concurred with Pius' actions, and during Vatican Council I, 8 Dec., 1869–1 Sept., 1870, defined the dogma of the infallibility of the pope while speaking *ex cathedra* on questions of faith or morals, 18 July, 1870.

DEFEAT OF LIBERALISM. The growing conservativism of the pope and the church hierarchy led to the division of the church, 1st in France and then elsewhere, into Liberal and ultramontane factions. In Germany the Liberal Munich school of theology led by Johannes von Döllinger (1799–1890) was challenged by the Mainz school. In England, Döllinger's disciple Lord Acton (1834–1902) and Richard Simpson (1820–76) faced increasing opposition from the hierarchy, while John Henry Cardinal Newman (1801–90), the leader of the Anglican converts, was regarded with great suspicion. By the end of Pius' reign the Liberal movement had been overcome, and papal authority in spiritual matters secured. The temporal power of the church was cut short, however, by the occupation of Rome by Italian forces, 20 Sept., 1870. The conservativism of the national churches was an important factor in the major church-state conflicts in Germany (*Kulturkampf*), 1871–90; in France, 1879–1914; and in Mexico, 1913–37.

THE CHURCH AND MODERN SOCIETY. Under Leo XIII (reigned 1878–1903) the church began a gradual adjustment to modern society. His encyclical *Aeterni patris,* 4 Aug., 1879, which established Thomism at the center of Catholic theology, was a step toward improving the education of the clergy. Building upon the teachings of Cardinal Manning (1808–92) of England and Bishop Ketteler (1811–77) of Germany, Leo directed the church toward a Catholic response to the problems of industrial society. The encyclical *Rerum novarum,* 15 May, 1891, announced the church's support of social justice, while the ideas of Christian democracy were given limited support in *Graves de communi re,* 18 Jan., 1901. Pius X (reigned 1903–14) amplified Leo's social doctrines and affirmed the ideas of Catholic Action under church control. Catholic Action was given its greatest impetus by the encyclical *Ubi Arcano Dei,* 23 Dec., 1922, issued by Pius XI (reigned 1922–39). In *Quadragesimo anno,* the 2nd of the great social encyclicals, 15 May, 1931, Pius XI pressed for the implementation of social reforms. This stance was taken up by subsequent popes, and in *Mater et Magistra,* 14 July, 1961, John XXIII (reigned 1958–63) brought the church's social doctrines up to date.

MODERNISM AND AFTER. Attempts to reconcile the teachings of the church with the findings of science led, in the 1890's, to the formation of a modernist movement. Alfred Loisy (1857–1940) challenged the doctrine of the inerrancy of the Bible, while a number of other French Catholics, looking to the church in America as a model, proclaimed the need for a free church in a free state. Despite Leo's attack on the modernists in the encyclical *Providentissimus Deus,* 18 Nov., 1893, and the establishment of the Pontifical Biblical Commission to supervise Catholic biblical studies, 1902, the movement flourished in Catholic intellectual circles. The definitive condemnation of modernism came in 1907 with the decree *Lamentabili san exitu,* 3 July, and the encyclical *Pascendi dominici gregis,* 8 Sept. A number of modernist leaders were excommunicated, and the movement was crushed by 1910.

Subsequent orthodox Catholic theology has followed along the path laid down by Leo XIII. The dogma of the Assumption of the Blessed Virgin Mary was set forth by Pius XII in *Munificentissimu Deus,* 1 Nov., 1950. The main current of theology has been Neo-Thomism, of which Jacques Maritain (b. 1882) and Étienne Gilson (b. 1884) are the leading exponents. Cardinal Augustin Bea (1881–1968) has been influential in broadening the permissible scope of scriptural interpretation. Attempts to formulate a "new theology" incorporating evolutionism, existentialism, and historicism were condemned, however, by Pius XII in the encyclical *Humani generis*, 12 Aug., 1950. Many of the writings of Pierre Teilhard de Chardin (1881–1955), which outlined a metaphysic of evolution, were banned from publication during his lifetime, but are now making an impact upon Catholic theology. John XXIII gave impetus to the ecumenical movement and summoned Vatican Council II, 11 Oct., 1962–8 Dec., 1965. Hans Küng (b. 1928), who has sought to reconcile Barth (p. 976 below) and Catholic theology on the doctrine of justification, was appointed official theologian of the Council. The Council evoked a number of liturgical innovations, and established the principle of collegiality, by which the pope shares power with the bishops of the church. With the publication, however, of the encyclical *Humanae vitae*, 29 July, 1968, which condemned all methods of artificial contraception, Pope Paul VI, whose reign began in 1963, may have set aside this principle.

Protestantism

EVANGELICALISM. The decisive moment in the rise of evangelicalism from its 16th-cent. pietistic origins was the beginning of the Methodist movement in England. Based on the teachings of John (1703–91) and Charles (1707–88) Wesley and George Whitefield (1714–70), the movement did not separate from the Anglican Church until American Methodists demanded their own clergy following the American Revolution. Presbyters were ordained by John Wesley for the American Church in 1784, and later for Scotland and England. Between 1795 and 1836 the separation from the Church of England was completed. Conflicts over leadership and methods led to secessions: the Methodist New Connection, 1797, the

Primitive Methodists, 1812, and the Bible Christians, 1818. Evangelical techniques spread to the Baptists and Congregationalists, who experienced revivals, as well as to the Church of England, where evangelicalism became the decisive force in the early 19th cent. Isaac Milner (1750–1820) and Charles Simeon (1759–1836) were the early religious leaders of the movement, and the Clapham Sect its philanthropic arm.

MISSIONS. Evangelicalism also gave impetus to new missionary societies. The Baptist Missionary Society, founded 1792, the London Missionary Society, 1795, the Church Missionary Society, 1799, the British and Foreign Bible Society, 1804, and the Methodist Missionary Society, 1813, were the main English movements. On the Continent, the Basel Mission was established in 1815, the Berlin and Paris Missionary Societies 1824, the Rhenish Missionary Society 1828, the Swedish Society 1835, Leipzig Society 1836, Bremen Society 1836, and the Norwegian Society 1842.

NORTH AMERICAN PROTESTANTISM. In North America the evangelical movement aided in the rapid growth of Baptist and Methodist denominations. It also gave birth to a number of benevolent and missionary societies, such as the American Board of Commissioners for Foreign Missions, 1810, the American Education Society, 1815, the American Bible Society, 1816, and the American Sunday School Union, 1824. The repeated evangelical revivals of the 19th cent. gave rise to a large number of sects. The Adventists were one offshoot that arose in response to the millennial prophecies of William Miller (1782–1849). The 7th-Day Adventist Church established by Ellen G. White (1827–1915) stemmed from Miller's preaching, as did the Church of Jesus Christ of Latter-Day Saints (Mormons) founded by Joseph Smith (1805–44) in 1830. However, after its movement to Utah in 1847 under the leadership of Brigham Young (1801–77), the Mormon Church diminished the adventist emphasis. The Jehovah's Witnesses were established as the Watch Tower Bible and Tract Society, 1879, by Charles Taze

Russell (1852–1916). The Christian Science Church, established in 1879 by Mary Baker Eddy (1821–1910), was a sect which based itself upon special knowledge and prayer healing. A revulsion from Calvinistic orthodoxy led to the foundation of the American Unitarian Movement, 1825, while the Universalists were established as a separate denomination in 1833.

ROMANTICISM AND ITS RESPONSES. The 19th-cent. reaction to the Enlightenment gave birth to romanticism, which in religious thought led to an emphasis upon the nonrational aspects of the human mind. The main figures of the romantic philosophy of religion were Immanuel Kant (1724–1804), Georg Hegel (1770–1831), and Hegel's opponent Friedrich Schleiermacher (1768–1834). Outside Germany the movement had its greatest impact in American transcendentalism. Within Germany it gave birth to a number of diverse responses. Lutheran orthodoxy denied the tenets of the romantic school, and instead revived confessionalism, which stressed doctrine, the sacraments, and church discipline. Its main spokesmen were Ernst Wilhelm Hengstenberg (1802–69) and Gottlieb von Harless (1806–79). Ferdinand Christian Bauer (1792–1860), the main figure of the Tübingen school, moved away from the speculation of Hegelianism to a closer analysis of the New Testament. Bauer stimulated the development of Biblical criticism, which flourished in the late 19th cent. David Friedrich Strauss (1808–74) and Ernest Renan (1823–92) were among the leading figures in the attempt to reconstruct the life of Jesus, as was Albrecht Ritschl (1822–89), who rejected the association of Christianity with any form of metaphysics, and the church historian Adolf von Harnack (1851–1930). With the publication of *The Quest of the Historical Jesus,* 1906, by Albert Schweitzer (1875–1965) the 19th-cent. delineation of Christ in ethical terms was replaced by one in theological terms.

THE OXFORD MOVEMENT. Following the passage of the Irish Church Act of 1833, the Oxford movement arose in England to assert the independent authority of the clergy as the successors of the apostles. The movement was led by John Keble (1792–1866); Edward B. Pusey (1800–82), the most famous of the English Tractarians; and John Henry Newman (1801–90). When Newman left the movement in 1845 to join the Roman Catholic Church, where he became the central figure in the revival of English Catholicism, the Oxford movement went into decline.

THE DEVELOPMENT OF A SOCIAL GOSPEL. Anglicans under the leadership of John Malcolm Ludlow (1821–1911) and Frederick Denison Maurice (1805–72) were among the 1st to respond to the conditions of industrial society. Their movement, Christian Socialism, flourished between 1848 and 1854. The Anglican Church took up the challenges of industrial society with the organization of the Guild of St. Matthew, 1877, and the Christian Social Union, 1889. The Y.M.C.A. was founded by George Williams (1821–1905) in 1844, while the Y.W.C.A. had its beginnings in 1855. Both organizations sought to combine religious and social objectives. English and American nonconformists were deeply involved in the temperance movement, and also in the efforts to reach the urban poor through the Salvation Army, organized in 1878 by William Booth (1829–1912), and the Volunteers of America, established by Booth's son Ballington (1859–1940) in 1896. In Germany the writings of Albrecht Ritschl, one of the founders of modern Liberal Protestantism, helped to provide a theological basis for the social gospel. The inspiration for a Christian social movement came, however, from leaders of the Inner Mission, such as Johann H. Wichern (1808–81) and Adolf Stöcker (1835–1909), and in the U.S. from such figures as Walter Raushenbusch (1861–1918).

SCIENCE AND RELIGION. While Biblical criticism provided the internal challenge to Protestantism, science provided the external one. After the publication of Charles Darwin's *Origin of Species,* 1859, the literal interpretation of Genesis was undermined. Anthropological studies of primitive societies challenged the concept of the universality of the moral code, while the rise of "social Darwinism" alienated large numbers of intellectuals from organized religion. Liberal theology attempted to accommodate the new doctrines of science, while American fundamentalism, which arrived at its views at a Bible conference at Niagara in 1895, rejected them.

THE RISE OF REFORMED CHURCHES. The conflict between church leadership, supported by the state, and evangelicalism led to a number of reformed Calvinist churches in the 19th cent. In Scotland about ⅓ of the clergy and laity of the Scottish Kirk broke away to form the Free Church of Scotland under the leadership of Thomas Chalmers (1780–1847) in 1843. The Scottish churches were not reunited until 1929. A revival in Switzerland led to the breakup of several of the established canton churches: the Free Church of Vaud was organized in 1849, the Free Church of Geneva in 1849, and the Independent Evangelical Church of Neuchâtel in 1873. The repercussions of this movement had their greatest effect in France, where the Reformed Church was sharply divided throughout the 19th cent. Following the separation of church and state in 1905, the Reformed Church divided into 3 churches. In the Netherlands the established Dutch Church was split by a secession in 1834 which led to the formation of the Christian Reformed Church. Another group broke away in 1886 and joined the Christian Reformed Church in 1892.

THE THEOLOGY OF CRISIS. Liberal theology, which had dominated Protestant thought in the last half of the 19th cent., was shattered by World War I. Optimism gave way to a revival of the teachings of Søren Kierkegaard (1813–55), and the theology of crisis became the dominant form of 20th-cent. Protestant theology. Karl Barth (1886–1968), the founder of the movement, emphasized that man and his religion stood under the judgment of God (the *Krisis*), and that God was approachable only through faith. Emil Brunner (b. 1889) broke with Barth to formulate a more personalistic approach to Christ, while Rudolf Bult-

mann (b. 1884) combined crisis theology with Heidegger's system of existentialism; he also stressed the need to "demythologize" the Gospel in order to make it relate to the situation of modern man. Reinhold Niebuhr (b. 1892), who has become increasingly critical of Barth's approach, was a pioneer of neo-orthodoxy in the United States. Paul Tillich (1886–1965) moved away from Barth's emphasis upon Biblical theology to elaborate a form of philosophical theology.

THE ECUMENICAL MOVEMENT. Although the ecumenical movement had antecedents in the 19th cent.—the formation of the Evangelical Alliance, 1846, and the organization of the World's Student Christian Federation, 1895—the movement effectively dates from an International Missionary Conference held at Edinburgh in 1910. The movement was given impetus through the 1925 Universal Christian Conference on Life and Work organized by Nathan Söderblom (1866–1931) and the World Conference on Faith and Order of 1927. Missionary conferences held at Jerusalem, 1928, and at Tambaram, 1938, brought in many of the Asian and African churches. The Oxford Conference on Life and Work, which promoted the development of lay institutions, and the Edinburgh Conference on Faith and Order were held in 1937. They laid the groundwork for the World Council of Churches, which was established at Amsterdam on 23 Aug., 1948.

Eastern Orthodoxy

DECLINE OF THE ECUMENICAL PATRIARCHATE. Until the early 19th cent. the heads of the various Greek and Slavic Orthodox churches of the Balkans were selected by the ecumenical patriarch at Constantinople. As these nations won their independence from the Ottoman Empire, their churches asserted the right to elect their own primates and to be self-governing. The Greek Church was declared autocephalous in 1833, the Serbian Church in 1878, the Rumanian Church in 1885, and the Bulgarian Church in 1908.

RUSSIAN ORTHODOX CHURCH.

In the 19th cent. the Russian Orthodox Church underwent a spiritual and theological revival. A form of evangelical awakening was inspired by the *startsi* or elders, intense ascetics credited with the gift of healing. The most important of the *startsi* was St. Serafim of Sarov (1759–1833). In theology there was a return to the patristic traditions and a reaction against western thought. The main Slavophile thinkers were Alexei S. Khomiakov (1804–60), Feodor Dostoevski (1821–81), and Vladimir S. Soloviev (1853–1900). Under the influence of Soloviev's teachings, Nicholas Berdyaev (1874–1948) and Sergius Bulgakov (1871–1944) reacted against Marxism and pioneered a renovated Orthodox theology in the 20th cent.

The Holy Synod, which acted as the government of the church, became more closely bound to the czarist regime as the 19th cent. progressed. After the Bolsheviks gained power in 1917, the church, which was seen as a bulwark of the monarchy, was subjected to intense persecution, 1918–27. During World War II, however, the government permitted the election of a new patriarch (the post had been vacant since 1925), and the church entered an era of limited toleration.

Judaism

CABALISM AND HASIDISM. Cabalistic philosphy gave rise to mysticism and to a number of messianic movements in 18th-cent. Europe. The most important of these was led by Jacob Frank (1726–91) and his daughter Eve (d. 1817). The mystical teachings of Cabalism were absorbed into the doctrines of Israel ben Eliezer (known as the Baal Shem Tov, 1700–1760), the founder of Hasidism. Opposition to Hasidism centered around Elijah, the Gaon of Vilna (1720–97), and the Misnagdim (the "Opponents"). During the 19th cent. this schism within the East European Jewish community gradually healed.

REFORMISM. The Jewish Enlightenment began in Germany under the leadership of Moses Mendelssohn (1729–86).

The challenges to Jewish life brought about by the breakdown of the ghetto system and the final emancipation of the Jews (beginning in France, 27 Sept., 1791, and spreading to Prussia, 1812 and 1848, England, 1858, Austria-Hungary, 1867, Italy, 1870, and Russia, 1917) led to Reformism as well as assimilation (to the Gentile world) and Zionism. Napoleon aided the spread of Reform Judaism through his sponsorship of the Grand Sanhedrin, 9 Feb., 1807. The Reform movement centered initially on Germany, where the 1st Reform synagogue was established in 1810. Talmudic Judaism was undermined in the writings of Abraham Geiger (1810–74) and Samuel Holdheim (1806–60), while the Reform Society of Frankfurt, in its Declaration of 1843, rejected the doctrines of the Talmud. The aims and practices of the movement were elaborated in rabbinic conferences held in Brunswick, 1844, Frankfurt, 1845, and Breslau, 1846. Milder forms of Reform Judaism spread to Britain in 1840, to the U.S., where the reform movement dates from the arrival in 1846 of Isaac Mayer Wise, and to France in 1907. Attempts to unite Reform congregations resulted in the formation of the Union of American Hebrew Congregations, 10 July, 1873; the Central Conference of American Rabbis, 9 July, 1889; and the World Union for Progressive Judaism, 10 July, 1926.

COUNTERREFORM. Reform was unable to make headway against Orthodox Judaism in Eastern Europe, the Middle East, or Africa. The Union of Orthodox Jewish Congregations, founded 8 June, 1898, became the spokesman for Orthodoxy in the U.S., while the Agudath Israel was established, 8 May, 1912, to function as the international authority in matters of Orthodox law. Attempts to define a middle ground between Orthodoxy and Reform gave rise to the neo-Orthodoxy of Samson Raphael Hirsch (1808–88) in Germany, and to the Conservative Judaism of Solomon Schechter (1850–1915) in the U.S. The United Synagogues of America, founded 23 Feb., 1913, affiliated Conservative synagogues in the U.S. and Canada. In 1922 Mordecai M. Kaplan (b. 1881) established the Reconstructionist movement in the U.S.

Islam

REFORMISM. The 1st Islamic reform movements were directed against the internal deterioration of the faith. The Wahabi (Wahhābi) movement, founded c. 1744 by Mohammed ibn-Abd-al-Wahab (Muḥammad 'Abd al-Wahhāb) (1703–87), rejected Sufism and demanded a return to early, puritanical Islam. The impact of Wahabi ideas led to the formation of the Faraidi sect under Shariat Allah (Shari'at Allāh), c. 1804, in India, but all other major Islamic reformers and movements have shown deep Sufi influence. In 1781 Ahmed al-Tijani (Aḥmad al-Tijānī) (1737–1815) founded the Sufist Tijaniya (Tijāniyya) brotherhood, which became an important force in the western Sudan during the 19th cent. Shan Wali-yullah of Delhi (1703–81) emphasized reform Sufism and a revival of Indo-Moslem power.

Although the Sufi doctrine of union with God was rejected by Ahmad ibn Idris (1760–1837), the Idrisiyya movement which he founded, as well as the other missionary orders influenced by him, were organized along the lines of Sufi *tariqas* (*tarīqas*). Of these movements the most important were the Sanusiya (Sanūsiyya), founded in 1837 by Mohammed ibn Ali al-Sanusi (Muḥammad ibn 'Alī al-Sanūsi) (1791–1851) in Cyrenaica, the Mirgha-niyya of Mohammed Uthman al-Mirghani (Muḥammad 'Uthmān al-Mirghani) (1793–1853), and the Rashidiyya of Ibrahim (Ibrāhīm) ar-Rashidi (d. 1874) in the Sudan and East Africa.

By the middle of the 19th cent. a new group of reformers were emerging who recognized that the West had to be confronted as well as Islam reformed in order for Moslem society to be fully regenerated. The main figure in the search for internal Islamic reform and defense from western penetration was Jamal al-Din al-Afghani (Jamāl al-Dīn al-Afghānī) (1839–97). Although his dream of Pan-Islam was not realized, his influ-ence survived in popular movements which combined Islamic fundamentalism and activist politics. Afghani also influ-enced Mohammed Abduh (Muḥammad 'Abduh) (1849–1905), the most important modern commentator on the Koran. Abduh, and also Sir Sayyid Ahmad Khan (Aḥmad Khān) (1817–98), the founder of Aligarh College (India) in 1875, strove to accommodate western thought to Islam; they brought about a revaluation of tradi-tional social ethics. Sir Mohammed (Mu-ḥammad) Iqbal (1876–1938) urged the incorporation of western learning and science as a means of resuming the heri-tage of Moslem civilization.

RISE OF NEW SECTS. In 1844 Sayyid Ali Mohammed ('Alī Muḥammad) of Shiraz announced that he was the Bab ("gateway" to knowledge) and began a new sect, Babism. After his death, the majority of his disciples followed Bahaul-lah (Baha 'ullah) (1817–92), who founded the Bahai (Baha'i) faith. Partially in reaction to the "Aligarh movement" the Ahmadiya (Aḥmadiyya) sect arose, 1889, when Mirza Ghulam Ahmad (Aḥmad), c. 1835–1908, received the 1st oaths of loyalty from his followers. Later he pro-claimed himself the Mahdi and Messiah in India. The Ahmadiya split in 1914, the majority forming the Qadianis and the minority the Lahore Ahmadiya.

Hinduism, Buddhism, and Shinto

REFORM OF HINDUISM. The impact of the West on India in the 18th cent. led initially to a large number of conversions to Christianity. But by the 19th cent. contact with the West tended to revitalize Hinduism through the teachings of a number of reformers. In 1828 Raja Ram-mohan Roy (1774–1833) founded the Brahmo Samaj based on the unitarian doctrines of the Upanishads. Although almost extinct today, the Brahmo Samaj under the leadership of Roy, Deven-dranath Tagore (1817–1905), and the latter's son Rabindranath (1861–1941) campaigned successfully against certain aspects of Hinduism, such as suttee (abol-ished 4 Dec., 1829), child marriage, and polygamy. Keshab Chandra Sen (1828–84) broke away from the Brahmo Samaj to teach a more Christian-oriented form of Hinduism in 1866. A return to the teachings of the Vedas was stressed in the Arya Samaj founded in 1875 by Dayananda Sarasvati (1824–83). Ramakrishna Paramahamsa (1834–86) stressed the mystical aspects of Hinduism. His teachings inspired Swami Vivekananda (1863–1902) to found the Ramakrishna Mission in 1897. Yoga was popularized by Shri Aurobindo Ghose (1872–1950), who aided in its spread to Europe and the U.S. Mahatma Gandhi (1869–1948) renewed interest in the Bhagavad-Gita in his campaigns for political and social reform.

BUDDHISM. The 5th Great Council was held in Mandalay, Burma, in 1871, and the Pali text of the canon was inscribed on marble slabs. Between 17 May, 1954, and 23 May, 1956, the 6th Great Council met at Rangoon, Burma, where the Tipitaka was recited in Pali. Steps were also taken to translate it into several modern languages.

SHINTO. As one of the first acts of the Meiji Restoration, Emperor Mutsuhito (1852–1912) disestablished Ryobu Shinto (a fusion of Buddhism and Shintoism) and established Shinto as the state religion of Japan on 30 Nov., 1868. On 15 Dec., 1945, the allied occupation government directed that Shinto be disestablished as the state religion.

PHILOSOPHY

German Idealism

At the end of the 18th and beginning of the 19th cents. a group of German philosophers, perhaps the most influential of modern times, took up and developed the philosophical system of idealism. Earlier expounded by George Berkeley (1685–1753), idealism was an assertion of the primacy of mind and of spiritual values over matter. It denied the existence of physical objects apart from man's perception and consciousness of them. Discontented with the Enlightenment philosophers' confidence in knowledge and science to explain all aspects of the world, Immanuel Kant and his followers made use of the idealist argument to reject utilitarian explanations and to demonstrate that there were some things that could not be known by means of reason.

KANT. Immanuel Kant (1724–1804) was born in Königsberg in East Prussia, where he spent his entirely uneventful and regular life. He was greatly influenced by Leibniz, Hume, and Rousseau and admired Newton. His 1st work was scientific: he wrote a theory of earthquakes and of the winds, and published *General Natural History and Theory of the Heavens,* 1755. He considered the physical sciences to be the true realm of reason and, beginning c. 1780, began to point out the limits of reason in other fields. In his *Critique of Pure Reason,* 1781, he attacked metaphysics, claiming that there was no way of gaining knowledge of the suprasensible world. Empirical evidence can never be employed to prove metaphysical concepts, such as the existence of God, freedom of the will, or the immortality of the soul. The nature of human experience remains uncertain, since the reality behind sense perception consists of unknowable "things-in-themselves." For Kant there were 2 distinct realms: sensations or phenomena, and reason. Our own mental apparatus orders sensations according to its intuition of space and time and by means of innate "categories." Thus we perceive a material world of objects existing in time and space; yet what we experience through our senses need not apply to the things-in-themselves, which are beyond the realm of experience (*Prolegomena to Any Future Metaphysics,* 1783). Kant thus demolished all intellectual proofs of the existence of God. Yet he found proof in the study of morals, which he called "practical reason" (*Critique of Practical Reason,* 1786). His argument ran as follows: since the moral law demands justice—i.e., happiness proportional to virtue—and since justice does not obtain for all in this life, then there must be a God and a future life. In the *Metaphysic of Morals,* 1785, he developed an ethical system, condemning actions—no matter how useful they might be—that were performed merely out of self-interest. Moral actions are performed out of a sense of duty; Kant's "categorical imperative" prescribed that each man act in such a way that he can will his actions to become a law for all men.

FICHTE AND SCHELLING. Kant's disciple Johann Gottlieb Fichte (1762–1814) drew more radical consequences from the idealist philosophy. Abandoning the things-in-themselves, he considered that all of experience is derived from the activity of the ego (*Introduction to the Theory of Knowledge,* 1797). He is best known for his *Addresses to the German Nation,* 1807–8, which prompted the surge of German nationalism leading to the defeat of Napoleon. Friedrich Wilhelm von Schelling (1775–1854) was Fichte's disciple. He turned from early theorizing about the ego (*Vom Ich als Prinzip der Philosophie,* 1795) to a "philosophy of nature." He considered the natural world to be just as real and important as the ego (*Ideen zu einer Philosophie der Natur,* 1797). Yet he did not desert idealism, and in 1800 produced a Kantian system of knowledge (*System des transzendentalen Idealismus*).

HEGEL. The most influential of the German idealists was Georg Wilhelm Friedrich Hegel (1770–1831). With the intention of making philosophy scientific, he constructed a system explaining the history of the world and of the philosophies and institutions produced by man. He considered the history of the world to be an evolution toward ever greater perfection. It was the progressive realization of "spirit" (*Geist*) in man. In philosophy, this meant an ever nearer approach to truth; in history, an ever greater realization of human freedom (*Phenomenology of Mind,* 1807; *Philosophy of Right,* 1821; *Philosophy of History,* lectures c. 1830.) This evolution proceeded, according to Hegel, by a dialectical process: inadequate ideas, sharply contrasted with each other, were continually being synthesized into new and slightly better ones. This process would repeat itself until the state of perfection was reached. Hegel spoke of a "spirit of the times" (*Zeitgeist*) which dominated each historical period. The prime movers of history were "world historical individuals."

MARX. During his lifetime, Hegel collected a great many disciples, among whom were conservatives as well as the radical "Young Hegelians." The most important of these latter was Karl Marx (1818–83), who based his revolutionary socialist theory largely on Hegelian precepts. (He was also influenced by French socialism and English classical economics.) Working with Friedrich Engels (1820–95), Marx accepted the evolutionary, dialectical view of history propounded by Hegel (*The German Ideology,* 1845–46). But he "stood Hegel on his head" by replacing "spirit" with matter (that is, economics) as the moving force in history ("dialectical materialism"). He saw the history of the world, not as the progression from one type of state to another (Hegel), but as a succession of modes of production—as the replacement of one class by another in the dominant role in society. The dialectical process would end only with the triumph of the working class and the end of private ownership of the means of production. Marx's aim was not merely to construct an abstract philosophical system explaining world history, but to use such a system in order to change the world.

REVIVALS OF IDEALISM. The influence of Kant and Hegel was often of a negative sort, eliciting violent attacks on their theories. But at the end of the 19th cent. there was a revival of idealism in England and in Italy. The group of neo-Hegelians at Oxford and in Scotland included Thomas Hill Green (1836–82), Francis Herbert Bradley (1846–1924), Bernard Bosanquet (1848–1923), and John Ellis McTaggart (1866–1925). In Italy, Benedetto Croce (1866–1952) expounded a "philosophy of the spirit."

Utilitarianism

Unlike the German idealists, the group of English philosophers known as utilitarians made no attempt to construct abstract philosophical systems. Rather, they formulated theories that they hoped would lead to the betterment of mankind. They belonged to the "philosophical radicals," a group of liberal Whigs who hoped to produce reforms by combining philosophy, economics, and politics.

Jeremy Bentham (1748–1832) and James Mill (1773–1836) developed an empirical theory of ethics which was later refined and adapted to new conditions by Mill's son, John Stuart Mill (1806–73). The basic theory was formulated by Bentham in *Introduction to the Principles of Morals and Legislation,* 1789. Utilitarian morality was based on hedonism, the doctrine that pleasure is the chief good in life and pain the chief evil. Bentham defined happiness as the greatest amount of pleasure and of freedom from pain. The rightness of an action was to be judged by the contribution it made to human happiness and to the decrease of human misery. Laws and political institutions were to be judged according to the same criterion. Coercion by the state was allowable only when the action of individuals did not lead to the greatest good. James Mill used the utilitarian principle to defend representative institutions (article on "Government" in the 1820 *Encyclopaedia Britannica*). John Stuart Mill attempted to broaden Bentham's system without destroying its fundamental principles. He insisted that certain kinds of pleasures (i.e., those of the intellect) were more important than other kinds: therefore the *quantity* of pleasure it produced was not an adequate measure of the rightness of action (*Utilitarianism,* 1863). He contributed to the study of logic (*System of Logic,* 1843) and to liberal political theory as well (*On Liberty,* 1859).

Positivism

Auguste Comte (1798–1857) was educated as a scientist and was influenced by the French socialist Saint-Simon (1760–1825). His great respect for the precision and certainty of scientific knowledge led him to reject metaphysics as meaningless. His philosophy of positivism, based only on verifiable propositions, was meant to make philosophy scientific. In his *Course of Positive Philosophy,* 1830–42, and *System of Positive Philosophy,* 1851–54, he expounded an evolutionary theory of the sciences. He named a new science, sociology, which would submit society and religion to empirical study. He propounded a "Law of 3 Stages" to explain the evolution toward perfection of each of the sciences. In the *theological* stage, men describe the world in terms of their knowledge of themselves, ascribing life to all they encounter. In the *metaphysical* stage, they abandon personalized agencies, yet retain entities which are beyond experience. In the final *positive* (or scientific) stage, they finally learn to trust only the data of experience. At the end of his life, Comte attempted to develop a theory of ethics without metaphysical precepts. He suggested a Religion of Humanity, in which the best of human qualities would be worshiped.

Schopenhauer and Nietzsche

Arthur Schopenhauer (1788–1860) was influenced both by Kant and by the study of Oriental religions. In *The World as Will and Idea,* 1818, he described 2 ways of looking at the world, corresponding to Kant's 2 realms: the scientist studies the world in terms of *ideas* produced by experience, while the philosopher can get beyond appearances by studying the forces of *will* at work in the world. Schopenhauer believed in a World Will of which each individual, as well as inanimate things, partakes. He was a pessimist, believing that the will, always demanding and never satisfied, causes pain to predominate over pleasure in human experience. He described 2 ways of deliverance from unhappiness: the contemplation of eternal ideas or the conduct of a saintly life.

Friedrich Nietzsche (1844–1900) was the son of a Protestant pastor and reacted violently against the piety of his family. He was a brilliant student of classical philology and received a professorship at the University of Basel at the age of 24. He was influenced by Richard Wagner, with whom he quarreled, and by Schopenhauer. He became insane in 1889, just as his philosophy began to gain recognition. He had great influence on literature and the arts as well as on philosophy.

Nietzsche's philosophy was developed from psychological speculation on morality and religion. His 2 volumes of aphorisms, *Human, All Too Human*, 1876–80, and *The Gay Science*, 1882, are full of psychological observations. He concluded that "the will to power" is the basic human drive. In *Thus Spoke Zarathustra*, 1883–84, he demonstrated this human drive to reach a higher, more powerful position. He was the 1st to describe *sublimation*—later a basic element in Freudian psychoanalysis—as the overcoming of one's passions and making them creatively useful. The rare individual who could do this Nietzsche called the "Overman" (*Übermensch*) : he alone became a creator, rather than a creature, and thus had no need of power over others. In *Beyond Good and Evil*, 1886, and *The Genealogy of Morals*, 1887, Nietzsche noted the relativity of ethical systems. He divided them into two types: master morality and slave morality. Master morality was joyous: it was imposed by a ruling class which delighted in its power. Slave morality, however, the morality of Christianity, was imposed out of resentment felt by a weak and servile class which used religious dicta to terrorize its superiors. While he did not approve a return to master morality, Nietzsche called for a revision of Christian morality, for a "transvaluation of values."

Bergson

Henri Bergson (1859–1941) was educated at the École Normale Supérieure and spent much of his career as a professor at the Collège de France. His philosophy of "creative evolution" had a considerable influence on the literature and thought of the 20th cent. He was a defender of metaphysics and developed a theory of the relation of life and matter. In *Time and Free Will* (*Essai sur les données immédiates de la conscience*, 1889), *Matter and Memory*, 1896, and *Introduction to Metaphysics*, 1903, he contrasted 2 mental faculties—intellect

and intuition. The intellect, viewing things from the outside, conceives of them spatially, as a succession of static moments. Even time is so considered. Intuition, a part of the individual's self-consciousness, does not measure by clock time, but by "duration" (*durée*) : it experiences an endless succession of states; it is aware of the constantly changing flow of consciousness. Bergson considered intuition to be a creative force which allows man to use his intellect to best advantage. He developed a philosophical theory of evolution in *Creative Evolution*, 1907. He believed that evolution proceeded, not by regular change, but by the *élan vital*, the vital impulse which brings new forms to life. He discussed 2 tendencies in the universe: a tendency to repetition and dissipation of energy, and the contrary thrust of life, constantly producing and renewing. In *Two Sources of Morality and Religion*, 1932, he applied these 2 tendencies to the study of social and religious groups.

Philosophy in the United States

William James (1842–1910) was a physician and psychologist before turning to philosophy. He wanted to use philosophy as therapy—to show men how they might lead better lives—and defended human initiative against such deterministic theories as Hegelianism and the evolutionary philosophy of Herbert Spencer (1820–1903) . He is best known as an exponent of pragmatism (*Pragmatism, a New Name for Some Old Ways of Thinking*, 1909) . The name pragmatism was coined by Charles Sanders Pierce (1839–1914) . The meaning of an idea was considered to be the sum of all possible consequences which might ensue from the truth of that idea. An idea without consequences was not an idea at all. James embraced this theory, considering ideas as plans of action which should be tested frequently and discarded if they did not work. He was willing to accept any hypothesis whose consequences were useful to life.

John Dewey (1859–1952) was very different from James, but he, too, was a psychologist and was interested in a philosophy that would affect culture and society. He developed out of his philosophy a system of education which was widely influential. His philosophical works include *How We Think*, 1910, *Human Nature and Conduct*, 1922, *Experience and Nature*, 1925, *The Quest for Certainty*, 1929, and *Logic, the Theory of Inquiry*, 1938. Dewey believed that the function of thought is problem solving: the value of an idea could be judged by the permanence of the belief or action to which it led. His educational theory stressed learning, not by memorization, but by problem solving, by thinking questions through and finding the most valuable solutions. He developed an ethical theory along the same lines: a new course of action had always to be judged by its degree of success in removing the causes of breakdown. Every idea was to be tested empirically, for Dewey had no interest in ideologies applied "from the top down."

George Santayana (1863–1952) and Alfred North Whitehead (1861–1947) were not born in the U.S., but they made considerable contributions to American philosophy. Santayana was born in Spain. He was educated at Harvard University and lived in the U.S. between 1872 and 1912. He was interested in aesthetics (*The Sense of Beauty*, 1896; *Interpretations of Poetry and Religion*, 1900) and in the use of the imagination. In *The Life of Reason*, 1905–6, he distinguished 2 major elements in man's nature, "impulse" and "ideation," which must unite in order for the individual to function properly. Impulse, he felt, is responsible for artistic creation; ideation, for wisdom. After leaving the U.S., Santayana devoted himself to theories of knowledge and metaphysics (*Realms of Being*, 1927–40). Combining realism and idealism, he decided that the existence of physical objects can never be proved but can be accepted on "animal faith" (*Scepticism and Animal Faith*, 1923). He asserted the existence of a realm of universals, which he called "essences."

Whitehead was trained in England as a mathematician and based his philosophy on logic and mathematics. He was invited to the U.S. in 1924 to teach philosophy at Harvard University, where he remained until his death. He believed that experience is felt as interconnected continua of feelings and not as separate elements, and he tried to describe the overlapping of these continua by means of topology. His most important works include *Principles of Natural Knowledge*, 1919, *The Concept of Nature*, 1920, *Science and the Modern World*, 1926, *Process and Reality*, 1929, and *Adventures of Ideas*, 1933.

Logical Analysis

Bertrand Russell (b. 1872) has achieved eminence in several fields: he wrote on mathematics, philosophy, political affairs, and the history of philosophy. Trained as a mathematician, he began studying philosophy because he wished to find some reason for believing in the truth of mathematical precepts. He was first drawn to Hegelian idealism, but became a realist under the influence of George Edward Moore (1873–1958), who emphasized the importance of common-sense beliefs and everyday language. Furthering the work of Gottlob Frege (1848–1925) in mathematical logic, Russell rejected traditional descriptions of mathematical thought and attempted to reduce mathematics to logical principles. In *Principles of Mathematics*, 1903, he analyzed mathematical terms, forming them into purely logical concepts; in *Principia Mathematica*, 1910–13, he and Alfred North Whitehead developed a system of logic from which propositions of mathematics could be deduced. His analysis of sentences was of great influence on the school of logical positivism.

Logical positivism (or logical empiricism) was developed by Russell's pupil Ludwig Wittgenstein (1889–1951) and by the members of the "Vienna Circle" (Moritz Schlick, 1882–1936; Rudolf Carnap, b. 1891; *et al.*). They were influenced by the mathematical logic of Frege and Russell and the antimetaphysical attitude of Ernst Mach (1838–1916). Their philosophy, which claimed to be scientific, was based on linguistic analysis. They allowed only 2 sorts of statements:

factual ones, which could be verified, and the "analytical" statements of definition used in logic. All ethical and metaphysical statements were ruled out as nonsensical violations of the proper use of language. The most important publications of logical positivism are Schlick's *Allgemeine Erkenntnislehre*, 1918, Wittgenstein's *Tractatus Logico-Philosophicus*, 1921, Carnap's *Logical Syntax of Language*, 1934, and *Language, Truth and Logic*, 1936, by Alfred Jules Ayer (b. 1910), who spread the philosophy in England. Carnap formulated the most radical version of the theory, ruling out as nonsensical not only metaphysics but most of the postulates of science as well. All of the logical positivists have more recently modified their views.

Phenomenology

Phenomenology was developed by Edmund Husserl (1859–1938). He carried forward the "intentional psychology" of his teacher, Franz Brentano (1838–1916), by creating a philosophy which aimed at the description of experience. He did not intend empirically to study consciousness, but rather to examine our perceptions and beliefs from the inside. He wished to study things as they appear in consciousness; whether objectively existing entities or purely imaginary ones was immaterial. His "phenomenological method," the investigator's suspension of belief in the natural world in order to examine his consciousness, has been widely used by existentialists. His major publications include *Logical Investigations*, 1900–1901, *Formal and Transcendental Logic*, 1929, and *Cartesian Meditations*, 1931.

Existentialism

The name existentialism is given to the theories of a widely varied group of philosophers who by no means form a school or agree in all their ideas. In general, existentialists assert the freedom and dignity of man, protesting against deterministic theories which place man at the mercy of mechanical or natural processes. They object to generalizations and to system building, nor do they wish to posit new dogmas, for they insist on the right of the individual to choose to believe and act as he desires. Thus, instead of writing philosophical treatises, some existentialists have preferred to express their ideas through informal essays and fiction. They assert that existence is absurd, for there is no ultimate explanation of why we exist. The existentialist dictum that "existence precedes essence" suggests the necessity for each man to make his own world and find his own meaning in life, rather than to accept traditional beliefs.

Much of existentialist theory was formulated in the late 19th cent., although its impact has been entirely on the 20th. Nietzsche, the Russian novelist Feodor Dostoevski (1821–81—*Notes from the Underground*, 1864), and the Danish religious thinker Søren Kierkegaard (1813–55 —*Concluding Unscientific Postscript*, 1846) were the 1st existentialists. Karl Jaspers (b. 1883) described the dangers to individualism of modern technological society (*Die geistige Situation der Zeit*, 1931). He retained his religious faith, but referred, not to God, but to "transcendence," an unknowable source of being (*Philosophie*, 1932). Martin Heidegger (b. 1889) was a student of Husserl and made use of phenomenology in his philosophy. In *Sein und Zeit*, 1927, he described man as cast into an unsympathetic world in which he tries to achieve purposes which are ultimately rendered meaningless in death. Jean Paul Sartre (b. 1905) described his atheist version of existentialism in the treatise *Being and Nothingness*, 1943; in his plays *The Flies*, 1943, and *No Exit*, 1944; and in the series of novels *Les Chemins de la Liberté* (begun 1946). Both he and Albert Camus (1913– 60—*The Stranger*, 1942; *The Plague*, 1947; *The Fall*, 1956; *The Myth of Sisyphus*, 1942: *The Rebel*, 1959) were profoundly influenced by their experiences during World War II. The defeat of France and the rise of resistance to the Nazis suggested to them the necessity for each individual to take responsibility for his fate. Gabriel Marcel (b. 1889) developed a religious form of existentialism.

Literature

BRITAIN, IRELAND, AND THE COMMONWEALTH

18th Cent.

POETRY. In most of Europe the literature of the 18th cent. was dominated by a classical revival, characterized by a devotion to reason, propriety, balance, and purity of form. The works of antiquity were revered and imitated. In England the outstanding poet of the neoclassical period was Alexander Pope (1688–1744), who welded the heroic couplet into a lethal weapon in a masterful series of satires beginning with *Essay on Criticism,* 1711. Other poets of importance in Pope's time were James Thomson (1700–1748) and John Gay (1685–1732). In the latter half of the century the neoclassical traditions were carried on by Oliver Goldsmith (1728–74), author of *The Deserted Village,* 1770, an attack on industrialization, and Thomas Gray (1716–71), whose *Elegy in a Country Churchyard,* 1751, celebrates rural life. Preromantic strains are discernible in the nature poetry of William Collins (1721–59), the melancholy "graveyard" verse of Edward Young (1683–1765), and the medieval ballads of Thomas Chatterton (1752–70). Also noteworthy in this period were George Crabbe (1754–1832), who offered a harsh, naturalistic view of village life, and Robert Burns (1759–96), the national poet of Scotland, who combined humor and lyricism in such memorable dialect poems as *To a Mouse,* 1785.

PROSE. Among 18th-cent. prose writers Pope's counterpart was Jonathan Swift (1667–1745), whose savage satires (particularly *Gulliver's Travels,* 1726) pilloried human life remorselessly. A more benign spirit ruled in the urbane essays of Joseph Addison (1672–1719), who collaborated with Richard Steele (1672–1729) on the famous journal, the *Spectator,* 1711–12, 1714. After 1750 the reigning sovereign of English letters was Samuel Johnson (1709–84). A powerful Latinate style, a moralistic, somewhat didactic bent, and a sober skepticism informed such great critical works as the *Lives of the Poets,* 1779–81. Other significant figures in the realm of nonfiction prose were James Boswell (1740–95), author of the *Life of Samuel Johnson,* 1791, the historian Edward Gibbon (1737–94), and the statesman Edmund Burke (1729–97).

THE NOVEL. The outstanding literary development of the 18th cent. was the emergence of the modern realistic novel. The chief innovators in this new genre were Daniel Defoe (1660–1731), author of such "autobiographical" histories as *Moll Flanders,* 1722; Samuel Richardson (1689–1761), whose *Clarissa Harlowe,* 1747–48, became the prototypical work of sentimentalism and middle-class morality; and Henry Fielding (1707–54), a bawdy but humane novelist who gave the world one of its great comic masterpieces, *Tom Jones,* 1749. Subsequent practitioners of the novel form included Tobias George Smollett (1721–71), the Gothic horror writer Ann Radcliffe (1764–1823), and the great humorist Laurence Sterne (1713–68).

19th Cent.

ROMANTICISM: POETRY. The romantic era in English literature spanned roughly the first ⅓ of the 19th cent. It represented a rebellion against the Industrial Revolution and a rejection of 18th-cent. neoclassicism. Politically, the romantics favored equality and social justice. Aesthetically, they discarded the principles of reason, propriety, and simplicity of form in favor of intuition, individualism, love of nature, and expansive, highly colored diction. The period began with the appearance of *Lyrical Ballads,* 1798, by William Wordsworth (1770–1850), in whose works nature is glorified as a moral teacher and poetry becomes "the spontaneous overflow of powerful feelings." Wordsworth's friend and collaborator, Samuel Taylor Coleridge (1772–1834), showed his fascination with the supernatural in such haunting, evocative poems as *The Rime of the Ancient Mariner,* 1797–98. Contemporaneously, a love of the past and a gift for narrative verse marked the poetry of Sir Walter Scott (1788–1824). Among the younger generation of romantic poets George Gordon Byron (1788–1824), Percy Bysshe Shelley (1792–1822), and John Keats (1795–1821) were the foremost figures. Byron, a social rebel, ran the gamut from agonized confessions to the great satiric epic *Don Juan,* 1819–24. Shelley declared his Neoplatonist sympathies in such poems as *Prometheus Unbound,* 1820, and *Ode to the West Wind,* 1819. Keats produced a series of rich, sensuous meditations on the nature of beauty, most notably *Ode on a Grecian Urn,* 1820, and *To Autumn,* 1820.

NONFICTION PROSE. Major contributions in nonfiction prose were made by Charles Lamb (1775–1834), whose gentle, humorous essays appeared under the name "Elia"; William Hazlitt (1778–1830), an accomplished stylist and sensitive critic; and Thomas De Quincey, best remembered for his autobiographical *Confessions of an English Opium Eater,* 1821.

THE NOVEL. The leading novelists of the period were Walter Scott, who displayed his impressive gift for historical romance in such works as *Quentin Durward,* 1823, and Jane Austen (1775–1817), the 1st great novelist of manners, whose delicately precise style and fine eye for nuance reached their apex in *Pride and Prejudice,* 1813.

VICTORIANISM: POETRY. The Victorian age is generally thought to have begun with the passage of the Reform Bill of 1832. As a literary era, it is marked by an interest in social reform, a widening breach between science and religion, and an extreme didacticism. In poetry, it produced at least 2 figures of the 1st rank, Alfred Tennyson (1809–92) and Robert Browning (1812–89). Tennyson's lyric poetry achieved a mellifluous, free-flowing beauty, while *Idylls of the King,* 1859, an extended treatment of the Arthurian legend, lamented the moral decay in Victorian society. Cultivating a much rougher poetic line, Browning imitated the fitful movements of the human mind in brilliant dramatic monologues like *Fra Lippo Lippi,* 1855. In contrast to Browning's rugged verse stood the lush postromanticism and medievalism of the Pre-Raphaelite school, particularly Dante Gabriel Rossetti (1828–82) and Algernon Charles Swinburne (1837–1909). Other poets of note in this era were William Morris (1834–96), Elizabeth Barrett (1806–61), the novelist George Meredith, and Matthew Arnold (1822–88), whose *Dover Beach,* 1867, announced the poet's melancholy disillusionment. In the late Victorian period the vigorous, infectiously rhythmical verse of Rudyard Kipling (1865–1936) made him world famous.

NONFICTION PROSE. Nonfiction prose of high distinction was produced by the historian Thomas Babington Macaulay (1800–1859); by Thomas Carlyle (1795–1881), a stern critic of his society; by John Ruskin (1819–1900), whose notions of art were set forth masterfully in *The Stones of Venice,* 1851–53; by John Henry Newman (1801–90), a penetrating religious thinker and eloquent stylist; and by Matthew Arnold, who advanced a classically oriented social criticism in *Culture and Anarchy,* 1869.

THE NOVEL. Victorian fiction soared to extraordinary height with the emergence of Charles Dickens (1812–70). *David Copperfield,* 1849–50, showed its creator's gift for robust characterization, good-natured humor, entertaining melodrama, and the exposure of social abuses. Other Victorian novelists followed Dickens' lead. William Makepeace Thackeray (1811–63) turned his powerful gift of comic irony on fashionable society in *Vanity Fair,* 1847–48. Charles Reade (1814–84) gave English literature one of its greatest historical novels, *The Cloister and the Hearth,* 1861. The Brontë sisters, Charlotte (1816–55) and Emily (1818–48), earned lasting fame with, respectively, *Jane Eyre,* 1847, and *Wuthering Heights,*

1847. George Eliot (pseudonym of Mary Ann Evans, 1819–80) excelled in the realistic depiction of provincial life, a talent best exhibited in *Middlemarch,* 1872. Of slightly less stature, Anthony Trollope (1815–82) also focused his attention on the provinces. More psychological than either Trollope or Eliot, George Meredith (1828–1909) studied the comic aspects of human behavior in *The Ordeal of Richard Feverel,* 1859. Thomas Hardy (1840–1928) sounded a much gloomier note, imparting a bleak, morbidly deterministic mood to such novels as *The Return of the Native,* 1878. The master romanticist among the Victorian novelists was Robert Louis Stevenson (1850–94), who combined romance and psychology in *The Master of Ballantrae,* 1889. Lesser figures in the realm of Victorian fiction include Edward Bulwer-Lytton (1803–73), Benjamin Disraeli (1804–73), and Charles Kingsley (1819–75).

20th Cent.

POETRY. Abandoning his career as a novelist, Thomas Hardy devoted his energies exclusively to poetry after 1895. The morbid determinism and harsh texture of his verse represent a distinct departure from Victorianism. Such a departure was also apparent in the verse of Gerard Manley Hopkins (1844–89), published posthumously in 1918 by the poet's friend and disciple, Robert Bridges (1844–1930). The religious intensity and metrical irregularity of Hopkins' verse appealed to the modern age, and his reputation has grown steadily.

Although somewhat marred by sentimentality, the poetry of A. E. Housman (1859–1936) achieved a classical purity of form and an exquisite precision of phrasing that won him a wide audience. Of slightly less stature were Rupert Brooke (1887–1915) and Wilfred Owen (1893–1918), 2 gifted poets whose careers were cut short by World War I. Numerous schools of poetry sprang up during the war, notably the imagists (an English version of the American movement founded by Amy Lowell), whose most prominent adherents were Richard Ald-

ington (1892–1962) and D. H. Lawrence. Imagism strove to eliminate abstractions from poetry and to employ an impressionistic technique. Concurrent with the imagists was the Georgian school, which sought escape from the unpleasantness of modern life in bucolic settings (*vide* W. H. Davies, 1871–1940).

The 2 most influential poets of the 20th cent. writing in English were the Irishman, William Butler Yeats (1865–1939) and the American-born Thomas Stearns Eliot (1888–1965). Yeats began as a lyric poet of deeply romantic sensibilities, but in the period preceding World War I underwent a period of disillusionment with his former beliefs and thereafter, in works like *Responsibilities,* 1914, his diction grew sparser and the content of his verse more intellectual. Most of his subsequent poetry, relying for philosophical framework on a system expounded in *A Vision,* 1925, showed a profound despair over contemporary life, a continual hardening of style, and a highly recondite symbolism.

In the 1930's a wave of Marxism swept across England, carrying on its crest C. Day Lewis (b. 1904), Stephen Spender (b. 1909), and W. H. Auden (b. 1907). The most important of these was unquestionably Auden, whose marriage of colloquialism and polished literary diction can be seen in poems like "Venus Will Now Say a Few Words," 1930.

Of the poets who achieved prominence in the post–World War II period, Dylan Thomas (1914–53), a master of lush lyricism, was probably the greatest. Other figures of note are Philip Larkin and John Wain.

ESSAYS AND CRITICISM. Predominant in the art of the essay during the Edwardian years, 1901–10, were the fervent Catholic Gilbert Keith Chesterton (1874–1936) and the elegant, urbane Max Beerbohm (1872–1956). In a more revolutionary vein, Herbert George Wells (1866–1946) provided lively and perceptive social criticism, while George Bernard Shaw turned his attention to everything from music criticism to economic problems with the same witty, delightfully imperious results.

FICTION. The naturalistic school of Zola revealed its impact on English writing in the works of George Moore (1852–1933), Arnold Bennett (1867–1931), and John Galsworthy (1867–1933). All 3 relied to a large extent on accurate chronicling of social details. Galsworthy, however, must be singled out for his uniquely evocative style.

The psychological novel found its proponents in Ford Madox Ford (1873–1939) and Joseph Conrad (1857–1924). Both were disciples of Henry James and, less directly, Turgenev. Emphasizing the inner life of his characters, Conrad sought to recreate their elusive experience through the use of flashback, fragmented narrative, and point-of-view techniques, and a heavily impressionistic style. *Lord Jim,* 1900, and *Nostromo,* 1904, are among his best works. Conrad's friend and sympathizer, Ford, employed his own variety of psychological realism, using jumbled time schemes and stream-of-consciousness in such works as *The Good Soldier,* 1915.

The spirit of liberalism that informed the writings of H. G. Wells found a very different spokesman in E. M. Forster (b. 1879). Forster's humane, compassionate temperament can be seen in the anti-imperialistic *A Passage to India,* 1924. Forster was part of a literary set known as the Bloomsbury Group which called for more emphasis on psychological realism. Next to Forster, Bloomsbury's most important writer was Virginia Woolf (1882–1941), whose novels ignored the social and physical side of experience, focusing exclusively on various states of the conscious mind.

However, the writers who broke most sharply with tradition were D. H. Lawrence (1885–1930) and James Joyce (1882–1941), who may be viewed as the 2 opposing poles in modern fiction. Both displayed a far-reaching disenchantment with modern life, but here the similarity ends. Lawrence, a visionary and impassioned primitive, pilloried the scientific and rational spirit of the age. His novels (e.g., *The Rainbow,* 1915, *Women in Love,* 1920) are written in an onrushing, romantic diction that seeks the mystical essence of the novelist's characters. By contrast Joyce's novels reveal a static, formalistic approach. A great innovator, Joyce moved from the lyrical, intensely personal *A Portrait of the Artist as a Young Man,* 1916, to the greater objectivity, intricate symbolism, and stylistic virtuosity of *Ulysses,* 1922, which in effect introduced the stream-of-consciousness method into English literature.

Among other, lesser novelists who felt equally alienated from their society were Aldous Huxley (1894–1963), who wrote a series of bitter, satirical novels on modern life; Evelyn Waugh (1903–66), also a satirist, whose mordant Catholic novels flayed society with a kind of witty cruelty; and Graham Greene (b. 1904), another Catholic, who produced a series of lean, tough novels about human frailty that employ some of the technique and framework of the "thriller."

The art of the short story found its most brilliant exponent in Katherine Mansfield (1888–1923). Miss Mansfield's delicate neurasthenic temperament expressed itself in such stories as "The Garden Party," 1922, where unsatisfied, Chekhovian longings are sketched with great refinement and attention to nuance. Elizabeth Bowen (b. 1899) exhibits a similar sensibility in novels like *The Death of the Heart,* 1938.

Since the end of the 1920's English literature has abandoned its former experimental qualities, emphasizing instead traditional forms of expression, a greater concern for objective reality, and moral consciousness. This is particularly true of the novel, where such figures as C. P. Snow (b. 1905) and Angus Wilson recall the ethical and social awareness of George Eliot. Exceptions to this trend are Iris Murdoch (b. 1919), whose novels often make use of bizarre, almost baroque elements, and Lawrence Durrell (b. 1912), whose lushness of style, exotic settings, and omnipresent symbolism set him off from his contemporaries.

CANADA. The outstanding poetic school in 19th-cent. English-speaking Canada was the "Confederation Group," in which C. D. G. Roberts (1860–1943) and William Bliss Carman (1861–1929) were major figures. Contemporaneously, Canadian fiction produced such writers as John Richardson (1796–1852) and William Kirby. In the 20th cent. Robert Service (1874–1958) became internationally known with his Yukon ballads (e.g., "The Shooting of Dan McGrew"), Stephen Leacock (1869–1944) achieved similar fame for his satires, and novelists Morley Callaghan (b. 1903) and Hugh MacLennan (b. 1907) became familiar to Canadian and non-Canadian readers alike.

AUSTRALIA. The adoption of the "bush idiom" as a literary style in the 1880's gave rise to the 1st uniquely Australian literature, specifically in the bush ballads of Adam Lindsay Gordon (1833–70) and, at the turn of the century, Henry Lawson (1867–1922). Lawson also displayed striking gifts as a short-story writer. In the realm of fiction Lawson is equaled only by the novelist Henry Handel Richardson (pseudonym of Henrietta Richardson, 1870–1946).

UNITED STATES

18th Cent.

POETRY. Though not a period of literary giants, the 18th cent. produced several writers of interest and importance. In Philadelphia a circle of neoclassicists grew up which included Thomas Godfrey (1736–63) and Francis Hopkinson (1737–91). In New England a group known as the "Hartford wits" became famous through the satires and mock epics of John Trumbull (1750–1831) and Joel Barlow (1754–1812). But the finest American poet of this century was the fiery patriot Philip Freneau (1752–1832), who, though an imitator of English verse styles, showed a certain originality in such efforts as the romantic *The Wild Honeysuckle*, 1788.

PROSE. Prose was well in advance of poetry during the 18th cent. William Byrd (1674–1744), a Virginia aristocrat, left behind diaries and several discursive studies of southern life. Benjamin Franklin (1706–90), a jack of all trades and master of many, won fame with his collections of homely maxims (e.g., *Poor Richard's*

Almanack, 1732–57) and his uncompleted *Autobiography* (begun in 1771), the 1st self-portrait by an American. Far from the serene capitalism and cheerfully middle-class ethics of Franklin, Jonathan Edwards (1703–58) revealed a stern Puritan temperament and great intellectual vigor. A fine prose stylist, his best-known work is the sermon *Sinners in the Hands of an Angry God*, 1741, while *The Freedom of the Will*, 1754, shows his consuming interest in philosophy. Other prose writers of note in the 18th cent. were William Bartram (1739–1823), author of travel literature from which Coleridge and Wordsworth borrowed, and Michel Guillaume Jean de Crèvecoeur (pen name J. Hector St. John, 1735–1813), a Frenchman who produced some interesting descriptions of life in America, including the famous essay *What Is An American?* Though not strictly speaking a literary figure, Thomas Paine (1737–1809) showed an impressive command of language in his impassioned political pamphlets (e.g., *Common Sense*, 1776).

19th Cent.

POETRY. In the 19th cent. American poetry came of age. William Cullen Bryant (1794–1878) wrote memorable nature poetry and Edgar Allan Poe (1809–49) superimposed a gloomy melodiousness on his Gothic subject matter. In Boston, Henry Wadsworth Longfellow (1807–82), Oliver Wendell Holmes (1809–94), and James Russell Lowell (1819–91) formed a group of poetically inclined Brahmins. John Greenleaf Whittier (1807–92) won immortality with homespun poems like "Barbara Frietchie." Of considerably greater stature were Emily Dickinson (1830–86), whose brief, fragile lyrics often departed from traditional prosody, and Walt Whitman (1819–92), who wrote a frank, virile free verse that revolutionized American poetry. In the South, Sidney Lanier (1842–81) achieved lasting fame.

FICTION. American fiction as a major force began with the delightful sketches of Washington Irving (1783–1859) and continued through the Leatherstocking frontier novels of James Fenimore

Cooper (1789–1851). In the same period, nonfiction prose of the highest order was written by the transcendentalists Ralph Waldo Emerson (1803–82) and Henry David Thoreau (1817–62). The American novel reached decisive greatness with the somber, guilt-ridden *The Scarlet Letter*, 1850, by Nathaniel Hawthorne (1804–64) and the cosmic whaling saga *Moby Dick*, 1851, by Herman Melville (1819–91). Shortly afterward the great humorist Mark Twain (pseudonym of Samuel Clemens, 1835–1910) proved himself a great novelist too with *The Adventures of Huckleberry Finn*, 1884. Meanwhile tales of local color were supplied by Bret Harte (1836–1902). The realistic novel was officially sponsored by William Dean Howells (1837–1920) and resulted in the psychological realism of Henry James (1843–1916) and the naturalism of Stephen Crane (1871–1900) and Frank Norris (1870–1902). Of these writers James bulks the largest. In *The Portrait of a Lady*, 1884, and *The Ambassadors*, 1902, he emerged as a master of the point-of-view technique, seeking to present the world through the expanding moral awareness of his characters.

20th Cent.

POETRY. American poets in the 20th cent. have produced a staggeringly rich body of work. The trail breaker was Edwin Arlington Robinson (1869–1935), a dry ironist through whose brilliantly chiseled verse blew the bleak winds of New England. Concentrating on the misfits and outcasts of modern life, Robinson painted a gallery of memorable character portraits. Another New Englander, Robert Frost (1874–1963), also broke ground for modern poetry, creating a carefully understated verse that crackled with sly humor and adroit colloquialisms. Outside New England a good deal of poetic activity was concentrated in the imagist school, whose members were H. D. (Hilda Doolittle, 1886–1961), Ezra Pound (b. 1885), and Amy Lowell (1874–1925). The imagists called for a sensuous verse freed of philosophical stuffing and built with clear, concrete images. Although imagism

left few poems of lasting value, it stimulated much experimentation. William Carlos Williams (1883–1963), employing a colloquial idiom and free-verse forms, chose prosaic subject matter and made it poetry. Beginning under the influence of the imagists, Wallace Stevens (1879–1955) went on to establish himself as a preeminent force in American poetry, cultivating an aloof, detached manner, an almost dandiacal elegance of diction, and a kind of neohumanistic philosophy. Coming of age in the 1920's along with Stevens were Marianne Moore (b. 1887), a creator of urbane, precisely worded verse; e. e. cummings (Edward Estlin Cummings, 1894–1962), whose lyrical and witty poems often made use of typographical effects; Harte Crane (1899–1932), who set out to create an epic about America. During this period the 2 most influential of modern American poets also came to the fore, Ezra Pound and T. S. Eliot (1888–1965). Breaking away from the imagists, Pound's poetry began to reflect a new and difficult diction, an interest in the literature of other countries, an antirational bent, and a disgust with modern society (e.g., *Hugh Selwyn Mauberley*, 1920). Eliot shared most of his friend's attitudes; his masterpiece, *The Waste Land*, 1922, is a panoramic view of modern life, heavily symbolic, incorporating numerous passages from other authors and other languages, and attempting to depict the spiritual aridity of the contemporary age. Contemporaneous with Eliot and Pound were the southern poets John Crowe Ransome (b. 1888) and Allen Tate (b. 1899), who developed their own tradition of sophisticated formalism and keen irony. To further enrich the 1st quarter of the century, several minor poets made their mark, among them Edgar Lee Masters (1869–1950), Carl Sandburg (1878–1967), Vachel Lindsay (1879–1931), Robinson Jeffers (1887–1962), Stephen Vincent Benét (1898–1943), and Edna St. Vincent Millay (1892–1950).

The Great Depression of the 1930's stimulated a new proletarian verse, but little of it reached the level of excellence achieved by the preceding generation.

Archibald MacLeish (b. 1892), beginning with an "invocation to the social muse," soon abandoned social themes for a more subjective form of verse. Of those poets 1st heard in the 1930's Muriel Rukeyser (b. 1913) and Louise Bogan (b. 1897) are among the best remembered. Following World War II, a highly introverted "confessional" school of poetry emerged; its best-known member is Robert Lowell (b. 1917). For the most part, postwar poets have been plagued by a growing alienation from the general public and a shrinking market for poems. It has become convenient to divide contemporary poetry into the academics—those poets connected with a university and writing a dry, abstract verse—and the underground poets—practitioners of a wild, unorthodox poetry usually hostile to the intellectual establishment. Theodore Roethke (1908–64) is an example of the 1st school, Allen Ginsberg (b. 1926) of the 2nd.

FICTION. The 20th cent. opened with the publication of *Sister Carrie*, 1900, by Theodore Dreiser (1871–1945); the frank realism and unflagging energy of this and other Dreiser novels compensated for their technical awkwardness. Working in the naturalistic tradition of Frank Norris, Upton Sinclair (1878–1968) published *The Jungle*, 1906, an exposé of the meatpacking industry. More sophisticated criticism of America was provided by the trenchant social satire of Sinclair Lewis (1885–1951), who took aim at the smugness and hypocrisy of the middle class with deadly accuracy. *Main Street*, 1920, and *Babbitt*, 1922, are typical of his better work. Edith Wharton (1862–1937) used the novel of manners to expose the tradition-bound mores and cruel codes of the American aristocracy. Willa Cather (1873–1947), a gifted regionalist, laid bare the greed of the West in *Death Comes for the Archbishop*, 1927. A different kind of realism flowed through the robust adventure stories of Jack London (1876–1916).

But aesthetically speaking, the real revolutionaries were the avant-garde writers who grew up in the 1st 2 decades of the century. Gertrude Stein (1874–1946), enthroned in her Paris salon, reigned as queen of experimental writing. Her influence was felt by such figures as Sherwood Anderson (1876–1941), who employed a bare, unadorned style to chronicle frustrated dreams; John Dos Passos (b. 1896), whose novels presented life in a jumble of narrative, headlines, and "newsreels"; and Ernest Hemingway (1898–1961), perhaps Miss Stein's greatest disciple. Rejecting the traditional forms of literary diction, Hemingway, in works like *The Sun Also Rises*, 1926, developed a lean, economical style aimed at communicating the most powerful feelings in the fewest possible words. The other great spokesman for what Miss Stein called the "lost generation" was F. Scott Fitzgerald (1896–1940), official biographer of the Jazz Age, whose haunting novel *The Great Gatsby*, 1926, expressed both the frenetic vitality of the 1920's and the author's romantic disillusionment.

Also a romantic, William Faulkner (1896–1962) found most of his inspiration in the sweat-soaked life of his native Mississippi, from which he carved a rich microcosm called Yoknapatawpha County. In such novels as *Absalom, Absalom!*, 1938, and *Light in August*, 1935, he portrayed the South as "a land primed for fatality," tragic and decadent, struggling to redeem itself from the curse of slavery.

Under the influence of Joyce and Lawrence, a rash of *Bildungsroman* appeared in America, each evoking the young manhood of its author. The best of these was *Look Homeward, Angel*, 1927, by Thomas Wolfe (1900–1938), a long, loose, ornately styled novel. The 1930's brought a new wave of social realism to literature, of which the Studs Lonigan trilogy by James T. Farrell (b. 1904) is a good example. But the best writer to emerge from this movement was John Steinbeck (1902–68), whose *The Grapes of Wrath*, 1939, stated eloquently the plight of migrant workers in California. A solitary figure during the 1930's was Nathanael West (1902–40), author of 4 short, bitter novels about the various myths and illusions manufactured by contemporary society. Another writer who stood apart from the social realism of the time was Katherine Anne Porter (b. 1890), whose lyrical short stories, written in a stream-of-consciousness style, emphasized psychology and symbolism.

Since World War II proletarian writing has given way to a fiction based on the problems of the individual. Alienation of man from society is a popular theme, appearing in such works as *The Catcher in the Rye*, 1951, by J. D. Salinger (b. 1919), *The Adventures of Augie March*, 1953, by Saul Bellow (b. 1915), and *Invisible Man*, 1952, by Ralph Ellison (b. 1914). The Salinger and Bellow works also indicate a trend toward picaresque plotting and a colloquial, often comic, prose style. In the 1960's "black humor," a type of grotesque satire, developed. *Giles Goat Boy*, 1966, by John Barth (b. 1930), is a prominent example. Simultaneously, Bernard Malamud (b. 1914), author of several brooding novels of Jewish life, found a large popular audience with *The Fixer*, 1966.

FRANCE

18th Cent.

THE ENLIGHTENMENT. For the most part French poetry lay fallow in the 18th cent., though the didactic works of Jacques Delille (1738–1813) showed definite skill, and the fervent verse of André de Chénier (1762–94) anticipated later developments in romantic poetry. The greatest contribution of the French Enlightenment was in the area of social thought, where Montesquieu (Charles de Secondat, 1689–1755) led the way with *L'Esprit des Lois*, 1748, a prodigious and influential study of political institutions. The leading man of letters in this century, however, was unquestionably Voltaire (François Marie Arouet, 1694–1778), whose voluminous output included short verse, epic poems, classical tragedies, essays, and historical works. A champion of reason and an unrelenting opponent of ignorance, intolerance, and outmoded institutions, Voltaire vented his rage most memorably in such satires as *Candide*, 1759, and *L'Ingénue*, 1767. In addition, he was one of the countless intellectuals who contributed to the *Encyclopédie*, 1751–80 (35 vols.), a work of staggering proportions whose aim was nothing less than the systematic organization of all learning. More than anything else it typifies the French Enlightenment, with its fierce confidence in the powers of knowledge and human progress. Others who devoted their time and wisdom to this great work were Denis Diderot (1713–84), Jean d'Alembert (1717?–83), and Claude Adrien Helvétius (1715–71). The most gifted of these was Diderot, whose philosophical essays, critical writings, and the brilliant dialogue *Le Neveu de Rameau*, 1762, have made his reputation secure. In philosophy the dominant figure of the 18th cent. was Jean Jacques Rousseau (1712–78), whose famous attack on society, *Contrat Social*, 1762, trumpeted the cause of the "natural man" and made its author world-famous. In his novel *La Nouvelle Héloise*, 1761, and his renowned *Confessions* the passionate and rebellious Rousseau prefigured the romantic sensibility. In the domain of the novel proper, the outstanding accomplishments of this period were the realistic *La Vie de Marianne*, 1731–41, by Pierre de Marivaux (1688–1763), the psychological *Manon Lescaut*, 1731, by the Abbé Prévost (1697–1763), and the wittily amoral *Les Liaisons dangereuses*, 1782, by Choderlos de Laclos (1741–1803).

19th Cent.

ROMANTICISM. During the Napoleonic era, 2 major literary figures emerged: François René de Chateaubriand (1768–1848) and Mme. de Staël (1766–1817). Chateaubriand eloquently reasserted the traditional Christian values, adopting a highly colored prose that made him known as the father of romanticism. De Staël, very much a daughter of the Enlightenment, defended democratic institutions in a series of critical works and romances. Three transitional figures, the poets Pierre Jean de Béranger (1780–1857) and Alphonse de Lamartine (1790–1869) and the philosopher Hugues Félicité Robert de Lamennais (1782–1854), helped pave the way for the French romantic movement. It arrived torrentially in the 2nd quarter of the century, bringing to the fore Victor Hugo (1802–85), Alfred de Musset (1810–

57), Alfred de Vigny (1797–1863), Théophile Gautier (1811–72), and Gérard de Nerval (pen name of Gérard Labrunie, 1808–55). In both verse and drama these revolutionaries abandoned classical rules in favor of unrestrained emotionalism and florid diction. Hugo, with his astonishing profusion of odes, ballads, and philosophical poetry, was the Promethean figure of this school. Sainte-Beuve (1804–69) was the guiding critical force of romanticism.

PARNASSIANISM AND SYMBOLISM. The transition from romantic to modern poetry was stimulated by Charles Baudelaire (1821–67) in his brilliantly evocative *Fleurs du mal,* 1857, in which the poet dwelt fondly on unsavory, forbidden experiences. In the wake of this work a new school, known as Parnassianism, arose. Led by such former romantics as Gautier and Leconte de Lisle (1818–94), the Parnassians raised the banner of art for art's sake, advocating purity of expression and the subordination of feeling to form. Sully Prudhomme (1839–1907), José María de Heredia (1842–1905), Paul Verlaine (1844–96), and Stéphane Mallarmé (1842–98) were among the young poets attracted to this movement.

Emotionally sterile, Parnassianism soon gave way to symbolism, the foremost practitioners of which were Mallarmé, Verlaine, and Arthur Rimbaud (1854–91). Making extensive use of symbols, these poets groped after strands of mysticism and strove to suffuse their work with the rich, mysterious qualities of music. An all-pervasive suggestiveness was their aim: to express the ineffable. A later phase of symbolism, 1880–85, known as the "decadent period," produced Jules Laforgue (1860–87). The influence of Mallarmé, Verlaine, Rimbaud, and Laforgue on modern poetry throughout the western world has been immense.

FICTION. In fiction the romantics were represented by the inexhaustibly prolific Hugo (*Les Misérables,* 1862); the tormented, introspective Benjamin Constant de Rebecque (1767–1830), author of *Adolphe,* 1815; the inventive Alexandre Dumas (1802–70), creator of such great adventure novels as *Monte Cristo,* 1845;

and the impassioned humanitarian George Sand (pseudonym of Amandine Dupin, Baronne Dudevant, 1804–76). Ranged in opposition to the romantics were great realistic novelists like Honoré de Balzac (1799–1850), Stendhal (pseudonym of Marie Henri Beyle, 1783–1842), and Gustave Flaubert (1821–80). Balzac displayed his withering skepticism and exceptional talent for characterization in the massive series *La Comédie humaine,* novels which explored every stratum of French society. Stendhal depicted the tragic unsuitability of the romantic temperament in post-Napoleonic France in *Le rouge et le noir,* 1831. Flaubert, something of a romantic himself, subordinated this side of his nature to a painstakingly classical style and a realistic point of view; *Madame Bovary,* 1857, is his greatest work. In the last third of the century realism hardened into naturalism, a mode more or less invented by Émile Zola (1840–1902), who sought to transform the novel into a scientific study of man and his environment (e.g., *L'Assommoir,* 1877). Naturalism also produced the outstanding short-story writer of the period, Guy de Maupassant (1850–93), a masterfully controlled craftsman and penetrating observer of human psychology. Alphonse Daudet (1840–97), another naturalist, also made his mark in the short-story form. A *fin-de-siècle* reaction against naturalism produced the ivory-tower aestheticism of J. K. Huysmans (1848–1907), whose most famous work is the influential *À Rebours,* 1884.

20th Cent.

POETRY. Though modern French poetry has not maintained the brilliance of the 19th cent., several figures of great interest have appeared. Chief among these is Paul Valéry (1871–1945), a symbolist who created a highly introverted and self-analytic verse. In the period preceding World War I, Valéry was joined by the Catholic prose poet Paul Claudel (1868–1955) and Charles Péguy (1873–1914), another Catholic, whose work displayed mystical and patriotic strains.

Surrealism, one of the most viable

movements in contemporary French poetry, had its roots in the pre-World War I verse of Guillaume Apollinaire (1880–1918), who attempted to follow the lead of the cubist painters and produce a thoroughly modern, antitraditionalist poetry. The founders of surrealism were André Breton (1896–1966), Paul Éluard (Eugène Grindel, 1895–1952), and Louis Aragon (b. 1897). Freudian psychology had a powerful impact on this new school, which sought to depict the activities of the unconscious mind by presenting experience in a series of disordered, dreamlike images. The interest in preconscious mental states encouraged "automatic writing." In the 1930's the best of the surrealist poets, Aragon and Éluard, abandoned the movement in favor of Marxism.

During World War II the threat of Nazism united the divergent strains in French poetry for a while, and patriotic verse abounded. Following the war, poets maintained their ties with popular sentiments for a time and then returned to a more personal and esoteric manner.

The best of the postwar poets are Pierre Jean Jouve (b. 1887), whose verse is dipped in a deeply felt pessimism; Saint-John Perse (Alexis Saint-Léger Léger, b. 1887), a highly cerebral poet with a disciplined style; and Jules Supervielle (1884–1960), an apostle of simplicity whose main gifts were wit and a sly charm. Also noteworthy in the contemporary period are Jacques Prévert (b. 1900) and René Char (b. 1907).

NONIMAGINATIVE PROSE. The spirit of self-analysis in the French temperament resulted in such autobiographical writings as the famous *Journal* of André Gide (1869–1951), with its lucid, penetrating style. Jules Renard (1864–1910), François Mauriac, and Julian Green issued similar works in this vein. Many novelists also turned their pens to translations, biography, and criticism. Marcel Proust translated John Ruskin's writings; Mauriac brought out a volume of perceptive reflections on his contemporaries; Romain Rolland (1866–1944) produced biographies of Tolstoy and Beethoven. Rolland's work, however, was transcended by an outstanding biographer of the modern period, André Maurois (Émile Herzog, b. 1885), whose studies of Hugo, Proust, and Balzac have won him a high place in French letters.

FICTION. The modern French novel has significantly outpaced the poetry of the period, contributing several Promethean figures. In the ranks of the titans one finds Marcel Proust (1871–1922), whose huge novel cycle, *À la recherche du temps perdu*, 1913–28, has already taken its place as one of the enduring classics of world literature. In this remarkable work Proust analyzes the fashionable society of his time, creating a world of infinite subtlety and nuance and filling it with characters whose lives seem no less genuine to the reader than his own. The governing theory of *À la recherche* is that experience is fully comprehended only when sorted out and scrutinized by memory.

André Gide, another luminary of the post–World War I years, was not a novelist of Proust's stature, but his intriguing fiction (*L'Immoraliste*, 1902) combined with his brilliant *Journal* made him an immortal in his own lifetime. He promulgated a doctrine of radical freedom in which man could free himself from all soul-destroying restraints.

The vogue of the novel cycle continued after the success of Proust's great work with *Les Thibault*, 1922–40, by Martin du Gard (1881–1958), which offers an extended family history. Jules Romains (b. 1885) contributed another such cycle in *Les hommes de bonne volonté*, 1932–47, based on the principle of "unanimism," a theory which held that one underlying factor forms the basis of all human life. The most popular novel cycle of the period (though far from the greatest) was Romain Rolland's *Jean Christophe*, 1904–12, which focuses on a composer of Beethovenesque genius.

World War I produced a substantial body of antiwar literature. The most gifted exponent of this mode was Georges Duhamel (1884–1966), whose *La Vie des Martyrs*, 1917, emphasizes the cruel absurdity of war.

Of the woman writers who appeared in the 1st quarter of the century, the most highly regarded is Colette (Sidonie

Gabrielle Colette, 1873–1954), whose brief, carefully polished stories generally deal with the turbulence of romantic love.

In the 1930's French writing took on an intensely political and social tone. On the left, the proletarian novel found passionate partisans in Charles Plisnier (1897–1952), a Belgian, and Louis Aragon. On the right, Louis Ferdinand Céline (Louis Fuch Destouches, 1894–1961) showed conservative, even fascist, leanings. His most famous work is the bleak *Voyage au bout de la nuit,* 1932.

The modern French short story owes much to the pen of Marcel Aymé (1902–67), whose sardonic humor has made him an international favorite. Others who have worked successfully in this form are Paul Morand (b. 1888) and Jean Cassou (b. 1897).

The working out of human destinies within a Catholic framework became the domain of François Mauriac (b. 1885), who drew his materials from bourgeois life in the provinces. Cultivating a classically pure style, Mauriac regarded the inevitable clash between body and soul with brooding compassion in such brilliant novels as *Thérèse Desqueyroux,* 1927, and *Le Noeud de vipères,* 1932. Second only to Mauriac among the Catholic novelists is Georges Bernanos (1888–1948), who presented the struggle for salvation in the starkest possible terms. His masterpiece is *Journal d'un curé de campagne,* 1936, an episodic study of a young cleric's struggles.

Humanism found its most eloquent voice in André Malraux (b. 1901), a Marxist who showed that he understood the human soul, singly as well as collectively. The best of his ideologically based novels is *La Condition humaine,* 1933. Following World War II Malraux renounced Communism. Also of humanistic leanings, but less political in orientation, Antoine de Saint-Exupéry (1900–1944) sought a transcendent reality in the exaltation of flying, a search beautifully described in *Vol de nuit,* 1932. More memorable, however, is his charming children's fantasy, *Le petit prince,* 1943.

Henry de Montherlant (b. 1896) carried on the traditions of French realism,

exhibiting a keen eye for social problems and a fine command of language. *Les Jeunes Filles,* 1938–39, may be singled out for special praise.

The existentialist school of philosophy, popular in France after 1930, exercised a profound influence on the world of letters. The most famous of the existentialist writers is Jean Paul Sartre (b. 1905), whose bleak view of a meaningless universe in which man must choose his own values is reflected in *La Nausée,* 1938. Simone de Beauvoir (b. 1908), a disciple of Sartre, established her reputation with *L'Invitée,* 1943. Generally associated with the existentialists, Albert Camus (1913–60) expounded his famous theory of an "absurd" universe in works like *L'Étranger,* 1942, in which the author's style is remarkable for its combination of lucidity and lyricism.

After World War II the avant-garde novel came into fashion in France. A revolt against the old forms took place and writers began to experiment with new methods of construction; the result was the so-called antinovel. The chief practitioners of this new mode are Nathalie Sarraute (b. 1900) and Alain Robbe-Grillet (b. 1922). In a lighter vein, the novels of Raymond Queneau (b. 1903) found favor in the 1950's.

CANADA. The most memorable poetry to come out of French-speaking Canada in the 19th cent. was the patriotic verse of Octave Crémazie (1822–79). In fiction, the novel *Les anciens canadiens,* 1863, by Philippe Aubert de Gaspé (1786–1871) was the outstanding work. After the turn of the century symbolist and Parnassian influences became pronounced in French-Canadian poetry; the formalistic verse of Jean Charbonneau is exemplary. Among contemporary novelists of importance are Claude Henry Grignon and Léo Paul Desrosiers (b. 1896).

GERMANY

18th Cent.

CLASSICISM AND STURM UND DRANG. In the early decades of the 18th cent., German classicism, under the leadership of the critic Johann Christoph

Gottsched (1700–1766), instituted a somewhat slavish imitation of French theories. Rebelling against French influence and demanding more room for personal inspiration, F. G. Klopstock (1724–1803) produced a body of ardently patriotic verse. His work helped spark a revival of interest in German antiquity, though no poets of the 1st rank emerged until the arrival of Goethe. Worthy of mention, however, is C. M. Wieland (1733–1813), author of several verse romances and one of the 1st to translate Shakespeare. A major force in the search for a national consciousness was the critic and playwright Gotthold Ephraim Lessing (1729–81), who rejected the French authority and looked instead to England and to classical Greece for aesthetic guidance, adapting both of these cultures to the needs of contemporary Germany. *Laokoon,* 1766, is his best-known critical treatise.

The 4th quarter of the 18th cent. was dominated by 2 movements, *Sturm und Drang* and classicism. The former represented an attempt to throw off the hegemony of rationalism. Radical individualism, *Weltschmertz,* and an emphasis on the primacy of feeling were some of the hallmarks of this new school. Its greatest disciple was Johann Wolfgang von Goethe (1749–1832), whose early lyrics set the tone for all *Sturm und Drang* literature. In fiction, too, it was Goethe's *Die Leiden des jungen Werthers,* 1774, that became the dominant work. It was in dramatic arts, however, that *Sturm und Drang* flourished most impressively. There Goethe was rivaled by Johann Christoph Friedrich von Schiller (1759–1805). The foremost critical spokesman for *Sturm und Drang* was Johann Georg Hamann (1730–88). Wild and undisciplined, the movement soon expended its energies and yielded to the chastening influence of a resurgent classicism, one which combined the old, idealistic yearning and violent individualism with a new sense of duty and control. The aesthetician Johann Gottfried von Herder (1744–1803) enunciated most of the major principles of classicism in his writing, particularly the notion of

Humanität (humanitarianism), which stresses the need of each country for an indigenous literature, one that draws on folklore and tradition. Abandoning *Sturm und Drang,* Goethe and Schiller soon became the leading forces in this classical school with a brilliant outpouring of plays and ballad poetry. In fiction, Goethe loomed equally large, contributing the immortal *Bildungsroman, Wilhelm Meisters Lehrjahre,* 1795–96.

19th Cent.

ROMANTICISM. Near the end of the 18th cent. German romanticism began to emerge, even as classicism was coming into full bloom. Rabid subjectivism, sentimental yearning for the unattainable, and an interest in the supernatural were among the characteristics that marked the romantic movement in Germany. Two separate schools existed, 1 founded in 1798 (in which Johan Ludwig Tieck, 1773–1853, was the leading figure) and 1 in 1804, whose best-known representative was Clemens Brentano (1778–1842).

After 1809 romanticism as an organized movement ceased to exist, although it survived in such solitary geniuses as Heinrich von Kleist (1777–1811), the Prussian dramatist and short-story writer, and the novelist E. T. A. Hoffmann (1776–1822). At the same time the classicism of Goethe burst powerfully on the world in *Faust,* Part I, 1808. Part II, 1832, brought the poet's powers to their apex.

In lyric poetry the 2 foremost names after 1835 were Eduard Mörike (1804–75) and Heinrich Heine (1797–1856). Heine was the leader of a movement known as "Young Germany," which lodged vigorous protests, literary and political, against the old order.

FICTION. After the death of Heine, German fiction began to outstrip poetry. A realistic regionalism appeared in such writers as Adalbert Stifter (1805–68), Gottfried Keller (1819–90), and Theodor Storm (1817–88).

Writers of a somewhat different stamp were the antibourgeois Wilhelm Raabe (1831–1910); Conrad Ferdinand Mayer (1825–98), author of several historical

Novellen; and Theodore Fontane (1819–98), who focused on social problems. Naturalism made itself felt at the end of the century in the poetry of Arno Holz (1863–1929) and the prose of Wilhelm von Polenz (1861–1903).

20th Cent.

POETRY. Germany's 1st major poet after the turn of the century was Stefan George (1868–1933), champion of aestheticism. His formalistic and somewhat esoteric verse shows him to be a descendant of the French symbolists. At the same time a spirit of classical control hovers over his poetry. A poet of equal delicacy, Hugo von Hofmannsthal (1874–1929) created a small but striking body of lyric poetry. Introspection and a sense of the evanescence of human experience dominate his verse.

The outstanding German poet of the modern period is Rainer Maria Rilke (1875–1926). A hypersensitive temperament is apparent throughout his work and also a strong lyrical impulse. Spiritual dilemmas generally form the subject matter of his poetry; an onrushing, almost rhapsodic flow of verse carries him through these dilemmas. World War I had a deadening effect on Rilke's creativity, but in 1922 his inspiration reawakened triumphantly, and he completed the *Duineser Elegien* and *Sonette an Orpheus.*

Another rich vein of poetic activity was the expressionist school, which called for a rebellion against traditional values and the materialism of modern Germany. Revolted by what they saw, the expressionist poets turned inward, attempting to depict states of mind in place of external reality. In their poems the logical structure is suppressed and bizarre images often predominate. The key figures in expressionist poetry were Georg Heym (1887–1912), Georg Trakl (1887–1914), Ernst Stadler (1883–1914), Heinrich Lersch (1889–1936), and Gottfried Benn (1886–1956).

The 3rd Reich brutally interrupted the development of modern literature in Germany. But following World War II a new group of poets appeared. Günter Eich (b. 1907) and Paul Celan (b. 1920)

reflect the shock and despair of postwar Germany in their deliberately fragmented, disconnected verse. Wilhelm Lehman (b. 1882), though belonging to an older generation, came into prominence after the war. Peter Huchel (b. 1903) has shown a gift for verse dealing with rustic life.

FICTION. At the turn of the century Vienna was one of the great cultural centers of Europe. Among the writers it nurtured was Arthur Schnitzler (1862–1931), a trenchant analyst of character and manners in the upper layers of Viennese society. A sharp sense of irony tempered his impressionistic portraits in such stories as *Die griechische Tänzerin,* 1904. Another astute critic of Austrian life was Robert Musil (1880–1942), whose massive novel *Der Mann ohne Eigenschaften,* 1930–43, recognized only after World War II, became 1 of the most highly regarded works of modern German literature.

The greatness of Rilke is counterbalanced in the novel by that of Thomas Mann (1875–1955). Influenced by Wagner and the symbolist movement, Mann interlaced his works with myths, leitmotifs, and symbols. His subject matter was usually the German *bourgeoisie,* whose decadence he portrayed with unparalleled profundity in his 1st great work, *Buddenbrooks,* 1901. A philosophical tone predominates in Mann's works, especially in his masterpiece *Der Zauberberg,* 1924.

Mann's older brother Heinrich (1871–1950) was a more outspoken critic of specific social and political corruptions. Later he exhibited a gift for the historical novel. By contrast the mystical, impressionistic works of Hermann Hesse (1877–1962) explored the interior life of man (e.g., *Demian,* 1919).

The expressionist movement had ramifications in the domain of fiction, whereas in poetry it dealt with alienation and sought to depict mental states. Though he later abandoned expressionism, Franz Werfel's (1890–1945) early works reveal the impact of this vital school. Simultaneously, however, a far greater novelist was at work. Franz Kafka (1883–1924) successfully objectified a series of frightening neuroses in his novels and stories, and described his painful isolation from the world of ordinary men. Guilt and anxiety are the ruling moods in Kafka's world, where large inscrutable institutions torment people for unstated offenses. In novels like *Der Prozess*, 1925, reality is distorted systematically, and the characters find themselves trying to deal rationally with an irrational universe.

German fiction became more objective during the 1920's with the founding of a movement called *Die neue Sachlichkeit*. Out of this school came Arnold Zweig (b. 1887), Erich Maria Remarque (b. 1898), and Hans Fallada (1893–1947). But technical innovation did not cease. Stream-of-consciousness was employed successfully in the novels of Hermann Broch (1886–1951), especially *Das Tod des Vergil*, 1945.

Since World War II literary activity has been heavy. Wolfgang Borchert (1921–1947) depicted the chaos and pessimism of postwar life. Max Frisch (b. 1911), a Swiss, Heinrich Böll (b. 1917), Günter Grass (b. 1927), and Uwe Johnson (b. 1934) are others who have made names for themselves in the field of the modern novel.

RUSSIA

18th and 19th Cents.

18TH CENT. Relatively little writing of the 1st rank was produced in Russia during the 18th cent., a period during which German, French, and English models were imitated shamelessly. Among those who showed some degree of originality were Mikhail Lomonosov (1711–65), a ground-breaking critic and poet; Gavriil Derzhavin (1743–1816), author of several remarkable odes; and Alexander Radishchev (1749–1802), whose work of social criticism, *Journey from St. Petersburg to Moscow*, 1790, marks the beginning of revolutionary literature in Russia. Also noteworthy were Nikolai Karamazin (1766–1826), who introduced numerous linguistic reforms and left some memorable fiction. Two of Karamazin's disciples, Vasili Zhukovski (1783–1852) and Konstantin Batzushkov (1787–1855), won fame as poets.

19TH CENT. The 1st great literary figure in Russian history was Alexander Pushkin (1799–1837), whose vigorous and original genius expressed itself in dramatic narratives, folk tales, and the great verse novel *Evgeni Onegin*, 1836. Second only to Pushkin during this era was Mikhail Lermontov (1814–41), a lyric poet of great distinction, while the metaphysical poetry of Fyodor Tyutchev (1803–73) made him another major figure.

In the 2nd half of the century a symbolist movement appeared in reaction against the dominance of realism in Russian letters that developed after 1850. Alexander A. Blok (1880–1921) was the leading figure of this movement.

In fiction, Lermontov, though chiefly a poet, nevertheless succeeded in giving Russia one of its 1st important novels, *A Hero of Our Times*, 1840. But the finest fiction of the period 1800–1850 was written by Nikolai V. Gogol (1809–52), a realist whose satires of provincial life reached their culmination in *Dead Souls*, 1842. Following Gogol's lead, Ivan A. Goncharov (1812–91) created one of Russia's great classics of realism, *Oblomov*, 1858.

From the 1850's onward, 3 extraordinary giants divide the laurels of Russian fiction. Ivan Turgenev (1818–83) carried on the traditions of Pushkin and Gogol in such triumphs of irony and compassion as *A Sportsman's Sketches*, 1847–52. Feodor Dostoevski (1821–81) de-emphasized the importance of external reality and concentrated on the spiritual and psychological turbulence of his characters. *The Brothers Karamazov*, 1880, is his masterpiece. Count Lyev Tolstoy (1828–1910) showed his broad human sympathies and his profound sense of historical movement in the great classic of world literature, *War and Peace*, 1869.

The outstanding master of the short-story form during the 19th cent. was Anton Chekhov (1860–1904), whose gently ironic tales undercut the hopeless dreams of their characters. Maxim Gorky (1868–1936), exponent of social realism, made his mark before the Revolution as a novelist and playwright, and went on to become a leading literary figure in the later Soviet state.

20th Cent.

POSTREVOLUTIONARY LITERATURE. After the Revolution a vigorous control over literary activity was exercised by the government, and literature was expected to reflect official Soviet values: confidence in Communism, love of the proletariat, and the importance of communal action.

POETRY. The new Marxist aesthetic produced poetic propagandists for the most part, but one figure, Vladimir Mayakovski (1884–1930), exhibited genuine poetic gifts. He was part of a "futurist" movement, which called for the abolition of all literary traditions and the creation of a new Soviet literature. He himself celebrated the Revolution and the Russian people in a highly colloquial free verse. The best of Mayakovski's numerous disciples is Nikolai Aseyev (b. 1889).

Although the majority of poets expressed the philosophy of the state, a few turned instead to subjective concerns. Chief among these, and perhaps the greatest Russian poet of the 20th cent., was Boris L. Pasternak (1890–1960). Pasternak began as a futurist, and produced 2 long narrative poems on social themes, but his natural tendencies carried him toward the lyric, where nature, religion, individualism, and eternal human values were the focus of his attention. Stylistically, Pasternak's poetry is unorthodox, but powerful rhythmic and melodic qualities are present. It has often been accused of obscurity by Soviet critics. Nikolai Tikhonov (b. 1896), another poet of independent temperament, mixed romance and realism in his multivarious outpouring of tales, ballads, and lyrics.

After the death of Stalin, the government's rigid control over literary activity was somewhat relaxed, and 2 highly individualistic poets, Yevgeny Yevtushenko (b. 1933) and André Voznesensky (b. 1931) appeared. In the late 1960's poets

and other creative writers found rather rigid controls re-imposed.

FICTION. Fiction under the Soviet regime has concentrated on social realism and is often marred by too blatant propaganda. At the same time, however, the influence of Russia's 19th-cent. masters has not been entirely obliterated. The spirit of Dostoevski is present in the writings of Leonid M. Leonov (b. 1899), who emphasizes character development (e.g., *The Thief,* 1927), and a Chekhovian tone pervades the fiction of Konstantin A. Fedin (b. 1892). Similarly, the novels of Aleksandr A. Fadayev (1901–56) reflect the influence of Tolstoy. Seeking to bridge the gap between the Russian masters and the new social realism, A. N. Tolstoy (1883–1945) wrote his memorable novel *The Road to Calvary,* 1920, the events of which span the pre- and postrevolutionary periods. Also noteworthy is the novelist Isaac Babel (b. 1894).

The writer who best succeeded in adapting the art of the novel to the demands of proletarian writing was Mikhail Sholokhov (b. 1905), whose 2 great works, *And Quiet Flows the Don,* 1940, and *The Don Flows Home to the Sea,* 1941, are epic novels of Russian life which display a skillful, Tolstoyan balance between panorama and character delineation.

In spite of the Marxist edict that literature must follow the party line, satires of Communist life have been permitted over the years, most notably in the case of E. I. Zamyatin (1884–1937), whose stories exposed the follies of bureaucracy. However, his extraordinary novel, *We,* 1924, was considered too subversive and was banned. Ilya Ehrenburg (b. 1891) and Mikhail Zoshenko (1895–1958) are 2 other writers who have worked well in the satirical manner.

The most famous Russian novel of modern times is undoubtedly *Doctor Zhivago,* 1955, by Boris Pasternak. This is a long, richly drawn work about the life of a young poet and doctor who witnesses the Revolution and its aftermath. The book was banned in Russia because of its implied criticism of Communism. Nevertheless, the period of de-Stalinization in Russia had at least made it possible to attack the abuses of the Stalin era, as can be seen in the famous *One Day in the Life of Ivan Denisovich,* 1962, by Aleksandr I. Solzhenitsyn (b. 1918).

ITALY

18th and 19th Cents.

18TH CENT. In the 1st half of the 18th cent. the Arcadians, a highly academic school of poets, held sway in Italy. The verse dramas of Metastasio (Pietro Trapassi, 1698–1782) were the finest products of Arcadianism. After 1750 a reaction against the aridity of the Arcadians brought the vigorous Sicilian Giovanni Meli (1740–1815) to the fore. Also crucial to the literary revival of this period was the cultural historian, Giovanni Battista Vico (1668–1744). A healthy, viable neoclassicism appeared in the odes of Giuseppe Parini (1729–99) and in the balanced, well-ordered verse of Vincenzo Monti (1754–1828).

Toward the end of the 18th cent. a new spirit of romanticism began to express itself. It is particularly evident in the poetry of Ugo Foscolo (1778–1827), which blends deeply felt patriotism, classical harmony, and romantic pessimism.

19TH CENT. In the 1st half of the 19th cent. the romantic and classical schools overlapped. The towering giant of Italian classicism was Giacomo Leopardi (1798–1837), whose lyrical poetry expressed in a lucid, masterfully controlled style a profound sadness over man's fate.

Alessandro Manzoni (1785–1873) was the leader of the romantic school in Italy. He is best known for *I promessi sposi,* 1825–26. Romanticism was closely allied with the *Risorgimento,* and the patriotic impulse was passionately indulged by writers like Giuseppe Mazzini (1805–72) and Francesco De Sanctis (1817–83).

In the latter part of the 19th cent. romanticism was abandoned and realism became the dominant trend. Among the poets Giosuè Carducci (1835–1907) reflected this new outlook, combining it with a revived classicism. But in prose, realism tended to be regionalism. The greatest prose writer of the period was the novelist Giovanni Verga (1840–1922).

20th Cent.

POETRY. Italian literature of the early 20th cent. gave the world of letters one of its most glamorous figures, Gabriele D'Annunzio (1863–1938), whose romantic verse sweeps the reader exultantly from nature to nationalism to self-glorification. Elsewhere in Italian poetry of the period, 2 major schools were discernible: the *"crepuscolare"* poets (e.g., Guido Gozzano, 1883–1916), who adopted a disenchanted malaise as their basic attitude, and the futurists (e.g., Filippo Marinetti, 1876–1944), who denounced all literary tradition and pursued a dynamic and violent modernism in their poetry.

During the Mussolini years the "hermetic" school came into the forefront, advocating a dry, abstract formalism (e.g., Giuseppe Ungaretti, b. 1888). Since World War II the futurist school has yielded to a more realistic approach, and Italian poetry has become more responsive to political and social forces.

PROSE. Though not strictly speaking creative authors, Benedetto Croce (1866–1952) and Giovanni Gentile (1875–1944) made enormous contributions to Italian literature. With the publication of *Estetica,* 1902, Croce established himself as one of the most influential aestheticians of the century. Gentile, one of Croce's disciples, produced several impressive studies of Italian authors.

In fiction the poet D'Annunzio was active, but without much distinction. More important work issued from such figures as Grazia Deledda (1875–1936), who faithfully recorded the way of life in Sardinia, and Alfredo Panzini (1863–1939), who cultivated a fine-drawn irony blended with precision of style. Of the writers who came into prominence during the Fascist era, the most unusual was Italo Svevo (pseudonym of Ettore Schmitz, 1864–1928), whose novel *La Coscienza di Zeno,* 1923, has gained an international audience. The novel of social protest found an able practitioner in Ignazio Silone (pseudonym of Secondo Tranquilli, b. 1900), whose anti-Fascist left-wing sympathies were set forth in *Pane e vino*, 1937.

After World War II a striking revival took place in Italian fiction. Cesare Pavese (1908–50) and Elio Vittorini (b. 1908) led the way with several vigorous, neorealistic novels. They were soon followed by Vasco Pratolini (b. 1913), who re-created working-class life with accuracy and compassion. Carlo Levi (b. 1902) extended his reputation far beyond Italy with *Cristo si è fermato a Evoli*, 1945. The postwar novelist of greatest renown, however, is Alberto Moravia (pseudonym of Alberto Pincherle, b. 1907), whose novels are marked by a cold, analytical detachment and well-realized sense of ennui.

SPAIN AND PORTUGAL

18TH CENT. A time of great intellectual awakening in Spain, the 18th cent. produced such enlightened critical forces as Ignacio de Luzán Claramunt (1702–54) and Benito Jerónimo Feijóo y Montenegro (1676–1764), both products of the French Enlightenment. In opposition to these rationalist and humanistic tendencies stood the truculently reactionary scholastic, Juan Pablo Forner (1756–97).

19TH CENT. Romanticism burgeoned briefly (and belatedly) in Spain, giving the country 1 important poet, José de Espronceda y Delgado (1808–42), but no novelists of the 1st rank. However, the fierce subjectivism and individuality of romantic poetry paved the way for the more enduring verse of Gustavo Adolfo Bécquer (1836–70) and Gaspar Núñez de Arce (1834–1903).

The growth of the Spanish novel was linked with regionalism. The greatest example of this tradition was José Maria de Pereda (1833–1906), whose novels chronicled the life of his native Santander with extraordinary verisimilitude and richness. In the next generation Emilia Pardo Bazán (1852–1921) carried realism

to naturalism in her studies of Galicia. Standing apart from regionalism and naturalism alike, Benito Pérez Galdós (1843–1920) gave his novels a broader scope, treating the entire Spanish nation and its recent history in a prolific flow of novels.

20TH CENT. Modern Spanish literature began with the "generation of 1898," which sought to rehabilitate a demoralized country. Among the poets of this period were the Andalusians Juan Ramón Jiménez (1881–1958) and Antonio Machado Ruiz (1875–1939). The subsequent generation, however, produced the best-known Spanish poet of this century, Federico García Lorca (1899–1936), whose lyrical verse draws heavily on the rhythms and themes of folk ballads. The surrealist poet Vicente Aleixandre (b. 1900) also produced much work of merit.

In prose the greatest spokesman for the generation of 1898 was the philosopher and essayist Miguel de Unamuno y Jugo (1864–1936). His influence on contemporary thought was rivaled only by José Martínez Ruiz (b. 1874) and José Ortega y Gasset (1883–1955). Among novelists of this generation, the outstanding figures are Pío Baroja y Nessi (1872–1956), a vigorous master of picaresque adventure; Ramón de Valle Inclán (1870–1936), an eclectic and imaginative writer; Ramón Pérez de Ayala (b. 1881), a satirical novelist; Gabriel Miró Ferrer (1879–1930), a creator of mystical, dreamy romances; and Vicente Blasco Ibáñez (1867–1928), whose novel *The Four Horsemen of the Apocalypse*, 1918, made him world-famous. Among the more prominent younger novelists is Camilo José Cela (b. 1916).

PORTUGAL. Dominating the 1st half of the 19th cent., Portuguese romanticism produced the poetry of Almeida Garrett (1799–1854) and the novels of Camilo Castello-Branco (1826–90). A rebellious movement known as the "Coimbra Group" and led by the poet Antero de Quental (1842–91) ruled the 2nd half of the century. Camilo Pessanha (1871–1926), a deeply subjective poet, and Aquilino Ribeiro (1879–1941), a skillful novelist, are 2 of the many figures who have emerged since 1900.

LATIN AMERICA

18th Cent.

CULTERANISMO AND NEOCLAS-SICISM. A classical movement took hold of Latin American letters in the 18th cent. with generally stultifying results. Numerous poets wrote exclusively in Latin, and a new term, *culteranismo,* was coined to describe their pomposities of style. But in the 2nd half of the century the currents of neoclassicism, emanating mainly from France, had an invigorating effect, and social critics began to appear. The most gifted of them were the Peruvian Pablo de Olavide (1725–1804), the Ecuadorian Francisco Eugenio de Santa Cruz Espejo (1747–95), and the Mexican Fray Servando Teresa de Mier (1765–1827). The only poet of note in this era was the bucolic Mexican, Manuel de Navarrete (1768–1809).

19th Cent.

ROMANTICISM. For 70 years following their emancipation the Latin American nations produced a literature of romanticism in which strong nationalistic sentiments predominated. The Argentine poet Esteban Echeverría (1809–51) is generally considered to have inaugurated this movement. Among the many Argentine poets who joined it were Olegario Víctor Andrade (1841–82) and Rafael Obligado (1851–1920). Elsewhere in South America romanticism begot an equally popular school of poetry; its members included the Chilean Salvador Sanfuentes (1817–60), the Bolivian Adela Zamudio (1854–1928), the Uruguyan Juan Carlos Gómez (1820–84), and the Mexican Fernando Calderón (1809–45).

Romanticism permeated the fiction of the 19th cent. as fully as it did the poetry, beginning in Mexico with José Joaquín Fernández de Lizardi (1776–1827) and continuing in Argentina with José Mármol (1817–71). Other novelists of a romantic stamp were the Uruguayan

Alejandro Magariños Cervantes (1825–93), the Ecuadorian Juan León Mera (1832–94), and the Colombian Jorge Isaacs (1837–95), author of the most famous novel in Latin American history, *María,* 1867. But the most impressive of the romantic writers was the Argentinian Domingo Faustino Sarmiento (1811–88).

The inevitable reaction against romanticism came in 1888 with the publication of *Azul,* a brilliant and influential book of poems by the Nicaraguan Rubén Darío (Félix Rubén García Sarmiento, 1867–1916). The influence of French symbolism and Parnassianism pervaded these rich, exotic poems.

BRAZIL. In Portuguese-speaking Brazil, 19th-cent. literature followed a predictably similar course to that of the other Latin American states. The period of romanticism issued in the patriotic verse of Domingos José Gonçalves de Magalhães (1811–82) and Antônio Gonçalves Dias (1823–64). In the 1880's romanticism gave way to Parnassianism and such ivory-tower "formalists" as Raimundo Correia (1860–1911) and Olavo Bilac (1865–1918) took over the leadership of Brazilian poetry.

A moreninha, by Joaquim Manuel de Macedo (1820–82), is considered to be the 1st Brazilian novel. But the 1st work of literary importance is *Memórias de um sargento de milícias,* 1854, by Manuel Antônio de Almeida (1830–61). The next step forward came with the cyclic novels of José Martiniano de Alencar (1829–77). These stages of development culminated in Joaquim Maria Machado de Assis (1839–1908), the greatest of all Brazilian novelists. Toward the end of the century, social realism made its appearance in the works of Aluízio Gonçalves de Azevedo (1857–1913) and others.

20th Cent.

MODERNISM. The modernism of Rubén Darío continued to dominate Latin American literature after the turn of the century. Among Darío's disciples were the Argentinian Leopoldo Lugones (1874–1938), the Colombian Guillermo Valencia (1873–1943), and the Mexican

Amado Nervo (1870–1919). However, Darío, who remained nominal leader of the modernist school, began to move away from it, returning to traditional forms and more humanistic concerns. At the same time, some of his followers, notably Lugones and Nervo, had passed into new phases of modernism. Perpetuating the earlier symbolist phase of *modernismo* was, among others, a group of women poets that included the Nobel prize winner, Gabriela Mistral (Lucila Godoy Alcayaga, 1889–1957), and Delmira Agustini (1887–1914). Also direct descendants of modernism were the Mexican Ramón López Velarde (1888–1921), a lyric poet; the Guatemalan Rafael Arévalo Martínez (b. 1884), a mystic; and the Cuban Nicolás Guillén (b. 1904), who made effective use of native techniques and rhythms in his verse.

VANGUARD MOVEMENT. After 1910 a general break with modernism took place. Mexico's Enrique González Martínez (1871–1952) and Uruguay's Julio Herrera y Reissig (1875–1910) struck out on their own, setting new styles and experimenting with new techniques. Along with Darío, Lugones, and Nervo, they anticipated the next move in Latin American letters, vanguard literature. Born of the nihilistic disillusionment that followed World War I and bred by the general turbulence of political and social institutions in South America, the vanguard movement espoused radical experimentation. Free verse, new forms, startling images, bizarre syntax—these were a few of the things the new literary rebels advocated. *Ultraistas* was the name given to these poets and writers, the most prominent of whom were César Vallejo (1895–1938) of Peru, Jorge Luis Borges (b. 1900) of Argentina, and Pablo Neruda (b. 1904) of Chile. The latter, creating verse of uniformly high quality and ranging from neoromanticism to surrealism, has established himself as the greatest of modern South American poets.

PROTEST LITERATURE. The political and social turmoil of Latin America ensured the primacy of social protest in the novel. The precursors of modern fiction were Chile's Baldomero Lillo (1867–1923) and Mexico's Federico Gamboa (1864–1939), naturalists in the Zola tradition. Later, somewhat more sophisticated writers emerged, including Mariano Azuela (1873–1952) of Mexico, whose *Los de abajo,* 1915, is a penetrating study of the Mexican Revolution, and José Rubén Romero (1890–1952), another Mexican. The passionate concern with social conditions swelled the growing *indianista* literature, a body of work dating from the 19th cent., which exposed the terrible plight of the Latin American Indian. In their novels and stories the Peruvian Enrique Lopez Albujar (b. 1872), the Bolivian Alcides Argüedas (1879–1946), and the Ecuadorian Jorge Icaza (b. 1906) took up the Indian's cause.

The painful process of modernization served as an additional spur to social and economic commentary. The inevitable abrasion between modern dynamism and old, settled ways was ably reflected in the fiction of the Argentinians Benito Lynch (1885–1952) and Ricardo Guiraldes (1886–1927), and of the Uruguayan Javier de Viana (1872–1927). The problems of urban life were examined in the memorable writings of Argentina's Manuel Gálvez (b. 1882) and Chile's Manuel Rojas (b. 1896) and Eduardo Barrios (b. 1884). While men sought to exploit the natural resources of Latin America in arid plain and dense jungle, the struggle was recorded by Horacio Quiroga (1878–1937) of Uruguay and José Eustasio Rivera (1889–1928) of Colombia.

Nor has the psychological novel been absent from Latin America, as the works of María Luisa Bombal (b. 1910) bear witness. At the same time, historical fiction found a skilled exponent in Enrique Rodríguez Larveta (1875–1961), and powerful social criticism has flowed from the pen of the Nobel prize winner, Miguel Asturias.

BRAZIL. In Brazil modern literary developments paralleled those of Spanish America with only a few exceptions. Poets like Bilac and Alberto de Oliveira (1857–1937) perpetuated the escapist tendencies of symbolism and Parnassianism after the turn of the century. But in 1922 came the Brazilian version of vanguard writing.

The *modernistas,* as the avant-garde authors were termed, proclaimed their revolt against tradition. The standard-bearer of revolution among poets was Mario de Andrade (1893–1945). Other *modernistas* of distinction were Manuel Bandeira (b. 1886) and Jorge de Lima (1898–1953). More recently, Vinícius de Morais (b. 1913) has come to the fore.

Brazilian prose in this century began on a high level with Euclides da Cunha (1866–1909), whose epic work *Os sertões,* 1902, set the tone for the protest writing that was to come. Regionalism and a search for native subject matter resulted in the "Northeastern school" of the 1930's, which focused on the problems of the Brazilian backlands. Among the key figures in this school were José Lins do Rego (1901–57), whose great "sugar cane" novel cycle has already become a classic, and Jorge Amado (b. 1912), a Marxist of almost hypnotic power. Departing from this general trend, the cosmopolitan and experimental Erico Veríssimo (b. 1905) has concentrated on the individual and his problems.

SCANDINAVIA

Sweden

18TH CENT. Voltaire's classicism and Rousseau's idealism were the major forces in 18th-cent. Swedish literature. The classical temper is evident in the satirical poetry of Olof von Dalin (1708–63), while Rousseau's influence is equally pervasive in the prose of Thomas Thorild (1759–1808). Standing apart from these trends were the lyric poet Carl Michael Bellman (1740–95), the philosopher Emanuel Swedenborg (1688–1772), and the scientist Carl von Linné (Linnaeus, 1707–78), whose travel books are remarkable for their lucid prose style.

19TH CENT. In Sweden the 1st half of the 19th cent. was dominated by romanticism, a movement in which the poet Per Daniel Amadeus Atterbom (1790–1855) and the critic Esaias Tegnér (1782–1846) were 2 of the leaders. The period from 1850 to 1875 witnessed the growth of realism in such writers as Fredrika

Bremer (1801–65) and, with the appearance of the great playwright August Strindberg, realism became naturalism. In the 1880's, however, a sharp reaction against naturalism resulted in a brilliant group of neoromantic writers that included Selma Lagerlöf (1858–1940) and Verner von Heidenstam (1859–1940).

20TH CENT. In the 20th cent. Sweden's realistic traditions re-emerged with such vigorous talents as Hjalmar Söderberg (1869–1941) and Hjalmar Bergman (1883–1930); the latter was a gifted psychological novelist who anticipated Sweden's greatest literary figure of this century, Pär Lagerkvist (b. 1891). Poet, playwright, and novelist, Lagerkvist portrays the spiritual crises of modern man unforgettably, though there is also a political strain in his works. The gifted poet Birger Sjölberg (1885–1929) was one of his followers.

The influence of American writers, especially Ernest Hemingway, resulted in a group called "The Young Five," of which the most important members were Artur Lundkvist (b. 1906) and Harry Martinson (b. 1904). Of equal importance are Eyvind Johnson (b. 1900), a realist who recorded the abuses of the industrial system, and Agnes von Krusenstierna (1894–1940), whose novels examined sexual problems with great sensitivity. Since World War II the interest in realism has grown even stronger.

Norway

18TH CENT. Due to the political unity that existed between Denmark and Norway in the 18th cent., a Dano-Norwegian culture developed, in which the outstanding figure was Ludvig Holberg (1684–1754), poet, essayist, and playwright. Simultaneously, a separatist movement spawned such poets as Jens Zetlitz (1761–1821) and Johan Nordahl Brun (1745–1816).

19TH CENT. Gaining its independence from Denmark in 1814, Norway sought a national consciousness. This search is reflected in the great romantic poet Henrik Arnold Wergeland (1808–45), from whose work a massive folk tale and ballad revival issued. At the same time, 1850–80, European realism was on the rise and these 2 forces combined to produce the fierce social protest of Henrik Ibsen and Björnstjerne Björnson (1832–1910), playwright, novelist, and poet. But the 1890's brought a revolt against realism in such neoromantic figures as Knut Hamsun (1859–1952).

20TH CENT. In modern Norway the "epic," a long series of novels about a particular region or family, became the dominant literary trend. The 1st of the epicists was Johan Bojer (1872–1959), who glorified the Norwegian fishermen. He was followed by Knut Hamsun, who, abandoning romanticism, began to write in this new mode. But the 2 greatest epic writers were Sigrid Undset (1882–1949), whose novels probed the role of women in the modern world, and Olav Duun (1876–1939), who concentrated on country life.

The best poets of this generation were Olav Bull (1883–1933) and Arnulf Överland (b. 1889), the former a charming lyricist, the latter a passionate, patriotic leftist. Överland's verse set the tone for the literature of the 1930's, which dwelt heavily on anti-Fascist themes. After World War II the best writings produced in Norway were reminiscences and accounts of the war.

Denmark

18TH CENT. During the 1st half of the 18th cent. lyric poetry of a high order flowed from H. A. Bronson (1694–1764) and Ambrosius Stub (1705–58). Both were surpassed, however, by Johannes Eurald (1743–81), whose verse exploited Scandinavian folklore extensively. Contemporaneously, the humorist Johann Herman Wessel (1742–85) created a striking body of satirical plays, poems, and stories.

19TH CENT. Like most of Europe, Denmark experienced a romantic period in the 1st half of the 19th cent., and a subsequent upsurge of realism after 1850. The best-known products of Danish romanticism are Hans Christian Andersen (1805–75) and Søren Kierkegaard (1813–55), while the famous critic, Georg Brandes (1842–1927), was the acknowledged leader of the realist movement.

20TH CENT. The outstanding Danish poets in the pre-World War I era were Johannes V. Jensen (1873–1950) and Jeppe Aakjaer (1866–1930), both masters of lyric verse. In the interwar period Tom Kristensen (b. 1893), Harald Bergstedt (b. 1877), and Nis Petersen (1897–1943) emerged as major poets. Influenced by the French symbolists, Kai Friis Möller (1888–1960) and Paul la Cour (1902–56) also made their reputations during this period. Among the new voices 1st heard after World War II, the lyric poet Ola Sarvig (b. 1921) may be singled out.

The 20th-cent. Danish novel flowered brilliantly in the fiction of Martin Andersen Nexö (1869–1954) and the poet Johannes V. Jensen, both realists working in the epic manner. After World War I, Jacob Paludan (b. 1896) and H. C. Branner (b. 1903) established themselves as significant psychological novelists. At the same time Karen Blixen (pseudonym Isak Dinesen, 1885–1962), a subtle ironist of international stature, came to the fore. In the post–World War II era, Erik Aalback Jensen (b. 1923) and Hans Jepsen (b. 1920) have made names for themselves.

LOW COUNTRIES

The Netherlands

18TH CENT. Imitations and translations of the French neoclassical literature dominated Dutch letters in the 18th cent. Exceptions to this situation were the realistic novels of Elisabeth Wolff-Bekker (1738–1804) and the preromantic poetry of Antony Staring (1767–1840).

19TH CENT. Romanticism in the Netherlands expressed itself through a movement called *reveil*, 1830–50. After a subsequent period of decline, a new renaissance blossomed, bringing with it such figures as the poet Willem Kloos (1859–1938). Standing apart from these trends was Eduard Douwes Dekker (1820–87), who, using the pseudonym Multatuli, produced *Max Havelaar*, 1860, a novel protesting Dutch treatment of the Javanese.

20TH CENT. Impressionistic verse, dominant in the 1890's, gradually gave way to a more reflective and symbolic poetry, as in the works of Frederik van Eeden (1860–1932) and Albert Verwey (1865–1937). Also of importance were the surrealist Martinus Nijheff (1894–1953) and the formalist Gerrit Achterberg (b. 1905).

The Dutch novel reached greatness in the naturalistic work of Louis Couperus (1863–1923). Following World War I a reaction against naturalism brought to the fore Arthur van Schendel (1874–1946), who emphasized spiritual struggles. A more recent novelist of genius is Simon Vestdijk (b. 1898).

Belgium

18TH CENT. Among 18th-cent. Belgian writers working in Flemish, the neoclassical essayist Karel Broeckaert (1767–1826) and the poet P. J. de Borchgrave (1758–1819) are 2 names that stand out. Among French-speaking writers in Belgium during this period, Prince Charles Joseph de Ligne (1735–1814) is remembered for his charming essays and memoirs.

19TH AND 20TH CENTS. Flemish literature in the 19th cent. produced only 1 important poet, Guido Gezelle (1830–99), and 1 memorable novelist, Hendrik Conscience (1812–83). But out of a revival at the turn of the century the novelist and essayist August Vermeylen (1872–1945) emerged and inspired such writers as the novelist Herman Teirlinck (b. 1879) and the poet Karel de Woestijne (1879–1929). Following World War I, successive waves of antitraditionalism, idyllic pastoralism, and naturalism swept through Flanders. Around 1930 the formalistic work of poets like Bert Decorte (b. 1915) began to appear. Among post–World War II authors of particular merit is Louis-John Boon (b. 1915).

Except for the great novelist Charles de Coster (1827–79), French writing in Belgium languished during the 19th cent.

until about 1880. At that time it experienced a rebirth under the leadership of Max Waller (pseudonym of Maurice Warlomont, 1860–89). The most significant poet to reach fame during this period was the symbolist Maurice Maeterlinck (1862–1949). In the years preceding World War I the impact of Maeterlinck's symbolism showed itself in the melodious verse of Albert Mockel (1866–1945). During the interwar period French novelists sought to break away from localism and universalize their fiction. Among the more successful were André Baillon (1875–1932), John Tousseul (pseudonym of Olivier Degee, 1890–1944), and Georges Simenon (pseudonym of Georges Sim, b. 1903).

EASTERN EUROPE

Finland

19TH CENT. Finland's 1st modern author of significance was Aleksis Stenvall (pseudonym Aleksis Kivi, 1834–72), whose novels and plays blend humor and psychological realism. Simultaneously, the art of poetry in Finland was advanced by A. Oksanen (pseudonym of August Engelbert Ahlquist, 1826–89). In the 1880's, 2 major novelists appeared, Minna Canth (1844–97) and Juhani Aho (pseudonym of Juhani Brofeldt, 1861–1921).

20TH CENT. At the turn of the century neoromanticism flourished in the lyric poetry of Eino Leino (pseudonym of Armas Eino Leopold Lönnbohm, 1878–1926), the finest Finnish poet of modern times. Leino's 3 closest rivals for this honor are Larin Kyösti (pseudonym of Kaarlo Kyösti Larson, 1873–1948), Otto Manninen (1872–1950), and Veikko Anteronen Koskenniemi (1885–1962). Among recent poets, Kaarlo Sarkia (1902–45) and Aaro Hellaakoski (1893–1952) are especially noteworthy.

While poetry was embracing romanticism, the novel was moving in another direction, toward the naturalism of Itmari Kianto (b. 1874) and Joel Lehtonen (1881–1934). Of the same generation but less realistic in approach, Aino Kallas

(1878–1956) produced memorable work in the novel and short-story forms. Frans Eemil Sillanpää (b. 1888) holds the distinction of being the only Finn to win a Nobel prize for literature, 1939. The best-known Finnish writer outside Finland is Mika Waltari (b. 1908), whose novel *Sinuhe, egyptiläinen*, 1945, became famous in English translation as *The Egyptian*. Of greater stature than Waltari, however, is the untranslated Volter Kilpi (1874–1939).

Poland

18TH AND 19TH CENTS. The impact of French neoclassicism is clearly discernible in 18th-cent. Polish letters, especially in the poetry of Ignacy Krasicki (1735–1801) and Stanislaw Trembecki (c. 1740–1812) and in the verse dramas of Franciszek Zablocki (1750–1821). Romanticism in Poland, emerging during the period of Russian domination, took the form of impassioned patriotism. The greatest of the romantic poets was Adam Mickiewicz (1798–1855). The Polish novel flowered most impressively after the rise of realism in the works of Boleslaw Prus (pseudonym of Aleksander Glowacki, 1847–1912). At the same time, Henryk Sienkiewicz (1846–1916) became known throughout Europe for his historical novels.

20TH CENT. At the end of the 19th cent. a reaction against realism set in, resulting in the symbolist movement known as "Young Poland." The outstanding poet of this school was the "decadent" Kazimierz Tetmajer (1865–1940). But for pure poetic skill Tetmajer was easily surpassed by Jan Kasprowicz (1860–1926), a lyric poet employing predominantly religious themes.

Polish independence, 1918, brought a new surge of poetic activity. The Skamandrite school cultivated bizarre new forms and irregular verse, which it used for exultantly patriotic themes. Julian Tuwim (1894–1953) was the leading figure. A still more radical school, the Vanguards, demanded the complete abolition of all old forms and traditions; the verse of Tadeusz Peiper (b. 1891) is typical of this school. During this era the great dramatic poet Karol Rostworowski (1877–1938) also emerged.

Among modern Polish novelists, few have attained greater stature than Stefan Zerowski (1864–1925), a master of social protest, and Wladyslaw Reymont (1867–1925), who recorded peasant life in epic terms. In the newly independent Poland, fiction was mainly realistic. Zofia Nalkowska (1884–1954), Marja Dabrowska (b. 1892), Jósef Wittlin (b. 1896), and Michal Chorománski (b. 1904) made important contributions to the novel of realism. An antirealistic strain existed also, however, as exemplified in the novels of Juljusz Bandrowski (1885–1944) and Stanislaw Wittiewicz (1885–1939), where the subject matter is often distorted almost to the point of surrealism. Historical novels were not without adherents; the best of them was by Zofja Kossak-Szczucka (b. 1890). During World War II much writing flowed up from the underground and the postwar period has seen a certain amount of literary productivity, most of it the socialist realism encouraged by the Communist rulers.

Czechoslovakia

18TH AND 19TH CENTS. Relatively little was produced in the way of literature in the 18th cent., although the enlightened scholarship of Josef Dobrovský (1753–1829) laid the foundations for the renaissance that was to come. Swelling powerfully in the 19th cent., this national revival reached its height in the romantic poets Karel Hynek Mácha (1810–36) and K. J. Erben (1816–70). Among novelists the quasi-realistic works of Božena Němcovâ (1820–62) have retained their appeal. A 2nd wave of romanticism, flowing from France after 1870, produced the lofty poetry of Jaroslav Vrchlický (1852–1912).

20TH CENT. The 20th cent. ushered in for Czechoslovakia a cultural revolution led by T. G. Masaryk (1850–1937), aimed at freeing the country from German influence. Out of this movement came Petr Bezruč (pseudonym of Vladimír Vašek, b. 1867) and R. X. Salda (1867–1937), who stressed the moral, reformative function of poetry. But the greatest poet of the period was Antonín Sova (1864–1928), a symbolist. He was followed by the mystic Otakar Březina (pseudonym of Václav Jebavý, 1868–1929), the "decadent" Jiří Lvovic (pseudonym of Josef Jiří Antonín Karásek, 1871–1951), and the realist Stanislav Neumann (1875–1947), a champion of vitalism. During World War I proletarian poetry was popular, but in the late 1920's and 1930's many poets turned away from social realism to surrealism. The leader of this movement was Vítězslav Nezval (b. 1900). Neoromanticism also sprang up in such poets as Martin Rázus (1888–1937).

Modern Czech fiction has chosen various modes. Vitalism produced the impressionistic novels of Fráňa Šrámek (1877–1952), while realistic writing was well represented by Josef Holeček (1853–1929) and Teréza Nováková (1853–1912); the latter documented peasant life vividly. Realism shaded into naturalism in the works of Karel Čapek-Chod (1860–1927), which describe middle-class life in Prague. Satire, too, was employed effectively by Czech writers, first by Viktor Dyk (1877–1931) at the turn of the century, later by Karel Čapek (1890–1938) and Jaroslav Hašek (1883–1923), whose novel *The Good Soldier Schweik* is an international favorite.

Hungary

18TH AND 19TH CENTS. The beginning of a great revival of Hungarian culture dates from the 18th cent., when such emerging figures as Ferenc Kazinczy (1759–1831) fought for the readoption of the Hungarian language, long neglected by the ruling Hungarian nobility, who had written in German or Latin. In the following century, with this revival at its height, nationalism shaped the most characteristic literature, the poetry of Sándor Petöfi (1823–49), János Arany (1817–82), and Mihály Vörösmarty (1800–55). In fiction, the historical novelist Mór Jókai (1825–1904) was pre-eminent.

20TH CENT. After the turn of the century a great revival took place in Hungarian letters, partly spurred by the vigorous periodical *A Het (The Week)*. In 1906 the lyric poet Endre Ady (1877–1919) burst into the literary world and quickly gained recognition as a major figure. Left-wing verse found a home in the new journal *Nyugat (The West)*. The interwar period was an especially rich one for Hungarian poetry, boasting as it did the militant verse of Attila József (1905–37) and the religious poetry of Lászlo Mécs (b. 1895). Little verse of importance was written in Hungary during World War II, but since then at least one voice has been heard, that of Gyula Illyés (b. 1902).

Modern Hungarian fiction began with *A Het*, where such writers as Zoltán Ambrus (1861–1932) appeared. Among novelists of this era, the greatest is Zsigmond Móricz (1879–1942), whose novels are realistic portraits of provincial life. Also of significance is Frigyes Karinthy (1888–1938). Generally speaking, the new wave in Hungarian writing was represented by the *Nyugat* group, which eventually gained recognition. However, the novelist Dezsó Szabó (1879–1945) is a solitary giant, as is Lajos Kassák (1887–1967), a chronicler of the proletarian world. In the interwar period memorable fiction was written by Lajos Zilahy (b. 1891) and Sándor Márai (b. 1900), who depicted middle-class life; Pál Szabó (b. 1893) and József Darvas (b. 1912), masters of social realism; and Péter Veres (b. 1897), who championed the cause of the peasants. Since the war social and economic forces have been emphasized in literature. Tibor Déry (b. 1894) has acquired the greatest reputation.

Rumania

18TH AND 19TH CENTS. The outstanding literary figures in 18th-cent. Rumania were the scholars Dimitrie Cantemir (1673–1723) and Ion Neculce (1672–1745). Toward the end of the century a Latinist movement, attempting to establish the Latin origins of the

Rumanian language, sprang up. It spurred much literary activity in the following century, including the lyric poetry of Mihail Eminescu (pseudonym of Mihail Eminovici, 1850–89) and the fiction of Ion Creangă (1837–89).

20TH CENT. An interest in folklore can be discerned in the poetry of Octavian Goga (1879–1938). Occidental influences were apparent in the symbolist poetry of I. Minulescu (b. 1881). Following World War I, the key poetic figures were the philosophical Lucian Blaga (b. 1895) and the lyrical Tudor Arghezi (b. 1880).

Rumanian fiction grew to prominence with the novels of Liviu Rebreanu (?1885–1943). Rebreanu was followed by such regional novelists as Cezar Petrescu (b. 1892), G. Mihaescu (b. 1894), and, most notably, the Transylvanian I. Agarbiceanu (b. 1892).

Yugoslavia

18TH AND 19TH CENTS. In the 18th cent. the ideas of the Enlightenment were developed steadily by the Serbian scholar Dimitrije Obradović (?1742–1811), the Croat satirist Matija Reljković (1732–98), and the Slovene poet Valentin Vodnik (1758–1819). In the 19th cent. the growth of the area's literature was inextricably bound up with the awakening of national consciousness, folk poetry, and western romanticism. The foremost romantic was the poet Sima Milutinović-Sarajlija (1791–1847). Realism followed, bringing with it the novelist Laza Lazarević (1851–90).

20TH CENT. Expressionist, surrealist, and symbolist influences are discernible in Yugoslav poetry after 1900. Among the leading poets are the Serbs Milan Rakić (1876–1938) and Aleksa Santić (1868–1924), the Croats Vladimir Nazov (1876–1949) and Vladimir Vidrić (1875–1909), and the Slovenes Oton Župančić (1878–1949) and Alojz Gradnik (b. 1882).

Fiction has not kept pace with poetry. Nevertheless, important work has been done by the Nobel prize winner Ivo Andrić (b. 1892) in Serbian, Vjekoslav Kaleb (b. 1905) in Croatian, and V.

Levstik (1886–1957) in Slovene. Other writers of importance are Krleža, Čopić, and DaviČo. The Macedonian language has also developed a unique literature, in which the novelist Slavko Janevski is a central figure.

Greece

18TH CENT. Literary activity was not great during the 18th cent., due to Turkish control of Greece. However, the didactic verse of Kaisarios Dapontis (1714–74), the patriotic poetry of Rhigas (1757–98), and the anacreontic efforts of Ioannis Vilaras (1771–1823) are worthy of note. In prose, important efforts at linguistic reform (anticipating later developments) were made by Adamantios Korais (1748–1833).

19TH CENT. In the aftermath of the revolution of 1821, the deeply patriotic Ionian school sprang up; its chief representatives were Andrea Kalvos (1796–1869) and Dionysios Solomos (1798–1857). In the 2nd half of the century, romanticism found an uninhibited voice in the Athenian poets of that period, but subsequently a new antiromantic school appeared in Athens, headed by Kostes Palamas (1859–1943). Allied with Palamas was Jean Psichari (Ioannes Psychares, 1854–1929), who revolutionized the Greek written language by his use of the vernacular.

20TH CENT. The pre–World War I period was marked by 3 major poets: Konstantinos Kavafes (1863–1933), a prophet of disillusionment and despair; Angelos Sikelianos (1884–1951), a melodious and powerful mystic; and Kostas Varnales (b. 1884), a Marxist with a deep sense of tragedy. After the war a group of disillusioned surrealist poets appeared, most notably Georgios Seferes (pseudonym of Georgios Seferiades, b. 1900).

Modern Greek prose lagged behind poetry until after World War I, although the prewar era produced such figures as Kostas Theotokes (1872–1923), who perfected the novel of social criticism, and Konstantinos Christomanos (1887–1911), a refined and subtle stylist. The greatest writer of this period was Gregorios Xenopoulos (1867–1951), a psychological novelist. During the interwar period several major authors emerged, among them Angelos Terzakes (b. 1907) and Elias Venezes (b. 1903). Nikos Kazantzakis (1885–1957), also a poet, gained an international reputation with novels like *Zorba the Greek*, 1943, and *The Last Testament of Christ*, 1960.

HEBREW AND YIDDISH

Hebrew

18TH AND 19TH CENTS. Beginning in 1750, a great renaissance in Hebrew letters swept Jewish communities in Europe. Known as Haskalah, this movement was initiated by Moses Mendelssohn (1729–86) and his disciples. Its influence was felt by Jews in Russia, Galicia, Germany, Italy, and elsewhere. In the 19th cent. it produced such poets as the contemplative Abraham Dob Lebensohn (1794–1879) and the fiery Jehuda Leb Gordon (1830–92). The 1st great novelist of the Haskalah was Abraham Mapu (1808–67), author of several historical novels. Mapu was surpassed, however, by Perez Smolenskin (1842–85), whose powerful novels depicted contemporary Jewish life. Among other writers of importance were Mordecai Feierberg (1874–99) and Judah Steinberg (1863–1908).

20TH CENT. At the close of the 19th cent. new spirits of realism and nationalistic yearning became pronounced in Hebrew letters. Among contemporary Hebrew poets, these trends can be seen clearly in the verse of Saul Chernikovsky (1875–1943), Jacob Kahn (b. 1881), and Jacob Fichman (b. 1882). Chernikovsky, the best of the 3, recreated Russian village life in striking Biblical language. Also of significance was C. N. Bialik (1873–1934), who gave memorable expression to the search for a modern Jewish identity. Later poets worthy of mention are Rachel (R. Blovstein, 1890–1931) and A. Shlonsky (b. 1900), a symbolist.

An emphasis on the Hebrew past had characterized much of the Haskalah literature. *Fin-de-siècle* and 20th-cent. writers abandoned this emphasis and turned their attention to modern Jewish life. Under the influence of the Yiddish novelist Mendele such writers as Ahad Haam called for a modern Hebrew culture centered in Palestine. Realistic short stories of high quality were produced by I. H. Brenner (1881–1921), G. Schofmann (b. 1880), and U. N. Gessin (1880–1913), all emigrants whose work is pervaded by a rootless melancholy. In Palestine there was a good deal of literary activity; the novels of A. A. Kabak (1881–1944) portray pioneer life there, and the Nobel prize winner S. J. Agnon (b. 1880), perhaps the greatest of modern Hebrew writers, has set his scenes in the Holy Land. Hebrew literature has continued to thrive in the state of Israel and has become more colloquial and cosmopolitan. In the U.S. a substantial body of Hebrew writing has arisen, most notably the poetry of Simon Halkin (b. 1899) and Eisig Silberschlag (b. 1903), the fiction of Abraham Shoar (1869–1939), and the essays of Abraham Goldberg (1883–1942).

Yiddish

The fountainhead of modern Yiddish literature is Mendele Mokher Sefarim (Sholem Abramovitch, 1836–1917), whose novels and stories drew a realistic portrait of Jewish life in Russia. Mendele was followed by the greatest of Yiddish humorists, Sholem Aleichem (Solomon Rabinowitz, 1859–1916), who successfully blended humor and pathos. Contemporaneously, the short-story writer and playwright I. Leibush Peretz (?1851–1915) brought a new universality to Yiddish letters. Among Peretz' disciples were Sholem Asch (1880–1957) and Abraham Reisen (1876–1953). Other Yiddish writers of prominence in the 20th cent. are Der Nister (pseudonym of Pinchas Kahanovitch (1885–?1948) in the Soviet Union and David Pinsky (1872–1959), Joseph Opatoshu (b. 1886), and the poet Morris Rosenfeld (1862–1923) in the U.S. The best-known novelist now writing in Yiddish is probably Isaac Singer (b. 1904).

CHINA

18TH CENT. Antiquarian trends were powerful in the Chinese literature of the 18th cent., with writers striving to imitate the great classical and medieval works. Especially praiseworthy is the fiction of Wu Ching-tzu (1701–54) and Ts'ao Chan (?1715–63), author of the famous *Hung Lou Meng* (*Dream of the Red Chamber*), a tragic love story written in the vernacular.

19TH CENT. With the opening of China to western influence, translations from European languages soon became common. Yen Fu (1852–1921) and Lin Shu (1852–1924) did especially memorable work in the field of translation. Among creative writers western models were widely imitated. The spoken rather than the literary language was adopted by the poet Huang Tsun-hsien (1845–1905), who made extensive use of folk songs and foreign materials. In prose, the leading figure was Liu E (1857–1909), whose *Lao Ts'an Yu Chi* was the most important in a series of picaresque novels.

20TH CENT. An ardent supporter of Huang Tsun-Hsien, Liang Ch'i-ch'ao (1873–1929) carried on the modernization of Chinese literature by cultivating a more flexible prose style and by introducing foreign expressions. This set the stage for the Literary Revolution of 1917, an antitraditional movement which championed the vernacular over the classical language and called for a new literature. The chief "revolutionary" was Hu Shih (b. 1891), whose persuasive articles appeared in the journal *Hsin Ch'ing-Nien* (*The New Youth*), edited by another key figure, Ch'en Tu-hsiu (1879–1942). With the publication of Hu Shih's masterful *Chung-kuo che-hsüeh Shih Ta-Kang* (*Outline History of Chinese Philosophy*), 1919, the Literary Revolution gained victory. The spoken language, *pai-hua,* became the accepted form of literary and journalistic expression. Among the poets to adopt *pai-hua* was Kuo Mo-jo (b. 1891), whose Marxist leanings were typical of the new writers. The outstanding

fiction of the period was written by Lu Hsün (pseudonym of Chou Shu-jen, 1881–1936), author of the famous story "The Diary of a Madman." Other writers of importance were Chou's brother, Chou Tso-jen (b. 1885), Mao Tun (b. 1896), and the woman novelist Ting Ling. Realism was the dominant trend in all these authors.

Under the rule of the People's Republic, Chinese literature has been strictly controlled through the Chinese Writers' Union, which tolerates little deviation from Marxist theories of art. In poetry the use of classical forms has been discouraged; in fiction socialist realism is the official mode of expression. Nevertheless, poetry of considerable merit has been written under the Communists, notably by Ko Pi-chou and by the party chairman himself, Mao Tse-tung (who has to a great extent ignored his own interdiction of classical form). In the genre of the novel, Choi Li-po (b. 1908) has excelled with such works as *Great Changes in a Mountain Village,* 1958.

JAPAN

18TH AND 19TH CENTS. The period 1700–1850 represented the culmination of a great renaissance in Japanese letters which had begun in the 1630's. Old verse forms such as the tanka were employed with great success by poets like Motoori Norinaga (1730–1801). Adapting the tanka to realistic subject matter, Okuma Kotomichi (1798–1868) and Tachibana Akewi (1812–68) broke new ground. At the same time, the haiku became a major genre in the hands of such new masters as Kobayashi Issa (1763–1827). In fiction, the 18th cent. produced such new forms as the *sharehon* (wit book) and *kokkeibon* (comic book). Jippensha Ikku (1765–1831) was a master of the latter mode. After 1800 the novelist Takizawa Bakin (1767–1848) made his mark. From 1853 on, western influences left their impact; the tanka and haiku were modernized by poets like Masaoka Shiki (1867–1902). In the 1880's translations of European narrative poems encouraged the Japanese to attempt poetry of unusual length. Meanwhile, a realistic brand of fiction developed in the works of Furabatei Shimei (1864–1909) and Natsume Soseki (1867–1916).

20TH CENT. The popularity of free verse and symbolist poetry after 1900 bore witness to continuing western influence. More traditional in its approach was the Asakasha school, founded near the end of the 19th cent. and including among its members Onoe Shibafune (1876–1957) and Sasaki Nobutsuna (1872–1963). Opposed to the Asakasha group was the Shinshisha school, calling for a new naturalistic verse that utilized the vernacular. Its leading figures were Yosano Tekkan (1873–1935), his wife Akiko (1878–1942), and Ishikawa Takubaku (1885–1912). Still another school of poetry that sprang up was the Negishi, which called for classical restraint and propriety. Masaoka Shiki was the founder of this group and Saito Mokichi (1882–1953) one of the chief members. Ranged against the Negishi were numerous younger poets of a revolutionary bent who sought to abandon all traditions. Kawahigashi Hekigodo (1873–1936) was the most famous of these young insurgents.

In fiction, a vast profusion of movements appeared after 1900. The realistic novel found able exponents in Tayama Katai (1871–1930), Masamune Hakucho (1879–1962), Kikuchi Kan (1888–1948), and, more fiercely, in the proletarian novels of Kobayashi Takiji (1903–33). Simultaneously, idealism was cultivated by Koda Rohan (1867–1947) and Tokutomi Roka (1868–1927), and by the Mita school, whose outstanding representative, Nagai Kafu (1879–1959), produced many brilliant portraits of the theatrical world in Tokyo. The idealists represented a more subjective, aesthetic approach to literature; some of them, notably Yokomitsu Riichi (1898–1947), became known as "neo-sensualists." Extending these trends even further, Tanizaki Jun-ichiro (1886–1965) advocated art for art's sake. Also a deeply subjective writer, Shiga Naoya (b. 1883) developed a loosely constructed autobiographical form called the "I novel," which has been widely adopted in modern Japan. From the younger generation have come such new voices in fiction as Dazai Osamu (1909–48) and Mishima Yukio (b. 1925). In 1964 Hiraoka Kiwitake (b. 1925) created a stir with the novel *The Sailor Who Fell from Grace with the Sea.*

INDIA

19TH CENT. The impact of English culture wrought profound changes in Indian literature. New forms were introduced, such as the novel and the short story, and numerous European authors were translated. Before these revolutionary changes exerted their effect, classical literature had been the dominant force, imposing on the writer a rigid series of conventions and a fixed literary language. Prose was not used as a literary medium, and poetry was expected to deal exclusively with religious and mythic subjects. In addition, the metrical schemes used in poetry were highly standardized. But all these traditions were discarded by progressive 19th-cent. writers, who adapted the vernacular, experimented with new meters and new forms, turned from religious to secular subjects, cultivated the novel, and used literature as a vehicle for social commentary.

20TH CENT. In the 20th cent. the demand for independence became a major literary theme. At the same time, the short story surpassed the novel in its appeal, and Indians assiduously studied European masters of this form. Generally speaking, the focus of attention in both novels and short stories was on economic and social injustice—against a backdrop of swelling patriotism. Once independence had been achieved, however, Indian literature was faced by a new problem: the immense diversity of languages and dialects, which prevented the creation of a truly national literature.

HINDI. The well-known journal *Saraswati* was a seminal force in modern Hindi literature, encouraging many young writers. *Saraswati*'s editor, Mahavivprasad Dwivedi (1868–1938), was also noteworthy for promoting a modernized version of Hindi. The way was then clear for Prem Chand (1880–1936), who became the leading Hindi novelist with such works as *Godan* (*Godān*), 1935. Also of impressive stature is Ilachand (Ilāchand) Joshi (b. 1902), a Freudian writer.

The 1st modern Hindi poet of importance was Bharatendu Harishchandra (1850–83). In 20th-cent. poetry, aestheticism was represented by Surykant Tripathi (1896–1961), social criticism by Yashpal (b. 1904), and experimental verse by S. H. Vatsyayan (known as Ajney, b. 1911).

URDU. The father of modern Urdu is Sir Sayyid Ahmad Khan (Khān) (1817–98), who organized a movement aimed at adapting western ideas to Islamic culture. In poetry the 1st modern figure was Mirza Ghalib (Ghālib) (1797–1869), while Anis (1801–74) proved himself a master of older forms. Soaring beyond these 2 (and all other rivals) Mohammed Iqbal (Muḥammad Iqbāl) (1873–1938) has taken his place as the greatest of Urdu poets.

Urdu prose found gifted practitioners in Altaf Hali (Altāf Hālī) (1837–1914), biographer, poet, and critic, and in Sarshar (Sarshār) (1846–1902), the novelist of Lucknow. After 1900 Prem Chand, who also wrote in Urdu, established himself as a major novelist and short-story writer.

BENGALI. Modern Bengali poetry began in the 1860's with the introduction of such metrical innovations as blank verse. The guiding figures in this movement were Michael Madhu Sudan Dutt (1824–73), Rangalal Bandyopadhyay (Rangalāl Bandyopādhyāy) (1826–77), and, most notably, Hemcandra Bandyopadhyay (Bandyopādhyāy) (1838–1903). Among recent poets Buddhadeva Bose (b. 1908) has produced much excellent work.

Modern Bengali prose dates from the journalistic work of men like Ishwarchandra Gupta (1806–58) in the 1830's. Their renovation of Bengali prepared the way for the unsurpassed fiction of Bankim Chandra Chatterji (1838–94) and the world-famous Rabindranath Tagore (1861–1941). Later writers of high achievement include Bibhuti Bhusan Banerjee (1896–1950) and Annada Sanka Roy (b. 1904).

GUJARATI. The modernization of Gujarati poetry and prose began with Narmadashankar (1833–86). Subsequent poets of impressive achievement were Narsimhrao Divatia and Kavi Nanalal Dalpatram. Gujarati prose reached its peak in the novel *Sarasvaticandra* (*Sarasvatīcandra*) by Govardhanram Tripathi (1855–1907) and in the works of K. M. Munshi (b. 1887) and Mohandas K. Gandhi (1869–1948).

MARATHI. Keshavsut (Krishnaji Keshav Damle, 1866–1905) is generally considered the father of modern Marathi poetry. In the 20th cent. the poetry of Bhaskar Ramchandra Tambe (1874–1941) is especially memorable. Marathi fiction came of age with the novelist Hari Narayan Apte (1864–1919) and further developed in the hands of Vaman Joshi (1882–1943) and of the outstanding short-story master Vishnu Sitaram Phadke (b. 1898).

A certain amount of literary activity has also taken place in the other Indo-Aryan languages: Assamese, Kashmiri, Oriya, Panjabi.

DRAVIDIAN LITERATURE. Dravidian literature has followed roughly the same course of modernization as the Indo-Aryan tongues: the use of nationalism as a literary theme, the adoption of the colloquial idiom, etc. The languages with the most extensive literatures are Tamil, Kanarese, Telugu, and Malayalam.

LITERATURE IN ENGLISH. Among the numerous Indian poets who have written in English are Sarojini Naidu (1879–1949), an ardent nationalist, and Sri Aurobindo (Aurobindo Ghose, 1872–1950), whose religious writings include an epic in blank verse. Modern Indian fiction in English has produced such outstanding works as *Coolie*, 1936, by Mulk Raj Anand (b. 1905) and *The Guide*, 1958, by R. K. Narayan, (b. 1906).

SOUTHEAST ASIA

BURMA. Modern Burmese literature dates from the introduction of western printing methods, c. 1875. Around the turn of the century the novel became an accepted literary form, and such writers as U Kyi and U Lat quickly made their mark. The foundation of the University of Rangoon, 1920, stimulated further literary activity. Fiction remained the dominant genre, and in 1936 *Tet Hpon-gyi* (*The Modern Monk*) by Thein Pe made a tremendous impact. Burmese independence, 1948, added a strongly nationalistic impulse to literature. Recent writers in whom this strain is pronounced are Min Aung and Ja-nè-gyaw Ma Ma Lay.

THAILAND. In the early part of the 19th cent., King Rama II produced a number of notable poetic works, chiefly romances in the traditional manner. *Pra Abhaimani,* by Soutorn Bhu, is a memorable fantasy also written during this period. After 1850 prose became a major form of literary expression. At the same time, court poetry continued to be written by such figures as Prince Bidyalongkorn, Jit Buradat, and King Chulalongkorn. The poem *Talengpai,* by Prince Paramanujit, has earned its author a high place in modern Thai poetry. Novelists of significance are Dokmaisod and Kukriddhi, author of *Phaiden* (*The Red Bamboo*).

INDONESIA. Contemporary Indonesian literature takes in a multiplicity of attitudes and styles. Among the writers working in Djakarta, eastern and western influences clashed sharply. Of this group Amir Hamzah became the leading poet in the 1930's and Armijn Pané the leading novelist. Prose itself had only appeared as a literary form in the 1920's with writers like Merari Siregar. An Islamic movement emerged in Medan, favoring extreme nationalism and calling for a religious revival. Simultaneously a Marxist school sprang up and produced a small body of proletarian literature. Among subsequent poets Chairil Anwar and Usmar Ismail displayed exceptional gifts. In the post–World War II period a new group of writers, known as the "generation of 1945," came into prominence. Some of this group's more outstanding members were Asrul Sani, Achdiat Mihardja, and Mochtar Lubis, whose novel *There Is No Tomorrow,* 1948, evoked much interest.

PHILIPPINES. The outstanding novel of the 19th-cent. Philippines was *Noli me tangere,* 1886, by José Rizal. Since the turn of the century Filipino authors have increasingly used English as their literary medium.

AFRICA

19th Cent.

INFLUENCE OF MISSIONARIES. European missionaries played a crucial role in the growth of modern African literature by developing written languages where only oral ones had existed before and by introducing the printing press. The missionaries also made numerous western works available to Africans through translations. Naturally, the Bible and other religious writings were translated first. Deeply influenced by these materials, western-educated Africans began to produce hymns, parables, essays, and didactic verse. Also crucial in shaping the sensibility of modern African letters was Africa's rich tradition of oral literature: chants, tales, folklore, drum histories, praise songs, and the like. Among the more prominent literary efforts of the 19th cent. were Tiyo Soga's translation of *Pilgrim's Progress* into Xhosa; *The Song of the Cross,* a religious poem by H. M. Mthakathi; and the "Great Discussions" by William Gqoba.

20th Cent.

SOUTH AFRICA. Bantu languages like Tswana, Xhosa, Zulu, and Sotho have been extensively cultivated as literary media. Poetry, though not the dominant literary mode in South Africa, has found gifted practitioners in H. I. Dhlomo, S. E. K. Mqhayi, and B. W. Vilakazi, whose *Isabelo Seka Zulu KaZulu,* 1935, is one of the landmarks of Zulu poetry. Bantu fiction began with Thomas Mofolo (1873–1948), whose historical romance *Chaka* (translated into English in 1931) celebrates heroic aspects of the African past. Another distinguished figure is Solomon T. Plaatje, who compiled Tswana proverbs, translated Shakespeare's plays into Tswana, and produced a series of historical novels.

The best-known African writers in South Africa, however, Ezekiel Mphahlele and Peter Abrahams, both write in English. They have, moreover, discarded the romantic tradition of Mofolo and Plaatje and replaced it with a fiction of social protest. This new realism is evident in Abrahams' impassioned novel *The Path of Thunder*, 1943, and Mphahlele's excellent short-story collection *The Living and the Dead*, 1961. Other writers of note are Alex La Guma and Richard Rive.

South African writers of European descent include Stuart Cloete, Nadine Gordimer, and Alan Paton. Paton will be remembered for his deeply felt novel *Cry, the Beloved Country*, 1948.

ENGLISH-SPEAKING WESTERN AFRICA. Poetry of excellence has been written in the Yoruba language by Ajayi Ajisafe and in English by the Nigerian Dennis Osadebay. Fiction is, however, the most popular literary genre. The father of Anglo-African literature in the region is Amos Tutuola, whose novel *The Palm-Wine Drinkard*, 1952, is widely read. Tutuola has been very successful at weaving folk tales and motifs into his works. Another Nigerian, Chinua Achebe, produced the powerful and celebrated novel *Things Fall Apart*, 1958, a study of the conflict between African custom and encroaching western patterns of life. After Achebe and Tutuola, 3 of the most respected West African writers are Cyprian Ekwensi, Wole Soyinka, and T. M. Aluko. In Sierra Leone, Abioseh Nicol has established himself as a leading short-story writer. Among women authors Efua Sutherland of Ghana is noteworthy.

FRENCH-SPEAKING AFRICA. In contrast to the other regions of the continent, poetry is more popular in the French-speaking areas than fiction. The most distinguished poet is Léopold Senghor (b. 1906; president of Senegal, 1962), author of 5 vols. of highly polished French verse, the 1st appearing in 1945. Senghor spent his *Wanderjahre* in Europe, where he drank in western culture and blended it with a passionate need to assert his African heritage. This need expresses itself in the theme of *négritude*—the nature and beauty of blackness—which runs through his poetry. Léon Damas (b. 1912) of French Guiana served the same term of expatriation as Senghor and employs similar themes. Among the many other African poets writing in French are Keita Fodeba of Guinea, Antoine Roger Bolamba of the Congo, and David Diop of Senegal.

The appearance of *Batouala*, 1921, by René Maran (b. 1887), which won the Prix Goncourt, marks the beginning of Afro-French fiction. Of no less importance is the Guinean Camara Laye (b. 1928), whose subtle allegory *Le Regard du roi*, 1954, is 1 of the masterpieces of African literature. Simultaneously, the Camerounian writer Mongo Beti made his mark, and another Camerounian, Ferdinand Oyono, has emerged as a gifted satirist.

PORTUGUESE-SPEAKING AFRICA. Literary activity in Portuguese-speaking Africa has resulted in a small body of work, mostly poetry. Among the chief characteristics of this poetry are a hatred of colonialism, a strong concern with social and economic problems, and the use of local dialects along with standard Portuguese. Oswaldo Alcantara, Onesimo Silveira, and Antonio Jacinto are among the most noteworthy figures.

MIDDLE EAST

Arabic

19TH CENT. After several centuries of intellectual stagnation during the period of Turkish domination, Arabic literature began to revive during the latter half of the 19th cent. This renaissance stemmed from an invigorating contact with western culture; it resulted both in a revival of interest in classical Arabic literature and in an effort to modernize Arabic letters along western lines. The classical school was led by the Lebanese Nasif al-Yaziji (1800–1871), who published a skillful imitation of al-Hartri's 12th-cent. Maqamat (Maqāmāt), a collection of picaresque stories. The modernization movement was spearheaded by the missionary schools, particularly in Beirut. Other cornerstones of modern Arabic literature were the publication of the 1st modern Arabic dictionary by Butrus al-Bustani (al-Bustāni) (1819–83); the introduction of printing presses and daily newspapers;

translations from European languages; and the founding of influential periodicals such as *al-Muqtataf* (*The Culled Ones*), 1877.

20TH CENT. Toward the end of the 19th and beginning of the 20th cent., western forms such as the novel, short story, and essay were adopted by Arabic men of letters. Poetry remained more closely bound by tradition. In contemporary literature the works of Tawfiq al Hakim (b. 1902), an Egyptian novelist and dramatist, have won great praise. His satirical mystery *Yanmīyāt Nā'ib fī al-Aryāf* (*The Diaries of a Country Magistrate*), 1937, is perhaps his best novel. Also of considerable importance is Taha (Tāhā) Husayn (b. 1889), another Egyptian, whose fiction and autobiography have been widely read. In the U.S. the Lebanese immigrant Kahlil Gibran (Jubrān Khālīl Jubrān, 1883–1931) has become well known for his volumes of prose poetry (e.g., *The Prophet*).

Persian

19TH CENT. In Persia the story of modern literature has been much the same as in the Arabic countries: the impact of the West, translation of European works, revived interest in the Persian classics, etc. In addition, Persian authors such as Qu'im Magam Farahani and Amir Kabir revealed a commitment to social reform as early as the 1820's. In the following years the use of fiction as a medium for social commentary was further stimulated by James Morier's *Hajji Baba,* 1834. Among others, Zain al-Abidin (al-'Abidin) drew much inspiration from this work.

20TH CENT. The Persian renaissance continued after 1900, assisted by the publication of numerous classical works under government auspices. The press also contributed to the revival by helping to render the language more colloquial and more flexible. In poetry the 1st blows for modernist verse were struck by such figures as Adib i Pishavari and Iraj Mirza. Among the more conservative poets, Parvin i I'tisami was an outstanding figure. Left-wing verse was represented by Ishgi and, more recently, by Lahuti. In the post–World War II period the names of Mohammed (Muhammad) Hussein Shahriyar (b. 1904) and Parviz Natel Khanlari (b. 1914) have become well known.

The Theater

GREAT BRITAIN AND IRELAND

18TH CENT. In the 18th cent. the English theater boasted several noteworthy figures, among them the novelist Henry Fielding (1707–54), who achieved both popularity and notoriety with such stinging political satires as *The Tragedy of Tragedies,* 1731. Another novelist (and poet), Oliver Goldsmith (1728–74), contributed one of the most entertaining comedies in the history of English drama, *She Stoops to Conquer,* 1773. However, the theater's most original genius during this century was Richard Brinsley Sheridan (1751–1816), whose polished, witty style cut deeply into the surface of upper-class hypocrisy. His gift for comic portraiture and command of the comedy of manners is best seen in such works as *The Rivals,* 1775, and *The School for Scandal,* 1777.

19TH CENT. During the 1st half of the 19th cent., however, the English theater produced little of value. It was not until the appearance of T. W. Robertson (1829–71), with a series of relatively realistic comedies, that Victorian England had a playwright of even historical importance. More significant were the translations of Ibsen that began to appear in the 1870's, gradually stimulating an interest in the drama of social criticism. Out of this interest were born the "problem plays" of Arthur W. Pinero (1855–1934), which focused on current social issues. Meanwhile comedy began to flourish again in the clever *divertissements* of Henry Arthur Jones (1851–1929) and rose to decisive greatness with the arrival of Oscar Wilde (1856–1900), whose deftness of situation and polished brilliance of dialogue are best exemplified in *The Importance of Being Earnest,* 1895, perhaps the finest drawing-room comedy ever written.

20TH CENT. Following the realistic tradition of Pinero, John Galsworthy (1867–1933) stressed social and economic problems in loosely constructed but moving plays. Simultaneously, Sir James M. Barrie (1860–1937) displayed his gift for charming, whimsical fantasy in such plays as *What Every Woman Knows,* 1908. The realistic, Ibsenite movement culminated in the towering genius of George Bernard Shaw (1865–1950). Brazenly didactic, Shaw bombarded his audiences with eloquent social protest and outrageous iconoclasm—though as often as not the playwright's iron hand came gloved in masterful wit and unrivaled command of rhetoric. His powers reached their pinnacle in *Man and Superman,* 1905, though lesser plays such as *Saint Joan,* 1923, and *Heartbreak House,* 1917, still raise him higher than any other English or Irish dramatist of the century.

Meanwhile a remarkable dramatic revival was under way in Ireland, where the Abbey Theater was founded in 1902. The Abbey mounted plays by W. B. Yeats, Lady Augusta Gregory (1859–1932), and, more notably, John Synge (1871–1909), whose *The Playboy of the Western World,* 1907, satirized Irish life in a kind of poeticized vernacular. There, too, the rough-hewn plays of Sean O'Casey (1881–1964) were performed (*The Plough and the Stars,* 1926).

After 1930 the quality and vigor of English drama fell off sharply. Exceptions to this were the smooth, craftsmanlike plays of Terence Rattigan (b. 1912) and the ambitious verse dramas of T. S. Eliot (who became a British subject in 1927). The best of Eliot's plays was *Murder in the Cathedral,* 1935. Following World War II a spirited revival in the British theater brought such "angry young men" as John Osborne (b. 1929) to the fore. *Look Back in Anger,* 1958, a furious broadside at the British Establishment, made Osborne world-famous. Still more

recently, Harold Pinter (b. 1930) has achieved success on both sides of the Atlantic with a series of plays that suggest undercurrents of horror beneath the conventional surface of life.

REPERTORY THEATER. England's repertory system is perhaps the most extensive in the world. Annie Horniman (1860–1937) founded the 1st modern English repertory theater in Manchester in 1907. At present there are about 50 such companies operating on a full-time basis; in the provinces one of the most respected of these is the Birmingham Repertory, founded in 1913. Generally speaking, a repertory company performs a play a week throughout the year; most British actors receive their early training in repertory. In London the major companies are the Royal Shakespeare, dividing its time between Stratford-upon-Avon and London, and the newly created, 1962, National Theater, subsidized by the government and under the direction of Sir Laurence Olivier (b. 1907).

UNITED STATES

DEVELOPMENT OF AMERICAN DRAMA. In the 19th cent. American drama was largely an imitative form, drawing both subject matter and technique from England. However, at the turn of the century a number of playwrights achieved conspicuous success on the American stage, among them W. V. Moody (1869–1910) and Clyde Fitch (1865–1909), the latter often having 2 or 3 hits running simultaneously. But American drama as a major art form arrived with Eugene O'Neill (1888–1953), whose plays, though often clumsy in language and construction, carried a full-blooded intensity that stunned audiences. A gloomy, morbid quality pervades all his work from *Beyond the Horizon,* 1920, the tragedy of a poetic dreamer, to *Mourning Becomes Electra,* a retelling of the *Oresteia,* to *The Iceman Cometh,* 1947, which deals with the inevitability of human illusion.

Although O'Neill bestrode the American theater for 3 decades, other playwrights reached considerable prominence as well. In the 1920's Sidney Howard (1891–1955) came forward with *They Knew What They Wanted,* 1925. He was followed by Robert E. Sherwood (1896–1955), George Kelly (b. 1889), and Philip Barry (1896–1949). Elmer Rice (1892–1967) assured his place in American literature with the expressionistic *The Adding Machine,* 1923, and the naturalistic *Street Scene,* 1929. Next to O'Neill the best playwright of this period was Maxwell Anderson (1888–1959), who revived the verse play in such works as *Winterset,* 1935. In the 1930's a theater of social consciousness became popular, and gave rise to Clifford Odets (1906–63) and Sidney Kingsley (b. 1906). Also coming to the fore in the 1930's were Lillian Hellman (b. 1905) and Thornton Wilder (b. 1897), whose *Our Town* has become an American classic. The 1940's produced 2 dramatists who surpassed all predecessors except O'Neill: Tennessee Williams (b. 1915), author of *The Glass Menagerie,* 1947, and Arthur Miller (b. 1915), whose *Death of a Salesman* is of great distinction. Among the younger playwrights, Edward Albee (b. 1928) is the best known.

THEATERS AND DRAMA GROUPS. The Theater Guild (founded in 1918) provided New York with a home for serious drama and helped spawn such figures as Eugene O'Neill and Maxwell Anderson. In spite of the impact of the depression, American drama continued to grow; the Group Theater, based on Stanislavski's acting system, was founded to cultivate new actors, and the Federal Theater Project created low-price theater for the mass audience. After World War II the Actors' Studio became famous for "method acting," a technique influenced by Stanislavski. New directors rose to prominence, among them Elia Kazan (b. 1909) and José Quintero. The expense of mounting Broadway productions stimulated the development of numerous "off-Broadway" theaters, e.g., the Circle in the Square, where revivals and less commercial plays could be produced. In recent years several repertory companies of note have appeared; the APA Co. in New York is the most widely admired.

MUSICAL COMEDY. The most original of American theatrical institutions is musical comedy, a unique blend of operetta, revue, and burlesque. *The Black Crook,* produced in New York in 1866, is generally considered to be the 1st musical. Among the subsequent landmarks are the sassy, infectious songs of George M. Cohan (1878–1942), the light operas of Victor Herbert (1858–1924), the witty, cosmopolitan lyrics of Cole Porter (1891–1964) and Lorenz Hart (1895–1943), the dynamic and inventive jazz rhythms of George Gershwin (1898–1937), and the sentimental but richly melodious shows of Richard Rodgers (b. 1902) and Oscar Hammerstein II (1895–1960). From the standpoint of musical sophistication and substance, Gershwin's *Porgy and Bess,* 1935, is probably the greatest work of this genre (though it is sometimes termed a "folk opera").

FRANCE

18TH CENT. The tragedies of Voltaire, lifeless imitations of Racine, dominated the French theater of the 18th cent., but quickly vanished from the boards with their author's death. Diderot also tried his hand at comedy with even less success. The only French playwright of lasting importance in this period was Beaumarchais (Pierre Augustin Caron, 1732–99), who achieved immortality with 2 ingenious comedies, *The Barber of Seville,* 1775, and *The Marriage of Figaro,* 1784, which served as the bases for operas by Rossini and Mozart, respectively. The same hero, a common barber, appeared in each, and his skillful handling of aristocratic intrigues represented to theatergoers a new and democratic, even revolutionary, note in French drama.

19TH CENT. The production of Victor Hugo's *Hernani,* 1830, inaugurated the romantic age in French drama. Classical rules of construction were abandoned, comedy and tragedy were mixed, and a new, extravagant emotionalism prevailed. Hugo's success was soon duplicated by Alexandre Dumas *père* (1802–70) in *La* *tour de Nesel,* 1832, by Alfred de Vigny (1797–1863) in *Chatterton,* 1835, and by Alfred de Musset in *Lorenzaccio,* 1833. A reaction against the excesses of the romantics came with the "well-made plays" of Eugène Scribe (1791–1861), which limited themselves to light, amusing situations. In a broader vein Georges Feydeau (1862–1921) perfected the bedroom farce. Meanwhile, serious theater in the 2nd half of the century thrived on the plays of Alexandre Dumas *fils* (1824–95), Henry Becque (1837–99), and Émile Augier (1820–89). Problem plays, such as those of Eugène Brieux (1858–1932), introduced a new realism into the theater. But the outstanding playwright of the period was the anachronistic Edmond Rostand (1868–1918), an impassioned romantic, whose *Cyrano de Bergerac,* 1898, tempered poetry with wit in an exquisite blend.

20TH CENT. The forces that shaped contemporary French theater were gathering at the close of the 19th cent. Maurice Maeterlinck's symbolic dramas made their impact, and in 1896 Alfred Jarry (1873–1907) produced his *Ubu-Roi,* a violent, heavily stylized burlesque of French society. Often considered the 1st modern French play, it anticipated much of the experimental theater that was to follow. In the post–World War I era French drama came into full bloom with such figures as Jean Cocteau (1899–1963), a leading surrealist, whose *Orphée,* 1926, showed him at his best. Also part of the flowering was Jean Giraudoux (1882–1944), who adapted classical situations to modern themes with disarming adroitness (*La Guerre de Troie n'aura pas lieu,* 1935). More recently, Jean Anouilh (b. 1910) has also made use of ancient myths; his best work varies from tragedy to comedy and his interpretations of historical figures are striking. Of slightly less stature, Armand Salacrou (b. 1899) has cast his bitter anti-bourgeois vision in several notable satires.

Several French novelists have successfully adapted their talents to the theater, among them François Mauriac and Henry de Montherlant. During and after World War II existentialism invaded the theater through the works of Jean Paul Sartre (*Les Mains sales,* 1948) and Albert Camus (*Caligula,* 1944). In the 1950's and early 1960's Samuel Beckett, an Irish dramatist writing in French, rose to prominence with such plays as *En attendant Godot,* 1952. The Theater of the Absurd, an antirealistic movement specializing in various forms of irrationalism, bubbled up in the exuberant comedies of Eugène Ionesco (b. 1912).

GERMANY

18TH CENT. The 1st German playwright of significance in the 18th cent. was Gotthold Lessing (1729–81), who left his mark on the theater of his time with the adept folk comedy *Minna von Barnhelm,* 1763, and the prose tragedy *Emilia Galotti,* 1772. Lessing was followed by Goethe, whose plays also had a tremendous impact on the drama of the period, though they survive more as literature than as theater. Among his more stageworthy works are the domestic drama *Clavigo,* 1774, and the tragedy *Egmont,* 1788. Better suited to the stage were the wild, romantic plays of Friedrich von Schiller, especially the prose melodrama *Die Räuber,* 1780–81, whose revolutionary fervor was imitated and echoed in the *Sturm und Drang* literature of the time. Schiller's most successful verse plays, the product of his later, classical period, were the tragedy *Don Carlos,* 1787, and the historical trilogy *Wallenstein,* 1798–99.

19TH CENT. In the 1st half of the 19th cent. the greatest German dramatists were Heinrich von Kleist, Franz Grillparzer (1791–1872), Friedrich Hebbel (1813–63), and Georg Büchner (1813–37), all tragedians. After 1850 the heroic operas of Richard Wagner (1813–83), especially the tetralogy *Der Ring des Nibelungen,* exerted a great force in the theater. From this pinnacle of romanticism the pendulum swing to naturalism was inevitable, and came with the social protest of Gerhart Hauptmann (1862–1946) in such dramas as *Die Weber,* 1892. Hauptmann's chief disciple, Hermann Sudermann (1857–1928), also made several notable contributions to naturalist drama.

20TH CENT. Sudermann and others carried naturalism into the 20th cent. (though Hauptmann himself abandoned it for various forms of experimental drama). However, in the post–World War I era expressionism came into the foreground, adopting an extreme form of symbolism and endeavouring to project states of mind into concrete externals. The leading expressionists were Georg Kaiser (1878–1945), whose *Von Morgen zu Mittag,* 1916, was produced throughout the world, Ernst Toller (1893–1939), and Frank Wedekind (1864–1918). Other dramatists who appeared in the 1st quarter of the century were Hugo von Hofsmannsthal, author of several verse dramas, and Arthur Schnitzler, whose impressionistic "playlets" dwell on sexual impulses. Meanwhile, in the vibrant Berlin of the 1920's, the greatest German playwright of the century, Bertolt Brecht (1898–1956), appeared. His *epische Theater* was, in its efforts to instruct the audience, both antiromantic and antirealistic. A confirmed Marxist, Brecht leavened his fine sense of theater with lectures on the corruption and dehumanization of class society. *Mutter Courage und ihre Kinder,* 1941, and *Das Leben des Galileo Galilei,* 1943, are among his best dramas.

In the period following World War II the most important work in German theater was done by 2 Swiss writers, the novelist Max Frisch and Friedrich Dürrenmatt (b. 1921). In 1962 Rolf Hochhuth, 1931, a German playwright, scored an international success with *Der Stellvertreter* (*The Deputy*), an attack on the papal policy toward Jews during World War II.

STAGING AND DIRECTION. The greatest director in modern German theater was without question Max Reinhardt (1873–1943), who departed from both the stiff, tradition-bound schools of acting and the new naturalistic movement. Between these 2 extremes Reinhardt found a middle way, which balanced color and theatricality with quasi-realistic acting styles. In the 1920's 2 of Reinhardt's followers, Leopold Jessner (b. 1878) and Erwin Piscator (b. 1893), helped to develop the new expressionist theater in

which stylization and symbolism predominated. After World War II Bertolt Brecht's theories of a didactic drama were pre-eminent, and his company, the Berliner Ensemble (East Berlin), is still the most famous in Germany.

SOVIET UNION

PREREVOLUTIONARY DRAMA. Of the 4 best-known Russian playwrights from 1800 to 1850, 3—Pushkin, Lermontov, and Gogol—worked chiefly in other genres. The 4th, Alexander Griboyedov (1795–1829), produced the delightful comedy *Woe from Wit,* 1822. In the 2nd half of the century the dominant dramatist was Alexander N. Ostrovski (1823–86), whose tragicomedies portrayed the author's fatalistic view of life with uncompromising realism. Among other novelists who worked successfully in the dramatic mode were Turgenev and Tolstoy.

Breaking away from the declamation and bathos of the classical acting styles, Stanislavski (Konstantin Alekseyev, 1863–1938) founded the Moscow Art Theater, 1898. There he developed a new naturalistic acting technique in which performers were expected to plumb the depths of the characters they portrayed and bring out the spiritual essence of each. Stanislavski immediately found the ideal material for his purposes in the plays of Anton Chekhov (*Uncle Vanya,* 1900; *The Cherry Orchard,* 1904), tragicomedies in which the characters discover the impossibility of happiness and the inevitability of longing for it. Tragedy for Chekhov was a gradual abrasion rather than a sudden blow. His key disciple was the novelist Maxim Gorky, whose still more gloomy, naturalistic plays include the famous *The Lower Depths,* 1902.

POSTREVOLUTIONARY DRAMA. Under the Soviet regime dramatists, like other authors, have been expected to express the values and beliefs of Marxist ideology and to help to educate the masses. State support for the dramatic arts resulted in the construction of many new theaters and in the expansion of old ones. Of the prerevolutionary playwrights, those who retained prominence were Gorky, Aleksei N. Tolstoy (1883–1945), and Anatol Lunacharski (1875–1933). Among the postrevolutionary figures were Aleksandr Afinogenov (1904–41), author of the propagandistic but penetrating *Fear,* 1930, and Nikolai F. Pogodin (1900–1962), whose didactic play *Tempo,* 1930, showed an understanding of mass psychology. During World War II patriotic anti-Nazi plays prevailed, the best of them being *The Russian People,* 1942, by Konstantin Simonov (b. 1915). Since the period of de-Stalinization began, greater freedom of artistic expression has been permitted, but no major dramatists have yet come forward.

ITALY

18TH AND 19TH CENTS. A great revival in Italian drama took place in the 18th cent., bringing to the fore the comic playwright, Carlo Goldoni (1707–93), and the tragedian, Count Vittorio Alfieri (1749–1803). Goldoni's droll portraits of native life resulted in such masterpieces as *Il Servitore di Due Patroni.* Alfieri projected his hatred of tyranny and his fiery patriotism into a series of preromantic tragedies, of which *Filippo,* 1787, is one of the best remembered.

During the *Risorgimento* patriotic dramas seemed to flow from every pen. The best of these nationalistic plays were those of Giovanni Niccolini (1782–1861), in which the author denounced tyranny and argued passionately for his country's unification. As the realistic movement engulfed Italian letters, a theater of social criticism began to appear, especially in the works of Fausto Martini (1886–1931), Giuseppe Giacosa (1847–1906), and Marco Paga (1862–1929), where adultery recurred as a major theme.

20TH CENT. At the turn of the century Roberto Bracco (1862–1943) became famous for his depiction of Neapolitan life. He was quickly eclipsed, however, by the poet and novelist Gabriele D'Annunzio, author of several spectacularly decadent and sordid dramas which won him a temporary international reputation. Also popular outside Italy,

chiefly for *La Cena del Beffe,* 1909, was Sem Benelli (1877–1949).

Both D'Annunzio and Benelli were overshadowed, however, by Luigi Pirandello (1867–1936), Italy's leading modern dramatist and a great force in the theater throughout the world. An intensely cerebral playwright, Pirandello challenged old assumptions about the sacredness of facts, arguing in his plays that truth is subjective and fragmentary. This point of view is set forth with particular ingenuity in *Cosi è (se vi pare),* 1917. *Sei Personaggi in Cerca d'Autore,* 1921, which demonstrates the impenetrability of truth and illusion, is Pirandello's masterpiece. The only recent Italian dramatist to approach major stature is Ugo Betti (1892–1953), whose plays concern themselves with the problems of moral responsibility.

SPAIN

19TH CENT. Romanticism invaded Spanish drama through the works of Francisco Martínez de la Rosa (1789–1862), Antonio García Gutiérrez (1813–84), and José Zorrilla y Moral (1817–93), whose play *Don Juan Tenorio,* 1844, is still performed. In the 1870's a wave of realism began to wash over Spanish drama. In *El Hijo de Don Juan,* 1892, the romantic José Echegaray y Eizaguirre (1832–1916) successfully mixed romanticism and Ibsenesque realism.

20TH CENT. Benito Pérez Galdós (1843–1920), primarily a novelist, further advanced the realistic movement in his didactic plays (e.g., *Alcestis,* 1910), which struck out at injustice and reactionary institutions. Less powerful than Galdós but far more sophisticated in dramatic technique was Jacinto Benavente y Martínez (1866–1954), Spain's greatest modern playwright. His early plays (e.g., *Gente Conocida,* 1896) quickly established him as a masterful satirist. Later he produced several highly imaginative fantasies and the impassioned melodrama *La Malquerida,* 1913, which extended his influence and reputation far beyond Spanish borders. After Benavente the most successful playwrights in modern Spain were the brothers Quintero, Serafín

(1871–1938) and Joaquín (1873–1944), whose unbroken flow of charming peasant dramas won them enduring popularity. Humor, pathos, and compassion are combined in such plays as *Papá Juan: Centenario* (performed in England and America as *A Hundred Years Old*). Also significant is Gregorio Martínez Sierra (1881–1947), who wrote *El Reino de Dios,* 1915.

In terms of international renown, Spain's leading playwright in the 20th cent. was the poet Federico García Lorca (1899–1936), whose romantic verse dramas (e.g., *La Casa de Bernarda Alba,* 1936) are widely performed. Other modern Spanish playwrights of importance are José Pemán (b. 1897), Jacinto Grau (b. 1877), and Enrique Poncela (1901–52).

LATIN AMERICA

MEXICO. The romantic movement provided a healthy stimulus for Latin American drama. In Mexico it resulted in the plays of Ignacio Rodríguez Galván (1816–42), of which *Muños, visitador de México* is the most outstanding. Other playwrights who felt the impact of romanticism were Fernando Calderón (1809–45) and José Peón y Contreras (1843–1907). Social protest emerged in the dramas of Maurice Magdaleno (b. 1906). The 20th cent. has thus far produced 2 figures of noteworthy achievement: Rodolfo Usigli (b. 1905) and Celestino Gorostiza (b. 1904). The growth of Mexican drama has been aided by the establishment of numerous *teatros debolsillo* (pocket theaters).

BRAZIL. Brazil's 1st significant dramas were written in the 2nd quarter of the 19th cent. Particularly memorable is the tragedy *Antonio José ou o Poeta e a Inquisicão,* 1838, by Domingo José Gonçalves de Magalhães (1811–82). In the same year Luis Carlos Martins Pena (1815–48) produced his enduring satire *O Juiz de paz na roca*. Some of the more important romantic dramatists were Francisco Pinheira Guimarães (1832–77) and João Franklin Távora (1842–88). In the contemporary period Brazilian drama has been enriched by playwrights like Joracy Camargo, whose *Deus lhe pague* is known throughout America, and Raoul Raoulian, author of the immensely successful *Robert the Irresistible*. Other significant names are Olwald de Andrade (b. 1890) and Claudio de Souza (b. 1876). The Brazilian government has contributed to the development of theater through various types of subsidy.

CUBA. In Cuba drama thrived in the 19th cent. but fell off sharply in the 20th. For a time, 1900–1910, *bufes cubanos,* a unique brand of political satire, were popular. In the 1930's a similarly indigenous musical form called *zarzuela cubano* found a wide following.

CHILE. Chilean theater boasts 2 figures of distinction, Acevedo Hernández (b. 1886), author of numerous folk plays and realistic dramas, and Armando Moock Bousquet (1894–1942), from whose prolific output of plays *Rigoberto,* 1935, may be singled out.

ARGENTINA. Of the Latin American countries, Argentina boasts the most flourishing theater. Although José J. Podesta (1858–1937) staged the popular *Juan Moreira* in 1886, most Argentine drama of importance began after the turn of the century. Then such plays as *La Piedra de escándolo,* 1912, by Martín Coronado (1850–1919) and *Sobre las ruinas,* 1902, by Roberto J. Payró (1867–1928) established their authors as important playwrights. The greatest modern dramatist in Argentina is the Uruguayan Florencio Sánchez (1875–1910), whose plays (*La Gringa,* 1904; *Barranca abajo,* 1905) depict the clash between old creole families and the new immigrant element. After Sánchez, the most significant figures are Samuel Eichenbaum (b. 1894), a perceptive student of psychology; Alberto Vacarezza (b. 1896), whose great tragedy *Tu cuna fue un conventilla,* 1920, became a long-run success; and Conrado Nalé Roxlo (b. 1898), author of *El pacto de Cristina,* 1945.

SCANDINAVIA

NORWAY. It is Scandinavia's distinction to have produced the 2 playwrights who mark the beginning of modern drama, the Norwegian Henrik Ibsen (1828–1906) and the Swede August Strindberg (1849–1912). With Ibsen began the tide of realism that was to sweep across Europe. Mixing ideas, poetry, and fierce social protest, Ibsen almost singlehandedly revived European drama. His 1st great success was *A Doll's House,* 1879, championing the cause of female emancipation, which stirred the most violent debates from London to Moscow. *Ghosts,* 1881, debunking the middle-class notion of respectable marriage, and *An Enemy of the People,* 1882, exposing small-town venality, were controversial landmarks in a stormy career.

The leading Norwegian playwright after Ibsen is Björnstjerne Björnson (1832–1910), another stern social critic who called attention to many contemporary ills. The most admired of his works is *Beyond Human Power,* 1883.

In the 20th cent. there were no Norwegian dramatists of Ibsen or Björnson's stature, though Gunnar Heiberg (1857–1929) and Nordahl Grieg (1902–43) produced a good deal of interesting work.

SWEDEN. In Sweden, Strindberg stood almost as high as Ibsen, though he evoked less controversy and earned less notoriety. A disturbed and deeply misogynistic personality, Strindberg pioneered the techniques of naturalistic psychology in such plays as *The Father,* 1887, and *Miss Julie,* 1888, where a morbid, almost pathological tone predominates. He was also a forerunner of the expressionist drama that was to flower more fully in the 20th cent. *The Dream Play,* 1890, and *The Spook Sonata,* 1890, with their fascinating evocation of dream states, set the tone for many later developments in modern drama. A contemporary Swedish playwright of international importance is the novelist Pär Lagerkvist.

EASTERN EUROPE

While the art of theater has not flourished in Eastern Europe as it has in Western, neither has it been inactive. Hungary's Ferenc Molnár (1878–1952) created a series of engaging comedies whose cosmopolitan tone has won them an international audience. *The Guardsman,* 1910, and *Liliom,* 1919, are his best-known works. In Czechoslovakia the Čapek brothers, Karel (1890–1938) and Josef (1887–1927), wrote several memorable plays, most notably Karel's *R.U.R.* and *Ze Života hmyzu,* 1921, written in collaboration. Produced in English-speaking countries as *The World We Live In,* this latter play was enthusiastically received.

CHINA

19TH CENT. In 19th-cent. China a traditional theater, relying heavily on stylization and convention, predominated. There were 2 types of plays, *wu* (military) and *wen* (civilian). The former usually dealt with heroism and warfare, the latter with domestic life; in the latter, reverence for the family and scholarly ability were emphatic virtues. Singing generally accompanied both types of drama. Other conventions included a relatively bare, curtainless stage, where a few simple objects signified a larger setting; rhythmical, dancelike movements by the actors; lush, colorful costumes; and the use of men in female roles.

20TH CENT. Under the influence of western drama a new realistic Chinese theater grew up alongside the old. Beginning in 1907, this "talking drama," as it was called, abandoned pure Chinese for the vernacular, *pai-hua,* and gradually spread throughout China. After the "Literary Revolution" of 1919 the new drama soon gained acceptance. It tended to focus on social and economic rather than psychological problems, and revolutionary groups soon seized on it as a medium for propaganda and indoctrination. It has continued to serve this function under the Communist regime. Traditional, conventionalized drama, however, has been allowed to survive—at least until it came under attack at the time of the Great Cultural Revolution. The quality of acting in modern China owed much to the impressive example of Mei Lan-fang (1894–1943).

JAPAN

18TH AND 19TH CENTS. Two traditional forms of extremely stylized drama were pre-eminent in the 18th and 19th cents. These were the No play, an aristocratic genre, and the Kabuki, a more popular form. In the 18th cent. the most distinguished dramatists to write for the Kabuki theater were Chikamatsu Monzaemon (c. 1652–1724) and Takeda Izumo (1688–1756). In the 19th cent. the most popular guardian of Kabuki tradition was the playwright Kawatake Mokuami (1816–93).

The No play was generally an episodic treatment of a Japanese myth or legend; the Kabuki drama, involving ritualistic songs and dances, presented plays of a more worldly nature. Both made use of music (often a flute and drums), a stage open to the audience on 3 sides, chanting and declamation of lines, an all-male cast, and resplendent costumes. The stagehands often mingled with the players during the performance, and as a rule acting was emphasized rather than plot or characterization.

20TH CENT. Both the No and Kabuki theaters (especially the latter) survived as viable genres in the 20th cent. But around 1900 a new naturalistic form of drama began to emerge, one that dealt with everyday life, allowed women to appear on stage, and used the spoken rather than the literary language. It was called *shimpa* (new school). Out of it evolved modern Japanese drama, whose 1st great spokesman was Tsubouchi Shuyo in *Shingakugekiron*, 1905, a treatise on the theater. The new movement which grew up around Tsubouchi contained divergent factions, among them the neo-realistic school of Kikuchi Kan and the idealistic school of Arishima Takeo. Influenced by western playwrights and the Moscow Art Theater, Hijikata Yoshi founded the Tsukiji Little Theater in Tokyo, 1924. Subsequently another actor, Ichiawa Chojuro, organized the Progressive Theater. The groups performed both traditional Kabuki and modern dramas of socialist realism. Because of its left-wing origins, contemporary Japanese theater has retained a strong impulse toward social protest.

INDIA

19TH CENT. The influence of British rule in India tended to foster a realistic westernized theater from the 18th cent. onward. However, after 1850 there was a revival of classical Indian theater through translations from the original Sanskrit into Bengali. This new theater was traditional in its combination of music and dance, artificial and conventionalized subject matter, symbolic stage settings, and stress on acting. Elaborate headdresses were worn to signify particular gods or heroes. Broadly speaking, 2 genres existed: *nataka,* dealing with the exploits of mythic figures, and *prakarama,* treating aspects of everyday life. The guiding theory, known as *rasa,* called for the evocation of an emotional response from the audience, who could thereby attain serenity.

20TH CENT. Classical drama has flourished in this century due, in great measure, to the efforts on its behalf of Sir Rabindranath Tagore. Government subsidies have also helped. Tagore, who adopted the classical form in such plays as *The King of the Dark Chamber,* 1914, is India's best-known modern playwright. English influence is largely represented by the popularity of Shakespeare, who is widely performed. The most popular theater at present is the Prithui, founded in 1943, which tours the country regularly. More modern in technique is the Theater Unit in Bombay, which performs in English, while the Gujarati Theater, also in Bombay, has shown a preference for plays of social criticism. Other dramatic groups are the Madras Theater, with a repertory of religious plays, and the Indian National Theater, which tours farms and factories. Among Indian dramatists writing in English, Bharati Sarabhai has achieved special distinction with plays like *The Well of the People,* 1943.

AFRICA

In recent years a formal African drama has begun to take shape. Various African dance troupes have toured Europe and the U.S., and the South African jazz opera, *King Kong,* created a sensation in London in 1962. In addition, numerous theatrical groups have been formed, most notably the Mbari Club in Nigeria and the Ogunmola Folk Opera. In South Africa a National Theater was founded in 1948 with a government subsidy.

Among African dramatists the most eminent are Wole Soyinka of Nigeria, whose plays (e.g., *A Dance of the Forest*) dramatize the impact of western culture on the African mind; J. P. Clark (b. 1935), also of Nigeria, who enjoyed a notable success with *Song of a Goat;* and B. H. Khakleta of Botswana.

Newspapers, Periodicals, and Journalism

GREAT BRITAIN

EARLY NEWSPAPERS. In London at the end of the 18th cent. the *Morning Post* (founded as the *Morning Post and Daily Advertising Pamphlet,* 1772) rose to prominence. The *Times,* begun by John Walter (1739–1812) in 1785, reached a circulation of 5,000 by 1815. The editorial genius of Thomas Barnes (1785–1841) helped make the paper a national institution. In 1880 the *Evening Standard* was begun and, in 1881, the *Evening News.* The *Daily Mail,* 1896, introduced numerous typographical innovations.

In the provinces the *Manchester Guardian,* 1821, won national fame as a Whig organ and exponent of liberalism. Other important provincial journals were the *Yorkshire Post,* 1854, the *Liverpool Daily Post,* 1855, and the *Birmingham Daily Post,* 1857.

A crucial event in the history of British journalism was the abolition of the stamp tax, 1855, part of the "taxes on knowledge." With the elimination of these taxes and the consequent rise of the "penny newspaper" (the 1st in London was the *Daily Telegraph and Courier,* later the *Daily Telegraph,* founded 1855), English newspapers burgeoned. Between 1855 and 1857 over 100 new papers were established.

Notable newspapers of the past century which expired through discontinuance or merger include *Morning Chronicle,* 1769–1862; *Daily News,* 1846–1930 (edited for a time by Charles Dickens); *Pall Mall Gazette,* 1865–1925; and *St. James's Gazette,* 1880–1903.

EARLY PERIODICALS. One of the earliest and most famous of British periodicals was the *Spectator,* published by Joseph Addison and Richard Steele. Half a century later Samuel Johnson brought out the *Rambler,* 1750-52, which won similar fame. Perhaps the greatest of British periodicals, the *Observer,* 1st appeared in 1791. During the 19th cent. 3 British periodicals achieved international renown: the *Edinburgh Review,* 1802, the *Quarterly Review,* 1809, and *Blackwood's Magazine,* 1817. The popular Sunday newspaper, *News of the World,* 1843, emphasized crime and sports.

20TH CENT. The *Daily Express,* 1900, founded by C. Arthur Pearson (1866–1921), became the 1st British paper to publish lead stories on the front page. Lord Beaverbrook (1879–1964) acquired control in 1922, and by 1966 the circulation had reached 4 m. In 1903 the *Daily Mirror* was established by Alfred Harmsworth (1865–1922), who made it the 1st halfpenny illustrated tabloid in England. The *Daily Sketch,* 1909, another illustrated tabloid, absorbed the *Daily Graphic,* 1869, in the 1920's, becoming for a time the *Daily Sketch and Graphic.* In 1911 the *Daily Herald* was established as an organ of the Labour Party. It passed into the hands of the T.U.C. (Trade

Union Congress) in 1929 and later, 1961, the *Daily Mirror* group (International Publishing Corp.) gained a controlling interest. In 1964 this group replaced the *Daily Herald* with the *Sun.* In the 20th cent. the *Times* has maintained its reputation as the most influential British newspaper. Alfred Harmsworth (owner from 1908 to 1922) introduced numerous modernizations, and George Geoffrey Dawson (editor, 1912–19 and 1923–41) provided an independent-minded editorial policy.

In the provinces the *Yorkshire Post, Birmingham Daily Post,* and *Liverpool Daily Post* have remained among the major organs. The *Manchester Guardian,* also one of the leading journals of opinion, became the *Guardian* in 1960 and began to appear in London as well as in Manchester.

Among the more important journals of opinion founded in the 20th cent. are the *Times Literary Supplement,* 1902, the *Listener* (a publication of the British Broadcasting Corp., founded 1929), and the cultural review *Encounter,* 1954.

FREEDOM OF THE PRESS. In the 18th cent. government harassment of the press was a frequent occurrence. John Walter, publisher of the *Times,* and the poet Leigh Hunt were among those who paid with jail sentences for having given offense to men of power. However, important victories in the struggle for the freedom of the press were: 1763, when John Wilkes (1727–97), publisher of the *North Briton,* was acquitted of "seditious libel"; 1771, when another libel case determined (though unofficially) the right of newspapers to publish parliamentary debates; 1792, when the passage of Charles Fox's libel law guaranteed a jury trial in cases of alleged defamation; and 1855, when the stamp tax was abolished.

Though not specifically protected by law, British journalists enjoy the protection of tradition. Apart from restrictions against libel (more stringent than those in the U.S.), sedition, blasphemy, etc., governmental interference in the workings of the press is practically nonexistent. As a result of this a broad spectrum of political opinion finds expression. However, charges of slackening standards and excessive concentration of ownership

prompted an investigation by a Royal Commission, 1949. As a consequence the industry began to exercise a self-regulating function through a body called the Press Council.

UNITED STATES

EARLY NEWSPAPERS. In 1783 the *Pennsylvania Evening Post,* founded by Benjamin Towne, became the 1st American daily. It was followed the next year by the *Pennsylvania Packet and Daily Advertiser.* During the same period most newspapers developed a vehemently partisan tone, acting as spokesmen for particular parties and distorting the news accordingly. Trumpeting the Federalist cause was the *Gazette of the U.S.,* 1789–1818, founded in New York by John Fenno, while Philip Freneau's *National Gazette,* 1791–93, a Philadelphia paper, briefly looked after the interests of the Jeffersonian Republicans. After 1800 some of the most influential party papers were the Washington *National Intelligencer,* 1800, organ of the Jefferson administration, and the New York *Evening Post,* 1801, controlled in its early days by Alexander Hamilton and edited from 1829 to 1878 by William Cullen Bryant.

PENNY PRESS. The advent of the "penny press" marked a new era in American journalism. Selling for a penny rather than the normal 6 c., these papers were noted for their small size, their appeal to low-income groups, their exposés of social abuses, and their use of human-interest stories. In addition, the emphasis on timeliness in the penny press resulted in the development of swifter and more efficient means of transmitting news.

The history of the penny press began with the establishment, 1833, by Benjamin H. Day of the New York *Sun.* Within a decade the *Sun* had 2 powerful competitors: the New York *Herald,* created, 1835, by James Gordon Bennett (1795–1872), and the New York *Tribune,* begun, 1841, by Horace Greeley (1811–72). Rivals for 30 years, Bennett and Greeley towered over all other editors, the former famous for innovations and organizational ability, the latter a renowned crusader and abolitionist. Elsewhere in the country, the penny (or twopenny) press was represented by the *Republican* (1844, Springfield, Mass.), the *Picayune* (1836, New Orleans), and the Baltimore *Sun*, 1837.

West of the Appalachians journalism arrived with the *Pittsburgh Gazette*, 1786. Among other important papers in the West and Midwest were the *Indiana Gazette*, 1808, the Chicago *Democrat*, 1833, the *Minnesota Pioneer*, 1849 (later the St. Paul *Pioneer*), the *Alta California*, 1849, and the Hawaii *Polynesian*, 1840–64.

During the Civil War rigid censorship was imposed on the press, and several papers were suspended, notably the New York *Daily News*, founded 1855, and the Chicago *Times*, founded 1854. In the Reconstruction era, such papers as the Chicago *Daily Tribune*, founded 1847, and the New York *Sun* emerged as powerful organs; the latter owed its greatness to the editorial genius of Charles A. Dana (1819–97). These years also saw efforts, largely successful, by many papers to free themselves from specific party ties.

BEGINNING OF MODERN JOURNALISM. Modern American journalism dates from the last quarter of the 19th cent., when Joseph Pulitzer (1847–1911) founded the St. Louis *Post-Dispatch* and, purchasing the New York *World*, transformed it into the most popular paper in the country. The *World* was lively and well written, set generally high standards of reportage, and involved itself in numerous crusades. Two of its rivals for the huge New York readership were the New York *Sun* and the New York *Herald*.

YELLOW JOURNALISM. After a youthful success with the San Francisco *Examiner*, William Randolph Hearst (1863–1951) came to New York in 1895 and bought the *Journal*. In its pages a new style of writing was born: yellow journalism. So called because of a Hearst comic strip, "The Yellow Kid," this term came to designate such journalistic techniques as a reliance on pictures, a Sunday supplement (with a special magazine and comics), stories of a lurid, sensational nature, and large headlines. A great rivalry developed between the Hearst and Pulitzer papers, with the *World* soon

perfecting its own brand of sensationalism in order to stay in the race. Elsewhere in the country the influence of yellow journalism made itself felt, and the impact of this style on American—and even world—journalism has been immense.

It was during this period, however, that a different kind of paper came to maturity in *The New York Times*. One of the world's great newspapers, the *Times* attained prominence under the editorship of Adolph S. Ochs (1858–1935), who emphasized dignity, objectivity, and conservatism, adopting the slogan "All the news that's fit to print." Maintaining extremely high standards of reportage in domestic and foreign affairs, the *Times* rose to a position of unrivaled prestige among American papers.

NEWSPAPER CHAINS. Newspaper chains became a prominent feature of American journalism at the end of the 19th cent. The 1st was the E. W. Scripps empire, which included the Cincinnati *Post*, the Kentucky *Post*, and the Cleveland *Press*. In 1922 the organization became Scripps-Howard, and soon added the Pittsburgh *Press* and the New York *Telegram*, which was later merged with the *World* and the *Sun*.

The most famous of the newspaper chains was William Randolph Hearst's, which began with the San Francisco *Examiner* and the New York *Journal*. On this foundation Hearst went on to build a journalistic empire that eventually included 40 daily papers. His personal power reached its apex in 1898, when the sensational jingoism of the papers he controlled created a favorable atmosphere for the U.S. declaration of war on Spain. Other organs he founded were the Boston *American*, 1904, and the Chicago *American*, 1900.

Second only to Scripps and Hearst was Frank Munsey (1854–1929), who in 1916 acquired the New York *Sun*, the *Evening Sun*, and the *Press*, merging the *Press* and the *Sun*. Munsey's career consisted largely of such consolidations. In 1924, for example, he combined the *Mail and Express* and the *Telegram*.

RISE OF THE TABLOID. Still another crucial chapter in the history of American journalism began at the turn of the century when the "tabloids" were born. Beginning with the redesigned New York *World*, 1 Jan., 1900, the tabloid soon came to be characterized by extensive use of photographs, a highly compressed style, and a small 4-column page. Most successful of the New York tabloids was the *Daily News*. Founded in 1919, it captured the largest readership of any daily in America.

In recent years there have been numerous discontinuances and mergers, particularly in New York. The number of New York dailies has diminished from 6 in the 1950's to 3 in the late 1960's. The most dramatic loss was the death of the *World Journal Tribune* (a merger of the *Journal American*, the *World Telegram & Sun*, and the *Herald Tribune*), 1967.

PERIODICALS. The 1st American periodical, Andrew Bradford's *American Magazine*, appeared in Philadelphia in 1741. Outstanding magazines founded in the years 1800–1850 were the *North American Review*, 1815–1940; the transcendentalist *Dial*, 1840–44; *Youth's Companion*, 1827–29; and the *Saturday Evening Post*, 1820. *Harper's New Monthly Magazine*, 1850, became the 1st quality magazine by introducing woodcut illustrations and imported English serials. The *Atlantic Monthly*, 1857, began under James Russell Lowell's editorship. The *Nation*, still a leading political organ, was founded in 1865.

In the 20th cent. the pre-eminent periodicals empire builder was Henry Luce, founder of *Time*, 1923, and *Life*, 1936. Huge success has also been enjoyed by the *Reader's Digest*, 1922. On a more sophisticated level, such "little magazines" as the *Little Review*, 1914–29, and the *Double-Dealer*, 1921–26, specialized in avant-garde writing, and helped to give new authors their first audience. *Poetry*, 1912, began as a little magazine and grew into an established literary organ. *The New Yorker*, founded in 1925 by Harold Ross and famous for both cartoons and advertisements, also became the most influential literary magazine in the U.S. Economic problems, however, have caused a steady shrinkage in the numbers of magazines published since World War

II, and mergers and discontinuances have been frequent.

FRANCE

EARLY NEWSPAPERS AND JOURNALISM. The 1st French daily, *Journal de Paris*, was founded in 1777 and survived until 1819. It was followed by *Journal des débats* (1789; discontinued, 1939) and *Moniteur* (*Gazette nationale, ou le moniteur universel*), founded in 1789, which provided official news. In 1826, one of France's best known papers, *Le Figaro*, came into existence. The appearance 10 years later of *La Presse*, founded by Émile de Girardin (1806–81), and *Le Siècle* marked the beginning of inexpensive papers aimed at a mass market. Within a few years *La Presse* could claim a readership of 20,000 and *Le Siècle* of 38,000.

The next major development in French journalism was the passage of the *Loi Tinguy*, a law stipulating that all newspaper articles had to be accompanied by their authors' names. A lasting result of this law is the high percentage of signed articles in French papers; journalists in France are generally better known to the public than in other countries.

The French halfpenny press was born when *Le Petit journal* was founded, 1863, by Moïse Polydore Millaud. Accentuating crime and scandal, *Petit journal* appealed to a mass audience and soon had countless rivals.

In the last quarter of the 19th cent. French papers began to shift their emphasis from analysis of political situations to a relatively objective presentation of the news. Factual reporting—especially extensive coverage of foreign affairs—gave rise to a new species of newspaper known as the *journal d'information*, of which leading examples were *Écho de Paris*, 1884, and *Le Matin*, 1884.

French provincial newspapers of the 19th cent. remained stubbornly independent of Paris, and often surpassed the Parisian journals in the collection of domestic news. Among those which became nationally famous were *La Dépêche* of Toulouse, *Le Petit Marseilles,* and *La Petite Gironde* of Bordeaux.

MODERN JOURNALISM. Modern French journalism has provided an unusually broad spectrum of political opinion. *L'Humanité,* 1904, was created by Jean Jaurès as a Socialist organ, but in 1920 became Communist and has continued to speak for the Marxist point of view. On the right *L'Action française* fought for the royalist cause after World War I, and in the political center *Le Quotidien,* 1919, struggled to preserve France's republican institutions.

At the time of the Nazi invasion Paris possessed some 25 dailies. This total was quickly reduced to 6, of which *Le Petit Parisien* and *Le Matin* (among others) continued to appear throughout the occupation with the approval of the Germans. Simultaneously, a defiant underground press was born, including such papers as *Combat* and *Libération.*

Following the liberation of France, 1944, only those papers which had resisted the Germans were allowed to continue: *L'Humanité, Le Populaire* (Socialist, 1920), *Le Figaro* (moderate), and *L'Aube* (Christian-Democrat). As a result many new papers sprang up. By the mid-1960's the 2 leading dailies were both of recent origin, *France-Soir* and *Le Parisien libéré. France-Soir* proved especially successful at adopting American-style emphasis on headlines, pictures, and accounts of crime. *Le Figaro* became famous for its coverage of literary and social activities, while *Le Monde,* another product of the postwar era, maintained very high journalistic standards and commanded a respect extending far beyond the borders of France.

PERIODICALS. The 1st French periodical was the *Journal des scavans,* founded in 1665. The 18th cent. saw the birth of numerous imitations of the English *Spectator,* the best being *Le Pour et contre,* 1733–40, written by the Abbé Prévost. In the 19th cent. France possessed one of the world's most famous cultural reviews, *Revue des deux mondes,* 1829–1944. During the same period *L'Illustration,* 1843–1944, achieved international renown for its pictures.

In present-day France *Paris-match,* 1949, a weekly illustrated magazine, and *Marie-Claire,* 1954, a woman's magazine, are especially popular, as is a French translation of *Reader's Digest. Réalités,* modeled on American magazines, is noted for its lush illustrations. In the cultural sphere, the *Revue de littérature, histoire, arts et sciences des deux mondes* came into being in 1948 to replace the old *Revue des deux mondes.*

GERMANY

EARLY NEWSPAPERS AND JOURNALISM. Notable German newspapers of the 18th cent. included the *Hamburgischer Correspondent,* 1714, the *Spener'sche Zeitung,* 1749, of Berlin, and the *Hamburger Nachrichten,* 1792. Renamed the *Berlinische Nachrichten,* the *Spener'sche* survived until 1827. During the period of Napoleonic domination the German press was used as a propaganda organ by the French. Even after the liberation of Germany, however, strict supervision of the press continued.

Among 19th-cent. German papers the *Allgemeine Zeitung,* 1798, was perhaps the most famous. Founded by Johann Friedrich Cotta (1764–1832) at Tübingen, it shifted its location during the next 50 years to Stuttgart to Augsburg to Munich. The intense revolutionary activity of the 1st half of the century found its voice in numerous short-lived organs. Also in sympathy with the insurgents were such established papers as the *Kölnische Zeitung,* 1804.

The period 1850–1900 was an era of phenomenal expansion in German journalism. Such papers as the *Frankfurter Zeitung,* 1856, became nationally famous, and by 1900 there were some 45 dailies in Berlin alone. It was also during this period that Leopold Ullstein laid the foundations of his great newspaper empire (known as the House of Ullstein) by purchasing the *Berliner Zeitung,* 1877.

20TH-CENT. NEWSPAPERS. *Der Tag,* founded in 1900, soon became a major Berlin daily, and this and other papers enjoyed extraordinary freedom (by previous standards) from government control under the Weimar Republic, 1919–32. During this period German newspapers were divided into the *Gruppenpresse* (organs of particular political, social, and religious movements) and a *Massenpresse* (the big-city dailies with a mass circulation and a more or less objective style of reporting). It was also at this time that several publishing empires grew up. The most notable of these was the House of Ullstein, which included the *Berliner Morgenpost*, the *Vossische Zeitung, Tempo,* and *BZ am Mittag* (formerly *Berliner Zeitung*).

Rivaling the Ullstein chain in size and power were the papers controlled by Alfred Hugenberg, leader of the Nationalist Party. These included *Der Tag* and the *Berliner Nachtausgabe,* 1924. Another combine, founded by Rudolf Mosse, included the *Berliner Tageblatt,* the *Volkszeitung* and the *Morgenzeitung.*

The nature of German journalism changed abruptly on the accession of Adolf Hitler, 1933. Freedom of the press was suspended unconditionally, Jewish newspaper owners were eliminated, and hundreds of papers ceased publication. The *Deutsche Nachrichtenburo* (DNB) was created to supersede all other news agencies. Hitler's personal organ, the *Völkische Beobachter,* 1920, became one of the leading papers in the country, together with such state-controlled journals as *Angriff,* 1927, and *Hitlerjugend.* As propaganda minister, Joseph Goebbels was absolute monarch of the German press.

In the postwar period, under allied occupation, a new German press was born. *Der Kurier* was founded by the French, *Telegraf* by the British, *Tagesspiegel* by the Americans, and *Tagliche Rundschau* by the Russians. After the establishment of the Federal Republic, many new papers were created, old ones reappeared, and occupation papers became permanent. In the late 1960's the largest readership in West Berlin had been attained by *Morgenpost* and *BZ am Mittag,* 2 revivified pre-Hitler papers. Of lower circulation but higher quality are *Der Tagesspiegel* and *Telegraf,* 2 surviving occupation papers. In East Berlin 8 daily papers flourish.

PERIODICALS. The earliest German periodical was *Acta eruditum,* 1682–1731. In the 18th cent. *Der Vernunftler,* 1713, and *Die lustige Fama,* 1718, achieved fame by adopting the style of Addison and Steele's *Spectator.* Later in the century C. M. Wieland's *Der Teutsche Merkur,* 1773–1810, was a leading literary periodical, while the *Jenaische Allgemeine Litterature-Zeitung,* 1804–41, became famous under Goethe's editorship. Political ferment bubbled up in the pages of the *Jahrbucher für wissenschaftliche Kritik,* 1827–46. In the 2nd half of the 19th cent. the *Deutsche Rundschau,* 1874, became an influential journal.

In the 20th cent. the status of the periodical press in Germany has varied with the political situation. In the post-World War II era, however, a certain stability was achieved, and by 1960 there were over 4,000 German periodicals, among them the *Deutschland Review,* 1949, *Spiegel,* 1947, *Die Besinnung,* 1946, and the picture magazine, *Zeit und Bild,* 1947.

SOVIET UNION

PREREVOLUTIONARY NEWSPAPERS. Although newspapers existed in Russia as early as 1703, the brutal repression enforced by successive czars stunted the growth of Russian journalism until the 19th cent. By then such papers as *Novaye Vremya* had become famous. Meanwhile, revolutionaries seized on the press as a means of disseminating their ideas, and the results included *Kolkol* (*Bell*), founded in London, 1857, by refugees, and *Novaya Zhizn* (*New Life*), established, 1905, by Lenin.

SOVIET JOURNALISM. After 1917 the Russian press became an arm of the government. By 1966 there were some 6,000 daily newspapers in the Soviet Union, some national, some issued by individual republics, and some municipal. These papers appeared in a total of 60 different languages, the chief ones being Russian, Byelorussian, Uzbek, and Ukrainian.

The foremost paper in the Soviet Union is *Pravda* (*Truth*), official organ of the Communist Party (1966 circ., 7 m.). Regional editions appear throughout the USSR. *Pravda* generally consists of from 4 to 8 pages, is conservatively designed, avoids sensationalism, and emphasizes politics, science, and education. Second only to *Pravda* in influence is *Izvestia* (*Spark*), the chief publication of the Presidium of the Supreme Soviet (1966 circ., 8.3 m.). Publications aimed at specific groups within the Soviet Union include *Trud* (trade unions) and *Selskaya Zhizn* (agriculture). The official Soviet news agency is *Telegrafnuye Agentstvo Sovietskovo Soyuza* (TASS), which provides both domestic and foreign news.

PERIODICALS. The 1st Russian journal was *Yezhemyesyatchnüya Sochinemiya* (*Monthly Works*), founded in 1755. Among the most popular of Soviet magazines today are *Krokodil*, a humorous publication often used to satirize the West, and *Novy Mir* (*New World*), a cultural journal.

OTHER EUROPEAN COUNTRIES

ITALY. Italy's largest paper is *Corriere della séra*, published in Milan. Other important dailies are *Unità* (Communist), Rome; *La Nuova Stampa*, Turin; and *Il Tempo*, Rome. In 1962 there were 95 Italian dailies. A unique aspect of the Italian press is the so-called *terza pagina*, or "3rd page," where cultural news is discussed.

SPAIN. By 1962 Spain was supporting over 100 dailies. At present the largest is *A.B.C.* Of the numerous papers in Madrid, *Ya* (Catholic) and *Arriba* (Falangist) are among the most popular. All Spanish papers are subject to strict government censorship.

PORTUGAL. Severe government repression has hampered the growth of a press in Portugal. The highest circulation in the country has been achieved by 2 dailies, *Diario de noticias* and *Diario*

Popular. By 1962 there were 25 dailies in Portugal.

BELGIUM. The biggest of the Belgian newspapers are issued in Brussels, *Le Soir* and *Het Laatste Nieuws*. In Antwerp the major organ is *Gazet van Antwerpen*. In 1962 there were 47 dailies, 18 of them Flemish, 28 French, and 1 German. In Belgium freedom of the press is constitutionally guaranteed.

NETHERLANDS. The largest Dutch paper is *Het Vrije Volk*, a Socialist paper published in Amsterdam, Groningen, Rotterdam, and Arnhem. *Het Parool* and *De Telegraaf* (both independent) are the next largest. The oldest Dutch newspaper is *Oprechte Haarlemsche Courant*, founded in 1656. There were 93 newspapers in the Netherlands in 1964.

DENMARK. Copenhagen's *B.T.* has the largest readership in Denmark, while the *Berlingske Tidende* is the oldest paper in the country and the most respected. Next in popularity is the *Politiken*, a Liberal organ. In 1962 there were some 81 dailies in Denmark.

SWEDEN. The 3 most popular dailies in Sweden are *Dagens Nyheter*, *Expressen*, and *Aftonbladet*, all originating in Stockholm. The oldest paper is *Norrkopings Tidningar*, founded in 1758. In 1962 there were more than 94 dailies in the country.

SWITZERLAND. The multiple languages of Switzerland appear to have encouraged the growth of newspapers. In 1962 there were no less than 127: 67.5% German, 26% French, and 4.5% Italian. *Tages-Anzeiger* is the largest Swiss paper.

AUSTRIA. One of the major Austrian papers today is the influential *Die Presse* (independent). Like most' present-day Austrian papers, it was founded after World War II. Earlier papers included the *Wiener Zeitung*, the official government newspaper, and the *Arbeiter Zeitung* (Socialist). Two organs represent the majority People's Party, *Österreichische Neue Tageszeitung* and *Das Kleine Volksblatt*, a tabloid.

GREECE. The poverty of modern Greece has prevented the development of a flourishing newspaper industry, though by 1964 there were no less than 95 dailies in the country. Athens is the center of activity, supporting over 20 dailies; of these *Akropolis* has the largest readership. Among the most distinguished papers are the Athenian *Kathimerini* and the Salonikan *Makedonia*.

FINLAND. The major paper is *Helsingin Sanomat* and the oldest is *Åbo Underrättelset,* 1824. In 1962 Finland had 91 dailies, 11% printed in Swedish.

EASTERN EUROPE. The press in the Communist states of Eastern Europe is, in general, in the service of party and government. In Czechoslovakia the official Communist organ, *Rudé Pravo,* has the largest circulation. Other important dailies are *Mladá Fronta* (*Youth League*) and *Prace* (*Labor*). In Hungary journalistic activity is centered around *Nepszabadság,* the party newspaper. In Rumania the trade unions are represented by *Munca,* the government by *Romînia Liberiă,* and the party by *Seînteia.* In Bulgaria the major newspapers are *Zemedelsko Znam* (Peasant Union), *Otechestven Front* (Fatherland Front), and *Rabotnichesko Delo* (Communist Party). In Yugoslavia newspapers are printed in 2 alphabets, Cyrillic for Serbia, Montenegro, and Macedonia, and Latin for Croatia and Slovenia. The party newspaper is *Borba.* Other leading organs are *Vjesnik* (Zagreb), *Oslobodjenje* (Sarajevo), and *Politika* (Belgrade). Of the Communist countries, Poland possesses the most independent press, and a relatively objective form of reporting prevails. The official party organ is *Trybuna Ludu,* while the highest circulation is possessed by *Express Wieczovny.*

LATIN AMERICA

EARLY NEWSPAPERS. The 1st regular newspaper in Latin America, *Gaceta de México,* appeared in 1722. *Diario de México* and *Diario de Veracruz,* both founded in 1805, were the 1st daily papers. Among the oldest journals still publishing in South America are *La Capital,* 1867, in Argentina, and *Diario de Pernambuco,* 1825, in Brazil. A major hindrance to the growth of journalism in the 19th cent. was censorship, exercised 1st by the Spanish and Portuguese authorities and later by the governments of the newly independent republics.

20TH CENT. In 1962 there were about 900 daily newspapers publishing in Latin America. The states which contributed most heavily to this total were Brazil (200 dailies), Mexico (140), Argentina (150), and Peru (60). The actual readership, however, of these numerous papers was rather low because of widespread illiteracy. At present a few papers, like *La Razón* and *Clarin* of Buenos Aires, reach a fairly large audience, but the majority of dailies do not sell more than 50,000 copies. The most famous journal in South America is undoubtedly *La Prensa* of Buenos Aires.

PERIODICALS. Among the major periodicals in Latin America in 1964 were Mexico's *Tiempo,* a news magazine modeled on *Time;* Argentina's *Veritas,* which stresses business reports; and Brazil's *O Cruzeiro,* a picture magazine with the largest circulation in the area. Latin American editions of *Life* and *Reader's Digest* are also popular.

ASIA

CHINA. Modern Chinese newspapers began in the 19th cent. The 1st paper intended for the general public was the English-language *Canton Register,* 1827. Other English-language papers followed, among them the *China Mail* of Hong Kong, 1845, with Andrew Shortrede as editor. Chinese-language papers began to appear in 1858 with a translation of the *China Mail* called *Chung Ngoi San Pao.* Soon afterward many Chinese-language papers were founded, the most important of these being *Shun Pao* of Shanghai.

The liberal constitution promulgated after the revolution of 1911 encouraged the growth of newspapers. By 1921 over 500 dailies were in existence. *Sin Wan Pao* of Hong Kong reached a circulation figure of c. 350,000, with *Shun Pao* not far behind. After the Communist takeover, 1949, all newspapers in China were subordinated to the party. By the late 1950's nearly 800 dailies were being issued throughout the country, the most important being *Jen Min Jih Pao* (*People's Daily*). The official news agency is Hsin Hua. Nationalist China supports 30-odd dailies, including 3 in English. The largest paper in Taiwan is *Chung Yang Jih Pao*.

JAPAN. The 1st Japanese newspaper was the *Shipping List and Advertiser,* 1861, of Nagasaki, an English-language journal. The 1st Japanese-language paper was *Shimbunshi,* 1864. After the Meiji Restoration, 1868, Japanese journalism began to burgeon, and newspapers sprang up in Tokyo, Yokohama, and Kyoto. The Tokyo *Nichi-Nichi,* 1872, and the Osaka *Mainichi,* 1876, were 2 of the most successful of the new papers. Meanwhile the coverage of foreign affairs was improved by the sophisticated Tokyo *Asahi* 1888, and Osaka *Asahi,* 1879.

After World War II Japanese newspapers were strictly supervised by the allied authorities. Gradually control was lessened, and by 1962 Japan could claim 100 dailies with a combined readership of 39 m. In Tokyo 3 papers dominate: *Yomiuri, Asahi,* and *Mainichi.* Also publishing in Tokyo is the *Nippon Keizai Shimbun* (the "Japanese *Wall Street Journal*"). In Osaka, *Asahi* and *Mainichi* are the largest papers.

INDIA. The 1st Indian newspaper, the *Bengal Gazette or Calcutta General Advertiser,* was launched in 1780 by James Augustus Hickey. It was followed the same year by the *Indian Gazette or Calcutta Advertiser,* which dealt mainly with East India Co. affairs. Vernacular papers began with the *Digdarshan,* 1818, published in Bengal. A prime mover in the journalism of this period was the religious leader Ram Mohan Roy, who started *Mirat-ul-Akhbar,* a Persian-language weekly, in Calcutta. Later he lent his support to *Banga Dutt* (*Bengal Herald*), whose multilingual editions included Persian, Hindi, and Bengali.

In 1962 India possessed 300 dailies—76 in Hindi, 42 in Urdu, 33 in English, and the remainder in other languages. Among English-language papers, the leading organs are the *Times of India* of Bombay,

founded in 1838; the *Amvita Bazar Patrika,* 1860, a Calcutta paper; and the *Tribune,* 1881, of the East Punjab. The largest non-English dailies are the Bengali *Ananda Bazar Patrika* of Calcutta and the Hindi *Naubharat Times* of New Delhi. Other prominent non-English dailies are the Tamil *Thanthi* and the Telugu *Andhra Patrika,* both of Madras.

OTHER ASIAN COUNTRIES. In Pakistan perhaps the most influential daily is *Dawn,* which appears in many languages. The *Pakistan Times* of Lahore is the leading English-language paper. In the Philippines the 1st regular newspaper was *Del Superior gobierno,* 1811, and the 1st daily, *La Esperanza,* 1846. At the present time the largest daily is the *Manila Times,* founded in 1848. In Indonesia the earliest paper was the *Bataviase Nouvelles,* a weekly founded in 1744. The leading journal today is *Indonesia Raya.* Burma's oldest paper is the *Hanthawaddy,* 1889. In Singapore, the *Straits Times,* founded in 1845, is still one of the leading papers, while in Malaysia the *Malay Mail,* 1896, retains its importance. In Ceylon the Sinhalese and Tamil tongues are represented by the *Dinamina* and *Thinakaran* respectively.

MIDDLE EAST AND AFRICA

TURKEY. The Turkish press has, in general, suffered from official restriction and governmental interference. The largest paper in the country is *Hürviyet* of Istanbul, a Turkish-language journal, but newspapers also appear in Greek, Armenian, English, and French. In Istanbul alone over 40 individual dailies are published, and in Turkey as a whole over 300 were in existence in 1962.

EGYPT. Although newspapers were printed for a short time on Napoleon's orders in 1798, the 1st permanent Egyptian paper was an official gazette printed in 1828 by Mohammed Ali. A true Egyptian press emerged in the 2nd half of the 19th cent., and by 1865 there were 12 papers in Cairo and 2 in Alexandria. The oldest and most influential Egyptian journal is *Al Ahram,* 1875, which pioneered the use of foreign correspondents and introduced linotypes with Arabic characters at the turn of the 20th cent.

OTHER MIDDLE EASTERN COUNTRIES. In Iran the 1st regular newspaper was *Rúznáma*, 1851, of Teheran, and the 1st daily, *Khulásatul-Hawádith*, 1898. At present *Ettela'at*, 1925, is the leader. In Lebanon, though journalistic activity was slight until recently, the country now supports more than 30 dailies, most of them in Beirut. In Syria, the press is of similarly recent origin, yet by 1962 there were c. 20 Arabic-language dailies in publication. In Iraq daily newspapers have existed since 1914, when the *Baghdad Times* (later the *Iraq Times*) was founded. In Jordan there are 6 dailies, and in Saudi Arabia, 2: *Al Bilad* and *Um Al Quarah*. In Palestine, the 1st Hebrew-language daily was *Haheruth*, 1909. After the state of Israel was established, journalism flourished, and by 1962 there were 23 dailies being published in, among others, the Hebrew, Yiddish, German, and Bulgarian languages. The largest Israeli paper is *Ma'ariv*, 1948.

SOUTH AFRICA. Journalism in South Africa dates from the publication in 1800 of the *Capetown Gazette* and *African Advertiser*. In the mid-20th cent. the most influential English-language papers are the *Cape Times*, 1876, the *Cape Argus*, 1857; and, in the Transvaal, the *Star*, *Rand Daily Mail*, and *Sunday Times*. Afrikaans-language papers include *Die Burger* of the Cape, *Die Vaderland* of Johannesburg, and *Die Volksblad* of Bloemfontein. The 1st African-language newspaper was the Xhosa *Imvo Zabantsundu*, 1884. More than 20 African-language papers exist today.

FRENCH-SPEAKING AFRICA. In Tunisia there are 5 dailies at present, 2 in Arabic and 3 in French; the largest is *L'Action*. In Algeria 7 dailies are published in French and Arabic; *L'Écho d'Alger* is the best known. In Morocco there are 11 dailies, in Spanish, French, and Arabic.

ENGLISH-SPEAKING AFRICA. In the mid-20th cent. 7 Arabic- and 2 English-language dailies were appearing in the Sudan; in Ghana, 5, all in English; in Nigeria, 22; in Kenya, 4; in Sierra Leone, 2; in Liberia, 1; and in Tanzania, 6.

In all of Africa, c. 1962, there were some 230 dailies in publication.

Cinema, Radio, and Television

CINEMA

SILENT FILMS. The foundations of the art of the motion picture were laid in several different countries. The American cinema was responsible for the following landmarks in silent film history: the "peepshow" kinetoscope, developed by Thomas Edison in 1889; the 1st narrative film, *The Great Train Robbery*, 1903; the creation and growth of the Nickelodeon; and the spectacularly successful *The Birth of a Nation*, 1915, and *Intolerance*, 1916, made by the father of American—and perhaps of world—cinema, D. W. Griffith (1875–1948). Griffith's dynamic, brilliantly edited films revolutionized cinematic technique and made "the movies" an art. His genius was equaled by

that of Charles Chaplin (b. 1889), whose combination of pathos and comedy in films which he wrote, directed, and starred in (e.g., *City Lights*, 1930) made him world famous.

Particularly vital also was the German school, where surrealism and the technique of the moving camera were combined to produce such masterpieces as *The Cabinet of Dr. Caligari*, 1919, for which the scriptwriter, Carl Mayer, was largely responsible. In Russia, a radically different theory dominated the cinema. Known as "montage," it called for a series of brief shots assembled, for rhythmic effect, into an over-all pattern. Its masters were Sergei Eisenstein (1898–1948) and V. I. Pudovkin (1893–1953); the former's *Battleship Potemkin*, 1925, has taken its place among the masterworks of world cinema. In Scandinavia, the greatest film maker of the silent era was the Dane, Carl Dreyer, who cultivated the close-up in his memorable *The Passion of Saint Joan of Arc,* 1929.

THE MODERN CINEMA. In the U.S., chiefly in Hollywood, Calif., the major technical innovations of the modern cinema were born: the 1st motion picture using a sound track beside the picture frames (*The Jazz Singer,* 1927), the invention of color movies (Technicolor, 1930's), and the development of wide-screen techniques (Cinerama, Cinemascope, 1950's). Generally speaking, American film makers have proved themselves masters of escapism, specializing in such genres as the melodrama, the "Western," and the musical, in which directors like John Huston, Preston Sturges, Vincente Minelli, and Fred Zimmerman have been prominent.

In Europe a new breed of directors appeared with the coming of sound, and succeeded in adapting spoken dialogue to the visual nature of the medium. Especially gifted in this respect was the Frenchman, René Clair, whose talents were best exemplified in *À Nous la liberté,* 1931. Clair's countryman, Jean Renoir, also made his mark in the early sound era. In 1944 Marcel Carné equaled the best work of both these men with his richly textured *Les Enfants du paradis.* Germany too remained in the vanguard as directors like Fritz Lang and G. B. Pabst came to the fore.

Following World War II international reputations were earned by Robert Bresson in France, Vittorio de Sica in Italy, Carol Reed in Britain, and the Spanish-born Luis Buñuel in Mexico. The 1950's gave birth to the "New Wave" in France, a school of young directors in which François Truffaut and Jean-Luc Godard were the principal figures. In Italy Michelangelo Antonioni came into prominence. The most impressive films of the decade, however, were those of the Italian Federico Fellini and the Swede Ingmar Bergman. The former's *La Strada,* 1954, and the latter's *The Seventh Seal,* 1956, were major landmarks in world cinema.

In Japan the most admired director was Akira Kurosawa (*Rashomon,* 1951). In the 1960's films from Eastern Europe, particularly from Poland and Czechoslovakia, attracted much attention.

RADIO AND TELEVISION

EUROPE. In Great Britain, radio broadcasting began in 1920 under an independent monopoly granted by the government to the British Broadcasting Co. (later Corp.), or BBC. Television, also controlled by the BBC, began in 1939, but lapsed during World War II. In 1954 commercial television was permitted under the supervision of an Independent Television Authority and operating alongside the BBC's revived service. In general, European radio and TV are organized along similar lines to the British: exclusive broadcasting privileges leased to a private co. or cos. and the individual set owner paying a regular annual license fee. European commercial radio broadcasting began in the 1920's and television in the 1950's. A smaller percentage of time has traditionally been devoted to advertising than in the U.S. In Eastern Europe, where commercial advertising is not employed, all communica-

RADIO AND TV SETS IN USE IN
SELECTED COUNTRIES, 1965–66
(million)

	Radio Sets	TV Sets
U.S.	240.0	61.8[a]
USSR	74.0	7.0
West Germany	26.0	12.0
Japan	20.0	20.0
U.K.	16.0	12.5
China (mainland)	15.7	.1
France	15.0	8.4
Italy	11.0	7.5
East Germany	5.6	1.6
Poland	5.4	1.0
Czechoslovakia	3.7	1.3
Sweden	2.9	2.0
India	2.1	b
South Korea	1.0	.04
Thailand	.16	.16

[a] Estimated number of viewers rather than sets, 1963 figure.

[b] TV used chiefly for educational purposes.

tions networks are owned and operated by government agencies.

UNITED STATES. Commercial radio in the U.S. began in the 1920's. By 1963 both standard (AM) and frequency modulation (FM) stations existed in abundance. Commercial TV appeared as a significant force only after World War II, but by the 1960's had become the foremost communications medium in the country, devoting the bulk of its program time to situation comedies, dramatic shows, Westerns, and other types of popular entertainment. All radio and TV stations and networks, though generally privately owned, are regulated by the Federal Communications Commission (FCC).

Music

EUROPE AND THE UNITED STATES

18th and 19th Cents.

1750–1827

CLASSIC PERIOD. Contributing to the evolution of new forms in music was the social and cultural unrest generated by the rationalist philosophy of the Enlightenment. Previously, the monumental forms of the baroque period, 1600–1750, had found their highest expression in the masterworks of Johann Sebastian Bach (1685–1750), whose major works include the B minor Mass, 1738; *Passion According to St. John,* 1723; *Passion According to St. Matthew,* 1740; and of Georg Friderich Handel (1685–1759) —*Messiah,* Dublin, 1742. These baroque composers were succeeded by a new generation of composers presaging the changing taste and ideas of the 2nd half of the 18th cent. Instrumental music, long subordinated to the dominance of vocal music, now emerged as the primary medium of expression. The classic sonata of 3 movements, later 4, developed from earlier models, crystallized in the genius of Franz Joseph Haydn (1732–1809) —104 symphonies for orchestra (No. 94, "Surprise," 1791; No. 100, "Military," 1794; No. 101, "Clock," 1794; No. 104, "London," 1794), 26 concerti, 84 string quartets. The emergent architectonic form served the composers of the classic period. Also by Haydn are 2 outstanding oratorios—*The Creation,* 1798, and *The Seasons,* 1801— which resemble their baroque choral and instrumental counterparts.

MOZART. The aesthetic and artistic ideals of the period are superbly exemplified in the compositions of Wolfgang Amadeus Mozart (1756–91). His works include 12 operas (*Marriage of Figaro,* K.492, 1786; *Don Giovanni,* K.527, 1787; *Magic Flute,* K.620, 1791, in German), 41 symphonies (No. 39 in E flat, K.543; No. 40 in G minor, K.550; No. 41 in C major, K.551), 35 concerti, much chamber music, sonatas for piano, and masses (Requiem, 1791). Originality, musical sophistication, charm, wit, and sentiment are expressed with elegance and refinement in compositions that balance and integrate form and content, music addressed to the aristocratic audience upon whom the composer depended for patronage. By 20th-cent. standards the orchestras were small, generally including strings, flute, oboe, clarinet (late Mozart), bassoon, trumpets, and horns. Trombones were introduced by Gluck and Mozart in their operas (and were 1st used in symphonic music by Beethoven in his 5th Symphony); also tympani.

BEETHOVEN. The classic period attained its climax in the works of Ludwig van Beethoven (1770–1827), whose works include 9 symphonies (No. 3 in E flat major, Op.55, "Eroica"; No. 5 in C minor, Op.67; No. 7 in A major, Op.92; No. 9 in D minor, Op.125, 1824, with chorus and soloists); 5 concerti for piano (No. 4 in G major, Op.58, and No. 5 in E flat, Op. 73, "Emperor"), violin concerto in D major, Op.61, 1806; 32 sonatas for piano alone; 10 sonatas for violin and piano; numerous chamber music works; masses

(*Missa Solemnis* in D major, Op.123, and Mass in C) ; and the opera *Fidelio,* 1805, rev. 1806. Beethoven infused the established forms with a dynamism of emotional energy and spiritual elevation that transcended the personal expression of his genius. In depth and range of expression he mirrored the spirit of the changing social, cultural, economic, and political climate of Western Europe which followed the French Revolution, and forecast the approaching romanticism of the 19th cent. The liberating influence of these changes affected the author's humanistic and individualistic approach to his art and broadened his attitude toward his audience, the new *bourgeoisie* that was emerging in the early stages of the Industrial Revolution.

1824–98

ROMANTICISM. The introduction of poetry into the classic symphonic form in Beethoven's 9th Symphony in 1824 marks a new era in the evolution of music. The verses of Schiller's *Ode to Joy* proclaiming the brotherhood of man, sung by a quartet of singers and a chorus, epitomized Beethoven's optimism about man's ultimate ability to resolve his problems.

Franz Peter Schubert (1797–1828) largely followed Beethoven's principles of form, yet imbued his 8 symphonies with his own exquisite sense of tender poetry, sensitive orchestral coloring, and characteristic harmonies and modulation, thereby bridging the period from classic to romantic. His symphonies include No. 7 in C major, "The Great," 1828, and No. 8 in B minor, "The Unfinished," 1822. Subsequent composers, though still influenced by the classic concept of form, tempered their symphonies with elements drawn from romanticism—broader melodic line; more complicated harmony, in some cases even chromatic; more involved and even cross-currented rhythms; and more elaborate and even more sensitive orchestration. Notable among these composers were Felix Mendelssohn (1809–47) —Symphony No. 3 in A minor, "Scotch," 1842; No. 4 in A major, "Italian," 1833; No. 5 in D minor, "Reformation," 1830–

32; Robert Schumann (1810–56) —Symphony No. 1 in B flat major, "Spring," 1841; No. 3 in E flat major, "Rhenish," 1850; No. 4 in D minor, 1841; Johannes Brahms (1833–97) —Symphony No. 1 in C minor, Op.68, 1876; No. 2 in D major, Op.73, 1877; No. 3 in F major, Op.90, 1883; No. 4 in E minor, Op.98, 1885; Anton Bruckner (1824–97) —Symphony No. 4, "Romantic," 1874; No. 7, 1881–83; No. 9, 1894; César Franck (1822–90) — Symphony in D minor, 1888; Peter Ilyich Tchaikovsky (1840–93) —Symphony No. 4 in F minor, 1877; No. 5 in E minor, 1888; No. 6 in B minor, "Pathétique," 1893; Antonin Dvořák (1841–1904) —Symphony No. 5 (now known as No. 9) in E minor, Op.95, "From the New World," 1893.

PROGRAM MUSIC. The *Symphonie fantastique,* 1830, of Hector Berlioz (1803–69) , with its autobiographical program and extravagant instrumentation, served as a model for much of the romantic program music to follow. Such music found its subject matter in extramusical sources, such as poetry, painting, folklore, and philosophy, and was given form in the 1-movement symphonic tone poems of Franz Liszt (1811–86) —*Tasso,* 1840–48; *Les Préludes,* 1845. Liszt's *Faust Symphony* (after Goethe) , 1850, comprises 3 movements, musical characterizations respectively of Faust, Gretchen, and Mephistopheles. Subsequently, Richard Strauss (1864–1949) intensified the form in a series of tone poems—*Aus Italien,* 1886; *Macbeth,* 1887; *Don Juan,* 1888; *Tod und Verklärung,* 1880; *Till Eulenspiegel,* 1895; *Also sprach Zarathustra,* 1896; *Don Quixote,* 1897; *Ein Heldenleben (Hero's Life)* , 1898. Other examples of pictorial orchestral music were provided by Mendelssohn's *Midsummer Night's Dream,* 1826; *Fingal's Cave,* 1832; *Ruy Blas,* 1839; and by symphonic suites such as *Scheherazade,* 1888, by Nicolai Rimsky-Korsakov (1844–1908) .

SMALLER FORMS. The romantic aesthetic, with its stress on personal emotion, found its proper medium in the lieder (art songs) of such outstanding composers as Franz Schubert—*Der Erlkönig,* D.328, 1815; *Gretchen am Spinnrade,* 1814; *Serenade,* D.889, 1826; as well as in song cycles, including *Die Schöne Müllerin,* D.795,1823; *Die Winterreise,* D.911, 1827; *Schwanengesang,* D.957, 1828; Robert Schumann—*Die beiden Grenadier,* 1840, and the song cycles *Frauenliebe und -leben,* Op.42, 1840, and *Dichterliebe,* Op.48, 1840; Johannes Brahms—*Vergebliches Ständchen,* Op.84, 1878–81; *Sapphische Ode,* Op.94, 1884; *Wiegenlied,* Op.49, c. 1868; and the song cycles *Magelone,* Op.33, 1861–68 and *Vier Ernste Gesänge,* Op.121, 1896; Hugo Wolf (1860–1903)—*Nachgelassenelieder (Youthful Songs)*; *Mörikelieder,* 1888; *Eichendorfflieder,* 1888; *Goethelieder,* 1889; *Spanisches Liederbuch,* 1890; *Italienisches Liederbuch,* 1891–96; Richard Strauss—4 sets of songs with orchestra, 1897–1921; 26 sets with piano, 1882–1929.

MUSIC FOR PIANO. The piano, invented by Bartolommeo Cristofori in Florence, c. 1710, improved by Broadwood (London, 1817) and Érard (Paris, 1821), with its fuller tonal resources, provided the 19th-cent. composer with an instrument of extraordinary range and possibilities for expression. It inspired a variety of new forms (mostly short), such as études, preludes, waltzes, mazurkas, polonaises, nocturnes, intermezzi, capriccios, rhapsodies, fantasies, etc. Foremost among the composers for the piano were Frédéric Chopin (1810–49)—*Fantasie* in F minor; ballads, waltzes, preludes, mazurkas, nocturnes, and, in larger forms, sonatas in B flat minor, 1839, and in B minor, 1844; Franz Schubert—6 *Moments musicaux,* 1823–28; 8 impromptus, 1827; *Wanderer Fantasie,* 1822; and 11 sonatas (A flat major, 1817; B flat major, 1828); Robert Schumann—*Album for the Young,* Op.68, 1848; *Scenes from Childhood,* Op.15, 1838; *Papillons,* Op.2, 1832; *Carnaval,* Op.9, 1834–35; *Symphonic Études;* Fantasy in C major, Op.17, 1836; and 3 sonatas; Felix Mendelssohn—*Songs in Short Words,* 8 vols., 1830–45; *Variations sérieuses,* Op.54, 1841; Franz Liszt—*Années de Pélérinage,* 3 vols., 1855, 1858, 1883; 12 *Études d'exécution transcendante,* 1852; *Deux études de concert: Waldesrauschen* and *Gnomenreigen,* 1849–63; *Deux légendes,* 1866; 20 *Hungarian Rhapsodies,* 1851–86; Johannes

Brahms—6 sets of variations; 3 rhapsodies (B minor, A minor, E flat major); intermezzi, capriccios, ballades; 3 sonatas.

MUSIC FOR SOLO INSTRUMENTS WITH ORCHESTRA. The piano with orchestra served as a vehicle for distinguished concerti (large form): Schumann—A minor, Op.54, 1845; Chopin—E minor, Op.11, 1833; F minor, Op.21, 1836; Liszt—E flat major, Op.22, 1857; A major, Op.23, 1863; Brahms—No. 1 in D minor, Op.15, 1858; No. 2 in B flat major, Op.83, 1881; Tchaikovsky—No. 1 in B flat minor, Op.23, 1875; Grieg—A minor, 1868, rev. 1907. Concertos for violin and orchestra include Mendelssohn—E minor, Op.64, 1844; Brahms—D major, Op.77, 1878; Paganini—No. 1 in E flat major, No. 2 in B minor; Tchaikovsky—D major, Op.35, 1878. Brahms also composed a double concerto for violin and cello in A minor, Op.102, 1887.

CHAMBER MUSIC. Piano quintets include Schubert—Quintet in A, "Die Forelle," 1819; Schumann—E flat major, Op.47, 1842; Brahms—F minor, Op.34, 1864; César Franck—F minor, 1879. Other distinguished chamber works (large form) include Schubert—string quartets in A minor, D.804, 1824; D minor, D.810, "Death and the Maiden," 1824–26; A major, D.887, 1826; string quartet in C, D.956, 1826; trio in B flat major, D.898, 1827; octet in E for clarinet, horn, bassoon, and string quartet, D.803, 1824; Mendelssohn—octet in E flat for strings, Op.20, 1825; piano trio in D minor, Op.49, 1837; Brahms—string quartets in C minor, Op.51, No. 1, 1873; A minor, Op.51, No. 2, 1873; B flat major, Op. 67, 1875; sextets in B flat major, Op.18, 1860, and in G major, Op.36, 1865; clarinet quintet (with strings) in B minor, Op.115, 1891.

CHORAL WORKS. Religious works for chorus and orchestra include Schubert—Mass in A flat, D.667, 1819–22; Mass in E flat, D.957, 1828; Mendelssohn—oratorios (influenced by Handel and Haydn), *St. Paul,* Op.36, 1838, and *Elijah,* Op.70, 1876; Berlioz—*L'Enfance du Christ,* 1854; Requiem (*Grande Messe des Morts*), Op.5, 1837; *Te Deum,* 1849; Liszt—*Hungarian Coronation Mass,* 1867;

oratorios, *Legend of St. Elizabeth,* 1857–62, and *Christus,* 1855–62; Brahms—*Ein Deutsches Requiem* (Protestant), 1866; Verdi—*Manzoni Requiem,* 1874. Secular works include Brahms—*Rhapsodie (Alto Rhapsody)*, Op. 53, 1869; *Song of Destiny,* Op.54, 1871; *Nanie,* Op.82, 1880–81; *Song of the Fates,* Op.89, 1882.

1762–1814

OPERA: CLASSIC PERIOD. Italian opera maintained its pre-eminence in the repertory of European opera houses throughout the 18th cent. The "reform" operas of Christoph Willibald Gluck (1714–87)—*Orfeo ed Euridice* (Vienna, 1762) and *Alceste* (Vienna, 1767)—represent an effort to avoid the abuses and excesses of Italian opera and to confine music to its proper function of serving poetry to express the plot. The official opera of the Austrian court remained Italian, the humbler *Singspiel,* with its folk subject matter in the vernacular, being relegated to less prestigious theaters. The trio of Italian operas by Mozart to librettos by Lorenzo da Ponte (1749–1838)—*Le Nozze de Figaro (Marriage of Figaro,* Vienna, 1786), *Don Giovanni (Don Juan,* Prague, 1787), and *Cosi fan Tutti (Thus Do They All,* Vienna, 1790)—and his German opera, *Die Zauberflöte (The Magic Flute,* Vienna, 1791), with libretto by Emanuel Schikaneder, have survived as musical masterpieces. Beethoven's only opera, *Fidelio,* originally performed in Vienna in 1805 with a French libretto and revised twice to a final German version performed in Vienna in 1814, has its roots in Mozart, but exemplifies Beethoven's unique dynamism.

1821–42

OPERA: ROMANTIC PERIOD. Founder of the German romantic opera was Carl Maria von Weber (1786–1826), whose *Der Freischütz (The Freeshooter,* Berlin, 1821) incorporated such characteristics as (1) romanticizing plots, using folklore and legend; (2) elements of the supernatural; (3) nature, wild and mysterious; (4) use of German folksongs to characterize the realities of contemporary life; (5) recurrent musical motives; and (6) brilliantly effective pictorial orchestration, defining a style Germans recognized as their own, and inspiring a developing tradition. Also by Weber were *Euryanthe* (Vienna, 1823), based on medieval romanticism, and the fairy opera *Oberon* (English libretto, London, 1826).

1842–82

WAGNERIAN OPERA. German opera reached its zenith with the controversial operas and music dramas of Richard Wagner (1813–83)—*Rienzi* (Dresden, 1842); *Der Fliegende Hollander (Flying Dutchman,* Dresden, 1843); *Tannhaüser* (Dresden, 1845); *Lohengrin* (Weimar, 1850); *Der Ring des Nibelungen: Das Rheingold* (1854, performed Munich, 1869), *Die Walküre* (1856, performed Munich, 1870), *Siegfried* (1871, performed Bayreuth, 1876), and *Die Götterdämmerung (Twilight of the Gods,* 1874, performed Bayreuth, 1876); *Tristan und Isolde* (1857, performed Munich, 1865); *Die Meistersinger von Nürnberg* (1867, performed Munich, 1868); and *Parsifal* (1882, performed Bayreuth, 1882). Wagner's concept of music drama, set forth in voluminous prose works, envisaged a composite or total art form through the fusion of poetry, music, dance, architecture and painting, and unity of stage and music direction. This concept utilized the art form as a vehicle of propaganda for advancing the German national state. Characteristics of Wagnerian music drama include (1) use of German mythology and folk material in later works; (2) use of "endless melody" (breaking down of the concept of 4-bar melody by avoiding final cadences); (3) chromatic harmony; (4) use of the orchestra as a psychological delineator; (5) use of leitmotif (leading motive) as a guide to identifying characters and situations; (6) increased technique of voice and instruments by enormously new demands; (7) enlarged number of instruments in the orchestra. *Der Ring des Nibelungen* was given for the 1st time in its entirety in

1876 at the Festspielhaus (Festival Theater), conceived, designed, and built under Wagner's direction expressly for the production of his music dramas (the 1st time this had been done in the entire history of music).

1797–1908

FRENCH OPERA. French opera was centered in Paris in the early part of the 19th cent. The grandeur and heroism of the French Revolution were favorite themes. Prominent composers were Luigi Cherubini (1760–1842) —*Médée* (Paris, 1797) in the classic tradition, and *Les Deux Journées* (1800, known in England as "The Water Carrier"), a good example of the *"reçue"* opera; and Gasparo Spontini (1772–1851) —*La Vestale*, 1807.

GRAND OPERA. Influenced by the rising generation of French playwrights (Eugène Scribe, 1791–1886; Victor Hugo, 1802–85; and others), grand opera often took for its subject matter pseudo-historical situations, directing battles and mob scenes toward overemotional effects. *La Muette de Portici*, 1828, by Daniel François Esprit Auber (1782–1871), opened the new era. Exerting enormous influence were Giacomo Meyerbeer (1791–1861) — *Robert le Diable* (1831), *Les Huguenots* (1836), *Le Prophète* (1849), *L'Africaine* (1864); Hector Berlioz—*Benvenuto Cellini* (1834–38), *Les Troyens* (1859), *Béatrice and Bénédict* (1862); and Jacques François Halévy (1799–1862) —*La Juive* (1835). An outstanding example of lyric opera was *Faust* (1859), by Charles Gounod (1818–93), while *Manon* (1884), by Jules Massenet (1842–1912), reveals a growing trend toward sentimentalism. Outstanding among composers in lighter vein was Jacques Offenbach (1819–80), whose many operettas influenced light opera for years to come—*Orphée aux Enfers* (*Orpheus in the Underworld,* 1858), *Les Contes d'Hoffmann* (*Tales of Hoffmann,* Paris, 1881). The operatic masterpiece *Carmen* (1875), by Georges Bizet (1838–75), a folk drama of extraordinary power, inspired the subsequent school of veristic Italian opera. *Louise* (1900), by Gustave Charpentier (1860–

1956), was a combination of naturalism, nostalgia, and lyricism.

ITALIAN OPERA. The most celebrated composer of Italian opera in the early 19th cent. was Gioacchino Rossini (1792–1868) —*Barber of Seville* (Rome, 1816), still a sparkling gem of Italian comic opera; *William Tell* (Paris, 1829), in the grand-opera tradition. *Lucia di Lammermoor* (Naples, 1831), by Gaetano Donizetti (1797–1848), is still a vehicle in the repertory for brilliant coloratura sopranos. Also surviving are Donizetti's 2 comic operas, *L'Elisir d'Amore* (Milan, 1832) and *Don Pasquale* (Paris, 1843). Still produced are Vincenzo Bellini's (1801–35) semi-seria opera, *La Sonnambula* (Milan, 1831), and the opera seria, *Norma* (Milan, 1831), both distinguished for their beautiful melodies. Arrigo Boito (1842–1918) completed 1 full opera, *Mefistofele* (Milan, 1868), but his reputation rests chiefly on 2 librettos for Giuseppi Verdi—*Otello* and *Falstaff*—and the libretto of *La Gioconda* (Milan, 1876) by Amilcare Ponchielli (1834–86).

VERDI. Giuseppi Verdi (1813–1901) outranked all composers of Italian opera. Originally following in the traditions of his predecessors, beginning with *Nabucco* (Milan, 1842), he quickly found his own style. Endowed with an unusually fertile gift of melody, using harmony, rhythm, and orchestration with a sure hand (the last never permitted to overshadow the vocal line), and possessing an extraordinary sense of the theater, Verdi composed operas epitomizing dramatic energy and passion. Throwing himself into the struggle of his people to escape the Austrian yoke, he chose subjects for his librettos that, despite the most rigorous censorship, carried meaning and inspiration to his compatriots—*Ernani* (Venice, 1844), *Luisa Miller* (Naples, 1849), and *Rigoletto* (Venice, 1851). The last, along with *Il Trovatore* (Rome, 1853) and *La Traviata* (Venice, 1853), are 3 of the most popular operas of all time. More ambitiously conceived were his operas of the middle period—*Un Ballo in Maschera* (*Masked Ball,* Rome, 1859), *La Forza del Destino* (St. Petersburg, 1862), and *Don Carlos* (Paris, 1867). Verdi composed his

greatest works in his later years—*Aïda*
(Cairo, 1871), commissioned by the
khedive of Egypt for the opening of the
Suez Canal; *Otello* (Milan, 1887) ; and the
opera buffa, Falstaff (Milan, 1892), which
appeared in the composer's 80th year.

RUSSIAN OPERA. Russian opera
properly begins with *A Life for the Czar*
(1836) and *Russlan and Ludmila* (1842)
by Michael Glinka (1804–57), who was
inspired by contact with poets and writers
of the national literary movement. Aleksandr Sergeyevich Dargomijsky (1813–69),
the other outstanding figure among the
Russian composers of his generation, produced *Esmeralda* (1847), *Russalka* (1856),
and *The Stone Guest (Don Juan,* 1872).
Of the Russian 5 (see below), 3 wrote
outstanding operas: Aleksandr Porfirevich
Borodin   (1833–87)—*Prince Igor*   (St.
Petersburg, 1890) ; Nicolai Andreyevich
Rimsky-Korsakov   (1844–1908) —*Mlada*
(1890), *Christmas Eve* (1895), *Sadko*
(1896), *Czar Saltan* (1896–98), *Kitezh*
(1904), *Le Coq d'Or* (1907) ; all of these
works made charming use of Russian
fairy tales and folk melodies, and were
attractively written for voice and brilliantly orchestrated; Modest Mussorgsky
(1839–81), the most distinguished of these
operatic composers, whose *Boris Godunov*
(1868–69) is a masterpiece and an extraordinary psychological study; and
Peter Ilyich Tchaikovsky (1840–93),
among whose 11 operas are *Eugene Onegin* (1884) and *Pique Dame (Queen of
Spades,* 1890).

OTHER OPERATIC COMPOSERS.
Other national operatic composers of
this period include Bohemian—Bedřich
Smetana (1824–84) —*The Bartered Bride,*
a comic opera which is a treasure trove of
folk song and folk dance; English—outstanding were the operettas of Sir Arthur
Sullivan (1824–1900), set to librettos by
Sir William Gilbert (1836–1911) —*H.M.S.
Pinafore* (1878), *Pirates of Penzance*
(1879), *Patience* (1881), *Iolanthe* (1882),
Princess Ida (1884), *The Mikado* (1885),
Ruddigore (1887), *Yeomen of the Guard*
(1888), *The Gondoliers* (1889) ; Austro-
German—the outstanding composer of
operetta in the German language was
Johann Strauss, the younger (1825–99),
also famous as a composer of waltzes, as
was his father Johann Strauss, Sr. (1804–
49), before him—*Die Fledermaus (The
Bat,* Vienna, 1874).

1854–1927

NATIONALISM. The compulsive desire
of various ethnic groups to assert their
own cultural identity found forthright
expression in music. Richard Wagner,
influenced by Carl Maria von Weber,
successfully unified music and drama,
imbuing his creations with a philosophic
concept that was seized by German nationalists (and was subsequently exploited in the 20th cent. in the USSR). In
at least 5 of his 1st 15 operas, Verdi chose
subjects that inspired Italian patriots to
fight Austria.

Nationalism found particular expression in the Russian group known as the
"Mighty 5": Aleksandr Borodin (1833–87)
—opera, *Prince Igor* (1890) ; César Cui
(1835–1918) ; Mily Balakirev (1837–1910)
—*Islamey* (1869) ; Modest Mussorgsky
(1839–81) —*A Night on Bald Mountain*
(1867), *Pictures at an Exhibition* (suite
for piano, 1874; orchestrated by Maurice
Ravel, 1935), song cycles *Sunless* (1874)
and *Songs and Dances of Death* (1875–
77), opera *Boris Godunov* (St. Petersburg,
1874; revised and orchestrated by Rimsky-
Korsakov, 1896, and also by Dmitri
Shostakovich, 1941), opera *Khovantchina*
(St. Petersburg, 1886) ; and Nicolai Rimsky-Korsakov (1844–1908), active as composer, collector of folk songs, orchestrator
and teacher, and author of *Foundations
of Orchestration* (St. Petersburg, 1913).
Rimsky-Korsakov's most widely played
orchestral works include *Capriccio Es-
pagnol* (Op.34, 1887), *Scheherazade*
(Op.35, 1888) ; his operas include *Sadko*
(Moscow, 1898) and *Golden Cockerel*
(Moscow, 1909). Russian folk song and
dance, although less consciously used, are
reflected in the music of Peter Ilyich
Tchaikovsky (1840–93), whose outstanding works include Symphonies No. 4 in F
minor, Op.36, 1877; No. 5 in E minor,
Op.64, 1888; No. 6 in B minor, Op.74,
"Pathétique," 1893; Violin Concerto in D
major, Op.35, 1875; Piano Concerto in B

flat minor, Op.23, 1875; programmatic works: the symphonic fantasy, *Francesca da Rimini,* Op.32, 1876; symphonic poems: *Romeo and Juliet,* 1880, and *Manfred,* Op.58, 1885; ballet music from *Swan Lake,* Op.20, 1876, *Sleeping Beauty,* Op.66, 1889, *Nutcracker Suite,* Op.71A, 1892; operas: *Eugene Onegin,* Moscow, 1879, and *Queen of Spades,* St. Petersburg, 1890.

Other Russian nationalist composers include Alexander Glazunov (1865–1936) —Symphony in C minor. Op.58, 1896; Violin Concerto in A minor, Op.82, 1904–15; Alexander Scriabin (1872–1915) —2 symphonic pieces: *Poem of Ecstasy,* Op.54, 1908, and *Prometheus: Poem of Fire,* Op.60, 1910; Sergei Rachmaninov (1873–1943) —Piano Concerto No. 2 in C minor, 1901; No. 3 in D minor, 1909; Symphony No. 2 in E minor, Op.27, 1907; Reinhold Glière (1875–1956) —Symphony No. 3, Op.42, "Ilya Murometz," 1911; ballet *The Red Poppy,* Op.70, Moscow, 1927; awarded Stalin prize twice, 1948 and 1950.

CENTRAL EUROPE. In Central Europe, the songs and dances of Poland were prominent in the piano music of Frédéric Chopin, while the Czech composers Antonín Dvořák and Bedřich Smetana gave distinct ethnic color to their music through the use of indigenous folk material. Smetana's opera *The Bartered Bride* (1866) is considered a folk masterpiece, and his *My Country* (1874–79), a cycle of 6 symphonic poems, includes the well-known epic of *The Moldau.* In addition, Franz Liszt used Hungarian gypsy tunes in his 20 *Hungarian Rhapsodies,* 1851–86.

SCANDINAVIA. Scandinavian nationalist and folk motifs are exemplified in the work of Edvard Hagerup Grieg (1843–1907), with his liberal use of Norwegian songs and dances; also Piano Concerto in A minor, 1868, rev. 1907, and 2 suites from Ibsen's *Peer Gynt,* 1888–91. Denmark is represented by Carl Nielsen (1865–91) —6 symphonies, 3 concertos, 2 operas. Intense Finnish nationalist aspirations are expressed in the tone poems of Jean Sibelius (1865–1957) —*En Saga,* 1892, and *Finlandia,* 1899, and in his 4 legends —*The Swan of Tuonela,* 1893; *Lemmin-*

kainen and the Maidens, 1895; *Lemminkainen in Tuonela,* 1895; *Return of Lemminkainen,* 1895—based on the Finnish folk epic *Kalevala.* Sibelius also composed tone poems—*Pohjola's Daughter,* Op.49, 1906, and *Tapiola,* Op.112, 1925—and the Finnish folk idiom is evident in his 7 symphonies, his Violin Concerto in D minor, Op.47, 1903, and his string quartet *Voces Intimae,* Op.56, 1909.

SPAIN. The colorful rhythms and exciting melodies of Spanish folk music are captured by Isaac Albéniz (1860–1909) — *Iberia,* suite of 12 pieces for piano, 1906–9; by Enrique Granados (1867–1916) —opera *Goyescas,* 1916; and by Manuel de Falla (1876–1946) —opera *La Vida Breve,* 1913; ballets *El Amor Brujo,* 1915, and *Three-Cornered Hat,* 1917; and suite for piano and orchestra *Nights in the Gardens of Spain,* 1916.

GREAT BRITAIN. British folk tunes and nationalism are easily recognizable in the music of Sir Edward Elgar (1857–1934) —*Enigma Variations,* Op.36, 1899; oratorio *The Dream of Gerontius,* Op.38, 1900; 5 *Pomp and Circumstance* marches, Op.39, 1901–30, of which No. 2 in D major is world-famous. Other distinguished British composers include Sir Arthur Sullivan (see above); Frederick Delius (1862–1934), who, though influenced by French impressionism and the Norwegian Grieg, used English folk idioms in his symphonic music—*Over the Hills and Far Away,* 1895; *Brigg Fair,* 1907; *In a Summer Garden,* 1908; *On Hearing the First Cuckoo in Spring,* 1913; and in his work for chorus and orchestra, *Sea Drift* (after Walt Whitman), 1903.

1872–1933

FRENCH NATIONALISM AND POST-ROMANTICISM. The founder of the French school of composition based on classical forms, yet featuring a symphonic and leitmotif treatment of lyric drama, was César Franck (1822–90). Among his outstanding works were his oratorios, *Redemption,* 1872, and *Les Béatitudes,* 1880; and his church music, *Mass for Three Voices,* motets, offertories, *Psalm 150.* His major orchestral works include the Symphony in D minor, 1888, and *Symphonic Variations for Piano and Orchestra*, 1885. In addition, he wrote chamber music— Piano Quintet in F minor, 1879; Sonata in A major for Violin and Piano, 1886; String Quartet in D major, 1889; and music for piano and organ, *Trois Chorales*, 1890, as well as songs.

Other outstanding French composers of the time were Vincent d'Indy (1851–1931) —*Symphony on a French Mountain Air*, Op.25, 1886; Symphony in B flat major, Op.57, 1903; symphonic variations, *Istar*, Op.42, 1896; Paul Dukas (1823–92), who survives through his brilliant orchestral scherzo, *The Sorcerer's Apprentice*, 1897; Édouard Lalo (1823–92), skilled violinist and violist—*Symphonie Espagnole* for violin and orchestra, 1875; Concerto in D minor for cello and orchestra, 1877; Emmanuel Chabrier (1841–94) —orchestral rhapsody *España*, 1883; Ernest Chausson (1855–99) —Symphony in B major, 1898; *Poème* for violin and orchestra, 1897; Camille Saint-Saëns (1835–1921), whose works still in the repertory include: opera *Samson et Dalila*, Op.47, 1877; Piano Concerto No. 2 in G minor, Op.22, 1868; Concerto for Cello and Orchestra, Op.33, 1873; tone poem for orchestra *Danse Macabre*, Op.40, 1874; Concerto in B minor for Violin and Orchestra, Op.61, 1880; Symphony in C minor for orchestra with organ and 2 pianos, Op.78, 1886; Gabriel Fauré (1845–1924) —*Requiem*, Op.48, 1887; chamber works: Violin Sonata in A, Op.13, 1876; Piano Quintet in C minor, Op.115, 1921; String Quartet in E minor, Op.121, 1924; incidental music to *Shylock*, Op.57, 1889; musical score for Maeterlinck's *Pelléas et Mélisande*, Op.80, 1898; Henri Duparc (1848–1933), outstanding as an exponent of the French art song—*Chanson Triste, L'Extase, L'Invitation du Voyage*.

FRENCH IMPRESSIONISM. The French impressionist movement came as a reaction against German romanticism. The French aesthetic spirit, deeply wounded by the defeat in the Franco-Prussian War, 1870–71, retreated into a twilight world best represented in painting by Monet, in poetry by Verlaine and Rimbaud, and in music by Claude Debussy (1862–1918). Debussy expressed his concern for mood, atmosphere, and color by means of forms of his own invention— freedom of rhythms; modal, pentatonic, and whole-tone scale patterns; suppleness of melody; harmony somewhat influenced by Wagner, yet original in concept. His orchestration was expertly coloristic and delicate in contrast to the broad, heavy, deep strokes and colors of the German school. His orchestral works include *Prélude à l'Après-midi d'un Faune*, 1894; 3 *Nocturnes*, 1899; *La Mer*, 1905; works for piano: *Estampes*, 1903; *Images*, 1905–7; *Préludes*, 1910–11; opera: *Pelléas et Mélisande* (after Maeterlinck's play), 1902; choral works: *L'Enfant Prodigue*, 1884; *La Damoiselle Élue*, 1888; *Le Martyre de Saint Sébastien*, 1911.

The other leading exemplar of this school was Maurice Ravel (1875–1937). Influenced by Debussy's impressionism, Ravel combined classic forms, clear-cut melodic line, substantive harmony, and more precise rhythms in his music. His numerous compositions include, for piano—*Jeux d'Eau*, 1901; *Sonatine*, 1905; *Gaspard de la Nuit*, 1908; *Pavane pour une Enfante Défunte*, 1899 (arranged later for orchestra); chamber music— String Quartet, 1903; Introduction and Allegro for harp, string quartet, flute, and clarinet, 1906; Piano Trio, 1915; Cello Sonata, 1922; Violin Sonata, 1927; ballets —*Daphnis et Chloé*, 1912; *Ma Mère l'Oye* (from suite for piano duet), 1915; operas —*L'Heure Espagnole*, 1907; *L'Enfant et les Sortilèges*, 1925; for orchestra—*Rhapsodie Espagnole*, 1907; *La Valse*, 1920; *Boléro*, 1928; Concerto for Piano (left hand alone) and Orchestra, 1931; Concerto for Piano and Orchestra, 1931; orchestral arrangement of Mussorgsky's *Pictures at an Exhibition*, 1922.

POSTROMANTICISM. The outstanding composers of the postromantic period were Gustav Mahler (1860–1911) in the field of the symphony and Richard Strauss (1864–1947), 1st in the tone poem and subsequently in German opera. Mahler encompassed in his symphonies lyricism (the folk songs and dance tunes of his native Bohemia permeate his music), the chromatic harmony of Wagner (somewhat refined), a loosening of the symphonic form, a characteristic polyphony, and extraordinary sensitivity and mastery of the orchestra, using full-scale orchestral resources and extended instrumental techniques. Inherent in his work is a deep religiosity and an attempt to communicate philosophic principles. His works include Symphony No. 1, "Titan," 1888; Symphony No. 2, "Resurrection," 1894; No. 3, 1895; No. 4, 1900; No. 8, "Symphony of a Thousand" for expanded orchestra, choir, 8 solo voices, double chorus, boys' chorus, and organ, 1907; *Das Lied von der Erde* for solo voices and orchestra, 1908; also many songs and song cycles.

Gifted with a fertile imagination, extraordinary dramatic sense, and a brilliant mastery of orchestral technique, Richard Strauss 1st achieved fame with his series of tone poems: *Don Juan,* 1888; *Tod und Verklärung,* 1889; *Till Eulenspiegel,* 1895; *Also Sprach Zarathustra,* 1896; *Don Quixote,* 1897; *Ein Heldenleben,* 1898; *Symphonia Domestica,* 1903. His most important operas are *Salome,* 1903; *Elektra,* 1909; *Der Rosenkavalier,* 1911; *Ariadne auf Naxos,* 1912; *Die Frau ohne Schatten,* 1919. Among the loveliest of his many songs are his last compositions, *4 Last Songs,* with orchestra, 1947.

1890–1958

ITALIAN OPERA TRENDS. The style of the period was primarily *verismo,* in which everyday life was presented realistically. Exemplars include Pietro Mascagni (1863–1945) —*Cavalleria Rusticana* (Rome, 1890) ; Ruggiero Leoncavallo (1858–1919) —*I Pagliacci* (Milan, 1892) ; Umberto Giordano (1867–1948) —*Andrea Chénier* (Milan, 1896) . Most important of Italian composers after Verdi was Giacomo Puccini (1858–1924) , whose operas, still outstandingly popular in the current repertory, reveal an unsurpassed ability to write for both voice and orchestra— *Manon Lescaut* (Turin, 1890) ; *La Bohème* (Turin, 1896) ; *Tosca* (Rome, 1900) ; *Madame Butterfly* (Milan, 1904) ; *The Girl of the Golden West* (New York, 1910) ; *Turandot* (completed by Franco Alfano, Milan, 1926) . Other operatic composers include Italo Montemezzi (1875–1952) —*L'Amore dei Tre Ré*

(Milan, 1913) ; Ildebrando Prizzetti (1880–1968) —*Murder in the Cathedral* (based on T. S. Eliot's play, 1958) . The leading Italian composer of symphonic music in this period was Ottorini Respighi (1879–1931) —*Fountains of Rome,* 1917, *Pines of Rome,* 1924, *Roman Festivals,* 1929—works incorporating Italian color with the impressionism of Debussy, the postromanticism of Strauss, and the brilliant orchestral technique of Rimsky-Korsakov.

U.S. COMPOSERS. In this period, U.S. composers reflected nationalist influences and impressionism. Although influenced by his German romantic musical training, Edward MacDowell (1861–1908) sought to express American nationalistic feeling in such works as Suite No. 2 ("Indian") for Orchestra, Op.48, 1895; *Woodland Sketches* for piano, Op.51, 1896; *New England Idyls* for piano, Op.62, 1902; Piano Concerto No. 2 in D minor, 1889. For his time an extraordinary innovator, Charles Ives (1874–1954) used polytonality, cross rhythms, quarter tones, dissonances (together with, on occasion, quite conservative harmony) , and consciously drew upon American folk subjects in his Sonata No. 2 for piano ("Concord, Mass., 1840–1860") , 1915; the symphonic piece *Three Places in New England,* 1914; Symphony No. 3, 1904, rev. 1911 (awarded Pulitzer prize, 1947) . Charles Martin Loeffler (1861–1935) , whose work was dominated by impressionist influences, left *A Pagan Poem* for piano and orchestra, 1905–6. Similar influences, along with motifs from Asia, are reflected in the works of Charles Tomlinson Griffes (1884–1920) —*White Peacock* from *Four Roman Sketches,* 1914; *Poem for Flute and Orchestra,* 1918; *Pleasure Dome of Kublai Khan,* 1919.

20th Cent.

1900–1968

NEW MUSICAL TRENDS. 20th-cent. music has been composed in the spirit of change. Although cognizant of tradition, composers have endeavored to write present-minded music, and even to project into the future. This point of view has manifested itself in different uses of the elements of music: melody seldom composed in symmetrical phrases, but frequently instrumental in concept, with jagged leaps rather than a consonant vocal line; harmony becoming increasingly complicated and dissonant; rhythms similarly more complicated and irregular; chromaticism, polytonality (simultaneous use of many keys), and atonality (absence of a tonal center) becoming common; form becoming freer, yet the old baroque and classic forms used; texture frequently polyphonic (many-voiced) instead of largely homophonic (melodically dominated); orchestration becoming more involved, yet expressive, with the techniques of older instruments and the human voice extended and newer, electronic instruments introduced; style affected by contemporary painting and literature—primitivism, objectivism, urbanism, sports, ballet, humor, satire—and resulting in neoclassicism, neoromanticism, neonationalism, and expressionism (the attempt of the artist to use the inner experience or subconscious as the only reality).

EXPRESSIONIST COMPOSERS. Expressionist composers include Arnold Schoenberg (1874–1951), best known for such 12-tone compositions, 1921–33, as the following: Five Pieces for Orchestra, Op.23; Suite for Piano, Op.25; Serenade for 7 Instruments and Bass Baritone, Op.24; Quintet for Wind Instruments, Op.26; String Quartet No. 3, Op.30; Variations for Orchestra, Op.31. His earlier nonatonal works include *Verklärte Nacht*, 1899, and *Gurre-Lieder*, 1901–2, and the more experimental music dramas, *Die Glückliche Hand*, Op.18, 1913, and *Pierrot Lunaire* for Sprechgesang and instruments, Op.21, 1912. Later more conservative works include Violin Concerto, Op.36, 1936, and *A Survivor from Warsaw* for narrator, male chorus, and orchestra, Op.46, 1947. Alban Berg (1885–1935), a pupil of Schoenberg, composed the operas *Wozzeck*, 1921, and *Lulu*, 1937; 3 Orchestral Pieces; Chamber Concerto for piano, violin, and 13 wind instruments; String Quartet; Lyric Suite for string quartet; and Sonata for piano. Anton von Webern (1883–1945), also a Schoenberg

pupil, used pointilist technique, frequent rests, and low dynamic level in his works, which include 6 Pieces for Orchestra, Op.6, 1909; 5 Pieces for Orchestra, Op.10, 1913; Symphony for Chamber Orchestra, Op.21, 1928.

NEOCLASSIC COMPOSERS. Prominent among the neoclassicists is Igor Stravinsky (b. 1882). His early works— *Fireworks for Orchestra*, 1908, and the ballet *Firebird*, 1910—reveal the influences of his teacher Rimsky-Korsakov, but he has been constantly evolving different styles. Other works include the ballets *Petrouchka*, 1911, and *Le Sacre du Printemps*, 1913. The larger part of his output falls into the neoclassic category: *Les Noces* (with chorus), 1923; *Histoire du Soldat* (with speaking voice), 1918; the operas *Rossignol*, 1914, *Mavra*, 1922, and *Rake's Progress*, 1951; opera oratorio *Oedipus Rex*, 1927; orchestral works: Symphony for Wind Instruments, 1920, Symphony in C, 1940, Symphony in 3 Movements, 1942; concertos, *Dumbarton Oaks*, 1938, Concerto for String Orchestra, 1946, Concerto for Piano and Wind, 1924, Violin Concerto, 1931; choral works: *Symphony of Psalms*, 1930, Mass, 1948, *Canticum Sacrum*, 1956, *Threni—Id Est Lamentationes Jeremiae* (in 12-tone technique), 1958; *The Flood* (ballet for pantomime with narrative, written for television), 1962.

Paul Hindemith (1895–1963) was associated with the idea of *Gebrauchsmusik* ("music for use"). His works include Sonata No. 3 for piano, 1936; 3 Sonatas for organ, 1937–40; Symphony in B flat for Band, 1951; *Ludus Tonalis* for piano, 1943; symphony *Mathis der Maler*, 1934; *Nobilissima Visione* for orchestra, 1938; *Symphonic Metamorphosis on Themes of Weber*, 1945; song cycle, *Marienleben*, 1923, rev. 1948.

Carl Orff (b. 1895) found the inspiration for his cantata *Carmina Burana* (Frankfurt, 1937) in the 13th-cent. song manuscripts which were discovered at the Bavarian monastery of Benedictbeuren. He has since incorporated that work into the triptych *Trionfi* (Milan, 1953) for soli, chorus, and instruments, with scenery.

Béla Bartók (1881–1945) was an avid

collector of Central European folksongs, the influences of which are prominent in his music. His compositions include an opera, *Duke Bluebeard's Castle,* 1911; ballet, *The Wooden Prince,* 1914–16; pantomime, *The Miraculous Mandarin,* 1919; set of studies for piano, *Mikrokosmos,* 1926–37; Rhapsody No. 1 for cello and piano, 1928; *Cantata Profana* for chorus and orchestra, 1930; Music for Strings, Percussion, and Celesta, 1936; Sonata for 2 Pianos and Percussion, 1937; Concerto for Orchestra, 1943–44; 6 string quartets; 2 violin sonatas; 3 piano concertos; and many arrangements of folksongs for voices and instruments.

Zoltán Kodály (1882–1967) also used much Hungarian folk material in his music, including *Psalmus Hungaricus* for chorus and orchestra, 1923, and the suite from his ballad opera *Háry Janos,* 1926.

NATIONALIST COMPOSERS. In the USSR art has always been a political concern, and artist and composer have been expected to adhere to the aesthetic credo of socialist realism. Composers who, despite political limitations, have achieved world recognition are Sergei Prokofiev (1891–1953) —Symphony No. 1 ("Classical"), Op.25, 1918; Symphony No. 5, Op.100, 1944; Symphony No. 6, Op. 111, 1944; Symphony No. 7, Op.131, 1952; Piano Concerto No. 3 in C major, Op.26, 1921; 2 violin concertos—No. 1 in D major, Op.19, 1914, and No. 2 in B minor, Op.63, 1935; opera *The Love for Three Oranges,* Op.33, 1921; orchestral suite from the movie *Lieutenant Kije,* Op.60, 1934; *Peter and the Wolf,* for narrator and orchestra, Op.67, 1936; ballet *Romeo and Juliet,* Op.64, 1935–36; Dmitri Shostakovitch (b. 1906), noted for 12 symphonies, including No. 1, Op.10, 1925; No. 5, Op.47, 1937; No. 7, Op.60, 1941; opera *Lady Macbeth of Mzensk,* 1934; ballet *The Age of Gold,* Op.22, 1930.

British composers who have developed characteristic British music, using British folk tunes and dances in their compositions, include Ralph Vaughan Williams (1872–1958) —*A London Symphony* (No. 2), 1914, rev. 1920; *Pastoral Symphony* (No. 3), 1922; Symphony No. 4 in F minor, 1935; Symphony No. 5 in D major,

1943; Symphony No. 8 in D minor, 1956; Symphony No. 9 in E minor, 1958; *Fantasia on a Theme of Thomas Tallis,* 1910; Gustav Holst (1874–1934) —orchestral suite *The Planets,* Op.32, 1916; Benjamin Britten (b. 1913) —operas *Peter Grimes,* Op.33, 1945, *The Turn of the Screw,* Op. 54, 1954, and *A Midsummer Night's Dream,* Op.64, 1960; choral works *A Ceremony of Carols,* Op.28, 1942, and *War Requiem,* 1962; orchestral work *The Young Person's Guide to the Orchestra,* Op.34, 1945.

Of the French composers who rebelled against French impressionism, the following are notable: Erik Satie (1866–1925) — *Ballet Parades,* 1917; and 3 composers of the group called *Les Six:* Francis Poulenc (1899–1963) —religious opera *Les Dialogues des Carmelites,* 1957; *La Voix Humaine,* 1958; Darius Milhaud (b. 1892) —ballet *La Création du Monde,* 1922; operas *Christophe Colombe,* 1930, and *Bolivar,* 1950; *Sacred Service for Synagogue,* 1947; Arthur Honegger (1892–1955) —*Pacific 231* ("Locomotive") for orchestra, 1923; oratorio, *Le Roi David,* 1921.

AMERICAN MUSICAL TRENDS. American jazz, which originated in New Orleans in the early part of the 20th cent., spread to northern cities of the U.S. by 1917, when "King Oliver" (1885–1938) moved his band to Chicago, followed in 1922 by Louis ("Satchmo") Armstrong (b. 1900), and since has had an enormous impact on world music. A blend of Afro-American songs, blues, and spirituals, ragtime, Appalachian folksongs, and religious hymns, jazz has passed through many transformations: boogie-woogie, swing, bop, cool jazz, and rock 'n' roll (from 1954), and is constantly being further transformed. Other outstanding jazz figures are Duke Ellington (b. 1899); Benny Goodman (b. 1909), who introduced the era of "swing" in the 1930's, along with such "swing" artists as Harry James (b. 1916) and "Count" Basie (b. 1904); "Dizzy" Gillespie (b. 1917), protagonist in the early 1940's of "bop"; and Dave Brubeck (b. 1920), popularizer of "cool" jazz. An annual jazz festival was established at Newport, R.I., in 1954.

ASIAN MUSIC. The Asian continent is home to so many diverse cultures that it is impossible to treat its music as a whole. Through the centuries there has been cultural exchange between ethnic and national groups, but despite such contacts there have emerged national styles of music that are distinct.

INDIA. The music of India is the oldest living music in the world and one of the most sophisticated. Based on the concepts of the *raga,* a melodic pattern with a distinctive ethos that serves both as scale and subject matter for composition, and of the *tala,* a rhythmic formula that gives organization to the music in time, Indian music has remained melodic-rhythmic in nature through millennia of development. It is thus quite different from the music of the western world, which, by contrast, is harmonic and polyphonic in concept. The continuity of the musical tradition in India was not affected by British rule, although the introduction of military music and European folk song occasionally intrigued an Indian composer and caused him to adapt a foreign tune to his native musical idiom. Both the Hindustani music of the north and the Karnatic music of the south trace their origin to the *Samaveda,* the musical version of the *Rigveda.* They are in agreement on fundamentals, though the nomenclature of *ragas* and *talas* differs. Today the difference between them is largely a matter of style. Instrumental music is more developed in the north.

The late 18th cent. gave birth to 3 great composers, Tyagaraja (1767–1847), Muthuswamy Dikshitar (1776–1835), and Syama Sastri (1762–1827), often referred to as "the Trinity." Their compositions (with texts in Telugu, Sanskrit, and Tamil), together with the works of Purandara Dasa (1484–1564), constitute the core of the Indian artist's repertory. It is in this period that the necessity for evolving an accurate system of notation arose. Earlier, music had been passed on by rote from master to pupil. In 1873 Tachur Singaracharlu began publishing graded books on music. The published works on Indian music in English by P.

Sambamoorthy (b. 1901) affected music education at all levels, not only in India, but throughout the world.

With the attainment of independence, 15 Aug., 1947, Indians took a new interest and pride in their musical heritage. National and state music academies (Sangeet Natak Akademi) were established for the recording, archiving, study, and publication of works from the various musical cultures—tribal, folk, and classical. State-government music schools, private academies, and the music departments of colleges and universities began to offer courses in history, theory, and practice of Indian music. The popularity of the cinema gave rise to a new genre, film music, which reflected considerable foreign influence.

CHINA. The long-established tradition of imperial interest in music was followed by the Ch'ien Lung emperor (ruled 1736–95), under whose auspices 128 chapters were added to *Lü Lü Cheng I,* 1746, an encyclopedia on music theory (including a chapter on western music), 1st published under the auspices of the K'ang Hsi emperor in 1713.

Ceremonial music (*ya yüeh*) flourished until the middle of the 19th cent., when continuous internal rebellion and invasions by western powers caused its decline. After the downfall of the Ch'ing Dynasty, 1911, the practice of *ya yüeh* was discontinued. Thus a great tradition, established in the Chou Dynasty and perpetuated by all major dynasties of the past, passed into oblivion.

Music drama (*k'un ch'ü*), which was developed by Wei Liang-fu in the middle of the 16th cent. and was already in a state of decline by the end of the Ming Dynasty, 1368–1661, enjoyed a revival during the Ch'ing, 1662–1911. In 1776 the Ch'ien Lung emperor summoned 4 provincial drama troupes to Peking, paving the way for the emergence of *Ching hsi* (the so-called Peking opera), which represented a merger of the various regional drama schools. However, *Ching hsi* did not achieve its great popularity until after 1821, when it gradually replaced the declining classical school, *k'un ch'ü,* as the predominating school of music drama in

China. Meanwhile, *k'un ch'ü* persisted as a revered classical drama school and later enjoyed a slow revival in its popularity after the revolution of 1911. A very popular collection, *O Yün Ko Ch'ü P'u,* was published as late as 1870.

In the field of solo and ensemble music, the *ch'in* (*koto* or *kin* in Japanese, and *kum* or *kumunko* in Korean), a fretted long zither, has maintained an uninterrupted tradition as the instrument cultivated by scholars and artists. Publication of treatises on the instrument and collections of its music have continued to the present. It has enjoyed some degree of popularity with the public since the revolution of 1911, an important publication, *Ch'in Hsueh Ts'ung Shu,* being compiled in 1911–31. The *p'i p'a* (*biwa* in Japanese), a short 4-stringed lute, has always been an important instrument in ensemble music and in certain types of dramatic music, but it did not emerge as a solo instrument until the early 19th cent. The 1st collection of *p'i p'a* music, Hua Ch'iu Ping's *P'i P'a P'u,* was published in 1819. A popular collection, Li Tsu Fen's *P'i P'a Hsin P'u,* appeared in 1895, and other collections have been published since the revolution of 1911. The *p'i p'a* now shares with the *ch'in* the 1st position among Chinese solo instruments.

A parallel interest in other instruments and ensemble music is represented by the publication of important treatises and collections, notably *Hsuan So Shih San T'ao* (*Thirteen Compositions for Strings*), 1782, and *Hsuan So Pei K'ao* (*A Study of Music for Strings*), 1814. This led to a revival of interest in ensemble music, particularly the type known as *szu cho* (music for strings and winds). Although not comparable with the great orchestral music of the past, *szu cho* nevertheless became a popular category in the so-called *kuo yüeh* (a modern term meaning "national," i.e., "traditional," music), and was encouraged by the government and by persons interested in preserving traditional music. During the Nationalist regime a strong effort was made to reform traditional music. The *szu cho* ensemble was expanded into the so-called *kuo yüeh t'uan* (national music orchestra). After the establishment of the People's Repub-

lic, 1949, this reform was intensified. Under the Communist regime all forms of traditional music, except *ya yüeh,* which is not a secular form, have been actively revived. Musicological research has been encouraged and an impressive number of publications in this field have appeared from the mid-1950's onward.

JAPAN. A spirit of nationalism in the Tokugawa period, 1603–1867, began to supplement the intercultural influences which had affected Japanese music in earlier times. Three new genres emerged —*shamisen, koto,* and *shakuhachi*—which were held in great esteem by the merchants and artisans in the cities. The *koto,* a long zitherlike instrument with 13 silk strings, each tuned by a movable bridge, was regarded as the 1st instrument for accompanying songs as well as being a solo instrument in its own right. The *shamisen,* a 3-string banjolike long-necked lute, was employed in 3 styles of music: *Uto-mono* (singing style), *Kotori-mono* (narrative style), and *Minyo* (folk song). The *shakuhachi,* an end-blown or vertical bamboo flute, played by itinerant Buddhist priests in the Middle Tokugawa period, was adapted to solo art music. At the close of the period the 3 instruments were joined together, thus establishing an ensemble style of music called *sankyoku* (3 instruments).

Gagaku, the ancient court music of Japan, represented a synthesis of Chinese, Korean, Indian, and indigenous influences. Established in the early half of the 9th cent., it has been preserved to the present day at the imperial court and in some shrines and temples, although it suffered a decline following the Meiji Restoration of 1868. The repertory today consists of instrumental ensemble (*Kangan*), dance music (*Bugaku*), songs, and ritual music for Shinto ceremonies. The latter category is restricted to religious use, but the remaining pieces are secular and are played at court ceremonies and banquets. At present the *Gagaku* orchestra is divided into 2 groups—saho (left) and uho (right)—the former consisting mainly of music from China and, to a smaller extent, from India, the latter of music from Korea and Manchuria. The instrumentation of Saho Kangan consists of ryuteki (flute), hichirick (oboe), sho (mouth organ), so (zither), biwa (lute), kakko (side drum), shoko (gong), and taiko (big drum).

Genres of traditional music which have been preserved into the present include shomyo (Buddhist chanting), biwa music,

nohgaku (music of the No drama), and kabuki music. The development of Japanese music has been influenced by the dominant position of vocal modes, and a teacher-student relationship which is a special feature of the music system.

Fine Arts and Architecture

PAINTING

1789–1830

THE CLASSIC-ROMANTIC PERIOD. In the late 18th cent. Paris, with its many painters and its regularly held salons, was the greatest European center of painting, though the latest wave of enthusiasm for antiquity which spread in the wake of the excavations at Herculaneum and Pompeii meant that Rome was still a source of inspiration for artists as it had been since the 17th cent. Jacques-Louis David (1748–1825), whose *Oath of the Horatii,* 1785, was a symbol of the new revolutionary virtues in ancient Roman form, won the coveted Prix de Rome, 1774, and spent several years there, returning to become the champion of the neoclassical ideal of academic drawing, composition, and highly finished surface, and of subjects drawn from classical sources. David had a powerful realist vision. His portraits set a new standard of vitality, and in such works as the *Death of Marat,* 1793, and the *Coronation of Napoleon,* 1808, he participated in a new expansion of history painting to include subjects of current political importance. But his dominant influence, made powerful through his high position under Napoleon and his studio teaching as well as by such works as *The Rape of the Sabines,* 1795–1800, was on the side of neoclassicism. Such immediate followers of David as François Gérard (1770–1837), Anne Louis Girodet de Roucy (1767–1824), and Pierre-Narcisse Guérin (1774–1833) maintained a smooth sculptural style and relieflike composition, often in subjects drawn from classical sources (Guérin's *Return of Marcus Sextus,* 1799; Gérard's *Cupid and*

Psyche, 1798), but increasingly influenced by romantic literature, as in Girodet's *Entombment of Atala,* 1808, derived from Chateaubriand. David's greatest pupil was Jean Auguste Dominique Ingres (1780–1867), who during a long life kept alive at least in theory the qualities of classical form and the tradition of the Academy. *The Apotheosis of Homer,* 1827, was an image of the classical tradition, though his great nudes (*L'Odalisque, Le Bain Turque*) betray a romantic intensity. For Ingres classicism was a bulwark against chaos, both personal and social. Like David, he was one of the greatest of portraitists; in fine pencil drawings as well as in paintings (M. Bertin, Mme. d'Haussonville) he recorded the character of the 19th-cent. *haute bourgeoisie.*

TRENDS IN ROMANTICISM. The new forces, beginning c. 1800, which challenged neoclassical principles and modified their practice grew gradually more powerful as the Napoleonic Wars exercised their unsettling effect throughout Europe. Some of the general characteristics of the new movement were (1) a feeling for the national past, with heroes taken from among the knights and princes of European history rather than from Greece or Rome; (2) a feeling for one's own locality, expressed in a new landscape realism; (3) a new value placed on the experience of strong dramatic feeling, whether in subject or in composition and color; and (4) a growing preference for the particular over the general, and for observation over formulas.

SPAIN. Francisco de Goya y Lucientes (1746–1828), coming out of the baroque tradition of Velasquez and Tiepolo, developed a powerfully anticlassical, expres-

sionist style which was one of the foundations of romanticism and ultimately of
modernism. Beginning as a bravura court
painter, his unsparing realism later overcame flattery in his royal portraits. His
Caprichos, 1796–98, reveal a wealth of
dark, unconscious imagery, as well as a
mastery of the etching medium. In the
series of etchings known as the *Disasters
of War*, 1810–13, Goya expressed his
horror of the French campaign in Spain
by vividly describing the wretchedness of
its victims, and his *Second of May*, 1813,
was a statement of the evil that mankind
inflicts upon itself. More than anyone else
of his time he made of painting a powerful
instrument for the expression of deep
emotions.

ENGLAND. The greatest contribution
of the English to the new era in painting
was in the development of landscape
painting, and the consequent interest in
qualities of light and atmosphere. Joseph
Mallord William Turner (1775–1851) began in the established English tradition
of fine topographic description, but became increasingly involved with the complex and ephemeral experience of light,
particularly of light and water (*Burning
of the Houses of Parliament*, 1833). His
later pictures (e.g., *Rain, Steam and
Speed*, 1844) are almost formless in the
traditional sense because the artist has
been true to the actual experience of the
dissolving of solid form by atmosphere,
light, and movement. Where Turner's
temperament inclined him toward the
drama of landscape and weather and
toward the exotic, John Constable (1776–
1837), who was imbued with a Words-
worthian reverence for the simplest natural facts, devoted himself to the quieter
subtleties of the English countryside, particularly around his Sussex home of East
Bergholt. His *Hay Wain*, shown at the
Salon in Paris of 1824, was an inspiration
to Delacroix and other French artists
because of the lightness of its palette,
which placed it in strong contrast to the
traditionally brown-toned studio landscapes of the time. In addition to their
oils, both Constable and Turner made
many studies and paintings in water
color, a medium highly suited to fresh
color, effects of light, and immediacy of

impression, and some of these qualities
were incorporated into their work in oil.
At this period in England the art of water-
color painting was highly developed, most
notably in the work of the Norwich
School—John Crome (1768–1821), John
Sell Cotman (1782–1842), Peter de Wint
(1784–1849), and many others. Richard
Parkes Bonington (1802–28) also came
out of this water-color tradition, and his
many paintings of French coastal scenes
formed a link between the English school
and the later development of atmospheric
painting in France. From an entirely
different milieu and exemplifying a quite
different attitude were William Blake's
(1757–1827) highly personal linear en-
gravings and water-color drawings used to
illustrate his own hermetic mythological
poetry as well as the works of Milton and
Dante. Other artists in England, including the Swiss Henry Fuseli (1741–1825),
George Romney (1734–1802), and John
Martin (1789–1854), though not vision-
aries like Blake, also responded to the
awakening interest of the period in early
literature. The works of Shakespeare, in
particular, who had long been the target
of classical critics, now provided themes
for many paintings.

GERMANY AND AUSTRIA. Romantic art in Germany combined a sharp
linear realism of technique with symbolism and religious nostalgia. Philipp-Otto
Runge (1773–1810) in his *Times of Day*,
1805–8, attempted like Blake to create a
personal cosmic symbolism, while Caspar
David Friedrich (1774–1840) used the
Christian symbolism of the Cross and the
Gothic church in order to express a sense
of the isolation of the soul in the world
(*The Cross on the Mountain, The
Ruined Abbey*). Frederick Overbeck
(1789–1869) and his disciples founded an
ascetic community of artists in Rome,
called the Nazarenes, whose ideal of the
stylistic and religious purity of Italian
painting before Raphael was to influence
a later generation of English artists.

FRANCE. Though trained by David,
Baron Gros (1771–1855) expressed the
romantic spirit in panoramic scenes of
contemporary battle (*Napoleon at Eylau*,
1808). In the *Pesthouse at Jaffa*, 1804,
Napoleon is seen as a national and reli-

gious hero rather than as a nobly classical one, and the viewer is not spared the details of the sick men's sufferings. Théodore Géricault (1791–1824) carried this intense psychological realism further in his studies of old and insane people and in his *Raft of the Medusa*, 1819, which made of a contemporary shipwreck a dramatic image of human courage and suffering. Géricault died young, and of the other young men of the rising romantic generation, who included Paul Delaroche (1797–1855), Ary Scheffer (1795–1858), and Eugène Deveria (1805–65), the greatest (though he disowned the term romantic) was Eugène Delacroix (1788–1863). Delacroix was imbued not only with classical literature but with the works of Shakespeare and Dante, Walter Scott, and Byron, and took his subjects from these (*The Barque of Dante*, 1824; *The Shipwreck of Don Juan*, 1841), as well as from medieval and classical history (*The Entry of the Crusaders into Constantinople*, 1841; *The Justice of Trajan*, 1840), and from his own experience in North Africa (*The Women of Algiers*, 1834; *The Lion Hunt*, 1855). He was one of the last great artists to decorate large public buildings with important paintings (The Chamber of Deputies, the Luxembourg Palace Library, the Church of St.-Sulpice). As a gentleman with high government connections who nevertheless despised the Academy (which long refused him membership because of the novelty and independence of his work), Delacroix was a kind of bridge between the older type of artist who served a patron and the modern artist whose independent creative spirit isolates him from society. For this reason as well as for his painterly style and his experiments in light and color, Delacroix was revered by succeeding generations of French artists. A remarkable writer, his *Journal* is a lucid and moving expression of wide-ranging artistic ideas and a valuable source for the cultural life of the period.

1830–60

TYPES OF REALISM. The mood of progressive mid-19th-cent. art focused increasingly on the observation and description of external facts, both physical and social. One of the legacies of romanticism with its expansion of the possibilities of feeling was a greater awareness of the conditions of life of the humbler classes, and a sense that neither the formulas of classical nobility nor the newer conventions of romantic heroism and drama could adequately convey the truth of actuality. Honoré Daumier (1808–79) is noted for his sympathetic portrayal of the working people of Paris (*3rd-Class Carriage*, 1862; *The Laundress*, 1861) as well as for his many lithographs, published in the journals of the day, which satirized by sharp observation and caricature the foibles of the *bourgeoisie*. Jean François Millet (1816–75) was primarily concerned with the life of the peasant, and his *Sower*, 1850, and *Angelus*, 1859, though considered subversive at the time, have become probably the most widely known images of the 19th cent., so popular indeed that they have obscured knowledge of the rest of Millet's work. Official opposition was even fiercer in its hostility to Gustave Courbet (1819–77), who aggressively flaunted political and social views which after the Commune of 1871 forced him into exile, and encouraged him to paint with powerful detail and in shocking size the rough country people of the *Stonebreakers*, 1849, and *The Burial at Ornans*, 1851. Courbet painted many landscapes, often of dark, unpeopled forest interiors, but is best known for large figure compositions, of which the most ambitious is *The Painter's Studio*, 1855.

BARBIZON SCHOOL. Landscape realism was developed by the painters who came to be known as the Barbizon School because they often stayed in the little village of Barbizon in the Forest of Fontainebleau outside Paris. Here they worked directly from nature under the inspiration of 17th-cent. Dutch and more recent English landscape painting. Jean Baptiste Camille Corot (1796–1875) perfected his lucid style in trips to Rome and the northern French countryside and, though his reputation was based on studio-made Salon paintings, his most lasting works were *plein-air* landscapes which created a convention of tonal harmonies and inspired many followers. The guiding spirit of the Barbizon group was Théodore Rousseau (1812–67), who, with a less classical, more northern feeling than Corot, typified in his paintings of various regions of France the movement away from the ideal landscape of Italy and toward the recording of particular motifs in the French countryside (*Village in Berry*, 1842, *Le Givre*, 1845, many paintings of Fontainebleau, Les Landes, the Auvergne, etc.). Other artists in this group were Charles Daubigny (1817–78), whose free touch earned him the kind of criticism later directed against the impressionists; Constant Troyon (1810–65), heavily influenced by the Dutch in his treatment of animals in their rural environment; Jules Dupré (1811–89); and Narcisse Virgile Diaz de la Peña (known as Diaz) (1808–76). All of the Barbizon painters were in varying degrees known to and admired by the generation that followed them, the impressionists. Two other painters, even more intimately associated with impressionism through their friendship with Monet, were Eugène Boudin (1824–98) and the Dutchman, Johann Barthold Jongkind (1819–91). Both of these men were noted particularly for their coastal scenes, in which low horizons, vast skies, and the flicker of light on water provided an opportunity for experiments with color as light.

ENGLAND. Outside of France the most notable type of realism was that of the Pre-Raphaelite painters in England. The young artists John Everett Millais (1829–98), William Holman Hunt (1827–1910), and Dante Gabriel Rossetti (1828–82) formed the Pre-Raphaelite Brotherhood in 1848, and for a few years thereafter produced pictures in which the intense rendering of detail was supported by a genuine moral conviction (Millais' *The Blind Girl*, 1856; Hunt's *The Awakening Conscience*, 1853). Their art greatly influenced later artists such as Ford Madox Brown (1821–93), and was defended by John Ruskin against accusations (by Charles Dickens and others) of crudeness and blasphemy.

LATER REALISM. The French artists were the pioneers of realism, which spread rapidly throughout Europe. In its later phases the style tended toward the dry and the literal, and was always at its best in modest genre and landscape subjects. In France the academic realism of Meissonier (1815–91) and J. L. Gérome (1824–1904) was the expression not of a deep personal vision but of the more trivial interests and fantasies of bourgeois society. The stronghold of such artists was the Salon, a large exhibition juried by members of the Académie des Beaux-Arts and held regularly in Paris. The Salon was taken by the public to be the arbiter of aesthetic taste and regularly refused to admit the most original works of the time.

1860–85

BEGINNING OF IMPRESSIONISM. Although impressionism as a critical (in both senses) term was not officially coined until the 1870's, the group of extraordinarily gifted artists who were associated with the movement came into their maturity in the 1860's.

MANET. Édouard Manet (1832–83), a bourgeois and even a dandy, and trained in the studio of the academic Thomas Couture (1815–79), consistently submitted his work to the Salon, where it was frequently refused. In 1863 he and other rejected artists—Camille Pissarro (1830–1903), Armand Guillaumin (1841–1927), the American James Abbott McNeil Whistler (1834–1903), and Jongkind—exhibited their works separately at what was called the Salon des Refusés, where Manet's *Picnic on the Grass* caused a public sensation, although in its combination of nude women and clothed men it was following a long-established Renaissance tradition. Manet's *Olympia*, shown in the Salon of 1865, also aroused the public, who could not tolerate the novel, contemporary treatment of what had been established as an idealized theme, the reclining nude. Manet's realism was fresh and direct. He had a remarkable gift for creating convincing form with great economy of stroke, and his subjects —contemporary Parisians in contemporary dress—made him what the poet Baudelaire had called for in his critical writing, the "painter of modern life" (*Concert at the Tuileries,* 1862; *Portrait of Zola,* 1868; *At the Café,* 1878; *The Bar at the Folies Bergère,* 1882).

DEGAS. His friend Edgar Degas (1834–1917), an admirer of Ingres and student of Renaissance painting who began his career by portraying traditional subjects (*The Young Spartans Exercising,* 1860; *Semiramis Founding a Town,* 1861), also developed into an acute observer of the contemporary scene in many penetrating portraits (*The Bellelli Family,* 1859) and in his paintings of the ballet, the racecourse, the café, and women bathing (*The Dancing Class,* 1874; *The Absinthe Drinker,* 1876). Degas, influenced by the Japanese prints which 1st appeared in Paris in the 1850's, and by experiments in photography, developed a new sense of pattern in his compositions and an asymmetrical cutting off of figures which creates the impression of immediacy (*Place de la Concorde,* 1873; *The Millinery Shop,* 1886). Neither Manet nor Degas considered themselves impressionists. Manet, though friendly with the group, joined none of their 8 group exhibitions held in Paris between 1874 and 1886; Degas participated in 7 of these but held himself aloof from what he considered the radical nature of the group.

THE IMPRESSIONIST STYLE. The general characteristics of the impressionist style, all of which became fundamental sources of modern painting, were (1) a lightening of the palette far beyond anything previously known; (2) a concentration on the relationship of light and color, so that form is created by many individual touches of color and hence traditional solidity is dissolved; (3) an increasing interest in the 2-dimensional surface of the picture rather than the 3-dimensional penetration into depth; (4) an apparently casual, over-all "scatter" composition; and (5) a concern with the life of leisure and private experience, whether among strolling city crowds and country vacationers or in domestic interiors and gardens.

MONET AND RENOIR. The most consistent and powerful of the impressionists was Claude Monet (1840–1926), whose *Impression—Sunrise* drew the con-temptuous term "impressionist" at the 1st group exhibition in 1874. Monet worked in the 1860's and 1870's with Auguste Renoir (1841–1919), painting brilliant *plein-air* landscapes on the Normandy coast and in villages along the Seine outside Paris. They often employed the same motifs (*La Grenouillère,* 1869; *The Duck Pond,* 1873; *The Seine at Argenteuil,* 1874). As early as 1873 Monet built a studio on a boat at Argenteuil, and for the rest of his long life he never ceased to study the effects of light and atmosphere, often in series which rendered the changing colors of the different times of day (*Haystacks,* 1893; *Rouen Cathedral,* 1894). His crowning works were the great *Water Lilies* paintings, created (between the late 1890's and his death) in a specially constructed water garden at Giverny, where he had settled in 1883. Renoir also continued to paint landscape, but with less intensity, and was always more interested in figure painting (*The Moulin de la Galette,* 1876; *The Boating Party,* 1879), and increasingly devoted to women and children (*Mme. Charpentier and her daughters,* 1878) and bathers from the 1880's until the end of his life.

OTHER IMPRESSIONISTS. The most genial of the impressionists was Pissarro, who produced many canvases of scenes of Paris and the Île-de-France, which changed little except for a period in the late 1880's, when he was influenced by the ideas of Georges Seurat. Other painters in or associated with the impressionist group were Alfred Sisley (1839–99), Frédéric Bazille (1841–71), Berthe Morisot (1841–95), the American Mary Cassatt (1845–1926), Jean Louis Forain (1852–1931), and Félix Bracquemond (1845–1914).

1885–1905

POST-IMPRESSIONISM. The 1880's saw a reaction against impressionism and a desire, variously expressed, for an art that would be more structured, more austere, less sensuous, and more spiritual. The belief that impressionism, with its interest in light and air, was an art of naturalism formed part of one of the most important processes of the modern revolution in art: the divorce of the painting from nature, the destruction of the idea of the "mirror of nature," the assertion of the autonomy of a work of art.

POINTILLISM. Georges Seurat (1859–91), fascinated by the scientific color theories of Chevreul and Rood, systematized the loose, varied, commalike strokes of the impressionists into a pattern of uniform, calculated spots of color with which he built up a relatively flat, highly simplified, and carefully composed pattern of shapes (*La Grande Jatte,* 1886; *Les Poseuses,* 1888; *Le Cirque,* 1890). Known as pointillism—though Seurat preferred the term divisionism—the style attracted many followers, who tended to apply Seurat's original method rather mechanically and without his compositional structure. Seurat's imitators included Paul Signac (1863–1935), Maximilien Luce (1858–1941), Henri Édouard Cross (1856–1910), and the Dutchmen Théo van Rysselberghe (1862–1926) and Henry van de Velde (1863–1957).

CÉZANNE. The greatest of the forerunners of modern painting was Paul Cézanne (1839–1906), who, after 1st working in a very intense romantic vein (*The Temptation of St. Anthony,* 1868), disciplined himself through impressionism and went on to develop an art in which strong feeling is controlled by form. He made of the impressionist brush stroke a sensitive, vibrant plane of pure color, with which he built structures at once solid and luminous. After the death of his disapproving father in 1886, he was able to work steadily in his native Provence, where he made many landscapes of the region, still lifes, and figure paintings. These works, with their visible structure of overlapping planes, express a new sense of what a painting is: not a finished product in which the artist's effort is concealed, but a dynamic object which conveys the experience of the artist responding and deciding. This structure and this dimension of time were later of great significance for the cubists.

VAN GOGH. For Vincent Van Gogh (1853–90) impressionism was not a discipline but a release, freeing him from his early dark Dutch palette (*The Potato Eaters,* 1885), but not taking him far enough for a man of his intense spiritual ardor. At Arles in the south of France he found the brilliant light he needed and, for a time, the hoped-for simplicity of man and nature. In the 2½ yrs. before his death by suicide he produced an extraordinary body of work marked by brilliant color, rich pigment laid on rapidly in swirling brush strokes, and powerful distortions of form (*L'Arlésienne,* 1886; *Cypresses,* 1889; *Crows over a Wheatfield,* 1890). Unknown in his lifetime—Van Gogh remains the archetype of the great but neglected artist—his work exerted a strong influence on later expressionist artists. Two other northern artists of the same generation, the Belgian James Ensor (1860–1949; *Entry of Christ into Brussels,* 1888) and the Norwegian Edvard Munch (1863–1944; *The Cry,* 1893), also created powerfully emotional images through exaggeration and distortion of form.

GAUGUIN. Paul Gauguin (1848–1903), like Van Gogh, despised Parisian sophistication—indeed, social convention of almost any kind—and sought simplicity, 1st at Pont-Aven in Brittany, later for a short disastrous period in Arles with Van Gogh, and finally, from 1891 until his death, in Tahiti. The strength and range of Gauguin's revolt against western society and art has been enormously influential. His life—beginning as a conventional stockbroker and Sunday painter, abandoning income and family for art, and finally leaving Europe entirely to seek the freedom of a primitive land—is a modern paradigm, and his art has given birth to many forms of antinaturalism. Gauguin's development out of impressionism was toward an increasing flattening of the picture surface, composing with strongly outlined shapes in brilliant colors, with a minimum of 3-dimensional modeling. His emphasis on the expression of feeling or idea rather than representation of nature allied him with the literary movement of symbolism, though he and his collaborator Émile Bernard used the term synthetism. Both in his actions and in his art Gauguin reached out toward cultures which had long been ignored as alien or crude—Romanesque Europe, the Near and Far East—and which have ever since his time exerted a strong influence on western art. Artists associated with and directly influenced by Gauguin were the Nabis, active in the 1890's: Maurice Denis (1870–1945), Pierre Bonnard (1867–1947), Édouard Vuillard (1868–1940), and the sculptor Aristide Maillol (1861–1944). Bonnard and Vuillard later developed their own personal styles of post-impressionist depiction of private, domestic interiors, known as intimism.

OTHER LATE-19TH-CENTURY PAINTERS. Other artists active at this time and associated with the antinaturalistic movement were Henri de Toulouse-Lautrec (1864–1901), whose combination of sharp observation and flat patterns revolutionized the art of the poster; Odilon Redon (1840–1916), who painted the imagery of dreams; Henri Rousseau (1844–1910), called "le Douanier" and the father of modern primitivism in painting; the Swiss Ferdinand Hodler (1853–1918); and the Viennese Gustave Klimt (1862–1918).

ART NOUVEAU. Much of the painting of the 1890's and particularly the work of Gauguin, is characterized by a highly developed surface pattern, often with curved and twisting shapes. This strong emphasis on the long, sinuous curve, the curve of a stem or a flame, was the basis of an extremely unified style, known variously as Art Nouveau, Jugendstil, and Style Moderne, which appeared all over Europe at the end of the 19th cent. Appearing perhaps earliest in England (Arthur Mackmurdo [1851–1942]; title page of Wren's *City Churches,* 1883) as a development of the Arts and Crafts movement, it soon went well beyond that movement's serious social aims in the art of Aubrey Beardsley (1872–98), whose extraordinary illustrations for *Siegfried, Salomé,* and *Lysistrata* exploit the possibilities of the long curve, the arabesque, and the pattern of black and white to a point at the extreme edge of refinement. A contemporary Dutch artist, Jan Tooroop (1858–1928), had something of Beardsley's feeling for curving, attenu-

ated, neurasthenic figures (*The Three Brides,* 1893).

Art Nouveau, resulting primarily from a revival of the craft of design, is found most of all in the decorative arts and in architecture. The poster, revived by Lautrec and the Nabis, became a universal expression of the style, whether or not designed by a well-known painter. New magazines—*Studio, Jugend, Simplizissimus, L'Art Décoratif, The New Art Club, Sezession, Les Vingt*—sprang up and made use of the new style in illustration and typography. Émile Gallé (1846–1904) in France and Louis Comfort Tiffany (1848–1933) in America made glass vessels and lamps which often took the actual form of growing plants. In Belgium, one of the earliest architectural sources of the style was Baron. Victor Horta's (1861–1947) house at 6 Rue Paul-Émile Janson in Brussels, where every element, iron stair railings, molding, floor patterns, is in the form of flowing tendrils. Perhaps the best-known examples of Art Nouveau are Hector Guimard's (1867–1942) stations of the Paris Métro, dating from 1900. Its most extraordinary manifestation is in the architecture of Antonio Gaudí (1852–1926) in Barcelona: Sagrada Familia, 1903–26; Casa Batiló, 1905–7; Casa Milá, 1905–7, with their elaborately worked surfaces, their sudden shifts of proportion, and their obsession—e.g., the undulating façade of the Casa Milá—with the curved line.

1905–45

THE NATURE OF 20TH-CENT. ART. Almost the only accurate generalization that can be made about 20th-cent. art is that it possesses no single, unified tendency. There are, however, dominant forces, and it is these which will ultimately characterize the period in historical perspective. Schools and movements multiply in this century, but there are certain fundamental elements: (1) a sharp reaction against the classical tradition of the West, and a ready acceptance of influences from the arts of Africa, India, Persia, the Pacific Islands—all the earlier arts in which realism is subordinate to expressive form; (2) a profound sense of the dimension of time: the role of speed, the rapidity of change, the relativity of point of view; (3) the notion of object-as-energy: things are no longer seen as solid impregnable surfaces but as microcosms of invisible universal energy, hence unstable and built of forms entirely new, having nothing to do with their visible surfaces; (4) the increasing significance of color, which ceases to be an attribute of things and becomes an independent substance with attributes and implications of its own; (5) the idea that the unconscious, both personal and collective, has a greater force than the rational will, hence the significance of unconscious imagery, spontaneous gesture, and chance; and (6) in the nonwestern world the universal influence of styles developed in the West, particularly the styles of abstraction which liberate the artist from local tradition and imagery.

EXPRESSIONISM. With roots in the work of Van Gogh, Munch, Ensor, and Klimt, expressionism as a movement emerged in Germany with the founding in 1905 of the group of artists called "Die Brücke": Ernst-Ludwig Kirchner (1880–1938), Erich Heckel (b. 1883), and Karl Schmidt-Rutloff (b. 1884). These artists, joined in 1906 by Emil Nolde (1867–1956) and Max Pechstein (1881–1955), looked for inspiration to the harshness of northern medieval art and to primitive African art, which now for the 1st time was looked at aesthetically. They were possessed by a strong social and religious antagonism against bourgeois society, and their subjects were often drawn from the lower depths and were expressed with brilliant acid color and violent, angular shapes. They particularly developed the art of the woodcut, creating simple, angular forms suited to the cutting medium. Other German and Austrian artists who worked in an expressionist style were Egon Schiele (1890–1918), Oskar Kokoschka (1886–1966), George Grosz (1893–1959), and Max Beckmann (1884–1950). The latter 2 in particular, with their savage imagery of German life between the wars, exemplified the characteristic expressionist content of moral concern

and fierce social criticism. Another significant European expressionist was the Polish Chaim Soutine (1894–1943), who, like so many artists at this time, was an *émigré* in Paris and whose imagery was largely French—still life, landscape, figure—but whose tensions and agonies were expressed in thick, swirling impasto and dislocations of form. Later important examples of expressionism on a large public scale were the murals done in Mexico and the U.S. by the Mexican painters José Orozco (1883–1949) and Diego Rivera (1886–1957), both of whom were deeply concerned with the social and political content of their work.

FAUVISM. The members of Die Brücke were much influenced by the work of a group of French painters who in 1905, when a number of them showed together for the 1st time in the Salon d'Automne in Paris, were dubbed "Les Fauves" or "The Wild Beasts": Henri Matisse (1869–1954), Georges Rouault (1871–1958), André Derain (1880–1954), Raoul Dufy (1877–1953), Maurice Vlaminck (1876–1958), Albert Marquet (1875–1947). With the exception of Rouault, who went on to create a Christian imagery involving prostitutes, evil judges, and the Man of Sorrows, these artists were far less concerned with social problems than were their German contemporaries. Their main objective was to develop the implications of the art of Seurat, Van Gogh, and Gauguin by the use of strokes of brilliant arbitrary color, often so separated as to leave empty canvas between, and highly simplified shapes, composed in a strong surface pattern. Fauvism as a movement was short-lived but, particularly in its use of color, it had a permanent effect on modern painting. It was Matisse who most consistently worked with the Fauve principles of color throughout his life. His late works were composed of organic shapes cut from papers which he had himself painted in brilliant saturated colors.

CUBISM. Cubism was probably the single most fruitful movement of the century, affecting as it did the development not only of painting but of sculpture and architecture as well. Both the form and the content of cubism were implicit in the late work of Cézanne, and the movement took root all over Europe at roughly the same time, wherever the new currents of thought were fertilized by knowledge of Cézanne's work. It was Pablo Picasso (b. 1881) and Georges Braque (1882–1963), however, who 1st seriously worked out the appropriate implications and gave form to the cubist vision. Picasso's *Demoiselles d'Avignon,* 1907–8, was the 1st major work in which solid form is broken into planes, in this case harsh and angular as though wrenched from stability. In the following year Braque and Picasso became close friends, and began to make paintings which were deliberately indistinguishable in their earth colors and their increasingly more complex network of interpenetrating planes. By 1912, they were composing pictures entirely with superimposed flat shapes, a structure emphasized by the invention of the collage, in which some of the shapes are actual pieces of newspaper, concert tickets, or printed wallpaper. This final destruction of traditional pictorial depth was fundamental to all future painting, and the collage became a new independent medium, widely practiced in the 1920's by the Dada group, in particular by the German Kurt Schwitters (1887–1948), and most recently giving birth to the contemporary form of the assemblage, in which collage moves from the realm of painting into that of sculpture. Picasso and Braque grew apart after 1914. Braque went on to make out of the cubist spatial structure a perfect medium for still-life painting, while Picasso used it for essentially expressionist purposes, as in his *Guernica* of 1937.

Among the Parisian contemporaries of Picasso and Braque were many artists who around 1910 began to experiment with cubist forms. These were the men who showed in the Salons and attracted critical attention and the term "cubism" to their work. (By this time in Paris independent Salons in which all artists were free to show their work had existed for 25 years. However, Picasso never showed there, but made his work known to buyers through the great dealer Daniel

Henri Kahnweiler. In this he again foreshadowed the future: after World War I the Salons declined in importance, and the present system of exhibitions held at dealers' galleries, publicized in the press and by critics, was fully established.) Albert Gleizes (1881–1953) and Jean Metzinger (1883–1956) were the theorists of the movement, interested, as was Jacques Villon (1875–1963), the leader of their group, in the simultaneity of vision in cubism—the seeing of all aspects of an object at once by the breaking of it up into shifting planes. Robert Delaunay (1885–1941), noted for his *Eiffel Tower* series, moved close to abstraction in his *Simultaneous Disks* of 1912; Fernand Léger (1881–1955) expressed a new enthusiasm for industrial life by constructing figures out of cylindrical, machinelike forms; Marc Chagall (b. 1887), a Russian fantasist, adapted the structures of cubism to his own expressive dislocations; and Marcel Duchamp's (b. 1887) *Nude Descending a Staircase* was one of the sensations of the Armory Show of 1913, which 1st brought to the U.S. the work of the European moderns. Other important cubists were Juan Gris (1887–1927) and Francis Picabia (1879–1953).

FUTURISM. An Italian movement, futurism was affiliated with cubism, both because its progenitors, Filippo Marinetti (1876–1944) and Gino Severini (1883–1966), were friends of the Parisian circle of cubists and because they used the style to express their progressive sense of time and motion. Other futurists were Giacomo Balla (1871–1958) and the sculptor Umberto Boccioni (1882–1916).

DER BLAUE REITER. Der Blaue Reiter (The Blue Rider), a group formed in 1911 in Munich by Wassily Kandinsky (1866–1944) and Franz Marc (1880–1916) and later joined by Paul Klee (1879–1940) was the center of the cubist style in Germany, most particularly in the work of Marc, who was killed in the War, and Klee, who made out of cubist structure his own cryptic, miniature style.

ABSTRACT PAINTING. Pure abstraction was the 1st of the modern movements not to receive its main impulse from Paris, though Delaunay and the expatriate Czech Franz Kupka (1871–

1957; *Disks,* 1912) contributed to its origin. The 2 major theorists and practitioners of abstraction were Wassily Kandinsky in Munich and Piet Mondrian (1872–1944) in Holland. Each arrived at abstraction around 1911 by a very different development and with very different results. Their work represents the 2 historic poles of abstract painting: the organic and the geometrical, the expressionist and the restrained, the romantic and the classic. Kandinsky's color abstractions, the 1st of which was perhaps done in water color, developed out of a richly colorful style that had been strongly influenced by the Fauves. They were composed of a variety of loose strokes and touches, all held together by color, tone, and movement. In 1912 Kandinsky's book, *Concerning the Spiritual in Art,* expounded his theories of the metaphysical meaning of color harmonies. Mondrian, on the other hand, coming out of Dutch realism and Art Nouveau, was greatly affected by cubism, and in a series of *Trees,* 1909–11, he moved from delicate realism through increasing linearity to a basic "plus-minus" pattern—gridlike, but so sensitively composed that it is never mechanical. With Theo van Doesberg (1883–1931) he founded in 1917 *De Stijl,* a revolutionary review of the arts which particularly attracted architects like J. J. P. Oud (1890–1963) and G. T. Rietveld (1888–1964), and whose name became attached to the severely rectilinear style of Mondrian and his followers, also called "neoplasticism." Mondrian had a monklike austerity and a belief in the value of utter purity, which led him to limit himself to the 3 primary colors, plus black and white, and to employ only right-angle forms. In 1940 he came to New York, where he experimented with smaller color areas, juxtaposed so as to create optical movement (*Broadway Boogie-Woogie*), and where his personality and art influenced young painters such as Robert Motherwell (b. 1915).

Kandinsky's own spontaneous style became more schematic and geometrized when he went in the 1920's to teach at the Bauhaus, the great German school of design founded by Walter Gropius in 1919 and later closed by Hitler. There the most powerful influences were the ideas of neoplasticism and the Russian constructivist Kasimir Malevich (1878–1935). Three of the major figures at the Bauhaus—Lyonel Feininger (1871–1956), László Moholy-Nagy (1895–1946), and Josef Albers (b. 1888)—all came in the 1930's to the U.S., where the latter 2 helped to revolutionize the teaching of art and design. Although Kandinsky never went to the U.S., his works were collected by the Guggenheim family and exhibited in New York in the 1940's, where they influenced a new generation of artists. Another influence was the teaching of the German artist Hans Hofmann (1880–1966), who taught in the U.S. from 1932, and whose work from 1940 on represented an effort at synthesis of the 2 poles of abstraction.

DADA AND SURREALISM. In 1916 a group of artists in Zurich taking refuge from the war—Jean Arp (1887–1966) and the poets Tristan Tsara and Richard Huelsenbeck—picked for themselves the nonsense word "Dada" to express their feeling that all traditional seriousness about high art was foolish. Picabia, Duchamp, and Max Ernst (b. 1891) later joined the group in Paris, and exhibitions were held in which the aim was to shock the beholder by displaying ordinary objects, such as urinals, and extraordinary objects, such as a mustachioed Mona Lisa, with all the solemnity of a work of art. The point was not to confer serious meaning on the objects so much as to satirize and destroy the notion of serious meaning in art as it had traditionally existed. Visitors were also assaulted by sudden blackouts, nonsense readings, and false disasters. In all these attitudes and actions the Dada group proved to be what they would certainly have disowned at the time—the founders of a tradition, now very active in the current international "scene" of Pop art and Happenings.

Surrealism, a term coined by the poet-critic Guillaume Apollinaire (1880–1918) in 1917, was developed in the 1920's in Paris by some of the Dada artists, together with André Masson (1896–1967), Joan Miró (b. 1893), Salvador Dali (b. 1904), Yves Tanguy (1900–1955), Giorgio di Chirico (b. 1888), and the French poets Louis Aragon, André Breton, and Paul Éluard. Philosophically the movement drew on Freudian ideas of the unconscious; pictorially it represented a reaction against the discipline of cubism and geometric art. One aspect of surrealism, exemplified by Dali, is the highly realistic rendering of impossible objects, or ordinary objects in extraordinary relations. This kind of surrealism continued to be practiced by the Belgian artists René Magritte (1898–1967) and Paul Delvaux (b. 1897). Another and more fruitful development was the invention of abstract organic forms, as in the work of Miró and Arp. Masson and Ernst contributed the influential idea of "automatic writing" (or drawing) as a significant record of spontaneous, subconscious gesture. Both Masson and Ernst lived in New York during World War II (Dali and Tanguy were also there, and Duchamp had lived in New York since 1920) and established important contacts with younger American artists, some of whom, like Arshile Gorky (1904–48) and William de Kooning (b. 1904), had themselves emigrated from Europe as young men.

1945–68

ABSTRACT EXPRESSIONISM. With the appearance of a group of artists known as the "New York School"—Mark Rothko (b. 1903), de Kooning, Franz Kline (1910–1962), Motherwell, Barnett Newman (b. 1905), Adolph Gottlieb (b. 1903), William Baziotes (1912–1966), Jackson Pollock (1912–1956) —American artists became for the 1st time full participants in the international artistic world. The U.S. had always, since John Singleton Copley (1738–1815), had a powerful tradition of realism, ranging from the mid-19th-cent. landscape and genre painters through Winslow Homer (1836–1910), Thomas Eakins (1844–1916), and Edward Hopper (1882–1967), but its role in relation to the

European discoveries since impressionism had been largely that of pupil and assimilator. Many things contributed to the change, the most immediate being direct personal contact for American artists with European modernists who expatriated themselves during World War II. What took place in the U.S. was a leap into abstraction that had the character of the Kierkegaardian leap of faith, full of exaltation and anxiety and of a strength sufficient to make itself felt during the postwar years as a genuinely new movement.

The work of Pollock, de Kooning, and Kline introduced a new conception of the canvas as an over-all field of force in which the drama of painting itself is enacted, and in which personal gesture is of primary significance. Rothko, Newman, and Gottlieb, working like the others on a new large scale, concentrated on the massive, single, contemplative image in which experimental color relationships play a major role. Postwar European abstraction developed along similar lines in the work of Pierre Soulages (b. 1919), Nicolas de Staël (1914–55), Hans Hartung (b. 1904), and others, but for the 1st time in interaction with American work rather than as inventor and master, and in countries outside France the impact of New York was often greater than that of Paris.

The various styles of abstraction, though personal and hence individually different, became in the aggregate a new international style, spreading rapidly due to the new mobility of travel, the ease of reproduction, and the growth of international loan exhibitions. Artists in Eastern Europe, particularly in Poland and Yugoslavia, were deeply influenced by the new abstraction as they tried to break away from the prescribed socialist realism which had been the official Soviet style since the early 1920's. At that time, after approving an initial burst of modernism connected with the Revolution, the Soviet government had reversed its position and suppressed the modern movement, causing the exile of such major figures as Kandinsky, Malevich, Pevsner, and Chagall. Abstract painting, which does in fact give visual expression to the modern sense of personal, emotional, and imaginative freedom and thus carries some of the most advanced values of individualistic western civilization, continues to be resisted by official-Communist culture, which asserts the supremacy of social over individual values. (Ironically, conventional opinion in the West, particularly in the U.S., has often regarded abstract art as dangerously "socialistic," imaginative freedom here being linked with anarchy and the destruction of traditional community values.) The new international style was also the model for artists outside the European tradition, whose struggle was not political but rather cultural, since they had to assimilate modernism to centuries-old traditional patterns. The results have of necessity been more imitative than inventive, but such figures as Japan's Zao-wou-ki (b. 1920) and Kenzo Okada (b. 1902) represent original contributions to modern painting.

The later 1950's saw a reaction against the dramatic, emotional content of abstract expressionism and toward a greater impersonality and objectivity in works of art. One aspect of this reaction, to be seen in the work of Robert Rauschenberg (b. 1925) and Jasper Johns (b. 1930), was the conferring of a new kind of aesthetic status on such common objects as mattresses and beer cans. This innovation was followed by the introduction of a whole range of themes derived from popular, commercial imagery by a group that came to be known as the "Pop" artists. Another trend was the development of hard-edge, or "post-painterly," abstraction by such figures as Ellsworth Kelly (b. 1923), Kenneth Noland (b. 1924), and Frank Stella (b. 1936), who use the traditional materials of paint and canvas but often combine modular units in constructivist fashion to create complex patterns of line, color, and shape. Their experiments in color relations link them to such older European figures as Victor Vasarely (b. 1908) and the Groupe de Recherche Visuel (founded in Paris in 1960), who work with the physical properties of light and color to create the optical illusion of actual movement on a surface. One of the convictions held by these artists is the importance of anonymity and impersonality. They also feel the need to relate their work to the discoveries of science.

SCULPTURE
1800–1910

NEOCLASSICAL SCULPTURE. In the 1st half of the 19th cent. sculpture was largely dominated by neoclassical style and subject matter. The two neoclassical masters, the Dane Bertel Thorwaldsen (1768–1844) and the Italian Antonio Canova (1757–1822), set a pattern which went unchallenged and continued to be practiced throughout the century by such men as James Pradier (1792–1852; *Atalanta at Her Toilet,* 1830) and Giovanni Dupré (1817–82; *Sappho,* 1857). The most characteristic sculptural expression of the period was the monument, usually publicly commissioned to honor a national hero. Numerous 19th-cent. monuments of this kind remain, but for the most part their creators have been forgotten. Among the most famous is the Arc de Triomphe, on which the central relief group, *Departure of the Volunteers,* 1836, by François Rudé (1784–1855), is a fine example of dramatic romantic expression in neoclassical form. The monumental tradition was carried on to the end of the century in such works as the Statue of Liberty, 1886, by Frédéric Auguste Bartholdi (1834–1904) and the *Adams Memorial,* 1891, by the American Augustus Saint-Gaudens (1848–1907).

On a smaller, more private scale were the portrait busts of David d'Angers (1788–1856) and the animal sculptures of Antoine Louis Barye (1795–1875). The most expressive sculpture of the midcentury was done by Daumier, who made many studies of figures and heads which he considered only as personal sketches and of which few have been preserved. Degas, too, made powerful little wax studies of dancers which he cast in bronze but did not exhibit. A gentle genre realism was practiced by Jules Dalou (1838–1902), while the Belgian,

Constantin Meunier (1831–1905), taking up sculpture after a career in painting, continued to create heroic images of the working man (*The Puddler*). Jean Baptiste Carpeaux (1827–75) produced classical sculpture, but with a new feeling of directness and realism; his stone group, *The Dance,* done for the Paris Opera House, 1865–69, had the compliment paid to it of a bottle of ink thrown at one of the nude figures, which were felt to be obscene not because of their nudity but because of their expressiveness.

RODIN. By far the greatest sculptor of the 19th cent. was Auguste Rodin (1840–1917). Formed essentially by a study of Michelangelo and by painstaking observation of nude models in movement and in repose, Rodin produced sculpture which in its monumentality climaxed the Renaissance figural tradition, in its dramatic realism expressed the 19th cent., and in its innovations foreshadowed the 20th. On the appearance of his 1st major piece, *The Age of Bronze,* 1877, Rodin was accused of having achieved such convincing realism by making a cast of a live young man; later objections were raised to the expressive realism of his *Burghers of Calais,* 1884–86, and to the insufficient dignity of his *Balzac,* 1891–98. In *Man Walking,* 1888, and other figures he used anatomical fragmentation as an expressive means, and the surface of his bronzes retains the rough marks of the sculptor's touch in clay.

1910–68

CUBISM AND CONSTRUCTIVISM.

Sculpture in the 20th cent. has had a development more closely related to painting than at any time during the preceding century. Leaving public commissions to the academic realist, modern independent sculptors have participated to the full in the visual revolution, i.e., in the denial of naturalism and the invention of new forms based on a new view of reality.

Much of modern sculpture has grown from the cubist vision, Picasso himself in his *Head* of 1910 having created volume out of angled planes. In Raymond Du-champ-Villon's (1876–1918) *The Horse,* 1914, form is entirely broken up and reconstituted into separate elements, which combine to express the movement rather than the surface appearance of the animal. This destruction of solid 3-dimensional form and reconstruction into multidimensional form was also accomplished in the years before World War I in the work of Alexander Archipenko (1887–1964), Henri Laurens (1885–1954), and Jacques Lipschitz (b. 1891). Their productions were created by a new method, by means of which a piece of sculpture was constructed out of separate pieces of material. Previously, the 2 traditional ways of making sculpture had been either to cut away from solid material or to mold the object, using a plastic material. The new method was 1st definitively followed by the Russian constructivists Vladimir Tatlin (b. 1885) and the brothers Naum Gabo (b. 1890) and Antoine Pevsner (b. 1886), all of whom were greatly influenced by cubism and by collage, itself a constructivist medium. Gabo's *Head,* 1910, is constructed of sheets of iron bent and folded like paper so that the hollows of space are an intrinsic part of the structure. Gabo and Pevsner soon made completely abstract forms out of such new materials as plastic, steel, and nylon thread, with such titles as *Translucent Variation on a Spheric Theme* (Gabo, 1937). Other notable constructivist sculptors are Julio Gonzales (1876–1942), David Smith (1906–65), and Richard Lippold (b. 1915).

KINETIC SCULPTURE.

Important contemporary developments resulting from the constructivist revolution include "kinetic" sculpture. Alexander Calder (b. 1898) began making wire "drawings in space" and in the early 1930's constructed the 1st mobile: a structure of flat iron shapes and wires so composed and balanced that it moves with air currents. Nicolas Schöffer (b. 1912) introduced the electric motor as the source of movement along with light, color, and sound in a kind of grand synthesis of the arts. Jean Tinguely (b. 1925) went beyond Calder's playful humor in his sardonic "meta-machines" which are intended to destroy themselves as they operate. The use of electronics for both movement and light has become an important area of investigation in kinetic sculpture today.

FOUND OBJECTS AND JUNK SCULPTURE. Probably the earliest *objet trouvé* in sculpture was the metal cheese-server in Picasso's *Glass of Absinthe,* 1912. The Dada artists originated the phrase, though their interest was in the nature of the object itself rather than in its transformation into part of a constructed sculpture. Picasso's *Goat,* 1950, is an example of the latter—a bronze casting of a lifelike animal figure constructed out of bicycle parts, toy cars, and other bits of junk. Eduardo Paolozzi (b. 1924) and Richard Stankiewicz (b. 1924) are 2 major figures whose sculpture is made in this way. Louise Nevelson (b. 1900) does not cast but builds directly with an enormous variety of objects, constructing hugh boxlike reliefs encased in wood, which approach the quality of a total environment.

ORGANIC SCULPTURE. Another trend in 20th-cent. sculpture was the concern not so much with space, movement, and mechanics as with the simplification of volume so as to bring sculptured forms closer to the basic forms and rhythms of nature. Biology rather than physics has been its inspiration. Constantin Brancusi (1876–1957), a Hungarian who worked in Paris from 1904, was influenced by cubist planarity but even more by archaic Mediterranean sculpture and his feeling for such natural phenomena as the egg and the water-polished stone. He advanced from his simplified heads of 1910–20 to the more completely abstract forms of the *Fish,* 1928, and *Bird in Space,* 1940. Amadeo Modigliani's (1884–1920) painting as well as his sculpture was influenced by Brancusi, whose close friend he was. Jean Arp (1888–1966) worked his way from organic shapes in cut paper and in relief toward sculpture in the round, the latter purely abstract, but with the smooth, irregular curving shapes of a snowdrift, a sleeping cat, or a nude woman. In England, sculpture was revitalized by Henry Moore (b. 1898), who like Brancusi has always used the traditional media of wood, stone, and bronze. He has progressed from purely formal organic shapes to an increasing interest in the human figure, which he has interpreted in terms of the natural rhythms of solid and void, convex and concave. His monumental reclining figures, made for an outdoor setting, take on the character of Mother Earth herself. Barbara Hepworth (b. 1903) makes abstract forms of wood and stone which express the movements of nature. In the postwar period Seymour Lipton (b. 1903) and Isamu Noguchi (b. 1904) have worked primarily in the organic mode.

EXPRESSIONIST SCULPTURE. Expressionist sculptors tend to be concerned with the human figure, distorted for emotional effect and spiritual meaning. Wilhelm Lembruck's (1881–1919) *Standing Youth,* 1913, uses elongation to express pathos and vulnerability. Alberto Giacometti's (1906–1966) bronze figures are reduced to the dimensions of a structure of nerves, while Germaine Richier (1904–1959) created the effect of the tearing apart of nerves and flesh. A very different kind of expressionism is found in the later works of Jacques Lipschitz, such as the *Minotaur,* where human and animal forces are expressed in heavy, curving, twisting shapes.

RECENT TRENDS. "Pop" sculpture is a reprise of Dada wit with a distinctly American flavor. It is characterized by a fusion of sculpture and painting (Jim Dine, Marisol) and by a desire to make of sculpture not a single object but a total environment (George Segal). In "minimal" sculpture, where the work is composed of flat, geometrical, or bulging organic forms, the impulse is essentially constructivist, both in technique and in the desire for impersonality. The Englishman Anthony Caro (b. 1924) has been an important originator in this mode.

ARCHITECTURE AND DESIGN

1800–99

19TH-CENT. REVIVALISM. 19th-cent. architecture was characterized by a series of revival styles: primarily neoclassical and pure Gothic in the 1st half of the century, and picturesque and eclectic mixtures of Neo-Renaissance and neo-baroque in the 2nd half. Some magnificent monuments have resulted: Charles Barry's Houses of Parliament in London, the Paris of Napoleon III, and the great museums and opera houses of Europe, as well as many buildings whose high degree of decorative articulation has come to be appreciated anew in modern times. For the progressive minds of the later 19th cent., however, such historicism became increasingly intolerable. The ardent Gothicist, Augustus Welby Northmore Pugin (1812–52), believed that architecture expressed the character of an age, and that the virtue of medieval society could be deduced from the beauty of its buildings; he concluded that the building of Gothic was essential for the spiritual health of modern society, which with the advent of industrialism had become mean-spirited and ugly. The creators of modern architecture agreed with his premise, but repudiated his conclusion; for them, only that society could be healthy which developed its own style out of its own conditions, materials, and aspirations. The desire to formulate a distinctive modern style of architecture resulted from a growing awareness of modernity shared by all the arts.

ARTS AND CRAFTS MOVEMENT. 19th-cent. sources of modern design were in their time completely unrelated and even antithetical: the English Arts and Crafts movement and the iron and steel constructions of the engineers. William Morris (1834–96), trained as an architect and painter and repelled by the cheap, ornate, inorganic quality of the textiles, utensils, and furniture produced by the factories of the 1850's, made the crucial decision to become, not a painter withdrawn from the crass world, but a designer and head of a firm of designers who would devote themselves to making objects of solid craftsmanship and honest design. Morris' medievalism and particularly his rejection of the machine put him at odds with his own theory of art for the people, but his stubborn belief that present-day society should produce valid design and his establishment of the dig-

nity of craftsmanship were very important to the following continental generation. With his architect friend Philip Webb (1831–1915) he designed his own home, The Red House, in 1859, also a model for the European modernists in its simple, undecorated forms and in the fact that conscious craftsmanship was applied to every detail of a middle-class home.

ENGINEERING STRUCTURES: IRON AND STEEL. At a time when architecture was defined as the ornamental part of a building, the new demands of industrial life were giving birth to purely functional structures, such as bridges and railway stations, in which the physical requirements and the nature of the materials determined the form of the structure. An impressive early example was the Clifton Suspension Bridge of 1836 by I. K. Brunel (1806–59), with its simple, sweeping curve and total lack of adornment. The same architect, with Sir M. D. Wyatt (1820–77), built Paddington Station in London, 1852–54, where glass supported by slender iron columns and ribs served to enclose the large space of the train shed. Joseph Paxton's (1801–65) Crystal Palace, built to house the 1st international exhibition (London, 1851), was a prophetic structure of prefabricated iron and glass parts, spanning an unprecedentedly enormous space. The skeletal structure and consequent lightness resulting from the load-bearing powers of the slender iron shafts and large quantities of non-load-bearing glass looked forward to one of the most characteristic forms of the 20th cent., the curtain wall. Probably the best-known 19th-cent. iron structure, also built for an international exhibition (Paris, 1889), is the Eiffel Tower. Designed by the French engineer Gustave Eiffel (1832–1923) as an open-work structure of small iron and steel beams, its upward thrust and sense of release from earth were very appealing to the constructivists.

THE SKYSCRAPER AND THE CHICAGO SCHOOL. Developments in steel manufacture by 1890 made possible the skeletal construction of the skyscraper, which was for a long time a primarily American phenomenon. Louis Sullivan's (1856–1924) Wainwright Building in St.

Louis, 1890–91, was the 1st in which the uniform gridlike appearance reveals the structure (despite the ornament and the top cornice, which are reminiscent of traditional masonry buildings). Other important industrial buildings in Chicago were the Marshall Field Wholesale Building of 1885, built by Henry Hobson Richardson (1838–86), a pioneer in the use of large, simple masses and an important influence on Sullivan; and Burnham and Root's Monadnock Block of 1890–91. Frank Lloyd Wright (1869–1959) was also associated with the Chicago school through his early studies with Sullivan, though his major contribution has been in the field of organic domestic architecture (Ross House, 1902; Bear Run, 1936).

Apart from steel, the most important modern material developed in the 19th cent., but not widely exploited until the 20th, was reinforced concrete, an aggregate which combines the compression strength of concrete and the tensile strength of steel. The French architect Auguste Perret (1874–1954) was the 1st to develop fully the possibilities of this new material (flats at 25 bis Rue Franklin, Paris, 1902–3; Notre-Dame du Raincy, Paris, 1922–23), which was further developed by his Swiss-born student Le Corbusier (Charles Édouard Jeanneret, 1887–1965) and the Italian engineer-architect Pier Luigi Nervi (b. 1891).

1900–68

EARLY MODERNISM. Apart from Perret, the major French contributor to early modernism was Tony Garnier (1869–1948), whose plans for an Industrial City were made as early as 1901, exhibited in 1904, and published in 1918. Garnier, with his statement that "in architecture, truth is the result of calculations made to satisfy known necessities with known materials," clearly states the case not only against Beaux-Arts academicism but against all historical architecture which embodies "false principles"—i.e., considerations other than the purely functional. This extreme position has never been consistently followed by modern architects, but it implies an attitude toward the past which the architects, like the painters, required in order to achieve their revolutionary changes. Garnier's designs were extraordinarily advanced in their conception of town planning, in their technical inventions (e.g., the cantilever principle), and in the flat, clear, uncluttered lines of the buildings.

British and Austrian architects were pioneers in the development of the new modern style which, in the effort to cast away the habits of eclecticism, strove toward simplicity of form and, where ornament was used, toward the invention of original ornamental forms. In the Glasgow School of Art, 1896–1907, by Charles Rennie McIntosh (1868–1928), there is no element drawn from period styles. The austere masses of the walls and the large plain windows are combined, in the interiors, with an intricate rectilinear design of pillars and galleries which look forward to abstract geometric painting. The interior wall designs of the Cranston Tea Room in Buchanan Street, Glasgow, 1897–98, with their slim, hieratic figures, establish a link with the Viennese designers of the Sezession, who subsequently invited McIntosh to Vienna, where he designed a Music Room for the founder of the Wiener Werkstätte. After McIntosh, British architecture, like American architecture generally after the Chicago Exhibition of 1893, fell back into a reaction against the new movements and a return to "neo" styles, while the most advanced work was being done by Austrian and German architects. The Viennese Joseph Hoffmann's (1870–1955) Convalescent Home at Purkersdorf, 1903–4, with its flat, unadorned lines, could easily be dated in the 20's, while his major work, the Palais Stoclet in Brussels, 1905, has the "streamlined" quality of the 30's. The Steiner House, 1910, in Vienna by Adolf Loos (1870–1933) could similarly be misdated. The older Viennese architect Otto Wagner (1841–1918), stimulated by the work of his followers, built the Post Office Savings Bank in Vienna in 1905, a building in which the structural facts of load-bearing vertical members and curtain wall (in this case a vaulted glass ceiling) are expressed with great visual clarity.

BEHRENS. The most important German architect of this period was Peter

Behrens (1868–1940), who expressed the reaction of the 1st decade of the 20th cent. against not only period styles but also the elaboration and the increasingly hothouse aestheticism of Art Nouveau, a reaction comparable in its seriousness and austerity to that of the cubist painters against the patterned decorativeness of the art of the 1890's. Behrens was influential not only through his buildings, such as the AEG Turbine Factory (Berlin, 1909), but through his emphasis on simplicity and excellence of design for all kinds of industrial products and through his effect on his disciples, among whom were 3 of the great architects of the century: Le Corbusier, Ludwig Mies Van der Rohe (1886–1969), and Walter Gropius (1883–1969).

THE BAUHAUS AND THE INTERNATIONAL STYLE. The work of Gropius before World War I (Fagus Factory, 1911; Model Factory for the Werkbund Exhibition, Cologne, 1914) developed the ideas of Behrens and established many of the principles of the 20th-cent. style—smooth lines, corners without visibly massive supports, walls of glass with only the slenderest of steel supporting beams—all adding up to a visual statement of technological mastery over new materials. In 1919 Gropius founded the Staatliche Bauhaus, a workshop and school, in which the style later christened by Alfred Barr as the "international style" was worked out not only in building (Gropius' Bauhaus at Dessau, 1925) but in typography, painting, and industrial design. The Bauhaus was the realization of William Morris' desire for high standards of design in ordinary objects, here enthusiastically applied to the products of the machine; and its style put a permanent mark on the 20th-cent. visual environment. Gropius' belief in anonymous group design and in the importance of relating architecture to actual social needs and problems (e.g., the importance of mass housing) were later adopted by the Architect's Co-operative which he founded in Cambridge, Mass.

MIES VAN DER ROHE. The director of the Bauhaus (at Dessau from 1930; moved to Berlin, 1932) until its closing under Hitler in 1933 was Mies Van der Rohe, who had planned the Wiessenhof Housing Exhibit of 1927 (including buildings by Gropius and Corbusier as well as by himself) in which models of future mass housing were displayed. His elegant Barcelona Pavilion, 1929—for which his famous Barcelona chairs were designed—was the prototype of the "glass box" which became so well known. Like Gropius, Mies went to America in the 1930's, and from his position at the Illinois Institute of Technology (whose building he designed, 1940) he influenced a whole generation of architects and designers. His spare, skeletal Seagram House in New York, 1955–58, is a recent example of his epigram, "less is more."

LE CORBUSIER. The 3rd of the great shapers of the 20th-cent. style was Le Corbusier, whose tremendous influence on architects has come not only from his buildings (Villa Savoie at Poissy, 1929–31; Swiss Pavilion at the Cité Universitaire of Paris, 1931–32; Unité d'Habitation at Marseilles, 1952; the Capital at Chandigarh, India, beginning 1950) but in his writings (*Vers Une Nouvelle Architecture*, 1923; *La Ville Radieuse*, 1925), in which he expressed his intense convictions about the classical purity of proportion in modern architecture and about the qualities of the machine as a model for architectural form. Le Corbusier, who was himself a Purist painter, is an outstanding example of the profound connection between the cubist and constructivist vision and that of the architects of the international style. Another example of this link is the Schröder House in Utrecht, Holland, built by Gerrit Rietveld (1888–1964) in 1923–24; Rietveld was a member of De Stijl, a group which grew out of cubism and included Mondrian and Van Doesburg, and the house, with its structure of lines and planes and lack of any fixed point of view from which to be observed, is a 3-dimensional translation of a De Stijl painting.

The most consistent exponent of the international style in the postwar world has been the firm of Skidmore, Owings, and Merrill, whose major designer is Gordon Bunschaft (b. 1909), but which has inherited the Gropius principles of group design. The Lever Building in New

York, 1950–52, was the 1st of a series of elegant glass office towers (Pepsi-Cola, Union Carbide, Chase Manhattan) that established the style (unfortunately often cheapened by its imitators) of American commercial building both at home and abroad.

EXPRESSIONISM. Expressionism in architecture is a rather vague term which can nevertheless be used to characterize those ideas and forms which stress sculptural shape and personal or organic feeling as opposed to an emphasis on rationality, technology, and objective geometrical proportion. It has its roots in the work of Gaudi; in the plans and drawings of the Italian Antonio Sant' Elia (1880–1916), whose Città Nuova project of 1914 aroused great interest; and in the work of Eric Mendelsohn (1887–1953) in Germany in the 20's (Schocken Department Store, Stuttgart, 1927). In the post-World War II period a reaction against the stringencies of the international style led to a renewal of expressionist feeling, even on the part of such creators of the classic style as Le Corbusier. Le Corbusier's Chapel of Notre-Dame du Haut at Ronchamp, 1950–54, with its swelling roof, fortresslike walls, and mysterious lighting from irregularly scattered windows, is a highly personal statement. So too is the soaring, sculptural TWA Building at Kennedy Airport, 1960, by Eero Saarinen (1910–61) the Finnish-American architect whose earlier General Motors Technical and Research Center (Warren, Mich., 1946–55) was a perfect Miesian glass box.

BRUTALISM. Brutalism is a term loosely derived from *béton brut,* or poured concrete, which is left with the rough cast marks of the wooden forms visible on the surface, and is therefore opposite in feeling to the smooth perfection of the glass curtain wall. Related qualities are the use of thick, massive forms, deeply inset fenestration, and a visual irregularity or complexity of structure such as that found in Paul Rudolph's (b. 1918) School of Art and Architecture at Yale University, 1964. Le Corbusier

again provides an example in his Maisons Jaoul at Neuilly, Paris, 1945–56. Another is the Richards Medical Research Building at the University of Pennsylvania, 1958–60, by the Estonian-born American Louis I. Kahn (b. 1901), whose powerful and unconventional personality has been, like Frank Lloyd Wright's earlier, an important influence on the generation of architects now coming to maturity. The work of the Finn, Alvar Aalto (b. 1898), is related to brutalism, though his use of native timber and brick in such buildings as the Technical College at Otaniemi, Finland, 1955, is more natural and organic than doctrinaire.

THE CONTEMPORARY INTERNATIONAL STYLE. It is, however, misleading to apply the term international style only to the classic modernism developed in the 1920's and 1930's, since the various more expressionistic postwar styles have also been international in scope. Because of its close link with modern technology and the abstract simplicity of its formal idiom, modern architecture has been relatively easily assimilated to a great many indigenous traditions, and important modern architects have emerged all over the world. An outstanding example of the fusion of traditional style with modern forms and methods is found in Japan, whose traditional architecture was itself an influence on modernism, particularly through the work of Frank Lloyd Wright. For example, Kenzo Tange (b. 1913), who belonged to a group of Bauhaus-trained architects in Tokyo in the 1930's, has built since the war a number of important buildings such as the Kurayoshi Town Hall, 1956, which uses form-marked concrete in a way that is both completely contemporary and reminiscent of the wooden temples of traditional Japan. Other outstanding examples of such assimilation of modern technology to indigenous traditions are the Ministry of Education and Health Building, Rio de Janeiro, the University of Mexico Library, Mexico City (with its mosaic decoration), and the Knesset, Jerusalem.

INDEX

70 71 72 73 10 9 8 7 6 5 4 3 2 1